THE
PULPIT COMMENTARY

THE
PULPIT COMMENTARY

Edited by

H. D. M. Spence

and

Joseph S. Exell

———

Volume 19
CORINTHIANS

Wm. B. Eerdmans Publishing Company, Grand Rapids, Michigan

THE PULPIT COMMENTARY

Edited by

H. D. M. Spence *and* Joseph S. Exell

This large-type edition republished
from new plates by

WM. B. EERDMANS PUBLISHING COMPANY
Grand Rapids, Michigan

January 1950

Reprinted January, 1953

Reprinted January, 1958

Reprinted March, 1962

PHOTOLITHOPRINTED BY CUSHING-MALLOY, INC.
ANN ARBOR, MICHIGAN, UNITED STATES OF AMERICA

I CORINTHIANS

EXPOSITION BY

F. W. FARRAR

HOMILETICS BY

DAVID THOMAS

HOMILIES BY VARIOUS AUTHORS

E. HURNDALL

C. LIPSCOMB

D. FRASER

J. R. THOMSON

R. TUCK

J. WAITE

H. BREMNER

THE FIRST EPISTLE OF
PAUL TO THE CORINTHIANS

—◆—

INTRODUCTION

—◆—

ST. PAUL AT CORINTH

ALONE, and much disheartened by the unfruitfulness of his sojourn, St. Paul left Athens after his memorable address in the Areopagus, and sailed to Corinth. In about five hours his vessel dropped anchor in the bright waters of the Saronic bay, under the pine woods and low green hills of Cenchreæ. A walk of about eight miles along the valley of Hexamili brought him to the city, nestling under the huge mass of its citadel—the famous Acrocorinthus, which flung its dark shadow over each of the city's double seas. In that city he spent more than a year and a half of his life.

The city of Corinth was no longer the old city so famous and so powerful in the days of the Peloponnesian War. After the decline of Sparta and Athens, she had held the hegemony of Greece, and had placed herself at the head of the Achæan league. In B.C. 196, Flamininus, after the battle of Cynocephalæ, had proclaimed at Corinth the independence of Hellas. But in B.C. 146 the city had been taken, its buildings committed to the flames, its treasures rifled, and its inhabitants massacred by L. Mummius. After it had lain in ruins for a hundred years the prescient eye of Julius Cæsar had recognized the beauty and importance of the site, and, wishing both to immortalize his own name and to call attention to his mythic descent from Venus—who, under her Greek name of Aphrodite, had been the patron goddess of the city—he rebuilt Corinth from its foundations; gave it the name of Julia Corinthus, and peopled it with a colony of veterans and freedmen.

With the advantage of its two harbours, Lechæum and Cenchreæ, and of the Diolkos, or land channel, over which ships were dragged to avoid the circumnavigation of Cape Malea, the town at once became important. It was "the bridge of the sea." Jews flocked to it for trade; Phœnicians, for commerce; Romans, in order to visit a place so famous and to buy "antiquities," genuine and spurious, for the Roman market; men of pleasure, to avail themselves of the immorality for which it soon became infamous. Greeks were attracted in large numbers by the renown of the revived Isthmian games. It was the Greeks who stamped their own character upon the majority of the inhabitants. They became proverbial for litigious shrewdness, intellectual restlessness, and, above all, sensual indulgence. The mixture of classes and nationalities in a seaport and emporium of commerce produces invariably an unfavourable effect, and Corinth—still continuing to be in a certain sense "the Star of Hellas," and the emporium of half the world—became known as the Vanity Fair of the Roman empire; alike the London and the Paris of the first century after Christ.

Into this city of six hundred thousand inhabitants—this seething mass of Jews, merchants, philosophers, ex-soldiers, retailers, and agents of vice— the lonely and suffering apostle found his way. With all their faults of head and of heart, these Greeks aroused his deepest interest. Evidently his stay in Corinth impressed his imagination. He draws many illustrations from their stadium, their races, their boxing matches, their courts of justice, their theatres, their garlands of Isthmian pine (ch. ix. 24, 27; iv. 9; ix. 25; 2 Cor. ii. 14—16; v. 10; ix. 25). He learnt to love the Corinthians with intense affection, though he never had to deal with any Church so inflated and so immoral, so indifferent to his sufferings, so contemptuous towards his teaching, or so tolerant of the opposition and the calumnies of his personal enemies and rivals.

The worst moral sins of the city were dishonesty, drunkenness, and above all, sensuality, which was directly due to the worship of Aphrodite Pandemos, and to the thousand female *hieroduli*, who were consecrated to her service. Against these sins again and again the apostle lifted up his voice (ch. v. 10; vi. 9—20; x. 7, 8; xi. 21; 2 Cor. vi. 14; vii. 1; xii. 21, etc.).

The chief intellectual faults were a litigious spirit, restless speculation, eager factiousness, and inflated vanity. To these St. Paul would not pander for a moment. Perhaps because he had learnt experience from the failure of his more recondite and philosophical address at Athens, he determined to discard all human wisdom and eloquence, and to preach the gospel in its uttermost and humblest simplicity, knowing nothing among them but Christ Jesus, yes, and Christ crucified (ch. i. 17, 23; ii. 1—5; 2 Cor. i. 18).

The volatile suspicious character of the people made the apostle feel the necessity for being most carefully on his guard. He was determined to set an example of the most lofty and disinterested self-denial. He had been trained to a trade, like every other Jewish boy, in accordance with a wise rule of the rabbis. His trade was the humble and mechanical trade of tent-making; and finding a Jewish compatriot named Aquila, who worked at this trade, with his wife Priscilla, he entered into partnership with them. They had been expelled from Rome by a decree of Claudius, in A.D. 52, and had probably been converted to Christianity by the unknown disciples who had founded the Roman Church. With them St. Paul formed a happy and lifelong friendship, and by toiling with them, he was able to earn a living, which was, however, so scanty that it often barely sufficed even for his simple wants (Acts xx. 34; ch. iv. 11, 12; ix. 4, 12; 2 Cor. vii. 2; xi. 9).

After a time he was joined by Silas and Timotheus, who not only aided him effectually in his mission work, but also brought a welcome supply for his needs from the Church of Philippi, the only Church from which he ever consented to accept pecuniary aid (2 Cor. xi. 9; Phil. iv. 15).

The mission was successful. Crispus the ruler of the synagogue was baptized, with all his house. The Jews, however, as a body, showed such determined opposition, that he had to leave their synagogue altogether and turn to the Gentiles. He went with his converts to a room near the synagogue, which was placed at his disposal by a proselyte named Justus, and there, amid much physical weakness and mental depression, he preached for many months. His labours brought about the conversion of many Gentiles (Acts xviii. 8), and the founding of Churches, not only in Corinth, but also at Cenchreæ and other towns of Achaia (2 Cor. i. 1; Rom. xvi. 1).

The Jews, filled with bitter hatred against him, seized the opportunity offered them by the arrival of a new proconsul—Marcus Annæus Novatus (Gallio), a brother of Seneca—to accuse him of acting contrary to Law. Gallio, indeed, dismissed their accusation with true Roman contempt; but the strong indignation of the apostle against his obstinate and infatuated fellow-countrymen breaks out in his First Epistle to the Thessalonians (1 Thess. ii. 14—16), the earliest of his extant Epistles, which, like the Second, was written from Corinth.

After staying for some time longer at Corinth, he sailed to Ephesus on his way to Jerusalem, and, returning from thence to Antioch, set out with Timothy and others on his third missionary journey. Fulfilling his promise that he would revisit Ephesus, he made that city his head-quarters for nearly three years (Acts xx. 31).

DATE AND DESIGN OF THE EPISTLE.

It was during the latter part of his residence in the Ionian metropolis— probably a little before Pentecost, A.D. 57—that he wrote his First Letter to the Corinthians. His intention had been to leave Ephesus shortly and to sail to Corinth. After a brief stay with the Church, he purposed to visit Macedonia, and then to return to Corinth, in order that, after a second visit, the Church might help him forward on his way to Jerusalem (2 Cor. i. 15—17). The news which he received from Corinth frustrated this plan He had informed them of it (apparently) in a lost letter, in which he had also given them a rule "not to company with fornicators," of which they had mistaken the due significance. But in ch. xvi. he had silently indicated his change of plan, and this had led his opponents to charge him with insincerity and frivolity (2 Cor. i. 17).

But the reason for this change of plan had been the account of the evil state of the Church at Corinth, which he had received, first from Apollos; then from a letter which the converts had addressed to him; and lastly from some members of "the household of Chloe."

From Apollos he must have heard generally that some of the brethren were only too likely to succumb to the perils of the heathendom by which they were surrounded; and he must have told the apostle that there was pressing need for him to meet the yearning wish of all the most faithful converts by paying them a visit as soon as possible.

The letter of the Corinthians themselves revealed the existence of some genuine perplexity and of many eager and unhealthy speculations.

1. They had asked many questions about marriage and celibacy; about second marriages; about mixed marriages; about the marriage of wards and daughters.

2. They wished for direction in the bitter disputes which had arisen between "the strong" and "the weak" on the question of "meats offered to idols."

3. They had asked whether men or women ought to appear in the assemblies with their heads covered or uncovered.

4. They had difficulties about the relative value of spiritual gifts, and the way to regulate the phenomena of glossolaly ("speaking with the tongue").

5. They were perplexed with material difficulties about the resurrection.

6. They asked about the collection for the poor in Jerusalem.

7. They invited Apollos to pay them another visit.

There were many points in this letter which gave ground for anxiety; but this was as nothing to the grief with which St. Paul heard the tidings brought by Stephanas, Fortunatus, and Achaicus—tidings which he should have heard from the Church, but which their letter had passed over with a reticence which was little honourable to their faithfulness and sincerity.

First of all, he learnt that the Church was rent by a deplorable party spirit. Apollos and others, especially some emissaries from or representatives of the mother Church of Jerusalem, had visited Corinth during St. Paul's long absence, and the consequence had been that various factions had rallied round different teachers. One party still adhered to the name of Paul; others preferred the stately rhetoric and Alexandrian refinements of Apollos; others claimed allegiance for the name of Cephas; and some Judæo-Christians, probably of the narrowest school, vainly wished to monopolize for their section the name of Christ himself.

Then grave scandals and abuses had been caused in the Church meetings by the forwardness of women, by the egotism of rival orators, and most of all by the disordered and almost insane abuse of the impulse to speak with the tongue.

Further, the very agapæ which were held in connection with the Eucharist had been shockingly disgraced and profaned by greed, selfishness, envy, gluttony, and even by the besetting Corinthian vice of intoxication.

Worst of all, uncleanness had not only found its open defenders but a considerable section of the Church, in its inflated sophistry, had condoned and abetted a case of incest so flagrant that the very heathen cried shame upon it.

It was under these almost heartrending circumstances that St. Paul wrote his First Epistle to the Corinthians. The Epistle, which is very characteristic of the apostle, is in many ways most deeply interesting, and especially for these reasons—

1. It shows the powerful self-control of the apostle in spite of his physical weakness, his distressed circumstances, his incessant troubles, and his emotional nature. It was written, he tells us, in bitter anguish, " out of much affliction and pressure of heart, . . . and with streaming tears " (2 Cor. ii. 4) ; yet he restrained the expression of his feelings, and wrote with a dignity and holy calm, which he thought most calculated to win back his erring children.

2. It gives us a vivid picture of the early Church before the days of its organization and episcopal government; and it entirely dissipates the dream that the apostolic Church was in an exceptional condition of holiness of life or purity of doctrine.

3. It shows how the most trivial details can be decided by great and solemn principles. Problems however dark, details however intricate, become under St. Paul's treatment both lucid and orderly in the light of eternal distinctness. St. Paul shows that the rule of charity and the voice of conscience are sufficient to decide all questions.

4. It is addressed to a Church predominantly Gentile, and thus shows us the method adopted by the greatest of Christian teachers when brought face to face with the problems suggested to the minds of converts from paganism.

AUTHENTICITY.

The authenticity of the Epistle is beyond all doubt. It is attested from the very earliest times, and among others by St. Clemens Romanus (A.D. 96), within forty years of the date when the letter was written. Alike the external and the internal evidence is so indisputable, that not a single writer of the smallest importance, however " advanced " his school of criticism, has ever ventured to question its cogency.

Many of the questions which are sometimes discussed by way of Introduction to the Epistle—such as the supposed unrecorded visit to Corinth, the nature of the factions, the matter and style, etc.—will be found discussed in the following notes.

CONTENTS.

The outline of the Epistle—owing to the circumstances in which it originated—is very simple. It is as follows:—

THE FIRST EPISTLE OF

PAUL TO THE CORINTHIANS

—◆—

EXPOSITION.

CHAPTER I.

The oldest superscription was probably, "To the Corinthians, the first (Πρὸς Κοριν-θίους πρώτη)." This is found in ℵ, A, B, C, D.

Vers. 1—3.—*The greeting.* An opening salutation is found in all the Epistles of St. Paul, and in every Epistle of the New Testament except the Epistle to the Hebrews and the first Epistle of St. John, both of which were more in the nature of treatises than letters.

Ver. 1.—**Paul.** After the beginning of the first missionary journey (A.D. 45) he seems to have finally abandoned his Hebrew name of Saul. **Called.** The word "called" is absent from A, D, E, and other manuscripts, but may have been omitted as superfluous. It occurs in the greeting of Rom. i. 1, but not in any other Epistle. The words might also be rendered "a called or chosen apostle." To be **an apostle.** He uses this title in every letter except the private one to Philemon, the peculiarly friendly and informal one to the Philippians, and the two to the Thessalonians, which were written before the Judaizers had challenged his claim to this title in its more special sense. The Epistle to the Romans is the first in which he calls himself "a *slave* of Jesus Christ" (comp. Phil. i. 1; Titus i. 1; Jas. i. 1; 2 Pet. i. 1; Jude 1). It was necessary for him to assert his right to the apostolate in the highest sense of the word, as one who had received from Christ himself an authority equal to that of the twelve (see ch. ix. 1—5; xv. 9; 2 Cor. xi. 5; xii. 11, 12; Gal. i. 1—19, etc.). **Of Jesus Christ.** In the Gospels the word "Christ" is all but invariably "*the* Christ," *i.e.* the Anointed, the Messiah. It is the designation of the office of Jesus as the promised Deliverer. We trace in the New Testament the gradual transition of the word from a title into a proper name. In the two names together our Lord is represented as "the Saviour," and the anointed Prophet, Priest, and King, first of the chosen people and then of all mankind. **Through the will of God** (comp. 2 Corinthians; Ephesians; Colossians; 2 Tim. i. 1). This *special* call to the apostleship is emphatically expanded in Gal. i. 1. The vindication of the Divine and independent claim was essential to St. Paul's work. It was not due to any personal considerations, but to the necessity of proving that no human authority could be quoted to overthrow the gospel which was peculiarly "*his* gospel" (see Gal. i. 11; Eph. iii. 8), of which one main feature was the freedom of the Gentiles from the yoke of Judaic bondage. **And Sosthenes.** The association of one or more brethren with himself in the greeting of his letters is peculiar to St. Paul. Silas and Timothy are associated with him in 1 and 2 Thessalonians; and Timothy, though so much his junior, in 2 Corinthians, Philippians, Colossians, and Philemon; doubtless he would have been associated with St. Paul in this Epistle had he not been absent (ch. iv. 17; xvi. 10). The practice arose partly from St. Paul's exquisite courtesy and consideration towards his companions, partly from his shrinking from mere personal prominence. It is owing to the same reasons that in the earlier Epistles he constantly uses "we" for "I," and sometimes when he can only be speaking of himself (1 Thess. ii. 18). But even in the Epistles to the Thessalonians he sometimes relapses from "we" into "I" (2 Thess. ii. 5). **Our brother;** literally, *the brother;* i.e. one of "the brethren" (comp. 2 Cor. i. 1). Of Sosthenes nothing whatever is known. He may possibly be the amanuensis whom St. Paul employed for this letter. Later tradition, which in such matters is perfectly valueless, spoke of him as " one of the seventy disciples, and Bishop of Colophon" (Eusebius, ' Hist. Eccl.,' i. 12). There is a Jewish Sosthenes, a ruler of the synagogue, in Acts xviii. 17; but it is only a vague conjecture that he may have been subsequently converted, and may have joined St. Paul at Ephesus. It is obvious that the persons named in the greetings of the Epistles were not in any way supposed to be responsible for their contents, for St. Paul begins with "I" in ver. 4. *Brother.* At this time there was no recognized title for Christians. In the Acts they are vaguely spoken of as "those of this way." Among themselves they were known as "the saints," "the faithful," "the elect." The name "Christians" was originally a nickname devised by the Antiochenes. In the New Testament it only occurs as a designation used by enemies (Acts xi. 26; xxvi. 28; 1 Pet. iv. 16).

Ver. 2.—**Unto the Church.** This form of address is used in 1 and 2 Thessalonians, 1 and 2 Corinthians, and Galatians. In St. Paul's later Epistles, for some unknown reason, he prefers the address " to the saints." These forms of address show the absence of any fixed ecclesiastical government. He does not in this Epistle address any "bishops" or "presbyters" whom he might regard as responsible for the growing disorders which prevailed at Corinth, but he appeals to the whole Church. The word *ecclesia*—signifying those who were "called out of the world," and so primarily applied to "the congregation of Israel"—came ultimately to mean "a congregation." The only apostle who uses the word "synagogue" of the Christian assemblies is St. James (ii. 2). **Of God.** Not the Church of this or that party leader. Some commentators give to these words an emphasis and importance which does not seem to belong to them. **Which is at Corinth.** So in 2 Cor. i. 2. In 1 and 2 Thessalonians he prefers the form, "the Church of the Thessalonians." "The *Church* at Corinth " was an expression which involved the sharpest of contrasts. It brought into juxtaposition the holiest ideal of the new faith and the vilest degradations of the old paganism. It was "a glad and great paradox" (Bengel). The condition of society at Corinth, at once depraved and sophistical, throws light on many parts of the Epistle. Cicero describes the city as "illustrious alike for wantonness, opulence, and the study of philosophy." Even **them that are sanctified.** The apostles could only write to Churches as being *really* Churches, and to Christians as being *true* Christians. In all general addresses they could only assume

that the *actual* resembled the *ideal.* They never conceal the immense chasm which separated the real condition of many members of their Churches from the vocation which they professed. They knew also that it is (as Calvin says) " a perilous temptation to refuse the name of Church to every Church in which there is not perfect purity." Ideally even the Corinthian Christians were redeemed by Christ's expiation, consecrated and sanctified by the work of the Holy Spirit. They could only be addressed in accordance with their ostensible position (see Hooker, ' Eccl. Pol.,' iii. 1; v. 68). Our Prayer-book is constructed on the same principle. The harvest is still a harvest, though amongst the corn there may be many tares. **In Christ Jesus.** The words, " in Christ," constitute what has been happily called "the monogram of St. Paul." The life of the true Christian is no longer his own. The Christ *for* him has become the Christ *in* him. His natural life is merged into a higher spiritual life. Baptized *into* Christ, he has become one with Christ. **Called to be saints.** (On this Christian calling, see Eph. iv. 1, 4 ; 2 Thess. i. 11; 2 Tim. i. 9; Heb. iii. 1 ; 2 Pet. i. 10.) They are called to be united saints, not schismatic partisans or members of antagonistic cliques. The description of what they were *ideally* is the more emphatic because he feels how much they had fallen away. **With all that . . . in every place.** Perhaps this may mean the same as 2 Cor. i. 1, " With all the saints that are in the whole of Achaia; " or the words may imply that St. Paul's exhortations are applicable to all Christians, wherever they may be and (as is expressed in the next clause) whatever may be their varying shades of individual opinion. It was well in any case to remind the Corinthians that they formed but a fraction of the Christian communities. Catholicity, not provincialism, makes the true Church of God. **Call upon the Name.** The Greek verb is here in the middle voice, not " who are called by the Name"(comp. Jas. ii. 7; Amos ix. 12, LXX.). It means, therefore, all who reverence the Name of Christ, all who adore their one " Lord " in the fulness of his nature (see Joel iii. 5; Acts ii. 21; Rom. x. 24 ; 2 Tim. ii. 22, etc.); in other words, " all who profess and call themselves Christians " (comp. Acts xxv. 11). **Their Lord and ours.** I connect these words, not with " place," as in the Vulgate, *In omni loco ipsorum et nostro*— which, however it may be twisted, can give no good sense—but with " Jesus Christ." It has been in all ages a fatal temptation of party Christians to claim a monopoly of Christ for themselves and their own sects, as though *they* only taught the gospel, and were the *only* Christians or the *only*

"Evangelicals." But Christ cannot thus be "parcelled into fragments" (see vers. 12, 13), nor has any party a right to boast exclusively, "I am of Christ." The addition, "and ours," could not be regarded as superfluous in writing to a Church of which one section wanted to assert an exclusive right in Christ.

Ver. 3.—**Grace to you and peace.** This is St. Paul's greeting in all the Epistles except the pastoral Epistles, in which he beautifully adds the word "mercy." It is a remarkable blending of the Greek and Jewish salutations. The Greeks said Χαίρειν, and to them the word "grace" involved the notions of joy and brightness and prosperity. The calmer and more solemn greeting of the East was, "Peace be to thee." The Church unites both forms of greeting—"grace," the beginning of every blessing; "peace," the end of all blessings; and into both she infuses a deeper meaning, that of a "joy" which defied all tribulations, and a "peace which passeth all understanding." **From God our Father and the Lord Jesus Christ.** God is the Source of "every good gift and every perfect gift." God is our Father as our Creator, and as the Father of our Lord Jesus Christ, in whom we become, in a higher sense, his children. Christ, in his mediatorial kingdom, is specially and immediately "our Lord," though that phrase, now so universal, only occurs (in its isolated form) in Heb. vii. 14. *Jesus Christ.* One of St. Paul's peculiarities of style is the constant reiteration of one dominant word. In the first nine verses of this Epistle, the Name "Jesus Christ" is repeated no less than nine times. "Observe," says St. Chrysostom, "how he *nails them down* to the Name of Christ, not mentioning any man, either apostle or teacher, but continually mentioning him for whom they yearn, as men preparing to awaken those who are drowsy after a debauch. For nowhere in any other Epistle is the Name of Christ so continually introduced. . . . By means of it he weaves together almost his whole exordium."

Vers. 4—9.—*The thanksgiving.* The thanksgiving is a feature in almost every Epistle of St. Paul, except the Epistle to the Galatians, in which he plunges at once into severe reprobation.

Ver. 4.—**I thank my God.** It is probable, from papyrus rolls in the British Museum, that the general form and outline of letters was more or less conventional. In St. Paul, however, this thanksgiving is the natural overflow of a full heart. It was no mere compliment or rhetorical artifice like the *captatio benevolentiæ*, or endeavouring to win the hearers by flattery, which we find in most ancient speeches. *My God* (Rom. i. 8).

Always; that is, constantly; on all occasions of special prayer. He could still thank God for them, though his letter was written "with many tears" (2 Cor. ii. 4). **For the grace of God.** The grace (χάρις) of spiritual life showing itself in many special spiritual gifts (χαρίσματα), such as "the gift of tongues." **Which was given you.** This is one of St. Paul's "baptismal aorists." He always regards and speaks of the life of the soul as summed up potentially in one supreme moment and crisis—namely, the moment of conversion and baptism. The grace given once was given for ever, and was continually manifested. **In Christ Jesus.** St. Paul regarded the life of the Christian as "hid with Christ in God," and of Christ as *being* the Christian's life (see Rom. vi. 23; 2 Cor. iv. 10, 11; Col. iii. 3, 4; 2 Tim. i. 1; 1 John v. 11, etc.).

Ver. 5.—**In everything**; *i.e.* of course, every gift which belongs specially to the Christian life. **In all utterance**; *i.e.* in all "eloquence" (λόγῳ), or perhaps "in all *doctrine*" (so Luther, Calvin, Meyer, etc.). The word for "utterance" is *rhema*; *logos* means "discourse" and "reason" (comp. 2 Cor. viii. 7). **Knowledge.** From the word *gnosis* is derived the name *Gnostic*, which was applied to so many forms of ancient heresy. There was danger to the Corinthian Christians in the exaggerated estimate of what they took for *gnosis*, and many of them were tempted to pride themselves on purely intellectual attainments, which were valueless for the spiritual life. St. Clement of Rome also, in writing to them ('Ep. ad Cor. i.') speaks of their "mature and established knowledge."

Ver. 6.—**Even as**; *i.e.* "inasmuch as." **The testimony of Christ.** The testimony borne to Christ by the apostle. The genitive is thus objective (*about* Christ), not subjective ("the testimony borne by Christ"). In reality, however, the meaning would be the same in either case, for if the apostles testified concerning Christ, so, too, Christ spoke in the apostles. **Was confirmed in you.** This does not merely mean "that the truth of Christianity was established among them," but that they were living confirmations of the apostolic testimony.

Ver. 7.—**So that ye come behind in no gift.** The "gifts" are here the *charismata*, graces, such as powers of healing, etc., which were the result of the outpouring of the Spirit. The sequel shows that they were rather outward than inward; they were splendid endowments rather than spiritual fruits. Yet even these were not wholly wanting, as we see from 2 Cor. viii. 7. The Greek may also mean "*causing you* not to be *conscious of* inferiority." **Waiting**; expecting, not fearing it. This was the constant attitude of the early Christians (Rom. viii. 19—25; Phil. iii. 20; Heb. ix. 20; 1 Thess. i. 10; Col. iii. 4; Titus ii. 13). Love for Christ's manifestation was a Christian characteristic (2 Tim. iv. 8). **The revelation.** Three words are used to express the second advent: *apokalypsis* (as here and in 2 Thess. i. 7; 1 Pet. i. 7, 13); *parousia* (as in Matt. xxiv. 3, 27, etc.; 1 Thess. ii. 19; Jas. v. 7, 8, etc.); and *epiphaneia*, in the pastoral Epistles (1 Tim. vi. 14; 2 Tim. i. 10; iv. 1—8; Titus ii. 13). St. Paul, however, only uses *parousia* six times in 1 and 2 Thessalonians, and once in 1 Cor. xv. 23. All Christians alike expected the return of Christ very soon, and possibly in their own lifetime (1 Thess. i. 9, 10, etc.; ch. xv. 51; Jas. v. 8, 9; 1 Pet. iv. 7; 1 John ii. 18; Rev. xxii. 20, etc.). Their expectation was founded on the great eschatological discourse of our Lord (Matt. xxiv. 29, 30, 34), and on his express promise that that generation should not pass away before his predictions were fulfilled. They *were* fulfilled in the fall of Jerusalem and the close of the old dispensation, though they await a still more universal fulfilment.

Ver. 8.—*Who;* clearly Christ, though his Name is again repeated in the next clause. **Shall also confirm you.** This natural expression of the apostle's yearning hope for them must not be overpressed into any such doctrine as "the indefectibility of grace." All honest and earnest students must resist the tendency to strain the meaning of Scripture texts into endless logical inferences which were never intended to be deduced from them. **Unto the end;** namely, to the end of "this age," and to the coming of Christ (Matt. xxviii. 20; Heb. iii. 6, 13; vi. 11). That ye be **unreprovable;** rather, *unimpeached* (*anenkletous*), as in Col. i. 22; 1 Tim. iii. 18; Titus i. 6. It is not the word rendered "blameless" (*amemptos*) in Phil. ii. 15 or in 2 Pet. iii. 14. A Christian can only be "blameless," not as being sinless, but as having been forgiven, renewed, sanctified (ch. vi. 11; Rom. viii. 30). **In the day of our Lord Jesus Christ.** This is the same as the *apokalypsis* or *parousia*. It is sometimes called simply "the day" (comp. ch. iii. 13; Acts i. 20; Joel iii. 4; 2 Thess. i. 10; Rev. vi. 17).

Ver. 9.—**God is faithful.** He will not leave his promises unfulfilled or his work unfinished (ch. x. 13; 2 Thess. iii. 3; Heb. x. 23; Rom. viii. 28—30). **Through whom.** By whom, as the moving cause and agent in your salvation. **Ye were called.** The calling was a pledge of the final blessing (Rom. viii. 30). **Into the fellowship of his Son.** Union (*koinonia*, communion) with Christ is the sole means of spiritual life (John xv. 4; Gal. ii. 20). Through the Son we also have fellowship with the Father (1 John i. 3). The perfect

sincerity of the apostle is observable in this thanksgiving. He speaks of the Church in general in terms of gratitude and hopefulness, and dwells on its rich spiritual endowments; but he has not a word of praise for any moral advance such as that which he so lovingly recognized in the Thessalonians and Philippians.

Vers. 10—17.—*Party spirit at Corinth.* This subject is pursued in various forms to ch. iv. 21.

Ver. 10.—**Now.** The particle implies the transition from thanksgiving to reproof. **Brethren.** This very title involves an appeal to them to aim at unity among themselves; and St. Paul, like St. James (v. 10), uses it to soften any austerity which might seem to exist in his language (ch. vii. 29; x. 1; xiv. 20, etc.). **Through the Name of our Lord Jesus Christ;** that is, by the whole idea of Christ's being and office—the strongest bond of union between true Christians (see the powerful appeal in Eph. iv. 1—6). **That ye all speak the same thing;** that is, "that ye may all with one mind and one mouth glorify God" (Rom. xv. 6). They were doing the very reverse—each glorifying himself and his party (ver. 12). **Divisions** (*σχίσματα*); "schisms" used of bodies within the Church, not of separatists from it (ch. xi. 18). The word is only used in this special sense in this Epistle. In Matt. ix. 16 and Mark ii. 21 *schisma* means "a rent;" in John (vii. 43; ix. 16; x. 16), "a division of opinion." There would be little or no harm in the *schismata* so far as they affected unessential points, if it was not their fatal tendency to end in "contentions" (*erides*) and "factions" (*haireseis*, ch. xi. 19). Corinth was a place where such divisions would be likely to spring up, partly from the disputatious vivacity and intellectual conceits of the inhabitants, partly from the multitudes of strangers who constantly visited the port, partly from the numerous diversities of previous training through which the various sections of converts had passed. **Perfected together;** literally, *repaired, reunited.* **In the same mind and in the same judgment;** that is, in what they think and believe (*voi*), and in what they assert and do (*γνώμη*). The exhortation, "be of one mind," in every sense of the word, was as necessary in the ancient as in the modern Church (Rom. xv. 5; 2 Cor. xiii. 11; Phil. i. 27; ii. 2; 1 Pet. iii. 8).

Ver. 11.—**It hath been signified unto me.** He had heard these saddening rumours towards the close of his stay in Ephesus. **By them** which are of the household **of Chloe.** The Greek only has "by them of Chloe." St. Paul wisely and kindly mentions his *authority* for these reports. Nothing is known of Chloe or her household. It has been conjectured that Stephanas, Fortunatus, and Achaicus, Corinthians who were now with St. Paul at Ephesus (ch. xvi. 16), may have been Chloe's slaves or freedmen. **Contentions.** These are the works of the flesh (2 Cor. xii. 20; Gal. v. 20; 1 Tim. vi. 4). The condition of the Church was the same when St. Clement of Rome wrote to them. He had still to complain of the "strange and alien and, for the elect of God, detestable and unholy spirit of faction which a few rash and self-willed persons kindled to such a pitch of dementation" ('Ep. ad Cor. i.').

Ver. 12.—**Now this I mean**; in other words, "what I mean is this." Their "contentions" are defined to be equivalent to "religious partisanships; " antagonistic adoption of the names and views of special teachers. **Each one of you saith.** That party spirit ran so high that they were all listed on one side or another. None of them were wise enough and spiritual-minded enough to hold aloof from parties altogether. They prided themselves on being "uncompromising" and "party men." *Saith;* in a self-assertive way (ch. iii. 21). **I am of Paul.** He shows his indignation at their partisanship by first rebuking those who had used *his own name* as a party watchword. He disliked Paulinism as much as Petrinism (Bengel). All the Corinthians would probably have been in this sense Paulinists but for the visits of subsequent teachers. At present the Paul party consisted of those who adhered to his views about Gentile freedom, and who liked the simple spirituality of his teaching. St. Paul rose above the temptation of considering that party spirit is excusable in our own partisans. He reproves factiousness even in the party of freedom. **And I of Apollos.** Apollos personally was absolutely loyal and honourable, but his visit to Corinth had done mischief. His impassioned oratory, his Alexandrian refinements, his allegorizing exegesis, the culture and polish of his style, had charmed the fickle Corinthians. The Apollonians were the party of culture. They had, as we see from later parts of the Epistle, exaggerated St. Paul's views, as expounded by Apollos, into extravagance. Puffed up with the conceit of knowledge, they had fallen into moral inconsistency. The egotism of oratorical rivals, the contemptuous tone towards weaker brethren, the sophistical condonations of vice, were probably due to them. Apollos, as we see by his noble refusal to visit Corinth under present circumstances (ch. xvi. 12), was as indignant as St. Paul himself at the perversion of his name into an engine of party warfare. (On Apollos, see Acts xviii. 24—28; xix. 1; Titus iii. 13.) Nothing further is known respecting him, but he is the almost undoubted author of the Epistle to the

Hebrews, which proves that he was of the school of St. Paul, while at the same time he showed a splendid originality in his way of arriving at the same conclusion as his teacher. **I of Cephas.** The use of the Aramaic name (ch. iii. 22; ix. 5; xv. 6; Gal. ii. 9), perhaps, shows that these Petrinists were Judaizers (though it should be added that St. Paul only uses the name "Peter" in Gal. ii. 7, 8). They personally disliked St. Paul, and questioned his apostolical authority. Perhaps the extravagances of the "speaking with tongues" arose in this party, who recalled the effects of the outpouring of the Spirit after Peter's great sermon on the day of Pentecost. **And I of Christ.** We trace the origin of this party to one man in particular (2 Cor. ii. 7), who was, or professed to be, an adherent of James, and therefore one of the more rigid Judaizers. He may have been one from the circle of Christ's earthly relatives—one of the Desposyni (see ch. ix. 5), and, like St. James, may have had views resembling those of the Essenes and Ebionites. If so, he was probably the author of the questions about celibacy and marriage; and perhaps he prided himself on having seen "Christ in the flesh." This party at any rate, like some modern sects, was not ashamed to degrade into a party watchword even the sacred name of Christ, and to claim for a miserable clique an exclusive interest in the Lord of the whole Church. It is the privilege of every Christian to say, " Christianus sum; " but if he says it in a haughty, loveless, and exclusive spirit, he forfeits his own claim to the title. This exclusive Christ party is, perhaps, specially alluded to in 2 Cor. x. 7—11. The view of Chrysostom, which takes these words to be St. Paul's remark—"But I belong to Christ," is untenable, and would make him guilty of the very self-assertiveness which he is reprobating.

Ver. 13.—**Is Christ divided?** Has Christ been parcelled into fragments? "Is there a Pauline, a Petrine, an Apollonian, a Christian Christ?" Whether you call yourselves Liberals, or Intellectualists, or Catholics, or Bible Christians, your party spirit is a sin, and all the worse a sin because it pranks itself out in the guise of pure religious zeal. This is more forcible than to take the clause affirmatively: " Christ has been parcelled into fragments." In either case we see "the tragic result of party spirit." **Was Paul crucified for you?** Again he rebukes the partisanship which attached itself to his own name. This showed a splendid courage and honesty. The introduction of the question by the negative μὴ expresses astonished indignation: " Can you possibly make a watchword of the name of a mere man, as though *he* had been crucified for you?" This outburst of feeling is very important, as proving the immeasurable distance which, in Paul's own view, separated him from his Lord. It is also instructive to see how St. Paul at once denounces the *spirit* of party without deigning to enter into the question as to *which* party of these wrangling "theologians" was most or least in the right. He did not choose to pander to their sectarian spirit by deciding between their various forms of aggressive orthodoxy. **Into the name** (comp. Matt. xxviii. 19).

Ver. 14.—**I thank God that I baptized none of you.** St. Paul, in his characteristic manner, "goes off at the word" *baptize*. He thanked God, not by way of any disparagement to baptism, but because he had thus given no excuse to the undue exaltation of his own name. Compare the practice of our Lord himself, in leaving his disciples to baptize (John iv. 2). The apostles would not have approved the system of wholesale baptisms of the heathen which has prevailed in some Romanist missions. **Save Crispus.** The ruler of the synagogue (Acts xviii. 8). Doubtless there were some strong special reasons why, in these instances, St. Paul departed from his general rule of not personally baptizing his converts. **And Gaius.** Gaius of Corinth (Rom. xvi. 23). It was one of the commonest of names. There was another Gaius of Derbe (Acts xx. 4), and another known to St. John (3 John 1).

Ver. 15.—**I had baptized.** The better reading, followed by the Revised Version, is, *Ye were baptized unto my name;* א, A, B, C.

Ver. 16.—**And I baptized also.** This he recalls by an afterthought, being, perhaps, reminded of it by Stephanas himself. **The household of Stephanas.** Stephanas and his house were the first converts in Achaia (ch. xvi. 5). When converts became more numerous, St. Paul ceased to baptize them personally (comp. Acts x. 48). **I know not.** The inspiration of the apostles involved none of the mechanical infallibility ascribed to them by popular dogma. He forgot whether he had baptized any one else or not, but this made no difference as regards his main argument.

Ver. 17.—**Sent me not to baptize, but;** that is, according to Semitic idiom, "not so much to baptize, as" (Matt. xxviii. 19). The word "sent" (*apesteilen*) involves the meaning "made me an apostle" (*apostolos*). The primary function of the apostles was "to bear witness" (Mark xvi. 15; Acts i. 8, etc.). **To preach the gospel.** St. Paul again "goes off" at this word, and dwells for eight verses on the character of his preaching. **Not in wisdom of words;** not, that is, in a philosophic and oratorical style. The simplicity of the style and teaching of the

apostles awoke the sneers of philosophers like Celsus and Porphyry. **The cross of Christ.** The central doctrine of Christianity, the preaching of a crucified Redeemer. **Should be made void.** The rendering of the Authorized Version is too strong; the cross cannot "be made of none effect." The word means "should be emptied" (comp. ch. ix. 15; 2 Cor. ix. 3; Phil. ii. 7; Rom. iv. 14); made void of its special and independent power. The words, "the cross of Christ," form the emphatic end of the sentence in the Greek.

Vers. 18—25.—*The nature of true Christian preaching.*

Ver. 18.—**For the preaching of the cross;** rather, *the word of the cross.* **To them that are perishing;** rather, *to the perishing;* to all those who are now walking in the paths that lead to destruction (2 Cor. ii. 15). To them it was foolishness, because it requires spiritual discernment (ch. ii. 14); and, on the other hand, human wisdom is foolishness with God (ch. iii. 19). **Foolishness.** It shows the heroic character of the faith of St. Paul that he deliberately preached the doctrine of the cross because he felt that therein lay the conversion and salvation of the world, although he was well aware that he could preach no truth so certain at first to revolt the unregenerate hearts of his hearers. To the Jews "the cross" was the tree of shame and horror; and a crucified person was "accursed of God" (Deut. xxi. 23; Gal. iii. 13). To the Greeks the cross was the gibbet of a slave's infamy and a murderer's punishment. There was not a single association connected with it except those of shame and agony. The thought of "a crucified Messiah" seemed to the Jews a revolting folly; the worship of a crucified malefactor seemed to the Greeks "an execrable superstition" (Tacitus, 'Ann.,' xv. 44; Pliny, 'Epp.' x. 97); yet so little did St. Paul seek for popularity or immediate success, that this was the very doctrine which he put in the forefront, even at a city so refined and so voluptuous as Corinth. And the result proved his inspired wisdom. That very cross became the recognized badge of Christianity, and when three centuries had elapsed it was woven in gold upon the banners and set in jewels on the diadems of the Roman empire. For had not Christ prophesied, "And I, *if I be lifted up,* will draw all men unto me"? **Unto us which are being saved;** who are on the way of salvation. The same present participle is used in Luke xiii. 23; Acts ii. 47; 2 Cor. ii. 15; Rev. xxi. 24. **It is the power of God.** Because the cross is at the heart of that gospel which is "the power of God unto salvation to every one that believeth" (Rom. i. 16; viii. 3), though many were tempted to be ashamed of it. It could never be a carnal weapon of warfare, and yet was mighty for every purpose (2 Cor. x. 4, 5).

Ver. 19.—**It is written.** This formula (ch. i. 31 ; ii. 9 ; iii. 19 ; ix. 9 ; x. 7 ; xv. 45 ; 2 Cor. viii. 15) is chiefly used in letters to Churches in which there were many Jews. This is a free citation from the LXX. of Isa. xxix. 14 (the same thought is found in Job v. 12, 13 ; see too Matt. xi. 25). The original ·passage refers to penal judgments from the Assyrians, which would test the false prophets of Israel.

Ver. 20.—**Where is the wise?** etc. (Isa. xxxiii. 18); rather, *Where is a wise man?* i.e. a scribe, etc., which is even more incisive. These questions are triumphant, like the "Where is the King of Hamath and of Arpad ? " The same impassioned form of speech recurs in ch. xv. 55 and in Rom. iii. 27. The questions would come home to the Jews, who regarded their rabbis and the "pupils of the wise" as exalted beings who could look down on all poor ignorant persons (*amharatsim*, or "people of the land"); and to the Greeks, who regarded none but the philosophers as "wise." **The scribe.** With the Jews of that day "the scribe" was "the theologian," the ideal of dignified learning and orthodoxy, though for the most part he mistook elaborate ignorance for profound knowledge. **The disputer.** The word would specially suit the disputatious Greeks, clever dialecticians. The verb from which this word is derived occurs in Mark viii. 11, and the abstract substantive ("an eager discussion ") in Acts xxviii. 29. If St. Paul has Isa. xxxiii. 18 in his mind, the word "disputer" corresponds to "the counter of the towers" (comp. Ps. xlviii. 12). Even the rabbis say that when Messiah comes human wisdom is to become needless. **Of the world**; rather, *of this age*, or æon. The old dispensation, then so rapidly waning to its close, was called " this age " (*olam hazzeh*); the next or Messianic age was called "the age to come" (*olam habba*). The Messianic age had dawned at the birth of Christ, but the old covenant was not finally annulled till his second coming at the fall of Jerusalem. **Hath not God made foolish the wisdom of the world?** rather, *Did not God* (by the cross) *stultify the wisdom*, etc. ? The oxymoron, or sharp contrast of terms—a figure of which St. Paul is fond (see 1 Tim. v. 6; Rom. i. 20, etc.; and my 'Life of St. Paul,' i. 628)—is here clearly marked in the Greek. The thought was as familiar to the old prophets (Isa. xliv. 25) as to St. Paul (Rom. i. 22); and even Horace saw that heathen philosophy was sometimes no better than *insaniens sapientia* (Horace, 'Od.,' i. 34, 2).

Ver. 21.—**In the wisdom of God; that**

is, as a part of his Divine economy. **The world through its wisdom knew not God.** These words might be written as an epitaph on the tomb of ancient philosophy, and of modern philosophy and science so far as it assumes an anti-Christian form (Luke x. 21). Human wisdom, when it relies solely on itself, may "feel after God," but hardly find him (Acts xvii. 26, 27). **Through the foolishness of the preaching.** This is a mistranslation. It would require *keruxeos*, not *kerugmatos*. It should be *by the foolishness* (as men esteemed it) *of the thing preached*.

Ver. 22.—**Jews ask for signs**; rather, *Jews demand signs.* This had been their incessant demand during our Lord's ministry; nor would they be content with any sign short of a sign from heaven (Matt. xii. 38; xvi. 1; John ii. 18; iv. 48, etc.). This had been steadily refused them by Christ, who wished them rather to see spiritual signs (Luke xvii. 20, 21). **Greeks seek after wisdom.** St. Paul at Athens had found himself surrounded with Stoics and Epicureans, and the same new thing which every one was looking for mainly took the shape of philosophic novelties (Acts xvii. 21).

Ver. 23.—**Christ crucified**; rather perhaps, *a crucified Messiah.* It was only by slow degrees that the title "the Christ," *i.e.* the Anointed, the Messiah, passed into the name Christ. **A stumbling-block.** They had for centuries been looking for a regal and victorious Messiah, who should exalt their special privileges. The notion of a suffering and humiliated Messiah, which reduced them to the level of all God's other children, was to them "a stone of stumbling and a rock of offence" (Rom. ix. 33; comp. Isa. viii. 14). These two verses, translated into Syriac, furnish a marked play on words (*miscol*, stumbling-block; *mashcal*, folly; *secel*, cross); and some have seen in this a sign that St. Paul *thought* in Syriac. **Unto the Greeks**; rather, *unto Gentiles*; א, A, B, C, D. **Unto the Jews . . . unto the Greeks.** Both alike had failed. The Jew had not attained ease of conscience or moral perfectness; the Greek had not unriddled the secret of philosophy; yet both alike rejected the peace and the enlightenment which they had professed to seek. **Foolishness.** The accent of profound contempt is discernible in all the early allusions of Greeks and Romans to Christianity. The only epithets which they could find for it were "execrable," "malefic," "depraved," "damnable" (Tacitus, Suetonius, Pliny, etc.). The milder term is "excessive superstition." The heroic constancy of martyrs appeared even to M. Aurelius only under the aspect of a "bare obstinacy." The word used to express the scorn of the Athenian philosophers for St. Paul's "strange doctrine" is one of the coarsest disdain (ἐχλεύαζον), and they called him "a seed-pecker" (Acts xvii. 18, 32), *i.e.* a mere picker-up of "learning's crumbs."

Ver. 24.—**Unto them that are called** (see Rom. viii. 28); literally, *to the called themselves.* **Both Jews and Greeks.** Henceforth the middle wall of partition between them is thrown down, and there is no difference (Rom. ix. 24). **Christ the power of God, and the wisdom of God.** These words are a summary of the gospel. St. Paul is the best commentator on himself. He speaks elsewhere of "the exceeding greatness of God's *power* to usward who believe, ... which he wrought in Christ" (Eph. i. 17—20), and of "all the treasures of *wisdom* and knowledge" as being "hid in Christ" (Col. ii. 3). And the world, once so scornful, has learnt that Christ is indeed the *Power* of God. When Rudolph of Hapsburgh was being crowned, and in the hurry no sceptre could be found, he seized a crucifix, and swore that that should be his only sceptre. When St. Thomas of Aquinum asked St. Bonaventura what was the source of his immense learning, he pointed in silence to his crucifix.

Ver. 25.—**The foolishness of God . . . the weakness of God;** the method, that is, whereby God works, and which men take to be foolish and weak, because with arrogant presumption they look upon themselves as the measure of all things. But God achieves the mightiest ends by the humblest means, and the gospel of Christ allied itself from the first, not with the world's strength and splendour, but with all which the world despised as mean and feeble—with fishermen and tax-gatherers, with slaves, and women, and artizans. The lesson was specially needful to the Corinthians, whom Cicero describes ('De Leg. Age,' ii. 32) as "famous, not only for their luxuriousness, but also for their wealth and philosophic culture."

Vers. 26—31.—*The method of God in the spread of the gospel.*

Ver. 26.—**For behold;** or, *consider* (imperative, as in ch. x. 18; Phil. iii. 2). **Your calling;** the nature and method of your heavenly calling; the "principle God has followed in calling you" (Beza); see Eph. iv. 1; Heb. iii. 1. **Not many wise after the flesh.** Those who hear the calling are alone the truly wise; but they are not wise with a carnal wisdom, not wise as men count wisdom; they have but little of the wisdom of the serpent and the wisdom of "this age." The Sanhedrin looked down on the apostles as "unlearned and ignorant men" (Acts iv. 13). "God," says St. Augustine, "caught orators by fishermen, not fishermen by orators." **Not many mighty;** *i.e.* not many persons of power and influence. Almost the first avowed Gentile Christian of the highest

rank was the consul Flavius Clemens, uncle of the Emperor Domitian. This was the more marked because *the Jews* won many rich and noble proselytes, such as the Queen Helena and the royal family of Adiabene, Poppæa the wife of Nero, and others. The only illustrious converts mentioned in the New Testament are Joseph of Arimathæa, Nicodemus, Sergius Paulus, and Dionysius the Areopagite. **Not many noble.** All this was a frequent taunt against Christians, but they made it their boast. Christianity came to redeem and elevate, not the few, but the many, and the many must ever be the weak and the humble. Hence Christ called fishermen as his apostles, and was known as "the Friend of publicans and sinners." None of the rulers believed on him (John vii. 48). It must, however, be borne in mind that these words apply mainly and primarily to the first age of Christianity. It was essential that its victory should be due to Divine weapons only, and that it should shake the world "by the irresistible might of weakness." After a time, the wisest and the noblest and the most powerful were called. Kings became the nursing fathers of the gospel, and queens its nursing mothers. Yet the ideal truth remains, and human power shows utter weakness, and human wisdom is capable of sinking into the depths of folly.

Ver. 27.—**God chose;** not, *hath chosen out.* We may remark, once for all, that there was no reason why the translators of 1611 should thus have turned the Greek aorists of the New Testament into perfects. In this and in many instances the change of tense is unimportant, but sometimes it materially and injuriously affects the sense. **The foolish things . . . the weak things.** So, too, the psalmist, "Out of the mouths of babes and sucklings hast thou ordained strength" (Ps. viii. 2); and St. James, "Hath not God chosen the poor of this world rich in faith?" (Jas. ii. 5).

Ver. 28.—**And the base things;** literally, *low-born, unborn;* "those who are sprung from no one in particular"—*nullo patre, nullis majoribus.* Nothing could be more ignoble in the eyes of the world than a cross of wood upheld by feeble hands, and yet before it "kings and their armies did flee and were discomfited, and they of the household divided the spoil." **And the things that are not.** The *not* is the Greek subjective negative (μὴ); things of which men conceived as not existing—"nonentities." It is like the expression of Clement of Rome, "Things *accounted as* nothing." Christianity was "the little stone, cut without hands," which God called into existence. We find the same thought in St. John the Baptist's sermon (Matt. iii. 9).

Ver. 29.—**That no flesh should glory.** For the weak instruments of God's triumphs are so weak that it was impossible for them to ascribe any power or merit to themselves. In contemplating the victory of the cross, the world could only exclaim, "This hath *God* wrought." "It is the Lord's doing, and it is marvellous in our eyes."

Ver. 30.—**But of him are ye in Christ Jesus.** *Ye* do not belong to the wise and noble. Your strength will consist in acknowledged weakness; for it is solely derived from your fellowship with God by your unity with Christ. **Who was made unto us,** etc. These words rather mean, "Who was made unto us wisdom from God—both righteousness and sanctification and redemption." The text is a singularly full statement of the whole result of the work of Christ, as the source of "all spiritual blessings in things heavenly" (Eph. i. 3), in whom we are complete (Col. ii. 10). **Righteousness** (see 2 Cor. v. 21). "Jehovah-tsidkenu—the Lord our Righteousness" (Jer. xxiii. 5). This is the theme of Rom. iii.—vii. **Sanctification** (see especially ch. vi. 11 and Eph. v. 25, 26). **Redemption.** One of the four main metaphors by which the atonement is described is this of ransom (λύτρον, ἀπολύτρωσις). The meaning and nature of the act, *as regards God,* lie in regions above our comprehension; so that all speculations as to the person to whom the ransom was paid, and the reason why it was indispensable, have only led to centuries of mistaken theology. But the meaning and nature of it, *as regards man,* is our deliverance from bondage, and the payment of the debt which we had incurred (Titus ii. 14; 1 Pet. i. 18; Matt. xx. 28; Rom. viii. 21—23). In all these cases, as Stanley well observes, the words have a double meaning—both of an inward act and of an outward result.

Ver. 31.—**As it is written.** A compressed quotation from the Septuagint Version of Jer. ix. 23, 24; 1 Sam. ii. 10. **Let him glory in the Lord.** The word rendered "glory" is more literally, *boast.* The reference is to Jer. ix. 23, 24; 1 Sam. ii. 10 (LXX.). The prevalence of "boasting" among the Corinthians and their teachers drove St. Paul to dwell much on this word—from which he so greatly shrinks—in 2 Cor. x.—xii. (where the word occurs twenty times), and to insist that the only true object in which a Christian can glory is the cross (Gal. vi. 14), not in himself, or in the world, or in men.

HOMILETICS.

Vers. 1—3.— *To feel, to be, and to desire.* "Paul, called to be an apostle," etc. This salutation of Paul suggests (1) *what all ministers should feel;* (2) *what all Christians should be;* and (3) *what all men should desire.*

I. WHAT ALL MINISTERS SHOULD FEEL. They should feel: 1. That they have a *call* to their mission. Paul did so. "Called to be an apostle of Jesus Christ through the will of God." No man will do his work effectively in any sphere unless he is assured in his own mind that he is called to it. The inner evidence of this call is *sympathy* with the work and *aptitude* for it. 2. That their call is *Divine.* Paul felt called "through the will of God." It is one thing to feel you have a call to a mission, and another thing to feel that call is Divine. The predominence of the sympathy and the pre-eminence of the aptitude will give this assurance. No man succeeds in any mission unless he feels called to it.

II. WHAT ALL MEN SHOULD BE. The description given of the persons addressed suggests what all men should be. What? 1. *Religiously social.* They should be identified with a religious community. "The Church of God which is at Corinth." All men should be in fellowship with the good, not isolated. 2. *Consecrated to Christ.* "Sanctified in Christ Jesus." Set apart to him, devoted to him, and thus "called to be saints." Called to live holy lives. "In every place call upon the Name of Jesus Christ our Lord." A reverent, conscious dependence on him everywhere. 3. *A catholic participation in Christ.* "Both theirs and ours." There are those who feel that Christ is their special property, they would monopolize him. An un-Christly feeling this. The feeling should be *our Christ.* "Our Father which art in heaven." There is no personal Christianity that is not catholic in spirit.

III. WHAT ALL MEN SHOULD DESIRE. "Grace be unto you, and peace, from God our Father, and from the Lord Jesus Christ." In this we have the highest philanthropy—a philanthropy that desires for man: 1. The highest *good.* "Grace and peace." If men have these they have all. 2. The highest good from the highest *Source.* "God the Father." Men need this good; Heaven only can bestow it.

Vers. 4—9.—*Exemplary gratitude and precious confidence.* "I thank my God always on your behalf," etc. Here we have two blessed states of mind—(1) *exemplary gratitude,* and (2) *precious confidence.*

I. EXEMPLARY GRATITUDE. "I thank my God always on your behalf." The gratitude here was: 1. *Unselfish.* "On your behalf." It is right and well to praise God for what he has done for us, but it is a higher and nobler thing to praise him for what he has done for others. No man rightly appreciates a blessing who does not desire others to participate in it. The sublimity of a landscape is more than doubly enjoyed when one or more stand by your side to share your admiration. 2. *For spiritual good.* "For the grace of God." (1) That grace which "enriched in all utterance and in all knowledge." Two splendid gifts these, where they are inspired by the "grace of God," and properly related. "Utterance," apart from "knowledge," is worthless and pernicious. Volubilities and garrulousness are social evils. "Knowledge" is of no value to others, unless it has effective "utterance." Knowledge, with a powerful natural oratory, will move the world; it has shivered dynasties, converted millions, and created Churches. (2) That grace which confirmed in their experience the testimony of Christ. Their spiritual experience confirmed the testimony. What higher gift than this—a personal realization of Christianity? (3) That grace which inspired them with a practical hope of the appearance of Christ. "Waiting for the coming of our Lord." 3. *An habitual state of mind.* "I thank my God always." It was not an occasional sentiment; it was a settled attitude of heart.

II. PRECIOUS CONFIDENCE. The apostle seems to have had confidence in three things in relation to Christ. 1. In his *perfecting character.* "Who shall also confirm you unto the end." So perfecting it that it shall be "blameless." All moral imperfections removed. 2. In his *appearing again.* "In the day of our Lord Jesus Christ." The day—when he will appear. This day is the day of days for humanity. 3. In his *granting them companionship.* "Unto the fellowship of his Son Jesus Christ our Lord." "Where I am there ye shall be also." Unshaken confidence in these things, how precious!

Vers. 10—13.—*The importance of spiritual unity.* "Now I beseech you, brethren, by the Name of our Lord," etc. Here the apostle comes to the grand object of writing this letter: it was to put an end to that party spirit that had riven the Church at Corinth into conflicting divisions. His remarks on this subject continue to ch. iv. 20. There are two things here which show the transcendent importance which he attached to *spiritual unity*—(1) *his solemn exhortation,* and (2) *his earnest expostulation.*

I. HIS SOLEMN EXHORTATION. "Now I beseech you, brethren, by the Name of our Lord Jesus Christ, that ye all speak the same thing," etc. What union does he seek? Not *ecclesiastical* union, conformity to the same system of worship. Not *theological* union, conformity to the same scheme of doctrine. Such unions cannot touch hearts, cannot weld souls. They are the union of the various parts of the machine, not the union of the branches of a tree. 1. The unity he seeks is that of *spiritual utterance.* "That ye all speak the same thing." Not the same thing in letter, but in life. Let the utterances be as varied as all the notes in the gamut, but let love, like the key-note, tune them into music. 2. The unity he seeks is that of *unity of soul.* "That ye be perfectly joined together in the same mind and in the same judgment." These include unity of the supreme sympathy and aim. Of such unity Christ alone is the Centre. Creeds divide; Christ unites. According to the laws of mind, all that love Christ supremely, though separated in person by distances immeasurable, are one in heart, one as planets are one, revolving round the same centre. This is the union that Paul sought; this is Divine socialism. No wonder that he was solemn in his entreaties. "In the Name of our Lord Jesus Christ" he asks it.

II. HIS EARNEST EXPOSTULATION. Divisions or schisms were rife and rampant in the Church at Corinth at this time. Some person of the name of Chloe, unknown to us, but evidently well known to Paul and his contemporaries of the Corinthian Church, brought these divisions under Paul's notice, told him of the contentions. We must, I suppose, assume that this Chloe was a good character, although, as a rule, the most unamiable persons are the most ready to parade the imperfections of others. Now, what were the divisions against which he protests? "Now this I say, that every one of you saith, I am of Paul; and I of Apollos; and I of Cephas; and I of Christ," etc. Their divisions consisted in rabid preferences for certain ministers. One party set up Paul as pre-eminent; another party set up Apollos as unapproached in excellence; others Cephas, or Peter; and others gave Christ the pre-eminence, and they were right. Now, to put down these divisions, these schisms, Paul expostulates with great vehemence. "Is Christ divided? Was Paul crucified for you? or were ye baptized in the name of Paul?" Party spirit has been the greatest curse to Christianity; it has filled Christendom with conflicting sects. Alas! that any professed minister of the gospel should defend the existence of separate sects and Churches. How often have I heard preachers on platforms compare the different denominations to regiments in the same army! Do regiments in an army fight one with another, and do they misinterpret the grand purpose of the campaign? However, so long as men have vested interests in sects, and live by denominations, I fear nothing but the crash of doom will destroy sectarianism.

Ver. 17.—*The world's greatest blessing and its greatest evil.* "Lest the cross of Christ should be made of none effect." Here we have—

I. The greatest BLESSING in the world. "The cross of Christ." By "the cross of Christ" the apostle did not mean, of course, the timber on which Christ was crucified, or any imitation of that in wood, brass, marble, gold, silver, or paint. He uses the word as a symbol, as we use the words "crown," "court," "bench," etc. He meant the eternal principles of which the cross of Christ was at once the effect, evidence, and expression —he meant, in one word, all that we mean by the gospel. And this, we say, is the greatest blessing in the world to-day. The human world lives under a system of mercy, and mercy pours on it every hour blessings innumerable. But no blessing has come to it, has ever been found in it, or will ever come to it, equal to the cross or the gospel. Look at it, for example, in only three of its many aspects, and you will be impressed with its incomparable worth. 1. As a *revealer.* The chief value of the material universe is, that it reveals the spiritual and the eternal; but the gospel reveals all that the material does of God and the universe with much greater fulness and effect. It presents the "image of the invisible God." All true theological doctrine and ethical science come to us through the cross. It is the moral light of the world. 2. As an *educator.* That in human life which is the most successful in quickening, evolving, and strengthening all the powers of the human mind is its chief blessing. The "cross of Christ" has done this a thousand times more effectively than any other agency. Art, government, science, poetry, philosophy, owe infinitely more to it than to any other agent in the world. The cross is to the human soul what the vernal sunbeam is to the seed; it penetrates, warms, quickens, and brings all its latent powers out to perfection. 3. As a *deliverer.* The cross is more than a revealer or an educator; it is a deliverer. The human soul is condemned, diseased, enthralled; everywhere it groans under the sentence of its own conscience. It languishes under a moral malady; it is fettered by lusts, prejudices, evil habits, and social influences; its deepest cry is, "O wretched man that I am, who shall deliver me?" The cross bears a pen to cancel the sentence, a balm to heal the wound, a weapon to break the fettering chain. Such, and infinitely more, is the cross. What would human life be without it? A voyage without a compass, chart, or star.

II. The greatest EVIL in the world. What is the evil? Making this cross of "none effect." That is "none effect" so far as its grand mission is concerned. Some effect it must have; it will deepen the damnation where it does not save. "We are unto God a sweet savour," etc. We offer three remarks concerning this tremendous evil. 1. It is *painfully manifest.* The fact is patent to all, that the cross has not to any great extent in Christendom produced its true effect. Though it has been in the world upwards of eighteen hundred years, not one-tenth of the human population know anything about it, and not one-hundredth of those who know something of it, experience its true effect. Intellectually, socially, politically, it has confessedly done wonders for mankind; but *morally,* how little! How little genuine holiness, disinterested philanthropy, self-sacrificing devotion to truth and God! How little Christliness of life! In all moral features, England is well-nigh as hideous as heathendom.[1] 2. It is *easily explained.* How is it done? The apostle in this verse indicates one way in which it could be done, that is, by "wisdom of words," by which we understand him to mean gorgeous rhetoric. What is called the Church has done it; that is, the assembly of men who profess to be its disciples, representatives, ministers, and promoters. The Church has done it: (1) By its *theologies.* In its name it has propounded dogmas that have clashed with reason and outraged conscience. (2) By its *polity.* It has sanctioned wars, promoted priestcraft, established hierarchies, which have fattened on the ignorance and poverty of the people. (3) By its *spirit.* The spirit of the Church, as a rule, is in direct antagonism to the spirit of the cross. The spirit of the cross is self-sacrificing love; the spirit of the conventional Church has been to a great extent that of selfishness, greed, ambition, and oppression. Malrepresentation of Christ by the Church is the instrument that has made the cross of "none effect." 3. It is *terribly criminal.* It is wonderful that man has the power thus to pervert Divine institutions and blessings; but such perverting power he has, and he uses it every day even in natural things. He forges metals into weapons for murder, he turns bread-corn into liquids to blight the reason and to damn the souls of men. Wonderful power this! and terrible is the crime in employing it for perverting the cross of Christ. A greater crime than this you cannot conceive of. Were you to turn all bread into poison, make the flowing rivers pestiferous, quench the light of the sun, mantle the stars in sack-cloth, you would not perpetrate a crime half so enormous as that of making the cross of Christ of "none effect."

CONCLUSION. Two questions. 1. What is the spiritual influence of the cross on us? Has it crucified unto us the world; destroyed in us the worldly spirit—the spirit of practical atheism, materialism, and selfishness? 2. What are we doing with the cross? Are we abusing it or rightly employing it?

Vers. 18, 19.—*Two classes of gospel hearers.* "For the preaching of the cross is to them that perish foolishness; but unto us which are saved it is the power of God. For it is written, I will destroy the wisdom of the wise, and will bring to nothing the understanding of the prudent." Instead of the "preaching of the cross," the New Version reads, the "word of the cross," and the word of the cross stands in contrast to the word of worldly wisdom. How great is the contrast! We have here two classes of gospel hearers.

I. The one is gradually PERISHING, the other is gradually BEING SAVED. The perishing and the saving are *gradual.* 1. There is a class in every congregation, perhaps, gradually *perishing.* They are gradually losing moral sensibility—contracting fresh guilt, etc. They are not damned at once. 2. There is a class in every congregation, perhaps, gradually *being saved.* Salvation is not an instantaneous thing, as some suppose.

II. To the one class the gospel is FOOLISHNESS, to the other the POWER OF GOD. 1. It is *"foolishness"* to them that are perishing, because it has no meaning, no reality. 2. It is a Divine *"power"* to them that are being saved. Enlightening, renovating, purifying, ennobling. The power of God stands in contrast with mere philosophy and cloquence.

Vers. 20, 21.—*Philosophy and the gospel.* "Where is the wise?" etc. The "wise" (σοφός) here refers specially to the sages of Greece. They were called at first "wise men," and afterwards assumed a more modest title, "lovers of wisdom," philosophers. The "scribe" refers to the learned among the Jews. The appeal of the text, therefore, is to the wisdom or the philosophy of the world, including that of the Greek or Jew. Here we have—

I. Philosophy CHALLENGED by the gospel. The apostle here challenges the wise men of the world to accomplish the end which the gospel had in view. That end was the impartation to men of the saving knowledge of God. Where, unaided, had it ever

---

[1] See 'Modern Christianity a Civilized Heathenism,' by the author of 'Fight at Dame Europa's School.'

succeeded in accomplishing this? Who amongst the wise will come forward to give one single instance?

II. Philosophy CONFOUNDED by the gospel. "Hath not God made foolish the wisdom of this world?" 1. By doing what philosophy could not do. "The world by wisdom knew not God." Though the pages of nature lay open to the eye, with God's signature on the whole, man failed to discover him. 2. By doing *by the simplest instrumentality* what philosophy could not do. The proclamation of the history of Jesus of Nazareth, and that by a few simple men regarded as the offscouring of all things, did the work. Hath not God in this way "made foolish the wisdom of the world"?

III. Philosophy SUPERSEDED by the gospel. "It pleased God by the foolishness of preaching to save them that believe." The preaching is not foolish in itself, only in the estimation of the would-be wise men. The great want of men is salvation—the restoration of the soul to the knowledge, the likeness, the fellowship of God. This want philosophy cannot supply; but the gospel does. It has done so, it is doing so, and it will continue to do so.

Vers. 22—25.—*Christianity viewed in three aspects.* "For the Jews require a sign," etc. Our subject is *Christianity*; and here we see it in three aspects.

I. As associated with a GREAT FACT. "Christ crucified." This fact may be looked at: 1. *Historically.* As an historical fact, it is the most famous, influential, and best authenticated in the annals of time. 2. *Theologically.* It unfolds the Divine, it rends the veil in the great temple of theological truth, and exposes the inmost and holiest sanctuary; it is a mighty expression of God's idea, government, and heart. 3. *Morally.* It is fraught with the most quickening, elevating, and sanctifying suggestions.

II. As associated with POPULAR OPINION. It was a "stumbling-block" to the Jew; it was "foolishness" to the Greek. It had not sufficient of the gorgeous *philosophical* ritualism for the speculative and pedantic Greek, nor sufficient of the gorgeous *religious* ritualism for the sensuous and bigoted Jew. What is it in popular sentiment now? To the millions it is nothing. They have formed no idea of it; they do not think about it. To the sceptic it is a *fable;* to the formalist it is a *creed* to be repeated, and a ceremony to be attended to on certain occasions, and nothing more.

III. As associated with CHRISTIAN CONSCIOUSNESS. "But unto them which are called, both Jews and Greeks, Christ, the power of God, and the wisdom of God." The Christian sees the highest wisdom in a system which, in saving the sinner, does four things. 1. Manifests the righteousness of the insulted Sovereign. 2. Augments the influence of moral government. 3. Maintains intact all the principles of moral freedom. 4. Develops, strengthens, and perfects all the original powers of the individual soul. He sees, too, the highest power in the difficulties it surmounts, the revolutions it effects, the deeds to which it stimulates, the hopes it inspires, and the deep fountains of pleasure which it opens up. He feels it is both wise and powerful. What is Christianity to us? As a fact, there it is in the archives of humanity, for ever independent of us; nothing will ever blot it out from the page of history. As a fact, though centuries old, it is more influential than ever. It will be a fact eternally. What is it to us? Is it folly and weakness; or is it wisdom and power? This is the question.

Vers. 26—29.—*God destroying the conventionally great by the conventionally contemptible.* "For ye see your calling, brethren," etc. These verses remind us of two facts.

I. EVIL EXISTS HERE UNDER CONVENTIONALLY RESPECTABLE FORMS. Evil is spoken of in these verses as the "wise" and the "mighty." In Corinth dangerous errors wore the costume of wisdom. Power was also on their side. Sages, poets, artists, statesmen, wealth, and influence stood by them, and they appeared "mighty." Men in England, as in Corinth, have robed evils in attractive costumes, and labelled them with brilliant names. Often, indeed, has religion itself been used as a means of covering vices, and of raising the vilest passions of the human heart into the spheres of worship. Everywhere evil assumes a respectable garb. 1. *Infidelity.* This great evil writes and speaks in the stately formularies of philosophy and science; borrows its sanctions from astronomy, chronology, criticism, and metaphysics. It is a "wise" thing of the world. 2. *Licentiousness.* This evil, which involves the utter neglect of all social obligations, and the unrestrained development of the base and vicious lusts of the soul, passes under the grand name of liberty. The vaunted religious liberty of England's population means often only power to neglect sacred ordinances, profane the holy sabbath, etc. 3. *Social injustice.* This is a demon which works in every sphere of life, leading the crafty to take advantage of the ignorant, the strong of the weak, the rich of the poor; and this does most of its fiendish work in the name of law. 4. *Selfishness.* This goes under the name of prudence. The man whose heart knows no throb of sympathy for another passes through life with the reputation of a prudent man. 5. *Bigotry.* This, which leads men to brand all who differ from them as heretics and doom them to perdition, wears the sacred name of religion. 6. *War.* This, which by the common consent of all Christian philosophers is the pandemonium where all evil passions of the human heart run riot in their most fiendish forms, is called glory. Thus here and now, as everywhere and ever, evil appears as the "wise" and the "mighty." That errors and evils should appear in respectable forms is one of the most unfavourable symptoms in all the history of man. Could we but take from sin the mantle of respectability that society has thrown over it, we should do much towards its annihilation.

II. GOD IS DETERMINED TO OVERTHROW EVIL BY CONVENTIONALLY CONTEMPTIBLE MEANS. "God hath chosen the foolish things of the world to confound the wise," etc. The "wise" and the "mighty" cannot protect evil. The agency to sweep evil away is here represented as "foolish," "weak," "base," "despised," and "things which are not." What does this language mean? 1. It does not mean that the *gospel* is an inferior thing. The gospel is no mean thing. It has proved itself the wisdom of God and the power of God. 2. It does not mean that the men appointed as its *ministers* are to be inferior. There are several things to show that the gospel ministry requires the highest order of mind. (1) The character of the *work.* What is the work? Not the mere narration of facts or the enunciation of the current opinions of men. No; it is teaching men in all wisdom. Teaching implies the impartation to others of what they are ignorant of, and that in such a way as will commend it to the common sense. (2) The character of the *system.* If a man is to teach the gospel, he must first learn it. What a system it is to learn! Simpletons call the gospel simple; but intelligence has ever found it of all subjects the most profound and difficult. The greatest thinkers of all ages have found the work no easy task. (3) The character of *society.* Who exerts the most influence upon the real life of the men and women around him? The man of thought and intelligence. If the gospel ministry is to influence men it must be employed by men of the highest type of culture and ability. (4) The *spirit* of the work. What is the moral spirit in which the gospel should be presented to men? Humble, charitable, forbearing, reverent. Such a spirit comes only from deep thought and extensive knowledge. (5) The character of the *apostles.* Where can you find greater force of soul than Paul had? more searching sagacity than James had? They were men of talent and thought. Away, then, with the thought that the words here afford any encouragement for an ignorant or feeble ministry. 3. What, then, do they mean? (1) That the *gospel was conventionally mean.* The Founder was a carpenter's Son. It was a "foolish" thing to the Greek, etc. (2) That the *first ministers were conventionally mean.* They were fishermen, clerks, tent-makers, etc. The system and its ministers, however, are merely *conventionally* contemptible, nothing more. These, like many other things that erring man regards as insignificant and mean, shall do a great work. From this subject we may infer : (1) *That, so long as evils exist in the world, great commotions are to be expected.* God has chosen this system to "confound and bring to nought" things that are. (2) *That the removal of evil from the world is, under God, to be effected through man as man.* The gospel is to make its way in the world, not by men invested with adventitious endowments, such as scientific attainments, etc., but by men as men endowed with the common powers of human nature, but these powers inspired and directed by the living gospel.

Vers. 30, 31.—*The union of the genuine disciple with his Master.* "But of him are ye in Christ Jesus, who of God is made unto us wisdom, and righteousness, and sanctification, and redemption : that, according as it is written, He that glorieth, let him glory in the Lord." Concerning this union—

I. It is MOST VITAL. "In Christ," not merely in his dispensation, in his school, in his character, but in himself, as the branches are in the vine. He is their life.

II. It is DIVINELY FORMED. "Of him are ye in Christ." Whom? Of God. It is the eternal Spirit that brings the soul into vital connection with Christ. "My Father is the Husbandman."

III. It is BLESSEDLY PRODUCTIVE. "Wisdom," "righteousness," "sanctification," and "redemption" come out of this union. What transcendent blessings are these!

IV. It is EXULTINGLY ADORING. "He that glorieth, let him glory in the Lord." It inspires the highest worship, it causes the soul to triumph in God himself.

HOMILIES BY VARIOUS AUTHORS.

Vers. 1—9.—*St. Paul and the apostleship.* First of all, HE ASSERTS THE DIVINE AUTHORITY OF HIS OFFICE, to which he was "called though the will of God." This profound sense of the *dignity* belonging to his vocation, as one sent of God, was a supreme principle of his nature; not an opinion, but a conviction, and a conviction too strong to be dislodged from its central seat in his mind by any assault of adverse circumstances. It must needs be subjected to manifold and severe *tests*, since in this way alone can a conviction be made available for the highest moral uses. Owing to his exceptional position, St. Paul underwent, in this respect, a series of peculiar trials which distinguish him from the other apostles, so that, while he shared with them the persecution incident to the apostolate in itself, he had an experience of its perplexities and sorrows, personal to himself, in the distinctive and supplementary attitude he was ordained to maintain. Like all men, he had fluctuant moods, the ebb and flow of emotion with its reflex influence on intellect and volition. His natural temperament was extremely sensitive, and it was aggravated by hardship and disease. The blood that warmed and the nerves that thrilled under the touch of outward agencies, had their counterpart in the sensibility of his spiritual life, and, accordingly, body and soul were in singularly close partnership in his nature, and acted and interacted very powerfully on each other. Yet, in spite of this liability to the moods of subjective sensations and internal impressions, the conviction of his call to be an apostle of the Lord Jesus, and to exercise his Divine endowments in a specific way, *stood altogether apart from the variations of ordinary thought and feeling,* and held its strength of consciousness unimpaired throughout his career. So strong and yet so beautiful; humility the ornament of its energetic vigour, so that while he starts with "Paul, called to be an apostle of Jesus Christ," he loses not a moment, but in the opening verse of the Epistle introduces "Sosthenes our brother." Not a trace of Sosthenes appears in the Epistle; the production is Pauline to the core; and yet St. Paul would associate with him "Sosthenes our brother." If St. Paul is about to rebuke intellectual pride and vanity, and condemn the evil partisanship that grows out of selfishness and disguises an inflated personality under the mask of homage to a great leader, what more fitting words can he utter on the threshold of his letter than "Sosthenes our brother," whose name was no battle-cry of faction? Naturally enough, this sense of unity in St. Paul's mind with all Christians finds immediate vent in addressing "the Church of God" at Corinth, "with all that in every place call upon the Name of Jesus Christ our Lord," adding with touching expressiveness, "both theirs and ours." A true sense of manhood is always known by its prompt and *hearty identification with the manhood of the race.* All growth and culture advance from the individual and the personal towards the universal, until at last—the providential work of development on earth accomplished—the narrow horizon that was quite sufficient for youth and early manhood, widens to the reach of the world. When we find this circumference, we find our real centre. Not otherwise can a man attain genuine individuality. For the light that blesses his eyes, for the air that feeds his lungs, for the food nourishing bodily strength, he is a debtor to the universe. And it is the aim of Christianity to call out and perfect the latent vigour of this instinct of race, and, but for its Divine office, the sentiment were impossible as a spiritual actuality. No wonder, then, that St. Paul announces to the mixed population of Corinth—to Romans, Greeks, Asiatics, in the Corinthian Church—the doctrine of grace for all, and emphasizes the gift as "both theirs and ours." The formative thought of the first chapter is thus intimated. To prepare for its enlargement, he reminds the Corinthians that it was as a Church and in their organic capacity they were "*saints;*" that, as members of Christ's body, they had been "enriched by him in all utterance, and in all knowledge;" and then proceeds to show that the faithfulness of God was pledged to their continued progress in this selfsame line of direction, viz. fellowship in Christ Jesus as the Son of God and Lord of humanity. Here, as everywhere in St. Paul's writings, the two ideas of the Divine and the human in Christ are assumed as the ground of our fellowship in him and with one another; brethren because disciples, one below because one above, the strength and purity and permanence of the tie between man and man in this fellowship being determined solely by our union in him. On no other basis could the word "fellowship" have taken its specialized place in the vocabulary of Christianity. The contents of the term outreach what we ordinarily mean by respect, confidence, intercourse, and like expressions, and signify a deep sense of equality, of the recognition of common rights and privileges, and of a sympathy that has its roots, not in the shallow soil of races and their latitude and longitude as geographical facts, but in One who was the Representative in a peculiar and exclusive manner of the human race. Fellowship is an acknowledgment of redemption. It is not union alone, but a vital unity, a communion of man with man, and as man by means of communion with God in Christ—a bond that exists between spirit and spirit through the common grace of the Holy Ghost, as the Executive of the Father and the Son in the heart of every believer. Who knew more of the intensity of race-blood, of its subtle force, of its open and virulent activity in all the practical questions of the age, of its perpetuated and unyielding traditions, of its frantic emergence on every occasion unless repressed by the arm of authority,—who understood this better than St. Paul, himself a notable example for years of its power to blind common sense and stupefy common instincts? And where was there a city of such miscellaneous activity of mind and such collisions of inherited beliefs and such ill-adjusted public life as this same Corinth—a huge reservoir for all the tributary streams of civilization that had washed down into its bosom whatever had survived of the degeneracy in Asia Minor, in Egypt, in Italy? Yet this St. Paul is the man to speak of fellowship, and this Corinth is the community to which he would address himself in behalf of the grace "both theirs and ours."—L.

Vers. 10—17.—*Divisions in the Church condemned.* The formative idea of the chapter is now brought into full view, viz. "There are contentions among you," and it is prefaced by the statement of a principle, to which St. Paul earnestly directs the attention of the Corinthians, viz. "that they be joined together in the same mind and in the same judgment," or "perfected together," the stress being laid, as before, on their corporate or organic character as a Church. These warring divisions were not matters merely or chiefly personal, but they involved the very heart and soul of the Christian community. No doubt their partisanship in the supposed interest of Paul, Apollos, and Peter, ay, of Christ himself, was very hurtful to them as individuals. But the point he urges is that their partisanship was a disjunction of their unity, and hence that this unity, which was designed to grow into perfection, was arrested by strife. And just here St. Paul strikes the great fact that men of the outside world judge of Christianity much more by the Church in its totality than by instances of individual character in the Church. History is full of exemplifications of this truth, from the times of Julian and Celsus to the age of Voltaire and Rousseau. Nor should this surprise us; for evidently there is a philosophy in it, however much the philosophy is abused by the wit and devices of men. Individuals are "members one of another," members of the body; but the body is the Church, and the organic life of the Church is the Divine witness to the glory of Christ made visible through the Church to the world. How quickly the apostle rises into fervid utterance, and how compact his words! "Is Christ divided? was Paul crucified for you? or were ye baptized in the name of Paul?" If his services to the Corinthian Church are to be perverted in this way, St. Paul can only thank God that he baptized but a few of them. At the moment, St. Paul hastens to assert his own high manhood by an utter refusal to be made an object of partisanship, and he does this in the only method possible to his argument, by confessing his obligations to Christ who had sent him "to preach the gospel."—L.

Vers. 18—31.—*How St. Paul regarded the preaching of the gospel.* By an easy movement he advances to the gospel, to the mode of preaching it as essential to its

Divine success, and thus reaches the climax of his reasoning in the first chapter. Other functions of his apostleship will come hereafter into view—the resolute disciplinarian, the firm administrator, the tender but unyielding executive of the Head of the Church. At present, however, one thing absorbs him, namely, the Divine institution of preaching. What is his foremost relation to these Corinthians? It is that of a preacher of Christ's gospel. And how had he preached it? "Not with wisdom of words"—not as a speculative thinker, not as a Greek rhetorician, not in the spirit of worldly eloquence—"lest the cross of Christ should be made of none effect." Two things are prominently set forth—the gospel and its manner of presentation; and Christ is in each of them, and in each of them alike, so that not only the substance of the gospel, but the mode of its exhibition, must conform to his sovereignty as the Head of the Church. All preaching of the gospel is not gospel preaching. Looking at the character in the light St. Paul viewed it, the preacher was an original creation of Christ, a new force ordained and anointed of him, and introduced by him for the proclamation of the gospel. It dated no further back than Pentecost; it was of universal adaptation; it was to command all languages, and speak to the simplest instincts, not of men, but of man as man; and this original creation, this new force, was to continue through all time, and never surrender its rights and prerogatives to any successor. And *the spirit and manner of fulfilling this grand office were thoroughly unworldly,* so much so, indeed, that, it would strike the Greek as "foolishness," and prove to the Jew "a stumbling-block." But in contrast with the Greek and his search after wisdom, and with the Jew in his love of national signs as the elect race of Jehovah, Christ was preached as "the power of God and the wisdom of God." The word "power" is not used except in connection with the preaching of "Christ crucified," and its value in the argument is assured by its specialty of application. All the aid of contrast and comparison is given to this one word. Power, God's power, is the designation of preaching Christ crucified. Over against it are put "not many wise men after the flesh, not many mighty, not many noble," and the array of dissimilarity is lengthened out by "foolish things," "weak things," "base things," and "things despised." But *what bearing has this condensed energy of a single idea and its rapid accumulation of phraseological forms on the partisanship of these Corinthians?* Has not the apostle wandered from the main idea of the chapter—the "contentions among you"? Nay, this very partisanship is the exact opposite of Paul, Peter, Apollos, in preaching the gospel, and they can never consent to this abuse of their position. Nay, further, it is in downright antagonism to "Christ crucified." There is no "power" in it, no "wisdom." It is the idolatry of the senses. It is the intellect of the senses repeating the folly of Greek and Jew in another but equally fatal shape. It is mere seeking to find themselves and their glory in man. Directly opposite to this, St. Paul argues, we preach "Christ crucified," so that "no flesh should glory in his presence." A great lesson it is in the true spirituality of Christianity as the only strength and safeguard of the Church. If Christ is "made unto us wisdom, and righteousness, and sanctification, and redemption;" if Christ become "the power of God" to our hearts in this fourfold form of the "riches of grace;" the root of all worldliness is destroyed, partisanship is at an end, because self-seeking is ended, and henceforth that Scripture has a very real import to us, "He that glorieth, let him glory in the Lord." A man may admire others for their own sakes, and this admiration may be very helpful. To admire others because our image is projected upon them can only augment our own weakness. Our praise in such cases is but the echo of our self-admiration, and echoes are dying sounds.—L.

Ver. 2.—"*Called to be saints.*" The term "saint" is, in common use, limited to certain classes of holy men. It is applied to the inspired evangelists and apostles; to the great doctors and martyrs of the early Church, especially to such as were "canonized;" and to the glorified in heaven. But the New Testament usage is more general. In the Acts and in the Epistles, Christians generally, otherwise designated "disciples" and "brethren," are also called "saints." In all except two of St. Paul's Epistles, the Christians to whom he writes are thus designated in the opening salutations. The appellation is one very significant and very instructive.

I. THIS DESIGNATION REMINDS CHRISTIANS OF WHAT THEY EITHER ONCE WERE OR

WOULD HAVE ,BEEN BUT FOR THE GRACE OF GOD. Properly and literally, a saint is one separated and consecrated, made holy by being called out of a sinful society and set apart and dedicated to God. In the case of most of those first thus addressed, it was literally the case that they had been "plucked as brands from the burning." Inhabitants of one of the most luxurious, voluptuous, and debased cities of the ancient world, these members of the Corinthian Church had been rescued and saved by the gospel of God's grace. If the case seems different with hearers of Divine truth in our own land and in our own day, still it must be borne in mind that Christianity alone has brought about such a result that God alone has made us differ.

II. THIS DESIGNATION REMINDS CHRISTIANS OF WHAT THEY ARE. 1. They are the creation, the "new creation" of God's Holy Spirit. His cleansing and regenerating power, symbolized in the purifying waters of baptism, has effected this great change. 2. They are accordingly consecrated unto God. In the Corinthian temple of Aphrodite, a thousand priestesses were "consecrated" as prostitutes, to the impure worship of the goddess of lust. In the Christian Church all members are devoted to the holy service of a holy God. 3. They are sanctified in character. Negatively, Christians are represented by this language as being freed from the bondage and service of sin. Positively, they are arrayed in the white garments of spiritual purity. Outward, ceremonial purity is insufficient; for Christ looks for and values the purity of the heart. 4. They are associated with a holy fellowship. The Church is a holy body, and an unholy member would be out of sympathy with the body to which it professedly belongs. Holiness is a "note" of the spiritual brotherhood.

III. THIS DESIGNATION REMINDS CHRISTIANS OF WHAT THEY WILL BE. They are inheritors of a holy kingdom. They look forward to immortal citizenship in that city into which entereth nothing that defileth, where holiness reigns perfectly and for ever, whose occupations of service and of praise are suited to holy beings and to a holy place. A prospect such as this is inspiring as well as delightful. The future casts its influence upon the present. "He that hath this hope in him purifieth himself, even as Christ is pure."—T.

Ver. 5.—*Enrichment in Christ.* Paul's view of the dignity of the Christian calling, of the privileges and honours of the Christian life, was both just and instructive, and may well assist us in our endeavour to live clear of and above the false and worldly standard with which we often meet. How could the grandeur and sacredness of our religious position be more effectively set before us than by this inspiriting language addressed by the apostle to the members of the Christian community at Corinth: "In everything ye were enriched in Christ"?

I. A PARADOX, WHEN WE REGARD THOSE WHO WERE THUS ADDRESSED. In the house of one Justus, a proselyte to Judaism, who had become a Christian—a house close by the Hebrew synagogue, in the wealthy, commercial, pleasure-seeking city of Corinth, there assembled in a large apartment a company of disciples of the Nazarene. Some were of Jewish, some of Gentile race. Most, though not all, of the brotherhood were poor, and few were learned or of high station. Perhaps the families of Crispus the president, of Justus himself, and of Chloe from Cenchrea, were the persons in the assembly of most consideration; for Aquila, Apollos, and Sosthenes were absent. Some of those assembled to hear the letter of the apostle, who was the founder of the Church at Corinth, were bondsmen, and few were persons of any note. When Titus and Trophimus, bearers of Paul's Epistle, accompanied by the Corinthians—Stephanas, Fortunatus, and Achaicus, who had also just come from the apostle then labouring at Ephesus—when these looked round upon the gathering of Corinthian Christians, they may well have started with astonishment as the language of the Epistle was read out, which described the abundant enrichment of these lowly, poor, unlettered disciples. Here was a company, including "not many wise men after the flesh, not many mighty, not many noble," but composed of the ignorant, the weak, the base, the despised of the world. A few Jewish merchants, a few handicraftsmen, a few slaves, a few industrious women, and perhaps a scholar or two, were declared to be "enriched in all things." It was a paradox; and it was a paradox which has been repeated again and again during the past nineteen centuries.

II. A POSSIBILITY, WHEN WE THINK IN WHOM THIS ENRICHMENT TOOK PLACE.

Nothing but the consciousness of a new life breathed into humanity, a new hope dawning upon the world, could account for these Corinthians being thus addressed by a teacher like Paul. The language is so sweeping and unqualified, and the statement is made with so much confidence, that we feel that something very remarkable must have occurred to account for Paul addressing such persons in such language. The explanation is to be found here—" *In him* " ye were enriched. It is in Christ that the wealth of God is placed at the disposal of the destitute children of men. 1. His Divine nature is a storehouse, a treasury of true wealth; in him all fulness dwells. 2. His ministry was an earnest of the greater blessings which should follow; for he was ever freely giving. 3. His death and sacrifice were the means of securing to us the fulness of God; he unlocked the treasury : " Though he was rich, yet for our sakes he became poor, that we, through his poverty, might be rich." 4. His ascension, so far from impoverishing the race he came to save, was the occasion of its enrichment. " He received gifts for men; " he poured out spiritual blessings from on high.

III. A FACT, WHEN WE CONSIDER THE ACTUAL SPIRITUAL POSSESSIONS ENJOYED BY MANKIND THROUGH JESUS CHRIST. As the sun enriches the earth with luxuriant fruit-fulness, as great men enrich a nation by their heroic deeds and saintly self-sacrifice, so does Christ actually bestow untold blessings upon this race. Referring to the Epistle, we observe that wisdom and knowledge, faith and healing, miracles and prophecy, tongues and interpretation, were among the special instances of wealth with which the early Church was dowered. Yet the same Epistle assures us that love is a greater gift than all these. " See that ye abound in this grace also." The fruits of the Spirit are the riches of the Church. The unsearchable riches of Christ are made over to his redeemed and renewed people. To them it was said, " All things are yours."

APPLICATION. There is nothing in the resources or the purposes of God, nothing in the heart of Christ, to limit the extent to which this spiritual wealth may be diffused.—T.

Ver. 9.—" *The fellowship of his Son*." Social ties are inevitable either for good or for evil; some are made for us and others are made by us. All religions have made use of the social tendency, the social necessity, which distinguish human nature. Christianity adapts itself to the highest form of the tendency. The Divine Christ has made himself the Associate, the Friend, the Brother of mankind.

I. THE FELLOWSHIP OF FAITH IN CHRIST'S REDEMPTION. The work of Christ was perfect in itself, but its benefits are only to be enjoyed through spiritual association and affinity with Christ. Union of heart and soul with Christ is the condition of true salvation. Christians are built on Christ as the foundation, grafted into Christ as into the vine, joined to Christ as to the body, partakers of Christ as of spiritual bread, friends with Christ as by a congenial attachment.

II. THE FELLOWSHIP OF SPIRIT WITH CHRIST'S CHARACTER. The frequent expression, " in Christ," shows what was the view of the Lord himself and of his apostles concerning the identification of the people of Jesus with their Lord. It is their aspiration to be like him, to have the mind which was in him. They are followers, disciples, imitators, representatives of him whose name they bear. Sympathizing with Christ's obedience and submission to the Father, they are practically and powerfully and beneficially affected by this sympathy.

III. THE FELLOWSHIP OF THE ACTIVE LIFE WITH THE WORK OF CHRIST. Christians recognize their Master's devotion to the highest interests of men, his unwearied efforts, his unflinching sacrifice. In communion with him they make their life one of service, of consecration. In *motive* the Christian life is service to Christ ; in *result* it is service to man. How many a life has been rescued by the cross from selfishness and from sin, and made a life of devoted and successful benevolence !

IV. THE FELLOWSHIP OF HEART AND OF ACTION WITH CHRIST'S PEOPLE. Union with the Head is the basis of communion with the members; yet by this last the former is fostered and perfected. Congeniality and sympathy of disposition and aim, worship and ordinances in common, mutual aid, conjoined endeavours and testimony,—these are the results, and, at the same time, the means of communion with Christ.

V. FELLOWSHIP PROSPECTIVELY IN CHRIST'S INHERITANCE. The Lord ever encouraged his disciples, who shared his humiliation, with the prospect that they should share his exaltation. It was his promise, "Because I live, ye shall live also;" it was his prayer, "Where I am, there may also my people be." Fellowship with such a Being cannot be for a season, it must be imperishable. To be "ever with the Lord" is the bright and joyous expectation of all who honour and who love his appearing. This shall be the crown of communion. Then in the fullest sense shall his disciples and friends be truly "partakers of Christ."—T.

Ver. 17.—*The mission to preach.* No man did so much as Paul to prevent Christianity degenerating into form. He had himself been galled by the bondage of the old dispensation, and he the more rejoiced in the liberty of the new. He upheld the spirit against the letter, the life against the ceremony. He did not depreciate baptism, for it would not have been easy to depreciate the ordinance and at the same time to honour the spiritual reality it symbolized. But others could and might administer the rite of purification; he was at liberty to leave this to them, in order to give himself the more devotedly to his own special and appointed work, the preaching of the gospel.

I. THE LANGUAGE EXPRESSES THE CONVICTION OF A DIVINE MISSION. 1. The Christian, and emphatically the Christian preacher, does not go his own way and do his own work in the world. He does not claim to direct his own steps. 2. Christ is the sender. To Paul he had said, "Unto whom now I send thee;" and Paul acknowledged concerning his commission, "I received it not of men." It is a high and sacred truth that we are *sent* men. The soul that awakens to a sense of the reality of life and hears the voice of God, proves its vitality by exclaiming, "Here am I; send me." Every Christian is, in a sense, a missionary, an apostle of Christ.

II. THE LANGUAGE ASSERTS THE VAST IMPORTANCE OF PREACHING. It is common amongst worldly men to undervalue this spiritual agency; they think more of political or physical power than of moral influence. What is preaching? It is the use of moral means towards a moral end. It is the presentation of truth to the understanding, of authority to the conscience, of persuasion to the heart. Above all, it is the use of a Divine weapon, though with an arm weak and ill adapted for a service so high. Our Lord himself was a preacher, Paul was a preacher, and preachers have been among the greatest moral factors in the history of all Christian nations. Preaching is the vehicle of a Divine blessing, the means towards a Divine and immortal result.

III. THE LANGUAGE LAYS STRESS UPON THE SUBSTANCE OF CHRISTIAN PREACHING. Paul felt himself called and qualified to preach *the gospel.* 1. This was good news. An argument may be reasoned, an oration may be declaimed, a poem may be sung, but that which has to be preached is *good news.* 2. It was good news from God. From any inferior source good tidings could scarcely have deserved the name. Man needed pardon, the principle and power of a new life, hope for the future; and these were blessings God alone could bestow. 3. It was good news concerning Christ. Thus to preach Christ and to preach the gospel were one and the same thing. For Christ was to man the wisdom, the power, and the love of God. 4. It was good news for all men. It brought liberty to the Jew and light to the Gentile, truth to the inquiring, comfort to the sorrowful, peace to the sinful penitent, and hope to the downtrodden and the slave.

APPLICATION. 1. The preacher may be reminded of his true vocation. 2. The hearer of the gospel may be reminded of his precious privilege and of his sacred responsibility.—T.

Ver. 18.—*The doctrine of the cross.* There is a holy zeal of indignation in the spirit animating this passage. Paul, the rabbinical scholar, not untinctured with Hellenic culture, must have felt it hard that the life he had voluntarily adopted often brought him into disrepute even amongst his intellectual inferiors. But he had chosen deliberately and in the sight of God, and no power on earth could make him swerve from his course. His own mind was satisfied that the gospel could do for man what no other power could effect, and his daily observation convinced him that in this judgment he was right. He could afford, then, to endure the scorn of men, for the doctrine he was promulgating was attested as the power of God.

I. THE SUBSTANCE OF THE DOCTRINE, OR WORD, OF THE CROSS. 1. The *cross* had to Paul no merely material and superstitious meaning. In after ages men heard much of "the true cross," and even now relics (supposed) of the instrument of our Saviour's sufferings are treasured and revered. The cross may be reproduced in shape, in ornament, in architecture, in posture, and there may all the time be no spiritual understanding of the cross. 2. Nor did a merely sentimental meaning attach itself in Paul's mind to the cross. Suffering, and especially the suffering of innocence, awakens sympathy, and people talk about the cross they carry, with no other apprehension of the meaning of the phrase. 3. But it was a symbol of Christ's sacrifice. Jesus bare the cross before he set out for Calvary; its shadow had been for years upon his soul. In his death upon the cross he bore our sins, and secured that his people should with him be crucified unto the world. Thus the tree of death became the sign of redemption and the law of life.

II. THE OFFENCE OF THE DOCTRINE, OR WORD, OF THE CROSS. 1. In itself. The cross was associated in men's minds with slavery, with guilt and crime, with suffering, with shame, with reviling, and with death. 2. In its position in the Christian scheme. To hope to convert the world by *preaching* seemed to many the vainest folly; by preaching *a person*, ridiculous; by preaching a person *judicially put to death*, insanity; by preaching *one crucified*, a moral obliquity and infamy. 3. There was a special reason why the Jews should resent this doctrine. They cherished a carnal love of splendour and power of a manifest and impressive kind, and the word of the cross outraged their sentiments. They looked for a temporal deliverer in the Messiah, and this expectation was disappointed in the gospel of the Crucified. 4. There was a special reason why the Gentiles, especially those of education and philosophical tastes, should take offence at the word of the cross. They disdained the barbarian and despised the Jew, and they contemned the form in which Christianity was proclaimed. They loved health, beauty and power, and had no sympathy with a religion which gloried in the Crucified, and appealed to the sinful and the wretched. Their taste for speculation and for novelty was not gratified by Christian doctrine, and the cross would fit into none of their schemes of the universe.

III. THE POWER OF THE DOCTRINE, OR WORD, OF THE CROSS. 1. The *source* of this power. It is Divine. The word of the cross expresses the Divine mind, shows God's estimate of human sin, exhibits the Divine righteousness, reveals the Divine love, and does all this on a human platform, so that we are enabled to appreciate the mystery of heavenly counsels. 2. The *sphere* of this power. Unbelievers cannot recognize it; they cannot but regard it as folly, for they are perishing in the sin from which it might deliver them. But all who are "in course of salvation" are living witnesses to the efficacy of the gospel. In a free moral nature, truth and love must be received in order that they may operate. 3. The *proofs* of this power. Compare it with any other power, and its superiority is manifest. What else can awaken the selfish, the sensual, and the obdurate to a sense of sin; can impel the low-minded and earthly to the pursuit of holiness; can guide and graciously constrain to a life of consecrated service; can enter a corrupt society as leaven, and can purify it as salt?—T.

Ver. 31.—*Glorying in the Lord.* The one condition of spiritual blessing, upon which Scripture universally insists, is humility. The lowly are assured of acceptance, and the proud and self-confident are condemned to rejection. The terms of Christianity correspond with the teaching of the Old Testament; for it is to the poor in spirit and to the meek, to the child-like in character and disposition, that the blessings of the new covenant are assigned. The same spirit which is a means of obtaining the blessings of Christianity is distinctive of those who possess these blessings. They have received all they enjoy from the free grace of God, and it is their delight to abase themselves and to exalt him from whom they have derived their spiritual privileges and prospects. They may glory, but it is not in anything which is their own; it is in him of whom and to whom are all things.

I. CHRISTIANS REPUDIATE ALL GLORYING IN SELF. 1. *In their own possessions and powers.* There is a natural tendency to think highly of self, and to depreciate our fellow-men and their gifts, and to forget our God the Giver of all. But the very fact that we are Christians is conclusive against the lawfulness of such moral habits. God has made us; Christ has redeemed us, and we are not our own. 2. *In the gifts of God's providence.* To boast of wealth, or nationality, or family, is to overlook the great question, "What hast thou that thou didst not receive?" 3. *In their privileges.* This the Jews were constantly in the habit of doing; they boasted that they were Abraham's children, and Moses' disciples, etc. If highly favoured by Christian privilege, let Christ's people be upon their watch lest they claim credit for what they owe to the free grace of God. 4. *In their attainments.* The Corinthians seem to have been in special danger of falling into this snare. Human learning and philosophy may very possibly become an occasion of stumbling and reproach. 5. *In their virtues.* This was the Pharisaic spirit, and should be checked by the remembrance that "we are unprofitable servants."

II. CHRISTIANS CULTIVATE THE HABIT OF GLORYING IN THEIR LORD. 1. This is a *just and reasonable habit.* Reflection assures every true and spiritual Christian that he is indebted to the mercy of God in Christ, first for his redemption from sin, and then for every grace, all help, all counsel, all comfort, through which he is what he is. Therefore in the Author of salvation and life he is bound to rejoice. 2. This is a *profitable habit.* To glory in the Lord is a sure preservative against ingratitude and murmuring, and will help in maintaining a cheerful and happy tone and temper of mind. It is, moreover, an evident and beautiful preparation for the employments of heaven. 3. This is a *habit for which we have the apostolic example and precedent.* It was the habit of Paul's mind to glory, not in man, but in God. He could glory in his own infirmities; he could glory in the blessing God bestowed upon his labours, though then he "became a fool in glorying." But this was the prevailing sentiment of his spirit: "God forbid that I should glory, save in the cross of Christ Jesus my Lord!"—T.

Vers. 1—3.—*Christian salutation.* I. CHRISTIAN SALUTATION SHOULD BE COURTEOUS. Christianity teaches the truest politeness. It seeks to eradicate the harsh and the brutal. Life is rough enough without our making it rougher; Christianity tends to smooth the ruggedness of life and to make it more kindly. Courtesy in others towards ourselves we greatly value; we have to be towards others what we would have them to be towards us. Paul's courtesy is evidently of the right type—it is *heart*-courtesy. Surface-courtesy is of little worth. Besides which it is *a lie.*

II. CHRISTIAN SALUTATION SHOULD BE GENEROUS. Paul's is not conceived in a carping spirit. There is a disposition to look upon the better side. The Corinthian Church afforded plenty of inducement to severity in an exordium. The apostle declined the temptation. ¡He knew the way to the human heart, and, whilst reserving needed rebuke, he saluted his Corinthian friends (and enemies) in a manner certain to impress them as charitable and large-hearted. Whilst strictly adhering to truth, we must, if we would win men, manifest a spirit of generosity. We are sometimes so terribly afraid of saying too much, that we say altogether too little. We are severely anxious to be just, and become really unjust. Large-heartedness is attractive, and wins; stinginess in sentiment is repulsive, and loses. Insistance upon the dark side often makes it darker. Men need encouragement as well as lecturing, and the exhibition of a noble, sympathetic, generous spirit is one of the most encouraging spectacles that men who are erring and imperfect can be called to look upon.

III. CHRISTIAN SALUTATION SHOULD BE CHEERFUL. Many burdens pressed upon the apostle's heart, but he nevertheless gives a cheery greeting to the Corinthians. To start with a groan is not propitious. We have *sometimes* cause for sorrow; we have *always* cause for joy if we are in Christ. To wave the black flag is to give but poor welcome. We are to rejoice in the Lord *always,* and in saluting our brethren we may well let this joy beam forth. Glumness and dismalness are not the chief of the Christian graces, though some seem to think they are. We are not looking forward to a *funeral,* but to a *wedding* —"the marriage supper of the Lamb." In Christian intercourse a little more brightness and gladness would not be out of place.

IV. CHRISTIAN SALUTATION MAY WELL BE EXTENSIVE. We are one family, and all the members have a claim upon our good wishes. Paul's greeting is not too selective; his sympathies go out to all who call upon the Name of the Lord. Some are very fond of saluting the rich, and have no fondness for saluting the poor. One might suppose that a serious mistake had been made in the non-calling of many wise and mighty and noble, for some of God's people seem to care for no others. Paul sent an equal greeting to the Corinthian believers; his sentiment was unaffected by poverty, ignorance, feebleness, or obscurity. Our love is apt to become cramped. The very best of us tend to

love the lovely Christian, and to give the cold shoulder to the unlovely. We need more of the Spirit of the One who came to help the sinful and the unattractive, and who " loved the world."

V. CHRISTIAN SALUTATION SHOULD NOT BE EMPTY. Much salutation says nothing and means it. Paul's salutation is very ample and full of significance. He desires for the Corinthians the *grace* or favour of God and Christ—the Divine love to be manifested towards them. " In his favour is life" (Ps. xxx. 5). All blessing from God to be their portion. And *peace* as the result of this—the inward assurance of the friendship of God, that sin is pardoned, that " all things are yours." Under the terms of the apostolic greeting all good, whether providential or spiritual, temporal or eternal, is included.

VI. CHRISTIAN SALUTATION SHOULD SAVOUR MUCH OF CHRIST. 1. Here Christ is frequently named; but in no affected or canting way. It is a pity that when men talk of Christ in friendly intercourse they so often become *intensely unnatural*. The holy naturalness of Paul when talking of his Master is refreshing. 2. Here is much of the spirit of Christ. The salutation breathes forth love, tenderness, unselfishness, great-heartedness, and intense sympathy.—H.

Vers. 1—9.—*The approach to rebuke.* The occasion of this letter was largely furnished by the need of rebuke. The Corinthian Church had erred grievously. To rebuke is frequently painful, but when called for it should not be shrunk from; not to rebuke under such circumstances is unalloyed cruelty. To rebuke, often painful, is *always perilous*. By maladroitness we may easily drive men from the right instead of drawing them to it. Unwise rebuke adds to the ill. We need to *prepare for rebuke* if when we reach it we would not deserve its infliction. Note the apostolic procedure. We have here one of the finest examples of preparing men's minds for well-deserved censure.

I. REMARK SOME GENERAL FEATURES OF THIS PREPARATORY ADDRESS. We find in it: 1. *Courtesy.* A graceful and gracious salutation. The apostle does not rush into harsh words. He shows no *eagerness to condemn*. Roughness and rudeness add no strength to admonition. 2. *Affection.* This pervades every sentence, and culminates in the opening of the tenth verse, " Now I *beseech* you," etc. Love keeps in check apostolic authority and righteous indignation. We shall not injure delinquents by *loving them very much*. Nothing can make rebuke more telling than administering before and after and with it, unaffected love. If men see that we are unwilling to rebuke them, they will be very much more likely to accept our rebuke. To *enjoy rebuking* is to demonstrate our total unfitness for it. 3. *Candour.* The condemnation is not to be wholesale. Some can see nothing but fault in those who err, but the apostle perceives excellences. He generously acknowledges spiritual attainment and endowment. To blind our eyes to the good is to make ourselves powerless to remove the bad. Many rebukes have worse than failed through lack of *strict honesty* in the rebuker. The " candid friend " has often proved very uncandid. 4. *Wisdom.* (1) He turns the thought of the Corinthians to their *oneness* (ver. 2). His message is to them as *one* people in Christ : " *The Church* . . . at Corinth "—not the *Churches.* The Church of *God*—not of *many leaders.* Presently he will have to censure them for lack of unity. (2) He prays that they may have more " grace." Soon he will show that they need it. The Church has been boasting of its man-power; Paul thinks its great need is God-power—enlightenment, guidance, help from above. (3) He desires that they may have " peace " from God—not without an eye to their divisions and quarrels. He is wisely preparing his way. 5. *Absence of pomposity* and of assumption of superiority. It is not the great man speaking to the infinitesimal; nor the spotless to the utterly depraved. *Paul gets as near to the Corinthians as he can.* He seems to remember that his Master was made " *in the likeness of men* " (Phil. ii. 7). " Come not near to me, for I am holier than thou," is likely to make people keep their distance and have nothing to do with us or our words. Not without wise humility has " Sosthenes our brother " a place in the salutation. 6. Yet the *apostolic authority is not lost sight of.* It may be well to show that we are entitled to rebuke— that we are not assuming an office to which we have no claim. Rebukes should come from proper quarters. Paul was the " apostle of Jesus Christ through the will of God." It was manifestly within his province to point out blemishes in the Christian Church and to reprove evil-doers.

II. NOTE HOW EARNESTLY HE STRIVES TO TURN THEIR THOUGHTS TO GOD AND TO

CHRIST. This is, perhaps, the most striking feature of these introductory verses. Read the passage and *note the extraordinary number of times mention is made of God and of Christ.* The connection of this with the coming rebuke is apparent. The Corinthians have forgotten God, and therefore they have gone astray. Christ has become less and less to them, and so they have sinned more and more. We quarrel with one another very easily when we get away from our Master. We grow carnal swiftly when God begins to pass out of our thoughts. With heavenly wisdom the apostle *floods the minds* of the Corinthians with thoughts of God and of Christ. If they can be brought into the light of the Divine presence they will see their corruption, and standing once again before Jehovah they will be made ready to receive and not to resent a deserved and much-needed rebuke. If they can be brought again well within the attractive influence of the marvellous self-sacrifice and love of their Lord, self-will will become crucified, pride humbled, and grateful life and service compelled. Note more particularly: 1. The apostle traces his apostleship to *Christ* and *God.* He stands before the Corinthians as the appointed representative of their Lord. The position he assumes was given to him by Christ through the will of God. We are what Christ makes us. 2. They are the Church of *God,* sanctified in *Christ Jesus,* and their oneness with all other Christians is through *Christ* (ver. 2). 3. All that they have received, and in which they glory so much, has come from *God* and from *Christ* (vers. 4—6). 4. Their right position is one of waiting for the revelation of *Christ* (ver. 7). 5. Their continuance in the faith and their perfection at last are made to depend upon *Christ.* 6. At first they were called by *God* into the fellowship of *Christ.* Memories of conversion-time are potent. Paul thus strives in every way to take the Corinthians to their Father and to their Lord. The battle of Christian rebuke is half won when gracious thoughts of God and Christ are revived. Erring Christians are likely to be brought to their senses when they are brought to their Master.

III. THE APOSTLE REMINDS HIS READERS OF CERTAIN THINGS, AND IN THIS WAY PREPARES THEM FOR WHAT IS TO FOLLOW. 1. *Their Christian profession.* They are sanctified or supposed to be. They are known as " saints," and therefore should live as such. 2. *Past mercies, privileges, honours.* (Vers. 4—7.) These are so many arguments to seek the Divine pleasure and not their own. And this can be done only by renouncing the evil and cleaving to the good. All the redeemed are laid under infinite obligation to live unto the Lord. 3. *God's faithfulness to them.* (Ver. 9.) A great argument that they should be exemplary towards him and his kingdom. 4. *What they are looking forward to.* (Ver. 7.) Soon they will be in the visible presence of Christ. We are not far from the judgment. Well may we bear rebuke *here,* that we may escape rebuke *there.*—H.

Vers. 10—17.—*Divisions in the Church.* How numerous these have been since Paul wrote! How many of them springing directly from human weakness, folly, or wickedness! How alien to the true spirit of Christianity, and to the prayer of Christ—" That they all may be one "!

I. A GREAT EVIL. Cause of: 1. *Weakness.* Co-operation hindered. Strength expended in opposing each other instead of sin and Satan. Great opportunity offered for Satanic attack. Unity is strength; division is weakness. 2. *Scandal.* The contempt of the world is not only experienced, but largely deserved. The Head of the Church is dishonoured. The renovator of society shows its own need of renovation. Satan has achieved a triumph in the very Church founded to overthrow him. 3. *Unchristian feeling.* Unity begets more love; division more hate. Church quarrels have often proved most bitter. A united Church is an Elim, a divided Church a Marah. 4. *Hindrance to unbelievers.* Conversions are stayed by Church divisions. Men seeking peace hesitate to cast in their lot with those who are flying at one another's throats. The strait gate is sometimes *quite blocked up* by bickering, quarrelling Christians. A crucified Christ invites, and a divided Church repels, the sinner. Men can find plenty of division, estrangement, hate, and fight in the world, without troubling to enter the Church. Church division is a serious stumbling-block to the unbeliever, and often causes him to continue an unbeliever.

II. ARISE FROM VARIOUS CAUSES. 1. Frequently, as among some at Corinth, *from favouritism* towards leaders in the Church. This favouritism may be: (1) In respect of

personal qualities or position.   Apollos was eloquent and captivating; Paul spiritual and simple; Cephas had peculiar charm through his long association with Christ, and represented the Jewish element to the minds of the Corinthians.   Instead of enjoying all the teachers in common, folly suggested division and monopoly, and thus loss all round.   (2) In respect of real or supposed doctrinal tendencies.   Some at Corinth, having a love for "wisdom of words" and the philosophies of men, would with their old and only half-discarded beliefs pleading powerfully, incline towards the brilliant scholar of Alexandria, who might seem to favour a more rationalistic system than that of Paul.   Others, with Jewish prejudices still strong, might shelter themselves under the name of Cephas, as they attempted to combine Christianity and Judaism by a large sacrifice of the former.   Then, as now, *men asked themselves what doctrines they liked,* and held to these.   Instead of seeking "the mind of the Lord," we are very prone to seek our own minds; and then, what wonder if there be "divisions among us"?   If truth were *sought* instead of *manufactured,* how much more unity of doctrine and practice there would be in the Church of Christ!   (3) Through the carnal disposition to exalt the servant unduly, losing sight of the Master.   *It is easier to follow men than to follow Christ.*   There is a good deal of the *heathen* in us: we love to have a god whom we can *see.*   We are much like the Israelites when Moses went up into the mount; and it is not, therefore, very surprising if we soon discover that our new teacher and guide is a gorgeous and resplendent calf.   Only Christ is fit to be supreme in our life.   Directly we put men in his place, we begin to follow that which is *imperfect,* and we draw its imperfection upon and into ourselves.   2. Sometimes, as with one section at Corinth, *from repudiation of all earthly leaders.*   "We are not of Paul, or of Apollos, or of Cephas; we are of Christ."   This position has been assumed in later times.   It possesses not a little plausibility, but investigation discloses its true character.   One has well said of the Corinthian section, "It was in no Christian spirit that they set up their claim to be of Christ."   That love to Christ is more than suspicious which ignores his accredited servants.   It is no great compliment to a king to reject his ambassador.   The apostle could say, "We are ambassadors for Christ."   Christ has a ministry which is not to be ignored.   As Christ's servants are never to be put in Christ's place, so the place of Christ's servants is not to be made void.   Not improbably these who claimed to be "of Christ" claimed to be the only Christians in Corinth.   It is possible to cry, "Lord, Lord!" very loudly, and to have none of the Spirit of Christ.   That man could know nothing truly of Christ who failed to recognize in the Apostle Paul a true servant of the great Master.

III. How to be dealt with.   1. In a spirit of *meekness.*   "I *beseech* you"—not "I *command* you."   Assumption and arrogance widen the breach.   2. In *love.*   "Brethren" —not reprobates, outcasts, heretics.   Hard words make hard hearts.   3. With *discretion.*   Paul shows discretion in not mentioning Cephas or Apollos after ver. 12.   He does not object more to the parties under their names than to the one under his own.   *It is most suggestive that he appears to castigate his own party chiefly.*   He objected to all *parties.*   For himself, he wanted only his *legitimate position.*   To rebuke our own followers for following us unduly and factiously is indeed a sign of grace in the heart, and of heavenly wisdom too.   4. With *candour.*   "Concealment and mystery sow distrust and destroy love."   5. By *turning thoughts towards Christ.*   A hidden Christ makes a divided Church.   If we saw the Master more clearly, we should see the right place of the servants better.   Paul beseeches, not for his own sake, but for Christ's sake.   He did not fear that this would encourage those who said, "We are of Christ."   He showed them *the real Christ.*   This was the best medicine for their spiritual ailment.   They had been *making a Christ* to go before them.   Many *false Christs* are worshipped and served.   6. By *argument.*   The reasonableness of unity.   Paul urges that Christ is not and cannot be divided, and that if the Corinthians are Christ's, they should not be divided either.   As there is only one Head of the Church, there should be only one body.   By divisions Christ will seem to be rent asunder.   Teachers are not centres of unity; for perfect unity there can be but one centre—that is, Christ.   7. By *taking a blameless course one's self.*   Paul will do nothing to foster division.   In his condemnation, as we have seen, he sacrifices his own party first, and ridicules the idea of the undue exaltation of himself: "Was Paul crucified for you?"   Many try to heal Church divisions by abasing their opponents and exalting themselves.   Paul is singularly clear in this matter; he sharply rebukes those who would transform Paul into Pope. Avoiding every occasion of increasing the evil, he rejoices that he has not baptized many Corinthians, lest this should be wrested into an attempt to acquire pre-eminence, and consequently dishonour fall upon the pre-eminent Christ. Some Church divisions may seem necessary: for example, when professors walk disorderly or embrace erroneous views. It may be then our duty to separate ; yet we should preserve the spirit of charity, and seek to be most loyal to Christ. But how many Church divisions are more or less after the Corinthian type!—H.

Vers. 17—25.—*The preaching of the cross.* I. THE CROSS IS TO BE PREACHED. The gospel cannot be preached unless the cross is. The cross is the central fact. The converging point of the Scriptures is found in "Christ crucified." Without the cross Christianity becomes meaningless and powerless. Salvation and the cross are indissolubly linked: the cross speaks of the shedding of blood, "and without shedding of blood is no remission" (Heb. ix. 22).

II. THE CROSS IS TO BE PLAINLY PREACHED. As "not many wise" are called, it is but reasonable that the unwise and simple-minded should be specially borne in mind. The offence of the cross is not to be lessened by "wisdom of words." Knowledge of the meaning of the cross is the deepest need of the world; all things should be subordinated to conveying that knowledge with utmost clearness and fulness. Men cannot be saved by eloquence, or philosophy, or learning; they can by the cross. "The great preachers have been natural orators, not rhetoricians or actors." The greatest care is necessary lest, by the character of our preaching, the cross of Christ should be made of none effect. Some preaching seems designed for the very purpose, and succeeds deplorably.

III. THE CROSS IS TO BE PREACHED, NOTWITHSTANDING ITS UNFAVOURABLE RECEPTION. Some, indeed, receive it with all gladness, but our obligation to preach it is not dependent upon its reception. We may always remember that the cross is what men *want*, though it may not be what they *wish*. 1. To the Jew the cross was a stumbling-block. He looked rather for a *military* than for a *martyr* Messiah—one who would deliver by sound of trumpet and sword, not by ignominy and death. If he is to believe, he must have signs from heaven (ver. 22), miraculous interventions, and not a reiteration of the event which was the greatest scandal to his mind, and most grievously shocked his prejudices and anticipations. The Jew put the cross *very low down.* We can make anything into a stumbling-block if we will only put it low enough. 2. To the Greek the cross seemed foolishness. That the great revelation for which he and the world had been looking so long should come through a crucified Jew, and be most closely associated with that crucifixion itself, appeared to him too absurd. He would have welcomed a philosopher with a new philosophy. He sought after wisdom—that is, *his* wisdom. In the cross there was too profound a wisdom for even his keen eye to discern, and so he called it folly. He thought the cross was shallow, because he was shallow himself, though he little suspected it. Further, he desired philosophic demonstration about matters of religion, and had a great horror of "faith." And his pride was wounded (and that which wounds our pride is always folly). That all must come to God by the same way, making a similar confession of sin and impotence, was in conflict with his most cherished ideas. The approach of barbarians to the cross made it a way of foolishness to the Greek. There are many "Greeks" now.

IV. THE CROSS IS TO BE PREACHED WITH THE KNOWLEDGE THAT IT OPERATES AS A GREAT TEST OF CONDITION. The character of its reception indicates the condition of those who hear. To some it is foolishness—but only to those that *are perishing. Only to them!* They are so utterly blind that the brightness of the cross is blackness. To others it is the power of God and the wisdom of God—and they are *the saved.* They are "both Jews and Greeks" (ver. 24). The new nature has conquered the old. All is changed when the heart is. These Jews sought for *power;* these Greeks sought for *wisdom ;* and *here* both were found when Jew and Greek responded to the Divine call. 1. We may well ask ourselves—What is the cross to us? The answer will indicate whether we are perishing or being saved. The preaching of the cross to us is a *personal test.* 2. In preaching the cross, we should strive and pray that it may not be foolishness to our hearers, knowing what this would indicate. 3. In preaching the cross, we must not be too disconcerted if men receive our message as one of foolishness. This will not indicate faultiness in the cross, but in those who hear its story, though of course there may be faultiness in our mode of telling that story.

V. THE CROSS IS TO BE PREACHED WITH THE REMEMBRANCE OF THE FAILURE OF EARTHLY WISDOM. Ancient schemes of philosophers having some external indication of wisdom, what has become of them? " Where is the wise? " etc. Where are the scribes and their improvements upon the Divine Law? God has made in the course of the ages all such " wisdom " to become folly—recognized folly. " The world by wisdom knew not God." Human wisdom gave the world no more piety, but much more pride. Human wisdom has failed most egregiously all along the line to redeem and regenerate men. Calvin bluntly says, " We must here carefully notice these two things—that the knowledge of all the sciences is mere smoke where the heavenly science is wanting, and man with all his acuteness is as stupid for obtaining of himself a knowledge of the mysteries of God as an ass is unqualified for understanding musical harmonies." If the cross fails, failure is universal.—H.

Vers. 26—29.—*The humble status of the Church.* I. THE FACT. Not many wise after the flesh, mighty, noble, numbered amongst the adherents of Christianity. This was true in apostolic days; it is largely true in our own. Christianity was not *established* by *world-power.* The Founder and his disciples were poor and of humble social position, and in the ranks of the early Christians were comparatively few possessing means, learning, or rank. Christianity has not been *preserved* or *promulgated* by world-power. This has sometimes been called to its aid, but the " call " has often been of *man* rather than of God. The " aid " has frequently been injury. The " arm of flesh " has hindered rather than helped. The Church should not snatch at world-power; this is not her strength. Sanctified learning, influence, and position are of great service; but these things *in themselves, unsanctified,* whilst to carnal judgment promising most signal advantage, often operate as an unmitigated curse.—We may inquire into the cause of the exclusion as arising from free-will. And we may be sure that no calling by God violates human responsibility. 1. *The wise after the flesh.* These, like the Greeks (ver. 22), are often so filled with human wisdom as not to care for Divine—so absorbed by seeking to know earthly things as to have little leisure for heavenly. Pride is fostered, and pride bars the way to Christ and to God. It is difficult for a very " wise " man to become " as a little child " (Luke xviii. 17). " Heaven's gates are not so highly arched as princes' palaces; they who enter there must go upon their knees." The wise after the flesh are apt to have stiff legs. When we seek earthly wisdom we should have a care of its tendency. Human knowledge is good, but it need be kept in its proper place, and that is not the *first* place. 2. *The mighty.* Often subjects of adulation; have so many at their feet that they find it difficult to sit at the feet of Jesus. Excessive self-reliance does not encourage Christ-reliance. A sense of sufficiency is very antagonistic to " God be merciful to me a sinner." The mighty are wont to be too mighty, so that they can do without Christ. The mighty know their might, whereas what men need is to know their *weakness.* 3. *The noble.* High places are slippery. The command of temptations is great. Wealth, which often accompanies position, multiplies snares. Lofty station often begets a sense of excellence; but to enter the kingdom we need to feel our lack of excellence. It is easy to be great among men and very little before God. Earthly nobility and heavenly are two orders—often in startling contrast. Note: Men strive eagerly to be wise after the flesh, mighty, noble, wealthy—and *all the while they may be building barriers between themselves and God.* How well to commit our ways to the guidance of *the unerring wisdom of God*; to ask him to " choose our inheritance for us " (Ps. xlvii. 4); to give or withhold as he sees best!

II. THE PURPOSE. Regarding the Church as weak and uninfluential, we might feel some despondency as to its future. " How is Christianity to get on? " might escape our lips. So men are often very anxious to take care of Christianity instead of being very anxious that Christianity should take care of them. There is a sense in which the idea of our *defending the faith* is monstrous and absurd—it is not we who defend the faith, it is the faith that defends us. The matter is cleared by the revelation of a Divine purpose. God designed: 1. *To show his power.* He would prove that feeble agencies in his hands are infinitely more mighty than the greatest and most influential not so placed.

A "bruised reed" in his hand is more than a sword in another's. Men think that "things seen" are powerful; that which is unseen is much more so. The foolish things confounded the wise, the weak things the mighty, the base and despised things the highly esteemed,—because *God* was in the former and not in the latter. How this was illustrated in the early Church!—the foolishness of preaching breaking down everywhere the "wise" philosophic systems; the weak disciples triumphing over the marshalled might of Rome ; a Church, boasting as its Founder a crucified peasant, and possessing little wealth, influence, or human learning, spreading on all hands, and destroying idolatries venerable in age and powerful in adherents. "God moves in a mysterious way." It is *God moving*. A Church is made, not by the men who come into it, but by *the God who comes into it*. The Church needs more *divinity*. Here is solace for the consciously weak. We cry, "Who is sufficient for these things?" There is but one answer—*God!* 2. *To humble human pride.* "That no flesh should glory in his presence." The pride of man budded at the Fall. The all-successful stratagem took this form : "Ye shall be *as gods*." This pride has been the curse of man's existence—it has separated him from God, and led to a fearful multiplication of transgression. When God works in man, a first effect is the abasement of pride. The pride of man which is altogether of *the devil*, has persuaded man that he is *God*. God, in the formation and continuance of his Church on earth, dealt a deadly blow against human pride, and showed how powerless were the mightiest things of man when confronted with Divine power working through the weakest. The lesson is that henceforth we are not to glory in men—neither in ourselves nor in others, but we are to glory in the Lord. When we are humbled at his feet, we are in our right posture ; when we acknowledge that with him alone are might and dominion and true wisdom, we are in our right minds.—H.

Ver. 30.—*What Christ is to the believer.* What is Christ to *us?* This is a great, an all-important question. The answer to it is an answer to all vital questions respecting our present and future. To God, Christ is much ; to the angels, much; to many men, *nothing*—a mere "root out of a dry ground" (Isa. liii. 2). What to us? To the believer Christ is—

I. WISDOM. This is the supply of a great want, for though in the world there is much talk of wisdom, there is but little possession. Every philosopher has come with the promise of wisdom, but how few with the fulfilment! The great questions of life have found no satisfactory answers in even the profoundest human systems. But Christ is made to us the truest wisdom. From him we learn what to choose, reject, pursue, enjoy, in daily life. He teaches *how to live.* He is the Revealer of God. We have glimmerings of the Divine Being, but we *know* him not until we know him through Christ. "Neither knoweth any man the Father, save the Son, and he to whomsoever the Son will reveal him " (Matt. xi. 27). He makes us wise in a true knowledge of God. Through him we are made wise *unto salvation.* He discloses to us the future, and at the same time he instructs us in the fitting preparation for it. The closer our union with Christ, the wiser shall we become ; the more of Christ we have, the more of wisdom we have. When the union is complete, we shall know even as we are known. This is a wisdom which will not come to nought (ch. ii. 6).

II. RIGHTEOUSNESS. Our natural state is sinful; our righteousnesses as "filthy rags," that is, complete unrighteousness. But when we receive Christ, his righteousness is imputed to us; as our Representative, the second Adam, he was righteous *for us* in his obedience to the Divine Law, and satisfied the claims of Divine justice in his death. So we cry, "The Lord our Righteousness." He took our sins and gave us his righteousness. This righteousness is (1) perfect, (2) accepted by God, and thus (3) of justifying efficacy.

III. SANCTIFICATION. We need not only righteousness *imputed,* but righteousness *realized* ; not only justification, but purification, regeneration ; not only a vital alteration in our relation to God, but a vital alteration *in ourselves.* "Verily, verily, I say unto thee, Except a man be born again, he cannot see the kingdom of God " (John iii. 3). Through Christ we receive the Divine Spirit, who renews us and *conforms us to Christ.* He transforms us into the likeness of Christ, and when our sanctification is complete, we shall be "like him." "If any man be in Christ, he is a *new creature*" (2 Cor. v. 17).

IV. REDEMPTION. Christ redeems us from the curse of sin, but here reference is to the final redemption from corruption, pain, peril, sorrow, death, the fruits of sin, which we shall experience at last if we are Christ's. This redemption includes the redemption of the body. How bright is the believer's prospect! Well may he "glory in the Lord." Note: 1. Christ is wisdom, righteousness, sanctification, and redemption, only to those who are *in him*. To be in Christ is to believe in him, to love him, to serve him, to follow him. 2. It is through God, of Divine grace alone, that we can be in Christ: "*Of him* are ye in Christ Jesus." God gave Christ; God calls us to find salvation and all blessing in Christ; and faith itself is the gift of God (Eph. ii. 8). As no man cometh unto the Father but by the Son (John xiv. 6), so no man cometh unto the Son but by the Father (John vi. 44). All the praise of our salvation must be rendered to God: "According as it is written, He that glorieth, let him glory in the Lord."—H.

Vers. 1—3.—*The salutation.* As usual in Paul's Epistles, this preface contains the name of the writer, the persons addressed, and a prayer for blessing. We have—

I. APOSTOLIC AUTHORITY. Paul's authority as an apostle was disparaged by some at Corinth, who regarded him as inferior to the twelve. Each of the opposing factions had its favourite teacher (ver. 12), and party spirit led them to decry all but their own. In opposition to this, the apostle opens his letter by presenting his credentials. As an apostle, he was: 1. *Called.* He had not taken this office of himself. 2. Called *by Jesus Christ.* He had not been elected by the Church, nor commissioned by any of the twelve, but had been directly appointed and consecrated by the Lord himself. "Not from men, neither through man, but through Jesus Christ, and God the Father" (Gal. i. 1). 3. Called *through the will of God.* This is the ultimate ground. His apostleship rests on Divine authority. In thus magnifying his office (Rom. xi. 13), Paul shows his own humility. Learn: (1) *Every true worker has a call to his work.* This is true of secular as of spiritual work. Natural aptitude, hereditary position, providential circumstances, may clearly indicate to each man his *calling.* For spiritual office there must be a spiritual call—the call of Christ. What mischief is done in the Church and in the world by men intruding into office without a call! (2) *The consciousness of this call is a source of strength.* Let a man be assured that he is doing the work assigned him by God, and nothing will stand before him; but if he doubts, he is weak. The apostle, the preacher, the missionary, the teacher, need above all to have this assurance. (3) *Look well to the credentials of all that profess to speak in the Name of Christ.* "Prove the spirits, whether they are of God" (1 John iv. 1). To follow a false prophet is as dangerous as the refusal to listen to a true one.

II. MARKS OF THE CHURCH. The description of those to whom Paul writes gives us some notes of the Church of Christ. Its members are: 1. *Called.* This designation is implied in the word translated "Church" (ἐκκλησία), which is the body of those that have been *called out* from the world. There is an outer and an inner call—the invitation of the gospel addressed to all, and the effectual call of the Holy Spirit in compliance with which the sinner arises and comes to Christ. This last is the call referred to here. Every believer has come out from his old position in obedience to a Divine summons. The work of grace in the heart is not a thing of constraint. It is a call addressed to men with such sweetly persuasive power that they cannot but come to him who calls (comp. ver. 9; 2 Tim. i. 9; Heb. ix. 15; 1 Pet. v. 10). 2. *Consecrated.* This is the root-thought in the words "sanctify" and "saints." The believer is separated from the world by the Divine call and set apart for God. Israel was the people of Jehovah, sacred to him. Animals devoted in sacrifice could never be turned to any common use. Even so Christians are "not their own" (ch. v. 19, 20), but "living sacrifices" unto God (Rom. xii. 1). They are "an elect race, a royal priesthood, a holy nation, a people for God's own possession" (1 Pet. ii. 9). What a powerful factor in Christian life should this thought of consecration be! Devoted in Christ Jesus unto God! 3. *Holy.* This follows naturally from the foregoing mark. Consecration and holiness are the elements of sanctification. Believers are called to holiness (1 Pet. i. 15). They are separated from the world in standing that they may be separated from it in character (2 Cor. vi. 14—18). The Church at Corinth existed in the midst of a community that was fearfully corrupt. How significant for them these marks of consecration and holiness! Their Christian life could not be safe if they did not hold themselves aloof from the evil around them, and regard themselves as holy unto the Lord. Believers now, as then, must keep themselves " unspotted from the world," for the sake of their spiritual health and their mission as the " salt of the earth." 4. *Prayerful.* They " call upon the Name of our Lord Jesus Christ." They worship him as Lord. This is the distinguishing mark of Christians everywhere. They " honour the Son even as they honour the Father " (John v. 23). The believer is a man of prayer. Jesus Christ is to him a living Presence, near to hear and help. He worships him in the manifested glory of his person and perfection of his work. A prayerless Christian is a contradiction in terms. 5. *One in a common Lord.* The Church Catholic is one in Christ. True unity does not consist in anything outward, as in a visible head, an identical creed, a uniform government; but in spiritual union with the Lord Jesus Christ. Hence geographical divisions, denominational differences, do not destroy the Church's unity. All believers are branches of the same vine (John xv. 5), members of the same body (ch. xii. 12). The diverging radii of the circle find their point of union in the centre. A rebuke to the spirit of faction so strong in the Corinthian Church. A warning against the narrowing influence of country or sect. The Church is not a mere club. The communion of saints is fellowship " with all that call on the Name of our Lord Jesus Christ." These marks suggest: (1) *The distinction between the Church visible and the Church invisible.* The Church *visible* consists of all that profess the religion of Christ, among whom there may be many that are not true believers. The Church *invisible* consists of all that are in living union with Christ the Head—all that have the marks here given. Paul addresses the actual Christian community at Corinth as " the Church of God," although it was disfigured by many corruptions. A field of wheat may have many weeds growing in it, but you still call it a field of wheat. The field as it is is a picture of the Church visible; remove the weeds so as to leave nothing but the pure wheat, and you have the Church invisible. There never has been a perfectly pure Church on earth. While striving to debar from her communion all that is manifestly unholy, absolute purity can never be laid down as a test of whether a Church is true or false. (2) *A test of Christian profession.* Have we the marks here specified? Have we been called? Are we consecrated? etc.

III. THE APOSTOLIC BENEDICTION. " Grace to you and peace." This is the usual form of the apostolic blessing (Rom. i. 7; 2 Cor. i. 2, etc.). Sometimes there is added " mercy " (1 Tim. i. 2; 2 Tim. i. 2); and in Jude 2 we have " mercy, peace, and love." Grace and peace include all the blessings of salvation. 1. *Grace.* The grace of God is a manifestation of love. It is the free kindness of God towards the guilty and ill deserving. Grace and Mercy are twin sisters sent forth by Love to bless sinful men. They come to us hand in hand, alike, yet different. Grace looks upon the guilty and speaks words of pardon; Mercy looks upon the miserable and stretches out the hand of pity. The idea of grace runs through the whole work of redemption from beginning to end. In purpose, plan, progress, perfection,—all is of grace. The prayer that grace may be to a Christian means that he may realize and make his own the grace of God in all the fulness of its manifestation. Grace as a principle in the heart, the inner working of the Holy Spirit, enables us to appropriate the grace of God in Christ. The apostolic wish covers the whole of the Christian life, more particularly: (1) The grace that *justifies.* We are " justified freely by his grace through the redemption that is in Christ Jesus " (Rom. iii. 24). " It is of faith, that it may be according to grace " (Rom. iv. 16). Faith brings us immediate pardon and acceptance with God for the sake of Jesus Christ; yet this is not always realized as a fact. The consciousness and comfort of this will not be enjoyed till it is seen how thoroughly it is of grace. (2) The grace that *sanctifies.* Sin as a polluting and perverting power must be overcome, and the fair features of our Father brought clearly out. This also is of grace. Christ was made unto us sanctification (ch. i. 30), and this becomes ours through the gracious operation of the Spirit (2 Thess. ii. 13; 1 Pet. i. 2). Grace reigns where formerly sin reigned (Rom. v. 21). (3) The grace that *strengthens* (2 Tim. ii. 1). (*a*) In service (Phil. iv. 13). (*b*) In temptation (Heb. ii. 18). (*c*) In trouble (2 Cor. viii. 9). (*d*) In death (Ps. xxiii. 4; ch. xv. 57). (4) The grace that *glorifies* (Ps. lxxxiv. 11). 2. *Peace.* Peace is the fruit of grace. It may be regarded as covering all the blessings which grace bestows. The angels sang of " Peace on earth " (Luke ii. 14), as the sum of the good things to be brought by the Prince of Peace. It includes: (1) *Peace with God.* (Rom. v. 1.) By faith we are justified, our sins being put away and we ourselves accepted as righteous; and thus we are "reconciled to God through the death of his Son" (Rom. v. 10). Henceforth there is friendship between us and God. We become sons of God (Rom. viii. 14 —17), and have "fellowship with the Father and with his Son Jesus Christ" (1 John i. 3). There is a mutual love between God and us, as between father and child. This leads to: (2) *Peace within ourselves.* The knowledge that we are reconciled to God begets an inward calm. We are filled with "peace in believing" (Rom. xv. 13). "The peace of God, which passeth all understanding, guards our hearts and our thoughts in Christ Jesus" (Phil. iv. 7). Christ gives us his own peace (John xiv. 27)— that ineffable oneness with the Father in which his own deep joy lay; and this peace rules in our hearts (Col. iii. 15). Such a peace springs only from reconciliation to God. "There is no peace unto the wicked" (Isa. xlviii. 22). Only when men discovered that the sun is the centre of our planetary system did all its parts move in harmony; only when our nature finds its centre in Christ is it truly at peace with itself. Grace and peace come to us "from God our Father and the Lord Jesus Christ." The gifts of grace come to us from God, but only through Jesus Christ. The inspired writers never hesitate to join the Name of Christ with that of God the Father. The true Godhood of our Lord is everywhere taken for granted, rather than formally asserted. How great must be the grace and the peace that come to us thus!—B.

Vers. 4—9.—*Thanksgiving on account of their gifts.* Paul, as is his wont, begins by congratulating the Corinthian Church on all that is good and praiseworthy in their character, and by expressing a confident hope for the future. This is just in itself,—tell a man his good points as well as his bad; and it is wise, for thus the good among them will be encouraged, and the evil will be the more disposed to listen to rebuke. Consider—

I. THEIR GIFTS (χαρίσματα). 1. They had the gift of "*all utterance,*" as appeared in their highly gifted teachers and preachers; and they had "*all knowledge,*" i.e. an intelligent apprehension of the truth. These two gifts are closely connected. There may be knowledge without utterance, in which case it is of profit only to the individual; and there is too often utterance without knowledge, to the hurt of speaker and hearer. This last is the plague of our time. Whoso feeds on empty words becomes lean. But how blessed is the union of thought and speech! Happy the Church that possesses spiritual insight into the mind of God, and the power of communicating this to the edification of others! 2. The other gift is that of "*waiting for the revelation of our Lord Jesus Christ.*" Faith rests on the first advent; hope looks onward to the second. The time of that great apocalypse has been left indefinite, even the Son being ignorant of it (Matt. xxiv. 36). Sometimes it is represented as very near ("at hand," Jas. v. 8; 1 Pet. iv. 7); while hints are dropped that this nearness is not to be taken according to our time-measurement (2 Pet. iii. 8). The purpose of this uncertainty is that we may watch and wait, look for and earnestly desire the day of the Lord (2 Pet. iii. 12). The apostles maintained this attitude of expectancy, and exhorted others to maintain it. It is noted here as a mark of true spirituality, and elsewhere the crown of righteousness is promised to all them that "love his appearing" (2 Tim. iv. 8). Apart from all points of dispute, the coming of the Lord a second time should exercise a powerful influence on the Christian's life. What a motive to holiness, a stimulus to work, a strength to endure affliction, is the thought, "The Lord is at hand"! "Amen: come, Lord Jesus" (Rev. xxii. 20). These gifts are: (1) *Of grace.* They are not natural endowments. They are given by the free, good pleasure of God. (2) Given *in Christ Jesus.* All fulness dwells in him, the fulness of the Godhead (Col. ii. 9). The gifts of grace come to us only through him (comp. ch. v. 3). To him, therefore, let us repair, that we may receive of his fulness. In him we are truly enriched ("made full," Col. ii. 10). (3) *A confirmation of the gospel.* The gospel is a *testimony* concerning Christ, not a system of doctrines. This was specially true of apostolic preaching: "That which we have seen and heard declare we unto you" (1 John i. 1—3); and it is true of all right preaching. There is a personal testimony to Christ and the power of his gospel unto salvation. This testimony is *confirmed* when it is believed and acted on. Faith and its fruits are the best evidences of Christianity.

"He that hath received his witness hath set his seal to this, that God is true" (John iii. 33).

II. ASSURANCE OF HOPE. These gifts of grace are pledges of future blessings. 1. *Confirmation unto the end.* (Ver. 8.) He who begins the good work in us will perfect it until the day of Jesus Christ (Phil. i. 6). God does nothing by halves. He not only brings up the sinner out of the horrible pit and sets his feet upon a rock, but he also establishes his goings (Ps. xl. 2). The Holy Spirit is the "earnest of our inheritance" (Eph. i. 14), the first instalment of the full heritage. "The God of all grace, who called you unto his eternal glory in Christ, . . . shall himself perfect, stablish, strengthen you" (1 Pet. v. 10). Observe the links of the chain in Rom. viii. 29, 30. All through life, onwards to the end of the world, will God deliver our feet from falling (Ps. lvi. 13). "The righteous also shall hold on his way, and he that hath clean hands shall be stronger and stronger" (Job xvii. 9). This confirmation is effected by the continued impartation of his grace to the believer. 2. *The object in view—"that ye be unreprovable in the day of our Lord Jesus Christ."* (Comp. Col. i. 22; 1. Thess. v. 23.) God will not stop short in his work of grace till it be fully completed. Meanwhile believers are unreprovable in Christ; no charge can be brought against them which he does not meet. Who shall impeach the perfection of his work for us? But we are not morally blameless in ourselves. Personal holiness is far from being perfect. In the day of Christ, however, this work shall be complete. The challenge, "Who shall lay anything to the charge of God's elect?" (Rom. viii. 33), will then apply to character as well as standing. God's ideal will be realized in us when we are holy as he is holy. What a comfort, amid conscious imperfection and sinfulness, to know that we shall one day be "set before the presence of his glory without blemish in exceeding joy" (Jude 24)! 3. *The security for this.* "God is faithful." Not our faithfulness to him, but his faithfulness to us, is the ground of our assurance. Having called us into the fellowship of his Son, all else will follow (Rom. viii. 30). (See next homily.)

Learn the duty of giving thanks for the blessing bestowed upon others. Our own joy shall thus be multiplied.—B.

Ver. 9.—*The faithfulness of God.* To be faithful is to be true to what one has promised or engaged to do. God has come into relation with the universe and the creatures he has made. He has revealed himself to us in various ways, declaring his will, and hence we can speak of his faithfulness. As the unchanging One, ever consistent with himself, he is true to all he has spoken. In all the departments of his working this great principle may be traced.

I. THE FAITHFULNESS OF GOD IS EXEMPLIFIED IN NATURE. What we call "the laws of nature" are not mere blind forces, beyond which we cannot see; they are simply the modes of the Almighty's working, the impress of his will upon creation. On what does the fixity of these laws rest but just the faithfulness of God? The movements of the heavenly bodies, the succession of the seasons, the production of like effects by like causes,—these have been uniform since the present course of things began. Upon this uniformity all human activity depends. The husbandman sows his seed, relying on the laws of growth. The sailor launches his vessel, believing that the waters will bear it up, and that the breeze will fill his sails. The chemist mixes his materials, knowing that they will combine according to the laws of chemical affinity. To the materialist these are ultimate facts, of which he has no explanation to offer; to the Christian they are so many evidences of the truth that God is faithful.

II. THE FAITHFULNESS OF GOD IS EXEMPLIFIED IN THE MORAL GOVERNMENT OF THE WORLD. On what principles does that government rest? Are the ten words of Sinai still in force as the statute-book of the world? Is that old announcement as true to-day as when it was uttered by the prophet (Isa. iii. 10, 11)?—"Say ye to the righteous, that it shall be well with him; woe unto the wicked, it shall be ill with him." Good and evil seem to us inextricably confused in this world. Bad men frequently get the best of life, while good men as often go to the wall. Is God faithful? Amid all apparent anomalies there is enough to show that he is on the side of righteousness, and that all his laws are working for that end. But we must not forget that he does not promise to strike the balance between good and evil in this life. Things are meanwhile in process, and the full result can be judged of only hereafter.

When the mists have rolled away from this world's ongoings, and everything is seen in its naked reality, the faithfulness of God will stand out in clear relief.

III. THE FAITHFULNESS OF GOD IS EXEMPLIFIED IN THE SPHERE OF GRACE. Here it shines with conspicuous lustre. All round the circle you may trace it; but a few illustrations will suffice. God is faithful: 1. *In regard to his promises.* They are "precious and exceeding great" (2 Pet. i. 4), because "he is faithful that promised" (Heb. x. 23). Not one of them shall fail of fulfilment. The great promise contained in the protevangel (Gen. iii. 15) took long centuries to reach its development, but the fulness of the time came at last, and the seed of the woman blossomed into the Christ. Similarly, every promise of God shall be fulfilled in its season. What Joshua said to Israel may be said to us when we have entered on the promised inheritance: "Ye know in all your hearts and in all your souls, that not one thing hath failed of all the good things which the Lord your God spake concerning you" (Josh. xxiii. 14). 2. *In regard to the pardon of sin.* "If we confess our sins, he is *faithful* and righteous to forgive us our sins, and to cleanse us from all unrighteousness" (1 John i. 9). A frank and full confession will always bring forgiveness, because God has pledged himself to this. What an encouragement to keep nothing back from him! His faithfulness and righteousness demand the pardon of the penitent child. 3. *In regard to temptation.* "God is faithful, who will not suffer you to be tempted above that ye are able," etc. (ch. x. 13; comp. 2 Thess. iii. 3). There is no promise to exempt believers from trial. Temptation will surely come to us, as it came to our Saviour; and in that hour our security does not lie in our own watchfulness or strength, but in the faithfulness of God. True to his word, true to the obligation implied in our effectual calling, he will always "deliver us from the evil." 4. *In regard to perfect holiness.* It is introduced in this connection here (vers. 8, 9) and in 1 Thess. v. 23, 24, "And the God of peace himself sanctify you wholly. . . . Faithful is he that calleth you, who will also do it." Having called us, he will complete the work thus begun. The faithfulness of God is the pledge that we shall at last be "holy as he is holy."

APPLY. 1. To Christians, as a ground of comfort. His faithfulness will carry you through every valley of death-shade, and bring you home at last. 2. To the ungodly, as a ground of warning. God is faithful to his threatenings as well as his promises.—B.

Vers. 10—17.—*The factions at Corinth.* The word translated "divisions" is the original of our word "schism," which means a "rent" as in a garment, and then a division in a society or a separation from it. These internal divisions had begun to show themselves at Corinth, if not in the form of regularly defined parties, at least as forces that were moving in that direction, and which, if not checked, might soon lead to open rupture. On what principles these divisions rested, we are left to gather from the watchwords of each. 1. The *Paul party* would consist for the most part of those who were the firstfruits of the apostle's labours at Corinth, and who asserted his full apostolic authority. Not content with this, they had ranged themselves under his name in opposition to others. They seem to have boasted of their liberty in respect of some things which gave offence to more scrupulous consciences, such as eating things sacrificed to idols, and to have treated uncharitably the more contracted views of the Jewish Christians. 2. The *Apollos party* is named after Apollos, who came to Corinth shortly after Paul's departure. He was "a Jew, born at Alexandria, an eloquent man, and mighty in the Scriptures" (Acts xviii. 24); and from his education in his native city he was probably well acquainted with Greek philosophy and literature. Hence his style of teaching was more learned and rhetorical than Paul's, and it attracted the more cultured among the Corinthians, who began to contrast it with the simple, unadorned style of the apostle. Agreeing in doctrine and spirit, the two teachers differed only in gifts and manner of teaching; but this did not prevent the would-be philosophers and rhetoricians of Corinth from using the eloquent Alexandrian's name as a party watchword. 3. The *Cephas party* was mainly composed of Jewish converts, unlike the two previous parties, which were made up of Gentiles. In it we recognize the representatives of that Judaizing tendency which Paul had so frequently to combat. Bringing with them their notions of Jewish prerogative, they sought to impose the Law of Moses even on Gentile converts, and to bind about the neck of Christianity the yoke of legalism. It was natural for this party to call themselves after the apostle of the circumcision, and to contrast his eminence among the twelve with the position of Paul; while they sought to make compulsory the stricter practice of their favourite apostle, in opposition to the greater freedom allowed by the apostle of the Gentiles. 4. The precise character of the *Christ party* is more difficult to determine. The most likely view is that they rejected all human authority, refusing to acknowledge Paul, or Apollos, or Cephas, or any other eminent teacher, and calling themselves simply by the name of Christ. They did this, however, in such a way as to degrade that Name to the shibboleth of a sect, and were thus as guilty as the others whom the apostle here condemns. Among the parties of our own day there are not wanting those who disparage an accredited ministry, and call themselves simply "Christians." In view of these factions consider—

I. THE EVIL OF PARTY SPIRIT. The existence of parties and differing schools of thought in the apostolic Churches leads us to search for some root in human nature whence they spring, and this we find in the limitations and varieties of mental constitution. No single mind can take in the whole of Divine truth so as to hold it in proper balance. There is sure to be a projection of one portion to the comparative obscuring of others,—a looking only at one side of the sphere while the other is out of view. Witness the variety to be found among the apostles. While there is no contradiction in the views of truth presented in their writings—all teaching the same fundamental doctrines—we cannot read them without observing that each lays stress on a different portion of the truth from the others. The difference between Paul and James, *e.g.*, is so evident that not a few shallow readers have pronounced them irreconcilable; while a comparison of both with John reveals other characteristics equally peculiar. And what is true of these inspired teachers is true of the Church in all ages. Christianity does not obliterate individuality. The Holy Spirit works on the lines already laid in nature, and thus the foundation is prepared for varying types of doctrine and life. This diversity is not a thing to be deplored, but rather to be rejoiced in. How high a purpose it is fitted to serve, our Lord showed in selecting apostles, each one of whom was different from his fellows. It needed minds of different hues to transmit the different rays of which the pure light is composed. And God still makes use of the many types of mind to hold up before the Church the many aspects of truth, thus enriching the general body of Christ and preventing it from becoming narrow and one-sided. This is the use of different schools and parties in the Church. They serve to give expression to the many-sidedness of the Christian faith and life. But how readily does this natural and useful diversity give rise to hurtful divisions in the body of Christ! We must not confound the factious spirit which Paul denounces with an enlightened attachment to one particular branch of the Church. We may prefer that branch to others because it appears to us the most scriptural in doctrine, government, and worship, without denying to other branches the marks of a true Church, or overlooking the part they play as members of the one body. Party spirit consists in elevating that which is peculiar to our own sect above that which is common to us with others, and thereby unchurching them. The progress of the kingdom of God in the earth is made subordinate to the success of our own denomination or faction. The spirit that wrought such mischief at Corinth has been busy in the Church ever since. The divisions of Christendom are the scandal of Christianity. It is not merely that the Church is everywhere split up into sections, but that this has led to party strife and jealousy. How much bitterness of feeling has it engendered! how much unchristian speaking! Men glory in their distinctive shibboleths more than in the great doctrines of grace which are our common heritage. The guns of one division of Christ's army are too often directed against another division, instead of being turned against the foe.

II. ARGUMENTS AGAINST IT. 1. *The Head of the Church is One.* "Is Christ divided?" There is no schism in Christ the Head; why should there be in the body? Why rend asunder that which was intended to be one? The members of the human body have different functions to discharge, but the one does not deny to the other its due place in the body (ch. xii. 12, etc.). So with the members of Christ's Church; all belong to the same body, which owns the same Head. The spirit of faction breaks up this unity into a monster of many bodies and many heads. There is but one Head and one body—one Christ and one Church. 2. *Salvation is not due to human teachers.* "Was Paul crucified for you?" Do you owe your redemption to him? If not, why should you call yourselves by his name? Party spirit raises the party name above that of the common Lord, thus putting the servant in the Master's place. It gives undue prominence to men, and virtually leads to idolatry. He who died for us must have no other put by his side, and no name but his own called over his chosen and ransomed Church. 3. *Party spirit is opposed to the true significance of baptism.* "Were ye baptized into the name of Paul?" The baptismal formula (Matt. xxviii. 19) implies that all thus baptized are to be regarded as devoted to him whose sacred Name is pronounced over them. It involves a vow of perpetual allegiance. The administrator of the ordinance, even though he is an apostle, is of no consequence in the case. Paul thanks God that it was so ordered that he baptized only a few persons at Corinth, and that thus no pretext was afforded for calling themselves by his name. His mission was not to baptize, but to evangelize. Baptism, therefore, is hostile to party spirit, since we are not baptized into the name of man, but into the Name of the Three-One. Hence, like the sister sacrament, it is a symbol and pledge and expression of the unity of the Church. That brother, from whom you differ so widely, was baptized into the same thrice-holy Name as yourself. "One Lord, one faith, one baptism" (Eph. iv. 5).

III. EXHORTATION TO UNITY. The apostle is not content with a negative, but sets before them the positive duty of unity. 1. *Unity of mind.* "That ye be perfected together in the same mind and in the same judgment" (ver. 10). Oneness of disposition and oneness of view, in opposition to the division that prevailed. This is to be cultivated by all Christians. It was a characteristic of the early Church: "And the multitude of them that believed were of one heart and soul" (Acts iv. 32). When the same Spirit is dwelling in men's hearts, it will appear in unity of sentiment, opinion, and purpose with regard to religion. 2. *Unity of utterance.* "That ye all speak the same thing." The inner unity should find an outward expression. Hence the utility of confessions of faith as a testimony to the truth held in common, and an evidence of unity in the faith. Short of this, however, there is implied harmony in the utterances of the Church as opposed to the party cries that were heard at Corinth. Men that are at heart one should take care lest their public statements convey an opposite impression. In every free and healthy Church there will be more or less discussion, in which difference of opinion on matters non-essential will be revealed; but this should be conducted in such a way as "to keep the unity of the Spirit in the bond of peace" (Eph. iv. 3). There may be a saying the same thing in Paul's sense, while there is no mechanical uniformity of expression. 3. *A powerful motive to unity.* "I beseech you through the Name of our Lord Jesus Christ." That Name is dear to all Christians, whatever other titles they may give themselves, and a regard to it is the strongest reason that can be urged for any course of conduct. If we love Christ and seek his glory, let us cease from strife, and regard all believers as our brethren. What Christian heart can resist such pleading?—B.

Vers. 17—25.—*Man's wisdom and God's.* The mention of baptism leads the apostle to speak of his preaching at Corinth. His mission was "not to baptize, but to preach the gospel," and he proceeds to vindicate his discharge of that mission as against those who preferred the "wisdom of this world."

I. THE THEME OF EVANGELICAL PREACHING. He calls it "the word of the cross;" "Christ crucified" (comp. ch. ii. 2). Here at Corinth, even more than elsewhere, Paul felt the necessity of adhering to the simplicity of the gospel and disclaiming the "wisdom of words" upon which others laid stress. The central point in his teaching was that which he delighted to sum up in the expression, "the cross of Christ." He did not keep the Crucifixion out of sight as a thing to be ashamed of, but gloried in it as the distinguishing feature of the good news he proclaimed. The humiliation and death of the Saviour of men, his "becoming obedient unto death, even the death of the cross" (Phil. ii. 8), is the very kernel of the gospel, the key which unlocks the mystery of his work. Paul might have told them of a purer morality than their moralists had taught, and a sublimer philosophy than Socrates or Plato had imagined; but this would at best have stirred only a few minds to new thought, and made a few earnest hearts feel that perfection was further off than ever. It was otherwise when he could speak to them of the cross of Christ, with all that it implied; for in this is the Divine answer to the great life-query which men had striven in vain to answer— How can man be just with God? Here is the One dying for the many, the Son of God suffering as a substitute for sinners, and thus salvation actually accomplished. To preach this was truly to bring glad tidings. The example of the apostle is a pattern for all preachers. Let us not think to recommend Christianity by hiding the cross or reducing it to a figure of speech, as if the death of Christ were merely a testimony to the sincerity of his life. Christianity without the cross is no real evangel to men. You may admire the spotless life of Jesus, rejoice in his wonderful teaching, bless him for his Divine philanthropy, and weep over his undeserved fate; but this would simply make him a greater Socrates or a greater Paul. It is his atoning death above all that makes him more to us than any of the illustrious teachers or martyrs of history. But while this is true, we must not suppose that preaching Christ means nothing more than a simple recital of the way of salvation. Paul's letters are virtually summaries of his oral teaching; and in them we see how the one theme expands into the whole circle of Christian truth, how Christ appears as Prophet, Priest, and King, and how the gospel is applied to the trials and duties of actual life. Let us not make narrow what God has made so broad. Let us not stunt and deform our spiritual life by feeding only on one kind of nourishment, and refusing the large provision he has made for us. We shall preach Christ aright only by exhibiting the fulness that dwells in him.

II. THE METHOD OF EVANGELICAL PREACHING. Whilst the main reference in this passage is to the theme of the preacher, there is also a reference to the manner in which that theme is presented. "Not in wisdom of words, lest the cross of Christ should be made void." We may preach Christ in such a way as to neutralize the gospel's peculiar power. 1. We may do this *by merely speculating about the death of Christ.* Philosophical essays on the work of Christ, and disquisitions on Christian doctrine, have their place and value; but they must not usurp the place of simple preaching. They appeal only to the intellect, whereas the sermon appeals to the heart and conscience as well. As a matter of experience, it is found that the style of preaching here condemned is productive of little spiritual fruit. 2. We may do this *by a rhetoric which hides the cross.* The gospel may be so adorned that men's attention is drawn to the gaudy trappings or to the preacher himself, instead of being fixed on the truth; and in so far as this is the case its influence is lost. The flowers with which we bedeck the cross too often hide it. The right idea of preaching may be gathered from the two words translated "preach" in this passage. The first means "to bring glad tidings"—the good news of a Saviour for sinners (εὐαγγελίζεσθαι, ver. 17); the second signifies "to proclaim as a herald" the facts of salvation and the invitations and promises founded upon them (κηρύσσειν, ver. 23). Evangelical preaching is a publication of the good news to men, a direct setting forth of Christ in all his offices. Thus presented, the cross is full of power to draw men to the Saviour (John xii. 32).

III. HOW THE GOSPEL APPEARS TO THOSE THAT REJECT IT. The preaching of the cross affects men according to their prepossessions. Bent of mind, education, sur-roundings, largely determine their attitude towards Christ. Two classes are mentioned by the apostle who rejected the gospel for two different reasons. 1. *The Jews.* "Jews ask for signs," *i.e.* they crave for some outward miraculous exhibition to call forth their wonder. "Master, we would see a sign from thee" (Matt. xii. 38) was their constant demand of Jesus; and, in so far as the demand was a legitimate one, it was complied with. Peter on the day of Pentecost could speak of Jesus of Nazareth as "a man approved of God unto you by mighty works and wonders and signs" (Acts ii. 22). The chief sign of all was the cross; but the Jews did not understand it. They stumbled at it as a "scandal," which they could not get over, and which seemed to them to say the opposite of what God intended. The cross was in their eyes the token of humiliation and shame. They looked for a Messiah attended by far different manifestations, and they would not believe in One who had been crucified. There are still those among us who, like the Jews, seek after signs. They crave for the outward, the visible, the sensational—for something to dazzle and startle. The Roman Catholic will go hundreds of miles to visit the spot where "our Lady" is supposed to have appeared, will gaze with devout reverence on the curdled blood of Januarius turning liquid before his eyes, and will touch with awe the relics of some saint, believing that they will cure his diseases. The Protestant, disdaining these superstitions, shows the same spirit in other ways. He may love the sensuous in worship and the sensational in preaching. He may run after the man who is an adept in oratorical jugglery, who knows the day and the hour when the world is to end, etc. Whatever is novel, unusual, popular, is sure to find such sign-seekers among its ardent supporters. To men of this temper the cross of Christ is still a "stumbling-block." For it speaks of humiliation, of obedience unto death, of a quiet unostentatious doing of the will of God; and this is the very thing such people feel to be distasteful. To go with Jesus into the garden, and there drink the cup God puts to our lips; to endure with him the contradiction of sinners, and be exposed to shame and hissing; to go after him, denying ourselves and bearing our cross;—this is the meaning of the sign. Is it any wonder if men stumble at it? 2. *The Greeks.* "Greeks seek after wisdom." The idea of a crucified Saviour was to them foolishness. Accustomed to the speculations of their own philosophers, set forth with learning and subtlety, these lovers of wisdom applied to the doctrine of the cross a purely intellectual test. It was in their eyes a new philosophy, and Jesus of Nazareth was to be tried by the same rules as the founders of their own schools. To these critical Greeks Paul had nothing to offer but the story of him who was crucified (compare our Lord's words to the Greeks, John xii. 23, etc.). The cross for them, as for the Jews, had but one language—it spoke of the lowest infamy; and to preach salvation by a cross would be in their view the sheerest absurdity. These Greeks have still their representatives in modern life. There are those who glorify human intellect, and think themselves capable of solving all mysteries. How many of our men of science seem to lose their heads when they come to speak of Christianity! They have nothing but a sneer for a "theology of blood;" and their quarrel with Jesus is that, after giving the world such splendid precepts, he should have imagined that he could save men by letting them crucify him. In forms less extreme than this the same spirit may be traced. Many hearers of the Word have more regard to the mental grasp of the preacher, the literary finish of the discourse, or the manner in which it is delivered, than to the scriptural and edifying character of the truth preached. The simple preaching of Christ crucified is to their thinking comparative folly. Let us not be carried away by this craving for wisdom. "When once the idolatry of talent enters the Church, then farewell to spirituality; when men ask their teachers, not for that which will make them more humble and Godlike, but for the excitement of an intellectual banquet, then farewell to Christian progress" (F. W. Robertson). Observe the apostle's statement with regard to these despisers of the cross: "In the wisdom of God the world through its wisdom knew not God." Men groped after him, but could not find him. It was part of the Divine scheme that the wisdom of the world should have free scope to work; and only when it had exhausted itself was the world ripe for the bringing in of the gospel. This was a part of the preparation for Christ. Human wisdom is still inadequate. It cannot save a single soul. Men perish as they speculate; men die as they frame theories of life. In God's view, man's wisdom is folly; in man's view, God's wisdom is folly. Which is the wiser?

IV. How THE GOSPEL APPEARS TO THOSE THAT RECEIVE IT. They are described as "called" (ver. 24), as "believers" (ver. 21), as "being saved" (ver. 18); each term presenting a different aspect of their condition. They are called by God out of the world into the fellowship of Christ; being called, they believe in him; and believing, they are in the way of salvation. There is no salvation without faith, and no faith without the calling of God by his Word and Spirit. Now, to all such Christ is "the Power of God, and the Wisdom of God." The Jew stumbled at the cross as a thing of weakness; the believer rejoices in it as a thing of power. It has done for him what all other appliances failed to accomplish. It has made him a new creature, bringing him out of darkness and death into light and life. Every one who has been cured by a particular medicine is a witness to the efficacy of that medicine; so every saved sinner bears testimony to the power of the cross. And there is wisdom here as well as power —"the wisdom of God." Christ crucified is not a philosophy, but a fact; yet through this fact there shines the highest wisdom. We can well understand how the Greek mind, once brought to the obedience of faith, would revel in this view of the cross. He would learn to see in Christ "all the treasures of wisdom and knowledge" (Col. ii. 3). In him "God is just, and the justifier of him that hath faith in Jesus" (Rom. iii. 26). In him we have the highest exemplification of that great law of the kingdom: "He that humbleth himself shall be exalted" (Matt. xxiii. 12). All that the ancient philosophies had been striving after—the knowledge of God, the nature of man, and the meaning of human life—is to be found in Christ and him crucified. Here is the centre of all knowledge, round which all else revolves in order and beauty. Here is the shrine where the wise men of the earth must fall down and worship—the touch-stone by which their speculations must be tried. Here is "the wisdom of God," outshining every other manifestation in creation and providence—that wisdom by which we become wise unto salvation.—B.

Ver. 24.—*Christ the Power of God.* The power of God is seen in nature and in providence, but here we have a new conception of it. Jesus Christ is that Power. In his person, as God manifest in flesh, there resides the potency of the Highest; but the apostle is here thinking mainly of him as crucified. In that cross, which seems to us the culmination of weakness, he sees the very power of God. Consider—
I. THE ELEMENTS OF DIVINE POWER TO BE FOUND IN THE CROSS OF CHRIST. 1. The death of Christ *manifests the power of God's love.* As soon as we understand the meaning of the cross, we cannot help exclaiming, "Herein is love!" Nor is it merely the *fact* of his love to men which it reveals, for this might be learned elsewhere; but it is the *greatness* of his love. It is the "commendation" of it (Rom. v. 8)—the present-ing of it in such a way as to powerfully impress us with its wonderful character. Here is the Son of God dying for sinners; and on whichever part of this statement we fix attention, it casts light on this marvellous love. (1) The Son of God! The strength of God's love to us may be gauged by the fact that he gave up to death his own Son. "God so loved the world that he gave his only begotten Son," etc. (John iii. 16); "He that spared not his own Son," etc. (Rom. viii. 32). What a power of love is here! Not an angel, nor some unique being specially created and endowed for the mighty task, but his one only Son. Human love has rarely touched this high-water mark. (2) For sinners! "While we were yet sinners, Christ died for us." Human measures and analogies fail us here. "Greater love hath no man than this, that a man lay down his life for his friends" (John xv. 13); but here is love for enemies. And love, not in mere sentiment, not in simple forbearance, but in self-sacrifice—love persisting in its purpose of salvation in the face of hatred and scorn. Thus on both sides the love of God is seen in power. And what a battery to play upon the hearts of men! 2. The death of Christ *manifests the power of his justice.* No reading of the cross that leaves this element out of account can explain the mystery. In a work the professed design of which is to restore men to righteousness, there must surely be no breach of righteous-ness; yet it is here put to a severe test. Is the Law impartial? Will it punish sin wherever it is found? What if the Son of God himself should be found with sin upon him? Shall the sword awake and smite the man that is God's Fellow (Zech. xiii. 7)? Yes; for he dies there as one "bruised for our iniquities." Surely justice must be mighty when it lays its hand on such a victim. If that modern description of God as a "power making for righteousness" is applicable anywhere, it is so here; for nowhere is he so severely righteous as in the working out of salvation for men. Nothing can more powerfully appeal to conscience than his treatment of the sinner's Surety; and nothing can more thoroughly assure us that the pardon which comes to us through the cross is righteous.
II. THE POWER OF GOD IN THE CROSS AS SEEN IN ITS PRACTICAL EFFECTS. Our readiest measure of any force in nature is the effect it produces, and in this way we may gauge the power of the cross. Take it: 1. In regard to *the powers of darkness.* "For this purpose the Son of God was manifested, that he might destroy the works of the devil" (1 John iii. 15; comp. Heb. ii. 14). The execution of this purpose is intimated in Col. ii. 15, "Having put off from himself the principalities and the powers, he made a show of them openly, triumphing over them in it [the cross]." It is as if ten thousand fiendish arms were stretched out to pluck him from that cross; but he strips them off him, and hurls them back into the abyss. It cost him much to win that victory, even

" strong crying and tears" and an agony of soul beyond all human experience; but the triumph was complete. 2. In regard to *the actual salvation of sinners.* To deliver a man from sin in all respects, undo its direful effects, and fit him to take his place among God's sons,—what power is adequate to this? Take Paul's own conversion, on which apologists have been willing to stake the supernatural character of Christianity. And every conversion presents substantially the same features. It is nothing less than a new creation (2 Cor. v. 17)—a calling of light out of darkness, order out of chaos, life out of death; and this is a more wonderful exercise of power than that which gave existence to the universe. The fair temple of God in the soul has to be built, not out of fresh-hewn stones, but out of the ruins of our former selves. A poor weak man is rescued from corruption, defended "against the spiritual hosts of wickedness in the heavenly places" (Eph. vi. 12), and presented at last without blemish before God,— what but Divine power can accomplish this? Add to this the exercise of this power in a countless number of instances. From the steps of the throne survey that radiant multitude, beautiful with the beauty of God and noble with the nobility of Christ, and the might of the cross will need no other proof. 3. In regard to *what he enables his people to do and suffer for his sake.* Take an active missionary life like that of Paul. Read such a catalogue of afflictions as he gives us in 2 Cor. xi. 23—33, and ask why a man should voluntarily undergo all these. Thousands have followed his example, meeting toil, privation, death, for their Lord's sake. Nor does the power of the cross shine less conspicuously in the sick-chamber. How many a Christian invalid exhibits a patience, a meekness, a cheerfulness, which can be found nowhere else!—B.

Vers. 26—31.—*Salvation all of God.* The apostle has shown, in the previous section, that the cross of Christ, which men count foolish and weak, is really the wisdom and the power of God. In proof of this he now calls their attention to the social status of the converts at Corinth. For the most part they were of no account in the world's esteem; but, though nobodies according to the flesh, they were raised to true dignity in Christ.

I. THE CHRISTIAN CALLING DOES NOT PROCEED ON THE PRINCIPLES OF THIS WORLD. "For behold your calling, brethren," etc. The Church at Corinth was composed chiefly of the poor and the illiterate. The philosophers and the rich merchants, the high-born and those who occupied positions of influence, had but few representatives among the disciples of Jesus. They were drawn in great part from those whom the world reckoned foolish, weak, base, and of no importance. And the case of Corinth was not singular. It is characteristic of Christianity to begin low down. The Lord Jesus himself was not born in a royal palace or nursed among the lordly of the earth. His birthplace was a stable, his home the simple dwelling of Joseph, his training-school the carpenter's workshop. His disciples were derived mainly from the labouring classes. One or two of the twelve may have been in easy circumstances, but none of them appears to have been of high birth; and outside this circle his followers, with the exception of Nicodemus and Joseph of Arimathæa, were almost entirely of the same class. From the beginning, therefore, the gospel found acceptance, not in the high places of the land, nor among the representatives of the learning and religion of the time, but among the plain, unschooled, unsophisticated people. "The poor have good tidings preached to them" (Luke vii. 22). Beyond the bounds of Palestine it was the same. The pride of wisdom and station closed the ear against the story of the cross. It did not flatter the wise or the great. It spoke to all alike as sinners needing a common salvation, and summoned all to repentance and faith. The result may be illustrated by comparing the reception of the gospel at Athens and at Corinth. In the metropolis of philosophy and art only a few were converted (Acts xvii. 16—34); in the capital of trade a large Church was formed. So also at Rome. The first and chief successes of the gospel were among the lower classes of society; and this was urged as an objection against it. Celsus jeers at the fact that "wool-workers, cobblers, leather-dressers, the most illiterate and clownish of men, were zealous preachers of the gospel, and particularly that they addressed themselves, in the first instance, to women and children." The proud Roman could not understand a religion which treated the slave as a man, and addressed itself equally to all. But the leaven thus put into the mass spread not only outwards but upwards. From slave to master, from plebeian to patrician, did the blessed influence pass, till at last the emperor himself was constrained to do homage to Jesus Christ. To a large extent the course of the gospel is the same still. In our own country the profession of Christianity is not confined to any class in society; but a living godliness is a plant of rarer growth. Among our men of science, our philosophers and poets, and our hereditary nobility, there are to be found eminent Christians, whose lives evince the power of the gospel over the finest intellects and the most exalted station; yet it is mainly among those less privileged that the Church is strongest. The greatest number of her members are to be found among the humbler classes, especially among those who have neither riches nor poverty, and who know the meaning of honest work. Illustrate also from the history of modern missions to the heathen.

II. REASONS FOR THE DIVINE METHOD. When men inaugurate any new scheme or system, they seek the patronage of great names in order to recommend it to the people; but the gospel of salvation was not proclaimed to the world under the auspices of kings and philosophers. This is referred to the *purpose of God* (vers. 27, 28), according to which all things proceed. More particularly the end in view is: 1. *The humiliation of human pride.* "That no flesh should glory before God" (ver. 29). Human wisdom and power are of small account in this matter. Salvation is all of God. Had he chosen the wise and the great, pride might have boasted itself before him; but in choosing the foolish and the weak, all ground of glorying is removed. This does not imply that the one class is of more value in God's sight than the other; nor does it put a premium upon ignorance and weakness. It means that the wise man will not be saved because of his wisdom, nor the nobleman because of his high birth, nor the rich man because of his wealth. All trust in these things must be *put to shame*, as is done when they that are destitute of them enter the kingdom of heaven more readily. In the eye of the gospel all men are equal, which means that some must be humbled, while others are exalted. It is always our Father's way to "hide these things from the wise and understanding, and to reveal them unto babes" (Matt. xi. 25). Pride is at once insulting to God and hurtful to man; and it is in mercy that he requires us to "become as little children" (Matt. xviii. 3). In like manner, the advance of the gospel in the earth is not to be promoted by an arm of flesh ("not by might, nor by power," etc., Zech. iv. 6). Christian work must not be undertaken for the aggrandizement of persons, or parties, or sects. The flesh must not be elevated to the dishonour of God. 2. *The advancement of the Divine glory.* Human pride is to be humbled, that the honour of salvation may belong to God alone. It is the prerogative of the Almighty to make his own glory the chief end of all he does. No created being can do so. For man and angel, happiness consists in seeking the glory of our Father in heaven. A life with self as the centre, self as the aim, must be a life of misery. Does not this explain the misery of Satan? "Better to reign in hell than serve in heaven!" It is otherwise with the Most High. To seek his own glory is simply to desire truth and reality. In the nature of things all praise is due to him alone who is the Alpha and the Omega of existence. Hence the glory of God coincides with the greatest happiness of men, in the matter of salvation as in other things. "He that glorieth, let him glory in the Lord."

III. THE RICHES IN CHRIST. Salvation is due entirely to God. It is *of him* that we are in Christ Jesus. The believer's union with Christ has been brought about by God Himself, who has given us all things in his Son. 1. *Wisdom.* "In him are all the treasures of wisdom and knowledge hidden" (Col. ii. 3). He reveals to us God—his nature and his will, his purpose and plan of grace. In the person and work of Christ; in his incarnation, life, teaching, atonement,—the wisdom of God shines out conspicuously. And in union with Christ we become truly wise. In him we have the key which opens all mysteries. We learn to know God and to know ourselves; and in him the broken fellowship between God and us is restored. The quest for wisdom, alike in its speculative and in its practical form, is satisfied only in him. 2. *Righteousness.* He is "Jehovah our Righteousness" (Jer. xxiii. 6). To be righteous is to be in entire consistence with the mind and Law of God; and *this* Jesus, as our Representative, was. He bore the penalty of our sins, and met the positive requirements of the Law; and thus wrought out a righteousness for us (2 Cor. v. 12; Gal. iii. 13; 1 Pet. ii. 24). When by faith we accept Jesus Christ as our Saviour, his work is reckoned to us, and we are received as righteous for his sake. 3. *Sanctification.* This includes the whole of the process by which we are restored to the image of God. Not only is the righteousness of Christ imputed to us, the character of Christ must also be reproduced in us; and this is the work of the Holy Spirit. It is his to illuminate, regenerate, purify; and the whole man thus renewed is consecrated to God. Every part of the nature—spirit, soul, body; every activity of thought, affection, desire, purpose; all are transformed and devoted to the noblest service. Justification and sanctification are the two sides of one whole, never to be separated. 4. *Redemption.* This denotes deliverance from all evil, enemies, afflictions, death. Soul and body shall be completely emancipated, and presented at last without blemish (Rom. viii. 23; Eph. v. 26, 27).

LESSONS. 1. To be emptied of self is a necessary condition of God's working in us and by us. 2. Give God all the glory of salvation. 3. Christ is the Source of all blessings. "In him ye are made full" (Col. ii. 10).—B.

Ver. 6.—"*The testimony of Christ.*" There are two kinds of testimony—the external and the internal; the revelation without and the revelation within; the written historical testimony that God has given us of his Son, and that which consists in the facts of Christian consciousness, the consciousness of one in whom he dwells. These are not to be regarded as separate and independent. The external record is vain until graven on the living heart; while there could be no such inward realization apart from the outward record, with all that helps to attest and substantiate it. The one is to the other as the river is to the bed in which it flows, as the echo to the voice that awakens it, as the musical harmony to the instrument by which it is produced. The revealed truth is made the instrument and channel of a hidden life. The written record becomes a vital experience. The testimony finds its answer in the living heart. Thus was the gospel word "confirmed" in the Corinthians, as in all who savingly receive it. Consider—(1) *The testimony;* (2) *the confirmation.*

I. THE TESTIMONY. It is the truth about Christ which formed the sum and substance of the apostolic message. The truth "as it is in Jesus." 1. *The message contains two elements—the historical and the doctrinal.* An unwarrantable separation is sometimes made between these. The attempt to sever the historic fact from some form of dogmatic teaching by which that fact is linked with the spiritual interests and needs of men, as the Divine answer to them, is irrational and vain. The fact contains within itself the doctrine. It is not a meaningless incident. What is the doctrine but just the articulate expression of its meaning? Take any of the recorded apostolic discourses—Peter's sermon on the day of Pentecost (Acts ii.), Paul's sermon in the synagogue at Antioch (Acts xiii.), or his summary of the gospel (ch. xv. 1—4)—they are none of them bare statements of historic fact. They glow with the living force of words that carry the historic fact home to the consciences and hearts of men as God's condemnation of sin and pledge of forgiveness and promise of the life everlasting. 2. *The authority of this message of mingled fact and doctrine lies in its divinity.* It is the testimony that "God has given us of his Son." The reason men disregard the appeals of the gospel is that they do not believe or feel this. Their diviner sensibility is so deadened by other than Divine influences, that they fail to recognize the approach of God to their souls. If they know that God is speaking to them how can they resist? "If we receive the witness of men, the witness of God is greater." We readily receive the witness of men. Our whole social existence proceeds on the principle of faith in the general veracity of those with whom we have to do. Why can we not carry up into the higher region a principle of action that in the lower we feel to be so salutary and necessary? Habitual distrust of one's fellow-creatures would be a dishonour done to our common nature, would poison the very springs of human life, and turn some of our purest joys to bitterness. And yet men cherish on the heavenward side of their being a cold, repellent spirit of unbelief that gives the lie to a God of infinite truth and righteousness and love. "He that hath received his testimony hath set to his seal that God is true" (John iii. 33); "He that believeth not God hath made him a liar," etc. (1 John v. 10).

II. THE CONFIRMATION. For the testimony to assert its authority in a way that cannot be gainsaid is one thing; for it to be practically and savingly efficacious is another. No man to whom the message has intelligibly come can escape the special

responsibility under which it places him. His whole position as an accountable being
is henceforth changed. He may affect to disown the claim, but the sovereign authority
of that claim is over him still, and he must answer for his neglect (John xii. 47).
The testimony accomplishes its end only when the Spirit of God writes it in living
characters on the "fleshy table of the heart."   How important a transition of thought
to pass from the region of words, ideas, outward revelations, to that of the perceptions,
affections, and energies of a personal life! Consider the confirmation : 1. *As regards
its effect on the believer himself*. "He that believeth on the Son of God hath the
witness in himself" (1 John v. 10). It has become emphatically his own.   The
Christ revealed to him is now "in him," a quickening, sanctifying power, "the hope
of glory," "a well of water springing up unto everlasting life." All life is self-asserting,
self-assuring. It proves and verifies itself. We don't question the reality of our
physical life. We know that we live *in living*. We think, feel, breathe, move, act—
therefore we live. So spiritually; in the sensibilities and energies that accompany
Christian faith we have sufficient proof of the power of Christ "to give eternal life to
as many as believe in him." And as no external evidence can supply the place of
this, so no outward assault of the forces of unbelief can have any real power against it.
"We know that the Son of God is come," etc. (1 John v. 20). This is what is wanted
to give firmness to men in these days of restless thought and unsettled opinion ; not
mere doctrinal safeguards, not theological rigidity, but the deep inward consciousness
of the life-giving power of Christ. 2. *As regards its effect on others*. The testimony
of Christ wins its victories in the world on the strength, not so much of historic or
miraculous or argumentative proof, but of what it is and what it can do. The fruits
of Christian character and deed are the mightiest of all arguments. Saintly, consecrated lives ;—it is these that give convincing force to the doctrine. "Ye are our
epistle," etc. (2 Cor. ii. 2, 3).—W.

Ver. 13.—*Divisions*. The "contentions" in the Church at Corinth, the report of
which had reached St. Paul, and which he here rebukes, were probably not the outgrowth of definite party divisions, but were individual differences as to who among
the great Christian leaders should receive superior honour. They were individual
strifes, however, that might develop into very serious divisions—schisms (σχίσματα)
that would utterly rend asunder the fellowship of the Church. It must have been
deeply painful to the apostles that they should thus be set in rivalry with one another,
as if they were seeking the ends of their own vain ambition, and still more that their
names should be permitted in any way to obscure the glory of the Name of their
Divine Master. "Is Christ divided?" The question suggests—
I. The essential unity of Christ. Consider different aspects of this unity. As
it regards : 1. *His own person*. In him we see the blending of the Divine and human
in one glorious personality, the balance and harmony of all conceivable forms of
moral excellence. No discord in his being, no flaw in his character, no failure in his
life; he stands before us in every light, on every side, a complete, symmetrical, and
perfect whole. 2. *His redeeming purpose and the means by which he effects it*. He
comes to deliver men from the power of evil, to turn them from their iniquities, to
restore them to fellowship with God. The end he seeks is the same for all. "There
is no distinction ; for all have sinned," etc. (Rom. iii. 22—24). And as all human
distinctions are lost in the common need of salvation, so in Christ the same possibility
of good is placed within the reach of all : "As through one trespass the judgment
came unto all men," etc. (Rom. v. 18). There is but one gospel message, and it is
"the power of God unto salvation to every one that believeth." 3. *The life with which
he inspires those who receive him*. In whomsoever it dwells this life is always one—
one in its affections and energies, in the laws of its development, in the fruit it bears,
in the ends to which it leads. The inspiration of a common spirit-life is the grand
uniting principle amid endless individual diversities. "By one Spirit we are all
baptized into one body," etc. (ch. xii. 13). 4. *His authority as the sole Head of the
Church*. There can be no divided authority. In the very nature of things, Christ
can own no rival. The body can have but one living head, the source of informing,
guiding, and controlling power. Its own unity lies mainly in the recognition of this :
"One Lord, one faith, one baptism," etc. (Eph. iv. 5, 6 ; ch. viii. 6 ; xii. 5).

II. THE EVIL OF EVERYTHING THAT VIOLATES THIS UNITY. The divisions of the Church of Corinth were deprecated by the apostle as an offence against the fundamental principles and laws of the Christian fellowship. All such divisions have certain marked features of evil. 1. *They exalt that which is subordinate and accidental at the expense of the vital and supreme.* The form of truth is placed above the spirit, doctrine above life, the instrument above the power, appearances above realities, the shadow above the substance—creeds, systems, men, above Christ (ch. iii. 4, 5). Examine them closely, and you find that all "contentions" in the Church mean this. 2. *They engender mutual animosities which are destructive of the fellowship of a common life.* Here lies the heart and core of the evil. Mere outward diversities are not so much to be dreaded. Schism is a thing of the spirit. It lies not in the formal separations that conscience may dictate, but in the fierce antagonisms that may unhappily, but not necessarily, grow out of them. Sectarianism consists not in the frank outspoken assertion of individual convictions, but in the bitterness and uncharitableness with which one conscience may assert itself against all other consciences. So that the very spirit of schism may inspire that passion for uniformity which would suppress individual liberty of thought and speech and action. The true schismatics are those who by their intolerance create divisions. Whatever tends to check the flow of spiritual fellowship violates the law of Christ. We do well carefully to watch against the estrangement of heart that difference of religious opinion and ecclesiastical practice too often generates, "giving diligence to keep the unity of the Spirit in the bond of peace" (Eph. iv. 3). 3. *They bring public dishonour on the Name of Christ.* That Name is the symbol of a Divine reconciliation—the reconciliation of man to man, as well as man to God. But in this case it is made the cause of separations. Christ came to bind men together in a true brotherhood; but thus he is made a "divider." "Where jealousy and faction are there is confusion and every evil work" (Jas. iii. 16). And thus the very essential principle and purpose of the Saviour's mission is falsified, and occasion is given to the enemy to blaspheme. Few things have a more disastrous effect in discrediting the Christian cause than the bitterness of contending parties in that Church which is "the pillar and ground of the truth." 4. *They squander and dissipate energies that ought rather to be devoted to active service in the Lord's kingdom.* Think of the waste of spiritual force these divisions involve! If half the enthusiasm mere partisanship has engendered had been expended on some real substantial work for the good of humanity and the glory of God, how blessed the results might have been! In one sense, of course, all zeal for truth, however subordinate the position of the particular truth may be, is for the good of humanity and the glory of God; but to be contending for the maintenance of comparatively trivial points of difference in violation of the spirit that ought to harmonize all differences, and of the grand responsibilities of the Christian calling, is to be guilty of "tithing the mint and the anise and the cummin, to the neglect of the weightier matters of the Law."

III. THE CURE FOR THESE EVILS. There is but one cure—to keep Christ in all the glory of his being and the supremacy of his claims habitually before our minds, and to open our hearts freely to the inspiration of his Spirit. This will raise us above the littleness and meanness of party strife. A lofty object of contemplation and a high moral purpose must needs have an elevating and ennobling influence on the whole man. It will subdue within us all base affections, will rebuke our personal vanity, will enlarge our sympathies, will chasten our lesser enthusiasms. We shall not be in much danger of helping by our influence to violate the unity of the great household of faith, when our souls are filled with the full-orbed glory of the undivided Christ. The expansive Spirit he gives will teach us to say, "Grace be with all them that love our Lord Jesus Christ in sincerity."—W.

Vers. 22—24.—"*Christ crucified.*" It is difficult for us to realize the deep-rooted strength of the prejudices the truth of Christ encountered on its first proclamation. One thing, however, is clear—while the apostles accommodated the mode of their teaching to those prejudices, they never so accommodated the teaching itself. Their doctrine was the same for all. They never thought of modifying it or softening down its essential peculiarities, to suit the taste of any. With reference to the *form* of his teaching, St. Paul says, "To the weak I became weak," etc. (ch. ix. 22); with reference to the *substance*, "Though we or an angel from heaven should preach any other gospel," etc. (Gal. i. 8). Jews and Greeks are the two broad classes under which these varieties of prejudice might be grouped; and here are their prominent characteristics. "Jews ask for signs." It was so in the days of Christ. "An evil and adulterous generation," etc. (Matt. xii. 39); "Except ye see signs and wonders," etc. (John iv. 48). And in the apostolic age the race everywhere manifested the same mental tendency. They were sign-seeking Jews. "Greeks seek after wisdom"—such wisdom as found a home for itself in their own philosophic schools. They knew no other. Thus each of these classes illustrated a particular aspect of the vanity of human nature; the one craving after that which would minister to the pride of sense, the other to the pride of intellect. For both Paul had but one message: "Christ and him crucified." Note—

I. THE THEME OF THE APOSTOLIC TEACHING. "We preach Christ crucified" (see also ch. ii. 2; Gal. iii. 1). This is the sum and substance of evangelical doctrine, the idea that filled the foremost place in the apostle's thought and supplied the chief inspiration of his heroic life. Not a little of the emphasis falls on the word "crucified." He preached Christ as the personal Redeemer of men, and that not merely as the great miracle-working Prophet of God, the moral Reformer, the Revealer of new truth, the Lawgiver of a new spiritual kingdom, the Example of a divinely perfect life, but as the Victim of death. It was in the death of Christ that the whole force and virtue of the apostolic testimony about him lay. What meaning did Paul attach to this death? The mere reiteration of the fact itself would be powerless apart from its doctrinal significance. If he had represented it simply as the crowning act of a life of devotion and self-sacrifice in the cause of God and of humanity, he would have placed the Name of Christ on the level of many another name, and his death on a level with the death of many another witness for truth and righteousness; instead of which a virtue and a moral efficacy are everywhere imputed to it, which cannot be conceived of as belonging to any other death, and which alone explain the position it occupies in apostolic teaching (see ch. v. 7; Eph. i. 7; ii. 14, 16; Col. i. 21; 1 John i. 7; ii. 2). Forgiveness of sins, spiritual cleansing, moral freedom, practical righteousness, fellowship with God, the hope of eternal glory,—all are set forth here as fruits of the death of Christ and our faith in it. St. Paul made it the one grand theme of his ministry, because he knew that it would meet the deep and universal needs of humanity. No other word would bring rest to the troubled conscience and satisfaction to the longing, weary, distracted heart of man; no other voice could awaken the world to newness of life out of the dread shadow of despair and death in which it lay.

II. THE RECEPTION IT MET WITH, from "Jews," "Gentiles" and "them that are called." 1. "*Unto Jews a stumbling-block*"—an offence, something "scandalous." On several special grounds Christ was such an offence to them. (1) The lowliness of his origin. (2) The unostentatious character of his life. (3) The unworldliness of his aims and methods. (4) The expansive spirit of his doctrine; its freedom from class and national exclusiveness. (5) The universality of the grace he offered. (6) Above all, the fact of his crucifixion. How could they recognize as their Messiah One who had died as the vilest of malefactors; died by the judgment of their rulers and amid the derision of the people; died by a death that above all others they abhorred? The cross, which Paul made the basis of human hope and the central glory of the universe, was to them "a stone of stumbling and a rock of offence." 2. "*Unto Gentiles foolishness.*" The Gentile world was pervaded by Greek sentiment. "Greece had now for more than a century been but a province of Rome; but the mind of Greece had mastered that of Rome." "The world in name and government was Roman, but in feeling and civilization Greek." Such a world scorned the "preaching of the cross" because: (1) It lowered the pride of the human intellect, both by its simplicity and by its profundity—so plain that "the wayfaring man though a fool" could understand it, too deep for the utmost stretch of thought to fathom. (2) It revealed the rottenness of the human heart beneath the fairest garment of civilization and culture. It made man dependent for all his light upon supernatural revelations, and for all his hopes of redemption on the spontaneous impulse of sovereign mercy. No wonder it was "foolishness" to proud Romans and polished, philosophic Greeks. And have we not around us now similar phases of aversion to the doctrine of "Christ crucified"? The spirit of the world is not the spirit of the cross. The one is carnal, vain, selfish, revengeful, self-indulgent; the other is spiritual, lowly, benevolent, forgiving, self-abandoning. The cross to every one of us means submission, humiliation, self-sacrifice, it may be reproach and shame; and these are hard to bear. It is hard to say, with Paul, "God forbid that I should glory," etc. The cross may occupy a prominent place in our creed, our worship, our sermons and songs, may decorate our churches, may be made a favourite instrument of personal adornment; but to have its spirit filling our hearts, moulding and governing our whole being and life, is another thing. 3. "*Unto them that are called,*" etc. The "called" are they who "are being saved" (ver. 18). In the case of all such the Divine purpose in the gospel is answered. They are called, and they obey the call. The heavenly voice falls on their ears, penetrates the secrecy of their souls, and there is life for them in the sound, because, like the still, small voice that breathed in the hearing of Elijah at the mouth of the cave, "the Lord is in the voice." The proof they have that the gospel is the embodiment of the power and wisdom of God is the infallible seal of the Spirit, the unanswerable witness of a Divine and heavenly life. Is it a "sign" that you ask for? Believe in Christ, and you shall have within you that mightiest of all wonders, the miracle of grace by which a soul is translated from darkness into light, and from the death of sin to the life of holiness. Is it "wisdom" you seek after? Believe in Christ, and he will unlock for you the unsearchable riches of the mind and heart of God.—W.

Ver. 7.—*The patience of hope.* "Waiting for the revelation of our Lord Jesus Christ." Old Testament worthies waited for the advent of Messiah and the consolation of Israel. New Testament saints wait for the second coming of the Lord, the completion of the Church in holiness, and its entrance into his glory at his appearing. They already possess Christ by faith. He answers for them in order to their justification, and he dwells in them in order to their sanctification. They love him as their Saviour unseen, and therefore they long to see him as he is. Men who are afraid of judgment hope for acquittal; men who are weary and worn hope for rest; men whose earthly course has been disappointing hope for a better world; but none of these wishes or expectations come up to the blessed hope which is distinctively Christian. We look for the Saviour. We wait for the apocalypse of our Lord.

I. THE GROUND ON WHICH WE CHERISH THIS EXPECTATION. It is simply the word of promise. In parables, and in plain statements also, Jesus Christ assured his disciples that he would return in an unexpected hour. At his ascension the heavenly messengers, "men in white apparel," said explicitly to the "men of Galilee" that "this Jesus" would return from heaven. Accordingly the apostles infused this hope into the early Church; all the Epistles refer to it; and the last book of the Bible closes with a repetition of the Lord's promise: "Behold, I come quickly;" and the response of the Church: "Even so, come, Lord Jesus!" We do not entertain any question of probability. For Christians the matter rests on a sure word of prophecy and promise, pledging the truth of the Son of God. If any persons are capable of believing that the Son of God spoke at random or kindled by his words expectations that are never to be fulfilled, we cannot prove to them that Christ will come again. But all who reverence him as One in whose mouth no guile was ever found, are bound to believe that he will be revealed in his glory; and all who love him will look for his appearing.

II. REASONS FOR OUR WAITING FOR THE LORD. 1. "We see not yet all things put under him," and we long to do so. Promises of universal sovereignty and honour made to Christ in the Psalms wait for fulfilment. Prayers of many generations made "for him" as well as through him, wait for the answer. Therefore the Church, believing the promises and continuing the prayers, above all, loving him to whom such things are promised and the ardour of such prayers is devoted, cannot but wait for the Lord as night-watchers wait for the morning. Ever since the Ascension, Christ has had, by appointment of the Father, "all authority in heaven and earth." The glory in heaven is hidden from us, but all may see that since the day of his ascension his Name has been rising continually above all other names known to mankind, and has so extended the area of its fame and influence that it is beyond question the mightiest name upon earth. Still Christ has many enemies. They are not yet made "his foot stool." And many of those who are called Christians are at heart indifferent to his cause, disobedient to his Word, apathetic about his kingdom and glory. Then the tribes and nations of the earth do not to any appreciable extent, even in Christendom, acknowledge or serve the Lord Jesus; and there are vast populations that have scarcely heard his Name. Even in our own country, one is struck with the avoidance of any express mention of him who is Lord of all, as Lord over us. In public documents, expressive of the national mind and will, there may be reference to "Almighty God," and to a superintending Providence—cold phrases of theism; but there is an apparent reluctance to name the Lord Jesus Christ, and to own submission to his Word. This is grievous to those who love him and know that he is the sole sufficient Healer of mankind. They take their part zealously in all movements to check injustice, to stay the fœtid streams of vice, to relieve misery, and to spread virtue and peace; but they lament that Christ is so little sought and honoured in the efforts of philanthropy, and they often cry to him in their struggle, "Lord, how long? When wilt thou return from the far country? When wilt thou take thy great power, and reign?" 2. We have such correspondence now with the unseen Saviour as makes us long for his bright presence. It is not fair or reasonable to put the revelation of Christ to us now by the Holy Spirit against the personal revelation to his saints at his second coming, and to ask which of them is the more to be desired. Each is to be desired in its season, and the first whets the longing for the second. If I have had pleasant and profitable correspondence for years with one whom I have not seen, but who is known to me by his wisdom and kindness; if he has done me more good than all the men whom I have seen, taught me, helped me, and stamped the impression of himself on my mind and heart; do I not long to see him face to face, and eagerly wait for a day when I may be nearer to him who has become indispensable to me, the very life of my life? Surely it is so between Christians and Christ. They have heard his words, received his Spirit, had much correspondence with him in prayer and the Lord's Supper, got much help from him in time of need. Though unseen, he has been far more to them than all the teachers and friends whom they have seen; and for that very reason they long to behold him. Their hearts can never be quite satisfied till they see the Lord. 3. We are weary of ourselves and ashamed of our faults, and therefore long to be perfected at his coming. It is true that the life of faith has deep wells of comfort, and Christians ought to be happy. It is also true that the abiding Spirit of Christ is able to keep his servants from sin, and to sustain them in a course of holy obedience. But it is useless to dispute the fact that we are all imperfect in character and faulty in service. We fall short of our best aims, blunder in our well-doing, spoil much good by faults of temper and even of manner, and are unprofitable servants. The best Christians, in whom perhaps we see no blemish, see in themselves sin and imperfection to the last. Now, we make no excuse for fault or inconsistency. We maintain that honest servants of Jesus Christ will aim daily and prayerfully at amendment, and endeavour to walk more closely with God. Still, there will always be some defect till the servants see their Lord. It is his coming that will give the signal for the perfecting of his people, and their complete transformation into his likeness. Such is the doctrine often taught by the Apostle Paul: "Unreprovable in the day of our Lord Jesus Christ" (ver. 8); "Unblamable in holiness before our God and Father at the coming of our Lord Jesus with all his saints" (1 Thess. iii. 13); "Without blame at the coming of our Lord Jesus Christ" (1 Thess. v. 23). There may here be added the prospect of the Lord's kind approval of diligent though imperfect service rendered to him, for which he will award a kingly recompense. But we do not much dwell on this, because the thought of getting anything from the King is not so dear to those who love him as the expectation of being made like him, purified as he is pure. Therefore the intense longing of the saints for the revelation of our Lord Jesus. (1) *Watch and be sober.* Extravagance of mind, glorying in the flesh, indulgence of inordinate desire, are not becoming in men who wait for the Lord. Be temperate in all things. (2) *Watch and pray.* Ask God to help your infirmities, and to deliver you from the spirit of slumber. Your lamps will not go out so long as you pray; for then you have a continual supply of oil. (3) *Watch and work.* The Lord followed up the parable of the waiting virgins with that of the trading servants. Blessed is the faithful and wise servant whom the Lord, when he comes, shall find doing the work assigned to him. The Master bids us not "prepare for death," as so many put it, but prepare to render account of our service to him at his return. Alas for the wicked and slothful servants in that day!—F.

Ver. 9.—*Sacred partnership.* "Ye were called into the fellowship of his Son Jesus Christ our Lord."

I. WHAT IS MEANT BY THIS FELLOWSHIP? It is something more than discipleship or even friendship. It is *partnership.* It is a form of the word which is used when the sons of Zebedee are described as "partners with Simon," and when the early Christians at Jerusalem are said to have "had all things common." St. Paul held that heathen worshippers of demons were sharers with the demons—made common cause with them; and that, on the other hand, the worshippers of God in Christ were sharers with Christ, and made common cause with him, having a common interest in the "day of grace," and destined to a common inheritance in the day of glory. He was theirs, and they were his. It was a partnership which God's purpose had contemplated from of old, which his Spirit had constituted, and which his faithfulness was pledged to maintain and defend. Fail not to observe the fulness of the designation —"his Son Jesus Christ our Lord." Christians are made sons of God by adoption, and, "if children, then heirs, heirs of God, and co-heirs with Christ." But the inheritance is not yet. This is the day of service, perhaps of suffering. Therefore let us consider the fellowship with the Father of which the Son Jesus Christ was conscious in the time of his service and sorrow on the earth; for the holy calling is into the fellowship of the Son. In the Gospel according to St. John it is shown that our Saviour had not only an unbroken communion of heart and purpose with the Father in heaven, but also a conscious participation with the Father. All things that the Father has were his. No practical line of division could be drawn between the Father's will and his will, the Father's works and his works. As in eternal essence, so also in operation, he and the Father were one. The Father was always with him. He spoke words which he had heard with his Father. He did works which were the Father's works, which indeed the Father dwelling in him performed. He received and kept men whom the Father had given to him out of the world. The very hatred which he encountered was the hatred of the world to the Father; and the glory for which he looked was glory with the Father above the reach of human scorn. Now, it is into participation with the Son as thus participating with the Father that Christians are admitted by adoption, in so far as it is possible for the human to share with the Divine. Made one with Christ through faith, they also have communion with him in the sense of having a common cause and interest with him. His Father is their Father, and his God their God. The same Spirit that rested on him is imparted to them. The same works that he did, they do also. The adversaries that they encounter hated him before they hated them. The path which he trod is the path for them also. His cause is their concern; and their cause is his concern. Nay, the very love with which the Father loved the Son is in and on them also; and their hope of glory is the hope to be with him and behold his glory. Thus the fellowship means more than friendship. It is participation with Christ. His disciples are in his work, waiting to enter into his rest; in his battle, looking to share his victory; and, if need be, co-suffering with him, long to be also co-glorified.

II. HOW IS THIS FELLOWSHIP CONSTITUTED? By the gracious call of God. The apostle spoke of the transfer of the Corinthian Christians from their old and sinful fellowships to a new and sacred one, proceeding on the true ideal and heavenly calling of the Church, notwithstanding actual defects and faults which he saw and reproved in the particular Christian community there, and in some of its individual members. Heathen society was in his view a region of darkness; Christian society a region of light. The one was a temple of idols; the other a temple of God. The one was the fellowship of Belial; the other the fellowship of Christ. The transition from the one to the other was by compliance with a call of God, which was a public call to all men in the mouths of preachers of the gospel, an effectual call of the Holy Spirit in all who believed and obeyed.

III. HOW IS THE FELLOWSHIP MANIFESTED, AND SO THE CALLING MADE SURE? 1. In resolutely breaking away from evil associations. Read in the Book of Proverbs how "the wicked join hand in hand," and young persons are ruined by casting in their lot with sinners who entice them. Read in this Epistle the homely saying that "bad company corrupts good manners." And depend on it that it is as needful as ever to shun the society of evil-doers and scoffers. The tendency of the time is to obliterate sharp distinctions on moral grounds, to suggest pleasant compromises, and get rid of all that is difficult or stern in the obligations of Christian consistency. But those who really obey the call of God in Christ Jesus have no choice but to follow the direction of his Word, cost what it may, and therefore must decline intimacy with such as make light of that Word, and must not be conformed to this world, but transformed by the renewing of their minds. 2. In adherence to those who retain and obey the doctrine once for all delivered to the saints. No other conditions should be required. To confine fellowship to those of our own party and of our own way of thinking all round indicates sectarian zeal or self-complacency rather than brotherly love. The Corinthians broke into parties and set up rival names. In their assemblies, and even at the Eucharistic Supper, individuals courted observation and scrambled for precedence over others. It was sadly inconsistent with the fact that God had called them to the fellowship of his Son. It is well to be warned in this matter, so as to have patience one with another, avoid party spirit, and cherish regard for all who, having the doctrine and Spirit of Jesus Christ, are and must be in the holy fellowship. 3. In exhibiting the disposition and mind of Christ. They who have a new life in union and communion with Christ must feel, speak, and act accordingly, putting away evil passions and all deceit, and putting on a meek, compassionate, and honest heart. In the third chapter of the Epistle to the Colossians St. Paul beautifully expounds this holy obligation, and imparts these two pregnant counsels: " Let the peace of Christ rule [arbitrate] in your hearts; " " Let the Word of Christ dwell in you richly in all wisdom."—F.

Ver. 21.—*Wisdom and foolishness.* " Seeing that in the wisdom," etc.

I. THE CONTRAST AT CORINTH. The Greeks could no longer boast of great soldiers or statesmen, for military and political power had deserted them and centred at Rome; but they had among them rhetoricians and philosophers, and still considered themselves intellectual leaders of the world. In this spirit they sat in judgment on the gospel. As to its treatment of the problems of sin and righteousness, they were not deeply concerned; but they were ready to weigh and measure it as a new philosophy, and thought it deficient in intellectual flavour, and quite inferior to the speculations of Greek teachers on the nature of God and of man, the order of the world, the beautiful and the good. St. Paul knew this feeling well, and felt the sting of such imputations, for he was an educated man; but with his usual frankness and manliness he faced this allegation of the supercilious Greeks, and with a sharp spear pricked the bubble of their self-conscious wisdom. Nay, he boldly maintained that what they thought wise was foolish, and what they thought foolish was wise. At the same time, he was too wary and too kind-hearted to irritate his readers by pointing the statement at Corinth, or even at Greece by name. He spoke of the wisdom of the world. Let all the wisdom to which the whole world had attained by human investigation into the things of God be gathered into a heap, and displayed in all the light that the world's best minds could cast upon it, and he would maintain that it was weak, dim, and futile as compared with that wisdom which he and other preachers of Christ could inculcate by the gospel. It was a large claim; but those who know " the wisdom of the ancients " best, and are most accurately acquainted with the ideas and usages of that old heathen world, will be the most ready to say that St. Paul had good ground for his assertion—that his claim was absolutely true.

II. THE CONTRAST TO-DAY. Contemptuous thoughts about the evangelical faith show themselves in many quarters. Men seem to forget that the intellectual advancement of modern society, of which they boast, and which they put forward as superseding old-fashioned Christianity, is itself mainly due to Christianity; that the great schools and universities of Europe all had their roots in religion; and that the very ideas which give tone and breadth to our civilization, the appreciation of the force of truth, and the sense of human brotherhood as something far above mere enthusiasm for one race and antipathy to all others, all have been engendered and fostered by our holy faith Ungratefully overlooking this, men stand to-day on an eminence which Christianity has cast up, and thence decry Christianity. Religion is pronounced weak and quite unprovable. It is not good enough for these very knowing people and hard thinkers! Yet nothing is more certain than that men have urgent need of God, and of those moral helps and profound consolations which are bound up with a knowledge of God and friendship with him. And the heart at times has a passionate cry, " Where is my God?" Put aside the money-bags, the clever schemes, the amusements, the newspapers, the scientific instruments, and the social engagements, and tell me this, O wisdom of the world! "Where is God my Maker? Is there not a Highest and Wisest and Best? And where is he? 'Oh that I knew where I might find him! that I might come even to his seat!'" What can the wisdom of this world reply? It does not deny Divine existence, though a good many persons are coldly doubtful and agnostic on the subject. But as in the first century any effective conception of the Divine was wearing out of thoughtful minds, and there was hardly any religious check on licentiousness and rapacity; so now there are mere vague and high-sounding phrases about the Almighty current among the worldly wise, without as much real faith in God as may restrain one fit of passion or dry one bitter tear. He is a force— personal or impersonal, no one knows; where seated, why operative, how directed, none can tell. Or, he is a dream of ineffable beauty and a fountain of ineffable pity; but how to reconcile this with the more severe aspects of nature and life baffles all the wisdom of the world. The sages are puzzled; the multitude know not what to think; and so the world by wisdom knows not God. But there is a better wisdom, and St. Paul has shown it to us. It may be well for some to watch the weary gropings and struggles of the world's wisdom, and speak or write on the evidences of Biblical theology and the Christian faith when they find a fit occasion. Yet those to whom the gospel is committed ought not, as a general rule, to turn aside to such discussions. They ought to preach often and earnestly, trusting to God's vindication of the wisdom of that which men call foolishness. "What will this babbler say?" they cried against St. Paul in Greece. "What will this heretic say?" they cried against Wickliffe in England, and afterwards against Luther in Germany. "What will this tub-thumper say?" they cried against Whitefield and Wesley—men who, under God, saved the moral and religious life of England. But however preachers may be mocked, the foolishness of preaching has abundantly shown itself to be wisdom by its results. Its seeming weakness covers real power. O wise babbler who says, " Christ crucified!"—F.

Vers. 22—24.—Apostolic preaching. St. Paul magnified the function of preaching. He could leave the baptism of converts and the details of Church business to others, but devoted himself to the proclamation and defence of the truth. No encounter of resistance or neglect could turn him away from preaching Christ, or make him ashamed of the gospel. His occupation gave him a deep and solemn joy.

I. THE SUBJECT OF PREACHING. "We preach Christ crucified;" not Christianity, but Christ; not even the Crucifixion, but the Christ crucified. There are many topics on which we may discourse, many questions we may discuss; but we ought to preach Christ. Indeed, our discourses and discussions have spiritual freshness and force only as they start from or lead up to this central object and inexhaustible theme. And "Christ crucified"—not his life and character and example only, but his dying "for our sins according to the Scriptures;"—it is this that brings peace to troubled consciences of men, and the strongest and most persuasive appeal to their hearts. Little does he know the calling of a New Testament preacher, or the secret of success in proclaiming the Word of truth, who contents himself with occasional and distant allusions to the great Sacrifice. The preacher's place is over against the cross.

II. THE PREJUDICE WHICH THIS PREACHING PROVOKED AND ENCOUNTERED. 1. The Jews required signs. Addicted as they were to much boasting over the signs and wonders wrought for their forefathers by the hand of Moses and other prophets, they demanded signs or prodigies in attestation of the gospel. It was a demand which our Lord always refused when it was urged on him, and one which the apostles did well to discourage. They were not thaumaturgists, but preachers of righteousness. Therefore the Jews believed not. To them Christ crucified was a stumbling-block. A Man whom their council had condemned for blasphemy, and whom the Roman authorities had put to death,—how could he be a Saviour? how could he be the Messiah? Why did not God save him from a miserable death if he delighted in him? Why did he himself not come down from the cross? So the Jews stumbled and fell through unbelief. And to this day they blaspheme the Nazarene as the Man who was hanged upon a tree. A similar prejudice shows itself among Gentile hearers of the gospel also.

Men who have little sense of sin dislike any distinct doctrine of Christ suffering for our sins. And men who think chiefly of power as the sign of Deity stumble at the statement that One who died with nails through his hands and feet was the Son of God and is the Lord of all. 2. The Greeks sought after wisdom. And to them the preaching of the cross seemed to be mere folly. It appealed to the consciousness of sin, which did not much trouble them; and it said nothing to the speculative understanding, hardly noticed those problems over which the philosophical schools of Greece had talked and disputed for generations. The same prejudice hinders many educated men at the present day from receiving the gospel. Is it high thought? What light can the fate of One who was unjustly crucified among the Jews long ago cast on the intellectual problems of to-day? The gospel seems to them unworthy of the serious attention of cultured persons. It may have its uses for the common people; but it has no philosophy, and so it is foolishness! But blessed are they who are not offended in Jesus. When the gospel is preached in the power of the Holy Spirit, it finds some receptive hearts. There are always some on whom the preaching is not wasted or lost.

III. THE GAIN WHICH ACCRUES TO BELIEVERS. They are described as "the called"— a phrase evidently not tantamount to "invited," for all are invited. By "them that are called" are meant those in whom the gospel finds reverence and faith. These are the called according to God's purpose. And see what Christ crucified is to them. 1. Are they Jews, or do they resemble the Jews in looking for signs of heavenly power? Lo! they have in Christ a power far greater than ever dwelt in Moses or Elias. He is the Power of God; and that not merely in the outward sphere in which the Jews desired to see signs and wonders, but also in the inward or moral sphere, where he has shown himself able to loose men from their sins, and to despoil evil principalities and powers, triumphing over them on the cross. Just because "crucified in weakness," he is mighty to save. And all believers of the gospel may know in themselves his sin-vanquishing and burden-bearing power. They need no further sign. 2. Are they disposed by nature, or education, or both, to seek after wisdom like the Greeks? Have they a restless, hungry mind? Here is the best provision for their want, if not for their curiosity. Christ is the Wisdom of God. The highest problems receive light from Christ crucified. Reconciliation of the claims of justice with the yearnings of mercy; justification of the transgressors of moral Law without detriment or dishonour to the Law itself; and the introduction of a new and better life through death, as wheat grows from seed that has died in the earth;—these are not small or easy problems, and they have no solution till we receive the gospel of Christ crucified. He who would make his own calling sure should seek the evidence in his own attitude of mind and heart towards Christ crucified. Is he in your eyes weakness or power? foolishness or wisdom? As the Power of God, has he subdued you to himself? As the Wisdom of God, is he the Light of life to you—the Wonderful, the Counsellor?—F.

Vers. 30, 31.—*All sufficiency in Christ.* "But of him are ye," etc. Here is central truth well compacted. And plain sermons on such texts ought to be frequently given, in order to feed the Church of God, which grows lean on mere fine phrases, sounding periods, controversial janglings, and vapid exhortations.

I. THE WAY OF BLESSING. It is obtained from the grace of God, and by a twofold action of his grace. 1. "Of God are ye in Christ Jesus." This union to Christ, engrafting into Christ, enclosure in Christ, is the root-secret of all spiritual blessing. And while we take action in fleeing to Christ, clinging to him, and making him our Refuge, this very action on our part is ultimately due to the drawing of the Father and the inward operation of the Holy Spirit. Therefore "of God" we are in Christ Jesus. 2. "Of God, Christ is made unto you" who believe, all-sufficient. It is according to God's good pleasure that the merits, riches, and perfections of Christ are made available to you. It is at all events conceivable that one might be saved in and through Christ, and yet receive only in part and scantily out of his fulness. But such is not the will of God concerning us. It is his purpose that we should be, not merely rescued from destruction, but enriched with heavenly blessings in Christ Jesus.

II. THE SUBSTANCE OF BLESSING. What Christ is to his own, who are in him: Wisdom, for they are foolish; Righteousness, for they are unrighteous; Sanctification, for they are unholy; Redemption, for they are lost as other men. 1. *Wisdom.* The early Christians were made wise, not after the type of Jewish rabbis or Greek sages, but as cast into a higher mould—the mind of Christ. And so also now. It must be confessed that some who profess and call themselves Christians speak and act foolishly; but the more Christian at heart one becomes, the more does he gain of a wisdom far beyond the keenest penetration of worldly minds, for he makes his estimates in the light of God, and learns to look on earthly things as from "heavenly places." Christ in us is Wisdom from above. 2. *Righteousness.* "There is none righteous, no, not one." The world can show men of strength, skill, valour, shrewdness, eloquence, erudition, enterprise; but where is the righteous man? Alas! there is not one. Nay; but there is One righteous. Jesus Christ was and is that "Just One." And as the wisdom ascribed to him is "the wisdom of God," so also the righteousness attributed to him is "the righteousness of God." This righteous One died for us, the just One for the unjust many. And in his restoration from the dead and return as the righteous One to the Father, there is the basis of acceptance for all who are "of God in him." So righteousness is imputed without works. Christ is made to us Righteousness. 3. *Sanctification.* "Holiness to the Lord" is not known, or even possible, without Christ. Yet "without holiness, no man shall see the Lord." Now, the apostle does not say that Christ is made to us Holiness; for this might seem to favour a doctrine of imputed holiness, which is full of peril. But he is made to us Consecration; so that in him we are constituted saints, separated from evil to the service of the holy God, and from him we derive purifying and sustaining grace for that newness of life to which we are called and pledged. 4. *Redemption.* There is no need to say "complete redemption," or "final redemption," as some menders of Scripture have been wont to do, because the thing in view is not "the redemption of the purchased possession," or the redemption of the body at the resurrection of the just; but the redemption which is now obtained by reason of the precious blood of Christ, because he gave himself a ransom for us. So we have decisive and conclusive quittance, both from guilt and from "the house of bondage." And here also Christ is all.

III. THE AIM AND ISSUE OF BLESSINGS SO CONFERRED. (Ver. 31.) That the saved may have confidence in the Lord, and ascribe to him all the praise and glory of their salvation. It is a good test of doctrine, whether it refers all sufficiency and renders all praise to God in Christ Jesus. It is a test of the heart, whether it delights to have it so. We mean not merely glory and thanks to God for sending the Saviour into the world—for so much is common to all types of Christian doctrine; but also glory and praise to God for bringing men into union with the Saviour, and so into personal possession of the blessings of salvation. It is reckoned a mark of a base spirit among men that it assumes credit to which it is not entitled, and ignores its obligations to others. But noble minds are the first to say that, for whatever they have accomplished, they were not sufficient of themselves, but had help of Divine providence, help of favouring circumstances, and help of their fellow-men. When grace is received from Heaven, how base and unthankful would it be to boast as if one had not received it! Some cannot give glory to the Lord, because they really are not in Christ; and some because, though perhaps in him, they do not trust in him with steady faith. Some too are always trying to be saved. They spend their lives in the channel of the Red Sea, sore afraid of the Egyptians. They never come up on the shore where the delivered sing to the Lord who has triumphed gloriously.—F.

Vers. 1—9.—*Paul's claim to apostleship.* The personal appearance and characteristic disposition of Paul, with the particular circumstances which led to the writing of this letter, and roused intense personal feeling, form a fitting introduction. Paul blends Sosthenes with himself in the salutation, partly because of this man's connection with Corinth (see Acts xviii. 17), partly as an answer to those who charged him with making too much of himself and his apostolic rights. By associating this name in the address, Paul intimates that he did not desire to make himself the sole guide of the Church, nor would he put himself before Christ in the thought of the people. The general idea of apostleship is *mission.* An apostle is a *sent* one, or a *commissioned* one It was applied to other than the twelve, or thirteen, usually so called; Barnabas and Silas coming under this classification. As applied to the "twelve" (either as including

Judas or Matthias), the term involves *personal knowledge of Christ* and *direct reception of the commission from him* (Acts i. 21, 22).

I. THE GROUND OF PAUL'S CLAIM. It could not rest on personal knowledge of Christ's ministry. We have no good reason for assuming that Paul ever saw Christ in the flesh. That, however, was not the more essential of the two qualifications. Paul had received a direct call to his office from the Lord himself. For the historical facts, see Acts ix.; xiii. 2. Such a direct call did not involve infallibility; but it did form a ground for feeling *personal confidence*, for speaking with *prophetic boldness*, and for exercising *measures of authority*. More especially when we find the "call" was followed up with signs of the Divine presence and approval in the *working of miracles*. Paul ever makes much of the directness of his "call." This point he most emphatically insists on when writing to the Galations (Gal. i. 1, 11, 12). It is characteristic of Paul's training and habit of thought, as a Jew, that even this "call" from Christ should be conceived only as *agency* carrying out the sovereign and holy "*will and purpose*" of God the Father. It was, through all the ages, a characteristic of pious Jews that they traced everything to God's supreme will, and saw that will working through all. Compare and illustrate by the Mohammedan conception of *Islâm*, or submission to the will of God.

II. THE SPECIAL FEATURES OF PAUL'S COMMISSION. It was in full harmony with, yet perfectly distinct from, that of the other apostles. Such distinction may be traced *in its sphere*. He was to go to the *Gentiles*, and find opportunities of labour among them. He was the pioneer of Christian missions to the Gentile world. But adaptation to this sphere and work involved a further distinction *in the subject of his commission*. There is a marked *individuality* in the *form* of Paul's presentation of the truth in Christ. We must give full recognition to that individuality, and its adaptation to the thought and life of the people among whom Paul laboured; but we should carefully guard against *exaggerations* which would set Paul's apprehension of the Christian truths out of harmony with that of the earlier apostles. Paul's leading subject may be thus stated: Christ is *risen*; then his life-work is *accepted by God*; and he is *living*, prepared for *direct* saving relations with all who look to him in *penitence* and *faith*. To enter into direct, personal, living relations with Christ is to find *perfect freedom* from all other religious or ecclesiastical bondages, old or new.

Apply by showing what is the call to Christian office and ministry now. There is a selection of men by Divine *endowment* and Divine *providence*. These two go together, and the *recognition* of them may be made by other than the man himself. Such a "call" still involves *teaching power, persuasive influence,* and *gracious authorities.*—R. T.

Ver. 2.—*What the Church is, and what the Church ought to be.* In introduction deal with the features of Christian life in towns and cities, as represented in Corinth, noticing its relation to *complicated civilization, diversity of sects, class distinctions, society evils,* and *intellectual pride*. Out of the population of such a town as Corinth Paul gathered what he calls a *Church*, and this body he regards *ideally* and *practically*. Here the full conception of what *it should be* is the prominent thing. His advice, given later on, applies to the Church as it *actually was*.

I. THE CHURCH IS A WHOLE, WITH A SPECIALITY. A whole, for it is *the* Church— the Church *of God*, who is One; and it includes "*all* that call upon the name of our Lord Jesus Christ in every place." We fittingly call it the "one holy Catholic and Apostolic Church." But it has a characteristic *speciality*. It can be *localized*. It can be the Church *at Corinth* or at any other place, but the localization does not break up the unity. It is but a condition of the *earthly sphere* which the Church must of necessity have, and need in no way destroy our sense of the complete oneness and wholeness of the Church. The tendency to *sectarian division* can best be checked by fuller presentations of the essential, ideal "wholeness" of Christ's Church. And the same truth alone gives efficient place to the conception of Christ's *living and universal rule*, with its related fact, the *unity and brotherhood of all believers*.

II. THE CHURCH IS A BODY ACTUALLY SANCTIFIED. The two senses in which the term "sanctified" may be used need careful consideration. It may mean "made holy;" and it may mean "set apart," or "consecrated," "devoted to one special object," and this latter is the more frequent and familiar use in Scripture, especially in the Old

Testament, where cities, lands, persons, and things were constantly "sanctified" in the sense of being devoted, or consecrated, to the Divine service. Manifestly the meaning "made actually holy" cannot be that required in our text, for this has never yet, in any age, been the fact concerning Christ's Church; and, indeed, the New Testament holds this forth only as the sublime attainment of the *future*. But it is true of each sincere member, and so of the whole Church, that they are sanctified in the sense of being "self-dedicated," "devoted to God," and so ideally a "holy people." A man *is* what he really wishes to be and endeavours to be; he *is* what he sets before himself as his highest attainment. Guard this truth against misrepresentation and misuse, and make it an incentive to the formation of high ambitions and patient effort for their attainment. Add that the pervading *element, atmosphere,* and *tone* of Christ's Church is *holiness*. Christ present brings the surroundings of the "holy," and we are "called unto holiness." So, ideally, Christ's Church is "sanctified."

III. THE CHURCH IS A BODY SEEKING TO BE PRACTICALLY WHAT IT IS MYSTICALLY. This opens the application of the subject. Our response to and acceptance of the call into Christ's Church puts us under a definite and distinct pledge and responsibility. We bind ourselves to win the *personal holiness* that will match our call and worthily follow it up. This involves due *self-watching* and *self-mastery*, as well as fitting use of the various "*means of grace*" provided for us. What we *ought* to be we shall be found every day *striving* to be, if we are true-hearted and sincere.

In conclusion, revert to the practical bearings of the *oneness* and *wholeness* of Christ's Church. It involves a tender and helpful common brotherhood in *rights,* in *sentiments,* and in *duties.* Such brotherhood is "becoming to saints," to those "called to be saints."—R. T.

Ver. 3.—*The Hebraic and the Christian salutations.* The formalities of politeness have deep meanings, and bear important relations to the social and moral life of cities and nations. The heathen benediction was *Salve,* or "Health to you." The modern salutation, "Good morning," or "Good day," is a brief assertion of national and individual faith in the *one God;* for it really means "God bless you to-day," and so is a perpetual witness against infidelity. The salutation in the text is a blending together of the characteristic points of the Hebrew and the Christian good wishes.

I. FROM THE HEBREW POINT OF VIEW, WHAT WAS INVOLVED IN WISHING "PEACE UNTO YOU"? "Peace" to the Hebrew was the word gathering up the blessings of the keeping of the Jehovah-covenant. If faithful to the claims of that covenant and to the spirit of that covenant, they would realize peace in the *heart,* in the *home,* and in the *state.* And to an *industrial* and *agricultural* people, "peace" would appear the most desirable of all earthly blessings, and the condition of enjoying all others. It may be noticed how the unsettled years of later Jewish history intensified the common desire and prayer for "peace." As the prosperity of the whole land was bound up in the faithfulness of *each member*, it was befitting that each should wish for the other that "peace" which can alone attend on righteousness. So the formality of the salutation covered a real anxiety for brotherly faithfulness to Jehovah.

II. FROM THE CHRISTIAN POINT OF VIEW, WHAT WAS INVOLVED IN WISHING "GRACE AND PEACE UNTO YOU"? The addition is most characteristic, seeing that Christianity declares the "*grace* of God that bringeth salvation." Man discovers that the adequate keeping of covenant, and so securing "peace," is not *within his own power.* It is this discovery that prepares him to welcome the revelation of *grace for his need.* With the *grace* he can attain the *righteousness* which ensures the *peace,* and so he recognizes that both the grace and the peace come *from God.* Then the wish of the early Christian is that a special manifestation of Divine grace may be made to the individual. The salutation, in effect, is this: May you enter fully into the blessings of the gospel, into the grace brought unto men in Jesus Christ; and so may you know the gospel peace, which you will find a hallowing influence resting on all your life! How may we put into modern Christian language the Pauline benediction? And how should we so watch over even the formalities of every-day speech that our common good wishes should be filled with rich and fervent *Christian meanings?*—R. T.

Ver. 3.——*The Father and the Lord.* From the Gospels it may be efficiently set forth

and illustrated that the *Father-name for God* was a most marked feature in our Lord's life and teachings. He seldom or ever used any other name; and a candid reader cannot fail to realize that in this "Father-name" must lie much of the secret of his mission. It may be further shown from the Epistles that his disciples caught his purpose; and, with great frequency, they use the names *Father* for God, and its correlate, *Son*, for the Lord Jesus. This appears in the text, but connected with a different name for the Lord Christ.

PAUL'S PREVAILING THOUGHT FOR GOD. The Father; our Father; the Church's Father. Towards realizing the aspects of the Divine Being that are gathered under this name, we gain help by considering the *natural associations and duties of paternity;* the idea of the *tribal patriarch as found in the early ages;* and the *prophetic qualifications of the sterner and governmental conceptions of God which are found in the Mosaic system.* If the Father-name for God be an essential, and a foundation of Christianity, as set forth by the Apostle Paul, then we must expect to find the entire Christian revelation *toned* and *conditioned* by this primary conception of the Divine Being and relations. This may be worked out and illustrated in connection with either of the primary Christian truths. And it may be pointed out that the term "Father" is properly *inclusive* of all *holy demands,* all *governmental authorities,* all *reverential relations;* but it is new and infinitely precious to the race, because it brings home the possibility of God's *individual and personal love to each member of it.* In that lies a great part of the attractive and persuasive power of Christianity.—R. T.

Vers. 4—7.—*Gifts are signs of grace.* The introduction will naturally deal with the fact, universally recognized, that talents and genius and particular endowments *come from God.* This was early declared in the call of Bezaleel and Aholiab, and was a familiar idea even to the heathen nations. It is one that needs fresh and frequent statement in our day. In the early Church there were both ordinary and special gifts, but the manifest Divine origin of the more special ones was designed to convince of the Divine source of *all* gifts, great and small.

I. THE GIFTS SPECIALLY ENTRUSTED TO THE CORINTHIAN CHURCH. They included everything that could be regarded as necessary to their maintenance and work as a Church. But only two things are mentioned here: 1. *Utterance.* 2. *Knowledge.* Both these were highly valued at Corinth, *rhetoric* and *wisdom* being eagerly pursued. Consequently, as the desire for these found expression and sphere within the Christian community, Paul properly leads them to recognize fully the *source* of such endowments. And to know the source is to recognize the responsibility of *using the gifts* only in the *Divine spheres* and in accordance with the *Divine will.* This may be pointedly applied to all the modern gifts and talents in Christ's Church; all are *from God,* all are *for God's use,* and all are to be used *on God's conditions.*

II. THE GRACE SEEN IN THE BESTOWMENT OF THE GIFTS. This may be recognized in the *honour* of receiving such *trusts,* and in the *adaptation* of the gifts to the various *needs* of the Church.

III. THE AGENT THROUGH WHOM THE GIFTS ARE BESTOWED. The living Lord Jesus Christ—"in Christ Jesus"—conceived as present with and presiding over the Church; dispensing to every man severally as he wills, for the general edification.

Apply by showing the *importance of gifts* in every age, the *proper modesty* of those who have the trust of gifts, and the *thankfulness and hope* we should cherish concerning those among us who are divinely endowed.—R. T.

Vers. 7—9.—*Christ coming, and Christ here.* The early Church conceived that the Lord Jesus Christ would return, in some material manifestation, *during their age.* Inquire how far this idea rested on the view they held of Messiah as an earthly Deliverer and Patriot-King. Their question, after our Lord's resurrection, "Wilt thou *at this time* restore again the kingdom to Israel?" indicated a bias and preoccupation of mind which even their Lord's ascension did not correct; and possibly this lingering misconception helped to form the idea of Christ's speedy second coming. It may be further shown that our Lord's assurances about his coming again might have been taken *literally,* though he so carefully sought to impress the *spiritual* bearing of his promises, and their fulfilment, mainly in the abiding and indwelling of the Holy Ghost.

With the conception of this speedy coming of Christ in their minds, the apostles regard the proper attitude of the Christian and the Church as being one of "waiting." Such waiting becomes a virtual "preparing;" it involves a care to have and hold all things ready, and this is a good sign of the faithful and diligent *servant*. "The attitude of expectation is thought of as the highest that can be attained here by the Christian. It implies a patient, humble spirit, one that is waiting for, one that is looking forward to, something nobler and better." The moral influence of a high and noble expectation may be pointed out. "Where your treasure is, there will your heart be also;" and it is certain that to *fitness for it* your life and conduct will be moulded. In these verses we find a double thought associated with the Lord's second coming.

I. PAUL'S THOUGHT OF CHRIST'S COMING TO REWARD. As he has been writing of "gifts" and their use in the Church, he must have in mind Christ's gracious *reward* of his faithful ones. Reward is proper from one occupying the position of *Master*. Rewards may be given for work that is far *short of perfection*. Rewards may be bestowed when no *absolute claims* can be made for them. Divine rewards can only be *gifts of grace*. The moral ends to be served by granting rewards are such as God may seek by such means. So it is rational and right that we should still watch, work, and use our gifts, in the full expectation of gracious recognition and reward in due season. Qualify, however, the expectation, by showing that the New Testament strives to impress on us that Divine and future rewards must be *spiritual*, not *material*; we are to have *crowns*, but they are crowns of *life, righteousness,* and *glory*.

II. PAUL'S THOUGHT OF CHRIST'S PRESENCE TO CONFIRM. Too much attention to Christ's coming would lighten the conviction of his real, though spiritual, presence *now* with the individual and with the Church. That presence Paul conceives as the *confirmation*, the *inspiration*, and the *security* of Christ's servants. In it they have their only, but their all-sufficient, *guarantee* that, amid frailties, temptations, and perils, they shall hold out unto the end, attaining unto the coming of the Lord. Either of these thoughts of Christ may prove misleading *if it stands alone*. Each tempers and qualifies the other. Both together keep us wisely looking *down* on our *work, beside us* at our *helper,* and *on* to our *reward*. The thought of "reward" makes us wonder how the Divine One will ever be able to testify to *our* "blamelessness and unreprovableness." Illustrate by David's appeal to his "integrity." We may be *genuine* and *sincere*. A standard of *consistency* may be pressed on us as *Church members;* but nothing less than the standard of *absolute purity* must be pressed on us as one day to stand in the presence of the glorified Christ.—R. T.

Vers. 11, 12.—*The spirit of faction.* Introduce by showing the various elements of which the Church at Corinth was composed. There are signs that some members were wealthy and learned, many were certainly poor, and probably many were slaves. Those who suddenly become wealthy are always in peril of showing masterfulness, and claiming undue authority and influence. Party feeling ran high in Corinth, and this, with the mixed character of the population, tended to break society into sects and schools. This affected the Church, and Paul received reports of the disposition to make parties within it, and so destroy the unity of the Church in Christ; such reports greatly distressed him, and they are in part the immediate occasion of his writing this Epistle. The subject of the verses before us we may take to be *Church unity—how it may be preserved and lost.* Our Lord and his apostles manifest a peculiar anxiety for the conservation of the unity of the Church, and appear to regard that unity as essential to the Church's *stability* and *growth* and *witness*.

I. CHURCH UNITY PRESERVED BY MAKING EVERYTHING OF CHRIST. He is the One living Head, the only Master and Lord. The common life of the Church is the life in Christ. The Church is a whole vine, made up of many branches, but Christ is the uniting and quickening *Life* in them all. The direct and immediate dependence of each individual upon the same Lord Jesus Christ is the one secret of maintaining the unity. We have "one Lord, one faith, one baptism." Then it follows that a man keeps in the unity as he *keeps up his dependence on Christ,* and the unity of the Church is realized only in the completeness of the *loyalty of its members to Christ*. And the one thing that mars the unity is the one thing that separates from Christ,

viz. *man's self-willedness.* The yielded will to Christ's living lead is not a *crushed will.* Such yielded personal wills to Christ ensure a mutual sympathy which will ever preserve brotherhood and unity in the Church.

II. CHURCH UNITY LOST BY MAKING TOO MUCH OF MAN. We are greatly helped by human teachers, but there is a constant peril of our making too much of them, and putting their *modes of setting* the truth in the place of the *truth itself.* Following after favourite preachers has always been, and still is, one of the weaknesses of Christian life and habit. In the early Church differences were observed in the teachings even of the *apostles* themselves, and preferences were easily based on these differences. The four Gospels have marked individuality, and the writings of the apostles which are preserved for us indicate that particular aspects of the truth gained prominence in the teachings of each of them. While this fact secures that we see all round the Christian revelation, it may easily be exaggerated and misused. It *is* when it is made the excuse for manifesting the *party spirit.* The gospel truth is a *many-sided unity;* the unity lies in the revelation of *one Christ;* the many-sidedness is involved in the various *relations to men* in which the one Christ stands. Paul put forward prominently "justification by faith," "the salvability of the Gentiles," and "Christian liberty." Apollos had a singularly attractive power of eloquence, and became a sort of "popular preacher." Peter became the centre round which the Jewish elements of the community gathered.

Apply, by showing the serious *moral evils* of sectarian feeling and partisanship; its influence on the man's *own Christian spirit* who may nourish it; its mischievous influence on the *community;* and the hindrance it presents to the *progress of the gospel.* "Nothing more certainly eats out the heart and life of religion than party spirit. Christianity is love; party spirit is the death of love."—R. T.

Ver. 13.—*The unique relation of Christ to the Church.* This is set forth because there was a manifest disposition at Corinth to make Christ a mere party leader. Some said, "I of Christ;" as if Christ stood on the same plane as Paul, Apollos, or Cephas. Bring out, with varied illustration, two points.

I. THE AGREEMENTS BETWEEN A TEACHER'S RELATION TO THE CHURCH AND CHRIST'S RELATION TO IT. Christ's teaching is *original,* man's is *derived.* Christ's authority is *supreme,* man's is only *delegated.* Christ is the Church's *Foundation,* the human teacher is but a *workman* engaged in the *superstructure.* Both *teach,* both *bear authority,* both are *builders.* The glory of the human teacher is that he can be a "co-worker together with Christ." In some sense human teachers may think of themselves as filling the vacant earth-sphere of the great Teacher, and carrying on his gracious mission. See Paul's plea, "Now then we are ambassadors for Christ." So far as they bear the Master's *spirit,* speak the Master's *truth,* and carry out the Master's *will,* we give them all *honour, attention,* and *obedience* for their Master's sake. We are "followers of them so far as they follow Christ."

II. THE DIFFERENCES BETWEEN A TEACHER'S RELATION TO THE CHURCH AND CHRIST'S RELATION TO IT. There are important distinctions and differences in the things in which both agree. And there are *positive distinctions,* things in which Christ stands absolutely alone. No other was "crucified for us." Into no other "name" were we "baptized." The relative positions of Christ and the ministry are indicated by the figures of the *Shepherd and the under-shepherds.* The careful and constant preservation of Christ's unique position in the Church, and relation to it, is the secret of the maintenance of all Church *order, unity,* and *peace.*—R. T.

Vers. 14—18.—*Paul's commission from Christ.* It did not concern *baptism,* but *preaching.* Rites are of value in relation to the Christian life and culture. But rites may be *overvalued,* and, instead of helping the apprehension of spiritual realities and duties, may be sought for their own sakes. This peril always lies in symbols. The commendation or the establishment of rites had no place in Paul's mission. They would have confused his presentation of the doctrine of "Christian liberty" under Christ; though *he* himself observed rites; and *we* are able to see how sacrament and ceremonial may be in full harmony with our freedom in Christ. The expression "baptized into the Name" needs explanation. Here "baptism" is the public act by

which our discipleship to a person is declared. Illustrate by the branding of cattle or slaves, or by the public declaration of having adopted a child as son and heir. Baptism is a voluntary taking on ourselves of a Name; from it we are called "Christians;" we *bear on us the Name* into which we were baptized, and are under pledge to *live in the spirit* worthy of that Name. With the administration of any rite Paul contrasts his call to preach the gospel. The nature of his call may be thus enlarged on. He was—

I. TO PREACH. A term used in the Acts as distinct from *teach.* "Daily . . . ceased not to teach and preach Jesus Christ." The figure in the word is that of the herald, whose duty is to go from place to place, and announce, or declare, a message, or proclamation. John the Baptist preached as a herald. When our Lord sent the apostles forth on a trial mission, he would instruct them in their work as preachers, "As ye go say, Repent; for the kingdom of heaven is at hand." Press, that *still* preaching is the authoritative *announcement* of God's mercy to men in Christ, and the *demand* at once to accept that mercy.

II. TO PREACH THE GOSPEL. The very essence of the gospel is given in John iii. 16. It has these points—*Man's need and helplessness; God's love and pity;* the effective *manifestation of that love in Christ;* the requirement of *faith in the Redeemer* thus set forth. The power that lies in the simple announcement of the gospel may be illustrated by the familiar story of Kajarnak the Greenlander and the early Moravian missionaries.

III. TO PREACH THE GOSPEL IN SIMPLICITY. Not with elaborations of "human wisdom," or as trusting to the artifices of "human rhetoric." Paul wanted no other power than that which lay in personal conviction and simple fulfilment of the duty imposed upon him. To him the persuasion and power of the gospel lay in its simplicity. He preached *Christ,* and strove to *draw men to him* in trust and love.

IV. TO PREACH THE GOSPEL EVEN IN THE ASPECT THAT MEN WOULD RESIST. He was not to hold back the story of the *cross,* however Jew or Greek may seem to be offended at it; he was to declare the whole gospel he had received; and he was to be quite confident that God *could* and *would* make it *power unto salvation.* In this we have the very essence of *missionary work* in every age. A kind of work that has its spheres both at *home* and *abroad;* and finds its agents in all who, having received the gospel, find an inward impulse urging them to *make that gospel known.*—R. T.

Vers. 19—25.—*The world's foolishness, and God's wisdom.* So far as we can understand the Divine dealings with our race, it appears that, for some four thousand years, God left the nations to a *free experiment.* They might find out for themselves what is the "chief good of man." The more civilized Gentile nations were interested in one form of the experiment, viz.—Can man find God, and all in God, *by the researches of his own wisdom?* At Corinth much was made of man's "wisdom." Therefore Paul deals with it, and shows that—

I. HITHERTO MAN'S WISDOM HAD FAILED. The various devices of *science, philosophy,* and *religion* may be reviewed; and the actually hopeless moral condition of Paul's age should be forcibly presented. There was prevalent *atheism; religion* was mocked at; *philosophy* was an amusement, and had become a mere logomachy, an arena for mere disputants; and there was *no satisfaction* for man's *mind* or *heart* anywhere. The foolishness of the world's wisdom was declared. Impress what must be the consequences always if man's wisdom is made *mistress,* and not kept *handmaid.*

II. HENCEFORTH MAN'S WISDOM MUST BE DISPLACED. It was *not* to be the Divine agency employed in the redemption of the world. That should be *revelation,* not man's discovery. A *manifestation,* in the earthly spheres, beyond human imagination. *A life and death,* in which human wisdom would see nought but weakness and shame. And the simple *heralding of a message,* the proclaiming of a fact and truth given, which the wise of this world would think any commonplace and ignorant person could do. Yet *God's wisdom* proves able to accomplish that in which man's wisdom failed. For the gospel preaching *does* bring God near to men, does bring home to them the knowledge of him and the love of him, and does give to men the *salvation, satisfaction,* and *eternal life* which they both need and seek.—R. T.

Vers. 26—30.—*Intellectual power and moral power : which does God chiefly honour and use?* Paul's point appears to be that the wisdom of God is declared in his using *moral* rather than *material* or *intellectual* forces in carrying out his great purpose of human redemption. The material forces had to be set aside in order that the moral forces might work without obstruction; therefore only the *simplest human agents* were chosen as the apostles and first preachers of the gospel. It is still true that *moral character* and *spiritual affinities* are the best fitnesses for Christian service. It may be well to compare the moral and the intellectual powers.

I. THEY ARE OFTEN CONNECTED IN THE SAME PERSON. There is no natural divorcement between them. They may be found in becoming harmony.

II. IN IDEAL MANHOOD THEY MUST BE SO CONNECTED. For the ideal man has all the faculties and powers of his nature proportionally and harmoniously cultured and developed.

III. IN ACTUAL FACT THEY ARE TOO OFTEN SEVERED. And this is the fact, mainly by reason of the disturbance and disorder of man's nature, which follows as the consequence of *sin*. *Self-will* tends to nourish those parts of our nature through which we may *gain human place and praise;* and so it fosters the material and intellectual at the expense of the moral and spiritual.

IV. GOD SETS MORAL POWER AT THE HIGHEST VALUE. And this he manifests and declares in every revelation he makes to men, passing by the " rich and great and wise " to exalt the humble and the meek. He honours *moral power* because of its *sphere*. It is character, and the influence of character, the force of the man himself, of what he *is*. And because of its *agent*. It is the soul, the man's *very self*, and not the *mind*, which is only something the man *has*. Then show what is the *true self-culture*.—R. T.

Vers. 30, 31.—*What Christ is to the heart that welcomes him.* The Revised New Testament makes a slight but important difference in the renderings. It reads, " Who was made unto us *wisdom from God,* and righteousness and sanctification, and redemption." This alteration suggests that the *wisdom* spoken of embraces and includes the three latter terms; some, however, prefer to regard *wisdom* as a fourth term, to be joined with the others. As the word may certainly be used to describe a part of Christ's gracious work in us, we may observe Christ's saving work in—

I. THE MIND-SPHERE. His revelation *enlarges knowledge*. His teachings give *practical guidance*. His Spirit leads *into all truth*. He is the only safe *Thought-Leader*.

II. THE RELATIONAL SPHERE. The word " righteousness " here seems to be equivalent to " justification," and to refer to our " standing as before God." Christ is our Righteousness, as our *Representative*, in whom God *sees us*, and whose infinite acceptability stands for us.

III. THE CHARACTER-SPHERE. Christ's righteousness we are under pledge to *win* and make *our own*. But *over the winning Christ presides*. And this his operation in the sphere of character we call *sanctification*. Here the idea of " making personally holy " is prominent, rather than that of " consecration " or " separation."

IV. THE CIRCUMSTANTIAL SPHERE. Conceived as surrounded with an environment of evil influences and temptations, the Church is in the hands of Christ for a *daily deliverance and redemption*. The full purpose of the Redeemer is not accomplished until we are *wholly rescued from self and from sin*. This is practically the *present* work of Christ in every heart and life that is *opened* and *kept open* to his gracious operations.—R. T.

EXPOSITION.

CHAPTER II.

Vers. 1—5.—*St. Paul's own method.*

Ver. 1.—And I; " I too;" I in accordance with God's method. **When I came to you.** The date of his first visit was in A.D. 52, and he had stayed a year and a half (Acts xviii. 11). He had since been (roughly speaking) " three years " (τριετίαν, Acts xx. 31)

at Ephesus. **Of speech or of wisdom.** I spoke to you neither oratorically nor philosophically. Hence the Apollos party, fond of the brilliant rhetoric of the young Alexandrian, spoke of Paul's speech as " contemptible " (2 Cor. x. 10). **The testimony of God**; that is, the witness borne to Christ by the Father (1 John v. 10, 11).

Ver. 2.—**I determined.** The unadorned

simplicity of my teaching was part of a fixed design. Not to know anything. Not, that is, to *depend* on any human knowledge. Of course, St. Paul neither means to set aside all human knowledge nor to disparage other Christian doctrines. His words must not be pressed out of their due context and proportion. Jesus Christ, and him crucified. Christ, in the lowest depth of his abasement and self-sacrifice. He would "know" nothing else; that is, he would make this the central point and essence of all his knowledge, because he knew the "excellency" of this knowledge (Phil. iii. 8)— knew it as the only knowledge which rose to the height of wisdom. Christ is the only *Foundation* (ch. iii. 11). In the person and the work of Christ is involved the whole gospel.

Ver. 3.—I was with you; literally, *I became* or *proved myself, towards you*, as in ch. xvi. 10. In weakness. St. Paul was physically weak and liable also to nervous weakness and depression (ch. iv. 7—12; Gal. iv. 13; 2 Cor. x. 1, 10; xii. 7, 10). He shows an occasional self-distrust rising from the consciousness of personal infirmities. This enhances our sense of his heroic courage and endurance. Doubtless this physical weakness and nervous depression were connected with his "stake in the flesh," which seems to have been an acute and distressing form of ophthalmia, accompanied with cerebral disturbance (see my 'Life of St. Paul,' i. 215—221). In fear, and in much trembling. Probably the words are even literally true, though they are a common phrase (2 Cor. vii. 15; Phil. ii. 12, 13; Eph. vi. 5). It must be remembered that in his first visit to Corinth St. Paul had gone through stormy and troubled days (Acts xviii. 1—12).

Ver. 4.—My speech and my preaching; the form and matter of my discourse. He would not attempt to use the keen sword of philosophical dialectics or human eloquence, but would only use the weapon of the cross. Was not with enticing words of man's wisdom; rather, *with persuasive words of wisdom* (the word *anthropines* is a gloss). This simplicity was the more remarkable because "Corinthian words" was a proverb for choice, elaborate, and glittering phrases (Wetstein). It is not improbable that the almost total and deeply discouraging want of success of St. Paul in preaching at Athens had impressed him more strongly with the uselessness of attempting to fight Greek philosophers with their own blunt and imperfect weapons. In demonstration of the Spirit and of power. So he says to the Thessalonians, "Our gospel came not to you in word only, but also in power, and in the Holy Ghost, and in much assurance." The

plain facts, so repellent to the natural intellect, were driven home with matchless force by spiritual conviction. The only heathen critic who has mentioned St. Paul's method is Longinus, the author of the treatise on 'The Sublime and Beautiful,' who calls him "a master of unproved dogma," meaning apparently that his force lay in the irresistible statement of the facts which he came to preach.

Ver. 5.—In the power of God. So in 2 Cor. iv. 7 he says that the treasure they carried was "in earthen vessels, that the excellency of the power may be of God and not of us."

Vers. 6—16.—*The apparent foolishness is the only wisdom.*

Ver. 6.—Howbeit. In this passage he shows that in reality a crushing irony lay in his description of the gospel as being, in the world's judgment, "weak" and "foolish." It was the highest wisdom, but it could only be understood by the perfect. Its apparent folly to the Corinthians was a proof of their blindness and incapacity. Among the perfect. The word either means (1) the mature, the full-grown, as opposed to babes in Christ (ch. iii. 1); or (2) the fully initiated into the mysteries of godliness (ἐπόπται, 2 Pet. i. 16). A wisdom not of this world; literally, *of this æon*. The word *kosmos* means the world in its material aspect; *æon* is read for the world in its moral and intellectual aspect. "The wisdom of this world is foolishness with God" (ch. iii. 19). Nor of the rulers of this world. Some have taken these "rulers" to be the same as "the world-rulers of this darkness," *i.e.* the evil spirits, in Eph. vi. 12 (John xiii. 27; Luke xxii. 53). Ignatius (?) seems to have understood it thus; for he adopted the strange notion that "the prince of this æon" (*i.e.* Satan) had been deceived and frustrated by the incarnation from a virgin, and the death on the cross (Ignat., 'Ad. Eph.,' 19). It means more probably "wisdom," as understood by Roman governors and Jewish Sanhedrists, who treated the Divine wisdom of the gospel with sovereign contempt (Acts iv. 27). That [who] come to nought; literally, *who are being done away with.* Amid all the feebleness of the infant Church, St. Paul saw empires vanishing before it.

Ver. 7.—In a mystery; that is, "in a truth, once hidden, now revealed." The word is now used for what is dark and incomprehensible, but it has no such meaning in the New Testament, where it means "what was once secret, but has now been made manifest" (Rom. xvi. 25; Eph. iii. 4, 9; Col. i. 26; 1 Tim. iii. 16). It implies the very reverse of any *esoteric* teaching. Hidden. It was "hidden from the wise and prudent, but revealed to babes" (Matt. xi. 25).

Before the worlds; literally, *before the ages ;* before time began. **Unto our glory.** The author of the Epistle to the Hebrews clearly states that "the future age" is in God's counsels subjected, not to the angels, but to man. But "our glory" is that we are "called to his eternal glory by Christ Jesus" (1 Pet. v. 10).

Ver. 8.—**Had they known it ;** literally, *had they recognized ; had they* got to know *it.* The apostles often dwell on this ignorance as being in part a palliation for the sin of rejecting Christ (see especially Acts iii. 17; xiii. 27; comp. Isa. ii. 1). Jews and Romans, emperors, procurators, high priests, Pharisees, had in their ignorance conspired in vain to prevent what God had fore-ordained. **The Lord of glory.** This is not a mere equivalent of "the glorious Lord," in Ps. xxiv. 10. It is "the Lord of the glory," *i.e.* "the Lord of the Shechinah" (comp. Eph. i. 17, "the Father of the glory"). The Shechinah was the name given by the Jews to the cloud of light which symbolized God's presence. The cherubim are called, in Heb. ix. 5, "cherubim of glory," because the Shechinah was borne on their outspread wings (see, however, Acts vii. 2; Eph. i. 17). There would have been to ancient ears a startling and awful paradox in the words "*crucified* the *Lord of glory.*" The words brought into juxtaposition the lowest ignominy and the most splendid exaltation.

Ver. 9.—**But as it is written.** The whole sentence in the Greek is unfinished. The thought seems to be, "But God has revealed to us things which eye hath not seen, etc., though the princes of this world were ignorant of them." Scriptural quotations are often thus introduced, apart from the general grammar of the sentence, as in the Greek of ch. i. 31. **Eye hath not seen,** etc. The Revised Version is here more literal and accurate. The quotation as it stands is not found in the Old Testament. It most resembles Isa. lxiv. 4, but also vaguely resembles Isa. lii. 15; lxv. 17. It may be another instance of a loose general reminiscence (comp. ch. xiv. 21; Rom. ix. 33). "Non verbum e verbo expressit," says St. Jerome, " sed *παραφραστικῶς eundem sensum* aliis sermonibus indicavit." St. Chrysostom regards the words as part of a lost prophecy. Origen, Zacharias of Chrysopolis, and others say that the words occurred in an apocryphal book, the 'Apocalypse of Elias,' but if so the apocryphal writer must have had the passage of Isaiah in his mind. Some regard the words as a fragment of some ancient liturgy. Origen thought that they came from the 'Revelation of Elijah.' They were also to be found in the 'Ascension of Isaiah' (Jer. on Isa. lxiv. 4), and they occur in the Talmud (Sanhedr. 99 a). In a curious

fragment of Hegesippus (circ. A.D. 150) preserved in Photius (Cod. ccxxxii.), that old writer indignantly repudiates this passage, saying that it is futile and "utterly belies (*καταψεύδεσθαι*) the Holy Scriptures and the Lord, who says, 'Blessed are your eyes which see, and your ears which hear.'" Photius cannot understand why (*ὅτι καὶ παθὼν*) Hegesippus should speak thus. Routh ('Rel. Sacr.,' 253) hardly knows how to excuse him; but perhaps if we had the context of the fragment we should see that he is attacking, not the words themselves, but some perversion of them by heretics, like the Docetæ. The phrase, "As it is written," decisively marks an intention to refer to Scripture. Neither have entered into the heart of man ; literally, *things which have not set foot upon the heart.* The general thought is that God's revelations (for the immediate reference is to *these,* and *not* to future bliss) pass all understanding. The quotation of these words as referring to heaven is one of the numberless instances of texts inaccurately applied.

Ver. 10.—**But God hath revealed them unto us.** They are secret no longer, but are "mysteries which now it is given us to know" (Matt. xiii. 11). **By his Spirit.** The Spirit guides into all truth (John xiii. 16). In ch. xii. 8—11 St. Paul attributes every gift of wisdom directly to him. **Searcheth.** "How unsearchable are his judgments!" (Rom. xi. 33). **Yea, the deep things of God.** This expression, "The depths of God," passed into the cant expression of the Gnostics, and it may be with reference to their misuse of it that St. John uses the phrase, "The depths of Satan" (Rev. ii. 24). "Oh, the depth," etc. ! (Rom. xi. 33).

Ver. 11. — **The things of God none knoweth.** Some manuscripts have not the same word (*οἶδεν*) as that rendered "knoweth" in the earlier clause, but "hath learnt" (*ἔγνωκεν*); comp. John xxi. 17; 2 Cor. v. 16. All that is meant is that our knowledge of God must always be relative, not absolute. It is not possible to measure the arm of God with the finger of man.

Ver. 12.—**The spirit of the world.** The heathen world in its heathen aspect is regarded as under the power of the devil (2 Cor. iv. 4; Eph. vi. 11, 12). **Freely given to us by God.** The word "freely" is here involved in the verb (*χαρισθέντα*) "graciously bestowed." It is different from the phrase used in "Freely ye have received," which is gratuitously (*δωρεὰν*, Matt. x. 8). All God's gifts are "without money and without price" (Isa. lv. 1), and not "to be bought with money" (Acts xviii. 20).

Ver. 13.—**Comparing spiritual things with spiritual.** The meaning of this clause is

very uncertain. It has been rendered, "Blending spiritual things with spiritual" (Kling, Wordsworth), *i.e.* not adulterating them with carnal admixtures (2 Cor. ii. 17; 1 Pet. ii. 22). "Interpreting spiritual things to spiritual men" (Bengel, Reichert, Stanley, margin of Revised Version; see Gen. xl. 8; Dan. v. 12, LXX.). "Explaining spiritual things in spiritual words." This meaning the Greek will not bear, but Calvin and Beza get the same meaning by rendering it, "Adapting spiritual things to spiritual words." It is doubtful whether the Greek verb (*sunkrinontes*) can be rendered "comparing," which comes from the Vulgate, *comparantes*. Wickliffe has the version, "Maken a liknesse of spyritual things to goostli men, for a besteli man persuyved not through thingis." The commonest sense of the word in the LXX. is "interpreting" (Gen. xl. 8, etc.), and the best rendering is, "Explaining spirituals to spiritual men." If it be supposed that the verb συγκρίνω acquired the sense of "comparing" in Hellenistic Greek (2 Cor. x. 12; Wisd. vii. 29; xv. 18), then the rendering of our Authorized Version may stand.

Ver. 14.—**The natural man.** The Greek word is ψυχικὸς (psychical); literally, *soulish*, i.e. the man who lives the mere life of his lower understanding, the unspiritual, sensuous, and egoistic man. He may be superior to the fleshly, sensual, or carnal man, who lives only the life of the body (σωματικὸς); but is far below the spiritual man (πνευματικός). St. Paul (1 Thess. v. 23) recognizes the tripartite nature of man —body, soul, spirit. **Receiveth not;** *i.e.* "does not choose to accept." He judges them by the foregone conclusions of his own prejudice. **Because they are spiritually judged.** The organ for the recognition of such truths—namely, the spirit—has become paralyzed or fallen into atrophy, from neglect; therefore the egoist and the sensualist have lost the faculty whereby alone spiritual truth is discernible. It becomes to them what painting is to the blind, or music to the deaf. This elementary truth is again and again insisted on in Scripture, and ignored by sceptics (Rom. viii. 6, 7; John iii. 3; vi. 44, 45; xiv. 17; 2 Cor. iv. 3—6). This verse is sometimes used to depreciate knowledge, reason, and intellect. On that abuse of the passage, see Hooker, 'Eccl. Pol.,' iii. viii. 4—11, an admirable passage, which Bishop Wordsworth quotes at length. It is, perhaps, sufficient to say that if God has no need of human knowledge, he has still less need of human ignorance.

Ver. 15.—**Judgeth all things.** If he can judge the higher, he can of course judge the lower. Being spiritual, he becomes intellectual also, as well as *more than* intellectual. He can see into the difference between the dream and the reality; he can no longer take the shadow for the substance. He can not only decide about ordinary matters, but can also "discriminate the transcendent," *i.e.* see that which is best even in different alternatives of good. "The *secret* of the Lord is with them that fear him" (Ps. xxv. 14). **He himself is judged of no man.** He may be judged, condemned, depreciated, slandered every day of his life, but the arrow-flights of human judgment fall far short of him. These Corinthians were judging and comparing Paul and Apollos and Cephas; but their judgments were false and worthless, and Paul told them that it was less than nothing to him to be judged by them or by man's feeble transitory day (ch. iv. 3). "Evil men," as Solomon said, "understand not judgment" (Prov. xxviii. 5).

Ver. 16.—**Who hath known the mind of the Lord?** "The Lord" is Jehovah (see Isa. xl. 13, LXX.; Rom. xi. 34). This is the *reason* why no one can judge the spiritual man in his spiritual life. To do so is like judging God. **We have the mind of Christ.** So Christ himself had told the apostles (John xv. 15); and St. Paul always claimed to have been taught by direct revelation from Christ (Gal. i. 11, 12). They had the *Spirit* of Christ (Rom. viii. 9), and therefore the *mind* of Christ.

HOMILETICS.

Vers. 1—5.—*A faithful picture of a true gospel preacher.* "And I, brethren, when I came to you, came not with excellency of speech," etc. These words may be regarded as a faithful picture of a true gospel preacher.

I. The grand subject of his ministry is the CRUCIFIED CHRIST. 1. Christ crucified, because he is the *highest revelation of God's love for man*. 2. Christ crucified, because he is the *most thrilling demonstration of the wickedness of humanity*. 3. Christ crucified, because he is the *grandest display of loyalty to moral rectitude*. This is the theme—a personal "Christ crucified;" not a creed or creeds written in books. He *himself*; not the theories of theologians about him.

II. The grand subject of his ministry is TO HIM SOUL-ABSORBING. "I determined not to know anything among you, save Jesus Christ, and him crucified." The man who has some paramount sentiment looks at the universe through it, ay, and values the universe so far as it reflects and honours that sentiment. Hence to Paul Christ was "all in all." All other subjects—political and philosophical—dwindled into insignificance in its presence; it swallowed up his great soul.

III. The grand subject of his ministry makes him INDIFFERENT TO ALL RHETORICAL CONSIDERATIONS. "I . . . came not with excellency of speech." In order to exhibit this theme to men, he never thought of brilliant sentences and polished periods and studied composition ; not he. The theme was independent of it, infinitely too great for it. Does the splendid apple tree in full blossom require to be decorated with gaudy ribbons? Christ crucified is eloquence, mighty eloquence. Tell the story of his life in plain vernacular, with the notes of nature, however rough, and in vital sympathy with its spirit; and your discourse will be a thousand times mightier than the orations with which Demosthenes shook the proud democracy of Greece.

IV. The grand subject of his ministry SUBDUES IN HIM ALL SELF-CONSCIOUSNESS. "I was with you in weakness, and in fear, and in much trembling." This Paul was naturally a strong, intrepid soul, but in the presence of this grand theme he felt weak and trembling. "Who is sufficient for these things?" he exclaims. Vanity in any man is a vile and disgusting incongruity, but in a preacher it is a thousand times worse. A vain preacher is an anomaly, an impostor. He has failed to realize the grand theme about which he prates.

V. The grand subject of his ministry INVESTS HIM WITH DIVINE POWER OVER MAN. "My preaching was not with enticing words of man's wisdom, but in demonstration of the Spirit and of power: that your faith should not stand in the wisdom of men, but in the power of God." There is as truly Divine power in the ministry of a true preacher as there is in the heaving of ocean or the rolling of planets; but a higher power withal, power over mind, it is "the power of God unto salvation."

"Would I describe a preacher such as Paul," etc.

(Cowper.)

Vers. 6, 7.—*The gospel : its description, preachers, and hearers.* "Howbeit we speak wisdom," etc. In these words we have three things concerning the gospel.

I. A DESCRIPTION OF ITS NATURE. Paul calls it the "wisdom of God." The wisdom of a system may be determined by two things. 1. *By the character of the end it contemplates.* A system which aims at an insignificant or unworthy end would scarcely be considered wise. What is the end the gospel aims at? The restoration in human souls of supreme sympathy with God. The absence of this sympathy is the cause of all the crimes, evils, and sorrows that curse humanity. 2. *By the fitness of the means it employs.* Though a system contemplate a grand end, yet if the means it employs are unadapted, it could scarcely be called wise. What are the means Christianity employs to generate this love for God in unloving souls? Ask what the souls destitute of this love must have in order to get it, and our answer will be three things: (1) a *personal* manifestation of God ; (2) a *human* manifestation of God; (3) a *loving* manifestation of God. These things we think essential in the nature of the case, and these three things the gospel gives. It is, therefore, emphatically the "wisdom of God."

II. A RULE FOR ITS PREACHERS. "We speak wisdom among them that are perfect." The apostle clearly means by the word "perfect" those in the Christian community who were more advanced in the knowledge of Christ, who stood most in contrast with those who are but "babes in Christ." One of these ideas may be attached to the language of the apostle. Either that he had an exoteric and esoteric doctrine for men, or that the most advanced Christian alone could discern the wisdom of his doctrine, or that he *adapted his teaching to the capacity of his hearers.* The last is the idea which I think we are to accept as the meaning. In another place he tells the Christians at Corinth that he had hitherto "fed them with milk, and not with meat, because they were not able to bear it." His conduct is, I take it, a *rule* for all true preaching.

III. AN OBLIGATION UPON ITS HEARERS. If the higher aspects of gospel religion can only be appreciated by those who are "perfect," those who have attained to a high stage of Christian knowledge, it is manifestly their duty to advance beyond the " first principles of the oracles of God." This duty hearers owe (1) to *themselves ;* (2) to their *minister ;* (3) to the *system of Christ.*

Vers. 8, 9.—*Spiritual ignorance the cause of immense evil and the occasion of immense good.* " Which none of the princes of this world," etc. The words lead us to look on spiritual ignorance—*i.e.* ignorance of God and our obligations to him—in two very opposite aspects.
I. As THE CAUSE OF IMMENSE EVIL. These " princes of the world," through ignorance, " crucified the Lord of glory." A greater crime was never perpetrated. It involved : (1) The grossest injustice. He was innocent. (2) The basest ingratitude. He did good, and good only. (3) The most heartless cruelty. They crucified him—the most excruciating death that infernal malignity could desire. (4) The most daring impiety. Whom did they treat thus? " The Lord of glory." How this spiritual ignorance was the cause of immense evil is evident from two considerations. 1. *Because it is in itself an evil, and like will produce like.* There is an ignorance that is a calamity. When mind and *means* are absent, ignorance is a calamity ; but when they are present, it is always a crime. These " princes" had both. Their ignorance was a sin, and sin, like virtue, is propagated. That this spiritual ignorance was the cause of evil is clear from the fact that : 2. Had it not existed, *such an evil could never have been perpetrated.* The words lead us to look at spiritual ignorance—
II. As THE OCCASION OF IMMENSE GOOD. Paul tells us that this Crucifixion introduced things that " eye had never seen nor ear heard." Divine pardon, spiritual purity, immortal hopes, are all things that come through the Crucifixion. From the subject learn : 1. *That the sinner is always engaged in accomplishing that which he never intended.* These " princes" did two things they never intended. (1) They ruined themselves ; (2) they served God. 2. *That whatever good a man may accomplish contrary to his intention, is destitute of all praiseworthiness.* What oceans of blessings come to the world through the Crucifixion ! Yet who can ever praise the crucifiers? 3. *That no man should act without an intelligent conception of what he is doing.* How many act from prejudice and blind impulse ! how few have a right conception of what they are doing !

Vers. 10—16.—*The gospel school.* " But God hath revealed them unto us by his Spirit," etc. *Because* man naturally craves for knowledge and deeply needs it, schools abound everywhere throughout the civilized world, especially here in England—schools of science, schools of philosophy, schools of art, etc. But there is *one* school that transcends all—the gospel school. Three facts are suggested concerning this school.
I. That here the student is INSTRUCTED IN THE SUBLIMEST REALITIES. " Deep things of God." Things, not words, not theories. " Deep things ; " deep because undiscoverable by human reason ; deep because they come from the fathomless ocean of Divine love. What are these deep things? The primary elements of the gospel, and the necessary condition of soul-restoration. These " deep things" we are here told are : 1. The *free gifts of Heaven.* " Freely given to us of God." 2. Freely given to be *communicated.* " Which things also we speak," etc. He who gets these things into his mind and heart, not only can communicate, but is bound to tell them to others, and that in plain natural language, free from the affectations of rhetoric, the language which the " Holy Ghost teacheth," language which is suggested by " comparing spiritual things with spiritual." Men think in words ; thoughts come dressed in their own language ; the intellectual thoughts have their own language, and spiritual thoughts have a language all their own.
II. That here the student is TAUGHT BY THE GREATEST TEACHER. Who is the Teacher ? The Divine Spirit himself, here called the " Spirit of God" and the " Holy Ghost." 1. This Teacher *has infinite knowledge.* " The Spirit searcheth all things." The word " searcheth " must not be taken, I presume, in the sense of investigation, but rather in the sense of complete knowledge. In the last clause of the next verse it is said, " The things of God knoweth no man, but the Spirit of God." He knoweth those things of God ; he knows them in their essence, number, issues, bearings, relations, etc. 2. This Teacher *is no other than God himself.* " What man knoweth the things of a

man, save the spirit of man which is in him? Even so the things of God knoweth no man, but the Spirit of God." The implication is that this Spirit is as truly God as man's mind is man. No one knows the things in man's mind but man himself; no one knows the "deep things of God" but God himself. "Who teacheth like God?" He knows thoroughly the nature of the student, and how best to indoctrinate that nature with his own "deep things."

III. That here the student MUST DEVELOP HIS HIGHER NATURE. "But the natural man receiveth not the things of the Spirit of God, for they are foolishness unto him: neither can he know them, because they are spiritually discerned." Man has a three-fold nature, designated by St. Paul as *soma, psyche,* and *pneuma*—body, soul, and spirit. The first is the animal, the second is the mental, and the third the moral or spiritual. This is the *conscience,* with its intuitions and sympathies, and this is the chief part of man, nay, the man himself, the core of his being, that which Paul calls "the inner man," the man of the man. Now, this part of the man alone can receive the "things of the Spirit of God." Set these things before the "natural man," his mere body; they are no more to him than Euclid to a brute. Set them before the mere psychical or intellectual man, and what are they? Puzzles over which he will speculate; nay, they are "foolishness unto him." Mere intellect cannot understand *love,* cannot appreciate *right.* It concerns itself with the truth or falsehood of propositions, and the advantages and disadvantages of conduct—nothing more. Moral love only can interpret and feel the things of moral love, the "deep things of God." Hence this moral *pneuma,* this spiritual nature, this conscience must be roused from its dormancy, and become the ascendant nature before the "things of the Spirit" can be "discerned," and then the man shall judge all things, all spiritual things, whilst he himself will not be judged rightly by any "natural man." "For who hath known the mind of the Lord?" Who, thus uninstructed, can "know the mind of the Lord"?

HOMILIES BY VARIOUS AUTHORS.

Vers. 1—5.—*How St. Paul preached the gospel.* A great truth is capable of manifold presentations. To be seen fully it must be viewed in various aspects, each of which is relative to the wholeness of the idea, while supplying to the student an increased sensibility to its excellence. Sir Joshua Reynolds speaks of his disappointment when he first saw the painting of the Transfiguration, but it grew upon him and educated his eye, the mind in the eye, to appreciate its sublimity. Hazlitt mentions a similar experience in his own case. Such impressions are not due to simple recipiency; the active intellect is aroused, and the thinker himself becomes a voluntary party to the object affecting him. Evidently, now, St. Paul's idea of preaching, as given in the first chapter, returned upon him and solicited further consideration. Accordingly, we find him in the second chapter detailing his personal history as a preacher while at Corinth, and, as usual in his Epistles, the autobiographical element discloses its presence in his logic. Whenever there was an important issue in his ministry, we see the man in the fulness of his proportions and look into his very heart, so that we are at no loss to understand the reason of his impassioned energy. In this instance he declares that he did not come to the Corinthians "with excellency of speech or of wisdom," as the world regarded speech and wisdom. But he was with them "in weakness, and in fear, and in much trembling." It was not the "weakness" of cowardice, nor the "fear" that brings a snare, nor the "trembling" that comes from an apprehension of criticism and hostility. Agitation and solicitude were the product of his fine sensibility, not rising from below, but descending from the highest realm of his being, the ideal of duty and responsibility so vast within him as to oppress the capacity of performance. A most blessed "weakness" this, the best possible assurance of truthful power, the most reliable token our latent nature offers as a promise of success. The throb of the engine in a huge Atlantic steamship sends its own quiver into every plank and bolt of the vessel. There is a "trembling" in all its compartments, but it is the trembling of power. St. Paul had no gift more remarkable than the gift of feeling to the utmost the doctrines of the gospel. Christ in him, Christ as the self of self, was the Christ he preached; and hence no discourse he ever delivered, no letter he ever wrote, affected others as much as they affected him. Effective speakers and writers are never on a level with their hearers and readers. They see more, feel more, than those whom they impress, and their personality is no small constituent in the effect produced. Rightly enough, St. Paul specializes " my speech and my preaching." The " *my* " means a man "determined not to know anything . . . save Jesus Christ, and him crucified." Self-exaltation he had none ; for self-exaltation is always a parody on the truthfulness of one's nature, and Christ was so real to St. Paul that he could not be other than real to himself in his ministerial work. And, in accordance with this fact, his manner of preaching the gospel is itself *evidential of the divineness of the gospel.* It was a "demonstration of the Spirit and of power." Of what avail that the " Jews require a sign, and the Greeks seek after wisdom " ? Give them the " sign " and the " wisdom : " what then ? The belief, or " faith," if you so call it, is the man's own product, standing in his own strength, the pride of his own intellect, the joy of his own vanity. Not so the doctrine of " Christ crucified." The way it comes to the soul proves its infinite truth. It does not approach a man on the sense side of his nature, but on the spiritual side. Unlike education and culture, which begin with the intellect of the senses and develop upward, Christianity arises from the instant of its initial contact with the human soul at the highest moral capacity, and recognizes this soul as it stands related to God its Father, to Christ its Redeemer, to the Holy Ghost its Convincer and Sanctifier. Man as the image of the natural universe is regarded subsequently. Therefore the emphasis of St. Paul on the "demonstration of the Spirit and of power," and therefore the strength and glory of faith, which stands, not " in the wisdom of men, but in the power of God."—L.

Vers. 6—13.—*Contents of the revelation.* But the apostle claims " wisdom" for the gospel. The counterfeit has been exposed, and the genuine coin is now presented. And how does he proceed to verify his right to use a term that, in the estimation of all thinkers, commanded respect and admiration ? He will honour the Word ; he will restore its meaning and clear it of obscurity, nay, expand its significance and invest it with a charm not known before. Solomon had used his splendid intellect to give the word " wisdom " a wide currency among his people, and Socrates had laboured for the Greeks in a similar way, each of them an agent of Providence, to teach intellect its legitimate uses and rescue it from bondage to the senses. And there was that old world in which these men, under very different circumstances and sharing very unlike illumination, had taught their countrymen what they knew of wisdom, and this remnant of its former state—the mere effigy of earlier grandeur—stood confronting St. Paul at Corinth, with its conceits, prejudices, and animosities, arrayed most of all against him, because he resisted so bravely its earthly arts and methods. From a far loftier standpoint than Greeks and Jews acknowledged, an infinite distance, indeed, between the disputants of either side, he preached wisdom that came from God— a wisdom long hidden and hence called " a mystery," but now revealed in the fulness of the times. Yet, during the ages when this wisdom had been concealed, when eye and ear and the subtlest imagination had been unable to probe the secret, when human thought had exhausted itself in vain research, and had sunk at last into unnatural content with its own imbecility,—through all this probation of intellect in the school of the senses, God had reserved " the hidden wisdom " for " our glory." The demonstration of man's utter weakness had to be made, and Judæa and Greece had been chosen to make it. Rome's task was to gather up the results and exhibit them in a solidified form; nor could there have been such a Rome as that of the Cæsars unless the experiment with the " wisdom of this world," and of the " princes of this world," had proved a failure disastrous in the extreme. That time had passed. And now this " hidden wisdom " had been made known as a spiritual certainty, which was nothing less than a " demonstration of the Spirit and of power." " There is a spirit in man," and it " knoweth the things of a man." Who can gainsay its consciousness ? Who can appeal from its testimony to anything higher in himself ? So too the Spirit of God " searcheth all things, yea, the deep things of God," and, furthermore, the Holy Spirit is given to our spirit so that we " might know the things that are freely given to us of God." Just before St. Paul had stated that the mystery, the hidden wisdom, had been held back for "our glory." And is not the truth of that statement now attested? Understand wherein "our glory" lies. It is in this—man has a spirit, and God communicates his own secret intelligence unto it in the shape of a "demonstration of the Spirit and of power." Not wisdom alone, not only perception and reflection, but realization and assimilation in the attending form of power, the act of the recipient of grace not being the functional act of a faculty, but of the whole mind; "comparing spiritual things with spiritual"—the spirit of the renewed man most fully conscious of itself, because of the presence of God's Spirit and the expansion thereby of its own consciousness. What a comparing power suddenly wakens! What an outreaching process begins! This capacity of comparing, beginning our development in childhood and continuing till old age, is one of the mind's foremost activities. It is susceptible of more culture than any mental property. The inventive genius of poets and artists, the skill of the great novelist, the discriminating power of the sagacious statesman, are alike dependent on the diversified energy of comparison. Accuracy of judgment, depth of insight, breadth of sympathy so essential to largeness of view, are mainly due to this quality. Give it fair treatment, and three score and ten years witness its beautiful efflorescence. But its spiritual uses are its noblest uses. "Comparing spiritual things with spiritual" is its grandest office. When the human spirit receives the Divine Spirit, what a glorious enlargement, by reason of the superaddition of "the things of God," to the domain of thought, emotion, impulse! Calmly the mind works on; its laws never disturbed, its strength invigorated, its ideal of greatness opened in fuller radiance, its range and compass widened by a new horizon, a motive power brought to bear it never knew, and the repose of strength deepening evermore in the peace of Christ.—L.

Vers. 14—16.—*Natural man and spiritual man.* The natural man, who had not been forgotten by St. Paul in the first chapter, now comes under closer inspection. We can see him from the point of view occupied in the second chapter. What is said of him? He "receiveth not the things of the Spirit of God: for they are foolishness unto him: neither can he know them, because they are spiritually discerned." Nature is represented here as very different from grace, and the difference has the breadth of contrast. Low and vulgar forms of nature are not enumerated, nor would it have been like the apostle to select his illustrations from exceptional cases of human depravity. Corinth could have easily supplied such instances. But the noticeable fact is that he avoids this sort of specification, and chooses his typical examples from "the wise," "the scribe," "the disputer of this world," yea, the very "princes of this world;" and these are they who lack all spiritual discernment, and in their blindness look upon the glorious gospel of Christ as "foolishness." And the portraiture is not finished till these "princes of this world" are sketched against the darkest of possible backgrounds, even the crucifixion of the Lord Jesus. It is not the brutal mob that he pictures on his canvas, but the best specimens, according to current opinion, of the mind and culture of the age. Against these—the guides of public sentiment and the accepted leaders of society, men of character and position—he directs his condemnation. And the grief of his heart is that these are the very men whose evil spirit has infected the Corinthian Church, and introduced vitiating elements long ago abandoned by believers as utterly inconsistent with morality and religion. The natural man of that day was not the creature of the day, not an accident of those volcanic times when the foundations of civil order were shaking, and even the majestic hills of Rome were threatened with upheaval. No; time and opportunity and ample means for development had been allowed; the fairest portions of the world had been given him for home and commerce; a thousand miles around the Mediterranean yielded everything that material civilization demanded; art and philosophy and government had afforded whatever the intellect of the senses craved; and Judaism had diffused itself far and wide, till even Stoicism had felt its influence. After all, however, the natural man has wound up the history of ancient culture by crucifying the Lord of glory; and now, the stain of holy blood upon him, he has learned nothing from his own experience, but persists in treating the gospel as "foolishness." Nor can it be otherwise so long as the man remains under the thraldom of nature. Anomalous it may seem, but it is none the less true, that nature is morally known to us as the opposite of spirituality; and, though a human spirit is in the man, it is wholly incapable of itself to see, to feel, to will, to act, as a spirit in anything that concerns the truly Divine functions of spirit. Hence the need of the Holy Spirit to create spiritual discernment, and hence the supreme distinction of the Christian is that he has a spiritual judgment. "The things of God" are not discovered by him, but are revealed unto his spirit by the Holy Ghost. The discovering intellect of man is a splendid endowment, and yet it is altogether limited to the senses and their connections, nor can it pass under any urgency beyond the sphere of the visible universe, and penetrate the secrets of the Almighty. If, indeed, he could discover them, he would not be a Christian believer; for the traits of the natural man would adhere to him and be merely enhanced by power thus exerted, and there would be less room than before in his capacious soul for intellectual docility, for childlike trustfulness, for the obedience of self-abnegation. And, therefore, the work of the Holy Ghost consists in teaching us to understand, to appreciate, to assimilate, the Divine truths disclosed by him; and, accordingly, what he reveals is not content to remain as ideas and dogmas, but seeks the inmost heart, allies itself with the instincts, and communicates to man a sense of himself and of the possibilities of character hitherto unimagined. Finally, St. Paul argues, "We have the mind of Christ" within us; and what better compendium of all embraced in spiritual discernment than this expression, "mind of Christ"? Far more than the truths he taught, and the practical lessons he enforced, is meant here; for it includes the entire method, the spirit, the aim, of his teachings, as imparting his own life to those believing in him. No moral principle, no doctrinal fact, no phenomenon of spiritual experience, now occupies ground and sustains relations to thought and volition and action that are independently its own. Not one of them is competent to self-existence. There is not, there cannot be, a single abstraction in Christianity. "The mind of Christ" is in every ethical truth, in every miracle, in everything that involves taste, sensibility, reason, conscience, affection; and the life in one is the life in all. To dislocate is to destroy. And this "mind of Christ," the apostle urges, is in us, and, by virtue of its abiding presence and infinite "wisdom" and "power," the breadth of contrast between the natural man and the spiritual man is fully brought out. After eighteen centuries, the distinction is as luminous as ever. The very words remain to us—"wisdom," "power," "foolishness"—and "the princes of this world" attest their ancient lineage. The "natural man" of our day has grown to large dimensions. Never had the senseman, the intellectual man, the man of physical civilization, so much to boast of; for he has well-nigh made good the claim of his sceptre to universal dominion. "Wisdom" was never so conspicuous. "Power" has been developed in a greater degree than its uses. And yet in this very hour, when destructive strength is the daily terror of mankind, and when liberty is ever threatening to riot in licentiousness, we see just what St. Paul saw in old Corinth; and the commentary on God's Word which the nineteenth century, like all centuries since Christ's advent, has written for our eyes, only enforces the truth that "the natural man" knows not God, and "receiveth not the things of the Spirit of God." In science and art, in government, in all sorts of internal sovereignty, "the natural man" has made a vast advance upon himself. But all this has brought him and his institutions and his well-being no nearer to "the mind of Christ."—L.

Ver. 2.—*None but Christ crucified.* What is personal is here, as throughout these Epistles to the Corinthians, remarkably combined with what is doctrinal. These are the utterances of a noble-minded and tender-hearted man, writing to fellow-men in whom he takes the deepest personal interest. Hence he writes of himself, and he writes of his correspondents; and to his mind both have the highest interest through their common relation to the Word of life. These Epistles are a *window* into the heart of the writer, and they are a *mirror* of the thoughts and conduct of the readers. How naturally, when thinking of present successes and discouragements, Paul reverts in memory to his first visit to Corinth! He has the comfort of a good conscience as he calls to mind the purpose and the method of that ministry. Human philosophy and eloquence may have been wanting; but he rejoices to remember that from his lips the Corinthians had received the testimony of God and the doctrine of Christ crucified.

I. THE ONE GREAT THEME OF THE APOSTOLIC AND OF ALL CHRISTIAN MINISTRY.

1. A Divine *Person* is exhibited. Christian preaching sets forth, not rabbinical learning, not Hellenic wisdom, not a code of morals, not a system of doctrine, not a ritual of ceremony, but a Person, even Jesus Christ. 2. An historical *fact* is related, even the *crucifixion* of him who is proclaimed. Everything relating to Christ's ministry was worthy of remembrance, of repetition, of meditation; but one aspect of that ministry was regarded, and still is regarded, as of supreme interest—the Cross, as preceded by the Incarnation, and as followed by the Resurrection. In his earliest Epistle Paul had written, "God forbid that I should glory save in the cross;" in one of his latest he taught that the incarnate Redeemer became obedient unto "the death of the cross." 3. *Religious teaching* of highest moment was based upon this fact regarding this Person. Thus sin was condemned, redemption was secured, a new motive to holiness was provided; for the cross of Christ was the power of God and the wisdom of God.

II. REASONS FOR EXCLUSIVE DEVOTION IN THE MINISTRY OF RELIGION TO THIS ONE GREAT THEME. 1. *A personal and experimental reason* on the part of the preacher. Paul had a personal experience of the excellence and power of the doctrine of the cross. The knowledge which he prized he communicated, the blessings he had received and enjoyed he could offer to others. So must it be with every true preacher. 2. *A more general reason*—the adaptation of the gospel to the wants of all mankind. For Christ crucified is (1) the highest revelation of the Divine attributes of righteousness and mercy; (2) the most convincing testimony and condemnation of the world's sinfulness and guilt; (3) the Divine provision for the pardon of the transgressors; and (4) the most effectual motive to Christian obedience and service. The same doctrine is also (5) the mighty bond of Christian societies; and therefore (6) the one hope of the regeneration of humanity.

APPLICATION. 1. Here is a model and an inspiration for those who teach and preach Jesus Christ. 2. Here is a representation of the one only hope of sinful men; what they may seek in vain elsewhere they will find here—reconciliation with God, and the power of a new and endless life.—T.

Ver. 4.—*Spiritual power*. Language like this sometimes refers to those special, supernatural gifts which were bestowed upon the members and officers of the Church in the apostolic days. But, as the apostle is speaking of the gospel of the cross of Christ and of its moral and spiritual effects, it seems reasonable to take the very strong expressions here employed as referring to the Divine vigour and energy accompanying the Word of salvation.

I. CHRISTIANITY IS THE DISPENSATION OF THE SPIRIT OF GOD. The Jews would have received it had it been a dispensation of miracle and prodigy; the Greeks, had it been a dispensation of rhetoric and philosophy. But God's Spirit has his own mode of operation, withheld from the apprehension of carnal natures. The same Spirit who abode upon the Saviour at his baptism, rested as the Spirit of truth and illumination upon the inspired apostles, and as the Spirit of power accompanied their word to the hearts of men. He is from above, as the Breath, the Wind, the Fire, the Dew, the Rain, the Dove of God.

II. HUMAN SOULS ARE THE FIELD OF THE OPERATIONS OF THE SPIRIT OF GOD. Christianity is no mechanical religion; its ends are not to be secured by any external conformity; it does not consist in buildings, ceremonies, priesthoods, etc. He only understands the nature of Christ's purposes who can join in the consecration and confession—

> "I give my heart to thee,
> O Jesus most desired;
> And *heart for heart* the gift shall be,
> For thou my soul hast fired.
> Thou hearts alone wouldst move;
> Thou only hearts dost love;
> I would love thee as thou lov'st me,
> O Jesus most desired!"

III. THE GOSPEL IS THE IMPLEMENT AND WEAPON OF THE SPIRIT OF GOD. God's Spirit approaches man's spirit in every true, pure, and lofty thought, in every revelation of pity, love, and sacrifice. But God's mind is made known with special reference to man's position and needs in "the truth as it is in Jesus." It is because the Spirit is in the Word that the Word is living and powerful, and sharper than the two-edged sword.

IV. FAITH AND REPENTANCE, OBEDIENCE AND HOLINESS, ARE THE POWER AND DEMONSTRATION OF THE SPIRIT OF GOD. Here we have "the witness of the Spirit," telling us that the source of such streams is above. Here we have "the fruits of the Spirit," telling us whence is the life which embodies itself in such results. Doubtless under the conviction of the Spirit there present themselves displays of feeling, deep and signal. But the great and reliable proofs of the presence and action of the Divine Spirit are to be sought in those moral effects which can be traced to no inferior cause. The weeds sow themselves; but an abundant and precious crop is witness to the skill and the energy of the husbandman.

V. RESPONSIBILITY IS INVOLVED IN THE PRESENCE OF THE SPIRIT OF GOD. 1. The preacher of the gospel is reminded that his reliance should be, not upon his own gifts, but upon the Word and Spirit of God. 2. The Church of Christ is admonished neither to "quench" nor to "grieve" the Holy Spirit. 3. The hearer of the gospel is warned that to refuse the gospel is to reject the Spirit; and deliberately, persistently, and finally to do so is to sin against the Holy Ghost.—T.

Ver. 7.—*The Divine mystery.* The Apostle Paul was accustomed to press into his service, as a Christian teacher, all the institutions and usages of the societies with which he was in any way and at any time associated. Thus in this passage he makes use of the Eleusinian mysteries, with which his readers were doubtless familiar, to set forth the profundity of the Divine wisdom, and the distinction and happiness of those who were initiated into the glorious secrets of Christianity. "We speak God's wisdom in a mystery."

I. THE SUBSTANCE OF THE MYSTERY. There is little reason to believe that the ancient Grecian mysteries had any substantial and valuable truth to conserve and communicate. Observe the contrast: the New Testament tells us of the purpose of God to save mankind; not Jews only, but Gentiles also, in the exercise of his wisdom and compassion.

II. THE HIDING OF THE MYSTERY. It is not for us to explain why a purpose so gracious should have been so long concealed. So it was. And for generations and ages the human race was unacquainted with the purpose which the Supreme had conceived in the counsels of eternity. We can see that the Law had been a "pedagogue" to bring the Jews, and philosophy to bring the Gentiles, to Christ. But the fulness of the time was known only to God.

III. THE REVELATION OF THE MYSTERY. This took place when Christ came and, in his ministry and sacrifice, made known the gracious designs of the Father, that all men should be drawn unto himself, and that the world might not be condemned but saved with an everlasting salvation.

IV. THE COMMUNICATION OF THE MYSTERY. This took place in the gospel. The fervour which Paul and his fellow-labourers displayed in the preaching of the glad tidings shows how deeply those tidings had sunk into their nature, and how precious the reception of them appeared to their enlightened minds. They unfolded what had been wrapped up; they brought to light what had been buried beneath the soil, even "the hid treasure;" they brought out from the deep sea that "pearl of great price" which is for the enrichment of every possessor and for the delight of every beholder.—T.

Ver. 8.—"*The Lord of glory.*" When the Jews and the Roman governor united in effecting the crucifixion of the Lord Jesus, neither party to the proceeding can be said to have understood and realized what was being done. The enemies and murderers of the Prophet of Nazareth saw neither the glory of his character and person more than very dimly, nor the glory of his redemption in any measure at all. Jesus himself had declared, "They know not what they do;" and Paul here says that, had they known the counsels of God, they would not have crucified Christ. This does not justify or excuse their act; for they certainly knew that they were putting to a cruel death One who was innocent and just. Christ is the Lord of glory—

I. IN RIGHT OF HIS OWN NATURE AND PERSON. This he himself asserted, when he spoke of the glory which he had with the Father before the world was. And such was the teaching of the apostles concerning him who was "the Emanation, the Effulgence, of the Father's glory, and the very Image of his substance."

II. IN VIRTUE OF THE CHARACTER OF HIS MINISTRY AND SACRIFICE. It is true that the life of Jesus upon earth was accompanied by lowly circumstances, and was not likely to dazzle the carnally minded. In his incarnation he emptied himself of his glory and took the form of a slave. Yet those who had eyes to see could look through the humiliation to the glory behind and within. And they have left their witness on record : " We beheld his glory, the glory as of the only begotten of the Father, full of grace and truth." Spiritual discernment recognized Divine glory even amidst the ignominy of the awful death of the Redeemer.

III. BY HIS EXALTATION AND THE EVENTS THAT FOLLOWED IT. The Resurrection and Ascension were the completion of the work which was begun by the Incarnation and the Sacrifice. If in the earlier of these movements constituting the redemptive work the glory was hidden, in the later it was conspicuously revealed. Jesus arose " in the glory of the Father ; " he ascended, " carrying captivity captive ; " he shed forth the gifts of the Spirit in royal profusion ; he occupies his immortal throne. To his people he is the eternal " King of glory."

IV. BECAUSE HE SECURES THE GLORIFICATION OF ALL HIS PEOPLE. Christ is described as " bringing many sons unto glory." The context refers especially to " our glory," i.e. to the heavenly happiness, dignity, and reign of those who have a part in Christ's redemption, who share his conflict here, and to whom it is assured that they shall be partakers of his majesty and of his dominion hereafter. The honour of Christ is bound up with that of his people. It is not intended that they shall behold his majesty and splendour from afar, as something to admire and to adore, but not to share. On the contrary, his glory shall be reflected upon them ; as the Lord of glory, he will admit them to participate in it, and this very participation shall be the means of its enhancement.—T.

Vers. 9, 10.—*The revelation of things unseen and unheard.* It may perhaps have been complained, though unreasonably enough, that Paul's compositions were lacking in logic, and his language in eloquence. There was in the substance of his teaching enough to compensate any deficiencies of such kinds. No sage communicated such wisdom, no poet such wonders, as he. Deep things, drawn by the Spirit from the ocean of God's unfathomable nature, were brought up, and were by him presented to the Church of Christ—to all who possess the spiritual capacity to recognize their meaning and to appreciate their worth.

I. CONSIDER WHAT THESE REVELATIONS WERE. In the original prophecy the reference was to marvellous and Divine deliverances wrought for Israel ; the apostle " accommodates" the prophet's language to his own purpose, to express the display of Divine wisdom and power evinced in the gospel, in which Christ is made unto his people wisdom and righteousness, sanctification and redemption. The privileges of the Christian calling enjoyed in the present are an earnest of the higher joys of the eternal future. The gospel manifests the favour and fellowship of God, assures of sonship and of heirship. It reveals Divine truth, and it imparts Divine grace.

II. OBSERVE HOW INACCESSIBLE THESE BLESSINGS WERE TO THE ORDINARY POWERS OF MEN. The eye can range over the surface of this beautiful earth, and can explore the glories of the majestic firmament. The ear has receptivity for the manifold sounds of nature and for the intricacies and the charms of music. The heart speaks often and profoundly : " A man's mind is sometimes wont to tell him more than seven watchmen that sit in a tower." But the revelations here alluded to are not like the features of nature, which are recognizable by sense, or like the inspirations of practical sagacity. The eye can see the works of God, but not the Artificer ; the ear can hear the voice of God, but knows not the Speaker ; the heart can echo the appeals of God, but these appeals must reach it from above.

III. REMARK THAT THESE REVELATIONS ARE MADE BY THE SPIRIT OF GOD HIMSELF. We possess a spiritual nature susceptible of Divine impression and appeal, and with this nature, created after his own likeness, the Father of spirits is in direct communication. Not that truth is miraculously conveyed; the Spirit takes the revealed facts and applies them to the mind, quickening and illumining the powers so that they receive and rejoice in the truth of God.

IV. PONDER THE CONDITION OF RECEIVING THIS KNOWLEDGE. The revelations are for those who *love* God. Not the great, or the wise, or the outwardly righteous are the recipients of Heaven's best blessing; but those who possess this moral and spiritual qualification. They who "wait for God," as Isaiah puts it; they who "love God," as it is phrased by Paul,—are the enlightened and the enriched. The spirit that is filled with gratitude and with love is thereby prepared to understand and appreciate the mysteries of Divine grace. The true love, which puts on the form of obedience, is the path to spiritual perfection. Love grows, and with it knowledge; and heaven is attractive because it is at once the abode of perfect love and the sphere of perfect knowledge.—T.

Ver. 16.—"*The mind of Christ.*" Some professed Christians have the *name*, and only the name, of Christ. Some are satisfied to have in sacramental bread what represents the *body* of Christ. "We," says the apostle, and all true Christians will in a lowly grateful spirit unite in the same profession—"we have the *mind* of Christ."

I. WHAT IS MEANT BY "THE MIND OF CHRIST"? His earthly ministry, his counsels and promises to his disciples, his willing sacrifice, revealed that mind; and that so fully and so clearly that we may justly say, *that mind* has become and is the richest heritage and possession of humanity. 1. His was the mind that *saw the truth*. He did not reason it out or accept it from authority; he looked it in the face; he was naturally and perfectly and always acquainted with it. 2. His was the mind that *loved the good*. It was through no fierce struggle that Jesus came to admire and to appreciate moral beauty; for goodness was natural to him and perfectly congenial and delightful to his being. 3. His was the mind that *chose the right*. The will of man is often vacillating and varying, and in some cases it persistently chooses evil. But throughout Christ's ministry, righteousness was not the law to which he submitted, but the very life he lived. There is no instance of his preferring the wrong; he was without sin. 4. His was the mind that *thought and planned and suffered for all men*. It is not a just view of the mind of the Lord Christ to regard it as personal character. For he was the Son of man, and took all humanity into the embrace of his great and comprehensive mind. He thought and spake of all men as most closely related to himself. To know his mind is to know alike the mind of man and the mind of God.

II. HOW CAN WE PARTAKE "THE MIND OF CHRIST"? When we consider what that mind was, we may well be all but hopeless of possessing and of sharing it. Yet it is his will that his mind should be ours, and he has made provision for our participation in, our appropriation of, his mind. 1. *We acquire knowledge* of that mind through the record of the gospel. His words, his miracles, his conduct, his sufferings, were all a revelation of his mind; pondering them, we come near to the thought, to the heart, of our Saviour. 2. *We receive with faith* the all-sufficient redemption he has effected. He is not only a Teacher, he is not only a Revelation of the Father; he is the Saviour. And it is in accepting the salvation which is through him that we are re-created in the likeness of his holy mind and nature. 3. *We do his will*, and learn that obedience is the method by which we attain to a more thorough sympathy with him. Thus a growing revelation on his part brings about a growing appropriation on ours.

III. HOW CAN WE PROVE OURSELVES TO HAVE "THE MIND OF CHRIST"? 1. By our judgment concerning spiritual things; for these are spiritually discerned by the disciplined, the sympathetic, mind. 2. By our life of loving service; for "if a man have not the Spirit of Christ, he is none of his."—T.

Vers. 1—5.—*Pauline preaching.* I. WHAT IT WAS NOT. 1. *It was not "with excellency of speech."* Paul did not come as a rhetorician; his utterances were not orations of highly wrought eloquence. He did not seek to make the gospel palatable by presenting it with "enticing words." His manner was simple and unaffected; his diction plain and easily understood. He did not aim to carry everything before him with a flood of words, neither did he, a preacher, seek fame as an orator. He had *a message* to deliver, and would not obscure it by many words; he dreaded lest anything should divert attention from its all-important terms. It is recorded of James II. that he once sat for his portrait to a great flower-painter, but so completely was the canvas filled with beautiful garlands of flowers, that the king himself was lost sight of. So many paint Christ in their sermons; when they preach Christ they preach everything except Christ. 2. *It was not the impartation of human wisdom.* Paul did not come as a philosopher; he came as a herald. He had certain facts and truths to proclaim, and he would not philosophize about them, at all events until they were accepted, for, until accepted, their true philosophy could not be understood. Human wisdom had failed; Paul brought something which would not fail. Paul was no enemy to human wisdom; he despised it only *as a means of human redemption;* it was very contemptible to him when it attempted to transcend its sphere.

II. WHAT IT WAS. It was the proclamation of " Christ and him crucified." This was pre-eminent, excluding philosophies and subordinating all other things. The apostle would not *know* aught besides; this should fill his consciousness. If the Corinthians would not receive *this*, he had nothing more for them; he must turn to others more willing. A myriad other things had been presented to them by philosophers and various teachers; all had failed. He would present Christ, and this Christ crucified, and stake everything upon the issue. That which was the sum and substance of Paul's preaching is, in much preaching, like the proverbial needle in the haystack—exceedingly difficult to discover at all. 1. His theme was : (1) The person of Christ. The subject of prophecy, of history, of the apostle's own knowledge. Christ the Sent of God. Christ the Son of God and the Son of man. (2) The office of Christ. Christ the Saviour of men. Exhibited as the Saviour especially in that tragedy of the cross, when " he was wounded for our transgressions, and bruised for our iniquities." 2. This was " the testimony of God" (ver. 1). The revelation of Divine wisdom. God had nothing greater or better to disclose to men than this. Well might the apostle pass by the wisdom of man, since he was entrusted with the wisdom of God. The " mystery " of God. Thought of in past eternal ages, long hidden from men, transcending the poor flights of boastful human intellect, but now plainly declared. Paul spoke not his own words or thoughts, but God's. 3. Note a special feature of his preaching : it was " in demonstration of the Spirit and of power." It was the utterance of certain truths with reliance upon the Divine Spirit to carry them to the heart. The apostle, in proclaiming the gospel, whilst using evidence and employing argument, relied upon the conviction of the Spirit. Words and human wisdom could not effect what he desired—conviction of sin, of the need of a Saviour, conviction that Christ was *the* Saviour, the *only* Saviour, the " Mighty to save." Paul preached waiting for the witness of the Spirit—*and that witness was given.* It is sometimes not given because it is not sought. All preaching without it is useless, and yet it is often the last thing thought of.

III. ITS ACCOMPANIMENTS ON THE OCCASION IN QUESTION. 1. *Weakness.* Possibly the " thorn in the flesh " was at that time specially harassing, or the apostle may have been in special bodily weakness. But perhaps he was deeply conscious of weakness and insufficiency when he viewed the magnitude and importance of his work. Corinth was a strong Satanic citadel to storm. 2. *Fear.* Under a sense of responsibility, and the issues at stake. Apprehension lest mistakes should be made, and evil done instead of good. It might be well if there was more of this " fear " in some modern preachers. 3. *Much trembling.* There was much commotion in the apostle's spirit—he was deeply agitated. With no " light heart " did he set about his work. A very pathetic picture! But *probably the best condition for the apostle under the circumstances.* This apostolic condition has not a little to do with apostolic success. The all-confident may suceed in the world, but they will fail sooner or later in the Church. Such a state as that of Paul's makes us feel that *we are nothing,* and that we can do nothing; *and then God works.* When we are weak, then are we strong (2 Cor. xii. 10). The despondencies, humiliations, emptyings, of Christian workers have frequently been the preludes of marked spiritual successes. We are often too strong and too confident for God to make any use of us.

IV. ITS AIM. 1. *The awakening of faith.* This preaching was not a performance for applause, but earnest work for an all-important, spiritual result. Nothing less than personal saving faith in Christ as the issue of his preaching could satisfy the apostle—

a faith which should indissolubly bind to Christ, and blossom into the excellences and beauties of the Christian life. 2. *Faith well founded.* Not standing in the wisdom of men (ver. 5). Not built upon beautiful words or fine-spun theories, but having the work of God in the heart as a sure foundation. The apostle desired *divinely wrought conviction and conversion.* So in his preaching he sought to *make all room for God.* He did not desire to be personally prominent; he swept away philosophies and the cunning arts of rhetoric, fixed the attention upon the God-sent Saviour and his victorious work upon the cross, and relied upon God to make this break down the opposition of the natural heart and to build up in the soul a steadfast, abiding faith in Christ. An important inquiry—What is our faith based upon? Do we know anything of the "power of God," the "demonstration of the Spirit"? The faith of not a few—such as it is—is based upon the imagination, eloquence, learning, or eccentricities of their ministers; upon the authority of their Church; or upon their own unsanctioned fancies.—H.

Vers. 6—16.—*True wisdom.* I. Is FOUND IN CHRISTIANITY. Paul has been speaking slightingly of "wisdom." Might lead some to suppose that Christianity was unwise, or at all events a one-sided system; that it was a religion for the heart only, and unfriendly to the intellect. The apostle guards against this damaging supposition by claiming true wisdom for Christianity. What he has been decrying is the ineffective wisdom of the world. Christianity is for the whole man. When a man is in a right condition, Christianity satisfies both his head and heart. Christianity is *the sublimest philosophy.* Its creed contains the profoundest truths, and under its influence we are placed on the high road to the solution of all that is mysterious in the universe. We are in alliance with, and under the teaching of, the Eternal Mind, which will at last lead us into all truth. An intricate piece of mechanism may baffle the intelligence of careful students, but those on terms of intimacy with the *inventor* may obtain from him a lucid and all-satisfactory explanation. God is the great Inventor of the universe, and all its puzzles are very plain things to him. Those who are on terms of sacred intimacy with him—not those who are estranged—are likely to enter into the higher knowledge of things. Christianity places us in this all-advantageous position. We are on the road of knowledge. One day we shall know even as we are known. Perhaps to the lost the disheartening puzzles and mysteries will continue evermore.

II. ITS CONTENT. The knowledge of God's redemptive work in its widest significance (ver. 7). Showing how man is restored to the Divine favour; his relation to God upon his recovery; the plan of his new life; shedding much light upon the Divine character and upon the Divine working in nature and in providence, since these are allied to and influenced by his working in grace; leading to the knowledge of many deep things of God (ver. 10), profound doctrines, etc. Man learns whence he came; the meaning of his present life; whither he goes; the cause of the disorders which he beholds in the world and realizes in himself; how this cause may be dealt with so far as he and others are concerned; how he and they may escape from its control and rise from it to God. Christianity solves now the mysteries attaching to *practical* moral and spiritual life. It shows man *how to live.* The Christ of Christianity could say, "I am the Way, the Truth, and *the Life.*" "In him was *life,* and the life was the light of men" (John i. 4). *Life-wisdom* was the wisdom the world needed; it was found in Christianity. The wisdom of the world was powerless to answer the *great* question of life—in this province it was mere folly. Christianity answered every question that *really required an answer;* and, in its marvellous plan of salvation, exhibited the sublimest wisdom, seeing that the Deity is hereby glorified and man's rescue from sin, ennoblement, purification, and present and future well-being are secured. When Paul expounded the doctrines of Christianity, he was not speaking folly, but setting forth the truest and highest wisdom the world had ever listened to; and those who truly embraced Christianity became "wise," seeing that they then possessed true views of God and of human life, and moreover yielded themselves to the control of an influence which would make them practically wise in every-day conduct. Let us realize that Christianity contains the *profoundest* wisdom. Men laugh at Christianity,—not because *it* is foolish, but because *they* are. Let us guard against being *laughed out of* Christianity; for if we are, we shall be laughed out of wisdom and laughed into folly.

III. ITS ORIGIN. 1. *Not of this world.* The true wisdom is heaven-born, not earth-born. The world is at enmity with God, and omits him from its schemes of wisdom; no wonder that these develop into utter folly. 2. *Not of the rulers of this world.* The world's great men did not produce Christianity; it sprang not from philosophers, rhetoricians, politicians, or conquerors. World-powers tend to come to nought and their wisdom with them (ver. 6). The true wisdom revealed in Christianity never entered the heads of the wise men of the world (ver. 9); it was alien to their natures and notions. They were natural; it was supernatural. 3. *God.* It is true wisdom because it is Divine wisdom; its origin proves its quality. It springs from the Supreme Mind; it conveys his thoughts; it reveals his purposes and acts. In Christianity the finite mind runs upon the lines of the infinite. The human occupies the standpoint of the Divine. We see with God's eyes. 4. *Ancient.* We speak of the wisdom of the ancients: this is the wisdom of the Ancient of days. Older than the worlds. Thought out by God in a past eternity. Conceived *then* for our well-being. Wondrous thought! Here Divine love takes its place by the side of Divine wisdom. For *us;* and *shall we miss it after all?* Because fools call it folly, shall we? It is the eternal wisdom, prepared for us before time was. It comes to us down through the ages unshattered, unshaken, by the assaults of the centuries.

IV. BY WHOM UNDERSTOOD. By the spiritual. It is spoken amongst "the perfect" (ver. 6), the spiritually minded, the matured. Every believer has some comprehension of it; but the more spiritual a man is the keener is his perception of its beauty and force, the greater his delight in it. The carnal understand it not. Once they were tested in its close and striking approach to them in the person of the Lord Jesus, but him they sought to destroy (ver. 8); and, *could they have done so,* they would have robbed the world of light and left it to interminable darkness. To the "natural man" the true wisdom is folly (ver. 14); *as the ordinary wisdom of men might seem to creatures of lower grade.* The spiritual man is exalted, and sees clearly what to the man beneath appears blurred, unsightly, puzzling, and undesirable. The carnal man has a valley view, and gazes through thick and distorting mists; the spiritual man has a mountain-top view, and the more spiritual he is the clearer is the atmosphere through which he looks. Many men who quarrel with Christianity should rather quarrel with themselves; the fault is not in it, but in them. *We* need alteration, not God's revelation. We must not think lightly of Christianity because many reject it; an imbecile throws away bank-notes. Honesty is good, but a thief will have none of it. A blind man has a poor opinion of pictures. When the mouth is out of condition, the sweetest meats are unsavoury. When God revealed the true wisdom in Christianity, he announced that it would be unappreciated by many, and *explained why this would be so* (Rom. viii. 7).

V. ITS POSSESSION AND EXERCISE BY THE SPIRITUAL. 1. *Possession.* (1) The spiritual possess the Spirit (vers. 10, 12, 16). This is the cause of their being spiritual. By nature we are all carnal—the children of darkness and of wrath. Our carnality is dissipated by the coming of the Divine Spirit into our hearts. He is light, we are darkness; the light chases away the darkness. The Divine Spirit commences the work of grace in our hearts and carries it on to the end. How eagerly should we open our hearts to this Divine Guest! How heedful should we be to the command, "Quench not the Spirit" (1 Thess. v. 19)! To quench the Spirit would be to involve ourselves again in the darkness from which we had escaped. (2) The Spirit reveals the true wisdom to the spiritual. We are taught of the Spirit. Here we tread the road of the highest and truest knowledge. "Who teacheth like him?" Here is the school for all Christians; only as they learn here do they learn truly. Men have boasted of their teachers. How many sat at the feet of Socrates, Plato, and Aristotle! and one very familiar to us sat at the feet of Gamaliel. But what an honour is reserved for the children of God to have as their Teacher the Holy Spirit! A Teacher, too, *always with us,* for he dwells within us; and *ever ready to instruct.* How diligent should we be in learning the lesson set for us by this Teacher! (3) The Spirit is qualified for this office. What a striking testimony to the divinity of the Holy Ghost we have in ver. 11! God is represented under the figure of a man; the Holy Ghost under the figure of the spirit of that man. How full the knowledge! how intimate the association! how indissoluble the connection!—*the two are one!* We are taught *by God,* and who can teach God's wisdom, the true wisdom, like *God himself?* 2. *Exercise.* The Spirit not only reveals wisdom to the spiritual, but makes them practically wise. As led by him, all their actions are wise; their foolish deeds are the fruits of refusing to be so led. (1) They compare spiritual things with spiritual (ver. 13). This expression is obscure. Some have thought the meaning to be, comparing passages of Scripture together, all being recognized as inspired by the Spirit, and one being expected to shed light upon the other. And surely such "comparing" is wise. Single-text men have a profound impression of their own wisdom, but no one else has. It has been well said that the best commentary on Scripture is Scripture. The Spirit has certainly made us wise when we have a special fondness for his own teaching. Men are apt to search everything before they search the Scriptures. We want more Bible students. Many know a good deal *about* the Bible, and very little *of* the Bible. The passage has been thought to mean, joining spiritual truths to spiritual (not worldly-wise) words, thus causing it to continue the thought of the preceding clause—upon which, by the way, adherents of the verbal inspiration theory lay much stress as supporting their views. As for ourselves, if we are wise, we shall certainly desire to be led by the Spirit, not only in thought, but in utterance. Preachers and teachers need to attend the Divine school of language. Words are a great power; they hinder or help according to their suitability. How many sermons of noble and useful thought have been thrown away because of unsuitable diction! How much truth has been suffocated under masses of verbiage! How much reproof, exhortation, incitement, has been made pointless by being expressed in carefully rounded periods! The edge has been taken off; the sword has been blunted. How often "eloquence" has hidden Christ! And further, how often false doctrine has been fostered by carelessness of expression! We need a "wisdom of words;" though not that false wisdom of words which Paul so vigorously condemned. The modern Church requires a "gift of tongues," and must look for it whence the ancient gift came. The ministers of Christ should speak "as the Spirit gives them utterance." (2) They form true judgments. In the degree in which they possess the true wisdom, according to the measure in which they are taught and led by the Divine Spirit. The reference is, no doubt, to matters moral and spiritual; but it must be remembered that all things in this life have a moral or spiritual bearing, and it is in this respect that the spiritual have true discernment. The truly spiritual man cannot be judged by the carnal. The carnal cannot form a true estimate of spiritual matters, because these are spiritually discerned (ver. 14). So that the world's judgment of the Christian, *per se*, need not distress him; it is the judgment of ignorance (see ch. iv. 3). This true wisdom, so priceless, is within the reach of all. By believing in Christ we may become "wise unto salvation," and, under the Spirit's teaching, wise for all time and for all eternity.—H.

Vers. 1—5.—*Paul the model preacher.* The apostle has shown that God does not save men by human wisdom, but by the preaching of Christ. He now declares that his own practice at Corinth was in accordance with this great principle. His example is a pattern for all preachers of the gospel.

I. THE MATTER AND METHOD OF PREACHING. Paul's business was to "proclaim the mystery of God," "even the mystery which hath been hid from all ages and generations; but now hath it been manifested to his saints" (Col. i. 26). The substance of that mystery is set forth in "Jesus Christ, and him crucified." The person and the work of Christ, what he was and what he did, constitute the great theme of the preacher. These two great heads cover all that is distinctively called *the gospel.* How is this to be preached? "Not with excellency of speech or of wisdom;" "not in persuasive words of wisdom." Not as a new philosophy to supplant the old; not as a well-reasoned argument, compelling the assent of the mind; not as a rhetorical display, taking captive the imagination. The temptation to seek to win men in this way is frequently great, as Paul felt it to be at Corinth, but it must not be yielded to. The preacher is the bearer of a Divine message to men which needs no adventitious helps (compare what is said above on ch. i. 17—25).

II. THE SOURCE OF POWER IN PREACHING. 1. *Self-distrust.* "And I was with you in weakness, and in fear, and in much trembling." Paul magnified his office and humbled himself. In presence of the forces arrayed against him and the great trust committed to him, he felt his own weakness. And if the great apostle trembled in view of his work, does it become any preacher of the gospel to be self-confident? Human power at its best can produce no spiritual result. The most highly gifted are impotent to convert a single sinner. To be confident in our own strength is to be weak; for this confidence prevents the exercise of Divine power. To be self-emptied, self-distrustful, consciously weak, is to be really strong; for then God can work by us. Whilst we preach the Word, we are to stand still in impotence and see the salvation of God. This is a negative source of power to the preacher, a keeping of the field clear to let the Divine force have full play. Here also the law holds, "He that exalteth himself shall be humbled; but he that humbleth himself shall be exalted." 2. *The presence of the Holy Spirit.* The apostle's preaching was "in demonstration of the Spirit and of power." The truth he uttered was carried home to men's minds and hearts by the Spirit of Christ, and consequently with a power of conviction which no force of reasoning could produce. Here lies the preacher's strength. Great results may be wrought by human power on a lower level: logic may convince the intellect, rhetoric may dazzle the imagination, pathos may touch the heart; but the Holy Spirit alone can convert, and *nothing short of conversion should satisfy us.* As the powder to the ball, as the strong arm to the sword (Heb. iv. 12), so is the Spirit to the Word. "Not by might, nor by power, but by my Spirit, saith the Lord of hosts" (Zech. iv. 6). This was the secret of the apostle's power, and all workers for Christ must depend on the same source of strength if they would "be strong and do exploits."

III. THE CHIEF END OF PREACHING. Paul aimed at producing faith in Christ, and he was careful that this "faith should not stand in the wisdom of men, but in the power of God." Belief in Jesus Christ may rest upon evidence addressed to the understanding, or upon the authority of a teacher or Church; and this is important in its own place. But such belief implies no more than a mental assent to certain facts or truths, and requires for its production nothing beyond the natural force of proof. The faith which saves is the product of the Holy Spirit working effectually in the hearers of the Word, and is based upon his "demonstration" of the truth. It is, therefore, a stable and abiding thing, upheld by him who produced it; and it is an operative thing, affecting the heart and life of the believer. The end of gospel preaching is to bring men to exercise this living faith. Let the preacher pray and work for this; let the hearer ask himself if he has obtained it.—B.

Vers. 6—10.—*Spiritual wisdom.* While disclaiming a gospel based on the wisdom of men, Paul is careful to show that he does not disparage true wisdom. The facts of Christianity are the embodiments of great principles; the story of the cross has behind it the sublimest philosophy. Hence the gospel is at once milk for babes and meat for men (ch. iii. 2); and a wise teacher knows how to adapt his teaching to the capacities of his pupils. Among the newly converted, the apostle confined himself to a simple presentation of truth; but among the "perfect," or more advanced, he exhibited that truth in its higher relations. The Epistles to the Romans and the Ephesians are examples of the wisdom which he communicated to the full-grown in the Christian Churches. The child and the philosopher find a common point of interest in Christ crucified.

I. THE CHARACTERISTICS OF SPIRITUAL WISDOM. These are set forth negatively and positively. 1. It is "*not of this world.*" It is not a natural product springing out of earthly soil. It is not the invention of this world's princes, the leaders of thought and the wielders of power, who control the ongoings of the age. They and their works belong to a state of things that is coming to nought. They have no place as such within the kingdom of God, and their wisdom shall perish with them. Christianity derived nothing from this source, and all attempts to improve upon it by human wisdom have been futile. 2. This wisdom is *of God.* The plan of salvation is a product of the Divine mind. At every step in it we mark his impress. Its conception as a whole, and all its details, speak of him. The characteristics here enumerated are in keeping with its Divine origin. (1) It is "a mystery." This is a favourite word with Paul in describing the way of redemption (cf. ch. iv. 1; Eph. i. 9; vi. 19, etc.). Some ancient religions had their so-called mysteries, into which their votaries required to be initiated; and the wisdom of God so far resembles these that it needs a Divine preparation in order to understand it. Mere natural reason cannot receive it; it must be revealed to us by God himself. (2) It "hath been hidden"—"kept in silence through times eternal, but now is manifested" (Rom. xvi. 25, 26). God's secret purpose of mercy has been revealed in the gospel. God has broken the silence and has spoken. (3) It was "foreordained before the worlds [ages]." Redemption is a forethought, not an afterthought. Before the world was, before man was made, before all time, the thought of God was upon sinners, and he purposed to save them. Follow the broad river of salvation back to the cross of Christ, back through all the stages of its development, and you come at last to the spring of infinite love in the heart of God. This great tree, which in the course of the ages has grown into strength and sent out many branches, has its roots in the timeless past, and its fully ripened fruits in the eternal future. Who shall overturn it (Rom. viii. 29, *et seq.*)? (4) It was foreordained "unto our glory." Here are the first and last links of the golden chain of redemption. Glory is the final completion of salvation, the full-blown flower of grace. God gives all his sons a "crown of glory," and for this his wisdom and power in Christ are working. The Divine origin of evangelical wisdom is confirmed by the treatment it received at the hands of men. When the hidden mystery was revealed in Jesus Christ, they knew it not. Even the Lord of glory had no charm in their eyes—"no beauty that they should desire him." The rulers of this world, the representatives of its wisdom and power, counted him worthy of a cross. And this has been the case whenever the gospel has encountered human wisdom. Acting on its principles, men have rejected Christianity and sought to crush it by force. Every day the same blindness is seen in those who do not embrace the Saviour, leading now to indifference and now to active hostility.

II. How SPIRITUAL WISDOM IS REVEALED. To give point to the contrast he has been drawing out, Paul quotes freely from Isa. lxiv. 4, to show whence our knowledge of heavenly wisdom is derived. "Whatsoever things God prepared for them that love him" is a beautiful description of the blessings of salvation—pardon, peace, renewal, life eternal. All these have been made ready in the working out of the scheme of redemption. During the Old Testament period they were in course of preparation, the great plan step by step unfolding itself, till in the fulness of the time the Christ appeared, to turn shadow into substance, prophecy into history. And these prepared blessings are for them that love him; for they alone can receive them. Love has an eye to see, an ear to hear, a heart to embrace, the things of salvation; and to love they are revealed. 1. The knowledge of these things *is not attained by the exercise of natural faculties*. (1) Not by sight: "Eye saw not." What wealth of beauty has God prepared for the eye! Sky and earth and sea teem with fair forms from the Creator's hand. Much knowledge comes to us through this noblest of our senses; but spiritual things lie in a region where it cannot enter. They belong to the *invisible* (2 Cor. iv. 18). (2) Not by hearing: "Ear heard not." Many sweet sounds in nature has God prepared for the ear. We learn much through the medium of words, spoken or written; but spiritual knowledge does not come thus. "Faith cometh by hearing," but hearing alone does not produce faith. The Pharisees heard Jesus, but they did not believe on him. The men of Athens and Corinth heard Paul, but how few understood his message! Thousands listen to the gospel again and again without entering into its real meaning. (3) Not by thought: "And which entered not into the heart of man." Wonderful things have been conceived by man. Think of the progress he has made in wresting from Nature her secrets (the sciences), and of the triumphs of inventive genius (telegraph, telephone, electric light, spectroscope, etc.). Think of the speculations of philosophers in their efforts to understand all mysteries, the dreams of poets in creating new worlds of imagination. But here is something which science could not discover, nor genius invent, nor imagination create. 2. *They are revealed to us by the Spirit of God*. It is his office, as the Spirit of truth, to guide us into all the truth (John xvi. 13). Spirit can be touched only by spirit. Our inner being lies open to the access of God, who can put his finger on its secret springs and move it as he pleases. The influence of one human mind upon another is similar to this. The process by which the things of God are made known to us is here called *revelation*. A twofold unveiling is requisite. The Holy Spirit presents the truth to our spirits, holds up before us Jesus Christ and his salvation; whilst at the same time he withdraws the veil from the mind, touching the closed eye and opening the deaf ear. Of

Lydia it is said, "Whose heart the Lord opened, to give heed unto the things which were spoken" (Acts xvi. 14); and Paul says, "It was the good pleasure of God to reveal his Son in me" (Gal. i. 15, 16). By this spiritual unveiling, and not by natural sense or reason, do the things of God become to us realities.—B.

Vers. 10—16.—*The Holy Spirit as the Revealer.* In this section the apostle develops more fully the subject of revelation through the Spirit of God. The things prepared by God for them that love him have not been discovered by human wisdom, nor can they be apprehended by natural reason. As they come from God, they are made known to us by God through the operation of the revealing Spirit.

I. THE COMPETENCE OF THE REVEALING SPIRIT. "For the Spirit searcheth all things," etc. He is competent to reveal to us the things of God, because he has a thorough knowledge of them. There is nothing in God that is hid from him, not even the "deep things." The nature, perfections, purposes of the Almighty are patent to his eye. This is explained by an analogy between the spirit of a man and the Spirit of God. "For who among men knoweth the things of a man," etc.? The depths of my being do not lie open to the eyes of others. They cannot observe the hidden motive, the secret desire, and all the movements that precede the formation of a purpose. They see only what is without, and from that infer what is within. But to my own spirit all that inner region is unveiled. I am immediately conscious of all that is going on within me. "Even so the things of God none knoweth, save the Spirit of God." We can see a little of God's working in the universe, and from that we can gather something of his mind; but we cannot by searching find him out. We can only make dark guesses at a few truths regarding him, whilst the matters of his grace are completely hidden from us. But the Spirit of God knows the things of God, as the spirit of a man knows the things of the man. He does not know them by inference. As dwelling in God and himself God, he knows them immediately, infallibly, and perfectly. The analogy is not to be pressed beyond this particular point. The apostle is not speaking of the relation between the Spirit and the Godhead, except in regard to the Spirit's perfect knowledge. From all this the fitness of the Spirit to be our Instructor in the things of God is manifest. The argument is not that he is superior to every other teacher, but that in the nature of things he is the only Teacher. He alone fully knows; he alone can fully reveal.

II. THE WORK OF THE REVEALING SPIRIT. The all-knowing Spirit, proceeding from God, is imparted to believers. As "the spirit of the world" works in the sons of disobedience (Eph. ii. 2), the Spirit of God dwells and works in the children of faith. His work appears in two ways. 1. *In teaching us to know the things of God.* "That we might know," etc. (ver. 12). The things prepared for them that love God are the free gifts of his grace. They have been provided at infinite cost, but to us they are given "without money and without price." These things are taught us by the Spirit, who, as "the Anointing from the Holy One," gives us to know all things (1 John ii. 20). How great a privilege to have such a Teacher! How far does it raise the Christian above the wise of this world! How accurate and assured should be our knowledge! And this knowledge is more than the apprehension of certain doctrines as true, or the persuasion that the gospel is God's way of salvation. We know his gracious gifts only in so far as we receive them. Justification and sanctification are verities only to the justified and sanctified. The way to spiritual knowledge is through faith and personal experience. 2. *In teaching us to speak the things of God.* Paul has in view, first of all, his own case. It was his work as a preacher to declare the glad tidings to men, and this he did, "not in words which man's wisdom teacheth, but which the Spirit teacheth." He was not left to his own unaided skill in choosing the forms under which he presented the truth. The Spirit gave him utterance as well as knowledge, taught him the very words he was to employ. This statement covers both his oral and his written teaching. Apart from theories on the subject, inspiration must be held to extend to the verbal framework of apostolic teaching, as well as to the teaching itself; yet so as to give free play to the writer's own form of thought and style of expression. He fitted spiritual truth to words suggested by the Spirit (this is one probable meaning of πνευματικοῖς πνευματικὰ συγκρίνοντες, ver. 13), and so interpreted spiritual things to spiritual men (according to another probable meaning). Does not this apply in measure to all speakers for Christ? The apostles had a special inspiration for their special work, but many in the Church at Corinth had a gift of utterance (ch. i. 5). May not preachers, teachers, writers, and all who tell the story of Christ crucified, expect similar help?

III. THE NECESSITY FOR THE REVEALING SPIRIT. This appears in the contrast drawn between the natural man and the spiritual man (vers. 14—16). The *natural* man (ψυχικός) is he who is in the fallen condition into which sin has brought mankind, and in whom the faculty of knowing Divine things (the spirit, πνεῦμα) is dormant. Such a man is not necessarily sensual or brutish, but he is earthly—all his movements being governed by the lower part of his incorporeal nature (ψυχή), and directed to selfish ends. The *spiritual* man (πνευματικός) is he in whom the spiritual faculty (πνεῦμα), by which we discern the things of God, has been wakened into life and activity by the Spirit of God. This quickened spirit, dwelt in by the Holy Spirit, becomes the ruling part of his nature, to which thought, desire, purpose, passion, are in subjection (compare the threefold division of human nature in 1 Thess. v. 23, which may be illustrated by the threefold division of the tabernacle—the holy of holies, the holy place, and the outer court). Hence: 1. "The natural man (1) *receiveth not the things of the Spirit of God: for they are foolishness unto him.*" He fails to understand them, and, not thinking that the fault is in himself, he rejects them as absurd. They cross his prejudices and overturn his cherished principles. The doctrine of the new birth seemed foolish to Nicodemus. Every unconverted hearer of the gospel confirms the truth of this statement. (2) *This rejection arises from spiritual inability.* "And he cannot know them, because they are spiritually judged." The natural man is destitute of the faculty by which spiritual things are discerned, as a blind man cannot judge of colour. The tints of the rainbow, the gorgeous hues of sunset, awaken no sensation in him; and for a like reason the glorious things of God's grace call forth no appreciative response from the natural man. How humbling to human pride and human wisdom! How great the need for spiritual illumination! 2. The spiritual man (1) "*judgeth all things.*" This may be taken broadly as covering all the matters on which the spiritual man is called to decide. He alone is in the position where all things are seen in their proper relations, for he alone gives the spiritual element its place of paramount importance. But the apostle has specially in view the things of salvation, which are perceived and appreciated only by the renewed man. His inner eye has been opened, and he now lives and moves in the region of spiritual things, where the natural man stumbles and falls. Many an unlettered, Spirit-taught Christian has a clearer insight into God's ways of grace than the man of mere learning. Hence every believer is called to exercise his own judgment as to Divine truth, and not to rest supinely on the judgment of another. The spiritual eye, like the natural, is given us to be used; and in the use comes greater clearness of discernment and accuracy of judgment. But: (2) "*He himself is judged of no man.*" A man with eyesight can judge of the matters of a blind man, but the blind man cannot judge of him. The spiritual man understands the language in which other men speak, but they do not understand his language. Paul understood Greek philosophy, but the philosophers did not understand him. "Thou art mad," said Festus (Acts xxvi. 24); "This babbler," said the Athenians (Acts xvii. 18); "Fool," said the Corinthians. None but a poet can criticize a poet; none but a painter can judge a painter; none but a believer can appreciate a believer. The spiritual man has the mind of Christ, of which the natural man is destitute; and for the latter to sit in judgment on the former would imply that he is capable of instructing the Lord.—B.

Ver. 7.—*The wisdom of God in a mystery.* The word "mystery" has a twofold meaning as used by the apostle. It means that which is concealed from men until the due time for its disclosure has come; and it also means that which in itself, by reason of its own inherent greatness, surpasses human comprehension. Both meanings are involved here. God's wisdom in the gospel, though foreordained before the worlds, had been "hidden" from the ages and generations of the past. As it would seem to be with many of the secrets of nature, there was the proper, the "appointed" time for it to be brought to light. The men of the earlier ages were as ignorant of it as our fathers even of the last generation were of many of the marvellous things that are now among the familiar facts of our social life, or as we are of what the triumphs of scientific discovery a hundred years hence shall be. Not that the discovery of this Divine wisdom is like a mere step in scientific development. It is a supernatural revelation. And now that it has been revealed, it is still a "mystery," too profound for any power of man to fathom. The apostle "speaks" it, handles it, deals with it, as a mystery—a mystery which even he himself cannot penetrate and solve (see also Rom. xvi. 25, 26; Eph. iii. 5; Col. i. 26). Having special regard now to this inherent characteristic of the gospel, note—

I. WHEREIN THIS ELEMENT OF MYSTERY CHIEFLY LIES. It lies in matters such as these. 1. The person of Christ (1 Tim. iii. 16). 2. The efficacy of his atoning sacrifice (Eph. iii. 9, 10; 1 Pet. i. 12). 3. The operation of his Spirit on the souls of men (John iii. 8). 4. The nature of the union between himself and his people (John vi. 53—63; Eph. v. 32). 5. The ultimate issues of his redemption (ch. xv. 51; 1 John iii. 2; Acts iii. 21).

II. CERTAIN CONSIDERATIONS THAT VINDICATE AND EXPLAIN IT. 1. That which is Divine must needs transcend the limits of human intelligence. 2. It shows Christianity to be in harmony with every other form of Divine revelation. 3. It accords with the progressive character of our present state of existence. 4. It serves to develop in us some of the noblest moral qualities. 5. It heightens our impression of the simplicity of those truths which are vital to our salvation. 6. It stimulates our longing for the brighter and better future (ch. xiii. 9, 12).—W.

Vers. 9, 10, 14.—*The revelation of the things of God.* It may be that we have here a free quotation of Isa. lxiv. 4. But whether a quotation or not, it expresses a principle true in every age. The great "things of God" have ever been beyond the reach of the unaided powers of man. What are these "things which God hath prepared for them that love him"? To apply this expression, as is sometimes done, merely to the glories and joys of the heaven of the future, is to narrow its meaning. Those heavenly things, indeed, are purely matters of faith, above sense, above reason, above experience, above the loftiest flights of imagination. The most suggestive teachings of Scripture, even the grand apocalyptic visions, do not enable us in the remotest degree to conceive of them.

> "In vain our fancy strives to paint
> The moment after death."

But the "deep things of God" here spoken of, "the things freely given to us of God" (ver. 12), are matters of present realization, facts of consciousness, and not merely anticipations of faith. They are those great moral and spiritual truths of which the Name of Christ is the symbol, and those privileges and joys which are the distinguishing marks of Christian life. Consider what is here asserted about them: (1) *Negatively—that the eye and the ear and the heart have not apprehended them;* (2) *positively—that they are revealed to us by the Spirit of God.*

I. THE NATURAL POWERS OF MAN CANNOT APPREHEND THESE THINGS. We may take the eye and the ear and the heart as equivalent to the whole sum of our natural faculties. They are those of the "natural man" as contrasted with the "spiritual" (ver. 14). Every faculty of our nature has its own proper sphere, the "things" that belong to it and with which it is conversant. Sense perceives material things, and, according to the delicacy of its organization, it appreciates the truth of these—beauty of form and colour, variety and harmony of sound, etc. Intellect moves in a region of abstract thought, entertains ideas, judges their relations, etc. Conscience deals with moral questions, determines the dictates of duty, the distinctions of right and wrong. The heart is the seat and tribunal of the affections, love and hate, desire and aversion, hope and fear. Each faculty has its particular part to play in the economy of our life. But when we come to the higher region of the "things of God," we find that which lies beyond the range of these mere natural powers. These Greeks of Corinth and Athens with whom Paul had to do were many of them men of fine native capacity and high culture, men of subtle thought and delicate sensibility. There were "princes" among them, men who had risen above their fellows in the particular departments of human interest for which nature qualified them. The ruler, the senator, the economist, could discern the exigencies of state, and judge matters of law and policy. The philosopher could weigh the evidences of science and thread the mazes of speculative thought. The poet knew what the "fine frenzy" of imagination meant, and could portray in glowing speech the changeful phases of human passion and life. The sculptor and painter had souls alive to the beauty of form and colour, and conversant with the canons of æsthetic taste. And no doubt there were among them men of tender feeling and noble character—benevolent citizens; honourable merchants; faithful, loving fathers, husbands, brothers, friends. And yet how utterly in the dark were they as to the real nature and character of the Deity, and the way of access to him; as to how their being might be redeemed from the power of evil; and how they might solve the mystery and soothe the sadness of death and of the tomb! There had been among them many

> "A grey spirit yearning with desire
> To follow knowledge like a sinking star,
> Beyond the utmost bounds of human thought."

But they could not gain the most distant glimpse of this higher knowledge. It was as a star that had not risen upon them and of the beauty of whose light they could not dream. Indeed, the shadow of their ignorance had settled down so deeply upon them that they had lost the hope of ever seeing the light. They could not recognize it when it came. Paul's preaching was "foolishness" to them. He was but one of the tribe of "babblers," a "setter forth of strange gods." His voice was like that of "one that crieth in the wilderness." It awakened for the most part no responsive echo, but died away upon the empty air. *The powers of the natural man are as ineffectual for any saving purpose now as ever they were;* as incapable of receiving the deep things of God as they were of discovering them. To be assured of this, we have only to remember to how large an extent the intellect of the age goes darkly and wildly astray from Christ; how men of scientific genius, dealing with the phenomena and laws of the universe, fail often to find in them anything Divine; and how many there are whose very natural virtues condemn them because they refuse to exercise on the heavenward side of their being affections that give so much charm to their lower earthly life. All this tells us that men must be inspired by a Power higher than any that is latent in their own nature before they can rise to the apprehension of Divine things and to the beauty and dignity of the life of God.

II. THESE THINGS ARE REVEALED TO US BY THE SPIRIT OF GOD. The Spirit is plainly spoken of here as a personal Being, entering into personal contact and converse with the human soul, imparting to it a faculty of spiritual apprehension which it would not otherwise possess. Note: 1. *The Spirit who inspired the apostles to deliver their gospel message prepared men rightly to receive and interpret it.* It was the same power in both (John xv. 26, 27; xvi. 13; vers. 4—8; 1 John ii. 20—27). 2. *This interpretive faculty is far less a matter of mental penetration than of spiritual sympathy.* This is seen in the contrast instituted between the "spirit of the world" and the "spirit that is of God." The spirit of the world is ever a captious, sophistical spirit, distrustful, carnal, vain, self-willed. The spirit that is of God is simple, lowly, loving, trustful, submissive, childlike. Coming from God, it is in true affinity with the mind of God, and with that Word which is the reflex of the thought and of the heart of God. When, in answer to the wondering question of the Jews, "How knoweth this man letters," etc.? (John vii. 15), Jesus answered, "My teaching is not mine," etc., he placed himself on a level which they also might occupy. Let them emulate his loving loyalty to the will of the Father, and they also shall "know." We must have something of the spirit of the well-beloved Son in us if we would rightly apprehend "the things that are freely given to us of God."—W.

Ver. 15.—*The judging faculty.* "He that is spiritual" is he in whom the Spirit of God dwells, pervading his spirit with a light and quickening it to a life above that of nature. This higher spirit-life has many marks of distinction. It is one of these to which the apostle here gives prominence. Two things are affirmed of the spiritual man—(1) *His power to judge;* (2) *his freedom from being judged.*

I. HIS POWER TO JUDGE. The attitude of mind suggested is an inquiring, critical, testing attitude—an attitude in which it holds its faith in abeyance until perfectly convinced that that which claims it is divinely true, "proving all things" that it may "hold fast that which is good." The spiritual man brings everything thus to the secret tribunal of his own soul. 1. *All forms of human teaching and influence*, the various ways in which men seek to guide our opinions and our conduct. "Believe not every spirit, but prove," etc. (1 John iv. 1). We may apply this to the whole action of the spirits of men upon us through the ordinary means of personal influence. The spirit of truth and the spirit of error, the spirit of good and of evil, come to us through these human channels; and our mental conditions, our daily habits of thought and life, are determined, often far more than we are aware of, in this way. The spirits of men are embodied in their works and words, and thus not merely when they are physically present with us, but when we have never seen them face to face, when oceans roll between us, when they have passed away to other worlds, we may feel their living touch upon our souls. Their sway over us is independent of the conditions of space and time. "Being dead, they yet speak." "They rule us from their urns." Their very names are instruments of persuasive spiritual power. The grand question in every such case is whether this power is on the whole favourable or otherwise to the cause of truth and righteousness. It is by some criterion of right and wrong in our own souls that this question must be determined, and what can the criterion be but the "spirit of power and of love and of a sound mind" that God gives? Books, sermons, newspapers, theories, systems of religious faith and ecclesiastical polity, the personal example and converse of others, the social sentiments and customs that prevail around us,—in short, everything that possesses a moral quality and wields a moral influence over us, must be subjected to this test. This is the Divine "right of private judgment," which in its highest aspect we cannot surrender if we would. 2. *The revelation of God*, coming to us as it does through human and natural channels, must needs be amenable to the same law. According to its own teaching, the Divine in us can alone discover and recognize the Divine element in it. "He that is of God heareth the words of God" (John viii. 47); "Every one that is of the truth heareth my voice" (John xviii. 37); "Ye have an anointing of the Holy One," etc. (1 John ii. 20). Men justly argue that the Bible, like every other book, must be brought to the tribunal of the "judging faculty." But what is that faculty? If they mean by it the Spirit of God given in his measure to every lowly Christian believer, the wondrous supernatural light that shines from heaven upon every soul that humbly and prayerfully looks up for it,—this is a principle to which all apostolic voices bear witness. But if they mean some native faculty, some light of natural reason, some power of spiritual discernment inherent in the very constitution of our being,—they are trusting to that which is the source of all confusion of thought and divergence of opinion, an *ignis fatuus*, which leads through mazes of uncertainty to the darkness of doubt and of despair. The religious sensibility in every man to which revelation appeals is one thing; the interpretive and verifying faculty, which is the special gift of the Spirit of God, which, indeed, *is* the Spirit of God in man, is another. How shall we know that we have this power? In one view of it it is a self-witnessing power, which no rival authority can gainsay; in another, it is a power that proves itself by its qualities and results. It is a lowly, loving, patient, trustful, obedient spirit. And its supreme characteristic is that it testifies to Christ as at once the Centre and Circumference of our highest thought, the Source and End of our noblest life. It is the "mind of Christ," and no "persuasion" can be in harmony with it that does not lead more or less directly to him.

II. HIS FREEDOM FROM BEING JUDGED. "He himself is judged of no man" who has not the same spiritual faculty. This follows as a necessary consequence of the superiority of his own gift. Take it in different ways. 1. *No such man can understand him.* The workings of his inner life, his deepest thoughts, affections, aspirations, conflicts, the powers that sustain and the principles that govern his whole spiritual existence,—these form a world into which the unspiritual man cannot enter. We are all mysteries to each other in the individuality of our being. Each lives in his own world, and the painful sense of solitude will often seize upon the thoughtful spirit. Imperfect sympathies arising from imperfect mutual acquaintance are among the saddest features of our social existence, and will often awaken strange longings for a state of being in which we "shall know even as also we are known." In no case is this separation so complete as between the spiritual and the carnal man. Here lies a gulf which no artifice, no arrangement of outward circumstances, can bridge over. When a good man's lot is cast among uncongenial society, he is driven in upon himself, on the silent satisfactions of his own soul. Like the Master, he "has meat to eat which the world knows not of." Many a tender spirit has felt thus isolated in the midst of those most fondly loved. An atmosphere of natural affection and all natural endearments of life surround them, but in the deepest reality of their being they dwell alone. 2. *He is not open, on the side of his religious thought and life, to the hostile criticism of any man.* How shall others "judge" that with which they have nothing in common, and the very essential meaning of which they cannot understand? 3. *No false influence from man can lead him fatally astray.* Who shall unsettle the faith or shake the steadfast-ness of one who is thus bathed in the light and rooted and grounded in the life of God? Who is he that shall bring again into bondage one whom the "law of the Spirit of life in Christ Jesus" has thus made free? Here lies the grand condition alike of mental assurance and moral strength.—W.

Ver. 2.—*The great theme.* The apostolic preacher considered what was most needful and profitable to his audience, not what would meet their curiosity or please their taste. So he, of deliberate purpose, gave prominence to a theme which the Greeks were disposed to scorn, but which they, in common with all sinners, needed to hear—Christ crucified. A modern preacher who would be faithful must keep his soul braced to the same determination: "*Not anything . . . save Jesus Christ.*" Not Christianity, but Christ; not a system, but the Saviour at the centre of it. "Whom we preach," etc. (Col. i. 28). "*And him crucified.*" That which appeared to men the indelible disgrace of Jesus of Nazareth has proved to be his great power over human conscience and his great attraction for the human heart. St. Paul had seen many proofs of this in his public ministry, and had felt the force of this in his own soul. And the chief theme of the apostle ought to be the chief theme still. A thousand things have changed in the world, but not the moral and spiritual exigency of man. The preaching of Christ crucified cannot grow obsolete. Take the following as reasons for determining to preach Christ and him crucified :—

I. REDEMPTION IS BY CHRIST CRUCIFIED. Whether it be redemption from "all iniquity," from "the curse of the Law," or from a "vain manner of life," it is distinctly ascribed in Scripture to the blood of Christ or to his death (see Eph. i. 7; 1 Pet. i. 18; Gal. iii. 13; Rev. v. 9). The dignity of his person, the purity of his disposition, and the holiness of his life gave value to his death; but it was by his death that he obtained eternal redemption for us.

II. PEACE OF CONSCIENCE COMES THROUGH CHRIST CRUCIFIED. No study of nature, no study of Scripture apart from the cross of Calvary, can relieve the distress of a conscience alive to the heinousness of sin and the imminence of judgment. Not even the contemplation of Jesus Christ in his spotless example can give any relief. How far are we from full conformity to him! We are more and more conscience-stricken till we behold him suffering for our sins, and then we have "peace by the blood of his cross."

III. DEATH TO SIN IS THROUGH CHRIST CRUCIFIED. We are baptized into his death, and, being buried with him, emerge in newness of life. Through faith we have moral identification with our Lord, and, dying to sin, as crucified with him, we live to righteousness, because he lives in us.

IV. THE SUPREME ARGUMENT OF LOVE IS IN CHRIST CRUCIFIED. At the cross God commends his love to us, and Christ proves himself the good Shepherd in giving his life for the sheep. The plea for love among Christians is thus put by St. Paul: "Walk in love, even as Christ also loved you, and gave himself up," etc. (Eph. v. 2).

V. THE SUPREME EXAMPLE OF PATIENCE IS IN CHRIST CRUCIFIED. (See 1 Pet. ii. 20—24.) Thus it is that many sufferers have learned submission from considering the unmurmuring endurance of the Lamb of God, who, under all the pressure of the last sufferings, made no complaint—"opened not his mouth."

VI. ENMITY TO HIS CROSS IS REPRESENTED AS A FATAL SIN. In Heb. x. 29 contempt of "the blood of the covenant" is referred to as deserving of the sorest punishment. In Phil. iii. 18, 19, St. Paul writes, not without tears, of the destruction which awaits those who are "enemies of the cross of Christ." Men are such enemies when, being self-righteous, they will not put their trust for salvation in Christ crucified; or when, being self-willed and earthly minded, they refuse the sanctifying power of the cross, and will not have their "old man crucified with Christ." It is no light matter or venial offence to ignore or despise the "one Sacrifice for sins." For all these reasons, the modern preacher should resolve as St. Paul resolved, and let no passing fashion of the time shake his resolution. Great works of God around us have a certain freshness and immortality. The flow of rivers, the surging of the sea, the course of the seasons, the splendour of the sun, and the bright order of the stars are the same now as when man first observed them. So also it is with the great work of God in Christ for our salvation, finished on the cross. Its wisdom and righteousness and love are as worthy of adoring praise to-day as they were in the days when apostles, prophets, and evangelists went to and fro among wondering cities of the East, determined to know nothing among the people save Jesus Christ and him crucified.—F.

Vers. 9, 10.—*The true wisdom.* Often in the Epistles there is a single word on which the whole discussion turns. In the letter to the Romans, it is "righteousness;" to the Colossians, it is "fulness;" to the Hebrews, it is "perfection." In the letter to the Corinthians, it is "wisdom." Those Greeks sought after wisdom. It was nothing to them that the gospel might relieve a troubled conscience or reform an unworthy life, if it did not correspond with their ideas of philosophy. But St. Paul had an answer to give them for which they were not at all prepared. He calmly affirmed that they were incompetent judges of a heavenly wisdom, and that in his gospel to the people there was a philosophy beyond their power of apprehension—"the manifold wisdom of God." Greek philosophy at its best sought to ascertain how man may, by knowledge and the pursuit of virtue, reach up towards the highest good. But the gospel taught that the highest Good had come down to dwell among men; and that, by union in faith to that highest Good, man becomes more than a philosopher—a saint.

I. THE INAPTITUDE OF MAN TO RECEIVE THE DIVINE WISDOM OF THE GOSPEL. This is expressed by a quotation from the Old Testament (Isa. lxiv. 4): "Eye hath not seen it." The reference is not, as in a well-known poem, to "the better land," but to the wisdom of God. When Jesus, the incarnate Wisdom, was on earth, many eyes saw him that could not discern the glory of God in him. And many an eye to-day sees the position of Christianity in the world, the width of its influence, and the dignity of its institutions, yet does not "see Jesus," and the things which God has prepared in Jesus for those that love him. "Ear hath not heard it." That organ which receives so impartially all communications fails to drink in the wisdom of the gospel. It is closed by earthliness of mind, till the power of God's Spirit unstops it, so to hear that the soul may live. "Neither have entered into the heart," etc. (ver. 9). The heart is hardened, as well as the eye closed and the ear stopped. The spirit of a man of itself knows only "the things of a man," conceives of wisdom and goodness after the manner and measure of man, and so fails to conceive the ways and thoughts of God, and the things which are freely given by him. So the apostle denied that a man untaught by the Spirit, even though he were a Greek, could rightly estimate the gospel. He could remind the disputers and rhetoricians of Greece that their philosophy might sound as jargon to the unlettered, who could not bring to it a sufficient intellectual appreciation. In like manner, the gospel which he preached might seem to them a jargon or a piece of "foolishness," merely because they were out of moral sympathy with it, and had not sufficient spiritual enlightenment to discern and value it. It was the same lesson which our Lord impressed on Nicodemus, "Except a man be born again, he cannot see the kingdom of God." He can see Churches, preachers, forms of service, but not the kingdom which is "righteousness, peace, and joy in the Holy Ghost," till he is born again.

II. THE REVELATION OF THE HEAVENLY WISDOM BY THE HOLY SPIRIT. 1. It was made known to holy apostles and prophets in the Spirit. By them it was communicated to the Churches. But all who heard them required the unction of the Spirit, that they might receive and know the truth. No one can say that this is unreasonable. Every kind of knowledge requires for its reception a healthy state of the human understanding; and, when it relates to morals, a healthy condition of the imagination, conscience, and affections, because of the effect which these have on the understanding. In like manner, spiritual things can be interpreted only to spiritual men. The all-searching Spirit of God must act on the spirits of men to whom the gospel is proclaimed, and so enlighten and empower them to receive "the deep things of God." Thus boasting is excluded at every point. Boasting of our righteousness is excluded by the work of the Son of God, all-sufficient for us; and boasting of our wisdom by the work of the Spirit of God, all-sufficient in us. By the Spirit all things are made new. Eye and ear and heart are new. The eye can see, the ear hear, the heart conceive, "the things which are freely given to us of God." What a dignity is this! What a joy! "We have received, not the spirit of the world, but the Spirit which is of God." We are taught of God, so as to enter with a new power of discernment into the secret of his covenant and the glory of his gospel.—F.

Ver. 2.—*The subject of the Pauline ministry.* The power of preachers is very various. Some depend on the rhetorical *form* in which they present their message. Their appeal is rather to feeling than to intellect, and they are stronger in the persuasive than in the instructive faculties. Very important spheres open to such men, though their work always needs careful and wise following up and supplementing. Others depend almost wholly upon the value of their *subject-matter,* and even fail to win the acceptance they might in consequence of their so entirely neglecting to culture rhetorical and persuasive forms of speech. In over-civilized people, such as were found at Corinth, there usually grows up a great passion for the merely rhetorical, as pleasing to the ear and to the artistic feeling. The Apostle Paul, in his zeal and intensity, despises all mere arts of rhetoric, and relies wholly on the grandeur of his theme, and the spiritual power with which its announcement is to be accompanied. His subject was—

I. A PERSON. "Jesus Christ." The first work of the apostles was to declare the Christian *facts,* which are the basis of the Christian system. Those facts concern the life, teaching, miracles, sufferings, death, and resurrection of the Lord Jesus Christ. Of all these things the apostles had precise and accurate knowledge, and concerning them they could render personal testimony. Of all these things they took care that adequate and satisfactory records should be preserved (2 Pet. i. 15, 16). But their interest did not lie in the mere facts, but in those facts as throwing light upon the *person,* the mission, and the Divine saving power of the Lord Jesus Christ. Salvation, they declared, comes by personal trust in Christ; and that he may be trusted he must be *known,* fully known. Therefore the apostle went everywhere preaching Christ, setting forth Christ, glorifying Christ, bidding men bow to him, confess to him, and receive forgiveness and eternal life from him. It is still true for us that the preaching of the Christian facts must set forth before men Christ, the person, and the unfolding of the Christian doctrines must glorify the "living Christ," who has all power to save.

II. THAT PERSON'S HISTORY. In view of the tendency to form myths and legends in those days, and to explain everything by theories of myth and legend in our days, it is important that we press the *historical* value of the records we have concerning Christ. It may be effectively urged that, apart from the question of the miracles, which demand a separate treatment, there is no feature of our Lord's life that is in any way unnatural, or likely to offend the historical faculty. No hero of the historic page can be received as real if a like acceptance be not given to the story of Christ; for the records we have of him will stand as well as any others the severest historical tests. In our day it is necessary to lay firmly again the old foundations of a real human life and human relations. We must begin with the "*Man* Christ Jesus." It may further be urged that, apart from higher considerations, the human history of the Lord Jesus Christ presents features of supreme and fascinating interest, as the records of a *child,* a *man,* a *teacher,* a *physician,* and a *sufferer.*

III. THAT PERSON'S WHOLE HISTORY. "And him crucified." The apostle might have been tempted to withhold portions of our Lord's story. His own intense Jewish feeling would make him revolt from having to preach salvation by One crucified. "We can scarcely realize now the stumbling-block which the preaching of a crucified Christ must have been to Jews and Greeks, the enormous temptation to keep the cross in the background, which the early teachers would naturally have felt, and the sublime and confident faith which must have nerved St. Paul to make it the central fact of all his teaching." He must have had a revelation of the glory of the mystery of the Crucifixion.

He must have seen how it "behoved Christ thus to suffer." He knew that this was the necessary completion of his earthly mission, the last earthly step, to be followed by a footfall in the "heavenly places" where he should receive authority and power to save. The "history" would be incomplete without the Crucifixion. The "mission" would have been altogether a failure without the Crucifixion. The Christian doctrine would be a moral scheme, and not a Divine salvation, without the Crucifixion.

IV. THAT IN WHICH CHRIST'S WHOLE HISTORY CULMINATED. St. Paul could not stay and rest in a human Christ, however attractive the records of his life and doings, or however quickening to human sympathy the story of his suffering death. He says, "Though we have known Christ after the flesh, yet now henceforth know we him [thus] no more." The earth-story culminated in this, viz. that he is exalted, a Prince and a Saviour. He is endowed with a present saving power. Crucified in weakness, he liveth by the power of God. From the cross he went to the throne, and St. Paul himself saw him at the right hand of God. St. Paul's subject was—The once-crucified Christ, who can save to the uttermost *now*.

Impress that men find shame in the Crucified until they can read the mystery of the cross; then they glory in the shame, glory even in the cross. There will always, for true Christian hearts, be darkness and sadness hanging all about the cross, and yet the darkness is dispelled with streams of holy, loving light, and the sadness of our sympathy passes, giving place to songs of joyous triumph.

> "We sing the praise of him who died,
> Of him who died upon the cross."

R. T.

Vers. 3—5.—*Personal weakness and spiritual strength.* In both the ordinary daily concerns and in the special religious service of life, a man may be *just himself alone,* confident in his own powers, self-centred, self-satisfied, reliant on his own health of body, vigour of mind, well-trained habits, quick judgment, and sound wisdom. Then, no matter how safe and strong he may seem to be, he is really weak; and, as life advances and testing-times take new and severer forms, his weakness will be proved and his pride effectively humbled. A man may even now be *moved and possessed by an evil spirit.* Still the solemn fact remains that man's soul lies open to malign spiritual influences, which work through the bodily lusts and passions. Then the man himself is weak indeed, and the alien force within him shows strength only unto things that are debasing and evil. A man may be *God's agent,* having the Spirit of God dwelling in him and working through him. Then, no matter what may be the bodily frailties or the untoward earthly surroundings, the man will be found really strong, efficient to all spiritual work, which the indwelling Spirit may move him to undertake. This last is St. Paul's experience. Men saw in him great human weakness. He felt within him great spiritual power, for he was the agent of the Holy Ghost.

I. THE IMPRESSION MADE BY ST. PAUL'S APPEARANCE. There can be little doubt that he was diminutive in stature, frail in health, unskilful as a rhetorician, and probably he was suffering from some disease or infirmity which made his appearance even unsightly. Of this his enemies were prepared to take undue advantage. The various descriptions of St. Paul's person should be considered, and the various theories concerning the special infirmity from which he suffered. Many of God's most devoted servants have, like Richard Baxter, Robert Hall, and many others, had to bear the heavy burden of constitutional disease, of intense physical suffering. But these things have been overruled, as in St. Paul's case, for good, so that they have become the very forces that have fitted the men for the nobler discharge of their great life-works.

II. THE CONSCIOUSNESS OF FRAILTY WITH WHICH ALL HIS WORK WAS DONE. There was not only the *fact* of suffering, but also the *feeling* of frailty. There was the sense of "fear," and there was much "trembling." He did not overmaster his trouble, but actually worked with it ever pressing upon him. "There was no self-confidence, nothing but self-mistrust, anxiety, the deepest sense of unworthiness" (comp. 2 Cor. x. 10; xi. 30; xii. 5, 7, 9, 10; Gal. iv. 13, 14). "There was a large element of that self-distrust which so noble and sensitive a nature would feel in the fulfilment of such an exalted mission as the preaching of the cross." We may to some extent realize at how great a cost Christian ministers master bodily infirmity in order to do us service for Christ's sake; but few can know how much intenser is the struggle with inward fear and hesitation, and with the overwhelming sense of unworthiness and unfitness. Only in the strength and grace of God are these diffidences and inward fears overcome.

III. The glorious results reached by St. Paul's work. These are implied in his appeal to the Corinthians that his work had been " in demonstration of the Spirit and of power." Those results were of two kinds—(1) conversions; (2) edifications. Men received Christ as St. Paul unfolded his claims and his love. The Church was built up in the faith through the Pauline instructions. Subsidiary results, such as overthrow of idolatry, and change of daily moral life and relations, may be further considered. The Corinthians were themselves among the most interesting results of his divinely inspired labours.

IV. The secret of his success in his openness to Divine lead. Men would have found it in his "accent of conviction," his intensity, his natural gift of leadership, the newness of his subject, the preparedness of the times, or the appeal to men's feelings; but none of these would have satisfied St. Paul. He would have said, when all had passed by, "You have not found out my secret." None of these explanations could satisfy any of us who carefully judged the phenomena. St. Paul was an endowed man. He was open to the Divine leadings. He was inspired by the Divine Spirit. God wrought with him, and these were the signs following. True spiritual work has still no other explanation. Men are mighty in the measure of their openness to the Divine lead. And the maintenance of this openness is the supreme anxiety of all earnest Christian workers. There must be, for all noble and lasting issues, the "demonstration of the Spirit."

Impress the mysterious power which some men have in conversation and in preaching; yet how often they are men or women of frail bodies, sensitive nerves, and wearying disease! They are under all kinds of disabilities; but these seem only to culture the higher spiritual power. Illustrate, e.g., McCheyne, Henry Martyn, F. Ridley Havergal, etc. This openness to the agency of the Holy Ghost is to be won. Our Lord taught us how. Such power comes through prayer and fasting: prayer, or closeness and intimacy of communion with God; fasting, or watchfulness, self-denial, and mastery of bodily passion. We may win the joy of being "co-workers together with God." —R. T.

Ver. 6.—*Who are the perfect?* The word is used in various senses in the New Testament. Our Lord applied it to God, saying, "Be ye therefore perfect, even as your Father in heaven is perfect." It is used to express what a Christian ought to be, and is pledged to be, and is striving to be, very much as the term "saints" is used in the Old Testament. Perfection, as presented by the apostles, is the idea, the aim, to be kept in the soul of the Christian, there to work as a perpetual inspiration to the seeking of perfection in the life. St. Paul presents the distinction between full-grown men and little children. The full-grown men are the perfect; they have reached the fulness, the standard of Christian manhood. St. John has a similar kind of expression; he addresses several classes—the fathers, the young men, the little children; viewing these as different stages on the way to the perfect, that "perfect" being kept as the thought and aim in the soul of each. In one passage we read, "That ye may be perfect and entire." The idea of "perfect" comes out more plainly when it is set beside another word. A man "entire" is one who has preserved or regained a lost completeness, or one in whom no grace is wanting that ought to be found in a Christian man; but a man really "perfect" is one who has attained his moral end, the standard according to which he was made; or one in whom no grace that ought to be found in a Christian is lacking, none are imperfect or weak, but all have reached a certain ripeness and maturity. St. Paul's idea of the "perfect," to whom he could speak freely the "wisdom," the higher spiritual mysteries of the gospel, may be considered under three figures—they are the *whole*, the *sound*, and the *full-grown*. It was not likely that the young Church at Corinth could furnish very many answering to this description; for most of them the simpler instruction in the commonplaces of gospel truth was still needful.

I. THE WHOLE; or the entire, the complete. Those having all the Christian faculties and graces, and all of them harmoniously cultured. The figure suggests the complete animal, with every limb well formed, and every organ efficiently working. Too often we find Christians who are incomplete; some sides of their natures are quite uncultivated, and some are over-cultivated; they are strong in some things, but weak in others. Just as we see in animals, there are Christian "monstrosities," one-sided growths, deficiencies of some important members. Wholeness, perfectness, requires the due culture of the large as well as the small graces and powers. And such "completeness," when reached, is a most important witness to Christ's grace, and appeal to men to seek their perfection through him.

II. THE SOUND; that is, the healthy. It is not enough that the different parts are present, and fitted together in good and practically efficient proportions; all the parts must be free from disease and full of vitality. Perfection demands *health* as well as completeness. Christians often fail of the standard by reason of sin-disease affecting various organs of their spiritual life, *e.g.* their prayer; their activity in Christian service; their watchfulness over personal habits, or their tendency to depression and doubt. St. John very tenderly writes to the well-beloved Gaius, "I wish above all things that thou mayest prosper and be in health, even as *thy soul prospereth.*"

III. THE FULL-GROWN; or the developed and matured, who have quite passed out of the infantile or childish stage. This is probably the precise form of the figure as it was presented to the mind of the apostle. He elsewhere speaks of adapting his teachings to the uncultured and unspiritual, making them like milk that is suited to the nourishment of babes. He means to press on the Corinthians that, while it is quite right that they should be babes, and as such be fed with the simplicities of Christian doctrine, it is not right that they should remain babes; they should reach Christian manhood, and want man's food of truth and mystery.

Impress how reasonable these views of the "perfect" are, and how contrasted with the vague and sentimental notions of an absolute freedom from sin, of which enthusiasts sometimes dream.—R. T.

Ver. 8.—*What would have prevented Christ's crucifixion?* Attention is directed to the second clause of the verse : "For had they known it, they would not have crucified the Lord of glory." From the point of view of merely worldly policy, the crucifixion of Christ was a profound mistake. Martyrdom never effects the objects sought by the persecutors. It tends rather to glorify, in the popular sentiment, the cause for which the martyrs died. "Not a single calculation of those who compassed the Saviour's death was destined to be fulfilled. Pilate did not escape the emperor's displeasure. Caiaphas (John xi. 50) did not save Jerusalem. The scribes and Pharisees did not put down the doctrine of Jesus." Christ's crucifixion may be regarded from several points of view. As we understand how it actually came about, we are prepared to consider what might conceivably have prevented it. 1. It occurred in the order of Divine providence. Every man's life is a plan of God. Each event is fitted, and its influence used or overruled. A man's incoming to life, and outgoing from life, are arranged by the Divine wisdom. The time, the place, and the mode of a man's death are Divine ordering. This is true of every man; it is recognized and made a secret of calm trustfulness for all the future by the Christian man; it is in sublime and glorious manner true of God's own Son, in the life on earth, which was a special Divine mission. 2. It occurred as a natural result of operating causes. In considering this point, we put on one side the Divine overrulings, make a fair estimate of the influence exerted by Christ's character, example, and teaching upon the various classes constituting the people among whom he lived and laboured. When national prejudices are duly weighed, and the character of the public sentiment concerning the expected Messiah, it no longer seems strange that our Lord excited an opposition which culminated in his death. 3. It occurred as a consequence of our Lord's own conduct. He did not, in any determined way, avoid those circumstances and situations which tended to bring about his death. He might, humanly speaking, have remained in Galilee, or hidden himself in Bethany, or fled from Gethsemane as the arresting party approached. Instead, we find him day by day following the Divine lead; in no way forcing his circumstances, though the issue of them was evident enough to himself.

His example in this has not been sufficiently considered, though it bears so directly on his characteristic submission, and on the virtue of his sacrifice as purely a voluntary act. Enemies of Christ endeavour to set this to his disadvantage, but a glorifying light shines upon it from the consideration that he knew the *cross* to be then and there the consummation of his earthly life as designed by the Father. Yet the apostle suggests that the cross might conceivably have been avoided. We can see three possible ways in which this might have been.

I. BY AN EXERCISE OF GOD'S SOVEREIGNTY. It might have pleased God to save mankind in another way. While we see the wonder and the grace of the way God did choose, we are not justified in affirming that it was the *only way* Divine wisdom could have devised. Or, in God's sovereignty, he might have read the perfect willingness and obedience of Jesus, and spared him the actual shame and pain of the cross. If such exercise of Divine sovereignty was not made, we may be sure that *concern for us* and for our full redemption made God send his "Lamb to the slaughter." That which was abstractly possible was impossible to him who "so loved the world" as to make even so extreme a sacrifice that it might be saved and won.

II. BY CHRIST'S WILFULNESS. He might have failed in obedience under this last and extreme test. He might have refused the cross, and put away from him his Father's cup. He was a free agent, and such wilfulness was possible. But the consequences would have been so serious as to be most painful for us to conceive. Man's salvation, though in part accomplished by our Lord's teaching and life, would at last have failed utterly. Christ could have won no saving power. He would have been no more than a Moses, a Zoroaster, a Socrates, or the Buddha; he could not have been the one only and all-sufficient Sin-bearer and Saviour.

III. BY THE RULERS' KNOWLEDGE OF WHO HE WAS AND WHAT HIS MISSION WAS. This is St. Paul's point here in the text. The rulers could only put Christ to death while deceiving themselves or deceived as to his character and claims. They could not have put Messiah to death. The whole hope of their race centred in him. But for that very reason their feelings were the more intense against a man of despised Nazareth, who claimed to be the Messiah, and, they thought, dishonoured the very idea of the Messiahship by his imposture. Had they known—had they seen his glory, they too would have bowed the knee to him, and crowned him with the many crowns. Had they known, they would have sought no false witnesses, nor started the cruel shout, "Crucify him! crucify him!" Often we go over in our thought *what might have been*, and wish things had been other than they were; and yet God so overrules for good that we may even rejoice in that they "crucified the Lord of glory."

From our meditations two things come impressively to view. 1. Our Lord's death was no accidental circumstance, but a Divine ordination; and this is true though the outworking of the events show what may be called the usual, or common, orderings of Providence. 2. Our Lord's death was entirely a voluntary act. His will was set on fully carrying out the Divine will, whatever of bearing, doing, or suffering that will might have in it. The virtue of the sacrifice lay partly in the sublime nature of the Victim; partly in the representative character he had taken; but partly also in the free surrender of his will and life to God, and the unforced voluntariness of his obedience, as tested by a painful and ignominious death. "By the which *will* we are sanctified."—R. T.

Ver. 9.—*The surprising freshness of the new dispensation.* The precise words, as quoted by the apostle, are not found in the Old Testament. They are probably Isa. lxiv. 4, given from memory and modified by the thought of phrases found in other parts of Isaiah. Only an unreasonable sentiment concerning verbal inspiration would make difficulty about the inexactness of quotations given from memory. The sense of a passage may be precisely indicated when the words are set in a different order and form. This text has often been used as the basis of elaborate descriptions of heaven, but such treatment is only possible when ver. 9 is separated from ver. 10. The apostle is plainly dealing with some glory which *has been* revealed and is now realized. He conceived of the Divine dealings with men as having been arranged in "ages," or "dispensations." We may thus distinguish the Adamic, Patriarchal, Mosaic, Davidic, Exilic, and post-Exilic. In the passage before us St. Paul shows, not merely that the Christian is *another* and a *succeeding* dispensation, but also that, in important respects, it differs from others, and is superior to others. Previous dispensations have given only faint suggestions of the surpassing glory of this one, just as Solomon's magnificent temple did but hint the exceeding glory of that later and spiritual temple, Christ's Church. We may dwell on some of those points in which the Christian revelation seems so new, so surprisingly fresh, so utterly beyond what human imagination could have conceived or human experience suggested.

I. RELIGION IS NOT A CEREMONIAL, BUT A LIFE. To a Jew this was so fresh a conception as to be even bewildering. A less thoughtful Jew would be in peril of cherishing the sentiment that religion was *only* a ceremonial, a round of ordinances, festivals, and sacrifices. And this view of religion had become the general and prevailing notion in the time of our Lord. A more thoughtful and pious Jew would connect personal godliness with outward ceremonial, and strive to culture an inner life of trust, obedience, and communion with the outward observance of rites and ceremonies. But the new thing revealed in Christianity is, that religion is, essentially and only, the soul's life, and that all ceremonial is mere expression and agency in the work of culture. The relations are manifestly reversed. Formerly there must be ceremonial, and there ought to be life; now there must be life, and there may be ceremonial. On fully maintaining these later relations, the health and vigour of Christianity must ever depend.

II. SALVATION BY A SUFFERING AND DYING SAVIOUR. This is indeed a fresh and surprising thing. Triumph is to lie in defeat. Glory is to blossom out of shame. A sublime mission is to be accomplished by a seeming failure. Life for men is to come forth out of death for Christ. It is the introduction of a new force, a moral force. Christ lifted up is to draw men. The story of the crucified One is to melt men into penitence, win their faith, and ensure such a love as shall make even self-sacrifice for Christ possible. Men knew before of love that would *work* for those it loved, and love that would *fight* for those it loved, and love that would *bear* for those it loved; but it was never that love should *die* such a death, not for the loved only, but for the ungodly and enemies by wicked works. "While we were yet sinners, Christ died for us."

III. SANCTIFICATION BY THE PRESENT POWER OF HIM WHO DIED. This is altogether new. Christ, as the exalted One, by his Spirit, is now carrying out his redeeming purpose in all hearts and lives that are open to him by faith. We do not struggle for righteousness by unaided personal efforts. Unseen, indeed, still the Living Christ is ever with us. Untraced, indeed, the mighty Spirit of Christ is ever working within us, sanctifying us wholly. And so, in face of all difficulties, perplexities, frailties, or hindrances to spiritual progress, we may calmly say, "If God be for us, who can be against us?" "Greater is he who is with us than all who can be against us."

IV. MAN THE DWELLING-PLACE OF GOD THROUGH THE SPIRIT. This is also new; for hitherto the common sentiment had been that God dwelt in places, on the mountain's crown, at the altar, in shining pillar-clouds, in tabernacle or in temple. Our Lord Jesus Christ, as the God-man, shows us that God can dwell in man and make man's body his temple. He can even dwell in us; and an apostle may plead with his people, saying, "Know ye not that your body is the temple of the Holy Ghost, which is in you?" Surely such an honour for us is beyond all that "eye has seen, ear heard, or heart conceived."

Illustrate that aged Simeon loved God and knew something of him, but he never could have dreamed what God had in store for him—even to hold the world's Babe-Saviour in his own trembling arms. What could Abraham, who saw Christ's day; or Moses, who spoke of the great prophet to come; or David, who sang of his Lord making his foes his footstool,—have really known of the Christian glories, the spiritual mysteries of the revelation in Christ? These spiritual things broke more and more clearly on the minds of Peter and John and Paul, until, in utter ravishment and wonder, they exclaimed, "Oh the depth of the riches both of the wisdom and knowledge of God! How unsearchable are his judgments, and his ways past finding out!"—R. T.

Vers. 12—14.—*Speech in the power of the Spirit.* The personal references in St. Paul's Epistles are suitable to the epistolary style of correspondence, and necessary as the vindication of a man who was seriously attacked and slandered. Generally his allusions are more or less directed to his claim as an apostle. Because this did not take precisely the same grounds as the claims of the earlier apostles, it was easy for his enemies to question and even deny his rights. St. Paul's chief argument is that the "signs of an apostle were wrought by him," and here, in our text, he urges that his teaching was manifestly inspired and sealed by the Holy Spirit, and that his apostolic claim was fully recognized by all "spiritual men." Wickliffe skilfully renders the last clause of ver. 13, " Maken a liknesse of spyritual things to goostli men."

I. The Divine preparation for apostolic teaching. 1. The apostle must have received the Spirit of God. Personal experience of regeneration, and personal openness to the Divine incoming, are absolute essentials to all Christian service as teachers, in older days and now, in the lesser spheres as well as the greater. Judas can teach nobody; only as "converted" can St. Peter "strengthen the brethren" or "feed the lambs." 2. He must know the things of God through the Spirit's teaching. Here the adequacy of the Spirit to be the renewed man's Teacher may be shown. (1) He knows God. (2) He knows man. (3) He has access to man's mind and heart, and an adaptation to each individual can be assured. The operations of the Divine Spirit as the renewed man's Teacher also require consideration. Generally it may be said that he unfolds the redemption-mystery in its practical details and applications. Our Lord's division of his work is that he teaches (1) of sin; (2) of righteousness; (3) of judgment. The true preparation for teaching is an inner spiritual life, a Divine indwelling and endowment, and these finding expression through the natural powers and relations. There is a full sense in which the true Christian teacher has still an inspired and sanctified speech, and therefore all the authority which the Divine Spirit can give.

II. The ministry of apostleship in human language. "Which things we speak." Speech is almost our best force for the communication of truth and for the impression of duty. It works by persuasion, not force. It has no physical, but wholly moral power. Yet history declares, in repeated instances, how human words can sway emotion and arouse to action; e.g. the Crusades. But man's words may be mere words, incapable of producing more than limited effects upon passion, sentiment, etc. They may have a Divine life in them, and so be mighty to break stubborn hearts, bow the wicked to penitence, draw men to God, and change the whole character of the life. Words which the Holy Ghost teacheth are mighty to pull down strongholds. By the "foolishness of preaching" men are saved and blessed. But the sphere of apostolic speech is clearly defined. Such a teacher speaks *spiritual things*; and it is indicated that he will speak in vain, save as men are *receptive,* spiritually toned, having the spiritual sensibility quickened. The merely *natural* man cannot receive God-inspired teachings. So there is at once a preparation of the teacher, and a preparation of those to whom his words are addressed. The practical duty of culturing Christian life and feeling, in order to gain the best blessing from our pastors and teachers, may be made the subject of an earnest and effective conclusion.—R. T.

Vers. 14, 15.—*The natural and the spiritual man.* This is not a common division of men, or one that can be recognized from a worldly point of view. The world knows learned men and ignorant men, rich men and poor men, but not natural men and spiritual men. This distinction is wholly made from the Christian standpoint, but it becomes the all-important one, in the presence of which all merely worldly classifications of men become insignificant. Modern theories of man's nature may be reviewed. Some regard man as composed of body and soul; others distinguish the rational soul from the spiritual and immortal nature, and divide into body, mind, and soul. This mode of regarding man may give clearness to the distinction in our text between the natural and the spiritual man; but the apostle would seem rather to have in mind the principles and spirit ruling the several men, and making the difference between them, and it does not seem likely that he held any particular theory of man's nature. It is sufficient that the two kinds of men—the natural and the spiritual—have been recognized in every Christian age, and are plain to our view now.

I. Compare the spheres of the two. Most of the spheres are common to both. (1) The physical sphere; (2) the relational sphere; (3) the social sphere; (4) the intellectual sphere. But to the natural man the intellectual is the highest department. He may have genius for literature, poetry, painting, sculpture; but he can never transcend the sphere of mind. "The natural man is he whose perceptions do not extend beyond the region of the intellect, the part of his being which he has in common with the animal creation." "The natural man is he in whom pure intellectual reason and the merely natural affections predominate." But though the natural man's sphere is thus limited, there is glorious fulness within the limits; the perfection of art is yet unattained; the possibilities of knowledge are far from exhausted, though the noble minds of the long ages have been occupied in study and research. We need not undervalue the natural man's sphere, so far as it goes. But the spiritual man enters a region altogether unknown to, and hopelessly closed to, the natural man. It is the sphere of the unseen, the eternal, the spiritual; in a word, of God and the things of God. Regeneration in the power of the Holy Ghost involves and includes an awakening of new sensibilities to Divine and eternal things. It is as if a man were endowed with some new senses, and found revealed to him what his fellow-men might not know. In this higher and further sphere man can alone find satisfaction for his full powers. It is an encircling sphere that hallows all the lesser ones in which he shares with his fellows.

II. COMPARE THE CONDUCT OF THE TWO. As a rule, the conduct of the natural man will be ruled and toned by considerations of self-pleasing. This may be tempered by goodness of the natural disposition, or by culture and self-mastery; but the tendency always lies towards bodily indulgence and power of sensual passion. The sky over such a man is low, and he fails to get the elevating of the high, vast, pure heavens. Another sentiment tones the conduct of the spiritual man. For him life is God's, the world is God's, he is God's; and there is no question with him as to what *he would like*; all his desire is to know what God would wish. His whole conduct must be in harmony with and must tend to work out God's purposes. For him there is no danger of deterioration. His sphere is exhilarating, his thought is inspiring, his progress is assured.

III. COMPARE THE FUTURE OF THE TWO. The natural man can have no future that is more than sentiment. His sphere is temporary. He must make what he can of the life that now is. His career has its limits *here* and its good things *now*. To the spiritual man life here is but a stage of the true life, a preparation-time for a nobler life, upon which he is soon to enter. That future ceases to be strange to him, as he fully realizes life in the Divine spheres now.

Impress the disabilities of the "natural man," and show how, by God's gracious provision, the "natural" may become "spiritual."—R. T.

EXPOSITION.

CHAPTER III.

Vers. 1—4.—*The carnal conceit of the spiritually immature.*

Ver. 1.—I . . . could not speak unto you as unto spiritual. Though softened by the word **brethren**, there was a crushing irony of reproof in these words: "You thought yourselves quite above the need of my simple teaching. You were looking down on me from the whole height of your inferiority. The elementary character of my doctrine was after all the necessary consequence of your own incapacity for anything more profound." **As unto carnal.** The true reading here is *sarkinois*, fleshen, not *sarkikois*, fleshly, or carnal; the later and severer word is perhaps first used in ver. 3. The word *sarkinos* (*carneus*), fleshen, implies earthliness and weakness and the absence of spirituality; but *sarkikos* (*carnalis*) involves the dominance of the lower nature and antagonism to the

spiritual. **As unto babes in Christ.** The word "babes" has a good and a bad sense. In its good sense it implies humility and teachableness, as in ch. xiv. 20, "In malice be ye babes;" and in 1 Pet. ii. 2, "As newborn babes, desire the sincere milk of the Word;" and in Matt. xi. 25. Here it is used in its bad sense of spiritual childishness.

Ver. 2.—I fed you with milk. The metaphor is expanded in Heb. v. 13, "Every one that partaketh of milk is without experience of the Word of righteousness; for he is a babe." The same metaphor is found in Philo; and the young pupils of the rabbis were called "sucklings" (תינוקות) and "little ones" (comp. Matt. x. 42). **Not with meat;** not with solid food, which is for full-grown or spiritually perfect men (Heb. v. 14). **For hitherto;** rather, *for ye were not yet*—when I preached to you—*able to bear it*. The same phrase is used by our Lord in John xvi. 12, "I have many things to say unto you, but ye cannot bear them now;" and he taught them in parables, "as they were able to bear it" (Mark iv. 33). **Not even now are ye able.** Though you imagine that you have advanced so far beyond my simpler teaching.

Ver. 3.—**For ye are yet carnal.** This is the reason for the spiritual dulness which your pride prevents you from recognizing. **Envying, and strife, and divisions.** The two latter words are omitted in some of the best manuscripts, and may have been added from Gal. v. 20. Partisanship and discord, the sins of the Corinthians—sins which have disgraced so many ages of Church history—are works of the flesh (Gal. v. 19), and involve many other sins (Jas. iii. 16), and are therefore sure proofs of the carnal mind, though they are usually accompanied by a boast of superior spiritual enlightenment. **As men;** that is, "as men, not as Christians." To walk as a mere ordinary human being is not to "walk in the Spirit" (Gal. v. 25); comp., "I speak as a man" (Rom. iii. 5).

Ver. 4.—**For when one saith, I am of Paul.** This is a proof that there were jealousies and partisanships among them. We again notice the generous courage of St. Paul in rebuking first those adherents who turned his own name into a party watchword. **Are ye not carnal?** The true reading is, "Are ye not men?" (א, A, B, C, and so the Revised Version); *i.e.* Are ye not swayed by mere human passions? The Spirit which you received at baptism ought to have lifted you above these mean rivalries. You ought to be something more than mere men. Religious partisanship is, in the eye of St. Paul, simply irreligious. He sets down party controversies as a distinct proof of carnality. Those who indulge in it are men devoid of the spiritual element.

Vers. 5—15.—*The one foundation and the diverse superstructure.*

Ver. 5.—**Who then is Paul?** The better reading is *what?* (א, A, B). The neuter would imply a still greater depreciation of the importance of human ministers. **Ministers.** The same word as that rendered "deacons" (*diakonoi*); "ministers of Christ on your behalf" (Col. i. 7). **Through whom ye believed.** "*Through.* whom," not "*in* whom" (Bengel). They were merely the instruments of your conversion. In the second Epistle (2 Cor. iii. 3) he calls them "the epistle of Christ ministered by us written . . . with the Spirit of the living God." **As the Lord gave to him.** The gifts differ according to the grace given (Rom. xii. 6).

Ver. 6.—**I planted.** St. Paul everywhere recognized that his gift lay pre-eminently in the ability to *found* Churches (comp. Acts xviii. 1—11; ch. iv. 15; ix. 1; xv. 1). **Apollos watered.** If, as is now generally

believed, Apollos wrote the Epistle to the Hebrews, we see how striking was his power of strengthening the faith of wavering Churches. Eloquence and a deep insight into the meaning of Scripture, enriched by Alexandrian culture, seem to have been his special endowments (Acts xviii. 24, 27). The reference of the word "watered" to baptism by Augustine (Ep. 48) is one of the numberless instances of Scripture distorted by ecclesiasticism. **God gave the increase** (comp. ch. xv. 10; 2 Cor. iii. 5). The thought of every true teacher always is, "Not unto us, O Lord, not unto us, but unto thy Name give the praise" (Ps. cxv. 1).

Ver. 7.—**Anything.** The planter and the waterer are nothing by comparison. They could do nothing without Christ's aid (John xv. 16), and were nothing in themselves (2 Cor. xii. 11). **But God that giveth the increase.** The human instruments are nothing, but God is everything, because, apart from him, no result would follow.

Ver. 8.—**Are one;** literally, *one thing.* God is the sole Agent; the teachers, so far from being able to pose as rival leaders, form but one instrument in God's hand. Their *relative* differences shrink into insignificance when the source and objects of their ministry are considered. **His own reward . . . his own labour.** In the lower individual sphere the work of teachers shall be fairly estimated and rewarded as in the parable of the pounds and talents (comp. John iv. 36; Rev. xxii. 12).

Ver. 9.—**God's fellow-workers.** Throughout the Bible we are taught that God requires the work of man, and that he will not help those who will do nothing for themselves or for him. The world was to be evangelized, not by sudden miracle, but by faithful human labour (Mark xvi. 20). **God's husbandry;** rather, *God's field,* or *tilled land.* The thought which he desires again and again to enforce is that they belong *to God,* not to the parties of human teachers. The word "husbandry" may also mean vineyard, and the metaphor is the same as in Isa. v. 1; xxvii. 2; John xv. 1; Matt. xiii. 3—30; Luke xiii. 6—9; Rom. xi. 16—24. **God's building.** This is one of St. Paul's favourite metaphors, as in vers. 16, 17; 2 Cor. vi. 16; Eph. ii. 20 —22; Rom. xv. 20; 2 Tim. ii. 19 (comp. 1 Pet. ii. 5; Rev. xxi. 14).

Ver. 10.—**According to the grace of God which is given unto me;** rather, *which was given.* Here, again, we have St. Paul's *baptismal aorist*—his habit of regarding his whole spiritual life as potentially summed up in the one crisis of conversion and baptism. This phrase is a favourite one with him (ch. xv. 10; Rom. xv. 15; Gal. ii. 9; Eph. iii. 2). **As a wise master-builder.** "Wise" only in the sense of subordinating every pretence of human wisdom to the will of God ; and here the adjective only applies to the wisdom required by a builder. In other words, "wise" is here equivalent to "skilful." Since Paul had received the grace of God for this very purpose, he was made "wise" by the knowledge of Christ (for the metaphor of building, see Matt. vii. 24 ; xvi. 18 ; Eph. ii. 21 ; 1 Pet. ii. 5). **The foundation** ; rather, *a foundation.* Though in truth there is but one foundation, as he proceeds to say, St. Paul always refused to build on the foundation laid by another (Rom. xv. 20). **Another.** Perhaps the special allusion is to Apollos.

Ver. 11.—**Other foundation can no man lay.** Any "other" gospel is not merely "another," but "a *different*" gospel (Gal. i. 9). **That which is laid** ; rather, *that is lying* (comp. 1 Pet. ii. 6). It has not been placed there (τεθέντα) by any human hands, but *lies* there by the eternal will. **Which is Jesus Christ.** "The *doctrine* of Jesus Christ is the foundation of all theology ; his *person* of all life." This is again and again inculcated in Scripture : Isa. xxviii. 16, "Behold, I lay in Zion for a foundation, a stone, a tried stone, a precious corner-stone, a sure foundation." On this rock the Church is built (Matt. xvi. 18 ; Acts iv. 11, 12 ; Eph. ii. 20).

Ver. 12.—**Gold, silver.** Perhaps St. Paul thought for a moment of the gorgeous metals and rich marbles used in the Corinthian temples, as well as in the temple at Jerusalem. But it is surely fantastic to suggest that his reference is an historical reminiscence of the melting of gold and silver in the burning of Corinth by Mummius, nearly two hundred years before. **Costly stones** ; *i.e.* costly marble from Paros, Phrygia, etc. **Wood, hay, stubble.** These words seem to symbolize erroneous or imperfect doctrines, which would not stand the test, and which led to evil practices. Such were the " philosophy and vain deceit," " the weak and beggarly elements," " the rudiments of the world," of which he speaks in Gal. iv. 9 ; Col. ii. 8. So in the Midrash Tehillin, the words of false teachers are compared to hay. The doctrines to which he alludes are not antichristian, but imperfect and human—such, for instance, as, " Humanas constitutiunculas de cultu, de victu, de frigidis ceremoniis " (Erasmus).

Ver. 13.—**Each man's work shall be made manifest.** The real nature—the worth or worthlessness—of each man's work, will be made clear sooner or later. **The day shall declare it.** "The day" can only mean " the day of our Lord Jesus Christ" (ch. i. 8), which would specially "make manifest the counsels of the hearts" (ch. iv. 5), and "judge the secrets of men" (Rom. ii. 16), and make all men manifest " before the judgment-seat of Christ" (2 Cor. iv. 10). **It shall be**

revealed by fire ; rather, *because it is being revealed in fire.* The phrase "is being" is called bad English, but some such phrase is positively needed to render the continuous present tense, which here expresses certainty, natural sequence, perpetual imminence. This tense is constantly used to express the continuity and the present working of Divine laws (comp. Matt. iii. 10). As the nominative is not expressed, it is uncertain whether "it" refers to "each man's work" or to "the day." Either gives an apposite sense (Mal. iv. 1 ; 2 Thess. i. 8). Some would make " he " (namely, Christ) the nominative, because " the day " means " the day of Christ ; " and in favour of this view they quote 2 Thess. i. 7, "The revelation of the Lord Jesus from heaven in flaming fire." But the ellipse of an unexpressed nominative is harsh. **The fire itself shall prove each man's work.** This is the " probatory " or testing fire of the day of the Lord, of which we read very frequently in the Fathers. The doctrine of purgatory has been in some measure founded on this verse (Council of Florence, A.D. 1439) ; but such a view of it cannot be maintained. The reader will find the subject examined and the quotations from the Fathers given in the writer's ' Mercy and Judgment,' p. 69. All that is said here is that the fire of Christ's presence—the consuming fire of God's love— shall *test* the work, not *purge* it. The fire is *probatory*, not *purgatorial*, and it is not in itself a fire of wrath, for it tests the gold and silver as well as the inferior elements of the structure. It is the fire of the refiner, not of the avenger.

Ver. 14.—**If any man's work shall abide.** St. Paul is speaking primarily of teachers, though, of course, his words apply by analogy to all believers. **He shall receive a reward.** One of the teacher's rewards will be his converts (1 Thess. ii. 19), who will be " his joy and crown of glorying " (Phil. ii. 16) ; another will be " a crown of glory that fadeth not away" (1 Pet. v. 2, 4 ; Dan. xii. 3) ; yet another will be fresh opportunities for higher labour (Matt. xxv. 23).

Ver. 15.—**He shall suffer loss.** He shall not receive the full reward to which he might otherwise look (2 John 8). **He himself shall be saved.** It is an inexpressible source of comfort to us, amid the weakness and ignorance of our lives, to know that if we have only erred through human frailty and feebleness, while yet we desired to be sincere and faithful, the work will be burnt, yet the workman will be saved. Some of the Fathers gave to this beautiful verse the shockingly perverted meaning that "the workman would be *preserved alive* for endless torments," "salted with fire" in order to endure interminable agonies. The meaning is impossible, for it reverses the sense of the word "saved;" and makes it equivalent to "damned;" but the interpretation is an awful proof of the distortions to which a merciless human rigorism and a hard, self-styled orthodoxy have sometimes subjected the Word of God. **Yet so as by fire**; rather, *through* or *by means of fire* (διὰ πυρός). We may be, as it were, "snatched as a brand from the burning" (Zech. iii. 2; Amos iv. 11; Jude 23), and "scarcely" saved (1 Pet. iv. 18). Similarly it is said in 1 Pet. iii. 20 that Noah was saved "through water" (δι' ὕδατος). The ship is lost, the sailor saved; the workman is saved, the work is burned.

Vers. 16—23.—*The peril and folly of glorying in men.*

Ver. 16.—**Know ye not**. The phrase is used by St. Paul in this Epistle to emphasize important truths, as in ch. v. 6; vi. 2, 9, 15; ix. 13, 24. Out of this Epistle it only occurs in Rom. vi. 16; xi. 2. **That ye are the temple of God.** "Ye," both collectively (Eph. ii. 21) and individually; "God's shrine;" not built for men's glory. The word "temple" in the Old Testament always means the material temple; in the Gospels our Lord "spake of the temple of his body;" in the rest of the New Testament the body of every baptized Christian is the temple of God (ch. vi. 16), because "God dwelleth in him" (1 John iv. 16; comp. John xiv. 23). In another aspect Christians can be regarded as "living stones in one spiritual house" (1 Pet. ii. 5). *The temple;* rather, *the shrine* (*naos*) wherein God dwells (*naiei*), and which is the holiest part of the temple (*hieron*).

Ver. 17.—**If any man defile the temple of God.** The verb is the same as in the next clause, and should be rendered, *If any man destroy the temple of God;* but the word is perhaps too strong, and the word "mar" or "injure" might better convey the meaning (Olshausen). The two verbs are brought into vivid juxtaposition in the original: "God shall ruin the ruiner of his temple." St. Paul was, perhaps, thinking of the penalty of death attached to any one who desecrated the temple of Jerusalem. Inscriptions on the *chêl*, or "middle wall of partition," threatened death to any Gentile who set foot within the sacred enclosure." **Which** temple **ye are**; literally, *the which are ye;* i.e. ye are holy. St. Paul is here referring to the Church of Corinth, and to the false teachers who desecrated it by bringing in "factions of destruction" (2 Pet. ii. 1). Ideally the Church was glorious, "not having spot, or wrinkle, or any such thing" (Eph. v. 27).

Ver. 18.—**Let no man deceive himself.** Like the other formula, "Be not deceived" (ch. vi. 9; xv. 33; Gal. vi. 7); "Deceive not yourselves" (Jer. xxxvii. 9); "Let no

man deceive you" (Matt. xxiv. 4; Luke xxi. 8; 2 Thess. ii. 3; Eph. v. 6; 1 John iii. 7). We are so liable to self-deception (1 John i. 8; Gal. vi. 3), as well as to being deceived by others (2 Tim. iii. 13), that there was need to repeat this warning incessantly. **Seemeth to be wise**; rather, *thinketh that he is wise*. He is referring specially to the Apollos party, who vaunted their esoteric knowledge, and so were "wise in their own eyes, prudent in their own conceits" (Isa. v. 21).

Ver. 19.—**The wisdom of this world.** Here the word for "world" is *kosmos*, in the last verse it was *aion*. *Kosmos* is the world regarded objectively; *aion* the world regarded in its moral and intellectual aspect. **He that taketh the wise in their craftiness.** This is one of the few references to the Book of Job in the New Testament. It comes from the speech of Eliphaz in Job v. 13, but St. Paul substitutes the words "clutching" (*drassomenos*) and "craftiness" (*panourgia*) for the milder *katalabōn* and *phronēsei* of the LXX.

Ver. 20.—**The Lord knoweth**, etc. A quotation from Ps. xciv. 11. St. Paul substitutes "the wise" for the "men" of the original, because the psalmist is referring to perverse despisers of God. *Dialogismoi* is rather "reasonings" than "thoughts." It is used in a disparaging sense, as in Rom. i. 21; Eph. iv. 17.

Ver. 21.—**Wherefore.** St. Paul, with this word, concludes the argument of warning of the previous section, as in ch. iii. 7; iv. 5; viii. 38; xi. 33; xiv. 39; xv. 58 (Wordsworth). **All things are yours.** It is always a tendency of Christians to underrate the grandeur of their privileges by exaggerating their supposed monopoly of *some* of them, while *many* equally rich advantages are at their disposal. Instead of becoming partisans of special teachers, and champions of separate doctrines, they might enjoy all that was good in the doctrines of all teachers, whether they were prophets, or pastors, or evangelists (Eph. iv. 11, 12). The true God gives us *all things* richly to enjoy (1 Tim. vi. 17).

Ver. 22.—**Whether Paul, or Apollos, or Cephas.** All were their servants for Jesus' sake (2 Cor. iv. 5). Instead of becoming partisans of either, they could enjoy the greatness of all. **Or the world.** The sudden leap from Cephas to the world shows, as Bengel says, the impetuous leap of thought. There is a passage of similar eloquence in Rom. viii. 38, 39. The "hundredfold" is promised even in this world (Mark x. 29, 30). **Or life.** Because life in Christ is the only real life, and Christ came that we might have life, and have it more abundantly (see Rom. viii. 38). **Or death.** To the Christian, "to live is Christ, and to die is gain" (Phil. i. 21). So that death is no more than

"The lifting of a latch;
Nought but a step into the open air
Out of a tent already luminous
With light which shines through its trans-
   parent folds."

Or things present, or things to come. "He that overcometh shall inherit all things" (Rev. xxi. 7), because Christ has received all things from the Father.

Ver. 23.—**And ye are Christ's** (see ch. vi. 19; xv. 23; Rom. xiv. 8; Gal. iii. 29). Christians possess because they are possessed by Christ (Meyer). Christ is our Master, and God our Father (Matt. xxiii. 10). **And Christ is God's;** because "Christ is equal to the Father as touching his Godhead, but inferior to the Father as touching his manhood." Hence in ch. xi. 3 he says, "The head of Christ is God;" and in ch. xv. 28, we read of Christ resigning his mediatorial kingdom, that God may be all in all. Perhaps St. Paul implies the thought that Christ belongs, not to a party, but to God, the Father of us all. But the ultimate climax from Christ to God is found also in ch. iv. 1; Rom. xv. 5, etc.

HOMILETICS.

Vers. 1—8.—*Reflections for Churches.* " And I, brethren, could not speak unto you as unto spiritual," etc. In these verses are three subjects worthy of the profoundest contemplation.

I. THE GRADUATING METHOD OF TEACHING. "And I, brethren, could not speak unto you as unto spiritual, but as unto carnal, even as unto babes in Christ. I have fed you with milk," etc. Truth is to be administered with a practical regard to the receptive powers of the student, just as the administration of bodily food must have regard to the digestive capacities of those who need it; "milk" for children, "meat" for men. This is Paul's metaphor; though men might live on milk, strong meat would kill children. There are truths in the gospel of such an elevated character, requiring so much intellect and culture to appreciate them, that to enforce them on the attention of mental and moral children would be positively to injure them. Christ practised this method of teaching. He had many things to say which his disciples could not bear. Had he preached to them the doctrines of the cross at first, they would have been shocked. When at one time they were merely intimated, they produced a kind of revulsion in Peter, and he exclaimed, "That be far from thee, Lord." This method of teaching shows: 1. That a minister that may be useful to one class of men may be unprofitable to another. 2. The necessity of all who would enjoy the higher teaching to cultivate their mental and moral powers.

II. THE CARNALITY OF CHURCHISMS. " For whereas there is among you envying, and strife, and divisions, are ye not carnal, and walk as men?" etc. By Churchisms I mean sectarianisms, denominationalisms, etc. What are Churches? The best Churches in Christendom to-day are but the organization of certain opinions concerning Christ and his gospel. Some men extol one class of opinion more than another, and they set up one Church in opposition to another, and so on. Paul says this is "carnal." Carnal, because it engrosses the soul: 1. In the *human* rather than the *Divine*. 2. In the *personal* rather than in the *universal*. 3. In the *selfish* rather than in the *self-denying*. 4. In the *transitory* rather than in the *permanent*.

III. THE UNITY OF ALL TRUE MINISTERS. "Who then is Paul? and who is Apollos? but ministers by whom ye believed," etc. Again, "He that planteth and he that watereth are one." 1. *One, notwithstanding the diversity of talents and kinds of labour.* Paul, Peter, and Apollos differed in many personal respects; they differed in the kind and measure of their faculties, in their temperaments and attainments; still they were one in spirit and aim. 2. *One in grand practical aim.* What were they working for? The spiritual cultivation of mankind. One planting, another watering, etc. Different kinds of labour, but still one. 3. *One in their connection with God.* (1) Whilst all depended on God for success, God gave the "increase." (2) All were co-workers with him; "labourers together with God." 4. *One in their ultimate reward.* "Every man shall receive his own reward according to his own labour." Each from the same God, each according to his work.

Ver. 9.—*God a Husbandman.* "We are labourers together with God: ye are God's husbandry," etc. The words lead us to look at God as the great Husbandman of human souls. As a husbandman—

I. HE IS THOROUGHLY ACQUAINTED WITH THE SOIL. 1. He knows its *original state*. The soil in its pristine state, with all its original powers, he knows. 2. He knows its *present condition*. Its present barren and wilderness state he understands. To him it seems like the "field of the slothful" mentioned by Solomon. It is stony, weedy, and thorny. 3. He knows its *tillable* capabilities. He knows what can be made of it, notwithstanding its present condition. He knows what every soul is capable of producing. He knows that some are far more capable than others. Some can become the majestic cedar, whilst others only the shrub.

II. HE HAS ALL NECESSARY INSTRUMENTALITIES. This stony, weedy ground requires certain well-contrived implements to work it into a fruitful condition. 1. He has them in the *events of life*. All the dark and painful circumstances in life are his implements to break up the fallow ground. All the pleasant and propitious are instruments for mellowing the soil. 2. He has them in the *revelations of truth*. There is Law and love, Sinai and Calvary. All are soul-culturing implements.

III. HE POSSESSES THE PROPER SEED. The seed he has to sow is good seed, and seed adapted to the soil. What is it? His Word. His Word is seed in many respects. 1. In *vitality*. Every seed has life in it. His Word is Spirit and life. 2. In *completeness*. The seed is complete in itself. 3. In *prolificness*. One seed in course of time may cover a continent. The Word of God is wonderfully fruitful.

IV. HE COMMANDS THE CULTURING ELEMENTS. The best agriculturists, who understand the soil, possess the best implements and the best seed, are thwarted in their efforts, because the elements are not propitious. God has command over the elements. He is the great Husbandman of souls, and we his husbandry.

Vers. 10—15.—*The true foundation of character.* "According to the grace of God," etc. The words suggest certain important thoughts concerning character.

I. That there is an ANALOGY BETWEEN THE FORMATION OF CHARACTER AND THE ERECTION OF A BUILDING. "If any man build," etc. It is like a building in three respects. 1. *In the variety of its materials.* Buildings are generally formed of a variety of materials—stone, wood, iron, etc. Moral character is built up by a variety of things—the impressions that are made on us, the emotions that rise in us, etc. 2. In the *unity of its design*. Every building is formed on some plan. One design shapes the whole. So with character. The master-purpose of the soul, whatever it may be, gives unity to the whole. 3. In the *function it fulfils*. Buildings are generally residences of some kind or other. The soul lives in the character. It is its home. In some cases the home is the mere sty of the animal; in some, the shop of the barterer; in some, the prison of the guilty; in some, the temple of the saint.

II. THAT CHRIST IS THE ONLY FOUNDATION OF A TRUE CHARACTER. "For other foundation can no man lay than that is laid, which is Jesus Christ." There are sometimes splendid edifices and poor foundations, and the reverse. All characters are based upon some one idea. 1. Some are based on the *sensual* idea; such as that on which the prodigal son started, etc. 2. Some are based on the *secular* idea. On this Judas, the young lawyer, and Demas built. 3. Some are based on the *ambitious* idea. Absalom, Haman, Herod, are examples. 4. Some are based on the *Christian* idea. What is that? Supreme sympathy with God; and this requires Christ. Christ is its Foundation, for he does two things to generate this supreme sympathy in the soul. (1) Demonstrates to man the propitiableness of God. (2) Reveals to man the moral loveliness of God.

III. THAT TO CHRIST, AS A FOUNDATION, MEN BRING WORTHLESS AS WELL AS VALUABLE MATERIALS. Some build edifices of "gold, silver, precious stones," and some of "wood, hay, stubble." 1. There are edifices *partially formed* of "wood, hay, stubble." (1) The mere *creedal* character is worthless. (2) The mere *sentimental* character is worthless. (3) The mere *ritualistic* character is worthless. All these characters are formed of "wood, hay, stubble"—things of no solidity, no value, no duration. 2. There are edifices *entirely formed of valuable* materials brought to Christ. They are formed of "gold, silver, precious stones." The profoundest thoughts, the strongest sympathies, the gold and silver of the soul, are connected with Christ.

IV. THAT THERE IS AN ERA TO DAWN WHEN ALL THE EDIFICES BUILT ON THIS FOUNDATION SHALL BE TRIED. "Every man's work shall be made manifest." Heaven has appointed a day for testing character. Individually, it is the day that dawns at the end of our mortal life; universally, it is the day that dawns at the end of this world's history. 1. This day will be *injurious* to those who have built on this foundation with *worthless* materials. (1) They will suffer loss—the loss of labour, opportunity, position. (2) Though they suffer loss, they may be saved—"saved, yet so as by fire." Though his favourite theories and cherished hopes shall burn like "wood and hay," yet he himself may survive the flames. 2. This day will be *advantageous* to those who have built on this Foundation with *right* materials. "If any man's work abide which he hath built thereupon, he shall receive a reward."

Vers. 16, 17.—*Humanity the temple of God.* "Know ye not that ye are the temple of God, and that the Spirit of God dwelleth in you? If any man defile the temple of God, him shall God destroy; for the temple of God is holy, which temple ye are." The apostle is writing not to those who were *spiritually perfect*; on the contrary, to those who were characterized by most salient moral defects. Yet he says, "Ye are the temple of God." Let us, therefore, look at man—

I. AS A DIVINE "TEMPLE." "The temple of God." In what respects a temple? 1. He is a special *residence* of God. God is in all material objects, but he is especially in moral mind. 2. He is a special *manifestation* of God. God is seen everywhere in this world, but never so fully as in the mind of man. "We are all his offspring," and we are like the Father in essence, conscience, freedom. 3. He is a special *meeting-place* with God. The temple at Jerusalem was God's *special* meeting-place with man. "There will I commune with thee." Man can meet with God in material nature, but not so fully and consciously as in mind. "The highest study of mankind is man."

II. As a Divine "temple" THAT MIGHT BE DESTROYED. "If any man defile [destroy] the temple of God." The destruction of a temple does not mean the destruction of all its parts, but the destruction of its *use*. Man might live for ever, and yet be destroyed as the temple of God, the special residence, manifestation, and meeting-place of God. Now, mark, this destruction, if it takes place, is not by God. He will not destroy the temple, only by *man*. "If any man defile [destroy] the temple." Alas! men are destroying this temple, *i.e.* destroying their natures as the temple of God. An awful work this!

III. As a Divine temple, the DESTROYER OF WHICH WILL BE DESTROYED BY GOD HIMSELF. "Him shall God destroy." Destroy, if not his existence, all that makes existence worth having or even tolerable. "He that soweth to the flesh shall of the flesh reap corruption." "The temple of God is holy," that is, *ideally* holy, ought to be holy.

Vers. 18—20.—*Worldly wisdom.* "Let no man deceive himself. If any man among you seemeth to be wise in this world, let him become a fool, that he may be wise. For the wisdom of this world is foolishness with God. For it is written, He taketh the wise in their own craftiness. And again, The Lord knoweth the thoughts of the wise, that they are vain." The "wisdom" here referred to is what Paul calls elsewhere "fleshly wisdom," the "wisdom of the world," or of *the age.* It is the same wisdom as he refers to in ch. i. 20. The "wisdom of this world" may be regarded as mere intellectual knowledge, applied to secular and selfish ends; however vast and varied its attainments, it is worldly in the apostolic sense; it is "earthly," "sensual," "devilish," not like the "wisdom which is from above," which is "first pure, then peaceable, gentle, and easy to be entreated, full of mercy and good fruits." In relation to this wisdom three remarks are here suggested.

I. It is SELF-DELUDING. "Let no man deceive himself. If any man among you seemeth to be wise in this world," etc. 1. This worldly wisdom deceives a man, inasmuch as it leads him to overrate the value of his *attainments.* He imagines that this kind of knowledge, "wisdom," is everything for a man. Hence the enthusiastic promotion of secular schools and colleges. But all such knowledge is of no value to man as man, and beyond his brief and uncertain earthly life. He deceives himself in its value. 2. This worldly wisdom deceives a man, inasmuch as it leads him to overrate his own *importance*. He is "vainly puffed by his earthly mind," as Paul says elsewhere (Col. ii. 18). Such a man imagines himself to be very great; he becomes a pedant; he "struts and stares and a' that."

II. It is SPIRITUALLY WORTHLESS. A man with this worldly wisdom must "become a fool, that he may be wise." Two things are here implied. 1. That with all his wisdom he is already really a "fool." He is a "fool;" for he looks for happiness where it is not to be found. Happiness does not spring from a man's brain, but from his heart; not from his ideas, but from his affections. Moreover, he is a "fool" because he practically ignores the chief good, which is love for, resemblance to, and fellowship with, the great God. Hence God esteems this wisdom as foolishness. "The wisdom of this world is foolishness with God." The most illustrious scholar, sage, orator, who is considered by himself and by most of his contemporaries to be a man of wonderful wisdom, to the eye of God is a fool.

III. It is ULTIMATELY CONFOUNDING. "It is written, He taketh the wise in their own craftiness." It must confound a man sooner or later, either (1) *here* in his *conversion*, or (2) *yonder* in his *retribution*.

> "Who are the wise?
> They who have govern'd with a self-control
> Each wild and baneful passion of the soul,
> Curb'd the strong impulse of all-fierce desires,
> But kept alive affection's purer fires;
> They who have pass'd the labyrinth of life
> Without one hour of weakness or of strife,
> Prepar'd each change of fortune to endure,
> Humble though rich, and dignified though poor,
> Skill'd in the latent movements of the heart,
> Learn'd in the lore which nature can impart,
> Teaching the sweet philosophy aloud
> Which sees the 'silver lining' of the cloud,
> Looking for good in all beneath the skies!—
> These are the truly wise."
>
> (Prince.)

Vers. 21—23.—*A call to the utmost expansiveness in religious sympathy.* "Therefore let no man glory in men. For all things are yours," etc. The attendants on a Christian ministry may be divided into two classes. 1. Those who esteem the doctrine because of the teacher. There are not a few in all congregations who accept doctrines simply because of the strong sympathies they have with the preacher. Paul seems to have thought of these when he wrote this chapter. He alludes to the men in the Church at Corinth who had been taken more with the teachers than with their doctrines. The other class of attendants on a Christian ministry are: 2. Those who esteem the teacher because of his doctrines. A man who preaches to them they feel is estimable only as he embodies and propounds the true doctrines of the gospel. The impropriety of glorying in teachers rather than in their doctrines is strikingly illustrated in these verses by three things.

I. THE UNIVERSE IS FOR THE CHURCH. "All things are yours." "All things," not some things. 1. The *ministry* is for the Church. "Whether Paul, or Apollos." There is no agency more valuable on earth than the Christian ministry; in every way it serves man—intellectually, socially, materially. But its grand aim is to restore the human spirit to the knowledge, image, and fellowship of its God. Why, then, should it glory in one form? Let those who like Paul take Paul, and be thankful, and not find fault with those who regard Apollos as the most effective preacher. 2. The *world* is for the Church. By the world we mean the earth, with all its beauties and blessings. In the sense of *legal* possession the world, of course, is not the property of Christians, nor is it the property of others. For he who claims the largest number of acres has but a handbreadth compared with its numerous islands and vast continents. Yet in the highest sense it is the property of the Christian. He feels an intense sympathy and oneness with God who created it. 3. *Life* is the property of the Church. "Or life." There are certain conditions in which we find men on this earth, in which they cannot be said to live. There are some chained in their cell, under the sentence of death; they have forfeited their life. There are others whose limbs are so paralyzed that they can neither speak nor move; life is not theirs. Morally, sinful man is as a criminal; he is under the sentence of death; he is dead in trespasses. But life is the Christian's; his sentence of death is removed; his moral infirmities are healed, and all his faculties and powers are alive unto God. 4. *Death* is the property of the Church. "Or death." What is death? Who shall define it? Who shall penetrate its meaning? The word has unfathomable depths of the wonderful and the terrible. But it is for the Christian; it is his. It delivers him from the imperfections of the present state; it frees him from all that is incompatible with his peace, his safety, and his advancement; it introduces him into the scenes, the services, the society, of a blessed immortality. It is his; it is the last step in the pilgrimage. 5. *General events* are the property of the Church. "Things present, or things to come"—an expression including all the circumstances of existence. "Things present," whatever their character, are ours. "Things to come:" what things are those? Now, if all these things are for the Church, why should any of its members give themselves up to any one particular ministry to the disparagement of others?

II. THE CHURCH IS FOR THE REDEEMER. "Ye are Christ's." There are two very different senses in which Christian men are Christ's. They are his: 1. By his *relationship to them*. He is the Creator of all. "By him were all things created." He is the Mediator of all. 2. By their *pledge to him*. They have pledged themselves to him as their moral Leader. They have vowed unqualified obedience to his teaching. If they have thus consecrated themselves to him as their great Teacher, how absurd to glory in subordinate and fallible teachers! Why live under the rays of the rushlight, when you can bask under the beams of the sun? Follow a Plato in philosophy, a Solon in law, a Demosthenes in eloquence, a Bacon in sciences, but no one but Christ in religion. Value the Calvins, the Luthers, the Wesleys, for what they are worth, but disclaim them as leaders.

III. THE REDEEMER IS FOR GOD. "And Christ is God's." Jesus, as a Mediator, is the Messenger and Servant of the Eternal. 1. Christ is God's *Revealer*. He is the Word of God, the *Logos*. (1) He reveals him in creation; (2) he reveals him in his personal ministry. 2. Christ is God's *Servant*. He came here to work out God's great plan of saving mercy.

Learn from this subject: 1. *The infinite worth of Christianity.* It gives all things to its true disciples. None of the "all things" specified here are possessed by those who are not his genuine disciples. The *ministry* is not theirs. If they attend preaching they are mere instruments in the hands of the preacher; they are carried away by the emotions of the hour. The *world* is not theirs, however large a portion of it they claim legally; the world uses them as its tools. *Life* is not theirs; it is forfeited to justice. They have no true enjoyment in it. *Death* is not theirs; they are its. "Through fear of death they are all their lifetime subject to bondage." "Things present and things to come" are not theirs; they are the mere creatures of circumstances. It is Christianity alone that makes all these things man's. It attunes the soul to the influences of God, as the Æolian harp is attuned to the winds; and every passing breeze in its history strikes out in music the anthem, "The Lord is my Portion, saith my soul." 2. *The contemptibleness of religious sectarianism.* How wretchedly mean and base does sectarianism appear in the light of this subject! The men who glory in their own theological peculiarities, ecclesiastical sect, and religious teachers, have never felt the grandeur contained in the text, that the universe is for the Church, the Church is for Christ, and that Christ is for God.

HOMILIES BY VARIOUS AUTHORS.

Vers. 1—4.—*Spiritual condition of these Corinthian partisans characterized.* These men were in a low state of Christian development, their growth in grace having been arrested by the jealousy and strife dominant in their midst. Under such circumstances, personal progress and Church progress were impossible. Individual self-assertion and arrogance could not but lead to the depreciation of others, nor could envious rivalries tolerate merit and worth in those whom it sought to crush. On the other hand, looking at the Church as an organic body, its virtue was a common stock, to be cherished, honoured, and diligently maintained by every one of its members. Its zeal was not a solitary flame burning on an isolated altar, but the combined warmth of many hearts. Diversity, too, is God's law, diversity reaching down into temperament, diversity in the highest realm of gifts, diversity of insight and experience, and this factious temper was fatal to diversity. Agreeably to the Divine method, diversity was preliminary to unity, and men were allowed free action of individuality, that the strongest and best elements of character, and especially its latent qualities, might be brought out and incorporated in the totality of the Church. A very miscellaneous world environed these Corinthians; the Christian community itself was made up of Jews, Greeks, and Romans; and the reasons were, therefore, exceptionally stringent that they should, as brethren, be very closely banded together in one mind, "the mind of Christ." Had they been a homogeneous people, circumstantial motives, which have a very important part to play in the scheme of providence, would not have been so imperative. But these dissensions involved their national peculiarities, and hence the antecedents of blood, the residuum of former bitterness, would surely come in to aggravate their animosities. They were "babes in Christ," and furthermore, they were "carnal;" and this infantile and carnal state, in which all growth had been stopped, was due solely to intestine discord. Had they considered what a grievous evil it was? Paul and Apollos, Tarsian and Alexandrian, had been put by no choice of theirs in a position very unenviable, nay, in despite of their earnest remonstrance. Leaders they were, leaders they must be, leaders of the Church; and on this very account, nothing could be more ill timed, nothing more abhorrent to their personal feelings, nothing so little like "the mind of Christ," as the attempt to make them heads of factions. Alas for such unwise friends, blocking up their way and multiplying the hazards, already enormous, of their ministry in Achaia! If this audacious effort continued, how could they withstand their enemies? The heart of St. Paul is stirred, and, in this chapter, it swells to the full compass of his apostleship. Intellectual heroism is needed now, and in that, as in the other qualities of an habitual hero, he is never wanting.—L.

Vers. 5—10.—*St. Paul's view of the ministry.* After declaring to the Corinthians that they were carnal in their estimates of God's ministers, the apostle exposes their folly in this particular, by assuring them that he and Apollos were but ministers, or servants, whom God had commissioned to labour in their behalf. Half-way work he never did. To show their error, and prove that it was a worldly sentiment disguised under a fictitious admiration, he sets before them the true idea of the ministry, as an instrument through which the Divine agency of the Holy Ghost operated. No one enjoyed proper sympathy and affectionate regard more than St. Paul, whose heart overflowed into everything that offered a channel for its diffusion. There is nothing about him of Cato, whose virtue runs into the fanaticism of hatred; or of Coriolanus, who looks upon the people as "if he were a god to punish, and not a man of their infirmity." Nevertheless, he guards his tenderness against effeminacy, nor will he accept the slightest tribute to himself at the expense of truth. The hardest thing in our nature to organize is impulse; and yet this man, whose sensibilities were so quick and strong (ch. iv. 14, 15; 2 Cor. ii. 13), could not tolerate the homage paid him by partisans. And in this spirit he asks, "Who then is Paul?" Only a medium used by the Spirit for their faith, and the medium itself valueless, except so far as the Spirit made it effective. Their very capacity to receive St. Paul's influence was the gift of God, and would they now turn the gift against the Giver? St. Paul's figures are not poetic, but practical, and his imagination is always the offspring of the reason; and hence the illustrative image—"I have planted, Apollos watered; but God gave the increase"—began and ended in a breath, with no delight in it beyond utility. Two conclusions follow: one, the entire dependence upon God for the increase; and the other, the co-working with him who is the only Source of the increase. Neither the sower nor the seed, however good, can secure the yield; this is from the great Husbandman, who apportions the result according to his sovereignty, and under conditions which St. Paul subsequently points out. The workman is rewarded for his labour; he does not create the reward, but receives it from God; nor could reward have any other basis than free and unmerited grace, seeing that we are co-workers with God. If this were not the law of nature and providence, it could not be a law of grace, nor could the figure of seed and sower have any logical force. But, at the same time, the workman under the gospel has a special relation to God, and, in a sense peculiar to the gospel, is a "co-worker." This is one of St. Paul's favourite ideas (see 2 Cor. vi. 1). It is not working, but co-working, that evidences the spirituality of the work and gains the recompense. Among the sources of deception, not one is so insidious as *our* work. The old man, long a servant of God, looks back upon his labours; his eye is tranquil now; it has grown to be a very honest eye; and nothing in the past surprises him so much as the mixture of self with work that he once thought was unselfish. Early manhood and middle life, if not absolutely incompetent to form a perfect idea of disinterestedness, are yet very prone to fall into a mistake on this subject. No doubt St. John imagined that he was doing Christ's work when he forbade the man casting out devils in Christ's Name; and, likely enough, St. Peter put a special value on his courage in the garden, when he drew his sword for the Lord's defence. If our tastes and self-will can be gratified, we are often ready to be enthusiastic workers for what we suppose is the cause of Christ. But God's rule is unyielding. You must labour according to his will, or the work will be rejected. And just here, his thought in transition to another aspect of the great topic, St. Paul brings into view the co-relationship of ministers and people, God being all in all. "We" and "ye"— "we" are co-labourers with God, and "ye" are not our husbandry and building, but God's. What claims he for himself? He is a builder, a master-builder, a wise one too; and he is free to assert it, because it is the utterance of humility, and humility is under obligation to speak the exact truth about itself, under-valuation being wrong, as well as over-valuation. The preface attests the spiritual purity of the avowal: "According to the grace of God which is given unto me," while the elaboration of the figure, taken from architecture, indicates more of the Grecian mode of illustration than the Jewish.—L.

Vers. 11—15.—*Workmen and their works.* St. Paul affirms that he had laid just such a foundation in Corinth as became a wise master-builder. Like a good architect, he had made sure of a solid basis, but had the edifice in process of erection been true to the corner-stone? There was but one Foundation—Jesus Christ—and a man might build rightly or wrongly on it in the materials used. The range of substances which might be employed in the superstructure was large. Large it must needs be, for, if the builders are many, the material must be manifold. Individuality in workmen must be respected, and, though the risks are numerous and great, yet Christianity can only adhere to its fundamental principle of each man as a man in himself. Brutus sacrificed his instincts to what he deemed patriotism in the murder of Cæsar; Rome taught her best men to have no conscience except what she dictated; but Christianity laid a stress on personality in the human will in order to secure the full activity of individual responsibility. Providence ordains our home and life in a very ample world. The amplitude is seen, not in its size nor in the mere variety of its objects, but in the endless adaptability to human tastes and dispositions. Despite the curse, this earth is a grand historic memorial of the original idea of humanity, and a prophecy likewise of a glory to be recovered. "The field is the world;" and this is true of every man in it, so true indeed that our connections with the great world are far more vital and operative on our destiny than we imagine. This, furthermore, is our discipline. We have a world from which to choose our resources, means, and opportunities, and hence the wonder of experience is the multitudinous additions ever making to the world we inhabit as our own world. Now, to each Christian, "the field is the world;" and therein he finds a vast miscellany—"gold, silver, precious stones," and they are side by side with "wood, hay, stubble." Redeemed man is treated by Providence and the Holy Ghost, not on the bare idea of what he is in an earthly condition, but also and mainly on the ideal of his capacity in Christ. And consequently, when St. Paul says (ver. 21), "All things are yours," he has only formally wrought out the truth involved in the workman's command of his diversified materials. Just because the worker is in such a vast and heterogeneous world, he must "take heed." Nothing short of spiritual discernment can protect him against woeful blunders. A hard worker he may be, a sincere and enthusiastic worker, but he must have Divine insight, and show himself " a workman that needeth not to be ashamed," and the work must be true and acceptable work, or his labour will inevitably perish. St. James is often referred to as the supporter and defender of the doctrine of work. From his point of view Christianity was the final outgrowth of Judaism, its culmination and crown, and, quite in accord with his instincts, he presents the work side of religion with a very vigorous emphasis. St. Paul, however, confines himself in the text *to the kind of work*, and puts forth his strength on a single line of thought. What is uppermost in his mind is the absolute need of spiritual insight. The practical man is in the eye of St. James, and he writes of " religion pure and undefiled " as its spectator and analyst among the actualities of the world. Cæsar, in the ' Commentaries,' is not more terse and compact, nor does he observe more rigidly the requirements of intensiveness as a mental law than St. James in his great monograph. Be it noticed, however, that St. Paul is viewing this matter as a branch or offshoot of a topic engrossing at the time his sympathies, and, consequently, he limits himself to the difference between work which shall be found worthy of reward and work undeserving of recompense. Two cases are before him—in the one the man is saved and his work rewarded; in the other, the man is saved and his work disallowed and destroyed. The latter suffers loss, but not the loss of his soul, and, though the ordeal be severe, the man is " saved, yet so as by fire." Now, this view of work, truthful in itself, was specially suited to these noisy, impulsive, erratic Corinthians. And may we not reasonably conjecture that he had the products of partisanship in his eye while writing of the fiery test? Looking at the world's history, we can scarcely fail to see that the fruits of factions are the most perishable things in civilization, and, in Church history, the fact is still more obvious. But the apostle has something further to say.—L.

Vers. 16—23.—*Believers as the temple of God.* Previously St. Paul had said, " Ye are God's building;" and now he adds, " Ye are the temple of God." Along with this comes the idea of sanctity : "The temple of God is holy, which temple ye are." If, then, these Corinthians were the temple of God, and if the Spirit of God dwelt in them, no stronger motive could bear upon them than the need of holiness ; and this holiness is a personal matter. " If any man "—whoever he be and whatever his gifts—" if any man defile the temple of God, him shall God destroy." The man's duties to the Church are duties to the Spirit of God in the Church ; and the purity of principle and affection, purity of motive and aim, purity of life, which he is bound to maintain,—in brief, his spiritual character, grows out of his relation to the Holy Ghost. " Know ye not" this fact—that the Church is much more than a society for mutual helpfulness, much more than a human institution, and most truly human when most Divine ? To violate this relation in such a way as to " defile the temple of God " is to incur a fearful punishment: " Him shall God destroy." Hitherto in the argument no such language had been used. Did the thought of the gross sin—the son taking the father's wife—cross his mind at the instant, and leave its darkness in his memory? Whether so or not, St. Paul knew of moral corruption in the Church as well as religious defection, and he reminded the Corinthians of their peril. Observe the change ; a man's work, if rejected, shall be burned, but he shall be " saved, yet so as by fire." Amid the danger, God will rescue him. But if a " man defile the temple of God, him shall God destroy." And now the exhortation: " Let no man deceive himself." And wherein lies the danger of deception ? It is in the " wisdom of this world." Intellect exposes us to dangers because it is the great organ of receptivity, by means of which the outer world finds unceasing access to our souls. Through the open avenues of the senses, myriad influences gain an entrance within and distribute themselves over every portion of our nature. Very many of them are unchallenged. Few men criticize their senses and hold them accountable for truth and fidelity in their momentous functions. What habits come from this facile power of sensuousness over the mind, we all understand, alas! too well. The natural man (animal man) has the world of sensation on his side. Instead of the body growing more and more into harmony with spirit and participating in its elevation, the opposite more commonly occurs, so that men become in large measure the creatures of the senses.

St. Paul had a very clear insight into this fact. No man makes so many references, direct and indirect, to the physiological connections of sin. As a writer of Scripture, the terrible truth of the " fleshly mind " is often before him, and from him we learn the supreme necessity of keeping the body *under*, lest we become *castaways*. " Castaways " are far more numerous than we take knowledge of. Short of downright materialism and its counterpart in sensual degeneration, we have innumerable evidences of the wreck of the spiritual nature. These nerves of ours—delicate threads that interlace the whole body and are frequently too fine for the eye—what a machinery for the hand of Satan, skilled by the practice of centuries, to play upon! We err when we confine our view of materialism to its professed advocates. We err also when we measure the sensualism of the age by its grosser forms. Far greater, far more harmful, and far more widespread, are the deleterious effects, often unrecognized, that work havoc among our spiritual sensibilities. It is this deadening of the intellect by the sensuousness that keeps itself aloof from overt sensualism which St. Paul so earnestly assails as " the wisdom of this world." Not seldom it boasts of morality, cultivates beauty, patronizes æsthetics, and abounds in animalized poetry and eloquence and science. Meantime it lends all its aid, acting through an army of auxiliaries, to encourage men in a bloated sense of self-sufficiency, until there is no felt need of God and still less of Christ. Most of all, this state of mind is inimical to the agency of the Holy Ghost upon the human heart, and consequently we find in our times a much more wilful and violent rejection of the Holy Ghost and a contempt for his gracious offices than hostility to the Father and the Son. Against this most evil and fatal habit St. Paul lifts a vehement remonstrance. And he was the only man of his day competent to this task. No rude Galilean was he; no obscure and unlettered person; but a cultured soul, whose endowments had been signalized before he went forth to convert an empire to Christ. "Become a fool"—a fool in the world's estimation—" that ye may be wise." It is " craftiness," argues the man who had experimentally known it all, and, furthermore, it ensnares itself in its own net. And hence glory not in man; there is no wisdom in it, no plea and no excuse for it, since " all things are yours." Party spirit shuts us up in narrow limits; Christianity gives the freedom of the world. Party spirit makes us the disciples of men; Christianity declares that we do not belong to Paul, Apollos, Peter, but that they belong to us, and all Divine in them ministers to the Divine in ourselves, so that our life superabounds by means of theirs. Nor is this all. The vast inventory embraces things as well as men: " The world, or life, or death, or things present, or things to come; all are yours." No room for pride here, since it is a common possession; no opportunity to thank God like the Pharisee that we are not as others are, for God's grace humbles the natural man, that it may endow and then exalt the Christian. If we undertake to be Christians of a particular sort, it is certain that we shall be cast in a very dwarfing mould, and get our colouring from a very earthly pigment. To be a true Christian is not to adopt the Name of Christ as the watchword of a sect or party, but to accept and venerate it as the watchword of humanity redeemed in the Son of man. Any other use of Christ's Name is essentially schismatic. All things are ours only so far as we are Christ's. And it is the Christ of God, the Son of God, the anointed Messiah, who was filled with the unction of the Spirit, and who said, " I do nothing of myself,"—it is this Christ who is ours. Seen in him, life redeems itself from everything low, groveling, and merely sensuous; and even the human body, whose wants and demands are the unmanageable factor in all civilization, and whose warfare against the Spirit is the most fearful hazard in moral probation, becomes, through Christ, the temple of the Holy Ghost. Spiritualize in this sense the human body; sanctify its large and beautiful capacity for a true sensuousness; organize its habits until it becomes almost the automaton of the Spirit, and self-denial, prayer, and praise, by virtue of the automatic and semi-automatic laws of the physical system, are well-nigh incorporated in the nervous functions. Ask art, science, philosophy, to attempt such a task, and would they set themselves to it? Political economy, physiology, hygiene, sanitary science, concern themselves much with the human body, and are entitled to honour for their interest in its welfare—welfare only, however, stopping very far short of genuine well-being. Let no word of ours be understood as depreciating these invaluable services. But, nevertheless, their field lies in a department of life comparatively humble—life as existence, as organic and vegetative, life as intellectual and moral, *not in life as spiritual*. Now, at this very point, the incomparable glory of Christianity demonstrates itself by a profound interest in the human body as a religious question, and, first and last, its words are, "temple of God." No wonder that St. Paul rises to the height of exultation. The eagle-wing smites the upper air in its buoyant strength, and the eagle-eye, catching a radiance unknown in the thick atmosphere of earth, commands the scope of a vast horizon. One of his grand powers was this instinct—shall we call it?—of exultation, always held in check till the Divine fulness of Christ and the sublimity of humanity in Christ kindled it into rapture. Nor is he ever more like himself nor ever nearer to us than in these moments—"such high hour of visitation from the living God."—L.

Vers. 6—8.—*Spiritual husbandry and growth.* A man, looking upon the world, sees according to his power of vision; *i.e.* not simply according to what he finds in it, but to what he brings to it. To the eye of the Apostle Paul, the world was a wilderness which might be made a garden. There was, he saw, rude, worthless growth to be extirpated, rich soil to be tilled, plants of worth and renown to replace the weeds. His prophetic eye beheld the desert rejoice and blossom as the rose. And to his mind Christians were plants, and Christian ministers were gardeners and husbandmen.

I. Spiritual cultivation needs human industry. There is need, in order to the progress and perfection of the work of God, of: 1. Intelligent and willing labourers. Men are employed by Divine wisdom to labour among their fellow-men. Saved, renewed, and consecrated labourers have ever been blessed in the work of securing a spiritual harvest. The olive-yard, and the vineyard cannot flourish and prosper without unstinted toil, vigilance, skill, and care; so is it with the garden of the Lord. 2. Divinely commissioned labourers. They work best for Jesus who have heard his voice saying, "Go, work to-day in my vineyard;" whom the authoritative Lord has addressed in his own commanding language, "Unto men I now send thee."

II. Spiritual cultivation demands a variety of character and ability in the toilers. 1. One class of labourers are especially adapted to the work of planting. There are Christian missionaries and evangelists who have the gift of awakening attention, arousing concern, eliciting inquiry, calling forth repentance, founding Churches even among the ignorant and degraded heathen. 2. Another class possess the grace of watering the plants already placed in the spiritual soil. These, as pastors and bishops, impart instruction, administer consolation, exercise guidance and control. Catechists and teachers carry on the work which missionaries have begun. 3. All classes co-operate towards the one great end in view. All true labourers are one in motive and in aim, in spirit, in mutual confidence and love. None may say to the other, "I have no need of thee." Each has his service, and none is more indispensable than another. 4. All are individually noticed, appreciated, and rewarded. "Then shall every one have praise of God;" "I will give unto every one of you according to your works;" "My reward is with me, to give every man according as his work shall be."

III. Spiritual cultivation depends for its efficiency and success entirely upon the blessing of the Lord. 1. From God comes the vitality of the spiritual plant; his is the gospel and his the Spirit, by whose co-operation the result is brought about. 2. From God comes the preparation of the labourer; whose intellectual gifts, whose emotional sympathy, and whose spiritual power are all alike of heavenly origin. 3. From God comes the living energy to which is owing the progress and increase of that which man plants and waters. Thus the excellency of the power is seen to be of God, and not of us.—T.

Ver. 9.—"*God's fellow-workers.*" God is ever working. Let this thought shame those foolish, worthless persons who deem it derogatory to labour. Not only when he fashioned this world and made it fit for our dwelling-place, not only when he created man, but always and everywhere is God working. The laws of nature are the operations of the Almighty, and he is working as well in the spiritual sphere as in the physical.

I. True Christians are spiritual labourers. Christian evangelists and pastors, teachers and bishops, are all working in prominent positions in the harvest-field of spiritual toil. But spiritual labour is the natural outcome of the spiritual life. Every sincere follower of Christ is seeking an end outside of himself—the promotion of the kingdom of righteousness and the glory of the Divine Master. Our hearts may rest in the Lord, but our hands work for him.

II. CHRISTIANS ARE FELLOW-LABOURERS ONE WITH ANOTHER. 1. There is difference in natural powers, in spiritual gifts, in ecclesiastical position, in length of service. 2. But there is unity in aim, in hope, in the relation all sustain to him by whose authority and for whose glory they toil. 3. And there is sympathy, mutual good will, and helpfulness. If there is defect here, it is a discredit to the common profession, a hindrance to the general usefulness, a grief to the one Lord.

III. CHRISTIANS ARE FELLOW-LABOURERS WITH GOD AS THEIR MASTER. 1. All are alike called by him who sends forth labourers into his harvest. He is independent of us, and it is to his grace we owe it that we are permitted to labour for him. 2. All are alike directed to labour for the one great end—the universal and immortal reign of truth and righteousness, holiness and love. 3. All are alike instructed by him as to the special means by which the one end is to be secured. He gives to every one the appropriate implement for his toil, the weapon adapted to his warfare. 4. All alike receive the needed strength and guidance from him, the spiritual impulse and power which gives efficacy to their service. 5. All rejoice that, whether they plant or water, the same Lord "gives the increase."

IV. CHRISTIANS ARE LABOURERS WITH GOD AS THEIR FELLOW-WORKER. This interpretation, whether justifiable or not grammatically, does not seem liable to a charge of irreverence. 1. In Christ Jesus, the Son of God, we have the supreme Exemplar of spiritual labour. "My Father worketh hitherto, and I work." Jesus calls us to do what he himself is doing. What power there is in his appeal, "Work, not only *for* me, but *with* me!" 2. The agency of the Divine Spirit is never withheld. The husbandman can only work effectually when God works with him by the agencies of nature; the mechanist, only when physical forces can be employed under his control, the physician, only when his treatment is in harmony with physiological laws. So the Christian labourer is successful, not through independence, but just because he avails himself of the co-operation of the Lord and Giver of life; because, in all devotion and diligence and humility, he endeavours to live and to toil as *a fellow-worker with God!*—T.

Ver. 11.—*The one Foundation.* There was a tendency on the part of the Corinthians to exalt their favourite teachers and leaders. Such exaltation could not but be at the expense of the Lord Jesus himself. In dissuasion from such a course of Church thought and practice, the inspired Apostle Paul puts in a just and clear light the relative positions of the teachers, the taught, and the great theme of all Christian instruction. He makes use of a familiar figure of speech, based upon the common craft of masonry. Christ is the *Foundation*; the people of Christ are the *stones* of the structure reared thereon; and the apostles and other teachers are *builders* of the spiritual edifice. It is of the Foundation that the text especially treats.

I. JESUS CHRIST IS THE FOUNDATION OF THE SPIRITUAL TEMPLE. 1. The temple is composed of human souls, fashioned into a Divine unity and endowed with a Divine life. 2. The temple is inhabited and inspired by the Holy Ghost consecrating and honouring it. 3. This temple has actually and historically been called into existence by the ministry and mediation of Jesus Christ, who has thus constituted himself its Foundation. As Son of God and Son of man, as the accepted Mediator, as the authoritative Teacher and rightful Lord, he is the Author and the Basis of the true Church.

II. THE PERFECT SUFFICIENCY OF THIS FOUNDATION. 1. Christ is a Foundation deep and strong enough to support the fabric reared upon him. No fear need be entertained as to the permanence of Christ's Church. It may be assailed by the storms of persecution, it may be threatened by the decaying force of time; but "the gates of Hades shall not prevail against it." It rests on Christ, and the Foundation standeth sure. 2. Christ is a Foundation broad and comprehensive enough to underlie the widest, stateliest structure. None who is conversant with the character, the designs, the promises of Jesus Christ, can question this. In our day, all systems that are narrow are doomed to contempt and destruction. This fate Christianity need not fear;

it has only to be true to the Divine Head and Lord, and nought can overturn it or even injure it.

III. The EXCLUSIVENESS OF THIS FOUNDATION. Upon this the text lays an especial stress. 1. No other is permitted by God. It would be dishonouring to the Father to suppose that his Son can be replaced or supplemented by any other; the sufficiency of the Divine provision does not admit of question. 2. No other is needed by man. 3. No other is possible. Any other than the Divine Foundation must be of man's appointment, must be indeed merely human. The apostle teaches that he and Apollos were only builders upon the Foundation, and could not therefore be the Foundation itself.

IV. The RELATIONS MEN SUSTAIN TO THIS FOUNDATION. 1. All Christians are represented as living stones built upon Christ. Each has his own place and his own use; but all are alike in this fact—they support themselves upon the strong foundation laid in Jesus. 2. All Christian pastors and teachers are building upon Christ. The question for them to ask is this: Are we building into the walls of the temple such material as will endure the test of trial and the test of time?—T.

Ver. 13.—*The test of fire.* "Fire is a good servant, but a bad master." The element is symbolical of proof and testing; for where it has its liberty and may do its work unchecked, there is little that can withstand its assaults and outlast its ravages. How many a city, like this Corinth itself, has been burnt, and laid for the most part in ashes, so that only the most substantial buildings have survived the conflagration! So shall all spiritual work, sooner or later, be tested and put to the proof. The means may seem severe, but the result shall be decisive.

I. The WORK. 1. It is spiritual, not material work, of which the assertion is made. All are builders, not only of their own character and destiny, but of the character and destiny of some associates. There is an awful solemnity attaching to this responsible work in which men are bound to engage. 2. Every man's work is in question, especially that of every professedly Christian labourer who aims to build in the temple of the living God. The learned and the illiterate, the sober and the enthusiast, the sanguine and the desponding,—all are teaching Christian doctrine, and are more or less exercising influence over human souls. 3. Work of every kind is included—genuine and pretentious, hasty and gradually progressive, sound and superficial.

II. The FIRE. This must be something universally applicable, since it is not represented as an accident befalling here and there one, but as an incident of every man's labour of every kind to pass through this fire. We shall not be wrong in terming it the fire of judgment, fire being the discriminating and decisive element. The fire may purify, and it may consume. It is possible that this fire may burn here and now; it is certain that it will burn hereafter, when God "shall try every man's work of what sort it is."

III. The TEST. There are circumstances and times which have no virtue of probation. There is weather in which the soundly built house, the well-found ship, cannot be distinguished from the most ill-planned and faultily constructed house, the most unseaworthy craft. But the storm tries both. And the fire of judgment puts to the proof the workmanship of the spiritual labourer. "Judge nothing before the time." "The day will declare it, for it shall be revealed in fire." None can evade this trial or deceive him who shall then cast all work into the furnace of his probation.

IV. The RESULT. It shall be unmistakable and decisive. 1. To the work which is sound and workmanlike glory shall accrue, and credit to the faithful and diligent labourer. The precious metals and the costly marbles shall be none the worse but rather the better for the test; their qualities shall shine out the more resplendent. 2. To the work which is bad destruction shall come; for the wood, hay, and stubble of false doctrine and of worthless profession shall be consumed and shall disappear. The builder may escape, though only as through the burning embers and the falling sparks. "If the righteous scarcely be saved, where shall the ungodly and the sinner appear?"—T.

Vers. 16, 17.—"*The temple of God.*" The temple at Jerusalem was holy, being constructed according to Divine directions, inhabited by the Divine glory, and consecrated by divinely appointed services and sacrifices. But that temple was local, temporary, and for a purpose. It was, in accordance with the Lord's prediction, destroyed and abolished before the generation which rejected him passed away. And it was not intended that it should be replaced by any material edifice. The spiritual temple was destined to supersede the material and to abide for ever. It is of this spiritual structure that the apostle here speaks.

I. The materials of which this temple is composed. "*Ye*," says the apostle, "are the temple." Not that the Corinthians were more than other Christians entitled to this honourable distinction ; for this language was addressed to all Christians. All Christ's people were and are living stones, each in its proper place, and all alike upon the one Foundation. How noble a conception ! how worthy of Christ himself, to whom the material was ever of secondary interest, and in whose view the spiritual was of supreme significance and value !

II. The presence by which this temple is consecrated. The first temple had been hallowed by the Shechinah-glory which hovered over the ark of the covenant. The second temple—the body of the Lord—had been consecrated as the dwelling-place of the mind of the Holy One. This third temple is the residence and the shrine of the Spirit of God. In his transforming, quickening, purifying power, the eternal Spirit penetrates his separated and consecrated society, and makes it growingly his own. His light and glory glow within it, so that its spiritual lustre excels that of the holy house at Jerusalem.

III. The worship which is in this temple offered. Here is the living oracle; here is the consecrated priesthood; here are the spiritual sacrifices. The offerings are those of willing obedience and grateful praise; the incense is the incessant worship which floats in fragrance fron the spirits of the just; the music that fills these courts is the anthem of adoration, the harmony of imperishable love. Worship is here not occasional, not frequent, but unceasing; there is no moment when this spiritual temple is not telling the praises of the Lord.

IV. The attribute by which this temple is characterized. "The temple of God is *holy*." This expression does not import simply a ceremonial and nominal holiness, but such a character as was both exhibited and required by the Lord Jesus himself. Holiness, not only of word and deed, but of purpose and desire, is required by him who searches the heart and tries the reins of the children of men—holiness such as the Holy Spirit alone can create.

V. The regard and treatment which this temple should receive. 1. It deserves to be regarded with reverence. Men treat with respect the palaces of kings. Of how much deeper a reverence is that true palace of God, that temple of the Holy Ghost, that home of Christ, deserving ! 2. It should not be defiled or destroyed. Every member of Christ's Church is called upon to purify himself, lest his impurity should dishonour the sacred edifice. "Holiness becometh thy house, O Lord, for ever !"—T.

Vers. 21—23.—"*All things are yours.*" These are great words; but if they were not so great they would here be out of place. Men are given to boast of their possessions; but the Christian's boast is in this respect larger and grander than any man's beside. Men are wont to glory in belonging to some select society, some great nation, some illustrious king; but the Christian glories in belonging to a greater than the greatest who owes his honour to this world. "All things" are his; and he is "Christ's."

I. Our property in all things. To Christians it may be said—it was said by the inspired apostle : 1. All *ministries* are yours; the dead and the living, the speaking and the writing, the official and the unrecognized. (1) The ministry of doctrine and of conversion, such as that of Paul, who planted. (2) The ministry of eloquence and of edification, such as that of Apollos, who watered. (3) The ministry of morality and zeal, such as that of Cephas. Each has his gift, and the Church is not for the ministry, but the ministry for the Church. 2. All *circumstances* are yours. (1) The world, which is ours by the gift of God and by the redemption of Christ. (2) Life is yours, in its opportunities and its manifold blessings. (3) Death is yours—not your master, but your servant and your friend. 3. All *times* are yours. (1) The present, in enjoyment, which is more the Christian's than it is the worldling's. (2) The future, in reversion, which has for him brightness, glory, and joy. The future can deprive the Christian of no real good; it must bring him advantages unnumbered.

II. CHRIST'S PROPERTY IN US. To Christians it may be said, "Ye are Christ's:" 1. By the purchase of his blood. For, "Ye are not your own; ye are bought with a price." 2. By his choice and ours. "I," says he, "have chosen you." And, "We love him because he first loved us." 3. By the inhabiting of his Spirit, whose gracious presence makes us his. It is not a case of mere property, but of spiritual affinity: "The Lord knoweth them that are his." 4. By our grateful and affectionate service. That Christians are his, it is their daily aim to prove, by their delight in his Word, their devotion to his cause, their obedience to his commands.—T.

Ver. 1.—*Carnal Christians.* I. MANY SUCH ARE FOUND IN THE CHURCH. Christians in whom Christianity is not *dominant.* They have a portion of the Spirit, but a very large portion of the flesh. They allow Satan to hinder them. The world has still much power over them and much attraction for them. They love Christ, but not enough to lead them to live very near to him. They are conspicuous chiefly for fault and failure. They reach the verge of Christianity and *stay there.* They desire "to be saved," and beyond this they have few spiritual longings. They are no credit to Christianity, but make it questionable in the eyes of the world. Spiritual dwarfs, who have not even the advantage of stimulating curiosity, seeing they are so numerous. II. THEIR RELATION TO THE FAITH. They are babes; but note—babes *in Christ.* It is better to be a babe in Christ than a full-grown man apart from him. Still, these are babes in Christ when they ought to be *men* in Christ. As babes, they are: 1. Of no practical use in the Church. They cannot be relied upon for service; they are not fitted for real work. In spiritual things they are weaklings. They draw upon the resources of the Church rather than add to them. They are encumbrances—sources of weakness rather than of strength. They require much looking after. *The Church has to nurse them when she should be converting the world.* Yet withal they often have a very high opinion of their own powers, and sometimes are exceedingly anxious to take up a great work—as anxious as they soon become to put it down again. Childish instability of purpose, as well as lack of spiritual power, prevents them from being useful. And work that is done after so carnal a manner that often it had better have been left undone. It is *child's* work, having in it more marring than making. 2. Not a source of joy. A babe in Christ delights the hearts of all true Christians—*when it ought to be a babe;* but continuous babyhood is monstrous and revolting. Carnal Christians are babes without promise; often it seems as though they would never get out of their spiritual long-clothes. They sadden the heart of their spiritual parent. They are *disappointments.* Hope deferred concerning them has made the heart sick. Neither to Christ, nor to man, nor to themselves, are they satisfactory. The Church which has many of them will have its share of spiritual depression. Carnal Christians are kill-joys. 3. Often fretful and peevish. Carnal Christians are often quarrelsome Christians. They are fault-finders, and if they cannot find faults they can always make them. Into the Church they bring ill temper, which is contagious, and thus they become the cause of not a little mischief. They have considerable destructive power. They have only enough Christianity to make them miserable. They are fractious and self-willed, and always want to have *their* way, whether it is a good way or an ill. 4. Fond of toys. They must have their playthings, even in Church. Things pleasing to the senses are the things pleasing to them. Ornate ritual, pretty pictures, gaudy decorations, elaborate but unsuitable music, have been brought into the Churches by those babes in Christ, carnal Christians. Where they have their way the sanctuary resembles nothing so much as a toyshop or an opera-house. 5. Not very open to reasonable appeal. They are wilful. Having very little knowledge, they believe that they possess all. They are hard-mouthed, and the bit of reason controls them but little. To argue with a babe is not promising, but it is quite as hopeful as to reason spiritually with a carnal Christian. III. CONSPICUOUS SIGNS OF THE CARNAL STATE. 1. *Jealousy.* Partisan spirit, rivalry, pride; in opposition to "in honour preferring one another." Leading to: 2. *Strife.* Active opposition instead of hearty co-operation. Creation of causes of strife; evident fondness for it. The carnal Christian is seldom at peace except when he is at war. Love of fighting other Christians rather than love of fighting Satan. The disciples at the table had a strife for pre-eminence, and thus showed their carnality.

Leading to: 3. *Division.* Estrangement, separation, hatred; instead of unity, peace, love. The carnal Christian's progress is very different to the true pilgrim's progress. 4. *Men-followers rather than Christ-followers.* The carnal Corinthians showed their carnality conspicuously in this respect. 5. *Arrest or retardation of development.* "Not even now are ye able" (ver. 2). If the carnal Christian does not go back, he tends to stand still. 6. *Weak spiritual digestion.* (Ver. 2.) Poor spiritual appetite. Little power of assimilation. Spiritual food does not seem *to feed* the carnal believer. He is lean. There are many religious dyspeptics.

IV. How to be dealt with. 1. *To be fed.* (Ver. 2.) Not to be neglected as of no account or cast out as evil. Whilst some of these babes may have little appetite, others of them may be noisy because they are hungry. To be *fed*; if the rod is not to be spared, still less are the spoon and cup. Carnal Christians are in the care of the Church, and must be dealt with kindly and helpfully, in the hope that, by the Spirit's working, manhood may be attained at last. 2. *With milk.* Food suited to their condition. With *milk*—*good* food; *unadulterated,* for they need the best—the "sincere milk of the Word." *Sweet* milk; for babes like sweetness, and *sour* milk can only injure them. With *milk,* which may nourish and strengthen; not with the vinegar of scolding condemnation, which some seem to favour. Not too much physic; abundance of milk. 3. *Not with meat.* This would choke them. Babes may cry for strong meat, but they must not have it. The Corinthians found much fault with the simplicity of Paul's teaching; but Paul knew what they needed, though they clamoured for something else. Not with the deeper things of God, which can be appreciated only by the matured (ch. ii. 6); but with the more elementary truths put in elementary forms. The carnal Christian can appreciate only the exterior parts of gospel truths; these must come first; the surface must be passed before the internal can be reached. So, though Paul did not *conceal* any doctrines from the carnal Corinthians, he could only carry them with him in his teaching *as far as they were prepared to go.* Milk is the simple religious view; meat, the profounder. The same doctrine can be presented as milk and meat; the carnal Christian only goes so far in comprehending it, the spiritual searches into its depths. The doctrine of Romish reserve is not sanctioned by Paul.—H.

Ver. 6.—*Man's work and God's.* I. Man's work. It is: 1. *Varied.* Paul speaks of planting and watering; may extend to the multiform operations of agriculture. We cannot all do the same work. Let us seek to do that for which we are fitted. *There is some spiritual work suited to each of us.* In agriculture all find employment, from the boy with his clapper scaring away the birds, to the presiding mind which controls all operations. If Christians do nothing it is because they want to do nothing. 2. *Important.* As in husbandry, unless we sow and water we may not look for a harvest, so as a rule in things spiritual. Never think that what you can do is *unimportant.* You may think *too little* of your work as well as *too much.* You will think too little if you think that your work may safely be left undone. 3. *Honourable.* Christian work itself,—*what can compare with it for an instant?* Further, in it we are "*God's fellow-workers*" (ver. 9). The Christian worker is one of God's nobility. 4. *Limited.* We can only do so much. We may sow and water, but not give the increase. It belongs to us to preach and teach, not to convince; to invite and warn, not to convert. *We cannot produce spiritual results.* We are not responsible for them. 5. *Not independent.* We cannot do our own work apart from God; it is "as the Lord gave to every man" (ver. 5). The seed that we plant is God's; the soil and water are God's; our powers employed are not "ours" but "God's." 6. *To be rewarded.* Upon just principles; according to the "labour" (ver. 8); according to faithfulness in the labour (Matt. xxv. 14—30). Not according to success. We cannot command this, though success usually follows faithful labour, and lack of success often means lack of diligence, or lack of something which should not have been lacking. *Many Christians have an unhappy facility in accounting for failure.*

II. God's work. 1. *Wonderful.* Deeply mysterious. How marvellous the development of the seed after it is planted! Before this expansion and multiplication of life science stands dumb and confounded. So with the seed of the Word in the human heart. What inexplicable working and result! Well may we bow in adoring awe before this mystery of Divine might. 2. *All-important.* The great need : without this, all nothing. If the increase comes not, of what service is it to plant and irrigate? If the Divine blessing rests not on our preaching and teaching, of what possible service can it be ? *Alas ! how often we forget this ! No harvest because God ignored.* 3. *Independent.* God is not in any way dependent upon us or others for the increase; neither is he for the sowing and watering. The storm-wind can be his seed-sower, the rains and the dews are his servants.

III. REFLECTIONS. 1. God's work and man's are usually conjoined. God works generally by means. Let us, therefore, see that our part is done. 2. As our part is important, let us do it with the utmost possible efficiency. 3. Let us ever remember that we are working in *God's field, and near to him,* under his observation, etc. 4. Let us never attempt to do God's part or take any of the glory when it is done. 5. Let us ever bear in mind the *relative* importance of God's work and ours. Our work is *nothing* in comparison with his ; we are *nothing* in comparison with him (ver. 7). 6. When we have done our part, let us look in faith to God to accomplish his. 7. Let us think little of man, much of God. 8. Let us never expect God's work from man. 9. As we work with and for the same God, let us cultivate unity.—H.

Vers. 10, 11.—*The great Foundation.* I. WHAT IT IS. It is Christ (ver. 11). He is the Foundation of: 1. *Christianity.* Its basis is conveyed in its name. It rests upon Christ. If he be removed, it falls to the ground in ruins ; if he be diminished (as in the denial of his divinity, for example), Christianity becomes weak and tottering. As Christianity is of Christ, so is it strong, abiding, glorious. 2. *The Christian Church.* Its doctrines and practice. How many other foundations have been laid for it from time to time ! how often there has been *an attempted union of other foundations with the one Foundation, Jesus Christ !* To tamper with this Foundation is perilous indeed ; *to add* to it is to deteriorate and to threaten the whole superstructure. The Christian Church should *look to her Foundation,* and clear away all that is not of Christ. No hurricane or storm will move her if she is on the Rock ; but if her dependence be upon the shifting sands of wealth, position, world-power, human learning, or other things of man, woe betide her ! 3. *Religious work.* How Paul made Christ the Foundation of his work amongst the Corinthians when he determined to know nothing but Christ and him crucified (ch. ii. 2)! When we teach we should teach Christ, when we preach we should preach Christ. Our work amongst men is not to be based upon our fancies or upon human theories, but upon Christ and his great redemptive work. We may amuse men with the fireworks of rhetoric or startling supposition, but the blaze will soon be over, and the old darkness will seem more intense than ever. If we want to bring abiding light to men, we must not divert them with pyrotechnic displays, but we must bring them to *the Sun*—the Sun of Righteousness. Much "religious work" is like a house *built upon nothing.* The marvel is, not that it should last so short a time, but that it should last *at all.* 4. *Godly life.* There is no sure foundation but this. Christ is the way to holiness. A life's labour after true excellence will be thrown away unless Christ be the Starting-point. We shall not reach God without Christ : " No man cometh unto the Father but by me " (John xiv. 6); "Without me ye can *do nothing.*" From Christ we receive power to live aright. Many seek to be godly that they may come to Christ, instead of coming to Christ that they may be godly. We have heard of the man who resolved to rear the house first and put in the foundation afterwards, but he was not a successful builder. 5. *National greatness.* A nation is truly great only in so far as it is based upon Christ and the principles which he expounded. The nations have perished one after another ; their greatness was spurious, and therefore they were ephemeral ; they rested upon that which *moved,* not upon that which is immovable—" The same yesterday, to-day, and for ever." When the nation arises which shall be founded upon Christ and his truth, its glory and greatness shall excel the palmiest days of Solomon, and it *shall abide.* Our duty as subjects is to remove from the national foundations all that is not of Christ. *Sacrifice* may be entailed, but never loss : *it is never loss to cast away the bad.*

II. HOW IT IS LAID. 1. *By human instrumentality.* At Corinth by Paul : " wise " (ver. 10) was he as a master-builder to lay this foundation, as well as wise in his manner of laying it. Here is marvellous honour conferred upon human creatures, that of laying the great foundation. We may participate in this vast privilege; we may have the high joy of laying the Foundation, Jesus Christ, in some unsaved souls. If archangels could envy, assuredly they would envy us this sublime, all-glorious work. How readily should we run to it! how gladly devote to it our every power! how unceasingly labour and pray until "Christ be formed in" those whose salvation we desire! 2. *Under Divine direction and by Divine help.* "What wisdom is here required! and of ourselves we are but foolish; what power! and we are weaklings. "Our sufficiency is of God." Only are we "wise master-builders" when we constantly look up for guidance and rely upon Omnipotence. If we do anything in this matter it can only be "according to the grace of God" (ver. 10). This grace must be sought. When received and made effective in our lives, all the glory of that which is accomplished must be ascribed to him from whom the grace has flowed.—H.

Vers. 10—15.—*Christian work and its testing.* I. CHRISTIAN WORK: 1. *Should be rightly based.* Christ is the only Foundation for the spiritual building. This Foundation may have been already laid for us by others where we are' called to labour: if so, we must see that we are building upon it; if it be not laid, by "the grace of God" (ver. 10) we must seek to lay it without delay. All our teaching must rest upon Christ. He is not only the Omega to be ended with, but the Alpha to be begun with. All our efforts will be fruitless unless identified with him. The well-constructed house built upon the sand perishes; so the most earnest and devoted labour is thrown away where Christ is ignored. The Christian builder should look carefully to his foundation. Whilst others build upon all sorts of things, he should build only upon Christ. 2. *Should be wisely ordered.* It is not enough to work; we must work wisely and well. Some seem to think that if they engage in Christian service, it is no matter how they engage in it; if the work be but done, it is no matter how it is done. Some of the most slipshod slatternly work under God's sun is done in God's Name and in connection with his kingdom. In other departments of life, care, watchfulness, anxiety, assiduity, are demanded; but in the religious sphere the thing is to get the work done somehow or other, and if it be but done somehow, all is likely to be well! Such careless builders sadly need the apostolic blast of warning: "*Let every man take heed how he buildeth*" (ver. 10). Christian work should be conformed to Christ in every particular. The superstructure should correspond to the Foundation. Epithets may go for little with us; in our teaching we should be just as "narrow" as Christ and just as "broad" as Christ. Our building will be of right dimensions if it is neither wider nor less wide than the Rock-foundation upon which it rests. As to being "old-fashioned," we need not greatly dread this if thereby we are more fully identified with our Lord; or "new-fangled," if thus we and our work are more truly after his mind. Christian work is *planned work.* As the architect has a plan for his work, so the great Architect has a plan for his work, and *for that part of his work which he entrusts to us to perform.* If we "take heed how we build," we shall take heed that we build only according to the Divine plan. Knowledge of this is to be sought in prayer and from the Divine Word. There is one way in which our life-work should be done; that way has been conceived by the Divine mind; we should seek a revelation of it. The Christian must not be his own architect. 3. In Christian work *right materials should be used.* It is not enough that we teach; we must teach the truth, and we must teach the truth *as it is in Jesus.* Our doctrine must be of Christ, and it must be *sound doctrine,* the "sincere milk" of the Word; the revelation of God, *unedited by man.* What *rubbish* has been and is taught by not a few! how much "wood, hay, stubble," placed in the great spiritual building! No wonder that the Christian soldier is so often worsted when he fights with gingerbread weapons. Shame upon men that, when the right material for labour is provided, they go hunting about for the wrong. The Scriptures are the great quarry and mine in which costly stones and gold and silver abound, and no zealous spiritual builder need lack who will search these mines.

II. CHRISTIAN WORK WILL BE TESTED. A solemn thought. *Our* work will be tested! When Christian work is done, *that is not the end of it.* It will be tried. Well may we ask: 1. *When?* On "the day," says the apostle. Christian work is tested on many days. Much of it does not stand the test of these days. But on *the* day—the day of days—the judgment day—all shall be *tested* and *finally* tested. "Each man's work shall be made manifest;" its *true character* will then be seen. "The day shall declare it" *as it is*, not as it has been thought to be. *Now* it may look well; but *then?* A veil now rests upon Christian work, then the veil shall be taken away; now the scaffolding obscures the building, then it shall fall, and then shall be seen "of what sort" the building is. The *final test* cannot be escaped from. 2. *How?* By "fire." (Not by the fires of purgatory; the apostle speaks of fire applied to *work*, not to *persons*,—not *remedial*, but *testing*.) The test will be *thorough, searching, perfectly efficient*. The false work will stand this test when hay and wood and stubble can abide unchanged in the flame; but not till then. Our work may look well now, but how will it bear the fire-test? 3. *By whom?* God. At the great day he will be Judge, and will try every man's work. *He will apply the fire-test.* He loves *truth* and hates *lies*, which we call *shams*. On that day he will manifest *the truth* concerning work done in his Name. Whatever it has seemed before, it will then seem *as it really is*. The careless and the false may well tremble at the thought of this ordeal; but the sincere and faithful may have confidence; for as no work then will be made to appear better than it is, *none will be made to appear worse*.

III. THE ISSUES OF THE TESTING OF CHRISTIAN WORK. 1. *As to the work tested.* Some will stand. The pessimists will then be ashamed; railers and mockers will then be silenced. There is some work (and who shall say that it is little?) which will approve itself to God, and stand the final and most searching trial. This, doubtless, will be the work done in Divine strength, and, whilst the doers of it will rejoice with exceeding joy, they will as assuredly cry, "Not unto us." Some work will not stand the test. As hay and wood and stubble are speedily consumed in the fire, so this work will perish in the last testing flames. To see a life-work destroyed in a day! A life lived and no fruit. No "Well done" because all has been ill done. And perhaps all through carelessness, sluggishness, self-reliance, inattention to the "mind of Christ." Sad, sad close of a "Christian course." 2. *As to workers.* Some shall "receive a reward;" their work has borne the test. Though they say truly that this reward is "unmerited," they shall have it. "Doth Job serve God for nought?" Certainly not; no man ever did or shall. We lose nothing by labouring for Christ; and note that we lose nothing by labouring *thoroughly* for him. We may lose by labouring *half-heartedly*—we may lose our reward. It is best every way to do our best in Christ's service. Some receive no reward. Their work perishes and they "suffer loss," but they themselves are saved, "yet so as by fire," *i.e.* barely, with difficulty. The reference is to those who hold fundamental truths (for they are supposed to build on the one Foundation, ver. 12), but who mingle with their teaching the wood, hay, and stubble of human notions. Strikingly are we here taught that salvation is not of works; for the works perish, but the salvation abides. Doubtless we must suppose that in such cases there is true Christian living and a real desire to do the Master's will; for these are necessary evidences of a saved, regenerate state; but the vital truth of salvation by faith is pointedly illustrated by the chief works of the life (upon which all would have been resting if salvation were of works) suffering ignominious rejection. Being saved "so as by fire" is in striking contrast to "the abundant entrance." May we have the ecstatic joy of the latter, and the holy gladness which comes from seeing that we have not "lived in vain"!—H.

Vers. 16, 17.—*God's temple.* Declared to be the Church of Christ. Each community of Christians is a temple of God. The old temple has perished; this is the new and the imperishable. The Christian Church has often been insignificant in numbers, wealth, position, earthly learning; men have despised her; judged by human standards she has appeared contemptible; but the Divine thought has been this—*the temple of God!*

I. RESEMBLANCES. 1. *Erected under Divine direction.* The old and new temples are of God; they express his thought and purpose. Believers who constitute the new temple become believers through him; for faith is the gift of God. They are gathered into the Church as spiritual stones, by his servants, under his direction, and each has an appropriate place. God is the Author of the constitution of the Church. 2. *Erected for the Divine glory.* The supreme object. Everything in the Church to be made subservient to this. To glorify God should be the life-object of the redeemed. And: 3. *Erected for the welfare of men.* The temple of old was for God and also for man. The Church has a great mission to the world. There is no conflict between the two objects. As the Church seeks to save the lost, she is most truly seeking to bring glory to God. Her *worship* is likely to be a mockery unless her *work* is faithfully performed. 4. *Set apart for God.* The Church should be *separate, holy, peculiarly God's.* "A peculiar people—a people for God's own possession" (1 Pet. ii. 9); "Ye are not your own." 5. *An object of beauty.* The beauty of holiness should clothe the Church. The world's admiration has often been commanded, in early days and since. And better still, God has approved. 6. *Of great variety in its parts.* Vast diversity in gift and condition, but one spiritual building. In the Christian Church there cannot, perhaps, be too much variety as there certainly cannot be too much oneness. 7. *The dwelling-place of God.* Not only *for* God, but God's dwelling-place. This was the glory of the Jewish temple—the Shechinah—the Divine presence. The Church's joy and glory are that "God is in the midst of her." He dwells not now in temples made with hands, though he does dwell in the temples made by the Divine hands. The ancient temple was unmeaning and useless without the presence of Jehovah. So is the Christian Church: "Ye also are builded together for a habitation of God through the Spirit" (Eph. ii. 22). 8. *From it true worship should arise.* Sanctuary worship, home worship, business worship, recreation worship, worship throughout all the life of those who constitute the temple. 9. *In it should ever be the great sacrifice.* Not the sacrifice of the Mass, but "Christ crucified" manifestly set forth. The temple of old would have been offensive to God without sacrifice, so we cannot be acceptable to him without the atonement. When the Church loses the cross she loses God. In every Christian community there must be a Calvary. And the true Jerusalem has not its Calvary "without the gate;" Christ crucified is central, chief, predominant.

II. PUNISHMENT FOR INJURY. Aaronic priests who violated the ancient temple were doomed to death; injurers of the Church of Christ will meet a terrible fate. In ver. 17 the Greek verb, which means "to bring into a worse state," is repeated; what we do to the Church, God will do to us—if we injure it, he will injure us. At Corinth the dividers of the Church were likely to become destroyers, and so God will "destroy." These are far more serious offenders than those named in vers. 12 and 15. God is jealous over his temple, and men may not do evil to it with impunity. Those who sin against it sin directly against him. Note: We may injure the temple of God in many ways. For example, by (1) false doctrine; (2) unchristian spirit; (3) personal unholiness; (4) conniving at unholiness in others; (5) failing to do our part; (6) failing to take our place in the Church.

III. HOW CAREFUL WE SHOULD BE IN ALL THAT CONCERNS THIS TEMPLE. In Church life and Church work. How serious are these! in them there is no room for trifling. Alas! how many are living in the Church, and even labouring in it, who seem to feel little or no responsibility! Let us realize what this Church is, and then assuredly with more care than the Aaronic priests shall we comport ourselves. To avoid offence and injury and failure, we shall need the wisdom that cometh down from above (vers. 18—20).—H.

Vers. 21—23.—*The believer's possessions.* I. WHAT THESE ARE. 1. *Ministers.* The Corinthians had made a strange mistake; they had been regarding ministers as *masters*, and choosing which they preferred to serve. In a singular loss of dignity (singular because many of them were not a little afflicted with pride) they had become ambitious of belonging to ministers, forgetting that ministers, *as such*, belonged to them. Ministers are the servants of the Church, and thus among the believer's possessions; instead of quarrelling over them, he should use and enjoy them. God has greatly enriched his people by sending to them many able and faithful ministers. Whilst these should be highly esteemed for their work's sake, their true relation to the Church should never be lost sight of. *They* should bear it in mind, and thus check any tendencies towards lordship. 2. *The world.* It is generally thought that the world belongs to the Wicked One and his children, seeing that it appears to be largely in their hands. This is a popular blunder. The world was *made* and is *kept* for the people of God. Unbelievers have *no right* to the things which they grasp. The ungodly hold their possessions upon a precarious tenure. They are very short leaseholders, or rather they are tenants-at-will. Believers are the freeholders, and at last " the meek shall inherit the earth." The child of God has not yet " come of age; " but his title is good, and now he enjoys as much of his inheritance as is good for him in his present state. But as believers look at the world they can say, " It is ours—all of it, and all things in it work together for our good." Cowper says—

> " The Christian looks abroad into the varied field
> Of nature, and, though poor perhaps compar'd
> With those whose mansions glitter in his sight,
> Calls the delightful scenery all his own.
> His are the mountains, and the valleys his,
> And the resplendent rivers; his t' enjoy
> With a propriety that none can feel
> But who, with filial confidence inspir'd,
> Can lift to heaven an unpresumptuous eye,
> And smiling say, 'My Father made them all.' "

3. *Life.* Without Christ there is nothing worthy of the name of *life.* *Life* is emphatically the believer's. What possibilities it has for him! how vast are his opportunities! Pity it is that some believers seem only half alive to this. The child of God has in life the experience most likely to benefit him: mercies, joys, trials, temptations, pains— all his, to do him good. The lives of others are also controlled for the welfare of the redeemed. 4. *Death.* Death, a precious possession. The entrance to the life immortal. Death conquered has become the believer's servant. Death, the dire loss of the impenitent, the great gain of the saints. The death of those outside the Church is ordered for the well-being of those within. God strikes down the foes of his people when the right hour has come. 5. *Things present.* The present order and movement in the world; all governments and powers; the march of the ages;—all these things are made subservient to the great work of redemption. " God moves in a mysterious way," *but always moves for his people.* 6. *Things to come.* Not only the present order of the world, but *the future.* Believers often tremble for what is coming; the Church quakes, for she dreads some future movement, glimmerings of which she can discern, perhaps, in the present. But God is in the future, giving that future to his people. All discoveries, all increase of knowledge, all progress, shall be for the weal of Zion : " The mouth of the Lord hath spoken it." And the believer reckons amongst things to come, the heavenly world, the life immortal, the higher service, the perfected nature, the unsullied joy. All these are his. How rich, how blessed, is he! 7. *All things.* Marvellous truth, that there is nothing of which he can say, " It is not mine."

II. SECURED BY THE BELIEVER'S CONNECTION WITH CHRIST. Believers are Christ's. His servants? yes; his friends? yes; but his " brethren," and thus " heirs " with him —" joint-heirs with Christ " (Rom. viii. 17). Christ is God's. All that the Father hath is the Son's. All that the Son hath belongs to those that are his; and this is " all things." What an amazing transformation, then, there is in conversion! The unsaved has nothing; the saved, " all things." Are we unutterably poor or infinitely rich? The question is answered when another is: " Are we Christ's?"—H.

Vers. 1—9.—*Christian teachers and their work.* The apostle has still in view the dissensions prevailing in the Corinthian Church. Throughout the first four chapters this subject is never absent from his mind, even when it is most in the background. The spirit of party, with the various phases of thought and life that found expression therein, suggests the several topics on which he enlarges.

I. THE CHRISTIAN TEACHER ADAPTS HIS TEACHING TO THE CAPACITIES OF HIS HEARERS. (Vers. 1—4.) Paul has already said (ch. ii. 6) that he " spake wisdom among the perfect," and here he presents the other side. 1. At Corinth he had to deal with *carnal Christians.* In the last verses of the previous chapter he has contrasted the natural man and the spiritual man, the latter alone being able to discern the things of the Spirit. Here the comparison is not between Christians and non-Christians, but between different classes of Christians, distinguished according to spiritual attainment. Every believer in Christ is a spiritual man as compared with those who do not believe;

but one believer may be carnal in comparison with another believer. The new nature may be weak and sickly and all but overlaid by the old. This was the case with the Corinthians, whose fleshliness of mind appeared in the prevalence of " jealousy and strife " and of party spirit. These things spring from the flesh (Gal. v. 20), wherever they are found. When the Church is rent by faction, and men think mainly of the aggrandizement of their favourite party, no further proof is needed of the reign of carnality. "The fruit of the Spirit is love, peace." A fleshly Christian ! What opposites must we unite in describing real character ! 2. They were as yet " *babes in Christ.*" Conversion is a new birth : young converts are new-born babes (1 Pet. ii. 2). They have in germ all that is to be found in the full-grown man ; but they are weak, dependent, immature. Young Christians have the rudiments of the Christian character in more or less clear outline, but only the rudiments. Infancy is beautiful in its season, and so is the young life of the new convert ; but out of season, its beauty is gone. A child with the years of a man is a monstrosity in nature ; an old Christian with the crudeness of a young convert should appear to us as great a monstrosity in grace. The "babe in Christ" is meant to develop into " a full-grown man, into the measure of the stature of the fulness of Christ" (Eph. iv. 13). 3. As babes, they must be fed "with *milk, not with meat.*" Infants and men must each have food suitable to their capacity. The doctrines of the faith may be presented in the form of milk or of solid food. Milk has in it all the nourishing elements to be found in strong meat, though in more diluted form. The facts of the gospel history contain all the truths of the most elaborate theological system ; a child can digest them in the one form, but not in the other. Every wise teacher will adapt his teaching to the capacity of his hearers. He will give to each only such food as he can receive and assimilate. He will not give solid food to infants, nor will he feed full-grown men merely with milk. The preacher should consider the wants of women and children, as well as of men, and adapt some part of the public service to them (comp. Heb. v. 12—14).

II. MINISTERS ARE GOD'S SERVANTS, NOT PARTY LEADERS. The childish condition of the Corinthians was shown in their party divisions. They gloried more in the leader after whom their faction was called than in Jesus Christ. To correct this the apostle presents the right view of spiritual teachers and their work. 1. *Ministers are but servants.* They are not heads of sects or schools, whose object is to gather disciples for themselves. They are servants of God, doing his work. Therefore they are not to be lifted above their position, as they are when they are regarded as masters in the Church ; nor are they to sink below it, as they do when they take the law from any other but God. 2. *Each minister has his own peculiar work.* " I planted, Apollos watered." Paul began the work at Corinth ; Apollos continued it. One minister is sent to preach the gospel to sinners, another to edify believers, another to teach the ignorant, another to comfort the sorrowful ; but all are contributors to the same great interest. The servant's work, however, is but a subordinate instrumentality. Planting and watering are the ordinary conditions of growth, but they do not of themselves cause growth. It is " God that giveth the increase." In the spiritual sphere, as in the natural, the life-giving power is Divine ; but in both cases this power usually works through human ministries. It is only in connection with diligent planting and watering that we can expect the increase. 3. *Each minister has his own peculiar reward.* All are one, inasmuch as all are servants of one Lord and engaged about the same work. Hence they are not to be set against each other as rivals. Their work is one, yet diverse ; and so is their reward. No faithful servant shall go without a recompense at his Master's hand ; but each shall receive his own, alike in kind and in degree. The principle that determines this is—" according to his own labour." It is not according to the fruit or result of our labour, but simply according to the measure of our labour. What reversals of human opinion are in store for us ! Men applaud success ; God praises fidelity. Many an obscure but faithful worker shall receive a greater reward than he who has been less faithful but more prominent and successful. 4. *Ministers are God's fellow-workers.* All God's servants are fellow-servants as workers for him ; but here the fellowship is carried still higher. We are workers along with God, who is pleased to associate us with himself in the great work of his kingdom. What a thought is this! (1) What dignity it gives to the Christian ministry ! It is to work with God. (2) How inspiring to the Christian worker ! Who would not labour when God is with him? (3) How sure the reward! Will God leave his fellow-workers without a due recompense?

III. BELIEVERS ARE GOD'S FIELD. The same idea is elsewhere expressed under the figure of a garden (Isa. lviii. 11) and a vineyard (Isa. v.). Consider: 1. *The Proprietor of the field.* The Church is *God's* field. It is not the Church of Paul, or Apollos, or any other; but "the Church of God, which he purchased with his own blood" (Acts xx. 28). It belongs to him; it exists for him; it is called by his Name. Hence the spirit of faction, which ranges parties and sects under the names of rival leaders, robs God of his glory as the Church's Lord. 2. *The labourers in the field.* These are apostles, evangelists, pastors, teachers, etc. (see above). 3. *The field itself.* (1) *Its original condition.* Wild, untilled, full of merely natural growths. Believers are originally a part of the world, living in a state of sin, under no gracious culture. (2) *The work bestowed upon it.* Preparatory work: trenching, ploughing, gathering out stones, fencing; and then the sowing of seed, planting, weeding, etc. Corresponding to this there is a preparation of heart for receiving the truth, an awakening to a sense of sin and need, a quickening into spiritual life, a culture of the new life into fulness and strength, etc. For these ends every true labourer works, but always in dependence on the power of the Holy Spirit, who alone can make our labour fruitful. (3) *Its produce.* The farmer looks for a return from his field in the form of fruit in harvest; God expects his Church to yield fruit to his glory. Christian character, life, usefulness, productiveness,—these are some of the returns for which the Lord of the field looks (comp. Luke xiii. 6—9; John xv. 1, etc.).—B.

Vers. 10—15.—*The Foundation and the superstructure.* Under the figure of a building, the apostle continues to speak of the work of Christ's ministers, and specially of his own labours at Corinth. As the first to preach the gospel there, he had laid the foundation, upon which the teachers that succeeded him were to build. The reference is primarily to doctrine, but the principles apply to work and life as well.

I. THE FOUNDATION. This is Jesus Christ the Mediator (Isa. xxviii. 16; 1 Pet. ii. 6). He is the Foundation *of truth:* the system of Christian theology is built upon him. All Christian teaching and preaching must have him for their basis. The entire structure of knowledge rests upon him who is the Source of all wisdom. He is also the Foundation *of life.* The Church is built upon him, believers being "living stones" in the great spiritual temple. In both these respects Jesus Christ is: 1. A *Divine* Foundation. "Behold *I* lay." The Church requires a basis laid by God himself. 2. A *sure* Foundation. No work of God can fail. Jesus Christ is a Foundation, not of sand, but of solid rock (Matt. vii. 24—27). It will bear any strain, even the weight of a world. 3. The *only* Foundation. This is the point emphasized here. Men build on other foundations when they rest their systems of belief on human opinion, or base their hope of heaven upon their own works, the merits of others, the general mercy of God, etc. But "other foundation can (δύναται) no man lay;" there is but one.

II. THE SUPERSTRUCTURE. Having found the true Foundation, we must "take heed how we build thereon." The work of ministers or of believers in general is here viewed as the superstructure. Two kinds of materials may be employed: "gold, silver, costly stones"—the beautiful and lasting materials, suited for a temple; or "wood, hay, stubble"—the baser and more perishable materials, fit only for a temporary house. Apply this to: 1. *Doctrine.* The "gold," etc., represents pure, scriptural teaching. Take Paul's Epistles, *e.g.,* as a noble structure of truth built on Jesus Christ. Such doctrine is precious and abiding, like its Foundation. The "wood," etc., represents human opinions and speculations put in the place of God's truth. In Paul's time, Jewish tradition, Gnosticism, etc.; in ours, Popery, Ritualism, etc. Such doctrines are not truly *edifying.* 2. *Life.* The "gold," etc., is a Christian life of the noblest kind, built out of faith, hope, love. Pure, unselfish, Christ-like character. Variety may be indicated in the three materials. *Gold* may denote the most brilliant service rendered by consecrated genius, heroic faith, patient suffering. *Silver* may indicate a work less brilliant, but useful—the honest doing of the Lord's will. *Costly stones*—marble or granite, *e.g.*—a life of solidity and strength, on which others may lean. Each of these classes has its own place and value. All are genuine. The "wood," etc., is a Christian life of the poorest kind. Dull as *wood,* with little spiritual insight. Swayed by

public opinion, as the *grass* by every breeze.   Barren as *stubble*, bringing forth little
to the glory of God.   What differences in the lives of Christians!   Gold or stubble :
which ?

III. THE FIERY TRIAL.   The true nature of our life and work is not always seen here.
We judge wrongly of others and of ourselves.   Men praise the wood as if it were gold ;
depreciate the gold as if it were wood.   But "*the day* shall declare it "—*Dies iræ, dies
illa*—the day of fire, when Christ comes to judge (Mal. iii. 2, 3 ; iv. 1 ; 2 Thess. i. 8).
Time tests but partially ; the thorough test is the judgment-fire.   Shall our work stand
that ?   1. *The edifice of " gold," etc., shall stand.*   Truth will come through the fire ;
so will a genuine, unselfish, Christly life.   Work for time perishes ; work for eternity
endures.   The fiery ordeal will only bring out more clearly its true quality.   The
builder shall receive a reward in seeing his work abide (Phil. ii. 16), in being recognized as a good workman (Matt. xxv. 21), and in wearing the crown of life (Jas. i.
12).   Observe, the reward is not for being on the Foundation, but for what is built
thereon.   Salvation is of free grace ; the reward is " according as his work " (Rev. xxii.
12).   2. *The structure of " wood," etc., shall be burned up.*   Error, falsehood, unreality ;
a life animated by a worldly, selfish spirit ;—these shall be consumed.   The builder is
glad to get away with his life, as one escapes from a house in flames, saved " so as
through fire."   Picture the consternation of the poor builder as he sees the fire doing
its awful work, and hears the crash of his life-structure !   He himself is saved for
Christ's sake, but his labour is lost.

LESSONS.   1. See to the nature of your life and work as Christians.   Apply specially
to Christian workers.   2. Be not satisfied with bare salvation at last.   Build with
materials that will endure.   Have an eye to the "full reward " (2 John 8).   3. If
many on the true Foundation shall be saved only " so as through fire," how shall they
escape that are building on a false foundation ? (1 Pet. iv. 17, 18).—B.

Vers. 16, 17.—*The temple of God.*   Paul again takes up the idea of a building and
gives it a new direction.   The noblest of all edifices is a temple in which architecture
finds its highest and worthiest employment.   Under this figure the apostle sets forth
sometimes the collective Church of Christ, sometimes the individual believer (ch. vi.
19 ; Eph. ii. 21).   Man was created to be a sanctuary of God, but this sanctuary was
overturned by sin.   It lay in ruins till the Lord Jesus came as the Restorer, whose
work it is to rebuild the ruined walls ; and now the temple is seen rising in its fair
proportions in the hearts of the regenerated, and in the spiritual house built of these
living stones (1 Pet. ii. 5).

I. BELIEVERS ARE GOD'S TEMPLE.   1. *God dwells in them.*   The temple at Jerusalem
was Jehovah's dwelling-place.   There he had his Shechinah in the cloud above the
mercy-seat and between the cherubim, and there he was worshipped.   Even so "the
Spirit of God dwelleth in you."   The Father and the Son make their abode with
the man who loves and obeys the Son (John xiv. 23), and this is effected by the Spirit.
This indwelling is the culmination of the work of grace within us.   The heart must
first be quickened, renewed, purified, ere the Holy Spirit can dwell in it.   How wonderful
a truth is this !   God in me !   It is not the dream of the pantheist, who calls me a
spark from the eternal fire—God dwelling in me because I am only a mode of the one
universal existence.   It is not the raving of the mystic, whose imagination has betrayed
him into a hazy confusion of ideas regarding his relation to God.   It is the utterance
of sober truth.   In me the creature—the new creature—God the Creator makes his
abode ; not, indeed, in the infinity of his being, as if our tiny vessels could contain the
ocean, yet really.   The little flower-cup has the sun dwelling in it all the day, though
he dwells in thousands besides ; and his presence is made known by the colour and
fragrance and growth of the flower.   The same Spirit of God who abides in the Church
abides in every true member of it ; and this abiding is revealed in the love shed abroad
in the heart, in the odour that breathes through the life, and in the gracious bending
of the nature to all that is righteous.   2. *They are holy.*   As the place where Jehovah
dwelt, the Jewish temple was holy—consecrated to him, and to him alone.   None but
an Israelite could tread the outer court ; none but the priests could serve in the holy
place ; none but the high priest could enter the holy of holies.   Believers are holy,
set apart for God and his service.   They are not a public street or common, which the

world may use as it likes; they are a sacred enclosure, marked off and devoted to holy uses. They are God's temple—body, soul, and spirit corresponding to the three divisions of the ancient tabernacle. This applies also to the Church, which is holy because dwelt in by God.

II. GOD'S TEMPLE MUST NOT BE MARRED. This follows from what has been said. If God dwells in believers, an injury done to them is done to his sanctuary. Consider: 1. *How the temple may be marred.* Sin in every form pollutes and injures the soul. It is an outrage on God's temple. The Holy Spirit cannot dwell with unholiness. More particularly: (1) *By setting up idols.* To place any person or thing beside God is to be guilty of idolatry. He will not dwell in the temple where other gods are worshipped; it is polluted (Isa. xlii. 8; 1 John v. 21). (2) *By throwing it open to all.* The temple was holy ground, which none but consecrated feet might tread. The heart of the believer is not to be flung open to the world or to unholy thoughts and desires; the Church is not to act on worldly principles, or employ carnal means, or seek secular ends. All such intruders defile God's temple (John ii. 14—17). 2. *The penalty threatened against those that mar God's temple.* He who defiled God's sanctuary was punished by death (Lev. xv. 31; comp. Numb. xix. 20). He who destroys God's spiritual temple shall himself be destroyed. The grieved Spirit will depart and spiritual death will ensue. A warning to Christians against espousing error, or practising sin, or cherishing party spirit. A warning to teachers lest, by preaching false doctrine or fomenting strife, they incur this awful punishment. How watchful should we be over our own hearts! How careful should we be in our treatment of fellow-Christians!—B.

Vers. 18—20.—*The way to wisdom.* "Wisdom" is one of the key-words of these early chapters of the Epistle. Here again the contrast between true and false wisdom appears in the form of a warning against self-conceit. "Let no man deceive himself."
I. TO BE WISE WE MUST FIRST BECOME FOOLS. The wisdom of this world has its uses within its own sphere, but it is no help to the understanding of the things of God. It is a hindrance which must be removed ere we can learn the Divine wisdom. We must divest ourselves of our fancied wisdom and become fools in our own eyes, in order to be spiritually wise. This is a general law. Pride or self-conceit in regard to any branch of knowledge or art is an effectual bar to progress. We must confess our ignorance in order to knowledge, our weakness in order to strength, our folly in order to wisdom. "He that humbleth himself shall be exalted." This truth holds: 1. *As to the beginning of the Christian life.* How often are anxious souls kept back from entering into peace because they will not renounce their own ideas of the way of salvation! Only when they submit entirely to God's way as little children do they enter the kingdom. 2. *As to progress in the Christian life.* Even after conversion we must be careful "to bring every thought into captivity to the obedience of Christ" (2 Cor. x. 5). We can grow in spiritual insight, in holiness, in patience, in power for service, in faith and hope and love, only by esteeming ourselves foolish and being content to sit as learners at the Lord's feet.
II. THE WISDOM OF THIS WORLD IS FOOLISHNESS. This explains why our own wisdom must be renounced. In the judgment of the All-wise it is folly. The speculations of men regarding God and our relation to him, however much of truth they contain, are yet on the whole vain, inasmuch as they fail to reach an adequate knowledge of him. Those who have worked the longest at the great problems of life are the readiest to confess this. One after another of the world's wise men have wrestled with them and passed them down to their successors unsolved. Or look at the schemes of men for the regeneration of the world. Education, æsthetic culture, the teaching of morality, social communism, religion made easy,—all have been tried and found wanting. None of them can redeem mankind from sin and restore them to their lost dignity. And in nothing do men seem so foolish as just in those things in which they think themselves wise. They are caught in their own net. Their schemes of salvation work their ruin.—B.

Vers. 21—23.—*The Christian's heritage.* Since the wisdom of men is foolishness, and even the ministers of Divine wisdom are but servants, all glorying in men is to be avoided. Boast not in this one or that, however eminent; for all such boasting is a degradation to one who is possessed of so rich an inheritance.

I. IT IS UNIVERSAL. "All things are yours." Man's original lordship over creation (Ps. viii. 6) has been lost by sin, but is now restored in Christ. All things exist for the Christian; all things co-operate for his good (Rom. viii. 28).

> "For us the winds do blow;
> The earth doth rest, heaven move, and fountains flow.
> No thing we see but means our good,
> As our delight, or as our treasure:
> The whole is, either our cupboard of food,
> Or cabinet of pleasure.

> "Oh, mighty love! Man is one world, and hath
> Another to attend him."
>
> (George Herbert.)

1. *All teachers* belong to the Christian. The Church was not made for Paul, or Apollos, or Cephas; but these have been given to the Church for its planting and watering and culture. The ministers of Christ are workmen employed in erecting God's temple. One lays the foundation, another hews the stones, another carves the ornaments, another does the carpenter-work, etc. All are working for the same end, each in his own department. Why should we set the one against the other, as if the mason were everything and the carpenter nothing? You have your favourite apostle: do not neglect the practical James, because you delight in the fervid, argumentative Paul; or the dogmatic Peter, because you love the calm, intuitive John. Learn from Christian men of various schools and denominations, whom God sends with a message to their generation. All are yours. 2. *The world.* This denotes the material universe and all its providential arrangements. However evil men may usurp possession meanwhile, it is the saints that inherit the earth (Matt. v. 5). It is maintained for their use, ordered with a view to their welfare, and in the end they shall be its sole possessors. The world, with all its forces and all its treasures, lies at their feet. All has been given to make life happier and better, and to help us to glorify our Father in heaven. 3. *Life and death.* The term of our sojourn on the earth, with all that it brings, is ours. Life is a mighty gift—a great field in which to sow eternal seed. It is ours for two great purposes—for *being* and *doing.* The culture of the new life within us, and the promotion of our neighbour's well-being,—in these two directions life is our opportunity. "To me to live is Christ." There are ways of promoting God's glory which are peculiar to this life, and which can never come to us again. *Death* also is ours as well as life. That grim, horrid thing, whose face strikes terror to the stoutest heart, and whose icy grasp freezes the fountains of life,—that, too, becomes our servant. As the sailor conquers the winds by making them propel his vessel, so death ministers to our advancement. "To die is gain." It releases from the pains, and toils, and conflicts, and limitations of this mortal state, and ushers us into the enjoyment of our inheritance. 4. *Things present and things to come.* The present and the future in the most comprehensive sense. Our actual lot is ours, whether it be easy or hard, pleasant or distressing. It is ours to serve us, if we will only let it do its work and turn it to the best account. The future is still hid from us, but it can bring us nothing which shall not work for our good. Whatever form the things to come may take, we are assured that they are ours.

II. THE TITLE IS GOOD. "Ye are Christ's; and Christ is God's." All things are ours only because we belong to Christ. He has recovered for man his lost sovereignty, and in him we receive what he has won for us. The crown is again placed on our heads; we become joint-heirs with Christ (Rom viii. 17), who is Heir of all things (Heb. i. 2). Apart from him we have no title. And belonging to Christ, we belong to God; for "Christ is God's." As the Son of God manifest in flesh for the redemption of his people, he is the Father's Servant, delighting to do his will; whilst at the same time he is the Father's equal (ch. xi. 3; xv. 28). Mark the successive steps of this great ladder of being. All things are subject to the saints; the saints are subject to Christ their Head; Christ as Mediator is subject to the Father.

LESSONS. 1. Be not subject to men; Christ is your Head. 2. How valid is the believer's title to his glorious heritage! 3. Reckon up your possessions in Christ; claim them as your own; and all earthly wealth and dignity will fail to dazzle you.—B.

Ver. 9.—"*God's husbandry.*" The leading truth in the context would seem to be this —that the most honoured and most successful worker in the kingdom of Christ is but as a helpless instrument through which the living power is pleased to operate, and that power is in God alone. The name of God, therefore, occupies the emphatic place in each clause of this verse. "*Of God* ye are the husbandry." This is spoken of the Corinthians, not so much as individual believers, but as an organized Christian society. Observe the view it gives us of—

I. THE NATURE OF A CHRISTIAN CHURCH. It is God's "tilled land." Not so much the process of husbandry, but the field in which the process is wrought out, is here intended. Every organized Christian society is the sphere of a spiritual culture analogous to that which goes on in the realm of nature, in the gardens, the vineyards, and the corn-fields. Two or three distinct elements of thought are suggested. 1. *There is the idea of a germ of Divine life implanted in the hearts of men.* The course of nature's husbandry proceeds on the law that when the seed-corn, in which the mysterious principle of vegetable life is hidden, is brought into contact with certain quickening and nourishing elements of the soil, it will germinate and be productive. The step of primary importance is the planting of the seed in the ground, because that establishes the necessary connection between the latent forces that combine to work out the desired result. So in the higher sphere of man's moral life. The "truth as it is in Jesus" is the productive germ, in which, beneath the husk of the literal verbal form, is hidden the very spirit and life of God. And the condition of its unfolding is that it should be brought into real, direct, living contact with the soul (Matt. xiii. 23; Jas. i. 21; 1 Pet. i. 23). There is no uncertainty in the result when the needful conditions are supplied. The Church is God's "tilled land." "The field is the world;" but then the world has its "wayside" and its "stony and thorny places;" the "good ground" is composed of those who, "in an honest and good heart," are prepared to receive the imperishable seed of the kingdom. 2. *The development of this germ by external culture.* The husbandry of the earth is man's effort to supply the most favourable conditions for the working out of nature's great productive law. Churches exist to promote, as far as possible, the operation of the spiritual law. Social life generally, with all its relations and activities, is no doubt intended by God to be helpful to this. We rise to the true, broad idea of religious culture only when we look on them all as auxiliaries to the great work of spiritual enlargement and enrich-ment. But the Church relationship, by all its conditions of fellowship, worship, and work, is specially fitted to accomplish this end. Spiritual culture is the primary purpose of its existence. The ideal may not always be reached. As the earth has its frigid and temperate and torrid zones, so Christian societies differ as to the kindliness of their soil and atmosphere for the development of the germs of spiritual life. But this is their Divine intent—that they should be nurseries of all truth and goodness, where everything that is best and noblest and loveliest in men may be fostered and brought to perfection. 3. *The production of the appropriate fruits.* All labour is for the sake of the "profit" that can be got out of it. Seed-sowing, "planting and water-ing," point on to the harvest. One harvest lays the foundation for another and a greater. The "increase" is the end of all. "Herein is my Father glorified, that ye bear much fruit" (John xv. 8). "These things [good works] are good and profitable to men" (Titus iii. 8). Churches exist for the production of the fruits of Divine goodness, with all the added force and fulness that social unity can give. They answer their end only so far as spiritual power goes forth from them, and they are felt to be centres and sources of blessing to the world, producing something that shall make it richer and happier than it would otherwise have been, something that shall never die.

II. THE RELATION BETWEEN DIVINE AND HUMAN AGENCY IN THE DEVELOPMENT OF THE LIFE OF THE CHURCH. "God's husbandry." Divine *proprietorship* is an important truth involved here, but Divine *activity* is no doubt the more prominent. The field not only belongs to God, so that none dare claim any kind of "lordship" over it; but it is one in which God is the great Worker. The process wrought out in it is the result of his productive power, and, as far as the vital part of it is concerned, of his alone. Man is nothing; God is "all in all" (ver. 7). But the instrument has its needful and proper place. God works out his beneficent ends through the intervention of man's own willing co-operation, and in this lies for man himself an infinite benediction. He might have made the earth to yield its fruits without any culture of ours; but would that have been a merciful arrangement? In those parts of the earth where there is the nearest approach to such a condition of things, human life is always found to be in a state the most degraded. Labour is the law of man's being. And though that labour, through the curse of sin, presents too often the aspect of irksome toil, yet still it is a "sublime necessity," the indispensable condition of physical health and happiness. In the spiritual sphere, too, God would have us to be "fellow-workers" with himself. He will not accomplish his beneficent purposes without us. He employs us as the channels and vehicles of his power. His working in us is the motive and the inspiration of our working for him. "Work out your own salvation with fear and trembling; for," etc. (Phil. ii. 12, 13). We can expect to see the blessed issue only when we place ourselves as ready and prepared instruments in his hands. But never may we forget that the power is his and not ours.

> "Should e'er his wonder-working grace
> Triumph through our weak arm,
> Let not our sinful fancy trace
> Aught human in the charm."

                                                                W.

Ver. 11.—*The one Foundation.* It is of the personal, not the doctrinal, Christ that the apostle here speaks—of Christ, not so much as the basis of a system of religious teaching, but as himself the living Foundation of living souls. Look at this Foundation in two or three different lights.

I. As THE GROUND OF THE SINNER'S HOPE OF SALVATION. "Neither is there salvation in any other: for there is none other Name," etc. (Acts iv. 12). The apostles never diverged in the slightest degree from this testimony. To have done this would have been to preach no gospel to men at all, but only to flatter them with a false, delusive hope. The reason of Paul's unyielding fidelity to the simplicity of his gospel message at Corinth and everywhere else, lay in his deep sense of the fact that, in whatever land or age or grade of social life a man may be found, whatever the level of his civilization or intellectual culture, "Christ crucified" can alone meet his spiritual necessities. And he would pay just as little respect to our dreams of self-sufficiency as he did to those of the men of his own times; for they have just as little solid ground to rest upon. Our nature is the same as theirs. Our spiritual needs are the same. There is the same insatiable craving within us, the same guilt on our consciences, the same seeds of corruption latent in our hearts, the same moral dangers besetting the pathway of our life. The same eternal spirit-world surrounds us, and we must confront the same "righteous judgment of God." What can we do but cast our souls, with all the wealth of their affections and the weight of their immortal interests, on Christ? What other "refuge" have we but the "hope set before us in the gospel"?

II. THE BASIS OF ALL TRUE SPIRITUAL ONENESS AND FELLOWSHIP AMONG MEN. The Church at Corinth had become a distracted and divided communion. It failed to maintain the "unity of the spirit in the bond of peace." St. Paul knew well where the secret of this lay. As a "wise master-builder," he saw at once that the breach, the disruption in the house was caused by some fault in its relation to the Foundation on which it was supposed to rest. In spite of all his care, the superstructure had not been based with sufficient firmness upon that. He calls them back to the principle and ground of their unity. They were divided because they had in some way wandered from it, had slipped off from it, lost their hold on it. The uniting principle had become less to them than the forces that rend asunder. *There is no real, living, lasting union among men, except on the basis of a common life in Christ.* There are appearances, shadows of it, approximations to it more or less near, but not the Divine reality. Think of those associations into which men enter for purposes of commerce, personal enrichment, science, pleasure, politics, philanthropy; the oneness of a nation in its devotion to the throne and constitution; of an army in the enthusiasm of its service; of a popular assembly under the spell of some commanding influence; the oneness even of a family, with its identity of interest and interchange of natural affection;—what are all these forms of unity compared with that of souls that are bound together in the fellowship of the eternal life of Christ, members of his body, and therefore "members one of another"? The true brotherhood, which men seek elsewhere in vain, they find in the Church ransomed by the blood of Christ and built on him as its eternal Foundation.

III. THE ROOT OF AN ENDURING PERSONAL RIGHTEOUSNESS. In what the apostle afterwards says of the different ways in which men "build," he probably has religious teachers and the quality of their teaching specially in view. But we may also apply it to the quality of a man's personal character and life. The picture is presented of one who, as regards the groundwork of his being, may be "in Christ," but whose practice is not altogether worthy of the sacred relationship—a loose fabric of "wood, hay, stubble." In the day "when every man's work shall be made manifest of what sort it is," how mournfully will the defective doings of the unfaithful servant, the careless slothful builder, be swept away before the consuming fire! "He shall suffer loss: . . . saved; yet so as by fire." And this suggests an opposite picture. There are those whose virtue has no living root in Christ, draws none of its inspiration from the faith of which he is the "Author and Finisher." It is a fabric symmetrical and fair to look upon, but it rests not on the true Foundation. It is not for us to judge any man. "To his own Master he standeth or falleth." But this we know—that the criterion by which Christ will judge us all "at that day" is the relation in which we stand towards himself, and "other foundation" of personal righteousness "can no man lay."—W.

Ver. 13.—*Proof by fire.* There can be no doubt as to what day it is that is here intended. It is that "great and dreadful day" of the Lord's coming to judgment, to which all Scripture bears more or less distinct prophetic witness—the day when the final issues of time shall be gathered up, and time itself shall melt into the measureless eternity. One special characteristic of the day is that then all human works will be put to the supreme and decisive test. Consider—

I. THE INSTRUMENT OF THE TEST. "The fire shall prove each man's work." 1. *Literal elemental fire.* It is the plain teaching of Scripture that the visible, material world around us shall undergo some wondrous transformation by fire, that out of the ashes of the old there may arise "the new heavens and the new earth, wherein dwelleth righteousness" (see Mal. iv. 1; 2 Thess. i. 8; 2 Pet. iii. 7, 10). And science confirms the possibility, if not actual probability, of such an issue. 2. *The fire of Divine holiness.* The elemental fire is but the outward symbol of moral judgment. It was for such judgment that Christ came into the world at first (Isa. x. 17; Mal. iii. 2, 3; Matt. iii. 11, 12). He will finally and completely fulfil in the last day this judicial function. The holy love of God, in its fiery antagonism to all evil, is incarnated in "that Man whom he hath ordained to be the Judge of quick and dead."

II. THE PURPOSE OF THE TEST. To make manifest "every man's work of what sort it is." To make manifest: 1. *The basis on which it rests.* Christ is the Source of all true saintliness of character and righteousness of life in men. Only as our souls are "rooted and grounded" in him can we build up a fabric of personal virtue that will stand the searching test of that day. "This is the work of God, that ye believe on him whom he hath sent" (John vi. 29). 2. *The spirit that inspires it.* The mere form of the work, the place and space it has visibly occupied on the stage of the world's history, is of comparatively small moment. The spirit that has animated it, this is its living substance, its essential quality. It is this that makes it of "the sort it is." 3. *The practical results of it.* Not all the works even of the best of men will bear the revealing light and the consuming fire of that day. When the good die, "their works do follow them," as grateful memories, as enduring fruits of goodness and of blessing to the world. And yet not all. There may have been works among them that were too much "of the earth, earthy." They perish with meaner things, not worthy of immortality. While in the case of some men it is as if all were lost; they leave no lasting memorials behind them, over which the living may rejoice; but like one flying from his burning house, escaping with bare life, they are "saved; yet so as by fire." Prove yourself and your work now by the Divine standard, "that when He shall appear you may have confidence, and not be ashamed before him at his coming."—W.

Vers. 16, 17.—*The New Testament temple.* Under the Old Testament, the temple of God was a house made with hands, a worldly sanctuary. The New Testament or dispensation reckons the people of God to be his temple, "the habitation of God in the Spirit." At Corinth there were many temples to the gods, but one temple of God. And the former were of dead stones, however beautiful to the eye. It is a common saying, "As dead as a stone." But St. Paul, with a fine audacity of thought, conceived of the latter—the temple of God—as formed of living stones, from the Foundation upwards.

I. THE CONSTRUCTION OF THE TEMPLE. The foundation of the whole Church God himself laid in raising up Christ from the dead. Whom men despised, he accepted; whom men slew, he quickened. And this living One is made "the Headstone of the corner." A "tried stone," too, thoroughly tested and proved to be sufficient. The foundation of the local Church at Corinth, Paul as a wise master-builder had laid, *i.e.* he had made known Jesus Christ as crucified and risen from the dead, and taught the Corinthian converts to rest on him. Eloquent Apollos followed; and, though a party formed itself under his name, saying "I am of Apollos," St. Paul never blamed the eloquent preacher for this or showed the least jealousy of his influence. On the contrary, at the end of the Epistle he promised to the Corinthians another visit from "our brother Apollos, . . . when he shall have convenient time." Any builder was welcome to continue the work and enter into St. Paul's labours, provided that he did not disturb the Foundation which had been laid and could not be improved, and that he took good heed how he built thereon. The duty of builders is first to gather men, even though they be dead stones, to Jesus Christ, that they may live; and then to build them together, or edify them in faith and love. For this the proper means are found in the exposition and application of the Word with tenderness, pointedness, comprehensiveness, fearlessness, and fidelity. The power is altogether of God. Paul planted, Apollos watered; but the Church at Corinth was not their husbandry, but God's. Paul laid the foundation, Apollos built on it; but the Church was God's building, not theirs. It is so always and everywhere. "Except the Lord build the house, they labour in vain that build it."

II. THE CHARACTERISTICS OF THE TEMPLE. 1. *Holiness.* "Holiness becometh thine house, O Lord, for ever." The temple built by Solomon was holy, or separated to sacred use; but when its holiness was outraged by the idolatrous images and altars afterwards placed within its courts, it still retained beauty, because it was material. But now that the temple is spiritual only, its holiness is its attraction. Corrupt the character, degrade the purity of the Church, and you destroy its beauty too. The holiness of the Church is produced and maintained by the Holy Ghost abiding therein. We have not "influences of the Spirit" as from a distance, but his personal presence. When the Lord Jesus stood in the house of God at Jerusalem, he said, "In this place is One greater than the temple." For once, the less contained the Greater. Now in every meeting of the saints is One greater than the Church, for the Holy Spirit is there. And it concerns his Divine honour to purify the place of his habitation. It is his high prerogative to consecrate; and the New Testament temple is throughout consecrated, not by man, but by the Spirit of God. And as it is in calling and consecration, so ought it to be in fact and in service—holy to the Lord. 2. *Unity.* We read not of temples, but of one temple. However men may arrange themselves ecclesiastically, God sees but one temple or Church in each city, as of old at Corinth or at Ephesus. Indeed, there is but one temple, one Body of Christ, in all the world. And the unity is not brought about by negotiation or legislation; it is wrought by God. "By one Spirit are we all baptized into one Body." We have nothing to do with making the unity; but we are to know, feel, and evince it, worshipping together with joy, helping and exhorting each other, working together for the glory of God and good of man, and partaking together of the same bread and the same cup, not as partisans, but as Christians, members of one Body, guided by one Spirit, and cheered by one hope of our calling. 3. *Variety.* There are various courts, wings, towers, and porticoes in this great building. To our minds there may seem to be confusion and incongruity; but the supreme Architect knows how to adjust and reconcile all in a building "fitly framed together." Variety is not desultoriness. The mere heaping of stones together gives no temple, far less the making of little groups or heaps here and there over a wide field. They must be built and knit together in love. And then, too, there is variety in the places assigned to individual Christians. Some "seem to be pillars." They are like those vertical columns which supported a horizontal entablature in those classical temples with which the Corinthians were familiar. Others must be content to fill a niche or fit into a corner. It is an honour to be anywhere in the spiritual house.

III. A WARNING AGAINST INJURING THIS TEMPLE. One may mar the temple by not taking heed to what he builds. It may be called very liberal and tolerant to make no distinctions, and bestow Christian privileges on all; but St. Paul would call it the building of "wood, hay, and stubble," which cannot abide the fiery trial that comes on every man's work. One may also mar the temple by introducing the temper of the market-place, and of the tables of the money-changers into its courts. Such things call again and again for censure and a whip of small cords. One may destroy the temple, *i.e.* aim blows at its very life, by striking at its holiness, its unity, or its variety. Not that any one can actually demolish it; for it is an ever-living Church: "The gates of hades shall not prevail against it." It is a capital crime against Christ and the Church, either (1) to bring unholy teachings and practices into the temple ("deeds of the Nicolaitanes, which I also hate," Rev. ii. 6); or (2) to disunite the living stones, striking the pick-axes of dissension and a "separating humour" into the temple wall; or (3) to forbid in a bigoted spirit all variety in Christian organization, and say, "The temple of the Lord are we," instead of looking with an eye of charity on all who love the Saviour and breathe his Spirit, saying, "The temple of the Lord are these."—F.

Vers. 21—23.—*A Christian's possessions.* It is a folly under the sun to live above one's means. It is the folly of very many Christians that they live spiritually far below their means of grace and godliness. They are like poor people who have come into a large estate, and cannot for some time adapt themselves to their altered position or comport themselves as befits their fortune. They still betray the narrow ideas and awkward manners of their former condition. So Christians are assured that they have unsearchable riches in Christ, but cannot elevate their ideas and modes of life to the high level of their spiritual privilege. They still betray the narrow estimates and unworthy habits of their time of unregeneracy and unbelief. To correct this tendency and raise the standard of Christian sentiment and conduct, let us look into this inventory of a believer's possessions, and the right or charter by which they are his.

I. THE PROPERTY. "All things are yours." It is at once real and movable estate. It has the most permanent character; and yet it may be taken by the Christian whithersoever he goes, and enjoyed anywhere. A man rich in this world's goods has necessary limits to his possessions. His real estate is irremovable and his personalty or movable wealth is perishable. But he whose riches are intellectual and spiritual has property everywhere. Cast him naked and shipwrecked on an unknown coast; yet he is rich. Spoil him of all earthly goods; reduce him to the very almshouse; and yet he is rich. When he has nothing, he still possesses all things. 1. *The Christian ministry,* represented by Paul, Apollos, and Cephas. The Church is not for the ministry, but the ministry for the Church. The Corinthian Christians did not belong to the great preachers here named, but the great preachers belonged to them. Often the isolation of particular flocks under their own pastors is carried to an extent which virtually brings the doctrine to nought, and gives them no enjoyment of other gifts bestowed by the Head of the Church for the perfecting of his saints. But some are best for planting, others for watering. Let ministers and teachers of the Word, variously qualified, be welcomed and cherished. All of them are yours. 2. *The world.* It is a bad master, but a useful servant. All things in it that are not sinful may be made serviceable to the happiness and progress of the Christian, and to the glory of God. "Use this world as not abusing it." 3. *Life,* with all its vicissitudes and possibilities, sorrow and joy, trial and success. It is quite different to the Christian from what it is to the non-Christian. He is never helpless, and need never be in despair; for he may be sure that the circumstances of his life are ordered by his heavenly Friend, the lines of his life are drawn according to the plan of his loving Saviour. 4. *Death*; which comes, not as a grisly terror, but to do a kindly office. Death, like life, just because it is not in the Christian's power, serves his best interests. "Whether we live or die, we are the Lord's." We may add—The death of friends is yours, soften-ing your heart. The death of enemies is yours, delivering you out of their hand. And as for yourself, Boston has said, "Death comes to the godly man as Haman to Mordecai, with royal apparel and the horse, and commission to do him honour, though with a sullen voice and unkind countenance." 5. *Things present*. The Christian has a promise that he will lack no good thing, and things that seem evil, wounds, losses, disappointments, all tend by the Divine blessing to exercise his faith and patience, and so to strengthen his soul. 6. *Things to come*. Of these we cannot speak. The sights we may see, the feelings we may experience, the changes we may witness, within a year or two, who can tell? How much less can we descant on things beyond? But enough to know that the future is ours. There will be no power among things to come which can separate us from the love of God.

II. THE SECURITY FOR ALL THIS PROPERTY. The Christian holds all through his relation to Christ, "the Heir of all things." "Ye are Christ's; and Christ is God's." Believers belong to Christ, as given to him by the Father, redeemed by him on the cross, effectually called and mystically united to him by the Holy Spirit. And Christ is God's, as the well-beloved of the Father, to whom all things are made subject both in heaven and earth. Now believers inherit through Christ, are co-heirs with him. It is because he is Heir and Lord of all, that all things are theirs. To quote an old divine: "The saints have nothing but through Christ; and whatsoever is his, is theirs. His God is their God; his Father, their Father; his blood, his merits, his Spirit, his victories, all the spoil he hath gotten, all the revenue and income of his life and death,—all is theirs." If men only believed that these things are so, that Christians have such treasures, and hold them by such a tenure, surely a motive of enlightened self-interest would urge them to the feet of Christ. Alas! all men have not faith. The current ideas of wealth and substance are quite unconnected with religion, which seems to many a good thing to die with, but rather a hindrance than otherwise in life. St. Paul's teaching tells a different tale. It is the Christless who, being without God in the world, are poor and indigent. It is those who are Christ's who, however poor in this world, are rich towards God.—F.

Ver. 1.—*The carnal mind*. In view of St. Paul's description of the immoralities and sensualities of the pagan peoples, given in Rom. i., and in special lists of prevailing iniquities, such as are given in Gal. v. 19—21, his sense of the hindrance the carnal mind presents to the reception of spiritual teachings can be fully apprehended. Probably the severest thing St. Paul said about the carnal mind is that it is "enmity against God: for it is not subject to the Law of God, neither indeed can be. They that are in the flesh cannot please God" (Rom. viii. 7, 8). Possibly a distinction between the "natural" man and the "carnal" man may be intended. The natural man is one "whose hopes and desires are bounded by the limits of the physical principle of life;" the carnal man is regarded as more or less under the influence of the sensual passions. But St. Paul seems to recognize that the Corinthian tendency to disputes and religious strife was a sign that the carnal principles were yet strongly working in them; and "an appetite for religious strife prevents us from discerning the deeper truths of the Christian faith." It is broadly true that the reception of spiritual truth mainly depends on the openness and preparedness and culture of those to whom such teaching is given. The teacher may indeed be *unskilful*, but more often the hindrance is that the hearer is *unspiritual*. The preparation of the teacher is considered to be essential, the prepara-tion of the taught is left to the accident of personal earnestness.

I. THE SIGNS OF THE CARNAL MIND. With the hints given above two signs may be fully dealt with and illustrated. 1. Inability to receive advanced spiritual instruction. Self-indulgence in meat or drink, inordinate pursuit of pleasure, the captivity of mind and heart to business schemes, the deteriorating influence of worldly ambitions,

—all destroy interest in Divine things, and take from us the very possibility of apprehending the higher mysteries of the kingdom. 2. A spirit of strife and division. It is never the best people in a Christian community who are the cause of strife. Contention and controversy are only interesting to those who are not really growing in likeness to and nearness to Christ. Schism and strife are sure signs of carnality. Men who get soul-visions of the *truth* never can want to contend over *words*. It would seem that St. Paul recognized signs of remaining carnality in the regenerate members of the Church, and found this to be a principal hindrance to the advance of his teaching. Such signs of the "carnal mind" are still observed by Christian pastors, and are the occasions of their deepest depressions and constant grief.

II. THE FOOD FOR THE CARNAL MIND. St. Paul does not neglect it or refuse to consider it. And it is remarkable that he does not deal with it by warnings or threatenings, but by food, and that of a kind carefully appropriated and adapted. So the physician deals with some classes of disease; he gives no medicine, but nourishes the general health, with a full expectancy that the renewed vitality will throw off, out of the system, the specific disease. St. Paul evidently thinks the real cause of carnality to be *low spiritual vitality,* want of capacity to digest and assimilate good strong food of truth. These religious men were, in regard to religious truths and principles, really only babes, and religious food suited to babes, to beginners, must be provided for them. They must have the "milk" of gospel simplicities until they are strong enough to take the "meat" of gospel mysteries. Only the milk was to be given with the purpose of nourishing the powers for better food. First principles duly apprehended would prepare the way for higher teachings.

Impress that in Christian congregations there is always a call for the gospel simplicities, but that call should not be continually made, as it so often and so sadly is, *by the same persons.* Milk prepares the way for meat. It may be earnestly urged that, after all these centuries of Christian teaching in the home and in the Church, there ought to be an earnest and a mighty cry for advanced and spiritual preaching of the great revealed mysteries of God in Christ. We ought to be "men."—R. T.

Vers. 5—7.—*Man's work and God's.* Explain the agricultural figure used in ver. 6. In the production of the year's harvest many different agencies are employed. Each man has work and his time for work, and upon man's labour the harvest in large measure depends. Yet sun, and wind, and rain, and atmosphere, and soil, are things quite as essential as man's work, but absolutely out of man's control. Year by year man ploughs, man plants, man tends, but *God gives the increase.* So in spiritual things, there is an important sphere for man's agency, but efficiency and result depend on the co-operating grace and blessing of God.

I. MAN NEVER CAN GET BEYOND MINISTRY. That is his duty, and that is his dignity. Even Paul and Apollos can be but "*ministers* by whom we believe." Man cannot control the plan into which his work may fit, or the issues which his work should reach. Man never can be independent, so as to take up anything and do it completely. He never has entrusted to him more than a piece or part, which, if well done, fits into other pieces and parts, entrusted to other men, and goes to complete the whole purpose that was in God's thought. And so no *honour* of results can ever attach to man the agent. Servants only ask praise for faithfulness, the honour of the work belongs wholly to the master whose thought and plan are thus wrought out. This feeling should ensure the sincere *humility* of all Christian teachers.

II. BEHIND MINISTRY IS ALWAYS MASTERSHIP. We serve somebody. "We serve the Lord Christ." But in the case of spiritual work, we may say that in God is more than mastership, there is presidency over and use of more important agencies than man's, though agencies related to man's, and working in with his. Spiritual agencies are as much out of our control as sun, or wind, or rain; yet God uses them, with ours, to win the increase. Man can never, by himself, accomplish any moral or spiritual service. Paul and Apollos could do much for the Church at Corinth, but they stand aside, and let men see how gloriously and effectively *God works.*—R. T.

Vers. 9—12.—*Foundations and buildings.* A curious and interesting blending of metaphors is found in ver. 9. "Ye are God's husbandry, ye are God's building." The sudden changing of metaphors is a characteristic of St. Paul's style; for instances, see ch. ix. 7; 2 Cor. x. 4—8; Eph. iii. 17; Col. ii. 6—7. The apostle now dwells fully on the architectural metaphor, and gives some thoughts of singular depth and importance on the true foundation for a noble life-work, and the kind of buildings which may hopefully be reared upon it. The apostle speaks of himself as a foundation-layer; reminds the Corinthians that it had been his work to commence or found Christian Churches; that this he had successfully done again and again during his missionary travels; and that the Corinthian Church had its first announcement of the gospel from him, and the first stones of its spiritual Church laid by him. He naturally felt jealous concerning the character of the members of that Church, and would have them such as would stand the testing of the great day.

I. St. Paul as a layer of foundations. Only the layer, not the maker. The Foundation was provided (ver. 11); with it not even an apostle could interfere. St. Paul was fitted for the work of laying it, or of commencing a Christian Church in new districts, (1) by his special gifts as a missionary; (2) by his having received a personal revelation from Jesus Christ, which gave intensity to his convictions; and (3) by his clear apprehension of the gospel message, and sympathetic power as a teacher. His personal and persuasive influence on his fellow-men needs to be taken into account. But St. Paul did not look upon the beginning of a Church or the conversion of a soul as any end of his work. Laying foundations involves a design for a building that is to be raised upon it, and the apostle kept up his relations with the Churches he was honoured to found, so that he might ensure that the building was being raised in a manner worthy of the Foundation, and in harmony with it. He had no greater joy than to know that "his children walked in the truth."

II. Other teachers as builders on the Foundation. St. Paul's call to the missionary work involved the necessity of removing from place to place, and prevented his personally watching over the uprising or growth of any one Church. This disability he often seriously felt, and it made him very anxious concerning the wisdom, skill, and character of those teachers who continued his work. That anxiety comes out in our text, and it made him appeal even to the individual Church member, urging him to see that, whatever might be the character of his teachers, his own personal character was being nobly and safely reared. The following points may be dwelt on:—1. *The builders of any one Church may be many.* There may be a long succession of pastors and teachers, with very various gifts and endowments; but each may, in his time and way, add to the symmetrical and harmonious growth of the building. Each must have done so up to the measure of his loyalty to Christ and openness to his Divine lead. Still the same variety and succession are maintained, and under the many builders' hands the great Church of the redeemed advances to its perfection. 2. *The materials used in the construction may differ.* Even of right materials there is diversity, represented by "gold, silver, precious stones." Some teachers are strong in Biblical exposition, others in enforcement of practical duties, and others in appeal to pious feeling; but all bear upon the harmonious uprising of the building. 3. *The architectural features may in parts differ.* The general design cannot be altered, but multitudes of details are left open. A Christian character and a Christian Church can have but one general form; but there may be decoration and tracery according to men's thought of the morally beautiful in the age in which they build, and the whole Church appears at last as a composite structure, combining all architectural thought and form. But *man's work*, in character or Church, must be subject to a final and fierce testing, and only the really substantial and good may hope to bear that test.—R. T.

Vers. 13—15.—*Final testings of our life-work.* In treating this passage it should be noted that the first and chief reference of it is to Christian *teachers* and their work, and that it can only in a second sense be applied to the ordinary Christian, and the kind of influence for good which he strives to exert. Still, a great principle is enunciated in St. Paul's counsel to the teachers, and we may give that principle a wide and general application. The apostle is, in this part of the Epistle, dealing with the tendency of the teachers at Corinth to overpress their individual apprehensions of the truth, and so to make *parties* under their lead, instead of carefully preserving the unity of the Church in the common truth "as it is in Christ Jesus." "The image, in these verses, is taken from what would meet the eye of a traveller in Ephesus, where St. Paul now was, or in Corinth, where his letter was to be first read. It is such a contrast as may be seen (though not in precisely the same striking form of difference) in London in our own day. The stately palaces of marble and of granite, with roof and column glittering with gold and silver decorations, and, close by these, the wretched hovels of the poor and outcast, the walls made of laths of wood, with the interstices stuffed with straw, and a thatched roof above. Then arose before the apostle's vision the thought of a city being visited by a mighty conflagration, such as desolated Corinth itself in the time of Mummius. The mean structures of perishable wood and straw would be utterly consumed, while, as was actually the case at Corinth, the mighty palaces and temples would stand after the fire had exhausted itself" (T. T. Shore). The point of the apostle is that, sooner or later, all earthly works come under severe and searching testings, which prove whether there is anything in them of permanent value, and destroy what had but a temporary use or was really worthless. There is a good and important sense in which the testing-day is a continuous day. We need not put the thought of the proving of our life-work off to some indefinite future. Every day tests and tries. Every night we may think that God weighs the day and its works in his perfectly adjusted balances. But the early Christian mind was very fully occupied with the idea of a particular day, on which Christ would appear and the judgment of mankind be completed; see 2 Cor. v. 10.

I. THE FIRE-TEST FOR ALL LIFE-WORK. Fire is conceived as: 1. The most *destructive* agent. 2. The most *searching* agent. Recent fires have shown how it can destroy even buildings of brick and stone. Illustrate from the great Chicago fire. 3. The most *purifying* agent. Illustrate its power to cleanse the dross from metals. Compare the two other cleansing agents noticed in Scripture—*water* and *blood*. Both these cleanse by a mechanical process; fire cleanses by a chemical process. Nowadays, in great cities and in regard to great buildings, the most anxious question is, " Will the walls etc., stand fire ?" We try to build places that shall be fire-proof. Fire fitly represents the searching power of God: " As fire does, so does God in the end thoroughly search out and destroy all that is vile or refuse, all that is not thoroughly genuine and durable." For passages associating fire-symbols with God, see Deut. iv. 24; ix. 3; Ps. l. 3; xcvii. 3; Isa. lxvi. 15, 16; Mal. iii. 2, 3; 2 Thess. i. 8; Heb. xii. 29. It may be shown that (1) time, (2) difficult circumstances, (3) afflictions, test our life-work, and act as the fire of God. Sooner or later, even in this life, men find out of what sort their work has been, but all mistake and delusion about the quality of our work will be swept away in the great revealing day of God.

II. THE REWARD FOR ALL WHOSE LIFE-WORK ABIDES THE TEST. The reward is really found in the *abiding*, the *permanent character* of the work. "Those who have built well shall have their reward in their work having survived the trial of the fire." F. W. Robertson points out the doctrine of the rewardableness of work, as taught in this passage. "All were one, on the one Foundation; yet St. Paul modifies this: they were not one in such a sense that all their work was equally valuable, for ' every man shall receive his own reward according to his labour.' It is incredible that the mere theologian, defending the outworks, writing a book on the evidences of Christianity, or elaborating a theological system, shall be as blessed as he who has hungered and thirsted with Christ, and like Christ suffered. Nevertheless, each in his own way shall gain the exact recompense of what he has done." On the doctrine of rewards, consider (1) the sense in which they are present; (2) the sense in which they are future; (3) how far we may think of them as material, and how far as moral; (4) their precise adaptation to the worker, and relation to the work he had done; and (5) their coming as a gift of grace, never as a claim of merit.

III. THE LOSS OF THOSE WHOSE LIFE-WORK WILL NOT ABIDE THE TEST. Their work will perish. It is proved to be " of the earth, earthy." It had no abiding spiritual character. Reference, no doubt, is to all so-called Christian teaching that has *mind* in it, *energy* in it, *individuality* in it, but not Christ in it, and Christ wholly. All work that only glorifies the worker must perish. Only work that glorifies Christ can stand the fire-test. Show with what care we should test our own work in God's sight, to be sure that no *self-seeking* has crept into it and spoiled it. "If we would judge ourselves we shall not be judged." But St. Paul, while writing such severe and searching things, makes most careful qualifications, so that none should be unduly discouraged. This is said for the comfort of sincere souls whose life-work has proved a failure. "He himself shall be saved; yet so as by fire." "He shall be saved, while all his work shall be destroyed, just as, to use St. Paul's metaphor, a builder escapes from his house which has been burnt over his head, and stands trembling yet safe, looking on his work in ruins." "Surely the 'smell of fire' may be said to pass on him who sees all those works which he so honestly believed to be for God vanishing as worthless stubble in the searching trial which will 'purge away all the dross' of our human doings, and leave only what is of real value in God's sight." Impress how entirely our human will should be lost in the Divine will, so that our Christian work should be in no sense at all *our work*, but entirely God's appointment for us, and wholly done under his guidance and in his strength. Work that has the self-seeking stamp on it will be sure to burn up. Precious stonework, gold and silver work, is work done wholly for Christ, in which the *self* does not appear. Let each man, then, test his ministry, his teaching, his influence, now, while he may correct his errors, and begin to do better things in a better spirit.—R. T.

Vers. 16, 17.—*The Church a temple.* It is usual to regard these verses as referring to the individual Christian, but the Epistle is addressed "unto the Church of God which is at Corinth," and we may profitably dwell on some thoughts suggested by the comparison; premising that the peculiarities of ancient temples are well understood. The central building of a structure called a temple was not a place of meeting or of worship, it was the sacred shrine or dwelling-place of the deity. Round this central building were grouped the courts in which worship was conducted. Eastern people are extremely jealous about the sanctity of their temples. The Christian system transfers the sanctity from the buildings to the body of believers, and even to the individual believer. All the sacredness which Jews felt to surround their temple at Jerusalem Christians ought to feel surrounds them and the Church; consequently each Christian should anxiously guard the Church, lest it should be injured by false teachings or defiled by the evil living of any of its members. No doubt St. Paul had chiefly in mind to warn all those teachers who were likely so to teach as to split the Church into divisions; for, in his thought, the Church is one great whole, and strife and party feeling are the very things that most seriously defile it.

I. THE CHURCH A TEMPLE, WITH AN INDWELLING DEITY. Compare the descent of God, in his symbol of fiery cloud, to take up his abode in Solomon's temple, with the descent of God the Holy Ghost—manifest through symbols of wind, fire, and tongues—to take up his abode in his Church, on the day of Pentecost. Observe how clearly St. Paul apprehended the truth of God's real and permanent presence with his Church, and how strongly he urges the consequent sanctity of the Church. It may be true that God is not *seen*, but he was not seen in the earlier shrines of tabernacle and temple. He is not therefore unknown or unfelt. Spiritual worshippers realized his presence in the older days; and spiritually quickened men and women feel his nearness now. How should we think of ourselves; how of each other; and how of the Church, if it be true that "God dwelleth with us, and is in us"?

II. THE INDWELLING DEITY UNIFIES AND SANCTIFIES THE WHOLE TEMPLE PRECINCTS. If he makes that innermost chamber the "holy of holies," because his cloud-symbol, his Shechinah-glory, rests there; his presence makes the outer chamber holy, and the courts all holy, and the altar and lavers and utensils all holy. And if Christ "dwells in our hearts," and makes them like the holy of holies, we must realize that he sanctifies all our being and all our relations; sanctifies mind, affection, will, body, so that the prophetic figure should be fulfilled, and in the Christian life and Christian Church *holiness* should be inscribed on the very "bells of the horses.". The one anxious endeavour of a Christian life is to get all the "courts" of our body-temple wholly sanctified.

III. THE OLD LAWS OF JUDGMENT ON THE DEFILEMENT OF GOD'S TEMPLE APPLY TO THE CHRISTIAN TEMPLE. Compare Exod. xxviii. 43; Lev. xvi. 2. The word used here, "defile the temple of God," is better read "destroy," as the opposite of "building up," which is the Christian teacher's duty. Ways in which a man may defile, or destroy, the temple of God, which he is himself, or which the Church is, may be detailed and illustrated. We may be sure that God will punish—does punish—all dishonour done to his spiritual temples.

Impress how the cherished thought of our temple-like sanctity would influence our daily life and conversation. As ever present with us, God seems to say to us continually, "Be ye holy; for I am holy."—R. T.

Vers. 18—23.—*The cure for the party spirit.* Having still in mind the difficulty occasioned by those who claimed to be superior teachers; and gathered parties round them, the apostle proceeds to show that merely human wisdom is in itself worthless for spiritual purposes, and, therefore, that the possession of it alone is no reason for the exaltation of the teacher who is endowed with it." A man over-confident in his superior knowledge is always a dangerous man. The most learned are always the most humble. "A child-like willingness to learn is the first step towards the true wisdom." To find the *cure* for the party spirit, we must search for the real root of its evil; just as the physician who would remove disease and restore health must discover precisely where the disease is seated and what are its essential features.

I. THE ROOT OF THE PARTY SPIRIT. It is precisely *self-satisfaction*, but it may take form as (1) pride of wisdom; (2) pride of place; (3) pride of birth; (4) pride of power. A man wants to be separate from his brethren and to be counted superior to them. The party spirit is not, however, only shown in the *leaders;* there are persons who are weakly willing to take sides and follow leaders, and he who *follows* may be quite as wrong and as mischievous as he who *leads.* The root of the evil, the *self-seeking spirit,* may be equally found in them both. Illustrate the evil of the party spirit by the silent, spreading, fatal influences of a cancer; and give cases of sectarian evil from Church history. In every age the Church has suffered from those who broke away from her unity, following this leader and that.

II. THE CURE OF THE PARTY SPIRIT. It is found in a full and worthy estimate of our rights, privileges, and possessions in Christ. If we enter into and maintain right relations with Christ, we shall certainly be delivered from any undue allegiance to men. Christ is Lord, and he is supreme; all teachers are but ministers, Divine agents, by whom we believe, and who are graciously used to help our spiritual joy. Christ alone is ours to *follow and obey,* ministers and teachers are ours to *use* and to *honour* for their works' sake. All are God's; all are in commission to Christ; all are in use, by him, for the instruction and edification of his Church; and therefore we ought to follow after no one of them, but only after Christ. "Let party spirit cease. Do not degrade yourselves by calling yourselves after the names of any man, for everything is yours—these teachers only exist for you. The enthusiasm of the apostle, as he speaks of the privileges of Christians, leads him on beyond the bare assertion necessary to the logical conclusion of his argument, and, enlarging the idea, he dwells, in a few brief and impressive utterances, on the limitless possessions—in life and in death, in the present life and that which is future—which belong to those who are united with Christ." F. W. Robertson finely dwells on the freedom from party following which those have who are supremely loyal to Christ: "Then it is that he is emancipated from circumstances; then, all things are his—this marvellous life, so full of endless meanings, so pregnant with infinite opportunities. Still more death, which *seems* to come to him like a tyrant commanding him when it will—death is his in Christ, his minister to lead him to higher life. Paul is his, to teach him freedom. Apollos his, to animate him with his eloquence. Cephas his, to fire him with his courage. Every author his, to impart to him his treasures. But remark, that St. Paul refers all this to the universal law of sacrifice: all things are ours on this condition—that we are Christ's. The law which made Christ God's has made us Christ's. All things are yours, that is, serve you; but they only discharge the mission and obey the law involuntarily that you are called on to discharge and obey voluntarily—the law to which Christ was subject, for Christ 'was God's.' So that, when the law of the cross is the law of our being—when we have learnt to surrender ourselves—then, and then only, we are free from all things: they are ours, not we theirs; we use them, instead of being crushed by them."

Conclude by showing the peril of nourishing the party spirit *in these days,* when particular aspects of doctrine are so hotly contested. There may be party feeling doing serious mischief within Christian communities, though it may not reach the length of separation or schism.   We need anxiously to watch against the *beginnings* of this evil in ourselves and in others.—R. T.

EXPOSITION.

CHAPTER IV.

Vers. 1—5.—*Judgments, human and Divine, respecting ministers.*

Ver. 1.—**Let a man so account of us.** Since it is inevitable that Christians should form some estimate of the position of their ministers, he proceeds to tell them what that estimate should be. Ministers are not to be unduly magnified, for their position is subordinate; they are not to be unduly depreciated, for if they are faithful they may appeal from frivolous human prejudices and careless depreciations to that only Judge and Master before whom they stand or fall. **Ministers;** here *hupēretas;* in ch. iii. 5 *diakonous.* They are *hupēretai* (in its derivation "under-rowers") in their relation to Christ; *diakonoi* in their relation to men. **Of Christ;** and therefore responsible to Him. **Stewards;** dispensers, subordinate distributors. These "agents" were higher slaves (Luke xvi. 1—8). **Of the mysteries of God.** The word "mysteries" means truths once hidden but now revealed; as in Luke viii. 10, "Unto you it is given to know the mysteries of the kingdom of God." In later patristic usage the word means "sacraments;" but St. Paul has expressly said (ch. i. 17) that his mission was to preach the gospel, not primarily to administer the sacraments. (For descriptions of the work of a minister according to St. Paul's lofty ideal, see the pastoral Epistles, and 1 Thess. ii. 7—11; Col. i. 25—29; Acts xx. 18—21, 24—28. St. Peter's is given in 1 Pet. iv. 10, 11; v. 2—4.) A minister is not to be estimated as a supernatural teacher, or a civil autocrat, or an infallible critic, but as an ambassador from Christ, who reveals to the "initiated" that which they could not otherwise know.

Ver. 2.—**Moreover.** The true reading (א, A, B, C, D, F) is ὧδε λοιπὸν, *here, moreover; i.e.* "on this earth." It may be required of him as a minister that he should be faithful, but if, being faithful, he is misjudged and depreciated, his appeal lies to a truer and loftier tribunal. **It is required.** This is the reading of א, A, C, D. Other manuscripts have "ye require;" but the sound of the two words in Hellenistic Greek would have been almost indistinguishable. **That a man be found faithful.** We have a right to demand that on trial he be proved to be honest and diligent. So our Lord has described the "faithful and wise steward" in Luke xii. 42, 43. What is required of ministers is neither brilliancy, nor eloquence, nor profound knowledge, nor success, but only—fidelity.

Ver. 3.—**But.** The Corinthians might have expected that the conclusion of St. Paul's remarks would be a recognition of their right to sit in judgment on his faithfulness; but it is, on the contrary, an expression of his complete indifference to their shallow and unfair estimate, and an appeal to the approval of his own conscience and to the judgment of the Lord. **It is a very small thing;** literally, *it is for the least.* **That I should be judged of you;** rather, *that I should be examined by you (anakrithō).* Technically the word *anakrisis* means "an examination preliminary to trial." **Or of man's judgment;** literally, *of man's day.* The brief day of human life is bounded by too narrow an horizon for accurate judgments. Many of the greatest and best men have felt, like Lord Bacon, that they must leave to other generations the right estimate of their characters, views, and actions. St. Jerome reckons the expression "day" for "judgment" among the "Cilicisms" of St. Paul (Jer., 'Ad Algas.,' 10), *i.e.* the expressions due to his early training in Cilicia. More probably (as Grotius thinks) there is a reference to the "day" fixed for earthly trials (*diem dicere*, equivalent to "to impeach"), and to the phrase "the day of judgment"—"the woeful day" of Jer. xvii. 16. The word "day" in all languages and idioms signifies "judgment" (Hammond). From *dies*, a day, comes the phrase "a diet." A "daysman" means an arbitrator. **Yea, I judge not mine own self.** Here, as in the previous clause and in ch. vi. 4, the verb is not *krinō*, I judge, but *anakrinō*, I examine. Thus the verse discourages all morbid self-introspection. It also shows that St. Paul is not arrogantly proclaiming himself superior to the opinion of the Corinthians, but is pointing out the necessary inadequacy of all human judgments. The heart is too liable to self-deceit (Jer. xvii. 9, 10) to enable it to pronounce a judgment with unerring accuracy. Hence neither a man's contemporaries nor the man himself can form any final estimate of him or of his fitting position, because their knowledge is too imperfect. History often reverses the decision of contemporaries.

Ver. 4.—**I know nothing by myself;** rather, *nothing against myself.* The phrase of the Authorized Version originally meant this, but is now obsolete in this sense. "I am sorry that each fault can be proved *by* the queen," says Cranmer to Henry VIII.

It is like the Latin *Nil conscire sibi*. The same phrase occurs in the LXX. of Job xxvii. 6. St. Paul says, "The verdict of my own conscience acquits me of all intentional unfaithfulness;" but this is insufficient, because God sees with clearer eyes than ours. "Who can understand his errors?" asks the psalmist (Ps. xix. 12); and the "secret faults" against which he prays are not hidden vices, but sins of which he was himself unconscious. It must be remembered that St. Paul is here only speaking with conscious integrity of his ministerial work. Nothing could have been further from the mind of one who elsewhere calls himself "the chief of sinners" than to claim an absolute immunity from every form of self-reproach. They who claim immaculate holiness can as little quote the sanction of St. Paul (ch. ix. 27; xv. 9; Eph. iii. 8; Phil. iii. 13, etc.) as of any other saint. The confessions of the holiest are ever the most humble. **Yet am I not hereby justified.** Because "every way of a man" is apt to be "right in his own eyes," but God pondereth the hearts, and therefore in God's sight "no man living is justified." St. Paul is here using the word in its legal rather than its theological sense. **He that judgeth me is the Lord.** This is a reason for serious awe and deep self-searching of heart (Ps. cxxx. 3; Job ix. 2). Yet also for hope and confidence when a man can, like the modern statesman, "look from the storm without to the sunshine of an approving conscience within." For God, being "greater than our hearts" (1 John iii. 21), may count "the long 'yes' of life" against the one "no," or the single faithless minute. Knowing whereof we are made, remembering that we are but dust, he looks on us

"With larger other eyes than ours,
To make allowance for us all."

Ver. 5.—Judge nothing. St. Paul, in the Epistle to the Romans, insists with some indignation on this duty of checking the tendency to vain depreciation, both because we have not the capacity for forming adequate judgments, and because censoriousness is a very common though thoroughly unchristian vice (Rom. xiv. 4, 10, 13). **Before the time.** The time is when God shall "judge the secrets of men" (Rom. ii. 16), and when "the day shall try every man's work of what sort it is" (ch. iii. 13). **Until the Lord come.** The advent is called in the New Testament sometimes the "epiphany," and sometimes the *parousia'* of Christ. The word used for "until" (*heōs an*) points to a time entirely indefinite. **Both**; rather, *also; i.e.* among other things. **The hidden things of darkness.** "All things are naked and opened unto the eyes of him

with whom we have to do" (Heb. iv. 13; comp. Eccles. xii. 14). God "shall illuminate the crypts of the darkness which naturally fills the self-deceiving heart." **The counsels of the hearts.** These may bear no scrutiny, even when the actions of the life have been made to look plausible enough. **And then.** God only "seeth in secret" (Matt. vi. 4), and therefore the praise and blame of men may in this life be equally unjust. **Shall every man have praise of God**; rather, *each one shall then have his praise* (i.e. such praise as he deserves) *from God*. Some of the Greek Fathers (*e.g.* Theophylact) here make "praise" a "word of intermediate sense," involving either praise or blame. But St. Paul says "praise" for two reasons—partly because he is thinking of faithful teachers like Cephas, Apollos, and himself, who were depreciated by rival factions; and partly because he, like other apostles, shows an invariable tendency to allude to the bright rather than to the dark side of judgment. The "praise from God"—the "Well done, good and faithful servant"—is so infinitely precious that it reduces to insignificance the comparative value of human praise or blame.

Vers. 6—13.—*Contrast between the inflated self-sufficiency of the Corinthians and the earthly humiliation of the apostles.*

Ver. 6.—Brethren. The occasional use of this and similar expressions ("beloved," etc.) often serves to strengthen an appeal, or, as here, to soften the sternness of a rebuke. **I have in a figure transferred to myself and to Apollos.** The meaning seems to be that St. Paul has prominently transferred to himself and to Apollos, or rather to the parties who chose their names as watchwords, the proof as to the sin and futility of partisanship which applied equally well to the parties which ranged themselves under other names. (For the verb "transfer"—more often "transform"—see 2 Cor. xi. 13, 14, 15; Phil. iii. 21.) He abstains purposely and generously from publicly naming the fuglemen of the antagonistic factions. **For your sakes.** By rebuking party spirit in his own partisans and those of the teacher who was most closely allied to himself, he robbed his remarks of all semblance of personality or bitterness. It showed his generous delicacy not to allude rather to the adherents of Cephas and the Judæan emissary. **Than ye might learn in us.** I made Apollos and myself instances of the undesirability of over-exalting human teachers, that by our case you might learn the general principle. **Not to think of men above that which is written.** The true reading is merely, *not above the things which have been written*, as though the words were a sort of proverb, like *Ne quid nimis* or Milton's "The rule of not too much" (μηδὲν ἄγαν). The word "to think" is omitted in the best manuscripts. The phrase, "which have been written," is of very uncertain meaning. It may refer generally to "the scriptural rule" that all boasting is wrong (Jer. ix. 23), or to the humble estimate of teachers which he has just been writing down for them. All his Old Testament quotations so far (ch. i. 19, 31; iii. 19) have referred to humility. Some see in it a reference to Matt. xxiii. 8, "Be not ye called Rabbi;" but it is uncertain whether St. Matthew's Gospel was yet written; and St. Paul never refers so directly to any written Gospel. Perhaps it is a sort of proverb, "Keep always to strict evidence;" "Say nothing which cannot be proved in black and white." The text, like so many others, has only a very remote connection with the sense in which it is usually quoted. **That no one of you be puffed up.** St. Paul was painfully impressed by this *inflation* of the Corinthians, and he often recurs to this word as a description of their vain conceit (ch. iv. 18, 19; v. 2; viii. 1; xiii. 4; 2 Cor. xii. 20). In other Epistles the word is only found once (in Col. ii. 18). **For one against another.** The expression is a profound one. The glorying in men (ch. iii. 21), undesirable in any circumstances, becomes the more pernicious because the exaltation of one set of teachers is almost invariably accompanied by mean and unjust depreciation of any who could be supposed to be their rivals. The Corinthian who was "for Cephas" would be almost certain to be, to some extent, "*against* Paul."

Ver. 7.—**Who maketh thee to differ?** literally, *Who distinguisheth thee?* He means that this glorification and depreciation of rival views and rival teachers sprang from unwarrantable arrogance. It involved a claim to superiority, and a right to sit in judgment, which they did not possess. **That thou didst not receive?** Even supposing that you have some special gift, it is a *gift*, not a merit, and therefore it is a boon for which to be thankful, not a pre-eminence of which to boast.

"Satan, I know thy power, and thou know'st
            mine,
Neither our own, but given. What folly,
            then,
To try what arms can do!"
                    (Milton, 'Paradise Lost.')

Ver. 8.—**Now ye are full, now ye are rich;** rather, *already ye have been sated, already ye grew rich.* There is a strong but healing irony in these expressions, and in the entire contrast between the comfortable, full fed, regal self-satisfaction of the Corinthians, and

the depression and scorn in the midst of which the apostles lived. The loving delicate irony is, in a different way, as effective as the stern denunciation of St. John: "Thou sayest, I am rich, and increased with goods, and have need of nothing; and knowest not that thou art wretched, and miserable, and poor, and blind, and naked" (Rev. iii. 17). St. Paul's satire is always akin to charity; it is never satire with no pity in it. **Ye have reigned as kings.** The word simply means "ye reigned." Like the Stoics, so each little Corinthian sectarian regarded himself as a king. "To reign" was, however, a proverbial phrase (like the Latin *vivo et regno*) for being "happy as a king." **Without us** (comp. Heb. xi. 40). The Corinthians were cultivated enough to appreciate the deep irony of the phrase, "We poor apostles have become quite needless to you in your lordly independence." **And I would to God ye did reign.** The words "to God" should be omitted. The loving heart of St. Paul could never long keep up a strain of irony. He drops the satire, and passes on to impassioned and affectionate appeal. **That we also might reign with you.** If the exalted eminence which you now only enjoy in your own conceits had been but real, then we, whose "hope, and joy, and crown of exultation you are in the presence of Christ" (1 Thess. ii. 19), should share the grandeur with you.

Ver. 9.—**For.** This word shows how different was the reality. **Hath set forth;** displayed as on a stage (2 Thess. ii. 4). **Us the apostles.** St. Paul identifies them with himself; but undoubtedly he had "laboured more abundantly than they all." **Last.** Servants of all; in the lowest circumstances of humiliation (comp. Mark ix. 35). **The apostles.** Not the twelve only, but those who might be called apostles in a wider sense, who shared the same afflictions (Heb. x. 33). **As it were appointed to death.** This daily doom is referred to by St. Paul in ch. xv. 30, 31; 2 Cor. iv. 11; Rom. viii. 36. Tertullian renders the word "veluti bestiarios," like criminals condemned to the wild beasts ('De Pudicit.,' 14). But the day had not yet come when Christians were to hear so often the terrible cry, "Christianos ad leones!" **A spectacle;** literally, *a theatre.* The same metaphor is used in Heb. x. 33. **To angels.** The word, when used without an epithet, always means *good* angels, who are here supposed to look down in sympathy (comp. Heb. xii. 22).

Ver. 10.—**We are fools for Christ's sake.** The irony is softened by the intervening sentences, and as regards the apostles there is no irony. St. Paul was called "a seedpecker" (*spermologos*) by the Epicureans and Stoics at Athens, and Festus in full court called him "mad." **Ye are wise in**

Christ. He could not say as before, "for Christ's sake;" for even though he is using the language of irony, "the pseudo-wisdom of the Corinthians had *other* motives." **We are weak.** The consciousness of physical and personal weakness weighed heavily on the mind of St. Paul in moments of depression (2 Cor. x. 10; xiii. 4). **Ye are honourable, but we are despised;** literally, *ye are glorious, but we are dishonoured.* The word "dishonoured" also means "disfranchised."

Ver. 11.—**Unto this present hour.** In these three verses he draws a picture of the condition of the apostles, especially of the trials to which he was himself subjected, on which the best comment is in 2 Cor. xi. 23—27. This letter was written from Ephesus, where he had so much to do and to endure (Acts xx. 31). **Hunger and thirst.** "In hunger and thirst, in fastings often" (2 Cor. xi. 27). **Are naked** (Matt. xxv. 36; Jas. ii. 15; and comp. 2 Cor. xi. 27). **And are buffeted.** The verb means literally, *are slapped in the face* (comp. 2 Cor. xii. 7). Such insults, together with scourgings, fell to the lot of St. Paul (Acts xxiii. 2, etc.) and the other apostles (Acts xvi. 23, 1 Pet. ii. 20), as well as to that of their Lord (Matt. xxvi. 57, etc.). It showed the utter contempt with which they were treated; for though St. Paul ought to have been exempt from such violence, both as a freeman and a Roman citizen, he was treated as vilely as if he had been a mere foreign slave. **Have no certain dwelling-place.** This homelessness was among the severest of all trials (Matt. viii. 20 ; x. 23).

Ver. 12.—**Labour, working with our own hands.** St. Paul supported himself by the dreary toil and scant earnings of a tent-maker, in the express determination to be no burden upon his converts (Acts xviii. 3; xx. 34; 1 Thess. ii. 9; 2 Thess. iii. 8; ch. ix. 6; 2 Cor. xi. 7, etc.). Such conduct was the more noble because all mechanical trades were looked down upon by the Greeks as a sort of *banausia.* And though it was repellent and mechanical work to be handling the strong-scented black goats' hair all day, yet by this labour he maintained not only himself but also his brother missionaries (Acts xx. 34). **Being reviled.** The early Christians were falsely accused of the most execrable crimes, so that the very name "Christian" was regarded as equivalent to "malefactor" (1 Pet. iv. 14, 16). **We bless.** Herein they obeyed the direct precept of our Lord (Matt. v. 44), as well as his example (Luke xxiii. 44; 1 Pet. ii. 23; iii. 9).

Ver. 13.—**Being defamed, we entreat.** The expression "we entreat" is very general. It may mean "we entreat men not to speak thus injuriously of us" (Calvin); or "we

exhort them to do right." **As the filth of the world.** The Greek word *katharmata* has a technical sense, in which it means "men devoted to death for purposes of expiation" (*homines piaculares*). The word *perikatharmata* has the sense of "sin offerings" in Prov. xxi. 18; Tobit v. 18. It is, however, doubtful whether this meaning of the word could have been at all familiar to Greek readers, and it is only in a very general and distantly metaphorical sense that the sufferings of God's saints can be regarded as, in any sense of the word, vicarious. It is better, therefore, here to retain the sense of "refuse" (*purgamenta*, things vile and worthless). **The offscouring of all things;** perhaps rather, *of all men.* The word *peripsema* means "a thing scraped off," and this word also was used in expiatory human sacrifices, where the formula used to victims thus flung into the sea, in times of plague or famine, was, "Become our *peripsema*'" ('Schol. on Ar.;' Plut., 456). Thus in Tobit (v. 18), Anna the wife of Tobias says, "Let the money be used as a *peripsema* for the child;" and Ignatius uses the phrase, "I am your *peripsema*." From this and the similar phrase in the Letter of Barnabas, "I am the *peripsema* of your love," it seems to have become a current expression of tenderness among Christians, "I am your *peripsema*." But in this case also it may be doubted whether the sacrificial idea was present in the apostle's mind. He is thinking of scenes which he had already faced and would have to face hereafter, when mobs shouted against him that he was "a pestilent fellow" (Acts xxiv. 5) and not fit to live (Acts xxii. 22).

Vers. 14—21.—*The practical steps which he intends to take with reference to these party divisions.*

Ver. 14.—**To shame you.** Such seems to be the meaning of the word, for it is so used in the LXX. (compare the use of the verb in 2 Thess. iii. 14; Titus ii. 8; and of the substantive in ch. vi. 5; xv. 34). **I warn;** rather, *I admonish.* St. Paul here gives the reason why he *cannot* write angrily or bitterly, even though he has used strong expostulation and keen irony. It is because he regards himself as their spiritual father (comp. 2 Cor. vi. 13; xii. 14, 15; 1 Thess. ii. 11).

Ver. 15.—**Ten thousand ;** *never so many.* The word in Greek is used indefinitely, but here implies a touch of impatience at the itch of teaching which seems to have prevailed at Corinth. **Tutors;** rather, *pedagogues,* in a technical sense. We have no exact equivalent in English to the *paidagogos,* the slave who led boys to school. The word also occurs in Gal. iii. 24, 25. The father loves most, and has the nearer and dearer claim. **In Christ.** So he says, "The Law was our *paidagogos to Christ.*" These guides or guardians were such "in Christ," *i.e.* in the sphere of Christian life. **Not many fathers.** St. Paul felt a yearning desire that his unique claim as the *founder* of their Church should not be so ungratefully overlooked, as though it were of no importance (comp. ch. iii. 6; ix. 1, 2; Acts xviii. 11). **I have begotten you.** The word is here only used in a secondary and metaphoric sense, as in Philem. 10; Gal. iv. 19. In the highest sense we are only begotten by the will of God, by that Word of truth (Jas. i. 18), to which he alludes in the words "through the gospel." The "second birth" is, however, a doctrine more dwelt on by St. John (iii. 3; 1 John iii. 9; v. 1, etc.) than by St. Paul, who, as Mr. Beet observes, only refers to it in Titus iii. 5.

Ver. 16.—**Be ye followers;** rather, *imitators.* He makes the same appeal in ch. xi. 1; Phil. iii. 17. Of course, he only uses his human example as a guide to them in the special virtues of humility, self-denial, and faithfulness (1 Pet. v. 3; Heb. xiii. 7). In the highest sense we can only be "imitators of God" (Eph. v. 1).

Ver. 17.—**For this cause.** Because, as your spiritual father, I naturally take the deepest interest in your well-being. **Have I sent;** rather, *I sent.* Timothy had started before this letter was despatched (Acts xix. 22), but he did not reach Corinth till after its arrival, because he had been unable to go by sea, and had to travel round by Macedonia. St. Paul, on hearing the grave news from Corinth, seems to have countermanded him (ch. xvi. 10, "*If* Timotheus come"), but was uncertain whether the messenger would reach him in time. The necessity for despatching *Titus* had been more immediate. **My beloved son, and faithful in the Lord;** rather, *who is my beloved and faithful child (teknon) in the Lord.* St. Paul had converted him, and felt towards him all the love of a father (1 Tim. i. 2; 1 Thess. iii. 2; Phil. ii. 20—22). **Shall bring you into remembrance of my ways which be in Christ.** The expression shows all St. Paul's delicacy. He is not sending the youthful Timothy as an authoritative teacher, since the Corinthians, fond of high pretension and soaring oratory, might scorn to show any submission to a shy and shrinking youth; but he is only sending him because, as his closest companion, Timothy would be best able to explain to them his plans and wishes in the organization of Churches.

Ver. 18.—**Are puffed up;** rather, *were*

puffed up; at the time that they made these disparaging comparisons of me with others. **As though I would not come to you;** rather, *as though I were not coming to you.* St. Paul was on the eve of starting for Macedonia on his way to visit them (ch. xvi. 5), but, owing to the grievous state of the Church, he subsequently changed his purpose (2 Cor. i. 15, 23). When he left them he had promised to return, "if God will" (Acts xviii. 21). His many enemies and critics were likely to say, "He is afraid to come himself, and so he sends Timothy." They flattered themselves that he was alarmed by their culture and intellectualism.

Ver. 19.—**I will come to you shortly** (Phil. ii. 24; 2 Tim. iv. 9). He came soon after writing the Second Epistle. At this time he was preparing to leave Ephesus (ch. xvi. 8); his actual departure was precipitated by the tumult (Acts xx. 1, 2). **If the Lord will.** The apostolic use of the phrase was something more than a mere form (Rom. xv. 32; Heb. vi. 3; Jas. iv. 15); it expressed a real and humble spirit of dependence. **Not the speech of them which are puffed up, but the power.** He will use his gift of spiritual discernment to discover whether the haughty self-assertion and sounding phraseology of these inflated partisans would not collapse when confronted with real authority. The "speech" was there in abundance; but was there anything genuine, any real spiritual force, behind it?

Ver. 20.—**The kingdom of God.** The Christian life, with all its attainments and all its hopes. **Is not in word, but in power.** It is not a matter of profession, or of eloquence, or of phrases, but of transforming efficacy. St. Paul always appeals for the corroboration of his authority to the signs and power of the Spirit (2 Cor. x. 45; Rom. xv. 19; 1 Thess. i. 5), to the "demonstration" of which he has already referred (ch. ii. 4).

Ver. 21.—**What will ye?** "The whole thing lies with you" (Chrysostom). **With a rod;** literally, *in a rod* - a not uncommon Greek phrase. The meaning of this expression is best seen from 2 Cor. x. 2; xiii. 10. **In love.** He would come to them "in love" in any case; but if they now rejected his appeals the love would be compelled to manifest itself in sharpness and stern deeds. **In the spirit of meekness.** Meyer here gives to the word "spirit" the sense of "the Holy Spirit," as in John xv. 26; 2 Cor. iv. 13; but the simpler sense of the term is almost certainly the true one.

HOMILETICS.

Vers. 1—7.—*A true and a false estimate of genuine ministers of the gospel.* " Let a man so account of us as of the ministers of Christ," etc. Here we have—

I. A TRUE ESTIMATE of genuine ministers of the gospel. 1. They are *servants of Christ.* " Let a man so account of us as of the ministers of Christ." There are some who regard ministers of the gospel as servants of their Church. The Churches guarantee their stipend, and they require that their dogmas shall be propounded and their laws obeyed. The paymasters, whether deacons, or elders, or the state, naturally expect subordination in their ministers. He who yields in any measure to such an expectation degrades his position, and is not in the truest sense a minister of Christ. He who is the true servant of Christ will feel and act as the moral master of the people—the leader and commander. " Obey them that have the rule over you," etc. There is no office on this earth so dignified and royal as that of the true servant of Christ. 2. As servants of Christ, they are *responsible.* " Stewards of the mysteries of God." The " mysteries of God " here mean the gospel, which in the second chapter is said to be " the hidden wisdom which God ordained before the world." The gospel is a mystery, not in the sense of absolute incomprehensibility, but in the sense of progressive unfoldment, both in respect to communities and individuals. It is a mystery to the man who at firsts begins its study, but as he gets on it becomes more and more clear. The true minister is entrusted with these " mysteries ; " he is to bring them out, translate them into intelligible ideas, and dispense them to the people. As a steward of such things, his position is one of transcendent responsibility. 3. As servants of Christ, they are *faithful.* " Moreover, it is required in stewards, that a man be found faithful." Fidelity is an essential attribute of a true minister. He must be faithful to his *trust,* not abuse it, but use it according to the directions of its owner. Faithful to its owner, in all things regulated by his directions. He must be faithful to his *hearers,* seeking no man's applause, fearing no man's frown, " commending himself to every man's conscience in the sight of God." 4. As servants of Christ, they are *independent.* " But with me it is a very small thing that I should be judged of you, or of man's judgment." Whilst no true minister will despise the favour or court the contempt of men, he will not be concerned about their judgment so long as he is faithful to his God. Paul gives utterance to this sentiment in order, no doubt, to reprove those preachers in the Corinthian Church who were seeking the praise of men. Paul seems to indicate here three reasons for this feeling of independency. (1) His own consciousness of fidelity. " For I know nothing by myself; yet am I not hereby justified." " The sense is," says a modern expositor, " I am not conscious of evil or unfaithfulness to myself; that is, in my ministerial life." It is well remarked by Calvin that " Paul does not here refer to the whole of his life, but only to his apostleship. And the sense is, ' I am conscious of integrity in this office. My own mind does not condemn me of ambition or unfaithfulness. Others may accuse me, but I am not conscious of that which should condemn me or render me unworthy of this office.' " (2) His confidence in the judgment of God. " But he that judgeth me is the Lord." I am content to abide by his judgment. If his judgment of me agrees not with my own judgment of myself, I will loyally submit. (3) His belief in a full revelation of that judgment. " Therefore judge nothing before the time, until the Lord come, who both will bring to light the hidden things of darkness," etc. Do not let us judge one another ; do not let us even trust too much to our own judgment of ourselves. Let us await Heaven's judgment. (*a*) There is a period appointed for that judgment, " Judge nothing before the time, until the Lord come." There is a " day appointed in which he will judge the world in righteousness." Ah! that day. (*b*) At that period there will be a full revelation of our characters. " Who both will bring to light the hidden things of darkness, and will make manifest the counsels of the hearts." (*c*) At that period, too, every man shall have his due. " And then shall every man have praise of God." " Praise " here does not mean approbation, but that every man shall receive his just due. Such considerations as these may well make ministers independent of the judgments of men, and regardless alike of their smiles and their frowns.

II. A FALSE ESTIMATE of genuine ministers of the gospel. " And these things, brethren, I have in a figure transferred to myself and to Apollos," etc. Paul here means to say that he spoke of himself and Apollos to show the impropriety of one minister being pitted against another. The members of the Corinthian Church had evidently formed an incorrect estimate of the true gospel minister. 1. They seemed to estimate ministers in *proportion as they met their views and feelings.* Every true preacher preaches the gospel as it has passed through his own mind, and as it passes through his own mind it will, of course, be more interesting to the minds most in harmony with his own experience, capacity, and sympathies. Hence, in the Corinthian Church, those who preferred Peter's preaching thought no one was like Peter; those who preferred Apollos' thought there were none like him; and so with Paul. It is so now. "There is no minister like our minister; all others are grades below." This is very false, for inasmuch as the great bulk of the community are more or less uneducated, unreflecting, and sensuous, the preacher who approximates most to their type of mind will attract the largest crowd and get the loudest hosannas. But is he on that account superior to others? By no means. Thus it is that some of the most inferior preachers are over-rated and the most elevated and devoted degraded; whereas all true ministers are "servants of Christ," the "stewards of the mysteries of God," and as such should be honoured. 2. They seemed to estimate ministers according to the *greatness of their natural endowments.* "Who maketh thee to differ from another?" etc. Between the natural endowments of Paul, Apollos, and Peter there was a great difference, and, indeed, between all ministers of the gospel there is a difference in natural endowments, and a great difference in the quality and measure of mind. But what of that? There is nothing in those natural endowments for boasting; for they all came from God. The man of the most far-reaching intellect, the most brilliant imagination, and transcendent genius has nothing which he has not received from that Spirit which distributes to every man according to his own will. No man or angel deserves credit on account of natural abilities.

CONCLUSION. "Let us strive," says F. W. Robertson, "as much as possible to be tranquil. Smile when men sneer; be humble when they praise; patient when they blame. Their judgment will not last; 'man's judgment,' literally, 'man's day,' is only for a time, but God's is for eternity. So, would you be secure alike when the world frowns its censure or its applause upon you? feel hourly that God will judge. That will be your safeguard under both. It will be a small thing to you to be judged of any man's judgment; for your cause will be pleaded before the Judge and the Discerner of all secrets."

Ver. 8.—*Apostolic treatment of vanity.* "Now ye are full, now ye are rich, ye have reigned as kings without us: and I would to God ye did reign, that we also might reign with you." Vanity is a state of mind at once the most *prevalent* and *detestable;* it is a plant that springs from self-ignorance, and is disgusting to the spectator in all its forms and fruits. See how the apostle treats it here.

I. With WITHERING SARCASM. "Now ye are full, now ye are rich, ye have reigned as kings without us." The Bible furnishes us with many instances of irony (see 1 Kings xviii. 27; Job xii. 2), but nowhere have we it in language more full and forceful than here. "Now ye are full," or "already are ye filled." You have had enough, you want nothing; "ye are rich" or "already ye are become rich." You are affluent in all gifts and graces. "Ye have reigned as kings without us." "Here are three metaphors, the first taken from persons filled with food, the second from persons so rich that they require no more, the third from those who have reached the highest elevation—obtained a throne." Paul seems to say to these conceited teachers that they were so great that they did not require such services as his. We scarcely know of a more effective way of treating vanity than by sarcasm. Treat the vain, swaggering man before you, not according to your judgment of him, but according to his estimate of himself. Speak to him as one as stupendous as he believes himself to be, and your irony will stab him to the quick. Sarcasm is often the instrument of a great manly soul when roused into indignation.

II. With A NOBLE GENEROSITY. "I would to God ye did reign, that we also might reign with you;" or, "I would ye did reign." Here the north wind of sarcasm gives way to the south breezes of love. What he means is a wish that they were as truly full, rich, and royal as they thought themselves to be. The irony of a Christly man, however pungent, is not malign, but generous.

Ver. 9.—*Man an object of angelic observation.* "For I think that God hath set forth us the apostles last, as it were appointed to death : for we are made a spectacle unto the world, and to angels, and to men." The margin reads "theatre" for "spectacle," from the Greek word θέατρον. The reference, in all probability, is to the ancient amphitheatre, whose arena was surrounded by circular seats, capable of accommodating thousands of spectators. In this arena trained athletes struggled for prizes in the ancient games; on such an arena Paul speaks of himself and fellow-labourers as struggling, the objects not only of human but of angelic spectators. The world is indeed a moral theatre, every man an actor, and disembodied spirits look on as spectators. "We are encompassed about," etc. Angels as spectators are *intelligent, interested, numerous, constant.* If the eyes of such intelligences are constantly upon us, what are the practical conclusions?

I. THAT OUR CONDUCT HERE CONCERNS THE UNIVERSE. No man lives unto himself; each unit is a link in being's endless chain. His actions must tell banefully or beneficently on the creation; hence all loving and loyal intelligences direct their attention to him with deep and unabating interest. Besides, men and angels are offsprings of the same Father, participators of the same nature, subjects of the same moral government. No wonder they are so concerned.

II. THAT OUR PART SHOULD BE CAREFULLY PLAYED. How doubly careful are our actors on the stage, in the presence of spectators distinguished for the highest genius, erudition, and artistic culture! It behoves every man to be cautious how he acts in the presence of his fellow-creatures, whether they are children or adults, plebeians or princes; but how much more cautious should he be when he knows that angels, whose pure natures loathe sin in all its forms, have their keenest gaze fastened ever on his life.

III. THAT THERE IS NO CHANCE OF CONCEALING OUR SIN. The attempt to cloak or dissemble our sins is absurdly futile. Whilst there is One who reads the heart, there may be millions who mark all our overt acts, whether wrought in darkness or in light.

IV. THAT WE MAY EXPECT HELP IN ALL HOLY ENDEAVOURS. Those celestial spirits are sent forth to minister to the heirs of salvation. They have received a Divine commission to bear us up, lest we dash our feet against a stone. In all ages they have rendered assistance to the good. They helped Abraham on the plains of Mamre, and Lot in his flight towards Zoar; they freed the apostle from the prison; they bore the spirit of Lazarus to the bosom of Abraham.

CONCLUSION. "Wherefore seeing we also are compassed about with so great a cloud of witnesses, let us lay aside every weight, and the sin which doth so easily beset us" (Heb. xii. 1).

Vers. 10—14.—*Paul's treatment of self-conceited teachers.* "We are fools for Christ's sake, but ye are wise in Christ; we are weak, but ye are strong; ye are honourable, but we are despised. Even unto this present hour we both hunger, and thirst, and are naked, and are buffeted, and have no certain dwelling-place; and labour, working with our own hands: being reviled, we bless; being persecuted, we suffer it; being defamed, we entreat: we are made as the filth of the world, and are the offscouring of all things unto this day. I write not these things to shame you, but as my beloved sons I warn you." Paul is still thinking of those teachers of the Corinthian Church who were "puffed up," inflated with conceit. He treats them here with—

I. AN IRONIC APPEAL. "We are fools for Christ's sake, but ye are wise in Christ; we are weak, but ye are strong; ye are honourable, but we are despised;" or, "ye have glory, but we have dishonour." "We are fools," we know nothing, "but ye are wise," you know everything; "we are weak," timid, and feeble, "but ye are strong" and fearless. "Ye are honourable," you have "glory," you are thought a deal of, you are extolled, but "we are despised," the "offscouring of all things." All this is sarcasm again, well deserved, and well directed. How would our little penny-a-liners feel if such a man as Thomas Carlyle were to stand before them and speak in this way? If they had any sense remaining, they would quiver into nothingness. How much more would those small pretentious teachers in the Corinthian Church feel this stroke of satire dealt out to them by the great apostle to the Gentiles!

II. A PERSONAL HISTORY. Here he refers to his *privations:* "Even unto this present hour we both hunger, and thirst, and are naked, and are buffeted, and have no certain dwelling-place"—without nourishment, without clothing, without the shelter of a home. Here he refers to his *labours:* "And labour, working with our own hands." Here he refers to his *persecutions:* "We are made as the filth of the world, and are the offscouring of all things." Then he refers to the *spirit* in which he endured the sufferings : "Being reviled, we bless; being persecuted, we suffer it; being defamed, we entreat." Now, why did he state all this? Not for the sake of parading his great trials and toils, but for the sake of bringing these proud teachers to their senses. They could not fail to acknowledge that he was an apostle—a pre-eminent minister of Christ; notwithstanding this, in the world he was treated with cruelty and contempt, he was poor and despised. What, then, had they to be proud of as ministers?

CONCLUSION. From this subject it is natural to ask—Who in the present age engaged in the Christian ministry are most likely to be of *apostolic succession ?* Those who are "full," and "rich," and royal, and "wise," and "strong," who pride themselves in all these things; whom the people favour and flatter? or those who, like the Apostle Paul, in the discharge of their ministry, endure privations, persecutions, and all in the magnanimous spirit of self-abnegation and generous forgiveness of enemies? Call no man a successor of the apostle who has not the *apostolic character.* To call a man a successor of the apostle who has not the apostolic character—manfully noble, Christly loyal, and withal self-sacrificing—is a mischievous imposture.

Ver. 15.—*Spiritual paternity.* "For though ye have ten thousand instructors in Christ, yet have ye not many fathers: for in Christ Jesus I have begotten you through the gospel." The subject of these words is *spiritual paternity,* and three remarks are suggested.

I. THAT ONE MAN MAY BECOME THE SPIRITUAL FATHER OF ANOTHER. What is it to become the spiritual father of another? 1. Something more than to become the father of one's ideas. There are men in society gifted with that intellectual vitality and vigour which enables them to generate the leading ideas in the minds of their contemporaries. This they do by their conversation, their speeches, their writings. But these are not spiritual fathers, they are mere schoolmasters or teachers. Coleridge and Carlyle are examples of this. 2. Something more than the author of a certain style of thinking. There are men in society who not only generate leading thoughts in the minds of their contemporaries, but, what is perhaps something higher, a style of thinking—a style characterized by precision, freshness, and force. Aristotle, Bacon, etc., are examples. But a spiritual father is one who is the father of man's *moral character,* one who generates in another his own spirit, sympathies, and aims, one who transforms the character of another into his own image.

II. THAT THE NOBLEST SPIRITUAL FATHER IS HE WHO BEGETS IN ANOTHER THE CHRISTLY CHARACTER. Many are the moral characters prevalent amongst men—the sensual, the sceptical, the selfish. The Christly character stands in sublime contrast to these; it is *disinterested, spiritual, Divine.* 1. The man who generates in others this character *imparts the highest good.* In the Christly character is harmony, kinghood, and paradise. To be like Christ is the highest end of being, it is the *summum bonum* of souls. 2. The man who generates this character in others *creates the highest mutual affection.* Far deeper and profounder is the affection subsisting between the spiritual father and his offspring than that which exists between the physical. Christ recognized this when he said, "Whosoever shall do the will of God, the same is my brother, and my sister, and my mother." Paul called Timothy his "beloved son ;" and elsewhere he speaks with inexpressible tenderness of his converts as his little children, with whom he travailed in birth (Gal. iv. 10).

III. THAT THE CHRISTLY CHARACTER IS ONLY BEGOTTEN IN OTHERS BY THE GOSPEL OF CHRIST. "I have begotten you through the gospel." *Natural religion* cannot do it; Judaism cannot do it; Mohammedanism cannot do it; heathenism cannot do it; no speculative creeds, no moral codes, no ritualistic religions can do it. The gospel alone is the power to generate in man the true Christly character; it is that transformative glass into which as we look we get changed into the same image from "glory to glory." CONCLUSION. Learn from this: 1. *The supreme interest of man.* What is that? —learning, wealth, fame? No; *Christliness.* He who has this has everything; all things are his. He who has not this has "nothing," says Paul. 2. *The grandest distinctions amongst men.* What are they?—sages, soldiers, sovereigns? No; *spiritual sires.* The man who generates in another the Christly character has done a greater work than any sage as sage, king as king, has ever done. Every man may and ought to become a spiritual father.

Vers. 16—21.—*Six subjects worth reflection.* "Wherefore I beseech you, be ye followers of me," etc. There are six noteworthy subjects in these verses.

I. A REMARKABLE REQUEST. "Be ye followers of me." Were Paul an ordinary man, such an exhortation would resound with arrogance; but he was a man of pre-eminent excellence, Christly in spirit, deportment, and ministry. There were three reasons why they should imitate him. 1. He was a *follower of Christ.* There was no living man who had followed his Master so closely. Elsewhere he says, "Be ye followers of me, as I also am of Christ." 2. He was their *spiritual father.* He had begotten them in the gospel; they were his moral offspring. They had numerous instructors, but he was their father; they gave them ideas, he gave them character. 3. He was *no partisan.* Other teachers amongst them became the leaders of parties, these parties were contending one with another; but Paul belonged to no party, he followed Christ, knew "nothing amongst men but Christ, and him crucified." Such a man was justified in calling on others to follow him. "Ministers," says an old writer, "should so live that their people may take pattern from them, and even after their copy; they should guide them by their lives as well as by their lips, go before them on the way to heaven, and not content themselves with pointing."

II. A HIGH TESTIMONY. "For this cause have I sent unto you Timotheus, who is my beloved son, and faithful in the Lord, who shall bring you into remembrance of my ways which be in Christ, as I teach everywhere in every Church." He is dear to me as a "son;" he is "faithful in the Lord;" he knows my "ways." High testimony this. And this is the man he promises to send to them. What for? That he might give them good reasons why they should be followers of him. I do not want you to follow me in the dark; I send him that he may throw light upon my ways everywhere, "in every Church." A man must have a high consciousness of rectitude who can trust the representation of his character to one who knows him as well as a son knows his father, and withal a man of incorruptible honesty.

III. A FOOLISH EXULTATION. "Now some are puffed up, as though I would not come to you." There were those in the Church at Corinth who were out of sympathy with Paul, and who had no desire that he should visit them, and as the "wish is father to the thought," when they heard he was coming they would not believe it. When the intelligence that he was sending Timothy to them reached them, they would be likely to say, "This proves the truth of our assertion; he is afraid to come himself, and so he sends Timothy." In this they seem to have rejoiced; they were "puffed up." Now, I call this a *foolish* exultation, because the visit of Paul to them was what they deeply needed, and was intended to confer on them the highest blessing. How often do we foolishly rejoice in deliverance from visitations fraught with priceless blessings!

> "Ye fearful saints, fresh courage take,
> The clouds ye so much dread
> Are big with mercy, and shall break
> In blessings on your head."
>
> (Cowper.)

IV. AN EXEMPLARY DECISION. "But I will come to you shortly if the Lord will," etc. Paul believed that God had a will concerning him, and that will determined his destiny. Hence on this he based all his calculations in life; all his plans and purposes were subject to that will. "If the Lord will." This is an exemplary decision. His will is not only absolute and righteous, but benevolent; therefore to acquiesce in that will is not only right, but wise. "Go to now, ye that say, To-day or to-morrow we will go into such a city, and continue there a year, and buy and sell, and get gain ; whereas ye know not what will be on the morrow."

V. A GLORIOUS SYSTEM. "For the kingdom of God is not in word, but in power." By this he means, I presume, the gospel ministry. It is a *divinely regal* "*kingdom ;* " it is not a thing of sentiments or ceremony; it is invested with Divine authority. It is not a thing of mere "*word ;* " it transcends all language, however logical in force or rhetorical in beauty ; it is "*power* "—the "power of God unto salvation."

VI. A SOLEMN PROPOSAL. "What will ye? shall I come unto you with a rod, or in love, and in the spirit of meekness ? " In any case I shall come as a father. Shall I come as a father to chastise you with a "rod," or with looks of "love " and words of commendation and sympathy ? God's minister is bound to deal with men according to their states of mind. His ministry to some must be as the severity of Sinai, with others as the tenderness of Calvary. Evermore is it true that the effects of Divine visitations depend on the spirit in which they are received, and what this spirit shall be is for man to determine. God says to every man, "What will ye? shall I come unto you with a rod, or in love, and in the spirit of meekness ?" This is the solemn proposal.

HOMILIES BY VARIOUS AUTHORS.

Vers. 1—7.—*Ministers as stewards.* The idea of the ministry as a Divine institution, set apart as a peculiar calling and charged with an infinite trust, cannot as yet relax its hold on St. Paul's mind. Tenacity of a great truth is not altogether a matter of our volition. At first the will has much to do in directing attention to a truth and keeping it fixed ; but in no long time, if the man has trained himself to reflect, and, above all, if he is an earnest man, the truth recurs by some process of self-suggestion. After a while, indeed, it happens with many who give themselves to profound investigations, that the subject gains a certain mastery over them, so that it costs more effort to dismiss it than was originally needed to concentrate attention. No capacity of the mind is so pliant as the capacity to be absorbed in an object of thought, and it seems independent of idiosyncrasy. Sir Isaac Newton and Sir Walter Scott both refer to the difficulty they had in discharging a topic from their minds if it had enlisted their interest. St. Paul had said much on the office of the ministry, but the theme was by no means exhausted. One aspect, a special one, remained, viz. *stewardship.* Ministers are "stewards of the mysteries of God ;" if so, fidelity is their highest duty, or rather the soul of every duty. If the preacher had to set forth so unpopular a doctrine as Christ crucified, so obnoxious to worldly culture, so alien to the civilization of the age, then this "foolishness of preaching " was a very urgent reason for faithfulness. What need of watchfulness here! "Who can understand his errors," and especially these errors? Apostles were "men of like passions" with others; and this very likeness, while fraught with dangers both obvious and occult, made them fit, under God, for their work. The idea of stewardship was familiar to these Corinthians, perhaps keenly so to some of them ; for in the business of that day much had to be entrusted to agents. Now, the master in such cases cannot give detailed instructions to his stewards, and hence a good deal must be left to their judgment. The hazard, let it be observed, is not on the side of the understanding ; no rare intellectual outfit was requisite in this instance ; the one supreme doctrine of Christ crucified had wisdom and power sufficient to impart truth of thought and emotion to all subordinate doctrines. But the danger lay in a want of fidelity. And had not St. Paul evinced this faithfulness while with these Corinthians? Yet, whether they admired or blamed, whether acquitted or condemned, what was that to him? "A very small thing was man's judgment ;" nor, forsooth, would he judge himself, but leave all judgment to the Lord Jesus. Spiritual discernment has its functions; insight is a glorious gift ; but the Lord reserves judgment to himself. That judgment awaits its day of revelation, when "the hidden things of darkness " and the "counsels of the hearts " shall be made manifest. Then, indeed, men shall see themselves as Christ sees them. Here, in this world, even in our most enlightened state, consciousness is partial. Much of a man lies far down in unillumined depths ; the secrets of motives and impulses evade his personal cognizance ; only in fragments can he realize himself; how much less can he comprehend others! And, " therefore, judge nothing before the time." Obviously, then, humility of judgment is not only an intellectual excellence but a spiritual virtue. It is a Divine discernment of our limitations, a Divine insight into the fact that there is an unconscious man no less than a conscious one in every human being, and that, meantime, fidelity stands free of all restrictions and abatements. Does fidelity look at office? It does not see popularity, honour, preferment, but duty, duty alone, duty ever; and this sense of duty, inspired and directed by the Holy Ghost, educates the man in tact and skill, in diligence and patience. Does fidelity look at others? It neither exaggerates nor depreciates them, nor can it regard them as rivals, since no man can possibly have a sense of rivalry who realizes Christ in the most essential fact of work, viz. *brotherhood*. And consequently, one of the many beautiful provisions of Christianity to secure fidelity is found in the brotherhood of Christians. Does fidelity look into its own heart? Even then infirmity clings to its energetic searching. On its good side it may be too self-exacting, morbid, harshly critical of itself; on its weak side it may be lenient and over-indulgent. And hence St. Paul, while conscious of knowing nothing against himself, declares, " Yet am I not hereby justified," and relies solely on the justification of Christ at that great assize, which, among all its wonders, shall surprise men most of all by its divinely revealed estimates of human character. " For your sakes," so he argues, " I have been thus explicit and emphatic, transferring these things to myself and Apollos," in order that the Corinthians might clearly see his own disinterestedness. This point assured, the way is open for remonstrance. Why are ye puffed up? If we are recipients; if Paul and Apollos are mere stewards of the Master's riches; if self-judgments and judgments of others are impossible to men under the limitations of consciousness and observation; if " the counsels of the hearts " keep out of sight and hold their latency intact for the final day; and if, meantime, fidelity is the supreme concern and adequate to call out and employ all the spiritual resources of our nature under grace; and, finally, if you owe all your means of acting on one another and the world to the brotherhood of the Church ;—why do ye stand arrayed in sharp hostility against one another and rend asunder the Lord's body ?—L.

Vers. 8—13.—*A vivid contrast.* Having shown that the Christian consciousness was a twofold realization of the worthlessness of whatever was its own, and the infinite worth of the " all things " in Christ, and having proceeded thence to the idea of stewardship and the urgent need of faithfulness, how can St. Paul withhold the stern application of such truths? Had it been a childish self-complacency with which he was dealing, we know how he would have treated it. But it was an active jealousy, a pompous arrogance, a virulent self-conceit, a carnal temper in which the natural man survived, that he had to combat. Now, therefore, he would show them what they were. The weapons of his warfare were not carnal, but, nevertheless, they were weapons, and withal such weapons as Elijah had employed, and even the Lord Jesus had not disdained to use. If, by means of contrast, we know everything external, and if thereby we know ourselves too and realize our identity by discriminating one mood of consciousness from another, it follows that irony has its legitimate place and may be sanctified to the best purposes. Men are acutely sensitive to its caustic probe, and, as they will not exercise it on themselves, its application is one of those offices, severe but humane, which must be performed on them. Is the conflict over and the victory won? Full and rich, lo! ye are reigning " as kings," and significantly enough, " without us," the apostles, the *sent* of God, in this movement. And what dominion is that from which we are excluded? Where are your apostles in this hour of your coronation as kings? " God hath set us forth "—a terrible contrast to their self-glorification—at this instant are we so set forth, like criminals doomed to death, and made a spectacle as in a vast theatre, " unto the world, and to angels, and to men." Alas! the only use just then to which the great Apostle to the Gentiles could put his knowledge of Greek games in the amphitheatre was in an outburst of indignation and sorrow. And then follows one of his characteristic sentences, in which impassioned feeling is quite as condensed as strong thought: fools, weak, despised, are we the apostles, while ye are wise and strong and honourable. The formal contrast is dropped, and now, how like the rapid summation of his experience to the sufferings of his Lord? Fidelity in suffering, fidelity to suffering, reconciliation to it, acceptance of its law as basic to his life, not an exceptional thing occurring at rare intervals as most of our sad experiences, but common and habitual, wounds unhealed and yet deeper wounds, "even unto this present hour." Hunger and thirst, nakedness, buffetings, homeless, refusing all remuneration and earning our own support, returning good for evil and blessing for cursing, objects of persecution, denied recognition as the friends of humanity and lovers of their kind, abused and vilified, ay, treated in the centres of this world's intelligence and refinement as "the filth of the world and the offscouring of all things," and no break or cessation, "unto this day." The sameness of these sufferings is twice mentioned, and the wondrous biography, first and last, is one chapter of woes. Over all stands a single motto, which came and could only come from Christianity: "For Christ's sake." At this juncture, call to mind a fact of some moment. Men are wonderfully individualized by sufferings. Considering how suffering abounds, it is noticeable that few truly regard themselves as providential sufferers, and realize in their experience the Divine discipline they are appointed to undergo. There is much selfishness in our ways of enduring the ills of life, in the uses made of affliction, and the habits of intellect and sensibility growing therefrom; and St. Paul strikes the heart of the subjects when he connects his sufferings with "Christ's sake." This gives an instant pathos to the recital and an instant nobility to the apostle as a sufferer. Furthermore, only for "Christ's sake" does he go into this affecting detail of the number, variety, and continuation of his sorrows. A noble sufferer like St. Paul could find no selfish pleasure in such an enumeration; nay, in itself it would be painful. Vain men, ignoble men, gratify their littleness in recounting what they have endured, and these pensioners of public opinion—it may be the public opinion of a very diminutive world—find their account in the illusory sense of sympathy. Far from this weakness—very far—was this heroic man, to whom it was a new suffering to tell his sufferings, but who, in the courage of humility, the most courageous of the virtues in a true man, was even ready to uncover a bleeding heart for "Christ's sake." We shall now see that his love for these erring Corinthians prompted him to make the narration of his sufferings.—L.

Vers. 14—21.—*Warnings of tenderness.* From mood to mood, yet in all, St. Paul had the same dominant zeal and affection in behalf of his converts. Rebuke was not with him a pleasure to which the natural man ministered, but a very painful duty that proceeded from conscience and kept sensibility unalloyed by animal passion. Herein he is distinguished from men who love authority because it is a signal of personal eminence and a means to make others feel their inferiority. A really superior mind never likes to dwell on the infirmities of ignorance and littleness in those below him. The mountain points upward, and the higher the summit the more is it lost in the heavens. "Who maketh thee to differ?" is always present as the interrogatory of consciousness in such a nature, and the answer thereunto, whenever a true man has to vindicate his authority and especially in rebuke, is as Divine as the question. The delicacy of the apostle and his depth of insight have not forsaken him in this trying hour, nor would he expose the vanity of such as made themselves leaders and assumed transcendent powers, save in a manifest spirit of self-abnegation. Manner is not a mere mode; it is a spirit; it is the very spirit of a man taking on a visible embodiment, and hence the rebuke administered by St. Paul is impregnated with the humility of his soul. There are men who commit

"Mischievous foul sin in chiding sin;"

but it would be a poor compliment to the apostle to say that he was not one of this class. What is most truly to his honour is his purpose to make the Corinthians sensible of the wrong to their better nature, and quicken from that side of their character the feeling of repentance. This brings out the sentiment of his soul in the words, "I write not these things to shame you, but as my beloved sons I warn you;" and again the master-thought of all his thinking recurs—Christ Jesus—in whom he had begotten them through the gospel, urging them to be imitators of Christ in him. To be genuinely serviceable, imitation must not be mechanical and servile, not be the literal copying of a pattern or model, but an education in the art of discriminating, and particularly a sense of the ideal in those whom we follow. For this reason, that they may be reminded of his " ways which be in Christ," he has sent Timotheus unto them. Prudence dictated this course. Circumstances were such as that absence would be his most effective presence—one of those occasions when a man's thoughts had better do their work unattended by the emphasis of eye and voice. But would they misinterpret this and attribute it to cowardice? "I will come to you shortly," leaving the time to the will of the Lord, for in executing a grave purpose it is not enough that we have the Spirit in our motive and aim, but we must wait patiently on the providence of the Spirit, which is often our best discipline. St. Paul's expectations were rarely fulfilled promptly,—instance his visit to Rome; hope grew more reverent by delay; and in no aspect is his career more interesting than in that which shows how postponed gratification of desire ennobled the desire itself and secured a larger good to others. Fruit must grow, ripen, mellow, especially inward fruits, and St. Paul prized the mellowing touch of time. Many a lesson he gives us unawares in psychology, many an insight into the philosophy of true feeling, many a revelation of the soul, which but for him would have been a "hidden mystery." But, while waiting for "time and place to cohere," he utters his opinions strongly as to those who are "puffed up." What an ever-recurring sense of cardinal principles! Great truths are never long out of sight, and hence the declaration, "The kingdom of God is not in word, but in power." Did he under-rate language? Nay; who ever spoke of language in a higher strain than he who did not hesitate to allude to his own preaching as not in the "words which man's wisdom teacheth, but which the Holy Ghost teacheth"? But the idle and impotent word, the word of swelling vanity, the word that dishonoured the Word,—for this he had only rebuke and condemnation. Such use was stolen use, the gift turned against the Giver, a redeemed gift wrested from the Redeemer, a recognized organ of the Holy Ghost taken from its only Sanctifier. For this must be said of language, that it is not merely or chiefly a medium of acting on others, but that it reacts on the man himself. Apart from its conventional functions, it is an instrument of communion with self, of stating self to self, of inspiring, while defining faculty to faculty in the mind's solitary cognizance of its own powers. Language is far mightier for introverted conception, for images that never escape the picturesque world in which they have their birth and life and death, for emotions and affections to which silence is the most precious of blessings—far mightier, we say, is language in this respect than in its economic uses. From the lexicon we learn the language that gives us intercourse with men. From our own souls and by conversing with them we learn the language by means of which we compare "spiritual things with spiritual." Even on the plane of common life, the former is confined to communication. Expression is a very different thing from bald communication. Expression is due to the ability of the Spirit to vitalize words by imparting its own life to them. Something individual, something distinctly personal, imparts itself in expression. Hyperboles are matters of fact to the inmost consciousness, and all eloquence and poetry are but symbols of what the soul sees and can only intimate in this half-articulate way. "I will know when I come"—so St. Paul reasons—"whether your speech is empty words, the wisdom which man's wisdom teacheth and is foolishness to God, or the power of the Spirit." This is the test—God's power. Only through that power can these Corinthians advance the kingdom of God; for only through it can they have oneness with Christ and fellowship with his disciples. Come to them St. Paul will—come to them as a father—the acknowledgment of them as sons, *beloved sons*, precedes him, and he will not forget his relation to them; but how shall he come? With a father's rod or in love? Will they relieve him of the necessity of discipline? And the thought of love lingers in his mind, amplifies itself, seeks fuller utterance, and the father's heart throbs once more in the associated clause—"the spirit of meekness."—L.

Vers. 1, 2.—*Spiritual stewardship.* In the Corinthian Church two errors were prevalent with regard to the apostolic and other ministries—there was a tendency to exaggerate the importance of the agents by whom the truth was communicated, and there was a disposition to set one of these agents up as against another; so that partisanship and sectarianism violated the Christian unity.

I. THE SUBORDINATE POSITION OF CHRISTIAN TEACHERS. None need deem it a degradation or an undue humiliation to stand where the apostle stood; indeed, Paul is an acknowledged and admired model to all who work for the kingdom. 1. They are, in relation to Christ himself, *ministers*. They serve him, and count it an honour so to do. For his sake, and in his Name, they act as servants to their fellow-men. 2. They are, in relation to the truth they promulgate, *stewards*. That is to say, the truth is not revealed by them, but to them; it is held not as their property, but as their trust; it is not appropriated to their own use, but dispensed by them for the benefit of others; they are not at liberty to do as they like with it—they are accountable to the Lord of all for the way in which they deal with it. 3. This being so, *faithfulness* is the virtue they are bound to cultivate and display. Whilst those who are independent are not especially bound to this duty, all who have derived from another, and are accountable to that other, are emphatically called to be faithful. Such is the position of all the ministers of Christ.

II. THE TRUE DIGNITY OF SPIRITUAL SERVANTS ARISES FROM THEIR RELATION TO THEIR LORD AND TO HIS WORD. There is a contrast between the service and the Master, between the stewardship and the mystery. The minister cannot think too lowlily of himself or too loftily of his theme and trust. 1. If they are ministers, they are ministers of *Christ*. An ambassador may be a person of lowly birth and feeble powers, but if he is an ambassador, his relation to his sovereign and the credentials and commission he has received entitle his message to peculiar consideration. And however the pastor, teacher, or evangelist may in himself be lacking in claims upon the respect of the superficial society called "the world," however he may be destitute of the shining gifts which command the admiration of the Church, still neither he nor those whose welfare he seeks are ever at liberty to forget that he is an ambassador from heaven, that he is commissioned and authorized by the King of kings. 2. If they are stewards, they are stewards of the mysteries of God. By mysteries the apostle meant truths which had in the past been hidden but were now revealed. Revealed in Christ, the Divine purposes of grace, salvation and life to all mankind, were published by the apostles and their fellow-labourers. And the declaration of the mind and heart of God was well worthy of being regarded as the impartation of a mystery compared with which all the wonders of Eleusis sank into insignificance. Of this Paul was conscious, and it would be well if every preacher of the gospel were ever to have this before his mind. We have this *treasure*, though "in earthen vessels." The solemnity of publishing Divine truth and the responsibility of hearing it are alike by these considerations brought very vividly before the mind. Thus are ministers unto some a savour of life unto life, unto others a savour of death unto death.—T.

Vers. 3—5.—*Judgment, human and Divine*. No man can work entirely with reference to his own labours and his own opinion of them. We all need to live under the sense that others are taking some notice of what we do; and with most there is danger of attaching exaggerated importance to human criticism. But it is well for us to cherish the feeling of the nearness and the supervision of the omniscient Searcher of hearts. In this passage St. Paul represents the effect which both human and Divine judgment should have upon the Christian's life.

I. THE JUDGMENT WHICH IS DEPRECATED. This is the judgment: 1. Of our fallible fellow-men. For they have not the necessary material or the due knowledge and opportunity for forming a just judgment. Men are influenced in the opinions they form of one another by their prejudices and prepossessions. We judge our friends too favourably, and are too severe in our censure of our opponents. Hence our Lord has warned us, "Judge not!" 2. That which is passed at this present time. This is the time for work, not the time for judging and for recompense. No man's work can be fairly judged until it is completed. And beside this, we cannot see life in its true proportions when we look at it from a point of view so near. To judge now is to judge "before the time."

II. THE JUDGMENT WHICH IS ANTICIPATED. 1. This is God's judgment. He will bring every work into judgment. His acquaintance with all who shall appear before his bar is perfect. His material for forming a judgment is complete. His mind is unclouded by human prejudices. He is infinitely just. 2. This shall take place upon our Lord's return. His *parousia* is what the Church looks forward to with affectionate interest and hope. Her children offer the frequent prayer: "That at thy second coming to judge the world we may be found an acceptable people in thy sight." For whilst the judgment shall be Divine; it shall be accomplished by " that Man whom God hath appointed to judge the quick and the dead." 3. This shall be accompanied by revelation. There are hidden things of darkness which must be brought to light; virtues and vices of which the world has taken little or no note, but which must be brought forward and taken into account, in order to a just decision and award. There are counsels of the heart to be made manifest; for whilst men necessarily judge by the conduct, God will take into account the secret intentions and motives of those who have laboured for him, both good and evil. 4. This will be by a perfect discrimination. The hypocrite shall be distinguished from the sincere, the diligent from the idle, the time-server and men-pleaser from the true servant of God. 5. This will be the occasion of recompense. The case of the utterly unfaithful is left out of view as irrelevant in this connection. But among the faithful it is presumed that there are degrees of fidelity; and every man shall have *his praise* from God. This implies that each has a special meed for special service; and it also implies that praise shall be accompanied by a substantial and everlasting recompense. It is well, therefore, to work " as ever in the great Taskmaster's eye," to avoid judging one's self, to be indifferent to the partial judgment of men, and to wait for the revelation and the awards of eternity.—T.

Ver. 7.—*All is of grace.* Paul's quick, impulsive mind here flashes out into indignation at the spectacle of partisanship and schism in the Corinthian Church. They who lay great stress upon individual human teachers and ministers are in danger of forgetting, perhaps already have forgotten, two things, viz. (1) that every minister and teacher has a special blessing for the Church; and (2) that all such agents are but messengers from the court of heaven, and distributors of the blessings of God.

I. WE MAY TAKE CREDIT TO OURSELVES ONLY FOR OUR WANTS AND FOR OUR CAPACITY. Why should any man be proud, when he remembers that he was born a helpless babe; that he was dependent upon the kind services of others for the preservation of life; that he has learned nothing which he was not taught; that he enjoys nothing except through the good offices of his fellow-men? And why should any Christian be " puffed up " with spiritual conceit, when he remembers that all he brought to the Scriptures, to the Church, to the Lord, was just his necessities and his capacity to receive spiritual blessings?

II. WE ARE INDEBTED FOR ALL THINGS TO HUMAN MINISTRATIONS. When we regard our circumstances, our worldly possessions, our education, our position in life, our family, our friends, this fact is obvious enough. But the same is true of our religious advantages, our spiritual blessings. The Bible was secured to us by human efforts and labours; the gospel was preached to us by human lips; the Church has been to us the fellowship of our human teachers and brethren; our religious knowledge has been conveyed to us by human interpreters; our piety has been inspired by human examples.

III. DIVINE MERCY HAS MADE HUMAN MINISTRIES SUBSERVIENT TO OUR SPIRITUAL WANTS. It is not wise or just to discriminate too nicely between human gifts and Divine. The human gifts are Divine gifts bestowed by human hands. It is the privilege of the devout and enlightened mind to look through the seen to the unseen; to recognize in every Christian helper and friend the messenger of God, the minister of Christ. The form, the voice, may be earthly, but there is behind a spiritual presence and a Divine power. It is the Giver of every good gift and every perfect gift who is so near.—T.

Ver. 9.—*A spectacle.* In the midst of his irony and sarcasm, Paul here reverts to the more natural habit of his mind. The self-exaltation and self-importance of the Corinthians were mingled with depreciation of the apostle, at least on the part of some. But alas! if his own converts, so deeply indebted to his labours and his care, could think slightingly of him, what earthly compensation could he expect for all the pain, hardship, contempt, and danger he cheerfully endured? Were not he and his fellow-apostles like gladiators doomed to be flung to the wild beasts—"a spectacle to the world, to angels, and to men "?

I. THE GRANDEUR AND SUBLIMITY OF THEIR POSITION DEMANDS OUR ADMIRATION. They were not as slaves cast to the lions. They were men who might have led a quiet and peaceful, and some of them an honourable and distinguished, life. But they gave their hearts to Christ, and having done so gave up all for him. There was no exaggeration in the apostle's language. On the contrary, he spoke the plain truth when he represented himself as standing before the universe as a witness to the Lord Christ. The position was one of dignity and moral impressiveness; the angels felt it then, and the world of humanity has come to feel it now.

II. THE PATHOS OF THEIR POSITION DEMANDS OUR SYMPATHY. We observe the bodily privations, the homelessness, the physical toil, the ignominy, the persecutions, the general contempt, which the apostles passed through; and we cannot observe all this unmoved. Doubtless it touched the heart of that Divine Saviour who was made perfect through sufferings; doubtless there were those who wept with their leaders when these were constrained to weep. Nothing in all human history is more profoundly affecting.

III. THE MORAL PURPOSE OF THEIR POSITION DEMANDS OUR APPRECIATION. The motives that induced Paul and his colleagues voluntarily to submit to such experience as they relate were two—fidelity to Christ and pity for men. Christ the Master had condescended himself to be upon the cross a spectacle to the world; and those who benefited by his redemption and shared his Spirit were ready to follow his example. They were the true followers of him who "endured the cross, despising the shame." And their aim and hope was to bring the world to the foot of the Saviour's cross. For this end they "counted not their life dear unto them." It was for the sake of their fellow-men that they consented to brave the scorn of the philosopher and the jeer of the multitude.

IV. THE MORAL LESSONS OF THEIR POSITION DEMAND OUR STUDY. 1. It is a rebuke to self-indulgence and ease. Shall we be satisfied and enjoy our ease in the midst of the world's errors and sins, when we call to mind the heroic and pathetic sufferings of our Lord's first followers? 2. It is a consolation under any contumely and discredit we may endure in the Christian profession and vocation for Christ's sake. "The like afflictions have befallen our brethren who are in the world." 3. It points on to the glory which shall be revealed. "Through much tribulation ye must enter into the kingdom of heaven." The apostles have ended their struggles, and now enjoy their victory; the Church militant will soon become the Church triumphant.—T.

Ver. 15.—*Children, tutors, and fathers.* Our religion makes use of all the many and various relationships that obtain among men to set forth and to assist us in understanding spiritual realities.

I. GENERALLY SPEAKING, CHRISTIANS MAY BE DESCRIBED AS CHILDREN. 1. Like the Corinthians, most members of the Church of Christ need constant and watchful care. Providence has appointed that children should be born more dependent than the offspring of the inferior animals upon parental attention and devotion. From infancy until the approach of manhood and womanhood, human beings stand in need of the supervision and assistance of their parents. So is it with the members of Christ's Church. They are in need of pastoral care and kindness, and without this are not likely either to grow in Christian character or to escape the assaults of their foes. 2. In addition to care, they need wise and fatherly counsel. It would be well if spiritual pastors bore in mind the inexperience of a large proportion of the flock. Paul was a faithful counsellor, and in writing to these Christians at Corinth he warned them very faithfully against the faults and errors they were in danger of falling into. Not with severity, but with directness and earnestness, he admonished his spiritual children, and entreated them to render obedience to his advice and directions. Even sincere disciples of Christ are often in peril by reason of their own want of knowledge and experience, and by reason of the temptations which beset them in this world. Hence the importance of such pastoral admonitions as those of which Paul here gives an example.

II. THERE ARE IN THE CHURCH OF CHRIST THOSE WHO MAY BE DESIGNATED SPIRITUAL FATHERS. At Corinth the apostle occupied a pre-eminently honourable and influential position. He claims in this passage to have been, what the history of the Acts shows that he was, the planter of the vineyard, the founder of the edifice, the father of the family. It was by his labours, his bravery, his perseverance, that the Christian community came into existence. In the highest sense, of course, the Father was God himself, who gives the Spirit of adoption to all his people. But instrumentally, the apostle was blessed by God, through the preaching of the gospel, to the begetting and birth, so to speak, of this congregation, this spiritual household. This relationship involved the obligation on their part to reverence, honour, obey, and gratefully to love and rejoice in, one to whom they were, under God, so immeasurably indebted. For his was a unique position with regard to them. No other could claim to stand in the same relation, and Paul was bold to tell them so. Still are there those who are honoured by the calling of God to this spiritual fatherhood; and such should meet with that respectful and grateful recognition which is the due of benefactors so signally favoured by God himself.

III. TUTORS AND INSTRUCTORS IN CHRIST OCCUPY IN THE CHURCH A POSITION ONLY INFERIOR TO THAT OF SPIRITUAL FATHERS. At Corinth the *charisma* of teaching seems to have been imparted and exercised in a measure almost embarrassing in its abundance. Paul speaks hyperbolically of the "myriads" of tutors who followed up his apostolic labours. The same Spirit bestows gifts in multiplicity and variety. Let Christians be grateful for all the "means of grace," and especially for the holy and devout ministrations of the learned, the wise, the sympathetic, and the strong. For thus is it appointed that the Church should grow in grace.—T.

Ver. 20.—*The power of the kingdom.* The Corinthians were given to words; they delighted in eloquence; they were addicted to disputations. The Apostle Paul, who fulfilled his ministry by language, written and spoken, was not the man to disparage words. But no man was more impatient of mere words—of words with no reality, no force, no conviction. He had reason to complain of his converts at Corinth, and was resolved to bring matters to an issue with them; and it should be a contest, not of barren verbiage, but of spiritual force.

I. THE NATURE OF GOD'S KINGDOM PROVES THAT IT CANNOT BE MERELY IN WORD. 1. A kingdom implies authority exercised, obedience rendered. Although a kingdom not of this world, not maintained and supported by human means, by laws and arms, still God's empire is a reality. Christ is the King and Head; his laws are binding and stringent, although the motives that inspire obedience are gratitude and love—his subjects are willing and submissive. 2. Such a kingdom is incompatible with the reign of words. To be a subject of Christ is not (1) to be merely by verbal assent, as by confirmation or any other form of admission to Church privileges, associated with the society of Christians; nor is it (2) to make any kind of profession; nor (3) to recite and maintain the great Christian creeds; nor (4) to utter words expressive of devotion. Men may make use of many and sacred words, and be none the nearer the kingdom of heaven. A nominal and verbal kingdom is weak and despicable; such is not the spiritual kingdom of our Lord.

II. THE ORIGIN AND NATURE OF THE POWER OF THE KINGDOM. 1. Words may be only from man; power is from God. All natural and physical power originates in him. But moral power is either good or evil; and the good only but always is from God. Christ is " the Power of God." 2. When we contemplate this spiritual power which pervades the new kingdom, what do we find it to be? The power of *truth*, the power of *goodness*, the power of *pity* and of *love*.

III. WHERE AND HOW THIS POWER DISPLAYS ITSELF. 1. Its seat is the soul; there it first enthrones itself, and thence it spreads until it pervades the whole nature, changing the beliefs, the feelings, the principles, and the habits. For "the kingdom of God is righteousness, peace, and joy in the Holy Ghost." 2. The power of this kingdom manifests itself through the whole realm of human nature and life; both by the forces, obstacles, and oppositions it overcomes, and by the results it produces. We observe these effects especially in (1) the newness of life which is characteristic of the kingdom, as emphatically in the case of the first disciples, brought out of Judaism and paganism into the marvellous light of the gospel; (2) in the social results, which were exhibited in the cities where the gospel took root, and where the sentiment of brotherhood proved a new power in humanity, sanctifying society within and attracting elements from without. (3) We have a proof of this power in the case of those martyrs who for

Christ's sake were content to lay down their life; for here we have evidently a new spiritual force, capable of inspiring with a fortitude in the cause of an unseen Lord which surpassed the heroic devotion of a Roman to his country's good. (4) The progress and perpetuity of this power stamps it as Divine, as the one great prevalent and successful force working in human society for its purification, its elevation, its lasting and highest welfare.—T.

Vers. 1, 2.—"*Ministers of Christ.*" I. WHAT THEY ARE. 1. *Ministers.* Not masters; servants, not lords. The word means literally "under-rower," or common sailor, and is generally used of the lower class of servants. Ministers are the *mere servants* of Christ; they have no authority save that which they may receive from him. "Be not ye called Rabbi" (Matt. xxiii. 8). A domineering despotic spirit is altogether out of place. If any will be chief, he must be servant of all. Many ministers have trouble with their Churches because of their own masterful spirit. Like Rehoboam, they do not heed the sage counsel, "If thou wilt be a servant unto this people this day, and wilt serve them, and answer them, and speak good words to them, then they will be thy servants for ever" (1 Kings xii. 7). Some of the Corinthians had unduly exalted their teachers (ch. i. 12); others, perhaps, had regarded them as utterly insignificant ("I of Christ"); Paul defines the legitimate position. Ministerial activity is hinted at; ministers are to be workers, not idlers. 2. *Ministers of Christ.* This makes their calling most honourable. They are servants of the Church, servants of their fellows, but not *primarily.* They serve the Church and their fellow-men because they desire to serve Christ. They are (1) appointed by Christ; (2) responsible to him; (3) to be judged by him; (4) to be devoted to him; (5) to speak in his Name; (6) to preach him and his redemption; (7) to rely upon his help; (8) to take orders from him; (9) not to originate, but to ascertain *his* mind. 3. *Stewards.* A position (1) of trust and confidence; (2) of influence; (3) of responsibility; (4) of some peril; (5) of much honour. 4. *Stewards of the mysteries of God.* "Mystery" in the New Testament does not mean something incomprehensible, but something beyond the reach of unaided human intelligence. The "mysteries of God" are thus "hidden" (ch. ii. 7) until revealed by him. They are the truths of the gospel—"the truth as it is in Jesus." Ministers have special charge concerning these truths—(1) to preserve them; (2) to dispense them. As stewards, they should be deeply impressed with (1) the vast importance of the "riches" entrusted to them; (2) the need of utmost care in discharging the duties of their office; (3) the awful issues to themselves and others if they are remiss. Many are satisfied if self-approved or if praised by others; but Paul looked to the judgment of Christ (ver. 4). We are not to be despondent if we are "unpopular" with men, so that we are approved by our Lord. Though "unpopularity" with men is very far from being an argument that we please our Master: "The common people heard him gladly," and probably would so hear us if we were more like him.
II. A NECESSARY QUALIFICATION. Faithfulness. This is a first requisite in those who are "stewards of the mysteries of God." Stewards must not use their lord's goods for their own advantage. What evils result from unfaithfulness in an earthly stewardship! who can estimate the evils flowing from an unfaithful ministry! A minister should be faithful: 1. *To Christ,* in (1) obedience, (2) love, (3) zeal, (4) devotion, (5) holiness. 2. *To his flock.* (1) Preaching unadulterated doctrine. Not corrupting the Word of God. Not substituting something else for it. (2) Rightly dividing the word of truth. (3) Reproving, rebuking, exhorting with all long-suffering and teaching (2 Tim. iv. 2). (4) Striving "to present every man perfect in Christ Jesus" (Col. i. 28).—H.

Vers. 3—5.—*Human and Divine judgments.* I. REFLECT THAT HUMAN JUDGMENT IS FALLIBLE. It is needful to remember this. Many laugh at "infallibility" when it affects a pope at Rome, but are much disposed to believe in it when it affects a pope at home. We should not forget that (1) our powers are limited; (2) our information often very defective; (3) our minds very subject to bias. Our fallibility should lead us: 1. To take heed how we pronounce *final* judgments. There are some things about which we should not judge at all, as altogether transcending our powers and province. About many things we are compelled to form judgments, and to act upon the judgments formed. But *finality* of judgment may often be profitably avoided. We should particularly observe this when our judgments affect : (1) The providence and dealings of God. (2) The character, motives, deserts, of our fellows. We see the deeds, and may pronounce upon them as such, but we must remember that the heart is hidden from us. (3) Certain matters connected with ourselves. It may be well to judge ourselves severely, since our tendency is to take too favourable a view of our own conduct. We may acquit ourselves when we ought to condemn ourselves. Implicit faith cannot be reposed in the voice of conscience; it may be perverted. Our judgment of ourselves should command our confidence only when we feel sure that our judgment agrees with God's judgment. 2. Not to be disconcerted if harshly judged by our fellows. If an enlightened conscience does not condemn, fallible human judgment should not greatly depress us. We should *value* human judgment, not *overvalue* it. Rightly estimated, it is under such conditions "a very small thing;" under all conditions, a very small thing compared with the judgment of God. To our own Master we stand or fall. So fallible is human judgment that often the best men have been counted the worst, and the worst the best.

II. REFLECT THAT DIVINE JUDGMENT IS INFALLIBLE. That judgment will be exercised upon us and all around us when the Lord comes; or rather, that judgment is *now* being exercised, and then will be declared. The day of the Lord will be a day of universal and infallible judgment. When the Lord comes: 1. Hidden things of darkness will be brought into the light. So much is hidden from us; nothing will be hidden from him. We judge from *part*; he sees *all*. No darkness can hide from him; no hiding can baffle him. 2. There will be *heart*-revelation. How carefully veiled the heart often is now! How different the *counsels of the heart* from the expressions of the lips and the actions of the hand! Heart-revelation must bring widespread condemnation. Yet may we not say also that often, if we had known the counsels of the heart, we should have more favourably estimated the conduct? The *whole man* will be disclosed at the day of the Lord. 3. There will be award. Praise will be administered—" due praise;" for so the rendering might be. Therefore *valuable*, for unmerited praise is of nothing worth. When God judges, the result will not be all condemnation by any means. There will be praise as well as blame—" due praise," and, let us not forget, "due blame." The reference, however, is not to *our salvation*, but to God's judgment of our conduct as his servants.

Live for the judgment of "the day of the Lord," not for the judgment of "man's day" (for so "man's judgment" may be rendered). The one "a small thing" indeed! The other how great! When the Lord comes, some praised of men will be censured, and not a few blamed of men will be praised.—H.

Ver. 7.—*Our indebtedness to God.* I. REFLECT UPON THE FACT. Are apt to forget it altogether. So anomaly is often presented of our quarrelling over "possessions" which do not belong to us, and boasting of that to which we have no title. The air we breathe, the world we dwell upon, our food, clothing, and shelter, our "prosperity" as we fondly call it,—these things are *lent* to us by God. So also our powers—yea, our very existence is not of ourselves, but of God. If we were to have taken away from ourselves all that we have received through the free benevolence of God, *what would be left?* Our salvation, our spiritual joys, our glad prospects, are also of him.

II. DUE REMEMBRANCE OF OUR INDEBTEDNESS WILL HELP TO CHECK PRIDE. We are apt to regard things as though *we had not received them*—as though they were our own *in some other sense than as received from God*. Thus we become proud of our attainments and belongings, and glory in ourselves as possessors, if not originators, and not in God. For the luxury of boasting we easily delude ourselves. A gracious recollection *of the actual state of the case* should do something in the way of shaking the throne of conceit and vain-glory. Pride is great folly as well as great sin, and when we indulge in it we have to smother our common sense. And of all pride, "spiritual pride" is the most reprehensible and the most absurd.

III. DUE REMEMBRANCE OF OUR INDEBTEDNESS MAY INCLINE US TO USE ARIGHT WHAT WE HAVE RECEIVED. Instead of *pride*, we should feel *responsibility*. Instead of boasting, we should desire to employ wisely and well the Divine benefaction. The things which we handle, see, and have, are not ours, but God's. We are stewards, and presently shall have to give an account of our stewardship. We should ask, For what are these things given? What does God wish us to do with them?

IV. DUE REMEMBRANCE OF OUR INDEBTEDNESS WILL TEND TO INSPIRE GRATITUDE AND LOVE. He distinguishes us by his bounty. All we receive is of pure benevolence ; we have done no work for it, we have not merited it. If only a little had been withheld, we should have lived in misery. Our joy and usefulness are dependent upon Divine gift. We thus get glimpses of the love of God, and, as he has first loved us, we should also love him.

V. DUE REMEMBRANCE OF OUR INDEBTEDNESS WILL TEND TO QUICKEN FAITH. How much God *has* done for us! We have not to *trust* for *that!* It has come to pass. And will not the Unchangeable continue to help us and to supply all our need? We have the promises, and the past tells us of no broken promise. Past experience should speak death to present doubt and fear.—H.

Vers. 8—10.—*Irony in religion.* I. SCRIPTURE WARRANTS THE USE OF IRONY IN CERTAIN CASES. Scripture is here fully at one with common sense and experience. There are certain conditions which can be most successfully touched by the shafts of ridicule : certain positions which can be carried most effectually by light artillery. In the Old Testament the folly of idolatry is often exhibited in ludicrous lights. Take, for example, Elijah's words on Carmel (1 Kings xviii. 27). Here Paul employs the weapon of satire. The Corinthians, in their carnality, conceived themselves to be at the very height of spirituality. They had attained already—and that without much knowledge of the daily cross. They had reached the goal suspiciously early. They were full; their knowledge was complete. They were rich; never were there such amply endowed Christians. They reigned as kings—none so high as they—monarchs of all they surveyed. And all this without the insignificant aid of such a very commonplace teacher as Paul! They had far transcended their early master. They were now so wise that he in comparison was quite a fool (ver. 10). They were strong, impregnable, triumphant; he evidently was weak, very weak still. Had he not been with them " in weakness, and in fear, and in much trembling " (ch. ii. 3) ? Was not that a very common condition for him to be in? Upon them crowded honour, dignity ; they were " all honourable men." He was despised and despicable; clearly they were in paradise. In the paradise of fools! and with majestic simplicity, but with keenest irony, Paul states the case as it appeared to them, and as it necessarily resulted from the position which they had assumed. If *that* did not open their eyes, they were blind for evermore. The Corinthians resembled the Laodiceans (Rev. iii. 17).

II. BUT IRONY IS A KEEN AND DANGEROUS WEAPON, AND SHOULD BE EMPLOYED WITH GREAT CARE. A suitable weapon for the hands of Paul, not of necessity for ours. Appropriate for some occasions, not for all. 1. Its use should be limited. We may easily run to excess. Irony is rather *a pleasant weapon* to use. Its employment in Scripture is not frequent. In this Epistle it is, indeed, used, but only occasionally. 2. It may profitably be accompanied by sober argument. So we have it here. 3. It should be employed in a spirit of love and with sincere desire to benefit. Not to make men ridiculous for the sake of making them so. Not for our own diversion. It should not be *bitter.* Paul was intensely solicitous to benefit the Corinthians; he had no pleasure in causing them pain. Note how in the midst of ironical utterances he expresses his fervent longing, " Yea and I would that ye did reign " (ver. 8). The object of his irony is to lead them from a mock kingship to a true.—H.

Vers. 11—13.—*The best and most useful often the most afflicted.* I. HISTORY AND PERSONAL OBSERVATION TEACH US THIS. Read Heb. xi. 35—38. Paul's case is a striking illustration. Note the (1) variety, (2) painfulness, (3) strangeness, of the apostolic afflictions. See also another list (2 Cor. xi. 23—27).

II. LET US LEARN THAT : 1. *Affliction is not always significant of Divine displeasure.* Often we have chastisement because of our sins, but sometimes sorrow comes to us when most firmly we tread the path of duty. Under such circumstances it should not dismay or depress us. 2. *Suffering—even severe suffering—is not always a valid reason for relinquishing active service.* Some people are too anxious to "retire." Work done under suffering is sometimes marvellously effective. Our woes fit us to deal with the woe-begone. When under great stress we feel that we can do nothing, we sometimes become Samsons; when we feel that we can do everything, we are generally mere Philistines. 3. *Much affliction need not necessarily be even a hindrance to us in our work.* Paul's sufferings did not make him less active in the cause of Christ. He abounded in toil whilst he abounded in sorrow. 4. *If affliction comes to us in the path of duty, it should not drive us from that path.* Most of Paul's sorrows were caused by his zeal and faithfulness. He *would* preach Christ. To choose an easier path would not have been wise for him—is not wise for us. 5. *Affliction is sanctified to God's faithful servants.* Beyond all doubt Paul was greatly the better for his many sorrows. Humanly speaking, he could never have been *Paul* without them. That which seems likely to hinder may help. Men who have to do much have generally to suffer much. Biography furnishes multitudinous illustrations of this. 6. *Extraordinary sufferings sometimes bear with them the promise of unusual usefulness.* Idlers have thus been made remarkably diligent, sleepers have been awakened, the worldly have become consecrated. The first true and inspiring view of Christian service has been obtained from the flame of the furnace. The apprenticeship of some "of whom the world was not worthy" has been served in the fires. Some great lives have *begun* with martyrdom. 7. *Affliction should be received in a spirit of meekness, even when it comes directly from men who have no reason to use us ill.* Paul, when reviled, blessed; when persecuted, calmly endured it, without after-retaliation; when defamed, he entreated (perhaps God to pardon his enemies). Herein Paul was like Christ. He employed conquering kindness. To imitate him will require much grace. *It is often much easier to take affliction from the hands of God than from the hands of men.*—H.

Vers. 14—21.—*Spiritual parentage.* I. A VERY TENDER RELATIONSHIP. Paul notices: 1. *The way in which the relationship is formed.* (Ver. 15.) The spiritual father (1) "begets" his children (2) in Christ Jesus (3) through the gospel. He finds them "strangers to the covenant of promise," strangers to Christ, strangers to the Church; but under the preaching of the truth they are led by the Spirit to lay hold of salvation: they become in Christ "new creatures," are "born again;" and he who has been the instrument employed in their conversion becomes their spiritual father. This relationship is a limited one, but nevertheless deeply interesting and important. 2. *That it differs from the relationship existing between a mere teacher and learner.* None can be to us what those are who have brought us to Christ. They have a peculiar claim upon our love and gratitude. "Ten thousand instructors make not one father." We may love our teachers, but they are not our parents.
II. THE DUTIES OF THE FATHER TO HIS SPIRITUAL CHILDREN. 1. *He should be watchful over them.* As Paul was. They need much care; they should not be left to shift for themselves. A pernicious opinion is rife, that when people are "converted" no further trouble need be taken about them. As though when a child is "born" it is to be cast adrift and left to take care of itself! No wonder that there are so many spiritual cripples, so many diseased, so many weaklings, and not a few religious imbeciles. Fathers should look after their spiritual children; as far as possible we should see that our converts, if not under ours, are under good influences. 2. *He should manifest a loving spirit towards them.* They should be peculiarly dear to him. In many ways they may try his patience, *but it should bear the trial.* He should *cherish* them. Paul fed the Corinthian babes with milk; he did not discard them because they were not what he would have had them to be. He did not indulge in undue severity; fathers are not "to provoke their children to wrath" (Eph. vi. 4). 3. *He should be faithful, ever inclining towards tenderness, but not sparing the rod when it is called for.* (Ver. 21.) Willing to rebuke when rebuke is necessary, but not *fond* of rebuking. Paul was gentle but decisive. He sought to nip evil in the bud. Foolish fondness lets the evil grow till it is too great to cope with. Correction must be wise, or it will be pernicious. Sometimes the placing of a faithful child amongst the unfaithful may be very efficacious for the latter. Paul sent Timothy (ver. 17). 4. *Acting and living so as to be a fit example.* We have no right to expect our spiritual children to follow us closely unless we are following Christ closely. Paul could say, "Be ye followers of me, even as I also am of Christ" (ch. xi. 1). He does not exhort them to follow him as a party leader, but to imitate

him as he sought to imitate Christ. He set a good example. It is what we *are* rather than what we *say* that has influence. Spiritual children have quick eyes.—H.

Vers. 1—5.—" *The ministers of Christ.*" The Corinthians were to be delivered from their tendency to glory in men,' by being taught to regard them as a part of their heritage. All teachers were for their use, not the particular one whom they chose as their party leader. Besides, a right view of the ministerial office should prevent all boasting in men.

I. HOW MINISTERS ARE TO BE REGARDED. They are: **1.** *Servants of Christ.* They are not "lords over God's heritage" (1 Pet. v. 3), the chiefs of the kingdom. Their true dignity lies in serving the Lord Jesus, from whom they take their orders. They have no authority beyond that which is committed to them. Nor are they the servants of men. Obedience to their own Master delivers them from subjection to every other (comp. on ch. iii. 5). **2.** *Stewards of the mysteries of God.* The Church is God's house, in which he alone is Master; apostles and other teachers being dispensers of the good things of the house, the great doctrines of the faith. Every man is a steward, being entrusted with the laying out of the gifts conferred upon him, and the improving of the opportunities put in his way. But this is true in a special sense of the Christian minister. He is entrusted with the dispensation of the Divine mysteries to men. He is not called to deal out his own things, but the saving truth of God, giving to each his portion of meat in due season. How responsible an office! This view of the Christian ministry should guard us against two common extremes. On the one side, *ministers are not lords*, endowed with a kind of supernatural power, and set to rule the consciences of men. On the other side, *ministers are not the servants of the people*, appointed to teach only some favourite type of doctrine. They are the servants of Christ, charged to deliver his truth, whether men will hear it or not.

II. FAITHFULNESS THE GREAT REQUISITE. Every steward must give account of his stewardship, and the chief thing required is fidelity. Men ask of a preacher, "Is he able, eloquent, attractive?" God asks, "Is he faithful?" Fidelity does not depend on the quality or quantity of the original gifts, but on the use to which they are put. The man with two talents receives the same reward as the man with five, because he has been equally faithful (Matt. xxv. 21, 23). Nor is fidelity measured by what men call success, since it is often incompatible with popularity. Let the much-gifted minister beware; let the little-gifted take comfort. "Well done, good and *faithful* servant."

III. THE MINISTER'S JUDGE. **1.** *Not the congregation.* It was a very small thing in Paul's view to be judged of men. The verdict of the people on a minister's discharge of duty is not to be lightly laid aside. If they praise, let us beware of being satisfied with this; if they condemn, let us the more thoroughly search ourselves. But from this verdict there must ever be an appeal to a higher tribunal. Men cannot read the motives that lie behind the outward act, nor can they gauge the proportion between a minister's powers and the use he makes of them. Their measure of fidelity must always be imperfect. **2.** *Not the minister himself.* The apostle disclaims being his own judge. He cannot charge himself with any remissness in duty, but he does not regard this as an unfailing proof of fidelity. He distrusts his own verdict. Let those who think themselves perfect ponder this statement. A good conscience is very precious, but let us not run into the folly of measuring ourselves by ourselves. Conscience is not the final judge in the matter. **3.** *The Lord is his Judge.* "Who art thou that judgest the servant of another? to his own lord he standeth or falleth" (Rom. xiv. 4). This is man's judgment-day; let us wait "until the Lord come, who will both bring to light the hidden things of darkness, and make manifest the counsels of the hearts." The verdict of that day will proceed upon a perfect knowledge of the whole case, and every steward shall receive the praise of God according to the just award of the Judge. Wherefore: (1) *Do all your work remembering that Christ is your Judge.* He knows your weakness as well as your strength, and sees the honest desire to serve him beneath many an apparent failure. (2) *Do not sit in judgment upon others.* Christ will judge his own servants.—B.

Vers. 6—13.—*Against self-conceit.* Party spirit leads to the undue exaltation of men. The head of a faction becomes a hero in the eyes of those that belong to it. Two evil consequences follow—pride, self-sufficiency, conceit, on the one hand; undue depreciation of others and boasting against them, on the other hand.   Against this hateful spirit the apostle has already presented a variety of arguments; and while speaking chiefly of himself and Apollos, he has in reality been teaching us how to regard all the ministers of Christ.   They are not to be exalted beyond the position assigned them in Scripture, nor are they to suffer themselves to be puffed up with pride one against another.

I. A COGENT ARGUMENT.   "For who maketh thee to differ?"   If we are better than our neighbours, or possess gifts which they do not possess, we have God to thank for it. This question should be asked in view of all earthly privileges—health, wealth, position, education.   More especially with regard to spiritual benefits.   Who maketh thee to differ from that reeling drunkard, that erring sister, that condemned felon, that poor imbecile, that blind heathen?   "By the grace of God I am what I am" (ch. xv. 10). The thoughts awakened by such an inquiry should silence all boastfulness, and call forth praise to him to whom we owe all.   Spiritual pride robs God of his glory.

II. AN IRONICAL PICTURE.   "Already are ye filled, already ye are become rich, ye have reigned without us."   You speak as if you had already attained perfection and participated in the millennial glory.   You are not only rich, but seated as kings upon the throne.   I would it were really so, for then we also might share in your glory; but alas! ye reign *without us*.   You fortunate ones are exalted, but we poor apostles are still suffering on the earth.   Thus does Paul hold up the self-conceit of the Corinthians to derision.   A warning for all time to those who run off with a part of the truth as if it were the whole.   Like the perfectionists of our day, these Corinthians had fallen into the delusion that they had reached the goal.   Spiritual pride is very subtle and very dangerous.   This picture is suggestive when viewed in connection with the low morality prevalent in the Christian community at Corinth.   Note here the legitimate use of irony, as in the case of Elijah (1 Kings xviii. 27) and Isaiah (xliv. 9, etc.).   Evil has its ludicrous side, and the exhibition of this is sometimes more effective than plain argument.   Irony, however, is a dangerous weapon, and needs to be handled with skill. The anger that pours ridicule upon an opponent must have behind it a heart of love, if its wounds are to prove wholesome.

III. A PATHETIC CONTRAST.   With the proud position of the Corinthians, Paul contrasts the suffering condition of himself and his brother apostles.   Consider: 1. *The general picture.*   "For, I think, God hath set forth us the apostles last of all, as men doomed to death."   He seems to have in view the exhibitions given in the amphitheatre, at the close of which criminals condemned to death were brought in to fight with wild beasts or with one another.   The sufferings of the apostles were a spectacle to the world, men and angels beholding them with interest.   And what was true of these servants of Christ is true in part of every believer.   We are wrestlers in the arena, fighting for dear life, with a myriad eyes upon us (comp. Heb. xii. 1).   2. *The details of the picture.*   Very touching is this description of apostolic life, supplemented by the fuller details in the Second Epistle (xi. 23—33).   Follow the steps of the homeless evangelist as he goes from place to place, earning his own bread while preaching the gospel, suffering many privations, exposed to many perils, and treated as the refuse of the world.   No wonder if men called him a fool.   Looked at from the outside, scarcely any life could appear more miserable; but all is changed when we know that it was lived "for Christ's sake."   Love to him made the fellowship of his sufferings a matter to boast of.   Are we willing to endure hardship for the Lord's sake?   Are we taking up the cross he lays athwart our path?

IV. A CHRIST-LIKE SPIRIT.   Suffering *for* Christ is also suffering *with* Christ.   He too was despised and rejected of men; and where he is there must also his servant be. In addition to this we have here suffering endured in the Spirit of Christ.   "Being reviled, we bless; being persecuted, we endure, being defamed, we entreat."   This was according to the Lord's commandment (Matt. v. 44), and after his example (1 Pet. ii. 23).   How really noble is such a life!   The truly strong man is he who can rise above the reproach and hate of men, and regard them with Christ-like compassion.   Contrast this humble following of Jesus with the proud boasting of the Corinthians.—B.

Vers. 14—21.—*The father and his children.*   The apostle has used sharp words, but they have been dictated by love. He has written as a father who desires the correction and not the shame of his children.

I. SPIRITUAL FATHERHOOD. 1. *How constituted.* "For in Christ Jesus I begat you through the gospel." Conversion is the beginning of a new life, the birth by which we enter on spiritual being. This change is wrought by the agency of the Holy Spirit, on the basis of Christ's redemptive work; the Spirit's instrument is the Word, the incorruptible seed (1 Pet. i. 23); and this Word is administered by servants of the gospel. In a subordinate sense, Paul could speak of himself as the father of the Corinthian Church, inasmuch as he was the means of introducing them to the Christian life. The relationship is a peculiarly tender one, carrying with it much honour and much responsibility. 2. *How distinguished.* "For though ye should have ten thousand tutors in Christ, yet have ye not many fathers." The teachers who succeeded Paul at Corinth, and of whom they made so much, were like pedagogues who superintended the education of children. Theirs was an important work, but it did not alter the fact that the apostle was their spiritual father. They built on the foundation which he had laid. There is no disparagement of those who minister to the culture of the Christian life, as compared with those who are instrumental in commencing it. The evangelist and the teacher have each his own place in the Divine economy. Yet the relation of spiritual fatherhood is one by itself, different from that subsisting between teacher and scholar. Often the two go together, the pastor being also the father. 3. *Implies the duty of admonition.* It is the part of a father to "reprove, rebuke, exhort," in all fidelity. Spiritual fathers must not be blind to the faults of their children. Love must patiently instruct, affectionately entreat, sharply chastise. Witness the paternal severity of the apostle in this Epistle as he "admonishes his beloved children." 4. *Implies the setting of a worthy example.* "Be ye imitators of me." The eyes of the children are towards the father, and they cannot help copying him. Example is powerful in all spheres, and most of all in a sphere so conspicuous as the Christian ministry. It confirms the truth taught, encourages believers, rebukes the ungodly, draws inquirers to the Saviour. Every servant of Christ should be able to say, "Follow me." Yet our imitation of other Christians, even the most eminent, has its limits. Men are imperfect, reflecting but brokenly the image of Christ; and no wise teacher will desire to see his own peculiar mannerisms reflected in his people. Human example is useful only in so far as it helps us to imitate Jesus.

II. SOLICITUDE FOR THE CHURCH'S SPIRITUAL INSTRUCTION. Like a true father, the absent apostle desires to further the spiritual growth of his converts, and with this view sends to them a personal deputy. 1. *The mission.* In order to promote their imitation of his humble, self-denying life, he sends a messenger to recall to them "his ways in Christ." The remembrance of a good man's life is a help to piety. The memory of some departed saint has often proved a guiding star. And so is the recollection of truth already learned. It is part of the preacher's work to press home old truths and deepen their hold of the heart and conscience. 2. *The missionary.* There was wisdom in sending a deputy, and in the choice of Timothy for the mission. As the apostle's "beloved and faithful child," he stood in the same spiritual relation to him as did the converts at Corinth. He could speak to them as a brother of their common father's doctrine and life. The visits of wise and faithful servants of Christ are often instrumental in reviving the Church's life.

III. APOSTOLIC VISITATION. 1. *Carried out in the face of detraction.* Those who sought to undermine Paul's authority asserted that he would not again venture to visit Corinth; but in spite of this he declares his intention of doing so. The servant of Christ needs courage. 2. *Subject to Divine direction.* "If the Lord will" (comp. Jas. iv. 15). Man proposes, but God disposes. All our plans for the future must be subject to his control. 3. *To test spiritual profession.* The proud boasters at Corinth were great in talk, and Paul wished to show whether there was reality behind it. For power is the chief thing, not mere speech. The kingdom of God, *i.e.* genuine Christianity, is not an affair of words, but of living power. "Our gospel came not unto you in word only, but also in power, and in the Holy Ghost" (1 Thess. i. 5). Profession must be tested by practice. A religion of the lip is vain without the religion of the life. 4. *Proceeds according to circumstances.* Whether Paul was to come with a rod or in love depended on themselves. The discipline of the Church takes its complexion from the character of the persons with whom it deals, being severe or tender, as the case requires. A combination of fatherly love and wisdom is required in those who are called to deal with the erring.—B.

Ver. 2.—*Faithful stewardship.* This is a principle approved alike of God and man. Stewardship implies responsibility, and responsibility demands faithfulness. The principle is applicable specially to the ministry of the Word. No responsibility like that of those who are called to keep watch and guard over the mysteries of God, to minister in Christ's Name the richest treasures of his grace. Note St. Paul's own profound sense of his responsibility. It was a comparatively "small thing" to him to be "judged of man's judgment;" but the consciousness of the righteous judgment of God was always present with him, and the anxiety to approve himself to him as one who "needed not to be ashamed" was perhaps the deepest and strongest emotion he knew. And the principle may be applied to everything that distinguishes us personally among men, and that puts any power for good into our hands (Parables of the Unjust Steward, of the Talents, etc.). Intellectual capacity, educational advantages, wealth, social position, power of speech, any kind of artistic or constructive skill, vigour of physical health, abundance of leisure time,—these and such as these are endowments that put the possibility of incalculable good within our reach, and for the use of which we must give account. All human life is a sacred stewardship. In every position in which Providence has placed us our fidelity is being put to the test, our loyalty to God and to conscience, to the eternal principles of truth and righteousness, to the sovereign authority of the Law of Christ. It is required of us that we should be faithful always and in everything. And if at heart we are faithful men, it will be seen to be so. Observe respecting this stewardship—

I. THAT IT IS INDEPENDENT OF WHAT SEEMS TO BE THE RELATIVE IMPORTANCE OF THE POSITIONS WE OCCUPY AND THE MATTERS WITH WHICH WE HAVE TO DEAL. What we call the trivial and commonplace affairs of life are quite as effectual a test of moral faithfulness as the greater; often more so. We are prone to treat lightly what seem to us to be "little things," and for that very reason they are often the truest revealers of our character. Our real dispositions come out most clearly in the way in which we deal with them, because then our behaviour is most spontaneous, unpremeditated, free from artifice. If you want to know what a man really is, don't judge of him as he appears on the broad open platform of public life, but follow him into his more private ways, and see how he speaks and acts when he feels himself to be beyond the ear and eye of the world, and in matters on which no great consequence seems to hang. It is quite possible to raise a purely artificial standard of moral obligation, and to magnify unwisely certain scruples of conscience. But a really conscientious man will be conscientious in everything. And as a feather or a straw will show which way the stream is flowing, so do the trivial circumstances of life reveal the moral drift of our being. (Note the bearing of this on the probation to which Adam was subject: "Thou shalt not eat," etc.) What is daily life to every one of us but a series of silent tests of our inward fidelity? We are hedged in by little restrictions, called to take upon us manfully the burden of many unwelcome duties; to suffer many abstinences, rebukes, selfmortifications. And when we are disposed to overstep the boundary, because at certain points it seems so narrow or so low, we show that we have not learnt the full surrender of the spirit of obedience. "Offending in one point" of the law of our allegiance, we betray a spirit that is "guilty of all." So as regards the right use of faculty and passing opportunities of doing good. The temptations that belong to a low order of personal faculty and a narrow range of personal influence are often greater than those that belong to the highest and the largest. You do nothing because the utmost you can do is so little; or you do carelessly and half-heartedly what, as it seems to you, for anything the world would really be the better for it, you might neglect to do at all. The spirit that dictates this is one that would trifle with the loftiest powers and abuse the noblest possibilities of life. "He that is faithful in that which is least," etc. (Luke xvi. 10).

II. ALL PRACTICAL FIDELITY IN THE STEWARDSHIP OF LIFE HAS A TENDENCY TO DEVELOP INTO HIGHER CAPACITY AND NOBLER DEED. Note here the power of habit. Accustom yourself with an earnest spirit to meet the claims of every-day duty as in the Master's sight, and you call to your aid a power and obey a law of life by which the highest moral victories shall ultimately be won. Let our children be trained to act from principle and not from mere passion or policy, to habits of self-surrender, to simple forms of Christian service, and they will become so habituated to the right way that when the heavier responsibilities of life begin to fall upon them they will be prepared bravely to meet them—the " yoke will be easy and the burden light." Thus is it given to us all to educate ourselves for what awaits us in the future. The Jews say of David that "God tried him first with those few sheep in the wilderness, and then, because he faithfully and bravely kept them, took him from the sheepfolds to feed his people Israel." Only use manfully whatever moral power you possess, and you need not fear any strain that shall ever be put upon it. Cast yourself freely upon your faith, and though it be now but as a " grain of mustard seed," it shall be mighty enough one day " to remove mountains."

III. SUCH FIDELITY LEADS TO BLESSED ISSUES IN THE GREAT FUTURITY. It is not given to us to trace the path of moral forces very far in this world. Our judgments are often at fault, our forecasts often strangely falsified. Only very imperfectly and with cautious hesitating steps can we follow the winding and widening stream of earthly issues. And who shall say how some of the unnoticed doings of every human life, and the results that grow out of them, will appear in the all-revealing light of the day when " God will bring every work into judgment and every secret thing, whether it be good or bad "? But of this we may be perfectly well assured, that to a lifelong endeavour to serve and please the Lord Jesus Christ there must be a blessed eternal reward. Let our life be a faithful one, a work faithfully wrought out in his Name, and we need not fear but that it will prove itself to be a life worth living and that ends well. " Be thou faithful unto death, and I will give thee a crown of life " (Rev. ii. 10).—W.

Ver. 20.—*Not in word, but in power.* The exact point of this affirmation is to be determined by the circumstances that called it forth. The apostle refers in the context to his personal adversaries in the Church at Corinth. They spoke against him, " puffed up" by the spirit of proud hostility. But he will come and put their pretensions to the test. He will "know, not their words" only, but the amount of real " power " that there is in them. This suggests the general relation of the " word " to " the power " in the kingdom of God as an organized fellowship. Seen in several particulars.

I. ITS MEMBERSHIP. Not a question of professed creed, or ritual observance, or forms of godliness; but of the energy of a Divine life in the soul, transforming the whole being of a man into a " new creature." " Except a man be born of water and of the Spirit," etc. (John iii. 5); " The kingdom of God is not meat and drink," etc. (Rom. xiv. 17); " In Christ Jesus neither circumcision," etc. (Gal. vi. 15).

II. ITS MINISTRY. Not by the utterance of mere forms of speech, the establishment of ecclesiastical systems, the multiplication of the means of Christian culture; but by the diffusion of the living force of truth, and the silent sovereign power of the Spirit of God. " It is the Spirit that quickeneth," etc. (John vi. 63); " Our gospel came unto you not in word only," etc. (1 Thess. i. 5).

III. ITS ADMINISTRATION. Not by hollow pretence, or blatant assumption, or self-constituted officialism; but by the authority that lies in real personal capacity, distinguished goodness, saintly character, effective spiritual power (1 Tim. iii. 1—7; Titus i. 7—9).—W.

Ver. 20.—*The kingdom is power.* The contrast between word and power is familiar to our minds. To say of a man that he is a stickler for the letter, a pedant about forms, a zealot for words, is to say that he is shallow and tiresome. A wise man looks beneath the skin and shape of things to their substance. An effective man goes in for power. Yet the world is governed by words as the expressions of thought and purpose. Education is conducted, opinion is formed, all human combinations of knowledge and practical force are got together, and held together, by means of fit words. The kingdom of God itself is introduced by the Word of testimony. What avails not is mere repetition of words after the manner of a charm, or " vain jangling " about verbal forms. Especially irksome must all such metallic clatter of words without profit have been to a man so much in earnest as St. Paul. No doubt there was much of it among the Christians at

Corinth, where to the minute pedantry of Jews was added the inveterate disputation of Greeks. The apostle wished to discourage their sharp word-contests, and gave notice that, on his next visit, he would probe the arrogant pretensions of certain talkers very closely. Their speech would avail them little if they failed in spiritual power. Such cautions against religious verbalism are needed constantly. Just because Christianity owes so much to true and faithful utterances, rests on testimony, and requires much teaching, it is peculiarly liable to be weakened by hollow, pretentious, or disputatious speaking. Therefore must we emphasize the futility of religious words without the informing Spirit of life and power. The great characteristic of the kingdom of God, as announced by Jesus Christ, and spread abroad by his apostles, was its penetrating and elevating dynamic. It had a quiet but potent energy. It could "turn the world upside down;" could break off Jews from self-righteousness and Gentiles from idolatry, abase the proud and exalt the lowly, make the wise simple and the simple wise. And what was this power? It was the force of truth, the diffusive element of light, the majesty of righteousness, the sublime persuasiveness of love. It was all this, and more. It was the heart piercing and enthralling energy of the Holy Ghost, working with and by the Word. God gave the increase. In the light of St. Paul's compact and weighty saying, look at—

I. THE KINGDOM OF GOD AMONG OURSELVES. We speak not of a particular Church, but of the kingdom moving forwards in the midst of Churches variously constituted and administered. Church usages and appointments may, and indeed must, change. It is not possible or desirable to reproduce in the nineteenth century, and in the West, the very Church of the first century in the East. But the kingdom of God must be, and is, the same. It is "righteousness, and peace, and joy in the Holy Ghost." Wherever these are found, they betoken the presence of a heavenly power. But a Church may appear strong, and yet be at heart cold and weak. It may be irreproachable in word and form, clothed with venerable traditions as some old wall is mantled with ivy; it may be exemplary in all the routine of prayer and preaching, and yet be barren and ineffective, because it has nothing but forms and words; and "the kingdom of God is not in word, but in power." It is quite impossible to overcome the world, abase the proud, sober the frivolous, arrest the mind that is busy with a thousand trifles, or lift up the spirit that has debased itself to avaricious deceits or to those fleshly vices which civilization cannot overcome, by words ever so well chosen, services ever so comely, forms of godliness ever so correct. What is wanted is the kingdom of God in power.

II. THE KINGDOM OF GOD ELSEWHERE—EVERYWHERE. Even if we take a very hopeful survey of missionary work, we must confess that Churches have been too languid in purpose, too pedantic in method, and in some places too jealous of one another, too ready to cry, "Lo, here!" "Lo, there!" It is the kingdom of God which should be preached; and if only its power comes to be felt, we might all keep our minds comparatively easy about the moulds into which new life may flow, or the forms under which Christian activity may organize itself throughout the world. It is a startling and mournful fact that in countries where our faith has been professed for centuries, we have yet to discuss the evidences of Christianity. Christian literature has reached an almost prodigious development; and Christian teaching and preaching are not scarce. Yet the world does not believe or obey the gospel. Surely there is a hiding of power. Rise up, Christians! gird up the loins of your mind. Be evidences of Christianity, known and read of all. There is no witness so luminous and so irresistibly convincing as that which comes from the practical effect of the gospel on the minds, consciences, dispositions, and conduct of the men and women who profess to believe it.—F.

Vers. 1, 2.—*The Christian teacher a steward.* The apostle here intimates what are right thoughts for Christian people to cherish concerning their teachers. He uses two words, "ministers," "stewards," the former of which is familiar, the latter needs some explanation. A minister is "one who serves," and no more honourable thought can be attached to the Christian teacher than that he *serves* Christ among his people, and serves the people for Christ's sake. Our Lord himself said, "I am among you as he that serveth;" and St. Paul says to his converts, "Ye serve the Lord Christ." We propose now to dwell more fully on the figure of the *steward.* A Christian teacher is to be thought of as a " steward of the mysteries of God." The word " steward " is used in England for a " land bailiff ; " but in the East it was employed for a person put in trust of all his master's goods—" such as was Eliezer in the house of Abraham (Gen. xxiv. 2 —12), and Joseph in the house of Potiphar (Gen. xxxix. 4). It was one of the main duties of such a steward to dispense their portions of food to the different members of the household (Luke xii. 42), to give the slaves or servants their " portion in due season." Compare the words " housekeeper," " house-ruler," " house-feeder," and see Matt. xxiv. 45. The apostle's point is that the Christian teacher is not to be esteemed for any particular qualifications which he may have of his own, but simply for his faithfulness in doing his work as the servant of God. Christian congregations may fall into either of two errors; the " Christian minister may be glorified, or made an idol of, in two ways —by party worship of the *man*, or by attaching a mystical or supernatural power to the *office.*" Both the minister himself, and those among whom he labours, do well to keep ever in mind that he is but a steward, only Christ's servant, to minister to them in Divine things. We consider, then—

I. THE STEWARD'S TRUSTS. " The mysteries of God." Mysteries were familiar things to those whom the apostle addressed. " The word ' mysteries ' is derived from a word signifying *to close, to shut*, and was in the old Greek civilization used to denote those rites which were only permitted to the initiated, and were kept a strict secret from the outside world. Of such a kind were the well-known Eleusinian mysteries, which were kept every fifth year at Eleusis, in Attica ; the rites of the Bona Dea, which were observed at Rome ; and those of Isis and Mithras, which were of Egyptian and Persian origin." It should be noticed that the word " mystery " is used in the Scriptures in two distinct senses : (1) for things that are hidden from the ordinary understanding; and (2) for things that in past times were unknown, but are now revealed to those who believe the gospel. The term is chiefly used in this latter sense. When St. Paul exclaims, " Great is the mystery of godliness," he means the " revealed mystery," of which he immediately speaks, even God, or Christ, being " manifest in the flesh." The *trust* of the Christian teacher is, then, the revealed mystery of the gospel, and this may be said to have three centres round which it gathers : (1) the Incarnation ; (2) the Sacrifice ; (3) the Resurrection. The Incarnation reveals the mysteries of God and of man ; the Sacrifice reveals the mysteries of sin and of redemption from sin ; and the Resurrection reveals the mysteries of immortality and of sanctification. So these are the great truths and trusts of which the Christian teachers are " stewards." Their work is to minister these truths, in all their varied adaptations and applications, to the people of their charge. Happy, indeed, are they who can close their ministry pleading as St. Paul did, " I have not shunned to declare unto you the whole counsel of God."

II. THE STEWARD'S RESPONSE TO HIS TRUSTS. " Found faithful." The thought of St. Paul seems to have been that due inquiry is made into the character and trust-worthiness of a man before he is put into the office of a steward ; as he elsewhere says, " Let them first be proved." But we may fairly include under his language the reasonable expectation that the man who is entrusted with a responsible position and work will be " found faithful " in his doing of it. Then we must inquire what should be the faithfulness of a Christian teacher, or indeed of the Christian man, to whom the gospel mysteries have been revealed. It should be manifest in three departments : 1. He must be faithful to his Master, God ; seeking his service only, and his glory only. 2. He must be faithful to the truths he has received ; carefully setting *them*, and not any mere ideas he may have about them, before the people ; and seeking to set the *whole* of them, and not merely portions in which he may be personally interested, before his congregation. 3. He must be faithful to the people to whom God may have sent him ; taking up the burden of their spiritual needs on his own heart ; feeling ever as did good Samuel Rutherford when he said, " God is my witness, that your salvation would be two salvations to me, and your heaven two heavens to me ! " Impress that the more deeply we feel the greatness of our trusts, as having had the great religious mysteries in part revealed to us, the more serious becomes for us the question of our " faithfulness ; " and the more shall we feel the need for solemn times of self-searching and self-criticism. It is an unspeakable honour to be entrusted with the " mysteries " of God and of Christ and of redemption from sin ; but all true and humble souls say with the apostle, " But who is sufficient for these things ? "—R. T.

Vers. 3—5.—*A threefold judgment of the Christian teacher.* The thought of the apostle is evidently occupied with the disposition of the Corinthians to form judgments for and against different Christian teachers, and to make parties by their preference for one over another. There seems to have been a critical habit, which was applied to the work of each minister; and such a habit is always found seriously to injure the work of our ministers, and fatally to influence that openness and receptivity of spirit on which due reception of Christian teachings depend. It may be especially pointed out that the habit of discussing the work of the clergy in our families, depreciating some of them, and unduly praising others, has a most mischievous influence on the younger members of our households. In this passage St. Paul strongly urges his indifference to any judgments that may be formed about him. He was simply but heartily trying to do Christ's work under Christ's lead, and he could wait for his Master to judge what had been the quality and the value of his work. He speaks of three kinds of judgment to which the Christian teacher may be subject.

I. MAN'S JUDGMENT. We must all do our work with the feeling that, at least, our fellow-men have their eyes upon us, and form their opinions concerning us. Illustrate how we form estimates of one another. When great men die, the judgments which their contemporaries formed of their work finds expression in numerous articles and books; and when the friends of simpler folk meet at their funerals, their talk shows how the tone and character of the dead man's life has been fully—sometimes fairly, and at other times unfairly—estimated. Now, such judgments of our fellow-men may be helpful to us when they find expression in our lifetime. (1) They are if they help to increase our sense of the seriousness of our duty; (2) they are if they lead us to know ourselves better, to see and to correct our mistakes; (3) they are if they make us more anxious to win men's approval by a higher faithfulness to our duty. But the thought of man's judgment may be mischievous if it (1) makes us nervously sensitive to merely human opinion; (2) if it makes us self-conscious; and (3) if it makes us in any sense or degree more anxious about the praise of men than the praise of God. We may value men's good opinion as an encouragement; we may consider men's severe judgments as helping us to see our faults; but we may not permit our settled life-work to be hindered by men's opinion, nor our hearts to be depressed by men's criticisms. We serve the Lord, not men.

II. SELF-JUDGMENT. St. Paul says, "I judge not mine own self." Show how important to all Christian workers is self-knowledge, and the power to fairly weigh and estimate one's own doings. So many fail because, while heeding everybody's criticism, they fail to criticize themselves. But wise and helpful self-judgments are (1) very dependent on natural disposition; (2) on particular bodily and mental moods; and (3) on the measure and degree of a man's self-love. The duty is plainly taught by the apostle when he said, "If we would judge ourselves, we should not be judged" (ch. xi. 31).

III. THE LORD'S JUDGMENT. "He that judgeth me is the Lord." That judgment is stricter than any man's, and than any which we can make concerning ourselves. These points may be illustrated as impressing the superiority of the Lord's judgment. (1) It is most searching; (2) it concerns even our motives; (3) it is infallibly correct; (4) it is going on every day now; (5) it is in measure revealed to us now; (6) it is in measure kept from us now, that our freedom may not be unduly limited; (7) it will be fully revealed to us by-and-by; and (8) on it our allotments of place and work in the "eternities" must entirely depend.—R. T.

Ver. 6.—*Differences according to grace received.* One can but be struck with the prudence and delicacy of the apostle in not mentioning the actual names of the party leaders at Corinth, but illustrating his principle from such more prominent names as his own, that of St. Peter, and that of Apollos. He avoids any charge of personality; and names only the greater leaders, that the Corinthians might learn not to be puffed up for *any* minister. All teachers are but men, and all are to be esteemed for the Divine gifts that may be entrusted to their charge. We may not "glory in *man*," only in *God*, who distributeth to each man severally as he wills, using this man and that for whatever service he may please. F. W. Robertson, speaking of the Christian ministry, well says, "The qualities which are requisite for the higher part of the ministry are—

great powers of sympathy; a mind masculine in its power, feminine in its tenderness; humbleness; wisdom to direct; that knowledge of the world which the Bible calls the wisdom of the serpent; and a knowledge of evil that comes rather from repulsion from it than from personal contact with it. But those qualifications which adapt a man for the merely showy parts of the Christian ministry are of an inferior order—fluency, self-confidence, tact, a certain histrionic power of conceiving feelings, and expressing them. Now, it was precisely to this class of qualities that Christianity opened a new field in places such as Corinth. Men who had been unknown in their trades suddenly found an opportunity for public addresses, for activity, and for leadership. They became fluent and ready talkers; and the more shallow and self-sufficient they were, the more likely it was that they would become the leaders of a faction." The correction of this evil is indicated in our text. The humble sense of grace received, and the burden of responsibility in so high a trust, should keep all Christian teachers in their right place. Recognizing the differences of men's gifts according to the grace they have received, we should value each man for what gift and grace he may have; but we should take care never to make contrasting estimates, nor allow ourselves to be " puffed up for one against another." The following points may receive illustration from other portions of St. Paul's Epistles, especially from the two to the Corinthians, and from those known as the "Pastoral Epistles " (1 and 2 Timothy and Titus) :—

I. THE DIVERSITY OF GIFTS ENTRUSTED TO CHRISTIAN TEACHERS. The work to which they are called is very various in its forms and demands. In the family there must be a variety of services, and ability for each; and in the state a variety of offices, and a fitness for each. So in the Christian Church. For its upbuilding there is needed the gift of architect, and carver, and mason, and labourer, and carpenter. The gift of the preacher differs from that of the teacher, and that again from the gift of the organizer. If we once fully admit that all gifts are *of grace,* and each an unspeakable honour and an overwhelming responsibility for him to whom it is entrusted, envy of each other would pass for ever away, and we should thankfully use each man for the service God has fitted him to render.

II. ALL DIVINE GIFTS ARE UNTO EDIFICATION. God never bestows anything on any man that he may get praise of men or worldly honour for it. All God's gifts are for *use.* All are entrusted to us for the *sake of others.* All bear upon the " fully furnishing of our fellow-men unto all good works."

III. ALL, TOGETHER, WILL BE FOUND TO MAKE UP A COMPLETE CIRCLE OF THE MEANS OF GRACE. We fail in : 1. The effort to bring out the various gifts of men into use. The Church is everywhere rich with the gifted *unknown,* and the gifted *idler.* 2. In the due recognition of the spiritual completeness which God, in his providential leadings, brings to our Churches. 3. In the consequent freeing of men from duties for which they are unfitted, that they may fully cultivate and use their special gift. Impress that the thankful recipiency and use of the Divine provisions for our spiritual needs should master all personal feeling towards individuals. We should honour the Master who arranges the gifts, and honour the servants only *for his sake.*—R. T.

Vers. 8—12.—*Suffering for others a proof of interest in their welfare.* Recall Paley's argument from the sufferings of the early Christians as to the sincerity of their belief. Similarly, St. Paul urges here that the troubles and persecutions which he and the other teachers had endured in ministering to the Churches, ought to convince the people of his love and zeal for their highest welfare ; and should also be felt to set him in such intimate and confidential relations with them that he might claim the right to reprove and correct. We all know that reproof cannot be easily or usefully accepted, save from those whom we know love us truly and sincerely seek our highest well-being. From these verses two subjects may claim consideration—

I. GOD'S MISSION FOR APOSTLES, LOOKED AT, KINDLES ENTHUSIASM. " We are made a spectacle unto the world, and to angels, and to men." Watching such a devoted, self-sacrificing, heroic life as that St. Paul lived ought to stir us up to enthusiastic efforts to follow so noble an example. Illustrate how the story of great martyrs and great missionaries has, in all ages, been used to inspire lesser men to noble things. " Lives of great men all remind us," etc.

II. GOD'S MISSION FOR APOSTLES, CARRIED OUT, AWAKENS SYMPATHY. (Vers. 11, 12.)

Fully detail the sufferings which St. Paul underwent, and the bodily frailty which made those sufferings so exceedingly trying (see 2 Cor. xi. 23—30). After our Lord in his closing sufferings, no man so awakens our tenderest sympathy as does the Apostle of the Gentiles. Illustrate how, in modern missions, the Pattesons and Livingstones have excited world-wide sympathy. Illustrate also how their constant sufferings made Baxter's and Robert Hall's continued and devoted labours so affecting to us. Or refer to the power, on his little audience, of Adolphe Monod's talks from his bed of suffering and death. St. Paul shows what made his sufferings so interesting to us—they were borne as submissive obedience *unto God* ; and as vicarious *for us* ; and this ought to give him a persuasive power and a full right to advise, and reprove, and correct, and warn, and teach.—R. T.

Ver. 16.—*Imitators of men.* The Revised Version of this passage reads, " I beseech you therefore, be ye imitators of me." It may, however, be disputed whether the word " followers " is not a better and more suitable one to express the apostle's idea. Mere *imitating* is the work of the unintelligent; it is represented by the mere reproduction of sounds and manners such as we have in the parrot or the monkey, or more fully in the child. For men, all mere imitations are either signs of mental and moral weakness, or they are the accidents attending on an intelligent acceptance of the *principles* which another man exhibits in conduct. We are not, in the limited sense of the word, even to *imitate* Christ ; we are to " copy his example," and to " follow in his steps ; " but when more fully and worthily apprehended, we find that what we really are to do is to " let that *mind be in us* which was also in Christ Jesus." In the passage now before us St. Paul has been speaking of his relationship to the Corinthian Christians. He was their father in Christ ; " For in Christ Jesus I have begotten you through the gospel." And he is really pleading with them to preserve the *family likeness* which should accompany such a relation. But it may be said—Are we ever justified in following or imitating our fellow-men ? We reply—Yes, so far as men are Christ-like, we may ; so far as they are more Christ-like than ourselves ; so far as they have reached any Christly virtue or grace beyond us, we may. And since there is a sense in which Christ must ever seem to us out of reach ; since of his virtue we must ever say, " It is high, I cannot attain unto it ; "—it may often be really helpful to us to see his virtue reflected in a fellow-man, and manifestly brought within the reach of human attainment. This may help us while we are weak, but when we more fully grasp the truth of our Lord's humanity, we shall realize that Divine virtues were shown by him in a human life precisely that we might feel the possibility of attaining them, and so seek to be " changed into his image." After dwelling on the " imitative faculty," its uses and abuses, consider that—

I. GOOD MEN MAY BECOME MODELS FOR US. Observe : 1. That in every age some men have risen above their fellows in moral virtues ; and some have been set in prominent positions so as to attract the attention of their fellows. 2. From the Scripture models which are preserved to us, learn : (1) That no merely human being can present his entire human life, the whole circle of his doings, for our imitation. " There is none righteous ; no, not one." Illustrate the sides of moral infirmity in all Scripture characters—Abraham, Moses, David, Hezekiah, Peter, Paul, etc. (2) That each becomes a model of some one characteristic feature ; *e.g.* Abraham of faith, Moses of disinterestedness, David of habits of personal piety, Paul of singular loyalty to the living Christ. So with modern saints, and the holy ones from our own circles ; in some one thing each is strong, and just in that one thing each may be a model.

II. GOOD MEN'S MODELS ARE, AT THE BEST, BUT IMPERFECT. Sensible of this, David says in his prayer before God, " My goodness extendeth not to thee ; but to the saints that are in the earth, and to the excellent." Even in the one thing in which they are strong, God can find weakness. When we most admire, we are compelled sadly to feel that the " trail of the serpent is over it all." So we must use men's examples as but incomplete copies of the Divine, and remember that our aim is to transcend any previous human attainments, and to be " perfect, even as our Father in heaven is perfect." Whatever there is in men that is imitable is but a reflection of Christ, and we may have shining on us what they have in measure caught, even the very light of Christ himself. We may " follow his example, who did no sin."

III. CHRIST IS OUR GREAT MODEL, AND MEN ARE MODELS ONLY SO FAR AS THEY BRING HIM NEAR AND GLORIFY HIM TO OUR THOUGHT. We must take this knowledge of them that they have been with Jesus, and have, in measure, caught his likeness. Impress that we may fully copy Christ's life, but only very seldom can we copy men's *actions;* we can only seek to be possessed and ruled by the same principles.—R. T.

Vers. 18—20.—*Speech and power.* These are by no means always associated together in the same man. Oftentimes they seem quite unable to dwell together. Speech is in inverse ratio to power. The free talker is seldom a vigorous thinker; and the boaster can never gain any real power by his extravagances. It seems that, at Corinth, there were some loud talkers, who depreciated St. Paul's authority, and endeavoured to destroy his influence. They made out that his "bodily presence was weak, and his speech contemptible;" and they mockingly said, "No doubt he writes very vigorous and terrible letters, but he is afraid to come himself." "These persons persuaded themselves that they had so undermined his reputation that he would not dare to come again to Corinth, and they grew more self-asserting in consequence." Paley notices an undesigned coincidence between this passage and 2 Cor. i. 15—17; ii. 1. There evidently had been some uncertainty about his visit, of which his opponents took undue advantage.

I. SPEECH WITHOUT POWER. A mere gift of fluent talk is granted to some men. It is seldom associated with vigorous mental power, and is a perilous gift because it can be so readily misused. Such speech may be pleasant to listen to, as is the murmur of a flowing stream. It may be popular; it may be exciting to mere sentiment; it may be boastful. Its influence is small and temporary. It bears very little relation to the correction of moral evils, or the culture of the godly life.

II. SPEECH WITH POWER. Speech which is (1) the utterance of thought; (2) which bears the "accent of conviction;" (3) which is carefully set in adaptation to the hearer; and (4) which is uttered in dependence on Divine leadings and inspirations. Here the word is used by St. Paul especially to mean "the power that is derived from Christ, which he himself possesses to influence the heart of man. It includes, no doubt, the power of working miracles, for, with one or two exceptions, the miracles of the gospel were manifestations of Christ's power to deliver humanity from the dominion of evil and its consequences." Speech with power is that kind of speech which directly influences the heart and the conscience, and leads to the fuller apprehension of truth, the conviction of sin, or the discovery of neglected duty. It may comfort, instruct, counsel, or warn. Dr. Horace Bushnell says, "Three distinct elements must be included in preaching which has the genuine power. (1) A descent to human nature in its lower plane of self-love and interested motive, and a beginning made with the conscience, the fears, and the boding expectation of guiltiness. (2) The due exhibition of the Christian *facts.* In the Apostles' Creed nothing is included but the simple facts of Christ's life. Too little by a thousandfold is made of these facts. How much easier to preach the decoction (doctrine), and let the dried herbs of the story go! It might be so if they were really dry; but since they are all alive, fresh and fragrant as a bank of roses, how much better to go and breathe among them, and catch the quickening odours! (3) The right conception of the gospel, and the fit presentation of it, under the altar-forms provided for it." And Canon Liddon, in his 'Bampton Lectures,' pp. 168, 169, has the following passage:—"Picture to yourselves a teacher who is not merely under the official obligation to say something, but who is morally convinced that he has something to say. Imagine one who believes alike in the truth of his message, and in the reality of his mission to deliver it. Let his message combine those moral contrasts which give permanency and true force to a doctrine, and which the gospel only has combined in their perfection. Let this teacher be tender, yet searching; let him win the hearts of men by his kindly humanity, while he probes, ay, to the quick, their moral sores. Let him be uniformly calm, yet manifestly moved by the fire of repressed passion. Let him be stern yet not unloving, and resolute without sacrificing the elasticity of his sympathy, and genial without condescending to be the weakly accomplice of moral mischief. Let him pursue and expose the latent evil of the human heart, through all the mazes of its unrivalled deceitfulness, without sullying his own purity, and without forfeiting his strong belief in the present capacity of every human being for goodness. Let him know ' what is in man,' and yet, with this knowledge clearly before him, let him not only not despair of humanity, but respect it, nay, love it even enthusiastically. Above all, let this teacher be perfectly independent. Let him be independent of the voice of the multitude; independent of the enthusiasm and promptings of his disciples; independent even when face to face with the bitter criticism and scorn of his antagonists; independent of all save God and his conscience. In a word, conceive a case in which moral authority and moral beauty combine to elicit a simultaneous tribute of reverence and of love. Clearly such a teacher must be a moral power." Impress that such teachers we should seek to find; such was the 'Apostle Paul; and under the power such can exert we may hope to grow into the " stature of the perfect man in Christ Jesus."—R. T.

Ver. 21.—*Adaptation the teacher's power.* Evidently St. Paul desired to be precisely adapted to those whom he would teach. The tone and the substance of his teachings would directly depend on their moral condition. As a faithful teacher, he tells them it must depend on *them* whether he came to them " with a rod, or in love, and in the spirit of meekness." A brief outline will sufficiently guide thought on this subject.

I. ADAPTATION INVOLVES KNOWLEDGE. 1. General knowledge of human nature. 2. Particular knowledge of those to whom we minister. 3. Sufficient knowledge of the measure of our authority and influence. 4. Practical knowledge of the corrective instruments which we may use.

II. ADAPTATION INVOLVES DISCERNMENT. 1. Discrimination of the precise condition in which those we influence are at the time. 2. Of the differences in which each one may stand related to the evil we reprove. 3. Of the limitations to which reproof may be wisely subject, and of the time when the tone may be changed to one of encouragement.

III. ADAPTATION MAY DEMAND SEVERITY. Which may be very trying to our feelings, and very difficult in view of our disposition; but must be made to characterize our relations, if we would be found faithful. The severity of gentle souls is the mightiest persuasive to goodness. It was quite out of St. Paul's way to be severe, but, for that very reason, we feel his severity the more.

IV. ADAPTATION PREFERS COMMENDATION. So St. Paul writes, urging the Corinthians to remove the evils before he comes, for he would so much rather have only kindly and encouraging things to say. Impress that, as we are to God, he must show himself to us. See Ps. xviii. 24—26. And in the same way, as we are in godly habits, in moral and spiritual condition, so—in precise adaptation—must our faithful teachers be.—R. T.

EXPOSITION.

CHAPTER V.

Vers. 1—8.—*Excommunication of an incestuous offender.*

Ver. 1.—**It is reported.** The abruptness with which the subject is introduced shows the intensity of St. Paul's feelings, and his indignation that he should have been left to hear of this crime by common report. The news had come to him " from those of Chloe's household." But St. Paul was not acting on mere " report." The Greek phrase *implies,* " It is notorious that there is uncleanness among you." St. Paul must have felt it to be a bad feature in the character of the Corinthian Church that they had not mentioned this gross scandal in their letter. **Commonly**; ;rather, *actually* or *absolutely.* Elsewhere in the New Testament the word only occurs in Matt. v. 24; ch. vi. 7; xv. 29. Tertullian renders it " in totum." St. Paul

has no need in this instance to name his informants. Every one knew of this scandal. **Fornication**; a general word for all kinds of impurity. **And.** The word involves an indignant climax, " Yes, and uncleanness of such a kind that," etc. **Is not so much as named.** The true reading is, *does not even exist.* This form of incest was, indeed, " named " among the Gentiles, for it forms the basis of the story of Hippolytus, the scene of which was in the neighbourhood of Corinth; but the feelings even of pagans were so shocked by it that Cicero alludes to such a crime in the words, " Oh, incredible wickedness, and—except in this woman's case—unheard of in all experience!" (' Pro Cluent.,' 5). At this very epoch Nero deepened the general execration against himself by the generally accepted suspicion that he had been guilty of a yet more flagrant crime. **Should have**; rather, *that*

X *a certain person has his father's wife.* Apparently this was some nominal Christian, who was living in open sin with his step-mother, and thereby braving the curse of Lev. xviii. 17; Deut. xxvii. 20. We gather from 2 Cor. vii. 12 that the father was living, and had also joined the Christian community. From the complete silence as to the crime of the woman, it must be inferred that she was a heathen. Whether she had been divorced or not does not appear, nor whether the offender was nominally married to her or not. **His father's wife.** He might have used the one Greek word for step-mother (μητρυιά), but the periphrasis might remind some of the heinousness of the sin, and of Lev. xviii. 8.

Ver. 2.—**And ye are puffed up;** perhaps rather, *And have ye been puffed up?* The "ye," being expressed in the Greek, is emphatic—"*ye,* the very persons whose horror ought to have been most intense." It might seem inconceivable that any community calling itself Christian would fall so low as to be puffed up at the existence of such an offence among them. There is, indeed, a subtle and close connection between arrogance and sensuality, and both are sometimes fatally linked to the conceit of religious knowledge without the reality. But not even a heathen community could have been "puffed up" on such grounds. Yet the Corinthians may have been "puffed up" with the conceited reasons which induced them to leave the offence unrebuked, because they boasted the possession of some spurious "knowledge." Perhaps they had seized some deadly notion of antinomian liberty, such as has existed at times among Gnostic sects, like the Ophites in ancient and the Anabaptists in modern days. Perhaps they sheltered themselves under the arrogant Jewish rule that all a man's conditions of life were altered by becoming a proselyte—that old relationships were for him entirely abolished; for the Jews held that a proselyte was like "a new-born child," and had begun life a second time (Bechoroth, f. 47, 1), and might marry any of his relatives. Such miserable sophisms would acquire fresh force from the universal impurity with which Corinthian society was stained, and which rendered it necessary for St. Paul in these Epistles to utter his most solemn warnings against every kind of sensuality (ch. v. 11; vi. 15—18; x. 8; xv. 33, 34; 2 Cor. v. 11, etc.). But besides all this, St. Paul's remark does not necessarily mean that their "inflation" was exclusively connected with Gnostic excesses, which bore on the case of this offender. It may mean, "Here is a gross fault in the midst of you, and yet—not *propter hoc,* but *cum hoc*—the characteristic of your religious factions is pride and

conceit." This was indeed Κορινθιάζεσθαι, "to play the Corinthian," in the worst sense of that proverbial taunt. Possibly the prominence or wealth of the offender may have led to a more easy condonation of his crime. Exculpatory sophism may have been suggested by self-interest. That; *i.e.* in order that, as a result of your godly sorrow, the offender might be removed from your midst. **He that hath done this deed.** The language of St. Paul, as always, is as delicate as clearness would allow. The fact that the verb is in the past aorist may perhaps allow us to *hope* that the offence, at any rate in its most aggravated forms, had ceased to be committed. The manner of the crime ("in such a way") seems to have been an aggravation of the crime itself. In this indignant verse we have, as Stanley says, "the burst of the storm, the mutterings of which had been heard in the earlier chapters." So intense was the effect produced by St. Paul's stern severity, that a great part of the Second Epistle had to be devoted to allaying the agitation which these words had excited (see especially 2 Cor. vii. 8—12).

Ver. 3.—**For I verily.** The broken structure of the verse shows the deep emotion with which it was penned—as it were with sobs. St. Paul contrasts the line which *he* means to take with the lax condonation granted by the Corinthian Church. **As absent;** rather, *being absent* or *though absent.* The *as* is omitted in the best manuscripts. **But present in spirit;** literally, *in the spirit;* but he is referring to his own spirit: "Bodily I am absent; but speaking as though my spirit were present in your assembly [comp. 2 Kings v. 26], I have already judged," etc. **Have judged already.** My decision was instantaneous and is final. **As though I were present.** My sentence is as clear as though I were at this moment standing in the midst of you. **That hath so done.** The verb is not as before, *poiēsas,* but *katergasámenon,* which is stronger, "the *perpetrator* of this deed." The "so" means "with all these circumstances of aggravation." The same verb is used in Rom. i. 27. The broken periods of the Greek reflect the emotion of the writer. The passage is as it were written with sobs (Wordsworth).

Ver. 4.—**In the Name of our Lord Jesus Christ.** The word "Christ" is probably an addition. The clause may either be taken with "when ye are gathered together," or with "to deliver" (comp. 1 Tim. v. 21). **With the power of our Lord Jesus.** Each clause adds solemnity to the scene in which St. Paul imagines himself as standing with them in the spirit, and joining with the assembly of the Church, and armed with the authority of Christ, while he pronounces on the offender the sentence on which he had already determined. That he could claim "the power of the Lord" resulted from his possession of the Holy Spirit, and the special commission to bind and to loose, to remit and to retain, on earth, which Christ had entrusted to the apostles (Matt. xviii. 18, 20; John xx. 23).

Ver. 5.—**To deliver such a one unto Satan.** Scripture nowhere defines the character and limits of such a sentence as this. By cutting off an offender from Church communion (2 Thess. iii. 14, 15), that is, from all the visible means of grace, he was for the time separated from spiritual influences, and was, therefore, so far handed over to Satan. The phrase is also applied to Hymenæus and Alexander, in 1 Tim. i. 20. It is very doubtful whether it was necessarily meant to involve such physical inflictions as fell on Ananias, Sapphira, or Elymas. It is, however, important to observe that the intention of the sentence, like the true intention of excommunication, when exercised in a right spirit (see Hooker, 'Eccl. Pol.,' iii. 1, § 13), was not wrathful, but merciful. It was, as Calvin says, "medicinale remedium"—"not for destruction, but for edification" (2 Cor. x. 8). Hymenæus and Alexander were handed to Satan, not for their final ruin and damnation, but with a kind and remedial purpose, "that they may learn not to blaspheme" (1 Tim. i. 20), and this offender with the express object "that his spirit may be saved." Had these facts been more deeply studied, there would have been a very different tone and spirit in many of the mediæval anathemas. *Such a one* (comp. 2 Cor. ii. 7). He seems to hold aloof from the man's very name. So "such as she" (τὰς τοιαύτας) is used of the adulteress in John viii. 7. **For the destruction of the flesh**; *i.e.* that all *carnal influences* in him might be destroyed. It is not his "body" which is to be destroyed, but the "flesh," the *jetzer ha-ra*, or "evil impulse," as the Jews called it. When this was destroyed, the body might once more become a temple of the Holy Ghost. **That the spirit may be saved.** The destruction of the lowest element of our human nature is the salvation of the highest; it is the cutting away of the dead corpse from the living soul. **In the day of the Lord**; when the Lord should judge the quick and the dead. The merciful intention of St. Paul is clearly developed in 2 Cor. ii. 6—11. He looked on God's judgments as *remedial*, not as solely retributive (ch. xi. 29—32). Here, as Chrysostom finely says, the apostle lays down, as it were, his laws to the devil, telling him how far, and how far *only*, he can proceed. The object of excommunication is to save the offender, and not to do the devil's work by

ensuring his eternal ruin. We can imagine how awful would be the solemnity of these words when they were first read aloud to the little Christian communities of Corinth. It was natural that they should produce an overwhelming excitement.

Ver. 6.—**Your glorying**; rather, *the subject of your boasting, the point on which you glorify yourselves.* The Greek word does not mean the act of boasting, but the thing of which we boast. **Not good.** The Greek word is not *agathon*, but *kalon*, an almost untranslatable word, which implies all moral beauty, and resembles the English word "fair" or "noble." When he says that it is "not good," he uses the figure called *litotes;* *i.e.* he employs an expression intentionally too weak, that it may be corrected into a stronger one by the involuntary indignation of the reader; as when Virgil calls the cannibal tyrant Busiris "unpraised." Hence the clause is equivalent to "the thing of which you are boasting is detestable." **Know ye not.** This clause is used by St. Paul in specially solemn appeals, and almost exclusively in these Epistles (ch. iii. 16; vi. 16, 19; ix. 13, 24). **A little leaven leaveneth the whole lump** (Gal. v. 9). The taint alluded to is not only the presence of the unpunished offender, but the general laxity and impurity displayed by their whole bearing in the matter (comp. the line of Menander quoted in ch. xv. 33, and the "root of bitterness" in Heb. xii. 15). (For the word "lump," see Rom. xi. 16.)

Ver. 7.—**Purge out therefore.** The word "therefore" is absent from the best manuscripts, and the abruptness is more emphatic without it. No doubt the metaphor was suggested by the fact that St. Paul was writing about the time of the Passover (Acts xvi. 8). The most essential requisite of the Jewish regulations, with which his whole training had made him so familiar, was the absolute putting away, and even destruction, of every trace of leaven, which was diligently sought for the day before the Passover began. The putting away of leaven was a type of sanctification. **The old leaven.** "Old" as belonging to their unregenerate and unconverted condition; a remnant of the day when they had been Gentiles and Jews who had not known Christ. The least *willing* tolerance of the taint would cause it to work throughout the whole society. **As ye are unleavened.** Leaven is the type of evil in its secret and corrupting workings. Ideally, Christians can only be addressed as "unleavened," *i.e.* as "purged from their own old sins" (2 Pet. i. 9); and it is the method of Scripture (indeed, it is the only possible method) to address Christians as being **Christians** *indeed*, and therefore in their *ideal* rather than their actual character. Some have taken these words to mean, "You are actually keeping the Passover, and therefore have no leaven among you;" but (1) the words cannot bear this meaning; nor (2) was St. Paul likely to appeal so prominently to a Jewish ordinance; and (3) he is thinking of the Christian Easter, and only borrowing a casual illustration from the Jewish Passover. **For even Christ our Passover is sacrificed for us**; rather, in the true reading, *for our Passover also was sacrificed—even Christ.* As Christians, the Gentile Corinthians certainly did not keep the Jewish Passover; but St. Paul reminds them that they too had a Passover—that for them, too, a Paschal Victim had been offered, whose sacrificial blood had been shed for their redemption (John i. 29; xix. 36; 1 Pet. i. 19). (Comp. Heb. xiii. 10, "We have an altar.")

Ver. 8.—**Therefore let us keep the feast.** Let us keep the Christian feast of Christ's resurrection in that spirit of holiness—of purging away sin from the midst of us—which was symbolized by the Jewish removal of leaven. **Not with old leaven.** For now ye are "in Christ," and, therefore, are a "new creation." Leaven is the type of hypocrisy (Luke xii. 1) in its secret workings, but more generally it is a type of every corrupting influence. **Of sincerity and truth.** "All that corresponds to an unsullied, uncontaminated, and genuine Christian character." The beautiful Greek word for "sincerity" means freedom from all admixture. It is, perhaps, derived from "testing in the sunshine," and is used by St. Paul in 2 Cor. i. 12; ii. 17. "Truth" means "reality."

Vers. 9—13.—*Correction of a mistaken inference which they had deduced from a former letter of St. Paul's.*

Ver. 9.—**In an Epistle;** rather, *in* the *Epistle;* in some former letter to the Church, which is no longer extant (comp. 2 Cor. x. 10). The attempt to get rid of so plain a statement, in the supposed interests of some superstitious notion that every line which an apostle wrote to a Church must necessarily have been inspired and infallible, is at once unscriptural and grossly superstitious. The notion that "*the* Epistle" intended is *this* Epistle is an absurdity invented in the interests of the same fiction. The only hypothesis which could give the least plausibility to such a view is that which makes this paragraph a postscript or marginal addition after the letter was finished; but there is little or nothing in favour of such a view. **Not to company with.** The Greek word is rather stronger: *not to be mingled up among* (comp. 2 Thess. iii. 14). The spirit of the injunction is repeated in Eph. v. 11, "Have no fellowship with the unfruitful works of darkness, but rather reprove them."

Ver. 10.—**Yet not altogether.** The words correct a false inference, and mean, "I did not intend absolutely to prohibit all communication with Gentiles guilty of this sin under all circumstances." **Of this world.** Those outside the pale of the Christian Church (comp. ch. iii. 19; 2 Cor. iv. 4). **Or with the covetous.** St. Paul often uses the Greek word in immediate connection with sins of impurity (ch. vi. 10; 2 Cor. ix. 5; Eph. v. 3; Col. iii. 3), and, though it does not exclude the connotation of greed and avarice (2 Cor. ix. 7; 1 Thess. ii. 5), it seems to have been used euphemistically of the deadliest form of heathen sensuality. The principle of selfishness may work equally in greed and in lust. **Extortioners.** The word may also mean "ravishers," but there is no reason to abandon the sense of "rapacious." **Idolaters.** This is the earliest instance of the use of this word, which does not occur in the LXX. No Christian could still be an open "idolater." So, unless we suppose that the expression has slipped in involuntarily, we must here give the word a metaphorical sense, as in Col. iii. 5. We must else be driven to suppose that there were some half-and-half Christians, like Constantine, who "feared the Lord, and served their own gods" (comp. ch. vi. 9; viii. 10; x. 7, 14; Eph. v. 5). **For then must ye needs go out of the world;** *for in that case* (as they had perhaps implied in their letter of questions to St. Paul) *ye would have been morally bound to leave the world altogether* and seek a new one. The Greek particle *ara* perhaps refers to the astonishment caused by their misapprehension of St. Paul's rule. The clause throws painful light on the condition of the heathen world. If all communication with "fornicators" was to be forbidden, the sin was so universal, especially at Corinth, that all intercourse with Gentiles would have become impossible. Even some who professed to be stern moralists among the heathen, like Cato and Cicero, looked on the sin as being, at the worst, quite venial, and even, under certain circumstances, commendable.

Ver. 11.—**But now I have written unto you.** The tense used is, perhaps, the epistolary aorist, and is therefore equivalent to "but now I write to you;" otherwise the sense is, "but what I *meant* in my letter was," etc. The position of the words rather favours this view. St. Paul expressly tells them in ch. x. 27 that he never intended to forbid all intercourse with heathens. They were not to be "taken out of the world," but to be free from evil (John. xvii.

15). **If any man that is called a brother.** The word "brother" was used before the name "Christian" was accepted by the members of the Church. **Or an idolater** (see ch. v. 10; x. 7, 14). He might call himself a Christian, and yet be in reality an idolater (Eph. v. 5; Col. iii. 5; Gal. v. 20; 1 John v. 21). **With such a one no not to eat.** If the phrase be pressed, it would involve exclusion from all privileges of the body, for the Holy Communion was celebrated in connection with the *agapæ*. But the general meaning is that of 2 Thess. iii. 6, "We command you . . . that ye withdraw yourselves from every brother that walketh disorderly."

Ver. 12.—**For what have I to do to judge them also that are without?** To pass sentence on heathens is no concern of mine; it is no part of my office. The phrase "them that are without" was originally a Jewish phrase. To the Jews all men were "outsiders" (*chitsonin*) except themselves. The phrase was adopted by Christians, but

in a less contemptuous sense (1 Thess. iv. 12; Col. iv. 5). We find a description of "those that were without"—"aliens from the commonwealth of Israel, and strangers from the covenant of promise"—in Eph. ii. 12. **Do not ye judge them that are within?** An appeal to their own practice and to common sense. Christian rules can, of course, only apply to Christian communities.

Ver. 13.—**God judgeth.** To that "judgment of God" (Rom. i. 29) Christians must leave them. They have no jurisdiction over them. The mention of "judging" forms a natural transition to the next chapter. **Therefore.** The word is omitted in the best manuscripts. The command is more abruptly forcible without it. **Put away from among yourselves that wicked person.** The command would come the more powerfully because it is a direct reference to the language of Deut. xvii. 7; xxiv. 7. The explanation, "Put away the evil one [*i.e.* the devil] from among you!" is adopted by Calvin, but is too general.

HOMILETICS.

Vers. 1—5.—*The socially immoral in Churches.* "It is reported commonly that there is fornication among you," etc. The greater portion of this chapter is taken up with one subject, that is, gross social immorality. The verses before us suggest three general remarks—

I. THAT THE SOCIALLY IMMORAL SOMETIMES FIND THEIR WAY INTO CHRISTIAN CHURCHES. It had been reported to Paul that there were some members of the Corinthian Church guilty of gross "fornication;" that one of the members had actually married his father's wife—not, however, his own mother, but his step-mother. Such a piece of immorality would be regarded with the utmost abhorrence, even through the whole Roman empire. Paul says that such a case was not "so much as named among the Gentiles." How such a character became a member of the Christian community is not stated. It is reasonable, however, to suppose that it was through imposition on the one hand and the lack of scrutiny on the other. It is to be feared that the admission of the socially immoral into Churches has in every age been too common. How many Churches are there in England entirely free from those who every day outrage the golden rule, "Do unto others as you would have others do unto you"? There are merchants that cheat their customers, lawyers that swindle their clients, doctors that take advantage of their patients, statesmen that deceive their constituents and in the name of patriotism promote their own selfish ends, masters and mistresses that oppress their servants, servants unfaithful to their employers. Ay, the Church is a field in which grows the tare as well as the wheat, a net in which there is the "unclean" as well as the "clean."

II. THAT CHURCHES IN THEIR INTERNAL RELIGIOUS DISPUTATIONS ARE IN DANGER OF OVERLOOKING THE SOCIALLY IMMORAL AMONG THEM. "And ye are puffed up, and have not rather mourned." Probably there were those in the Church who were proud of the membership of this incestuous man; perhaps he was an orator, or had a long purse, or was a person of great social influence. We have known joint stock swindlers who have been made chairmen of religious meetings, and who have been cheered to the echo. Party feeling was so strong, and religious disputation so rife amongst them, that such immoralities escaped their notice. Who is the best preacher? what is the sound doctrine? what are the ceremonies to be observed? Such questions as these were all-absorbing amongst them. Moral character was a secondary thing, theories and beliefs primary. This has ever been too much the case in Christian Churches. Creeds are more thought of than character, doctrines than doings, heretics dreaded more than rogues. Some of the worst men morally I have ever known have been prominent members of Churches. Hence the saying, " Sooner trust a man of the world than a professor of religion."

III. THAT THE EXCLUSION BY THE CHURCHES OF SUCH MEMBERS FROM THEIR MIDST IS AN URGENT DUTY. A true Church is a community of Christly men, and the presence of such characters in it is an outrage. The verses teach: 1. That their expulsion *should be practised with the utmost zeal.* It would seem that no sooner did Paul hear of this abomination than he determined to put an end to it. " For I verily, as absent in body, but present in spirit, have judged already, as though I were present, concerning him that hath so done this deed." As if he had said, " Though absent from you, as soon as I heard it I determined to get such a vile character expelled forthwith from the community ; " and to do it when they were gathered together " in the Name of our Lord Jesus Christ," that is, by the authority and power of Christ. Paul seems to burn with zeal in the matter. Zeal is not an uncommon thing in Churches : in some cases and seasons it becomes a glowing passion ; but, alas ! it is too often concerned more with the tenets of creeds and the interests of sects than with purity of life in its members. 2. That the expulsion should be practised with the utmost zeal, *not to destroy, but to save the offender.* " Deliver such a one unto Satan for the destruction of the flesh, that the spirit may be saved in the day of the Lord Jesus." Satan was regarded as the origin of all physical evils, and the meaning here may be—deliver the immoral person over to the sufferings of excommunication. But what for ? Not to destroy him, but " that the spirit may be saved." All punishment should be refor-mative—should be inflicted to correct, not to crush. " Brethren, if a man be overtaken in a fault, ye which are spiritual, restore such a one."

Vers. 6—13.—*The true Church a feast.* " Your glorying is not good," etc. There are numerous Churches, but only *one true* Church, viz. that community of men who possess the Spirit and exemplify the character of Jesus Christ. These verses lead us to look upon the true Church—

I. In its INTERNAL ENJOYMENTS. It is called here a " feast." Truly the association of such Christly spirited men is a " feast " of the sublimest kind, a feast to each and all. A " feast : " 1. Because it contains the choicest elements for spiritual *nourishment.* The quickening, elevating, and suggestive ideas current in such fellowship, current, not only in language, but in looks, and bearing, and acts, and spirit, constitute the soul-banquet, a " feast of fat things," etc. 2. Because it contains the choicest elements for spiritual *gratification.* A feast implies not merely nourishment, but pleasure and delight. What is a higher delight than the loving intercourse of kindred souls, free interchange of the most lofty thoughts and purest sympathies, loving souls flowing and reflowing into each other ? The true Church is not a moody, melancholy assemblage, speaking in sepulchral tones, and singing doleful dirges ; it is the brightest and most jubilant fellowship on earth. " These words have I spoken unto you, that your joy may be full ; " " Rejoice, . . . and again I say, rejoice."

II. In its EXTERNAL RELATION TO THE UNGODLY. 1. There is a connection with ungodly men that it *must* avoid. They must not be admitted to its " feasts." " Purge out therefore the old leaven, that ye may be a new lump, as ye are unleavened. For even Christ our Passover is sacrificed for us." As the Jews put away leaven at the celebration of the Passover, so all corrupt men must be excluded from the Church feasts. Christ is its Passover, its Feast. It is suggested that the presence of corrupt men at the feast would be *contagious.* It would be likely to act as " leaven " through the com-munity. As leaven kneaded into a lump of dough spreads from particle to particle, fer-ments in its process, spreads through the whole, and assimilates all to its own character, so a bad man's spirit may work through the community of the good. Therefore, because it is so contagious and pernicious, exclude it. " Therefore let us keep the feast, not with old leaven, neither with the leaven of malice and wickedness ; but with the unleavened bread of sincerity and truth." No Church that has such leaven in it, whatever its intellectual, social, or spiritual advantages, has any reason for exultation. " Your glorying is not good," says Paul : " know ye not that a little leaven leaveneth the whole lump ? " Be grave, be serious, look well to the moral character of your members. 2. There is a connection with ungodly men that it *cannot* avoid. " I wrote unto you in an Epistle not to company with fornicators: yet not altogether with the fornicators of this world, or with the covetous, or extortioners, or with idolaters; for then must ye needs go out of the world." You cannot avoid contact and some kind of intercourse with the ungodly men outside. You cannot attend to the temporal affairs of your life without them. Nor can you discharge your spiritual obligations without going amongst them. As a Christian you are bound to go amongst them, to correct their mistakes, to enlighten their darkness, to reprove their wrongs, and to endeavour to "turn them from darkness to light, and from the power of Satan unto God." Over such you have no legal control, you can exercise no jurisdiction; they are without. You have no power to exclude them from your neighbourhood or your country; they are to be left alone in that respect. "Them that are without God judgeth." But if you find such characters inside the Church, you are to deal with them. "But now I have written unto you not to keep company, if any man that is called a brother be a fornicator, or covetous, or an idolater, or a railer, or a drunkard, or an extortioner; with such a one no not to eat." Observe here: (1) Sin in man takes various forms. Paul adds to the incestuous man, the "fornicator," the "covetous" man, the "idolater," the "railer," the "drunkard," the "extortioner;" all have to be avoided. Sin is to be avoided whatever form it takes; and it takes many forms. What is a temptation to one man is not to another. Hence one is tempted to be a "fornicator;" another a miser, "covetous;" another an "idolater," worshipping false gods; another a scorner, a "railer;" another a "drunkard," intemperate; another an "extortioner," overreaching, overexacting, tyrannic. (2) In whatever forms this "leaven" shows itself, it must not be tolerated for a moment. It must be excluded at once.

HOMILIES BY VARIOUS AUTHORS.

Vers. 1—5.—*Excision of a flagrant offender from the Church.* No haste was evinced by the apostle to reach a question that gave him much anxiety. Among the striking phenomena incident to mind as connected with body, the rate of movement in ideas is worthy of notice. Certain classes of ideas, such as those associated with instinctive action, are very rapid. And equally noticeable is the fact that thoughts involving the spontaneous intellect are more swift than those belonging to the volitional intellect. And, moreover, the same man thinks with more rapidity in some moods than in others. We all know how the physical heart is accelerated in its beat and how the lungs breathe faster under certain circumstances; and, beyond doubt, there is a co-relation in these phenomena between mind and matter. Now, at first sight, this fact may not strike us, but, on a nearer view, we see that intellectual and moral discipline is very intimately bound up therewith. Take the case of St. Paul in the matter under consideration. Here was a scandal in the Corinthian Church, a case of incest, a son taking his father's wife, publicly known, so shocking as to be under the ban of heathenism. A man such as St. Paul, intense, full of impulse, with a temperament eager to act on the spur of the moment—a man whose sensations instantly turned into sensibilities, and whose thoughts naturally tended to immediate words and deeds,—this man, in one of his most anxious seasons as an apostle, holds his painful solicitude in check and will not utter his heart till the way has been fully prepared. Rare self-control this, and most honourable—all the more so, indeed, as he had other grounds for just indignation. But he was writing "for Christ's sake," and this was enough. He will not hurry to relieve his overfull mind. Other things had to be said first. The glory of his Lord as the Wisdom and Power of God, the Divine idea in the ministry, the broad contrast between preaching the gospel and all utterances merely human, the evil of partisanship, the humiliation and suffering of the apostles, and especially his fatherly care over sons disturbing the peace of the Christian household,—all these truths were to be set forth, illustrated, enforced, before he entered on practical questions. Is there not something here worthy of reflection? The world's practicalness is not very tolerant of general ideas and their elaboration. With it, brain and hand are near neighbours; its thoughts and actions hasten into alliances. If a proper degree of precaution be used, this is unquestionably a wise general rule. There is indeed

" A tide in the affairs of men,
Which, taken at the flood, leads on to fortune ;"

but the same representative thinker of humanity warns us that when we "mean to build," we should " survey "

> " The plot of the situation, and the model;
> Consent upon a sure foundation."

Promptness is not always the synonym of prudence, and where one Hamlet wastes excessive sensibility on mere ideas and their images, so that "enterprises lose the name of action," scores of men wreck themselves in an opposite direction. Between these extremes, St. Paul was happily poised. He had mastered principles, he understood details by virtue of these principles, and he was an exception even among great leaders, because he saw very deeply into the springs of action. So that when he came to deal with the case of the notorious offender among the Corinthians, a broad space had been cleared for himself. The ideal of the Church, of the ministry, of Christianity itself, had been resplendently displayed. Thought had been elevated, feeling quickened, selfishness put to shame, and a state of mind created in himself, and we may hope in his brethren, favourable to fortunate issues. How much these Corinthians needed just such instruction, and, more particularly, what obligations were laid upon them by Christianity to be humble, we see plainly enough in this chapter. "Instead of expelling the offender with mourning and shame, you—oh, strange mystery of the invariable connection between sensuality and pride—have been inflated with sophistical excuses about the matter" (Dr. Farrar). And yet, all the while, though this wickedness is an outrage on common decency, and in shameless contempt of public opinion, at which even paganism would blush, St. Paul approaches the subject from the standpoint of Christianity. He never takes a lower way when the higher is possible. For with him it is a cardinal principle that the higher includes the lower; this is his method of thought; and agreeably thereunto he is the profoundest of intellectual philosophers, even in his exposure of the meagreness and vanity of the world's reasonings. So that we see in this instance that he felt himself set for the defence of true reason, no less than of genuine religion, working down to the instinct of the reason as he worked down to the depths of consciousness in all else. The reality of the position, the solemnity of the transaction, the whole body of circumstances, rise with instant vividness before the eye of the mind, never so much an eye as when outer vision is suspended. Away in Ephesus, the apostle had brooded over this severe trial so taxative to skill and patience, since the roots of the horrible evil were as a cancer spreading its poisonous fibres through the body. Night and day it clung to him, and, wherever he went, some new rumour of the disgrace awaited his heart. Ionia was as Achaia. So long had he dwelt upon it, so many prayers had gone up to God for enlightenment and guidance, so agonizing had been the wrestlings of his spirit, that he was as if on the spot. "Absent in body," says he, "but present in spirit," and I have "judged already, as though I were present" with you in the body. And thus ideally in their midst, the whole procedure not only before the Church, but the Church participating in the judicial act, he himself a witness and an actor, and Christ Jesus with them in the power of the Spirit, this shocking offender must be delivered to Satan. Not only had the Church been dishonoured by the guilty man, but they themselves had shared the sin and the reproach by neglecting to exercise that discipline which was one form, and a very important form, of the kingdom that was "not in *word*, but in *power*." Deliverance to Satan means excommunication from Christian fellowship. How much more is implied it is difficult to determine. Taking the passage in its immediate bearings and in connection with the general tenor of the Scriptures, it would seem to indicate that the culprit was surrendered to the power of Satan, by whose influence he had already been corrupted; his own will consenting to the depravation. This act of the Church gave him over to the malignant agency of Satan, and in so doing fulfilled a Divine judgment. Yet it contemplated besides a merciful discipline. The punishment was punishment since it was "for the destruction of the flesh," and coincidently a disciplinary process that "the spirit *may be saved* in the day of the Lord Jesus." Mercy and truth meet together here, and righteousness and peace kiss each other. The door of repentance is not closed; still less is the possibility of reconciliation forestalled. Christ demonstrates himself in and through the Church, his representative, as Christ the Judge. But it is Christ, Head of the Church, not Christ, the Judge of the nations, on the throne of the last day. Suffering in the body was ordained for the well-being of the spirit. Natural laws, if violated, revenge themselves on the violator. Apparently, however, much more is meant in this instance. The culprit had gone beyond natural law. A member of the Church, and nominally retaining his place among those "called to be saints," he had sacrificed, in a most ruthless manner, those spiritual relations which are to the immortal man more sacred and enduring than any and all other ties. If his vice, reeking and dripping with the foulest slime of earth, had invaded the spiritual realm of Christ's kingdom, the act of excommunication cannot pause at simple excision. Nay; of that other world, whose mysteries envelop us—a world of spirit and spirits within the world of the senses—the offender and the Church and St. Paul were inhabitants, and, hour by hour, the realities of life were most real in this occult domain. *There*—the great secrets lie, the secret sources of motive and purpose, of strength and weakness, and of life and death. *There*—we get our tragedies, so that Shakespeare found it impossible to write 'Macbeth' without "supernatural solicitings," and even the Platonic Brutus must face the vengeance of the other world in the tent near Sardis. And *there*—this judgment allies itself with Satanic agency in subordination to Christ's authority. And *there*, finally, over all, is infinite tenderness; and, though ruin might be wrought on the outward man, seeing that his sin was specially heinous and involved in a signal way the most terrible retributions of an outraged body, yet it remained possible that his spirit might be "saved in the day of the Lord Jesus."—L.

Vers. 6—13.—*Supplementary views and explanations.* Was nothing necessary except to get rid of the offender? That was to be done, but something else was quite as much of an exigency. Here, then, we see the extent to which the enormous evil had spread, for the whole Church had been infected. If the vice had assumed in one man the completest form of social iniquity, what was the state of the atmosphere in which this was possible? Such corruption was not sporadic: the whole air was poisoned; and in this state of things nothing short of a general purification would suffice. For, in the midst of this widespread taint, you are breathing out your complacent self-conceits. Glorying (boasting) is not good. To glory in a time like this of your privileges, gifts, eloquence, devotion to leaders, is a wretched delusion, bad enough under any circumstances, incomparably worse now, because of the immense contrast between your state of mind and your actual condition. This is St. Paul's argument. But his logic is not content to be logic only. Buoyant and flexible as are his reasonings, he must have the help of metaphors, since all our greatest thoughts tend to perfect themselves by means of the imagination. Beyond the illustrative imagination (for he is very utilitarian in the use of images) he seldom goes, and he is especially given to the habit of using the interrogatory imagination. "Know ye not that a little leaven leaveneth the whole lump?" *Purge* it out—an earnest word; cleanse and purify by ridding the Church of its moral defilement, and so complete the work begun in the excommunication of the incestuous man. It is "old leaven," the relic of the natural man, and it threatens to destroy the new man of Christ's kingdom. For what now is the Divine ideal of a Christian? A new creature in Christ. And what the ideal of the Church? A new brotherhood of humanity in Christ. Therefore, purge out the old leaven, and be *a new lump*, remembering that even discipline executed in Christ's name has its dangers, and may divert us from attention to our own spiritual condition. Inasmuch, then, as St. Paul looked on the excision of the ungodly member of the Church, and the internal purification of the Church in all its members, as branches of one and the same duty, he presses his argument under the idea of a new lump—not a mere outer reform, but a thoroughgoing inward renewal by the grace of the Spirit. Such language could have emanated from no man who had not been a religious Jew. Nor could it have proceeded from one who was simply a spiritual Jew. It was a Christian thinker, a thinker of catholic insight, who saw into Judaism from the cross of Calvary, when that cross and its Divine Sacrifice had the great darkness under which they stood cleared away by Pentecost. Once St. Paul had understood the scrupulous removing of the leaven by the Jews from their homes in a very different way. Once he had seen in the Passover and kindred institutions a life-giving and perpetual force. Now, however, the images lingered in his thoughts, only to remind him that Christians were "unleavened," and that all the leaven of impurity must be put away from them. For them the Paschal Lamb had been slain, and in the Victim's death they had redemption. "Let us keep the feast;" our consecrated life a festival of gladness, and our thanksgiving continually ascending to God. And how shall this long and sacred festivity be observed? No external demonstrations are mentioned. Could the Jew conceive of a festival 'like this? Would not the pomp and show of national reunions, the booths and palm boughs, the cheer of open-air life, and the music and domestic joy of the congregated caravans, rush upon him with their thrilling recollections? And would not the Greek, whose senses were so finely attuned to whatever was beautiful in material nature, and whose very birthright was the luxury of existence beneath skies and amid landscapes that seemed to pour their sympathies into his bosom,—would not he recall the theatre and the games? And yet St. Paul tells them of a festival which the renewed soul may keep without any of these things, and be supremely happy. "The old leaven," especially "the leaven of malice and wickedness," must be excluded, and the feast must be kept "with the unleavened bread of sincerity and truth." The evil in our nature must be destroyed, and, in its place, must be had the genuine excellence which has been tried and proved, and the harmony that comes from self-control because the human will is controlled by the indwelling Spirit of God. Virtues such as sincerity and truth need society, and, assuredly, society needs them. Eager to communicate and in turn to receive, what shall be the law of their intercourse with mankind? Fellowship is a Christian designation that cannot have its meaning in the world. But Christians are in the world, and a very important element in its life. To deny its associations and segregate themselves from others is to commit a species of suicide. On a former occasion St. Paul had written an Epistle touching this subject. But he had been misunderstood, and now he would rectify their error. They had blundered, not he. And now he sets the matter clearly before them by impressing on these Corinthians that there was not only a distinction between the Church and the world, but likewise between the good and the evil in the Church itself. Tares must grow with the wheat, but that was no reason why they should treat the tares as wheat. Fornicators in the Church or out of it were fornicators, and the brethren were not to keep company with them. And hence his explicitness, "not to company" with any man who was a fornicator, though he might be "called a brother." Nor does he stop here. Covetous men, idolaters, railers, drunkards, extortioners, they were not to associate with on such terms of social companionship as would be symbolized by eating with them. How could he as an apostle judge those who were without? If he did not do this, could they suppose that he meant to require it of them? The outer world must be left with God. And now St. Paul returns to the matter engrossing his solicitude: "Put away from among yourselves that wicked person." If, indeed, Christ is our Paschal Lamb; if through that offering of expiation and reconciliation in itself for ever perfect and by us realized in pardon and renewal and sanctification, life becomes an Easter of glad thanksgiving; we must make this sincerity (purity) and this truth (harmony) visible to the world in our social sympathies. Bodily sins are easily condoned among men: beware of that evil. Extortion and covetousness grow out of the idolatry of the senses, and they must not be countenanced by familiar association. How modern is this Epistle! No thought had St. Paul of us and our century, but these words of his rise from their local connections and assume universality of application. Corinth is at our doors, because its spirit is in all unsanctified hearts. And yet—thanks to the grace of the Spirit—in all the foremost civilizations of this age and over a wider space than ever before, the Paschal Lamb is precious to thousands. Since the days of the apostle, human life has expanded its outward area. Myriads of things, unknown to it then, are its possession and strength and glory now. Two wonderful enlargements have gone on—that of the universe to our comprehension, and this of the globe and the world to which we belong. And, in the midst of all the widening, specially in the fuller opening of human sympathies and the growth of human intercourse, the blessed festival of Christian life repeats its ancient joy and multiplies the participants of its Divine gladness.—L.

Vers. 1, 2.—*Impurity in the Church.* There could scarcely be stronger internal evidence of the genuineness of this Epistle than is supplied by this very painful chapter.

Real circumstances alone could account for the devotion of a considerable portion of this document to such a theme as is here treated. The solicitude and indignation of the apostle are highly characteristic; whilst the insight afforded into the moral state of the Corinthian congregation is obviously one which only unmistakable facts can justify and explain. Moral lessons of high value may be deduced from the apostle's treatment of a distressing subject.

I. WE OBSERVE THE DEBASED MORAL SENTIMENTS AND PRACTICES WITH WHICH CHRISTIANITY HAD TO CONTEND. We need not go to the moralists, the satirists, the poets of classical literature, in order to form a judgment as to the corruptions which prevailed among the nations previously to the promulgation of Christianity. The New Testament, especially St. Paul's writings, are a sufficient witness. We have the opportunity of learning, through our travellers and missionaries, how largely the state of the heathen world at the present time corresponds with that of pre-Christian paganism. 1. The passage before us furnishes an example of fornication, which was scarcely thought to be a vice, and indeed was a religious observance among the voluptuous society of Corinth. 2. But the case was one of aggravated adultery and incest, which the moralists of antiquity admitted to be crimes, but which it surprises us to find, even in an individual case, in one of the early Christian communities. Such, however, was the moral condition for which our Divine religion brought a remedy.

II. WE REMARK THE LAXITY ON THE PART OF A CHRISTIAN COMMUNITY WHICH COULD TOLERATE SUCH OFFENCES AGAINST MORALITY. 1. The Church at Corinth allowed the offender to remain unreproved in their midst, as though nothing had happened which called for especial notice and vigorous and immediate action. 2. They did not even mourn, did not distress themselves, did not make the event an occasion of humiliation and mourning; which showed a sad insensibility to the evil. 3. So far from this, at the very time when their fellowship was so disgraced, they were "puffed up," boasting themselves of their spiritual gifts and intellectual distinction!

III. WE GRATEFULLY NOTE THE PROTEST OF THE INSPIRED APOSTLE AGAINST THE CONDUCT BOTH OF THE OFFENDER AND OF THOSE WHO TOLERATED HIM. It may occur to some readers of the Epistle to ask—Is not the very fact that such sin existed and was suffered in the bosom of a Christian society a proof that Christianity had little real, moral, beneficent power in the world? Wherein was this Church at Corinth better than any heathen society? Could a worse state of things exist without than that which admittedly existed within? The answer to this objection is obvious and sufficient, and is very instructive to us. 1. The conduct of the offender was in direct violation of the laws upon which the society to which he nominally belonged was built. Purity was, as much as justice or benevolence, a fundamental law of the Christian kingdom. 2. This conduct was also in flagrant contrast and antagonism to the spirit and life of the Divine Founder of that religion which was professedly received by these Corinthian Christians. Jesus was the model of purity of heart, and his life and character were sinless, holy, blameless. 3. The inaction and tolerance which were blamable in the congregation were inconsistent with their well-known duty. The Christian Church is not a club, whose members are at liberty to receive and reject whomsoever they choose. It is a society of which Christ is the Head and Lord, and is bound to receive those who possess his Spirit, and to reject those who openly and unmistakably grieve and outrage that Spirit. The members of the Church were termed "the holy," or "saints;" and although all were and still are in character far short of the designation they bear, there can be no question as to the inconsistency of a life of incest with a Christian profession. 4. The case called for the stern interference of the apostle, as an authority over the Churches. His language was intended to quicken the conscience, to enlighten the judgment, to call forth the action, of those who were very negligent and culpable. It was a new thing in heathendom that such a stand should be made as that which was on this occasion made by the apostle of the Gentiles. 5. Further, the action of the Church, when brought to a proper state of mind, was such as to show that one great end of the existence of Christian societies was the promotion of moral purity. The excision of the members was necessary to the preservation of the health of the body. 6. The ultimate repentance and restoration of the offender is a proof to us that the Christian Church was designed to promote, not only the purity of the pure, but the recovery of the lapsed. In this the Church showed herself to be penetrated with the compassionate Spirit of her Divine Master and Head.—T.

Ver. 3.—"*Absent in body, but present in spirit.*" Much as Paul loved his converts in the city of Corinth, he could not, at the period when he wrote this Epistle, think of visiting them. Their conduct in the matter treated in this chapter so distressed his pure and affectionate heart, so disappointed his expectations, that he felt constrained to remain absent from them. But in so doing he was not showing any lack of interest in their Christian life or their Church proceedings. Quite the contrary; he was content to stay away because, as the text makes evident, he knew there was a sense in which he was really with them.

I. THE SPECIAL INSTANCE OF THIS PRINCIPLE FURNISHED IN THE CASE OF PAUL AND THE CORINTHIANS. In what senses could the apostle deem himself to be with these Corinthian Christians "in spirit"? 1. By his *teaching*. He had long laboured in word and doctrine in this great centre of Greek commerce and literature, and amongst this company, of whom not many were wise or noble, but many were called and washed and sanctified by the gospel of Christ and by the Spirit of God. His teaching laid the foundation upon which Apollos and others had built. And we know enough of that teaching to be sure that it included many precepts and motives to holiness. This instruction had sunk into the hearts of the spiritually susceptible, and by it the apostle yet spake of this society, summoning them to a holy life, and bidding them maintain a standard of social purity. 2. By his *authority*. Paul never forgot that he was an inspired apostle of the Lord. He spake by the Spirit of the Lord, and his counsels were not those of human wisdom merely, but of celestial authority. What the Corinthians were directed to do they were to do in his name, and with the assurance that their action would be sanctioned by the Divine Head of the Church. In vindicating the purity of Christian communion, in cleansing the Bride of Christ from any stain of the world that had fallen upon her white robe, the Corinthians were to feel that the apostle was with them, inspiring and corroborating their lawful necessary action.

II. THE GENERAL OPERATION OF THIS PRINCIPLE IN THE LIVING CHURCH OF CHRIST JESUS. 1. The great Saviour and Founder of the Church is absent in body, but present in spirit. He himself assured his disciples that it was good for them that he should go away, for that thus the Comforter should come. And the spiritual and universal and perpetual presence of the great Head of the Church is thus delightfully and graciously secured. 2. The action of Christ's Church, when in accordance with the express and plain instructions of our Lord and of his inspired apostles, must be recognized as prompted by his Spirit and sanctioned by his authority. In the application of this principle there are and will be many differences among the people of Christ, but with regard to the principle itself there should be no diversity or hesitation. We do not see his form or hear his voice; but we cannot question his spiritual presence. And he is at hand, not only to teach the disciple, to comfort the sufferer, to counsel the perplexed, but to impart a Divine authority to the actions and to the discipline of those who rely upon his Word and do his will.—T.

Vers. 6, 7.—"*Purge out the old leaven.*" The apostle sought the illustrations with which he enforced Christian doctrine and duty from every source, Hebrew and Gentile alike. In this passage he derives, from the practices of his countrymen during the festival of the Passover, a figure by which he brings before his readers the necessity of moral purity in life and in fellowship. As the Jews were accustomed at the approach of the feast to search out every scrap of leaven to be found in their houses, that they might duly keep the Feast of Unleavened Bread, so were the Corinthians exhorted to clear themselves of all moral taint, that they might be a people meet for the fellowship and the service of the holy Redeemer.

I. THE IDEAL STATE OF THE CHRISTIAN HEART AND OF THE CHRISTIAN SOCIETY IS ONE OF PERFECT FREEDOM FROM ALL TAINT OF SIN. It was a high and noble aim that which the Divine Founder of Christianity set before him—the formation of a society which should be pure with his own purity, *i.e.* both of life and of heart. It is to such an aim that he himself, and after him his inspired apostles, encourage all Christians to aspire: "Be ye therefore perfect, even as your Father in heaven is perfect."

II. THERE IS A LEAVEN OF SINFUL INFLUENCE IN HUMAN NATURE AND IN HUMAN SOCIETY WHICH ENDANGERS THE PURITY OF THE CHURCH. 1. The presence of such a leaven was very painfully manifest in the society at Corinth. But where is the Christian community which is absolutely pure? There are societies which make great professions in this matter; but their "glorying is not good." Where is the individual Christian in whose nature there is no trace of the old, worldly, sinful, corrupt humanity? The purest and the best are foremost to acknowledge that this is so. 2. Leaven furnishes an illustration of the diffusive, contagious, corrupting power of sin. A little leaven leavens the lump. A sin tolerated, a sinner countenanced, in a Christian society, may imperil the general purity. "One sickly sheep infects the flock;" "Behold how great a matter a little fire kindleth!" These and other proverbial intimations of the power of this principle are sufficient to put us upon our guard. Each heart is aware of the secret temptations to evil to which it is most exposed; and perhaps every one's experience can show how evil habit grows when unchecked and indulged.

III. THE DIVINE SUMMONS REQUIRES THAT THE LEAVEN OF SIN BE REMOVED THAT THE MASS MAY BE PRESERVED IN PURITY. 1. The case of the Corinthians reminds us that the excision of an offending member may be necessary in order to vindicate Christian purity and to protest against the encroachments of sin. The old leaven must, in this sense, be "purged out." 2. There is, however, a wider application of this principle. Corruption creeps into every nature, into every society. And the apostle here enjoins that we submit to no truce, to no compromise with sin, but that, for the sake of our own spiritual and eternal interests, we keep a watch upon ourselves, lest the sour leaven steal in unobserved, and corrupt our nature ere we be aware of its operation, or at all events its power. Holiness becometh the house of the Lord for ever.—T.

Ver. 7.—"*Christ our Passover.*" The connection of this illustration with the passage in which it occurs is obvious. The Jews commenced the Feast of Unleavened Bread with the slaying, roasting, and eating of the Paschal lamb. Now, the apostle has been urging the Corinthians to moral purity, and has enjoined them to put away the leaven of wickedness, and keep the feast with the unleavened bread of sincerity and truth; and, as a motive to do this, he reminds them that the Christian dispensation is as a spiritual Passover, which commenced with the sacrifice of "the Lamb of God who taketh away the sin of the world." The Paschal lamb is regarded as a symbol of Christ.

I. IT COMMEMORATED A GREAT DELIVERANCE. The Israelites were reminded by the Passover feast of the bondage from which their ancestors had been delivered when they were brought out of Egypt "with a high hand and a stretched-out arm." The nation had been emancipated from the tyranny of the Pharaohs, and had been spared the doom of the first-born of the people of the land. Christ's redemption set his people free from the tyranny, the bondage, the unrewarded toil, the darksome night, the dreary hopelessness, of sin; and brought them out into the freedom, the light, the gracious privileges, the glorious hopes, of the gospel.

II. IT WAS SLAIN AS A DIVINELY ORDERED SACRIFICE AND OFFERING. Put to death by the head of the family, the lamb was taken to the priest, who sprinkled its blood upon the altar and burned its fat, according to the ordinance. Although the lamb was offered yearly, it was in the first instance that it was regarded most strictly as a sacrifice. Christ was offered once only; "There remaineth no more offering for sin." Yet the Eucharist is a perpetual memorial of the great Sacrifice of Calvary. It is by the willing, accepted, vicarious sacrifice of our Redeemer that mankind have been reconciled and consecrated unto God.

III. IT WAS PARTAKEN BY THE FAITHFUL WORSHIPPERS IN THE PASCHAL MEAL. It was in this way that every Hebrew family was reminded of its share in the covenant mercy and faithfulness of the Eternal. As they ate the lamb in the appointed way, and with the appointed observances and accompaniments, the children of Israel were led to appropriate, in faith and obedience, the spiritual provision which the God of their fathers had made for them. In like manner the members of the spiritual common-wealth of Israel "eat the flesh and drink the blood of the Son of man," taking Christ as the nourishment of their souls, and appropriating the strength, the wisdom, the grace of God himself. In the sacrament of the Supper, they who eat and drink in faith participate in the provisions of Divine bounty and love.

IV. IT WAS SUGGESTIVE OF INDIVIDUAL, OF HOUSEHOLD, OF NATIONAL, PURITY. In connection with the Paschal meal, several circumstances may be noted. The lamb was without blemish; the house was freed from leaven; all were careful to avoid ceremonial defilement. These arrangements symbolized " holiness unto the Lord," and they remind us that those who regard the Christ of God as their Passover are bound by every sacred consideration to seek that purity of heart, that sanctification of nature, which can alone render a man and a society acceptable to a holy and heart-searching God.—T.

Ver. 8.—*The Christian festival.* The apostle seems to represent the whole of the Christian life as one long Passover festival and solemnity, and to invite his readers to unite with him in an appropriate and perpetual observance.

I. THIS FESTIVAL IS BASED UPON THE SACRIFICE AND REDEMPTION OF CHRIST JESUS. As the events connected with Israel's emancipation from Egypt constituted the foundation of the national and religious life of the Hebrews, so we Christians date our fellowship, our standing, our privileges from the redeeming and mediatorial work of our Divine Saviour. Apart from him there would have been no foundation for our new life and hallowed communion; he accounts for all, and is himself " all and in all."

II. THE OBSERVANCE OF THIS FESTIVAL MUST CORRESPOND WITH THE PURPOSE AND WITH THE CHARACTER OF OUR LORD. " The leaven of malice and wickedness" has no place in the household of faith and holiness. As the Israelites ate the unleavened bread during the celebration of the Passover festival, so are Christians called to make their daily spiritual feast upon the purity, the sincerity, the truth which are the appropriate aliment of the consecrated Israel of God. In the Church which Christ has purchased with his precious blood, nothing impure, corrupt, defiling, should be tolerated. The Eucharistic meal should impart something of its character to all meals; and the holy and public observances of the Church should cast something of their glow and beauty upon the daily employments of the Lord's consecrated people.

III. THIS IS AN UNBROKEN AND PERPETUAL FESTIVAL. The times and seasons, the sabbaths, new moons, and festivals, which were observed among the Jews, were doubtless designed to inculcate the practice and to familiarize with the idea of holiness. And they were intended to prepare for the dispensation which teaches that all days and all scenes, all relationships and all actions, are holy unto God. The spiritual festival to which Christians are bidden is one which never ends, the viands of Divine grace are never exhausted, the fellowship of the saints never wearies, and the Master of the banquet never departs.—T.

Vers. 9—11.—*The limits of fellowship.* " No man liveth unto himself." Attempts have been made to build a science of human nature and a scheme of human life upon the foundation of the individual existence, but such attempts have failed. Man is born into society and lives in society, and is inexplicable apart from society. For good or for evil we are with one another. " As iron sharpeneth iron, so a man sharpeneth the countenance of his friend;" " Evil communications corrupt good manners;" " He that walketh with wise men shall be wise."

I. CHRISTIANS ARE NOT LIMITED TO THE SOCIETY OF THEIR FELLOW-CHRISTIANS. St. Paul possessed no small measure of what has been humorously called " sanctified common sense." He saw clearly and at once that if a man set out with the determination to have no intercourse with those of different principles and sentiments from himself, he would be driven in consistency to " go out of the world." So far from forbidding such intercourse, he permitted it, and even in some instances encouraged it. 1. The example of the Lord Jesus and of his apostles sanctions intercourse with general society. Jesus talked with persons of all sorts and conditions, accepted invitations to the houses of strangers, and even of enemies. And we find the apostles seeking introduction to Jews and Gentiles, to the virtuous and the vicious. 2. Such conduct exercises a power of attraction over all who are affected by it. The assumption of superior sanctity repels, whilst the kindly sympathy of neighbourhood, the good offices of social life, may lead to a desire to know and enjoy the blessings of the gospel. 3. Opportunities occur in social intercourse for introducing, either directly or indirectly, the truths of religion. It is not always the public proclamation of the truth which reaches the heart of the careless and ungodly. "A word spoken in season, how good it is!" Many have had reason for lifelong gratitude towards such as have in a casual way taken advantage of the opportunity to commend the gospel to their souls.

II. Christians are restrained from free intercourse with fellow-professors whose conduct is unworthy of the name they bear. 1. It must not be supposed that we are confined to the fellowship of those whose character is mature and blameless. This would be to set up in the Church an aristocracy of the worst kind. 2. Those whose company is forbidden are such as, by manifest and flagrant violation of the moral law, prove the utter insincerity of their profession to be followers of Christ. 3. The reasons for this prohibition are obvious. (1) It could scarcely be other than injurious to our own moral nature to be intimate with those whose life belies their creed, whose hypocrisy is unmistakable. (2) Such intimacy would be interpreted by the world as meaning that in our esteem it is of little consequence what a man is, if he only professes to be Christ's. (3) And there can be no question that to cultivate the friendship of a hypocrite would tend to encourage him in his sinful course; whilst to withdraw from his society might lead him to repentance.—T.

Vers. 1—7.—*Church discipline.* I. Flagrant sin is not to be tolerated in the Church. Though the precepts of Christianity are most pure, professors are sometimes impure. The Corinthian Church furnished a deplorable example. The sin of one of its members was a sin which was "not even among the Gentiles." Occasionally occurring among them, but exceptional even in such debased communities; held in general reprobation, not countenanced by their laws. Into the purest society a great impurity may creep. But in the Church of Christ no such iniquity must be winked at. To permit its continuance would be : 1. *To imperil the spiritual life of the whole community.* "Know ye not that a little leaven leaveneth the whole lump?" Sin has great *spreading* power; it is marvellously *aggressive.* 2. *To bring contempt upon the Church.* The Church has often to endure contempt, but she should never *deserve* it. 3. *To annihilate the Church's influence for good.* How can she fight against evils without, if she tolerates them within. 4. *To grieve the Head of the Church.* What an anomaly for the Church to foster or be indifferent to the sins which pierced her Lord ! 5. *To invite the judgment of God.* For transgression the ancient Church was cast away, and shall the Church of the new dispensation escape if she gives herself to folly and sin ?

II. To be dealt with : 1. *By the Church.* 2. *The flagrant offender to be excluded.* For slight offences warning may suffice, but serious lapses call for serious remedies. Sufficient recognition of the sin (as in excommunication) may be well, not only for the Church, but for the transgressor. If the Church think lightly of his misdemeanour, he will probably think lightly of it also. Inferentially we gather that the social position, wealth, influence, of the offender do not come into the account. The law of the Church is the same for rich and poor, high and low. 3. *With hope of the offender's reclamation.* In the case at Corinth the guilty one is, in Paul's language, to be delivered "unto Satan for the destruction of the flesh." The meaning probably is that Satan shall have power to deal with him somewhat as he did with Job (Job ii. 4—7) and with Paul himself (2 Cor. xii. 7); that the sin shall be followed by suffering; the evil-doer, outside the Church, being placed in the hands of Satan, "the god of this world," not absolutely, but largely, so far as bodily affliction is concerned. Satan is represented in Scripture as causing bodily pain (see Luke xiii. 16). This deliverance to Satan was a power delegated to the Corinthian Church by Paul, who, as an inspired apostle, possessed it. The *object* of the deliverance to Satan was that "the spirit might be saved in the day of the Lord Jesus." The *means,* "the destruction of the flesh," not the destruction of *the body,* which is to have a place in the resurrection, but by affliction of the body the destruction of that "flesh," that carnality, that corrupt nature, which cannot inherit the kingdom of God. It is charitable to hope that affliction may fall, even heavily, upon flagrant transgressors in the Church. This may lead them to repentance and to a holier life. Exclusion from Church fellowship is to have this object in view. The severance is with a view to reunion, either below or above. We give up fellowship, but not hope. Our expectation and prayer should be that those excluded may be found in a saved condition in the day of the Lord Jesus. We should not exclude out of vindictiveness, nor with spirit of final judgment, nor in despair of God's grace. Note: It is a very solemn thing to be excluded from the visible Church of Christ. This places us *visibly* in the kingdom of Satan, and we know not how much more fully under Satanic influence. The Church is a shelter and refuge appointed by God; we should be careful how we forfeit our place in it. But, however sad our severance from the Christian Church may be, the *real sadness* is *in the sin which causes that severance.*

III. CHURCH DISCIPLINE A CAUSE OF CHURCH SORROW. 1. *Incompatible with boastfulness.* A cause of humiliation. Whilst we are vainly glorying, the devil is doing his work diligently, and the result will presently appear. Those who are "puffed up" are preparing for a great abasement. Corinthian joy is the herald of sorrow. 2. *Grief for the excluded one.* Once a brother—a brother greatly beloved, perhaps—and now? 3. *Grief tending to self-examination on the part of those still in fellowship.* (1) Possibly the lapsed one was not cared for as he should have been. (2) The evil was not checked, perhaps, when it was in the bud. There may have been opportunities to save from actual and open transgression. (3) The evil, perhaps, was rather fostered; indirectly, at all events, by too light an estimate of its heinousness. This may have been so at Corinth; in a city so notoriously corrupt some believers may have entertained lax views of profligacy. If we have in any way helped a brother to fall, how keen should be our regret! (4) The offender may have been led away by the careless living of some in the Church. Or (5) may have been influenced by the general tone of the Church. At Corinth, no doubt, the many divisions and the much glorying in men bred an unhealthy Church atmosphere.—H.

Vers. 7, 8.—"*Our Passover.*" What the Jews had, we have—only with fuller and richer significance. They had the foretastes, the shadows; we have the substance. The events in their history point forward to the greater events in ours. They had a Passover, and so have we; and theirs was a prefiguration of ours.

I. CHRIST IS OUR PASSOVER. 1. *He was typified by the Paschal lamb.* Often called the "Lamb" (for example, John i. 29; Rev. v. 12). (1) *Appointed by God.* Israel's Passover was "*the Lord's* Passover" (Exod. xii. 27); "*My* sacrifice" (Exod. xxiii. 18). Jesus is the "Christ," the Anointed of *God.* "It pleased the Lord to bruise him." Here is our confidence, that *our* Passover is *the Lord's* Passover, appointed and approved by the Eternal: "My beloved Son, in whom I am well pleased." Salvation by the cross is *God's plan* of salvation; it must, therefore, fully commend itself to God. (2) *Innocent.* Here is the pathos of the cross. He died not for his sins, but for ours. He had not transgressed, but we had, and *therefore* he died. (3) *Without blemish.* "With the precious blood of Christ, as of a lamb without blemish" (1 Pet. i. 19). Keen unfriendly eyes were upon Christ, but the reluctant verdict was "no fault." "Holy, harmless, undefiled, separate from sinners" (Heb. vii. 26). (4) *Slain.* Christ *crucified.* The converging point—"Without shedding of blood there is no remission." The Paschal lamb was slain by those for whose welfare and safety it was appointed; *so Christ was crucified by men whom he came to redeem.* No bone broken (comp. Exod. xii. 46 with John xix. 36). (5) *The blood sprinkled.* The blood *shed* is not enough, it must be *applied.* The blood of the Paschal lamb was applied with a bunch of hyssop, a type of "faith" which, though apparently small and insignificant, brings the blood of Christ into saving contact with the heart. (6) *The flesh eaten.* We have to feed upon Christ. "My flesh is meat indeed." The Passover was a feast; the idea of *enjoyment* is involved. So those who feast upon Christ obtain truest happiness. The Paschal lamb was eaten by the Israelites with loins girded, shoes on feet, staff in hand; so the followers of Christ, when they become such, confess themselves to be strangers and pilgrims upon the earth. The lamb was eaten *in Egypt.* So we are saved as *sinners*; we have not to come up out of the Egypt of corruption. We have not to *get ourselves ready* for Christ; we are *ready* when we are lost and desire to be found of him. Many are hindered by their "unworthiness;" they want to be holy before they seek salvation, which means that the patient desires to be cured before he sends for the doctor. And *he comes to us*; we do not come to him,—we are *in Egypt* when we first behold the Lamb of God. (7) *The whole eaten.* We have not to take *a part* of Christ. We have to accept the *full terms* of salvation, not those only that most please us. Christ and his cross as well as Christ and his crown. (8) *Eaten with bitter herbs.* So repentance should accompany faith. We should have bitter sorrow for bitter sins. Our sins were very bitter to him. We have never tasted sin fully—only *a part of* it, the *sweeter* part of it. He tasted the bitter part for us. 2. *Identified with deliverance from wrath and bondage.* (1) *From wrath.* The destroying angel was abroad, and smote every house unprotected by the sprinkled blood. So the wrath of God falls upon the rejecters of Christ, but those upon whose hearts and consciences the blood of Christ is sprinkled are preserved from the stroke of Divine justice. At the cross "righteousness and peace have kissed each other" (Ps. lxxxv. 10). The blood of the Paschal lamb made the Israelite perfectly safe; we are made so by the blood of Christ. (2) *From bondage.* The Passover and the Exodus are indissolubly united. So in our spiritual history. When God pardons, the bondage of Satan is destroyed. We are no longer slaves of the devil, but children of God. And this becomes manifested; justification and sanctification, joined by God, are not put asunder. We begin a new life; we depart from our old master; we "spoil the Egyptians," for we bring everything with us out of the old life that is worth bringing; and our faces are set towards the new Jerusalem, the everlasting home of the redeemed.

II. The influence of our Passover on our life. At the Passover the Jews were exceedingly anxious to get rid of every particle of leaven (Deut. xvi. 4); so all who can call Christ their Passover should search and purify their hearts. As the Feast of Unleavened Bread followed the slaying of the Paschal lamb, so the unleaven of righteousness, of godly life, should *abide* with all who have part in the great Passover. This is "keeping the feast." It is then a *feast,* a time of joy to the believer, when all leaven of "malice and wickedness" is excluded. The "unleavened bread of sincerity and truth" is not only wholesome, it is surprisingly *sweet.* The influence of Christ's death is not only towards *salvation,* but towards *holiness.* If we are his we must depart from evil. We must have works as well as faith—the former a natural outcome of the latter. The one is not without the other—the Passover and unleavened bread go together. Profession by all means, but certainly practice as well. We must show that we are out of Egypt by a repudiation of Egyptian manners. "Christ our Passover;" "For to me to live is Christ."—H.

Vers. 9—13.—*Converse with the ungodly.* I. In our ordinary life we must associate more or less with the impure and godless. Our legitimate business leads us among such, our duties as citizens and subjects as well. If we kept ourselves entirely apart, we should have "to go out of the world." 1. Christianity is not designed to drive us "out of the world." We are to live *among men* righteously. Here we have an argument against monasticism, which is "going out of the world" to escape from its evils. 2. Our Lord and Master mixed freely amongst men. 3. We have many opportunities of witnessing for Christ when we come in contact with men of the world. This should never be lost sight of; private Christians thus may become ministers and missionaries. And they may thus reach classes beyond the ordinary aggressive means. Christians should *live the gospel* amidst a crooked and perverse generation. 4. Still, we must recognize the peril of such association with ungodly men. Duty may call us to mix with worldlings, but duty will never call us to shut our eyes to the danger of doing this. The hunter may be right in running into peril, but he can't be right in refusing to recognize the peril, and *in making no provision for it.* When we go into the world we should go *armed.* "The whole armour of God" should be our panoply. We should not go *alone;* we may go *with Christ* if the path be the path of duty. Prayer, watchfulness, God-reliance, not self-reliance, should be remembered. We are then not only in an enemy's country, but the enemy is around us and will soon attack. "Be ye also ready:" many have been unready, and have been sorely wounded of the archers. *Go not further into the world than duty bids you.*

II. But we are not to associate with a professed Christian who walks disorderly. The case is here altered. Those outside are as strangers to us, though we mix among them; this one we know and have been identified with. Those outside are left to the judgment of God; we have no part in judging them. But we have in the case of an offending brother. As members of the Church, it is our duty to sit in judgment upon him (vers. 4, 5), and, if the offence be sufficiently serious, to expel him. Henceforth, until he repents we-are not to have fellowship with him, not even to eat with him, but to show him by our conduct what has been expressed in the Church's decree, viz. that he is separated until repentance and amendment. If this were not so: 1. *The force of Church discipline would be seriously weakened.* It would become largely unmeaning. It would be very idle, as well as scandalously contradictory, to cut off from fellowship and to admit to it at the same time. 2. *The effect upon the offender would be lessened.* Church discipline does not lose sight of *his* welfare; it is directed towards his recovery and restoration. But if it is to produce this effect it must be *felt.* It cannot be felt if practically it is destroyed. 3. *It would seem as though the evil were lightly esteemed.* This would bring a great scandal upon Christianity. It would not only expose it to contempt, but *justify contempt.* 4. *There would be much peril to the other members of the Church:* (1) In the association. There is often more peril in associating with a false professor than with an open evil-doer. (2) In the conviction that they could sin with comparative impunity so far as the Church was concerned. We may ask—What kinds of sin involve such separation? The apostle gives a list of transgressors. (1) *Fornicators.* The unclean; professing purity, practising impurity. (2) *The covetous.* Those who make a god of the things of sense. Heart-idolatry. (3) *Idolaters.* Probably those who, professing to serve the only true God, identified themselves very closely with idolaters, joined in their feasts and sacrifices, and so became partakers of their guilt. There are many professors now who pay homage to " the god of this world." A little wholesome Church discipline might not be altogether thrown away upon some of these. (4) *Railers* or *revilers.* Those who say they have a clean heart, but keep a foul mouth. (5) *Drunkards.* Those who claim to be akin to Christ, and yet sink themselves lower than the brutes. (6) *Extortioners.* Greedy, grasping souls, who overreach and cheat others, but who overreach and cheat *themselves* pre-eminently. We may not company with these; we may *pray* for them, we may labour for their recovery. We may do so gratefully, humbly, remembering that we stand because Divine grace upholds us.—H.

Vers. 1—6.—*Church discipline.* From the subject of the party divisions at Corinth, the apostle passes on to consider other evils which had come to his knowledge. The first is a case of incest, in which a member of the Church had married, or was cohabiting with, his step-mother; and this incestuous person was permitted to remain in the Christian community. Such a case gives us a glimpse into the sad condition of Corinthian society. This heterogeneous population was exposed to three influences that were decidedly adverse to a high morality: extensive commerce, involving contact with the vices of foreigners and developing luxurious living; the Isthmian games celebrated in the neighbourhood; and the worship of Venus. The Church that was drawn from such a community could not escape the infection of its low moral tone. Many weeds were already in the soil into which the good seed was cast. We can thus understand how in such a society so gross a case as this might arise.

I. SPIRITUAL PRIDE AND GROSS SIN ARE OFTEN FOUND TOGETHER. The Corinthians were puffed up because of their fancied attainments (ch. iv. 8), whilst this awful wickedness was tolerated among them. Spiritual pride is a distemper sure to beget other grosser evils, whether in individuals or Churches. It dims the spiritual eye and blunts the moral sense, and thereby leads to a fall. Perfectionism content to dwell with incest!

II. THE EXERCISE OF DISCIPLINE. 1. *Its warrant.* Every society has the right to reject members whose character is inconsistent with its constitution and ends. This is true of the state, as of private associations; and the same right is not to be denied to the Church. As a healthy body throws off disease which finds a lodgment in an unhealthy one, so a healthy Church will not tolerate in its bosom open transgressors. The true ideal of the Church is not collective, but selective—not embracing all men as such, but only those who have been called out from the world (ἐκκλησία). The dividing line is not absolute—there will always be tares among the wheat; but some line there must be. And this inherent right is confirmed by Divine injunction (Matt. xviii. 17). 2. *Its form.* In this case the Church is to assemble, Paul himself being present in spirit, and in the Name of the Lord Jesus " to deliver such a one unto Satan " (comp. 1 Tim. i. 20). This probably points to something more than simple excommunication, perhaps to bodily suffering or death, which the apostles in certain instances had the power of inflicting (Ananias and Sapphira, Acts v. 1—11; Elymas, Acts xiii. 11). Apart from the specialties of this case, it is plain that disciplinary dealing with scandalous members is to take the form of exclusion from the fellowship of the Christian society; and this is to be the solemn act of the Church, either collectively or by duly appointed representatives. Such a judicial sentence, pronounced in virtue of the power conferred by the Lord Jesus, should carry with it great weight; and that it may have its due effect on the mind of the offender, let there be joined with it brotherly dealing and prayer. 3. *Its ends.* (1) As regards the individual, the censures of the Church have in view his true well-being. The deliverance to Satan has for its object the destruction of the flesh and the ultimate saving of the spirit. How it brings this about may be learnt from the case of Peter (" Satan asked to have you," Luke xxii. 31); from Paul's thorn in the flesh (" a messenger of Satan," 2 Cor. xii. 7); and especially from the experience of Job (Job i. 12). The sifting of the adversary drives away the chaff; his buffeting makes us feel our need of heavenly grace; his infliction of loss and disease weans from the world and teaches submission to the will of God. Such discipline is not a pleasant thing for the erring one. The patient does not like the surgeon's knife; but if it cuts out a cancer or amputates a diseased limb, and thereby saves the whole body, it is endured for the sake of the good it effects. Better that the flesh be scorched by the fire of chastisement, if thereby the soul be saved in the day of Christ. We may gather from 2 Cor. vii. 8—12 that in this case the severe discipline produced the desired effect. (2) As regards the Church, discipline is a protective measure. This one flagrant sinner, suffered to remain amongst them, would act as a corrupting leaven upon the rest. Others would be emboldened to pursue similar courses, until at length the disease would infect the whole body.—B.

Vers. 7, 8.—*The Christian life a Paschal feast.* The mention of leaven recalls to the apostle's mind the Jewish Passover, in connection with which the putting away of leaven was strictly enjoined. A most careful search was made for every remnant of the forbidden substance, especially in later times, when every hole and corner was ransacked with candles. What was done then with leaven should be done now with that of which leaven is the type (comp. Exod. xii.). I. CHRIST OUR PASCHAL LAMB. Note the main points of correspondence between the type and the antitype. 1. The lamb was to be " *without blemish.*" Jesus Christ was " holy, guileless, undefiled, separated from sinners " (Heb. vii. 26); " a lamb without blemish and without spot " (1 Pet. i. 19). 2. The lamb *was slain.* It was a sacrifice, the victim's life going for the life of the people. Jesus Christ was crucified for us, " bearing our sins in his body upon the tree " (1 Pet. ii. 24). 3. *The blood of the lamb was sprinkled* " on the two side posts and on the upper door-post of the houses." It was not enough that the blood was shed, it must also be put as a mark on the door. " And when I see the blood, I will pass over you " (Exod. xii. 7, 13). Even so the blood of Jesus Christ must be applied to each individual sinner ere it can avail to deliver from the condemnation. Personal faith in him appropriating his atoning sacrifice, is the hand that dips the hyssop in the basin and sprinkles the blood on the house. 4. The lamb *was to be eaten that night by the household.* Its blood was their protection, its flesh their food. Jesus Christ is our Life as well as our Atonement. The believer sheltered by his blood draws his nourishment from him (John vi. 51). II. THE CHRISTIAN LIFE AN UNLEAVENED FESTIVAL. 1. It is *a festival.* " Let us keep the feast." There is no special reference to the Lord's Supper, but to the whole Christian life. What the Paschal week was to the Jew, the believer's life is to be to him. It is to be (1) consecrated to God, and (2) spent in grateful remembrance of God's redeeming mercy. All through let us keep festival in view of the Lamb slain, with the joy of those who have been delivered from bondage. 2. It is to be kept *without leaven.* All sin is to be purged out. The Christian is ideally unleavened. Theoretically no leaven was to be found in the houses of Israel during the Passover, although some of it might escape the most diligent search; and so believers, as they stand in Christ, are dead to sin. This is the high calling which we are to make our own by putting away all sin. Let us be in reality what we are in idea (1 Pet. ii. 9)—let us be a holy people. Every form of vice and wickedness must be cast away as inconsistent with our

unleavened condition, and only " the unleavened bread of sincerity and truth " be found
in our homes. A pure, transparent, honest life, corresponding in all things to the
truth, becomes those who rightly " keep the feast."—B.

Vers. 9—13.—*The intercourse of Christians with the world.* In a former letter, now
lost, Paul had given the Corinthians instructions not to mix themselves up with persons
of evil character. These instructions had been misunderstood, and the apostle now
explains what his meaning was.
I. CHRISTIANS ARE NOT TO AVOID NECESSARY INTERCOURSE WITH THE WORLD. Society
at Corinth was corrupt. Every law in both tables was habitually transgressed, and to
avoid meeting such transgressors was impossible. And this is true of the world as it
now is outside the Church. You have to do business in it. and to deal often with men
whose character is immoral. You cannot help forming relationships with them, and
being associated with them in many ways. But while this is a necessity of our situation
in a wicked world, true Christians will not make companions of such sinners. Duty
may take you into unpleasant and dangerous localities, but you do not remain there
of choice. Whilst you are in the world, as the followers of Christ you are not of it.
II. PROFESSING CHRISTIANS OF EVIL CHARACTER ARE TO BE SHUNNED. Remembering the condition of Corinthian society, we are not astonished to find such sins as Paul
here mentions appearing in the Church. A so-called Christian living in the practice of
these or similar iniquities, thereby proves himself to be no Christian at all. There
must be no fellowship with such persons, no eating and drinking with them as if they
belonged to the Church. They are to be put out of the Christian society. This applies,
not only to the judicial act of the Church, but also to the conduct of individual members
towards offenders. There must be a holy abhorrence of the sin as defiling the body of
Christ, and a careful keeping of our garments clean. Not, however, with the mistaken
aim of having a perfectly pure Church; for discipline can take cognizance only of open
and scandalous sins. Nor are we to act in a censorious or Pharisaic spirit. Along with
hatred of the sin let there be a Christ-like compassion for the sinner.—B.

Vers. 7, 8.—" *Christ our Passover.*" At no point is the relation between Christianity
and the old economy of the Law more profoundly interesting and significant than at
that which is indicated in this passage. Of the Passover it is emphatically true that
it was as a "shadow," of which the substance, the body, is in Christ. The memorial
of that grand Divine interposition by which the Hebrews passed out of their primitive
state of miserable subjection to a foreign power into that of a free and independent
people with Jehovah as their King, it also foreshadowed the great redemption of the
Church, and the establishment of that eternal kingdom of which Christ is the living
Lord. Consider—(1) *The analogy*; (2) *the exhortation based on it.*
I. THE ANALOGY. "Christ our Passover." Both in the type and in the antitype
we have: 1. *A vicarious sacrifice.* The slaying of the Paschal lamb, which was the
leading feature in the whole Passover festival, was clearly of this nature. The lamb
was a blameless creature, the very emblem of simple, guileless innocence. It had no
share in the sins and sorrows of the people. Unlike them, it needed no redemption.
It was the victim of their necessities. It suffered death for their sakes, died to serve
the interests of their life. The broad mark of resemblance, in this respect, between
the lamb and Christ is the very heart and core of the meaning of the text. In him
we see the highest expression of that great law of self-sacrifice which pervades the
universe, and of which the slaying of the Paschal lamb (as, indeed, the slaying of every
lamb) was one of the lower forms. " Not for himself was he cut off;" " Wounded
for our transgressions;" "Slain for us." The innocence of the lamb, and especially
the fact that it was "without blemish," the very flower of the flock, was typical of
his sinless perfection, his absolute exemption from the evil that belongs to us. While
its patient yielding up of its life dimly imaged forth the sublime self-surrender of his
love, when, for our sakes, he "offered himself without spot unto God." 2. *The
instrument of a great deliverance.* The sprinkling of the blood on the door-posts of
the Israelites was both the condition of their safety and the sign and pledge to them
that they were safe (Heb. xi. 27). There could be no fitness in the phrase, "Christ
our Passover," except as meaning that the blood of Christ is to us the means of an

infinitely greater deliverance. Salvation from death for the human race, through the virtue of his death as its Representative and Head, is the fundamental truth of the Christian system. On this truth rests the whole fabric of the kingdom of God among men. It is a kingdom founded, built up, consummated, glorified, by the power of a crucified Redeemer. We are reminded how—

> " All the souls that are were forfeit once,
> And he who might the vantage best have took
> Found out the remedy."

" We have redemption through his blood," delivered by it from " the power of darkness." And the destroying angel cannot touch the house that has taken shelter under the shield of its efficacious grace. 3. *The pledge and seal of a consecrated life.* The first Passover marked the beginning for the Hebrews of a new and distinctly national existence. However slow they may have been to recognize the full meaning of this, the most prominent feature of their position ever after was that principle of separation and consecration to the Lord, of which the blood of the Paschal lamb was the symbol and the seal. Special emphasis is given to this by the fact that the Passover was at first a purely family observance. Its moral influence began at the very fountain-head of national life—the family circle. It was thus the memorial of a covenant that existed before the Law, before the priesthood ; and may well be regarded as prefiguring a grace that is independent of all national and ecclesiastical conditions, all Churches, priesthoods, ritual orders—the bond of the fellowship of the elect and reconciled children of God. Thus is participation in Christ, " our Passover," the beginning of a new life, the seal of a new Divine relationship, the charter of spiritual freedom, the pledge of personal consecration, the passport to citizenship in the eternal kingdom of God.

II. The exhortation. " Wherefore let us keep the feast, not with the old leaven," etc. The seven days' Feast of Unleavened Bread followed the slaying of the Paschal lamb. In " the feast " the apostle may possibly have indirect reference to that sacred observance of " the Lord's Supper," in the institution of which he himself developed the Jewish Passover into its simpler Christian form (Luke xxii. 15, 16). This also, though no sacrifice, is both a memorial and a prophecy. " As often as ye eat," etc. (1 Cor. xi. 26). But the reference is far broader. It indicates the life-long feast of Christian fellowship and service. We are reminded: 1. *That the value of all the solemnities of our religion*—sabbaths, sacred seasons, special Divine manifestations, acts of worship, etc.—*lies in the influence they exert on our personal character and conduct.* Let our daily life be a " sacrament," a solemn yet joyous Passover of love, and gratitude, and trust, and praise. 2. *That in order to this we must be "purged from our old sins."* The evil of the past must be resolutely abandoned. " Malice and wickedness " cast out from our dwellings, that " sincerity and truth " may take their place. Simplicity of mind, singleness of heart, honesty of purpose,—these are the cardinal Christian virtues, the very " bread and staff of life " to all Christian strength and nobleness.—W.

Vers. 7, 8.—*The Passover and the Lord's Supper.* The Lord's Supper is not the Passover; but the one sprang from the other, and is to Christians what the other was to Hebrews, the memorial of redemption.

I. The meaning of these ordinances. In the Passover were two parts, closely connected and yet distinct. 1. The sacrifice of an unspotted lamb. 2. The feast on the sacrifice kept by each household. Under the established ritual in Israel, the former was rendered at the sanctuary. It required an altar, and the hand of an authorized priest or Levite. The latter was within the domestic circle. It required no other celebrant than the head of a household. There was no altar, but a family table. The service was not propitiatory, but commemorative and social. The Lord's Supper can never be clearly understood if these two elements are superstitiously confused together. There is an exhibition, not a renewal, of the sacrifice of Christ. The altar has been served, and its occupation is gone. We have no more need of altar on earth, or sacrificing priest. Christ our Passover " has been sacrificed." What remains is the feast of commemoration and communion; and for this a table only is wanted, with one to preside and lead the service, not a priest to interpose between the Christians and Christ. But while these two things are not to be confounded, they are not to be put apart in our thoughts. It is not enough to say of the Lord's Supper that it is a social pledge of Christian friendship and a common hope. It may not be dissociated from the impressive thought and fact of Christ's atonement for our sins; and we cannot regard those who deny the propitiatory character and value of the Lord's death as competent to administer or partake of the Lord's Supper. The Passover was a family service, because it commemorated the redemption of a nation which was reckoned in tribes according to families. The Lord's Supper is observed by groups, congregations, or organized companies of Christians, because it commemorates the redemption of the Church which is arranged and reckoned in congregations or groups, all forming one "household of faith."

II. The COMMUNICANTS. "Let *us* keep the feast." No alien or uncircumcised person might partake of the Paschal supper; but all the congregation of Israel was charged to observe this ordinance, for redemption was not the privilege of the few, but the joy of the whole nation. And for the occasion, distinctions of rank and opulence within the nation were ignored. As all classes had shared the bondage, so were all classes to share the joy of redemption. Let all who have redemption through the blood of Christ "keep the feast" of the Lord's Supper, and that in obedience to his command, not as and because they think proper, but as and because the Lord has appointed it in his Church. And let no difference of rank, wealth, or social position be recognized. The eminent and the obscure, the rich and the poor, the master and the servant, are at this, if at no other table, to eat of the same bread and drink from the same cup. Such as are aliens from the faith, or uncircumcised in heart, are not entitled to communicate.

III. The DISPOSITIONS WHICH OUGHT TO CHARACTERIZE COMMUNICANTS. The Passover was the Feast of Unleavened Bread. Hence the apostle's charge, "Purge out the old leaven." We know that the Jews were extremely punctilious in this respect, and searched their houses minutely, lest in a dark corner some particle of leaven might lie unsuspected; for leaven was regarded as a symbol of corruption and of the self-propagating power of evil. With similar earnestness should Christians examine themselves, and so eat and drink of the Lord's Supper. Away with the old leaven; the tendency to corruption which belongs to the old life is sin. Away with malice and wickedness; purge out even the smallest fragments of unholy disposition and temper, and keep the feast with sincerity and truth. The Corinthians were required to prove their sincerity by excluding from communion a certain "wicked person," whose conduct had brought reproach on the Christian name. So must we be ready at all times to prove our sincerity by renouncing fellowship with unrighteousness and concord with Belial. They were also required to have "truth in the inward parts," and so are we. We fall short of that strength of faith, fervour of love, and depth of humility which would well become communicants at the holy table of our Lord; but at all events we may bring, and ought to bring, to the feast hearts honest and true. "Lord, thou knowest all things." Thou knowest our shortcomings, perversities, stupidities, follies, prejudices, errors, and faults; but "thou knowest that we love thee." We are not at thy table playing a part or affecting devotion to thee in order to be seen of men. Far from us be such ghastly hypocrisy! Ours be the unleavened bread of sincerity and truth.—F.

Vers. 2—5.—*Right feeling towards erring brethren.* There have been a great variety of forms in which men have attempted to associate religion and immorality. Multiplied explanations and excuses have been given, if so be the indulgence of the immoral may be maintained; but it remains as searchingly true as ever it was, that into the kingdom of our Lord and Saviour—here or yonder—nothing entereth that "defileth, or worketh abomination, or maketh a lie;" and that every Christian man should know how to possess the vessel of his body in sanctification and honour, not being "conformed to this world, but transformed by the renewing of his mind." He is to "come out from the world, and to be separate, and in no wise touch the unclean thing." There were special forms of sensuality characteristic of and encouraged by paganism; but the sin into which the member of the Christian Church at Corinth had fallen was one which would be utterly repudiated and condemned by Gentile and Jew alike. It was one wholly subversive of family and social relations; and anything approaching to the toleration of it in the Christian Church would seriously imperil its character, and give at least apparent ground for the shameful accusations which its enemies brought against it. For the Levitical law upon the matter, see Lev. xviii. 8. In advising the Church as to its mode of dealing with this erring brother, there is an unusual severity in the apostle's language; and this is accounted for rather by the attitude which he understood the Church had taken towards the offender, than by his sense of the enormity of the offence. St. Paul's supreme jealousy was ever concerning the purity, good order, and moral worth of the Churches. He seems to have highly valued *character*—in the individual and in the Church—as being the best witness among men for Christ. He strongly affirmed the absolute necessity of the connection between morality and Christianity, and based his argument on this foundation-principle—our whole being, spirit, mind, and body, is the Lord's; and this whole being is redeemed in Christ, and is to be, in actual fact, wholly won and held for Christ. It may also be noted, in introducing the subject, that our idea as to the purity, unity, and model order of the early Church is quite a fanciful one. Probably there was no separate Church of those times that came anywhere near realizing the Christian ideal. We consider, from these verses, two things.

I. THE SIN OF A CHRISTIAN PROFESSOR. It may be shown: 1. *Whence it may come.* (1) from relics of old evil; (2) from circumstances reviving old feeling; (3) from neglect of due self-watchfulness and culture; (4) from undue fulness of eating and drinking; (5) from the friendship of those who may lead astray; (6) from sudden influx of bodily passion; and (7) from actual occasions of temptation. Though regenerate in will and life-principle, the Christian must never forget that he is not free from the relics of evil in his nature and habits, or from the influence of evil in his surroundings; and therefore he constantly needs the counsel, "Watch and be sober." It should be especially pointed out that the most perilous temptations to which Christian professors are subject are those which come *suddenly*, reaching them at moments when some unguardedness or some self-confidence lays them open to assault. 2. *How it may gain its support.* Here only one point is dwelt on. The apostle is anxious about the perversion of Christian doctrine to the excusing of sin. In many ways what is known as the antinomian spirit has been made the excuse of sin. It cannot be too constantly affirmed that, so far from releasing its members from the claims and obligations of the moral Law, Christianity presses them with tenfold urgency, for it demands an obedience that shall not be merely formal, but one that concerns motive and feeling and will. See the teaching of our Lord in Matt. v. 17—48.

II. THE RELATION OF FELLOW-PROFESSORS TO SUCH SIN. No doubt, at Corinth, each individual Christian would strongly and decidedly condemn this erring brother, but party spirit was so rife in the Church, that some took his side, and laboured to find excuses for him, or to secure the continuance of his membership. It is still found most difficult to carry out the due discipline of the Church, seeing that party feeling gathers round even the drunken, the dishonest, and the immoral. It is, indeed, important that all judicial action should be taken by the Church itself, and that individuals should not have independent authority to exclude or to punish, but only right of speaking and of acting in the Church's name. St. Paul urges: 1. That every effort should be made to cherish and to inculcate right sentiment concerning the sin. 2. That action should be taken which would clear the Church of any suspicion of complicity in or approval of the sin. It must be made quite plain that the sin is the sin of an individual, and is an outrage on the Church's principles and purity. 3. And the action must be taken in such a way as may hopefully bear on the recovery of the sinner from his sin. This appears to be the idea of St. Paul in the figure of "delivering to Satan." The sinner was to be given over for a while to suffer the miserable consequences of his sin, but only in the hope that he would be humbled and brought to penitence and confession; and this seems to have been the result in the case of the Corinthian offender.

In conclusion, press that (1) the moral purity of the Christian Church should be the supreme anxiety of every member of it; and (2) that the maintenance of such purity is quite consistent with the fullest Christian charity, which, through all its dealings, keeps steadily in view the reformation of the offender.—R. T.

Ver. 5.—*The very sufferings of Christian sinners may be overruled unto sanctifying.* On the precise meanings and references of the terms and figures used in this verse, the exegetical portion of the Commentary should be consulted. Some suppose that a temporal judgment, sickness, or loss, followed on the excommunication of this offender (as in the cases of Ananias, Elymas, etc.), and that such suffering became disciplinary, and resulted in the man's full moral recovery. " As a man soweth, thus shall he also reap ; " and we need only explain the term " deliver unto Satan " as meaning, leave the man to the consequences naturally and necessarily following on his sin ; the very first of these consequences being his separation from Christian fellowship and Christian privileges. " It should be carefully noticed that it is not the *body*, but the *flesh*, that is, the carnal appetite, that is to be destroyed by the chastisement." F. W. Robertson says, " Here the peculiarly merciful character of Christianity comes forth ; the Church was never to give over the hope of recovering the fallen. Punishment, then, here is remedial. If St. Paul punished, it was that the 'spirit might be saved in the day of the Lord Jesus.' And hence (putting capital punishment out of the present question) to shut the door of repentance upon any sin, to make outcasts for ever, and thus to produce *despair*, is contrary to the idea of the Church of Christ, and alien from his spirit." Unfold and illustrate both from Scripture and modern life—

I. How CERTAINLY ALL SIN, UNCHECKED, BEARS ITS FRUITAGE OF SUFFERING. There may be even prolonged delay, and consequent presumption in keeping on in sin. But the suffering comes at last ; it is certain as the returning harvest. Take two cases. 1. The familiar one of the drunkard. Want cometh, on him and his, as an armed man. 2. The dishonest. A man placed in a position of trust embezzles secretly for years ; at last, just as his children are on the threshold of manhood and womanhood, ruin and shame come on them ; flight, desolation, misery, and the exile's poverty for him. Man cannot take " fire into his bosom and not be burned ; nor can he touch pitch and fail to be defiled." The laws of heredity being now better understood, we can feel more deeply how a man's sins can carry a burden of suffering, even to the innocent unborn generations.

II. How, FOR THE ERRING CHRISTIAN, SUCH NECESSARY SUFFERING OR SUCH DIRECT DIVINE JUDGMENT MAY BE REMEDIAL. Illustration may be taken from David's experience, as indicated in his words, " Before I was afflicted I went astray, but now will I keep thy Word." Explain the process by which, under God, suffering influences the views and feelings of the erring Christian ; but point out carefully how suffering affects differently the good and the bad man. It tends rather to harden the bad, because it seems to him mere loss and disability. It softens and humbles the Christian, because by him it is known as the heavenly Father's chastening hand. Show how the sanctifying discipline of suffering is shown in the very story of our human race. The " day of the Lord Jesus " may be conceived as the time when a man's life-story is complete ; then it can come into consideration and judgment. Then it may be seen that, through all the sufferings that followed upon the soilings, " the spirit has been saved." Press that " delivering over to Satan " does not put the erring one out of Christ's loving thought and care, and therefore it should never put him out of our Christian interest and prayer and sympathy. We must ever keep his welcome back awaiting him.—R. T.

Ver. 6.—*The lesson of the leaven.* It is very confidently affirmed that *leaven* is *always* used in a bad sense in Scripture, and is the illustration of the working of evil principle. Some forcing of Scripture is, however, necessary if a bad sense must be always found ; and while we must admit that leavening is, in measure, a corrupting process, we should also recognize that the permeating influence of leaven may be used to illustrate the advance and extension of good principle. Undoubtedly it is the tendency of evil to propagate itself rapidly, and infect all around it, on which the apostle here dwells—a tendency which may be also illustrated by the insidious spreading of contagious and infectious disease. It may be helpful to give some account of the character and action of " leaven." Hugh Macmillan says, " It consists of myriads of the cells of the common green mould in an undeveloped state. If a fragment of the dough with the leaven in it be put aside in a shady place, the cells of the fungus in the leaven will vegetate, and cover the dough with a slight downy substance, which is just the plant in its complete form. The swelling of the dough, and the commotion which goes on in the leavened mass, are owing to the multiplication of the plant-cells, which takes place with astonishing rapidity. By this process of vegetation, the starch and sugar of the dough are converted into other chemical products. But it is only allowed to go to a certain length, and then the principle of growth is checked, by placing the dough in the oven and baking it into bread. Leaven is thus a principle of destruction and construction—of decay and of growth—of death and of life. It has two effects, which are made use of as types in Scripture. On the one side, the operation of leaven upon meal presents an analogy to something evil in the spiritual world; for it decays and decomposes the matter with which it comes into contact. On the other side, the operation of leaven upon meal presents an analogy to something good in the spiritual world; for it is a principle of life and growth, and imparts a new energy and a beneficent quality to the matter with which it comes in contact." Archbishop Trench says, "In some passages, the puffing up, disturbing, souring propetries which leaven has are the prominent points of comparison; in others, its warmth, its penetrative energy, the power which a little of it has to lend its own savour and virtue to much wherewith it is brought in contact."

I. LEAVEN IS A FIGURE OF MORAL EVIL IN THE CHURCH. It suggests (1) the insidious nature, (2) the rapid propagation, (3) the corrupting influence, of evil. "Observe, the evil was not a matter of example, but of contagion. Such a one as this incestuous man—wicked, impenitent, and unpunished—would infect the rest of the Church. Who does not know how the *tone* of evil has communicated itself? Worldly minds, irreverent minds, licentious minds, *leaven* society. You cannot be long with persons who by innuendo, double meaning, or lax language, show an acquaintance with evil, without feeling in some degree assimilated to them, nor can you easily retain enthusiasm for right amongst those who detract and scoff at goodness." The corrupting influence of evil in the Church may be illustrated from the history of the great heresies, more especially those which have been started by immoral and unworthy men.

II. SUCH MORAL EVIL IS SURE PRESENTLY TO ATTRACT PUBLIC ATTENTION. And so it brings a wrong estimate of the Church, and excites prejudice against it. The Church has most gravely suffered, in every age, from her unworthy members, who have been only too readily regarded, by outsiders, as the Church's representatives. "The student of history will remember how dexterously Gibbon contrives to throw discredit upon Christianity by enlarging upon the shortcomings of the early Church, and by evading the comparison between its moral elevation and the shocking demoralization of heathen society."

III. SUCH MORAL EVIL HAS A DANGEROUSLY ACTIVE AND PERVASIVE INFLUENCE. "It leaveneth the whole lump." It spreads in the soil as the roots of bindweed. Therefore, as, in preparation for the Paschal feast, the Jews carefully and minutely searched for every particle of leaven, to turn it out of their houses, so must the Christian Church watch lest any bad person come into its membership, and must strictly exclude those who may take bad ways after joining its membership, lest their evil influence should be found to pervade the whole lump. The very first symptoms and indications of moral evil demand resolute dealing, and should be immediately met by the strong yet charitable discipline of the Church. In simple language, suited for children, the poet expresses the danger dealt with in this homily.

> "One sickly sheep infects the flock,
> And poisons all the rest."

R. T.

Ver. 7.—*The Christian Church as unleavened.* "As ye are unleavened." The idea of the Church is of a pure and unadulterated and uncorrupted mass, and every individual member of the Church is under obligation to aid in securing and maintaining the purity. The Church must put out, purge out, and keep out, the very relics of the old leaven. Reference is made in the figure which St. Paul uses to the Jewish custom of searching for leaven, which was probably retained in the apostle's time. "Because Scripture speaks of 'searching Jerusalem with candles' (Zeph. i. 12), they used to carry out this custom of searching for leaven with great strictness, taking a candle and 'prying into every mouse-hole and cranny,' as St. Chrysostom says, so as to collect even the smallest crumb of leavened bread, which was to be placed in a box or some place where a mouse could not get at it."

I. THE CHRISTIAN CALL TO BE UNLEAVENED. "Ye are not called unto uncleanness, but unto holiness." The apostles were especially called to witness to a truth by word of lip; but, while each member was equally called to speak for Christ, the testimony of the Church, as a whole, was to be the testimony of its purity. Its very aim was to be to keep itself separate and free from the evils and defilements of the world. Show how far the modern Church may be regarded as having forgotten the Divine call unto "uncorruptness."

II. THE CHRISTIAN PERIL OF BECOMING LEAVENED. A peril coming (1) from without, in the attractions of worldly pleasure and success; (2) from within, by the defection of individuals, and their evil influence, or by the unwatchfulness and neglected spiritual culture of many. When Christians cease to find their joy in God, they easily seek for it in the world and in worldly things.

III. THE CHRISTIAN CARE TO KEEP UNLEAVENED. This care should characterize each for himself, and each for the other. And it should ever be regarded as the great life-burden of the Christian and the Church. It must cost constant watchfulness and effort; and he who would be pure must learn how to deal sternly with himself.—R. T.

Ver. 7.—*Christian fellowship a Passover feast.* The sentence, "Even Christ our Passover is sacrificed for us," appears to be suddenly inserted in the paragraph, without any immediately evident connection with it. Such connection we seek to discover, and then we would press home that particular duty which the apostle is so earnestly urging upon the Corinthian Church. Exactly rendered, St. Paul's words are, "For also Christ our Passover is slain." There is no word for "even;" the words "for us" are not found in some of the best manuscripts; and the order of the words is very carefully arranged, so as to throw the stress of the sentence on the term "is slain." The apostle has some point to impress by this fact, "Christ *is* slain:" he is not "about to be slain," or "being slain;" it is an accomplished, completed, historical fact, "he is slain;" "he has been slain." From a reference in one of the later chapters, we find that St. Paul wrote this Epistle to the Corinthians just about the time of the Passover; his mind was occupied with the associations of this feast, and so, in a very natural way, he took his illustration from it. Reverting to the original appointment of the Passover, we observe that the Lord designed to come in one last and overwhelming judgment on the rebellious Egyptians. God's people dwelt in the very midst of them, but no Divine judgments hung over *them.* Still, it was necessary that, by some sign, the Israelites' houses should be distinguished from others. The observance of an appointed sign would prove the obedience of Israel, and clearly mark the judgment as Divine. The point in the matter to which St. Paul now directs attention is, however, this—the slaying of the lamb was the *beginning* of the Feast of the Passover, or of Unleavened Bread. If the lamb was killed, the feast-time had plainly begun (see Exod. xii. 18), and no *leaven* ought to be found in their habitations. This is the thing on which the apostle fixes for the enforcement of his counsel. It is as if he had said, "This is the time of the Christian feast of the unleavened. 'Christ our Passover *is* sacrificed;' the purity-time *has therefore come.* Our feast is not indeed for seven days only, but for our whole life. We too are under the most solemn responsibilities; pledged to lives of holiness; bound to cleanse out every relic of the old leaven of sin and self-will, urged by every persuasion to 'perfect holiness in the fear of God;' and set upon 'possessing our vessels in sanctification and honour.'" We must be practically what we are theoretically, a new and regenerated society. Dwelling on the Christian suggestions of the text, we notice—

I. THE SLAYING OF THE CHRISTIAN PASSOVER LAMB. Limit the thought on this to the one thing that is prominently in the apostle's mind. The word "Passover" is used by him for that seal which marked the Israelites off from the Egyptians, so that the destroying angel might pass over their houses. The blood of the lamb, sprinkled on the lintel and posts, was the sign that marked them as the Lord's obedient people, the objects of his grace, experiencing then a preservation which was to be followed by a glorious deliverance. This feature of the old Passover may be pressed on the Christian Church. The apostle says, "You too are marked off as God's; for you the Passover

Lamb has been slain; on you the blood has been sprinkled; for you the great deliverance has been wrought; you are actually now sealed over, as a Christian Church, unto God, by the blood of the everlasting covenant."

II. THE RESPONSIBILITIES OF THOSE SPRINKLED WITH THE PASSOVER BLOOD. As sealed over to God, Israel was bound to realize what was involved in *their side* of the covenant into which they had entered. On God's side, the covenant pledged fatherly interest, unceasing care, gracious provision for all need, and the fulfilment of certain defined promises. On man's side, it pledged obedience, service, and above all else, *separation* from the world, and *purity*. God impressed his claim to this purity by instituting the seven days of unleavened feast immediately on the sealing of the covenant, enjoining that what they did symbolically for seven days they were in moral and spiritual manner to do *all* their days. St. Paul applies this to the Corinthian Christians, who had, as it were, entered fully into covenant with God, seeing that Christ, their Passover, had been slain. They too should remember to what moral life and conduct they were pledged. They must realize a spiritual separation from evil; holiness becometh the people of God.

Press that each of us should seek to realize the *responsibilities* of our Christian standing. This is the time when, in home, and family, and society, and business, and the Church, we have to remember that we are "called unto holiness." Christ *is* sacrificed, and this is the time of "feast of the unleavened."—R. T.

Vers. 7, 8.—*Keeping the Christian feast of the unleavened.* Give, in introduction, a careful description of the old Passover. Observe especially that (1) there was a sacrificed lamb; (2) that its blood became a protection and a sign; (3) that the meat of the lamb was partaken of together; (4) that all the food was unleavened; and (5) that the loins were girt ready for a journey. Then show how this old Passover may be regarded as realized in the Christian feast. 1. Jesus is the slain Lamb. 2. His blood is the Church's protection and sign. 3. His truth and love—that is, he himself—is the Church's food. 4. The spirit in which we share our Divine food is that of sincerity and truth, which is represented by the "unleavened." 5. We share as those who belong to the heavenly, and therefore say, "This is not our rest." Press that the presence of the leavened, the guileful, and the sinner spoils the simplicity and purity of our Christian feast.—R. T.

Vers. 9—13.—*The Christian law of association with evil.* Two points require to be illustrated and enforced.

I. COMMON, EVERY-DAY LIFE-ASSOCIATIONS WITH EVIL HAVE TO BE MAINTAINED, in (1) family; (2) business; (3) society. Yet in all these the earnest Christian need never find it difficult to make a firm witness for truth, righteousness, and charity.

II. SPECIAL RELATIONS OF FRIENDSHIP WITH EVIL WE MAY NOT MAKE. We may not (1) for our own sake; (2) for such friends' sake; (3) for the sake of others who may observe our friendship, and, above all, (4) for Christ's sake, who said, through his servant, "Come out from among them, . . . and touch not the unclean thing, and I will receive you."—R. T.

EXPOSITION.

CHAPTER VI.

Vers. 1—11.—*Litigation before heathen courts forbidden.*

Ver. 1.—**Dare any of you?** rather, *Dare any one of you?* It is in St. Paul's view an *audacious* defiance of Christian duties to seek from the heathen the justice due from brother to brother. **A matter;** some ground of civil dispute. **Against another;** *i.e.* against another Christian. When one of the litigants was a heathen, Christians were allowed to go before heathen law courts, because no other

remedy was possible. **Go to law before the unjust.** The "unjust" is here used for "Gentiles," because it at once suggests a reason against the dereliction of Christian duty involved in such a step. How "unjust" the pagans were in the special sense of the word, the Christians of that day had daily opportunities of seeing; and in a more general sense, the Gentiles were "sinners" (Matt. xxvi. 45). Even the Jews were bound to settle their civil disputes before their own tribunals. The ideal Jew was *jashar*, or "the upright man," and Jews could not consistently seek integrity from those who were not upright. *A fortiori*, Christians ought not to do so. **Before the saints.** All Christians were ideally " saints," just as the heathen were normally " unjust." If Christians went to law with one another before the heathen, they belied their profession of mutual love, caused scandal, and were almost necessarily tempted into compliance with heathen customs, even to the extent of recognizing idols. Our Lord had already laid down the rule that " brothers " ought to settle their quarrels among themselves (Matt. xviii. 15—17).

Ver. 2.—**Do ye not know ?** The word " or " should be supplied from ℵ, A, B, C, D, F, etc. Bishop Wordsworth points out that this emphatic question occurs ten times in these two Epistles (ch. iii. 6; v. 6; vi. 2, 3, 9, 15, 16, 19; ix. 13, 24), and only twice in all the rest (Rom. vi. 16; xi. 2). It was a fitting rebuke to those who took for knowledge their obvious ignorance. It resembles the " Have ye not so much as read ?" to Pharisees who professed such profound familiarity with the Scriptures. **That the saints shall judge the world.** So Daniel (vii. 22) had said, " The Ancient of days came, and judgment was given to the saints of the Most High." Our Lord had confirmed this promise to his apostles, " Ye also shall sit upon twelve thrones, judging the twelve tribes of Israel " (Matt. xix. 28). Various modes of evading the literal sense have been adopted, but even in the Book of Wisdom we find, " They [the righteous] shall judge the nations, and have dominion over the people" (Wisd. iii. 8). All speculation as to the manner and extent in which the saints shall share in the work of Christ as Judge of the quick and dead, are obviously futile. **Shall be judged ;** literally, *is being judged*— the present points to the future, as though that which is inevitable is already in course of fulfilment. **To judge the smallest matters ;** literally, *of the smallest judgments.*

Ver. 3.—**That we shall judge angels.** Angels, *i.e.* some who belong, or once did belong, to that class. The statement furnishes no data for further speculation. It can hardly mean " evil spirits," for where the word is entirely unqualified it always means good angels ; otherwise we might refer it to the " angels which kept not their first estate " (Jude 6). It is impossible, and not straightforward, to explain away the word " angels" as meaning Church officials, etc., or to make the word " judge " mean " involve a condemnation of them by comparison with ourselves." All that we can say is that " God chargeth even his angels with folly, and in his sight the very heavens are not clean " (Job iv. 18) ; and that " to angels hath he not subjected the world to come"

(Heb. ii. 5). We must take the plain meaning of the apostle's words, whether we can throw any light on his conceptions or not. The only alternative is to suppose that the word means "those who *once* were good angels," but *are now* fallen spirits. It was so understood by Tertullian, Chrysostom, etc. **How much more** ; rather, *to say nothing of.* The accurate rendering of these verses is a matter of some difficulty, but not to an extent which affects the material sense, or which can be explained without a minute knowledge of Greek.

Ver. 4.—**If then ye have,** etc. The verse implies that civil disputes might naturally occur among them. What he is here reprobating is their objectionable method of settling them. **Set them to judge who are least esteemed in the Church.** This implies an utter scorn of trivial quarrels about personal rights. Surely the lowliest, the most unregarded members of the Church —those of no account—have wisdom enough to decide in such small matters. Thus when there arose a murmuring between Hebrews and Hellenists about the daily distribution to widows, the apostles, thinking that they had much more important work in hand than the adjustment of such jealousies, left the whole matter in the hands of the seven deacons. Some understand "those held of no account in the Church " to mean heathens ; but he is here forbidding them to bring their quarrels before the heathens. Of course, ideally, *none* ought to be "despised " or " held of no account " in the Church ; but St. Paul is here speaking relatively, and with reference to the views of the Corinthians themselves, and not without irony. The perfect participle, " those who have been set at nought," perhaps means persons of proved inferiority of judgment.

Ver. 5.—**I speak to your shame.** He adds this to account for the severe irony of the last remark. **Not a wise man among you.** Among *you*, who set yourselves up as so specially wise ! **To judge** ; rather, *to decide.*

Ver. 7.—**Now therefore** ; rather, *Nay more, already.* **Utterly** ; rather, *generally,* "altogether," "looking at the question as a whole." **A fault.** The word means "a defect," or possibly "a loss" (Rom. xi. 12, "the diminishing"). Your going to law is an inferiority or deficiency ; you ought to know of "a more excellent way." **Why do ye not rather take wrong ?** Strange as such advice would sound to heathens, who prided themselves on the passionate resentment of injuries as though it were a virtue, this had been the distinct teaching of our Lord : " Resist not evil " (Matt. v. 39).

Ver. 8.—**Nay, ye do wrong and defraud.** Thus they violated a rule which Paul had laid down to the Thessalonians (1 Thess. iv. 6), and incurred God's anger.

Ver. 9.—**Know ye not**; rather, *Or know ye not*, as before. Are you defying God, *or* does your sin arise from mere ignorance? **The unrighteous**; better, *that wrong-doers*, the verb being the same as "ye do wrong" in ver. 8. Perhaps the Corinthians thought that they would be saved by the mere fact of having been admitted into God's kingdom (the Christian Church in all its highest privileges) by baptism. St. Paul here lays down, as distinctly as St. James does, that faith without works is dead, and privileges without holiness are abrogated. The spirit of his warning is the same as that of Jer. vii. 4, "Trust ye not in lying words, saying, The temple of the Lord . . . are these;" or that of St. John the Baptist, "Say not unto yourselves, We be Abraham's sons." Christians have often been liable to the temptation of underrating the peril which results from the falling asunder of action from knowledge. There can be no greater danger than that of talking slightingly of "mere morality." Religion is not an outward service, but a spiritual life manifested by a holy living. **Be not deceived.** So our Lord says, "Let no man deceive you" (Mark xiii. 5; comp. 1 John iii. 7). St. Paul uses the warning very solemnly again in ch. **xv.** 33 and Gal. vi. 7, and St. James in Jas. i. 16. The self-deception of merely verbal orthodoxy is the most dangerous of all. **Neither fornicators.** The first four classes of sinners were specially prevalent at Corinth, where, indeed, impurity formed part of the recognized cult of the local Aphrodite (comp. 2 Cor. xii. 21). Lists of these "works of the flesh," which were the all but universal curse and stain of heathendom, occur also in Gal. v. 19—21; 1 Tim. i. 10, etc.; Col. iii. 5—7.

Ver. 10.—**Nor thieves**, etc. (see Rev. xxii. 15).

Ver. 11.—**And such were some of you**; literally, *and these things some of you were.* As Gentiles, many of them had been "dead in trespasses and sins" (Eph. ii. 1). (For a similar contrast of the change wrought by the Spirit of God, see Titus iii. 3—7.) **But ye are washed.** The voice and tense in the original differ from those of the following words. This cannot be accidental. It is better, therefore, to render, *But ye washed away your sins;* i.e. ye, by your baptism, washed away those stains (Acts xxii. 16). The very object of Christ's death had been that he might cleanse his Church "by the washing of water by the Word." **But ye are sanctified, but ye are justified;** rather, *but ye were sanctified, but ye were justified,* namely, at your conversion. By "sanctified" is meant, not the progressive course

of sanctification, but the *consecration* to God by baptism (Wickliffe, "halowed"). (For what St. Paul meant by justification, see Rom. iii. 24—26.) **In the Name of the Lord Jesus**, etc. This clause and the next belongs to all the three previous verbs. **Of our God.** In the word "our" is involved that appeal to Christian unity of which he never loses sight throughout the letter.

Vers. 12—20.—*The inexcusable sin and shame of fornication.*

Ver. 12.—**All things are lawful unto me.** The abruptness with which the phrase is introduced perhaps shows that, in the letter of the Corinthians to St. Paul, they had used some such expression by way of palliating their lax tolerance of violations of the law of purity. By "all things," of course, is only meant "all things which are indifferent in themselves." They erroneously applied this maxim of Christian liberty to that which was inherently sinful, and thus were tempted to "make their liberty a cloak of viciousness." St. Paul, as Bengel observes, often, and especially in this Epistle, uses the first person *generally* in gnomic or semi-proverbial sentences (ch. vi. 15; vii. 7; x. 23, 29, 30; xiv. 11). **But.** This is St. Paul's correction of too broad a formula. **Are not expedient.** St. Paul illustrates this in ch. viii. 8—10. We have no right to do even that which is innocent, if it be disadvantageous to the highest interests of ourselves or others. "He alone," says St. Augustine, "does not fall into unlawful things who sometimes abstains by way of caution even from lawful ones." **Will not be brought under the power.** The play of words in the original might be imitated by saying, "All things are in my power, but I will not be brought under the power of any." In other words, "boundless intemperance" may become a tyranny. The pretence of moral freedom may end in a moral bondage.

"Obedience is better than freedom? What's free?
The vexed foam on the wave, the tossed straw on the sea;
The ocean itself, as it rages and swells,
In the bonds of a boundless obedience dwells."

I will be master even over my liberty by keeping it under the beneficent control of law and of charity.

Ver. 13.—**Meats for the belly**, etc. The argument of the Corinthians about the indifference of eating "meats" which were merely ceremonially unclean was quite tenable. Things Levitically unclean might be essentially pure, and both food and the body which lives thereby are things "which perish in the using" (Col. ii. 22). **Shall**

destroy; *shall bring to nought.* This would occur when the physical body becomes a spiritual body, like that of the angels of God (ch. xv. 51, 52). How vile, then, is it to make a god of the belly—only to sleep and feed! **Both it and them.** There shall be no need for *the belly* when men "shall hunger no more, neither thirst any more" (Rev. vii. 16); and the meat alluded to is "meat which perisheth" (Luke xv. 16). **Now the body is not for fornication, but for the Lord.** The argument, therefore, which would class this sin as a matter of indifference, as was the Levitical distinction between different kinds of food, at once fell to the ground. Food was a necessity, and the stomach was formed for its assimilation. Fornication is not a venial but "a *deadly* sin." It is not a natural necessity, but a consuming evil. The body was created for higher ends— namely, to be a temple of God. "God hath not called us unto uncleanness, but unto holiness" (1 Thess. iv. 7). **And the Lord for the body.** Therefore our members ought to be used "as instruments of right-eousness unto God" (Rom. v. 13), and our bodies presented as a living, holy, reason-able, acceptable sacrifice to him (Rom. xii. 1). The end of our existence is "to serve God here and enjoy him for ever hereafter."

Ver. 14.—**God hath both raised up the Lord.** St. Paul always grounds man's resurrection] and immortality on the re-surrection and ascension of Christ (see ch. xv.; 2 Cor. iv. 14; Rom. vi. 5, 8; viii. 11).

Ver. 15.—**Members of Christ.** We find the same metaphor in ch. xii. 12, 27; Eph. v. 30. The Church is often alluded to as "the body of Christ" (Eph. i. 23; Col. i. 18; ii. 19, etc.). Elsewhere the union between Christ and Christians is described by the metaphor of a tree and its branches; a building and the stones of which it is composed (Eph. ii. 21, 22). **God forbid.** An admirable idiom to express the real force of the original, which means, "May it never be!" (for the *rationale* of the Greek phrase, I may refer to my 'Brief Greek Syntax,' p. 135). It occurs in Rom. iii. 4, 6, 31; vi. 15; vii. 7, 13; ix. 14; xi. 1, 11; Gal. ii. 17; iii. 21. The formula, which involves the indignant rejection of some false con-clusion, is characteristic of the second group of St. Paul's Epistles, but especially (as will be seen) of the Epistle to the Romans.

Ver. 16.—**What, know ye not, etc.?** The clause is used to explain and justify the strong expression which he had used in the previous verse. It involves an argument against the sin which is the most original and impressive which could have been used. To this passage especially is due the tone taken by Christians as to these sins, which differed so totally from that taken by

heathen. **They two.** The words do not occur in Gen. ii. 24, but are always so quoted in the New Testament (Matt. xix. 5; Mark x. 8; Eph. v. 31). **Saith he.** This is a vague Jewish formula of quotation, adopted to avoid the needless introduction of the sacred Name. "He" is "God" in Scripture. **Shall be one flesh**; rather, *shall become.* This ap-peal to Gen. ii. 24 (Matt. xix. 5) is equiva-lent to the rule that no intercourse between the sexes is free from sin except under the sanction of marriage.

Ver. 17.—**That is joined unto the Lord.** This phrase, indicating the closest possible union, is found in Deut. x. 20; 2 Kings xviii. 6. **Is one spirit.** There is a "mystical union," not only "betwixt Christ and his Church," but also between Christ and the holy soul. Hence, to St. Paul, spiritual life meant the indwelling of Christ in the heart—the life "in Christ;" so that he could say, "It is no more I that live, but Christ that liveth in me" (Gal. ii. 20; iii. 27; Col. iii. 17).

Ver. 18.—**Flee fornication.** In the battle against sensual sins, there is no victory except in absolute flight, for the reason which immediately follows, namely, that these sins have their dwelling in that body which is part of our being, and which yet they tend to destroy. They make a man his own deadliest enemy. **Every sin . . . is without the body.** Some have supposed that this cannot apply to gluttony and drunkenness, which they therefore class with fornication; but even in those sins, as in suicide, the *cause* of and *incentive to* the sin is external, whereas the source of unclean-ness is in the heart and in the thoughts, which come from within, and so defile the man. Other sins may be *with* and *by means of* the body, and may *injure* the body; but none are so directly against the sanctity of the whole bodily being as fornication. **Sinneth against his own body.** By alien-ating it from the service of him to whom it belongs; by incorporating it with the degradation of another; by staining the flesh and the body (Prov. v. 8—11; vi. 24—32; vii. 24—27); by subtly poisoning the inmost sanctities of his own being. St. Paul is here thinking mainly, however, if not exclusively, of the *moral* injury and defile-ment.

Ver. 19.—**That your body is the temple** (or rather, *a sanctuary*) **of the Holy Ghost.** He has already said that the Church is a shrine or sanctuary of the Holy Ghost (ch. iii. 16); but here for the first time ex-pression is given to one of the deepest and newest truths of Christianity (comp. 2 Cor. vi. 16). Three great epochs are marked by the use of the word "temple." In the Old Testament it means the material temple, the sign of a localized worship and a separated people; in the Gospels our Lord uses it of his own mortal body; in the Epistles it is used (as here) of the body of every baptized Christian, sanctified by the indwelling Spirit of God. **Ye are not your own.** We cannot, therefore, use our bodies as though they were absolutely under our own control. They belong to God, and, "whether we live or die, we are the Lord's" (Rom. xiv. 8).

Ver. 20.—**Ye are bought with a price.** That price is the blood of Christ, wherewith he purchased the Church (Acts xx. 28; Heb. ix. 12; 1 Pet. i. 18, 19; Rev. v. 9). This metaphor of ransom (ch. vii. 23; 2 Pet. ii. 1) has its full and absolute applicability to man. The effect of Christ's death for us is that we are redeemed from slavery and prison, and the right of our possession is with Christ. Thus by various metaphors the effects of redemption are revealed to us on the human side. When we unduly *press* the metaphor, and ask *from whom* we were purchased, and *to whom* the price was paid, we build up scholastic systems which have only led to error, and respecting which the Church has never sanctioned any exclusive opinion. The thoughts touched upon in this verse are fully developed in the Epistle to the Romans. **Glorify God;** by behaving as his redeemed children, and therefore by keeping yourselves pure. In these few brief words St. Paul *sums up* all he has said, as he did in ch. v. 13. **In your body.** The following words, "and in your spirit, which are God's," are a perfectly correct and harmless gloss, but are not found in the best manuscripts, and are foreign to the drift of the passage. Your body is a temple, and in that temple God must be honoured. (As Augustine says, "Dost thou wish to pray in a temple? pray in thyself. But first *be* a temple of God.") "Unchastity dishonours God, and that in his own temple (Rom. ii. 23)" (Meyer). In these clauses St. Paul has touched on three subjects which occupy important sections of the remainder of the Epistle, namely, (1) the relation between the sexes (ch. vii.); (2) the question of idol-offerings (ch. viii.); and (3) the doctrine of the resurrection (ch. xv.).

HOMILETICS.

Vers. 1—8.—*The ideal Church a tribunal.* "Dare any of you, having a matter against another," etc.? In our sketch on the preceding verses we looked on the true Church as a *feast.* Here we have to look on it as a *tribunal,* a court of judicature, where disputes are to be settled and grievances redressed. It would appear that questions arose among the Corinthian Christians that required settlement—questions of wrong done to persons or to property, and that too the litigious spirit was so rife in their midst that they took their grievances to the heathen courts. For this the apostle reproves them. "Dare any of you, having a matter against another, go to law before the unjust, and not before the saints?" Three remarks about the ideal Church as a tribunal.

I. IT IS SUPERIOR TO OTHER TRIBUNALS ON THE EARTH. 1. It is a court *formed of morally righteous men.* This is implied in the words, "Dare any of you, having a matter against another, go to law before the unjust, and not before the *saints?*" Saints, or just men, form the tribunal. In worldly courts of judicature men are judged by legislative enactments or judicial decisions. Not so in this court. It is a court of equity, a court that tries cases not by statutory precepts, nor by ecclesiastical laws, but by scriptural principles, and these principles as they are embodied in the teaching of him who delivered the Sermon on the mount. The true Church is his representative and administrator. 2. It is a court whose *jurisdiction is universal.* "Do ye not know that the saints shall judge the world?" In many ways men of Christly lives are judging the *world* now. Their ideas of right and wrong, between man and man, and man and God, form that standard of character to which the consciences of men are constantly appealing, and to which they are forced to bow. All men at last will be judged by the character of Christ, and the Church is the representative of that character. "The words I say unto you, they shall judge you in the last day." Not only does this Church-tribunal judge the world, but judges *angels* also. "Know ye not that we shall judge angels?" Redeemed humanity is in some respects higher than angelic natures. It has passed through greater changes and is brought into closer connection with the Divine. They who have in them the spirit of absolute justice in the highest measure are the best judges of character. In modern courts this spirit is often very feeble, and in some cases extinct. Hence the sad blunderings about the interpretation of statutes and the decisions of judges. But the spirit of absolute justice reigns in the true Church.

II. IT IS A TRIBUNAL FOR THE SETTLEMENT OF ALL DISPUTES. Paul intimates that it is to judge disputes on the "smallest matters," and of "things pertaining to this life." These expressions seem to comprehend all disputes—not merely religious, but secular; not only disputes on great subjects, but disputes on minor subjects as well. The instinct of Christly justice which inspires it peers into the heart of all moral conduct. It has an "anointing from the Holy One, by which it knows all things." The more spiritually pure a man is the more readily will he detect the wrong. Only a few years ago some of our judges occupied twelve months or more, at an enormous expense to the nation, in order to find out whether a man was an impostor or not. To a mind full of moral justice an impostor is detected instinctively and at once. No logic can read the hidden principles of a man's heart. Christ knew "what was in man," and those highly imbued with his Spirit are to some extent gifted with the same insight.

III. DISPUTANTS WHO WILL NOT HAVE THEIR CASES SETTLED IN THIS COURT ARE JUSTLY LIABLE TO REPROACH. 1. Reference to another court is *unwise*. "If then ye have judgments of things pertaining to this life, set them to judge who are least esteemed in the Church." The meaning is that any other court to which the case is taken is of no account in the estimation of the Church—it is a morally inferior institution. The tribunal of man in comparison to Christ's tribunal is a truly contemptible thing. You Christians degrade yourselves by taking disputes to such tribunals. "I speak to your shame. Is it so, that there is not a wise man among you?" It is a shame to you to have your disputes carried to such tribunals, a shame that you cannot settle your disputes among yourselves, that "brother should go to law with brother, before the unbelievers." 2. Reference to another court is *wrong*. "Now therefore, there is utterly a fault [a defect] among you, because ye go to law one with another." Better than to do this, better than to go to a worldly tribunal to settle your disputes, better you should suffer wrong than take your grievance into the worldly courts. "The Church has principles," says Robertson, "according to which all such matters may be set at rest. And the difference between the worldly court of justice and the Christian court of arbitration is a difference of diametrical opposition. Law says, 'You shall have your rights;' the spirit of the true Church says, 'Defraud not your neighbour of *his* rights.' Law says, 'You must not be wronged;' the Church says, 'It is better to suffer wrong than to do wrong.'"

Vers. 9—11.—*Genuine reformation.* "Know ye not that the unrighteous shall not inherit the kingdom of God? Be not deceived: neither fornicators, nor idolaters, nor adulterers, nor effeminate, nor abusers of themselves with mankind, nor thieves, nor covetous, nor drunkards, nor revilers, nor extortioners, shall inherit the kingdom of God. And such were some of you: but ye are washed, but ye are sanctified, but ye are justified in the Name of the Lord Jesus, and by the Spirit of our God." Reformation of some kind or other is an object most earnestly pursued by all in every land who are alive to the woes and wrongs of life. Some of the reformations sought are of a questionable utility; none will prove of any essential and permanent service but that presented in the text. The reformation is—

I. A REFORMATION OF THE MORAL CHARACTER OF MANKIND. "Know ye not that the unrighteous shall not inherit the kingdom of God? Be not deceived: neither fornicators, nor idolaters, nor adulterers, nor effeminate, nor abusers of themselves with mankind," etc. Sin, which may be defined as *self-gratification*, is here presented in a variety of forms—"fornication," idolatry, avarice, intemperance, etc. All these manifestations are hideous developments of the same ungodly principle, self-gratification. The principle of sin, like holiness, is one and simple, but the forms are multifarious. Now, these morally corrupt classes we are here told were changed; they were "washed," and "sanctified," and "justified," which, stripped of figure, means, they were changed in the very root and fountain of their character. They were, to use Scripture phraseology, *converted, regenerated, created anew* in Christ Jesus to good works. The reformation was not *doctrinal, ecclesiastical,* or *institutional,* but *moral.*

II. A REFORMATION INDISPENSABLE TO A HAPPY DESTINY. What is the only happy destiny for man? To "inherit the kingdom of God." What is the "kingdom of

God"? Righteousness, peace, joy in the Holy Ghost. It is the reign of truth, purity, light, harmony, and blessedness. To "inherit" that empire, to be in it, not as occasional visitors, but as *permanent* citizens, holding fellowship with its Sovereign, and mingling with the great and the good of all worlds,—this is our high destiny. For this we were made, and for nothing lower. Hence Christ urges us to "seek first the kingdom of God and his righteousness," which means—come under the Divine reign of truth and right. Now, there is no getting into this kingdom without this moral reformation. All who have not undergone this reformation are excluded.

III. A REFORMATION EFFECTED BY THE REDEMPTIVE AGENCY OF CHRIST. "And such were some of you: but ye are [were] washed, but ye are [were] sanctified, but ye are [were] justified in the Name of the Lord Jesus, and by the Spirit of our God." This means that they had been cleansed from all moral foulness, "washed;" that they had been consecrated to holiness, "sanctified;" that they had been made right in their being and relationships, "justified." And all this, how? "In the Name of the Lord Jesus, and by the Spirit of our God." This is the reformative measure, the gospel; nothing on this earth will effect this moral change but this. Not the enactments of legislations, not the creations of genius, not scientific systems. I disparage none of these, but they cannot effect this reformation of soul, the reformation which humanity wants, a reformation without which all other reformations are but reformations on parchment, a change in mere outward forms of life. "Marvel not that I said unto thee, Ye must be born again." "Without holiness no man shall see the Lord."

Vers. 12—20.—*Christianity in relation to the body.* "All things are lawful unto me, but all things are not expedient," etc. It would seem that there were those in the Church at Corinth who regarded Christianity as giving them a kind of liberty to do whatsoever they wished. Some of them having left Judaism with its various restraints, and others paganism, which also had restrictions, they were too ready to push the doctrine of religious liberty, as proclaimed by Paul, far beyond its limits. The apostle here states, perhaps in answer to a question on the subject, that there is a limitation to Christian liberty. He says, "All things are lawful unto me, but all things are not expedient." As the liberty which they seemed to covet was a liberty in relation to the gratifications of bodily appetites, he takes occasion to state certain things in relation to the body. His remarks suggest to us the *relation of Christianity to the human body.* We observe—

I. THAT IT RECOGNIZES ATTENTION TO THE NATURAL NEEDS OF THE BODY AS PROPER. "Meats for the belly, and the belly for meats." This means the body has appetites, and there are provisions intended and fitted to satisfy them. Christianity allows man to partake of those provisions in nature necessary to satisfy and strengthen his physical nature. To act thus is to act in harmony with the constitution of nature. All animal existences act in this way. Christianity, instead of requiring you to starve the body by fastings, and to exhaust its energies by painful pilgrimages and self-mortifications, says, "Eat and be satisfied, eat and be strong, take care of your bodies. If you choose to eat the meat offered to idols to allay your appetites and to invigorate your frames, well, eat it." Feeding the body, however, Christianity regards, though proper, as very temporary; both the food and the body must perish. They are not like spiritual existences and spiritual supplies, that have regard to an immeasurable hereafter. "All flesh is grass."

II. THAT IT RECOGNIZES INDULGENCE IN THE GRATIFICATIONS OF THE BODY AS WRONG. "Now the body is not for fornication, but for the Lord; and the Lord for the body." This is not a necessity of the body, like eating and drinking, but an immoral indulgence of its propensities. Man should attend to his bodily propensities as *reliefs*, not as gratifications. He who attends to his physical propensities in order to get pleasure out of them, sinks lower than a brute, violates the laws of his nature, degrades his being, and offends his God. Hence intemperance, whether in eating or drinking, is a moral outrage. The crime and curse of men in all ages have been seeking happiness out of the gastric, the sexual, and other propensities of their physical being.

III. THAT IT RECOGNIZES THE PROPER TREATMENT OF THE BODY AS IDENTIFYING IT WITH CHRIST. 1. It is a *property* of Christ. It is "for the Lord; and the Lord for the body." It is not ours; we are its trustees, not its proprietors; we hold it "for the

Lord," and we should use it according to his directions. It is his will that it should
be used by the soul to convey from the external universe quickening and hallowing
impressions of the Divine, and used to express and develop the holy thoughts and
purposes which such impressions should produce. It is to let in God to the soul and
to reveal God to our race. 2. It is a *member* of Christ. "Know ye not that your
bodies are the members of Christ?" If we are genuine Christians, he regards even
our bodies as having a vital connection with him. He had a human body, and that
human body raised to heaven is the model into which our bodies shall be changed.
This being so, the prostitution of the body to sensual indulgence of any kind is an
incongruity and an outrage. "Shall I then take the members of Christ, and make them
the members of an harlot? God forbid. What? know ye not that he which is joined
to an harlot is one body? for two, saith he, shall be one flesh. But he that is joined
unto the Lord is one spirit," etc. 3. It is a *temple* of Christ. "What? know ye not
that your body is the temple of the Holy Ghost which is in you, which ye have of
God?" Christ, by his Spirit, claims the body as a temple, in which he is to *dwell*, be
revealed and *worshipped*. It is his property. "Ye are bought with a price; therefore
glorify God in your body, and in your spirit, which are God's." The language here is,
of course, figurative. It does not mean that there was a strictly commercial transaction
in the redemption of man, a literal *quid pro quo*, for the thing spoken of pertains to
spiritual interests and relations, and not to commerce.

HOMILIES BY VARIOUS AUTHORS.

Vers. 1—11.—*Civil relations and Church membership; litigation before heathen
courts.* The chapter opens abruptly. "Dare any of you"—a strong expression of disapproval—"having a matter against another, go to law before the unjust?" Judaism
had taught the Jews not to go before Gentile judges with a lawsuit against their
brethren; the Romans had accorded to the Jews the right to settle their disputes among
themselves, and Christians at that time might avail themselves of this rule (Lange).
But St. Paul, true to his ruling method, views the matter from Christian ground and
treats it solely on the principles of the gospel. The argument in the preceding chapter
concerned social relations, the present argument applies to civil relations, and yet they
are sympathetic in his mind. Emotion is an associative force, and often establishes or
rather discloses connections of ideas not perceptible in the "dry light" of intellect.
In both these arguments the underlying sentiment is the same, viz. the dignity of
Christian character and the supremacy of its obligations over interest, custom, usage,
and every form of self not compatible with the generous spirit of sacrifice "for Christ's
sake." Bear in mind, then, in reading St. Paul's Epistles, that if at times you lose the
compactness of logic and its tenacious unity, you are always sure to find that more
interior tie which binds thought to sentiment and displaces order for the gain of a
higher method. Method, rather than order, marks the thinker whose vocation is to
instruct the mass of mankind. Saints, as saints exist in the ideal of Christianity,
"shall judge the world." They are to rule with Christ, to share his glory, and be
acknowledged by the universe as participants in the final triumph of his mediatorial
authority. If so, the mediatorial honour in future prospect has a certain scope of present
activity, since it could not be *then* unless it were *now*. Of the character of these
functions and the circumstances incident to their display, what know we? They fall
under that law of reserve which the Lord Jesus spoke of when he said, "Of the times
or the seasons, which the Father hath put in his own power," we are kept ignorant, and
are the better for the ignorance. Details of great facts may intensify the intellect of
sense, and work damage to the higher mind. If Christ was the Son of man, and as such
filled the sphere of humanity, while admitting as such the limitation of his knowledge
in one direction, viz. "of that day and hour knoweth no man," surely we need not
perplex ourselves as to specific theories bearing on this subject. Christianity lays the
stress on intelligence rather than on information, and, in fact, assures us that restraint
is essential in our condition to equable development. St. Paul argues from the future
to the present; thus, "shall judge the world, . . . shall judge angels;" and the conclusion
is emphasized,—"how much more things that pertain to this life!" On this ground

of the spiritual superiority of the saints in Christ, he claims that the judgment of believers may now be most advantageously exercised. It is a training in the school of Christ, and the discipline, while varied, is adapted to the highest good. Does St. Paul mean to put earthly tribunals under the ban? By no means. Again and again he sought their protection against Jews and Gentiles, and, if Roman law had not befriended him, his apostleship as men reason would have had a speedy termination. Who was more explicit and earnest than he in urging the doctrine that human government was a Divine ordinance, and as such to be obeyed and honoured? And who among statesmen and philosophers ever saw as deeply into the nature and functions of sovereignty as an essential element of the idea of man in the scheme of the universe? In law, in its administration of justice, in its protection of persons and property, in its power to verify and conserve the multitudinous interests of society, he recognized the right arm of Providence. The sense of providence must be social no less than individual, must transcend geographical bounds, and embrace the human family as a family of "one blood," or it failed of its office. So, then, he has no issue with law and its adjudications as such. But the uses of the law by Christians; the common and facile resort to it in order to gratify covetousness, pride, ambition, revenge, and any and every form of selfishness;—that is the grave matter before his mind. "There is utterly a fault among you," a weakness, a repudiation of noble sentiment, a departure from the idea of the true self in Christ, "because ye go to law one with another" before unbelievers; brother arrayed against brother; and [this exposure of a mutilated unity, with its accompanying evils, made in the presence of men whose criticisms would be only too eager to detect and magnify your imperfections. This is one aspect of the matter. But you gain your rights. Ay, and rights may be purchased too dearly. Go to law and get your rights; and then, as you retire from the seat of judgment, think of what you leave behind you—what losses of sentiment, trust in others, hope of humanity, brotherliness of heart, perchance even integrity and honour. Right and rights, how often they part company, and the one is the burlesque, the shame, the bitter contempt of the other! "Rather take wrong;" it is altogether a manlier thing, if done for Christ's sake. Lord Erskine, when at the bar, once said to Dr. Parr, "Accommodate the difference amicably. . . . I can scarcely figure to myself a situation in which a lawsuit is not, if possible, to be avoided." This is another aspect of the matter. Alas! there is an aspect yet sadder. Law is used as a means to inflict a wrong. "Ye do wrong, and defraud, and that your brethren." What gigantic wrongs have been perpetrated under the name of law, we all know; but who can tell how far this spirit, which uses justice to accomplish injustice, has gone forth into all the relationships of men, and vitiated life among the sacred retreats of home and the Church? The depravity of man's lower nature is fearful, not because it is cruel and brutal, but because it is continually re-enforced and invigorated by the depravity of his higher nature. What is true of the individual in this respect is true also of society. History and our own observation warrant the statement that the grossest perverters of law and justice have been found among those who were wealthy, or in high office, or otherwise influential. Their example, in very many instances, has worked downward, just as certain poisonous gases, too heavy to ascend, have infected the air on a level with us. Then follows a question containing its own answer: "Know ye not that the *unjust* shall not inherit the kingdom of God?" His impassioned formula, "Be not deceived," introduces a catalogue of immoralities that shut out men from God's kingdom, in which we have a startling revelation, common with St. Paul, of bodily sins. "Such were some of you." But how different now!—*washed, sanctified, justified,* in the Name of Christ, and by the Spirit. Would they fall back into their heathenish practices? Within the compass of a few verses, St. Paul gives us principles that permeate civil society no less than religious. If carried out, we should have much less law and much more equity, and both law and equity would be immense gainers by the change. The tendency of the argument is the thing to notice. That tendency is to give men a true spiritual conception of themselves, and to develop their thought of self in accordance with God's thought of them. The sense of public justice may compel us to resort to law, but this will not conflict with St. Paul's idea. On the other hand, any abuse of an institution, whether governmental or domestic, whether ecclesiastical or earthly, is an abuse of manhood, and on this truth he expends the force of his reasoning. In these verses, as in the previous chapters, arguing, denouncing, exhorting, pleading,—it is the voice of a grand doctrine and a lofty trust and a sublime hope that we hear. And we hear it in the midst of strife and turbulence, out of the depths of a heart most sorrowful and yet "always rejoicing," and able to command itself and its faculties and resources whenever and wherever needed.—L.

Vers. 12—20.—*The human body and its relation to Christ.* Among the objects about him proper for use and enjoyment—those objects which accorded with his nature and position as a redeemed man—was there anything from which he was excluded? "All things are lawful unto me," and, in this sense, liberty and law are identical, the measure of the one being the measure of the other. If law is of God, so is freedom; if the former is the expression of the Divine will and character, so is the latter; and if man is the image of Christ in law, so is he in freedom. Observe, then, that it is not law and liberty as existing in a perfect world that the apostle is considering, but as found in this mixed and disordered world, in which probation is going on to its eternal issues. Ideally "all things are lawful," and yet, because life is a discipline, how could it be otherwise than that liberty should be abridged? One of the main purposes of probation is to discipline the will, to choose for itself among a multitude of objects addressing our sensibilities. Scores of things appeal daily to our senses, and, if all our sensations are converted into desires, thence into motives, thence accepted by volition, and made a part of ourselves, then certainly this is not freedom for the ends of moral discipline, but freedom for simple and universal gratification. Freedom in St. Paul's view is not a final cause, it is a means; and he would have the Corinthian remember that one of their greatest obligations was to restrain this freedom. The freedom itself had a large range as to the objects allowed its use and enjoyment. Should it cover the whole area of activity? Nay, says the apostle, this would be bondage in another form. "I will not be brought under the *power* of any," for "all things are lawful unto me," which is to say, "all things are in my power," and I will exercise my *power* by imposing limitations on self-indulgence. Of course, then, this restraint put on individual freedom is our own voluntary act. Such is the stress laid on personality that a man's Christian virtue must be specifically his own, and recognized by infallible signs as his own. Development is a common duty, self-development segregates a man from his fellows that he may grow in a given way. Self-denial is a common duty, but under this law of individuality in using our freedom, self-denial assumes a variety of shapes, and becomes wonderfully potential in human affairs by the diversity it presents. In this view the self-denial of A is no guide for B. The special form of your self-denial may not commend itself to me, nay, it may be hurtful to me; and, assuredly, it will lose its virtue if I adopt it merely because it is yours. And hence the value of example in this respect is not to create a slavish imitation on the part of others, but to set forth the worth inherent in the spirit of self-denial. If this principle, so boldly urged by St. Paul, had been faithfully adhered to, it would have saved the Church from many inconsistencies. Private opinion, while it is content to be such, may be over-stringent, and yet do no great harm. But in many cases it exceeds the limits of individuality and takes shape as the tyranny of public opinion. Morbidness is rarely satisfied till it acquires notoriety before the eyes of men, and so it comes to pass that we have ecclesiastical agitation and legislation about many things—for instance, amusements—concerning which no exact standard can be set up for everybody. If we could have an exact standard, it would not compensate for the loss of personal freedom, since this is precisely one of those matters in which self-denial owes all its excellence to the restrictions that it imposes upon itself. St. Paul's emphatic "*I*" in this connection is the "*I*" of every redeemed man, and accordingly, as a universal prerogative, this exalted characteristic of individuality is most carefully guarded. And how is it guarded? To say nothing of what Christian freedom is in itself as delegated by God in Christ, and conditioned widely different from Adam's sovereignty in Eden; to say nothing of its original limitations by the Divine Law, and the fixed barriers over which it may not pass, and, if true to itself, cannot pass; what is this liberty but a glorious privilege to be made still more glorious by our own self-enacted laws of restraint? It is a new limitation peculiar to man. It is a limitation which each man under the grace of the Spirit originates and executes in attestation of his own endowments as God's redeemed servant, It is sonship in its most beautiful and tender form—the

"Abba, Father," which is not heard in the responses of the Church, nor in hymns of social worship, but is an utterance that rises to God in those hours when loneliness is a supreme joy. I have the power; I will not use it; I will deny myself its exercise, and I will do it because "all things are not expedient." What other eye save his own could penetrate those mysteries, from which he draws reasons and motives for particular acts of self-denial? Mysteries, we say; for many an advanced believer yields in this phase of experience to half-awakened instincts and undefined impulses. How can ministers of the gospel, how can Churches in their official capacity, get at the knowledge of what is wisest and best in those matters that belong to the very highest attributes of personality as the ground of individuality? "Let every man be fully persuaded in his own mind." "Fully persuaded" he can never be unless he use his liberty untrammelled. If you dogmatize and legislate, the *full persuasion* cannot be the outcome of "*his own mind.*" If God can trust him, why not you? The safeguard has been provided—it is *expediency*. And this sense of expediency or of fitness and propriety is a conservative and prudential force, which operates to check all excesses, and binds about the man the golden *cestus* of moderation. Expediency is never self-willed and arbitrary. It presides over tastes and the minor moralities no less than over the more prominent virtues; nor does it trifle with trifles nor disdain the helps of look and tone and manner, but is cardinal to whatsoever reflects the man upon his associates. Keenly alive to discriminations, it educates us to know the best from the merely good, and, by its fine tact and subtle sagacity, goes on swift wing to the noblest objects. It considers, as though it were a part of itself, the welfare of others, and thus becomes a guarantee that a man's liberty shall not invade the rights of his fellow-man. And remembering that "all things" are his only so far as he is Christ's, he realizes that it is "no more I that live, but Christ liveth in me." Then St. Paul proceeds to dwell on the sanctity of the human body—a favourite topic, on which he expends much thought. In the third chapter he had discussed it, and in subsequent passages, every one of them singularly clear and vivid, he recurs to this great topic. Here the leading idea is that our bodies "are the members" of Christ's body. "The body is for the Lord, and the Lord for the body." And hence St. Paul, in his concrete method of thinking, refuses to separate, even in thought, body and soul, as they are connected with redemption. Matter and mind are perfectly unlike; they are known to us only by their infinite contrariety; and yet matter and mind meet and unite as body and soul, and the union is human nature. These two substances grow each in its own way, the natural union at birth becoming closer and yet closer as years progress, and the body subordinating itself more and more to the mind's service. In the mature man—the mechanic, the accountant, the artist, the poet, the philosopher—a vast advance has occurred in the nearness and adaptability of the corporeity to the wants, demands, and aspirations of the spirit. If the providential idea in education and culture be fulfilled, the co-operative activity constantly increases, each forward step a step for both, and the law of development taking effect in mutuality of advantage. Still more fully is this fact brought out in Christian experience. St. Paul's figures on this subject stand for facts. Bodily appetites cease to be mere animal instincts. They are elevated and purified. If Christ was raised from the dead, so too our bodies shall be raised, for the companionship of mind and matter as soul and body is not a transient but an eternal fact. One may speak of being "here in the body pent" and of the "body of humiliation" (vile body), but the idea of body as an investiture of spirit and an auxiliary to its functions is a part of the original scheme of humanity, and will have its complete development in the future life. Little do we realize that the resurrection-man is now in a process of training as to his corporeal form. This training is double—mental and material—and hence, while it is true that certain physical functions will expire and be known no more, yet the effects of their experience will survive in the soul itself. "A *spiritual* body" is assured us by Christianity and confirmed to us by Christ's resurrection; and, agreeably to this doctrine, the present growth of body into the mind's service, the tuition of the senses, the reduction of the nerves to the will, the command which is acquired over the lower organs, all indicate that the resurrection-man of body and spirit is now in process of formation. If this is true; if the resurrection is not only a prospective glory but a realization now going on by means of the present ennoblement and sanctification of the human body; and, furthermore, if Christ's education of his own body to the offices he filled as Teacher, Miracle-Worker, Philanthropist, Redeemer, etc., as to the spirit actuating him, an example to his followers;—then surely we have the weightiest of reasons for regarding the body as the "temple of the Holy Ghost." Greek philosophy had abused the truth that all creatures are for man, and that he is the measure of all things. Professing Christians had followed a carnal philosophy in the application of this truth. And now that St. Paul has rescued it from its perversions and set it in its proper light, he may well urge the conclusion, "Ye are bought with a price: therefore glorify God in your body, and in your spirit, which are God's." Could anything more timely, more momentous, more significant of the aim of Christianity as it respected the social regeneration of mankind, have been said by St. Paul? The sin of the body; that one sin which surrenders the body to another and degrades it as nothing else can degrade; that sin of sins, which debauches the body where it ought to be purest, and sinks lowest that which should be highest;—could its wickedness be set forth in stronger language than when he speaks of the body as the tabernacle, in which not only the soul but the Holy Ghost dwells? "Which ye have of God," and therefore "not your own," but "bought with a price." And yet this redeemed possession, the purchase of Christ's blood, a member of his mystical body, a tabernacle of the Spirit, alienated, abused, prostituted to the most shameful and the most fatal of all vices. Of nothing is it so true as of this vice, that we become like that with which we associate. Association is assimilation, and, in this case, assimilation is the most dreadful form of desecration. These verses (18—20) contain, as has been suggested (Alford), the germ of the three weighty sections of the Epistle about to follow. And we do well to enter into their meaning and implore the grace of God to assist us, lest we fail to receive the profound impression sought to be made. It is useless to blink the fact that among Christian nations and in the nineteenth century this colossal vice of a desecrated human body is the Satanic citadel of iniquity. Take all the vices and sins on earth, aggregate them in one huge bulk, and the misfortunes, evils, catastrophes, tragic disasters, put together, would not outweigh the consequences morally and socially viewed of this enormity. Half of the man goes straight and quick into the hands of the devil, and the other half, unless God interpose, follows on in a fascination of blindness exceptional among illusions. God help us! For verily "*vain*," in this instance, "is the help of man." We need a much larger and bolder discussion of the religion of the human body; and if writers and preachers would study the art of doing this work, the Church and the world would be vast gainers. Any way, this is open to us all, viz. to lay a much greater stress than is commonly done on the dignity, worth, and glory of the human body as seen in the light of Christ's teaching. Full justice is not done this subject, not even approximative justice, and, therefore, no wonder the body is disparaged, vilified, tolerated by many as a nuisance, and immolated by thousands as a creature of appetite and lust. "Bought with a price," the blood of the Lord Jesus paid for it—a glorious thing to be bought and not too precious a ransom paid, and now sprinkled by that blood and hallowed by the indwelling Spirit. Oh what intenseness of soul should go into the pleading, "Glorify God in your body"!—L.

Vers. 1—8.—*Litigation; or, How shall Christians settle their differences and disputes?* Remarkable is the insight which this Epistle affords us into the interior life of a Church of the first age. We seem to be brought into the presence of remarkable virtues and of remarkable faults, and are impressed with the incongruity of the picture. One thing is certain, that human nature was then what it is now, and that Christianity offers the one Divine remedy for individual and for social ills.

I. IT IS TO BE EXPECTED THAT DIFFERENCES AND DISPUTES WILL ARISE WITHIN THE BOUNDARIES OF CHRISTIAN COMMUNITIES. The occasions are manifold; the conflict of interests and of opinions and of tastes will account for not a few. It is irrational to suppose that human nature can be at once transformed from the condition of the self-indulgent pagan, for example, to the position of a mature and holy servant of God. There are to be found in the Church on earth persons occupying every point intermediate between these extremes; and among such "offences will come."

II. IT IS SCANDALOUS THAT SUCH DISPUTES SHOULD BE BROUGHT BEFORE A HEATHEN

TRIBUNAL. The Greeks were an especially disputatious and litigious race. It was natural enough that those who in the days of their heathenism had been accustomed to refer their disputes to the judges of the city should still carry any differences that might arise into the same courts. But reflection, as the apostle urges, must have made manifest the unwisdom of such a proceeding. Christianity proclaimed itself a religion of peace and love; and its adherents spoke of one another as brothers; whilst it was known that the great Lord had enjoined the forgiveness of injuries, and had himself set an example of such forgiveness. It is clear that for Christians to go to law with one another before the tribunals of the heathen was to create a scandal, and to bring both the religion and its professors into contempt. The same reasonings apply wherever, in our own day, the powers that be are unchristian, and the followers of Jesus are but as leaven in the mass of heathenism.

III. Every Christian society contains within itself elements capable of dealing with such emergencies. According to the apostle's teaching, the "saints" shall be assessors with the Lord Christ in the judgment of the world and of angels; and those destined to fulfil functions so majestic may surely be entrusted with the settlement of trivial disputes. It is best if the two persons between whom a misunderstanding has arisen can compose their differences with no outside assistance; if this cannot be done, it is well to call in the aid of a Christian of calm, impartial character and of large experience, with a common agreement to accept his award without murmuring. There is surely a large opportunity for the exercise of the virtues of wisdom and justice in such directions as these. Much bickering and heart-burning might be avoided were there a sincere and general desire to act upon the counsels of the apostle. The courts of justice, even in Christian countries, might thus be relieved of much of their business, to the advantage of the whole community.

IV. The best preventive of quarrelling is a disposition to suffer injuries rather than to resent or even to redress wrong. There is something very startling and very grand in the apostle's sudden, unexpected questions, "Why not rather take wrong? why not rather be defrauded?" These are "counsels of perfection." The alternative already suggested is good; but this is better far, however it be opposed to the inclinations of "the natural man." Christ has given us an example of suffering wrong. From the world we are bound, if it be so ordered, to accept with patience language of contumely or treatment of injustice. And it is suggested that, even amongst those who are fellow-members of the same body, there may be mutual forbearance, there may be a patience amounting to magnanimity, a renunciation of rights which shall make it clear of how little importance are all those matters upon which it is possible for good men to differ.

> " Learn how sublime a thing it is
> To suffer, and be strong ! "

T.

Ver. 11.—*Past, present, and future.* In the two preceding verses the apostle has described, in terse, plain terms, the awful vices to which the heathen inhabitants of Corinth were addicted. To his enlightened mind the kingdom of Satan and the kingdom of God were diametrically opposed; and the test by which Paul judged them was the test of moral character—a test which the reason and conscience cannot but approve. The apostle knew from what a slough some of his Corinthian converts had been delivered, and he points the contrast between the kingdom in their person and history.

I. A blessing as respects the past: the Christian is washed from moral foulness. The language of this passage must have gone home with power to some hearts : " Such were some of you ! " They had indulged in sins of the flesh and of the spirit, in vices which were deemed pardonable, and in vices which were deemed vile, in transgressions against their own nature and against society. Some had been notorious and flagrant, others ordinary, offenders. But all had contracted moral defilement. And what had Christianity done for them? What has it done for all to whom it has come? It has purified them from their old sins. " Ye were washed." The lustration of baptismal waters was a symbol of the purification wrought in the spirit by the redemption of Christ, by the Holy Spirit of God.

II. A blessing as respects the present : the Christian is renewed in holiness.

Forgiveness and cleansing from impurity may justly be regarded as the means to an end; *i.e.* to hallowing or sanctification. This is the positive, to which the other is the negative, side. Set free from vice and crime, the subject of the Divine power of the cross comes under a new and inspiring influence. The Holy Spirit creates the nature afresh. No inferior power is adequate to produce a change so vast. It is a proof of the Divine origin and adaptation of Christianity that it attempts and achieves a task so superhuman. These moral miracles of sanctification constitute an evidence of Christianity which is to many minds the most conclusive of all.

III. A BLESSING AS RESPECTS THE FUTURE: THE CHRISTIAN IS JUSTIFIED FROM CONDEMNATION. The expression employed refers to the government of God and our relation to it. Justification is acquittal at the bar of the righteous Judge. By anticipation Scripture represents this acquittal as already pronounced in the case of those who have accepted the terms of salvation. For such the Name of Jesus Christ avails, and in such the Spirit of God graciously works. Justification is conferred now; but the full benefit of it will appear by contrast in the day of judgment.

APPLICATION. 1. The question is suggested to every hearer of the gospel—Could the apostle have used this language with reference to *me?* Are the signs of this mighty change manifest in *my* life? 2. The reflection is suggested to those who have experienced this moral transformation—How wonderful and how effectual is the grace of God! How vast is the debt of gratitude we owe to the Father who loved us, the Saviour who redeemed us, the Holy Spirit who sanctifies us!—T.

Vers. 12—16.—*The sanctity of the body.* At Corinth idolatry assumed a most imposing, luxurious, and voluptuous form. It is quite in accordance with all we know of the opulent and pleasure-loving inhabitants of and visitors to "the star of Hellas," that those controversies and scandals which are dealt with so fully in this chapter should arise in a Christian society planted by the apostle at Corinth. It should be more especially noticed that there is a sufficient reason for the remarkable fact that sexual matters should be treated more fully in this Epistle than in any other part of the New Testament. The apostle in this passage demolishes the sophistical arguments and excuses by which certain professed Christians at Corinth were disposed to defend the practice of fornication. It was said that matters relating to the bodily life were indifferent to the moral welfare of men, that as an enlightened man will eat this food or that, irrespectively of any superstitious prejudices, inasmuch as food and the digestive system are naturally in co-relation with each other, so he will satisfy the sensual appetites of his body in whatever way may be convenient and agreeable to him. Against this doctrine of devils Paul here argues, not on grounds of asceticism, but on grounds which must be conceded as secure by the moral and especially by the Christian thinker.

I. THE GROUNDS UPON WHICH CHRISTIANITY ESTABLISHES THE SANCTITY OF THE BODY. As here presented, they may appear to some readers to be mystical, but in fact they are in harmony both with the facts of human nature and with the great doctrines of the New Testament. 1. *The Lord Christ and the body of man are "for" each other.* In his incarnation Christ has assumed the human body, in his ministry he has honoured it, in his death he has redeemed it. Not the soul only, but the body, is God's creation, and the object of Christ's regard, and partaker of the benefits of his mediation. As the Lord is for the body, so is the body for the Lord. 2. *More particularly, the bodies of Christians are members of Christ.* The ransomed and renewed humanity is one glorious whole, one Divine organism, the Lord Jesus being himself the authoritative Head. If the Head, the informing Spirit, is holy, must not also the subordinate members be also pure and consecrated? 3. Christ having been raised from the dead, it is appointed that *the body of every follower and friend of Christ shall share in this resuscitation and exaltation.* In what way this shall take place is immaterial to the argument. The spiritual renewal is the earnest of the high and immortal resurrection of the whole man. These things being so, the body of the Christian standing in relation so intimate to the glorious and holy Mediator and Lord,—is there any consistency between such a connection with the King of saints and a life of filthy sensuality? The incompatibility is apparent and undeniable.

II. THE PRACTICAL CONSEQUENCES WHICH FOLLOW UPON THE CHRISTIAN DOCTRINE OF THE BODY. These are broadly distinguished into two classes. 1. *Food is a matter of indifference.* Many weak Christians laid great stress upon clean and unclean food; some objected to eat what had been or might have been offered to idols. Now, the apostle claims all this as a province of Christian liberty. Diet was a matter "without" the body. All things were lawful. Those who ate and those who refrained from eating were forbidden to despise one another; for both alike were called upon to act in this matter "as unto the Lord." 2. *Impurity is absolutely forbidden.* There is a vital difference between the satisfaction of hunger and the gratification of the sexual appetite. This latter is only permissible within the boundaries of holy matrimony. Fornication is an abuse of the body, a defilement of Christ's members, an insult to the Lord himself, whose property it not only takes by theft from him, but hands over to a harlot. This is very plain speaking on the part of the apostle. But it is just; and if it was necessary in those days, it is equally necessary now. Physiology is often invoked to sanction vice; but it is well to listen to the nobler and purer counsels of the apostles, which are not more in harmony with the loftiest ethics than they are with the soundest conclusions of physical and of social science.—T.

Ver. 17.—*Christ and his people are one.* It was the wont of the apostle to associate the commonest duties of life with the highest motives drawn from spiritual realities and relations. In dissuading from the sin of impurity, he might have adduced considerations drawn from physical laws or from social conditions; but it is more in harmony with his convictions and habits to appeal to the loftiest principles of the Christian religion.

I. THE BOND WHICH UNITES CHRISTIANS TO THEIR LORD. It is a personal relation which is here asserted, and evidently not one of mere external association, but of vital and spiritual union. 1. *It is a bond of faith.* "Whom not having seen," etc. Christians receive with cordiality the gospel concerning Christ; they receive Christ himself to dwell in their hearts by faith. 2. *It is a bond of love.* They are joined to him as the bride to the bridegroom, in a spiritual affection, in love "stronger than death." 3. *It is a bond of affinity.* Drawn to Jesus as sinners to the Saviour, they remain with him as friends congenial in character, in disposition, and in aims.

II. THE CONSEQUENT UNITY BETWEEN CHRISTIANS AND THEIR LORD. They are "one spirit." 1. They are in *a spirit of subjection* to the Father, whose will and law are authoritative and supreme. 2. They are one in *the love of all that is holy and morally admirable.* The sympathy that exists is sympathy with regard to matters of the highest moment, with regard to the principles that animate and the aims that dignify the moral life. 3. They are one in *the bonds of an immortal fellowship.* Christ's prayer for his people was, "That they may be with me where I am"—a prayer which the Father is graciously and constantly answering.

III. THE PRACTICAL PROOFS OF THIS UNITY. 1. *A repugnance on the part of Christians to all which is repugnant to their Lord;* as *e.g.* those vices to which allusion is made in the context, practised by the heathen, but hateful to those who name the Name of Christ. 2. *A cultivation of the spirit of brotherly love.* The "one spirit" must needs be a spirit of true love, linking together the members of the mystical body of Christ, and disposing them to a sympathetic and harmonious action.—T.

Vers. 19, 20.—*A purchased possession.* Every noble character and life is based upon self-renunciation. A man, in order to make his mark upon the world, must lose himself in some great cause, that *e.g.* of his country, of science, of art, of humanity. Is there an all-absorbing aim in which men generally may justly lose themselves? If there be, it must be the highest, all-comprehending, perfectly and lastingly satisfactory. Christians have found this secret: they live to God in Christ. They are not their own, for they are bought, they are owned by the Son of God.

I. THE STATE OF BONDAGE FROM WHICH CHRISTIANS ARE RANSOMED. 1. There was a time, a state, in which they thought themselves "their own." They followed their own desires and went their own way. 2. But in reality they were in bondage—to the Law and its sentence of condemnation; to sin and its cruel fetters; to Satan and his wretched service. 3. The power of evil then fostered the delusion of liberty, flattered pride and fostered selfishness, all the while drawing tighter and tighter the chains of spiritual bondage.

II. THE LIBERATOR TO WHOM CHRISTIANS ARE INDEBTED FOR THEIR REDEMPTION. They were ransomed: 1. By One whose laws and service had been forsaken and despised. 2. By One without whose help bondage would have been eternal. 3. By One upon whom we sinful men had no claim based upon right and justice. 4. By One whose heart was moved with pity by the sad spectacle of our slavery. 5. By One who graciously resolved to do and to suffer all that might be involved in the work of our deliverance.

III. THE COST AT WHICH CHRISTIANS WERE RANSOMED FROM SLAVERY AND PURCHASED AS THE FREE BONDMEN OF GOD. 1. It was a price which no mere man could by any possibility have paid. 2. It was a price which could not be reckoned and estimated in any earthly or human equivalent. 3. It was a price in order to pay which it was necessary that the Son of God should become incarnate, and empty himself of his glory. 4. It was a price which consisted in "the precious blood of Christ."

IV. THE OBLIGATIONS WHICH THIS PURCHASE AND REDEMPTION LAY UPON CHRISTIANS. These may be regarded in two aspects. 1. *Negatively.* "Ye are not your own." Your heart is not your own, but Christ's; your thoughts are not your own, but his who liveth in you; your time is not your own, but is redeemed for the Redeemer; your abilities and influence are not your own, but are to be consecrated to him to whom you owe both them and the bias which has been given them; your property is not your own, but his who claims your all. 2. *Positively.* "Glorify God therefore." The praise is due to him who in his own mind conceived the purpose of redemption. The service is due to him whom to love is of necessity to serve. All the faculties of our nature and all the opportunities of our life may well be laid, as a consecrated offering, upon the altar of God, whose we are, not only by right of creation, but by right of grace and redemption, whose we are by every tie, and whom we are bound to serve as the best expression of our gratitude and the best exercise of our liberty.—T.

Ver. 20.—"*Glorify God.*" "The heavens declare the glory of God." Hosts of angelic and glorified spirits give "glory, honour, and thanksgiving unto him." "All nations whom he hath made shall come and glorify his Name."

> "And shall man alone be dumb
> Till this glorious kingdom come?
> No! the Church delights to raise
> Psalms and hymns and songs of praise."

I. ON WHAT GROUNDS SHOULD CHRISTIANS GLORIFY GOD? This is a reasonable service, a reasonable requirement. 1. God has a natural right over us, *i.e.* by his creative power and providential care. "Man's chief end," says a famous Catechism, "is to glorify God." 2. Redemption is the great reason adduced why Christians should glorify God. This is the doctrine of the context. The claim of purchase is added to the claim of creation.

II. FROM WHAT MOTIVES SHOULD CHRISTIANS GLORIFY GOD? 1. From a remembrance of the danger and ruin consequent upon any other end in life. Exemplified in Scripture history, as in the instance of Belshazzar, to whom it was said, "The God, etc., hast thou not glorified," and in the instance of Herod, who "gave not God the glory." 2. From a grateful acknowledgment of the love and grace to which they are indebted for their redemption. The ransom and redemption do indeed avail for all men; but multitudes are insensible to the loving-kindness of the Lord. They who have tasted and seen that the Lord is good are prompted by their experience to yield themselves to the service of their Saviour. 3. From a desire to secure their own highest happiness. They have learned how every other principle of life fails to yield a deep and lasting satisfaction; and now they are learning, by happy experience, how truly blessed is the life which is unto the Lord of love and glory. This is exemplified in the history of this very Apostle Paul. 4. From a delight in the Divine commands. It is an invitation, but it is also a behest: "Glorify God." And nothing is so congenial to the Christian as what is enjoined upon him by his Lord's authority.

III. IN WHAT MANNER MAY CHRISTIANS GLORIFY GOD? 1. By praise. "Whoso offereth praise glorifieth me." "Confess that Jesus Christ is Lord, to the glory of God the Father." Public, cordial, unceasing praises should ascend from every company of the redeemed. 2. By obedience and service; and that not only of spirit, as is presumed, but of body, as is here expressed. The occasion of this chapter, the prevalence of sensual sin, seems to give an especially appositeness and force to this admonition, "Glorify God in your body." That which had been the instrument of unrighteousness and uncleanness, becomes, through the redemption of Christ, the instrument of obedience and holiness.—T.

Vers. 1—8.—*Christians and the law courts.* How far are Paul's exhortations applicable to believers in the present day? Amongst the ancients, laws were often unjust, judges venal, and frequently certain objectionable formalities, such as adjuration by false deities, had to be observed. In our own land and time these things happily are not as of old. Yet even amongst us there are laws tainted with injustice, and there is not a little in our modes of legal procedure which is objectionable. Legal proceedings are sometimes necessary. Paul appealed to Cæsar. And our duty to society may render it incumbent upon us not to allow an evil-doer to escape. Nevertheless litigation between professing Christians—
I. Often presents a melancholy spectacle. 1. *The principals frequently receive injury.*—Not in pocket only; and in this respect he who gains the suit is generally little better off than he who loses. But morally and spiritually. Anger is excited, and ill feeling, if not positive hatred, towards the opponent. There is the direst temptation to take every possible advantage. The legal atmosphere is largely of the earth, earthy, and does not engender the state of mind needful for the beautiful but very heart-searching petition, "Forgive us our trespasses as we forgive them that trespass against us." The prayer, "Lead us not into temptation," may indeed be offered, for the man who loves legal contests requires no *leading* into temptation, since he runs into it headlong of his own accord. 2. *Brings scandal upon the Church.* Both as (1) to its lack of wise men capable of forming a true judgment; (2) to the real condition of its members. The world judges all by those it sees. Irritated, if not vengeful, litigants will be taken as samples fairly representing the "Church of the redeemed." Thus: 3. *Christianity itself becomes lowered in the estimation of men.* To them it will seem as though the religion of peace, forbearance, unity, and love had failed at its very head-quarters. So: 4. *A great injury is done to the world.* By prejudicing it against the truth whereby alone it can be saved. Faulty Christian conduct drives men away from Christianity itself. Professors of religion have made many atheists.
II. Much litigation might be avoided by: 1. *Desiring only the right.* Men who want their due *and a little more* rush to the courts. Many who think themselves very just are very unjust in their desires. It is very easy to become unjust *almost unconsciously.* If men would only judge *their own cause* justly there would often be an end of the dispute. It is astonishing how many men fail in forming a fair estimate of their own claims: there seems an almost invincible tendency to exaggeration. We should sternly educate ourselves in principles of justice. We should judge our own cause impartially, *as though it were not our own.* 2. *Being content oftentimes to take less than our due.* The law promises to us all that we can claim, but we should not always seek all that we can claim. A spirit of sacrifice is not unchristian. "Suffering wrongfully" is not altogether deprecated in Holy Writ. Even if we are smitten on the cheek, our Master does not counsel to instantly cast our assailant into prison, and to keep him there until he has paid the last farthing of damages. Forgiveness, disposition to pass by injury, the most charitable view of an opponent's motives and conduct,— these things are "of Christ." 3. *Not making great matters of little.* If theoretically we deem ourselves justified in going to law, we may well ask ourselves the question— Is the matter in dispute worth disputing, and worth causing the evils likely to arise therefrom? 4. *Remembrance of our relationship.* "All ye are brethren." If Christians, we are trying to do the same work, to follow the same Lord, to serve the same God, to reach the same home. Is the contemplated litigation consistent with this relationship, and is it likely to promote "*brotherly love*"? And here we must avoid becoming prejudiced against our opponent. *Opposing us,* being on the other side, often makes all the difference. If on our side, a man is evidently a Christian, consistent, a credit to the community; but if against us, he is very apt to be everything objectionable. So some have a very easy conscience in going to law against a brother, because before

doing so they have mentally ejected him from the brotherhood on account of his numerous delinquencies. 5. *Submitting the matter in dispute to the arbitration of Christian brethren.* Earnestly does the apostle recommend this course. He seeks to arouse the spiritually dormant Corinthians by the sarcastic supposition that, with all their boasted wisdom, they have not a man sufficiently wise to arbitrate in a case of dispute between two brethren. He unfolds a startling truth respecting believers, viz. that hereafter they shall judge (1) the world (ver. 2); (2) angels (ver. 3). This declaration has much mystery attaching to it, but it accords with Christ's promise to his disciples, that they should sit upon twelve thrones and judge the twelve tribes of Israel (Matt. xix. 28; see also Rev. iii. 21). And Jude tells us (ver. 6) that fallen angels are reserved for future judgment. We get thus a glimpse of the future exaltation of the redeemed. Having shared in the shame of Christ, they will share in his glory and power. He is the great Judge, but they will be identified with him in judgment. "I in them, and they in me." As the Law on Sinai was ordained by means of angels, so the saints shall administer the kingdom of their Lord. (1) If believers are to exercise such exalted functions hereafter, they should on earth be able to judge many of the causes of their brethren, and to do so with fairness and impartiality. Some are shy of arbitration, because sometimes it has had *very little justice* in it. (2) In thus administering justice below, believers are preparing themselves for the duties of the life to come. Such work should not be slighted; it is in the highest degree *educational.* It should be performed with all possible care. Injustice done to others is always injury done to ourselves.—H.

Vers. 9—11.—*Our inheritance in peril.* I. WHAT OUR INHERITANCE IS. "The kingdom of God:" present, but chiefly future. Of which Peter speaks (2 Pet. iii. 13), "We, according to his promise, look for new heavens and a new earth, wherein dwelleth righteousness." Heaven, and the heavenly life, and the heavenly joys; the "rest that remaineth for the people of God;" the nightless, sinless, curseless, painless land; the "many mansions" of the Father's house; the eternal home, where we "shall see his face." This inheritance is in a certain sense the inheritance of all, since Christ died for the sins of the world. The gospel invitation is addressed to all. *We disinherit ourselves.*

II. SINS WHICH HINDER US FROM INHERITING THE KINGDOM OF GOD. 1. *Sins of sensuality.* Brutal lusts; unholy indulgence. Amongst the ancients (and also amongst the moderns too) vices existed which must not be so much as named amongst the decent and pure. 2. *Idolatry.* If we serve false gods, how can we expect a reward from the true God? Some have keen eyes for injuries done to men; idolatry is a pre-eminent sin against God. And we may be thorough idolaters whilst we are professed Christians. What is that which occupies the throne of our heart and of our life? Is it an idol or is it God? 3. *Theft, covetousness, extortion.* These may be grouped together. They do not seem so heinous as the foregoing, but they are associated with them—and through them, equally with the others, *may the inheritance be lost.* Such sin shows that our heart is not right either towards man or God. And the three are much upon a par. Yet many a man would be horrified at the thought of being a thief who is not at all horrified at being undoubtedly covetous and extortionate. *How names betray us!* Why, what is covetousness but theft in the bud? And extortion is theft —unmitigated theft—in the blossom! Many a man steals mentally, and is as guilty as if he stole actually; for nothing but the restraints of society and the dock keep his hands still. And he passes for an honest man! Many a theft is committed in a court of justice before the very eyes of judge and jury, and sometimes with the assistance of a bewigged counsel; for example, *when a man is striving to get more than his due.* 4. *Drunkenness.* This curse of our land—what men lose by it! Health, respect, friends, position, home, wealth—and *the kingdom of God.* 5. *Foul language.* Reviling, railing, sins of the tongue. Foul lips which speak of a foul heart, for the sweet fountain sends not forth bitter waters. Sins such as these entail the forfeiture of the great inheritance. Plainly are we here taught that a nominal faith can never save us. All the *profession* in the world cannot carry us an inch towards the promised land. It is the old pagan notion that religion consists in outward observances and not *in heart and life.*

III. THESE HINDRANCES MAY BE REMOVED. Here is consolation for great sinners—and who are small ones? When a man is deeply convinced of sin he is often tempted to despair. Can I, the unclean, the immoral, the foul-mouthed, the foul-hearted, enter into the kingdom of ineffable holiness? It seems impossible. But after detailing some of the vilest acts of which humanity can be guilty, the apostle turns upon the Corinthians and says, "And such were some of you." Of greatest sinners God has sometimes made greatest saints. If the heart be contrite, there is no cause for the abandonment of hope. The barriers which are insuperable to man can be cast down by the might of God. In our sin we need look to God, for none besides can aid us. Our sickness is beyond all skill save that of the great Physician.

IV. THE MANNER OF REMOVAL. The apostle speaks of " washing "—the great need of the defiled—and then directs attention to its twofold character. That the impure may enter into the all-pure kingdom of God, two things are necessary. 1. *Justification* —which we receive through Christ (ver. 11). He took our place; he bore our sins; he made atonement for us. Our sins are imputed to him; his righteousness is imputed to us. Through him God can be just and yet the Justifier of the ungodly. " With his stripes we are healed; " " The blood of Jesus Christ his Son cleanseth us from all sin " (1 John i. 7); he is able to save " to the uttermost; " " Though your sins be as scarlet, they shall be as white as snow " (Isa. i. 18). 2. *Sanctification*—which we receive through the operation of " the Spirit of our God " (ver. 11), the Holy Ghost. Justification is that which is done *for* us; sanctification is that which is done *in* us. Yet one is not without the other. By the Divine Spirit we become " born again," " born of the Spirit," made pure inwardly; our affections purged, our desires corrected, our spiritual being controlled and purified (see John iii. 3).

V. A CAUTION IMPLIED. "And such *were* some of you." Are ye becoming so again? We need beware of " going back " to those things which once barred our access to the kingdom of God, and which will do so again if indulged in. Our great inheritance may be lost after all! It will be, unless we " endure to the end." How earnest, anxious, prayerful, watchful should we be lest we " come short "! There is One who is " able to keep us from falling " (Jude 24). " Cleave unto the Lord your God " (Josh. xxiii. 8).—H.

Ver. 12.—*The lawful and the expedient.* I. IT IS IMPORTANT TO ASCERTAIN WHAT IS LAWFUL FOR US IN LIFE. All things indifferent (*i.e.* not evil in themselves) are lawful for the Christian. He has the widest liberty. He is not under the restriction of the older economy. To him " every creature of God is good " (1 Tim. iv. 4), and to be received with thanksgiving. The Christian must abide within the limits of the lawful. Nothing that seems expedient *outside* of the lawful must be touched by him. He is under the rule of righteousness, and must not allow himself in aught that is unright-eous. Note: Nothing is *really expedient* outside of the limits of the lawful, but many things *may appear to be so.*

II. BUT ANOTHER QUESTION HAS TO BE ANSWERED BEFORE CONDUCT CAN BE DETERMINED, VIZ.—WHAT IS EXPEDIENT WITHIN THE LIMITS OF THE LAWFUL? The Christian must not use his liberty *indiscriminately;* he must consider probable results. The end does not justify the means, but the end often determines whether means (justifiable in themselves) shall be used or not. Means, good enough in themselves, may under certain conditions lead to most undesirable ends; those ends foreseen determine for the believer that those means shall not be employed. *The Christian has to select the truly expedient out of the truly lawful.* It has been well said, " Unlawful things ruin thousands, lawful things (unlawfully used) ten thousands." And also, " Nowhere does the devil build his little chapels more cunningly than right by the side of the temple of Christian liberty." A Christian, before availing himself of his liberty, had need ask such questions as the following:—1. *What will be the effect upon myself?* Shall I be made less spiritual, less useful, less pleasing to God? All that we do we do more or less " unto ourselves." We mould ourselves very largely by what we allow to ourselves. 2. *What will be the effect upon my liberty?* Liberty may commit suicide. Undue indulgence of *liberty* results in *slavery.* Paul was intensely anxious " not to be brought under the power of any;" even lawful, thing. It is of the greatest importance to the moral health and needful freedom of the soul that it should not be in subjection to any appetite or desire, however innocent. 3. *What will be the effect upon my fellows?* Will it aid or hinder them? "No man liveth unto himself." Every man is "a man of influence." Innocent things to us may be by no means innocent things to others. By example we may lead men to destruction, whilst we withal escape. "If meat make my brother to offend, I will eat no flesh while the world standeth" (ch. viii. 13). 4. *How will my conduct appear to God?* Is this that I propose to do, not only good in itself, but *the best thing* for me to do at this time? Whatever the Christian does, he is to do to the glory of God, even in matters of eating and drinking. Can I do *this* to the glory of God? The familiar question, "*Is it wrong* to do this or to go thither?" is often both misleading and utterly irrelevant. The answer to the question may be "No." *Then the fallacious reasoning follows,* "If it is not *wrong,* I may do it without sin." Stop! that is unsound logic. The thing *thoroughly right* may be *unutterably wrong!* "All things are lawful unto me, but all things are not expedient," and the Christian is bound by every obligation to do that which is expedient within the realms of the lawful. He must do *what is best;* to do aught else is to sin. What he *ought to do,* and what he *may do lawfully,* are often two very different things. "Ye are not your own; for ye are bought with a price" (vers. 19, 20).—H.

Vers. 13—19.—*Duties to the body.* Christianity concerns itself about man's body as well as about man's soul. Christianity is a religion for *man*—for a *whole man.* When considering matters of religion, we are apt to leave the body too much out of account. Our remissness might be corrected if we remembered how large an influence the body has upon the mind and soul.

I. CONSIDER WHAT CHRISTIANITY SAYS ABOUT THE BODY. It is: 1. *For the Lord.* (1) For his service and glory. We may serve Christ with our body. We may glorify God with our body (ver. 20). With *our whole being* we should serve the Lord. Our body should be "set apart" for God. How much more useful many would be if they did but cultivate physical health! Their uncared-for bodies become grievous burdens and woeful hindrances. Disorder in the body is contagious, and often spreads to mind and soul. Athletics, rightly ordered, lie within the realm of religion. The man who, not neglecting other duties, seeks to make his body thoroughly strong and vigorous, is more pious, not less. With others, diseases the fruits of old sins, abide and greatly check them in active service for God. (2) The body of the Christian is a member of Christ (ver. 15). Closely united to the great Head. He took our nature—not only our spiritual and mental nature, but our *bodily* nature. We are one with him in our whole being. (3) Purchased by Christ. When he redeemed man he redeemed man in his entirety. Our bodies have a part in "the great salvation." And at what a price was the purchase made! 2. *A temple of the Holy Ghost.* Solemn thought! How true— yet how often forgotten! Whilst in the body, God dwells in us. The body is the outer framework of the sanctuary of the Divine Spirit. It is thus consecrated for a high, holy, and sacred purpose. It is God's possession and dwelling-place, like the temple of old. Thus: 3. *It is not our own. Then we must not deal with it as though it were.* It has been bought by Christ, and should be freely and fully surrendered to him. When we give him our heart we should give him our body also. *Many forget to do this.* 4. *Cared for by God.* "The Lord is for the body." He preserves, feeds, clothes, shelters, guards it. How soon it would perish if uncared for by him! 5. *To be raised.* The resurrection of *the body* is a cardinal doctrine of Christianity, and insisted upon at great length by the apostle in the fifteenth chapter of this Epistle. We are but too apt to ignore this, and practically to conclude that at death we shall part with the body for ever. We think it worthless, but God does not. He will raise it in a glorified form. Its present constitution will be greatly changed, as the apostle intimates in ver. 13. The time will come when the body will not be sustained, as it now is, by meats. It will be a "glorious body" (Phil. iii. 21), a "spiritual body" (ch. xv. 44).

II. THESE TRUTHS RESPECTING THE BODY SHOULD: 1. *Greatly ennoble it in our estimation.* It is not to be thought lightly of or treated with contempt. Ancient philosophy taught hatred of the body, but ancient philosophy is not Christianity. We must not despise the body; this is a dire mistake often perpetrated. The body has a great part to play both here and hereafter. It has been an occasion of sin—often is a burden; but it is in the hands of God, and he will fully redeem and glorify it. It is his workmanship, thrown much out of gear by evil; but he shall rectify its defects, and make it "meet for the inheritance." 2. *Lead us to use it most carefully.* Being precious in God's sight, purchased by Christ, tenanted by the Divine Spirit,—shall we deal with it as though it were a common thing? There is one sin mentioned by the apostle which injures the body grievously, and utterly outrages the Divine intent concerning it. Let us guard carefully against this and kindred evils; *terrible will be the punishment of those who defile the temple of the Holy Ghost, and who prostitute to base uses the "members of Christ."* Pure body, pure mind, pure soul;—may this trinity of blessings be ours !—H.

Vers. 1—8.—*On going to law.* Among other evils at Corinth calling for correction, a litigious spirit had begun to show itself, fostered doubtless by the unpleasant friction of parties. Brother went to law with brother before the heathen tribunals, and the Christian name was thereby brought into ill repute. For this the apostle rebukes them, and assigns weighty reasons why they should settle their disputes otherwise.

I. THE JUDICIAL FUNCTION OF THE SAINTS. All judgment has been committed to Christ (John v. 22), and in the exercise of this function his saints are associated with him. Suffering with him here, they shall reign with him hereafter (2 Tim. ii. 12), a kingdom being given to them (Dan. vii. 22; Matt. xix. 28); and when he comes again he will be accompanied by them in glory (Jude 14, 15). In this capacity they shall judge, not only mankind, but also the angels. Whether the apostle has in view good angels or bad, it is not essential to inquire; the point is that the judicial dignity of the saints is so great that they shall sit in judgment even on angelic beings. How wonderful an honour! Meantime we share in the humiliation of our Lord. The saints are not exalted to the judgment-seats of the earth. They walk here as kings in disguise, unknown by a world that lets itself be governed by the prince of darkness. Even now they exercise a judging influence, their holy lives condemning the ungodly around them; but the full manifestation of their judicial function is reserved for the time when Jesus comes in power. Oh, it will be a bright day for this world when holiness is exalted to the throne and all the evil of earth and hell is summoned to its bar, when the moral confusion meantime prevailing shall give place to the fair order of the reign of righteousness! What manner of persons ought they to be who are appointed to judge the universe of men and angels?

II. THE RIGHT SETTLEMENT OF DISPUTES BETWEEN CHRISTIANS. 1. *Do not take them to a heathen court.* To seek redress from unbelievers is an offence against Christian dignity. If the saints are to judge the world, why go to this same world for judgment? These pagan magistrates shall yet stand at your bar; why demean yourselves by standing at theirs? The question comes, how far this rule is binding upon us. Are we forbidden in every case to go to law with a brother? Looking strictly at the case of a quarrel between two Christians, the spirit of the apostolic rule is certainly of permanent obligation. While our courts of law are free from many of the objectionable features of heathen tribunals, they are not so thoroughly Christian as to justify believers in appealing to them, especially when redress may be had otherwise. And it is as unseemly for brother to sue brother at law as for members of the same family. Paul's appeal to Cæsar cannot be cited against his prohibtion here; for it was not a going to law at his own instance, but an appeal from one court to another where justice was more likely to be done. 2. *Refer them to Christian arbitration.* If the saints are to judge the world and angels, surely they are capable of deciding in matters pertaining to this life. Refer the quarrel to some wise Christian brother possessing the confidence of both parties, and let him judge. Arbitration has much to recommend it, even in matters purely civil; and in the case supposed, it tends to promote brotherly kindness, while securing the ends of equity. This does not warrant any judicial interference of the Church in matters properly belonging to the state. She is not to be "a judge or a divider" in secular affairs (Luke xii 14). It is in disputes arising between her own members that she is to adopt this method of friendly settlement.

III. THE AVOIDANCE OF DISPUTES. If quarrels between Christians arise, let them be settled as directed; but why should they arise? "Why not rather take wrong? why not rather be defrauded?" This is the spirit of our Lord's teaching (Matt. v. 38—40), which goes to the root of the evil. Instead of insisting on your legal pound of flesh, it is better to suffer yourselves to be wronged. This is the sublime unselfishness of Christianity. Unworkable? On this principle Jesus acted (1 Pet. ii. 23), and Paul (ch. iv. 12); and in proportion as it pervades society will wrong-doing cease. There is something higher than mere rights, something diviner than legal justice; it is to "endure griefs, suffering wrongfully," in the spirit of him who won his triumph by the cross. Thus willing to suffer injustice, while careful to do no wrong, disputes will be avoided.—B.

Vers. 9—11.—*Before and after: two pictures.* The apostle reminds them that wrong-doing of every kind excludes from the kingdom of God, and that consequently their quarrels and litigation are bringing them into danger. They are forgetting the meaning of their conversion.

I. OUR ORIGINAL CONDITION. Though this dark picture is meant to represent sinners at Corinth, its general features are universally applicable. 1. *Sin is various, yet one.* The branches are many, but they grow out of the same root. "For out of the heart come forth evil thoughts, murders," etc. (Matt. xv. 19). They are all "works of the flesh" (Gal. v. 19—21), conceived in the heart and brought forth in the life. Some are sins directly against God; some against our neighbour's person, estate, good name; some against ourselves. Let us not excuse ourselves by looking on another's sin, and thanking God we are free from that. In some other form it besets us, and "Whosoever shall keep the whole Law, and yet stumble in one point, he is become guilty of all" (Jas. ii. 10, 11). How awful a thing is sin! Let it work its way, and it will utterly corrupt soul and body, the family and society. Every man has in him by nature the seed whence these fruits of Sodom grow. 2. *The practice of sin excludes from the kingdom of God.* Between such sins and the kingdom there is an absolute contradiction. The kingdom is righteousness (Rom xiv. 17), and these are forms of unrighteousness. Religion and morality, faith and works, creed and conduct, go together. "Regenerate thieves! regenerate libertines! regenerate extortioners! There is a horrible contradiction in the very thought" (F. W. Robertson). Let us guard against deception here. No amount of outward observance can atone for an immoral life. "Without are the dogs" (Rev. xxii. 15).

II. OUR CHANGED CONDITION. At conversion all this is changed. We become new creatures, the old things passing away (2 Cor. v. 17). Three aspects of this change are mentioned. 1. *Washing.* Sin is pollution, and from this we are cleansed by the blood of Jesus (1 John i. 7), "Through the washing of regeneration and renewing of the Holy Ghost" (Titus iii. 5). This is set forth in baptism, and it was a prominent idea in the Old Testament ritual (Exod. xl. 30—32; Ps. li. 7). 2. *Sanctification.* Devoted to sin once, we are now consecrated to God. We are separated from the world and devoted to the service of Christ. 3. *Justification.* The guilt of sin is removed, and we are accepted as righteous in Christ on the ground of what he has done for us. And this many-sided blessing of salvation is procured for us by the Lord Jesus Christ, and applied to us by the Spirit of our God.

Compare these two pictures and: 1. *Ask which of them represents you.* Have you been washed, sanctified, justified? Is there a "but" in your spiritual history, dividing the new from the old? 2. *Learn your indebtedness to saving grace,* and be humble and grateful. 3. *Have done with sin in every form.* It is a return to the condition from which you have been delivered. "Put off the old man with his doings."—B.

Vers. 12—20.—*Abuse of Christian liberty.* It appears that the principle of Christian liberty, "All things are lawful for me," had been greatly abused by some in the Church at Corinth. It was cited in defence of fornication, as well as of eating all kinds of meats. They confounded it with the philosophical maxim that man is the measure for himself; from which they drew the conclusion that the sexual appetite may be gratified in the same indiscriminate way as that of hunger. This pernicious abuse the apostle corrects, first by setting the doctrine of Christian freedom in its true light, and then by presenting a variety of arguments against the sin of fornication.

I. CHRISTIAN LIBERTY, ITS GROUNDS AND LIMITS. "All things are lawful for me." Under the old dispensation there was curtailment of freedom in respect of meats and drinks and days; but this is now removed. In Jesus Christ the believer is restored to dominion over the creatures, all things being put under his feet (Ps. viii. 6; Heb. ii. 7—9). "All things are yours" (ch. iii. 22). The world and its contents exist for the sons of God, to subserve their welfare. But this large freedom has obvious limitations. 1. *The limit of expediency.* Many things in our power may not be for our good, either in themselves or because of special circumstances. This is true of foods, and of many forms of work and pleasure lawful in themselves. Here, too, the good of others comes into view as a limiting consideration. The exercise of my liberty must be tempered by a regard to the welfare of my brother (ch. viii. 13). Apply this to certain forms of amusement, the use of wine, etc. 2. *The limit imposed by the duty of preserving our liberty.* "I will not be brought under the power of any." "Every creature of God is good" (1 Tim. iv. 4), but only when used as a servant. We must not suffer ourselves to be brought into bondage to anything. Music, *e.g.*, is a legitimate and healthful enjoyment, but I must not become its slave.

II. THE SIN OF FORNICATION. 1. *Fornication is not warranted by the analogy of meats.* "Meats for the belly, and the belly for meats." The one has been created for the other. The stomach demands food, and all kinds of food have been made for the stomach; hence it is lawful to eat whatever is good for us. But there is no similar adaptation between the body and sensuality. The one was not made for the other. Again, both the belly and its food belong to a transitory condition of things. Both shall be brought to nought when this present world-age is completed, and the natural body becomes the spiritual body. But the body shall not thus perish; it has an eternal destiny. In both these respects, therefore, the analogy fails; and fornication cannot be defended as a case of nature. 2. *It takes away from Christ that which belongs to him.* The Christian's body is the Lord's. (1) It exists for him, and he for it. The relation is mutual. Christ redeems, sustains, rules, and glorifies the body; the body is subject to him for his service. (2) It is a "member of Christ" (ver. 15). Our bodies are essential parts of ourselves, and as such belong to Christ's body (Eph. v. 30). The same Spirit dwells in him and in us (ver. 17); the life of the Head is the life of the body and its members. How awful the sin of prostituting that which is a member of Christ! 3. *It is inconsistent with the eternal destiny of the body.* The relation of the body to Christ is abiding. He who raised the Lord Jesus from the dead will also quicken our mortal bodies (Rom. viii. 11), raising them to a glorious life in him (comp. ch. xv.). The resurrection of the body tells us that it is not to be treated as a temporary thing, belonging only to this stage of existence. It is not to be destroyed like the belly and meats, but is united to Christ for ever. Fornication, therefore, degrades the body, inasmuch as it is thereby treated as the instrument of a perishable appetite. 4. *It is in its own nature degrading.* The act itself is a union with the vilest characters (ver. 16). Think of the dignity of the Christian's person as a member of Christ, standing in everlasting union with him; and with what holy horror should we regard this sin! [5. *It is peculiarly a sin against the body.* (Ver. 18.) "Drunkenness and gluttony are sins done *in* and *by* the body, and are sins *by abuse of* the body; but they are still without the body—introduced from without, sinful *not* in their *act*, but in their *effect*, which effect it is each man's duty to foresee and avoid. But fornication is the *alienating that body which is the Lord's, and making it a harlot's body*; it is sin *against a man's own body*, in its very nature—against *the verity and nature* of his body; not an *effect on* the body from participation of things without, but a *contradiction of the truth* of the body, wrought *within itself*" (Alford). The awful effects of this sin are frequently written in characters of fire in the physical system. 6. *It is a profanation of the Divine temple.* The body is "a temple of the Holy Ghost" (ver. 19). What was said before of the believer is here said of the body (ch. iii. 16, where see homily). The body is the outer court of the temple, but still a part of it, and therefore holy. Dare we admit unholy feet to tread this court? Dare we profane the sanctuary by devoting it to sacrilegious uses? Will the Spirit of God continue to dwell in a polluted temple? 7. *It contradicts the Divine proprietorship of the body.* Believers are not their own, but the purchased possession of God, bought for himself with precious blood (ver. 20; Acts xx. 28; 1 Pet. i. 18, 19). Our bodies are not our own to do with them as we please. We are God's bondservants, bought for the purpose of serving and glorifying him (1 Pet. ii. 9). How weighty an argument for entire devotion to God's service! Love to our redeeming God is the only sufficient motive for a holy life. "Glorify God *therefore* in your body."

LEARN: 1. The sacredness of the body. 2. The extent of sanctification—it reaches to the utmost circumference of our being (1 Thess. v. 23). 3. *Flee* fornication. Victory here is to be won by flight, not by fight (Gen. xxxix. 12). 4. Watch against everything that might lead to this sin.—B.

Ver. 12.—*Free, and yet not free.* The first step to a right understanding of this passage is to observe that the "all things" of which the apostle speaks are things in themselves indifferent (ἀδιάφορα), not things in which any vital principle of morality or point of Christian doctrine is involved. Nothing could be "lawful" to him that was in its essential nature unlawful. There are matters in which the question of right and wrong is fixed, absolute, changeless; and there are others in which it is variable, conditional, determined by circumstances. It is of the latter that he speaks. He is consciously raised above the bondage of mere conventional or traditionary distinctions of clean and unclean, sacred and common, etc. A man is free from the restraint of external law when he has the spirit of it in his heart. All things are lawful to him when the governing principle of his life is that "love which is the fulfilling" of all holy law. The singularity of this declaration is that, while the apostle asserts his freedom, he at the same time surrenders it. He asserts it by voluntarily submitting to that which seems to be a denial of it. There is something paradoxical in this. But are we not familiar with many similar paradoxes? External nature is a marvellous combination of what seem to be conflicting elements—laws that limit, forces that balance each other, processes that run in opposite directions. What a strange commingling is there in the world around us of beauty and deformity, economy and waste, order and disorder, life and death! Divine providence presents the same characteristics. The wheels of the great providential plan move in different, often contradictory, directions; but the sovereign Spirit that controls and guides them develops from them one grand result. What is every man's daily history, in the common relationships of life, but a perpetual working and counterworking of what seem to be incongruous principles? He loses that he may win, serves that he may rule, stoops to conquer, sacrifices liberty in one direction that he may secure it in another, denies himself to please himself, suffers that he may enjoy, dies that he may live. No wonder there should be a similar balancing and limiting of seemingly discordant principles in the sphere of Christian doctrine and Christian life. Two views of personal freedom are here given.

I. FREEDOM LIMITED BY THE THOUGHT OF MORAL ADVANTAGE. That is in the highest sense "expedient" which is morally right and good. A thing may be "lawful" and yet, considering all the conditions of the case, not desirable, because unprofitable. Legitimate enough in itself, it may have bearings and involve consequences that are neither right nor good. In such a case a man of fine Christian sensibility will feel that, while perfectly free in one sense, in another sense he is not free. His conscience and the sympathies and affections of his religious life will restrain his use of that freedom. There is something dearer to a noble soul than even liberty. The thought of the higher profitableness of a thing should be more to us than the thought of its abstract lawfulness. Freedom is not in itself an end, but the means to an end above and beyond itself. To seek after "whatsoever things are true, honest, just," etc., even though it may involve us in many penalties, is better than to be always jealously maintaining our exemption from the bonds of external restraint. One of the finest examples of this principle is supplied by our Lord's payment of the temple tax (Matt. xvii. 24—27). Though "the children were free," yet, lest there should be "offence," he will pay the claim and work a miracle to provide the means of payment. The Sonship that relaxed one law only made the other the more sacred and binding. The apostolic Epistles are full of illustrations of the same principle (ch. ix. 14, 15, 19—22; Gal. v. 13; 1 Pet. ii. 16). Never are we so loftily conscious of our Christian freedom, and never is that freedom so manifest, as when, for some high end, we choose to forego it.

> "A life of self-renouncing love
> Is a life of liberty."

II. FREEDOM CONTROLLED BY THE CONSCIOUSNESS OF MORAL POWER. "I will not," etc. This is self-assertion of the right order; the manly use of the power by which it is given us to determine our own course, and not allow it to be left at the mercy of outward influences, or to be determined for us by the persuasive force that happens to be the strongest. As a mere act of self-discipline, this is good; for the will, like any other faculty, grows by use, and self-mastery by the power of a resolute will is the basis of all moral excellence. Think what differences there are among men in this respect. The secret of success or failure in the lower interests of human life lies mainly here. It depends far less on native talent, favourable circumstances, etc., than it does on the energy of a self-regulating will. This power is necessary to give due effect to any other power. Many a man has noble qualities both of mind and heart—quick intelligence, wise judgment, warm enthusiasm—but lacks the steadfast will that would bind them all together, giving unity and strength to his character and effective force to his endeavour. According, however, to the greatness and strength of this faculty, so is the danger of its being misdirected—like the forces of nature, water, steam, electricity, etc. Self-will is blind, lawless, immoral, and therefore not really free. Moral freedom lies in the mastery of a will that determines for the right, chooses to move in harmony with the Divine will, the "will that is holy and just and good." Learn chiefly two grand lessons. 1. That things lawful and innocent in themselves may become evil by being allowed to gain an undue mastery over us. 2. That our only effectual preservative against this is the resistive energy of a will inspired by the Spirit of the well-beloved Son.—W.

Ver. 19.—*Divine ownership.* One of the most elementary principles of Christian thought and life is expressed in these words: "Ye are not your own." The sense of Divine ownership rather than self-ownership is the inspiration of all Christian dignity and strength. Consider—

I. THE NATURE AND GROUNDS OF THIS PERSUASION. There is a sense in which it is true of all men that they are not their own. It is a necessary inference from the fact that they are created and dependent beings. But more than this is meant here. As a mere truth of natural religion, it is lifeless and profitless. As in so many other cases, it must be elevated to the level of a Christian doctrine, linked with, set in the light of, the great facts that belong to the "record God has given us of his Son," before there can be any efficacious force in it. As a reality of Christian life, then, this Divine ownership rests on two distinct grounds. 1. *Purchase.* "Ye were bought with a price." The apostle refers to a historic fact of the past, viz. the personal self-surrender and sacrifice of Jesus, the Son of God, for the redemption of men. This, with all that it involved of obedience, humiliation, and suffering even unto death, was the "price" that bought us. We may differ in our abstract ideas as to the nature of the atonement, but this *fact* is to the Christian mind indisputable. "The Son of man came to give his life a ransom for many" (Matt. xx. 28); "Christ hath redeemed us from the curse," etc. (Gal. iii. 13); "Redeemed with the precious blood of Christ," etc. (1 Pet. i. 19). Like the noble Roman youth who, as tradition tells, leaped full-armed into the yawning chasm because the city could only be saved by the sacrifice of her best treasure, so did Jesus, the "well-beloved" of heaven, the noblest treasure of earth, the "only-begotten of the Father," the Head and Chief of our humanity, yield up his life to redeem the life of the world. He gave himself for us. "He suffered, the just for the unjust, that he might bring us unto God." Not that there was any essential moral efficacy in the mere fact of suffering, but that that suffering was the measure of our value in the sight of infinite and eternal Love. Pure love invests its object with a value in comparison with which all that belongs to itself is as nothing. The heart in which it dwells finds its deepest satisfaction in the joy of another. Saving another, itself it "cannot save." All tender human relationships are meant to develop in us this Divine sensibility. How spontaneously does all the thought and care and passion of the mother's soul, the deep exhaustless wealth of her being, flow out towards her child! She loses herself to find a dearer self in him. How instinctively, at any risk, does she shield him from danger! With what sublime self-forgetfulness does she surrender her own ease and comfort, to toil through the livelong day, and watch through the weary night, and let her very life ebb slowly and silently away, that she may find a deeper joy, a better life, in nourishing and saving his! So has it been with Christ's more than human, more than mother's love. "Herein is love," etc. (1 John iv. 10). It is the memory and consciousness of this, and all that it means, that produces in us a profound impression that we are "not our own." Of all the forces that move the spirit to grateful self-surrender, none so mighty as this sense of personal obligation to redeeming love. "The love of Christ constraineth us," etc. (2 Cor. v. 14).

> "Love so amazing, so Divine,
> Demands my soul, my life, my all."

2. *Possession.* "Your body is a temple of the Holy Ghost." The context requires that we give to this a strictly individual application. It is spoken here, not of the Church as the Body of Christ, "the fulness of him that filleth all in all," but of the physical personality of each individual member of that body. And it is spoken of as a simple, unquestionable element of Christian knowledge and consciousness. "What, know ye not," etc.? The heathen have had their ideas of Divine "possession;" but their possession has been exceptional, transitory, fictitious, the device of priestcraft, the wild dream of mystic superstition. Here the Divine possession is real, reasonable, permanent, fruitful of blessed issues. If we could only realize it more, not with anything like the wildness of a dangerous fanaticism, but with the calm quiet dignity of a spirit that is consciously walking in the light of God, what strength and beauty it would give to our life! Imagine the awful sanctity with which the temple of old must have been invested to the view of the worshipping people as soon as the heaven-kindled fire came down, and "the glory of the Lord had filled the house." With what higher sanctity still should we clothe the being of a man in whom the Holy Spirit dwells! Shall not "Holiness unto the Lord" be the acknowledged, manifest, and all-pervading law of his life?

II. THE PRACTICAL RESULTS OF IT. "Glorify God therefore in your body." This is something more than a mere passive, negative abstinence from evil. It is the consecration of the powers of our nature to all holy service, the active expression of the inner Divine life in all possible forms of well-doing. It implies: 1. *Conscious spiritual freedom.* Christ delivers us from all kinds of degrading moral bondage when he thus redeems us and makes us his own for ever. And "where the Spirit of the Lord is, there is liberty." Spiritual freedom lies in willing personal subjection to him who is our rightful Lord. Self-hood in all its forms and phases is the slavery, the paralysis, and death of the soul. Live in and for yourself, as if you were "your own," and you have a very hard and oppressive taskmaster. Live unto the Lord, and you are most truly and joyously free. 2. *The mastery of the spiritual over the fleshly part of us.* The apostle has in view a special and most important aspect of the sanctity of the body. But we may take this word "body" as symbolizing the whole form and fashion and habit of the outward life. From the inner shrine of a spirit that has thus become the Lord's, the glory will stream forth through all channels of self-revelation. The very outskirts of our being, the very lowest part of our nature, will be sure to be lighted up, spiritualized, beautified by it. We are apt to think of the body as being necessarily the encumbrance and the foe of the spirit. This is not a Christian way of thinking. Rather let us regard it as an instrument that God has wisely constructed, "fearfully and wonderfully made," and through which the holy energy of the spirit may serve his purposes and do him honour.—W.

Ver. 11.—*Great sinners saved.* It has been alleged that the early Christians were gathered from the mere rabble and offscourings of the ancient world. Gibbon remarks, with his usual sneer, that "the missionaries of the gospel, after the example of their Divine Master, disdained not the society of men, and especially of women, oppressed by the consciousness and very often by the effects of their vices." But it is not the fact, and it is not fair to insinuate, that the Church was formed from the mire of society. The gospel then, as now, influenced in some measure all ranks of society, all orders of mind, and all grades of moral culture. Yet it is not to be concealed, and indeed it is to the credit of the gospel, that it brought newness of heart and life to some of the most profligate inhabitants of the ancient cities where it was preached. Not only in Judæa had it saved the very harlots; but in the licentious cities of the heathen, as Ephesus, Corinth, and Rome, it had rescued persons who were steeped in sensual vice. "Such were some of you," writes the apostle to the members of "the Church of God at Corinth." He had put down a terrible catalogue of sinners, who were not to inherit the kingdom of God. "Such were some of you; but you are so no longer: I recognize the mighty change."

I. THE THREEFOLD CHANGE. 1. "*Ye were washed.*" "Ye washed yourselves." A definite fact, as much so as the washing of Naaman in the river which took away his leprosy. Such is the way of Divine grace. The thought of man's heart is that his sins may be rubbed out, or the traces worn out by lapse of time, or that by repentance and amendment of life they are atoned for. But nothing removes sin except washing. "The blood of Jesus Christ cleanses us from all sin." 2. "*Ye were sanctified.*" After the washing comes the anointing with holy oil. They who are cleansed are consecrated and set apart for Divine use. This is sanctification of the Spirit, which is imparted freely and at once to those who receive the gospel, though it is only gradually realized in experience and practice. 3. "*Ye were justified.*" Being defiled, ye were cleansed; being profane, ye were hallowed; and being unrighteous, ye were justified. You are no longer under condemnation, but being regarded as "in Christ," you are reckoned righteous in him. And this too is an accomplished fact in God's grace. Know it well, for it is the charter of your acceptance, and the warrant of your peace.

II. THE PHILOSOPHY OF THIS CHANGE. 1. "*In the Name of the Lord Jesus Christ.*" Warnings of the consequences of vice, expositions of the beauty and advantage of virtue, can do little in such cases as are indicated here. It was not for want of sages to sound the praise and discuss the nature of virtue that the Greeks of Corinth had been so vicious. But no change was wrought upon them till the Name of the Lord Jesus Christ was published. Here was not a sage turning fine sentences, but a Saviour who could save men from themselves, and make them sons of God. In this Name it was, and to this day it is, that the soiled are washed, the unholy sanctified, the guilty justified. 2. "*And by the Spirit of our God.*" For it is that Spirit who convinces men of their sins, and who brings and unites them to the Saviour, in whom they are made new creatures. What condescension in that pure and Holy Spirit, to come near to such vile persons as the previous verse describes, and transform such sinners into saints!

III. THE LESSONS SUGGESTED. 1. *That no sinner's case is too desperate for the gospel remedy.* Christianity can do more than develop germs of goodness where they exist. It has a new-creating energy, and can inspire good motives and feelings where there seemed to be nothing but evil, evil continually. There is no case so sunk and lost as to baffle the power of Christ's Name and the Holy Spirit's quickening grace. We do not make light of moral gradations. It is a thing to be thankful for, if one has been preserved from gross sin. It is a thing to be bitterly lamented, if one has committed, even in thought, such sins as the apostle enumerates. But the most moral man has something on his heart to be ashamed of before God. And the immoral have grievous confessions to make. Let the shame and grief be felt; they are wholesome for the soul. But let no one despond or despair. The Divine grace which brings salvation is no perquisite of the higher and middle classes of sinners. It goes down through all degrees to the lowest depth of human sin and misery. The Name of the Lord Jesus Christ is a shield for the most unclean. The Spirit of our God can renew those who are dead in trespasses and sins. 2. *That a Christian is to be known by what he is, not what he once was.* Many seem to have no real conception of the transforming power which the Holy Spirit exerts on those who truly receive the gospel; and, accordingly, when one who was known to be a sinner begins to confess the Saviour's Name, many virtuous persons shake their heads suspiciously, and sometimes wag their heads reproachfully, and relate all that they have heard, however vaguely, of such a person's faults, as though they must cleave to him for ever. Thus the old sins are kept hanging as a perpetual reproach over the head of the new recruit to the Christian army, just as though there were no washing possible, no sanctification, no justification. But how unreasonable is this! Is it not from the ranks of sinners that the ranks of the saints have always been filled up? Is there not a significant "*but*" in our text, indicating the transition from the old state to the new? And is it not true in life, as well as in Scripture? You tell me what this person *was*: I bid you see what this person *is*, and glorify God, whose grace works such blessed changes among the children of men. Make not the conversion of a sinner more difficult than it need be, by your suspicions. Reserve your strictest judgments for yourself.—F.

Vers. 1—8.—*The relations of Christians to public law.* The apostle here deals with a fresh mistake made by the Corinthian Christians. In view of the extensive commercial interests of Corinth, we can well understand that disputes constantly arose which could only be settled by the common law courts. St. Paul does not intend us to infer that these law courts were unjustly conducted, or that, in ordinary matters and under ordinary circumstances, recourse may not be had to them. He only points out that the new feeling and sentiment which they should have and cherish, as Christian disciples, would be opposed to the litigious spirit, and fill them with an anxiety to set things right with their brethren rather than to struggle for the securing of their own rights. He glances, further, at the misconception which the surrounding heathen would form of such indications of quarrelling among the Christians. "We can well understand how detrimental to the best interests of Christianity it would be for the Christian communion, founded as it was on principles of unity and love, to be perpetually, through the hasty temper and weakness of individual members, held up to the scorn of the heathen, as a scene of intestine strife." The principle laid down by the apostle led in later times to the appointment of "courts of arbitration." Of these we have historical evidence in the middle of the second century. It has been pointed out that the proper illustration of St. Paul's principle should be sought, not in a Christian country, but in a heathen country where Christians may happen to reside. On his principle, as it may now be applicable to us, we propose to dwell.

I. ST. PAUL THROWS NO SLIGHT ON PUBLIC LAW. How are we to regard law? Is it the arbitrary command of a ruler? Or is it a national code created by the gifts of some legal genius, some Lycurgus or Justinian? Is it not rather a nation discovering the importance of the protection of its persons and property, mutually agreeing to the adoption of rules for the securing of such protection, and putting the applications of such rules into the hands of certain individuals, called kings, judges, or magistrates? So for a people to disobey the laws is more truly rebellion against themselves, against their best interests, than against their rulers; and every individual in a nation is bound both to honour and to keep the law. St. Paul would fully recognize this, and intend no disrespect by what he says concerning it. We should observe that he carefully distinguishes the sphere of law to which he refers. Explain the difference between the "criminal" and "equity" courts at our assizes. St. Paul deals with matters of dispute, with equity questions, not with crime. And he very properly urges that such disputes usually rest on "strong feeling," "misunderstanding," etc., and consequently can be best dealt with from *within* the Christian brotherhood, which can recognize "feeling," and help its members to overcome "faults." Elsewhere he urges full obedience to the "powers that be." But he pleads that the Christians only confessed their failure from the Christian spirit when they could not give way one to the other, but were compelled to get outsiders and heathen to tell them what was just and right. So still we may say there are only a *few things* in respect of which Christians are justified in going to law, and they concern wholly the interpretations of national law in relation to rights of property. For these it is sometimes necessary to get an authoritative decision. Happily, the principle of arbitration is spreading in trade disputes and in national differences. Christians will hail the day when arbitration, the handmaid of *peace*, gains her rule in every land, and men and nations "learn war no more."

II. ST. PAUL ASSUMES THE AUTONOMY (SELF-RULE) OF CHRIST'S CHURCH. He would have them fully understand that, as a Church, they were quite competent to manage their own affairs—all their affairs, and certainly all internal disputes. Show on what frequently declared and comprehensive principles the apostle's argument is based. 1. The Church of Christ is a society. 2. It is a separated society, standing free from the world; *in* it, but not *of* it. 3. It is a complete society; the Head and the members together make up a "whole body." 4. It is a society resting on a common basis, the "life in Christ," not on a common opinion, nor on a common order, but on a common life, which makes it as *one family*. 5. It is a society under a living Head. It endures as "seeing him who is invisible;" and it is a spiritual realization of the "theocracy," or direct practical ruling of the Divine Lord. 6. It is a society with judicial functions. Show that the Church has disciplinary powers which it may bring to bear on the moral offender (as at Corinth); and consultative powers which it may employ to settle family, trade, or society disputes. 7. It is a society with a character, one of whose leading features is "mutual forbearance"—a self-denying regard rather for the welfare of others than for our own. In such a society it would be manifestly inappropriate for any member who had a contention with a fellow-member to "go to law before the unjust." The high Christian feeling finds expression in St. Paul's intense language, "Why do ye not rather take wrong? why do ye not rather suffer yourselves to be defrauded?"—R. T.

Vers. 2, 3.—*The judgment of the saints*. The Christian disciples are called "saints," not because they are actually *holy*, but because they are (1) consecrated to God; (2) separated for the world; (3) under moral obligation to seek for and attain personal holiness. St. Paul here speaks of them as "saints," to remind them that they hold their Christian standing by virtue of their *character*, that their "*goodness*" was to be their power. The word "judge" should be treated as the equivalent of "govern;" it does not, as used by St. Paul here, merely mean "give legal decisions." Illustrate by the work of the judges in ancient Israel; they were virtually rulers of the country.

I. THE SAINTS' JUDGMENT OF THE WORLD. F. W. Robertson says, "Successively have force, hereditary right, talent, wealth, been the aristocracies of the earth. But then, in *that* kingdom to come, goodness shall be the only condition of supremacy." For the idea of our sharing with Christ in the judgment, at his second coming, see Dan. vii. 22; Matt. xix. 28; Luke xxii. 30. It is better, however, to impress the point that the actual presence of good men in the world, in society, is a constant testing and showing up of the evil of the world.

II. THE SAINTS' JUDGMENT OF ANGELS. This must refer to evil angels (comp. 2 Pet. ii. 4; Jude 6). We may, however, treat it as an intense expression of the apostle's, uttered under the deep impress of all that might be involved in the spiritual union of Christ and his people. Christ rules the angels, and so do we, since we are in him. "It is better to regard the passage as a climax arising out of the apostle's intense realization of the unity of Christ and his Church triumphant—a point which seems ever present to the mind of St. Paul when he speaks of the dignity of Christianity. In this sense, redeemed humanity will be superior to, and judges of, the spiritual world."

III. THE SAINTS' JUDGMENT OF EVERYDAY MATTERS. The argument of the apostle is that, if they recognize their high standing and privilege, and the power and responsibility of judging such external things as the "world" and the "angels," they ought also, and much more anxiously, to recognize their power to rule and judge all small matters arising within the Christian fellowship. What must be their condition if they could not find among themselves an efficient arbitrator? Illustrate by our Lord's advice to his disciples in relation to their disputes. (1) The two disputants were to confer together; (2) if that failed to settle the difficulty, then two or three witnesses might be brought into the conference; if that also failed, then (3) the matter was to be told to the Church, and its decision sought. The apostle does but find adaptation for the comprehensive principle which was laid down by Christ, and can be equally adapted by us in the perplexities and misunderstandings of Church and social life.—R. T.

Ver. 9.—*Inheriting the kingdom*. "Know ye not that the unrighteous shall not inherit the kingdom of God?" The phrases "kingdom of heaven," "kingdom of God," are familiar enough to the New Testament reader, as synonyms for the new, the Christian dispensation. The apostles seem to use the term for a kingdom which, they conceive, will be set up at Christ's second coming and the "restitution of all things." There is an important sense in which we are to recognize that the "kingdom" is actually now established; but it need not interfere with our cherishing the high hope of a day when that kingdom shall be fully perfected, and in some glorious way declared to be the kingdom of the world become the kingdom of God. The figure contained in the word "inherit" is taken from Israel's long journey through the deserts to the promised land, which was a country to be "inherited." Under careful limitations, the figure may be carried over into Christianity, and the Christian may be spoken of as "seeking a city which hath foundations, whose builder and maker is God." We are "heirs of salvation," which is "ready to be revealed in the last time." John Bunyan makes his pilgrim talk persuasively to Pliable, and say, "There is an endless kingdom to be inhabited, and everlasting life to be given us, that we may inhabit that kingdom for ever," etc. For gracious moral purposes, for the furtherance of his sanctifying work, God would have us think of the privileges of salvation as both realized now and to be realized more fully by-and-by. This St. Peter states with the utmost plainness in his Epistle (1 Pet. i. 3—6). A present keeping and a present joy are directly associated with the "lively hope" of an "inheritance incorruptible, undefiled, and fading not away." Consider, then—

I. THE POWER OF A PROMISED FUTURE. That is, its bearing on the Christian (1) spirit, (2) character, (3) opinions, (4) conduct. Hope is one of man's most important moral forces; strong according to the reasonable grounds upon which it rests. A man is never lost until he has lost hope. A man can rise up out of the uttermost disability and distress so long as he can imagine a brighter future, and fix his hope on it. Explain the relation in which "faith" stands to "hope," so that it may give us a sense of the present possession of that we hope for. "Faith is the substance of things hoped for, the evidence of things not seen." Also show the influence of hope as: 1. Producing a restful feeling, a contentment with present circumstances. Illustrate from St. Paul, who could say, "I have learned in whatsoever state I am, therewith to be content," but only because he could also say, "There is laid up for me a crown of righteousness." 2. An inspiration to patient and earnest endeavour. Thousands are kept at work by the hope of *success*. The value and strength of the inspiration depend greatly on the character of the hope. How great, then, must be the inspiration of the Christian hope! and how practically purifying, seeing it is the hope of perfect and everlasting *righteousness!* "We shall be like him; for we shall see him as he is."

II. THE INFLUENCE OF A SENSE OF RIGHT TO THE PROMISED FUTURE. That right we have; but it is not of merit or of mere birth, it is wholly by grace, and belongs to our *new* birth through the Spirit. Still, we have a distinct sense of *right*; and that we ought to keep and to cherish, recognizing that varying moods of feeling, or conditions of frame, can in no way affect our standing and our rights. "If we believe not, yet he abideth faithful: he cannot deny himself;" "Fear not, little flock; for it is your Father's good pleasure to give you the kingdom." Illustrate by the influence of the sense of *right* and *possession* which the husband and wife have in each other. Also by the spirit of *noblesse oblige*, which gives tone and character to all the sayings and doings of the young heir. Also by the claim to nobility which the Roman felt was laid on him by his Roman *rights*, in whatever country he might reside. If we have a right of heritage in God's everlasting and holy kingdom, we are under a constant impulsion to "walk worthy of our vocation."—R. T.

Ver. 11.—*Recalling grace received.* We should be always prepared to make direct personal applications of Holy Scripture; and the skill of applying general principles to particular cases is one of the proper results of Christian culture and experience. This, however, often involves accommodation and modification. Principles which Scripture illustrates in particular instances need adaptation when referred to new and different cases; and we should clearly apprehend that Scripture does not propose to provide mere *examples* for a bare imitation, but rather *principles* which are so truly human that they may be applied to the varying conditions and circumstances of every age and clime, so that the sacred Word has really been written "for our sakes, on whom the ends of the world are come." At first sight, the passage now before us does not seem suited to us. The list of sins here given is not ours; it is essentially pagan. We do not even know what some of these words stand for; and to say to us, "Such were some of you," rouses a feeling of indignation and opposition. Yet if we can reach beyond the mere terms to the spirit and principle of the apostle's appeal, we shall find it bears its message also to us. St. Paul is really dealing with what is consistent for a Christian; and he puts it in this way, "What is in true harmony with one who is washed, sanctified, and justified?" We can settle every difficult question by asking—Is the thing befitting a sanctified man? And to realize our Christian standing becomes the best resistance of evil.

I. RECALL YOUR SELF-SEEKING PAST. "Such were some of you." Apply to the Corinthians. Indicate something of the luxury and vice of Corinthian society. For them it was a marvellous change to become pure and sober-minded Christians. We think that we have no such review; most of us have no experience of violent and open forms of ungodliness. But if we look a little deeper, may we not see that those Corinthian sins were but the forms for that age of the universal sin and self-seeking of mankind? They all mean just this—man, asserting his independence of God, throwing off all bondages of authority, and seeking his own will and pleasure. Then we can see that the same root of evil has been in our past; and we must not let the mere refinement of modern terms for sin blind us to the fact that, in us, is the same heart-evil (see Eph. ii. 1—3, 10—12). In the light of this fact of depravity review your past, see the stain of self-seeking, and then you will feel that St. Paul may say even to you, "And such were some of you."

II. ESTIMATE YOUR CHRISTIAN STANDING. "Ye are washed," etc. We need not fear to do this; since it is a standing of *grace*, our so doing need not nourish any pride or self-reliance. Our "standing" is set under three figures. 1. *Washed*; or perhaps the translation should be, "Ye have got yourselves washed." The figure for putting away old sins and sinful habits. 2. *Sanctified*. The figure for having consecrated yourselves; being separated unto holy uses; and we are *sealed* in such consecration, by the gift and abiding presence of the Holy Ghost. 3. *Justified*. The figure for our being, as washed and consecrated, received into gracious relations of acceptance with God. The order of the terms seems to be singular, but, when rightly understood, it is seen to be correct: (1) put away sin; (2) devote yourself to God; (3) receive the sense of acceptance. And this is our present Christian standing; we are *clean, consecrated*, and *accepted*. And all is *through grace*.

III. RENEW YOUR SENSE OF RESPONSIBILITY. For to such a "standing" something is becoming. The apostle wants us so to *feel* this that we should not require any telling. We are under obligation to live such a life as would worthily express our thankfulness for grace received; such a life as would manifestly harmonize with our standing. We are called with a holy calling. But we have to find out what precisely is "holy" and "good" in our times. Everything that is pure, true, self-denying, good, and kind we may be sure is becoming to our Christian standing. Nay, we may come in from all mere general terms, and we may say, "A life for Christ, and a life like Christ's,—these are the 'becoming' for all those who have received his salvation." "What manner of persons ought ye to be in all holy conversation and godliness?"— R. T.

Ver. 11.—*What we were and what we are.* The early Churches were gathered out from corrupt heathenism, and this was sadly sensual and immoral. This occasioned difficulty in dealing with the Churches. The question had to be met—Is moral defilement absolutely incompatible with the Christian profession? Show how this question is answered *now*, in our day, and by the Apostle Paul in his day. Now the answer is sadly uncertain, especially if moral delinquency happens to be joined with riches. By St. Paul it is answered with a noble firmness and fidelity. Take two topics for consideration.

I. OUT OF THE SELF-LIFE. Show that the characteristic of a Christian is his deliverance from the slavery of the self-rule. Then all yieldings to self and passion must, for him, be wrong.

II. INTO THE CHRIST-RULED LIFE. This process is conceived under three forms and by two agents. (1) Washing; (2) sanctifying; (3) justifying. The two agents are (1) the Lord Jesus; (2) the Spirit of our God. Then it follows that an entire yielding to the pure impulses and guidances of God's indwelling Spirit in all the life and all the relationships and all the conduct is for every Christian the right and the necessary thing.—R. T.

Ver. 12.—*The lawful and the expedient.* "All things are lawful for me; but not all things are expedient." This is the statement of a general principle, which may be thus expressed: when a man is renewed in Christ Jesus, he becomes a law unto himself, his regenerate conscience sufficiently attests what is lawful and what is expedient. The apostle is applying the principle to two subjects of discussion which were closely connected with the heathen worship: (1) whether it was lawful for Christians to eat food which had been offered in sacrifice to idols; (2) whether it was permissible to overlook, in Christians, indulgence in the sin of fornication. It seems that, because St. Paul affirmed the right of Christian liberty in relation to the heathen food, his enemies declared that he also held loose notions concerning Christian immoralities. St. Paul, therefore, makes it quite clear that the liberty which he claims is a reasonable liberty, duly toned and tempered by a quickened and sensitive consciousness of what is becoming and what is right. "There is such a thing as becoming the very slave of liberty itself. If we sacrifice the power of choice which is implied in the thought of liberty, we cease to be free; we are brought *under* the power of that which should be *in* our power." "Starting from the doctrine of Christian liberty taught by Christ (John viii. 32, 36), and proclaimed with one mouth by his apostles (Rom. viii. 2; Jas. ii. 12; 1 Pet. ii. 16), they declared that the Christian was bound to a 'service' which was 'perfect freedom.' St. Paul accepts the principle, but with limitations. No actions were *in themselves* unlawful, he was ready to admit, provided (1) that they were in accordance with God's design in creation; (2) that they were calculated to promote the general welfare of mankind; and (3) that we were masters of our actions, not they of us." We here consider the *lawful* and the *expedient*, and we observe that—

I. EVERY MAN MUST RECOGNIZE THIS DISTINCTION. In all the practical relations of life it comes up to view continually; in the home, in the business, and in society, a man has constantly to say, "I may, but I will not. I have an absolute right to do it, yet for others' sakes I must not do it." Observe that the *expedient* is not here the *self-serving* or the *time-serving*. A man's limitations are not, first of all, his own personal interests, but (1) the sense of the fitness of things; and (2) the well-being of others. Illustrate the distinction as applied to such questions as the use of strong drinks; modes of keeping sabbath; limits of permissible amusements, etc.

II. THE DISTINCTION NO MAN FINDS SO SEARCHING AS DOES THE CHRISTIAN. By reason of (1) his sensitiveness to what is in harmony with the Christian profession; and (2) his charitable consideration of even the *weaknesses* of others. He is most jealous of himself, lest he should cast a stumbling-block in his brother's way. The subject can be efficiently illustrated from the details of modern Christian life. And the following passages sufficiently suggest the practical application of the subject:—"Ye are called unto liberty; only use not liberty for an occasion unto the flesh, but by love serve one another;" "Be not conformed to this world, but be ye transformed by the renewing of your mind." Our Lord Jesus could demand absolute liberty; all things were lawful to him, because, his will being wholly right, his choices and preferences and decisions were fully according to God's will. A man must be *right* before we can give him liberty.—R. T.

Ver. 19.—*The temple-body and its sanctity.* The idea of the old temple was not that of the modern church, which is a building in which men may gather to worship God. The old temple was a shrine for Deity to dwell in; and this Divine presence in the central shrine was conceived as hallowing the entire temple buildings, right through to the outer courts and gates. Nothing might enter the precincts that defiled or worked abomination. Illustrate from Solomon's temple, and the extreme jealousy with which the Jews regarded the sacred place. Two points may be dwelt on as working out the figure of the text.

I. THE DEITY IN THE SHRINE SANCTIFIED ALL THE COURTS MAKING UP THE TEMPLE BUILDINGS.

II. THE DEITY IN THE SHRINE SANCTIFIED THE VERY CITY AND LAND. So, if "Christ dwells in our hearts by faith," if our souls know his Divine presence,—then all the forces and powers of our body are consecrated, and ought to be hallowed. Our whole life, in its narrower and in its wider circles of relationship, must be thought of as sanctified, treated as pure, made and kept ever "clean," ever "holy."—R. T.

Ver. 19.—*The Christian has no personal rights.* This assertion may be made both concerning *himself* and concerning the *things* which he is said to possess. Three points claim consideration.

I. THE CHRISTIAN IS NOT HIS OWN. Before conversion he may have so thought of himself. The essence of conversion is a voluntary surrender of will and life to Christ.

II. HE IS A BOUGHT ONE. And he dwells with holy satisfaction on the "precious blood" which was as it were his purchase money (1 Pet. i. 18, 19).

III. HE IS A BOND-SLAVE TO CHRIST. Held indeed by purchase rights, but quite as truly held by the entire and willing surrender of a thankful love. Therefore in all the Christian *is*, in all the Christian *has*, and in all the Christian *can be*, he is under solemn obligation to glorify God, who is his Lord. And the Lord whom he serves, and who holds sole right in him and his, he is permitted to apprehend and recognize as his gracious Master, the glorified "Man Christ Jesus," whose service is perfect freedom and holiest joy.—R. T.

EXPOSITION.

CHAPTER VII.

Vers. 1—40.—*Answers to the inquiries of the Corinthians respecting marriage.*

Vers. 1—11.—*The lawfulness of marriage, and its duties.*

Ver. 1.—Now concerning. This refers to questions of the Corinthians (comp. ch. vii. 25; viii. 1; xii. 1). It is **good for a man not to touch a woman.** The word used is not *agathon*, good, but *kalon*, fair; "an excellent thing." In ver. 26 he limits the word by the clause, "good *for the present necessity.*" There is no limitation here, and it is probable that St. Paul is quoting the actual words of the letter which he had received from Corinth. There had sprung up among them some antinomians, who, perhaps by perverting his own teaching or that of Apollos, had made liberty a cloak of lasciviousness. In indignant reaction against such laxity, others, perhaps, with Essene proclivities, had been led to disparage matrimony as involving an inevitable stain. Gnosticism, and the spirit which led to it, oscillated between the two extremes of asceticism and uncleanness. Both extremes were grounded on the assertion that matter is inherently evil. Ascetic Gnostics, therefore, strove to destroy by severity every carnal impulse; antinomian Gnostics argued that the life of the spirit was so utterly independent of the flesh that what the flesh did was of no consequence. We find the *germs* of Gnostic heresy long before the name appeared. Theoretically, St. Paul inclines to the ascetic view, not in the abstract, but in view of the near advent of Christ, and of the cares, distractions, and even trials which marriage involved in days of struggle and persecution. Yet his wisdom is shown in the cautious moderation with which he expresses himself. The tone of the letter written by Gregory the Great to Augustine with reference to similar inquiries about Saxon converts is very different. The example of St. Paul should have shown the mediæval moralists and even the later Fathers how wrong it is "to give themselves airs of certainty on points where certainty is not to be had." *Not to touch a woman.* St. Paul means generally "not to marry" (comp. Gen. xx. 4 [LXX.]). Celibacy under the then existing conditions of the Christian world is, he admits, in itself an honourable and morally salutary thing, though, for the majority, marriage may be a positive duty. He is not dreaming of the *nominal* marriages of mediæval ascetics, for he assumes and directs that all who marry should live in conjugal union.

Ver. 2.—Nevertheless. In this single word St. Paul practically refutes all the dangerous and unwarrantable inferences drawn by St. Jerome and others from the previous clause. St. Jerome argues: "If it is good for a man not to touch a woman, it must be bad to do so, and therefore celibacy is a holier state than marriage." He also says, "I suspect the goodness of a thing which the greatness of another evil enforces as a lesser evil." Such reasoning shows: 1. The danger of pressing words to the full extent of the logical inferences which may be deduced from them. 2. The errors which always arise from arguing upon isolated texts dissevered from their context, and from all consideration of the circumstances under which they were written. 3. The necessity of following the guidance of the Holy Spirit when he shows, by history and experience, the need for altering precepts with reference to altered conditions. There is in celibacy a moral beauty—it is *kalon ;* there are cases in which it becomes a duty. But in most cases marriage, being no less a duty, as St. Paul proceeds to show, is even fairer and more excellent. Neither state, the wedded or the unwedded, is in itself more holy than the other. Each has its own honour and loveliness, and can only be judged of in connection with surrounding circumstances. Those who make St. Paul judge slightingly of marriage contradict his own express rules and statements (Eph. v. 24, 31, 32; 1 Tim. ii. 15), and make him speak the current heathen language of heathen epicures, who, to the great injury of morals, treated marriage as a disagreeable necessity, which was, if possible, to be avoided. If the " it is a good thing " of St. Paul in ver. 1 were to be taken absolutely, it would have to be corrected (1) by the example of Christ, who beautified with his presence the marriage at Cana (John ii. 1, 2); (2) by the primeval law which said, " It is not good for man to be alone " (Gen. ii. 18); and (3) by the fact that marriage is the chosen analogue of the relation between Christ and his Church. But the very phrase he uses, as will be seen by reference to ch. ix. 15; Matt. xv. 26; Rom. xiv. 21, etc., is a *relative* not an *absolute* one, and St. Paul uses it here concessively, but with the object of pointing out limitations which almost reversed it. To avoid **fornication**; rather, *because of fornication;* i.e. because of the many forms of impurity which were current everywhere, but especially at Corinth. Some have argued that St. Paul takes a " low " and " poor " view of marriage by regarding it only in the light of a remedy against fornication. The answer is : 1. That the reason which he assigns is a true reason in itself, and with reference to the masses of mankind; for which reason it is adopted by our Church in her Marriage Service. 2. He is addressing those who were living in a corrupt and semi-heathen atmosphere. 3. He is not here speaking of the idealized and spiritual aspect of marriage, but only of large practical necessities. When he speaks of marriage as a high Christian mystery (as in 2 Cor. xi. 2; Eph. v. 22—33), he adopts a very different tone. **Let every man have**. A rule, not a mere permission. He here implies the truth that married love bears no analogy whatever to the *vagæ libidines* of those who live like "natural brute beasts." In marriage the sensuous impulse, by being controlled and placed under religious sanctions is refined and puri- fied from a degradation into a sacrament. Instead of being any longer the source of untold curses to mankind, it becomes the condition of their continuance and an element in their peace, because it is then placed under the blessing of God and of his Church. Ver. 3.—**Due benevolence**. An euphe- mistic and needless modification by the copyists of the pure and simple expression of St. Paul, which, as shown by the best manuscripts, is " her due "—*debitum tori.* St. Paul is evidently entering on these subjects, not out of any love for them, but because

all kinds of extreme views—immoral in- difference and over-scrupulous asceticism— had claimed dominance among the Corin- thians. Ver. 4.—**The wife hath not power.** Marriage is not a capricious union, but a holy bond. " They two " become " one flesh." Ver. 5.—**Defraud ye not.** St. Paul pur- posely leaves the expression general. Primarily he is thinking of " the due " or " the power " which each has over the other, as is shown by the next verse; but he does not confine the expression to this. **Except** it be; literally, *unless by chance.* The exception he regards as something possible, but not normal. **For a time.** By this and the next words he disparages, by anticipation, the celibate and separate married lives which, in a corrupt age, were so much and so unwisely admired in the ascetic saints of the Middle Ages. Temporary separation for special reasons had been recognized from the earliest times (Exod. xix. 15; 1 Sam. xxi. 4). **Ye may give yourselves**; rather, *ye may have leisure.* The verb is in the aorist, which shows that the " leisure " contem- plated was for brief periods, not during continuous years. It was altered to the *present* by the officious copyists, who believed in external and mechanical rules of holiness. **To fasting and prayer.** " Fasting " is an asce- tic interpolation, not found in ℵ, A, B, C, D, F. On this interpolation, and perhaps on the analogy of the rule given by Moses at Sinai (Exod. xix. 15), rose the practice of married persons living apart at Lent (Stanley). **Come together again.** The prepossessions of ascetic scribes have again tampered with the text. The true reading is, " *be* together again " (ἦτε), not " *come together* " (συνέρ- χησθε). **For your incontinency;** rather, *because of.* Their past lives and their present temptations were a warning that they could not lay on themselves burdens which God did not require. They should not strive

" . . . to wind themselves too high For sinful man beneath the sky."

Violent, unnatural, self-tormenting, repres- sions beyond what God demands, and adopted without reference to the strength or the circumstances of individual natures, only tend, as all ascetics have confessed, to increase rather than to diminish the force of sensual temptations Ver. 6.—**I speak this.** The " this " applies to his advice in general, but especi- ally to the last verse. **By permission.** This phrase is generally misunderstood. It does not mean that *St. Paul was permitted* though not commanded to give this advice, but that his gentle advice was given " by way of permission" to Christians, not "by way of injunction." He means to say that he leaves the *details* of their lives, whether celibate or married, to their individual consciences, though with large-hearted wisdom and charity he would emancipate them from human and unauthorized restrictions. The clause is not, therefore, a parallel to the restrictions on the authority of his utterances, such as we find in vers. 12, 29, 40, and in 2 Cor. viii. 10; xi. 17.

Ver. 7.—**For I would.** The verb here used is *thelo* (will). In 1 Tim. v. 14 he says, "I prefer (*boulomai*) that the younger women marry." **Even as I myself**; endowed, that is, with the gift of continence, which would (in the expected nearness of Christ's coming) render marriage needless, and the condition of man like that of the angels in heaven, who neither marry nor are given in marriage. **His proper gift.** The "gifts" alluded to are the "graces" (*charismata*) of the Holy Spirit; and the grace of perfect continence does not exist equally in all (Matt. xix. 11). **One after this manner, and another after that.** The remark is general, but also has its special application to continence and marriage (Matt. xix. 12).

Ver. 8.—**To the unmarried**; including widowers. In my 'Life of St. Paul,' i. 75 —82, I have given my reasons for believing that St. Paul was a widower. **It is good for them.** It is an expedient, honourable, and morally "beautiful thing," but, as he so distinctly points out further on, there might be a "better" even to the "good." **Even as I.** In the unmarried state, whether as one who had never married, or, as I infer from various circumstances, as a widower (so too Clemens of Alexandria, Grotius, Luther, Ewald, etc.); see my 'Life of St. Paul,' i. 169). Tertullian and Jerome (both of them biassed witnesses, and with no certain support of tradition) say that St. Paul was never married.

Ver. 9.—**If they cannot contain**; rather, *if they have not continency.* **Let them marry.** In 1 Tim. v. 14 he lays down and justifies the same rule with reference to young widows. **It is better to marry than to burn.** The original tenses give greater force and beauty to this obvious rule of Christian common sense and morality. The "marry" is in the aorist—"to marry once for all," and live in holy married union; the "burn" is in the present—"to be on fire with concupiscence." Marriage once for all is better than continuous lust; the former is permitted, the latter sinful.

Ver. 10.—**And**; rather, *but.* **Unto the married**; to *Christians* who have already married. **I command.** This is an injunction, not a mere permission as in ver. 6. **Not**

I, but the Lord. Because the rule had been laid down by Christ himself (Mark x. 11, 12; Matt. v. 32; xix. 6; Luke xvi. 18). **Let not the wife depart.** By divorce or otherwise. The wife is mentioned, perhaps, because the Christian wife, in the new sense of dignity and sacredness which Christianity had bestowed upon her, might be led to claim this spurious freedom; or perhaps the Christian women of Corinth had been more impressed than their husbands by the Essene notions of purity. The exception of divorce being permissible in case of fornication is assumed (Matt. v. 32; xix. 9).

Ver. 11.—**If she depart.** The reference throughout the verse is to separation due to incompatibility of temper, etc.; not to legal divorce.

Vers. 12—16.—*Directions about mixed marriages.*

Ver. 12.—**To the rest.** That is, to those who are married, but are heathen. They were the remaining class about whose duties the Corinthians had made inquiry. **Not the Lord.** The Lord had made no express reference to such cases, since it had been no part of his mission to lay down minute details which would be duly settled from age to age by the wisdom taught by the Holy Ghost. **She be pleased to dwell with him.** It is assumed that, if she did *not* please, the poor Christian convert would have no protection of his rights; pagan courts would regard conversion as a sufficient reason for breaking off marriages.

Ver. 13.—**Let her not leave him.** The verb is the same as in the clause rendered "let him not *put her away*."

Ver. 14.—**Is sanctified**; literally, *has been sanctified*, the status has been rendered (so to speak) theoretically clean. **By the wife**; literally, *in the wife.* The bond is still holy; its holiness rests *in* the believing wife or husband. The reasoning would remove any scruples which Jewish Christians might derive from Deut. vii. 3, etc. **By the husband**; rather, *in the brother.* The liberty implied by these remarks, contrasting so strongly with the rigid rules laid down in the days of Ezra (Ezra ix.; Neh. ix.) recall the change of dispensation. **Unclean**; *i.e.* not placed in immediate covenant relation to God. **But now are they holy.** This does not necessarily imply that they were baptized as infants, but only that they were hallowed as the fruit of a hallowed union. See the remarkable words of Malachi (ii. 15). "If the root be holy, so are the branches" (Rom. xi. 16).

Ver. 15.—**If the unbelieving depart.** The sense of the word rendered "depart" is rather "wishes to be separated." **Is not under bondage**; literally, *has not been enslaved.* Our Lord assumes one cause alone—unfaithfulness—as adequate for the disruption of the marriage tie; but he was not contemplating, as St. Paul is, the case of *mixed* marriages. **To peace;** rather, *in peace.* Peace is to be the sphere in which the calling comes, and in which it issues. Milton, in his 'Tetrachordon,' quotes Maimonides to the effect that "divorce was permitted by Moses to preserve peace in marriage and quiet in the family." Similarly, a voluntary separation might be the only possible means of preserving moral peace where the union was between souls separated from each other by so vast a gulf as those of a pagan and a Christian.

Ver. 16.—**For what knowest thou, O wife,** etc.? The meaning is as follows:—You may, perhaps, plead that, by refusing to sever the union, the believing partner may convert the unbelieving; but that possibility is too distant and uncertain on which to act. St. Peter does indeed show that so blessed a result is possible ("That, if any obey not the Word, they also may be won . . . by the conversation of the wives," 1 Pet. iii. 1); but he is only speaking of cases in which the unbelieving husband did *not* wish the union to be dissolved. The ancient misinterpretation of the passage (due to neglect of the context and of the argument as a whole) viewed it as an argument *for* mixed marriages, founded on the chance of thereby winning souls. Most misinterpretations of Scripture have done deadly harm; this one, however, has been overruled for good, and led, as Dean Stanley points out, to such happy marriages as that of Clotilde with Clovis, and Bertha with Ethelbert of Kent.

Vers. 17—24.—*Corroborative instances of the duty of remaining in the state wherein each was called.*

Ver. 17.—**But;** literally, *if not.* The phrase introduces a caution. The *rule* is that the circumstances of our lives are regulated by the providence of God, and must not be arbitrarily altered at our own caprice. Christ allotted his portion to each Christian, God hath called each man; that lot and that call are to guide his life. "Quâ positus fueris in statione mane" (Ovid). **Hath distributed;** rather, *apportioned.* **So ordain I in all Churches.** He proceeds to give specific instances to which his rule applies.

Ver. 18.—**Being circumcised.** The first instance he gives is that of Judaism and paganism. The circumcised Jew is to remain circumcised; the uncircumcised Gentile is not to undergo circumcision. **Become uncircumcised.** The Hellenising Jews in the days of the priest Menelaus (1 Macc. i. 15; Josephus, 'Ant.,' xii. 5, 1) had discovered a process for obliterating the appearance of circumcision; such persons were known as

masoochim. St. Paul does not permit the adoption of this course. In the rebellion of Barcocheba many obliterated the sign of circumcision, and were afterwards, at great danger to themselves, recircumcised. ('Yevamoth,' fol. 72, 1). **Let him not be circumcised.** This rule was of much more practical significance than the other. The early fortunes of Christianity had been almost shipwrecked by the attempt of Jewish rigorists to enforce this odious bondage on the Gentiles, and their deliverance from it had been due almost solely to St. Paul. It was his inspired insight which had swayed the decision of the synod at Jerusalem (Acts xv.); and at a later period his Epistle to the Galatians was the manifesto of Gentile emancipation. He proved that after Christ's death "circumcision" (*peritomè*) became to Gentiles a mere physical mutilation (*katatomè*) (Phil. iii. 2).

Ver. 19.—**Circumcision is nothing.** The Jews regarded it as everything; and to make this assertion at so early an epoch of Christian history, required all the courage of St. Paul, and proved his grand originality. He was the first to prove to the Jews that circumcision had become a thing intrinsically indifferent, which might, under some circumstances, be desirable (as in the case of Timothy), but could never be reckoned among essentials. **And uncircumcision is nothing.** The same sentence occurs three times in St. Paul, summing up, as it were, the liberty which it had cost him endless peril and anguish to achieve. Each time he concludes it with a weighty clause to show what *is everything:* "Circumcision is nothing, and uncircumcision is nothing, but *the keeping of the commandments of God*" (ver. 19); ". . . but *faith which worketh by love*" (Gal. v. 6); ". . . but *a new creation*" (Gal. vi. 15). **But the keeping of the commandments.** So St. John says, "Hereby we do know that we know him, if we keep his commandments."

Ver. 20.—**Let every man abide in the same calling,** etc. In accordance with this general principle, which illustrates the distinction between Christianity and violent social revolutions, St. John the Baptist had not bidden publicans or soldiers to abandon their callings, but to do their duty in that state of life to which God had called them (Luke iii. 12—14). The "calling" alluded to is not what is described as "a vocation," a calling in life, but the condition in which we are when we are *called by God* (comp. ch. i. 26; Eph. i. 18; iv. 1).

Ver. 21.—**Being a servant.** This is the second instance of the rule. One who was converted whilst he was a slave is not to strive over-anxiously for freedom. The word "emancipation" sometimes seems (as in the letter to Philemon) to be "trembling on Paul's lips," but he never utters it, because to do so would have been to kindle social revolt, and lead to the total overthrow of Christianity at the very commencement of its career. Our Lord had taught the apostles to adapt means to ends; and the method of Christianity was to inculcate great principles, the acceptance of which involved, with all the certainty of a law, the ultimate regeneration of the world. Christianity came into the world as the dawn, not as the noon—a shining light, which brightened more and more unto the perfect day. **Care not for it.** Do not be troubled by the fact, because in Christ "there is neither bond nor free" (Gal. iii. 28), and because earthly freedom is as nothing in comparison with the freedom which Christ gives (John viii. 36). **But if thou mayest be made free, use it rather.** The words may mean, (1) "use freedom"—avail yourself of the opportunity of emancipation; or (2) "use slavery"—be content to remain a slave. In favour of the first interpretation is the fact that there is nothing extravagant or fantastic in Christian morality; and that, considering what ancient slavery was—how terrible its miseries, how shameful and perilously full of temptations were its conditions—it sounds unnatural to advise a Christian slave to remain a slave when he might gain his freedom. Yet the other interpretation, *remain a slave by preference*, seems to be required: 1. By the strict interpretation of the Greek particles. 2. By the entire context, which turns on the rule that each man should stay in the earthly condition in which he first received God's call. 3. By the fact that even the Stoic moralists—like Epictetus, who was himself a slave—gave similar advice (Epict., 'Dissert.,' iii. 26; 'Enchir.,' x. xxxii.) 4. By the indifference which St. Paul felt and expressed towards mere earthly conditions (Gal. iii. 28), as things of no real significance (Col. iii. 22). 5. By his appeal to the nearness of the day of Christ (vers. 29—31). 6. By the preponderance of high authorities—Chrysostom, Theodoret, Luther, Bengel, De Wette, Meyer, Alford, etc.—in favour of this view. 7. By its parallelism to the advice given to Christian slaves in 1 Tim. vi. 2, where they are urged to serve Christian masters all the more zealously because they were brethren. 8. Lastly, all the apparent harshness of the advice is removed when we remember that St. Paul was probably thinking only of *the Christian slaves of Christian masters*, between whom the relation might be as happy as that of Philemon to the forgiven Onesimus.

Ver. 22.—**Is the Lord's freeman**; rather, *freedman*. Clearly the entire bearing of this verse favours the view which we have

taken of the previous verse. **Christ's servant.** The sharp antithesis of this verse was often present to the mind of the early Christians. They knew that the bondage of Satan was so crushing that mere earthly bondage was, in comparison, as nothing; and that the liberty wherewith Christ has made us free, though it might seem to take the form of service, was the sole perfect freedom. The freedmen of sin are the most hopeless slaves; the servants of God alone are free (see Rom. vi. 22; 2 Tim. ii. 26; 1 Pet. ii. 16).

Ver. 23.—**Ye are bought with a price;** rather, *ye were bought*, namely, by Christ; and the price paid for you was his blood (see ch. vi. 20; 1 Pet. i. 18, 19). **Be not ye**; rather, *become not*. **The servants of men.** There is a grand play of words in the advice to them *not to become slaves*, at the very moment when he is advising them to continue in slavery. In that which the world called "slavery" the Christian slave might enjoy absolute liberty. The price which a master paid for them was but an unmeaning shadow; they had been bought once and eternally by an infinitely nobler price, and that purchase was the pledge of absolute emancipation.

Ver. 24.—**Therein abide with God.** The verse is a summary and reiteration of the advice contained in the whole paragraph. "With God;" literally, *by the side of God*; "as in God's sight;" "doing service as to the Lord;" "for conscience towards God." The words sum up the essence of all apostolic counsels to Christian slaves in Eph. vi. 5—8; 1 Tim. vi. 1, 2; Titus ii. 9, 10; 1 Pet. ii. 18, 19, etc.

Vers. 25—40.—*Advice respecting the unmarried.*

Ver. 25.—**Now concerning virgins.** This is doubtless another reference to questions contained in the letter from Corinth. **No commandment of the Lord.** Christ had never directly dealt with this subject. **I give my judgment.** The word "commandment" is rendered in the Vulgate *consilium*, and the word "judgment" *præceptum;* and thus, as Stanley points out, has originated the modern Romish distinction between "precepts" and "counsels of perfection," which, however, have clearly no connection with the real meaning of the passage. **To be faithful.** As a steward of his Word, which is the first essential of true ministry (1 Tim. i. 12). "Faith makes a true casuist" (Bengel).

Ver. 26.—**I suppose.** St. Paul only states this modestly, and somewhat hesitatingly, as his personal opinion. **For the present distress;** rather, *on account of the pressing necessity;* in the urgent and trying conditions which at the present moment surround the Christian's life, and which were the prophesied "woes of the Messiah" (Matt. xxiv. 3, etc.). **For a man;** rather, *for a person*—whether man or woman. **So to be;** that is, "unmarried." The words are not improbably a quotation from the Corinthian letter. Otherwise we might explain the "so" to mean "*as he is*—whether married or unmarried."

Ver. 27.—**Seek not a wife.** It is entirely alien from St. Paul's purpose to take this as an abstract or universal rule. He gives his reasons for it as a *temporary necessity.*

Ver. 28.—**But and if thou marry, thou hast not sinned.** This advice merely touches on the question of expediency, not on questions of absolute right and wrong. **Such.** Those who marry. **Trouble in the flesh.** Their marriage will in these days necessarily involve much trouble and discomfort. Common experience shows that in days of "trouble and rebuke and blasphemy" the cares and anxieties of those who have to bear the burden of many besides themselves, and those dearer to them than their own selves, are far the most trying. Perhaps St. Paul was thinking of the "Woe unto them that are with child, and to them that give suck in those days," of our Lord (Luke xxi. 23). **But I spare you.** I desire to spare you from adding to the inevitable distress which will fall upon you in "the great tribulation" —"the travail-throes of the Messiah," which we all expect.

Ver. 29.—**But this I say.** I will not dwell on those coming trials, but will only remind you that they are imminent, and that when they come all earthly distinctions will vanish into insignifiance. **The time is** short; literally, *the season has been contracted;* in other words, "The end of all things is at hand" (1 Pet. iv. 7). The word *sunestalmenos* cannot mean "disastrous." The verb is used for "folding up" in Acts v. 6; "Tempus in collecto est" (Tertullian). **It remaineth, that.** The reading and punctuation are here uncertain. The best reading seems to be "The time has been shortened henceforth, in *order that*," etc. The very object of the hastened end is that Christians should sit loose to earthly interests. **As though they had none.** They would thus be nearer to the condition of the "angels in heaven."

Ver. 30.—**They that weep,** etc. Earthly sorrow and joy and wealth are things which are merely transient and unreal when compared with the awful, eternal, permanent realities which we shall all soon have to face.

Ver. 31.—**As not abusing it;** rather, *as not using it to the full*—not draining dry the cup of earthly advantages (comp. ch. ix. 18). Like Gideon's true heroes, we must not fling ourselves down to drink greedily of the river of earthly gifts, but drink them sparingly, and as it were with the palm of the hand. **The fashion of this world passeth away.** So St. John says, "The world passeth away, and the lust thereof" (1 John i. 18). It is but as the shifting scene of a theatre, or as a melting vapour (Jas. iv. 14).

Ver. 32.—**But I would have you without carefulness.** In these words he reverts to ver. 28, after the digression about the transiency of earthly relations. If they were "overcharged . . . with cares of this life," the day of the Lord might easily "come upon them unawares" (Luke xxi. 34).

Ver. 33.—**Careth for the things that are of the world.** St. Paul's language must not be extravagantly pressed. It only applies absolutely to times in which the conditions are the same as they then were. The "anxious cares" which marriage involves may be more innocent and less distracting than those which attack the celibate condition; and when that is the case, marriage, on St. Paul's own principle, becomes a duty. Thus some of the best and greatest of our missionaries have found their usefulness as God's messengers vastly increased by marriage, in spite of the awful trials which marriage often involves. The apostles and brethren of the Lord felt the same. St. Paul's opinions here are, as he tells us, *opinions only*, and admit of many modifications. Advice given to men and women when Christians believed that the Lord was coming, perhaps in that very age, to judge the world, is not universally applicable to all ages. In St. Paul's later Epistles he does not revert to this advice, but assumes that marriage is the normal condition.

Ver. 34.—**There is difference** also, etc. The reading, punctuation, and exact sense are surrounded with uncertainty, which does not, however, affect the general meaning. This is probably given correctly in our English Version. He implies that the married woman must of necessity be more of a Martha than a Mary. Nevertheless, two things are certain : (1) that God intended marriage to be the normal lot; and (2) that marriage is by no means incompatible with the most absolute saintliness. It is probable that most, if not all, of the apostles were married men (ch. ix. 5). The spirit of St. Paul's advice—the avoidance of distraction, and the determination that our duty to God shall not be impaired by earthly relationships —remains eternally significant. Another common way of punctuating the words is, "The married man cares . . . how he may please his wife, *and is divided* [in interests]."

Ver. 35.—**For your own profit.** My advice turns simply on questions of expedience. **Not that I may cast a snare upon** you. He does not wish to " fling a noose" over them to win them over to his own private views, and entangle them in rules which they might not be able to bear. **That which is comely.** Seemliness ; "the *beauty* of holiness" (Rom. xiii. 13). **Without distraction.** The phrases used in this clause make it probable that St. Paul had heard how Martha was "anxious" and distracted (περιεσπᾶτο) about much serving, while Mary sat at Jesus' feet (Luke x. 39—41).

Ver. 36.—**Uncomely.** If any father thinks, by keeping his virgin daughter unmarried, he is acting in a way which may cause sin or scandal, then let him permit her to marry her suitor. The word "uncomeliness" is terribly illustrated in Rom. i. 27. (For "comely," see ch. vii. 25; xii. 24.) **His virgin.** Obviously a daughter or ward. **Pass the flower of** her age. If she be more than twenty years old, which the ancients regarded as the *acme* of the woman's life. **And need so require.** If there be some moral obligation or necessity in the case. **Let them marry.** The "them" means the virgin and her unmarried lover.

Ver. 37.—**Steadfast.** The general meaning of the verse is that the father, who, from high motives, remained unshaken in the resolve to dedicate his daughter (as Philip did) to the virgin life, doeth well, though neither Jews nor pagans thought so. **Having no necessity.** Because the maiden did not wish to marry or was not sought in marriage.

Ver. 38.—**Doeth well.** Because "marriage is honourable in all." **Doeth better.** Obviously not *morally*, because, if one course

be *morally* better than another, we are bound to take it; but "better" with reference to expediency in "the urgent necessity" which rested on the Christian world in that day. It is quite clear that, if these words *are* meant to disparage matrimony in comparison with celibacy, or to treat celibacy in the abstract as a holier state that marriage, they have been set aside by the universal practice and theory of the Christian world. But, as we have seen, they are expressed by St. Paul only as a relative and diffident opinion. It is remarkable that not one word is said as to the choice of the virgin herself in the matter, which is one of the most essential points on which the decision must turn. St. Paul, no doubt, assumes the acquiescence or preference of the maiden as one of the elements in the absence of any "need" for her marriage; but also he writes after lifelong familiarity with the all but absolute control exercised by Jewish parents over their youthful daughters.

Ver. 39.—**Only in the Lord.** The second marriage of the Christian widow *must* be a holy and a Christian marriage (2 Cor. vi. 14).

Ver. 40.—**Happier.** Freer from cares, distractions, and entanglements. **If she so abide.** If she *remain* a widow. **I think also that I have the Spirit of God ;** rather, *I think that I also,* as well as the other teachers who have claimed spiritual authority for the rules they have given you about these subjects. The claim to authoritative decision is obviously less emphatic than it is in ch. xiv. 37; still, it is an expression of personal conviction that he *has* the Spirit, not an implied doubt of the fact.

HOMILETICS.

Vers. 1—14, 25—28, 32—40.—*Paul's conception of marriage.* "Now concerning the things whereof ye wrote unto me," etc. All that Paul here says of marriage is in answer to some communication which the Church had addressed to him on the subject, and what he says he declares is not "of commandment," that is, not by Divine authority, but by "permission." All Scripture is therefore not inspired, even all the counsels of St. Paul do not seem to have been so. So desirous did he seem to be that all he says on this subject should be regarded as coming from himself without any inspiration of God, that he declares it not only in the sixth verse, but also in the twenty-fifth verse, in which he says, "I have no commandment of the Lord." My purpose now is to gather up from all these verses Paul's personal ideas of marriage. His idea seems to be—

I. That marriage is not a DUTY BINDING ON MANKIND. It is not a moral obligation, like "Thou shalt love the Lord thy God," etc. He says, "It is good for a man not to touch a woman" (ver. 1); again, "I would that all men were even as I myself" (ver. 7); and again, "It is good for them if they abide even as I" (ver. 8). In referring to the widow, he says, "She is happier if she so abide, after my judgment : and I think also that I have the Spirit of God" (ver. 40). So Paul seems to teach that the question of marriage is optional, not obligatory. Some may feel that celibacy is best for them, then let them remain single; others think that marriage is the most desirable state, then let them enter into that relationship. Now, it does strike one as something marvellous that this condition of life on which the very continuation of the human race depends should remain thus open and optional. Suppose that to-day every individual of the human race determined not to enter into this relationship, and to have no intercourse with the opposite sex, sixty years hence, at most, the race would be extinct; no man, woman, or child would be found on the earth. The earth would be as it once was, without a man, a school without a student, a theatre without a spectator, a temple without a worshipper. The answer to the question which some may give is this, that there is no reason for a written command on this subject—it is a law of nature. God does not command us to eat and drink, because it is not necessary—the law of our nature urges us to it. For the same reason he does not command us to marry. However, so it is, and it is a wonderful thought that upon the volition of this generation on this question, depends the continuation or non-continuation of the race.

II. That marriage is PRIMARILY FOR SPIRITUAL ENDS. "The unbelieving husband is sanctified," etc. (ver. 14). The view given of the end of marriage in the Marriage Service, viz. the "procreation of children," is evidently not the idea that Paul had, and it is a somewhat degrading one. Paul's idea throughout seems to be that the grand purpose of marriage is mutual spiritual influence, correcting faults, removing unbelief, establishing faith, serving the Lord. Those who enter on this relationship from fleshly impulses and with fleshly ends misunderstand the ordinance and are never truly married. There is not only no union of soul, but an inner division. True marriage means such a mutual spiritual affection as welds two souls into one moral personality.

III. That marriage INVOLVES MUTUAL OBLIGATIONS THE MOST SACRED. 1. *Mutual benevolence.* "Let the husband render unto the wife due benevolence: and likewise also the wife to the husband." Benevolence, a hearty well-wishing, each wishing the well-being of the other. The New Version drops the word "benevolence." 2. *Mutual identification.* "The wife hath not power of her own body, but the husband: and likewise also the husband hath not power of his own body, but the wife." The both are one. The equal rights of wife and husband are everywhere recognized in the Bible. 3. *Mutual honesty.* "Defraud ye not one the other." Deception is inimical to the true union of souls. Nothing cuts united hearts asunder so easily and effectively as artfulness and deception. 4. *Mutual forbearance.* "If any brother have a wife that believeth not, and she be pleased to dwell with him, let him not put her away. And the woman which hath an husband that believeth not, and if he be pleased to dwell with her, let her not leave him" (vers. 12, 13). Should difference of opinion on religious subjects crop up, should the faith of one or the other in religious matters be shaken or wane, forbear, do not separate on that account, for the right may correct the wrong, the believing correct the unbelieving. 5. *Mutual concession of personal freedom.* "But if the unbelieving depart, let him depart. A brother or a sister is not under bondage in such cases: but God hath called us to peace" (ver. 15). If the wife feels it in her conscience to be a duty to leave her husband, he should not coerce her, nor should she employ compulsion, should he feel it his duty to withdraw.

CONCLUSION. Such are roughly and briefly some of Paul's personal opinions on the question of marriage. They seem to be on the whole wise and just. We have made marriage a civil contract, and we bind two persons together for life who never possessed those mutual affinities which are the essence of marriage. The essence of marriage is this—the strongest mutual sympathies and aims that one being can have for another ; the bond of marriage is the solemn mutual pledge. Those who are thus married are united by a cord stronger than adamant, finer than the finest web, too weak to fetter, yet too strong to break.

Vers. 15—24.—*Abide in Christliness, whatever the condition in life.* "But if the unbelieving depart, let him depart," etc. As St. Paul seems desirous that most of his utterances in this chapter should not be regarded as the language of inspiration, but rather that of his own private judgment (for twice he gives the assurance), we may be justified in criticizing his opinions. His opinions here refer to three conditions in man's existence on earth : matrimonial life, ecclesiastical connection, and domestic slavery ; and concerning each of these, he says, "Let every man abide in the same calling wherein he was called." Now, if by "calling" here he means that condition of life in which we find ourselves, *irrespective* of our choice, or into which we have entered by *depraved* choice, I can scarcely think that his principle here can be accepted. Apply it for example to—

I. MATRIMONIAL LIFE. If two persons have entered into this, of all relationships the most solemn, whose temperaments, beliefs, tendencies, tastes, and habits are soon found to be so antipathetic as to produce nothing but constant quarrellings and mutual miseries, are they to "abide" in that state? If Paul means this, we cannot accept his counsel, for such unions are not marriages at all. But he does not mean that, for in the fifteenth and other verses of this chapter he seems to authorize a separation. "But if the unbelieving depart, let him depart. A brother or a sister is not under bondage in such cases." Chain two vessels together on the ocean, allowing them to be some yards or even feet apart, and in the storm they will soon tear themselves to pieces and go down into the depths. But if you so rivet them together that the twain will be one, they will be mutual helps, and they will stand the tempest. So in marriage. Unless the two souls are so tightly riveted or clasped together by the strongest mutual affection, it is better to separate. If they are only joined by a chain forged by civil or ecclesiastical law, the speedier that chain is snapped asunder the better for both. Philanthropy is justified in promoting the divorce of such, and in this age methinks, it will find plenty of this merciful work to do.

II. ECCLESIASTICAL CONNECTION. "Is any man called being circumcised? let him not become uncircumcised. Is any called in uncircumcision? let him not be circumcised." Does Paul mean by this—If you find yourself in an ecclesiastical system which has worthless or pernicious rites and ceremonies, abide in it, make no effort to abolish the unspiritual institutions? If you are in a Church which exalts ceremonies and creeds, works for money and by money, and thus misrepresents the sublime genius of the gospel, continue where you are? If he does, we cannot accept his advice. But he does not mean this, for it is opposed, not only to his own teaching, but to his own religious life.

III. DOMESTIC SLAVERY. "Art thou called being a servant [slave]?" Does Paul mean—If you find yourself the legal property of another, and treated by your master as mere goods and chattels, make no effort to break your bonds and to win your freedom? If he meant this, we repudiate his doctrine; it strikes against those aspirations for liberty, which are as deep as the human soul and as wide as humanity. But he does not mean this, as the history of his life and the genius of his teaching show. What, then, does he mean? The principle, "Let every man abide in the same calling wherein he was called," he here lays down in connection with these three things— matrimonial life, ecclesiastical connection, and domestic slavery. And if he means by "calling," condition of life, it cannot apply to either. But by "calling" Paul does not mean this. "'Calling' here must not be regarded in the modern sense of profession or condition of life; it is nowhere so used in the New Testament, but always signifies God calling to us (see Rom. xi. 29; Eph. i. 18). Continue to be Christians of the kind which God's call to Christianity made you. If you were circumcised, and so God's call into the Christian Church made you a circumcised Christian, continue so; don't do anything which would seem to imply that some other change in addition to your call was necessary to complete your admission to the Church." Understanding the "calling" here, as I do, to be personal religion, or Christliness, which is elsewhere called the "heavenly calling," Paul's advice to abide in that state, in whatever relationship or condition we are found, is intelligible and right. In relation to *matrimony*, it will then mean this—Though you feel your conjugal relation to be such a bondage and misery that you break away from it, sever your connection with your partner, don't fail to "abide in your calling" or in your religion. Whatever your domestic grievances and storms and separations, hold fast to your religion. Though you lose your wife or your husband, hold fast your religion, your "calling." In relation to *ecclesiastical connections*, it will mean this—Whether you are "circumcised" or uncircumcised, whether you continue in your old Church connections or break away from them, "abide in your calling," your religion; that is something that is independent of all ecclesiastical institutions and ceremonies, can live with or without them. In relation to *domestic slavery*, it will mean this—Whether you are satisfied with your bondage, and settle down in it, or struggle to break your fetters and rise into full freedom, "abide in your calling," your religion. Personal Christianity may exist in all conditions of life; it is independent of family relations, independent of ecclesiastical institutions, independent of social distinctions, whether slave or master, rich or poor, and where it exists it should be retained amidst all changes and at all costs. "Abide in your calling."

Vers. 22—24.—*Personal Christianity for the bond and the free.* "For he that is called in the Lord, being a servant, is the Lord's freeman: likewise also he that is called, being free, is Christ's servant. Ye are bought with a price; be not ye the servants of men. Brethren, let every man, wherein he is called, therein abide with God." Although the remarks in our previous sketch include these three verses, there is sufficient meaning in them to justify, if not to require, a separate notice. Understanding, as before intimated, the expression, "called in the Lord," and again, "abide with God," to mean *personal Christianity*, the verses include three general truths.

I. That personal Christianity may be possessed BY THOSE IN SLAVERY AS WELL AS BY THOSE IN FREEDOM. "For he that is called in the Lord, being a servant [a slave], is the Lord's freeman." Slavery under the Greek and Roman governments was an established institution. In Corinth slaves abounded. Many of these had been converted by the gospel, and were in connection with the Corinthian Church. Naturally enough, some would desire their emancipation, and the more so as Christianity gave them a sublime sense of their manhood. Paul's advice is not to be too anxious on the subject of their enfranchisement, but rather to be anxious to "abide" in their "calling," their religion. Christianity is for man as man, not for him as rich or poor, erudite or rude, bond or free, but for him as a man; it comes to him as outward nature comes to him, with equal freeness and fitness for all. The physical, civil, or ecclesiastical condition of a man, therefore, in this life is no excuse for his not becoming a Christian: though bound in chains, his soul is free—free to think, to resolve, to worship, and it is with the soul that Christianity has to do. Hence religion in slavery is not an uncommon fact. Slaves were members of many of the first Churches, and religion reigned amongst a large number of those who were held in bondage in the Southern States of America.

II. That the possession of personal Christianity, whether by the bond or the free, INVESTS MAN WITH THE HIGHEST LIBERTY. He is the "Lord's freeman," whoever he is; the Lord has emancipated his soul, however firmly manacled his bodily limbs. All the inner chains that bound his soul, to mere earthly influence, fleshly pleasures, and sinful pursuits, are snapped asunder, and he revels in the liberty wherewith "Christ makes his people free." What freedom like this freedom from the dominion and consequences of moral wrong? This is the "glorious liberty of the children of God."

> "He is the freeman whom the truth makes free,
> And all are slaves besides."

III. That the possession of the highest liberty LESSENS NO MAN'S MIGHTY OBLIGATION TO SERVE CHRIST. "Ye are bought with a price; be not ye the servants of men." All creatures are the property of the Creator. No creature owns itself. The highest angel has nothing in him that he can call his own. Man is not merely the property of God on the ground of creatureship, but on the ground of Christ's interposition. "Ye are not your own: ye are bought with a price: therefore glorify God in your body, and in your spirit, which are God's." This being the case, however free and independent of men, you must ever be the servant of Christ; serve him heartily, faithfully, loyally, and for ever. His service is perfect freedom, his service is heaven.

CONCLUSION. See how Christianity is to work out necessary reformations for the world, not by force but by influence, not from without but from within, by working from the centre to the circumference. "There are," says F. W. Robertson, "two mistakes which are often made upon this subject: one is the error of supposing that outward institutions are unnecessary for the formation of character, and the other that of supposing that they are all that is required to form the human soul. If we rightly understand the duty of a Christian man, it is this—to make his brethren free inwardly and outwardly: first inwardly, so that they may become masters of themselves, rulers of their passions, having the power of self-rule and self-control; and then outwardly, so that there may be every power and opportunity of developing the inward life; in the language of the prophet, " to break the rod of oppression, and let the oppressed go free."

> "Who are the free?
> They who have scorn'd the tyrant and his rod,
> And bow'd in worship unto none but God;
> They who have made the conqueror's glory dim,
> Unchain'd in soul though manacled in limb,
> Unwarp'd by prejudice, unawed by wrong,
> Friends to the weak, and fearless of the strong;
> They who could change not with the changing hour,
> The self-same man in peril and in power;
> True to the law of right, as warmly prone
> To grant another's as maintain their own;
> Foes of oppression wheresoe'er it be;—
> These are the proudly free."

HOMILIES BY VARIOUS AUTHORS.

Vers. 1—11.—*Views concerning marriage : the institution in itself and in relation to circumstances, obligations, and duties.* We have seen what a meeting-place Corinth was for the schools of philosophy and Judaism—a sort of metropolitan Coliseum, in which the gladiators of intellect were in unceasing combat. Neither Rome, nor Athens, nor Jerusalem, afforded such a field of contention as this proud and sensual city, where worldly culture and elegance existed side by side with commercial wealth and luxury. Now, we know what occurs when the waters of the Gulf Stream, bearing northward its immense store of heat from the Gulf of Mexico, come in contact off Newfoundland with the Polar currents, and what a vast bank of fog rises from the condensation of warm vapour in a cold atmosphere. This may symbolize what was going on in Corinth at this time. A century before, the world had been agitated by the ideas and schemes of Julius Cæsar, the foremost man of his age, and quite as great a revolutionizer of men's ways of thinking as of political institutions. Imperialism was now in the ascendancy, and the nations were ostensibly a nation—a colossal Rome. But the quickening of thought remained, and this inured to the advantage of Christianity. There was not only external tranquillity, but the precise kind of tranquillity which St. Paul needed ; and, though local disturbances often arose and at times violent commotions, yet the Roman law was his best earthly friend. At Corinth he had taught and preached and founded a Church. For three years he had been absent, and, meantime, what collisions had set in, and, amidst the surging to and fro of opinions and prejudices and enmities, what disorders had been tolerated! Over everything and everywhere was felt the chilly mist, a twilight to some, a midnight to others, a bewildering gloom to all. This, however, was providential. Teachers must remand pupils to themselves. Such a new and singular force as St. Paul was in the world—such pre-eminently as he had shown himself in Corinth by his opposition to the views of Greeks and Jews, and by his uncompromising zeal in behalf of the distinctive tenets of the gospel—must be suffered to do its work independently of his presence and immediate oversight. And we now see in this chapter, more fully than before, what conflicts of intellect and passion were in progress, what strange alienations had transpired, and how far gone many of his disciples were from the path in which he had expected their feet to tread. Had anything escaped this billowy sweep of strife? It was even dashing against the institution of marriage, which men had agreed to honour as the most important and the most venerable of earthly interests. Incest had been tolerated in the Church, and St. Paul had found it necessary to argue on the highest religious ground against the sensual evils of fornication. Of late we have heard much concerning a scientific basis of morality. If, however, we follow St. Paul, who never contradicts history, we see that even enlightened instincts cannot be trusted when withdrawn from the guidance and support of the Holy Spirit. Men may theorize as they please. One thing, nevertheless, is certain, and that one thing is, that whenever practical men deal with social questions, they accept St. Paul as the thinker of humanity. Even instincts need

God to control them. Proceeding to discuss the questions submitted to him by the Corinthians, he begins this chapter by considering marriage in that aspect which was under debate just then at Corinth. Marriage in the abstract is only in view so far as recurrence is necessary, in the conduct of the argument, to the fundamental principles inseparable from the relation. He treats it, in view of existing circumstances, as a matter to be decided by expediency, each one judging what is best. Whether the unmarried shall be married or not must be determined by themselves in the light of their personal organization, and by the indications of Providence and the Spirit. Freedom within the bounds of law is freedom to deny the use of lawful rights and privileges—so St. Paul had just argued—and marriage comes under this provision. But here as everywhere, "let every man be fully persuaded in his own mind," and so reverential is he in his attitude towards humanity, that in the application of expediency to marriage, he will go no further than offer advice. Under the circumstances, it was the only proper course for him to adopt. No sympathy could he feel with the reaction against marriage in itself, which had set in more than a century before among the Romans, and, while an effect, was also a cause of the widespread demoralization of the age. Doubtless the cares of a family in that troubled period, and the supposed nearness of Christ's advent, had their influence on his mind, and yet he is well aware that, in the lowest view of marriage, it was a protection against vice. Too well he knew the evils which were cursing society because of the popular free-thinking on this subject. For five hundred and twenty years not a divorce had been known in Rome, but we may form some idea of the effect of class wealth and debauching leisure if we recall the facts that in the last days of the republic, Cato of Utica, a religious fanatic in his way, had separated from his wife because a friend wished to marry her and, after his friend's death, had made her his wife again. "On the whole," says Mr. Lecky, "it is probable that the Roman matron was from the earliest period a name of honour; that the beautiful sentence of a jurisconsult of the empire, who defined marriage as a lifelong fellowship of all Divine and human rights, expressed most faithfully the feelings of the people; and that female virtue shone in every age conspicuously in Roman biographies." But a deplorable change had set in, such a change that Augustus had found it necessary to take measures for the encouragement of marriage. Nowhere was this corruption more rife than in Corinth, that only repeated on a larger scale the social enormities daily witnessed at Baiæ, Herculaneum, and Pompeii. Now, in this state of free-thinking, with its attendant wickedness, St. Paul's duty was not without embarrassment. Towards the evil itself and its utter grossness his course was plain enough. On the other hand, there were questions of casuistry to be considered. Marriage as a safeguard of virtue, marriage as a union of hearts, marriage as the highest type of human oneness, marriage in its spiritual import—all involved in it as a Divine institution and as the basis, vitality, security, of all other institutions—this was realized then and always in his apostleship. But there were pure and honest-minded persons among his Corinthian converts, who were troubled by doubts and misgivings, and to whom duty was by no means clear. The instincts of nature had something to say, ond their voice was entitled to a hearing. And, at the same time, prudence and conscience were not to be dogmatically silenced. St. Paul saw what to do, and he did it. He was profoundly sensitive to principles, he was thoroughly sympathetic with persons, and his judgment was the product of a wise consideration of gospel truth and of the facts at Corinth with which he was dealing. There is an ideal view to which he refers in the opening verse of this chapter, but the practical view in contrast with it is that, in order to be guarded against temptation and escape falling into the worst of social sins, "Let every man have his own wife, and let every woman have her own husband." For, as Neander says, "we must not overlook the fact that Paul is here, not treating of marriage in general, but only in its relation to the condition of things at Corinth, where he feared the effect of moral prejudices concerning celibacy." Nor does he hesitate to say, "I would that all men were even as myself," and yet he qualifies this by stating that "every man hath his proper gift of God," a gift of grace, "one after this manner, and another after that; " so that, whether married or single, the "*gift of God*" must be recognized, since, as Bengel remarks, "that which in the natural man is a natural habit, becomes in the saints a gift of grace."—L.

Vers. 12—28.—*Mixed marriages.* "To the rest," those cases in which one party was a believer and the other not (mixed marriages), "speak I, not the Lord." Yet, while St. Paul does not claim to expound and apply a formal law, he must not be considered as abnegating for the time his apostolic office and giving an opinion simply personal. The decision pronounced here is a very weighty one, and obviously it is an utterance of God's will. "If any brother hath a wife that believeth not," what shall he do? That depends on the wife herself. The initiative step is not with the husband: "If she be pleased to dwell with him, let him not put her away." So of the wife with respect to her husband. Obviously, then, personal will is contemplated, and the difference between marriage where both parties are Christians, and marriage where only one party is a Christian, lies in the fact that, in the latter instance (mixed marriages), the continuance of the relationship is contingent on the adaptiveness of the parties each to the other and their ready disposition to be a mutual source of happiness. The will of the Lord is that they keep together, and they should endeavour to fulfil this will, but if controversies exist and the true ends of marriage are not only not met, but cannot be met, then at the option of the wife, the husband may put her away. The converse holds good, so that in the case of either party, individual will may interpose a bar to the continued union. "God hath called us to peace." In such a solemn act, no wilfulness, no passion, no worldly and selfish motives, must have place. "*Peace*," and "peace" only, can warrant the step. And in connection with "*peace*" he presents two views, one antecedent, the other subsequent, to the statement, that "a brother or a sister is not under bondage in such cases." A Christian husband or wife *sanctifies* the marriage tie, and accordingly it was pleasing to God that the relationship should be perpetuated. "I am not the rose," says a Persian proverb, "but I live with the rose, and am therefore sweet." What grace comes to us through the tender associations of life, much of it unconscious, silent and secret, asking no leave, provoking no resistance, floating into us on the air and mingling with our blood, sweetening and purifying we know not how, and all the more precious because our agency is for a while quietly set aside, and the Spirit of the blessed Jesus asserts his Divine supremacy! "Your children," too! The declaration is strong and unequivocal: "They are holy." Age was before the Fall; childhood came after; and childhood had not been possible but for the promise of the "Seed of the woman" antedating her other offspring. "Of such is the kingdom of heaven." Baptism does not create this holiness, but acknowledges its existence, and testifies, on the part of God and on behalf of the Church, that "your children" are in Christ and therefore "holy." What a motive this, that the marriage relation in these "mixed marriages" should be maintained! What an appeal to instinct, to memory and hope, to all the truest and noblest sentiments which are the strength and stay of home! All the grandest influences of Christianity come from the heart of Christ to our hearts; and whenever intellect is perplexed and doubts arise and logic confesses its weakness, we fall back on the great, sure, primal instincts of the heart, and work thence and upward into light and assurance. "Your heart shall live for ever," and because it shall "live for ever," it lives now amidst intellectual conflicts and bewildering questions with an inherent testimony to Christ and his truth such as could only spring from the immovable consciousness of its immortal birthright. Turn now to the subsequent statement contained in the sixteenth verse. Hatred and contentions may arise; if incurable, "peace" must be had by separation. But St. Paul is exceedingly anxious to prevent a severance of the marriage tie, and hence appeals to the believing husband or wife to continue in the holy relationship in view of the possible salvation of the unbelieving partner. By some learned men this interpretation is contested. According to their view, St. Paul meant to express uncertainty, to throw doubt on the sacred utility of the marriage union with regard to its prospective bearing on the salvation of the unbelieving party, and virtually to advise the believer to look after his or her own spiritual interest. This is not like St. Paul. It is not in accord with his generous solicitude to impress upon the parties the sanctity of their union. It is at variance with the declaration that Christianity recognizes the *sanctification* of the unbelieving party by the believing. It conflicts with his statement concerning the "holy" children, or at least abates much of its force as a reason why the marriage should not be disrupted. Congruity must be maintained, and congruity in this instance—so it seems to us—demands that this verse, "What knowest thou," etc., should be construed in close sympathy with the context. A break here would not only be at the expense of the general argument, but a violation of unity at its most essential point, viz. as a *nexus* between what precedes and what follows. Understand what the time was. Outwardly the sceptre of Rome ruled, tranquillity was maintained, and the disturbances which came on some years later scarcely gave a threatening sign of their approach. But, notwithstanding this condition of things, the foundations of society were undermined, and the instincts of men, though unable to foresee the changes that were to occur, were conscious of impending revolutions. Unrest was common, and unrest never appears alone. A host of apprehensions, an undefinable dread, a disposition to exaggerate dangers, never fail to attend it. St. Paul's disciples could not escape this atmospheric feverishness, and consequently one of his solicitudes was to keep them contented with their allotments in life. If Christianity proposed to regenerate human society, one of the conditions on which this vast result rested was: "Let every man abide in the same calling wherein he was called" to be a Christian. Whether circumcised or uncircumcised, let him remain satisfied. Was he a servant? "Care not for it: but if thou mayest be made free, use it rather." Providence that had the past on its side was the best providence for them. "Therein abide with God." Was not this contentment one of the elements of that sanctification in marriage, and one of the means of holiness in children, and again one of the agencies for the furtherance of the Spirit's work in the unbelieving husband or wife? To this one point all the lines of his thought converge, viz. let peace be your object, and, in order to attain it, be contented with your position. Beyond question, St. Paul ardently desired to see certain of these positions changed, but he would not have his disciples to be agitators and revolutionizers. Is this a plea for blind conservatism, for an Oriental lethargy, for an unaspiring and unhoping slavishness to things as they were? Does the argument forestall progress? Nay, at that very moment a mighty revolution was going on in society. Christianity guarded all rights and interests; Christianity protected the marriage institution; Christianity, in due time, would make the slave a freedman. But "My thoughts are not your thoughts, neither are your ways my ways," and Christianity must be left to do its work according to God's method.—L.

Vers. 29—40.—*Apostolic counsels for the times, and general principles applied now as before.* Some minds are so organized as to be peculiarly open to those impressions which the local and circumstantial produce on thought and feeling. If these become excessive, they are almost sure to trench on principles. Such persons are devotees of sectionality; their prudence is shrewd, but not sagacious; intelligence is narrowed down to time, place, and immediate results; and expediency is with them "the previous question." St. Paul was not one of these men. Other minds, fond of abstractions and habituated to cloistered thinking, lose the helps of the senses and especially that very important culture, derived from contact with the open world, which teaches us to adjust principles to measures and measures to occasions. Expediency is seldom in their view. St. Paul was not one of these men. A marked fact about his conversion to Christianity was that he ceased to be an intellectual extremist; not only his opinions and convictions were radically changed, but likewise his method of looking at all things. We see in this chapter a man who adheres firmly to his ideal of the Christian Church, and, at the same time, a man who is thoroughly sensible of the uses of expediency. With him, nothing that Christ had settled could be unsettled. Nothing wrong could be expedient, and, in every case, expediency was to render homage to fundamental principles, so that the Spirit of Christ should manifest its purity and beauty. Such an expediency is always morally safe, because it rests, not on self-gratification, but on self-denial. This is the temper of his argument in the paragraph now under notice. "No commandment of the Lord;" and yet "my judgment" as an apostle is entitled to respect and confidence; the truth none the less a truth, and worthy of this consideration because the utterance of one who had "obtained mercy of the Lord to be faithful." That great transparency was not then glowing as in special hours with the resplendency behind it; but the same Divine illumination was there, and every line, touched by the almighty hand, faithfully represented the original. "Mercy to be faithful;" fidelity to truth just as much in advice and counsel as in direct and authoritative command; ay, this is "mercy" indeed, since it shows the dignity of spiritual intellect, and what importance men should attach to its daily offices in life. "The time is shortened:" here is his starting-point; and this abridged time is applied instantly to a certain state of mind, which St. Paul would have his converts to cultivate with regard to the world and its relations. Future time is not ordinary future time. It has been *narrowed*, in order that you Corinthians and all other believers may have an intenser conception of opportunity, a deeper sense of Christ in time, and so learn to look upon human existence under this aspect of its solemnity. First of all, the domestic relation; this most beautiful, tender, and noble of all earthly relationships, whose spirit refuses to be limited by what its loving arms embrace, and is ever reaching towards a loftier ideal, and even when its arms are paralyzed still symbolizes alike in memory and hope the immortality of affection,—this holy relation must be made holier by the fact, "the time is shortened." If true of this, it is true of all else. Sorrow may be, to some extent, pure and noble, and yet, unawares to ourselves, it may contain a selfish element, and, in the degree this is present, we mourn over ourselves as losers rather than over the object lost. A sorrow truly pure and noble hides its tears from the world, takes up the cross of daily work, feels its loneliness and bears it silently, and toils on with serene patience. To be a Divine discipline—the most purifying and exalting of which we are capable—it must loosen us from earthly things and raise our hearts to God. The death of others, even of our dearest friends, is thus overruled by Providence, as the death in some measure of our pleasure-loving nature. "Perfect through suffering" was said of Christ, and in so far as we realize perfection, it is only attained in this way. Our joy must not engross us so as to impair our lively sense of things spiritual. Business must leave us free for meditation and devout exercises. And in whatever way we use the world, whether the world of home, of culture, of trade and commerce, or of professional activity, it must be used in moderation and with due regard to its moral significance. "The earth hath he given to the children of men," that they may be more than earthly. "All things are yours," that ye may thereby be richer in Christ Jesus. Viewed in this light, it may not be proper to say that these things are "means of grace," but they are helpers and auxiliaries to goodness, and give us no small furtherance in the life Divine. Much, very much, in this world is capable of a most blessed utility. Much of it will live for ever, not in itself, but taken into us and assimilated and glorified. Bodily, how much that is bodily, is ever becoming eternally mental and spiritual! It is the immortal soul, born of God, redeemed by Christ, sanctified by the Holy Ghost, that saves material nature from being a picturesque show and a deceptive sham. Plentifully, indeed, she meets our physical wants, quite as lavishly our wishes, generously too our tastes, and yet, while guaranteeing her economic and intellectual uses with a royal magnificence, she is looking beyond and afar, and her thought is of the blessings that are imperishable. "The body is . . . for the Lord;" and through the pathways of the body, the gates of the senses, the "vaults," the "galleries," and "passage-ways" that physiology assures us exist beneath the grey matter of the upper brain;—through these as highways what vast processions are daily moving heavenwards! Beauty and sublimity have not terminated their offices when they have flashed to the canvas of the painter or breathed themselves into the marble of the sculptor. Poetry has not finished her task when she has found a Dante, a Shakespeare, a Milton. Music has not been exhausted in the act of creating Mozart and Beethoven and Mendelssohn. Every one of these influences is what it is in itself, because of man's immortality. The training we get in the body and through the body, such as the subjugation of the material organization to the organism of the man, the clear common sense won by experience from toil and enterprise, the swift energy, the mastering will of achievement, the patience of endeavour, the heroism that works and waits, and the discipline of the social and rational man,—all this complicated training, which suffers no constituent of manhood to evade its grasp, has a reference distinctly providential to the future man. The idea of a Christian probation as altogether different from other conceivable probations, and as standing specifically by itself in the dispensations of the universe, runs through all the economic arrangements of our world. And hence the words of St. Paul, "Use this world as not abusing it," using it not to the full of the senses and the intellect and the sensibilities as if it were all, but using it as a world even now moving from beneath your feet, and which has no permanency except in the moral and spiritual impressions left by it upon your souls. " The fashion of this world passeth away ; " the whole structure, the modes of existence, the relations of existence in their variety and multiplicity, all present objects, the totality which no mind can compute,—all this is in motion, the duration has been shortened, and the end is near at hand. Reviewing this argument of the apostle, may we not claim that it presents time in a light altogether new, that its estimate of duration is something intrinsically different from that measured by the time-keeper of the heavens, and that it inspires our sense of successional moments in a way peculiar to itself? Nothing in us is more closely connected with the external framework of the universe than our sensibility to time. Yet, while this natural capacity is subjected to an outward machinery, it is also dominant over that machinery, so that an instant may be expanded into an hour or an hour into days. In this respect, moods assert a mastering force, emotions are well-nigh omnipotent, and the heavenly orbs take their motions from our pulses. If Christianity took no knowledge of this phenomenon of experience, it would be strangely exceptional to its method of operating on man, which allows no recess of his being to remain unvisited by its light and warmth. Its teaching is, " The time is shortened," and it makes its doctrine available to practise us in the highest moral wisdom, using the world without abusing its relations. Now, it is worthy of notice that the civilization of our century has advanced in no direction more remarkably *than in victory over time.* The era opened with the steam-engine, and has progressed with the telegraph and telephone, and, in each case, the triumph has been in a fuller control of time. Time has been shortened and yet lengthened, so that we do in weeks what our grandfathers required years to accomplish. Time has been intensified. To-day in Europe is to-day in the backwoods of America, and the yesterday of China and Egypt is a part of the breakfast table-talk of this morning. Obviously, sensuous life, in its connections and sympathies, gets the most, at present, of this stimulation. One, however, who takes a broad view of providence, cannot think that the tendency of this increased sensuousness is necessarily downwards into sensualism. For, indeed, Christianity is often most active where we least suspect its presence, since the " kingdom of God," in civilization as in all else, " cometh not with observation." This enhanced sensuousness, if we read aright the signs of the times, is gathering together a vast fund of raw materials for transformation into a more capacious and robust Christian manhood. Within the realm of natural law, Christianity is signalizing its power more and more, and the day is not distant when " uniformity," " evolution," " homologies," will have a wider and profounder interpretation than they have now. " The earth helped the woman ; " it still helps the woman ; and age by age the apocalyptic wonder reveals fresh wonders. Silently, unobserved by the multitude, hidden even from scientific thinkers, God is reclaiming nature for his Son ; and he who, eighteen hundred years ago, multiplied bread for the hungry, healed diseases, and established his claim as the Lord of nature, is making ready to reaffirm that sovereignty in a manner more resplendent than by miracles. And as to this matter of shortened and intensified time, who but the Lord Jesus as Son of man was the first sublime instance of ascendancy over the limitations of time? Thirty years of seclusion, three years of work, young manhood cut short in its prime, and yet those three years giving birth to centuries which, amid manifold evils, have yet steadily progressed in the direction of a regenerated humanity. *For him, indeed, time was shortened,* and his is the perfect example of using the world without the slightest abuse. And just in the proportion we have his Spirit, shall we feel that the soul has a calendar of days unknown in the chronometry of the material universe.—L.

Ver. 2.—*Christianity and marriage.* The human mind is influenced by the law of action and reaction, and hence human opinion tends to extremes. Corinth was a city famous, or rather infamous, for its licentiousness; not only was society corrupt; religion sanctioned and spread the prevalent moral corruption. No place was more remarkable for the union between splendour and impurity. When a Christian community was formed at Corinth, it was natural enough that some of the old leaven of sensuality should appear and threaten to corrupt the mass. Hence the tolerance of fornication and, in one case, even of adultery and incest. But what is remarkable is that in the very same society there should be a faction or a tendency of thought and sentiment in the direction of asceticism. There were those who represented all sexual intercourse as impure, and beneath the dignity and unworldliness of spiritual men. Paul himself, though his language was afterwards coloured by sectarian transcribers of his Epistle, was evidently somewhat inclined to severity in his judgment upon the relations between man and woman. Yet in this verse he honours and authorizes the estate of marriage.

I. MARRIAGE IS AN INSTITUTION AND RELATIONSHIP BASED UPON THE DIVINE COMMAND. This cannot be questioned by those who accept the Scriptures as credible and authoritative. The primeval commandment stands upon record, and witnesses both against the unrestrained and licentious intercourse which some have defended as natural, but which is really unnatural and debasing, and also against the ascetic doctrine, to which now and again religious societies have inclined, that all sexual feeling is sinful. It is noticeable that our Lord Jesus himself repeats and sanctions the original commandment as to the lawfulness and inviolability of marriage.

II. THE EXPRESS COMMAND IS IN HARMONY WITH THE CONSTITUTION AND NATURAL ADAPTATION OF THE SEXES. There is nothing arbitrary and meaningless in the provisions of the moral law. That law is written upon the heart and conscience, upon the very bodily frame of man, and is not simply uttered in the voice of the Divine Lawgiver. Whoever studies the human constitution in body and in mind cannot fail to recognize and admire the adaptation which is embodied in the sacred ordinance of matrimony.

III. MARRIAGE IS PROMOTIVE OF SOME OF THE BEST AND PUREST AFFECTIONS OF HUMAN NATURE IN THOSE WHOM IT UNITES. There is no institution which so emphatically strikes at the very root of selfishness. The man is weaned away from the too common practice of self-gratification; the woman has called forth all the latent affection and devotion of her being; and the family becomes the sphere of self-denial and self-sacrifice, of mutual forbearance and helpfulness. That such is always the case is not asserted; but such is the proper, and to a very large extent the actual, tendency of this institution. True, there are those among the unmarried who cherish love which animates them to many labours; but there is no room for comparison between the virtues of the married and the unmarried, inasmuch as, amongst men, those who shrink from marriage usually do so avowedly to escape serious obligations and to indulge unbridled desires.

IV. MARRIAGE IS THE BEST PRESERVATIVE AGAINST VICE AND THE BEST AID TO VIRTUE. Paul seems to have admitted the contention of his Corinthian correspondents, that in some cases it was expedient to avoid marriage, and that such a course might be admirable in the passionless and peculiarly spiritual. But what in modern English is called "common sense" was very strong in the apostle, and he gives a very plain reason for a very plain precept. In the presence of the voluptuousness of Corinth there could be little need for many words; Paul's words are few and pungent. And whilst human nature is what it is, his counsels will hold good, and those of superfine and ascetic moralists will be discredited by the facts of human life.

V. BY MARRIAGE ARE SECURED THE WELFARE OF SOCIETY AND THE PROSPERITY OF THE CHURCH. The family is the true unit in human society, and the enemy of marriage is the enemy of humanity. It is in the family that virtuous and honourable citizens are bred and reared, and there principles are instilled which are at the foundation of national stability. And the old saying is equally true, that by marriage heaven itself is replenished. It is hence that the Church draws its members and its officers; it is here that the natural life and the eternal life are alike commenced and nurtured.—T.

Ver. 7.—*Distinct gifts.* Paul had peculiar natural powers, adapting him for a life of consecration and a life of service. But it was a beautiful feature in his character that he did not expect or wish all Christians to resemble himself in all things; such resemblance might be naturally pleasing to him, but his was too noble a nature to constrain him to see and judge all through his own medium. In fellow-labourers he recognized adaptation for usefulness, and was evidently convinced that the distribution of Divine gifts was appointed by the wisdom and beneficence of the great Head over all things to the Church.

I. HUMAN ENDOWMENTS ARE DIVINE GIFTS. It is characteristic of a religious and devout mind to look up to the Source and Author of all. If to God we are to attribute the providential favours we enjoy, shall we suppose that even higher gifts are to be traced to an inferior source? Inspiration enabled our great teachers to see the Giver in the gift. The word here used is indeed often used to denote those special super-natural powers, such as healing, tongues, prophecy, which were bestowed upon members of the primitive Church for a season and for a purpose. But the context shows that those gifts which are ordinary are as justly to be traced to the favour and bounty of Heaven as those which are extraordinary. Indeed, it may asked of every Christian, " What hast thou that thou didst not receive? "

II. DIVINE GIFTS ARE BESTOWED UPON MEN IN GREAT DIVERSITY AND VARIETY. " Every man hath his proper gift of God." It is so in bodily constitution—one has muscular strength, another constitutional endurance, a third manual dexterity, etc. It is so in temperament—one is calm and wise, another is tender and sympathetic, a third is impulsive and commanding. It is so in intellectual character—one reasons with force, another persuades with fervour, a third speaks with eloquence. Where are two leaves of the forest alike, or two faces indistinguishable? So in the Church of Christ—one has the gift to rule, another the gift to teach, another the gift to console. One is fitted for a pastor, another for an evangelist. One is called to a public position, another is adapted to the service of the one Redeemer in private life.

III. THESE GIFTS ARE COMPLEMENTARY TO ONE ANOTHER, AND IN THEIR EXERCISE CO-OPERATE TO THE GENERAL GOOD. None can be spared. There is generosity, but no lavish waste, in the liberality of the Divine Giver. On the other hand, there is no deficiency, no grudging and withholding. Pray for the qualified workman, and the work shall not be left undone for want of the necessary helper. Because all things are Christ's, all things are ours. One supplies another's lack, and mutual sympathy and common ministrations subserve the general good.

PRACTICAL LESSONS. 1. Gratitude should be cultivated as due to him who is Giver of all. 2. Pride should be repressed; for if one has his gift he has to remember that it is a gift bestowed in grace. 3. Forbearance and toleration are requisite. It is vain to expect all gifts to centre in the same person, to look for what God has not bestowed, to complain because a man has " his proper gift " and only that.—T.

Ver. 16.—*Earthly relationships sanctified to heavenly uses.* There were several obvious and powerful reasons why a Christian husband or wife should not leave a partner who was married in days when both were unbelievers, and who had not experienced con-version from heathenism or Judaism to Christianity. And to some extent the same reasons hold good when one has passed from merely nominal to real and spiritual Christianity. 1. An obligation has been undertaken from which only flagrant immo-rality can liberate either party. 2. Children may have been born during the union, whose welfare depends upon its continuance. 3. Affection may have sprung up which it would be a cruel outrage to suspend or check. And then, in addition, there is the reason given in the text. 4. The continuance of the union may make the Christian husband or wife the minister of spiritual blessing to the "unconverted" consort.

I. AN ATTRACTIVE REPRESENTATION MAY BE FURNISHED OF THE CHRISTIAN CHARACTER. The standard of moral excellence presented in the Word of God is indeed singularly high and admirable. But morality in a book is one thing, morality embodied in the life is quite another thing. Morality proclaimed from a pulpit is far less impressive than morality speaking from the domestic hearth. There are such virtues as truth, meekness, pity, patience, and charity, which are peculiarly Christian; and the exhibition of these is likely to lead to the inquiry—Whence come these traits of character? What is the secret of a life so different from the life of the selfish and the ungoverned? How many a husband has been won to Christ, beholding in his Christian wife a "a chaste conversation coupled with fear"!

II. AN UNCONSCIOUS INFLUENCE IN FAVOUR OF TRUE RELIGION MAY BE EXERCISED BY ONE PRAYERFULLY SOLICITOUS FOR THE SALVATION OF A SPOUSE. Who can know, unmoved, that a dear consort is seeking his spiritual welfare? There is a tone imparted to the intercourse of daily life by the habit of intercessory prayer. And there is a dignity, a gentleness, a spirituality, of manner and of language, which cannot escape the observation of such as are associated in the tenderest intimacies of life. There is no desire and prayer so all-penetrating and all-influential as the desire and prayer for the spiritual and eternal welfare of those who are nearest and dearest, united by the most sacred and endearing of earthly ties.

III. AN OPPORTUNITY IS GIVEN IN THESE RELATIONSHIPS FOR EXPRESS INSTRUCTION AND PERSUASION WHICH MAY ISSUE IN SPIRITUAL GOOD. In many instances it may be unwise to make a special and formal effort to convince and to persuade; it may be better to leave religion to tell its own tale and do its own work. But cases do occur in which Providence makes an opening for an effort. Stanley's remark upon this verse is well worth quoting: "The verse so understood has probably conduced to the frequent instances of the conversion of unbelieving husbands by believing wives. Even the stern severity of Chrysostom relaxes in its presence into the declaration, 'that no teacher has such an effect in conversion as a wife,' and this passage, thus interpreted, probably had a direct influence on the marriage of Clotilde with Clovis, and Bertha with Ethelbert, and consequently on the subsequent conversion of the two great kingdoms of France and England to the Christian faith." There are few Christian ministers who from their own observation could not tell of similar instances in lowlier life, where God has blessed the influence of wife to husband, or of husband to wife, so that they have become heirs together of the grace of life. Whilst, on the one hand, the mere hope of exercising such influence should never lead a man or a woman to marry an unbeliever, on the other hand, when unequal unions have been formed, the possibility opened up in this verse should lead to wise and affectionate effort, and to earnest and unwearying prayer.—T.

Ver. 19.—*Obedience is everything.* One great result of the introduction of Christianity into the world was to diminish the importance of trifles and to elevate great things into their due prominence. True religion thus acts by restoring to all things their due proportions, by putting all things in their due perspective. In religions of human device the greatest stress is laid upon what is valueless and things of supreme moment are ignored. In nothing is the religion of Christ more signally in contrast with and in advance of the religions of the heathen than in this vital point.

I. THE INDIFFERENCE OF OUTWARD POSITION AND OBSERVANCE. The great distinction in the time of the apostles and in the society in which they moved was the distinction between Jews and Gentiles, or, as it was the custom to express it, between the circumcision and the uncircumcision. But this distinction stands before us as representative of all external lines of demarcation, of all parties sundered by associations and observances amongst men. When the apostle says that circumcision and uncircumcision are "nothing," he uses very strong language, but he thus sets forth the insignificance of a man's birth, religious associations, reputation in this world, compared with his personal character. A lesson this which we find also in his Epistle to the Galatians, who, like the Corinthians, were assailed by false teachers who sought to substitute formality for spirituality. The inference is valid from this instance to all instances embraced in the general principle. It is to be observed that this apostolic teaching has two applications. 1. Those who insist upon forms are blamed for their narrowness. 2. Those who insist upon the neglect of forms are equally blamed for their intolerance. Neither one way nor the other is it allowable for one to dictate to another or to boast over another. The temperaments, habits, education, opinions, of Christians will probably decide whether or not they incline to express their religion in ceremonies or to dispense with such.

II. THE ALL-IMPORTANCE OF AN OBEDIENT HEART AND LIFE. When it is affirmed that circumcision and uncircumcision are "nothing," it is suggested that the keeping of the Divine commandments is *everything*—that this is the one thing of supreme importance. 1. There is implied the evangelical *motive* to Christian obedience. Certainly Paul was the last to teach that the mere outward compliance and conformity were sufficient. The prohibitions of the Law may be observed, yet the Searcher of hearts is not satisfied if the soul be not surrendered and devoted to him. And our Lord Jesus has very clearly and pointedly shown the relation between motive and practice in his saying, "If ye *love* me, keep my commandments;" "Ye are my *friends*, if ye do whatsoever I command you." 2. There is implied the supreme and righteous *authority* of God. It is too common, in representing the Creator as the Bestower of all gifts and as the Source of all grace, to overlook the very important and scriptural view of God as the just Governor and King of men. He has a right to command; all his ordinances and directions are in perfect harmony with the eternal and flawless moral law. It is not merely a superior power, it is a rightful authority to which we are bidden to submit, and to this our own reason and conscience unequivocally testify. 3. There is implied the *universal range* and sphere of the religious life. Not in an occasional act, not in an exceptional observance, lies our conformity to the Divine will. The commandments of God apply to the whole moral life of man, leave nothing untouched, unblest—they are "exceeding broad." All the activities of our nature and all the aspects of our life are contemplated and included in this comprehensive condition of true religion. The Jew and the Gentile, the young and the old, the learned and the illiterate, however they may be related to ceremonial observances, are all one in this— all can recognize the obligation to Christian obedience, and all can find in their several positions and avocations and relationships abundant opportunity for practically and cheerfully fulfilling the obligation they are alike in acknowledging.—T.

Vers. 22, 23.—*Freedom and bondage.* To the mind of the apostle spiritual and immortal relations seemed so vast and momentous that they dwarfed those relations which are earthly and temporary. It may appear to some readers of this passage of the Epistle as if Paul did not attach enough importance to the conditions of life in which Christians may find themselves. But the fact is that the friendship of Christ and the hopes of eternity were so real and precious to him that all beside seemed insignificant; whilst the uncertainty attaching to the period of the present dispensation was so present to his mind that he could not concern himself very feelingly with what might so soon for ever pass away.

I. THE BONDMAN'S FREEDOM. It is well known how very large a proportion of the Roman empire were slaves, and how pitiable was the condition of the whole class, how wretched and hopeless the condition of a large portion of the class. We cannot wonder that the gospel of Jesus Christ found so cordial and grateful a welcome from the bondmen in many cities of the empire. In many instances Christianity actually ameliorated the lot of the slave; in many more it enabled the unfortunate to bear their trials with patience, and to look beyond them to the glorious liberty of the children of God. The Epistle to Philemon gives us an insight into the relations between a Christian master and a Christian slave. What was the secret of the change which began so auspiciously, and which has proceeded so surely and so beneficially with the lapse of centuries? That Christianity had from the first a tendency to put an end to such inequality, none can doubt. But deeper than the social movement was a spiritual energy which displayed itself in the individual life. Liberty of spirit compensated the yoke of bondage. The humblest slave cherished the assurance that he was the Lord's freeman. This honourable distinction, the privileges and immunities it brought, the hopes it inspired, made the heart contented and the life tranquil and bright. The same process may take place in cases very different, yet allied. There are in every state of society those whose position is lowly and whose earthly prospects are cheerless, who may nevertheless enjoy the conviction that the Lord, the Son, has made them free, so that they are free indeed, in the enjoyment of a spiritual liberty and all its privileges and anticipations.

II. THE FREEMAN'S BONDAGE. The passage contains a twofold paradox: it presents us with a slave enfranchised, and with a freeman in bonds. If the poor slave was encouraged not to allow his chains to tie him in spirit to the earth, the freeman was reminded that, "called in the Lord," he was captive to a Divine will and consecrated to a Divine service. 1. *The cause and explanation of this servitude.* The Christian is reminded that he is "bought with a price." Brought into a new bondage by the purchase of a Saviour's blood, he is no more his own. Thus Christ and his sufferings are represented as the source of the new obligations which the ransomed have contracted. 2. *The negative side of the change thus effected.* It is a grand and stirring appeal of the apostle: "Be not ye the servants of men." Alas! what multitudes subject themselves to a base thraldom, in accepting the chains of human slavery, whilst they disdain the easy yoke of the Redeemer! But it is the prerogative of the

Christian to be superior alike to human judgment and to human authority. 3. *The positive side.* He is "Christ's servant" who is called in the Lord, although free in a civil sense. From Paul's own biography we are able to form a judgment as to the value which he set on Roman citizenship. But his highest honour was to subject and devote his powers to his Saviour. So far from there being any degradation, any ignominy in such service, it is most honourable, most illustrious. Yet it must be something more than a name; it involves the bringing, not of the life only, but of every thought, "into captivity to the obedience of Jesus Christ."—T.

Vers. 29—31.—"*The time is short.*" There is, and there ought to be, a marked difference between the conduct of the Christian and that of the unbeliever. This difference originates primarily in the new principles with which the mind of the disciple of Christ is possessed and by which it is governed; the faith and gratitude towards the Saviour which constitute and mark the man a Christian make him a new man. Yet there is another, beside this loftiest reason, for the outward differences. To this the apostle here refers; the rapidly approaching end of the present dispensation, when really expected, must exercise considerable influence over the Christian's life. I. The transitoriness and perishableness of the present state and of all that pertains to it is a powerful motive over the Christian's mind and life. The apostle puts this matter in two lights. 1. The *time* is short, contracted into a small compass. This must be taken in connection with the eternity of God, with whom "one day is as a thousand years, and a thousand years as one day;" and also in connection with the mortality of man, whose days on earth are as a shadow, whose life passes as the swift ships. The season, or dispensation, in which our earthly work is to be done and our earthly witness borne, is fleeting. "The day and the hour knoweth no man;" yet our Lord's language is ever, "Watch!" 2. "The fashion of this world passeth away." It is like a cloud-shadow on the sea, a wind-wave on the corn, a meteor in the sky. Of this pathetic truth all human history is a proof, and the events of every generation an illustration that to the reflective cannot fail to be impressive. Nothing continueth in one stay. The first Christians seem sometimes to have been possessed with the conviction that the end of the age and the advent of the Lord were very near. Nearer still are they to us, who are admonished to live under the influence of the sublime expectation. II. Human life abounds with opportunities for exhibiting the practical power of this principle and motive. 1. *Human relationships are influenced by the considerations adduced.* The apostle refers especially to marriage, because it was the question concerning the expediency of matrimony which occasioned the introduction of the great principle of the passage. On account of present uncertainties and the pressure of the time, Paul thought it well for some Christians not to marry, and for the married to be on their guard against absorption in family cares. 2. *Human emotions should be moderated by the same considerations.* There is no room for extreme joy or sorrow when the events which occasion these feelings are themselves upon the wing. The emotions are not forbidden, but excessive indulgence of them is deprecated. 3. *Human business cannot be allowed to be too absorbing;* for property will soon be valueless, and the world itself will vanish and be no more seen. How obvious the duty to hold earthly possessions with a light hand, and to use the world and all it contains with a wise discretion, and to avoid misusing what is so little able to afford a lasting satisfaction!—T.

Vers. 1, 2, 7—9 25—35.—*Celibacy and marriage.* The Corinthian Christians had written to the apostle for direction respecting the relative desirability and incumbency of single and wedded life. Probably some of them regarded marriage as *obligatory*, and others perhaps looked upon it as *an evil.* Amongst Gentiles there was at this period a strong tendency towards celibacy. The reputation of Corinth was, moreover, unenviable for wantonness and uncleanness. There was therefore great need for full and explicit statement, supplemented by apostolic authority. I. The apostle declares each state to be lawful. This is apparent from the two opening verses of the chapter. In itself it is no sin to marry; it is no sin to remain unmarried. Perhaps specially to those regarding marriage as obligatory, the apostle says "It is good [expedient, profitable] for a man not to touch a woman;" and to those all for celibacy—speaking generally, "Let every man have his own wife." Both conditions are honourable. We are left to choose between the two. But rules are laid down for guidance.

II. CHOICE BETWEEN THE TWO SHOULD BE LARGELY DETERMINED BY CONDITION AND CIRCUMSTANCE. From vers. 1, 7, 8, 38, it has been too hastily concluded by some that Paul decidedly favours celibacy *per se*. But ver. 7 is ambiguous, and is thought by not a few to refer to the gift of continence, which qualifies a man for single or wedded life, as circumstances may determine; and the other verses, together with this verse, must not be dissevered from ver. 26, *which qualifies the whole chapter*. Paul has vividly before his mind the surroundings of the Christian Church in his own age. What was expedient in the "present distress" might not be desirable under other conditions. And similarly, the "better" might cease to be so under changed circumstances. We read elsewhere (Heb. xiii. 4) that "marriage is honourable in all." And it is the Apostle Paul himself who elevates marriage to the loftiest position by employing it as a type of the union between Christ and believers (Eph. v. 25—32). It is also the same apostle who pronounces the prohibition of marriage to be one of the signs of the great apostacy (1 Tim. iv. 3). "It is not good that the man should be alone" (Gen. ii. 18). On Paul's communication to the Corinthians it has been aptly said, "The truth is that the apostle writes to the Corinthians as he would do to an army about to enter on a most unequal conflict in an enemy's country and for a protracted period. He tells them, 'This is no time for you to think of marriage. You have a right to marry. And in general it is best that all men should marry. But in your circumstances marriage can only lead to embarrassment and suffering.'" This is putting the matter *bluntly*. Perhaps it goes a little beyond the apostle's expressed counsel, yet it shows *the drift* of his advice. It would seem that choice is to be determined by: 1. *Condition or qualification*. Celibacy is not commended to any except those who have the gift of continence. To many it would prove a snare—an occasion of the most serious evil. It is not at all "good" for the generality, since most men do not possess the necessary qualification. Thus the almost universal injunction in the second verse follows and qualifies the commendation in the first. Even under adverse temporal circumstances it may thus be better for some to marry. The apostle is most cautious upon this point, and is in great contrast to Romanists, who relegate to celibacy the entire priesthood. 2. *Circumstances*. The "present distress," because of the sorrows, perplexities, and sufferings which it occasioned in so large a degree to those having upon them the responsibilities of married life, inclined the apostle to commend celibacy to those qualified to practise it. We have here valuable suggestions. Marriage is not to be rashly entered upon. Temporal surroundings and prospects are to be taken into account. Prudence is to be observed in affairs matrimonial. What woeful results have followed imprudent unions! Many who fall into love seem to fall out of their senses at the same time. Not a few regard marriage as a goal to be reached at all hazards. They display infinitely more anxiety to get to *it* than they do to get to *heaven*. Evidently they regard it as a most perfect paradise, but when they reach it by the road of folly they generally find that there is a serpent in that garden as in the one of old.

III. THE APOSTLE DIRECTS OUR THOUGHTS TO THE RELATIVE ADVANTAGES OF THE TWO STATES. 1. *Celibacy has less care attaching to it, especially in troublous times.* The unmarried have more leisure to attend to the things of the Lord. The married must concern themselves more about things temporal, and this may prove a distraction injurious to higher duties. A loving wife tends to occupy her mind very largely about her husband, and a loving husband about his wife. There is danger here lest the claims of One who should be far more to us than husband or wife be neglected. This is especially so in days of persecution and of violent and sudden change. The beloved object may be threatened with suffering; the price of escape may be unfaithfulness to God. Here is the pinch; felt terribly in days of darkness. It is easier for many to suffer themselves than to see their dear ones suffer. And we are apt to excuse conduct which has for its object the welfare of another—when we should be bound to condemn it if we only were concerned. Shall I see my wife and children exposed to nameless insult and hideous cruelty, or forswear the faith? This was the dread alternative set before many a married man in the days of Paul. As we have seen, a celibate may devote himself *entirely* to the Lord and his service. I do not understand the apostle to say that this is *impossible* in one who is married, but that human claims *may* come into conflict with Divine. In happy peaceful times the conflict might never arise; in days of persecution it might be severe. Note: There is here no commendation of monastic or isolated celibacy. The apostle would doubtless expect the celibate to exhibit his devotion to God very largely by works of usefulness amongst his fellow-men (as in the case of Paul himself). Observe: The single state is not to be sneered at. It has special opportunities. Those who adopt it from right motives are worthy of all esteem. And those who are compelled to it by circumstances, if they use its advantages, are to be held in honour. Frequently, however, they are considered the fittest objects for ridicule. Yet "old maids" are sometimes the best of maids. And men unfettered by wedded responsibilities have frequently been patterns of excellence and usefulness. 2. *Marriage is the safer condition morally.* (Ver. 2.) It is freer from temptation. It is the condition appropriate for a large number. And let us not forget that *God* has so made us that the generality find their true place in the domestic circle (ver. 7). "It is not good that the man should be alone" has very extensive application. Marriage is needful for the replenishing of the earth. There are some who under *any* external circumstances will find it easier to serve God in the married state. Marriage is a great support and source of strength to many. The home influence is felt wherever a man journeys, and often upholds him in good resolution, and animates him when despondent. It expands his sympathies. It draws him out of himself. Celibacy presents many perils even for those who are naturally qualified for it. Tendencies towards narrowness, selfishness, lack of sympathy, have to be carefully guarded against. Domestic life of the right kind supplies an antidote. And in the home and in its duties we may truly serve God. When we *rightly* "care" for those near and dear to us we are offering acceptable service to the Most High. The home may and should be a true sanctuary. It will be seen that this applies chiefly to quiet times. In times of disturbance and insecurity, "home" exists often only as a name, and the advantages of married life are turned into serious disadvantages. Its powers for good assume then the form of perils. Finally, whichever state we choose, we must ever remember the "shortness of the time" (ver. 29), and must not settle down in this world as though it were our abiding-place. Eternity has opened upon our view. For that we are chiefly to live. With an eye to that we must determine our conduct and choices. Time, in which we marry and are given in marriage, is but a *flash* (though it is the flash of *preparation*); eternity is our *life.*—H.

Vers. 2—6, 10—17.—*Marriage: its nature and duties.* I. NATURE. 1. *It is the union of one man and one woman.* (Ver. 2.) Polygamy and polyandry are rigorously excluded from the sanction of the Christian faith. The former was tolerated by God in early times, but never enjoined or commended. The first union, in Eden, was of the Christian order. The wisdom of the dictum of Christianity has been exemplified by universal experience. All other arrangements are prolific of evils. 2. *It is a union for life.* (Ver. 39.) No hint is given of temporary wedlock. 3. *It is a bond not to be lightly severed.* (1) Not by difference of faith (vers. 12, 13). A converted husband or wife might plausibly argue that it was undesirable to further consort with a heathen. The prohibition illustrates the permanence of the marriage bond. Continuance in the marriage state is obligatory under such circumstances. "But to the rest speak I, not the Lord," does not signify that Paul is not speaking the mind of the Lord, but that he is conveying something which Christ did not communicate whilst among men. "Yet not I, but the Lord," in ver. 10 means that Paul was only repeating what Christ had previously taught. The apostle in ver. 14 advances an argument for the continuance of such a marriage. The unbelieving one is sanctified by the believing, *i.e.* brought within the covenant, within the pale of Christianity. Not saved or converted, for see ver. 16, but as all Jews were sanctified, brought under the old covenant, although "he is not a Jew which is one outwardly" (Rom. ii. 28). In this sense the children of Christian parents are "holy," and, according to the apostle's statement, equally so when one parent is heathen. (2) Not by taste or caprice (ver. 10). (3) Not by temporal exigencies (ver. 27). These might very lawfully *prevent* marriage, as Paul teaches, but they could not *annul* it. (4) Not by anything except wilful desertion (ver. 15) and adultery, as taught by Christ (Matt. **v.** 32). Paul's teaching does not conflict with Christ's. It is not lawful *to put away* except for adultery; the apostle adds that if the believing party be, without just cause, put away, he or she is free. But this meaning of ver. 15 is somewhat open to question. Note : There may be *separation* without the annulling of the marriage obligation. The apostle supposes such a case (ver. 11), and enjoins that no second marriage be entered upon, since the first still remains in force. 4. *It is an exclusive union.* It is to *avoid* fornication (ver. 2). 5. *Those who enter upon it must do so prudently.* This is developed in the apostle's argument as to the respective advantages of celibacy and marriage. And : 6. *In the Lord* (ver. 39) *will apply to all cases.* Marriages are to be *continued* with the ungodly, but not to be *commenced.* Of our choice we are not to be " unequally yoked." We are not to marry in order to convert. Many do this and, soon discover their mistake. They are like the woman who journeyed to Rome to convert the pope, but instead of converting his holiness, his holiness converted her !

II. DUTIES. 1. *The body of one is to be surrendered to the other.* (Ver. 4.) Cohabitation may be suspended for a time by mutual consent, for special purposes, but with distinct recognition of speedy reunion. Care must here be exercised, lest temptation be occasioned. There is no command for this temporary separation; it is permitted, not enjoined or even recommended. 2. *Mutual pleasing.* (Vers. 33, 34.) This, referred to as a natural result, may be regarded as an implied injunction. Corroborated by Eph. v. 21—25. It is evidently needful. But it has limits; we must not displease God in order to please husband or wife. 3. *The highest spiritual interests of one to be sought by the other.* (Ver. 16.) A special case is supposed, which, however, opens up a wide question of home influences. How earnestly should we desire the salvation of those most closely united to us ! How terrible the thought of final separation ! The home presents the best opportunities of winning the ungodly to Christ. Not by *words* so much as by *life.* The influence is *very continuous,* and is exercised by those nearest and often dearest. Still, much grace is needed for such a ministry as this. Faults, jealously concealed in public, are often undisguised and freed from check in the household. We may do great harm as well as great good in the home; we may drive from Christ as well as draw towards him. The converted husband or wife is *the pastor* of the unconverted. Solemn responsibility ! Care for the higher interests involve care for the lower. *In all things* those united in marriage should seek each other's good. This will involve much—(1) self-restraint, (2) self-denial, (3) unselfishness, (4) patience, (5) true affection.—H.

Vers. 20—24.—*Christianity and slaves.* Christianity found slavery in existence. Proceeded upon wise lines for its extermination. Not by revolutionary violence. Worked from within rather than from without. Inculcated moral principles which, when fully realized and practically observed, involved the doom of slavery. Such passages as Matt. vii. 12 are in point. Occasionally there is more direct attack, as in the condemnation of men-stealers in 1 Tim. i. 10. What message had Christianity to the slaves ? It said—

I. SERVE GOD AS YOU ARE. As a slave you may do a good and important work. Your condition has *some* special opportunities. It will be something for the world to see a pious, conscientious, faithful *slave.* This you can be, for with all shackles you may be " the Lord's freedman." A lesson for us. We often try to *change our condition* instead of *glorifying God in it.* All men seem to have fallen into the wrong places ! For all men seem intensely anxious to change their condition. The powers, opportunities, time, of not a few are practically absorbed in this endeavour. And the craze is continuous. When the change is secured, *another change is desired,* and so on interminably. Men are used up in this insane struggle. It is not necessary to change our condition before we can do anything. The true way to the more favourable condition may be our glorifying God in the less favourable. The sterling piety of a slave became a strong protest against slavery itself. In *various conditions* the world needs to see *the same faith* and *the same life.* A man need care *comparatively* little about his external condition in this world, who is freed from the bondage of Satan and who tastes the liberty wherewith Christ makes his people free. *That* is nothing compared with *this. No human shackles can bind the soul.* The slave with all his bonds could not be hindered from coming to Christ. No one can stop us. Not all men. Not all devils. Not all adverse circumstances. We can come if *we will*, whoever or whatever we are or in whatsoever condition. The responsibility is upon our shoulders. None shall say at last that they *could not* come. God hath not permitted man so to bind his fellow that the journey to the cross is an impossibility.

II. IF YOU CAN OBTAIN YOUR FREEDOM BY RIGHTEOUS MEANS, DO SO. Not "do evil that good may come." But embrace any legitimate opportunity, for as a freedman you have generally more opportunities of service and less perils. When freed, you may make it more apparent, perhaps, that you are "Christ's bondservant." To us: seek a freer position when opportunity is presented, since in that you may more abundantly serve God. That is the object which you must ever have in mind. Let not the freer position be for self, but for God. A more *comfortable* condition is not always a more *useful* one. When we are taking off one shackle we may be putting on another. It may be a heavier one.

III. DO NOT BECOME SLAVES. It may be your duty to *continue* slaves, not to become such. This would be throwing away most important advantages. You are Christ's, bought with a price; have by choice no other bonds upon you than your Master's. To us: never seek a position in which service to Christ may be prejudiced. Here is a crucial test. 1. A rise in the social scale may impair our usefulness. The new house may tax our purse and check our charity, the numerous engagements our time, the atmosphere our piety. We may become "bondservants of men," and very miserable ones. 2. A more lucrative post may entail loss rather than gain—greater occupation of time, larger demands upon our strength, even the shortening of our lives. All such things come into the account. 3. The removal to a more pleasant place of residence may mean the arrest of Christian activity. People remove from where they are wanted to where nobody wants them. God places them in the field to labour, where there is much to be done, but they contract a fondness for mountain air and scenery, and off they go, leaving their appointed work to take care of itself. And when they get to the mountain of delights there is nothing for them to do but to grumble, and this, it must be acknowledged, they do with most unflagging zeal. Christians seem to think they are their own masters, and can come and go for little reason or for none, and without any reference to the great work to which every Christian is pledged, viz. seeking to extend the kingdom of Christ among men. "My Father's business" should be first with the disciple, as it was with his Lord. Instead of this, it is often practically lost sight of altogether, and people go without a thought or care from where the Father's business is urgent and almost overwhelming in importance, to where in comparison it can be prosecuted only upon a most limited scale. Men listen to the "call" of inclination, not to the "call" of God (note vers. 20, 24). We must ever beware of running into bonds. Many of these are golden. Not the less binding. In whatever circumstances we may be placed we must refuse to be such bondservants of men as to impair our relation to God. *At all costs*, in every condition, his will and glory must be supreme.—H.

Vers. 36—40.—*Duties of parents to children as to marriage.* The apostle's words apply directly to daughters only. Among Jews and Greeks the disposal of the daughters of the family rested with the father. What is said, however, may extend very largely to sons as well.

I. MARRIAGE IS NOT TO BE INSISTED UPON. It too commonly is in many circles, especially in the case of daughters, and thus becomes prolific of evils. The apostle rather commends the father who does not give his daughter in marriage (ver. 38). Doubtless with an eye to the "present distress," but assuredly in opposition to any forcing of the inclination, and to any notion that marriage is *universally* desirable. It is not the parent's wish so much as the child's which should be consulted. Spheres should be opened for unmarried females. This has been done largely of late years, but a greater extension is one urgent need of the times.

II. CONSENT TO MARRIAGE IS NOT TO BE CAPRICIOUSLY WITHHELD. (Ver. 36.) The dread of refusal of consent has often led to rash acts involving much subsequent suffering. Parents often blame their children for marrying without consent when they should blame themselves for withholding it. Some parents seem to think that their convenience and predilections are the chief things concerned, as though it were *their* marriage and not their child's.

III. THE CHILD'S WISHES SHOULD BE CONSULTED. This seems to be involved in "Let them marry," as though a specific attachment was supposed. "Having no necessity" (ver. 37) and "behaveth himself uncomely" (ver. 36) bear also upon this point. Certainly obtains in case of widows (ver. 39). The child's wish, not only as to marriage itself, but as to the one with whom a union is proposed should never be left out of account. Parental counsel and guidance are wise and well; parental compulsion is gross folly. Consent to marriage may be withheld, and must be, if there are sufficient grounds, but to in any way force a union is to pave the way for misery, if not for something worse. Modern usages much more favour consultation of the child's wish than ancient, but in some circles there seems to be a tendency to revert to barbaric customs. In the land where there are no slaves, daughters are in many cases as truly sold to the highest bidder as was ever an African upon an American auction-block. When parental selfishness and folly run to such lengths, divorce courts are likely to be in great request and never to lack causes.

IV. CHRISTIAN PARENTS SHOULD DESIRE THE MARRIAGE OF THEIR CHILDREN "ONLY IN THE LORD." Alas! how many professedly Christian parents seem to have but little regard for this! Position, wealth, influence, titles,—if these, or any one of them, can be attained, there is not only satisfaction but jubilation. Yet what possible joy should there be to a Christian parent in giving his child to be the lifelong companion of an enemy of Christ? He may not be able *to prevent* such a union, but to rejoice in it is quite another matter. A suitor's *spiritual position* should be weighed as well as his *temporal*. A union with an unbeliever may promise much, as men judge, for this world, but it promises very little for the next. Such marriages are not "made in heaven," nor can they be expected to lead thither. But a godly husband wonderfully aids the spiritual life of a godly wife, and *vice versâ* ; and they walk well together, because they are "agreed." Mixed marriages seem generally to end in an "agreement" to give up attendance at the house of God on the sabbath, and to care nothing for the God of the house during the week. Yet many parents scarcely consider for a moment whether they are giving their daughter to a child of God or to a child of the devil. And sons are congratulated if they succeed in making "a good match," which is very possibly one of the *worst* matches they could have made. Parents should give the supreme place to the *spiritual* interests of their children.—H.

Vers. 1—9.—*Celibacy and marriage.* Hitherto the apostle has been treating of abuses in the Church at Corinth, which had come to his knowledge, either through the household of Chloe (ch. i. 11) or through common report (ch. v. 1). He passes now to deal with certain matters regarding which the Corinthians had asked his advice by letter; and the first of these is marriage, with other related subjects. While treating the whole chapter homiletically, the preacher will do well to exercise a wise delicacy in introducing many of the points to a mixed congregation.

I. CELIBACY. The preference apparently given to celibacy in this chapter calls for careful consideration. 1. *In what sense is it called "good"?* It is not good in the sense of being in itself and always superior to marriage. Elsewhere Paul speaks of the married state with the greatest respect, as an image of the union between Christ and his Church (Eph. v. 23—25), and gives it as a mark of the false teachers of later times that they "forbid to marry" (1 Tim. iv. 3). The law of consistency, then, bids us interpret his statements here as in no sense depreciatory of the Divine ordinance of marriage. A single life is good in the sense of being in itself honourable, and in certain circumstances expedient. The apostle's "good" here must always be read in view of the "not good" of Gen. ii. 18. 2. *When is it to be preferred to marriage?* Leaving out of view considerations of physical health, which in some cases may render marriage imprudent or even culpable, three answers to our question may be gathered from this chapter. (1) In circumstances of peculiar distress (ver. 26). Such trouble had either come upon the Corinthians or was near at hand, that Paul judged it better for them to keep clear of such engagements as would only increase their suffering. In times of persecution or dearth it may be wise not to marry. (2) When called to some peculiar service for the Lord. This was Paul's case. Other apostles, indeed, were married, but in view of vers. 32, 33, we may suppose that the apostle of the nations judged it best for his peculiar mission to remain unmarried. Celibacy may be preferred "for the kingdom of heaven's sake" (Matt. xix. 12). (3) Both these considerations must be taken along with a third presented in ver. 7. If a man has not the gift of continency, there is in that a clear indication that it is his duty to marry (ver. 9); if he possesses this gift, then he is free to give weight to other reasons which may turn the balance in favour of celibacy. Even then, however, the higher ends of wedlock are not to be over-looked. 3. *It is not to be made obligatory.* The Church of Rome ascribes a peculiar excellence to the celibate state, as fitted to promote greater sanctity. Hence her cultivation of monastic and conventual life, and the imposition of celibacy on the clergy. There is no warrant for this in the teaching of the apostle here; while experience testifies to the dreadful evils to which it leads.

II. MARRIAGE. 1. Marriage is *a safeguard against incontinence.* The apostle is not here treating of marriage in general or presenting it in its higher aspects and bearings. The pure union of man and woman in wedlock is a communion of soul and body in love, a fulfilment of the Divine intention clearly expressed in our nature. Husband and wife thus united "in the Lord"—the one being the complement of the other, and set "like perfect music unto noble words"—are joined by a bond so holy, so exalted, so mysterious, that it is the earthly reflex of the spousal union between Christ and his Church. Still, the use here referred to by the apostle is not to be overlooked, especially in view of such licentiousness as prevailed at Corinth. God never bids us eradicate any natural appetite, as asceticism does, but provides for its gratification in a way consonant to our nature and destiny. 2. *It implies the rendering of conjugal duty.* (Vers. 3, 4.) The one party exists for the other, and for the other alone—the twain having become one flesh (Gen. ii. 24). 3. *Marriage is a union between one man and one woman.* In polygamy the true idea of marriage is lost. The original appointment was the union of two persons only, Adam having only one Eve; and the departure from this was due to sin. The testimony of Scripture, alike in precept and in its purest examples, is all in favour of monogamy (Gen. ii. 24; Matt. xix. 4, 5; 1 Tim. iii. 2); and the statements of the apostle here take this for granted. The domestic bliss of which poets sing is not to be found in the homes of polygamy.

> "Here Love his golden shafts employs, here lights
> His constant lamp, and waves his purple wings,
> Reigns here and revels."
>
> ('Paradise Lost,' iv. 763—765.)

> " Domestic happiness, thou only bliss
> Of Paradise, that has survived the Fall! ...
> Thou art the nurse of virtue; in thine arms
> She smiles, appearing, as in truth she is,
> Heaven-born, and destined to the skies again."
>
> (Cowper's 'Task.')
>
> B.

Vers. 10—16.—*Divorce: mixed marriages.* Having spoken of celibacy and marriage, and having presented considerations for their guidance in the choice of the one or the other, the apostle proceeds to speak of persons already married. And here two different cases are dealt with: (1) *Where both the parties are Christian;* (2) *where one of the parties is Christian and the other heathen.*

I. WHERE BOTH PARTIES ARE CHRISTIAN. In this case the Lord Jesus, in his recorded teaching, had already given a decision, and Paul refers them to his words (*vide* Matt. v. 32; xix. 9). 1. *The marriage bond is indissoluble.* It is a union for life, which cannot be broken up without sin. It is not to be dissolved at the mere will of the parties, nor for any frivolous reason. This perpetuity arises from the relationship itself, as well as from the Divine appointment. Husband and wife are ideally one, and their separation is the disrupting of a bond which has no parallel in this world. An additional sacredness attaches to the marriage covenant in the case of Christians, who invoke the blessing of God upon their union. 2. *Separation is not to be final.* The case supposed is that of a wife leaving her husband on the ground of harsh and cruel treatment or for some similar reason. The cause of separation may or may not be sufficient to justify it, but in either case it must not be regarded as severing the marriage tie. Only two alternatives are open. The wife thus separated must remain unmarried, since a new union would imply that the previous one was null and void; or she must be reconciled to her husband and return to live with him. This last is in every way the desirable course, and every means should be used to bring it about. Husband and wife cannot go apart without sin and scandal to the Christian name, and their religious profession requires them to reconsider their position and remove every barrier to reunion. The apostle is not here speaking of adultery, which is of itself a dissolution of the marriage bond and a sufficient ground for divorce (Matt. xix. 9), but simply of the general rule that married persons are bound to each other for life. With what prayerful deliberation should such a union be contracted! A step that cannot be retraced should not be taken without thought.

II. WHERE ONE OF THE PARTIES IS CHRISTIAN AND THE OTHER HEATHEN. The case supposed is not that of a Christian entering into wedlock with a heathen spouse, which Paul in another place forbids (2 Cor. vi. 14); but the case where one of the parties, already married, is converted to Christianity. This must have frequently happened in the early history of the Church, just as it is of constant occurrence in modern missions among the heathen. How does this complication affect the sanctity of the marriage bond? Is it not a union of the dead and the living, between whom there is a great gulf? The Lord Jesus had given no utterance on the subject of mixed marriages, and therefore the apostle gives his inspired judgment regarding it. If the unbelieving partner is content to remain, the Christian partner is not to seek a separation. If the unbelieving partner refuses to remain, the Christian partner is not to hinder separation. 1. Consider the case *where the unbelieving partner is content to remain.* The Christian spouse is not to seek a separation as if the marriage were unholy; "For the unbelieving husband is sanctified in the wife, and the unbelieving wife is sanctified in the husband" (ver. 14). The apostle does not mean that an unbeliever, in virtue of conjugal union with a believer, becomes personally holy; but that he or she is thereby consecrated or hallowed. As the altar sanctifies the gift that is laid upon it (Matt. xxiii. 19), so the Christian reflects something of his own character upon everything connected with him. His property, his business, his family, are all in a sense holy, as belonging to one who is in covenant with God, and are under his special protection. Hence the pagan husband or wife is a privileged person on the ground of union with a Christian spouse. The tares in the wheat-field are sacred for the sake of the wheat (Matt. xiii. 29); the ungodly men in Israel were privileged because they belonged to a holy nation. The reason adduced by Paul in support of this position is very significant. "Else were your children unclean; but now are they holy" (ver. 14). It was an accepted maxim that the children of such mixed marriages were born within the Church. This principle was recognized among the Jews, as the case of Timothy shows (Acts xvi. 1—3). But if the children of such a marriage are reckoned holy, the marriage whence they spring cannot be unholy or inconsistent with the Law of God. "If the root is holy, so are the branches" (Rom. xi. 16); and, conversely, "If the branches are holy, so is the root." The children take their standing from the Christian parent, who is regarded as the nobler of the two. 2. Consider the case *where the unbelieving partner refuses to remain.* In this case the Christian partner is not to insist on maintaining the union, but to let the other depart. For: (1) "The brother or the sister is not under bondage in such cases." The marriage is not to be dissolved at the instance of the believing partner; but if the other refuses to remain, the contract is no longer binding. It would be a case of bondage if the one were held to a union which the other has wilfully broken up. (2) "God hath called us in peace." The gospel was not intended to produce variance and strife in families; and if this is to be the result of the heathen partner continuing to dwell with the Christian, it were better to let him have his wish and live apart. From the very centre of life out to its circumference, God desires us to live in peace. (3) The Christian partner is not to prevent the departure of the other, in the hope of being instrumental in his or her conversion. This is at best uncertain, and peace is not to be hazarded therefore. And if such a union is not to be maintained for the sake of a possible conversion, much less is it to be contracted with that view.

REMARKS. 1. This passage is generally adduced as the Bible warrant for the view that *wilful desertion is a sufficient reason for divorce*. Such desertion is a *de facto* rupture of the marriage bond, and stands on the same footing as adultery. 2. *The evil of mixed marriages*: (1) Render impossible the complete fellowship of husband and wife. (2) Break up domestic peace. (3) Prevent family religion. (4) Interfere with the religious training of children. "Be not unequally yoked with unbelievers."—B.

Vers. 17—24.—*Christianity and the relations of life.* From the special case with which he has just dealt, the apostle proceeds to lay down a general principle. To understand the need for this, we have only to remember the circumstances of the time and the bearing upon these of the doctrines of the gospel. To many minds Christianity must have appeared to be revolutionary in its tendency. It proclaimed the equality of all men in the sight of God, the temporary nature of earthly things, the approaching advent of the Lord Jesus Christ, when a new era was to dawn; and men who drank in these views as the new wine of life were apt to become intoxicated. They were ready to cast off family obligations, disrupt social ties, and break up every earthly relationship. Against this tendency Paul here warns them. Christianity was not meant to revolutionize society in this violent way. On the contrary, it adapts itself to every position and relation in life in which men may be placed.

I. A GENERAL RULE. This rule is thrice repeated with slight variations (vers. 17, 20, 24). "Let each man abide in that calling wherein he was called." 1. *The Christian view of life.* (1) It is a distribution of God—a lot. Our station, occupation, relationships, are of Divine appointment. He assigns us our lot (Ps. xvi. 5, 6) and determines the bounds of our habitation (Acts xvii. 26). (2) It is a calling. Our true work in the world is that to which the voices of Providence call us. If we are where we ought to be, we should look upon our occupation as a real vocation of God. 2. *The Christian's duty in relation to his lot or calling in life.* The general rule is—Remain where you are. This follows from the view of life just presented; for it is our duty to abide by the Lord's appointment, and conversion does not necessarily change our secular vocation. If he finds you at the plough, or at the desk, or engaged in trade, or in the married state, or in the service of another,—serve him where he finds you. Christianity is a hardy plant that thrives in every clime. Do not imagine that if you were in a different line of things it would be easier for you to follow Christ. Nothing is more needed in our day than a consistent exhibition of Christian principle in the common walks of life—the family, the workshop, the office, the exchange, etc. Let your light shine where it is first kindled, continuing there "with God" (ver. 24). To this rule, however, there are two obvious exceptions. (1) When we discover that our occupation is inconsistent with the Law of God. A wrong course of life, such as a business which cannot be conducted on Christian principles, should be abandoned at once. It is not a "lot" or a "calling" of God. (2) When there is a clear call to a position of greater usefulness, presenting fuller opportunities of serving the Lord. Thus the apostles left their boats and nets to follow Jesus. Thus many a young man is called to leave his secular occupation and give himself to the ministry of the Word.

II. ILLUSTRATIONS OF THE RULE. To show how the rule applies, Paul takes two illustrative examples—the one from religious position, the other from social position. 1. *Circumcision.* If a Jew is called, let him not attempt to efface the mark of the covenant; if a Gentile is called, let him not think it needful to be circumcised. To do otherwise in either case would be to attach a value to external forms which they do not possess. Paul's own practice in circumcising Timothy (Acts xvi. 3), and refusing to circumcise Titus (Gal. ii. 3, 4), throws light upon this. To have acted otherwise in the case of Timothy would have been to attach importance to the *omission* of the rite, since one of his parents was a Jew and the other a Greek. To have allowed it in the case of Titus, whose parents were both Gentiles, would have been to attach importance to the *performance* of the rite, and so to submit to the yoke which the "false brethren" sought to impose. By acting as he did he showed that both circumcision and uncircumcision were to him matters of indifference. *Religion is not an affair of outward ceremonies, but of spiritual obedience.* Comp. ver. 19 with Gal. v. 6 and vi. 15, in all which the first clause is the same. In opposition to such matters of ritual observance, he places: (1) "Faith working through love;" (2) "A new creature;" and (3) "The keeping of the commandments of God." These are the great essentials of Christianity (see Stanley, *in loc.*). 2. *Slavery.* If there is any institution to which we should have expected Christianity to show itself hostile, it is just this. Slavery strikes at the root-idea of humanity, denying to man his proper dignity as a person; and is therefore in collision with the axiom on which the gospel proceeds, that " He made of one every nation of men" (Acts xvii. 26). At the time when Paul wrote, it was the great " open sore" of the world, and was frequently accompanied with great hardship and cruelty. Yet he does not counsel the Christian slaves—a numerous class—to rise in rebellion and throw off their bondage. He bids them " care not for it " (ver. 21). Freedom, indeed, is to be preferred if you can obtain it; but you can serve God as a bondservant as truly as if you were free. It was not by dint of hacking and cutting that the fetters were to be struck off, but by a surer and more excellent method. As the frost-fetters of winter give way before the warm breath of spring, so Christianity was to loosen the bonds of the slave wherever it came. And this principle was to regulate individual action. For : (1) *It makes no difference to your Christian standing whether you be bond or free.* You were bought with a price, and so redeemed from the bondage of sin and Satan in order to serve Christ. Hence, though you are a bond-servant, you are really the Lord's freedman; and though you are outwardly free, you are really Christ's bondservant. Man must serve, but he cannot serve two masters. Our Redeemer delivers us from Satan, so that we are now free; but this freedom shows itself in the service of our new Master. " Let my people go, that they may serve me," is still the Lord's demand. (2) *The service of Christ is true freedom.* It delivers us from every other spiritual service. Christian liberty is compatible with outward slavery, but not with subjection to men in spiritual things. Here we must not call any man " master." How often do Christians become bondservants of men! We fall into this error when we shape our views and conduct according to tradition, or party, or school, or the popular voice, instead of simply asking, " What saith the Lord?"—B.

Vers. 25—40.—*Concerning virgins and widows.* Paul now passes to another question referred to him, viz. the marriage of virgins and widows. This has been briefly touched upon already (ver. 8), and is now dealt with more in detail. Here also the apostle has no express commandment of the Lord to adduce, and he therefore proceeds to give his own inspired judgment on the matter, "as one that hath obtained mercy of the Lord to be faithful." This judgment is not in the form of explicit injunction, but of an advice given in view of existing circumstances.

I. ADVICE TO THE UNMARRIED OF BOTH SEXES. In the previous sections the apostle has argued against the disrupting of social ties, even when these are of so unpleasant a character as being bound to a heathen spouse or subject to the yoke of slavery. Here he gives similar counsel, advising against a change of condition. This applies to married persons, who are not to seek a dissolution of the bond; but especially to the unmarried, whom he advises to remain as they are. This advice does not proceed from a disparagement of marriage in itself or from an absolute preference of celibacy (comp. homily on vers, 1—9, above), but is based upon special reasons which are afterwards mentioned. 1. *The present distress.* (Ver. 26.) This may refer to persecution already commenced, as that under Nero (A.D. 64), or to the troubles which were to usher in the second advent (comp. Matt. xxiv.). In view of this impending crisis, it is better not to marry. The apostolic advice will hold in all similar cases; as when a soldier is called to dangerous military duty, or a man is approaching death, or during the prevalence of famine and pestilence. 2. *Tribulation in the flesh.* (Ver. 28.) This arises out of the external distress, which bears more hardly upon the married than the single. It is to spare them this affliction that Paul advises the unmarried to remain as they are. 3. *The shortness of the time.* (Ver. 29.) Here again the apostle has in view the advent, which seemed to be drawing near. Marriage belongs to a transitory condition of things—the passing fashion of this world. Life is short, just that our affections may not be set on earthly things. They that have wives must soon leave them, and the remembrance of this should render marriage or celibacy a matter of comparatively little moment. 4. *The cares incident to the married state.* (Ver. 32.) The husband is bound to protect and provide for his family, and in troubled times this causes much anxiety. Husband and wife, moreover, have to consult each other's wishes, considering how they may please each other. From these cares the unmarried are free, and can therefore consider "the things of the Lord" with less division of heart. This does not mean that marriage is less favourable to holiness than celibacy : experience warrants no such statement. The apostle compares the two conditions only in respect of their freedom from worldly care, and in this the unmarried have the advantage. It does not lie in his way to indicate counterbalancing benefits belonging to the married state. His aim is to deliver us from distraction in attending upon the Lord (ver. 35). We are not to be like Martha, " cumbered about much serving," "anxious and troubled about many things; " but like Mary, sitting with undivided heart at the Lord's feet (Luke x. 38—42).

II. ADVICE TO FATHERS REGARDING THEIR UNMARRIED DAUGHTERS. In the East, marriages are arranged by parents much more exclusively than with us, and hence the obligation here laid on the father of judging when it is becoming for his daughter to marry. Very much depends upon the Christian wisdom of parents in this matter. How often are the highest interests sacrificed for the sake of a union that offers worldly attractions! Faithful and prudent parental guidance may prevent an unholy alliance and lead to a happy union " in the Lord." The point before the apostle now is the direction of fathers as to when they may grant, and when withhold, permission for their daughters to marry. 1. *When permission to marry should be granted.* (Ver. 36.) Generally, when the refusal would lead to anything unseemly. In particular, if the daughter has come to full marriageable age, if she and her lover are bent upon the union; in that case, for the father to enforce celibacy would be to put temptation in his daughter's way. The general advice not to marry because of present distress, is over-borne by stronger considerations (see ver. 2); and in view of these the father will do well to put no barrier in the way. 2. *When permission may be withheld.* The father is required to look at all the circumstances of the case, and judge accordingly. The elements determining his judgment will be such as these : (1) The presence or absence of such considerations as have been mentioned in the previous case ; (2) the tempera-ment or inclination of the daughter in reference to marriage ; (3) her fitness for the service of the Lord in the single state ; (4) her general well-being, both temporal and spiritual. If in view of these elements he judges it best for his daughter not to marry, he may properly resist the solicitations of suitors who desire to have her to wife. That is, he is at liberty to give effect to the apostolic preference of celibacy in respect of the necessities of the time.

III. ADVICE TO WIDOWS. This proceeds on the same lines as the advice to unmarried persons. The wife whose husband has "fallen asleep" (κοιμηθῇ, ver. 39; comp. 1 Thess. iv. 13, 14, and our *cemetery*) is no longer bound (comp. Rom. vii. 1—3), but is free to remarry if she chooses. The only restriction is that she marry "in the Lord," *i.e.* that she marry a Christian, and that her whole conduct in the matter be in keeping with her profession. Yet here also the apostle advises against a second marriage, on grounds already adduced in the case of virgins. A widow may marry again, but she will be more free from care and trouble if she remain as she is.

REMARKS. 1. *The application of abiding principles is modified by changing circumstances.* This must be remembered in considering how far the advice given here is generally applicable. What is prudent in a Christian country, with a settled government, and at peace, may be imprudent where the conditions are the reverse. There is a wide sphere for the exercise of true wisdom in the practical conduct of such matters. 2. *Christians should marry " only in the Lord."* On its lower side, marriage is the same to all men, irrespective of creed and character; but the Christian is called to consider the interests of his higher life. He is to enter upon this relationship as a follower of Christ, and seeking therein the glory of God.—B.

Vers. 29—31.—*The shortness of the time.* Very impressive is the apostle's manner in always rising above the mere details of duty to great ruling verities. Throughout this chapter there is a constant reference from rules to principles, and nowhere is this more conspicuous than in these verses.

I. THE CHRISTIAN VIEW OF THIS LIFE. 1. " *The time is shortened.*" The apostle seems to have in view the coming of Christ, of which the troubles of the time appeared to be the harbingers. Any day the " sign of the Son of man " might be seen in the heavens, so brief was the interval. Long centuries have rolled away since then, and the strained eyes of the Church have not yet beheld that sign. Still, the utterance of the apostle is not mistaken. Though the horizon that bounded his vision has been widening with the ages, the time is still short. For us the practical truth is that our life-span here is brief, whether its boundary be the Lord's coming to us or our going to him. (1) The time is short as compared with other periods. Brevity is a relative thing, according to the standard of measurement. The present average of human life is brief compared with the limit of "three score years and ten;" this term is brief compared with that of the antediluvians; the years of Methuselah are but an handbreadth compared with the duration of the earth; and this again is as nothing compared with eternity. Life seems long in prospect, short in retrospect. "Few and evil" (Gen. xlvii. 9) is ever the old man's plaint. (2) The time is short as compared with our life-task. Every true ideal of life seems to mock the little space we are given to reach it. "Art is long and time is fleeting." We learn little more than the alphabet of knowledge. We have but placed a few stones on the building when our work-day is over, and we leave the structure to be completed by others. What can we accomplish in one short life for the perfecting of our Christian manhood, the extension of Christ's kingdom, the redemption of our fellow-men? But let us not either lower our ideal within attainable limits or fold our hands in despair. The true work of this life, stripped of its temporary form, is carried over into the life to come and continued there. 2. "*The fashion of this world passeth away*" (ver. 31). It is like a scene in a theatre—vanishing while you gaze on it. (1) This is true of external nature. All is in a condition of flux; there is nothing permanent. The face of the earth, the boundaries of sea and land, even the everlasting hills,—all have changed and are changing. And at last, when the day of the Lord comes, "the earth and the works that are therein shall be burned up" (2 Pet. iii. 10). (2) This is true of human life.

> "All the world's a stage,
> And all the men and women merely players."
> ('As You Like It,' act ii. sc. 5.)

Within a single lifetime what changes do we see! Nations rise and fall; governments come and go; public men play their parts and then pass out of sight. How few of the friends of our youth and manhood remain with us till old age! New actors are ever coming on the stage and the old disappearing. The customs of society, modes of living, the whole environment of life, are like so many shifting scenes. (3) This is true of ourselves. The seven ages (see reference above) are the seven acts of our little life-drama; and each successive age brings its characteristic habits of mind. Standing amid all this transitoriness, where nothing is stable and abiding, we need to hold by the Unchanging in order to keep our balance.

II. THE PURPOSE OF GOD IN THE BREVITY OF LIFE. The time has been shortened that we may sit loosely to all earthly things. Their temporary character is to be remembered in all our relations to them. This is illustrated in several particulars. 1. *The married life.* "That those that have wives may be as though they had none." The apostle does not say that celibacy is a more spiritual condition than marriage. There is no asceticism in his teaching here or elsewhere. The married are to be as the unmarried, remembering that marriage is one of those things that are passing away. While loving husband and wife, we are not to forget that the time is short. This stage of existence is but preparatory to another, where "they neither marry nor are given in marriage" (Luke xx. 35). 2. *Sorrow.* "Those that weep, as though they wept not." Tears are not forbidden to the Christian. This is no stoical precept, bidding us refrain from weeping as inconsistent with our dignity. Grief is human, and all that is purely human Christianity encourages. "Jesus wept" (John xi. 35). The liker we are to him, the more tender of heart, the more sympathetic shall we become. But we are to weep remembering that the time is short. Sorrow also is transitory. It must not master us or break our hearts. Whatever touches the spring of tears—bereavement, loss, pain, the sufferings of others—belongs to this temporary condition of things. "Weeping may endure for a night, but joy cometh in the morning" (Ps. xxx. 5); "And he shall wipe away every tear from their eyes," etc. (Rev. xxi. 4). Therefore weep as though you wept not. 3. *Joy.* "Those that rejoice, as though they rejoiced not." Christianity does not frown upon earthly happiness. It is the part of Satan to represent the religious life as one of gloom, and the teaching of some Christians gives colour to the falsehood. Nature, literature, the arts, society, domestic fellowship,—all may pour their tributaries into the stream of our gladness. None should enjoy God's world like God's own child. But here the tempering thought comes in—" The time is short." Even this is not our highest joy, for it springs from a source that will soon be dried up. The " joy unspeakable and full of glory " (1 Pet. i. 8) belongs to the region of faith, and flows from those things which faith alone apprehends. Apply this to amusements. Pure and wholesome entertainments are to be encouraged, especially for the young. But whatever will not bear the thought of the brevity of life is not good for a Christian. Instead of the sword of Damocles or the death's head, the believer moderates his joy with the thought that " the Lord is at hand." 4. *Possessions.* " Those that buy, as though they possessed not." Christians are not forbidden to engage in trade or merchandise with a view to the acquisition of property. Every lawful calling is open to them. They are not prohibited from possessing wealth. The real question is—What place has it in the heart? Earthly possessions are to be held under the recollection that they belong to a transitory state of things. The man of substance is to sit loosely to what he possesses, not forgetting that " the things which are seen are temporal" (2 Cor. iv. 18). 5. *The use of the world.* " Those that use the world, as not abusing it." All that God gives us of this world is to be used as ministering to our need. The thing to be guarded against is the wrong use of it. It is to be our servant, not our master. God has put it under our feet (Ps. viii. 6), and we must keep it there. We abuse the world (1) if we seek it as the chief good of life, or (2) if we use it so as to hurt or hinder our spiritual life.—B.

Ver. 24.—*Quietness of spirit.* St. Paul knew how to hold the balance between the stirring forces of Christianity, and its calming, soothing power. He exemplified the combination in his own character; for he was ever moving yet never restless, ever aspiring yet always content, ever fighting, and that not as one that beats the air, and yet always breathing and making peace. The application of Christianity to actual conditions of society in ancient Greece raised many questions on which the Corinthian Church needed apostolic guidance. Such were the continual obligation of marriage after husband or wife had become a Christian; the question whether Judaism should yield to Gentilism, or *vice versâ*, in the new community; and the problem of domestic slavery. St. Paul had no express command from the Lord Jesus on such matters, but guided, as he firmly believed, by the Spirit of God, he handled these three points with rare wisdom and foresight.

I. THE LESSON FOR THE FIRST CENTURY. The introduction of the Christian faith into such cities as Corinth could not but operate as a disturbing, unsettling force. It was therefore the duty of the Christians to avoid as far as possible giving alarm to rulers, by abruptly or violently assailing the forms of life and the established institutions round about them. If their religion should present itself to the eye of observers as mainly an agitation or social revolution, it would be put on a false issue, and would give to its adversaries a strong argument for its suppression. Therefore, though the apostle hated all social injustice, he perceived and taught that precipitate action, even with the best intentions, would be a serious mistake; and that the only sound policy was to work on men's consciences and subdue their hearts, and gradually lift them up into a condition of moral feeling and a love of righteousness which could no longer brook such institutions as Greek and Roman slaveholding. On this topic, therefore, he checked impatience. The first thing needful was to bring Jesus Christ into every station and walk of human life. When Christ should dwell among and in men, society would take to new moulds by an inward necessity, not from any outward dictation. This was the best course to be taken even with regard to slavery. The endurance of it was hard; for St. Paul wrote at a period when the rich in Greece and Italy were cruel and contemptuous to their slaves, and it was possible for a Roman emperor to give their flesh to feed his pet fishes. But the institution was so familiar to the public mind that it was regarded as indispensable; and so Christianity was not to assail it directly, but to teach masters to give to their slaves what was just and equal, and slaves to be faithful and honest in service. If a slave could get his liberty, he was to take it joyfully—" use it rather." If not, he was to abide with God in that calling. His spirit was with God in a far loftier sphere than could be conceived of by the heathen master, who probably treated him with scorn. The Christian slave was the Lord's freeman.

II. THE LESSON FOR THE NINETEENTH CENTURY. 1. *Negatively.* (1) This text must not be quoted to require or justify adherence to a questionable calling or occupation. A Christian may find himself in a trade or business which offends his now enlightened conscience and is hurtful to his fellow-men : he may be in a place or appointment which requires him to practise deceit or minister to vice. Then he must leave it, because in such a place it is not possible to "abide with God." At the same time, such abandonment of one's situation or means of livelihood must be only under real stress of conscience, and not merely because the work is hard or troublesome. (2) This text must not be quoted to retain Christians in ecclesiastical positions which they see to be at variance with the Divine Word. The presumptive evidence always is in favour of one's continuing in that Church in which he obtained mercy from the Lord, and it is foolish and ungrateful to leave it so soon as he sees a flaw or fault in it. He who cannot live in a Church that has faults will have an unhappy Christian career, and end probably in a small clique of impracticable persons like himself. At the same time, one must avoid the other extreme of refusing to consider what is or is not in harmony with the Law of Christ, and sheltering or defending abuses which ought to be confessed and corrected. Such a mode of acting puts a stop to all Church reformation. Of small faults we do not speak; but serious errors and abuses we should try to remove. If we fail, we must change our position in order to "abide with God." (3) This text must not be quoted to check human aspirations. It is not to be implied that, because a man was poor at the time of his conversion, he must always be poor ; or if he was a servant, must continue a servant to his dying day. Christianity gives no countenance to the idea that the ranks of society should be stereotyped, and no one allowed to rise above the station in which he was born. There is a wriggling anxiety to gain personal importance which is not worthy of a Christian ; but if, by honest industry or conspicuous ability, one should rise in position and influence, the thing commends itself to good feeling and to reason. Therefore it cannot be condemned by Christianity, which is pervaded by good feeling and is supremely reasonable. 2. *Positively.* The text sets a wholesome check on self-regarding ambition. The great problem of life is not how to step up from one calling or station to another, but how, in this calling or that station, to abide in communion with God and advance his glory. No doubt, one position appears to great advantage over another, for happiness and for usefulness; but the difference is seldom so great as appears. That which has outward facilities has special risks and anxieties, and that which has disadvantage in one respect has compensation in another. But to "abide with God," not when apart from our worldly calling, gathered into a church on a holy day, but in our calling,—this is the problem. To have him with us and in us by the Holy Spirit ; to walk up and down in his Name ; to work and to rest as in his sight; to have his light shining on our path ; to have his grace working in us both to will and to do ; to have our labour lightened, our care relieved, our leisure sweetened, by his love! This, indeed, is life—high life. Oh, to abide in our calling calmly with God—our minds and hearts open to his impulse and direction—our wills submissive to his ! This is what will baffle the tempter and silence the gainsayer, by proving that our religion is no mere selfish hope of future enjoyment, but a power deep-seated in the soul, which can conquer passion and covetousness, and diffuse over the life a sweet serenity. To quote an English poet of the sixteenth century, now little known—

> " He most of all doth bathe in bliss
> That hath a quiet mind."

                                                                                            F.

Ver. 32.—*Free from cares.* I. NOTE THE PRECISE MEANING AND DRIFT OF THIS SHORT SENTENCE. It refers to the anxieties of married life. Neither in Old Testament nor New is any disrespect shown to the state of matrimony. St. Paul himself, when writing of the reciprocal duties of life, gives most sympathetic counsels to husbands and wives; and, far from placing marriage in an unfavourable light as compared with celibacy, describes it as a sign of the sacred union of Christ and the Church. But, in this part of his letter, he is replying to a question put to him from Corinth regarding the course most expedient in the special circumstances of the time, *i.e.* in view of impending persecution and distress.   Should unmarried persons marry at such a time?   Should parents give their daughters in marriage?   Should married Christians, if joined to heathens, remain in the marriage bond?   These questions the apostle deals with, giving his opinion, not for all time, but for a time of trouble.   It was no sin, or even fault, in any one to marry; but it would be wise to form no new ties at such a crisis, not to burden one's self with new anxieties.   In this sense the text is not for us, except in special emergencies and exceptional circumstances.   It is hardly needful to say that a man who is about to start on a dangerous expedition, or one who is involved in serious pecuniary difficulty, or one who has some arduous task to accomplish by a given date which will require incessant attention, ought not to marry.   Men in such conditions ought not to drag another into their difficulties or dangers, nor should they gratuitously add to their own anxieties.   Let them keep their minds undistracted, and defer marriage to some easier and more auspicious day.

II. Deduce a principle which will apply to all occasions.   It is this : the Christian life ought not to be hampered with cares.   Well for it to move on simple lines, as much as possible free from distraction and solicitude.   Novelists and poets have said much against over-anxiety and the black curse of care.   Spenser describes care as forging iron wedges day and night.

> "Those be unquiet thoughts that careful minds invade."

Shakespeare says—

> "Care is no cure, but rather corrosive,
> For things that are not to be remedied."

Another writes of "low-thoughted care."   And it is easy to show that it clouds the judgment and defeats itself by restlessness and over-anxiety which betray men into ruinous mistakes.   But after all that has been said against care, it is not shaken off— no, not by those moralists and poets themselves.   Every man we meet has some vexing care about money, or reputation, or health, about the conduct or misconduct of others. We want some deeper teaching and some stronger help.   We have both in and from our Master Jesus Christ—the most profound teaching and the most timely and effectual help. 1. *The life without care.*   Our Lord spoke of it in the Sermon on the mount. His disciples should not be anxious about food, or raiment, or the possible mishaps of to-morrow.   Such wisdom they might learn from the birds and from the flowers, that are fed and clothed by God.   If it be rejoined that the life and wants of birds and flowers are very much more limited than ours, who have to run so many risks and are vulnerable at so many points, the reply is obvious.   We ought so to conduct our lives as to keep our grounds of anxiety at the lowest possible limit; in short, to simplify our habits, restrain our self-tormenting bustle, and, reducing our external wants, give more voice to those which are inward and spiritual. 2. *The model of that life.*   It is Christ himself; for the perfect Teacher lived all his doctrines, practised all he preached. The way of human life which the Son of God selected, and to which he adhered, was the best for the purpose of developing a model humanity. We pass over the station in which he was born, because we have no discretionary power over our own birth.   But we take note of this, that he grew up in a home of piety, remote from those excitements and temptations that render our modern town-bred youth so precocious.   He had a quiet time among the hills and valleys round Nazareth, to let his thoughts grow large and his character acquire deliberate strength.   Then, when the time was ripe for opening his prophetic mission, he kept his personal life as simple as possible, and allowed no room for anxieties on his own account.   He also surrounded himself with friends who were of simple habits and little worldly ambition.   He taught them as they walked from one village to another or rowed their boat upon the lake, and did good everywhere without a particle of ostentation.   And so he went on to the end, implicitly trusting and obeying the heavenly Father who had sent him and was always with him.   Thus was he always calm and self-possessed.   No dust of brooding care lay upon his heart.   And, indeed, it was because he held himself so free of petty entanglements, that he could be and was so engrossed with the work which the Father gave him to do.   Easily satisfied as to food, and raiment, and lodgings, and things that perish, he devoted all the strength of his thought and purpose to the supreme object for which he had come into the world. It may be urged that this, though admirable in him, is really no model for us. We cannot lead anything like that simple, untrammelled, unconventional life of which we read in the Gospels. Now, no one alleges that in form we can live as our Saviour lived, or his servant Paul. But we do maintain that Christians ought to catch the spirit and principle of the life of Christ, and therefore should not let artificial wants multiply or needless anxieties entangle their hearts. Unless pains be taken to prevent it, life becomes in modern times very much of a *grind*—heart-wearing and perplexing. Our bones and brains are weary. Our time slips away from us, and with all our fagging, we find our work drag. We are caught in the tyrannical grasp of the conventional, and go on in a laborious fashion, not happy, certainly not Christ-like. They are the wisest and the happiest who lay down simple lines for themselves, reducing the cumbrousness of the outward life in order to cultivate more fully the inward life of faith, hope, and charity. 3. *The principle of the care-renouncing life.* It is faith in God. Let us cast our care on him, for he cares for us. On this principle the Man Christ Jesus walked, believing that the Father heard him always and compassed his path. On this principle he assured his followers that the very hairs of their heads were numbered. On this principle have all patient and humble Christian lives been sustained. "The Lord is my Shepherd; I shall not want." The thirty-seventh psalm teaches it well. Art thou anxious about temporal wants? "Trust in the Lord, and do good; so shalt thou dwell in the land, and verily thou shalt be fed" (Ps. xxxvii. 3). Art thou keen and eager for a lawful object? "Delight thyself also in the Lord; and he shall give thee the desires of thine heart" (Ps. xxxvii. 4). Art thou concerned about the issue of a matter? "Commit thy way unto the Lord; trust also in him; and he shall bring it to pass" (Ps. xxxvii. 5). Art thou hindered or discouraged by the success of unscrupulous rivals? "Rest in the Lord, and wait patiently for him, fret not thyself" etc. (Ps. xxxvii. 7). With these simple directions laid to heart and obeyed, one may go through the greatest vicissitudes and most exhausting toils with a spirit cheerful and serene.

> "There are, in this loud stunning tide
> Of human care and crime,
> With whom the melodies abide
> Of th' everlasting chime,
> Who carry music in their heart
> Through dusky lane and wrangling mart,
> Plying their daily task with busier feet,
> Because their secret souls a holy strain repeat."

F.

Vers. 1—7.—*Advice on details of Christian conduct.* In dealing with these verses, it should be noticed: 1. That, concerning such matters of practical detail, St. Paul gives his *advice*, he does not lay down authoritative *commands*. 2. The apostle's mission concerned principles, not details, which are properly regarded as well within the control of cultured Christian thought and judgment. Inspiration is wisely limited to subjects which, for any reason, are out of ordinary human reach. None of us need precise authoritative guidance of the common incidents and relations of life. We can ourselves sufficiently apply Christian principles. 3. Principles are better left without minute applications, as they can then be variously adapted to the differing conditions of society in each age. 4. St. Paul, when induced to give advice, takes care to bring out and impress the related principle; and, if possible, he presents his own example for imitation. The principles with which he deals in these verses concern: (1) The subordinate position of woman. On this matter details would be very unadvisable, as will be fully seen if we contrast the Eastern and Western, the ancient and modern, sentiments about the place and work of woman. (2) The mastery of bodily passion in the power of the sanctified will. This is enough, and we can make all necessary applications. "Each one of you should know how to possess the vessel [of his body] in sanctification and honour." (3) The duty of using for the service of others, and in no way misusing or abusing, any form of capacity with which we may be endowed (ver. 7).—R. T.

Vers. 8—16.—*The marriage tie.* When Christianity spread abroad among the heathen, very often, in a family, " one would be taken and another left," and much family and social difficulty was made when a heathen husband or a heathen wife was converted, and the other partner remained in heathen darkness. There could be no doubt that Christianity demanded separation from heathenism, and even declared a social connection with heathen people to be morally perilous; and it might very readily be inferred that this applied to the heathen husband or the heathen wife, and that divorce from them should at once follow upon Christian profession. It seems that the heathen in ancient times held the marriage bond very loosely, as do the heathen in many countries now. There is no more fruitful source of national immorality than ease in procuring divorce. Christianity has exerted such an ennobling influence on the European nations, in part because it has testified so firmly to the sacredness of the marriage bond. Christianity treats marriage as the main foundation of moral relations, and the proper preventive and cure of social evils. The relation must, therefore, be anxiously sustained, and almost every other consideration must be made subservient to its maintenance. Its various claims must be duly met; its various duties must be properly performed: 1. For the Christian partner's own sake, whether the other be Christian or not. If not, then maintaining faithfully the marriage relation will prove a spiritual discipline. 2. For the sake of the children of the mixed marriage, over whom the Christian partner can exercise a holy influence. 3. And even for the heathen partner's sake, since he or she may be won by the " chaste conversation " and holy example of the fellow-partner. Impress that the principle applied to marriage has wide applications. Whatever our spheres and relations may be, the man in Christ ought to master and mould and use them by the force of his new life in Christ.—R. T.

Ver. 14.—*Christian baptism.* " But now are they holy."
I. WHAT IS IMPLIED IN THIS STATEMENT. It is an acknowledgment of their virtual Church membership.
II. THE BEARING OF THIS DOCTRINE ON THE BAPTISM OF INFANTS. By this act of baptism the Church (1) expresses its own evangelical faith; (2) recognizes the children as belonging to God and to Christ; (3) testifies its confidence in their present spiritual safety; (4) pledges itself to train them up in the culture of the Lord.
III. GENERAL INFERENCES CONCERNING CHRISTIAN BAPTISM. 1. It is only an external sign. 2. Where persons are not baptized as infants, they should not afterwards be submitted to the rite except as intelligent believers in Christ. 3. As to the mode of baptism, it may be performed in any decent, possible way. 4. It may be administered by any one qualified or appointed to represent the Christian Church. 5. It should be consummated by an early admission to the Lord's table. 6. The duty of those who were never baptized in infancy.—R. T.

Ver. 24.—*Abiding as called.* Observe the peril of Christianity, as it spread among the nations, disturbing the social conditions, customs, and relations. Yet Christianity never directly attacks social evils, war, slavery, etc. There was also a constant danger of men's conceiving Christianity as a ceremonial and outward, and not as a spiritual and inward, religion. Our Lord had constantly to resist the expectation that he would prove a new Maccabeus, a national Messiah. And so the apostles had to assert constantly that Christianity is not, first of all, an ordering of conduct, but a life, an inward spiritual thing, that can gain expression in all circumstances and through all relations. A man may " abide " in whatever state he is when " called," seeing that he can *there* live out the Christian spirit and the Christian life.
I. THE LORD'S CALL. Notice: 1. Its form. It comes through human agency. 2. Its effectuality. It is accompanied by the witness and the sealing of the Holy Ghost.
II. THE CONDITIONS IN WHICH THE LORD'S CALL MAY FIND US. Illustrate: 1. The personal conditions, as suggested by the distinction of circumcised and uncircumcised. 2. The relative conditions. We may be bond-slave or freeman, master or servant.
III. THE CHRISTIAN'S DUTY IN RELATION TO THE CONDITIONS HE IS IN WHEN CALLED. As a rule, he had better remain in them. The new life in Christ should not make men restless concerning their circumstances. It is always a far nobler thing to conquer

circumstances of disability by the power of Christian principle and Christian life, than merely to change our circumstances, and shake ourselves free from the disability.

Press, in conclusion, that *God's presence* is not conditioned by any outward positions in which we may be placed. He dwells with contrite hearts everywhere, and pays no heed to the presence or absence of the brand-marks of the slave.—R. T.

Ver. 24.—*Religion and business.* The apostle, in this and the connected chapters, is giving to the Corinthian Christians a variety of counsels respecting the various relationships of life which they were called to sustain. The gospel of Jesus Christ, which brings its influence first to bear on the *individual*, next exerts its power on the family and social relations; and we can well understand how, in those early days, a number of serious practical questions would arise and demand consideration. One of these questions concerned the condition of servitude, serfdom, in which many of the early converts were placed. The apostle points out that personal religion is independent of calling or of social position. Whatever our earthly lot may be, we can be truly *godly* as we fulfil it; and St. Paul recommends that every one should continue in the business which he happened to be pursuing when the grace of God came to him, provided it was an honest and honourable business. His one counsel is that, whatever may be their place or their work, they should therein abide with God, in fellowship with God, in obedience to the will of God, in openness to the leadings of the Spirit of God, and in reliance upon the daily strength of God. Regarding the text in this light, it may direct us to consider the practical influence of Christianity on a man's business. We dwell on three points. 1. Religion is above business. 2. Religion comes into business. 3. Religion must not be lost in business.

I. RELIGION IS ABOVE BUSINESS. "Seek ye *first* the kingdom of God, and his righteousness." "What shall it profit a man if he gain the whole world, and lose his own soul?" 1. Religion is above business in its *character*. Its interests are different; its aims are different; its prevailing spirit is different and nobler. It is the heavenly occupation and the heavenly spirit. 2. Religion is above business in its *demands*. Business calls for the exercise of mind and skill; it asks the culture of our bodily powers—it develops skill of hand, promptness of judgment, keenness of insight, and perseverance in effort. It goes even further than this, and calls out certain moral qualities, the more simple and natural qualities, such as honesty, integrity, diligence, and truthfulness. But religion demands more, even purity, unselfishness, a fine consideration for the well-being of others, rightness of motive, and the inspiration of a supreme purpose to glorify God. Business does not touch the *affections*. Yet we are only cold, grasping, self-seeking creatures, if life and conduct are not toned by affections; and the religion which purifies and nourishes our affections must be above business. 3. Religion is above business in its *issues*. Business results are a certain measure of worldly comfort in our home, a share of the pleasures which the world can afford, and a position of respect and influence among our fellow-men. What more than this can the most successful business bring? It wins nothing that can go through the "great gates" with us. Its issues have rather to do with quantity than with quality; they are bounded by life, and have no out-reachings into eternity. Religion is above it, since "godliness hath both the promise of the life that now is, and of that which is to come." Religion shines down on common life all the golden rays that make the beauty of the present prospect, and it assures us that all it can shed *now* are but a few scattered rays of an "exceeding and eternal weight of glory," which will shine for ever on the "good and faithful servants."

II. RELIGION COMES DOWN INTO BUSINESS. Because it is higher than business, it claims to take it up into its grasp and glorify it, breathing its own noble spirit into all business relations. Some men do not hesitate to say that religion and business occupy separate spheres. Ward Beecher says, "How hateful is that religion which says, 'Business is business, and politics are politics, and religion is religion'! Religion is using everything for God. But many men dedicate business to the devil, and shove religion into the cracks and crevices of time, and make it the hypocritical outcrawling of their leisure and laziness." 1. Religion comes into business as a new force, nourishing diligence. William Jay used to say that Christian tradesmen ought to be the *best* tradesmen, and Christian servants should be the *best* servants, and he would sometimes quaintly add,

"There's many a good woman who is not a good *washer*-woman." 2. Religion comes as a Divine help in bearing disappointment and loss. Many by the troubles of business life are made reckless and hard. It is a great thing that religion, in a world where "man is born to trouble," should help us to suffer well. 3. Religion comes into business to elevate our standards of honesty and uprightness. We need not affirm that integrity is only connected with religion; but we may fully admit that the high standards are maintained by religion, and that it stands foremost among the forces that preserve business morality. 4. And religion comes into business as a spirit attempering business relations. It makes men more gentle, considerate, and gracious towards others; and elevates the tone of masterhood and servanthood, establishing mutual helpfulness as the ruling feature in all relationships.

III. RELIGION MUST NOT BE LOST IN BUSINESS. This it may be in two ways. 1. By excess of ambition and exertion preventing due attention to religious duties and personal culture (see 2 Tim. ii. 4). 2. By the wealth-getting spirit spoiling the Christian spirit. Illustrate by our Lord's saying, "How hardly shall they that have riches enter into the kingdom of heaven!"—R. T.

Vers. 29—40.—*An argument from the shortness of the time.* It is impossible to understand a large number of the apostolic allusions unless we recognize the early Church conception that the Christian dispensation would be very brief, and in all probability closed and completed in the first century, by the expected reappearance of the Lord Jesus Christ. This idea certainly prevailed among the disciples. To some extent at least it was shared by the apostles; but it is evident that they found it necessary to check a tendency to extravagance and fanaticism, and in some quarters the sentiment was allowed to nourish an antinomian spirit, which seriously imperilled the Christian morality. The notion of our Lord's second coming in some kind of earthly manifestation could only have been entertained by those who failed to understand that the words which he spake were "spirit and life," and were to be spiritually understood. "The letter killeth, the spirit giveth life." Yet there is a proper sense in which the Christian should be impressed with the "shortness of the time." Life at the longest is but brief. Life, in comparison with eternity, is but as a passing breath to the long day. To the Christian, life is so full of solemn claims and responsibilities that it seems impossible to fulfil them all in the narrow limits of an uncertain earthly career. The apostle argues here that a sense of the "shortness of time" should influence—

I. OUR HUMAN RELATIONSHIPS. Having this particular influence on them, that it prevents our being wholly absorbed in them, and helps us to the right use of them. St. Paul's principle is that we should "use this world as not abusing it." Here Christianity stands between the worldly spirit and the narrow religious spirit. The worldly spirit says, "Time is short; take your fill; live while you can." The narrow religious spirit says, "All the pleasure here is a snare, and dangerous; keep out of it altogether." In opposition to this narrow spirit, Christianity says, "Use the world;" and in opposition to the worldly spirit, "Do not abuse it. All things are yours. Take them and use them; but never let them interfere with the higher life which you are called on to lead. 'A man's life consisteth not in the abundance of the things which he possesseth'" (F. W. Robertson). Illustrate, in relation to wives, the early notions of the value of celibacy, and show that the married state can be preserved without interfering with the soul's culture, and that, indeed, the married state is found, for most men, singularly helpful to the religious life.

II. OUR HUMAN JOYS AND SORROWS. Explain what an amelioration of both is found in the fact that they are strictly limited. Joys soon fade. Affliction is but for a moment. For both the "time is short," and we need not, therefore, be unduly affected by either. We may gratefully accept the pleasure and patiently bear the trouble; for "we soon fly away" to be at rest.

III. OUR EARTHLY TOILS. St. Paul argues, from the shortness of the time, that "those who buy" should be "as though they possessed not." Resisting the tendency to fix thought and heart on what we can gain, and realizing that we can take nothing of it away with us. Moderation and sobriety may well mark our very acquisitions. The energy that wins success needs to be kept within reasonable bounds. Though not in precisely the sense in which St. Paul used the term, still for us also the "time is short," and we may therefore wisely sit loosely from all earthly things, and remember that where our treasure is there will our heart be also, and that, as Christians, our treasure is *in heaven.*—R. T.

Ver. 31.—*The passing world.* "For the fashion of this world passeth away." The figure used by the apostle is that of a shifting scene in a theatre. We may better realize the figure by applying it to a moving panorama. On, on it goes, ever new scenes coming into view, moving across, and then passing for ever away. Such life appears to us when we can seem to step aside and look at it. Sometimes it has been likened to the river, which bears the vessel on from the harbour among the hills, down past ever-varying scenes, and out into the great ocean. Poetic souls are touched with a fine melancholy as they see the "stately ships pass on," and feel how each resembles a human life. Time is short; the voyage is brief, and the ocean is so vast, so unexplored, so unknown. "The word 'fashion' has not here the popular meaning which has been generally assigned to it. It does not refer to those customs and conventionalities which vary in different nations and different ages,—all these pass away; but the word refers here to all that is external upon earth; all that has form and shape and scenery; all that is visible in contradistinction to that which is invisible." Work out and illustrate two things.

I. It is only the fashion of the world that passes away. This we should feel if we could rightly understand what the "fashion of the world" is. Clearly distinguish between the "essence" and the "accident" of a thing. It may be quite true that the "essence" escapes us; it is beyond our present vision. But we can realize it in thought. We know that within appearances are undying realities, and that appearances may change and pass, but the reality is eternal. Phenomena are but the utterance of eternal things, so that under our present sense-limitations we may know something of them. This is best apprehended by reference to the Lord Jesus Christ, who was "God manifest" in our sense-spheres. The mere fashion of him, as the Fellow-man, with whom we might have *sense*-relations, may pass away—it did pass away—but such passing in no way touched the reality of his abiding presence with us. So we seem every day to be losing things, but we only lose the *fashion* of them, the outward show. Whatever they have really been to us, for good or for bad, they are still, and they shall be for ever. We ourselves must presently pass away; but it is only the *fashion* that passes; we remain. With reverence it may even be said of us, that "our years are throughout all generations." Then we can loose from our grasp the merely "seen and temporal," if we have for our possession the "unseen and eternal."

II. It is the reality of the world that is abiding. If we can only find out what that reality is. And surely it is this—the character of the beings that pass under its thousandfold influences. There is nothing else that is abiding. The physical world is ever changing and passing away. We talk of the everlasting mountains, while they are crumbling and being washed down into the plains. "He that doeth the will of God abideth for ever," and he alone. The reality of the world is just that unseen spiritual sphere in which Christ's soul and the Christian soul lives. You may call it earth or call it heaven, according to the *fashion* in which it is apprehended. So the apostle urges his practical point—Do not even try to satisfy your souls in the merely sensuous spheres that so surely *pass away.* Break all these bonds of the sensual, if you are now bound with them. Keep away from these bonds of the sensual, if in any form they are likely to entangle you. Live in the Spirit. "Walk in the Spirit; and you will not fulfil the lusts of the flesh."—R. T.

EXPOSITION.

CHAPTER VIII.

Vers. 1—13.—*The relation of love to knowledge with respect to the question of eating idol-offerings.*

Ver. 1.—**As touching things offered unto idols.** This was doubtless one of the questions on which the Corinthians had asked for advice. We judge from the tone of the questions to which St. Paul here replies that the majority of the Corinthians, being liberal in their views, held that it was a matter of perfect indifference to eat idol-offerings; and that, in acting upon this conviction, they contemptuously overrode the convictions of those who could not help thinking that when they did so they committed a sin. The practical decision of the question was one of immense importance. If it were unlawful under any circumstances to eat idol-offerings, then the Gentile convert was condemned to a life of Levitism almost as rigorous as that of the Jew. The distinction between clean and unclean meats formed an insuperable barrier between Jews and Gentiles. Wherever they lived, Jews required a butcher of their own, who had been trained in the rules and ceremonies which enabled him to decide and to ensure that all the meat which they ate should be clean (*tâhôr*), not unclean (*tamê*). They could touch no meat which was not certified as free from legal blemish or ceremonial pollution by the affixed leaden seal on which was engraved the word "lawful" (*kashar*). But Gentiles had always been accustomed to buy meat in the markets. Now, much of this meat consisted of remnants of animals slain as sacrifices, after the priests had had their share. So completely was this case, that the word "to sacrifice" had come to mean "to kill" in Hellenistic Greek. Theophrastus, in his 'Moral Sketches,' defines the close-handed man as one who, at his daughter's wedding feast, sells all the victims offered except the sacred parts; and the shameless person as one who, after offering a sacrifice, salts the victim for future use, and goes out to dine with some one else. The market was therefore stocked with meat which had been connected with idol-sacrifices. The Christian could never be sure about any meat which he bought if he held it wrong to partake of these offerings. Further than this, he would —especially if he were poor—feel it a great privation to be entirely cut off from the public feasts (*sussitia*), which perhaps were often his only chance of eating meat at all; and also to be forbidden to take a social meal with any of his Gentile neighbours or relatives. The question was therefore a "burning" one. It involved much of the comfort and brightness of ancient social life (Thucydides, ii. 38; Aristotle, 'Eth.,' vii. 9, § 5; Cicero, 'Off.,' ii. 16; Livy, viii. 32, etc.). It will be seen that St. Paul treats it with consummate wisdom and tenderness. His liberality of thought shows itself in this—that he sides with those who took the strong, the broad, the common-sense view, that sin is not a mechanical matter, and that sin is not committed where no sin is intended. He neither adopts the ascetic view nor

does he taunt the inquirers with the fact that the whole weight of their personal desires and interests would lead them to decide the question in their own favour. On the other hand, he has too deep a sympathy with the weak to permit their scruples to be overruled with a violence which would wound their consciences. While he accepts the right principle of Christian freedom, he carefully guards against its abuse. It might have been supposed that, as a Jew, and one who had been trained as a "Pharisee of Pharisees," St. Paul would have sided with those who forbade any participation in idol-offerings. Jewish rabbis referred to passages like Exod. xxxiv. 15; Numb. xxv. 2; Ps. cvi. 28; Dan. i. 8; Tobit i. 10, 11. Rabbi Ishmael, in 'Avoda Zara,' said that a Jew might not even go to a Gentile funeral, even if he took with him his own meat and his own servants. The law of the drink offering forbids a Jew to drink of a cask if any one has even touched a goblet drawn from it with the presumed intention of offering a little to the gods. Besides this, the Synod of Jerusalem had mentioned the eating of idol-offerings as one of the four things which they forbade to Gentile converts, who were only bound by the Noachian precepts (Acts xv. 29). But St. Paul judged the matter independently by his own apostolic authority. The decision of the synod had only had a local validity and was inapplicable to such a community as that of Corinth. St. Paul had to suffer cruel misrepresentation and bitter persecution as the consequence of this breadth of view (Acts xxi. 21—24); but that would not be likely to make him shrink from saying the truth. This treatment of the subject closely resembles that which he subsequently adopted in Rom. xiv. **We know that we all have knowledge.** It is very probable that this is a semi-ironical quotation of the somewhat conceited remark which had occurred in the letter from Corinth. No doubt there was a sense in which it might (theoretically) be regarded as true; but it was St. Paul's duty both to disparage this kind of knowledge and to show that, after all, there were some among them who did *not* possess it (ver. 7). **Knowledge puffeth up.** The brief energetic clause, "Knowledge puffeth up; love buildeth up," shows the strong feeling with which the apostle enters on the discussion. There is a wide distance between theoretic knowledge and heavenly wisdom (Jas. iii. 13—18). "He who is full is rich; he who is puffed up is empty" (Stanley). "The first person puffed up was the devil" (Beza). **Charity edifieth.** There is no reason whatever for the rendering of ἀγάπη sometimes by "love," sometimes by "charity." The fondness for variation which led King James's translators to do so only obscures the identity of thought which prevails among all the apostles respecting the absolute primacy of love as the chief sphere and test of the Christian life. *Edifieth.* Helps to build us up as stones in the spiritual temple (ch. iii. 9; Rom. xiv. 19; Eph. iv. 12). "If because of meat thy brother is grieved, thou walkest no longer in love" (Rom. xiv. 15).

Ver. 2.—**If any man think that he knoweth anything.** Humility is the test of true knowledge, and love the inevitable factor in all Christian knowledge. The conceit of knowledge is usually the usurped self-assertion of an imaginary infallibility. We only know "in part," and our knowledge, having at the best a purely relative value, is destined to vanish away (ch. xiii. 8). **As he ought to know.** True knowledge has in it an element of moral knowledge, and saintliness *is* knowledge and supersedes the necessity for formal knowledge. Love is knowledge which has passed into heavenly wisdom. The student may say to the mystic, "All that you see I know;" but the mystic may retort, "All that you know, I see."

Ver. 3.—**If any man love God, the same is known of him.** We should have expected the sentence to end "the same knows him." St. Paul purposely alters the symmetry of the phrase. He did not wish to use any terms which would foster the already overgrown conceit of knowledge which was inflating the minds of his Corinthian converts. Further than this, he felt that "God knoweth them that are his" (2 Tim. iii. 19), but that, since we are finite and God is infinite, we cannot measure the arm of God by the finger of man. Hence, although it is quite true that "Every one that loveth is begotten of God and *knoweth God*" (1 John iv. 7), yet in writing to those whose love was very imperfect, St. Paul deliberately chooses the passive form of expression as in Gal. iv. 9, "Now that ye have known God or are rather *known of God.*"

Ver. 4.—**We know that an idol is nothing in the world.** After his brief but pregnant digression on the nature of *true* knowledge, he returns to these questions, and probably once more quotes their own words. They had given this reason for open and public indifference with respect to meat offered to idols. With respect to idols, three views were possible to Christians : either (1) that they were "demons"—the spirits of deified dead men; or (2) that they were evil spirits —a favourite view among the Jews (ch. x. 20; Deut. xxxii. 17; 2 Chron. xi. 15; Ps. cvi. 37; Rev. ix. 20); or (3) that they were merely dead images corresponding to nothing

at all (Isa. xliv., etc.). **That there is none other God but one.** This belief is the signature of Judaism, according to their daily and oft-repeated *shemâ* (Deut. vi. 4, etc.).

Ver. 5.—**For though there be that are called gods.** The verse is a limitation of the phrase which perhaps he had quoted from their letter. There are, indeed, demons, and there are created things, like the host of heaven and the powers of nature, which are called gods and pass for gods. **Gods many, and lords many.** Perhaps a passing allusion to the use of *elohim*, gods, for men in great positions, and to the habitual deification of Roman emperors even in their lifetime. The title "Augustus," which they all had borne, was to Jewish ears "the name of blasphemy" (Rev. xiii. 1), implying that they were to be objects of reverence. Indeed, the worship of the Cæsars was, in that strange epoch of mingled atheism and superstition, almost the only sincere cult that was left.

Ver. 6.—**But to us.** The "but" means "nevertheless." We Christians only regard these "gods," "lords," and "idols" as non-existent, except so far as they correspond to created and material things. **The Father.** Not only by creation and preservation, but much more by redemption and adoption, and as the Father of our Lord Jesus Christ (Rom. viii. 15; Gal. iii. 26). **Of whom** are **all things.** All things, even including the gods of the heathen, "visible and invisible, whether they be thrones, or dominions, or principalities, or powers; all things were created by him and for him, . . . and by him all things consist" (Col. i. 16, 17). **And we in him;** rather, *into* or *for him.* He is the End and Goal as well as the Author of our existence. **One Lord.** The only real "Lord," though the Roman emperors often took the title, and one of them—Domitian—insisted on the use of the expression, "*Dominus Deusque noster*" ("Our Lord and God"), as applied to himself (Suetonius, 'Domit.,' 13). **By whom** are **all things.** "By whom," as the Agent of creation and redemption (John i. 3, 10; Heb. i. 2). **And we by him.** "By him," as the Mediator and the Giver of life (Rom. xi. 36, "Of him, and to him, and through him are all things").

Ver. 7.—**There is not in every man that knowledge.** A correction of the somewhat haughty assertion of the Corinthians in ver. 1. **With conscience of the idol;** literally, *by their consciousness of the idol.* In eating meat offered to any god whom they had been accustomed to worship, "being used to the idol," as the Revised Version renders it (reading "by familiarity with," συνηθεία for συνειδήσει) cannot dismiss from their minds the painful sense that, in eating the idol-sacrifice, they are participating in the idol-worship. **Their conscience being weak** is defiled. Being Gentiles who till recently had been idolaters, the apparent participation in their old idolatry wore to them the semblance of apostasy. The thing which they were eating was, in its own essence, indifferent or clean, but since they could not help esteeming it unclean, they defied a conscientious doubt, and so their conduct, not being of faith, became sinful (Rom. xiv. 14, 23). St. Paul admits that this was the sign of a conscience intellectually weak; but the weakness was the result of past habit and imperfect enlightenment, and it was entitled to forbearance and respect.

Ver. 8.—**But meat commendeth us not to God**; rather, *will not recommend us.* God would think none the better of them for eating idol-sacrifices, even though they asserted thereby a freedom which was the reward of clear insight. This verse will serve to show why "fasting" is nowhere rigidly *enjoined* on Christians. If fasting is a help to our spiritual life, then we should practise it, but with the distinct apprehension of the truth that God will think none the better of us merely because we eat less, but only if the fasting be a successful means of making us more pure and more loving. If the Bible had been in the hands of the people during the Middle Ages, this verse would have rendered impossible the idle superstition that to eat meat in Lent was one of the deadliest sins, or that there was any merit whatever in the Lenten fast except as a means of self-improvement and self-mastery. This verse says expressly, "We lose nothing by not eating; we gain nothing by eating."

Ver. 9.—**Lest this liberty of yours become a stumbling-block**; rather, *this power* or *right of yours.* To lead any one to do that which *he* thinks to be wrong is to place a stone of stumbling in his way, even if *we* do not think the act to be wrong. For we make men worse if by our example we teach them to act in contradiction of their conscience. "Let your motto be *forbearance*, not *privilege*, and your watchword *charity*, not *knowledge.* Never flaunt your knowledge, seldom use your privilege" (Evans).

Ver. 10.—**Sit at meat in the [an] idol's temple.** To recline at a banquet in the temple of Poseidon or Aphrodite, especially in such a place as Corinth, was certainly an extravagant assertion of their right to Christian liberty. It was indeed a "bowing in the house of Rimmon" which could hardly fail to be misunderstood. The very word "*idoleum*" should have warned them. It was a word not used by Gentiles, and invented by believers in the one God, to avoid the use of "temple" (ναὸς) in connection with idols. The Greeks spoke of the "Athenæum," or "Apolloneum," or "Posi-

deum;" but Jews only of an "*idoleum*"—a word which (like other Jewish designations of heathen forms of worship) involved a bitter taunt. For the very word *eidolon* meant a shadowy, fleeting, unreal image. Perhaps the Corinthian Christians might excuse their boldness by pleading that all the most important feasts and social gatherings of the ancients were held in temples (comp. 1 Macc. i. 47; x. 83). **Be emboldened;** rather, *be edified.* The expression is a very bold paronomasia. This "edification of ruin" would be all the more likely to ensue because self-interest would plead powerfully in the same direction. A little compromise and complicity, a little suppression of opinion and avoidance of antagonism to things evil, a little immoral acquiescence, would have gone very far in those days to save Christians from incessant persecution. Yet no Christian could be "edified" into a more dangerous course than that of defying and defiling his own tender conscience.

Ver. 11.—**Shall the weak brother perish.** The fact that he was "weak" constituted a fresh appeal to pity. It made him more emphatically one of "Christ's little ones," and Christ had pronounced a heavy malediction on all who caused such to offend. But if there is this "ruinous edification" upon the trembling and sandy foundation of a weak conscience, what could possibly follow but a gradual destruction? The *tense* is the present (the *præsens futurascens*), "and he who is weak, in thy knowledge, *is perishing*"—"the brother for whose sake Christ died." The order of the original often gives a force to the words, which it is difficult to reproduce, as here. The word "is perishing" becomes very emphatic by being placed first in the sentence. "Destroy not him with thy meat for whom Christ died" (Rom. xiv. 16). *Perish; terrificum verbum. Clarius.* He could use no word which would more effectually point his warning.

Ver. 12.—**And wound their weak conscience**; rather, *and in smiting their conscience which is weak.* "What," asks St. Chrysostom, "can be more ruthless than a man who strikes one who is sick?" Was it not a cowardly exercise of liberty to strike the conscience of the defenceless? It is another form of "defiling" (ver. 7) the conscience, but brings out the *cruelty* of such conduct. **Ye sin against Christ.** Because Christ lives and suffers in the persons of the least of his little ones (Matt. xxv. 40, 45; Rom. xii. 5, etc.).

Ver. 13.—**Make my brother to offend.** "Make to offend" is, in the original, the verb "scandalize." The word for "meat" means any kind of food. **Flesh.** The particular subject of discussion here. "I will," says St. Paul, "abstain from flesh altogether rather than by eating it lead a weaker brother into sin." **While the world standeth.** The same expression is elsewhere rendered "for ever." Literally it means *to the æon*. St. Paul is often led into these impetuous expressions of the depth of his feelings. The reader will find the whole question argued in a similar spirit in Rom. xiv. 19—22. Lest; namely, in the case supposed. In reality there was no need for taking so severe a pledge of abstinence.

HOMILETICS.

Vers. **1—3.**—*A twofold knowledge.* "Now as touching things offered unto idols, we know that we all have knowledge. Knowledge puffeth up, but charity edifieth. And if any man think that he knoweth anything, he knoweth nothing yet as he ought to know. But if any man love God, the same is known of him." Here a new subject is introduced. Paul had already touched on four difficult points in connection with the Corinthian Church—points on which it seems some of the members had written to him for information. One referred to matrimony, another to ecclesiastical ritualism, another to slavery, and another to the eating of meats that were offered to idols. Meats used for sacrificial purposes in the heathen temples were, according to custom, offered in Corinth for sale as food. In that Church there were some who had scruples about the eating of such meat, and some who had not. Paul's counsel was sought on that subject, and in this chapter he supplies it. In this sketch I shall confine my attention to the *twofold knowledge* to which he here refers.

I. A PRIDE-GENERATING KNOWLEDGE. "Knowledge puffeth up." By this knowledge he means, I presume : 1. A knowledge that is *merely intellectual*—a stock of mental conceptions concerning the various objects brought under attention : they might be material or spiritual, those referring to body or those referring to mind, to the creature or to the Creator. Now, such knowledge, even though it be of a theological and ecclesiastical character, tends to self-conceit. 2. A knowledge that is *essentially superficial*. Mere intellectual knowledge has a tendency to generate pride, and the more superficial that knowledge the stronger its tendency. The men who go furthest into the essence of things, take the widest view of the domain of knowledge, enter furthest into the arcana of nature, will be the least disposed to self-elation. The greater the scientist the more humble of his class.

II. A MAN-EDIFYING KNOWLEDGE. "Charity edifieth. And if any man think that he knoweth anything, he knoweth nothing yet as he ought to know. But if any man love God, the same is known of him." It appears from this : 1. That " charity," or love to God, is the *true* knowledge. Love is the life and soul of all science. Mere intellectual knowledge, however great, is a tree without sap, without moral beauty or strengthening fruit; love is the root of the universe, and you must have love rightly to interpret it. 2. That this true knowledge *builds up* the soul. It "edifieth." It builds it up, not as a house is built up, by putting dead stones and timber together, but as the oak is built up, by the world-appropriating force of its own life, compelling outward nature to deepen its roots, extend its bulk, multiply its branches, and push it higher towards the heavens. 3. That this true knowledge *ensures the approval* of God. "If any man love God, the same is known of him." The word "known" must be taken in the sense of approval. In the last day, Christ will say to those who have not this love, "Depart from me : I never knew you," that is, never approved of you. This love for God in the heart converts the tree of intellectual knowledge into the tree of life.

Vers. **4—13.**—*Aspects of responsibility.* "As concerning therefore the eating of those things that are offered in sacrifice unto idols," etc. This paragraph suggests three general remarks.

I. THAT THE MORAL OBLIGATIONS OF ALL MEN ARE DETERMINED BY THEIR RELATION TO THE ONE GOD AND HIS SON. "As concerning therefore the eating of those things that are offered in sacrifice unto idols, we know that an idol is nothing in the world, and that there is none other God but one." There are many objects in the world that men call gods, and treat as gods, but they are really nothing, their existence imposes on them no moral obligation. There is One, however, and only One, from your relation to whom there grows up all moral obligations. "One God." Monotheism is demonstrated by all nature, by all consciences, as well as by the Bible. 1. He is a *Father*. "The Father, of whom," etc. The Creator of the universe, but the Father of spirits; *spirits* are his offspring. 2. He is the *Source of all things*. "Of whom are all things." The mighty universe and all it contains are but streams from him, the Fountain of life. 3. He is *our End*. "We in him," or "unto him," more properly. The supreme End of our existence and Object of our love. In connection with him there is another, "one Lord Jesus Christ." This one Lord Jesus Christ was not only his creative Agent, "by whom are all things," but his *redemptive* Agent, the Mediator between God and men. And we by him," or "through him." As Christians, we are what we are through him. Now, the will of this one God, as coming through Christ to us, we are morally bound to fulfil. An obligation this which not only can never be abrogated, but never modified by any circumstances, age, or revolution.

II. THAT WHAT MIGHT BE WRONG FOR ONE MAN TO DO MIGHT NOT BE SO FOR ANOTHER. The apostle teaches that those in the Corinthian Church who had reached the conviction that an idol was nothing in the world, and that consequently there was no harm to them personally in eating of the sacrifices that were offered to idols, would commit no wrong in doing so. The meat itself had not been corrupted because it had been offered to idols, it was as good as any other meat, and as their consciences were not against it there would be no wrong in them participating in it as food. On the other hand, those who had a superstitious idea that they ought not to touch the meat they saw the priests feeding upon in heathen temples, would commit wrong in using it as food. "Meat commendeth us not to God: for neither, if we eat are we the better; neither, if we eat not, are we the worse." The right or the wrong depended on *each man's conscience*. That which is against a man's conscience may not be against the eternal law of right, but is against his own sense of right, and therefore should be avoided; and that which is in accord with a man's conscience, though it may not be in accord with the principles of absolute rectitude, would not be wrong to him. Though sincerity is not a virtue, it is always relatively binding; insincerity is always an absolute sin. Thus what is relatively wrong to one man is not so to another. Here is the principle, "Whatsoever is not of faith is sin." "To him that knoweth to do good and doeth it not, to him it is sin." Therefore, "let every man be fully persuaded in his own mind."

III. THAT TO OFFEND THE CONSCIENCE OF A GOOD MAN, HOWEVER WEAK, IS A WRONG IN ALL. "Take heed lest by any means this liberty of yours become a stumbling-block to them that are weak." Respect for the weak consciences of good men: 1. May *require self-denial on our part*. A truly enlightened and healthy minded Christian may feel at perfect liberty to do that from which a weak-minded disciple would recoil with horror. The apostle, for example, might have felt at perfect liberty to sit down in heathen temples, and feast on meat that had been offered to idols, for his great soul had risen up out of the letter and form of religion, concerning meats, and drinks, and cere- monies, and statutory laws, and exulted in that "liberty wherewith Christ makes his people free." Therefore any restriction in such matters would involve more or less self- denial, and this Paul willingly accepted, rather than "offend" a "weak brother." On this principle it becomes all to act. Men who have reached the higher stages of Christly life may feel at liberty to do many things; but if they are surrounded by good people whose consciences are in the strongest antagonism to all such things, it is their duty to deny themselves of such liberty. 2. Is urged on the *strongest considerations*. (1) The lack of it may inflict serious injuries on the weak. (*a*) It may "become a stumbling-block to them that are weak." This means, I presume, an occasion of sin. Their faith may be shaken, and they may become apostates; and, more, (*b*) they may be "emboldened," encouraged to do the wrong. Without your moral strength, imitation of you will be pernicious. (*c*) It may ruin them. "And through thy knowledge shall the weak brother perish, for whom Christ died?" Christ died for all, tasted death for every man; yet his death, it seems, does not necessarily ensure the salvation of any. What a solemn thought, that the conduct even of an advanced Christian may lead to the spiritual ruin of others! (2) The lack of it is a sin both against the weak brethren and against Christ. "When ye sin so against the brethren, and wound their weak conscience, ye sin against Christ." 3. Is exemplified in the *sublime resolve of the apostle:* "If meat make my brother to offend, I will eat no flesh while the world standeth, lest I make my brother to offend." Here is benevolent expediency, the strongest ground on which the temperance reformation can be wisely and effectively advocated. In this sublime utterance you have the self-sacrificing and magnanimous spirit of the gospel. Give up all rather than ruin souls. Such an utterance as this is characteristic of Paul. "But I could wish that I myself were accursed for my brethren's sake, my kinsmen according to the flesh."

CONCLUSION. Where, in the state or in the Church, can you find a man who approaches in spirit the sublime philanthropy of Paul? In the state we have men who call themselves reformers, who grow eloquent in proclaiming the rights of man and the glories of liberty; but can you find either in their speeches or deeds the matchless spirit of philanthropy, beaming and booming in these words of the apostle?—"Wherefore, if meat make my brother to offend, I will eat no flesh while the world standeth." Are not our reformers, alas! more or less traders and hirelings? Where even in our Churches do we find preachers aglow with this unconquerable love for man? And yet this is Christianity, this is what the world wants, what it must have ere it can be morally redeemed. "There never did," says Sir Walter Scott, "and never will, exist anything permanently noble and excellent in a character which was a stranger to the exercise of resolute self-denial. Teach self-denial, and make its practice pleasurable, and you create for the world a destiny more sublime than ever issued from the brain of the wildest dreamer."

HOMILIES BY VARIOUS AUTHORS.

Vers. 1—13.—*Strength and weakness; knowledge and love.* The discussions contained in this chapter relate to "things offered unto idols." Bear in mind that idolatry was not then simply a religious system, but a system immensely extended and covering a corresponding surface of political, social, and business interests. At all points it touched individuals and families, and was connected with feasts, entertainments, and etiquette. "Most public entertainments and many private meals were more or less remotely the accompaniments of sacrifice" (Stanley). How far might knowledge assert itself and put on independency? What was the true use of expediency? And what the offices of conscience? And to what extent must the strong be tender and considerate towards the weak? Two parties existed on this subject in Corinth: the one that rested on Christian liberty, and, believing that "an idol is nothing in the world," demonstrated its adhesion to this belief by buying and eating meats sacrificed to idols, and even went to the excess of attending the feasts "in the idol's temple;" the other party looked upon such conduct with abhorrence. If, now, Christianity had been a mere scheme of human thought, an elaborate philosophy, a poetic inspiration, it is obvious that no such earnest dispute could have arisen. If, again, St. Paul had contemplated the subject on the ground only of abstract and theoretical principles, following out the logic that "an idol is nothing," and claiming the full freedom guaranteed by the assumption, a very different chapter from this would have been written. But see how he approaches the matter. His first step is to check the liberalists, and he does it efficaciously, for he convicts them of pride and recklessness on the side of intellect. Intellect he does not condemn, but its wrong use. His condemnation is founded on the fact that the intellect arrogantly claims to be the mind, to be the equivalent of the man himself, and, consequently, shuts off the recognition of anything except knowledge. St. Paul's position at the outset is, "*Knowledge puffeth up,* but charity edifieth." It is vigorously stated and is accompanied by evident impulse. The "knowledge" referred to is knowledge isolated from its rightful and essential associations, the knowledge of a truth, and yet without its checks and balances—an engine lacking safety-valve and governor. No matter how valuable the knowledge may be in itself; call it insight, call it what you please; if it abuse itself in its use, it loses its worth. Selfishness vitiates its excellence, and makes it doubly harmful, pernicious to the possessor, and obstructive of benefit to him on whom it acts objectively. Men are prone to exaggerate knowledge as knowledge. They say, "Knowledge is power." So it is, but whether the power be for good or evil depends on the man behind the knowledge. Think of the intimate connection between the intellect and the body, and how much more it is affected thereby than other portions of the mind; think how tangled it often is in the nerves, and imprisoned in the cells of the brain,—and can you wonder at the distrust that wise men have of its functions, unless controlled, and that sternly, by principle and sentiment? What subtle poisons creep into the blood and thence into thought! A slight imprudence in eating, a bad dream last night, a household worry or a business vexation, disturbed breathing or accelerated heart-action, and the intellect is warped and enfeebled. Do what we may to curtail the evils, infirmities cling to all its activities. Yet much may be done, and it is done in no other way than that suggested by the apostle. "Charity [love] edifieth [buildeth up]." By this he means that the heart must be under the influence of grace, and thus inspire the intellect so that it may be delivered from its selfishness and especially its self-conceit. And so fully has Christianity indoctrinated all our best thinkers with this idea, that they have come to believe that wisdom is the conjoint product of right thought and true feeling. "If any man love God, the same is known of him," and the knowledge here predicated of God has a reflex agency on the man's knowledge. Instead of being "puffed up," instead of an immoderate and unjustifiable use of his Christian freedom, instead of a vaunting display of his superiority to prejudice and ignorance, he is regardful of the scruples of others, and, while aware of the difference between them and himself, turns the difference to the account of humility and forbearance. The idol is nothing, but its nothingness is no reason for insensibility to the claims of weak brethren on his manly sympathies. For the great doctrine of "one God, the Father, of whom are all things, and we in him," is so profoundly realized, that human brotherhood is its complement in his character and conduct. "One Lord Jesus Christ, by whom are all things, and we by him," the Mediator of the natural universe, in whose sovereignty all laws and institutions and objects have their reason and end; the Mediator of the spiritual universe, who has consummated the manifestation of humanity in the person and work of the Holy Ghost;—this Jesus of Nazareth, who is the Christ of God and Lord over all, has so embodied the fatherhood of God and the brotherhood of humanity in his own incarnation and office, that henceforth the grandeur of the one is the strength and joy and glory of the other. St. Paul loses no opportunity to enforce this supreme truth. Does he argue in behalf of Christian liberty? Here is his basis. Does he plead for expediency? Here is his warrant. Does he harmonize them as coexisting and co-operating sentiments? They are mutually supporting because their possessor has the knowledge which comes from God in Christ. From this sublime height he is never long absent. Thitherward is he always tending, nor will he decide any question, whatever its bearings, with a judgment detached from the great truth Christ taught: "I in them, and thou in me, that they may be made perfect in one." All, however, have not this knowledge. The insight of some is partial and confused, "whose Christian faith is not yet so emancipated from the religious convictions of their old heathen state, and who are still in the bonds of their former conscience, moulded by heathen ideas" (Dr. Kling). Having this "conscience of the idol," looking upon the idol as a reality, and forbidden by his conscience to eat the flesh offered to an idol, the "weak brother" is offended. The meat itself is a matter of indifference, nor are you the "better" or the "worse" for the mere act of eating. A grave question, however, lies at the back of the action. It concerns "this liberty of yours," and the spirit actuating your mind in doing this thing. "Take heed;" this liberty may degenerate into a haughty self-valuation, may become a "stumbling-block," and may induce the "weak brother" to imitate your example, and thus sacrifice his conscience under your influence. Though the conscience be weak, it is conscience; it is his; its authority over him is sacred; obey it he must. Worse than all, your conduct, taking effect upon him, may imperil the salvation of a man, "for whom Christ died." Enlighten his conscience all you can; help to make it truthful as well as sincere; but, meantime, "take heed" lest sympathy and conventionality embolden him to err. "Weak" now, you will only weaken him the more if your liberty mislead him. The only element in him out of which strength can grow is the conscience. Use your freedom so as to liberate, not to enslave, this highest authority in our nature. Use your knowledge to illuminate, not to darken, this divinest of all the organs personal to the soul, through which truth reaches the man. Use your Church relation to build up and not pull down your brother, that you may be a co-worker with God and with his conscience in making him a "temple of the Holy Ghost." Then comes the utterance of great-heartedness—the declaration that he will eat no such meat for ever if it make his brother to offend. This was no sudden effervescence of sentimentality. It was genuine sentiment. It was organic to the man's nature. Impulse was strong because conscience was stronger. The current of feeling was no cataract leaping from a rocky bed into rocky depths, and dashing itself into foam, but a mighty river that could not become too full for its banks.—L.

Ver. 1.—*Knowledge and love.* In the Divine Being himself both knowledge and love are perfect; he is light; he is love. Man, made in God's image, is capable of both; but his knowledge is and must be very limited and partial, whilst he has vast capacities for love. Not only so; as the apostle here teaches, love is better than knowledge, for whilst this puffs up, that edifies. We recognize this superiority in several particulars.

I. IN ITS INFLUENCE UPON THE INDIVIDUAL'S OWN CHARACTER. Paul's observation convinced him that this was the case. There were at Corinth those who boasted of their knowledge, of their intellectual powers of discrimination, of their superiority to the ignorant vulgar. But these very persons, although Christians in name, were very far from displaying the character of Christ himself, evincing little of consideration and forbearance towards their fellow-believers. In fact, they were "puffed up," their knowledge inflating them, but imparting to them no real stability or vigour of character. On the other hand, such as were animated by the purifying and elevating principle of love were, by the action of that principle, delivered from selfishness and self-seeking. They were "edified," *i.e.* built up, as a temple in stately proportions, upon a secure and ample foundation. This is a generalization, the justice of which is borne out by the experience of the Church of Christ. A show of knowledge is often unlovely when compared with the reality of love, which imparts a beauty and a radiance to the character beyond what human effort and culture can possibly bestow.

II. IN ITS INFLUENCE UPON HUMAN SOCIETY. It has been maintained in our own day (by Mr. Buckle) that moral beliefs have no influence in the development of society, which is due to the advance of scientific knowledge. But facts are in contradiction to this theory. Learning, science, art, are all good in themselves; but they give no guarantee that they shall be wisely and beneficially used, and they may be far from a blessing to society. But where compassion and benevolence are prevalent and ruling principles, there society feels the benefit of their operation. The Church is maintained in peace and harmony; the world around is profited by the self-denying efforts made for the amelioration of its condition. We have only to compare the condition of ancient Rome with that of modern England to be assured of this.

III. IN ITS ACCEPTABLENESS TO GOD. We are not to understand that our Divine Ruler is indifferent to the progress of knowledge. "That the soul be without knowledge is not good." And there is a kind of knowledge which is near akin to love: to know God is life eternal. But mere intellectual activity, mere speculative acquaintance with truth, are vain and worthless in his sight to whom all things are known from the beginning. But love, as it is the highest expression of the Divine nature and character, is peculiarly congenial and acceptable to God. With the loveless soul God has no sympathy; but the soul that is on fire with love to God and man is preparing to dwell in the everlasting radiance which makes and blesses heaven.—T.

Ver. 3.—*Intimacy between God and man.* As the passage treats of man's knowledge professed, supposed, and real, we should expect in this verse to find a statement regarding man's knowledge of God. And by some the second clause of this verse has been interpreted in this sense. If this somewhat strains the language, and if it is necessary to understand that we have here an assertion that the lover of God is known by God, all the same the apostle must be acknowledged here to affirm a spiritual intimacy between the human spirit and the Father of spirits.

I. THE CONDITION OF THIS INTIMACY. 1. It is a condition which could scarcely occur to man apart from revelation. Men fear God, reverence God, worship God, seek to avert the wrath of God; but to love God is not an exercise of mind which seems congruous to the relation between the Creator and his creatures. 2. It is a condition which Christianity renders possible and natural. By revealing God as love, by bringing that love home to the heart in the incarnation and the sacrifice of the Son of God, Christianity makes a claim upon human love. The manifestation of affectionate interest and benevolence in a way so remarkable, so unique, is sufficient to account for a new relationship, and for new emotions corresponding therewith. 3. It is a condition capable of universal fulfilment. "If *any man* love God." There are many whose natural powers of body aɴd of mind are very limited. But there is none who has not the capacity for love. There may be a moral unpreparedness, but this may be overcome. The Gentile as well as the Jew, the illiterate as well as the learned, are capable of loving the Author of salvation.

II. The character of this intimacy. Love is represented as leading to, as involving, knowledge. 1. On the side of God himself. This is the explicit statement of the text: "The same," *i.e.* the man who loves, "is known by him," *i.e.* by God. Knowledge is, in Scripture, according to a Hebrew idiom, often used as equivalent to favour; even as we say we know a person intimately, meaning in the knowledge of friendship. Of course, the Omniscient knows all his creatures; but he has a friendly, fatherly, affectionate, intimate knowledge of those who love him. He reads the language of their hearts. "The Lord knoweth them that are his." He knows them to watch over and keep, to guide and govern, to strengthen and to save them. 2. On the side of man. This is the implicit statement of the text; for he who in the sense affirmed is known by God also knows God. How true it is that he who loves God knows him too! There are many respects in which we cannot know our earthly, human associates, unless we are drawn to them by the cords of love. Love opens the doors of knowledge. It creates that sympathy which gives intensity to the intuitive gaze of the soul. Thus it is that, whilst many learned and philosophic minds are ignorant of the Deity, there are to be found, among the lowly, the ignorant, and the feeble, those who, with hearts quickened and softened with grateful love, live in a hallowed intimacy with him who is the Father of their spirits and the God of their salvation.—T.

Vers. 5, 6.—*The unity of God.* The Apostle Paul had been trained in the monotheism which had from the first been the belief of the Hebrew race, and from which they had not for centuries previous to his time ever swerved. But as a preacher of Christianity, a religion which aspired to world-wide empire, he was constantly brought, especially as the apostle of the Gentiles, into contact with the worshippers of idols, both philosophic and popular. And he was often called to be the counsellor of those who, although called out of heathenism, still lived in a heathen atmosphere and were entangled in consequence in not a few practical difficulties. In discussing for the benefit of these Corinthian questions of conduct arising out of their necessary association with those who practised heathen customs, Paul took his stand boldly and uncompromisingly upon the great religious doctrine of the unity of God.

I. The unity of God is contrasted with polytheistic belief and worship. 1. The deities of the heathen are *called* gods. They are *called*, but they are not; it is a delusion. "An idol is nothing in the world." The grand denunciation of the Hebrew psalm occurs to the mind: "Eyes have they, but they see not," etc. 2. These deities are deemed "gods" and "lords." They were and still are, in heathen lands, deemed superhuman, supernatural, and are invested by the imagination with some claims to the homage, reverence, and service of intelligent men. 3. They are in number many, every river and grove having its deity. It is well known that the heathen had even their household gods, *e.g.* the Romans their *lares et penates.* 4. They have their several localities and ranks and realms of dominion. They are "in heaven," as the superior Olympian deities; or "on earth," as those inferior *numina* which haunt this lower world, nymphs and fauns and dryads, etc. Such was the system which Christianity found, with which Christianity came into conflict.

II. The unity of God furnishes a centre and an aim for the new religious life of men. 1. In himself he is "the one God, the Father." In itself this was a glorious revelation; and in Jesus Christ provision was made for its wide promulgation and acceptance. 2. He is the Creator and Upholder of all; "Of whom are all things." 3. And especially he is the great Object of our faith, love, and devotion. We are "for, ... unto him." It is at this point that the great revelation of the new theology becomes the great motive of the new religion. Polytheism distracted the minds of the worshippers, and made it impossible that faith in God should become the inspiration of a new and better life; for it was a question—What measure of reverence and of service shall be offered to this deity, and what to that? But Christianity revealed one God, in whom are all perfections, and who is not only the Creator but the moral Governor and Saviour of mankind. They who live to serve this God have an elevating, purifying, powerful aim in the conduct of their life.

III. THE UNITY OF GOD FURNISHES THE NOBLEST MOTIVE TO THE NEW RELIGIOUS LIFE. 1. The one God is made known by the one Lord Jesus Christ. It is a misunderstanding of the Scripture doctrine to conceive of this view of the Redeemer as conflicting with the monotheism which is the glory of the Bible revelation. The one Lord reveals the one God, as the Word reveals the Utterer, as the Son reveals the Father. 2. Christ is the universal Mediator, "by whom are all things." This is the doctrine of John as well as of Paul. And we may well understand the moral as well as the physical creation to be included. For all the blessings which the Father destines for humanity he has resolved to confer by Jesus Christ. 3. We as Christians are what we are "through him." As in the former clause we recognized the great *aim,* so here we recognize the great *means* and *motive* of the new, the distinctively Christian life. The Divine nature and mediation of Immanuel, so far from obscuring our belief in the unity of God, is the best and strongest and most effectual support of that doctrine. Even as Jesus himself said, "He that hath seen me hath seen the Father;" and "No man cometh unto the Father but by me."—T.

Vers. 8, 9.—*Christian liberty.* No doubt Paul was regarded as the great champion of liberty. The apostles at Jerusalem were more under the influence of the old Judaism; Paul, the apostle of the Gentiles, gained a larger spirit of tolerance through his association with men of various races and habits. The Spirit of God set him free from restraints by which many good men were fettered. To him the party of knowledge, of emancipation, of liberalism, would naturally look for countenance and encouragement, when scruples about trifling matters of outward observance perplexed the conscience and threatened to divide the Church. And, so far as his views of religion were concerned, Paul was with this party; yet, as this passage reminds us, in his view, religion had one side turned towards God, and another side turned towards men, and he would not have this second side overlooked.

I. THE INDIFFERENCE, AS A MATTER OF PRINCIPLE, OF OUTWARD OBSERVANCES. 1. *The general doctrine.* It is not what we eat or abstain from eating that God regards, that God will judge us by. The reasons for this doctrine are obvious. (1) The nature of God, who is a Spirit, and in whose view what is spiritual is of overmastering and supreme interest. Priests in their pettiness may think matters all-important which in God's sight are trifles light as air. (2) The nature of man, who is a reasonable and spiritual being, and whose highest welfare cannot consist in what food enters into his body and what food he refrains from partaking. (3) The nature of Christianity, which is a spiritual religion, and seeks to take possession of human nature and so to influence human life. It is not a religion of feasts and fasts, but a religion of faith, hope, and love. 2. *The special application of the doctrine.* The query propounded by the Corinthians is fairly answered. It is as though Paul had said, "So far as God is concerned it makes no difference at all whether you belong to the scrupulous party, and refrain from eating meat which may possibly have been offered in idol sacrifice and worship, or to the liberal party, and, despising such distinctions, eat whatever is purchased in the market or placed upon the table. These habits of yours cannot make you either better or worse, cannot commend you to God or involve you in his displeasure; he looks at something very different from such things." So with parallel cases; matters may have importance as regards the Church, as regards human society, which are utterly unimportant as regards our relation to God.

II. THE DANGER OF CARRYING CHRISTIAN LIBERTY SO FAR AS TO INJURE OUR FELLOW-MEN. A Christian in these early days might be himself quite superior to the small scruples by which his neighbours were influenced. But, at the same time, he might be justly called upon to consider his weak brethren, and not to put an occasion of offence in the path of any. The best things may be abused, and it is often so with liberty. Paul cared not a whit for idol feasts and sacrifices, and, had he considered only himself, he would have eaten meat that had been presented in an idol-temple; but he cared for his brethren, and he cared for them all the more if their knowledge was slight, their faith feeble, their apprehensions of spiritual realities obscure. He would not break the bruised reed; he would rather abstain than injure a brother's conscience. It was a grand view of Christian duty this which Paul took; a noble resolution this which Paul formed. A lesson to the whole Church of God in all the various phases of experience and trial through which it is called to pass. Let Christians think first, indeed, of their own position in the sight of the heart-searching God. But let them not omit to think of their relation to their brethren in Christ, and let them so act that none may be troubled in conscience or caused to fall by reason of any want of consideration and sympathy, by reason of any disposition to push liberty to too great an extreme. God is our Lord; yet his people, however feeble, are our brethren. Their interests are dear to our hearts, and our intercourse with them is to be guided not only by wisdom but by charity.—T.

Ver. 11.—*The brother's claim.* It seems as though Paul treated of this case of conscience at inordinate length. Perhaps this would be so were it not that, in disposing of this difficulty, the apostle was really disposing of many other difficulties which should emerge in the course of the centuries. Principles are laid down in this "casuistical" portion of the Epistle which are applicable to Christian conduct in varying states of society and throughout all time.

I. The danger to Christian brethren of the unrestrained indulgence of liberty. Let a Christian man consider only what will commend him to God, what is in accordance with his right and liberty; and what will be the result? This passage makes this very evident, showing that for an enlightened Christian to partake of food offered to idols may prove prejudicial to weak brethren, who take such conduct as a sanction of idol-worship and of idolatrous practices generally. No doubt this is a misconception, but it is a misconception which is likely, which is certain, to happen. Thus the man of weak conscience, of little enlightenment, has his nature defiled and hardened, and, according to the very strong expression of this verse, is in danger of perishing. An awful, unforeseen, consequence to follow upon the indulgence in Christian liberty. The possibility of such a consequence is in itself sufficient to make a liberal Christian pause lest he should carry his liberty too far.

II. The great Christian motive which restrains the exercise of liberty. The apostle calls upon the enlightened Corinthians to consider *who he is* whose welfare and salvation are endangered by the course supposed. 1. He is a *brother*. Who will say, "Am I my brother's keeper?" On the contrary, the spiritual bond that unites the people of Christ one to another is so close and precious that anything that threatens its permanence should be regarded with suspicion and dread. 2. Not only so; he is one *for whom Christ died*. Observe the contrast which is so powerfully presented in this language. The Lord of glory died to ransom and to save each disciple and friend of his; submitted for his sake, not to inconvenience and restraint, but to sufferings, to the cross, to the grave. And shall any follower of the Lord Jesus treat with contempt even the weakness and prejudice of one whom the Lord of glory so pitied that he gave up his own life to save? Who are we that we should act in a manner so contrary to the action of our Divine Lord and Leader? Let him be our Example, as in other things, so in this; let his self-sacrifice be our model and motive, that with a sympathizing and affectionate disposition we hold dear the security and well-being of every Christian brother, however ignorant and however feeble. So far from assisting in the ruin, be it ours to promote the salvation of every member of the spiritual family, every sheep, every weak and helpless lamb, of the vast flock of that good Shepherd who laid down his life for his sheep.—T.

Ver. 12.—"*Sin against Christ.*" It is a proof of the personal and intimate character of the relation between Christ and his people, as that relation was conceived in the primitive Churches, that it should be the very climax of reproach against any professed Christians because of any course of action they followed, to charge them with sin against Christ. It is surely obvious that language like this could not be used of any merely human teacher or leader. One who was on the one hand so closely united to the Divine Father and on the other hand so truly a Son of man, as Jesus, Immanuel, could alone be spoken of thus. It was not possible to go further in expostulation than by the use of such language as this, addressed to those who considered too little the conscience of a weak brother, "Ye sin against Christ." To act without due sympathy, consideration, and charity towards a brother Christian is to sin against Christ, because it is—

I. To OFFEND AGAINST CHRIST'S COMMANDMENT. Our Lord's great commandment, his new commandment, his oft-repeated commandment, was a commandment to his disciples to love one another. He even went so far as to make obedience to this law of charity a test and note of discipleship: "By this shall all men know that ye are my disciples, if ye have love one to another." A disregard for the feelings, the conscience, the spiritual health, of a Christian brother was an evident and flagrant violation of the Lord's great precept, and was therefore "sin against Christ."

II. To CONTRADICT CHRIST'S EXAMPLE. Our Lord did not enjoin a spirit or conduct which he did not exemplify in his own life. Whoever reads the record of that life must observe that his spirit in dealing with his disciples was one of forbearance, consideration, pity, and benevolence. He washed his disciples' feet; he bore with their infirmities and their slowness to understand him; he pitied and instructed their ignorance; he overlooked and forgave their cowardice and desertion; in a word, he laid himself out in every way for their spiritual good. How then could any Corinthian, how can any other professing Christian, be a follower of the blessed Lord, if he display an inconsiderate, contemptuous, unforgiving spirit towards a brother in Christ? In so doing he sins against the Master.

III. To INJURE CHRIST IN THE PERSON OF ONE OF HIS LITTLE ONES. Jesus laid down this principle with great clearness when he identified himself with his own, assuring us that what was done—good or ill—to his little ones he should, in the judgment, regard as done unto himself. The Head is insulted when the member is injured; the King is aggrieved when his subject is attacked; the Shepherd is smitten when his sheep are scattered. Whosoever is indifferent to the welfare of the Lord's servant sins against that Lord himself, and shall not be held guiltless. Christ expects all his people to act as if he were present in the person of every one whom he loves and for whom he died.—T.

Vers. 1—11.—*The two guides—knowledge and love.* I. THEY ARE BOTH EXCELLENT. This requires no proof. The apostle who sat at the feet of Gamaliel, would have been the last to speak slightingly of real knowledge. We are made capable of an ever-increasing knowledge. How much knowledge has been the means of accomplishing in this world! Ignorance is but a "fool's paradise;" "Knowledge is power." And how excellent is love. How dull and sad this world would be without it! How much more prolific in crime and evil even than it now is! One's only regret about love is that there is so little of it. It is the world's great want. Herein heaven and earth contrast, seeing that there is much love there and little here. The triumphs of knowledge are great, but greater are the victories of love.

II. THEY ARE COMPLEMENTARY. One is not without the other. 1. Knowledge without love leads to (1) pride; (2) intolerance; (3) selfishness; (4) injury to others; (5) many blunders in thought, feeling, and action. Knowledge is not enough for a people. We may have abundance of knowledge, and yet be very unwise, very injurious, and very unlovable. 2. Love without knowledge leads to moral catastrophe. It is impossible to predict what conduct may result from mere affection. Knowledge is necessary to determine within what limits we may rightly act. Knowledge can decide for us what is "lawful." Love determines what, within the circle of the lawful, we should choose. Knowledge and love united lead to that more perfect, that penetrating, that *true practical* knowledge, the opposite of which Paul describes in ver. 2. True love controlling sound knowledge leads to a *deeper insight*—in other words, to a truer knowledge. For example, a man may know God as God; may have some conception of the Divine attributes, etc. But when he *loves* God his knowledge makes incalculable strides; he now knows God so much more fully and truly that his former knowledge is little better really, and *no better practically*, than crass ignorance. Knowledge

" puffeth up ; " by itself it is sometimes *worse* than ignorance. Love, not acting without knowledge, but on the lines of knowledge, " buildeth up."

III. A SPECIAL CASE IN ILLUSTRATION. The Corinthians had written to the apostle respecting their liberty to eat meats which had been offered to idols. The portion of victims not consumed upon the idol-altars belonged partly to the priests and partly to the offerers. Much of this meat found its way to the public markets, or was consumed in private houses, at social gatherings, or at feasts in the temples. Christians would be often tempted to partake of these idol-meats. 1. The apostle shows that knowledge alone would be a very unsafe guide in such a matter. An enlightened mind would perceive that meats were in themselves the same, whether offered or not offered to idols; and knowing also that " meat commendeth us not to God: for neither, if we eat, are we the better; neither, if we eat not, are we the worse;" would consider the matter as purely indifferent, and to be determined solely by inclination. But here mere knowledge would lead to error. Love, which concerns itself about *others*, steps in and says, " Take heed lest by any means this liberty of yours become a stumbling-block to them that are weak." All do not realize the nothingness of the idol, or the fact that idol-meats are unchanged by idol-contact. Their immature and weak condition leads them to conclude that the idol is something, and to them the eating of idol-meats is an act which identifies them with idol-worship. Thus the partaking by the more enlightened may prove both a *scandal* and a *temptation* to the unenlightened. Knowledge says, " Do all that you have a right to do ; " Love says, "Consider others, especially the weak." Knowledge alone leads to contempt of the weak and ignorant, and to indifference as to how they are affected : but Love champions the cause of those who specially need consideration and help. Knowledge does not take into account the weak brother, but Love yearns over his welfare, and forgets not that Christ died for him. Love kindled at the cross flames forth in Christ-like self-sacrifice. Love, directing its glance around, sees that the highest interests of those for whom Christ died may be imperilled if the claims of liberty be too rigidly enforced ; and so she leads men to the choice of that " better part," self-sacrifice for the welfare of others. This is the " shining way " once trodden by the feet of the Son of God. This is the path of the *truest knowledge ;* for here we learn not only what we *may* do, but what in the highest sense we *ought* to do. 2. The apostle has here no occasion to show that love without knowledge would prove a faulty guide. But it evidently might. Love might lead the weak and ignorant to eat the idol-meats, so as to please those more enlightened, and so as not to be a check upon their desires. We need, for safe guidance, the twin guides, knowledge and love.—H.

Ver. 6.—"*One God . . . one Lord.*" I. THE ONE GOD. The oneness of Deity is here emphasized. It is insisted upon throughout the Scriptures. The true Israel, ancient and modern, has been monotheistic. The conflict, contradiction, confusion, and absurdity, conspicuous enough in the polytheistic systems, find no place in Judaism or Christianity. The oneness of Deity is confirmed by (1) nature, (2) providence, (3) the moral sense. The one God is : 1. *The Source of all things.* " Of whom are all things." He is the great Originator ; all things sprang from his creative touch. We know not *how*—the manner is not revealed to us, the *fact* is. God may have left much to man's scientific instinct to discover ; he may have intended not a little to remain enshrouded in mystery. We may travel reverently along the lines of true knowledge until they cease for us ; then the great truth remains still for our enlightenment and comfort. The march backward of science is towards *unity ;* revelation began with it. 2. *The End of all things.* " We unto [not 'in'] him." What is here asserted of some of God's works (" we ") applies to all (see Col. i. 16). All things were created " unto " God ; the object of their existence terminates in God, they show forth his glory, they subserve his purposes. The whole universe looks God-wards. So far as intelligent creatures do not find the end of their existence in God, so far as they do not seek the Divine glory, so far they fall out of harmony with the rest of creation and bring failure into their lives. We are not created for ourselves, but for God ; we should therefore " glorify God in our bodies, and in our spirits, which are *his* " and *for him.*

II. THE ONE LORD. This is Jesus Christ—the " Son of man " and the " Son of God." We are here taught that the Head of the Christian Church was the active Power in creation. *Of* the Deity, as such, were all things ; *through* the one Lord, the second person in the Deity, were all things. Some have been led by this verse to question the divinity of Christ: it appears to *teach it* in a very impressive and convincing manner. The administrative, mediating position occupied by Christ is indeed recognized, but the assertion that *"through"* him *all things were* seems scarcely susceptible of a fair interpretation if his divinity be excluded. Moreover, this very expression, "through him," is applied elsewhere to God as such (see Rom. xi. 36; Heb. ii. 10). And the expression which we have here applied to God, "unto him," is in Col. i. 16 applied to Christ. The apostle is speaking to the Corinthians about idols as "gods and lords." These were all regarded as *deities.* In carrying over the same terms to the realm of Christianity, there is nothing in the statements made which should lead us to regard "Lord" as less Divine than "God."

III. THE SPECIAL RELATIONS SUBSISTING BETWEEN BELIEVERS AND THE ONE LORD AND ONE GOD. 1. *Believers are "through" Jesus Christ.* As creatures, they are amongst the "all things" which are said to be "through" him. But the additional statement, "we through him," indicates a very special relationship. Believers are such through Christ; they believe on him. Through Christ they are separated from the "all things" and made a "peculiar people." All that distinguishes them from others in condition and prospect is "through" him. He is their "Alpha and Omega." He created all things, and they are his new creation—a creation of a higher order and with sublimer ends. Apart from Christ believers are nothing; through him they become "heirs of God." As through Christ in the realm of nature the chaos became order and beauty, so through Christ men pass from the disorders of a lost state into the excellences and glories of a redeemed and consecrated existence. 2. *Believers are "unto" God.* All things are, but believers are in a very special sense. This is "through" Jesus Christ. As all the creation under the administration of Jesus Christ is "unto God," so in a peculiar and lofty sense are believers. They show forth the Divine glories as none other of the human race can. They reflect the Divine love manifested in the transcendent work of redemption. They are presented to God as the fruits of the Divine grace. Their "life is hid with Christ in God." They are "not their own." Their lives are devoted to the Divine service. They are "servants of God." Once rebellious, they are now obedient; once defiled, now purified; once lost, now saved "unto God." Here is pre-eminently the believer's condition; he is emphatically "unto God." Is this so with us? If we are saved by Christ, *for what, to what,* are we saved? Some seem to be saved *for nothing in particular!* Many are satisfied with being "saved," and never ask, "Saved for what?" 3. *God is the Father to believers.* In a certain restricted sense he is the Father of all. We are all his offspring. But in a spiritual sense God is not the Father of all. Of certain unbelievers Christ said, "Ye are of your father the devil." God cannot be our *Father* unless we are his *children.* There must be the double relationship or none. Some are willing enough for God to be their Father, but not willing at all to be his *children!* But the true believer has received the adoption and cries, "Abba, Father." High privilege indeed! How it speaks of care, and support, and protection, and guidance, and teaching, and love! How *near* to God we are brought when he becomes *our Father!* Our origination is in the mysterious Deity; we are fashioned by the hands of Christ; amid the infinities of creation receiving existence for the Divine glory, we seek our own, and become blots on the universe otherwise so fair; "through" Jesus Christ we become changed, redeemed; by him we are led back to God, and see as life's supreme object the glory of God, now brought so much nearer to our grasp; and as we reach the dread presence of the Eternal, whence all things come, we lift up our eyes and behold "our Father." This also is "through Christ." God is the Father of Jesus Christ, and Jesus Christ has become our Brother. If Christ be our Brother, his Father is our Father.—H.

Ver. 13.—*The great argument for abstinence.* I. ARGUMENTS IN FAVOUR OF ABSTI-NENCE OFTEN RUN UPON SUCH LINES AS THE FOLLOWING :—1. That from which we are enjoined to abstain is asserted to be dangerous to ourselves, since we may be led to indulge to excess. Or : 2. Is injurious to ourselves, physically, morally, or spiritually. Or : 3. Is pure waste, bringing with it no real benefit. Or : 4. Is intrinsically wrong.

II. SUCH ARGUMENTS FREQUENTLY LACK COGENCY. 1. The fourth will have no application to the large class of things indifferent in themselves, and it is generally in respect of such that the war is waged. 2. The second and third will generally be open to question. The difficulty of proof is great. Facts, apparently conflicting, will be adduced, and where knowledge is limited and imperfect, the contest is likely to continue, the advantage now seemingly being on one side and then on the other. 3. The first seldom carries conviction, since every man deems it an impossibility for him to fall. Every one else may be weak, but we are certainly strong. The argument against often acts as a temptation, for when human nature is warned of peril it often delights to show how brave and steadfast it can be.

III. THE APOSTOLIC ARGUMENT. 1. The apostle enlarges the view so that others are included as well as ourselves. Abstinence is not for ourselves *alone,* sometimes not for ourselves *at all,* but for our fellows. " Look not every man on his own things, but also on the things of others." Whether we realize it or not, we always decide for more than one. We are units, but united units. We cannot legislate merely for that little area which we ourselves occupy. 2. The apostle recognizes the influence of example. Mentally, we instantly assent to this ; practically, we generally deny it. Our words are a spider's web ; our acts are a cable. Men do what we *show* them, not what we *tell* them. And we cannot persuade men that we are strong and that they are weak ; they will believe the opposite with very little persuasion. Men are like sheep : though the shepherd calls and the dog barks, if one sheep leads the way the others will follow, though it be over a precipice. 3. The apostle asserts the obligation of self-sacrifice for the welfare of others. That which is " indifferent " becomes anything rather than indifferent if our indulgence in it is likely to cause injury to our fellows. We are not only to think of others, but to deny ourselves for others. Our sacrifice will often seem very small indeed compared with their possible loss. Here is an argument which will stand where many others fall. It has special force for Christians. (1) They have a great example of self-sacrifice in their Master. They are to imitate him. " He saved others ; himself he cannot save." He " *gave himself* for us." The apostle seems to suggest a comparison of Christ's sacrifice with the sacrifice which he desired the Corinthians to make. Christ *died* to save men : you are called upon to sacrifice *what* that men may not fall away from salvation : *how little* compared with *how much !* And to those not making the required sacrifice : Christ died to save the weak brother ; you, to gratify your appetite, are causing him to perish. (2) They have a more impressive view of the issues involved in the fall of a fellow-creature. (3) Their non-abstinence may be a sin against a fellow-Christian (ver. 11). The fall may be, not of an unbeliever, but of a brother, associated in Christian fellowship and service. And thus be (4) a sin against the brethren (ver. 12) ; against the Church, bringing scandal and disgrace through a brother's fall. And also (5) a sin against Christ (ver. 12). For Christ and Christians are one—he the Head and they the members. (6) They have in their ears certain suggestive utterances of their Master's ; such as, " Inasmuch as ye have done it unto one of the least of these my brethren, ye have done it unto me " (Matt. xxv. 40) ; and, " Whoso shall offend [' cause to stumble,' as in text] one of these little ones which believe in me, it were better for him that a millstone were hanged about his neck, and that he were drowned in the depth of the sea " (Matt. xviii. 6).—H.

Vers. 1—13.—*On the eating of sacrifices offered to idols : liberty and expediency.* Another of those questions which troubled the Christian community at Corinth comes up here for consideration. To understand the difficulties connected with it we must bear in mind that the religious worship of the pagans entered largely into their social life. The victims offered in sacrifice to the gods were not entirely consumed on the altar. A portion went to the priests, and the remainder was either given to the poor or sent to the public market. Thus not only the feasts in the temples, but also private meals, were brought into close connection with idolatrous worship ; and the Christians could never be sure that the meat they purchased had not formed part of a sacrifice. It is easy to see how this interweaving of religious with social life would occasion complications and perplexities as to practical duty. To the Jewish converts the eating of things sacrificed to idols would be an abomination. Among the Gentile converts two classes may be discerned. 1. There were those who had been completely emancipated from their old ideas regarding the heathen divinities. To their view these divinities were mere creatures of the imagination, having no real existence ; and accordingly they felt themselves quite free to partake of the sacrificial flesh when set before them. 2. There were those who could not get rid of the idea that an idol was a reality, and that consequently everything connected with the system they had abandoned was polluted. Thus the question became an important one, and the decision of it had an interest, not only for the Church at Corinth, but also for other Churches where the same difficulties had arisen (comp. Rom. xiv.). But it may be asked—Had this matter not been already settled by the council at Jerusalem (Acts xv.)? The apostle himself was present on that occasion, and we naturally ask why he does not simply refer to the Jerusalem decree, instead of proceeding to give a judgment of his own in some respects opposed to it. The answer is to be found in a right view of the grounds on which that decree proceeded, which were grounds of expediency. The Gentile converts were enjoined to abstain from things sacrificed to idols, out of regard to the feelings of the Jewish converts among whom they were located. But this reason did not hold good in a Gentile community like Corinth; and consequently the whole subject had to be considered on its merits and in view of the altered circumstances. The question in itself is no longer a living question for the Church, but there emerge in connection with it great abiding principles which never lose their value.

I. KNOWLEDGE AND LOVE. The apostle prefaces his treatment of the question "concerning things sacrificed to idols," by a statement regarding the relative value of knowledge and love. 1. *Knowledge by itself puffeth up.* Knowledge without love inflates the mind with conceit. Take the knowledge of God. You may read what is written on the pages of nature and of Holy Scripture, so as to know a good deal about him; but if there be no outgoing of heart towards him, you do not really know him. What you have learned of God will lead to a false exaltation, inasmuch as you rest in it as sufficient instead of advancing to a personal acquaintance with him. Or take the case in hand. The knowledge of the nullity of idols led many of the Corinthians to think themselves superior to their brethren, who could not shake themselves clear of the notion that an idol had a real existence. They were filled with conceit, which, being untempered by love to others, led them to please only themselves. 2. *Love leads to true knowledge and true edification.* The way to knowledge is through love. This is true of the knowledge of God. "If any man loveth God, the same is known of him" (ver. 3). "Every one that loveth is begotten of God and knoweth God. He that loveth not knoweth not God; for God is love" (1 John iv. 7, 8). Love gives itself away to the object beloved, opens out the nature to receive impressions, and puts all it has at the service of the loved one. Love to God brings us near to him, and gives us experience of his gracious dealing, while he in turn opens himself to us. It is only where mutual love exists that there is a mutual revelation of heart to heart; and this holds good, with necessary limitations, of our relation to God. We know him only in proportion as we love him, and even his knowledge of us turns upon love. "The Lord knoweth them that are his" (2 Tim. ii. 19), in a way that he knows no others. Our knowledge of God is more correctly his knowledge of us; for all we can know of him here is but the alphabet of that more perfect knowledge which comes with perfect love (comp. ch. xiii. 12). Now, the knowledge that comes through love is not an empty thing, puffing up the soul as a bubble, but a solid thing, imparting strength and stability. It *builds up* the spiritual temple within with the stones of truth. The lesson is—You can know God only by loving him, and the measure of your love will be the measure of your knowledge. 3. *Conceit of one's knowledge is a sure evidence of ignorance.* The man who is proud of what he knows has no adequate view of the greatness of the object. The more we really know the more humble do we become. This is true of secular knowledge, but especially of Divine knowledge. The glimpses we get of God lay us in the dust. He who is puffed up because he has gathered a few pebbles on the shore has never looked out on the great ocean of truth.

II. THE LIBERTY THAT COMES THROUGH KNOWLEDGE. (Vers. 4—6.) Returning now to the question in hand, the apostle shows how the faith of the enlightened Christian suggests a ready answer. 1. *The idols which the heathen worship are mere nonentities.* Their so-called gods, with which they have filled the heaven and the earth, have no real existence. There is no Jupiter, no Mars, no Venus. They are simply creatures of the imagination, having nothing corresponding to them in the universe. This view of the pagan divinities finds frequent expression in the prophets, who ridicule them as mere vanities (comp. Isa. xliv. 9; Jer. x. 3; Ps. cxv. 4). How melancholy a picture does this present of the condition of those who know not the true God! Men must worship, and so strong is this impulse that they first create the objects of worship and then bow down before them. It is the blind groping of the human mind after the Most High—a creature, with dreamy recollections of a lost glory, stretching out suppliant hands towards a silent heaven. 2. *There is but one living and true God.* This is the Christian's simple creed. (1) Instead of "gods many," "to us there is one God, the Father, of whom are all things, and we unto him." This Supreme Being is the Creator and Primal Source of all things, our Father in heaven, for whose glory we exist. This is the fundamental doctrine on which all true religion rests, and which at once takes the ground from pagan polytheism. It also strikes against all modern idolatries which are practised in Christian lands: hero-worship, mammon-worship, etc. (2) Instead of "lords many," there is "one Lord, Jesus Christ, through whom are all things, and we through him." There is but one Governor of the universe, into whose hands all power has been committed, Jesus the Messiah, by whose agency all things were created, and in whom we are made new creatures. This is the second article of our holy faith. Instead of the endless series of gods and demigods, who were supposed to hold sway over different parts of the universe, "there is one God, one Mediator also between God and men, himself man, Christ Jesus" (1 Tim. ii. 5). 3. From this the inference is plain *that eating or not eating of things offered to idols is a matter of indifference.* If an idol has no real existence, it cannot defile that which is presented to the image in the temple. The flesh which formed part of a sacrifice is neither better nor worse on this account, and may be used without scruple. Thus the enlightened Christian is freed from the entanglement of such petty questions, which belong to the bondage of legalism rather than the liberty that is in Christ. How important is a full acquaintance with Divine truth! How good it is to be free from prejudice, and to receive the whole truth as to our standing in Jesus Christ! But such knowledge is dangerous if it stands alone.

III. LIMITATIONS TO LIBERTY ARISING FROM CHRISTIAN LOVE. (Vers. 7—13.) An enlightened view of the nature of heathen divinities delivers the Christian from questions as to the lawfulness of eating what had first done duty as a sacrifice; but all Christians are not thus enlightened. There were at Corinth believers, converts from heathenism, who could not get rid of the idea that the idols they had formerly worshipped had a real existence, and who consequently regarded the flesh used in sacrifice as polluted. A due regard to the case of these weaker brethren will modify the use of their Christian liberty by the stronger. 1. *Consider their case.* Their conscience was weak, inasmuch as it could not rise to the conviction that an idol is nothing, and was therefore troubled with scruples as to the lawfulness of partaking of a thing sacrificed to an idol. Hence such persons could not eat without defiling their conscience, *i.e.* without the feeling that they had done wrong. This carries with it principles that have an important bearing upon Christian ethics. It is wrong for a man to do what his conscience tells him is wrong, or what it does not clearly approve. The thing in itself may be good, but if you are in doubt about it you are thereby debarred from doing it. The dictates of conscience are always imperative, but with this there goes the duty of seeing that conscience is instructed. Comp. Rom. xiv. 23, where Paul is treating of the same subject: "He that doubteth is condemned if he eat, because he eateth not of faith; and whatsoever is not of faith is sin." Apply this to some forms of amusement, doubtful practices in trade, extravagant living, etc. It is not enough to plead the example of others, if you are in doubt regarding their rightness. "Let each man be fully assured in his own mind." Do not disregard the faithful voice within your bosom, even when it speaks in whispers. 2. *The eating of such things has no religious significance.* Neither the use nor the abstinence from use commends us to God or affects our standing before him. To abstain from eating for the sake of weak brethren is not to surrender any spiritual benefit. It is a matter of indifference. "The kingdom of God is not eating and drinking" (Rom. xiv. 17). Observe *the class of matters* to which alone the apostle's reasoning is meant to apply. They must be such as involve no religious principle—cases where accommodation to the weakness of others does not imply the sacrifice of truth or duty. In such cases we are free to consider the condition of our brethren, and to regulate our conduct by a regard to them. 3. *The strong must not use their liberty so as to put a stumbling-block in the path of the weak.*

If a weak brother, who had doubts about the eating of sacrificial flesh, should by the example of another be emboldened to eat also, in that case he would sin and his conscience be defiled. The more enlightened Christian would thus be the occasion of stumbling to his brother, bringing him into danger of perishing altogether, and would thereby sin against Christ who died for him. Rather than do anything that might lead to this result, the apostle declares, "If meat maketh my brother to stumble," etc. This is the principle of *Christian expediency*, of which Paul is the great exponent, and which enters so largely into the believer's practical life. It has its root in love, which leads us to "bear one another's burdens, and so fulfil the law of Christ" (Gal. vi. 2). It is an outcome of that spirit of self-denial which dwelt in him. "Now we that are strong ought to bear the infirmities of the weak, and not to please ourselves. Let each one of us please his neighbour for that which is good, unto edifying. For Christ also pleased not himself" (Rom. xv. 1—3). In applying this principle, note : (1) It applies only to things in themselves indifferent. Where true Christian liberty was in danger, Paul refused to yield (Gal. ii. 3—5). (2) It is not to be confounded with mere time-serving or man-pleasing. (3) Each Christian must judge for himself how this principle requires him to act in special circumstances. Total abstinence from strong drink for the sake of others is a good example of its application.—B.

Ver. 1.—*Knowledge and love.* There is a great difference between being "puffed up" and being "built up." The one implies something pretentious and plausible, but hollow and unreal. It means show without substance, size without solidity, inflation without real enlargement. The other implies the gradual accumulation of substantial materials, on a firm basis, to some useful and enduring result. Now, the apostle would have the Corinthian Christians determine the question of personal duty concerning attendance at feasts in honour of idols, or eating of meat offered in sacrifice, on far other ground than any supposed sagacity of their own. All, no doubt, had "knowledge." But there is a higher criterion of judgment than this. Love is a better guide in such matters than knowledge. In all these things let it be that delicate regard for the feelings and interests of others which love implies, rather than any abstract ideas about their own liberty, that determines their conduct. Hence the broad principle, "Knowledge puffeth up, love edifieth." Consider—

I. THE KNOWLEDGE THAT PUFFETH UP. The case contemplated is one in which the purely intellectual element in the determination of moral questions is divorced from right feeling. It is a knowledge ideal and speculative, not vital and spiritual. The knowledge of the theologian, the logician, the casuist ; not that of the man whose reason and conscience and heart are alike alive unto God. The characteristic of this knowledge is that it makes men vain, conceited, self-asserting, "thinking more highly of themselves than they ought to think." A true knowledge of the things of God has no such tendency as this. "If a man thinketh that he knoweth anything," etc. (ver. 2). Real knowledge in the spiritual sphere is beyond the reach of one who is destitute of humility and love. Even in the realm of purely secular science, true knowledge does not make men vain. The lives of such men as Newton, Herschel, Faraday, etc., illustrate the truth of this. They were men of lowly, childlike spirit. They stood reverently, as with bared head and unsandalled feet, before the infinite mystery of the universe. It is the novice, the mere tyro in learning, the man of shallow thought and narrow view, who is proud of his attainments, dogmatic and self-asserting. How much more will it be so in matters purely spiritual, belonging to a region into which our science cannot climb! Take St. Paul himself as an example. While he moved within the narrow circle of Jewish tradition and prejudice, he was probably the very type of personal vanity. His Pharisaic pride was not only that of legal blamelessness, but of theological culture. Had he not sat at the feet of Gamaliel ? Who could teach him what he did not know ? It is a portrait of himself that he paints in those half-sarcastic words: "If thou bearest the name of a Jew, and restest upon the Law," etc. (Rom. ii. 17—20). But when the light from heaven shone upon him, how was the loftiness of his pride laid low! He "became a fool that he might be wise." Moreover, this mere theoretic knowledge is as profitless in its effect on others as it is to one's self. It becomes disputatious, "gendering strifes about words," etc. There is no "edifying" quality in it. It does not make men one whit the nobler, purer, more gracious in heart and life. It in no way promotes the reign of those Divine principles of "righteousness, peace, and joy in the Holy Ghost," in which the kingdom of God consists.

II. THE LOVE THAT BUILDETH UP. Take love here in the highest and broadest sense, as including love to God and love to man. These are but two sides and aspects of the same affection. It is an essentially religious affection. There are tender sensibilities and generous sentiments which give a natural grace to human character quite apart from all religious thought and feeling. They may prepare the way for the awakening of this Divine affection, but are not to be confounded with it. Only by personal fellowship with Christ can we rise into the atmosphere of a pure, unselfish, all-embracing love like his. Love builds up the temple of God. The separate personality of every Christian, and the complex, many-membered personality of the whole redeemed Church, are the dwelling-place of God, prepared by gradual enlargement and adornment to be the fitting shrine of his glory; and it is the office of love to promote this process. It is the effective power in the development and perfecting of personal Christian character and social Christian life. In confirmation of this, think of it: 1. *As the essential spirit of all other graces.* It gives them their highest, richest quality. It is the life, the beauty, the strength, the very soul, of them all. Consider the position love occupies in the circle of the Divine attributes. Truth, justice, purity, goodness, etc., are attributes of the Divine character; but "God *is* love." A similar position does love occupy in the ideal character of his true children. We are such poor, fragmentary, distorted reflections of the Divine beauty that even in the best of us this truth is too often obscured. Personal Christianity assumes many forms—the gentle and the severe, the reserved and the demonstrative, the meditative and the practical, the punctilious and the free; but this is the essential spirit of all its forms. It is true to the Divine ideal only so far as this spirit breathes through all its moods. 2. *As the bond of Christian unity.* Keenness of spiritual insight, zeal for truth, fidelity to conscience, may of themselves have a separating effect; but love draws and cements men together in a real fellowship of life. Differences in opinion, modes of thought, ecclesiastical usage, etc., become of comparatively small account, "so love at heart prevail." 3. *As an incentive to all real Christian activity.* It is the distinction of Christianity as a Divine method of moral culture that it bases practical and social virtue on this foundation, casts it freely on the prompting and sustaining power of love. "Love is the end of the commandment, the fulfilling of the Law." Get your soul filled with love, and you will never want for an effectual motive to all noble living. As the materials of the building arrange themselves and rise into their finished form in obedience to the thought and will of the architect; as the notes fall, as if by an instinct of their own, into their due place according to the inspiration of the musician; as the words flow in rhythmic cadence in answer to the mood of the poet's genius; as the grass and the flowers and the corn grow by the spontaneous energy of the creative and formative mind that animates them all;—so will you rear for yourself the structure of a beautiful and useful Christian life, if your heart is filled with love. 4. *As the mightiest of all instruments of blessing to others.* By the sweet constraint of his love Christ wins the hearts of those for whom he died. By the almightiness of his love he will ultimately conquer the world and build up that glorious temple to his praise—a redeemed humanity, a creation ransomed from the curse. Let his love be the inspiration of our life, and we wield a moral force akin to his; we share his work, his triumph, and his joy.—W.

Ver. 1.—*Knowledge and love.* Revised Version, "Knowledge puffeth up, but love edifieth;" Greek, "buildeth up." This remark is made at the outset of the consideration of a new topic. It embodies a principle upon which Christians may safely act in any of the practical difficulties that may arise. The precise matter which engaged the apostle's attention only concerns us historically. It hardly represents any kind of difficulty that is likely to arise in modern society. "In Corinth and other cities meat was offered for sale which had been used for sacrificial purposes in the heathen temples, having been sold to the dealers by the priests, who received a large share of the sacrifices for themselves, or by the individuals who offered them, and had more remaining of their own share than they could use themselves. Thus a Christian might unconsciously eat of meat, either at the house of a friend or by purchasing it himself in the public shambles, which had been previously brought in contact by sacrificial use with an idol." Exactly how to treat such a matter it was not easy to say. Some had no compunctions in partaking of such food. Others had very troublesome scruples; and only too readily contentions might arise over such a small and insignificant question. Some would say strongly, "We *know* that an idol is nothing, and so he cannot defile the meat." Such persons would be likely to laugh to scorn the feebleness and superstitions (as they would call them) of the weaker brethren. Their knowledge would "puff them up," and make them positive and inconsiderate; whereas the "charity" which "endureth all things, and thinketh no evil," would make them gentle and considerate, ready to put their own ideas aside if pressing them unduly seemed to offend the weaker brethren. This is the point to which our attention is directed.

I. KNOWLEDGE TENDS TO PUFF UP. This is a *fact*, attested by the experience of all ages, and well within our own observation at the present time. There is often a positiveness, a dogmatism, and a contempt of others about persons who have a little knowledge, which may properly call for an apostle's reproof. We must, however, remember that fulness of knowledge is almost always attended with humility, considerateness, and cheerful readiness to serve. It is a *little knowledge* that has the injurious influence. A man may pride himself on the limited pond in his own grounds, but he must feel humbled when he stands before the boundless ocean, and knows that powers are too small and life too short for him to exhaust the infinite stores. But the point which St. Paul helps us to impress is that knowledge puffs up because it keeps a man *thinking about himself*. It is always what *I* have read, what *I* know; and the egotistic sphere is the most dangerous for any of us to dwell in. "Look not every man on his own things, but every man also on the things of others."

II. LOVE TENDS TO BUILD UP. This may be applied both to the *man* and to the *Church*. Self-seeking and self-worship so engross a man's attentions that the interest of others cannot be served, little things are easily magnified into difficulties, and dissension and dispute are fostered. But "love," "charity," cares more for others than for self; concerns itself about the general well-being; asks about everything—what influence it will have for good or for evil; and puts strong restraints upon personal feelings and preferences, if pressing them against the opinions of others would cause contention. Love is set upon "edifying," upon "culturing," upon "up-building," upon preserving that "peace" in which alone souls can thrive and grow. So St. Paul earnestly urges that *love* ought to rule and decide in all our Church relations and practical difficulties.—R. T.

Ver. 3.—*Knowing God, and being known of God.* The construction of this sentence is peculiar. We expect the apostle to say that the man who *loves* God is alone the man who can be said to *know* God. There is, however, in his words the under-thought of the identity between knowing God and being known of him. Olshausen says, "The knowledge of God presupposes the being known of him: the soul will not vivify with life from above until God has drawn nigh." It may be noticed that St. Paul, in "dealing with inquisitive and argumentative people like the Corinthians and Galatians, takes care to invert the phrase, so as to exclude all glorifying on the part of man." The statements of the Apostle John, in 1 Epist. iv. 7, 8, should be compared with this. Fixing attention on the two terms, "knowing God;" "being known of God," observe—

I. HOW THESE ARE RELATED. Are they two parallel things, or does the one follow after and result from the other? If we take this latter view, which of the two comes first? Show that the *knowledge* of God is an impossibility for unaided man. This impossibility is shown (1) from the facts of man's depraved and distorted nature; (2) from the statements of Holy Scripture, "No man, by searching, can find out God," etc.; and (3) from the actual experiences of men, as individuals or as nations. Four thousand years of experiment left God still virtually the "unknown God." God must graciously come near to us, reveal himself to us, manifestly concern himself for us, and show that he knows us, or we can never get to apprehend him. And this he has done in the manifestation of his Son. And this he does still in a gracious individual response to the open and trusting soul. If we are known of God, taken into his special regard, and favour; if he "lifts upon us the light of his countenance,"—then we can be said to know him. But the knowledge comes always by Divine condescension to us, not by the unaided efforts of our intellect. Our Lord put this truth under another figure when he said, "No man can come unto me except the Father which hath sent me draw him." Those whom God knows, in the sense of "approves," "reveals himself to," are those alone who, in any high, proper, spiritual sense, can be said to "know God."

II. Whereon both these are based. "If any man love God." Our best knowledge comes by love, not by intellect. The mutual knowledge of husband and wife, of mother and child, come not by mental study of each other, but by the relations and revealings of love. And so alone can we know our heavenly Father. Let him come near to us in gracious communions, and our hearts will surely find out how precious he is. "We shall see him as he is." Bodily vision will not be needed, for souls can see. Intellect may stand back, for *love* can see and feel and know. It will be observed that the *love* of which St. Paul here speaks is seen, not on its sentimental but on its practical side. It is the *charity* which takes due account of the frailties of others, and acts with the desire to help them. Charity is the varied expression of the love cherished in the heart; somewhat as obedience is the expression of faith. Faith is seen in good works, and love is seen in charity. John Tauler, the mystic, suggestively says, "Rightly is God called the 'Master of love,' for he rewards love; he rewards with love; and he rewards out of love." See the Revised Version on Luke ii. 14, "On earth peace among men in whom he is well pleased," or "men of good will"—of love, or charity. Impress how earnestly we should seek that disposition and character which will bring God near to us, and so give to us the saving apprehension of him. "We love him because he first loved us." And we can judge of our love to God by our feeling concerning our brother; for "If a man say, I love God, and hateth his brother, he is a liar;" "And this commandment have we from him, That he who loveth God love his brother also."—R. T.

Vers. 5, 6.—*Not gods, but God.* Two primary and foundation truths of religion were committed to the keeping of the Jews as a nation. They were revealed to, and fully apprehended by, Abraham, and were the reason for his separation from his polytheistic surroundings in the country of the Chaldees, and for the subsequent remarkable isolation of his descendants in the small, compact, yet central country of Palestine. Those two truths were—the *unity* and the *spirituality* of God. "God is one;" "God is a Spirit." It is the first of these truths which St. Paul here reaffirms, in view of the pagan conception of many deities and divinities; and there can be no doubt concerning the clear-cut testimony which Christianity makes to the truth of the Divine *unity*. There is only one God, whose favour and reconciliation we have to seek, and whose claim to obedience and service we must meet. It is true that Mohammedanism also affirms the unity of God, but it adds the questionable statement, "and Mahomet is his prophet." Christianity does indeed declare that there are "three persons in one God;" and that "Jesus Christ is the Son of God;" but both these truths are to be held, and can be held, consistently with our faith in the Divine unity. We have to avoid the perils of tritheism, and of conceptions of the divinity of Christ which fall short of his essential Deity; for "the Word was God;" "God manifest in the flesh." In the verses before us we have—

I. The common notion of gods and lords. "As there be gods many, and lords many." Paganism peopled earth and sea and sky with different orders of divinities, and imagined gods presiding over mountains, streams, and flowers; over flood and pestilence and fire; over virtue and over vice; over families and nations. Illustrate by the impressions made upon St. Paul when he first entered Athens. The place seemed to him crowded with idols, "given over to idolatry." There was a regular hierarchy; and probably a dim notion of one supreme god to whom the rest were subordinate, but as these lesser gods and lords stood in direct and close relations with men, it was inevitable that *they* should get all the worship. Illustrate from what is observed in heathen lands now; especially where heathenism is associated with learning and civilization, as in India. Show what complicated social questions arise in that country out of the conflicting claims of the multitudinous gods and lords; and the painful uncertainty which men in idolatrous countries must feel as to whether they have propitiated the *right god*, or left an offended one still to execute his vengeance. In contrast with elaborate heathenism, the worship and service of the one God is simple and satisfying. Fear God, and there is no one else to fear.

II. THE CHRISTIAN NOTION OF "GOD" AND "LORD." The two words may be taken to include the Divine Being as an *Object of worship*, and as our *practical Ruler*. Our God is at once the highest Being we can conceive, who rightly claims our reverence; and the very centre of all authority, to whose will we must wholly bow. But the two terms may be used to indicate the oneness, yet distinction, of the Father and the Son. The term "lord" suggests the immediacy of Christ's relations to us. So the word "God" may stand for the *essential* being; and the word "Lord" for the *mediatorial* being. 1. *The essential being—God.* Four points are here noticed by St. Paul. (1) God is *one*. (2) He is the Father—that relation being the most suitable for representing him, because it includes the personal interest of his love for each one of his creatures, which such words as "King," "Ruler," "Judge," "Moral Governor," do not. (3) All things are of him. He is the one and only Creator of things and of men. And (4) we are witnesses for him, who are bound to hold firmly, and show forth fully, this first truth of the one Father-God. 2. *His mediatorial being.* Under this term we apprehend the one God as the Lord Jesus Christ, and we are to see that he is practically (1) our present Lord and Ruler; (2) our only Mediator in his manifestation of himself in our flesh and upon our earth; and (3) our Christian standing and Christian hope are only in him and by him. Fully embracing this truth of the Divine unity, we shall be wholly delivered from the fear of offending the "gods many or lords many," whether they be fellow-men or imagined divinities.—R. T.

Ver. 9.—*Our dealings with weak brethren.* Our liberty may become a stumbling-block to others, and against this we must be constantly on our guard. There will always be around us some "weak brethren." 1. They may be *intellectually* weak, really unable to grasp more than the simplicities of the truth, and readily thinking that what they can neither understand nor appreciate must be error. There is also such a thing as mental bias, which prevents men from appreciating or receiving more than some particular side of truth. And this mental bias is often the affliction of men who are otherwise intelligent; and it becomes the occasion of much religious bigotry. 2. They may be weak *in conscience.* Instead of firmly attesting what is right and what is wrong, their conscience may only present scruples and questions and doubts. It is the same thing to say that they have little power of *decision;* and feel restless and uncertain, and weakly full of fears, when a decision is made. 3. They may be weak *through the relics of old habits.* A man cannot immediately separate himself from all his surroundings; and it was very difficult for Gentile Christians to shake off their heathen notions. Missionaries now, in heathen lands, are gravely perplexed by the lingering sentiments and habits of their converts. And in Corinth many could not get out of the idea that meat offered to an idol must be defiled and unfit for their eating as Christians. So it may be shown that there are "weak brethren" with us still; some who are offended with higher truths, which they are intellectually unable to reach; others who have scruples about what is permissible to Christians in social life, and yet others who fix narrow limits to the observance of the sabbath, and other details of Christian conduct. Now, St. Paul lays down some of the principles on which we should deal with these "weak brethren."

I. THE PRINCIPLE OF FIRMNESS. More especially if our brother's weakness in any way imperils the truth. Concessions to our weaker brethren may go to the fullest length so long as they concern only our personal relations with them. But we may concede nothing if our brother's weakness puts in peril vital truth. Then we must be firm and stand our ground, and claim our full liberty to receive whatever truth God may be pleased to give us. And it is even found, in practical life, that our brother's weakness in matters of detail is best met by a firm and intelligent resistance. We need to be especially careful that our dealings with our brethren shall in no way foster and encourage their weakness. Modes of keeping sabbath, or relations of Christians to public amusements, will furnish necessary illustrations.

II. THE PRINCIPLE OF HELPFULNESS; wherever we stand in such relations to the

" weak brethren " as may give us a power of influence upon them. If we condescend to them, it can only be that we may lift them out of their weakness into strength. Such helpful influence we may exert (1) by direct teachings; (2) by our own personal example. Others may see that what they call " our liberty " in no way injures our spiritual life, and seeing that may best help them to correct their mistakes.

III. THE PRINCIPLE OF SELF-SACRIFICING CHARITY. Actually depriving ourselves of pleasures, and what we think to be both permissible and good things, in order that we may be no hindrance or injury to others. Illustrate in the case with which St. Paul is dealing here; and show how many good Christians nowadays abstain from such things as balls and theatres because they are anxious not to set a stumbling-block in the way of others. Our practical difficulties in life apply to things *indifferent*; and in such matters it is proper that we should regulate our conduct by the effects which it may have *on others*. The true Christian spirit would lead us to say, " Rather let me suffer by abstaining from what I should enjoy, and could do without any personal injury, than let my brother suffer, either by the judgment which he would form of my doings, or by his imitating my example to his own serious hurt."—R. T.

Ver. 13.—*The law of Christian self-restraint*. No more perplexing questions are presented to the Christian than those which deal with the limitations of his Christian liberty. Were the Christian man alone in the world, or were he assured that his actions would in no way influence those around him, there are many personal enjoyments in which he could freely indulge, and he would have little call to self-restraint. He would at least be a " law unto himself," and need make no laws for himself upon consideration of others. But none of us can live under such conditions. We are not only a " spectacle unto men and angels," but every act of ours bears influence on some one, affecting others either for good or for evil. And this fact we must take into solemn account. The relationships of life are main sources of our pleasure, but they bring us all our responsibilities, and, though our conduct in all essential things is to be determined only by what is *right*, in all matters that are left to our decision we are bound to consider how *others* will regard our conduct; and we should even take into account how they may misunderstand and misrepresent, and so make mischief out of our actions. It is true that " the fear of man bringeth a snare," but it is also true that the *love* of man, and sincere desire for the blessing of others, will always help us to form good judgments concerning what is prudent and advisable. Sincere hearts are full of anxiety lest, by any personal indulgences or needless displays of superior moral strength, they should " sin against the weaker brethren." It should be observed that upon things doubtful God lays down no direct rules. The Christian man is expected to make his own wise laws of self-restraint. If he be sincere and earnest he will make for himself two supreme laws.

I. THE LAW OF CHARITY TOWARDS OUR BROTHER. That is, in every disputable or doubtful case he will give the advantage to his brother, and act taking into account even his weaknesses. It should be clearly understood: 1. That when, in a spirit of charity, a Christian man puts himself under strong restraints, he does not *alter his views* of the weakness of his brother's difficulty or of the possibility of his own acting or enjoying without personal injury. The very point of his Christian virtue is that, while recognizing the rightness of the thing *for himself*, he refrains for the sake of others. There would be no virtue in his self-restraint if he changed his opinion as to the rightness of the act. He holds his own opinion, but in Christian love he yields to the opinion of another. 2. We may also see that, when the Christian puts himself under restraint for the sake of a weak brother, it is that he may gain influence upon him that shall lift him up out of his weakness. It can be no part of Christian duty to condescend to a brother's weakness, and leave him weak. If St. Paul refrained from eating the meat that had been offered to idols, it was in the hope of presently getting the weak brethren to see that, since an idol is " nothing at all," he cannot defile any meat. Our charity does not concern the particular case, but the *entire well-being* of our weaker brother. 3. It may further be shown that the restraints under which the Christian man puts himself, by the persuasions of his brotherly love, may be severe and trying at first, but become easier after a while, and will often turn into blessing for himself at the last. This may be efficiently illustrated in the case of a man giving up all alcoholic drink for the sake of helping a brother who is in peril from the enticements of the drink-demon. If he be of a social disposition, it may cost him a great deal to give up long-settled habits, but he may prove, in both health and means, that the self-restraint of Christian charity can become a blessing to him who manifests it, as well as to him for whose sake the sacrifices have been made. God ever graciously secures to us the rewards of right-doing, and makes "charity twice blessed."

II. THE LAW OF LOYALTY TO CHRIST. Our one supreme purpose must be to *serve him*, and he has told us that what is done unto "the least of the brethren" is "done unto him." We think that, in the greatness of our loyalty, we would do anything for Christ, and put ourselves under any kind of restraints, were he really here with us in the flesh. But he puts our loyalty under a severe test when he says, "Do to your weak brother, do for your weak brother's sake, just what you would have done for me." We think we could go without meat, or put away drink, at once and for ever, if Jesus wished. It is Christ's wish that is expressed to us when we are led to see that our "liberty" is injuring a brother; and our Lord counts it loyalty to him when we restrain ourselves for a brother's sake. St. Paul makes this plain. To offend against a weak brother, to refuse proper limitations of our own liberty when such limitations would help a brother, is to sin against Christ, even against Christ who—at the uttermost self-sacrifice—even died that he might save and sanctify the weak brother. Conclude by showing that the appeal may be made to us, in relation to this matter, which is made by the writer of the Epistle to the Hebrews in a more general way, "Ye have not yet resisted unto blood, striving against sin." In how few of us the self-restraints of Christian charity can be said yet to have reached the sublime heights of *self-sacrifice!*—R. T.

EXPOSITION.

CHAPTER IX.

Vers. 1—27.—*The rights and the self-denial of an apostle.*

Vers. 1—14.—*An apostle's right to maintenance.*

Ver. 1.—**Am I not an apostle? am I not free?** The order of the best manuscripts is, *Am I not free? am I not an apostle?* St. Paul designed in this chapter to show that he was not only *giving a precept*, but *setting an example*. He told the "strong" Corinthians, who had "knowledge," that they should be ready to abnegate their rights for the good of others. He now wishes to show them that, in a matter which affected his whole life, he had himself abnegated his own rights. Being free and an apostle, he could, if he had chosen, have claimed, as others had done, a right to be supported by the Churches to which he preached. He had thought it more for their good to waive this claim, and therefore he had done so at the cost (as appears in many other passages: ch. iv. 12; Acts xx. 34; 1 Thess. ii. 9) of bitter hardship to himself. But St. Paul practically "goes off" at the word "apostle." It was so essential for him to vindicate, against the subterranean malignity of hostile partisans, his dignity as an apostle, that in asserting that authority he almost loses sight for the time of the main object for which he had alluded to the fact. Hence

much that he says is of the nature of a digression—though an important one—until he resumes the main thread of his subject at ch. xi. 15. **Have I not seen Jesus Christ our Lord?** Doubtless he mainly refers to the vision on the road to Damascus (Acts ix. 3, 17; ch. xv. 8), though he received other visions and revelations also (Acts xviii. 9; xxii. 14, 18; 2 Cor. xii. 1, etc.). He had probably not seen Christ during his life on earth (see my 'Life of St. Paul,' i. 73—75). The words are added to remind them that those who boasted of personal knowledge and relation with Jesus—perhaps the Christ party—had no *exclusive* prerogative. **Are not ye my work in the Lord?** I am not only *an* apostle, but emphatically *your* apostle (Acts xviii. 1—11; ch. iv. 15).

Ver. 2.—**Unto others.** If the emissaries from Jerusalem or the Petrine party do not choose to regard me as *their* apostle or an apostle at all, yet at any rate I am *yours*. Doubtless; rather, *at least, at any rate.* **The seal of mine apostleship.** Your conversion attests the genuineness of my claim, as a seal attests a document. Thus baptism is the seal of conversion (Eph. iv. 30; comp. Rom. iv. 11; John iii. 33).

Ver. 3.—**Mine answer;** literally, *my defence;* the word "examine" is the word used for a legal inquiry. The Corinthians had as it were placed him on his defence at the bar of their criticism. **Is this.** That I was the cause of your conversion. In 2 Cor. xii. 12 he refers to other proofs of his apostolic power.

Ver. 4.—**To eat and to drink.** To be supported by those to whom we preach (Luke x. 7).

Ver. 5.—**To lead about a sister, a wife.** There can be no doubt that this represents the true reading, and that the meaning is, "We have power to lead about, that is, to travel in company with, some Christian sister to whom we are married, and who is supported at the expense of the Church." This plain meaning, however, involving the assertion that the apostles and desposyni (" the Lord's brethren ") were married men, was so distasteful to the morbid asceticism which held celibacy in a sort of Manichæan reverence, that the scribes of the fourth, fifth, and later centuries freely tampered with the text, in the happily fruitless attempt to get rid of this meaning. They endeavoured, by putting the word in the plural or by omitting " wife," to suggest that the women whom the apostles travelled with were " deaconesses." Augustine, Tertullian, Ambrose, and others explain the verse of "ministering women" (Luke viii. 2, 3). The false interpretation avenged itself on the bias which led to it. Valla adopts the wilful invention that the apostles, though married, travelled with their wives only as sisters. Such subterfuges have eaten away the heart of honest exegesis from many passages of Scripture, and originated the taunt that it is a "nose of wax," which readers can twist as they like. It was the cause of such shameful abuses and misrepresentations that at last the practice of travelling about with unmarried women, who went under the name of "sisters," " beloved," " companions," was distinctly forbidden by the third canon of the first Council of Nice. Simon Magus might unblushingly carry about with him a Tyrian woman named Helena; but apostles and true Christians would never have been guilty of any conduct which could give a handle to base suspicions. They travelled only with their wives. *A sister.* A Christian woman (ch. vii. 15; Rom. xvi. 1; Jas. ii. 15, etc.). *A wife;* i.e. as a wife. **Other apostles.** This is a positive mistranslation for "*the rest of the* apostles." It might be too much to infer positively from this that *every one* of the apostles and desposyni were married; but there is independent evidence and tradition to show that at any rate most of them were. **The brethren of the Lord.** They are clearly and undeniably *distinguished from* the apostles. According to the Helvidian theory (to which the plain language of the Gospels seems to point), they were sons of Joseph and

Mary. This is the view of St. Clement of Alexandria in ancient times, and writers so different from each other as De Wette, Neander, Osiander, Meyer, Ewald, and Alford, in modern. The theory of Jerome, that they were cousins of Jesus, being sons of Alphæus and Mary, a sister of the Virgin, is on every ground absolutely untenable, and it was half dropped even by St. Jerome himself, when it had served his controversial purpose. The theory of Epiphanius, that they were sons of Joseph by a previous marriage, is possible, but incapable of proof. It comes from a tainted source—the apocryphal Gospels (see my ' Early Days of Christianity,' ii.). **Cephas.** St. Paul also uses the Aramaic name in Gal. ii. 9. Peter's wife is mentioned in Matt. viii. 14 and in the tradition of her martyrdom (Clem. Alex., ' Strom.,' vii. § 63).

Ver. 6.—**And Barnabas.** Like St. Paul, Barnabas was in every respect a genuine apostle, by the Divine call (Acts xiii. 2; Gal. ii. 9), though not one of the twelve. He seems to have continued in his separate mission work the practice of independence which he had learnt from St. Paul. This allusion is interesting, because it is the last time that the name of Barnabas occurs, and it shows that, even after the quarrel and separation, Paul regarded him with love and esteem. **To forbear working.** To give up the manual labour by which we maintain ourselves without any expense to the Churches (Acts xviii. 3; 2 Thess. iii. 8, 9). If, then, St. Paul toiled at the dull, mechanical, despised, and ill-paid work of tent-making, he did so, not because it was, in the abstract, his duty to earn his own living, but because he chose to be nobly independent, that the absolute disinterestedness of his motives might be manifest to all the world. For this reason even when he was most in need he would never receive assistance from any Church except that of Philippi, where he had at least one wealthy convert, and where he was beloved with a peculiar warmth of affection.

Ver. 7.—**Who goeth a warfare, etc. ?** In this and the following verses he adduces six successive arguments to prove the right of a minister to be supported by his congregation. 1. From the ordinary laws of human justice (ver. 7). 2. By analogy from the Law of Moses (vers. 8—10). 3. *A fortiori,* from the obligations of common gratitude (ver. 11). 4. From their concession of the right to others who had inferior claims (ver. 12). 5. From the Jewish provision for the maintenance of priests (ver. 13). 6. By the rule laid down by Christ himself (ver. 14). *Goeth a warfare.* Analogy from the payment of soldiers (2 Cor. x. 4). **At his own charges.** The word used for " cost " means literally *rations* (Luke iii. 14; Rom. vi. 23). **Planteth a vineyard.** Analogy from the support of the vine-dressers (Matt. ix. 37). **Feedeth a flock.** Analogy from the support of shepherds (1 Pet. v. 2). The two latter classes of labourers are paid in kind in the East to this day.

Ver. 8.—**Say I these things as a man?** Am I relying exclusively on mere human analogies? The same phrase occurs in Rom. iii. 5; Gal. iii. 13. **Saith not the Law.** The verbs used for "say" (λαλῶ) and "saith" (λέγει) are different: "Do I *speak* [general word] these things as a man? or *saith* [a more dignified word] not the Law," etc.?

Ver. 9.—**In the Law of Moses** (Deut. xxv. 4). He uses the same argument again in 1 Tim. v. 19. **The mouth of the ox that treadeth out the corn;** rather, *an ox while treading out the corn.* The flail was not unknown, but a common mode of threshing was to let oxen tread the corn on the threshing-floor. **Doth God take care for oxen?** Certainly he does; and St. Paul can hardly mean to imply that he does not, seeing that tenderness for the brute creation is a distinguishing characteristic of the Mosaic legislation (Exod. xxiii. 12, 19; Deut. xxii. 6, 7, 10, etc.). If St. Paul had failed to perceive this truth, he must have learnt it at least from Ps. cxlv. 15, 16; Jonah iv. 11. Even the Greeks showed by their proverb that they could pity the hunger of the poor beasts of burden starving in the midst of plenty. It is, however, a tendency of all Semitic idiom verbally to *exclude* or *negative* the inferior alternative. St. Paul did not intend to say, "God has *no* care for oxen;" for he knew that "his tender mercies are over all his works:" he only meant in Semitic fashion to say that the precept was much *more* important in its human application; and herein he consciously or unconsciously adopts the tone of Philo's comment on the same passage ('De Victim Offerentibus,' § 1), that, for present purposes, oxen might be left out of account. The rabbinic Midrash, which gave this turn to the passage, was happier and wiser than most specimens of their exegesis. St. Paul sets the typico-allegorical interpretation above the literal in this instance (comp. 1 Tim. v. 18), because he regards it as the more important. It is a specimen of the common Jewish exegetic method of *à fortiori* or *à minori ad magus.* Luther's curious comment is: "God cares for all things; but he does not care that anything should be *written* for oxen, because they cannot *read*"!

Ver. 10.—**Altogether.** It is probable that St. Paul only meant the word to be taken argumentatively, and not *au pied de la lettre.* This application (he says) is so **obviously the right** application, that the other may be set aside as far as our purpose is concerned. In the margin of the Revised Version it is rendered "Saith he it, *as he doubtless doth,* for our sake?" **In hope.** St. Paul's large experience of life, and his insight into character, sufficed to show him that despairing work must be ineffectual work. The spring and elasticity of cheerful spirits is indispensable to success in any arduous undertaking.

" Life without hope draws nectar in a sieve,
And hope without an object cannot live."

Ver. 11.—**If we.** The *we* is in both clauses emphatic, to show that the argument applied directly to St. Paul's own case. **Is it a great thing.** An argument *à fortiori.* If *ordinary* labour is not undertaken gratuitously, is the *spiritual* labourer to be left to starve? St. Paul always recognized the rights of preachers and ministers, and stated them with emphasis (Gal. vi. 6; Rom. xv. 27), although from higher motives he waived all personal claim to profit by the result of his arguments.

Ver. 12.—**If others.** St. Paul felt a touch of natural indignation at the thought that these Corinthians submitted to the extremest and haughtiest exactions from other teachers who had been loud in the statement of their own pretensions, while his own claims were shamefully disparaged, and he was even left, with perfect indifference, to suffer real privation. We shall find the full expression of his wounded sensibilities in 2 Cor. xi. 1—15. **We have not used this power.** This strong climax here asserts itself before the time. It anticipates ver. 15. **Suffer.** The same word, which also means "to contain without leaking," is used in ch. xiii. 7; 1 Thess. iii. 1, 5. **All things.** Any amount of privation and distress. **Hinder the gospel of Christ.** By giving any handle for malicious misrepresentations as to our being self-interested. The word for "hindrance" means etymologically "cutting into," *i.e.* an impediment on a path, etc.

Ver. 13.—**They which minister about holy things.** Jewish priests. He adds his two final arguments—since the right which he is pleading has its own intrinsic importance —before proceeding to the example which he set in order to prevail on the strong *to give up their rights and their liberty,* when need was, for the sake of the weak. **Live;** literally, *eat,* or *feed.* The Zealots used this excuse for themselves when they broke open the temple stores in the siege of Jerusalem (Josephus, 'Bell. Jud.,' v. 13, § 6). **Of the things of the temple.** They shared in the victims offered (see Numb. xviii. 8—13; Deut. xviii. 1). **Partakers with the altar.** Only certain portions of certain victims were allowed them.

Ver. 14.—**Hath the Lord ordained** (Matt. x. 10; Luke x. 7). The reference has special interest, because it shows that St. Paul was at least orally familiar with the discourses of Christ. Indeed, there is nothing impossible or improbable in the supposition that some of these were already being circulated in manuscript. **Should live of the gospel.** If, that is, they desired and had need to do so. He does not say, "to live of the altar," because Christians have no "altar" except in the metaphorical sense in which the cross is called an altar in Heb. xiii. 10.

Vers. 15—23.—*Self-denying ordinance of St. Paul.*

Ver. 15.—**I have used none of these things.** None of the forms of right which I might claim from these many sanctions. He is appealing to his own abandonment of a right to encourage them to waive, if need required, the claims of their Christian liberty. His object in waiving his plain right was that he might give no handle to any who might desire to accuse him of interested motives (ch. ix. 4; Gal. vi. 6, etc.). **Have I written**; rather, *do I write;* the epistolary aorist. **That it should be so done unto me.** Do not take my argument as a hint to you that you have neglected your duty of maintaining me, and have even seen me suffer without offering me your assistance. **Better for me to die.** Not "to die of hunger," as Chrysostom supposes, but generally, "I should prefer death to the loss of my independence of attitude towards my converts." **Than that any man should make my glorying void.** The Greek is remarkable. Literally it is, *than my ground of boasting—that any one should render it void.* Another reading is, *better for me to die than—no one shall render void my ground of boasting.*

Ver. 16.—**I have nothing to glory of.** He is desirous to remove all appearance of haughtiness from his tone. There was, he says, no merit involved in his preaching the gospel. He did so from the sense of overwhelming moral compulsion, and he would have been miserable if he had tried to resist it. **Necessity is laid upon me.** "We cannot but speak" (Acts iv. 20).

Ver. 17.—**If I do this thing willingly.** The word rather means "spontaneously," "without compulsion." He was preaching willingly, but still it was in obedience to an *irresistible* behest (Acts ix. 6, 15). **I have a reward.** The reward (or rather, "wage") of such self-chosen work would be the power to fulfil it (comp. Matt. vi. 1). **Against my will;** rather, *involuntarily,* "under Divine constraint." **A dispensation.** He was appointed a "steward" or "dispenser" of the gospel, and could only regard himself at the best as "an unprofitable slave," who

had done merely what it was his bare duty to do (Luke xvii. 10). There is no merit in yielding to a *must.*

Ver. 18.—**What is my reward then?** The answer is that it was not such "wages" as would ordinarily be considered such, but it was the happiness of preaching the gospel without cost to any. **I abuse not;** rather, *I use not to the full,* as in ch. vii. 31. It may be said that this was a ground of boasting, not a reward. It was, however, a point to which St. Paul attached the highest importance (1 Thess. ii. 9; 2 Cor. xi. 7—12; Acts xx. 33, 34), and he might therefore speak of it, though almost with a touch of half-unconscious irony, as his "fee." There is no need to adopt the construction suggested by Meyer: "What is my reward? [none] that I may preach gratuitously;" or that of Alford, who finds the reward in the next verse.

Ver. 19.—**For though I be free;** rather, *though I was free.* He has voluntarily abandoned this freedom. The true rendering of the verse is, *For being free from all men* [Gal. i. 10], *I enslaved myself to all.* In acting thus he obeyed his own principle of not abusing his liberty, but "by love serve one another" (Gal. v. 13).

Ver. 20.—**Unto the Jews I became as a Jew.** When, for instance, he circumcised Timothy (Acts xii. 3) and probably Titus also (Gal. ii. 3; see 'Life of St. Paul,' i. 412, *sqq.*); and he was continuing this principle of action when he took the vow of the Nazarite (Acts xxi. 21—26), and called himself "a Pharisee, a son of Pharisees" (Acts xxiii. 6). **To them that are under the Law.** That is, not only to Jews, but even to the most rigorous legalists among the Jews. It should be carefully observed that St. Paul is here describing the innocent concessions and compliances which arise from the harmless and generous condescension of a loving spirit. He never sank into the fear of man, which made Peter at Antioch unfaithful to his real principles. He did not allow men to form from his conduct any mistaken inference as to his essential views. He waived his personal predilections in matters of indifference which only affected "the infinitely little."

Ver. 21.—**To them that are without law, as without law.** In other words, I so far became to the heathen as a heathen (Rom. ii. 12), that I never wilfully insulted their beliefs (Acts xix. 37) nor shocked their prejudices, but on the contrary, judged them with perfect forbearance (Acts xvii. 30) and treated them with invariable courtesy. St. Paul tried to look at every subject, so far as he could do so innocently, from their point of view (Acts xvii.). He defended their gospel liberty, and had intercourse with Gentile converts on terms of perfect equality (Gal. ii. 12). **Not without law to God.** Not even "without law" (*anomos*) Much less "opposed to law" (*antinomos*), though free from it as a bondage (Gal. ii. 19). The need for this qualification is shown by the fact that in the Clementine writings, in the spurious letter of Peter to James, St. Paul is surreptitiously calumniated as "*the lawless one.*" Even the Gentiles were "not without law to God" (Rom. ii. 14, 15). So that St. Paul is here using language which base opponents might distort, but which the common sense of honest readers would prevent them from misinterpreting.

Ver. 22.—**To the weak.** His whole argument here is a plea for condescension to the infirmities of weak converts. A similar condescension to their prejudices might be necessary to win them to Christianity at all (ch. viii. 13; "We that are strong ought to bear the infirmities of the weak, and not to please ourselves," Rom. xv. 1). St. Paul often touches on our duties to weak brethren (ch. viii. 7; Rom. xiv. 1; 1 Thess. v. 14; Acts xx. 35). **All things to all men.** He repeats the same principle in ch. x. 33, "I please all men in all things, not seeking mine own profit, but the profit of many, that they may be saved;" and once more, at the end of his course (2 Tim. ii. 10). This condescension laid him open to the malicious attacks of religious enemies (Gal. i. 10). But not on that account would St. Paul ever be led to abandon the fruitful aid of that universal sympathy and tolerance which is one of the best tests of Christian love. **That I might by all means save some.** He adds this explanation of the motive of his condescension to various scruples (συγκατάβασις) lest any should accuse him of men-pleasing, as some of his Galatian opponents had done (Gal. i. 10). In his desire to win souls he acted with the wisdom and sympathy taught by experience, suppressing himself.

Ver. 23.—**And this I do.** The better reading is, *and I do all things.* **For the gospel's sake.** This is a wider feeling than even "for the elect's sakes" of 2 Tim. ii. 10. **With you.** The "you" is not expressed in the original, where we only have "a fellow-partaker [συγκοινωνὸς, Rom. xi. 17] of it." But the word illustrates the deep humility of the apostle.

Vers. 24—27.—*Exhortation to earnestness as a corollary from the principles here stated.*

Ver. 24.—**Know ye not that they which run in a race run all?** They as Corinthians would well know the full bearing of every illustration derived from the triennial Isthmian games, which were the chief glory of their city, and which at this period

had even thrown the Olympic games into the shade. The words "in a race," are rather, *in the stadium.* The traces of the great Corinthian stadium, where the games were held and the races run, are still visible on the isthmus. This metaphor of "the race," which has pervaded the common language of Christianity, is also found in Heb. xii. 1; Phil. iii. 14; 2 Tim. iv. 7. **The prize.** The *bravium* was the wreath given to the victor by the judges. The Christian prize is that of "the high calling of God in Jesus Christ," towards which St. Paul himself was pressing forward.

Ver. 25.—**That striveth for the mastery;** rather, *that strives to win in a contest.* St. Paul never allows his converts to dream of the indefectibility of grace, and so to slide into antinomian security. He often reminds them of the extreme severity and continuousness of the contest (Eph. vi. 12; 1 Tim. vi. 12). **Is temperate in all things.** One good moral result which sprang from the ancient system of athleticism was the self-denial and self-mastery which it required. The candidate for a prize had to be pure, sober, and enduring (Horace, 'Ars Poet.,' 412), to obey orders, to eat sparely and simply and to bear effort and fatigue (Epict., 'Enchir.,' 35) for ten months before the contest. **A corruptible crown.** A fading garland of Isthmian pine, or Nemean parsley, or Pythian olive, or Olympian bay. **An incorruptible;** "unwithering" (1 Pet. ii. 4); "amaranthine" (1 Pet. v. 4); "a crown of righteousness" (2 Tim. iv. 8); "a crown of life" (Jas. i. 12; Rev. ii. 10; comp. also 2 Tim. ii. 5; Rev. iii. 11).

Ver. 26.—**Not as uncertainly.** My eye is fixed on a definite goal (2 Tim. i. 12). **So fight I** (Rom. vii. 23; Eph. vi. 12; 2 Tim. iv. 7); literally, *so box I.* **Not as one that beateth the air;** rather, *as not beating the air.* Not what the Greeks called "a shadow-battle." I strike forthright blows, not feints, or blows at random.

Ver. 27.—**I keep under my body, and bring it into subjection;** literally, *I bruise my body, and lead it about as a slave.* The word tamely rendered "keep in subjection" means literally, *I smite under the eyes.* The pugilistic metaphor is kept up, and the picturesque force of the words would convey a vivid impression to Corinthians familiar with the contests of the Pancratum, in which boxing with the heavy lead-bound *cæstus* played a prominent part. The only other place in the New Testament where the word occurs is Luke xviii. 5, where it seems (on the lips of the unjust judge) to have a sort of slang sense. How St. Paul "bruised his body" may be seen in 2 Cor. vi. 4, 5; Col. iii. 5; Rom. viii. 13. It was not by absurd and harmful self-torture, but by noble labour and self-denial for the good of others. **When I have preached to others, I myself should be a castaway.** "Lest"—such is the meaning of the metaphor—"after proclaiming to others the laws of the contest (as a herald), I should myself violate those conditions, and be not only defeated as a combatant, but ignominiously rejected from the lists and not allowed to contend at all." The metaphor is not strictly adhered to, for the herald did not personally contend. No candidate could compete without a preliminary scrutiny, and to be "rejected" was regarded as a deadly insult. The word "rejected," "reprobate"—here rendered "a castaway"—is a metaphor derived from the testing of metals, and the casting aside of those which are spurious. That Paul should see the necessity for such serious and unceasing effort shows how little *he* believed in the possibility of saintly "works of supererogation, over and above what is commanded." "When the cedar of Lebanon trembles, what shall the reed by the brookside do?"

HOMILETICS.

Vers. 1—21.—*The leading characteristics of a truly great gospel minister.* "Am I not an apostle? am I not free?" etc. Taking these verses as a whole, they illustrate some of the leading characteristics of a truly great gospel minister, and I offer the following remarks:—

I. The greater the minister of Christ, the MORE INDEPENDENT OF CEREMONIAL RESTRICTIONS. Paul was one of the greatest, if not *the* greatest, ministers of Christ that ever existed. He was an apostle, and had "seen Christ"—a qualification that distinguished him as a minister from all, but eleven others, that ever lived. Besides this, his natural and acquired endowments placed him in the very first rank of reasoners, scholars, and orators. He was brought up at the feet of Gamaliel, etc. But see how this great minister regarded the mere conventionalities of religious society. "Am I not an apostle? am I not free?" He refers in all probability to the preceding chapter, which treats of the eating of meat offered to idols, and concerning which he says, "If meat make my brother to offend, I will eat no flesh while the world standeth." As if he had said, "I am free to eat that meat, and free to reject it; I am not bound by any conventional custom or ceremonial law, for I am 'an apostle.'" Now, it may be laid down as a universal truth that, *the greater a gospel minister, the more independent of ceremonies.* Indeed, the greater the **man**, always the more independent he is of forms, fashions, customs. Hezekiah called that which his countrymen worshipped "Nehushtan"—a piece of brass. Cromwell called that glittering insignia of authority on the table of the House of Commons, and at which most of the members, perhaps, trembled with awe, a "bauble." Thomas Carlyle called all the pageantry of office and the glitter of wealth "shams." Burns called the swaggering lordling a "coof." How much more would a man like Paul—who possessed that spirit of Christ which gave him an insight into the heart of things—look down, not merely with indifference, but with contempt, upon all that the world considered great and grand! The more Christly inspiration a man has, the more he will discern degradation on thrones and pauperism in mansions. A famous French preacher began his funeral address over the coffin of his sovereign with these words, "There is nothing great but God." To the man whose soul is charged with the great ideas of God, all the distinctions amongst men are only as the distinctions existing among the various bubbles on the flowing stream. Some are a little larger than others, some are tinged by the sunbeam, and some are pallid in the shade; but all have the same common nature, and all, breaking into the abyss, are lost for ever. "Am I not free?" says Paul. A grand thing this, to be free from all the conventionalities of society and the ceremonies of religion. What cared Elijah for the kings of Syria, or Israel, or Judah? Nothing. Agrippa trembled before the moral majesty of Paul, even in chains. Oh for such ministers as Paul in this age of hypocrisies and forms!

II. The greater the minister of Christ, the HIGHER THE SERVICE HE RENDERS TO SOCIETY. What high service did this great minister St. Paul render to the members of the Corinthian Church! "Are not ye my work in the Lord?... The seal of mine apostleship are ye in the Lord." Ye are, as far as ye are Christians, "my work." I converted you; I turned you away from idols to the one true and living God, from the kingdom of Satan to the kingdom of Christ. No work on earth equal to this. "He that converteth a sinner from the error of his ways," etc. This work which I effected in you "in the Lord," or by the Lord, is a demonstration of my apostleship. What work again, I ask, approaches this in grandeur and importance? It is the work of creating men "anew in Christ Jesus;" it is the work of establishing that moral empire in the world, which is "righteousness, peace, and joy in the Holy Ghost." *The man who succeeds in accomplishing this work* thereby *demonstrates the divinity of his ministry.* Hence Paul says, "Mine answer to them that do examine me is this." Those that question or deny my apostleship I refer to the spiritual work I have accomplished; "this is my answer," my defence. Truly it might be said of Paul, "No man can do the works that thou doest, except God be with him." The only way by which we can prove ourselves true ministers is, not by words, but by spiritual works.

III. The greater the minister of Christ, the MORE INDEPENDENT HE IS OF THE ANIMAL ENJOYMENTS OF LIFE. "Have we not power to eat and to drink? Have we not power to lead about a sister, a wife, as well as other apostles, and as the brethren of the Lord, and Cephas?" Paul claims the privilege to eat and drink as he pleased, and to marry or not according to his pleasure, to be a celibate or a benedict. Perhaps some of the members of the Corinthian Church questioned Paul's apostleship because he was not married. Those who belonged to Peter's party—who was a married man—would be likely to say, "Paul cannot be an apostle, for Cephas, who is an apostle, has his wife, whom he takes about with him in the prosecution of his mission." And then the "brethren of the Lord," too, they have their wives. Paul's reply to this is virtually, "I have the power and the right to all connubial privileges and comforts, the right to feast at banquets, and to form domestic relations; but I forego them, I am independent of them, I have higher tastes and sublimer sources of enjoyment. 'For me to live is Christ.' He is the all and in all of my soul." The more brain and Christly inspiration a man has, the less carnal, and the less carnal the more independent of material enjoyments.

IV. The greater the minister of Christ, the MORE CLAIM HE HAS TO THE TEMPORAL SUPPORT OF THOSE WHOM HE SPIRITUALLY SERVES. The apostle goes on from the sixth to the fourteenth verse to say that he and Barnabas would be right if they were to forbear working for their livelihood, and claim their temporal support from those to whom they spiritually ministered. He goes on to indicate several reasons why he had a claim to their temporal support. 1. *The general usage of mankind.* "Who goeth a warfare any time at his own charges?" etc. He draws three illustrations from human life to show the equity of the principle—from the soldier, the agriculturist, and the shepherd. 2. *The principle of the Jewish Law.* "Say I these things as a man? or saith not the Law the same also?" etc. On a space of hard ground called a threshing-floor the oxen in Jewish times were driven to and fro over the corn thrown there, thus separating the husk from the grain. "God," says Matthew Henry, "had therein ordered that the ox should not be muzzled while he was treading out the corn, nor hindered from eating while he was preparing the corn, for man's use, and treading it out of the ear. But this law was not chiefly given out of God's regard to oxen or concern for them, but to teach mankind that all due encouragement should be given to those who are employed by us or labouring for our good, that the labourers should taste of the fruit of their labours." "Doth God take care for oxen?" Yes. He enjoined that the mouth of the working ox should not be muzzled, but should have food to eat. Is not man greater than the ox? And shall he work and be deprived of temporal supplies? 3. *The principles of common equity.* "If we have sown into you spiritual things, is it a great thing if we shall reap your carnal things?" They had given to them far higher things, infinitely more important than the temporal support which they required. He who gives to his race Divine ideas gives that which alone can secure the progress of humanity, both in temporal and spiritual good. True ideas destroy bad institutions and create good ones. 4. *Other apostles and their wives were thus supported.* "Or I only and Barnabas, have not we power to forbear working?" ... If others be partakers of this power over you, are not we rather?" This language implies that all the others who worked amongst them obtained their temporal support. Why should not we? Have we done less? Is our authority inferior? 5. *The support of the Jewish priesthood.* "Do ye not know that they which minister about holy things live of the things of the temple? and they which wait at the altar are partakers with the altar?" "The first part of the passage refers to the general principle that the priests who were engaged in the temple services were supported from the various offerings which were brought there; and the second clause more definitely alludes to the particular fact that, when a sacrifice was offered on the altar, the sacrificing priests as well as the altar had a share of the animal." 6. *The ordination of Christ.* "Even so hath the Lord ordained that they which preach the gospel should live of the gospel" (see Matt. x. 10). "Should live of the gospel," not grow rich on the gospel, but have from it that which is needful for subsistence. Looking at all that Paul says on that question here, and at the immense service that a true minister renders to society, the conviction cannot be avoided that no man has a stronger claim to a temporal recompense for his labour than a true gospel minister. Albeit no claims are so universally ignored. What Churches in these modern times tender to their ministers as an acknowledgment of their service is regarded as a charity rather than a claim. Charity, indeed! Call the money you pay to your butcher, baker, lawyer, doctor, charity; but in the name of all that is just, do not call that charity which you tender to the man who consecrates his entire being and time to impart to you the elements of eternal life.

V. The greater the minister of Christ, the MORE READY TO SURRENDER HIS CLAIMS FOR THE SAKE OF USEFULNESS. Great as were the claims of Paul, he magnanimously surrenders them all in order to become more useful. He would not feast at banquets, enjoy conjugal life, or take payment for his services, lest his usefulness should be in the least impaired. "But I have used none of these things: neither have I written these things, that it should be so done unto me; for it were better for me to die, than that any man should make my glorying void." I would sooner die than be dependent on you for a livelihood. Grand man! He stood before his congregations and said, "I have coveted no man's silver, or gold, or apparel. Yea, ye yourselves know, that these hands have ministered unto my necessities, and to them that were with me."

Vers. 22, 23.—*Moral identification with others a qualification of the evangel.* These verses and the context are sometimes taken as expressive of the *accommodating* spirit of the apostle in his endeavours to save men. Hence he is regarded as acting in a somewhat Jesuitical way, pretending to be what he was not, coming down to the prejudices of men, and taking them as it were by guile. Such a view of the apostle is utterly untrue. From his very constitution, to say nothing of his Christianity, he could not bend to any temporizing expediency. There was nothing of the Jesuit or the diplomatist in him. All that he means, I think, by the words is that he endeavoured to put himself into the place, or rather into the views and feelings, of those whom he endeavoured to win to Christ. He transmigrated himself, so to speak, went into their souls, clothed himself with their feelings, and argued from their standpoint. Now, this way of influencing men is both right and wise. As a debater, whether in politics, philosophy, or religion, he only acts fairly and with power who endeavours to put himself into the very position of his opponent, to look at the points in dispute from the opponent's standpoint, with the opponent's eyes, and through the opponent's passions. Such a man becomes mighty in debate. This is what Paul did. He made "himself all things to all men." In arguing with the Jew he made himself a Jew in feeling, with the Greek a Greek in feeling, with a slave a slave in feeling, with a master a master in feeling. Thus he was a philosopher when he spoke to the Athenians, and a Jew when he spoke to the Jews. Now, we regard this power of *moral transmigration,* this power of passing into another man's soul and taking another man's experience, as an *essential qualification* for a *successful evangel;* and this power implies at least three things.

I. A HIGHLY IMAGINATIVE TEMPERAMENT. The phlegmatic man, whose nature is incapable of taking fire, who moves with the creeping legs of logic rather than on the wings of moral intuition, would find it all but impossible to realize another man's experiences. He could not be a dramatist. He could not show another man to himself. No one can enter into the experience of another only on the strong warm current of social sympathy. Hence no young men should be encouraged to assume the work of the Christian ministry who have not that fervid imagination, that glowing temperament, that constitute a dramatic genius.

II. A KNOWLEDGE OF HUMAN LIFE. It is necessary that we should make ourselves thoroughly acquainted, not merely with the outward circumstances of the men we seek to influence, but with their *inner* life—their moods of thought, their habits of mind, their leading passions, their strongest proclivities. This requires study of men, not as they appear in books, but as they appear in their circle ; and men, not in the mass, but in their individual character and idiosyncrasies. Can an Englishman so know a Hindoo, a Chinese, or a Japanese, as to put himself into his experience ? I trow not.

III. A PASSIONATE LOVE FOR SOULS. Nothing but the constraining love of Christ can invest man either with the disposition or the power for such a work—a work requiring self-sacrifice, patience, tenderness, invincible determination, and hallowed devotion. This is what gave Paul the power to be "made all things to all men." "I please all men in all things," he says, "not seeking mine own profit, but the profit of many, that they may be saved."

CONCLUSION. The work of a moral redeemer is, of all works, the greatest and the most arduous. There is no work in all the departments of human labour that requires such high qualifications as the work of bringing souls to Christ.

Vers. 24—26.—*The Christian race.* "Know ye not that they which run in a race, run all, but one receiveth the prize ? So run, that ye may obtain. And every man that striveth for the mastery is temperate in all things. Now they *do it* to obtain a corruptible crown; but we an incorruptible. I therefore so run, not as uncertainly ; so fight I, not as one that beateth the air." The Christian life is a race, and we are exhorted to run that the prize may be obtained. "So run." How ?

I. Run in the PRESCRIBED COURSE. The course is marked out and measured. The starting-place is at the foot of the cross, and the goal is planted in the grave.

II. Run WITHOUT INCUMBRANCE. "Lay aside every weight," all worldly cares, and inordinate sympathetic embarrassing prejudices, and fettering habits.

III. Run WITH ALL POSSIBLE CELERITY. Shake off sloth and languor, stretch every muscle and limb, throw the whole force of your being into the effort.

IV. Run WITH UNTIRING PERSISTENCY. Pause not, nor loiter a moment until the end is obtained. "So run, that ye may obtain."

Ver. 27.—*Hell after preaching.* "But I keep," etc. These are terrible words, and they teach at least three things.

I. THAT DELIVERANCE FROM HELL DEMANDS THE MOST EARNEST SELF-DISCIPLINE. "I keep under my body." I subdue the flesh by violent and reiterated blows. The reason for this mortification of the flesh is, "lest that by any means, when I have preached to others, I myself should be a castaway." Self-discipline may be said to consist of two things. 1. *The entire subjugation of the body to the mind.* The body was intended to be the organ, the servant, and the instrument of the mind, but it has become the master. The supremacy of the body is the curse of the world and the ruin of the man. 2. *The subjugation of the mind to the Spirit of Christ.* Though the mind governs the body, if the mind is false, selfish, unloyal to Christ, there is no discipline. The mind must be the servant of Christ in order to be the legitimate sovereign of the body. These two things include spiritual discipline.

II. THAT THE NECESSITY OF THIS SELF-DISCIPLINE CANNOT BE SUPERSEDED BY THE MOST SUCCESSFUL PREACHING. "When I have preached to others." Paul had preached to others. He had preached to many in different lands, preached earnestly and successfully, preached so that thousands were converted by his ministry, preached so as no one else has ever preached; yet his preaching, he felt, did not do the work of self-discipline. Indeed, there is much in the work of preaching that has a tendency to operate against personal spiritual culture. 1. Familiarity with sacred truths destroys for us their charm of freshness. 2. A professional handling of God's Word interferes with its personal application. 3. The opinions of audiences, favourable or otherwise, exert an influence unfavourable to spiritual discipline. In connection with all this, Satan is especially active in opposing the growth of spiritual piety in the preacher's tone. So that there is a terrible danger that, whilst the preacher is cultivating the vineyards of others, he is neglecting his own.

III. THE MOST SUCCESSFUL PREACHING MAY BE FOLLOWED BY ULTIMATE RUIN.

" I myself should be a castaway ! "—rejected! Who shall fathom the meaning of this word? A successful preacher a " castaway "—be rejected! The Tophet of him who has offered mercy to others which he has despised, urged truths on the credence of others that he has disbelieved, enforced laws on others which he has transgressed, will burn with severer fires and peal with more awful thunders. A magnifying-glass held in a certain position by the hand of a child may convey sufficient fire through it to wrap the neighbourhood in conflagration, albeit the glass through which the fire has passed remains unheated, cold as flint. So a man may convey to others the rays of the sun of Righteousness, and yet his own heart remain cold as ice. Truly a terrible fact this.

HOMILIES BY VARIOUS AUTHORS.

Vers. 1—14.—*How St. Paul regarded his apostleship and its rights.* To induce the Corinthians to deny themselves the exercise of a liberty they had in things indifferent, St. Paul had made the argument in the eighth chapter. Liberty was amenable to conscience, knowledge secondary to love, and love was the constructing or building-up power of the new spiritual edifice. Not one of these could be spared, for they were all constituents of manhood in Christ; but they must be adjusted to one another under the supremacy of love. If one had a true reverence for his own conscience, he would reverence conscience in others. The conscience of another might be weak, and he might pity the weakness, and yet this pity, if genuine, would not allow scorn or contempt. The argument was a lesson in patience and forbearance, a lesson in self-abnegation, and a lesson, furthermore, in responsibility for our example. So far as the immediate issue is concerned (meats offered to idols and participating in feasts held in heathen temples), the logic is direct and conclusive. At no moment does the apostle confine himself to individual rights on the part of such as had enlightened views as to the nothingness of idols. He looks also at community-rights and discusses a special duty on the ground of general interests. Here, as in the former chapters, the community-man, the community-Christian, is before him; and he shows the great characteristic of a teacher in the fact that his business is to mould a body of men into unity. Of what value are minds of large endowments, in their social relations, if they stand for a narrow and cramped individualism? If a man has a finer eye than others, it is that he may see further into the needs of the race. If he has more ardent sympathies, it is for their wider outgoing. Genius is nature's protest, not against ordinary talents, but against the littleness and selfish absorption of individuality. And so far, genius is an instinctive yearning in the direction of a world-wide appreciation and love, and is one of those innumerable parables in which Christianity lies imbedded till the human mind can be prepared to receive it. Now, St. Paul was the foremost representative, in a certain sense, of this community-idea, and, unquestionably, Corinth put its strength and compass to a very severe test. At his time of life, at that era in his ministry, and from just such a mixed people, this grand sentiment of universality was destined by Providence—so we may conjecture—to undergo a thorough discipline. Each truth has its own peculiar test. Some truths need a hotter furnace than others to separate the human dross and bring out the refined gold. If, then, St. Paul was experiencing a special mental and spiritual training in respect to this transcendent doctrine, we have an insight into his mode of argument, and even into the style of his illustrations and enforcement. Identified with his doctrine, he himself merging, as it were, his personality in its nature and operations, his own fortunes bound up inseparably with its fortunes,—how could he avoid citing his own example to confirm the views he so fervently advocated? One paragraph, at least, must be given to his individual portraiture as a community-man, a race-man, intent with his whole heart on bringing a world to the Lord Jesus. And he had sprung to this high level of his own experience and history when he said in the thirteenth verse of the previous chapter, " I will eat no flesh," etc. On that ground, remote as it was from that occupied by some of his Corinthian friends, he was perfectly at home; he knew his strength in God; he saw precisely what to say of grace and its workings in his soul, and how to say it with unanswerable force—straightforward, vivid, incisive. The movement of thought, even for him, is uncommonly rapid. Sentences are short; the words simple, intense, and closely linked. Interrogation abounds. He is an apostle; a free apostle; an apostle who saw not Christ in his humiliation, and never knew him after the flesh, but has seen him in his glorification, and dates his conversion from the spectacle of his Divine exaltation; and, last of all, an apostle whose success among the Corinthians ("my work in the Lord;" "the seal of mine apostleship") has vindicated and verified his claims as Christ's chosen servant. Self-assertion becomes under some circumstances a very important duty, and, if self be surrendered to God, there is no way more effective to exemplify humility. One who can ascend to a height so lofty, and stand among the sublimities of the universe apart from self and even dead to self, is a far greater man in the moral scale than one who, on the low plain of this world, merely foregoes his selfishness and acts disinterestedly to comply with an earthly contingency. Full of the infinite and eternal, St. Paul's thoughts are God's thoughts finding tone and accent in his utterance. There is no faltering, no nice qualifyings, no hesitating apprehension lest self should insinuate its pretensions. But the view given of himself is large, massive, and, for its purpose, strikingly complete. Men cannot speak of themselves in such a strain unless an utter self-forgetfulness be precedent. A thinker's illustrations show what hold a thought has on him. In this instance St. Paul's illustrations are significant as well as diversified. Soldiers in the field, husbandmen in the vineyard, shepherds with their flocks, supply his imagination with analogies to establish the right claimed by himself "to eat and to drink," "to lead about a sister, a wife, as well as other apostles," and "to forbear working." On all grounds, natural and civil and religious, he maintains the right, and then advances to Old Testament authority. "Doth God take care for oxen?" Yea, not only for their sakes as animals, but for man's benefit, the providence over the lower creation being tributary to the providence that looks to man's welfare as the final earthly cause of all arrangements in the kingdom of nature. Yea, verily, we are in the song of the bird and the muscle of the horse and the fidelity of all domesticated creatures, as surely as in the grass and the cereals and the luscious fruits of the ground. Most true it is that—

> "More servants wait on man
> Than he'll take notice of; in every path
> He treads down that which doth befriend him
> When sickness makes him pale and wan.
> Oh, mighty love! Man is one world, and hath
> Another to attend him."

The prefigurations and the wondrous homologies are all from below, so that whatever may be found by industry, by science and art, in the amplitude and beneficence of material things and of animal existence, are but so many prophecies of man's natural position of headship. Yet what incompleteness were in all this, and what a mockery of man's exaltation, if it were all!—a vast pyramid enclosing a mummy—a magnificent temple, like the heathen temples, in which you walk through portico and corridor and hall to confront at last a worthless image in stone. To perfect this idea of man shadowed forth beneath him and ever advancing towards him, there must be a counterpart. The counterpart is the archetype above. It descends to man in Christ—Son of man because Son of God. "For our sakes, no doubt, this is written;" and all the writings, below and above, on the earth's strata, in the Holy Scriptures, are alike in this: "*for our sakes.*" It is all a unity or it is all nothing. And this power of manhood St. Paul declares to belong to him, and vested to the full in his apostleship. If, now, St. Paul had exhorted the Corinthians so urgently to obey the dictates of conscience in a matter clearly harmless, and thus avoid a wrong to the weaker brethren and a wrong to their own souls; and if he had avowed his own inflexible resolution to "eat no flesh" (the meat of which he had been speaking) "for ever;" it was a fit occasion to testify to his own self-denial for the sake of the gospel. The solace of domestic life, the special tenderness of close sympathy, the offices of watchful affection, ministerial support, "carnal things" that might have lightened the burden of poverty and made his toil much easier,—these were cheerfully resigned. Others allowed themselves these aids and comforts; he refused them, one and all. From the common order of apostolic life he would stand aside in his own isolated lot, and "*my gospel*" should have in his own career the most forcible demonstration of his glorious individuality. And then, recollecting the law of the temple service which provided for the support of the priests, he would strengthen the analogical argument already presented in favour of his rights. At every touch the individual portrait of the community and race-man glows more vividly on the canvas. The contrast had cost him much. Poverty, loneliness, sorrow, had been intensified, but there it was—a contrast with the soldier, the husbandman, the shepherd, the priest, the apostles—self-assumed and a perpetual obligation—"lest we should hinder the gospel of Christ."—L.

Vers. 15—23.—*Reasons for this self-denial.* The rights had been resigned, the power to use his privileges had been unused, and the obligation, self-assumed, was to be perpetual. Did any one suspect otherwise? "Better for me to die" than this matter of boasting should be taken from me. No ground for boasting existed in the mere preaching of the gospel; but he could claim and did claim that, in renouncing his right to a support and making other exceptional sacrifices, he was entitled to the boast of preaching a free gospel. A woe is upon him if he preach not the gospel, a necessity he cannot evade while true to his moral nature, and yet a necessity which he will transmute and glorify by his magnanimity in serving without remuneration. Rights; what were they? Where there was such an overpowering sense of the goodness of God and the grace of Christ as had been manifested in his personal salvation and in conferring upon him the apostleship, "better die" than measure duty by mere equivalence of action. Out of the depths of gratitude the man rises, not to the attitude of an apostle, but an apostle who felt with the utmost intensity the obligations of sentiment no less than those of principle. Freely had he received, and freely would he give, so freely indeed as to part with a portion of freedom and to gain by his loss; and in this and by means of this he had his reward. Relinquishing his rights and descending to the condition of a slave, he accommodated himself to the infirmities and prejudices of others so as to save the greater number. Whenever he could evince his regard for the Jewish nation and conform to its customs and usages without compromising Christianity, he became "as a Jew unto the Jews." Nor did he limit his concessions to his own countrymen, but he became "all things to all men," never yielding the truth, never compromising a principle, never making conscience subservient to prudence, never finding the supreme law of action in any utility, and always resolute to concede points only indifferent and equally resolute to maintain that things indifferent involved no moral obligation. And why all this? There were two reasons for it: one was for the good of the large number, "gain the more;" and the other was the benefit to himself—a fellow-"partaker with you" in the blessings of the gospel. "Up to this point he has been speaking of his self-denial for the sake of others; here he begins to speak of it for his own sake. It is no longer 'that I may save some,' but 'that I may be a partaker of the gospel with you'" (Stanley).—L.

Vers. 24—27.—*Self-denial urged in view of the heavenly crown.* Power is no self-guiding instinct in itself. To be true power, it must be directed by something higher than its own nature. A vast fund of power is laid up within us, and of it two things may be said, viz. *the amount of power* abstractly considered is far greater than we can use; and, again, *our available power* must be held under check. As to the former, capacity in every man exceeds ability, and much of our education consists in converting capacity into actual ability. And this latency of power serves another purpose, inasmuch as it is a reserved fund held for an emergency. At times, sudden calls are made on our energies, drafts at sight, which demand extraordinary effort. Feats of physical strength are then performed which are amazing. The same is true of the mind; we witness its faculties, under some tremendous pressure, yielding a wisdom, a patience, a persistency, that surpass all expectation. On the other hand, our available power that can be brought any moment into play must be restrained, or injury results. The harm is manifold. It is pernicious to others. Power antagonizes the power of our fellow-men much oftener than it conciliates, and, acting as a repellent instead of an attractive force it destroys unity, which is the great end of all existence. Nor is it less hurtful to the man himself, for, in pushing his power to extremes, he exhausts the very ability concerned in using the power. An undue use of power, therefore, overtaxes others and ourselves. And, accordingly, St. Paul takes both these facts into consideration, advancing from self-denial for the sake of others to self-denial for his own good, and in this way perfecting the argument. Was he not a philosopher of profound insight in this method of mental procedure? Dismiss, for an instant, the view of him as a Christian apostle, and look at him as an ethical thinker. To induce men to practise the self-denial of power, he marshals all the social and sympathetic virtues to its aid; brings pity and compassion as humane instincts to its service, enlists the imagination and its sensibilities as a higher form of emotional energy, and crowns the ascending series of influences by conscience and moral affection in behalf of our fellow-men. This is the first training of self-denial. Thence it proceeds to its other task. It gathers up its strength and resources, and turns them to its self-culture. Was this the method of Stoicism? Was not the method of Stoicism the precise opposite of this? If Seneca had observed this law of culture, would not his exile have presented a very different spectacle? If Marcus Aurelius had trained himself to discern the image of humanity in others, instead of looking into the mirror of Stoicism to see his own image, could he have been guilty, a man of such beautiful and noble virtues, of persecuting Christianity? Return to St. Paul as a Christian apostle. The true philosopher is here, but not complacently studying his own image in the glass that Stoicism held up before its disciples. What he first sees is the Christ of humanity in others, who, in a religious sense, are bone of his bone and flesh of his flesh. And there is an expression of pain on the brow, and of the sorrow of the heart in his fixed eye, as he realizes that these men are not fully conscious of their relationship to Christ, and therefore very imperfect in their appreciation of others and themselves. But he comprehends them in Christ, and he can bear their infirmities since his love is no mere æsthetic sentiment. Now, then, he can show the extent of that self-denial required to attain the reward of the gospel. Of course, this must be done by figurative language, images being the perfection of language and most necessary when spiritual things are to be made clear. Naturally enough, the Grecian games occurred to him; and as the pomp and splendour of these national shows passed before him, was it the gathered multitude, the high enthusiasm, the thrilling suspense, the heart of Achaia throbbing with pride and exultation, that enlisted his interest? What a sense it was to the senses, and even more than to the senses, as Greeks interpreted its meanings! The very landscape lent a charm to the contests, and conspired with the Corinthian citadel, the sloping hills, the marble seats, and the eager crowds, to perpetuate the historic memories of a vanished Greece. Even here, degenerate as the age was, moral elements were at work. A better past had not left itself without a witness in the present. Recollections of ancestry, traditions of virtue and heroism, honourable emulation, an energetic will, hard and continuous discipline for ten months, were associated with the occasion. But St. Paul's mind was engrossed by the symbolism of the Isthmian games. The metaphor of the racecourse attracts his attention. The preparatory training, the diet, the willing temperance and moderation, the regimen of the athlete, and the studious care to observe the conditions of success, furnish a forcible illustration of what was essential to those who would run the Christian race and win an immortal crown. Between the two there is a resemblance. Between the two there is a vast dissimilarity. "They do it to obtain a corruptible crown; but we an incorruptible." Once more, St. Paul introduces himself; he is an earnest athlete bent on victory; all his energies are in training and have long been in training; and, changing the figure at this point, the boxer is mentioned: "So fight I, not as one that beateth the air"—not as one who wastes strength in random strokes, but one whose blows are delivered with skill and an achieving purpose. And now, just as one who has toiled up to some mountain summit brings back to the plain a finer light of beauty in his eye and a larger play of strength in the muscle of the heart, so St. Paul returns from the figurative to the literal with his thought enhanced in vigour. "I keep under my body, and bring it into subjection"—"buffet the body," "beat it," and "bring it into bondage." What! is the body a contestant against us? Is it an adversary to be bruised and beaten, made to know its place? So indeed St. Paul argues in respect to his own body, and the fact in his case is the fact in all cases. *Ideally*, the body is the soul's helper, furnishing the soul with very many true and lofty ideas, giving it much it could never have if disembodied or in an organization less sensuous, and securing it a grandeur of development not possible otherwise. *Practically*, the body is so sensitive to itself, so in love with its own enjoyments, so enslaved to its lusts and appetites, that it must be kept under and brought into subjection. The law is very plain. It has to be obeyed in some measure by every one. If the epicure is nothing but an epicure and always an epicure, nature is soon in violent revolt. To be an epicure, he must have some prudence in his indulgence, and order times and seasons into the service of his pleasures. To be students, poets, artists, philosophers, ay, to be mechanics, tradesmen, farmers, we must put the body *under* by asserting, in a certain degree, the inherent superiority of the mind. For the most part, however, there are reactions, fearful in some, hazardous to all. Suppose, now, that the gross forms of sensuality or even the fascinating forms of sensuousness, are held under mastery. What then? Is the Divine ideal of the body realized? Nay; the body may be made a most efficient and admirable servant to the business man, to the student, to the artist, to the philosopher, and may answer all the earthly and social ends of the intellect and the natural affections, *and yet be an undeveloped human body.* Only in conforming to spiritual relations, only in sharing Christ's humanity, *can it be developed.* Faith, hope, love, Christian principles, Christian sentiments, Christian impulses, are just as requisite to form and shape the material body to the companionship of the redeemed spirit, as food, air, sleep, are necessary for its physical existence. The argument of St. Paul implies all this, nor could it imply less and be congruous with his purpose and aim. And, therefore, when he says, "I keep under my body, and bring it into subjection," he means to say, "I am not making my body less a part of the universe, but more a part thereof, and I am lifting this lower nature towards the higher, and developing my body in the direction of the nature and functions of the resurrection body."—L.

Vers. 1, 2.—*Signs of apostleship.* Why should Paul, departing from his usual custom, speak here of himself and of his claims? Undoubtedly because in this Christian society at Corinth there were those, prompted by Judaizing teachers, who called in question his apostleship, his equality with those who had been the companions of Jesus in his ministry, and had received their commission before his ascension. Wishing to incite the Corinthians to self-denial, Paul put himself forward as an example of this virtue. But to make this example effective, it was necessary that he should assert and vindicate his position and rights. If he had no special commission from Christ, there was no virtue in renouncing privileges which were never his. That an apostle should live as he did—a life of celibacy and manual labour—for the Church's good, was very significant. Such was Paul's position; he sets out, therefore, by establishing his apostolic claims and position.

I. THE VISION OF THE LORD CHRIST. Not that every one who saw Jesus became an apostle; but that none became an apostle who had not seen him, who had not received the commission from his lips. In all likelihood, some of Paul's opponents at Corinth had contrasted the past history of the apostle of the Gentiles with that of the twelve, to his disadvantage. The others, it was well known, had seen the Lord; but was it certain that Paul had been so favoured? Now, Paul would not submit to an imputation which must needs weaken the authority of all he might say or do. He had seen the Lord on the way to Damascus, had heard his voice, and had by him been then entrusted with a special commission to the Gentiles. It was not simply that Paul had seen Jesus; he had been endowed with his Spirit and with his authority. He was not preaching the gospel at the instigation of his own inclinations, but in obedience to a command laid upon him by the highest authority.

II. SUCCESS IN APOSTOLIC LABOUR. The craftsman proves his ability by the work he does; the sailor by his navigation of the vessel; the soldier by his bravery and skill in war. So the apostle acknowledges the justice of the practical test, and subjects himself thereto accordingly. There may be a shade of difference in the meaning of the words employed. 1. Paul appealed to his *work.* Labour is misspent when no results ensue. But this man's labour had not been in vain in the Lord. Jews and Gentiles had been brought to the faith of Christ and to the hope of life eternal. 2. The workmanship of the apostle was also his *seal,* i.e. it bore the mark, impress, and witness of his own character and ability and office. A competent judge, looking to the Churches Paul had founded, would admit them to be evidence of his apostleship. 3. It is observable that the signs were manifest in the very community in which his authority was questioned. There is irony and force in the appeal made to the Corinthians, whether they themselves were not, in their own Christian position, proof of Paul's apostleship. Whoever raised a question, whoever offered opposition, the Christians of Corinth should certainly have honoured the founder of their Church and the bearer of the gospel to their souls.—T.

Vers. 11, 12.—*Rights asserted and foregone.* No passage in Paul's writings more reveals to us the nobility of the man's nature than this. As we read, we feel that such a character could not fail to command the admiration and sympathy of all who were capable of appreciating it. The apostle's abilities were great; but his moral qualities towered more loftily above those of other men, even than did his intellectual powers. Such a servant of God was well fitted to be the first and the greatest preacher of Christ to the nations; for he so shared the mind of the Master, that they who saw, heard, and knew him must have been brought by such experience very near to the Saviour whose Spirit he possessed and whose gospel he preached. I. THE JUST RIGHTS THE APOSTLE ASSERTED. Paul claimed that, like other teachers, he had a claim upon his scholars for recompense and support. 1. He supported this by striking illustrations. The soldier has his rations provided by his country on whose behalf he fights; the vine-dresser eats of the produce of the vineyard; the shepherd shares in the profit of the flock which he feeds; the husbandman who ploughs, sows, and threshes does so in the expectation that he shall eat of the corn he grows. 2. He adds an argument from Scripture. Ingeniously does he apply the principle involved in the humane regulation which forbids the ox to be muzzled when it treads out the corn. A principle which holds good even with regard to cattle is surely valid when applied to men, to Christian labourers. 3. He urges the superiority of the advantages bestowed by the teacher over those which he is justified in expecting by way of acknowledgment if not of return. They who receive spiritual things may surely yield carnal things. 4. This right Paul claims for all ministers and evangelists, himself included. II. THE NOBILITY OF SPIRIT WITH WHICH THE APOSTLE WAS WONT DELIBERATELY TO FOREGO THESE RIGHTS. 1. Observe the fact. The apostle had acted upon this principle from the beginning. An open statement like this could not have been made had it not corresponded with the actual and well-known facts of the case. 2. Consider what this purpose involved, viz. hard manual labour. Like every Jew, Paul had been taught a trade; he wove the Cilician goats' hair into the fabric used for tents and sails, etc. It was a tax upon his energies whilst he was thinking, writing, and preaching, to spend part of the day in hard, rough toil. 3. Remember the exception; from the Macedonian Churches, for a special reason, Paul had consented to receive a liberal gift. 4. The motive which animated Paul deserves attention. It was not pride. There was a personal motive; whilst preaching was a necessity in his case, so that he could take no credit and make no boast for his ministry, he willingly gave up his right to maintenance, that he might have the pleasure of a voluntary sacrifice, a ground of lowly glorying. And there was an official motive; his design was to remove any hindrance out of the way of the progress of the gospel. It might be thought by some that he preached for gain, and such a supposition would render his hearers suspicious and unreceptive. That this should not be the case, he chose to forego his rights, that the obvious disinterestedness of his conduct might support and render effective the gospel which he proclaimed.—T.

Ver. 16.—*The obligation of preaching.* The sincerity of the strong emphatic language of the apostle in this passage is not to be questioned. His whole life is a proof that it was with him as he here affirmed. A law, a vow, was upon him; and there was no discharge, no intermission, until his fight was fought and his course was run. I. THE SPECIAL OBLIGATION LAID UPON THE APOSTLE. 1. *In what it originated.* There is no room for doubt upon this point. Christ himself had met Paul on the way to Damascus, and at the same time that he shed Divine light upon the mind of the persecuting Pharisee Saul, he converted him into the apostle of the Gentiles, and gave him the "marching orders" upon which he was henceforth to act. "Depart: for I will send thee far hence unto the Gentiles." The tones of that voice rang in his ears throughout the whole of the ministry which was thus inaugurated. 2. *How it was fulfilled.* The record makes it plain that the obligation was not only recognized, but practically fulfilled, in a spirit of cheerfulness, gratitude, confidence, and devotion. Such is the explanation of a life so different from the ordinary life of men; a life which Paul himself acknowledged to be one of toil, of privation, of suffering, and persecution. " Necessity was laid upon him." In Asia and in Europe, to Jews and to Gentiles, he offered with warmth and cordiality the unsearchable riches of Christ. 3. *The opening which this obligation left for voluntary devotion and sacrifice.* Paul says plainly that he had no choice as to preaching; preach he must; woe is to him if he refrains from doing so! Yet his ardent, generous nature desired to do something over and above what was required. This was the explanation of his refusing to receive pay and maintenance from his converts. He had a right to this, even as his fellow-labourers; but he put this right in abeyance; he voluntarily declined what he might have claimed, and thus left himself somewhat in which to glory.

II. THE GENERAL OBLIGATION LAID UPON THE CHURCH OF CHRIST. The acknowledgment here made by the apostle is one which may appropriately be made by the whole Church of Christ. 1. *An obligation of authoritative command.* The Lord Jesus, who is the Saviour of the world, is the Monarch of his Church. His order is, " Go ye into all the world, and preach the gospel to every creature." It is only open to us either to dispute his authority or to obey his direction. 2. *A moral obligation of gratitude.* Jesus himself has unfolded the law : " Freely ye have received; freely give." If we have a just sense of our indebtedness, first to the love and sacrifice of Christ, and then to the self-denying labours of those whom he has sent to labour for our spiritual good, we shall feel the gracious constraint leading us to such efforts as he himself has enjoined. 3. *An obligation enforced by many illustrious examples of devotion.* They who read of the heroic enterprises of Christian evangelists, and of the noble fortitude of Christian martyrs who have died at the hands of those they sought to save, may well gird themselves to the labours to which they are invited by the spirit of benevolence, as well as commissioned by him whose authority is ever binding and whose recompense is ever sure.—T.

Vers. 19—23.—*Ministerial pliancy and adaptation.* In great natures we sometimes meet with a remarkable combination of firmness and yielding. To do a great work in this world, a man needs a powerful will, a resolution not easily moved, at the same time that he displays a flexibility of disposition, and a readiness to adapt himself to different characters and to changing circumstances. Without the determination which approaches obstinacy, he will not keep the one aim before him; without the pliancy needed in dealing with men, he will not be able to secure the aim. Thus the same Apostle Paul who said, " This one thing I do," is here found professing that it was his principle and his practice to become all things to all men.

I. INSTANCES OF MINISTERIAL ADAPTATION. Paul's was a very varied life and ministry; he was brought into association with all sorts and conditions of men. Himself a Jew by birth, he was yet the apostle of the Gentiles, and he was equally at home with those of either race. Himself a scholar, he was prepared to deal with rabbis and with philosophers; yet he delighted to minister to the rudest barbarians. In this passage Paul mentions three instances of his pliancy. 1. To the Jews he was a Jew, *i.e.* he openly honoured the Divine Law given to Moses; and not only so, in certain circumstances he observed the ceremonies of his nation. This is evident in his circumcising Timothy, and in his shearing his hair and fulfilling a vow. 2. To those without the Law, outside its pale and regimen, he became as one of themselves, *i.e.* he was superior to many of the petty prejudices and indifferent to many of the customary observances of his fellow-countrymen. How he adapted himself to the Greeks may be seen from his preaching upon the Areopagus at Athens. 3. To the weak he became as weak; *e.g.* in the matter treated in the preceding chapter, he had shown his consideration and condescension in refraining from eating what might possibly be ceremonially defiled.

II. THE PURPOSES SOUGHT BY THIS COURSE OF MINISTERIAL ADAPTATION. He was " free " in so far as, by refusing support from his converts, he left himself at liberty to act as he thought fit; yet he made himself " a slave " for the sake of those whose welfare he sought. The aim he set before him was one which justified the use of the means he describes. 1. He desired to *gain* some. Whatever he might lose, it was his hope and purpose to " win souls "—a rich recompense and an abundant compensation for all his losses. 2. He desired to *save* some. This is a stronger expression, for it implies the peril to which the hearers of the gospel were exposed whilst they remained in unbelief, and it implies the happiness, security, and dignity to which those were brought who received the Word. 3. He did what he did *for the gospel's sake.* For his own advantage he would never have submitted to all which he willingly endured because of his attachment to the truth in Christ Jesus. 4. Yet there was a *personal* aim before him. He hoped to be partaker himself with his converts of the blessings of the great salvation. His own interests were bound up with theirs, and it was ever his hope to share in the joys of that time when "he that soweth and he that reapeth shall rejoice together."—T.

Vers. 24, 25.—*The Christian race.* Nothing could be more natural, more effective, than an allusion of this kind, occurring as it does in a letter to residents at Corinth. The Isthmian games, celebrated in the neighbourhood of their own city, were to the inhabitants of this famous place a matter of the greatest concern and interest. The gathering of representatives from all parts of Greece to witness the athletic contests which took place in the stadium of the isthmus, gave dignity and solemnity to the occasion. And the honours accorded to the victors were so highly coveted that there could have been but few of the ambitious young men of Achaia, indeed, of the whole of Hellas, who were not fired with a desire to distinguish themselves in these contests. No wonder that Paul should stimulate his own zeal and that of his Christian friends and disciples by reminding himself and them of the efforts and the sacrifices which were willingly undertaken for the sake of a perishable crown.

I. THE COURSE. The marble stadium of the isthmus serves as a picture to us of the course to which Christians are summoned. The Christian course is one of faith and obedience, of love and patience, of devotion to God and benevolence toward men.

II. THE SPECTATORS. It was the presence of the illustrious from every part of Greece which gave such peculiar dignity to the Olympian and the Isthmian games. In the Christian race, they who run are encompassed by a "great cloud of witnesses"—the Church militant and triumphant, the glorious angels, and the Divine Lord himself looking on with the deepest interest, and perhaps justifiable anxiety.

III. THE COMBATANTS. We are not to restrict these to apostles, to preachers, to public labourers for Christ. Every disciple is a spiritual athlete, is called upon to run the race, to maintain the struggle. No room in the course for the indolent and inactive.

IV. THE DISCIPLINE AND PREPARATION. It is well known that for many months the athletes who aspired to the victor's wreath were obliged to undergo severe discipline, under the guidance and care of a skilful trainer, who required them to deny themselves many pleasures, to endure much fatigue, hardship, and suffering. Paul reminds us of the necessity of being temperate in all things, of bringing under the body—buffeting it with many blows. The Christian life is not one of ease and self-indulgence; it is one of strenuous effort and self-denial. They who strive for masteries must strive lawfully, must accept and obey the Divine conditions of the course.

V. THE EFFORT. The "one" combatant who received the prize did so as the result of great effort, strenuous and persevering. For neither apathy nor weariness were compatible with success. "So run," says the apostle, meaning that we are to imitate, not those who fail, but him who succeeds and conquers. What need, in living unto Christ, is there of diligence, of watchfulness, and above all of endurance!

VI. THE PRIZE. At the isthmus this was a chaplet of pine leaves, which soon faded. Yet its possession was coveted, and was counted a reward for the training and the toil. How much more should the Christian be animated by the prospect of an eternal inheritance and an amaranthine crown!—T.

Ver. 25.—"*An incorruptible crown.*" There was an ardour of temperament, a resoluteness of purpose, in the constitution and moral life of Paul, which made the imagery of this passage peculiarly congenial to his soul. He was fired with a sacred ambition, and he sought to inspire his hearers and readers with something of his own enthusiasm. His glowing imagination could realize something of the glory gained by the successful athlete who was welcomed with honour in his native state, whose statue was shaped in marble by some illustrious sculptor, and whose praise was embalmed in verse deathless as that of Pindar. How much more must he, with his cleared moral perceptions, his elevated spiritual aims, have sympathized with the prospects which inspired all true Christian athletes, who endured an earthly strife and hoped to gain a heavenly diadem !

I. The Giver of the crown. Christ has himself contended, suffered, and overcome; on his head are many crowns. He is the Lord of the course and the conflict. Coming from such hands, the recompense must be infinitely precious. He sweetens the gift he bestows by words of gracious approval. He counts the crowns of his people as his own.

II. The wearer of the crown. He who is to partake the throne, the triumph, must first share the strife and bear the cross of Jesus. The crown of thorns comes before the crown of victory and empire. They who shall hereafter triumph are they who now and here strive and suffer, endure and hope. Their contest must be lawfully conducted and strenuously maintained. It is they who are " faithful unto death " to whom is promised the fair crown of life.

III. The value of the crown. It is a gift, and not a reward to which there is a just' claim ; there is no case of merit here. At the same time, it is an expression of satisfaction and approval, and coming from Christ has in consequence a peculiar value to his people. The Isthmian wreath was in itself of no worth; its value lay in the witness it bore to the wearer's prowess. But the Christian's crown is not only a token of Divine approbation ; it is accompanied by substantial recompense, especially by promotion to rule and authority. He who is crowned is made " ruler over many things."

IV. The imperishableness of the crown. It is not a material crown, like the wreath of fading leaves. It is a crown of righteousness and of life, and is consequently in its nature immortal. It is worn in the land of incorruption and of immortality, It blooms perennially in the atmosphere of heaven.

Practical lessons. 1. Here is an appeal to the aspiring. Why seek earthly distinctions which must pass away, when within your reach is the unfading crown of glory? 2. Here is an inspiration and stimulus to the Christian combatant. Why grow weary in the race, why sink faint-hearted in the contest, when there is stretched forth, before and above you, the Divine and imperishable crown of life ?—T.

Vers. 1—15.—*The support of the ministry.* Paul recognizes a ministry set apart.

I. The right of ministers to claim adequate support from their people. Enforced by : 1. *Analogy.* (1) The soldier who gives his services to his country receives maintenance. (2) The planter of a vineyard eats of its fruit. (3) The shepherd finds the means of his support in the flock which he tends. The Christian minister is a soldier, fighting the battles of the Lord and of his Church ; a labourer in the vineyard of Christ, planting, watering, pruning, training; a shepherd, watching over the sheep and lambs of his flock, seeking the wandering, correcting the rebellious, leading, feeding, etc. 2. *The Mosaic Law.* (1) The ox treading the corn was unmuzzled, that he might feed as well as toil (ver. 9; Deut. xxv. 4). The apostle claims that this was commanded more with an eye to *men* than to *oxen* (ver. 10). (2) The priests and Levites lived on the things of the temple. Here the parallel becomes more striking. The ministers under the old dispensation were supported out of the offerings of the people : why should not the ministers of the new be also ? Moreover, this obtained amongst men generally. Even the heathen perceived its fitness. 3. *Common sense.* It is *reasonable* that those who give up their time, energies, and gifts to the service of the Church should be supported by it. This is seen more strikingly when we remember that what is *received* by the Church is of infinitely more value than what is *given:* " If we have sown unto you *spiritual* things, is it a great thing if we shall reap your *carnal* things ? " The Church is not a loser, but a great gainer. What blessings God has bestowed in the past through the channel of a faithful ministry ? What may he not in the future, to ourselves, our friends, our children ? 4. *The express ordination of Christ.* As though the preceding strong arguments were not strong enough, this the strongest and altogether unanswerable one is added. The Head of the Church commands, He sees what is fitting and best. We run counter to his mind if we do not yield prompt and willing obedience. Whatever *we* may think, this is what *he* thinks (Matt. x. 10; Luke x. 8). Ministerial support: (1) Should be rendered cheerfully. Grudging or tardy gift in such a matter is semi-disobedience to Christ, and not a little dishonouring to the givers. (2) Should not be regarded as an equivalent for what is received. A minister is not *paid* for what he does. He is not in receipt of a *salary*. This is a degrading view of the whole matter. A minister is *supported*, whilst he lays himself out for the spiritual profit of those amongst whom his lot is cast. (3) Should be sufficient. A due estimate of the advantages derived from a faithful ministry will prompt to a *generous* support, so that, amid many spiritual cares, temporal anxieties may not unduly press. A Church failing to adequately support its ministers, whilst possessing the ability to do so, inflicts much injury upon its ministers, *but much more upon itself*. Matthew Henry says, "A scandalous maintenance makes a scandalous ministry."

❡ II. THE RIGHT MAY PROFITABLY BE WAIVED UNDER CERTAIN CIRCUMSTANCES. 1. To remove prejudice. 2. To prove disinterestedness, showing that we are not actuated by love of lucre. 3. To gain more independence, which may be desirable under certain conditions of Church life. 4. To make a strong position for one's self when unjust charges are apprehended. The Apostle Paul would not give the least advantage to his enemies. 5. For any other reasons which promise profit to the interests of Christ's kingdom. If thereby we can "gain the more" (ver. 19). There is nothing derogatory in a minister supporting himself. It is a pity that there should be so much absurd prejudice against it. A marvel of incongruity that the title of "Rev." should be bestowed upon the minister who is supported by his people, and denied to the minister who follows the lead of the apostolic tent-maker! that the one should be welcomed to certain associations and circles, and the other kept at arm's length! Not that the title of "Rev." is appropriate for any; yet if ever a man deserved such a designation, I suppose it was the very apostle, who, according to modern notions, disqualified himself for it. As to privileged societies, men of good sense need scarcely worry themselves about being excluded from those which would have blackballed the apostle of the Gentiles.—H.

Vers. 16, 17.—*Compulsory gospel preaching.* I. THE TRUE MINISTER BECOMES SUCH NOT BY MERE CHOICE OR PREDILECTION. Preaching the gospel is: 1. Not easy. 2. Often disheartening. 3. Its joys come rather after triumph over natural inclination. 4. Too responsible to be undertaken without authority.

II. THE TRUE MINISTER BECOMES SUCH BECAUSE OF: 1. God's command. Uttered to heart—a "Divine call," corroborated by suitability, confirmed by blessing on labours. 2. Claims of fellow-creatures. 3. Conscientious promptings towards service.

III. THOSE CALLED TO THE MINISTRY DARE NOT REFUSE. "Woe is unto me, if I preach not the gospel!" To refuse would involve: 1. God's displeasure. 2. The blood of our fellows resting upon us. 3. The non-employment of gifts, and the consequences of this.—H.

Ver. 22.—*Soul-saving.* The great apostle of the Gentiles was a singular man and lived a strange life. Some looking at him pronounced him to be a fool; others, a madman. He seemed, indeed, strangely destitute of that wisdom which places self-interest in the front, and incites to the pursuit of position, power, and the praise of men. When brought to a knowledge of the truth, the future apostle relinquished the course which he had mapped out, and his association with Gamaliel and the great teachers. He commenced with gigantic self-sacrifice: why? He desired to save souls. He became a great traveller—from city to city, town to town, village to village, he went on untiringly: why? To save souls. He underwent extreme sufferings (2 Cor. xi. 24—29)—to save souls. He exposed himself constantly to danger and death—to save souls. With the Jew he banished from his mind all Gentile tendencies—to save the Jew. With the Gentile he severed himself from all Jewish partialities—to save the Gentile. He was willing to be anything or nothing, to do this or that, if by any means he might "save some." Soul-saving had become a master-passion of his soul. He was in the world for it. Everything must be subordinated to it.

I. WHY WAS PAUL SO DESIROUS TO SAVE SOULS? He remembered: 1. *The value of the soul.* Of this he had the deepest conviction. To him the soul of man was the most precious thing in the world. Whilst men were seeking to save all other things, he would seek to save *this*. All other gain was as loss compared to *the gain of a soul*. 2. *The fate of the lost soul.* He saw the unsaved soul *going down*, getting further and further from God, becoming viler, ripening for hell. The fearful words of his Master rang loudly in his ears. He *believed them*, he did not refine them down until they meant nothing. He saw the souls "cast out;" he heard the dread "Depart;" the "weeping and wailing and gnashing of teeth" sounded in his heart; and he resolved that, as an instrument in the Divine hand, he would do his utmost to "save some." 3. *The future of the saved soul.* (1) In this life. Tending upwards; becoming purified; increasing in joy, peace, usefulness; indissolubly united to God. (2) In the next life. "With Christ." The fulness of joy. Every soil of sin removed. All powers becoming developed. The "higher ministry" commenced and continuing. 4. *The glory of Christ.* This was *supreme* in the apostle's mind. The *Master* was *first*. Paul was pre-eminently a "Jesus Christ's man." Soul-saving redounded to the honour and praise of his Lord. Christ had come "to seek and to save that which was lost." The purpose of the Master became the all-absorbing desire of the servant. Paul saw that his Master was glorified by the victories of the cross. So in season and out of season the apostle preached "Jesus Christ and him crucified" that he might "save some." He lived, laboured, suffered, for the day when "the multitude which no man could number" should sing to the praise of Christ the sweet stanzas of the "new song." The love of Christ constrained him.

II. Note some ways in which Paul sought to save souls. 1. *He used all means at hand.* (1) Preaching. He had a *definite object* in preaching. (2) Conversation. He could preach well to a congregation of one! (3) Writing. What a gift he had for "Epistles"! Letter-writing with a view to saving souls is an excellent means, but it requires dexterous use. Paul could not "drivel," or be "goody-goody," or "talk cant." Many religious letter-writers can. Hence the contrast between ancient and modern epistles. (4) Prayer. He "bowed his knees." Stiff-kneed preachers often have stiff-necked people. (5) Living the truth. Here, perhaps, lay the transcendent power of Paul. He not only prayed, wrote, talked, preached,—*he was*. Satan is more afraid of the gospel in the concrete than of the gospel in the abstract. 2. *He complied with prejudice and prepossession.* If we would make others like ourselves in things essential, we must first make ourselves like them in things indifferent. Paul tells us that to the Jew he became a Jew—remembered Jewish feeling, looked at things from a Jewish standpoint, accorded with Jewish observances. To the Gentile he became a Gentile—accommodating his utterance, manner, form of thought, mode of presenting the truth, to Gentile predilection. You can talk to a man more easily if you stand on the same platform with him. To the weak Paul became as weak; not insisting upon his liberty or ruthlessly running counter to imperfect conceptions. In fact, he asserts that he became "all things to all men" in order to realize his supreme object. Personal predilections must be sacrificed, and unpleasant restraints submitted to, if we would do effectively the greatest work under heaven. An unbending preacher will preach to unbroken hearts. An insistence upon our rights and privileges is a short method, often adopted, of ruining all hopes. A spirit of holy compliance, a disposition to stand *just alongside* the one we would gain,—these are potent. *We often bar and bolt the very door that we are trying to unfasten.* Often we forget that we are speaking to very imperfect men, and that we are very imperfect ourselves. Compliance must, of course, not be unlimited. (1) We must exercise discretion. We must abide in the realm of "the lawful," and select what will be truly "expedient." Sound judgment need be exercised. We must look to probable results. (2) We must never sacrifice the right. Paul was most compliant in things indifferent, but most unyielding in things essential. When he yielded he not only confined himself to things indifferent, but made it to be understood that the things were indifferent. When they were regarded as essential he refused to comply. This is strikingly illustrated in his permitting the circumcision of Timothy, but resisting that of Titus. 3. *He practised great self-sacrifice.* He did not think of *himself*, but of those he sought to gain. We have seen how willing he was to sacrifice his personal predilections. He went further. (1) In some instances he sacrificed his maintenance, supporting himself by the labour of his own hands. (2) He sacrificed his personal ease and comfort. (3) He sacrificed much of his freedom—he made himself "servant unto all" (ver. 19). A man who is prepared for illimitable self-sacrifice can do much. No sacrifice is too great for the attainment of Paul's life-object. Christ laid down his life for it. He who bore the great cross spoke of crosses for his followers. His ministers often have heavy ones, but it is worth while to carry them, if by doing so we become instrumental in *saving souls*. Souls saved will be our "joy and crown" at last. What vast possibilities life presents, when we think that in it we may be the means of saving souls! This applies to all Christians. Every saint should toil for the salvation of men. All the sorrows endured and sacrifices made will seem like "the dust of the balance" when we see our spiritual children welcomed home.—H.

Vers. 24—27.—*Spiritual athletics.* Paul compares the Christian life to a foot-race and to a boxing contest. These were familiar to the Corinthians, being conspicuous features of the celebrated Isthmian games. A wise teacher speaks through things known of things unknown. Christ spoke in parables. Passing events may be made the vehicles of abiding truths. The *secular* may often illustrate the *sacred*. There is no loss of dignity or impropriety in such modes of instruction. Some people are shocked by references to everyday life; but such people ought to be shocked. Homely garb sometimes wins the readier admittance. Note some points of resemblance.

I. CHRISTIAN LIFE IS A PASSAGE—FROM SIN TO HOLINESS, FROM EARTH TO HEAVEN. It is *a daily movement.* We need beware of stumbling-blocks, of straying from the right course, of indulgence which may hinder, of violation of laws, of loitering, since the time is short.

II. CHRISTIAN LIFE IS A CONTEST WITH ENEMIES. The "race" does not fully illustrate it. We have opponents, many and resolute. We have a trinity against us as well as for us—the world, the flesh, and the devil. We have not only to "run," but to "fight."

III. FOR SUCCESS ARE NEEDED: 1. *Preparation.* For athletic contests how much "training" has to be undergone, often very painful and wearying! Our preparation for Christian life is arduous and long, but it does not commence *before* we enter upon Christian life, but *as* we enter, and continues until the close. We "train" *as* we run and *as* we fight. 2. *Earnestness.* No indifferent competitor was likely to win in ancient races or boxing contests. Indifference kills Christian life. The half-hearted go not far from the starting-point. Many have only enough earnestness to "enter" for the race and fight; as soon as they have "entered," they think all is done. 3. *Striving.* To be amongst the runners is not enough; we must exert our powers; we must call into activity all our energies. We must not be as those who "beat the air," but as those who beat their enemies. Christian life is real, with issues of infinite importance. It is not for exhibition of skill, but for stern work. "Strive [agonize] to enter in at the strait gate." Paul would have each Christian to be as the winner, who "spent himself" in snatching the victory (ver. 24). We do not hinder others from attaining, and for this we may be not a little thankful; but we each need to use the utmost effort. 4. *Patience.* Christian life is not soon over. At first we may do well, but when difficulties arise we shall be *tested*. Some who run fastest at first run slowest at last. Our all-wise Master spoke of "enduring to the end." 5. *Watchfulness.* Lest we trip. Lest our enemy gets an advantage. The great Preacher's text was often "Watch!" 6. *Resolution.* If we are to endure to the end, we shall need stern resolve. Fixedness of purpose is an essential for Christian life. We should determine in God's strength to go on, whatever may lie in our path: to fight on, no matter what enemies confront us. Christian life demands courage and fortitude; we must not be too easily frightened. 7. *Concentration.* "This *one thing* I do." The "whole man" must be given to religion. Some professors are "called off" from the race, and lose it. They lower their guard, for their hands must be about earthly things, and then their enemy overthrows them. 8. *Continuity.* This tries many. If religion were spasmodic, they could be religious. There are many "now-and-then" Christians. People like to be pious at intervals. 9. *Mortification of the flesh.* Ancient athletes knew, as their modern brethren do, what this means. The victor was "temperate in all things." A pampered body meant disappointment, disgrace, loss. Paul said, "I keep under [I buffet, I bruise] my body." Our lower nature must be dealt severely with. Indulgence is disaster; we must practise self-control, self-denial, self-sacrifice. 10. *Confidence, but not excess of confidence.*

Confidence that will prompt to exertion, not confidence which kills effort. "Lest . . . I myself should be a castaway."

IV. SUCCESS MEETS WITH REWARD. Contrast the crowns of earth with the crown of heaven. Many do so much for a corruptible crown, and we so little for an incorruptible one. A garland of leaves and a day's popularity: paradise and life eternal.

V. MANY SPECTATORS WITNESS THE CONTEST. The eyes of the ungodly are upon us. Fellow-Christians watch us closely. The angels behold us, and are "ministering spirits" to us. Perhaps victors of the past, perhaps those who have failed in race and fight, watch us. The King sees us—the Judge—he who holds "the crown of righteousness" for those who have "fought a good fight" and "finished the course." "Wherefore seeing," etc. (Heb. xii. 1, 2). When we think of the race and fight, we should ponder Phil. iv. 13, "I can do all things through Christ which strengtheneth me."—H.

Vers. 1—3.—*The marks of apostleship.* This chapter grows out of the noble utterance of self-denial with which the previous one closes. The apostle illustrates and enforces the duty of curtailing our liberty in things indifferent for the sake of weaker brethren, by a reference to his own example in foregoing the right of maintenance by the Church. Was he not free? Had he not all the rights belonging to Christians, unfettered by obligations to men? Nay, more, was he not an apostle? At Corinth, as elsewhere, there were some who questioned the full apostolic authority of Paul, on the ground that he was not one of the twelve; and his self-denial seems to have been turned into an argument against him. It was insinuated that he refrained from asking the support of his converts, as the other apostles were in the habit of doing, because he was conscious of his inferiority. It is apparently for this reason that he here presents the marks of his apostleship.

I. HE HAD SEEN JESUS THE LORD. There is no evidence that he had seen Jesus in the days of his flesh, but the reference is mainly to the appearance near Damascus (Acts ix. 4—6). On that occasion the Lord met him and gave him his commission as an apostle; and this was regarded as an essential mark of apostleship in the highest sense, as we see from the election of Matthias (Acts i. 22; comp. ch. xv. 8). In this respect the apostles can have no successors. The office was a special and temporary one, needful for the planting and organizing of the Church, and was intended to expire with the men who held it. Having set the house in order, they were to deliver the keys to the ordinary servants who were left in charge. Still, every one whom Christ sends forth to do his work must first have had the sight of him that faith gives. Only when we have beheld him in his glory, invested with "all authority in heaven and on earth," and heard from his lips the call to go forth, shall we feel ourselves clothed with power as his ambassadors (comp. Isa. vi.; Matt. xxviii. 18, 19).

II. THE CORINTHIAN CHRISTIANS WERE THE SEAL OF HIS APOSTLESHIP. Whatever reason others might have for questioning his standing, they at least had none; for as the instrument of their conversion, he could point to them as "his work in the Lord." The power which accompanied his preaching, and which had wrought so mighty a change in them, was a proof that he had not run unsent. This of itself did not prove apostleship in the high sense in which Paul claimed it, but it proved that the Lord was with him. This kind of evidence requires to be adduced with caution, inasmuch as it is difficult for us to estimate the real success of a ministry; but where there are unmistakable proofs of the conversion of sinners and the edification of saints, we are warranted in viewing these as the seals of our mission. In seeking these high ends, we are doing truly apostolic work. Happy the minister who can say to his congregation, "Ye are my work in the Lord"!—B.

Vers. 4—18.—*Ministerial support.* Having vindicated his claim to be reckoned among the apostles of Christ, Paul proceeds to assert his right to a temporal maintenance at the hands of those to whom he ministered. The other apostles received support, not only for themselves, but also for their wives: why should he not make the same claim? Though he was unmarried, and though he had hitherto supported himself by the labour of his own hands, this did not invalidate his right. Consider—

I. THE RIGHT OF MINISTERS TO A SUITABLE MAINTENANCE. This is upheld by various arguments and analogies. 1. *The labourer is worthy of his reward.* Three instances are adduced in illustration (ver. 7). (1) The soldier. The duty of fighting for his country throws the burden of his support upon others. Why should it be otherwise with the Christian soldier (2 Tim. ii. 4)? (2) The husbandman. His labour is rewarded by the fruit. The minister of the gospel is also a husbandman (ch. iii. 6—9). (3) The shepherd. Does he not receive the milk of the flock, partly for food and partly for exchange? Why should not the Christian pastor, who tends the flock of Christ, have a similar return (1 Pet. v. 2)? The principle in these instances is that every occupation in common life yields support to the worker, and that he does not require to go beyond it for daily sustenance. In like manner, the minister of the gospel is entitled to an adequate maintenance without having to resort to secular work to supply his wants. 2. *The teaching of the Mosaic Law.* "Thou shalt not muzzle the ox," etc. (ver. 9; Deut. xxv. 4; comp. 1 Tim. v. 18). What was the meaning of this injunction? It shows, indeed, the care of the Lawgiver for the brute creation, but it is only a particular application of a great principle. The Law has regard for oxen, not for their own sake, but for the sake of him to whom they are in subjection. And if even the labouring ox was to be fed, how much more should the plougher and the thresher work in hope of partaking! The Law of Moses thus confirms the teaching of natural analogy, that the labourer is to be maintained by his work. 3. *The fairness of the claim.* "If we sowed unto you spiritual things," etc. (ver. 11). In every case the sower expects to reap; but there is more than this in the apostle's argument. The preacher of the gospel sows spiritual things—those great truths that minister to the spirit: is it a great matter if he looks for carnal things in return—those things that minister only to the flesh? If he is the instrument, in God's hand, of saving the souls of his hearers, what amount of gold can be an adequate recognition of the service rendered? 4. *Analogy of the Jewish priesthood.* (Ver. 13.) The rule was that they who served at the altar should receive a portion of the sacrifices and other gifts that were constantly brought to the temple. A sufficient support was thus secured; and the Divine sanction implied in that ancient rule applies equally to the case of the Christian ministry. 5. *The express ordinance of the Lord Christ.* (Ver. 14.) When he sent forth his apostles to preach, he said, "Get you no gold, nor silver, nor brass in your purses; . . . for the labourer is worthy of his food" (Matt. x. 9, 10). This was their marching order. They were to depend on the offerings of the people among whom they laboured; and the reference here shows that this was no temporary arrangement, but that it was intended to be the New Testament rule for preachers of the gospel. Instead of having to turn aside to secular pursuits, they are to be free to give themselves wholly to their work. By these various arguments the apostle establishes the right of ministers to claim support at the hands of the Christian people, and the corresponding duty of the people to contribute that support. Both the right and the duty have been but imperfectly recognized by the Church. This will appear if we consider: (1) *The average rate of ministerial support.* Compare this with the incomes of men in the other learned professions or in mercantile pursuits. (2) *The manner in which giving to the cause of Christ is frequently regarded.* How many either give with a grudge or do not give at all! The evil resulting is twofold— spiritual loss to the individual, and a crippling of the Church in her work. Not until all the tithes are brought into the storehouse will the Lord open the windows of heaven and pour out a blessing (Mal. iii. 8—10).

II. THE RENUNCIATION OF THIS RIGHT. (Vers. 15—18.) Strongly as Paul insists upon his right to temporal maintenance, it is not with a view to urge his claim upon the Corinthians, but to bring into clearer relief his renunciation of it. That he preached the gospel free of charge was to him a matter of boasting which he would rather die than be deprived of. It was no glory to him that he was a preacher; for, as a steward put in trust with the gospel, this was his simple duty. But it was no part of his stewardship to labour without support; and this, accordingly, was a proof of his sincerity in which he was entitled to boast. In this act of self-denial he had a reward in making the gospel entirely free, and in securing that on this ground no hindrance should be put in its way (ver. 12). Here some practical considerations emerge. 1. *How a minister of the gospel should bear himself towards pecuniary support.* There are cases in which he may forego his right, especially where he sees that this renunciation will tend to the advancement of the gospel. Usually, however, it is his duty to accept a stipend at the hands of the Christian people, and that for the reason which led

Paul to decline it. To receive a reasonable maintenance is to be in the best position for devoting one's self entirely to the ministry of the Word. But at all times it should be manifest that the servant of Christ does not act from mercenary motives. The shepherd is not to tend the flock for the sake of the fleece. "Not yours, but you," should be his motto (2 Cor. xii. 14). 2. *The obligation to preach the gospel.* "Necessity is laid upon me." There is a Divine *must* in the case of every true preacher, as there was in the case of Jesus (comp. Mark viii. 31; Luke iv. 43; xix. 5; John iii. 14). The love of Christ, not less than the command of Christ, constrains him. It is with him as with the prophet: "Then I said, I will not make mention of him, nor speak any more in his Name. But his word was in mine heart as a burning fire shut up in my bones, and I was weary with forbearing, and I could not stay" (Jer. xx. 9). 3. *The doctrine of reward.* The apostle's statement regarding the reward he expected for his optional renunciation of support has been adduced by popish divines in support of their doctrine of supererogation; but it will not bear such an application. The distinction he makes is between what was plainly a part of his bounden duty as a steward, and what seemed best for the furtherance of the gospel in his peculiar circumstances. In one sense it was a matter for his own choice whether he should accept a temporal maintenance, but this is not the sense required by the Romish argument. Whatever promises to conduce to the furtherance of Christ's kingdom, becomes thereby a duty to the apostle; for "to him that knoweth to do good, and doeth it not, to him it is sin" (Jas. iv. 17). There is no act which is not included under love to God and love to man. There is no self-denial to which the love of Christ should not prompt us. The gospel doctrine of reward does not rest on any theory of supererogation, but rather on the principle that God is pleased to recognize the fidelity of his servants.—B.

Vers. 19—23.—*The principle of accommodation.* Paul's resolve to preach the gospel without charge was but one instance of the general rule which guided his life. Though under obligation to none, he yet became the servant of all—"all things to all men." He accommodated himself to the Jews (ver. 20), as when he circumcised Timothy (Acts xvi. 3) and purified himself in the temple (Acts xxi. 26). He accommodated himself to the Gentiles (ver. 21), by refusing to impose the Law of Moses (Gal. ii. 5) and by meeting them on their own ground (Acts xvii. 22—31). He accommodated himself to the weak (ver. 22), as when he abstained from meat because of their scruples (ch. viii. 13). Consider—

I. ACCOMMODATION AS A RULE OF MINISTERIAL PRACTICE. There is a high sense in which every minister of Christ is called to become "all things to all men." We are to adapt ourselves to the circumstances, modes of thought, and even the harmless prejudices of those among whom we labour. In dealing with human souls, we must not stand upon points of etiquette, but be ready when occasion requires to sacrifice our preferences and sometimes our rights. This principle will cover matters of dress and modes of living, as also our choice of recreation and amusement. William Burns, missionary to China, adopted the Chinese dress that he might the more easily gain access to the people. On the same ground we shall present the truth in language which our hearers understand, whether they are children or adults. This happy faculty of adaptation has frequently proved of great service to the gospel.

II. LIMITS TO BE OBSERVED IN FOLLOWING THIS RULE. The highest things may frequently be mistaken for the lowest. Christian accommodation may be confounded with time-serving, but nothing is more unlike. The man whose principles are flexible, who trims and carves to serve his purpose, who is a devout Christian in this company and a railing scoffer in that, may be said to be "all things to all men;" but such a man is a mere jelly-fish character, a mass of moral pulp. For such accommodation as Paul practised there is needed the highest principle, the strongest consistency; and in order to this, certain limits are to be observed. 1. *It must not lead us to do or tolerate that which is sinful.* This limit is transgressed by Jesuit missionaries when they suffer their converts to retain part of their old idolatrous worship. 2. *It must not lead us to keep back any essential truth because it is unpopular.* This were cowardice and infidelity to our trust. 3. *It must not lead us to do anything which would compromise the Christian name.* "Let not your good be evil spoken of" (Rom. xiv. 16).

III. MOTIVES THAT PROMPT US TO FOLLOW THIS RULE. These are: 1. *A desire to save others.* It is not a wish to please men, but a desire to remove every hindrance to the reception of the gospel. With this end in view, we shall not find it difficult to become "all things to all men." A human soul is not too dearly won at the cost of a little self-sacrifice. In this aspect the rule we are considering is but a faint copy of the great accommodation—the incarnation and work of Jesus Christ. 2. *A regard to our personal salvation.* (Ver. 23.) Paul connects his work "for the gospel's sake" with his being a "joint partaker" of its blessings. In work for the good of others we must not be unmindful of our own good; and there is nothing more conducive to our spiritual benefit than faithful, self-denying service for Christ. "Continue in these things; for in doing this thou shalt both save thyself and them that hear thee" (1 Tim. iv. 16).—B.

Vers. 24—27.—*The race for the prize.* The thought introduced in ver. 23, that Paul's self-denial had a reference to his own salvation as well as the salvation of others, is here carried on and applied generally to all Christians. The imagery is derived from the Isthmian games celebrated in the neighbourhood of Corinth, and therefore well known to his readers. These games occupied a place in the national life of Greece corresponding to that occupied by the great yearly festivals in the life of Israel. There is no reference to them in the Gospels, as they were unknown in Palestine, but more than once they are used in the Epistles as a metaphorical representation of the Christian life (comp. Phil. iii. 14; 2 Tim. iv. 7, 8; Heb. xii. 1). Consider—

I. THE RACE. The stadium presented an animating spectacle. At this end stand the competing athletes, awaiting the signal to start; at the other end is the judge, holding in his hand the prize; whilst all around, rising tier upon tier, are the seats crowded with spectators. The Christian life is a race for the great prize offered by God to the successful runner. At conversion we take our place in the racecourse and have our names proclaimed by the herald. The leading ideas in the figure are: 1. *Progress.* "Forgetting the things which are behind, and stretching forward to the things which are before, I press on," etc. (Phil. iii. 13). 2. *Earnestness.* The Christian life is one of strenuous effort—every muscle strung, every faculty called into exercise. No place for lukewarmness or indifference here. 3. *Concentration.* "One thing I do." The runner, with eye on the goal and all else out of view, bends his whole strength to this single effort. Dissipation of energy, the *multa* rather than the *multum*, is a source of weakness in spiritual life. "One thing is needful." 4. *Endurance.* "Let us run with patience" (Heb. xii. 1). To faint or fall is to lose the prize. The cross must be borne to the end. Nothing but "patient continuance in well-doing" will conduct us to the goal (comp. Jas. i. 12).

II. CONDITIONS OF SUCCESS IN THE RACE. To run well we must run as the successful racer. The end in view must be clear: we must know what we are running for ("not uncertainly"). Here specially emphasize the preparatory condition—*self-restraint.* The athlete under training was required to avoid excess in eating and drinking, and every form of fleshly indulgence. The Christian athlete must practise a like temperance if he would run his course with success. In this point of view the body is the antagonist with which we contend, and which must be buffeted and bruised rather than suffered to gain the mastery over us. How many Christians are hindered in their spiritual course by lack of self-restraint! The worship of comfort, the love of luxury, not to speak of such indulgences as are clearly sinful, cause many to lag in the race. An intemperate use of, or affection for, things in themselves good, is a most insidious snare in the path of spiritual advancement. Bodily mortification is not spirituality, but it is often helpful towards its attainment. The Christian runner must lay aside every weight as well as every sin (Heb. xii. 1).

III. THE PRIZE. This consisted of a chaplet of leaves—olive, parsley, pine. In addition, the name of the victor was celebrated in a triumphal ode and a statue was erected to his memory. It was a great honour—one of the greatest in a land where the gymnastic art was so highly appreciated; and even Roman emperors (Nero, *e.g.*) did not hesitate to enter the lists. But at best it was, like all earthly honours, corruptible. These crowns would quickly fade, that applause would soon cease. The prize for which the Christian contends is *an incorruptible crown.* It is the "crown of righteousness" (2 Tim. iv. 8), the "crown of life" (Jas. i. 12; Rev. ii. 10), the "crown of glory" (1 Pet. v. 4). To have righteousness and life in perfection is our true glory, and this is the very crown of our being. A crown composed of such materials cannot fade away. All the trees in that country are evergreen. What an object to fill the eye and fire the soul! A proud moment when the successful runner had the chaplet of leaves put on his brow! A grander moment for the Christian athlete when the pierced hand of Jesus places on his head the crown of glory! And if men endure so much and strive so earnestly for the corruptible, how much more should we endure and strive in order to obtain the incorruptible!

REMARKS. 1. The human side of the Christian life is strongly emphasized in the figure of the race; but along with this we must take the other side of the truth. Without the grace of God we cannot run. Mark the striking combination in Phil. ii. 12, 13. 2. Notice the apostle's self-distrust. He is not ashamed to confess that he brings his body into subjection, "lest by any means, after that I have preached to others, I myself should be rejected." Compare such outbursts of confident assurance as Rom. viii. 38, 39, and 2 Tim. i. 12, and regard the one as the complement of the other. Self-diffidence goes hand-in-hand with genuine assurance. A lesson for all Christians, and especially for all preachers.—B.

Ver. 16.—*Compulsory service.* The apostle here affords us a passing glimpse of his own state of mind in reference to his high calling as a "preacher of the gospel." The revelation of the secret workings of an earnest human spirit must needs be deeply interesting to us, and most of all in the case of a man of such noble nature as Paul, and in reference to a matter of such supreme moment. We could scarcely have a finer view of the ministry of the Word, a finer model of right thought and feeling about it, than is presented in these simple but lofty words. Chiefly three elements of feeling are here expressed.

I. A SENSE OF THE DIGNITY OF THE PREACHER'S OFFICE. The preaching of the Word is evidently regarded here as a fixed and permanent institution of the Church, a work to which men are divinely called to consecrate themselves, and from which they may draw the necessary support of their life (ver. 14). And the fact that Paul disavows all self-glorying on account of it, implies that there is that in the office which might lead a man unduly to exalt himself. But what is the real nature of its dignity? It is very different from that which belongs to social rank or any kind of worldly distinction. Much mischief springs from losing sight of this difference. Ever since the time when a halo of worldly glory began to be thrown around the witness for Christ, and the ideas of social elevation, priestly supremacy, large emolument, luxurious ease, came to be associated with it, it has been degraded by the intrusion of false motive, and by being made the prize of a purely carnal ambition. The dignity Paul recognizes in it is that which is inherent in all high and holy service; the honour he would have paid to it is that which is due to a faithful discharge of sacred responsibility. The dignity of the preacher's function lies in such facts as these: 1. *It brings a man,* more than any other office does, *into habitual contact with the mind of God and with the realities of the invisible world.* Not that he who sustains it has in this respect a privilege denied to others. Every path of human life may be thus gilded and gladdened by the heavenly glory. But it is his special business, by habits of thought and prayer, to become more deeply conversant than other men with the revelations of God and the things unseen and eternal. And the fact that his work demands that mind and heart should be ever dwelling in such a high spiritual region, imparts a greatness and dignity to it surpassing that of all others. 2. *It brings him into a purely spiritual relationship with his fellow-men.* Other human relations are more superficial. The world recognizes no bonds of union but such as grow out of the passing interests and experiences of this present life. To the preacher of the gospel, as such, the secular aspect of the position men occupy is nothing as compared with the spiritual. He "knows no man after the flesh." He has to do with the nobler, the immortal part of them, "to watch for their souls as one that must give account." 3. *It leads on to eternal issues.* All the grandeur of the endless futurity overshadows it. None of our earthly businesses have reference merely to the issues of time. Lines of moral influence are connected with them that stretch out into the great hereafter. But this is specially the case with the work of the Christian teacher. It must have infinite developments. It is the seed-sowing for an eternal harvest. It is to every man "none other than the savour of life unto life, or of death unto death."

II. THE SENSE OF PERSONAL UNWORTHINESS. "Though I preach the gospel, I have nothing to glory of." The conscious dignity of his office is coupled with deep humility. "Who is sufficient for these things?" (2 Cor. ii. 16). Paul's humility, indeed, was not that of the man who is always doubting his right to the position he occupies, and fitness for the work he is doing. He knew that he bore the stamp and seal of a Divine commission. . And every true preacher of the Word must in a measure share this feeling. If a man has no conscious or acknowledged fitness for the work, he has no business to undertake it. But it must needs be that, in hours of calm reflection, in the solitude and silence of the night, he will often lie

"Contemplating his own unworthiness."

Many things will serve to humble him. 1. The thought that he is but an instrument in the hands of God (ch. iii. 5—7). 2. The fact that, in proclaiming the mercy of God to sinners, he has to look upon himself as the foremost of those who need that mercy (1 Tim. i. 15, 16). 3. The light the Word he preaches continually sheds on the evils of his own heart and life. 4. The sense of the subtle spiritual dangers that beset his sacred calling. 5. The fear "lest that by any means, having preached to others, he himself should be a castaway" (ver. 27).

III. A SENSE OF MORAL CONSTRAINT. "Necessity is laid upon me," etc. The apostle felt that he had been invested by the risen Lord with a very solemn stewardship, and that he dared not be unfaithful to it. The heaviest of all "woes," the woe of a remorseful conscience, the woe of a spirit that has fallen from the height of a glory that might have been its own for ever, would fall upon him if he did. His would be the misery of being basely untrue to himself as well as to his Divine Master. There are two kinds of moral "necessity"—the necessity of an external force and that of an internal: the necessity of an outward law, backed by some form of outward penalty; and the necessity of an inward impulse, backed by the sacred fear of inward shame and loss. It was this latter kind of necessity of which he was supremely conscious. It was consistent with perfect moral freedom, because it was of the nature of a resistless force in the depths of his own soul, the decision of his own will, the impulse of his own heart. The will of God had imposed this stewardship, this "dispensation of the gospel," upon him. He had been separated unto it from his very birth (Rom. i. 1; Gal. i. 15). And God's will had become his will, God's purpose his purpose. The manifested love of Christ had become a constraining power within him, leading his whole being into captivity, drawing forth every energy of his nature in a holy and joyous service. This kind of "necessity" is the loftiest principle by which any human spirit can be actuated. Never is a man so great, so free, so royal, so divinely blessed, as when he is intelligently conscious of it. This is the true inspiration of gospel ministry. The harvest is great. May the Lord of the harvest "send forth labourers" thus inwardly constrained to serve him!—W.

Ver. 22.—"By all means save some." Two points present themselves for our consideration here—(1) The end the apostle had in view; (2) the method by which he sought to secure it.

I. THE END. "To save some." What does he mean by this? What to him was the salvation of men? 1. It certainly means deliverance from a dread future calamity. "The wrath to come," "the perdition of ungodly men," was to St. Paul no dream, but an awful reality. It was worth all possible effort and self-sacrifice to save men from it. If he had no other impulse than that of mere human sympathy to move him, we have here a sufficient explanation of the enthusiasm of his zeal. It is often said that if Christian people really believed the future that is before multitudes of their fellow-creatures to be so dark and dreadful as they say it is, they could never rest as they do in their own natural or spiritual satisfactions. They would rather be beside themselves with a frantic agony of sympathetic sorrow and desire to save. There is truth in this. The easy indifference with which too many of us regard the condition and prospects of the godless world around us, belies the reality of our faith. Our conceptions of what the solemn issues of the future shall be may differ. Some, after anxious and earnest thought, may have arrived at the conclusion that to forecast the nature or the duration of the penalty that will then fall on the transgressor is beyond our province, and that we can only take the language of Scripture as it stands, without attempting to penetrate the haze of dreadful mystery that hangs around it. But the broad and certain facts of the case are such as may well affect us far more deeply than they do, and bring forth in us far richer and more abundant fruits of practical beneficence. It is to be feared that doctrinal controversy about the future tends to weaken rather than deepen and strengthen our impressions. We lose in speculation and debate the practical earnestness the subject itself might be expected to awaken. St. Paul lived in the clear light of the future. His soul was thrilled by the sense of its tremendous reality. And though its issues probably were no more distinct and definite to his apprehension than they are to ours, yet his faith in their certainty was such as to stir up all the noble energies of his being in the endeavour to save his fellow-men. 2. But the foresight of the future was far from being the only thing that moved him; *it was a present deliverance from a present calamity that he had in view.* To save men now from the evil that enthralled and cursed them, ruining their Godlike nature, darkening all the glory of their life,—this was the end he sought. He was no visionary. It was no object of remote and uncertain utility, but one of most practical and immediate urgency at which he aimed. Whatever its bearing on the future may be, the influence of the gospel on the present passing life of men is so benign and blessed that our utmost zeal in diffusing it is fully justified. If we think of nothing more than the superficial social changes that Christianity has introduced, how it is at this very hour the prolific root of all social progress in every land, we see here an ample reward for all the sacrifices that have ever been made for its extension. But beneath all this there lies the fact that, as sin is the ruining, destroying power in man's nature and life, it must needs be a Godlike purpose that seeks to deliver him from it (Matt. i. 21; Acts iii. 26). "That I may by all means *save some.*" He could not hope for all, but if "some" only yielded to his persuasive word, it would be a blessed recompense. This is the inspiring hope of every true preacher and worker for Christ. The net is cast, the arrow is shot at a venture; the issue is not now made manifest. But a seemingly profitless work may be linked indirectly with results that are very great and glorious. Waves of spiritual influence, from a narrow circle, travel out where none can follow them. While there are those who shall find at last that the "great and wonderful things" they supposed they had done in the name of Christ are little recognized, there are others who will be amazed to discover that their lowly endeavours have yielded fruits of which they never dreamed. And to "save some," to be able to lay some trophies at the Master's feet, will be a blessed reward.

II. THE METHOD. "I am become all things to all men." It is remarkable that words which express the highest nobleness of an apostolic spirit should have come to be used by us in familiar discourse as descriptive of a type of character and mode of conduct that is mean and despicable. It is suggestive of the behaviour of one who has no steadfast principle, no honest outspokenness; the mere obsequious time-server, full of smiles and gilded insincerities; who, to serve his own ends, can put on any face that suits the occasion;

> "A man
> Versed in the world as pilot in his compass,
> The needle pointing ever to that interest
> Which is his lode-star, and who spreads his sails
> With vantage to the gale of others' passion."

There was nothing of this sort in Paul. Nothing could be more abhorrent to his spirit than a time-serving policy or a habit of smiling, plausible deceit. These words from his lips simply indicate that his strong desire to save men and win them to Christ led him to enter as much as possible into their circumstances, to place himself on their level. Thus would he disarm their prejudices and bring his heart into sympathetic contact with theirs. Thus would he commend to them the love of him who "was made under the Law that he might redeem them that were under the Law;" who for our sakes became poor, that we through his poverty might be made rich." Examples; Acts xvi, 3; xvii. 22—31; xxi. 26.) The lesson for all Christian preachers and workers is this : Cultivate a broad and generous human sympathy. In dealing with men in various conditions—doubt, error, poverty, sorrow, temptation, subjection to the power of evil—put yourself as much as possible in their place, if you would hope to guide, or comfort, or save them.—W.

Vers. 24—27.—*Running and fighting.* The crown of eternal life is here set forth as the issue of successful conflict with difficulties and foes. It would seem as if all Divine excellence must needs present itself to our minds as the negation of opposite forms of evil. We cannot think of God but as the "Light" that contends with our darkness, the "Fire" that consumes our corruption. God's Law is but the Divine restraint of our wayward propensities, the Divine rebuke of our transgressions. The Divine life in the soul is an energy that reveals itself in ceaseless struggle with forces that would otherwise destroy it, a perpetual battle with the powers of death. Heaven is victory, the rising up of the soul out of the region of trial and strife and suffering to its true destiny and inheritance in the glorious presence of God. Look at this passage as suggesting certain conditions of success in this spiritual conflict.

I. CONCENTRATION OF THOUGHT ON THE PRIZE AS A MATTER OF INTENSE PERSONAL INTEREST. "All run, but one receiveth," etc. The analogy here instituted is not complete, inasmuch as in the Christian race all who "run with patience" will attain. But it serves to enforce the need of great fixedness of thought and purpose, as if each runner felt that only one could win, and he would be that one. There is nothing narrow, envious, selfish, in this. A great difference lies here between the heavenly and the earthly striving. He must be a man of very elevated spirit who is able to rise entirely above the narrowing influence of secular rivalry. In urging his way to success along the crowded thoroughfares of the world, a man almost inevitably thrusts some one else aside. The gigantic system of commercial competition means this. And it is an important problem of social life to determine how one may claim as he ought that personal inheritance in the world that God has placed within his reach, and yet not fall into the sin of a selfish violation of the rights of others. There is no room, however, for anything of this kind in the spiritual race and warfare. Mutual emulation is mutual profit. The success of each one is to the advantage and the joy of all. Strive to win the heavenly crown as if you alone could wear it, and the more intensely earnest you are in your striving, the more does your example inspire your fellow-combatant, the more do you become a fount of healthful influence, a source of enrichment and blessing to all around you.

II. SELF-RESTRAINT AND SELF-DISCIPLINE. The severe physical discipline to which the athletes subjected themselves was gladly borne for the sake of the "corruptible crown" they sought to win. Not that the perishable wreath of wild olive encircling the victor's brow was in itself the thing he cared for. It was but the symbol of something else. To be conscious of the mastery, to have his name proclaimed by the herald before the assembled multitude as one who had conferred honour and renown on his family, his tribe, his country,—that was his reward. So that the very ephemeral character of the crown made it the more striking witness to the nobility of man's nature, to the truth that he can never find his satisfactions in the region of sense ; they belong, after all, to the super-sensible, the ideal world. Every form of ambition greater than the apparent object will account for or warrant, is proof of this. The enthusiasm that magnifies its objects beyond their real dimensions, and invests them with a fictitious charm, is always a significant memorial of man's relation to a higher and a better world. At the same time, this striving for the corruptible crown reminds us how vain often are the rewards of earthly ambition, and how the price men pay often for their successes is a very costly one. They surrender that which is far more precious than the thing they gain. They "spend their money for that which is not bread, and their labour for that which satisfieth not." In "seeking to save their life, they lose it." The law of the heavenly race is the reverse of this. As the unsubstantial, the delusive, the perishable, is relinquished, the soul wins for itself the "inheritance incorruptible, and undefiled, and that fadeth not away." You lose the lower life to gain the higher. "Temperate in all things." Let not the word "temperance" have to our minds a limited and exclusive meaning, one which, however important, does not cover the whole field of its Scripture applications. The Christian is called to be temperate alike in all his thoughts, emotions, words, and ways; in his joys and sorrows, his schemes and activities, his personal indulgences and personal mortifications; in his worldly ambitions, and even in the zeal of his religious life. But "the flesh" must needs be the chief occasion for the exercise of this self-regulating grace. "I buffet my body, and bring it into bondage." Nothing could be more expressive of that subjugation of our lower nature by which we can alone win the crown of the spirit. Not that there is any essential virtue in mere physical austerities and mortifications.

> "Pride may be pampered while the flesh grows lean."

Asceticism is no natural outgrowth of Christianity, but rather of its unnatural alliance with that pagan philosophy which regarded matter and spirit as essentially antagonistic principles. Christ teaches us to honour the body that God's wonder-working hand has framed, and that he makes the temple of his Spirit. But then do we most honour the body when we make it most thoroughly the submissive servant of the soul's diviner purposes, confronting it, meeting it full in the face, as it were, with the swift violence of our holy purpose, when it dares to obstruct the spirit in its path to the heavenly crown.

III. The confidence that springs from faith. "Not as uncertainly, not as beating the air." Vivid realization, unwavering assurance,—this was the secret of Paul's strength. The prize of his high calling stood out clear and luminous to his view. He had no misgivings as to the reality of it. It filled the whole field of his vision with its glory, and the whole energy of his nature was consecrated to its pursuit. We must rise above the chilling, paralyzing mists of doubt, and see the heavenly crown clearly before us, if we would have there to be any real vigour in our spiritual striving. "This is the victory that overcometh the world, even our faith."—W.

Vers. 26, 27.—*A good servant of Jesus Christ.* It was quite in St. Paul's manner to support his exhortations to Christian service by adducing his own example and experience. Those who were not acquainted with him might misconstrue such references and set them down to a vain-glorious spirit, but no one could do so who knew how fully and fervently this apostle ascribed all that he was and did as a Christian to the grace of Jesus Christ. "Not I, but the grace of God which was with me." "Not I, but Christ liveth in me."

I. Illustrations of Christian service. 1. St. Paul was as a runner in the Isthmian games, and so ran "not uncertainly." Suppose one to attempt that course without his mind made up as to the reason why or the goal to which he should run, moving without spirit or purpose, looking to this side and to that; he could take no prize. One must have a clear course and a definite aim in the race which is set before the servants of Christ. 2. St. Paul was as a boxer in the arena, and fought not as one "beating the air." The poet Virgil has the same expression in describing a boxer who missed his antagonist: "Vires in ventum effudit" ('Æneid,' bk. v. 446). To do so is to waste force. He fights well who plants his blows skilfully and makes them tell. The apostle was a man of peace, but he needed boldness and firmness, as well as love and patience, for his hard service. He had journeys to make, trials to bear, testimonies to raise, controversies to conduct, difficulties to adjust, calumnies to refute, sorrows to assuage—a great and arduous career; and, by the grace of God, he put all his force into it, ran his race of duty with ardour, fought his fight of faith with resolution.

II. Training and discipline for such service. "I buffet my body, and bring it into subjection." He who would subdue evil in others must suppress it in himself. Now, the apostle found that the gospel was hindered, not so much by intellectual objection, as by moral depravity. The flesh lusted against the spirit. He had felt this in himself, and knew that the flesh prevailed by fastening on the organs of the body and inducing indulgence or excess. So he brought himself into good training for active Christian work by bruising the body and "mortifying its deeds." He would not surfeit or pamper it, lest he should stupefy the soul. This is something quite different from that "neglect of the body" which St. Paul elsewhere mentions among the superstitions of a delusive piety. To deprive the body of necessary food and sleep is to disable the powers of the mind in hope of purifying the soul. Such has been the practice of men and women in the ascetic life, and at one time it took the form of a frenzy, when the Flagellants traversed a considerable part of Europe in long processions, with covered faces, chanting penitential hymns, and continually applying the scourge to one another's naked backs. Those fanatics meant well, and, indeed, supposed that they were following the Apostle Paul. But to such foolish and cruel actions few of us are prone at the present day. Our danger lies on the opposite side. We do not hold the body sufficiently under control. We give it ease and luxury and ornament; we allow dangerous scope to those cravings and passions which have a physical basis, and so our spiritual life languishes, and we can put no glow of feeling or strength of purpose into the service of Christ. Corinth was a city notorious for profligacy. The Christians there must have known that, if a young athlete did not hold himself apart from the vices of the place, he could win no distinction in the public games. Every such competitor had to resist indulgence, and bring his frame to a firmness of muscle and a full strength of vitality which would enable it to bear the fatigue and strain of the Isthmian contests. In like manner St. Paul, for a higher purpose, restrained and governed himself, cultivated simplicity in the tastes and habits of his outward life, studied to keep himself in spiritual health and vigour, that he might run well and fight well for his heavenly Master.

III. AN EYE TO CONSEQUENCES. To sustain his purpose, St. Paul kept in view the prize of success and the disgrace of failure. 1. *The prize would be an incorruptible crown.* In desiring this, the good servant is not open to any charge of selfishness or vain-glory. He thought of no prize, conceived of no praise or glory for himself which was not wrapped up in the praise and glory of Jesus. He had no desire to sit by himself on a high seat, with a chaplet or garland on his brow, drinking in his own praises. To see the people who had been converted to Christ through his labours safe in the kingdom would be to him a crown of rejoicing. And to see Christ praised and magnified would be to the good servant a great recompense of reward. 2. *The disgrace of failure would be the Master's disapproval.* How mortifying for one who had been a herald to others to be excluded at last as unworthy of a prize! Paul had preached to others, and called them to the Christian race, like the herald at the public games of Greece, who proclaimed the rules and conditions of the contest, and summoned runners or combatants to the lists. Alas for him if, through self-indulgence or want of thoroughness in his ministry, he should be disapproved by the great Judge at the close of the day! It is quite a mistake to infer from this that St. Paul was still uncertain about his ultimate salvation, and afraid of being cast away in his sins. That would, indeed, be strange and perplexing in the face of his strong expressions to the contrary in such passages as Rom. viii. 38, 39; 2 Tim. i. 12. The question here is not of a sinner's salvation, but of a believer's service—of doing well or ill in ministry; and fear of failure was and always is the obverse side of the desire of success. St. Paul was a very favoured servant of Christ, but it was none the less necessary for him to remember the need of diligence and self-government in view of the day when the Master will call all his servants to account, and either reward or disapprove them at his coming. Indeed, the remembrance of this is needful for all of us as a caution against presumptuous and careless living. If the doctrine of salvation by grace be taught alone, men are apt to abuse it, and become spiritually conceited and morally heedless. The corrective is the call to service. "If a man serve me, him will my Father honour." Be not *half-hearted.* So run as to attain: so fight as to overcome. Be not *faint-hearted.* Pray as you run: pray as you fight. "They that wait on the Lord shall renew their strength."—F.

Vers. 1, 2.—*The rights of apostleship.* One of St. Paul's chief difficulties arose from the efforts of his enemies to disprove his claims to apostleship. There does not seem to have been in the early Church a common understanding as to what constituted an apostle, and it was readily observed that the grounds of St. Paul's claim differed from the grounds on which the older apostles claimed. This, indeed, was but a surface appearance of difference, and did not reach the heart of the matter; but it sufficed to give the enemies of St. Paul an opportunity of questioning his authority, and even of asserting that, in the extravagance of his self-esteem, he had assumed a position and office which in no sense belonged to him. It will be seen from his letters that he was very jealous of his position as an apostle, and persisted in claiming the rights which belonged to the office. We may, therefore, recall to mind the general grounds on which he believed himself to be an apostle, and the more special signs of his apostleship which ought to have commended his claim to the Corinthians. St. Peter, on the occasion of filling the betrayer's place, had declared a condition of apostleship for which he gives no kind of authority. According to his idea (Acts i. 21, 22), "Of the men therefore which have companied with us all the time that the Lord Jesus went in and out among us, beginning from the baptism of John, unto the day that he was received up from us, of these must one become a witness with us of his resurrection." Probably St. Peter was led to this idea by our Lord's appointment of the apostles as his *witnesses*, and he conceived that an apostle must have a complete knowledge to be a true witness. But the essential condition of apostleship is rather to be found in the direct pershnal call to the office by the Lord Jesus Christ himself. Each one of the first twelve our Lord personally called. St. Paul he directly and personally called. No man can claim the office. The number can never be increased, unless Christ should be pleased to make himself manifest again, and call men to the office. St. Paul saw the Son of man, and heard his voice, and received his direct call, when smitten by the light near Damascus. Where there had been this direct personal call of Christ, there would surely be a seal of the call in a Divine endowment of miraculous power. This the first twelve apostles had, and this it is certain St. Paul also had. This, then, was the general ground of his claim; but he further urges upon the Corinthians that they had special reasons for accepting him as an apostle. The power of Christ which had come to them through him carried its own testimony. "The seal of mine apostleship are ye in the Lord." God had witnessed to him by crowning his labours with success; and the Corinthians had *felt* his apostolic power. Now St. Paul had to vindicate his personal dignity and liberty and right as an apostle. He had persisted in working for his own living at the trade of the tent-maker, in which he had been brought up, and his malicious enemies argued that he did so because he felt that he could not press his claim to maintenance, as did the other apostles. "The followers of St. Peter, with malicious ingenious logic, argued from this practice of St. Paul that his dignity and authority were thereby proved to be somewhat inferior to that of St. Peter and the Lord's brethren, who were supported by the Christian Church." In this chapter St. Paul declares his apostolic liberty and rights, especially in three matters.

I. His RIGHT OF ENTERING INTO SOCIAL RELATIONSHIPS. St. Peter had a wife. Other apostles were married men. And St. Paul might have been had he chosen to be. If he voluntarily refrained from entering into this social relation, because of the limitations which its responsibilities would entail on him, and because of the itinerant character of his labours, no one need assume that he abandoned his rights or failed to recognize them. Had he so minded, he could have made both wife and family chargeable to the Churches, and the burden those who loved him would gladly have borne. Voluntary abstention from the pressing of a man's rights ought never to be construed as the surrender of those rights. So St. Paul lays down the true and only principle upon which the celibacy of the clergy can be recognized. Every clergyman has the *right* to "lead about a sister, a wife," but any clergyman may refuse to exercise his right, and may voluntarily set his own liberty in bonds, if he thinks that he may thus gain a higher power in the service of his Divine Lord. The principle is equally applicable in the life of the ordinary Christian. Abridgments of liberty are oftentimes necessary, and yet more often advisable, but they never involve abandonments of rights. Constantly the Christian man says, "I may, but I will not—I will not for Christ's sake."

II. His RIGHT OF WORKING FOR INDEPENDENT MAINTENANCE. This was certainly a peculiarity in St. Paul, and no doubt other teachers felt it to be a kind of reproach upon them. But St. Paul never argues that it was a necessary duty for others. Any other man might feel it a duty, just as he did; but he had no intention of making his conduct in this respect even an *example*. He was placed in peculiar circumstances; he was of a singularly sensitive temperament; he laboured among all classes, and was anxious to keep away everything that might be made a reproach of the gospel; he was determined to make his motives quite clear, and so he would receive from the Churches no maintenance, only, in times of necessity, some kindly and helpful gifts. Now, we need not even say that St. Paul was right in this. He had an unquestioned ministerial claim to support in carnal things. We can only say he had a right also to exercise his liberty, and work for his own living, if he chose so to do. Those who work for their living may serve Christ in the preaching of his gospel; and those who preach his gospel may work for their living, if they prefer so to do.

III. HIS RIGHT OF CLAIMING THE DUE REWARDS OF HIS WORK. (Ver. 7.) This is urged by three figures: the support of the soldier in war; the partaking of the fruitage of his vineyard by the vine-dresser; and the sharing of the milk, given by the cattle, by him who has them in charge. The true rewards of Christian service for others are (1) their loving confidence and esteem; (2) the expressions of that love in their holy lives and labours; and (3) the more personal expressions of their love in gifts and care and kindly concern for the temporal well-being of their teachers.—R. T.

Vers. 7—12.—*The duty of supporting the ministry.* The separation of certain members of the Christian Church to the specific work of the pastor, the teacher, or the missionary, may be said to have begun at the election of the " seven," commonly called " deacons," which is narrated in Acts vi. 1—6. Then certain persons gave themselves up to the study and ministry of the Word and to prayer. The question how they were to be fed and supported was at once met by the members of the Church, who, in response to a natural and reasonable demand, and in full accordance with the principles and practices of the Mosaic dispensation, made provision for their material necessities. Our Lord, in sending out his disciples on their trial mission, had laid down the principle that they should not supply their own material wants, because " the labourer is worthy of his hire." Much has been said in recent times against an organized Christian ministry, dependent on the good will of the several Churches they may serve; but the Scripture cannot be read with unprejudiced mind, and the reader fail to perceive that " they who preach the gospel should live of the gospel." In the verses now before us St. Paul urges the duty of supporting the ministry by three lines of argument and illustration.

I. BY COMMON WORLDLY ILLUSTRATION. 1. The soldier, who, if he fights the battles of his country, reasonably expects his country to provide for his maintenance and his comfort. 2. The vine-dresser, who expects to reap in fruitage the reward of his labours in the vineyard. 3. And the keeper of a flock, who day by day lives upon the milk of the flock. These illustrations only touch the general principle that the worker has a claim to a portion at least of the results of his labour. The illustration of the soldier is the one most to St. Paul's point, because, while doing a special kind of work for us, he looks for our care of his temporal necessities. So the minister, in doing a spiritual work for us, commits to us the care of his " carnal things."

II. BY SCRIPTURE RULES. (Ver. 9.) The law is taken from Deut. xxv. 4. The figure is that of the oxen, who were driven to and fro over a hard space of ground, called a threshing-floor, on which the corn-stalks were spread, so that by their " treadings " the grain might be separated from the husk. Those oxen were engaged in doing work for the good of others, and it was only fitting that they should be provided for while they laboured.

III. BY THE RITUAL LAWS OF THE OLDER MOSAISM. (Ver. 13.) Priests and Levites had special maintenance, and this almost entirely by the offerings and good will of the people. They had certain towns allotted for their residence, certain portions of the sacrifices for their food, and certain tithes for the supply of their other necessities, and such a regulation could in no sense be regarded as an unreasonable burden. St. Paul even declares, upon his apostolic authority, that " Even so hath the Lord ordained that they which preach the gospel should live of the gospel." When we have sufficiently proved that the material support of a spiritual ministry is one of the first duties of the Christian professor, we are prepared to argue and to illustrate further that a *generous, liberal, hearty,* and even *self-denying* provision is comely and noble; and that in securing such generous provision our thankful love may find a most fitting expression.—R. T.

Vers. 15—23.—*St. Paul an exception.* He wishes it to be understood that he does precisely what he thinks to be right, but does not wish the peculiarity of his conduct to be made a model for others. There are things in life concerning which each man must make his own individual stand, upon which he may find himself compelled to take an individual and exceptional line. And he may do this without opposition to others, without making himself in any way objectionable. St. Paul found sufficient reason for the adoption of a singular course of conduct in relation to his apostleship or ministry. He would receive nothing in a way of payment or reward from the Churches among whom he laboured. His reasons probably were: 1. That the older apostles never quite approved of his work, and he found it better to act in an independent way, and make no one responsible for his modes of work, or the advanced truths which were given him to teach. 2. That he was, throughout his missionary labours, keenly watched by active and bitter enemies, who were ever ready to misrepresent his conduct, and fashion accusations against him. He well knew how promptly they would seize on his receiving payments, and declare that he was mercenary, and only preached for selfish ends. 3. That he had, in his hands, a kind of skill—that of tent-making—which he could readily turn to account wherever he went. Probably it was the second of these reasons that more particularly influenced him. It was most important that he should give his enemies no opportunities or advantages against him; and he would even refuse some of his rights and privileges, if the assertion of them could be made into a hindrance of his work. The point to be considered from his exceptional conduct is the force of the double law that must rule a Christian life. We must ask both what is *lawful* and what is *expedient*, both what is *necessary* and what is *becoming*. We must beware of forcing our *rights*, as they may stand by the rule and by the law; and we should see that our personal and individual conduct must be ordered so that the impressions which others receive from it shall be helpful to them and to the Church. We must watch against even unintentionally causing offence and hindering Christ's work.—R. T.

Vers. 20, 21.—*Under the Law and without Law, both to be one for Christ.* The apostle is illustrating what we may call the "Christian law of accommodation," and is urging (1) the objects for which such accommodation may be permitted; and (2) the careful limitations under which such accommodation must be put. There can be no accommodation of Christian principle and truth. The sphere for it is (1) the expression of principle in adaptation to persons and circumstances; and (2) things indifferent, such as the wearing of Chinese dress by English missionaries in China, which might seem to have the appearance of disguise, but may be advisable in order not to shock the conservative prejudices of the race. Still, in application to modern life, accommodation, with full preservation of principle, is demanded, and is the secret of gracious and kindly relations in the family, in society, and in the Church. So St. Paul submitted to "take vows," "and be at charges," in accordance with Jewish regulations; and so he accommodated himself to Greek notions, as at Athens, by references to philosophy and poetry. For some illustrations of his method of action, see Acts xvi. 3; xviii. 18; xxi. 26; xxiii. 6; xxvi. 4, 5, 6, 22, 27; and also Gal. ii. 3, 12, 14. In the verses, observe the explanatory parenthesis in ver. 21, which is a kind of apology for the use of the term " without Law." See St. Paul's argument in Rom. ii. 14, 15. Gentiles might be so regarded by the Jews, who were under well-recognized Mosaic rules, but they were really under the living law of Christ, to whom they had yielded heart and life. We notice that—

I. MEN ARE CLASSED BY THEIR RELATIONS TO LAW. The term "law" may be applied to: 1. The natural conditions under which God has created us and set us. These are known, more or less distinctly, to every man. 2. Particular laws, directly revealed to certain nations of men. Reference here is to the particular revelation of law made to the Jews, which was rendered necessary, (1) to secure their isolation from other nations; and (2) to aid them in holding fast the special trust of two truths—the unity and the spirituality of God—which had been committed to their charge. That Law given to the Jews was (1) civil, (2) ceremonial, (3) moral. The moral law alone was of permanent obligation; and it was precisely the same moral law that was, in other forms and terms, revealed to the entire human race. The civil and ceremonial laws of Mosaism were but a fence around the moral law, and an aid to keeping it. St. Paul recognized no permanent obligation in it. But seeing he had to do with men who exaggerated the importance of this formal law, he would stand with them on their level, and hope to raise them up to his. The secret of all good teaching, and of all high spiritual influence, is condescending to the level of those whom we would uplift and bless.

II. MEN REGARDED AS INDEPENDENT OF LAW. That is, of particular and ceremonial law. The mass of mankind never came under the shadow of Mosaism. Yet they too were "God's offspring," for whom he surely cared, and to whom, in wise and gracious ways, he had also revealed his will. Such men came under (1) natural law, written in the conscience ; (2) under social laws, tabulated by rulers and governors; and, (3) when they became Christians, they voluntarily put themselves under Christ's living rule, which is the everlasting law of God, finding present daily adaptations precisely to us. To these St. Paul brought the gospel, and he persisted in dealing with them just as they were. He would not require them to come under Jewish yokes in order to gain a Christian standing through Mosaism.

III. MEN DEALT WITH ON THEIR COMMON STANDING-GROUND. The gospel knows nothing of such peculiarities as "under Law" or "without Law." It recognizes only two standings of men before God. 1. *Sinners.* And to men, as such, it brings a message of forgiveness and eternal life. 2. *In Christ.* And to them it brings its varied unfoldings of Christian duty and of Christian privilege. Impress the limits of the adaptations made by the Christian worker.—R. T.

Vers. 24—27.—*The laws of the Christian race.* The illustration used in these verses is one which St. Paul frequently employs, and we cannot but think that he must have actually seen some of these games, for the impression made by them on his mind is that which comes from personal observation and impression rather than from knowledge through books. There is special force in his allusions to the games in writing to the Corinthians, because the set of games known as the Isthmian were held in the isthmus on which Corinth stood. For details of the games, reference may be made to the exegetical portion of this Commentary, and to the articles in classical and Biblical cyclopædias. They cannot be precisely compared with anything that we have in modern times, because they were regarded by the Greeks as great national and religious festivals. Dean Stanley, writing of these Isthmian games, says, "This was one of the festivals which exercised so great an influence over the Grecian mind, which were, in fact, to their imaginations what the temple was to the Jews and the triumph to the Romans." St. Paul refers to the game in order to enforce his exhortation to self-restraint, and we may find three great practical laws commended by him.

I. THE LAW OF TRAINING. "For thirty days previous to the conflicts the candidates had to attend the exercises of the gymnasium, and only after the fulfilment of these conditions were they allowed, when the time arrived, to contend in the sight of assembled Greece." The training was very severe, conducted upon carefully prescribed rules, and designed to nourish vigorous physical power and precise skill for the kind of contest in which the man was to engage. We are to apply the illustration to moral and religious culture. Observing: 1. How God applies the law of training in the preparation of his servants for their work ; as by sending Joseph into bondage; Moses to the Egyptian court and the Horeb desert; David into the wilderness of Judah ; our Lord into the scenes of temptation ; and St. Paul into Arabia. The providential dealings with men are meant to afford opportunities of training for their life-work. 2. How men are required to meet the "law of training" by making personal efforts to secure fitness for the work to which they are called, such training taking the general form of soul-culture, and the specific forms of adaptation to work. Anything that is worth our doing is worth our preparing to do well.

II. THE LAW OF TEMPERATENESS. (Ver. 25.) We are wont to associate this law only with drinking. It applies to all the passions of the body, indulgences of the appetite, and relationships of the life. The Grecian philosopher says, "Wouldest thou conquer at the games ? Thou must be orderly, spare in food, must abstain from confections, exercise at a fixed hour whether in heat or cold, and drink not cold water nor wine." Applied to moral and religious life, the law requires us (1) to avoid the haste and hurry that plucks from us rest, and quiet, and calmness, and meditative moods; (2) to keep from those religious excitements which are characteristic of our times, but unfriendly to real spiritual growth ; (3) to take up Christian work with a seriousness that will ensure "patient continuance in well-doing;" (4) to keep Christian habits, of reading, visiting, etc., under judicious control, so that we may not be brought under the power of any. Everything is at our service and for our use, within careful limits, and these limits no rules can fix, only our own good judgment decides them.

III. THE LAW OF SELF-MASTERY. (Ver. 27.) This reminds us that training means *trial*, and temperateness means severe and painful dealings with self. "The Christian career is not merely a *race*, but a *conflict*; and a conflict, not only with others, but with one's self. St. Paul had to contend with the fleshly lusts of the body, the love especially of ease, the indisposition to hardship and toil so natural to humanity." The contest of life is between the regenerate will and the enslaved and corrupt body with its inclinations and motions (see Rom. vii.). St. Paul says that the renewed will must hold the body in subjection and service. But such complete self-mastery is the product of long struggle. He who fully gains it has won the moral race, and may receive the "incorruptible crown."—R. T.

Ver. 27.—*The relation of personal consistency to public labours.* The expression used by the apostle here, and translated, "I keep under my body," is literally, "I strike under the eye; I beat black and blue" (comp. Luke xviii. 5). Mastery of the body, repression of the lusts and indulgences and evil inclinations of the body, a strong hand upon the "self," are necessary to ensure "consistency;" yet what is the worth of a Christian teacher whose life tells one story and his lips another? St. Paul contemplates with horror the possibility of his preaching the gospel to others, and, by reason of his personal inconsistencies, proving at last a "castaway." No amount of religious profession, no fervour in religious work, no mere utterance of religious sentiment, can avail without personal and practical consistency of life. On this point we dwell further.

I. THE SENSES IN WHICH PERSONAL CONSISTENCY AND PUBLIC LABOUR ARE DISTINCT THINGS. It may be urged that the question is one of *gifts* for a particular work, and not of personal character. It may be said that we do work with the skill and power entrusted to us, and the good workman may be personally of good or bad character. However true that may be in common life—and we should be prepared to contest its truth even there—it cannot possibly be true in the religious spheres, because all Christian work is the impress of the *man himself*, is inseparable from the force which his character gives to it. Exactly what we ask for in religious spheres is not mere truth, but truth with some stamp of personal conviction upon it; not mere duty, but duty pressed on us by the force of some holy example. The true preacher is the man who bears in on us the force of his own life and feeling. The true teacher is the man who can win our confidence in himself. The true visitor benefits and blesses the poor and the sick by the restings and comfortings of his own quick sympathies, that come from sanctified character. So in the religious spheres there can be no separation between holy character and faithful labour. Show that, just here, serious mistake is made, and much seeming service is unacceptable to God and of no real value to men.

II. THE POSSIBILITY OF THE INCONSISTENT MAN DOING GOOD WORK. In view of what has been said in the previous division, it would seem to be an impossibility, but those remarks may be limited to the higher forms of Christian work and the exertion of spiritual influence. Scripture teaches us, by its examples, that God claims the service of even ungodly men, and deigns to work by them. Of Cyrus God says, "I girded thee, though thou hast not known me," etc. But perhaps there is no distress in life like that which we feel on finding that those who have helped us in our religious life fail morally. When such distress comes to us, we are almost ready to make shipwreck of our faith.

III. THE FORCE ADDED TO ALL GOOD WORK BY THE CONSISTENT CHARACTER OF THE WORKER. Reviewing the influences for good which have rested upon our life, we can but feel that the holiest and mightiest and best have come from consistent and holy men and women, who bore upon us the force of saintly character, and whose memories still keep us true and faithful. When McCheyne died, a note was found unopened on his study table. It was from some one who had recently been brought to God through his preaching, but the note said it was not so much the truth that had impressed, as the sincerity and holy fervour of the preacher. It is the great secret of the highest work. What a man *is* tells more for the honour of God and the blessing of men than merely what a man *does*. So we may be warned by the apostle, and take heed lest, while working for others, we ourselves should prove "castaways."—R. T.

EXPOSITION.

CHAPTER X.

Vers. 1—14.—*Warnings against over-confidence in relation to idolatry and other temptations.*

Ver. 1.—**Moreover**; rather, *for*. He has just shown them, by his own example, the necessity for strenuous watchfulness and effort. In continuance of the same lesson, he teaches them historically that the possession of great privileges is no safeguard, and that the seductions, even of idolatry, must not be carelessly despised. Although the connection of the various paragraphs is not stated with logical precision, we see that they all bear on the one truth which he wants to inculcate, namely, that it is both wise and kind to limit our personal freedom out of sympathy with others. The reading "but" (δὲ, morever) is probably a correction of the true reading (γὰρ, for), due to the failure to understand the whole train of thought. **I would not that ye should be ignorant.** This is a favourite phrase of St. Paul's (ch. xii. 1; 2 Cor. i. 8; Rom. i. 13; xi. 25; 1 Thess. iv. 13). The ignorance to which he refers is not ignorance of the facts, but of the *meaning* of the facts. **All our fathers.** He repeats the "all" five times, because he wishes to show that, though "all" partook of spiritual blessings, most (ver. 5) fell in spite of them. He says, "our fathers," not only because he was himself a Jew, but also because the patriarchs and the Israelites were spiritually the fathers of the Christian Church. **Were under the cloud.** The compressed Greek phrase implies that they *went* under it, and remained under its shadow. The "cloud" is the "pillar of cloud" (Exod. xiii. 21), of which David says, "He spread a cloud *for a covering*" (Ps. cv. 39). The Book of Wisdom (x. 17) calls it "a cover unto them by day," and (xix. 7) "a cloud shadowing the camp." **All passed through the sea** (Exod. xiv. 22).

Ver. 2.—**Were all baptized.** This reading, though well supported, may, perhaps, be a correction for the middle, "they baptized themselves," *i.e.* accepted baptism. The passing under the cloud (Exod. xiv. 19) and through the sea, constituting as it did their deliverance from bondage into freedom, their death to Egypt, and their birth to a new covenant, was a general type or dim shadow of Christian baptism (compare our collect, "figuring thereby thy holy baptism"). But the typology is quite incidental; it is the moral lesson which is paramount. **Unto Moses**; rather, *into*. By this "baptism" they accepted Moses as their Heaven-sent guide and teacher.

Ver. 3.—**And did all eat the same spiritual meat.** As the cloud and the Red Sea symbolized the waters of baptism, so the manna and the water of the rock symbolized the elements of the other Christian sacrament, the Lord's Supper. The manna might be called "a spiritual food," both because it was "angels' food" (Ps. lxxviii. 25; Wisd. xvi. 20) and "bread from heaven" (Ps. lxxviii. 24; John vi. 31), and also because it was a type of "God's good Spirit," which he "gave to instruct them" (Neh. ix. 20). St. Paul only knows of *two* sacraments.

Ver. 4.—**The same spiritual drink.** The water from the smitten rock might (Exod. xvii. 6; Numb. xx. 11) be called a "spiritual" drink, both as being a miraculous gift (comp. Gal. iv. 29, where Isaac is said to be "born *after the spirit*"), and as being a type of that "living water" which "springs up into everlasting life" (John iv. 14; vii. 37), and of the blood of Christ in the Eucharist (John vi. 55). These "waters in the wilderness" and "rivers in the desert" were a natural symbol of the grace of God (Isa. xliii. 23; lv. 1), especially as bestowed in the sacrament through material signs. **They drank**; literally, *they were drinking*, implying a *continuous* gift. **Of that spiritual Rock that followed them**; rather, literally, *of a spiritual following Rock.* This is explained (1) as a mere figure of speech, in which the natural rock which Moses smote is left out of sight altogether; and (2) as meaning that not the rock, but the water from the rock, followed after them in their wanderings (Deut. ix. 21). There can, however, be little or no doubt that St. Paul refers to the common Jewish Hagadah, that the actual material rock did follow the Israelites in their wanderings. The rabbis said that it was round, and rolled itself up like a swarm of bees, and that, when the tabernacle was pitched, this rock came and settled in its vestibule, and began to flow when the princes came to it and sang, "Spring up, O well; sing ye unto it" (Numb. xxi. 17). It does not, of course, follow from this allusion that St. Paul, or even the rabbis, believed their Hagadah *in other than a metaphorical sense.* The Jewish Hagadoth — legends and illustrations and inferences of an imaginative Oriental people — are not to be taken *au pied de la lettre.* St. Paul obviates the laying of any stress on the mere legend by the qualifying word, "a *spiritual* Rock." **And that Rock was Christ.** The writings of Philo, and the Alexandrian school of thought in general, had familiarized all Jewish readers with language of this kind. They were accustomed to see types of God, or of the Word (*Logos*), in almost every incident of the deliverance from Egypt and the wanderings in the wilderness. Thus in Wisd. x. 15 and xi. 4 it is Wisdom —another form of the *Logos*—who leads and supports the Israelites. The frequent comparison of God to a Rock in the Old Testament (Deut. xxxii., *passim*; 1 Sam. ii. 2; Ps. xci. 12, etc.) would render the symbolism more easy, especially as in Exod. xvii. 6 we find, "Behold, I [Jehovah] will stand before thee there upon the rock in Horeb."

Ver. 5.—**With many of them**; rather, *with most of them*. They were overthrown in the wilderness. A quotation from the LXX. of Numb. xiv. 16. All but Caleb and Joshua perished (Numb. xxvi. 64, 65; comp. Jude 5). In Heb. iii. 17 the word used is "they fell."

Ver. 6.—**These things were our examples.** If this rendering be adopted, perhaps "examples" is the best equivalent of the original *tupoi*, as in Phil. iii. 17, "Walk so as ye have us for an example (*tupon*)." It may, however, mean "types," *i.e.* foreshadowing symbols, as in Rom. v. 14, where Adam is the "figure" (*tupos*) of Christ. But, in spite of Alford's decisive rejection of it, the rendering, "Now in these things they proved to be figures of us," is at least equally probable. **To the intent.** Of course, the events had their own immediate instruction, but the example which they involved was the ulterior purpose of their being so ordained by the providence of God. **As they also** lusted. (For quails, Numb. xi. 4, 33; and see Ps. xcv. 7—11.)

Ver. 7.—**As** were **some of them.** As in the case of the golden calf, the worship of Moloch, Remphan, Baal-peor, etc. In the prominent instance of the calf-worship, they (like the Corinthians) would have put forth sophistical pleas in their own favour, saying that they were not worshipping idols, but only paying honour to cherubic emblems of Jehovah. **To play.** The word is, perhaps, used euphemistically for the worst concomitants of a sensual nature-worship (Exod. xxxii. 3—6), which resembled the depraved and orgiastic worship of *Aphrodite Pandemos* at Corinth.

Ver. 8.—**Commit fornication.** This sin was not only an ordinary accompaniment of idolatry, but often a consecrated part of it, as in the case of the thousand *hierodouloi*, or female attendants, in the temple of Aphrodite on Acro-Corinthus. **Three and twenty thousand.** The number given in Numb. xxv. 9 is twenty-four thousand. We cannot give any account of the discrepancy, which is, however, quite unimportant.

Ver. 9.—**Tempt Christ** (see the note on ver. 4). Christ is here identified with the angel which went before the Israelites, whom they were specially warned not "to provoke," because "my Name is in him" (Exod. xxiii. 20, 21). Another reading is "the Lord." "Christ" may have come in from a marginal gloss. On the other hand, since "Christ" is the more difficult reading, it was, perhaps, the more likely to be altered by copyists. The word for "tempt" means "tempt utterly," "tempt beyond endurance." **As some of them** (Exod. xvii. 2, 7; Numb. xiv. 22; xxi. 5, 6). **Of serpents**; rather, *perished by the serpents*, viz. the "fiery serpents" of the wilderness (Numb. xxi. 6).

Ver. 10.—**Neither murmur ye** (Numb. xiv. 2, 29; xvi. 41, 49). The Corinthians *were* at this time murmuring against their teacher and apostle. **Of the destroyer.** All plagues and similar great catastrophes, as well as all individual deaths, were believed by the Jews to be the work of an angel whom they called Sammael (see Exod. xii. 23; 2 Sam. xxiv. 16; Job xxxiii. 22; 2 Macc. xv. 22). In the retribution narrated in Numb. xvi. 41, etc., fourteen thousand seven hundred perished.

Ver. 11.—**For ensamples**; literally, *by way of figure*; typically. The rabbis said, "Whatever happened to the fathers is a sign to their children." The thought is the same as in Rom. xv. 4, "Whatsoever things were written aforetime were written for our learning." The example in this instance would come home more forcibly from the sickness and mortality then prevalent among the Corinthian Christians (ch. xi. 30). **The ends of the world**; rather, *of the ages*. The expression is in accordance with the view which regarded the then epoch as "the close or consummation of the ages" (Matt. xiii. 39; 1 Pet. iv. 7, "The end of all things is at hand;" 1 John ii. 18, "It is the last time;" Heb. ix. 26; Matt. xiii. 39).

Ver. 12.—**Take heed lest he fall.** The Corinthians, thinking that they stood, asserting that they all had knowledge, proud of the insight which led them to declare that "an idol is nothing in the world," were not only liable to underrate the amount of forbearance due to weaker consciences, but were also in personal danger of falling away. To them, as to the Romans, St. Paul means to say, "Be not highminded, but fear" (Rom. xi. 20).

Ver. 13.—**But such as is common to man**; rather, *except such as is human*; i.e. such as man can bear. The last verse was a warning; this is an encouragement. Having just heard what efforts even St. Paul had to make to run in the Christian race, and how terribly their fathers in the wilderness had failed to meet the requirements of God, they might be inclined to throw up every effort in despair. St. Paul, therefore, reminds them that these temptations were not superhuman, but were such as men *had* resisted, and such as *they* could resist. **God is faithful.** He had called them (ch. i. 9), and since he knew "how to deliver the godly out of temptations" (2 Pet. ii. 9), he would surely perform his side of the covenant, and, if they did their parts, would stablish and keep them from evil (2 Thess. iii. 3). **Also.** The mode of deliverance shall be ready simultaneously with the temptation. **A way to escape**; rather, *the way to escape.* The way to escape is different in different temptations, but for each temptation God would provide the *special* means of escaping it.

Ver. 14.—Wherefore. As a result of the whole reasoning, which has been meant to inspire the weak with a more liberalizing knowledge, and the strong with a more fraternal sympathy. **Dearly beloved.** The word "dearly" should be omitted. **Flee from idolatry.** The original implies that they were to turn their backs on idolatry, and so fly from it.

Vers. 15—22.—*The inherent disgracefulness of any tampering with idolatry.*

Ver. 15.—I speak as to wise men; judge ye what I say. An appeal to their own reason to confirm his argument (comp. ch. xi. 13), perhaps with a touch of irony in the first clause (ch. iv. 10; 2 Cor. xi. 19). The word for "I say" is φημι, I affirm.

Ver. 16.—The cup of blessing. A translation of the name *côs haberachah* (comp. Ps. cxvi. 13), over which a blessing was invoked by the head of the family after the Passover. The name is here transferred to the chalice in the Eucharist, over which Christ "gave thanks" (ch. xi. 24; Matt. xxvi. 27). There seems to be a close connection between the idea of "blessing" (*eulogêsas*, Matt. xxvi. 22; Mark xiv. 22) and "giving thanks" (*eucharistêsas*, 'Luke xxii. 19), and here, as always, St. Paul and St. Luke resemble each other in their expressions. **The communion of;** literally, *a participation in.* By means of the cup we realize our share in the benefits wrought by Christ's precious bloodshedding. The cup is at once a symbol and a medium. **The blood of Christ;** of which the wine is the sacramental symbol. By rightly drinking the wine, we spiritually partake of the blood of Christ, we become sharers in his Divine life. **The bread;** perhaps rather, *the loaf,* which was apparently passed from hand to hand, that each might break off a piece. **Is it not the communion of the body of Christ?** The best comment on the verse is John vi. 41—59, in which our Lord taught that there could be no true spiritual life without the closest union with him and incorporation into his life.

Ver. 17.—We being many are one bread, and one body. It is easy to see how we are "*one body,*" of which Christ is the Head, and we are the members. This is the metaphor used in ch. xii. 12, 13 and Rom. xii. 5. The more difficult expression, "*we are one bread,*" is explained in the next clause. The meaning seems to be—We all partake of the loaf, and thereby become qualitatively, as it were, a part of it, as it of us, even as we all become members of Christ's one body, which that loaf sacramentally represents. Some commentators, disliking the harshness of the expression, render it, "*Because* there is one bread, we being many are one body;" or, "For there is one bread. We being many are one body." But the language and context support the rendering of our version; and the supposed "physiology" is not so modern as to be at all surprising.

Ver. 18.—Partakers of the altar. It is better to render it "Have they not *communion with the altar?*" for the word is different from that in the last verse. The meaning is that, by sharing in the sacrifices, the Jews stood in direct association with the altar, the victims, and all that they symbolized (Deut. xii. 27). And St. Paul implied that the same thing is true of those who sympathetically partook of idol-offerings.

Ver. 19.—What say I then? What is it, then, which I am maintaining (φημι)? **That the idol is anything.** St. Paul repudiates an inference which he had already denied (ch. viii. 4). **Is anything.** Has any intrinsic value, meaning, or importance. In itself, the idol-offering is a mere dead, indifferent thing. Of itself, the idol is an *eidolon*—a shadowy, unreal thing, one of the *elilim*; but in another aspect it was "really something," and so alone could the rabbis account for phenomena which seemed to imply the reality of infernal miracles ('Avoda Zarah,' fol. 54, 2; 55, 1; and see note in 'Life of St. Paul,' ii. 74).

Ver. 20.—But. The word rejects the former hypothesis. "[No I do *not admit* that], but what I say is that," etc. **They sacrifice to devils, and not to God.** The word "demons" should be used, not "devils" (Deut. xxxii. 17). The argument is that, though the idol is nothing—a mere stock or stone—it is yet the material symbol of a demon (see Ps. xcvi. 5; cvi. 37; Baruch iv. 7). So Milton—

"And devils to adore for deities;
Then were they known to men by various names,
And various idols through the heathen world, . . .
The chief were those who, from the pit of hell,
Roaming to seek their prey on earth, durst fix

Their seats long after next the seat of
God,
Their altars by his altar, gods adored
Among the nations round."
(' Paradise Lost,' i.)

St. Paul uses a word which, while it would
not be needlessly offensive to Gentiles,
conveyed his meaning. The Greeks themselves called their deities *daimona*, and St.
Paul adopts the word; but to Jewish ears
it meant, not " deities " or " demigods," but
" demons."

Ver. 21.—**Ye cannot.** It is a *moral* impossibility that you should. **The Lord's table.**
This is the first instance in which this
expression is used, and it has originated the
name. **The table of devils** (see Deut. xxxii.
37). In the fine legend of Persephonê, she
might have been altogether liberated from
the nether world if she had eaten nothing
since her sojourn there; but unhappily she
had eaten something, though it was only
the few grains of a pomegranate; and hence
she must leave the upper air, and become
the Queen of Hades.

Ver. 22.—**Do we provoke the Lord to
jealousy?** (Deut. xxxii. 21, " They have moved
me to jealousy by that which is not God ").
The expression, " a jealous God," is used in the
second commandment with express reference
to idolatry, as in Exod. xxxiv. 14, 15. **Are
we stronger than he?** Can we, therefore,
with impunity, kindle his anger against us?
" He is . . . mighty in strength : who hath
hardened himself against him, and hath prospered ? " (Job ix. 4).

Ver. 23—ch. xi. 1.—*Directions about eating idol-offerings, founded on these principles.*

Ver. 23.—**All things are lawful for me**
(see ch. vi. 12). The " *for me* " is not found in
א, A, B, C, D. St. Paul repeats the assertion
and its limitations, because he has now proved
their force. He has shown that Christian
liberty must be modified by considerations
of expediency and edification in accordance
with the feelings of sympathy and charity.

Ver. 24.—**But every man another's wealth.**
The addition of the word " wealth " is very
infelicitous. Rather, as in the Revised
Version, *but each his neighbour's good* (comp.
ver. 33 and Rom. xv. 2).

Ver. 25.—**Whatsoever is sold.** By this
practical rule of common sense he protects
the weak Christian from being daily worried
by over-scrupulosity. If a Christian merely
bought his meat in the open market, no one
could suspect him of meaning thereby to con-
nive at or show favour to idolatry. It would,
therefore, be needless for him to entertain
fantastic scruples about a matter purely
indifferent. The fact of its forming part of an
idol-offering made no *intrinsic* difference in
the food. **Shambles;** rather, *food-market.* Ask-

ing no question for conscience sake. Do not
trouble your conscience by scruples arising
from needless investigation (ἀνακρίνων)
about the food.

Ver. 26.—**For the earth is the Lord's** (Ps.
xxiv. 1). Consequently, " Every creature of
God is good, and nothing to be refused, if it
be received with thanksgiving " (1 Tim. iv.
4). The text formed the ordinary Jewish
" grace before meat." **The fulness thereof.**
The plenitude of its created furniture—
plants, animals, etc.

Ver. 27.—**Bid you** to a feast. It is assumed
that the feast is to take place in a private
house, not an idol-temple (ch. viii. 10). **Ye
be disposed to go ;** rather, *ye wish to go*, with
an emphasis on the " wish," which, as Grotius
says, perhaps implies that the *wish* is not
particularly commendable, although the
apostle, in his large-hearted tolerance, does
not actually blame it. The rabbis decided
very differently. " If," said Rabbi Ishmael,
" an idolater makes a feast in honour of his
son, and invites all the Jews of his town,
they eat of the sacrifices of the dead, even
though they eat and drink of their own "
(' Avodah Zarah,' fol. 18, 1). There are many
passages of the Talmud which raise the
suspicion that the rabbis are *purposely*
running counter to the teaching of the New
Testament.

Ver. 28.—**But if any man say unto you.**
Who is the " any man " is left undefined.
Perhaps some " weak " Christian is meant,
who happens to be a fellow-guest. **This
is offered in sacrifice unto idols.** The true
reading is probably, *hierothuton*, sacred
sacrifice, not *eidolothuton*, idol-sacrifice.
Perhaps there is a touch of delicate reserve
in the word, implying that the remark is
made at the table of heathens, who would be
insulted by the word *eidolothuton*, sacrificed
to *idols*. Whoever the interlocutor is supposed to be—heathen host or Christian
guest—the mere fact of attention being drawn
to the food as forming part of a heathen
sacrifice is enough to make it your duty to
give no overt sanction to idolatry. In that
case, therefore, you ought to refuse it. It will
be seen how gross was the calumny which
asserted that St. Paul taught men to be
indifferent about eating things offered to
idols. He only taught indifference in cases
where idolatry could not be directly involved in the question. He only repudiates
the idle superstition that the food became
inherently tainted by such a consecration
when the eater was unaware of it. In later
times, when the eating of such offerings was
deliberately erected into a test of apostasy,
he would have used language as strong
against every semblance of compliance as
any which was used by St. John himself
or by Justin Martyr. Difference of time and

circumstances necessarily involves a difference in the mode of viewing matters which in *themselves* are unimportant. **For the earth is the Lord's.** It is doubtful whether the repetition of this clause is genuine. It is omitted by all the best uncials.

Ver. 29.—**Conscience, I say, not thine own, but of the other.** You may be well aware that *you* intend no sanction of idolatry, but if the other *supposes* that you do, you wound his conscience, which you have no right to do. Your own conscience has already decided for itself. **For why is my liberty judged of another** man's **conscience?** These words explain why he said "conscience not thine own." The mere fact that another person *thinks* that we are doing wrong does not furnish the smallest proof that we *are* doing wrong. We stand or fall only to our own Master, and our consciences are free to form their own independent conclusion. Perhaps in this clause and the next verse we have an echo of the arguments used by the Corinthian "liberals," who objected to sacrifice themselves to the scruples of the weak. The independence of conscience is powerfully maintained in Rom. xiv. 2—5.

Ver. 30.—**For if I.** The "for" should be omitted. There is no copula in the best manuscripts. **By grace.** The word may also mean "with thankfulness" (comp. Rom. xiv. 6, "He that eateth, to the Lord he eateth, *for he giveth God thanks;*" 1 Tim. iv. 3, "Meats which God hath created to be received with thanksgiving;" compare our phrase, "saying *grace*"). Another view of these clauses interprets them to mean "You should refrain because, by not doing so, you give occasion to others to judge you"—a rule

which has been compared with Rom. xiv. 16, "Let not your good be evil spoken of." Whichever view be taken, it is clear that *theoretically* St. Paul sided with the views of the "strong," but *sympathetically* with those of the "weak." He pleaded for some concession to the scrupulosity of ever-morbid consciences. He disapproved of a defiant, ostentatious, insulting liberalism. On the other hand, he discouraged the miserable micrology of a purblind and bigoted superstition, which exaggerated the importance of things external and indifferent. He desiderated more considerateness and self-denial on the one side; and on the other, a more robust and instructed faith. He would always tolerate the scruples of the weak, but would not suffer either weakness or strength to develop itself into a vexatious tyranny.

Ver. 31.—**All.** There is much grandeur in the sweeping universality of the rule which implies that all life, and every act of life, may be consecrated by holy motives. **To the glory of God.** Not to the glorification either of your own breadth of mind or your over-scrupulosity of conscience, but "that God in all things may be glorified" (1 Pet. iv. 11).

Ver. 32.—**Give none offence.** Of course St. Paul means "give no offence in unimportant, indifferent matters" (comp. Rom. xiv. 13). "Offence" means "occasion of stumbling." The word only occurs in Acts xxiv. 16; Phil. i. 16. **Nor to the Gentiles;** rather, *nor to the Greeks.*

Ver. 33.—**That they may be saved.** All the sympathy, tolerance, forbearance, which I try to practise has this one supreme object.

HOMILETICS.

Vers. 1—15.—*The ages.* "Moreover, brethren, I would not that ye should be ignorant, how that all our fathers were under the cloud, and all passed through the sea; and were all baptized unto Moses in the cloud and in the sea; and did all eat the same spiritual meat; and did all drink the same spiritual drink: for they drank of that spiritual Rock that followed them: and that Rock was Christ. But with many of them God was not well pleased: for they were overthrown in the wilderness. Now these things were our examples, to the intent we should not lust after evil things, as they also lusted. Neither be ye idolaters, as were some of them; as it is written, The people sat down to eat and drink, and rose up to play. Neither let us commit fornication, as some of them committed, and fell in one day three and twenty thousand. Neither let us tempt Christ, as some of them also tempted, and were destroyed of serpents. Neither murmur ye, as some of them also murmured, and were destroyed of the destroyer. Now all these things happened unto them for ensamples: and they are written for our admonition, upon whom the ends of the world are come. Wherefore let him that thinketh he standeth take heed lest he fall. There hath no temptation taken you but such as is common to man: but God is faithful, who will not suffer you to be tempted above that ye are able; but will with the temptation also make a way to escape, that ye may be able to bear it. Wherefore, my dearly beloved, flee from idolatry. I speak as to wise men; judge ye what I say." From this passage several things may be inferred concerning the ages of human history.

I. THE MORAL RELATIONSHIP of the ages. Paul teaches here that the age of the Jew in the wilderness sustained a twofold relation to men of all future times—the relation of a representative and of an admonisher. 1. It was a *representative*. Things that happened in the wilderness happened as "ensamples." (1) Their blessings were "ensamples." Their "pillar" represented the Bible. Their baptism unto Moses represented the dedication of Christians to the religion of Christ. Their manna and their water from the rock represented Christ—the Bread and Water of spiritual life. (2) Their imperfections were "ensamples." Their lusts, idolatries, frivolity, discontent, represent the sins to which men are liable through all Christian times. (3) Their punishments were "ensamples." Thousands died in the wilderness in consequence of their sins, and this represents the fact that sin and misery are indissolubly connected. 2. It was an *admonisher*. "They are written for our admonition." The principles embodied in their history are of universal application. They are: (1) The special care which God exercises over those who commit themselves to him. (2) The tendency of the depraved heart to go wrong. (3) The inviolable connection between sin and suffering.

II. THE DIVINE SUPERINTENDENCE of the ages. It is here taught that God employs one age as a minister to another. He is in all ages. He makes the events that happened to the Jews in the wilderness thousands of years ago minister to the good of men of all future times. This fact: 1. Should restrain us from hasty judgments of his providence. 2. Should impress us with the seriousness of life.

III. THE GROWING RESPONSIBILITY of the ages. "Upon whom the ends of the world are come." The patriarchal was succeeded by the Mosaic, the Mosaic by the Christian. The Christian is the last. All the past has come down to us: 1. Through *literature*. Books bring down to us the poets, the sages, the orators, the preachers of past ages, etc. 2. Through *tradition*. Were there no books, one generation would impart its thoughts, spirit, art, institutions, to another.

IV. THE COMMON TEMPTATION of the ages. "There hath no temptation taken you but such as is common to man," etc. Men through all times have been subject to similar temptations. (1) All men are *temptable*. (*a*) Men are *constitutionally* temptable. All moral creatures in the universe are temptable, even the highest angel. There is no virtue where there is no temptability. (*b*) All men as fallen creatures are *specially temptable*. Having yielded to temptation by the law of habit, they have gained a tendency to do this, and this tendency is ever on the increase. (2) All men are in *tempting circumstances*. In heaven there may be no incentives to wrong, no seductive influences. Earth is full of the tempting. The passage here teaches us two things. 1. *That our temptations require great caution.* "Wherefore let him that thinketh he standeth take heed lest he fall." The Jews in the wilderness had great privileges. Inspired men were with them. Supernatural manifestations surrounded them; God himself was specially with them. Yet they yielded to their temptations, and they fell. Wherefore let all "take heed." Privileges are no security. 2. *That our temptations must be resisted.* They are *resistible*: (1) Because God does not allow any temptation to happen to us that outmeasures our power of resistance. "He will not suffer you to be tempted above that ye are able." He is in all the events of life. He proportions the burden to the back. If temptations came outstripping our capabilities of resistance, our yielding to them might be a calamity, but would not be a crime. Such a case, I presume, never happens in the history of man. The righteous God would not allow it to transpire. (2) Because if we are in earnest in our resistance, he will enable us to escape. He "will with the temptation also make a way to escape, that ye may be able to bear it." "There is no valley so dark," says an old expositor, "but he can find a way through it, no affliction so grievous but he can prevent or remove or enable us to support it, and, in the end, overrule it to our advantage."

CONCLUSION. 1. Do not suppose that the *advantages of past times were greater than ours*. There are men who are constantly referring us to the past, saying the former times were better than the present. Of all the ages that are past, what age had the advantages of this? Not the patriarchal; for under it the Deluge came. Not the Mosaic; for under it came the ruin of Jerusalem and the destruction of the Jewish commonwealth. Not the apostolic; for in it grievous heresies arose and moral abominations grew rife. 2. Do not suppose that the *type of excellence reached by our ancestors is high enough for us.* We ought to be more noble than the old patriarchs, more enlightened and Christ-like than the best Christians of apostolic times.

> On us, great God, on us are come
>   The ends of rolling time;
> We would begin each opening day
>   With gratitude sublime.
> Men after men have come and gone,
>   Myriads have passed away;
> But thou hast lived unchanged, O God,
>   And brought us to this day.
>
> The past, an ocean under thee,
>   Bore onward thy great plan,
> And every billow, as it broke,
>   Was fraught with good to man.
> The dispensations under which
>   Our fathers lived and died
> Were only, as compared with ours,
>   Dim daybreak to noontide.
>
> "A goodly heritage" have we,
>   Ages of choicest lore;
> What "kings and prophets long'd" to see
>   Are ours for evermore.
> The great men of the past are ours,
>   To help us on life's way;
> The Sun of Righteousness we have,
>   To flood our hearts with day.
>
> All that past times have given us
>   May we employ aright,
> And live a grand and godly life,
>   Full worthy of our light.
> We follow in the awful march
>   Of all the mighty dead.
> Eternal Father, succour us
>   When all our years have fled!

Vers. 16—22.—*The Christian feast.* "The cup of blessing which we bless, is it not the communion of the blood of Christ?" etc. The text undoubtedly refers to the feast which Christ instituted the night on which he was betrayed, and the words lead us to look at that feast in two aspects.

I. As a MEDIUM FOR SPIRITUAL COMMUNION. "The cup of blessing which we bless, is it not the communion of the blood of Christ? The bread which we break, is it not the communion of the body of Christ?" The shed blood and broken body of Christ are here regarded, and must ever be regarded, as the effects and expressions of his self-sacrificing love. His "flesh" and "blood" mean *his spiritual life.* What was that *spirit-life* that animated and controlled him? *Self-sacrificing love.* This made him Christ, marked him off from all other men that ever lived; it was the very "body" and "blood" of his soul. When we are commanded, therefore, to eat his flesh and drink his blood, it means that we *are to take his spirit into us,* his spirit of self-sacrificing philanthropy. This spirit is, indeed, the only true food for souls. It alone answers the two great purposes of food—it gives *strength* and *satisfaction.* No man can become morally strong, or morally satisfied, without appropriating the self-sacrificing love of Christ. Now, in the true spiritual celebration of this feast, there is a twofold "communion." 1. A "communion" of the disciples with Christ. They drink in his spirit, and by a living sympathy are brought into a close and tender fellowship with him. Christ comes in to them and sups with them, and they with him. We are always bringing those with whom we have the strongest sympathy into our inmost being. 2. A "communion" of the disciples with one another. "For we being many are one bread, and one body: for we are all partakers of that one bread." "This verse explains how the breaking of the bread was the significant act, which expressed, sacramentally, the communion of the body of Christ. There is one bread, it is broken in many pieces, and as we all (though each receives only a fragment) partake of the one bread, which, unbroken, consisted of these pieces, we, though many individuals, are one body, even the body of Christ, with whom, as well as with each other, we have communion in that act." All who have a supreme sympathy for one common object will, by a law of their nature, be brought into communion one with another. All hearts will throb with one great feeling, all thoughts will flow into one common channel. Thus all true Christians are *united* one with another, as all the planets are united by circling round one centre, and deriving therefrom a common impulse, a common life, and a common order.

II. AS THE EXCLUSIVE PRIVILEGE OF CHRISTIANS. Paul speaks in these verses of two other feasts. 1. The feast of the Jewish priesthood. "Behold Israel after the flesh." The Jewish sacrifice was divided, a portion offered on the altar, and a portion taken and eaten. 2. The feast of the idolatrous heathen. "What say I then that the idol is anything, or that which is offered in sacrifice to idols is anything?" etc. The heathen had their feasts; they partook of that which they offered to their gods. But the spirit manifested in the partakers of both of these feasts—Jewish or heathen— *would exclude from the feast which Christ ordained.* In the one there was only a formal respect for Jehovah, and in the other, for demons and evil spirits. "But I say, that the things which the Gentiles sacrifice, they sacrifice to devils, and not to God: and I would not that ye should have fellowship with devils." None are to be admitted to Christ's feasts who are not in vital sympathy with him. "Ye cannot drink the cup of the Lord, and the cup of devils."

Vers. 23—33.—*Gospel casuistry.* "All things are lawful for me, but all things are not expedient," etc. These verses teach us the following lessons:—

I. A GOOD MAN MAY HAVE A RIGHT TO DO THAT WHICH MAY NOT ALWAYS BE EXPE-DIENT FOR THE SAKE OF OTHERS. "All things are lawful for me, but all things are not expedient: all things are lawful for me, but all things edify not." What has not a good man a right to? He has a right to go wherever he pleases, to eat whatever he pleases, to dress as he pleases, for a good man will be actuated evermore from a good motive. But for him to use his full right would manifestly be often inexpedient and even pernicious to others. "Things lawful" for him would not always be things that would "edify," build up, souls in reverent faith and true worship. Therefore, it is not always right to stand upon our rights, it is right to conciliate and yield for the sake of others.

II. SMALL SCRUPLES ON MINOR MATTERS SHOULD NOT BE ENCOURAGED. 1. If you are over-scrupulous about what you eat, it will interfere with your participation in the provisions which nature has made for you. "Whatsoever is sold in the shambles, that eat, asking no question for conscience sake." Some of the meat which had been used for sacrificial purposes in heathen temples was afterwards exposed in the markets for sale. If it is good meat, it is not the worse for human food because used in sacrifice. Your nature is exhausted, it requires replenishment; you are hungry, there is the food hung up for sale; buy it, do not let superstitious feelings interfere with the claims of nature. How wretched and wan some of our co-religionists look, because their scruples keep them from food! 2. If you are over-scrupulous about the beliefs of men, you will be deprived of social enjoyments. "If any of them that believe not bid you to a feast, and ye be disposed to go; whatsoever is set before you, eat, asking no question for conscience sake." Free, genial, hearty social intercourse is one of the greatest blessings of this life. Our Saviour came "eating and drinking," but if you are over-scrupulous about the credenda of your host and his provisions, you sacrifice all this and injure your nature. Remember always that the world was given for your enjoy-ment. "The earth hath he given to the children of men." "All things are yours."

III. A DEFERENCE TO THE CONSCIENCES OF OTHERS SHOULD ALWAYS BE RENDERED. "If any man say unto you, This is offered in sacrifice unto idols, eat not for his sake that showed it, and for conscience sake," etc. When at the table with meats spread before you which have been sacrificed to idols, and a fellow-guest conscientiously abstains from touching them, and he reminds you of the fact, then, out of deference to his weak conscience, do not you touch them. However delicious they may appear, however fragrant in aroma, however hungry you may be, out of regard to that weak brother's conscience deny yourself. The most sacred thing under these heavens is the conscience. The weakest conscience should be respected; to wound the conscience is to wound the man. What are meats and drinks in comparison with a human conscience?

IV. SUPREME REGARD FOR THE GLORY OF GOD SHOULD RULE US IN ALL. "Whether therefore ye eat, or drink, or whatsoever ye do, do all to the glory of God." "These words embrace all life. The definite acts of eating and drinking are mentioned expressly, as they are the subject immediately under consideration. They are, however, to be regulated by the same principle which guides all true life. The modern idea of some acts being religious and some secular is neither here nor elsewhere recognized by St. Paul. No act of life is in itself either religious or secular. The quality of each act depends on the spirit which guides it and the motives from which it springs. The commonest thing may be done in a highly Christian spirit; the greatest deed may spring from a low and selfish motive. A religious act done in a secular spirit is secular; a secular thing done in a religious spirit is religious. This is the first great principle of Christian life."

V. THE GOOD OF OTHERS, AND NOT THE GRATIFICATION OF SELF, SHOULD BE OUR CONSTANT AIM. "Let no man seek his own, but every man another's wealth." "Give none offence, neither to the Jews, nor to the Gentiles, nor to the Church of God: even as I please all men in all things, not seeking mine own profit, but the profit of many, that they may be saved."

HOMILIES BY VARIOUS AUTHORS.

Vers. 1—13.—*Subject continued; arguments from the Old Testament; warning against false security.* Reference had been made in the preceding chapter to the law of Moses respecting oxen, and to the priests of the temple, for whose support there was a special provision. But St. Paul had introduced a striking illustration from Grecian life to show the importance of earnest and exact discipline in matters pertaining to the soul's salvation. The body, with its infirmities and sins, was a very serious danger, and, unless kept under by the power of grace, would acquire mastery over the spirit. Even he, though an apostle, might become "a castaway." The terrible liability was before him as a personal thing, the idea lingered and demanded a fuller emphasis, and how could he contemplate himself without considering the hazardous exposure of his brethren? Every fibre of his private heart was a public tie that bound him to others, and hence he could not see his own peril and be blind to the peril of the Church. Under the pressure of this anxiety, his mind reverts to the history of the Jewish Church. Historical examples are very powerful, and where could he find them except in the Old Testament? Grecian games pass out of view, and the stately procession of wonders, beginning in the deliverance of the elect race from Egyptian bondage and progressing through the events of the desert, moves before his eye. "Our fathers" indicates how true he was to ancestral blood, and this warm-hearted sense of country, in which patriotism and piety interblended, exemplifies the origin and tenacity of the feeling that prompted him in the previous chapter to put in the foreground this fact, "Unto the Jews I became as a Jew." Let us remember that his peculiar state of mind at the moment took its colouring from one single thing, viz. the hazards of moral probation because of the body. How predominant this idea was appears in the instances enumerated to show the unfaithfulness of God's people to their covenanted engagements. Such words as "lust," "lusted," "eat and drink," "rose up to play," "commit fornication," are significant of his intense feeling, and they are as reverberations from what was to him an awful term— "*castaway*," "rejected," "fail shamefully of the prize." According to his conception, brain and nerves, all the facts of the physical organism, had to be taken into account in looking at the practical side of Christianity. And it was a practical question, because it rested on a broad generalization of man's place, order, and destiny in the universe. No empiric was he, but a thinker of most penetrating insight, far in advance of his times, in advance too of our century; and while he was not a psychologist nor a physiologist in our sense of the terms, yet no man has ever seen so clearly, so deeply, into the principles underlying psychology and physiology in their relations to spiritual life. His own personal experience turned his thoughts to this study. Providence made him this sort of a student, and the Holy Ghost enlarged and sanctified his investigations. Such thinkers generally come as precursors to scientists and philosophers; but St. Paul was much more than a precursor, for we find in him, not merely a knowledge of facts, but of truths, and a facility in applying them altogether remarkable. What a volume on this subject lay open in his own consciousness! A temperament of singular impressionableness; a natural activity that sprang quite as much from the interaction of his mental faculties and their quick sympathy with one another as from the accesses of the outer world; feeble health, and yet that kind of weakness in certain functions which is sometimes connected with other organs of great strength, and is consistent with astonishing power of endurance; the "thorn in the flesh, the messenger of Satan to buffet" him; add to all this the manner of life he led, and the physical sufferings that enemies inflicted on him;—and how could he help being reminded what a factor the body was in his manhood and apostleship? Think of the effect on the associating and suggestive faculty, on the imagination, on his use of language both for thought and expression, that this mass of disturbed sensibility must have produced, and for which there was no earthly anodyne. Observe, moreover, how the wisdom of God manifests itself in the temperament of this man and its specific discipline. Probably temperament is the secret of individuality, but whether so or not, it must be reckoned as of no little significance as to the influence of the books we read, the teachers that instruct, and the other countless agencies which make up the total of educative forces. Now, in this particular, mark the contrast between St. Peter and St. Paul. The fisherman of Galilee, healthy, robust, abounding in the instinctive joyousness of natural sensations, trustful to an extreme of his emotions, pliant towards himself, singularly impulsive; what a problem was in that temperament and its physiological laws, when the Lord Jesus began to educate his nerves, arteries, brains, for discipleship, and through the disciple to develop the apostle of the "Rock" and the "Keys"! Yet it was done, and done thoroughly, so that the changed body of St. Peter is quite as noteworthy as the changed mind, the same body but functionally subdued to a well-governed organism. During the forty days between the Lord's resurrection and ascension, the man and the apostle emerged from the chrysalis. At Pentecost, what a commanding figure he presents! No haste, no spasmodic action, now, but equipoise and cool wisdom and the courage of repose. In temperament, no less than in official position, St. Peter is the antecedent of St. Paul. And their difference herein, according to providential ordination, was carried out in their training and culture, so that diversity, jealous of its rights in all things, is only self-insistent for the sake of prospective unity. Now, St. Paul wishes to put this subject of danger on the bodily side of human life in the strongest possible light for his own benefit and that of the Corinthians. What then? A nation rises before him. By the arm of Jehovah, Egypt has been smitten, the Red Sea has opened a pathway to their triumphant march, and waves and winds have chanted the anthem of a victory in which they had no share. And this nation "passed through the sea," and "were all baptized unto Moses," as their mediatorial leader, "in the cloud and in the sea." Nay, more; the typical idea is still further wrought out, and baptism and the Lord's Supper are conjoined. "All did eat the same spiritual meat; all did drink the same spiritual drink;" the meat and drink were from above; the Holy Ghost was present as the source of the miracles and the Divine Agent of blessing; the "spiritual" is insisted on, for "that Rock was Christ." There was a revelation to the senses and there was a revelation to the spirit. To deny the supersensuous element is to destroy the force of the analogy, since it is not a resemblance to the imagination alone, but a real likeness to the reason, Christianity and its sacraments being prominent in St. Paul's view. It was not, then, a mere miracle to the body and for the body. It was likewise a supernatural demonstration, a gracious influence from the Holy Ghost, a prelusive blessedness brought within reach of experience in that dispensation of types and shadows. It was not our spirituality; nevertheless, it was spiritual, since "that Rock was Christ." Our Lord said in his Capernaum discourse, just after his great miracle that fed thousands, "Your fathers did eat manna in the wilderness, and are dead. This is the bread which cometh down from heaven, that a man may eat thereof, and not die." Did not the miracle, wrought so lavishly for the public, wrought without solicitation, seem to the excited multitude a sign that Christ was the national Messiah their hearts craved to have? Next day, he disenchanted them by sweeping away the secular illusion and telling them plainly, "I am that Bread of life." The contrast between the manna of the wilderness and the bread of life was stated and enforced at a time, in a way, under circumstances, calculated to secure its object. It did not effect its purpose. "From that time many of his disciples went back, and walked no more with him;" and henceforth the popular expectation of a worldly Messiah was a waning moon in a darkening night. And this contrast was recognized by St. Paul even while adhering most closely to the parallelism. On the ground of the parallelism, he argues the eminent privileges of the Jews, the opportunities enjoyed, the Divine manifestation, the spiritual influence secured to the nation in the desert. They failed to understand and appreciate their position. Appetite, lust, idolatry, overcame them; "they were overthrown in the wilderness," and so swift was God's wrath and so overwhelming, that there "fell in one day three and twenty thousand." Here was a supernatural economy; here was a religion that provided for bodily necessities, and even gave "angels' food;" here, at the same time that the claims of a true and proper sensuousness were divinely met, a "spiritual" agency was established and administered—here, in the solitudes of sand and rock, where the chosen people were alone with God, and where neither day nor night was allowed to wear its accustomed face because of the presence of the pillar-cloud of glory; and yet amid such displays of the providence and Spirit of God, men fell into idolatry, murmured against God, tempted him, and perished under miraculous judgments. It is not simply a lesson from individuals to individuals. It is a warning from a community to a community. Vice as personal, vice as social, vice as an epidemic in the air,—this is the vice of bodily degradation as it exhibits its raging enormity in lust, fornication, and idol-worship. "These things were our examples," "for ensamples," "written for our admonition, upon whom the ends of the world are come," the coalescence of the ages in the grand demonstration of Christianity as the completed revelation to mankind of God in Christ. "Wherefore . . . take heed." We have more light, larger privileges, nobler opportunities, but there is no mechanical security in these things. The crisis-age has come, the crisis-trial has come with it. "Wherefore let him that thinketh he standeth take heed lest he fall." To encourage their holy endeavours, he assures them that there is no fatality in temptation. Oftentimes it happens that men are morally disabled before the struggle, before an incitement to do evil has fairly set in. By this proneness to believe in fate, they surrender in advance. Remote causes are frequently more potent than proximate causes, and many a man has been the victim of a false philosophy of morals long before he has fallen as an actual prey to Satan. Bodily sins have something in them which renders their subjects uncommonly liable to this destructive belief, and "I could not help it; I cannot help it," are words that easily rise to their lips. But the doctrine of St. Paul is a protest against such a demoralizing idea. "No trial has come upon you beyond man's power to bear" (Conybeare and Howson). "God is faithful." The laws of the universe and their administration, the presence of the Spirit as the universal Helper, and the glory of Christianity as the consummation of the ages, are so many Divine assurances that no man is doomed beforehand to fall into the snare of the devil. Satan himself is only Satan, man's adversary, within certain limits. God holds him in check. At first, the influence of evil takes effect on the involuntary nature, sensations are awakened, passions excited, but it becomes a temptation when these lower instruments are brought to bear on the consent of the will. "God is faithful" to the human will. There is nothing in man which is so constantly quickened and energized as a defensive force. And, furthermore, as a positive and aggressive force, what resources are at its command! If temptation is subtle and insinuating, who knows the number and variety of the Spirit's secret avenues to the will? There is always "a way to escape," and this way is provided by our heavenly Father, who is evermore answering the prayer, "Lead us not into temptation, but deliver us from evil."—L.

Vers. 14—33.—*Argument further enforced; fellowship with Christ by means of the*

communion ; idolatrous feasts a communion with demons ; law, expediency, conscience.
"Wherefore," says St. Paul, as a deduction from the foregoing argument, "my dearly
beloved," his heart kindled anew towards his brethren, *"flee from idolatry."* This
dread of idolatry is the key to what follows. Idolatry, in those days, was a sin that
included all sins, and Corinth was behind no city in the charm and splendour it threw
around this iniquity. Bodily indulgences of the worst sort were notorious. Throughout
Greece, Corinth was the common synonym of the most shameful vices, and that too,
not in despite of idolatry, but as a constituent of religious worship, especially of Venus.
Art among the Greeks had done its utmost to destroy the uglier features of the old
heathenism, had called beauty and culture into the service of the priests and the
ceremonial of the temples, and had succeeded in making the æsthetic a reproach to pure
taste and a mocking insult to every moral virtue. Corinth was a leading centre of all the
corrupting and lascivious influence of idolatry, and hence St. Paul's tender and fervent
entreaty, "My dearly beloved, flee from idolatry." The connection with his foregoing
argument is clear. If the athlete must subject himself to a severe and protracted
discipline ; if God's elect race so largely perished in the wilderness by reason of
transgression ; if any and every temptation may be successfully resisted, so that
neither the throng of evil-doers nor the show and fascination of a pompous idol-worship
can be an excuse for sin ;—with what force could he urge, "Flee from idolatry"! St.
Paul knew the strength of his appeal. And he credited these Corinthians with insight
sufficient to see this strength, for he bade them hear him "as wise men," and "judge"
what he said. Is he satisfied to leave the argument at this stage? Observation
of current facts, historical examples preserved from oblivion for their warning, God's
faithfulness, have been brought to bear on the question ; and yet, so far from being
content to dismiss the subject, he resumes it with new vigour of thought and a
deepened intensity of emotion. The language changes. Few or no metaphoric words
occur. Throughout the paragraph, it is the vocabulary of pure feeling and impassioned
earnestness that he employs, for the imagination has retired from its task and left
the heart to consummate the work. He begins with the sacrament of the Lord's
Supper, binding the argument to the point whence he had digressed at the opening
of the ninth chapter. "This liberty of yours," he had said, "might prove ruinous to
weak brethren 'for whom Christ died,'" and therefore such an abuse of freedom
was a sin "against the brethren" and a "sin against Christ." What is the special
connection of the Lord's Supper with the completion of the argument? Obviously
the position it occupies in the logic of the case is one of eminence, St. Paul having
reserved it for his conclusion. It would seem that he had before his mind one
particular and engrossing idea in relation to the Supper, which, although perfectly
consistent with other ideas of the sacrament, and, indeed, essential to their import,
was detached at the moment and set forth with very distinct and commanding
prominence. It is the idea of the *communion.* "Cup of blessing," "bread which we
break," the thanksgiving, the faith and love exercised, the recollected obligations, the
spiritual conception of "the blood" and "the body of Christ" as means of an inward
holiness ; are not these a communication, a participation, an entering into Christ's
death, a true and real fellowship with him as "the Lamb of God that taketh away
the sin of the world"? If so, it means separation from all evil compliances and from
all dangerous associations. "Separate from sinners" was a distinguishing fact in
Christ's life ;" not only "holy, harmless, undefiled," but, by his *separation* from men,
exhibiting in the fullest and most effective way the three characteristics mentioned.
Near, very near, to all about him, and yet the nearer he was the further removed
he stood in the dignity of his person and the exclusiveness of his office, so that
the mysterious awe which invested him was profoundly felt by his friends even while
ignorant of his nature and mediatorship as Son of God and Son of man, and on various
occasions acknowledged by his enemies. And this *separateness* appeared even more
conspicuously in his vicarious and propitiatory death. His life was a new revelation
of life ; his death was a new revelation of death. "Separate" was that death from
all deaths actual and possible. He spoke of it as he never spake of aught else involving
himself. He had feelings concerning it that he never indicated as touching other
personal interests. For its loneliness and secret agony, for its public dishonour and
humiliation, for its apparent triumph of his foes and its seeming discomfiture of

himself, for its Jewish and Roman and world-wide aspects, for its self-sacrifice, for it as the divinely ordained means to reconcile God to man and man to God, he prepared himself as one who realized the infiniteness of the act. Previously to the great passion-hour, nature had given him, of her own accord, no recognition of his Divine majesty. It was his act, not hers, when miracles transpired. But, at his death, she put forth the power of her attestation to the fact that he was "separate from sinners," and by the darkness, and the earthquake, and the opened graves, and the rent veil, signified that, "Truly this man was the Son of God." Now, in St. Paul's view, partaking of the Lord's Supper is partaking spiritually of the blood and body of Christ, and if so, it is communion with him, *the communion*—a special form of confessing him, a particular and most solemn act of acknowledging him as our Redeemer and Lord, in a word, *a sacrament*. Wine and bread are symbols; but the sacrament must not be limited to ordinary symbolism. It is a fact, a vital and absolute fact, a Divine reality, to the believer's soul, a spiritual realization of Christ. Nothing magical and superstitious, nothing mechanical, nothing that derives virtue from priest and cere-monials in the form of sacerdotal consecration, belongs to its nature, use, and end. It is simple, it is personal to the faith and love of the humble disciples of the cross, it is sublime because so perfectly spiritual in the union and fellowship with Christ which it is intended to secure. But is this all? By no means; it is communion and fellowship among believers. "We are all partakers of that one bread." Now, there are common ties among Christians that grow out of their relation to one another in Christ considered as Son of man. If he was Philanthropist, Benefactor, Friend, Healer, Teacher, Inspirer, he has left us an example that we should follow in his steps, and this example is beautifully potent when we co-operate in these beneficent duties. Yet there is a higher expression of our union when we partake of the Lord's Supper, since this recognizes his atoning death as the bond that makes us one. And as Christ's works of power and mercy throughout Galilee and Judæa went forward and attained their fullest manifestation in the atonement of Calvary, so our sympathies with one another and harmonious activity in daily acts of kindness must be ratified and sealed by being "partakers of that one bread." Jesus said, "And I, if I be lifted up from the earth, will draw all men unto me." No such drawing power did he claim for his miracles, nor for other marvellous forces that radiated in every direction from him as the great Centre of blessing in his day to the poor, the diseased, the demoniac. Where he is mightiest we are most mighty; for it pleased him, in varying the manifestations of his omnipotence and adapting them to the different instincts of man as he dealt one by one with these primal qualities, it pleased him, we say, to leave similar channels of activity for us to occupy. Therefore it is that the cross lifts us up into a higher companionship with one another. Even in common life, there is no such reconciler as death. A corpse in a divided household is a peace-maker. We are all brothers at a funeral. The presence of death lingers not in the senses, nor pauses in the imagination, nor rests in the understanding, but goes down into the great original instincts, where the sense of humanity lies embedded under the shadow of the infinite. Of what immeasurable value, then, is the death of Christ as a uniting influence in behalf of brotherhood! And what an appeal the communion makes to that social sentiment which is so precious to Christianity! And who can go in a devout frame of mind to the table of the Lord without feeling that "life's poor distinctions vanish here," without a larger consciousness of the Divine loveliness of forbearance, and of patience with others, and of forgiveness of enemies, and of the blessedness unspeakable and full of glory in charity when charity as "the greatest" possesses intellect, heart, and life? God be praised for such hours! Finer spheres than sun and planets measure their coming, their stay, and their going. Nor does the argument rest at this point. "To partake of a Jewish sacrifice as a sacrifice, and in a holy place, was an act of Jewish worship" (Hodge). Here are "our fathers," "Israel after the flesh," and they were "partakers of the altar;" and here are we, to whom "the ages" have brought their light and privileges and been perfected in the epoch of Christianity, and who "are all partakers of that one bread." Shall we be found feasting in idol-temples? This is heathenish idolatry, this is communion with devils, this is fatal to brotherhood, this is treachery to the Lord Jesus Christ. What do I say? Do I declare that the idol is anything or the sacrifice anything? I, Paul, say to you, that ye cannot "drink the cup" consecrated to the Lord and "drink the cup" consecrated by the heathen to their demons—deities to the Gentiles, evil spirits to Jews and Christians. For this use of the cup is an acknowledgment of fellowship with these "evil spirits," and a fraternization with their worshippers. Such conduct is utterly unjustifiable; it will "provoke the Lord to jealousy," and to a jealousy like that when wedded love has proved faithless to its holy vow. And can ye Corinthians withstand such a devouring flame of anger? Then he recurs to the statement made in ch. vi. 12, "All things are lawful," etc., and reaffirms the ethical principle of restraint on personal liberty. And with the mightier impulse which has just accented its deep tones of warning, the thought of expediency widens its application. What is the great tap-root of all our evils? Selfishness. And this selfishness assumes manifold forms, intellectual and social, physical and commercial. Subtle one moment and palpable the next; disguised and then open; endless in shifts and turns; inexhaustible in resources; skilled in every variety of means; sharp, vigilant, unwearied; its five senses multiplied in its unnumbered agents;—what save Christianity, would entertain such a hope of the human race as to warrant the strong utterance, "Let no man seek his own, but every man another's wealth"? This is laying the axe to the root of the gigantic tree with its trunk and branches. Anything less than unselfish love will not satisfy the argument at this stage. Whither has the fiery logician been? Where has he arrested his course and paused to meditate and analyze? The death of Christ and the memorials of that death, fellowship with his sufferings, communion with the "great High Priest that is passed into the heavens;" and, along with this theme, the communion with brethren and the burdening sense of that unity of believers which all great souls aspire to, but have to mourn over as a postponed reality;—such were the truths that had engaged the strength of his intellect and the ardour of his feelings. Could he tolerate the idea of one making himself the supreme object of consideration? Could he think of a man in Christ shutting himself out of the very heart of Christ? Only in such words as these can he appease the yearnings of his nature: "Let no man seek his own, but every man another's wealth." Suppose, then, that these Corinthian Christians were at a private feast, enjoying the hospitality of a friend; would it be proper for the man of scruples to inquire into the meats? Nay, this is not a "communion," though a social union, and hence you are at liberty to eat; "asking no question for conscience sake." Sentiment has its obligations no less than conscience, and, in fact, conscience is honoured when you remember that "the earth is the Lord's, and the fulness thereof." If, however, some one says to you, "This is offered in sacrifice unto idols," the matter takes another aspect. For the sake of a brother guest whose scruples are wide awake, do not eat. It is his conscience that your conscience is to respect, and therefore abstain. If a weak brother were to ask you to do something or avoid something for the sake of his conscience that your own conscience would not suffer you to do or to forbear, resist him and by no means comply. Weakness may be yielded to simply as the infirmity of another, but if it become dogmatic and aggressive, seeking to impose its restraints on our convictions, Christianity never requires of us to submit to such meddling dictation. Condescension to an infirm mind is very proper and commendable, provided it do not make us infirm. Easy compliances of this lax sort are dangerous snares. In the one case, the compliance is on principle; in the other, the non-compliance is on principle; and, in each instance, conscience is upheld. Then the apostle rises again to a broad, general truth, "Do all to the glory of God." For this statement, that extends the sentiment of a spiritual mind over all duties, he had already prepared the way. Twice had he said, "The earth is the Lord's, and the fulness thereof," and, in the third chapter of the Epistle, he had declared, "All is yours." We are not like trees that can only grow in certain soils and climates. We are not like animals that are found exclusively on this or that continent. We are not creatures limited to their immediate surroundings. To form a human soul, a world and a universe of worlds are needed. Influences acting on us are not counted and tabulated by the intellect of the senses. These senses shut us up in the body. They are for to-day and for appropriating what is at hand. Intellect is under stern limitations. Yet the sphere of the inner life is for ever widening beyond the sphere of sensuous existence, and on the eyes of "three score and ten" the stars shine with a home-light unknown to young manhood. Growth is within, but there is no self-nutrition. All the materials that nourish and build up the man come from without, and, hence, it is not by looking merely at ourselves and our capacities, but by regarding the world and the universe as furnishing the occasions and supplying the means of development, that we learn to measure our ability by the gaace of God stored up in all things for our enrichment. Where we are interprets what we are. Now, in view of this, St. Paul lays down the principle, "Whether . . . ye eat, or drink, or whatsoever ye do, do all to the glory of God." The range is immense; the world is not to be cut up into fragments, and the "glory of God" identified solely with them; but, as the primary condition of glorifying him, we are to believe that his Divine presence is in whatever he has created. There is nothing speculative and remote in this doctrine. How are we to glorify God? By being most truly human; by realizing that others are a part of ourselves and we a part of them; by acting on the truth that individuality attains its perfection in brotherhood; and therefore we should "please all men in all things." Nothing selfish must appear in it; "not seeking mine own profit." Nothing of effeminacy, nothing of calculating acquiescence, must taint its purity, and we must please others for their *profit, that they may be saved.*—L.

Ver. 4.—"*That spiritual Rock.*" There is no need, in explaining this passage, to suppose a reference on the part of the writer to the Jewish fable that the rock in question was rolled along with the advancing camp of Israel through the wilderness of wandering, and that upon the chant of the chiefs, "Spring up, O well!" the water gushed forth for the supply of the thirsting tribes. There seems to be no need even to adopt the common supposition that water sprang miraculously from rocks at every station of the wonderful journey. It is enough to accept the plain record that the miraculous event did happen, once at the commencement and once towards the close of the pilgrimage of the chosen people. The apostle's mind was filled with memories of the consecrated nation, and so clear before that mind was the unity of the two dispensations, that it seemed most natural to him, in drawing a parallel between the Israelites and the Corinthian Christians, to assert that the spiritual Rock was Christ—the Source and Author of all blessings in every period of history and in all circumstances of humanity. The assertion may be regarded—

I. HISTORICALLY. As a matter of fact, the Word, the Wisdom of God, was the Angel of the Church in the wilderness. It is the privilege of the Christian to trace his Saviour's presence throughout the whole of human history. He who was the Rock of salvation to the tribes ready to die from thirst, is the same to all mankind in every age. His presence never removes and his grace never fails. He is Jehovah, the Rock of eternal ages.

II. SPIRITUALLY. Evidently the apostle draws his readers' attention to the supply of other than physical necessities. To Israel and to the Church of this dispensation of grace the Lord Christ is the all-sufficient channel of Divine mercy and blessing. 1. *Generally speaking*, there is an obvious aptness in the similitude. (1) As a Rock, Christ is distinguished by stability, and is not to be shaken or removed. (2) He has heights for refuge into which his people can flee, a stronghold and security to all who put their trust in him. (3) As the rock has cliffs and clefts for shadow and for shelter from the great heat in a dry and thirsty land where no water is, so Christ screens the soul from fiery temptations and distresses. 2. *Specially*, and upon the suggestion of the incident referred to, it must be remarked that Christ is the Rock because he is the Source of living waters. This is no doubt the central thought of the passage, and the resemblance is very striking and very full and rich. Thus it is apparent: (1) That Christ supplies an urgent need. It was in the sorest extremity of the nation that the rock was smitten and yielded the streams which the dry desert knew not; and, in like manner, the need of humanity was distressing and urgent when the Divine Rock gave forth the springs of life eternal. (2) The supply came from an unexpected source. What so unlikely as the hard rock of the desert to yield rivulets of limpid water? And who that saw Christ in his humiliation, who grew up "as a root out of a dry ground," could imagine what stores of blessing were in his sacred being? (3) From Christ proceeds satisfaction for all spiritual wants. These are the thirst of the soul, which desires knowledge, favour, peace, refreshment, and joy,—all which is included in the phrase "eternal life." "If any man thirst," says Jesus, "let him come unto me, and drink." He has promised "living water, of which whoso drinks shall not thirst again." The dying revive, the thirsting are satisfied, the weary are refreshed, the labourers are cheered, as they together draw near to the spiritual fountains which flow from Christ. (4) The blessings which proceed from Jesus proceed in an enduring and unfailing stream of supply. Generations drink at the same spring, and quench their thirst, only to commend the living fountain to all succeeding ages.

III. SACRAMENTALLY. The allusion is unmistakable to the communion of the Lord's Supper. Both the streams in the wilderness and the cup of the Eucharist symbolize the spiritual participation, which is the privilege of those to whom the Word of the Lord is addressed, in the supply afforded by the Divine and living Rock. The voice of heaven reaches our grateful ear: "Eat, O friends; drink, . . . O beloved!" The superiority of the new covenant is manifest: the Israelites drank of water; Christ is not only the Stream of water in the desert, he is the Cup of wine at the banqueting table. "The cup of blessing which we bless, is it not the communion of the blood of Christ?"—T.

Ver. 6.—"*Our examples.*" The force of example, both to encourage and to deter, is familiar and admitted. The principle is used in education, in the arts, in government and law. It is justly believed that a readier and deeper impression is produced by living characters and real events than by abstract propositions. The principle is employed by religion. The Bible is full of examples of sin, punishment, repentance, virtue, reward. The Old Testament has been termed the picture-book accompanying and illustrating the lessons of the New Testament. The text assumes the special applicability of the history of Israel in the wilderness to the spiritual instruction, first of the Corinthians, and then also of all professed Christians. Paul points and emphasizes his appeals to diligence, purity, cheerfulness, etc., by referring to the well-known incidents of the journey of Israel from Egypt to the land of promise.

I. ISRAEL IN THE WILDERNESS IS AN EXAMPLE OF WARNING. 1. Against *murmuring,* which, it is to be feared, never appears to many Christians to be of the nature of sin, and against which accordingly many are not upon their guard. But murmuring is against Divine appointment, and is therefore against God himself. 2. Against *sensuality.* Into these it was not surprising that Israel should fall, having only just escaped from Egypt, and being surrounded by the licentious heathen. And what more important and necessary than a caution against defiling and destroying the temple of the Holy Ghost? 3. Against *rebellion.* Israel again and again rebelled against Moses the servant of God, and against Jehovah himself. And Christians need to be reminded that to violate God's Law, to defy the authority of God's inspired apostles, to resist the Divine message of God's ministers, is treason, and cannot go unpunished. 4. Against *unbelief.* This was the sin which lay at the root of the others, as is shown in the Epistle to the Hebrews. It contrasts with that childlike faith which is becoming in the privileged people of the Lord. All such conduct, as we may learn from the Old Testament narrative referred to, is observed, disapproved, and censured by the omniscient Ruler. It is tempting Christ. We are reminded of the possibility and of the culpability of such sin.

II. ISRAEL IN THE WILDERNESS IS AN EXAMPLE OF ENCOURAGEMENT. If we look at the human side, the lesson is one of warning; but if we regard the Divine side, there we see much to cheer, animate, and inspire us. We remark: 1. Divine *guidance.* As Israel was led by the pillar of cloud and of fire, so will all who look up and commit their way unto the Lord, experience his directing grace. 2. Divine *care, bounty, and goodness.* As Israel ate of the manna from heaven and drank of the streams from the rock, so that, when earth failed, heaven interposed, in like manner will the beneficence of God satisfy the wants of all who in necessity and straits call upon him. 3. Divine *protection.* As Israel's foes were discomfited, as threatening dangers were averted, so shall a way of escape and a door of deliverance be provided for all who trust in a gracious and redeeming God. The arm of flesh may fail, but the arm of Omnipotence shall prove ready and victorious. 4. The final *possession of the promises.* God led his people to the land he promised to their fathers; not immediately, not by a way they knew, not without difficulties, hardships, contests, yet surely, safely, victoriously. Those who are "on their way to God" may well be animated by such recollections, and by the light they cast upon the position and the hopes of the Christian. Heaven may seem to us " the land which is very far off; " yet faith can bring it near and make it ours even now.

> " E'en now by faith I see thee,
> E'en now thy walls discern,
> To thee my thoughts are kindled,
> And strive and pant and yearn."

T.

Ver. 9.—*Tempting Christ.* Whether we read here " the Lord," or " Christ " the meaning is the same. The relation of Israel to Jehovah was parallel, was identical, with the relation of Christians to their Lord Christ. If we are loyal to our King Jesus, then we are in the position of the Hebrews when they reverenced and served the Lord their God; if we are traitors to him whom we call Master and Lord, then we stand in the same condemnation as rebellious Israel. The language of the apostle implies that there is danger lest we presumptuously test, by our unbelief, ingratitude, and rebellion, the forbearance and the grace of him whose we profess to be, whom we profess to serve.

I. THE WAYS IN WHICH WE ARE IN DANGER OF TEMPTING CHRIST. 1. Some hearers of the gospel tempt the Lord by neglecting his gospel as unimportant and unnecessary. 2. Some by deferring that adhesion and devotion to Christ which his authority and circumstances require. 3. Some Christians tempt the Lord by their longings for the sins from which he came and died to deliver them. As the Israelites lusted for the flesh-pots of Egypt, so it is to be feared there are Christians who cast a longing eye upon the sinful and worldly pleasures from which they should be delivered. 4. Some by their ingratitude, murmuring, and rebelliousness. As at Corinth there were those who were dissatisfied with the simplicity of the gospel, those who resisted the authority of the apostle, those who had little sympathy with the Christian spirit of self-denial; so in the Church are there not a few whose temper and conduct are such as to put to the utmost trial the long-suffering and forbearance of the Lord.

II. THE REASONS TO BE FOUND IN CHRIST HIMSELF WHY HIS PEOPLE SHOULD NOT TEMPT HIM. 1. They are bound to honour and obey him as the Son of God. 2. They are bound to acknowledge his claims upon their gratitude, love, and service. 3. They may well be affected by the touching spectacle of his patience and long-suffering. Has he not " borne with their manners in the wilderness "? Can they any longer subject him to a trial so unjust and so cruel?

III. THE REASONS RELATING TO THEMSELVES WHY CHRIST'S PEOPLE SHOULD NOT TEMPT HIM. 1. Continuance in unbelief and rebellion will certainly harden the heart, and unfit and indispose for his service. 2. The blessed and sacred opportunity which life affords for grateful consecration and obedience will pass by unimproved. 3. An example of the kind deprecated will tend to embolden others to persevere in irreligion and in iniquity. 4. It must not be forgotten that, although Christ is a Saviour, he is also a Judge. His forbearance will not last for ever. Where he cannot acquit, he must and will condemn. Men may try Christ too long and too far. Sentence may be deferred, but it will be pronounced and it will be executed. After all, it is not so much the case that we are testing and trying Christ, as that he is testing and trying us. Now is the time of our probation. How do we endure when he puts us to the proof?—T.

Ver. 10.—" *Neither murmur ye.*" Many were the occasions upon which Israel in the wilderness murmured against their God. They murmured against the manna and longed for flesh; against the authority and appointments of Moses and Aaron; against the reports which the spies brought concerning the land of Canaan; against the difficulties which beset them and the foes who encountered them upon their journey. No wonder that their gracious and forbearing Ruler exclaimed, " Forty years long was I grieved with this generation." The conduct of the chosen people in this respect is by the apostle brought under the notice of the Corinthian Christians as recorded for their advantage, to serve as a warning and a corrective to themselves. And there is no congregation in which there are not those who stand in especial need of the inspired admonition, " Neither murmur ye."

I. HUMAN LIFE ABOUNDS WITH OPPORTUNITIES AND TEMPTATIONS TO MURMUR. 1. There are such as are common to the human lot. There may be mentioned among these—infirmity and suffering of body; the brevity of its life, and its consequent insufficiency for carrying out favourite schemes or studies; the limitation of the mental powers and of knowledge; the imperfections of human society, civil, social, and religious. 2. There are such as may, at any time, be special to individuals. Some are called upon to endure personal sufferings and privations; others, sorrows and bereavements; others, unremitting toil; others, uncongenial occupations; others, calamities and disappointments; others, very limited opportunities; others, trials and persecutions for Christ's sake. All these may be occasions for murmuring, and sometimes those who are thus tried must need special grace to refrain from complaints, and to cultivate a cheerful, grateful, submissive spirit.

II. THE MURMURING HERE CENSURED IS A CERTAIN SINFUL KIND OF DISSATISFACTION AND COMPLAINT. The admonition may be misunderstood. The apostle does not exhort us to be fatalistically contented with whatever actually exists, to be silent in the presence of human wrongs and ills, to be careless and indifferent as to the improvement and amelioration of the condition of society. But we are warned against rebelling against God, complaining of his ways, and resisting his will. Circumstances may be displeasing and uncongenial to us, yet they may be permitted by the wisdom and goodness of God. The spirit of discontentment and rebellion must be repressed, and language expressing it must be silenced.

III. THERE ARE CONSIDERATIONS WHICH MAY ACT AS DISSUASIVES AND CORRECTIVES. 1. The injurious moral effect of murmuring. This is undeniable; we recognize its effect upon: (1) The murmurer himself, whom it renders unhappy, using up energies which might be otherwise and well employed, and unfitting him for the service of God. (2) Upon society generally; for the habit is most contagious, and is one which produces a very depressing effect upon all who yield to it and upon all who listen to their dismal complaints. 2. The dishonour done to God's providence. In fact, to murmur is to call into question, or at all events to cast some suspicion upon, God's wisdom, goodness, purposes of benevolence concerning us, and interest in and care for us. 3. Christ's example should deter his followers from murmuring. How cheerful was his demeanour! how acquiescent was he in the humiliation of his lot! how patient in suffering! how submissive in death and sacrifice! Followers and disciples of Jesus are inconsistent indeed when they give way to a spirit of complaint. 4. Murmuring is inconsistent with the proper exercises of religion. It cannot contribute to obedience; it is not consistent with giving of thanks and with praise; it is not the fruit of prayer. 5. The hope of the future should banish murmuring. The occasions for complaint—the trials of the earthly life—will soon be over. Let them have their way and do their work now. The prospect before us is one which may well inspire a contented, patient, uncomplaining disposition and habit.

PRACTICAL LESSONS AND APPLICATION. 1. The admonition of the text is the voice of Divine authority: how dare we resist it? 2. It is the voice of wisdom and reason: why should we resist it? 3. It is the voice of love and persuasion: how can we resist it? "Be careful for nothing, but in everything, by prayer and thanksgiving, let your requests be made known unto God."

> "Some murmur, when their sky is clear
> And wholly bright to view,
> If one small speck of dark appear
> In their great heaven of blue;
> And some with thankful love are filled
> If but one streak of light,
> One ray of God's good mercy, gild
> The darkness of their night.

> "In palaces are hearts that ask,
> In discontent and pride,
> Why life is such a dreary task.
> And all things good denied.
> And hearts in poorest huts admire
> How love has in their aid
> (Love that not ever seems to tire)
> Such rich provision made."
>   (Trench.)

Ver. 12.—*The danger of self-confidence.* To "stand" is to be and to continue upright in the Christian life, and they truly stand whose character and habits agree with their profession. To "fall" is to act with inconsistency, to yield to the tempter, to stumble over the stone of offence, to be caught by the snare which is spread; and this, either temporally or permanently. Life is a probation, and is as much so to the Christian as to others. The apostle puts all his readers upon their guard, reminding them that this is a scene, a period, of probation, and that the true preparation is not to be found in self-confidence and boastfulness, but in watchfulness, humility, and prayer. "Let him that thinketh he standeth take heed lest he fall."

I. THE DISPOSITION AGAINST WHICH THIS ADMONITION IS DIRECTED. It is self-confidence. 1. *Reliance upon outward privileges.* As Israel was a chosen nation, so Christians are God's "peculiar people;" and there is danger lest this should be adduced, perhaps to one's self, as a ground for presumption and arrogance. 2. *Reliance upon personal strength and purity of character.* A man is assured that he can take good care of himself, that no temptation can overtake and overmaster him, that he is clad in armour proof against the fiery darts of the wicked. No need to warn him; he is safe! 3. *Boastfulness.* The man who thinks himself so secure is likely to glory in his own position, his strength of character, his superiority to infirmities,—to make a loud profession, and to regard the timid with a compassionate disdain.

II. THE PERILS ACCOMPANYING SUCH A DISPOSITION. Paul knew how necessary and appropriate was his counsel; his own experience of human nature and life, elevated and cleared by a Divine inspiration, led him to this most wise and salutary admonition. 1. Such a peril is suggested by the facts of human nature. It is supposed that there is an inflated, unguarded state of mind; that a violent and sudden temptation comes in the way; and that there follows an unexpected and grievous fall. That a self-confident spirit is more dangerous because more liable to temptation than a lowly spirit, distrustful of self, is well known to all who have experience of human nature. Those who boast of sinlessness are on the verge of sin. 2. Notable examples recorded in Scripture prove the assertion now made. Hazael was indignant at the very supposition that he could be guilty of barbarities and cruelties such as the prophet foretold; but when the temptation came, he fell into the snare. Peter was vehement in his protestations, "Though I die with thee, I will not deny thee!" Yet when he was tempted by cowardice, he denied his Lord.

III. THE EFFECTUAL REMEDIES AGAINST A SPIRITUAL FALL. If self-confidence is of no avail, where is safety to be found? 1. In self-abasement and distrust. 2. In a simple trust in the protecting, preserving, delivering power of God. 3. In watchfulness; for the Christian soldier must never be off his guard; he must arm himself, watch, and withstand his foe. 4. In prayer, which is a confession that we are exposed to danger, and is a waiting upon God and seeking his providential interposition and his spiritual aid.—T.

Ver. 13.—*Temptation.* With warning the inspired teacher conjoins encouragement. The self-confident are admonished lest their high opinion of themselves should be the occasion of their fall. And, in the next verse, the timid are cheered by the assurance that, although they must be tempted, a Divine Deliverer shall appear upon their behalf, and they shall be led in the path of safety. This is an assurance consolatory to all who are desirous to turn the discipline of life to high spiritual account, and especially to the doubtful and the diffident.

I. TEMPTATION IS PERMITTED BY GOD. 1. Seeing that it is allowed by Providence to be an incident of human life, none need expect to escape. The young are tempted by the pleasures of sense and of society; the old by avarice and the love of ease; the learned by self-confidence; the great by ambition; the pious and the useful by spiritual pride. 2. There is in this very fact an element of consolation. To every tempted soul it may be said, "Your case is not peculiar; all the good have attained to goodness by passing through the fiery furnace of affliction and persecution, of doubt and spiritual conflict." Christ himself was sorely tempted, and the disciple is not above his Lord. It is the common lot, in which we have fellowship with one another and with Christ.

II. TEMPTATION IS WITHSTOOD THROUGH THE FAITHFULNESS OF GOD. 1. God has undertaken to defend and deliver his servants: "He knoweth how to deliver the godly out of temptation." The faithfulness of a true and unchanging God is the anchor by which the tempted shall ride out the fiercest storm. 2. God effects this by the instrumentality of his Word. This is "the sword of the Spirit." When Jesus was beset by the adversary, he warded off every thrust by the power of the Scripture. 3. God encourages his people to call upon him in the day of trial. The sentry does not advance to meet the approaching foe; he falls back, and gives warning to the garrison and the commander. So, when tempted, should we arise and call upon our God.

III. TEMPTATION IS ITSELF TEMPERED BY AN OVERRULING PROVIDENCE. It shall not exceed our powers of endurance and resistance. It may be subtle; it may be sudden; yet the watchful, prayerful soul shall repel and overcome. The dart which would pierce the unarmed falls broken from the coat of mail; the flaming torch, which would explode the powder did it fall into a powder magazine, drops harmless into a pool of water; and the Ruler of all can both moderate the force of the onset and impart strength to stand in the evil day.

IV. TEMPTATION IS, IN THE CASE OF GOD'S PEOPLE, ACCOMPANIED BY A MEANS OF ESCAPE. The same God who delivered Daniel from the lions' den, and Peter from the prison, makes a path of safety for all who trust in him. The experience of every Christian verifies this assurance. The story of the soul is the same as the story of the Church; dangers and distresses ever recur, but they ever afford to the Divine Lord an opportunity for revealing his compassion, and for effecting an interposition and securing a deliverance. It is only when Christ's followers have entered the gates of heaven that they will be beyond the reach of the tempter's arm.—T.

Ver. 15.—*The judgment of the wise.* The apostle, being specially and divinely inspired, claimed to have authority in the Church of Christ. Yet it is observable that he did not require an unintelligent and unreasoning assent to his doctrine and counsel. If his words were true and right, he had the reason and the conscience of the rational and the spiritual upon his side. Hence the frankness and fearlessness of his appeal. If Paul took such a position, his language may well be adopted by teachers and preachers of Christianity, who, whatever their abilities, piety, and zeal, do not profess to enjoy the special and supernatural guidance vouchsafed to an apostle.

I. THE SPIRIT AND METHOD PROPER TO THE CHRISTIAN PREACHER AND TEACHER. 1. He should not speak as to the ignorance of the ignorant, as if his aim were to take advantage of, to impose upon, persons whose slender knowledge, ability, and opportunities incapacitated and forbade them to receive and appreciate the truth. 2. He should not address himself to the credulity and superstition of men; for there are too many who are content to believe upon the authority of man, when they ought to inquire with regard to what comes to them whether it comes with the authority of truth, of God. 3. He should not appeal to the selfish interests or the selfish fears of men; for these are methods which are certain to produce an immediate and powerful effect, but are unlikely to work real good. 4. But he should speak as unto wise men, inviting their attention and inquiries. Christ and his apostles proceeded upon this method; they appealed to the thoughtfulness, the conscience, the right feelings of those whom they addressed. Compare the language of Scripture with that of arrogant priests, of domineering pastors, of superficial revivalists; and what is the result of the comparison? It is to produce the impression—How just, temperate, thoughtful, reasonable, convincing, persuasive, are the arguments, expositions, and appeals of Scripture!

II. THE SPIRIT AND METHOD PROPER TO HEARERS AND READERS OF THE WORD. 1. Let them cultivate wisdom; for it is to wise men that the Word of God is addressed. In the Old Testament, especially in the Proverbs, there are innumerable eulogies of wisdom, and the sons of men are entreated to listen to the voice of wisdom, to cherish, seek, and pray for it. And in the New Testament, our Lord's discourses evince the same appreciation of this quality of mind. Christ commends the *wise* man who built his house upon the rock, the *wise* virgins who took oil in their vessels, the *wise* and faithful servant who did his Lord's will, the disciples who are *wise* as serpents. Not a pretentious and proud spirit, but the wisdom of humility, is the preparation for the kingdom; the wise of this world, the wise in their own conceit, are not in the way for the blessing. 2. Let them judge the religious teaching they receive. This admonition of St. Paul's is a copy of that of Christ himself: "Why even of yourselves judge ye not what is right?" It was an admonition which the apostle seems often to have repeated: "Prove all things;" "Judge ye if it is not unseemly," etc.; "We who are spiritual judge all things." There is abundant material for judging, in nature and in revelation; there are canons and counsels of judgment which all may use; and each Christian has a certain ability and opportunity to judge for himself. Happily the most really important matters are the least difficult to judge. 3. Let them judge with a view to practical conduct and under a constant sense of responsibility. We are not called upon to judge other men, but to judge of what relates to our duty as followers of Christ Jesus. The questions for us to decide are questions of pressing moment for ourselves. The responsibility of deciding such questions cannot be shifted from our shoulders to those of others. The messenger and minister of Christ speaks as unto wise men; as wise men let the hearers of the Word hear, judge, and act.—T.

Vers. 16, 17.—*Communion.* This passage and another in the following chapter would in themselves suffice to prove the antiquity of the Lord's Supper. And as this Epistle is of undisputed genuineness, it may be taken as established that the Eucharist has been observed in an unbroken chain from its institution by the Founder of Christianity down to our own days. Important light is cast by these two verses upon the spiritual and social significance of the Supper of the Lord.

I. THE HOLY COMMUNION IS A DISTINCTIVE BADGE OF THE CHRISTIAN CHURCH. It is only by recognizing this fact that we understand the introduction of a reference to it in this place. St. Paul was anxious to dissuade the Corinthian Christians from participating in the idolatrous festivals of the heathen. And he brings forward, with this end in view, the distinction between heathenism and Christianity in their characteristic festivals and observances. The Jews had their Passover, the Greeks their *eranoi*, the early Christians their *agapæ*. The peculiar and distinctive observance of the Christians was, however, the Eucharist. The Corinthians were justly reminded that they must take their stand, that they could not be upon both sides, that they must not at the same time frequent the idol-feasts and sit down at the table of the Lord Christ. And this distinction still substantially holds good. And young people especially may justly be urged to take their stand upon the Lord's side and pledge themselves to Christian fidelity in the ordinance distinctive of the Church of Christ.

II. THE HOLY COMMUNION IS A MEANS BY WHICH CHRISTIANS COMMEMORATE THE DEATH OF CHRIST AND PARTAKE OF ITS SPIRITUAL BENEFITS. 1. Prominence is given to our Lord's death by the mention of his body and his blood. In the following chapter St. Paul expressly reminds his readers that in the sacrament they show (proclaim) his death—until he come. 2. But for his purpose the apostle, in this place, lays special stress upon communion in the Lord's body and blood. Amidst all the diversities of opinion and controversies which have arisen with regard to this sacrament, it may, perhaps, be affirmed that to spiritually minded Christians of all Churches, the observance of the Lord's Supper has been an act of obedience to Christ, and the means of spiritual union and fellowship with him. The true participation in the Lord's death is the privilege of the lowly, believing, reverent communicant. Necessary as are food and drink for the sustenance of the bodily life with its functions and activities, equally necessary is it for the spiritual health of the Christian that he should receive Divine nourishment—that he should feed by faith upon the Son of God.

III. THE HOLY COMMUNION IS A SIGN AND A MEANS OF CHRISTIAN FELLOWSHIP. This passage casts light, not only upon the work of Christ and upon the individual appropriation of the benefits of that work, but also upon the character, constitution, and purposes of the Church. It is observable that great stress is laid upon communion, *i.e.* upon the common interest in the one Saviour and the one salvation, and the mutual regard of interest, confidence, and brotherly love, which is the proper consequence of union to Jesus. The one cup, the one bread, of which all partake, are the symbol of a spiritual unity. Nay, Christians are actually denominated, in virtue of their unity with their Lord and with one another, "one bread, one body." The language must have been startling when first employed; it sounds very strong, even to us who are familiar with it. Yet it expresses the simple and literal truth. A unity which no power on earth could effect, and which no thinker could have conceived, is in course of realization, through the one Saviour and the one Spirit; and of this the Holy Communion is a divinely appointed and effectual witness.—T.

Ver. 23.—*Expedience and edification.* Like a true rhetorician, as (in the best sense) Paul was, he took up the positions of his opponents, and turned them to good account for his own cause. Those of the Corinthians who adopted the laxer view and practice with reference to association with idolatry, put forward the natural and unquestionable plea—All things indifferent in themselves are lawful for a Christian. "True," answered Paul, "it is so; none has more than myself insisted upon this principle : you learned it from my lips. Yet it does not follow that, because an action is lawful, it is also expedient or edifying; and in all his conduct the Christian has to consider this." Judged by this standard, conduct may be disapproved which by the other standard might be vindicated.

I. THE LARGE LIMITS OF CHRISTIAN LIBERTY. The Christian religion is not one which lays down exact and minute laws for the regulation and guidance of human life. It provides principles, and leaves their application to the individual. There is thus large scope for the exercise of Christian wisdom. This arrangement is an incidental proof of the Divine origin of Christianity; and it is also in harmony with the universality of its intended diffusion. There are no local or temporary elements in this religion, which is the religion of God, the religion of humanity.

II. CONDUCT THAT APPROACHES THE EXTREME LIMITS OF WHAT IS LAWFUL MAY BE INJURIOUS TO THE INDIVIDUAL AGENT HIMSELF. 1. It may promote a selfish disposition and habit of mind. He who says, "I am enlightened; I am not bound by rules ; I can neglect such and such usual observances; I can indulge in such and such practices;" and all because he is living under a dispensation of liberty, and all things are lawful to him, will probably confirm the natural selfishness which he should aim at repressing. 2. Such conduct may also gradually deteriorate the religious character. There are those who need the assistance and the restraint of rules; and although these may not be laid down by inspired authority, they may be very expedient, and their neglect may be very prejudicial to the spiritual life.

III. THE TOO FREE USE OF LIBERTY MAY BE UNEDIFYING AND HURTFUL TO CHRISTIAN SOCIETY. 1. It restricts the range and the operation of sympathy. If Christians are members one of another, then, if one member suffers, all suffer with it. But where the only question is, "What may I do?" and, "What must I do?" instead of, "How may I act for my brother's welfare?" there an element of discord is introduced into society, for "all seek their own." 2. It encourages some to conduct which their conscience condemns, and so indirectly leads them into sin. So it was at Corinth, where the freedom with which some Christians partook of things offered to idols emboldened the scrupulous to partake when their conscience condemned them, and brethren were thus led into sin by the inconsiderateness of those who deemed themselves the strong. Well is it to ask, concerning any proposed conduct of a doubtful character, not only, "Is it lawful?" but, "Will it tend to the edification of those for whom Christ died?"—T.

Ver. 24.—*Unselfishness.* Cases of perplexity and difficulty as to the separate actions of Christians may often be decided by the application of a general principle. If we possess this, and both know how to bring it to bear and have the disposition and purpose to do so, we shall not be at a loss as to how to conduct ourselves in the circumstances and relations of practical life. This will serve us better than a code of laws, a book of casuistry, a human oracle. How could we desire a nobler law than this, which was laid down for the guidance of the Corinthians in deciding upon their intercourse with heathen neighbours?—"Let no one seek his own, but every one his neighbour's good."

I. A CAUTION. "Let no one seek his own." 1. Now, this is a very necessary caution, for that which is here condemned is what most persons are in danger of doing, and what even society encourages men to do, and praises them for doing. 2. And such action is even sanctioned by a certain view of religion. Under pretence, perhaps with a sincere intention of promoting their own salvation, men sometimes overlook the claims of others upon their interest and services. Thus monks and hermits and other selfish religionists have retired from the world, to make sure of their own spiritual welfare. 3. Yet it is not intended to forbid or censure a due attention, on the part of every Christian, to his own welfare, bodily and spiritually. There have been those who in bitter anguish have exclaimed, "They made us keepers of the vineyard, but our own vineyard have we not kept." One thing ought we to do, yet not to leave the other undone.

II. A RULE. "Let every one seek his neighbour's good." 1. It is a rule which expressly applies to all. Whatever a person's position in the family, in the Church, in society, he is equally under obligation to self-denial, benevolence, and helpfulness. "Bear ye one another's burdens." 2. There is abundant scope in human society for such unselfish effort. There are the ignorant to instruct, the sad to console, the miserable to relieve, the young to protect, the sinner to restore, etc. 3. The rule may be especially obeyed by spreading the gospel of Jesus Christ. The want of the gospel being the root of human ills, the supply of the gospel is the radical cure. Paul's missionary life was a proof that it was in this light he regarded his brethren of this sinful race ; in his toils and his sufferings he was ever seeking the good of all.

III. A MOTIVE. This is not expressed, but it is implied; for the apostle wrote as a Christian, and assumed the action and operation of distinctively Christian principles. 1. The example of Christ's life and death was an example of unselfishness; in all he did and said he left us an example that we should follow in his steps. 2. Christ's love and sacrifice constitute the moral power of benevolence. He died for us that we might live for others—first to him, and then to those for whom he died. His death is the death of selfishness ; for this sin was nailed to his cross. 3. It is assumed that, in the conflict with natural selfishness, and in the new and holy life of benevolence, we seek and receive the aid and guidance of the Holy Spirit of God.—T.

Ver. 31.—*The aim of the Christian's life.* Nothing is more characteristic of Paul's mind than the way in which, upon every suggestion, he ascends to great principles. He begins with what it seems must be a homely and practical and almost trivial discussion concerning idol-feasts. But now and again, before he quits the subject, he rises to some sublime truth and principle. What could be a grander precept in itself, what could be worthier of acceptance by all rational beings, not to say all sincere Christians, than the command of the text ?—"Do all to the glory of God."

I. THE PRINCIPLE IS TO BE EXPLAINED. 1. What is the glory of God ? It is the bringing into prominence of his attributes, the working out of his purposes, and this especially by intelligent and voluntary beings. It is the gratitude which all owe, the obedience to which all are summoned, which show forth God's glory. 2. How can men do aught to God's glory ? Not surely by the mere invocation of God's Name, so common and customary among Jews and Mohammedans. But they may fall in with his purposes, reverence his laws, recommend his service, utter his praise.

II. THE PRACTICAL APPLICATION OF THE PRINCIPLE IS TO BE EXHIBITED. 1. It is so minute and searching that it extends to the most ordinary and trivial acts of life. Even eating and drinking are included ; probably they are mentioned here upon the suggestion of meals partaken in common with idolaters. "Epictetus, on being asked how any one could eat so as to please God, answered, 'By eating justly, temperately, and thankfully.'" If a heathen moralist could take so noble a view of religion, shall Christians sever their daily life and its manifold occupations from the high aims and sacred motives of their lofty vocation in Christ ? 2. It is so vast that nothing escapes it. It is universal in its operation, "embracing all things." No interest in life is so wide, no relationship so sacred, no occupation so honourable, as not to come under this principle, which can give dignity and sweetness to all the functions of human life.

III. THE ADVANTAGES OF THIS PRINCIPLE ARE TO BE URGED. 1. It delivers him who adopts it from miserable and debasing self-seeking. How many there are who do all things to the glory of self ! And what a degrading and deteriorating influence does such an aim exercise over the character of those who adopt it ! On the other hand, to live for God is to rise at a bound above the murky atmosphere of earth into the serenest air of heaven itself. 2. It conduces to the well-being of society. When all men seek their own, society is afflicted with discord and is threatened with dissolution. When all seek their Maker's honour, this common aim and endeavour tend to sympathy, harmony, co-operation. 3. It is an aim in life just and satisfying to the mind—the right aim and motive, and the only one of which we shall never repent and never feel ashamed. 4. It is a stable and eternal aim. With this design and hope the angels serve and wait and praise in heaven. And the glorified saints who have finished their course on earth, when translated to the presence of God, may change place and occupation, but the end and aim of their being remains the same, for it is capable of no improvement, of no elevation.—T.

Ver. 33.—*Benevolence.* Paul recommended to the Corinthians that course of conduct which he followed himself. As a religious teacher, he practised what he taught. And the lessons of his lips and of his pen were enforced with a tenfold power by the actions of his life. In nothing was this more observable and undeniable than in his devotion to the welfare of others, and his habit of adapting himself to all men, in order that he might win some for Christ.

I. THE CONDUCT ABJURED. Paul sought not his own profit; and he dissuades Christians generally from doing so. By this we are to understand that our own profit is not to be the one ruling principle of our life. Certainly it is not wrong to seek our own spiritual welfare and eternal salvation; for this we are responsible, to this we are called. But having found Christ ourselves, we are not to make our personal advantage our one and only concern. They who seek such an end always fail; none are more stunted in spiritual growth than those whose only thought is how they may obtain abundant nourishment for themselves. Christians must be prepared to sacrifice religious advantages and enjoyments, when such a sacrifice is demanded in the interests of their fellow-men.

II. THE RULE ADOPTED. Paul's rule, which he commends to us, was to "please all men." This might easily be misunderstood, for nothing is baser than a habit of pandering to the passions and courting the favour and humouring the prejudices of all we meet with. But there is a pliancy and adaptation of character and demeanour, which flows from and expresses sympathy, and which is a sure road to most men's hearts. It is no degradation to condescend to the simple and illiterate, to enter into the thoughts and pursuits of the scholarly, to talk the languages of the foreigner, to share the ways and the life of any man, in innocence and without duplicity. It was by this habit, carried to excess, that the Jesuits gained their hold upon individual natures and upon general society. And it is by this habit, rather than by great powers of thought or of speech, that successful servants of Christ usually achieve their success.

III. THE AIM SOUGHT. 1. It respects "the many." This is just like the large heart of Paul, who in this was a true follower of Christ himself. The Lord's purpose is to draw "all men" unto himself; his prediction, that "many" shall come and sit down in his kingdom; and his commission: "Preach the gospel to every creature." He gave his life a ransom "for many;" his blood was shed for "many;" he bare the sins of "many." 2. It is their immediate "profit" or advantage. What he concerned himself not about, as far as he himself was concerned, he anxiously sought for others. 3. The final aim is the salvation of mankind; a purpose and hope which may well justify, and indeed all but compel, self-denial and effort; for salvation includes all blessings of which human nature is capable, and the prolongation, the perpetuation, of those blessings throughout a glorious eternity.—T.

Vers. 1—12.—*Old Testament pictures.* Painted from life. Painted for our inspection and instruction. Painted by the genius of inspiration.

I. A PICTURE OF PRIVILEGE. The privileges of the Israelites were, like our own, multifarious. Five are here enumerated. 1. *The Israelites were all "under the cloud."* They were thus *signally protected by God.* *He* was in the cloud; "The Lord went before them by day in a pillar of a cloud, to lead them the way; and by night in a pillar of fire, to give them light" (Exod. xiii. 21). Divine protection is a great privilege. How safe we are if God keeps us! Of themselves, the Israelites were peculiarly helpless and defenceless; but they were stronger than the strongest because God was with them. Our great ally is God. 2. *They all "passed through the sea."* Special deliverance was theirs. Menaced by fearful danger, they were required merely *to walk on,* and they *walked out of* the peril. They were hedged in, but God made for them a path through the waters. God always leaves one safe way for those whom he favours. God helps us when we are at our wits' end. Everything fails, but God never fails. 3. *They were all "baptized unto Moses."* They became his disciples—were under his leadership; he, under God, was their ruler and head. A great privilege, for Moses was a prince among men. Association with such a man, divinely commissioned for his great work, was no slight mark of God's favour. We are baptized unto a greater than Moses. The "cloud and sea" were their baptism, typifying the "water and Spirit" of ours (John iii. 5). 4. *They were all fed.* A table was spread for them in the wilderness—and a *good* table too; God does not half-starve his children. No ordinary fare was theirs; it was "spiritual meat." It was not coarse; it was "angels' food" (Ps. lxxviii. 25). It was "spiritual," being derived from the great Spirit; *God* fed them. This meat had, therefore, a message for *their spirits,* as well as sustenance for their bodies; it spoke of the love of God; it was thus still further "*spiritual* meat." Moreover, it pointed to the bread which should by-and-by come down from heaven (John vi. 35), of which it is now our privilege to partake, and which the pious Israelite fed upon by faith. 5. *They were all supplied with drink.* "They drank of that spiritual Rock that followed them, and that Rock was Christ." The water which came to them was from God, and was thus like the meat, "spiritual;" and, if intelligently received as from Divine love, quenched spiritual as well as physical thirst. But we are told that "that Rock was Christ." Not only did it foreshadow him, who *was smitten* that the waters of salvation might flow out to a perishing world (Isa. liii. 5), but from him came the supply of the physical wants of the Israelites. He, having had all things connected with the administration of the world committed to him, was with the people of God in the wilderness and ministered to their needs. The expected Messiah was in their midst as Ruler and miraculous Worker; yet then, as afterwards, he was hidden from their eyes. The spiritual Rock "followed them;" Christ ministered to their physical and spiritual need *continuously.* Divine favours never fail the believer. Always in the wilderness here, but always cared for.

II. A PICTURE OF TRANSGRESSION. As five special privileges are enumerated, five instances of transgression are recorded. 1. *They lusted after evil things.* They were not content with the good things provided by God. They complained of the manna and longed for the flesh-pots of Egypt. That these were identified with their bondage seemed to matter to them but little. Professors of religion sometimes hanker after old delights, though these are associated with their earlier years of disobedience and sin. The provisions of God's house are "light bread;" they want the more tasty dishes of the world. The Corinthians were tempted by meats identified with idol-worship; they were in danger of imitating the sin of Israel. Egypt-tastes cling to us; we should mortify them. 2. *They became idolatrous.* Almost insensibly, but very truly. When they made the golden calf, they no doubt intended it only as a symbol of deity, and designed to worship the true God through it (Exod. xxxii. 5), but they began by disobedience to an express command (Exod. xx. 4, 5), and they terminated in gross idolatry and in many evils often connected with it. They went near to the fire, and were burned. People do not become idolatrous instantly, but by steps. The Israelites were impatient, had a great sense of their own importance and of their privileges, cast off restraint—and fell. On the spot where they had solemnly promised obedience they transgressed. The danger of the Corinthians was similar. They did not *intend* to worship idols when they inclined towards the sacrificial feasts of the heathen, but this was the practical peril, and those who participated in these feasts were in danger of becoming apostates nigh to the very spot which had witnessed their confession of Christ. We should not seek to go to the end of our tether; under the strain the tether may break. Those who seek to go as far as they may, often go much further. Liberty and licence live next door to each other. 3. *They fell into immorality.* False worship leads to false life. Idolatry to the Israelites was the door of sensuality (Numb. xxv. 1—9). It threatened to be so to the Corinthians. First idol-recognition, then participation in idol-rites, many of which were scandalously impure. It might be difficult to draw the line; not *theoretically* perhaps, but *practically.* And the temptation to go further would assuredly be strong. When we get away from God, corruption soon masters us. On the devil's ground the devil has great power. We laugh at the danger, but the author of the danger laughs at us. How low the privileged may fall! The chosen people have become as moral scum and refuse. 4. *They tempted God.* Or Christ, as the Angel (Exod. xxiii. 20) and Administrator of the Divine kingdom. By their sinfulness they tried the forbearance of God—they provoked him. Their unbelief and disobedience strained his long-suffering to the utmost. This was a great sin. The Corinthians were in peril of committing it by verging towards idolatry and living as much like men of the world as they dared. We should ask, not only what effect our conduct may have upon ourselves, but *how it affects God.* It may arouse the Divine anger. It was to those who provoked him that God sware " they shall not enter into my rest." 5. *They murmured against God.* And this murmuring was of no insignificant character. It was an impugning of the Divine character—a charge of evil against the infinitely good. The reference may be to Numb. xiv. 2 and to Numb. xvi. 41. The justice, the wisdom, and the love of God were assailed; and what could be a greater crime? " Murmuring;" we say and think but little of it. What creatures of words we are! The charge against God was none the less evil that it was indirect—it was made directly against Moses and Aaron. In Numb. xvi. 41 the Israelites say, " Ye have killed the people of the Lord," though it must have been patent to all that Moses and Aaron had nothing to do with the actual death of Korah and his company. The Israelites' sin was made no better by the cowardice which prompted them to make a charge against men, which they *intended* for God, but dared not make against him. The Corinthians, many of them, murmured against Paul, and perhaps would murmur more after his sharp rebukes. Now, here was a question suggested for them, " Against whom are you really murmuring?" A pregnant question for us. We may half unconsciously veil our attacks upon God by directing them against our fellows. But after all, *what is it we find fault with?* Is it of man, confined to him? *Or is it of God, coming to us through men?* We should ponder what is involved in making charges against God *indirectly.* Note: Privilege cannot " keep us from falling." It cannot hold us up. Though numbered amongst God's people and participating in Divine favours, we may perish. Though we have sailed over many spiritual seas, we may yet " make shipwreck of faith." We need to be watchful and diligent, lest *we* become " castaways." The peril of the Corinthians under higher privilege than that of Israel was so clearly foreseen that these things were written for their admonition (ver. 11), and these " examples " of privilege and fall were for their eyes to behold (ver. 6). They are for ours also, for upon us, with them, " the ends of the ages are come " (ver. 11). Especially do those need to beware who are over-confident. " Let him that thinketh he standeth take heed lest he fall " (ver. 12). Some are so sure, that they run into temptation and perish. Self-confidence leads to disaster, God-confidence to security.

III. A PICTURE OF PUNISHMENT. Great privilege—great sin—great punishment. Jehovah will " by no means spare the guilty." Condign punishment followed Israel's transgression. God's stern messengers to her were : 1. Sword; as Exod. xxxii. 27. 2. Plague; as Numb. xvi. 44—49 and xxv. 9. 3. Serpents; as Numb. xxi. 6. 4. Other death-heralds, followed by the overthrow in the wilderness of those who had sinned (vers. 5, 10). " God is not mocked : for whatsoever a man soweth, that shall he also reap " (Gal. vi. 7). As privilege cannot save us from sin, neither can it save us from punishment. God's justice was *impugned*, but it was not *impaired*; those who murmured against it felt its stroke. How gracious is God to those who submit themselves and are obedient! how terrible to those who *dare* him! If his chosen people did not escape, " how shall we escape?" Our fall will be greater, as our privileges are. " Of how much sorer punishment, suppose ye, shall he be thought worthy, who hath trodden under foot the Son of God, and hath counted the blood of the covenant, wherewith he was sanctified, an unholy thing, and hath done despite unto the Spirit of grace ?" (Heb. x. 29). These are three companion pictures to be hung in our gallery and to be often studied.—H.

Ver. 13.—*The hour of temptation.* I. TEMPTATION COMES TO ALL. It came to the writer of this Epistle, to all the apostles, to Christ himself. It has come to the great and good in all ages, as well as to the insignificant and evil. It will come to us. The conditions of our life on earth make it unavoidable. It must not be regarded as indicative of Divine disfavour or as an evil altogether. The salutary effect of the hour *of* temptation has often been shown in the hour *after* temptation. Many who have fallen "into manifold temptations" have been led to "count it all joy" (Jas. i. 2).

II. To BE TEMPTED IS NOT TO SIN. We need to remember this. Some sensitive natures conclude that they must be very sinful *because* they are so much tempted, whereas multiplicity of temptation is often *rather* an evidence of faithfulness and integrity. The strongest attacks are made upon the strongest forts. Satan does not waste his ammunition. He would not be so earnestly seeking to capture us if we were already completely his captives. Repeated temptation argues the existence of *resistance*. Sin is *consent* to the temptation. Where there is *no acquiescence* there is no sin. The greatly tempted Christ was the perfectly sinless Christ.

III. TEMPTATION IS NOT COMPULSION. Some dread temptation, because they think it will *force* them to that which is evil. *But since the world was, no man has ever been compelled to commit a single sin*. Satan has no power of compulsion. Indeed, to be "compelled to sin" involves a contradiction in terms; if we are *compelled*, there can be no *sin*. We could not be *responsible* if we were under compulsion. Temptation at its strongest is only *inducement*. Satan said to Christ, "Cast thyself down;" he can say no more to us; he cannot cast us down. Here the responsibility of sin comes in. Every sin that we commit is *voluntary*. *We* do it—no one else.

IV. GOD'S GRACIOUS PROVISION FOR HIS TEMPTED PEOPLE. 1. *He will not allow them to be unduly tempted*. Our *temptations* are under his control. His eye is upon us whilst we are tempted. His hand is stretched out. His voice says, "Thus far." Though he never tempts us in an evil sense, every temptation is *weighed by him* before it reaches us. He is faithful to his covenant with believers (1 Thess. v. 24). 2. *He will provide the appropriate means for dealing with the temptation*. A "way of escape," not necessarily from the temptation, but from the *peril* of it. As with Job, Daniel, Paul (2 Cor. xii. 8, 9). "*The* way of escape" as it should be rendered—the precise way in which the temptation should be *received, borne, resisted*. This way of escape comes with the temptation: when the temptation comes, *this* comes also; to the true believer the two are inseparable. With the sickness comes the cure, with the shaft the shield. In temptation we should look to God; from him cometh our help. When the enemy comes in like a flood, he lifts up the standard against him. The promise is only to those who are in alliance with God. Others *go down* under temptation, not because they are *compelled*, but because to the invitation from without there is a quick response from within. We should enter into covenant with God through Christ; then we shall be in his hands who can "keep us from falling" and who *will*.—H.

Vers. 14—22.—*Wariness in Christian walk*. A burning question amongst Corinthian Christians was whether they were justified in partaking of sacrifices offered to idols. With this the apostle deals in several parts of these Epistles. Note the course of his argument here.

I. HE LIFTS THE VEIL FROM IDOLATRY. He is quite willing to allow that an idol is nothing in itself, and that meats offered to an idol are in themselves as though they had not been so offered. But he thrusts upon the attention the startling truth that, when men professedly sacrifice to idols, they really sacrifice to devils. "They sacrificed unto devils, not to God; to gods whom they knew not" (Deut. xxxii. 17). 1. *The character of many of the heathen deities was Satanic*. The conception of the worshippers was largely a conception of the character of devils. 2. *Paganism is a part of the Satanic kingdom*. It is not of the true God, and what is not of him is of the devil. There are but two masters. Pagan worship is the worship of the false, and the false is of Satan, not of God. Behind every idol, because it is an idol, lurks a devil. The dumb image and the supposed deity associated with it are but masks hiding the face of the fiend. An idol is nothing; yes, but "nothings" are generally the veils of very palpable "somethings." *Beware of the nothings of life*; they are most dangerous because least dreaded. 3. *When any objects are worshipped in the place of God, the devil-kingdom is served*. Idolatry of whatever sort involves "sacrifice to devils." All sin is homage and offering to Satan, the "god of this world." The truth applies when pure things, as well as when impure, are substituted for God. Satanic interests are advanced; a sacrifice is laid upon the altar of darkness.

II. HE SHOWS WHAT PARTAKING OF HEATHEN SACRIFICES INVOLVES. 1. *To all*. As the sacrifice is virtually offered to devils, partaking of it when it is in the form of a sacrifice—this would not apply to meat sold in the shambles (ver. 25) or to meat at a friend's house (ver. 27)—involves fellowship with devils. Established by reference to: (1) Jewish sacrifices. Those who partook of these sacrifices identified themselves with Jehovah and his altar. To partake of Jewish sacrifices was to proclaim one's self a Jew and a follower of Israel's God. So to partake of sacrifices offered to devils was to identify one's self with the service of devils and to have communion with them. (2) The Lord's Supper. When the bread and wine are partaken of, there is a profession of attachment to him whose flesh and blood are thus set forth—of fellowship with him, of association in his service, of union with him. The union set forth is so close that it unites those who gather at the table (ver. 17). The Lord's Supper pre-eminently identifies us with Christ. At his table we may look for the closest fellowship. Similarly at the table of devils men are closely associated with these evil spirits. 2. *To Christians specially.* It is an attempt to serve God and his greatest enemies. This is what it amounts to *really*, though not necessarily with full realization of the fact on the part of the participants. (1) A moral impossibility. Ye cannot serve two masters, especially masters diametrically opposed. "Ye cannot drink," etc. (ver. 21). (2) A horrible spectacle. That those who have been so near to Christ should get correspondingly near to Satan and his angels. That *as* they have been to their Lord, *so* will they be to his foes. (3) A great provocation to the Lord. Our God is "a jealous God" (ver. 22). Men might plead that they did not even think of idols or devils whilst they partook. But it was a public act, and God would regard its true import. A great provocation that his people should do this *outwardly;* and the *outward* would surely affect the *inward* sooner or later. (4) An act of great folly. Running into extreme danger. "Can a man touch pitch and not be defiled?" We should not see how near we may get to sin, but how far we may keep away. The exercise of our "liberty" may lead us to bondage. Tempting *God;* "Are we stronger than he?" (ver. 22).—H.

Ver. 26.—*The great Proprietor.* I. REALIZE AND REMEMBER THE FACT OF GOD'S UNIVERSAL PROPRIETORSHIP. It is easy to say that all things are God's, but difficult to adequately grasp and to retain this in our minds. We yield a ready acquiescence, are but little impressed because the truth is cloudy to us, and then go our way thinking, speaking, and acting, as though God did not own a square foot of ground in the universe! Yet all things are his—the earth and its fulness, small things and great, "our possessions" and the possessions of others, things consecrated to him and things unconsecrated, creatures who obey and creatures who disobey,—all are his.

II. GOD'S PROPRIETORSHIP MAKES THE WORLD MORE BEAUTIFUL. 1. His possessions become associated with himself. We prize certain things because they belong or belonged to our dear ones. All around us has been and is God's. Interesting in themselves, their interest is increased without limit as the whisper comes to us, "They are all *God's* and of God." 2. As his proprietorship springs from his creation of all things, we may be able to trace his mind in objects around us, to see the marks of his fingers, to behold his skill and power. He will be reflected to some extent in his works. 3. He has purposes in connection with his possessions. Everything was made for some end. We may discern some of these ends. We may know that the principle is universal, and may thus be stimulated to seek for further knowledge. 4. Brings good cheer into a world where there is much to sadden. Not the earth *was* the Lord's, but the earth *is* the Lord's. It is still in his hands. Here is light amid dense darkness. The world has not slipped from the grasp of the Eternal—he holds it *now.*

III. GOD'S PROPRIETORSHIP SHOULD INFLUENCE OUR USE OF THE WORLD AND THE THINGS THEREOF. If all things are God's, they should not be used (1) thoughtlessly, (2) irreverently, (3) selfishly, (4) injuriously, (5) contrary to his revealed will, (6) to the dishonour of his Name.

IV. GOD'S PROPRIETORSHIP EXTENDS TO OURSELVES. If "the earth is the Lord's, and the fulness thereof," *we* are his. 1. We are not our own. 2. Let us not think, feel, speak, or act as though we were.

V. IF WE ARE REDEEMED, WE SHARE IN GOD'S PROPRIETORSHIP. As children do in the possessions of their father. If we are in Christ, God is our Father. We have received the adoption of children. We are "heirs of God and joint-heirs with Christ."

How rich is the condition of the poorest believer! how exalted the status of the humblest! The way to power, dignity, and wealth is the way of the cross; for thus we become the inheritors of all things. "All things are yours."—H.

Ver. 31.—*The great rule of life.* I. WHAT IT IS. To seek the glory of God. There have been and are many life-rules; this alone is flawless. Many have themselves as life-ends. Some enjoin us to make the welfare of others our life-object, and preach to us "the greatest happiness of the greatest number," which would prove a very high and excellent object to aim at were it a little less obscure and a little more practicable; but it would not be *high enough* even then. God must be the Sun of our system, not ourselves or others. Then order and well-being result, but otherwise confusion, contradiction, chaos. When we truly seek God's glory, neither our own interest nor that of others will be prejudiced, but the reverse. This life-rule is: 1. *Reasonable.* As *creatures*, we should live to our Creator. All we have, and all we are, belong to God; it is intensely reasonable that they should be used for his pleasure. 2. *Beneficial.* It fulfils the object of our creation. If that object be frustrated, God is robbed, others are injured, and we cannot profit. Our life must be according to the Divine intent, or it will become pernicious all round. 3. *Joy-bringing.* We are "out of gear" until our lives are thus ordered. We may gain excitement, but we shall lack solid satisfaction. The joy of heaven arises from the fact that those in it live *for God;* heavenly *joy* comes to earth where heavenly *life* comes.

II. TO WHAT IT APPLIES. The answer is brief—*to everything.* It is a rule for *all* life, for *every part* of life. Note particularly that it applies to small things as well as great, to so-called secular things as to sacred. But the distinction is destroyed—*it makes all things sacred.* It saves anything *from becoming insignificant* by giving it this supreme significance, "the glory of God." It makes everything *interesting* and *useful.* The apostle particularizes such acts as eating and drinking—the most familiar and commonplace. A man should eat and drink so as to be fitted for serving God. How many by gluttony and wine-bibbing are unfitted! "Sunday religion" is a flagrant violation of the apostolic precept. Obedience will make our piety *continuous,* and there is no piety which is not so. How different our lives would be if this commandment were ever in our thoughts! What a check it would prove to self-seeking and to sin generally! How much we should have to discontinue because such things could not possibly be done to the Divine glory! How strangely beautiful our lives would become if we yielded a full obedience!

III. WHAT IT INVOLVES. 1. *Conversion.* However it may be with others, we to whom the gospel has come cannot live to the glory of God if we reject Christ. Apart from Christ we are the enemies of God. Our lives may be moral, but the rejection of Christ is like poison mixed with good food—resulting in a poisonous mass. We must come to God in the appointed way before we can serve him. There is a parallel passage to the text: "Whatsoever ye do in word or deed, *do all in the name of the Lord Jesus*" (Col. iii. 17). We must start at Calvary. We must be converted to God before we can glorify him. "They that are in the flesh cannot please God" (Rom. viii. 8). 2. *Direct service offered to God.* In worship. In Christian enterprise and labour. If we use the smaller opportunities of bringing glory to God, we shall not neglect the greater. The man who serves God in his home and business will seek to serve him also in the Church and in spheres of Christian usefulness. The man who professes to serve God on *one* day out of seven is more than open to suspicion, and so is the man who professes to serve God on *six.* 3. *Duties to ourselves.* Our duties to ourselves are our duties to God. We cannot glorify God unless we observe his laws, and many of these are directed towards our personal well-being. By self-improvement, by growth in grace, by increase in physical, mental, and spiritual health, we may glorify our Father who is in heaven. 4. *Duties to others.* The first and second commandments (Matt. xxii. 37—39) are indissolubly united. When we *truly* serve men we serve God. We may glorify God by seeking to advance the true interests of our fellow-creatures. Under the guidance of this principle, we shall: (1) Not offend men's consciences (ver. 28). (2) Not hinder them in their spiritual life or cause them to sin (ver. 32). (3) Earnestly seek their salvation (ver. 33). (4) Be willing to practise much self-denial (ver. 33).—H.

Vers. 1—4.—*Ancient types.* These incidents of patriarchal history were typical of what belongs to the Christian age (ver. 11). A "type" is one of two things—it is either a figure and prophecy of something to come, the antitype, in which the idea of the type finds its full and complete unfolding; or it is the example and representative of a class, combining and setting forth most distinctly the characteristics of that class. Both these meanings may to some extent be involved here, but we take the latter to be the more prominent and the more important. To say that these incidents mystically foreshadowed the "sacraments of the Christian Church," or that they are "a standing testimony to the importance of the Christian sacraments as necessary to the member-ship of Christ" (Alford); or to attempt to gather from them definite teaching as to the mode and order of those sacraments,—all this is to subordinate the inner truth and meaning of the subject to the mere accidental form. We take these incidents as typical of principles rather than ordinances, of living truths rather than of the ritual forms in which those truths may be embodied. There are three representative facts here.

I. THE CLOUD AND THE SEA. (For the narrative of the crossing of the Red Sea and the movement of the cloud, see Exod. xiv.) From this it would appear that the Israelites, in a very literal sense, passed "under the cloud and through the sea," *i.e.* through the bed and channel of it, through its very depths. The cloud was to them emphatically "a guide, a glory, a defence," and the divided sea the instrument of their deliverance—the grave of their enemies, but to them the gate into a region of freer, nobler life. See here a beautiful memorial of the grand truth of God's perpetual guidance and guardianship of his people. The Divine providence of human life, specially of all consecrated life, was thus made visibly, palpably manifest to the men of that age. The providence that assumes a variety of forms but is always animated by one and the same spirit; the providence that arranges circumstances and determines issues, that both marks out and clears the way, that shields from harm and avenges it, that interposes difficulties and also removes them, that leads into danger and then makes a way of escape; the ever-watchful, kindly, faithful providence of an all-wise Father, a gracious and almighty Redeemer;—it is this that we here see typically repre-sented. The miraculous apparition or incident, which in its very nature was local and temporary, did but bear witness to the universal and abiding fact. It is in accordance with our advanced position in the history of the kingdom of God that we should be thrown more entirely on the exercise of our faith for the apprehension of this, as of every other Divine truth. But the wing of the same beneficent providence is over us, though we have no such significant symbol of it. The overshadowing cloud leads us, often in "a way that we know not,"—it may be into the entanglement of mountain difficulties, through deep waters of sorrow, over waste wildernesses of unrest; but always in the right way, the way that is best fitted to "prove" us and to develop in us the needful moral qualities. And it is a way signalized often by unexpected deliverances. The mountains are not found to be so terrible as they seemed. The waters divide when we step down into them. The very wilderness abounds with fruits of tender, succouring love that we could scarcely have known if we had never entered it. The angel of the Lord still goes before his people as in the days of old—

> "Leader of faithful souls and guide
> Of all who travel to the sky."

II. THE BAPTISM UNTO MOSES. We regard this as referring to nothing in Christian baptism beyond the essential idea and principle of it. As a formal rite, there was nothing in the experience of the Israelites in coming out of Egypt that bears the remotest resemblance to it, and it is a waste of ingenuity to attempt to find out such a resemblance. But what is the essential moral meaning of this rite? It is consecration, dedication. It is a sign and a pledge, the avowal of a faith, the oath of an allegiance. In passing "under the cloud and through the sea," the fathers became the avowed followers of Moses. It was the pledge, the sign, the seal, of their allegiance to him as God's anointed "leader and commander of the people." And his leadership of that emancipated host did but dimly shadow forth Christ's headship of his ransomed Church (Heb. iii. 5, 6). As the uprising of that host, with all its tribes and families, at the call of Moses, was the formal pledge of submission to him, so our assumption of the sacred name of "Christian" commits us to the responsibility of following and obeying Christ. The supreme fact in the history of all the ages is God's redemption of the human race by Jesus Christ his Son. Through him God enters into a new relation to humanity. In him humanity rises into its true freedom and dignity. By him the kingdom of God upon earth is established, consummated, led on through varying fortunes to final victory and glorious everlasting rest. "The Head of every man is Christ." He bears to every man the triple relation of "Prophet, Priest, and King." Shall not this historical covenant relation of the fathers to Moses teach us seriously to consider how far we are worthily maintaining our true personal allegiance to *Him*?

III. The spiritual meat and drink. The word "spiritual," as applied to the manna and the water from the rock, refers to their supernatural origin, rather than to their essential quality. They were not the result of ordinary physical causes, but the direct and miraculous product of an unseen spiritual power. Whether, in saying the rock "followed them," the apostle gives countenance to a fanciful Jewish tradition or not, this deeper truth is sure—"that Rock was Christ." Both the manna from heaven and the water from the rock were shadows, the substance, the "body," of which is in Christ (John iv. 13, 14; vi. 32—35, 49—51). Here, again, is an old-world witness to that grand truth which is at once the centre and the circumference of the whole circle of Divine revelations—that in Christ alone is there life for the souls of men. He alone can satisfy their hunger and allay their thirst; he alone can nourish and build up the fabric of their being unto a blessed immortality. Faintly gleaming through those ancient types and figures, as in the morning twilight, it is to us the glorious, full-orbed revelation of the gospel day—life from God for a perishing world through Jesus Christ his Son. "This is the record," etc. (1 John v. 11). *The providence, the lordship, and the life-giving power of Christ* are the three great truths that we find typically represented in these historical memorials. How nobly did the lives of many of our fathers bear witness to their faith in these truths! The world in which they moved may have been strangely different in its outward aspects from ours, but the substantial realities of human life were the same.

"The old order changeth, giving place to new;"

but the vital principles that underlie that order change not. As regards the Divine relationships and the essential needs of our being, we stand just where our fathers did. We are encompassed by the same almighty power and love. We pass through the same kind of discipline, are exposed to the same dangers, realize the same deliverances, bear the same burdens of responsibility. We live by the same spiritual food, are saved by the same mercy, redeemed by the same atoning sacrifice. "All flesh is as grass, and all the glory of man as the flower of grass," etc. (1 Pet. i. 24, 25).—W.

Ver. 31.—*Eating and drinking to the glory of God.* The particular questions with which the apostle here deals may be of comparatively little interest to us, but, as usual in such cases, he brings to bear on them principles that affect the moral life of man in every age. So far as he speaks of the right or wrong of eating that which has been offered in sacrifice to idols, or attending heathen festivals, he is treating of what may have been of great moment to Corinthian Christians in apostolic times, but does not much concern us now. When, however, he says, "All things are lawful for me," etc.; "Let no man seek his own," etc.; "The earth is the Lord's," etc.; "Whether therefore ye eat, or drink, or whatsoever ye do, do all to the glory of God," he is laying down laws that are of universal and eternal obligation. Our aim must be to distinguish this vital and enduring element from all that is local and temporary; to extract from that which may seem foreign to our interest those Divine lessons that bear on the deepest realities of our individual and social life. Here, then, lies one grand condition of all true nobility of character and deed. Every man is great and honourable in proportion as he makes the "glory of God" the definite and conscious aim of his existence. "Whether therefore ye eat or drink," etc. Note respecting this apostolic exhortation—

I. The ground on which it rests—the absolute sovereignty of God's claims. The twofold character of this Divine right is recognized. 1. *Natural proprietorship.* "The earth is the Lord's," etc. (vers. 26, 28; Ps. xxiv. 12); "Of him, and through him, and to him, are all things : to whom be glory for ever" (Rom. xi. 36). The end of all creatural existence must needs be the glory of him who created it. In proportion as we recognize the fact that all the springs of our being are in God, that all the faculties of our nature, all the resources, materials, and relations of our life are from him, we shall feel that our existence answers its true end, life is worth living, just so far as it fulfils his purposes. 2. *Personal redemption.* There is a more tender but not less powerful claim established by that marvellous act of grace of which the "table of the Lord," with its "cup of blessing" and its "broken bread," is the perpetual memorial. "Ye are not your own, ye are bought with a price," etc. (ch. vi. 19, 20). Here is a proprietorship superadded to that of the original and natural relation. See the fatherhood of God as it appears in the cross of Jesus, and the sovereignty of his claims comes home to you, not with the mere force of natural authority, but with the resistless persuasiveness of unparalleled self-surrendering love.

II. THE SENSE OF MORAL FREEDOM IN US TO WHICH IT MAKES ITS APPEAL. The essential dignity of our nature is implied in this assertion of God's claims over us. The inferior creatures show forth his glory by fulfilling the ends for which he has created them, but their service is rendered by a law and necessity of their being which they have no power to resist. The myriad forms of lower life that people the earth and air and sea cannot but obey the instincts of their nature, and in that blind, instinctive obedience the end of their existence is attained. To us alone belongs the mysterious, self-regulating power by which it lies with ourselves to determine whether we will respond to the Divine appeal or refuse to do so. These inferior creatures of God, all of which in themselves "are good" (1 Tim. iv. 4), are intended to be the instruments of our higher purpose. We are "crowned with glory and honour" above them all, that we may interpret their voices and utilize their powers in presenting to him our living tribute of gratitude and love and service. Our daily life, in its deeper moral meaning, proclaims how far this is really the case with us. As every new day dawns upon us, God throws it upon us afresh to decide whether we will "use the world" as we ought to use it by living to his glory, or will "abuse it" by following the impulses of our own self-will and serving the idols of our own imagination or carnal appetite.

III. THE FAMILIAR COMMONPLACE FIELD OF INTEREST IN WHICH IT IS TO BE FUL-FILLED. "Whether ye eat or drink," etc. The simplest materials of our life are to be consecrated to his service, and the meanest doings of life are to be made designedly a tribute to his praise. We greatly err if we imagine certain things to be so purely physical or so trivial as to have nothing to do with the sublimer interests and responsibilities of our being. You learn the deepest truth of things only when you come to see spiritual principles and laws and issues enshrined in them; that every-thing, in fact, in the root of it, in its inmost heart and core, is spiritual, and bears some relation to that higher part of us which will endure for ever. No doubt life is for the most part an aggregate of many little things. To some it may seem but a monotonous round of trivialities—the same things done day after day in the same way and to the same end, and that an end of very little moment. But may not the noblest principles of moral feeling and life, as motive powers, be underlying these seemingly insignificant activities, and making them really great? Infuse something of the wealth of a devout and godly soul into them, and the meanest doings of your life become no longer mean. That inner, invisible greatness of holy thought and feeling makes them great. There is no motive so lofty but it may be brought to bear upon the so-called trifles that make up the story of our days. The minutest movements of the material world around us are effected by the same forces as govern the most majestic.

> "The very law that moulds a tear
> And makes it trickle from its source,
> That law preserves the earth a sphere
> And guides the planets in their course."

So may the grand motives of reverence for God and love to the Saviour give shape and beauty, consistence and harmony, to everything we do. And then, he who "seeth not as man seeth," who recognizes none of our distinctions of great and small, will accept it as a welcome tribute to his praise. The poor widow's consecration of her "two mites" to the Lord's treasury, the "cup of cold water" given to the disciple in the name of a disciple, the simplest act of real Christian service and self-sacrificing love,— these are as pleasing to him as the heroism of a Paul compassing sea and land with painful toil and travail that he may win souls, or a Luther daring the dark powers of earth and hell in his brave witness for the truth. Learn to fill your common everyday life with the inspiration of a high and holy purpose. This will make it far other than it seems to be, more real, more satisfying, less like a mere feverish pursuit of unsub-stantial shadows. It will then become a thing of imperishable beauty and worth. Its outward incidents will be but as the scaffolding within which the structure of a holy character and glorious destiny is being raised. The outer form of it will be a matter of small concern to you so that that interior work is going on well. Take this spiritual view of things, and yours shall be indeed a consecrated life, in which every work you do will be as a " sacrament," and every step you take will lead you nearer to your home in God.—W.

Vers. 3, 4.—*Meat and drink for God's people.* By a few master strokes of his pen St. Paul indicated the typical significance of Israel's life in the wilderness. His object in these allusions to the Old Testament was to correct party spirit among the Greek Christians of the first century, by showing that, like the tribes of Israel in the old time, the people of Christ are one in respect of their redemption and consolation in him. As all the Hebrew fathers were delivered from slavery in Egypt, so all the Christians are delivered from the bondage of the flesh. As all of them were baptized unto Moses in the cloud and the sea, so all the Christians have been baptized into Christ by death and burial with him. As all of them ate of the manna from the Lord, so all Christians have the same spiritual food ; and as all of them drank of the water from the smitten rock in Horeb, so all Christians drink of the same spiritual Rock, which is Christ. Thus what God did for Israel, he did for all ; what he gave to Israel, he gave to all that people. It was the fault of the people that this unity was broken. " Some of them were idol-aters ; " " some of them committed fornication ; " " some of them tempted the Lord ; " " some of them murmured." Christians should mark this, and beware lest any of them, through temptations to idolatry, fleshliness, or wilfulness, forfeit what the Lord has provided for all of them without respect of persons. Here are the necessaries of the spiritual as of the natural life—food and drink, bread and water.

I. SPIRITUAL FOOD. The Israelites got manna as a direct and free gift from God. Christians receive Christ as " the true Bread which came down from heaven," a direct and a free gift from God. The bread is his flesh which he has given for the life of the world ; *i.e.* Christ nourishes his people through the efficacy of his atonement. Who-soever heartily believes in Christ crucified eats by faith of the flesh which is heavenly bread. The emphasis in this passage lies on the words, " They all did eat the same." In the wilderness, every family of the whole redeemed nation ate daily of exactly the same bread with every other family. Moses himself partook of the manna, and so did the lowest of the people. There was no difference between the princes of Israel and the feeblest in the tribes, between the old people and the children, or between masters and servants. All partook of the same daily bread. So there is the same Christ for all of us. Believers have the same life and the same support or staff of life. No matter what social and intellectual distinctions may be among us, or what varieties of view on secondary points ; in this we are at one, that we have the same spiritual food. And we show this when we all partake together of the Lord's Supper.

II. SPIRITUAL DRINK. The water from the rock at Horeb not only supplied the immediate want, but was of use to the tribes of Israel for many days. Now, that rock signified Christ. Jehovah said to Moses, " I will stand before thee there upon the rock in Horeb." So God is now before us in Christ Jesus, able and willing to satisfy all the poor and needy whose hearts faint and " fail them for thirst." Christ as the Rock smitten is a Fountain of life, available to us now, and not now only, but all our lives long. As the bread resolves itself into the flesh, so the stream also into the precious blood of Christ. We eat the flesh and drink the blood of the Son of man, according to his own teaching at Capernaum. Thus we are again brought to the fact and virtue of the atonement. That which it would be gross and intolerable to eat and drink after a literal and carnal manner, is, after a spiritual manner, full of sweetness and strength. And again, the emphasis is on the participation by all Christians of the same spiritual drink, which is symbolized in the Lord's Supper. "The cup of blessing which we bless, is it not the communion of the blood of Christ?" Other Scriptures follow more closely the idea of water gushing from a rocky fountain. As the blood of Christ signifies his atonement, so the water is a sign of the communication of the Holy Ghost. By the former our Lord gives peace to the conscience; by the latter, cleansing and healing to the heart. Christ, our Rock, spoke more than once of his power to impart to all comers the water of life (John iv. 10—14; vii. 37—39). And now, as from a height above the plain on which his people still walk as pilgrims, our Saviour in heaven gives this water to the thirsty. To it all are welcome. Water is no luxury for the few, but an acknowledged universal necessary of life; and so a participation of the Spirit of life in Christ Jesus is no privilege of a few superlative Christians, but necessary to the inward life of every one who is a Christian at all. "If any man have not the Spirit of Christ, he is none of his." How can a rock follow? The rock in Horeb did not move from its place, but followed the people in the stream which issued from it and flowed through the lower levels of the wilderness. So Jesus Christ remains at God's right hand; yet is with us always in the continual efficacy of his shed blood and the continual fellowship of his Holy Spirit. The fountain never runs dry. We never find anything less than fulness in him. And there is no need to go on a long pilgrimage to our sacred well. The Rock follows us.

III. How TO GET THIS NOURISHMENT. By grace, through faith. When the children of Israel saw the manna, they "wist not what it was." Then Moses told them from God what it was, and bade them gather it, "every man according to his eating." So now, men do not know of themselves what Christ is; but it is preached or proclaimed as from God that this is the true Bread. Take, and eat, and live. Why should any household be without the heavenly Bread? When the rock was smitten, no one stood by but Moses and the elders, who had gone in advance of the host. One can imagine those elders hastening back to the camp, and calling aloud to the several tribes, "Water! water! Ho, every one that thirsteth, come to the waters!" Shall we who have found life and peace in Jesus Christ hold our peace? Nay, but we call to every thirsty soul, "Come, and drink, and live."—F.

Ver. 2.—*Baptism unto Moses.* The expression used here is a singular and suggestive one, and one that seems to require an enlargement of our associations with the term "baptized." "Were all baptized unto Moses in the cloud and in the sea." It may be noted that more precisely the passage should read, "all baptized themselves unto Moses." St. Paul sees, in the incidents of the crossing of the Red Sea under the guidance of the pillar-cloud, a symbol of that Christian *confession* which puts us wholly under the redeemings and guidings of the Lord Jesus Christ. For the incidents, see Exod. xiv. 21, 22. The point is that the "fathers," the "Israelites," voluntarily dedicated themselves to the leadership of Moses when they went through the waters at his command. They came up out of the waters, on the further shore, a new people, devoted to Moses as the earthly ruler representing Jehovah. "The Israelites were baptized '*unto Moses*' because, by passing through the cloud and the sea, they had become connected with him, dependent on his commands and guidance." F. W. Robertson well points out the reason for the warnings here given. "The peril of the Corinthian Church lay in their false security. They were tempted to think that all things were safe to do, because all things were lawful. They were ready to rest satisfied with the knowledge that they were God's people and God's Church. Now, the apostle shakes this sense of their safety by reminding them that the ancient Church of Israel fell, although it had the same privileges; therefore he infers that spiritual privileges are not perfect security. Now, the argument by which he proves that the privileges of ancient Israel were similar to theirs is remarkable. That people had a baptism as well as they, and a spiritual food and drink. Baptism is the solemn profession of our Christianity; and the passing through the Red Sea was the Israelites' profession of discipleship to Moses." Here, then, baptism is the symbol of confession, or profession; it is the act by which we voluntarily yield ourselves to the leadership of another. This may receive four illustrations.

I. COMPARE JOHN'S BAPTISM. Observe the connection between John's teaching and John's rite. Those who accepted his teaching yielded themselves to his leadership by

the act of submitting to his rite.   He led them to a change in their ideas and expectations of Messiah which should have prepared them to recognize in him a spiritual
Saviour—a Saviour from sin.   Through voluntary submission to John's baptism, they
publicly confessed themselves to be John's disciples.

II. COMPARE OUR LORD'S BAPTISMS.   It does not appear that he personally baptized
any one; but his disciples did so in his Name.   Here, again, the act was a public and
outward acknowledgment or confession of the Messiahship of Christ, and a voluntary
submission to his rule and law.   It was the faith of the disciple gaining expression in
a solemn public act.   It brought the disciple under our Lord's leadership, just as following Moses into the sea involved full submission to his guidance.

III. COMPARE ST. PAUL'S TEACHING ABOUT BAPTISM.   It is always with him the
equivalent of confession.   It is confession by an *act* rather than by a *word*.   Such
confession St. Paul declares to be an absolute necessity for salvation.   With characteristic
point and force, he even makes it as necessary as faith, saying in Rom. x. 9, "If thou
shalt confess with thy mouth the Lord Jesus, and shalt believe in thine heart that God
hath raised him from the dead, thou shalt be saved."   And from this St. Paul argues
that we are now, by our own consecration, "under law to Christ."   "We serve the
Lord Christ."

IV. COMPARE PRESENT-DAY DISCIPLESHIP.   The rite is perhaps less regarded, but that
which it stands for is still essential.   Impress that the following things are the proper
stages of religious experience :—1. Repentance, with due forsaking of sinful ways.
2. Faith in Christ as able to grant forgiveness and to give life.   3. Confession of Christ,
by some form of voluntary and public testimony.   4. Full and submissive practical
obedience to his rule and law in everyday life and conduct.—R. T.

Vers. 3, 4.—*The spiritual meat and drink.*   Give account of the historical facts to
which the apostle refers.   It seems as if he had in mind also the Jewish tradition that
the rock—*i.e.* a fragment broken off from the rock smitten by Moses—followed the
Israelites through their journey.   St. Paul sees, in that symbol of the Divine presence
and providing, an aid towards our realizing the gracious abiding presence of the Lord
Jesus Christ with his Church.   His point here is that God's people, in the olden times
and still, are divinely *led* and divinely *fed ;* so no excuse for apostasy can be found in any
"straitening in God."

I. DIVINELY LED.   By God in the pillar-cloud that loomed dark against the clear
sky by day, but shone like fire at night, and moved or rested to direct the people's
journeyings.   By God's power through the Red Sea, whose waters were held back,
making a great pathway over the dried sands.   The fact of such leadings ought to have
bound the people to Jehovah in everlasting bonds.   Then show what is the answering
Christian fact to this, and how, when we are brought to Christ, a new light shines upon
the wondrous providences of our whole lives, and so we feel freshly bound to our Lord,
and say—

"Jesus, still lead on,
Till our rest be won."

II. DIVINELY FED.   By God in the provision of the manna day by day.   By God in
the smitten rock, that provided in a miraculous manner for them when natural supplies
failed.   Such daily signs of Divine presence and care ought to have held them fast to
daily obedience and service.   Then we may realize that (1) the manna answers to
Christ, the Bread of life for us; and (2) the water answers to Christ, the Rock sorely
smitten for us.   And then we should feel how, in the daily provisions of Christ's grace
in the supply of all our need, we are bound to his service, daily urged to "yield ourselves unto him, and our members instruments of righteousness unto his service."—R. T.

Ver. 11.—*Ensamples from the wilderness-life.*   The words of this verse may be better
rendered, "happened unto them *typically.*"   "The real point of the passage is—These
things which occurred to them are to be looked upon by us, not merely as interesting
historical events, but as having a typical significance.   Their record remains as a standing warning that great privileges may be enjoyed by many, and used by them to their
destruction."   In introducing this subject, dwell on the mission of history and biography

in relation to education and culture. If science and mathematics bear most powerfully on *mental* training, history and biography are the most important agencies in *moral* culture. As the poet Longfellow says—

> " Lives of great men all remind us
> We may make our lives sublime."

There is an important sense in which there is "nothing new under the sun." Circumstances, situations, and the relations of men to them, constantly repeat themselves; with sufficient variety, indeed, to give individuality and to impress responsibility, but with sufficient sameness for us to recognize the adaptation of the warning or the example *to us*. One age can become thus a power upon another, but the power is related to general principles rather than to minute details. So the records of ancient and Eastern life, given to us in Holy Scripture, become a gracious power on us. The records have been written for our admonition, upon whom the "ends of the age" are come. The story of ancient Israel, especially in the forty years of its wilderness-life, is for the most part one of warning. As such, the apostle here calls it to mind. We may find in it warning of four possible perils.

I. YIELDING TO BODILY PASSIONS. In all ages there are found indications of man's danger from the corrupt inclinations of his own body. Adam and Eve sinned by yielding the conscience of duty to the bodily inclination ; and brought upon the race an undue force of carnal passion, which makes the life-conflict to win righteousness a heavy and a hard one for every man. Some have felt this so deeply that they have thought virtue must come by the crushing down of the body, the absolute repression of all its inclinations. This is the inspiring thought which has driven men into hermits' caves and monkish cells ; but it is a truer conception of life that regards the body as providing the very conditions of our moral trial ; and the problem for us to work out is the conquering and efficient using of every power and faculty. The Christian triumph is to know how to "possess the vessel of our body in sanctification and honour." This may be illustrated from the perils of the Corinthian Christians, who had to live in the midst of a society where bodily pleasure reigned supreme. The passions by which we may be overcome are : 1. *Self-indulgence ;* over-responding to the appetites for (1) food, (2) drink, (3) society, (4) pleasure, (5) learning, (6) art. All for our use and for our good ; but all may be unduly pursued, to our moral peril. 2. *Sensuality ;* the passions which bear relation to our life-associations. It is important to learn, from the example of the Israelites, and from the usual scenes at pagan and heathen festivals, that unusual excitement in religion fosters the sensual passions into undue strength.

II. YIELDING TO IDOLATRY. It may seem as if no such peril could be near to us in these Christian times. But the Apostle John starts us upon searching thoughts of our own dangers when he says, "Little children, keep yourselves from idols." For us now, (1) children may be idols ; (2) friends may be ; (3) success may be ; (4) our house and home may be ; (5) our pursuits may be ; for an idol is anything in a man's life which succeeds in pushing itself before God.

III. YIELDING TO PRESUMPTION. (Ver. 9.) David shows a remarkable insight of his own frailty when he prays, "Keep back thy servant also from presumptuous sins ; let them not have dominion over me." This is the subtle peril of advanced and experienced Christian life. A man may take advantage of God ; presume upon what is his will, without asking him ; and even may put God to the test ; these being sure signs of lost humility and lost childlike dependence. It was the sin of Rebekah ; she presumed on the promise made her concerning Jacob, and so was set upon trying to fulfil the promise by schemes of her own.

IV. YIELDING TO COMPLAINING. (Ver. 10.) A peril that comes to us all when the circumstances of life will not go "according to our mind." Troubles and disappointments and failures are Divine testings of our professed *trust ;* and for us to complain and fret and murmur is plainly to show lost submission and lost trust. He never complains who holds firmly the assurance that "all things work together for good to them that love God."—R. T.

Ver. 12.—*Self-security is insecurity.* Over-confidence in a religious profession is one of the most perilous of Christian faults. He who presumes upon his position and his privileges is only too likely to be unwatchful of his conduct. A solemn lesson is learned from the wilderness-life of God's people Israel. Though so honoured, so guarded, so guided, and so provided for, only a very few of those who came out of Egypt kept their faithfulness and were permitted to enter the "promised land." "It is not sufficient to have beeen admitted into the Christian covenant; we need watchfulness in order to use our privileges aright" (Rom. xi. 20). I. Distinguish between the man who "standeth" and the man who "thinketh he standeth." 2. The man who "standeth" is not, necessarily, in any danger of falling. 3. The man who "thinketh he standeth" has just cause to fear. So we are led to understand that a man's moral peril never lies merely in the circumstances in which he is placed; never merely in his outward surroundings, but always in his *inward moods*—in his conditions of mind and feeling, and the relations in which they set him towards outward circumstances. Our standing or our falling depends on our heart-rightness. Anywhere we might stand if but our heart be right with God. Everywhere we must fall if we fail to "keep our heart with all diligence." And what may we regard as the one essential thing in heart-rightness? Surely it is the *humility* that keeps us ever leaning hard on our strong Lord, hiding in him when calamities come nigh, doing all things only "through him that strengtheneth us." It may be urged, in conclusion, that the falls of the self-secure and over-confident are usually sudden, violent, and overwhelming falls; though even these may be only permitted to break down the over-confidence and to humble them under God's mighty hand.—R. T.

Ver. 13.—*The commonness of our temptation.* "No temptation taken you but such as is common to man." In Christian experience there is constant fresh surprise at the forms which temptation can take ; and one of our gravest difficulties arises from our fear that the forms are special to us—such as no others have known. We are thus led to think that we must battle with the temptation alone, since we can hope to gain no real help from the sympathy or the experience of our Christian brethren. It is a great joy to us when we find out that all the ages are linked together in a common experience of the possible forms of temptations. Human nature is the same in every age and every place. The corruption of human nature shows itself in the same forms among all classes. Even in what we think to be quite subtle and peculiar forms of sinful inclination and passion, we are really but sharing a common experience ; our temptation is one that is common to men. Again and again, as life advances, we find this out, often with a great surprise; and, although the finding it out does not relieve us from the conflict with the evil, it does relieve us from the strain of feeling that our experience is unique, our tempter a hitherto unconquered one. We seem to gain new strength when we can say, "Our brothers have mastered this very foe many a time; and God has adapted his grace to those tempted just as I am over and over again." The Revised Version gives a somewhat different turn to the sentence : "There hath no temptation taken you but such as *man can bear* ;" i.e. such as is fairly within the limitations of a human and earthly experience.

I. TEMPTATION IS A COMMON HUMAN EXPERIENCE. It is a necessity of our probationary state; it is the condition of our changing the mere innocence of ignorance for the virtue that comes by knowledge and will. If God were pleased to give us, as moral creatures, the discernment between right and wrong, with a distinct understanding that he stood by the right, then he must set his creatures in the midst of circumstances which would test their good will towards the right. So, in one sense, temptations around us, taking their thousandfold forms, make the battle and the bitterness of our human life. But, in another sense, our surrounding of temptation is but the great sphere in which we are to win holiness and virtue. None of us can get out of the way of temptation. It goes with us where we go, because God will not leave us alone : he wants us to be *holy*.

II. CHRISTIAN LIFE IS NOT EXEMPT FROM TEMPTATION. It cannot be too fully shown that becoming a Christian never alters a man's circumstances; it only alters *his relation to the circumstances*. The laws of life rule on for the Christian and the unrenewed man ; and, from his higher position, the Christian has still to see all virtue wrung from the tempter. Temptation may even take more subtle and perilous forms for the

Christian. His new thought and feeling may even discover temptations where duller souls would miss them.

III. THE RELATIONS IN WHICH GOD STANDS TO TEMPTATION, AS AFFECTING THE CHRISTIAN. Here three points need treatment. 1. God modifies the temptation to the *bearing power* of the man to whom it comes. We may be sure that God will "not suffer us to be tempted above that we are able." 2. God will provide the necessary *escapes* either *from* or *through* the temptation. 3. God comforts with gracious *promises* and assurances, to which he is ever faithful. "God permits the temptation by allowing the circumstances which create temptation to arise, but he takes care that no fate bars the path of retreat." Then "all that a Christian has to do is to live in humble dependence upon him, neither perplexed in the present nor anxious for the future." —R. T.

Ver. 16.—*The communion of souls in Christ.* These words are uttered in illustration of an important practical principle, which St. Paul is urging as sufficient to guide the Corinthians safely through many of the difficulties of the Christian life. Explain the question, which threatened to break up the unity and peace of the Church at Corinth, whether "a Christian man was justified in eating meat which had been offered in sacrifice to idols." Show under what circumstances of social life this question arose, and the different ways in which persons of different temperament were disposed to treat it. St. Paul in no way encourages superstitious notions, but he pleads that consideration for others and Christian charity will readily decide our conduct in every case that may arise. Having had to refer to the heathen feasts, he is led to think of the one Christian feast. He says that is a sealing of the union of all who love the Lord Jesus Christ; it is a joint partaking as it were of the redemption, and so a community of sentiment and feeling and life which involves that each member shall be concerned for the highest well-being of the others, and willing to put his own preferences aside if they stand in the way of his brother's good. We have two subjects here brought before us,— (1) The reality of the communion of souls in Christ; and (2) the value of a symbolical feast which will assert that communion.

I. THE REALITY OF THE COMMUNION OF SOULS IN CHRIST. The word "communion" is often applied to the intercourse of friendship, the fellowship of two kindred souls between whom there is a recognized community of sentiment and feeling. The word is applied to our privilege of access to God; we are said to have communion with God, with his Son Jesus Christ, and with the Holy Ghost. But the term would be more precisely applied to that feeling of mutual interest which two persons have in each other because of their common interest in some object, or common love to some third person. We may not even be personally known to each other, but if we are both interested in the same thing, and working for the same ends, we have "communion" with one another. Illustrate that this is the basis on which societies and associations of men are formed. Those who have the same love to the Lord Jesus Christ feel that they are bound to one another; they gather themselves into Churches that they may have "communion" with each other. Christianity demands love to a Person. It sets forth one Person, the *One* who is worthy to receive the devotion of every soul. Usually, indeed, if two love one person, there rises a deadly jealousy and hatred between them, but that only springs from the fact that both cannot possess the object of their affection *in the same sense;* but even here on earth there are many cases in which two may love the same person, and find their common love brings them nearer to each other. You may fall into conversation with a fellow-traveller, and may find that you both know and love some third person, and at once all strangeness passes, and you converse together as do long-known friends. Now, the Lord Jesus Christ can be as much to one believer as to another. He can be *all* to each one, and so there need be no jealousy, but mutual love for Christ may make it easy for us to love each other. But our text significantly calls our communion the "communion of the *blood* and *body* of Christ;" and this we must try to understand. In the story of the heathen gods there is generally some one *incident* which is regarded as specially characteristic of each one, and from which he may even take his name or fashion his symbol. Something of the same kind may be observed in Scripture and modern biographies. There is some event of the life which is regarded above all others as revealing the man. Thus we have in the Bible, Jacob the supplanter, Moses the meek, impulsive Peter, etc., the qualifying terms recalling some characteristic incident. In the reference of the text to the "body and blood of Christ" we have something of the same kind. Everything in the life of Jesus is of supreme concern to us, but the Christian heart has always regarded the "body-breaking and blood-shedding" as the characteristic incident, the one so peculiarly significant as revealing the person, the spirit, and the mission of the Lord Jesus. That "body and blood" reveal to us these things—duty, love, self-sacrifice. This trinity expresses the very essence of Christ's religion. And "communion in the body and the blood" is the fellowship of those in whom the essential spirit of Christianity is found; who are toned and ruled by *duty*, out of their sonship to God; by *love*, because the "love of Christ is shed abroad in their hearts;" by *self-sacrifice*, because the spirit of their Master has become theirs. Those who have thus "communion in the body and the blood" can enter into the meaning and power of that "cup of blessing which we bless," and of that "bread which we break."

II. THE VALUE OF A SYMBOLICAL ACT WHICH WILL ASSERT THAT COMMUNION. As in everything, so in respect of symbols, two extremes are possible, and both are to be avoided. He is *un*human who thinks he may refuse the help of any symbol. He is *too* human who multiplies symbols, glorifies symbols, until *they* occupy all his thought, and he has no room for the realities of which they should testify. Symbols of spiritual things will be not only useful, they will be necessary, so long as we are in the body. We have embraced *spiritual* truths, but they came to us in symbolic words; they are represented to us in symbolic acts. There can be no question as to our *need* of symbols; the only questions concern their character and their kind. Our Lord met our need in the institution of the "Lord's Supper," the "communion of the body and the blood." We are drawn into a great and tender fellowship as we share together the one loaf, as we make affirmation of our common life in Christ; and our communion finds fitting expression in a gentle patience with our brother's failings, a loving consideration for even our brother's prejudices, and a cheerful willingness to put our own preferences aside, if they grieve or hinder our brethren.—R. T.

Ver. 24.—*The primary law of Christian association.* "Let no man seek his own, but every man another's wealth;" the word "wealth" being here used in the general sense of "well-being," and, more especially, "moral well-being" (comp. Rom. xv. 1—3; Phil. ii. 4). Here is given to us—

I. THE PRIMARY LAW OF HUMAN ASSOCIATION. It is the law of brotherhood which leads us to regard our brother's interests as of more importance than our own. Show how such a law universally working would, of necessity, make a heaven of earth. But it may be said, "Are we not to care for ourselves, and consider our own interests?" We shall not need to do so if, while we care for our brother's well-being, that brother is as anxious to put his own aside that he may secure ours. In the *mutuality* of our service will lie our common safety, and our common blessing. To this height, of a practically working brotherliness, Christianity is seeking to uplift the world.

II. THE HINDRANCES TO THE WORK OF THIS LAW PUT BY HUMAN SELFISHNESS. Sin repeats before God, age after age, the words of the self-seeking Cain, "Am I my brother's keeper?" An exaggeration of the distinction between "mine and thine" keeps men separate from each other, and makes the separation take all sorts of forms of class-distinction.

III. THE RESTORATION OF THE LAW TO ITS FULL POWER THROUGH THE ADOPTION OF THE CHRISTIAN PRINCIPLE. What shall bring men together in mutual helpfulness? Try society schemes, bonds of commerce, ameliorations through education and science. None of these can reach the very root of selfishness. But if we could win a supreme love for Christ and full consecration to him, we would be sure to "love our brother also;" and find out practically how to "seek another's wealth."—R. T.

Vers. 31—33.—*All for God will be all for men.* "Do all to the glory of God;" and then it will not be difficult for you to "please all men in all things . . . seeking the profit of many, that they may be saved." "No act of life is in itself either religious or secular. The quality of each act depends on the spirit which guides it and the motive from which it springs. The commonest thing may be done in a high Christian spirit. The greatest deed may spring from a low and selfish motive." "The glory of God, that is to be the end of all your actions." And St. Paul ventures to affirm that the man who holds a supreme purpose—to glorify God, will be found the kindest, most generous, and most helpful man by all his fellow-men.

I. THIS IS AN ACTUAL FACT. The truly pious are the truly philanthropical. Illustrate from the general influence of Christianity in securing care for the suffering and the poor; and from individual cases, such as those of Howard, Wilberforce, Nightingale, etc.; appeal may also be made to cases within our personal experience. A weak recognition of the claims of the brotherhood is one of the surest signs of a frail, unnourished piety.

II. IT IS REASONABLE THAT THIS SHOULD BE THE ACTUAL FACT. This may be argued: 1. From the impression of the fatherhood of God which the Christian gains. If he turn his eyes down from up-looking to the Father, he cannot fail to see the *Father's children*. 2. From the growth of Christian life, which is a changing into God's image, until we come to think about his children as he thinks, and to work for them as he works. 3. From that simple, unquestioning obedience to God's will which would surely characterize us if we really held all for God and were set upon securing "his glory."—R. T.

EXPOSITION.

CHAPTER XI.

Ver. 1.—**Followers of me**; rather, *imitators of me;* follow herein my example, as I follow Christ's. What Christ's example was, in that he too "pleased not himself," he sets forth in Rom. xv. 1—3; and the general principle of self-abnegation for the sake of others in Phil. ii. 4—8. This verse ought to be included in ch. x. It sums up the whole argument, and explains the long digression of ch. ix. **As I also am of Christ.** This limits the reference to his own example. I only ask you to imitate me in points in which I imitate Christ.

Vers. 2—16.—*Rules and principles respecting the covering of the head by women in Church assemblies.*

Ver. 2.—**Now**; rather, *but, on the other hand.* **That ye remember me in all things, and keep**, etc. This is probably a quotation from their letter. He thanks them for this kind message, but points out one particular in which their practice was not quite commendable. **The ordinances.** The word literally means *traditions,* but is here rightly applied to rules which he had *delivered* to them. The Vulgate has *præcepta.* The word is used in Matt. xv. 2 of the rules and precedents laid down by the rabbis.

Ver. 3.—**But I would have you know;** rather, *but I wish you to know.* **That the head of every man is Christ.** St. Paul, as was customary with him, applies the loftiest principles to the solution of the humblest difficulties. Given a question as to what is right or wrong in a particular instance, he always aims at laying down some great eternal fact to which the duty or decision is ultimately referable, and deduces the required rule from that fact. The head-

ship of Christ is stated in Eph. i. 22; iv. 15; and its application to the superiority of man is laid down also in Eph. v. 23. The subordinate position of the woman is also stated in 1 Tim. ii. 11, 12; 1 Pet. iii. 1, 5, 6, etc. This, however, is merely an ordinance of earthly application. In the spiritual realm "there is neither male nor female" (Gal. iii. 28). **The head of the woman is the man.** In Christ the distinctions of the sexes are done away. It was, perhaps, an abuse of this principle which had led the Corinthian women to assert themselves and their rights more prominently than decorum warranted. **The head of Christ is God.** That Christ is "inferior to the Father as touching his manhood," that his mediatorial kingdom involves (so far) a subordination of his coequal Godhead, has been already stated in ch. iii. 23, and is further found in ch. xv. 27, 28. This too is the meaning of John xiv. 28, "My Father is greater than I."

Ver. 4.—**Prophesying**; that is, *preaching.* **Having** his head covered. This was a Jewish custom. The Jewish worshipper in praying always covers his head with his *tallith.* The Jew (like Orientals generally) uncovered his feet because the place on which he stood was holy ground; but he covered his head by way of humility, even as the angels veil their faces with their wings. Æneas is said by Servius to have introduced this custom into Italy. On the other hand, the Greek custom was to pray with the head uncovered. St. Paul—as some discrepancy of custom seems to have arisen—decided in favour of the Greek custom, on the high ground that Christ, by his incarnation, became man, and therefore the Christian, who is "in Christ," may stand with unveiled head in the presence of his Father. **Dishonoureth his head.** He dishonoureth his own head, which is as it were a sharer in the glory of Christ, who is Head of the whole Church. "We pray," says Tertullian, "with bare heads because we blush not." The Christian, being no longer a slave, but a son (Gal. iv. 7), may claim his part in the glory of the eternal Son. The head was covered in *mourning* (2 Sam. xv. 30; Jer. xiv. 13), and the worship of the Christian is joyous.

Ver. 5.—Or prophesieth. Although St. Paul "thinks of one thing at a time," and is not here touching on the question whether women ought to teach in public, it appears from this expression that the rule which he lays down in ch. xiv. 34, 35, and 1 Tim. ii. 12 was not meant to be absolute. See the case of Philip's daughters (Acts xxi. 9 and ii. 17). **With her head uncovered.** For a woman to do this in a public assembly was against the national custom of all ancient communities, and might lead to the gravest misconceptions. As a rule, modest women covered their heads with the *peplum* or with a veil when they worshipped or were in public. Christian women at Corinth must have caught something of the "inflation" which was characteristic of their Church before they could have acted with such reprehensible boldness as to adopt a custom identified with the character of immodest women. **Dishonoureth her head.** Calvin, with terse good sense, observes, "As the man honours his head by proclaiming his liberty, so the woman by acknowledging her subjection."

Ver. 6.—Let her also be shorn. Not a command, but a sort of scornful inference, or *reductio ad absurdum*. **If it be a shame for a woman to be shorn or shaven.** When a woman was tried by "the ordeal of the water of jealousy," her head was uncovered by the priest (Numb. v. 18). To be shorn or shaven was a sign of mourning (Deut. xxi. 12), and was a disgrace inflicted on adulteresses.

Ver. 7.—He is the image and glory of God. Because he reflects and partakes in the glory of Christ, who is the effulgence of God and the impress of his substance (Gen. i. 27; Ps. viii. 6; Heb. i. 2). **The woman is the glory of the man.** As moonlight is to sunlight, or as the earthshine is to the moonshine. Man reflects God; woman, in her general nature in this earthly and temporal dispensation, reflects the glory of man.

Ver. 8.—But the woman of the man. An allusion to Gen. ii. 21, 22.

Ver. 9.—But the woman for the man. As is expressly stated in Gen. ii. 18.

Ver. 10.—To have power on her head. A great deal of irrelevant guesswork has been written on this verse. Under this head must be classed the idle attempts to twist the word *exousia*, power, or authority, into some other reading—an attempt which may be set aside, because it is not sanctioned by a single manuscript. We may also dismiss the futile efforts to make *exousia* have any other primary meaning than "authority." The *context* shows that the word has here a *secondary* sense, and implies *some kind of covering*. The verse, therefore, points the same lessons as Gen. xxiv. 64, 65. This much may be regarded as certain, and this view is adopted by the steadfast good sense of our English translators, both in the Authorized and Revised Versions. The only question worth asking is *why* the word *exousia* had come at Corinth, or in the Corinthian Church, to be used for "a veil," or "covering." The simplest answer is that just as the word "kingdom" in Greek may be used for "a crown" (comp. *regno* as the name of the pope's tiara), so "*authority*" may mean "*a sign of authority*" (Revised Version), or "a covering, in sign that she is under the power of her husband" (Authorized Version, margin). The margin of the Revised Version, "authority over her head," is a strange suggestion. Some have explained the word of *her own* true authority, which consists in accepting the rule of her husband; but it probably means *a sign of her husband's authority over her*. Similarly the traveller Chardin says that in Persia the women wear a veil, in sign that they are "under subjection." If so, the best comment on the word may be found in the exquisite lines of Milton, which illustrate the passage in other ways also—

"She, as a veil, down to the slender waist
    Her unadorned golden tresses wore . . .
    As the vine curves her tendrils, which
    implied
    Subjection, but required with gentle sway,
    And by her yielded, by him best received."

The fact that Callistratus twice uses *exousia* of "abundance of hair" is probably a mere coincidence, resembling the Irish expression "a power of hair." Nor can there be any allusion to the isolated fact that Samson's strength lay in his hair. The very brief comment of Luther sums up all the best of the many pages which have been written on the subject. He says that *exousia* means "the veil or covering, by which one may see that she is under her husband's authority" (Gen. iii. 16). **Because of the angels.** In this clause also we must set aside, as idle waste of time, the attempts to alter the text, or to twist the plain words into impossible meanings. The word "angels" cannot mean "Church officials," or "holy men," or "prophets," or "delegates," or "bridegroom's men," or anything but angels. Nor can the verse mean, as Bengel supposes, that women are to veil themselves because the angels do so (Isa. vi. 2), or (as Augustine says) because the angels approve of it. The only question is whether the allusion is to good or bad angels. In favour of the latter view is (1) the universal tradition among the Jews that the angels fell by lust for mortal women, which was the Jewish way of interpreting Gen. vi. 1, 2. This is the view of Tertullian ('De Virg. Vel.,' 7) in writing on this subject. A woman, in the opinion and traditions of Oriental Jews, is liable to injury from the *shedim*, if she appears in public unveiled; and these evil spirits are supposed to delight in the appearance of unveiled women. The objection to this view, that *angeloi* alone is never used of evil but always of good angels, is not perhaps decisive (see ch. vi. 3). The verse may, however, mean (in accordance with the Jewish belief of those days) that good angels, being under the possibility of falling from the same cause as their evil brethren, fly away at once from the presence of unveiled women. Thus Khadijah tested that the visitant of her husband Mohammed really was the angel Gabriel, because he disappeared the moment she unveiled her head. On the whole, however, the meaning seems to be, *out of respect and reverence for the holy angels, who are always invisibly present in the Christian assemblies.* (On this point, see Luke xv. 10; Eph. iii. 10; Heb. i. 14; xii. 1; Eccles. v. 6; Ps. cxxxviii. 1 [LXX.]; Tobit xii. 12. See Latimer's 'Sermons,' p. 253). "Reverence the angels" is St. Chrysostom's remark.

Ver. 11.—**Nevertheless.** The verse is meant to correct any tendency on the part of men to domineer. Man and woman are "all one in Christ Jesus" (Gal. iii. 28).

"The two-celled heart, beating with one full stroke—
Life."

Ver. 12.—**By the woman;** that is, "born of a woman" (Job xiv. 1). **But all things of God.** And all things also "through him and to him," made by him, and tending to him as their end (Rom. xi. 36).

Ver. 13.—**Is it comely, etc.?** An appeal to the decision of their instinctive sense of propriety.

Ver. 14.—**Doth not even nature itself teach you?** "Nature" here has much the same sense as "instinct."

"His fair large front and eye sublime declared
Absolute rule; and hyacinthine locks
Round from his parted forelock manly hung
Clustering, *but not beneath his shoulders broad :*
She, as a veil, *down to the slender waist*
Her unadorned golden tresses wore."
(Milton, 'Paradise Lost,' iv. 304.)

Ver. 15.—**It is a glory to her.** Because it is at once beautiful and natural; and as Bengel says, "Will should follow the guidance of nature."

Ver. 16.—**But if any man seem to be contentious.** St. Paul cuts the question short, as though impatient of any further discussion of a subject already settled by instinctive decorum and by the common sense of universal usage. "Seem to be contentious" is (like the Latin *videtur*) only a courteous way of saying "*is contentious.*" If any of you wish to be disputatious and quarrelsome about this minor matter of ritual, I must content myself with saying that he must take his own course (for a similar use of the euphemistic "seem," see Phil. iii. 4; Heb. iv. 1; Jas. i. 26). **We have no such custom.** The emphatic "*we*" means the apostles and the leaders of the Church at Jerusalem and Antioch. *Such custom.* Not referring to "contentiousness," but to the women appearing with uncovered heads. **Neither the Churches of God.** If you Corinthians prefer these abnormal practices in spite of reason, common sense, and my arguments, you must stand alone in your innovations upon universal Christian practice. But catholic custom is against your "self-opinionated particularism."

Vers. 17—34.—*Discreditable irregularities at the Eucharist and the agapæ.*

Ver. 17.—**Now in this that I declare** unto you I praise you not; rather, as in the Revised Version, *But in giving you this charge, I praise you not.* A reference to the "I praise you" of ver. 2. **Ye come together.** As he advances, his rebukes become more and more serious; for the present reproach does not affect a few, but the Church assembly in general.

Ver. 18.—**First of all.** The "second" rebuke is not clearly stated, but is no doubt meant to refer to the abuses in "speaking with the tongue." **In the Church;** rather, *in congregation,* or *assembly.* The reference is not to a particular building. The Lord's Supper was administered frequently (originally every day, Acts ii. 46), and often in private houses. **Divisions;** *schisms* (ch. i. 10, 12). Here, however, he is referring to cliques and quarrels at the love-feasts. **Partly. I cannot think,** he says, in a tone of kindness, that these reports are *wholly* false. There must be *some* ground for them, even if the facts have been exaggerated.

Ver. 19.—**There must be also heresies among you.** It results from the inevitable decrees of the Divine providence. "It is impossible but that offences will come" (Luke xvii. 11). *Heresies.* The word does not mean "erroneous opinions," but *party factions.* Originally the word only means "a choice," and is not used in a bad sense; but since the opinionativeness of men pushes "a choice" into a "party," and since it is the invariable tendency of a party to degenerate into a "faction," the word soon acquires a bad sense (see its use in Acts v. 17; xv. 5; xxiv. 5, 14; xxviii. 22; Gal. v. 20; Titus iii. 10; 2 Pet. ii. 1; and Gieseler, 'Church Hist.,' i. 149). The mutually railing factions, which in their Church newspapers and elsewhere bandy about their false and rival charges of "heresy," are illustrating the virulence of the very sin which they are professing to denounce—the sin of factiousness. **That they which are approved may be made manifest among you.** Similarly St. John (1 John ii. 19) speaks of the aberrations of false teachers as destined to prove that they did not belong to the true Church. Good is educed out of seeming evil (Jas. i. 3; 1 Pet. i. 6, 7). *Approved;* standing the test (*dokimoi*), the opposite of the "reprobate" (*adokimoi*) of ch. ix. 27.

Ver. 20.—**Into one place.** There were as yet no churches. The Lord's Supper was held in private houses. **This is not;** or perhaps, *it is not possible.* **The Lord's Supper.** The fact that there is no article in the Greek shows the early prevalence of this name for the Eucharist.

Ver. 21.—**For in eating;** rather, *in your eating.* **Every one.** All who have themselves contributed a share to the common meal. **Taketh before** other **his own supper.** It is as if they had come together only to eat, not to partake of a holy sacrament. The abuse rose from the connection of the Lord's Supper with the *agape*, or love-feast, a social gathering of Christian brothers, to which each, as in the Greek *eranoi*, or "club-feasts," contributed his share. The abuse led to the separation of the *agape* from the Holy Communion, and ultimately to the entire disuse of the former at religious gatherings. **One is hungry.** The poor man, who has been unable to contribute to the meal which was intended to be an exhibition of Christian love, looked on with grudging eyes and craving appetite, while the rich had more than enough. **Is drunken.** "St. Paul draws the picture in strong colours, and who can say that the reality was less strong?" (Meyer). Calvin says, "It is portentous that Satan should have accomplished

so much in so short a time." But the remark was, perhaps, dictated by the wholly mistaken fancy that the Church of the apostolic days was exceptionally pure. On the contrary, many of the heathen converts were unable at once to break the spell of their old habits, and few modern Churches present a spectacle so deplorable as that which we here find in the apostolic Church of Corinth. It is quite obvious that Church discipline must have been almost in abeyance if such grave scandals could exist uncorrected and apparently unreproved.

Ver. 22.—**To eat and to drink in.** The object of the *agape* was something higher than the mere gratification of appetite. Though not a sacrament, it was an accompaniment of the Lord's Supper, and was itself intended to be a symbolical and sacred meal. **Despise ye the Church of God?** The congregation of your fellow-Christians. **Shame;** rather, *disgrace*, or *put to shame.* **Them that have not.** It would be natural to supply "houses." But the commentators found it difficult to suppose that any of the Corinthians had not "houses to eat and to drink in." Hence most commentators give to the phrase its classic sense, in which "those who have" means the rich, and "those who have not," the poor. They seem, however, to have forgotten that slaves at any rate could hardly be said to have "houses of their own," and it is certain that not a few of the Corinthian Christians were slaves. **I praise you not.** As in ver. 17, this is an instance of what is called *litotes*, a mild expression, suggesting a meaning much stronger than the words themselves. **For.** He is about to give his *reason* for thus strongly blaming their irregularities.

Ver. 23.—**I have received;** rather, *I received.* He thus refers the revelation to some special time, and this seems to point to the conclusion that he is not referring to any account of the institution of the Lord's Supper, which may have been given him by St. Peter or one of the twelve, but to some immediate revelation from Christ. The terms in which he describes the institution of the Eucharist resemble most nearly those of St. Luke, who may very probably have derived his information from St. Paul. This passage should be compared with Matt. xxvi. 26—29; Mark xiv. 22—25; Luke xxii. 19, 20. **Was betrayed;** rather, *was being betrayed.*

Ver. 24.—**When he had given thanks.** The same word is used in St. Luke (εὐχαριστήσας), and is the origin of the name Eucharist. St. Mark and perhaps St. Matthew have "having blessed it" (*eulogesas*). Hence the Eucharist is "this our *sacrifice of praise* and thanksgiving." **Take, eat.** These words are omitted by all the best uncials. **Which**

is broken for you. The word "broken" is of doubtful authenticity. Some manuscripts have "given," and one (D) a milder word for "broken," as though to avoid any contradiction of John xix. 36, where, however, the word is "shall not be *crushed*." Since the participle is omitted altogether by ℵ, A, B, C, there can be no doubt that it is a gloss, and accordingly the Revised Version reads, "which is for you." The "broken" is nevertheless involved in the "he brake it," which was a part of the ceremony as originally illustrated. The breaking of the bread ought not, therefore, to be abandoned, as in the case when "wafers" are used. **This do.** St. Luke also has this clause, which is not found in St. Matthew or St. Mark. The variations show that it was the *main fact* which was essential, not the exact words spoken. **In remembrance of me.** The words may also be rendered, *for a memorial of me*, or *to bring me to your remembrance*.

Ver. 25.—**When he had supped** (see Luke xxii. 27). The cup, like the *côs ha-berachah*, was given after the meal was ended. **The new testament;** rather, *the new covenant*. The Greek word *diathēkē* is indeed a "will," or "testament;" but in the LXX., on which the Greek of the apostles was formed, it always stands for *berith*, covenant. The Jews knew nothing of the practice of "making wills" till they learnt it from the Romans. The *only* passage of the New Testament (an expression derived from this very passage through the Vulgate) in which *diathēkē* means a "testament" is Heb. ix. 16, where the writer reverts for a moment only to this signification of the word to introduce a passing illustration. **In my blood.** The cup was a symbol of the blood of Christ, because the gospel covenant was ratified by the shedding of his blood. The Jews had an absolute horror, at once religious and physical, of tasting blood. This was the reason why the Synod of Jerusalem forbade even to the Gentiles the eating of "things strangled." If the apostles had not fully understood that our Lord was only using the ordinary language of Semitic imagery, and describing only a sacramental symbol, the words, "This is my blood," would have thrilled them with horror and repulsion.

Ver. 26.—**Ye do show the Lord's death.** The word literally means, *ye announce*, or *proclaim*, with reference to the repetition of the actual words used by our Lord. It will be seen that St. Paul does not lend the smallest sanction to the "unfathomable superstition" of a material transubstantiation. **Till he come.** Accordingly the antiquity and unbroken continuance of this holy rite is one of the many strong external evidences of the truth of the gospel history. The ἄν is omitted in the Greek, to indicate the certainty of Christ's coming. The same Greek idiom is hopefully and tenderly used in Gal. iv. 19.

Ver. 27.—**And drink** this **cup.** This ought to be rendered, *or drink this cup*. It seems to be one of the *extremely* few instances in which the translators of our Authorized Version were led by bias into unfaithful rendering. They may have persuaded themselves that the apostle *must* have meant "and;" but their duty as translators was to translate what he *said*, not what they supposed him to have meant. What he meant was that it was possible to partake in a wrong spirit either of the bread or the cup. King James's translators thought that, by rendering the word *or*, they might seem to favour communion in one kind only. St. Paul's meaning was that a man might take *either* element of the sacrament unworthily. **Unworthily.** We are all "unworthy"—"unworthy so much as to gather up the crumbs under Christ's table;" yet not one of us need eat or drink *unworthily*, that is, in a careless, irreverent, defiant spirit. **Guilty of.** He draws on himself the penalty due to "crucifying to himself the Son of God afresh," by "putting him to an open shame."

Ver. 28.—**Let a man examine himself.** The verb means "let him *test* his own feelings;" put them to the proof, to see whether they be sincere or not. He must "wash his hands in innocency," and so come to God's altar (see Matt. v. 22, 23; 2 Cor. xiii. 5). **And so.** Soberly, that is; seriously, humbly, and with due reverence.

Ver. 29.—**Unworthily.** The word is not genuine here, being repeated from ver. 27; it is omitted by ℵ, A, B, C. **Eateth and drinketh damnation to himself;** rather, *eateth and drinketh judgment to himself.* There is reason to believe that the word "damnation" once had a much milder meaning in English than that which it now popularly bears. In King James's time it probably did not of necessity mean more than "an unfavourable verdict." Otherwise this would be the most unfortunate mistranslation in the whole Bible. It has probably kept thousands, as it kept Goethe, from Holy Communion. We see from ver. 32 that this "judgment" had a purely merciful and disciplinary character. **Not discerning;** rather, *if he discern not*, the Lord's body. Any one who approaches the Lord's Supper in a spirit of levity or defiance, not discriminating between it and common food, draws on himself, by so eating and drinking, a judgment which is defined in the next verse.

Ver. 30.—**Many are weak and sickly among**

you. St. Paul directly connects this general ill health with the abuse of the Lord's Supper. It is not impossible that the grave intemperance to which he alludes in ver. 21 may have had its share in this result; but apart from this, there is an undoubted connection between sin and sickness in some, though not, of course, in all cases (John v. 14). **Many.** The word is different from the previous word for "many," and means a larger number—"not a few," "a considerable number." **Sleep;** *i.e. are dying.*

Vers. 31, 32.—**For if we would judge ourselves,** etc. These verses are very unfortunately mistranslated in our Authorized Version. They should be rendered (literally), *For if we discerned* (or, *discriminated*) *ourselves, we should not be undergoing judgment* (namely, of physical punishment); *but, in being judged by the Lord* (by these temporal sufferings), *we are under training, that we may not be condemned with the world.* The meaning is that "if we" (St. Paul here identifies himself with the Corinthians) "were in the habit of self-discernment—and in this *self*-discrimination is involved a discrimination between spiritual and common things—we should not be undergoing this sign of God's displeasure; but the fact that his judgments are abroad among us is intended to further our moral education, and to save us from being finally condemned with the world." Discernment (*diakrisis*), by saving us from eating unworthily (Ps. xxxii. 5; 1 John i. 9), would have obviated the necessity for penal judgments (*krima*), but yet the *krima* is disciplinary (*paideuometha*, we are being trained as children),

to save us from final doom (*katakrima*). Unworthy eating, then, so far from involving necessary or final "damnation," is mercifully visited by God with temporal chastisement, to help in the saving of our souls. "Blessed is the man whom thou chastenest, O Lord" (Ps. xciv. 12; Heb. xii. 5—12).

Ver. 33.—**Wherefore.** He now briefly sums up the practical remedies for these discreditable scenes. **My brethren.** Introduced, as often, into a stern passage to show that the writer is only actuated by the spirit of love. **Tarry one for another.** This would prevent the scrambling greediness which he has already condemned in ver. 21.

Ver. 34.—**And if any man hunger, let him eat at home.** A reminder of the *sacred* character of the *agape* as a symbol of Christian love and union. **Unto condemnation;** rather, *judgment.* In Greek, the same word (*krima*) is used which in ver. 29 is so unhappily rendered "damnation." But even "condemnation" is too strong; for that is equivalent to *katakrima.* **The rest;** all minor details. It is not improbable that one of these details was the practical dissociation of the *agape* from the Lord's Supper altogether. Certainly the custom of uniting the two seems to have disappeared by the close of the first century. **When I come;** rather, *whenever.* The Greek phrase (ὡς ἂν) implies uncertainty. The apostle's plans for visiting Corinth immediately had been materially disturbed by the unfavourable tidings as to the conditions of the Church.

HOMILETICS.

Vers. 1, 2.—*Imitation and commendation.* "Be ye followers of me, even as I also am of Christ. Now I praise you, brethren, that ye remember me in all things, and keep the ordinances, as I delivered them to you." In these words we have—

I. THE PRINCIPLE ON WHICH THE CHARACTERS OF MOST MEN ARE FORMED. "Be ye followers of me, even as I also am of Christ." Men are imitative beings, and, from a law of their nature, those whom they most admire and with whom they most associate, they become like in spirit and in character. The request of Paul here, at first sight, seems somewhat arrogant: "Be ye followers of me." No man has a right to make such an unqualified claim on another. Hence Paul puts the limitation, "Even as I also am of Christ." The apostle undoubtedly refers to the preceding verses, in which he speaks of himself as *not seeking his own pleasure or profit, but that of others.* This Christ did. We are told that he "pleased not himself." He means to say, "Be like me in this respect, as I in this respect resemble Christ." Here is the principle that should regulate our imitation of men; imitate them just so far as they resemble Christ. Children should not imitate their parents, pupils should not imitate their teachers, congregations should not imitate their ministers, only so far as they resemble Christ.

II. A COMMENDATION OF MERIT WHICH MANY ARE RELUCTANT TO RENDER. "Now I praise you, brethren, that ye remember me in all things, and keep the ordinances, as I delivered them to you." In some things, if not in all, some of the Corinthian Christians pleased Paul, did what he considered right—they remembered him, and practically attended to his directions. There was much in them with which he could find fault, and did find fault, but so far as they did the proper thing he praises them. To render generously credit where credit is due is the characteristic of a great soul, but one which others have not. I take it to be a duty to render credit where credit is due; but how seldom is this attended to! In domestic matters how it is neglected! A *wife* will go on loyally and lovingly attending to the wants and wishes of her husband, and perhaps not from one year to another does she receive from him one word of hearty commendation. So with *servants* and masters: the employer, when he has paid the stipulated stipend to the most useful of his *employés*, feels he has done his duty, and gives not a word of commendation. So with *ministers* and their congregations. How many ministers are there in every Church, who give the best fruits of their cultivated minds, and, by their sweating brain and agonizing prayers, produce discourses every week admirably suited to serve the highest interests of their congregations; and yet seldom receive one generous word of hearty commendation for all their toils! Miserable criticisms they will get in abundance, but nothing else. Verily, I believe that no social service is more important, and at the same time more neglected, than the yielding of a *generous commendation to the truly commendable.*

Vers. 3—16.—*The man and the woman.* "But I would have you know," etc. Although there are some things in these verses that perhaps no one can rightly interpret, and that may have been written as personal opinion rather than as Divine inspiration, there are two or three points in relation to man and woman interesting and noteworthy.

I. THERE IS BETWEEN THEM A SUBORDINATION IN NATURAL RELATIONSHIP. "But I would have you know, that the head of every man is Christ; and the head of the woman is the man; and the head of Christ is God." The principle of subordination, it would seem, prevails throughout the spiritual universe; one rising above another in regular gradation up to God himself. God is over Christ, Christ is over man, man is over woman. "For the man is not of the woman; but the woman of the man. Neither was the man created for the woman; but the woman for the man." The *ideal* women and the *ideal* men are here, I presume, meant. It is because the man is supposed to have more brain and soul than the woman that he is the master; but in cases—and they are not few—where the woman is the greater, the greater in intellect, heart, and all moral nobleness, she, without her intention or even wish, will necessarily be the head. In the Marriage Service, the woman at the altar is called upon solemnly to vow to *obey* her husband. I confess I have often been struck at the incongruity of this, when I have seen a little-chested, small-brained man standing by the side of a woman with a majestic brow and a grand physique, when she is called upon to vow obedience to such a man.

II. THERE IS BETWEEN THEM AN INDEPENDENT OBLIGATION IN RELIGIOUS SERVICES. "Every man praying or prophesying, having his head covered, dishonoureth his head. But every woman that prayeth or prophesieth with her head uncovered dishonoureth her head," etc. It is here implied that both the man and the woman are to prophesy, teach, and pray; *not one instead of the other*, but each independently. However closely related the man and the wife may be, however dependent one is on the other, neither can perform the spiritual and religious obligations of the other. There is no sharing of duty here, no shifting of personal obligation; each must stand alone before God.

III. THERE IS A DIFFERENCE BETWEEN THEM IN OUTWARD ASPECT. There are two points here concerning the difference. 1. *A difference in the way in which they are to appear in public.* The man is to appear with an uncovered head, the woman with a covered head. "If the woman be not covered, let her also be shorn: but if it be a shame for a woman to be shorn or shaven, let her be covered. For a man indeed ought not to cover his head." The woman's head is to be covered with her hair or a veil, or both. Who shall divine the meaning of the tenth verse?—"For this cause ought the woman to have power on her head because of the angels." To me this is utterly incomprehensible. Probably there were at Corinth women who shaved off their hair in order to obliterate the distinction of sex: shameless women. 2. *This difference is adventitious rather than natural.* Is there any reason in nature why a man's head should be uncovered and a woman's covered; why one should wear long hair and the other short? No such thing seems reasonable; the uncivilized tribes know nothing of it. The reason can only be traced to custom. And is not custom second nature? "Doth not even nature itself teach you, that, if a man have long hair, it is a shame unto him?" But original nature does not seem to teach us that, but custom and conventional propriety. Hence Paul says, "If any may seem to be contentious, we have no such custom;" by which he means, I understand, that, whoever may contend to the contrary, such a custom—as that woman should pray and preach with uncovered heads—was not known by Paul in other Churches, and that the Church at Corinth should not allow it.

Vers. 17—22.—*Religious institutions: their abuse.* "Now in this that I declare unto you I praise you not," etc. Three practical truths may be fairly deduced from this paragraph.

I. That attendance on the institutions of religion may prove pernicious rather than beneficial. "Now in this that I declare unto you I praise you not, that ye come together not for the better, but for the worse." The apostle in this verse censures the Corinthians that they came together to the Lord's Supper, and were made "worse" rather than "better." Men cannot be made religious; an irresistible moral force is a contradiction in terms, an impossibility in fact. Hence it comes to pass that the highest redemptive forces on man often conduce to his ruin. The gospel proves in the case of all hearers either the "savour of life unto life, or of death unto death." Pharaoh's heart was hardened under the ministry of Moses, and the hearts of the men of Chorazin, Bethsaida, and Capernaum were hardened under the ministry of Christ.

II. That assembling together for religious purposes does not necessarily imply unity of soul. "For first of all, when ye come together in the Church, I hear that there be divisions among you; and I partly believe it. For there must be also heresies among you, that they which are approved may be made manifest among you." The factious and schismatic spirit seems to have existed in the same Church and even at the Lord's table. It does not follow that, because people are brought together in the same religious assembly or Church, that they are united together in spirit. Two people may sit in the same pew, hear the same discourse, sing the same hymns, partake of the same bread and wine, and yet in soul be as remote from one another as the poles. No real spiritual unity can exist where there is not a supreme affection for the same being. Christ is the only uniting Centre of souls.

III. That the very best institutions on earth are often sadly perverted by men. For many reasons the Lord's Supper may be regarded as one of the best ordinances. But see how it was now perverted. It was made the means of gluttony and drunkenness; men used it as a common feast. "When ye come together therefore into one place, this is not to eat the Lord's Supper. For in eating every one taketh before other his own supper: and one is hungry, and another is drunken." Are not men constantly perverting Divine institutions, Churches, Bibles, the Christian ministry, etc.?

Vers. 23—34.—*The Lord's Supper.* "For I have received," etc. These verses give an account of what is called the Lord's Supper. This supper was instituted by Christ himself the night in which he was betrayed, while he was observing the Passover with his disciples. On that night he virtually directed the minds of men from all Jewish ritualism and centred them on himself. "Do this in remembrance of *me*." True religion now has to do with a *Person*, and that Person is Christ. In reading the words of the apostle here, there are four things which strike us with amazement.

I. That any should doubt the genuineness of Christianity. Here is an institution that was started the night previous to our Saviour's crucifixion, which was attended to by the Church at Jerusalem after the day of Pentecost, celebrated by various other apostolic Churches as recorded in the Acts of the Apostles, and which Paul says here he "received from the Lord." From the apostolic age down to this hour, through eighteen long centuries, it has been attended to by all the branches of the true Church. Since its origin hundreds of generations have passed away, many systems have risen and disappeared, nations have been organized, flourished, and broken up; but this ordinance continues; what for? To commemorate the great central fact of the gospel, viz. that Christ died. Is there any other fact in history sustained by evidence half so powerful as this?

II. THAT ANY SHOULD MISINTERPRET THE ORDINANCE. Here we are distinctly told that it is to "show the Lord's death." No language can more clearly show that it is purely commemorative. There are three abuses of this institution. 1. The *gustatory.* Some of the Corinthians thus used it. They introduced a love-feast to immediately precede it, probably because a Jewish feast preceded its first celebration. This led to gluttony and other evils. The members of the Corinthian Church were converts from heathenism, and they had been accustomed in their heathen festivals to give way to gluttony and intemperance. Many of them, from the force of old habits, were tempted to use the Lord's Supper in this way. 2. The *superstitious.* There are some who believe that, after the words of consecration are pronounced by the priest over these elements, the elements become literally the "body and blood of the Lord." This is transubstantiation. Others who would not go thus far still superstitiously regard the ordinance as a mystic medium through which grace is poured into the soul of the recipient. Fearful abuse this! 3. The *formalistic.* There are those who partake of the bread and wine merely as a matter of form and ceremony. We evangelical Christians are not guilty of the first nor of the second, but we may be of the third. The text tells us it is to "show" or to teach'; it is an educational ordinance.

III. THAT ANY SHOULD SAY THE INSTITUTION IS NOT PERMANENT IN ITS OBLIGA-TION. The apostle tells us distinctly that it was to "show the Lord's death till he come." When will that be? Not just yet. The human world seems to be only in its infancy, and Christianity only just beginning its work. The billows of a thousand ages may break on our shore before he comes. On to that distant point the obligation is binding. There are some professing Christians who think themselves too spiritual to observe such an ordinance. These very spiritual ones, to be consistent, should avoid all *scientific* studies, for science has to do with material forms; its principles are all embodied, are made palpable to the eye and ear. They should also avoid all *Biblical* studies, for Biblical truths are for the most part embodied in material facts and forms. Christ himself was "flesh and blood."

IV. THAT ANY ACQUAINTED WITH THE BIOGRAPHY OF CHRIST SHOULD NEGLECT IT. Consider: 1. That it is to *commemorate* the world's greatest Benefactor. It is to keep Christ in the memory of man. Here is a Benefactor that has: (1) Served the world in the highest way. He has delivered it from sin and death. (2) Served it by the most unparalleled sacrifice. He sacrificed his life to the work. (3) Served it with the most disinterested love. 2. That it is *enjoined* by the world's greatest Benefactor. He himself has enjoined it: "Do this in remembrance of me."

HOMILIES BY VARIOUS AUTHORS.

Vers. 1—16.—*Apostolic injunctions with regard to Church services.* Though the Corinthians deserved blame in some things, they were entitled to praise in that they had generally observed St. Paul's directions. Despite their departure from certain of his instructions, he could say, "Be ye followers of me, even as I also am of Christ;" by which he recognized that they had discernment enough to see the Lord Jesus in his personal and official character, and a sufficient brotherly sympathy to imitate his example. His commendation is hearty: "Ye remember me in all things, and keep the ordinances, as I delivered them to you." With this preface, short but conciliatory, he takes up his first topic, viz. the headship of man in the natural and spiritual order, established by Providence and maintained by the Spirit in the Church. In his writings, natural facts are ever reappearing in new and diviner connections, as if they had undergone a silent and wonderful transfiguration, and had been glorified in light and beauty. Instinct had always acknowledged the subordination of woman to man, nor, indeed, is the instinct of sex conceivable in the absence of this element in its nature. But St. Paul is careful to lay his doctrinal foundation on the fact "that the head of every man is Christ," assured that the ultimate strength of all truth is in its spirituality. Be it a law, a principle, a motive, an end, "other foundation can no man lay." Critics may entertain widely different estimates of the man, may be as broadly separated as M. Renan and Dr. Farrar, and yet none can deny that St. Paul had this incomparable advantage, namely, a great centre, from which he saw all objects that engaged his attention. His method is fully brought out in the third verse: the head of the man is Christ; the head of the woman is the man; the head of Christ is God—a statement clear, compact, exhaustive. One moment he is dealing with the relationship between man and woman: Eden rises to his view, the sleeping Adam wakening to find Eve at his side, "the woman of the man," and "the glory of the man;" and the next moment he is contemplating the Trinity in its economic and immanent relations. Yet from this sublime height of Christ's exaltation at the right hand of the Father there is no break when he descends to discuss woman's behaviour in Church assemblies. The principle involved keeps him on ground far above dress and decorum as such, and, indeed, he will not touch the matter at all until he has set forth the dignity of its associations. Let us be careful, then, lest we err by supposing that St. Paul looked upon dress and decorum, in this instance, as simply convention- alities based on whims of taste and caprices of opinion. Conventionalities they were in a certain sense, but conventionalities to be respected and observed. In brief, they were customs that had a moral meaning. If a woman appeared in public unveiled, she was deemed immodest. To wear a veil was a sign of womanly delicacy, and hence, if she went to a public assembly without her veil, she acted shamelessly. To be consistent, argues St. Paul, "let her also be shorn," and so assume the mark of a disreputable woman. A woman acting in this way sets public opinion at defiance; and as public opinion in many things is public conscience, and as such the aggregated moral feeling of a community, no woman could do this thing and not shock all right sensibility. Besides, the veil is a sign of subordination and dependence. Refusing to use this covering of the head was a mark of insubordination and independence. A symbol it was, but to cast off the symbol was to repudiate the thing signified. This was not all. If uncomely, it was also unnatural; "for her hair is given her for a covering." The argument has one passage (ver. 10) which is confessedly difficult to understand, but this does not detract an iota from the general directness and force. St. Paul's purpose is unmistakable—to set forth the order of God's economy in the relative positions of man and woman to each other, and the entire unity of their relation to God in Christ. Man's authority is guarded against all excess, and woman's dependence is beautified by delicacy, retiringness, and trustful love. So high an estimate is put on her character and attitude, that even her personal appearance, as to attire and demeanour, is a matter of moment, involving the honour and happiness of her husband, and intimately blended with the conservatism of society and the influence of the Church. Nor is the apostle's manner of appeal to be overlooked. A great truth may be conveyed to the mind, while nevertheless the mode of its communication, left to hap-hazard impulse, or, forsooth, in downright contempt of the mind's laws, may work an amount of harm for which the truth itself is no compensa- tion. Rest assured that so discerning a man as St. Paul, whose eye took its seeing from sensibility no less than from reason, would not violate manner when he was discussing the worth of manners. Rest assured, too, that he would seek a very firm basis for the logic of his judgment. That such was the fact, "Judge in yourselves" demonstrates. At the very moment that he distinctly recognizes public opinion as public conscience, and counsels deference to its *dicta* as divinely authoritative, he yet addresses human intuitions. "There is a spirit in man, and the inspiration of the Almighty giveth them understanding." No other truth save this could have availed Elihu when he came to the perplexed Job and his well-meaning but very mistaken friends, and, as a mediator, prepared the way to close the controversy. No other truth than the "spirit in man" and its "inspiration of the Almighty" can qualify any man to mediate where intellectual conflicts interblend with the moral and spiritual instincts. Inspiration in its highest form makes no war on inspiration in its lower form, since the inspiration that gives original truth, and that openness and sympathy which receive it, are both from God. St. Paul preached a gospel that commended itself to every man's conscience in the sight of God, and he acted in the same frame of mind when he treated of decorum and showed wherein manliness and womanliness consisted. Customs and habits vary; he goes back to the sense of custom and habit permanent in the soul. He is not afraid of human instincts. Although he knows how they miss their way and sadly blunder in working out themselves through the mists and clouds of the intellect, yet trust them he will, nor can he suffer others to disparage their office. This inward consciousness the Holy Spirit acknowledges, and to it he brings light and warmth, in order that the intuitive judgment may be supplied with the conditions of its best activity. It is, indeed, a part of our fallen nature, but, notwithstanding that, it is a Divine remnant, and only awaits God's voice to utter its response. The dark lumps of coal when dug from the earth give no sign of the sunbeams hidden in them, but, on being ignited, they attest their origin. Therefore, argues the apostle, "judge in yourselves," since there is no knowledge of God unaccompanied by a knowledge of ourselves. Only let your judgment be in the Lord; for only in him can man and woman be seen in the perfection of their mutuality. After all, then, may we not say, in view of this argument no less than of all his methods of thinking, that St. Paul is peculiar among the apostles by his insight into the natural economy of the universe, the apostle of nature as well as of grace, because each was a portion of the same vast scheme of Providence? According to his view, the human race was in Christ from the beginning, and Adam's federal headship took its whole meaning from the pre-existence of Christ, as the Creator of man.—L.

Vers. 17—34.—*Special consideration of the Lord's Supper; uses of self-judgment.* And what is St. Paul's mood of mind now? "I declare unto you" (command you), and "I praise you not," since I hear of "divisions" among you, and "I partly believe it." "Heresies [sects] *must* be among you," for in the present state of our nature there is no way to develop the good without the evil manifesting itself. The evil has its uses; the evil is not a cause but an occasion of good; the evil is overruled by the Holy Ghost and turned to the advantage of the Church; the evil does not change its character and become a good, but is instrumentally employed to subserve other and very different purposes than itself contemplates. Thereby the genuine advocates of truth are made to appear, and truth itself is brought out in a more luminous aspect. The standpoint is that God is not only the Author of the institutions of the Church, but their Divine Guardian. The institutions are not left to themselves, nor are circumstances outside of them surrendered to their own operation, but God himself is in the workmanship of his hands, and presides over all external things, so that his providences are in behalf of a providence which has a supreme object and end. Now, the Lord's Supper is a holy sacrament, and St. Paul approaches the discussion of it in a very marked way. We understand him to claim a direct revelation from the Lord Jesus on this subject, and, by virtue thereof, to "declare," or command, as he states in the seventeenth verse. Truth is truth, whether mediately or immediately received. Yet we do know that there are circumstances under which truth affects us in a manner singularly personal. Only one such scene as that "near Damascus" is reported in the New Testament, and only one such unique individuality as that of St. Paul is recorded for our instruction. So that we are moving in the line of all the precedents of his career when we suppose that this account of the supper was communicated directly by the Lord Jesus to the apostle of the Gentiles. In a previous discussion (ch. x.) he had referred to a specific aspect of the supper as a communion or participation. Beyond this the argument then in hand did not require him to go. Now, however, he is full and explicit as to details—the time when it was instituted, the circumstances, the manner of the Lord Jesus, the formula employed; so that nothing might escape observation, but the utmost depth and solemnity of impression be secured. "In remembrance of me" is the heart of the holy ordinance—the "remembrance" of the broken body and the shed blood—the penalty of the violated Law endured, satisfaction offered to the Lawgiver, the sense of justice met in the human heart, the love of God expressing itself as the grace of God, and the means therewith provided for the sense of God's grace to be awakened and developed in the human heart. Memory is the power in man this holy institution addresses. "In remembrance of me." Now, looking at memory in its position among the mental faculties, we may perchance get some light on the words just quoted. Memory is a very early and energetic activity of the mind. It begins our development and is the chief stimulant of progressive development. It is the spinal column of the faculties. Sensation, perception, imagination, associative and suggestive functions, reasoning and conclusions reached, are all very intimately identified with its operations. Memory is the first of the intellectual powers to attain perfection, as judgment is the last, and this law of rapid maturity would seem to indicate, by its exceptional character, that memory sustains a very near relation to the growth of our moral nature. It is clear that the Lord Jesus adopted the method of storing facts in the minds of the twelve apostles, and leaving them in latency, the truths in these facts being reserved for subsequent realization. And it is equally certain that one of the chief offices of the Holy Ghost, as the Executive of the Father and the Son, was " to bring all things " to their " remembrance." Naturally, indeed, a past was formed in the memories of the twelve, but *it was made a spiritual past* by the Divine agency of the Spirit as a Remembrancer. Furthermore, the apostles were to be witnesses, or testifiers : " Ye also shall bear witness ; " but the importance of the Spirit as a Remembrancer exhibits itself in this, that, out of the miscellaneous mass of facts deposited in the memories of the twelve, a *selection* was to be made, for, according to the fourth Gospel, there were " many other things which Jesus did " that were not " written," while those " written " were such as were adapted to Christian faith. It seems, then, that memory was inspired by the Holy Ghost in accordance with the principle contained in the words, " These are written "—only these—" that ye might believe that Jesus is the Christ, the Son of God ; and that believing ye might have life through his Name." Aside, however, from the apostles, is there not a principle here which is recognized by the Spirit in all its gracious administrations ? Memory is ordinarily *the starting-point* in religious life when that life becomes positive and decided. It enters largely into conviction for sin and into repentance. Further back than recollection extends, impressions of God's goodness and the need of Christ for pardon and peace were made on the soul, and there they lay like old deposits in the strata of the globe, till the Holy Ghost uncovered them to our consciousness. God keeps for us his witness in this faithful register of the past. Without being Platonists on the subject of reminiscence, or accepting all that Wordsworth teaches in the grand ' Ode on Intimations of Immortality from Early Recollections of Childhood,' we may well believe that memory is the master-organ through which grace is imparted to men. A simple hymn of Dr. Watts's or Mrs. Barbauld's learned in childhood ; the little prayer, " Now I lay me down to sleep ; " and most of all, " Our Father which art in heaven," taught by a mother's lips ; our first sight of death ; our first walk in a graveyard ;—come back to us in after years, and suddenly the hard grip of the world on our hearts is relaxed, and the " little child is set in the midst " of life's scenes, and we know that Jesus has set it there for our restoration to its long-lost image. No wonder, then, that it should have pleased the Lord Jesus to make the Holy Supper an institution appealing to memory. There, in that upper room, a few hours on earth remaining to him, the past three years with his disciples were gathered in a few most solemn moments. The righteousness of his perfect life of obedience, all he had taught and done and suffered, had come into this final interview, and were going forward into his expiatory death. The motive and blessedness of the act in the celebration of the Eucharist are drawn from " In remembrance of me." Christ in all his fulness, Christ in his one personality as Son of God and Son of man, Christ in the entire compass of mediation, is in this " *me*." At the same time, the act shows forth the " Lord's death till he come," and accordingly is prospective. As a natural fact, memory is the great feeder of the imagination, and is ever exciting it to picture the future. Except for memory, the imagination could not exist, or, if existing, would be a very imperfect because torpid faculty. As a religious organ, the medium as we have seen of the Spirit, the memory stimulates the imagination and qualifies it to " show the Lord's death till he come." St. Paul mentions *first* the " remembrance " in connection with the broken body and again with the blood, and *then* comes the idea of showing, or proclaiming. Of course, the supper had to be a memorial before it could be an anticipation, but the order involves more than chronological sequence. It is an inner order of ideas, and it states, we think, with force and precision the relativity of these ideas. If this analysis be correct, then the determinative idea in the institution is its memorial character (*remembrance*), and by this idea we are to judge its nature and influence. Yet not alone by this abstractly viewed, since memory is supplemented by imagination and its vivid sense of futurity. From this point of view we understand why St. Paul should protest so strongly against the shocking abuse of the Lord's Supper among the Corinthians. With this feast, instituted and consecrated by Christ himself, its purpose being to bring him back into their midst and to enable them to realize his coming again, the two ideas being closely joined,—with this tender remembrance and expectation they had associated sensual pleasures, eating and drinking to excess, separating themselves into classes, despising the Church of God, and bringing condemnation upon themselves. What of Christ was in all this? Instead of memories of his sacrificial death, instead of their personal recollections of his providence and grace in their behalf, instead of touching and humbling recallings of how he had dealt with each of them, what utter forgetfulness, what a closing up of every avenue of the past opening into the present, and what a concentration in the animal gratifications of the hour! Instead of anticipation and joyous hope, looking to the Lord's coming, what blindness to all but the transient festivities of the carnal senses! On this account (therefore) "many are weak and sickly among you, and many sleep." The reference is not to the weakness and sickliness that follow the violations of natural laws, nor is the sleep the falling asleep in Jesus, but a punishment sent from God and executed under the directive agency of providence. Just in proportion as a man realizes Christ in the past will he realize him in the future. Just in the degree that he loses him from the past of his own heart, in that same degree will he vacate the future of his glorious image. The present is all, and it is all of the senses. And when God arises to judgment, as in the case of the Corinthians, what a sudden intensity surcharges the present, the blessedness of the old yesterdays and the awaiting to-morrows all extinguished, and the immediate moments, once so fugitive and so eager to glorify themselves by larger additions, lingering now and lengthening in the keener consciousness of pain and remorseful anguish! "Judge yourselves," O Corinthians! Examine your hearts; return to your memories and expectations; go to the cross of Christ and learn the lesson of its self-sacrifice; condemn and punish yourselves for the guilty past; and make this discipline of self a chastening for future well-being. But let no true and humble soul be tortured by the thought of eating and drinking "unworthily," and thereby incurring "condemnation." Whoever comes to the Lord's Supper after a close self-examination aided by the Spirit, and brings to it a meek and trustful mind; whoever repairs to it after he has communed with his memories of Christ's goodness to him,—will be a worthy participant in the sacred rite, and may surely expect the seal of God's approbation. A Christian child may understand the essential idea and spirit of the institution. And yet it has connections that transcend all thought, and the soul of every devout communicant welcomes the mysterious glory with which it is invested. Charles Wesley sings for every believer when he says—

> "His presence makes the feast,
> And now our bosoms feel
> The glory not to be expressed,
> The joy unspeakable."

L.

Ver. 1.—*Imitation.* The personal feelings of the apostle come out in these Epistles to the Corinthians perhaps more than in any other of his writings. This may well have been because at Corinth his authority was questioned, and other teachers were by some exalted as his rivals or superiors. That he should resent such treatment from those who were under peculiar obligations to him we can well understand; and it is very natural that he should be led all the more boldly to vindicate his apostolic character and to assert his apostolic authority. There is self-confidence of a just and warrantable kind in the admonition and challenge of this language: "Be ye imitators of me."

I. THE PRINCIPLE TO WHICH THE APOSTLE HERE APPEALS—IMITATION. 1. It is a principle natural to all mankind. Most conspicuous is it in the case of children and young people, and in the case of the uncivilized and untutored, who cannot easily acquire knowledge through symbols, but who learn arts with great facility through imitation. 2. Its range of operation is as extensive as the nature of man. We trace it in exercise in the bodily life, for multitudes of acts and of arts are acquired by those who carefully copy the proceedings of others. We trace it in the mental life: ways of thinking, of regarding life generally and one's fellow-men in particular, moral judgments and habits,—all are owing largely to imitation. 3. It is of set purpose employed in all education; for the discipline and culture of the young is almost dependent upon the operation of this interesting and most powerful principle of human nature.

II. THE GREAT AND GENERAL USE WHICH CHRISTIANITY MAKES OF THIS PRINCIPLE. 1. In the Holy Scriptures, especially of the New Testament, men are summoned to be followers, imitators of God, in all his moral perfections. It is represented that the excellences which are supreme and glorious in him may inspire us with the desire and resolve to copy and to acquire them in our measure for ourselves. 2. Jesus Christ is set before us as the especial Object of our reverence, as the highest Model for us to study and to imitate. It is possible that, through our reverence for him as our Divine Saviour, we may lose sight of the fact that he is also our human Exemplar. We are summoned to grow up in all things unto him. 3. Yet this grace of imitation is to be ours, through our response to the love of Jesus and our participation in the Spirit of Jesus. It is not a mechanical, but a spiritual, intelligent, living process. We must love with the love of admiration, sympathy, congeniality, in order that we may be changed into the same image.

III. THE SPECIAL APPLICATION PAUL MAKES OF THIS PRINCIPLE. 1. Religion permits us to study human models of excellence and to aim at conformity with such. Thus the author of the Epistle to the Hebrews sets before his readers illustrious examples of faith, as a practical and powerful principle governing and inspiring human nature and life. And here Paul requires of the Corinthians that they should be imitators of him. How many Christians in all ages have been fired with this noble ambition! And how wonderfully has it proved for the advantage of the Church and of the world that it has been so! 2. The limitation set to this principle: "Even as I also am of Christ." This was an acknowledgment of the Lord's supremacy; in copying Paul, the Corinthians were only to be copying Christ, as it were, at one remove. 3. The extent to which this imitation was designed to go. Surely they might, and we may, be imitators of the apostle, in his love to Christ, in his devotion to Christ's cause, in his affliction for Christ's people, in his obedience to Christ's laws, in his willingness to suffer for Christ's sake, in his wise forbearance with the infirmities of the brethren, and in his overflowing and very practical brotherly kindness and charity. In these respects it is not possible to follow Paul without at the same time following Christ.—T.

Ver. 2.—*Apostolic authority and traditions.* In using language so imperious to all seeming as this is, St. Paul spake as an *apostle,* i.e. as one sent and commissioned by the Divine Head and Ruler of the Church. That he should use such language at all is very instructive and significant to all who read the Epistles and desire to receive them in the appropriate and intended spirit.

I. APOSTOLIC INDIVIDUALITY AND AUTHORITY ASSERTED. "That ye remember *me.*" What an assumption is here of importance and peculiar authority! It was Paul's great concern that his converts should remember Christ: does he here set himself up as a rival of the Lord? By no means. But he claims to be the minister, the ambassador of Christ to the Churches, whose words are to be received as the words of one speaking by the Spirit of Christ. Readers of the New Testament are by such language reminded that the inspired writers, through their personal, intimate, official relation to Christ, have a claim upon the respectful attention and the cordial faith of those who profess to be Christ's.

II. THE OBSERVANCE OF INSPIRED TRADITIONS ENJOINED. In Christianity there is an element of law and an element of liberty; and these two elements are in harmony each with the other, the two being necessary in order to the completeness of the dispensation. In some passages even of this Epistle stress is laid upon freedom; whilst in this verse stress is laid upon subjection. Traditions, communications, of a religious kind had been committed by the apostle to these Corinthians. What were these? 1. Traditions of *doctrine.* It was from Paul's lips that many of them had first heard the gospel; to him all were indebted for the systematic exposition of its glorious truths. 2. Traditions of *precept and conduct.* This letter is itself full of such; for Paul combined, in a remarkable and admirable manner, the functions of the teacher of truth and those of the ethical instructor. 3. Traditions of *discipline*. As soon as societies were formed, it became necessary to draw up and promulgate regulations for the internal government and ordering of such societies. They naturally looked to inspired apostles for directions how to proceed, and they did not look in vain. The context shows us how dependent the first Churches were upon apostolic guidance for the maintenance of their order and the administration of their offices and affairs.

III. SUBJECTION TO APOSTOLICAL DIRECTIONS COMMENDED. We gain here an insight into the very mixed character of the members of the primitive Churches. Much in their conduct is in this very Epistle censured with something like severity; yet praise is not withheld where praise is due. There is a kind of praise which is dangerous, which involves insincerity on the part of those who offer, and fosters pride on the part of those who receive it. Yet the general fault amongst men and amongst Christians is unduly to withhold praise. Such commendation as this of the apostle could not but encourage and stimulate to a cheerful and resolute obedience to the injunctions of apostolic and Divine authority.—T.

Ver. 3.—*The hierarchy*. Before entering upon particular counsels with regard to the attire of the two sexes respectively in the Christian assemblies, St. Paul lays down a great general principle, from which, rather than from custom or from experience, he deduces the special duties devolving upon the members of Christ's Church. The case upon which he was consulted, and upon which he gave his advice, has lost all practical interest, and is to us merely an antiquarian curiosity; but the great principle propounded in connection with it holds good for all time.

I. THE APPOINTED SUBORDINATION OF WOMAN TO MAN. There is a sense in which there is equality between the sexes. In Christ Jesus there is neither male nor female. The gospel is intended for and is offered to both men and women. Both are equally dear to him who died for all. As in Jesus' earthly ministry he wrought cures and expelled demons for the relief of women, and as he chose certain women as his personal friends, and as he willingly accepted the affectionate and generous ministration of other women; so in the dispensation of the Spirit he numbers women amongst his people, and honours them by promoting them to his service. There is, so to speak, spiritual equality. But domestic and social equality is quite another thing. In the household and in the congregation there must be subjection and submission. "Order is Heaven's first law." "The head of the woman is the man." And this notwithstanding that many men are base and unworthy of their position and calling; notwithstanding that many women are not only pure, but noble and well fitted for command.

II. THE ARCHETYPE IN SPIRITUAL AND HEAVENLY RELATIONS TO WHICH THIS ORDER CONFORMS. 1. Man is not supreme, though invested with a limited authority. "The head of every man is Christ." He, the Son of man, has the primacy over this humanity. In wisdom and in righteousness, in power and in grace, the Lord Jesus is superior and supreme. The law is revealed in him and administered by him. Every man is morally bound to subjection and submission to the Divine Man. And he is Head over all things to his Church. This is the truth, the ideal, the purpose of eternal wisdom; though, alas! often misunderstood, or forgotten, or denied by men. 2. Even in the Godhead there is an official subordination of the Son to the Father; "the head of Christ is God." This language takes us into the region of heavenly things, of Divine mysteries. But it reveals to us the fact that the universe is one great hierarchy, of which not every member is mentioned here, only certain leading dominant notes being successively sounded in the celestial scale. Men may suppose that order and subordination in human society, civil and ecclesiastical, are merely expedients for peace and quietness. But it is not so; there is Divine archetype to which human relationships and affairs conform. Let there be non-conformity to this, and there is discord breaking in upon the harmonious minstrelsy of the spiritual universe. Let there be conformity, and the sweet concert proves that earth is in tune with heaven.—T.

Ver. 7.—*Man the image and glory of God*. The Bible is the book of paradoxes; and, if it were not, it would not correspond with the facts of human nature and history. Nowhere do we find such an exposure of human sin and such denunciations of human guilt as in the Scriptures. And, on the other hand, nowhere do we meet with such majestic representations of man's grandeur and dignity. There is a depth in this simple but inspiring language which we cannot fathom; but we may remark some particulars in which it is verified by facts.

I. MAN IS GOD'S IMAGE AND GLORY IN HIS FORM AND FEATURES. This seems to be asserted in this passage. Why must not man's head be veiled when in the sacred assembly he draws near to the Father of spirits, the Lord of the universe? Because "he is the image and glory of God." This does not imply that the Divine Being possesses a body as man does. No such anthropomorphism is suggested in the text. But so far as matter can be moulded into a form which shadows forth the Divine majesty, it has been so fashioned in the construction of the human frame and features. High thoughts, noble impulses, pure desires, tender sympathy, these—the glory of humanity—are written upon the countenance of man.

II. IN HIS INTELLECTUAL AND MORAL ENDOWMENTS. This is probably what is meant by the declaration in Genesis that God made man in his own image. In his capacity to apprehend truth, in his recognition of moral excellence, in his power of will, man resembles his Maker. And there is no way by which we can arrive at a knowledge of God in his higher attributes other than by the aid of the nature with which he has endowed us, and which he has declared to be akin to his own.

III. IN HIS POSITION OF SUBORDINATE RULE OVER THE CREATION. The psalmist asserts that God crowned man with glory and honour, and set him over the works of his hands, putting all things under his control. Thus did the Lord of all delegate to his vicegerent an authority resembling his own.

IV. IN THE BROTHERHOOD OF JESUS CHRIST. The assumption of human nature by the eternal Word was only possible because man was originally made in the Divine image. It is wonderful to find language so similar used concerning man and concerning the Son of God, who is described as "the emanation from the Father's glory, and the very image of his substance." The Incarnation seems a necessity even to explain the nature of man; it casts a halo of glory and radiance around the human form, the human destiny. For the Incarnation was the condition, not only of a Divine manifestation, but of the redemption of humanity; and Christ's purpose was to bring many sons unto glory.

V. IN HIS FUTURE OF ETERNAL BLESSEDNESS. All things which show forth God's glory are passing and perishing. Man alone of all that is earthly is appointed for immortality. The mirror that reflects so bright a light shall never be broken; the glory which man receives from heaven and returns to heaven shall never fade.—T.

Ver. 20.—"*The Lord's Supper.*" The abuses and disorders which prevailed in the Corinthian Church served as an occasion for an apostolic exhibition and inculcation of a more excellent way. Incidentally, we are indebted to them for the account given by the apostle of the original institution, and for instructions as to the proper observance of the ordinance. The designation here applied to the distinctive observance of the Christian Church is one of beautiful simplicity, and suggests an exposition of the acknowledged nature and benefit of the ordinance.

I. THE DIVINE AUTHORITY OF THE LORD'S SUPPER. 1. It is an ordinance of Christ, and its observance is consequently an act of obedience on the part of his people. It is not a service of man's device; the Lord himself has said, "Do this." 2. It is a tradition of apostolic times. Paul professed to have "received from the Lord that which he delivered." The sacrament was accordingly celebrated within a generation of Christ's own lifetime, and has been celebrated in unbroken continuity from that time to our own. 3. It was in the first century a regular observance of the Christian societies. This is apparent from the way in which it is mentioned in this Epistle; it is treated as something actually existing, although in some cases misunderstood and abused. And as Paul writes, "As oft as ye," etc., it is presumed that the observance took place regularly and frequently.

II. THE DOCTRINAL SIGNIFICANCE OF THE LORD'S SUPPER. 1. It is a memorial of Christ, and especially of his death. He himself appointed that it should be observed "in remembrance of" himself and of his sufferings whose body was broken and whose blood was shed for his people. 2. It is a Eucharist, or service of thanksgiving. The Institutor of the ordinance "gave thanks," or "blessed," probably upon the suggestion of the cup of which the Jews partook during the Paschal meal. The sacrament is a reminder of all the benefits which we have received from God, and especially of the "unspeakable gift." 3. It is a symbol and means of spiritual nourishment. Spiritually, the communicants eat the body and drink the blood of their Saviour, partaking and feeding upon Christ by faith. The real presence of the Redeemer is experienced in the heart of the faithful recipient. 4. It is a bond of fellowship and brotherhood. Hence called a communion, or *the* communion, as the appointed means and manifestation of a true spiritual unity. The brethren of the family are seated at one table, they join in one meal or sacred feast, they eat of one loaf and drink of one cup.

III. THE SPIRITUAL PROFIT OF THE LORD'S SUPPER. 1. It is a divinely appointed means of increased and more vivid fellowship with the unseen Redeemer, who in this service draws near to those who draw near to him. 2. It is a profession of faith, attachment, and loyalty, the admitted and enjoined method of declaring upon which side we stand in the moral conflict which rages, under whose banner we have enlisted, and whom we purpose loyally to serve. 3. It is a testimony to the unbelieving world around. The death of Christ is proclaimed, not only to those within, but to those without. More effectively than by words, men are reminded that the grace of God and the salvation of Christ have come very nigh unto them.—T.

Ver. 26.—*The Church's proclamation.* What so fitted to rebuke those who profaned the Supper of the Lord, what so fitted to arouse them to a sense of their high calling, as a solemn declaration like this? The noisy, greedy, quarrelsome gatherings which seem at Corinth to have been associated with the professed observance of one of the highest mysteries of the Christian faith, naturally awakened the indignation and the reproaches of the apostle. Recalling them to a sense of the dignity of their position as witnesses to God in an ignorant and sinful world, the apostle summons the Corinthian Christians so to eat the bread and drink the cup of the Eucharist as to declare to all the sacred tidings of a Redeemer's death.

I. THIS SACRAMENT IS A COMMEMORATION OF THE PAST. The Lord's death was an admitted fact; and if anything was needed to establish the historical fact, the existence of this ordinance was sufficient and more than sufficient for the purpose. But men may forget and lose sight of an event which they do not dream of denying. And it seemed good to Divine wisdom that the crucifixion and sacrifice of the Son of God should be held in everlasting memory by means of this simple but most significant observance. It was not simply as an historical fact that the death of Christ was to be recorded, but as a Christian doctrine. Christ's was a redeeming, atoning, reconciling death; and as such was cherished in everlasting memory by those who profited by it, who owed to it their eternal hopes.

II. THIS SACRAMENT IS A PROCLAMATION TO THE PRESENT. "Ye set forth, or proclaim, the Lord's death," says the apostle. And from his expression, "as often," it may be inferred that periodically and frequently the primitive Christians kept the feast, remembering and declaring that "Christ our Passover is slain for us." There is something very affecting and at the same time very inspiring in this representation. From generation to generation and from age to age the sacrament of the Lord's body and blood publishes salvation to mankind, telling of him who tasted death for every man, and in his cross reconciled the world unto God. It is an aspect of the Holy Communion which should not be left out of sight, upon which great stress should be laid; for some, whom words may fail to reach, may have their hearts opened to the grace and love of Christ by witnessing the silent yet eloquent declaration concerning the Saviour which is presented when the members of Christ's Church partake of the symbols of their redemption.

III. THIS SACRAMENT IS A PREDICTION OF THE FUTURE. "Till he come!" Our Lord, in instituting the ordinance, had turned the gaze of his disciples towards the future, speaking of drinking wine new in the kingdom of God. And here the eye of faith is pointed on to the glory which shall be revealed when he who came to die shall come to judge, shall come to reign!

> "And thus that dark betrayal night,
> With the last advent we unite
> By one bright chain of loving rite,
> Until he come!"

T.

Vers. 1—16.—*Decency in public worship.* When we appear before God we should observe the greatest propriety. Externals should not be lost sight of, for they are *significant.* Often they are indicative of inward condition. The apostle had occasion to blame the women of Corinth for laying aside the veil—the mark of modesty and subjection—in public assemblies. On the ground of the abolition of distinction of sex in Christ, they claimed equality in every respect with men, and the right to appear and act as men did. Whilst women, they would be as men. Equality as believers they had a right to claim, but they forgot their "subjection in point of *order, modesty,* and *seemliness.*" When women leave their proper sphere, it is never to rise, but to fall. Men-women are failures. In the apostle's argument valuable truths are enunciated.

I. He DEFINES MAN'S POSITION. 1. *Man is the head of the woman.* (Ver. 3.) Woman is subordinate to man, is largely dependent upon him. He is her natural guide, defender, supporter. Authority lies with him, not with her. "I suffer not a woman to . . . usurp authority over the man . . . for Adam was first formed, then Eve" (1 Tim. ii. 12, 13). Woman is the "weaker vessel" (1 Pet. iii. 7). She is to be "in subjection" (ch. xiv. 34). This is after the Divine order, and any subversal of it is sure to lead to injurious results. 2. *The head of man is Christ.* (Ver. 3.) Man is not a monarch; he is subordinate to the God-Man as his Head. Man can only act aright as head of the woman when he recognizes Christ as his Head. The apostle does not mean to intimate that Christ is not the Head of the woman as of the man. He is pointing out the order in the Divine economy, and "by the term 'head' he expresses the next immediate relation sustained." Man is subordinate to Christ; woman is subordinate, though not in the same sense, to man as well as to Christ. To further illustrate the Divine order, the apostle states that: 3. *The head of Christ is God.* That is, of Christ the *God-Man.* There is nothing here which conflicts with the doctrine of the divinity of Christ or of the equality of the Son with the Father. Rather is there here additional evidence of the former, since the distinction between the position of man and woman obtains where there is identity of nature. Christ is here spoken of as he assumed "the form of a servant." Christ in his mediatorial capacity is lower than the Father (John xiv. 28). 4. *Man is the Image and Glory of God.* (Ver. 7.) Man was made in the likeness of God (Gen. i. 26). How great is the dignity of human nature! But how that dignity is lost *when God is blotted out of a man!* How eagerly should fallen creatures seek recovery, that the blurred image may be restored to its original beauty, and the impaired glory made once more lustrous! Through the Son of man, the ideal Man—declared to be "the brightness of his glory and the express image of his person"—this may be effected. The apostle does not intend to convey that woman is not in many respects the image and glory of God, but that man is this "*first* and *directly,* woman *subsequently* and *indirectly.*" Man represents the authority of God; he is the ruler, the head.

II. He DEFINES WOMAN'S POSITION. 1. *She is subject to man as her head.* She sprang from him (ver. 8). She was created for him (ver. 9). Still, there is mutual dependence: "Neither is the man without the woman, neither the woman without the man" (ver. 11). "In the Lord"—this is of Divine appointment. And man and woman constitute complete humanity—one supplying what the other lacks; and thus forming in Christ "the Bride," the Church redeemed by his blood. And further, although at first woman sprang from man, now the man is of the woman (ver. 12). But "all things are of God"—man and woman. Man has a *real* but *qualified* supremacy; *so* qualified as to save woman from any *humiliation,* and to allow her a position of peculiar dignity and beauty. 2. *She is the glory of the man.* (Ver. 7.) Woman is not directly the glory of God; she does not directly represent God as the head of creation—she rather is man's representative, as man is God's. She is the glory of man directly, of God indirectly. Man is the sun, woman the moon (Gen. xxxvii. 9).

III. His CONCLUSIONS AS TO PROPRIETY OF DRESS IN PUBLIC WORSHIP. 1. *That man should not have his head covered.* The covering would indicate subjection, which, in relation to those joining with man in public worship, was not man's true condition. There he appeared as "the image and glory of God," representing the Divine headship, and to assume the badge of subjection would be to "dishonour his head." This may mean to dishonour his own head by placing upon it something unsuitable, or to dishonour Christ, the Head of man, who has placed man in his position of honour. We should not usurp a higher position than God has appointed for us; we should not take a lower. Our best place is where God places us. 2. *That woman should have her head covered.* The veil was a recognition of subordination and an indication of modesty. To discard it was to claim man's position and thus to dishonour man, her head—or to dishonour her own head by depriving it of a mark of propriety and even of chastity. For by discarding the head-covering a woman put herself in the class of the disreputable. It was but a carrying out of the principle involved for a woman to have her head shaved (vers. 5, 6), which was sometimes done in the case of those who had forfeited their honour, and became thus a brand of infamy. Thus a woman snatching at the position of man would descend far below her own. An apparent rise is sometimes a very real fall. The apostle enforces his argument by: (1) An appeal to nature (vers. 14, 15). Paul evidently thinks that there is accord between the kingdom of nature and of grace. Both are from one hand and one mind, and conflicts between the two may be very apparent, but can never be real. Nature gives the man short hair and the woman long; here is a natural distinction which should be observed, and which indicates that woman specially needs the head-covering. Or by nature the apostle may mean what obtains among men who are not instructed by revelation. Among many of the heathen the wearing of the hair long by men was ridiculed, but long hair for women was generally recognized as appropriate. (2) The presence of angels in Christian assemblies (ver. 16). Earth looks on, but heaven also. Woman should have the symbol of power, of subjection to man, upon her head, because any usurpation of improper position or flaunting boldness would be offensive to these heavenly visitors. (3) Apostolic authority (ver. 10). Where reasoning fails, authority must utter her voice. Paul always preferred to convince rather than to compel. But he possessed the right to determine when the contentious persevered in contention. The regulation was according to the mind of an inspired apostle, and was observed by Churches founded by himself or other like-minded leaders. In estimating the teaching of the passage, we must discriminate between the *necessary* and the *accidental*. The principle is that women should be so attired as to indicate, or at all events so as not to conflict with, their rightful position. Amongst those to whom the apostle wrote, the veil was the symbol of modesty and subordination. Because women in Western Churches are not so attired, it does not follow that they are acting antagonistically to the apostle's precept, though it will be admitted by most that the preposterous head-gear of many female worshippers, in our own land calls loudly for reform, and is frequently an outrage upon all propriety and a sarcasm upon womanly modesty. I do not understand that the apostle has here specially in view the praying and preaching of women in public assemblies—this he deals with further on in the Epistle (ch. xiv. 34, etc.); but he is now insisting upon what is appropriate in the attire of woman (and incidentally of man) on public occasions. His primary reference is to public worship, and surely when we come to "appear before God," we ought to be most specially anxious that everything about us shall be decent and in order. Whilst nothing that is outward can compensate for absence of the inward, that which is external is often an index of the internal, and has its influence upon the internal.—H.

Vers. 17—22.—*Some hindrances to the right observance of the Lord's Supper.* Holy institutions may become unholy by perversion. That which is bestowed upon us as a peculiar blessing may prove a very real curse by misuse. The ordinance of the Lord's Supper is for our spiritual help and joy, but we may "come together not for the better, but for the worse." This was so with many of the Corinthians. They had conjoined to the Lord's Supper the love-feast. To this feast each brought his provision, the rich bringing more, so as to supply the deficiencies of the poor. From this supply the bread and wine required for the Lord's Supper were taken. These feasts were the occasions at which the evils reprobated by the apostle occurred. The poor were despised and neglected, the congregation became divided into cliques, some communicants were hungry, and others had drunk to excess. The apostle insists that, under such circumstances, it was impossible to observe aright the sacred feast of the Lord's Supper. Note some hindrances to right observance thus suggested.

I. PRIDE. At the Lord's table all are equal. Conventional distinctions disappear. There is one Lord, and "all ye are brethren." Arrogance and conceit, always out of place and intolerable, are most strikingly so where all should be humbled and subdued. It is not for us to think there how excellent we are, but how vile, and to admire the amazing grace which rescued us from the dominion of sin. Instead of despising others there, we should rather despise ourselves for our sins which crucified Christ, and we should feel, like Paul, that we are "the chief of sinners." It is utterly impossible for a proud heart to rightly show forth the death of him who was meek and lowly. It is preposterous and absurd to attempt it.

II. SELFISHNESS. How can the selfish have communion with the infinitely unselfish One! If we have a self-seeking, grasping, greedy spirit, what part can we have with him who "gave himself for us"? How alien to the spirit of Christ is the spirit of selfishness! If we sit with it at the table of the Lord, we sit there as Judas did.

III. ESTRANGEMENT. Christ calls us ever to union, and most specially and pathetically at his table, where we eat of the one bread (ch. x. 17). To cherish a spirit of disunion is to run directly counter to one of his commands at the moment when we profess to observe another. And the spectacle of estrangement at the Lord's Supper must be one of utmost offensiveness in the Divine sight, as it is one of greatest scandal in the eyes of men. If we seek to be one with Christ, we must also seek to be one with the brethren. He is the Head; we are the members of his body. How utterly incongruous to be disunited at that feast which specially sets forth our union with Christ and with one another!

IV. HATRED. This in some form generally accompanies division. But where is the place for hatred at the feast of dying love? God is love, Christ is love, and we are—hatred. How can two walk together unless they are agreed? What reason our Saviour had to hate us! "He was despised and rejected of men," crucified by men; and yet he loved men, and at his table his love is specially set forth. How can we there cherish our animosities, for which we have such little cause! "We know that we have passed from death into life, because we love the brethren. He that loveth not his brother abideth in death" (1 John iii. 14). The Lord's Supper is a song of love; hatred at it is a terrible discord.

V. GLUTTONY. Some of the Corinthians loved their meat more than they loved their brethren. They ate greedily, not even tarrying for others to arrive. A singular carnality for so spiritual a season. Men with the manners and unrestrained appetites of beasts are scarcely fit for the table of Christ. Sensuality and spirituality are at opposite poles. Those who abandon themselves to gratify the lower nature sacrifice the higher. "Man shall not live by bread alone."

VI. DRUNKENNESS. It seems scarcely credible that any should have drunk to the excess of intoxication at the love-feast so intimately associated with the Eucharist; but it is to be feared that this was so. And there are degrees of intoxication, so that the danger of imitating the Corinthians in this matter may not be so remote from some as they imagine. There is a great deal of semi-intoxication. And if this sin be not committed immediately before the Lord's table is approached, undue indulgence at all is surely a fatal hindrance to right observance. No drunkard shall inherit the kingdom of heaven. And no drunkard, whilst he cleaves to his degrading habit, is entitled to a place at the Lord's table.

VII. IRREVERENCE. There must have been vast irreverence in the Corinthians rebuked by Paul, or such abuses could never have obtained amongst them. There may be as much irreverence in us, though we do not commit the same sins. Anyway, to approach the Lord's table irreverently is to instantly demonstrate our unfitness. There we should be filled with godly fear, and our hearts should be subdued to greatest devoutness and awe as we marvel over the justice of Jehovah, the amazing sacrifice of Christ, and the tender ministry of the Divine Spirit, whereby we who were once afar off are brought nigh.—H.

Vers. 23—26.—The sacred feast. Paul's description is singularly beautiful. His information apparently came directly from Christ (Gal. i. 12). Additional importance attaches to the observance of the Lord's Supper, since an express revelation was made to the great apostle of the Gentiles. The supper was for the Gentile world as well as the Jewish. Its institution was associated with the preaching of the gospel throughout the world.

I. ITS INSTITUTION. By the Lord Jesus (ver. 23). 1. *Personally.* Evidently important in his eyes. Specially precious to us because instituted personally by our Master. Appropriate; for he in his great redemptive work is set forth. Christ is "all in all" at his table. As Christ was present at the first celebration, he should be looked for at every celebration. 2. *Under most affecting circumstances.* "The same night in which he was betrayed;" *whilst betrayal was proceeding—and this known to him.* (1) He thought of others rather than of himself. Might have been expected to think of his sufferings; he thought of our needs. He had sorrow, but no selfish sorrow. The unselfishness of Christ is here shown in unrivalled beauty. (2) His love was not quenched by treachery. The betrayal by Judas did not dry up his fount of affection. When treachery was at its height, love was at its height also. When men are most anxious to injure us, we should be most anxious to do them good. (3) His sacrifice was not arrested by hate. The multitude were hotly against him when he prepared to give himself for them. Outside the upper room and inside in the breast of Judas there was bitter hate, but Christ was not checked in his purpose for an instant. He resolved to *go on* and to fulfil all that had been foretold respecting him, and so he quietly and calmly instituted the supper which should in every after age testify to incomparable self-sacrifice under all—adverse conditions. If we would be like Christ, hostility must not hinder sacrifice.

II. ITS MODE. 1. *Thanksgiving.* Thanksgiving for the bread and wine. We should not "say grace" but really "give thanks." Perhaps to teach us that our thanksgivings should ascend for what the bread and wine typify. 2. *Bread.* (1) Symbolic of Christ's body. Not actually his body, seeing that that was intact and before the eyes of the disciples. If Rome's teaching were true, the disciples would have required a very lengthy explanation to enable them to grasp the meaning. We have no such explanation recorded; we might have expected it in this place, if anywhere. (2) Broken. Many see in this a symbol of the violent death of Christ. But the better rendering of ver. 24 is, "This is my body which is for you." Breaking the bread was, I rather think, the mere adoption of a custom suited to the kind of bread used at that time in Palestine. We read, "A bone of him shall not be broken." (3) Eaten. Indicating that we are to feed upon Christ spiritually, to appropriate, to assimilate, him. 3. *Wine.* Symbolic of Christ's blood shed for the remission of sins. Partaken of to indicate the application of the blood of Christ to our hearts and consciences. The blood must not only be shed, it must be applied.

III. ITS SIGNIFICANCE. 1. *Remembrance of Christ.* Of his dying love specially; and of his life, lordship, etc. 2. *Communion with Christ and with each other.* (See ch. x. 16, 17.) 3. *A feast.* We feed upon Christ spiritually. As bread and wine support the body, so he supports the soul. There is a physical symbol and a spiritual reality. Joy should be one element in the observance; it is a feast, not a funeral. 4. *A covenant.* We enter into covenant with God for pardon, peace, service, and the covenant is ratified by the blood of Christ typified by wine: "This cup is the new covenant in my blood." The Hebrews entered into covenant with God when the blood of the heifer was sprinkled upon them; they bound themselves to obedience, and God bound himself to bestow the promised blessings; so when we receive the cup, we commemorate the covenant which we have entered into with God through the shed blood of Christ and the covenant which he has entered into with us. 5. *Proclamation of Christ's death.* Christ's death is the great central fact shadowed forth. The cross is exalted. Not a new sacrifice offered, but the old yet ever-new sacrifice of Calvary commemorated and shown forth. 6. *A pledge of the Lord's second coming.* "Till he come." He *will* come, and it is not for us to say, "My Lord delayeth his coming." He will come not too soon and not too late. "Till he come" we must be watching.

IV. ITS INCUMBENCY. "This do in remembrance of me." A dying command. Some believers have many excuses for not coming to the Lord's table; they do not find one here: "*This do.*" Last requests of loved ones are held precious: should not the request of this loved One be also? In this command our welfare is consulted as in all Divine commands laid upon us. We *lose much* if we refrain from doing this in remembrance of our Master—much spiritual joy, enlightenment, strengthening, and not a little usefulness. The Lord's table is the Elim of Christians; we act foolishly if we fail to embrace opportunities of resting beneath its palm trees and drinking from its many wells of living water.—H.

Ver. 24.—*Remembering Christ.* The Lord's Supper is very specially a feast of *remembrance.* Is there in it a suggestion that we are very prone to forget Christ? This is, alas! our tendency, and here we are in strange contrast to our Lord. He needs nothing to keep us in his remembrance; he ever thinks of his people. In the institution of the Lord's Supper he thinks of our forgetfulness, of its perils, of its certain sorrows. He remembers that we are prone not to remember him. What should we remember concerning Christ?

I. HIS HOLY SPOTLESS LIFE. What a life that was! The greatest and best of human leaders have been marked by defects, but our Leader was "without blemish." In the lives of heroes there is always something which we should be glad to forget; but there is *nothing* in the life of Christ. Jealousy, hatred, malice, and all uncharitableness could find in him "no fault." Many great men have grown small, many holy men questionable in character, many honoured men dishonourable, under the ruthless criticism of modern times; but not Jesus of Nazareth. The fiercest light has been focussed upon his earthly course; the brains of sceptic and of scoffer have been racked in prolonged endeavour to discover the flaw; *but it has not been discovered yet!* The voices of all the centuries cry, "Without fault!" "Holy and undefiled!" "Separate from sinners!" Well may we remember that life.

II. HIS TEACHING. When compared with Christ, all the other teachers of the world seem to have nothing to teach *upon matters of high moment.* At best they *guess,* and often they guess folly. He teaches with the authority of knowledge; all other teachers seem hidden in the valley, imagining what the landscape may be. He alone has climbed the hill and *beholds* what he speaks about. We need to remember, more than we are accustomed to do, the utterances of the world's great Teacher. Seekers after knowledge should be careful lest after all they miss the richest mine of truth. Learned scoffings and atheistical ribaldries are naught but devil-blinds to hide from our view the beautiful form of truth as it is in Christ. In him "are hid all the treasures of wisdom and knowledge" (Col. ii. 3). When God broke the dread silence upon the Mount of Transfiguration it was to exclaim, "This is my beloved Son: *hear him.*" The Holy Ghost was promised as One who would "bring to remembrance" what Christ had declared. Through the Lord's Supper, as a means, the Divine Spirit works now for this end.

III. HIS MIRACLES. These speak eloquently of his power. Nature bows before her God. How weak the mightiest of the earth are compared with this mighty One! When the kingdom of Christ is about to be overwhelmed and shattered and generally annihilated by blatant wiseacre warriors, with their sceptical pea-shooters and atheistical popguns, I laugh as I remember that it is the kingdom of *Christ* which is being assailed! We do well to bear in mind what *Christ did* when he was upon earth, and then to say quietly to ourselves, "The same yesterday, to-day, and for ever." What he did, he can do; what he was, he is. His miracles illustrated his beneficence. They meant the supply of human need, the binding up of wounds, the restoration of the outcast, the arrest of sorrow, the wiping away of tears, the cheer of lonely hearts. We must remember his miracles; they show so truly *what the Christ was.* With all his omnipotence, how gentle and tender!

IV. HIS DEATH. This was the grand culmination of his life; it gave to him the great title of Saviour; to it the Lord's Supper specially points. We must remember him as the One who laid down his life for us, who bore our griefs and carried our sorrows, who was wounded for our trangressions and bruised for our iniquities, who died the just for the unjust that he might bring us to God. The Lord's Supper leads us to Calvary—through the motley crowd, past the weeping Marys, beyond the penitent thief, to the central figure in the Judæan tragedy, and there we see *salvation!* "Mercy and truth are met together; righteousness and peace have kissed each other" (Ps. lxxxv. 10). Remembrance of Christ's death will mean remembrance of *our sinfulness.* And when we remember that "he endured the cross, despising the shame," we may ask ourselves the suggestive question, "What would be our present condition and prospect if he had not done so?"

V. His resurrection and ascension. The Lord's Supper was for the remembrance of Christ both after he had died and after he had risen from the dead. We must not forget the dying Christ; but neither must we forget the *triumphing* Christ. The resurrection of Christ is the counterpart of the cross ; one is not without the other. The Lord died, but the Lord is risen indeed. He came to this world in abasement; he lived so, he died so, but he did not depart so. He rose from the dead, *and ever liveth*. We remember the dying Christ, but we remember also the living Christ, exalted at God's right hand, our Advocate, preparing our heavenly home, looking down upon us, present with us by his Spirit. We remember the reigning Christ, the One who has completed his glorious redemptive work, who has triumphed openly, and we remember him thus " till he come."

VI. His marvellous love. Shown in every incident and every instant of his course. In his coming ; in his words, deeds, spirit ; and pre-eminently in his sufferings and death. God is love; Christ is God; Christ is love.

VII. His personality. Not only what he said and what he did, *but what he was*. All his acts and words of beneficence and love were only *expressions of himself*. They were but manifestations of what dwells in perpetual fulness in his heart. Remember *him*. " This do in remembrance of *me*." This is a *dying request. Are we observing it ?* The dying request of him who " *gave himself* " for us.—H.

Vers. 27—29.—*Perils at the Lord's table.* A frequent question, " Who should come to the Lord's table ? " Many have come who ought not to have come *as they were ;* not a few have been deterred from coming who were quite suitable. Many have not pondered sufficiently the duty of observing the Lord's Supper ; many have been alarmed by certain expressions contained in this passage.

I. Glance at the scene. It lies in gay, voluptuous, immoral Corinth. A city magnificent externally ; abased and abandoned internally. A meeting of Christians in some private house, light amid darkness, truth surrounded by error, holiness in the centre of corruption. The gathering is for the love-feast and the Supper of the Lord. A love-feast, alas ! in which love is largely absent ; a Supper of the Lord in which the Lord is strangely dishonoured. The light is dimmed, the truth is alloyed with error, the holiness is defiled by guilt. There are divisions (ch. i. 11, 12) ; there are pride, selfishness, irreverence (vers. 21, 22) ; there is even drunkenness (ver. 21) ; yea, even further, the hideous head of immorality is raised in the midst of this little Christian society (ch. v. 1). This Epistle arrives from the founder of the Church—a letter smiting Corinthian transgression and transgressors hip and thigh. Picture the scene !

II. Glance at certain words and their meanings. 1. *Damnation.* This word has so terrified some that they have never been able to summon sufficient courage to obey the dying command of their Lord. They have supposed that an unworthy participation in the sacred feast would seal their doom and consign them to perdition without remedy. But the word does not justify such a view. Instead of " damnation," we should read, as in the Revised Version, " judgment." And ver. 32 explains what " judgment " means : " When we are judged, we are *chastened* of the Lord, *that we should not be condemned with the world.*" Judgment here means " chastisement," and note particularly that this chastisement is sent *to prevent us from being condemned with unbelievers.* What follows upon unworthy participation at the Lord's table, if we are believers, is not something to destroy us, *but something to prevent us from being destroyed.* If we will not benefit by the chastisement, if under it we harden our hearts like Israel of old, then we shall be cast away. The sin of unworthy participation is great, and the correction will be severe, but neither is what some sensitive natures have dreaded. 2. *Unworthily.* Note that the apostle speaks of the unworthiness of the *act*, not the unworthiness of the *person*. To say, " I am unworthy," is doubtless to speak the truth, but it is *irrelevant*. Unworthy persons may participate worthily. Nay, further, only those who feel that they are unworthy are in a right state to sit at the table. The self-righteous are never " fit." The supper is for *penitent sinners ;* for such as Paul, " the chief of sinners." But the act may be unworthy, and that from many causes. Anything that hinders us from " discerning the Lord's body " (ver. 29) will cause us to eat and drink unworthily. We have to recognize the bread and wine as emblems of that body, as set apart to show this forth, and therefore to be dealt with solemnly, thoughtfully, reverently. We must enter into the meaning of the feast, and through the outward reach the inward and spiritual. At the supper we do not halt at the emblems ; we have fellowship with Christ, we remember him, we renew our vows, we profess to be his followers, we show forth his death "till he come." Now, many things may hinder us from doing this, and thus cause us to eat and drink unworthily ; such as : (1) Thoughtlessness, leading to irreverence. (2) Ignorance of the meaning of the ordinance. This may be very culpable ignorance. (3) Unconverted condition. Quite unfit for supper because have not received what it sets forth. (4) Worldly spirit. "Ye cannot serve God and mammon." We may be trying, and thus be *charging Christ with falsehood*, even as we approach his table. (5) Unbrotherly feeling. That which separates us from believers is very likely to separate us from Christ. (6) Immorality. If we hug sin, we cannot embrace the Saviour. Such unworthy participation involves : (1) Guilt. We become guilty of the body and blood of the Lord, seeing that our sin is concentrated upon that observance which specially sets these forth. (2) Punishment. "For this cause many are weak and sickly among you, and many sleep" (ver. 30). Present chastisement, and, if this prove inefficacious, future and final punishment.

III. A REMEDY. This is not to see that "we are good," according to a very current expression and impression. In one sense we can never be "fit." It is to examine or prove ourselves by (1) appeal to conscience, (2) God's Word, (3) God's Spirit. And what we have to ascertain is whether we (1) repent of sin, (2) believe on the Lord Jesus Christ, and (3) are seeking to live in the fear and love of God. If we are right upon these points, we need have no dread in approaching the Lord's table, but rather draw near in joy and confidence and in anticipation of large spiritual blessing.

IV. A WARNING. Remark that none are here told to absent themselves from the Lord's table. Not even the Corinthians most blamed, an apparent exception being the immoral person (ch. v. 1), and he was excluded only until he had shown repentance for his sin (2 Cor. ii. 7, 8). The reason is that to abstain from the Lord's Supper is to sin. We ought to be "fit," in the true sense of the expression. There is only one place which is right for us, and that is at the table. We *may* be wrong in coming ; we *must* be wrong in staying away. To refrain is to condemn ourselves at once. "This do in remembrance of me" is one of the most sacred of commands. If we are bound to break it because of our carnal and lost state, we do but multiply transgression. We are *not bound*, for we may escape from the condition which unfits us, and then draw near with boldness and with hope. There is a false humility restraining many from coming to the Lord's Supper; it is a *very false* humility and a very deceptive humility —it is the adding of another sin. Away from Christ we are altogether wrong, and in escaping from one sin (coming to the table whilst unconverted) we only fall into another (disobeying the dying command of Christ). There is every obligation resting upon us to repent, believe, and live to God ; then we are fitted to discharge the other obligation, "This do in remembrance of me." Failure in the one involves failure in the other, and our condemnation is increased. There is no *right place* for the unbeliever.—H.

Vers. 31, 32.—*The chastisement of believers.* The apostle has been speaking of disorders at the Lord's table and of the Divine judgments which in Corinth had followed upon the profanation of the sacred feast. He now pursues the latter theme and discourses upon the afflictions which sometimes fall upon the people of God.

I. ITS INFLICTOR. We may well ask, "Where do our troubles come from?" The chastisement of his people comes from God. "Whom the Lord loveth he chasteneth" (Heb. xii. 6). *God is behind the sorrow.* Reflect that : 1. *He sees sufficient cause for the chastisement.* This shows that there *is* sufficient cause. He never sends a trouble without a *cause*, and never without a *sufficient* cause. We may not see the cause, but he does. 2. *He might destroy instead of chastising.* There is *mercy* in the visitation : had there been wrath only, there had been destruction, not chastisement. 3. *He may destroy.* If chastisement does not bear fruit unto repentance, we shall be cut off as was Israel of old. Here is a solemn warning against resisting and resenting Divine chastisement. If we stiffen our neck and harden our heart, we shall be broken with a "rod of iron." We are in the hands of the *Omnipotent;* let us beware of folly and impiety. 4. *Chastise-*

ment is a message from God. We should *listen,* We should *learn* what the Lord our God has to say to us. We shall find in the chastisement a *command ;* it is for us to obey that command. We shall discover in it a *promise ;* it is for us to embrace it.

II. ITS CAUSE. Always sin in some form or other. Sin is the only possible cause. God does not afflict us "willingly" or for his "pleasure," but for our profit. We fall into sin and he whips us out. So when a believer transgresses he cuts a rod for his own back. Is it God who chastises us? More truly, we chastise ourselves. Our sin puts the rod into God's hand. We cry out *when we have hurt ourselves* if we cry out when we are under the chastisement of God.

III. ITS BENEVOLENCE. It is sent in love. It is a *good* gift, not an evil one. God has not changed in sending it ; he is still love. Here the special object of Divine chastisement is beautifully conveyed : "That we should not be condemned with the world." Many think that their afflictions will destroy them ; the afflictions are sent that they *may not be destroyed.* We feel that we shall sink under our troubles, but they are sent *that we may not sink.* We cry out "Poison !" but it is "medicine,", sent to keep us from being poisoned. God troubles his people now, that he may not trouble them hereafter. He smites them gently now, that he may not smite them then with the arm of destruction. They stand near the precipice and the rod falls upon them to drive them back. In heaven, perhaps, we shall bless God more for our earthly chastisements than for our earthly joys. Chastisement is sour to take, but sweet when taken. It is a nut hard and rough of shell, but goodly in kernel. It is the love of God transfigured into darkness by the black shadow of our sin.

IV. HOW WE MAY AVOID THE NECESSITY OF IT. "If we would judge [or, 'discern'] ourselves, we should not be judged." If we dealt with ourselves, there would be no need for God to deal with us. If we would avoid the *chastisement,* we must avoid the *sin.* If the *cause* be destroyed, we need not fear the *effect.* If the Corinthians had examined themselves, they would have avoided the irregularities of which they became guilty. They were careless, unwatchful, and so they fell, *and when they fell they opened the door of chastisement.* We may keep that door shut if we "walk with God," as Enoch did. The only way to escape the rod is to escape the necessity of it, and that is to escape the sin.—H.

Ver. 3.—*The headship of Christ.* "The head of every man is Christ." It may be of the man as distinct from the woman that the apostle here speaks, but the truth asserted is one in which all human beings, without regard to sexual or any other distinctions, are alike interested. The relation in which we each and all stand to Christ, or rather in which Christ stands to us, is one that surmounts and absorbs into itself every other relationship. As the vault of heaven surrounds the world, and the atmosphere in which it floats envelops everything that lives and moves and has its being in it; so does the authority of Christ embrace all that belongs to the existence of every one of us, and from it we can never escape. The supremacy here indicated has certain distinct phases.

I. EVERY MAN SEES HIS OWN HUMAN NATURE PERFECTED IN CHRIST. Manhood is perfectly represented in him. He is the Crown and Flower of our humanity; its realized ideal, "*the Man*"—the complete, consummate, faultless man—"Christ Jesus." Not a development from the old stock, but a new beginning, the Head of the "new creation." The ideal of humanity, defaced and destroyed by the Fall, was restored again in the Incarnation. "The first man is of the earth, earthy: the second man is the Lord from heaven" (ch. xv. 47). Adam was formed in the image of God—a sinless, symmetrical, perfect man. But he lost the glory of his first estate, and became the father of a degenerate humanity that could never of itself rise again to the original level, however long the stream of its succeeding generations might roll on. Christ, the God-Man, in the fulness of time, appears—true, perfect manhood linked in mysterious union with Deity, the "Firstborn among many brethren; " "Partaker with the children of flesh and blood," that he may "lead many sons to glory." We must look to him, then, if we would know what the possibilities of our nature are, what we ourselves may and ought to be. It is curious to note how different, as regards physical form and feature, are the artistic conceptions one meets with of the person of Jesus; what various degrees of serene majesty and tender sorrow they express. Some of them, perhaps, exaggerate the element of tenderness at the expense of that of power. They none of them, it may be, answer to our own ideal. And we conclude that it is vain to think of representing upon canvas the mingled splendours—the heavenly lights and earthly shadows—of that wondrous face in which

> " The God shone gracious through the Man.

But we are scarcely in danger of error in any honest and intelligent *moral* conception of Christ. The glorious Original appears too plainly and luminously before us. "Behold the Man!"—the consummate type of all human excellence. Do we really admire and adore him? Do we admire everything that we see in him; every separate lineament and expression of his countenance? Would we have all men, specially those with whom we have most to do, to be like him? Is it our desire to be ourselves fashioned at every point exactly after such a Model? This is involved in a true recognition of the headship of Christ over ourselves and every man.

II. THE SPRING OF THE HIGHER LIFE FOR EVERY MAN IS CHRIST. However we may deal with the subtle questions suggested here respecting the original constitution and prerogatives of man's nature, one thing is plain—that nature now has no self-recovering power of life in it. It has in it rather the seeds of decay and death. "In Adam all die." The second Adam, the Lord from heaven, is a "quickening Spirit." In him the power of death is overmastered. Through him God pours into our being the stream of a new and nobler life, a life in which every part of it, both physical and spiritual, shall have its share (John v. 21; vi. 47—50; xi. 25, 26; 1 John v. 11, 12). The Fountain-head of a blessed, glorious immortality for every man is he. Looking abroad over a languishing, dying world, he says, "I am come that they might have life, and that they might have it more abundantly." And there is not a human being on the face of the whole earth who is not personally interested in this Divine revelation of the Life eternal.

III. THE SUPREME LAW FOR EVERY MAN IS CHRIST. We are all necessarily under law. It is not a question as between law and no law that has to be decided. The question is—What shall be the law that we voluntarily recognize? What shall be the nature of the governing force to which we yield ourselves? Shall it be true, righteous, beneficent, Divine? or shall it be false, usurping, fatal, Satanic? There is no middle course. God would have us make our own free, unfettered choice. Our whole daily life is actually a choice of servitude, and it is emphatically our own. The true servitude is the service of Christ. All holy law is summed up in his authority. He is the proper, rightful Lord of every human soul. He demands the unreserved allegiance of every man. His claims are sovereign, absolute, universal. They admit of no qualification, and from them there is no escape. As well think by the caprice of your own will to render your body superior to the laws of matter, to defeat the force of gravitation, to escape from your own shadow, as think to shake off the obligation of obedience to Christ when once you have heard his voice, and he has laid his royal hand upon you.

IV. THE REST AND HOME OF EVERY MAN'S SOUL IS IN CHRIST.

> " Oh, where shall rest be found,
> Rest for the weary soul?"

We scheme and toil to surround ourselves with earthly satisfactions, but the secret of a happy home on earth is that the spirit shall have found its true place of safety and repose. And Christ only can lead us to this. O blessed Lord Jesus, thou Friend and Brother and Saviour of every man, bring us into living fellowship with thyself!

> " Here would we end our quest;
> Alone are found in thee
> The life of perfect love, the rest
> Of immortality."

                                                                W.

Vers. 23—26.—"*The Lord's Supper*." St. Paul had not been an eye-witness of the sacred incident that he here relates. Nor had he gained his knowledge of it by the report of others. He had "received it of the Lord." At what time and in what way this took place we know not. We may, perhaps, best attribute it to that remarkable transition period immediately after his conversion, the "three years" that he spent in Arabia and Damascus before he went up to Jerusalem and began his apostolic ministry (Gal. i. 17, 18). We can well believe that it was during that time of lonely, silent contemplation that the grand verities of the gospel message were divinely unveiled to him; and this may have been among the things that he then "received of the Lord." The simplicity of the way in which he describes the institution of this sacred rite is in perfect harmony with the simplicity of the gospel record. One can only wonder how it can have been possible for such an incident to be turned, as it has been, into a weapon of sacerdotal pretence and spiritual oppression. The too prevalent neglect of the observance has, no doubt, to a great extent been the natural and inevitable result of this abuse. The false or exaggerated use of anything always provokes to the opposite extreme. We may urge its claims on the Christian conscience and heart by looking at it in three different aspects—as a *memorial*, as a *symbol*, and as a *means of spiritual edification.*

I. A MEMORIAL. "This do in remembrance of me." "As often as ye eat this bread, and drink the cup, ye proclaim the Lord's death till he come." Christ's own words set it forth as an act of personal remembrance, Paul's as a time-long witness to the great sacrifice. Taking the two together, it appears as a memorial of "Christ and him crucified "—of himself in all the truth and meaning of his earthly manifestation, of his death as the issue in which the fulness of that meaning was gathered up and consummated. We may regard this memorial in its relation both to those who observe it and to those who observe it not; as a method of keeping the fact of Christ's self-surrender vividly before the minds of those who believe in him and love him, and as a testimony that appeals with silent eloquence to a thoughtless, careless world. In this respect it resembles other Scripture memorials (Gen. xxii. 14; xxviii. 18, 19; Exod. xii. 24—27; Josh. iv. 20—24; 1 Sam. vii. 12). And when we think how easily things the most important fade away from our memories while trifles linger there, and sacred impressions are obliterated by meaner influences, we may well recognize with devout thankfulness the wisdom and love which ordained such a mode of perpetuating the remembrance of the most momentous of all events in human history, while, in spite of all its perversions, the simple fact of the continuance of such a sacred usage of the Church is a proof that it rests on a Divine foundation.

II. A SYMBOL. It represents visibly that which in the nature of things is invisible. Not merely is bread a fitting emblem of the Saviour's body and wine of his blood, and the breaking of the one and the pouring out of the other of the manner of his death; but the service itself symbolizes the personal union of the soul with him, the method alike of its origin and its support. It bears witness, as in a figure, to the deeper reality of the life of faith. It sets forth, in the form of a significant *deed*, what our Lord set forth in the form of metaphoric *words* when he said, "Except ye eat the flesh of the Son of man," etc. (John vi. 53—58). And in both cases "it is the Spirit which quickeneth." Mysticism has thrown its false halo, its bewitching glamour, around these Divine words; and the sacred ordinance that would otherwise have made its simple appeal to the insight of the Christian understanding and the tenderness of the Christian heart has become mere food for superstition. But there is no Scripture warrant whatever for this. From the gross materialism of the Romish "Mass" to the subtler refinement of thought that regards the Lord's spiritual presence as being in some mystic sense inherent in the bread and wine, speaking of the sacrament being "administered," as though it had some occult virtue in it, a kind of spiritual medicament conferred by priestly hands, and "taken" by the faithful for their souls' healing, —all these shades of opinion alike substitute a physical mystery for a spiritual truth, and engender a superstitious faith that fixes its attention on the material emblems and something that is supposed to be true of *them*; rather than the intelligent faith that discerns the unseen Saviour through them, very much as we look through our window upon the golden glory of the setting sun without thinking of the transparent medium through which we behold it (see 'Christ the Bread of Life,' J.McLeod Campbell, p. 21, *et seq.*).

III. A MEANS OF SPIRITUAL EDIFICATION. Here lies the Divine reason of the memorial and the symbol. It is more than a "transparent medium" through which the soul may gaze upon the crucified Christ; it is a channel of spiritual influence by means of which the soul's fellowship with him may be deepened and strengthened. It accomplishes this end, not by any magic power that it may wield over us, but by virtue simply of the influence it is naturally fitted to exert on mind and conscience and heart, and by the grace of that good Spirit whose office it is to testify of Christ. We may be fully alive to the dangers that lurk in the use of all symbolic religious rites, the danger especially of attributing to the sign an efficacy that lies only in that which is signified. And we may see in this the reason why the rites of Christianity are so few. But what Christian heart can be insensible to the high spiritual value of an observance such as this? Moreover, the obligation is plain. "Do this," says our dying Lord, "in remembrance of me." May not such an appeal be expected to draw forth a ready response from any soul that has ever "tasted that he is gracious"? Its being the behest of love rather than the stern requirement of law, makes it doubly imperative, while the simplicity of the deed it enjoins makes it doubly efficacious as a bond of affection and a vehicle of moral power. We all know what a charm there is in even the most trivial memento of those whom we have loved and lost, especially if it be some object with which the personal memory is most closely associated by familiar daily use, some little thing that tender hands we can no longer grasp and a loving voice that is now for ever still have bequeathed to us. With what a glow of grateful affection will the sight of it sometimes suffuse our hearts! How near does it bring the departed to us again! How closely does it draw us into sympathy and fellowship with their personal life! And shall not this be expected to be pre-eminently true of these simple memorials of our loving, suffering, dying Lord? The realization of this, however, must always depend on something in ourselves. The influence we receive from the outward observance will depend on what we are prepared to receive, *i.e.* on what we bring to it in the conditions of our own inward thought and feeling. It will never of itself create right feeling. Come to it with a worldly spirit, with a divided heart—cold, careless, carnal, frivolous, prayerless, or in any way out of harmony with the Divine realities it represents—and you can expect to find no uplifting and inspiring power in it. You are not likely to "discern the Lord's body." Christ is never further from us than when we desecrate sacred scenes and services by our discordant mental and moral conditions. But come with your soul yearning after him, and he will unveil to you his glory and fill you with the joy of his love. "Let a man prove himself, and so let him eat of the bread, and drink of the cup."—W.

Ver. 2.—*Christian ordinances.* We do well to boast of our freedom in Christ. It is a sign of the elevation of our religion above others that it does not need to drill its votaries by a constant discipline of prescribed rites, ceremonial shows, and verbal repetitions. It loves simplicity and spontaneousness, and the life which it fosters needs not to be guarded and hedged by minute regulations, but is developed in a chartered holy liberty. At the same time, Christianity has concrete forms, and the Church received at the beginning ordinances, or directions, to keep. The Apostle Paul had delivered these to the Church at Corinth.

I. NEGATIVELY. 1. *They were different from the ordinances of the old covenant.* The rites and statutes connected with animal sacrifice, distinctions of meats, regulations about dress and divers washings, were suited to the time in which they were instituted, and served to impress on the Hebrew mind great thoughts of God, of sin, and of righteousness, and to impregnate life in the house and labour in the field with religious suggestions. But with Jesus Christ a new era came. The restrictions and rites of the ceremonial law, ceasing to be necessary, lost their obligation. Moral inculcations, whether through Moses or through subsequent prophets, of course remained, and were enlarged and emphasized by the Master and his apostles. But the Church, after some struggle and sharp controversy, discerned and asserted her freedom from the sacerdotal and ceremonial ordinances by which the house of Israel had been bound. 2. *They were not the traditions of Jewish rabbinism.* Our Lord spoke strongly against the bondage into which the Jews of his time had been brought by "traditions of men," which had no Divine sanction, but had acquired, under the rabbinic and Pharisaic *regimé*, a fictitious authority. Such traditionalism tended to weaken the honour due to the authentic Law, and its continuance was entirely opposed to the doctrine of Christ. 3. *They must not be confounded with the traditions of later Christian origin.* A tradition which cannot be traced to Christ or his apostles, and which is without support in the New Testament, cannot claim any countenance from this text. Alas! how Christians have become the servants of men and of prescribed usage! As the Jews have overlaid and burdened their religion with a huge mass of Talmudic and Kabbalistic traditions, so have the Greek and Latin Churches all but ruined their Christianity by admitting ecclesiastical tradition to a place alongside of Holy Writ in the rule of faith.

II. POSITIVELY. The traditions which the Corinthians were exhorted to keep were the instructions which the apostle, under the guidance of the Spirit of Christ, had himself delivered to the saints; and they had authority, not by coming down from remote antiquity and passing through many hands, but by coming directly from one whom the Lord had fitted and appointed to found Churches, and to set their affairs in order according to his mind and will. The directions specially referred to here had regard to the fellowship of believers and the worship rendered in the assembly of God. He had taught that the assembly was the true temple, wherein the Holy Spirit dwelt, and this temple was to be full of praise. The believers were to come together, not so much to pray for salvation, as to worship God their Saviour, and give thanks for the remission of sins and the hope of glory. Then the teaching about the Lord's Supper came in, for it is the centre and crowning act of Christian worship; and this had been ordained at Corinth by St. Paul. " I received of the Lord that which also I delivered [ordained] to you." So the apostle, while commanding the adherence of the Corinthians to his directions, took the opportunity to give more explicit instruction, and correct some abuses which had already crept into the Church. 1. The separation of the sexes, which sacerdotalism desires, was to be ignored in this service. Alike during the time of praying and prophesying, and during the Eucharistic Supper, men and women were to mingle together, because in Jesus Christ " there is neither male nor female." And yet a distinction between the sexes, in the interest of purity and modesty, was to be duly marked. 2. The precious feast of unity and love ought not to be marred by party spirit or by selfishness and excess. Irreverence and greediness might appear at feasts in the precincts of the heathen temples; but in the holy temple of God his redeemed should have discernment of the Lord's body, and a grave fraternal remembrance of him. " Let a man examine himself, and so let him eat of that bread, and drink of that cup."—F.

Vers. 18, 19.—*Words of evil omen.* In a good English dictionary, the term " schismatic " is thus explained: " One who separates from a Church from difference of opinion." The Bible makes no reference to an individual schismatic; nor does it apply the word " schism " to separation from the Church. " Heresy " is defined in the dictionary as " the taking and holding of an opinion contrary to the usual belief, especially in theology." Such, no doubt, is according to ecclesiastical usage; but the Scripture means by a " heresy " a sect or faction, not apart from but within the Church: " Heresies [factions] among you."

I. A SCHISM IS A RENT IN THE MIDST OF THE CHURCH, marring the enjoyment and expression of its essential unity. If a piece of undressed cloth were put to an old garment, a schism would occur. Not that the garment would fall into two parts, but that it would show an unseemly rent. A division of opinion among the people who heard our Saviour is called a schism; and the same word is used to denote the discord in the crowd when St. Paul appeared before the council at Jerusalem. The only Church of all those to which St. Paul wrote, which had schisms within it of such seriousness as to give him anxiety and call for animadversion, was the Church at Corinth; but by these he did not mean the action of parties breaking off from the primitive Church in that city, and forming rival Churches or separate denominations. They were parties in the Church dissenting or differing from one another. This will appear the more clearly if we mark the remedies which the apostle prescribed, viz.: 1. To speak the same thing, and be perfectly joined together in the same mind and the same judgment. To speak the same thing was to exalt the one great Name of the Lord Jesus, and not to take party names, saying, " I am of Paul; I am of Apollos." And to be perfectly joined in the same mind—the mind of Christ, and the same judgment—the judgment of his Spirit, while it never precluded activity of investigation and discussion, certainly implied that the normal condition of the Church should be one of concord, and not one of countless variations and opposing views. 2. To keep the Lord's Supper as the apostle instructed them. The Corinthians were charged not to partake of the sacred supper as of a common meal, lest they should "come together to judgment." They were to keep the feast with reverence, and with discernment of the Lord's body. They were also to show brotherly kindness, not as partisans, but as brethren, coming together and waiting for one another at the festival of love. 3. To bear in mind the doctrine of the mystical body, and, as members therein, to have the same care one for another. To have schisms or alienations would be to separate limbs that had need of each other, and so to vex and impede the whole body of Christ. At the present day, wherever parties are formed in a particular Church with hostile feelings and a desire to weaken one another, there is schism, in the New Testament sense of the word. And wherever, within the Church general, or communion of saints, there is an elevation of party names, and a setting up of party or denominational communions, making the Lord's Supper "their own supper," there is schism.

II. A HERESY IS AN AGGRAVATED FORM OF A SCHISM, AND DENOTES A SEPARATIST PARTY OR A SECT. We read of "the heresy of the Sadducees" (Acts v. 17), and "the heresy of the Pharisees" (Acts xv. 5). The Christians were charged with forming a new heresy or sect—"the heresy of the Nazarenes." It was in this sense, and not at all in the sense of heterodoxy, that St. Paul admitted that he worshipped the God of his fathers, "after the manner which they called heresy." The Jews at Rome, agreeing to hear the apostle on the faith of the Nazarenes, remarked, "As concerning this heresy, we know that it is everywhere spoken against." Thus the term undoubtedly denoted a faction, not a mode of thought or form of doctrine, true or false; but in the Church it took from the beginning an unfavourable meaning. A heresy was a faction which carried out a schism to actual separation, and was animated in doing so by a proud, unruly spirit. Accordingly, heresies are classed with variances, strifes, and seditions, among "the works of the flesh" (Gal. v. 20). "A man that is a heretic," therefore, means, not an errorist, but a separatist. We do, indeed, read in 2 Pet. ii. 1 of "heresies of doctrine;" but the reference is to the conduct of introducers of strange doctrine as forming a separate party. "Many shall follow their pernicious ways." We have seen that direction was given for the prevention of schism. It was also given for the correction and removal of heretics. Titus was instructed to admonish a heretic once and again. If admonition failed, Titus was to reject or shun him as a mischief-maker among brethren. We live in a time of great confusion. Church unity is misunderstood; Church liberty is abused; and Church discipline is relaxed—is, in some quarters, almost obsolete. Let every one look to his own spirit and conduct. As a Christian, you are a Churchman. Never join a sect or faction. Never lift the mere banner of a party. Belong to the Church of God, which was born of the Holy Ghost on the day of Pentecost. For actual instruction and united worship, you must be in some one particular part of that Church; abide in that which is in your judgment the best constituted and administered; but never take your chamber for the whole house, or any particular Church for the Church universal. Bear a brotherly heart and countenance towards all who love the Lord, that, so far as your influence extends, there may be no schism in the body. Deplore the existence of splits and divisions as an evil; yet remember that it evolves some good—"that they who are approved may be made manifest among you." Oh to be approved of him who knows what spirit we are of, and to be manifested as no heretics, but faithful members of Christ and loving children of God!—F.

Ver. 1.—*The limitation set on the following of good men.* "Of me, even as I also am of Christ." The apostle calls to the same personal following, without the qualification, in ch. iv. 16. This first verse of ch. xi. should be the closing verse of ch. x., as it really completes the exhortation which is there given. "The apostle refers to his own example, but only to lead his readers up to Christ as the great example of One who 'pleased not himself' (Rom. xv. 3). His own example is valuable inasmuch as it is the example of one who is striving to conform to the image of his Lord." Recall David's very striking expression in Ps. xvi. 2, 3, "My goodness extendeth not to thee [O God]; only to the saints that are in the earth." We consider—

I. THE IMPULSE OF SAINTLY EXAMPLES; or, expressed in simple terms, of recognized goodness in our fellow-men. Distinguish between the life-missions of *talented* men and of *good* men. The "talented" may seem to be out of our range, the "good" never are. The weakest, poorest, humblest among us may be "good." God has taken care to provide the saintly ones in every age. He sets some such in every sphere of life. We all know of men and women better than ourselves who act on and inspire us. They exert these influences; they persuade us that (1) goodness is beautiful; (2) that goodness is attainable. Then it is the bounden duty of all men and women who fear God and love the Lord Jesus Christ to culture personal character, become saintly, and gain the power to witness for Christ by a holy example.

II. THE IMPERFECTION OF ALL SAINTLY EXAMPLES. None of them are perfect and complete. It is human to err. All the saintly ones fall short of the full standard of humanity as shown to us in Christ. This point is suggestive of abundant illustration taken: 1. From Scripture. There is only one man mentioned in Scripture who even seems to have been perfect. It is Enoch; and we cannot be sure concerning him, seeing that the records of his life are gathered up into only one or two brief sentences. Abraham, Joseph, Moses, Elijah, David, etc., are all frail, fallible men, whose very sides of goodness and strength are at times exaggerated so as to become evil. 2. From experience and observation. We know that those who seem to us most heroic and saintly are deeply sensible of their own failings and shortcomings, and we cannot have to do with them long before finding occasion for the exercise of our charity in relation to their conduct. Even the Apostle Paul could not permit us to make himself our standard. He knew too well what hastiness of temper sometimes overcame him, and how greatly he had to struggle with the body of sin. We can be followers of no man, if he stands alone. We can only follow a fellow-man as he may be in some point a reflection of and suggestion of Christ, the manifested God. Consequently only Christ can be our absolute Exempler. We can be followers of him; we may put the whole force of our natures into following him; we may let no fellow-man stand before him. Show that the enemies of Christ could have easily gained their end if they could have found a stain upon his moral character, a word spoken or a thing done which the conscience of mankind could distinctly recognize as unworthy of ideal manhood. None such have ever been found during the nearly nineteen centuries of Christianity. The things usually made into moral charges are abundantly capable of explanations that redound to Christ's honour, or belong to the mystery of his Divine birth and mission. But, while we admit that no man can be to us a full exemplar, we may recognize that good men do catch measures of the goodness of the Christ whom they serve, and are examples for us so far as they are Christ-like. It is possible for us to go a little further even than this, and admit a certain special and peculiar power upon us exerted by purely human examples, which, by reason of their very frailty, tone and temper and shadow for us, and in adaptation to our weakness, the over-splendour of the Christly and Divine. It is most practically helpful to us that we may be followers of such a brother man as St. Paul, so far as he follows Christ and reflects the full Christliness with a human tempering suited to our feeble sight. Then it follows that what St. Paul thus is to us we may be to others.—R. T.

Ver. 2.—*The Christly traditions.* "Keep the ordinances," or, as given in the margin, "the traditions." St. Paul had given in his ministry "ordinances" of three kinds. 1. Regulations for the government of the Church. 2. Statements concerning doctrine. 3. Statements concerning historical facts. Illustrate the use and misuse of the term "traditions." Show that the traditions of Christ, in the sense of the records preserved, in memory or in writing, of his life, ministry, miracles, death, and resurrection, are the basis on which the Church is built. Christianity is not a revealed *religious system*, as Mosaism was. It is the revelation, in an individual man, of that divinely human life which was God's thought when God made man in his image, but which man spoiled by the assertion of his rights of self-will, and consequent separation of the Divine from the human. All Christian doctrine rests on the ideal humanity which Christ exhibited. All Christian duty is the effort to reach and express that ideal. So Christianity is strictly an historical religion; and yet the historical is only the body which manifests to us, and sets in relation with us, and permanently preserves for us, the spiritual and the mystical. Then we ought to be anxious about the adequate remembrance of and knowledge of the traditions of Christ. Show how these are attacked and defended. 1. They are the walls that keep the city. 2. They are the body which manifests the life. 3. They are the material through which alone the spiritual can be apprehended. Notice and duly impress two points. (1) The fourfold care with which the Christly traditions have been preserved for us. (2) The elaborate and precise way in which the apostolic teachings support the traditions.—R. T.

Vers. 2—16.—*Laws of order in Christian assemblies.* The subject dealt with in this passage is the appropriate conduct and dress of the women in Christian assemblies. That, however, was but a matter of present and passing interest, one standing related to the customs and sentiments of a particular age. Our concern is not with the details of apostolic advice, but with the *principles* upon which St. Paul deals with a particular case. " Every circumstance which could in the least degree cause the principles of Christianity to be perverted or misunderstood by the heathen world was of vital importance in those early days of the Church, and hence we find the apostle, who most fearlessly taught the principles of Christian liberty, condemning most earnestly every application of those principles which might be detrimental to the best interests of the Christian faith. To feel bound to assert your liberty in every detail of social and political life is to cease to be free—the very liberty becomes a bondage" (Shore). "It appears that the Christian women at Corinth claimed for themselves equality with the male sex, to which the doctrine of Christian freedom and the removal of the distinction of sex in Christ (Gal. iii. 28) gave occasion. Christianity had indisputably done much for the emancipation of women, who in the East and among the Ionic Greeks (it was otherwise among the Dorians and the Romans) were in a position of unworthy dependence. But this was done in a quiet, not an over-hasty manner. In Corinth, on the contrary, they had apparently taken up the matter in a fashion somewhat too animated. The women overstepped due bounds by coming forward to pray and prophesy in the assemblies with uncovered head " (De Wette). St. Paul gives advice which bears upon the maintenance of due order in the Christian assemblies. Taking this as the subject illustrated, we observe the following points:—

I. ORDER MUST BE BASED ON FIRST PRINCIPLES. Here on the designed relationship of man and woman. The new law of the equality of the sexes must be dealt with in a manner consistent with the earlier principle of the natural dependence of the woman on man. " Observe how the apostle falls back on nature. In nothing is the difference greater between fanaticism and Christianity than in their treatment of natural instincts and affections. Fanaticism defies nature. Christianity refines it and respects it. Christianity does not denaturalize, but only sanctifies and refines according to the laws of nature" (F. W. Robertson).

II. ORDER MUST BE ARRANGED BY CHRISTIAN PRUDENCE, which acts by persuasion rather than by force, avoids any over-magnifying of little differences, and makes due allowance for individual peculiarities. Prudence can recognize that the preservation of peace and charity is of greater importance than the securing of order, and order may wait on charity.

III. ORDER MUST BE ADAPTED TO EXISTING CUSTOMS. No stiff forms can be allowed in Christian assemblies. Social and national customs and sentiments have to be duly considered. Illustrate from the necessary differences of administering the ordinance of baptism in different countries, or from the diversities of Church order in heathen lands that receive the gospel. There can be unity of principle with variety of detail.

IV. ORDER MUST BE ACCEPTED BY EVERY MEMBER LOYALLY. This is the condition of working together in every kind of human association. A man's individuality may properly find expression in the *discussion* of what shall be done; but he must sink his individuality in order to help in carrying out the order that is decided on.

V. ORDER BEARS DIRECTLY UPON SPIRITUAL PROFIT. It injures to have the Church's attention diverted to forward women. Order relieves the minds of the worshippers, so that full attention may be directed to spiritual things. In quietness, in rest of mind and heart, the soul finds the time to enjoy and to grow. Distracted by the *material*, due attention cannot be given to the spiritual. Illustrate from the anxiety with which harmony, beauty, and order were sought and preserved in the older Jewish ritual.

Amid all those formalities worshipping souls could be still, and in the stillness find God.—R. T.

Vers. 17—19.—*Sectarian feeling within the Church.* "There be divisions among you." "There must be also heresies [sects] among you." Distinguish between the divisions which lead to the formation of separate sects, and the sectarian feeling which may disturb the harmony and the work of a particular Church. The apostle refers not to sects dividing the Church into parts, but to parties and party feeling within an individual Church. Such party feeling tells most injuriously on spiritual profit and progress. "St. Paul must be understood as saying that, not only will there be dissension and divisions among Christians, but that some of them will go their own way in spite of the instructions both in doctrine and practice delivered to them by Christ's apostles." We may illustrate the sources from which sectarian feeling within the Church is likely to arise.

I. SECTARIANISM FROM SOCIAL CLASSIFICATION. Christianity assumes the absolute equality of all men before God. But so far as Christianity is an organization, it is bound to recognize and make due account of class distinctions. These become a constant source of difficulty, the ground and occasion of much offence.

II. SECTARIANISM FROM FAMILY DISPUTES. Within the same class there arise jealousies, misunderstandings, and heart-burnings. The Church is too often made the sphere for the expression of such ill feeling.

III. SECTARIANISM FROM PERSONAL DISPOSITION. Such as that of Diotrephes, "who loved to have the pre-eminence." Suspicious, masterful, or conceited men are the most fruitful sources of Church dispute and division. The evil man in Church life is the man who "looks only on his own things, not on the things of others."

IV. SECTARIANISM FROM INTELLECTUAL DIFFERENCES. Such should never occur, because the true unity of a Church is its common life in Christ, and not its common opinion about Christ. The life must be always the same, and so it can be a basis of union. Opinions must differ according to variety of capacity and education. Impress that, if the causes of sectarianism cannot be wholly removed, their influence may be overruled by the culture of high Christian life and sentiment.—R. T.

Ver. 23.—*St. Paul's claim to direct revelation.* "For I have received of the Lord that which also I delivered unto you." "The whole structure of the passage seems to imply that what follows had been received by St. Paul directly from Christ, and that he is not appealing to a well-known tradition." "The method of communication (whether in a trance, or state of ecstasy, or any other supernatural manner) does not appear to cause either doubt or difficulty to those to whom the apostle conveyed the information thus miraculously bestowed on him." Illustrate St. Paul's distinct claim to apostleship on the ground of a direct call and revelation from the Lord Jesus. If St. Paul had a distinct revelation on the matter of the Lord's Supper, we must regard it as a divinely instituted ordinance or sacrament. The verses following our text become for us an authentic explanation, given by the risen Christ, concerning his sacrament. We fix attention on the proofs that St. Paul had received a direct Divine revelation. Three points may be dealt with in illustration.

I. THE BEGINNING OF HIS CHRISTIAN LIFE WAS A REVELATION. See the remarkable vision and communication on his approaching Damascus.

II. THERE WERE TIMES DURING HIS LIFE OF DIRECT REVELATION. As at Troas; on the journey to Jerusalem; when in prison; during the storm and shipwreck; and as narrated in 2. Cor. xii.

III. HE RECOGNIZED HIS KNOWLEDGE OF THE FACTS OF CHRIST'S LIFE AS DIRECTLY COMMUNICATED. He had no personal acquaintance with Christ; he was not dependent on the narratives of apostles and disciples, save in part. Christ told him his story by vision and revelation. And St. Paul goes even further, and declares that the gospel which he preached, the views of truth and duty which were characteristic of him, he received from no man; all came by direct revelation of the Lord. A special interest, therefore, attaches to the Pauline teachings.—R. T.

Ver. 26.—*The Lord's Supper a showing forth.* Considering how much has been made of the sacrament of the Lord's Supper by the Christian Church it is remarkable that the passage connected with this text should be the only apostolic teaching we have respecting its observance. We have in the Gospels the records of the incident from which it takes its origin, but though we should have expected St. Peter or St. John to give us complete counsels for its observance, neither of them refers to it. St. Paul alone deals with it, and it is a singular thing that he makes no allusion to it when writing to Timothy and Titus, and seeking to fit them, and others through them, for their pastoral work. It even seems that, but for the accident of an abuse creeping into the Corinthian Church, we should have been left entirely without apostolic precedent or instruction concerning it. Our text, and the verses connected with it, contain hints of the way in which the Lord's Supper was then observed; indications of the kind of abuses likely to creep in; and teachings concerning those great principles which were to regulate its management. We can clearly see that it was then a meal, not a service; a feast, not a fast; a communion, not an administration; a means of remembrance, and not a mystical presence. Our Lord kept the ordinary Passover meal, and into one of the customary incidents of it he put a new and spiritual significance. Now, see what actually occurred in the early Church. Those having a common faith naturally sought fellowship together. The Eastern idea of fellowship is partaking of the same food together. In this way grew up the *agapœ*, or love-feasts, and these seem to have been observed in all the Churches that were founded. These *agapœ* could easily be con-nected in thought with our Lord's last meal with his disciples, and on the closing part of them a special significance was probably made to rest. When Christianity touched Western life, the old Eastern *agapœ* naturally dropped away. Feeding together is not so familiar a sign of fellowship in the West as in the East. So in the West a part of the meal was retained and became a sacrament, a service, and a mystery. St. Paul helps us to understand the special significance put into a part of the meal. It was a *showing forth*; but we ask—

I. A SHOWING FORTH OF WHAT? 1. *Of a fact of history:* the "Lord's death." Remember that St. Paul usually goes on to the Resurrection, as revealing the significance of the death. The Lord's death is shown forth in (1) the *substance* of the sacrament— bread, which is crushed in the mill before it can become food; wine, which is trodden in the wine-press before it can become drink; (2) the form of the food in the sacrament —it is broken, and poured out. Impress the importance of keeping up the remem-brance of this fact, (*a*) as affirming the actual historical character of the Gospel records; (*b*) as keeping for the death of Christ its central place in Christian doctrine; (*c*) as renewing, on men's souls, the special moral influence of Christ, the life-persuasion, the "constraining" of his cross. 2. *Of a fact of faith:* "Till he come." That is "shown forth" in keeping up the observance, and in the manifest fact that he is now sensibly absent. We declare that the only president of the feast is Christ, as spiritually present. The importance of showing forth this fact is seen in its (1) testifying to the resurrec-tion and present life of Christ; (2) in its affirming the foundation of the Church to be faith, not doctrine, or knowledge, or experience; and (3) in its renewing the Church's great hope, and witnessing to the reality and value of things unseen, future, and eternal.

II. A SHOWING FORTH TO WHOM? 1. *To God;* as assuring him that we value his great Gift. 2. *To ourselves;* as quickening our own feeling, remembrance, and spiritual life. 3. *To our fellow-Christians;* as bidding them rejoice with us in the common salvation which we all share. 4. *To the world;* as testifying that the despised "spiritual" is nevertheless the "true" and the "eternal." In conclusion, show the value of symbolic helps in religious life, and the claim that rests on us to show forth Christ's death, if we have faith in him and the hope of his coming again.—R. T.

Ver. 27.—*Sacramental unworthiness.* The special thought here is the evil of looking at the Lord's Supper as if it were a mere eating and drinking time. It is a symbolic time; it is a spiritually feasting time. It is a time when the wants and demands of the body are to be put wholly aside. It is a soul-time. He eats unworthily who stays with any bodily partaking of mere emblems, and fails to fill his soul with living bread—with him who is the "Bread of life." The following points are so simple and suggestive that they only need statement:—We eat, at the sacrament, *unworthily;* 1. When we eat *without suitable remembrance.* "The Son of man knew our nature far too well (to trust us without such helps). He knew that the remembrance of his sacrifice would fade without perpetual repetition, and without an appeal to the senses; therefore by touch, by taste, by sight, we are reminded in the sacrament that Christianity is not a thing of mere feeling, but a real historical actuality. It sets forth Jesus Christ evidently crucified among us" (Robertson). 2. When we eat *without spiritual insight,* and so fail to recognize the holy mystery of the symbols. 3. When we eat *without devout feeling* duly nourished by preparatory seasons of quietness, meditation, communion, and prayer. 4. When we eat *without thankful love* cherished for him who gave his very life for us. 5. When we eat *without holy resolves,* to which gratitude ought to urge us. Impress the penalty of the unworthy eating. (1) It is as if a man were really scorning Christ and putting him to shame. (2) It is a piece of deception, for participation presupposes spiritual relations. The man who eats "unworthily" is guilty, that is, he is amenable to punishment; and spiritual punishments, though they may creep up very slowly and come on very silently, are fearful punishments: they are the hardened heart that cannot feel, the deluded mind that can perish in self-deceptions.—R. T.

Ver. 28.—*Moral fitness for communion.* Explain the Scottish custom of "fencing the tables" at sacramental seasons, that is, of guarding the tables from the approach of unworthy persons. There has grown up round the expression, "Let a man examine himself," a kind of self-searching, as a Christian duty, which could hardly have been in the thought of the apostle. It has come to be considered the right thing that, at stated seasons, the Christian should subject his whole inner life, his thoughts, his views of truth, his frames of mind, and his varied feelings, to examination; testing them by the most familiar and admired models of Christian experience. Many of us know what it is to attempt this painful and difficult work, and perhaps we know also the heavy penalties which follow the attempt; the oppressed moods into which our souls get, the killing outright of all Christian joy, the morbid pleasure found in dwelling on the *evil* phases of our experience, and, above all, the subtle self-trust which it engenders, until we awake to find that we have been led away from simple, childlike reliance on Christ to an attempted confidence in our own frames and feelings and experiences. St. Paul distinctly enjoins the duty of examining one's self, but if we take his counsel in connection with the circumstances and doings of those to whom his counsel was given, we shall see what was the sphere of self-examination to which he referred. The evils which the apostle deals with are plainly the relics of the old heathen life gaining strength again, such strength as to imperil this most solemn Christian ordinance. There were class rivalries, one pressing before another; the rich were making ostentatious display; the poor were grasping at the best food; self-indulgence, gluttony, were so manifest that few could realize the special religious significance of the closing part of the feast, the common sharing of the bread and wine of memorial. St. Paul, having this in mind, urges that a man must examine into his morals, his habits, his conduct, his relationships, and his duties, and gain a moral fitness for partaking of the bread and of the wine of memorial. We consider—
I. THE MORAL LIFE THAT IS IN HARMONY WITH HOLY COMMUNION. One important element of the Christian spirit is sensitiveness to the tone, the character, the genius, of Christianity. We ought not to have to ask, "What is consistent?" We should *feel* what is becoming, what is worthy of our vocation. The cultured, spiritually minded Christian, who is "transformed by the renewing of his mind," finds himself resisting all wrong, disliking all that is unlovely, shrinking from everything that is untrue, and gathering round him all that is kind and lovely and of good report. His life he seeks to set sounding through all its notes in full harmony with the key-note of the gospel. But we should see that our moral life is to be tested by Christianity when that religion is at its highest point of expression, and that we find in the Eucharistic feast. We must test ourselves by the ideal which we imagine as realized at the Lord's table. Then we say : 1. That there must be a very clearly cut and marked separation from the larger social evils of our time. 2. There must be a firm stand in relation to the questionable things of our time, the things that seem to lie on the border-land between good and evil. 3. There is further required a wise ordering of family relationships, and an efficient restraining of personal habits. Our communion-times, when the holy

quiet is around us, when the fever and the bustle of life are stilled, and our glorious, pure, white Lord comes so near to us, bring out to view the stains of secret fault.

II. THE RESPONSIBILITY OF SECURING THE HARMONY BETWEEN THE MORAL LIFE AND CHRISTIANITY IS THROWN UPON THE CHRISTIAN HIMSELF. The question of supreme importance to us is this, "Will we let the Christ-spirit that is in us nobly shape our whole life and relationship? Will we so fill everything with the new life that men shall find the Christ-image glowing everywhere from us? Will we be thoroughly in earnest to live the holy life?" The old idea was, win the soul for Christ, and let the body go—the helpless body of sin and death. The truer idea is that we are to win our bodies for Christ, our whole life-spheres for Christ. And the burden lies on us. God will win no man's body or life-sphere *for* him. He will win them *with* him. God will help every man who sets himself manfully to the work. The sanctification of a believer is no accident and no miracle. The law concerning it is most plain : "Work out your own salvation with fear and trembling, for it is God who worketh in you to will and do of his good pleasure." The responsibllity lies on us of "putting off the old man with his deeds," and the responsibility lies on us of "putting on the new man." The goodness and graces of the Christian life are to be won; they are not mere gifts. Gentleness of speech and manner, lowly mindedness, meekness of self-denial, tender consideration for others, glistening purity of thought and heart, strong faith, glowing love, and ardent hope; the inexpressible loveliness of those who have caught the spirit of Christ; the charming bloom—richer far than lies on ripened fruit—that lies on the word and work of the sanctified;—all these are to be *won*. We must want them, set ourselves in the way of them, wrestle and pray for them, put ourselves into closest relations with Christ so that they may be wrought in us by his Spirit. And communion-times bring all these claims so prominently before us. Brotherhood, holiness, forgiveness, charity, mean then so much; and our attainments seem so few, so small, in the light of the ideal Christian life. Let a man examine himself; find his evil and put it away; find what is lacking, and seek to gain it, and so attain the moral fitness for sharing in the Holy Communion.—R. T.

EXPOSITION.

CHAPTER XII.

CH. XII.—CH. XIV.—ON SPIRITUAL GIFTS, AND THE DANGER WHICH AROSE FROM THE ABUSE OF THE "GIFT OF TONGUES."

Vers. 1—11.—*On spiritual gifts in general.*

Ver. 1.—**Now concerning spiritual** gifts; rather, *things spiritual.* The context, however, shows that St. Paul is thinking almost exclusively of the gifts (*charismata*) of the Spirit. **I would not have you ignorant** (see ch. x. 1). The Corinthians had doubtless inquired in their letter as to the views of the apostle on this important and difficult subject.

Ver. 2.—**That ye were Gentiles.** The undoubted reading is, *that when ye were Gentiles.* The sentence is then in form an *anacoluthon;* in other words, it is not grammatically finished. The ancients were much less particular about these small matters of precision and symmetry than the moderns; and writers who are deeply moved by their subject, and hurried along by the strength of their feelings, often fall into these unfinished constructions (see Rom. ii. 17—21; xv. 25—27; Gal. ii. 6; 2

Thess. ii. 3, etc., in the Greek). **Dumb idols.** This characteristic of idols (Hab. ii. 18; Ps. cxv. 5; cxxxv. 16) is fixed upon to show that their "oracles" were mere falsity and pretence. We find an illustration of the epithet in the statue of Isis at Pompeii, where the ruined temple shows the secret stair by which the priest mounted to the back of the statue; and the *head* of the statue (preserved in the Museo Borbonico) shows the tube which went from the back of the head to the parted lips. Through this tube the priest concealed behind the statue spoke the answers of Isis. **Even as ye were led;** rather, *howsoever ye might be led,* as in the Revised Version. The Greek phrase shows that, under the oracular guidance of dumb idols, the Gentiles had been, as it were, drifted hither and thither "as the winds listed."

Ver. 3.—**Wherefore.** Their previous condition of Gentile ignorance rendered it necessary to instruct them fully respecting the nature and discrimination of the *charisms* of the Spirit. **By the Spirit of God;** rather, *in the Spirit;* i.e. in the state of spiritual exaltation and ecstasy. The phrase is a Hebrew one to describe inspiration. **Jesus** accursed. It may well seem amazing that the Corinthians should need instructing that such awful language could not be uttered by any one speaking "in the Spirit of God." It is evident, however, that such expressions *had* been uttered by persons who were, or seemed to be, carried away by the impassioned impulse which led to "glossolaly." (It is better to use this technical word in order to dissipate the cloud of strange misconceptions as to the true nature of this *charism*.) So terrible an outrage on the conscience of Christians could never have passed unchecked and unpunished, except from the obvious inability of the young community to grapple with the new and perplexing phenomena of an "inspiration" which appeared to destroy the personal control of those possessed by it. Among Jewish converts glossolaly was regarded as a form of that wild mantic "inspiration" of which we find some traces in Jewish history (1 Sam. x. 10, 11; xviii. 10; xix. 23, 24, etc.), and which was alluded to in the very name *Nabô*, which implied a boiling energy. Among Gentile converts the glossolaly would be classed with the overmastering influences of which they read, or which they witnessed, in the Sibyls, the Pythian priestesses, and the wild orgiastic devotees of Eastern cults. They would not like to call any one to task for things spoken in a condition which they regarded as wholly supernatural. As to the speakers, (1) some of them, not being sincere, might have really fallen under the influence of impulses which were earthly and demonish, not Divine; (2) others, not duly controlling their own genuine impulse, may have been liable to the uncontrolled sway of utterances for which they were at the moment irresponsible; (3) or again, being incapable of reasoned expression, they may have audibly expressed vague Gnostic doubts as to the identity of the "Jesus" who was crucified and the Divine Word; or (4) they may have been entangled in Jewish perplexities rising from Deut. xxi. 23, "He that is hanged" (which was also the expression applied by Jews to the crucified) "is accursed of God;" or finally, (5) by some strange abuse of the true principle expressed by St. Paul in 2 Cor. v. 16, they may have asserted in this fearful form their emancipation from the acknowledgment of Jesus "after the flesh." Similar phenomena—the same intrusions into worship of downright blasphemy or of blasphemous familiarity—have constantly recurred at times of overwhelming spiritual excitement, as for instance in the adherents of the "everlasting gospel" in the thirteenth century, and in various movements of our own day. *Is accursed*; rather, *is anathema*. The word corresponds to the Hebrew *cherem*, which means "a ban," and "what is devoted or set apart by a ban;" and to the Latin *sacer*, which means not only "sacred," set apart by holy consecration, but also "devoted to destruction." **No man can say that Jesus is [the] Lord, but by [in] the Holy Ghost.** It involved a strong rebuke to the *illuminati*, who professed a profound spiritual insight, to tell them that no man could make the simple, humble confession of the divinity of Jesus (for "Lord" is here an equivalent of the Hebrew "Jehovah") except by the same inspiration as that which they so terribly abused. There is a very similar passage in 1 John i. 2; but there the "test" of the inspiration is a confession of the humanity of Jesus as against Gnostics, who treated his human life as purely phantasmal. Here the test is the confession of his divinity as against Jews and Gentiles. (For a parallel passage, see Matt. xvi. 17, "Flesh and blood hath not revealed it unto thee.")

Ver. 4.—**Diversities.** This word is used in each of these verses. **Gifts**; *charismata*; endowments imparted by the Holy Spirit. The word is rendered "free gift" in Rom. v. 13. **The same Spirit.** The gifts of the Spirit are not uniform, but display diversity in unity. Just as the sunlight playing on different surfaces produces a multiplicity of gleams and colours, so the Holy Spirit manifests his presence variously, and even sometimes with sharp contrasts, in different individualities.

Ver. 5.—**Administrations.** Different individuals render different services, and even apply the same gifts in different ways, as we see in Rom. xii. 6—8. **The same Lord.** Who, as Head of the Church, directs all ministries and assigns all functions.

Ver. 6.—**Operations.** Manifestations of Divine power. **The same God which worketh all in all.** God is the Source of all gifts in all men. He is the Sun of the whole universe, and always in the meridian; and from him, as the Father of lights, flows every good and perfect gift (Jas. i. 17). It will be seen that this is one of the many passages which teach with perfect clearness the doctrine of the Trinity in unity. *All in all* (for this expression, see ch. xv. 28; Eph. i. 23). There are very similar passages descriptive of the diversity in unity of God's dispensations, in Eph. iv. 4—6, 11, 12; Rom. xii. 6—8; 1 Pet. iv. 10, 11.

Ver. 7.—**To profit withal.** With reference, that is, to the *general* profit.

Ver. 8.—**The word of wisdom . . . the word of knowledge.** In modern usage, "knowledge" is the learning which we by use and effort acquire; "wisdom" is the insight which gradually dawns upon us from thought and experience. In the language of the New Testament, the distinction between the two words is not so clearly marked, but "wisdom" seems to belong more to the human *spirit*, and "knowledge" to the *intellect*. The "discourse of wisdom" would be that which sets forth the truth of the gospel persuasively to work conversion (ch. ii. 6, 7); the "discourse of knowledge" would be that which enters into the speculative and theoretical elaboration of systematic theology. The first might find its illustration in the 'Imitatio Christi;' the second in the 'Summa Theologiæ.'

Ver. 9.—**To another.** Various attempts have been made to classify the gifts thus enumerated, as: 1. Intellectual. (1) The word of wisdom; (2) the word of knowledge. 2. Pertaining to exalted faith (*fides miraculosa*). (1) Healings; (2) miracles; (3) preaching; (4) discrimination of spirits. 3. (1) Tongues; and (2) their interpretation. These attempts are not very successful. St. Paul probably uses the phrases "to one" and "to another" (ἀλλῳ δὲ . . . ἑτέρῳ δὲ) merely for variety of style (as in Heb. xi. 35, 36), with no very definite classification in view, as he does not mention all the *charisms* (see ver. 28). **Faith.** Faith in its highest energy, as a supernatural power; the faith that removes mountains (Matt. xvii. 19, 20). **The gifts of healing.** Not, that is, by medical knowledge, but by supernatural power (Mark xvi. 18; Acts v. 15, 16; Jas. v. 14, 15).

Ver. 10.—**The working of miracles;** literally, *active efficacy of powers;* such as "the signs of an apostle," to which St. Paul himself appealed in 2 Cor. xii. 12, which included "wonders and mighty powers" (comp. Rom. xv. 18). **Prophecy.** Not "prediction," but elevated and inspired discourse; the power of preaching to edification. **Discerning of spirits;** rather, *discernings,* or *powers to discriminate between true and false spirits.* It was necessary in those days of intense enthusiasm and spiritual awakenment to "test the spirits, whether they be of God" (1 John iv. 1). There were such things as "deceitful spirits" which spoke "doctrines of devils" (1 Tim. iv. 1; Rev. ii. 1, 2; see ch. xiv. 29). **Divers kinds of tongues.** There is no need for the word "divers." The particular variety of the ecstatic, and often entirely unintelligible, utterance known as "the tongue" differed with the individuality or temperament of the speaker. Recent lines of research, by that historical method which can alone furnish correct results, have led to the conclusion that, whatever may be thought of the "tongues" on the day of Pentecost (which is a separate question), the "tongue" spoken of (for the most part with *relative* disparagement) by St. Paul as a *charism* of the Spirit was closely analogous to that wild, rapt, unconscious, uncontrollable utterance which, with vary-

ing details, has always occurred in the religious movements which stir the human soul to its utmost depths. The attempts to explain the word "tongues" as meaning "foreign languages," or "the primeval language," or "poetic and unusual phraseology," etc., are baseless and exploded. The notion that by this gift the early Christians knew languages which they had never acquired, is not only opposed to the entire analogy of God's dealings, but to every allusion in the New Testament (except a *primâ facie* but untenable view of the meaning of Acts ii. 4) and to every tradition and statement of early Christian history. The apostles (so far as we have any record of their missionary work in the New Testament) had not the slightest need to acquire foreign languages. Since Palestine was at this epoch bilingual, they could all speak Aramaic and Greek, and therefore could address Jews and Gentiles throughout the civilized world. Every single allusion which St. Paul makes to this subject excludes the possibility of the supposition of a miracle so utterly useless and meaningless, so subversive of every psychological consideration, and so alien from the analogy of all God's methods, as the talking in unacquired foreign languages by persons who did not understand them. **The interpretation of tongues.** Sometimes, but not always (ch. xiv. 13), the speaker, on relapsing from his ecstasy, was able to express his outburst of unintelligible soliloquy in the form of reasoned thought. When he was unable to do so, St. Paul ordains that another should convey in ordinary language the impressions left by the inspired rhapsody (ch. xiv. 27—29).

Ver. 11.—**One and the selfsame Spirit.** The unity of the source from which all the *charisms* flowed ought to have excluded the possibility of a boastful *comparison* of gifts, and all depreciation of those gifts which, because they were less dazzling, were deemed inferior. St. Paul afterwards shows that the less dazzling might be infinitely the more valuable for purposes of spiritual edification.

Vers. 12—31.—*The Church compared to a body and its members.*

Ver. 12.—**As the body is one, and hath many members.** To this favourite image St. Paul reverts several times (Rom. xii. 4, 5; Eph. iv. 11—16; Col. ii. 19). It is probable that he was familiar with the image from the fable of Menenius Agrippa, who had used it as a plea for civil unity (Liv., ii. 32). **So also is Christ.** Christ and the Church form one body, of which Christ is the Head; one Vine, of which Christians are the branches (John xv.); one building, of which Christians are the living stones.

Ver. 13.—**By one Spirit;** rather, *in one*

Spirit. The diffusion of one spirit is the element of unity. **Are we all baptized;** rather, *we were all baptized.* **Whether** we be **Jews or Gentiles, whether we be bond or free.** Moreover, as these were national and social differences, they were all obliterated by baptism, which made us all equal members of one holy brotherhood (Gal. iii. 28). **Have been all made to drink into one Spirit.** The word "into" is probably spurious. We have all been given to drink of one Spirit, which is as the outpouring of living water (Acts x. 45; John vii. 37).

Ver. 15.—**If the foot shall say,** etc. So Seneca says, "What if the hands should wish to injure the feet, or the eyes the hands? As all the members agree together because it is the interest of the whole that each should be kept safe, so men spare their fellow-men because we are born for heaven, and society cannot be saved except by the love and protection of its elements" ('De Ira,' ii. 31). And Marcus Aurelius: "We have been born for mutual help, like the feet, like the hands, like the rows of upper and lower teeth. To act in opposition to one another is therefore contrary to nature" ('Enchir.,' ii. 1). And Pope—

" What if the foot, ordained the dust to tread,
Or hand, to toil, aspired to be the head?
What if the head, the eye, or ear repined
To serve mere engines to the ruling mind?
Just as absurd for any part to claim
To be another, in this general frame," etc.

Ver. 17.—**If the whole body** were **an eye,** etc. In the body there is between the members an identity of common interest and a perfection of separate functions. All are not equal in strength and delicacy, but each is happy, and each is necessary to the well-being of all. There could be no better image of the ideal relation of Christians to each other and to the Church.

Ver. 18.—**As it hath pleased him.** Not arbitrarily, but in furtherance of one wise and beneficent design, so that each may be honoured and indispensable, and therefore contented in its own sphere.

Ver. 19.—**And if they were all one member, where** were the body? The interests of the individual must never overshadow those of· the Church. In the Church, as in the body, the hypertrophy or the atrophy of any one member is injurious, not only to itself, but to the whole.

Ver. 21.—**I have no need of thee.** A rebuke to the pride of those who thought their own gifts to be exclusively valuable.

Ver. 22.—**Are necessary.** This is the point of the fable of the belly and the members.

Ver. 23.—**Which we think to be less honourable.** The shelter and ornament of clothing are used to cover those parts of the body which are conventionally regarded as the least seemly. The whole of this illustration is meant to show that rich and poor, great and small, high and low, gifted and ungifted, have all their own separate and indispensable functions, and no class of Christians can wisely disparage or forego the aid derived from other and different classes. The unity of the members in one body corresponds to "the unity of the Spirit in the bond of peace" which should prevail in the Church.

Ver. 25.—**No schism in the body.** What is exclusively called "schism" is not necessarily such. There may be difference of fold in the one flock. There may be no real discord or dissension, though there may be varieties of ecclesiastical government. Unity, as the whole argument shows, does not demand the existence of uniformity. That **the members should have the same care one for another.** Thus the early believers "were of one heart and of one soul;" and the moment that a complaint arose that one of the weakest and smallest interests was neglected, the supposed neglect was amply remedied (Acts iv. 32; vi. 1—6).

Ver. 26.—**Whether one member suffer, all the members suffer with it,** etc. St. Chrysostom illustrates this verse by saying that if a thorn runs into the heel, the whole body feels it and is troubled; and that, on the other hand, if the head is garlanded, the whole man is glorified.

Ver. 27.—**Ye are the body of Christ, and members in particular.** Each Church is a sort of microcosm of the whole Church. St. Paul does not mean that the Corinthian Church is a member in the body of all the Churches, but that each Corinthian Christian is a member of the Church.

Ver. 28.—**Hath set;** rather, *appointed.* **First apostles.** Apart from the twelve (Luke vi. 13) and Paul and Barnabas, the name was in a lower sense extended to leading and eminent Christians, especially to those who had taken part in founding or ruling Churches (Rom. xvi. 7). **Prophets.** Wise spiritual preachers. It is instructive to note that St. Paul places the gifts of wisdom and knowledge which these preachers require above those which we are apt to regard as exclusively miraculous. The "wonders" stood in a lower, not in a higher, position when compared with the ordinary gifts of grace. **Teachers.** Those who have the minor gifts of instruction and exposition (Acts xiii. 1). **Helps.** All the services rendered by the power of active sympathy; by the work of deacons, sisters of mercy, etc. (Acts vi. 3, 4). The word occurs in 2 Macc. viii. 19; Ecclus. xi. 12, and the corresponding verb in Acts xx. 35; 1 Tim.

vi. 2 ; Luke i. 54 ; see Rom. xvi. 3. **Govern-ments.** Powers of leading and organization. **Diversities** [kinds] **of tongues.** Ranked as *last* in value. They are emotional gifts, which had only a very subordinate part in the work of edification, and are, therefore, placed below the gifts of knowledge, of power, and of practical life, which sum up the previous enumeration.

Ver. 29.—**Are all apostles?** etc. It is God's providence which " has appointed divers orders in his Church," and has "ordained and constituted the services of angels and of men in a wonderful order."

Ver. 31.—**Covet earnestly;** literally, *be zealous for, strongly desire.* That which we aim at we usually attain; and we should aim at that which really *is*, not at that which

seems, the most splendid *charism*. **And yet show I unto you a more excellent way.** The "more excellent way" is the way of love, which he sets forth in the next chapter, and which lies open to all Christians without distinction. The verse means either, "And further" (besides bidding you aim at the better gifts), "I show you *one supreme way of attaining them;*" or, "And I show you a still more eminent way." I bid you desire the best gifts, and further show you a truly royal road (*viam maxime vialem*), a road *par excellence*, which leads to their attainment. The way of love would lead to them, and it was itself the best of them. "All the way to heaven lies through heaven, and the path to heaven is heaven."

HOMILETICS.

Vers. 1—31.—*The Christly assembly.* "Now concerning spiritual gifts," etc. All throughout this chapter refers to the *Christly assembly.* I use this word in preference to the word "Church," for what are now called Churches are not always assemblages of genuine Christians. Overlooking the more minute parts of this remarkable chapter, and taking a broad glance at the whole, there are three important subjects very suggestive and capable of amplification, which are discoverable. These are that every member of this Christly community has *passed through a radical change ;* that every member has *received special endowments from God ;* and that every member should regard these endowments as *parts of a vital whole.*

I. Every member of this Christly community has PASSED THROUGH A RADICAL CHANGE. "Now concerning spiritual gifts, brethren, I would not have you ignorant. Ye know that ye were Gentiles, carried away unto these dumb idols, even as ye were led." The change here spoken of, it is to be observed, is a change from the spirit of the Gentiles, or the world, to the Spirit of Christ. The most radical change that can take place in a man is a change in his *predominant disposition*, or moral spirit. Such a disposition is in truth man's moral heart. This change is here described: 1. *Negatively.* No man who has experienced it has anything irreverent or profane in his spirit towards Christ. "No man speaking by the Spirit of God calleth Jesus accursed." 2. *Positively.* "No man can say that Jesus is the Lord, but by the Holy Ghost." "Can say," not of course merely the words, for all could easily do that, but with the heart and life. This change is the production of the Divine Spirit—of "the Holy Ghost." Now, no man is a member of the true Church who has not experienced this transformation ; who has not renounced the spirit of the world and come under the control of the Spirit of Christ. There are such who are found in connection with no conventional Church, and there may be conventional Churches where no such are found. All such, however, wherever found, belong to the Church of the "Firstborn written in heaven."

II. Every member of this Christly community has RECEIVED SPECIAL ENDOWMENTS FROM GOD. "Now there are diversities of gifts, but the same Spirit," etc. (vers. 4, 12). Without pausing to interpret the meaning of these endowments, I simply remark that they seem capable of being divided into three classes: (1) Those of *intellect.* "Wisdom," "knowledge," etc. (2) Those of "*faith*," operating faith in words, in deeds, and in "discernment." (3) Those of *language.* "Tongues," speaking and interpreting. Now, all responsible men have *intellect* of some kind and amount. All men have *faith* of some sort. Man has an instinctive *tendency* to believe; hence his credulity is proverbial. And he is *necessitated* to believe; he could not carry on the business of life without faith. All men also have a *language* of some kind or other. What, then, do we mean when we say that the endowments here refer to intellect, faith, and language? Simply this, that the man who has come into possession of the Christly

Spirit and purpose, and is thus a member of the genuine Church, will receive (1) a new force and elevation of *intellect*; (2) a new object and energy of *faith*; (3) a new style and emphasis of *expression*—a new tongue. This great variety of endowments reveals: 1. The *sovereignty* of the Spirit. Why did he bestow any at all? Still more, why so different to different men? The only answer is because it pleased him so to do. "He worketh all things after the counsel of his own will." 2. The *affluence* of the Spirit. All these great and varied spiritual and mental endowments came from him. He is the inexhaustible Fountain, not only of all life, but of all spiritual endowments. 3. The *benevolence* of the Spirit. All these varied endowments bestowed for what purpose? To "profit withal." All for the highest usefulness; spiritual happiness is the end of the creation. Since all our endowments are the free gifts of God, there is no reason for those of the humblest to be dissatisfied, nor for those who have the most splendid to be exultant.

III. Every member should regard these endowments as PARTS OF A VITAL WHOLE. The whole is here called the "body of Christ." As the soul resides in the body, directs the body, reveals itself in the body, so Christ in the true Church. "For as the body is one, and hath many members, and all the members of that one body, being many, are one body, so also is Christ," etc. Great is the variety in the various faculties, organs, and parts of the human body. Some are larger and more comely than others, but each, even the most insignificant and uncomely, are equally essential. "Those members of the body, which seem to be more feeble, are necessary," etc. How preposterous would it be for one vital part of the body to contend with another for importance and supremacy! Yet not more absurd than for one member of a Church to contend with another. This is Paul's argument against the divisions that were rampant in the Corinthian Church.

> " What if the foot, ordained the dust to tread,
> Or hand, to toil, aspired to be the head?
> What if the head, the eye, or ear repined
> To serve mere engines to the ruling mind?
> Just as absurd for any part to claim
> To be another, in this general frame:
> Just as absurd to mourn the task or pains,
> The great directing Mind of all ordains.
> All are but parts of one stupendous whole,
> Whose body nature is, and God the soul."
>
> (Pope.)

HOMILIES BY VARIOUS AUTHORS.

Vers. 1—31.—*Spiritual gifts.* A transition occurs here to a class of topics most important and interesting, since they involve the character and glory of the new dispensation. It was the special economy of the Holy Ghost which St. Paul was now to consider. All along we have had an insight into mistakes and disorders, into disputes and wranglings and, at times, into shameful vices. A quarter of a century had little more than passed since Christ ascended to the throne of the Father as the God-Man of the universe, and the Spirit had descended as the promised Paraclete. Yet what strife and confusion! The marvellous gifts were strangely misunderstood. Once these Corinthians—so the apostle reminds them—had been Gentiles, "led away unto dumb idols, howsoever they might be led." But for them the age of "dumb idols" had ended and the great dispensation of speech had opened. No man sharing this speech from heaven—"speaking by the Spirit of God"—could call "Jesus accursed;" and only such as were enlightened and directed by the Holy Ghost could say from the heart of love and faith that "Jesus is the Lord." At the outset, this principle is laid down as fundamental to the economy of gifts; *it is a Divine economy; it is the dispensation of the Holy Ghost.* Something was gained when this was made clear. Inspiration was no wild, spasmodic, frantic thing. It was not individuality unloosed and driven into gross eccentricity. Whatever mysteries were connected with these manifestations, there was a grand system to which they appertained, and it was upheld, applied, administered, by the Holy Ghost. Such, then, is the position assumed, and it commands the whole question. This done, the places occupied by different parties, the diversity of gifts, their number and multiformity, the relativity of each to a controlling general idea, and the unity sought as a final end, could be ascertained. Naturally, then, *diversities of gifts would be the first to attract attention.* Difference between objects begins our perceptive education, difference in our moods of mind cultivates our consciousness, difference must be seen before the higher intellect can perform the processes of abstraction and generalization. Accordingly St. Paul starts with "diversities of gifts." It was not a new idea. The Prophet Joel had it substantially, along with the conception of universality, when he spoke of prophesyings, of dreams, of visions, and declared that servants and handmaids should rejoice in the possession of this power. Christ had closed his earthly revelation of the Father by unfolding the manifoldness of the Spirit's office. Pentecost had made good the promise, and had shown as the firstfruits of the harvest the recovery of the world's languages to the service of Christianity. St. Paul, however, handles the idea in a way altogether new. Genius passes old truths through its transforming brain, and they charm the world as fresh and wondrous disclosures. Inspiration honours individuality; nothing treats the personality of the man with such respect; and hence St. Paul's specialization of the fact of diversity. Mark how he treats it. *Gifts themselves,* as relative to men who are their recipients, are very unlike. Capacity in each case is a pre-existent fact of providence, and the Spirit consults providence. But in the next place, *gifts are ministries,* and the diversities (distributions) are for various spheres. Functional work is of many kinds, offices have each its speciality, and, as earthly industry must achieve its results by division of labour, so the economy of the Holy Ghost must differentiate one form of energy from another. Ministers are servants, and these ministries are serving forces. And again, the gifts are represented as *operations* by whose effects, as incorporated in society, the kingdom of God is built up. "These are not to be limited to *miraculous* effects, but understood commensurately with the gifts of whose working they are the results" (Alford). If, in other passages of Scripture, the person of the Father or of the Son is prominently displayed, the personality of the Holy Ghost, as proceeding from the Father and the Son, is here set forth with a distinctness and emphasis characteristic of his relations to the plan of salvation. Just before (ver. 3), St. Paul had declared the presence of the Holy Ghost in the confession of Jesus as Lord, and the name, by which he was known among men (Jesus of Nazareth) and recognized in his trial, condemnation, and crucifixion, is borne up from earth and glorified in his exaltation. And here he is the "same Spirit" in the opening thought, "diversities of gifts." There are "differences of administrations," but the "same Lord;" "diversities of operations," but the "same God that worketh all in all;" nor will the apostle specify the fulness of the Spirit's gifts and the greatness of his presiding agency over the Church without connecting him with the Father and the Son. The mystery of the Trinity remains. But the doctrine becomes a very real and practical fact, and, as such, assimilable in Christian experience, when thus identified with grace in all its workings through the Church. And so true is this that the very mystery is essential to the effect the doctrine produces, by forming an infinite background, against which the fact stands in relief. Under these circumstances, mystery commends itself, not simply to reverence, but to experimental appreciation. Reason, if made conscious of its own instinct, finds a basis for itself and a vindication of its functions in the exercise of faith, and, by means of this illumination, reason is assured that the faculties of the human mind have their laws and are bound in obedience thereunto, because the law of mystery is the primal law whence they draw their life and support. No marvel, then, that the apostle presents God the Father, God the Son, and God the Spirit with such prominence in the initial stage of his argument on spiritual gifts. Most closely is the doctrine identified with the experimental and practical truths he was about to enforce. From no lower source than the mystery of all mysteries will he bring the awe, the sense of responsibility under trust, and the greatness of Church duties arising from the diversities of gifts. It is not this or that gift alone, nor this or that office-bearer alone, nor this or that outwrought result alone, but their union in one economy and their combination in a totality, which he wished to emphasize. Most impressively is this done by presenting Father, Son, and Spirit as the one God of these diverse gifts, the Trinity itself being the very ground and source of the diversification. The broad scope of the diversities in the Church is indicated in the statement that the "manifestation of the Spirit is given *to every man* to profit withal." The character of the Divine communication to "every man" is defined by the word "*manifestation*," which expresses the agency of the Spirit in these human instruments. First of all, the Spirit is manifested *to* the man and then *through* the man. As a condition precedent to his office, the man has an experience, and it consists in his own conscious knowledge that God has come to his soul and imbued it with the Spirit. Herein, herein only, lies his capacity for usefulness; herein his safeguard against failure. And the measure of the one manifestation is the measure of the other; for in the degree that a man feels his own soul alive to God will he impart vitality to his ministrations. Preacher, Sunday school teacher, Bible reader, tract distributer, Paul on Mars' Hill or in the prison at Rome, Bunyan writing in gaol, Hannah More at Barleywood, John Pounds with his ragged school; no matter what the manifestation, as to where made and how modified by individuality, it is divinely human to its subject before it is made divinely human in him as an instrument. Finally, the broad scope (*every man*) and the quality of the influence (*manifestation*) are carried forward to the object and end, viz. *to profit withal*. For the common advantage these gifts were bestowed; the greater the bestowment, the nearer its human connections; and the more of a recipient the man, the more of a man must he be in the outgoings of his intelligence, love, and zeal in behalf of others. "Who maketh thee to differ from another? and what hast thou that thou didst not receive?" Such was the argument (ch. iv.) to check partisanship in the Corinthian Church; but in this passage, "to profit withal" is exhibited in its positive aspect as the inspiration of motive and purpose and end of all Christian working. Is it not, then, remarkable that Christianity approaches man at a point where he is most sensitive to self, and where he is quickest and boldest to assert his unyieldingness to the claims of others, and at this very point to demand of him "the common profit"? Make any analysis of human nature you please, pride of intellect is the most lordly of all its imperious qualities. Particularly in the case of fine gifts, men who are the possessors of them are instinctively disposed to assert a despotic sway over others, or, if not that, to indulge a feeling of self-gratulation and its counterpart of self-isolation because of their superiority. Yet it is just here Christianity requires humility and enforces the claims of a most vigorous sympathy. How this "common profit" is to be subserved, St. Paul proceeds to show in vers. 8—11. There is no large accumulation in one man, no fostering of the spirit of self-aggrandizement no such exaltation of one as to prove a humiliation to another. Talents are divided out, and each talent bears the seal of God, and comes authenticated, not to the intellect, but to the spiritual sense of a redeemed manhood. Go through this catalogue as drawn out by the apostle; dwell on the significance of each specification; avail yourself of the helps afforded by our most critical scholars in the explication of "*wisdom*" as intuition, of "*knowledge*" as acquired information, of "*faith*" as transcending its ordinary limits as the grace of salvation, of the "*gifts of healing*" as adapted to various diseases, of the "*working of miracles*" as time and occasion called for, all these *charisms* proceeding from the same Spirit; continue the enumeration that includes "*prophecy*" or the illumination of the mind by the Spirit and the exalted activity of its faculties, after that the eye of watchful judgment, "*discerning of spirits*," so as to discriminate between genuine inspiration and its alloys and counterfeits, then the "*divers kinds of tongues*," and the power to interpret or translate the unknown language; and all these the works of "one and the selfsame Spirit" that distributes the *charism* to each one in harmony with the law of individuality, and, at the same time, exercises the Divine sovereignty so that the distribution is made "severally as he will" (Alford, Hodge, Lange); and when you have thus expanded your views to the dimensions of this spiritual provision for the Church and the exquisite symmetry of its organism, tell us if any interest possible to man's present attitude, if any craving of true life in its mortal and immortal relationships, if any outreachings toward the infinite when body, soul, and spirit have interblended their instincts, and become one in the heir-

ship of an eternal inheritance, have been left neglected or meagrely provided for?
To bring this variety and unity more vividly before the Corinthians, St. Paul employs
a most apt illustration taken from the human body as an organism. Already he
had argued the diversity of gifts in adaptiveness to the capacities and wants of the
Church. Left at that point, the argument would have been incomplete. It was
needful to see what the Church itself was as an organization, and how its wholeness
stood related to its individual parts. In the earlier portion of the Epistle he had
combated the unhappy tendency towards an excessive individualism. Theoretic
speculations had been kept out of sight, and practical questions, lying within immediate range and urgently demanding treatment, had been scrutinized. Was the
work done when domestic morals had been pleaded for, when social companionships
were set in a true light; when the betrayals of a lax and over-accommodating
sympathy in public intercourse were exposed; when the corruptions growing out of
an abuse of love-feasts and extending to the Holy Communion had been faithfully
dealt with; when, in addition thereunto, he had expounded the Divine import and
sacredness of the Lord's Supper? Was the work done when he had opened the
treasures of grace and taught his brethren how the Divine munificence had enriched
their souls? Was he content to stop after delineating the correspondence between
the bestowments of the Spirit in his multiformity of gifts, and the complexity of
the Church as the witness to the Trinity? By no means was the subject exhausted.
Specific as he had been—direct, resolute, pungent—how much remained to be said
(as we shall see hereafter), to reflect back on what had been said, and bring out
half-latent meanings of truths stated which the argument, in its direct connections,
did not exact of his logic at the instant! At this point, then, he introduces a
felicitous illustration. It is done in a business-like style. Image it can scarcely
be called, since it has no poetic element addressed merely to the æsthetic sense,
and is quite as much the product of the reason as of the imagination. We have
spoken of St. Paul as one who studied the human body and was profoundly interested
in considering its present and prospective condition in the light of the Christian
revelation. The illustration here used extends through a large portion of the
chapter, and, as a figure, is for him elaborated with unusual fulness and painstaking.
Evidently it is not a creation of the moment, for there is not a mark of sudden
impulse. Tracing the analogy between the Church and the human body, and recognizing the Spirit of the earlier creation in this later and more glorious one, the
inspired author evinces that delight in similarity of relations which is the infallible
sign both of high endowment and broad culture, and he proceeds with a quiet and
steady gait till the ground has been fully traversed. 1. *The human body is an
organism.* It is "*one*, and hath many members." By an organism we understand " a
whole consisting of parts which exist and work each for all and all for each; in other
words, which are reciprocally related as means and end" (Dr. Kling). The principle
of life is a principle of organization, weaving a form for itself, shaping that form to
itself, and impressing thereupon its own distinctive image. The principle assumes
various organizations—simple in some, complex in others—and, in every case, the
life-power is the animating and determinative force. "So also is Christ" (ver. 12).
In the Church, which is his body, Christ is the constituting Power. He is its Life,
and without him it is nothing. Through the Spirit he maintains those operations
which impart vitality to all the institutions and agencies of the Church. "By
one Spirit are we all baptized into one body" (ver. 13), whether "Jews or Gentiles;"
such is the almighty energy of the Holy Ghost in begetting vitality and transforming
national and race distinctions into its own likeness, that they are made one. This
is also true of "bond or free." The characteristics of individuality as to races and
social positions remain, but whatever is incapable of unity is removed and the
organism subdues to itself every element and constituent it adopts. All are made
"to drink into one Spirit." Viewed externally, we see Jews and Greeks, bond and
free, with their peculiarities derived from the past and respected as the signs of
Providence in the ages preparatory to Christ's advent. A rich and picturesque
mosaic is thus presented by the Church. Along with this, the Church is also a
type of the future man, from whom all selfish antagonisms have gone and over
whom the sentiment of brotherhood is supreme. 2. *The human body has various*

correlated parts. "For the body is *not one* member, but *many*" (ver. 14). Each constitutent or "member" must be recognized as something in itself, as having an autonomy, as created for a distinct function and ordained to do its own special work. Not else could the body be worthy of its place as the head of the physical world and represent the mind of man. In this wondrous organism, which may be likened to a community, every cell is an independent activity, a citizen with rights of its own and entitled to protection against all hostile influence. The fable of Menenius is introduced, and the classic reader of our day is reminded of Coriolanus as the representative of the haughty patricians and yet more of the haughtier statesman, and of the fierce contempt felt for the people. St. Paul has given due prominence to this idea of each organ as performing its functions and as essential to the whole. If the unity is brought about from within, then it follows that every member must share the animating principle. Food must be provided for blood, blood must nourish the organs, the organs must be tributary in specific ways to the organism, or the organism must perish. So in the Church, different men are different organs. Such are the numerous offices of the Holy Ghost as the Executive of Father and Son; such are his relations as Remembrancer, Testifier, Convincer; that there must needs be much diversity of gift; and hence there are gifts of healing, helping, governing, extraordinary faith, and "divers kinds of tongues." Light is distributed in colours, and colours in tints and hues, and tints and hues multiply themselves in minute differences. Sound breaks up in notes. Form assumes multitudinous shapes and attitudes. The ocean rolls in restless lines and the earth curves to a curving sky. "Not one member, but many," and the manifoldness in the magnificence of the universe is repeated, as far as may be, in the complexity of the human organism, and, in turn, this exists for the Church. But: 3. *Reciprocity of action must be fully maintained.* The organs of the body are distinct but not separate, since they combine in one organism and are subordinate to a unitary result. They are supplied with blood by the same heart and they are all dependent on nerves running from nervous centres. Spinal cord, medulla, cerebellum, cerebrum, are local in position, but not local in function. Not an organ, though independent in structure and functional operation, can insulate itself and be independent of the whole. Our pleasures and pains alike testify to this dominant mutuality. A beautiful landscape is not limited to the retina; a musical sound enters the rhythm of heart and lungs, and the ear is only a fragment of the joy; so that localized sensibility, however intense, becomes generalized feeling. The special senses exist for a sensorium. St. Paul regards the body, therefore, as an assemblage or confederation of organs, and enlarges (vers. 15—26) on the idea in its several aspects. The section has been fitly spoken of as a "colloquy in a highly dramatic style." The body itself is thoroughly dramatic. It represents and interprets mind. It acts the soul. Downward it may go and imitate the beast, even descend below the beast. Upward it may go, and go so high that the faces of Moses and St. Stephen glow with a light never on shore or sea. Now, this colloquy presents one member of the body arrayed against another and vainly asserting its independence. If a discontented foot envy the hand, or the ear envy the eye, "is it therefore not of the body," participating in its rights, enjoying its privileges, ennobled by the organism? They are for the sake of each other, so that "the eye cannot say to the hand, I have no need of thee: nor again the head to the feet, I have no need of you." Furthermore, in the case of *feeble* organs, does the body turn vindictively against them?—in the case of those *less honourable*, are they despised? in the case of the *uncomely parts,* are they treated with contempt? Nay, in the well-ordered commonwealth of the body, where the instincts, endowed by the Almighty with a measure of his sovereignty, retain their sway, parts that are feeble, less honourable, less comely, appeal to pity and sympathy and taste to be cheered and comforted. The whole glandular system, though assigned to the functions of secretion and excretion, is yet a wonderful provision for emotion, not only for emotion as respects others, but as self-regarding and self-relieving. A whispered need of assistance from the very humblest organ is heard in every recess of the corporeal structure. Temple it is even in ruins, and its ministers, inhabiting dim vaults and mysterious crypts, hear the prayer for compassion and aid, and hasten to give sympathy and assistance. Beyond all this, what vicarious work the organs do in their considerate kindness to one another? No doubt we are open to the charge of reading between the apostle's lines and of going beyond his intended meaning. Be it so; on the lines or between them, no matter, if the philosophy and spirit of the thought be observed. St. Paul's inspiration was for our day as well as his own, and perhaps it would not be very extravagant to say that the Christian scholarship of the nineteenth century sees depths in some of his conceptions that he never saw. For it is the nature of inspiration to be ever unfolding its manifoldness of meaning, holding tenaciously to its original ground, and yet pressing back its horizon to embrace fresh territory, and thus making itself a specially quickening power to successive ages. One thing, however, is very clear, namely, St. Paul saw the analogy between the Church and the human body. By virtue of the connection of its organs, he takes occasion to urge on the Church very weighty and solemn duties. Mutual forbearance, respect, honour, must be sacredly cherished. The organic life of the Church makes it Christ's body. "Ye are the body of Christ, and members in particular." The main thought is restated and re-enforced as to apostles, prophets, etc. (vers. 28—30); and surely nothing has been left unsaid which could convince and persuade the Corinthians that their spiritual organization was not a thing to take care of itself, nor to be trusted to hap-hazard, nor to be surrendered to self-appointed leaders. It was a life, a sphere, a discipline and culture, a joy and blessedness, for all. Were the weakliest among them to be overlooked as useless? If there were poor widows with only two mites to cast into God's treasury, they had their place and vocation. If there were little children, their looks and ways told of the kingdom of heaven. Were there uncomely parts? Grace was strong enough to do them abundant honour. One of the invaluable blessings of Church life is to show respect and regard for such as society excludes from its esteem, and alas! too often treats with disdain, and thereby dooms them to a fate more wretched than poverty. In honouring them, the Church teaches these persons to honour themselves, and that, once secured, improvement outward and inward is made far easier. In brief, wherever anything was lacking, there "more abundant honour" should be bestowed. And why all this? That none be neglected, that all be partakers of one another's sufferings and pleasures, and that the community be indeed a communion of one heart and mind. "That there should be no schism." This was the dread that hung over St. Paul: "schism;" this was the terror that darkened his path far more than the enemies and persecutors that pursued his steps. "Members should have the same care one for another." Brotherhood should sanctify individuality, and consummate and crown all the gifts of the Divine Giver. What a wonder this, to set before a city like Corinth! What an ideal to lift up in its resplendent glory in a period such as the first century! And this by the "ugly little Jew," a wandering tent-maker, who had nothing and would have nothing to commend him to the carnal philosophy and popular tastes of the age, and who could only speak from his own soul and the Spirit in that soul to the souls of men. Yet the doctrine of Christ's headship of humanity was his stay and strength, and the gifts of the Holy Ghost were his tokens and pledges of victory for his cause. He would have others share his assurance and participate with him in the infinite blessedness. Therefore, he argues, "covet earnestly the best gifts," and the *best way* to secure these *best gifts* he will proceed at once to show them.—L.

Ver. 12.—*Spiritual unity.* If this be a true representation, what an honour, what a happiness it is to be a Christian! It is to be joined to the Lord of life and glory, and to be associated with the noblest, the purest, the best of mankind.

I. IN WHAT RESPECTS CHRIST AND HIS MEMBERS ARE ONE. The expression used by the apostle is remarkable: "So also is Christ." He says, "Christ;" yet he means Christ's people; from which it appears that, in the view of the apostle, as in the view of the Lord himself, all who are his are identified with and comprehended in his own Divine personality. 1. This is a fact which is exhibited in various manners and especially by various metaphors. Not only are Christ and his people the Head and the body; they are the Vine and the branches, the Foundation and the stones, the organism and the Soul. 2. The union as spiritual is formed and sustained by faith. There are sacramental symbols of the union, but the real and vital connection is of spirit with spirit, *i.e.* is of faith. As mutual, it is depicted by the Lord himself, when he says, "I in you, and you in me." 3. The character and the aim of the Head and the members are identical. "As he is, so are we in this world."

II. IN WHAT RESPECTS CHRIST'S MEMBERS ARE SUBORDINATE TO HIM. 1. He is the Giver of the life which his people have in common with him. 2. He is the Source of authority, issuing the commands which govern their activity. 3. He is the Centre of harmony; they who are his revolve around him as planets round the sun; and their orbits resemble one another, because all are drawn by the same attractive force. 4. He confers upon them the glory which is their prerogative—the moral glory which is conferred here and now, and the glory to be revealed hereafter.

III. IN WHAT RESPECTS CHRIST'S MEMBERS ARE RELATED ONE TO ANOTHER. All are "one body." 1. Their dependence upon the one Head is the same. The unity is not simply in the organization; it is in the life. 2. They are bound by Christian law and drawn by Christian impulse to mutual affection and confidence. Love is the law of Christian social life, as in the following chapter is so exquisitely shown. 3. They have each his several service to render to the one Master; the gifts are alike consecrated, the ministrations are alike devoted, to the Divine Lord. 4. They have mutual ability and obligation to help. As in the body each member, each sense, supplies the other's lack of service, so in the Church it is not simply the case that the gifted and the powerful render help to others less favourably endowed, but the feeblest and the most obscure may render some service for which his brethren may have reason to be for ever grateful. 5. In the blessings conferred by the Church upon the world around, each may be said to supply the other's deficiency; and the work of evangelization, in which each performs his proper part, is advanced by the cordial co-operation of all whom Providence has qualified and grace has inclined for the work.—T.

Vers. 15, 16.—*Contentment is better than envy.* Where party spirit is rife, as it was in the Corinthian Church, there is always danger of hatred, envying, and jealousy. The rebuke to these dispositions, administered by the apostle, is founded upon the deepest principles of Christianity. The Church is not a club which each member joins for his own advantage and convenience, but a body in which each member is incorporated for mutual co-operation in common subjection to the Divine Head.

I. THERE MUST NEEDS BE, IN RELIGIOUS AS IN CIVIL SOCIETY, DIFFERENT POSITIONS CORRESPONDING TO VARYING GIFTS AND SERVICES. As the body needs all its members, they must occupy their appointed positions for which they are severally fitted and to which they are severally called. It is so in the Church of God; and, according to the office filled, the duties performed, will be the position occupied in the regard and esteem of men.

II. THOSE IN INFERIOR POSITIONS SHOULD REMEMBER THAT INFERIORITY IN THE VIEW OF MEN IS NOT NECESSARILY SUCH IN THE SIGHT OF GOD. That there *is* a scale of excellence cannot be questioned, but that God's graduation agrees with man's is not to be for a moment supposed. He judgeth not as man judgeth. Not always do those who fill most space in men's eyes stand first in the view of God.

III. AN ENVIOUS SPIRIT IS PRODUCTIVE OF THE UTMOST MISERY TO HIM WHO CHERISHES IT. All painters and poets who have dealt with the subject have agreed in depicting envy as consumed and tortured with wretchedness. The envious man cannot enjoy his own blessings or exercise his own powers, for the sight or thought of what he deems the choicer blessings or the rarer powers of his neighbour.

IV. ON THE OTHER HAND, A CONTENTED SPIRIT IS PRODUCTIVE OF TRUE HAPPINESS. When "the sun of sweet content" has risen in the eyes, the light is upon every feature. A holy and calm conviction that his lot is ordered by Divine wisdom gives a deep peace, an abiding cheerfulness, to a good man's life. If one were to have regard only to his own happiness, he would do well to beware of discontent.

V. IT IS TO BE REMEMBERED THAT AN APPARENTLY LOWLY SERVICE MAY BE IMPORTANT AND EVEN ESSENTIAL. The foot has not so complex a structure, has not the same adaptation to a varied service, as the hand; yet, with no power of locomotion, the man would be crippled and pitiable, notwithstanding the marvellous manual mechanism of which he is master. The ear does not afford the same range of know-ledge, perhaps not the same gradation of pleasure, as the eye; but the man who loses hearing is shut out from many of the joys and very much of the information which this life affords. And in the Church of Christ, what work has been done by the lowly, the feeble, the illiterate! and in how many cases do they put to shame the gifted and the eminent!

VI. IF THE TRUST BE SMALLER, THE RESPONSIBILITY WILL BE LESS. Instead of looking up to the great, the learned, the eloquent, and sighing because we have not their gifts, let us be grateful that we have not their account to render. To whom much is given, of him will much be required.—T.

Ver. 21.—*Respect is better than contempt.* In previous verses the apostle has expostulated with those in lowly stations and with inferior gifts who give way to the temptation to repine because of what is their own and to envy the higher position and the larger gifts of others. In this verse he exemplifies his justice and impartiality, rebuking those who despise such as are beneath them in mental or spiritual endow-ments.

I. PRIDE FOLLOWS UPON FORGETFULNESS OF THE DIVINE SOURCE OF ALL GIFTS. The man who looks down upon his fellow-Christian virtually boasts of whatever he himself has which he deems a ground of superiority. Now, this is in contradiction to the precepts of the Bible and the spirit of Christ. "What hast thou that thou didst not receive? Who hath made thee to differ?"

II. CONTEMPT IMPLIES FORGETFULNESS OF THE RULE OF DIVINE PROVIDENCE. Can we say to a brother, "I have no need of thee"? whilst we remember that the Head of the Church has stationed him where he is, and has given him what he possesses? To question his place in the Church, his function in the body, his service to the Head, is to dispute the wisdom and the authority of Christ himself.

III. CONTEMPT IS SELF-DESTRUCTIVE. It rebounds upon the head of him who casts it at his neighbour. For the fact is that we are members one of another in such a sense that each one's efficiency and usefulness is to a large extent dependent upon those of his brethren. In the figure used by the apostle, the eye and the head in which it is so pre-eminently and regally stationed, are taken as representing the great and notable among the members of a Christian society. And it is laid down as evident that they cannot say to hand, to foot, to the trunk and all the vital organs, "I have no need of you." For the fact is, they have such need. The well-known fable of Agrippa may be quoted, as in Shakespeare's 'Coriolanus,' in illustration and proof of the mutual dependence of all parts of the organism. So is it in the Church of God. The great controversialist, the great episcopal administrator, the great Biblical scholar, the great church builder, are all doubtless and undeniably of great importance, and fill a large place in men's eyes. But the obscure pastor, the lowly Scripture reader, the unnoticed Bible woman, the patient and unrewarded teacher of the young,—these and many others like them are the rank-and-file of the army, and cannot be dispensed with. To look down upon them with disdain would be a proof of folly as well as of sinful self-conceit. Happily, the truly great are ever foremost to recognize the value of the labours of the humble, ever foremost to do them honour. They know full well that their own work would fall to pieces were it not for the unnoticed work of others who may be less known to fame.

IV. MUTUAL RESPECT IS PROMOTIVE OF SPIRITUAL UNITY. Let there be murmuring among the lowly and disdain among the great, and there follows at once a "schism." But when each renders due honour to his brother, the society is compacted, and is made strong for its united work and witness in the world.—T.

Ver. 26.—*Sympathy.* The desirableness and preciousness of sympathy are unques-tionable. Selfishness is the curse of human nature and human society. There is a tendency towards absorption in individual interests, pleasures, and sorrows, which needs to be counteracted. Sympathy is as natural a principle as selfishness, though not so strong. Christianity tends to strengthen it for the conflict; and in the new humanity the love of the Saviour awakens and fosters regard for all those for whom Christ died.

I. CHRIST HIMSELF IS THE DIVINE FOUNDATION OF SYMPATHY. 1. Christ's words are the *law* of sympathy. It was he who uttered admonitions which have been so potent to affect the heart and influence society; *e.g.* "Do unto others," etc.; "Love one another," etc. And his apostles' words are his; *e.g.* "Bear ye one another's burdens;" "Look not every man," etc.; "Rejoice with them," etc. 2. Christ's life was the *model* of sympathy. In the Gospels we behold him sympathizing with sufferers, mourners, doubters, and inquirers, the ignorant and uncared for, sinners who repented of sin, and others. He is still the High Priest touched with a feeling of our infirmities. 3. Christ's cross is the *motive* to sympathy. It presents the Redeemer suffering with and for mankind; and those who can say, "He gave himself for me," feel the constraint of the cross, the love of Christ. 4. Christ's Spirit is the *power* of sympathy—an unseen, but mighty and gracious force.

II. THE VAST RANGE OF CHRISTIAN SYMPATHY. 1. The whole Church of the Redeemer demands its exercise. Christians are members of the one body, and subject to the one Head. Their mutual relations to one another are consequent upon their common relations to their Lord. Hence their interdependence and sympathy. When the head is crowned, the whole body is glorified; when the eyes brighten, all the features respond; when a limb aches, the whole frame is depressed. In such sympathy the body is a picture of the Church as it should be, and as it is just in proportion as it is pervaded by the Spirit of the Lord. 2. The whole race of mankind is included in its scope and action. Christianity alone can attack human isolation, and serve as the bond of universal brotherhood. The wanderers have to be gathered into the fold, and to this end they must first be pitied and yearned over and sought.

III. THE MANIFESTATIONS OF CHRISTIAN SYMPATHY. These are especially: 1. Sympathetic suffering with the sad and distressed, as opposed to indifference or malicious pleasure in others' misfortunes. 2. Sympathetic joy in the advancement and honours of others, as opposed to envy and jealousy. 3. Sympathetic action; for emotion leads to practical interposition and help. Aid, gifts, self-denying effort, may prove the reality of the feeling expressed in words.

IV. THE ADVANTAGES AND BLESSINGS OF CHRISTIAN SYMPATHY. 1. To those who display it, it is advantageous as developing and fostering spiritual qualities. 2. To those who partake of it, whose cheerfulness is augmented and whose sorrows are relieved. 3. To society in general, which is thus leavened by Christian spirit and influence.—T.

Ver. 27.—*Body and members.* At Corinth there was much of the spirit of self-assertion: "I," said one, "am for Paul!" "I," said another, "for Apollos!" "I," said a third, "for Cephas!" This was a selfish partisanship; and with it was conjoined a disposition on the part of many to magnify their own gifts and powers and to depreciate those of their neighbours and fellow-members. To all this the apostle furnishes the true corrective. Let Christians but regard themselves in the true light, as Christ's body collectively, and as individually living members of that body, and then inconsiderateness, selfishness, envy, and jealousy will flee away.

I. COLLECTIVELY, CHRISTIANS FORM THE BODY OF CHRIST. Not, of course, the body of flesh and blood which he assumed and wore; not the bread and wine of the Eucharist, which he called his body and blood; but the human representation of his presence which he has left on earth. 1. This assertion cannot be made of any one outward, visible, organic society. All these, because composed of human beings and consequently of imperfect and faulty characters, and because doubtless including within their boundaries unspiritual persons and hypocrites, are themselves far from reaching the Divine ideal. If one "visible" Church cannot claim to be the body of Christ, neither, for the same reason, can any association of such communities. They may be admirable, and their existence may be most important for the conservation of the gospel and the evangelization of the world, but they are not to be confounded with the body of Christ. 2. But it is true of the Church as it exists in the view of the omniscient Lord. The spiritual Church, sometimes called invisible, because its boundaries cannot be traced by human eyes, is penetrated by Christ's Spirit, is a living witness to his mind and doctrine, and is ever offering a service of obedience to his will. In these respects it is the *Body*, of which Christ himself is the living, inspiring, directing Soul.

II. INDIVIDUALLY, CHRISTIANS ARE MEMBERS OF CHRIST. 1. This comes to pass through individual spiritual union with him. Though each Christian is indebted beyond measure to the teaching, influence, and spirit of the consecrated society in which he has been trained, still a spiritual process must, through the reception of the means of grace, take place in his conscious nature. 2. Each Christian has his several functions to discharge in the Church and for the Lord. There are diversities of gifts and consequent diversities of ministries; and this diversity is itself a witness to the individual, the personal nature of the membership of every one in him who is the Source of all true blessing and power. 3. All co-operate for the same end. That this is so is evident; and how can it be so, except as a result of such common subjection to the one Head as secures the mutual harmony and co-ordination of all the members? Each is selected for his own part and qualified for his own position.—T.

Ver. 28.—"*First apostles.*" There are degrees of eminence, not only in the state, but in the Church. In the hierarchy which Heaven has appointed, the highest station was occupied by a class of men, few in number, eminent in qualifications, and honourable in office. Their functions were special, being in some particulars incapable of transmission to successors. In what did this pre-eminence consist? The answer to this question may serve to increase the reverence with which we receive their teaching and submit to their authority.

I. THE PRE-EMINENCE OF THE APOSTLES IS OWING TO THE DIGNITY AND MAJESTY OF THE LORD WHO GAVE AND SENT THEM. Christ himself was sent, and came forth from God. He had "all power in heaven and in earth," and he had consequently authority to commission the twelve and those associated with them. There was an authority in his word sending them forth, which they at once recognized and obeyed.

II. TO THE PURPOSES FOR WHICH THEY WERE SENT. Their mission was to preach Christ, to make converts, to gather those converts together into societies, to govern and administer the affairs of the congregations, to provide instruction in doctrine by speech and by writing, and to make provision for the permanent welfare of the whole Church. Such a mission was in many respects peculiar and unique; those entrusted with it could not but come first in the hierarchy.

III. TO THE POWERS WITH WHICH THEY WERE ENTRUSTED. To their natural gifts spiritual endowments were added; and over and above these were the supernatural possessions and trusts peculiar to their age, such as the gifts of tongues, of miracles, of healing, etc. Above all there was Divine inspiration, displayed in their supernatural wisdom both in doctrine and in government. From the day of Pentecost these men were entrusted with every high and sacred qualification which could tend to the suitable discharge of the honourable and responsible duties of the apostolate.

IV. TO THE BREADTH OF THEIR COMMISSION. Though so few, they may be said to have portioned the world among them. They were sent to neighbours and to strangers, to Jews and to Gentiles, to cities and to villages, to the civilized and to barbarians. To a commission so vast and extensive there attached honour altogether special and unrivalled.

V. TO THE WONDERFUL RESULTS OF THEIR APOSTOLIC LABOURS. The immediate and rapid spread of the gospel was such as could not have been anticipated by human wisdom, and such as has not been paralleled in after ages. They laid the foundations upon which the toilers and builders of after ages have reared a glorious superstructure.

APPLICATION. 1. Let hearers of the gospel consider the claims upon them of such a message as that communicated by ambassadors so gloriously authenticated as were the apostles of the Lord. 2. Let those who labour for Christ feel the summons which is addressed to them by the spirit and the example of predecessors so illustrious and so efficient.—T.

Vers. 1—11.—*The spiritual gifts of the Church.* I. THESE ARE VERY VARIOUS. In the early Church there were many supernatural gifts, in fulfilment of the prophecy, "And it shall come to pass afterward, that I will pour out my Spirit upon all flesh; and your sons and your daughters shall prophesy, your old men shall dream dreams, your young men shall see visions" (Joel ii. 28), and of the more remarkable utterance of Christ, "These signs shall follow them that believe; In my Name shall they cast out devils; they shall speak with new tongues; they shall take up serpents; and if they drink any deadly thing, it shall not hurt them; they shall lay hands on the sick, and they shall recover" (Mark xvi. 17, 18). We have in this passage an enumeration of some of these gifts. The "word of wisdom"—further disclosure of Divine wisdom in redemption. The "word of knowledge"—ready utterance of truth already revealed. "Faith"—not for salvation, but for the performance of miracle in any special case. "Gifts of healing"—restoring the sick miraculously. "Working of miracles"—generally, or those of more striking character. "Prophecy"—here probably not inspired teaching of matters already revealed, but the foretelling of events. "Discerning of spirits"—power to determine between God's operation and Satan's or man's. Peter's dealing with Ananias and Sapphira furnishes an illustration. "Kinds of tongues" —speaking various languages or in the "unknown" spiritual language (ch. xiv. 2). "Interpretation of tongues"—interpreting the foregoing. In the modern Church there are many spiritual gifts, though we do not speak of them as supernatural. As the former were fitted for the needs of former days, so the latter are for the requirements of the present age. The variety of the gifts in each case is stamped with Divine wisdom and is of large advantage; for (1) there are various positions to be filled; (2) various work has to be done; and (3) one gift often supplies the defect of another.

II. Their object is one—"to profit." (Ver. 7.) They are not: (1) *For mere display.* (2) *For personal aggrandizement.* They are: (1) *For the welfare of the Church.* (2) *For the welfare of the individual members.* (3) *For the welfare of the world.* The Church has a large mission to those outside her pale. She is made rich very largely that she may make them rich. She is placed in a world-parish, that she may carry the gospel of the grace of God to all within the bounds. Her strengthening and enrichment are for the world's weal; her special endowments fit her for this grand enterprise. (4) *For the glory of God.* This is the *ultimate object.* As the Church's endowments come from God, so should they return to him. The Church is for itself, is for the individual, is for the world,—but these only comparatively; supremely and specially the Church is for God. And all her gifts and graces should redound to the Divine honour and glory.

III. Their origin is one—God. They should be used, then: 1. *With reverence.* Our qualifications for Christian service as truly come from God as the ancient gifts of tongues or miracles. We feel that the latter should have been used very reverentially; not more so than the former: both are equally of God. We are God-endowed now as truly as were any of the early Christians, and God-endowments should be used with utmost reverence. 2. *With care.* Lest the good gift be perverted by ill use. Our gifts may do as much harm if wrongly used, as good if rightly used. 3. *With diligence.* The *value* of the earlier gifts we can easily perceive; we need to realize that modern gifts are *equally valuable* for modern times. If we felt the value of that which is entrusted to us, we should be more likely to use it diligently. "Stir up the gift of God which is in thee" (2 Tim. i. 6). 4. *With the thought that they will have to be accounted for.* These are talents, and the reckoning day will surely come. The time is short in which they can be used. The need of their employment is stupendous. Let none suppose that they are unendowed. "To every man his work;" and never yet was work given without gift for the work.

IV. Their distribution is of one—of God. (Ver. 11.) The choice of our spiritual gifts does not rest with us. What rests with us is the right employment of those we possess. To murmur because we are not endowed as others are is worse than foolish; it is criminal, for it impugns the wisdom and the goodness of God. Some five-talent men will do nothing because they are not ten-talent men. They mourn and complain because of what they lack, and certainly they appear to have a large lack—of common sense. We are not the Lord; we are servants, and the great Spirit "divideth to every man severally as he will." Let us take our talents thankfully, use them diligently, and never wrap them up in the napkin of repining and discontent. Our condition was once akin to that of the Corinthians, who were carried away unto "dumb idols" (ver. 2). From the idolatry of sin we have been brought into the Church of the Redeemed, and made the worshippers and servants of the true God. Abounding gratitude should leave no room for the faintest murmur. In truth we have nothing to murmur over, but everything to be devoutly thankful for.

V. THEIR TEST IS ONE. They are tested by their relation to Christ (ver. 3). Spurious gifts may appear, or good gifts may be perverted. In early days the test of utterance was, "What saith it of Christ?" Did it declare him to be anathema—accursed? Then it declared itself to be not of God. "By their fruits ye shall know them." And this test applies to all spiritual gifts ancient and modern. Unless they tend to the exaltation and honour of Christ, they are not what they profess to be. If genuine, they are under the control and administration of the Holy Ghost, and he who was sent to glorify Christ (John xvi. 14) will never abase and dishonour him. If men have all other credentials, yet cast reproach upon the Head of the Church, we must instantly reject their testimony and regard them as charlatans. Here is the supreme end of our spiritual gifts—"that he may be glorified." "Try the spirits."

VI. THEIR CONTROL AND EXERCISE ARE ONE. They came from God and they are still in the hands of God. They are very various, but they are unified in the One who gave them and the One who directs their use. "Diversities, . . . but the same Spirit, . . . the same Lord, . . . the same God" (vers. 4—6). The control and exercise of spiritual gifts are of the Triune Jehovah—"God," "Lord," "Spirit." When our spiritual gifts are rightly employed, *God works through us.* As we have the gifts from God, so it is *only as we have God with the gifts* that they can be rightly and usefully employed. *We are channels for Divine power to run in.* Our impotence apart from God is strikingly shown in ver. 3, "No man can say that Jesus is the Lord, but by [or, 'in'] the Holy Ghost." We may use the words, but we cannot feel their power, receive their truth, or bear the effective witness to Christ, apart from the Divine Spirit. How ennobled and inestimably precious do spiritual gifts appear in this light! How careful should we be not to resist the working of God through us! And we may profitably remember that he uses the smaller gifts as well as the larger; nay, sometimes uses the former the more. The more dazzling gifts are not always the most useful.—H.

Vers. 12—27.—*The body of Christ.* A striking figure. Christians are not separate, unrelated units; they are compacted together and form one whole, which is "the body of Christ." Of this body Christ is the Head (Col. ii. 19)—the central controlling and directing Power, and each believer is some member of the body. In this passage the apostle is speaking of the members of the body rather than of the Head—of Christians rather than directly of Christ. Note—

I. THE NUMBER AND VARIETY OF THE MEMBERS. This makes the body rich and beautiful. In scenery and in paintings we do not love monotony. A fair landscape possesses almost infinite variety of tint and form; that is not a painting which is composed of one colour, however brilliant. The Church is enriched by the diversities in condition, age, ability, of its members. Yet though one member differ strikingly from another, all are *equally* of the body (ver. 15). We must not despair because we are unlike some other Christians; if all the members of the body were as even the chief and most honoured members, the symmetry, usefulness, and beauty of the body would be greatly impaired (ver. 17). We must not seek to occupy a place for which we are not fitted. We are admitted to the body of Christ by God, and *he places us* (ver. 18). *We* must not move; if we are to be moved, *he* will move us. To choose a place for ourselves would be to put ourselves out of place.

II. THE VARIED DUTY. This explains the variety of place and power. The Church offers the utmost variety of work; there is something suitable for every capacity. As in the body all parts and members perform their special and appropriate duties, so in the Church each believer has his appointed task: "To every man his work." Some are troubled because they seem to be "inferior" members; but note, *an inferior member can often do its work better than a superior member could do that work.* Each member is specially adapted to perform its functions; each Christian in the Church is specially fitted for the performance of his duties. *No man can fill your place as you can.*

III. THE INTIMATE CONNECTION. In the human body what vital union there is between the several parts! There should be a corresponding connection between the members of the body of Christ. Christians are not to be like grains of sand, or isolated trees, or detached houses. We admit that our union with Christ should be real; equally real should be our union with fellow-believers. The anomaly of Christians not speaking to each other, of the rich and poor being separated from common fellowship, is by this figure shown to be monstrous. The member of the body which will have no fellowship with other members is preparing to be lopped off. Our union with Christ cannot be very intimate if we have none with his followers. "A new commandment I give unto you, That ye love one another" (John xiii. 34).

IV. THE COMMON IMPORTANCE. Not the *equal* importance. All are important, but not equally so. But the least attractive and the least demonstrative may be the most important. The heart is more important than the tongue. Many of the Corinthians were madly elated with the gift of tongues; but there is something greater and better than *talk*. The lungs are more important even than the hand. The modest and unobtrusive are often of more value than those who ever will come to the front. And where true discernment obtains the former are likely to receive "more abundant honour" (ver. 23). Apparent *feebleness* is no criterion; some of the feeblest saints have been the strongest. And some of the weakest members of the body are much more necessary to its well-being than the robust (ver. 22). And further, as it is an instinct of nature to adorn the less comely parts of the body (ver. 23), so in the Church, if a right spirit prevails, the humblest and least attractive will receive special care and attention. The sick child is the mother's favourite. All members are thus important. No member of the Church of Christ is non-important except he makes himself so. And as with the physical body, the body of Christ cannot afford to dispense with the services of a single member, however obscure.

V. THE COMMUNITY OF FEELING. (Ver. 26.) Sympathy should abound amongst Christians. "Bear ye one another's burdens." Every Christian should be a good Samaritan. Imagine one hand rejoicing in or being indifferent to the laceration of the other. Our union with believers should be so intimate and real that when they suffer we suffer, that when they are blessed we are. Their health is our health, their strength is our strength. Christians should remember that Christ pronounced a second commandment as well as a first. When true fellowship is attained we "rejoice with those who do rejoice, and weep with those who weep."

VI. THE HARMONIOUS WORKING. How beautifully this is illustrated in the physical body! So amongst Christians there is no necessity for collision. Contests indicate faultiness and derangement. If all did their appointed work in the appointed way, there would be completest harmony. And the more harmony the better working. What waste of power has been caused by divisions and strife! Note: One perverse member may do much harm. In machinery, if one part fails to perform its function, fracture and extensive derangement may ensue. There should be no schism in Christ's body (ver. 25). The Church, the body of Christ, has a vast, complicated, infinitely important work to do: how essential that there should be the truest co-operation, the utmost faithfulness in discharge of duty, on the part of its members!

VII. THE MUTUAL DEPENDENCE. (Ver. 21.) Christians are not independent of each other: *they should not seek to be so.* We are not the body of Christ *individually*, but we are *collectively*. We are not set to stand alone, but with others. We can help others and be helped ourselves. Another's work may be needful for the success of ours, ours for the success of another's.

VIII. THE COMPLEMENTARY CHARACTER. One supplies just *what* the other lacks. So that if all supply what they can, the body becomes perfect in working. The eye needs the ear; both the hand; all the foot.

IX. THE UNITY AMIDST DIVERSITY. "Many members, but one body" (ver. 20). In the body there is the greatest variety, but the greatest unity; one life pervades the whole. So with the Church—the members are one in Christ, vitally united to the one Head, pervaded by the one Spirit, joined in one baptism, sitting at one Supper of the Lord, engaged in one work, and going forward to the same destiny. There is the great spiritual life-principle which pervades all true believers and makes them *one*.

X. THE VITAL UNION WITH THE HEAD AND SUBORDINATION TO IT. We may survive severance from some members of the body; we cannot severance from the head. We perish unless we are vitally joined to Christ. And as with the physical body, the head must rule or all sorts of disorders will be occasioned. We must be united to Christ as servants to a Master. He is the Head of the body; we are the members. It is for him to direct, it is for us to obey. Some seem sorely tempted to exercise lordship over

Christ; they are wise above what is written. Were it polite to give them the appellation, we might well call them *disloyal fools.* Disloyal, because insubordinate to their Lord; fools, because they not only disorganize the work of the body and injure the other members, but are in the surest way of bringing immeasurable evils upon themselves.—H.

Ver. 12.—*The body of Christ.* The analogy the apostle here uses is broadly true of the whole fellowship of redeemed and regenerate souls—" the Catholic Church throughout all the world," which acknowledges Christ as its living Head. It also applies to the Corinthian Christians as a local society, a part of the grand whole. The principles on which the constitution of the whole depends are supposed to be illustrated in that of each particular part. The comparison of the Church with a living body is not one that we find in the teachings of Christ himself; but he employed an essentially similar image when he said to his disciples, " I am the Vine, ye are the branches " (John xv. 5). Whether we take the figure of the body or of the tree, substantially the same ideas are presented. There is in each case an organization animated by a mysterious principle of life. And the hidden life is the cause of the organization, determines it, shapes it " after its kind." The life is the formative principle. The growth of the body or of the tree is not by addition from without, but by development from within. The materials that nourish and build it up lie without, but it is the life that appropriates them, assimilates them, transforms them into its own substance, turns them to its own proper uses. So with the form of Christian society. We believe in no " visible Church " which is not the spontaneous result of the free play of the Divine Spirit in the minds and consciences and hearts of men. Its beliefs, its worship, its fellowship, its work, all have real worth in them just so far as they are the spontaneous expression of the Spirit that dwells within, and no further. Note respecting the Church—

I. ITS UNITY. As the body with its many members is one, " so also is Christ." Here is unity in variety; variety of parts with a principle of unity underlying them, flowing through them, binding them into one connected whole. And Christ is that uniting power. It is the " body of Christ." The body that was " prepared " for him when he became " God manifest in the flesh " (Heb. x. 5)—the human body in which the " fulness of the Godhead " dwelt, which grew from infancy to manhood, which was crucified and then transformed in the imprisoning tomb,—this body has been withdrawn from the earth. Men see it no longer. It is glorified and immortalized " within the veil." But he has taken to himself another body, in which the Divine energy dwells, through which the Divine beauty reveals itself, which he is leading on gradually to a perfect manhood—" the measure of the stature of the fulness of Christ." That body is his Church. And just as the unity of our physical frame lies in the indwelling soul which holds all its parts together, and without which they would soon lose their organic form and dissolve into their primary elements, so the unity of the Church is the presence of Christ by his Spirit in the whole and in every part (ver. 13). The sentient life pervades every fibre of our frame. Enthroned in the centre, it throbs and glows in the remotest part. But the members have no separate and independent life in themselves. Let any one of them be severed from the rest, and it is senseless, powerless, dead. So is it with our souls in relation to him who is to the spiritual body both as the heart and the head, the inspiring energy, and the living bond of unity. "Apart from me ye can do nothing," etc. (John xv. 5). Thus it comes to pass that union with Christ and union with the Church, in the deepest and truest sense, are one and the same thing. The old dictum, " Out of the Church no salvation," has profound truth in it; but not as they imagine who by the " Church " mean any outward organization that is of human origin and under human control. The papal doctrine asserts, " Where the Church is, there is Christ." We rather say, " Where Christ is, there is the Church." To be in personal fellowship with him is to have a " part and lot " in it of which no power in the universe can ever rob us. This is the principle of unity—the living Christ dwelling by his Spirit in each and all.

II. THE RELATION ITS MEMBERS BEAR TO EACH OTHER. " The body is not one member, but many." The context shows that the apostle has not mere number but variety also in view, variety as of the hand and the foot, the ear and the eye. The relation between Christian men is spiritual, not formal; one that lies in community of thought and affection and aim, not in any kind of external resemblance. (Note the difference between a body, a living organism, and any mere inert mass the particles of which are bound together simply by mechanical force or even by chemical affinity.) In every form of human society it is the sense of individuality combined with the sense of mutual sympathy that constitutes the real cementing principle. It is a fellowship of life that binds men together, and not the constraint of outward circumstance. The oneness of a family lies, not in the fact that its members dwell together under the same roof or bear the same name, but in the common sympathies and affections that grow out of their natural kinship. The oneness of an army lies in the enthusiasm of its devotion to the common cause, far more than in the force of military discipline. The oneness of a nation is not the mere accident of its coming within one geographical boundary, but the spirit of loyalty and patriotism that pervades its citizens. So in the Christian commonwealth, we cannot be too careful to distinguish between its formal aspects and associations, and those relations that are internal and spiritual and in which the living and enduring reality of it lies. The fact of men forming themselves into a visible society, calling themselves by the same name, meeting in the same place, consenting to the same creed, using the same language, joining in the same modes of worship, doing the same work, does not make them one in Christ. These are but the outward signs and symbols of unity. They may be the mocking semblances of it. They have no value unless they represent what is real and spiritual and divinely true. In this unity of spiritually related parts, *each member has its own proper place and function*, and the beauty and harmony of the whole structure lie in its faithfully fulfilling it (Eph. iv. 16). We best serve the interests of others when we are most simply and honestly "ourselves;" when we think our own thought, speak our own word, do our own deed; when the whole outward form and habit of our Christian life is just the natural outcome of what is deepest and truest within us. Anything that tends to weaken the sense of individuality; anything that prompts us to play a part that is not "our own," anything that tends to obliterate natural differences and reduce all to one common level of artificial sameness,—is altogether evil (vers. 17—19). Some parts of the body are small, hidden, apparently insignificant. But those who are best acquainted with its structure know well that they are not for that reason the less important and even essential. Let them fall out of their place or cease to discharge their function, and it may be the whole frame would suffer dislocation or sink into decay. The true Christian spirit will teach us never to make light of our position, or the sphere we fill, or the influence it is given us to wield. It will make us "content to fill a little space," so that our Lord may but be glorified. And if true to the light that shines within us, and to the noblest impulses of which we are conscious, we only faithfully do our work in lowly allegiance to him and loving helpfulness towards our fellows, we may find in the end how true it is that "God hath given more abundant honour to that part that lacked" (ver. 24).

III. THE ENDS FOR WHICH IT EXISTS. The body is created to be the vehicle and organ of the indwelling soul, the channel through which its hidden virtues shall reveal themselves, the instrument by means of which it may work out its nobler purposes. The Gospel records in no way satisfy our curiosity in reference to the physical form and feature of Jesus. But we may be very sure of this, that the body in which he appeared was a fitting vehicle for the Divine soul that inhabited it. It was as a transparent medium, through which the radiance of the spiritual beauty within must often have streamed forth in a way that commanded the honour and admiration of men. Let the Church be true to its high calling, so shall the glory of the indwelling Christ shine through it upon the dark world, drawing all men to him. Upon every section of the Church, and every individual member of the body, according to its measure, this responsibility rests.—W.

Ver. 21.—*Mutual service.* These words indicate, not only the principles that ought to govern the Church of Christ, but also the Divine order and law of all human society. The New Testament Church, like the ancient Jewish commonwealth, bears a representative character. We have to regard it, not only as a spiritual fellowship distinct from the world, united by a different bond, ruled by different laws, inspired by a different spirit, living a different life, advancing to a different destiny, but also as a fellowship that is called to illustrate before the world the Divine idea of social human life. Taking this broader view of the passage, observe—

I. THE WAY IN WHICH CHRISTIANITY RECOGNIZES SOCIAL DISTINCTIONS. These are suggested by the "eye," the "hand," the "head," and the "feet." The distinctions that exist among men are of various kinds—natural and acquired, essential and conventional. There are distinctions intellectual, moral, educational, national, official, circumstantial. All these are recognized in some way or other by the religion of Christ. But they do not receive from it precisely the same recognition. They are not recognized by it to the same extent. There are certain social distinctions that are far too deeply rooted in the instinctive tendencies of our nature, or in the moral necessity of things, ever to be obliterated. If they could be levelled in one age they would inevitably rise again in the next. If levelled in a violent and repressive way, they only spring up afterwards in some exaggerated and extravagant form. The French Revolution began with glorious dreams of "liberty, fraternity, and equality;" it ended in a "Reign of Terror" in which every man's hand was against his brother, in a military despotism that crushed the hopes and energies of the people in the dust, in social separations broader and deeper than had been known before. The religion of Christ is in no way antagonistic to those radical and natural tendencies—it does but mould and regulate them. It seeks to control, but not to crush them, wisely to direct the current, but not to stay its course. Revolutionary as it is in its purpose and workings, it is truly conservative, gradually transforming the whole life of man, but demanding no violent changes, developing the form of the nobler future out of the crude, imperfect, and misshapen past. Hence what seems to some the strange silence of apostolic teaching in reference to many of the dark facts and phases of the social life of the world as then existing—slavery, polygamy, military tyranny, oppressive laws, etc. The chief lesson for us here, however, is this—that in the body politic, the living frame of society, each man according to his distinction has his own special function and special work to do. There is the *eye*—the discerning, perceptive, observant power; the *head*—the regulative, guiding, governmental power; the *hand*—the operative faculty, the power that does the finer and more skilful work of the world; and the *feet*—the part of the frame that bears the heavier burdens, does the drudgery, endures in the way of physical toil the more painful pressure of life. Each member has its own particular work to do, and which another cannot do. The eye cannot handle, the hand cannot see, the head cannot bear the heavy burdens, the feet cannot direct. There are men of fine speculative, philosophic thought, but who have little practical capacity; a nice discernment of the truth of things, but no power to embody even their own ideas in real and substantial forms. Again, there are men of great administrative ability, quick for all the practical business of life, "born to rule" or to manage affairs; place them where you will they will soon assert their power, and others will recognize it and follow their leading. While there are also men to whom physical toil is a natural instinctive delight, and whom the educational influences of life never have fitted or, perhaps, could fit for any other function. Distinctions that grow thus in a natural way out of radical qualities in men Christianity recognizes. Also those that belong to the parental and family relations, or that may be necessary to assert the majesty of law (Rom. xiii. 1—6). But as to any further distinctions, any that rest upon a purely fictitious and conventional basis, having no foundation in nature, which merely feed the lust of power and the pride of life, it would seem to acknowledge none.

II. THE LAW OF MUTUAL DEPENDENCE THAT GOVERNS ALL PARTS OF THE SOCIAL FRAME. The conditions of our life in this world involve us all, in a thousand subtle ways, in the obligation to serve one another, and subject us all, whether we will or not, to the law of self-sacrifice. All nature, in its purely physical aspects, is framed on this principle.

> "Nothing in the world is single,
> All things, by a law Divine,
> In another's being mingle."

Every form of physical existence draws its life from those beneath it, and in its turn has to surrender its life to them. The lower forms exist for the higher, the highest can never assert its freedom from the law of dependence on the lowest. So in the complex system of human life, no grade in the social scale, no order of faculty, no kind of "interest," can claim exemption from the common bond. Take *e.g.* the relation that exists between the men of thought and the men of action, the theoretical and the practical. They are apt to think and to speak slightingly of each other; the one intolerant of being brought continually to a merely utilitarian test, the other always ready with the charge of speculative dreaming. This is a mistake. God has set the one over against the other, "that the one without the other should not be made perfect." Thought without action is worthless. Yet it is thought that rules the world, and if there were no "eye" to guide it the labour of the "hand" would soon cease. So also of social conditions. The tendency sometimes seen in those upon whom the burdens of toil and privation press most heavily, to look up enviously, suspiciously, and even defiantly towards those who occupy a higher level, may be very senseless; but, on the other hand, what more false and irrational than the tone of lofty superiority that social distinction sometimes assumes? Can the head, then, say to the feet, "I have no need of you"? What would become of the loftiest dignities of the world if there were none to bear the heavier burdens and do the rougher work of life? From what do the fairest forms of our civilization spring, our comforts and indulgences, and all the thousand pleasant associations of our life? of what are they the fruits, but of patient, life-consuming labour in field and factory and mine? All the bright and beautiful things of the world, all the pride and glory of man's existence in it, have their roots more or less directly in the base earth. The eye and the head, with all their fine sensibility and lofty faculty, can do nothing without the hands and the feet. Christianity gives the utmost sanctity and force to this lesson. It is in the light of the incarnation, the sympathetic humanity, the lowly life, the beneficent ministry, the sacrificial death, of the Lord Jesus that we see what a wondrous bond of brotherhood it is that unites the whole human family together, and that we learn to understand the great law that God has formed us all to "live not unto ourselves." The gospel makes us more keenly sensible of our obligations than of our rights, of what we owe to others than of what they owe to us. It inspires us with the spirit of him who was "among us as one that serveth" and who "gave his life a ransom for many."

III. THE GROUND ON WHICH WE OUGHT TO PAY SPECIAL HONOUR TO OUR FELLOW-MEN. The Law of Christ teaches us to reverence our common humanity in all its conditions. "Honour all men. Love the brotherhood. Fear God. Honour the king" (1 Pet. ii. 17). These utterances would seem to embrace all the points of Christian duty in this respect. But the whole drift of the apostle's teaching, in this as in so many other places, is to the effect that special honour is due to the faithful discharge of personal responsibility. Whatever station men occupy, whatever function they perform, it is the profitable use of faculty for the common good that confers upon them the noblest distinction.

> "Honour and shame from no condition rise;
> Act well your part; there all the honour lies."

W.

Vers. 1—3.—*The presidency of the Spirit.* This passage does not direct us to this general topic, but to one particular point in relation to it. The presidency relates to, covers, and hallows every feature and every expression of Christian life and worship and fellowship. The whole life of the regenerate man is directly and fully within the Spirit's lead, so that he cannot even speak—if he be a Christian indeed—without the inspiration, the guidance, the toning, of the indwelling Holy Ghost. The apostle is giving these Christianized Gentiles a test by which they might know whether they had indeed the sealing and sanctifying gift of the Spirit. They could tell even by the character of their utterances. These found expression for the cherished feeling; and such was the natural depravity of man that they might be sure no man cherished admiring and loving thoughts of Christ, and found expression for them by saying, "Jesus is Lord," save as he was inwardly moved by the Holy Ghost. If it be true of so simple an expression of the Christian life as that, it is surely true of all other expressions. It is even the glory of the Christian man that nowhere and in nothing is he independent. The "Great-heart Guide" is always with him. He speaks, he acts, as moved by the Holy Ghost. St. Paul is led to the impression of this point by the false notion that might be so easily taken up—the notion that only great gifts and talents are under the presidency of the Spirit; that he bears no immediate and precise relation to the common life. The question of practical concern for each one of us is this—How much of daily life can we recognize as being in God's lead, and under the Spirit's presidency? In answer we may say—

I. THE SPECIAL THINGS OF A MAN'S LIFE ARE IN THE SPIRIT'S LEAD. This may be opened by dwelling on: 1. The special things of personal *experience*. 2. Of Christian *employment and use of gifts*. 3. Of *relationship and opportunity*. 4. Of *confession and witness*, as in the case of apostles and martyrs.

II. THE COMMON AND LITTLE THINGS OF A MAN'S LIFE ARE IN THE SPIRIT'S LEAD. The "three-fourths of life which is made up of conduct." Our sayings, our doings in home and in business. Every act which can express *character* is of interest to the sanctifying Spirit, and may be done, should be done, in his leadings and inspirations. —R. T.

Vers. 4—6.—*Diversity and sameness.* "Although conversion is identical in every case, yet afterwards there are spiritual gifts which vary according to individual capacity and character, but they all come from the one Spirit. There are varieties of ministration in which those spiritual gifts are employed, and the same Lord is served by these various ministries." Nature shows us the diversified forms and expressions of the common life. Science admits the diversity, and seeks to recognize the one great principle, the life, that lies within them all. The diversity lies in the expression in our human spheres. The sameness lies in the source, for all things are of God.

I. DIVERSITY IN THE CHRISTIAN CHURCH. There are: 1. *Diversities in endowments, or "gifts."* Meyer's division of the early Christian gifts is suggestive. (1) Gifts which have reference to intellectual power: divided into (*a*) the word of wisdom; (*b*) the word of knowledge. (2) Gifts which depend upon special energy of faith: divided into (*a*) the faith itself; (*b*) operating in deeds, healings, miracles; (*c*) operating in words, as in prophetic utterances; (*d*) operating in distinguishing true and false spirits. (3) Gifts which relate to tongues: divided into (*a*) speaking with tongues; (*b*) interpreting tongues. 2. *Diversities in the service required*, or in "ministrations" (margin, *ministeries*), that is, forms in which service may be rendered to Christ and his members by his disciples. 3. *Diversities in the modes of fulfilling the service*, or in the ways in which individual character and ability may find expression in carrying out various Christian duties. If many Christian men are engaged in the same form of service, each one will impress his individuality upon his method of doing it. No two workmen work exactly alike. In Christ's Church there is full, free room for all kinds of diversity and variety. No man's personal peculiarities need be crushed; all may be of use; only each man must see to it that the expression of his individuality, and the use of his gift, do not become in any way a hindrance or an offence to his fellow-workers. Diversity is fully compatible with harmony and unity.

II. SAMENESS IN THE CHRISTIAN CHURCH. There is one source of all Christian gifts; one president over the using of all Christian gifts; and one end to be served by the employment of all Christian gifts. "The unity of the source is strongly insisted upon, to put an end to the mutual jealousy of the Corinthians. And it is remarkable that each person in the blessed Trinity is introduced to emphasize the argument, and in contrary order (as Estius remarks), in order to lead us step by step to the one Source of all. First, the Spirit, who bestows the 'gifts' on the believer. Next, the Lord, to whom men render service in his Church. Lastly, God the Father, from whom all proceeds, whose are all the works which are done to him and in his name." The following points may be illustrated:—There is sameness (1) in the distributer of gifts; (2) in the purpose contemplated by the distribution; (3) in the grace ready for those who are using the gifts; (4) and in the dependence of every one who has a gift upon the aid and leading of the Divine Spirit. Impress that the whole attention of the Christian should be occupied with the *one* motive and the *one* source of inspiration. All other motives and inspirations can but fulfil—can but be modes of operation for the one great motive and inspiration, which is that the Spirit of God dwelleth in us, sealing us as Christ's, teaching us all truth, and leading us in all duty.—R. T.

Vers. 12—26.—*The law of order in the human body.* For other cases in which this simile is employed, see Rom. xii. 4, 5; Eph. iv. 16; v. 30; Col. ii. 19. The human body presents a very striking illustration of (1) diversity of gifts, each member having its own endowment and use; (2) unity amid diversity, since each member shares the common life; (3) mutual dependence, as each member is efficient for its particular use only with the aid and support of all the others. "Unity, not unvarying uniformity, is the law of God in the world of grace as in that of nature. As the many members of the body compose an organic whole, and none can be dispensed with as needless, so those variously gifted by the Spirit compose a spiritual organic whole, the body of Christ, into which all are baptized by the one Spirit." Using the human body for illustration of the Church regarded as Christ's body, it may be shown that—

I. IT IS A WHOLE. Evidently for it there was a plan, an ideal. It is a complete thing. It has its appointed parts; nothing whatever can be added to it, and nothing can be taken from it. Though it may be unrealized as yet, God sees his Church to be, as perfect, a whole.

II. IT IS A VARIETY. The sides of the body seem to match, but even the left and the right have their special functions. Every limb and member and joint has its individual mission. And so in the Church of Christ. No two of its members are really alike, and each has his fitted place and appointed work.

III. IT IS A SET OF RELATIONS. No member having any powers or abilities by itself; doing its own particular work only with the aid of all the other members. The whole being set in mutual dependence and helpfulness.

IV. IT IS A HARMONY. So long as each part and portion does its own particular work efficiently and well. Schism in the body is disease, common helplessness, and the beginnings of death.

V. EACH MEMBER CAN ONLY DO ITS PART BY VIRTUE OF THE COMMON LIFE. Use our Lord's illustration from the vine and the branches. The member must abide in the body, and the branch in the vine. Apply in each case to the Christian Church, and impress that, in the body and in the Church, there can be (1) no unnecessary part; (2) no idle member; and (3) no dishonourable or unhonoured portion; since each has its particular use for the good of the whole.—R. T.

Ver. 26.—*The common bearing of a Christian Church.* "Whether one member suffer, all the members suffer with it." "This is a matter of the most ordinary experience in the human body. A pain in any portion, even the most remote from the seats of life, affects the whole. A glance at history will show us that it is the same with the body politic. Whatever is physically, morally, or spiritually injurious to any one portion of society, or of the Church of Christ, is sure in the long run to produce injury, moral and spiritual deterioration, to the rest." "So whatever tends to exalt the character and purify the aims of any one class in society, is sure in a greater or less degree to affect every other. If the one thought is calculated to alarm us by calling our attention to the infinite mischief which may be wrought by one act of thoughtlessness or selfishness, it is an immense encouragement to be reminded by the other that no work for good, undertaken from unselfish motives and carried out in an unselfish spirit, can possibly be without effect." Chrysostom says, "When a thorn enters the heel, the whole body feels it and is concerned; the back bends, the belly and thighs contract themselves, the hands come forward and draw out the thorn, the head stoops, and the eyes regard the affected member with intense gaze." John Howe says, "It is a most unnatural thing to rejoice in the harm of another. In the body, when one member is suffering, all the members suffer with it. And to delight in the harm of others is as contrary to the spiritual nature which is diffused in the true body of Christ, as if the head or any other member should rejoice that the hand or foot is in pain." Two points may be fully treated. 1. As suffering in any part of the body disturbs the whole frame, exciting sympathetic feeling in the most distant parts, so suffering, and even more truly sin, in the lowest and lowliest member of a Christian Church, affects, injures, and grieves the whole. Every member ought to suffer and sympathize with the sufferer or the sinner. 2. As pain elsewhere in the body is really a sympathetic effort to relieve local pain, so sympathetic pain in other members of the Church finds its proper use in the help afforded, and relief given to the suffering or sinning member.—R. T.

Ver. 27.—*The Church Christ's body.* (Comp. vers. 12, 13.) Recall our Lord's own figure of the vine. The branches are the body through which the vine-life finds its expression. Compare the *human* body which our Lord took upon him in his incarnation, which was the means of showing the Son of God to men, and setting him in relation with men, with the *Church* body which our Lord took when he ascended from this world, and became a living and spiritual Christ, which is the means of showing Christ to men *now*, and maintaining his relations with them. Illustrate the two following points by the comparison of the human body with the Church body of Christ :—

I. EVERY PART OF CHRIST'S BODY SHOULD MAKE ITS OWN IMPRESSION. Dealing with the human Christ, we show how every part, every feature and phase of his earthly manifestation, had its own power and influence. We are obliged to separate part from part for consideration. Sometimes we dwell on his moral character, or on his habits, or on his speech, or on his actions, or on his endurances. Taking his life piece by piece, we find meaning, mission, use, everywhere. And so with the Church, as Christ's body or earthly manifestation now—each part, each person, has characteristic place and influence. Each must make its or his own impression. From this impress the demand which Christ makes for loyal service from each part of his Church body ; every member must be a faithful member.

II. THE CHURCH BODY, AS A WHOLE, MUST MAKE ITS IMPRESSION. Besides any precise impression produced by dwelling on any phase of the human life of Christ, there is a special impression which the whole figure of Christ makes upon us. Illustrate by the feeling of Christian people on seeing Dore's full-sized picture of " Christ leaving the prætorium." So the Church can get its proper impression on men only as it becomes a full unity, the one catholic and apostolic Church. For the securing of the Church wholeness, and its presentation to the world as Christ's complete body on earth, all earnest hearts will ever strive and pray.—R. T.

Vers. 28—30.—*The order of offices in the Christian Church.* " Apostles " are set in the first place or rank, because they were called to their office by the Lord Jesus Christ himself; they had immediate personal knowledge of his life and character and teachings; and they were the actual founders and practical rulers and referees of the Church. Next come the " prophets," who were not persons merely endowed with the power of foretelling future events, but persons to whom direct revelations and communications from God came, and so were empowered to enlighten the Church upon the mysteries of the faith and upon the claims of duty. Compare the older Jewish prophets as directly inspired teachers. Then " teachers," regarded as those with ordinary powers of intellect, and the natural gifts of instructing others, who educated and trained the Church in Christian doctrine. After that " miracles," or the power of working miracles. This is set on a new and lower range, perhaps, because only exercised occasionally, and so not comparing with the more regular and orderly arrangements for the Church's culture. " Miracles " are distinguished from " gifts of healings," which we are to suppose were traceable to personal power on nervous systems, of which there seem to be modern instances. " Helps " may refer to such minor services as succouring the needy, tending the sick, etc. What the apostle meant by " governments " is very difficult to decide. Stanley thinks that reference is intended to the faculty otherwise known as " discerning of spirits." The word used, however, means " guiding the helm of affairs," and reference may be to those officers who managed, or ruled, the temporal affairs of the Church, and answered, in some measure, to the elders, or rulers, of the synagogue. " Tongues " St. Paul puts last ; for, from other passages, we know that he did not greatly value the mere power to express Christian feeling in ecstatic and incomprehensible language, or in some foreign and unknown tongue. He thought that it could bear a very feeble relation to the Church's edification unless it were properly interpreted. St. Paul constantly urges the variety of the gifts entrusted to the Church, and the common honourableness of them all ; but he as earnestly impresses upon us that, from the human standpoint, and in view of the preservation of order and efficiency in Church relations, the gifts must set men in different positions, and bring on them different forms and degrees of responsibility. Three things may be unfolded.

I. SOME GIFTS NECESSITATE POSITIONS OF AUTHORITY. The man of gifts, as an apostle or as a ruler, can only use his gifts in offices of authority. So now a man may have the gift of organizing or of managing men, or the gift of mastership and business; then such men we must all be willing to set in the high places.

II. OTHER GIFTS AS TRULY NECESSITATE POSITIONS OF DEPENDENCE. They are gifts of dependence and service. They can only be put to use in lowly places. Those having them can only be faithful in what men may call lesser places. Ambition in men is limited by their gifts. A right ambition leads a man to press for the position in which he can use his gifts. A wrong ambition sets a man upon seeking offices and positions for which he has no gifts.

III. EVERY MAN IN THE CHURCH OF CHRIST SHOULD HAVE HIS OFFICE BY VIRTUE OF HIS GIFTS, AND NOT OF HIS CLAIMS OR OF HIS AMBITIONS. The true idea of selection for office is the discovery of the men among us with the gifts related to the office. The injury of the Church comes by the pressing of men into offices upon other than this ground. God provides the fitted ones; we too often fail to wait on him for the right men, and foolishly fill Church offices on other than Divine grounds. The inquiry for each one to put to himself is first this: "What are the gifts entrusted to me?" And then this: "What is the sphere in which I may find exercise for these gifts?" The most honourable place that any man can occupy is that which is precisely fitted to his gifts, whether to man's view it seem to be lowly or seem to be high.—R. T.

Ver. 31.—*The comparison of gifts and graces.* The most important aspect of religion is the practical one. It is a power working for good upon the whole of our human natures, effecting vital changes, and moulding our conduct and conversation to the pattern of a new model; a Divine power, quickening every right and good faculty our natures may possess, and consecrating to God their exercise; a power seeking to crush and kill all wrong within us and about us, checking every form of evil influence. The great Redeemer takes possession of our natures that he may fit them to be his own abode. And no view of Christ's work should be so precious to us as that which represents him, amid daily scenes and by daily sanctifyings, changing the desolated mansion of our nature into a palace of divinest purity and beauty, wherein the King of kings may dwell. This gracious work may be represented as the culture of the Christian graces, and our text reminds us how much more important for us are the graces of Christian character than the gifts of Christian ability. By a "gift" we understand something which enables us to *do*; by a "grace," something which enables us to *be*. A gift is something, as it were, put into our hands, that can be used by us; a grace is some change effected in our very natures, which makes us unquestionably better men and women. We observe the distinction more clearly in the similar words, "talent" and "character." Our text suggests that graces are better than gifts—they are "the more excellent way;" and even gifts are worth very little save as they are united with graces. It is very remarkable that St. Paul should be the one to set graces above gifts; since in personal endowments he surpassed all the other apostles.

I. WHAT HAVE GRACES AND GIFTS IN COMMON? 1. They have a common Divine origin. The apostle said of himself, inclusive of his great mental powers and cultivated capacities, and also inclusive of his beautiful moral qualities and high spiritual attainments, "By the grace of God I am what I am." 2. Graces and gifts have a common purpose to effect. Both are for the use of "edifying." That word is made from a Latin term which means "to build up," and it brings before us the Pauline figure of Christian life as a temple in course of construction. We seem to see the gathered stones and material; we watch the toiling workmen; we discern some indications of the design of the eternal Architect; and, whether we be men of gifts or men of graces, we must not be mere lookers-on; we must be adding something, either to the stability or the beauty of that uprising building. If we have gifts, we are to put them to use in kindly and wise actions, helping our brothers to carry their burdens, or teaching them how best to lay stone upon stone. If we have graces, then we are enabled to exercise a holy influence on those around us, inspiring and inspiriting their souls; throwing a Divine fragrance, like that from the flowers of paradise, over all our intercourse with others; helping our fellows to work more heartily and bear more cheerily. 3. Graces and gifts are alike in this—they both can grow and both can suffer loss.

II. WHAT HAVE GRACES WHICH GIFTS HAVE NOT? 1. Graces have power to come to all and enrich all. In any very large sense gifts can only come to the few. We almost feel as if we could count up the men and women who, in each department of gift, have risen high above their fellows. We have a special name for such—we call them "geniuses," and we know that real genius is very scarce. But we may all have great graces; they are like the beams of God's sweet sunlight, that fall alike on the castle that crowns the hill and on the cluster of cottages that gathers at its foot. 2. Graces are better than gifts, because they last for ever. The things which we *have* must one day drop out of our hands; the dead hand holds nothing. What we are in ourselves we must be for ever, we cannot cease to be when death severs the mortal from the immortal. 3. Graces are better than gifts, because they have the power of working always. Gifts are dependent on men's wills, and those wills are so often wholly self-ruled. We very seldom can get the full benefit of the gifts of the gifted. If a man be a gracious soul, he cannot help working for his fellow-men and for Christ. The glory of our graces is just this—they are either independent of our wills, or they are simply and gloriously triumphant over our wills. Be beautiful, be gentle, be humble, be true, be generous, in a word, be Christ-like; let only your soul be filled with the graces of the Spirit, and you will become, you cannot help becoming, one of God's most constant and most efficient workers, in nursery and kitchen, in home and friendship, in office and shop, in society and in the Church. Could we see deeply into the reality of things, we should be ready with one voice to acknowledge that goodness is the true greatness, and our supreme concern would be to become beautiful for Christ. —R. T.

EXPOSITION.

CHAPTER XIII.

Vers. 1—13.—*The supremely excellent way of Christian love.* This chapter has been in all ages the object of the special admiration of the Church. Would that it had received in all ages the loftier and more valuable admiration which would have been expressed by an acceptance of its lessons! Tertullian says that it is uttered "with all the force of the Spirit" (*totis Spiritus viribus*). It is a glorious hymn or pæan in honour of Christian love, in which St. Paul rises on the wings of inspiration to the most sunlit heights of Christian eloquence. Like the forty-fifth psalm, it may be entitled "A Psalm of Love." Valcknaer says that the "oratorical figures which illuminate the chapter have been born spontaneously in an heroic soul, burning with the love of Christ, and placing all things lower than this Divine love." In vers. 1—3 he shows the absolute *necessity* for love; in vers. 4—7 its characteristics; in vers. 8—12 its eternal permanence; in ver. 13 its absolute supremacy.

Ver. 1.—**Though I speak with the tongues of men and of angels.** The case is merely *supposed.* The tongues of men are human languages, including, perhaps, the peculiar utterance of ecstatic inspiration with which he is now dealing. It is, perhaps, with reference to this latter result of spiritual exultation, at any rate in its purest and loftiest developments, that he adds the words, "and of angels." It is unlikely that he is referring to the rabbinic notion that the angels only understood Hebrew, and not Aramaic or other languages. The words are meant to express the greatest possible climax. The most supreme powers of utterance, even of angelic utterance—if any of the Corinthians had or imagined that they had attained to such utterance—are nothing in comparison with the universally possible attainment of Christian love. It is remarkable that here again he places "tongues," even in their grandest conceivable development, on the *lowest* step in his climax. **And have not charity.** It is deeply to be regretted that the translators of the Authorized Version here introduced from the Vulgate a new translation for the sacred word "love," which dominates the whole New Testament as its Divine key-note. Greek possesses two words for "love." One of these, *eros*, implying as it did the love which springs from sensual passion, was dyed too deeply in pagan associations to be capable of redemption into holier usage. It is characteristic of the difference between paganism and Christianity, that Plato's eulogy in the 'Symposium' is in honour of *eros*, not of anything resembling *agapē.* The apostles, therefore, were compelled to describe the ideal of the gospel life by another word, which expressed the love of esteem and reverence and sacred tenderness—the word *agape.* This word was not indeed classical. No heathen writer had used it. But the verb *agapaō*, corresponding to the Latin *diligo*, and being reserved for this loftier kind of love, suggested at once the substantive *agape*, which, together with the similar substantive *agapesis* (Jer. xxxi. 3, etc.), had already been adopted by the LXX. and by Philo and in Wisd. iii. 9. The word is thus, as Archbishop Trench says, "born in the bosom of revealed religion" ('New Testament Synonyms,' p. 41). The Vulgate chose *caritas* (whence our "charity") to express this love of reason and affection, the dearness which reigns between human beings, and between man and God. This word, like *agape*, is absolutely unstained with any evil association. If "charity" had been *exclusively* used for *agape*, no objection need have arisen, although "love" is English while "charity" is Latin. But it was an unmixed evil that, by the use of two different words for the same Greek word, English readers should have been prevented from recognizing the unity of thought on this subject which prevails among all the books of the New Testament (Matt. xxii. 37—40; 1 Pet. i. 22; 1 John iii. 14; iv. 7, 8, etc.). To argue that the word "love" in English is not unmingled with unhallowed uses is absurd, because those uses of the word have never been supposed for a single moment to intrude into multitudes of other passages where "love" is used to render *agape*. Who has ever dreamed of objecting on such grounds to the favourite hymn?—

> "Faith and Hope and Love we see
> Joining hand-in-hand agree;
> But the greatest of the three
> And the best is Love."

It is true that Lord Bacon admired "the discretion and tenderness of the Rhenish Version" in using the word "charitie," "because of the indifferencies and æquivocation of the word [love] with impure love." But that objection, if it ever existed, has now been done away with by the use of "love" in such a multitude of other pure and lofty passages of Holy Writ. It is, therefore, a great gain that the Revised Version restored to this passage the word "love," which had been used by Tyndale, Cranmer, and the Geneva Bible. For in modern English usage the word "charity" is almost confined to "almsgiving," and that of a kind which is often made an excuse for shirking all real self-denial, and for *not* acting up to the true spirit of love. Christian love is always and infinitely blessed, but the almsgiving which has usurped the name of "charity" often does more harm than good. **I am become as sounding brass, or a tinkling cymbal;** more literally, *I have become booming brass, or clanging cymbal.* My "tongues" without "love" become a mere discordant, obtrusive, unintelligible dissonance. The Greek word for "clanging" (*alalazon*) is an onomatopœia, like the

Hebrew name for cymbals, *tseltselim* (Ps. cl. 5).

Ver. 2.—**Prophecy.** The power of lofty utterance belonged to Balaam and Caiaphas; yet it availed them nothing without love. "Lord, Lord," exclaim the troubled souls at the left hand, "have we not *prophesied* in thy Name?" Yet he answers them, "I never knew you." **All mysteries.** Though I can speak of the secrets of God once hidden but now revealed (Matt. xiii. 11; Rom. xvi. 27; ch. ii. 7; Eph. iii. 3, etc.). **And all knowledge.** Insight into the deeper meanings of Scripture, etc. **All faith.** Not here meaning "justifying faith," or "saving faith," which can no more exist without showing itself in works than light can exist without heat; but *fides miraculosa*, reliance on the power to work wonders. Judas, for instance, must have possessed this kind of faith, and it was exercised by "many" who will yet be rejected because they also work iniquity (Matt. vii. 21—23). **So that I could remove mountains.** It has been supposed that this must be a reference to Matt. xvii. 20; xxi. 21. It is, however, much more probable that, if St. Paul derived the words from our Lord, they came to him by oral tradition. And the inference must in any case be precarious, for the phrase was so common among the rabbis that "remover of mountains" was one of their admiring titles for a great teacher. **I am nothing.** No expression could involve a more forcible rebuke to intellectual and spiritual pride.

Ver. 3.—**And though I bestow all my goods to feed** the poor. The five words, "bestow to feed the poor," represent the one Greek word *psōmisō*, and after all do not give its force. It is derived from *psōmion*, a mouthful, and so means "give away by mouthfuls," *i.e.* "dole away." It occurs in Rom. xii. 20 for "feed." Attention to this verse might have served as a warning against the often useless and sometimes even pernicious doles of mediæval monasteries. Much of the "charity" of these days is even more uncharitable than this, and shows the most complete absence of true charity; as for instance the dropping of pennies to professional beggars, and so putting a premium on vice and imposture. **To be burned.** The reading is extremely uncertain. The change of a letter gives the reading, *that I may glory* (καυχήσωμαι for κανθήσωμαι). Perhaps the scribes thought that "death by burning" was as yet (A.D. 57) an unheard-of form of martyrdom, though it became but too familiar ten or twelve years later in the Neronian persecution. St. Paul was, however, probably referring, not, as some have supposed, to *branding*, which would have been expressed differently, but to the ease of the "three children," in Dan. iii. 23, where the LXX. has, " They gave their bodies *into the fire ;* " or to the various tortures and deaths by fire in 2 Macc. vii. At the burning of Ridley and Latimer, Dr. Smith chose this verse for his text. Its applicability is on a par with millions of other instances in which Scripture has been grossly abused by employing its letter to murder its spirit, and by taking it from the God of love to give it to the devil of religious hatred. The burning of a saint was a singular specimen of the Church's "love." **It profiteth me nothing;** literally, *I am nothing benefited.* A consideration of this verse might have shown the Christians of the early centuries that there was nothing *intrinsically* redemptive in the martyrdom into which they often thrust themselves.

Vers. 4—7.—*The attributes of love.*

Ver. 4.—**Suffereth long, and is kind.** Passively it endures; actively it does good. It endures evils; it confers blessings. **Envieth not.** Its negative characteristics are part of its positive perfection. Envy—"one shape of many names"—includes malice, grudge, jealousy, pique, an evil eye, etc., with all their base and numerous manifestations. **Vaunteth not itself.** The meaning would probably be most nearly expressed by the colloquialism, *does not show off.* It does not, for instance, "do its alms before men to be seen of them" (Matt. vi. 1). The Latin *perperus,* which is from the same root as this word, means "a braggart," or "swaggerer." Cicero, speaking of a grand oratorical display of his own before Pompey, says to Atticus, "Good heavens! how I *showed myself off* (ἐνεπερπερευσάμην) before my new hearer, Pompeius!" ('Ad. Att.,' i. 14). **Is not puffed up.** Has no purse-proud or inflated arrogance. "Love," therefore, is free from the characteristic vice of the Corinthian Church (ch. iv. 6, 18, 19; v. 2; viii. 1).

Ver. 5.—**Doth not behave itself unseemly** (see ch. xii. 23; xiv. 40). Vulgar indecorum is alien from love, as having its root in selfishness and want of sympathy. "Noble manners" are ever the fruit of "noble minds." "Be courteous" (1 Pet. iii. 8). **Seeketh not her own.** Self-seeking is the root of all evil (ch. x. 24, 33; Phil. ii. 4; Rom. xv. 1, 2). **Is not easily provoked.** The word "easily" is here a gloss. The corresponding substantive (*paroxusmos,* whence our "paroxysm.") is used of the "sharp contention" between Paul and Barnabas (Acts xv. 39). Love, when it is perfected, rises superior to all temptations to growing *exasperated,* although it may often be justly indignant. But, as St. Chrysostom says, "As a spark which falls into the sea hurts not the sea, but is itself

extinguished, so an evil thing befalling a loving soul will be extinguished without disquietude." **Thinketh no evil;** literally, *doth not reckon* (or, *impute*) *the evil.* The phrase seems to be a very comprehensive one, implying that love is neither suspicious, nor implacable, nor retentive in her memory of evil done. Love writes our personal wrongs in ashes or in water.

Ver. 6.—**Rejoiceth not in iniquity;** rather, *at unrighteousness.* The rejoicing at sin, the taking pleasure in them that commit sin, the exultation over the fall of others into sin, are among the worst forms of malignity (Rom. i. 32; 2 Thess. ii. 12). The Greeks had a word, ἐπιχαιρεκακία, to describe "rejoicing at the evil" (whether sin or misfortune) of others (Prov. xxiv. 17); *Schadenfreude,* "malignant joy" (Arist., ' Eth.,' ii. 7, 15). It is the detestable feeling indicated by the remark of La Rochefoucald, "that there is something not altogether disagreeable to us in the misfortunes of our best friends." **Rejoiceth in the truth;** rather, *with the truth.* There are many who "resist the truth" (2 Tim. iii. 8); or who "hold the truth in unrighteousness" (Rom. i. 18); but love accepts it, keeps it pure, exults in all its triumphs (Acts xi. 23; 2 John 4).

Ver. 7.—**Beareth all things** (see on ch. ix. 12). Endures wrongs and evils, and covers them with a beautiful reticence. Thus love "covereth all sins" (Prov. x. 12; 1 Pet. iv. 8). **Believeth all things.** Takes the best and kindest views of all men and all circumstances, as long as it is possible to do so. It is the opposite to the common spirit, which drags everything *in deteriorem partem,* paints it in the darkest colours, and makes the worst of it. Love is entirely alien from the spirit of the cynic, the pessimist, the ecclesiastical rival, the anonymous slanderer, the secret detractor. **Hopeth all things.** Christians seem to have lost sight altogether of the truth that hope is something more than the result of a sanguine temperament, that it is a gift and a grace. Hope is averse to sourness and gloom. It takes sunny and cheerful views of man, of the world, and of God, because it is a sister of love. **Endureth all things.** Whether the "seventy times seven" offences of a brother (Luke xvii. 4), or the wrongs of patient merit (2 Tim. ii. 24), or the sufferings and self-denials and persecutions of the life spent in doing good (2 Tim. ii. 10). The reader need hardly be reminded that in these verses he has a picture of the life and character of Christ.

Vers. 8—13.—*The eternal permanence of love.*

Ver. 8.—**Never faileth.** The word "faileth" (ἐκπίπτει) has two technical meanings between which it is not easy to decide. 1. It means, technically, "*is never hissed off the stage* like a bad actor," *i.e.* it has its part to play even on the stage of eternity. This is its meaning in classic Greek. 2. It means "*falls away*" like the petals of a withered flower (as in Jas. i. 11; comp. Isa. xxviii. 4). Here, perhaps, the meaning is not technical, but general, as in Rom. ix. 6 and in the LXX. (Job xxi. 43). But the reading may be simply πίπτει (falleth), as in א,‎ A, B, C. **They shall fail.** This is not the same word as the one on which we have been commenting; it means "shall be annulled" or "done away;" and is the same verb as that rendered in the next clauses by "vanish away," " be done away " (ver. 10), and "put away" (ver. 11). Thus in two verses we have the same word rendered by *four* different phrases. No doubt the effect of the change sounds beautifully to ears accustomed to the "old familiar strain;" but it is the obvious duty of translators *to represent*, not *to improve upon*, the language of their author. In the Revised Version the same word is rightly kept for the four recurrences of the verb. **Tongues.** Special *charisms* are enumerated to show the transcendence of love. **Knowledge.** This shall be only annulled in the sense of earthly knowledge, which shall be a star disappearing in the light of that heavenly knowledge which shall gradually broaden into the perfect day.

Ver. 9.—**We know in part.** The expression applies directly to religious knowledge, and should be a rebuke to the pretence to infallibility and completeness which is sometimes usurped by religious men.

Ver. 10.—**That which is in part shall be done away.** It will be lost in perfectness when we have at last attained to "the measure of the stature of the fulness of Christ" (Eph. iii. 14).

Ver. 11.—**I understood as a child, I thought as a child;** *I felt as a child, I reasoned as a child.* **But when I became a man, I put away childish things;** *now that I am become a man, I have done away with childish things.* No specific time at which he put away childish things is alluded to, but he means that "manhood" is a state in which childishness should have become impossible.

Ver. 12.—**Through a glass;** rather, *through* (or, *by means of*) *a mirror.* Our "glasses" were unknown in that age. The mirrors were of silver or some polished metal, giving, of course, a far dimmer image than "glasses" do. The rabbis said that "all the prophets saw through a dark mirror, but Moses through a bright one." St. Paul says that no human eye can see God at all except as an image seen as it were behind the mirror. **Darkly;** rather, *in a riddle.* God is said to have spoken to Moses "by means of riddles" (Numb. xii. 8; Authorized Version, "in dark speeches"). Human language, dealing with Divine facts, can only represent them indirectly, metaphorically, enigmatically, under human images, and as illustrated by visible phenomena. God can only be represented under the phrases of anthropomorphism and anthropopathy; and such phrases can only have a *relative*, not an absolute, truth. **Then;** *i.e.* "when the perfect is come." **Face to face.** Like the "mouth to mouth" of the Hebrew and the LXX. in Numb. xii. 8. This is the beatific vision. "We know that, when he shall appear, we shall be like him; for we shall see him as he is" (1 John iii. 2). "Now we walk by faith, *not by sight*" (2 Cor. v. 7). **Then shall I know even as also I am known;** rather, *then shall I fully know even as also I was fully known*, viz. when Christ took knowledge of me at my conversion. Now, we do not so much "know" God, but "rather *are known of God*" (comp. ch. viii. 3).

Ver. 13.—**And now.** The "now" is not temporal (as opposed to the "then" of the previous verse), but logical. It sums up the paragraph. **Abideth.** These three graces are fundamental and permanent; not transient, like the *charisms*, on which the Corinthians were priding themselves, but which should all be "annulled." **Faith, hope, charity.** It might be difficult to see how "hope" should be permanent. But if the future state be progressive throughout eternity and infinitude, hope will never quite be lost in fruition. Even "within the veil," it will still remain as "an anchor of the soul, both sure and steadfast" (Heb. vi. 19). **The greatest of these** is **charity;** more literally, *greater than these is love.* St. Paul does not explain *why* love is the greatest and best of the three. Various reasons may be given. 1. Love is the greatest, because it is the root of the other two; "we *believe* only in that which we love; we *hope* only for that which we love." 2. And love is the greatest because love is for our neighbours; faith and hope mainly for ourselves. 3. And love is the greatest because faith and hope are human, but God is love. 4. And love is the greatest because faith and hope can only work by love, and only show themselves by love. Thus love is as the undivided perfection of sevenfold light. Faith and hope are precious stones of one colour, as a ruby and a sapphire; but love, as he has been showing us throughout the chapter, is a diamond of many facets.

HOMILETICS.

Ver. 1.—*Eloquence without charity.* "Though I speak with the tongues of men and of angels, and have not charity, I am become as sounding brass, or a tinkling cymbal." Two introductory truths are suggested by the context. 1. *That there is great diversity in the talents with which Heaven has endowed mankind.* There are "diversities" of gifts. Whilst it is true that the apostle refers especially to miraculous gifts, those very gifts have their equivalents amongst men now. True, we have no miraculous gifts of tongues; but we have great linguistical scholars, men who are the masters of many languages. Though we have no miraculous gifts of prophecy, we have men of such a far-sighted sagacity as to discern the signs of the times, and foretell events destined to occur on the earth. Though we have not the miraculous gifts of healing, modern medical science invests some men with a healing power in some respects approaching the miraculous. In sooth, the unmiraculous endowments of the present day, exhibited in the various evolutions of art, science, philosophy, are more than an adequate compensation for the loss of the miraculous endowments of apostolic times. Some men are distinguished by one faculty and some by another. Some by the faculty of *creating* thought, some by the faculty of *combining* thought, some by the faculty of *oratorically presenting* thought. These faculties exist in various degrees of strength; in some they are dwarfish, in some gigantic. 2. *That without charity the highest kind and degree of talent is of little worth.* Indeed, in this chapter Paul says, in relation to the highest faculties, and to the highest services, that without this charity man *himself* is nothing : "I am nothing." Now, the text directs attention to one particular faculty, and that is *eloquence.* "Though I speak with the tongues of men and of angels." Angels speak. Perhaps Paul had heard their oratory when he was caught up into heaven. He means, though he had eloquence of the highest type, without charity, it would be utterly worthless. Two thoughts are suggested.

I. That it is POSSIBLE FOR ELOQUENCE OF THE HIGHEST TYPE TO EXIST WITHOUT CHARITY. Why say, "possible"? It has ever existed and still exists, dissociated from this charity, this queen of virtues, or rather this root of all moral excellence. 1. We find it in party *politics.* Read the party speeches delivered at the hustings or in the House of Commons. Some of those speeches are fashioned after the highest models of oratory, and delivered with all the graces of the art, but utterly destitute of charity. They beat with selfish ambition and burn with envious spleen. 2. We find it in party *theology.* Some of the discourses on polemic theology are, in all the attributes of true eloquence, unexcelled if not unmatched; but how destitute of charity! They are all aglow with acrimonious zeal for certain dogmas of the brain. 3. We find it in party *Churchism.* During the month of May men appear on the platform of Exeter Hall who have spent many a laborious day, or week, it may be, in preparing a speech on behalf of some cause, before whose brilliancy the author hopes all other speeches will pale their fire. Read the most eloquent of these speeches; and for the most part how destitute of charity! Sect zeal reigns in all. The Protestant damns the Catholic, the Evangelical the Ritualist, the Church sneers at Dissent, and Dissent at the Church, and all agree in consigning pagans and heathen of every grade to nethermost perdition. The spirit of all the speakers, as a rule, at those busy manifestations of eloquence, is, "We are the wise men, and wisdom will die with us; the temple of the Lord, the temple of the Lord, are we."

II. That eloquence of the highest type without charity is UTTERLY WORTHLESS. It is as "sounding brass, or a tinkling cymbal." The word ἀλαλάζον, from ἀλαλή or ἀλαλά, a war-cry, properly denotes a loud cry or shout, such as is used in battle. Whilst the sound is anything but pleasant, the material is comparatively worthless, made of two pieces of common brass. The idea is *worthlessness.* Take the speech of a man whose idea of eloquence shall excel the theory of Quintilian, and whose practice shall excel that of Demosthenes himself; what is it if it has not charity? Paul would say, "brass," giving out a mere clanking sound. 1. It is worthless in *itself.* What would you give for two little pieces of brass forming a cymbal? Whatever their marketable value may be, for musical purposes they are not worth a "penny whistle." What worth is there in an organism unless it has life? and what worth is there in sentences, however eloquent, unless they have charity? There is no moral worth in any act or word apart from charity. In the sight of Heaven all else is mere rubbish. Without it, I with all my endowments, services, sacrifices, says Paul, am "nothing." 2. It is worthless in its *influence.* The sounds you get out of the "cymbal" are not musical, and they produce rather an irritating than an inspiring or calming influence upon the listener. What moral good can speeches without charity accomplish? They may shed some light upon the intellect, correct some error, but they have no power to win the soul of a man. They often irritate, but never soothe. Bigoted partisans are attracted by the clankings of their brass, but men pass by them as by a Punch and Judy show. Eloquence without charity is like the roar of a winter's north-easter, irritating and destructive; but eloquence with charity is like the quiet south-wester in spring, warming all things into life and touching all things into beauty.

Vers. 2, 3.—*Man-worth.* "Though I have the gift of prophecy," etc. 1. The greatest thing in the universe is *mind.* All material systems would lack completeness and meaning were there no mind to observe, study, and worship the great Invisible. 2. The greatest thing in mind is *love.* Here the apostle teaches that whatever a human intelligence may be, if it is destitute of love it is nothing. What is this love without which humanity is nothing? It is not the *gregarious* sentiment which links us to and gives us an interest in our species. This is an instinct common to animal existence. We regard this element as a blessing, not a virtue. Nor is it *theological* love—the affection which one has for his own faith and sect, but which will look coldly and hardly on all besides. This is a demon working under the mask of an angel. It reduces the gospel to a dogma and man to a bigot. Nor is it *sacerdotal* love—the love which speaks from ecclesiastical chairs, consecrated altars and seats of political power, but whispers no accents of sympathy for the physical and social woes of the race. We call this priestly selfishness, not manly love. What, then, is love? We may describe it—for we cannot define it—as a *generous moral sympathy for the race springing from love to the Creator.* This is, in fact, the love that only can confer real worth on humanity. We observe—

I. That man without this love is nothing spiritually in relation to NATURE. We say *spiritually ;* for we assume, of course, that the spiritual is the man. Whatever does not minister to this, does not minister to him. Nature has three kinds of pleasure to impart—the sensuous, the intellectual, and spiritual. The last is the highest in the scale, and arises from a warm and living sympathy with the being, character, and purpose of the Creator of all. It is nature looked at through the heart, through the self. It is not sensation, but inspiration; not philosophy, but poetry; not the letter of a science, but the spirit of life. These are the highest joys of nature and the only real joys for man as man. To impart these is nature's highest function. But are they not confined entirely to the children of love? As nature would be nothing to the body of a man were his senses scaled up, and nothing to the intellect of a man whose reflective faculty was paralyzed, so it is nothing to the *soul* of a man who has not a loving heart. To the sensual nature is *gratification*, to the thinker it is *theory*, to the loving it is *heaven.* True it is, then, that without love "I am nothing" in relation to the spiritual enjoyment of nature.

II. That man without this love is nothing spiritually in relation to the PROVIDENCE THAT IS OVER US. If I have not love, I am nothing to providence. It ministers no *real* good to me as a spiritual existent—as a man. As the mortally diseased must say, "I am nothing to the health-giving economy of nature," so the unloving may truly say, "I am nothing in relation to the spiritual blessings of providence." But love in the heart makes providence a minister for good, and for good only. Like the bee, it transmutes the bitterest fruit into honey. "All things work together for good."

III. That man without this love is nothing spiritually in relation to CHRISTIANITY. Love alone can interpret love. Christianity is a revelation of love, and none but the loving can rise to its meaning. Theology is one thing, Christianity is another, the one is a "letter," the other is a "spirit." Love is the single eye of the soul, and it fills the whole body with the light of life. Still more that which renders us incapable of entering into its meaning unfits at the same time from applying its provisions. It is a system of great and precious promises. But of all the sons of the earth is there one who, uninspired with love, dare apply a single promise? They are for the children of love, and them only. Without love, then, I am nothing in relation to Christianity.

IV. That man without this love is nothing spiritually in relation to the COMMUNITY OF THE GOOD. There is a great social system in the universe—a city, a Church, a family. There are myriads of beings who mingle together as citizens, fellow-members of one Church, a family. Wherever they exist they have the same bond of union, the same condition of friendship, the same principle of inspiration, and the same standard of worth. What is that? In the great community of the good love is every-thing. "If I have not love, I am nothing to this community. Thou art learned, but though thou shouldst speak with the tongues of men and of angels, and have not charity, thou art as sounding brass or a tinkling cymbal." Thou art gifted; prophetic genius is thine; thou art conversant with the arcana of science; thou hast faith too, orthodox, vigorous, and earnest; but though thou hast the "gift of prophecy," and understandest "all mysteries and all knowledge," and though "thou hast all faith, so that thou couldst remove mountains, and hast not love, thou art nothing." Thou art liberal; but "though thou bestowest all thy goods to feed the poor, and though thou givest thy body to be burned, and hast not charity, it profiteth thee nothing." (Extracted from *Homilist*, vol. viii. p. 433.)

Vers. 4—8.—*The immortality of love.* "Charity never faileth," etc. Amongst the many things which Paul predicates in this chapter concerning "charity," or love, is its permanence.

I. It will "never fail" as an ELEMENT OF MORAL POWER. Love is the strongest force in the soul. 1. It is the strongest *sustaining* power. Our present state is one of trial and sorrow. Burdens press on all, in all grades of society. Godly love is the best sustaining power under all. All Divine promises are made to the loving. 2. It is the strongest *resisting* power. We have not only burdens to oppress, but enemies to conquer and destroy. If love preoccupies the soul, temptations are powerless. 3. It is the strongest *aggressive* power. We have not only to bear up with fortitude under trials, and to resist with success temptations, but we have battles to fight and victories to win. Love is at once the inspiration and the qualification for the warfare. There is nothing so aggressive in the moral world as love. Man can stand before anything sooner than love. As a sustaining, resisting, aggressive power, love will "never fail."

II. It will "never fail" as a PRINCIPLE OF SOCIAL UNITY. Deep in the heart of man is the desire for union with his fellow. He wishes to flow with the race as waters with the stream. His ingenuity has been taxed for ages in the invention of schemes for union. Love alone can secure this; love only is the unifying force. We are only one with those we love with the moral affections of our nature. But we can only love the lovable. Love in the moral empire is what attraction is in the material. Love "never faileth" as a principle of social unity.

III. It will "never fail" as a SOURCE OF SPIRITUAL HAPPINESS. Love is joy. 1. *It expels from the mind all elements unfavourable to happiness.* 2. *It generates in the mind all the elements of spiritual joy.*

Vers. 9, 10.—*Partial knowledge.* "We know in part." Partial knowledge is of four kinds.

I. There is a partial knowledge that is a NECESSITY. The knowledge of the highest intelligent creature must by the *necessity* of nature be partial. What he knows is as nothing compared with the knowable, still less with the unknowable. "Who by search-ing can find out God?"

II. There is a partial knowledge that is a CALAMITY. Our *necessary* ignorance is not a calamity; on the contrary, it is a benediction. The necessarily unknown acts as a stimulus to our intellectual faculties. But our ignorance of things that are really knowable must be ever more or less a disadvantage. Ignorance of true ethics, of political economy, agriculture, laws of health, beneficent rules of conduct, true religion, entails incalculable injuries. Ignorance of these things is the night, the winter, of intellect.

III. There is a partial knowledge that is SINFUL. A partial knowledge of our moral condition, the claims of God, the means of redemption, where a fuller knowledge is attainable, is a *sin*. Ignorance of Christ in a land of churches and Bibles, is a sin, and that of no ordinary heinousness. It is a *calamity* to the heathen; it is a *crime* to us.

IV. There is a partial knowledge that is BENEFICENT. Our ignorance of our future is a *blessing*. Were the whole of our future to be spread out before us, with all its trials and sorrows, and all the circumstances connected with our death, life would become intolerable; it is mercy that has woven the veil that hides the future.

CONCLUSION. Our partial knowledge should make us *humble, studious, undogmatic. devout.*

Ver. 11.—*A child in time, a man in eternity.* "When I was a child, I spake as a child, I understood as a child, I thought as a child: but when I became a man, I put away childish things." From all the writings of Paul you cannot select an extract more beautiful, significant, and valuable than this chapter. It touches that which is the root of the universe, the heart of God, and the fountain of all virtue and blessedness—*love*. The subject of the words under our notice is the *Christian a child in time, a man in eternity.*

I. This is the case in relation to SPEECH. "When I was a child, I *spake* as a child." Though·the word "child" here properly denotes a babe, the apostle evidently uses it with no such limitation, for an infant neither speaks, thinks, nor understands. He denotes by it the human being in the first stages of intelligence and voluntary action. The speech of a child is often marked by incoherence and unintelligibility. It is irrelevant, disconnected, and broken. So is the speech of the sagest and most eloquent Christian here as compared with his language in eternity. The Christian's speech in eternity will be characterized: 1. *By clearness.* Our speech here, like that of children, is often unintelligible, mere jargon. The reason is that our conceptions are cloudy, half formed, and ill defined. Obscurity of language, either oral or written, is the result of confusion in thought. Clear speech requires a clear head. In heaven thoughts are clear and complete as balls of radiant crystal. 2. *By reality.* Our speech here, like that of children, is frequently nothing more than the vehicle of mental fantasies and conjecture. Words only embody and reveal the unsubstantial dreams of the mind. But speech in eternity is the organ of *reality*. Words there are things. They are truths made vocal. 3. *By comprehensiveness.* How meagre the vocabulary of a child! Our speech here, like that of children, is limited to a very small range of things. When it conveys truth, the truths are but very few; and they relate to a mere speck in the great universe of intelligence. Not so in heaven. The soul will range over the whole domain of facts, receive true impressions of all, and speak them out. 4. *By sublimity.* Our speech here, like that of children, is not of the most exalted and soul-inspiring character. The best only talk of the rudiments of truths which have become more or less theological platitudes. In heaven speech will be the vehicle of the most soul-inspiring and soul-uplifting realities. Every word will be electric, every sentence radiant and quickening as the sunbeam.

II. This is the case in relation to UNDERSTANDING. "I understood as a child." The Christian's understanding here is like that of a child in several respects. 1. *In feebleness.* The child's intellect, like his body, gets strength by nutriment and exercise. In the first stages it is very feeble. It is incapable of any great effort. It is thus with the Christian here. We say of such a man, "He has a great intellect." But in reality the greatest is very weak. How little the effort that the greatest intellect can make in search of knowledge! What a small amount of truth can the most vigorous hold within his grasp! In heaven the understanding will be strong, unencumbered by matter, unchecked by disease, unclouded by sin. It will grow young with age and strong with exercise. 2. *In sensuousness.* A child's understanding is under the control of the senses. It judges by appearances; it is taken up with the forms of things. Is it not so with the Christian? He is prone to "mind earthly things," "to judge after the flesh." The theology and the ritualism ·even of the most spiritual are coloured by sensuousness. The hell and heaven of Christendom are sensuous worlds. 3. *In relativeness.* The child judges of all things by their relation to himself. His father may be an author thrilling the intellect of his age, or a statesman directing the destinies of a nation, but the child knows nothing of him in those relations. As a father only he knows him. So with the understanding of a Christian. His conceptions of God are purely relative—Redeemer, Father, Master. Thus only is he regarded. Of what he is in himself, what he is in the universe, what he is in immensity, he understands nothing. In eternity we shall "see him as he is." 4. *In servility.* The child yields his understanding up to others, often allows it to be used as "clay in the hands of a potter." So it is often with Christians here. They are not generally independent in their inquiries. They put themselves in the hands of Churches and priests, and call them masters. Not so in heaven. Each with a full consciousness of his individuality will be independent in his investigations and conclusions.

III. This is the case in relation to REASONING. "I thought as a child." In the margin the word *reasoned* is put for "thought." The child reasons. Logic is not mere art, it is an instinct in human nature. How does the child reason? 1. From an *insufficiency of data.* Having neither the power nor the opportunity of making an adequate observation and comparison, he draws his conclusions from passing impressions and unfounded conjectures. Thus it is often with the Christian here. His knowledge of the facts of God and the universe on which he reasons, is so limited that his conclusions are often inconclusive and puerile. The grave and pompous discussions of our most learned theologues on the ways of God must appear to the ear of an angel as absurd as the prattle of children on the affairs of kingdoms does to us. 2. From the *impulse of desire.* In all cases the wish is the father to the thought. It is too often so with Christians here. Their likings control their logic. Not so in heaven. How sublime the difference between the Christian in time and the Christian in eternity! How vast the disparity between the *speech, understanding,* and *reasoning* of Saul, the little Jewish boy, and "Paul, the aged," the great theologian and sublime apostle! This is only a faint type of the difference between the Christian here and the Christian yonder.

CONCLUSION. This subject teaches: 1. *The educational character of this life.* The true view of this life is that it is a school for eternity. Here all souls are in a state of pupilage. Some are deriving the true advantages from the discipline, and some are not. Whilst thousands leave this school from year to year unimproved, incorrigible, utterly unfit for the services of eternity, worthless to God and the universe, others are being made "meet for the inheritance of the saints in light." Brother disciples, be reconciled to this state. School-days are not always the most pleasant. There are restrictions, disciplines, and studies, more or less painful. Struggle on till you "put away childish things," all that is childish in speech and understanding and reasoning. We shall leave this school soon for the family mansion and the grand inheritance. 2. *The organic unity of man through all the scenes and stages of his being.* Though the man here talks and judges and reasons very differently to what he did when a child, he is nevertheless the same being. He is but the child more fully developed. He is but the sapling grown into the tree. It is so with the Christian in the other world. He is the *same* being as he was here, he is but the child grown into the man, freed from "all childish things." Man in heaven is but the child matured. We shall never be greater than men. Whatever is brilliant and great for us in the future will be but the development of the germs that slumber in us now. 3. *The necessity of modesty in the maintenance of our theological views.* In the light of this subject, how preposterous it is for poor frail, fallible man to set himself up as an authority in theological matters, to assume the priest, the bishop, the pope! "I do not know," says Sir Isaac Newton, "what I may appear to the world; but to myself I seem to have been only like a boy playing on the seashore, and diverting myself by now and then finding a smoother pebble or a prettier shell than ordinary, while the great ocean of truth lay all undiscovered before me."

Ver. 12.—*The body the dark medium of spiritual vision.* "For now we see through a glass, darkly," etc. It needs no illustration to show that our vision of spiritual things is very dim. The *cause* of this is our subject—the medium is dark, that medium is the body. Through the five senses we gather all the lights that flash on our consciousness and form within us ideas. But why is it dark?

I. The body tends to MATERIALIZE THE CONCEPTIONS OF THE MIND. We "judge after the flesh."

II. The body tends to SWAY THE DECISIONS OF THE MIND. The desires of the flesh often move and master the soul.

III. The body tends to CLOG THE OPERATIONS OF THE MIND. Business, sleep, refreshment, exercise, disease,—all these interrupt the soul. Our visions of spiritual things being so dim: 1. *None should pride themselves in their knowledge.* 2. *None should arrogate infallibility of judgment.* 3. *All should anticipate higher and fuller visions.* When the medium is removed, we shall see "face to face."

Ver. 13.—*Love the greatest power in mind.* "And now abideth faith, hope, charity," etc. Love is here brought into comparison with two other great things in mind—faith and hope.

I. The CORRESPONDENCE between these three. The words imply: 1. That they are all *great*. The apostle speaks of the "greatest." "Faith" is a great thing. It implies reason, truth, and the investigation of evidence. It is a great thing in business, in science, in society, as well as in religion. "Hope" is a great thing, too. It implies the *recognition* of good, a *desire* for good, and an *expectation* of good. It makes the greatest trials of the present bearable by bringing into the spirit the blessedness of the future. 2. That they are all *permanent*. There "abideth" faith and hope. In virtuous souls they are as lasting as life, as lasting as mind itself.

II. The SUPERIORITY of one over the others. "The greatest of these is charity." Why is it the greatest? 1. It is a virtue in *itself*. There is no moral virtue in faith and hope. They are, under certain conditions, necessary states of mind. But love—disinterested, godly love—is in itself a virtue. 2. It is that quality which *alone gives virtue to all other states of mind*. Where this love is not, faith and hope are morally worthless. 3. It is that state of mind by which *the soul subordinates the universe to itself*. The loving soul alone can interpret the universe. 4. It is that state of mind which links the *spirit to all holy intelligences*. Love is the attractive power that binds all holy spirits together. 5. It is that state of mind which *includes the highest faith and hope*. Love implies the both. 6. It is that state of mind *which is in itself happiness*. Love is happiness. We cannot say so of either faith or hope. 7. Love is the most *God-like state of the soul*. God is not faith or hope; "God is *love*." The Eternal does not believe or anticipate, but he does love—he *is* love. Love is the life of the soul. It warms every vein and beats in every pulse.

HOMILIES BY VARIOUS AUTHORS.

Vers. 1—3.—*Negative view of love.* Again and again, in St. Paul's writings, we have an epistle within the Epistle. Thus, the summation of practical duties (Rom. xii.), the argument on the resurrection (ch. xiv.), and the portraiture of love in this chapter. By this means we get a well-defined view of the object without losing its connections. It is not as if we were looking at the Peak of Teneriffe rising out of the loneliness of the sea, but rather a Mont Blanc, one with the Alps, and yet a solitary form of majesty. Grandeur, as distinct from beauty and sublimity, requires some degree of isolation so as to produce an adequate impression. Here, then, the apostle makes a space for this grand delineation, every feature of which may be seen in concentrated light, and not a thing allowed to distract the eye. This is in itself a call to attention, a summons to the activity of our whole nature, and, in accordance herewith, he presents something more than a mere sketch or profile of love. It is a complete portrait. The features are individually given, and, at the same time, the expression which combines them in a most striking unity. First, then, *we have the supreme excellence of love* in contrast with the worthlessness of other gifts unaccompanied by its presence. Great stress was laid at that time on the gift of tongues. We are all inclined to set a high value on an exceptional endowment of speech. Eloquence passes for much even in a rude age; the North American Indian and the barbarous tribes of Asia acknowledge its power, while cultivated society is never stinted in admiration of its influence. And the possessor of it seldom fails to exaggerate its worth. Stated roughly, eloquent men appear to have a peculiar intensity of consciousness as respects this gift. They are singularly open to the seductions of popular applause, so much so, indeed, that the public approval which a scientific man, or a statesman, or a military hero would be unharmed by, is often ruinous to an orator. Not the common air, but the breath of the multitude, fragrant with adulation, feeds his lungs. This it is that arterializes his blood and sends it hot and poisonous to his brain. Of course, these Corinthians were the very persons to overvalue the gift of tongues. It was in the channel of their tastes and traditions. But the apostle teaches them that this wonderful power holds a subordinate rank. He does not depreciate it; no, he appreciates it to the full: "tongues of men" are associated with "the tongues of angels;" and yet, without love, the endowment is as "sounding brass, or a tinkling cymbal." What is it but mere noise, an idle tumult of the air? Unless love to God and man attend the gift, restrain its selfishness, destroy its vanity-making tendency, and sanctify it to the welfare of others, it is worthless. But the second verse enlarges the thought. One may have the gift of prophecy and use his intellect with amazing skill and force so as to excite and captivate his hearers, and this, too, under the teachings of revelation; and, further, one may have insight into Divine secrets, and "understand all mysteries," and have them at command as "knowledge;" yet what is he without love? Can it be possible that this resplendent power could exist, and that other light kindled by love be utterly wanting? Observe, it is "all" mysteries and knowledge; the man explores every height and depth, and he has the freedom of the universe. Nay, superadd *all faith*, so that material nature falls in homage at your feet and the "mountains" remove in obedience to your will; but of what avail this expenditure of mighty energy, where the holiness of love is lacking? If, then, the man endowed with universality of utterance—"tongues of men and of angels;" and if the prophet with his clear and broad insight into the counsels of God, and before whose eye the panorama of distant events moves as a spectacle of to-day; if the miracle-worker who transcends all natural capacities and exercises the delegated power of Jehovah in producing supernatural phenomena;—if these men and their gifts are compared to "sounding brass and tinkling cymbal," and verily are "nothing;" and though they are known as apostles, prophets, miracle-workers, heroes of faith, instruments of the supernatural: if all these are nothingness itself without love, can anything more be said to intensify the excellence of love as a Divine principle and sentiment and impulse? The third verse answers this question. Charity, almsgiving, philanthropy, even self-sacrifice at the stake, here come into view. How far may one go in the benevolent appropriation of earthly property and yet fall below the highest motive? St. Paul replies that he may "dole out" all he owns, do it gradually, do it cautiously, do it to the exhaustion of his resources, yet do it unmindful of that sovereign law which gathers into itself all other laws and imparts to them a virtue that makes them Divine. Nor is this all. One may have the philanthropic idea and sensibility so largely developed as to accept martyrdom, have the courage to face it unblenched, and to endure it with fortitude; but he may surrender life without the highest love. Love may be there —love of a truth, love of a cause, love of humanity—not necessarily *the love*, however, here under discussion; and hence, this distinctive Christian love, which includes the Divine and the human, being absent, the martyrdom is not for Christ's sake, and consequently is nugatory as to its Christian character. "It profiteth me *nothing*." If, now, such a doctrine as this rested on a ground solely ethical, we confess our inability to see how it could be accepted as a trustworthy view of human nature. Logic in itself has no fundamental principle from which it can be deduced. Philosophy as such, and as confined to what it finds in our constitution, would be compelled to reject a conclusion so alien to its spirit. On the other hand, the doctrine may be easily and heartily received on the score of Christian logic and philosophy. For, in the scheme of Christianity, human nature is a revelation from God. It is the Divine thought of this nature which we are to embrace, to cherish, to act upon. And if we admit, as we ought to do in the presence of such satisfactory evidence, that God has spoken to man of man, and disclosed to him the once hidden mystery of himself, as well as that other and infinitely greater "hidden mystery" of his redeeming purpose in Christ—if we acknowledge this, then we cannot impeach the wisdom, the justness, the stern truthfulness, of St. Paul's argument. The argument assumes that Christianity is of God, and, as such, advances to this point, namely, Christianity alone gives a full and complete view of our nature. Its ethical teachings, their reasons and motives and ends, are founded in Christ and in his relations to us. Our relations to him and to one another are subsequent considerations, and take their quality and bearings simply, solely, altogether, from him, the "Image of the invisible God," and the "Firstborn of every creature." Inasmuch, then, as the ideal of our nature is not as we see it in and by our own unaided consciousness, but in and by a consciousness illuminated and guided by the Holy Ghost, how could it be otherwise than that new intuitions occur, and that demands are made on us never imagined before? On this foundation St. Paul stands when he affirms that those endowments which charm, those splendid gifts that win enthusiastic admiration, even self-sacrifice itself at the bidding of earth-born instincts, are *nothing* without *that love* which is purely a responsive affection, or, as St. John expresses it, "We love him because he *first* loved us."—L.

Vers. 4—7.—*The nature and operation of love.* The negative view having been presented, the apostle considers the *nature and operations of this love.* And one characteristic of it, he puts in the foreground of its excellences. *It can suffer.* A virtue that cannot suffer is hardly a virtue at all. Certainly it is not a virtue that can lay the least claim to divineness. Wedded love, parental love, philanthropic and patriotic love, have to undergo a discipline of pain and sorrow even to *symbolize* the higher affection of Divine love. This holy love, of which this chapter is so laudatory, derives its very essence from the "Man of sorrows." Short of realizing, in its measure, the agony in the lonely garden and the yet lonelier cross, it dare not, it cannot stop, since only there is its test found. A beautiful æstheticism, moral, perchance semi-spiritual, may follow the lowly Jesus of Nazareth through the windings of his Galilean and Judæan journeys, cling reverently to his person, spread the palm branches in his pathway, and shout its glad hosannas to his Name, and, after all, "forsook him and fled" may be the final record of its weakness. Only when he rises to the sacrificial height of his anointing as the Christ of God's Law and the Christ of God's love, and bears our sins in his own body on the tree—only here, where Jehovah "lets the lifted thunder drop," can the human soul be reconciled first to its own disciplinary sufferings, and learn afterwards, by many conflicts with self, to glory in the cross. But love not only suffers, it "*suffereth long.*" It is patient—patient towards others, and, what is quite as important, patient with itself. And under all its sufferings, instead of being irritable, it is kind. Unsanctified suffering is usually morbid. It broods over its ills; it magnifies its afflictions; often, indeed, it makes us misanthropic. Sweetness of temper and tender outgoings of sympathy are not the common results of painful experiences, but the fruits of the Holy Spirit in them. Fortitude may be shown, and it may be naught but homage at the shrine of self. This love is of God. It takes to its heart God's thought of suffering as chastening, as correction, as the supreme moral necessity of a probationary life, through which we must pass to get any deep knowledge of ourselves. For it is never pleasure, but pain, that holds the key to the secret chambers, where the latent man awaits the voice of God bidding him arise and gird himself with immortal strength. Now, what effect on this love would ensue from suffering that had become habitual and wrought patience and silent enduringness into character? By suppressing a morbid regard for self and quickening the sympathies that give width to the inner life, what would be the specific result on the relations sustained to others? These Corinthians, as we have frequently noticed, were pulling down one and putting up another, were thoroughgoing partisans, were censorious and depreciatory towards those with whom they were disinclined to affiliate. What change for the better would love bring about? St. Paul answers, "*Love envieth not.*" Observe how quickly he turns again to the negative aspects of this "supremely excellent way," and what vigour is imparted to the argument. At every step, contrast aids him by suggesting what love excludes, while its true qualities are set in bolder relief. Envy is pain at the sight of superior excellence in another, and is always a mark of blinding selfishness. According to one's temperament, it is displeasure or something worse, and usually contains an element of hatred.

> "Men, that make
> Envy and crooked malice nourishment,
> Dare bite the best."

Of course it leads to strife. It is a fruitful cause of schism, and as schism was a terrible evil in the apostle's view, he could not fail to show its utter inconsistency with this cardinal virtue. Along with this he says, "*Love vaunteth not*"—a similar idea to the foregoing as to its bad temper, but unlike as to its mood of exhibition. Reference is here made to the foolish display of self-importance after the manner of a swaggerer or braggart. Next comes the statement, "Is *not puffed up*," not inflated or swollen by self-conceit; this is followed by, "*Doth not behave itself unseemly*"—is not uncourteous, but studies propriety of manner, and shows the instinct of a right demeanour, from which all good breeding proceeds. The art of behaviour is manifold. It is amenable to circumstances and classes, variable as to outward manifestations, suiting language and other demonstrations to the claims of occasion, and, in all this, its root-principle is the same if it be truthful and sincere, since it loses sight of self and ministers to the happiness of others. Christian manners are the offspring of a Christian manner; the manners are external, the manner is internal; so that here, as in all else, form is created by spirit. The tones of the voice, the look of the eye, the muscular play of the countenance, are not physical facts only, but expressions and languages that have modulation, accent, emphasis, direct from the soul. Thus attended, our words take on other, fuller, more inspiriting meanings than those drawn from the dictionary; so that a man's face, figure, gesture, attitude, give a personal import to what emanates from his heart. If one compares the spiritual expression in the face of a Madonna by Raphael with the mere sensuous beauty of the face as depicted by antique art, he sees at once that Christianity has affected art to such an extent as to modify the laws of representation. "Expression is the vivid image of the passion that affects the mind; its language, and the portrait of its situation" (Fuseli). It is not extravagant to claim that Christianity has so far changed *physiological expression* as to spiritualize, and thereby to heighten, its quality and force. But why limit the change to art? The fact is that Christianity has had its effect—a very distinctive and appreciable effect— on what may be termed *the physiology of manner*, in the intercourse of society. We seldom think of it. We rarely number this among the myriad advantages Christianity has brought to man. Yet the fact is indisputable that Christianity has given to the human voice tones of strength and tenderness never before known, and to the human eye a depth of power, of stillness, of pathos, that, without its grace, had been impossible. Nor can we doubt that this is one of the numerous ways it has adopted to establish a closer relation between mind and matter, *and educate the body for the glory of the resurrection*. Passing from decorum while yet retaining the general idea in his grasp, St. Paul now mentions the unselfishness of love: "*Seeketh not her own.*" If its deportment is never obtrusive, but always becoming; if it never uses its gifts to remind others of their inferiority, but orders its manners so as to avoid everything which might tend to inflame envy; it goes still further, and manifests its disinterestedness as the soul of the "supremely excellent way." To pursue its own honour and aggrandizement, as if it had a sole proprietary interest in itself and could only exist by existing for its own reputation, influence, happiness, is forestalled by its nature and operations. The "all things" are not *its*, but "yours," and "ye," one and all, "are Christ's." So he had argued in the third chapter. The echo of the great truth comes back again and again, and once more it is heard in this verse. What St. Paul has just said of love as suffering long, and as kind, as not envying and vaunting, nor conceited and indecorous, are as so many stepping-stones to "seeketh not its own." Would it have anything in the universe for itself alone? If so, the very thing itself, the universe itself, would be changed into another thing and another universe, and be no more a joy and a blessedness, but a restraint and an evil and a curse. Instead of a palace, a prison; instead of sublime disinterestedness, sordidness and ceaseless descent in degradation; instead of an ideal in Christ, the idea of virtues as bare commercial utilities, and of the soul as a commodity valued by the market-place. Have anything alone? This were loneliness indeed. It were grievous, it were misery, to be isolated even by goodness and greatness from the heart of humanity. It is painful to a true man to be reminded of his superiority at the expense of others, and whenever one welcomes this sort of homage and glorifies himself, he loses truth of manhood. To thank God that we are "not as other men are" is sheer Pharisaism, and all such thanksgiving is worship of self. Love has not a wish, a desire, an aim, an aspiration, bounded by the limits of itself; and as Jesus prayed, "That they all may be one; as thou, Father, art in me, and I in thee, that they also may be one in us," so is the prayer of the soul in all its greatest moments, and when the cross is nearest by, that it may be one with others, as it longs to be one with Christ and the Father. Every inch that a majestic oak goes upward or spreads laterally, down go its roots; further and wider they spread themselves out, tree above and tree below, preserving, each in its way, proportion and symmetry. And so with love. Reaching that high development indicated by capacity to suffer and yet be kind, by victory over envy and ostentation, and the transformation of daily manners into spiritual grace and beauty, it has so enlarged itself as to afford ample room even for the most generous and magnanimous emotions. It wants to be good and to be better, but *where is the best?* And as the years move on and the soul grows, this thought comes to be uppermost, "There is a better world;" and not alone in a better nature, and as a better being, but *in a better world*, it looks for its perfection. A world of love is its demand. The negative idea is still further unfolded in the words, "*Is not easily provoked*," or, "Is not provoked" (Revised Version). Much of peevishness, of anger, of resentment, springs from wounding the imaginary being whom we call by our name, fondle with our caresses, and idolize in our vanity. This deformed self, though apparelled in gaudy drapery and lifted to an exalted pedestal, is but too conscious of its blemishes and flaws, to be tolerant of criticism or amiable under exposure of its imperfections. It is quick to take umbrage. It is full of suspicion and keenly alive to neglect, real or supposed. A chronic ailment, this self-conceit feels any fluctuation of circumstances and is acutely sensitive to wind and weather. On the other hand, love is not provoked; its temper is not quick, nor are its words hasty. How can it be otherwise, when it "*thinketh no evil*"? By governing its thoughts, it obtains that rare virtue of intellect which consists in no small degree of a mastery over associations and suggestions, and that is probably the most signal triumph of mind over its physical connections. "Imputeth not the evil" (Dr. Kling); "Taketh not account of evil" (Revised Version); and whereas the "evil" is real and palpable, it refuses to bear it in mind, and, by fixing attention and keeping it fixed on the wrong, to aggravate the impression. Here, as everywhere, mark the unity in our constitution. One cannot have a sore finger, or toothache, or painful limb, that the affection is not enhanced by directing thought to it. The blood is inflamed the more, and the nervous susceptibility augmented. So it is with the mind. Can we wonder, then, that St. Paul's insight detected the relation between thinking of injury or injustice, and the moral effect on character? And, finally, as to these repeated negatives, love "*rejoiceth not in iniquity*," or, "in unrighteousness," but "rejoiceth in [or, 'with'] the truth." It exults not at the overthrow and prostration of others. The downfall of another, even if that other made himself a rival, is no gratification. A human soul, a redeemed spirit, sank in that fall, and love cannot rejoice in such a calamity. "*Rejoiceth in* [or, 'with'] *the truth*." Love has been personified all along; truth is here personified. Love approaches moral truth, offers its congratulations, enters into its success, shares its joy. So, then, St. Paul approaches the close of this paragraph by the beautiful picture of love and truth side by side, and happy in the purity and glory of their fellowship. Looking back on the course of the argument, we see love as a meek and gentle sufferer, the traces of pain on its face, yet a sweet and holy reconciliation to the pangs long borne. We see kindness imprinted on the countenance. We discover no sign of envy, of pride and vanity, of overweening self-regard, and, wherever the figure moves, its grace and charms are not blurred by unseemly demeanour. Most of all, its eye has an outward look, as if offering its heart to the service of others. And while unpleasant things occur, and wrongs are perpetrated, it is not made angry, nor does it nurse malice and resentment, nor rejoice at the retributions that overtake iniquity. Joy, indeed, it has, but its gladdest hours are those when love clasps hands with truth, and when "seeketh not its own" finds its highest realization in fellowship with truth. But the positive side of love must now be presented. It "*beareth all things*," that is, "hides to itself and to others" (Bengel), conceals or covers up the infirmities of others, which envy, pride, malice, would not expose, but delight in the exposure. A virtue is most glorious when it courts silence and prizes it as a beatitude. Unwitnessed patience and heroism are grandest when the soul asks no recognition, but abides with its consciousness alone in God. In his four statements in ver. 7 this quiet bearing of the imperfections of other people is first mentioned. And with what expressiveness of diction! "Beareth *all* things." That passive strength which bears life's burden is no sudden, still less an early, acquirement. It is a slow growth. Time, as a co-worker with grace, has much to do with its excellence. Years only can give it maturity and years full of providence. Consider, too, what a co-education of the body is implied here, what a subduing of recreant nerves, what a check on the blood, what refusals to obey sensations, before one can learn the art of silence as to the faults that annoy and often vex. If it is thus that Christian character is rounded off, we cannot doubt that it is not attainable except through a tedious and protracted experience. But does this bearing with the faults of others comply with the requirements of social duty? Nay, says the apostle, love "*believeth all things.*" It searches for good qualities in men who are disagreeable and even repulsive, and whatever its diligent scrutiny can bring to light amid the mass of infirmities overlaying better traits, yields it genuine pleasure. Colour-blindness is not confined to the physical eye. Individuals who are sensitive to the faults of others, and habituated to criticizing them, are generally more affected by nervous annoyance than by conscience, and it commonly happens with such that they seldom look for any redeeming goodness. To estimate the force of circumstances, to study motives, to make charitable allowances, are alien to their tastes and temper. On the contrary, the instinct of love is to believe that others are better, or, at least, may be better, than they seem. So that while love is an heroic believer, it is also a wise doubter, and gives the unhappy idiosyncrasies of men the benefit of its doubts. Because of this, it "*hopeth all things.*" Right believing is an expansive force in the intellect. It is a quickener of imagination. It finds reasons for confidence unknown to him who has the conceit of scepticism, and cherishes it for its own sake, and prides himself on it as a sign of intellectual acumen. Faith acts on the emotions. These two, imagination and sensibility, stimulate hope, that in turn rises above the senses and comprehends, to some extent, the mighty forces engaged on the side of goodness. The power of God in Christianity makes its way slowly to the heart, while Satanic influence is demonstrative to the eye. Hope is not left to itself, but is taught of Christ, who, in the days of his flesh, looked beyond humiliation, obloquy, death, to the glory waiting to invest him. So, then, we may say that large views and large hopes go together, and the grace that "believeth all things" also "hopeth all things." But is a great hope immediately gratified? Never; if it were it would lose its greatness. Hope is a beautiful education, and it is this by holding back its fulfilment and thereby expanding the soul's capacity for the fullest gratification. Hope must have time and opportunity to develop the sense of enjoyability in us before it bestows the reality. Each day of postponement goes onward to the day of realization, which is thousands of days in one. But it educates us in other forms. The delay of hope to meet our anticipations tests our strength and patience. Has the hope a firm hold on our souls? If so, its possessor "*endureth all things.*" Through doubt and darkness, amidst adversity, despite opposing circumstances, love is persistent, and its persistency is the measure of its power. When we reach this ability to endure, waiting in serene patience, submissive to God's will, content with to-day for what it is in itself, anticipating a coming joy, but leaving its birth-hour to him who keeps the times and seasons for himself,—when we attain this point of experience, we are near the boundary of earthly growth. Passive excellence, such as that pointed out by the word "endureth," seems to be the final work of the Holy Ghost in the human heart. Fitly, therefore, St. Paul finds the climax of expressions (ver. 7) in "endureth all things." True, "beareth," "believeth," "hopeth," are alike related to "all things" with "endureth," and yet this is obviously the consummation of the idea pervading the apostle's mind. Fitly so, we have said, since men are accustomed to regard endurance as the mark of the highest power. It is a trained and balanced power. Body, soul, and spirit are present in the fulness of its strength. There is no disquiet in those sensibilities that are ever creating ripples on the surface of life. There is no agitation in those great depths that once heaved under the fury of the storm. Enduring love has entered into rest, and the repose is God-like.—L.

Vers. 8—13.—*Permanence of love.* Why is it that the numerous objects around us are transient? On every side they appeal to us, connect themselves with hope and fear, enter into our business, awaken enterprise and ambition, and even inspire ardent love; yet they are ever passing away. Now, there must be a discipline in all this, and Christianity assures us what it means. It is that we may be trained in the midst of evanescence for that which is permanent. And this presupposes that there is not only an immortal soul in man, but that, by reason of his present organization and its relations, certain of his functions and acquirements are purely temporary, while others are to live for ever. In fact, there are functions and acquirements which do not wait for the death of the body. They fulfil their purpose and expire long before age overtakes us. Yet, says Wordsworth—

> "Not for this
> Faint I, nor mourn nor murmur; other gifts
> Have followed, for such loss, I would believe
> Abundant recompense."

It is in the spirit of a true and noble Christian philosophy that this great moral poet of the century sees no cause to "mourn nor murmur" because our nature has a *rejecting instinct*, which, as God ordains, throws off and leaves behind it tastes and habits that were once very useful as well as precious. Keeping in mind, then, that this rejecting instinct is an organic part of our constitution and has its allotted functions to discharge, we can appreciate all the more St. Paul's line of thought in the closing verses of this chapter. "*Love never faileth.*" Its existence, activity, manifestation, will be perpetuated. The wonderful spiritual gifts of which he had said so much—prophecy, the ability to speak with tongues, knowledge—these should cease to exist. Although they proceeded from the Holy Ghost and were mightily instrumental for good in the incipient work of the Church, yet, nevertheless, they were to terminate. Scaffoldings were they all, useful as such, subserving most important ends, but mere scaffoldings, that could no longer remain when the edifice had been finished. What, then, is the ideal of the Church? It is not splendid endowments, for they are doomed to extinction, but the love "that never faileth." Whether the passing away of these gifts refers to the apostolic age or to "the age to come," matters nothing, since the idea of their discontinuation, rather than of the time it should occur, is foremost in St. Paul's mind. Imagine, then, his conception of love, when he could contemplate the Church as a vast body laying off these mighty accompaniments of its career, and yet, so far from being weakened, would be girded afresh with a power more resplendent and display it in a form infinitely more majestic. Disrobed of these habiliments, its contour would appear in the perfection of sublimity; its anatomy as an organism would be, as it were, transparent; the whole framework, the various parts, the ligaments binding them together, the circulating life-blood, would disclose the single animating principle of love. Would it startle the Corinthians to learn that even knowledge should vanish away? "We know in part, and we prophesy in part." All knowledge cannot be meant, for love itself includes much knowledge, and, in its absence, would be simply emotional intensity. To possess the mere faculty of knowing would be worthless, if the mind could not retain the contents of knowledge and make them a portion integrally of itself. What the apostle teaches is that such knowledge as stands related to the present state and time, and grows directly out of imperfect human development, and shares the condition of all things earthly, is short-lived and must terminate. Tongues shall cease, but the gift of speech shall not be lost. And he explains himself by saying that the gifts relating to prophecy and tongues were only partial, were exclusively adapted to a preliminary state of experience and activity, and completed their purpose in a temporary spiritual economy. We are here under specific, no less than general limitations, and, in certain directions, we are restrained more than in others. What the Spirit looks to is not knowledge alone, but to its moral aspects as well; to humility, meekness, self-abasement, when the intellect is strongest, freest, and boldest; nor will he expand the understanding and its expressional force for their own sakes, but develop them only so far as subservient to an object higher than their immediate ends. Partial information, partial command of our mental faculties, partial uses of even the wisdom we possess—this is the law of limitation and restraint, under which the complex probation of intellect, sensibility, volition, aspiration, and outward activity, works out immeasurable results. Therefore, he argues, we now know and prophesy "in part;" at the best, we are fragmentary and incomplete; and yet this imperfection is connected with a perfect system and leads up to it. The perfection will come; the existing economy is its foreshadowing; nor could knowledge give any rational account of itself, nor could prophecy and tongues vindicate their worth, if the fuller splendours, of which these are faint escapes of light, were not absolute certainties of the future. Only when the "perfect is come" shall that which is "in part" be "done away." Institutions founded in providence and upheld by the Spirit are left to no chance or accident as to continuance, decay, extinction. God comes into them, abides, departs, according to the counsel of his will. If he numbers our days as living men, and keeps our times in his hand; if only his voice says, "Return, ye children of men;"—this is equally true of institutions. For the dead dust, man makes a grave; but the life of individuals, institutions, government, society, even the Church, is in God's keeping, and he alone says, "Return." How shall St. Paul set forth the relation of the partial to the perfect? A truth lacks something if it cannot be illustrated, and a teacher is very defective in ability when he cannot find a resemblance or an analogy to make his meaning more perspicuous and vivid. Truth and teacher have met in this magnificent chapter on ground reserved, we may venture to say, for their special occupancy and companionship. The great teacher sees the sublimest of truths in a glowing light, and most unlike Paul would he be if no illustration came to hand spontaneously. Is there something in the more hallowed moments of the soul that suddenly reinstates the sense of childhood? "When I was a child" in the heathen city of Tarsus, the capital of a Roman province; the mountains of Taurus and the luxuriant plain and the flowing Cydnus near by; the crowded streets and gay population and excited groups of talkers pressing on eye and ear; the festivals of paganism; the strange contrasts of these with the life in his Jewish home; his training under the parental roof; the daily reminders of the Law and the traditions of the Pharisees;—what thoughts were they? Only those of a child, understood and spoken as a child. No ordinary child could he have been. Providence was shaping him then for an apostle, so that while the holy child Jesus was growing "in wisdom and stature" amid the hills of Nazareth and in the nursery of the virgin mother's heart, there was far away in Cilicia a boy not much younger, who was in rearing there, under very unlike circumstances, to be his chosen apostle to the Gentile world. Yet the boy Saul was but a child, and thought and spake "as a child." But is childhood disallowed and set off in sharp contrast with manhood? Nay; childhood is of God no less than manhood as to quality of being. What is contrasted is the *childishness* in the one case and the perfected *manhood* in the other. So that we suppose the apostle to mean that whatsoever is initial, immature, provisional, in the child, has been put away to make room for something better. The better implies the good, a *childish* good, indeed, and yet a good from the hand of God however mixed with earthly imperfections. Another movement occurs in the leading thought. Can one think of knowledge without an involuntary recurrence of the symbol of light? The symbol has quite supplanted the thing signified, and the *enlightened* man is more honoured than the *knowing* man. St. Paul proceeds to say, "Now we see through a glass, darkly;" the revealed Word of God is conveyed to us "in symbols and words which but imperfectly express them" (Hodge, Delitzsch); and yet, while there is a "glass" or mirror, and the knowledge or vision of Divine things is "darkly" given, there is a real knowledge, a true and blessed knowledge, for "we see." Enough is made intelligible for all the purposes of the spiritual mind, for all spiritual uses, in all spiritual relationships of comprehension, conscience, volition, affection, brotherhood; enough for probation, responsibility, culture, and lifetime growth. What in us is denied? Only curiosity, excessive appetencies of the faculties, habits of perception and judging superinduced in the intellect by the sensational portion of our nature,—these are denied their morbid gratification. A *plethora* of *evidence* is denied that faith may have its sphere. Over-strength and over-constraint of *motive* are denied that the will may be left free. Violent impulses of *feeling* are denied that the heart may be intense without wild and erratic enthusiasm, treasuring its life of peaceful blessedness in unfathomable depths like the ocean, that keeps its mass of waters in the vast hollows of the globe and uses the hills and mountains only to shape its shores. On the other hand, what is granted to the mind in the revelation of Divine truth? Such views of God in Christ as the soul can realize in its present condition and thereby form the one master-habit of a probationary being, viz. *How to see God in Christ*. At present, we can only begin to see as by reflection in a mirror; and, as in the education of the senses to the finer work of earthly life the cultivation of the eye is the slowest and most exacting, the longest, the most difficult, and that too because the eye is the noblest of the special senses, so learn we, and not without much patient exertion, and oft-repeated efforts to see God in Christ as made known in his gospel and providence and Holy Spirit. Yet the mirror trains the eye and prepares it to see God through no such intervening medium. The promised vision is open, full, immediate. We shall see him "*face to face*," says St. Paul. "We shall be like him; for we shall see him as he is," declares St. John. And then partial knowledge shall expand into perfect knowledge, and we shall know after a new and Divine manner, for nothing less than this is the assurance: *Know as we are known.* "Glorious hymn to *Christian love*," as Dr. Farrar calls this chapter, what shall be its closing strain? "And now abideth" (remains or continues)—the same duration as compared with the evanescence of extraordinary gifts being ascribed to the three—"and now abideth faith, hope, love, these three; and the greatest of these is love." Who can doubt it after reading this chapter? Here it stands beside the great gifts of the "tongues of men and of angels," and of the prophetic insight, and of miracle-working, and of philanthropy and martyrdom, and, amid this splendid array, *love is greatest.* In what it does, it is *greatest.* In what it is, it is *greatest.* Here, finally, it is grouped with faith and hope, and yet the light that irradiates its form and features from the glory of God in the face of Jesus Christ is a lustre beyond that of the other two, because the "greatest of these is love."—L.

Ver. 1.—"*Love.*" The word rendered "charity" in the Old Version, and "love" in the Revised Version of our New Testament, is not a classical substantive. It is emphatically a Christian term. And this need not be wondered at; for as the virtue itself is one, if not created, yet developed by Christianity, it is what might have been expected to find that the thing gave rise to the name. This chapter has been called a psalm of love, and is admired both for its elevated thinking and its melodious diction, whilst to such as are imbued with the true Christian spirit it is especially congenial and delightful.

I. MISCONCEPTIONS HAVE TO BE REMOVED. *E.g.*: 1. The use of the word "charity" is ambiguous. It is often used as equivalent to tolerance, as in the phrase, "the judgment of charity;" and often as synonymous with "almsgiving," as in the sad proverb, "Cold as charity." Neither of these uses meets the requirements of the text. 2. "Love" is also an ambiguous word, being commonly applied to the feeling of attraction and attachment between young people of opposite sexes—a usage which evidently has no applicability here.

II. THE NATURE OF CHRISTIAN LOVE HAS TO BE EXPLAINED. 1. It is between one human being and another. The question is not of reverent love to God, but of the mutual feelings of those endowed with the same spiritual nature. 2. It is a sentiment, and there is no love where there is simply a principle of action, cold and unimpassioned. 3. It is a sentiment which governs conduct, restraining men from injuring or slandering one another, and impelling them to mutual assistance.

III. THE SOURCE OF CHRISTIAN LOVE HAS TO BE TRACED. 1. Its true and ultimate origin is in the nature of God, who is love. 2. Its introduction among men is chiefly owing to the Lord Jesus, who was the gift of the Father's love, whose whole ministry to earth was a revelation of love, and whose benevolent conduct and sacrificial death were the fruit of love. 3. Its individual power and social efficacy are owing to the presence and operation of the Spirit of God. Not without significance is love mentioned first in the inventory of the fruits of the Spirit, which are these: *love*, joy, peace, etc.

IV. THE EXCELLENCY OF CHRISTIAN LOVE HAS TO BE EXHIBITED. This is done in this chapter, systematically, in several ways. 1. It is superior to the supernatural gifts generously bestowed upon the Church in the first age. 2. It is the motive to dispositions and actions of the highest degree of moral beauty. 3. It will survive all that is most prized by man as intellectually precious and desirable. 4. It is superior even to gifts, or rather graces, so lovely and admirable as are faith and hope.—T.

Ver. 1.—*Love and language.* It would seem that, of all gifts, the gift of speech, and especially that variety of it known as the gift of tongues, was most prized by the Christians of Corinth. Probably for this reason the apostle puts this in the forefront, when he compares other possessions and virtues with the grace of love.

I. IN WHAT THE SUPERIORITY OF LOVE OVER SPEECH CONSISTS. 1. In the fact that the gift of tongues draws attention to the possessor himself, whilst charity goes forth from him who cultivates it to others. The gift in question was one splendid and dazzling. Whether it consisted in a power to speak intelligibly in foreign languages, or in the pouring forth of sounds—articulate, indeed, but not corresponding with any language known to the auditors—in either case it was a brilliant faculty, drawing all eyes to the speaker and all ears to his voice. On the other hand, the affectionate ministrant to the wants of his poor or afflicted neighbours would usually go his way unnoticed and unadmired. It is better that a man should be drawn out, as it were, from himself, than that his attention should be, because the attention of others is, concentrated upon himself. 2. In the fact that the grace of love is far more serviceable to the Church and to the world than the gift of tongues. There was a purpose subserved by this gift—it impressed carnal listeners, it was a proof to the Church itself of a special Divine presence. But love led men and women to sympathize with one another, to minister to the wants of the needy, to raise the fallen, to strengthen the weak, to nurse the sick, to comfort the bereaved, to rear the orphan. Thus its fruits vindicated its supremacy. 3. In the fact that the Lord Jesus loved, but never spake with tongues. 4. In the fact that the gift of tongues is but for a season, whilst love is indestructible and eternal.

II. By what comparison the superiority of love is illustrated. The gift without the grace is likened to the sounding of brass, to the clashing of a cymbal of bronze. There is noise, but it is *vox et præterea nihil*; there is no melody and no meaning. On the other hand, love is like a strain of exquisite music vibrating from the strings, warbling from a flute, or pealing from the pipes of an organ; or, better still, it is like the clear bell-like voice of a boy in some cathedral choir, rendering an immortal passage of sacred poetry to an air sounding like an echo from the minstrelsy of Paradise. The former arrests attention; the gong when struck produces a shock; but the latter sweetly satisfies the soul, then soothing and refreshing the spirit's longings for a heaven-born strain, and leaving behind the precious memory of a melting cadence.—T.

Ver. 2.—*Love and knowledge.* Different gifts have attractions for different minds. To the Corinthians the *charisms* of language seem to have had an especial charm and value. It might be supposed that those possessions here mentioned—prophecy, unravelling of mysteries, and knowledge, especially of spiritual things—would have a deeper interest for such a one as Paul. And that he did prize these is not to be questioned. Yet such was his appreciation of love, that in this eulogium of it he sets it above those half-intellectual, half-spiritual gifts.

I. These gifts are in themselves valuable. There is nothing here said to disparage the gifts. On the contrary, they are introduced in a way which witnesses to their excellence. Prophecy is the speaking forth of the mind of God—a function the most honourable the mind can conceive. To understand and reveal mysteries would universally be acknowledged to be a high distinction. Knowledge ranks high in connection with a religion which addresses man's intelligence. All these are, so to speak, aspects of religion peculiarly congenial to a thoughtful Christian, and peculiarly advantageous to a Christian community.

II. But it is possible that these gifts may be of no value to the possessor. That is, in case they be unaccompanied by love. The purely intellectual character is the unlovely character. The man may be the vehicle of truth, and yet the truth may pass through him without affecting his character, his spiritual position. Who does not know such men—men of Biblical scholarship, sound theology, great teaching power, yet loveless, and because loveless unlovely? To themselves they may be great men, and in the view of the Church; but in reality, and before God, they are *nothing*!

III. It is love which makes these gifts valuable to their possessor. How needful love is to impart a spiritual flavour and quality to these great endowments, is clear enough, *i.e.* to every enlightened mind. 1. Love infuses the spirit in which they are to be used. How differently the man of intellect or of learning uses his powers when his soul is pervaded by the spirit of brotherly love, every observer must have noticed. "Let all your things be done in charity" is an admonition appropriate to all, but especially so to the man of genius or of ability. 2. Love controls the purpose to which they are to be applied. Not for self-exaltation, not for the advancement of a great cause, but for the general welfare, will love inspire the great to consecrate their talents, according to the mind and method of the great Master himself.—T.

Ver. 2.—*Love and faith.* St. Paul was so emphatically the apostle of faith, that it is hard to believe that he wrote anything approaching to disparagement of that great and efficacious virtue. If he devoted a great part of his chief Epistle—that to the Romans—to an exhibition of the power of faith, it is not likely that here or anywhere he should write one word which could cast faith into the shade. And, in fact, the reference of the apostle in this passage is not to faith in Christ as a Saviour, but to that special faith in a special promise which was the means of enabling the possessor to perform great marvels—in the figurative language of Scripture, to remove mountains.

I. This language is not in disparagement of the faith which works by love. It is always taught in Scripture that faith precedes love; the heart must find Christ and rest in him and live from him, in order that it may love him. Confidence in a personal Saviour revealed in his words and life, in his sacrifice and triumph, will certainly awaken affection, more or less ardent according to the temperament and history of the individual believer. Strong faith is fitted to enkindle warm love.

II. We are taught that "gifts" are not always a sign of piety. The faith which was so much admired and coveted in the primitive Church was confidence in a certain definite promise of the Lord of supernatural aid to those whose position rendered such aid expedient. The removal of mountains is, of course, a figure for the vanquishing of difficulties, and probably for the performance of miracles. It would seem that there were in the early Churches some who possessed this gift who had not the spiritual qualifications which were far more to be desired. And it is not to be denied that even now there are in all Christian communities men largely endowed with gifts of administration, learning, and eloquence, who yet are lacking in those first qualities of Christian character which are a sign of the Spirit's indwelling. Far more to be desired is simple faith in the Saviour than the faith which removes mountains and dazzles multitudes.

III. These lessons are enforced by the consideration that Paul possessed both supernatural gifts and fervent charity, and was well able to compare the two. Never were wonders, miracles of moral power, wrought more manifestly, more repeatedly, than in the ministry of the great apostle of the Gentiles. If any had reason to boast, he had more. Yet to him his love to the Saviour, and his devotion to those for whom that Saviour died, were of far more consequence and value than all his supernatural gifts.

"Love is the brightest of the train,
And strengthens all the rest."

T.

Ver. 3.—*Love and almsgiving.* Of all the comparisons between love and other qualities, gifts, or practices, this is the one which sounds most strange to our ears. For in our minds charity and almsgiving are so closely associated that it scarcely seems possible that they should be placed in contrast one with the other. Yet so it is; and every observer of human nature and society can recognize both the insight and the foresight of the apostle in this striking, almost startling comparison.

I. Almsgiving may originate in inferior and unworthy motives. The apostle supposes an extreme case, viz. that one should give away all his substance in doles to the poor; and he gives his judgment that such a course of action may be loveless, and, if loveless, then worthless. For it may proceed from : 1. *Ostentation.* That this is the explanation of many of the handsome and even munificent gifts of the wealthy, we are obliged to believe. A rich man sometimes likes his name to figure in a subscription list for an amount which no man of moderate means can afford. The publication of such a gift gratifies his vanity and self-importance. His name may figure side by side with that of a well-known millionaire. 2. *Custom.* A commentator has illustrated this passage by reference to the crowds of beggars who gather in the court of a great bishop's palace in Spain or Sicily, to each of whom a coin is given, in so-called charity. Such pernicious and indiscriminate almsgiving is expected of those in a high position in the Church, and they give from custom. The same principle explains probably much of our eleemosynary bestowment. 3. *Love of power.* As in the feudal days a great lord had his retinue and his retainers, multitudes depending upon his bounty, so there can be no question that individuals and Churches often give generously for the sake of the hold they thus gain upon the dependent, who become in turn in many ways their adherents and supporters.

II. ALMSGIVING MAY IN SOME CASES BE INJURIOUS. In fact, it often is so. 1. To the *recipient.* The wretch who lives in idleness on rich men's doles is degraded in the process, and becomes lost to all self-respect, and habituated to an ignominious and base contentedness with his position. 2. To *society* generally. When it is known that the man who begs is as well supported as the man who works, how can it be otherwise than that demoralization should ensue? The system of indiscriminate almsgiving is a wrong to the industrious poor. 3. To the *giver.* For such gifts as are supposed, instead of calling forth the finer qualities of the nature, awaken in the breast of the bestower a cynical contempt of mankind.

III. NEVERTHELESS, TRUE CHARITY MAY EXPRESS ITSELF IN GIFTS. The man who doles away his substance in almsgiving, and has all the while no charity, is nothing; but if there be love, that love sanctifieth both the giver and the gift. For he who loves and gives resembles that Divine Being whose heart is ever filled with love, whose hands are ever filled with gifts.—T.

Ver. 3.—*Love and self-immolation.* It would seem that Paul had some anticipation of the approaching developments of Christian society. There is no ground for believing that, at the time when he wrote, any member of the Church of Christ had suffered at the stake for fidelity to principle and to faith. Such martyrdoms had occurred in Palestine, when the enemies of Jehovah had been triumphant and had wreaked their vengeance upon the faithful Jews. And even before Paul's decease, in Rome itself, Christians came to be the victims of the infamous Nero's brutality, and perished in the flames. Stronger language could not be used to set forth the superiority of love to zeal, fidelity, and devotion than this of St. Paul: "Though I give my body to be burned, and have not love, it profiteth me nothing!"

I. THE READINESS TO DIE, AT THE STAKE OR OTHERWISE, FOR CHRIST'S SAKE, IS GOOD. As the three Hebrew children were content to be cast into the burning, fiery furnace, as the faithful Jews died at the stake under the persecution by Antiochus Epiphanes, as Polycarp at over four score years of age gave his body to be burned, as the holy Perpetua suffered this martyrdom with willing mind, as in our own country at the Reformation many suffered in the fires of Oxford and Smithfield, so have multitudes counted their lives as not dear to them for the blessed Saviour's sake. It cannot but be that such sacrifice of self, such holy martyrdom, ever has been and is acceptable to Christ, who gave himself for us. For he himself has said, "Blessed are they which are persecuted for righteousness' sake: for theirs is the kingdom of heaven."

II. THE ABSENCE OF LOVE TAKES AWAY EVEN FROM THE VIRTUE OF MARTYRDOM. There is a story of a Christian of Antioch who, on his way to martyrdom, refused to forgive and be reconciled to a brother Christian. Such a case is an exact example of the zeal without love which the apostle here pronounces worthless. If Christian charity be absent where zeal is present, there seems reason to fear that the motives which induce to self-immolation are pride, self-glorification, and an inflexible obstinacy. If there be not love to Christ's people, there is no real love to Christ: "He that loveth God loves his brother also." It is strange to think that self-delusion may go so far that men may suffer martyrdom without being truly Christ's. Yet so it is. And we may be reminded, from the possibility of this extreme case, how readily men deceive themselves and suppose that they are influenced by truly religious and distinctly Christian motives, when all the while *self* is the pivot upon which their whole conduct revolves. And it may be suggested to us how inexpressibly essential, in the judgment of our Lord and his Spirit, is that grace of love, the absence of which cannot be atoned for even by a passage through the fiery flames of martyrdom.—T.

Vers. 4, 5.—*Love and our fellow-men.* In this panegyric of charity, we find, (1) in vers. 1—3, a statement concerning the indispensableness of charity to the Christian character, (2) in vers. 3—7, a list of the fruits of charity; and (3) in the remainder of the chapter, a declaration of the eternity of charity. The second and third of these divisions contain a very pictorial personification of this delightful grace; the lovely features and beaming smile of charity shine upon us, and win our hearts. Several of these clauses exhibit the effects of the indwelling of Christian love upon the intercourse of social life.

I. LOVE IS LONG-SUFFERING AS OPPOSED TO IMPATIENCE. There is no possibility of mixing with human society without encountering many occasions of irritation. Human nature is such that conflicts of disposition and of habits will and must occur. It is so in the family, in civil life, and even in the Church. Hence impatience and irritability are among the most common of infirmities. And there is no more sure sign of a disciplined and morally cultured mind than a habit of forbearance, tolerance, and patience. But Christianity supplies a motive and power of long-suffering which can act in the case of persons of every variety of temperament and of every position of life. "Love suffereth long."

II. LOVE IS GRACIOUS AND KIND AS OPPOSED TO MALICE AND ILL WILL. There is no disposition known to human nature which is a more awful proof of the enormity of sin than malevolence. And the religion of the Lord Christ in nothing more signally proves its divinity than in its power to expel this demoniacal spirit from the breast of humanity. In fact, benevolence is the admitted "note" of this religion. The sterner virtues, as fortitude and justice, were admired and practised among the heathen, and celebrated by the moralists of antiquity. These and others were assumed by Christianity, which added to them the softer grace of love—love which justifies itself in deeds of benignity and loving-kindness.

III. LOVE IS OPPOSED TO ENVY AND JEALOUSY. These are vices which arise from discontent with one's own condition as compared with that of others, and are justly deemed among the meanest and basest of which man is capable. Christianity proves its power of spiritual transformation by suppressing, and indeed in many cases by extirpating, these evil passions from the heart, and by teaching and enabling men to rejoice in their neighbours' prosperity.

IV. LOVE, AS OPPOSED TO ANGER, IS NOT PROVOKED WITH THE CONDUCT OF OTHERS. This must not be pressed too far, as though anger in itself were an evil, as though there were no such thing as righteous indignation. Christ himself was angry with hypocrites and deceivers; his indignation and wrath were aroused again and again. But the moral distinction lies here: to be provoked with those who injure us or pass a slight upon our dignity and self-importance, is unchristian, but it is not so to cherish indignation with the conduct of God's wilful enemies.

V. LOVE KEEPS NO ACCOUNT OF EVIL RENDERED. This trait in the character of the Christian is very beautiful. It is customary with sinful men to cherish the memory of wrongs done to them, against a day of retribution. Love wipes out the record of wrong-doing from the memory, and knows nothing of vindictiveness or ill will.—T.

Vers. 4, 5.—*Love and self-abnegation.* Where there is sincere Christian love, that grace will not only affect for good the intercourse of human society, it will exercise a most powerful and beneficial influence over the nature of which it takes possession; changing pride into humility, and selfishness into self-denial. And this is not to be wondered at by him who considers that for the Christian the spiritual centre of gravity is changed—is no longer self, but Christ.

I. LOVE DESTROYS BOASTFULNESS. It "vaunteth not itself." In some characters more than in others there is observable a disposition towards display. There may be real ability, and yet there may be the vanity which obtrudes the proofs of that ability; or there may, on the other hand, be an absence of ability, and yet the fool may not be able to conceal his folly, but must needs make himself the laughing-stock of all. Love delights not in the display of real power or the assumption of what does not exist. How can it? When love seeks the good of others, how can it seek their admiration?

II. LOVE IS OPPOSED TO PRIDE. It "is not puffed up." The expression is a strong one; it has been rendered, "does not swell and swagger," "is not inflated with vanity." The explanation of this is clear enough. The pretentious and arrogant man has a mind full of himself, of thoughts of his own greatness and importance. Now, love is the outflowing of the heart's affection in kindliness and benevolence towards others. He who is always thinking of the welfare of his fellow-men has no time and no inclination for thoughts of self-exaltation, aggrandizement, and ambition. It is plain, then, how wholesome, purifying, and sweetening an influence Christianity introduces into human society; and how much it tends to the happiness of individuals, cooling the fever of restless rivalry and ambition.

III. LOVE IS INCONSISTENT WITH ALL UNSEEMLINESS OF DEPORTMENT. There is an indefiniteness about the language: "Doth not behave itself unseemly." Possibly there is a special reference to the discreditable scenes which were to be witnessed in the Corinthian congregation, in consequence of their party spirit, rivalry, and discord. But there is always in every community room for the inculcation of considerateness, courtesy, self-restraint, and dignity. And the apostle points out, with evident justice, that what no rules or custom can produce is the spontaneous and natural result of the operation of Christian love.

IV. LOVE IS, IN A WORD, UNSELFISH; *i.e.* "seeketh not her own." Here is the broadest basis of the new life of humanity. Love gives, and does not grasp; has an eye for others' wants and sorrows, but turns not her glance towards herself; moves among men with gracious mien and open hands.—T.

Ver. 6.—*The joy of love.* There is, perhaps, no test of character more decisive than this: in what is the chief pleasure of life placed? Where is satisfaction of the soul? Whence does joy proceed? If Christianity is indeed a revolutionary religion, it will effect a change here—in this vital respect. Even in St. Paul's time, it appeared that with Christianity a new force—the force of love—had been introduced into humanity, a force able to direct human delight into another and purer and nobler channel than that in which it had been wont to flow.

I. JOY NO LONGER FLOWS FROM THE PRESENCE AND PREVALENCE OF UNRIGHTEOUS-NESS. It seems to attribute a fiendish spirit to human beings to suppose that they can anywhere and at any time be found to rejoice in wrong-doing and unrighteousness. Yet it is, alas! possible for sinful men to take a malignant pleasure in the prevalence of sin; for it is the proof of the power of the moral forces with which they have allied themselves, of the victory of their own party. The iniquity of others serves to support and justify their own iniquity. And it must be borne in mind that there are cases in which designing men profit by deeds of unrighteousness, take the very wages of iniquity. Against such dispositions Christian love must needs set itself; for when iniquities prevail, happiness and hope take wings and fly away.

II. JOY FLOWS TO THE CHRISTIAN HEART FROM THE PROGRESS OF TRUTH AND RIGHTEOUSNESS. Truth is the intellectual side of righteousness, and righteousness the moral side of truth. There is, accordingly, a real antithesis between the two clauses of the text. 1. This joy is *akin to the joy of God.* The Father rejoices over the repenting and recovered child, the Shepherd over the restored, once wandering, sheep. "There is joy in the presence of the angels of God over one sinner that repenteth." And they who themselves are enjoying peace and fellowship with a reconciled God cannot but participate in the satisfaction with which that holy Being views the progress of truth and religion among men. 2. It is *sympathetic with the gladness of the Saviour* in the accomplishment of his gracious purposes. As Christ sees of the travail of his soul, he is satisfied; for the joy set before him, *i.e.* in the salvation of men, he endured the cross. And all who owe salvation to what Jesus did and suffered for man must needs experience a thrill of gratification when a rebel is changed into a subject by the grace of God. 3. It springs from *the triumph of that cause which of all on earth is the greatest and most glorious.* Every noble soul finds satisfaction in witnessing the advance of truth from the dim dawn towards the full meridian day for which he, in common with all God's people in every age, is ever toiling, hoping, and praying.—T.

Ver. 7.—*Love and the conduct of life.* We are born into, and we live in the midst of, a system, vast and incomprehensible. Man is related to a thousand circumstances, and his moral life depends upon the principles which govern these relationships. It is by a sublime and spiritual intuition, itself an evidence of a Divine commission and apostolate, that St. Paul discerns the truth that love, when it takes possession of the

Christian's nature, relates him anew and aright to "all things," *i.e.* to the whole system in which he finds himself, and of which indeed he forms a part.

I. LOVE "CONCEALETH ALL THINGS." The word is one which, perhaps, cannot be confidently interpreted. But it may and probably does mean "conceal" or "cover." And so rendered, how appropriate is it in this place! What so characteristic of true charity as the habit of covering up and concealing the faults and infirmities of our brethren? It is a difficult exercise, especially to an acute and candid mind; but because we see an error it is not necessary to publish it. There may be good done and harm avoided by hiding good men's infirmities and the human defects which are to be found even in an excellent cause.

II. LOVE "BELIEVETH ALL THINGS." There is no point at which the wisdom of this world and the wisdom which is of God come more violently into conflict than here. To worldly men it seems the height of folly to proceed in human life upon the principle of believing all things. This is, in their view, credulity which will make a man the prey of knaves and impostors. Now, the words of the text must not be taken literally. They commend a disposition opposed to suspicion. A suspicious man is wretched himself, and he is universally distrusted and disliked. Where there is reason to distrust a person, even charity will distrust. But, on the other hand, charity cultivates that strain of nobleness in character which prefers to think well of others, and to give credit rather than to question and disbelieve.

III. LOVE "HOPETH ALL THINGS." Here again we have portrayed a feature of Christian character which it needs some spiritual discipline and culture to appreciate. A sanguine disposition is often distrusted, and not unjustly. But we may understand that temper of mind which leads us to hope good things of our fellow-men, and to view with confident expectation the progress of the truth over their nature.

IV. LOVE "ENDURETH ALL THINGS." This is to most men the hardest lesson of all. Many will cheerfully work from love, who find it no easy matter to suffer calumny, coldness, hatred, persecution, in a loving spirit and for Christ's sake. But we need the spirit of Divine charity to overlook all the assaults of men, and to pray for those who despitefully use us. This can and may be done when the whole nature is inspired with love to God and love to man.—T.

Ver. 8.—"*Love never faileth.*" Prophecies, tongues, knowledge,—these were all matters of immense importance in the Christian community at Corinth, whose members prided themselves upon their discernment, their intellectuality, their gifts. And they were not unimportant in the view of that one of the apostles whose mind was both more highly endowed by nature, and more sedulously and effectively disciplined by study, than was the case with his brethren. But let these excellent and beautiful things be brought into comparison with Christian love, and they vanish as the stars of night when the sun arises in his splendour and power.

I. THE CESSATION AND VANISHING OF INTELLECTUAL GIFTS. 1. What they were. They seem to have been supernatural gifts, highly prized by their possessors, and eagerly coveted by the members of the Christian societies generally. "Prophecy" was the faculty of uttering forth Divine truth. "Tongues" were supernatural utterances, probably of various kinds. "Knowledge" is here used in a special sense, equivalent to a peculiar spiritual illumination. Such were the gifts of which these Corinthians were wont to boast. 2. Why it is appointed that these gifts shall cease. Because they were bestowed to serve a temporary purpose, when the barque of Christianity had to be launched upon the sea of human society, when Christian doctrine needed a special introduction and a special authentication. There are certain parts of a plant which serve to protect it for a season, which disappear when the plant is mature. A scaffolding may be useful for a time; but when the building is completed, it has done its work, and is taken down and carried away. So with these gifts; good for a temporary purpose, they may be dispensed with when that purpose is attained.

II. THE UNFAILING LIFE OF LOVE. 1. Love is the special and permanent characteristic of the Christian economy. Observe its exemplification in such characters as the apostles Paul and John. And notice that whilst the special gifts referred to have passed away, charity remains the distinctive feature of the Church of Christ in all its varying circumstances and ministrations. 2. Love is permanent in the heavenly and eternal state. If faith shall then become trust without misgiving, and hope expectation without uncertainty, love shall then be adoration without coldness, affection without interruption. Love shall be supreme, and the great Centre of worship and adoration shall call forth all the affection of the countless host, whilst the members of that vast and glorious society shall find room for the infinite exercise of this peerless grace.

III. THE EXPLANATION OF THE SUPERIORITY AND SUPREMACY OF LOVE. 1. What calls it forth is permanent; there is no limit to the appeal for love made by the conscious universe and by its Lord. 2. What fosters and feeds it is permanent; there is no limit to the supply of the Spirit, the power, the grace, of God.—T.

Vers. 9, 10.—*The partial and the perfect.* Christianity is an intellectual religion as distinct from religions of ritual and ceremony. It is propagated and maintained by preaching and by teaching. It encourages inquiry, study, science. And, accordingly, there is some danger lest those who seize upon this characteristic of Christianity should give way to the temptation of spiritual pride. It is well that the infirmity and imperfection of our knowledge should be brought vividly before our minds, as it is in this passage. At the same time, provision is made against discouragement by an assurance that the partial and transitory shall be succeeded by the perfect and the eternal.

I. OUR APPREHENSION AND COMMUNICATION OF TRUTH IS PARTIAL. 1. This is a result of the limitation of our powers. This may be a doctrine humbling to human pride, but it is not to be disputed. It should be observed that the apostle speaks of himself as well as of private Christians; and from this we infer that revelation and inspiration are alike conditioned by the very limited powers of man. 2. It is a result of the limitation of our opportunities. We can only know what is brought before us; we cannot create truth. It pleases God that only glimpses and whisperings of Divine truth should be afforded to us. Our knowledge is therefore partial, as is the measure of truth which its Author sets before us. 3. It is a result of the brevity of our life. Human life is short as compared with the universe in which it is passed, and which has so many sides of contact with our understanding. And if nature cannot be known in all its fulness by even the most diligent student, how shall revelation be mastered in a lifetime? There is a religious side to every truth of fact, and the man of science, if a Christian, need never be at a loss for material for religious contemplation and emotion.

II. THAT WHICH IS PARTIAL IS DESTINED TO PERISH. It cannot be meant that any truth shall cease to be truth, that any aspect of religion once justified shall so change its character as to be disowned. We have known Christ, and such knowledge is not transitory, for it is eternal life. But special gifts, like the variety of prophecy known in the primitive Church, served their purpose, and were no more. Our systems of theology, our presentations of doctrine, our modes of homiletic, are adapted, more or less, to our age and circumstances, but they are only for a season. Partial knowledge may be useful whilst perfect knowledge is impossible; but only then.

III. FOR THE PERFECT SHALL COME TO ABOLISH THE PARTIAL. The star shall not disappear because lost in the dense black cloud, but because it shall melt in the splendour of the day. Our prospect is not one to inspire melancholy; or if a shade of pensiveness pass over the soul in the prospect of the disappearance of what is so familiar and so dear, that pensiveness may well give way to content and hope when we look forward to the glory which shall be revealed.—T.

Ver. 11.—*The babe and the man.* The half-informed and the immature in character are sometimes puffed up with conceit and pride; whilst humility often comes with a higher wisdom and a riper experience. The Corinthians were crude and unformed; the apostle was enlightened and inspired; yet they were puffed up with spiritual pride, whilst he was lowly in heart and free from arrogance. Hence this language, which is poetry and piety at once.

I. THE LITERAL FACT OF HUMAN NATURE AND LIFE. Childhood has its own speech, its prattle and babble; the babe utters inarticulate noises, the child speaks words, but with indistinctness and with many mistakes. Childhood has its own feelings, some of them very deep when inspired by trivial causes; feelings succeeding one another with rapidity in striking contrast. Childhood has its own thoughts, sometimes upon the most mysterious themes, always with little knowledge of the thoughts of others; thoughts unfounded, unjustifiable; thoughts, too, which may be developed into a larger and richer experience. Now, he who becomes a man puts aside these infantile ways. His language is articulate, perhaps elegant and precise, perhaps copious and poetical. His feelings are less easily roused, but they are deeper and more lasting. His thoughts range over heaven and earth, the past and the future; they "wander through eternity."

II. THE ANALOGY OF THE SPIRITUAL LIFE BASED ON THIS FACT. This the apostle suggests and leaves his readers to work out in detail. There is an obvious resemblance between the life of the individual upon earth and the larger, longer life of the soul. As is childhood to manhood, so is this present state of being to the immortality beyond. This being so, there is a measure of probability that the resemblance extends where we cannot follow it. This is the argument of analogy; alike in many points, alike probably in more. 1. The future will be a development and expansion of the present. The speech and the feeling, the thoughts and the judgments, of the man are based upon those of the child. They are not radically different. Even so our earthly faith and hope and love, our earthly consecration, obedience, and praise, are the germ of the experiences and services of the heavenly sanctuary. Heaven will witness the manhood of that intelligent piety, that devotion of heart and energy, of which earth has witnessed the infancy and childhood. 2. The future will immensely transcend the present. Great as is the difference between the acquirements of the child and those of the man, greater will be that between the religious knowledge and experience of earth, and what is reserved for us hereafter. It is vain for us to suppose that in this present state we can form any conception of the glorious future. We are now God's children, and we know not what we shall be. This we know: "We shall put away childish things."—T.

Ver. 12.—"*Face to face.*" He who looked into and, as it seemed, through the brazen disc saw a dim reflection of his own or his brother's features, or a misty representation of the landscape. But he who sees face to face sees, as by an immediate intuition, with nothing to hinder a perfect knowledge of perception. The comparison opens up to us a wonderful and most inspiring view of the perfection of the future, the heavenly state.

I. TRUE OF OUR KNOWLEDGE GENERALLY. The apostle speaks without any words limiting the application of his statement to religious realities. Man's pride of knowledge, notwithstanding his intellectual powers are limited in their range and in their efficacy. Some of the causes of this limitation we can see, and we can well believe that in another and higher state they may be removed. The senses or other avenues of perception may be multiplied in number and intensified in power. It may be that words—which are the medium of much of our knowledge—may be replaced by symbols more definite and instructive. Our feebleness of attention and application may be replaced by a vigour not possible in this body. Many things now known by inference may then be known by intuition. And whilst there may be a change in our own natural capacities and faculties, there may be also an enlargement of the material presented to our minds. And the search after truth may be more pure and disinterested as well as more vigorous. We are all aware that purity of heart is a condition of apprehending moral and spiritual truth; this condition will in heaven be perfected, and corresponding results may be expected.

II. TRUE ESPECIALLY OF WHAT MAY BE CALLED OUR RELIGIOUS KNOWLEDGE. 1. Of religious truth. This we now know sufficiently for all practical purposes; but we are often conscious that we see but glimpses and hear but whispers of the great truths upon which our higher life and deathless hopes depend. The progress made by the child as he advances to spiritual maturity is probably as nothing compared with the advance to be made by the Christian when the veil of sense and time falls off. The mysteries by which the mind has often been perplexed shall be revealed; the harmony of truths we could not reconcile shall be apparent; the reasons of regulations we could not understand shall become plain. The world, ourselves, society, life, all are now full of enigmas. Eternity shall provide the solution. 2. Of our knowledge of God in Christ. We do know Christ, and, notwithstanding the objections of philosophers, we have a real though very partial and inadequate knowledge of God himself;

for Christ said, " He who hath seen me hath seen the Father also." There have been special revelations of God to specially favoured members of the human family; but hereafter, the vision shall be open, it shall be for all the purified and glorified. " We shall see him as he is." " We shall know [God] even as we are known." Well is this called " the beatific vision : " to behold and know him who is infinite in nature, eternal in existence, perfect in all moral attributes.

III. TRUE ALSO OF OUR KNOWLEDGE OF OUR SPIRITUAL KINDRED AND BRETHREN. There are many circumstances which hinder us from enjoying more than a superficial acquaintance with some of our nearest kinsmen and our daily associates. But in heaven there shall be no disguise, no restraint, no separation. Misunderstandings shall vanish; we shall see " face to face." Imagination pictures, upon the suggestion of this principle, the fellowship of pure delight to be enjoyed with all " saints," in " the assembly and Church of the Firstborn, whose names are written in heaven."—T.

Ver. 12.—*Now, and then.* Divine knowledge is the truest riches of the intellect; Divine love, the dearest wealth of the heart. Love is greater than all gifts; greater than tongues and than prophecy, which shall pass away; greater even than knowledge, which here is but partial and progressive. How natural that St. Paul, whose mind was eager for knowledge, and whose life was so largely devoted to communicating it, should linger for a moment and think of knowledge such as it now is and such as it is destined hereafter to be!

I. THE PARTIAL KNOWLEDGE OF THIS PRESENT STATE. " We see as through a mirror, in an enigma." 1. *Earth is a mirror dimly reflecting God's attributes.* The glory, beauty, adaptations of nature, all speak of God. There is a reflection, and the wisdom, the power, the goodness, of the Creator may be recognized. Yet it is a dim reflection ; lightning, tempest, and earthquake, sickness, anguish, and death, perplex the mind of the reflective observer. There is no complete and adequate solution here. 2. *Life is a mirror dimly reflecting God's government.* No careful, observant mind can fail to trace an overruling Providence in human life, in the life of the individual, and in the life of the nation. Yet the reflection of a perfectly wise and righteous government, it must be admitted, is dim. We cannot always " justify the ways of God to men ; " the heart often sinks at the sight of prosperous wickedness, of the slow progress made by truth and righteousness. The kingdom of God seems near us ; but we ask, " Is it here ? " 3. *Revelation is a mirror dimly reflecting God's purposes.* There has been doubtless a progressive removal of the veil which hides God from us. Yet this revelation has been chiefly for practical purposes. We look into revelation to satisfy our inquiries concerning the Divine nature, concerning the eternal life, and there meets our view a dim manifestation. We see, but we see " in an enigma."

II. WHY THE FUTURE STATE IS ONE OF CLEARER, FULLER KNOWLEDGE. 1. *There may be a reason in ourselves.* Spiritual childhood will develop into manhood; the imperfections of the body, the infirmities of human nature, the prejudices of the earthly life, will disappear, and our vision will be purged. 2. *A reason in the character of our knowledge.* The processes here and now are slow, hesitating, inferential. Hereafter it would seem that we shall know by intuition much which now we learn mediately and with much liability to error. 3. *A reason in the manifestation itself.* More material will be offered to our faculties ; clearer light will beam upon us. In the vaster dominion then accessible, of which only a province is now within our reach, there will open up to the glorified as in a blaze, a sphere of Divine knowledge. 4. *A reason in the circumstances and the society of heaven.* Here opportunities are restricted ; there they will be illimitable. Here fellowship is imperfect; there the society of glorified saints and blessed angels will be fitted to stimulate and encourage the soul by sympathy with all its lofty quests and aspirations. 5. *A reason in the prolonged opportunity of eternity.* The reflection often forces itself upon us : " Art is long, and time is fleeting." There is no time for the dimness to pass off the mirror upon which, as we gaze, we breathe. Yonder infinite opportunity invites the ardent spirit to intermeddle with all knowledge ; we feel that we can but lose ourselves in a prospect so vast, illimitable, and glorious.

III. WHAT IT MAY BE EXPECTED WILL HEREAFTER BE CLEARLY KNOWN. 1. The past of our existence will then be seen in due perspective, and will be plain to the mind looking back upon it. 2. Light shall be cast upon the mysteries of earth and time. What has been perplexing and inexplicable when beheld so near at hand shall be clear and unmistakable as the appointment of Divine wisdom and love, when looked down upon from yonder heights. 3. Christ himself shall be then seen "as he is," so as even his dearest and most congenial friends cannot know him now. "Then face to face," to be "changed into the same image, from glory to glory."—T.

Ver. 13.—"*The greatest of these.*" Paul has often been called the apostle of faith, in distinction from John, the apostle of love. This declaration, therefore, coming from Paul is the more valuable. No doubt what he saw of the Corinthian Christians, who disputed much concerning gifts, natural and supernatural, made the apostle specially sensible of the supreme necessity of charity. What men *are*—their character—is of more importance than what they *have*—their abilities. Paul was not the man to disparage faith, which holds so high a place in his writings, nor hope, which was so prominent a feature of his character. But the higher the estimation in which he held these virtues, the loftier was the position to which he raised the grace of love when he pronounced it the greatest and the most enduring of all virtues.

I. BECAUSE OF ITS NATIVE SOURCE AND ORIGIN. God cannot exercise faith or cherish hope; but he not only has love, he *is* love. Our virtues are largely creature virtues; this is the great attribute of the Creator himself.

II. BECAUSE OF ITS SUPREME MANIFESTATION TO MANKIND IN THE PERSON AND WORK OF CHRIST. The Lord Jesus brought down the love of the Father to this world of ignorance, error, and sin. He revealed Divine love, which was indeed the motive of his advent, but which was also the prevailing and undeniable characteristic of his ministry, and the secret explanation of his willing and sacrificial death.

III. BECAUSE IT IS THE SPECIAL LAW OF THE LORD JESUS. His "new commandment" was this: "Love one another." And he made obedience to this commandment the great test of discipleship: "By this shall all men know that ye are my disciples, if ye have love one to another." What takes so pre-eminent a place in the mind of the Monarch, what stands so obviously supreme among his laws, must necessarily be regarded by his loyal subjects with an especial reverence.

IV. BECAUSE IT IS THE END TO WHICH THE OTHER VIRTUES ARE MEANS. Faith is not an end; it is faith in a Divine Deliverer and in his promise of salvation; it is the means towards life eternal. Hope is not an end; it is hope of final and eternal fellowship with God; it is the means to steadfastness and to heaven. But love is an end in itself. Charity is the bond of perfectness; beyond this even Christianity cannot carry us. As the grace of faith and the grace of hope realize their purpose when they produce the grace of Christian love, it is obvious that the virtue which is their final purpose is greater than they. And this conviction is confirmed when we consider that, of all virtues, love is usually the most difficult and the last to be acquired. There have been confessors and martyrs whose faith was firm and whose hope was bright, who yet did not arrive at the acme of perfect love. This is the test and the crown of spiritual maturity.

V. BECAUSE OF ITS SUPREME UTILITY. Society needs above all things to be penetrated with the spirit of charity, sympathy, and brotherly kindness. This is the radical cure for all its ills—this, and only this. What gravitation is in the physical realm, that is love in the moral. Without it, all is disorder and chaos; with it, all is regularity and beauty. It represses hatred, malice, envy, and uncharitableness; it cultivates considerateness, pity, gentleness, self-denial, and generous help.

VI. BECAUSE IT IS THE PECULIAR ELEMENT OF HEAVENLY BLESSEDNESS. Disputes have arisen as to whether or not faith and hope are found in heaven. But there is no difference of opinion as to the prevalence and eternity of the grace of love. For—

"Love is heaven, and heaven is love!"

T.

Vers. 1—3.—*Life without love.* I. THE APOSTLE DECLARES THE NOTHINGNESS OF LIFE WITHOUT LOVE. He supposes some extreme cases. 1. *The acquisition of all languages*; the utmost facility of expression; the most splendid eloquence. He does not even limit to humanity, but adds, "and of angels," to show that *no acquisition in this direction* at all meets the case. The Corinthian Church was peculiarly proud of its "gift of tongues;" its love was not so conspicuous. Our glorying is often false glorying. That which is most praised is not always the most praiseworthy. We are apt to prize most what we should prize least. To *talk* is not the chief thing; to *be* is far more important. Talking power without love is noise without music, sounding brass, clanging cymbals. Heavenly language would lose its heavenliness without the royal grace. 2. *The most extensive knowledge.* Knowledge of the future, human knowledge, knowledge of the secret purposes of the Most High. To *know* is not enough. If the knowledge of the head does not rightly affect the heart it is thrown away. Knowledge is a splendid weapon, but it is in dangerous hands if it is not in those of love. We may know Christ—know very much about his person, his character, his work—and yet not be his. "Many will say to me in that day, Lord, Lord, have we not prophesied in thy Name? . . . then will I profess unto them, I never knew you" (Matt. vii. 22, 23). Balaam, Caiaphas, and Judas are illustrations. 3. *Startling faith.* Judas wrought miracles; but how less than nothing, judged by true standards, was he! What profit if other mountains be removed and the mountain of selfishness be left! How sad to get so near the cross and to catch nothing of its spirit! Here is faith without the chief of works, which alone can prove its genuineness and power. Here is a faith which does not work by love, and is useless except for boast and display. 4. *Abounding charity.* The worth of charity lies not in *what* we give, but in *how* we give. The object for which the gift is bestowed does not determine its value; the motive prompting the gift does. We may give "all our goods," and that to "feed the poor," and yet perform no virtuous action. We can give lavishly from motives which rob our charity of all its charitableness. Men who give without love do not *give;* they *invest.* It is not a spiritual act; it is a *commercial speculation.* They invest and expect a large return—it may be of distinction or applause, or something similarly self-tending. 5. *Unlimited self-surrender.* Though the body be given to the flames, yet all may be "nothing." A man may go to the stake for Christianity, and yet know nothing truly of Christ. There is a self-sacrifice which is no self-sacrifice. Man has fallen so low that he has originated false and worthless martyrdoms. In later centuries the history of the Church was blotted by some who sought martyrdom from motives of notoriety and vain-glory. The martyr's crown may be sought by those who have not the martyr's spirit. The martyr is made, not by the burning of the body, but by the love which binds the truth to the heart, and will not let it go at any cost.

II. WHY IT IS THAT LIFE WITHOUT LOVE IS NOTHING. 1. Nothing can compensate for the moral quality. The motive is more than the deed. *To do* is nothing compared with *to be.* The internal is greater than the external. 2. Unless we have love we cannot be brought near to God. *God is love.* Love is of the Divine essence. If we are destitute of love we are destitute of that which is most conspicuous in God. When the great archangel fell he fell *out of* love. When we get power we *do not grow away from Satan,* nor when we get knowledge, nor when we do unusual deeds from selfish motives. When we get *love* we do. Love is never attributed to Satan; "love is *of God.*" As we have love, so far we are like God. Satan has power, knowledge, and is doubtless willing to sacrifice much to secure his own ends; if we have these, without love, we tend to grow *into devils.* Love is a redeeming, consecrating quality, which, pervading deeds, gives to them a new and God-like character.—H.

Vers. 4—7.—*Some characteristics of love.* The apostle gives a very beautiful description of some of the qualities of love. True love is—

I. PATIENT AND UNCOMPLAINING. It: 1. "Suffereth long," under provocation and injury. 2. "Is not easily provoked." Is not irritable—not allied to anger. 3. "Beareth all things." Is willing to bear burdens that others may be free. Rather hides than advertises injuries received. Does not revenge. 4. "Endureth all things." Neglect and persecution in a calm and Christian spirit.

II. KIND. Willing to perform good offices for others. Desires to be useful, obliging, helpful. Is kind after much suffering and ill usage. Is kind when showing mercy. Some show mercy *unkindly,* and utterly spoil the beauty of the deed.

III. HUMBLE. (Ver. 4.) Does not lead to vaunting, as the possession of supernatural gifts did amongst the Corinthians. Is not puffed up with pride, which is closely related to party zeal, as in those at Corinth who cried, "I am of Paul, and I of Apollos," etc. Does not seek to win praise or applause.

IV. UNSELFISH. "Seeketh not her own." Loses sight largely of self. The Corinthians cried, "I . . . I . . . I," because they had little love. Love is not filled with thoughts of her own rights; she thinks rather of the *rights of others*. "Envieth not." Is not jealous of the endowments of others; recognizes that "God hath set the members every one of them in the body, as it hath pleased him" (ch. xii. 18).

V. DECOROUS. (Ver. 5.) Keeps within the bounds of propriety; is courteous. Absence of love leads to gross disorders, as at the Lord's table at Corinth (ch. xi. 21, 22).

VI. CHARITABLE IN JUDGMENT. "Thinketh no evil." Does not delight to impute motives. Does not make the worst, but the best of things. Does not gloat over the evil done.

VII. PURE. "Rejoiceth not in iniquity [or, 'unrighteousness'], but rejoiceth with the truth" (ver. 6). Is not in sympathy with evil. Is not pleased to see it, but pained. When the truth triumphs, love rejoices.

VIII. TRUSTFUL. "Believeth all things" (ver. 7). Is not suspicious. Does not esteem *doubt* and *distrust* the chief virtues. Believes all that can with a good conscience be believed to the credit of others.

IX. HOPEFUL. "Hopeth all things" (ver. 7). Hopes when others without love have ceased to hope; is loth to regard any as hopeless. Hopes for good rather than for bad from men. Is not allied to despondency and despair. Is anchored in God and hopes on. Thus sweetly does the apostle chant the praises of true Christian love.—H.

Ver. 12.—*Now—then.* I. OUR PRESENT IGNORANCE. Our knowledge of Divine things (for these are here chiefly referred to) resembles that which we obtain of natural objects when we see them "through a glass," or rather "reflected in a mirror." And ancient mirrors, of which the apostle speaks, were by no means so perfect as modern ones. Made of imperfectly polished metal, they gave but a very defective representation of objects reflected. The imperfection of our present knowledge is thus strikingly illustrated. We see now "darkly," or "in an enigma," and the enigma often puzzles us not a little. Our present ignorance arises from: 1. *Imperfection in the mirror.* Though the Scripture be inspired of God, yet it reveals *plainly* only *necessary* truth. Other truth is set forth in figure or is barely hinted at. So that we do not find by any means in God's Word a solution of all mysteries. We see much in it—we may see *all that we need to see*; but it is still a book of mystery, a mirror which only partially reflects the great realities. Then *the mirror is often blurred.* (1) Defects and errors in translation if we read only in our mother tongue; and if we have the modern "gift of tongues," it is often difficult to determine the precise meaning of a word or passage. (2) Defects in exposition on the part of teachers. Other mirrors, such as nature and the course of human events, furnish us with knowledge of Divine things; but these mirrors, in the hands of men, and under the influences of evil, have become warped and misshapen, consequently the reflections are more or less distorted. We have further to reflect that no mirror could perfectly reflect what we desire to know. 2. *Imperfection in our vision.* We do not by any means see all that is reflected. Now dust is in our eyes, and now tears, and we see comparatively little. We have many ophthalmic disorders which impair our sight. 3. *Dimness of the light in which we live.* The haze of sin is around us; the atmosphere is darkened by evil; the beams of the Sun of Righteousness have to break through much fog. 4. *We move as we gaze.* Our life is rapid. We snatch hurried glances at things Divine. We do not see as much as we might see. The most of us might get longer seasons of quiet contemplation if we would. Not a few need to learn the wisdom of sacrificing the little for the great; alas! so many sacrifice the great for the little. We *must* do this and that and the other; and we never pause to ask the question—*Why must we?* It comes to this piece of folly—we must do the little and trivial; there is no need for us to do the great and the all-important! For these and other reasons our present condition is largely one of ignorance. Still we should be thankful (1) that we see something; (2) that we can see enough for life and duty.

II. Our future knowledge. Hereafter things will be changed. No longer shall we see in a mirror darkly, but "face to face." Our life will not then be a *study of reflections*. The atmosphere will then be purer. Our vision will be corrected and perfected. Earthly distractions will cease. Then remark how perfect our knowledge will be. *Our knowledge of truth will be like God's knowledge of us*: "Then shall I know even as also I am known." God sees us through and through, and is acquainted with all our ways; so hereafter shall we know those things which are now perplexing mysteries to us. The insoluble will then be solved, the contradictories reconciled. In our sphere then we shall be "perfect as our Father in heaven is perfect" (Matt. v. 48). We shall know God more truly; for "we shall see him as he is." Note: The path of piety is the path of knowledge. The promise of the solution of great mysteries is made to the godly. Part of the torment of the lost may consist in the distraction occasioned by mysteries which for them have no promise of solution. This is the cause of not a little suffering and sorrow here; it may be such a cause hereafter, and a more intense cause. Believers are sometimes ridiculed for credulity, fancifulness, indifference to "facts." But believers are on the way towards the very highest knowledge and the completest grasp, in all their significance, of the greatest facts of the universe. Now we are but children, and concerned with things which, in comparison with "things to come," are childish (though in the child and the childish things there are the true germs of what in fuller development belong to the man and manly things); hereafter we shall become men, and put away childish things (ver. 11).—H.

Ver. 13.—*The three graces.* These are faith, hope, love.
I. Their excellence. 1. *Faith.* Unites us to Christ; secures our forgiveness, justification, sanctification, final and complete redemption. It is the great power in our present life: "The just shall live by faith." 2. *Hope.* Brightens the present by brightening the future. In distress we have hope of deliverance; in sickness, of restoration or translation to the painless life; in sin, of holiness; in sorrow, of joy; in the world, of heaven. Without hope, how could we live? And the Christian's hope is the brightest and most joy-bringing conceivable. 3. *Love.* What a wilderness the world would be without love! Society would disintegrate; families would be wrecked; nations would fall. Love is the salt which checks the tendencies toward corruption. And love in its highest relation—love to God—elevates and purifies us, and brings to us the purest delights of which this life is capable.
II. Their continuance. "Now *abideth*." We may be devoutly thankful for this. Sometimes we are prone to regret that what we call the "extraordinary gifts" of the Church have ceased (ver. 8); but if *instead of losing these we had lost the others*, how infinitely impoverished we should have become! Faith, hope, love: these are sufficient for all our present needs. Miraculous gifts ceased because it was *best* for them to cease. They were suited to the infancy of the Church; but the necessity for them having passed away, they have disappeared. The spiritually miraculous gifts of faith, hope, and love abide evermore with the Church in this world.
III. The chief of the three. "The greatest of these is love." 1. *Longer continuance.* Hereafter faith will be lost in sight and the objects of present hope will be attained. Now "we walk by faith, not by sight" (2 Cor. v. 7). "Faith is the substance of [or, 'assurance of'] things hoped for" (Heb. xi. 1.) "We are saved by hope: but hope that is seen is not hope: for what a man seeth, why doth he yet hope for?" (Rom. viii. 24). As the special gifts of prophecy, miracles, and tongues disappeared when they would no longer have proved of service, so hope and faith will cease when their appointed task is finished, and love alone will reign on through the everlasting ages. Confidence in God will not cease, of course, nor the looking forward to further delights and Divine blessings; but these do not answer to the faith and hope which are ours in this world of darkness. Faith and hope mean to us, now, effort, struggle, difficulty; these things will "pass away." 2. *More useful to others.* Faith saves *us*; hope cheers *us*; love sends us out after our fellows. The former are chiefly self-tending; the latter is expansive. Still faith is the root of love, and our hope makes us more helpful, but love, pre-eminently and most directly, is concerned in the welfare of those around us. 3. *Makes us like God.* God is *not* faith; God is *not* hope: "God *is* love." As true love grows in us, God grows in us. When true love is impressed upon us, the Divine image is re-impressed (Gen. i. 26).—H.

Vers. 1—3.—*Charity puts the acceptableness on all gifts and works.* The Revised Version renders " charity " as " love." Explain " charity ; " distinguish from " almsgiving," and from the love that is connected with human relationships. If we could intelligently use the word " charity " to express God's love for us, we should be able to use it intelligently of the love which we have, as Christians, for each other, and of the love that must tone and temper the use of all Christian gifts. Charity is the considerateness and care for others which finds expression in self-denial for their welfare. Charity is the spirit in a man which leads him to put others before self. Our Lord's life on the earth was a life of charity ; love for men, longing for their highest good, and readiness to suffer, if by suffering he could do them good, are its characteristic features. *His* charity is commended to us. It has been said that the " English word 'charity' has never risen to the height of the apostle's argument." At best it does but signify a kindly interest in, and forbearance toward, others. It is far from suggesting the ardent, active, energetic principle which the apostle had in view. And though the English word " love " includes the affection which springs up between persons of different sexes, it is generally understood to denote only the higher and nobler forms of that affection, the lower being stigmatized under the name of " passion." Charity, then, is to be regarded as the tone and motive to which God looks ; things, actions, are accepted by him, not for their own sakes, but for the sake of the spirit and character for which they find expression. The one acceptable feature to God, in all human action and relationship, is *charity*, and this the apostle illustrates by his panegyric on love.

I. MAN'S ACCEPTANCE OF GIFTS AND WORKS ACCORDING TO THEIR APPEARANCE. " Man looketh on the outward appearance, but the Lord looketh on the heart." Only in a very imperfect way can we estimate the motives of others. Our attention is occupied by incidents, and we form our impressions from the things actually done. Consequently our estimates are always incomplete and often unworthy ; we misconceive what is really great and what is really little, and give our acceptance and our praise to things which will not endure the Divine searching. Of men who stand high in the esteem of their fellow-men for their excellent talents and their good-looking works, it must in truth be said, " Thou art weighed in the balances, and found wanting." " Thy heart is not right in the sight of God."

II. GOD'S ACCEPTANCE OF GIFTS AND WORKS ACCORDING TO THE SPIRIT AND THE MOTIVE WHICH UNDERLIE THE APPEARANCE. That motive God knows and judges perfectly. To him it is the real man. The appearance, the action, never deceives him. Man's show of virtue is fitly estimated. Upon God's estimate there are " many first who shall be last, and many last who shall be first." To true hearts it should come as an abounding satisfaction that while our fellow-men may misconceive us, God never does. He " knoweth us altogether." And we can confidently appeal from the judgment of men to the judgment of God.

III. THE CHRISTIAN DUTY OF GAINING FULL DELIVERANCE FROM THE MAN STANDARD OF LIFE, AND UPLIFTING TO THE DIVINE STANDARD. Growing likeness to God—which is the Christian sanctifying—should involve our seeing things as God sees them, and judging and appraising them on God's principles and in God's ways. Illustrate this subject by the apostolic references to the gift of tongues ; from the gift of prophecy ; from the apparent fervour often seen on religious lives that are not deeply toned ; from cases of mere generosity of natural disposition ; and even from cases of martyr-endurance which may be mere bravado, and not, to the heart-searching One, humble, fervent loyalty and love.—R. T.

Vers. 4—8.—*The grace of charity.* When we speak of charity (ἀγάπη) it is in the sense attached to the word in the New Testament. We do not speak of promiscuous and impulsive almsgiving, in which there is often but the veriest morsel of charity, and which, in our condition of society, is almost an unmitigated evil, tending as it does to the maintenance of an indigent and pauperized class. We do not speak of that kind of natural affection (ἔρος) which binds men together with the ties of family and friendship. Charity, as a grace of the gospel, is altogether larger and more comprehensive than these things. It is first the love of the whole human race, as being the objects of the love of God, our common Father, and the redeemed of his mercy. Then it is this spirit of love, ever seeking for us, and ever finding expression in, acts of generous kindness, thoughtfulness, and good will. In its larger, nobler meaning, charity is something peculiarly Christian ; something that springs up only in that soul which has felt the love of God in its own redemption.

I. CHARITY IS THE GREATEST OF GRACES IN THE WIDTH OF ITS SPHERE. Other graces have particular things with which they are more intimately concerned; special parts of our life on which they throw the light of their charm; special times in which they operate. But charity covers the whole life and relationships of the Christian ; his inner thoughts, his uttered feelings, his conduct and intercourse, the associations of the family and society, and also his relations with the dependent, the poor, and the suffering. Look at some of the spheres thus irradiated with the golden light of charity. 1. *The sphere of a brother's opinions.* "Believeth all things." Many find it easy to be charitable towards their brethren in almost everything except their opinions. Think of the bitternesses, separations, and conflicts arising from differences of political opinion, from differences of denominational opinion, from differences of theological opinion. In these matters what a sad worldful of uncharity we have to mourn over. We cannot, indeed, with the utmost stretch of charity, receive all opinions; it is impossible to delude ourselves into the acceptance of all forms of doctrine, as though all may be true. Not in that sense does charity enable us to "believe all things." Charity is a grace exercised concerning *persons* holding opinions, not concerning opinions separated from the persons holding them. The religious questionings which agitate the hearts of our fellow-men are altogether too solemn, the yearnings of the human heart everywhere after the standard of righteousness, the pardon of sin, the peace of God, and light beyond the grave, are altogether too serious and anxious, to permit us to speak of any one—of the Catholic, or the Unitarian, or the Hindoo, or the Mohammedan, or the island savage—save in terms of deepest and most sincere sympathy. 2. *The sphere of a brother's failings.* "Beareth all things." How ready we are to push right down a brother who has begun to slip! What strong things we say about the faintings and errors of others! How loudly we talk about the imperfections in the character and conduct of others! How easily we forget our own "beams," and, with malicious delight, swell out the "motes" in our brothers' eyes! Charity teaches us to say nothing at all about our brother if we cannot say something good. 3. *The sphere of a brother's sorrows.* "Seeketh not her own." Perhaps we may call this the principal sphere of charity, as it is certainly the easiest. There is so much of natural feeling to help us in this case, while in other cases our natural feelings may be opposed to our charities. What a peculiarly earthly and human sphere of charity this is ! There are no sufferers lying on sick-beds for us to tend in heaven ; no hungry ones for us to feed ; no imprisoned ones for us to visit ; no naked ones for us to clothe. Perhaps the exercises of charity in the midst of worldly sorrows are intended to prepare us for the yet higher charities of the eternal world. Charity finds so extensive a sphere for its present operations because so little of human sorrow is simple, so often it is complicated—complicated by peculiarly distressing circumstances, complicated by poverty, by mental anguish, etc. For sorrows pure and simple there may be no more needed than sympathy ; for sorrow complicated with other kinds of trouble there is needed charity, which takes up sympathy into itself, and goes on to express itself in generous gifts and kindly deeds. 4. *The sphere of a brother's sins.* "Rejoiceth not in iniquity." If charity towards a suffering brother is the easiest effort, charity towards a sinning brother is the hardest. It is very hard to be charitable towards one who has sinned, when the sin touches *others* rather than ourselves. It is the Divine triumph to be charitable when the wrong is done to ourselves.

II. CHARITY IS THE GREATEST OF THE GRACES BECAUSE OF THE DIFFICULTY WITH WHICH IT IS ATTAINED. It is so difficult because of the separating influence of *sin*. Sin broke up the fellowship of the human family, and filled the world with opposing interests. Charity has to heal up these great wounds, and temper these opposing relations, and make the human family one again. Charity cannot be won by any of us save as the issue of a constant, earnest struggle. Charity is only the final result of a day-by-day endeavour to think charitably of others, and act charitably towards them in their opinions, their failings, their sorrows, and their sins.—R. T.

Ver. 12.—*The nature of the future knowledge.* "Then shall I know even as also

I am known." Better read, "I was known," *i.e.* known or apprehended of Christ. St. Paul's thought appears to be that soul-culture brings the true, full knowledge and power. A man knows only in the measure of the progress of the work of Divine grace in him; and what we may call perfect knowledge can only come when we are ourselves morally perfected, wholly sanctified, through the grace that is in Christ Jesus. Two points claim consideration.

I. THE NATURE AND LIMITATIONS OF MAN'S PRESENT KNOWLEDGE. It is dependent on our senses. Show that this means that our knowledge is limited to the spheres with which our senses stand related. Even transcendent and so-called supernatural things cannot be conceived until set under sensible forms and figures. We can only transcend nature by the help of nature. The senses limit even the imagination. It may be shown that God's world is set ready for just the creatures he has put in it; and if any other than the sensible world is to be opened to us, we must be changed, renewed, regenerated, and so new sensibilities and capacities must be given and developed. Illustrate that the world of science is the proper sphere for men who have only senses and intellect. It is a vast sphere, a wonderful sphere, but only a limited sphere; and since researches or observations within it are dependent on the frailty of the instruments used, no absolute truth of science can ever be obtained. Illustrate from the observations of astronomers. No conclusion can be affirmed with absolute certainty because the disturbing conditions of the atmosphere can never be perfectly estimated in connection with any experiment. Then add to this frailty of the senses the influence of sin on man when his attention is directed to moral questions. No man can hope, of himself, to attain the perfect moral truth. Illustrate from the sadly mixed systems of all the great classical or modern moralists, and plead that the key to all truth is the vision of God which comes with the soul's conversion and regeneration. Here on earth a man knows nothing aright until he knows God, as manifested in the person of his Son.

II. THE NATURE AND LIMITATIONS OF MAN'S FUTURE KNOWLEDGE. It will not be imprisoned in sense forms or figures. It will come by soul-faculties, of which our bodily senses are but suggestive types. It will come out of new spheres and new relations. It will take new thought-forms. It will replace observation by insight, so it will need no verification. It will bear relation to moral character, and not to intellectual endowments. It will be the apprehension men may gain, when the blinding influence of sin and self-love are wholly passed away, and spiritual insight has no clouds or veils to pierce through. But man's future knowledge, however wonderful it may be, must still be limited, for ever it can but be the knowledge of a created being. He can never know God, never know more than God may be pleased to reveal of himself and of his ways.—R. T.

Ver. 13.—*The immortality of all graces.* "Now *abideth* faith, hope, charity, these three." The word "abideth" is significant, as applied to each of the three great graces. While so much must "pass away," why may faith, hope, and charity be said to abide? Because they are the dress of souls, not of bodies. They are things belonging to character, not merely to conduct. Souls pass through into new spheres of existence, taking with them all that is peculiar to them. We shall step into the eternal world with just the clothing of character—the garments of faith, love, and hope—which we had put on our spirit in our mortal sphere. More or less distinctly we all have an idea that faith and hope are powers peculiar to our present mortal and earthly condition. We think we shall no longer need them when we have reached to heaven. We think that only love, charity, will go with us there. Yet can it be that we shall ever get past "faith"? Is "sight" anything more than another and a higher form of "faith"? Shall we ever lose "hope"? As long as we remain creatures, not creators, we shall surely have to believe and hope and love.

I. THE IMMORTALITY OF LOVE. We may infer this from the abiding character of love in this life. All kinds of love tend to abide; they even strive to increase and grow. Life may greatly change with us, multiplied sorrows may come to us, but there are some who love us, whose love keeps on, and can neither change nor pass. True mother-love abideth. True wifely love abideth. True friendship-love abideth. We go out into the eternal world with such love folded like holy robes about our spirits.

And that kind of love which we call Christian love—charity—has the same power of abiding. Let it but be gained in the early days of our Christian life, and it will stay and grow, widening and adorning the Christian spirit down to its time of passing through. If love thus abides in Christian life, can it be possible that death, which is but the servant of Christ—Christ's hall-porter or gate-keeper—should be able to master it, overcome it, and finish it? But we may further argue the immortality of love from every view of the heavenly state that is presented to us, and every conception we can form of it. It is the place of union; the uniting bond must be love. It is a home; the one sanctifying power in a home is love. It is the place where God is all in all, and "God is love." Those whom God teaches to love he teaches to love for ever.

II. THE IMMORTALITY OF FAITH. What is the proper idea of faith? It is the relation in which we ought to stand to things above us, higher than we are. It is our "evidence of things not seen." As long as there is anybody in the world wiser than ourselves, we shall have to *believe* what they say. Get the very wisest man that ever lived on earth, if there is in heaven one spirit wiser than he, he will have to believe— to take on trust—what the wiser spirit may say. And the holiest archangel must believe what the all-wise God may say. Change them as we may, know as we are known, grow with giant strides as the eternal hours pass by, still we can never overtake or outgrow God. As long as we are creatures we shall be, in knowledge as well as in power, below our Creator. While we keep our being we shall have to believe—we shall have to trust. If we have the true spirit wrought in us, we shall never want to get beyond faith. For the creature it is the highest blessedness that he is found willing to trust. To wish to see is to rebel. It is to wish to be God, and take the place of God. Enough for us to be for ever the children of God, and it is a very foolish child who wants to get beyond trust. Heaven is so beautiful, because we shall there be children at home for ever; perfected in faith, in childlike trust, and safe in the protection and the shadow of the eternal Father. We are learning to believe by the experiences of our human lives, but it would be a sad thing if we were only learning something which we should lose when we came to die, even if we exchanged it for something better. Of this we may rest assured, that in learning to trust we are learning for the heavenly and immortal spheres.

III. THE IMMORTALITY OF HOPE. In this life hope seems to change, but in reality it abides, only changing its objects. The old man hopes quite as truly as the young man, though not with the same passionate intensity. The change into the eternal spheres is more evident to the senses, but it is not more real, than the change from the boy to the man; surely in his second, glorified, manhood man will keep his power of hoping, only setting it on new and higher and eternal things. If we are still to grow in the eternal world, we must have something ever before us and above us to hope for. If we know that we may become wiser, truer, stronger, holier than we are, we cannot keep from hoping that we may become such. And heaven cannot possibly be a mere stereotyping of the sanctifyings wrought through our Christian life on earth. In seeking, then, for faith, hope, and charity, we are seeking the heavenly treasures, the things that are abiding and eternal. They are the "treasure in the heavens, which faileth not."—R. T.

EXPOSITION.

CHAPTER XIV.

Vers. 1—25.—*The gift of preaching superior to the gift of tongues.*

Ver. 1.—**Follow after charity**; literally, *chase; pursue.* The word is one of which St. Paul is fond (Rom. ix. 30, 31; xiii. 13; xiv. 19; Phil. iii. 12, 14; 1 Tim. vi. 11, etc.). **And desire**; rather, *yet be zealous for.* **But rather that ye may prophesy**; *and yet more strive after the gift of sacred preaching.*

Ver. 2.—**In an unknown tongue.** The interpolation of the word "unknown" in

our Authorized Version is quite unjustifiable, and shows the danger of giving way to the bias of mere conjectures. Probably it is this word, not found in the original, which has given rise to the perplexing, unhistoric, and unwarranted theory that "the gift of tongues" was a power of speaking in foreign languages. **Speaketh not unto men.** Because, as a rule, no one understands anything that he says. The word literally means "hears." It may, perhaps, imply that no special attention was given to those who gave way to these impulses of utterance. The whole of this chapter proves in a most striking way the close analogy between "the tongue" and the impassioned soliloquies of inarticulate utterance which were poured forth in tones of thrilling power among the Montanists, and in modern times among the Irvingites. **In the spirit.** It is uncertain whether this means "in his own spirit," or "in the Spirit of God," *i.e.* as a result of inspiration. Probably the former (John iv. 24; Rom. viii. 13, etc.). Perhaps, however, the two imply the same thing. The spirit is the one Divine part of our human being, and when a man is a true Christian his spirit is in union with, is as it were lost in, the Spirit of God. St. Paul recognizes the true tongue—for it might be *simulated* by hysteria and even by mere physical imposture—as a result of inspiration, that is, of the overpowering dominance of the human spirit by a supernatural power. Nevertheless, he points out the extreme peril of yielding to or self-inducing these emotions public, or in leaving them uncontrolled. **Mysteries.** Secrets revealed possibly to him, but unrevealed by this strange "tongue" to others.

Ver. 3.—To **edification, and exhortation, and comfort.** The "to" should be omitted. His words build up the Christian soul, by rousing its efforts and consoling its sorrows. The "Son of prophecy" (Barnabas) is, as Stanley points out, also "a Son of consolation" (Acts iv. 36). "Support" (*paraklesis*) involves "comfort," *i.e.* strength and calm.

Ver. 4.—**Edifieth himself.** When the "tongue" was genuine, and under due control (ver. 32); when it avoided the physical and orgiastic manifestations by which a sort of spiritual possession was indicated in the ancient oracular shrines; when the self-consciousness was not wholly obliterated,—a sense of ennobling conviction would be produced by this spiritual outpouring. Those who have experienced the emotion describe this very result. They felt enlarged and elevated—their whole being was for a time expanded—by this emotion. **The Church.** Primarily the body of assembled Christians which he is addressing, and through them the Church of God in general.

Ver. 5.—**I would that ye all spake with tongues.** The language of *relative* disparagement which St. Paul uses throughout these chapters may lead us to regard this with surprise. Yet it is perfectly intelligible. Montanus truly said that each human spirit is like a harp, which the Holy Spirit strikes as with a *plectrum*, and which yields itself to the mighty hand by which the chords are swept. We have seen all along—and history has in various ages confirmed the impression, on every occasion when these phenomena have been reproduced in seasons of great spiritual revival—that the external *symptoms*

may be imitated with most dangerous and objectionable results both to the speaker and to others. But when the expression is *genuine*, the fact that the tides of the Spirit can thus sweep through the narrow channels of individuality is in itself a sign that the spirit of the man is alive and not dead; and thus he is an evidence of God's power both to himself and to others. Those who have heard "the tongue" have told me that its force, melody, and penetrative quality produced an impression not to be forgotten. When we see the stuffed and stopped-up hearts and lives of thousands of frivolous and worldly money-worshippers, we might well echo St. Paul's wish. **Greater.** Not of necessity greater absolutely or morally, but greater in the fact of his wider and deeper usefulness. **Except he interpret.** From this we infer that sometimes, when the passion had spent its force, the speaker in the tongue could give rational explanation of the thoughts and feelings to which he had given ecstatic utterance.

Ver. 6.—**Except I shall speak to you either by revelation, or by knowledge, or by prophesying, or by doctrine?** My "tongue" will be useless to you unless I also speak to you of what I know by *revelation*, or by my *thoughtful study*, which may take the form of *preaching* or of *teaching* (ch. xii. 28).

Ver. 7.—**Even things without life giving sound.** Even musical instruments—flute or harp—dead instruments as they are, must be so played as to keep up the distinction of intervals, without which the melody is ruined and the tune is unrecognizable. Much more is this the case with the human voice.

"How sour sweet music is,
When time is broke and no proportion kept!"

The indiscriminate use of the tongue is here compared to the dissonance of jarring and unmodulated instrumental sounds. In harmony there must be due sequence and intervals of sound.

Ver. 8.—**If the trumpet give an uncertain sound.** A spiritual exhortation should be like the "blowing of a trumpet in Zion;" but if, as in "the tongue," the trumpet only gave forth an unintelligible blare, its sounds were useless.

Ver. 9.—**Words easy to be understood;** rather, *distinguishable speech.* **Ye shall speak;** rather, *ye shall be* (all the time) *speaking.* **Into the air.** Mere pulses of useless inarticulate breath, spoken *ins Blaue hinein.* Philo has the word *aeromuthos,* one who speaks to the wind.

Ver. 10.—**It may be.** A mere expression of uncertainty as to the exact number (comp. ch. xv. 37). It is one of the very few instances where even the verb which implies "chance" is recognized. The word "chance" itself (τυχή) does not occur in the New Testament. **So many kinds of voices.** This does not seem to mean "so many languages." The Jews always asserted that the languages of the world were seventy in number. It seems to mean "classes of expressive sounds." **None of them is without signification.** The words rendered "without signification," literally mean *dumb.* The meaning must either be that "nothing—no creature—is dumb," or that "every class of sounds has its own distinct meaning."

Ver. 11.—**A barbarian;** in other words, *unintelligible,* according to the definition of the word by Ovid—

"Barbarus hic ego sum, quiâ non intelligor ulli."

Unto me; rather, *in my eyes.*

Ver. 12.—**Even so ye.** A general form of conclusion from the previous remarks. **Of spiritual gifts**; literally, *since ye are zealots of spirits.* **That ye may excel to the edifying of the Church**; rather, *seek them to the edifying of the Church, that ye may abound.* The same word is used in Matt. v. 20 ("exceed"); ch. viii. 8 ("are we the better").

Ver. 13.—**Pray that he may interpret;** either, *so pray as to be able to interpret,* or, *pray with the object of afterwards interpreting.* The meaning, "pray to have the power of interpretation given him," seems excluded by the next verse.

Ver. 14.—**My understanding is unfruitful.** I am only aware that I *am* praying. I have no definite consciousness as to what I say.

Ver. 15.—**What is it then?** A phrase like the Latin *quorsum hæc?* What is the purport of my exhortations? **I will sing.** This shows that the glossolaly sometimes took the form of singing. **With the understanding also.** When we worship or sing we must indeed "worship in spirit," but also worship and "sing praises with understanding" (Ps. xlvii. 7; John. iv. 24).

Ver. 16.—**That occupieth the room of the unlearned;** that is, "one in the position of an ordinary worshipper, who has no spiritual gifts." An *idiotes* is a private person; one who does not possess the skill or the knowledge which is immediately in question. **Say Amen;** rather, *say the Amen.* The custom of ratifying prayer and praises with the "Amen" of hearty assent and participation existed in the Jewish (Deut. xxvii. 15. Neh. v. 13; Rev. v. 14; Philo, 'Fragm.,' p. 630) as well as in the Christian Church (Justin Martyr, 'Apol.,' ii. 97). The sound of the loud unanimous "Amen" of early Christian congregations is compared to the echo of distant thunder.

"Et resonaturum ferit aethera vocibus Amen."

Being the answer of the congregation, the "Amen" was regarded as no less important than the prayer itself.

Ver. 17.—**Well.** It is good and honourable for thee to utter the voice of Eucharist; but if this be done in the unintelligible tongue, what does the Church profit? **The other.** The "layman" or "ungifted person."

Ver. 18.—**I speak with tongues;** rather, *with a tongue.* **More than ye all.** This is exactly what we should expect of the emotional, impassioned nature of St. Paul, who was so wholly under the influence of the Spirit of God. But it is clear from all that he has been saying that, while the personal and evidential value of this gift of yielding his whole being to the spiritual impulse, which expressed and relieved itself by inarticulate utterance, was such as to make him "thank God" that he possessed it, he must either have exercised it only in private gatherings or must have always accompanied it by interpretation.

Ver. 19.—**Yet in the Church.** In any public assembly of Christians. **Five words.** No disparagement of the prominence given to glossolaly could be more emphatic. "Rather half of ten of the edifying sort than a thousand times ten of the other" (Besser). **That . . . I might [may] teach others also.** The word rendered "teach" is rather *instruct,* the root of our "catechize" (Luke i. 4; Rom. ii. 8; Gal. vi. 6, etc.).

Ver. 20.—**Be not children in understanding;** rather, *in your minds.* Your tendency to overvalue glossolaly shows you to be somewhat childish. It is remarkable that this is the only verse of the New Testament in which the common Greek word "mind" (*phrēn*) occurs. **Howbeit in malice be ye children;** better, *but in wickedness be babes.* The Authorized Version misses the climax involved in the change of the word. The Christian should always be childlike (Matt. xi. 25; xix. 4), but never childish (ch. xiii. 11; Eph. iv. 14). **Be men;** rather, *become* or *prove yourselves full-grown;* literally, *perfect.*

Ver. 21.—**In the Law.** The quotation is from Isa. xxviii. 11, 12, but the term "the Law" was applied generally to the Old Testament, as in John x. 34; xii. 34; xv. 25; Rom. iii. 19). **With men of other tongues,** etc. The application of this Old Testament quotation furnishes one of the many singular instances of quotation which prove that the Jews often referred to the *words* without any direct reference to their context or original meaning. He here wishes to show that glossolaly had little or no value except as an evidence to unbelievers, and illustrates this by Isa. xxviii. **11, 12.** Now, in that passage Isaiah tells the drunken priests, who scornfully imitated his style, that, since they derided God's message so delivered to them, God would address them in a very different way by the Assyrians, whose language they did not understand; and that even to *this* stern lesson, taught them by people of alien tongue, they would remain deaf. In the original, therefore, there is not the least allusion to any phenomenon resembling the "gift of tongues." But the mere *words* of a scriptural passage always came to Jews with all the force of an argument, independently of their primary meaning; and it was enough for St. Paul's purpose that in Isaiah the allusion is to unintelligible utterance, and to the fact that the teaching which it was meant to convey would be in vain. **And other lips.** St. Paul does not quote the LXX. The Hebrew has "with stammerings of lips and another tongue will he speak" (comp. Deut. xxviii. 49).

Ver. 22.—**Wherefore.** In accordance with this illustration. **Not to them that believe.** ·Because *their* belief depends on other and far deeper grounds. Serveth. This word is wrongly supplied; it should be, *is for a sign.* **Not for them that believe not.** Because there is nothing necessarily startling in preaching. It might, indeed, produce conviction in the unbelieving (ver. 25), but it was not a special "sign." "The unbelieving" are those who used to drop in at the Christian services out of curiosity.

Ver. 23.—**All speak with tongues.** He does not necessarily mean that all are speaking *at once*; though, amid these strange scenes of self-asserting enthusiasm, even that was not wholly impossible; but he means, "if there be nothing going on except glossolaly." **Will they not say that ye·are mad?** This has often been the actual impression produced by these phenomena upon those who stand aloof from the spiritual influences which cause them. On the day of Pentecost the exaltation of the disciples caused mockers to charge them with drunken exhilaration (Acts ii. 13).

Ver. 24.—**All prophesy.** If one after another speak the word of spiritual exhortation. **He is convinced of all, he is judged of all**; literally, *he is being convicted by all, he is being examined by all*; in other words, each address is calculated to awaken conviction in him and to search his heart. Thus the address of St. Peter pierced the consciences of his hearers, when the glossolaly even of Pentecost produced no effect beyond that of irreverent wonder (Acts ii. 37). It is easy to see that the style and method of worship in the assemblies of Christians at this early epoch resembled

that now prevalent among Quakers. The teaching was not left to recognized pastors, but any Christian might speak who had gifts which moved him to address his brethren. The externals of worship are of no eternal signifiance, but are best left to be moulded by the requirements of time and place, with reference to the teachings of past experience. No doubt St. Paul's depreciation of glossolaly led to its rapid disappearance when it had done its work of being "a sign to unbelievers." But if ancient modes of worship were too independent of rigid conditions, modern modes are, on the other hand, too stereotyped and inelastic.

Ver. 25.—**The secrets of his heart.** "The Word of God is quick and powerful, and sharper than any two-edged sword, . . . *and is a discerner of the thoughts and intents of the heart*" (Heb. iv. 12). **Falling down on his face.** An Oriental, mode of showing humility and deep conviction (Isa. xlv. 14 ; 1 Sam. xix. 24). It does not furnish the shadow of an excuse for the encouragement of catalepsy by the mechanical excitement of revivalism. **That God is in you of a truth.** St. Paul is probably thinking both of Isa. xlv. 14 and Zech. viii. 23, where similar phrases are used.

> " Truth from his lips prevailed with double sway,
> *And fools, who came to scoff, remained to pray.*"
>
> (Goldsmith.)

Vers. 26—33.—*Rules to check disorderly self-assertion in Christian assemblies.*

Ver. 26.—**How is it then?** The same phrase as in ver. 15. **Every one of you hath a psalm**, etc. We see here a somewhat melancholy picture of the struggling self-assertion of rival claimants to attention. **A doctrine**; rather, *a teaching*, The glossolaly had probably been promoted by Syrian enthusiasts, perhaps of the Petrine party; the egotism of oratory and itch of teaching now described (Jas. iii. 1) may have been developed in the Apollonian party. **Unto edifying.** The object is moral improvement, not idle self-display, not the ostentation of individual gifts (ch. xii. 7, 8, 10). To this he recurs again and again (ch. iii. 9; xiv. 3, 5, 12; 2 Cor. v. 1; x. 8; xi. 19; xiii. 10; and the verb frequently). The substantive, as used by St. Paul, only occurs again in Romans (xiv. 19; xv. 2), and in Ephesians (ii. 21, etc.).

Ver. 27.—**And that by course**; rather, *and that in turn.* He does not allow more than one glossolalist to speak at a time, and not more than three at the most in any one service. This rule alone tended to extinguish the disorderly exhibition of "tongues." To control the passion which **leads to it is,** sooner or later, to stop the manifestation—a result which St. Paul would probably have been the last to regret, when its purpose had been accomplished.

Ver. 28.—**Let him keep silence.** The "him" refers to the glossolalist, not to the interpreter. **To himself.** In his private devotions (as St. Paul himself seems to have done); not in the public assembly.

Ver. 29.—**Two or three.** If more than two or three preached, the congregation would get weary. **Let the other judge**; rather, *let the rest discriminate* the value of what is said. "Prophesyings" are not to be despised, but we are only to hold fast what is good (1 Thess. v. 20, 21), and we are "to try the spirits" (1 John iv. 1). St. Paul is not encouraging the Corinthians to the censoriousness of conceited and incompetent criticism, but only putting them on their guard against implicit acceptance of all they hear; which was a very necessary caution at a place where so many teachers sprang up.

Ver. 30.—**Let the first hold his peace.** It would be easy enough to judge whether the revelation vouchsafed to his neighbour was more pressing and important than his own address.

Ver. 31.—**Ye may all prophesy**; rather, *ye all can*; that is, "if you have the gift of prophesying." St. Paul has already implied that at every assembly there would be *idiotai*, unendowed worshippers, who only came to profit by the gifts of others, and that "all" are not prophets (ch. xii. 29). **May be comforted**; rather, *may be exhorted* or *cheered.*

Ver. 32.—**And the spirits of the prophets are subject to the prophets.** Into this golden aphorism St. Paul compresses the whole force of his reasoning. The articles are better omitted: "Spirits of prophets are under the control of prophets." Mantic inspirations, the violent possession which threw sibyls and priestesses into contortions—the foaming lip and streaming hair and glazed or glaring eye—have no place in the self-controlling dignity of Christian inspiration. Even *Jewish* prophets, in the paroxysm of emotion, might lie naked on the ground and rave (1 Sam. xix. 24); but the genuine inspiration in Christian ages never obliterates the self-consciousness or overpowers the reason. It abhors the hysteria and simulation and frenzy which have sometimes disgraced revivalism and filled lunatic asylums.

Ver. 33.—**Of confusion.** The word is rendered "commotion" in Luke xxi. 9; "tumult," in 2 Cor. vi. 5 and xii. 20. "Confusion" is, as St. James says (iii. 16), the result of envious and pushing egotism. **But of peace**; which cannot coexist with inflation and restlessness. **As in all Churches of the saints.** The clause probably belongs to this verse, not to the following. It is a reflection on the exceptional turbulence and disorder which disgraced the Corinthian Church.

Vers. 34, 35.—*Rules about the public teaching by women.*

Ver. 34.—**Let your women keep silence in the Churches.** St. Paul evidently meant this to be a general rule, and one which ought to be normally observed; for he repeats it in 1 Tim. ii. 11, 12. At the same time, it is fair to interpret it as a rule made with special reference to time and circumstances, and obviously admitting of exceptions in both dispensations (Judg. iv. 4; 2 Kings xxii. 14; Neh. vi. 14; Luke ii. 36; Acts ii. 17; xxi. 9), as is perhaps tacitly implied in ch. xi. 5. **But . . . to be under obedience** (Eph. v. 22; Col. ii. 18; Titus ii. 5; 1 Pet. iii. 1). Christianity emancipated women, but did not place them on an equality with men. **As also saith the Law** (Gen. iii. 16; Numb. xxx. 3—12).

Ver. 35.—**Let them ask their husbands.** Here again St. Paul is dealing with general rules.

Vers. 36—40.—*Appeal and summary.*

Ver. 36.—**What?** An indignant exclamation. **Came the word of God out from you?** Are you the authors of the Christian system, that you are to lay down rules about it? No rebuke was too strong for the pretensions of these Corinthians. **Or came it unto you only?** Is no one to be considered but yourselves? Have you no respect for Christian custom? and that when you were by no means the first Gentile Church in Europe (1 Thess. i. 8)?

Ver. 37.—**If any man think himself to be a prophet.** Test your pretensions by the capacity to recognize that I have been speaking to you what Christ approves and requires (comp. 1 John iv. 6). **Or spiritual.** He has already said that to most of them he could only speak as carnal (ch. iii. 1).

Ver. 38.—**Let him be ignorant.** The formula seems to fall under the idiom which refuses to say anything more about a subject ("If I perish, I perish;" "What I have written, I have written;" "He that is filthy, let him be filthy still," etc.). The readings vary considerably ("He is ignored;" "He has been ignored;" "He shall be ignored;" "Let him be ignored"). These other readings would be a statement of retribution in kind—of God "sprinkling penal blindnesses on forbidden lusts." But the reading of our translation is on the whole the best supported, and means that to invincible bigotry and ignorant obstinacy St. Paul will have no more to say (Matt. xv. 14; 1 Tim. vi. 3—5).

Ver. 39.—**Wherefore.** The final conclusion. **Covet . . . forbid not.** The power to preach is to be desired; all that can be said of glossolaly is that it is not to be absolutely forbidden so long as the conditions which St. Paul has laid down for its regulation are observed. But glossolaly is hardly possible under conditions of order, decorum, and self-suppression, and we are not surprised that we hear no more of it in the Church, but only in the wild excitement of fanatical sects. The suppression, however, of the startling manifestation by no means necessarily involves any enfeeblement of the inspiring conviction from which it sprang. The brawling torrent which "foams its madness off" is lost in the calm and majestic flow of the deep river.

Ver. 40.—**Let all things.** The "but" of the original should not be omitted. It is a final caution against the abuse of the permission accorded in the last clause. **Decently;** that is, "with decorum." Thus Milton uses the term—

". . . and held
Before his *decent* steps a silver wand."

In Rom. xiii. 13 and 1 Thess. iv. 12 it is translated "honestly," *i.e.* honourably. **In order.** Time, proportion, regulation, self-suppression, are as necessary in worship as in "the music of men's lives."

HOMILETICS.

Vers. 1—28, 34—40.—*Grace and gifts.* "Follow after charity," etc. There are many separate verses in this chapter implying or suggesting thoughts capable of being wrought out into sermonic sketches, but my purpose now is to take a homiletical glance at the whole. The following general propositions will bring all the parts into a logical connection :—

I. THE GRACE OF CHARITY IS SUPERIOR TO ALL ENDOWMENTS. I say "charity," for I prefer the word to the word "love," which the New Version gives as the substitute. "Charity" implies the highest forms of love—compassion, sympathy, benevolence. "Follow after charity, and desire spiritual gifts." Whatever other endowments you may possess or desire, do not neglect the cultivation of charity. The remarks of the illustrious F. W. Robertson are so admirable on this point that I transcribe them here. In showing the difference between a grace and a gift, he says, "A grace does not differ from a gift in this, that the former is from God and the latter from nature. As a creative power, there is no such thing as nature; all is God's. A grace is that which has in it some moral quality, whereas a gift does not necessarily share in this. Charity implies a certain character, but a gift, as for instance that of tongues, does not. A man may be fluent, learned, skilful, and be a good man ; likewise, another may have the same powers, and yet be a bad man—proud, mean, or obstinate. Now, this distinction explains at once why graces are preferable. Graces are what the man *is* : but enumerate his gifts, and you will only know what he *has*. He *is* loving; he *has* eloquence, or medical skill, or legal knowledge, or the gift of acquiring languages, or that of healing. You only have to cut out his tongue or to impair his memory, and the gift is gone. But, on the contrary, you must destroy his very being, change him into another man, and obliterate his identity, before he ceases to be a loving man. Therefore you may contemplate the gift separate from the man, and, whilst you admire it, you may despise him. As many a gifted man is contemptible through being a slave to low vices or to his own high gifts. But you cannot contemplate the grace separate from the man—he is lovable or admirable according as he has charity, faith, or self-control. And hence the apostle bids the Corinthians undervalue gifts in comparison with graces. 'Follow after charity.' But as to gifts, they are not ourselves, but our accidents, like property, ancestors, birth, or position in the world. But hence, also, on the other hand, arises the reason of our due admiration of gifts : 'Desire spiritual gifts.' Many religious persons go into the contrary extreme : they call gifts dangerous, ignore them, sneer at them, and say they are of the world. No, says the apostle, 'desire' them, look them in the face as goods ; not the highest goods, but still desirable, like wealth or health. Only remember, you are not wealthy or good because of them. And remember, other people are not bound to honour you for them. Admire a Napoleon's genius, do not despise it, but do not let your admiration of that induce you to give honour to the man. Let there be no mere hero-worship, that false modern spirit which recognizes the force that is in a man as the only thing worthy of homage. The subject of this chapter is, not the principle on which graces are preferable as gifts, but the principle on which one gift is preferable to another : ' Rather that ye may prophesy.' Now, the principle of this preference is very briefly stated. Of gifts, Paul prefers those which are useful to those that are showy. The gift of prophecy was useful to others, whilst that of tongues was only a luxury for self. The principle of this preference is stated generally in the twelfth verse : 'Even so ye, forasmuch as ye are zealous of spiritual gifts, seek that ye may excel to the edifying of the Church.'"

II. Some endowments are superior to others. In the fifth verse the apostle says, " Greater is he that prophesieth than he that speaketh with tongues." In this chapter it is taught that the *didactic* faculty is greater than the *linguistic*. Sense is better than sound, ideas are better than words. Ideas are the seed of character and the soul of history. Of all classes of ideas, religious ideas, ideas in relation to God, are the most salutary and sublime. A man may pronounce " sun," " universe," " God," in fifty different languages, and he is not necessarily richer in ideas concerning these than the man who can only speak them in his own vernacular. It often happens that the man who has the most aptitude in acquiring languages, and the most fluency in pronouncing them, has the least capacity either for attaining or communicating great ideas. But the language of which the apostle is here speaking seems to have been of a very peculiar sort—an unintelligible vocal utterance. It was, perhaps, the inarticulate voice of new and strong emotions—an *emotional language*. It is not *necessary* to consider this gift as miraculous. We are so constituted that when there rises up in our souls a strong rush of tender emotions, we feel utterly incapable to put them into words. Sometimes they choke us. If expressed at all, they can only be in the quivering lip and the gleaming eye and the convulsive chest. No stranger or stronger emotions can enter a man's soul than those which Christianity awakens when it first takes possession of him. The groans, the sighs, the rapturous shouts, cannot be interpreted. Albeit they are a " gift," a gift of a high type, inasmuch as they are the expression of the most priceless states of soul. Such have been manifested in all great revivals of religion. In my younger days I have heard such untranslatable sounds under the mighty sermons of grand old Welsh preachers. The words imply that these " tongues," unintelligible vocal sounds, are valuable. " I would that ye all spake with tongues, but rather that ye prophesied." They are valuable : 1. *Because they are symptomatic of a new spiritual life.* You can talk about the facts of history, the principles of science, and the doctrines of theology, but not about the deepest and divinest things of the heart. They only come out in " groanings that cannot be uttered." 2. *Because in them the soul expresses its devotions.* " If I pray in an unknown tongue, my spirit prayeth, but my understanding is unfruitful." It is delightful to think of the human soul, generally so immersed in the selfish and the sensuous, bathing itself in the rising tides of spiritual emotions. 3. *Because by them the religious sympathy of the unbelieving is often excited.* " Wherefore tongues are for a sign, not to them that believe, but to them that believe not." Sounds expressive of human emotion often strike potently on the heart of the listener. The emotions of others, revealed either in sounds or " signs," groans, sighs, or tears, seldom fail to strike the deepest chords in the hearts of others. Take the most thoughtless man into some vast congregation in Wales, when all the people are singing their plaintive hymns in strains of weird music, and he will not be long, even if he understands not the language, before he feels the influence. Deep emotion often speaks in the " unknown tongue." Unsyllabled speech is often the mightiest. There are melodies that carry into the soul that which no word can express.

III. The highest endowment is the ability for spiritual teaching. " Even so ye, forasmuch as ye are zealous of spiritual gifts, seek that ye may excel to the edifying of the Church." " I thank my God, I speak with tongues more than ye all." What do I mean by " teaching " ? Not the mere impartation of the facts of the gospel, but rather the indoctrinating of the soul with its primary elements and spirit—taking the spirit of the truth out of the letter and transfusing it into the souls of men. On this subject the apostle's language suggests three remarks. 1. *That the gospel gives to its genuine disciples intelligent convictions that should be communicated to others.* This is certainly implied in the words, " Forasmuch as ye are zealous of spiritual gifts, seek that ye may excel to the edifying of the Church." He who has accepted the gospel in reality becomes instinct with mighty and irrepressible ideas—ideas which he " cannot but speak," for " necessity is laid " upon him to do so. They are given to him to communicate, not to monopolize, and on their communication the spiritual life, growth, and perfection of mankind depend. Paul assumes in the whole of these verses, not only that the members of the Corinthian Church *ought* to do so, but that they *did* so. " How is it then, brethren? when ye come together, every one of you hath a psalm, hath a doctrine, hath a tongue, hath a revelation, hath an interpretation. Let all things be done unto edifying." 2. *That these intelligent convictions can only be conveyed to others by intelligible language.* " Now, brethren, if I come unto you speaking with tongues, what shall I profit you, except I shall speak to you either by revelation, or by knowledge, or by prophesying, or by doctrine ? " The apostle proceeds to say that mere " sound " is not worth much. " Things without life," such as the " pipe " and the " harp," produce sound. Nay, more, unless the sound gives out clear and distinct ideas, it is not only useless, but injurious. " If the trumpet give an uncertain sound, who shall prepare himself to the battle? " If in battle the trumpet does not sound clearly the " advance " or " retreat " when intended, it is worse than useless. " So likewise ye, except ye utter by the tongue words easy to be understood, how shall it be known what is spoken ? for ye shall speak into the air." Whatever might be the *unintelligible utterances*, whether an unvernacular language or the unsyllabled expressions of emotion, he indicates their inadequacy without interpretation to convey to the hearer intelligent convictions of gospel truth. 3. *That the use of a language which the listener cannot understand should not be indulged in.* (1) Not in public devotion. " For if I pray in an unknown tongue, my spirit prayeth, but my understanding is unfruitful," etc. (vers. 14—16). Unintelligible utterances in public devotion fail to excite in the assembly a spirit of united worship. " How," in such a case, " shall he that occupieth the room of the unlearned say Amen at thy giving of thanks, seeing he understandeth not what thou sayest ? " So far as the individual himself is concerned, it does not matter with what tongue he speaks, or whether he speaks at all. " For thou verily givest thanks well, but the other is not edified." (2) Not in public ministration. Alas ! it is to be feared the language of many a sermon is an " unknown tongue "—to illiterate audiences, many syllabled, strangely compounded, high-sounding, technical language. Such language gratifies the vanity of the speaker, but wastes the time and tires the patience of the hearer. " I thank my God, I speak with tongues more than ye all : yet in the Church I had rather speak five words with my understanding, that by my voice I might teach others also, than ten thousand words in an unknown tongue." The apostle goes on to indicate that such unintelligible utterances in the Church are : (*a*) Childish. " Brethren, be not children in understanding : howbeit in malice be ye children, but in understanding be men." They who prize such utterances are infants in knowledge. (*b*) Useless. " In the Law it is written, With men of other tongues and other lips will I speak unto this people." As if the apostle had said, " Remember, there was a time in Jewish history when unintelligible language was a sign sent by God, but it proved unavailing so far as concerned the conversion of Israel." (*c*) Confounding. " If therefore the whole Church be come together into one place, and all speak with tongues, and there come in those that are unlearned, or unbelievers, will they not say that ye are mad ? " (*d*) To be of any service, they must be interpreted. " If there be no interpreter, let him keep silence in the Church; and let him speak to himself, and to God."

Vers. 29—33.—*Paul's idea of the Christian Church in assembly.* " Let the prophets speak two or three, and let the other judge," etc. From these words we may infer that Paul considered—

I. That the Christian Church in assembly, on the SAME OCCASION, MIGHT HAVE SEVERAL SPEAKERS TO ADDRESS THEM. " Let the prophets [or, ' teachers '] speak two or three." " For ye may all prophesy one by one." If this be so : 1. Should Christian teaching be regarded as a *profession ?* It is so now : men are brought up to it, trained for it, and live by it, as architects, lawyers, doctors. Surely preaching the gospel should no more be regarded as a profession than the talk of loving parents to their children. 2. Is the Church justified in confining its attention to the *ministry of one man ?* In most modern congregations there are some Christian men who, by natural ability, by experimental knowledge and inspiration, are far more qualified to instruct and comfort the people than their professional and stated minister. Surely official preaching has no authority, either in Scripture, reason, or experience, and it must come to an end sooner or later. Every Christian man should be a preacher. Were the half-hour allotted in Church services for the sermon to be occupied by three or four Christly men, thoughtful and reverent, with the capability of expression withal, it would not only be far more interesting, but more profitably spent than now.

II. That the Christian Church in assembly might ALLOW ONE OF ITS GODLY MEN TO RISE AND SPEAK ON THE INSPIRATION OF THE MOMENT. "If anything be revealed to another that sitteth by, let the first hold his peace." This does not mean, I presume, that the one who is speaking is to be interrupted, but that after he has delivered his message another, if he felt truly inspired to do so, might rise and address the audience. May it not be that under every discourse there might be some one or more in the audience so divinely excited with a rush of holy thought, that he craves for an utterance, not for his own sake, but for the sake of others; and why should he not have the opportunity? What an interest such an event would add to a religious service!

III. That the Christian Church in assembly SHOULD SUBMIT THE UTTERANCES OF ITS TEACHERS TO A DEVOUT CRITICAL JUDGMENT. "Let the other judge," or, as the New Version has it, "Let the others discern [or, 'discriminate ']." The people were not to accept as a matter of course all that the prophets or teachers spake to them; for even were they inspired, they were not infallible. They were to act as it is said the Bereans did, who "searched the Scriptures daily whether those things were so." Ah me! if congregations were so to act, there would soon come an end to the crudities, the assumptions, and the dogmas of modern pulpits.

IV. That the Christian Church in assembly SHOULD IN ALL ITS SERVICES MAINTAIN ORDER. "And the spirits of the prophets are subject to the prophets. For God is not the author of confusion, but of peace, as in all Churches of the saints." It is a characteristic of a true teacher that, however full of inspiration, he can so master his impulses as to prevent confusion. This should always be done, "for God is not the author of confusion, but of peace." Notwithstanding all the liberty of teaching, all the enthusiasm of the new life, where Christianity reigns there will be no disorder; all will be peace. There is an order in dead mechanism, and there is order, too, in the roar of ocean and in the thunderstorm. All that is Divine is under law.

HOMILIES BY VARIOUS AUTHORS.

Vers. 1—5.—*Love controls zeal in behalf of spiritual gifts.* In the opening verse we have three ideas, viz. love as a virtue to be diligently sought and practised, spiritual gifts as objects worthy of desire, and prophesying as a gift among gifts to be especially prized. "Rather that ye may prophesy" is the formative thought of this chapter, and it must be kept in view by the reader, since it is explicit or implicit in every associated idea. But this leading thought is closely connected with the twelfth and thirteenth chapters, and this also must be considered by the reader. To understand the reasoning of the apostle in the fourteenth chapter and sympathize with the fervour of his exhortation in the "rather that ye may prophesy," remember that he is contemplating prophecy from the standpoint of love. How else, forsooth, could he regard it, either in the logic as bearing on intellect, or in the appeal as applied to experience, or in their united effect on Christian character? Prophecy, in the light here presented, is not simply a revelation of God's will and wisdom to others, but likewise a revelation of love as a conscious influence pervading, inspiring, controlling the soul of the prophet or teacher. It is a voice from God himself by the Spirit. It is a Divine voice, moreover, in tones and accents most truly, most thoroughly, human, because of tender sympathy with the needs of its fellow-men and their dependence on it for guidance, help, furtherance, in the salvation of their souls. One of the aspects of love as the "greatest" instantly comes before the eye. Prophecy, in the case of the man so gifted, is an organ of his love, so that he teaches, not to enjoy the activity and brilliance of his intellect, or make in any way a demonstration of himself, but solely to benefit his fellows. Actuated wholly by brotherly sentiment, he comes down from the pedestal of complacent self-regard, and values his endowment in the degree that he is able to take the common level, and thereby instruct and console his brethren. Why, then, should the argument in this chapter follow the eulogy on love so closely? One reason —the chief reason—we may suppose to be that the gift of "tongues" was overvalued, and, as a consequence, the capacity to teach was depreciated. Without disparaging the "tongues" when rightly used, St. Paul lays a very proper stress on teaching, and gives it the preference, on the ground that it allows a fuller, freer, more effective manifestation of love. " Now abideth faith, hope, love, these three; but the greatest of these is love." And so, too, now abide the "spiritual gifts," the gifts in general, "tongues" and "prophecy" in particular, but the "greatest of these" is "prophecy." The parallelism is complete. And how easily St. Paul glides from the chapter on love as the greatest among virtues to the chapter on teaching as the greatest among gifts! One would have supposed that, after such an effort of analytic and descriptive intellect and its interblending with emotional outgoings, there would be a rebound, a pause for nature to recover from an intense exertion; but this is not apparent. The strong man is still strong, the eye beams as brightly and the hand moves as firmly as before, and the eulogist of love passes into the eulogist of prophecy with no change other than that which the nature of the new topic necessitates. The argument in ver. 2 takes an antithetic form. There is speaking in an unknown tongue. The speech is not a communication of wisdom to others, but a mysterious activity that exalts the speaker above the ordinary sphere of self-consciousness and is ecstatic. "No man understandeth him." There is the outward hearing on man's part, but no inward hearing. God is the only listener who comprehends him: "He speaketh . . . unto God;" "In the spirit he speaketh mysteries." The mysteries are things "which are hidden from the hearers, and sometimes also from the speaker himself" (Alford). Was language a sublimer function than we have comprehended? Are there uses of expressional power of which we know nothing? Are there utterances of intuition beyond our power to grasp? Is there some one vast generalization of speech as interiorily related to pure reason, under which, as fragmentary forms of embodied thought and as representations of the functional energies of the mental faculties, all the utilities of speech are classified? We cannot tell. 1. All we know is that the speaker here under notice speaks from his "spirit;" intellect, emotion, the entire nature, are simultaneously excited. Barriers between the faculties are broken down; speech is no longer merely philosophic, or poetic, or impassioned, but it is in some occult way the articulation of the spirit in its wholeness. No man ever said anything that he could look upon as the complete expression of himself. Before he utters his greatest thoughts, he is very hopeful of doing full justice to them; afterwards he is half abashed, deplores his shortcoming, and gazes with a feeling somewhat reproachful on the ideal that retreated afar. Now, in the instance St. Paul has in view, the speaker is under the perfected sway of his spirit, and he transcends the limits of habitual consciousness. 2. All we know is that this exceptional speaker utters "mysteries." And the "mysteries," out of whose deep solitudes the voice comes, remain mysteries; neither word nor tone, neither look nor gesture, gives any solution of the meaning. The secrets have taken on sound, but the sense is concealed, and the very sound is a deeper silence. And has not such silence its uses? Is it a mere image to the fancy that Milton gives when he so finely personifies Silence in paradise as pleased with the song of the "wakeful nightingale"? Or when Thomson breathes the invocation: "Come, then, expressive Silence, muse his praise"? And, in the present case, the sound falls back into silence, but, nevertheless, the "unknown tongue" is among "spiritual gifts," and fills its sphere in the spiritual economy of Christ's universe. What, then, is the object of St. Paul's argument? It is a question of comparative worth that he discusses. These Corinthians are fascinated by the "tongues," and, in their passion for high excitements, have been led to exaggerate beyond bounds the ecstatic singularity of the "unknown tongue." This unhappy craving for morbid and tumultuous agitation, this delight in sensations and emotions, threatened the decay, ay, the destruction of spirituality. It was the spirit of man, indeed, but the spirit borrowing the impulses of the lower man, instead of holding itself aloof from a depraving alliance with ungoverned blood and nerves. The remedy of the evil was in a proper estimate of the gifts as relative to brotherhood and helpfulness of others. Therefore, "desire . . . rather that ye may prophesy." And wherefore? That ye may "speak unto men" with three ends in view, namely, *edification, exhortation, comfort.* To edify is to build up the whole framework of Christian character; to exhort is to incite to duty by timely, appropriate, and effectual motives; to comfort is to show tenderness of fellow-feeling and be partners of the cares, burdens, and sorrows of others. What a blessed prerogative, to go forth from the isolations of intellect and from the selfish exclusiveness that our own anxieties and sufferings not infrequently bind upon us, and impart ourselves in large sympathies to such as in their weakness need our strength! "Himself;" there the benefit lies. Lifted to a lofty height, borne upward from one sublimity to another, rapt and entranced, it is still *himself* that is the party concerned. There may be quickening and ennobling; the immense realm within the soul, where the surprises of possible consciousness are dormant, may suddenly yield their resources and give the soul a new and astonishing sense of itself; yet, despite of all such results, it is *himself,* first and last. But he "that prophesieth edifieth the Church." A community gets the benefit, not the mere man "himself." Is St. Paul depreciating the speaking with tongues? Hear his hearty wish: "I would that ye all spake with tongues." In perfect consistency with this testimony to the worth of the tongues, he adds that he desires for them more ardently the gift of prophecy. Why this more fervent wish? Because the prophet or teacher is *greater* than the speaker with tongues not interpreted —*greater* because he builds up and inspirits and cheers his brethren more than the mystical speaker with "an unknown tongue;" *greater* because "it is more blessed to give than to receive."—L.

Vers. 6—13.—*Argument continued and illustrated.* Greater is the teacher than the speaker in a tongue not interpreted, was the statement of the apostle in the fifth verse. Suppose, then, that even he were to address these Corinthians "with tongues;" would not the edification be confined to himself? There would be no exception in his case, none in his favour as the apostle of the Gentiles, and hence his usefulness, no matter what he might say, would be at an end, for lack of interpretation. "What shall I profit you?" The profit is only possible by means of doctrine and knowledge. Tongues unexplained convey no doctrine and knowledge, and hence, as relative to the hearers, are nugatory. For instance, there are musical instruments, "pipe or harp," that have a language in the broad sense of the word, and convey their meanings if skilfully used. The instrument in the hands of an intelligent performer, though in itself "without life," yet receives life as it were from him who knows how to handle it. A dead thing, yet his breath or his touch imparts a representative vitality to its sounds, and you hear in those sounds the sentiments and emotions of the soul. What a range they have, rising and falling by turns, exulting, sorrowing, shouting, wailing! To effect this, there must be "a distinction in the sounds;" the instrument must obey its laws, and the laws are dictated by the art of music. And he argues further, that a trumpet in battle can give such discriminating sounds as to direct the movements of soldiers. The commanding officer, though distant, speaks to the trumpeter, and the trumpeter conveys the order through the trumpet. A thing "without life," and yet it outreaches the compass of the living voice and is fully understood, for it gives no "uncertain sound." Musical instruments are interpreters. Their utility exists in their intelligible modulations. If it were otherwise, they would but confuse and bewilder. The comparison is promptly applied. "So likewise ye," with all your admiration for "tongues" and your disposition to give them pre-eminence among the gifts, are indulging in a wild and incoherent display, unless you "utter by the tongue words easy to be understood." *Words* are not sufficient; they must be *words easy to be understood.* The capacity of the hearer, the humblest in the congregation, must be thoughtfully regarded, otherwise they are to him idle rhapsodies; "ye shall speak into the air." If neither "pipe," nor "harp," nor "trumpet" give an "uncertain sound," still less could it be said of human voices (languages) that they are unintelligible. "Many kinds are in the world, and none of them without signification." Varieties exist. The surface of the globe is not more diversified than language, and yet, as the globe is one, so are these languages one, although very unequal as to capacity for the conveyance of ideas. But is the "tongue" like these voices? If not, then he that speaketh in this way is a barbarian; and would you barbarians in your Christian relations, outside foreigners, you and your fellow-citizens in the commonwealth of Christ shut out from intelligible communication with one another? We can see, while reading St. Paul's argument, what force it contains. Pentecost had restored what Babel had destroyed; the ambitious tower that was to reach so high had been arrested by confusion of tongues; men had scattered from one great centre, and human centralization had been stopped in the evil form threatened. Pentecost had enabled men to co-operate; all languages could now be used as vehicles of making known the gospel, and the builders could work together on the temple of the Church. Pentecost, however, was here annulled, and Corinth was making ready to scatter her Christian population, to alienate them from community of impulse and aim, and changing the members of the Church in this respect into barbarians to one another. "Even so ye," declares the apostle, who are "zealous of spiritual gifts," should esteem it your first concern to edify the Church. "Wherefore," he adds in application, let the speaker in an unknown tongue "pray that he may interpret." Whatever construction may be given this difficult passage, it is certain that St. Paul intended to teach the Corinthians the absolute insulation of this sort of speech, its essential characteristic as opposed to the true function of language, and the complete exclusion of its possessor from the fellowship of the outward world.—L.

Vers. 14—22.—*Further enforcement of the argument.* At this point in the discussion St. Paul refers to the distinction between the spirit and the understanding. Such a distinction must be recognized or his argument has no basis in the nature of the human mind, and, if there be no foundation in the laws of the mind for this difference between Spirit and understanding, the operations of the Holy Spirit in the two forms under notice are inconceivable. Man has a spirit—a power of introversion that withdraws itself from the avenues of outward activity; a capacity of absorption in its own thoughts and feelings as self-related; a susceptibility to receive Divine influence as an experience restricted to its own intuitions and making the man himself the supreme object. Man, too, has an understanding, and its functions are to connect him with other men. But is there an impassable gulf between the two? Certainly not; the spirit may co-operate with the understanding. Left to its own ecstatic freedom, the spirit may soar and shine, but the flight is in loneliness and the resplendency unwitnessed. In this condition the body indicates occult activities that we do not comprehend, and its physiological expressions are, in a certain sense, "unknown tongues." On the other hand, this state may be translated from the *unknown* into the *known* by means of the understanding, and thus the latter, which was previously "unfruitful," becomes fruitful of thought and emotion in others. Prayer and praise will thus be mutual to spirit and understanding in the original party. No longer will these be dissevered forces, but coalescent for the common good, and the "unlearned" can intelligibly say, "Amen." What is worship without this true "Amen"? Response there must be; heart must go up to God with heart; and the glad "Amen" will be the assurance of this beautiful mutuality. The value of this single word cannot be measured. What a history it has! Far back in Hebrew life, when the psalms gave voice and sentiment to the thanksgiving of the nation; further back yet, when Israel wandered in the desert; in the land of promise, in the lands of captivity; heard in the acknowledgment of chastening and in the celebrations of returning light and hope; temple and synagogue, homes and booths, war and peace, repeating its loud echoes; and descending through the Christian ages with a deeper and more touching import, and everywhere an utterance precious to faith and sympathy, whether in lowly kirk or magnificent cathedral;—what a past this word preserves! "True or faithful," how could its meaning but survive in the long struggle of truth and fidelity for triumph in the world? And what honour comes to it when Christ himself is represented in the Apocalypse as the "*Amen*, the faithful and true Witness"! No marvel, then, that St. Paul felt the thrill of this "Amen" when he said that, though he spoke "with tongues more than ye all," yet he would "rather speak five words" with his understanding, and so teach others, than "ten thousand words in an unknown tongue." No higher estimate than this was ever put on practical wisdom. The best and profoundest utilitarian is the man who advocates utility on this high ground. St. Paul argued so warmly in behalf of the "understanding" because he felt so deeply the glory of the human "spirit." Hence the exhortation: "Brethren . . . in understanding be men," and this manliness is enforced by an appeal to Jewish history (Isa. xxviii. 11), wherein is seen the threatened judgment of Jehovah on those who despised the simplicity and truthfulness of Old Testament teaching. Then comes the significant "wherefore," followed by two ideas: (1) the tongues are a "*sign*" from God, and meant for unbelievers who have not hearkened to his words; and (2) prophesying or teaching was a sign to believers, a token of blessing, an earnest for the future, a proof of God's interest in them; a sign in the one case of impending evil, in the other of good in immediate realization and good in future store. Would he not rather preach a gospel to belief than to unbelief? a gospel to hope in preference to apprehension? a gospel of exceeding great and precious promises, instead of a gospel of exceeding great and awful threatenings? "Five words" to enlighten, cheer, inspire, the heart of belief and love outweighed "ten thousand" addressed as a rebuke and a warning to men who had willed not to hearken to God's voice.—L.

Vers. 23—32.—*How a spectator would regard the tongues; the gracious effects of prophesying; interpretation or silence.* Suppose that the whole Church were to assemble in one place (argues the apostle), and all "speak with tongues;" the unchecked energy pouring itself forth in many and discordant volumes, each speaker borne away on the mighty tide of his own transport; no one considerate of another; the ear scarcely cognizant of the sound issuing from the lips, the eye insensible to the impression made on a beholder;—suppose such a state of things occurring in the Corinthian Church, and, amid the disorder and commotion, the "unlearned" (those unacquainted with the meaning of the exhibition) or the "unbelievers" (such as were not converted to Christianity) were to make their appearance and look upon the scene; would they not think them "mad"? Instantly he reverses the supposition. The work of teaching is in progress, and the Church is receiving the doctrines, duties, consolations, of the gospel in appropriate methods of instruction. A person, who is unlearned or unbelieving, enters the assembly. He hears, is able to understand, is "convinced of all" and "judged of all." The word reaches his inmost consciousness, and he is revealed to himself. Perception, reflection, self-scrutiny, judgment, conscience, are aroused by the Holy Spirit, and for the first time, perchance, he listens to the voice of his own instincts in the articulations of others. It is usually through some mediating soul that God makes us known to ourselves. In our darkness the light is reflected as that of the moon on the night, and the sunrise and the day follow afterwards. And, in this case, the unlearned or unbeliever has the "secrets of his heart made manifest." The throne of judgment is set within; the hour is calm and meditative; the man is brought to the bar; and the ministering servants of the eternal Judge are here with their testimony. Most of all, the Divine Agent is here, of whom Jesus Christ said, "He shall testify of me." Step by step the trial advances. Memory speaks from the past, fear speaks of the future. The sense of guilt is awakened, "and so falling down on his face," overpowered by his convictions, "he will worship God, and report that God is in you of a truth." How is this? In the one case, there is an impression of madmen; in the other, God is felt to be with these men. In the former, religion was an unintelligible thing; in the latter, it was comprehensible. Recall the power of the "five words" spoken to the understanding, *versus* the "ten thousand" uttered in rhapsody, and the secret is explained. What, then, is the practical inference? "If, when you are met together, one is prepared to sing a hymn of praise, another to exercise his gift of teaching, another his gift of tongues, another to deliver a revelation, another an interpretation" (Conybeare and Howson); shall any of God's gifts be suppressed or discarded? Room for all, need for all, blessings for all, blessings in all, exist; and none must be suffered to fall into desuetude or cast away as useless. Let each have time and opportunity, subject to one inflexible condition: "Let all things be done unto edifying." *Edify* has had emphasis after emphasis in the conduct of the argument, and surely the Corinthians can be at no loss to understand its meaning. But St. Paul will particularize. Edification allows the use of tongues. Edification requires, however, that the tongues be used in order and under strict propriety. The order and propriety are specified: "If there be any who speak in tongues, let not more than two, or at the most three, speak (in the same assembly); and let them speak in turn; and let the same interpreter explain the words of all" (Conybeare and Howson). How important the interpreter was is obvious, for he says, "If there be no interpreter," let him who speaks in tongues "keep silence in the Church." Will this destroy his devotional spirit? Nay; he may still commune silently with himself and with God. Prophets may also "speak two or three," but edification holds them likewise under rule. "Let the others judge." Inspired teachers were amenable to the Church in the persons of those who possessed the gift of discernment as a specialty from the Holy Ghost. Furthermore, edification demands, that if the Spirit suddenly and powerfully act on "another that sitteth by," let the latter be heard. "One by one;" this is the method of edification, "that all may learn, and all may be comforted." For this was a matter under each prophet's personal control. In him the "spirit" and the "understanding" were harmonious. Consciousness kept its serene poise. There could be no reach of thought beyond the jurisdiction of the will, no passion for undue excitement, no verging towards hysterical emotion. And as heart and lungs maintain their beautiful relativity, and thus secure the maximum of health and vigour to the body, so "spirit" and "understanding" act in the prophet with no jar or jostle, but in perfect accord. For the "spirits of the prophets are subject to the prophets."—L.

Vers. 33—40.—*Concluding views.* If edification was to be the rule of conduct in everything, it is plain that the prophets must govern themselves. No matter how sincere and truthful their zeal, or how honest and excellent their purpose, feelings, and even the best feelings, must be held under firm restraint. They had this power, and it was from God; for he is "not the author of confusion, but of peace, as in all Churches of the saints." St. Paul directs further that "women keep silence in the Churches." If the Corinthians objected to this injunction, what right had they so to do? Usage in the Christian community as a whole was to be observed; local peculiarities offensive to the spirit and tastes of the body of Christ were not to be indulged. How could they claim exemption from a rule recognized everywhere? Were they the original Church? or did their position warrant any exclusive customs at variance with established custom? To enforce this view and the argument in the chapter, he asserts in the strongest manner that he spoke from Divine inspiration. "No more direct assertion of inspiration can be uttered than this" (Alford). If any one deny this inspiration, no controversy must be had with him. "Let him be ignorant," and, perchance, he may be self-convicted of his error. Then the idea which has been so prominent in his mind is introduced again in the words, "covet to prophesy." Had he not made good its claim to a pre-eminent excellence? By the concurrent "Amen" of approval and sympathy, by his own special delight in this gift, by the manliness connected with its exercise, by the effect on spectators, by the capacity of self-government which accompanied its activity and the culture given to volition and feeling, he exhorts his brethren to desire fervently this means of usefulness. What a momentum has the argument acquired before it comes to a close! Vapours rise from large tracts of territory, float in the air, run together, condense in clouds, and then descend in fruitful blessing to the fields. Far inland a stream begins its flow, gathers rivulets and creeks into its channel, and, before it reaches the ocean, has drained half a continent. St. Paul omits nothing essential to the greatness of his argument. From the Hebrew Scriptures, from musical instruments, from the "many kinds of voices in the world," from the laws of the human mind in respect to the difference between "spirit" and "understanding," he has drawn materials to enlarge and vivify the presentation of his doctrine. In other connections (Rom. xii.; Eph. iv.) we find him urging substantially the same view, pressing on the conscience and heart of the Church the individuality of gifts, and, at the same time, showing their worthlessness unless blended in unity. The most truly gifted, the most nobly endowed man, is portrayed in this chapter with singular distinctness, and this man is the prophet. Yet, he adds, "forbid not to speak with tongues;" let them be regulated, not discarded —a lesson widely applicable in the management of Church affairs. A genuine orthodoxy is always tolerant, charitable, and heartily disposed to make much allowance for idiosyncrasies in others. Many persons are content with love in their hearts. Intellect is left to itself. But the really orthodox man is a Christian in his method of thinking, and in many a thing not to his liking, ay, repellent to his tastes and sensibilities, he makes a special point to remember the "forbid not." The last constituent of a man to feel the thoroughly subduing grace of God is the intellect. Often when the animal nature has been conquered, often when the coarser struggles of life are all over, this besetment of dogmatic and tryannical intellect remains as the final entrenchment of evil. Orthodoxy is an admirable thing. It is beautiful and even glorious to feel the oneness of our beliefs with the greatest and best thinkers of the Church; but if truth of thought be exaggerated at the expense of truth of feeling and truth in external relations, it is truth despoiled of its supreme charm, and therefore the wisdom of the "forbid not." One who knows that he shall live for ever must needs feel, if he is a cultivated man, that a long past is not simply at his back, but is a part of himself, and that the parentage of much of the wisest and best in his soul lies in ancient years. Sympathy with the past is a foremost element in a charitable intellect. And he has also a keen fellow-feeling with forms of belief current in his own times. The sense of immortality widens his embrace of the present, and the "forbid not" is a welcomed dissuasive when he is tempted to the most disagreeable and pernicious form of vanity, viz. self-insistence. Only one thing remains for the apostle to say on the topic that has elicited so much wisdom and fervour from his soul : "Let all things be done decently and in order." And, doubtless, it commended him to the true-minded among the Corinthians as it has done ever since, that he should be so considerate of behaviour. There is an art of Christian behaviour, and St. Paul would have us make a conscience of it, and not leave it to mere taste and sentiment. It is not a distant and impracticable ideal. It is not the possibility of a few. But it is simply a cultivated sense of decency and order, and as such within the reach of all.—L.

Ver. 3.—*The purposes of prophesying.* There was a marked difference of judgment between St. Paul and his Corinthian converts with regard to the relative value of speaking with tongues and of prophesying. The Corinthians were disposed to set too high a value upon the more brilliant and startling gift; its novelty and singularity seem to have so impressed them with admiration that, in comparison with it, gifts which appealed to sober reason sank into insignificance. Paul, however, who himself spake with tongues, maintains the superiority of the rational and moral endowment over that which surprised the sense and dazzled the imagination. He does this most successfully by exhibiting in this verse the purposes of prophesying.

I. EDIFICATION. A prophet is one who speaks from God and for God, to his fellow-men. The prophets of the old covenant came before their fellow-countrymen with messages which they prefaced by the declaration, "Thus saith the Lord." In the new dispensation, there seems to have been at first an order of prophets, but in addition to these there were many who upon occasion uttered forth the mind of God. Now, since human nature is dependent upon truth, upon spiritual motive, upon personal influence, for the realization of the designs of the Creator, it is clear that a true prophet is one who apprehends those designs, and seeks their accomplishment by means ordered by Divine wisdom. Character and moral life require building up, *i.e.* upon a divinely laid foundation, by the use of divinely provided material, so that the edifice may assume form, proportions, beauty, in consonance with the idea of the great Architect. Hence the importance given in the New Testament to that element in prophecy denominated edification. No individual can become full grown, no society can be at once progressive and secure, where this department of ministry is lacking.

II. EXHORTATION. It must never be forgotten that the communication of knowlege is not the whole of ministry; that religion is not altogether a matter of the intellect; that human life is not simply one long lesson. Man is so framed that he is bound to action, and that he needs inducements, directions, encouragement, with a view to such action as shall be acceptable to his Maker and Saviour. Especially do the young, and converts whose principles are not fully formed, whose habits are not yet established, need frequent admonition. St. Paul reminds us that this also is part of the prophetic office and ministry.

III. CONSOLATION. If the necessity of exhortation follows upon the characteristics of human nature, the necessity of consolation arises from the circumstances of human life. Stronger than human philosophy, and tenderer, the consolations of Christian prophecy are able to bind up all wounds, and to cheer all sad and downcast hearts.—T.

Ver. 15.—*The two elements in devotion.* Religious exercises have always consisted mainly of praise and prayer. If there be a Deity, then from him we have received all we possess and enjoy, and to him, therefore, our natural feelings and our reason alike urge us to present sacrifices of thanksgiving. And since we are altogether dependent upon his favour and his faithfulness, we shall not omit to offer supplications and intercessions to the Giver of every good gift. Now, Christianity falls in with this natural view of religious observances, and raises these offices, which are too often perfunctorily performed, into a higher atmosphere, penetrating and sanctifying them with a new spirit.

I. IN PRAYER AND PRAISE THERE IS AN ELEMENT OF EMOTION AND COMMUNION. Human nature is so constituted that it is capable of great excitement, and Oriental nature, as is well known, is peculiarly sensitive to impressions and susceptible of enthusiasms and hallucinations. Now, religion, which consists in the relation and intercourse of the soul with the unseen, has peculiar power to raise some natures to a high pitch of excitement. The gesticulations, the self-inflicted tortures of devotees, the religious campaigns and wars of the East, are illustrations. Even at Corinth, a Grecian city, though largely frequented by Orientals, manifestations of enthusiasm were common in the Christian society. Paul himself was sometimes transported, in a trance, into unfamiliar and celestial regions of experience. He has not a word to say against those religious exercises which took place in "the spirit," *i.e.* which consisted in highly wrought feeling, in a consciousness of the presence of God, and which manifested themselves in the utterance of musical sounds reducible to no law or system, and of words unfamiliar sometimes to both speaker and hearers, but evidently an outpouring of fervent though vague and unformed prayers.

II. IN PRAYER AND PRAISE THERE IS AN ELEMENT OF THOUGHT, REASON, AND LANGUAGE. No doubt it often happens that this element preponderates. Where psalmody and common prayer are prepared beforehand, where there is a form of devotion, it is obvious that the understanding is engaged. Words are necessary in order to clear and articulate thought. It may be urged that there are higher moods of the spirit which cannot be interpreted by articulate speech. And this must be admitted. Yet the ordinary moods of the spirit have chiefly to be considered; and of these we may say, they are capable of being formulated in the conceptions of the understanding, in the phraseology of speech. And thus will devotion be most widely diffused and most profitably promoted, and Church worship be rendered most generally intelligent and fervent, and so most acceptable to God.—T.

Ver. 20.—*Babes, not in mind, but in malice.* There is in the style of St. Paul's admonitions a happy mingling of suavity and severity. A proverb reminds us that a hand of steel may be covered by a glove of velvet. The apostle will have no compromise with the errors, follies, and injurious judgments of the Corinthians; yet he speaks to them in language of gentleness and persuasion, addresses them as "brethren," and entreats them to act with wisdom and considerateness.

I. CHILDISHNESS OF JUDGMENT AND OF CONDUCT IS BLAMABLE. There is all the difference in the world between *childlike* conduct, *i.e.* conduct partaking of the true, proper, ideal character of the child, and *childish* conduct, *i.e.* conduct on the part of men which resembles the follies and frivolities of the infantile age. When the Corinthians preferred dazzling gifts to Christian graces, they were like children to whom a painted sweetmeat is dearer than a substantial treasure. And such a disposition is still exhibited by those to whom a splendid ritual, imposing learning, social eminence, are more admirable than a Christ-like spirit, a gentle, unobtrusive, self-denying habit.

II. CHILDLIKE FREEDOM FROM MALICE AND ALL VICE IS COMMENDABLE. Our Lord himself lays it down as one—indeed, as the chief—condition of entrance into his kingdom, that his disciples should become as little children. He taught this his favourite doctrine both by word and by symbols. This has ever been a stumbling-block in the way of the vain, the proud, the self-seeking, and it has been brought as a reproach against the religion of the Lord Jesus. Yet the morally cultivated have seen, in the condition laid down by him who was "meek and lowly in heart," a condition worthy of God and beneficial to humanity. Alas! in human society how much is there to corrupt the primitive simplicity of childhood! Sacred and precious is the spiritual power which restores the bloom of spring, the brightness of morning, the dew of youth.

III. MANLINESS OF UNDERSTANDING IS WORTHY OF HUMAN EFFORT AND ASPIRATION. If it is the glory of childhood to act upon pure, fresh, unsophisticated impulse, it is the glory of manhood to deliberate, to weigh motives and inducements and authorities, and to decide reasonably and justly. Well had it been for the Christian Church had it always been guided by the counsels of the thoughtful and the wise. There is abundant room for a manly understanding to show itself in the reasonings of the theologian, the policy of the bishop, the appeals of the preacher, the counsels of the pastor. And there is a far wider scope for the exercise of sanctified manliness of intelligence in the varied departments of human society, civil as well as ecclesiastical. It is the glory of Christianity that whilst it stoops to the child, it rises to the man, and aids him to realize the intellectual and spiritual prerogatives of manhood.—T.

Vers. 24, 25.—*The conviction of the unbeliever.* In estimating the gifts of intelligent prophecy on the one hand, and the gifts of tongues on the other, the apostle tests their respective value by their practical utility. It could not be denied that one great end of the existence of the Christian Church was, as it still is, the instruction of the ignorant and the reformation of the sinful. It is clear that at Corinth, and at other places where Christian communities existed in the first age, there was already a constant intercourse between the Church and the world. Attracted by curiosity, or driven by spiritual wants and hopes, the unbelieving heathen and Jews would sometimes attend the Christian assemblies. This being so, Paul asks, What must be the effect upon such persons, first of such an exhibition of supernatural powers such as the Corinthians delighted in, and secondly of the proclamation of the truths and promises of the gospel? His own answer is that, whilst the speaking with tongues may amaze, it will probably be set down as ranting; whilst the utterance of God's Word will sometimes issue in the enlightenment, conviction, and salvation of the sinner. Surely a sufficient and decisive test!

I. THE MEANS OF THE UNBELIEVER'S CONVERSION. This is represented as prophecy, *i.e.* the uttering forth by man, as God's messenger, of God's mind and will. And in the case supposed by the apostle, evidently the declaration concerns the sinful state and the spiritual needs of man, the merciful purposes of God, the provision of pardon, renewal, and eternal life, through the Saviour Jesus Christ. Prophecy, so understood, has never ceased in the Church of the Lord Jesus. His ministers prophesy when they give witness to him, when they publish the gospel and its gracious invitations.

II. THE PROCESS OF THE UNBELIEVER'S CONVERSION. The question arises—How does the Christian prophecy affect the mind and heart of the ignorant and unbelieving hearer? According to the representation of the apostle, the word evinces its own divinity by making the sinner known to himself. And there can be no more generally convincing and conclusive evidence of the authority of religion than is afforded by the fact that the preaching of the gospel reveals man to himself in his true state and position. The truths of the gospel are the utterances of him who formed the human heart. The candle of the Lord searches even the dark places of man's nature, and that which is hidden is brought forth to light. The conscience-stricken sinner realizes his guilt and danger, and his need of a Divine Deliverer. He is convinced, examined, judged, by the several messages which penetrate his nature. The secrets of his heart, his iniquities, his sorrow and penitence, his aspirations for a better life, are all made manifest.

III. THE RESULTS AND SIGNS OF THE UNBELIEVER'S CONVERSION. 1. His enmity to God and to God's truth is utterly vanquished. He falls down, contrite and submissive, like him who cried, "God, be merciful to me a sinner." 2. His enmity is exchanged for reverence and worship. Before, he may have adored the false gods whom he has been trained to revere; now and henceforth there is for him but one God, the Saviour of all men. 3. He acknowledges the Divine presence in the Church. Had he listened only to "tongues," he would have deemed the speakers to have raved. But listening to words of grace and truth, the convert acknowledges that in meeting God's people he has met with God, and their assembly has become to him, as it has become to multitudes, "the house of God, and the gate of heaven."—T.

Ver. 33.—*A God, not of confusion, but of peace.* True religion teaches us to refer all questions to the highest tribunal, and to ask, not merely—What is agreeable and expedient? but—What is the will of God? At Corinth many disorders had arisen; men spake with tongues and without interpreters, two or three prophesied at the same time, women appeared unveiled and spoke in the assemblies. Now, there were many reasons why such things should not be. But in this verse St. Paul adduces the highest of all reasons. Christians are the servants of God, and God is the God, not of confusion, but of peace; his people, therefore, should banish from their assemblies all that conflicts with the nature and the ways of their supreme Lord.

I. THAT GOD IS NOT THE AUTHOR OF CONFUSION, BUT OF PEACE, IS APPARENT FROM HIS WORK AS A CREATOR. The more nature is studied the more does it become apparent that it is the workmanship of an Intelligence proceeding according to order. "Order is Heaven's first law." Indeed, men of science affirm the universal presence of *law* through the whole realm of nature. By law they mean uniformity; and to those who believe in a Lawgiver the regularity with which the processes of nature are conducted is an evidence of the working of mind, and mind acting in accordance with the highest reason.

II. AND FROM HIS METHOD IN REVELATION. He who studies the Scriptures as a whole is struck with this—that they unfold a plan, unfold it gradually and regularly, according to a scheme of which the profound wisdom is apparent, although not fully apparent to a creature-mind. The truth was revealed first to a family, then to a nation, then to a race. "The Law was given by Moses, but grace and truth came by Jesus Christ." The Bible is a marvellously organic whole; in its diversity is discernible a unity and harmony which only a Divine mind could impart.

III. AND FROM THE WORK OF REDEMPTION. The whole motive of the economy of grace was to avert the confusion which had invaded, and threatened to overwhelm, this sinful humanity. To hush the moral discord, to introduce peace on earth,—such was the lofty purpose contemplated and fulfilled in the incarnation and the sacrifice of the Son of God.

IV. AND FROM THE INSTITUTION OF CIVIL SOCIETY. It is observable that social and political life are in the New Testament frequently attributed to God, the Author and Giver of all good. Jesus himself bade his disciples "render to Cæsar the things that are Cæsar's." And Paul taught that "the powers that be are ordained of God," enjoining loyalty and submission as a Christian duty.

V. AND FROM THE CONSTITUTION AND GOVERNMENT OF CHRISTIAN CHURCHES. Is it credible that the God in all whose ways order is so apparent, who, in the several spheres accessible to our observation, proceeds upon methods of regularity, and harmonizes all forces to fulfil his commands, should reverse his procedure in that realm which is the highest and noblest of all? Is Divine order to be confined to the physical and political spheres, and banished from the Church? It cannot be, and it is not so. Christ appointed and authorized apostles; apostles constituted Churches, ordained officers of various kinds and grades, and gave instructions for the conduct of worship, of business, of charity. If then, there be confusion, in any professedly Christian community, that confusion is traceable, not to Divine wisdom, but to human folly. In proportion as the Spirit of Christ lives and works in any society, in that proportion will subordination, co-operation, peace, and unity prosper and prevail.—T.

Ver. 38.—*Abandonment to ignorance.* Paul was a man who humbled himself but magnified his office. For himself, he was less than the least of all saints; but officially and in apostolic influence and authority, he was not behind the chiefest of the apostles. Of course there were in the primitive Churches men who acknowledged neither his authority nor the authority of any other than themselves. And when the apostle gave utterance to his judgment, it was with the knowledge that his judgment would not pass unchallenged. There is something of indignation and something of sarcasm in his reference to those who resisted his opinions and decisions. And there is wisdom as well as an admirable display of just impatience in his language: "If any man is ignorant, let him be ignorant."

I. OPINIONATEDNESS AND IGNORANCE OFTEN GO TOGETHER. A little experience convinces us that those who cling the most tenaciously to their own opinions, their own habits, are not always men of the soundest judgment. To resist evidence and authority is no sign of soundness of mind and power of intellect. Some are obstinate because they are blind to all testimony and evidence but that which is acceptable to their own prejudices.

II. THERE ARE THOSE WHOM NO EVIDENCE CAN CONVINCE AND NO AUTHORITY OVER-AWE. If all men were candid and dispassionate, and habituated to follow the clear white light of reason, human life and human society would be very different from what they actually are. Our Lord Jesus was forbearing and patient with those who opposed themselves to him; but even he confessed that there were those who loved darkness rather than light because their deeds were evil. Young and sanguine ministers of religion often begin their work with an inward persuasion that they have only to place the truth fairly and fully before men, in order to their conviction and conversion. But experience teaches them that it is not so; that there is a moral obduracy which is proof against all efforts.

III. IT MAY BE WISE TO ABANDON TO THEIR LOVED IGNORANCE THOSE WHO WILL NOT BE ENLIGHTENED. An affectionate and benevolent mind will be very slow to adopt such a course. And it cannot be adopted without the hope and prayer that, when ordinary and human methods have failed, it may please God to employ some methods unknown to finite wisdom, to secure the wished-for result. Even the Creator himself seems to act upon the principle here exemplified, at all events for a season and a purpose: "Ephraim is joined unto idols: let him alone."

IV. THERE IS BETTER EMPLOYMENT FOR THE TIME OF CHRISTIAN LABOURERS THAN THE ENDEAVOURS TO ENLIGHTEN THE INVINCIBLY IGNORANT. There are the young, the ardent inquirers for truth, the candid and open-minded, the earnest and prayerful, all anxious for more light, for lessons of truth, counsels of wisdom, encouragement, and admonition. In such directions there is abundant scope for effort, with the confidence that labour will not be in vain. Why spend years in tilling the rock or sowing the iceberg, when virgin soil awaits the plough and promises to reward the toil of the spiritual husbandman?

V. THERE IS A PROBATION AND A JUDGMENT APPOINTED BY GOD, TO WHICH SUCH CHARACTERS MUST NEEDS BE LEFT. It must be remembered by the Christian labourer that he is not one of the governors of the world. This reflection will not harden his heart against the unbelieving; he will leave such in the hands of One who is far more wise and far more merciful than the wisest and the most merciful of men.—T.

Vers. 1—19.—*Usefulness.* I. THE DESIRE FOR SPIRITUAL GIFTS IS LEGITIMATE AND PRAISEWORTHY. 1. *We must not rest content even with the possession of love.* We must seek qualification for making that love effective. Inactive love is both suspicious and useless. If we have a true love for men, we shall seek to be helpful to them, especially in their spiritual life, and to this end we shall seek all possible means for conveying to them the knowledge of the love of God and the truth as it is in Jesus. Spiritual endowments will aid us in this. The miraculous gifts in the early Church were bestowed with this object in view; and so are modern gifts. 2. *Spiritual gifts are to be most earnestly sought.* Whilst pointing out abuses to which gifts in the early Church were liable, Paul nevertheless commends these gifts as worthy of the keenest desire, for if rightly used they were productive of the most valuable results. So now, in every way, we should seek qualifications for the service of Christ in the world. Some of these must be natural to us, but not a few may be acquired; and by diligence the small gift may be made great. Prayer, study, earnestness, are channels through which spiritual endowment and spiritual power ever tend to flow. Not to desire spiritual endowment is to show that we are unspiritual and lazy. A master desire of our soul should be to be equipped for service. God can do this thing for us. He can sharpen the bluntest instrument, and give strength to the weakest.

II. WHAT GIFTS WE SHOULD MOST EARNESTLY DESIRE. Not (1) *the most brilliant,* (2) *the most remarkable,* (3) *the most rare,* (4) *the most praised,* (5) *the most mysterious,* (6) *those which are only enough to serve our own ends and supply our own needs;* but (7) *the most useful* (ver. 19). To win applause or to excite wonder is but the poorest of poor ends to attain. We should long to effect something for others. To lay out ourselves for ourselves is not to serve our fellows or our Master at all. That which startles most may be least valuable; that which calls forth most remark may be most barren. The apostle had to rebuke the childish Corinthians who were captivated by the strange gift of speaking in foreign languages—a gift most precious when foreigners speaking these languages were addressed, but valueless when they were absent. Yet the Corinthians, forgetting that the gift was bestowed for its special usefulness, exercised the gift and gloried in it when its usefulness was impossible! Here were selfishness and pride conjoined to supernatural endowment! *What penetrating power has evil!* It seems to touch everything, even the holiest, most God-like things, that man touches! Here is the touchstone which tries our work—Is it truly *useful?*

III. MARKS OF USEFUL GIFTS. 1. *Plainness.* We want to make men *understand* Divine truths; we should then assuredly use "great plainness of speech." Our speech should be "easy to be understood" (ver. 9). What a mass of preaching and praying has been lost because it was too ornate, or high-flown, or expressed in incomprehensible language! The ability to speak so that no one can understand us is a gift which should be earnestly desired by fools only. Some men are so profound that they are quite unfathomable, even to themselves. They dig the well so deep that they drown themselves in it. Possibly some avoid plainness intentionally, because they want no one to perceive the poverty of the portion which they are dealing out. They place nothing in many wrappers, with the fond expectation that it may pass for something amongst the ignorant. But such trickery is unworthy of the servants of the Most High, and would be called knavery if it were practised by a pedlar. The Romish Church is greatly censurable for continuing the use of Latin in her services, which is a "tongue unknown" of the people. 2. *Clearness.* No mean endowment is required so as to speak with lucidity upon scriptural topics. We need to *think clearly* ourselves. Hearers often do not understand because preachers do not. We may expect to be useful according to the measure in which we make clear to others Divine truths; and we must never forget how peculiarly prone men are to misapprehend these. A clear statement is like a piece of music played correctly; an involved and obscure one is like music in which the notes are all jumbled together without reference to order or time. Both may have exactly the same notes, but what a contrast! 3. *Force.* Like the sound of the trumpet when well blown (ver. 8). Life and vigour are needed in our utterances. We must not weaken the message which we deliver. If we would lead men heavenwards there must be power in our appeals. Our aim should be, not to tickle men, but to incite them. Force may be quiet; often is. But there is much quietness in which there is no force. Noise is not force, but earnestness and passion are generally its accompaniments. 4. *Certainty.* The trumpet-blast which directs must not waver. A halting, uncertain testimony is generally worse than useless. Some are so "gifted" that they are certain of nothing. One should not desire such gifts. Notwithstanding all boast about them, they carry much more folly than wisdom, and the devil's hand is more manifest in them than God's. We have *truth*—which is not an uncertain thing; one of the most precious and most useful gifts is a *certain grasp* upon that which is of the very essence of certainty.—H.

Ver. 15.—*How we should sing and pray.* I. AN IMPORTANT MATTER, SINCE SINGING AND PRAYER CONSTITUTE THE CHIEF PARTS OF PUBLIC WORSHIP.

II. THE "EXTERNALS" OF SINGING AND PRAYER ARE NOT OF THE FIRST IMPORTANCE. 1. Music. 2. Eloquence. 3. Form.

III. THE RIGHT METHOD. 1. *With the spirit.* Intellectual worship alone is very imperfect. It is cold, formal, not stimulative. Our emotional nature should take part. We should make melody in the heart, and should be deeply stirred in heart as we approach the Deity. To this end we must pray and sing "with the Holy Spirit;" the Holy Ghost must fall upon our spirits, and we shall then become acceptable worshippers who "worship the Father in spirit and in truth." 2. *With the understanding.* As the intellectual alone is not sufficient, neither is the emotional. The whole man should engage in the acts; even the body taking its subordinate part. Man, being an intelligent creature, should worship intelligently; should realize (1) to whom he speaks, (2) what he utters, (3) what he is.

IV. A TOO COMMON METHOD. 1. Without realization of the worshipped. 2. With inattention to the sentiments expressed. 3. With souls unmoved.—H.

Ver. 20.—*Mind and Christianity.* I. RELIGION IS NOT MERE SENTIMENT. II. RELIGION DEMANDS THE EXERCISE OF MENTAL POWERS. III. THE MORE DEVELOPED THE MIND BECOMES UNDER GRACIOUS INFLUENCES, THE MORE USEFUL, HAPPY, AND HONOURED WILL THE POSSESSOR BECOME. 1. Better fitted to labour for God's glory. 2. For the advancement of mankind. 3. Will become himself more firmly established in the truth. (1) The grasp of revealed truth will be more tenacious; (2) the conception of the Divine character loftier; (3) the realization of personal duty clearer and stronger. IV. CULTIVATE THE MIND. 1. *Store it.* 2. *Exercise it vigorously.* Generally minds are wrecked by too little effort, not by too much. 3. *Discipline it carefully.* 4. *Keep it ever under salutary influences.* Lest you become wise in your own conceit. Pride has great facility for entering by the door of knowledge.—H.

Vers. 23—25.—*Conversion prepared for.* I. CONVERSION EFFECTED BY MEANS. 1. The door of the sanctuary should be an open one (ver. 23). Restrictions and hindrances to attendance should be swept away. Non-churchgoers are often such through the action of churchgoers. 2. Means should constantly be employed in the sanctuary. The gospel should be preached. The presence of "unbelievers" should constantly be borne in mind, and of those altogether "unlearned" in the truth. Casual hearers should not be forgotten; the bow drawn at a venture has often done signal execution. II. PROBABLE MEANS OF CONVERSION. 1. *Order and propriety in the sanctuary.* The *building* itself should not be regarded as altogether unimportant. *There are some church buildings in which it is very difficult to be converted!* Wherever practicable, a suitable structure should be secured; not bare and ugly, to repel, nor unduly ornate, to distract. And the services should be well ordered and decorous, else some coming in may suppose that we are "mad." But dulness and coldness are not decorous. Vigour and enthusiasm are in the highest degree proper. If we want to move others we must be moved ourselves. There can be great freedom in the service without overstepping bounds. Modern Christian services tend to be too stilted, formal, frigid, unemotional. 2. *Church worship.* Song and prayer have won not a few from the kingdom of Satan. But the song service is sometimes a hindrance to edification; the music attempted is such as no angel could learn, and, for the matter of that, such as no angel would ever want to! Song, which should quicken, may freeze; and a freezing soul is very difficult to convert. Sanctuary song should be united song. In heaven the host sings, not a selected choir. Prayer should be earnest, real, intelligible. There are such things as mock prayers—prayers without any praying in them. Prayers of words and time; nothing in them except letters and minutes. Often too many of these. 3. *The preaching of the gospel.* This, the pre-eminent means, should be: (1) *Intelligible.* Not over the heads of the people. (2) *Sensible.* Not under their heels. If the sermon is despised, the gospel may be. (3) *Direct.* "He is convinced [or, 'reproved'] of all" (ver. 24). It is meant for him. There is something in the gospel which suits every condition. We are apt to take the edge off by general indefinite utterance. (4) *Searching.* "The secrets of his heart are made manifest." Preachers need acquaintance with human life; they should mix among men, and not live as recluses. Then under Divine influence they will be able to apply the gospel so searchingly that often hearers will think somebody has told the preacher the secrets of their lives. (5) *Scriptural;* or it may be preaching, but not preaching *the gospel,* and no conversion can be looked for. III. TESTS OF THE SUITABILITY OF MEANS. 1. *What do the unbelieving and ignorant think of the means employed?* Some will indeed scoff, but what will the common-sense and sincere ones think? What *ought* they to think? 2. *What results follow?* What are the effects of our services and work? We say no man can be responsible for results. This, in one sense, is a great truth, and in another a great lie. Do men under our ministrations fall down in contrition and humility, worship God, and declare that God is amongst us of a truth? If they do not, there is something amiss; and if we look for that something in ourselves and in our modes of work, we shall probably look in the right place. We must not ruin the usefulness of means by regarding them as anything more than means. To rest in them alone is suicidal. We need the power of the Holy Ghost. For this we should yearn, agonize, pray, as we humbly obey the command "not to forsake the assembling of ourselves together," and to " preach the gospel."—H.

Vers. 26—33, 40.—*Decency and order in the Church.* I. REFLECT UPON WHAT THE CHURCH IS. 1. *It is the " Church of the living God "* (1 Tim. iii. 15). In its worship it worships the Eternal. It is the depository of his truth. It is the "temple of God" (ch. iii. 16). 2. *It is the Church of Christ.* " My Church " (Matt. xvi. 18). It (1) bears his Name ; (2) is the place of his presence (Matt. xviii. 20 and xxviii. 20) ; (3) redeemed by his blood (1 Pet. i. 18, 19) ; (4) his body (ch. xii. 27) ; (5) identified with him by the world ; (6) the chief means by which his Name is made known in the earth ; (7) it is light derived from him shining in a dark place. 3. *The abiding-place of the Holy Ghost.* (Ch. iii. 16.) 4. *The great instrumentality for the conversion of the ungodly.*
II. THE IMPORTANCE OF EVERYTHING CONNECTED WITH THE CHURCH BEING AS FREE FROM FAULT AS POSSIBLE. Impropriety and disorder in the Church (1) dishonour God ; (2) grieve Christ ; (3) tend to quench the Spirit, and (4) to make the Church powerless for its mission.
III. WHAT VAST RESPONSIBILITY RESTS UPON THOSE WHO VIOLATE THE APOSTOLIC COMMAND. (Ver. 40.) God is a God of peace, but in this way he is made to appear a God of confusion and disorder (ver. 33).—H.

Vers. 34, 35.—*Women in the Church.* I. WOMEN HAVE A PLACE IN THE CHURCH. Christianity exalts woman. It found her degraded ; it ennobles her. In Christ there is neither male nor female (Gal. iii. 28).
II. WOMEN HAVE MANY MINISTRIES CONNECTED WITH THE CHURCH. If excluded from some positions, how many are still open to woman ! In not a few of these she is unrivalled by the other sex. If woman *may* not do some work, man *cannot* do other. Christianity has opened to woman a most wide sphere of usefulness. It is quite an open question whether the Church has received more help from men or women ; not a few would say from women. The Church owes a vast debt to the holy women who have been enrolled amongst her adherents.
III. WOMEN ARE DEBARRED BY THE APOSTLE FROM SPEAKING IN CHURCH ASSEMBLIES. On the ground of propriety. Does not accord with woman's true position. This position indicated in the Law (Gen. iii. 16), and laid down in the eleventh chapter of this Epistle. It had been foretold, " Your sons and your daughters shall prophesy " (Joel ii. 28), and in Acts xxi. 9 we read of four daughters of Philip who prophesied ; but in neither case is anything said of prophesying in public and mixed assemblies. The apostle does not prohibit women from prophesying, but only from prophesying *in public.* This, according to his view, would conflict with modesty and with woman's rightful position, and would lead to many evils. It is an evasion to discriminate between women speaking in *Church meetings* and women addressing general congregations. The apostle's objection was to the *public* character of the act, and when he is speaking of "meetings of the Church " in this very chapter, he is referring to gatherings to which unbelievers had access (ver. 24).
IV. WOMEN'S INSTRUCTION ENCOURAGED. To supplement instruction of the sanctuary, women may ask questions at home of their husbands. It may be said—What are those to do who have no husbands ? Emphasis seems to rest upon " their own " (Revised Version) rather than upon " husbands." It would be acting in the spirit of the apostle's injunction for the unmarried to ask their relatives or personal friends. There seems no possible reason why an unmarried woman should be allowed to speak in public mixed assemblies whilst a married woman is debarred, but rather the reverse. 1. *We have here incidentally indicated a special and most important sphere of woman— the home.* A beautiful temple for the exercise of woman's ministry. Oratorical females are frequently poor housewives. 2. *A suggestion that husbands should be well furnished with religious knowledge.* The head of the house should not be an empty head. If he glories in a superior position, he should realize its responsibilities. But many people like their office more than its duties. 3. *Evidence that women are not in the religious sphere to be mere automata.* They are not to be the dupes of priests. They are to think, ask questions, understand. They are not to be kept in ignorance. Intelligent

service is expected from them. Highest culture is as open to them as to men. There is nothing unwomanly in being well informed.—H.

Ver. 3.—*Christian prophesying.* In our day a "prophet" is one who predicts future events, but in the older times the word included much more than that. Old Testament prophets were religious teachers who revealed the will of God, and expounded the Word of God. Moses was a prophet, but his chief work was religious teaching. John the Baptist was a prophet, but he appeared as a preacher of repentance and of righteousness. New Testament prophets were the teachers or preachers of the Word—men to whom God had given special insight into his Divine truth, and a happy faculty of imparting that truth to others. The verse now before us describes the proper results that are to be reached by the prophecy, or ministry, of the Word. The gift of prophesying, or preaching, is the most useful and most practical of all the gifts. Other gifts direct attention to the man who possesses them ; this gift makes a man a blessing to others, for he may speak to "edification, and exhortation, and comfort."

I. The proper sphere of the Christian prophet. Theoretically our pastors are separated unto the ministry of the Word; practically the office is very sadly confused, and our pastors are brought into the most hindering and injurious contact with common worldly things and inferior Church duties. The Pauline idea is, that God has bestowed a variety of gifts upon his Church, and the true conception of his Church is only realized when each man uses faithfully his own gift without interfering with the gifts of others. The work of the Christian pastor is precisely this—by teaching and preaching to cultivate the spiritual life of believers. They should nourish so high and so vigorous a life and activity in the members of the Church as that each one might become, in his place, a light of God, a power for God; each one, in his own way, a holy force bringing in other souls to Christ. It does not matter what other work a pastor may do well, whether it be visiting or governing or writing, he is not faithful to his call and to his office unless by preaching he can speak to men "unto edification, and exhortation, and comfort." It would be a time of holiest revival for the Church of Christ, if her ministers might say, "For all other forms of work, look you out men from amongst you, full of the Holy Ghost and of faith, but we will give ourselves to the Word of the Lord and to prayer." If ministers could be more truly separated to their own proper work, they would bring, out of the deserts of holy stillness and quiet, the most heart-stirring views of truth and the noblest spiritual influences. Moses came forth in power from the lonely wilderness. Elijah burst out as a sudden flash of Divine fire from the privacies and hidings of the desert. Our Lord himself had a scene of lonely stillness and struggle on the threshold of his ministry, and his story tells of nights on the desolate mountain brow, or in the shady garden outside the city. The Christian prophet can only come forth aright into his sphere, if he dwells in the "secret place of the Most High, and abides under the shadow of the Almighty."

II. The proper influence of the Christian prophet within his sphere. His sphere is the Church. He is to be a spiritual power upon its members. That is work enough for any man. To do it aright he must know all the forms and influences of human sorrow ; he must understand, and find the antidote for, all the subtleties, devices, and diseases of temptation and of evil ; he must win the power to sympathize in every joy that gladdens, and in every sorrow that clouds, the Christian heart. He must be able keenly, critically, to estimate the spirit of the age, "the signs of the times," the tone of social, moral, and religious life, so as to judge aright of the atmosphere in which Christian life has to be lived. He must have a wide acquaintance with the history of Christian thought, and with the books exerting present influence upon the Christian mind. He must be deeply read in the mystery and meaning of God's great Book, so that, "like a scribe instructed to the kingdom, he may bring forth out of his treasury things new and old." Surely all this is a full life-work for any man. Observe the specific terms by which St. Paul describes the Christian prophet's influence. 1. *Edification*—a term bearing immediate relation to Christian growth. There is to be growth, under pastoral influence, in knowledge, in character, in the great grace of self-denial, in control over the bad passions and inclinations of a corrupt nature, and growth in practical devotedness to all works of charity. Upbuilding on all these sides must be continued, if the plan of the Divine Architect is to be seen gaining completion in the temple of our life. 2. *Exhortation*—a term bearing relation to Christian dangers, failings, and temptations. Warnings, revelations of the evils of sin, searching pictures of the common experience of frail men, calls to neglected duties—these are " exhortations," and a faithful ministry must deal largely with them. It must reach the worldly minded, the almost drunken, the man whose hands are stained with dishonest or ungenerous deeds, the injurer of the widow and the fatherless, the selfish, the proud, the unforgiving. He must " warn all the wicked from the error of their way." 3. *Comfort*—a term bearing relation to Christian sorrows. The pastor's words are to be holy words of quiet, tender memories of past goodnesses, gentle whispers of the stability of the God of Abraham and Isaac and Jacob, which may lift suffering souls up to their rest in the bosom of the heavenly Father, and lull the tired heart into a sweet sleep upon the "everlasting arms." What would Christian life be without its *comfortings?* It is no little thing that our pastors can bring balm for wounded hearts; leaves for the healing of bruised hearts; whispers of the eternal love for doubting hearts; and upliftings for downcast, tear-filled eyes, so that they may see the great High Priest " touched with the feeling of our infirmities," and " tempted even as we are."—R. T.

Ver. 5.—*The Church's edification the object sought in the trust of Christian gifts.* "That the Church may receive edifying." In classifying the Christian gifts, talents, and endowments, the first broad distinction to be made is between such as direct attention to the possessor, and such as give the possessor a gracious power of influence on others. Gifts which glorify the man who has them are not to be despised; but the apostle conceived that gifts which take men out of themselves, and only find their exercise in the help and blessing of others, are rather to be sought. The man who can speak in ecstatic language or in an unknown tongue, may seem to be supremely endowed, and men may be disposed to envy his gift; but it only draws attention *to him*; it only excites feeling; it bears no relation either to intellectual or moral culture. It serves its ends, and possibly these are simply to call attention to Christian preaching, and bring men into relation with the Christian teachers. The question which decides our estimate of the value of the different gifts is this—How does each bear upon spiritual profit; upon the *edifying* of the Church? "The teacher of religious truth to others, who thereby builds up the whole edifice of the body of Christ, is a greater one than he who is himself benefited by being possessed of profound but uncommunicable emotion." Opening this point, we notice—

I. THE INTEREST OF THE INDIVIDUAL IN THE CHURCH. The Church is a body made up of units; but it is not a mere aggregation of units; every unit is related vitally with every other unit, and in mutual helpfulness a common life is maintained. Schism comes when the interest of the individual is centred in *self*. The useless members of a Church are those who are satisfied to *get*, not to *give*. Each member ought even to nourish his own personal piety with a view to aid the healthiness and vigour of the whole body. Illustrate by the modern discovery of the formation of living beings from germ-cells. These do not lie side by side; they divide and form new cells, so that every single cell may be said to be in the whole creature, interested in the vitality of the whole.

II. THE PROOF OF THAT INTEREST IN THE DEVOTION AND USE OF INDIVIDUAL GIFTS. Gifts are not personal privileges, signs of special favour to individuals; they are always trusts committed to individual members of the Church for the use and benefit of the whole. A man only looks at his gift aright when, in the presence of the Church, he says, "This gift is for you; I hold it for your use. Find me the sphere in which I may serve you best in the use of the gift." How sublime the riches and strength of Christ's Church would be if each endowed man and woman would lay his gifts on the altar of the Church's service!

III. THE CULTURE AND PROGRESS OF THE CHURCH ARE ONLY SECURED BY SUCH DEVOTION AND USE OF GIFTS. Illustrate by taking the separate endowments and fitting them to their parts of the Church's edifying. Take: 1. The æsthetic or artistic gift; show how it bears upon the culture of the Church's sense of the beautiful, helping thus to worthy conceptions of one side of the Divine nature. 2. The musical gift; showing how it bears upon edifying by the relief of overcharged feeling, and aids in knitting the Church together by the common expression of common emotions. 3. The preaching and teaching gift; which stands related to mental culture, intellectual edification. 4. The literary gift; which in these days becomes the great defensive agency, by which the evils of the Church are kept off from her, so that she may duly thrive and grow. Others may be mentioned, or subdivisions of these may be taken. Press the importance of encouraging in each member full loyalty to the Church; and show that this becomes a valuable agency in spiritual edification, because it ensures the full and self-denying devotement of all the members' powers to the Church's well-being. The true and full upbuilding of a Church includes many things, great and small, and so there is need for the use of what we estimate as lesser and greater gifts.—R. T.

Vers. 7—11.—*Christian intelligence the medium of Christian growth.* The point presented in these verses appears to be that the Church is not really *edified,* save as the teachings presented to it appeal to the *understanding.* "Everything for use, and everything in its place, is a rule, the apostle is saying, that holds in spiritual gifts and exercises, as in everything else. If you speak with tongues, let it not be as only making strange noises, but let some one interpret, that the tongues may edify, and not be sounds without a meaning. It will not do for Christians to be more unmeaning and idle in spiritual gifts than even things without life themselves, the pipes, and harps, and trumpets, and drums of music; for these, when they give a sound, give it with distinctions that have a meaning and a power, else they are nought to us. Are voices and tongues to be less intelligent and significant than tubes of unconscious horn or metal?" (H. Bushnell, D.D.). Inquire: 1. How far it is true that all influences bearing upon the edification of the Church must appeal to the understanding. So far as edification includes right views of truth and right feelings about truth, the fitting acceptance of a Divine revelation, and the worthy expression of the principles declared in that revelation, the appeal must be to the mind. 2. Under what limitations must this statement be set. John Howe ('Works,' vol. ii. p. 75) says, "Nor do I believe it can ever be proved that God *never* doth immediately testify his own special love to holy souls, without the intervention of some part of his eternal Word, made use of as a present instrument to that purpose, or that he always doth it in a way of methodical reasoning therefrom." God usually works through the understanding, but he may use influences which bear at once upon heart and emotion. It must be observed, however, that such influences are but of temporary benefit, if they are not duly supported by intellectual considerations and mentally established principles. 3. Argue from these points the value and importance of an adequately educated and fully cultured ministry; showing, and efficiently illustrating, the relations of such an instructive ministry to (1) family piety, (2) liberal apprehensions of revealed truth, (3) social intercourse of Christian people, and (4) sober Christian activities.—R. T.

Ver. 20.—*The Christian both a child and a man.* The apostolic counsel here given bears immediate relation to the exaggerated estimate of the value of the "gift of tongues" which prevailed in the Church at Corinth. "Their conduct in exalting these 'tongues,' against which he has been warning them, is a proof that they are yet children in knowledge. They ought to be full grown; the only thing in which they ought to be children is *evil*, and in that they cannot be too young, too inexperienced; they should be merely 'infants.'" There is a sense in which all Christians must be children. There is a sense in which all Christians must be "men," "perfect," "full grown." To express the thought of the apostle in a sharply defined sentence—"Be childlike, but not childish." Refer to Bible sentiments about children. It seems always impressed with the little idea of evil which young children have. Take a thousandfold forms of human sin and transgression, and you will find that the little child can form no conception of the meanings of the terms in which you express them. The young child is the type of simplicity and innocence. But, in this passage, the apostle is rather thinking of the friendliness of children, of their readiness to forgive; they seldom or ever are found "bearing malice." Illustrating the point that the Christian should be both a *child* and a *man*, we notice—

I. WHAT CHILD-CHARACTERISTICS SHOULD WE FIND IN A CHRISTIAN? George Macdonald, in a Christmas sermon, given in 'Adela Cathcart,' very suggestively says, "It is as if God spoke to each of us according to our need: My son, my daughter, you are growing old and cunning; you must grow a child again, with my Son, this blessed birth-time. You are growing old and selfish; you must become a child. You are growing old and careful; you must become a child. You are growing old and distrustful; you must become a child. You are growing old, and petty, and weak, and foolish; you must become a child—my child; like the baby there, that strong sunrise of faith and hope and love, lying in his mother's arms in the stable." The characteristics of child-nature which ought to be found, nourished into the fulness of beauty, in Christian hearts and lives are such as these—each will prove suggestive of illustration—(1) receptivity; (2) submissiveness; (3) obedience; (4) trustfulness; (5) absence of self-consciousness; (6) hopefulness; (7) simplicity; (8) forgiveness. "If these things be in you and abound, they make you that you shall neither be barren nor unfruitful in the knowledge of our Lord Jesus Christ" (2 Pet. i. 8).

II. WHAT MANLY CHARACTERISTICS SHOULD WE FIND IN A CHRISTIAN? A man differs from a child in this, that what he is he is by *force of will*, and not as a mere accident of his being. What in a child we properly call *innocence*, in a man we call *virtue*. The proper manly characteristics are such as (1) self-control; (2) cultured intelligence; (3) energy; (4) prudence; (5) charity; (6) generous estimate of motives; (7) self-sacrifice. It is true that the Christian estimate of the manly is not precisely that which the world favours. The world has ever chiefly extolled the *active* virtues, and associated the *passive* virtues almost exclusively with womanhood. But in the Lord Jesus Christ has been presented to us the perfect type of manhood: we can conceive or wish nothing higher or more sublime; and we find the passive and active virtues fully represented and harmoniously blended in him. The world's best thought of manhood and womanhood meet in him; and so woman and man can make him their ideal. Nothing can be sublimer for a life-aim than to seek to be a *child* as Jesus was, and, at the same time, to be a *man* as noble as Jesus was.—R. T.

Ver. 20.—*The power of Christianity on intellect.* This text directly encourages the cultivation of intellect, and supposes that Christianity will exert a practical and helpful influence on such cultivation.

I. CHRISTIANITY WILL HELP TO MAKE US INTELLECTUAL MEN. Christianity recognizes no model, ideal man, save one whose whole circle of faculties has been duly developed, and certainly that noble part, the mind. It presents to us its ideal man in the person of Jesus Christ; there we see what it proposes to bring all men up to, and behold, in the very beginnings of Christ's life we read that "he grew in *wisdom* and in stature," exhibiting a surprising intelligence, which astonished the great doctors in the temple. A willingly ignorant Christian is an anomaly, a strange being, an imperfection, essentially incomplete; he has not felt, or he has resisted, the full force of the Christly principles and requirements. 1. Christianity comes into the world to restore man from his fallen condition. Man's self-willed fall involved his *mind* as well as his will, and the restorative applies to the fallen mind. The mind suffered sadly, lost its guiding truth, lost its harmonies, lost its place of rule, which was usurped by the passions of the body. 2. History confirms the relation of Christianity to intellect. Illustrate times of Wickliffe and Luther, etc. 3. The Christian services and duties help the intellect. Other religions are mostly ceremonial, making only routine demands. Christian services are essentially spiritual things, applications of mind to God's written Word, contemplations of Divine and heavenly realities, ordering of the thoughts so as to fashion them into prayers; these, and many other things, actually, by their own direct influence, storing and training the mind. The public Christian worship is intelligent. Its praises are expressed in the words of cultivated poets. Our Bible is the utterance of learning as well as of inspiration. Our preaching is the product of study and thought, and its appeal is made to the understanding as well as to the heart. 4. Christianity, with its revelations and doctrines, provides the very best food for the mind. It is the highest of sciences. It is the philosophy of the Infinite and the Absolute—it is the science of God. 5. Christianity makes the cultivation of the intellect a matter of direct counsel. It bids us "with all our getting get understanding," and assures us that "wisdom is to be chosen rather than riches." And the apostle complains that the believers do not mentally grow as fast as they should—that he has to feed them with the milk of first principles, when they ought to be able to take the strong meat of the Christian mysteries. If this be the relation of Christianity to mind, then two things are manifest. (1) Those men are utterly wrong who sneer at religion as a weak thing, and affirm that there is an antagonism between reason and revelation. (2) We are quite in the spirit of the religion which we profess, when we do our utmost to take our stand honourably among the intellectual men of our day. Our very religion helps us " in understanding to be men."

II. CHRISTIANITY PREVENTS OUR BECOMING INTELLECTUALLY PROUD MEN. It does so: 1. By announcing mysteries that are at present unfathomable by the human intelligence. 2. By making clear the distinction between speculation and knowledge. 3. By setting forth prominently its teaching of man's entire dependence on the Divine help. If we know anything, we know it only as God's revelation to us.

III. CHRISTIANITY KEEPS US FROM BEING ONLY INTELLECTUAL MEN. The mind may be cultivated and the morals neglected, so that a man may become dry, and cold, and hard, and unlovely. Men may be mentally vigorous and morally weak; intellectual giants, but slaves to passion. Christianity keeps men from this (1) by proposing to harmonize man's whole nature by beginning with the regeneration of his heart; and (2) by carefully developing the character and the moral qualities. Asking the love of the soul for God manifested in Jesus, it quickens and strengthens and nourishes every moral good, every moral power, and helps a man to grow healthily on every side of his nature, so as to develop into the "stature of the perfect man."—R. T.

Ver. 24.—*Preaching to unbelievers.* Previously the apostle had shown that the proper sphere of the Christian prophet was the teaching of the Church, so that its members might be *edified, exhorted,* and *comforted.* Now he intimates that this is not the only influence exerted by Christian prophesying; it has its power also on the "unbeliever" and the "unlearned." In the early Church the claims of *worship* were met by attendance on the temple and synagogue services, and the Christian meetings were, at first, simply gatherings for edification and prayer; so *preaching* and *teaching* were the prominent features of them. Gradually worship and edification became united in the Christian meetings, and a Christian cult, as well as Christian doctrine, was formulated. Then a greater publicity was given to the meetings; unbelievers were allowed to come in, and the preaching came to bear direct relation to *them.* We observe that—

I. A FAITHFUL MINISTRY WILL BE A POWER ON UNBELIEVERS. It may seem that a ministry adapted to believers is not suited for the arresting, convincing, and converting of the impenitent; and this is made a complaint against those who occupy the pastoral office. It may be advisable that for this particular work a class of evangelists, or missioners, should be raised up, but it may fairly be urged that in the regular Church ministry there should be, and may be, a real converting power. For: 1. *Faithful preaching is the exertion of spiritual power;* and this all must feel and respond to, in greater or less degree. When God speaks to men by tempests, plague, or famine, every one must feel it more or less; all must hear the voice. An assembled congregation is for the time shut in with God, and all must feel, in some degree, caught by the power of God. We have many cases, in history and within experience, in which the results have been much grander than the means used could indicate. Illustrate by the day of Pentecost, times of revival, seasons of hallowed emotion in Christian services. These are times of spiritual power which all must feel, times of life or of death to men. 2. *Faithful preaching will liberate and arouse the human conscience.* The preaching which fills believers with a new sense of God will arouse the conscience of unbelievers to the conviction of his existence and claims. The preaching that reveals the deep horror, the moral helplessness, and the final ruin of the sinner, will stir the conscience of all who hear it. The things that lull the Christian conscience to sleep are the very things which lull to sleep the sinner's conscience. Men's "refuges of lies," from which they have to be driven, are much the same. 3. *Faithful preaching must include the aspects of truth directly suited to reach the unbeliever.* He who would "declare the whole counsel of God" must be often dealing with the simplest foundation-truths. He speaks to many weak, unlearned believers, who cannot bear "strong meat," and so he must be very often laying down the groundwork of hope; and every sermon may thus gain its helpful adaptation to unbelievers. We have to be constantly presenting such great first principles as these : " All have sinned, and come short of the glory of God." God is the Father of all the human race. He finds expression for his Fatherhood in a gracious redemption of his erring children. The Divine Spirit is the source of all goodness in man. Jesus is the only, but he is the all-sufficient Saviour. Apart, then, from those direct appeals which ministers may be at times constrained to make, their whole preaching should prove a power unto salvation.

II. A FAITHFUL MINISTRY WILL EXERT A PARTICULAR KIND OF POWER ON UNBELIEVERS. Vers. 24, 25, speak of three things : (1) impression ; (2) knowledge of self ; (3) sense of God. 1. *Impression.* " He is convinced of all." He is interested, seized, held to thought, even, it may be, against his will. The trifles that agitated him are gone ; his purpose in coming is forgotten ; he is impressed, held by the force of preached truth. Illustrate by scenes in the itinerant labours of George Whitefield or John Wesley. 2. *Knowledge of self.* " Secrets of heart made manifest." Sometimes the minister seems to us as if he knew all about us. He brings to memory our wrong-doings. He reveals to us our bad motives, our heart-wrongness. We see the corruptness of our inclinations and purposes. We feel convicted of the master-sin of ungodliness. 3. *Sense of God.* (Ver. 25.) The merely shadowy thought of God becomes substance, the idea becomes reality. In the sanctuary God seems to come out of the dim distance and look us in the face. God's claims and relations go searchingly through our souls. God's love and redemption seem to be great glories far up out of our reach. The minister's sense of God is borne in upon us, compelling us to say, " God ! What is God to me ?" So sabbath preaching is the savour of life or of death to us all. Under its influence are we being won to God ? If not, what shall we say ? O guilty will, that decides not for Christ ! O mournful worldliness, that plucks men back from the very threshold of life !—R. T.

Vers. 34, 35.—*Woman's place in Christian worship.* Three points may be taken for due explanation and enforcement.

I. The Eastern, Jewish, and pagan sentiments concerning the public position and relations of woman.

II. The practical difficulties which arose when women were converted to Christianity, and became conscious of personal religious life, and the endowment of spiritual gifts.

III. The ways in which St. Paul's teachings on this subject require to be modified in adaptation to Western civilization, and the wiser, better conceptions of woman's mission, which are happily characteristic of modern times.—R. T.

EXPOSITION.

CHAPTER XV.

Vers. 1—58.—*The doctrine of the resurrection.* This chapter, and the thirteenth, on Christian love, stand out, even among the writings of St. Paul, as pre-eminently beautiful and important. No human words ever written have brought such comfort to millions of mourners as the words of this chapter, which form a part of the Burial Service of almost every Christian community. It is the more deeply imprinted on the memory of men because it comes to us in the most solemn hours of bereavement, when we have most need of a living faith. The chapter falls into six sections. 1. The evidence of Christ's resurrection (vers. 1—11). 2. The resurrection of Christ is the foundation of our faith in the general resurrection (vers. 12—19). 3. Results to be deduced from Christ's resurrection (vers. 20—28). 4. The life of believers an argument

for the resurrection (vers. 29—34). 5. Analogies helpful for understanding the subject (vers. 35—49). 6. Conclusion and exhortation (vers. 50—58).

Vers. 1—11.—*The evidence of the resurrection of Christ.*

Ver. 1.—**Moreover.** The δὲ of the original merely marks the transition to a new topic. **The gospel.** He here uses the word with special reference to the Resurrection, which is one of the most central and necessary doctrines of the " good tidings," and which always occupied a prominent place in St. Paul's preaching (Acts xvii. 18 ; xxiii. 6), as well as in that of all the apostles (Acts i. 22 ; iv. 2 ; 1 Pet. iii. 21). **Ye have received ;** rather, *ye received.* The " also " is emphatic. The Corinthians had not been like Christ's " own," who "received him not " (John i. 11).

Ver. 2.—**By which also ye are saved;** literally, *ye are being saved.* It is as if some surprise was expressed at the necessity for again making known to them a gospel which (1) he had preached and (2) they also received; and (3) in which they now stood fast (Rom. v. 2; Eph. vi. 13); and (4) by means of which they were now in a state of safety, they were of the class of *sozomenoi* (Acts ii. 47). **If ye keep in memory what I preached unto you.** The order, which is peculiar, is, "In what words I preached to you, if ye hold [it] fast." Possibly the "in what discourse" depends on "I make known to you." The duty of "holding fast" what they had heard is often impressed on the early converts (ch. xi. 2; 2 Cor. vi. 10; 1 Thess. v. 21; Heb. x. 23). **Ye have believed;** rather, *ye believed;* i.e. ye became believers. **In vain.** The word may either mean "rashly," "without evidence," as in classical Greek; or "to no purpose," "without effect," as in Rom. xiii. 4; Gal. iii. 4; iv. 11. In this case they would have received the seed in stony places (Matt. xiii. 21).

Ver. 3.—**First of all**; literally, *among the first things*; but this idiom means "first of all." It does not occur elsewhere in the New Testament, but is found in Gen. xxxiii. 2; 2 Sam. v. 8 (LXX.). This testimony to the Resurrection is very remarkable, because: 1. It is the completest summary. 2. It refers to some incidents which are not mentioned in the Gospels. 3. It declares that the death and resurrection of Christ were a subject of ancient prophecy. 4. It shows the force of the evidence on which the apostles relied and the number of living eye-witnesses to whom they could appeal. 5. It is the *earliest* written testimony to the Resurrection; for it was penned within twenty-five years of the event itself. 6. It shows that the evidence for the Resurrection as a literal, historical, objective fact, was sufficient to convince the powerful intellect of a hostile contemporary observer. 7. It probably embodies, and became the model for, a part of the earliest Creed of the Church. **For our sins**; literally, *on behalf of.* The passage is remarkable as the only one in which "on behalf of" is used with "sins" in St. Paul. In ch. i. 13 we are told that he died "on behalf of *us*" (Rom. v. 8; see 2 Cor. v. 21; 1 Pet. ii. 24). The expressions involve the image of Christ as a Sin Offering for the forgiveness of sins. **According to the Scriptures.** The chief passages alluded to are doubtless Isa. liii. 5, 8; Dan. ix. 26; Ps. xxii.; Zech. xii. 10; together with such types as the offering of Isaac (Gen. xxii.) and the Paschal lamb, etc. Our Lord had taught the apostles confidently to refer to the Messianic interpretation of the Old Testament prophecies (Luke xxiv. 25, 46; Acts viii. 35; xvii. 3; xxvi. 22, 23; John ii. 22; xx. 9; 1 Pet. i. 11).

Ver. 4.—**And that he rose;** rather, *that he had been raised.* The burial was a single act; the Resurrection is permanent and eternal in its issues. **According to the Scriptures** (Ps. xvi. 10; Isa. liii. 10; Hos. vi. 2; Jonah ii. 10; comp. Matt. xii. 40; xvi. 4; Acts ii. 31; xiii. 34).

Ver. 5.—**Was seen of Cephas** (Luke xxiv. 34). The appearances to the women (John xx. 14, etc.) are omitted, as being evidential rather to the apostles than to the world. **The twelve** (John xx. 19, 26). Some officious scribes have in some manuscripts altered the word into "the eleven." But "the twelve" is here the designation of *an office*, and great ancient writers are always indifferent to mere pragmatic accuracy in trifles which involve nothing. To witness to the Resurrection was a main function of "the twelve" (Acts ii. 23; iii. 15; x. 40, etc.).

Ver. 6.—**Above five hundred brethren at once.** We cannot be certain whether this memorable appearance took place in Jerusalem or in Galilee. It is, however, most probable that this was the appearance on the mountain (Matt. xxviii. 16, 17; comp. Matt. xxvi. 32). **Of whom the greater part remain unto this present.** This sentence—a confident contemporary appeal to a very large number of living witnesses, by one who would rather have died than lied—is of the highest evidential value. It shows that the Resurrection was not "a thing done in a corner" (Acts xxvi. 26). **Fallen asleep.** The beautiful and common word for death in the New Testament (Matt. xxvii. 52; John xi. 11; Acts vii. 60, etc.). Hence the word "cemetery"—"a sleeping-place."

Ver. 7.—**Seen of James.** The "James" intended is undoubtedly the only James then living, who was known to the whole Christian Church, namely, "the Lord's brother," the author of the Epistle, and the Bishop of Jerusalem (Gal. ii. 9; Acts xv. 13; xxi. 18). James the son of Zebedee had by this time been martyred, and James the son of Alphæus was never much more than a name to the Church in general. There is no mention of this appearance in the Gospel; but in the Gospel of the Hebrews was a curious legend (preserved in St. Jerome, 'De Virr. Illust.,' ii.) that James had made a vow that he would neither eat nor drink till he had seen Jesus risen from the dead, and that Jesus, appearing to him, said, "My brother, eat thy bread, for the Son of man is risen from the dead." The truth of the appearance is strongly supported by the fact that James, like the rest of the Lord's "brothers," "did not believe" in Christ before the Crucifixion, whereas *after the Resurrection* we find him and the rest of "the Lord's brothers" ardently convinced

(John xii. 3—5; Acts i. 14; ix. 5, etc.). **Of all the apostles** (Acts i. 3; Luke xxiv. 50). James the Lord's brother was only an apostle in the wider sense of the word.

Ver. 8.—**He was seen of me also.** The reference undoubtedly is to the vision on the road to Damascus (Acts ix. 5; xxii. 14; xxvi. 16). **As of one born out of due time;** literally, *as to the abortive-born.* The word means "the untimely fruit of a woman," a child born out of the due time or natural course; and hence "diminutive" and "weakly." The Greek *ektroma* is represented by the Latin *abortivus.* St. Paul, when he remembered the lateness of his conversion, and his past persecution of the saints, regards himself as standing in this relation to the twelve.

Ver. 9.—**For.** This and the next verse are an explanation of the strong and strange term which he had applied to himself. **The least of the apostles.** In St. Paul there was a true and most deep humility, but no mock modesty. He knew the special gifts which he had received from God. He was well aware that to him had been entrusted the ten talents rather than the one talent. He could appeal to far vaster results than had been achieved by the work of any other apostle. He knew his own importance as "a chosen vessel," a special instrument in God's hands to work out exceptional results. But *in himself* he always felt, and did not shrink from confessing, that he was "nothing" (2 Cor. xii. 11). The notion that he here alludes to the meaning of his own name (*Paulus,* connected with παῦρος, φαῦρος, equivalent to "little") is very unlikely. In Eph. iii. 8 he goes further, and calls himself "less than the least of all saints," though even there he claims to have been the special apostle of the Gentiles. **Because I persecuted the Church of God.** This was the one sin for which, though he knew that God had forgiven him (1 Tim. i. 13), yet he could never quite forgive himself (Gal. i. 13). In my 'Life of St. Paul' I have shown from the language used, that this persecution was probably more deadly than has been usually supposed, involving not only torture, but actual bloodshed (Acts viii. 4; ix. 1), besides the martyrdom of St. Stephen. We can imagine how such deeds and such scenes would, even after forgiveness, lie like sparks of fire in a sensitive conscience.

" Saints, did I say? with your remembered faces;
   Dear men and women whom I sought and slew?
Oh, when I meet you in the heavenly places,
   How will I weep to Stephen and to you!"

Ver 10.—**By the grace of God I am what I am.** And therefore he was "in nothing behind the very chiefest apostles." However humbly he thought of himself, it would have been mere unfaithfulness to disparage his own work (2 Cor. iii. 5, 6). **I laboured more abundantly than they all.** Because God wrought effectually in him (Gal. ii. 8). The word used for "labour" implies the extreme of toil (Matt. vi. 28; Phil. ii. 16), etc. **But the grace of God.** "It is God that worketh in you" (Phil. ii. 13; Matt. x. 20; Col. i. 29).

Ver. 11.—**Whether it were I or they;** namely, who preached this gospel to you. It is not his *immediate* object to maintain his independent apostolic claims, but only to appeal to the fact of the Resurrection which was preached by all the apostles alike. **So.** In accordance with the testimony just given (vers. 4—8). **We preach.** There are in the New Testament two words for "preaching." One is often rendered "prophesy," and refers to spiritual instruction and exhortation. The other, which is used here, is "we proclaim," or "herald" (*kerussō*), and refers to the statement of the facts of the gospel—Christ crucified and risen (ch. ii. 2; Acts iv. 2; viii. 5). Besides these, there is the one word for "to preach the gospel," or "evangelize."

Vers. 12—19.—*The resurrection of Christ is the basis of our faith in the general resurrection.*

Ver. 12.—**Now if Christ be preached that he rose from the dead.** St. Paul sees that if *One* has risen from the dead, the fact of that miracle, taken in connection with the rest of the gospel, furnishes Christians with a sufficient proof that they shall rise. "For," he had already said to the Thessalonians, "if we believe that Jesus died and rose again, even so them also which sleep in Jesus will God bring with him" (see the same argument in Rom. viii. 11). **That there is no resurrection of the dead.** These deniers of the resurrection are usually called "the Corinthian Sadducees." After the state of social and moral laxity of which we have been reading, we can scarcely be surprised at the existence of *any* disorder or anomaly in the Church of Corinth. Yet it comes with something of a shock on our paralyzed sense of astonishment to read that some of these Christians actually denied a resurrection! The fact at once proves two remarkable truths, namely, (1) that the early Christian Church had none of the ideal purity of doctrine which is sometimes ecclesiastically attributed to it; and (2) that there was in the bosom of that Church a wide and most forbearing tolerance. We have no data to enable us to determine what were the **influences which led to the denial** of the resurrection. 1. They can hardly have been Jewish. The mass of Jews at this time shared the views of the Pharisees, who strongly maintained the resurrection (Acts xxiii. 6). If they were Jews at all, they could only have been Sadducees or Essenes. But (1) the *Sadducees* were a small, wealthy, and mainly political sect, who had no religious influence, and can certainly have had no representatives at Corinth; and (2) the *Essenes*, though they had considerable influence in Asia, do not seem to have established themselves in Greece, nor are we aware that they were hostile to the doctrine of the resurrection. 2. Probably, then, they were Gentiles. If so, they may have been (1) either *Epicureans*, who disbelieved in a future life altogether; or (2) *Stoics*, who held that the future life was only an impersonal absorption into the Divine. Both these schools of philosophers "jeered" at the very notion of a bodily resurrection (Acts xvii. 32). In 2 Tim. ii. 18 we read of some, like Hymenæus and Philetus, who erred, saying " that the resurrection was past already." These teachers were incipient Gnostics, who *spiritualized* the resurrection, or rather said that the term was *only* applicable to the rising from the death of sin to the life of righteousness. The Corinthian doubters seem from the arguments which St. Paul addresses to them, to have been rather troubled with *material* doubts which they may have inherited from their Gentile training.

Ver. 13.—**Then is Christ not risen.** If the possibility of a resurrection be *generically* denied, it cannot in any instance be true. Yet you admit as Christians that Christ rose! and his resurrection "has begotten us again to a lively hope" (1 Pet. i. 3; see 2 Cor. iv. 14; 1 Thess. iv. 14; John xiv. 19).

Ver. 14.—**Vain.** You accepted our proclamation (*kerugma*), yet it would be utterly void if its central testimony was false. The word translated " then " has a sort of ironic force—" after all," or " it seems." The whole argument is at once an *argumentum ad hominem* and a *reductio ad absurdum*. **Your faith is also vain.** For it would be faith in a crucified man, not in the risen Christ.

Ver. 15.—**We are found.** The word means, " we are proved to be," convicted of being false witnesses. **False witnesses of God**; *i.e.* concerning *God*. St. Paul does not shrink from the issue. It is not one—it could not be one—between truth and *mistake*, but between truth and *falsehood*. **We have testified of God that he raised up Christ**; rather, *the Christ*. "This Jesus hath God raised up, whereof we all are witnesses" (Acts ii. 32; iv. 33; xiii. 30).

Ver. 16.—This verse is a repetition of **ver. 13,** to emphasize the argument that the Christian faith in the Resurrection rests not on philosophic theory, but on an historic fact.

Ver. 17.—**Vain;** rather, *frustrate*. The word used (*mataia*) is different from the word used (*kenē*) in ver 14. **Ye are yet in your sins.** Because a *dead* Redeemer could be *no* Redeemer. Christ's resurrection is the pledge of his Divine power. He was "raised for our justification" (Rom. iv. 25). It is only "as a Prince and Saviour" that "God hath exalted him to give repentance and forgiveness of sins" (Acts v. 31; Rom. v. 10).

Ver. 18.—**Which are fallen asleep in Christ.** Christians whose bodies have sunk into the sleep of death. **Are perished.** A notion which he feels that Christians must reject as utterly impossible. All that goodness, faith, tenderness, love, have not been dissolved to nothing.

Ver. 19.—**If in this life only we have hope in Christ.** The word to which " in Christ " should be joined is uncertain; the order of the original is, " If in this life in Christ we have hoped only." The " only " seems therefore to qualify the whole sentence : " If we have merely *hoped* in Christ, and that only in this life." **We are of all men most miserable**; literally, *we are more pitiable than all men.* The remark only has an *absolute* bearing when Christians really are suffering from persecutions, as they did in St. Paul's day (2 Cor. i. 5; 2 Tim. iii. 12). But to some extent all Christians have to bear their cross, and if all that they give up and suffer is sacrificed to a delusion, they deserve most pity in *one* sense, because they have been most conspicuously befooled. In *another* sense they are still the happiest of men; for their delusion, judged by its fruits, is more blessed than the dreary blank which is the only alternative.

Vers. 20—28.—*Results to be deduced from the fact of Christ's resurrection.*

Ver. 20.—**But now.** Since the supposition that Christ has not risen involves so many suppositions which you will rightly reject as absurd, we may assume the eternal fact that Christ has been raised. And **become the firstfruits of them that slept.** As the wave sheaf (Lev. xxiii. 10), which was the firstfruits of the harvest, is also a pledge of the harvest, so Christ is the firstfruits and pledge of the resurrection of all mankind.

Ver. 21.—**By man came death** (see Rom. v. 12, 17; vi. 21, 23).

Ver. 22.—**As in Adam all die.** All of us partake of Adam's nature, and are therefore liable to the death which that nature incurred as the law and condition of its humanity. **In Christ shall all be made alive.** It is St. Paul's invariable habit to isolate his immediate subject; to think and to treat of one topic at a time. He is not here thinking directly and immediately of the resurrection in general. In this verse, writing to Christians who are "in Christ," he is only thinking and speaking of the resurrection of those who are "in Christ." That any can be *nominally* "in Christ," yet not *really* so, is a fact which is not at present under his cognizance; still less is he thinking of the world in general. In other words, he is here dealing with "the resurrection of life" alone, and not also with the "resurrection of judgment" (John v. 26—29). Still, as far as his words alone are concerned, it is so impossible to understand the phrase, "shall all be made alive," of a resurrection to endless torments, that his language at least *suggests* the conclusion that "the principle which has come to actuality in Christ is of sufficient energy to quicken *all men* for the resurrection to the blessed life" (Baur, 'Life of St. Paul,' ii. 219).

Ver. 23.—**In his own order.** The word in classic Greek means "a cohort." Here it must either mean "rank" or be used as in St. Clement ('Ad. Cor.,' i. 37), in the sense of "order of succession." **They that are Christ's.** "The dead in Christ" (1 Thess. iv. 16). **At his coming.** The word here used for the second Advent is *Parousia*, which means literally, *presence*. It is implied (apparently) both here and in 1 Thess. iv. 15—17; Rev. xx. 5, that there shall be an interval—how long or how short we do not know—between this resurrection of the just and the final resurrection. But all the details are left dim and vague.

Ver. 24.—**The end.** That "end of all things," beyond which the vision of Christian eschatology does not look. **When he shall have delivered up the kingdom to God.** The "kingdom" delivered up is not that of the coequal Godhead, but the mediatorial kingdom. The Divine kingdom "shall have no end" (Luke i. 33, etc.), and "shall not pass away" (Dan. vii. 13). But the mediatorial kingdom shall end in completion when the redemptive act has achieved its final end. **When he shall have put down;** rather, *shall have annulled* or *abolished.* **All rule.** Because then "the kingdoms of the world" shall all "have become the kingdoms of our Lord and of his Christ" (Rev. xi. 15).

Ver. 25.—**He must reign.** He must reign in his mediatorial kingdom as the God-Man. **He hath put.** The "he" probably means Christ himself (comp. Ps. ii. 9; Heb. x. 13), though it makes no real difference in the sense if we understand it of God, as in Ps. cx. 1.

Ver. 26.—**The last enemy** that shall be destroyed is death. This rendering might imply that other enemies should still exist, though Death should be the last who would be destroyed. The original is more forcible, and implies, "Last of enemies doomed to annulment is Death;" or, as in Tyndale's version, "Lastly, Death the enemy shall be destroyed;" or, as in the Rhemish Version, "And at the last, Death the enemy seal be distried." The present, "is being annulled," is the *præsens futurascens*, or the present of which the accomplishment is regarded as already begun and continuing by an inevitable law. Death and Hades and the devil, "who hath the power of death," are all doomed to abolition (2 Tim. i. 10; Heb. ii. 14; Rev. xx. 14).

Ver. 27.—**But when he saith.** The "he" refers to God. This indirect method of quotation is common in the rabbis. The reference is to Ps. viii. 7 (LXX.), and the words, spoken of man in general, are here Messianically transferred to the federal Head of humanity, the ideal and perfect God-Man, Jesus Christ. (For the fuller explanation of the matter, see Heb. ii. 5—10.) **He is excepted, which did put all things under him.** So our Lord says, "All things are delivered unto me *of my Father*" (Matt. xi. 7). The universal dominion of Christ is also insisted on in Eph. i. 20—22; 1 Pet. iii. 22.

Ver. 28.—**Then shall the Son also himself be subject,** etc. The words can only be taken as they stand. The attempts to explain them have usually been nothing but ingenious methods of explaining them away. Of these the one usually adopted by the Fathers is the limitation of the statement to Christ's human nature (John v. 26, 27, 30) and mediatorial kingdom, just as we find in ch. xi. 3, "The head of Christ is God." We can easily "darken counsel by words without knowledge" in dealing with this subject, and hide an absolute ignorance under a semblance of knowledge; but anything and everything which we can say in "explanation" of this self-subjection of the Son to the Father is simply involved in the words which follow. **That God may be all in all.** "All things in all things" or "all things in all men." The words involve a complete and absolute supremacy. It is quite an easy matter for commentators to say that the scope of the words "must be confined to believers," if they chose to make "all" mean "some." Such methods often lead to an irreligious religionism and a heterodox orthodoxy. The reader will find the same phrase in Col. iii. 11. I confine myself to the comment of the profound and saintly Bengel: "There is implied something new, but also supreme and eternal. All things, and therefore all men, without any interruption, no created thing claiming a place, no enemy creating opposition, shall be subordinated to the Son, the Son to the Father. All things shall say, 'God is all things to me.' This is the consummation; this the end and summit. Further than this not even an apostle can go."

Vers. 29—34.—*Arguments from the practices and lives of Christians.* The three arguments used in these verses are: If there be no resurrection: 1. Why do some of you get yourselves baptized on behalf of your dead friends? 2. Why do we face lives of daily peril? 3. How would it be otherwise possible to resist Epicurean views of life?

Ver. 29.—**Else what shall they do which are baptized for the dead,** etc.? This clause can have but one meaning, and that its obvious one, namely, that, among the many strange opinions and practices which then prevailed, was one which was entirely unwarranted—but which St. Paul does not here stop to examine—of persons getting themselves baptized as it were by *proxy* for others who had died. Doubtless some of the deaths alluded to in ch. xi. 30 had happened to persons who had been cut off before they were actually baptized; and their friends had as it were gone through the rite *in their stead*, in the hope of extending to them some of its benefits. It is argued that St. Paul could not possibly mention such a practice without reprobation; but that is an *à priori* assumption not warranted by St. Paul's methods (see ch. x. 8; xi. 6). He always confines his attention to the question immediately before him, and his present object is merely to urge a passing *argumentum ad hominem.* There is nothing at all surprising in the existence of such an abuse in the medley of wild opinions and wild practices observable in this disorganized Church. It accords with the known tendency of later times to postpone baptism, as a rite which was supposed to work as a charm. We also find that the actual practice of baptism on behalf of the dead lingered on among Cerinthians (Epiph., 'Hær.,' xxviii. 7) and Marcionites (Tertullian, 'De Resurrect.,' 48; 'Adv. Marc.,' v. 10). Tertullian accepts the words in their obvious sense in his ' De Præscr. Hær.,' 48, but accepts the absurdity of "the dead" meaning "the body" ("pro mortuis tingui est pro corporibus tingui") in his book against Marcion (v. 10). St. Chrysostom tells us further that the proxy who was to be baptized used to be concealed under the bier of the dead man, who was supposed to answer in his name that he desired to be baptized. How perfectly natural the custom was may be seen from the fact that among the Jews also a man dying under ceremonial pollution was cleansed by proxy.

The "interpretations" of this verse are so numerous that it is not even possible to give a catalogue of them. Many of them are not worth recording, and are only worth alluding to at all as specimens of the wilful bias which goes to Scripture, not to seek truth, but to support tradition. They are mostly futile and fantastic, because they pervert the plain meaning of the plain words. It is a waste of time and space to give perpetuity to baseless fancies. Such are the notions that "for the dead" can mean "for our mortal bodies" (Chrysostom); or "for those about to die" (Estius, Calvin, etc.); or "over (the sepulchres of) the dead" (Luther); or "to supply the vacancies left by the dead" (Le Clerc, etc.). Equally unwarrantable are the "explanations" (?) which make those who are being "baptized" mean those who are "passing through a baptism of suffering" (!). Not a single argument which is worth a moment's consideration can be urged in favour of any one of these, or scores of similar views. If we are to get rid of everything that is surprising on the ground that it is "immensely improbable," we may as well discard Scripture at once, and reconstruct early Christian history out of our own consciousness. It has been very usual to represent it as we think that it ought to have been, and not as it was. The disuse of this vicarious baptism among orthodox Christians may have been due to the discouragement of it by St. Paul when he went to Corinth, and "set in order" various erroneous customs (ch. xi. 34).

Ver. 30.—**Why stand we in jeopardy every hour?** The verb means "Why do we incur peril?" The best comment on it will be found in 2 Cor. xi. 26. Cicero says ('Tusc. Disp.,' i. 15) that "no one would be so mad as to live in labour and perils if our instinctive anticipation of future life were taken away."

Ver. 31.—**I protest.** The particle of adjuration here used (νή) is found nowhere else in the New Testament. **By your rejoicing.** This is an erroneous translation. The words mean "by my glorying in you." St. Paul's one subject of earthly glory, his "hope, and joy, and crown of rejoicing," was the conversion of Churches (Rom. xv. 16, 17). **In Christ Jesus our Lord.** His boasting was not a worldly boasting, but was sanctified by its reference to the work of Christ. **I die daily.** St. Paul "died daily " a double death—the ever-deepening death unto sin and unto the world; and the daily death of sufferings borne for Christ's sake (see 2 Cor. iv. 10, 11). It is the latter to which he here alludes. "For thy sake are we killed all the day long" (Rom. viii. 36).

Ver. 32.—**After the manner of men.**

The phrase is a qualification of the strong metaphor, "I fought with beasts." It is equivalent to "humanly speaking." This is Chrysostom's view. It is the most reasonable, and accords with the use of the phrase in Rom. iii. 5; Gal. iii. 15. Meyer, however, explains it to mean "with mere human motives." **I have fought with beasts.** Not literally, for in that case he would have mentioned it in 2 Cor. xi. as one of his deadliest perils, and it must have been recorded by St. Luke in his full account of St. Paul's life at Ephesus. A Roman citizen was legally exempt from this mode of punishment. The word points to some special peril incurred in resisting the hostility of the worshippers of Artemis (Acts xx. 19), but *not* to the tumult in the theatre, which did not happen till after this letter was despatched (ch. xvi. 8, 9). The metaphor is not uncommon. Thus in 2 Tim. iv. 17 St. Paul alludes to Nero (probably) as "the lion." David often compares his enemies to wild beasts (Ps. xxii. 21, etc.). When his jailor informed Agrippa of the death of Tiberius, he did so in the words, "The lion is dead." St. Ignatius writes of the ten soldiers who were conducting him to Rome as "ten leopards." Epimenides, in the line quoted by St. Paul in Titus i. 12, spoke of the Cretans as "evil wild beasts," and the pseudo-Heraclitus gives this same uncomplimentary title to these very Ephesians. **Let us eat and drink; for to-morrow we die.** Perhaps the "if the dead are not raised" belongs to this clause. He means that such an Epicurean maxim, if never *excusable*, would at least be *natural*, if men could only look to life in the present. The sentiment is found on the lips of the despairing and the sensual alike in Isa. xxii. 13, and in the writings of the heathen (Horace, 'Od.,' i. 4, 13 —17, etc.). St. Paul would be all the more familiar with it because it formed the infamous epitaph of a statue of Sardanapalus, which he must have often seen in his boyhood at Anchiale, near Tarsus. It represented the debased king as snapping his fingers, and using almost these very words. It is strange that similar passages should be found even in the Talmud. Shemuel said to Rav Yehudah, "Seize and eat, seize and drink; for the world is like a wedding feast (soon over)" ('Eiruvin,' fol. 54, 1).

Ver. 33.—**Be not deceived.** Do not be led astray by such specious maxims. They can only arise from that too great familiarity with the heathen against which I have already put you on your guard. **Evil communications corrupt good manners.** An iambic line from the 'Thais' of Menander, and perhaps taken by Menander from a play of Euripides. More accurately it means "evil

associations corrupt excellent morals." According to the best reading ($\chi\rho\eta\sigma\tau\grave{a}$, not $\chi\rho\eta\sigma\theta'$), St. Paul does not quote it as an iambic, and in itself it does not offer the least shadow of proof that St. Paul was familiar with classic literature. It is just such a line as he might have seen carved on the Hermæ of any Greek town, or preserved in any chrestomathy or gnomology which may have chanced to pass through his hands. His other classic quotations (from Epimenides, Titus i. 12; and Aratus or Cleanthes, Acts xvii. 28) are of the same common and proverbial character. It is very unlikely that he would have deliberately quoted from the immoral play of a corrupt comedian like Menander. (For the sentiment, see 2 Tim. ii. 16—18.)

Ver. 34.—**Awake to righteousness.** The word rendered "awake" means "awake at once from a drunken sleep." This verb does not occur elsewhere in the New Testament. The word rendered "awake" in Eph. v. 14 and Rom. xiii. 11 is a different one. The metaphor, however, occurs in the simple verb in 1 Thess. v. 6, 8; 2 Tim. iv. 5; 1 Pet. v. 8, etc. The word rendered "to righteousness" is literally an adverb, *righteously*. It may mean "as is fit." **And sin not.** Here the present tense, "be not sinning," is contrasted with the instantaneous aorist, "awake." **Have not the knowledge.** The original is stronger, "have an ignorance." They have not a vacuum of nescience, but a *plenuum* of ignorance. **I speak this to your shame**; rather, *I am speaking to shame you.* The object of all I am saying is to excite your shame—not, as in some previous instances, "to spare you."

Vers. 35—49.—*Material objections answered.*

Ver. 35.—**But some man will say.** The objection is that of some philosophical materialist. The resurrection of the *body* was a difficulty alike to Sadducees and Gentiles. St. Paul meets this difficulty by natural analogies, which are intended to show that the resurrection-body, though identical with the mortal body so far as the preservation of personal identity is concerned, is yet a glorified body, so that the objections urged on the ground that it is impossible to preserve the same material particles which have passed into dust, are beside the mark. St. Paul gives no sanction to the coarse physical conceptions of the resurrection which described the human being as rising (to use the words of the Christian poet Prudentius) "with every tooth and every nail." **How are the dead raised up?** This question is one which, of course, admits of no answer. **And with what body do they come?** literally, *with what kind of body?* St. Paul, while he only answers the question indirectly and *by analogy*, implies that the resurrection-body is the same body, not so much by way of material identity as of glorified individuality.

Ver. 36.—**Thou fool.** The expression is too strong, and it is unfortunate that in English it seems to run contrary to the distinct censure of such language by our Lord. But here the Greek word is *aphrōn*, "O unreasonable!" (the nominative is used for the vocative) ; Vulgate, *insipiens;* Wickliffe, "unwise man." It is merely a reproach for neglecting to exercise the understanding. The word "fool!" (*mōre*) forbidden by our Lord (Matt. v. 22) has quite a different meaning, and implies quite a different tone. It involves moral depravity or obstinacy (Matt. vii. 26 ; xxiii. 17, etc.). The milder *aphrōn* is used in 2 Cor. xi. 16, 19; xii. 11 ; Eph. v. 17; and by our Lord himself. **That which thou sowest.** The "thou" is emphatic. It merely means "Even the analogy of human sowing ought to remove thy difficulty." The growth of the seed shows that there may be personal identity under a complete change of material conditions. **Is not quickened, except it die.** The mataphor is used by our Lord (John xii. 24, "Except a grain of wheat fall into the earth and die, it abideth by itself alone ; but if it die, it beareth much fruit "). It is also found in the Talmud.

Ver. 37.—**Not that body that shall be.** This deep remark should have checked the idly and offensively materialistic form in which the doctrine of the resurrection is often taught. **But bare grain.** Wickliffe, "a naked corne." In this passage, almost alone in all his Epistles, St. Paul, who does not seem to have been at all a close observer of external phenomena, uses metaphors drawn from natural life. His usual metaphors are chiefly architectural and agonistic—derived, that is, from buildings and games. That he was not a student of nature arose, no doubt, partly from his Semitic cast of mind, but chiefly from his being short-sighted, and from his having spent most of his early life in large cities. **It may chance;** *if it so happen* (see note on ch. xiv. 10). The English word "chance" occurs but four times in the whole Bible (1 Sam. vi. 9 ; Eccles. ix. 11). In Luke x. 31 the words rendered "by chance" mean rather "by coincidence."

Ver. 38.—**But God giveth it a body.** The material body of each living organism results from those laws of assimilation which God has made a part of His secret of life. They are not the life, only the instrument and expression and manifestation of the life. The "life" is the individual identity. The life of Hamlet is not in its essence the physical life of "the machine which is to him Hamlet," but the spiritual life which is *linked* on earth to that perpetual flux of material particles which we call the body, but is independent of those particles. **As it hath pleased him;** literally, *as he willed.* And in the word "as" lies the scope for all theories about the part played by what are called "natural laws." Their action is a part of God's will. **To every seed his own body.** Each of the seeds sown is provided with a body of its own, which is not identical with the seed, but results from the germ of life in the seed.

Ver. 39.—**All flesh is not the same flesh.** In other words, animal organisms differ from each other, just as do the vegetable. **Another . . . of beasts.** "The germinal power of the plant transmutes the fixed air and the elementary base of water into grass or leaves, and on these the organic principle in the ox or the elephant exercises an alchemy still more stupendous. As the unseen agency weaves its magic eddies, the foliage becomes indifferently the bone and its marrow, the pulpy brain and the solid ivory. That which you see is blood, is flesh, is itself the work, or shall I say the translucence of the invisible energy which soon surrenders or abandons them to inferior powers (for there is no pause nor chasm in the activities of nature) which repeat a similar metamorphosis according to their kind : these are not fancies, conjectures, or even hypotheses, but facts" (Coleridge, 'Aids to Reflection').

Ver. 40.—There are **also celestial bodies, and bodies terrestrial.** The words are often misunderstood. The "celestial bodies" are not the sun, moon, and stars of the next verse—for that would be a false antithesis to "bodies terrestrial"—but bodies (or organisms) which belong to heavenly beings, such as the resurrection-body of our Lord and of glorified saints, or even in some sense of angels (Matt. xxii. 30).

Ver. 41.—There is **one glory of the sun.** "Then shall the righteous shine forth as the sun" (Matt. xiii. 43). The point of the illustration is the difference between the earthly and the resurrection body ; not the supposed differences between the saints themselves in glory. *This* is not a question under consideration, and St. Paul, as we have seen, is not in the habit of mixing up half a dozen different questions in the same immediate argument. St. Augustine says of the saints, "Their splendour is unequal; their heaven is one." This may be very true, but to deduce it from this verse is to press into the argument an illustration used for another purpose. Tertullian's comment is very unhappy. He makes "men" mean servants of God ; "beasts," Gentiles ; "birds," martyrs; "fishes," *those who have been baptized;* the "sun," *Christ;* the "moon," the

Church, etc. One **star differeth from** another **star in glory.** All the righteous shall shine as " the brightness of the firmament and ... as the stars for ever and ever" (Dan. xii. 3), and their future bodies shall differ from their present, as one star differs from another.

Ver. 42.—**So also is the resurrection of the dead.** In like manner the dead, when raised, shall have bodies which differ from their body of humiliation (Phil. iii. 21). **It is sown in corruption.** "Dust thou art, and unto dust shalt thou return" (Gen. iii. 19). **It is raised in incorruption.** The word means strictly, " incorruptibility." The resurrection-body will not be subjected to earthly conditions (Luke xx. 35, 36).

Ver. 43.—**It is sown in dishonour.** "The awful and intolerable indignity of dust to dust." **In glory.** "Though ye have lien among the pots, yet shall ye be as the wings of a dove, that is covered with silver wings, and her feathers like gold" (Ps. lxviii. 13). The expression shows that, throughout, St. Paul is thinking exclusively of the resurrection *of the saints.*

Ver. 44.—**A natural body.** The adjective is the word ψυχικόν, which is so difficult to translate; it means a body only animated by the *psyche*, or natural life. The word is sometimes in our Authorized Version rendered "carnal." **A spiritual body.** The apparent contradiction in terms is inevitable. The thing meant is a body which is not under the sway of corporeal desires or of intellectual and passionate impulses, but is wholly dominated by the Spirit, and therefore has no desire or capacity to fulfil the lusts of the flesh. **There is.** The better supported reading (א, A, B, C, D, F, G), is, *if there is a natural body,* etc. The existence of the one is no more impossible than the existence of the other.

Ver. 45.—**The first man Adam was made a living soul** (Gen. ii. 7). **The last Adam.** A rabbinic expression also for the Messiah. **A quickening Spirit.** "The Son quickeneth whom he will" (John v. 21; comp. vi. 23). The best comment on the expression will be found in Rom. viii. 2, 11. Christ is "a quickening," *i.e.* a life-giving, "Spirit," here mainly in the sense that we shall only be raised by "the power of his resurrection" (John v. 24, 25), but also in the sense that his Spirit dwelleth in us, and is our true Life.

Ver. 46.—**That was not first which is spiritual.** The imperfect precedes the perfect.

Ver. 47.—**Earthy.** Made of "the dust of the ground" (Gen. ii. 7). **Is the Lord from heaven.** The words "the Lord" are a gloss, not found in א, B, C, D, E, F, G. The verse remarkably resembles John iii. 31, and probably oral reminiscences of our Lord's discourses were current among the apostles long before the Gospels were written. Tertullian attributes the insertion of "the Lord" to Marcion.

Ver. 48.—**As is the earthy, etc.** Men resemble their first parent Adam; Christians, their spiritual Redeemer, Christ (Phil. iii. 20, 21).

Ver. 49.—**We shall also bear the image of the heavenly** (for the fact, see Rom. viii. 29; 1 John iii. 2). For "we shall bear," the best manuscripts (א, A, C, D, E, F, G, etc.) read "Let us bear." Our reading is, however, supported by B, and this is just one of the cases in which manuscript evidence (or as it is called "diplomatic evidence") has a minimum value, and other evidence (paradiplomatic) is decisive. For (1) the pronunciation of the indicative and subjunctive at that time was almost identical, because in conversation the vowels seem to have been much slurred; and (2) there was a universal tendency to substitute hortative for direct forms, with a view to edification (as in ch. xiv. 15; Rom. vi. 2, 8; 2 Cor. v. 11, etc.). Here the exhortation would ruin the texture of the argument.

Vers. 50—58.—*Conclusion and exhortation.*

Ver. 50.—**Now this I say.** This sums up my meaning. **Flesh and blood.** Our mortal nature and human organism; our "earthly house of this tabernacle" (2 Cor. v. 1; Luke xx. 35). **Inherit incorruption.** A body liable to corruption, with all its loathly accompaniments, cannot enter into the "inheritance incorruptible, and undefiled, and that fadeth not away" (1 Pet. i. 4).

Ver. 51.—**I show you a mystery.** I make known to you a truth now made known to me by revelation. **We shall not all sleep, but we shall all be changed.** There is a great diversity of readings in this verse, noticed even by St. Jerome and St. Augustine. St. Jerome says that all the Latin manuscripts had "we shall all rise," and that the Greek manuscripts wavered between "we shall all sleep" and "we shall not all sleep." Some Greek manuscripts had "we shall all rise, but we shall not all be changed." This reading cannot be right, for it contradicts the next verse. There is little doubt that the reading of the Authorized version is right. It accounts for all the variations. They arose from a desire to shelter St. Paul from an apparent mistake, since he and his readers *did* all sleep. But (1) St. Paul may have written under that conception of the imminence of Christ's personal return which he expresses in 1 Thess. iv. 15—17, where he evidently imagines that the majority of those to whom he was writing would be of those who would be "alive, and remain unto the coming of the Lord;" or (2) even if he no longer entertained that expectation, the "we" may naturally apply to the continuity of the Christian Church. For in 2 Cor. iv. 14 he uses "us" of those who shall die and be raised. The universal expectation of the immediate return of Christ in the first century rose (1) from their non-apprehension of the truth that the close of the old dispensation *was* the "coming" to which our Lord had primarily referred in his great eschatological discourse (Matt. xxiv. 34), and (2) from the fact that watchfulness was intended to be the attitude of the Church, and the day and hour of Christ's coming were kept absolutely unrevealed (Matt. xxiv. 36; xxv. 13).

Ver. 52.—**The trumpet shall sound.** The Lord, he says, in 1 Thess. iv. 16, "shall descend from heaven with . . . the voice of the archangel, and with the trump of God." The trumpet is, of course, only a natural symbol. It is also found in rabbinic writers, and in the Old Testament (Zech. ix. 14), as well as in Rev. xi. 15. **We shall be changed.** The dead shall be changed by resurrection, the living by transition, into a glorified body. St. Paul, dealing with the essence of the question as it bore on the difficulties of his readers, says nothing here (1) of those who will arise to judgment, or (2) of any intermediate condition. As to the former question, he scarcely ever alludes to it with any definiteness, but seems with deliberate choice to contemplate the final and absolute triumph of good (Rom. viii. 19—23; xi. 30—36). To the intermediate state he does not here allude. He is here only speaking of death and glorious resurrection. In 2 Cor. v. 1—4 he says all that he has to say on this latter question. It was not prominent in the minds of the early Christians, who, as Calvin says, were awaiting the return of Christ "from hour to hour."

Ver. 53.—**This mortal must put on immortality.** When we are "clothed upon" by our "house from heaven," and have put off "this tabernacle," in which we groan being burdened, then "mortality will be swallowed up of life" (2 Cor. v. 3, 4, where we also find the metaphor of a *robe* of immortality, mixed up with the metaphor of a building).

Ver. 54.—**Death is swallowed up in victory.** A free citation from the Hebrew of Isa. xxv. 8. The words "into victory" are the LXX. rendering in other passages (Amos i. 11; viii. 8) for the Hebrew *la-netsach*, for ever. The metaphor, "is swallowed up," implying "the swallowing of the all-swallower," is found in the rabbis (comp. Heb. ii. 14, 15).

Ver. 55.—**O death, where is thy sting?** A triumphantly fervid exclamation of the apostle, loosely cited from Hos. xiii. 14.

The apostles and evangelists, not holding the slavish and superstitious fetish-worship of the dead letter, often regard it as sufficient to give the general sense of the passages to which they refer. **O grave, where is thy victory?** In the best-attested reading (, A, B, C, D, E, F, G), "death" is repeated, and in the best manuscripts this clause precedes the last. But if the reading, "O Hades," were correct, our translators, since they held it here impossible in accordance with their views to render it by "hell," ought to have taken warning, and seen the pernicious inapplicability of that rendering in other places where they have used it to express this same Greek word. Here "Hades" has probably been introduced into the Greek text from the LXX., which uses it for the *Sheol* of the original.

Ver. 56.—**The sting of death is sin.** Because death is the wages of sin (Rom. vi. 23). Death is represented as a venomous serpent. **The strength of sin is the Law.** The best comment on this expression is to be found in the Epistle to the Romans; see especially Rom. iv. 15; vii. 10—12. It must be admitted that this passing allusion to a distinct doctrine does not seem, at first sight, to harmonize with the glorious unity of the subject. No one can read it without a slight sense of *jar*, because it seems to introduce the element of dogmatic controversy. But this sense of incongruity is removed when we remember how intensely St. Paul felt that man is confronted with the horror of a broken Law, which at once reminds him of a Being infinitely holy, and of his own self-condemnation (Rom. vii.; 2 Cor. iii.). It is the sense that the Law in its deathful aspect is annulled, and the sinful soul delivered, which prompts the outburst of the next verse.

Ver. 57.—**Thanks be to God, which giveth us the victory.** The victory consists in the defeat of death by the Resurrection, and the forgiveness of sin through Christ's atonement, and the nailing to his cross of the torn and abrogated Law which made us slaves to sin and death (Col. ii. 14). "In all these things we are more than conquerors through him that loved us" (Rom. viii. 37). **Through our Lord Jesus Christ.** Who, by fulfilling the Law, has robbed it of its condemning power (Rom. viii. 1), and by his death "hath destroyed him that had the power of death, that is the devil" (Heb. ii. 14, 15).

Ver. 58.—**Therefore.** Seeing that you ought not to despair, but to share in this confidence of triumph. **Steadfast.** Firmly fixed in *your own* conviction (Col. i. 23; 2 John 9). **Unmoveable.** By others (Eph. iv. 14). **Abounding in the work of the Lord.** Doing diligently and ungrudgingly the work of your lives, which is *his* work. **That your labour is not in vain.** The thought of the verse is the same as that of Gal. vi. 9, "And let us not be weary in well doing; for in due season we shall reap, if we faint not."

Some general facts are very observable in this glorious chapter. 1. One is that St. Paul does not meet doubt by angry denunciation, or by crushing it with the iron mace of impatient authority. What would now be thought of Christians who denied the resurrection? Doubtless they were not mere speculative deniers of the resurrection, like Hymenæus and Philetus (2 Tim. ii. 17), but recent Gentile converts, who could not get over their pagan difficulties. Yet St. Paul meets them by personal appeals, by helpful analogies, by lofty reasoning, by the glowing force of inspiring convictions. Instead of taking refuge—*more ecclesiastico*—in anathema and excommunication, he meets error by the counter-presentation of ennobling truth. 2. Another noteworthy fact is that St. Paul's hope of the resurrection rests, like all his theology, on the thought that the life of the Christian is a life "in Christ." 3. A third is his superiority to false analogies—like those of the butterfly and the phœnix—which sufficed many ancient reasoners. Even Christian writers like St. Clement of Rome

continued to appeal to the phœnix as a proof of the resurrection. The greatest ancient thinkers—like Tacitus—believed in the existence of that fabulous bird, and even in the genuineness of a specimen of it which had been exhibited at Rome. Was there no "grace of superintendency" at work which prevented the sacred writers from adopting the universal error of their day? Had St. Paul appealed to the phœnix, centuries of Christian writers would have continued to maintain the existence of that creature; and science, laughing the belief to scorn, would (most unjustly) have made any allusion to it a proof of mental weakness, and of the falsity of the doctrine which it was supposed to prove. 4. A fourth point to be observed is the wisdom with which St. Paul holds himself aloof from speculative fancies. He does not, like Plato, appeal to the doctrine of "reminiscence" (*anamnesis*), or of unfulfilled ideas. He does not, like Kant, build any argument on man's failure to obey "the categorical imperative" of duty. He points to the sinless Man—to the fulfilled idea of Christ. His argument, which all could understand, is summed up in the words, "Ye are Christ's, and Christ is risen." Your resurrection from the death of sin to the life of righteousness is a pledge of your participation in Christ's resurrection from the grave.

HOMILETICS.

Vers. 1—11.—*The apostolic gospel.* "Moreover, brethren," etc. On all hands we hear persons talk about the "simple gospel." And it appears to us that, in the majority of cases, the expression means nothing more than a few crude notions which the speaker has received, or possibly formed, about the gospel. Some men's "simple gospel" is an offence to reason, a dishonour to God, and a curse to Christianity. The passage under review presents to us Paul's "simple gospel." And let us look at Christianity as here indicated. We observe—

I. THAT CHRISTIANITY IS BASED UPON HISTORICAL FACTS. It is not founded upon human reason—upon any of its primitive axioms or logical conclusions. It is not founded upon human imagination; it is neither an ingenious hypothesis to account for any phenomena, nor a poetic myth to adumbrate any truth. It is based on facts. 1. These facts are *personal*. They are connected with a person, and that person is not Socrates, Plato, nor Cæsar, but one whom Paul calls Christ. It is founded upon the personal history of one, and but one, individual, and that is Christ. 2. These facts are *few*. He "died," he was "buried," and he "rose." These facts are compendious facts; they imply many more, and may be reduced even to less. The resurrection of Christ involves the whole; and in the subsequent verses of this chapter, Paul uses it as such. 3. These facts are *well attested*. After his resurrection, Paul tells us here that he "was seen of Cephas," of "the twelve," then of "five hundred," and then of "me also." No facts on record are better attested than these.

II. THAT CHRISTIANITY IS DESIGNED FOR THE REMOVAL OF EVIL. Why did these facts take place? What is the aim of the whole? He "died for our sins." The great end of Christianity is to "put away sin" from the world, to put it away from the hearts, literature, institutions, customs, and governments of mankind. Let sin be put away, and all evil is put away; natural evil is but the effect of moral. *Philosophically*, there is no system on earth suited to destroy man's sinful disposition and to change his heart but Christianity, and *historically* nothing else has ever done it. Let the fact ring louder and louder through the world, that the grand end of Christianity is not the formation of creeds, however correct, nor the organization of societies, however scriptural; but it is to "put away sin."

III. THAT CHRISTIANITY IS TO BE PREACHED WITH THIS DESIGN. "By which also ye are saved, if ye keep in memory [hold fast] what I preached unto you," etc. Paul preached that they might be saved, but they could only be saved as they renounced and hated sin. The passage suggests three ideas in relation to Paul's preaching with this view. 1. He preached Christianity convincingly. He says, "The gospel which I preached unto you, which also ye ... received." They believed his gospel; then he must have convinced them by arguments. Christianity in preaching is to be commended "to every man's conscience." 2. He preached Christianity *scripturally*. He showed those facts in the light of the Scriptures, "according to the Scriptures." 3. He preached Christianity *humbly*. The expression "born out of due time" evidently indicates his humility; and then in the next verse he says, "For I am the least of the apostles, that am not meet to be called an apostle," etc. We thank God for such a system as this—a system built not on propositions, but on *facts, personal, few in number*, but *well attested*. Such facts are most palpable and attractive; a system which cures the evils of the moral world by taking away its sins. Let it be preached, as Paul preached it—convincingly, scripturally, and humbly.

Vers. 12—19.—*Terrible conclusions resulting from the denial of two great gospel facts.* "Now if Christ be preached that he rose from the dead, how say some among you that there is no resurrection of the dead? But if there be no resurrection of the dead, then is Christ not risen: and if Christ be not risen, then is our preaching vain, and your faith is also vain. Yea, and we are found false witnesses of God; because we have testified of God that he raised up Christ: whom he raised not up, if so be that the dead rise not. For if the dead rise not, then is not Christ raised: and if Christ be not raised, your faith is vain; ye are yet in your sins. Then they also which are fallen asleep in Christ are perished. If in this life only we have hope in Christ, we are of all men most miserable." In this paragraph the apostle refers to two great facts *fundamental* to Christianity, and *peculiar* to it as a system of religion. The one is the *general resurrection* from the dead, and the other is the *resurrection of Christ* himself. In order to make clear Paul's process of reasoning here, I see no better way than to exhibit the conclusions which he draws from the *denial* of these facts.

I. Conclusions resulting from the denial of the GENERAL RESURRECTION OF THE DEAD. These conclusions are threefold. 1. *The non-resurrection of Christ.* "If there is no resurrection of the dead, then is Christ not risen." If you can demonstrate the impossibility of men coming to life again after they have been buried, then you prove, of course, that Christ has not risen. What is true of the whole is true of all the parts. If no man can rise from the dead, then Christ is still numbered amongst the dead. There were evidently men in the Church at Corinth who, like the Sadducees, denied the doctrine of a future resurrection. Hence Paul informs them that doing so is tantamount to the denial of the resurrection of Christ from the dead, which fact he had proclaimed amongst them. 2. *That departed Christians are no more.* "Then they also which are fallen asleep in Christ are perished." They also, as well as others. If dead men do not rise, then our fellow-disciples who have departed this life, and who believed in a risen Christ, are no more. Those thousands who from the day of Pentecost accepted Christ, lived according to his teaching, and who quitted this world, have perished. Can you believe it? Are they quenched in eternal midnight? 3. *That there is no more pitiable condition in this life than that of Christians.* "If in this life only we have hope in Christ, we are of all men most miserable." How many things are implied in this language! It is implied that there are men in a pitiable condition on this earth; it is implied that the pitiable condition exists in different degrees; it is implied that the degrees of pitiableness are regulated by hope. Man is always hoping; man is always, therefore, enduring one of the greatest elements of suffering, viz. disappointment. It is implied that the hope of a Christian, if false, will make him of all men the most to be pitied. (For an amplification of these points, see *Homilist*, vol. xi. p. 61.) Of course it is not intended to teach that, apart from the resurrection of Christ, man has no evidence of a future state, nor that, on the supposition that there is no future life, the practice of virtue is not to be preferred to that of vice. It is implied that the higher the object of our hope, and the more of the soul that goes into it, the more overwhelmingly crushing will be the disappointment. The man who has thrown his whole soul into Christianity, and who reaches a point where he is convinced of its imposture, is at that moment " of all men the most miserable."

II. Conclusions resulting from the denial of CHRIST'S RESURRECTION FROM THE DEAD. There are three conclusions here resulting from the denial of this fact. 1. *That apostolic Christianity is vain.* "If Christ be not risen, then is our preaching vain, and your faith is also vain." It is vain, void, an empty phantom, a worthless fiction. The resurrection of Christ was the foundation stone in the temple of Paul's teaching. Take that stone away, then it falls and becomes worthless rubbish. But not only is preaching vain, and your faith vain, we ourselves are "false witnesses." We are impostors. Can you believe this? What motives have we to impose? The supposition either that they taught falsehood, that the disciples believed falsehood, or that they were "false witnesses," is eternally inadmissible. Hence Christ did rise from the dead. 2. *That the faith of the disciples was vain.* "Your faith is also vain." What a wreck of faith is involved in the denial of Christ's resurrection! Then (1) faith in the *credibility of historic testimony* is vain. On what stronger historical testimony can any fact rest than that of the resurrection of Christ? Then (2) faith in the *accuracy of philosophic deduction* is vain. The rapid progress of Christianity in the Roman empire in its first stages, and its subsequent influence throughout the world, reveal a mass of phenomena which you cannot account for if you deny the resurrection of Christ. Then (3) faith in the *moral value of character* is vain. Did a nobler character than Christ's ever exist? And yet if he rose not, then is he an impostor. Then (4) faith in the *righteous government of God* is vain. If a being so transcendently excellent as Christ is to be crushed for ever in the grave, where is the justice of Heaven? Verily, if our faith in the resurrection of Christ is vain, of what worth is any faith? 3. *That the followers of Christ are still in their sins.* It is here implied that faith in Christ can alone take men out of their sins. This is a fact grounded on history, consciousness, and the gospel. But the Christians at Corinth were conscious that they had got out of their sins, to a certain degree at least. "Such were some of you; but ye are washed," etc. Consciousness the highest ultimate argument, protested against Paul's hypothesis that they were still in their sins; hence it goes to verify the fact of the resurrection of Christ.

Vers. 20—23.—*The resurrection of Christ.* "But now is Christ risen from the dead, and become the firstfruits of them that slept. For since by man came death, by man came also the resurrection of the dead. For as in Adam all die, even so in Christ shall all be made alive. But every man in his own order : Christ the firstfruits; afterward they that are Christ's at his coming." These verses lead us to contemplate the resurrection of Christ as an established fact, as a significant fact, and as an influential fact.

I. AN ESTABLISHED FACT. Paul asserts this fact with a spirit of triumphant certitude. This fact is established : 1. On the *testimony of the most competent witnesses.* A competent witness is one who has a thorough knowledge of the facts whereof he affirms, and such an invincible love for truth as would render it utterly impossible for him to misrepresent them. The apostles were witnesses of this type. 2. On the very *existence of Christendom.* What gave birth to that domain amongst the peoples of the race called Christendom? The *gospel;* and the truth of the gospel rests on the resurrection of Christ. 3. On the *consciousness of genuine disciples.* Such consciousness attests that they are "not in their sins," that they have got more or less free from their thraldom and dominion, and they feel that this deliverance came from the gospel.

II. A SIGNIFICANT FACT. "Now is Christ risen from the dead, and become the firstfruits of them that slept." The reference here is to the "firstfruits" of the harvest which were offered by the priests unto the Lord (see Lev. xxiii. 12—19). Those firstfruits were both an earnest and a sample of the full harvest at hand. Hence Christ's resurrection was regarded : 1. As a *pledge* of the resurrection of those who were dead. As he rose so will all rise. 2. As a *pattern* of the resurrection of those who were dead. The sheaf waved before the Lord was a specimen or sample of what remained in the field to be gathered in. "Our vile bodies shall be fashioned and made like unto his glorious body."

III. An INFLUENTIAL FACT. "For since by man came death, by man came also the resurrection of the dead. For as in Adam all die, even so in Christ shall all be made alive." Between the influence of Adam and that of Christ on the race, there is a *resemblance* and a *contrast*. 1. A *resemblance*. The resemblance is in its *extensibility*. Though Adam's influence upon the race may be more extensive at present than that of Christ, it is not more *extensible*. It has in it the power of extending over the whole race down through all times, and it will so do. 2. A *contrast*. The influence of the one is *destructive*; the influence of the other, *quickening*. "As in Adam all die, even so in Christ shall all be made alive." If by death here bodily death is meant, then the idea is that Christ will quicken to life all that have died. But what does it mean to be *in* Adam and *in* Christ? There is, at any rate, one sense which we can understand in which we are in them; that is, in the sense of *character*. Without figure all men live in the characters of others—children live in the character of their parents, pupils in their masters, the present generation in the preceding. The characters of the men of past ages constitute the moral atmosphere of existing men. In Adam's character, the character of *selfishness, carnality, unbelief*, all unregenerate men live to-day; his principles pulsate in all hearts. In the character of Christ, in his *self-sacrificing love, spotless purity*, and holy *reverence*, all the godly live to-day. Now, those who live in the character of Adam must die, not merely in the sense of the dissolution of the soul from the body, but in the more awful sense of the dissolution of the soul from God; whereas those who live in the character of Christ live by a vital connection with the eternal Fountain of all life. The influence of Adam's character on the race is destructive; that of Christ's is quickening and restorative. "All shall be made alive." Shall there be a universal restoration?

Vers. 24—28.—*Christ resigning his administration.* "Then cometh the end," etc. By the "end" here, I presume, is to be meant the redemptive reign of Christ. It means that when Christ, in the exercise of his mediatorial government, has subjugated all the powers of moral evil, he will deliver up his commission to God, who will then be acknowledged as the absolute Ruler of all. The following are some of the truths that the passage suggests:—

I. That the GOVERNMENT OF OUR WORLD IS ADMINISTERED BY CHRIST. The New Testament is full of the doctrine that Christ reigns over our world. This doctrine explains several otherwise inexplicable things in the history of man. 1. *The perpetuation of the human race on the earth.* Death was threatened on Adam the same day on which he should sin. He sinned, and died not that day, but lived for centuries, and became the father of an immense and ever-multiplying family. And why? The Biblical doctrine of mediation is the only principle that explains it. 2. *The coexistence of sin and happiness in the same individual.* Under the government of *absolute* righteousness, we should antecedently expect that such an association would never exist. We are told that there is perfect happiness in heaven, and we can understand it, because perfect holiness is there. But here there are sin and happiness, comparative holiness and great suffering. The mediative government is the only principle that explains this. 3. *The offer of pardon and the application of remedial influences to the condemned and corrupt.* Under a righteous government how is this to be explained? It is explicable only on the ground that "he is exalted to be a Prince and a Saviour," etc.

II. That Christ conducts the government of our world IN ORDER TO PUT DOWN ALL HUMAN EVILS. There are two classes of evil referred to here. 1. *Moral.* "All rule, all authority and power." *Sinful principles are the moral potentates of this world.* Christ's government is to put them down from governments, Churches, books, hearts, etc. 2. *Physical.* "The last enemy that shall be destroyed is death." Death is the totality of physical evils. Christ will destroy this.

III. That when these evils are entirely put down, CHRIST WILL RESIGN HIS ADMINISTRATION INTO THE HANDS OF THE EVERLASTING FATHER. The time will come when moral evil shall be entirely exterminated from the earth, and when death shall be swallowed up in victory. Christ, having finished the work that was given him to do, resigns his office. "Then cometh the end."

IV. That when Christ shall have resigned his administration, GOD "WILL BE ALL IN ALL." What does this mean? 1. He will treat all men after this on the ground of their own moral merits. From the Fall up to this period, he had treated them on the ground of Christ's mediation; but now, the mediation removed, each man shall reap the "fruit of his own doings." 2. All men after this will subjectively realize the absolute One as they have never before. The atmosphere of their nature purified, he shall appear within them as the central orb, making the finite manifest and glorious in the conscious light of the Infinite.

Ver. 29.—*The Church-world.* " Else what shall they do which are baptized for the dead, if the dead rise not at all?" etc. There is a Church-world—a world inside, the general world of mankind, and in many respects distinct from it; a community of men whose principles, spirit, aim, character, and destiny distinguish them from every other class of human society. They are called a "chosen generation, a royal priesthood, a holy nation, a peculiar people." They are united to each other as stones in one building, as branches in one root, as members in one body. The text presents this Church-world to us in three aspects.

I. AS THINNED BY DEATH. The text speaks of those who are "baptized for the dead." Death was in the Church in the days of the apostle, and it has been ever since. The great law of mortality which extends over men in general enters this realm and operates here. The spiritual intelligence, the moral virtues, the godly devotions, and the social usefulness of this Church-realm constitute no barrier to the entrance of death. There is, however, great difference between the aspects and effects of death as he appears and works in the world of mankind. 1. He appears in the Church-world as the *messenger of mercy*; outside, as the *officer of justice.* Outside he appears to men as the stern officer of insulted justice, to drag the criminal to retribution; here as the messenger of heavenly mercy, to snap the chains of the prisoner, to terminate the trials of the afflicted, and to introduce the disciples of Christ to the joys of immortality. 2. He leaves behind in the Church-world *consolation for the survivors,* but outside *unmitigated sorrow.* What have the widow of the wicked husband, the child of the ungodly parent, to console their bereavement? Nothing. Death leaves the social wounds he has created in the outside world to bleed and rankle without any balm. Not so in this Church-world: here is abundant consolation. " Sorrow not as those that are without hope."

II. AS REPLENISHED BY CONVERSION. " What shall they do which are baptized for the dead?" This is confessedly an obscure expression, and has given rise to many and conflicting interpretations. Some say that Paul refers to an old custom in the Church of vicarious baptism, that is, baptizing survivors for those who had died without having received the ordinance of baptism; others, that the word " baptism " is to be taken in the metaphorical sense in which our Saviour sometimes employed it, as representing overwhelming sufferings (Matt. x. 20; Mark x. 39); and that Paul meant to say, " Why should men be baptized with such sufferings, if there be no resurrection of the dead? " Others say that the baptism spoken of is the baptism of the Spirit, and refers to conversion of the soul by the Spirit of God. There are many other opinions, but this is not the place for critical inquiries. I accept the last-mentioned idea, namely, *conversion.* By those who are " baptized for the dead " I understand those who, from pagan darkness, were converted by the gospel and were admitted into the visible Church, there to fill up the place of those who, by martyrdom or otherwise, had been called away by death. The new convert then took the place of the departed saint. Thus *conversions in the Church replenish the losses caused by death.* No sooner is one Christian removed from his station than another is raised up by God to supply the loss. Since the apostolic day, what myriads of able preachers, evangelists, theologians, reformers, and distinguished saints have passed away! Still the Church goes on, and their places are all occupied. As Joshua succeeded Moses; Elisha, Elijah; Eleazar, Aaron; so one man is ever raised up in the Church to take the place of another. This succession: 1. Affords a lesson to us for *humility.* The man of most brilliant talents, distinguished position, and extensive usefulness in the Church has nothing whereof to flatter himself; however important he may be, the Church can do without him. When he falls, others are ready to step into his place, having been baptized for the dead. 2,

Affords a lesson to us for *encouragement.* God's redemptive plan will go on, whatever happens to individual agents. "He has buried his workmen," says Charles Wesley, "but carries on his work." Let us learn to trust God rather than his most distinguished servants. The treasure is only in "earthen vessels"—vessels that must crumble.

III. As LIVING IN HOPE. "What shall they do which are baptized for the dead, if the dead rise not at all?" This language implies that the hope of a future state, of a resurrection, was a vital thing in the experience of the Church, and so it has ever been, so it is, and so it ever will be. The Church lives in hope. It reckons "that the sufferings of the present time are not worthy to be compared with the glories that shall be." It is "waiting for the adoption;" it is looking "for the blessed appearing." We must not mistake Paul's meaning, however. He does not mean to say that the religion of Christ is of no service to men if there be no future state. Let us answer his two questions—the what and the why. 1. *What* shall they do? We venture to reply, not renounce religion, but continue faithful for ever. Should there be no future, Christian virtue is good. You will lose nothing by it should you be annihilated; in that case you will not feel the disappointment, but you will gain immensely by it, even in the present life. "Godliness is profitable unto all things." 2. *Why* are they, then, baptized? We answer, because the claims of religion are independent of the future state. Were there no heaven, no hell, we should be bound to be truthful, honest, benevolent, God-loving.

Vers. 30, 31.—*Daily dying.* "Why stand we," etc.? The apostles, in their efforts to extend the gospel, endured great afflictions and involved themselves in terrific perils, and if there be no future life, Paul asks, why should they have done so? "Why stand we in jeopardy every hour?" Why should we thus "die daily"? But there is a daily dying in the case of every man.

I. There is a daily dying that is INEVITABLE to humanity. 1. There is a daily dying of our *corporeal frame.* In each human body the seed of death is implanted, the law of mortality is at work. The water does not more naturally roll to the ocean than the human frame runs every moment to dissolution. Life streams from us at every pore. This fact should teach us: (1) That worldly-mindedness is an infraction of reason. What a monstrous absurdity it is to set our supreme affections upon objects from which we are departing every moment. As the ship of the emigrant in full sail is bearing him every moment further and further from his native shore, so destiny is bearing every man further and further from his connection with this earth. No anchor can stop this ship of destiny. (2) That sorrow for the departed should be moderated. Why indulge in grief for those who are gone? Their departure was in obedience to the resistless law of their nature, and that same law is daily bearing us whither they are gone. (3) That Christianity is an invaluable boon to mortals. It does two things; it teaches us that there is a future world of blessedness, and points us the way by which that blessed world is reached. 2. There is a daily dying of our *social world.* We live not only with others, but *by* them. Without society we might *exist,* but *live* we could not. Our contemporaries are the objects of our sympathies, the subjects of our conscious life; they engage our thoughts, they affect our hearts, they originate our motives, they stimulate our conduct, and all this is much of our life. But this social world in which we live, and by which we live, is dying daily. The social circumstances which feed our life are changing every day. The thoughts, the love, the grief, the anger, the fear, the hopes, which were once elements of life to us, have passed away because the objects of them have gone. 3. There is a daily dying of our *mental motivity.* The motives that influence us to action are elements of life, and they are constantly dying. For example, the leading purpose that a man has is, for the time, one of his strongest motives of action, but the leading purpose of every man is a dying thing. It is dead as a motive both when it is frustrated, as is constantly the case, and also when it is fully realized. A realized purpose has lost its motivity. Thus we die daily in mind.

II. There is a daily dying that is OPTIONAL to humanity. This optional death is of two kinds, the criminal and the virtuous. 1. There is the *criminal.* There are noble things in man that are dying daily, for which he is responsible. In the depraved soul, sensibility of conscience, generosity of impulse, elasticity of intellect, freedom of thought, spirituality of feeling—these, that constitute the highest life of man, die daily in the corrupt soul. The sinner is constantly murdering these, and their blood cries to Heaven for vengeance. "To be carnally minded is death." 2. There is the *virtuous*. There are certain things that men should and ought to crucify—selfishness, sensuality, love of the world, etc. The highest life of man is a daily dying to all that is mean, false, mercenary, unspiritual, and uncharitable. The apostle felt this when he said, "I," that is, my carnal self, "am crucified with Christ;" nevertheless, "*I*," that is, my spiritual self, "live," etc.

Vers. 32, 33.—*Beasts at Ephesus.* "If after the manner of men," etc. The words lead us to consider four subjects.

I. A LOW JUDGMENT of human nature. "Beasts at Ephesus." There is no good reason for supposing that Paul meant literally beasts. By wild beasts he means men gross and savage in wickedness. Paul was not alone in classifying such men with irrational brutes. John the Baptist called some of his hearers "vipers," and the great Preacher compared some such men to swine. The Bible speaks of wicked men in two stages lower than humanity. 1. The *sensual*. The sensual state is a state where the senses rule the soul. Are not the mass of men in this state? 2. The *devilish*. Men have the power of getting lower than the beasts. By the faculty of imagination they can kindle their passions into a diabolical heat, and by bringing the elements of nature into new combinations they can generate and nourish unnatural appetites.

II. A FIERCE STRUGGLE for human nature. "I have fought with wild beasts at Ephesus." Like all the apostles of truth, Paul fought with men *for* men. 1. The battle was *inevitable to his mission*. He was the messenger of truths which struck directly against their prejudices, habits, greed, etc. 2. The battle was most *benevolent on his part*. Love, not anger, was its inspiration. He fought *for* them by fighting against their prejudices and their sins. 3. The battle was most *unequal in circumstances*. Numbers, authority, wealth, and influence were all arrayed against one. A penniless foreigner fought against the whole city. In moral battles numbers are an inferior consideration. One man in truth may conquer a nation in error.

III. A GREAT PROBLEM for human nature. "What advantageth it me?" On the assumption that there is no future life, what advantageth it all this struggle for truth? The apostle does not say either that there would be an advantage in a godly struggle for truth, were there no future life, nor that such a struggle was to be conducted with a view of advantage. He puts the question, and leaves it to be answered. Our answer will be: 1. That on the assumption that there is no future life, godliness will be of *physical* advantage to man. The habits of life promoted by Christianity are conducive to bodily health and longevity. 2. That on the assumption that there is no future life, godliness will be of *mental* advantage to man. It generates sentiments, starts trains of thought, etc., which yield to the mind a happiness which nothing else on earth can afford. 3. That on the assumption that there is no future life, godliness will be of *social* advantage to man. Christianity has proved itself to be infinitely the best system for promoting the peace of families, the order of society, the prosperity of nations.

IV. A SOLEMN TENDENCY of human nature. "Be not deceived: evil communications [company] corrupt good manners." Man is a social being; he lives *in* and *by* society. Observe: 1. There is "evil company" in the *social world*. There are those who are drawn together in fellowship simply on the ground of evil doctrines, dispositions, plans, purposes, pleasures, etc. 2. There is an *instinct* in "evil company" to *corrupt*. Evil is a self-propagating power. Those who have yielded to temptations become the tempters of others. 3. There is a *susceptibility* in most *to be corrupted*. Hence the exhortation, "Be not deceived." "He that walketh with wise men shall be wise; he that is the companion of the fool is foolish." Feltham well says, "One rotten apple will infect the store; the putrid grape corrupts the whole sound cluster. If I have found any good companions, I will cherish them as the choicest of men, or as angels which are sent as guardians to me. If I have any bad ones, I will study to lose them, lest by keeping them I lose myself in the end."

Ver. 34.—*Moral resurrection.* "Awake to righteousness," etc. Observe—
I. THE CONDITION FROM WHICH MAN IS SUMMONED. It is represented by a "sleep."

What is this moral sleep? There are three points of resemblance in this condition that warrant the figure. 1. *Insensibility.* How insensible is man in sleep! He has lost all consciousness. The great world of life is shut out from him. So it is with the moral sleeper. There is a world of realities round the sinner, of the most grand and solemn description. Yet he is dead to all. He is not conscious of his spiritual being. He does not feel that he has a soul. 2. *Fictitiousness.* If the mind of the natural sleeper act, it is in a world of pictures. Objects flit before it that have no real existence. The life of the moral sleeper is highly fictitious; it is a life of dreams; it is a great lie. 3. *Transitoriness.* Sleep is not a permanent state. It has its seasons. And so it is in relation to the soul. There is a dark spiritual night brooding over the moral sleeper, but there is a spiritual morning for every moral sleeper to awake in.

II. THE STATE INTO WHICH WE ARE SUMMONED. "Awake to righteousness," or "wake up righteously."

III. THE VOICE BY WHICH WE ARE SUMMONED. This may be regarded as God's voice to man in all times and in all lands. *Wake up to the right.* To the right in politics, commerce, religion, and in all departments of life. Realize the right, embody the right. The crime and curse of humanity is that it is gone from the right.

Vers. 35—44.—*The resurrection-body.* "With what body do they come?" The question which Paul puts into the mouth of the ancient sceptic assumes the fact of a general resurrection of mankind. And why should we not assume this fact? "Why should it be thought a thing incredible with you that God should raise the dead?" Incredible! Has not he who has engaged to do it all-sufficient power? Scepticism parades the difficulties connected with the work of the resurrection. Let them be a million times more than the fancy of the infidel can figure to himself, will they amount to anything as an argument against its accomplishment? Nay, the *difficulty of a work should always be estimated by the capacity of the agent engaged to perform it.* What is impossible for one being to perform, can be achieved by another with the greatest facility. Where Omnipotence is the agent, the talk about difficulties is manifestly absurd. What would baffle and overmaster the combined power of all created existences, Almightiness can effect by a single fiat. "Is there anything too hard for the Lord?" Incredible! Changes are constantly going on in the creation bearing some resemblance to the event. Spring is a resurrection of buried life. Unnumbered graves, some that have been sealed for centuries, are opened every hour by the warm touch of the vernal ray. Incredible! It meets the universal longings of the human heart. The cry of all generations is this: "We would not be unclothed, but clothed upon, that mortality might be swallowed up in life." The world's heart waits "for the adoption, to wit, the redemption of the body." Incredible! It is unmistakably stated in that gospel which has been demonstrated Divine. To the question, "If a man die shall he live again?" we have in the Bible replies the most varied, expressive, and full. The subject of the general resurrection is a very extensive one; it has many branches, and touches a vast variety of truth. In the light of the apostle's statements, I infer the following answers to this question:—

I. With a body not IDENTICAL WITH THAT WHICH DESCENDED TO THE GRAVE. "Thou fool, that which thou sowest is not quickened, except it die," etc. Not a few of the advocates of the doctrine of the resurrection have exposed it to the ridicule of the sceptic and the contempt of the philosopher by representing the resurrection-body as the literal re-organization of the buried dust. To work upon the passions of the unreflecting and the vulgar, the sensuous poem and the declamatory pulpit have given representations of the resurrection most extravagant in their materiality and their grossness. The particles of the buried body, which through the course of centuries have undergone innumerable transformations, and been separated from each other wide as the poles asunder, are described as coming together in the last day to take the very same place in that very same body as was conveyed to the grave. In poetry we have an example in such lines as Blair's—

> "Now monuments prove faithful to their trust,
> And render back their long committed dust;
> Now charnels rattle, scattered limbs, and all
> The various bones, obsequious to the call,

> Self-moved, advance : the distant head, the feet
> Dreadful to view, see, through the dusky sky
> Fragments of bodies in confusion fly ;
> To distant regions journeying there to claim
> Deserted members and complete the frame."

Science, of course, laughs all this to scorn. It tells us how the human body, as to the particles that compose it, is in a state of perpetual flux ; that portions of it are streaming off every moment from every pore ; that at the end of seven years not one atom shall be found in the body which was there in the beginning, and that at the end of seventy years a man will have had no less than ten different bodies. It tells us how that no sooner is the body dead, than the various particles begin to liberate themselves from each other, and in the course of time mix themselves up as parts of other existences ; how they form the grass upon which the cattle browse, flow in the stream, and become the fruit and flesh on which their children live. So that, in the course of ages, the same particles might have formed the frames of a thousand different men. It tells us, moreover, that millions of men have had no graves. In some of the Oriental nations the dead are not buried, but burned, and in the process of combustion the greater portions of the body pass into invisible gases, and are lost in the immensity of the atmosphere, while the handful of ashes that remain are borne away on the four winds of heaven. Now, it is our happiness to know that not on this point, any more than on any other, does the Bible teach what true science repudiates. "That which thou sowest, thou sowest not that body that shall be." There is a difference between the dead seed sown, and the living plant that springs from it. You drop into the earth a bare grain, and what comes up? Not a bare grain, but a green stalk, which grows, perhaps, to a tree with many branches, rich foliage, lovely blossoms, and delicious fruits. There is not a particle on that tree of the bare grain that you buried. It will be thus with the resurrection-body ; it will not be the bare grain that was put into the earth, but something else, that will come up. The resurrection-body will be no more identical with the buried one than the majestic tree of the forest is the same in particle or bulk as the acorn from which it sprang. "With what body do they come?" The apostle enables us to reply further—

II. With a body that WILL HAVE SOME ORGANIC CONNECTION WITH THAT WHICH WAS DEPOSITED IN THE DUST. The plant, though very dissimilar to the bare grain, has a vital connection with it. It grows out of it, and is of the same order ; there is an unbroken *continuity*. If the resurrection of the body from the grave means anything, it must mean that something from the old body comes up and takes a fresh form. What else is meant by such expressions as this : "All that are in the graves shall hear the voice of the Son of man and come forth"? It is true that this connection between the buried and the raised body is far more inexplicable than the connection between the buried grain and the up-growing plant, or between the chrysalis and the moth. In neither of these cases is life really extinct ; death is only apparent. There is an unbroken continuity traceable from the smallest seed to the mightiest tree, from the embryo in the shell to the monarch of the air. But no continuity is *traceable* between the raised and the buried man ; there seems an awful break. Still it exists. Whatever theories are accepted as satisfactory, we hold to the scriptural fact that the new body will have an organic connection with the old ; otherwise, the resurrection of the body is nothing but a pure fiction. Further, in answer to the sceptic's question, "With what body do they come?" the apostle's language enables us to give another reply.

III. With a body WHICH GOD IN HIS SOVEREIGNTY WILL BESTOW. "God giveth it a body as it hath pleased him." 1. That God clothes life. "To every seed his own body." There is no doubt that in the universe there is life unclothed by matter. It may be so with the angels : it is so, I trow, with God himself. It is true we know nothing of life only by its clothing. Around us there may be immeasurable oceans of naked life, but we only know something of the embodied. No science has yet told us what life is. 2. That God clothes life with the fittest body. "All flesh is not the same flesh." Life has boundless varieties, but God gives to each its fitting body. Paul points to the life of "beasts," and "fish," and "birds ;" to each he has given bodies. The hare and the elephant, the wren and the eagle, the minnow and the leviathian, all have bodies fitted to the peculiarities of their distinctive life. 3. That God clothes life according to his own pleasure. " Giveth it a body as it has pleased him." He chose the form, the hue, the gait of each life. Our resurrection-body will be as it " hath pleased him." Then it will be *beautiful*, for he is the God of all taste, the Fountain of all beauty, the Standard of all æsthetics. Then it will be *useful*, for he is the God of benevolence. Exquisitely suited to our present sphere are the bodies through which he streams into us the most exquisite sensations, and through which we convey and work out the best things within us. It will be *glorious*. " There is one glory of the sun, and another glory of the moon, and another glory of the stars :" so also with the resurrection of the just. Once more, to the question of the sceptic the apostle answers—

IV. With a body THAT SHALL BE A VAST IMPROVEMENT UPON THE OLD ONE. " It is sown in corruption." Between the buried body and the resurrection-body we have a series of antitheses, showing the vast superiority of the one to the other. 1. The one is *corruptible*, the other is *incorruptible*. " It is sown in corruption ; it is raised in incorruption." Our present frames are frail and dying. The resurrection-body will be incorruptible ; it will be deathless as the immortal spirit itself. 2. The one is *degraded ;* the other is *glorious.* Our present corporeal system is dishonoured, but it is raised in glory. How great the difference between the corrupting seed and the stately plant and full-blown flower ! 3. The one is *weak*, and the other is *powerful.* How feeble is our present body ! It is not like the oak that can stand the storms of centuries, but like the frail flower that withers in an hour. It is raised in power—power that shall never fatigue with labour or wear out by time. 4. The one is *natural ;* the other is *spiritual.* The present body is called a " natural body," probably because it is more the organ of the animal than the spiritual ; and the future body the spiritual, because it will be the organ of the intelligent and immortal mind. Man has in him two principles of life— the animal, which connects him with the material and local, and the *rational*, which connects him with the spiritual and the infinite. The body of the one falls at death, and will be required no more ; the perfected body of the other will be taken up at the resurrection, and will be continued for ever. What is death to him who has this hope ? Not the king of terrors, but the angel of immortality bearing to him the passport of an ever-blessed future.

Ver. 36.—*Man : his birth, death, and resurrection.* " Thou fool, that which thou sowest is not quickened, except it die." I shall take the verse as suggesting three great facts in man's existence.

I. MAN'S BIRTH. The text suggests—I do not say it was intended to teach—that man's *birth is a sowing of his existence in the earth.* The sowing of the grain of which the apostle speaks is not, I think, so analogous to the burial of his body as to the birth of his existence. The sowing of the grain takes place *before* its death. It dies after it is sown. But in the burial of the body the man has previously died. *Birth*, and not burial, then, must be considered as sown. Man, at birth, is sown into the earth like seed, in two respects. (1) The seed existed before it was sown ; man existed before he was born. (2) The seed required sowing in order for its development. Man required *birth* into this world in order for the development of his powers. What the soil is to the seed the external universe is to the soul—the developing agent. As a seed, however, man differs from all other germinant existences on this earth in several respects. 1. *He has a self-formative power.* The germs of all other life run into forms by the necessity of their nature. The grain has no power of determining what shape it shall take in its growth ; man has. Man has the power of determining whether he shall grow into a *beast*, a *fiend*, or an *angel*. 2. *He has boundless possibilities.* All other germinant existences on earth exhaust themselves in their growth. The time comes when they reach their culmination and decay sets in. Not so with man. He is a seed that shall grow for ever. At birth, then, we are sown into this world—immortal seeds we all are which the hand of the great Husbandman scatters over the earth.

II. MAN'S DEATH. His death is here represented as a reduction of the body to earth, not the reduction of himself. " That which thou sowest is not quickened, except it *die.*" In the grain it is not the *germ*, but the *husk*, the shell, which dies. The wrappage of the germ was made to rot. Nothing was necessary to the development of the life which it contained. The human *body* is the mere shell and wrappage of the man. It was made to die. Death is an essential element in the constitution of the world. It is in all material existences. It has been said that one-seventh of our earth's crust is comprised of limestone, and limestone contains the sepulchres of departed existences. We feed on death, and by our own death become food for future existences. The husk is not the germ, the body is not the man. It is his house that must crumble, it is his garment that must wear out.

III. MAN'S RESURRECTION. What is his resurrection? *A springing-up of his being from the earth.* After the death of the grain there is a resurrection of the seed that comes forth into new forms of life and beauty. It is not the husk that rises, but the germ. After the burial of the body the *man* comes forth into new life. The body rots, the man rises. Whether Paul refers here to the resurrection of the *body* from the grave or not, one thing is clear, that at death there is a real resurrection of the soul. As when the husks of the seed rot in the earth the seed itself is quickened, so when the body falls into the dust the soul springs forth into new life—a life of woe or bliss, according to its moral character. There is a resurrection, a standing-up of every soul at death. "The dust returns to dust, the soul to God who gave it." Will the body itself rise from the grave after it has gone to dust? It may, and we see some evidence to enable us to cherish the cheering hope. Whether this be a delusion or not, one thing is certain—the soul rises up at the fall of the body to its dust, and this is a most real and solemn *resurrection*. We "know that when the earthly house of this our tabernacle is dissolved, we have a building of God above, a house not made with hands, eternal in the heavens."

Ver. 41.—*Diversity in the heavenly inhabitants.* "One star differeth from another star in glory." The idea of Paul unquestionably is that there is as great a variety amongst redeemed men in the celestial world as there is in the orbs of heaven, that saint differs from saint as star from star in the midnight vault. We offer three remarks on this subject. Such a variety is—

I. A FACT WELL SUSTAINED. 1. *It is sustained by all analogy.* Variety reigns through every part of nature, not only in celestial, but in terrestrial spheres. No two objects are exactly alike. This variety reveals the illimitable inventiveness of the Divine mind, and gives to the universe its eternal freshness and transporting charms. 2. *It meets the instinctive love for the new in human souls.* All souls loathe monotony and crave for the fresh. A dead uniformity would crush out its life. 3. *It agrees with the varieties found amongst men here.* No two minds are alike here. They differ in the kind and measure of faculty, differ in the educational processes through which they have passed, differ in the positions which they occupy in relation to all objective truths and realities. Is it conceivable that all these varieties can be lost in the higher world, that all souls will run into a common mould? 4. *It accords with the general teaching of the Scriptures.* Paul speaks of the temple of the good as composed of gold, silver, and precious stones. Christ refers to Abraham, Isaac, Jacob, as sustaining the most honourable positions at the heavenly feast. Ay, ay, there must be varieties there. There are the speculative in mind and the practical, the imaginative and the logical, the intuitive and the philosophical; there are those who have been advancing in intelligence and power for millenniums, and those who have just commenced their heavenly studies, with those of every intervening stage. Such a variety is—

II. ESSENTIAL TO SOCIAL BLESSEDNESS. Suppose a society, all of whose members shall be exactly alike in temperament, in experience, in attainments, in articles of faith, in modes of thought, and in forms of expression. Could there in such a circle be any social enjoyment? What one thought, all thought; what one felt, all felt: why, such a state of things would be incompatible, not only with social enjoyment, but with social life. The monotony would become intolerable. The utmost variety in speculative thought is compatible with unity of heart; and the larger variety in spiritual temperament and conception in any circle—where all hearts are one—the higher the social enjoyment. Most unwise, most unrighteous, most impious, have been the attempts of ecclesiastics to force on all men the same system of thought and form of worship. Such a variety is—

III. CONSISTENT WITH THE HIGHEST UNITY. "One star differeth from another star in glory." 1. Whatever variety in the stars, they have *one centre.* Some larger, some smaller, some dimmer, some brighter, some moving more quickly, and some more slowly, yet all move round the same central orb: so with sainted souls. Whatever their diversities, they revolve round one great centre—God. God in nature and God in Christ. 2. Whatever variety in the stars, they are controlled by one law. Attraction moves all, regulates all, keeps each in its place and speed. One law, the law of love, rules all sainted souls above, however illimitable their varieties. 3. Whatever variety in the stars, they fulfil one mission. They all catch the light from the central orb, and flash their borrowed radiance abroad through all their spheres. So with souls above. They are all the recipients and reflectors of Divine light and love.

Ver. 45.—The two Adams. "The first man," etc. A specification of some of the points between the two Adams of resemblances and of dissimilarity will suggest a line of spiritual thought at once interesting, instructive, and practical.

I. THE RESEMBLANCE. 1. The existence of each rose not in the ordinary course of nature. Neither came by the ordinary laws of human generation. The first was formed out of the dust of the earth, and derived his spirit from the breath of God. The second was conceived of the Holy Ghost. The pedigree of each is unparalleled in the history of the race. 2. The existence of each commenced free from the slightest taint of sin. The first was created in the image of God; all his faculties were well balanced and free from all bias to wrong. The latter was "harmless, undefiled, separate from sinners." 3. The existence of each had a nature capable of temptation. Temptability is an attribute of all created intelligences. Where there is no power to go wrong there is no virtue in keeping right. The first Adam was tempted, and he was conquered; the second was tempted, and he triumphed. 4. The character of each exerts a momentous influence upon the whole race. The character of the first generated a moral atmosphere in which myriads of his posterity were born and brought up—an atmosphere of sensuality, ambition, selfishness, unbelief, etc. The character of the second generated a moral atmosphere into which his true disciples enter by faith in him—an atmosphere that is morally salubrious, sunny, and invigorating. He who lives in the first atmosphere is still in Adam and is earthly. He who lives in the second atmosphere is Christly and is spiritual.

II. THE DISSIMILARITY. 1. The one had a sublimer connection with God than the other. Adam at first was a Divine man, the offspring, representative, and steward of God. The second was God-Man. God was in him in a special sense, unfolding truths, working miracles, and reconciling the world unto himself. He was God "manifested in the flesh." The one yielded to the devil; the other conquered him. The first gave way to the tempter; the second stood against him, resisted him, and bruised his head. 2. The one possessed a higher type of moral excellence than the other. The character of the first was innocence, not holiness. Holiness implies intelligence, convictions, efforts, habits, etc. This had not Adam; hence he gave way to the first and simplest temptation. This holiness Christ had in the sublimest degree; and he triumphed over principalities and powers of evil, and made a "show of them openly." 3. The influence of the one upon the race has been infinitely pernicious, that of the other infinitely beneficent. The first planted that upas, whose pestiferous branches have spread over all the men that have been and that are, and whose poisonous fruit all have tasted and been injured. The other planted that tree of life, which is growing day by day, and is destined to grow until its branches, bearing fruit for the healing of the nations, shall spread over the world and give life to all. 4. The moral influence of the one is destined to decrease, of the other to increase. Though the moral influence of the first Adam has been universal and imperial for ages, and is so still, it is destined to contract in its dimensions and to weaken in its power. The influence of the second, on the contrary, is to widen its sphere and increase its power, until it shall encompass the wide world, and strike the highest moral inspirations into all souls. "Where sin abounded, grace will much more abound." The kingdoms of our God shall become the kingdoms of his Christ, and he shall reign for ever.

Vers. 46—49.—The two grand types of character. "Howbeit that was not," etc. The words show—
I. That man has set before him TWO MORAL IMAGES OR TYPES OF CHARACTER—the "earthy" and the "heavenly." These two are essentially distinct in the spring and

spheres of their activities. 1. The one is *sensuous*, the other *spiritual*. The earthly man is material, partially developed, and gross. (1) In his views of *happiness*. All his pleasures are of a sensuous order. (2) In his views of *wealth*. He knows of no man that is rich but he who possesses worldly property. (3) In his views of *dignity*. The only honourable man to him is he who occupies the highest worldly position, and who moves in the mere pageantry that dazzles the sensual eye. He is, in one word, a man of the flesh. He sees only the fleshly, appreciates only the fleshly, enjoys only the fleshly. On the contrary, the other is *spiritual*. He lives behind the visible phenomena, realizes the spiritual, the eternal. To him the invisible is the only reality, moral excellence the only wealth and dignity. Though in the world, he is not of the world. He has his citizenship in heaven. 2. The one is practically *selfish*, the other is *benevolent*. The earthly man is controlled in everything by a regard to his own pleasures and aggrandizements. Self is the centre and the circumference of all his activities, at once the lord of his faculties and the god of his worship. All outside of himself—even the universe itself—he values so far and no further than as it serves him. On the contrary, the heavenly man is benevolent. The social element within him controls the egotistic; his personal feelings are submerged in the ever-rising seas of sympathy with humanity and God. Like Christ, he "pleases not himself," and, like Paul, he would be "accursed" to help others. 3. The one is practically *atheistic*, the other is *godly*. The earthly man sees nothing but natural law, order, etc. "God is not in all his thoughts." The universe to him is only an eternal or a self-produced and self-regulating machine, a house that either has never had a builder or whose builder has deserted it. The other—the heavenly man—sees God in all; like the psalmist, sets him before him; like Enoch, walks ever with him. Such are the two images or types of character that are set before every man.

II. That man DOES BEAR THE ONE, HE SHOULD BEAR THE OTHER. Account for it how you like, every man, in the first stages of his life, bears the image of the "earthy." He is sensual, selfish, godless. This fact, which is too obvious to need or even to justify illustration, is at once the crime and the calamity of the race. But whilst we do bear this image at first, we should strive to bear the other. "We shall also" (or as Dr. Davidson renders it, "let us also") "*bear the image of the heavenly.*" Let us do it: 1. Because it is *right*. This heavenly image, embodying all virtue, realizes the soul's highest ideal of excellence. It is just that for which we unconsciously hunger, and for which we shall hunger for ever unless we get it. 2. Because it is *practicable*. (1) We have the model in its most imitable form. Christ is the model. He was pre-eminently spiritual, benevolent, godly; and never was there a character more imitable than Christ's—the most *admirable*, the most *transparent*, and the most *unchangeable*. We can never imitate a character that we cannot understand, admire, and find always the same. Christ was all this. (2) We have the means in the most effective forms. The gospel reveals the model, supplies the motives, and pledges the spiritual influences of heaven. 3. Because it is *urgent*. To do this is the grand mission of life. Unless the work is fulfilled, our existence becomes a failure and a curse. To pass from the "earthy" to the "heavenly," is to pass from darkness to light, from sin to holiness, from Satan to God, from Pandemonium to Paradise.

CONCLUSION. Here is a test of character. Conventional evangelism concludes that all who adopt certain tenets, join certain sects, and attend to certain religious ordinances are of the heavenly type and fold. A tremendous mistake is this! Without unchangeableness, it must be confessed that the vast majority of what are called Churches bear the image of the earthly; they are selfish, sensuous, and practically godless. Here also is a guide for preachers. Unless you get men from the earthly to the heavenly type of life, what boots your sermons, with all their ratiocination and rhetoric? Get their souls out of the earthly into the heavenly, and in the heavenly go on building up a character suited to the higher hierarchies of being.

> "So build we up the being that we are.
>   Thus drinking in the soul of things,
> We shall be wise perforce : and while inspired
> By choice, and conscious that the will is free,
> Unswerving shall we move, as if impelled
> By strict necessity—along the path

> Of order and of good. Whate'er we see,
> Whate'er we feel, by agency direct
> Or indirect, shall tend to feed and nurse
> Our faculties, shall fix in calmer seats
> Of moral strength, and raise to loftier heights
> Of love Divine, our intellectual soul."

(Wordsworth.)

Vers. 50—54.—*Corporeal transformation.* "Now this I say, brethren, that flesh and blood cannot inherit the kingdom of God; neither doth corruption inherit incorruption. Behold, I show you a mystery; We shall not all sleep, but we shall all be changed, in a moment, in the twinkling of an eye, at the last trump: for the trumpet shall sound, and the dead shall be raised incorruptible, and we shall be changed. For this corruptible must put on incorruption, and this mortal must put on immortality. So when this corruptible shall have put on incorruption, and this mortal shall have put on immortality, then shall be brought to pass the saying that is written, Death is swallowed up in victory." Paul here speaks of a bodily transformation that is indispensable, certain, instantaneous, and glorious.

I. Here is a transformation that is INDISPENSABLE. "This I say, brethren, that flesh and blood cannot inherit the kingdom of God." Its indispensability is not for this state of things, but for the state of bliss in the celestial world. "Flesh and blood," of course, means our mortal nature. "Cannot inherit the kingdom of God," the heavenly world. He does not say why it cannot—whether the state of the atmosphere, or the means of subsistence, or the force of gravitation, or the forms and means of vision, or the conditions of receiving and communicating knowledge, or the nature of the services required. He does not go into reasons, but boldly states the fact that it could not be. "Flesh and blood" can no more exist yonder, than the tenants of the ocean can exist on the sun-burnt hills. In such corporeal transformations there is nothing extraordinary, for naturalists point us to spheres of existence where they are as regular as the laws of nature.

II. Here is a transformation that is CERTAIN. "Behold, I show you a mystery." The word "mystery" here does not point to the unknowable, but to the hitherto unknown. What the apostle means is—I state to you as a fact that which has not hitherto been fully known, viz. that "we shall all be changed." "We shall not all sleep." Had Paul an idea either that he himself would escape death, or that the resurrection-day was just at hand? If he had, he here shows himself, as in some other places, not infallible, but otherwise; for he did die, and at that period the resurrection-day was far away in the abysses of the future. His words, however, clearly teach: 1. That some would be living when the day dawned. "As it was in the days of Noah, so shall it be in the days of the Son of man: they ate, they drank," etc. 2. That both those who were living in the earth and sleeping in the dust would undergo corporeal transformation. "We shall all be changed."

III. Here is a transformation that is INSTANTANEOUS. "In a moment, in the twinkling of an eye," that is, in the shortest conceivable period. At a moment when the living population least expects it, the blast of the "trumpet" shall be heard, and the transformation be effected. "The day of the Lord will come as a thief in the night," etc.

IV. Here is a transformation that is GLORIOUS. "For this corruptible must put on incorruption, and this mortal must put on immortality." The transformation is from mortality to immortality, from the dying to the undying; "death will be swallowed up in victory." "The idea," says one, "may be taken of a whirlpool or maelstrom that absorbs all that comes near it." The sense is, he would remove or abolish death for ever from mankind.

Ver. 53.—*The mind exchanging the mortal for the immortal.* "And this mortal must put on immortality," etc. Paul uses this language in relation to the *body.* What he means, I presume, is that the mortal shall be *exchanged* for the immortal. To put on "immortality" upon mortality is scarcely conceivable. But the receiving of the immortal *instead* of the mortal is what we can appreciate, and what we may well desire. When the apostle calls upon us elsewhere to put on the "new man," he means exchange the "old man" for the new—the old moral character for the new and Christly character. It may be both lawful, I think, and perhaps useful to use the words in another sense than that in which Paul employs them. We may apply them not to the material part of human nature, but to the *mental* and *moral*. And because such an application may prove suggestive of practical thoughts, we shall now view them in this light. There is much in the human mind, in its ideas, principles of action, character, etc., that is essentially mortal, and that must sooner or later be exchanged for the immortal. We observe, then—

I. That what is mortal in its SYSTEM OF THOUGHT must be exchanged for the immortal. All errors of judgment are mortal; they are perishable, and sooner or later must perish. And what system of human thought is not intermixed with ideas not true to fact? 1. Look at systems of *philosophy*. Many old systems of philosophy have already died out, because of the errors that were found in them; and existing systems, because they are often contradictory one to another, reveal their errability, and consequently must die. What is changing is mortal. All schools of psychological science, the sensational, the idealistic, the mystic, and the eclectic, are shifting as the clouds. It will not, it must not be always so; the mortal must "put on" the immortal, the true must take the place of the false in the realm of thought. 2. Look at systems of *theology*. How contradictory one toward another in many things are most of the systems of theology now prevalent! And what is worse, how contradictory are they to some of the most vital things embodied in the life and teachings of Jesus as recorded by the four evangelists! Many of the old systems have died. Some are dying now, and all will sooner or later die; for they are rotten with error. The mortal must "put on" the immortal. Human souls will one day have the "truth as it is in Jesus."

"Our little systems have their day;
They have their day, and pass away."

II. That what is mortal in the ELEMENTS OF HUMAN CHARACTER must be exchanged for the immortal. Analyze the character of unrenewed men—alas! the vast majority, not only of the human race, but even of professing Christians—and you will find moral principles that must die out if there be a God of justice and benevolence in the universe. Such principles, for example, as avarice, envy, pride, malice, ambition, and selfishness, which is in truth the root of all evil. The human mind was never formed to be inspired, or indeed to be influenced in any measure by these. The fact that they are antagonistic to the moral constitution of the human soul, to the character of the Maker and Manager of the universe, and to the order and well-being of all, show that they must sooner or later die out of existence. I have the hope that human souls will one day put off this mortal and "put on" the immortal—"Righteousness, joy, and peace in the Holy Ghost," etc. "Marvel not that I say unto you, Ye must be born again."

III. That what is mortal in the INSTITUTIONS OF HUMAN LIFE must be exchanged for the immortal. 1. Our *political* institutions are mortal. Human governments are constantly dying. They spring up and flourish for a certain time, and then are swept from the earth. The unwisdom in their method of management, the unrighteousness of some of their laws, the avarice, the tyranny, and haughtiness of those in power, and their constant fattening upon the over-taxed millions, give mortality to governments. Man will one day put off these mortal governments and put on the immortal, the government of common sense, common justice, common benevolence. Men are craving not for the aristocratic or democratic, but for the theocratic, the reign of God, which is the reign of honesty and love. "The kingdoms of this world will one day become the kingdoms of our Lord," etc. 2. Our *ecclesiastical* institutions are mortal. Whether they are Papal, Episcopal, Wesleyan, or Congregational, they are more or less mixed with error and must die. The great "cloud of witnesses," the Church of the Firstborn, reached their blessed destiny before churches or chapels existed. "God is a Spirit: and they that worship him must worship him in spirit and in truth." Indeed, whatever institutions, political, ecclesiastical, or social, that have in them a mixture of error, unwisdom, and injustice, must be exchanged for the immortal, namely, a "kingdom that cannot be moved."

IV. That what is mortal in the types of HUMAN GREATNESS must be exchanged for the immortal. In all men there is, in more or less intensity, a thirst for greatness, but their ideas or types of greatness widely differ. Some see the highest greatness in the millionaire, some in the triumphant conqueror, some in the man with a crown on his head, some in the fools who boast of their ancestry and their high-sounding titles. But such types of greatness as these are utterly false. They agree neither with reason nor the conscience of humanity. Because they are false they are mortal, and they will have to be exchanged for the immortal. The time will come when men will regard Christ as the only true type of greatness. They will give him the "Name above every name." In all things in their daily life and conversation, he will have the pre-eminence.

CONCLUSION. What a glorious change awaits humanity! St. Paul speaks of the resurrection of the *body*, an event which is confessedly mysterious: it may be far, far distant, and this we have no power to hasten or impede. But there is a more glorious resurrection—a resurrection of the human soul from the false, the unrighteous, the impure, to the true, the right and the holy—a resurrection, thank God, taking place every day in the world, and a resurrection which all men may either hasten or impede —their duty the former, their crime the latter. "Awake to righteousness and sin not."

Vers. 55—57.—*Death in idea.* "O death, where is thy sting?" etc. These words, which are a shout of victory evoked by what has preceded, suggest to us the popular and the Christian ideas of death. Notice—

I. THE POPULAR IDEA. The language implies that the bulk of the race view death not as the writer did; that the idea to them had a "sting" a "victory," and a connection with felt guilt. 1. The popular idea has a *sting*. "O death, where is thy sting?" This is a vivid personification of the last enemy. The world sedulously shuts up its heart against the idea; but there is not an individual into whose bosom it does not force its way at times, and like a serpent it *stings*. There is no idea that stings an ungodly man like the idea of death. 2. The popular idea has a *victory*. It not only stings like a serpent, but crushes like a conqueror. I speak not of the victory which death obtains over the body, but I speak of a more crushing "victory" than this—a victory over the soul. Whenever the idea takes possession of a worldly mind, it is a victory; the soul is prostrated, the man is unmanned. 3. The popular idea has a *felt connection with sin.* "The sting of death is sin; and the strength of sin is the Law." The sinner's sense of guilt will be according to his knowledge of Law, and the terror of death will be according to his sense of guilt. It is felt guilt that gives a "sting" and "victory" to the idea of dying. All that is horrific in the idea starts from a sin-stricken conscience. Such, then, is the popular idea of death. Wherever, whether in Christian or heathen lands, in ancient or modern times, Christianity is not received in its moral significance and spirit, you find it.

II. THE CHRISTIAN IDEA. 1. The idea has *neither* "sting" nor "victory." "O death, where is thy sting? O grave, where is thy victory?" By implication they once existed, but they are gone. 2. The Christian idea has, instead of "sting" and "victory," *rapture and triumph.* "Thanks be to God, which giveth us the victory." The victor has become the victim; the anguish of the sting has given place to the ecstasy of the song. 3. The Christian idea comes to man *through one medium.* The old terrific and popular idea of death has given way to a bright and a glorious one, "through our Lord Jesus Christ." How does Christ give this idea? By *awakening in the soul a new spiritual life.* But how does a new spiritual life do this? Because it involves the following things:—(1) *A stronger sympathy with the God of our destiny than with any other being.* Where there is a moral oneness with that God in "whose hand our breath is," there never can be any dread of death. But a dread of God must give a dread of death. (2) *A stronger sympathy with the spiritual than with the material.* Much of the fearfulness of death springs from the idea of separation from the dear objects of our attachment. Wherever, therefore, the supreme attachments are on the material, the idea of death must be distressing on account of the separation it involves; but where the *most* sympathy is with the unseen and the eternal, death will be regarded, not as severing connections, but as uniting them in closer fellowship. (3) *A stronger sympathy with the future world than with the present.* Where the prevailing sympathies of the soul are with the Divine, spiritual, and the future, the idea of death will be bright and jubilant. This threefold sympathy, then, is essential in the nature of things to the existence of this felicitous and triumphant idea of death.

Ver. 58.—*The work of works.* "Therefore, my beloved brethren, be ye steadfast, unmovable, always abounding in the work of the Lord, forasmuch as ye know that your labour is not in vain in the Lord." "Therefore." This is the practical conclusion of the sublime argument which Paul had conducted on the resurrection, in the preceding verses. All true doctrines lead to practice. "Therefore"—because death is not your end, because you are to live body and soul in a future state—" be ye steadfast."

I. The work of soul-restoration is SPECIALLY DIVINE. It is "the work of the Lord." The work of the Lord is illimitable. The universe is his handiwork, and all its movements are his operations. Providence is his work. But the "work" referred to in the text, viz. the spiritual restoration of mankind, is in a special sense his. It is his great work. Isaiah speaks of it as a creation that will eclipse in glory the material universe. Jesus always spoke of it as the great work. 1. Think of the *preparation* for this work. Four thousand years were occupied, involving a long series of sacrifices, priests, seers, miracles, as preliminary. 2. Think of the *sacrifices* made to accomplish this work. Christ came into this world, and the Incarnate lived, suffered, and died here, etc. 3. Think of the *unceasing agency of the Divine Spirit* in order to effect this work. He is always striving with men from age to age and in all lands. 4. Think of the *wonderful results* of this work. Millions of lost souls redeemed to the knowledge, image, fellowship, and service of Almighty God. What is the value of one soul? What is the influence that one soul can exert on the universe? This, then, may emphatically be called the "work of the Lord." It is the field which he—the great Husbandman—has been cultivating. He will make it one day his choicest garden. It is the temple which he—the great Architect—has been building; it will excel in glory all former structures. It is the "new creation" which he is accomplishing; before it will pale into dimness all other productions.

II. The work of soul-restoration DEMANDS THE MOST EARNEST EFFORTS OF MANKIND. "Steadfast, unmovable." There are some works of the Lord in which we cannot engage. We cannot help to control the ocean, guide the stars, or even create a blade of grass, but here we are "labourers together with him." 1. Our labour must be *invincible.* The two words, "steadfast" and "unmovable," express this. So many are the impulses within, so many are the forces without, opposing the work, that nothing but an invincible determination can carry us through. We must have a purpose strong enough to bend and subordinate everything to itself. "This one thing I do," says Paul. 2. Our labour must be *abounding.* "Always abounding." The spirit of this work should reign in us, everywhere and at all times. As the parental element inspires the mother, and mingles with all her domestic arrangements and pleasures, so this spirit must inspire us and mingle with all our undertakings. It should sweeten our daily toil and breathe into our recreations and amusements. The distinction between the secular and the spiritual is a theological fiction. Religion in a man is either everywhere or nowhere, everything or nothing. Labour and business, as well as the gospel, are means of grace. As the life of the plant requires the tempest to bend its fibres, as well as the calm to yield it repose, so the religious life requires for its development the rough element of worldly business as well as the smoother influences of spiritual devotion.

III. The work of soul-restoration MUST INEVITABLY SUCCEED. "Forasmuch as ye know that your labour is not in vain in the Lord." There are two kinds of vain labour. 1. That which aims at a *worthless end.* Therefore, if it succeeds, it is useless. 2. That which is directed to a good end, but *can never realize it,* simply because it is too indeterminate and feeble. But here is a work that must succeed. Every true thought, every earnest prayer, every godly deed, carry in themselves success. As all the elements and forces of this world go to build up a new stratum around the globe's surface, for geologists of coming ages to study, so all that I do and think and say in the work of the Lord goes to give blessedness to my being. Inasmuch, therefore, as you cannot fail in this work, labour.

IV. The work of soul-restoration will FULLY REALIZE ITS SUCCESS IN THE FUTURE

WORLD. "Therefore," says Paul, "were this life our all, our spiritual labour might be considered vain." What boots our striving after knowledge, our efforts to build up a noble character, if the grave be our end? But there is a future, and in it there is a full reward. All the waters of holy thought and effort we now receive into our being go to make a well within us that shall spring up to everlasting life.

HOMILIES BY VARIOUS AUTHORS.

Vers. 1—4.—*Introduction.* "Moreover" indicates a change of subject. "Declare unto you," or remind you, is somewhat emphatic. What St. Paul brings to memory are certain fundamental ideas which he does not hesitate to call "the gospel," the glad tidings of God to the world. It was the same gospel he had preached unto them, the same they had accepted, the same in which they stood. By it these Corinthians were saved, present and future, if they adhered to their faith, unless indeed their faith was "in vain." Was this faith a vain thing? Was it possible that it was an illusion? How could this be when they had embraced it, stood in it, felt its power to save, and rejoiced in its blessedness? The power of this gospel lay in these facts, viz.: Christ had died, had been buried, had been raised from the grave; and these had occurred for a special purpose and agreeably to pre-announcement of Divine revelation. What was the specific object of Christ's death? He died "for our sins." In this he was the Christ of God, the Messiah, the Anointed, the Jesus of Nazareth, who, as "the righteous Servant of the Father," was ordained to "bear their iniquities." It was not, then, a common death. It was not a death brought about as to its main end by the disappointment of his nation because he had refused to be a secular king. It was not the death of a martyr. Worldly influences, earthly agencies, Satanic power, appear in the immediate and circumstantial connections of his crucifixion. His arrest was an act of human violence; his trial was twofold, Jewish and Roman; his execution was Roman; and yet all this array of man's hate and skill and successful wickedness passes out of sight, and is lost in a view infinitely higher. Judas could not have betrayed him, Caiaphas and the Sanhedrim could not have condemned him, Pilate could not have given him over to the Pharisees and Sadducees, unless Christ himself had permitted them to control the manner and incidents of his death. The death itself, as to its motive, spirit, and aim, occupies the whole mind of the apostle. Man and man's instrumental relation to it fade from view, and it is with him a vicarious, expiatory, propitiating death, deriving its reason, character, and value from a single consideration—a death *for our sins*. On no other basis could he regard the gospel as glad tidings. And how had the knowledge of this as a doctrinal reality come to him? He had "received" it from Christ himself, who had appeared personally to him at midday. The historical facts of his death, burial, and resurrection had been known to him; for Saul of Tarsus could not have been ignorant of these things as events involving the nation. Mysteriously, too, he had felt their impression in vague ideas, in vaguer fears; out of unconscious depths, sounds had throbbed as strange pulsations on the inner ear; and so sharp had been the call to thought and reflection, as for the Lord Jesus to remind him on the way to Damascus that he had been kicking against the goads which had pierced his conscience. His conversion was sudden and marvellous. Sudden and marvellous it could not have been but for the long and acute goading that had opened his heart to the hand of the Divine Healer. Yet this preparatory work of conviction was all within himself, under the Spirit's agency. What he knew of Christ's death was not from the historical fact alone, but from the doctrinal truth couched in the fact, and this saving truth he had *received*. It was a revelation to his soul, a direct and assuring manifestation from the Lord Jesus. To be an apostle, he needed this immediate communication from heaven, this peculiar intensifying of conviction and conversion. Means and methods suited to others were not adapted to his case. Notorious as he had been in the championship of the national Church—the forlorn hope of Sadduceeism and Pharisaism, the young hero whose fanatical strength was adequate to replenish the wasting and well-nigh exhausted forces of the Sanhedrim—it was not for him to go over to Christ in some quiet way by meditation, by laborious inquest of soul, by those high resolves which often have their birth from the womb of solitude. No; he must be signally converted, for his own sake and for the sake of others. The change was a momentous affair in the history of the Jewish Church no less than the Christian Church, and, accordingly, he speaks of himself as having " received " the grace of God in an exceptional manner. But were human means disowned? Was naturalness set at nought or even depreciated? Not so; what he "received" was altogether in unison with the true creed of Israel as contained in the records of her national faith. " According to the Scriptures," argues he, was the truth of Christ's death which I "received." Above the effulgence that flashed from the Syrian noon upon his eye, there was another light, and it spread all over Pentateuch, Psalms, prophecies. What, indeed, Gamaliel stood for, but was not; what Sadducee and Pharisee ideally meant, but utterly failed to make real; what priest and scribe had been designed to represent, but had hidden under carnal observances; what temple and sacrifices had been set apart to commemorate and prefigure, but had obliterated in sign and symbol;—all these were now illumined. "According to the Scriptures," which he had learned when a boy in Tarsus, and had come to Jerusalem that he might enlarge and perfect his knowledge of these holy writings; "according to the Scriptures," which St. Stephen had expounded before the Sanhedrim when the shadow of death retreated before the glory descending upon the youthful saint from the " Son of man standing on the right hand of God;" " according to the Scriptures" that Ananias had explained to him at Damascus, when " there fell from his eyes as it had been scales," and, in no long time, the inner eyesight was made clear and strong. Thus it was that providence in the past became providence in the present, the Holy Ghost alike in each, and Tarsus, Jerusalem, and Damascus brought, though seemingly so wide apart, into the unity of his soul's development. Verily, a wondrous scheme of personal history, recognizing home and parents, life in "no mean city," life in the metropolis that was venerated as the glory of the elect nation, life in the leadership of an assault on the young Church, and for ever memorable in her annals because of the crown of martyrdom then first won; a marvellous interweaving of the natural and supernatural as warp and woof in one and the same fabric. Back to the original promise spoken in Eden that the seed of the woman should bruise the serpent's head; back to the early institution of sacrifice, and thence on to the organization of the Divine idea in a most solemn and august ceremonial that allowed no day to escape its impressive symbolization; all through penitential psalms and instructive prophecies. The great doctrine was present everywhere that "without shedding of blood there is no remission," that " he hath borne our griefs and carried our sorrows," and that " the Lord hath laid on him the iniquity of us all." No emaciating criticism here; no destructive intellect; no disposition inclining St. Paul to obscure Christ in the shadow of the Jewish nation, and minimize his figure to the smallest dimensions consistent with any faith at all. No such taste and temper had this man, fresh from the schools and master of the theology of his times. Nor is it other than one of his very marked peculiarities, that he so frequently cites his thorough and familiar acquaintance with the Scriptures, and that from first to last in his Epistles, he is quite as much a commentator of the Old as an exponent of the New. The two grand hemispheres of religious thought formed one globe in him. From the one to the other, he passed with unobstructed step. Over the immense domain, divided and cut up to so many other minds, adverse or even hostile sections to not a few honest souls; over all this stretch of diversified territory, there was to St. Paul the very perfection of unity. His footsteps never missed their pathway; his eye never lost a landmark. For him, Christ was in Eden, in Abraham, Moses, David, Isaiah, Hosea; and the Old Testament was what it was and all it was because Christ was in every one of its doctrines and institutions. The present Christ to him—the Christ of Damascus, and Arabia, and Jerusalem, and Athens, and Ephesus, and Corinth—was the Christ of the past, and he was this because he was the " Lamb slain from the foundation of the world." Is it likely, then, that we shall find too much of Christ, and especially as it respects the legal bearings of his death, in the Old Testament? Clearly St. Paul did not think so. "According to the Scriptures" was prefatory, and essentially so, to the logic, sentiment, fervour, of the grand argument he was about to make. What was this argument to be? A defence—*the defence*—of the doctrine of the resurrection of the human body. Observe now that the historical fact of the Lord's resurrection was not in debate. No one of the Corinthians denied or even doubted that. What, then, was in controversy? This it was, viz.: Did the doctrine involved in the Lord's rising from the dead apply to all? Was there to be a general resurrection? From this point of view, we see why in the present case he laid such stress on his dying for our sins. It was not death as an ordinary termination of life, but death considered in this exclusive instance as an atoning death, as a vicarious and expiatory offering, as a complete and perfect satisfaction to law and justice. It is this death that stands so closely related to his resurrection, and through it to our resurrection. Taking merely an ethical view of the matter, and confining ourselves to what Jesus of Nazareth taught, and to the example of moral excellence he set before men, we can see no reason why he should have risen. He added nothing to morality, nothing to example, nothing to a high and self-sacrificing manhood, by returning to life and reappearing at sundry times to his disciples during the forty days. On the other hand, looking at his death as penal— "for our sins"—we can understand why, if he was "delivered for our offences," he should be "raised again for our justification." Without the resurrection, we could not be assured whether he died simply and solely as a good man, the best of men, or as the Son of God to expiate our sins. If, indeed, law and justice have been satisfied by the sacrifice, let them express in an authoritative and sovereign manner, clear of all liability to misapprehension, and assuring to the most eager solicitude, that the penalty has been paid and a full pardon for guilt in man made possible. Precisely this was accomplished by Christ's resurrection, and thus the scars of Calvary, preserved upon his person, were shown to the disciples as the signs of victory over "hell and death." He rose, furthermore, on "the third day." Though it was not Christ's habit to fix times and seasons, yet he was careful to settle the day of his resurrection. Again and again he announced the date of the event. Friends, in their overwhelming dismay, forgot it, or if some remembered it, as the two who journeyed to Emmaus, it was clouded by grief and distrust. Foes remembered it and provided a guard for the sepulchre, and his foes were the first to know that he had risen, and that, too, from their own soldiers. There was no ethical reason for him to rise on the third day or on any other day, but, viewing his death as penal, its purpose instantly answered when he died, we can see congruity between the two facts, "the third day" being his own appointment and a proof that he had died, not as a mere man, but as the eternal Son of God. St. Paul repeats, "according to the Scriptures," i.e. Christ's resurrection had been foretold. "Thou wilt not leave my soul in hell, neither wilt thou suffer thine Holy One to see corruption" (Ps. xvi. 10). Christ's death, burial, and resurrection hold together, and their congruity is determined by the fact that "the chastisement of our peace was upon him, and with his stripes we are healed." To these truths the apostle gave prominence in the opening of his argument. Logically, they had to assume that commanding position, and emotionally they could have no other. And therefore, "first of all," he delivered these doctrines. They took precedence of all else; they were the data for everything in Christianity; they were "the gospel." So that if he was about to dwell on a topic which should evoke his power to the utmost, nor leave a faculty of his mind disengaged nor a sensibility unmoved, he would "first of all," as he had done in his preaching, rest his whole cause on Christ dying and rising as the Redeemer of the human race.—L.

Vers. 5—11.—*Apostolic testimony to Christ's resurrection, and testimony of others.* A prominent feature of Christ's plan was to train the apostles to be his witnesses. Conceive what this involved: on their part, a discipline of the senses as inlets of the mind, close and patient attention, constant revisals of impressions, contentedness under mystery, boldness of statement, heroism in adhering to testimony. Along with these qualities, an experience of the truth in Christ as a transforming power was to impart a peculiar character to all they affirmed, so that Christ Jesus, living, dying, risen, exalted, glorified, was to be seen in them as well as through them. On the part of Christ, what condescension and sympathy, what painstaking, what persistent efforts, were necessary to make these rude Galileans competent to the duties of testifiers! "Ye also shall bear witness, because ye have been with me from the beginning." To be *messengers* was not enough; they were to be witnesses also, for the "Holy Ghost shall come upon you: and ye shall be witnesses unto me both in Jerusalem, and in all Judæa, and in Samaria, and unto the uttermost parts of the earth." These men felt that they were Christ's chosen witnesses, and that their testimony was the chief agency employed by the Spirit to save the world. It was natural, then, for St. Paul to begin his argument on the resurrection of the body by calling attention to the fact that the risen Christ "was seen of Cephas, then of the twelve." For the space of forty days he manifested himself at intervals to their senses, and during this intermediate period—a special dispensation to the disciples, differing widely from all that went before or came after—their education as witnesses, and particularly as witnesses of his resurrection, was carried on to the verge of completeness at Pentecost. In fact, Pentecost was the forty days consummated. And was this great training merely in the historical fact that he had risen? Forty days were not needed for this. Twenty-four hours after he had reappeared, all the twelve, except St. Thomas, were firm believers of the fact. But they were to feel the connection between his resurrection and death as spiritual truths of the highest moment, truths of the Divine government, truths of holy sentiment, and thus fitted for the full dispensation of the Holy Ghost at Pentecost. "Did not our *heart burn* within us, while he talked with us by the way, and while he opened to us the Scriptures?" The heart, the burning heart, the heart of saving faith,—this is the distinctive type of experience now, and, *for the first time, Christian emotion* as to its essential quality is brought into notice. St. Paul enumerates the witnesses: St. Peter, the twelve, the five hundred brethren, St. James; and adds, "all the apostles." Then he mentions himself: "Last of all, he was seen of me also, as of one born out of due time." Could he speak of this in the way simply of historical summation? Not he; memory was too active, feeling too acute, humility and gratitude too profound, for a bare logical statement. In an instant, the devout soul hastens to acknowledge what it never lost an opportunity of expressing—its sense of God's mercy in calling him, a persecutor of the Church of God, to the apostleship. "By the grace of God"—words often abused since he used them, but most sacred and glorious as he uttered them—"by the grace of God I am what I am." That grace had not been bestowed in vain; nor does he hesitate to say that he had "laboured more abundantly than they all," and then "*I*" sinks out of sight, and it is all of grace. Notice the stages of the idea: born untimely; least of the apostles because he was guilty of persecution; the only man among them who stood against this dark background, but the light in the foreground is the more resplendent for that; not ashamed to confess his utter unworthiness in order to magnify the grace of God, and this grace deserving the entire honour of the more abundant labour. What an insight into the man! If, as we suppose, the hours when this chapter was written were extraordinary even in his wonderful mental history; if there was a fuller and closer interblending of his faculties than he had ever experienced; if human knowledge and culture then brought to inspiration their largest and richest tribute, and if inspiration brought to them its mightiest quickening;—what could be more striking than the fact that in this very period of exaltation, when intellect was in the splendid array both of its endowments and acquisitions, and when the power of speech had suddenly possessed itself of new facilities of expression, he cannot proceed without pausing to bow his heart in adoration before the God of grace! Uppermost, indeed, was the thought of him who had "died for our sins," and the glory of Christ risen as personal to him and his apostleship was the grace shown to him as a persecutor of the Church of God. And we who read his glowing words, what finer privilege can the unfoldings of the human soul in literature give us, what privilege so fine as this in which the apostle of the Gentiles, rising above the levels of all common experience, speaks from a height which would be the abode of silence save that humility would offer its homage to the grace of Christ! The nobility of the man displays itself here; for, though labouring "more abundantly than they all," yet he claims no more than to be one of the witnessing company of the apostles. After all, it is not the individual testimony of St. Peter, St. James, St. Paul, but the concurrent and united evidence, that is the important fact. Years intervened between the forty days and the scene on the road to Damascus, and he comes with his later testimony to join the group of the earlier witnesses. "Whether it were I or they"—we are all agreed as to the appearance of the risen Lord—"so we preach, and so ye believed."—L.

Vers. 12—34.—*Denying the resurrection from the dead, and what the denial involves.* Some of these Corinthian Christians denied that there would be a literal resurrection. They understood little or nothing of the idea of the body, of its uses intellectually and morally regarded, and of its partnership with the soul in all that concerned present probation and future reward. What had Grecian philosophy taught them? That the body was the seat of evil. What had Grecian art taught them? To admire the body for sensuous purposes as a gratification to æsthetic tastes. And what had idolatrous worships shown them? The body degraded to the lowest vileness. Yet, indeed, Christianity had assured them that the body was "the temple of the Holy Ghost," and, no doubt, St..Paul in his former preaching had instructed them in the sanctity of the body, "according to the Scriptures." But here they were explaining away the doctrine, and entirely unaware of what they were doing. "It was not materialism, but an ultra-spiritualism, which led the Corinthians into error" (F. W. Robertson). "Fascinated, perhaps, by its plausible appearance of spirituality, glad to get rid of the offence of a carnal and material immortality, and fain to take refuge in the more refined idea of the soul's recovered independence of the body here, and its entire emancipation from the body hereafter" (Dr. Candlish). Whatever the influences at work upon their minds, the results were obvious to St. Paul. And to convince them of what a fatal error they had fallen into if their disbelief were logically carried out into its consequences, he proceeds to inquire of them how it was that Christ could be preached among them as One risen from the dead, if there were no general resurrection. What consistency was there in believing that the Lord of humanity had risen, Lord of its body no less than of its soul, and yet this humanity in the race must be dislocated, body and soul sundered for ever, and soul alone be the survivor of death? This is the starting-point, Christ the Representative, the federal Head, the Image of humanity as well as the Image of God. If there be no general resurrection, "then is Christ not risen." The argument is from a broad, universal principle to a particular case under that principle, the former being the resurrection of man, and the latter that of the Son of man. By legitimate inference, therefore, supposing there were no resurrection for man, Christ was still in his grave. "*Christ not risen!*" What follows? Apostolic "preaching is vain, and your faith is also vain." This is pressing the matter home with startling energy. But how could the logical consequence be otherwise? Christ Jesus, Son of God, had assumed man's physical nature, had been born of a woman, had eaten and drunk and grown like other men, had conformed to the laws of human corporeity, had been "made under the law" of providence, and taken all its requirements upon himself; and hence, if "made like unto his brethren," he rose from the dead just as he had been incarnated, *under the general law of humanity.* From the beginning to the end, no break occurred in his career; *it was human throughout,* and just as human when he rose from the grave as when born of the Virgin Mary. To be sure, a glory beyond the human was in him and around him—the glory of the eternal Sonship—but the human was never lost or swallowed up, never even obscured, by the mysterious awe of the Divine investing him. In this view of the matter, Christ rose because he was a man among men, and by virtue of a law which found in him its highest manifestation, just as all other laws of humanity had realized in him their sublimest expression. But what of our preaching as apostles? If he has not risen (risen he cannot be unless there is a general resurrection), then "we are found false witnesses of God." Nothing else but *false witnesses,* "because we have testified of God that he raised up Christ: whom he raised not up, if so be that the dead rise not." Deluded men we cannot be; victims of excited and overwrought senses; innocent enthusiasts;—all this is impossible; and we are downright deceivers. Is this credible? Go back and read the roll of testifiers: St. Peter and the twelve, the outstanding fact of their testimony being Jesus and the resurrection; then the five hundred brethren, next St. James, and I myself. Can you Corinthians believe a thing as absurd as this, that we are all *false* witnesses? So much for apostolical preaching. He had put their preaching as apostles and the faith of these Corinthians in the same category; they were each "vain," that is, "empty, groundless, unreal" (Kling). Now, then, he urges that if there be no resurrection, "Christ is not raised." If Christ be not risen, what object has your faith? To believe in his atoning death, you must believe in the necessary sequel and counterpart of that death, his resurrection, since the two facts are inseparably united. Admit his death, deny his resurrection, and "ye are yet in your sins." Is this credible? On the hypothesis of no literal resurrection, three things up to this point of the argument have been made clear, viz. Christ's death was in vain, apostolic preaching of Christ crucified was in vain, and Christian faith was in vain. What a new Ecclesiastes is here! "Vanity of vanities, all is vanity." But was this all? If a denial of man's resurrection necessitated the rejection of Christ's resurrection; if the loss of his resurrection swept away his atonement, seeing that there was no proof of its validity, and hence no assurance of pardon and peace; if the nullification of the atonement destroyed the value of preaching and the worth of believing;—could there be any addition to the amount and quality of these dreadful consequences? Yes; the train of evils following this new doctrine of no resurrection was lengthened out still further; for "they also which are fallen asleep in Christ are perished." All departed Christians are lost. There is no heaven for them, and the touching words, "fallen asleep in Jesus," are mocking rhetoric. Again, the thought recurs—*Was this credible?* Another vanity must be superadded: affection for the departed, the tenderest and holiest of all human feelings, that which perfects the love unable to obtain its complete growth while the object lived to the eyes and was clasped in the arms; this most beautiful and noble affection is idle sentimentality, for they have "perished." At this point something more than logical reasoning is involved. The deepest instinct of the soul in its human relationships is in issue. Is this instinct a cheat, a falsehood? We, the apostles and the five hundred brethren, are not the only "false witnesses," but your nature, the very core of your nature, is a deceit and mockery. You have lost your Christ and his apostles, lost your faith, lost your friends. Nothing precious is left; you dare not trust your firmest instincts. "Most miserable!" Could there be a greater torture? "If in this life only we have hope in Christ, we are of all men most miserable." The hope of being with him hereafter, of seeing and enjoying him, of becoming more and more like him,—this is our heaven of anticipation; the crown is "a crown of righteousness;" the eternal reward is nearer and fuller communion with him. But this hope is all vain. Himself uncrowned, himself left to the dishonour of the grave, what can Christ be to you and what relief afford you—you of all men most wretched? Other men resign themselves to their dreams of earthly joys, seek the pleasures of sense and find them, fall down and worship Satan and get their kingdoms of power and wealth and passion. These you have denied yourselves and put far from your pursuits. Heaven has been enough for you. But lo! this heaven is a vain hope, a fleeting creature of fancy, and you are the victims of a supreme folly, the lowest on earth in hopeless misery. This mournful picture is not allowed to detain the eye, for St. Paul immediately says (ver. 20), "Now is Christ risen from the dead, and become the firstfruits of them that slept." There is the fact of his resurrection; there is also the doctrinal import of the truth with respect to believers; so that after showing the absurdity of the opposite view, he now lays down a positive assertion in conformity with the first stage of his argument. Christ has risen, but in what character and relation? The answer is, "The Firstfruits of them that slept." A vast harvest is in the future, and he is the Firstfruits. Was not the first sheaf a specimen of the matured field, a thank offering to the God of providence, a pledge of the full ingathering? In all things he was to have "pre-eminence," and consequently in this, that he was "the first begotten of the dead." Previous resurrections had occurred, but in no sense were they "firstfruits," since no representative or mediatorial character appertained to them, nor did they involve the idea of a Divine covenant. The significance of Christ's return to life is that, having been "reconciled to God by the death of his Son, much more, being reconciled, *we shall be saved by his life.*" The specialty of his vicarious sacrifice gives specialty to his resurrection, which is the beginning of his exaltation to be a Prince and a Saviour, "for to give repentance to Israel, and forgiveness of sins." And in this, humanity appears historically no less than prospectively: "Since by man came death, by man came also the resurrection of the dead." It is, in each instance, a race-fact he is contemplating, and he sees the race as existing in the natural headship of Adam and in the spiritual headship of Christ. "As in Adam all die" a natural death, "even so in Christ shall all be made alive"—restored to existence as it consists in the union of soul and body. Further on, St. Paul specializes the difference between Adam and Christ; here and in the context, it is the similarity of attitude towards the human family which he presents. To see the unlikeness, we must first see the resemblance, and, accordingly, he institutes a parallel between the two, Adam and Christ, as preparatory to the divergence which he introduces when discussing other aspects of the resurrection. The union of body and soul, by which human nature is constituted, belongs in itself to the natural order of the universe, and therefore offers a common platform on which Adam and Christ alike stand, the one as causing death, the other as the restorer of life forfeited. St. Paul never loses sight of nature and natural order. Everything that he says of Christianity either asserts or implies something back of Christianity. If, as often happens, he describes it as a scheme of restoration, *there is always an original system*, vast in reach and compass, to which it is subordinate. And if, as frequently occurs, he is showing that "where sin abounded, grace did much more abound," reference is still had to a primary or normal condition as having been transcended by substituting a higher for a lower form of life. In congruity with this habitual method of thought, fundamental to all his other habits of mind, and without which he could not have been the thinker he was, he traces here the resemblance of Adam and Christ in their respective headships of the human family. But has Christ such an identification with our race as to put his resurrection, time and circumstances considered, on a level with our rising from the dead? No; he stands alone. "Every man in his own order." There is an order, a rank, a succession, and the headship of Christ is attested as before in the figure of the "firstfruits." "Afterward they that are Christ's at his coming;" the long interval between the first and second coming of Christ illustrating his majesty as the risen Lord, and ripening a harvest worthy of him as the "firstfruits." If, then, the ages are to witness the success of his power as "a Prince and a Saviour," and if the final demonstration of his glory as exalted to the right hand of his Father be reserved for the resurrection of his saints and its attendant events, this result must be of the nature of a consummation. Viewed as *a system within a system*, it must be limited by conditions, must have instruments and agencies, must have various adjustments of means to ends, and the ends in turn accommodated to ulterior purposes, all which go forward to an era of grandeur. A perpetual scheme of this kind is inconceivable. It involves the trial of certain definite and clearly announced principles, the co-working of God and man, the test-operation of peculiar motives and sentiments; in brief, the idea of probation in the most educative and august shape it could assume. Are we the only learners in this school? Worlds have brotherhood as well as men, and the network, too delicate for any eye to see all the filaments even here, is spread over spaces unmeasured by the visible firmament. It is a mediatorial economy under which we live, nor can any reader of the New Testament doubt that the universe is affected in some way, though the manner and extent are mysteries, by this mediatorial rule. Inasmuch, then, as it is mediatorial, this system cannot be permanent, and hence "every man in his own order" presents the conception of a successional development, which must, at some period, reach its crisis and pass away. "Then cometh the end, when he shall have delivered up the kingdom to God, even the Father; when he shall have put down all rule and all authority and power." What is it that shall terminate? The previous verses (20—23) throw some light on this subject. Humanity is represented therein as to its contrasted forms, and these forms are Adam and Christ. Contrast is our chief mode of knowing objects in this world, and we are unceasingly dependent on its activity. It is a mark, however, of the weakness of our faculties and the limited sphere in which they are confined. Now, these contrasted forms of humanity as embodied in Adam and Christ shall vanish away, because they belong to our knowing "in part" and are only disciplinary for that "which is perfect." All the conflict between our nature in Adam and our nature in Christ having ended, and its connections with preternatural agents having come to a close, and that close triumphant on the side of the Lord Jesus, every sign of this sort of *rule, authority, and power*, shall disappear from the universe. We may venture to suggest that some hint of this is given in the forty days. The posthumous life of the risen Christ has dropped off the outward marks of its former rule, authority and power. No discussions are held with scribes and Pharisees; no snares are laid to entangle him; no repelling on his part the charges of sabbath-breaking, confederation with Beelzebub, and blasphemy in claiming to be the Son of God; but the battle has closed, and the Victor fresh from the grave is victor over Sanhedrim and Herod and Pilate, and henceforth the Holy Spirit orders the struggle between the forces of good and evil. But on a far wider arena, and with an infinitely grander display of majesty, will the Lord Jesus Christ consummate his victory over earth and hell when he resigns to God the Father his delegated sovereignty as the Mediator. As in the forty days no winds and waters were to be stilled, no demoniac crossed his path to call forth his power, no exertion made in the exercise of authority and rule over those inimical to his divinity, but conflict was swallowed up in conquest; so now, the end having been attained of mediatorial government and all opposition put down, what befits him so royally as to resume the ancient characteristics of his Sonship as the second Person in the holy Trinity and take the glory of eternal ages back, long ago resigned, to his bosom? Does this require that his humanity shall be laid aside? By no means. Turn again to the forty days. Humanity then manifested in him a semi-glorified state. Over time and space he was conqueror, nor was he amenable to any law of flesh and blood, but enjoyed the immunities of a "spiritual body." Yet, notwithstanding, he was most human, and in his voice the old tones were tenderer and sweeter, so that Mary knew him when he spoke her name, and in his manner there was a more precious condescension, which St. Thomas felt when he exclaimed, "My Lord and my God." The human body as it goes downward towards the brutes loses its native properties as the companion of the soul. The human body as it goes upward towards God increases its capacity to enshrine amd show forth the spirit. What limit exists to this capacity, we know not. But we may well believe that Christ's humanity, though the Mediatorship cease to exist, will be associated for ever with his Sonship. And under what conditions shall this termination of the Mediatorship occur? When the "*last enemy* shall be destroyed." And that enemy is *death*. This closes the protracted warfare. It began with his victory over the grave, it ends with his triumph over all graves. "*Death itself there dies.*" By the subjection of the Son to the Father, we understand, then, that it is the incarnate Son who is thus subordinated, and that this interferes in no way with the human relation sustained to his people. Less than Son of man he can never be, any more than less than Son of God. But just as his semi-glorified state during the forty days endeared him all the more to the disciples, and that too while they felt him removed from the old forms of social contact, so this last and most resplendent display of Christ's Godhead will elevate the humanity of his saints into a fuller assimilation to himself. The new distance will be only a new nearness, for God shall be "all in all." The next verse (ver. 29) introduces an abrupt change: "Else ['since' or, 'again'] what shall they do which are baptized for the dead, if the dead rise not at all?" Various interpretations have been put on this obscure passage, none of them free from difficulties. "Posthumous baptism by proxy," or the baptism of a living person for a friend who had died unbaptized; baptism in the sense of "being immersed in sufferings;" or, again, as signifying "a vicarious occupancy of the position once filled by a deceased person;" or, once more, as applied to all believers,— are the leading explanations offered. Whatever the meaning is of being "baptized for the dead"—whether it was a superstitious custom which had sprung up in the Church and was condemned by the apostle, or, the ordinary and proper use of this sacrament— it is not necessary for us to determine in order to see its connection with the argument. In any view of the matter, baptism was an unmeaning thing, if there were no resurrection. Solemnize it as they might, practise it with reference to the affectionate memories of the dead, administer the holy rite altogether with respect to the living, but, nevertheless, the living and the dead were in the same category, unless there were a resurrection. Why are we risking so much by our baptism as a profession of Christian faith? Why this useless and irrational "jeopardy"? Plainly enough, jeopardy has a Divine meaning for the living—a meaning, too, that every grave illustrates and enforces, if baptism is a sacrament—and, unquestionably, we do well to incur the risks, provided there be a general resurrection. But the dead body, what of that? And the living body, what of this? I write to you, Corinthians, of no disembodied existence. I write of no immortality of spirit as spirit. I have nothing to do with that. Baptism has nothing to do with that; our memory of the dead is no abstract memory of their souls, but of body and spirit as forming their human nature. And now, if baptism recognize the union of body and spirit, and symbolize the redeemed sanctity of each, there is good reason for jeopardy; otherwise none at all. By his love for this Church, by his joy in its members, he protests that his own jeopardy is so great as to warrant the statement, "I die daily." Outward circumstances beset him with so many perils and the inward pressure was so heavy and constant, as that he suffered like a dying man, day by day. To particularize; if (metaphorically) he had "fought with beasts at Ephesus," what advantage was it if the dead rise not? Was he facing all these terrible risks, hour by hour, to preach a gospel that left Christ imprisoned in the sealed grave of the Sanhedrim, and that it was vain to preach and vain to believe, and that made baptism a nullity? Was it for this that he underwent so much distress? "Let us eat and drink." If the body has no part or lot in the grace of Christ, and has no future, let us make the most of its enjoyments in the present life. " To-morrow we die." No punishment can be inflicted on the body hereafter, since it has no hereafter; "Let us eat and drink." And yet beware; deception is always possible, and deception is certain in this instance. " Evil communications corrupt good manners; " so that poet and apostle, Menander and St. Paul, are at one as it respects association and intercourse, and their effects on practical life. Then follows the warm exhortation: "Awake to righteousness"—" an exclamation full of apostolic majesty " (Bengel)—" and sin not." Such views as he had condemned came from a want of the knowledge of God. More than this, it was humiliating that such errors were found among the Corinthians. "I speak this to your *shame.*" The argument, as conducted to its present point, has included a number of particulars, each luminous in itself, each reflecting light on the general course of the idea foremost in his mind; and from the wide range, reaching to the end of the mediatorial kingdom, he returns to himself as daily dying for the sake of these truths. On the other side, what is the landing-place? It is, in Epicurean morality and practice, the deception and corruption and shame of "Let us eat and drink; for to-morrow we die." And as he comes back from this extensive circuit of thought, convictions far more profound than earthly logic, and emotions deeper than earthly love, press themselves into utterance while he reminds these Corinthians how far astray they had gone, " not knowing the Scriptures nor the power of God."—L.

Vers. 35—50.—*Objections to the resurrection; replies thereto; conclusions involved.* How far has St. Paul come on the path he has been treading? Beginning with the "many infallible proofs" of the forty days, and adding the appearance of the Lord Jesus to him, he had convicted those of an absurdity who denied a general resurrection. On various grounds, the view they held was incredible. The moral consequences of their belief were set forth. True logic and pure morality condemned their departure from that "righteousness" which only exists by virtue of "the knowledge of God." If the one class of thinkers whom he had answered had etherealized a fundamental, historic fact into a sheer fiction, so that a great truth was utterly lost, another class of thinkers stood arrayed against the doctrine itself, and refused its acceptance on the score of its unreasonableness. Nature, they claimed, was on their side. Nothing that died lived again. The whole economy of the material world was opposed to it. A grave was a grave for ever. Heaven and earth bore witness that death was death, and could never be other than death. Now, the body is a part of the physical kingdom, and, as such, has well-known properties, and is subject to certain laws. Well, he will discuss it on their ground. In the previous branch of the argument, the basis was "according to the Scriptures," and he had constant occasion to say, Christ, Christ Jesus, Christ Jesus our Lord, Christ as the Firstfruits, Christ in contrast with Adam, Christ as Mediator, Christ as the second Person in the Trinity. But there is a change, a noteworthy change, now, and for some verses Christ is not named. *According to nature,* or by analogy, the argument has to proceed if the objectors are met. The new stand-point is promptly taken, and St. Paul and the philosophical critics are face to face. Who are these that have gathered before the eye of his imagination in that humble room in Ephesus, the proud and lordly city, whose commerce connected it with every land, and whose wealth was the wonder and envy of the world? Near by was the magnificent temple of Artemis, renowned over Ionia and far beyond, safe too in its renown, since no art of man could surpass its pillars of Parian marble, its doors of cypress-wood, its roof of cedar resting on columns of jasper, and the great master-pieces of painting and sculpture by which it had been enriched. Likely enough, one who could quote from Menander, Aratas, and Epimenides, knew something of Anacreon, Thales, Heraclitus, and others associated with Ionia and Ephesus. Would not some of these illustrious thinkers rise before his vision when he began to meditate on the questions growing out of the relations between soul and body, questions on which Greek intellect had expended its subtlest power of investigation? And would not that memorable day in Athens flash back upon him from Mars' Hill, when he confronted the philosophers with the doctrine of the resurrection, some mocking, others saying, "We will hear thee again of this matter"? However this may have been, it is certain that St. Paul understood perfectly the objections made by Greek philosophy to the resurrection, as to the "how" and "with what body"—the general and the specific bases of Greek hostility to the doctrine so near his heart. To answer the two interrogatories— "how?" and "with what body?"—is the work now in hand. St. Paul had just closed an appeal by the sharp cry of "Awake to righteousness," as if intent on arousing the Church from stupor. Now, however, he begins with "Thou fool," or rather, "*Fool*," expressing no harshness, but simply the want of wisdom. The analogy is stated at once: "That which thou sowest is not quickened, except it die"—reminding one of similar words spoken by the Lord Jesus (John xii. 24). The seed you sow has to die, to pass into decay and dissolution, its component parts separated, before the germ can disengage its life and begin to sprout. Like that seed, your body dies. Like that, your body by dying enters on a condition preparatory to living. If life thus proceeds from dissolution, the general question "how" is met by the likeness between the decay of the seed and the body. The body of the seed dies, but it has a principle of life which springs thereby into active existence. Then, the contrast having been first presented between death and life, he advances to the second point: "With what body do they come?" *Not the old body*; nothing can be clearer than that, for the destruction of the former body supplies the conditions for the process of deliverance from decay, and institutes the work of quickening. And what is the issue of the new process? It is a new body, for "thou sowest not that body that shall be;" if thou didst, what reality would be in the sowing; what foundation for the hope of the husbandman; what work for the providential agency of nature? On the supposition of the same body in the seed-grain dying and growing, the resemblance would be to *sleep* rather than *death*, and, consequently the analogy as here used would break down at the start. Hence the statement so essential to the parallelism: "thou sowest not" the future body, but a body for transformation. It is "bare grain" which is put into the ground. This is your work as a husbandman; but God is there to perform his part, and "God giveth it a body as it hath pleased him." Admitting that God gives the new body according to his pleasure, does it follow that this act is arbitrary because it is sovereign? Is nature set aside? Are the former laws that made that seed the kind of seed it was, overthrown under the sod? Is it death to the economy of production, or is it production for reproduction? And he answers, God giveth "to every seed his own body." On the one hand, the continuity of nature is preserved, the particular character of the seed is not lost; and, on the other hand, the new growth is something unlike that which dies, for God has given it a different body. Similarity and contrast are both maintained. Is the identity destroyed? *Nay.* Is there a distinction between the body that dies and the body that lives? *Yea.* Identification must not conflict with dissimilarity; dissimilarity must not antagonize identification. Seen in this light, the change is one of form. Before death, there was body living; in death, body decayed and resolved into its elements; after death, body reconstructed. *The identity lies in the fact of body; the difference in the substance, properties, and form of body.* If so, what is there incredible in the resurrection? By analogy, it is a possible event. Nature authenticates a principle which *may* find application to the human body; and if you ask, "With what body do they come?" the reply is that it will be a new body, one of a higher form, one from him who "giveth to every seed his own body." Observe, then, the fact of the resurrection is not rested on analogy. The use of the analogical argument here is not for that purpose. Christ's resurrection establishes the fact of a general resurrection. But this having been assured, analogy is employed to show the consonance thereof with reason, by pointing out a correspondence between it and the germination of seed. And how beautiful as well as truthful is this use of nature! Enlightened from another source, even by the Spirit of God, St. Paul is in a position to see the God of nature as the God of the resurrection. He goes to nature and asks, "*Have you anything like this?*" And she points him to the growing harvest, a few months ago "bare grain," and says, "*So thall thy dead live!*" Our heavenly Father has not been content to give us great facts alone, but has superadded images, analogies, illustrations ; and the grander the truth, the more clear and copious its kindred associations. That sense of correspondence which exists in us all, and is a mainstay of our convictions, is continually addressed by him, and by thousands of ties he binds together his Word and his works. Inspired teachers exhibit their wisdom in the way they read and interpret nature. Scripture is not written for minds shut up in themselves, the order and grace of the universe hidden from them. Sensational consciousness is just as much a part of religion as spiritual consciousness, and, accordingly, an eminent teacher like St. Paul honours his office by appealing to nature. He wrote for the senses no less than for the spirit, and hence we find him (ver. 39) widening the scope of analogy. And whither shall he tend ? What is the objective point aimed at ? The identity of the resurrection-body with the dust and ashes of the grave—is that the goal of his thought? *Nay and yea.* Look on the gross side of identification, on the interminable disputes about bones and material particles, and the answer is *nay.* Look on the higher and far truer side of identification, and the answer is *yea.* As to the first, had the advocates of the dust and ashes theory existed in his day, he would perhaps have said, "Fool !" Happily for us, we know that identity as applied to the body means the persistent adhesion to the same idea in the plan and purpose of organization, so that while the particles of matter in the corporeal structure are ever coming and going, and are as short-lived as the ephemera of a summer day, such is the law of constancy beneath this variation that identity is no wise disturbed. St. Paul first takes up *diversity of animal organisms.* To show that the question is not about the retention and revivification of former *con-stituents* of the *body,* but a question solely of *body and its capacity* to assume such a form as God might be pleased to give, he states, "All flesh is not the same flesh." Men, beasts, fishes, birds, differ in flesh. It is all flesh, but very unlike. What then ? If body be capable of such variety in bodies, if you have such an interval as appears between man and bird, what limit will you put on body as to organization ? Creative power is manifested in matter as matter ; creative power makes its most wonderful manifestation in the countless shapes and adaptations of matter. And, accordingly, St. Paul's meaning is that you cannot argue from the structure and particles of the body here to the organization of a spiritual corporeity. But you can believe in new and higher forms, since "all flesh is not the same flesh." How far, then, has the argument progressed? To this landing-place : body here, body hereafter, body capable of a nobler type of existence. But he proceeds to use another illustration. Hitherto he has been mundane in his view ; now he enters on the upper realm. Celestial bodies, bodies terrestrial, exist in the universe, and do they present contrasts on a far broader scale than those we see in the flesh of men and other animals? Ay ; the diversity now is *one of glory.* Celestial and terrestrial bodies share different degrees of glory. The sun is a sun in its glory, and its splendour is its own. Moon and stars have their glory, and by this unequal distribution of radiance they impress us when we gaze on the firmament. Just here, then, the movement of the apostle's mind takes a sudden spring. It bounds afar, and it is no longer form, no longer seed and harvest, nor animal organisms, but it is the *splendour of form* that absorbs his contemplation. Long ago the royal psalmist had poured forth his wonder and adoration in the nineteenth psalm, that sublime hymn which chants "the glory of God" in the firmament and keeps the throbbing pulses of the human heart in the rhythm of the universe. And now—the eye dilated and the resplendency full upon it—hearken to the instant utterance : "So also is the resurrection of the dead." "Sown in corruption "—earth and its earthliness ; "it is raised in incorruption"—earth and its earthliness left in the grave. "Sown in dishonour"—its humiliations all upon it, and demanding speedy removal from sight and commitment to darkness lest it be loathsome; "it is raised in glory," and bears a likeness to him whose "countenance was as the sun shineth in his strength." "Sown in weakness"—always in a state of infirmity and as a corpse, "powerless and unable to resist corruption" (Bloomfield) ; "it is raised in power," and made capable of receiving plenitude of energy from the will of the spirit and answering all possible uses of mind. "Sown a natural body"—as in life so in death, a part of the material order, and subjected to its conditions, and never able to escape its limitations, so "natural" that this very apostle, "caught up to the third heaven," had to suffer "a thorn in the flesh" that he might not be "exalted above measure,"—"it is raised a spiritual body," and, if once a body that represented the soul, now a body that is in perfect sympathy with spirit as the highest organ in man for communion with God. The last antithesis is so important as to demand restatement: "There is a natural body, and there is a spiritual body." Notice that the term "body" as used here derives its import as to its character or quality, not from anything in itself, but from its subsidiary relations, in the one case being "natural," "psychical," as connected with the soul, and, in the other, as contradistinguished from the "psychical" or "soul-body," represented as the "spiritual body." What does the clear discrimination made by the apostle between the two forms of body require of us? A primary recognition of the difference between soul and spirit as determinative of the difference between the body natural and the body spiritual. Without entering into metaphysics, we may remark that the soul is that form of mind which connects man with the senses and the outer world of the senses, while the spirit is that form of mind which connects man with unseen and eternal objects. If this distinction were not real—a distinction that often develops in the feeling of most painful contrariety—how shall we explain our consciousness; how understand the amazing inconsistencies into which we fall; how give any account of moods and transitions, reactions, and rebounds? The fact of difference is plain to every student-thinker: the nature of it is difficult, perhaps impossible to make obvious in language. Is there not a poetry that finds access to the innermost life, and a poetry that goes no further than the external intellect and its correlated sensibilities? And of painting, sculpture, music, eloquence, are there not everywhere two vividly marked divisions, so that while the one kind is very palpable to the soul, the other is felt rather than known, and works by hints and intimations more than by communications actually defined? Still more as to persons: who has not known some individuals that always called forth by their presence the best within him? whereas there were others whose tones and looks were solicitations to evil? Only a few consciously note these experiences, and still fewer analyze them, but assuredly they are facts of life, and life would be barren of its most advantageous suggestions, were it otherwise. Now, it is this difference between soul and spirit which St. Paul employs to give the contrast in the verse: "There is a natural body, and there is a spiritual body." In this world, the body is so organized as to correspond to the soul; in the resurrection, the new corporeity will represent the spirit. Would you see how a great Christian thinker weaves into one pattern thoughts from nature and from Scripture? Ver. 45 presents St. Paul in these words: "It is written." Nature, though prolific of types, shadows, parables, cannot long detain him, and now he returns to the Mosaic account of the creation in the first and second chapters of Genesis. "Adam was made a living soul" (ch. ii. 7). Animal he was in corporeal organization, placed at the head of the animal kingdom, sovereign over all creatures and things, and, moreover, much else, for he was the image of God in his reason, intelligence, and moral nature. He had a soul in him, and, it was God's breath. It was therefore God-like. It was a capacity for whatever was good about him, and for whatever was best above him, in the order of creation to which humanity belonged. But he was put on trial, and he failed; his capacity sank instead of rising; it narrowed and shrank within the body, and then and there ended the possibility of the "living soul" having as such a Divine history of progress and perfect development. We are leaving St. Paul, however, who remarks, in juxtaposition to the statement touching Adam, "the first man," that "the last Adam was made a quickening [life-giving] spirit." How intimately associated in his mind were the two, Adam and Christ, is seen in the fact that he is the only Biblical writer who calls Christ by the name of Adam; while, at the same time that they stand in such close connection with humanity, the contrast between them is forcibly given. What Adam was is expressed in "living soul" as the starting-point or initiation of human nature, the designation expressing the predominant aspects of his earthly position and his candidacy as a being in God's image for a much loftier development. By the "life-giving spirit," we understand Christ in the power and glory of his resurrection, when "he led captivity captive, and gave gifts unto men," chief of which was the Holy Ghost. The "natural" precedes the "spiritual;" and what a philosophy of the universe opens in this single idea! The natural in law and government, the "do this and live," the special rule and the special test, the appeal to the senses and the sense-intellect, and the primal guardianship of conscience by means of fear over moral interests—the natural in social relations—the natural in the motives to obedience and the uses of God's grace and the offering of worship —must lead the way, since by no other method apparent to us could humanity attain its high destiny. "Afterward that which is spiritual." First the natural, afterward the spiritual,—this is the order in everything that concerns man. Every one of his attributes, such as perception, reasoning, volition, faith, love, obeys this paramount law; and the miracle of life is, whenever the Divine plan is carried out, that man is seen, as Milton describes the lion in Eden, extricating himself from earthly entanglements and winning his freedom. St. Paul multiplies the forms of this idea. "Of the earth, earthy," was Adam; "the second man is of heaven;" and as we bear here "the image of the earthy" in body and soul, so shall we bear "the image of the heavenly." Slowly the likeness of Adam fades even now under the fashioning hand of God. Natural law is made subservient to spiritual law, so that while the senses decay and the other animal functions abate more or less, the diviner sensibilities acquire the vitality thus disengaged and expand with new vigour. Providence co-operates with grace. And thus, line after line, lineament after lineament, disappearing from the "living soul," and also from the lower functions of the body, there comes out in its stead "the image of the heavenly." Our growing years, if we are consecrated to God, are all on the side of Christ, and are all helpers and auxiliaries to prepare us for the fulness of spiritual life in a spiritual body.—L.

Vers. 51—58.—*Concluding argument and exhortation.* If "flesh and blood" is "corruption," and cannot inherit "incorruption," what then? Educate the present body to the offices of the mind; let every function do its legitimate work, and every organ be faithful to the organism; refine, beautify, ennoble it by all natural and providential agencies; it is, nevertheless, "flesh and blood," and inherits "corruption." No such corporeal structure could go to heaven unchanged. The earthly body of Jesus Christ, which was fully adequate to the pre-resurrection state of humiliation, sorrow, death, and fitted him to show forth the Father, had yet to be changed by the resurrection before he, though "holy, harmless, undefiled," could ascend to the dominion of the universe. If, then, our "flesh and blood" be so debased by its mortality, by its animal connections, by its habits and functions, "Behold, I show you a mystery," a truth once concealed but now revealed by the Spirit, that those who are alive when Christ comes at the last day "shall all be changed." No graves shall open to receive and then restore them. Land and sea shall give up their dead, and, simultaneously therewith, the living shall be instantly transformed, rising out of their mortality and corruption into immortality and incorruption. What a scene here for picturesque description! But the apostle was too wise and reverent to indulge his imagination. The sublimity gathered no images about itself. Words for its splendid conceptions were not asked, nor were poetic transports suffered to obtrude on the awful glory of the hour. Yet there was speech, yet there was rapture, and the utterance and the feeling partook in full measure of the grandeur of the occasion. It was not the voice of imagination and its emotions, but the voice of pure and devout passion that exclaimed, "O death, where is thy sting? O grave, where is thy victory?" The battle has been fought, the victory won; and the victory is most glorious in this, that it is the gift to God to us, and a gift "through our Lord Jesus Christ." For what would a deliverance from mortality and debasement be to a Christian if won by his own arm, and what would heaven be if it were an outgrowth and final efflorescence of earthly culture and progress? "Through our Lord Jesus Christ:" this is the joy of the triumph, and this the heart of heaven. And "therefore" follows with the exhortation to his beloved brethren to be constant, enduring, abundant in the Lord's work, since they were well assured that their devotion to this labour, with its burdens, cares, and sacrifices, could not be "in vain in the Lord." It is a "*therefore*," indeed, and such a one as he had never had an opportunity to use before, nor would ever find just such an occasion to repeat. The thanksgiving, the tender appeal, the entire outburst, stands alone among all those effusions with which his grandest hours are imperishably associated. It has happened again and again that in some grave crisis of a nation, or when the fortunes of the human family seemed to be touching an epochal period, there has been some Demosthenes or Burke to plead for the hope of a better future for the state; or some Savonarola, Luther, Knox, Milton, to lift up a prophetic voice in behalf of the Church. But it fell to the lot of St. Paul to write the fifteenth chapter of the First Corinthians, to make an argument proof against every assault, to set forth the argument with such force and in such amplitude as to bring nature from the vegetable and animal kingdoms about us and from the remote heights of the firmament, so as to put her testimony in alliance with his logic in favour of the most precious of all truths, the doctrine of a perfected and immortal humanity in the Lord Jesus Christ. Nor can it be irreverent in us to borrow the language of his own exultant faith and say, "Thanks be to God, which giveth" to Christianity the "victory" over materialism and false spiritualism. Body is the meeting-ground of matter and mind; they have met, they have united; they separate to meet again in a nearer and holier fellowship, and they meet to be together for ever. Soul is spirit in its rudimentary life, in the childhood of thought and beauty and affection, in a state of trial and discipline, but its instincts, greater incomparably than its abilities, show their prophetic outreachings towards the infinite and eternal. So far as our dim reason can perceive, a fully developed spirit could not exist in a mortal body, nor a soul exist in an immortal body. Soul and body, each "natural" for this life; spirit and a "spiritual body" for the kingdom of God." "Thanks be to God."—L.

Vers. 1—58.—*The exposition and defence of the resurrection.* This chapter stands, as it were, by itself in the Epistle, and indeed in the Scripture. The Gospels relate the fact of our Saviour's rising from the dead; but St. Paul in this passage, remarkable alike for closeness of reasoning, for fervour of eloquence, and for elevation of spiritual treatment, writes as the theologian of the resurrection. In opposition to false teachers who had arisen in the Corinthian Church, the apostle maintains the fact of Christ's resurrection to be the basis of Christian faith, practice, and hope; and especially deduces from the historical event the expectation of a glorious immortality, then and ever the possession of the Church, and destined to be the possession of humanity.

I. THE FACT OF CHRIST'S RESURRECTION IS PROVED AND PREACHED. (Vers. 1—11.) This is here exhibited as: 1. The substance of Christian preaching. 2. The fulfilment of Old Testament predictions. 3. Verified by the witness of the apostles and of five hundred brethren. 4. Attested by Paul himself. 5. Believed and professed by the whole Church of the Redeemer.

II. INFERENCES FROM THIS FACT. (Vers. 12—28.) 1. *Destructive inferences.* (Vers. 12—19.) The resurrection of Jesus is represented as conflicting with and altogether overthrowing the belief inculcated by false teachers, that the dead rise not. 2. *Constructive inferences.* (Vers. 20—28.) The Lord Christ, as a risen Saviour and King, is represented as the Firstfruits of the spiritual harvest, and as the supreme Governor and Controller of the universe.

III. CONFIRMATIONS OF THE DOCTRINE OF THE GENERAL RESURRECTION FROM THE DEAD. (Vers. 29—49.) 1. Christian practice, and especially the endurance of opposition, persecution, and martyrdom, can only be accounted for by the power of a belief in worlds to come. Nothing is more evident than that the apostle himself, and many of the early Christians, came under the influence of this new and mighty power, making of them nothing short of new men. 2. Natural analogies support the doctrine of the resurrection. Especially the analogy of the seed sown from which vegetable life takes its rise, and to which the harvest of fruit is traceable. The manifest order subsisting in nature, and the progressive revelation of God himself, are in harmony with the Christian's hope.

IV. THE GLORIOUS PROSPECTS OF CHRIST'S PEOPLE. (Vers. 50—57.) 1. *The mystery told.* The inheritance of incorruptible and immortal blessedness. 2. *The triumph foretold.* Man's worst foes, sin and death, shall be vanquished, and that by the might of the Divine Conqueror, Christ.

V. CONSEQUENT EXHORTATION TO STEADFASTNESS. (Ver. 58.) Against apathy on the one hand, and enthusiasm on the other hand, Christians are warned. Labour is not in vain, for its fruits shall be reaped in eternity. Steadfastness and diligence are the appropriate attitude and habit of those who, believing that their Lord has risen, themselves look forward to the Divine, immortal life of heaven.—T.

Vers. 1—4.—*The apostolic doctrine.* It is interesting and valuable to have in these words from St. Paul's own pen a confirmation of the statements of the inspired historian,

St. Luke, regarding the preaching by which the first moral victories of Christianity were achieved.

I. THE SUBSTANCE OF APOSTOLIC DOCTRINE. Paul disclaims any pretension to a ministry of human learning or wisdom; he here as everywhere relies upon the *facts* which form the substance of his preaching and teaching. 1. The apostles proclaimed the death and burial of their Lord. These, indeed, were unquestioned historical facts, yet they lay at the basis of all their subsequent teaching, alike of doctrine, of promise, and of precept. 2. In conjunction with this they preached the resurrection of Christ. Whilst none denied that Jesus of Nazareth had been crucified, there were many who received the proclamation of his resurrection with incredulity and ridicule. But, however their preaching might be received, the apostles never wavered in their declaration that their Lord had risen from the grave. 3. These events were represented as a fulfilment of Old Testament prophecy; what had happened was "according to the Scriptures." To the Jews such a representation would appeal with peculiar power; and the Gentiles would recognize in it the unity of the dispensations of God. 4. The purpose of these events was represented as being the pardon and abolition of the sins of those who believed. The explanation of this "mystery" was a matter of inspired doctrine; but the fact was published abroad to all who would hear the Word.

II. THE RECEPTION OF APOSTOLIC DOCTRINE. 1. In the case of true converts, this was not vain, unreasonable, frivolous. There are those who are ready to receive every new doctrine; and some such professed adherence to Christianity without any sufficient acquaintance with the truth, without examining its credentials, without counting the cost of their decision. But sincere Christians act reasonably and deliberately in their acceptance of the Word of life. 2. True converts were stable in their faith. Such is the teaching of this passage: "Wherein ye stand;" "Ye hold it fast." Deliberate acceptance and adhesion may be expected to be followed by tenacious retention of the truth. Stability in faith and godliness is the condition of the enjoyment of true blessing.

III. THE ULTIMATE AIM AND RESULT OF APOSTOLIC DOCTRINE. No reader of the New Testament can suppose that the first preachers of the gospel intended simply to convey information. Theirs was a moral, a spiritual aim; they sought the salvation of their fellow-men—their deliverance from the curse, the bondage, the love of sin. Why was St. Paul so anxious that his hearers and his readers should receive and retain his teaching? It was because in his heart there glowed the flame of benevolence, because he desired above all things that his fellow-creatures should be rescued from the bondage of sin, and should rejoice in the liberty of the sons of God, and because he believed that this blessed result could be brought about only by their cordial reception of the gospel which it was his privilege and joy to preach.—T.

Ver. 6.—"*Some are fallen asleep.*" Sleep is a metaphor for death, which has been employed by the heathen poets, and by the rabbinical writers, as well as by the inspired penmen of the Old and New Testaments. But Christianity has given to the figure an especial sanction and an especial appropriateness.

I. OUR LORD HIMSELF HAS SET THE EXAMPLE OF DESIGNATING DEATH AS SLEEP. In speaking of Jairus's daughter, he said, "The maiden is not dead, but sleepeth;" and of Lazarus he said, "Our friend Lazarus sleepeth." As on both these occasions he was misunderstood, it would seem that the usage was not a familiar one. But as he spake, it was natural and right that his disciples also should speak.

II. DEATH TO THE CHRISTIAN IS SLEEP, FOR IT COMES AT THE CLOSE OF THE DAY'S TOIL. "After life's fitful fever he sleeps well," is language which Shakespeare uses with reference to the murdered Duncan. But how far more appropriate is such language when used with reference to those who have served God faithfully and diligently during many years, and who rest from their labours! "David, after he had served his own generation, fell on sleep;" and the expression is one suitable in application to every true servant of the Divine Lord.

> "How blest the righteous when he dies!
> When sinks a weary soul to rest,
> How mildly beam the closing eyes!
> How gently heaves the expiring breast!"

III. DEATH TO THE CHRISTIAN IS SLEEP, FOR IT IS THE LIBERATION OF THE SPIRIT FROM EARTH AND ITS COMMUNION WITH HEAVEN. The body of the slave or of the exile may be still and silent in slumber, and the spirit may in the visions of the night wander to the congenial scenes of home, and may imagine the renewal of broken ties and the resumption of suspended joys. And in this sleep is the emblem of that death through which Christ's people, absent from the body, are present with the Lord. On earth and in the life of the body, during the walk of faith, it sometimes seems that the beloved Saviour is far away, and that eternal joys are imaginary and remote. But when the frame sinks into the slumber of dissolution, the spirit wings its flight to the land where Jesus is, and where are pleasures for evermore.

IV. DEATH TO THE CHRISTIAN IS SLEEP, BECAUSE IT IS FOLLOWED BY THE GLORIOUS AND EVERLASTING AWAKENING. " An eternal sleep " is the expression of the heathen poets, not of the Christian teacher. On the contrary, the whole argument of this chapter is to banish such a notion, and to substitute for it one far more bright and blessed and far more true. Even the ancient prophet foretold that many of those who sleep in the dust of the earth shall awake to everlasting life. And we know that " Christ hath been raised from the dead, the firstfruits of them that are asleep." It shall be an awaking which shall fill the saints with surprise and satisfaction and infinite joy, and which shall be a new and marvellous revelation of the love and life of God to natures purified and glorified.—T.

Vers. 9, 10.—*Humility and self-assertion.* No writer is more given to paradox than the Apostle Paul. An eager, impulsive nature is wont to realize vividly every side of truth that is presented, and seems consequently to fall into inconsistencies. But such a nature is usually remarkably sincere and trustworthy. Such was the case with the apostle, and no candid reader can doubt that the language of the text represents the real facts of the case.

I. AN ASSERTION OF PERSONAL HUMILITY. 1. Paul occupied a singular position among the apostles, inasmuch as he had not, like the others, been privileged to enjoy the society of the Divine Lord during his earthly ministry, but had been called by Christ long after the Ascension. 2. Paul took shame to himself because he had persecuted the Church of God, which had been constituted through the labours and zeal of the other apostles and their colleagues. On these two grounds he deemed himself the least of the apostles, and even unworthy of the apostolic name. Such humility is rare; it secures the approval of him who regards the lowly and raises them up, who exalts the humble and meek; it commends itself to the Master who requires a childlike spirit as a condition of entrance into the kingdom, and who pronounces a blessing upon the meek.

II. A CLAIM OF OFFICIAL EMINENCE. 1. The apostolic office and dignity are attributed to the free favour of the Giver of all. " By the grace of God I am what I am." This was in accordance with Paul's own teaching that " God hath set some in the Church, first apostles." An honour like this, functions such as it involved, authority such as was connected with it, could come only from God. It is well for every servant of Christ to accustom himself deliberately and constantly to trace up his possessions and his trust to the Divine Lord and Author of blessing. 2. Paul acknowledged that the gifts bestowed upon him had been diligently and faithfully employed. Grace had been given, and grace had been found not vain or void. That is to say, opportunities, advantages, endowments, had all been used in such a manner as that they had been continued and increased. Growing years had brought enlarged powers and enlarged usefulness and influence. 3. Paul claimed pre-eminence in labour. His calling, as the apostle of the Gentiles, involved long journeys, many hardships and privations and perils. His ardent temperament, his burning love to his Lord, his grateful and consecrated disposition, led him to undertake and to perform more than had been undertaken and performed by others. It was a necessity alike of his position and of his temperament. Yet it is observable that he no sooner claimed to be first in toil, than he reminded himself that what he did was not his doing, but the fruit of God's grace towards him. If humility passes into self-assertion, self-assertion returns to humility.—T.

Ver. 17.—*A vain faith.* It often happens that men accept certain notions without realizing what they involve. So it seems to have been with those Corinthian Christians who lent too willing an ear to the false teachers who denied the resurrection of the dead. The apostle was justified in pointing out to such that their surrender of this great doctrine and revelation involved virtually the denial of the resurrection of Christ, and that this involved the denial of some of their most cherished beliefs and hopes. What the Lord Christ was to them he was because he was the risen and triumphant Saviour. To take away their faith in such a Saviour was to render their faith vain.

I. FAITH IN CHRIST'S DEITY LARGELY RESTS UPON THE FACT OF HIS RESURRECTION. 1. If Jesus had not risen from the dead, his own recorded predictions would have been falsified. On several occasions he had foretold that his violent death should be followed on the third day by his resurrection. Had this not taken place, his word would have been discredited, and all confidence in his Deity would naturally have been destroyed. 2. If Jesus had not risen from the dead, he would have been proved inferior to death. The argument of the apostle was a very powerful and effective argument—that, being not only David's Son, but David's Lord, it was not possible that he should be holden by death, that his body should see corruption. But had he remained in the grave, a very different impression concerning his nature would necessarily have been produced upon the minds of his disciples, and the world could never have been convinced of his Messiahship and divinity.

II. FAITH IN CHRIST AS A SAVIOUR RESTS UPON THE FACT OF HIS RESURRECTION. 1. This appears in the customary publication of the gospel by the inspired apostles. They preached that Jesus was "raised to be a Prince and a Saviour, to give repentance unto Israel, and remission of sins." 2. The resurrection of Christ is a token of the acceptance by the Father of that redemptive work of Christ whereby forgiveness is secured to those who believe. And it is the condition of the exercise of those mediatorial functions which are still discharged in the court of heaven, the presence of God. 3. The resurrection is a spiritual power in the hearts of those who believe it, a power of newness of mind, of holiness, of life immortal. They who die with Christ unto sin, and are crucified with him unto the world, risen with Christ, live in his heavenly and resurrection life.

III. FAITH IN CHRIST AS THE FIRSTFRUITS OF THE GENERAL RESURRECTION RESTS UPON HIS RISING FROM THE TOMB. There is observable a marvellous contrast between the hopelessness of the heathen and the confidence of Christians in the prospect of death. To those who believe the gospel, the victory of Immanuel over death and the grave is the pledge of the final triumph of the good, is their consolation when they are bereaved of their Christian kindred and associates, is their confidence and inspiration in the prospect of their own departure to be with Christ.—T.

Ver. 20.—*The firstfruits of life.* There is a perceptible change in the tone of the apostle's writing just at this point. He has been reasoning upon the supposition, adopted by some even among the Corinthians, that the dead rise not, and showing that, if such is the case, the resurrection of Christ is a fable, and the faith of Christians vain and their hopes baseless. This course he has taken to show to his readers the awful consequences of the false doctrine introduced among them. But he suddenly breaks off, and commences in another strain. After all, the supposition discussed is incredible. For as a matter of fact, of history, of certainty, Christ *has* risen from the dead, and in doing so he has become the Firstfruits of them that slept.

I. CHRIST'S RESURRECTION PRECEDES THAT OF HIS PEOPLE. The doctrine of the future life, obscure in the earlier periods of revelation, was made known with growing clearness as ages passed on. But it was Christ who "brought life and immortality to light through the gospel." Not only by his explicit teaching, but by his own victory over the grave, did our Saviour bring to mankind an assurance of eternal life. And, in point of time, he led the way for his faithful followers and friends.

II. CHRIST'S RESURRECTION IS EVIDENCE OF THE DIVINE AND QUICKENING POWER WHICH SHALL RAISE HIS PEOPLE AFTER HIM. The presence of a Divine power of life was manifest when, on the third day, the Lord of glory rose victorious from the tomb. If before it was doubtful whether in the universe there resided such a life-giving energy, such doubt was now dispelled. The same Divine might which raised the Leader can raise the followers too. The sun which has ripened the sheaf which is presented as the firstfruits of the harvest has warmth and vital geniality to mature the crop that clothes the vastest plain ; and the Spirit of life which quickened the crucified One will raise up us also to be glorified with him.

III. Christ's resurrection is unto the same blessedness of life which is appointed for his people. Our Lord did not rise to renew the humiliation and the sufferings of this earthly existence ; he rose a Conqueror to live and reign in glory. And the purpose of infinite grace is that, where the Master is, there also shall his disciples and servants be. We may share his weakness and his woe, but we shall share also his might and his blessedness ; we may bear his cross, but we shall also wear his crown.

IV. Christ's resurrection is the earnest of his people's immortal life. "Death hath no more dominion over him." And those for whom he both died and rose again live in him and live for ever. "There shall we ever be with the Lord." "They go no more out." It is to the glory of the Lord and Husbandman when the firstfruits are brought into the temple and offered upon the altar. But the glory of that day shall be yet greater when the harvest shall be completed, and when the garner of God shall be filled with the rich spiritual produce of the earth.—T.

Ver. 25.—*The reign of the Redeemer.* Even in his earthly humiliation, Christ was a King. Once the devil offered him the kingdoms of the world ; once the people would have taken him by force and have made him their King. Such secular dominion he sought not, neither would accept. Yet he entered Jerusalem in royal state ; before Pilate he confessed himself a King ; and over his cross it was written, "This is Jesus of Nazareth, the King of the Jews." Little notion had men during his ministry of the nature and extent of that dominion which should one day be his. Yet the apostles came to understand that not only the prophetic and the priestly, but also the kingly dignity and office, were appointed for him whose gospel they proclaimed.

I. Christ's right to reign. This is grounded upon : 1. His Divine nature and authority. 2. His moral right and qualifications. 3. His definite appointment by the Father. 4. His mediatorial sufferings and sacrifice.

II. The subjects of Christ's kingdom. They are spiritual and willing subjects. He cares nothing for a pretended loyalty or a merely outward obedience. His aim is to gain a dominion over human hearts, and thence to rule human society.

III. The foes whom Christ's reign subdues. These he is to put under his feet. They may be enumerated : 1. Ignorance. 2. Error. 3. Superstition. 4. Irreligiousness and worldliness. 5. Vice, crime, and sin. 6. All false and corrupt religions.

IV. The means by which Christ's reign is advanced and his foes subdued. 1. The weapons are the truths of the gospel, the exhibition of the righteousness and love of God. 2. The agency is that of believing, sympathizing, and consecrated natures. The kingdom comes by the labours and the courage and enterprise of the spiritual subjects. 3. The power is that of the Holy Spirit of God.

V. The period of Christ's reign. 1. It commenced at our Lord's ascension, when he was "raised to be a Prince and a Saviour," "from henceforth expecting," etc. 2. It has been constantly advancing, the kingdom has been extending its boundaries, and the number of the subjects has been multiplying. 3. It will not terminate until victory shall have been gained over every foe. "Thy throne is for ever and ever." Only when all opposition is vanquished, shall the Son himself yield the dominion, and God shall be all and in all.—T.

Ver. 33.—*Evil company.* This is one of several instances in which inspired writers have incorporated in their own compositions the language of current literature. The adoption of a line from Menander is a witness to the harmony between human reason and Divine revelation. From whatsoever source proceeding, truth and justice, wisdom and prudence, possess a Divine authority. We are encouraged to use the wisdom of so-called "profane" writers even in enforcing spiritual truth.

I. Infidelity and immorality are often associated. It would be unjust to charge all unbelievers with vice ; but there is no injustice in pointing out that the natural tendency of infidelity is both to shake the foundations of virtue and to snap the restraints upon vice. If there be no righteous God, no moral law, no future retribution, all sanctions to virtue and uprightness of heart and conduct are removed, except such as are imposed by civil society. Where external penalties are removed, or where they can be evaded, it is not reasonable to expect that the bulk of men will deny themselves, check their appetites and passions, and practise the difficult virtues of justice, chastity, and benevolence. And it cannot be concealed that in most cases the prevalence of infidelity opens the flood-gates of all iniquity. The Corinthian false teachers seem to have taught that, the body being perishable, sins of the flesh are immaterial and unimportant, and thus to have given countenance to the maxim of Epicureanism, "Let us eat and drink; for to-morrow we die."

II. INFIDELITY AND IMMORALITY ARE CONTAGIOUS AND CORRUPTING. By appealing to what is base and selfish in human nature, the champions of error and self-indulgence lead especially the young who come under their influence away from the stern steep road of virtue into "the primrose path of dalliance." None are more contemptible than those blasphemers and voluptuaries who, having grown grey in the service of Satan, make it their aim to corrupt and debauch the young and inexperienced. By casting aspersions upon religion, by insinuating doubts, by representing the pleasures of sin, and, above all, by an example of irreligion, profanity, and vice, such persons make themselves a moral plague and pestilence in human society.

III. INFIDELITY AND IMMORALITY SHOULD THEREFORE BE DISCOUNTENANCED AND ESCHEWED. For the sake of our own welfare, for the sake of the family, the Church, and society, it is needful that we should be upon our guard against those evil associations which have a tendency to corrupt even good manners and morals. And, on the other hand, those whose influence has been exerted against the cause of virtue and religion may well be reminded that they cannot perish alone, that their example will probably be injurious and even ruinous to others; so that if there remain in them any spark of pity and unselfishness, they may well be entreated to immediate and sincere repentance, for the sake of others as well as of themselves.—T.

Vers. 36—38.—*Death and quickening.* Although the apostle deems himself to have established the fact of the resurrection of the dead, by proving the resurrection of the Saviour, and by showing that the resurrection of Christ's people is a consequence of their Lord's resurrection, he is quite sensible of the difficulties attaching to this belief. These are difficulties which all have felt, and with which many sincere believers find themselves often confronted. Believing the fact, we know not how to render it to our own minds; the manner of the fact is inconceivable, or at all events unimaginable. The apostle endeavours to assist us in the effort either to overcome the difficulty or reasonably to acquiesce in its partial continuance. He makes use of natural analogies. The world is full of mysteries; and we may trace some mysteries which are common to nature and to revelation.

I. THE CREATOR, WHO APPOINTS THE DEATH OF THE SEED AS PREPARATORY TO THE LIFE OF THE PLANT, MAY APPOINT THE DEATH OF THE EARTHLY BODY AS THE PREPARATION FOR THE LIFE OF THE HEAVENLY BODY. The analogy is sometimes misunderstood, and it is supposed that, according to Paul, the dead body of the man is really the seed of the resurrection-body. This is not the case. But the apostle is evidently reasoning as did our Lord when he said, "Except a corn of wheat," etc. The death of the seed followed by the life of the plant is a figure of the death of the Saviour followed by the prevalence of his doctrine, and the vast extent of his personal, mediatorial influence. And so here, we are reminded that God's ways are not as our ways, that it pleases him to bring life out of death, and that he is able to make death the step towards a new and higher life.

II. THE CREATOR, WHO GIVES TO EVERY SEED A BODY OF ITS OWN, CAN PROVIDE THE GLORIFIED SPIRIT WITH A VESTURE AS SUITABLE TO THE HIGHER STATE AS OUR EARTHLY ORGANISM IS SUITABLE TO THE PRESENT LIFE. There is a great disparity between the grain of corn and the plant of wheat when green in spring or golden in harvest-time; a greater disparity still between the acorn and the giant oak of the forest. One seed gives life to a fragrant, radiant, delicate flower; another to a rich and luscious fruit; another to a lordly tree. One seed is more adapted to a temperate climate, another to the tropics; one grows best upon the mountain slope, another in the sheltered vale.

The resources of Omniscience and Omnipotence are strikingly apparent in the prodigality, diversity, and adaptation of vegetable life. Such considerations are a rebuke to our incredulity, which arises from an undue conceit of our own wisdom, and a lack of just humility. We may ask, "How are the dead raised? and with what body do they come?" All nature supplies the answer, inasmuch as it tells us that the Creator and Lord of all is never at a loss for means to execute his purposes and to fulfil his promises. When the time comes for this body to be laid aside, to be taken down, there shall be provided for the glorified and happy spirit "a house not made with hands, eternal in the heavens."—T.

Ver. 45.—"*The last Adam.*" The apostle has supported the Christian belief in the resurrection by adducing natural analogies, and these will always possess a certain measure of force for intelligent and reflective minds. But it is observable that he returns to what is the strongest ground of belief in the future life and all which it involves, viz. the personal relation of the Christian to his Divine and mighty Lord. The foundation of our hope is in the assurance of our Saviour, "Because I live, ye shall live also."

I. THE DESIGNATION OF CHRIST: THE LAST ADAM. This, though a rabbinical expression applied to the Messiah, has a truly Christian signification. 1. It implies our Lord's true humanity; he was a descendant of our first parents, and he was the Son of man. 2. It implies his federal headship, his representative character, and his peculiar authority. There is a new humanity created afresh for the glory of God; and of this the Lord Christ is the one rightful Ruler and Head.

II. THE DESCRIPTION OF CHRIST: A LIFE-GIVING SPIRIT. 1. This is in contrast with the description of the first Adam, "a living soul," so called in the book of Genesis. From our progenitor we have inherited the body and the animal and rational nature for which that body is a suitable vehicle. 2. This is indicative of the prerogative of Christ to impart a new and higher spiritual life to humanity. We receive from him by the bestowal of his Spirit a nobler being, a being which allies us to God, and which fits us for the occupations and the joys of heaven. "In him was life." He did not however possess life only to retain it as his own, but in order to share it with his people. "I," said he, "am come that they might have life, and that they might have it more abundantly." 3. This is explanatory of the revelation of resurrection and immortality. The nature we inherit from Adam fits us for earth; the nature which we receive from Christ fits us for heaven. Adam is "the earthy," and they who dwell on earth share his earthy being and life; Christ is "the heavenly," and they who are made in his likeness and who share his character and spirit are qualified for celestial and eternal joys.—T.

Ver. 49.—"*The image of the heavenly.*" According to the reading of the original which is adopted, this passage bears an indicative or an imperative meaning. If imperative, then it is an admonition to cultivate and perfect in our character and life, even now upon earth, the moral and spiritual image of the Divine Lord. If indicative and future, then it is an assertion that, in the coming time, the time of celestial glory, Christians shall bear the image of the heavenly.

I. WHOSE IMAGE IS THIS? The answer to this question cannot be doubtful. The heavenly One, whose image Christians are to reflect, can be none other than the Divine Lord himself. There is a measure in which this resemblance is attained even upon earth, and many admonitions are addressed to Christians, to cultivate moral resemblance to their great and glorious Head. But in the future state hindrances to assimilation shall be removed; and "we shall be like him; for we shall see him as he is" (1 John iii. 2). As St. Paul expresses it elsewhere, we shall be "changed into the same image." So that the apostles agree as to what shall constitute the peculiar privilege and glory of the coming state of felicity.

II. IN WHAT DOES THIS IMAGE CONSIST? 1. It is a spiritual likeness, consisting not in the similarity of form or feature, but in that of character, of moral life. 2. It is a likeness in true holiness. God's holy Child or Servant, Jesus, is the model of all purity and perfection, and to be like Christ is to be holy even as he is holy. 3. It corresponds to God's original intention as to what man should be. He at first created man in his own image; and although that image was marred by sin, grace restores it; and the great Father and Lord of all beholds his original conception realized in the regenerated and glorified humanity.

III. BY WHOM IS THIS IMAGE PARTICIPATED? 1. Properly speaking, it will be apparent in all those who by Divine grace are brought upon earth to the enjoyment of Christian character and privilege, and who are led safely home to glory. It is the family likeness by which the spiritual children are identified. 2. There is a wider sense in which all the holy intelligences who people heaven may be considered as bearing this image. There are those who have *not* borne the image of the earthly, who from their creation have been citizens of the heavenly Jerusalem, in whom appear the spiritual lineaments which are the mark of a Divine parentage and the earnest of a blessed immortality.

APPLICATION. That this image may be borne in all its brightness and beauty hereafter and above, its first rudiments must be traced here. The life of faith, obedience, and aspiration is the divinely appointed preparation for the glories and felicities of heaven. And no religion is of worth which does not form and cherish the spiritual likeness which alone can qualify for the employments and the society of heaven.—T.

Vers. 54—57.—*The victory of immortality.* In this, as in some other passages of St. Paul's writings, logic breaks into rhetoric, prose into poetry, reasoning into fervid exclamation. Anxious to convince, the apostle was nevertheless of a temperament too fervid to be restrained within the boundaries of argument. And when his soul was lifted up above the level of human thought, when inspiration carried him into the third heaven, then he could no longer discourse; but discourse kindled into song. If there is any passage in his writings fitted to fan the burning fire of feeling into the flame of enthusiasm, it is the sublime argument by which he seeks to give definiteness, point, certainty, and attractiveness to the life to come.

I. THE GREAT CHANGE TO BE EXPERIENCED. Our earthly state is characterized by corruptibility and immortality. That this is so is indeed a rebuke to human vanity, yet it is unquestionable. An apostle terms our earthly vesture, "this body of our humiliation," and the designation is just. We live a dying life, carrying within us the seeds of our mortality. Vast and wonderful to contemplate is the change which shall take place in the passage from time to eternity. Incorruption and immortality shall be the vesture of the saved and glorified. The apostle, bearing about in his body the marks of the Lord Jesus, must have anticipated with joy the promised release from earthly infirmities and sufferings, from all the troubles to which the burden of the body exposes the servant of Christ.

II. THE GREAT VICTORY TO BE WON. According to the view of St. Paul, there are three great enemies with whom the Christian has to contend, and conflict with whom mars the happiness and breaks the peace of this earthly condition. They are the Law, sin, and death. Sin is the goad with which death makes a thrust at the Christian soldier, and it is the Law which makes sin so sharp, powerful, and formidable a weapon. Over all these the glorified Christian has obtained a victory, in the might and by the grace of the Lord Jesus Christ. Anticipating the conquest, the Christian, even here and now, rejoices in the assured defeat and discomfiture of his formidable foes. He seems already to drag them in triumph at his chariot-wheels, already to be more than conqueror through Christ who loved him.

III. THE GREAT THANKSGIVING TO BE CELEBRATED. 1. The Source and Author of victory is God himself. No power but his could have defeated foes so mighty, so malicious and so crafty. 2. The Mediator of victory is the Lord Jesus Christ, who first conquered *for* us, and then conquers *in* and *with* us. His crucifixion, followed by his resurrection, gave the death-blow to our enemy. This conviction may well give us courage in carrying on the spiritual war, and in looking forward to its issue with confidence and hope.

> "Hell and thy sins resist thy course,
> But hell and sin are vanquished foes;
> Thy Jesus nailed them to the cross,
> And sang the triumph when he rose."

T.

Vers. 1—8.—*The gospel which Paul preached.* I. IT WAS A RECEIVED, NOT AN ORIGINATED, GOSPEL. " For I delivered unto you first of all that which I also received" (ver. 3). He tells us that he received it by "the revelation of Jesus Christ" (Gal. i. 12). He had the more confidence in it that it was not of himself, and we have also. It came from the very central Source of all. Paul's gospel *of* Christ came *from* Christ. Some preachers of the gospel are so able that they feel bound to originate. They throw a new light upon the truth instead of the old light. They preach, as they consider, a magnificent gospel, but it is unfortunately " of man," and thus worthless. Man can do many things, but he cannot make a gospel. When he tries he advertises his folly. With Paul, we should get as near as we can to the fountain-head—the streams are apt to become contaminated.

II. TWO CONSPICUOUS FEATURES. 1. *The atoning death of Christ.* Paul preached constantly, untiringly, supremely, the atonement (see his strong expression, ch. ii. 2). He laid greatest emphasis upon the *death* of Christ. The *life* was beautiful, full of teaching; but in the *death* was the propitiation for sin. He died for our sins; our sins were so great that they required *his death* ! " He bore our sins in his own body on the tree." And the death of Christ did not come suddenly upon the world. It was " according to the Scriptures:" foretold by the prophets, as, for example, by Isaiah in the fifty-third chapter of his book. He had no sins of his own to die for; he died for *ours.* He " gave *himself*" for us. 2. *The resurrection of Christ.* This was the demonstration of the efficacy of his death, a proof that he conquered and was not conquered. The real triumph achieved in his death was manifested by his resurrection. A pledge of our resurrection through him. A token of his acceptance by God. (1) The apostle laid stress upon the fact that Christ died. It was no swoon. A real death, and then a real resurrection. He " died" and " was buried" (ver. 4). He rose " the third day," so that for a day and part of two others he was in the sepulchre. Some afterwards denied the actual death of Christ, and thus made void his resurrection. The apostle here anticipates their attack. (2) That his resurrection accorded with prophecy. It was " according to the Scriptures " (see Ps. xvi. 10). (3) That his resurrection was well attested by witnesses. Paul does not give here all the appearances of Christ after his death, but a selection. (*a*) Appearance to Peter (Luke xxiv. 34). (*b*) To the twelve. Called by the familiar name " the twelve," though Judas was gone (Luke xxiv. 33—36). (*c*) To five hundred brethren. Possibly in Galilee, where intimation of his appearing had been given, and may have been widely known, occasioning a large gathering of his followers (Matt. xxvi. 32 and xxviii. 10, 16). (*d*) To James. Probably James who presided over the Church at Jerusalem. (*e*) All the apostles (John xx. 26 or Acts i. 4). (*f*) To St. Paul. As of one born out of due time. The least of the apostles. A grand array of evidence, and yet not all. The writer and speaker could bear personal testimony. Most of the five hundred were alive and could be interrogated. Others had " fallen asleep" in hope of a glorious resurrection through him who had appeared to them after his own death and burial.

III. RESULTS. 1. *Men received it.* (Ver. 1.) It arrested their attention. It convinced their judgment. It moved their heart. It was adapted to human want. It glorified ordinary life. 2. *Men were saved by it.* (Ver. 2.) It was the power of God unto salvation. Conscience was satisfied. Life was purified and ennobled. Christ was followed. God was feared and served and loved. Death lost its terror. " After death " was paradise. 3. *Men stood in this gospel.* (Ver. 1.) As long as they held to it they stood, and having done all, stood. Through it came a power which was " able to keep them from falling." Have we received this gospel ? Do we stand in it ? Are we saved through it ? We need " hold it fast" (ver. 2, New Version)—*grip it* and *keep gripping it.* A mere assent will lead to " letting it slip." It has no power to save unless we hold it and it holds us.—H.

Vers. 9, 10.—*Traits of Christian greatness.* I. HONESTY. How faithfully Paul speaks of himself! How candidly he acknowledges the circumstances connected with his apostleship! Yet he had the greatest reason to magnify his authority to the Corinthians. They were ready, many of them, to twist anything to his disadvantage. But he is not moved by this. To him the end does not justify the means; he must have " means" perfectly unquestionable. His candour and truthfulness are striking.

He is a man of transparent honesty, as every Christian man should be. Whether honesty be the best policy or not, it is the only Christian policy.

II. CONTRITION. As a man becomes spiritually great, he has keener regret for old delinquencies. Paul cannot forgive himself for persecuting the Church of Christ. That act becomes more glaring in its sinfulness the nearer he draws to the "Light of the world." Little saints—little sins. No sin is little except to the purblind. The more perfect our acceptance before God, the more perfect our condemnation of ourselves.

III. BOLDNESS. Paul does not shrink from testimony or deed. People may call him "a turncoat," but not now being a child, he has put away the childish thing of being appalled by epithets—epithets which, in his present condition, can really mean only praise, whatever they may be intended to mean. A man who has true and high "fear of God" has little fear of man. The truly great in Christian life are afraid only of being afraid to witness for Christ. Christian courage is a fine quality.

IV. DILIGENCE. The truly great Christian is a hard worker. He must do something for his Lord, whatever his circumstances. If he be stretched on a sick-bed he will toil there, in conversation or prayer, or in repressing anything that may dishonour Christ, such as irritability, repining, etc. Many professors can believe anything and do nothing. A ton of their piety would be dear at the cost of a bad farthing. There are some microscopic saints, who ever want "to be fed," but all their feeding seems to come to nothing. Instead of being "labourers in the vineyard," they are only pickers of the grapes. The great Paul was a great worker; he "laboured more abundantly than they all." If we would be great we must be diligent. "The hand of the diligent maketh rich" (Prov. x. 4).

V. LOVE. This is very apparent in Paul's case. His heart is going God-ward with the penning of every word. His contrition was related to his love. He felt that he had been forgiven much, and so he loved much. Love to God made him diligent, and perhaps in no one was love to man more strikingly exemplified than in this apostle. As we grow great we grow in love, because, as we grow spiritually great, we grow like God, and God is love. If our religion does not mellow and soften us and extend our sympathies, we have got hold of the wrong religion.

VI. HUMILITY. We cannot be great unless we are little. To go up we must go down. The true Christian is one who has become a "little child." Paul ascribes everything to God's grace, nothing to himself. This was a very true and accurate division; it represented things as they really were. The great Christian sees things as they are; the little Christian, as they are not, but as he would like them to be. The little Christian thinks himself to be a great Christian, and the great Christian thinks himself to be a little one. As we rise, God seems greater and greater, and we little and still more little, until at last he becomes "all in all" and we become "nothing." There is a greater gap between God and Gabriel in Gabriel's thought than between God and Judas in Judas's thought. We cannot boast of our salvation, for God has saved us; nor of our works, for his grace has wrought them through us.—H.

Vers. 12—19.—*Did Christ rise?* I. A GREAT QUESTION. Everything connected with "after death" is of high interest to us, but this, whether the professed Messiah and Saviour burst the bands of death or was held captive by them, is of the very highest moment. Christ rested his claims upon his resurrection; if it failed, they failed. His rising from the tomb was the demonstration of his Divine Sonship (Rom. i. 4). His witnesses were to be witnesses of his resurrection, as of an all-important event (Acts i. 22). His resurrection was the seal of the power of Calvary. It gave authority to all his teaching. It corroborated the antecedent miracles.

II. A DISPUTED QUESTION. Disputed from the first, when the absurd rumour was spread that his disciples had stolen his body away in the night, and that men sound asleep had witnessed the depredation! Around this central point of Christian faith have surged floods of controversy. It was and is natural that the citadel of Christianity should be fiercely attacked. Every conceivable supposition has been made to explain away the evidence. But this remains, that greater miracles have to be taken for granted by deniers than by believers. Our faith need not be shaken one whit by the onslaught; the truest and best things in the world have ever been the favourite targets of the devil and his archers.

III. A VITAL QUESTION. With the answer Christianity stands or falls. This the apostle willingly admits. Note what amongst other things is involved in the denial of the resurrection of Christ. 1. *The falsity of the witnesses.* (1) Yet everything these witnesses say and do has the savour of sincerity. They live lives of humility, purity, unselfishness; and in support of the asserted fact of the resurrection are willing to die. Yet if they knew their statement to be false, they had nothing to gain, but everything to lose, by making it. (2) They must have been false, not deceived. The circumstances of Christ's repeated appearances, as narrated by the evangelists, render it inconceivable that the witnesses should have been victims of illusion or imposture. (3) False witnesses of God. Their sin was directly against the Eternal. They blasphemously asserted that he had done what they knew he had not. (4) Their condition was most deplorable; ver. 19, "If we have *only hoped* in Christ in this life, we are of all men most miserable." For we have said it is not *hope* of Christ's resurrection that we possess, but our solemn testimony in God's sight has been that we were *personal witnesses* of the resurrection of Christ. Our claim has been, not *hope*, but *certainty.* Now, if we only have the former whilst we have professed to possess the latter, how great is our criminality! how miserable is our condition! how dread must be our future! We have been guilty of the basest misrepresentation in a matter of the highest moment. Other interpretations of ver. 19 seem to involve, what most Christians will strenuously deny, that if Christianity be a delusion, the condition of the believer in the present life is more miserable than that of the unbeliever. 2. *All preaching of the gospel is vain.* Instead of the proclamation of the truth, it becomes the dissemination of a lie. It is empty, unreal, has no basis. The gospel so rests upon Christ's resurrection that, when one succumbs, the other must share the same fate. 3. *Faith is vain.* It must be useless to trust to one whose word has already failed. To build our hopes upon one whose most solemn assertion has fallen to the ground would be nothing but sheer madness. The "Lord Jesus Christ," indeed, disappears, and we have left, as the object of our faith, only one like to ourselves. 4. *Living believers are unsaved.* Christ, we read, "was raised for our justification" (Rom. iv. 25); but if he did not rise, we are not justified. In penalty and power sin still attaches itself to us. And yet we feel that the burden has gone and that the power is broken! How can these things be? 5. *The dead in Christ are perished.* Not annihilated, but *before God without a Mediator!* God and the future remain if Christ did not rise, but those who have fallen asleep in Christ, believing on him, have found in him no help, have found through him no pardon. With all their sins upon them, they have entered into the presence of their Maker and Judge. What a relief to turn to the confident utterance of Paul, "But now is Christ risen from the dead" (ver. 20)! How thankful should we be for the clear, satisfactory, conclusive evidence of Christ's resurrection which we possess! And careful should we be not to hold loosely, or to deny, some doctrine which may seem of comparatively small importance, because we cannot understand it fully or because it conflicts with our prejudices. Much more may be involved than we think of. Some of the Corinthians denied the resurrection of the body, but appear to have been willing and desirous to accept the rest of the gospel revelation. They, perhaps, did not see how the single denial destroyed the whole fabric. But Paul shows that if the resurrection of the body be denied, the resurrection of Christ must be, and that this involves the destruction of the claims of Christ as the Messiah and Saviour and the entire overthrow of the gospel.—H.

Vers. 20—28.—*The resurrection.* I. ITS CAUSE. Christ—the second Adam. Through the first Adam, death; through the second Adam, the resurrection from the dead. We see how much depends upon Christ, how much upon his resurrection. Through him we expect to rise; but if he did not rise, how can we rise through him? "But now is Christ risen," and so our prospect is unclouded. He has passed through the grave to make a way for us. He found the bonds of death strong; we shall find them *broken.* He lives, and through him we shall live also. He has conquered the grave whilst in our nature, and now holds it as conquered for us to pass through.

II. ITS UNIVERSALITY. "As in Adam *all* die, even so in Christ shall *all* be made alive." Adam was the first head and representative of the human race; he fell, and one of the consequences of his fall was the grave for all men. Christ was the second

Head and Representative, and through him comes to all the race deliverance from the grave. In neither has the personal, responsible act of men, apart from their representative heads, a place. The disadvantage through Adam and the advantage through Christ come to all men, apart from their choice or desert. But this only applies to physical death and the recovery from that death. Personal sin and personal repentance and faith have issues unaffected by the general headship of Adam and Christ. The just and the unjust die through Adam; the just and the unjust rise through Christ: but they do not rise to the same future. What follows upon personal transgression and impenitence will be borne in the body delivered from death; and, similarly, that which follows upon personal repentance and belief in Christ.

III. Its ORDER. 1. *Christ.* First, as the cause. He is "the Firstfruits"—the earliest and the most costly and the most precious of the harvest. And also the pledge of the general harvest. He is the Firstfruits presented and accepted, and we who are in him shall ,be accepted also, for we shall be "like him." 2. *The saved.* "They that are Christ's." This is after the resurrection of Christ; how long after we are not told. But it will be "at his coming." In his first advent we have redemption; in his second advent, resurrection. "The Lord himself shall descend from heaven with a shout, with the voice of the archangel, and with the trump of God: and the dead in Christ shall rise first" (1 Thess. iv. 16). 3. *The rest of mankind.* "Then cometh the end"—the end of the resurrection—the rising of those that remain, as well as the end of the dispensation. The lost have the place of least honour. They were "first" in many things in life, but now they are "last."

IV. Its MODE. 1. *By the sound of a trumpet.* (Ver. 52; see Matt. xxiv. 31.) The dead shall hear, for the summons shall be of God. Those who stopped their ears on earth will not then be able. "The hour is coming, in the which all that are in the graves shall hear his voice, and shall come forth; they that have done good, unto the resurrection of life; and they that have done evil, unto the resurrection of damnation" (John v. 28, 29). 2. *Sudden.* This seems to be suggested by ver. 52. The change of the living will be sudden; the change of the dead also. Men generally die slowly; they will be raised from the dead instantly. The dead have been long in gathering—how many centuries have passed, how many more, perhaps, to come!—but probably in "the twinkling of an eye" will they be delivered from death. This strikingly illustrates Christ's power over the grave—how completely he has conquered, and holds in subjection, death.

V. Its VICTORY. It will be a triumph. It will show forth the victorious might of Christ. He triumphed in his own resurrection; that triumph will be consummated in the completion of the resurrection, when all, of every race and colour, are raised by his power.

VI. Its CONCOMITANTS. The following seem here to be *closely* connected with the final resurrection:—1. *The universal victory of Christ.* He shall conquer, and conquer all that now oppose him. "All rule, all authority and power," must fall before him. All enemies shall presently be under his feet. The powers of evil now seem great and strong, the kingdom of righteousness comparatively small and feeble; but at that day Christ will be King, and to him "every knee shall bow." 2. *The destruction of death.* The destroyer shall be destroyed. The shock of the great resurrection will be too much for his kingdom. The death-bonds long since broken by Christ shall then be burnt. Man's mortality shall cease for ever. Death shall die and know no resurrection. 3. *The delivering up of the kingdom by Christ to the Father.* Christ, as Mediator and Administrator of the kingdom of God, will then have completed his special work, and the *direct* rule of God *as God* will be reinaugurated. Christ will still remain as God-Man, the Head of his own people, and as one in the Godhead will participate in the Divine reign. 4. *The subjection of the Son to the Father.* As he was before his mediatorial work began. One with the Father ("I and my Father are one") in nature, but voluntarily subordinate as a son to a father. The Son as such will not be conspicuous in rule as now, but *God* will be "all in all." The united Deity will reign as one, and in the Deity the Son is subordinate in position to the Father.—H.

Vers. 29—34.—*Some things that follow upon the denial of the resurrection.* I. THE

FOLLY OF SELF-DENIAL AND SUFFERING FOR CHRISTIANITY. These must be branded as imbecile; yet they have ever seemed most sublime. But if there be no resurrection (the resurrection of the body being vital to the gospel and all its hopes, as Paul has shown in preceding verses of this chapter), the argument for such conduct fails. Why order one's life for a future which will never be realized? Why suffer for a lie as though it were a truth? There were some who had been "baptized for the dead"— an obscure expression, but probably meaning baptized to take the place of those who had suffered martyrdom. Why should these court so stern a fate if Christianity were a deception? The apostle had "fought with beasts at Ephesus"—probably figurative, to express his contest with beastlike men. He "died daily" in his faithfulness to his commission as a preacher of—*what?* Ah! upon the *what* depended everything. According to the answer, Paul was an utter fool or a marvellously heroic saint. If there was no resurrection, and if therefore the gospel fell to the ground, he was undoubtedly the former.

II. THE REMOVAL OF RESTRAINTS FROM INDULGENCE AND VICE. The denial of the doctrine of the resurrection involved the denial of the gospel, and with this perished the hope of salvation. Christians thus became as men of this world, having no bright hope of the hereafter. Consequently the check upon natural appetite was removed. Common sense would seem to favour a life of Epicurean pleasure. If there be no hope concerning the world to come, let us make the best of the world that now is: "Let us eat and drink; for to-morrow we die." "Soul, thou hast much goods laid up for many years: take thine ease, eat, drink, and be merry." The apostle is not supposing that there is no future existence. By "the resurrection" in this chapter he means the resurrection of the body, but he shows that with the rejection of this doctrine Christianity is destroyed, and here he is showing that if Christianity be destroyed the incentives to a pure and virtuous life are removed. His thought seems to be that, apart from Christianity, there is nothing in the world which will constrain men generally to live great and noble and self-denying lives. And this is a matter for our most serious reflection. If Christianity be done away with, what is there which will restrain men from indulgence and vice? No other religion can compete with Christianity; if it falls, all religion is doomed. Can philosophy do the practical work required? Alas! it is possible to be a very excellent philosopher and a very poor moralist. Will general education restrain men? It will, when cleverness and goodness mean the same thing, but not before! Will art and refinement effect what is needed? The palmiest days of art have been the days of most glaring obscenity, and refinement has shown over and over again how easily it allies itself with brutal lust. If Christianity falls, the prevailing doctrine amongst men must be, "let us eat and drink; for to-morrow we die."

II. CAREFULLY SHOULD WE GUARD AGAINST EMBRACING THIS FATAL OPINION. We may find difficulty in believing the doctrine; we shall find disaster in rejecting it. 1. *The apostle notices one thing very likely to lead us astray.* "Evil communications [or, 'evil company'] corrupt good manners"—a line borrowed from the Greek poet Menander. "Can a man touch pitch and not be defiled?" Many mix amongst the ungodly, confident in strength, and *fall.* We need remember that, in our present state, *we are more easily influenced towards the wrong than the right.* Our minds are not equally poised. There is already a bias. Strange that those who are so bold to venture into the atmosphere of moral evil shun that of physical evil. A professing Christian will company with an arrant unbeliever, but not with a man suffering from small-pox. 2. *Sin must not be yielded to.* (Ver. 34.) Those who live in sin easily persuade themselves of the truth of anything which they would like to be true. As denial of the resurrection leads to sin, so sin leads to the denial of the resurrection. Sin blinds the intellect as well as corrupts the heart. 3. *If we have been at all betrayed, we should at once seek to recover our position.* "Awake to righteousness," or, "awake up righteously." We are more than half asleep if we deny that for which there is abundant evidence. We need to rub our eyes or to ask the great Physician to touch them. "Awake," or "be sober." The condition of those who deny the resurrection is one of carnal intoxication. In denial our faces are towards evil; in assent and reception we turn towards righteousness. "Righteousness" in the world depends, according to the apostle, upon the reception of this doctrine, because with it stands or falls Christianity itself. 4. *Denial involves ignorance of God.* (Ver. 34.) To the Sadducees, who denied the resurrection, Christ said, " Ye do err, not knowing the Scriptures, nor the power of God" (Matt. xxii. 29). Men say, God *cannot* do this thing; but with him "all things are possible." True knowledge of God marvellously helps our faith. We doubt and question, not because we know so much, but because we know so little. The Corinthians boasted much of their knowledge; here Paul charges them with gross ignorance.—H.

Vers. 35—41.—*The resurrection of the body.* This doctrine has presented the greatest difficulties to many minds. Here faith has frequently found one of its severest tests.

I. BUT WE OUGHT NOT TO BE STAGGERED BY ANY FACT WHICH IS THE SUBJECT OF DIVINE REVELATION. God will assuredly justify himself and fulfil all his promises. Though we do not see how he will do so, *he* does. He sits higher than we do. When Ezekiel was asked, " Can these bones live ? " he did not reply, " It is utterly preposterous and absurd," but " O Lord God, thou knowest ; " and when God asserted that they could and should, Ezekiel obediently prophesied upon and unto them (Ezek. xxxvii. 3). Our Lord's words should ever ring in our ears, " With God all things are possible " (Matt. xix. 26).

II. CONSIDER THE IMPERFECTION OF OUR PRESENT KNOWLEDGE. How very little we know ! Our knowledge is extremely *superficial ; we know no one thing thoroughly.* Our knowledge is extensive in this sense, that we know a *very little* about a *great many* things. How ignorant we are of the nature of *matter, spirit, life!* How unfit to dogmatize ! yet how ever ready to do so ! Like children, we say, " It can't be ; " and we speak with infinite confidence because *we cannot understand* how it can be. The theory *cannot be made up* out of our superficial information. The mountain won't go into our bucket !

III. THE LIMITATION OF OUR FACULTIES. Our powers are very great viewed in one aspect, very little indeed viewed in another. As long as we possess only our present faculties we shall do well to guard against the flippant use of "impossible."

IV. HOW SOME DIFFICULTIES CONNECTED WITH THE RESURRECTION OF THE BODY MAY BE REMOVED. We have two indicated in this passage. 1. *How can the dead live ?* If our bodies *die*, are placed in the grave, dissolve, mix up with surrounding earth, is it not incredible that they should live again ? " How can these things be ? " The apostle has a very pertinent retort. He directs the objector to a very familiar operation and result. Seed is sown in the ground, a living plant springs up. The seed placed in the ground apparently perishes. As placed in the earth it is seen above it no more. Much of its substance decays and unites with the ground in which it lies. And yet there is the plant of *the same nature*, and called by *the same name.* There is here death and then life. In fact, *only* as the seed is sown, *only* as it seems utterly to perish, decompose, and be hopelessly lost—*only* this is the beautiful result attained. So the death of this body may be necessary (speaking after the manner of men) to the beauty and glory of the resurrection-body. That which seems to be a *difficulty* may be an *essential link* in the chain—essential, that is, unless a special miracle is wrought, as may be in the case of those alive at the coming of Christ (ver. 52). They will be " changed " suddenly—we know not how, through what process. Christ's body, which saw no corruption, was evidently changed. Paul does not assert that sowing seed and its result are parallel in all points to the death and resurrection of the body. He uses it as a helpful illustration. If our experience did not cover the sowing of the seed and the upspringing of the plant, perhaps our faith would be as greatly tried, if we were called upon to believe in *its* possibility, as we are now in the case of the resurrection of the body. 2. " *With what body do they come ?* " One common form of this difficulty is—how is it possible for us to have at the resurrection the same particles in our body which we now have ? Apart from the dissipation of these particles in the earth or sea, *they may actually belong to the bodies of a great many different people!* Amongst cannibals, for example. And amongst civilized people as well ; for animals and plants receive in various ways particles which once helped to constitute human bodies, and these animals and vegetables being eaten, the particles in question become constituents of other human bodies. How can this apparently insuperable difficulty be met ? Simply by saying that it is a difficulty originated by the objector, and has no basis in Divine revelation. We are not told that the earthly body and the resurrection-body shall consist of the same particles. In fact, the apostle seems expressly to combat such a notion; for he says, "*Thou sowest not that body which shall be*" (ver. 37), and in ver. 50, "Flesh and blood cannot inherit the kingdom of God." But then, if not the same particles, what particles? what form? The apostle meets this by reference to the Divine power as now seen in creation: "All flesh is not the same flesh." There are celestial bodies—the organisms of angels—bodies, yet greatly differing from the terrestrial bodies. The light of the "lamps of the firmament" greatly varies in glory and beauty. So there will be great contrast between the body *now* and *then*. God by what he has done shows what he can do, and so this part of the difficulty vanishes. But the greater part remains. If the resurrection-body has not the same particles now possessed, how can it be *the same*, and how can there be any fitness in speaking of the *resurrection* of the body? Our experience supplies a sufficient answer. *Sameness of particles is not essential to identity.* The particles in our present body are in constant flux. At no two moments do we possess precisely the same: we are always throwing off some and taking on others; and, separated only by the interval of a few years, science leads us to conclude that the body has lost all the old particles and is constituted entirely of fresh ones. Yet bodily identity does not disappear. The resurrection-body will be identified with our present body. As with the seed, to each a "body of its own" (ver. 38). Identity is in this life a great mystery to us; we cannot tell now what is necessary to it. But there is nothing in our partial knowledge of it which should lead us to doubt the doctrine of the resurrection of the body. With larger knowledge apparent difficulties doubtless would disappear. The resurrection-body will be very different to the present whilst identified with it. God will give a body as it shall please him (ver. 38). Note: It is no mark of wisdom to deny the resurrection of the body. The inspired apostle addresses the denier as "Thou fool." Many priding themselves in wisdom tumble into the morass of folly.—H.

Ver. 40.—*The two glories.* The apostle appears to be referring to the differences between the organisms—the spiritual bodies—of the inhabitants of heaven and the bodies of human beings on earth. But in a wider sense we may understand his statement that "the glory of the celestial is one, and the glory of the terrestrial is another." The glory of things belonging to a fallen world is one; the glory belonging to things of an unfallen world is another. The things of man fallen contrasted with the things of the God-Man unfallen. The natural as opposed to the spiritual.

I. THE GLORY OF THINGS TERRESTRIAL. 1. *Slight.* Showy, but delusive. Money, human learning, earthly power, worldly pleasures,—these are attractive, but the glory of the best of them is small. Innumerable testimonies have been borne to this fact, difficult for those to credit who are captivated by the gaudiness which they mistake for glory. 2. *Marred.* When we *speak* of earthly things we think of them in their highest perfection; our conception is apt to be ideal. Experimentally we find that the natural glory is greatly marred. 3. *Uncertain.* The flame flickers and darkness is threatened. Much depends upon our health, surroundings, position, as to whether things terrestrial have glory in relation to ourselves. Changes are often sudden and complete, and that which erewhile we pronounced glorious becomes simply detestable. That which pleases us to-day may disgust us to-morrow. Alas! with things terrestrial there is no improvement upon intimate acquaintance. 4. *Brief.* At best the glory is short-lived. The sun soon goes down. When most needed the glory often disappears. 5. *Unsatisfying.* Something more glorious is ever craved for. The more glorious may be expected from that which is of the earth, and when not found in it, the disappointment is often bitter. Earthly things have a firework glory.

II. THE GLORY OF THINGS CELESTIAL. 1. *Great.* Solid and substantial, not flashy. This is natural, for they are of God. In their glory there is more of substance than of shadow. 2. *Not fluctuating.* They are fixed stars, not meteors. There is in them certainty. They are stable. 3. *Increasing.* In our experience. We discover fresh glory ever. In things terrestrial we soon come to the end of the tether; in things celestial we never do. We ever find more to excite our wonder and to cause us delight. 4. *Eternal.* The glory abides undimmed, and shall blaze forth for ever. We are immortal, and as long as we endure shall the glory of those celestial truths which Christ reveals to us. 5. *Satisfying*. The cry of the soul is responded to. There is no disappointment. The feeling of unsupplied want vanishes. At last the soul is at rest.

III. THINGS CELESTIAL MAY BE SECURED IN THE LIFE TERRESTRIAL. Christ brings them to us here. The "strait gate" admits us to them. The Holy Spirit reveals them. In Christian worship and work we begin to enjoy them.

IV. THE RELATIVE GLORY SHOULD INFLUENCE OUR CHOICE. When we may have the better, it is folly to choose the worse. We may have both if we will not be absorbed unduly by the inferior. But amidst the glory of the terrestrial we have to choose the glory of the celestial, and to place it first. This is the better part. Moses is a splendid example of wise choice, and Abraham, and Paul, who counted all terrestrial things but loss that he might secure the celestial.—H.

Vers. 42—53.—*The resurrection-body*. Limited to resurrection-body of redeemed, for we know not what will be that of the lost. Of the former in our present state we can know comparatively little. Still some valuable and cheering truths respecting it are revealed.

I. IT WILL BE : 1. *Incorruptible*. Our body now is corruptible, tending towards decay and dissolution, bearing the marks of injury, disease, age. It becomes more corruptible at death. But the resurrection-body will have no such tendencies, be subject to no such influences. 2. *Glorious*. Our present body is a body of dishonour. The marks of the curse of sin are upon it. In the grave it becomes very inglorious. Paul calls it " our vile body" (Phil. iii. 21). The resurrection-body will be in striking contrast—a body of glory and beauty, like unto the glorious body of the Son of man. 3. *Strong*. Now our body is weak, subject to enervating sickness, and when "sown" as a corpse is the very perfection of weakness. But the resurrection-body will possess fulness of strength, abundant energy, never-diminishing vitality. 4. *Spiritual*. Our present body is dominated by the animal soul; it is fitted for life in the lower world; it is an organism of flesh and blood (ver. 50); it is "of the earth, earthy." It is a "natural" body. But the resurrection-body will be " spiritual," moulded by the Spirit, an organism adapted to the higher and spiritual life.

II. THOUGH SO DIFFERENT FROM, IT IS IDENTIFIED WITH, OUR PRESENT BODY. It is a new body and yet identified with the old. Not the same particles or form, yet *our* body. Note the apostolic expression : " It is *sown*; . . . it is *raised*." Much mystery is here. But perhaps the seed developing into a living plant conveys as much of the truth as we are capable of comprehending.

III. WE RECEIVE IT THROUGH THE SECOND ADAM, CHRIST. Through the first Adam we have our present body, and, through his sin and our own, not a few of its imperfections. The first Adam was a " living soul," endowed with an animal soul, the living principle of the body. His body was adapted for the lower life—for a life on earth. He was " of the earth, earthy." But the second Adam is a *life-giving Spirit*. If we are in him, he quickens our mortal body into glorious immortality. Through him we receive the spiritual body suited for the higher life. Contrasted with Christ, the characteristic of the first Adam is animal life,—the characteristic of Christ is spiritual life. We inherit from Adam what he had and was. So also we inherit from Christ what he had and was. The difference between the first Adam and the second causes the difference between our body now and our body at the resurrection.

IV. CIRCUMSTANCES ATTENDANT UPON ITS BESTOWAL. It will be assumed suddenly at the second coming of Christ. "The trumpet shall sound, and the dead shall be raised incorruptible " (ver. 52). The living will be "changed " " in the twinkling of an eye " (see 1 Thess. iv. 16). No slow process, as in the development of the present body, but suddenly we shall be " clothed upon."

V. WE SHOULD BE INTENSELY GRATEFUL FOR THIS GLORIOUS GIFT. This poor body we may be glad to lose. Certainly its imperfections. But what a life may we anticipate when we are " clothed upon with our house which is from heaven "! To be free from weakness, weariness, pain, decay, most of all from carnal cravings and fleshly lusts ; to have abounding energy, perfect health, pure desires, and great and completed powers ;—what service and pleasure we shall be capable of! This is " of the Lord." Is he our Lord? When we die shall we die in " Christ "? Can we humbly lay claim to this great gift as true, though imperfect, servants of the Master ?—H.

Vers. 54—57.—*Victory on the last battle-field*. I. WE HAVE MANY BATTLES TO FIGHT, BUT THE ONE MOST DREADED IS THE LAST—THE CONTEST WITH DEATH. Life is a series of contests. The battles of childhood are by no means insignificant, and they are many. In every succeeding stage of life contests continue. Life is a changing but unbroken fight. The final contest is usually the most feared. Then generally (1) the body is very weak; (2) in much pain; (3) thoughts of separation from loved ones and familiar scenes rack the mind; (4) life-opportunities are seen to be at an end; (5) a sense of loneliness is experienced; (6) we stand upon the margin of another world; (7) the time for rendering up the life-account is nigh; (8) we approach our final destiny; (9) we meet God.

II. IMPORTANCE OF THE ISSUE. 1. If we do not triumph, it is an evidence that we are still under the dominion of sin. Death is of sin (Rom. v. 12), and if death is not conquered, sin is not. "The sting of death is sin" (ver. 56). Death conquers only because sin conquers. If sin be slain, death will be powerless. 2. If we are "in sin," we are "without Christ." 3. If we are without Christ, we are without a Redeemer. 4. If we are without a Redeemer, we perish. The death-contest is a *great test* of our condition.

III. THE CERTAIN TRIUMPH OF THE CHILD OF GOD. 1. *Asserted*. "I will ransom them from the power of the grave; I will redeem them from death: O death, I will be thy plagues; O grave, I will be thy destruction" (Hosea xiii. 14). That which is so dreaded by many should not be feared by the believer. He has a Divine promise of victory. 2. *Explained*. (1) The triumph comes "through our Lord Jesus Christ." It is not to be achieved by our prowess. We have no strength for the conflict; our sufficiency is of him. Like Mary, we shall meet Christ at the sepulchre. Through him we shall conquer. Well may we offer heartfelt thanks to God (ver. 57), for "God so loved the world," etc. (2) He satisfied the demands of the Law. "Sin is of the Law;" the Law condemns. Christ passed under the Law for us—bore the penalties of the broken Law; so that those in him are brought from under the Law. "There is therefore now no condemnation to them which are in Christ Jesus" (Rom. viii. 1). "The sting of death is sin; and the strength of sin is the Law;" but we are not under the Law if we are in Christ. "Forasmuch then as the children are partakers of flesh and blood, he also himself likewise took part of the same; that through death he might destroy him that had the power of death, that is, the devil; and deliver them who through fear of death were all their lifetime subject to bondage" (Heb. ii. 14, 15). (3) He has risen from the grave. The power of his redemption is thus confirmed. His dominion over death is demonstrated. 3. *Exulted in*. Before the battle begins, the child of God may rejoice in coming victory. And well may he do so, for this will at the same time illustrate his faith in his Redeemer and brighten all his earthly course. That which was dreaded as a disastrous defeat is rejoiced in as a glorious and all-important victory. 4. *Often illustrated*. Christian biography is rich in death-triumphs. Thomas Rutherford in the last fight exclaimed, "He has indeed been a precious Christ to me; and now I feel him to be my Rock, my Strength, my Rest, my Hope, my Joy, my All in all." When Paul heard the bugle-call to the last of his many battles, he cried, "I am now ready to be offered up," etc.

IV. AN ARGUMENT FOR THE UNSAVED. Victory on the last battle-field comes alone through Christ. Without him our life will close in disaster and ruin. Suddenly the conflict may come upon us.—H.

Ver. 58.—*Preparation for the death-triumph*. The apostle has been speaking of the believer's triumph in the final contest with death. This is assured, for it is "through our Lord Jesus Christ" (ver. 57), who is "the same yesterday, to-day, and for ever;" but, though assured, it needs to be prepared for. Salvation is of Christ, yet we have to "work out our own salvation with fear and trembling;" and "they that endure to the end shall be saved." So we need to make constant preparation for the last battle, that when it comes we may be ready and may be found clad in "the whole armour of God."

I. THE APOSTLE URGES BELIEVERS TO ABIDE IN THE FAITH. 1. *We must be "in the faith."* Only thus can we anticipate triumph. Unless we know Christ we shall not know the death-victory. If we are not in the faith, death will triumph over us, and the marks of death's triumph we shall bear in all our future. 2. *We must be steadfast in the faith.* Not halting between two opinions—of one mind to-day and of another to-morrow. We must choose decisively and be faithful to our choice. "Unstable as water, thou shalt not excel." That soldier is not worth much who has much loyalty to-day and none to-morrow. Vacillation in Divine things is a poor preparation for death. We must be steadfast (1) to Christ personally ; (2) to his doctrine— including doctrine of resurrection, which Paul has specially in mind ; (3) to holy living. 3. *We must be unmovable in the faith.* Not turning aside ourselves, nor allowing others to turn us. Enemies will try to turn us—our great enemy pre-eminently. But we must be like limpets on the rock, which cling the more tenaciously the more we seek to dislodge them. Yet with these little creatures a *sudden* blow will generally remove them. *So we must "watch."* In such an hour as we think not the fierce temptation may come. We must hold to Christ and pray Christ to hold to us. He is able to keep us from falling.

II. THE APOSTLE URGES BELIEVERS TO BE DILIGENT IN THE LORD'S SERVICE. 1. *We should engage in the work of the Lord.* Some may think they had better concentrate their thoughts altogether upon themselves ; woo delightful frames of mind ; listen much to some captivating preacher ; "sit and sing themselves away to everlasting bliss." Spiritual selfishness is a poor preparation for the last fight. Many Christians pamper themselves and become hopeless spiritual invalids. We must cultivate personal piety, but we may do this largely by robust Christian work. We need *exercise.* The spiritual sedentary life is prolific of spiritual ills. A Church of do-nothings is always a hospital full of sick and complaining folks. Besides, the need of service is great, and the Master calls. 2. *We should abound in the work of the Lord.* We should not do as little as we can for Christ, but as much. How he "abounded" in work for us ! It is the man who abounds in his work who is most fit to leave it ; the diligent servant is the one most ready to meet his Lord. If we wish to be victorious over death by-and-by, we had need to be victorious over sloth and self-seeking and indulgence now. 3. *We should always abound in the work of the Lord.* Our work is not to be by fits and starts ; our consecration must be life-consecration. Always on the same side, always serving the same Master. 4. *We have much encouragement ever to abound in the work of the Lord.* "Our labour is not in vain in the Lord." (1) We may know this : (*a*) By promise. "My word shall not return unto me void." (*b*) By reason. The gospel, according to our judgment, meets the needs of men, and is likely to be accepted by not a few. (*c*) By experience. Our own, perhaps ; past work speaks in its results. The experiences of others ; what vast effects have followed upon devoted service ! (2) It is not in vain ; for : (*a*) It pleases God. *The true servant is never unsuccessful.* He is always successful in pleasing his Master ! (*b*) It has its effect upon those immediately concerned. We say in natural things every cause produces its appropriate effect : so in spiritual. The result that we desired may not follow, but there has been an effect, as we shall perceive hereafter. (*c*) It blesses ourselves. Few things are likely to do us so much good. (*d*) It will assuredly bring its reward. But our labour must always be "in the Lord"—in his Name, in dependence upon his power, in prayer for his help, in desire for his glory.—H.

Ver. 1.—*The large use of the term "gospel."* The general meaning of the term "gospel" is "good news," "glad tidings." It is "God's spel," or "word." All that is connected with the Lord Jesus Christ may properly be called *good news*, and the word "gospel" may be thought of as including it all. There is, indeed, a tendency to limit the term to a portion only of our Redeemer's work, which needs to be resisted. The gospel is treated as if it were only the message of our Lord's sacrificial death. But that is, evidently, not the matter that is at all in the mind of the apostle when he wrote to the Corinthians of the "gospel which he preached unto them." He was thinking of the "gospel of the resurrection," and of those truths which rest upon the risen rather than upon the dying Redeemer. We plead, therefore, for a full comprehensive application of the term "gospel," as including—

I. THE GOSPEL OF THE INCARNATION. The "good news" that God is willing to take upon himself our human nature ; to become a man among men ; and to show to us that humanity is not hopelessly depraved, but is still within reach of the redemptive power of God. The "good news" that God's love is no mere sentiment, but a holy pity leading him to make effort and sacrifice in accomplishing the purposes which love can fashion.

II. THE GOSPEL OF THE MIRACLES. The "good news," thus illustrated for us is that there is no ill from which humanity suffers, no bitter and terrible and seemingly hopeless consequence of sin, which Divine love and power cannot reach. Even death itself, man's last enemy, is well within God's control. And the "good news" that God, in his gracious Fatherhood, is as mightily and wonderfully caring for us every day, as Jesus was caring for sick sufferers and imperilled disciples and bereaved friends.

III. THE GOSPEL OF THE HOLY LIFE. The "good news" that a man has actually lived here upon the earth "holy, harmless, undefiled, and separate from sinners." And that he will not only show us how to live as he did, but will give us the grace for so living. He left us the "example that we should follow his steps," but he gave us also to be partakers of that Divine nature in which alone the following of the example becomes possible.

IV. THE GOSPEL OF THE SACRIFICE. The "good news" that our sins have been borne for us; acceptable sacrifice for them has been offered. The demands of infinite righteousness have been adequately met. The hindrances to reconciliation have been effectually removed. And men now have "peace with God through Jesus Christ our Lord."

V. THE GOSPEL OF THE RESURRECTION. The "good news" that God has signified his full acceptance of his Son. The "good news" that he who died for our sins lives to carry out his purpose of grace in our hearts. The "good news" that Christ "had risen again in order to communicate to us that new and Divine life whereby our own resurrection should be assured—a life which should make the human body, though laid in the grave, a seed from whence, in God's own good time, a new and more glorious body should arise." It is the gospel in this large and inclusive sense which has to be preached to men, and not a doctrine formulated by men respecting one part only of the "good news of God." They only preach the true gospel who can say with the apostle, "I have not shunned to declare unto you the *whole counsel of God*."—R. T.

Ver. 2.—*Salvation a present process.* Precisely rendered, the first sentence of this verse would read, "By which also ye are being saved." St. Paul applies, in his writings, the best corrective to the imperfect, and indeed false, notion that human redemption is a thing completed, a thing done outside of and separate from men, a something which they are to receive as if it were a mere gift provided for them apart from their own exertions. St. Paul clearly saw that redemption is a moral work ; its proper sphere is a man's mind and heart and life. It is a process, and it has to be carried on right through a man's earthly history. There is a sense in which it may be said that we *are saved*, but there is a much truer and deeper sense in which it may be said that we are *being saved*. One of the most striking expressions of the Pauline idea of salvation as a present process, carried on within us, is found in Rom. v. 10: "For if, when we were enemies, we were reconciled to God by the death of his Son, much more, being reconciled, we shall be saved by his life." Some adequate notion of the Pauline thought of salvation may be obtained by dwelling on the following three representations :—

I. THE BEGINNING OF SALVATION IS THE RECEPTION OF THE GOSPEL. Observe how the Christian teachers first demanded faith in the person of the Lord Jesus Christ. That is the beginning. We must accept of Jesus as the Sent of God, the Son of God, and the Saviour from sin. That beginning may be (1) intellectual,—a persuasion, upon due evidence, that Christ is the Saviour ; or it may be (2) emotional,—a constraint of love to him who condescended, bore, and suffered so much for us, and whose personal history is such a fascination. Here is the initial stage, "Dost thou believe that Jesus is the Son of God ?" You cannot be on the Christian platform at all unless you can give to that question a simple and hearty affirmative. But this is only a beginning. A man is not saved upon such a faith as that. There must be advance to spiritual apprehension of the relation in which Jesus stands to the individual and the individual may stand to him.

II. THE STATE OF SALVATION IS STANDING IN THE GOSPEL. It is apprehending that the Lord Jesus Christ has, by the perfection of his obedience and the sublime merit of his sacrifice, made a new standing-ground before God for us. That he represents us. That he wins a place before God, and a relation with God, for us. That his personal rights are not exclusively personal, but are rights which he shares with us, or allows us to share with him, and we are "accepted in the Beloved." In the presence of *law* claim, we stand as "justified." In the presence of *God's* claim to perfect obedience, we stand, in Christ, as righteous. In the anticipations of a judgment day, we stand as already acquitted; for us "there is now no condemnation."

III. THE PROCESS OF SALVATION IS GIVING THE GOSPEL FREE ROOM TO WORK IN MIND, AND HEART, AND RELATIONS, AND LIFE. The gospel being conceived, not primarily as a set of principles, and duties, and counsels, but primarily as the spiritual and abiding presence of the Lord Jesus Christ with us, using truths, principles, experiences, duties, thoughts, and counsels, as need be, for the carrying on of his gracious work of moral perfecting. "This is the will of God, even your sanctification;" and we lose the holiest interest in that sanctification when we fail to realize that the Lord Jesus Christ is now actually present with us, carrying on and presiding over this work. We are *being saved*; and the exceeding solemnity of our common everyday life lies in this—Christ is in it, working at our salvation. The apostle therefore urges upon us that we must hold in quick and living memory the gospel of the present, working Saviour—risen that he might carry on to its full completion his redemptive work—and that to believe in vain is to profess belief, but give the faith no power to open our soul and life to the redeemings of the risen, living, and ever-present Saviour.—R. T.

Ver. 3.—*Death for sins.* "How that Christ died for our sins." Here history is bound up with theology. The historical fact is that Christ died. More carefully considered, the historical fact is that he died for no sins of his own, but was put to death by the malice and sin of bitter enemies. The theological fact which is bound up with the historical fact is that in some sense—mysterious, spiritual, mystical, but nevertheless most real and most true—he died *for* sin, in respect of sin, in gracious Divine relations to the pardon and removal of sin. It will be necessary to discuss fully the conceptions that are possible under this term *for*—for sin. Our preference for either one of the conceptions will depend on the school of theology to which we belong. *For* may mean *in place of*, or *in respect of*, or *on account of*, or *with a view to the removal of*. Scripture teachings should be appealed to to fix what is the proper and precise meaning. The following may be consulted:—Old Testament: Gen. xxii.; Deut. ix. 24 —26; Ps. xxii.; Isa. liii.; Zech. xii. 10. New Testament: Matt. xx. 28; Mark x. 45; Rom. v. 8—10; ch. i. 18; v. 7; viii. 11; 2 Cor. v. 14, 15; 1 Tim. ii. 6; 1 Pet. i. 19. The subject may be fully treated under three headings, and, as it should be a scriptural rather than a theological study, the statement of the headings should suffice.

I. OLD TESTAMENT ANTICIPATIONS OF THE DOCTRINE OF DEATH FOR SINS.

II. OUR LORD'S OWN TEACHINGS RESPECTING HIS DEATH FOR SINS.

III. APOSTOLIC VIEWS CONCERNING THE DEATH FOR SINS.

If the Scripture passages be fully and fairly considered, it will be felt that the commonly accepted theological notions of our Lord's atonement for sin, need to be broadened and widened, and made inclusive of various possible relations. No one aspect of the death for sins need be conceived of as antagonistic to another. In the many-sidedness of the relation lies the depth and the glory of the truth.—R. T.

Vers. 4, 5.—*Veritable death and veritable resurrection.* Men in all ages have recognized that the truth of Christianity depends upon the historical verity of our Lord's resurrection from the dead. Consequently, attacks of various kinds have been made upon the fact. It has always been felt that this was the key of the Christian position. We may summarize the attacks thus: 1. Men denied the reality of our Lord's death. 2. Then they argued that the only resurrection possible to man is a spiritual regeneration and conversion. 3. By-and-by men said that the resurrection was no fact, only a myth that grew up, fashioned by the wishes of a credulous band of disciples. 4. And then the scientific people thought to bury the old truth for ever out of reach, by declaring that the resurrection of bodily forms which have once decayed is simply impossible; all decaying matter goes to the formation of fresh life, and the bodies of dead men really become, over and over again, constituents of the bodies of living men. But the question which concerns us first of all is not—How can these things be? but—

Is there sufficient evidence and proof? The matter may be beyond present explication, but it is not therefore untrue, nor can we be justified in refusing to accept an adequately sustained historical fact, because the fact is surrounded with scientific and moral difficulties. True science bids us accept without questioning every well-ascertained fact. Now, the verses before us declare two facts: (1) Christ really died; (2) Christ really rose from the dead. We affirm that we have—

I. ADEQUATE PROOF OF THE REAL DEATH. Illustrate: 1. The nature of the death, from ruptured heart. 2. The testing spear-thrust. 3. The distinct attestation of the Roman centurion, and subsidiary testimony of the Roman soldiers, who did not break our Lord's legs. 4. The actual burial in the tomb.

II. ADEQUATE PROOF OF THE REAL RESURRECTION. 1. Scripture antecedent cases show the possibility of resurrection from the dead. Our Lord's resurrection does not stand alone. 2. The various appearances of our Lord. 3. His special manifestation to St. Paul.—R. T.

Ver. 20.—"*Christ the Firstfruits.*" In the previous verses the apostle has fully illustrated this point, that the consequences of rejecting the truth of the resurrection are altogether more serious than any that can conceivably attend belief. If Christ be not risen, then our faith is vain, preaching is vain, even the apostles are false witnesses, the dead in Christ have perished, and we are yet in the misery and the peril of our sins. Our text is the revulsion from such an awful picture. It cannot be so. It must be true that "Christ is risen from the dead, and become the Firstfruits of them that slept." In speaking here of firstfruits, the apostle takes the general, rather than the special Old Testament, idea of them, though the fact of his writing at the time of the Passover no doubt suggested the figure.

I. FIRSTFRUITS SHOW THE POSSIBILITY OF HARVEST. So Christ, as a human being, showed the possibilty of resurrection. Imagine that the fields had never waved with harvest, and that in this spring-time the seeds were first sown. How men would watch for the result! Some stalks may be ripened early in the sheltered warm corner. It is enough to rest our hearts: we know there *can* be golden grain waving over all the field. So the grave-field is sown with the living seeds; and Christ is a seed sown among them. Lo! long before the others, one single blade appears. And the one says, "Wait patiently awhile." Man can rise. One day the grave-fields of earth will be rich with the golden harvests of the resurrection-life. This firstfruit comes to tell us that it *can* be so.

II. FIRSTFRUITS ASSURE OF THE CERTAINTY OF HARVEST. So Christ, as the representative human Being, assures the certainty of resurrection. Take a handful of seeds —say a handful of seemingly dead seeds from a mummy-case. Try if they have life by placing one of them in the soil. If one lives, all will live. It is a firstfruit which pledges a harvest. So it is with Christ. The relation in which he stands to men makes him the test of their resurrection. "If a man die, shall he live again?" Who shall answer that question? Is there a living and undying germ in that body which we bury out of our sight? Try. Take one and let it be representative. Take the Man Christ Jesus. Describe his burial, and the glory of the Easter morning when he rose. But on what grounds do we affirm that what is true of one will be true of all the others? It may be urged that one instance often suffices to establish a law. But, further, God's Word declares that Christ occupied a special place in relation to man. He was constituted his Representative. The human race has two heads, Adam and Christ. One covers the race for death, and one for life—the eternal life. Did all die in Adam? Then, verily, all shall be made alive in Christ. And *certainty* is added to bare *possibility*, and death has lost its great terror.

III. FIRSTFRUITS UNFOLD THE CHARACTER OF THE HARVEST. So Christ, as the model Christian, declares the character of the resurrection. Christ bore relation to the whole world; he is representative *Man*. But he bore a special relation to his own people; he is the representative *Christian*. Therefore we have two things in his resurrection: (1) the bare fact; (2) the glorious character of the fact. Firstfruits show the character of coming harvest. Illustrate by our thoughts and fears as we see the firstfruits thin, blighted, speckled; or standing well, clean, strong, and full. What hope, then, is there in Christ's resurrection, regarding him as the Firstfruits from the dead?

What will our coming life be if it is like his during the forty days he tarried with us? 1. Christ's forty days showed that the new life will be beyond the limiting conditions of humanity. It will be to our old life as flower to seed. 2. Christ's forty days showed the new life will have the old recognitions and the old sympathies. Jesus was in feeling the same. 3. Christ's forty days showed the new life to be a deathless and eternal life. This is the truth of the ascension. Once out of the death-grasp, death is done away. Impress (1) the importance of all moral seed-sowings, as directly bearing on the resurrection-life; (2) the duty of fixing firmly our oneness to Christ, our Representative and Head; (3) the joy of cherishing a good hope of the great awaking.—R. T.

Vers. 21—23, 45.—*The two Adams.* In introducing this subject, set forth, explain, and illustrate the distinctions between the relations in which man stands to God as an individual, as bound together in the membership of a community or nationality, or as a specially constituted race. In all matters of government and order God is pleased to deal directly with the individual, but mediately and representatively with families, with citizens, and with races. In these cases some individual stands before God, to deal with him in behalf of those he represents, and the results of his dealing affect all those in whose name he goes forth. Illustrate by the sentiment that was cherished in tribes. The whole tribe was carried, as it were, by the sheikh, or chief, and affected, for good or evil, by his action. Or illustrate by the notion of a champion, as found in Roman history. He stands for the army, and by his conduct carries defeat or victory for them all. Similarly the ambassador, or plenipotentiary, pledges the nation to the peace or settlement which he makes in its name, and every individual really makes the peace in him whom the nation sends forth to stand for them. Upon this familiar fact and truth the idea of the two Adams is based. We must remember that men may be classified in various ways—physically, locally, intellectually, morally, or spiritually, and under each classification men can act both directly and by representation. As a spiritual race of beings, man has had, at different times, two race-heads, the first and the second Adam.

I. The first Adam regarded as a race-head, or representative. Show how the race is bound up in him. Whether or not he be the actual race-father, this is certain, "God has made of one blood all nations to dwell upon the earth," and the blood is Adam's, the type is Adam's, the whole bodily and mental functions are precisely Adam's, and God is pleased to deal with the race through this Adam, making him the race's test-man, and laying the race under the burdens that were laid upon him. If we force the idea of our individuality into an undue strength, we shall resist the idea that any man can carry us with him so as to win for us blessing or woe; but if we duly estimate the solidarity of the human race, and what this involves for the *good* of the race, we shall be willing to accept the idea, and the consequences, of this mediation or representation. The standing of humanity before God is settled by the standing of Adam. The disabilities of humanity come as the disabilities of Adam, the consequences of his failure. It may even be that what we call *death*, as distinguished from simple *change* and *passing*, is due to Adam's fall. And our very character may be said to be deteriorated through Adam's triumphant wilfulness. We do not say that our relations with the first Adam are limited to these representative ones, but we do say that these are the prominent relations, and those which enable us to apprehend the similar relations of the Lord Jesus Christ.

II. The second Adam regarded as a race-head, or representative. Observe that the first Adam was directly *born of God*, not of any previous human being; and so, we are taught, was the Lord Jesus, though his full kinship with our humanity is brought home to us by his having a human mother. He, then, is a fitting new Race-Head, and God is pleased to deal with him in our name, and his dealings with him cover, carry, and include us, as those for whom he stands. Work out: 1. How Christ stood for us as penitent sinners, and won for us full pardon. 2. How Christ presented, in our name, perfect obedience, and won for us full acceptance. 3. How Christ asked for us life eternal, and gained the unspeakable gift. He is himself the type and the model of the new human race, the race that hates sin, and loves righteousness, and seeks God; and every one of us who makes Christ stand for him thereby pledges himself that he will give himself no rest until he is in everything just what Christ represents him to be. And so " in Christ shall all be made alive."—R. T.

Ver. 26.—*Man's last enemy.* For each individual death is the last enemy, in the sense of being the worst, the one unconquerable enemy; and it is the last in time, so far as time concerns our earthly sphere. The apostle's thought is, that he who has proved himself able to mate and master death, by his own resurrection, must be able to master sin, all the evils which sin brings, and all the lesser consequences of sin's reign. Christ's miracles of raising the dead, as well as his own resurrection, confirm his power to mate and master man's greatest enemy. Scripture teaches us to regard our Lord's resurrection as a final and irremediable conquest of death for us and on our behalf (see Acts ii. 24; vers. 21, 55, 56; Eph. iv. 8; 2 Tim. i. 10; Heb. ii. 14; Rev. i. 18). By that resurrection he abolishes death, and gains the mastery over all that death symbolizes to us.

I. CHRIST IS THE CONQUEROR OF DEATH ITSELF. It was no design of Christ's to destroy death altogether, and pluck from it its commission to the human race. He left it still to bite, but took away its sting, its hopelessness, and its relation to human sin. We shall die though Christ has conquered death; but death has now become the messenger of our Saviour, who would call us to himself, not the foe who drags us down to our doom. Even while this may be said, it must be admitted that death keeps a bitter enemy, dreaded still by men, even Christian men. We are impressed with the certainty of its coming. "There is no discharge from that war." The exceptions have been so few, and they have been made on such distinct grounds, that none of us can hold one moment's hope that we shall escape it. There is the humbling power of an irresistible destiny hanging over us all. And the certainty is blended with a most painful uncertainty as to the time or mode of its appearing for us. Death may be lurking in every journey. Morning, noon, and night it chooses for its visits. It "reaps the bearded grain," and the scythe sweeps down also " the flowers that grow between." Death can also put on repulsive and hideous forms. It can come as accident, as loathsome disease, as plague. And the separations it makes from loves and friendships add greatly to the bitterness with which we think of it. No wonder that so many of us are " all our lifetime in bondage, through fear of death." Then he who would be the Saviour of men must do something to deliver men from the power and fear of death. He must deliver men from that part of death which has come as a consequence of sin. In our human nature he submitted to death, when it grasped him in its most dreadful forms; but when he was fairly in its grasp, he lifted up his power—as Samson, when he awoke, snapped asunder the cords that bound him—he broke asunder the bars and gates; he " led captivity captive;" and rose, showing us our foe conquered, his arrows broken, his sting gone. Looked at now from Christ's point of view, the aspects of death are all changed. It is still " certain," but only because the Father wants all his children gathered safely home. It is still " uncertain," but only because such uncertainty is an important part of the Father's training. It puts on " repulsive forms," but only because Christian love needs severe testings. It involves " separations," but earthly separations are necessary to perfect the unities of heaven, whence they go no more out for ever. So, for the Christian, death is already virtually destroyed.

II. CHRIST IS THE CONQUEROR OF THAT WHICH DEATH SYMBOLIZES TO US. Scripture personifies death, and makes it the embodiment of all human ills. " Sin, when it is finished, bringeth forth death," some kind of death. All trouble is a little death; all disease is a little death. These things are symbolized in physical death. 1. Death is our ideal of *loneliness.* It is our great lonely time. Our best beloved must stand back from the gate while we go through alone. There are many lonely times in the course of our lives. Times when friends forsake; times of doubt; times of grief. But Christ, in mastering death, the height of loneliness, mastered all lesser phases of it for us. He is with us in death, and we know that we can be nowhere alone—he is with us. 2. Death is the ideal of all bad, untoward circumstances. We think of it as the sad time, when all things seem to be against us. But life is full of such times. Still, our Lord is the Master of all circumstances, and however wild and wanton the storms of life may seem, he holds the helm, and will bring us through to the desired haven. 3. Death is the great sorrow, the ideal of all sorrows. But to him who rose from the dead it is given to wipe the tear from every eye, to quiet every heaving heart, and shed abroad the "peace that passeth understanding." For the disciples of Christ death—the bitter, stinging thing death—is gone; and there is nothing whatever left now in the world that can be overwhelming. Christ conquered all our foes when he conquered death.—R. T.

Ver. 28.—*The close of the Mediator's mission.* This is a passage of almost extreme difficulty, because fitting into a general scheme of the universe which we find it very difficult to understand, and because dealing with a future so transcendent and sublime as to be beyond the grasp of our imagination. Treated theologically, and fitted into any redemptive scheme, as drawn out by human intellect, the passage is a perplexity. Treated meditatively, and for the sake of its spiritual suggestions, we may be guided by the following brief passage from F. W. Robertson, which seems to be a key to unlock the apostle's high imaginings:—"The mediatorial kingdom of Christ shall be superseded by an immediate one; therefore the present form in which God has revealed himself is only temporary. When the object of the present kingdom of Christ has been attained in the conquest of evil, there will be no longer need of a mediator. Then God will be known immediately. We shall know him, when the mediatorial has merged in the immediatorial, in a way more high, more intimate, more sublime, than even through Christ." "There rises before the prophetic vision of St. Paul the final triumph of Christ over all evil, over all power, and the Son giving up to the Father the kingdom of this world, which in his humanity he conquered for the Father as well as for himself. Christ, laying the spoils of a conquered world at the foot of the throne of the Father, shows, by that supreme act of self-sacrifice, that in his office as Redeemer he came, not to do his own will, but the will of the Father." In dealing with a passage which seems to concern the sublime and mysterious relations of the Divine Trinity, our spirit cannot be too serious and devout and reverent; yet we may humbly try to understand what God has been pleased so graciously to reveal. Probably the point of the apostle in this passage cannot be apprehended until we can see that the distinctions of the Trinity are, so far as we are concerned, revelational, and made known to us as a part of God's gracious and redemptive purpose. The apostle does not bring us into the presence of what neither he nor we could mentally grasp, the eternal constitution and distinctions of the Divine nature.

I. THE REVELATION OF THE SON IS TEMPORARY. That is, of the Son regarded as the mediatorial and redemptive Agent. There is a doctrine of the eternal Sonship of Christ, but with it this passage does not deal. God may employ on his mission a servant or a Son. In either case the mission is defined in character and limited in time. Whatever Jesus, as the Son of God, came to earth to do, it was a precise mission, having a temporary character. It had two stages. 1. One of earthly manifestation. We know how that was limited to a few years, and at its close he passed, accepted, into heaven. 2. One of spiritual influence. Within that we live, but it is no more abiding than the other, and our text describes its close.

II. THE REVELATION OF THE HOLY GHOST IS DEPENDENT ON THAT OF THE SON, AND IS ALSO TEMPORARY. He is the redemptive Agent who follows up and applies the work of Christ; and is only needed while the redemptive work has to be done. Here, again, no reference is intended to the sublime operations of God of a spiritual kind apart from those exerted in the redemption of man.

III. THE POINT OF THE PRESENT REVELATION OF GOD TO US IS THE RECOVERY OF MAN'S WILL AND HEART TO GOD. It is a moral purpose that is sought. The recovery first of the man himself, and then of his surroundings. This is fully argued in the passage from which the text is taken, and in Rom. viii.

IV. WHEN THE REDEMPTIVE DESIGN IS FULLY ACCOMPLISHED, THE MEDIATORIAL OFFICE MAY CEASE. But it only ceases because the end it sought is reached, the mission is fulfilled, and the mediatorial office can be lost in the glory of the relationships into which it will have brought man, and all human relations. "When the last hindrance, the last enemy, is removed, which prevents the entire entrance of God into the soul, we shall see him face to face, know him even as we are known, awake up satisfied in his likeness, and be transformed into pure recipients of the Divine glory. That will be the resurrection."—R. T.

Vers. 29—32.—*Baptism for the dead.* The apostle evidently alludes to some custom of the early Church, or some sentiment that prevailed concerning a custom which has not come down to us. "The only tenable interpretation of the passage is that there existed amongst some of the Christians at Corinth a practice of baptizing a living person in the stead of some convert who had died before that sacrament had been administered to him. Such a practice existed amongst the Marcionites in the second century, and still earlier amongst a sect called the Cerinthians. The idea evidently was that whatever benefit flowed from baptism might be thus vicariously secured for the deceased Christian." It was plainly what we should call a superstitious custom, and we are not to understand that St. Paul gives it his sanction—he only recalls the fact of the custom, and uses it for the purpose of his argument. F. W. Robertson objects to the association of such a custom with St. Paul's argument, saying, "There is an immense improbability that Paul could have sustained a superstition so abject, even by an allusion. He could not have spoken of it without anger." It may be that the apostle simply refers to the baptism of trial and suffering through which the disciples had to go, which often involved even death. A very needless enduring of suffering and death if there was no resurrection-life beyond. This is certainly more in harmony with the other arguments adduced in the chapter. Not only have those who are fallen asleep in Christ perished, if there be no resurrection, but they very needlessly endured suffering and trial. The underlying idea evidently is, that Christians are baptized into a life which is full of peril, trial, persecution, and martyrdom. They must look in the face, and fully accept, the possibility of death to seal their faithfulness. But how absurd it would be to voluntarily accept such a burdened and suffering life, if this life were all! Surely, then, the heathen were far wiser who said, "Let us eat and drink; for to-morrow we die." Why should the apostle be in "jeopardy every hour"? why should he die daily? save that he held fast the sure hope of being made partaker of his Lord's resurrection, if he was made partaker of his sufferings. This point may be more fully opened and illustrated by dwelling on three separate thoughts.

I. BAPTISM INTO CHRIST IS BAPTISM INTO SUFFERING. It may be shown (1) that this was the fact in apostolic days; (2) it has been the fact in every Christian age, sometimes more and sometimes less manifestly, and (3) though it may take on milder forms, it is still as true as ever that "they who will live godly must suffer persecution," and "through much tribulation we must enter the kingdom." It may be argued that there is even a necessity for this, if the exclusive demands of the Christian profession are estimated in view of the antagonistic claims of the world, in which Christian profession finds a sphere.

II. BAPTISM INTO SUFFERING MAY BE EVEN UNTO DEATH. Of this God keeps illustration for every age. There are no martyr ages. Men die for Christ by overwork, by exposure, by peril, nowadays, as truly as when our fathers burned at stakes and died in prisons. The Martyns, and Williamses, and Browns, and Pattisons, are the proofs that still baptism into Christ may mean baptism unto death.

III. SUFFERING MAY BE BORNE, AND DEATH MAY BE ENDURED, THROUGH FAITH IN THE RESURRECTION. *There* is a sufficient sustaining motive. Without a clear and full belief in the life beyond, men may well say that Christians are mad to put themselves under such painful limitations and endure such accumulated suffering. "If the future were no Christian doctrine, then the whole apostolic life—nay, the whole Christian life—were a monstrous and senseless folly. Grant an immortality, and it all has meaning; deny it, and it was in Paul a gratuitous folly." Impress what baptism into Christ pledges for us now. Show what forms of trial and suffering it may involve for us now. And urge what a sublime light of meaning on present trial is shed from the Christian revelation of the resurrection-life, with Christ.—R. T.

Ver. 33.—"*Evil communications.*" This sentence is taken from a work by Menander, and may be regarded as an indication of St. Paul's acquaintance with classical literature. Too much, however, must not be made of this, because so sharply defined a sentence might very well have become a common proverb, and the apostle may only have known it in this form. As a proverb it was designed to embody the truth that evil words are dangerous. The constant repetition of an immoral maxim may lead to immoral life. "Words that seem harmless, because they float lightly like thistledown,

may bear in them a seed of evil which may take root and bring forth evil fruit."
The apostle used it in reference to the mischievous moral influence of those who deny
the resurrection. It was, to the apostle's view, positively immoral to assert that the
resurrection is only spiritual; that sin belongs only to the body, and so will pass away
with its death. Dealing with the proverb in its more general applications, we note—

I. MAN CANNOT AVOID CONTACT WITH EVIL MEN. We must meet them in business,
and in all the various forms of life-association; and we cannot keep ourselves free
from their contaminating influence. We are like transplanted trees; the bad atmosphere
for us is all around us, and the question is whether our vitality is strong enough to
thrive even under the bad influence. Illustration of this point is very abundant and
ready to hand. It applies to evil thought as well as evil life.

II. MAN MAY AVOID FRIENDSHIP WITH EVIL MEN. We can put firm limitations on
the character of our relationships. Much of the practical wisdom in ordering our life
is shown in doing so.

III. MAN MAY BE PRESERVED FROM THE INFLUENCE OF EVIL MEN. Mainly in
three ways. 1. By due watching and care. 2. By adequate culture of the spiritual
life into vigour and strength. 3. By cherished dependence upon the guardings of
Divine grace. A man may be *in* the world, and not *of* it.

IV. MAN MAY BE A CORRECTIVE POWER ON EVIL MEN. Man may stand in three
relations to evil. 1. He may yield to it. 2. He may stand aloof from it. 3. He
may master it. The last is at once the relation that is safe; and the relation to which
the Christian man is called, and for which he is endowed.—R. T.

Vers. 39—44.—*Enlarged conceptions of the term "body."* The general idea of "body"
is a material form so set in relation to a material world, by its senses and sensibilities,
that a spiritual being using such form, or body, can dwell in the material world. Then
there can be all sorts of bodies, according to the relation which has to be borne in this
material world, or the relation which has to be borne in other worlds which we may
call material or spiritual. We only suggest points of thought, scarcely venturing
to set them in order for public homily or sermon. 1. Within our present earth-
sphere the term "body" is comprehensive. The apostle speaks of bodies of bird, fish,
beast, men,—in all cases the body being determined by the relation to the material
world which is desired; but we can properly speak of distinct body, or form, in relation
to intellectually moral or spiritual life. These are within the bodily form, but can
be conceived as distinct from it. 2. There is no necessary reason for limiting the
term "body" to our earthly sphere. Wherever any spirit is, if it desires relation with
any form of created existence, it must have a form, a body, for the purposes of that
relation. The various conceptions we may have of body beyond our earth-sphere need
careful study. It may further be shown how the diversities of body, and bodily
capacity, help us to understand the possibility of different degrees of glory, and yet
in each case a fulness of glory. Happiness is *here* varied and limited by capacity. It
must be thus varied and limited anywhere. How the term "spiritual" can be applied
to body we may be helped to apprehend by three things: (1) the angelophanies of
the Old Testament; (2) the incarnation of the Son of God; (3) the forty days which
our Lord spent in the resurrection-body.—R. T.

Vers. 55—57.—*Death's sting and strength.* Death, as being the worst, is regarded
as the representative of all human woes. Give the common and familiar sentiments
about death, its sadness, its bitterness, its hopelessness, its terrible forms, its lasting
separations, which prevail amongst men and even among Christians. And yet, what
is death, but the soul putting aside on the shelf the tool which it has long used, but
now has done with, because its work is finished? Still, philosophize as we may; get
up on a high Christian platform as we ought; win the keen spiritual insight if we
will; the fact remains that death has its sting, and we all feel it and live in the fear
of it.

I. WHAT IS THIS STING? It is the conscience of sin; the fear of our just deserts;
the conviction that due avengements of wrong-doing must come in the life beyond.

II. WHAT IS THE STRENGTH OF THIS STING? It is the revealed Law of God, which,
we are sure, has its sanctions. It must take cognizance of our sin. Its punishments

cannot have earthly limitations. Show that the redemption in Christ Jesus plucks death's sting away, because it quiets and satisfies the *Law*, and forgives and removes the *sin.*—R. T.

EXPOSITION.

CHAPTER XVI.

Vers. 1—18.—*Directions and arrange-ments.*

Ver. 1.—**Now concerning the collection for the saints.** "The saints" are here the poor Christians at Jerusalem (Rom. xv. 26). The subject weighed much on St. Paul's mind. First, there was real need for their charity, for at Jerusalem there was as sharp a contrast between the lots of the rich and poor as there is in London, and the "poor saints," being the poorest of the poor (Jas. ii. 5), must have often been in deep distress. Not many years before this time, in the famine of Claudius, (Acts xi. 27—30), Queen Helena of Adiabene had kept the paupers of Jerusalem alive by importing cargoes of dried grapes and figs. Besides the periodical famines, the political troubles of Judæa had recently increased the general distress. Secondly, the tender heart of St. Paul was keenly alive to this distress. Thirdly, it was the only way in which the Gentile Churches could show their gratitude to the mother Church. Lastly, the Apostle St. Paul had solemnly promised the apostles at Jerusalem that he would remember the poor (Gal. ii. 10). Hence he frequently alludes to this collection (2 Cor. viii., ix.; Rom. xv. 26; Acts xxiv. 17, etc.). The enthu-siastic communism of the earliest Christian society in Jerusalem had soon ceased, being, as all experience proves, an impossible experiment under the conditions which regulate all human life, and it may have aggravated the chronic distress. **As I have given order;** rather, *as I arranged.* **To the Churches of Galatia.** Not in his extant letter to the Galatians, but either in a visit three years before this time (Acts xviii. 28), or by letter. It appears from 2 Cor. viii. 10 that St. Paul had already asked for the con-tributions of the Corinthians. "To the Co-rinthians he proposes the example of the Galatians; to the Macedonians the example of the Corinthians; to the Romans that of the Macedonians and Corinthians. Great is the power of example" (Bengel). **Even so do ye.** The aorist implies that they should do it at once.

Ver. 2.—**Upon the first day of the week.** *This* verse can hardly be said to imply any religious observance of the Sunday, which rests rather on Acts xx. 7; Rev. i. 10; John xx. 19, 26. **Lay by him in store.** The Greek phrase implies that the laying up

was done *at home,* but when the money was accumulated, it was doubtless brought to the assembly and handed over to the presbyters. As God **hath prospered him**; rather, *what-soever he has been prospered in;* i.e. all that his prosperity may permit. **That there be no gatherings when I come;** rather, *that, when I come, there may then be no collections.* When he came he did not wish his attention to be absorbed in serving tables.

Ver. 3.—**Whomsoever ye shall approve by your letters, them will I send.** It is difficult to see why the translators rendered the clause thus, unless they disliked to face the certainty that the apostle must have written many letters which are no longer extant. The true rendering is, *Whomsoever ye approve, these I will send with letters.* The letters would be letters of introduction or commendation (Acts xviii. 27; Rom. xvi. 1; 2 Cor. iii. 1) to the apostles at Jerusalem. **Your liberality;** literally, *your grace or favour;* i.e. the token of your voluntary affection.

Ver. 4.—**If it be meet that I go also.** Unless the collection were a substantial proof of the generosity of the Gentile Churches, it would be hardly worth while (ἄξιον) for St. Paul to go too. **With me.** St. Paul would not take this money himself. His "religious" enemies were many, bitter, and unscrupulous, and he would give them no possibility of a handle against him. He makes such arrangements as should place him above suspicion (2 Cor. viii. 20). It turned out that the subscription *was* an adequate one, and St. Paul accompanied the Corinthian delegates (Rom. xv. 25; Acts xx. 4). The thought that they might visit Jerusalem and see some of the twelve would act as an incentive to the Corinthians.

Ver. 5.—**When I shall pass through Mace-donia;** rather, *when I have passed through Macedonia.* **For I do pass through Mace-donia;** rather, *for I mean to pass through Macedonia.* We learn from 2 Cor. i. 15, 16, that it had been St. Paul's intention to sail from Ephesus to Corinth, thence, after a brief stay, to proceed to Macedonia, and on his return to come again for a longer stay at Corinth on his way to Judæa. He had in an Epistle, now lost (see ch. v. 9), announced to them this intention. He changed his plan because, in the present disgraceful state of disorganization into which the Church had fallen, he felt that he could not visit them without being compelled to exercise a severity which, he hoped, might be obviated by writing to them and delaying his intended visit. Nothing but his usual delicacy and desire to spare them prevented him from stating all this more fully (2 Cor. i. 23; ii. 1). Mistaking the kindness of his purpose, the Corinthians accused him of levity. He defends himself from this charge in the Second Epistle, and he carried out the plan which he here announces (2 Cor. ii. 13; viii. 1; ix. 2, 4; xii. 14; xiii. 1).

Ver. 6.—**Yea, and winter with you.** This he did (Acts xx. 3—6). **That ye may bring me on my journey.** The "ye" is emphatic. The acceptance of this favour at their hands was a proof of affection. It was the custom in ancient days to accompany a departing guest for a short distance (Rom. xv. 24; Acts xv. 3; xvii. 15). **Whithersoever I go.** St. Paul well knew that some uncertainty must attach to his plans. As it was, he had to change his plan at the last moment. He had meant to sail from Corinth, but, owing to a plot to assassinate him, he was obliged to go overland round by Macedonia (Acts xx. 3).

Ver. 7.—**For I will not see you now by the way;** rather, *I do not wish to pay you a cursory visit now,* as I had originally meant to do. **If the Lord permit.** The Christians made a rule of adding these phrases in sign of dependence upon God (ch. iv. 19; Acts xviii. 1; Jas. iv. 15; Heb. vi. 3).

Ver. 8.—**I will tarry at Ephesus until Pentecost.** It is possible that this intention was frustrated by the riot stirred up by the silversmiths (Acts xix. 23—41). But, in any case, he stayed at Ephesus *nearly* as long as he intended, for the riot only occurred when he was already preparing to leave (Acts xix. 21, 22).

Ver. 9.—**A great door and effectual.** A wide and promising opportunity for winning souls to God. The metaphor of "a door," perhaps suggested by our Lord himself, was common among Christians (2 Cor. ii. 12; Col. iv. 3; Acts xiv. 27; Rev. iii. 8). **Many adversaries** (Acts xix. 1, 8, 9, 19, 20).

Ver. 10.—**Now if Timotheus come.** St. Paul had already sent on Timothy (ch. iv. 17), with Erastus (Acts xix. 22), to go to Corinth by way of Macedonia, and prepare for his visit. But possibly he had *countermanded* these directions when he postponed his own visit. In the uncertainties of ancient travelling, he could not be certain whether his counter-order would reach Timothy or not. It appears to have done so, for nothing is said of any visit of Timothy to Corinth, and St. Paul sent Titus. **Without fear.** Timothy must at this time have been very young (1 Tim. iv. 12). As a mere substitute for St. Paul's personal visit, he would be unacceptable. In every allusion to him we find traces of a somewhat timid and sensitive disposition (1 Tim. v. 21—23; 2 Tim. i. 6—8, etc.). He may well, therefore, have shrunk from the thought of meeting the haughty sophisters and disputatious partisans of Corinth. **As I also do.** "As a son with the father, he hath served with me in the gospel" (Phil. ii. 22). St. Paul felt for Timothy a deeper personal tenderness than for any of his other friends, and the companionship of this gentle and devoted youth was one of the chief comforts of his missionary labour.

Ver. 11.—**Let no man therefore despise him.** His youth and modesty seemed to invite a contempt which was only too consonant with the character of the Corinthians. **I look for him with the brethren.** There was a reason for adding this. The Corinthians would see that any unkindness or contempt shown towards Timothy would at once be reported to St. Paul. Who "the brethren" are is not mentioned, for in Acts xix. 22 we are only told that Timothy was accompanied by Erastus. Perhaps St. Paul means with the brethren who conveyed this letter (see ver. 12), and who, as he supposed, would meet with Timothy at Corinth, or fall in with him on their return to meet St. Paul in Macedonia. One of these brethren must have been Titus (2 Cor. ii. 13; vii. 6, 7), and there were two others.

Ver. 12.—**As touching our brother Apollos;** rather, *but as touching Apollos, the brother.* It seems clear from this that the Corinthians, in their letter, had requested that this eloquent and favourite teacher might be sent to them. **I greatly desired him to come unto you;** rather, *I besought him much.* There were at Corinth persons malignant enough to have suggested that Paul had refused their request; that he would not send Apollos to them out of jealousy of Apollos's superior oratory, and of the party which assumed his name. St. Paul anticipated this sneer. His nature was much too noble to feel the least jealousy. Both he and Apollos here show themselves in the purest light. **His will;** literally, *there was not will.* The word "will" most frequently means "the will *of God,*" but if that had been the meaning here, the word would have had the article. It is used of human will in ch. vii. 37; Eph. ii. 3; 2 Pet. i. 21. Here it means that Apollos had decided not to come at present, obviously because his name had been abused for purposes of party faction (ch. iii. 5). This was all the more noble on his part because he seems to have been a special friend of Titus (Titus iii. 13). St. Paul would gladly have sent his two ablest and most energetic disciples to this distracted Church. **When** he shall have convenient time; rather, *when a good opportunity offers itself to him.* Whether Apollos ever revisited Corinth or not we do not know.

Ver. 13.—**Watch**, etc. The brief impetuous imperatives show a sudden burst of emotion as he draws to a close. The next clause seems like an after-thought. Watchfulness (1 Thess. v. 6; 1 Pet. v. 8; Rev. iii. 2; xvi. 15), steadfastness (Phil. i 27), and strength (Eph. vi. 10; Col. i. 11; 2 Tim. ii. 1), and love (ch. xiii.; 1 Pet. iv. 8, etc.) were frequent subjects of Christian exhortation. The verb which expresses Christian manliness ("Play the men!") occurs here only. It is found in the LXX. of Josh. i. 6. They needed, as Chrysostom says, all these exhortations, for they were, in Christian matters, drowsy, unstable, effeminate, and factious.

Ver. 14.—**Let all your things be done with charity**; rather, as in the Revised Version, *Let all that ye do be done in love.* This is equivalent to the "Above all things, have fervent love among yourselves," of 1 Pet. iv. 8.

Ver. 15.—**Ye know the house of Stephanas.** This paragraph seems to have been written lest the Corinthians should be angry with Stephanas, Fortunatus, and Achaicus—who, perhaps, were slaves of the household of Chloe—for having carried to St. Paul their ill report (ch. i. 11). **The firstfruits of Achaia.** For which reason St. Paul had baptized Stephanas and his house (ch. i. 16). In Rom. xvi. 5 *Epænetus* is called "the firstfruits of Achaia," but there the reading ought to be, *of Asia.* **Have addicted themselves**; rather, *they set themselves.*

Ver. 16.—**That ye submit yourselves unto such.** Slaves though they may be in earthly rank, recognize their Christian authority as good men and women (see Eph. v. 21; 1 Tim. v. 17). The verb used for "submit yourselves," or, "set yourselves under," is the same as in the previous verse.

Ver. 17.—**Of the coming**; rather, *at the presence of.* They were now with St. Paul in Ephesus. **Fortunatus.** A Christian of this name also carried the letter of St. Clement to Corinth. **That which was lacking on your part.** This sounds like a reproach in the Authorized Version, but is quite the reverse. It should be rendered, *the void caused by your absence.* The same word occurs in 2 Cor. viii. 13, 14; ix. 12; xi. 9, etc. The nearest parallel to the usage here is Phil. ii. 30.

Ver. 18.—**My spirit and yours.** They refreshed *my* spirit by telling me all about you, sad though much of the news was; and *yours* by this renewal of our mutual intercourse (comp. 2 Cor. vii. 13).

Vers. 19—24.—*Salutations and autograph conclusion.*

Ver. 19.—**The Churches of Asia.** Proconsular Asia. There was a constant interchange of voyages between the western coast of Asia and Corinth. **Aquila and Priscilla.** This admirable Christian husband and wife had no small share in founding the Churches both of Corinth and Ephesus. Being St. Paul's partners in trade, he spent much time with them. (For all that is known of them, see Acts xviii. 1, 2, 26; Rom. xvi. 3, 5.) *Priscilla.* Most of the uncials have the shorter form, Prisca. In some manuscripts (D, E, F, G) and versions (*e.g.* the Vulgate) we find the addition, "with whom also I am lodging." **The Church that is in their house.** The time for large common churches for public worship had not yet arrived. Hence, when the Christian community numbered more than could meet in one place, the congregations were held in separate houses (Rom. xvi. 4, 15; Acts ii. 46; Col. iv. 15; Philem. 2).

Ver. 20.—**All the brethren.** The Ephesian Church in general. **With an holy kiss.** The kiss of peace is mentioned in Rom. xvi. 16; 2 Cor. xiii. 12; 1 Pet. v. 14. It was a sign of the reconciliation of all dissensions. But the abuse of the practice and the hideous heathen calumnies which it helped to perpetuate, led to its abolition. In the Roman Church a shadow of it still remains in the custom of the congregation kissing the *pax* after the priest has kissed it. The custom still continues in the *Christos voscress* of Easter Day in the Greek Church, when—

"See! the bearded faces kiss each other:
Every Russian Christian loves his brother.
Serf or noble, each to-day may claim
Friendly kiss in that all friendly Name."

Ver. 21.—**With mine own hand.** Every one of St. Paul's Epistles, except that to the Galatians (vi. 11), seems to have been written by an amanuensis. The blaze of light in the vision on the road to Damascus seems to have left him with acute and permanent ophthalmia as his "thorn in the flesh;" and this would naturally disincline him to the physical labour of writing. When he did write, his letters seem to have been large and straggling (Gal. vi. 11). But this was an age in which documents were frequently falsified by designing persons, and this seems to have happened to St. Paul after he had written his very first extant letter. After warning the Thessalonians not to be frightened "by epistle *as from us*" (2 Thess. ii. 2), he adds, at the close of the letter, that henceforth he intends to authenticate every letter by an autograph salutation (2 Thess. iii. 17; Col. iv. 18; Rom. xvi. 22). To this bad and dangerous practice of forgery is due the energetic appeal of Rev. xxii. 18, 19. A similar appeal to copyists, couched in the most solemn language, is found in Irenæus ('Opp.,' i. 821, edit. Stieren), and at the end of Rufinus's prologue to his translation of Origen's 'De Principiis.'

Ver. 22.—**If any man love not, etc.** This sentence (as in Col. iv. 18; Eph. vi. 24) is part of the autograph salutation. The verb here used for "love" (*philō*) was perhaps suggested by the word for "kiss" (*philēma*). The word generally used for "love of God" is *agapæ* (Eph. vi. 24), which implies less warmth, but deeper reverence. But this passage is full of emotion. **Let him be Anathema.** The word only occurs elsewhere in Acts xii. 3; xxiii. 14; Rom. ix. 3; Gal. i. 8, 9 (comp. Matt. xxvi. 74, "to curse"). It is the equivalent of the Hebrew *cherem*, a ban (Lev. xxvii. 29; Josh. vi. 17, etc.). I cannot pretend to understand what St. Paul means by it, unless it be "Let personal love to Christ be the *essential* of Christian fellowship, and let him who has it not be regarded as *apart from the Church*." Commentators call it "an imprecation," or "malediction," and say that it means "Let him be devoted to God's wrath and judgment." That language is, indeed, very like the language of religious hatred and religious usurpation in all ages, but it is the very antithesis to the general tone of the apostle. *If* this were the meaning, it would seem to resemble the very spirit which Christ himself severely rebuked as the Elijah-spirit, not the Christ-spirit. But I do not believe that, even in a passing outburst of strong emotion, St. Paul had any such meaning. For (1) the Jews used *cherem*, not only of the severer form of excommunication (*shem atha*), but even of the milder and by no means severe *temporary* form (*nidui*); and (2) it cannot be *more* severe than "handing over to Satan" (ch. v. 5; 1 Tim. i. 20), which was merciful in its purpose. **Maran-atha;** two words, *the Lord cometh;* like the Jewish *shem atha,* "the Name cometh," or, "the Lord comes." It seems to be an appeal to the judgment of Christ, and may possibly have been an allusion to Mal. iv. 6, the words with which the Old Testament ends (see Jude 14, 15).

Ver. 23.—**The grace of our Lord Jesus Christ be with you.** This is a *gnorisma*, or "badge of confidence," which, in one or other of its forms, is found at the end of all St. Paul's Epistles. Here it is the same as in 1 Thess. v. 28. "With you *all*" is added in 2 Thess. iii. 18; Rom. xvi. 24; Phil. iv. 23. In Galatians and Philemon we have "with *your spirit.*" In the pastoral Epistles and Colossians, "Peace be with you." In Eph. vi. 24 it is confined to those "who love the Lord Jesus in sincerity." In 2 Cor. xiii. 14 alone we have the full "apostolic benediction."

Ver. 24.—**My love be with you all in Christ Jesus.** Added as a last proof that, if he has written in severity, he has also written in love. **Amen.** Perhaps genuine, though omitted by B, F, G.

The superscription to the Epistle, rightly omitted in the Revised Version, does not possess the smallest authority, and is absolutely erroneous. It contains two positive misstatements, which show with what utter carelessness these superscriptions were written in the later manuscripts. The Epistle was *not* written from Philippi (a mere mistaken inference from ch. xvi. 5), but from Ephesus (ch. xvi. 8), and was not conveyed by Timotheus.

HOMILETICS.

Vers. 1—4.—*Christian philanthropy.* "Now concerning the collection for the saints," etc. At the outset three truths are suggested. 1. *That in the highest theological discussion the urgency of practical benevolence should never be overlooked.* Immediately after the apostle had passed through the discussion on the doctrine of the resurrection of the dead, he says, "Now concerning the collection." Practical benevolence is for many reasons more important than the grandest theological doctrine; it is doctrine demonstrated, exemplified, and reduced to utility; it is the blossom run into fruit. 2. *That the grandest institutions are likely to break down in a world of depravity.* The young Church at Jerusalem adopted the principle of Christian socialism. As many as were possessors of land or houses sold them, and brought the prices of those sold "and laid them down at the apostles' feet," and distribution was made to every man according as he had need. A magnificent social system this, a system suited to bind all classes and races of men into the unity of a loving brotherhood. But the swelling tide of human depravity soon bears it away; for here we find Paul urging a collection for the poor Christians at Jerusalem, many of whom were shut up in prison, and those of them who were released reduced to abject destitution,—hence the collection. How many magnificent schemes for the world's good are constantly being dashed to pieces by the black billows of popular depravity! 3. *That the practical sympathy for human suffering which Christianity generates is a Divine element.* Here are Galatia and Corinth drawn in sympathy for one common object, and that object was "suffering saints at Jerusalem." These people lived widely asunder, and were separated by many striking peculiarities, but here they meet together. This is the Divine principle that will one day draw all men together in Christ. Our subject is Christian philanthropy, and here we have—

I. ITS CLAIMS ZEALOUSLY ADVOCATED. "Now concerning the collection." Paul was the advocate, and his advocacy glows with zeal. We find that in this matter he proposes the Galatians as an example to the Corinthians, the Corinthians an example to the Macedonians, and both as an example to the Romans (2 Cor. ix. 2; Rom. xv. 26). Were it not for the earnest advocacy of Christly men, the probability is that the Divine element of pure and practical social sympathy would become extinct. It is the living ministry of the gospel that keeps it alive, and in this it fulfils the grandest of all missions.

II. ITS OPERATIONS WISELY DIRECTED. Paul directed: 1. *That the contributions should be personal.* "Let every one of you lay by him in store." No one was exempted, however poor; the widow's mite was acceptable. If no coin, then give service. 2. *That the contributions should be systematic.* "Upon the first day of the week." Begin the week with deeds of practical benevolence. 3. *That the contributions should be religious.* "As God hath prospered him." This was the principle to rule the amount. Were this principle acted upon, some of the men who subscribe their ten thousand pounds, and who are lauded the world over as philanthropists, would be found to be churls after all, and those who subscribed their few shillings would appear as princes in the domain of practical charity. But, alas! how men reverse this principle! *The more they have the less they give.*

III. ITS CONTRIBUTIONS HONESTLY DISTRIBUTED. "And when I come, whomsoever ye shall approve by your letters, them will I send to bring your liberality unto Jerusalem. And if it be meet that I go also, they shall go with me." It is your duty to see that what you have subscribed shall be honestly distributed, and for this purpose, send men as your almoners, and if it seems necessary to secure the honest distribution, I will go with them. How sadly is this duty frequently neglected! *How much money given for charitable purposes is dishonestly used and misappropriated every year!*

Vers. 5—9.—*God's will the rule, and spiritual usefulness the end of life.* "Now I will come unto you when I shall pass through Macedonia," etc. Two remarks are suggested.

I. GOD'S WILL SHOULD BE THE RULE OF LIFE. "But I trust to tarry a while with you, if the Lord permit." The text tells us that Paul had made a plan to visit the Corinthians, to "tarry a while" with them, and to spend the winter with them, after he had passed through Macedonia, and tarrying at Ephesus until the Pentecost; but see, he rests this plan (no doubt dear to his heart) on the Lord's will—"if the Lord permit." 1. There is a *belief* implied here. The great truth implied in this expression of Paul's is that God is in the *history of individual man.* He is not merely in the great material universe, in angelic hierarchies, in human empires, communities, Churches, families, but in the *individual* man himself. He is not too absorbed in the vast for this, not too great for this. Paul believed that God was interested in him personally, and that he arranged for him personally. There is something sublime, bracing, and ennobling in the thought that God knows me, cares for me, arranges for me. 2. There is an *acquiescence* implied here. "If the Lord permit." This means, "I have no will of my own." As if he had said personally, "Consulting merely my own will, I should like to winter with you, my Corinthian friends, but I subordinate my will to the will of my God. I feel myself in his hands, and am ready to act in everything according to his arrangements."

II. SPIRITUAL USEFULNESS SHOULD BE THE AIM OF LIFE. "But I will tarry at Ephesus until Pentecost. For a great door and effectual is opened unto me, and there are many adversaries." Three remarks are here suggested. 1. That wherever the gospel signally triumphs, great opposition may be anticipated. Paul was now at Ephesus, where he had laboured for a considerable time, and with such signal success that a deep and widespread opposition was excited, even to passion (see Acts xix. 9—20). It has ever been so: wherever there has been a great revival of religion there has been unusual opposition. The latent enmity of the serpent is ever roused by the dissemination of spiritual light. Christ kindled a fire upon the earth. 2. That opposition to the gospel often affords specially favourable opportunities for the labour of the evangelist. "For a great door and effectual is opened unto me, and there are many adversaries." Religious excitement is ever more favourable to the spread of religion than religious monotony. You stand a better chance of converting an earnest sceptic than a traditional religionist. Excitement opens a "door." 3. That the true evangelist will be stimulated in his labours rather than discouraged by opposition. Instead of quitting Ephesus, where there were so many adversaries, Paul says, "I will tarry at Ephesus until Pentecost." Little souls are dismayed by difficulties, great souls are roused to action by them. Difficulties awaken their courage, stimulate their activities, and marshal their faculties for battle.

Vers. 10—12.—*Wholesome teaching for the older ministers.* "Now if Timotheus come, see that he may be with you," etc. Taking these verses as the foundation for an address to the senior ministers of the gospel, we say to them—

I. SHOW A TENDER REGARD FOR THE INTERESTS OF YOUNG MINISTERS. "Now if Timotheus come, see that he may be with you without fear: for he worketh the work of the Lord, as I also do." Timothy was young in years and in the faith as well; a man, too, perhaps of delicate frame and nervous temperament, and probably not distinguished by any great gift, natural or attained. In Corinth there were men of philosophic fame, brilliant genius, and oratoric force. He would perhaps feel somewhat abashed in the presence of such; hence the considerate counsel which Paul addresses to the Corinthians to treat him kindly, not to "despise him," nor in any way to dispirit him. Alas! it is not an uncommon thing for elder ministers to disparage the younger ones, and often treat them with disrespect, and even rudeness.

II. RISE SUPERIOR TO ALL MINISTERIAL JEALOUSIES. If Paul had been capable of feeling jealousy towards any brother minister, it would have been towards Apollos. He seems to have been a man of distinguished ability and splendid eloquence. Moreover, he was very popular in Corinth, greatly admired and extolled by not a few, perhaps more popular even than Paul himself, the head of one of the factions of the Church against which Paul had been contending. Had he been jealous, Paul would have kept him out of Corinth as long as he could, and have treated him as a rival, instead of which he says, "As touching our brother Apollos, I greatly desired him to come unto you with the brethren." Jealousy amongst ministers of the gospel, though a most antichristian sentiment, is not a very uncommon thing; nay, it is rife, and shows itself often in detracting innuendoes and symbolic looks and shrugs.

III. BE NOT DISPLEASED IF INFERIOR BRETHREN ACQUIESCE NOT IN YOUR DESIRES. Both the Christian experience and ministerial ability of Apollos were inferior to that of Paul. Notwithstanding this, he did not comply with Paul's request: nor did Paul seem displeased. "His will was not at all to come at this time: but he will come when he shall have convenient time." If Paul had no authority to enforce his wishes on his brethren, how arrogant it seems for any uninspired minister to attempt it! The only authority which one genuine minister has over another is the authority of superior intelligence, experience, and moral force.

Vers. 13, 14.—*The demands of Christianity on its adherents.* "Watch ye, stand fast in the faith," etc. Here are certain demands which Christianity makes on all men.

I. A demand for VIGILANCE. "Watch ye." A military metaphor this, derived from the duty of those who are stationed to guard a camp or to observe the motions of an enemy. There were many evils, as we have seen, in the Corinthian Church—dissensions, heresies, inchastities, intemperances, etc. Hence the necessity of watchfulness. But where do not evils abound? Hosts surround us all, hence, "*Watch ye.*" "Watch and pray," says Christ.

II. A demand for STABILITY. "Stand fast in the faith." Do not be vacillating, wavering, "tossed about by every wind of doctrine." Strike the roots of your faith deep into the soil of eternal realities. Firmness is no more obstinacy than the stony rock is the deep-rooted oak.

III. A demand for MANLINESS. "Quit you like men." Be courageous, invincible, well equipped, manly. Be an ideal man; you can be nothing higher than this, nothing greater. There are great philosophers, great poets, great statesmen, great orators, great warriors, who are *small* men, if men at all, leagues away from the ideal. *A great functionary is often a very small man.* "Quit you like men." Be heroes in the strife. Here is—

IV. A demand for CHARITY. "Let all your things be done with charity" or love. Man's life consists of many acts, many "things done." Activity is at once the law and the necessity of his nature. He only really lives as he acts; inactivity is death. But whilst the acts of men are numerous and varied, the animating and controlling spirit should be one, and that spirit is love.

Vers. 15—18.—*Our duty to the truly useful.* "I beseech you, brethren," etc. The subject of these verses is our duty to the truly useful, and—

I. FOR THE TRULY USEFUL WE SHOULD CHERISH THE HIGHEST RESPECT. There are three useful persons that Paul mentions here. "Stephanas." He was one of Paul's first converts of Achaia; he and his house were baptized by Paul, and he and his family were "addicted" to the ministries of love. "Fortunatus and Achaicus" are also mentioned here. To these three personages Paul calls the special attention of the Corinthians, and that because they were useful. They had all ministered to Paul. The latter had supplied to him what the Corinthians had neglected, and they refreshed both his spirit and theirs; hence for this he says, "Acknowledge ye them that are such." *The truly useful are the truly honourable.* A man is to be honoured, not because of his ancestry, his office, his wealth, but because of what he is morally, and what he does generously in the way of helping the race. The philanthropist is the true prince.

II. WITH THE TRULY USEFUL WE SHOULD HEARTILY CO-OPERATE. "That ye submit yourselves unto such, and to every one that helpeth with us, and laboureth." 1. Co-operate with *useful men.* 2. In your co-operation *let them take the lead.* They have proved themselves worthy of your co-operation.

Vers. 19, 20, 23, 24.—*Salutations.* "The Churches of Asia salute you," etc. On these salutations we cannot do better than transcribe the remarks of F. W. Robertson:— "We make a remark respecting salutations generally. This Epistle has many, but they are not so numerous as in that to the Romans. In both of them individuals are mentioned by name. It was no mere general assurance of attachment he gave them, but one of his personal knowledge and affection.

"I. ST. PAUL'S PERSONAL CONSIDERATIONS WERE NOT LOST IN GENERAL PHILAN-THROPY. That because he entertained regard for the Churches, and for bodies of men, he did not on this account ignore the individuals composing them. It is common enough to profess great interest and zeal for humanity whilst there is indifference all the time about individual men. It is common enough to be zealous about a cause, about some scheme of social good, and yet to be careless respecting individual welfare. But St. Paul's love was from Christ's own Spirit. It was love to the Church generally, and, besides, it was love to Aquila and Priscilla. And is not this, too, the nature of God's love, who provides for the universe, and yet spends an infinity of care on the fibre of a leaf?

"II. THE VALUE OF THE COURTESIES OF LIFE. There are many minds which are indifferent to such things, and fancy themselves above them. It is a profound remark of Prescott's that 'liberty is dependent upon forms.' Did not the solemn, slow change in the English constitution, and our freedom from violent submersions, arise from the almost superstitious way in which precedent has been consulted in the manner of every change? But what is of more importance to remember is, that love is dependent upon forms, courtesy of etiquette guards and protects courtesy of heart. How many hearts have been lost irrecoverably! and how many averted eyes and cold looks have been gained from what seemed perhaps but a trifling negligence of forms!"

Vers. 21, 22.—*A negative crime and a positive punishment.* "If any man love not," etc. The words contain two things.

I. A NEGATIVE CRIME. "If any man love not the Lord Jesus Christ," etc. We make three remarks on this state of mind in relation to Christ. 1. It is *unreasonable.* There is everything in him to call out the highest love. There are three kinds of love to which we are susceptible, and which are incumbent on us—*gratitude, esteem,* and *benevolence.* The first requires a manifestation of kindness; the second, of moral excellence; the third, a purpose for the common good. Christ manifests all these, and therefore deserves our highest love. 2. It is *ascertainable.* We can soon ascertain whether we love Christ or not. There are infallible criteria. For example, the chief object of love will always be (1) the engrossing subject of thought; (2) the attractive theme of conversation; (3) the source of the greatest delight in pleasing; (4) the most transformative power of character; and (5) the most identified with our conscious life. 3. It is *deplorable.* This love is the only true regulative power of the soul. Where this is not, all the powers of our nature are misemployed, and all is confusion.

II. A POSITIVE PUNISHMENT. "Let him be Anathema Maran-atha." These words intimate two things concerning the punishment. 1. Its *nature.* "Let him be Anathema." The word expresses some terrible amount of suffering. It is one of Paul's strong words to express a terrible evil. Excommunication from all that is pure and good and happy is undoubtedly involved. The soul cut off from Christ, its Centre, Root, Fountain, Life, is utterly destroyed. 2. Its *certainty.* "Maran-atha," which means, "The Lord will come." This word is probably introduced by Paul in order to convey the certainty of the destruction of those who "love not the Lord Jesus Christ." Paul had written the other part of this letter by an amanuensis, but to write these terrible words he takes up the pen himself. "The salutation of me Paul with mine own hand." He felt the utmost recoil of heart for those who "love not the Lord Jesus Christ," and had the most overwhelming idea of the misery to which such will be exposed. Men are accursed, not merely because they hate Christ, rebel against his authority, and profane his ordinances, but because they *do not* love him.

HOMILIES BY VARIOUS AUTHORS.

Vers. 1—5.—*Charity; its systematic mode of exercise.* If these Corinthians shared the thoughts and emotions of St. Paul on love, on the uses of gifts, and on the resurrection, they were well prepared to have practical duties urged on their immediate attention. At that time "the collection for the saints" was a very important matter. These saints were poor disciples in Jerusalem, who needed foreign help, the Church in that city being unable, because of impoverishment, to render them adequate assistance. Furthermore, it was important as a means of spiritual discipline. Giving to others, and especially to the household of faith, is an acknowledgment of God in Christ, a testimony to brotherhood, and an active co-operation with providence, the last being a duty we are particularly liable to forget. The religion of providence, the sense of Christ in providence, and the sentiments thereby inspired, is a weak influence in many professing Christians, and it is certainly very desirable that we should have the mind of the Spirit on this subject. Apart from these reasons for "the collection for the saints," the evidential value of the act appears in this, that in about a quarter of a century a Christian community had grown up in the Roman empire, had spread over much of its territory, and had the means and the heart to aid poorer brethren. Nor must we fail to notice that Jerusalem was an object of much interest to Galatia and Corinth. The days of adversity were gathering upon her, but she was Jerusalem, and to no one more of a Jerusalem than to St. Paul. His zeal in her behalf won upon the sympathies of the Gentiles, and they were ready to join him in this work of the Lord. Observe, then, that he enters into no argument to prove the obligation of charity. This is presupposed to exist. The sentiment, too, is alive, the impulse is awake and operative. He makes no doubt of their readiness to co-operate with him. What he wishes to do is to organize the sentiment and impulse. Habits are the safeguards of good inclinations, habits are the most conservative of forces, and habits, after having been made by us, get the mastery and make us. Habits are as necessary for Churches as for individuals, and, therefore, he will have these Corinthians to do this work methodically. "As I have given order to the Churches of Galatia, even so do ye." Notice the apostolic method. It required a fixed time—"the first day of the week," the Lord's day. Would not the day cultivate and hallow the feeling? Are the associations of a given time for a given task unworthy of consideration? The heavens and the earth are obedient to periodicity, the human body is an organism of periodicity, the sabbath is an institution of periodicity, and benevolence cannot be a habit in the best import of the term unless it have stated periods of activity. Therefore, "the first day of the week." It was to be done by "every one." It was to be done individually and privately—"lay by him in store." And, again, it was to be performed with reference to accumulation, set apart, added to, kept in store. Finally, there was to be an examination of their daily business; intelligence was to be exercised, prudence and piety were to go hand in hand, and this was to be done in a religious spirit—"as God hath prospered him." Now, this looks as if St. Paul had given much thought to this matter. It was charity, not as mere charity, nor as a spasmodic impulse, nor as a thing of imposing occasions, but charity organized and habitual, regular as the sabbath, incorporated into the sanctity of the day, a product of the week's review, a commemoration of God's goodness in prospering their business; it was this sort of charity he directed them to practice. They practised many virtues in this one virtue. Too much of benevolent giving involves nothing beyond our sympathies and the wants of others. It is an education of the hand, the purse, the soul. But what of the spirit's higher culture? What of the calling into play the spiritual nature that was going forward to robe itself in a spiritual habiliment at the resurrection? The essence of this lay in the thought of God as prospering the man for the sake of others as well as for his own sake. Business, then, was not simply personal, it was relative also, and charity, no less than utility, entered into it as a component. What, now, is St. Paul's idea of making money? It is acquiring the means of your own support and of contributing to the relief of those in want. It is making wisdom and openness of heart and fraternity of sentiment, while making money. It is making the religion of brotherhood while making money. If the Corinthians would adhere to this plan, there would be no need of collections when he came, as the work would have been done already. Was not this one way of being steady, unmoved, "always abounding in the work of the Lord," and would it not prove by its self-action that it was not "in vain in the Lord?" And was it not one way, and a great way, of demonstrating that there was a business in religion as well as a religion in business? Throughout his statement of the matter, you see the apostle's large-mindedness. The cheerful giver is portrayed, the man who naturalizes and domesticates charity; nothing is said of tithes and tithing; it is Christianity and Gentile Christianity alone that is in view, and, instead of Jerusalem being a centre of power or metropolitan sovereignty, Corinth and Galatia are sources or head-springs of blessing to her. What a stride forward this, in the evangelization of the world! We may know that the end draweth nigh, when the money of the world—the stronghold of sin and Satan—is recovered for Christ. St. Paul had faith in the sentiment of these Corinthians. Disorderly as were some of their practices, shameful indeed, loose as was their Church discipline, erroneous certain of their tenets, yet, despite of all, they had the root of the matter in the willing mind of love, so that when he visited them, he would have nothing more to do than to accredit their messengers and commend them to the Church in Jerusalem. Come to them he would; and, if the collection were liberal, he might deem it advisable to accompany their messengers to Jerusalem. And what a spectacle it suggests at this distance to us, who can recall the old-time enmity between Jew and Gentile, and have the offset in a scene as beautiful as that presented by a delegation from Corinth, bearing its gifts to a suffering and down-trodden people!—L.

Vers. 6—18.—*St. Paul and his purposes; his friends; earnest exhortation.* If the apostle were before us in his Epistles as an inspired man of genius only, whose intellect teemed with great thoughts, and whose heart was absorbed in supplying fervency to those thoughts, his hold upon us would be weakened. The man has nothing about him of the intellectualist. Among the varieties of mind and character that have arisen from time to time in the development of humanity, turn for a moment to the ideal of an apostle, and tell us if the conception of such a person is not something unprecedented, an idea altogether original with Christianity. A new and most marvellous form of a public man—not a representative man, not a typical man, in no sense either the one or the other, since the man antedated the Church and had no continuation in the Church after its opening century. Take your ideals of philosopher, poet, military chieftain, statesman, ruler, and tell us what resemblance these bear to the character St. Paul sustained and the office he filled. Or take the worthiest dignitaries of the Church, and follow the procession as it moves, now in splendour and then in gloom, from the hills of Rome, over the Alps, through the forests of Germany, by the Rhine and the Rhone, over England, Scotland, and America, and see how they compare with him who fought with beasts at Ephesus and died daily. Quite as remarkable as the conception of this ideal was its realization in St. Paul from his conversion to his death. Look at the matter in another connection. What is the final test of greatness viewed in relation to society? Is it not the ease and freedom of access to the common heart of humanity, the magical power to create sympathy and fellowship, the God-like capacity to pass through the shallow feelings of admiration and conventional honour—often more of a tribute to our own vanity than to the worth of others—and to gain entrance to the depths of truthful affection? Beyond doubt, this was St. Paul's greatness. Just from an argument, that must have put an extraordinary pressure even on his great abilities, and which was well calculated, as all intellectual men know, to make him insensible, or at least indifferent, at the moment to the details of life, he is not forgetful of his brethren, but hopes to pass the winter in their midst. "A flying visit" (*by the way*) will not satisfy his love. But, for the present, he must "tarry at Ephesus." Why he would stay in this city, he states—"a great and effectual door is opened unto me;" the field of usefulness is large and promises vast results. Stay he would, moreover, because "there are many adversaries." Adversaries were the men to convert; if not that, to silence; but, any way, he will not desert a post of duty to gratify his desire to see the Corinthian brethren. If the Lord will permit, he will refresh himself among them, but, for a time, he will face the worshippers of Diana and bear the brunt of persecution. Then he thinks of the young Timotheus. If he visit you according to his expectation, be thoughtful of his youth, be specially considerate of his modesty, and see that his stay among you is "without fear," disturbed by none of your rivalries and factions. Honour him for his work's sake, for "he worketh the work of the Lord, as I also do." "Let no man therefore despise him;" on the contrary, "send him on without annoyance, with good understanding, and kindly affection," that he and his travelling companions may come unto me. Again, some of the partisans at Corinth might suspect him of jealousy as to Apollos. The name of the eloquent and holy man had become a watchword of strife. Lest they should do St. Paul this dishonour, he tells them of the affectionate relations between them; nor will he say *my* brother, but "*our* brother Apollos*,*" whom he wishes "greatly" to visit the Church at Corinth. But see! One of those sudden changes which originate in the soul, which pass from the soul into the nerves, and from the nerves into the muscles—one of those quick escapes from memory and stored-up emotion—occurs, and what an intenser expression settles in the muscles about the eyes, and in the eyes themselves! There is a break in the thought. Two verses intervene before the main idea is resumed. And it could hardly have been otherwise. It is nature to the life; it is St. Paul in the very soul of his temperament. It was scarcely possible for the apostle to mention Apollos without being reminded of the unhappy divisions at Corinth, for we can neither think nor feel except by means of association and suggestion. Each faculty, each sensibility, is an individual centre of these activities. No wonder, then, that there is an abrupt transition, all the more true to the laws of mind because abrupt. "Watch ye." Ah! if there had been Christian watchfulness in the Corinthian Church, what criminations, what reproaches, what humiliations, had been averted! To be a man, one must be apprehensive of the dangers ever lurking in ambush; must have the sentinel spirit and habit, and must exert it every moment. "Stand fast in the faith." Occasional watching will not do; steadfastness must go along with watchfulness, and fortify you against the wiliest assault. "Quit you like men." No manhood can live without courage; be manful. Fighting is your safety, business, profession; fight like men, fight on, fight to the end. "Be strong," or as it is in Eph. iii. 16, "Strengthened with might by his Spirit in the inner man." But fight how? There are many sorts of fighting—business fighting, professional fighting, legislative fighting, alas! even Church fighting. And there they are, each class of fighters with his particular weapons and his code of warfare. Only in this are they all alike, viz. the fighter gets the help of the animal soul. Beastly fighting he abhors; the fighting which brings hot blood and excited nerves and quick breathing into service, he admires, encourages, and depends upon for victory. *Not so* is St. Paul's view. "Let all your things be done with charity"—love, and, after his grand discourse on "love," an allusion is enough. To have a gentlemanly intellect in our fighting is a rare thing and a great thing, but to have a loving intellect in fighting for what we believe to be truth is much rarer and infinitely greater. Christian fighting is a very unusual excellence. From this emotional digression, he returns to "the house of Stephanas." This family were "the firstfruits of Achaia." How he likes the figure! St. Paul had baptized this household. They have "addicted themselves to the ministry of the saints." What the precise ministry was, we know not, but we know that it was a kind, beautiful, noble service, for it was rendered to the "saints." Think of the manifold ministries that Christianity set a-going. It is Anno Domini, say, 57. Christianity has in its Churches men of the generation that saw Christ die, that beheld him risen, that witnessed Pentecost. Jerusalem, though approaching her overthrow, still shows the temple where he taught, the spot where he was crucified, and the grave where he was buried. In this short space of time, what numerous workers have entered on careers of beneficence! From the apostles downward through all grades of kind and loving agencies, mark the variety, the diffusion, the heterogeneous civilizations, the unity, the accordant response, the consecration, pervading these Christian ministries. Mark it, we say; for it is a solitary phenomenon, up to this time, in human annals. Mark it, we repeat; for all the antagonistic forces of the world are in league to crush it, and they are reinforced and augmented by Satanic power. Take a single specimen, the household of Stephanas. No information is given as to his social position, no mention made of the sphere or spheres of usefulness filled. Enough to know, it was a "ministry" and a blessed one, since it was "a ministry to the saints." Yet we may picture that Corinthian home in the midst of a mongrel and licentious population, keeping alive the fervour of its love and the purity of its private heart, watching, standing fast in the faith, courageous and strong, and abounding in the work of the Lord. We may be sure that the poor, the sick, the infirm, were duly cared for and helped, and that the home itself was devoted to hospitality. Now, says the apostle, "submit yourselves unto such." There are two kinds of submission—one to authority, the other to influence. We need both. We need law, we need grace. Law and grace are coexisting constituents in modern civilization so far as Christianity has permeated, and, in our times, influence has assumed a very significant relation to government and society. We are governed much more by influence than authority. St. Paul urges that Stephanas and his household be respected and honoured, their wishes consulted, their judgments followed. And not only they, but "every one that helpeth with us and laboureth." Stephanas, Fortunatus, and Achaicus had come from Corinth and visited St. Paul at Ephesus, and "they have refreshed my spirit and yours." They had been sent as representatives of the Corinthian Church. The comfort and cheer were mutual; let them be acknowledged (valued, recognized) for these good offices. Wise instruction this; to be influenced by excellence in others, and *submit* our minds to such a gracious power, is the strongest of all evidences that we are on the path of culture and piety. For it has pleased God our Father, not only to reveal himself in Jesus our Lord, but he manifests himself also in those who are Christ's. Discipleship is a revelation and an inspiration. All the ministries are of God. They are his presence, his helpfulness, his glory, among the habitations of men. And whether it be the "ministering spirits sent forth to minister for them who shall be heirs of salvation," or the lowly ministrations that fall in the silent dew and breathe in the hidden violet, they are alike from him who "worketh all in all."—L.

Vers. 19—24.—*Closing words.* The salutations follow: first, from the Churches of Asia; then from Aquila and Priscilla, honoured names in the Churches; again from the Ephesian brethren. Let them renew their fellowship and pledge their love again " with a holy kiss." The work of the amanuensis over, St. Paul adds the salutation from himself with his own hand, " The salutation of me Paul." And the words follow, " If any man love not the Lord Jesus Christ, let him be Anathema," let him become accursed ; "Maran-atha," the Lord comes. Between the greeting " of me Paul " and " the grace of our Lord Jesus Christ be with you," followed immediately with " my love be with you all in Christ Jesus. Amen," this utterance of intense feeling occurs. What his tone of mind was, we understand fully from the chapter, which expresses confidence, hope, and brotherly affection. What his emotions were at the instant, we know from the salutation which precedes and the benediction which succeeds the Anathema Maran-atha. The warning is terrible, but it is one of love and tenderness. Had he been less conscious of the obligation to love the Lord Jesus Christ, less sensible of its immeasurable worth to the soul, less aware of the stupendous folly and guilt of rejecting it ; or if the profound sense of that love had not been present in the full blaze of his own consciousness ;—then, peradventure, words less stern and denunciatory might have been used. As it is, he speaks from the same high level of love to God and man, and the sentence of condemnation has its preface in a greeting and its sequel in a benediction. So closes this wonderful Epistle. Writing under the zenith of his years, if we rate those years by the chronology of his preaching and pen, St. Paul comes before us in its successive pages as one whose temperament, nervous vigour, observation, culture, experience, had been so far co-ordinated and interblended as to fit him, in an eminent degree, to give birth to this production. Never did a human soul exhibit its individuality more perfectly through all its organs of expression. Those organs are varied in every man. They were singularly diversified in the apostle. He cannot reason long without waking other forces of utterance. Imagination, in its form of relativity rather than its creative quality, is stirred into activity. Most of all, impassioned emotion is quickly evoked. And, in this Epistle, the transitions from one topic to another, and from one aspect of a topic to its contrast, are vivid tokens of his superabundant energy. Much is left without minute elaboration. Hints are given that might be expanded into essays and disquisitions. But he was not writing these ; he was writing apostolic letters, and " first and last and midst" he adhered to his plan and method. Judging from his recorded speeches, he is quite as much or more of a speaker when writing than when addressing a multitude. The spirit in him is often impetuous and finds it easy work to loose itself from restraints. Keenly conscious of himself, still more keenly conscious of Divine truth in himself, his personality is as nearly merged in his apostleship as we can conceive possible, and hence it is Paul, the servant of the Lord Jesus Christ, who has the pre-eminence in all the manifestations of his genius and character. This Epistle, a manual of Church order, an epitome of cardinal principles adapted to the ever-changing externality of Church life, presents many a germ-idea for future development. Not one of his Epistles bears so directly on certain questions of the day. If we study the human body from the Pauline point of view, we shall be rid very soon of those dangerous teachings which some of our physiologists are pressing on popular acceptance. If we follow St. Paul, we shall know more of the human soul than most of our philosophical systems teach us. There are no " wandering mazes " here in which men are " lost," but over every realm he traverses, light gathers as he advances, and the splendour always hangs its noon where the radiance is most wanted. Christ is the Power of God and the Wisdom of God. Christ is therefore his Power and Wisdom, wherever the duties of the apostleship have to be discharged and its sorrows have to be endured. The day has not come for this Epistle to be fully understood and appreciated. Science has many years of apprenticeship to serve before it can reach the plane of thought on which St. Paul stood. And our Christian thinkers have much to learn before culture and piety can open to them the hidden treasures of this Epistle. As true Biblical criticism advances, the profundity of this letter to the Corinthians grows more apparent, and we feel in our day, as was never felt, before the amazing compass of its power. Here are ideas which wait on time and have given as yet scarcely more than a fragment of themselves to our foremost scholars. Here are latent inspirations that will one day astound the world. Nothing that he wrote has a better-grounded assurance of a great future, and when that future shall come, the world will have a far juster sense of its indebtedness to St. Paul as a grand teacher.—L.

Vers. 1—4.—*Church gifts.* There are few interests in human life which can be separated from the consideration of money. Money is the first necessity of governments, and it is the sinews of war. In business, in professional life, in industrial pursuits, pecuniary considerations are prominent, perhaps paramount. It is no otherwise in religion; and, however some superfine Christians may object to associating anything so base as money with what is the loftiest of human interests, no way has been found of excluding money matters from the Church of Christ. Indeed, as Christianity claims to affect and to control all that is human, there seems no possibility of excluding anything so important as money from its range.

I. THE PURPOSES TO WHICH CHURCH GIFTS SHOULD BE DEVOTED. The contributions gathered in Achaia, Macedonia, and other places, at the instance of the apostle, were for the poor Christians of Jewish race at Jerusalem. There is no reason to suppose that all the methods and practices of the primitive Churches were unexceptionable. We have to deal with aims, with impulses and principles, not with details of method and administration. And we cannot question that the relief of the poor, and especially of the Christian poor, is a lawful and becoming means of displaying practical brotherly love. Wisdom, discrimination, ought indeed to be exercised, but for the direction and not for the extinction of liberality.

II. THE METHOD IN WHICH CHURCH CONTRIBUTIONS SHOULD BE MADE. From this passage, containing principles of apostolic authority, we learn that such setting apart of our substance to benevolent and ecclesiastical purposes should be: 1. Periodical. Some have, indeed, held that the words of the apostle especially sanction the devotion of money as an observance peculiarly appropriate to the Lord's day. In any case, regularity is enjoined. 2. In proportion to means. There is both common sense and Christian feeling in the apostle's direction as to the measure of liberality. The poor man gives of his poverty, and the rich man of his wealth; whatever is consecrated being regarded as an acknowledgment that all is from God. 3. In preparation and accumulation. To avoid a sudden levy or collection upon the apostle's arrival, he recommends that each shall lay by him in store, so that the product may be ready to hand when the day comes that it is wanted.

III. THE WAY IN WHICH CHURCH GIFTS SHOULD BE APPROPRIATED AND ADMINISTERED. Paul showed his wonted wisdom in the arrangements he suggested. 1. Personal ministration should be employed. Everything, especially everything connected with money, should be open and above-board. The givers choose the bearers of the gift. 2. The manner of apportionment should be altogether above any possibility of suspicion. Of such precautions Paul has set us an admirable and excellent example.—T.

Ver. 9.—*The open door and many adversaries.* Ephesus evidently had, as a scene of labour, many attractions for the ardent and fearless spirit of the Apostle Paul. Its vast population, its devotion to idolatry, the excitability of its inhabitants, all rendered it a congenial field for such a worker. And the opposition he encountered and the danger he braved, it is plain from the narrative, made him feel the city all the more to be an honourable and attractive post for a bold and faithful soldier of Jesus Christ.

I. THE OPPORTUNITY OF SERVICE FOR CHRIST REPRESENTED IN THIS FIGURATIVE LANGUAGE. A door offers the means of admittance to a house, and an open door invites approach and entrance. In Scripture a door is often used to express the opportunity to do God's will and advance his cause. So here, the apostle represents by this figurative language the summons which Providence addressed to him to evangelize this great city of Asia Minor. The citizens and visitors were numerous, the idolatry and vice which prevailed were flagrant, human sorrows and difficulties and temptations abounded; so that there was abundant room for evangelistic and pastoral labour. Further, there seems to have been in some quarters a remarkable and gratifying readiness to hear the gospel of Christ.

II. THE HINDRANCES TO SERVICE FOR CHRIST HERE ALLUDED TO. 1. Observe from what quarters it came. The narrative in the Book of the Acts makes it evident that opposition to Christian preaching arose from both Jews and Gentiles. On different grounds sinful men oppose the truth. It always has been so. It was so in the time of our Lord, and the disciple, the servant, must not expect or desire to be above his

Master. 2. Observe what forms it took. Slander and secret misrepresentation was one way in which adversaries sought to hinder the truth. And another was open hostility and violence. This we know to have been put in motion at Ephesus against the apostle. The ignorant and impassioned mob was stirred up to oppose the work of Paul; in this sense, at all events, he fought with beasts at Ephesus.

III. THE COMPATIBILITY OF GREAT OPPORTUNITIES AND MANY ADVERSARIES. It is certainly a paradoxical statement. Yet reflection will show that there is no real inconsistency. 1. Hindrances, calumnies, serve to draw attention to any cause, and the gospel is sure to profit by anything which leads men to inquire into it. 2. These obstacles serve to test the quality of the labourers, and to bring out courage and resolution and patience where such qualities are required. 3. They always answer a valuable purpose in testing the sincerity of the converts. Times of persecution are times of testing.

IV. THE ATTRACTION THIS COMBINATION HAD FOR THE APOSTLE. 1. It called forth and employed his many and remarkable powers. 2. It enabled him to realize his fellowship with his Master. 3. It promised great results of spiritual good.

APPLICATION. 1. Enter in, Christian labourers, at every open door! 2. Be fearless of adversaries!—T.

Ver. 13.—*The word of command to Christian soldiers.* Now and again we meet with passages in the New Testament which remind us that Christianity does not lose sight of the sterner virtues. Certainly our religion has brought the softer and more amiable virtues into honour and prominence; but we should make a mistake did we suppose that for the severer excellences of character it finds no place.

I. THE CHRISTIAN LIFE IS A SCENE OF WARFARE. It is an opportunity for bearing witness to the grace of God, an opportunity for faithful and diligent service. But this is not all. Who can, in any station of life, sincerely endeavour to live as a Christian, without finding out that life is a campaign, a scene of discipline, of conflict? Surely the language of the New Testament in which we are addressed as soldiers of the cross, is not mere poetry, the utterance of imagination!

II. THE FOES WHOM THE CHRISTIAN IS CALLED TO ENCOUNTER ARE SPIRITUAL. As the apostle expresses it elsewhere, "We wrestle not with flesh and blood, but with principalities and powers," etc. Whether at Corinth or at Ephesus, or in modern London, or far away beyond the seas, he who is bent upon doing the will of God must needs make up his mind to face the adversary. Many are the forms assumed by the foe of souls, many his devices, great his craft and power. In his temptation, our Divine Lord and Leader, the Captain of our salvation, himself faced the enemy, and withstood his repeated and various assaults.

III. OUR POSITION OF DANGER CALLS FOR THE EXERCISE OF THE SOLDIER-LIKE VIRTUES OF COURAGE AND ENDURANCE. 1. *Watchfulness;* lest the soldier be surprised at his post, and fall a victim to his foe. What stress our Lord and his apostles have laid upon this attitude of vigilance! If we know ourselves, our weakness, our liability to sin; if we know the resources of our enemies—we shall feel the necessity of watching, lest we enter into temptation. 2. *Steadfastness* in the faith; lest we be tossed to and fro by our indecision and vacillation. Persecution and prosperity are alike in this, that they expose us to this danger. 3. *Manliness* is, no doubt, in contrast to the spirit of effeminacy and sloth. "Quit you like men!" is the ringing battle-cry of one whose own life illustrated the precept. 4. *Strength* is needed in such a combat, in which only the weapons of warfare which are not carnal are mighty through God to the pulling down of the strongholds.

IV. DIVINE GRACE ALONE CAN EQUIP AND UPHOLD THE SOLDIERS IN THIS HOLY WAR. This great truth is always, when not expressed, in the background, when admonitions to vigilance and courage are addressed to Christians. It is not to be supposed that in our own strength we can comply with requirements so stringent and conduct a warfare so perilous. But "if God be for us, who can be against us?" The warfare is not ours, but God's, and his are the weapons and his the might, even as his is the glory of the victory.—T.

Ver. 14.—*Love a principle of action.* We may regard love as a sentiment. It is such; and yet its place in the economy of human nature and life is not fully described when thus much is said. For it is one of the most powerful practical principles of our being. Human love can effect great things. And Divine love is the motive which God himself has appointed for the renewal and salvation of our humanity. And this same emotion becomes in Christian society an elevating, purifying, regulating, and transforming power. It is thus that it is regarded in the text.

I. THE MODEL OF THE LIFE OF LOVE IS TO BE FOUND IN THE LIFE OF CHRIST. Who that reads the incomparable story of our Lord's earthly ministry can be insensible to this fact, which distinguishes that ministry from, and raises it above, every other life and work this world has witnessed? Love gleamed from his countenance, spoke in his tones, flowed from his presence, wrought by his hands. And love led him to his cross.

II. THE AUTHORITY FOR THE LIFE OF LOVE IS TO BE FOUND IN THE WORDS OF CHRIST. Again and again did the Saviour enjoin upon his disciples the virtue of brotherly love. It was his new commandment. It was his test of discipleship. Love to God and love to man constituted, according to him, the sum of obedience, righteousness, religion.

III. THE UNIVERSAL APPLICATION OF THIS PRINCIPLE. It is too common to regard Christian charity as a grace to be displayed in certain relations and upon certain occasions. But this is not the New Testament idea. Love is to govern the whole life, and is to permeate the Christian society. There is no limitation in the language of the text: "Let all that ye do be done in love!" It is a lofty motive, a far-reaching principle. The precept is doubtless one not easy of application so general. Yet nothing less than its universal adoption and prevalence can satisfy the Lord of the kingdom.

IV. THE ADVANTAGES ACCRUING TO THE CHURCH FROM THE ADOPTION OF THIS PRINCIPLE. How different is the selfish principle adopted by the unchristian world, is at once apparent. This is a new, an antagonistic principle, yet, in its proper influence, the principle which is to pacify strife, to harmonize conflicting interests, to breathe new life into human society. "All ye are brethren" was the Master's explicit declaration concerning the members of his Church. "See how these Christians love one another!" was the exclamation of a surprised and admiring world.

V. THE IMPRESSION PRODUCED UPON THE WORLD BY THE PRACTICAL EMBODIMENT OF THIS PRINCIPLE. The world is doubtless impressed by the novelty, the beauty, the celestial dignity, of Christian doctrine. Yet the expression of that doctrine in the life of brotherly love is more effective; and the realization of Christ's idea, the fulfilment of Christ's law, will do more than all preaching to convince the world of the Divine mission of the Christ.—T.

Vers. 15, 16.—*Service and honour.* As the family that had first in Achaia received the gospel, Stephanas and his household were regarded by the apostle with peculiar interest and affection. The manner in which they are introduced in this passage is highly instructive and suggestive.

I. THE VOCATION TO SPIRITUAL MINISTRY. 1. Its first condition is sincere personal adhesion to Christianity. Stephanas and his household were converted, baptized, and well instructed in the Christian faith. It was when they had become penetrated with the Spirit of Christ that they were impelled to holy and devoted service. We cannot expect men and women to become unselfish labourers for the welfare of their fellow-men, until they have come under the new and Divine motive and power. 2. Christian ministries are of many and very various kinds. These vary with the capacity and opportunity of the labourers, and the necessities of those whose welfare is sought. Too limited a view of ministry is frequently taken; the fact is, that whatever service men render to their fellow-men, for the sake of Christ, is a Christian ministry. Not only the preaching of the gospel, but the instruction of the young, the nursing and healing of the sick, the showing of kindness and hospitality, the supporting with generosity of benevolent undertakings, all fall into this class. 3. Services of such kinds involve both labour and co-operation. His people find a pleasure in offering to Christ, their Lord, that which costs them something. And they delight to help one another; some leading and others following, but all setting before them the same end, and toiling in the same spirit. 4. Ministering "unto the saints" is an especial form of acceptable service. From the beginning Churches have cared for their widows, and for their poor and aged members. The household of faith has a peculiar claim upon the sympathy and affection and liberal support of the Saviour's friends.

II. THE HONOUR AND SUBJECTION DUE TO THOSE ENGAGED IN SPIRITUAL MINISTRY. 1. They should be treated with especial regard and gratitude. Paul himself honoured the good Stephanas and his like-minded wife and household, and he reminded the Corinthians that a family among themselves so distinguished in the annals of the Church, and so dear to the apostle's heart, should be esteemed highly in love for their work's sake. 2. They had a claim upon such as were in a position to render them help in the good cause. Doubtless it was the case at Corinth, as elsewhere, that the burden was too readily left upon the shoulders of those disposed to bear it. But this ought not to be. "When one man is seen working hard for Christ, his neighbour should put to himself the question, "Can I help my brother, relieve him of some pressure, or render his labour more effective?" 3. Submission is, in many cases, a duty in Christian Churches. There are those whom we should be ready not only to work *with* but to work *under*.—T.

Ver. 18.—*Spiritual refreshment.* The three honoured members of the Christian society at Corinth who came to Ephesus, came officially as a deputation to consult the inspired apostle upon matters of faith and practice. But their visit was not simply official; for all three were personally attached to Paul, and their sentiments of affection were reciprocated by the fervent nature of the apostle of the Gentiles, whose largeness of heart was even more conspicuous than his keenness of intellect. The grateful language in which Paul acknowledges the benefit he had received from intercourse with his visitors, is suggestive of thought regarding the refreshment of spirit which is one happy result of Christian associations.

I. THE NEED ALL SOMETIMES FEEL OF SPIRITUAL REFRESHMENT. 1. Work may be burdensome, and even oppressive, and may weigh down the soul as well as the body. 2. Trials, desertion of friends, disappointment in fellow-labourers, etc., may distress the soul and dispose to melancholy. 3. Living much alone and in one's own occupations is wearisome to the spirit; the energies flag; the quality of work suffers; gloom takes possession of the life. These and many other causes render it most desirable that the thirsting, fainting spirit should be reanimated by some suitable influences.

II. THE APPOINTED AGENTS OF SPIRITUAL REFRESHMENT. Letters and books are precious, but in the case before us they are inadequate. Living companionship, the society of those like-minded with ourselves, alone can meet the requirements of the case. Not only so; sympathizing friends have a peculiar power of restoring the equilibrium of the soul. Sympathy was what Paul sought and valued. It is hard to do even work for Christ without the smile and word of encouragement which our brethren in the Lord are able to give us.

III. THE MEANS OF SPIRITUAL REFRESHMENT. The presence of Christian friends is much; but their conversation, the opening of their hearts, the inquiry concerning our labours, successes, and failures,—these are all much to be desired. Not only the communication of knowledge and advice from our superiors, but the friendly conversation of our equals, and even the sympathy and heart-revelation of those in some respects beneath us, may prove truly recruiting to our energies and restorative to our spirits.

IV. THE RESULTS OF SPIRITUAL REFRESHMENT. 1. Depression gives place to cheerfulness. 2. Weariness gives place to vigour. 3. Sluggishness gives place to vivacity. 4. Despondency gives place to hope. 5. Inefficiency gives place to successful labour. 6. Doubt gives place to living confidence. In all is seen the operation of that Spirit of grace who does not disdain to work in and through the lowliest of Christ's sincere disciples and friends.—T.

Vers. 19, 20.—*Christian greetings.* In St. Paul's Epistles personal messages occur in juxtaposition with doctrinal statements and arguments and moral counsels. Their occurrence makes us feel the true humanity of this method of religious communication;

we gain an insight into the heart, not of the apostle alone, but of his fellow-labourers and friends. And we cannot but admire the evident power of Christianity to hallow and ennoble, to refine and bless, the relations subsisting among friends.

I. FROM WHOM, AND TO WHOM, ARE THESE GREETINGS? 1. Individuals are named. Of Aquila and Priscilla we know that they were regarded by Paul as his dear friends and trusty fellow-labourers. Wherever they went they carried the gospel, they formed a circle of Christian friends, they provided a home for workers and a gathering-place for worshippers. 2. Households join in the greetings. This is evidently the case, whether we regard the expression "Church in the house," as applying to the Christian family and their dependents and guests, or to a party wont to assemble in a certain house for mutual edification and common worship. 3. Churches send salutations. The Christian congregations of Asia Minor were linked together in bonds of mutual confidence and affection, and expressed their feelings by the medium of the apostolical letter. This practice authorizes communications between Churches and groups of Churches, as promotive of brotherly love.

II. OF WHAT KIND? 1. They are fraternal. In the salutation those who send the messages are termed brethren. Not as fellow-professors of one faith, but as members of one family, did these primitive Christians exchange their greetings and good wishes and prayers. 2. Cordial and affectionate. Salutations are often matters of form, and are then cold and all but meaningless. The holy kiss, which was the custom in those primitive communities, was a sign of the warmth and sincerity of the good feeling which prevailed. 3. Mutual; for they were admonished to greet one another. "All ye," Christ had said, "are brethren;" and we see how true an attempt was made to comply with his commands, and to realize his descriptions.

III. UPON WHAT BASIS? Not upon the basis of mere courtesy, or of common interests or expediency, but upon a specially Christian basis; the greeting was "in the Lord." By this we must understand: 1. In fulfilment of the Lord's command, who had so often and emphatically enjoined the cherishing and manifestation of brotherly love. 2. In imitation of the Lord's conduct, who himself, in all his communications with his friends, had been wont to display that love which he desired to witness among his followers. 3. Under the influence of his Spirit, whose presence and gracious operations make themselves felt by the diffusion of courtesy, good will, and kindness.—T.

Ver. 22.—*The absence of love to Christ.* There are those who, not having known Christ, have had no opportunity of loving him. But of all who have heard and read of Christ, we may say that the one test of their character and their position lies in their feeling with regard to him, with all which that feeling involves. The apostle's warm heart could tolerate no indifference, no neutrality, here. The Lord Jesus must be not only respected, but loved. And not to love him proves that the nature is insensible to all that is good and Divine—involves its own condemnation and curse and misery.

I. THE ABSENCE OF LOVE TO CHRIST. Where there is no love to the Lord Jesus there appears to be: 1. A want of appreciation of his perfect moral character. If Jesus be known by a holy and sympathetic nature, he will appear to such a nature "the chief among ten thousand, the altogether lovely." Who can gaze upon the sinless and pure, the just and kind, the meek and patient Jesus, and be unaffected by the spectacle? Only those for whom moral excellence and beauty have no charms. 2. A deep sensibility to his infinite compassion. For it must be borne in mind that the Saviour's disposition and ministry, and especially his sacrifice, have a personal relation to ourselves. It was for us men and our salvation that he lived a life of poverty and contempt, that he deigned to die a death of agony and shame. To withhold the heart's best love from One who endured the cross for us argues a callousness of nature beneath the level of common humanity. 3. A base ingratitude for all he has done and is doing on our behalf. Even those who are indifferent to the Lord Jesus owe him a vast debt for the benefits which, by his mediation, he has conferred upon the human race, and for the forbearance with which they have individually been treated. If ingratitude to earthly friends and benefactors be base, how shall the heinousness be described of ingratitude to the Son of man?

II. THE CURSE AND CONDEMNATION INVOLVED IN INDIFFERENCE TOWARDS CHRIST. 1. We can trace this in the moral degradation which such insensibility occasions. Not to love the worthiest and the best is to debase our nature. Character is largely moulded by love; and they who turn away from the love of Immanuel choose death. 2. The condemnation of concience is inevitable. Its voice may be stifled for a season, but it will be heard, and that voice must needs utter a censure of no feeble or ambiguous kind. The judge is within, and cannot be escaped; that judge will charge the sinner with hating him who was and is supremely worthy to be loved, and the accusation is self-evidencing and brings its curse. 3. The judgment of the Lord may tarry, but it will surely come. The Lord himself is at hand, to deliver those who love him, but to execute a righteous sentence upon the unbelieving, the unloving, the unspiritual.—T.

Vers. 1—4.—*Concerning the collection.* I. THE NECESSITY OF GIVING. 1. *For maintenance of public worship in our own community.* Churches should aim at self-support. Assuredly there should be no unwillingness to give where we ourselves reap the advantage. And often the return, being spiritual, infinitely exceeds all that we part with. 2. *For various works which have for their object the dissemination of the truth or the relief of the needy.* Gospel at home is good, but we must see that the gospel is sent abroad. There are many societies aiming to reach the heathen in this land and in other lands; ready support should be rendered. " Go ye into all the world," etc. (Matt. xxviii. 19). Relief of the destitute is a bounden duty of the Christian. Here we have a beautiful example. The apostle is no doubt referring to the distressed believers in Jerusalem and Judæa (Rom. xv. 26). The largely Gentile Church is incited to aid the largely Jewish. This will form a new bond, and do the double work of relieving suffering and breaking down prejudice. Our charity should know no limits but the limits of need and ability. 3. *For givers individually.* Christians who do not give do not grow. The cultivation of charity is the cultivation, not of one grace, but of many. It is usual to plead the needs of others; *our personal need of giving is a strong argument.* Parting with some ballast prospers our voyage, and, instead of imperilling our safety, increases it. Right giving is great gaining. We cannot be like Christ unless we give. He " gave *himself* for us." 4. *For the Church.* That Church which is not a giving Church will not be a prospering Church. A spirit of charity in a religious community exercises a gracious influence upon everything that that community attempts, and is ever prompting fresh efforts. Church charity should be wide. There is such a thing as Church selfishness. A Church may bestow too much thought upon itself. High shutting-in walls are not good for gardens. 5. *For the glory of God.* Giving manifests the power of the Christian faith. It is a very powerful testimony in the eyes of the world. The world is apt to scoff at profession, even at worship; but this practical outcome often startles, and has sometimes staggered, the world. It is a great instrument of conversion. Moreover, every gift should be a direct offering to God. We must see in the hand of the needy the treasury of the Lord. The Master often sits over against that treasury. II. THE APOSTOLIC SUGGESTIONS. 1. *Setting apart each week.* This is very convenient for many. It also ensures *frequent* and *regular* giving. Further, and what is of far more importance than is generally thought, *it facilitates our knowing how much we give.* Those who do not know how much they give *think they give three times as much as they really do.* Perhaps the most certain way to increase our giving would be to keep a strict account of how little we give! Setting apart each week would provide us with a store from which we could draw as necessity arose. We are ready for the collection in the sanctuary when we have first made the collection in the home. 2. *On the first day of the week.* How appropriate a time! Associated with so many hallowed memories, and pre-eminently with the completion by his resurrection of *Christ's great gift to us.* His charity should be the inspirer of ours. A beautiful act for a holy day. How could we refuse to give *then*, or how could we give *grudgingly* ? 3. *The amount of gift to be determined by the measure of prosperity. All gifts are not expected to be of the same value.* " She hath done what she could " was the Master's gracious expression of approval. Note: Our prosperity is of God. *He gives that we may give.* If we take all to ourselves, we are robbers, not Christians.

And in so far as we do not give what we know he would have us to, we are *defrauders* of God. He *trusts* us with so much: let us see that we do not abuse the trust. Stewards are we, not proprietors. Christ's commendation of the widow's two mites is abused by some well-to-do folks; they always aim to give that amount. Alas! when the chill of adversity comes to many men it kills at once all offerings to the Lord— retrenchment " begins at the house of God "—and when prosperity comes they give but the old sum, which in the altered circumstances is a beggarly and disgraceful offering. 4. *All to give. All have received.* The widow gave " all her living." None are too poor to give something. Every Christian should be a giving Christian; it is a part of his Christianity. The gift of a Church is specially valuable when it is a gift of all its members. And right giving is such a joy, that when the most destitute part with something for Christ's sake they do not lose *now*, but gain. When we give we get. 5. *Giving is to be voluntary.* It is to be *giving.* The apostle does not propose to make an assessment. The matter is left between the individual and his God. Giving is valuable only as it springs from the heart. Where compulsion (and there are many sorts) begins, there charity ends. The beauty of Christ's offering was that it was voluntary. No man took his life from him; he laid it down of himself. III. Gifts should be carefully administered. Charity is greatly checked if suspicion arises that gifts do not reach their intended destination. The apostle uses great care here. He arranges that those who give should elect custodians of their gifts, who might bear the offering to Judæa. The loose way in which some Churches manage their finances tends to lessen liberality. *A Church should keep its accounts more carefully than a bank!* The administration of a Church's gifts is no mean work. The apostle offers to take part in it, if this shall seem well. Not alone—lest some should take opportunity to slander: ministers cannot be too careful in money matters. But with others he is willing even to journey to Jerusalem.—H.

Vers. 5—9.—*Words to those who travel.* I. We should always be on our Master's business. This we may be if we are engaged in " secular " affairs. Every part of life is to be consecrated to God. A Christian is *a Christian always, and a servant* always. Everything *may be* consecrated. Whether we eat or drink, or whatever we do, we may do all to the glory of God. Secular engagements become truly sacred if in them (1) we act justly; (2) seek to please God; (3) avoid injury to our fellows; (4) endeavour to display a Christian spirit. To do this as we travel, we should (1) preserve a prayerful frame of mind; (2) watch vigilantly for temptations. These are often very numerous and strong when we are away from our usual surroundings, and not amongst those who know us. We should embrace every opportunity of doing good. Not only to men in things temporal, but also in things spiritual. At last it will seem marvellous to some that their " charity " and " love " extended only to men's lower needs. II. Our movements should be ordered of the Lord. 1. *In secular affairs we should seek the mind of the Lord.* He who can help us in the great can help us in the small. There is nothing too insignificant to pray over. 2. *In sacred affairs we need ever say, " If the Lord permit." " D.V."* on a bill amounts to little; we need it engraved on the heart. 3. *Those who, evangelizing, pass from place to place will do well to study the conduct of their apostolic prototype.* (1) He did not think a difficult post meant a post to be abandoned as speedily as possible. Some are all for running away. They are ever " seeking rest," but they are ever " finding none." There is no " rest " out of the path of duty. (2) He was not overwhelmed by a little opposition, nor by much. Many adversaries being there was a reason why he should be there. Where the enemy is strongest, there the loyal soldiery should be strongest. (3) He read in an open door the mind of the Lord directing him to remain. He did not read this in (a) comfort, (b) applause, (c) remuneration, (d) predilection. Some communities have attempted to stereotype the mind of the Lord in a three years' pastorate; this looks more like the mind of man than the mind of the Lord. Some divines can only hear *certain* " calls ' of the Lord; it is to be feared that these " calls " are, after all, nothing more than the echoes of their own voices.—H.

Vers. 13, 14.—*A fivefold exhortation.* This the Corinthians needed. It fitly comes near the conclusion of the Epistle, summarizing much that has gone before. The

Corinthians tended towards false security, reliance upon gifts and teachers; so the apostle says, "Watch ye." They were wavering in adhesion to the gospel which Paul preached; so he says, "Stand fast in the faith." They were but "babes" (ch. iii. 1); so the apostle incites them to seek more of the qualities of manhood: "Quit you like men." They were enfeebled by false doctrine, Church abuses, irregularity of spiritual life; so he says, "Be strong." They were more remarkable for jealousy, rivalry, contempt, pride, than for the pre-eminent Christian grace; so Paul says, "Let all that ye do be done in love." Corinthian perils are our perils. Corinthian failures may be our failures—perhaps are. Let us heed the apostolic exhortation to—

I. WATCHFULNESS. 1. *Against dangers from without.* False teachers, bad examples, unholy influences, Satanic attacks. We who are of the day should be awake. 2. *Against danger from within.* We often tempt ourselves, often deceive ourselves, often injure ourselves. Our greatest enemy is within, not without. It is the traitor in the camp who does the mischief. 3. *For opportunities of usefulness.* Our day is short. Soon the final account must be rendered. We have many opportunities, but they never wait for us. We must watch for them, and catch them as they come. Opportunities have no resurrection. 4. *For the coming of Christ.* The Master himself enjoined this: "What I say unto you I say unto all, Watch" (Mark xiii. 37).

II. STEADFASTNESS. We have *to abide in* the faith. He that "endureth to the end" shall be saved. Lack of steadfastness (1) hinders our spiritual growth; (2) mars our usefulness; (3) imperils our salvation; (4) is a stumbling-block to others; (5) a great offence to Christ; (6) spoils our spiritual joys.

III. MANLINESS. Christians should be robust. They are not always to be children in the faith. They need a manly temper, (1) to contend with difficulties; (2) to bear up under opposition; (3) to endure temporary defeat. Christians should be bold and fearless. Every Christian should be a courageous Christian. The service in which we are engaged is grand beyond conception—the issues how momentous! "Quit you like men!"

IV. STRENGTH. Does it seem strange that we are *commanded* to be strong? Some will say we can only be what we are, and it is worse than futile to say to a weak man, "Be strong." But Paul said, "When I am weak then am I strong." When we are bidden to be strong, then we often feel most our weakness; but *then* we go to the Strong for strength. The Lion of the tribe of Judah can give to us a lionlike might. As to means: if we would be strong we must (1) abound in prayer (2) and in work —using all the strength we have; (3) avoid evil influences—not be more than duty calls us in pestilential worldly atmospheres; (4) seek solid knowledge of things Divine; (5) strive against sin.

V. LOVE. Love should rule *all* our *thoughts, purposes, words,* and *acts.* We are nothing if we are without love (ch. xiii.). This is the key to the preceding exhortations. If we have a real living love towards God and man, it will become easy to live in watchfulness; we shall not want to relinquish our faith; our Christian manliness will rapidly develop; and we shall be strong, for we shall be *like God.* "God is love." Love is salt; it will preserve from corruption our whole spiritual life.—H.

Ver. 15.—*Ministering to the saints.* I. A VERY NEEDFUL WORK. Many of God's children are poor children. The saints who presently shall inherit all things, at present often lack the necessaries of life. Not a few of God's choicest servants are afflicted, and need sympathy and aid. Persecution for the faith should be counteracted as far as possible by careful ministration. In early days imprisoned saints were specially cared for by those at liberty. "Remember those who are in bonds." In modern forms of persecution aid is equally needful. Many need to be "taken by the hand." "As we have therefore opportunity, let us do good unto all men, especially unto them who are of the household of faith" (Gal. vi. 10).

II. A VERY HONOURABLE AND BEAUTIFUL WORK. Angel-like: they are "ministering spirits, sent forth to minister for them who shall be heirs of salvation" (Heb. i. 14). Christ-like: "The Son of man came not to be ministered unto, but to minister" (Matt. xx. 28). At last the Lord will say, "Inasmuch as ye have done it unto one of the least of these my brethren, ye have done it unto me" (Matt. xxv. 40). Many do not rightly estimate this " high calling." True love for the brethren (a sign of our salvation, 1 John iii. 14) will make us diligent in this service.

III. A WORK WHICH CAN BE EXERCISED IN MANY WAYS. Thus suited to the abilities and opportunities of a large number. Many are idle in our Churches because they can find nothing to do. *Let them look in this direction.* Visiting the sick, condoling with the bereaved, relieving the destitute, cheering the depressed, securing rest for the over-worked, guiding the perplexed, encouraging despondent workers (ministers, sabbath-school teachers, etc.),—how many might find a suitable sphere in such holy ministries as these!

IV. A WORK WHICH MERITS RECOGNITION ON THE PART OF THE CHURCH. Those who engage actively in such service as this should be : 1. Highly esteemed. It is no slight service which they render. They do much to elevate the tone of the Church; much to preserve it in peace and content; much to stimulate its zeal. 2. Encouraged. The work is trying. Those who seek to encourage others often need very much encouragement themselves. 3. Aided. This is probably what the apostle means by " Submit yourselves unto such." " As they serve you, do you serve them." Above all, no obstacles should be put in their way.

V. A WORK VERY BENEFICIAL TO THOSE WHO ENGAGE IN IT. "They who water others shall themselves be watered." Here when we give we take. We grow rich by bestowing. Christians stagnate because they think of themselves. Saints take so much care of themselves that they become spiritual invalids. We may " sit under " our own ministry with great profit. A sure way of getting to heaven is resolving that some one else shall get there. Labours for others make us blind to our own troubles. If our ears are filled with the cries of the needy, we shall not be able to hear the croakings of sceptics or the evil prognostications of Satan. True ministering to the saints is truest ministry to ourselves.—H.

Ver. 22.—*Those who do not love Christ.* I. THERE ARE SUCH. Alas! how many! Not those who have never heard of him, but those who have heard much of him—those before whom the great revelation of Christ has been spread out. Not those who have been brought up under sceptical influences, but those who have been trained in Christian homes. How many of those to whom Christ has been made known as fully as he can be to any who have not received him, yet do not love him! This is (1) strange, (2) saddening, (3) explicable only upon belief in the extreme virulence of sin.

II. THE HEINOUSNESS OF THEIR SIN. Consider: 1. Christ is altogether lovely and lovable. There is nothing in him to check love, but everything to encourage it. 2. He has never done the slightest evil to any man. 3. He has relinquished heaven for men. 4. He has humbled himself to assume human nature for men. 5. He has lived for men. 6. He has died for men. 7. He is willing to redeem men from all things evil, and to ensure to them all things good. Not to love such a Being as this is the chief of crimes. No tale of guilt could be sterner. It is a fearful revelation of the " carnal heart," which is enmity against God and Christ, instead of love.

III. THEIR DOOM. They are " anathema "—accursed. Their crime merits completest condemnation. *If they can be guilty of this, they can be guilty of anything.* Their sentence is " everlasting destruction from the presence of the Lord ; " their home, with " the devil and his angels." Their *choice* is to be accursed. They choose the curse rather than the blessing which Christ waits to bestow. They choose the curse rather than the One who alone can deliver them from it. They are *now* accursed; their *present condition* is this condition, and their future condition will be this unless they " turn to the Lord."

IV. A SOLEMN QUESTION—DO WE LOVE CHRIST? 1. Not—Do we *admire* him? He is admired even by atheists. 2. Not—Do we abstain from hostility towards him? 3. Not—Do we take his name upon our lips, observe his day, meet with his people? 4. Not even—Do we work for him? 5. But—Has he touched our heart? Do we *love* him? Christ is the *great test* applied to human hearts. The issue reveals *condition, character, prospect.*—H.

Vers. 1, 2.—*The law of Christian giving.* It is interesting to note that one of the first and most natural expressions of the Christian spirit was a consideration of the needs of the poorer members of the Church, and a readiness to share what good things were possessed with them.   Of this spirit Barnabas is presented to us as offering the highest example (Acts iv. 36).   His thought and feeling in this matter had very probably influenced his companion St. Paul.   We can well understand that the Jewish Christians, dwelling in the holy city, would be placed under great disabilities.   Many of them were very poor; their opinions would prevent their obtaining the ordinary charities; perhaps they found it even difficult to secure remunerative labour; and, when times of famine and distress came, they would be the first to suffer.   When Christianity was proclaimed freely to the Gentiles, there was this grave danger to face; the separation between Jew and Gentile might be kept up within Christianity, and the conception of one Church—one flock under one Shepherd—might fail to be realized.   To correct this tendency, St. Paul sought to keep up the sympathy of the newer Gentile with the older Jewish Church, and guided the expression of such sympathy, letting it take the form of collections and money gifts. In the passage now before us the principles upon which Christian giving should be regulated are indicated.   They concern—

I. The claim of all to a share in Christian gifts.   Nothing that a man possesses is his own.   Money, talents, position, influence,—all are Divine gifts and trusts; none are sent for the man's sake alone who receives them.   He is only made an agent for ministering God's good gifts to others.   The whole Church has its claim to share in whatever good things any of its members possesses.   It should be impossible to find, among Christians, an unrelieved sufferer, or a helpless, poverty-stricken beggar. We must distinguish between charity and the meeting of the family claims of our brethren in the Lord.   It is not charity, it is duty, it is faithfulness, that leads us to share what is entrusted to us with those who share in the same salvation, and who have the same " good hope through grace."   We do not speak of charity among brothers and sisters of the same family, and the right view of Christian giving is taken only when the Christian Church is regarded as a family.

II. The need for preparation by previous storing.   The claims upon us only come at times, but they do come at times in forms quite beyond our meeting, if we have made no preparations.   And there is the further danger that when, through circumstances of distress, our feelings are unusually moved, we act from impulse, not from principle.   So St. Paul urges that the separation of shares for the needy brethren be made regularly, as a matter of duty; that a proportion of all our acquisitions be regularly set aside and stored up for due occasions, and that so we keep our brethren and their needs constantly in mind.

III. The time most suitable for such storing.   " First day of the week."   The Lord's day.   The memorial day of the Lord's resurrection; which, we cannot doubt, had become the Christian day for worship.   When minds were directed more especially to Christian privileges and duties, the separations and storings would be more liberally done, and would be made acts of worship.   It seems probable that the amounts thus regularly laid by were not stored privately, but made offerings at public worship, and stored by the treasurers.

IV. The rule that regulates the amount stored.   Many have argued for a tenth, but it was not in St. Paul's way to fix any limitations upon the free expression of Christian feeling.   He does not mean to suggest any proportion by his law, " As God hath prospered him."   Really he means, " Let your separation for others be according to your sense of God's goodness to you."   And this he suggests because, while the due provision for the poor is of grave importance, it is even more important that our storing and giving should be a means of grace to ourselves, an agency of spiritual culture.   Practically it is found that brotherly and generous regard for our needy fellow-Christians bears most directly on the efficiency of our own graces and the culture of the true Christian spirit.   " The liberal soul is made fat."—R. T.

Ver. 3.—*The relations of Gentile to Jewish Churches.*   Apart from the historical interest of this subject, which was one of the chief causes of anxiety to the apostle, it may be studied as illustrating for every age the principles on which older and younger Churches, richer and poorer Churches, can be brought into practical union and fellowship.   Then the topic for consideration becomes this—How can the idea of the

Christian brotherhood be applied to Churches? As introductory it may be well to show, concerning the duty of brotherliness, (1) its ground; (2) its character; (3) its examples; (4) its natural forms of expression. These may be treated in connection with the personal and individual relationships of life, and also in connection with the social and Church relationships. Then in practical detail, varying according to the sentiments and associations of the Christian bodies to which we may belong, we may consider—

I. BROTHERLINESS AS EXPRESSED TO EQUAL CHURCHES. In this case the brotherliness will take such forms as : 1. Fellowship in worship. 2. Mutual aid in enterprise and work. 3. Due watchfulness of each other's honour and spiritual health. 4. Anxious repression of all jealousies of each other's successes. 5. Manifestations of sympathy in times of Church depression or sorrow. Among equal Churches there is little opportunity for the charity of material help.

II. BROTHERLINESS EXPRESSED TO INFERIOR OR DEPENDENT CHURCHES. Besides those already dealt with, there should be these further expressions. 1. Careful conservation of the rights of the dependent Church. 2. Readiness to give material and moral help, as occasion demands. 3. Avoidance of superior airs or assumptions of authority. 4. Use of all opportunities that may be offered for the manifestation of sympathy. While it is true that times of calamity find special occasions for brotherliness, it is also true that those in any way dependent on us would not have us wait for the trial-times. True Christian brotherhood wants to find utterance for itself every day, and to fill all the ordinary associations of life with its helpful spirit.—R. T.

Ver. 9.—*The mission of our hindrances.* "There are many adversaries." In life we always find that the "open door" and the "many hinderers" go together. Very seldom can we have the one without the other. For the use of the term "door" as a figure for "opportunity," see Acts xiv. 27; 2 Cor. ii. 12; Col. iv. 3. For the narrative which illustrates the expression here used, see Acts xix. 19, 20. Of hindrances affecting St. Paul, we may think of (1) his own frail health; (2) the difficulties and dangers of travelling; (3) the wilfulness sometimes shown by his travelling companions; (4) the sudden and unexpected claims of the Churches altering his plans; (5) the persistent and watchful opposition of his Jewish enemies; and we may even add (6) the sometimes strange and trying limitations put by the guiding Spirit, as in Acts xvi. 6, 7. That which was so evidently true of St. Paul is the common experience of God's servants; and we must accept the conditions, and win virtue out of the very limitations.

I. GOD'S PROVIDENCE IS EVER MAKING OPEN DOORS FOR US. This is true in educational life, and in business life. Every man sooner or later gets his turn and opportunity. But we observe how true it is both of personal Christian life and of Church life. God sets before us open doors, shows us spheres of service which we may occupy. And such we enter upon with great hopes and expectations, assuming that if Providence has so manifestly opened the door, the path within *must* be straight and plain and easy. This we find is not always true; for—

II. GOD'S PROVIDENCE IS ALSO EVER MAKING HINDRANCES. 1. Often health fails at the moment of opportunity. 2. Sometimes the will to do it fades when the opportunity for doing appears. 3. Events as providential seem to block the path just inside the open door. 4. The work involves labour which seriously taxes energy and faith. 5. Too often we faint and fail, and prove the greatest hinderers of our work. We must fully accept the fact that, here on earth, God has put open doors and hindrances together, that the combination might nurture and develop the noblest qualities in his servants. —R. T.

Ver. 14.—*The limitation of the robuster virtues.* "Let all your things be done with charity." The connection in which this sentence stands suggests the topic. The apostle had been calling the Christians at Corinth to manliness, strong and vigorous action, watchfulness, and firm holding of the faith. He knew well how readily firmness could become stubbornness, and strength roughness. The strong may forget the rights of the weaker brethren, and the manly may fail to realize that full manliness which includes womanly tenderness and gentleness. Therefore, in an all-suggestive sentence, he says, " Temper the whole of your relations with charity, heavenly Divine charity," which "hopeth all things, endureth all things, and thinketh no evil." Chrysostom's note on these verses brings out a somewhat different association. It is as follows:— "Now in saying these things, he seems, indeed, to advise; but he is reprimanding them as indolent. Wherefore he saith, *Watch*, as though they slept; *stand*, as though they were rocking to and fro; *quit you like men*, as though they were playing the coward; *let all your things be done with charity*, as though they were in dissensions. And the first caution refers to the deceivers, viz. *watch, stand*; the next to those who plot against us, *quit you like men*; the third to those who make parties and endeavour to distract, *let all your things be done with charity*, which thing is the bond of perfectness, and the root and fountain of all blessings." In the teaching both of our Lord and of his apostles, the passive and gentle graces were so constantly commended that the enemies of Christianity might easily, and with some show of reason, say that it was a weak, unmanly thing, with yielding and patiently enduring and quietly waiting, as its chief and characteristic virtues. Therefore St. Paul makes so much of his point, that Christianity was the only force that could really and harmoniously culture the full manhood. Only this is true—the supreme grace of Christianity is *love, charity*, and it must tone and qualify and direct all other graces, all expressions of character in action. Consider—

I. THE TENDENCY OF HUMAN NATURE TO CORRUPT EVERYTHING. All the good things men may possess or attain are in constant peril of running over into extremes and exaggerations. Observe two points. 1. A man's strong side becomes inspired by self-will, and spoiled. 2. Some sides are unduly cultured by expression, and the whole character is put out of harmony and fair balance. Self-reliance, which has a small place in every good character, becomes corrupted into self-conceit; and so of other features of character.

II. HOW FAR IS THIS HUMAN-NATURE FORCE KEPT IN THE REGENERATE? It might seem that St. Paul's counsel only suited the worldly, and was hardly needed by the Christian. But we have to accept the fact, which both observation and experience attest, that the renewal of the principle on which our life is conducted does not involve an immediate deliverance from the ordinary deteriorating influences which affect men. Christian men's very graces may become so exaggerated as to be really vices. Strong-willed men may "love to have the pre-eminence," and be masterful and inconsiderate. The Christian life in a man ought to hold the evil tendency in strong bonds, but we cannot get free from the evil influence while we dwell in a body and are surrounded by earthly scenes.

III. HOW DOES THE CHRISTIAN SPIRIT AFFECT THIS EVIL? Apply especially to the robuster virtues. Manliness is liable to become masterfulness. Those who can watch come to despise the weak ones who must sleep. The strong try to force the frail to go at their pace, and easily quarrel with them when they cannot. Now, the Christian spirit proposes one effective triumph over all these evils. Tone all your life and relations with charity, which is, as treated in the New Testament, precisely *this*—consideration for *others* rather than *self*. All the evil comes out of thinking of and glorifying self, and the conquest surely comes by thinking of and glorifying others: getting the mind of Christ, who "pleased not himself."—R. T.

Ver. 15.—*The natural right of priority.* "The firstfruits of Achaia." We need not think of the household of Stephanas as being actually the first converts St. Paul made in the Peloponnesus, as apparently another person is spoken of in the same terms in Rom. xvi. 5: "Salute my well-beloved Epænetus, who is the firstfruits of Achaia unto Christ." The meaning need only be that the household of Stephanas was among those brought to Christ at St. Paul's *first* missionary visit. The apostle had an affectionate regard for his first converts in new spheres, as may be illustrated in the case of Lydia at Philippi. The interest we always feel in first things can be illustrated by way of introduction. 1. Firstborn children. 2. First forms of enterprise. 3. Firstfruits of our labour, etc. Natural feeling gives all first things prominence; and the Old Testament history and religion rested on the recognition of the rights of the firstborn and the interest of first things. They are the key to the life; the strong impress of the character. They are like the first proofs of an engraving; every line is sharply defined in them. They may become the reproach of our weaker after-doings, for they show what we did actually attain once, and prove that we could, through life, have done better. It is, however, the hope and promise of first things on which we now propose to dwell.

I. FIRST THINGS ARE DONE WITH INTENSE FEELING. Illustrate from the youth beginning business life; the man entering on a new undertaking; the missionary going forth to his new sphere, etc. Men brace themselves up to deal with new things. They have no experience to tell them what amount of strength the new work will demand, so they are likely to put too much into it. A vague but arousing wonder clings all about new things, and imagination makes them bigger and better than they are. At first we fail to estimate difficulties, qualifications, hindrances; we start out like Israel, and expect to reach our Canaan quickly: so all our hearts go out into our first things. And happily life is full of them, especially early life, and they exert a most gracious influence on us, for they again and again lift us out of ourselves and above ourselves.

II. FIRST THINGS HAVE A NATURAL PRE-EMINENCE. Of this the position and rights of the firstborn sons are but the illustration. First things are felt to have a representative character; they are the natural leaders of all that come after them—the specimens and examples of their sort. In all the spheres of life we give prominence to beginnings. When a servant comes to a new situation, the master or mistress watch the first actions to see "how they will frame." When a convert joins a Church, the pastor give prominence to the first forms in which Church responsibilities are met. Turning their thoughts back to their hopeful "first things," the apostle reproaches his converts thus: "Ye did run well; who did hinder you?"

III. FIRST THINGS HAVE PROMISE FOR THE FOLLOWING THINGS. As firstfruits have for harvest. The harvest need not be worse than the specimen firstfruits, but it may be much better. A man's first work need not be his *maximum* standard, but it ought to be his *minimum* standard. A first result may tell of *power*, and power always holds the promise of what culture can make it. Or, applying the point in relation to our text, one convert made in a new sphere of Christian labour holds the promise of a great ingathering; as we find at first one star in the darkening evening sky, which is the "glorious prospect of millions more."

IV. FIRST THINGS KEEP PROMINENT PLACE IN OUR MEMORY. Illustrate our first school; first steps in business life; first love; first communion; first convert to Christ by our influence; first sickness; first success in life, etc. The most treasured things in our memory are these first things of life; and, as such, their moral mission is (1) to aid us in the review of life, by fixing attention upon points; (2) to remind us that the spirit of energy in which we take things up is the spirit in which we should carry them through; and (3) to show us that we need the Divine help for "patient continuance in well-doing," as much as we remember we needed it for our anxious beginnings.—R. T.

Ver. 19.—*The Church in the house.* This expression is used concerning Aquila and Priscilla, who had been the apostle's friends at Corinth (Acts xviii. 1—3). A similar reference is found in Rom. xvi. 3—5; 2 Tim. iv. 19. At the time of St. Paul's writing this Epistle, Aquila and Priscilla were with the apostle at Ephesus, and it is probable that they opened their house or lodging as a place of worship for the Christian foreigners or strangers who happened to be visiting Ephesus. Some, however, think that St. Paul uses the term "Church" as equivalent to that of "family," or household, probably including servants, children, and workpeople connected with their business. The word "Church" appears to have been used with some variety of meaning, the associations of the term only gradually becoming settled into those with which we are familiar. The first suggestion of the word is a gathering or assembly. But this implied some purpose or design for which people met together. It might be a family object, or a political, or a social, or a religious object. Any assembly called for a purpose could be properly spoken of as a "Church." We know that it was applied to the political meetings of the Greeks; and it may also have been used for the synagogue meetings of the Jews, for these must be the "Church" to which our Lord referred, when he required his disciples to tell their disputes, or injuries from their fellows, to the "Church." We need to be on our guard against forcing words to bear their modern ecclesiastical meanings when we find them employed in the New Testament. The simple historical fact is that persons lent their rooms or their houses for the Christian congregations to worship in, and so the term "Church" is first used for the Christian friends who met for worship in any place. It subsequently became used for (1) the building in which the friends met; and (2) for the entire body of persons who thought alike and worshipped alike. The "Church" became the "body of Christ." In the treatment of this subject we only give suggestive lines along which thought and illustration may run, because the associations of different Christian bodies with the term "Church" now differ so greatly that detailed treatment would involve the introduction of disputable points.

I. THE SIMPLEST CONCEPTION OF A CHURCH. It is a meeting or assembly. As such it can only be applied to an organized body or to a material building by a figurative use of the term. No ideas of size, quantity, or number seem necessary to its realization. Two or three agreeing to meet for worship or work may properly be called a Church.

II. ITS CLOSE ASSOCIATION WITH A HOME. The "Church in the house" is here spoken of. It is interesting to note the historical fact that the Christian assemblies first sanctified homes. They did not need at first to find any architectural expression, or to fix architectural associations, or to use architectural aids. Home life found a sufficient sphere.

III. ITS FUNDAMENTAL FEATURES. Really only this—family religion extended to embrace the family friends. However the growth of the Church may have overshaded its first idea, we must admit that it began with family worship, and developed on the lines of household religious requirements, not presuming at first to affect either the synagogue or the temple demands. This family origin of the Christian Church needs to be more fully studied.

IV. THE LINES OF ITS PROBABLE DEVELOPMENT. These were fixed by (1) increase of numbers; (2) growth of wealth, bringing with it artistic sentiment and desires; (3) securing of freedom from persecution, and admission of citizen rights and liberties; (4) rise of a distinction between priesthood and laity, and the consequent development of a ritual in which the distinct priesthood could be employed. Impress in what sense the older idea of a "Church in the house" can even now be maintained.—R. T.

Ver. 22.—*The Christian anathema.* "Let him be Anathema Maran-atha." These words have no very evident connection. *Anathema* means "accursed." *Maran-atha* appears to mean, "The Lord is at hand." It can only be regarded as an exclamation. On it see the Expository portion of the Commentary. "*Anathema* is the Greek term representing the Hebrew *cherem,* or devoted to destruction, and indicates the excommunication practised in the Christian Church. The early Christians exercised discipline on offending members in lesser or greater forms. The greater is called *Anathema.* They regarded themselves as distinctly warranted in cutting off members from their body by our Lord's words (Matt. xviii. 17); and in using for such excision the term 'Anathema,' they appealed to Paul's employment of the word in Gal. i. 8. They regarded the anathema as cutting off a man from the way of salvation; so that unless he received the grace of repentance he would certainly perish. The word is uniformly used in the Septuagint Version as the equivalent of *cherem;* and it seems reasonable to suppose that where it occurs in the New Testament Scriptures it is to be understood in the deeper sense as relating to the spiritual condition, and not merely to exclusion from Church privileges." Modern anathematizing is chiefly illustrated by the acts of the Roman Catholic Church; the sentiment of modern life is unfavourable to the exercise of Church discipline in any of the Protestant communities.

I. THE PARTIES ST. PAUL ADDRESSED. The Church at Corinth; regarded as a company who made profession of love to Christ, and pledged themselves to live in accordance with Christ's will and example. Those who did *not* love Christ, or failed to realize the Christly spirit and purity, were not merely inconsistent—they were unfaithful and unworthy; they were even exerting a mischievous influence, as do dead flies in pots of ointment.

II. THE CONDITION IN WHICH SOME PROFESSED MEMBERS MIGHT BE FOUND. A condition involving *hypocrisy,* the sin against which our Lord spoke most severely. So impossible of rectifying and correcting, because so often connected with self-deception. Show how such a condition can be tested and discovered. The great test is the life, the practical conduct. The man who has lost the ruling motive of the "constraining love of Christ," will soon tone his conduct and relations with mere self-pleasing, and there will be first the pleasurable, then the questionable, and only too possibly these will lead on to the immoral, as in the case referred to at Corinth.

III. THE TREATMENT WHICH UNWORTHY MEMBERS SHOULD RECEIVE. Not excision, as a mere act of judgment; this man can have no right to do to his fellows. But excision as a matter of tender regard for the soul of the sinner; and as a discipline designed to effect his restoration. Final removal from Christian fellowship no Christian Church has power to arrange. Temporary removal may be the best and most hopeful means of arousing conscience and securing penitence. St. Paul gives minute directions in 2 Thess. iii. 14, 15, "Note that man, and have no company with him, that he may be ashamed. Yet count him not as an enemy, but admonish him as a brother" (see also 2 Cor. ii. 5—7).—R. T.

HOMILETICAL INDEX

TO

THE FIRST EPISTLE OF

PAUL THE APOSTLE TO THE CORINTHIANS

———◆◇◆———

II CORINTHIANS

EXPOSITION BY

F. W. FARRAR

HOMILETICS BY

DAVID THOMAS

HOMILIES BY VARIOUS AUTHORS

D. FRASER   J. R. THOMSON
C. LIPSCOMB   R. TUCK
            E. HURNDALL

THE SECOND EPISTLE OF
PAUL TO THE CORINTHIANS

INTRODUCTION

Very little is needed by way of introduction to the Second Epistle; for it is, in fact, a sequel to the First.

The apostle's departure from Ephesus had been precipitated by the tumult, in which, as appears from various scattered references, he had incurred extreme danger of his life. He went straight to Troas, still eager to preach the gospel of Christ. He had told Titus to meet him there; and it was the first place where he could hope to receive any tidings as to the reception by the Corinthians of his first letter—a point respecting which he was painfully anxious. But either St. Paul arrived at Troas earlier than the time appointed, or the journey of Titus had been delayed. St. Paul was preaching with success—"a door was opened for him in the Lord;" but the anxiety to which he found himself a prey rendered it impossible for him to continue his mission. Seeking some relief for the intolerable oppression of his spirit, he hurried to Macedonia, and there, perhaps in Philippi, he first met Titus. The meeting at once relieved the tension of his feelings, and caused an outburst of joy. For the tidings which Titus had to tell were good. He had been cordially received. The First Epistle had caused among the Corinthians an outburst of salutary grief, of yearning affection, of holy zeal. They had listened to the apostle's message with fear and trembling. The offender had been promptly and even severely dealt with. The news appeared at first to be so encouraging that St. Paul, with deep thankfulness, determined to send Titus, with "the brother whose praise is in the gospel," to finish the good work which he had begun, and to arrange about the collection for the poor saints at Jerusalem. And as, this time, Titus was not only ready but anxious to go, St. Paul began to dictate the letter of which Titus was to be the bearer.

But little by little the apostle learnt—what perhaps Titus, out of kindness and sympathy, might not have deemed it necessary at once to tell him—that there was another side to the picture. His change of plan about the double visit had given rise to a charge of levity, and many remarks most injurious to his character had been industriously disseminated, especially, it would seem, by some Jewish emissary. His opponents hinted at his cowardice in not coming; his vacillation and insincerity in changing his mind; the conscious inferiority which made him abstain from any claim to maintenance; the meanness of his aspect; the baldness and simplicity of his speech; the fact that he had no commendatory letters from Jerusalem; his dubious position as regards the Law. They insinuated doubts about his perfect honesty. They charged him with underhand guile, and fraudulent or self-interested designs with reference to the collection. They even ventured to hint their doubt as to his perfect sanity. Such charges would have been hard to endure at any time. They were so especially at a time when the apostle was suffering overwhelming distress—a combination of fears without and fightings within, which produced a mental and physical prostration. It became a duty and a necessity, however distasteful, to defend himself. Personally he neither required nor cared for any self-defence. But before God in Christ he felt bound to clear his character from these detestable innuendoes, because they were liable, if unnoticed, to hinder his work both in Corinth and in other Churches; and his work had on him a sacred claim. Hence, though nothing was more repellent to his sensitive humility than any semblance of egotism or boasting, he is driven by the unscrupulosity of his opponents to adopt such a tone of self-defence that the word "boasting" occurs in this Epistle no less than twenty-nine times. He neither could nor would appeal to any letters of commendation or to any certificate from his brother apostles, because he had received his own apostolate direct from God; and hence he is forced to appeal, on the one hand to his visions and revelations, and on the other hand to the seal of approval which in every way God had set to his unparalleled activity and devotion.

These circumstances sufficiently mark out the characteristics of the letter.

1. It entirely differs from the First Epistle. That is a letter in which he dealt with practical and speculative difficulties, answering the inquiries and correcting the abuses of a most unsatisfactory Church. The Second Epistle is the impassioned self-defence of a wounded spirit to erring and ungrateful children. It is the apostle's *Apologia pro vitâ suâ.*

2. Hence, as *hope* is the key-note of the Epistles to the Thessalonians, *joy* of that to the Philippians, *faith* of that to the Romans, *heavenly things* of that to the Ephesians, *affliction* is the one predominant word and thought in the Second Epistle to the Corinthians.

3. As Bengel says, "It reminds us of an itinerary, but interwoven with the noblest precepts." "The very stages of his journey," says Dean Stanley, "are impressed upon it—the troubles at Ephesus, the anxiety of Troas, the consolation of Macedonia, the prospect of moving to Corinth."

4. It is the least systematic, as the First Epistle is the most systematic, of all St. Paul's writings.

5. It is the most emotional, and therefore in some respects—in its style, expressions, and causal connections—the most difficult of St. Paul's Epistles. The labouring phraseology, the interchange of bitter irony with deep pathos, the manner in which he is haunted and possessed and mastered by word after word which seizes his imagination—now " tribulation," now " consolation," now " boasting," now " weakness," now " simplicity," now " manifestation "—only serve to throw into relief the frequent bursts of rushing and impassioned eloquence. The sorrow and tenderness displayed are a measure of the insolence and wrong which called out in the concluding chapters so stern an indignation.

6. At the end of the ninth chapter there is a sudden, startling, and complete break in the whole manner and tone of the Epistle. The remainder (ch. x. 1—xiii. 10) seems to be written in a mood so wholly different from that of the former, that some have even (though needlessly) supposed that it really was a separate Epistle. Vehement though suppressed indignation, scathing irony, strong denunciation, commanding authority, take the place of the pathetic tenderness and effusive thankfulness which are predominant in the previous chapters. This phenomenon of a tone suddenly changed is found in other writings both sacred and secular, and may be accounted for by circumstances under which the apostle wrote.

7. The analysis of the Epistle in minor details will be found in the notes. The main divisions are: ch. i.—vii., hortatory and personal, with an undercurrent of calm apology ; ch. viii., ix., directions and remarks about the collection; ch. x.—xiii., impassioned defence of himself and his apostolic position against the calumnies of his enemies.

THE SECOND EPISTLE OF
PAUL TO THE CORINTHIANS

EXPOSITION

CHAPTER I.

Address and greeting (vers. **1**, **2**). Thanksgiving for the comfort sent to him by God, wherein, as in his affliction which rendered it necessary, they sympathetically shared (vers. 3—11). He has earned a right to their sympathy by his sincerity (vers. 12—14). His change of purpose with respect to a visit to Corinth, with digression on the unchangeableness of the gospel (vers. 15—22). Explanation of his reasons (ver. 22—ch. ii. 4).

Ver. 1.—**By the will of God** (see 1 Cor. i. 1). In the face of Judaizing opponents, it was essential that he should vindicate his independent apostolate (Acts xxvi. 15—18). **And Timothy.** Timothy had been absent from St. Paul when he wrote the First Epistle, and Sosthenes had taken his place, whether as amanuensis or merely as a sort of joint authenticator. **Our brother**; literally, *the brother*, as in 1 Cor. i. 1. The brotherhood applies both to St. Paul and to the Corinthians; there was a special bond of brotherhood between all members of "the household of faith." **The saints.** Before the name "Christians" had come into general use, "saints" (Acts ix. 13) and "brethren" were common designations of those who were "faithful in Christ Jesus" (Eph. i. 1). **In all Achaia.** In its classical sense Achaia means only the northern strip of the Peloponnesus; as a Roman province the name included both Hellas and the Peloponnesus. Here St. Paul probably uses it in its narrower sense. The only *strictly* Achaian Church of which we know is Cenchrea, but doubtless there were little Christian communities along the coasts of the Corinthian gulf. To the Church at Athens St. Paul never directly alludes.

This letter was not in any sense an encyclical letter; but even if it were not read in other communities, the Corinthians would convey to them the apostle's greeting.

Ver. 2.—**Grace be to you and peace.** On this pregnant synthesis of the Greek and Hebrew greetings, see 1 Cor. i. 3; Rom. i. 7.

Ver. 3.—**Blessed be God** (Eph. i. 3). This outburst of thanksgiving was meant to repress the relief brought to the overcharged feelings of the apostle by the arrival of Titus, with news respecting the mixed, but on the whole good, effect produced at Corinth by the severe remarks of his first letter. It is characteristic of the intense and impetuous rush of emotion which we often notice in the letters of St. Paul, that he does not here state the special grounds for this impassioned thanksgiving; he only touches upon it for a moment in ch. ii. 13, and does not pause to state it fully until ch. vii. 5—16. It is further remarkable that in this Epistle almost alone he utters no thanksgiving for the moral growth and holiness of the Church to which he is writing. This may be due to the fact that there was still so much to blame; but it more probably arose from the tumult of feeling which throughout this letter disturbs the regular flow of his thoughts. The ordinary "thanksgiving" for his readers is practically, though indirectly, involved in the gratitude which he expresses to God for the sympathy and communion which exists between himself and the Church of Corinth. **Even the Father of our Lord Jesus Christ.** The Greek is the same as in Eph. i. 3, where, literally rendered, it is, "Blessed be the God and Father." The same phrase is found also in 1 Pet. i. 3; Col. i. 3. The meaning is not, "Blessed be the God of our Lord Jesus Christ, and the Father of our Lord Jesus Christ" (although the expression, "the God of our Lord Jesus Christ," occurs in

Eph. i. 17; comp. John xx. 17), but "Blessed be God, who is also the Father of our Lord Jesus Christ," and who is therefore "*our* Father" by adoption and redemption, as well as our God by creation. **The Father of mercies.** This corresponds to a Hebrew expression, and means that *compassionateness* is the most characteristic *attribute of* God, and *emanation from* him. He is the Source of all mercy ; and mercy

"Is an attribute of God himself."

He is "full of compassion, and gracious, long-suffering, and plenteous in mercy and truth" (Ps. lxxxvi. 15). "The Law," says the Talmud, "begins and ends with an act of mercy. At its commencement God clothes the naked ; at its close he buries the dead" ('Sotah,' f. 14, 1). Thus every chapter but one of the Korân is headed, "In the name of God the Compassionate, the Merciful ; " and it is an Eastern expression to say of one that has died that "he is taken to the mercy of the Merciful." Comp. "Father of glory," Eph. I. 17 ; 1 Cor. ii. 8 ("of spirits," Heb. xii. 9 ; "of lights," Jas. i. 17). The plural, "compassions," is perhaps a plural of excellence, "exceeding compassion" (Rom. xii. 1), and may be influenced by the Hebrew word *rachamim*, often literally rendered by St. Paul "bowels." The article in the Greek ("the Father of *the* compassions") *specializes* the mercy. **The God of all comfort.** So in ch. xiii. 11 God is called "the God of love and peace ; " Rom. xv. 5, "the God of patience and of comfort ; " ii. 15, "the God of hope." This word "comfort" (unfortunately interchanged with "consolation" in the Authorized Version) and the word "affliction" (varyingly rendered by "trouble" and "tribulation" in the Authorized Version), are the key-notes of this passage ; and to some extent of the whole Epistle. St. Paul is haunted as it were and possessed by them. "Comfort," as verb or substantive, occurs ten times in vers. 3—7 ; and "affliction" occurs four times in succession. It is characteristic of St. Paul's style to be thus dominated, as it were, by a single word (comp. notes on ch. iii. 2, 13 ; iv. 2 ; see note on ch. x. 8). The needless variations of the Authorized Version were well intentioned, but arose from a false notion of style, a deficient sense of the precision of special words, and an inadequate conception of the duties of faithful translation, which requires that we should as exactly as possible reflect the peculiarities of the original, and not attempt to improve upon them.

Ver. 4.—Who comforteth us. The "us" implies here, not only St. Paul and Timothy, but also the Corinthians, who are one with them in a bond of Christian unity which was hitherto undreamed of, and was a new phenomenon in the world. St. Paul always uses the first person in passages where he is speaking directly of individual feelings and experiences. In other passages he likes to lose himself, as it were, in the Christian community. The delicate play of emotion is often shown by the rapid interchanges of singular and plural (see vers. 13, 15, 17 ; ch. ii. 1, 11, 14, etc.). The present, "comforteth," expresses a continuous experience, with which the Christians of the first age were most happily familiar (John xiv. 16—18 ; 2 Thess. ii. 16, 17). **In all our affliction.** The collective experience of affliction is sustained by the collective experience of comfort. **That we may be able to comfort.** Thus St. Paul takes "a teleological view of sorrow." It is partly designed as a school of sympathy. It is a part of the training of an apostle, just as suffering is essential to one who is to be a sympathetic high priest (Heb. v. 1, 2). **In any trouble.** The original more forcibly repeats the words, "in all affliction." **Wherewith we ourselves are comforted.** By means of the comfort which God gives *us*, we can, by the aid of blessed experience, communicate comfort to others.

Ver. 5.—**As the sufferings of Christ abound in us ;** rather, *unto us.* "The sufferings of Christ" are the sufferings which he endured in the days of his flesh, and they were not exhausted by him, but overflow to us who have to suffer as he suffered, bearing about with us his dying, that we may share his life (ch. iv. 10). The idea is, not that he is suffering in us and with us (though the truth of his intense sympathy with his suffering Church may be shadowed forth in some such terms, Matt. xxv. 40—45 ; Acts ix. 4), but that we have "a fellowship in his sufferings" (Phil. iii. 17) ; Gal. ii. 20, "I have been crucified with Christ ; " Heb. xiii. 13, "Bearing his reproach." Our sufferings are the sufferings of Christ because we suffer as he suffered (1 Pet. iv. 13) and in the same cause. **Aboundeth by Christ.** If his sufferings, as it were, overflow to us, so too is he the Source of our comfort, in that he sendeth us the Comforter (John xiv. 16—18).

Ver. 6.—**And ;** rather, *but.* The verse expresses the additional thought that the comfort (*i.e.* encouragement and strengthening) of the apostle, as well as his affliction, was not only designed for his own spiritual training, but was the source of direct blessing to his converts, because it enabled him, both by example (Phil. i. 14) and by the lessons of experience, to strengthen others in affliction, and so to further their salvation by teaching them how to endure (Rom. v. 34). The affliction brings encouragement, and so works endurance in *us*, and, by our example and teaching, in *you*.

Ver. 7.—**And our hope of you is steadfast;** literally, *And our hope is steadfast on your behalf.* The variations of text and punctuation in the verse do not materially affect the sense. The meaning is "And I have a sure hope that you will reap the benefits of our common fellowship with Christ in his affliction, and of the comfort which he sends, because I know that you have experienced the sufferings, and am therefore sure that he will send you the strength and the endurance. The close connection of tribulation and Divine encouragement are found also in Matt. v. 4; 2 Tim. ii. 12; 1 Pet. v. 10. The interchange of the two between teacher and taught is part of the true communion of saints (comp. Phil. ii. 26).

Ver. 8.—**For we would not, brethren, have you ignorant.** This is a favourite phrase with St. Paul (Rom. i. 13; xi. 25; 1 Cor. xii. 1; 1 Thess. iv. 13). **Of our trouble;** rather, *about our affliction.* He assumes that they are aware what the trouble was, and he does not specially mention it. What he wants them to know is that, by the help of their prayers and sympathy, God had delivered him out of this affliction, crushing as it was. **Which came to us in Asia.** Most commentators refer this to the tumult at Ephesus (Acts xix.); and since St. Paul's dangers, sicknesses, and troubles are clearly *understated* throughout the Acts, it is possible that the perils and personal maltreatment which were liable to occur during such a season of excitement may have brought on some violent illness; or, again, he may have suffered from some plots (1 Cor. xvi. 9, **32**; Acts xx. 19) or shipwreck (ch. xi. 25). In Rom. xvi. 4 he alludes again to some extreme peril. But St. Paul seems systematically to have made light of external dangers and sufferings. All his strongest expressions (see Rom. ix. 1—3, etc.) are reserved for mental anguish and affliction. What he felt most keenly was the pang of lacerated affections. It is, therefore, possible that he is here alluding to the overpowering tumult of feelings which had been aroused by his anxiety as to the reception likely to be accorded to his first letter. To this and the accompanying circumstances he alludes again and again (ch. ii. 4, 12; vii. 5, etc.). The sense of "comfort" resulting from the tidings brought by Titus (ch. vii. 6, 7, 13) is as strong as that expresed in these verses, and the allusion to this anguish of heart is specially appropriate here, because he is dwelling on the sympathetic communion between himself and his converts, both in their sorrows and their consolations. **That we were pressed out of measure, above strength;** literally,

that we were weighed down exceedingly beyond our power. The trial seemed too heavy for him to bear. The phrase here rendered "out of measure" occurs in ch. iv. 17; Rom. vii. 13; 1 Cor. xii. 31; Gal. i. 13; but is only found in this particular group of letters. **Insomuch that we despaired even of life.** This rendering conveys the meaning. Literally it is, *so that we were even in utter perplexity* (ch. iv. 8) *even about life.* "I fell into such agony of mind that I hardly hoped to survive." Generally, although he was often in perplexity, he succeeded in resisting despair (ch. iv. 8).

Ver. 9.—**But;** perhaps rather, *yea.* The word strengthens the phrase, "were in utter perplexity." **We had the sentence of death in ourselves.** The original is more emphatic, "Ourselves in our own selves we have had." Not only did all the outer world look dark to me, but the answer which my own spirit returned to the question, "What will be the end of it all?" was "Death!" and that doom still seems to echo in my spirit. **The sentence;** rather, *the answer.* The word is unique in the LXX. and the New Testament. **In ourselves.** Because I seemed to myself to be beyond all human possibility of deliverance. **That we should not trust in ourselves.** There was a divinely intended meaning in my despair. It was meant to teach me, not only submission, but absolute trust in God (see Jer. xvii. 5, 7). **Which raiseth the dead.** Being practically dead—utterly crushed with anguish and despairing of deliverance—I learnt by my deliverance to have faith in God as one who can raise men even from the dead.

Ver. 10.—**From so great a death.** From a state of dejection and despair, which seemed to show death in all its power (see ch. iv. 10—12). **And doth deliver.** Perhaps a pious marginal gloss which has crept into the text of some manuscripts. **We trust;** rather, *we have set our hope.* **That.** This word is omitted in some good manuscripts, as also are the words, "and doth deliver." **He will yet deliver us.** This implies either that the perils alluded to were not yet absolutely at an end, or St. Paul's consciousness that many a peril of equal intensity lay before him in the future.

Ver. 11.—**Ye also helping together by prayer for us.** St. Paul had a deep conviction of the efficacy of intercessory prayer (Rom. xv. 30, 31; Phil. i. 19; Philem. 22). **By the means of many persons;** literally, *from many faces.* Probably the word *prosōpōn* here has its literal meaning. The verse, then, means "that from many faces the gift to us may be thankfully acknowledged by many on our behalf." God, he implies, will be well pleased when he sees the gratitude beaming from the many countenances of those who thank him for his answer to their prayers on his behalf. The word for "gift" is *charisma*, which means a gift of grace, a gift of the Spirit (1 Cor. xii. 4).

Vers. 12—14.—*Vindication of his right to their sympathy.*

Ver. 12.—**For our rejoicing**; rather, *for our boasting is this.* My expression of confidence in your sympathy with me may sound like a boast, but my boast merely accords with the testimony of my conscience that I have been sincere and honest to all, and most of all to you. **The testimony of our conscience.** To this St. Paul frequently appeals (Acts xxiii. 1; xxiv. 16; Rom. ix. 1; 1 Cor. iv. 4). **In simplicity**; rather, *in holiness.* The best reading is ἁγιότητι (א, A, B, C, K), not ἁπλότητι. "Holiness" seems to have been altered to "simplicity," both on dogmatic grounds and because it is a rare word, only occurring in Heb. xii. 10. **And godly sincerity**; literally, *sincerity of God;* i.e. sincerity which is a gift of Divine grace (comp. "peace of God," Phil. iv. 7; "righteousness of God," Rom. i. 17). For the word used for "sincerity," see note on 1 Cor. v. 8. **Not with fleshly wisdom** (comp. ch. ii. 17; 1 Cor. ii. 4), **but by the grace of God.** The preposition in both clauses is "in." The grace of God was the atmosphere which the apostle breathed, the sphere in which he worked. **We have had our conversation.** We lived and moved. The word "conversation" originally meant "mode of life," and is used to translate both *anastrophe* and *politeuma*, which means properly "citizenship." The exclusive modern sense of "conversation" is not earlier than the last century. **In the world**; *i.e.* in my general life as regards all men. **More abundantly to you-ward.** Sincerity, holiness, the signs of the grace of God, were specially shown by the apostle towards the Corinthians, because they were specially needed to guide his relations towards a Church which inspired him with deep affection, but which required special wisdom to guide and govern. The fact that, in spite of all his exceptional care, such bitter taunts could still be levelled at him, shows that he had not been mistaken in supposing that no Church required from him a more anxious watchfulness over all his conduct.

Ver. 13.—**For we write none other things unto you**, etc. Remarks like these obviously presuppose that the conduct and character of St. Paul had been misrepresented and calumniated. The perpetual recurrence to a strain of self-defence would have been needless if some one—probably Titus—had not told St. Paul that his opponents accused him of *insincerity.* Here, therefore, he tells them that he is opening out his very heart towards them. What he had to say to them and of them was here set forth without any subterfuges or *arrières pensées.* He had nothing *esoteric* which differed from *exoteric* teaching. It is a melancholy thought that even such a one as Paul was reduced to the sad necessity of defending himself against such charges as that he intrigued with individual members of his Churches, wrote private letters or sent secret messages which differed in tone from those which were read in the public assembly. **Or acknowledge**; rather, *or even fully know;* i.e. from other sources. The paronomasia of the original cannot be preserved in English, but in Latin would be "Quæ legitis aut etiam intelligitis." **And I trust . . . even to the end**; rather, *but I hope that, even unto the end, ye will fully know—even as ye fully knew us in part—that we are your subject of boast.* After telling them that they have in this letter his genuine and inmost thoughts, he adds that "even as *some of them* (for this seem to be implied by the 'in part') already knew well that the mutual relations between him and them were something wherein to glory, he hopes that they will appreciate this fact, even to the end." He *knows* that some honour him; he hopes that all will do so; but he can only express this as a hope, for he is aware that there are calumnies abroad respecting him, so that he cannot feel sure of their unbroken allegiance. Such seems to be the meaning; but the state of mind in which St. Paul wrote has evidently troubled his style, and his expressions are less lucid and more difficult to unravel in this Epistle than in any other. **To the end.** The expression is quite general, like our "to the last." He does not seem *definitely* to imply either to the end of his life or to the coming of Christ, which they regarded as the end of all things, as in 1 Cor. i. 8; xv. 24; Heb. iii. 6.

Ver. 14.—**In part.** Not as a whole Church. Some only of the Corinthians had been faithful to his teaching and to himself. (For the phrase, see Rom. xi. 25; xv. 15, 24; 1 Cor. xi. 18; xii. 27; xiii. 9.) **Rejoicing**; rather, *ground of boast*, as in ch. ix. 3; Rom. iv. 2, "whereof to glory;" 1 Cor. v. 6. In ver. 12 the substantive means "the *act* of rejoicing." The word is characteristic of this group of Epistles, in which it occurs forty-six times. **Even as ye also** are ours. This clause takes away all semblance of self-glorification. In 1 Thess. ii. 19, 20 and Phil. ii. 16 he expresses the natural thought that a teacher's converts are, and will be in the last day, his "crown of exultation." Here alone he implies that they may glory in him as he in them. The thought, however, so far from being egotistical, merely indicates the intense intercommunion of sympathy which existed between him and them. He does but place himself on a level with his converts, and imply that they mutually gloried in each other. **In the day of the Lord Jesus** (see on 1 Cor. iii. 13).

Vers. 15—22.—*His change of purpose in n t visiting Corinth.*

Ver. 15.—**In this confidence.** In reliance on the mutual respect and affection which exists between us. **I was minded.** The stress is partly on the tense : " my original desire *was.*" When speaking of matters purely personal, St. Paul generally reverts to the first person. **To come unto you before.** I meant to visit you, first on my way to Macedonia, and again on my return from Macedonia, as explained in the next verse. **A second benefit;** rather, *a second grace.* There is another reading, χαρὰν, joy, and the word χάρις itself sometimes has this sense (as in Tobit vii. 18), but not in the New Testament. Here, again, there is no boastfulness. St. Paul, filled as he was with the power of the Holy Spirit, was able to impart to his converts some spiritual gifts (Rom. i. 11), and this was the chief reason why his visits were so eagerly desired, and why his change of plan had caused such bitter disappointment to the Corinthians. The importance of the Church of Corinth, its central position, and its unsettled state made it desirable that he should give them as much as possible of his personal supervision.

Ver. 16.—**To be brought on my way** (see note on 1 Cor. xvi. 6) **toward Judæa** (1 Cor. xvi. 4—6).

Ver. 17.—**When I therefore was thus minded.** Without saying in so many words that all this plan was now given up, he proceeds to defend himself against the charges which had been evidently brought against him by his opponents. The Corinthians were aware that he no longer meant to come to them direct from Ephesus. They had certainly been informed of this by Titus, and he had indeed briefly stated it in 1 Cor. xvi. 5. Their disappointment had led some of them into angry criticisms upon the " indecision " of the apostle, the more so because he had (out of kindness, as he here shows) spared them the pain of expressing his *reasons.* **Did I use lightness ?** Was this change of plan a sign of "the levity" with which some of you charge me ? **Or the things that I purpose, do I purpose according to the flesh,** etc. ? Every phrase in this clause is of ambiguous meaning. For instance, the " or " may imply *another* charge, namely, that his purposes are *carnal,* and therefore capricious ; or it may be the alternative view of his conduct, stated by way of self-defence—namely, " Does my change of plan imply that I am frivolous ? or, on the contrary, are not my plans of necessity mere *human* plans, and therefore liable to be overruled by God's will ? " Thus the meaning of the " or " is doubtful, and also the meaning of " *according to the flesh.*" Generally this phrase is used in a bad sense, as in ch. x. 2 and Rom. viii. 1 ; but it may also be used to mean " in a human way," as in ch. v. 16. **That with me there should be yea yea, and nay nay.** There is probably no clause in the New Testament of which the certain sense must be left so indeterminate as this. (1) The Authorized Version gives one way of taking the clause. The grammar equally admits of the rendering. (2) *That with me the yea should be yea, and the nay nay.* Whichever rendering we adopt, it may be explained in accordance with the view indicated in the last note. " I was not showing the levity which my opponents speak of, but my purposes are necessarily mere human purposes, and therefore my 'yes' and 'no' can be only 'yes' and 'no' when I make a plan. My 'yes' or 'no' may be overruled by the Spirit (Acts xvi. 7) or even hindered by Satan, and that more than once (1 Thess. ii. 18)." " With me," *i.e.* as far as I am concerned, I can only say " yes " or " no ;" but *l'homme propose, Dieu dispose.* His intended double visit to them was prevented, not by any frivolity of his, but, as he afterwards shows, by their own unfaithfulness and his desire to spare them. There is yet a third way of taking it which involves a different meaning—" In order that with me the 'yea yea' may be also 'nay nay.'" Am I inconsistent ? or, are my purposes merely carnal purposes, in order that my " yes yes " may be, as far as I am concerned, no better than " no no "—like the mere shifting feebleness of an aimless man ? A fourth way of taking the clause, adopted by St. Chrysostom and many others, is, " Do I plan after the flesh, *i.e.* with carnal obstinacy, so that my ' yea ' and ' nay ' must be carried out at all costs ? " This suggestion can hardly be right; for St. Paul was charged, not with obstinacy, but with indecision. The phrases, " yea " and " nay," as mentioned in Matt. v. 37 and Jas. v. 12, throw no light on the passage, unless indeed some one had misquoted against St. Paul our Lord's words as a reason for adhering inviolably to a plan once formed. Of these various methods I adopt the first, because it seems to be, on the whole, most in accordance with the context. For on that view of the passage he contents himself with the remark that it cannot be inconsistency or levity on his part to alter plans which are liable to all the chance and change of ordinary circumstances ; and then tells them that there was one part of his teaching which has nothing to do with mere human weakness, but was God's everlasting

" yes ; " after which he explains to them the reason why he decided not to come to them until he had first visited Macedonia, and so to give them one visit, not two.

Ver. 18.—**But as God is true ; rather,** *but God is faithful,* whatever may be (1 Cor. i. 9 ; x. 13 ; 1 Thess. v. 24 ; 2 Thess. iii. 3 ; 1 John i. 9). **Our word towards you,** etc. The verse should be rendered, *But God is faithful, because* (faithful herein, that) *our preaching to you proved itself to be not yea and nay.* Whatever you may say of my plans and my conduct, there was *one* thing which involved an indubitable "yea," namely, my preaching to you. In that, at any rate, there was nothing capricious, nothing variable, nothing vacillating. St. Paul, in a manner characteristic to his moods of deepest emotion, "goes off at a word." The Corinthians talked of his "yea" and "nay" as though one was little better than the other, and neither could be depended on ; well, at any rate, *one thing,* and that the most essential, was as sure as the faithfulness of God.

Ver. 19.—**For.** This is a proof of what he has just said. His preaching was as firm as a rock ; for, tried by time, it had proved itself a changeless "yea," being a preaching of Christ, the same yesterday, to-day, and for ever. **By me and Silvanus and Timotheus.** They are mentioned because they had been his companions in the *first* visit to Corinth (Acts xviii. 5), and he wishes to show that his preaching of Christ had never wavered. "Silvanus" (1 Thess. i. 1 ; 2 Thess. i. 1) is the "Silas" of Acts xv. 22. He disappears from the New Testament in this verse, unless he be the "Silvanus" of 1 Pet. v. 12. **Was not yea and nay, but in him was yea.** "Became not (proved not to be) yes and no (in one breath, as it were, and therefore utterly untrustworthy), but in him there has been a yea." The perfect, "has become," means that in him the everlasting "yes" has proved itself valid, and still continues to be a changeless affirmation (Heb. xiii. 8).

Ver. 20.—**For all the promises of God in him** are yea ; rather, *For so many as be the promises of God, in him is the yea.* All the promises of God find in him their unchangeable fulfilment. He was "a minister to confirm the promises" alike to the Jews and the Gentiles (Rom. xv. 8, 9) ; and "the promise of the eternal inheritance" can only be fulfilled in him (Heb. ix. 15). **And in him Amen.** The true reading is, "Wherefore by him also is the Amen to God, uttered by us to his glory" (‎א, A, B, C, F, G, etc.). In Christ is the "yea" of immutable promise and absolute fulfilment ; the Church utters the "Amen" of perfect faith and grateful adoration. Here, as in 1 Cor. xiv. 16, we have a proof of the ancientness of the custom by which the congregation utters the "Amen"

at the end of praise and prayer. But as the "yea" is in Christ, so it is only through him that we can receive the grace to utter aright the "Amen" to the glory of God.

Ver. 21.—**Now he that stablisheth us.** They will have seen, then, that steadfastness not levity, immutability not vacillation, has been the subject of their teaching. Who is the Source of that steadfastness ? *God,* who anointed us and confirmed us, and you with us, into unity with his Anointed. **With you.** We partake alike of this Christian steadfastness ; to impugn mine is to nullify your own. **In Christ** ; rather, *into Christ,* so as to be one with him. They are already "*in Christo*;" they would aim more and more to be established "*in Christum.*" **Who anointed us.** Every Christian is a king and priest to God, and has received an unction from the Holy One (1 John ii. 20, 27).

Ver. 22.—**Who hath also sealed us.** We cannot be deconsecrated, disanointed. Still less can the confirming seal be broken. He continues to dwell on the conception of the unchangeableness of God and of the gospel into which he had been incidentally led by the charge of "lightness." **The earnest of the Spirit.** The promises which we have received are not mere promises, they are already so far fulfilled to us and in us as to guarantee hereafter their plenary fruition. Just as in money bargains "earnest money," "money on account," is given, in pledge that the whole will be ultimately discharged, so we have "the earnest of the Spirit" (ch. v. 5), "the firstfruits of the Spirit" (Rom. viii. 23), which are to us "the earnest" or pledge money that we shall hereafter enter upon the purchased possession (Eph. i. 13, 14). We now see the meaning of the "and." It involves a climax—the promise is much ; the unction more ; the seal a still further security (Eph. iv. 30 ; 2 Tim. ii. 19) ; but beyond all this we have already a part payment in the indwelling of the Present of God (Rom. v. 5 ; viii. 9 ; Gal. iv. 6). The word *arrabon,* rendered "earnest," has an interesting history. It is very ancient, for it is found (‎עֵרָבוֹן) in Gen. xxxviii. 17, 18, and comes from a root meaning "to pledge." It seems to be a Phœnician word, which had been introduced into various languages by the universality of Phœnician commerce. In classical Latin it is shortened into *arrha,* and it still exists in Italian as *arra,* in French as *arrhes.* The equivalent Hebrew figure is "firstfruits" (Rom. viii. 23).

Ver. 23.—**Moreover I call God for a record** ; rather, *But I call God for a witness.* At this point, to ch. ii. 4, he enters for the first time on the kindly reasons which had led him to forego his intended earlier visit. He uses a similar adjuration in ch. xi. 31 ; and although these appeals (comp. 1 Cor. xv.

31; Rom. i. 9; Gal. i. 20) may be due in part to the emotional fervour of his temperament, yet he would hardly have resorted to them in this self-defence, if the calumnies of his enemies had not gained much credence. The French proverb, *Qui s'excuse s'accuse*, is often grossly abused. The refutation of lies and slanders is often a duty, not because they injure us, but because, by diminishing our usefulness, they may injure others. **Upon my soul.** Not "to take vengeance on my soul if I lie," but to confirm the appeal of its honesty and integrity. By the use of such "oaths for confirmation," St. Paul, no less than other apostles, shows that he understood our Lord's rule, "Let your communication be, Yea, yea; Nay, nay," as applying to the principle of simple and unvarnished truthfulness of intercourse, which requires no further confirmation; but not as a rigid exclusion of the right to appeal to God in solemn cases and for good reasons. **To spare you.** This postponement of the intended visit was a sign of *forbearance*, for which they should have been grateful. After all that he had heard of them, if he had come at all, it could only have been "with a rod" (1 Cor. iv. 21). **I came not as yet.** The rendering is erroneous. It literally means "I no longer came," *i.e.* I forbore to come as I had intended.

Ver. 24.—Not for that we have dominion over your faith. The expression, "to spare you," might have been resented as involving a claim "to lord it over their faith." He had, indeed, authority (1 Col. iv. 21; ch. x. 6; xiii. 2, 10), but it was a purely spiritual authority; it was valid only over those who recognized in him an apostolic commission. St. Peter, no less than St. Paul, discourages the spirit of ecclesiastical *tyranny* (1 Pet. v. 3). **But are helpers of your joy.** We are fellow-helpers of your Christian joy, and therefore I would not come to cause your grief. *That* was how I desired to spare you. The object of my visits is always "for your furtherance and joy of faith" (Phil. i. 25). **For by faith ye stand.** The expression is not a mere general principle, but explains his disclaimer of any desire "to lord it over their faith." As far as their "faith" was concerned, they were not to blame; *that* remained unshaken, and was independent of any visit or authority of St. Paul. But while "in respect of faith ye stand" (Eph. vi. 13), there are other points in which you are being shaken, and in dealing with these I should have been obliged to take severe measures, which, if I postponed my visit, would (I hoped) become unnecessary.

HOMILETICS.

Vers. 1, 2.—*The will of God.*   "Paul, an apostle of Jesus Christ," etc.   Here are three subjects of thought.

I. THE SUPREME LAW. "By the will of God." 1. God has a *will*. He is, therefore, personality, free and intelligent. His will explains the origin, sustenance, and order of the universe. His will is the force of all forces, the law of all laws. 2. God has a will in relation to *individual men*. He has a purpose in relation to every man, every man's existence, mission, and conduct. His will in relation to moral beings is the standard of all conduct and the rule of all destiny. Love is its primal fount or mainspring.

II. THE APOSTOLIC SPIRIT. Judging from what Paul says here, we observe : 1. The apostolic spirit involves subjection to Christ. "An apostle of Jesus Christ." Christ is the moral Master; he the loving, loyal servant. 2. The apostolic spirit is that of special love for the good. He calls Timothy his "brother," and towards "the Church of God which is at Corinth, with all the saints which are in all Achaia," he glows with loving sympathy. Love for souls, deep, tender, overflowing, is the essential qualification for the gospel apostolate or ministry.

III. THE CHIEF GOOD. 1. Here is the highest good. "Grace and peace." He who has these has the *summum bonum*. 2. Here is the highest good from the highest Source : "From our Father, and from the Lord Jesus Christ."

Vers. 3—5.—*The God of Christianity.*   "Blessed be God, even the Father," etc. The God of nature is revealed in nature as the Almighty and the All-wise. "The invisible things of the world are clearly seen, being made visible by the things that are seen, even his eternal power and Godhead." But God in Christianity appears in three aspects.

I. AS THE FATHER OF THE WORLD'S REDEEMER. "Blessed be God, even the Father of our Lord Jesus Christ." Jesus Christ is the world's Redeemer, and the world's Redeemer is the Son of God. "This is my beloved Son, in whom I am well pleased."

II. AS THE SOURCE OF MAN'S MERCIES. "The Father of mercies, and the God of all comfort," or the merciful Father. Mercy implies something more than mere benevolence; it is a modification of goodness; it implies sorrow and suffering. God is good to all, but he is merciful to the afflicted—he compassionates and comforts them. God in nature does not appear as the God of mercy and comfort for the fallen and the lost.

III. AS THE COMFORTER OF AFFLICTED SAINTS. "Who comforteth us in all our tribulation, that we may be able to comfort them which are in any trouble," etc. The best of men have their tribulations here. Most, if not all, the men who have entered heaven have passed through much tribulation. 1. He comforts his afflicted people " in all their tribulations." Whatever the nature and variety of affliction, he has suitable and adequate comfort to bestow. Moral remorses, worldly losses, social bereavements,— he has a healing balm for all. 2. He comforts his afflicted people, that they may be able to administer comfort to *others*. "That we may be able to comfort them which are in any trouble." Affliction is necessary to qualify us to sympathize with and administer comfort to others. "They comfort others who themselves have borne," says Sophocles. By affliction Christ qualified himself to comfort others. "We have not a High Priest that cannot be touched with the feeling of our infirmities," etc.

Vers. 6—11.—*Personal sufferings.* "And whether we be afflicted, it is for your consolation," etc. The words suggest a few remarks concerning personal sufferings.

I. THEY ARE OFTEN EXPERIENCED IN THE BEST OF ENTERPRISES. What a glorious enterprise Paul and his fellow-apostles were engaged in!—nothing less than the restoration of mankind to the knowledge, image, and friendship of the great God. Yet how great their sufferings! "We were pressed out of measure, above strength, insomuch that we despaired even of life." [1]

II. THEY ARE EVER NECESSARY FOR THE RENDERING OF THE HIGHEST SERVICE TO MANKIND. "Whether we be afflicted, it is for your consolation and salvation, which is effectual in the enduring of the same sufferings which we also suffer." The apostle here teaches that his sufferings and those of his colleagues were *vicarious*. He and his co-labourers incurred them in their endeavours to extend the gospel, and they had the "consolations" which came to him, qualified him to sympathize with and administer comfort to all who were in the same trying condition. Paul could say to the sufferers at Corinth—We were in sufferings and were comforted; you are in sufferings and may participate in the same comfort. If you are partakers of the same kind of suffering, that is, suffering on account of your religion, you shall also be partakers of the same comfort. Suppose a man who had been restored from a certain disease by a certain specific were to meet another suffering under a complaint in all respects identical, and were to say to the man—I can not only sympathize with you, but I can assure you of that which will cure you, for it has cured me;—this, perhaps, may serve as an illustration of the apostle's meaning here; and this every true Christian man who has suffered can say to all—I was in your condition, I was restored; I can sympathize with you, and I urge the same means of restoration.

III. THEIR DETAILMENT PURELY FOR THE GOOD OF OTHERS IS JUSTIFIABLE. Paul says, "We would not, brethren, have you ignorant of our trouble." There is a wonderful tendency in men to parade their sufferings and their trials, to spread them out before men, in order to enlist their sympathy and excite commiseration. This is selfish, is not justifiable. Christ—perhaps the greatest of all sufferers—never did this: in this respect, "he opened not his mouth." But to declare sufferings in order to benefit others, to give them courage and comfort, and to establish between you and them a holy unity in the Divine cause, this is right, this is what Paul does here. He does it that they may believe in his sympathy and seek the comfort which he himself experienced.

IV. THEIR EXPERIENCE OFTEN PROVES A BLESSING TO THE SUFFERER. They seem to have done two things for Paul. 1. *To have transferred his trust in himself to trust in God.* "We had the sentence of death in ourselves, that we should not trust in ourselves, but in God." Paul no doubt felt that he was brought near unto death, to the

[1] See a sketch of Paul's trials, ch. xi. 23, 29.

very extreme of suffering, and that led him to look away from self, to put his trust in God. When affliction does this it is indeed a blessing in disguise. When it detaches us from the material and links us to the spiritual, takes us away from self and centres us on God, then, indeed, it worketh out for us a "far more exceeding and eternal weight of glory." 2. *To have awakened prayers by others on his behalf.* "Ye also helping together by prayer for us, that for the gift bestowed upon us by the means of many persons thanks may be given by many on our own behalf."

Ver. 12.—*Conscience and the inner life of man.* "For our rejoicing is this, the testimony of our conscience, that in simplicity and godly sincerity, not with fleshly wisdom, but by the grace of God, we have had our conversation in the world, and more abundantly to you-ward." Three remarks are suggested.

I. WHAT IS GOING ON IN THE SOUL CONSCIENCE OBSERVES. This is implied in its "testimony." The eye of conscience pierces into the deepest secrets of motives, and is cognizant of all our hidden impulses, thoughts, and aims. We may appear sincere to others, but hypocrites to conscience; hypocrites to others, but true to conscience. Conscience is the best judge.

II. WHATEVER IS GOOD IN THE SOUL CONSCIENCE APPROVES. 1. Paul's conscience approved of his *inner principles*—his "simplicity" or holiness, and "sincerity." On these elements it has ever smiled and will ever smile, but not on "fleshly wisdom," carnal policy, and worldly expediency. 2. Paul's conscience approved of his *external demeanour.* "We have had our conversation in the world, and more abundantly to you-ward." His outward conduct was the effect and expression of his inner life. Conscience smiles on every holy deed, however mean in the sight of men.

III. WHATEVER IS JOYOUS IN THE SOUL CONSCIENCE OCCASIONS. "Our rejoicing is this," or, "our glorying is this." Where there is not an approving conscience there is no real, moral joy. Its "well done" sets the soul to music; with its approval we can stand, not only calm and serene, but even triumphant, under the denunciations of the whole world. Dr. South says, "Conscience is undoubtedly the grand repository of all those pleasures which can afford any solid refreshment to the soul; when this is calm and serene, then properly a man enjoys all things, and, what is more, himself; for that he must do before he can enjoy anything else. It will not drop but pour in oil upon the wounded heart; it will not whisper but proclaim a jubilee to the mind."

Vers. 15—22.—*Possessions of a genuine Christian.* "And in this confidence," etc. These verses may be regarded as indicating what every genuine disciple of Christ—that is, every Christly man—possesses *now* and *here.*

I. HE POSSESSES MORAL STABILITY. Paul is here writing on the defensive; indeed, the whole tone of his letter is apologetic. Because he did not visit the Corinthians according to his first promise, they perhaps pronounced him fickle, vacillating, untrue to his word. Against this he protests. "And in this confidence I was minded to come unto you before, that ye might have a second benefit; and to pass by you into Macedonia, and to come again out of Macedonia unto you, and of you to be brought on my way toward Judæa." Here he admits his intention and his promise, but in reply says emphatically, "When I therefore was thus minded, did I use lightness?" etc. He claims stability, and the stability which he claims is possessed by all true Christians. 1. *A stability of purpose.* "As God is true, our word toward you was not yea and nay." What we said we meant; there was no equivocation, no "yea" and "nay" in the same breath. In defending his veracity: (1) He makes an asseveration. "As God is true," or as God is faithful, we meant to perform what we promised. (2) He indicates an incongruity. "For the Son of God, Jesus Christ, who was preached among you by us, even by me and Silvanus and Timotheus, was not yea and nay, but in him was yea. For all the promises of God in him are yea," etc. He means to say that the gospel which he had preached to them necessarily bound him to faithfulness. Christ, in whom he lived and for whom he laboured, was the grand Reality, the "Amen," the Truth. The idea of a man in Christ being unveracious, untruthful, was preposterous. An untruthful man cannot be a Christian. This the apostle means and declares. 2. *A stability of character.* "Now he which stablisheth us with you in Christ, and hath anointed us, is God." The stability he claims for himself he accedes

to all the Christians at Corinth. How blessed to have the heart fixed, their character
"in Christ" established, "rooted and grounded in love"!

II. HE POSSESSES DIVINE CONSECRATION. He that "hath anointed us is God."
Among the Jews in olden times, kings, priests, and prophets were set apart to their
offices by anointing them with oil; hence here the word "anointed" means they were
consecrated by God to a Christly life and labour. A truly Christian man is divinely
consecrated, not to a mere office, but to the noblest character and the sublimest mission.
As such he has God's seal on him, "who hath also sealed us."

III. HE POSSESSES A PLEDGE OF THE HIGHEST PROGRESS. "Given the earnest of
the Spirit in our hearts." "Let us," says F. W. Robertson, "distinguish between an
earnest and a *pledge*. A *pledge* is something different in kind given in assurance of
something else, as when Judah gave his staff and ring in pledge for a lamb which he
promised should be given afterwards. But an *earnest* is part of that thing which is
eventually to be given, as when the grapes were brought from Canaan, or as when a
purchase is made and part of the money is paid down at once." There is no finality
in the life of goodness; it passes on from "strength to strength," from "glory to glory."
In every step, after the first, up the celestial mountains, the scenes widen and brighten,
and the breezes become more balmy and invigorating as we advance. He who has the
Christly life within has already Paradise in germ.

Vers. 23, 24.—*A threefold theme.* "Moreover I call God for a record," etc. In these
verses we have three things worthy of note.

I. THE FULFILMENT OF A PROMISE ADJOURNED. "Moreover I call God for a record
upon my soul, that to spare you I came not as yet unto Corinth." Paul here, in the
most solemn way, assigns the reason why he had adjourned his promised visit to
Corinth. It was not for his personal convenience, or from a change of purpose, or from
any indifference towards them, but on the contrary, out of tender regard to their
feelings—"to spare you I came not." Knowing the prevalence of the spirit of schism
and disorder which had crept into the Church, he shrank from the exercise of that
discipline which of necessity would inflict great pain. Hence, hoping that the admonishing letter which he had addressed to them would have the effect he desired upon
them, he delayed. Surely a love so generous, so pure, and exquisitely sympathetic,
would justify, if not the breaking of a promise, the postponement of its fulfilment.
Regard for the feelings of others, it has been said, is the grand characteristic of the
"gentleman." Anyhow, it is an essential element in personal Christianity.

II. AUTHORITY OVER THE FAITH OF OTHERS DISCLAIMED. "Not for that we have
dominion over your faith." Had we desired to set up a lordship over you, we might
have hastened to you at once, but we respected your feelings, and sought your happiness. The authority which Paul here disclaims has been assumed by priestly ecclesiastics in all times. It is the very spirit of priestism. The minister, whoever he may
be, to whatever Church he belongs, who endeavours to make men believe that his own
personal ministry, or the ministry of his denomination, is the special ministry of heaven,
and essential to the salvation of mankind, has in him the intolerant spirit of the priest,
he seeks dominion over the faith of men, he would restrain liberty of thought, and
subject the minds of men to his credenda. These men, whether Papists or Protestants,
Churchmen or Nonconformists, outrage the spirit of the mission they have received,
and inflict untold mischief on the minds of men.

III. THE TRUE WORK OF A GOSPEL MINISTER. "But are helpers of your joy." He
is a helper, not a lord; a helper, not a substitute. A true minister is: 1. To help men
to *think* aright. To think aright is to think on the right subject, in the right way.
2. To help men to *feel* aright. Feel aright in relation to self, mankind, the universe,
and God. 3. To help men to *believe* aright. "By faith ye stand." Spiritually men
can only "stand" by faith, and the work of a true minister is to help people to
"stand" by "faith" on the right foundation. When will ministers come to feel that
they are the spiritual "helpers" of the people; to help them, not by doing their work
for them, but to assist them in working for themselves?

HOMILIES BY VARIOUS AUTHORS.

Vers. 1, 2.—*Salutation.* It is a greeting from Paul, an apostle of Christ Jesus, and from " Timothy our brother," instead of Sosthenes, as in the First Epistle. It is to the Church of God at Corinth, with all the saints in the whole of Achaia, all connected in the province with the central Church at Corinth. " Beginning at Jerusalem "—the holy city was to be the starting-point. Antioch, Cæsarea, Thessalonica, Corinth, Ephesus, Rome, were to be early reached by the gospel. Community-centres were to become Church-centres, so that the social idea of Christianity should have prompt and impressive development. As usual with St. Paul, " Grace be to you and peace," opening and closing with the word so comprehensive, so precious, " grace."—L.

Vers. 3—11.—*Thanksgiving in the midst of tribulation ; uses of sorrow ; comforting others ; personal references.* The ascription begins with " blessed," the strongest term the apostle could employ as representing the highest and strongest emotions, the head-word in the vocabulary of gratitude and praise, found in the Old and New Scriptures, and common to Jews and Gentile Christians. " Blessed ; " the best in us acknowledging the God of grace, an anthem in a single utterance, and embodying the whole nature of man in reverence and adoration. " Blessed be God, even the Father of our Lord Jesus Christ ; " not only God, but the Father of our Lord Jesus Christ, and a Father to us in him. What significance Christ gave to the word " father " we all know. It is the root-word of the Lord's Prayer, every ascription and every petition being but an offshoot from " Our Father which art in heaven." So of the entire Sermon on the Mount ; it is the motive to trust Providence, the reason to be like God, the ground of brotherhood, the inducement to forgive those who offend us, the inspiration of each duty, each sacrifice, and the joy and strength of each beatitude. So of the last conversations and discourse—all of the Father and of the Son in him, and the disciples in the Son. So after the Resurrection, " My Father and your Father." St. Paul rejoiced in the word. Nor did he hesitate to use on Mars' Hill the quotation, " We are also his offspring," and from this point of view expose the error and sin of idolatry. And wherever he comes to give it the fulness of its import, as in Rom. viii., his heart overflows with feeling. Here (ver. 3) he is also the " Father of mercies, and the God of all comfort," and no matter how the mercies reach us and what their nature and connections, they are from the Father as the God of all comfort. Physical and spiritual blessings, a visit from Stephanas, the return of Titus, good news from Corinth,—all alike are mercies from the Father, the God of all comfort. One may lose himself in the omnipresence of Jehovah and be overwhelmed by its sublimity, but it is a very practical doctrine with the apostle, a constant reality, and he feels it deeply because he feels it always. " Not far from every one of us." How can he be, when " we live and move and have our being " in him ? We say these great words, but with what little consciousness of their massive import ! Reason tries in vain to comprehend omnipresence ; imagination labours and sinks under its images ; while the humble and docile heart accepts the grandeur of God's presence in immensity as the grandeur of his nearness in all the affairs of life. " God of all comfort " because " Father of mercies ; " the mercies very welcome to him just then in that sore emergency, and the fatherhood of God in Christ unspeakably dear. It enlivened the sense of special providence in his soul ; it was the Comforter whom Christ had promised as more than a compensation for his absence, and while this Comforter was never taken from him, yet, as occasion demanded, his Divine manifestations were augmented. Just as we need human sympathy, assurances of human friendship and love, more at some times than at others, so need we the Consoler, and to this varying want he adapts himself in the infinitude of his power and tenderness. No soul is saved, we may suppose, on an unvarying plan ; no soul is cheered and strengthened by a rigid monotony of spiritual influence. " The wind bloweth where it listeth," a zephyr, a breeze, a gale, but in all the wind. " So is every one that is born of the Spirit." " Blessed be God," not only for " mercies " and " comfort," but for them in particular adaptations to seasons and experiences that doubly endear the gracious offices of the Paraclete. Now, these words of praise naturally lead us to expect a justification of their special utterance, and we have it immediately. " Who comforteth us in all our tribulation," and for what purpose?   Titus and Timothy had brought him much cheer and consolation, and why?   Was it just to revive his drooping spirit?   Just to assuage his personal pain, soothe his unquiet nerves, invigorate his tone of mind?   Nay; consolation was not selfish.   Happiness is not exclusively or even mainly for its possessor. " Doth God take care for oxen? "   Yea; for the owner of oxen too in his providence over the beast.   The tribulation had not fallen on St. Paul because of anything peculiar to him; it was vicarious; and the comfort had been granted, not in his behalf alone, but that he might know how to console others.   This is his statement: " That we may be able to comfort them which are in any trouble."   If the Holy Ghost is the Comforter, we are his agents, and, just as the gospel of doctrine reaches you from him through us, so too the gospel of consolation comes to your hearts through our hearts.   Look at what the apostolic office meant.   Far more than preacher, organizer, administrator, leader, champion, was included in its high duties and arduous responsibilities.   To console was one of its greatest tasks.   Everywhere the dejected were to be lifted up, the discouraged animated, the afflicted taught to hope.   To be a physician to suffering souls was a ceaseless requisition on St. Paul.   Think of what it entailed on such a man as he.   Think of but one aspect of the matter—tension of sensibility.   The exhaustion consequent on the unceasing strain upon sensibility is the hardest of all things to bear.   It opens the door to all manner of temptations.   It is the crucial test of manly fortitude.   Now, the quality of emotion has much more to do with the exhaustion of the nervous system than the quantity.   Every preacher knows that a funeral occasion on which he has to officiate is a severer tax on his nerves than half a dozen ordinary pulpit services.   The more solemn, and especially the more pathetic, the circumstances, the more rapid and complete the subsequent exhaustion.   Think now of what St. Paul had to endure in this kind of apostolic experience, and that too without a respite; how many thorns rankled besides " the thorn in the flesh; " and how many hearts bled in that one bleeding heart of his.   Just now, moreover, he was suffering greatly on account of the Corinthians. This will appear hereafter.   The main point before us is—How was he qualified to be a consoler?   What his discipline, what his education, for this beautiful and holy service? Ah, Tarsus and Jerusalem, Gamaliel, all other teachers, pass out of view in this deepest and most personal of all culture, and the Holy Ghost and the man are the only parties to the work.   " By the comfort wherewith we ourselves are comforted of God."   Talking from the intellect is in such a case of no avail.   A man must have been a sufferer, must have felt Christ in his sufferings, must have abounded in these " sufferings of Christ," as St. Paul designates his afflictions, before he can be fitted to minister unto others.   Only sorrow can speak to sorrow.   Notice the correspondence in the degree; if the sufferings of Christ abounded, so "our consolation also aboundeth by Christ."   "By the sufferings of Christ abound in us" ("unto us," Revised Version), we understand the apostle to mean his fellowship with Christ in suffering the ills and sorrows that came upon him as an apostle and as a man because of his spiritual union with Christ.   Mediation in all its offices, in the peculiar and exclusive work of Christ as the one Reconciler and Healer, in the subordinate and imperfect operations of human sympathy, is essentially painful.   And allowing for the infinite distinction between the Divine Sufferer and human sufferers, there is yet a unity in suffering predicable of Christ and the members of his mystical body.   For it is the capacity to suffer which is the dignity and glory of our nature.   We are God-like in this quality.   It is the basis of all grand excellence, nor can our innate love of happiness nor any other ideal of our being have its fulfilment except through that kind of sorrow which Christians undergo in the Man of sorrows. Ver. 6 emphasizes this fact.   If we are afflicted, argues he, it is for your good, that we may be instrumental in your salvation, and that grace may abound to you because of what we endure.   And, furthermore, it was for their present consolation; it was " effectual; " the example of their distressed apostle operated to strengthen and establish them, and the consolation wherewith he was sustained availed to animate their souls. For this reason, his hope of them was " steadfast."   Corruptions were among these Corinthians; God's judgments had overtaken them because of their free-thinking and laxity of morals; they were punished, they were chastened; but, in the midst of all, St. Paul was encouraged to hope for their stability and growth in grace, seeing that they were not only sympathizers but participants both in the suffering and in the consolation he himself experienced for their sakes.   Two points here come into view : first, the apostle was in great distress on their account, and they shared with him this peculiar burden of grief; and, secondly, the supporting grace which God had given him was not confined to his soul, but overflowed (abounded) in their souls. What a great truth is this! There are times in our history as believers when, if left without the support of Church relations, we should be overcome by temptation. In such hours God shows us the worth of membership in the Church; grace comes to us through their affections, and brethren in Christ are our best friends in the flesh. The human, or rather the Divine in the human, saves us when all else would be ineffectual, and thus it is that associates and companions in the faith co-operate with other "ministering spirits sent forth to minister for them who shall be heirs of salvation." And what a meaning this imparts to the Holy Communion, wherein we express, not only our remembrance of Christ's suffering and death, but our fellowship with his sufferings in others! Keep in mind how sorrow ennobles us. Is it the silence and loneliness, the self-examination, the penitence, the amendment, in which the divinest fruits of chastening appear? These are not ultimate results. It is not alone what the discipline of pain makes us in ourselves; it is not the individual man, but the social man, that is under God's plastic hand, and who, while learning to "bear his own burden," is also learning a lesson far more difficult, to bear another's burden and "so fulfil the law of Christ." Who are they that practise the "so"? Who are the burden-bearers—those that carry the ignorance, perverseness, folly, misfortune, troubles, of other people on their hearts? Only such as have known Christ as he suffered from taking "our infirmities" and bearing "our sicknesses," and who have been taught by the Holy Spirit that the mediating life to which we are called as the highest sphere of life is possible only by means of personal affliction. Was Bunyan immured in Bedford jail on his own account or for the world's benefit? Was Milton blind for his own sake or for England's? How could 'Pilgrim's Progress' or 'Paradise Lost' have been produced except in obedience to the law—partakers in suffering, partakers in consolation? St. Paul proceeds to the illustration. Of his general sufferings we have a definite idea. How he was misrepresented by his enemies, how he was charged with meanness and cowardice, how he was vilified for his self-denial, how the Judaizers pursued him with merciless zeal, we all know. We know, too, how his heart was moved by the deplorable state of things at Corinth. Now, it is quite true that the endurance of trouble prepares us to bear a new trouble; but it is true also that trouble increases the sensitiveness to pain, and hence, in a succession of sorrows, the last, though not in itself the heaviest, is virtually such because of the sensibility involved. This was St. Paul's condition. At this very conjuncture, when a phalanx of evils threatened, he had one particular trouble, of which he says, "We would not, brethren, have you ignorant of our trouble which came to us in Asia." What it specifically was, we know not. He tells us, however, that it was exceptional even in his sad life; for he was "pressed [borne down] out of measure," and again, "above strength" (human resistance inadequate to bear the load), so much so that he saw no way of escape, life hung in peril, "we despaired even of life." In that dreadful hour all seemed over. Such hours do come to the best and noblest of God's servants. Body gives way, heroism is weakened, faith is half shorn of its strength. It is the eclipse of all light, the hour of darkness and of the Prince of darkness; the very soul seems to put off its better attributes, and life to its core appears an unreality. St. Paul "had the sentence of death" in himself. Was there any "lower deep"? Yet in this season of terrible experience a Divine lesson was being taught him, and it was "that we should not trust in ourselves." Had he not learned it long ago? Yes; in part, but not in this precise shape nor in this degree. The capacity to suffer is peculiar in this, that its development requires a manifold experience. One trouble is not another trouble; one grief is not another grief. Affliction that reaches a certain sentiment or a particular section of our nature may leave other sentiments and sections altogether untouched. Every quality within must go through this ordeal. The loss of money is not the loss of position and influence, the loss of friend is not the loss of a child, the loss of a child is not the loss of a wife. Each affection must pass through the refiner's fire. Nay, the very instincts must share the purification ordained for such as are to be made "perfect through suffering." Every link must be tested, must be thoroughly known, before the chain can be formed. What the issue was in St. Paul's case he informs us, and it was this—all self-reliance was taken away, and, in utter hopelessness, his heart was committed to God with his life, even the God "which raiseth the dead." Could anything represent his marvellous deliverance except the resurrection? "Who delivered us from so great a death;" it was an act of omnipotence, and as signal as raising the dead. After this era in his career imagine his consciousness of God's power in him. There it was—part and portion of his being, thought of his thought, feeling of his feeling, separable never from the existence of self. Had the crisis passed? Yea; but maligners and intriguers and foes were still on his track; the half-Christianized Pharisee nursed the old grudge against him, and the Judaizer, who believed in no gospel of which the Law of Moses was not a vital part as a requisite to salvation, was as inveterate as ever in cunning and in the arts that undermine. Yet what a potency of assurance lies in sorrow! After this season of trial, St. Paul, who was very apprehensive of mischief from this Judaizing source, and most serious mischief, and who felt his own ministry more imperilled at this point than at any other, must have had an unwonted degree of heavenly strength imparted to his spirit. Is it not likely, indeed, that it was a period of special education for this struggle with the Judaizers? May it not have been that, while in Ephesus, Troas, Macedonia, the principal warrior on the side of Christianity and free grace had his armour refitted and burnished for the dangers newly impending? It is on record that he was revived and reinvigorated; for he speaks of God as one who had not only "delivered," but "doth deliver," and "in whom we trust that he will yet deliver us." "So great a death" had been escaped; why might he not hope for future and triumphant victory? Would not these Corinthians be brethren indeed? "Ye also helping together by prayer for us;" the joy of deliverance from his enemies would not be complete unless they were "partakers;" not even would he have triumph at the price of selfishness, but self in them and self in him must be one; and, therefore, the recurring plural, "we" and "us." "By the means," or through the agency of "many persons," the future deliverance, "the gift bestowed upon us," will be secured, and what then? It would be no private and personal thanksgiving on his part. Instead of that, "thanks may be given by many on our behalf." His joy would be their joy; their joy his joy; and, in their mutual thanksgiving, all would see that a common sorrow had been overruled for a common glory.—L.

Vers. 12—24.—*Defence of himself; character of his preaching.* "On our behalf" were the closing words of the preceding verse, and St. Paul would now impress upon the Corinthians that he was worthy of their confidence and affection. And yet, further, if their regard had been manifested by intercessions in his behalf, he wished to assure them that he had in his own mind a blessed witness to the truth and sincerity of his apostolic work. Conscience was this witness. It testified that, "in simplicity and godly sincerity" ("godly honesty and singleness," "a plain, single mind"), and without any carnal wisdom that is begotten of selfish intellect, and under the control of grace determining the matter and manner of his preaching, he had shown his character and done his work at Corinth. This was his "rejoicing;" it was inward, it was from God; it applied to his "conduct in the world," and especially to his labours among the Corinthians. Were they not the witnesses of all this? How could he be charged with duplicity? They read his heart in the letters written to their Church, and acknowledged his open and frank dealing. Certain persons were sharply censorious, questioning his integrity, attributing baseness to his motives, but some had testified to his "simplicity and godly sincerity," and rejoiced in his apostleship. And they and he would be united in this bond till the end, the day of the Lord Jesus. The day was already anticipated, and even now the "rejoicing" was a foretaste of its bliss. Such was his pleasure in them that he had been anxious to visit Corinth and confer "a second benefit," and so enlarge his usefulness in their community, and bind their hearts and his in a fellowship closer, firmer, tenderer. Two visits had been intended. Circumstances had changed his purpose. Was he, then, light-minded, fickle, irresolute? The explicit statement of the reason is delayed, but, while not assigning at the moment the cause of postponing the visit, he meets the charges of his enemies by speaking the stern, strong language of that internal authority, the conscience, to which he had just referred. Was he playing the part of a trifler and deceiver by raising expectations he never meant to fulfil? Was he carnally minded, saying, "Yea, yea, and nay, nay," so emphatically?

If he had this shifting and variable intellect (so said his enemies), what dependence was to be placed in such an apostle? Then the solemn protestation breaks forth, "As God is true, our word toward you *was not yea and nay.*" It was our purpose to come to you, but it was changed in the spirit of the gospel, and just as certainly as the preaching of Christ in this gospel was "*yea,*" just so certainly was our conduct in this matter in the "yea" of the gospel, *i.e.* truthful and reliable. All God's promises were made to be kept, and they are "yea" in Christ and we are "yea" in him. The response of the Church is "Amen," and it glorifies God through our instrumentality. All is in the Spirit of Christ—our preaching, promising, and living. God has made us firm and strong in Christ, has given us the unction of his Spirit, so that while Jesus of Nazareth was by distinction the Anointed, and received the Holy Ghost without measure, he has taken us, apostles and believers, unto himself, and conferred on us the gifts of grace. We are "sealed;" the mark is evident that we belong to Christ, and this "earnest" or pledge is "in our hearts." On the broad ground of his apostolic ministry and fidelity to its obligations, St. Paul makes his first defence as to sincerity and consistency. The charge of his adversaries, that he was guilty of double-dealing, is without foundation. His teaching and its results were proofs beyond question that he was anointed to his work, and these believers were the acknowledgment, the "Amen," that certified the fact. Why did he defend himself, at first, in this general way? Why not come at once to the specific reason for not visiting Corinth as he had promised? The reason is obvious. These Judaizers were striking at his apostleship, and the true issue between him and them turned on this point. What did they care about the assurance that he was coming to Corinth? This was a small matter. The main thing with his opponents, in their fiery zeal, was to overthrow the power of his ministry among the Gentiles by heaping contempt on his character and conduct. St. Paul saw this clearly, and hence his line of argument. He appealed to his ministry, to its fruits, most of all to the fact that the "yea" here was "yea," and the "Amen" of all converted souls was the endorsement of its success. And having met these slanders precisely in the form they were designed to affect him, he proceeds to tell the Corinthians why he had failed at the time to make them a visit. Hoping that his letter would lead them to see their grievous errors and induce them to repent and amend, he had deferred the journey to Corinth. "To spare you I came not as yet unto Corinth." The "rod" of severity (1 Cor. iv. 21) might not be needed, it would not if they administered the proper discipline in the case of the incestuous man and rectified the disorders in the Church. Had he not asked them to decide whether he should come to them "with a rod, or in love and in the spirit of meekness"? In this spirit of tender conciliation he had waited to see the issue. And now, vindicating his action in this matter, he solemnly appeals to God to be a witness against his soul if he had not spoken the truth. "I call God for a record upon my soul." Was not the case very clear? In what stronger light could it be put? There was the testimony of conscience, the seal of God, the unction and the earnest, the *yea* and the *Amen*; and here, last of all, the calling on God to testify against him if he had been untruthful. But, writing as he was under the consciousness that every word would be subjected by his adversaries to a merciless criticism, he would explain that he claimed no "dominion" over their "faith." In fact, they were steadfast in the faith, and his only wish was to be a helper of their joy. Thus ends the first chapter of the Second Epistle to the Corinthians. It is personal in an uncommon degree, a revelation of the man and the apostle in one of the critical periods of his career. Yet it is not a new revelation, but rather a fuller disclosure of what had been previously seen in part. No man can be known in one attitude and aspect. To see him in a single light and from a fixed angle of observation is impossible. Sculptors and painters, in representing men, work under this limitation. They select a characteristic expression, a dominant appearance, an historic moment. But not so with the historian, the poet, the dramatist. St. Luke in the Acts gives us St. Paul in various positions; but St. Paul is his own biographer, and, in this chapter, admits us to the privacy of his heart. Throughout the Second Epistle we shall enjoy this inner communion with him, and feel every moment the heart that throbs beneath the words.—L.

Ver. 1.—"*An apostle by the will of God.*" Paul claims to be what he is, not by his own choice, not by the favour or nomination of his fellow-men, but by the Divine will.

There were special reasons why he should so think of himself; the *office* to which he was called was special, for he was a commissioned apostle; and the *manner* in which he was called to that office was marvellous, supernatural, and miraculous. But the principle contained in this language applies to every Christian; whatever we are, whatever we do, we are, we do, by the will of God.

I. THIS IS EMPHATICALLY A CHRISTIAN PRINCIPLE. Our Lord Jesus lived a life of conscious obedience, for he came to do, not his own will, but the will of him who sent him. And he calls his disciples to a like life of subjection to the Divine will, by his precious blood redeeming them from self-will and summoning them to recognize the will of God in their salvation.

II. THIS PRINCIPLE APPLIES TO THE OCCUPATION OF EVERY CHRISTIAN. This may not be easy for the follower of Christ at once to see and believe. He looks back upon the time when he decided upon his business or profession, and he remembers that he was guided to a large extent by his own tastes and interests and by the advice of friends. But reflection will assure him that Providence is discernible in very familiar and ordinary means. And the appointment of God is to be observed, not only in the life of the statesman, the reformer, the missionary, but also in the life of the lowliest of Christ's disciples. It is not the scale upon which actions are performed that associates them with the Divine will, but the motive, the moral quality, the spiritual tendency. What is your calling? Are you a servant, a mechanic, a tradesman, a lawyer, a surgeon, a magistrate? In any case, if you are a Christian, and are in the path of duty, you are what you are, not simply through circumstances or through choice, but through the will of God. This principle has an obvious reference to *spiritual* work, for such is manifestly assigned by heavenly wisdom. The will of God calls the Christian labourer to witness, to work, and to endurance.

III. CONSIDER WHAT THIS PRINCIPLE IMPLIES ON THE PART OF GOD. It implies that the great Creator and Lord of all is conscious of all the affairs of all his people. He is not merely interested in their affairs; he exercises his will with reference to them. His will is not arbitrary or tyrannical; it does not override our liberty, for it is in harmony with justice and with kindness. Yet it has a supreme moral authority.

IV. CONSIDER WHAT THIS PRINCIPLE IMPLIES ON OUR PART. 1. The belief that we are what and where we are by the will of God gives dignity and grandeur to our life. It exalts the Divine will, yet it places us in a position of honour, as workers together with God. 2. It requires us daily to ask, "Lord, what wilt thou have me to do?" and then to bring our actions into harmony with the Divine will. 3. It induces a habit of cheerfulness and content. If we are not just what and where our will would choose, be it remembered that our Father has appointed our lot. What joy and strength must come to him who is convinced that his daily life is assigned and regulated by the will of the Eternal and Supreme!—T.

Vers. 4—7.—*Comfort, Divine and human.* The human heart is so sensitive, and the human lot is so sorrowful, that it cannot excite surprise when it is found that religion lays great stress upon the provision for true and lasting comfort which Divine wisdom furnishes and offers to the pious. And whilst the consolations of friendship and of philosophy are superficial, those of Christianity go down to the depths of the nature and extend throughout the whole period of life.

I. THE SUPREME AUTHOR OF SPIRITUAL COMFORT. Instead of looking merely to the earthly streams, the apostle goes straight to the living Fountain. 1. The universal sufficiency of this Divine consolation. God is the God of *all* comfort, and he comforts us in *all* our tribulation. For he is omniscient and knows all our sorrows: "He knoweth our frame; he remembereth that we are dust." He is infinitely sympathetic: "In all our afflictions he is afflicted." 2. Divine comfort abounds by Christ. Christ is all to his people. If, then, we share his sufferings and benefit by them, the ministration of his consolatory grace is enjoyed by us who recognize him as upon the mediatorial throne.

II. THE MINISTERS OF DIVINE COMFORT TO THEIR FELLOW-MEN. The apostle says of himself here what in a measure may be said of all true pastors. 1. They are qualified for this office by their participation in those sorrows which are the common lot of humanity. 2. By their experimental participation in the sufferings of the Redeemer.

They know something of that pain which human sin inflicted upon Christ's heart, and something of that sympathy which showed itself in Christ's tears and sighs. 3. By their interest and affection cherished towards those for whose spiritual welfare they are concerned. III. THE RECIPIENTS OF SPIRITUAL COMFORT. 1. In order to the enjoyment of true consolation, Christians must submit themselves with humility and resignation to the will of God. 2. If they have committed sin or neglected duty, they must not expect consolation except through contrition and repentance. 3. By whatever ministrations consolation may be administered, in order that it may be received aright, it must be sought from the God of comfort. and it must be sought in the Name and for the sake of Christ.—T.

Ver. 11.—*Intercessory prayer.* The grateful mind of the apostle recognized in the deliverance which had come to him at Ephesus the answer to the intercessions of the Corinthians on his behalf. Looking back upon affliction, illness, danger, he sees that a Divine hand has brought him out of adversity; yet he acknowledges his debt to those who had pleaded for him at the throne of grace. " Prayer moves the arm that moves the universe." Seeking the continuance of this intercessory application, he hopes great things from it in his future life and ministry.

I. FOR WHOM SHOULD INTERCESSORY PRAYER BE OFFERED? For all men doubtless, yet especially for certain classes. 1. For those who represent their brethren in devoted labour in Christ's cause. 2. Especially for all the public officers of the Church, for bishops and pastors, evangelists and teachers. They need it; for their responsibility is great and their difficulties are many, whilst their discouragements and disappointments are often sore.

II. WHO SHOULD OFFER INTERCESSORY PRAYER? The answer is emphatic and instructive: "*the many,*" i.e. the whole Church in the person of all its members— privately, in the family, and in an especial manner in the great public and solemn assemblies upon the Lord's day and other appointed seasons. The gatherings of worshippers should be composed of " the many," and everything should be done to secure the attendance of large numbers at the services of the Church.

III. WHAT BLESSINGS SHOULD BE SOUGHT IN INTERCESSORY PRAYER? Surely that the Christian labourers, whose case is remembered, may be made devoted, efficient, and successful. That they may be diligent in toil, faithful to their trust; that they may be cheered and comforted amidst their difficulties; and that their labour may not be in vain in the Lord.

IV. WHAT ADVANTAGES MAY BE EXPECTED FROM INTERCESSORY PRAYER? The expression, " helping together," seems to point to good results widely diffused. 1. To him who labours, the strength which comes from sympathy and the strength that comes from the abundant bestowal and outpouring of the Holy Spirit. 2. To him who prays, reflected blessings, such as ever abound to those who live, not for themselves, but for others. There is a reaction, a rebound of spiritual blessing, and they who water others themselves are watered. 3. To the world, a hallowed impression, as it sees how its salvation is near to the hearts both of those who labour and of those who pray for its enlightenment.

V. WHAT ULTIMATE RESULT MAY BE ANTICIPATED AS CERTAIN TO FOLLOW INTER- CESSORY PRAYER? *Thanksgiving* on the part of many; thanksgiving to God, who alike prompts the petition, qualifies the labourer, and gives his benediction to make all effort successful. Thanksgiving, here sincerely though imperfectly on earth, and hereafter perfectly, eternally in heaven.—T.

Vers. 18—20.—*The promises of God.* If Paul, in delaying his promised visit to Corinth, had seemed chargeable with levity and fickleness, he was not really thus guilty. Such qualities were alien from his Christian nature. And not only so; they were contrary to the character of the God he worshipped, the Saviour he preached; contrary to the promises of the gospel he believed—which they had received through his ministry. Thus the personal reference suggests the statement of a great Christian doctrine.

I. GOD IS GRACIOUS AND GIVES PROMISES. 1. Revelation is one long promise; it consists, not merely of commands and admonitions, but of assurances of favour and of help. Herein it proves its adaptation to the nature and to the needs of men. There were promises addressed to our first parents, to Abraham, to Moses. 2. The one promise distinctive of the old covenant was the promise of the Saviour, the Servant of the Lord, the Desire of all nations. In promising the Christ, Jehovah did indeed virtually promise all spiritual blessings to mankind. 3. The one promise of the new covenant is the promise of the Holy Spirit, in whom is grace and help for all human want and need. 4. The promises of God extend beyond this life into eternity, and include the vision of our Saviour and the possession of an immortal inheritance and home.

II. GOD IS FAITHFUL AND FULFILS HIS PROMISES. 1. Of this his unchangeableness and omnipotence are the certain pledge. What his fatherly goodness assures, his inexhaustible resources will realize. 2. The gifts of his Son and of his Spirit are the proof of his faithfulness. All his promises relating to these gifts have been already made good, and none who receives them can doubt his power and willingness to fulfil what yet remains. 3. The promises of individual guidance, protection, and aid cannot be falsified. "Ye know in all your hearts, that not one thing hath failed of all the good things which the Lord your God spoke concerning you." 4. Our confidence in Divine faithfulness may be tried, but cannot be disappointed. The stream sometimes disappears and flows for a space underground and unseen; but it is there, and soon emerges in beauty and power. So with the purposes of God; they may be hidden and delayed, but they shall all be accomplished.—T.

Vers. 21, 22.—*The Spirit in the heart.* The signs of an apostle were abundantly manifested in the case of St. Paul. Some of these signs were outward and visible; the wonders which he wrought and the labours which he fulfilled were evidences to many of his high calling. There were other signs which were rather internal, revealed in his own spiritual nature and life. These were precious to himself, whether they were recognized or not by others.

I. THE ANOINTING OF THE SPIRIT. 1. This rite received a significance from its employment under the old covenant in the designation of the prophet, the priest, and the king. 2. This significance is enhanced by the application to the Son of God of the official appellation, the Christ, *i.e.* the anointed One, the Being consecrated and commissioned by the Eternal. 3. The anointing claimed by the apostle is the qualification, by a supernatural and spiritual power, for holy and responsible office.

II. THE SEALING OF THE SPIRIT. 1. By this sealing the apostle was stamped with the mark which was the sign of Divine property in him. 2. And he was thus inwardly and graciously authenticated as the Lord's messenger to men. By the seal we understand the mark set upon the moral nature, the character, indicating Divine possession and Divine authority.

III. THE EARNEST OF THE SPIRIT. The other operations of the Holy Ghost relate to this present state; this refers to the future. 1. The Spirit within the heart is the earnest of a fuller indwelling; they who receive the Spirit are assured that they shall be "filled with the Spirit." 2. The earnest of a clearer revelation. The light shall brighten until the dawn shall be succeeded by the splendour of noonday. 3. The earnest of a richer, purer joy. The measure in which gladness is experienced in the present is a foretaste of the joy which is unspeakable and full of glory. 4. The earnest of an eternal inheritance. They who are possessed by the Spirit and pervaded by his gracious influences have within them both an anticipation of heaven and a preparation for heaven. To whom the Lord gives the pledge, he will give the redemption; to whom he gives the promise, he will give the glorious fulfilment and the eternal possession.—T.

Ver. 24.—*Helpers of joy.* Even when the immediate effect of the apostle's language and action was to produce heaviness and grief of spirit, the real and ultimate design was to awaken and to intensify spiritual joy. A benevolent nature can find no pleasure in the infliction of suffering; yet it may be that, as was the case with these Corinthians, the way of sorrow and repentance is the only path which can lead to true and lasting gladness.

I. THE CAUSES OF CHRISTIAN JOY. It is well known what the world calls joy—pleasure, mirth, exhilaration of spirits, occasioned by festivity and by prosperity. But the Scriptures represent, what Christian experience supports, that there are purer sources of nobler joy. 1. The joy of spiritual deliverance, known by those who are emancipated from the bondage of sin, ignorance, and error. 2. The joy occasioned by Divine favour. The psalmist appreciated this when he exclaimed, "Lord, lift thou up the light of thy countenance upon us; thou hast put gladness in my heart more than in the time that their corn and their wine increased." 3. The joy of anticipating the gracious and final approval of God.

II. THE MANIFESTATIONS OF CHRISTIAN JOY. 1. The most natural sign of spiritual gladness consists in the abundant utterance of thanksgiving and praise. "Is any merry? Let him sing psalms." 2. Where there is inward joy there is happy and energetic labour for Christ. "The joy of the Lord is your strength." Whilst a gloomy disposition cripples the energies of the worker, gladness within expresses itself in cheerful toil. He works well who "sings at his work."

III. THE WAYS IN WHICH THE CHRISTIAN MINISTER MAY HELP HIS PEOPLE'S JOY. 1. By presenting those Divine truths which are the spring and source of joy. 2. By fortifying their minds against all that would disturb and spoil their joy. 3. By providing for them outlets, in worship and in work, for the expression of the joy that is in them. 4. By encouraging all those special exercises which will promote joy. 5. By exhibiting to them the privilege of rejoicing, as a Christian virtue, and admonishing them to spiritual gladness as a happy duty: "Rejoice in the Lord alway, and again I say, Rejoice."—T.

Ver. 1.—" *Saints.*" A beautiful title frequently conferred upon the people of God in Scripture. They are called *believers*, since they exercise faith in Christ; *disciples*, as they place themselves under the teaching of Christ; *servants*, as they are pledged to do his bidding; *children*, as they are adopted into the family of God; and *saints*, since they are to live holily—" That ye may be blameless and harmless, the sons of God, without rebuke [blemish], in the midst of a crooked and perverse nation, among whom ye shine as lights in the world " (Phil. ii. 15). Christian saintship lays emphasis upon Christian holiness. 1. Upon *present* Christian holiness. It is not that we are to be saints in heaven only, but saints on earth. And we can have no well-founded expectation of being holy *there* unless we are holy *here*. It is the easiest thing in the world to be holy in the future! All are saints next year. But who is a saint *now*? The true child of God is—must be, or he cannot be a true child of God. 2. Upon *universal* Christian holiness. All real believers are real saints. Not so with the Romish Church, which canonizes a certain number, some of them very strange ones. Not as in our New Testament (erroneously continued in the Revised Version), *Saint* Matthew, *Saint* Mark, etc., as though these were saints because of their eminence in the Church. *All* Christians are saints. The idea of a Christian as a *believer* and *nothing more* is preposterous and utterly unscriptural. If a man believes, we want to know what his belief has done for him—what effects it produces. If it *does nothing*, it *is* nothing. Belief, says one, unites me to Christ. Very good; but Christ ridiculed the idea of a branch being united to the true Vine without bringing forth fruit. Belief, says another, alters my condition; being in Christ by faith, I am a "new creature." Excellent; but if you *are* a "new creature," let us *see* that you are, else we shall be apt to think that you are the *old creature* with a *new name*. "Faith, if it hath not works, is dead " (Jas. ii. 17). A *true* belief is ever followed by holiness. This, however, only suggests how much *false* belief there must be. True belief is something like the firing of a loaded cannon. If there be true firing the shot will be propelled. So, if we truly believe, we shall be propelled along the course of holiness. It would be but a poor thing if Christianity made us something very excellent in another world, and left us just as it found us in this. Holiness is, no doubt, progressive. But love of holiness, desire of holiness, striving after holiness, and some realization of holiness, are the possession of every true child of God.

I. HOLINESS IN HEART. Not the mere approval of holiness. Many applaud holiness who do not *possess* it and who do not *want to possess* it. It must reign in the centre of our being. A child of the devil has unholiness reigning in his heart, but a child of

God has holiness upon the heart-throne. "Behold, thou desirest truth in the inward parts; and in the hidden part thou shalt make me to know wisdom. . . . Create in me a clean heart, O God; and renew a right spirit within me" (Ps. li. 6—10). Holiness must *begin* in the heart; a holiness *tacked on to us* goes for very little. Many commence with *outward* reformation, when what they need is *inward*. The holiness of not a few is *very indifferent fruit hung on to the branches of a dead tree*. It is the pushing round of the hands of a clock which has no works behind the dial-plate. Mere external holiness is of nothing worth; God looks upon the heart. External saintship is the most miserable of shams.

II. HOLINESS IN THOUGHT. Some pass for holy livers who are very unholy thinkers. But if the heart be pure the thoughts are likely to be. Christ attached the same guilt to evil thinking as to evil doing (Matt. v. 28). It is not what we do, but what *we want to do!* Moreover, evil thinking is the father of evil doing. A child of God may be overtaken by a fault, sudden temptation may carry him away; but to think evil, to plan or purpose evil, is against the genius of his life. We should watch carefully our thoughts.

III. HOLINESS IN WORD. No man could tame the tongue, so God came to tame it. The true saint is pure in speech. The true saint speaks *holily*, not *cantingly*. Whenever a man speaks after a sanctimonious, shuffling, canting fashion, he is speaking under the inspiration of the devil. Some religious talking is peculiarly unholy; it sickens and disgusts; it is enough to turn the stomach of leviathan. But those who thus talk think they are infinitely pious, imagining probably that God Almighty measures his people's faces to ascertain how much grace there is in their hearts, and accounts them holy in proportion to their ability to pour forth unmeaning, impertinent or pretentious twaddle. We should speak holily, and then we shall be as far removed as we possibly can be from speaking sanctimoniously. And we should remember *the power of words*.

IV. HOLINESS IN DEED. Our actions will, as a general rule, show what we are, especially our *unstudied* actions. The true child of God is not only holy in profession, but in practice. The good tree will bring forth good fruit. Men judge us chiefly by what we *do*. The saint desiring the honour of God will let his light so shine that men may see his good works, and thus be led to glorify the Father in heaven. We shall not persuade either man or God that we *are* saints unless we *act* as saints. A *secret* holiness is no holiness. If we alone know that we are holy, we may be quite sure that we are unholy.

V. HOLINESS IN THE SPIRIT OF THE LIFE. The child of God is to have the fragrance of holiness pervading his life. The general bent of his life will be holy. To aid in the attainment of holiness we have : 1. *A Pattern*. Christ. He was "without fault." We are to seek to be *like him*. "As he which hath called you is holy, so be ye holy" (1 Pet. i. 15). 2. *A Helper*. The Holy Ghost. To (1) dwell within us ; (2) sanctify us; (3) aid us in every emergency. Without holiness our prospect is dark ; for "without holiness no man shall see the Lord" (Heb. xii. 14).—H.

Vers. 3—7.—*True comfort*. I. ITS SOURCE. God. Some seek comfort in reflecting that their case is no worse than that of others, that things will improve, that "it can't be helped ;" in attempted forgetfulness; in exciting and dissipating pleasures; in unmeasured complaint and repining. But the child of God goes to his Father. God is the God of comfort; he is "the God of *all* comfort" (ver. 3). All true comfort is of him. From God as "the Father of mercies" (ver. 3). All mercies are of him, and this great mercy of comfort amongst others. Comfort is a *mercy* ; it is of grace, not of right. Our sin has bred our sorrow, and we might have been left to it. But through the *mercy* of God we have abundant solace. As our comfort comes through mercy, we are not surprised to find that it comes "through Christ" (ver. 5), *the incarnation of the mercy of the Most High*. It is of the God who is "the Father of our Lord Jesus Christ" (ver. 3). It is thus associated with our redemption. It is for those who can say "*our* Lord Jesus Christ ;" *his* Father is then *their* Father. God's children shall be comforted; for they are the children of the One who is the sole Source of all true comfort.

II. ITS BESTOWAL. It comes to us when most needed. 1. *In affliction*. The world's consolations, such as they are, are offered to us when we least need them. Affliction finds few friends; but it finds one Friend. In the dense darkness the Christian has light in his dwelling, like Israel in Egypt. When the child of God is sick and troubled, his Father comes to him. 2. *In all our affliction.* (Ver. 4.) No affliction is beyond the reach of Divine comfort. God does not desert us in any trouble. Human comfort often aggravates our sorrow. When we are sore stricken we can bear no other touch but God's. We are sinking, but "underneath are the everlasting arms." Infinite in power; infinite also in consolation. 3. *In proportion to our affliction.* (Ver. 5.) God weighs all our troubles. He knows our sorrows. "As thy days so shall thy strength be." He is acquainted with our need, and will he not supply it? We may reckon upon sufficient Divine consolation in all our sorrows; very especially so when those sorrows have been directly brought upon us by our steadfastness in the faith, our loyalty to Christ, our faithfulness to God. Each martyr had a martyr's portion of comfort as well as of pain. And so with Paul, whom we may regard as a long-lived martyr, dying daily, yet living through the death-blows and comforted under them.

III. Its object. We are comforted for our peace and happiness, but here we learn that we are comforted for *our usefulness* also. Like the apostle, we are comforted of God that we may comfort others. Divine comfort enables us to do this; for: 1. We can then speak from experience of the efficacy of Divine comfort. 2. We can direct to the Source of comfort. 3. We can testify to the Divine faithfulness in bestowing comfort. 4. The salutary influence of sorrow comforted by God will make us efficient comforters. Only those who have tasted trouble are fitted to minister to the troubled. And of these only they who have been divinely comforted can truly comfort. Such will be just unlike Job's comforters. Christ was perfected as a Comforter by his sorrows, and by the Divine consolation which kept him from sinking under them. We are brought down and then lifted up again, that we may be made meet for this service. And great will be our joy if we see those comforted by us patiently enduring (ver. 6) their tribulation.

IV. One of its effects. Gratitude, mingled with adoration. "Blessed be the God," etc. (ver. 3). We shall thank God: 1. That he has comforted us. 2. That through this we have been enabled to comfort others. No stinted praise should we offer for such mercies. We shall all regard the first as great, but gracious spirits will regard the second as greater.—H.

Vers. 8—11.—*In the depths and out of them.* I. The emergencies of the people of God. God's children are often afflicted children. Far from escaping trial, it is frequently multiplied to them. Through much tribulation they enter the kingdom; with much tribulation they often abide in it whilst on earth. For them the furnace seems not seldom to be made "seven times hotter." Children of sorrows follow the "Man of sorrows." Like the apostle, they are sometimes "pressed out of measure," "weighed down exceedingly" (ver. 8), until their own power collapses. It is uncertain to what special exigency Paul refers, but in such straits was he that even his brave heart despaired of life. Happy are we if, like him, we do not in such tribulation despair of God. When our strength fails, his is untouched. As easy is it for him to deliver us when we are in great peril as when we are in little. God knows nothing of *emergency*.

II. The lessons of trial and peril. Very numerous—to teach us our weakness, to induce the pilgrim spirit, to bend our will to God's, to rouse us from lethargy, etc. One chief lesson noted here is to lead us to trust in God (ver. 9). He "raiseth the dead," and can do all things for us. Our perfect helplessness is demonstrated, and then faith lays hold of God's perfect helpfulness. Creatures become nothing, especially that very little creature, ourself. The soul cries out for God, and can rest upon nothing but omnipotence. This is Christian life—despairing of our own power, confident in God's. God sometimes keeps us in the fiercely hot furnace until he sees us walking therein by the side of the Son of God (Dan. iii. 25). Before we felt the fire we thought we could walk alone. God shakes us until he has shaken all the self-trust out of us. Self-confidence is poison; trial is intended to destroy that poison. When everything seems to fail us but God, then we lie at his feet.

III. Providence does not exclude prayer. (Ver. 11.) In our extremity we can do one thing—we can cry to God. The afflicted believer should say, "This one thing 1 do." 1. *Our own prayer.* Christians should not be dumb dogs. The command to pray is bound up with the command to trust. Prayer is *proof* of a trustful spirit. A confidence in God which makes us too lazy to call upon him is a confidence which will get more blows than blessings. We may be kept in the fires till we find our voice. 2. *The prayers of others.* The apostle evidently believed in the efficacy of intercessory prayer (ver. 11). He regarded such prayer as very real "help." Confidence in God's help which excludes confidence in spiritual help from our fellows is not so pleasing or honouring to God as some imagine. He has ever honoured "united" prayer. The prayers of saints are very precious and very prevailing as they ascend from the golden altar. God was very willing to deliver Peter out of prison, but he gave to the saints at Jerusalem the great honour of praying him out (Acts xii. 5). The prayers of righteous men avail much. God loves not only solo praying, but choral praying.

IV. Prayer answered in providence calls for praise. (Ver. 11.) Oftentimes, alas! we are so pleased with our deliverance that we forget to thank God for it. We say "Thank you" to every one except God. These things ought not so to be. When God hears us once in supplication, he should hear us once again in thanksgiving. Deliverances by God call for "songs of loudest praise." When prayer has been answered, praise should be exceedingly full and hearty. We do not prevail in prayer because we *did—and were unthankful.* When many have prayed and have been answered many should give thanks. We must have united praise meetings as well as united prayer meetings.—H.

Ver. 12.—*The testimony of our conscience.* I. The favourable testimony of conscience is a great support in the hour of trial and suffering. Affliction brought upon us directly by our own folly or sin is as wormwood for bitterness. Suffering is then greatly intensified by the reproaches of conscience. We feel that we are reaping only as we have sown. But when conscience acquits us we gain great moral support. The pressure of the heaviest burden is relieved; in the darkest day there is then some light. We may be "cast down," but we are "not destroyed" (ch. iv. 9). Sometimes the approval of conscience is enough to turn our sorrow into gladness, and to lead us to rejoice when otherwise we should have greatly lamented. We may glory in this without vain-glory. Paul was greatly comforted in his tribulations by a conscience which witnessed to the integrity of his conduct. II. The favourable testimony of conscience can be secured only by holy living. 1. Like the apostle, we must live in: (1) *Simplicity.* Singleness of purpose. Holiness: refraining from evil; walking ever before God. Though we shall not, it may be, be absolutely pure, we may abstain from all *wilful* transgression. (2) *Sincerity.* We must be true, honest, guileless, straightforward. Godly sincerity—*God-like* sincerity—*thorough;* a sincerity which comes from God. (3) *Not in fleshly wisdom.* A wisdom which has selfish aims, which is not particular about the means employed, a wisdom which ignores God. 2. This must apply to all our life. Our conversation in the world must be the same as in the Church. Some live double lives. It is no wonder that they have little peace of mind. Their conduct is ruled by *place* rather *principle.* We must be the same amongst the enemies of God as amongst his friends. III. We can live so as to secure the favourable testimony of conscience only by the grace of God. We may "sear" conscience, dull it, so that its voice may be scarcely heard; but if free, unfettered, it will assuredly condemn unless we are in alliance with the Eternal. We cannot live a life of which the healthy conscience will approve apart from him. We may lay down excellent plans for life, but we shall have to lay them down unless we get strength from the Strong One. The apostle had to say, "By the grace of God I am what I am" (1 Cor. xv. 10). Of ourselves we can do nothing—except sin. Our sufficiency is of him. He causes us to triumph. We cause ourselves to fail. We can walk "*in* the grace of God" only "*by* the grace of God."—H.

Vers. 17—20.—*Unchangeableness.* I. The unchangeableness of Christ. He is "the same yesterday, and to-day, and for ever" (Heb. xiii. 8). Paul, compelled by circumstances to alter his plans, and charged with fickleness, dreaded lest inconstancy should be associated with his Master or with the doctrines of the gospel. He passes rapidly from a defence of himself to defend that which is of so much more importance. Well would it be if we were equally jealous of the honour of Christ, equally anxious that through us no shadow should fall upon his glory. Christ is unchangeable as (1) a Saviour, (2) a Teacher, (3) an Example, (4) an Advocate, (5) a Master, (6) a Friend.

II. THE UNCHANGEABLENESS OF GOD. Illustrated by the fulfilment of Divine promises in Christ (ver. 20). Not one jot or tittle has fallen to the ground. In Christ is the " yea "—the affirmation, the accomplishment of Divine promise. True believers acknowledge this; "through him is the Amen" (ver. 20, new version); they say " Amen " to the Divine faithfulness which they see so strikingly illustrated in Christ. This is " to the glory of God." The glory of his character is proclaimed. God is not inconstant. A promise made by him is, to all intents and purposes, a promise fulfilled. This unchangeableness applies to all Divine dealing. Threat will as certainly be fulfilled as promise. Many believe in the *semi-unchangeableness* of God. They think he will fulfil all that they wish to be fulfilled, and kindly dispense with the remainder. They *make their own god*, as the heathen do.

III. THE UNCHANGEABLENESS OF CHRISTIAN DOCTRINE. Christian doctrine is certain, definite, abiding. It is not " yea " to-day and " nay " to-morrow (ver. 18). As there is no change in Christ, there is no room for change in statements respecting him. The apostle was assured that what he promulgated was *the truth* about *the Truth.* To change from that would have been to embrace error. If we change our utterances concerning the Saviour, we are justified only in so far as our prior statement was erroneous. The " old gospel " is the gospel for all new times. In Christianity the truest progress is to *go back*—to go back to what God himself revealed. As we do that, " more light will break from God's Word." But note, it will break *from God's Word,* not from the poor constellations of human wisdom. *There,* in the Word, we have the doctrine, which, like him in whom it centres, is " *the same* yesterday, and to-day, and for ever." There is no development in Christian doctrine as the ages roll on. There may be much development in our knowledge of it. The *same doctrine* is to come from the lips of all preachers at all times. The doctrine preached by Paul was preached also by Silvanus and Timothy (ver. 19).

IV. THE UNCHANGEABLENESS OF THE TRUE BELIEVER. This is relative, not absolute. But in proportion as we resemble Christ we shall become unchangeable— unchangeable in principle, in bent of mind, in love of holiness, in life-purpose, etc. We are not to be fickle, but steadfast. Men are to find us ever the same in loyalty to Christ, in devotion to his service. Paul was charged with lightness, instability of purpose (ver. 17); but it was a false charge. He altered his movements that he might not be altered himself. The same principles which led him to form his plans led him to change them. Change in them was evidence of unchangeableness in him. Inconstancy and inconsistency were grievous charges in apostolic eyes.—H.

Vers. 21, 22.—*Four privileges of the believer.* I. TO BE ESTABLISHED IN CHRIST. Brought into ever closer union with him. More and more firmly settled in faith. Increased in knowledge of him and of his doctrine. Made constant to Christ. Developed in likeness to him. Perfected increasingly along all the lines of Christian character. A work continuous; so Paul uses the present tense. The Christian's course is like that of the shining light, which shineth more and more unto the perfect day. Not all at once is he at his best. The seed of the kingdom takes time to develop. The points of contact at first may be few; but we are to be established " into " Christ. Believers should seek closest association with their Lord. True self-interest does not prompt the question—How far may we safely keep from Christ? but—How near to him may we draw? " Abide in me . . . if a man abide not in me, he is cast forth as a branch, and is withered " (John xv. 4—6).

II. TO BE ANOINTED. The believer is made like his Lord. Christ was the Anointed ; so therefore is the believer anointed. Christ was the Anointed of God ; so by God is the believer also anointed. Christ was anointed as King and great High Priest; so as king and priest is the believer anointed—" a royal priesthood " (1 Pet. ii. 9). Christ was anointed for a special life and a special work; so is the believer. It is not for nought that we receive our anointing from the Holy One (1 John ii. 20). We are consecrated, set apart, to carry out the Divine purposes. Christ was anointed with the Holy Ghost (Acts x. 38); so is the believer. With the anointing comes the power to realize the purpose of the anointing (1 John ii. 27). Here is great privilege, but at the same time great responsibility. Are we fulfilling the design of our anointing?

III. TO BE SEALED. Believers are sealed by the reception of the Holy Ghost (Eph. i. 13 and iv. 30). This is the Divine mark or seal put upon them. This sealing: 1. *Indicates proprietorship.* Believers have God's seal upon them because they are God's. He lays claim to them. They are in a most special sense *for God.* " Ye are not your own." 2. *Authenticates.* The genuineness of a believer is guaranteed by this mark. If he is sealed, then he is of God, though in some things he may seem eccentric. No spurious goods pass under this brand. Yet imitations of the Divine seal are many, so that we have need to " try the spirits," to ascertain whether they are truly of the Holy Spirit. The true seal authenticates us to ourselves. " The Spirit himself beareth witness with our spirit that we are children of God " (Rom. viii. 16). Our assurance springs from the Divine sealing. Dreamings, frames and feelings, and fancies, even opinions of others, are as nought compared with the witness of the Spirit. 3. *Invests with authority.* That which bears the royal seal has weight and authority among men; and those who bear the Divine seal are intended by God to exercise large influence over their fellows. They have the weight and authority of accredited servants of God. Not lightly are they to be esteemed; not contemptuously are their words to be received. So far as they are true to their sealing, they are of God, and are to be regarded as his messengers. 4. *Preserves.* Safety is often ensured by the human seal, always by the Divine. If God has marked us for his own, none shall pluck us out of his hand. Though the universe should rise up against a sealed saint, it should ingloriously fail; for the Divine seal is the pledge that Omnipotence will defend the sealed. God is not mocked. What he has set apart for himself he will have, and who shall say him nay? The saints are safe, for they are sealed of God. 5. *Testifies to value.* We seal only that which we value. And yet there may be no *intrinsic* value in that which is sealed. In itself it may be of no account; but we seal it because we can use it for some important purpose. So with the believer. Of himself he is nothing and less than nothing, and vanity. The sealing is no teacher of pride. He is sealed of God, not because he is excellent or of himself of any service, but because God in his infinite grace designs to make him so. The seal praises, not us, but God, who of us can make that which will redound to his glory and accomplish his purposes.

IV. TO BE ENDOWED WITH THE EARNEST OF THE SPIRIT. The Divine Spirit with which believers are sealed is the "earnest money," the pledge of that which has yet to come. The expression refers to that part of the purchase money which was paid in advance as a security for the remainder. Of what, then, is the possession of the Divine Spirit a guarantee? 1. Of yet fuller possession of the Spirit. 2. Of complete salvation. The "firstfruits" of the Spirit a pledge of the great harvest (Rom. viii. 23; Eph. i. 13, 14). 3. Of fulfilment of all Divine promises. 4. Of our enjoyment of the eternal inheritance. The heaven is begun. No great heaven above for those who have no lesser heaven below. This pledge of the future does not conflict with diligence and faithfulness in Christian walk. These are the signs of the possession of the Divine Spirit—a mirror in which alone we may see the reflection of the great privilege we claim. The holier we are in inner and outer life the more clearly shall we see what we possess. If we walk unholily the mirror will reflect only sin and condemnation. The perseverance of saints is saints persevering.

V. THE SOURCE OF THESE PRIVILEGES. God. We are debtors for these vast mercies. In them we are "enriched by him." Knowing the Source, we shall know where to seek for those things which are "more precious than rubies."—H.

Ver. 5.—*Christian suffering.* It is correct to say that Christ suffered in order that we may not suffer, died that we may never die. "Christ suffered for us." But it is also correct to say that Christ suffered in order that we may suffer with him, and, following him in the path of self-denial and patience, may be with him in his kingdom and glory. The apostles Paul and Peter regarded sufferings for Christ as continuations of the sufferings of Christ, and always looked, and taught their brethren to look, along a vista of trial and affliction toward the happy issue of being glorified together with Christ at his appearing. *As members of the body of Christ we suffer.* As the natural body of Christ suffered in the days of his flesh, so now the mystical body, the Church, suffers in these days of the Spirit. It must have its agony and bloody sweat before the end comes; blows of contempt, scourging, buffeting; and must have its "bones sore vexed," as were those of his body on the cross; sore vexed, but not broken: "A bone of him shall not be broken." *As witnesses for the Name of Christ we suffer.* While walking and witnessing in the acceptance and power of his resurrection, we must be identified with him as the despised and rejected One. We are in collision with the spirit of the world, and the more firmly we lift our testimony against it the more the sufferings of Christ abound in us. In primitive times men suffered as Christians, for no other offence than the confession of the Saviour's Name. The council of the Jews arrested the apostles Peter and John, and put the deacon Stephen to death, on this charge. The cultivated Pliny, when Proconsul of Bithynia, about forty years after the death of St. Paul, is shown, by his correspondence with the Emperor Trajan, to have regarded the very fact of being a Christian as a crime worthy of instant punishment. Christian faith was in his eyes nothing but "an absurd and excessive superstition," and the noble constancy of the Christians under threats and torture "a contumacious and inflexible obstinacy." So the witnesses for our Lord suffered in Bithynia under the illustrious Trajan, as well as in Italy under the infamous Nero, and throughout the empire under the cruel Domitian and Diocletian. But it sustained them to know that they were fulfilling the sufferings of Christ. His grace was sufficient for them. On them rested the Spirit of glory and of God. Such discipline continues, though without actual peril of life. Faithful Christians suffer many things, at many points, and from many quarters. And when they suffer for the Church it is a continuation of our Lord's unselfish suffering. So St. Paul endured all things for the Lord's sake and the sake of the elect. He used the expression, "I fill up that which is behind of the afflictions of Christ" (Col. i. 24), in reference to his inward anxiety and "agony" for those at Colosse and Laodicea, who had not seen his face in the flesh. His anxiety for their confirmation in the mystery of God was a sort of supplement to the deep struggle of the Saviour in behalf of multitudes, Paul included, who had not seen and could not see his face in the flesh. The apostle had no thought of adding to the sufferings of Christ in respect of their expiatory virtue, but rejoiced that he was permitted to follow his Master in this same path of affliction and solicitude for the Church. All sowers of "the incorruptible seed" have to sow with tears. And hearers of the Word are most profited when they receive it "in much affliction, with joy of the Holy Ghost." Three views may be taken of those afflictions which are distinctively Christian. 1. They are for the Lord, incurred and endured for his Name. So were the afflictions of Christ for the Name and glory of the Father. The world hated both him and his Father. 2. They are for the good of the Christian sufferer—tribulations that work patience, chastisements for his profit. So were the afflictions of Christ for his own good. "Though he were a Son, he learned obedience by the things which he suffered." 3. For the sake of his brethren, or for the good of the Church, which is edified through the self-denial and godly patience of individual believers in successive generations. So were the afflictions of Christ for the Church which he redeemed, and in which he now succours them that are tempted. The present time, then, is one of communion with our Lord in suffering. Let four advices be given to those who suffer with a good conscience—for well doing and not for evil doing.

I. HAVE A CARE ONE FOR ANOTHER. Trouble may make men sullen and self-engrossed. Correct this tendency by remembering that you are not isolated persons, but parts of the body of Christ, and so members of one another. If you suffer, bear yourselves so that others may be confirmed by your faith and patience. If they suffer, suffer with them, help to bear their burdens, condole in their sorrow, minister to their necessity. "Weep with them that weep."

II. LEARN PATIENCE FROM "THE MAN OF SORROWS." It ought to cure peevishness and wilfulness to read the story of our Lord's passion, and consider the meekness of him "who endured such contradiction of sinners against himself." See how St. Peter sets before suffering saints the example of their Master (1 Pet. ii. 20—23).

III. LOOK FOR STRENGTH TO THE SYMPATHIZING SAVIOUR. In the present connection between Christ and Christians the Scripture marks a distinction. The saints suffer with Christ; Christ sympathizes with the saints. The word for the former is συμπασ-χεῖν: the word for the latter is συμπαθεῖν. The Head is raised above suffering, but sympathizes with the distressed and bruised members, and loves to supply consolation and relief. "Our consolation also aboundeth by Christ." He makes us strong, even in the hour when our hearts are jaded and our spirits faint. The crook in the lot, the thorn in the flesh, the buffeting in the world, the disappointment in the Church,—he knows it all, and he can bear us through it all.

IV. REJOICE IN THE HOPE OF HIS COMING. There is a deep wisdom of God in the long-drawn affliction of Christ and the Church. Glory comes out of the dark womb of trouble. How long the travail must be God only knows. Jesus Christ suffered till he was perfected, and then God exalted him. The Church must suffer and struggle till she is perfected and God exalts her too. And the glory that awaits her is that of her Beloved. As the Church enters into his sufferings, so is she to enter into his glory. This is the day for faithful service and saintly patience. The coming day is that of honour and reward, "that, when his glory shall be revealed, ye may be glad also with exceeding joy."—F.

Ver. 9.—"*The sentence of death in ourselves.*" St. Paul had just recovered from a depression of spirit under which his frame, never very robust, had been bowed down almost to the grave. He was no Stoic. No spiritual man is. Regenerate life brings quickened sensibility. The new heart is both deep and rapid in its appreciations, and feels intensely both joy and sorrow. St. Paul had not lost faith or comfort in his distress. He trusted in the living and life-giving God. All spiritual men find that faith thrives when they have to endure hardness. If they occupy places of ease or walk on sunny heights, they look down into the sorrows of life and call them dark and dismal. But when their path lies through the valley on which death-shadows fall, they lift their eyes to the hills whence help comes. The hills are near and strong, and the sky above reveals its golden stars. It is in houses of comfort that we often find doubt and discontent; but Divine serenity floats over the tried saints, and the secret prayers of God's stricken ones have the sweetest tones of hope. The reason of this is not obscure. If your chamber is full of light by night, and you look out through the window, you discern little or nothing—all is dark. But if your chamber be in darkness, and you look forth, you see the moon and stars ruling the night, the trees standing as solemn sentinels in the valley, and the mountain casting a broad shadow on the sea. So, when you have worldly ease and pleasure, heavenly things are very dim to you. But, when the world is darkened, heaven brightens, and you trust in God who raises the dead. There is a heathen conception of death which makes all vigorous life shrink and recoil. The dead are thought to go away into a mournful stillness, or move through the air and haunt lonely places, as pallid shades or ghosts. There is also a Hebrew conception of death which sufficed in the time of the Old Testament, but falls quite short of what is now brought to light by the gospel (see Ps. cxv. 17; Isa. xxxviii. 18, 19). But Christ has delivered from the fear of death. Every believer in Christ may enter into the consolation of St. Paul. If he is in sickness and has a sentence of death in himself, or sees that sentence written on the wan countenance of one whom he loves, he is not without a strong solace. It is not the mere philosophical tenet of the immortality of the soul, which implies an endless being, but by no means attains to the Christian doctrine of eternal life. It is faith in God who raises the dead. Father Abraham had this comfort when he strode up the hill, with the knife to slay and the fire to consume in sacrifice his dear son, "accounting that God was able to raise him up even from the dead; from whence also he received him in a figure." We read of certain Hebrew women who through faith "received their dead brought to life again." We remember one instance in the ministry of Elijah, and another in that of Elisha. In those times it was an object to live long in the land which Jehovah God had given to his people; and so it was a blessed resurrection to be restored so as to prolong one's days on the earth. In the beginning of the gospel a few such cases are reported. We allude to the ruler's daughter, the widow's son, Lazarus, and Tabitha or Dorcas. But the gospel being fully unfolded, and the hope laid up in heaven made known, there are no more instances of restoration to mortal life. To depart out of the world and be with Christ is far better than to remain in it. So the resurrection for which we wait is that of the just at the appearing of Jesus Christ. When we believe in God who raises the dead, the first and chief reference is to his having raised up the slain Jesus (see Rom. iv. 24; x. 9; 1 Cor. xv. 15). This is in the very heart of the gospel, and this carries with it the sure and certain hope of the resurrection of " the dead in Christ." "God hath both raised up the Lord, and will also raise up us by his own power." The sentence of death which St. Paul had felt was not executed till years had passed; but it was well to be forearmed. Ere long, warned or unwarned, we all must endure death, if the Lord tarry. And before we die we may have to see the sentence carried out in others whom we love and for whom we must go mourning. There is no help in facing death but that which comes of faith; there is no comfort in regard to those who have endured it but in the belief that they are already with God, "breathers of an ampler day," and in the hope that he will raise them up complete and glorious at his coming.—F.

Ver. 19.—*Christ is "yea."* The apostle defended himself against imputations of levity and self-contradiction. He did not lightly form or change his plans. He did not bandy about "yea and nay." The serious theme of his ministry was some security for its grave and consistent treatment. At the present day one hears a good many complaints of vagueness and vacillation in the pulpit. Preachers are said to use ambiguous phrases, propound shifting opinions, and leave their hearers unsettled and perplexed. They seem to have no certainty in their own minds, and therefore cannot convey a sure and straightforward gospel to others. Their word is "yea and nay." Now, there may be reason for hesitancy on some topics of religion. It may be a great deal wiser than absolute assertion. But as to the main theme of gospel preaching there should be perfect certainty; for the very essence of it is the setting forth of Jesus Christ, the Son of God. He is the True One, and ought to be proclaimed with firmness, consistency, and "much assurance." The Greeks were fond of speculation. At Athens they inquired after some new thing. At Corinth they were fickle and disputatious. On such a people the calm certainty of St. Paul's preaching must have fallen with surprise. It was testified that Jesus, who had taught in Judæa, but never even visited Greece, and who had been crucified at Jerusalem, was the Son of God; that he had ascended to heaven, and would judge the world on an appointed day. This was not submitted to the critical acumen of the Greeks for their examination and approval. It was delivered as truth, and not as a lie—yea, and not nay. Jesus, the Son of God, was the grand Reality in a world of delusions, and the grand Essence in a world of shadows. Such had been the teaching of St. Peter and the other apostles at Jerusalem, of Philip at Samaria, and of the Cypriote and Cyrenian brethren who first delivered the testimony at Antioch. No one was more clear or more intent upon this than St. Paul. Though his powerful mind could easily have dealt with many questions that would have interested the Greeks, he resolved to adhere to the simple testimony to Jesus, the Son of the living God. It may be said that, though this was right and needful in the world which St. Paul looked upon, and is right and needful still among Jews and heathens, it is not necessary in Christian countries. But alas! it is necessary. Countries called Christian are still very ignorant of Christ; all of them need full, definite, and firm preaching of the Son of God. There is nothing like it for delivering men from their sins, and drawing them away alike from the arid sands of unbelief and from the marshy places of superstition. But the testimony must be delivered with unfaltering heart and voice; for it is the preaching of the Yea, the Faithful and True—a pillar that cannot be shaken, a foundation that cannot be moved. Heathenism was full of contradiction, incoherence, and contrast. Its gods conflicted with each other and its oracles were uncertain. It was and still is a thing of "yea and nay." Buddhism, in some respects an improvement on the heathenism which it supplanted, after all amounts to a mere dreary nihilism. One who had studied it carefully (Sir J. Emerson Tennant) said of Buddhism that, "insufficient for time and rejecting eternity, the utmost triumph of this religion is to live without fear and to die without hope." This is not "yea," not even "yea and nay," but a perpetual dismal "nay." In Christendom, too, something like it appears. There is a weary scepticism which a famous writer described as "the everlasting No." Partly it is a shallow fashion, partly it is a real plague and misery of the generation to have "nay" only in regard to the unseen. God is not. The Bible is not. The devil is not. Heaven is a dream. Hell is a fable. Prayer is useless.

Faith is a fond fancy. So the mist wraps men in its chilly fold. Against all this we place the everlasting Yea. Jesus Christ is God's mighty and loving Yes to the children of men. And whatever the differences among our religious communities, in this testimony all are at one. The Son of God is he who can give light to the darkened mind, rest to the weary spirit, warmth to the frozen heart. In him desire is satisfied, apparent contradictions are reconciled, or hope is given of solutions by-and-by, for which we can well afford to wait. Some contrast the Christian faith unfavourably with the physical sciences. They say that it is full of mysticism and loose conjecture, whereas the sciences proceed by rigorous induction of facts observed, collated, and scrutinized. In the former we are asked to walk on air; in the latter, every step we take is on sure and solid ground. This we totally deny. There is no fair and proper test of historical and moral truth to which our holy religion refuses to be subjected. We have the well-authenticated records spoken and written by those who saw and heard Jesus Christ. We have the best reasons for trusting their testimony; and in the words, and works, and character, and suffering of Jesus, in his reappearance after death, and in the whole influence which he has exerted over millions of men for nearly nineteen centuries, we have overwhelming proof that, while human, he is superhuman— he is the Son of God. It is science that has to change its voice, not religion. It has to modify its assertions, correct its conclusions, and reconsider its theories; but Jesus Christ is "the same yesterday, and to-day, and for ever;" and the gospel which proclaims him brings to us the Divine "yes" to which we have only to respond with the human "yes" of an unwavering faith. The Saviour asks, "Believest thou that I am able to do this?" Be ready with the answer, "Yea, Lord."—F.

Ver. 20.—*The certainty of Divine promises.* I. ALL THE PROMISES OF GOD. From the first (Gen. iii. 15) which points to the Saviour's first coming, to the last (Rev. xxii. 20) which assures us of his second coming, these are all very good. Their range is vast, their bounty large, their comfort sweet and strong. They bring balm to our wounds, help to our infirmities, rest to our weariness, encouragement to our prayers. They are "exceeding great and precious." Scattered as the promises are over the Bible, they should be searched out and read with an intelligent regard to the time when they were given, the persons to whom they were addressed, and the nature of the dispensation under which they were issued. They are profitable in a general sense as exhibiting the Divine character and mind, and they convey individual comfort to those who, in express terms or by fair inference from the express terms, are indicated in particular promises. These comprehend assurances of (1) temporal welfare; (2) free pardon; (3) a renewed and obedient heart; (4) the indwelling of the Holy Spirit; (5) the return of the Lord and our gathering to him in his glory. These are the keys to open all doors in the dungeons of Doubting Castle and set captives free. These are the strong withes that bind the holiest affections of men, or the cords and bands let down from above, which they hold as they skirt the precipices of moral danger and climb the steep places of duty. These are the stepping-stones across waters of despondency, on which pilgrims may pass dry-shod to the happy shore.

II. THE SECURITY OF ALL THOSE PROMISES IS IN JESUS CHRIST. No Divine promises are made to us out of Christ, and no promise in him can fail. This arises from: 1. The constitution of his mediatorial Person. He is very God and very man: God who is true and cannot lie, in union with a guileless Man who had no deceit in his mouth. 2. The nature of his mediatorial offices. As he is the Prophet, all the promises of Divine teaching and enlightenment are secure in him. As he is the Priest, all the promises of pardon, of acceptance in worship, and of salvation to the uttermost are secure in him. As he is the King, all the promises of the subdual of sin and of deliverance from spiritual adversaries are secure in him. 3. The covenant relations of Christ to his people. They are so comprehended in him or represented by him that all the promises made to him are for their help and consolation, and all the promises made to them are for his glory. So are they assured of pardon through him, eternal life in him, the Holy Spirit of him and by him, and the new heavens and new earth with him who is the Amen, faithful and true.

III. THE END IN VIEW IN THE SURENESS OF THE PROMISES. "For glory to God through us." It is glorifying to him that we go to the promises for solace and live on the promises by faith. It was when Abraham believed a promise, and was strengthened in faith, that he gave glory to God. And this way of glorifying our God is open to all of us. Let us not stagger at his promises, but believe his love and rely on his faithfulness. He cannot deny himself. Glory be to the Father, who promises to be a Father to us, and to take us for his sons and daughters! Glory be to the Son, in whom all things are ours by free grace, and God himself is not ashamed to be called our God! Glory be to the Holy Ghost, for the anointing, the sealing, and the earnest in our hearts (vers. 21, 22)! The promises of God being established in Christ, we too who believe are established in Christ by the Holy Spirit, and so the promises are ours. What will you do who have no hold of the promises, no hearty faith in the Divine Promiser? For you there is no bright future; for the inheritance is by promise of free grace in Christ Jesus. Yet we do not ask you to believe a promise. Strictly speaking, there is no promise to men who are not in Christ. But Christ himself is set before you and offered to you. Believe on the Name of the only begotten Son of God, according to the tenor of the gospel. Then all things will be yours. The promises of grace and glory are for you; for they are all yea and amen in Jesus Christ our Lord.—F.

Ver. 24.—*The apostolic ministry.* I. APOSTOLIC TESTIMONY. Our religion is based on facts seen and known, abundantly verified and honestly related. Of these facts apostles were the chosen witnesses. When they spoke to their countrymen, the Jews, they showed how those facts concerning Jesus of Nazareth fulfilled Old Testament types and prophecies of the Christ. But the real foundation which they laid everywhere was one of fact. Jesus had died and God had raised him from the dead. Of these things they were absolutely sure, and on their testimony the Church was built. On this it is well to lay emphasis. From one side there comes an insidious suggestion to cease from asserting the miraculous nativity and the actual bodily resurrection of Jesus Christ as historical facts, and to content ourselves with the elevation of ideas and sweetness of culture which are associated with his Name. To this we cannot listen, because we cannot live in a house without foundations, and we do not believe that the ideas and influences of Christianity can long remain with us if we part with the historical Christ to whom the apostles bore witness. From the opposite side we encounter another danger. The facts which were testified by apostles and prophets are overlaid with masses of theological statement and niceties of controversial distinction. Not the Redeemer is preached, but the scheme of redemption; not the death of Christ, but the doctrine of atonement; not his resurrection, but the tenets of the schools regarding the results secured by his "finished work." Now, we do not for a moment disparage theology, systematic or polemical, or forget that St. Paul put much theology into his letters to the Churches; but it is a thing taught and argued, not witnessed. We must adhere to our point, that the gospel is a proclamation of facts, and the Church rests on a foundation of facts, certified by the apostles as competent and chosen witnesses—facts, however, not dry and barren, but significant, suggestive, full of profound meaning and intense spiritual power. St. Paul was careful to assume no higher place in regard to the gospel than that of a faithful witness. He delivered it just as he had received it, "by the revelation of Jesus Christ." He told the Galatians that, if he himself should be found at any future time proclaiming any other gospel, or if an angel from heaven should do so, he was not to be listened to—he was to be accursed. Any perversion of that gospel which had been delivered from the beginning would be sufficient to discredit an apostle as a false apostle, an angel as a fallen angel.

II. APOSTOLIC AUTHORITY. The apostles had authority to "bind and loose," to direct and administer in the early Church. On fit occasions they exerted such authority, and none of them more firmly or wisely than Paul. But they forbore as much as possible to press mere authority even in matters of order and discipline, and they dislaimed any right of dominion over the faith of their fellow-Christians. The Apostle Paul in particular is never found demanding attention or obedience to his teaching on the ground of his official dignity. Many signs and special miracles attended his ministry and confirmed his word; but he never posed as a worker of wonders in order to awe the minds and compel the submission of his hearers. His aim was to manifest the truth to the consciences of men. In founding the Corinthian Church he had "reasoned,' "persuaded," "testified," and "taught the Word of God" (see Acts xviii.). His own statement is, "I declared unto you the testimony of God" (see 1 Cor. ii. 1—5). The object of St. Paul in thus refraining from any assertion of a right to dictate was to build the faith of the Church, not on apostles, but on God. He would not say, "Believe because we bid you, and whatever we tell you." He was one of a band of witnesses to Jesus Christ the Lord; but, once those facts were believed with the heart, the disciples in every Church stood for salvation on the same ground with the apostles themselves, and had the same confirmation of the truth by the Holy Spirit.

III. LESSONS FOR THE MODERN MINISTRY OF THE WORD. For the propagation of the gospel there must still be witnesses; for the edification and peace of the Church there must be teachers, helps, governments, overseers. But none of these have a right to "lord it over God's heritage;" least of all may they lord it over the faith of their brethren. If the apostles of the Lamb disclaimed such dominion, how much more should they who have ministries to fulfil in the modern Churches of God! It is preposterous to connect apostolic dignity or the glory of apostolic succession with pomp and lordliness and the assertion of official superiority. It is apostolic to serve diligently and suffer patiently, to preach the truth in love, and to teach the things which concern the Lord Jesus Christ, but seeking no honour or glory from men. The object of the ministry in regard to those who are without is to bring them to repent and believe the gospel. The object in regard to those who are within the household of faith is to promote their joy and health. 1. "In faith ye stand." This is not submission to a human authority, but allegiance of heart to God in Christ Jesus. In emotions, opinions, anxieties, conjectures, there is no standing. Only by faith is the heart fixed, the mind established, in this world of change and disappointment, solidity imparted to the character, and calm courage breathed into the soul. Want of faith or decay of faith accounts for restlessness, weakness, rashness and inconstancy. The heart is "tossed and not comforted." The will is yielded to selfish desires and uneasy impulses. But "we have access by faith into the grace wherein we stand." 2. Those who minister to the faith of Christians increase their joy. The apostles were intent on this (see Rom. xv. 13; Phil. i. 25, 26; 1 Pet. i. 8; 1 John i. 4). And every true minister of Christ will find, with St. Paul, that his own spiritual life is bound up with the steadfastness and liveliness of those whom he instructs in the truth.—F.

Ver. 1.—"By the will." In this assertion, "an apostle of Jesus Christ by the will of God," St. Paul briefly summarizes the claim to apostleship which he elsewhere argues, and which he so earnestly vindicates in a later portion of this Epistle. He carries the question to the final court of appeal, declaring that the primal source whence comes all call to office in the Christian Church is the "will of God." It matters not how that "will" may be expressed; whether, as to the older disciples, in the call of their Master to apostleship, or, as to St. Paul, by direct revelation from heaven. The only point of interest is this—Have sufficient signs of the Divine will concerning us been given to carry conviction to our minds? And what is the proper influence which the recognition of the will of God concerning us should have as we hold and fulfil the duties of the office? Such a conviction is—

I. A MAN'S HUMILIATION. It makes him nothing and God all. It sets him down among the ministries that God may use as he wills. But it brings to him a holier humiliation than that. It bows him down under the greatness of the trust he bears, oppresses him with the honour that is laid upon him, makes him feel his helplessness and unworthiness, as may be illustrated in the hesitations and humble expressions of Moses and Jeremiah when they were called of God. The healthiest humility is that wrought by a great and solemn trust.

II. A MAN'S INSPIRATION. It gives him an idea and an object in his life. It moves him with the power of a great purpose. It calls him to high endeavour. It wakens into bright activity every faculty and power of his nature. It urges him with the sense of duty. It delivers him from the weakness that ever attends a conflict of motives. It holds out before him the reward of the faithful.

III. A MAN'S STRENGTH. In the power of the conviction that he is where God would have him be, and is doing what God would have him do, a man can overcome and dare all things. St. Paul's own endurances are inconceivable save as we can feel that he had this strength. Especially illustrate from his wearying controversy with the Jewish party. They said evil things of him, but this was his strength—he knew that he was an apostle *by the will of God.*—R. T.

Ver. 4.—*Comforted, and therefore comforters.* It may seem strange that the Bible, and Christian ministers following its example, should deal so frequently and so largely with troubles and afflictions. You sometimes half suspect that Christian people must have a larger share of earthly sorrow than falls to the lot of others. We may admit a sense in which this is true. The higher susceptibilities of the Christian man, his clearer vision of unseen things, and his separateness from the world, do seem to involve some special kinds of suffering from which the heedless and the godless are free. The influences on personal character and on individual life, wrought by God through the sorrows he sends, are often presented. In the passage now before us the apostle puts another side of their influence. Our afflictions and our comfortings become a *blessing to others.* " That we may be able to comfort them which are in any trouble." Our sorrows have by no means exhausted their stores of blessing when they have dispelled *our* doubts, delivered us from *our* dangers, and cultured *our* characters ; they have stores of blessing left in them still, with which, through us, to enrich and comfort *others.* This may be set before us in two of its aspects.

I. OUR AFFLICTIONS AND COMFORTINGS ARE THE SOURCES WHENCE COMES OUR FITNESS FOR INFLUENCING OTHERS. It may be a question beyond present solution, what exact share have the sorrows of our past lives had in the formation and nourishment of our present abilities for Christian work and influence ? And yet surely no man can reach middle life or old age, and feel the respect in which he is held, his power to comfort and help others, and the value that is set upon his judgment and counsel, without recognizing how much of that fitness for influence has come out of his experience of sorrow. Precisely what qualities are nourished by particular forms of trouble we may not be able to decide, but the whole result we can estimate, and there is not one true Christian who would hesitate to say, " Blessed be God for the afflictions of my life ; yes, even for those which bruised and almost broke my heart, because, as sanctified by God, they have fitted me to sympathize with and to comfort others." Experience brings power. But the Christian's experiences are not of griefs only ; they are of griefs *together with Divine comfortings,* and these together bring a peculiar kind of power. This may be illustrated from any of the spheres of Christian influence. 1. Take the power of a Christian's ordinary conversation. We can discover in the very tones of the voice the holy subduedness that tells of some great woe that has put into the words and the voice that humbleness and gentleness. How often this tone of the stricken ones has had its power upon us ! 2. Take the special efforts which are made, by conversation, for the conversion and instruction of others. 3. Take any endeavour to express sympathy with those who may now be suffering under God's mighty hand. How different are the consolations offered by stricken and by unstricken ones ! The unstricken can find beautiful words, and be truly sincere as they utter them. But the stricken ones can express unutterable things in silence and look. Send the long-widowed woman to cheer the newly widowed. Send the mother who has children in heaven to comfort the mother who sits so still, with broken heart, bending over the baby's coffin. The plant of healing sympathies grows and blossoms and fruitens out of our very wounds and tears and deaths. Then it will but be reasonable to expect that, if God has high places of work for us, and valuable influence for us to exert, he will need to bring us through great and sore troubles. St. Paul recognizes this necessity in our text. How his life was filled with anxieties and sorrows we seldom worthily estimate. Great soul ! He did not care to be always talking about himself ; only once or twice does he lift the veil and show his secret history ; but there —in much affliction awaiting him everywhere, and the comfortings of God abounding in all—is the explanation of his mighty and gracious influence. He was " comforted of God that he might be able to comfort them which are in any trouble." The same truth shines out even more clearly from the life and cross of our Lord Jesus Christ. He is able to succour because in all points tempted. Lifted up, " he draws all men unto him." Gaining his influence by his own sufferings borne in patience and faith. Winning power to save and help the world by dying an agonizing death, and knowing, in the uttermost needs of a dying hour, the gracious comfortings of God.

II. Our afflictions and comfortings gain for us all the power of a noble example. In the previous part of the subject our *conscious* efforts to help and bless others have been chiefly considered ; but the good man's influence is by no means to be limited to them. There is an *unconscious* influence, less easily calculated, but more mighty, reaching more widely, blessing as does the bracing air of the hills, or the fresh blowing of sea-breezes, or the face of a long-lost friend. And this kind of power to bless belongs peculiarly to those who have come out of God's tribulations and comfortings. 1. Estimate the moral influence of those in whom afflictions have been sanctified upon men who are living with no sense of spiritual and eternal things. 2. Estimate their influence on doubting and imperfect Christians. 3. Estimate the influence of such persons on children. You may have thought that your afflictions have set you aside from your work. Nay, they have just lifted you up to the trust of some of God's highest and best work. Tribulation worketh patience, experience, and hope. It matures the finer elements of character. But it does more—it fits us for work, for higher influence on others, enabling us to set before men all the power of a noble example. Our afflictions and comfortings are really our clothing with the soldier's dress, our putting on the soldier's armour, our grasping the soldier's weapons, our drilling for the soldier's service, that we may be good soldiers of the cross. Each one of us may become a Barnabas, a son of consolation. Comforted of God, let us learn to comfort others.—R. T.

Ver. 5.—*Christ's sufferings renewed in his disciples.* " For as the sufferings of Christ abound in us." We have expressed here a characteristic and familiar thought of the apostle's—the one which brought to him the fullest and deepest consolations. It is true, but it is too easily apprehended to be all the truth, that St. Paul's sufferings, borne in fulfilling his ministry, were Christ's sufferings because a part of his service ; but the apostle evidently reached the unspeakably precious and inspiring view of Christian suffering which sees it to be Christ's, because it is essentially *like* his—it is vicarious, it is borne for others. He says, " Whether we be afflicted, it is for *your* consolation and salvation . . . or whether we be comforted, it is for your consolation and salvation." St. Paul would know " the fellowship of Christ's sufferings, being made conformable unto his death ; " even to that death in its vicariousness, as a sublime self-sacrifice for the salvation of others. For the thought that in our sufferings, of whatever nature, we share Christ's sufferings, comp. ch. iv. 10 ; Phil. iii. 13 ; Col. i. 24 ; 1 Pet. iv. 13. All vicariously borne suffering is Christly ; it is the kind of which he is the Leader and the sublime Example ; it is even necessary, as attendant on all human efforts to bless others. Every one who would help another must take into account that he may have to suffer in doing it. Illustrate by the doctor, or the man who tries to save, from water, or fire, or accident, a fellow-creature. He may even perish in so doing. The Christian may cherish this supreme comfort—he may become to others, in measure, what Christ is to him. He may become the inspiration of vicarious service. His Christly example may act on men as Christ's example acted on him. If it might be so, St. Paul was willing to suffer. It may be shown and illustrated that such Christ-like enduring has—

I. A teaching power on others. It brings its revelations of God and brotherhood. It opens mysteries. It impresses the evil of sin.

II. An elevating power on others. It lifts men up to bear their own sufferings well, when we can show them the Christ-likeness of ours.

III. A comforting power, since it shows, not only how God's grace can abound, but also how God can turn even what we think evil into gracious agency for blessing. Sufferers still can strengthen, help, and save others.—R. T.

Vers. 8—11.—*The sanctifying influence of nearness to death.* In God's providence he brings his people sometimes to the " border-land," and, after giving the expectation, and almost the experience, of death, he leads them back to life and labour and relations again. Of this Hezekiah is the prominent Bible example. The sufferings through which the apostle had passed are not here detailed, and there is found much difficulty in deciding to what experiences he refers. Some think he recalls the tumult in Ephesus, which Dean Stanley shows was a more serious affair than Luke's narrative alone would suggest. Others think that some time of grievous and imperilling sickness is alluded to. And the apostle's mind may go further back to the stoning at Lystra, when he was left for dead (see Acts xiv. 19). It has been remarked that "the language is obviously more vividly descriptive of the collapse of illness than of any other peril." The point to which we now direct attention is that the sufferings imperilled life and brought him to the full contemplation of death—brought him to the "border-land;" and he gives the Corinthians some account of his feelings and experiences at the time, and tries to estimate some of the spiritual results then attained. They are these—

I. A FEELING OF SELF-HELPLESSNESS. Man never feels that fully until he faces death. He knows that no resolution, no energy, no sacrifice, can ensure his "discharge from that war." He can do nothing, and that most humiliating conviction may be a part of our necessary experience. Somewhere in life we need to be brought up before a great sea, with mountains around and foes before, much as Israel was when led forth from Egypt. It is good for us to feel helpless, utterly helpless, and then to hear the voice saying, "Stand still, and see the salvation of God."

II. DELIVERANCE FROM SELF-TRUST. Some sort of reliance on ourselves is necessary in order to meet the claims of life aright, and do its duties faithfully. Some measures of self-reliance blend with the Christian's trust in God all through his life of activity and service. Seldom, indeed, are full surrender to God, and entire conformity to his will, and simple reliance on his care, really won; and the experience of nearness to death alone breaks away the last bonds binding us to self, and enables us to "trust wholly." Life, after visiting the "border-land," may be wholly the "life of faith upon the Son of God."

III. FULL CONFIDENCE IN THE CONTINUING AND ABOUNDING OF DIVINE GRACE. This follows from so extreme an experience of what "almighty grace can do." Short of the experience of death, we may doubt whether "grace" can meet us at every point of our need; whether there really are no complications of circumstances which may over-master grace. A man may say—Grace can meet many needs, *but* not just this condition or this particular frailty. A man brought back from the "border-land" has won an impression of God's power and mercy that enables him to look forward to life and feel that God's efficient grace can be with him everywhere and in everything. It is St. Paul, who "had the sentence of death in himself," who was a personally delivered man, and who spoke of God as being able to make all grace abound towards us, so that we, having all sufficiency in all things, might abound unto every good word and work (ch. ix. 8). Death is the climax of all human woes, and he who can deliver from death can master all our troubles and "make all things work together for good." In concluding, show that the sanctified influence of his extreme experience may be seen in the tone and spirit and manner of the Christian thus brought back from the "border-land;" but that there is great danger of misusing even such Divine dealings with us, as Hezekiah seems to have done. A man restored from imperilling sickness may *presume* on the very mercy which has been so gloriously manifested in his case. We should take as our model such an experience as that of the Apostle Paul.—R. T.

Vers. 11, 12.—*The gracious influence of prayerfulness and sympathy on suffering souls.* The apostle wanted his friends to know of his sufferings so that he might have—

I. THEIR SYMPATHY IN THE TROUBLES. Very tenderly beautiful is the way in which St. Paul, while turning to God for his great consolations, yet yearns for the sympathy of those among whom he laboured. He liked to have some of them with him. He was a most brotherly and sympathetic man, and could neither suffer nor rejoice alone. In this he illustrates what is the great want of all warm natures; they yearn for sympathy, and we may render noble service who can give such sympathy in response to them. It is help and healing for stricken ones that we can "weep with those who weep."

II. THEIR PRAYERS FOR HIS PRESERVATION. A man in trouble longs for the feeling—at which men may easily scoff, but which is nevertheless a most real and helpful feeling—that he is upheld by the prayers of those that love him. None of the difficulties about prayer in relation to material changes need meet us when we speak of prayer in relation to *spiritual* influences. We ought to pray for the preservation of our friend's life when he is in peril from disease, but we do this with uncertainty as to what the will of God is, and so with full submission to whatever the decisions of that will may be. We pray that our suffering friends may be inwardly upheld, comforted, and strengthened, and in such prayers we know what the will of God must be. Sympathizing prayers have a really gracious influence on suffering souls, and surely bring down Divine blessings on them.

III. THEIR THANKSGIVINGS WHEN HE WAS RESTORED. The apostle could not rejoice alone. He wanted others to help him sing both of "mercy and judgment." From this subject arises, as the point of practical impression, the question—How can we help our suffering brothers and sisters? Even the Lord Jesus wanted sympathy, and the uplifting of others' prayers for him, when he was in the agony of Gethsemane; and so do his brethren. In what ways can such sympathy and help find expression? Neither utterances of sympathy nor earnest prayers can suffice instead of, and as an excuse for, not rendering practical helpings, but they will be found to inspire such practical efforts; for those whom we take on our hearts to pray for we are most likely to take into our hands to help.—R. T.

Vers. 12—14.—*The conscience-testimony.* "For our rejoicing is this, the testimony of our conscience." This passage may be thus paraphrased: "It is this which causes such a perennial flow of joy and consolation into my heart amid all my anxieties and distresses. I can feel in my conscience that what knits us together in sympathy is a Divine and not a human bond. On my part there is the inspiration from above, on yours the verifying faculty which enables you to recognize the truth of what I deliver to you." Now, no man ever needs publicly to appeal to the testimony of his conscience unless he is misjudged, misrepresented, maligned, or slandered by his fellow-men. He may, however, be placed in such circumstances that he can make no other appeal than to the consciousness of having acted in sincerity and uprightness. Such a testimony may not be accepted by others, but the ability to render it brings rest and peace to a man's own heart. St. Paul was at this time greatly suffering from mis-representations and slanderings; and so was David, in the older time, when he turned with such passionate intensity to God, saying, "Judge me according to mine integrity, and according to my righteousness which is in me." The worst hurt a true and faithful man can receive is the misjudging of his sincerity. F. W. Robertson says, "Met by these charges from his enemies, and even from his friends, the apostle falls back on his own conscience. Let us explain what he means by the testimony of conscience. He certainly does not mean 'faultlessness,' for he says, 'Of sinners I am chief.' And St. John, in a similar spirit, declares that none can boast of faultlessness: 'If we say that we have no sin, we deceive ourselves.' And here St. Paul is not speaking of his own personal character, but of his ministry; and again, he is not speaking of the blame-lessness of his ministry, but of its success. No; it was not faultlessness St. Paul meant by the testimony of conscience, but this—integrity, moral earnestness in his work; he had been straightforward in his ministry, and his worst enemies could be refuted if they said that he was insincere." Now, the conscience-testimony may be said to include self-approval before self, self-approval before man, and self-approval before God.

I. SELF-APPROVAL BEFORE SELF. Treat conscience as the exercise of a man's judgment concerning the right and wrong of his own conduct—a man's self-appraise-ment. A man may be calm amid all storms of slander or persecution who can feel that he is consciously sincere, and that he has been true to himself. Carefully distinguish this from mere self-satisfaction, and from the pride that leads a man to "think of him-self more highly than he ought to think." A man's moral strength depends upon his self-approval when conscience makes its searching estimate of conduct and of motives. A man is only weak when his conscience upholds his accuser.

II. SELF-APPROVAL BEFORE MAN. 1. A man is often compelled to take action which he knows men are likely to misconceive and misrepresent. He can only do so with the assurance that he is right. 2. Men are corruptly disposed to put a wrong con-struction on the actions of their fellows, and every man must take this into account who occupies prominent or public positions. He dares not waver or change to try and meet everybody's wishes. He can but fall back upon the testimony of his own conscience.

III. SELF-APPROVAL BEFORE GOD. He, being the Searcher of the heart, knows the very secrets of motive and feeling, and it may seem as if there could not be any " self-approval" in his presence. And yet God's Word teaches us that God looks for sincerity, expects it, and knows that we can reach it. Perfect we cannot be; sincere we can be. " If we would judge ourselves, we should not be judged." David may even speak of his integrity before God. And the height of a man's moral strength is only gained when he feels consciously sincere in the Divine presence, but is truly humble even in the consciousness and says, " Search me, O God, and know my heart; try me, and know my ways."—R. T.

Vers. 21, 22.—*The sealing and earnest of the Spirit.* The figure used in the passage is taken from the custom, common to nearly all lands, of affixing marks to a man's peculiar property. That mark was frequently a seal, with a characteristic device. The shepherd has some mark which he places on each of his sheep, so that if any one of them strays away it may at once be known as his. And so Christ, the good Shepherd, has a mark by which he knows, and would have all men know, the members of his flock. That mark is the seal of the Spirit. The meaning of the term is explained by a passage in Rev. vii. The angel demands a little delay until he shall have " sealed the servants of God in their foreheads." That is, by a distinctive mark, the sons of God are to be separated from the world, stamped as God's chosen ones. And as that shall then be done by a glorious name, blazoned on the forehead ; as it was done, in the older time, to Israel, by a blood-sprinkled lintel; so now it is done by the gift of the great Comforter and Friend, the Holy Spirit of promise. The presence of the Spirit pledges the fact of our reconciliation to God, and so it seals us. That Spirit may work *on* ungodly men and *by* ungodly men, but he cannot properly be said to work *in* ungodly men. His is an influence *on* them from without; his dwelling *in* the heart is the assurance that the great change has taken place. A man must be " born again" ere he can be the dwelling-place of the Spirit. " The Spirit witnesseth with our spirit that we are the children of God." And it is not possible to overstate either the dignity or the safety that attends such a sealing. God stamps his people by giving them his own presence. It is not enough to affix a mark, not enough to entrust to guardian angels. Satan may conceivably overcome them, and sin may blot out the mark. God would give his people no other seal than his own omnipotent presence. Divinest seal! No human hands can tear that from our soul. It can only be lost by our own self-willed acts. We can pluck off the seal. We may grieve the Spirit away. None can deny the livery of the eternal King, with which we are clothed, but we may ourselves choose another service and strip off the King's dress. What the sealing and earnest of the Spirit are may best be illustrated by the experiences of the apostolic company when the Spirit first came in Pentecostal power and glory. The disciples were waiting at the throne of grace, waiting for the fulfilment of the as yet mysterious promise of the Lord. It was the early morning, when a sweeping sound of wind came about the house, and filled the room where they were sitting. Presently dividing tongues of flame rested on their heads, and they felt new power thrilling within them. Those were the symbols of the Spirit's sealing them for their great missionary service. In this new might a surprising change passed over them. They were ignorant Galilæans; now they could speak so as to be understood by people of all tongues; now they were swayed with feelings that raised timid disciples into moral heroes and noble witnesses and faithful martyrs. That was the first sealing of the Spirit, and it does but illustrate how still God takes us as his, gives to us his Spirit, secures us by a Divine indwelling, and inspires us with Divine motives and impulses.—R. T.

EXPOSITION.

CHAPTER II.

Continuation of his reasons for not coming to them direct from Ephesus (vers. 1—4). Their treatment of the incestuous offender (vers. 5—11). His thankfulness at the news which Titus had brought from Corinth (vers. 12—17).

Ver. 1.—**But I determined this.** The division of chapters is here unfortunate, since this and the next three verses belong to the paragraph which began at ch. i. 23.

The verb means, literally, "I judged," but is rightly rendered "determined," as in 1 Cor. ii. 2; vii. 37. He is contrasting his *final decision* with his original *desire*, mentioned in ch. i. 15. **With myself;** rather, *for myself;* as the best course which I could take. **That I would not come again to you in heaviness.** The "again" in the true reading is not placed immediately before the verb, but it seems (as Theodoret says) to belong to it, so that the meaning is *not* "that I would not pay you a *second* sad visit," but "that *my second visit to you* should not be a sad one." There have been interminable discussions, founded on this expression and on ch. xiii. 1, as to whether St. Paul had up to the time of writing this letter visited Corinth *twice* or only *once*. There is no question that only one visit is recorded in the Acts (xviii. 1—18) previous to the one which he had paid to this Church after this Epistle had been sent (Acts xx. 2, 3). If he paid them a second brief, sad, and unrecorded visit, it can only have been during his long stay in Ephesus (Acts xix. 8, 10). But the possibility of this does not seem to be recognized in Acts xx. 31, where he speaks of his work at Ephesus "night and day" during this period. The assumption of such a visit, as we shall see, is not necessitated by ch. xiii. 1, but in any case we know nothing whatever about the details of the visit, even if there was one, and the question, being supremely unimportant, is hardly worth the time which has been spent upon it. If he *had* paid such a visit, it would be almost unaccountable that there should be no reference to it in the First Epistle, and here in ch. i. 19 he refers only to one occasion on which he had preached Christ in Corinth. Each fresh review of the circumstances convinces me more strongly that the notion of *three* visits to Corinth, of which one is unrecorded, is a needless and mistaken inference, due to unimaginative literalism in interpreting one or two phrases, and encumbered with difficulties on every side. *In heaviness.* The expression applies as much to the Corinthians as to himself. He did not wish his second visit to Corinth to be a painful one.

Ver. 2.—**For if I make you sorry.** The verse may be rendered, "For if *I* pain you, who then is it that gladdens me except he who is being pained by me?" The "*I*," being expressed in the original, is emphatic, and the verse has none of the strange selfish meaning which has been assigned to it, namely, that St. Paul thought "the grief which he had caused to be amply compensated for by the pleasure he received from that grief." It has the much simpler meaning that he was unwilling to pain those who gladdened him, and therefore would not pay

them a visit which could only be *painful* on both sides, when the normal relation between them should be one of *joy* on both sides, as he has already said (ch. i. 24). The singular, "he who is being pained by me," does not refer to the offender, but to the Corinthians collectively. **Who is he then, etc.?** The "then" in the original is classically and elegantly expressed by καί, *and* (comp. Jas. ii. 4).

Ver. 3.—**And I wrote this same unto you.** *And I wrote.* He meets the tacit objection. If you shrink from causing us pain, why then did you write to us in terms so severe? The "I wrote" may be what is called the epistolary aorist, and will then be equivalent to our "I write:" "What I *write* to you now has the very object of sparing you a painful visit." If the aorist has its more ordinary sense, it refers to the First, and not to the present Epistle; and this seems the better view, for the "I wrote" in ver. 9 certainly refers to the First Epistle. *This same thing;* namely, exactly what I have written (whether in this or in the former Epistle). The words, "this very thing," may also, in the original, mean "for this very reason," as in 2 Pet. i. 5, and like the εἰς τοῦτο in ver. 9. *Unto you.* These words should be omitted, with ℵ, A, B, C. **When I came.** The emphasis lies in these words. He preferred that his letter, rather than his personal visit, should cause pain. **In you all.** It is true that in the Corinthian Church St. Paul had bitter and unscrupulous opponents, but he will not believe even that they desired his personal unhappiness. At any rate, if there were any such, he will not believe that they exist, since "love believeth all things, hopeth all things" (1 Cor. xiii. 7).

Ver. 4.—**For.** He proceeds to assign the anguish which his First Epistle had caused him as a proof of his confidence that, as a body, they loved him as he loved them. If they had regarded each other with indifference, his letter would not have been written to them, as it were, in his heart's blood. **Out of much affliction and anguish of heart.** The word for "anguish" means "contraction," "pressure," "spasm" (Luke xxi. 25). The expression may seem far too strong to be accounted for by the tone of the first letter. Hence some have supposed that he is referring to some other letter now lost; and others that ch. x.—xiii. of this letter, where the whole tone of affection and tenderness suddenly changes into one of impassioned irony and indignation, really belonged to this intermediate letter. There is no need, however, for these hypotheses. In 1 Cor. v. 1—vi. 11 he had spoken of the errors of the Church with strong reprobation, and the anguish with which he wrote the letter may have been all the more deeply felt because, in expressing it, he put on his feelings a strong restraint. **With many tears.** I wrote "out of" anguish, and that anguish showed itself through the tears which bathed my cheeks as I wrote. Such tears, says Calvin, "show weakness, but a weakness more heroic than would have been the iron apathy of a Stoic." It must, however, be remembered that, in ancient times, and in Southern and Eastern lands, men yielded to tears more readily than among Northern nations, who take pride in suppressing as far as possible all outward signs of emotion. In Homer the bravest heroes do not blush to weep in public, and the nervous, afflicted temperament of St. Paul seems to have been often overwhelmed with weeping (Acts xx. 19, 31 ; 2 Tim. i. 4). **Not that ye should be grieved.** The "not," by a common Hebrew idiom, means "not only," "not exclusively." His object in inflicting pain was not the pain itself, but the results of godly repentance which it produced (ch. vii. 11). **The love.** In the Greek this word is placed very emphatically at the beginning of the clause. **More abundantly.** I loved you *more* than I loved other converts, and the abundance of my love will give you a measure of the pain I felt. The Philippians were St. Paul's best-beloved converts ; but next to them he seems to have felt more personal tenderness for the members of this inflated, wayward, erring Church than for any other community, just as a father sometimes loves best his least-deserving son. There was something in the brightness and keenness of the Greek nature which won over St. Paul, in spite of its many faults.

Vers. 5—11.—*The results of his letter in their treatment of the incestuous offender.*

Ver. 5.—**But if any have caused grief.** The word "pain" or "grief" which has been so prominent in the last verses, naturally reminds St. Paul of the person whose misdoings had caused all this trouble. The "any" is in the singular. **He hath not grieved me, but in part,** etc. Of the various ways of taking this verse, the most tenable seems to be this : "If any one has caused pain, he has not pained *me* but partly (not to weigh down too heavily) *all* of you." St. Paul is denying that the feelings with which he had written his severe letter were due to mere personal sorrow or indignation. In writing he felt for the wrong done to *them*, to the whole Corinthian Church, at least as much as for the smart of his own grief and disappointment. The word "partly" is introduced, as St. Chrysostom says, to soften the expression, "he has grieved *you all*." It will then mean "to a certain extent." The words, "that I may not overcharge," or rather, as in the Revised Version, "that I press not too heavily," assign the reason for the modifying clause,

"in part." When St. Paul says that this man's conduct had *even* to *any extent* grieved the whole community, his words may seem to conflict with 1 Cor. v. 2 ; but he is thinking, not of the immediate condonation of the offender there alluded to, but of the agony of subsequent repentance which his letter had awoke in the whole (or practically the whole) community (ch. vii. 11). The phrase, "that I press not too heavily," refers then to the offender : "I will not say outright that he has grieved not *me, but all of you*, because I do not wish to bear too hard on him" (comp. 1 Thess. ii. 9 ; 2 Thess. iii. 8), "but I will say that he has grieved you and me alike to some extent." The phrase, "in part," occurs also in Rom. xi. 25.

Ver. 6.—**Sufficient to such a man is this punishment.** What the punishment was we do not know, but of course the Corinthians knew that what St. Paul had directed them to do was to summon the Church together, and there, by excommunicating the man, "to hand him over to Satan." But this handing over to Satan was, as we have seen, designed solely for a merciful purpose, and to awaken his repentance, so as to secure his ultimate salvation (1 Cor. v. 4, 5). Whether the Corinthians had done exactly as St. Paul bade them is uncertain ; but whatever they had done is here acquiesced in by St. Paul, and even if (as we may suspect) they had dealt more leniently with the offender than he originally intended, he here not only refrains from urging them to use greater severity, but even exhorts them to a still more absolute condonation. St. Paul's object had not been that they should take a particular course of action, but that they should bring about a desired result. The result had been achieved, and now the matter might rest. *To such a man.* St. Paul mercifully abstains from recording his name or from thrusting him into unnecessary prominence before the assembly in which the letter would be read. The apostle evidently entered into the Jewish feeling that there is a criminal cruelty in needlessly calling a blush of shame into a brother's face. *This punishment.* The word *epitimia*, which occurs here only in the New Testament, but is also found in Wisd. iii. 10, means "punishment," as in later Greek, and is not used in its classical sense of "rebuke" (Vulgate, *objurgatio*); but the mildness of the word, perhaps, implies that the Corinthians had not resorted to the severest measures. **Which** was inflicted of **many ;** rather, *by the majority*. The verb is expressed in the original, and St. Paul seems to allude to the steps taken, whatever they were, with a certain dignified reticence. It is obvious that there were still some opponents of St. Paul in the Church, who retained in this matter their "inflated" sentiments of spurious independence; and this may, perhaps, have driven others into too rigid an attitude of severity.

Ver. 7.—**Contrariwise**; *i.e.* contrary to the line taken or to the view expressed by the severer portion of the community. **Rather.** The word is omitted in A and B. **To forgive** him. The word is used of the mutual attitude of gracious forbearance which ought to exist among Christians ("Forgiving one another," Eph. iv. 32; Col. iii. 13), so that they might be not only Christians, but as Gentiles ignorantly called them, *Chrestians* ("kind-hearted," Eph. iv. 32). **And comfort**; *i.e.* "strengthen," "encourage." The "*him*" is omitted in the Greek, with the same delicate, compassionate reticence which leads St. Paul to speak of this person as "a man of such of a kind." In Gal. vi. 11 St. Paul suddenly breaks off the course of his remarks to give similar advice in a tone of peculiar solemnity; and in 2 Thess. iii. 15 he warns against any *excess* in the severity which he enjoins in the previous verse. **Such a one.** Like the indefinite "one" in 1 Cor. v. 5. In the Greek it is compassionately placed last in the clause. **Should be swallowed up.** The same metaphor, of being swallowed in an abyss, occurs in 1 Cor. xv. 54. In 1 Pet. v. 8 it is said that Satan is ever striving to "swallow up" men. **With overmuch sorrow**; rather, *with the*, or *his*, *excessive grief*. Despair might drive the man to suicide, or apostasy, or the wretchlessness of unclean living.

Ver. 8.—**To confirm your love toward him**; literally, *to ratify towards him, love*.

Ver. 9.—**For to this end also did I write.** This is another reason which he gives for the severe tone of his First Epistle. It was written (1) to avoid the necessity for a painful visit (ver. 3); (2) to show his special love for them (ver. 4); and (3) to test their obedience. **The proof of you.** Your proved faithfulness (ch. viii. 2; ix. 13; xiii. 3; Rom. v. 4); your capacity to stand a test.

Ver. 10.—**To whom ye forgive any thing.** In the original there is a conjunction, "but." It would, perhaps, be pressing it too much to imply that their "forgiveness" showed that they had not accurately stood the test of perfect obedience; yet it is difficult to read the whole passage without suspecting that St. Paul, while by temperament he leaned to the side of mercy, is here showing a spirit of generous self-suppression in accepting the course which the Corinthians had followed, although it had, in some way or other, diverged from his exact directions. *To whom.* Obviously, again, a purposely indefinite reference to the incestuous person. **I forgive also.** The

power of "binding" and "loosing," of "forgiving" and "retaining," had only been given to the apostles representatively and collectively, and therefore to the Christian Church (John xx. 23) in its corporate capacity. The Corinthian Church had in this case decided to forgive, and St. Paul ratifies their decision. **For if I forgave any thing, to whom I forgave it.** The reading here varies between ὅ, *what*, and ᾧ, *to whom*, which in dictation might be easily confused. The order of the words also varies. The best reading seems to be expressed by the version, "For what I also have pardoned, if I have pardoned anything (I have pardoned it) for your sakes." This represents the reading of א, A, B, C, F, G, etc., and is followed by the Revised Version. There seems to be here an intentional vagueness, and reference to circumstances of which we are not informed, which might, perhaps, have given room for wounded feelings in any one less magnanimous than St. Paul. The line he took in this matter was taken for their sakes—that is all he says, he adopted it as the best *relatively*, whether it was *absolutely* the best or not. **In the person of Christ**; literally, *in the face of Christ*; which seems to mean "in the presence of Christ," as though he were looking on at what I did (comp. ch. i. 11; iii. 7, 13, 18; iv. 6). It may be doubted whether the word *prosōpon* ever means "person" in the New Testament, except in a secondary sense.

Ver. 11.—**Lest Satan should get an advantage over us**; literally, *lest we should be overreached by Satan*, which would have been the case if our severity had resulted in the desperation of the offender, and not in his deliverance (comp. 1 Cor. v. 5). **We are not ignorant of his devices.** So too in Eph. vi. 11 we are told of the "crafty wiles of the devil."

Vers. 12—17.—*Outburst of thanksgiving for the news brought by Titus.*

Ver. 12.—**Furthermore, when I came to Troas.** "Furthermore" is too strong for the "but" of the original. There is an apparently abrupt transition, but the apostle is only resuming the narrative which he broke off at ver. 4 in order that he might finish the topic of the painful circumstance in which his First Epistle had originated. *To Troas.* Not "the Troas." St. Paul had to do with the city, not with the district. The city (now *Eski Stamboul*), of which the name had been changed from *Antigonia Troas* to *Alexandria Troas*, was at this time a flourishing colony (*Colonia Juris Italici*), highly favoured by the Romans as representing ancient Troy, and therefore as being the mythological cradle of their race. He visited it on his being driven from Ephesus after the tumult, a little earlier than he would naturally have left it. He had visited Troas in his second missionary journey (Acts xvi. 8—11), but had left it in consequence of the vision which called him to Macedonia. He now stopped there on his journey through Macedonia to Corinth, which he had announced in 1 Cor. xvi. 5. **And a door was opened unto me of the Lord;** literally, *and a door had been opened to me in the Lord;* i.e. and I found there a marked opportunity (1 Cor. xvi. 9) for work in Christ. Some commentators, in that spirit of superfluous disquisition and idle letter-worship which is the bane of exegesis, here venture to discuss whether St. Paul was justified in neglecting this opportunity or not. Such discussions are only originated by not observing characteristic modes of expression. St. Paul merely means "circumstances would *otherwise* have been very favourable for my preaching of Christ; but I was in such a state of miserable anxiety that I lacked the strength to avail myself of them." He was no more responsible for this state of mind, which belonged to his natural temperament, than he would have been responsible for a serious illness. To say that he *ought* to have had strength of mind enough to get the mastery over his feelings is only to say that Paul ought not to have been Paul. The neglect to use the opportunity was a "hindrance" which might in one sense be assigned to God, and in another to Satan. Moreover, that the opportunity was *not* wholly lost appears from the fact that St. Paul found a flourishing Christian community at Troas when he visited it on his return from this very journey (Acts xx. 6, 7), and that he stayed there at least once again, shortly before his martyrdom (2 Tim. iv. 13). Indeed, it was probably at Troas that his *final* arrest took place (see my 'Life of St. Paul,' ii. 569, 576). *Of the Lord;* rather, *in the Lord;* i.e. in the sphere of Christian work.

Ver. 13.—**I had;** literally, *I have had.* The perfect vividly realizes the scene through which he had passed. **I had no rest.** St. Paul had evidently told Titus to come from his mission to Corinth and meet him at Troas. But either St. Paul reached the town earlier than he intended, or Titus had been delayed. Now, the apostle was so intensely eager to know how his rebukes had been received—the name of "Corinth" was so deeply engraven on his heart—he could so ill endure the thought of being on angry terms with converts which he so deeply loved, that the non-appearance of Titus filled him with devouring anxiety and rendered him incapable of any other work. **In my spirit;** rather, *to my spirit.*

It was the loftiest part of St. Paul's nature —his spirit—which was utterly incapacitated from effort by the restlessness of his miserable uncertainty about the Corinthian Church. The disclosure of such feelings ought to have had a powerful influence on the Corinthians. We see from 1 Thess. iii. 5, 9 that St. Paul yearned for tidings of his converts with an intensity which can hardly be realized by less fervent and self-devoted natures. **I found not Titus my brother.** Not only "*the* brother," but "*my* brother;" the man whom in matters of this kind I most trusted as an affectionate and able fellow-worker (ch. vii. 6; viii. 6; xii. 18). Titus, though not mentioned in the Acts, is the most prominent person in this Epistle, and it is evident that St. Paul felt for him a warm affection and respect (ch. vii. 13, 15; viii. 16, 17; 2 Tim. iv. 10). **Taking my leave of them;** *i.e.* of the Christians in Troas. The word for "taking leave" is also found in Mark vi. 46. **Into Macedonia.** As he had intended to do (1 Cor. xvi. 5; Acts xx. 1). He had doubtless told Titus to look out for him at Philippi, and expected to meet him there on his way to Troas.

Ver. 14.—**Now thanks be unto God.** The whole of this Epistle is the apostle's *Apologia pro vitâ suâ,* and is more full of personal details and emotional expressions than any other Epistle. But nothing in it is more characteristic than this sudden outburst of thanksgiving into which he breaks so eagerly *that he has quite omitted to say what it was for which he so earnestly thanked God.* It is only when we come to ch. vii. 5, 6 that we learn the circumstance which gave him such intense relief, namely, the arrival of Titus with good news from Corinth about the treatment of the offender and the manner in which the first letter had been received. It is true that this good news seems to have been dashed by other remarks of Titus which, perhaps, he withheld at first, and which may only have been drawn from him, almost against his will, by subsequent conversations. But, however checkered, the main and immediate intelligence was good, and the apostle so vividly recalls his sudden uplifting out of an abyss of anxiety and trouble (ch. vii. 5) that the mere remembrance of it awakens a thankfulness to God which can only find vent by immediate utterance. *Now thanks be unto God.* The order of the original is more forcible, "But to God be thanks." The remembrance of his own prostration calls into his mind the power and love of God. **Which always causeth us to triumph;** rather, *who leadeth us in triumph.* The verb *thriambeuo* may undoubtedly have this meaning, on the analogy of *choreuo,* I cause to dance, *basileuo,* I cause to reign, etc.; and other neuter verbs which sometimes have a factitive sense. But in Col. ii. 15 St. Paul uses this word in the only sense in which it is actually found, " *to lead* in *triumph;*" and this sense seems both to suit the context better, and to be more in accordance with the habitual feelings of St. Paul (Gal. vi. 17; Col. i. 24), and especially those with which these Epistles were written (1 Cor. iv. 9—13; ch. iv. 10; xi. 23). St. Paul's feeling is, therefore, the exact opposite of that of the haughty Cleopatra who said, Οὐ θριαμβευθήσομαι, "I will not be led in triumph." He rejoiced to be exhibited by God as a trophy in the triumphal procession of Christ. God, indeed, gave him the victory over the lower part of his nature (Rom. viii. 37), but this was no public triumph. The only victory of which he could boast was to have been utterly vanquished by God and taken prisoner "in Christ." **The savour of his knowledge.** The mental vision of a Roman triumph summons up various images before the mind of St. Paul. He thinks of the streets breathing with the fragrance of incense offered upon many a wayside altar; of the tumult and rejoicing of the people; of the fame and glory of the conqueror; of the miserable captives led aside from the funeral procession to die, like Vercingetorix, in the *Tullianum* at the foot of the Capitoline hill. He touches on each of these incidents as they crowd upon him. The triumph of L. Mummius over the conquest of Corinth had been one of the most splendid which the Roman world had ever seen, and in A.D. 51, shortly before this Epistle was written (A.D. 57), Claudius had celebrated his triumph over the Britons and their king Caractacus, who had been led in the procession, but whose life had been spared (Tacitus, 'Ann.,' xiii. 36). *The savour of his knowledge;* i.e. the fragrance of the knowledge of Christ. **By us.** The details of the metaphor are commingled, as is often the case in writers of quick feeling and imagination. Here the apostles are no longer the vanquished who are led in procession, but the spectators who burn and diffuse the fragrance of the incense. **In every place.** Even at that early period, not twenty-five years after the Crucifixion, the gospel had been very widely preached in Asia and Europe (Rom. xv. 18, 19).

Ver. 15.—**We are unto God a sweet savour of Christ.** The undeveloped metaphor involved in these words is that "we and our preaching diffuse to God's glory the knowledge of Christ which is as a sweet savour." The apostles are identified with their work; they were as the incense, crushed and burned, but diffusing everywhere a waft of perfume. St. Paul is still thinking of the incense burnt in the streets of Rome during a triumph—"Dabimusque Divis Tura benignis" (Horace, 'Od.,' iv. 2. 51)—though his

expression recalls the "odour of a sweet smell," of Lev. i. 9, 13, 17 (comp. Eph. v. 2); see on this passage the excellent note of Bishop Wordsworth. **In them that are saved, and in them that perish**; rather, *among those who are perishing and those who are being saved* (comp. Acts ii. 47). The odour is fragrant to God, though those who breathe it may be variously affected by it.

Ver. 16.—**The savour of death unto death;** rather, *a savour from death to death.* To those who are perishing, the incense of the Name of Christ which our work enables them to breathe, seems to rise from death, and to lead to death. They (for here again the outlines of the metaphor shift) are like the doomed captives, who, as they breathed the incense on the day of triumph, knew where that triumph would lead them before the victors can climb the Capitol. To them it would seem to bring with it not "airs from heaven," but wafts from the abyss. So Christ was alike for the fall and for the rising again of many (Luke ii. 34). To some he was a Stone of stumbling (Acts iv. 11; Rom. ix. 33; 1 Pet. ii. 8), which grinds to powder those on whom it falls (Matt. xxi. 44). This contrast between the intended effect of the gospel as the power and wisdom of God, and its *accidental* effect, through man's sin and blindness which converts it into a source of judgment, is often alluded to in the New Testament (1 Cor. i. 18, 23, 24; John iii. 19; ix. 39; xv. 22, etc.). St. Paul is fond of intensified expressions, like "from death unto death," as in Rom. i. 17; "from faith to faith," etc. (comp. iv. 17). **Savour of life unto life;** rather, *a savour from life,* as before. It came from the Source of life; it is issued in the sole reality of life. Similarly the rabbis spoke of the Law as "an aroma" alike of death and of life. "Why are the words of the Law likened to princes (Prov. viii. 6)? Because, like princes, *they have the power to kill and to give life.* Rava said to those that walk on its right, the Law is a medicine of life; to those that walk on the left side, *a medicine of death*" ('Shabbath,' f. 88, 2; 'Yoma,' f. 72, 2). Everything is as a two-edged sword. All Christian privileges are, as they are used, either blessings or banes (Wordsworth). **And who is sufficient for these things?** St. Paul always implies that nothing but the grace of God could enable him to discharge the great duty laid upon him (ch. iii. 5, 6; 1 Cor. xv. 10).

Ver. 17.—**For we are not as many**; rather, *as the many.* This clause is introduced to show how much courage and effort the work requires. "The many" might, by Greek idiom, mean "the majority." The apparent harshness of the assertion that the majority of teachers in the apostolic age dealt untruly with the Word of God, led to the substitution of οἱ λοιποί, the rest, in some manuscripts (D, E, F, G, L). But "the many" here means "the many antagonists of mine," who preach a different gospel (Gal. i. 6). It must be remembered that conceit, Pharisaism, moral laxity, and factions were all at work in the Corinthian Church. **Which corrupt.** The Word means who are merely " trafficking with," "adulterating," "huckstering," the Word of life. The word occurs in the LXX. of Isa. i. 22; Ecclus. xxvi. 29; and Plato applies the same metaphor to the sophists, who peddle their wisdom about ('Protag.,' p. 313 d). The substantive *kapēlos* means "a retail dealer," and especially a vintner, and the verb *kapēleuo* is always used in a bad sense,

like the English "to huckster." Such deceitful dealers with the gospel are described in 2 Pet. ii. 3, and in one of the Ignatian letters they are called *Christemporoi*, Christ-traffickers. Such were those who altered the perspective of the gospel, lowered its standard, and adulterated it with strange admixtures. Their methods and their teaching are constantly alluded to in these Epistles (1 Cor. i. 17, 31; ii. 1—4; and ch. x. 12, 15; xi. 13—15, etc.). **But as of sincerity, but as of God.** Like one who speaks from the sincerity of his heart (ch. i. 12; iv. 2) and by the inspiration of God (1 Cor. xiv. 25). **Before God speak we in Christ.** The *sphere* of our teaching as of our life is Christ; and our work is done

" As ever in our great Taskmaster's eye."

HOMILETICS.

Vers. 1—11.—*The uniting force of Christian love.* "But I determined this with myself," etc. The subject which these words suggest is the uniting force of Christian love. We see it here uniting all its subjects in a common sympathy, a common punishment, and a common forgiveness. Here is Christian love—

I. Uniting all its subjects in a common sympathy. "But I determined this with myself, that I would not come again to you in heaviness. For if I make you sorry, who is he then that maketh me glad, but the same which is made sorry by me?" The language of Paul in the first four verses implies that the "heaviness" of one would be the heaviness of all, the sorrow of one the sorrow of all, the grief of one the grief of all, the joy of one the joy of all. And this is what Christian love does in all its subjects, wherever it exists. To whatever Church they belong, it gathers them together in one, it binds them together as attraction binds the material universe into one magnificent and harmonious system. What one feels all feel, all affections are drawn to a common centre, all hearts point to a common home. The pulsations of all throb in harmony and make music in the ear of God.

II. Uniting all its subjects in a common punishment. "But if any have caused grief, he hath not grieved me, but in part; that I may not overcharge you all. Sufficient to such a man is this punishment, which was inflicted of many." In the whole passage from vers. 5—10 Paul's reference is to that incestuous person of whom he wrote in his First Epistle (see 1 Cor. v. 1—5), and whose excommunication or "punishment" he secured. The retribution which that man received was not the work of any one of them, but all joined in it. They all sympathetically concurred in it, and thus it was inflicted on many. They all loathed the same wrong and all endured the same punishment. *True punishment for wrong is the work of love, not vengeance.* Therefore punishment is not for destruction, but for restoration. The punishment that destroys the criminal is Satanic, not saintly; devilish, not Divine. Restoration is the work of love, the work of God. This is here distinctly stated. "So that contrariwise ye ought rather to forgive him, and comfort him, lest perhaps such a one should be swallowed up with overmuch sorrow." It would seem from the language of the apostle that the punishment they had inflicted on this guilty person had produced a deep penitential sorrow—lest he "should be swallowed up with overmuch sorrow." His punishment had answered its purpose, therefore restore him and "confirm your love toward him."

III. Uniting all its subjects in a common forgiveness. "To whom ye forgive anything, I forgive also." As if Paul had said, "You and I are so united in loving sympathy that those whom you forgive I forgive." Observe here three things. 1. That *forgiveness is the prerogative of Christian love.* There is no love that has the true spirit of forgiveness but Christian. It is the highest form of love; higher than gratitude, esteem, adoration. It is the "new commandment." 2. That in the exercise of forgiveness there is a *consciousness* of Christ. "For your sakes forgive I it in the person of Christ." He who has Christly love in him has the very consciousness of Christ, feels as he feels, "one in the presence of Christ." How often does Christ urge his genuine disciples to proclaim forgiveness where there is genuine repentance! "Whatsoever is loosed on earth shall be loosed in heaven." 3. That the forgiving spirit *thwarts the purposes of the devil.* "Lest Satan should get an advantage of us; for we are not ignorant of his devices." Forgiveness is not, then, the prerogative of priests, but the prerogative of Christian love. A truly Christly man represents Christ—stands, so to say, in his stead ; and "Christ hath power on earth to forgive sins."

Vers. 12—16.—*The preaching of the gospel.* "Furthermore, when I came to Troas," etc. The subject of these verses is the preaching of the gospel. Notice—

I. THE DIFFICULTIES CONNECTED WITH IT. "Furthermore, when I came to Troas to preach Christ's gospel, and a door was opened unto me of the Lord, I had no rest in my spirit, because I found not Titus my brother: but taking my leave of them, I went from thence into Macedonia." Just at the time when the apostle was about opening his mission at Troas, and the prospect of usefulness seemed most suitable, he encountered a serious difficulty, and that difficulty was the absence of Titus, whom he fully expected. The disappointment cost him such great anxiety that he resigned his purpose, retired from the scene, and wended his way in another direction. Strange that an inspired man should have met with such a disappointment, and stranger still that a disappointment should have so disheartened him that he relinquishes for a time the grand message with which Heaven had especially entrusted him. Antecedently we might have supposed that a man going forth in a true spirit to preach the gospel would encounter no difficulties, that Heaven would sweep away all obstructions from his path; but not so. Perhaps no class of men encounter more difficulties in their mission than ministers. Many become so baffled, confounded, and depressed that, like Jeremiah, they exclaim, "I will speak no more in thy Name."

II. THE TRIUMPHS ACHIEVED BY IT. "Now thanks be unto God, which always causeth us to triumph in Christ, and maketh manifest the savour of his knowledge by us in every place." The grandest of all victories is the victory over sin. He who conquers the moral foes of one soul achieves a far grander triumph than he who lays a whole army dead upon the battle-plain. There is no grandeur, but infamy, in the latter conquest. It is here taught that these victories were achieved whenever they preached. "Always causeth us to triumph." Wherever they preached, "in every place," and always through God, "thanks be to God." He is the Author of their victory; he constructed the weapon, he instructed the soldiers, he inspired and gave effect to the strokes.

III. THE INFLUENCES RESULTING FROM IT. "For we are unto God a sweet savour of Christ, in them that are saved, and in them that perish." Observe: 1. The *manward* aspect of gospel preaching. (1) It quickens some. "To the other the savour of life unto life." (2) It destroys others. "To the one we are the savour of death unto death." These effects occur wherever the gospel is preached. 2. The *Godward* aspect of gospel preaching. "We are unto God a sweet savour of Christ." Whatever the results of preaching, baneful or beneficial, it is acceptable to God if rightly discharged. Ay, the preaching of the gospel is *the cause of immense good and the occasion of great evil.* Like the waters of the sea, the light of the firmament, the breeze of the atmosphere, it is the Divine cause of good; but man, through the perversity of his nature, may make it the occasion of his ruin.

IV. THE SOLEMNITY CONNECTED WITH IT. Paul felt its solemnity and exclaims, "Who is sufficient for these things ?" Who, of himself, is "sufficient" to expound the meaning of the gospel, to exemplify the spirit of the gospel, to inwork into human souls the eternal principles of the gospel ? Paul adds in another place, "Our sufficiency is of God."

Ver. 17.—*The way in which the gospel should be preached.* "For we are not as many, which corrupt the Word of God: but as of sincerity, but as of God, in the sight of God speak we in Christ." The words suggests the way in which the gospel should be preached.

I. WITH CONSCIOUS HONESTY. "As of sincerity." This is a state of mind in direct antagonism to all duplicity. No man who is not true to his convictions and to himself can preach the gospel. He must be a true man who would preach truth, a loving man who would inculcate love. To have conscious honesty he must preach his own *personal convictions* of the gospel, not the opinions of others.

II. WITH CONSCIOUS DIVINITY. "As of God, in the sight of God." 1. He must be conscious that God *sent* him. From God, not from schools, sects, Churches, or ecclesiastics, but direct from God himself. 2. He must be conscious that God *sees* him. "In the sight of God." This consciousness will make him humble, earnest, fearless, caring nothing for the frowns or smiles of his audience.

III. WITH CONSCIOUS CHRISTLINESS. "Speak we in Christ." To be "in Christ" is to be in his character, in his Spirit. "The love of Christ constraineth me," etc. He who is conscious of the Spirit of Christ within him will be free from all self-seeking, all sordid motives, all cravings for popularity and fame.

HOMILIES BY VARIOUS AUTHORS.

Vers. 1—11.—*Further explanations and directions touching matters just discussed.* The most copious writer in the New Testament is the man whose inward constitution and life are most fully brought into view. If the fact itself is noteworthy, the art of its management is even more significant. Didactic treatises would have excluded this method of blending the abstract and the concrete, and therefore the epistolary form which St. Paul adopted. What do we mean by this form? Much more, indeed, than a facile and graceful way of communicating facts and truths. In the Epistle we have the personality of the writer interblended with doctrine, duty, experience; so that in St. Paul's case we have not merely the gospel as a body of facts and truths, but the gospel in the consciousness of a leading exponent, and, in some respects, the most prominent representative of certain phases of that gospel. Gentile Christianity, as distinguished from the earlier Judaic Christianity, could never have been understood except for this intermingling of Christianity as a system and Christianity as a life in the history of our apostle. Both the conditions met in him as they met in no other apostle. The two things must not be confounded. Many in our day fall into this error and speak of Christianity as if it were only "a life." It is *a life*, but it is something else besides and something antecedent to *life*. Now, the epistolary style, and still more its method of thought, allow full play to the wholeness of Christianity. Its dogmas are preserved. Its experimental and practical forces are maintained. Its individuation is provided for. And thus, while seeing the system, we see also its life in the soul. If the psalmist, King David, is the signal representative of formal and spiritual Judaism in the Old Testament, St. Paul is the corresponding figure in the New Testament. At this point we are able to estimate the very great and specific value of the Second Epistle to the Corinthians. Beyond any of his writings, this unfolds the author, and does it with such masterly skill and on so comprehensive a scale as to give a twofold insight into his system and life. What an extension of the "Acts"! No St. Luke could have done this. It was the "Acts" in their secret head-springs in the man, and the man only could record what they were. The account of his personal feelings is resumed in this chapter. Not only for their sakes, but for his own, the visit had been postponed, since he was unwilling to come in sorrow. The "rod" would have been painful to him; they were to exercise discipline under the directions of his letter and thus forestall an occasion of grief to him. If he had made them sorry, who but they could give him joy? This was the reason for his writing, the reason too of deferring his visit; and thus the two things had been designed to co-operate in one result. A controversy is like a disease; the mode of treatment must be varied to suit its stages. No doubt personal presence, conversations, direct appeals, are best at some times for adjusting difficulties; at other times, letters are preferable. The discernment of the apostle prompted him to write and then to await the effect; and it was all in the interest of peace and for his and their consolation. Inspired by this confidence, he had written them a severe rebuke. It was a most painful duty; it was a duty, however, of love; and because of this coincidence, conscience and affection being at work in his soul, he had suffered most keenly. " Out of much affliction and anguish of heart I wrote unto you with many tears." The great soul was not afraid of words nor of the critics of words. He had a rare kind of courage. It was the boldness to say *how much* he thought and *how much* he felt, and to send forth his words laden with the meanings they had for him, that they might convey exactly those meanings to others. The love was not overstated, for it was a father's love towards the children of his heart: " More abundantly unto you." Evidently his paramount aim is to assure the Corinthians of his warm affection for them. Other feelings are held in abeyance; no mention now of suspicions, jealousies, backbitings, and other wrongs, by which he had been tortured; only the love, the impassioned love, he cherished for those whose sorrow and joy were his sorrow and joy. How naturally the way is prepared for what follows! "If any have caused grief [referring to the incestuous person], he hath not grieved me, but in part, that I may not overcharge you all." The Revised Verson, " If any hath caused sorrow, he hath caused sorrow, not to me, but in part (that I press not too heavily) to you all." Conybeare and Howson, " As concerns him who has caused the pain, it is not me that he has pained, but some of you (some, I say), that I may not press too harshly upon all." Many commentators read it thus : " If any have caused grief, he hath grieved not me, but more or less (that I be not too heavy on him) all of you." What is the point of interest is the light in which St. Paul now regarded the offender and the punishment inflicted upon him. Punishment had been punishment; it had expressed righteous indignation, upheld official order, vindicated the holy authority of law. It had been effectual in bringing the flagrant sinner to repentance and had proved a warning to others. But were the effects to stop here ? A great work had been done and yet other results were possible—were most desirable. Precisely here the far-sighted wisdom of St. Paul attracts our admiration. Discipline of a mechanical or of a military kind is cheap enough. True reformatory and saving discipline is a costly thing, requiring forethought and afterthought, the looking " before and after," which has won its place among the aphorisms of statesmanship. Much fruit falls and rots just as the ripening season approaches. Special care was needed, so the apostle argued, lest Satan should spoil the wholesome act in the sequel. " Sufficient to such a man is this punishment, which was inflicted of many." " Sufficient " leads the sentence. And the " many " has its weight, since in nothing is the power of the *many* so much felt as in condemnation.

> " There is no creature loves me,
> And if I die, no soul shall pity me."

This is Gloster perfected in King Richard. St. Paul urges the forgiveness of this gross offender. On the contrary, " Ye ought rather to forgive him, and comfort him, lest perhaps such a one should be swallowed up with overmuch sorrow." Make evident your love to him; so he beseeches them. If he is restored to their affection, this would prove that the Church was " obedient in all things." All through he keeps the dignity and authority of the Church in commanding view, and, as he had laid a most solemn duty on its conscience, so now he recognizes its high relationship in the matter of reconciliation. Would the brethren forgive him ? So would he, and that too in the most impressive manner—" in the sight of Christ." The reasoning of the apostle at this point ought to make a most profound and lasting impression on Christian thinkers. Sincere motives and upright intentions do not always preserve good men from terrible blunders in administering Church discipline. All unawares, the imagination exaggerates, right feeling becomes jealous of itself, motives are looked at askance, a spurious consistency sets up its tyrannical claims, and, in no long time, law parts company with authority, and equity is crushed by justice. No attitude in which St. Paul appears before us is so finely characteristic of high manhood as when he pleads for extreme thoughtfulness and tender consideration in the use of legitimate power. Who ever suffered from the numberless forms of injustice as he did ? Who died daily as he did ? The " beasts " at Ephesus were not merely such as do physical violence, but in their utter want of all moral sensibility to truth and right. Yet this was not the worst. Ask a man who has had a large experience in public life what has occasioned him the greatest amount of vexation, and he will tell you that it was the misrepresentation and carping criticism and wilful littleness of spirit pursuing him continually which had most embittered his career. St. Paul was subjected to these annoyances through all the middle period of his apostolic life. And what did he learn from them? To be distrustful of his own heart, to keep an open and vigilant eye on his infirmities, to be specially guarded as to the ambitious uses of power, and to foreclose every avenue to his soul through which an entrance might be effected of a fanatical temper in rebuke, in the management of Church troubles, and in the relation sustained to the other apostles. In the case of the Corinthian offender we see his lofty bearing. Ready to forgive, glad to forgive, yet he waits till he can say to the Church, " If ye forgive anything, I forgive also." And hear his reason, " Lest Satan should get an advantage of us : for we are not ignorant of his devices." Never could he have been St. Paul, apostle of the Gentiles, without this intense conception intensely realized of Satan as an infernal agent of prodigious power and unceasing activity. In his theology, in his way of looking at men and things, in his calculation of the forces to be met in the great conflict, it would have been inexplicably strange had he ignored or depreciated this gigantic spirit of evil. Elsewhere we have his allusions to Satan in other aspects of his character. Here he is the schemer, the wily plotter, the adroit strategist, observant of every movement, and on the alert for every opportunity. St. Paul was not afraid to acknowledge that in this matter at Corinth Satan might even yet turn things to his advantage. Recall the words (1 Cor. v. 5), " To deliver such a one unto Satan, for the destruction of the flesh ; " and yet they were to labour and intercede " that the spirit may be saved in the day of the Lord Jesus." And now, this repentant and forgiven man, should they not save him from the snares of Satan?—save themselves, too, from being over-reached by the arch-enemy of Christ and all goodness?—L.

Vers. 12—17.—*Coming to Troas ; disquietude ; defence of his apostleship.* Quite abruptly St. Paul mentions that he came to Troas. Why he left Ephesus he does not say, but we infer it was because of his anxiety to see Titus, and hear from him how his letter to the Corinthians had been received. There was a fine opening at Troas to preach the gospel, and yet he was greatly disquieted as Titus did not meet him. " Taking my leave of them, I went from thence into Macedonia." Here he met Titus, though, in the excitement of joy, he fails to state it. The sudden outburst of gratitude, " Thanks be unto God," expresses his exultation over the good tidings Titus had brought from Corinth, so that here, as is frequently the case, we get the outward history of events from the biography of the apostle's heart. All he had expected, and even more, had been realized, and he breaks forth in thanksgiving.

> " Ye that in waters glide, and ye that walk
> The earth, and stately tread or lowly creep,
> Witness if I be silent, morn or ev'n,
> To hill or valley, fountain or fresh shade,
> Made vocal by my song, and taught his praise."

St. Paul was not a silent man in his happiness. No depth of emotion satisfied him unless it could be imparted to others. On this occasion his soul found utterance in thanking God, " which always causeth us to triumph in Christ." A military triumph rises before him ; the victorious general is returning to the capital ; the long procession moves before his eye ; and, in the train, the captives brought home are conspicuous. Such a captive is the apostle following the chariot of his Lord. " Yet (at the same time, by a characteristic change of metaphor) an incense-bearer, scattering incense (which was always done on these occasions), as the procession moves on " (Conybeare and Howson). Christ is the fragrance ; " we are unto God a sweet savour of Christ." Whether men are saved or lost, Christ is Christ, and the fragrance cannot perish. There will be a " savour of death unto death " and a " savour of life unto life ; " but, in either issue, the glory of God's government is maintained. For, so far as we can see into the relations of Christ to man and of man to Christ, the fundamental fact in each aspect of the subject is human freedom. Of his own free-will Christ took upon himself our flesh and blood, suffered, and died ; and of our own free-will, made such by him and acted on as such by the Holy Spirit, we accept his atonement. If we reject the offered mercy, the act of our rejection testifies to the infinitude of the mercy, and the " savour of Christ " is none the less " sweet " in itself.

"And who is sufficient for these things?" Here is no one-sided gospel, that accommodates conscience to taste, and allows a compromise between duty and inclination. Here is a gospel that is the "savour of death unto death" and of "life unto life." Who is competent to maintain its stern truthfulness by preaching both these doctrines? The test of a faithful minister lies in the wise and earnest use of each class of facts. Is anything so difficult? Take the natural intellect; take the natural affections; take language as the vehicle of expression; and by what power of culture can a preacher be found who can set forth the gospel in its twofoldness of "death unto death" and "life unto life"? St. Paul, in the seventeenth verse, answers the question as to sufficiency. Now, as always, it is not simply the gospel which is the power and wisdom of God, but his way of preaching it. He declares that "many corrupt the Word of God;" not of this number is he. And where does the danger of corruption exist? In not holding with a balanced mind the "death" and the "life," so as to shun over-statements and under-statements in each instance. To preach after St. Paul's manner, one must have *sincerity*—the truth unmixed with human speculations; he must preach what God has revealed as to his Law and its righteousness, no more, no less; and he must preach it in Christ, himself in Christ, his gospel in Christ, and so preach as to spirit and temper and manner that the fragrance shall breathe in all his words.—L.

Vers. 3, 4.—*Sympathy in grief and joy.* How far from a formal or mechanical ministry was that of the apostle! He entered into the circumstances and the feelings of those for whom he had laboured. Nothing which affected their interests was indifferent to him. Some in his position would have said, "We have done our duty; it is no affair of ours how they act; why should we trouble ourselves regarding them?" Not so St. Paul. When the Corinthians acted unworthily, his sensitive heart was distressed; when they repented, that heart bounded with joy. This was not altogether the effect of natural temperament; it was the fruit of true fellowship of spirit with his Lord.

I. THE SPIRIT OF SYMPATHY IS THE SPIRIT OF CHRIST AND OF CHRISTIANITY. In the earthly life of our Saviour we behold evidences of this spirit. He rejoiced in men's joys; he wept by the grave of his friend; he sighed and groaned when he met with instances of unspirituality and unbelief. It was pity which brought him first to earth and then to the cross of Calvary. Similarly with the precepts of the New Testament. The lesson is often virtually repeated, "Rejoice with those who do rejoice, and weep with those who weep."

II. THE SPIRIT OF SYMPATHY IS SOMETIMES THE OCCASION OF SORROW. 1. The spectacle of a professing Christian falling into sin awakens commiseration and distress in the mind of every true follower of Christ. 2. The spectacle of a Christian conniving at sin, or regarding it with comparative unconcern, is painful in the extreme to one solicitous for Christian purity. 3. Sorrow, from whatever cause, awakens sorrow in a mind sensitive as was that of Paul.

III. THE SPIRIT OF SYMPATHY IS SOMETIMES THE OCCASION OF JOY. Even amidst personal difficulties and opposition encountered in his ministry Paul was not indifferent to the joys of his converts. And when those whose conduct had pained him came to a better mind and afforded him satisfaction, he rejoiced with them in their happiness. If there is joy in the presence of the angels of God over one sinner that repenteth, surely he most resembles the Father of spirits and his immediate attendants whose heart is lifted up with exhilaration and delight by anything that manifests the growth and victory of the Divine kingdom upon earth.—T.

Ver. 11.—*The devices of Satan.* The course of St. Paul with regard to the Christian Church at Corinth was one of great difficulty. A flagrant case of immorality demanded his decided interference. Yet he wished to deal, both with the offender and with those who made too light of his offence, in such a way as not to endanger his personal influence over the Corinthian Christians generally. If he were too lax or too severe, in either case he would give his enemies an opportunity to malign him. And he knew that there were Judaizing teachers who were ready to attribute the immorality to Paul's doctrines of grace. So that the apostle trod a very difficult path, which Satan had set with snares on either hand. He needed to be on his guard against the insidious machinations of the enemy, and he gave the Corinthians to understand that such was his attitude.

I. SATAN'S DEVICES ARE MANY AND VARIED. The resources of an earthly foe ought not to be under-estimated by a general who would gain the victory; and if the tactics vary with circumstances, vigilance and self-possession, courage and care, are all needed. Satan besets Christians with many temptations; if he cannot tempt them into conscious sin, he will endeavour to entrap them into some error of judgment and conduct which may give him an advantage over them.

II. SATAN'S DEVICES ARE SKILFUL AND CRAFTY. In the temptation of our Lord this was abundantly manifest, and the Saviour gave his disciples to understand that they would be called upon to endure the assaults of the same unsleeping foe. Against his ever-varying tactics, against his all but inexhaustible resources, it becomes, therefore, every Christian soldier to be upon his guard.

III. SATAN'S DEVICES ARE THE MEANS OF SNARING MANY OF THE UNWARY. Some who once ran well have been hindered. Some who have resisted one enemy have fallen beneath the attack of another. The annals of every Church, however pure, tell of those against whom the adversary has directed his blows only too successfully. "Let him that thinketh he standeth take heed lest he fall."

IV. SATAN'S DEVICES NEED TO BE WITHSTOOD WITH WATCHFULNESS AND PRAYER. It is something not to be ignorant of them. The unwary and unthinking are entrapped through very ignorance. Yet knowledge is no sufficient protection. A distrust of our own ability and a reliance upon superior power and wisdom are indispensably necessary in order to safety and deliverance. Well may the inspired counsel be received with gratitude and acted upon with diligence, "Put on the whole armour of God, that ye may be able to stand against the wiles of the devil."—T.

Ver. 12.—*An open door.* Men are prone to think what doors are open to them to enter, through which they may pass to their own profit, or advancement, or pleasure. Paul's was an unselfish and benevolent nature. He was a true follower of Christ, who came, not to do his own will, and not to be ministered unto, but to minister. Again and again, in the course of his life, his heart was gladdened by the spectacle of a door of holy service set open before him by God's providence, inviting him to enter in and in the name of the Lord to take possession.

I. THE OPEN DOOR LEADS TO OPPORTUNITIES OF WORK FOR CHRIST. To the true Christian this is more desirable than aught beside. Paul went nowhere but some door opened before him. A synagogue was open; he entered it, and reasoned out of the Law or the prophets. A market-place thronged with citizens afforded him opportunity for preaching the true God and the eternal life. Even a prison door, when it closed upon him, did not shut him off from human souls. It is well that Christians should think, not so much of their own interests, as of the service of their Master.

II. THE OPEN DOOR IS SET OPEN BY DIVINE PROVIDENCE. "Opened of the Lord" is the apostle's expression. We may not see the hand, but we should not ignore it. When God himself makes a way, his doing so is a command to his people to adopt and to follow it. When he opens, "no man can shut."

III. THE OPEN DOOR IS A DOOR OF PROMISE TO THOSE WHO WILL ENTER IN. Why is the door set open? Is there no purpose in this? Surely it is a want of faith to hold back when the Lord himself so manifestly encourages his servants to "go in and possess the land."

IV. THE OPEN DOOR WILL BE SHUT AGAINST THOSE WHOSE NEGLIGENCE OR DISOBEDIENCE HINDERS THEM FROM ENTERING IT. As the door of salvation will be closed against those who fail to enter in, so the door of service will be shut to exclude those who turn aside when the hand of God has opened it and has beckoned them to enter, but has beckoned them in vain.—T.

Vers. 14—16.—*The solemnity of the ministry.* A Roman triumph, to which the apostle refers in this passage, was the most magnificent of earthly pageants. The conqueror, in whose honour it was given, was an illustrious commander, who had defeated an enemy or gained a province. The route traversed by the triumphal procession lay through Rome to the Capitol itself. The spectators who feasted their eyes upon the sight were the vast population of the city. Before, the victor passed onwards the captives taken in the campaign, and the spoil which had been wrested from the foe. Behind, followed the army, flushed with victory and rejoicing in the insolence and pride of military might. The conqueror himself, mounted aloft upon his car, was the centre of observation and attraction. Every mark of honour was paid to him. Sacrifices were offered by the priests to the gods to whose favour victory was ascribed. Incense-bearers marched in the procession, and fragrant clouds ascended, floating in the air and mingling with the shouts and with the strains of martial music. And in the temples sacrificial offerings were accompanied by the presentation of the odorous incense.

I. The triumphs of the gospel. The warfare of the Word is against the sins of the rebels who have defied the authority of the Most High. In apostolic times the progress of the gospel, though often opposed and often checked, appeared to the view of Paul as a triumphal progress. God, who had triumphed over the enemies whom he converted into his friends and companions, made them, as his representatives, triumph in their turn, and admitted them to share his triumph over the enemies of truth and righteousness.

II. The incense-bearers in the triumphal train. There is a prodigality of wealth in the imagery here employed. Paul and his fellow-ministers were themselves both captives and also incense-bearers—"unto God a sweet savour of Christ." As the Son of the Eternal is infinitely acceptable to his Father, so those who share his mission and purpose, and faithfully publish his gospel, are well-pleasing to him, as the odour of the fragrant incense to the nostril.

III. The accompaniments and results of the gospel triumph. These are twofold and opposed. 1. To the perishing the ministry is a sentence of death. Some captives were taken aside and put to death in cold blood as the procession approached the Capitoline hill. The incense to such was deadly—an odour premonitory of a violent and miserable death. Thus the proclamation of the gospel, in itself an unspeakable blessing, is actually the occasion of the condemnation of unbelievers, who reject and despise it. 2. To those in course of salvation the ministry is a message of life. Welcome and pleasant alike to God and man, the glad tidings of redemption tell of life to those whose desert is death. A welcome and delightful fragrance to the saved, it promises participation in the glorious victory and the eternal reign of the Divine Redeemer.—T.

Ver. 14.—*The triumph.* The emotional and susceptible nature of the Apostle Paul was quick to recognize either opposition or success. And when it occurred to him, in the providence of God, to meet with instances in which his message was gratefully welcomed and he himself was cordially appreciated, his heart was filled with joy, and he was eager to utter forth gratitude and praise. When elated with prosperity in his evangelistic work, he felt that God was always making him to triumph. His spiritual successes were to him more glorious than the triumph which the victorious general enjoyed upon his return to Rome, when he ascended the Capitoline hill, with his fellow-warriors in the procession and his captives in his train. What an inspiration do these words of the apostle afford to those who are engaged in the service of the Saviour, and are experiencing the vicissitudes of earthly ministry!

I. If there is warfare, there will be victory. The Christian life is a warfare, involving effort, danger, and resistance. Much more manifestly does this figure apply to those who preach the gospel, especially as evangelists among the heathen, the degraded, the unbelieving. Such stand in need both of spiritual courage and of spiritual weapons. And in the stress of the conflict, in the noise and tumult of warfare, it is well for them to remember that the issue is not uncertain, that conquest is close at hand.

II. If there are enemies, they will become either captives or, better still, allies and fellow-soldiers. When spiritual opponents are many and daring, and when their onset is sore and perhaps alarming, the heart of the soldier of Christ may sometimes sink within him. But he is required to estimate the fortunes of the war, not by human probabilities, but by Divine predictions. Of those who oppose themselves none shall prevail. Some shall be vanquished and put to shame. Others shall confess the justice and the grace of Christ, shall lay down the arms of rebellion, shall enlist in the spiritual host, shall take to them the armour of God.

III. If there is disappointment, there will be recompense. Paul knew often enough what it is to be cast down. The higher the hope, the bitterer the sorrow when that hope is frustrated. It sometimes happens that, where the Christian warrior spends all his strength, and attacks the enemy with courage and perseverance, there he experiences the most humiliating rebuff. Then let him be assured that different experience is in store for him. Foes shall yield, whose stubbornness, it seemed to him, no power could subdue. Victory shall be to the faithful and to the brave.

IV. IF THERE BE A SHARING OF CHRIST'S CROSS, THERE SHALL BE ALSO A SHARING OF HIS THRONE. Our Lord, the Captain of our salvation, knew by experience the power of the enemy. And can it be expected that with us all will be prosperous? Shall we not be followers of him, and know the likeness of his death? Thus shall it be given to him that overcometh to sit down with him upon his throne.—T.

Ver. 16.—" *Who is sufficient?* " Those to whom the ministry of the gospel of Christ is merely a profession, who regard the offices of religion as a routine, who consider chiefly such emoluments and advantages as may be connected with it, read these words with astonishment and without sympathy. But those who think as Paul thought of the ministry, with a wondering amazement at the grace of God and at the provision made in Christ for the passage of that grace to man, those who realize the preciousness of the soul and the solemnity alike of life and of eternity, cannot but cherish a conviction that, for a service so high and holy as the ministry of God's Word, no human qualification can suffice.

I. THE INSUFFICIENCY OF HUMAN POWER. To understand this we must regard: 1. The deficiencies of the human agent. No minister has an adequate view of the Saviour he preaches; none has a sufficiently keen sympathy with the souls of his fellow-men; none has a power of persuasion commensurate with the necessities of the case; none has the burning zeal for God which was perfectly displayed by Christ alone. 2. The peculiar difficulties of the work to be accomplished. The ignorance, the levity, the prejudices, the wilfulness, the gross sinfulness of men,—all must be taken into account if we would have a just conception of the magnitude of the great task which is entrusted to the Christian minister.

II. THE SUFFICIENCY OF DIVINE GRACE. 1. This is revealed to those, and to those alone, who are sincerely conscious of their own powerlessness and the inadequacy of all human aid. 2. God's own commission is an assurance that he will not withhold the assistance needed. The work is his; his is the call and his the authority. 3. God, by his Spirit, assists all lowly and faithful agents in his service, strengthening the feeble, so that by their means, however seemingly inadequate, great results are accomplished. 4. By the same invisible but marvellous agency God overcomes the obstacles encountered in the sinner's heart, and makes the word of man effectual because the vehicle of the power and grace of Heaven.—T.

Ver. 4.—*The pains of rebuking.* I. THESE ARE VERY REAL TO GRACIOUS NATURES. Some delight to castigate; but they are not gracious or noble—they are rather fitted to feel the rod than to wield it. An affectionate parent often suffers more than his chastened child; a faithful pastor than the rebuked Church member. Paul said that if he came to Corinth he would not spare; before he came, he did not spare himself. There was grief at Corinth, but as much or more in Macedonia. Joy in causing suffering is a mark of degradation. We condemn pleasure obtained from cruel sports; pleasure obtained from wounding minds is even more barbaric and revolting. We may feel compelled to rebuke, and that sharply. We can never be justified in extracting joy from the suffering occasioned.

II. WHEN REBUKE IS PAINFUL TO THE REBUKER IT IS MORE LIKELY TO PROVE EFFICACIOUS TO THE REBUKED. 1. *There is evidence of qualification to rebuke.* The rebuke does not spring from personal feeling. 2. *Undue harshness will be avoided.* 3. *A gracious tenderness is likely to permeate the severest rebuke.* 4. *If known to the rebuked, a salutary influence will be exercised.* Nothing is more irritating or hardening than to be rebuked by one who evidently enjoys his office. But if the one who points out our fault is evidently deeply pained himself, we must be very obdurate if we are insensible to such an appeal. The wayward child is conquered, not by the rod in his mother's hand, but by the tears in her eyes.

III. The object of right rebuking is not the pain of the rebuked. This should ever be kept in mind. We are not judges to pass sentences of mere punishment. We may grieve our fellows, but only for their good. We may cause pain, but only as a means to something else. Castigation is a beginning, not an end. We have effected nothing except failure if we have merely caused sorrow. It is a thankless task indeed merely to make men sad. It is a noble one to make them sad that we may make them holier.

IV. Right rebuking is evidence of much love. Not to suffer sin upon our neighbour is a great duty ; but the best natures are apt to shrink from reproving. Great love will compel them, as it did Paul. We often cannot show our love more conclusively. It may not at once be apparent to men, but it will to God—and to men by-and-by. The strongest evidence of Paul's love for the Corinthian Church was exhibited in the rod which he held over it. So of God himself : those whom he loves he chastens. (Heb. xii. 6).—H.

Vers. 5—11.—*Restoring the backslider.* I. Church discipline should be administered by the Church. "This punishment which was inflicted by the many " (ver. 6). Not by an individual, be he the pope himself, nor by priests or clergy, but by the whole body of the individual Church or a majority of its members. A Christian has a right to be judged by his peers.

II. Church discipline should ever have in view restoration. Its object is not to punish the offender so much as to do him good, and at the same time to preserve the Church's purity. Church discipline should not be regarded as a *final act* towards the backslider, but with it should ever be associated prayers and hope that the severance may be brief. The Church rejects that she may accept ; she casts out that she may receive back again. So Church discipline should never be of a character to hinder repentance or to render restoration impossible.

III. Church discipline should be administered with great discretion. 1. On the one hand, it may be too slight and not produce suitable effects. 2. On the other, it may be so excessive as to drive the offender to despair. 3. In either case Satan will gain an advantage (ver. 11), which he is ever seeking and has often found when the Church or its leaders have attempted the delicate task of discipline. The Church's discipline of persecution and intolerance has served the devil's purposes admirably in many a dark century. And the Church's discipline of indifference and false charity has done similar service in many a century boasting of its light and breadth of thought and liberty.

IV. Penitence on the part of an offender is a strong argument for prompt restoration to fellowship. The duty of restoration is not so fully recognized as it might be. Often it is the predilection of the powers that be, rather than the condition of the offender, which determines whether he shall be restored or not. But when the honour of the Church has been vindicated, and the offender is undoubtedly contrite, the way of duty is clear. A Church which will not restore *then*, deserves to be excommunicated itself.

V. Restoration is not to be to toleration, but to love. The love is to exist whilst the discipline is being inflicted. It is to manifest itself unreservedly when discipline is removed. Many are restored to suspicion, coldness, contempt—a restoration which paves the way for a more fatal fall. If God forgives some professing Christians as they forgive others (and this is their frequent prayer), their share of the Divine forgiveness is likely to be a very slender one.—H.

Vers. 14—17.—*The constant triumph of the faithful minister.* I. He triumphs because wherever he goes he makes known God and Christ. This is a true triumph. If he succeeds in doing this he has a great success—the success of performance of duty and of fulfilment of the Divine will. Moreover, the kingdom of God is almost certain to be extended. Apparent failure, when more closely examined and tried by the test of time, will often be found to be success.

II. His triumph is not dependent upon the reception of his message. 1. *To some his word is a savour from death unto death.* The Christ proclaimed is to them a *dead* Christ, and his gospel lifeless and powerless, leading them only to denser spiritual death. This is very disheartening when viewed under one aspect. But Christ is preached, the work is acceptable to God, the Divine mercy is vindicated, and the responsibility of the disastrous issue rests solely on the rejecters. The excellence of the truth is demonstrated by its rejection on the part of the vile and sin-loving. 2. *To others his word is a savour from life unto life.* Here the triumph is unquestioned by all. A living Christ is recognized, and one who has life-giving power.

III. HE TRIUMPHS ONLY AS HE IS FAITHFUL. For only so does he honour God and set forth the truth as it is in Jesus. The faithful minister: 1. Does not corrupt the Word of God (ver. 17). Many do (1) by false interpretation, (2) bias, (3) insinuation, (4) omission, (5) addition. Prompted by (1) gain, (2) applause, (3) carnal preferences. 2. But (1) distrusts himself, crying, "Who is sufficient for these things?" (2) uses utmost sincerity; (3) gets his message from God—"of God" (ver. 17); (4) speaks as in the sight of God; (5) speaks in Christ, in communion with him as the Head.

IV. HIS TRIUMPH IS OF GOD. He is led in triumph by God (ver. 14). God has triumphed over him, and now God triumphs through him. His sufficiency is of God (ch. iii. 5). He has no power when he only has his own; he has all power when he has God's.—H.

Vers. 1—4.—*The sorrow of faithful love.* The apostle has still in mind the unfaithful member who had brought so sad a disgrace upon the whole Church. His conduct in the matter, especially in changing his mind when he was fully expected at Corinth, had been misrepresented, and made the occasion of accusations against him as a fickle-minded, self-willed man. He therefore here explains why he did not visit Corinth while it remained uncertain how the offending member would be treated. He had no thought but for the truest well-being of the Corinthian Church. He could not leave them to go on in sin. He could not bear to think that those whom he had instructed in Christ were indifferent to sin. Love, feeling sorrow for the sinning member and for the dishonoured Church, cannot be satisfied without earnest warnings about the sin and efforts to remove it. Such efforts carry and express both the sorrow and the love. Illustrate by the patient, gracious pleadings of God with sinning and backsliding Israel, as given in the prophets Isaiah, Jeremiah, and Hosea.

I. SUCH SORROWING LOVE CAN PERSONALLY SUFFER. Here it led the apostle to act in a way which brought to him the bitterest form of suffering, even the suspicion and mistrust of his very friends. Even that he would bear, if but his desire for the spiritual welfare of the Corinthian Church could be realized. "Men might think that it had cost him little to write sharp words like those which he has in his mind. He remembers well what he felt as he dictated them—the intensity of his feelings, pain that such words should be needed, anxiety as to their issue, the very tears which then, as at other times, were the outflow of strong emotion. Those who were indignant at his stern words should remember, or at least learn to believe this, and so to see in them the strongest proof of his abounding love for them." The heart of St. Paul was in this matter as the heart of him who said, "As many as I love I rebuke and chasten." Illustrate what a pressure on personal feeling it is for the parent or teacher to chasten. They often suffer much more than do those whom they feel called to smite. Even the misunderstanding, and even the temporary hatred, of those whom we would benefit, must be borne, in our earnest endeavours to deliver them from the dominion and defilement of their sins.

II. SUCH SORROWING LOVE CAN DEAL SEVERELY WITH THE SINNER. It is never love to pass by sin. It is no true love that touches the sin too lightly and gives inefficient and unworthy apprehensions of it. St. Paul seemed to be too severe. He could not be. The case called for an extreme of severity. It was not merely that the offence was an open and scandalous one, but, what was even worse, the Church seemed to be pervaded by a false sentiment concerning it, and manifested no distress in having the guilty member among them. In some way, St. Paul felt, he must arouse them to a sense of their shame. Strong language, refusal to give them a personal visit, anything that would waken a sense of sin, were necessary. It had been the time for sternest rebuke. And still love needs to use severity. For some forms of sin the gentler persuasions are inefficient; men must be roughly shaken out of their self-confidences, and their pride must be humbled and broken. The Church of modern days so gravely fails of her witness and her duty because she has no " discipline," no severe dealings for her grave offenders. She has no love to burn against transgressors.

III. Such sorrowing love can show fine consideration for the feelings of others. Paul did not wish to make his second visit to Corinth in grief, and if he had carried out his first plan that would have been the almost inevitable result. He would wait, delaying his visit, so that he might have the chance of seeing them with a smile on his face, after receiving the tidings of their heeding his warning and putting away the sin. " The second reason St. Paul alleges for not coming to Corinth is apparently a selfish one—to spare himself pain. And he distinctly says he had written to pain *them*, in order that *he* might have joy. Very selfish, as at first it sounds ; but if we look closely into it it only sheds a brighter and fresher light upon the exquisite unselfishness and delicacy of St. Paul's character. He desired to save himself pain because it gave them pain. He desired joy for himself because his joy was theirs. He will not separate himself from them for a moment ; he will not be the master and they the school ; it is not *I* and *you*, but *we* ; ' my joy is your joy, as your grief was my grief.' " Do we love enough to rebuke and punish those whom we love ?—R. T.

Vers. 5—11.—*The Church's dealings with unworthy members.* " The main defence of the apostle against the charge of fickleness in the non-fulfilment of his promise was that he had abstained from going to Corinth in order to spare them the sharp rebuke he must have administered had he gone thither. A great crime had been committed ; the Church had been compromised, more especially as some of the Corinthians had defended the iniquity on the ground of liberty, and St. Paul had stayed away after giving his advice, that not he, but they themselves, might do the work of punishment. He gave sentence that the wicked person should be put away, but he wished *them* to execute the sentence. For it was a matter of greater importance to St. Paul that the Corinthians should feel rightly the necessity of punishment, than merely that the offender should be punished." We notice—

I. The sinner within the Church grieves the whole Church. If one member suffer, all the members suffer with him ; and if one member sin, the whole Church ought to feel grieved and distressed by the sin. St. Paul argues that, if a Church fails to clear itself of complicity with the wrong of its members, the guilt of such wrong attaches to it as well as to him. No man within Christ's Church can be alone in his sin, for we are "members one of another." The judgment of the Church may be the means of winning the penitence of the erring member.

II. The sinner when penitent should find the love and forgiveness of the whole Church. In relation to him there should be harmonious and united Church action. Yet, in actual fact, the wrong-doing of individuals too often creates party feeling. Some take the side of the wrong-doer and prevent the full exercise of Church discipline.

III. Such forgiveness of the Church may express God's forgiveness. It is only becoming, and only efficient, as following upon God's forgiveness. And it has its special use in being the earthly assurance of the Divine forgiveness and acceptance. The Church can *give* no absolution ; it can only find expression for the absolution which God has already granted to the penitent, and add its forgiveness of the wrong so far as it disturbed Church relations. In the proper expression of Church feeling towards moral offenders, the Apostle Paul, as a recognized Church leader, herein sets an efficient example. He is as jealous for the Church's honour and mercifulness as he is for the restoration of the penitent offender.—R. T.

Ver. 11.—*Satanic devices within the Church.* The reference here made to Satan must be regarded as figurative. It should not be used as an argument for the existence of a supreme evil spirit, however the existence of such a spirit may be assumed. St. Paul has elsewhere used the figure of " delivering unto Satan " (1 Tim. i. 20). By this we are to understand a solemn excommunication or expulsion from the Church, possibly with the infliction also of some bodily disease. The offender was to be left to feel all the physical and social consequences of his wrong-doing, in the hope that, through suffering, he might be brought to a sense of his sin. Satan is thought of as the power which leads men into vice and then torments them when they have followed the leadings. The apostle conceives of God as overruling the very sin, and consequent suffering, for good, through them bringing the sinner to a hopeful penitence and humility of heart. There was, however, this danger to be recognized and guarded against. Satan might, as it were, outwit the Church, in its dealing with erring members, and make the suffering following on sin produce *remorse* rather than *repentance*. "Penitence works life, remorse works death. The latter is more destructive even than self-righteousness, for it crushes, paralyzes, and kills the soul." There must consequently be a judicious limitation of the punishment, and a watchfulness for the first opportunity of showing mercy and granting restoration. "Not to release the offender from the bondage when he was truly penitent would be to afford the enemy of souls an opportunity of which he would not be slow to avail himself. Nothing is so likely to plunge a man into every kind of crime as despair." For St. Paul's experience of Satanic schemes, devices, and strategy, comp. ch. xii. 7; 1 Thess. ii. 18; Eph. vi. 12. We may treat the subject in its wider and more general applications if we illustrate the following and other ways in which Satan may be said to get advantage within a Church :—

I. By OVERMASTERING INDIVIDUAL MEMBERS. Failure does not come to the Church as a whole, but to individuals in it. All are exposed to temptation and evil. We must be in the world, and Christian men may yield themselves to the power of the "lust of the flesh, the lust of the eye, and the pride of life." Some of the gravest of our Church anxieties arise from the moral failure of individual members. Illustrate cases occurring in youth-time ; but especially cases in men's middle life, when the passions for wealth, sensuality, or drink often gain an overmastering energy. Show also the force that may be gained by the *suddenness* of the temptation, and by the condition of spiritual *unwatchfulness* in which the man may be found. The forms of failure which we usually find are dishonesty, immorality, or self-indulgence in meat or drink. But, by the law that those in the Church are members one of another, the failure of one is the shame, and should be the distress and grief, of all. Satan disturbs and injures a whole Church if he can gain influence over one member ; and to do this is ever "one of his devices."

II. By SECURING THE HARSH AND UNLOVING TREATMENT OF THOSE WHO FAIL. Perhaps it would be true to say that Satan never more certainly gets the advantage over Churches than when he makes them exaggerate punishment, overpress discipline, and fail to temper judgment with mercy. The action of a Church must be exactly in harmony with the action, when he was with us on earth, of the Church's Lord. He was quick and keen to discern sin. He was swift and severe to punish sin. But he was watchful for signs of gracious influence effected by the punishment, and ready at once to restore and forgive the penitent. He never "breaks the bruised reed or quenches the smoking flax." Man's punishments are always in danger of running to excess. Man cannot judge motives or read hearts, and so he too often fails to recognize soon enough when discipline has accomplished its work. Explain the evil influence exerted by unwillingness to forgive members of a family or of a Church ; and show that a most mischievous conception of God himself, and wrong relations with him, would follow if we were not quite sure that he is "ready to forgive."

III. By MAKING A CHURCH INDIFFERENT TO THE MORALITY OF ITS MEMBERS. Laxity, carelessness about purity of life, uprightness of relations, and consistency of conduct, often do creep into Churches, and they are among the most grievous of "Satan's devices." Illustrate from the evil work done by Carnal Security, in the town of Mansoul, as described in John Bunyan's 'Holy War.' The evil influence is felt, not only by the erring brethren, who come under no kind of correction, but are left to go on in sin, until "sin, when it is finished, bringeth forth death ; " but also by the Church, which is defiled before God by the taint on its good name, and which fails to be duly sensitive to the Divine honour. Illustrate by the lesson that was taught in the failure of Israel at the siege of Ai, when the "accursed thing" was in their camp.

IV. By PERSUADING A CHURCH TO MAKE ITS FORGIVENESS A FORMALITY, NOT A FULL RESTORATION. Too often this grave mistake is made : the offender is formally restored to membership, but he is not really taken back into the love and trust of the brethren, and he receives no signs of restored confidence and no help back to goodness. He is a blighted man, and it seems to him that his slip or fall can never really be forgotten, never really be wiped out, and therefore he must hang down his head among the brethren to his dying day. The Church's forgiveness and restoration must be like God's, a help to the erring one towards realizing the glorious completeness of God's forgivings, forgettings, and restorings. For he casts our sins behind his back, and into the depths of the sea. " As the punishment of man is representative of the punishment and wrath of God, so the absolution of man is representative of the forgiveness of God." Impress, in conclusion, the extreme painfulness of the possibility that, in regard to her discipline, the Christian Church may be out-manœuvred by Satan, and come really to do his work.—R. T.

Vers. 12, 13.—*Providential doors.* Introduce by describing the leading instances of providential deliverance, care, and guidance in the life of the Apostle Paul. Especially dwell on the cases in which his life was preserved from peril and from the plots of his enemies. The reference made in our text is rather to the gracious way in which his missionary journeyings and missionary spheres had been opened before him ; and the illustration may be taken from the singular way in which doors were opened and shut, when the Divine will was for the apostle to preach the gospel in Europe (see Acts xvi. 6—9). For the figure of a "door" for an "opportunity," see 1 Cor. xvi. 9 ; Rev. iii. 8. The truth of the Divine providence ordering our lives is not one that is so familiar to us as it was to our fathers. Possibly our warmer thought of God's fatherly care has taken the place of the colder conception of an impersonal providence. Still, it may be well to revive the older notion and make it glow with Christian sentiment and feeling.

I. The ordering of providence for everybody. Irrespective of religious state and relations. Illustrations of this are found in all times of danger, disease, or calamity. Some are taken and some are left. We constantly read of remarkable providential escapes.

II. The speciality of providence for Christians. It may in part be that Christians more readily recognize the hand of God in their rescuings and guidances, but we may also believe that God gives a special protection to his own. Such a belief may be a great comfort to us, but it must be kept from becoming exaggerated and extravagant. The Christian cannot always be preserved, because his suffering may be for the good of the whole.

III. The attitude in which Christians should stand towards the ever-active providence. It may be shown to include (1) earnest watchings ; (2) patient waitings ; (3) prompt actings ; (4) full and unhesitating obediences ; and (5) thankful rejoicings. —R. T.

Vers. 15, 16.—*The twofold issues of a preached gospel.* Heroes, in the older days of the apostle, were usually great generals, leaders of mighty armies, conquerors of other nations—men whose " glory " came from desolated cities, down-trodden races, wasted harvests, and crushed and bleeding hearts. And such heroes were permitted to have a " triumph," as it was called. A triumphal procession was arranged in their honour, and to this event the Roman generals looked as to the very goal of their ambition. Magnificent and thrilling scenes they must have been. The general was received, at the gates of the imperial city, by all that was noble and grave and venerable among the officials, and he was led from the gate through the crowded and shouting streets to the Capitol. First marched the ancient men, the grave senators of the Roman council, headed by a body of magistrates. Then came the trumpeters, making the air ring again with their prolonged and joyous blasts. Then followed a long train of carriages and frames laden with the spoils brought from battle-fields or plundered from conquered cities, the articles which were most remarkable for their value, or rarity, or beauty being fully exposed to view. There might be seen models of the forts or cities which had been captured ; gold and silver statues, pictures, handsome vases, and embroidered stuffs. Then came a band of players on the flute, and then white bulls and oxen destined for sacrifice; and incense-bearers, waving to and fro their censers, and sending forth their sweet savour. Then were seen caged lions and tigers, or monstrous elephants, or other strange creatures, brought as specimens from the captive lands. And then the procession filled with pathos, for there followed the leaders of the conquered foe, and the long train of inferior captives, all bound and fettered, and altogether a sad and humiliating sight. At last came the great conqueror, standing in a splendid chariot, drawn by four milk-white horses, magnificently adorned, the conqueror bearing a royal sceptre, and having his brow encircled with a laurel crown. After him marched his great officers, the horse-soldiers, and the vast army of foot-soldiers, each one holding aloft a spear adorned with laurel boughs.   And so the procession moved on through the crowded, shouting streets until it reached the Capitoline hill.   There they halted, dragged some of those poor captives aside to be killed, and then offered their sacrifices and began their triumphal feast.   St. Paul's mind was evidently full of such a scene as this, and he took his figures from it.   He says that God permits us, as apostles and ministers, always to triumph with Christ.   We are, through grace, always conquering generals.   But St. Paul fixed his thoughts chiefly on those miserable, naked, fettered captives, who were going on to death.   He could not help thinking—What was the sound of the clanging trumpet and the piping flute to them—poor hopeless ones?   What was the savour of sweet incense in the air to them—poor agitated ones?   Some among them may indeed have had the promise of life, and to them the savour of the incense would be sweet; it would be " life unto life."   But so many of them knew what their fate must be; they dreaded the worst; they trembled as they came nearer to the ascent of the hill; and as the wind wafted the savour of the incense to them they could but sadly feel that it was a savour of "death unto death."   And the apostle thought of his life-work of preaching the gospel.   It was even thus with the savour of the gospel-triumph.   To some it was *death*, to others it was *life*.   Not, indeed, at the arbitrary will of some proud general, but as the necessary issue of the relations in which men stand to a preached gospel; for "he that hath the Son hath life, and he that hath not the Son of God hath not life, but the wrath of God abideth on him."

I.   THE PROPER RESULT OF A PREACHED GOSPEL IS LIFE.   It was God's gracious purpose that men, "dead in trespasses and sins," should have life, and have it more abundantly.   In his Son Jesus Christ life and immortality are brought to light.   In the early days God set before men life and death, and, with all holy persuasions, urged them to choose life and good.   This was the one absorbing purpose and endeavour of the Lord Jesus.   While he was here he was ever doing one thing—quickening life, restoring life, renewing life: the life of health to those afflicted, of reason to those possessed with devils, of knowledge to ignorant disciples, and even of the body to those smitten and dead.   And the apostles carried his gospel forth into all the world as the light and life of men.   Dwell upon the significance and interest of the word "life," and explain the new life in Christ Jesus, which the Christian enjoys.

II.   THE MOURNFUL RESULT OF A PREACHED GOSPEL OFTEN IS DEATH.   Our Lord used forcible but painful figures to express the death of the impenitent and unbelieving: " outer darkness;" " wailing and gnashing of teeth;" " worm that never dies;" "fire that none may quench."   We must feel the force of these things, for no man can worthily explain them.   This "death" was the mournful issue of a preached gospel when the Son of man was himself the Preacher.   Foolish Gadarenes besought him to depart out of their coasts, and leave them to their night and death.   Hardened Capernaum, exalted even to heaven in privilege, must be thrust down to hell.   St. Paul must turn from bigoted and prejudiced Jews, and go to the Gentiles, leaving the very children of the covenant in a darkness that might be felt.   He who came to give life is practically found to be a Stone of stumbling and a Rock of offence.   Five foolish virgins put their hands about their flickering lamps as they cry against the closed door; and this is the simple, awful ending of their story, " The darkness took them."   We do see men hardened under a preached gospel now.   Illustrate by the dropping well at Knaresborough.   Water ought to soften and melt, but these waters, falling upon things, encrust them with stone, and even turn them into stone.   Such may have been the droppings of the " water of life" upon us.   There are only these two issues.   The gospel must either take us by the hand and lead us up into the sunlight or it must bid us away down into the dark.   Only two issues, but what issues they are!   Life!   As we think of that word, all joy, light, and heaven come into our view.   Death!   As we speak that word, all darkness, woe, and hell come into our thoughts.   " Who indeed is sufficient for these things?"—even for the preaching of a gospel which must prove to be a " savour of life unto life or of death unto death."—R. T.

Ver. 17.—*Conscious simplicity and integrity.*   "The word for ' corrupt,' formed from a word which signifies ' huckster,' or ' tavern-keeper,' implies an adulteration like that which such people commonly practised.   We, says St. Paul, play no such tricks of trade with what we preach; we do not meet the tastes of our hearers by prophesying deceits. The very fact that we know the tremendous issues of our work would hinder that." God's gospel word, the message of eternal life in Christ Jesus, may be adulterated or corrupted in three ways. 1. By mixing up with it foreign, inharmonious, merely human, teachings. 2. Or by making the gospel revelation into a stiffened, formal creed, over the precise terms of which we may wrangle and dispute. 3. Or by displacing the true motive in preaching it, and giving place to low aims, and purposes of merely selfish ambition, and longing for the praise of men. The appeal of the text has its special force when we remember of what things the Judaizing party accused the apostle. St. Paul's enemies forced this appeal from him. Usually it is enough that the sincere and true man should keep on his faithful way, little heeding the opinions or accusations of others, trusting the care of his reputation to God. But occasions do arise when something like public vindication becomes necessary, and a man is called to assert his conscious integrity. Of this we have two very striking instances recorded in Scripture. Samuel, when set aside by the mistaken longing for a visible king, felt deeply hurt, though more for the insult thus offered to Jehovah, the ever-present but invisible King, than for his own sake. He pleaded thus with the people: "I have walked before you from my childhood unto this day. Behold, here I am: witness against me before the Lord, and before his anointed: whose ox have I taken? or whose ass have I taken? or whom have I defrauded? whom have I oppressed? or of whose hand have I received any bribe to blind mine eyes therewith? and I will restore it you" (1 Sam. xii. 2, 3). And David, misunderstood and slandered, turns to speak to God in the hearing of the people, and says, "Judge me . . . according to my righteousness, and according to mine integrity that is in me" (Ps. vii. 8). Consider—

I. THE GREAT GOSPEL TRUST. 1. On the one side, the trust of Divine revelation and message. Illustrate by the direct communications of the Divine will made to the ancient prophets. These they were expected to deliver with all simplicity and completeness, and without making any additions of their own to them. 2. On the other side, the trust of men's souls. The world was given to the apostles as the sphere in which their gospel message was to be delivered. Such a trust demanded seriousness, sincerity, and holy zeal. It should ever call out the best that is in a man.

II. THE PERIL OF ITS INJURY THROUGH THE GUILE OF THE SELF-SEEKER. Men will surely take their impressions of *it* from the character of the men who preach it. If we get a soiled idea of the gospel preacher, as an insincere, self-seeking man, it is only too likely that we shall have a soiled and stained image of the gospel that he preaches in our minds. Men can make golden glowings or deep shadows rest on the gospel that they declare, the message which they have in trust.

III. THE FORCE OF IT AS PRESERVED WHEN THE AGENT IS GUILELESS AND SINCERE. The stream gets no foulness as it flows through him. Illustrate how men of transparent character and beautiful piety put honour on religion. The commendation of Christ's gospel to men is (1) the pure and stainless Christ himself, and then (2) the graciousness and charm of his servants who are like him. The force behind gospel preaching is the *life* of the men who preach. The simple-minded, sincere, uncorrupted man may positively make additions to the practical power of the gospel upon men. Distinguish, however, between simplicity and moral weakness, and also between guilelessness and ignorance. The simplicity required is "unity" as opposed to "double-mindedness;" it is being wholly for God. - R. T.

EXPOSITION.

CHAPTER III.

Defence against the charge of self-recommendation, which St. Paul does not need (vers. 1—3). His sufficiency comes from God (vers. 4—6), who has made him minister of a covenant far more glorious than that given to Moses (vers. 7—11). This ministry needs no veil upon the face (vers. 12, 13), such as to this day darkens the hearts of the Jews (vers. 14, 15), though it shall one day be removed (vers. 16—18).

Vers. 1—11.—*St. Paul's ministry is his sufficient letter of commendation.*

Ver. 1.—**Do we begin again to commend ourselves?** The last verse of the last chapter might be seized upon by St. Paul's opponents to renew their charge—that he was always praising himself. He anticipates the malignant and meaning smiles with which they would hear such words. The word "again" implies that this charge had already been brought against him, perhaps in consequence of such passages as 1 Cor. ii. 16; iii. 10; iv. 11—14; ix. 15—23; xiv. 18, etc. Such passages might be called self-laudatory and egotistical, were it not that (as St. Paul here explains) they arose only from a sense of the grandeur of his office, of which he was the almost involuntary agent, used by God as it seemed best to him. Hence he says later on (ch. vii. 18) that self-praise is no commendation, and that the true test of a man is God's commendation. The verb "I commend," technically used in the same sense as our "commendatory letters," occurs also in Rom. xvi. 1. **Or need we**, etc.? The reading, ἢ μὴ, thus translated, is better supported than εἰ μὴ, *unless*, which would have a somewhat ironical force. The μὴ in the reading ἢ μὴ implies, "Can you possibly think that we need," etc.? Generally, when a stranger came to some Church to which he was not personally known, he carried with him some credentials in the form of letters from accredited authorities. St. Paul treats it as absurd to suppose that he or Timothy should need such letters, either *from* the Corinthians or *to* them. **As some.** He will not name them, but he refers to the Judaists, who vaunted of their credentials in order to disparage St. Paul, who was too great to need and too independent to use them. We can hardly, perhaps, realize the depth and bitterness of antagonism concealed under that word "some" in 1 Cor. iv. 18; Gal. i. 7; ii. 12. It is not meant that there was anything discreditable in using such letters (for Apollos had used them, Acts xviii. 27), but the disgraceful thing was that St. Paul should be disparaged for not bringing them. **Epistles of commendation.** The phrase, ἐπιστολαὶ συστατικαί—"introductory letters"—was familiar in later Greek. In days when there were few public hostels, and when it was both a duty and a necessity for small and persecuted communities like those of the Jews and Christians to practise hospitality (Rom. xii. 13; Heb. xiii. 2, etc.), it was customary both for synagogues and Churches to provide their friends and emissaries with authentic testimonials. Otherwise they might have been deceived by wandering impostors, as, in fact, the Christians were deceived by the vagabond quack Peregrinus. We can easily see how the custom of using such letters might be abused by idle, restless, and intriguing persons, who have never found it very difficult to procure them. We find traces of their *honest* use by Phœbe, by Silas and Jude, by Apollos, by Mark, and by Zenas, in Rom. xvi. 1; Acts xviii. 27; xv. 25; Col. iv. 10; Titus iii. 13; and of their unfair use by certain Judaists, in Gal. i. 7 and ii. 12. Nothing can more forcibly illustrate the necessity for St. Paul's protest against the idle vaunt of possessing such letters, than the fact that, *more than a century afterwards*, we find malignant innuendoes aimed at St. Paul in the pseudo-Clementines, under the name of "the enemy" and "Simon Magus" and "a deceiver." He is there spoken of as using letters from the high priest (which, indeed, St. Paul had done as Saul of Tarsus, Acts ix. 1, 2); and the Churches are warned never to receive any one who cannot bring credentials from James; so deep-rooted among the Judaists was the antagonism to the independent apostolate and daring originality of the apostle of the Gentiles! Dr. Plumptre quotes Sozomen ('H. E.', v. 16) for the curious fact that the Emperor Julian tried to introduce the system of "commendatory letters" into his revived paganism. **Or letters of commendation from you.** The substitution of "letters" for "epistles" is an instance of the almost childish fondness for unnecessary synonyms, which is one of the defects of the Authorized Version. The true reading probably is "to you or from you" (א, A, B, C). The word "commendatory" (*sustatikōn*) is omitted in A, B, C. *Or from you.* It was worse than absurd to suppose that St. Paul should need those *literæ formatæ* to a Church of which he was the founder; and nothing but the boundless "inflation" which characterized the Corinthians could have led them to imagine that he needed letters *from* them to other Churches, as though, forsooth, they were the primary Church or the only church (1 Cor. xiv. 36).

Ver. 2.—**Ye are our epistle.** Their very existence as a Church was the most absolute "commendatory letter" of St. Paul, both *from* them and *to* them (comp. 1 Cor. ix. 2, "The seal of mine apostleship are ye in the Lord"). **Written in our hearts.** The expression has no connection with the fact that the high priest bore the names of Israel graven on the jewelled Urim, which he wore upon his breast. St. Paul means that others may bring their "letters of commendation" in their hands. *His* letter of commendation is the very name and existence of the Church of Corinth written on his heart. **Known and read of all men.** The metaphor is subordinated to the *fact*. All men may recognize the autograph, and in it were read the history of the Corinthian converts, which was written on the apostle's heart, and which therefore rendered the notion of any other letter of commendation to or from them superfluous and even absurd. The play on words (*epigignōsko* and *anagignōsko*) is similar to that in ch. i. 13.

Ver. 3.—**Manifestly declared.** The fame and centrality of Corinth gave peculiar prominence to the fact of their conversion. **The epistle of Christ ministered by us.** The Corinthians are the epistle; it is written on the hearts of St. Paul and his companions; Christ was its Composer; they were its amanuenses and its conveyers. The development of the metaphor *as a metaphor* would be somewhat clumsy and intricate, but St. Paul only cares to shadow forth the essential fact which he wishes them to recognize. **Not with ink, but with the Spirit of the living God;** *i.e.* not with visible or perishable materials, but spiritual in its origin and character. The notion of "the finger of God" naturally recalled the notion of "the Spirit of God" (comp. Matt. xii. 28 with Luke xi. 20). **Not in tables of stone.** God's writing by means of the Spirit on the heart reminds him of another writing *of God* on the stone tablets of the Law, which he therefore introduces with no special regard to the congruity of the metaphor about "an epistle." **But in fleshy tables of the heart.** The overwhelming preponderance of manuscript authority supports the reading "but in fleshen tablets—hearts." St. Paul is thinking of Jer. xxxi. 33, "I will put my Law in their inward parts, and write it in their hearts;" and Ezek. xi. 22, "I will take the stony heart out of their flesh, and will give them a heart of flesh." The tablets were not hard and fragile, but susceptible and receptive. Our letters of introduction are inward not outward, spiritual not material, permanent not perishable, legible to all not only by a few, written by Christ not by man.

Ver. 4.—**Such trust.** The confidence, namely, that we need no other recommendation to or from you. **Through Christ.** Who alone can inspire such confidence in myself and my mission (1 Cor. xv. 10). **To Godward;** *i.e.* in relation to God; towards whom the whole Being of Christ is directed (John i. 1), and therefore all the work of his servants (Rom. v. 1).

Ver. 5.—**Not that we are sufficient of ourselves.** He here reverts to the question asked in ch. ii. 16. He cannot bear the implication that any "confidence" on his part rests on anything short of the overwhelming sense that he is but an agent, or rather nothing but *an instrument*, in the hands of God. **To think anything as of ourselves.** He has, indeed, the capacity to form adequate judgments about his work,

but it does not come from his own resources (ἀφ' ἑαυτῶν) or his own independent origination (ἐξ ἑαυτῶν); comp. 1 Cor. xv. 10. **But our sufficiency.** Namely, to form any true or right judgment, and therefore to express the confidence which I *have* expressed. **Is of God.** We are but *fellow-workers* with him (1 Cor. iii. 19).

Ver. 6.—**Who also.** Either, "And he it is who;" or, "Who besides *this* power, has made us adequate ministers." **Hath made us able ministers;** rather, *made us sufficient ministers.* **Of the new testament;** rather, *of a fresh covenant* (Jer. xxxi. 31). The "new testament" has not the remotest connection with what we call "The New Testament," meaning thereby the book—which, indeed, had at this time no existence. The word "testament" means a will, and in this sense implies neither the Hebrew *berith* nor the Greek *diatheke*, both of which mean "covenant." In one passage only of the New Testament (Heb. ix. 16, 17) does *diatheke* mean a "testament" or "will." For the thought, see Eph. iii. 7; Col. i. 25; 1 Tim. i. 11, 12. **Not of the letter, but of the spirit.** In other words, "not of the Law, but of the gospel;" not of that which is dead, but of that which is living; not of that which is deathful, but of that which is life-giving; not of bondage, but of freedom; not of mutilation, but of self-control; not of the outward, but of the inward; not of works, but of grace; not of menace, but of promise; not of curse, but of blessing; not of wrath, but of love; not of Moses, but of Christ. This is the theme which St. Paul develops especially in the Epistles to the Romans and the Galatians (see Rom. ii. 29; iii. 20; vii. 6, 10, 11; viii. 2; Gal. iii. 10; v. 4, etc.). *Not of the letter.* Not, that is, of the Mosaic Law regarded as a yoke of externalism; a hard and unhelpful "thou shalt" and "thou shalt not;" a system that possessed no life of its own and inspired no life into others; a "categoric imperative," majestic, indeed, but unsympathetic and pitiless. Both the Law and the gospel were *committed to writing;* each covenant had its own *book;* but in the case of the Mosaic Law there was the book and nothing more; in the case of the gospel the book was nothing compared to the spirit, and nothing without the spirit. *Out of the spirit.* That is, of the gospel which found its pledge and consummation in the gift of the Spirit. The Law, too, was in one sense "spiritual" (Rom. vii. 14), for it was given by God, who is a Spirit, and it was a holy Law; but though such in itself (*in se*) it was relatively (*per accidens*) a cause of sin and death, because it was addressed to a fallen nature, and inspired no spirit by which that nature could be delivered (see

Rom. vii. 7—25). But in the gospel the spirit is everything; the mere letter is as nothing (John vi. 63). **For the letter killeth, but the spirit giveth life.** This is one of the very numerous " texts " which have been first misinterpreted and have then been made, for whole centuries, the bases of erroneous systems. On this text more than any other, Origen, followed by the exegetes of a thousand years, built his dogma that the Scripture must be interpreted allegorically, not literally, because "the letter" of the Bible kills. The misinterpretation is extravagantly inexcusable, and, like many others, arose solely from rending words away from their context and so reading new senses into them. The contrast is not between "the outward" and the inward sense of Scripture at all. "The letter" refers exclusively to "the Law," and therefore has so little reference to "the Bible" that it was written before most of the New Testament existed, and only touches on a small portion of the Old Testament. *Killeth.* Two questions arise. (1) *What* and *whom* does it *kill?* and (2) *how* does it *kill?* The answers seem to be that (1) the letter—the Law regarded as an outward letter—passes the sentence of *death on those who disobey it.* It says, " He who doeth these things shall live in them ; " and therefore implies, as well as often says, that he who disobeys them shall be cut off. It is, therefore, a deathful menace. For none *can* obey this Law with perfect obedience. And (2) the sting of death being sin, the Law kills by directly leading to sin, in that it stirs into existence the principle of concupiscence (Rom. vii. 7–11 ; 1 Cor. xv. 56 ; Gal. iii. 10, 21). *But the spirit giveth life.* This contrast between a dead and a living covenant is fundamental, and especially in the writings of St. Paul (Rom. ii 27—29 ; vii. 6 ; viii. 11 ; Gal. v. 8 ; 1 Cor. xv. 45). The Law stones the adulteress ; the gospel says to her, " Go, and sin no more."

Ver. 7.—**The ministration of death.** The ministration, that is, of the Law, of " the letter which killeth." St. Paul here begins one of the arguments *a minori ad majus* which are the very basis of the Epistle to the Hebrews. **Written** and **engraven in stones ;** literally, *engraved in letters on stones* (Exod. xxxi. 18). The reference shows that, in speaking of "the letter," St. Paul was only thinking of the Mosaic Law, and indeed specifically of the Decalogue. **Was glorious ;** literally, *occurred in glory,* or, *proved itself glorious.* In itself the Law was "holy, just, and good" (Rom. vii. 12), and given " at the disposition of angels " (Acts vii. 53) ; and its transitory glory was illustrated by the lustre which the face of Moses caught by reflection from his inter-

course with God (Exod. xxiv. 16). **Could not steadfastly behold the face of Moses** (Exod. xxxiv. 29, 30). St. Paul has been led quite incidentally into this digression in the course of defending himself by describing the nature of his ministry ; but it bore very definitely on his general purpose, because his chief opponents were Judaists, whose one aim it was to bind upon the Church the yoke of Mosaism. That they could not " behold " the face of Moses is the *hagadah,* or traditional legend, derived from Exod. xxxiv. 30, which says that " they were afraid to *draw nigh* to him. The reader may recall the beautiful lines of Cardinal Newman—

" Lord ! grant me this abiding grace—
Thy words and saints to know ;
To pierce the veil on Moses' face,
Although his words be slow."

Because of the glory of his countenance. This circumstance is so often alluded to as to have become identified with the conception of Moses. The Hebrew words for " a ray of light " and " a horn " are identical ; hence, instead of saying that his face was " irradiated," the Vulgate says, *Cornuta erat ejus facies ;* and even in our version of Hab. iii. 4 we find " And he had *horns* [*i.e.* 'rays of light'] coming out of his hand." To this is due the mediæval symbol of Moses with horns, as in the matchless statue by Michael Angelo. **Which glory was to be done away.** The Greek might be expressed by "the glory—the evanescing glory —of his countenance." It was not " *to be* done away," but from the first moment they saw it it began to vanish. The verb " to do away," implying annulment, and the being abrogated as invalid, is a characteristic word in this group cf Epistles, in which it occurs twenty-two times. This illustrates the prominence in St. Paul's thoughts of the fact that the Law was now " antiquated " and " near its obliteration " (comp. Heb. viii. 13). But in dwelling on the brief and transient character of this radiance, St. Paul seizes on a point which (naturally) is not dwelt upon in Exod. xxxiv.

Ver. 8.—**The ministration of the spirit.** That is, " the apostolate and service of the gospel." **Be rather glorious.** A contrast may be intended between the ministration of the letter, which " became glorious," which had, as it were, a glory lent to it (ἐγενήθη ἐν δόξῃ), and that of the spirit, which *is,* of its own nature, in glory.

Ver. 9.—**The ministration of condemnation.** The same antithesis between the Law as involving "condemnation" and the gospel as bestowing " righteousness " is found in Rom. v. 18, 19. **The glory ;** perhaps, rather, *a glory ;* a stronger way of describing it as

" glorious." **Of righteousness.** Involving the further conception of "justification," as in Rom. v. 21 ; i. 16, 17 ; iv. 25 ; v. 21.

Ver. 10.—**For.** He proceeds to show that the latter ministration was far more superabundant in glory. **That which was made glorious,** etc. Many various interpretations have been offered of this text. The meaning almost undoubtedly is, " For even that which has been glorified [namely, the Mosaic ministry, as typified by the splendour of his face] has not been glorified in this respect [*i.e.* in the respect of its relation to *another* ministry], because of the surpassing glory [of the latter]." In other words, the glory of Mosaism is so completely outdazzled by the splendour of the gospel, that, relatively speaking, it has no glory left ; the moon and the stars cease to shine, they " pale their ineffectual fires " when the sun is in the zenith. The phrase, " in this respect," occurs again in ch. ix. 3 and 1 Pet. iv. 16.

Ver. 11.—**For.** An explanation of the " surpassing " glory of the later covenant founded on its eternity. **That which is done away;** rather, *that which is evanescing;* "which is being done away," as in ver. 7. **Was glorious . . . is glorious.** The expression is varied in the Greek. The brief, the evanescent covenant was " through glory," *i.e.* it was a transitory gleam; the abiding covenant is "in glory ;" *i.e.* it is an eternal splendour. It is, however, a disputed point whether St. Paul intended such rigid meanings to be attached to his varying prepositions (Rom. iii. 30, ἐκ πίστεως . . . διὰ τῆς πίστεως: v. 10, διὰ τοῦ θανάτου . . . ἐν τῇ ζωῇ: Gal. ii. 16, ἐξ ἔργων . . . διὰ πίστεως: Philem. 5, πρὸς τὸν Κύριον . . . εἰς τοὺς ἁγίους). **That which remaineth.** The final, eternal, unshakable gospel (Heb. xii. 27). **Is glorious;** literally, *is in glory.* Christ is eternally the Light of the world (John i. 9; ix. 5); and Moses and Elias derived all their permanence of glory by reflection from this transfiguring light.

Vers. 12—18.—*The confidence inspired by this ministry, and the veil on the hearts of those who will not recognize it.*

Ver. 12.—**Such hope.** A hope based upon the abiding glory of this gospel covenant. **Plainness of speech.** The frankness and unreserved fearlessness of our language is justified by the glory of our ministry. It was impossible for Moses to speak with the same bold plainness.

Ver. 13.—**And not as Moses.** We need not act, as Moses was obliged to do, by putting any veil upon our faces while we speak. And here the image of " the veil " as completely seizes St. Paul's imagination as the image of the letter does in the first verses. **Put a veil;** literally, *was putting,*

or, *used to put,* a veil on his face when he had finished speaking to the people. **That the children of Israel could not steadfastly look to the end of that which is abolished;** rather, *that the children of Israel might not gaze on the end of what was passing away.* The object of the veil, according to St. Paul, was to prevent the Israelites from gazing *on the last gleam of the covenant.* In other words, he did not wish them to be witnesses of a *fading* glory. It is preposterous to imagine that St. Paul is here casting any blame on the conduct of Moses, as though he acted fraudulently or delusively. Moses was aware, and even told the people, that his legislation was not final (Deut. xviii. 15—19), but it would be quite natural that he should not wish the people to witness the gradual dimming of the lustre which, in St. Paul's view, was typical of that transitoriness. It seems, however, that St. Paul is here either (1) following a different reading or rendering of Exod. xxxiv. 33; or (2) is adopting some Jewish *hagadah;* or (3) is giving his own turn to the narrative, as the rabbis habitually did, by way of *midrash,* or exposition. For from the narrative of Exodus we should not gather that it was the object of Moses to hide the disappearance of the splendour, but rather to render the light endurable. In our Authorized Version the verse runs, " *till* Moses had done speaking with them he put a veil on his face;" but the meaning of the original may be, "*after* he had done speaking with them," as the LXX. takes it and the Vulgate. *The end.* To interpret this of *Christ,* because of Rom. x. 4, is an instance of the superstitious and unintelligent way in which systems are made out of a mosaic of broken texts. The foolish character of the interpretation is shown when we consider that it involves the inference that Moses put a veil on his face in order to prevent the Israelites from seeing Christ! But this attempt to illustrate Scripture by catching at a similar. expression applied in a wholly different way in another part of Scripture, is one of the normal follies of scriptural interpretation.

Ver. 14.—**Their minds.** This word is rendered " devices " in ch. ii. 11; "minds" in ch. iii. 14 and iv. 4; and "thought" in ch. x. 5. It means that their powers of reason were, so to speak, petrified. **Were blinded ;** rather, *were hardened.* The verb cannot mean " to blind." By whom were their minds hardened? It would be equally correct to say by themselves (Heb. iii. 8), or by Satan (ch. iv. 4), or by God (Rom. xi. 7, 8). **The same veil.** Of course the meaning is "a veil of which the veil of Moses is an exact type." The veil which prevented them from seeing the evanescence of the light which shone on the face of Moses was symbolically identical with that which prevented them also from seeing the transitory character of his Law. It had been as it were taken from his face and laid on their hearts (see Acts xiii. 27—29; Rom. xi.). Many commentators have seen in this verse a reference to the Jewish custom of covering the head with the *tallith*, a four-cornered veil, when they were in the synagogues. But this is doubtful, since the *tallith* did not cover the eyes. More probably his metaphor may have been suggested by Isa. xxv. 7, "And he will destroy in this mountain the face of the covering cast over all people, and *the veil* that is spread over all nations." **Untaken away.** There are two other ways of rendering this verse: (1) "For until this very day at the reading of the old covenant the same veil remaineth unlifted; which veil is done away in Christ," as in the Revised Version; or (2) "The same veil remaineth, it not being revealed that it is done away in Christ," as it is taken by Chrysostom and many others, and in the margin of the Revised Version. The latter seems to be the better view. It is not the veil, but the old covenant, which is being done away in Christ. To the Jews that truth still remained under a veil. The present tense, "is *in course of* annulment," might naturally be used until the utter abrogation of even the possible fulfilment of the Mosaic Law at the fall of Jerusalem. **In the reading of the old testament;** rather, *the old covenant.* There is no allusion to the Old Testament as a *book*, but the phrase is equivalent to "Moses is read" in the next verse. (On this obduracy of the Jews, see Rom. xi. 7, 8, 25.)

Ver. 15.—**When Moses is read** (Acts xv. 21). **The veil;** rather, *a veil;* a veil of moral obstinacy, which prevents them from seeing the disappearance of the old covenant, as effectually as the veil on the face of Moses prevented them from seeing (as St. Paul viewed the matter) the disappearance of the transitory lustre on the face of Moses.

Ver. 16.—**When it shall turn to the Lord.** The nominative of the verb is not expressed. Obviously the most natural word to supply is the one last alluded to, namely, "the heart of Israel." The verb may have been suggested by Exod. xxxiv. 31. **Shall be taken away;** literally, *is in course of removal.* The tenses imply that "the moment the heart of Israel shall have turned to the Lord, the removal of the veil begins." Then "they shall look on him whom they pierced" (Zech. xii. 10); "He will destroy in this mountain the face of the covering cast over all people, and the veil that is spread over all nations" (Isa. xxv. 7).

Ver. 17.—**Now the Lord is that Spirit.** The "but" (Authorized Version, "now") introduces an explanation. To whom shall they turn? To the Lord. "But the Lord is the Spirit." The word "spirit" could not be introduced thus abruptly and vaguely; it must refer to something already said, and therefore to the last mention of the word "spirit" in ver. 8. The Lord is the Spirit, who giveth life and freedom, in antithesis to the spirit of death and legal bondage (see ver. 6; and comp. 1 Cor. xv. 45). The best comment on the verse is Rom. viii. 2, "For the law of the *spirit of life in Christ Jesus* hath made me free from the law of sin and death." All life and all religion had become to St. Paul a vision of all things in Christ. He has just said that the spirit giveth life, and, after the digression about the moral blindness which prevented the Jews from being emancipated from the bondage of the letter, it was quite natural for him to add, "Now the Lord *is* the Spirit to which I alluded." The connection in which the verse stands excludes a host of untenable meanings which have been attached to it. **There is liberty.** The liberty of confidence (ver. 4), and of frank speech (ver. 12), and of sonship (Gal. iv. 6, 7), and of freedom from guilt (John viii. 36); so that the Law itself, obeyed no longer in the mere letter but also in the spirit, becomes a royal law of liberty, and not a yoke which gendereth to bondage (Jas. i. 25; ii. 12)—a service, indeed, but one which is perfect freedom (Rom. v. 1—21; 1 Pet. ii. 16).

Ver. 18.—**But we all.** An appeal to personal experience in evidence of the freedom. **With open face;** rather, *with unveiled face;* as Moses himself spoke with God, whereas the Jews could not see even the *reflected* splendour on the face of Moses till he had shrouded it with a veil. **Beholding as in a glass.** This is *at least* as likely to be the true meaning as "reflecting as a mirror," which the Revised Version (following Chrysostom and others) has substituted for it. No other instance occurs in which the verb in the middle voice has the meaning of "reflecting," and the words, "with unveiled face," imply the image of "beholding." They are, in fact, a description of "the beatific vision." An additional reason for retaining the translation of our Authorized Version is that the verb is used in *this* sense by Philo ('Leg. Alleg.,' iii. 33). **The glory of the Lord.** Namely, him who is "the Effulgence of God's glory" (Heb. i. 2), the true Shechinah, "the Image of the invisible God" (Col. i. 15). **Are changed into the same image.** The present tense implies a *gradual* transfiguration, a mystical and spiritual change which is produced in us while we contemplate Christ. **From glory to glory.** Our spiritual assimilation to Christ comes *from* his glory and issues in a glory like his (1 Cor. xv. 51; comp. "from strength to strength," Ps. lxxxiv. 7). (For the thought, comp. 1 John iii. 2.) **As by the Spirit of the Lord.** This rendering (which is that of the Vulgate also) can hardly be correct. The natural meaning of the Greek is "*as by the* [or, *from*] *the Lord the Spirit.*" Our change into glory comes from the Lord, who, as St. Paul has already explained, is the Spirit of which he has been speaking. No such abstract theological thought is here in his mind as that of the "*hypostatic* union," of the Son and the Holy Spirit. He is still referring to the contrast between the letter and the spirit, and his identification of this "spirit" in its highest sense with the quickening life which, by the gift of the Holy Spirit, we receive from Christ, and which is indeed identical with "the Spirit of Christ."

HOMILETICS..

Vers. 1—5.—*Soul-literature.* "Do we begin again to commend ourselves?" etc. In the early Church it was customary for the member who was travelling into another locality to take with him a letter of commendation from the Church to which he or she belonged. The apostle says he did not require such a document from the Corinthian Church, as some others did, for they themselves were letters written on his own heart; and his ministry was a letter written on their hearts also. They were the living "epistles of Christ, . . . written not with ink, but with the Spirit of the living God; not in tables of stone, but in fleshy tables of the heart." Our subject is soul-literature, or Christianity written on the heart; and I offer five remarks.

I. Christianity written on the soul is CHRISTIANITY IN THE MOST LEGIBLE FORM. There are some whose caligraphy is difficult to decipher and whose thoughts are difficult to understand; their ideas are misty and their style involved; but what is written on the *soul* is written so clearly that a child can make it out.

II. Christianity written on the soul is CHRISTIANITY IN THE MOST CONVINCING FORM. Books have been written on the evidences of Christianity; not a few by the ablest men of their times, such as Paley, Lardner, Butler. But one life permeated and fashioned by the Christian spirit is a far more convincing power than any or all of their most magnificent productions. He who has been transformed by Christianity from the selfish, the sensual, and corrupt, into the spiritual, the benevolent, and the holy, furnishes an argument that baffles all controversy and penetrates the heart.

III. Christianity written on the soul is CHRISTIANITY IN THE MOST PERSUASIVE FORM. There are many books "persuasive to piety," and many of them very powerful; but the most powerful of them are weak indeed compared to the mighty force of a Christly life. There is a magnetism in gospel truth embodied, which you seek for in vain in any written work. When the "Word is made flesh" it becomes "mighty through God."

IV. Christianity written on the soul is CHRISTIANITY IN THE MOST ENDURING FORM. The tablet is imperishable. You may put truth on paper, but the paper will moulder; put it into institutions, but the institutions will dissolve as a cloud; put it on marble or brass, but these are corruptible.

V. Christianity written on the soul is CHRISTIANITY IN THE DIVINEST FORM. The human hand can inscribe it on parchment or engrave it on stone, but God only can write it on the heart. "The Spirit of the living God." Paul was but the amanuensis, God is the Author.

Ver. 6.—*The ministry of the letter and the ministry of the spirit.* "The letter killeth, but the spirit giveth life." Notice—

I. The twofold MINISTRY. "Ministers . . . not of the letter, but of the spirit." What does this mean? Not the two dispensations, the Mosaic and the Christian; for both alike had "letter" and "spirit." Nor does it mean a double interpretation of the Scripture, the literal and the spiritual. It means, I think, the word and the thought, the sentence and the sentiment. Christianity has both "letter" and "spirit." If it had no "letter," it would be unrevealed, a thought shut up in the mind of God; if it had no "spirit," it would be but a hollow sound. The words point to two distinct methods of teaching Christianity. 1. *The technical method.* Who are the technical teachers? (1) *The verbalist.* There were men in the Corinthian Church who thought much of words. "The words of man's wisdom," high-sounding sentences, oratoric periods, they scrupulously studied. The spirit of thought is so subtle that it goes off in the attempt to give it grand verbal costume. (2) *The theorist.* Those who throw into a logical system the ideas they have derived from the gospel; he who exalts his system of thought or creed and makes it a standard of truth is a minister of the " letter." The grandest system of theology can no more contain the whole truth than a nutshell can the Atlantic. (3) *The ritualist.* Men must have ritualism of some kind. What is logic but the ritualism of thought? art but the ritualism of beauty? rhetoric but the ritualism of ideas? civilization but the ritualism of the thoughts of ages? But those who represent those symbols as supernatural powers and mystic media of saving grace are ministers of the "letter" rather than of the "spirit." 2. *The spiritual.* What is it to be a minister of the "spirit"? He is a man more alive to the grace than the grammar, to the substance than the symbols of revelation. He is a man who has a comprehensive knowledge of those eternal principles that underlie all Scriptures, and has a living sympathy with those eternal elements.

II. The twofold RESULTS. "The letter killeth, but the spirit giveth life." 1. The result of the *technical* ministry. It "killeth." (1) *The verbalist kills.* It was said by Burke "that no man understands less of the majesty of the English constitution than the *nisi prius* lawyer, who is always dealing with the technicalities of precedence." And truly no man understands less of the gospel than he who is constantly dealing with its verbalities. Words in religion, when taken for realities, "kill," kill inquiry, freedom, sensibility, moral manhood. (2) *The theorist kills.* He who preaches his own little creed instead of the gospel of God kills souls. The Jews formulated a theory concerning the Messiah from their Scriptures. In their theory he was to appear in such a form, do such a work, reach such a destiny. He came, but did not answer to their theory, and they rejected him and were damned. Man's theory of the gospel is not the gospel, any more than pneumatical science is the life-breathing atmosphere. (3) *The ritualist kills.* He who exalts even the authorized ritualism of the gospel, such as baptism and the Lord's Supper, to say nothing of the unauthorized rites, kills souls. The ceremonial Church has ever been a dead Church. The ministry of the "letter" then "killeth;" it reduced the Jewish people to the valley of dead bones, entombed the souls of Europe for many a long century. 2. The *result* of the spiritual ministry. "The spirit giveth life." "It is the spirit that quickeneth; the flesh profiteth nothing; the words that I speak unto you, they are spirit, and they are life." "The spirit giveth life"—life to the intellect, conscience, sympathies, the whole soul.

CONCLUSION. How little of this soul-life we have in congregations! Creed-life, sect-life, Church-life, we have in abundance; but where is soul-life, the life of holy love, earnest inquiry, independent action, spiritual freedom in relation to all that is Christ-like and Divine?

Vers. 7—11.—*Divine revelation more glorious in Christ than in Moses.* "But if the ministration," etc. At the outset three facts are noteworthy. 1. The infinite Father has made a special revelation of himself to his human offspring. 2. This special revelation of himself has mainly come through two great general sources— Moses and Christ. 3. The special revelation of himself, as it came through Christ, far transcends in glory the form it assumed as it came through Moses. The essence of the revelation is the same, but the forms differ, and the form it assumes in Christianity are the most glorious. There are two facts here.

I. That the special revelation as it came through MOSES WAS GLORIOUS. It was so glorious that "the children of Israel could not steadfastly behold the face of Moses." Four things impress us with its glory as revealed in Moses. 1. *The wonderful display of divinity attending its manifestation on Mount Sinai.* The expression, "the face of Moses," refers to this (Exod. xxxiv. 1). What wonderful things Moses saw and heard during the forty days he was on the mount! "The Lord rose up and came from Seir with ten thousand of his saints," etc. 2. *The magnificence of its religious scenes and celebrations.* The temple, how splendid! the priesthood, how imposing! the psalmody, how inspiring! "Glorious things are spoken of thee, O thou city of God." 3. *The stupendous miracles that stand in connection with it.* The wilderness was the theatre of magnificent manifestations—the pillar, the manna, the flowing rock, the riven sea, etc. 4. *The splendid intellects which were employed in connection with it.* Solomon, Eiijah, Daniel, David, Ezekiel. For these reasons Divine revelation as it came through Moses was truly glorious.

II. That although this special revelation was glorious as it came in connection with Moses, it was MORE GLORIOUS as it came in connection with CHRIST. "How shall not the ministration of the spirit be rather glorious?" etc. Confining our illustrations on this point to the passage before us, we observe: 1. *The Christian form of revelation is more likely to give life than the Mosaic.* In Moses it was the "ministration of death." The Jews exalted the "letter" that "killeth" above the "spirit that giveth life," and they got buried in forms. In Christ the revelation is the gospel in life. 2. *The Christian form of Divine revelation is more emphatically spiritual than the Mosaic.* It is here called the "ministration of the spirit." In Moses it was associated with numerous forms and ceremonies; in Christ there are only two simple rites, and the spirit throbs in every sentence. 3. *The Christian form of Divine revelation is more restorative than the Mosaic.* The apostle speaks of the one as the "ministration of condemnation," of the other as the "ministration of righteousness." Maledictions thunder in the former, beatitudes in the latter. 4. *The Christian form of Divine revelation is more enduring than the Mosaic.* "For if that which is done away [which passeth away] was glorious, much more that which remaineth is glorious." Judaism is gone; Christianity is the "Word of God, which abideth for ever." It is the final revelation of Heaven to our world.

Such, then, is a brief illustration of the apostle's position; and the subject, in conclusion, serves several important purposes. 1. It serves to *expose the absurdity of making Moses the interpreter of Christ.* It has been common with professing Christians to look at the New Testament through the spectacles of Moses, and thus to Judaize Christianity. Much in popery, much, alas! in old puritanism, much even in modern theology, is but Christianity Judaized, a going back to the "beggarly elements." 2. It serves to *show the wrongness of going to Moses to support opinions which you cannot get from Christ.* You can support war, slavery, capital punishment, by going to Moses; but you cannot find the shadow of a foundation for these in Christ. 3. It serves to *reveal the glorious position of a true gospel minister.* To show this was the object of the apostle in the text. The position of Moses, David, Isaiah, and all the great teachers under the old administration was glorious, but it is scarcely to be compared with the position of him who preaches that Christ of "whom Moses and the prophets did write."

Vers. 12—18.—*The gospel as a transcendent benefactor.* "Seeing then that we have such hope," etc. Amongst the invaluable services which the gospel confers on man, there are four suggested by the text. It gives him moral courage, spiritual vision, true liberty, and Christ-like glory. It gives him—

I. MORAL COURAGE. "Seeing then that we have such hope, we use great plainness [boldness] of speech: and not as Moses, which put a veil over his face, that the children of Israel could not steadfastly look to the end of that which is abolished," etc. This means that, seeing the revelation we have of God in Christ is not so terrible as his revelation in Moses, we have "great boldness." We need have no superstitious fear or dread. Unlike the Jews, who were afraid to look at the Divine radiance on the face of Moses, who trembled at the manifestation of God on Sinai, and who lacked the courage to look at the fact that their system was a temporary one, passing away; we have courage to look calmly at the manifestations of God and the facts of destiny. We use "great boldness." He who has the spirit of Christianity in him has courage enough to look all questions in the face, and to speak out his convictions with the dauntless force of true manhood.

II. SPIRITUAL VISION. "But their minds were blinded: for until this day remaineth the same veil untaken away in the reading of the Old Testament; which veil is done away in Christ." The "veil" of Moses was on his face, some material used for the moment and then withdrawn, but the "veil" referred to here was that "veil" of prejudice and traditional notions which prevented them from seeing when Paul wrote that the old dispensation has passed away before the brightness of the new. The souls of unrenewed men are so veiled by depravity that they fail to see anything in the great universe of spiritual realities. The spiritual is no more to them than nature is to men born blind. Now, the gospel is the only power under God that can take the "veil" from the soul, and enable us to see things as they are. Its grand mission is to open the eyes of the blind, etc.

III. TRUE LIBERTY. "Where the Spirit of the Lord is, there is liberty." By the "Spirit of the Lord" here is meant the Spirit of Christ, his moral temper ; and wherever this is, there is freedom. 1. Freedom from the *bondage of ceremonialism*. 2. Freedom from the *trammels of legality*. 3. Freedom from the *dominion of sin*. 4. Freedom from the *fear of death*. The Spirit of Christ is at once the guarantee and the inspiration of that liberty which no despot can take away, no time destroy—the "glorious liberty of the children of God."

IV. CHRIST-LIKE GLORY. "But we all, with open face, beholding as in a glass the glory of the Lord," etc. 1. The glory of Christ was the glory of moral excellence. He was the "brightness of his Father's glory." 2. The glory of Christ is communicable. It comes to man through transformation "changed into the same image." 3. The glory of Christ which comes to man is progressive: "from glory to glory." The gospel alone can make men glorious.

HOMILIES BY VARIOUS AUTHORS.

Vers. 1—6.—*No letters of commendation needed ; his converts were epistles.* In the close of the last chapter St. Paul had spoken of men who corrupted the Word of God (retailed it as a commodity for their own profit), and he had put himself and his ministry in contrast to them. Likely enough, this would provoke criticism. The quick interrogation comes—Was he commending himself, or did he need letters of commendation to them and from them ? "Ye are our epistle;" written on his heart, known and read of all men—an epistle coming from Christ, and produced instrumentally by him as Christ's agent; not written with ink, but by the Spirit; "not in tables of stone, but in fleshy tables of the heart." With regard to the figure, it is probable that there was not another occasion in his life when it would have occurred to his imagination. Circumstances conspired with his state of mind to produce it, and one can almost trace the sequence of associations out of which it came. What solicitude the former Epistle had given him! What would be the effect ? Amid his thanksgiving to God (ch. xi. 14) it was a matter of joy that he had written this letter, and he could now see God's hand very clearly in its production. Was not that Epistle a new and additional proof that he was Christ's apostle ? Yet what was that Epistle, written with ink, to this "epistle of Christ," recorded on the soul, a part of itself, a part of its immortality ? It was "manifestly declared" that they were Christ's epistle, and it was equally clear that this epistle was due to his ministration. "Ministered by us." Had they not given a new and striking evidence of the two facts, viz. Christ the Author of the epistle written on their hearts, and he the apostle, the ministerial agent of the work ? It was a fresh motive to confidence: "Such trust have we through Christ to God-ward." Are we boasting of the late success of our Epistle—of our former successes ? Nay; how can we be "sufficient of ourselves," or rely on our own wisdom and strength, when we have just confessed that we wrote to you "out of much affliction and anguish of heart, with many tears," and while the period of suspense lasted we were unfitted for our work, and at last, no rest in our spirit, we left Troas for Macedonia so as to see Titus the sooner ?. Nay; "our sufficiency is of God." It is he who also "hath made us able ministers of the New Testament." And wherein differs this new covenant from the old ? Already he had spoken of "tables of stone" as contrasted with "fleshy tables of the heart," and the antithesis is resumed and further elaborated. The covenant is *new*, it is of the *spirit*, it is of the spirit that *giveth life*. Opposite in these particulars was the old covenant, the Mosaic Law, its ministers being chiefly engaged in executing a system of rules and ceremonials, adhering in all things to the exact language, and concerning themselves in no wise beyond the outward form. The external man with his interests and fortunes occupied attention. A nation was to exemplify the system, and therefore, by necessity, it largely addressed the senses, borrowing its motives and enforcing its penalties from a consideration of objects near and palpable. If we read Rom. vii. we see what St. Paul meant by "the letter killeth." On the other hand, the dispensation of the spirit "giveth life." The antithesis is stated in the strongest possible form—death and life. This, accordingly, was the apostle's "sufficiency," a spiritual wisdom for enlightenment, a spiritual power for carrying out his apostolic plans, and an attained spiritual result seen in the recovery of Gentiles from the degradation of idolatry, and in the freedom of Jews from the bondage of the Mosaic Law.—L.

Vers. 7—11.—*Ministry of the Old Testament compared with that of the New, and the superiority of the latter shown.* He speaks now of the "ministration of death," not of it as the ministry of the letter; and yet it was "glorious." Compared with the revelation made to Enoch, Abraham, Jacob, it was "glorious." Whether witnessing to the unity of God or to his providence over an elect race, it was an illumination, or splendour, unequalled in the centuries before Christ. Tribes were organized as a nation, bondmen transformed into free men ; and, despite their proclivity to heathenish idolatry, they came finally to hold and defend the doctrine of one God, their Jehovah, their Lord of hosts, their Benefactor and Friend, as the doctrine underlying all their hopes and aspirations. The sanctity of human life which the great lawgiver made the foundation of his system, the rights of persons and property, the obligations of brotherhood among themselves, duties to the poor and the stranger, duties to their nation, reverence for the sabbath and its worship, obedience to God in the minutest things, were taught them with a precision and a force that largely succeeded in producing the only phenomenon of its kind in history —a nation educated in the sense of God, of his presence in their midst, and of his providence as an unceasing and omnipotent agency in their homes and business. What a "glory" there was in their literature we all know. No psalmody is given in the New Testament; none was wanted ; inspired poetry reached its full measure of excellence in King David and his poetic successors; and the Christian heart, whether in prayer or praise, finds much of its deepest and most devout utterance in these ancient Judæan hymns. Reproduction is the test of enduring greatness. In this respect the genius and piety of David stand unrivalled. Whenever men worship God, he is the "chief singer" yet; nor have we any better standard by which to try the merit of our religious poetry and music than the similarity of their effect upon us to that produced by the Psalms of David. Last of all in the order of time, first in its importance, what a "glory" in him born of the Virgin Mary! On this system St. Paul made no war. What he antagonized was the misunderstanding and abuse of the system in the hands of Pharisees and Sadducees, and, especially in the shape it assumed among the Judaizers at Corinth and in Galatia. He calls the old covenant "glorious," a word he never uses but in his exalted moods of thought. True, it was "written and engraven in stones," but by whose hand? Even "the face of Moses" was more than the Israelites could bear, "for the glory of his countenance." The splendour irradiating Moses was transient—"which glory was to be done away;" but it did what it was intended to do by demonstrating where he had been and on what mission. Yet—the glory acknowledged—it was "the ministration of death." All the sublimity was that of terror, none that of beauty, when Sinai became the shrouded pavilion of Jehovah. "Whosoever toucheth the mount shall be surely put to death." This external characterization was a symbol of its condemning power. "When the commandment came, sin revived, and I died." It was not in the language of the Law that David prayed, "Cast me not away from thy presence, and take not thy Holy Spirit from me;" nor in sympathy with the Law that Isaiah spoke of the Anointed One, "The Spirit of the Lord God is upon me;" but in contemplation of grace beyond Law, and therefore *extra* to the ordinary workings of the Mosaic economy. A provision existed for these spiritual anticipations, and it was a part of its excellence, the highest part, that it had on a few minds this prevenient influence. Still, the distinctive feature stands, "a ministration of death;" and to the hour when Jerusalem and her temple fell, Sinai was the mount that could not be touched without death. It had a glory, a derived and subordinate glory, and the glory itself was to die. Certain qualities of Hebrew mind under the system, methods of thought, poetic modes of looking at nature, cultivated instincts of providence, yearnings for spirituality, were to survive and attain their completeness ; but the system was to end by the law of limitation organic in its structure. Now, on this basis, the glorious economy of which Moses was the minister, and the transientness of its duration, St. Paul builds an argument for the superior glory of the gospel. It is the "ministration" of the Holy Ghost. It is "the ministration of righteousness." Under the economy of grace the righteousness of God was first secured. That done, the justice of God appeared in the sinner's justification. And in this justification the converted man realizes that sense of demerit and guilt which arises in his personal instinct of justice, is met and satisfied ; while, at the same time, gratitude and love are awakened by the unmerited goodness of God in Christ. The two stand together. They are inseparable in the constitution of the universe. They are inseparable by the laws of the human mind. The joy of the one is vitally blended with the gladness of the other ; so that if the renewed heart feels its indebtedness to the mercy of God in Christ, it feels also that its salvation rests on the vindicated righteousness of God in Christ. It is what Christ is to the Father that makes him precious as the Christ of his faith, hope, and love. Most fitly, then, St. Paul presents the antithetic emphasis on *condemnation* and *righteousness.* Condemnation and righteousness are legal terms. The element of similarity in their common relation to Law is clearly recognized. Without this common element the antithesis could have no meaning. The dissimilarity is thus made vivid. "Much more doth the ministration of righteousness exceed in glory." Each is a "ministration," each a "ministration" of "glory," but the "ministration of righteousness doth exceed in glory." The idea is explained and strengthened yet further. A favourite thought of the Jews, and particularly of the Pharisees, was the perpetuity of the Law. After the Exile, this was the stronghold of patriotism, sentiment, and religion. On no other ground could Pharisaism have acquired its popular ascendency. This was the battle it was ever fighting for the nation—the dignity of the Law as seen in its permanent utility, since only thereby could Israel attain her true destiny and far surpass her ancient renown. Of course the anti-Pauline party at Corinth had much to say on St. Paul's view of the Law. Here, then, is an opportunity for him to defend his ministry. The point now is that the Mosaic ministration had no glory "in this respect," that is, in respect to the succeeding dispensation, which had entirely obscured its lustre. The once stately figure was not erect, but prostrated ; it was disrobed of its gorgeous vestments ; it wore no longer the breastplate with its precious stones ; its glory had departed ; and all this "by reason of the glory that excelleth." If so, then how transcendent the splendour of the Spirit's dispensation? "If that which is done away was glorious, much more that which remaineth is glorious." In the former Epistle he had written of various glories—one of the sun, another of the moon, still another of the stars, the radiance distributed over immeasurable spaces and among orbs widely different, each preserving from age to age its own distinctive splendour, every ray of light imaging the world whence it issued. A firmament was before his eye in its circles of magnificence. But now the glory, on which in other days he had looked with so much pride as a Pharisee, had passed for ever from his sight. Yet, so far from feeling that there was loss, he exulted in the infinite gain, because "of the glory that excelleth."—L.

Vers. 12—18.—*Boldness of speech ; the two ministries ; from "glory to glory."* Dwelling on the superior excellence of the gospel, it was natural for the apostle to speak of his hopefulness (such hope) and of the effect thereof on his ministry. He had spoken of his trust (ver. 4), and now he expresses the hope which filled his soul from "the intervening vision of the glory of his work" (Stanley) and its future results. He uses "great plainness of speech"—unreservedness, without disguise, boldness (the last conveying his meaning most fully). The "able ministers of the new covenant" were also bold, having no reason for concealment, but every reason for openness and candour. From the beginning of the Spirit's dispensation this boldness had characterized apostolic preaching. St. Peter, who had shown such cowardice in the high priest's palace, evinced the utmost fearlessness at Pentecost. It was a spectacle of wonder to the Sanhedrim. "When they saw the boldness of Peter and John . . . they marvelled ; " and what was the explanation of their courage? "They took knowledge of them that they had been with Jesus." Immediately thereafter we hear of prayer offered by the Church that "with all boldness " they may speak God's Word. Boldness, at that time, was a virtue in request, and not one of the apostles failed to meet its requisitions. At this point the contrast between the Law and the gospel presents a new aspect. Moses had veiled his face, "that the children of Israel could not steadfastly look to the end of that which is abolished." The veil concealed the evanescence of the brightness and was symbolic of that judicial blindness which fell upon Israel. "Their minds were blinded," or hardened, so that their perceptions were not in accordance with facts; impressibility was lost, feeling was callous. "Until this day remaineth the same veil untaken away in the reading of the Old Testament." The punishment continued. What were the old Scriptures but a sealed book to most of the Jews in the apostle's day? and now, after eighteen centuries, how palpable to us the confirmation of his words in the ignorance and the delusions of the Jews touching the spiritual import of their sacred books! "Until this day" has a meaning for us it could not have had to St. Paul's contemporaries. Time has done nothing or next to nothing to remove the darkness enveloping Jewish mind. Shrewd, intelligent, sagacious, in everything else; distinguished on nearly every arena of commercial and professional life; often foremost among men in matters as widely separated as music and statesmanship;—they yet present the strangest of contrarieties in adhesion to prejudices almost two thousand years old, and that too while evincing an adaptiveness to every form of civilization and to all the modifications going on in the current activities of the age. Find them where you may, they are pliant to circumstances. Not a national mould can be mentioned in which their external character cannot be cast, and yet, while this plasticity is such that we have Russian, Italian, German, Spanish, French, English, American, Jews, and withal the individual nationality apparent, there is the same religious blindness of which St. Paul wrote long ago. Their land, homes, institutions, the objects that come before us when we think of Judæa and Galilee, have passed from their grasp; but they hold fast to the shreds of their ancient beliefs, nor can any power relax their hold. Now, surely, this is inexplicable on the ordinary grounds of human experience. No law of the mind, no law of society, can explain the phenomenon. Such a spectacle as the Jews present of retaining their attachment and devotion to a skeleton religion, from which the soul has departed, is unique in the world's history. St. Paul solves the enigma; it is providential, it is punitive; "*until this day* the veil is untaken away." Two statements follow: (1) the "veil is done away in Christ;" (2) but, though done away in Christ, "even unto this day, when Moses [his writings] is read, the veil is upon their heart." Only in and through Christ have we the power to see Christ in the Old Testament. Only in Christ risen and glorified, only in him as sending the Holy Ghost, can we understand the relations of Moses to the gospel. "Then opened he their understanding, that they might understand the Scriptures"—a post-resurrection matter altogether and coincident with the preliminary gift of the Holy Ghost during the forty days. Yet, while asserting that Moses has been unveiled, and that his testimony to Christ, as the end of the Law to every believer, has been made clear and simple, nevertheless, the veil remains. The idea would seem to be, "The veil remains not taken away in the reading of the old covenant, it not being unveiled to them that it (the old covenant) is done away in Christ" (note in Lange's 'Commentary'). But was there not room for hope? Already, in thousands of cases, the veil had been removed. A blinder and more rabid Pharisee than St. Paul lived not in Jerusalem, and he had had the veil taken away. The work was going on. One day it would be completed and Israel would know her Messiah. "When it shall turn to the Lord, the veil shall be taken away." We, in the present day, read this third chapter of the Second Corinthians in a fuller light than even our immediate ancestors. The events of the nineteenth century have shown us how near the Jews are to the heart of Providence. Taken as a body of people, they are advancing in wealth, in culture, in certain elements of social power, at a rate beyond the average progress of races. Christian thinkers cannot look at these facts without seeing much more than material prosperity. Providence is the historic antecedent of the Spirit. The prophets of God in our age are not Elijahs and Elishas, but events that revolutionize thought and silently change the hearts of nations. But this turning to the Lord (ver. 16) must be explained as to its Divine Agent, and the nature, thoroughness, and growing excellence of the work be set forth. *Its Divine Agent.* He is the Holy Ghost. Not only did Christ teach that he depended on the Holy Spirit for his anointing as the Messiah, and that the unction proceeding thence was the strength and inspiration of his earthly work ("The Spirit of the Lord is upon me"); not only did he refer everything to the fulness of the Spirit in him ("I do nothing of myself"); not only did he wait for its baptismal descent upon him before entering on his ministry, and acknowledge his presence in his miracles and teaching ("If I cast out devils by the Spirit of God," etc.; "The words I speak unto you, I speak not of myself"); but, in the most solemn hours of his existence, death just at hand, he taught the disciples to expect the Spirit as his gift, stating what would be his offices as Remembrancer, Convincer, Witness, Glorifier, and in all the Comforter. This was to be their outfit for discipling all nations, for victory over themselves as to all self-seeking and self-furthering emotions, for triumph over all opposing forces. This was to be the means of realizing him as their glorified Lord, so that they should know him no more after the flesh, but after the Spirit. Now, we must not fail to notice that we are indebted to St. Paul for a very full portrayal of the actual work of the Spirit in the Church. One may call him the historian of the Spirit, the thinker who, under God, discerned his blessed operations in their variety and compass, the writer who put them on record for the illumination of the Church in all ages, the man who laid bare his own soul in extremities of sorrow and in moments of supreme happiness so that we might have his theology of the Holy Ghost in its experimental results. From him, then, we have not only the completest doctrinal instruction on this most vital subject, but likewise the flesh-and-blood view superinduced upon the anatomy of theological truth; witness this third chapter: yet this is only one among his many-sided presentations of this topic. Observe, however, this chapter fills a special place in his system of teaching. Step by step he had been approaching a point at which he could demonstrate the pre-eminent excellence of the gospel. Charity had been delineated once and for ever; the resurrection had been argued on a method and in a manner unusual with him; so too the economy of the Church as a society divinely planned. In this third chapter all his prominent ideas coalesce in one great master-truth, viz. the dispensation of the gospel as the ministry of the Spirit. The phrase, "ministry of the Spirit," is itself remarkable. It includes, in a certain sense, the ministry of Moses, while differentiating the old covenant from the new. It takes in all ministries, apostolic, ordinary, and the numerous kinds of the ordinary. If we have lost some of these as they existed in St. Paul's day, how many have we gained as original to later times and generic to circumstances called into existence by England and America in the eighteenth century—the century of a constellation of epochs in the firmament of history? "Now the Lord is that Spirit." Everywhere, in everything, the Lord Jesus Christ is the Dispenser of its manifold influence. "Being by the right hand of God exalted, and having received of the Father the promise of the Holy Ghost, he hath shed forth this, which ye now see and hear." It is the doctrine of Pentecost. It is the miracle and grandeur of Pentecost. Yet St. Peter does little more than state the fact. The doctrinal elaboration waits for St. Paul, and these two Epistles furnish the opportunity. *Nature, thoroughness, and growing excellence of the Spirit's work.* It is *liberty.* "Where the Spirit of the Lord is, there is liberty." Liberty from the pedagogy of the Law; liberty from the tyranny of the carnal intellect; liberty from that national domination which in the case of the Jews offered such a solid resistance to the gospel; liberty from Gentile idolatry; liberty from every agency that wrought evil in the soul of man. "If the Son therefore shall make you free, ye shall be free indeed." But it was the glorified Son who was to make men free by communicating the Holy Ghost. It is a revelation of God in Christ and Christ in the Spirit of the consciousness and conscience of men, and therefore *thorough.* It addresses his consciousness as one who has the capacity to think, feel, judge; and it addresses his conscience as to how he should think, feel, judge, as touching his obligations and as enforcing them by an immortality of reward or punishment. By the truth of the gospel, by the Spirit accompanying that truth and rendering it effective, consciousness is enlightened, cultivated, enlarged. The man sees much in himself he never saw before. And his moral sense or conscience, that mightiest of the instincts, is instructed and guided so as to represent the Spirit. It is in the soul a Remembrancer, a Convincer, a Witness, a Glorifier of Christ, a Comforter. And under this twofold development which is brought into unity by the Spirit of truth and love, the work of grace extends to all the man's faculties. The intellect, the moral sensibilities, the social affections, lift up the physical man into themselves, and grow together into the spiritual man. Not an appetite, not a passion, not an attribute, of body or soul is left neglected. The ideal is "body, soul, and spirit" consecrated to Christ, living, working, suffering, so that "whatsoever ye do in word or deed, do all in the Name of the Lord Jesus." And its *growing excellence* is seen in this, that in harmony with its freedom and its development of spiritual consciousness and conscience, it has an unveiled face. The eye is open and unhindered. Nothing intervenes between it and the glory of the Lord. True, it sees only in a mirror; it sees by reflection; it sees the image merely—the image of God in Christ, the image of humanity in Christ, the God-Man, the one perfect Man of the human race. We see him in the New Testament, in the Gospels and Epistles, in the Acts of the Apostles and in the Apocalypse, the *acts of Providence* future and final. We see him in all his relations and aspects—the babe of Mary, the boy of Nazareth, the carpenter's son, the public Man, Teacher, Benefactor, Healer, Helper, Friend. Every page of the New Testament is as a burnished surface whereon he is presented to the eye of faith as a manifestation of God's righteousness and love, while he exhibits also the guilt and condemnation of man. "The glory of the Lord" is thus brought to view amidst the scenes and circumstances that instruct us in daily life. It is on a level with our comprehension. It finds the same kind of access to our sympathies that human qualities have in ordinary intercourse. "I beseech thee, show me thy glory," was the prayer of Moses, and the Lord answered and made all his goodness pass before him. What Christ's glory was in Moses, in the Psalms and prophecies, in his incarnation and atoning death, in his glorification; what it has been, is now, and will be;—all this we have in the Scriptures of the Spirit and in his Divine offices to sanctify the Word. If we behold as in a mirror, is the image distorted, confused, inoperative, ineffective? Nay; it is with "open face" that we look, and the result is we "are changed into the same image from glory to glory." Faith is the organ of vision, and faith is essentially transforming by its power to make what is an object of thought and feeling the most effectual of subjective influences. It takes the object from the outer world, separates it from the limitations of sense and intellect, disconnects the object from whatever is darkening and enervating, and secures to it fulness of activity. Faith is the purest, truest, noblest, form of belief. It is belief of things unseen and eternal, revealed to us by God and testified unto by the most honest and faithful witnessess the human race could furnish. To give us a Peter, a John, a Paul, as testifiers, the world was under providential training for many centuries and especially its elect race, whose ancestor, Abraham, inaugurated the career of the nation by an act of faith the most pathetic, the most sublime, the most illustrious, in the annals of mankind. It is not only a belief of things invisible as disclosed by a Revealer and assured by witnesses, but likewise a belief created, directed, and sustained in personal consciousness by the agency of the Holy Ghost. Hence its power to conform us to the Divine image as displayed in Christ, and hence also its progressive work. Not only are we changed, but we are changed "from glory to glory." "The righteousness of God is revealed from faith to faith," so that we realize more and more clearly the consistency of the Divine righteousness in our justification, and the righteousness formed in our souls by the Spirit. We know why we are pardoned and by whom renewed, and, as we advance into new stages of experience, the past work of grace is rendered more and more intelligible. Current experiences leave much unexplained. Infancy, childhood, youth, in religious life are not fully comprehended till the interpretative light of manhood is thrown back upon them. "*From glory to glory*;" this is true of every Christian virtue. At first we are timid in confessing Christ before the world; the cross is heavy; self-denial is often very painful; the remains of the carnal mind are yet strong enough to resist when some onerous task is put upon us; but in time we gain strength, and in time are able to run and not weary, to walk and not faint. It is "from strength to strength," as the psalmist sang long ago. Take the virtue of patience; what years are needed to acquire it in any large degree! St. Peter says, "Add to your faith, virtue," etc.; keep up the supply, and exercise all diligence in building up one virtue by means of another. Again, "Grow in grace;" if growth stops, grace stops. "*From glory to glory*." Temptations that had to be fought against, and sometimes ineffectually, twenty years ago, trouble us no longer. Infirmities are less infirm. Mysteries that used to perplex have ceased to disturb. People whose presence was an annoyance can be borne with. Irritations, recurring daily, have lost their power to ruffle the temper. Many a crooked way has been made straight, many a rough place smooth, many a darkened spot bright, to our steps. "*From glory to glory*." Grace has worked its way down into our instincts and begun their fuller development. Thence comes the white light so grateful to sight and so helpful. It is reflected upon the intellect, the sense-organs, the outward world, and dissipates the occasional gloom that falls upon us when Satan's "It is written" obscures our perceptions, or when the logic of the sense-intellect gathers its mists about our pathway. Blessed hours of illumination are those which attend the later stages of grace penetrating the depths of instinct. Doubts are over; for we know whom we have believed. "*From glory to glory.*" Gradually our hearts are detached from the world, and, while its beauty and love and tenderness are none the less, they are seen as parts of a higher life and a remoter sphere. Afflictions, once "grievous," yield "the peaceable fruit of righteousness;" for the "afterward" has come, and what an "*afterward*"! To be reconciled to the cross of pain; to glory in the cross of the Divine Sufferer; to die to self as we die when the Man of sorrows becomes the Christ of our instincts; to say, "Thy will be done" with no half-way utterance, but from the heart, and submit not only willingly but gladly to whatever it may please Providence to ordain;—this indeed is proof that we have advanced "*from glory to glory.*"—L.

Ver. 2.—"*Our epistle.*" Paul did the work of his life partially by his voice, but to no small extent by his pen. His compositions which have come down to us, and by which we chiefly know him, are epistolary. His letters were admitted, in his own time, and even by his enemies and traducers, to be weighty and powerful. But in his own view the best of all his epistles—those which most unmistakably witnessed to his apostleship—were the characters, the new lives, of those who by his ministry had received the gospel of Christ. Whether as *amanuenses* who had indited these spiritual epistles, or as *tabellarii*, or letter-carriers, who had charge of them, and delivered them to human society, the apostles "ministered" their converts, who attested their skill and fidelity. At the expense of complicating the figure, Paul observes of the Corinthians that they were written in the hearts of himself and his colleagues. The lesson of the text is that *Christians are ever authenticating the ministry of faithful preachers of the gospel.*

I. MEN MAY READ IN THE HEART AND LIFE OF THE CONVERT THE DIVINE COMMISSION OF THE MINISTER. There are such proofs of the divinity of the doctrine in its effects upon the character and conduct of its sincere recipients as point up to the heavenly authority by which the agents were appointed and authenticated.

II. AND THE FAITHFULNESS AND ZEAL OF THE MINISTER. Paul had a good conscience with regard to the manner in which he had discharged his sacred and benevolent service to his fellow-men. Especially was this the case with his ministry to the Corinthians. In his First Epistle to them he had written, "If I be not an apostle unto others, yet doubtless I am to you; for the seal of mine apostleship are ye in the Lord."

III. AND THE ADAPTATION OF THE MINISTRY TO THE NEEDS AND THE CIRCUMSTANCES OF MEN. Events proved that to Jew and to Gentile, to men of every class and character, the gospel of Christ was the power of God unto salvation. This Church at Corinth was as an epistle written in various languages, in various styles, addressed to all nations and to all conditions of men, and assuring them that the apostles of Christ were laden with treasure which was able to enrich and to bless the world.—T.

Ver. 3.—"*Epistles of Christ.*" Some teachers had visited the Christians of Corinth, who boasted of the letters of introduction they brought with them, authenticating their commission and their ministry. Paul needed no such epistles; for the members of the Church were themselves *his* epistles; and better still, they were not only his, they were *Christ's* epistles, manifestly and undeniably such. The same may be said of all true disciples and followers of the Lord Jesus; it is an honourable and an inspiriting designation.

I. THE WRITER—CHRIST. Many great men, especially great thinkers, have perpetuated their influence and have served their race by their writings. As poets, philosophers, or moralists, they have made a place for themselves in the mind of humanity. The greatest of all, the Divine Man, wrote nothing. It is greater to be than to write; and the Lord Jesus simply lived and worked, suffered, died, and conquered. He could not compress and limit his mind within the compass of a treatise or a volume. He left his evangelists and apostles to write of him; his earthly manifestation thus spoke a universal language. Yet, in a sense, he has always been writing, and he is writing now. He is still daily issuing epistles to the world.

II. The epistle—Christians. As a friend and counsellor, when on a journey and at a distance, communicates by letter with those who need his guidance and the assurance of his interest, so our Lord, though he has ascended on high, is ever sending epistles to the children of men. Every Christian upon whom he impresses his own will, character, and purposes, thus becomes Christ's communication to the world, written by his hand, and authenticated by his autograph. Every individual is a syllable, every congregation a word, every generation of believers a line, in the ever-lengthening scroll, which approaches its close as the ages near the end.

III. The tablet—the heart. God does not write on stone, as men did in ancient monumental inscriptions, or as he once did on the tables of the Law. Nor on waxen tablets, as men wrote of old with the stylus, in notes of ordinary business or friendship. Nor on parchment or papyrus, as perhaps these Epistles of Paul were written. But Christ writes on tablets that are hearts of flesh. The expression, adapted from the Old Testament, is an impressive one. In the Proverbs, Wisdom invites the young man to write her precepts upon the tablets of his heart. By Jeremiah the Lord promised to write his Law upon his people's heart. Christ takes the human soul and works upon it, and engraves there his own characters, sets down there his own signature, and sends the human nature—so written upon—into the world, to tell of himself, to convey his thought, his will.

IV. The agency—not ink, but the Spirit of God. As in the processes of nature we see the operation of the living God, so in grace we discern spiritual hand-writing. The Spirit of God most deeply reaches and most blessedly affects the spirit of man. The Spirit carries truth and love home to the heart with an incomparable power. He writes upon the soul in deep, legible, sacred, and eternal characters.

V. The handwriting and substance of the epistles. What difference there is in the appearance and in the matter of the letters we daily receive! They vary in handwriting, in style, in tone, in matter, according to the character of the writer, the relation of the writer to the reader, the business upon which they treat. But there is something characteristic in all—all tell us something of our correspondents, and of their mind and will. So is it with these living epistles described in the text. Every epistle tells of the Divine Writer, bears witness to the Lord from whom it emanates, is evidently written in his handwriting, and reveals his mind and heart. Every epistle must be so authenticated by his signature that it cannot be suspected to be a forgery. Spirituality, holiness, obedience, meekness, benevolence,—these are the proofs that the epistle is the composition of the Christ. This is to be manifestly, unmistakably, declared.

VI. The readers—all men. There is some writing which only a few can read; the characters may be ill written and illegible, or they may be in cipher, or the language may be scientific and technical. There are letters of private business or of personal friendship, only intended for certain individuals. But there is literature, such as the Bible or the law of the land, intended for the instruction and benefit of all. So, whilst there is religious language only fully understood by the initiated, by a select class—e.g. doctrines, meditations, prayers—there is language intended for all mankind. The Christian character and life can be read with profit by all men. They can comprehend the virtues which adorn the Christian, and which are the manifest signs of the Lord's spiritual presence. If we are truly Christ's, then his handwriting will be legible to all men, and all men who know us may gain some advantage through reading what the Divine hand has inscribed upon our nature.—T.

Vers. 6—11.—*The old and the new.* The warm and affectionate nature of the apostle had embraced the religion of Christ with a fervour, an attached devotion, exceeding even that which he had shown in his earlier days towards the dispensation in which he had been nurtured. Not that he had lost any of the reverence, the affection, he had cherished towards the covenant which God had established with his Hebrew ancestors; but that the new dispensation was so glorious to the view of his soul that it shed its brightness upon the economy which it replaced. The contrast drawn here seems almost depreciatory of that Law which was "given by Moses," when that Law was brought into comparison with the "grace and truth which came by Jesus Christ."

I. The new is better than the old. If God is a God of order, if progress characterizes his works, if development is a law of his procedure, then it is only reasonable to believe, what we find to be the case, that that which displaces and supersedes what was good is itself preferable and more excellent.

II. THE SPIRIT IS BETTER THAN THE LETTER. Yet " the letter " was adapted to the childhood of the race, and was indeed necessary for the communication of the spiritual lesson to be conveyed from heaven. But Christianity cannot be compressed into any document; it is itself a spirit, unseen and intangible, but felt to be mighty and pervasive.

III. RIGHTEOUSNESS IS BETTER THAN CONDEMNATION. The old covenant abounded in prohibitions and in threats of punishment. The Law, when broken, as it incessantly was broken, is a sentence of condemnation to all who are placed under it. But it is the distinctive honour of Christianity that it brings in a new, a higher, an everlasting righteousness. It has thus more efficacy than the most faultless law of rectitude, for it supplies the motive and the power of true obedience.

IV. LIFE IS BETTER THAN DEATH. " The soul that sinneth, it shall *die* "—such is the import of the old covenant, which thus ministered death to those who were under it. "The gift of God is eternal *life* through Jesus Christ our Lord "—such is the evangel of the new covenant to mankind. Death is the emblem of all that is dark, dreary, and repulsive ; life is fraught with brightness, beauty, joy, and progress. Well might the apostle rise to fervid eloquence when depicting the incomparable moral excellence and beauty of the covenant of Divine grace. And justly might he deem his office one of highest honour and happiness, as bringing salvation and a blessed immortality to the lost and dying sons of men.

V. ETERNAL GLORY IS BETTER THAN TRANSITORY AND PERISHABLE SPLENDOUR. There was a glory in the scene and circumstances amid which the Law was given ; there was a glory in that code of piety and rectitude which was then conferred upon the chosen nation ; there was a glory in the illumined countenance of the great lawgiver when he came down from the mount. But this glory was for a season, and indeed it almost lost its title to be spoken of as glory, by reason of the glory that excelleth. The ministration of the Spirit, of righteousness, that which remaineth, this is encompassed with a halo, an aureole, of spiritual and heavenly splendour which shall brighten until it merges in the ineffable glory of eternity.—T.

Vers. 15, 16.—*The veil.* The historical incident in this passage makes way for the allegorical representation. When Moses came down from the mount he veiled his face that the people might not see his features and might not witness the fading of his celestial glory. And Paul affirms that a similar veil conceals the countenance of the great prophet and lawgiver when his writings are publicly read in the hearing of his countrymen. In many ways the Pentateuch is a witness to the Messiah, even Jesus. But over the Pentateuch, as read, there rests a veil which hinders the Jews from penetrating to the spiritual, the prophetic, meaning of the inspired writer. Moses testified of Christ ; but to the unenlightened the writings of Moses prevent any perception, any vision, of the Divine Lord. A similar veil keeps many from apprehending the truth which is so near them.

I. IN WHAT DOES THE VEIL CONSIST ? Especially in prejudice and in unbelief. As the Israelites were so persuaded of the incomparable excellence of the Mosaic Law that they could not discern the higher revelation to which that Law was designed to lead, so oftentimes men's minds are so preoccupied with their own notions of religion, of righteousness, etc., that they are not prepared to give heed to the Divine manifestation and appeal.

II. WHAT DOES THE VEIL HIDE ? The covering referred to in the context hid the face of the lawgiver ; but the veil of error and of unbelief conceals the countenance of Christ, the revelation of Divine attributes, purposes, and promises. What it would be most for our interests to behold we may, by our sin and folly, obscure from our own view. See what we may, if we behold not the light of God's glory in the face of Jesus Christ we forfeit the highest privileges of which we are capable.

III. HOW IS THE VEIL REMOVED ? The answer is very simple, " When it shall turn to the Lord." That is to say, the obstacle to spiritual vision lies with ourselves and not with Heaven. Repentance, or the turning of the heart away from sin, is the condition of true enlightenment. Whilst the mind is occupied with itself and its own inclinations and fancies, the spiritual glory of the Saviour is not discernible. It only needs that, under the guidance of the Spirit of God, the mind should look away from self to Christ, in order that at once the scales should fall from the eyes of the beholder, and the veil should drop from the face of the Redeemer, and a true *re-velation* should take place.

IV. WHAT DOES THE REMOVAL OF THE VEIL EFFECT? 1. The transitory character of preparatory dispensations is clearly discerned; the veil being dropped, it is seen that the glory of the older covenant has gone. 2. The true glory of Christ and of Christianity is made manifest; the new covenant appears in all its splendour, unfading and eternal.—T.

Ver. 17.—*The spirit of liberty.* If there are two words especially dear to St. Paul, they are these—the *spirit* as distinguished from the form and the letter, and *liberty* as distinguished from religious bondage.

I. MAN'S NEED OF LIBERATION. 1. Sin is bondage, however he may confuse between liberty and licence. There is no slave so crippled and so pitiable as is the bondman of sin. 2. Man's happiness and well-being depend upon his deliverance from this spiritual serfdom. 3. No earthly power can effect this great enfranchisement.

II. THE DIVINE LIBERATOR. Many of the designations applied to our Lord Jesus imply this character and function. He is the Saviour, who saves from the yoke of sin, the doom of death; the Redeemer, who ransoms from a spiritual captivity, who pays the price, and sets the prisoner free. "The Lord is the Spirit;" *i.e.* the work of redemption was wrought by Jesus in the body, and is applied and made actual to the individual soul by the unseen but mighty and ever-present Spirit, in whose operations the Lord Christ perpetuates his action and achieves his dominion.

III. THE ESSENCE OF SPIRITUAL LIBERTY. It is irrespective of personal condition; for the slave can enjoy its sweets, even when his clanking chains remind him of his earthly bondage. It is emancipation from the curse and penalty of the Law, as this oppresses every sinner who is at all aware of his real condition. It is freedom from what St. Paul calls the dominion of sin. It is the glad consecration of all powers to the service of the Divine Redeemer. It is "the glorious liberty of the children of God."

IV. THE FRUITS OF FREEDOM. 1. *Obedience*, strange and paradoxical as the assertion seems, is the consequence of the gracious enfranchisement of the soul. The service of the heart, which cannot be rendered in bondage, is natural in the state of emancipation. 2. *Joy* is natural to the emancipated slave, who realizes the dignity and the blessedness of freedom. 3. *Praise* of the Deliverer never ceases, but ascends in unintermitting strains to the Author and Giver of spiritual and everlasting liberty.—T.

Ver. 18.—*The glorious transformation.* An exulting joy seems to have moved the soul of the apostle, when he meditated upon the present immunities and honours, and upon the prospects of future blessedness and glory which, through Christ, belong to all true believers and followers of the Lord. A kind of spiritual exhilaration pervades and exalts his spirit, and adds eloquence and poetry to his enraptured language.

I. UNINTERRUPTED VISION. The figure of the veil continues to haunt the mind of the inspired writer, even after it has answered the purpose of its first introduction. Associating his brethren in the faith with himself, he affirms, concerning Christians, that the veil was in their case removed, so that for them was actually realized a wonderful approach to the unseen Saviour. Before their enlightenment by the Spirit of God, the scales were upon their eyes and the veil was before their countenance. Now, in Heaven's light they see light. The sin, the prejudice, the unbelief, which hid the Saviour from their view, have been removed, and nothing comes between the soul and its Saviour.

II. SPIRITUAL REFLECTION. Instead of the countenance being concealed by a veil, it is, in the case of true Christians, converted into a mirror, which receives and then reflects the rays of light. Thus the glory of the Lord, which is ever manifested in nature, and which shone in the face of our incarnate Redeemer, is gathered up and given forth by the renewed and purified character of the Christian. This is a moral process. A spiritual nature alone is capable of attracting and receiving such light, alone is capable of giving it forth in uncontaminated, though reflected, rays. Thus the disciple mirrors the Teacher and the servant mirrors the Lord. We are living representatives of the Divine Head.

III. GLORIOUS TRANSFORMATION. Faith in Christ and fellowship with Christ are the forces which produce assimilation to Christ. The image which is beheld seems to infix itself upon the mirror-like soul that receives it. The life of faith thus serves to carry on a gradual process of spiritual assimilation. The *progression* is denoted by the phrase, "from glory to glory," by which we understand, not earthly splendour, but spiritual excellence and perfection. And the *agency* is indicated by the expression here used, "as by the Lord the Spirit." Because he is the Spirit, the Lord has access to the heart, and renews, hallows, and glorifies the nature to which he makes himself graciously and divinely known. And there seems to be no limit to this most blessed process. In fact, the future state appears to offer the most amazing scope for its continuation: "We shall be like Christ; for we shall see him as he is."—T.

Ver. 3.—*The Christ-letter.* The people of God are set forth under various figures in Scripture. For example—as corn ripening for harvest; as Lebanon's cedars, standing like rocks under fiercest blasts; as stars fixed in heavenly places; as the sun climbing the heavens, enlightening the world; as purified gold, fit for the King; as jewels flashing forth tints of loveliness, prepared for regal crown; as vine branches richly laden; as pomegranates and figs, sweet and refreshing; for might, the lion and eagle; and, great paradox, for weakness, the defenceless sheep and lamb; for humility, the lily; for dignity, the palm tree; for usefulness, the salt of the earth. Here, as "the epistle of Christ." A singular but impressive title. And this sets forth what each individual believer should be—a Christ-letter. We have been accustomed to regard epistles as certain books of the Scripture or letters passing between men. The apostle leads us to this thought— *men are epistles.* Apart from nature and providence, we have regarded the Bible as God's only book. Now we are directed to other books of God, volumes of redeemed humanity. We speak of the Epistles of Scripture as inspired; men who are the epistles of Christ are inspired by the same Spirit. Of the former we think as testimonies for God, for Christ, for religion; the latter are equally so. And, as though God were not content with giving to mankind silent and secluded epistles, he has placed in the midst of the world *living* epistles, moving amongst men, unobscured, ever beheld and perused. We regard the Scriptures with reverence. What a thought that we, if we are truly of Christ, constitute part of the great Scriptures of God! The Bible we esteem as sacred; if of Christ, we are sacred, appointed to bear a like witness to the verities of the Christian faith. It would seem as though there could scarcely be a more honourab'e designation than this—"the epistle of Christ." If we are to be the epistles of Christ—

I. GOD MUST WRITE OUR LIVES. The epistle, to be worth anything, must be dictated by God. We say Paul's Epistles, Peter's Epistles, John's Epistles; but, if this adequately represents them, they are nothing. If they are anything, they are *God's* Epistles—God's Epistle to the Corinthians and to the Romans, and so on. So with us. If we are epistles of Christ, we must be "of God," "written, not with ink, but with the Spirit of the living God" (ver. 3); and the writing must be, not on "tables of stone" *for* us, but in "tables that are hearts of flesh" *within* us. The work of the Divine Spirit in our natures and in our lives can alone make us epistles of Christ. This is the highest form of human life, when it is *made* by God, day by day, hour by hour—the will of God finding expression in conduct, thoughts, motives, being. Free-will is the glory of man, received by the fiat of the Eternal; but the noblest act of free-will is its voluntary subjection to the will of God. We are highest when we are willing to become most completely the *servants* of God. Satan tempted our first parents to pass from under the will of God by the promise, "Ye shall be as gods." There was wonderful deceit here. The temptation *found them* as gods, it *left them* as devils. To live otherwise than in subjection to the will of God is to go down. The way upward is, "Not my will, but thine, be done." To consult the Divine wish in all our undertakings, to follow the Divine instruction in all our deeds, to wait upon the Divine purpose in our whole being and course, is for *God to be writing our lives.* How different, alas! is our experience! How often we have taken the pen out of the Divine hand, that we ourselves might write a little! How often, by our wilfulness, our self-seeking, our sin, we have rendered the Divine writing blurred, and the manuscript of our life blotted and defaced! How often have our foolish insertions entirely altered the meaning of what the Divine fingers were tracing! What chaos, confusion, disaster, have come into the epistle of our life because it has been largely of ourselves and not of God! How poor has been the influence of the life-letter because it has not been inspired of the Holy Ghost!

II. OUR LIVES WILL THEN TESTIFY OF CHRIST. This must be our supreme aim if we desire to be epistles of Christ. He is to be the one conspicuous feature in our life and being. Epistles we are to be, which, when men read, they shall find that they are *reading of Christ.* Many professing Christians are anything but epistles of Christ. There are some very great epistles of doubt, read and known of many men, telling us that they do not claim apostolical succession, and proving this with conclusiveness by being anything but fully persuaded in their own minds; epistles of dismalness, epistles of idleness, epistles of delay, epistles of change, epistles of frivolity, epistles of self, epistles of quarrelsomeness, and others who seem to be epistles of nothingness. In contrast to the true consistent believer—Christ manifested in his actions, Christ breathed forth in his influence, Christ the utterance of his life. To him *" to live is Christ."* If we are the epistles of Christ: 1. *We must allow men to read us.* We must not be too reserved. We must not hide our light. 2. *We should not be too forward.* Much talk of our attainments and graces will convince most men that we have not any. A book is not instructive which has the most of the printing outside. 3. *Men will be willing to read us when very unwilling to read the Epistles of the Scriptures.* There are two things which men are very fond of reading—their newspaper and each other. The true epistle of Christ is likely to have wide circulation and large usefulness.—H.

Ver. 6.—*The new covenant.* I. A COVENANT OF THE SPIRIT. The old covenant, the Law which came by Moses, was the "letter"—precepts laid down to be literally obeyed, fixed and rigid, external and ritual. The new covenant, the gospel, is the covenant of love, of spiritual obedience. The Jew, under the old covenant, could not be exempted by any piety of spirit from the letter of the legal ordinance; but under the new covenant the spirit of the observance is chief. The old covenant did not supply the inward power producing obedience—it was something outside of man, imposed *upon* him. But the new covenant has for an essential feature the power of God operating in the heart, leading to newness of life. The old covenant approached man from without, the new covenant works from within. One is "letter"—external; the other is "spirit"—internal.

II. A COVENANT OF LIFE. In the old covenant there was the holy Law and the command to fully obey it: "The Law is not of faith; but, The man that doeth them shall live in them" (Gal. iii. 12). The old covenant demanded perfect obedience: "Cursed is every one that continueth not in all things which are written in the book of the Law to do them" (Gal. iii. 10). Thus the old covenant tended to condemnation and death, because fallen human nature failed to keep the perfect Law of God. The "letter" of unswerving righteousness convicted man of sin, and then "killed" him. Not that the Law was evil, but that it showed the evil in man. "The wages of sin is death." The Law, by discovering sin, showed *that the wages were due.* The old covenant thus left man condemned, and, if man was to be justified and restored, there was urgent need of a new covenant. We find, thus, that the old covenant is ever pointing to the new, and that the design of the former was to lead to the latter: "The Law was our schoolmaster to bring us unto Christ" (Gal. iii. 24). Moreover, the Jew possessed the new covenant as well as the old, though not so fully unfolded as we have it. Men condemned by the old covenant lived the life of faith upon the Son of God who was to come, and thus participated in the life-giving principle of the new covenant. This new covenant is a covenant of life: 1. Because Christ has perfectly fulfilled the Law of God on man's behalf, and to man this perfect obedience is imputed. Condemnation is thus avoided. Life is secured for man by man's Substitute. 2. Man's personal transgressions are atoned for by the sacrifice of Christ. 3. The Holy Ghost is given to kindle spiritual life in man, to sanctify his nature, to bring him at last into full accord with the perfect Law of God.

III. A COVENANT NOT TRANSITORY. The old covenant has passed away. The new covenant puts men in a position with relation to God which is an everlasting one. Death and the next world will not call for the abrogation of this covenant, nor any changes occurring during the residence of the human family in the world. The old covenant was imperfect; it demanded something beyond itself; it was designed to do this. There is no such element in the new. It is complete; it calls for nothing outside of its own provisions.

IV. A COVENANT OF SURPASSING GLORY. This arises largely from points already noticed. 1. Its spiritual character. 2. Its issues in bringing life, not death, to fallen man. 3. Its enduring character. 4. Its direct initiation and administration by the Son of God. "The Law was given by Moses, but grace and truth came by Jesus Christ" (John i. 17). The inauguration of the old covenant saw the face of Moses illumined. The new covenant came with the transfiguration of Christ. 5. Its marvellous revelation of Divine *love*. The old covenant laid the emphasis upon Divine righteousness; the new, whilst displaying with untarnished lustre this attribute of Deity, exhibits pre-eminently the love of God.—H.

Ver. 15.—*The veil on the heart.* The veil which Moses put on his face (Exod. xxxiv. 33) obscured its brightness. The apostle seizes upon the event, so familiar to readers of Jewish history, to illustrate moral blindness, and especially the moral blindness of Jews in his own day. As moral blindness is subjective, he speaks of the veil, not upon those things which are obscured, as in the case of the face of Moses, but as upon the heart. Upon the *heart*, because in spiritual matters the inability does not spring from the head, but from the heart. This veil upon the heart—

I. OBSCURES THE GLORY OF THE OLD DISPENSATION. It did so to Jews in Paul's day; it does so to Jews now. The true glory of the old covenant lay in its foreshadowing of the new. It was a covenant of types and shadows. Underlying its legality was a deep spirituality. The Law condemned, and only condemned, but the "Law" was not the whole of the old covenant. Associated with the Law was the embryo of the gospel. And unveiled hearts looked through condemnation and shadow and type to the delivering Messiah, by whom men could be justified by faith and not by works. But the veil upon the heart caused the Jew to regard the old covenant as complete in itself, and to disregard the deeper spiritual meanings of its provisions. From him its true glory was thus hidden. A rigid system became much more rigid. The wings of a dispensation rising to something higher were clipped. A hard, narrow creed was substituted for an expansive and noble theology.

II. HIDES CHRIST. It did so when Christ came. When the Messiah appeared, veiled hearts failed to recognize him. The Jews would have welcomed a Messiah who came to continue Judaism as Judaism was understood by them. But the development of Judaism into Christianity, the fruition of the old covenant in the new, had no charms for them; on the contrary, it was obnoxious to them in the highest degree, as spirituality is ever to a carnal nature. In the Christ they could not see the Christ. He was not *their* Christ, and by facile logic was thus demonstrated to be no Christ at all. "Their minds were blinded" (ver. 14). From many to-day Christ is thus hidden. To them "a root out of a dry ground" is as beautiful as he. They think the fault is in *him*, but it is *in themselves*. False conceptions of the objects, duties, and pleasures of life possess them, and are the coloured media through which Christ is looked at. They see a darkened, shorn, maimed Christ; the *true* Christ is hidden from them.

III. CAUSES MEN TO REST IN SELF-RIGHTEOUSNESS. This was the only way of justification which was apparent to the Jew upon whose heart the veil rested. The veil shut out all, except legalism. So with many now. It is *their* righteousness, not the righteousness of Christ, to which they look. They seek to save themselves, not to be saved by another. Each is a Messiah to himself. But poor rest is secured. The voices of old sins make themselves heard, and to their clamour no satisfactory response is forthcoming. Present power to do right is found lacking. This is not to be wondered at, seeing that the Source of all true spiritual power has been abandoned. Piety becomes either a vague dream of the future or a dismal formality of the present.

IV. KEEPS MEN UNDER CONDEMNATION. The Law of God condemns, and if only the bare Law is seen there is no deliverance. Self-righteousness, if attained to in perfection, would not cancel past sentences on sin. But self-righteousness practically is ever self-unrighteousness, and, instead of atoning for sin, continuously increases it. The most moral man has but the cheerless vision of a broken Law imperiously demanding its penalties.

V. THE VEIL IS REMOVED AS WE TURN TO THE LORD. (Ver. 16.) When the Jew, led by the Spirit, believed on Christ, the veil, which had obscured his vision of the old covenant, and which had thus perverted his being and life, was removed. He saw then the true significance of the old economy, and perceived that Christ, in his own person and work, constituted the very fulfilment of the Law. Old things passed away, all things became new. The veil is destroyed for ever as we come to Christ. The apostle has, no doubt, in his mind the action of Moses: "When Moses went in before the Lord to speak with him, he took the veil off" (Exod. xxxiv. 34). Our turning to the Lord is a sign that the veil is rent in twain like the veil of the temple, and as we reach the Lord and are taught by the Divine Spirit, the veil vanishes, obscurity gives place to brightness, and we marvel that we ever could have been as we once were. When Moses came out from the presence of the Lord he again assumed the veil, but he is not here an example to us; for we are not to come out again, but to abide with Christ, to be "for ever with the Lord."—H.

Ver. 18.—*The great change.* I. WHAT THIS CHANGE IS. Into the Divine likeness. This, which was lost through the Fall, is recovered in the gospel. Believers become like Christ, who is the Brightness of the Father's glory, and the express Image of his person (Heb. i. 3). The change is not merely of opinion, or feeling, or even conduct, but a change of *being*. It is not something connected with ourselves, but our very selves which are changed, and changed so as to be like Christ. 1. *A marvellous change.* For before men believe, they are singularly unlike Christ. By nature like Satan; by grace like Christ. 2. *An all-desirable change.* For ennoblement, peace, joy, usefulness.

II. THE MANNER OF THE CHANGE. It follows upon turning to the Lord (ver. 16). As Moses, standing before God, was singularly changed in countenance, so that his face reflected the Divine glory, so we are changed as we are turned towards Christ, as we turn towards him in penitence and faith and in desire to be his. The figure of a mirror is employed. 1. We may read "reflecting as a mirror," and then the idea conveyed will be that, as Christ shines upon us, as he acts upon us, we become changed. Or: 2. If we read "beholding as in a mirror," the thought will be that, as we gaze upon Christ as he is reflected in the mirror of the gospel, we become like him. Both thoughts are correct, though it is by the Divine action we are changed, our looking upon Christ being only the means by which the Divine action reaches us.

III. A SPECIAL FEATURE OF THE CHANGE. Progressive—"from glory to glory." The change is often gradual. There is a great fundamental change at conversion. A condition of "glory" is reached, but there is a glory beyond this. We "grow in grace." At first we are "babes in Christ," but we develop into the stature of perfect men in him (Eph. iv. 13). Conversion is but the first stage. Many seem to think that it is the final one. Justification is enough for them; sanctification is not in their thoughts. But this is not the salvation of Christ. We are saved for holiness, for usefulness, for the service of God, and as we continuously gaze upon Christ in faith, and as his power falls upon us, we pass into a further "glory."

IV. A CONDITION OF THE CHANGE. Our face unveiled. And here face stands for heart. The veil occasioned by the old enmity, by prejudice, by misconception, by ignorance, must be removed. This will be so with all who in sincerity turn to the Lord. "When it shall turn to the Lord, the veil shall be taken away" (ver. 16). The more completely our face is unveiled the more rapidly shall we pass from "glory to glory." We should strive to remove all that is likely to hinder our development into the likeness of Christ. Anything that comes between ourselves and him will do this. Heart-veils are of very various patterns.

V. THE STRIKING USEFULNESS OF THE CHANGE. Adopting the reading "reflecting as a mirror," we see that: 1. Those who turn to the Lord reflect the glory of the Lord. They show forth Christ. Men take knowledge of them that they have been with Jesus. They reflect the redemptive glory of Christ. They exemplify the power of his salvation. They are monuments upon which is inscribed "Christ, and him crucified." They reflect the love of Christ in Christian activity. Having been saved themselves, they desire the salvation of all around them. What a thought, that we may reflect Christ! 2. As they seek to reflect Christ the change progresses. It is when we are diligent in the Master's business, when we consecrate ourselves to him, when we strive to set him forth in daily life, that we become changed into his image. As we strenuously endeavour to be like him we become like him. Our endeavour to reflect him is responded to by the change in us which enables us to reflect him. Reflecting his glory as a mirror, we are changed into the same image.

VI. THE WORKER OF THE CHANGE. The Holy Ghost, "the Lord the Spirit." Christ working by his Spirit, who takes of the things of Christ and reveals them unto us. "The Holy Spirit, whom the Father will send in my Name" (John xiv. 26). The work is Divine; it calls for Divine power. We cannot work this change, yet we can "turn to the Lord," that it may be worked.—H.

Vers. 2, 3.—*A living letter*. Apollos had carried to Corinth written credentials (see Acts xviii. 27; xix. 1). Why had Paul not done so too? He claims that he needed them not. The converts in that city were themselves his credentials. His appeal to the Corinthians on this point proceeds on a principle easily understood and often applied. The best testimonial a teacher can produce is the proficiency of his pupils. The most satisfactory evidences of the skill of a physician are the patients who have recovered health under his care. The convincing proofs of the competency of a gardener are the prosperity of the plants and the abundance of flowers and fruits which he produces from the ground. So was the Church at Corinth itself the best diploma or commendation of the apostle who had founded it and watched over it (see 1 Cor. iv. 14—16). A good teacher needs no letter of commendation to his own pupils, or a father to his own children. Seizing the idea of a letter, and showing that the Corinthian saints themselves formed the only letter he needed to produce, St. Paul used this as an illustration in two forms. 1. The Christians at Corinth were written on his heart, for they were dear to him (ch. vii. 3; Phil. i. 7). And this was no secret. The tie of affection between St. Paul and the Corinthian brethren was "known and read of all." 2. Christ had written upon their hearts what served as a powerful letter of commendation for his servant Paul. Let us pursue the second use of the metaphor. A Church is an epistle of Christ, open for all men to read.

I. THE AUTHOR OF THE LETTER. This is Christ. Whatever Divine thoughts are given to human minds, or spiritual impressions are stamped on human hearts, proceed from Christ. And it is true of Churches in all ages. As Christ is the living One, he is ever writing new epistles—in harmony with those which were written at the beginning—and yet new and fresh and suited to the current time.

II. THE AMANUENSIS. At Corinth this was Paul. In modern Churches it is the faithful ministry of the Word. The epistle is not invented or dictated by us, but "ministered by us." The mind of Christ is thereby conveyed to and impressed on the company of believers.

III. THE TABLETS. They are not of stone, but of the heart. The ministration of death was written and engraven on stone in the form of ten commandments. The more glorious ministration of the spirit and of righteousness is inscribed on the convictions and affections of living men. The law of Christ is put into the inward parts and written on the heart. For this end, too, the Lord knows how to soften the tablets, to make the heart tender and warm, and so susceptible of the instruction and impression of the Word. Oh to have a still heart, not restless, that the writing may be plain, and to have a lowly heart, not hard, that the engraving may be deep!

IV. THE MANNER OF WRITING. "Not with ink." St. Paul's letters were so written, as were those of other apostles (2 John 12); and by ink of the scribe and the printer have they been preserved and propagated. But for writing on the heart perishable material is unsuited. Jehovah wrote the Law on the tablets of stone with his own hand; and on the tablets of the human heart Jesus Christ writes, using ministry as he pleases in the process with the finger or power of God—"the Spirit of the living God." And so, in all times and all Churches of the saints, the application of the truth is by the living Spirit.

V. THE THING WRITTEN. It is the mind of Christ. Ye "have learned Christ, and the truth as it is in Jesus." There is no higher truth to learn, no better message to carry.

VI. THE PUBLICATION OF THE LETTER. It is "manifestly declared," and may be known and read of all men. This is said of the Church collective, for such is the temple of

God and such is the epistle of Christ—an argument surely for Christian consistency and for brotherly concord, that the sacred epistle may not be rendered unintelligible. If each member of a Church abide in his place, and all together dwell in peace and walk in the truth, there is produced an epistle of Christ which puts the gainsayer to silence. Thank God that even a faulty Church or blotted epistle has something of a Divine element, some impression and expression of Christ! The obligation which lies on the Church may be pressed on each member thereof. Would that Christ were more apparent and more legible in Christians! Let your character be a consistent representation or epistle of your Lord, and let it be an original, not a copy of some other man's religion, but a genuine production of Jesus Christ by "the Spirit of the living God." If you go to the Lord justifying yourself and accusing others, he will only write on the ground ; but if you with a penitent heart accuse yourself, he will write on you his grace and truth. Hereafter, when you have overcome, he will write on you his new Name.—F.

Ver. 6.—*The letter and the spirit.* The contrast between letter and spirit is in Scripture peculiar to the pages of St. Paul (see Rom. ii. 29 ; vii. 6). The subject specially occupied him, as the champion of Christian liberty and a profound thinker on the relations of the Old and New Testaments.

I. THE CONTRASTED TERMS—LETTER AND SPIRIT. A more frequent opposition is between flesh and spirit (see John iii. 6; vi. 63; Rom. viii. 1—13 ; Gal. v. 16—25). The distinction is obvious between a fleshly and a spiritual disposition, and the alternative is shown to be one of life or death. "To be carnally minded is death ; but to be spiritually minded is life and peace." But, by letter and spirit must be intended things of which it is possible for men to be ministers. St. Paul was a minister, not of the letter, but of the spirit ; and the context shows that by letter he meant the old covenant, and by spirit the new. Not that there was nothing but letter in the one and nothing but spirit in the other. The contrast is between predominant characteristics ; and characteristically, though not exclusively, the old covenant was letter and the new covenant was spirit. Therefore the latter excelled in glory. The old economy, or testament, is not spoken of with disrespect. It was adapted in the wisdom of God to the training of the Hebrew people as his chosen nation. It was not a mere dead writing, but had a meaning in it which was Divine. The very term "letter" implies some import or significance. And there was enough in the Old Testament to educate the minds of men in religious ideas, and bring home sacred obligations and hopes to their hearts. But it is called "the letter" because that which bulked largely in it was a code of law and a handwriting of ordinances. In its prescription of law it was to sinful men a ministration of death ; and in its ritual of worship it was inferior to that holy liberty which we now enjoy in everywhere worshipping the Father in spirit and in truth. The old covenant had shadows, the new has substance ; the old had rudiments and elements, the new has perfection ; the old had patterns of heavenly things, the new has heavenly things themselves ; the old was a dispensation of dimness as of light seen through a veil, the new is one of unveiled faces and God's marvellous light. The new economy, or testament, while characteristically one of "spirit," is not altogether without letter. As every soul must have a body, and every essence a form, in order to be known among men, so has the spirit of the New Testament embodiment and exact expression. But here lies the contrast. Pre-Christian religion contained a small proportion of spirit and life in a large bulk of letter and ordinance. Christianity has a large proportion of spirit and life in a bulk of law and form as small and light as possible. The teachings of Christianity are facts and principles, not propositions and restrictions ; its institutions are simple outlines, not precise ceremonies; and its laws are moral sentiments, not minute mechanical directions.

II. THE EFFECTS WHICH FLESH AND SPIRIT SEVERALLY PRODUCE. The letter, void of spirit, kills. The spirit, in whatever form or letter conveyed, gives life. We must still be on our guard against making that absolute which is intended only as a strong comparative. We must not say or suppose that under the Mosaic economy there was nothing but condemnation, bondage, and death. Beneath and within the letter which had such prominence, there was spirit ; and men who knew how to penetrate the letter got the spirit, and with it got life. But the more that men made of mere traditional letter and form, the less they knew of the spirit of liberty and the power of godliness.

Most apparent was the killing power of the letter in that generation of Hebrews to which Paul himself belonged. They gloried in circumcision, but had it in the flesh only, and not in the heart. They sought life by the law of works, and fell under its condemnation. The more devoted they were to religious peculiarities and ceremonial restrictions, the more did a shadow of death cover them. They clung to the types and would not recognize the Antitype. They trusted to a covenant which had exhausted its use and was passing away. So this letter-worship destroyed spiritual life. Israel after the flesh fell under a ministration of death. On the other hand, in that new dispensation, of which St. Paul was such an earnest minister, and in which spirit predominates, there is abundance of the grace of life. True that, under this dispensation also, a formalist or one who is self-righteous may turn the life into death. Externalism and traditionalism are as powerless as ever to make alive. But, when the letter which in some manner is indispensable to mortal worshippers is kept in due subordination, the spirit gives life, and the ministration of righteousness is exceeding glorious. And the Lord is that Spirit. The Lord is the Life-giver and the Life.

III. LIGHT CAST BY THIS STATEMENT ON SUNDRY QUESTIONS. 1. On the interpretation and use of certain precepts and usages mentioned in Scripture. Reverence for antiquity is good, is in some degree essential to historical Christianity; but there is a pedantry about the forms of things which is unintelligent and unspiritual. To correct this we must always distinguish between letter and spirit, and bear in mind that, in the long course of time and in altered conditions of society, there not only may be but must be circumstantial changes of form and expression in order to the conservation of spirit and truth. Apply this to (1) the precept of turning the cheek to the smiter; (2) that of washing one another's feet; (3) the forbiddal of lawsuits between Christians; (4) the salutation with a holy kiss. 2. On the corruptions of Christianity. Some harm, no doubt, has been done by the endeavour to abstract the spirit of the gospel too much from its letter, and to dispense altogether with definite forms of doctrine and service. But a greater danger has shown itself on the opposite side. The most formidable corruptions of Christianity have resulted from magnifying letter over spirit, and giving to our religion an imposing exterior while its heart fainted and all but perished. The great bane of the Church has been in the direction of exaggerated ceremonial and tyrannical insistence on outward usage and form. 3. On the propagation of the gospel. The old dispensation was not intended for world-wide diffusion; but the new has a gospel for all nations, and is meant to live in every climate and among all the tribes and races of mankind. But of its ever reaching its consummation we should despair if it were a religion of unbending, unelastic literalism, and committed itself to the maintenance of dry and rigid forms. We take courage when we remember that "the kingdom of God is not in word, but in power;" that the emphasis in Christianity lies on its active, spiritual, penetrating force; and that the Lord himself "is that Spirit." We do not set Christian form against heathen form, but preach Christ Jesus the Lord. The letter and the ritual will appear quickly enough, and may be expected to vary in a Church of all nations. What we should be most concerned about is the world-wide proclamation of him in whom all nations of the earth are to be blessed.—F.

Ver. 18.—*The Christian transfiguration.* When Moses, the minister of the Law, communed with God, his countenance became irradiated, and, on his return to the people of Israel in the camp, he was obliged to put a veil over his face. But that radiance did not last long. It faded from the prophet's countenance; and this is taken to illustrate the passing away of the glory of all that legal ministration. The Jews who rejected that gospel which St. Paul preached were still occupied with the Law. Moses stood before them still; and, when Moses was read, they failed to see that the lustre had faded from his face. Yet it was so. Not that the Law was at fault or obscure; not that Moses misled or clouded their minds. The veil was no more on his face, but on their hearts; and so they persisted, and the bulk of that nation still persist, in trusting to Moses and rejecting the more glorious ministration by Jesus Christ. The anti-Christian Jews are dimly reading the words of their lawgiver instead of rejoicing in the light of the Lord. But "we all," whether Jews or Gentiles in the flesh, who have believed the gospel, enjoy a ministration of righteousness and glory.

I. THE GLORY OF THE LORD. Moses said to Jehovah, "I beseech thee, show me thy glory." And he had some vision of the Almighty, and heard Jehovah God proclaim his Name as he passed by; but the God of Israel said, "Thou canst not see my face." Now this, which was impossible under the old covenant, and which was thought of by the faithful as the blessing of a future state (Ps. xvii. 15), is not only possible but actual under the new covenant. Christ is the Image of the invisible God. We see the glory of God in the face of Jesus Christ. He who of old surrounded himself with clouds or dwelt "in the thick darkness" now reveals himself brightly in his Beloved. The New Testament is, more fully than the Old, a revelation. God is revealed in a manner surpassing all the partial disclosures among the Jews, and correcting all the vain imaginations among the heathen. The holy Child was Immanuel, God with us. The Man who lived so purely, spoke so wisely, and suffered so patiently, revealed the unseen God; and God was glorified in him. So the apostle regarded Christianity as the breaking forth of new light on the human race, and that the very radiance of God in Jesus Christ his Son. So let us regard it. Truly the light is good—the inner light of the New Testament—the glory of the Lord.

II. CONTEMPLATION OF THAT GLORY. We behold it as one looks upon a mirror on which an object out of his reach is reflected. Our Lord has ascended to the Father, and we do not see him face to face in the present life, but we look on the Divine testimony, and, as we look, we gain "the excellency of the knowledge of Christ." In order to this, two things are necessary. 1. We must have our faces unveiled. The veil is prejudice or unbelief. The ignorance of God, long spread over the earth, is described by a prophet as "the covering cast over all people, and the veil that is spread over all nations." The removal of that covering or veil results in the turning of nations to the Lord. Alas! readers of the New Testament may be as blind to its true meaning and beauty as any Jews were in reading the Law. A vague light, perhaps, comes through the veil, but there is no clear discernment of that glory of the Lord which gives to the New Testament its surpassing power and value. St. Paul knew this well, and felt himself unable to make all men see what he saw. From some who heard him his gospel was hid. It was and is the preacher's duty to manifest and proclaim the truth; but blinded minds and veiled hearts could, and still can, defeat the testimony. St. Paul himself had once been very blind. When light shone in the face of the martyr Stephen as he stood before the council, "as it had been the face of an angel," Saul of Tarsus was only bewildered and irritated, and he consented to Stephen's death. Soon after, on his way to Damascus, a strong light from heaven shone round about him, and the voice of the Lord reached his ear. Some holy light through the veil fell on his countenance, but the veil was not yet removed, and the Pharisee was not yet a Christian. Illumination came to him when, at the word of the disciple Ananias, the eyes of his body, which had been blinded by the sudden effulgence on the way, were opened, and at the same time the eyes of the inner man were freed from the scales of unbelief, and God shone into his heart. 2. We must form a habit of beholding that glory. We do not presume to say what amount of blessing may be gained through even a rapid or occasional glance cast on the Lord Jesus; but what the apostle intends is an habitual and daily contemplation of that "brightness of the Father's glory." No study of books, acquaintance with doctrines, or observance of rites can do for us what is done by the habit of "looking to Jesus."

III. THE TRANSFORMING POWER OF SUCH CONTEMPLATION. "Changed into the same image." A moral metamorphosis is wrought, not magically as by a spell or charm, but in the manner proper to a moral nature, by the moulding influence of a new habit of thought and affection. This proceeds on the well-known principle that, whatever we look upon with frequency and with congenial feeling, stamps itself on our minds and characters. He who looks upon evil becomes evil. He who occupies himself with trifles grows trivial. He who associates with the wise grows wise. He who admires the good himself becomes good. So likewise he who beholds the pure and gracious image of God in the face of Jesus Christ is changed insensibly into that image, learns to think the thoughts of God and to exhibit the mind of Christ. Two important features of this great change are indicated in the text. 1. It is a progressive one. "From glory to glory." No doubt, if we could abide continually under the radiance of Christ, his glory would transform us more rapidly and completely than is the experience of average Christians. And we must not dwell on the idea of gradualness so as to excuse a low level of Christian attainment. But the truth lies here, that, as we receive out of Christ's fulness grace for grace, so are we transformed into his likeness from glory to glory, the light of the Lord gaining upon us and dispelling all the darkness until we are "light in the Lord." 2. While this change follows a law of moral influence, it is produced by the active operation of a Divine power—"as by the Lord the Spirit." The reference is to the Lord Jesus as "a quickening Spirit," who is here brought into contrast with Moses, the minister of the killing "letter." At the same time, we know from other Scriptures that the Lord pervades his Church on earth and renews men in his own image by the gracious presence and work of the Holy Ghost. Without this doctrine of spiritual operation, both direct and indirect, we fail to apprehend the transforming power of a pure Christianity. Note in conclusion : 1. *The connection between faith and character.* Some raise a cry that faith leads to mysticism and genders dispute, while nothing is wanted, nothing is to be valued, but an exemplary character and a good life. But what if such character and life are best attained by the habit of faith in the Lord Jesus Christ ? It might as well be said that it is of little consequence whether a man can see or is blind, so long as he walks and works well. He cannot walk or work well unless he can see. No more can one walk or act like Christ unless he looks to him in faith. Others raise a different cry. They are all for faith, and yet show no conformity to Christ. All such boasting is vain. The effect of beholding the glory of the Lord is to be changed into the same image. If there is no such change the faith is only in imagination, not in heart. 2. *The far reach of the principle of assimilation to what we habitually and willingly behold.* In this way are Christians conformed to Christ in this present time. But the principle carries much further. It is thus that the saints will be glorified with Christ at his appearing. "We know that, when he shall appear, we shall be like him ; for we shall see him as he is." 3. *The evil case of those who see in Christ "no beauty that he should be desired."* They miss both the way of peace and the way of holiness. Alas! when the gospel is set before them, the veil lies upon their hearts. They can see something to be admired in the wisdom of sages and the courage of heroes, and yet see nothing in the Son of God. They may look on nature with admiring eye, and see " the glory in the grass and splendour in the flower ; " but Jesus Christ is to them "as a root out of a dry ground." Lord, remove the veil! Shine into these hearts with power !—F.

Vers. 1—3.—*The best commendation.* It was an early custom in the Christian Church for teachers to carry with them "letters of commendation" when they passed from town to town. Of this custom we have an indication in Acts xviii. 27, "When Apollos was disposed to pass into Achaia [Corinth], the brethren [of Ephesus] wrote, exhorting the disciples to receive him." And the thirteenth canon of the Council of Chalcedon ordained that "clergymen coming to a city where they were unknown, should not be allowed to officiate without letters commendatory from their own bishop." It seems to have been made a charge against the apostle that he never presented any credentials, but assumed an authority for which he had no warrant. The apostle is here replying to such a charge, and his plea is that, having so manifestly received the greater commendation of God's witness with his work, he in no sense can need man's good word. His converts were the best possible commendation. His *letters* were those written by God as truth on human hearts. From the Christian standpoint the only satisfactory proof of call to ministry is the Divine seal set on the work of the ministry. It was the plea of St. Peter, when accounting for his admitting the Gentiles into the privileges of the Christian Church, that the " Holy Ghost had fallen upon them, even as upon us at the beginning." And that was felt to be an all-sufficient attestation of the work which St. Peter had done. In the same way St. Paul pleads that spiritual results had followed his ministry among the Corinthians. God had set his seal upon it, and that was his wholly satisfactory commendation, and the basis of any authority he claimed. Speaking in a figure he says, " The Corinthians are an *epistle.*" He regards Christ as the Author, and himself as the amanuensis. The characters of this epistle were preserved by no visible or perishable medium, but by the invisible operation of the Spirit. We consider—

I. THE USEFULNESS OF HUMAN COMMENDATIONS. Such are found to be necessary in the intercourse of nations. The ambassador is duly furnished with his credentials ; and the representative of the business firm carries with him his authority to act in the name of the firm. So it is found of practical value that clergymen and ministers going to other districts or countries should have such attestation as will win for them the confidence of those to whom they may happen to minister. Several questions of interest arise in connection with this subject. 1. From what central bodies, or from what individuals, should such letters of commendation come? 2. What should they properly concern? And can they ever wisely go beyond the attestation of personal character and ministerial efficiency? Men must be judged by their works rather than by the opinion which others may have formed concerning them. Still, in every age, Churches have needed to be guarded against plausible but unworthy men, who force themselves into positions of influence unawares. And this has been the special trouble of all smaller Churches, and those existing apart from Christian organizations. Every ordinary man should depend for his acceptance upon his letters of recommendation.

II. The limitation of the demand for such letters. Sometimes they are merely vexations. The demand for them is a mere piece of officialism. Some men so stand before the world that no letters about them can be necessary. And the letters may only concern (1) character, (2) efficiency. They should not deal with disputable opinions. A full and fair estimate of character is sufficient to give confidence that a man's work will be honest and faithful. Commendations of so-called "orthodoxy" or "heterodoxy" can never be anything but mischievous. We may commend the man; we had better take care not to commend his opinions. Of these let those to whom he ministers be the judges.

III. God's ways of making such letters wholly unnecessary. From the case of St. Paul we learn that God may so manifestly show his acceptance of a man and a man's work that no other credential can possibly be necessary. A man's labours and successes may sufficiently declare that he is a man of God, a messenger of God. Illustrate by such cases as Luther, Whitefield, Brainerd, etc. We must well apprehend that, because a thing is *unusual*, it is not therefore *untrue*. And in every age men have been raised up whose strongly marked individuality leads them to take fresh lines of thought and of work. Men may hesitate to give such men their credentials; it is enough if God manifestly accepts them.—R. T.

Vers. 4—6.—*The power, and the agency it uses.* The apostle here dwells upon the confidence he has in the Corinthian Church as the all-sufficient commendation of his ministry and apostleship. But he will take no honour to himself over his successes at Corinth. He had but been the agent, and the power and sufficiency were altogether of God. St. Paul was always before *men* firm, confident, bold; but always before *God* humble and dependent. The expression, "through Christ to God-ward," probably means "that our eyes are directed towards God, the Source of our confidence, and that it is through Jesus Christ alone that we possess the right thus to lean on him." Illustrate, from Old Testament Scriptures, the Jewish habit of mind which referred all events to God's direct working, confounding the cause with the agency. For instance, God is said to harden Pharaoh's heart, and to send a lying spirit among the prophets. Such direct reference of all things to God is characteristic of the imaginative, uncultured, superstitious ages; but, in intelligent form, it is found in Christianity. There is no confusion of power and agent, but behind agency the "power" is fully and humbly recognized. This we further unfold, noting the following points:—

I. In Christianity the man still works. God proposes to save the world by man. He does not use miracle, but deals with men as moral beings, subject to various moral influences arising from their relations one to another. Every man is a force upon his fellow-man. Some, by reason of particular positions and endowments, exert great influence on other men. It is at once true that man must be saved by man, and that man cannot be saved by man. The paradox is not a difficult one to explain from the Christian point of view. Christianity asks, therefore, from every man three things. 1. The consecration of his talents and trusts. 2. The sanctifying of his relationships. 3. And the faithful use of his opportunities. True of man in his ordinary life-spheres, this is more especially true of man as occupied in the Christian ministry.

II. In Christianity the man is only agent. He has no sort of independent authority. He is not fittingly likened to the plenipotentiary, who has a matter wholly committed to his judgment and decision. The Christian minister or worker is never

free of his close and intimate relations with God. His "sufficiency" is never of himself.
1. He works *for* another, and has no self-seeking ends to gain. 2. He works at the
will of another, holding himself ever in attitudes of dependent and submissive obedience, saying continually, "Lord, what wilt thou have me to do?" 3. He works in
the *strength* of another, leaning upon the "everlasting arms." Taking these as characteristic features of the Christian ministry, it will be readily shown in what a marked way
they contrast with the spirit of the self-depending and self-seeking worldly man.
III. IN CHRISTIANITY THE MAN IS ACTUALLY ENDUED WITH DIVINE POWER. "Our
sufficiency is of God." It is this truth that needs such distinct assertion for the sake
of the Christian worker himself, as well as for the sake of those to whom his work is a
witness. The Christian is a man quickened with a new life; it is that "new life"
which finds expression in his working. The Christian is a man sealed by the Holy
Ghost, who dwells in him, and that Holy Ghost is his secret strength and inspiration.
Two figures may be contrasted. The water flowing in pipes, and the sap flowing in the
branch. The latter is the only figure that efficiently represents the relation of power
and agency in the Christian worker, and it is the figure used by our Lord himself. The
union and relation are such that, while the full manhood is retained, and even nourished
into vigour, the vitality, the real force behind the manhood, and the direction of all
details of action, are God's. The Christian conceives of himself as not even able to
think anything as of himself, much less to do anything. He is "strong in the Lord,
and in the power of his might."—R. T.

Ver. 6.—*The letter and the spirit.* It does not appear that St. Paul had in mind
the different senses in which Scripture can now be read. Such distinctions as the
literal, the allegorical, and the mystical belong to modern times. The apostle is contrasting the Old Testament with the New. The older revelation consisted of exact
directions for the guidance of life and conduct. The new revelation consists of principles
and examples by the help and application of which a man may guide his own conduct.
But, while this distinction is carefully noted, it should be observed that, in the older revelation, there was both letter and spirit, and devout souls recognized and lived in the light
of the inner principles, the spiritual truth which precise injunctions did but illustrate.
F. W. Robertson says, "It was the business of Moses to teach maxims, and not principles; rules for ceremonial, and not a spirit of life. And these things—rules, cere-
monials, maxims, law—are what the apostle calls here the *letter*. Thus, for instance,
truth is a principle springing out of the inward life; but Moses only gave the rule:
'Thou shalt not forswear thyself.' It is impossible not to see how plainly inadequate
this rule is to all that truth requires; for he who scarcely avoided perjury may have
kept nevertheless to the letter of the Law! Again, love is a principle; but Moses said
simply, 'Thou shalt not kill, nor steal, nor injure.' Again, meekness and subduedness
before God,—these are of the Spirit; but Moses merely commanded fasts. It was in
consequence of the superiority of the teaching of principles over a mere teaching of
maxims that the ministry of the letter was considered as nothing." "The difference
between the old covenant and the new was that the former *prescribed*, the latter
inspired; the former gave written precepts, the latter the power to fulfil them; the
former laid down the rules, the latter brought man's heart into the condition in which
such rules became a part of his nature." In an educational point of view the letter
must come first, the child must have precise direction of his conduct, and only through
this will he be helped to grasp principles, and apply them himself to his conduct and
duties. So that we must not undervalue the letter, but give it a proper place as a
stepping-stone to higher and better things. The distinction between the letter and the
spirit may be illustrated in a variety of spheres.
I. IN THE EARLY MOSAIC RECORDS. The imaginative and the historical records of
the first ages. Perplexities and difficulties abound when we force literal meanings. The
first principles of morals and religion come to view when we read the spirit of them.
II. IN THE JUDAIC RELIGIOUS SYSTEM. That does seem to be a round of formal
injunctions, covering all the various family, social, and religious relations of the people,
and yet our Lord taught us, in his sermon on the mount, to find spiritual principles
within it. He showed that the spirit of hate underlay the sin of murder, and the
spirit of purity assured the maintenance of right marriage relations.

III. In the teachings of the prophets. It was almost the one essential thing in their work that they were to set free the spirit of the older revelation, which was in danger of being overcrushed by the letter of commandment and ceremonial rule. It may even be shown that, in the prophets, there was a tendency to undervalue the *letter*, in the earnestness of their effort to get a right value set on the *spirit* of obedience.

IV. In the life and gospel of the Lord Jesus. Illustrate by our Lord's parables, and by his teaching as in John vi. 63.

V. In the apostolic ministry. Especially illustrated in St. Paul's teachings respecting the relation of the Judaic and Christian systems, and equally illustrated in St. John's revelation of the inner and mystical meanings of the Christian truth and requirements. Conclude by showing how this distinction is still applicable to modern religious teaching. 1. The "letter" is needed. In some stages of religious experience and attainment precise directions are the best helps. 2. The mere "letter" may still be exaggerated, so as to become a mischievous bondage. 3. The true teacher uses the formal "letter" only to carry the "spirit." But the higher teaching of the very spirit of Christianity demands from the teacher a very marked and cultured spirituality, or spiritual insight.—R. T.

Vers. 7—11.—*The old covenant and the new.* In some sense it may be said that teachings respecting the relations between the older revelation in Judaism and the newer revelation in Christianity were special to the Apostle Paul. On this point he had direct revelations from Christ, and the liberal form which his teachings took exposed him to the peril of being misunderstood and misrepresented, and brought persecutions around him. No man could be found more truly loyal to the older revelation than the apostle of the Gentiles, but while he honoured it he saw clearly that it had its day and its mission. That day had now passed; that mission had been fulfilled. The older covenant had made open and plain the way for the new, and it was loyalty to the old for Paul to accept fully the new, in which it found its fulfilment, its completion, its glory; for the ministration of Jesus and the Spirit is but Judaism glorified, the gospel of the letter passed into the gospel of the spirit. Three contrasts are here dwelt upon. The old covenant and the new are conceived as—

I. A ministration of death and a ministration of life. St. Paul had said (ver. 6) that the "letter killeth." He meant that it crushed hope and effort, since no man could reach a perfect obedience. The old covenant condemned all who failed even in the least thing. It provided no *life*, no strength in which obedience could become possible. On the other hand, the new covenant provided a new life for the will and a new grace unto obedience. The old crushed down heart and hope, and made a man cry out, "I cannot." The new cheered him, lifted him up, and made him say, "I can, through him who strengtheneth me."

II. A ministration of condemnation and a ministration of righteousness. The old covenant said, "Thou shalt not," and it denounced its penalties on the offenders. The new covenant says, "Thou shalt," holds before us the model life of obedience lived by the Lord Jesus, and provides grace unto changing us into his image.

III. A ministration that was passing and a ministration that was permanent. (Ver. 11.) The older covenant was of necessity transitory. It had but a temporary and preparatory mission. The new is abiding, for there can be nothing higher than or beyond that spiritual righteousness which is its sublime aim to accomplish.—R. T.

Ver. 17.—*The liberty of the Spirit.* "The apostle assumes, almost as an axiom of the spiritual life, that the presence of the Spirit gives freedom, as contrasted with the bondage of the letter—freedom from slavish fear, freedom from the guilt and burden of sin, freedom from the tyranny of the Law." Distinguish carefully between liberty and licence. Whether a man can have and use liberty depends entirely upon what a man *is*. Some men are better in bonds; they must be in bonds; their fancied liberty is but a delusion. The point urged by the apostle is that the man who is renewed in Christ Jesus can be safely trusted with his full liberty, because he is established in principles, and upheld by a power which guarantees that he will put his liberty into reasonable and righteous limitations. We observe some of the reasons why "where the Spirit of the Lord is, there is liberty."

I. BECAUSE THERE IS LIFE. A new life, a Divine life. Life can always be allowed its free and natural expression. It is disease that must be set in limitations and bondages. The forces and expressions of *life* are evenly and harmoniously balanced; and order is preserved when life is permitted to be free. The expressions of the Christian life, the life of the Spirit, can only be true and beautiful and good.

II. BECAUSE THERE IS FREEDOM FROM BONDS. That is, from the bonds of formal rules. The Spirit establishes *principles*, and so frees us from *rules*. God's laws are written by the Spirit in our minds and on our hearts. Illustrate by the passing away of schoolboy commands and regulations when manhood has come and principles are established.

III. BECAUSE THERE IS KNOWLEDGE OF THE RIGHT. This the indwelling Spirit guarantees, because he takes of the things of Christ and reveals them unto us. He is our inward Monitor, our Teacher as well as our Comforter. Illustrate by the perplexity of life if we must control it by fashion and custom, deciding what we may eat and what we may not eat; what we may enjoy and what we may not enjoy; what is consistent and what is inconsistent. The Spirit shows the right; it is liberty to act on its great principle that we must everywhere be (1) true to God, and (2) helpful to our brethren.

IV. BECAUSE THERE IS DESIRE FOR THE RIGHT. He who is without the Spirit may "know the better but follow the worse." That is saying he is in bondages of self-will and evil which he cannot break. The indwelling Spirit controls the will and affections so that we desire what is right, and therefore are free to follow the *right* of which we may know.

V. BECAUSE THERE IS QUICK SENSITIVENESS TO THE WRONG. So that it is detected and its slavery resisted. The liberty of the Spirit is such that it cannot be taken at unawares. From these considerations plead for the importance of keeping our minds and hearts ever open to the Spirit's love and lead, as the secret of maintaining the only liberty that is worth calling such. For the liberty that is assured to man by the gospel, see John viii. 32; Rom. vi. 18, 22; viii. 2; Jas. i. 25; ii 12; 1 Pet. ii. 16. —R. T.

Ver. 18.—*The vision of God in Christianity.* This passage contains evident reference to an incident occurring in the life of Moses. He had tarried on the mount for forty days, in some mysterious manner within the immediate radiance of the Divine glory, holding some very near, yet very secret, fellowship with God. We might expect to find an influence from such converse resting on Moses' spirit ever after, and we could not wonder if some traces of it were left upon his very face. Such was the case. Unknown to himself, the skin of his face shone, and when the people of Israel saw it they were afraid to come near him. Partly to shadow the glory from them, and partly, as St. Paul tells us in this chapter, that they might not see the glory fade and die away, he covered himself with a veil. This glory on the face of Moses had two great lessons in it for the Jews and for us. 1. That the vision of God has a transforming power on human souls. 2. And that this glory of Moses was a symbol of the passing and preparatory character of the Old Testament dispensation. St. Paul's argumentative use of his reference to Moses may be thus traced. He is exalting his office as a minister of the new covenant. He argues that if a glory was shed upon the ministration of the Law, a Law written in letters and graven upon stones, much greater must be the glory which rests upon the ministration of the Spirit, which ministration is permanent. Being the minister of this more glorious covenant, St. Paul says he may speak and act with boldness, without disguise. He need not spread a veil over his face, as Moses did, in order that the sons of Israel might not see the end of that fading brightness. And this reminds him that, when he wrote, the minds of Israel were still blinded, a veil was on their hearts, so that they imagine the glory lies still on Moses and his system; they cannot see that the older covenant has done its work, that the Law has given place to love. When their hearts turn to the Lord Jesus, the veil is rent away; they have the vision of the Lord the Spirit; their bondage gives place to freedom. "We all, while with face unveiled we behold in a mirror the glory of the Lord, are ourselves transformed continually into the same likeness; and the glory which shines upon us is reflected by us, even as it proceeds from the Lord the Spirit." Two questions invite attention. 1. How is the vision of God granted to us? 2. What influence does the vision of God exert?

I. How is the vision of God granted to us? Man can never find rest for head or heart save in God. The deepest longing of every human soul is the vision of God. Idolatry is the expression of the desire to find and see God. Humanity in all ages is knit together as one man in this cry for God. Illustrate by references to Enoch, Abraham, Jacob, Moses, David, Job, Isaiah, Stephen, and the Apostle John, who says, " We know that, when he doth appear, we shall be like him; for we shall see him as he is." These, indeed, are all cases of *good* men, but the universal efforts to make a religion show that all men are alike in this, they would behold the glory of God. The vision is given us: 1. By the inner ministration of the Spirit. This is the meaning of the " open face, unveiled." St. Paul had just said, " We use great plainness of speech; " that is, in our ministry we can speak with freedom and boldness, without any disguise or veil, because we are ministers in the *power of the Spirit.* So, he would say, we all need no veil, we have openness, to behold the glory of the Lord in the leadings of the Spirit; for " where the spirit of the Lord is, there is [this] liberty; " veils are removed, hindrances are taken away, we can " behold as in a glass the glory of the Lord." 2. By the outward mirror of the Christ. " Beholding as in a glass." God's actual glory can be seen by no created eye; it must be reflected—it can only be seen as mirrored. We cannot look on the sun; we can see its image in a pool, we can find its reflected glory in the tinted flowers, and in the glorified clouds of the sunset. So our pained, strained, spiritual eyes rest delightfully upon the " Man Christ Jesus," who is the " Brightness of the Father's glory, and the express Image of the Father's person." The infinite excellences of the Divine character are exhibited in Christ in a form comprehensible by men. What the virtues and moral excellences of God are we could never know, but Christ shows them to us as if they were the graces and virtues of a man. Illustrate thus God's holiness, justice, mercy, and love.

II. What influences does this vision of God exert? " Changed into the same image." Moses could not see God and be the same man that he was. It changed his soul somewhat into the Divine likeness, even as his face lost its natural expression and shone with the glory. The sight of God is ever a transforming sight. It is seen to be so in the case of the transfiguration. The disciples saw our Lord's very raiment white and glistering, and glory all overspreading his frame. When a man sees God there is an inner change, of which that is the symbol. Illustrate by the way in which a close and trustful friendship makes the friends grow alike. As the Christian man maintains his daily relations with Christ the mirrored God, as he " dwells in the secret place of the Most High," he finds a transforming and transfiguring work is being carried on: the mind of God is coming to be his mind; the work of God is coming to be his work; the very life of God is coming to be his life. And this further result comes. They who are changing into the likeness of God are gradually reflecting the glory of God out upon men. They are becoming themselves, in turn, mirrors of God, glasses in which men may behold the glory of the Lord. We hardly know which is the more gracious and surprising—the change that is wrought in us by the constant communion of God and our souls, or the infinite condescension which permits us, in our earthly lives, to be light-bearers for God, mirrors to reflect the glory and attraction of his saving grace, so that men may be won to him. Conclude by showing (1) that the heart must be a veiled heart which resists the ministration of the Spirit; (2) that from such a veiled heart must ever be hidden the glory of the redeeming God.—R. T.

EXPOSITION.

CHAPTER IV.

The glory of the gospel ministry (vers. 1—6), which sustains the hearts of Christ's ministers among all weaknesses and trials (vers. 7—15), especially by the faith in things unseen (vers. 16—18).

Ver. 1.—**Therefore.** Because of the freedom and open vision of the gospel. **As we have received mercy.** Gratitude for a mercy so undeserved (1 Tim. i. 13) makes us fearless and vigorous in a ministry so glorious (Acts xx. 23, 24). **We faint not.** The word implies the maintenance of a holy courage (1 Cor. xvi. 13) and perseverance (2 Thess.

iii. 13). It occurs again in ver. 16, and in Luke xviii. 1; Gal. vi. 9; Eph. iii. 13.

Ver. 2.—**But have renounced**; rather, *but we renounced.* We renounced them once and for ever at our baptism. **The hidden things of dishonesty**; literally, *of shame;* meaning, of course, of all that causes shame. Disgraceful as may be calumnies of my Jewish opponents, I have said farewell for ever to everything for which a good man would blush. "Honest" was originally like the Greek word καλὸς, a general expression for moral excellence, as in Pope's line—

"An honest man's the noblest work of God."

Fletcher's—

"Man is his own star, and the soul that can Be honest is the only perfect man."

In craftiness. The word implies all subtle, cunning, underhand dealing (ch. xi. 3), and it is clear from ch. xii. 16 that St. Paul had been charged with such conduct. The word is both used and illustrated in Luke xx. 23. **Handling the word of God deceitfully.** He has already repudiated this charge by implication in ch. ii. 17, and he was always anxious to maintain an attitude of transparent sincerity (ch. i. 12) by uttering the truth and the whole truth (ch. ii. 17; Acts xx. 27), and not adulterating it. He had to meet such insinuations even in his first extant letter (1 Thess. ii. 3). **By manifestation of the truth.** The constant recurrence to this thought shows the apostle's anxiety to remove the suspicion, created by the attacks of his opponents, that he had an *esoteric* teaching for some (ch. i. 13), and kept some of his doctrines in the background. "The truth" cannot be preached by the aid of lies. The prominence of the word "manifest" in this Epistle is remarkable. St. Paul seems to be haunted by it (ch. ii. 16; iii. 3; iv. 10; v. 10, 11; vii. 12; xi. 6). **Commending ourselves.** This is the only form of self-commendation or of "commendatory letter" for which I care. There is evidently a reference to the same verb used in ch. iii. 1. **Before God** (see ch. ii. 17; vii. 12; Gal. i. 20). These solemn appeals are meant to show that it would be morally impossible for him to act as he was charged with acting. If he can assert his own integrity he will do so only as consciously in the presence of God.

Ver. 3.—**But if our gospel be hid.** This is added to avoid the semblance of a contradiction. He has spoken of "*manifestation* of the truth," and yet has spoken of all Jews as unable to see it because they will not remove from their hearts the veil which hides it from them. How can "a veiled gospel" be a "manifested truth"? The answer is that the gospel is bright, but the eyes that should gaze on it are wilfully closed. Similarly in ch. ii. 16, he has compared the gospel to a fragrance of life, yet to the doomed captives—"to the perishing" —it comes "like a waft from the charnelhouse." A better rendering would be, *But even if our gospel* (1 Cor. xv. 1; Rom. ii. 16) *is a veiled one, it is veiled only among the perishing* (comp. 1 Cor. i. 18). *Be hid;* rather, *has been veiled.* **To them that are lost**; rather, *to the perishing* (see note on ch. ii. 15).

Ver. 4.—**The god of this world**; rather, *the god of this age.* It is, as Bengel says, "a great and horrible description of the devil." He is not, however, here called a god of the kosmos, but only of the *olam hazzeh*, the present dispensation of things as it exists among those who refuse to enter that kingdom in which the power of Satan is brought to nought. The melancholy attempt to get rid of Manichean arguments by rendering the verse "in whom God blinded the thoughts of the unbelievers of this world" is set aside by the fact that the terrible description of Satan as "another god" (*El acheer*) was common among the rabbis. They knew that his power was indeed a derivative power, but still that it was permitted to be great (Eph. ii. 2; vi. 12). In John xii. 31 (xiv. 30) our Lord speaks of him as "the ruler of the kosmos." **Hath blinded**; rather, *blinded.* The verb here has no other meaning than "to blind," and is quite different from the verb "to harden," rendered by "to blind" in ch. iii. 14 with the same substantive. They are blind from lack of faith, and so being "unbelieving" they are "perishing" (Eph. v. 6), seeing that they "walk in darkness" (John viii. 12) and are in Satan's power (Acts xxvi. 18). "Blindness of heart," says St. Augustine, "is both a sin and a punishment of sin, and a cause of sin." **The light of the glorious gospel of Christ**; rather, *the illumination of the gospel of the glory of the Christ.* The word *photismos* in later ecclesiastical Greek was used for "baptism." **Who is the image of God** (ch. iii. 18; Col. i. 15; Heb. i. 3). **Should shine unto them**; or, as in the Revised Version, *should dawn upon them.* The other rendering, "that they should not *see* the illumination," gives to the verb *augazō*, a rarer sense, only found in poetry, and not known to the LXX.

Ver. 5.—**For we preach not ourselves.** There is no glory or illumination on *our* faces, and we have no personal ends to gain, nor are we "lords" over your faith. This is, perhaps, meant as an answer to some charge of egotism. **The Lord**; rather, *as Lord* (Phil. ii. 11; 1 Cor. xii. 3). **Your servants**; literally, *your slaves* (1 Cor. ix. 19). **For**

Jesus' sake. So Christ had himself desired (Matt. xx. 27).

Ver. 6.—**Who commanded the light to shine out of darkness.** The argument of the verse is that God, who created the material light (Gen. i. 3) and who is the Father of lights (Jas. i. 1) and sent his Son to be the Light of the world (John viii. 12), did not shine in our hearts for our sakes only, or that we might hide the light under a bushel for ourselves, but that we might transmit and reflect it. There is an implied comparison between the creation of light and the dawn of the gospel light, and each of these was meant for the good of all the world. The verse should be rendered, if we follow the best manuscripts, "Because it is God, who said, Light shall shine out of darkness, who shone in our hearts for the illumination of the knowledge of the glory of God." **In the face of Jesus Christ** (see ch. ii. 10; iii. 7). Probably, however, there is a reference to the glory of God, not as *reflected* from the face of Christ, but as concentrated in and beaming from it (Heb. i. 2).

Vers. 7—15.—*Glory of the ministry in the midst of its weakness and suffering.*

Ver. 7.—**In earthen vessels.** The glorious light which we have to show to the world is, like Gideon's torches, carried in earthen pitchers. The word *skēnos*, vessel, is used in Mark xi. 16, and "vessels of earthenware" in Rev. ii. 27. St. Paul, in Acts ix. 15, is called "a vessel of election," whence Dante calls him *lo vas d' elezione*. Man can never be more than an earthen vessel, being frail and humble, and the metaphor specially suits an apostle of Christ (see 1 Cor. ii. 3—5; 2 Tim. ii. 20). But when he takes the Word of life from the earthen pitcher and waves it in the air, it illuminates all on whom the light shines. No commentator seems to have seen the probable allusion to Gideon's pitchers. It is the "light," of which he has been speaking exclusively in the last verses, which constitutes the "treasure." Those who suppose that the "treasure" is gold or silver or something else of value, refer to Jer. xxxii. 14, and Herod., iii. 103; Pers., 'Sat.,' ii. 10. **The excellency**; literally, *the excess* or *abundance*. **Of God, and not of us**; rather, *of God, and not from us.*

Ver. 8.—**Troubled**; *afflicted*, as in ch. i. 4. **On every side**; *in everything*. **Distressed**; rather, *driven to straits*. **Perplexed, but not in despair.** In the original is a beautiful paronomasia, which might, perhaps, be represented in English by "pressed, but not oppressed." Literally the words mean, *being at a loss, but not utterly at a loss*. In the special anguish of trial of which he spoke in ch. i. 8 (comp. ch. vii. 5), he was indeed for a time "utterly at a loss," reduced to utter despair; but in the normal conditions which he here describes he always, as it were, saw *some* outlet out of his worst perplexities.

Ver. 9.—**Not forsaken.** St. Paul, like the author of the Epistle to the Hebrews, knew by blessed experience the truth of the promise, "I will never leave thee nor forsake thee" (Heb. xiii. 5, 6). **Cast down.** Flung to the ground, as in some lost battle; yet not doomed, not "perishing." "Though he fall, he shall not be utterly cast down, for the Lord upholdeth him with his hand" (Ps. xxxvii. 24).

Ver. 10.—**The dying of the Lord Jesus**; literally, *the putting to death* (Vulgate, *mortificatio*). This is even stronger than ch. i. 5. It is not only "the sufferings," but even "the dying," of Christ of which his true followers partake (Rom. viii. 36, "For thy sake are we killed all the day long"). St. Paul, who was "in deaths oft" (ch. xi. 23), was thus being made conformable unto Christ's death (Phil. iii. 10). Philo, too, compares life to "the daily carrying about of a corpse," and the Curè d'Ars used to speak of his body as "ce cadavre." **That the life also of Jesus**, etc. The thought is exactly the same as in 2 Tim. ii. 11, "If we be dead with him, we shall also live with him."

Ver. 11.—**For Jesus' sake.** St. Paul, as Bengel says, constantly thus repeats the name of Jesus, as one who felt its sweetness. The verse contains a reassertion and amplification of what he has just said. **In our mortal flesh.** This is added almost by way of climax. The life of Jesus is manifested, not only "in our *body*," but even by way of triumph in its lowest and poorest element. God manifests life in our dying, and death in our living (Alford).

Ver. 12.—**So then.** In accordance with what he has just said. **Death worketh in us, but life in you.** The life of us apostles is a constant death (Rom. viii. 36); but of this daily dying you reap the benefits; our dying is your living; our afflictions become to you a source of consolation and joy (ch. i. 6; Phil. ii. 17).

Ver. 13.—**We**; rather, *But we*. **The same spirit of faith.** The spirit manifested by the psalmist in the quotation which follows. It is from Ps. cxvi. 10, a psalm which corresponded with St. Paul's mood because it was written in trouble sustained by faith. And this faith inspires him with the conviction that, after "the body of this death," and after this death in life, there should begin for him also the life in death. St. Paul says nothing as to the authorship of the psalm, which probably belongs to a period far later than that of David. The words are from the LXX., and seem fairly to represent the disputed sense of the original.

Ver. 14.—Which raised up the Lord Jesus (see 1 Cor. vi. 14). **Shall raise up us also.** The thought is again expressed in Rom. viii. 11. As he is here alluding mainly to the resurrection from the dead, it is clear that he contemplated the *possibility* of dying before Christ's second coming (comp. 1 Thess. iv. 15). **By Jesus.** The reading supported by nearly all the best manuscripts is "*with* Jesus" (א, B, C, D, E, F, G), which perhaps appeared unsuitable to the copyists. But Christians'are "risen with Christ" here (Col. ii. 12; iii. 1); and in another sense also we rise *with* him, because the Church is "the body of Christ" (1 Cor. xv. 23). **Shall present us with you.** So St. Jude speaks of "God our Saviour" as able "to present us" before the presence of his glory (Jude 24, 25).

Ver. 15.—All things are for your sakes. St. Paul has already implied that his life is not his own (ch. i. 6; comp. 1 Cor. iii. 22, 23), and he recurs to the same thought in Col. i. 24, and repeats once again towards the close of his life: "I endure all things for the elect's sakes" (2 Tim. ii. 10). **Might . . . redound.** The verb *perisseuo* may mean either "I abound" or "I make to abound" as in ch. ix. 8 and Eph. i. 8. Here there is a similar thought to that expressed in ch. i. 11, and the best rendering is, *In order that the Divine favour, being multiplied through the greater number* (of those who share in it), *may make the thanksgiving* (which it excites) *abound to the honour of God.*

Vers. 16—18.—*The Christian minister is upheld by hope.*

Ver. 16.—Therefore. Knowing that our daily death is the pathway to eternal life (ver. 14). **We faint not** (see ver. 1). **Though;** rather, *even if.* **Our outward man.** Our life in its human and corporeal conditions. **The inward man.** Namely, our moral and spiritual being, that "new man which is renewed in knowledge after the image of him that created him" (Col. iii. 10). **Is renewed;** literally, *is being renewed;* i.e. by faith and hope. **Day by day.** The Greek phrase is not classical, but is a reminiscence of the Hebrew.

Ver. 17.—For our light affliction, which is but for a moment; literally, *for the immediate lightness of our affliction.* **Worketh for us.** Is bringing about for us, with all the immeasurable force of a natural and progressive law. **A far more exceeding and eternal weight of glory;** literally, *in excess unto excess.* For the phrase, "to excess"—characteristic, like other emotional expressions, of this group of Epistles—see ch. i. 8; Gal. i. 13. The word "eternal" is in antithesis to the "for a moment." The "weight" is suggested by the "lightness," and possibly also by the fact that in Hebrew the word for "glory" also means "weight." The general contrast is found also in Matt. v. 12; 1 Pet. v. 10; Heb. xii. 10; Rom. viii. 18. The frequent resemblances between this Epistle and that to the Romans are natural when we remember that they were written within a few months of each other.

Ver. 18.—While we look not at the things which are seen. The Greek suggests more of a reason, "Since we are not gazing at things visible" (see ch. v. 7). **Things which are not seen.** The negative is the *subjective* negative. It expresses not only the fact that now these things are not seen, but that it is their *nature* to be unseen by the bodily eyes. **Temporal.** That is, temporary, transitory, phantasmal, a passing world; for which reason we do not fix our gaze or our aim upon it. **But the things which are not seen** are eternal. The clause is important, as showing that eternity is not a mere extension of time, but a condition qualitatively different from time. The "things eternal" exist as much now as they will ever do. We are as much living in eternity now as we ever shall be. The only difference will be that we shall then see him who is now unseen, and realize the things which now are only visible to the eye of faith. This is one of the passages of St. Paul which finds a close parallel in Seneca ('Ep.,' 59). "*Invisibilia non decipiunt*" was, as Bishop Wordsworth tells us, the inscription put at the end of his garden arcade by Dr. Young, the poet.

HOMILETICS.

Vers. 1, 2.—*The character and work of a true minister of Christ.* "Therefore seeing we have this ministry," etc. These words present to us a true minister of Christ as he is in himself and in his labours, that is, his character and work.

I. HIS CHARACTER. It is here suggested that his character is marked by three things. 1. *Its strength.* "Therefore seeing we have this ministry, as we have received mercy, we faint not." Having in mercy such a gospel as this to preach, we are not disheartened. "We faint not;" on the contrary, we are courageous. The character of every minister of Christ should be marked by strength—strength of conviction, strength of principle. 2. *Its purity.* "But have renounced the hidden things of dishonesty," or rather, of "shame." Every element and form of sin is a thing of "shame," a thing which makes the conscience blush. Falsehood, inchastity, meanness, selfishness, dishonesty, are all things for shame and disgust. A true minister has renounced all these things, he is thoroughly cleansed of them. 3. *Its straightforwardness.* "Not walking in craftiness." No attribute of character is more common, at the same time more morally ignoble and anti-Christian, than artfulness or stratagem. Ministers of religion are frequently charged with this " craftiness," and the charge is, alas! too often true. The craft of priests is notorious. Now, a true minister is free from this; he is a man of frankness, candour, transparent honesty.

II. His work. How does he fulfil his mission? The answer is given here: 1. *Negatively.* "Not handling the Word of God deceitfully." It is thus handled when it is used to support a system, to advance a sect, to exhibit self, to gain a living and to win popularity. He is not a true minister who does this. 2. *Positively.* "By manifestation of the truth commending ourselves to every man's conscience in the sight of God." (1) He appeals to the conscience of humanity. "Every man's conscience." Elsewhere Paul calls conscience the " inner man ; " it is in truth the man of the man, his moral self. It is thus he addresses himself, not merely to the passion, or to the imagination, or to the intellect, but to that which underlies and permeates every spiritual faculty of man. (2) He appeals to the conscience of humanity through the truth. " By manifestation of the truth." What is the " truth "? " The Word of God." And that word, not as literature, but as life, the life of Christ. He is "*the* Truth." It is " truth as it is in Jesus," not in creeds or Churches that he addresses to the conscience. (3) He appeals to the consciences of humanity, through the truth under the felt inspection of Almighty God. " In the sight of God." The man who preaches the truth under a consciousness of the Divine eye will be free from (*a*) fear, (*b*) affectation, and from (*c*) dulness.

Vers. 3, 4.—*The condition of unregenerated men.* " But if our gospel be hid," etc. These words give an appalling view of ungodly men.

I. They are blind to the gospel. " If our gospel be hid [or, ' veiled ']." Men have different organs of vision. There is the *bodily* eye : the gospel is not " hid " from that —they can see the volume that contains it, they can see the print, and perhaps read its chapters. There is the *intellectual* eye to discover its sense and discern its meaning. There is the *spiritual* eye, the conscience which discerns the moral significance of things ; this is the eye which alone can see the gospel, its real essence. And this is the veiled eye, the eye of conscience is closed, so that the gospel is no more discerned than the bright heavens are observed by the man who is born blind.

II. They are perishing in sin. " It is hid to them that are lost," or veiled from them that are perishing. Soul-ruin is a *gradual* process. Souls are neither ruined nor saved at once. The wicked are "*going* into everlasting punishment;" they are not hurled there at once; step by step they proceed. With every sin their sensibility of conscience is perishing, their power of will is perishing, all the better tendencies of their nature are perishing. It matters not how strong in body, how prosperous in wealth, how elevated in society, they are perishing. Startlingly solemn this!

III. They are victimized by Satan. " In whom the god of this world hath blinded the minds of them which believe not." Observe : 1. Satan is not a principle, but a personality. 2. Satan has immense dominions. " The god of this world." Satan is a personality that has access to human souls. He enters men, acts on their springs of thought and fountains of feeling. 3. Satan is a personality whose action on the soul is essentially pernicious. " The god of this world hath blinded the minds of them which believe not." He closes the moral eye of the soul, "lest the light of the glorious gospel of Christ, who is the Image of God, should shine unto them."

Ver. 5.—*Preaching.* " For we preach not ourselves," etc. Here is—
I. A sad possibility in preaching. What is that? To " preach ourselves." To preach ourselves is to propound our own notions, to exhibit our own talents, genius, and learning, to parade our own productions. It is to put self, not Christ, in the front. In these days the egotism of the pulpit has become all but intolerable.
II. A glorious theme for preaching. " Christ Jesus the Lord." 1. Preach him

as the Mediator between God and man. He whose grand mission it is to reconcile man to his Maker. 2. Preach him as the great Example for man's imitation. He who embodies the ideal of human perfection and blessedness.

III. The RIGHT SERVICE in preaching. "Ourselves your servants for Jesus' sake." The true preacher is : 1. The servant of souls. 2. The servant of souls inspired by love for Christ. "Servants for Jesus' sake."

Ver. 6.—*True soul-light.* "For God, who commanded the light to shine out of darkness, hath shined in our hearts, to give the light of the knowledge of the glory of God in the face of Jesus Christ." There are two lights in the soul. There is the *light of nature.* This light consists of those moral intuitions which Heaven implanted within us at first. These intuitions are good enough for angels, did for Adam before he fell; but now, through sin, they are so blunt and dim that the soul is in moral darkness : "The light that is in thee is darkness." The other light is that of the *light of the gospel.* This comes because the light of nature is all but gone out, and comes as essential to our spiritual well-being. This is the light to which the passage refers, the new soul-light. The words call attention to three facts concerning it.

I. IT EMANATES FROM THE HIGHEST SOURCE. "God, who commanded the light to shine out of darkness, hath shined in our hearts." The reference is here to the creation (Gen. i. 3). It reminds us : 1. Of *antecedent darkness.* The state of the soul before this light enters it is analogous to the state of the earth before God kindled the lights of the firmament. It was cold, chaotic, dead. In what a sad condition is the unregenerate soul ! 2. Of *almighty sovereignty.* "Let there be light"—"Let light be, and light was." The luminaries of the firmament were kindled by the free, uncontrolled, almighty power of God. So it is with real spiritual light. It comes because God wills it. Everywhere he " worketh according to the counsel of his own will."

II. IT REVEALS THE GRANDEST SUBJECT. Light is a revealer. All the hues and forms, beauties and sublimities of the earth would be hid from us without the light. What does this soul-light reveal? "The light of the knowledge of the glory of God." Gospel light entering the soul makes God visible as the eternal Reality, the Fountain of being, and the Source of all blessedness. Where this gospel light is not, the soul either ignores or denies him; or, at most, speculates about him, and at best has now and then flitting visions. But under the radiance of the gospel, God is the *Reality* of all realities, the *Fountain* of all existences, the *Root* of all the sciences. In this light they see God, and through him they see and interpret his universe.

III. IT STREAMS THROUGH THE SUBLIMEST MEDIUM. "In the face of Jesus Christ." There is undoubted allusion here to what is said of Moses (ch. iii. 13) when the Divine glory was reflected on his face, and produced such a splendour and magnificence that the children of Israel could not steadfastly look upon it. The sense here is that, in the face or the person of Jesus Christ, the glory of God shone clearly, and the Divinity appeared without a veil. This light coming through Christ, "who is the image of the invisible God," is : 1. *True* light. He is the Truth. 2. *Softened* light. The soul could not stand the light coming directly from the infinite Source; it is too dazzling. Through the medium of Christ it comes so softened as to suit our weakness. 3. *Quickening* light. It falls on the soul like the sunbeam on the seed quickening into life.

Ver. 7.—*The true gospel ministry.* "But we have this treasure," etc. The words lead us to consider the true gospel ministry in various aspects.

I. As CONTAINING AN INESTIMABLE TREASURE. The gospel is a system of incalculable worth. The most valuable things in nature are employed to represent it— water, light, life, etc. There are four criteria that determine the worth of a thing— *rarity, utility, duration,* the *appreciation of the highest authorities.* All these applied to the gospel demonstrate its surpassing value.

II. As THE SERVICE OF FRAGILE MEN. "In earthen vessels." To whom have the inestimable truths of the gospel been entrusted for exposition, enforcement, and distribution ? Not to angels, but to frail and dying men. 1. They have frail *bodies.* They are subject to infirmity, exhaustion, decay, etc. 2. They have frail *minds.* The most vigorous in intellect is weak, the most lofty in genius is feeble, the most enlightened is ignorant.

III. As DEVELOPING A DIVINE PURPOSE. "That the excellency of the power may be of God, and not of us." The grand reason why frail men are employed to preach the gospel is that the glorious renovating and soul-saving effects may evidently appear as the work of God, and not of man. When sermons prove effective in converting souls, it is not because of the originality of their thought, the force of their logic, the splendour of their rhetoric, or the majesty of their eloquence, but because of the Divine power that accompanies them. " Not by might, nor by power," etc.[1]

Vers. 8—12.—*Trials in the cause of Christ.* " We are troubled on every side," etc. Three remarks are suggested.

I. That THE TRIALS ENCOUNTERED IN THE CAUSE OF CHRIST ARE SOMETIMES VERY GREAT. Hear what Paul says about his trials: " We are troubled on every side." He speaks of himself as hemmed in by enemies, pursued by enemies, stricken down by enemies, and dragging about with him, as it were, a living corpse. It may be laid down as a principle, that the man who is earnestly engaged in any righteous cause in this world will have to encounter trials. The old prophets had their trials, some of them were insulted, some incarcerated, some martyred. So with John the Baptist, and so with the apostles, so with the confessors, reformers, and genuine revivalists.

II. That, HOWEVER GREAT THE TRIALS ENCOUNTERED, THEY ARE NOT BEYOND BEARING. The apostle says that although " troubled on every side, yet not distressed," or straitened; though " perplexed," or bewildered, yet not benighted; though "persecuted," or pursued, yet not " forsaken," or abandoned; though " cast down," or stricken down with a blow, yet not perishing. The idea is that he had support under his trials; they did not entirely crush him. The true labourer in the cause of Christ, however great his trials, is always supported : 1. By the *approbation of his own conscience.* 2. By the *encouraging results of his own labours.* 3. By the *sustaining strength of God.* " As thy days, so thy strength shall be."

III. That THE RIGHT BEARING OF THESE TRIALS SUBSERVES THE GOOD OF SOULS. 1. In the right bearing of these sufferings the sufferer reveals the life of Christ to others. " Always bearing about in the body the dying of the Lord Jesus." Rightly endured sufferings bring the sufferer so near to the sufferings of Christ that he is in a sense a sharer of those sufferings, and hence in them the life of Jesus is made manifest. Who that has witnessed the true Christian languishing on the bed of suffering and death has not seen the spirit of the life of Christ revealed? 2. In the right bearing of these sufferings the sufferer promotes in himself and others the Christian life. " For we which live are always delivered unto death for Jesus' sake, that the life also of Jesus might be made manifest in our mortal flesh. So then death worketh in us, but life in you." " God," says Dean Alford, "exhibits death in the living, that he may also exhibit life in the dying."

Ver. 13.—*The speech of true faith.* " We having the same spirit of faith," etc. The world is full of speech. Human words load the atmosphere. All the speeches may be divided into three classes. 1. Speech *without* faith. Vapid and volatile talk. 2. Speech with *wrong* faith. Wrong faith is of two descriptions. (1) Faith in wrong subjects. Men believe errors. (2) Improper faith in right subjects. Weak wavering, etc. 3. Speech with *true* faith. Take the true faith as faith in Christ. In him, not in *propositions concerning him,* propositions either including doctrines or facts. I offer three remarks concerning the speech of this faith.

I. IT IS INEVITABLE. The man who truly believes in Christ feels that "necessity is laid upon him," that he " cannot but speak the things seen and heard." Such is the influence of faith on man's social sympathies that his emotions become irrepressible.

II. IT IS RATIONAL. How much speech there is in connection even with the religion of Christ that clashes with the dictates of human reason, and is an insult to common sense! But he who really has faith in Christ can give reasons for his convictions in language clear as the day. It is the lack of true faith that makes our sermons hazy.

III. IT IS STRONG. True faith in Christ is the strongest of all convictions, and a strong conviction will always have a strong utterance. The words will be free and full.

Vers. 14, 15.—*Soul-inspiring facts.* "Knowing that he which raised up the Lord Jesus," etc. There are four glorious facts here.

I. That Christ was raised from the dead. "Knowing that he which raised up the Lord Jesus." "No fact in history," says Dr. Arnold, "is more firmly established by argument than this."

II. That the genuine disciples of Christ will also be raised. "Shall raise up us also by [with] Jesus, and shall present us with you." Raised as he was raised, and all be presented together.

III. That all things are for good to the good. "All things are for your sakes." "We know that all things shall work together for good," etc. "All things are yours."

IV. That all things in life should result in the true worship of God. "That the abundant grace might through the thanksgiving of many redound to the glory of God." It is only in worship that the soul can find the free and harmonious development of all its spiritual powers. Worship is heaven. It is not the means to an end; it is the sublimest end of being.

Ver. 16.—*Soul-growth.* "For which cause we faint not," etc. Observe at the outset: 1. Man has a duality of nature—the *outward* and the *inward*; the latter the man of the man. 2. The decayableness of one of the natures. "Our outward man perisheth." This is constantly going on. 3. The constant growth of the inner nature. "The inward man is renewed day by day." Soul-growth implies three things.

I. Soul-life. Dead plants and dead animals can no more grow than stones. The inner man unrenewed is morally dead; its life consists in *supreme sympathy with the supremely good.*

II. Soul-nourishment. No life can live upon itself. The appropriation of outward elements is essential to sustentation and growth. Moral and spiritual truths are the nutriment of souls.

III. Soul-exercise. All life seems to require exercise. Even the productions of the vegetable world cannot grow without it; though they cannot move themselves, they are moved by the breezes of heaven. Animal life requires it, and the soul must have it in order to grow. It must "exercise itself unto godliness." "They that wait upon the Lord shall renew their strength."

Vers. 17, 18.—*The afflictions of Christly men.* "For our light affliction, which is but for a moment, worketh for us a far more exceeding and eternal weight of glory; while we look not at the things which are seen, but at the things which are not seen: for the things which are seen are temporal; but the things which are not seen are eternal." These words suggest a few thoughts concerning the afflictions of Christly men.

I. They are comparatively "light" and "momentary." They are "*light:*" 1. Compared with what they deserve. 2. Compared with what others have endured. 3. Compared with the blessedness that is to follow. They are *momentary*, "but for a moment." Momentary compared (1) with the enjoyments of this life; compared (2) with the interminable blessedness of the future.

II. That, though light and momentary, they work out glorious results. They issue in what? "A far more exceeding and eternal weight of glory." What is the affliction to the glory? 1. The one is "light;" the other is weighty. Put all the afflictions of the whole Church against the everlasting glory of one Christly soul, and how light! 2. The one is momentary; the other is eternal. "Eternal weight of glory." But the result is not only an eternal weight of glory, but "far more exceeding." No expression could be stronger than this. The apostle here seems to struggle after the strongest language to express his idea of the transcendent blessedness that awaits the Christly man.

III. That they work out these glorious results by the realization of spiritual and eternal realities. "While we look not at the things which are seen . . . for the things which are seen are temporal." Observe: 1. That there are things *invisible to the bodily eye that can be seen by the soul.* There are two classes of invisible things: (1) those that are *essentially* invisible, such as thoughts, spirits, God; and (2) those that are *contingently* invisible, such as those things that are visible in their nature, but, through minuteness, distance, or some other cause, are at present invisible. It is to the first of these that the apostle refers—things that are essentially invisible to the bodily eye. The soul can see thoughts, moral intelligences, and the great God. 2. That the things that can be seen only by the soul *are not temporal, but eternal.* We talk about the everlasting mountains, eternal sun, etc.; but there is nothing that is seen is lasting—all is passing away. Moral truths are imperishable; spiritual existences are immortal; God is eternal; these are things belonging to a kingdom that cannot be moved. 3. That the things that are seen only by the soul are the things that, if realized, will *make this mortal life issue in transcendent good.*

HOMILIES BY VARIOUS AUTHORS.

Vers. 1—6.—*Glory of the apostolic ministry; how its duties were discharged.* It is still "this ministry." The question, "Who is sufficient for these things?" has been answered in part by a statement of his "sincerity" and "plainness of speech," and he now proceeds to speak of his courage and steady zeal. "We faint not," allowing no difficulties or dangers to dishearten us. But what was the nature or spirit of this resolute energy? Energetic men, brave men, who are bent on their purpose, are not always choice or chary of the means employed to gain their ends. "Hidden things of dishonesty," plots, schemes concocted in secret, were renounced, nor did he in any way adulterate the gospel. Not only did he preach the Word, but he delivered it as received from the Lord Jesus. The mirror was kept clean and bright, so as to reflect the image. Of course, he contrasted himself with his opponents, who used intrigues to acquire influence. If certain men handled the Word of God deceitfully, he was not one of that number, for his single aim was; "by manifestation of the truth," to commend himself "to every man's conscience in the sight of God." Divine truth, such as the gospel contained, was a manifestation, a showing of its real and intrinsic character, to the only faculty competent to receive it as a self-evidencing system; and that faculty was the conscience. Reason lies back of all our reasoning, and is greater and truer than our formal logic. Instinct antedates experience, and is the condition precedent to experience. And these instincts with their intuitions constitute their own evidence and form the basis of all knowledge. St. Paul argued that the spiritual doctrines of the gospel, if faithfully presented to the conscience, would be recognized and accepted by conscience as the truth of God. History is history; testimony is testimony; judgment is judgment; conscience is conscience; and he will not disparage any one of these to exalt another, but will keep each in its place according to the constitution of our nature. Yet the human mind, made in God's image, must be master of its impressions, sovereign over its motives, lord of itself when most obedient to God; and, accordingly, it must have a conscience to witness "magisterially," as Bishop Butler puts it, for the authority of God. It was not to worldly taste and selfish intellect St. Paul appealed in preaching the gospel, nor to low and mercenary feelings of any kind, but to the conscience as the supreme sense of right in man. And was this all? Nay; they commended themselves, their persons, their private and public lives, their experience and conduct, to the consciences of others. Witness what we are, what we do, how we live, as well as what we preach, was St. Paul's argument. No man enjoyed true appreciation and love more than he; but, most of all, he sought the testimony of their conscience that he was their servant for Christ's sake, and was in no respect crafty and dishonest in his relations to the brethren. Private character and public character are, alas! too often disjoined, and not seldom are opposites; but St. Paul thought that gifts and graces should go together. What he professed as an apostle he would practise as a man, and in each respect he would commend himself to conscience. On no account would he have the confidence and regard of the Church except so far as he impressed this purest and safest kind of human judgment. And he did this most solemnly, "in the sight of God." Observe, then, it was not to their consciousness but conscience, to which his ministry, character, and life appealed. Nor was this limited to the Church. It was exhibited before all, believers and unbelievers, a savour of life, a savour of death. The manifestation of the truth would commend itself to *every* man's conscience; and yet the general verdict of conscience would be accepted and acted on by some, while it would be opposed and disobeyed by many. But who were the rejecters? "If our gospel be hid, it is hid to them that are lost" (who are now perishing), not finally lost, but at present unsaved, their day of grace not over, salvation yet possible. The state spoken of is one of mental blindness, which includes the want of spiritual perceptions and the darkness of the understanding. Conscience is instructed, but the intellect overpowers conscience. Conscience is on the side of truth; intellect on the side of the senses. Conscience entreats, warns, condemns, in the name of God; intellect is sophistical and imperious in behalf of the carnal man. And the intellect is thus alienated from its rational subordination to a ruling conscience by a usurper who is Satan, "the god of this world." Men have allowed him to assert sovereignty over them, have made him "a god," and have yielded to his wicked agency what belongs to the one God. They have robbed God to give him power over their bodies and souls. Without this clear and vivid recognition of the personality, the activity, the prodigious energy of Satan, the theology of St. Paul would have no consistency, no logical coherence, no adaptiveness to the convicting and renewing work with which he associates it. With him, human depravity is not an abstract thing, an isolated thing, but part and parcel of a vast system of evil, an immense empire of untruth, deception, fraud, cruelty, of which Satan is head and front. Is unbelief powerful? Satan is behind it. Are the lusts and appetites of the flesh tyrannic? Satan is the tyrant. Are men blinded to their interest and well-being? By him, "god of this world," are they blinded. One who estimates human depravity solely by what it is in itself will have a very different view of its actual character in experience and outworking from one who looks at it as an instrumentality in such hands as Satan's. In the former case it is the man indulging in depravity for his own gratification—he personally and individually and directly is its motive, impulse, and end; in the latter there is a kingdom and a despotic ruler, whose objects are furthered by widening his dominion and enhancing his sway. St. Paul is explicit. Satan is the blinder, and he is the blinder as "the god of this world." And he blinds the minds of men, "lest the light of the glorious gospel of Christ, who is the Image of God, should shine unto them." Turn to the close of the previous chapter and read of the "open face," of the reflected "glory of the Lord," of the assimilating power of the "image," of its transforming wonder in changing "from glory to glory." And now take this awful contrast—a fallen angel, a dethroned principality and power, the "god" among his hierarchies, the "god" of a world where men are on probation for an immortality of good or evil, and this "god" of darkness busy everywhere to hide the only light that reveals Christ as the Image of God. Here is this light in the history of Christ's life, death, resurrection, exaltation. It is glorious. It is preached as a "glorious gospel;" it is preached by men who have "renounced the hidden things of dishonesty," and who themselves, by their candour, integrity, purity, commend themselves to every man's conscience under the eye of God. But Satan exerts all his skill and influence, controls myriad agencies, works continually and works so successfully that the minds of many are blinded by unbelief. Destroy belief and you destroy the soul. And this is the Satanic might of evil, the climax of all his influence, that the blindness with which he shrouds the soul is the blindness of unbelief. Can he think of "the glorious gospel of Christ" and not be humbled? "We preach not ourselves, but Christ Jesus the Lord; and ourselves your servants for Jesus' sake." And now the idea which has occupied so much of his attention—the veiled face of Moses, the open vision of Christ, the image of the Father in him, the glory that excelleth, the ministry as a manifestation of glory, Christian growth as an expansion from one degree of resplendency to another till it reaches "the perfect day," and the contrasted blindness of unbelievers who are under Satan's power,—this idea, so suggestive, attains its final expression in the sixth verse. God had once said, "Let there be light, and there was light." It was the opening grandeur of creation; but was this all? This was to be the permanent symbol of God, the source and centre of more associations and suggestions than any other object in the material universe, a creative force to the imagination of metaphor, image, and illustration that cannot be measured. And, as such, St. Paul uses it when he says that "God, who commanded the light to shine out of darkness, hath shined in our hearts." What fuller embodiment could the thought take than "the light of the knowledge of the glory of God in the face of Jesus Christ"?

"Light," "knowledge," "glory of God," "face of Jesus Christ,"—what a collocation of sublime ideas!—L.

Vers. 7—18.—*Ministers in their weakness and strength; present affliction and future issues.* There is the ever-recurring contrast. It is now the ministry as a "treasure," and this treasure is "in earthen vessels." We understand the apostle to refer to the body when speaking of the "clay vessel," the contrasted elements being the glory of the ministry as a Divine illumination and the fragile human form in which it was contained. It was thus that "the excellency of the power" was seen to be "of God, and not of us." Not only was it the power of God, but of "exceeding greatness" (Kling), and while the "surpassing might" demonstrated itself in the gracious and widespread effects of the ministry, it was also obvious in the physical support given in the midst of such unprecedented labours and trials. To illustrate this "surpassing might" (Conybeare and Howson), St. Paul adduces his own experience. As it respects the "earthen vessel:" 1. Troubled on every side. 2. Perplexed. 3. Persecuted. 4. Cast down. 5. Always dying; bearing about in the body the dying of the Lord Jesus. As it respects the "excellency of the power:" 1. Not distressed. 2. Not in despair. 3. Not forsaken. 4. Not destroyed. 5. Life of Jesus made manifest in our mortal body. These ideas of suffering are taken from the body. 1. Pressed or hemmed in on every side. 2. Benighted on our path. 3. Pursued in a conflict. 4. Thrown down and expecting to be killed. 5. The dying of the Lord Jesus never absent as a bodily impression. This is the second of those vivid pictures St. Paul has given of his personal life, the first being found in 1 Cor. iv. 9—13. There is a marked difference between the two representations, the former referring to the contrast between himself and the self-sufficient Corinthians, while the latter sets forth the contrast between "the glorious gospel" and the weakness of its ministration by means of men. Here the prominence is given to the similarity of his own life to that of Christ, "that the life also of Jesus might be made manifest in our mortal flesh." Had he spoken in the previous Epistle of self-denials and voluntary sufferings over and above "other apostles," going on a warfare "at his own charges," planting a vineyard and eating not "of the fruit thereof," a shepherd who "eateth not of the milk of the flock"? No such allusions (except in the reference made in the twelfth verse) are found in this chapter. Before him, in full view, is the career of Jesus of Nazareth, his resignation of the comforts of earth, the homelessness and other privations he endured, and he, the apostle of the Gentiles, is conformed in outward or physical aspects to the sufferings of Christ. Still more, the life of Christ's resurrection and exalted glory appears in him, and this life, so manifested in "our mortal flesh" and the more signally exhibited because of infirmities and afflictions, is for their benefit. "Death worketh in us, but life in you." But is death a shadow, a discouragement, a paralyzing terror? Nay; the life imparted to the Corinthians through him returned from them to his own soul. He believed and spoke; they heard and believed. Furthermore, he had another consolation, the hope of a resurrection, when he and they should be presented by Christ to the Father for final acceptance. Yes; the fellowship would be immortal as well as glorious. "All things are for your sakes," whatever had befallen him, and this "abundant grace," extended to an ever-enlarging number, would swell the volume of thanksgiving to God. In his mind "the glory of God" is never associated with narrow bounds, never with a few, always with the "many"—"through the thanksgiving of many redound to the glory of God." This is his manhood; largeness in everything; breadth of thought and sentiment for this world and the future! a manhood that could breathe in nothing smaller than a universe. How much he is worth to us in this particular! On this account "we faint not." Nothing had power to dishearten his spirit or depress his efforts. The burden rallied the strength; the heavier the weight the more energetic the resistance. Another contrast—*outward* man, *inward* man : man in each. St. Paul, who is the theologian of the Bible on the subject of the body no less than of the soul, is here in one of his favourite moods, and, as usual, his philosophy (if we choose so to regard his discernment) is as profound as his piety. "Though our outward man perish." It cannot but perish. "Dust thou art, and unto dust shalt thou return." The body exists for no independent purpose, it is for the soul, and the ideal of the soul determines the ideal of the body's history. It eats, sleeps, works, for the soul. It decays for the sake of the soul. Now, this decay which the apostle is considering, we may look at in the light of modern physiology.   St. Paul is no teacher of physiology or of science in any form, but he mentions facts, which we can interpret by aid of recent science.   What, then, do we know of decay as a bodily law?   We know it is a law co-existent and co-operative with our physical life.   It sets in early, goes on continuously, and ends only when the body dies.   It is *a succession of decays.* Viewed in this light, decay is a function of activity or a sequel to activity, and, accordingly, *a condition of renewal.*   Exercise the arm like a blacksmith, and it rapidly wastes matter.   Exercise the brain as a student, and certain constituents are constantly thrown off and expelled from the system.   Yet, in all this, there is reproduction and even growth.   *The decay has an order ;* it proceeds from the less serviceable to the more useful functions.   Early in life, animal sensations are in excess.   The outer world floods the young senses, and no image is painted on the brain that is not a copy of something external.   But this abates.   It lessens by providential law.   The spirits decline in boisterousness ; perceptions are not so vivid ; reflectiveness increases ; and the pulse is more of a pulse of thought, will, emotion.   What we can spare best is the first to decay.   Long before eye and ear show signs of failing other organs begin to advertise their decline.   And hence the decay proceeds as to time and method in such a form *as to answer the ends of the body in its relation to the soul.*   Seldom are there violent changes.   No great revolutions occur.   Little by little the alterations go on, so that the mind is insensibly accommodated to them.   Agreeably to this law, decay contributes till late in life to the development of the mind.   Not until decay has accomplished higher ends does it tend towards dissolution.   Gently, indeed, the hand of the Father touches the frail tenement, here a nerve and there a muscle, so as to make it less a body for the earth and more a body for the soul.   *Physiologically,* therefore, there is a basis for St. Paul's *theology of the body.*   Now, physiologists may say, as some of them have said, that their science has nothing to do with religion, and, forsooth, this in one sense may be true.   But it is certain that Christianity has a good deal to do with their science. Nor, indeed, have we to look further than the text for proof of the fact that, while St. Paul was doing nothing more than unfolding the glory of the gospel, one or more of the rays of that splendour shone on facts which science is only just now beginning to understand.   But the inner man, what of him ?   *"Renewed day by day."*   We have seen that Providence uses decay for restoration and even enhancement of power, and moreover, not until physical development has attained its *maximum* in respect to mind, does it happen that decay operates towards dissolution.   Outward and inward—both the man, as we have said—and yet the differencing adjectives are very expressive.   Look at the outside of a tree, the rough bark adapted to the hard usages of wind and weather, and fitted to enclose and protect the fibre and circulating sap.   So of the body.   It is a sheath to the soul, preserving its freedom from being overpowered by the outward world and guaranteeing self-direction to its activity.   More than this, body is a developing instrumentality of mind, and, in this respect, fulfils the special purpose of Providence. Nevertheless, the soul has its own prerogatives.   It is God's image, and, as such, witnesses to its own nature as infinitely different from matter.   We call it *soul* because it is perfectly unlike body.   We call it *spirit* because "God is a Spirit."   Such words as *body, soul, spirit,* stand alone and contain the truth of all truths.   Now, the apostle urges this contrast ; body decays and dies, spirit under the influence of the Holy Ghost is renewed daily.   Spirit has a capacity for interminable growth.   *Day by day,* a clearer knowledge of itself, a keener penetration of consciousness, a deeper sense of sinfulness in its nature, and, anomalously enough, while gaining a victory more and more over particular sins, having an acuter conviction of inbred sin.   *Day by day,* the world falling away from its senses, and yet, amid the decay of sensuousness, a continual ascension of delight and gladness as the spirit loses its hold on merely æsthetic beauty and enters more fully into moral beauty, so that, while the body becomes more and more the "temple of the Holy Ghost," the earth grows into a sanctuary of God, where the hours fail not to observe their ritual of worship and the air is never so hushed as not to breathe praise to God.   *Day by day ?*   Ah! are there not idle days, apparently useless days, even days when prayer and holy service seem a burden ?   Doubtless ; but we must not conclude that these seasons are altogether unprofitable.   If we are learning nothing else, we are learning how weak and impotent we are, and how unreliable are our constitution and habits except we have daily renewing grace.   God leaves us to ourselves sometimes, that we may find out what company we keep when he is absent. *Day by day*, the most precious of all is a growing nearness to the Lord Jesus Christ. We can recall the time when he was mainly to our young souls a traditional Christ. We knew him by the hearing of the ear and by the sight of the eye. Voices there were that spoke of him and commanded our listening. Faces there were that shone with unearthly light and touched our eyes to a reverent gaze. They are gone now. Sorrow has done its work, and, if that be done, all other work is made effective for spiritual progress. How real he becomes when we suffer as Christians! In the loneliness that comes with all profound grief, what a personal Christ is he to our hearts! Hearts, we say, for the revelations of sorrow, the fullest and grandest ever made to the soul, are all revelations of the blessed Jesus to the affections. Once we could not have thought it possible, but, in later years, the secret of the Lord is with us, and we commune with him as friend with friend. The wonder now is, how we could ever live an hour without this sense of sonship possessing the soul. "Out of the depths" we have learned to say, "Abba, Father," and then we can rejoice with "joy unspeakable and full of glory." The outward man perishing, the inward man renewed day by day, how would such a man as St. Paul look upon trial and adversity? We know more of the nature, variety, and depth of his sufferings than of any one among the saints of the New Testament, and yet he calls his *affliction light*. It is also "but for a moment." Why he spoke in this way is made clear at once, for the light and momentary affliction is working for his benefit, fulfilling a purpose, executing a design, and this is a "far more exceeding and eternal weight of glory." These words are best left to private meditation. "Glory" in contrast with "affliction," "weight" with "light," "eternal" with "moment," and then the "exceeding," the "more exceeding," the "far more exceeding;" we honour the sublimity most by thoughtful silence. And this working, which is now going on by means of Christ's presence in affliction and derives no merit from him, is so far realized by the apostle that he cannot look upon the things about him other than as transient. It is not the mere decay of the outward man nor the evanescence of the world's glory that produces in him this exalted state of mind. The point of view is altogether different. From the height of spiritual life as essentially eternal life, he glances at the panorama of the world as it passes by, but his look—the fixed eye, the earnest gaze—is on the things which are eternal. For him this eternity has already begun; and while every new grief and every repetition of an old sorrow "worketh" a deeper feeling of the spiritual and eternal life within, he is equally well assured that each one adds something to the accumulated glory of the heaven awaiting him as an apostle of the Lord Jesus.—L.

Ver. 2.—*Truth and conscience.* In these comprehensive words of the apostle is revealed the true power of the Christian minister. This is represented as consisting of three several elements.

I. THE INSTRUMENT WHICH IS ENTRUSTED TO THE CHRISTIAN MINISTER TO WIELD. 1. In itself it is the truth. All truth is precious and powerful. But *the* truth, as it is in Jesus, is supreme in moral, spiritual power. The truth of God's righteousness and love, as they are united and harmonious in the gospel of Christ, is the greatest moral force which has entered and wrought in our humanity. It has power to convince the judgment, to convert the heart, to control the will, to constrain the life. 2. This truth exercises its power by simple manifestation. It does not need our apologies or defence, our ornaments or recommendations. It does its work best when it is simply allowed to shine by its own light, to take its own course.

II. THE MATERIAL UPON WHICH THE CHRISTIAN MINISTER HAS TO WORK; *i.e.* "every man's conscience." Some religious teachers appeal to men's interests, others to their fears, some to their superstition, others to their vanity. But the true appeal is to the conscience. "Why even of yourselves judge ye not what is right?" "I speak as unto wise men, judge ye what I say." Other principles of action address themselves to inferior parts of human nature, and produce proportionate results. But Christian truth aims high, calls forth into action the noblest faculties of the soul. Literally translated, the phrase is, "to every conscience of men," which seems to suggest that, whether the conscience be enlightened or crude, sluggish or active, it is evermore, when aroused, a witness to God's Word. The truth and the conscience are alike of Divine origin, and they are adapted the one to the other. What the truth utters the conscience echoes.

The preacher of righteousness may be assured that to his words there is always a response in human hearts.

III. THE SPIRIT IN WHICH THE CHRISTIAN MINISTER USES THE DIVINELY FASHIONED IMPLEMENT WHICH OPERATES UPON THE DIVINELY FASHIONED NATURE. It is "in the sight of God." He who works thus will work honestly, faithfully, earnestly. And his work will be profitable to men and acceptable to God.—T.

Vers. 3, 4.—*The gospel veiled.* Those things which are intended for man's welfare are often so perverted by sin that they become the occasion of the greatest evils. So that it is proverbial that the best things, when abused, prove to be the worst. The gospel of Jesus Christ, when it is received aright, is a power to enlighten, bless, and save. But to those who reject and despise it the gospel becomes the occasion of condemnation and destruction.

I. THE INVISIBLE AND SPIRITUAL POWER THAT VEILS THE GOSPEL FROM THE EYES OF MEN. The expression used by the apostle is very strong; he attributes this mischievous act to " the god of this world," apparently a personal principle of evil working in human society and in human hearts. Elsewhere we are reminded of the might of the evil one, who is designated " the ruler of this world," " the prince of the power of the air."

II. THE MEANS BY WHICH THE EYES OF MEN ARE VEILED. These are many, and are craftily adapted to the varying characters and habits of men. 1. *Sensuality* often incapacitates for spiritual vision; for the more it makes a man sensitive to the attractions of carnal pleasure the more it hinders his spiritual apprehensions and dulls his spiritual vision. 2. *Worldliness* fills the whole horizon of vision with the things of earth and time, and thus shuts out the shining of the true light which is from heaven. 3. The *pride of human reason*, which fancies itself to be independent and all-powerful, obscures in the case of many the rays of Divine truth which often reach the lowliest and the least esteemed among men.

III. THE EFFECTS WHICH THIS BLINDNESS PRODUCES IN THE MINDS OF MEN. 1. The glad tidings are regarded with indifference. 2. Christ himself, the very " Image of God," is contemplated with aversion and repugnance. There is no spiritual sympathy to draw the soul to the holy and the gracious One; his very features are regarded through a distorted medium. 3. All spiritual excellences lose their charm, fail to awaken to admiration and emulation. 4. The true condition in which they lie is altogether ignored and denied by the spiritually blind. 5. For lack of light they perish; the spiritually and wilfully blind doom themselves to death.—T.

Ver. 5.—*The theme of preaching.* Christianity was first diffused by the proclamation of the living voice, and the same method has always held the most prominent position in the history of the Church and especially of its missions. Yet the success of this method has been in proportion to the prominence which preachers give to their theme in comparison with their own individuality.

I. THE THEME THE APOSTLE DISCLAIMS. " We preach *not ourselves.*" 1. *I.e.* not about ourselves, as is the way with many. Not our own speculations, our own theories, our own fancies. Not even our own experiences in the religious life. 2. For it was felt by the modest and the wise that such preaching could only be to offer, in many cases, weakness, folly, and ignorance; in all cases human imperfection, and infirmity, to men who know quite enough of all this, and who stand in need of what is superhuman and Divine.

II. THE THEME IN WHICH THE APOSTLE GLORIES. 1. Christ as an *historical* Person. It was and still is necessary, in the first place, to inform the hearers of the gospel of the actual facts of our Lord's earthly manifestation—his incarnation, his ministry, his humiliation and obedience, his sufferings and death, his resurrection and exaltation. All good, sound doctrine is based upon fact. 2. Christ as a *Divine* Person; *i.e.* the Lord. He is to be preached as being what he declared himself to be—one with the Father, the King of angels and of men. It is such an all-sufficient Friend and Helper that man needs.

> " If thou wert less than One Divine,
>   My soul would be dismayed ;
> But through thy human lips God says,
>   ' 'Tis I ; be not afraid ! ' "

3. Christ as a *Mediator*, complete in all the qualifications needed to discharge the duties of all the offices he sustains. 4. Christ as a *living* Person—One who has not ceased to interest himself in men because he is no longer among them in bodily form; but One who, as represented in the Apocalypse, is living with and for those whom he died to save.

APPLICATION. There is danger lest those who accept this view of the apostle should be content with the mere reiteration of Christ's name. Be it remembered that Christ should be preached as to the *intelligence* and to the *heart* of men.—T.

Ver. 6.—*The light of spiritual knowledge.* Nature is a parable by means of which the Creator and Lord of all is ever teaching us concerning himself and his will. All the vast forces and sublime objects of nature have their spiritual analogues. So is it, as appears from this passage, with light, which typifies the truth, the gospel of God. We learn—

I. WHENCE THE LIGHT COMES. Physical light comes from the sun, and the sun was kindled by the Creator. He said, " Let there be light, and there was light." So all intellectual and moral light is from the Father of lights. He is light, and in him is no darkness. " He clotheth himself with light as with a garment." Our souls find their full enlightenment and satisfaction in the revelation of his mind, which is as the rising of the sun upon our benighted nature.

II. WHAT THE LIGHT IS. In the apostle's view this is " the knowledge of the glory of God." If this be so, God is not the Unknown, the Unknowable. The glory of the Eternal is not so much in his power and wisdom as in his moral attributes, his holiness, and love. The revelation of the Divine character is as light to his intelligent creation. It is welcome, cheering, illuminating, reviving.

III. WHERE THE LIGHT SHINES. "In the face of Jesus Christ." In our Lord's resurrection this light shone visibly from his face, as it had done on the occasion of his transfiguration. But really and spiritually it is always streaming forth; for Christ is himself the " Emanation of his Father's glory." Behold his face when teaching: the light of Divine knowledge is upon it. When pitying and healing the sufferer, the light of Divine compassion and love is there. When patiently enduring insult, upon it rests the lustre of majestic sweetness. When dying on the cross, the light of sacrificial victory is kindled on the features. When uttering his royal commands from heaven's throne, " his countenance is as the sun shineth in his strength."

IV. WHITHER THE LIGHT PENETRATES. "Into your hearts," says the apostle. As the sunbeams only awaken the sensation of light when they fall upon a receptive and sensitive eye, so the revelation of God's character implies a receptive and responsive heart. Though light ever shines from Christ, multitudes have no benefit or enjoyment from it. When the heart turns like the sunflower to the light, then the day dawns within, and the whole spiritual nature comes to bask in the light of God.

V. WHY THE LIGHT SHINES. In answer to this may be summed up the whole spiritual purpose and significance of the Christian revelation. 1. That we may *perceive* it. It is, alas! possible to hide from the light at noonday. But those who welcome the heavenly light rejoice in it, are guided by it, and know its power to inspire hope eternal. 2. That we may *walk* in it. " Walk ye in the light of the Lord;" " Walk in the light while ye have the light." For God's truth is profitable to all men, having the faculty of directing those who will be led by it into paths of wisdom, peace, and life. 3. That we may reflect it. The light of God is not absorbed by the soul that receives it. It is shed upon those who are around. Christians are " the light of the world "—are " light-bearers," through whose agency the earth is to be filled with the radiance of spiritual and immortal noon.—T.

Ver. 7.—*Spiritual treasure.* In this Epistle Paul speaks more frankly and warmly than in any other of his compositions of the ministry which was the work of his life. It is observable, however, that, in treating of this ministry, whilst he uses the most honourable terms in characterizing the office, he displays the utmost humility in what he says of himself.

I. PRICELESS TREASURE. 1. What it is. It is " the light of the knowledge of the glory of God in the face of Jesus Christ." It is the truth which Paul declared, the gospel which he preached, the mystery which he unfolded. The promise of free pardon for sin, of a new law and power for life, was what the apostles were privileged to convey to mankind. This is still, as it was then, the true wealth of the world, which enriches the mind and heart of man. 2. Upon whose authority this "treasure" is so described. This is the highest authority, that of the Divine Christ, who designates his gospel the "true riches," "the treasure hid in the field," "the pearl of great price;" who reminds us of "treasure in heaven;" who tells us that "where our treasure is, there will our heart be also;" who counsels to buy of him "gold tried in the furnace." 3. What makes this treasure so valuable? It is unvaryingly satisfying: it is inexhaustible; it is enduring, and not like the "riches that take to themselves wings;" it is accessible to all, so that the poor in this world, having it, are "rich in faith."

II. EARTHEN VESSELS. 1. Explain the figure. As Eastern kings stored their gold, silver, and jewels in earthen jars, so a plain casket may hold a costly jewel, a miry soil may yield an abundant crop, a battered ship may carry a precious freight, a lamp of clay may give a brilliant light, a mean book as to appearance may contain noble thoughts. So it is no objection against the gospel that those who preach it are in many respects unworthy of an office so dignified. 2. Exhibit its application. Christ was apparently a peasant, a carpenter's son; yet he was the Son of God most high. The apostles were fishermen, toll-takers, tent-makers; yet they were the heralds of salvation to mankind. The upper rooms where the early disciples met were not comparable to heathen temples, but they were scenes of Divine communion. Among those who frequented the assemblies where Christian ordinances were observed were not many noble or great, but there were inheritors of the kingdom of God. The apostle was deeply conscious of defects and weakness, was often distressed by humiliations and persecutions and contempt. His frail body, his fallible judgment, his imperfect character, his lowly and harassed condition, all contrasted with the preciousness of the gospel which was deposited in his heart and ministered by his labours. If it was so in the case of St. Paul, how much more manifestly was it so in the case of those far less gifted and far more burdened with infirmity!

III. DIVINE GREATNESS. To what purpose was this arrangement which the apostle here describes? He himself gives the true reason. 1. That all Christian labourers may feel their littleness and their weakness. 2. That they may recognize the exceeding greatness of the spiritual power of God. 3. That they may give Heaven the glory, alike for what they receive and for what they impart.—T.

Vers. 17, 18.—*Divine discipline.* In this pathetic and sublime passage Paul reveals to us his own spiritual experience. And the great lesson which he conveys for the fortifying of Christian faith and endurance, and for the inspiration of Christian hope, comes home to the heart with tenfold power, because it is so manifestly a lesson which he himself is learning, through the stress of earthly sorrow and the lapse of laborious years.

I. THE REVEALED PURPOSE OF DIVINE DISCIPLINE. Though oftentimes men fail to recognize the truth, there is in reality a purpose in human life, a purpose wise, beneficent, Divine. 1. The *means*: affliction. By this is intended here what is endured in Christ's service; as, for example, by missionaries and evangelists. Yet in the case of the true Christian affliction of every kind partakes of this character. The apostle says of affliction that it is "light" in quality, and that it is "momentary" in the time of its incidence. This is evidently a matter of comparison; for it is only when compared with the "weight" and the "eternity" of glory that earthly affliction can be denominated light and transitory. 2. The *end*: glory. This is future; for the present state is not characterized by this quality, save as a stormy day may be diversified by rays of light which break through the riven clouds. It is Christ's glory, such as that into which he entered when he had accomplished his vicarious sufferings. And, being such, it is weighty and eternal.

II. THE CONDITIONS UPON WHICH THE CHRISTIAN PROFITS BY DIVINE DISCIPLINE. In this passage God's part and ours are interwoven together. We can only receive the advantage by submitting to and falling in with the intentions of God. It is not a matter of course that the afflicted should be the better for their painful experience. 1. What is seen, what is known by sense, must be regarded and dealt with as of inferior importance, as soon to pass away. Men are prone to exaggerate the events of this perishing life; but Christians must see them as they appear to God.   2. The regards must be steadily fixed upon the unseen; *i.e.* upon the Christ who has gone before us, and who is apprehended in the exercise of faith; upon the heaven which is to be rest to the weary, joy to the sad, relief to the burdened; upon the God who, though invisible, is "near unto all who call upon him," and is the true Life of all holy souls. It must be remembered that these realities, in which Christians are deeply, supremely interested, are eternal.   Over them decay, time, and death have no power; of them the glorious things of earth can give but the promise and the earnest.   3. Thus shall strength be experienced to endure what is appointed for us to bear on earth; and thus shall an aspiring hope anticipate the glory which shall hereafter be revealed.—T.

Vers. 1—6.—*How men should preach.* I. WITH FAITH. Many preach *with despair* and prepare the way for failure. We should reflect that the preaching of the gospel is the divinely appointed way for saving men. We are likely to have success if we lay hold of God when we seek to lay hold of men. Our own salvation furnishes abundant evidence of the Divine power to save. "God shined in our hearts" (ver. 6); "We obtained mercy" (ver. 1). What God has done for us he can do for others. And we have the Divine promise that the Word shall not return unto God void. "Light shall shine out of darkness" (ver. 6). We must seek a faith which will prevent us from fainting even when the outlook is darkest (ver. 1). If we have not faith, how can we expect our hearers to have it?

II. WITH COURAGE. We must not faint because of foes. Many an assault upon strongholds has failed because of half-heartedness and cowardice. Preachers should be very bold and very brave. We have nothing to be ashamed of in our message. Shall the devil's work be done more bravely than Christ's? Shall the highest service on earth be marked by vacillation and timidity? "But that with all boldness, as always, so now also Christ shall be magnified in my body, whether it be by life or by death" (Phil. i. 20). The Church would be more aggressive if she were more courageous. Preachers should have stout hearts as well as tender ones.

III. WITH PERSEVERANCE. We must not faint because of difficulties. Discouragements are many, but persistency will bury them all. The preacher's motto must be, "On! on! on!" He must spend and be spent in the service. After the manner ascribed to British soldiers, Christ's soldiers must never know when they are worsted. "Line upon line, precept upon precept." Many things come to the preacher who can wait and work.

IV. WITH GREAT HONESTY AND SINCERITY. "Not walking in craftiness" (ver. 2). The preacher who wants his hearers to walk in holy ways must not walk in devious ways himself. He must not be a trickster. Some seem willing to do anything to please; but the object of the ministry is not to please. Meat cut with a dirty knife is likely to become unsavoury, and the gospel administered with knavish arts will lose its beauty and power.

V. WITH PURE DOCTRINE. "Not handling the Word of God deceitfully" (ver. 2). "Manifestation of the truth" (ver. 2). Christ gives us pure doctrine to preach, and woe unto us if we adulterate it! We must not season it to the tastes of the carnal, or keep back portions likely to offend influential sinners.   1. We preach in the sight of God. How, then, dare we tamper with his truth!   2. We are to commend ourselves to every man's *conscience.* Nothing but preaching *the truth* will do this. We may commend ourselves to men's fancies by preaching our own, and to their predilections by trimming doctrines according to their demands; but only by preaching pure doctrine shall we reach the *consciences* of men. Theological juggling may please men not a little; gospel doctrine will convict them. To our own Master we stand or fall. 'Tis a poor thing to please men if we displease him. Let Luther's caustic saying, "Counterfeits of money are burned, but falsifiers of God's Word are canonized," be never so true, the preacher must adhere to the doctrine delivered to him, though he lose all earthly things by doing so. In a heterodox world nothing is so likely to be so popular as heterodoxy.

VI. WITH PURITY OF LIFE. "We have renounced the hidden things of shame" (ver. 2). If we preach we should practise. Christianity is often weak because Christians are inconsistent. Men want to *see* the gospel as well as *hear* it. A preacher must live as well as talk. A man cannot preach *without himself.* There is always more in the pulpit than the sermon—there is *the man.* We inevitably wonder what the gospel has done for the gospel preacher when he so earnestly recommends it to us. And *life* has a strange power of revealing itself *in preaching.* It *peeps out.* If the preacher has a Judas-life it will betray him sooner or later. But when *the man* speaks as well as his sermon, a mighty influence is exerted. The light must shine in our own hearts and lives (ver. 6).

VII. WITH DISCERNMENT AS TO CAUSES OF NON-SUCCESS. The apostle teaches that those who reject the gospel when faithfully proclaimed are those whose minds are blinded by the god of this world (ver. 4). They have yielded themselves so utterly to evil influences that the gracious message of God through Christ fails to interest or arouse them. They are "perishing." Their rejection of the gospel says nought against the gospel or against the manner of its promulgation. The fault is not in it or in the preacher, but in themselves. It is well for a preacher to realize the possibility of such cases, so that undue discouragement may be avoided when they are met with.

VIII. WITH HUMILITY AND SELF-SUBORDINATION. 1. Preachers are not to preach themselves (ver. 5). A man may very easily preach himself even when he takes his text out of the Bible. There is not a little temptation sometimes to ministers to preach themselves. "Let him that thinketh he standeth take heed lest he fall." 2. Preachers are to be servants for Jesus' sake (ver. 5); servants of those to whom they preach. Not only servants of Christ, but servants *of men*—"*your* servants"—for Christ's sake. The preacher who would win souls must sacrifice self. For acoustics it is well for the pulpit to be above the people, but not otherwise. He who would catch fish must not be seen.

IX. WITH LOYALTY TO CHRIST. (Ver. 5.) Preachers must be true in all things to him from whom they have received their commission. They must believe in him, love him, follow him, preach him, live him, obey him, and in all things seek to glorify him.—H.

Ver. 7.—"*Earthen vessels.*" I. GOD HAS CHOSEN AS MINISTERS OF HIS GOSPEL "EARTHEN VESSELS." 1. *Not angels or other celestial beings.* Not heavenly vessels, but earthly. 2. *Men.* (1) Frail; (2) imperfect; (3) lowly; (4) weak; (5) unimposing.

II. THESE EARTHEN VESSELS ARE HELD IN THE DIVINE HAND. 1. *They are thus preserved.* "He had in his right hand seven stars" (Rev. i. 16). Often they seem in peril. "Pressed on every side . . . perplexed . . . pursued . . . smitten down" (vers. 8, 9); but the vessel is not allowed to be broken until it has done its work. 2. *They are thus useful.* (1) They are in the Divine hand to be filled. (2) They are in the Divine hand to be poured forth from. (3) They are in the Divine hand sometimes to be shaken, and the shaking of the vessel often makes the contents more efficacious.

III. A GREAT TREASURE IS COMMITTED TO THE EARTHEN VESSELS. The treasure is the truth as it is in Jesus—the great gospel message. Christ's ministers are vessels to hold this treasure and to dispense it to those to whom they minister. 1. Ministers have not to originate what they convey. It is given to them by their Master. The vessel is filled by a Divine hand from a Divine source. 2. Ministers have not to convey themselves to their people. The people do not want the vessel, but its contents. "We preach not ourselves" (ver. 5). An earthen vessel is poor food for folks to live upon, and poor medicine for a sin-sick soul to be cured with. The "vessel" must be "the servant" (ver. 5). Even an alabaster box may well be broken that the precious ointment may be poured forth. 3. The contents are apt to taste of the vessel. This must be avoided as much as possible. The less of ourselves and the more of Christ that we convey to men the better. The contents must change the vessel, not the vessel the contents. The preacher must be Christ's as well as his message. "We also believe, and therefore speak" (ver. 13).

IV. THE CONTRAST BETWEEN THE EARTHEN VESSELS AND THEIR CONTENTS. A treasure; and what a treasure! For it how long the world has been waiting! What marvels it has to work! What wonders it has wrought! And committed to "*earthen* vessels"! No royal vessels for this royal gift. What honour to the vessels chosen! A minister of Jesus Christ!—how poor all other titles are compared with this!

V. THE OBJECT OF THE DIVINE CHOICE. 1. *The uninterrupted working of the Divine power.* An "earthen vessel" can do nothing but receive and pour forth. What egregious folly for a minister of Christ to seek to enter into partnership with his Lord for the production of a theology! The earthen vessel cannot do anything, and should not attempt to. 2. *The glory of the Divine Being.* No glory *can* attach to the mere earthen vessel. God is "all in all." This should be the desire of every servant of God. Many, it is to be feared, are robbers of God in this matter. They snatch at the glory to which they have not the smallest claim.

VI. THE FUTURE OF THE EARTHEN VESSELS. They will be raised up (ver. 14). 1. *Made glorious.* "This mortal must put on immortality." "As we have borne the image of the earthy, we shall also bear the image of the heavenly" (1 Cor. xv. 49). The "vile body" will be exchanged for a "glorious body." We shall be made like Christ. The earthen vessels will be transformed into the likeness of him who filled them. The change is taking place whilst the earthen vessels are in the earthly service. "Though our outward man is decaying, yet our inward man is renewed day by day" (ver. 16). But when we see him as he is we shall be like him. 2. *Fitted for higher service.* Heavenly activities. We know not how closely associated the earthly service is with the heavenly, how much the one may depend upon the other, how much the one will influence and shape the other. Let us make the earthly service as true and perfect as we may.—H.

Vers. 16—18.—*Heavy affliction made light.* Paul's troubles were exceedingly heavy. So the troubles of many believers have been and are. The sufferings of saints often seem severer than those of sinners. For them the furnace is made seven times hotter. But Paul with his heavy sorrows speaks of them as light, and speaks of them as they really seemed to him to be under the conditions to which he refers. No affliction could well be heavier than his, and yet it was light. So is the believer's—

I. WHEN HE CONSIDERS DURING HOW SMALL A PORTION OF HIS LIFE IT HAS TO BE BORNE. It is but "for a moment." Not so long as a second contrasted with a thousand years. Eternity makes time short. Our troubles are like Pharaoh's horsemen—they cannot pass the Red Sea of death. In this *flash* of our existence we may weep, but in the ever-continuing life of heaven we shall rejoice.

> " There shall I bathe my weary soul
> In seas of heavenly rest,
> And not a wave of trouble roll
> Across my peaceful breast."

Our cross is borne but for a moment, our crown for ever.

II. WHEN HE CONTRASTS THE PRESENT BRIEF TROUBLE WITH THE ETERNAL WEIGHT OF GLORY. True thoughts of heaven prevent exaggerated views of earthly sorrows. When the future is shut out we can easily sit down and lament, but when faith sees the "inheritance incorruptible and undefiled, and that fadeth not away" (1 Pet. i. 4), our present griefs dwindle into insignificance. "For I reckon that the sufferings of this present time are not worthy to be compared with the glory which shall be revealed" (Rom. viii. 18). Why should we be disquieted so much by *these* things when *those* are so near? Shadows hang heavily over us until the sunshine of the coming glory breaks through the clouds, and then the shadows flee away. Why should we concentrate thought upon the short present when the long future is so fair? If we think much of the home, the journey homewards will seem short, and the troubles of the way of little account. Every hour of sorrow brings us an hour nearer the land that is sorrowless. And what shall we possess there? The apostle strives in vain to find language sufficiently strong to describe even what he on earth could perceive of heaven —" more and more exceedingly an eternal weight of glory " (ver. 17).

III. WHEN THE MEANING OF PRESENT TROUBLE IS REALIZED. To the true child of God: 1. It may mean the destruction of the outward man, but it assuredly means the renewal and development of the inward. It is not even present injury—it is present good. It is medicine, not poison. 2. It prepares us for the coming glory. The fire consumes the dross, the knife cuts away the diseased part, the chisel strikes off that which would impair the beauty of the statue. The apprenticeship of sorrow fits us for the long service of glory. Through much tribulation we enter the kingdom and are prepared for its duties. The joys of heaven are dependent on the sorrows of earth; without the latter we should not be ready for the former. "Tribulation worketh patience," etc. (Rom. v. 3). 3. Whilst suffering cannot in any way merit salvation, affliction rightly endured shall not be without reward. If we fight the fight of faith, and endure hardness as good soldiers of Jesus Christ, we shall receive a crown of righteousness which fadeth not away. "If we suffer we shall also reign with him" (2 Tim. ii. 12).

PRACTICAL. 1. *Faint not.* Many faint because they see no reason why they should not faint. Yet all reasons point the Christian to patient endurance. If we lose heart we lose strength. To despair is to charge our Master with unfaithfulness. Seek to be a good swimmer in the sea of trouble, and if the waves go over you, still faint not, foi soon you will rise to the surface again, and see that the shore is nearer. 2. *Be not much concerned about the things of this life.* (Ver. 18.) These are perishing. The imperishable are our better portion. Look not at the things which are seen; they are not worth looking at. "Set your affection on things above" (Col. iii. 2.) 3. *Look at things unseen by the carnal sense, but clear to faith's vision.* (Ver. 18.) God, Christ, holiness, usefulness, spiritual joys, the new Paradise,—these are "eternal."—H.

Ver. 5.—*Not self, but the Lord.* Two imputations had been cast on St. Paul during his absence from Corinth, and to each of these this verse contains a reply. It had been said that he sought commendation; and he answered that he set forth, not himself, but his Lord. It had been said that he tried to domineer over the Churches; and he answered that he was a servant of the Church for Jesus' sake.

I. THE PROMINENCE GIVEN TO THE LORD. "We preach not ourselves." By this disclaimer is not meant that the apostle excluded all reference to his own faith or experience, and maintained an altogether impersonal tone while delivering Christian testimony and instruction to the Churches. Extant specimens of his preaching and writing indicate the contrary. St. Paul freely spoke of his own experience of the mercy of God and sustaining grace of Christ, of his faith and hope, his sorrow and joy. So have all wise and successful ministers of the Word of life shown their own hearts to the people as holding the gospel precious. They have said, "What we preach to you we ourselves know and believe; what we commend to your acceptance we have ourselves accepted and proved; so we come before you, not merely as messengers by whom tidings are sent, but also as witnesses who can testify that those tidings are true." The apostle spoke and wrote freely of himself, but did not preach himself, *i.e.* did not set himself before the people as the leader or the Saviour. It was the fault of those factious teachers at Corinth, who tried to disparage the authority of St. Paul, that they commended themselves, taught their own speculations, eyed their own advancement, and drew away disciples after them. This was what the apostle disclaimed and abhorred, and what all preachers of the gospel must scrupulously, and even jealously, avoid. It is positively fatal to spiritual success to project one's self before the people instead of setting forth the all-sufficiency of Christ Jesus, the living Essence of the gospel. Some one complained to the excellent William Romaine of his constantly preaching Christ; and he answered, "We have nothing else to preach;" *i.e.* we preach nothing separate from him or disconnected with him. All sound doctrine converges towards, and all acceptable obedience issues from, the excellency of the knowledge of Christ. "Preach the Law," the Jews demanded of Paul; and he preached Christ, the end of the Law to every believer. "Preach wisdom," cried the Greeks; and he preached Christ as the Wisdom of God. "Preach practical virtues and good conduct," cry many modern critics and monitors; and we must preach Christ in order to make hearts new, and so make lives pure and upright from the roots. It is not enough to teach the existence of God, his attributes of being and character, his all-controlling providence, or even his universal fatherhood. We preach Jesus, the Teacher, the Healer, the Saviour, the Son of God. We preach him as Christ, the Messiah announced in ancient prophecy, who should suffer many things and so enter into his glory. And we preach Jesus Christ as Lord. He is Lord of all. He is Lord both of the dead and of the living. He is Lord "to the glory of God the Father." Do any think this impracticable? Do they point to the ignorance that has to be removed, vice to be restrained, selfishness to be corrected, and count it a mere waste of time to speak so much of a Personage who lived, and the things which he said and did in Judæa ever so long ago? Do they ask, "What good can this do?" We are bold to answer—If this will not do good, nothing will. Moral directions and monitions cannot lift men out of themselves or raise them above low levels of thought and conduct. There must be some new and near relation to God, some help from heaven; and this is gained only through faith in Jesus Christ the Lord. In no other way have been produced powerful and permanent transmutations of human character. In no other way are men rescued from evil habits and made good, and kind, and just, and pure. Therefore we will persist in preaching what Paul preached.

II. THE PLACE TAKEN BY THE APOSTOLIC PREACHER. We do not wish to lord it over the Church. "We are your servants for Jesus' sake." The factious teachers at Corinth sought their own advancement, and, judging St. Paul by themselves, alleged that he assumed more authority than he was entitled to, and wished to play dictator to the Churches. The sensitive and generous heart of the apostle acutely felt the imputation. He was, indeed, bound to assert his apostolate, but, absorbed as he was with the thought of his Saviour's authority as Lord, he abhorred the idea of claiming lordship over God's Church, and was careful to describe himself as a servant, and to associate with himself by name such fellow-servants as Silas and Timothy. Much more are modern ministers of the Word, while maintaining the reality and dignity of their ministry, to beware of anything that savours of lordly assumption. They are servants of the saints for Jesus' sake. Not for the sake of men, or for any inducement or remuneration which men can offer. They are not *employés* of the people, engaged by them to do their religious work, and responsible to them for their conduct. In fact, they are servants of the people, and yet the people are not their masters. One is their Master, even Christ; and they serve the Church under his orders and for his sake. So Jesus Christ himself became the Servant of all because he was God's elect Servant. Among his followers it is always better and nobler to serve than to be served. What an example Paul showed as a servant for Jesus' sake!—wearing out his frame in severe and dangerous travels and voyages, caring for all the Churches, praying for them, writing to them, visiting and revisiting them, running all risks, enduring all things— even that which was hardest of all, the ingratitude and fickleness of those to whom he had ministered—that he might fulfil the service which had been assigned to him by the Lord Jesus. Others might spare themselves, but he never did. "I will most gladly spend and be spent for your souls." It is a high standard; but we do well to keep lofty models before us, and try to rise to them according to the necessity and opportunity of our own time, and the ability which is given to us of God.—F.

Ver. 6.—*Light of the knowledge of Divine glory.* The Christianity of St. Paul was not a formulated religion, but the revelation or unveiling of God in his Son our Saviour

I. THE GLORY OF GOD IN THE FACE OF JESUS CHRIST. In that face, turned so graciously on the sons of men, is not merely the glow of human sympathy and pity, but the ineffable glory of the most high God. There is no thought here of the comparison sometimes made between the Divine glory in creation and that glory in redemption. The contrast still in the apostle's mind is between the Law and the gospel. He recalls the glory of God that once shone on the face of Moses as he descended from the holy mount; and he sets above it the glory in the face of Jesus Christ. The lustre on the prophet's countenance was transient, and its effect on the people was only to agitate them and make them desirous to have it softened by a veil. But Christ is the permanent and gracious Image of God; and he reveals it, not to drive men away in terror, but to save them and change them into the same image.

II. THE KNOWLEDGE OF THE GLORY OF GOD IN THE FACE OF JESUS CHRIST. Without this the salvation in the gospel profits us not. We can determine nothing about the benefit which may be derived from or through Christ by those who have had no opportunity to hear of him or know him. That will be as God sees meet. But to us who have the gospel, the blessing must come through spiritual knowledge. If knowledge of law and ordinances could save, Paul would have been saved while he was a Pharisee; but he entered not on a state of salvation till he gave up all for the excellency of the knowledge of Christ. Taught by his own experience, he commended this knowledge to others. It was his daily care and effort to spread abroad that know-ledge. And its propagation in the early ages of Christianity seemed like a fulfilment of the ancient prophecy that " the knowledge of the glory of the Lord shall cover the earth as the waters cover the sea."

III. THE LIGHT OF THE KNOWLEDGE OF THE GLORY OF GOD IN THE FACE OF JESUS CHRIST. God was light. The nations, estranged from him, sat in darkness. In Judæa there was a lamp for his Name, but it was dim. Pharisaic pride and Sadducean scepticism threatened to put it out. Then the true Light came into the world. And now, as Christ becomes known in the Spirit to this man or that, he lights up both mind and heart. There is to every believer a revelation of the Lord. It is a light above all other lights—calm, pure, searching, gladdening. And the shedding abroad of the light of Christ and the love of God is always by the operation of the Holy Ghost. Thus " the excellency of the knowledge" of God in Christ is imparted by " the excellency of the power " of the Spirit.—F.

Ver. 7.—*The lamp in the pitcher*. This verse is often quoted to express human insufficiency for the ministry of the gospel. It deserves to be quoted, for, if St. Paul felt so deeply his powerlessness without God, how much more should this feeling influence ordinary ministers of the Word of life !

I. THE TREASURE. Paul, working in the factory making tents, or passing through the street undistinguished by dress or retinue, may have been taken for a poor artisan. But he was conscious of possessing a treasure by the use and distribution of which he, while poor, made many rich. It was no store of silver or gold. It was not even the treasure of intellectual eminence, the wealth of a large and lofty mind ; for, though he had this, he could not impart it to others. It was the ministry of righteousness and liberty whereby he communicated to his fellow-men " the unsearchable riches of Christ." There is no need to draw a distinction here between the ministry which is the topic of the whole context and the light of knowledge which is the immediately preceding subject. In the apostle's thought these are intimately and necessarily combined and together constitute the treasure. It was as an illuminated man that he showed the light to others. And so at this day, only a man in whom the true light shines can be a minister of Christ. But who has the light may spread the knowledge of the glory of God, and has a treasure better than silver and more to be desired than fine gold.

II. THE EARTHEN VESSELS. It was and is the custom of Orientals to keep valuables and money in jars which might be hid, and, in case of danger, might be buried under-ground. A mere earthen jar might thus contain an enormous treasure. Alluding to this, St. Paul pointed to his own body, hard pressed by labours and afflictions. His bodily presence was weak. He had no external advantages for making an impression on either Jews or Greeks. Yet in such an earthen vessel was contained a treasure beyond all computation, and not needing to have its worth enhanced by adventitious surroundings. If we think of the treasure as one of light—the light of the knowledge of God's glory—there is a story in the Old Testament which may illustrate the phrase. The followers of Gideon had their lamps in pitchers, or earthen vessels, when they stole a march on the invaders from Midian, and, with sound of trumpet and loud war-shouts, fell upon their camp. So, by the light in earthen vessels, with the trumpet-notes of their testimony, did the apostles and other early preachers assail and defeat those opposing powers of the world that would have laughed at their weakness. It is still the same. Gospel victories are gained, not by a great array of human might, but by the treasure of light in earthen vessels, and by the shout of faith that makes appeal to Heaven.

III. THE POWER. " That the excellency," etc. This corresponds to the previous expression, " excellency of the knowledge," and both illustrate an Hebraic form of the superlative. The excellency of the power was that surpassing energy which, in St. Paul's time, attended the ministry of the gospel, and bore down the most formidable opposition. The contrast between the power of the ministry and the weakness of the ministers struck the apostle in thinking of his own early labours at Corinth (see 1 Cor. ii. 1—5). It is a remarkable, and in some respects a mortifying, fact that the modern Christian ministry, with all its advantages of special training, public respect, and perfect protection by law, shows less of conscience-convincing and heart-compelling power than the primitive ministry did when it was surrounded by difficulty and threatened with death. When it seemed weak, it was strong; and now that it seems strong, it is weak. As some explanation of this, it is only fair to admit that the modern ministry in Christendom has no longer the charm which lies in novelty. It has to be exercised where the terms and facts of our religion are already known, and the Holy Bible is the most widely circulated book. And when it goes to fresh fields, as India, China, or Japan, it has this disadvantage as compared with the apostolic ministry, that in those countries there is no such preparation for the gospel as there was in the countries and cities which were visited by St. Paul. The settlements of Jews, and the very considerable number of proselytes who knew the Old Testament in the Greek Version, and looked for a Messiah, gave an important facility to the Christian preacher, who formed out of them an intelligent nucleus round which to gather his converts from among the heathen; whereas now preachers must go to heathen communities that know not their language, and are wedded to religious conceptions quite different from those in which the missionaries have been trained, and, if there be Christians living among the heathen, holding office or in pursuit of commerce, too often they impede rather than promote the success of the gospel. All this may be recognized, and still it is true that the ministry might and should exert much more spiritual power everywhere than it does. Let prayer be made for this, since the power belongs to God, and only he can enable the ministers of his Word to overcome the dulness of religious routine as well as the hardness of anti-religious prejudice; to sober the frivolous; to abase the proud; to arrest minds that engross themselves with trifles, and recover those that have debased themselves with fleshly vice or avaricious deceit; to wound and to heal; to warn and to win; to kill and to make alive. Oh for power to prevail, to search the breasts of men, to make conscience start and hearts quiver, to reprove sin, to shatter vain excuses, to kindle new resolves and hopes! We cannot do it; but he who supplied all-sufficiency to St. Paul can supply it to us. "Our sufficiency is of God."—F.

Ver. 9.—"*Cast down, but not destroyed.*" In ministering the Word, we need to play, if we may so speak, on various instruments of music. We take the silver trumpet when we would utter "the joyful sound." We take the harp when we show forth God's praise. What shall we take for encouragement and comfort to the weary? As a great poetess has it—

> "Experience, like a pale musician, holds
> A dulcimer of patience in his hand."

Let us play on the dulcimer. A good man struggling with adversity has been the subject of many moral reflections. We want to go further than the moralist, and show how the man of God is preserved in time of trouble. What heroism in the immortal Jew of Tarsus! All the sharp ordeal through which he passed—his personal disadvantages, the disparagement by false apostles jealous of his influence, the coldness of former friends when he was in bonds at Rome, the hardship and misconstruction under which his great work had been done,—all served only to bring out more fully the singleness of his aim and fortitude of his spirit—

> "And give the world assurance of a man."

"Struck down, but not destroyed." Trouble threw him down, as one wrestler might throw another in the arena; but the cast was not mortal. He revived, for Christ lived in him. Nay; his sufferings increased his usefulness. No follower of Christ ever made such an impression on mankind, or did so much for the gospel, as this troubled, persecuted, perplexed, cast-down Paul of Tarsus. Times have changed. Religious liberty prevails. Gross forms of persecution for confessing Christ are prevented by law and condemned by public sentiment. But it does not follow that the course of a faithful Christian is made easy. It is often beset with difficulty, broken, and uneven. Good men are "cast down;" and it is painful to have the skin grazed, even when the bones are not broken. Under such disappointing experiences feeble souls are apt to become more timid and more querulous, while bolder natures grow selfish and cynical. These last, if they have been struck down when grappling with something to them impracticable or forbidden, resolve to knock others down, and, if need be for their own interest, trample on them. But natures that are sweet and sound learn wisdom, consideration for others, and knowledge of themselves through hard experience. And hearts that trust in God have this joy in the worst defeat, that they are not, they cannot be, destroyed. Life is not wrecked by every trouble or by a score of troubles. A mistake may be the very making of a man, if he knows how to correct it. If the way is blocked in one direction, other paths are open. And if helpers fail and friends forsake, God still lives. We do not, indeed, conceal from ourselves that some overthrows cannot be quite remedied in this world; some losses are irreparable on earth, just as some diseases are incurable. But no Christian needs to be inconsolable. If he be stripped of ever so much that he valued, his best treasure remains, and is above the reach of worldly vicissitude. There is a good part which shall not be taken away. Thus life is always worth living. For a brave man it cannot be utterly wrecked by misfortune. For a devout man it cannot be shattered, though once and again struck down to the ground. The good Shepherd restores the soul. But many are the uses of adversity. Remember your faults and correct them; your mistakes, and avoid them; but do not waste time in vain regrets or temper in weak complaints. What purpose does it serve to brood over disappointment and "feed with sighs the passing wind"? How much better to gird up your purpose and make the best of what is left to you of time, strength, and opportunity! You may yet stand all the more firmly because of that casting down. The ill you have suffered may lead to higher good. "Though the outward man perish, the inward man is renewed day by day." God knows how to give—

"Secret refreshings that repair your strength,
And fainting spirits uphold."

F.

Ver. 16.—*Inward renewal and outward decay.* The contrast here is not that which the apostle draws elsewhere between the flesh and the spirit, or the old man and the new. That is a moral distinction. But this is between the physical and the spiritual in man, the outward and palpable on the one hand, the inward and impalpable on the other. These are intimately connected. They have a constant sympathy. An aching body jades the mind; an aching mind jades the body. A healthy body invigorates the mind; a cheerful mind sustains the body. Each affects and is affected by the other. Yet there is sometimes witnessed a glorious mastery over outward disadvantages by the force of the inward man. The heroic mind is firm, even when the physical frame is shattered. And nothing is so productive of this heroism as faith. They who have "the same spirit of faith" as was in Paul "faint not."

I. OF INWARD RENEWAL. The case in view is that of a regenerate man. It is assumed that spiritual life has been received. And now it is shown that "the washing of regeneration" is followed by "the renewing of the Holy Ghost." Good men are liable to fits of inward fainting, languor, and emotional deadness, when they are in great danger of being overcome by temptation. Therefore they need to pray often for a stronger life. "Renew a right spirit within me." 1. *Wherein* is the inner man renewed? "In righteousness and holiness of truth" (Eph. iv. 24). And so in all spiritual strength—the power of resistance to sin, of self-denial, of patience, and of generous charitable action. 2. *Whereby* is the inner man renewed? By the power of God; by the energy of the Holy Ghost. It is he who, with the Word of truth, makes vivid demonstration of righteousness to the conscience, strengthens holy purpose in the will, and gives fervour to devout affections in the breast. 3. *How often* is the inner man renewed? "Day by day." Not that all days are alike. As a nation has its special dates in history, days by which its future has been moulded, on which its decisive battles were fought or its independence was won, so may a Christian man have his dates more or less clearly marked, outstanding and precious days by which his spiritual history has been determined, on which his fight of faith was well fought, and his liberty in Christ became established and sure. But while we recognize special days or eras of spiritual progress, we are disposed to say that in grace, as in nature, the ordinary is, after all, more expressive of Divine goodness than the extraordinary, and more essential to our welfare. The daily revival and maintenance of spiritual life is a better and greater thing than any occasional and exceptional blessing. "He holdeth our souls in life." The strength, moral as well as physical, which is daily expended is also daily restored. John Bunyan makes the Christian pilgrim see a man secretly feeding with oil a fire on which another cast water, and the fire burned "hotter and hotter." The Interpreter explained it of Christ's secret and constant renewal of the sacred fire in "the souls of his people."

II. Of the relation which inward renewal may bear to outward decay. St. Paul was conscious of two changes—an outward descent to feebleness and earth, and an inward ascent to firmer strength and higher vitality. 1. *The inward defies the outward.* "*Though* our outward," etc. The constancy of the believing heart is all the more triumphant because of the feeble or decaying frame. What might of spirit has shown itself in tender women under acute suffering! What force of character and splendour of patience in men who scarcely had a day without bodily pain! 2. *The inward renewal is often helped forward by the outward decay.* It pleases God to further the spiritual life of his children in ways that are hard to flesh and blood. Indeed, we seldom see a keen relish for the things of the Spirit of God, a weaned spirit, a holy fervour—while the outward man is quite at ease and commands every gratification. There is need of trouble in the outer sphere to exercise and quicken the inner life. Bengel, near the end of his course, said to a friend, "Illnesses serve to quicken and enlarge us in spirit after we have been dwindling. When our spiritual lamp burns dimly, it is often because its wick needs retrenching; and retrenchments are made from time to time upon the outward man by sickness and affliction." Thus it is not merely "though," but also sometimes "because," our outward man perishes that our inward man is renewed. What a sad case is theirs whose outward man decays while there is no spiritual life in them! Time passes, health fails, life ebbs away, and there is nothing to put against it. The outward man perishes and the inward man perishes too. But why will ye die? The Lord wishes not that any should perish, but that all should come to repentance.—F.

Ver. 18.—*Seeing the unseen.* I. The habit of mind here described. The apostle speaks, not of an act or effort, but of a steady mental habit which he had formed—an intentness of regard in a particular direction. He describes it in a form that sounds paradoxical, but the thing meant is well known to all experimental Christians. The things seen and not seen in this passage are not the visible and invisible by mortal eyes, as in Rom. i. 20. The things not seen in the verse before us are so, not because they cannot be seen, but because the time has not yet come for their manifestation. The things seen, from which St. Paul turned away his eyes, were the toils and afflictions endured by him as a servant of Christ. The things not seen were the rewards of faithful service at the coming of the Lord—the "weight of glory." And the habit here indicated is that of looking off from labours and sufferings to the glorious appearing of the Lord, and the bright "recompense of reward." It is the highest form of looking on the cheerful side of things. As this is a habit, it must be formed by degrees and by reiterated efforts. By bending the mind as much as we can towards the future with Christ, we must train it to habitual expectation and desire.

II. The reason assigned for forming this habit. "For the things which are seen are," etc. St. Paul reflected that "the sufferings of the present time" were, after all, of short continuance. The affliction he endured was only for a moment as compared with the eternity before him. So he felt that he would outlive and triumph over all his trials. They were temporal, and so could not reach into the life beyond or mar the hope laid up for him in heaven. Was not this the way with the Divine Master himself? For the joy set before him, he endured the cross, despising the shame. And so should all who are his bear the cross and endure patiently, because the time will not be long and the things not seen are eternal.

III. The benefits which accompany or flow from this habit when formed. 1. *Elevation of the tone of life.* Life is as its motives are; and the motives come from the convictions, fears, and hopes that are strongest in the mind. A superficial religion has not power enough to cleanse the heart or ennoble the principles of conduct. But a formed habit of regarding the things eternal as those to which we hasten must raise and refine the character. "Every one who has this hope in him purifies himself, even as he is pure." And this is no selfish hope, no egotistical ambition. It is the hope of being crowned along with all who love his appearing, and of being rewarded along with all the faithful servants of the King. 2. *Consolation in hardship and adversity.* Even when a lamp is not near enough to cast a clear light on our path, it is cheering to see it in a murky night; and so are we comforted as we look for the glory with Christ. We move towards it over ever so rugged a path. We steer towards it over ever so restless a sea. If we look at the things which are seen, the waves and the threatening rocks, we lose strength and courage; but with the eye fixed on the light of that blessed hope, we make straight for the harbour. 3. *Preparation for departure hence.* It is appointed to men to die. To take no thought about this appointment, and to occupy the mind with only the things that are seen, forgetting their transience, is to play the part of a fool. The wise man is he who, while fulfilling the duties of the passing time, looks much and steadily into the future, and so, when he departs, goes, not into regions unknown, but to the Saviour, whom he has loved and served, to wait with him and with all the saints for the resurrection and the glory.—F.

Vers. 1, 2.—*Full confidence in the power of the truth.* "By manifestation of the truth commending ourselves to every man's conscience in the sight of God." The great work of the Christian ministry is to set forth before men *the truth.* But we are not to understand by that term *all* truth or *any* truth. Reference is precisely to that truth about God, and his relations with men, which had been partially revealed before, and was fully disclosed in Jesus Christ the Saviour. That special truth had been committed to the trust of the apostles. They were to proclaim it freely to men, as they had or could make opportunity. And they were to be sure that God would make that truth his *power* unto men's salvation. Referring to the work of the modern ministry, it has been well said that we have not so much " to tell the truth as to make the truth tell." The apostle, in these verses, reminds us of some things that are necessary if we would efficiently set forth the gospel truth.

I. PERSEVERANCE. "We faint not." There must be no shrinking back in face of difficulties, no losing heart because things will not go smoothly, no wearying in our well-doing. St. Paul himself gave the noble example of what he enjoined. He did not count his life dear to him so that he might finish his course with joy. Succeed or fail, in strength or in weakness, he was "instant in season and out of season."

II. SIMPLICITY. The faithful minister will absolutely refuse all merely sensational aids to his work. He will wholly separate himself from worldly and guileful schemes for accomplishing his ends. He will refuse in any way to "do evil that good may come." It had been made an accusation against the apostle that he had shown craftiness and guile in his dealings with the Churches. This charge he most vigorously rebutted, and was led to urge that guilelessness is essential to the faithful minister, whose conduct and motives may be searched through and through. Illustration may be taken from the ministry of the Lord Jesus. He resorted to no arts, or schemes, or tricks, either of speech or of conduct. His work was simple. It was the living of a life, the delivery of a message, a genuine effort to bless and save men.

III. FAITH. In the witness which the truth ever makes, and the response to it which is always given by men's consciences. We may preach with this confidence—conscience will surely acknowledge the claim of God, and the guilt of sin, and the need of redemption. Men may indeed silence conscience and put away the truth, but we always have this assurance—the best and deepest in every man responds to our message.

IV. THE CONSCIOUSNESS OF BEING UNDER GOD'S EYE. "In the sight of God." That Divine presence the minister realizes as the fulfilment of Christ's words, " Lo, I am with you alway, even unto the end of the world." There is a hardness and coldness about the idea that we should work "as ever in the great Taskmaster's eye." There is warmth, tender sympathy, and inspiration in the assurance that the spiritual " Man, Christ Jesus," is with us everywhere.

In conclusion, such points as these need careful treatment. 1. Is this confidence in the power of the truth justified by experience? 2. Does Christ's truth ever really stand in peril? 3. If so, from what sources or in what directions does the peril come? Agencies and organizations and human moulds imperil it, and in every age men are raised up who can set Christ's truth free from our human limitations and bondages.

The true revival is the freeing of the truth to win its own good way. We can have no ground for glorying comparable to this—"the Word of God is not bound."—R. T.

Ver. 4.—*Christ as the Image of God.* "The glorious gospel of Christ, who is the Image of God." From 1 Cor. xi. 7 we learn that there is a sense in which *man* is the "image and glory of God." In Col. i. 15 the Son of God is spoken of as the "Image of the invisible God, the Firstborn of every creature." The word used in our text is exactly equivalent to our word "likeness." "An image, or likeness, is a visible representation of an object. So Christ, in his humanity, is a visible representation of the unseen God. No revelation of the wisdom and power of God that man has received can compare with that made in the life, death, and resurrection of the incarnate Son." The point to which we ask attention is this—the gospel sets forth the glory of *Christ.* But, when it is rightly viewed, this is found to be the setting forth of the glory of *God.* For God can only be known in image and symbol; and this is the perfect and wholly satisfactory image, precisely adapted to our human faculties and necessities. Jesus Christ is the "Brightness of the Father's glory, and the express Image of his person." His sonship is the earthly presentation of the Divine fatherhood. The Son is the very image of the Father. Philips Brooks well says, "This is the sum of the work of the Incarnation. A hundred other statements regarding it, regarding him who was incarnate, are true; but all statements concerning him hold their truth within this truth—that Jesus came to restore the fact of God's fatherhood to man's knowledge, and to its central place of power over man's life. Jesus is mysteriously the Word of God made flesh. He is the Worker of amazing miracles upon the bodies and the souls of men. He is the Convincer of sin. He is the Saviour by suffering. But, behind all these, as the purpose for which he is all these, he is the Redeemer of man into the fatherhood of God." Christ brings the light of God's fatherly love to shine on prodigal and sinful sons; that light wakens the old son-spirit in their hearts, and wins them home, in penitence and faith, to their heavenly Father. And just this is the mission of Christ and his gospel—to shine God's light into men's souls.—R. T.

Ver. 6.—*Light from God and light on God.* The new Revised Version makes an important alteration in this verse, reading it thus: "Seeing it is God, that said, Light shall shine out of darkness, who shined in our hearts, to give the light [or, 'illumination'] of the knowledge of the glory of God in the face of Jesus Christ."

I. LIGHT FROM GOD IN CREATION. (Gen. i. 3.) The following points may be illustrated. 1. All material light, as a warming, life-giving, beautifying agent, is from God. 2. All moral light, as the intimation of what is good and right in the relationships of men, is from God. 3. All revelational light, as the unfolding of the mysteries belonging to God and his claim and mercy, must come directly from himself. On spiritual things man can have no knowledge, save as God is pleased freely to give it; and, on these higher themes, all light must be tempered to the capacity of those on whom it shines.

II. LIGHT ON GOD IN CHRIST. Calvin says of this verse, "A notable place, whence we learn that God is not to be investigated in his unsearchable height, for he inhabits the light unapproachable (1 Tim. vi. 16), but to be known as far as he reveals himself in Christ. . . . It is more useful for us to behold God as he appears in his only begotten Son than to investigate his secret essence." The face of Christ is said to reveal the glory of God, as the shining of Moses' face told of the splendour about the mount where he had been with God. But the glory of God is his redemption-work. That showed (1) pity, (2) love, (3) wisdom, (4) holy purpose; and all these we find in the face of Jesus Christ. Illustrate the power of expression, and the power of revealing thought and heart, that are in the human face, and then show how the face of the Lord Jesus reveals to us the "heart of God." Before Christ came God was a half-known, if not an unknown, God. And the incomplete conceptions of him involved, too often, imperfect and unworthy conceptions. We now know the "true God and eternal life" in the face of Jesus, his manifested Son—or rather, his manifested Self. —R. T.

Ver. 7.—*Heavenly treasure in earthen vessels.* "It was the practice of Eastern kings, who stored up their treasures of gold and silver, to fill jars of earthenware with coin or bullion" (see Jer. xxxii. 14). To this custom allusion is made. St. Paul says that in these frail bodies of ours, with their limited faculties and powers, in these "earthen vessels" we have that priceless treasure, the knowledge of the glory of God as a Redeemer. Cecil says, "The meanness of the earthen vessel which conveys to others the gospel treasure takes nothing from the value of the treasure. A dying hand may sign a deed of incalculable value; a shepherd's boy may point out the way to a philosopher; a beggar may be the bearer of a valuable present." Three points claim attention.

I. THE TREASURE. This may be regarded as (1) a revelation, (2) as a gospel, (3) as a life. In either respect, the personal Christ being the very Centre and Essence of it, *he* is properly the Treasure. Christ himself is our most sacred Trust. We have the one Saviour for men committed to our care. Then how jealously we should guard the treasure! and how wisely we should put it to use!

II. THE NEED FOR THE CONVEYANCE OF THIS TREASURE. For it is not to be stored up in hiding-places, but somehow made the treasure of all men. It is a spiritual treasure, and needs some kind of material conveyance. Christ himself must be ministered to men by his disciples.

III. THE VESSELS FOUND FOR THE DUE CONVEYANCE OF THE TREASURE. Humbly spoken of as *earthly*, or as mere earthenware. Enlarging upon them beyond St. Paul's immediate thought in the use of the term, we may show (1) their frailty; (2) their fitness, especially in that they do not take away the honour that is due to the treasure by directing attention to themselves; (3) their safety, since God, who guards the treasure, will guard the vessel that holds it; (4) their usefulness, as the human agency commends the heavenly truth; and (5) their reward, for God will surely commend those who, in such a trust, are found faithful.—R. T.

Ver. 10.—*Suffering showing forth character.* It has been said that "affliction" is the one predominant word in the Second Epistle to the Corinthians. And perhaps no other Epistle is so charged with wounded personal feeling and reminiscences of varied suffering. This may be explained by the circumstances under which this letter was written. Perhaps we do not sufficiently realize how much personal suffering, from disease and bodily infirmity, the apostle had to endure; and yet this is evidently the key to many of his intense expressions. Either from constitutional weakness, or in consequence of his many exposures, he had upon him some painful and humiliating form of disease, which was incurable; and this his enemies made the occasion of scorn and insult, until they wounded him to the very quick, and drove him to the throne of grace, seeking, with threefold importunity, to have the "thorn in the flesh" removed. When we apprehend this, we begin to feel the meaning of our text; he was "always bearing about in the body the dying of the Lord Jesus:" pain, disease, suffering—like a daily dying—brought on him in the fulfilment of his ministry for the Lord Jesus. But St. Paul never dwelt long on the merely sad side of things, and so he goes on to say— Even if our life on earth be like the dying of the Lord Jesus, this also is true, through our very suffering and dying, the life of Jesus is made manifest in our mortal flesh and earthly spheres. "St. Paul felt that every true human soul must repeat Christ's existence. He could bear to look on his decay; it was but the passing of the human; and, meantime, there was ever going on within him the strengthening of the Divine. Pain was sacred, since Christ also had suffered. And life became grand when viewed as a repetition of the life of Christ."

I. ST. PAUL'S CONCEPTION OF OUR LORD'S LIFE. It had been a daily dying which nevertheless showed up himself, in the glory of his character and spirit. The dying manifested to men the life that was in him. St. Paul had, probably, never seen Christ in the flesh, but it was given to him, by his fellowship of suffering, to understand better than all the rest what a suffering Saviour Jesus was. It is St. Paul who writes so much about the *cross* of the Lord Jesus. He dwells oftener than any other early teacher upon our Lord's death, but when you apprehend his meaning, you find that he looked upon Christ's whole life as a dying. He saw that Jesus was every day dying to self, dying with shame, pain, exhaustion, conflict, and agony. And you do not read Christ's life aright unless you can see in it what St. Paul saw, even humiliation, limitation, suffering, burdening it every day. But that was not all St. Paul's conception of Christ. In that, standing alone, he could have found no rest, no inspiration. He saw also this, that our Lord's sufferings were just the dark background that threw out so perfectly, with such well-defined lines and graceful forms, his noble spirit, his Divine character, his sublime sonship, his blessed life. And so he could speak calmly, even triumphantly, of the suffering Saviour, and glory in the dying of the Lord Jesus, through which the life of Jesus found its highest and best manifestations. How much a picture depends upon its background! Fill the front with the most exquisite figures or landscape, still all the tone and character and impression of the figure will depend upon its background. You may so paint as to leave the forms and figures indistinct and uncertain. You may throw out into prominence the special thought or truth which you seek to embody in form; your picture may be calm morning, hot noonday, flushed evening, tender twilight, or gathering night, according to your background. St. Paul felt what shadows of suffering and woe lay all behind that life of his Lord; but they helped him to see the glory of Christ himself; they seemed to bring out so clearly the Divine and blessed life that was in him. Illustrate by the language of Isa. liii. and Phil. ii. 5—11. Also from the scenes of Gethsemane and Calvary. The Captain of our salvation was made perfect, to our view, through suffering.

II. St. Paul's conception of his own life. He could wish nothing better for himself than that what was true of Christ might be true of him, and that his sufferings, too, might show up his character and help to make him a blessing and a power for good. St. Paul never could glory in mere suffering. Suffering is grievance and loss. But if they could be like Christ's sufferings, not merely borne for him, and in the doing of his work, but actually like his, and ordained by God to be the same to him, and to others through him, as Jesus' sufferings did! The apostle felt he could glory in that. And this is the view of suffering that we also need to gain. Our troubles and sorrows are as the dying of the Lord Jesus. Once laying hold of this, we find that we have one thing to be supremely anxious about—it is that our dying shall show up Christ's life in us, shall make the Christly virtues and graces manifest in our mortal flesh. We have our sorrows. Does our character shine out clearly on the darkness of them? Do men see and feel our "whiteness" by the contrast of them? Are we beautiful with a Divine patience, and fragrant with a Divine sweetness, in the very darkness? On the background of our pain do men see our submission? In the hour of our disappointment do we show up to men our trust in God? When heart and flesh fail does the sanctifying Spirit of Christ make our very faces glow with the heavenly light? Is it true of us that the "life of Jesus is manifested in our mortal flesh"?—R. T.

Ver. 16.—*The outward and the inward man.* For the word "perish" in this verse, the Revised Version reads "is decaying." "Outward man" is the body, "inward man" is the soul, so far as the terms may be understood by anybody. "Outward man" is the whole sphere of the senses and the flesh; "inward man" is the whole sphere of the moral, the spiritual, the Divine, the eternal, so far as the terms may be apprehended by the quickened and regenerate of mankind. The "outward man" is man related to the "seen and temporal;" the "inward man" is man related to the "unseen and eternal." And what the apostle so plainly says in our text is this—the "outward man," the material framework of the body, and the whole circle of purely human and earthly relations, are yielding to a gradual process of decay, and soon they must all pass away. But the "inward man," the spiritual life, the very man himself, is day by day rising, through successive stages of renewal, to yet higher life. And the very decayings of the body and of the earthly surroundings bear directly upon the nourishment and growth of the soul's life, and so upon the soul's future. This is the thought which is set before us for our consideration, and we begin with that familiar truth on which the statement of the text rests.

I. Body-life and soul-life both depend on nourishment, on food. This is the law of all created life. Angels live on angels' food. Souls live on appropriate souls' food. And bodies live by meat and drink and air. Science tells us that bodily life, health, fatness, and vigour directly depend on the character and quantity and appropriateness of the food supplied. Given vitality and freedom from active disease, and any bodily result that is desired can be obtained by giving flesh-forming, or bone-forming, or brain-making foods. And the health, the vigour, and the work of our soul's life just as directly depend upon the food with which it is nourished. Would you get more good work out of your souls? Then you must feed them better. Do you expose your souls to much peril? Then you must improve and increase their food. We may speak of the soul's life as being *faith* and *love,* and as having for its natural expression *worship* and *work.* Then the soul's food which we provide must bear, in the most direct and efficient way, on these four things. Here is a most practical problem for each one of us to solve in our daily life—What will nourish into the fullest health and strength my soul's faith and my soul's love? What will strengthen the soul's brain and heart for holy worship, for prayer and praise, and the soul's muscle and nerve for holy work? As life unfolds there come to us all times of special stress and strain. Business has its unusual anxieties. Home has its unusual cares. Decisions of grave importance have to be made, and we too easily forget at such times that we need better soul-food; we must be oftener at the secret sources of spiritual nourishment; we must find out how strong they can become who eat of the tree of life, who partake of that Bread of life which satisfies, and that "flesh and blood" which are "meat indeed and drink indeed."

II. NOURISH THE BODY-LIFE HOW WE MAY, IT IS WEARING DOWN TO DECAY AND DEATH. "The outward man perishes." "The fashion of this world passeth away." All the feeding, all the nourishing, all the fresh air, cannot keep the bodily powers working over-long; for soon the sight grows dim, and the hearing fails, and the taste palls, and the hands tremble, and the breath goes hard, and the limbs totter, and then the golden bowl is broken at the fountain, and man goeth to his long home, and the mourners go about the streets. There is a fixed limit beyond which the body cannot go. None of us can with impunity exert ourselves beyond the limits of our physical strength, for gradually, as the years pass on, our vital force is lowered, our recuperative power fails, the body is really decaying and wasting down to helplessness and death. But why should we trouble because we cannot feed these bodies of ours into a strength that shall resist disease and old age, and make our years last through all the generations? They are not *us.* They are but the machinery, the agency, the sphere, of our sublime moral trial. They may last no longer than is needed for the perfecting of the trial. I shall not want this frail body, with its limited senses and relations, nor shall I want this "ower sin-burdened earth," when God sees that my moral trial is over; when he has found out, by this practical experiment, what I really am. I can see them both pass away, and enter God's spiritual and incorruptible body—the glorified counterpart of this body I now have—which is fashioned akin to the "new heavens and new earth, wherein dwelleth righteousness."

III. NOURISH THE SOUL-LIFE, AND IT WILL GROW ON FOR EVER. For there are no forces that can touch the regenerate soul to destroy it. "I give unto them eternal life," He said who brought life and immortality to light by His gospel, " and they shall never perish, neither shall any man pluck them out of my hand." Law, Satan, sin, temptation, worldly atmospheres, death, and hell cannot hurt the soul whose vitality is well nourished and maintained. Take food for the body, and its service is soon spent. Take food for the soul, and its service never can be spent; it becomes a permanent element of good; it has gone to the making of character, which death has no power to touch. There are, indeed, varieties of religious experience, ups and downs of religious feeling. We may encrust our lives with worldliness, we may feed our souls with nothing but the luxuries of human pleasure, and if we do so we must suffer, and bitterly suffer. Great diseases and calamities may come to us as cleansing and correcting processes. But God will not let the soul-growth be permanently hindered. If we will not make the soul thrive by the food of truth, and duty, and worship, and prayer, and fellowship, then he will make it thrive by the medicine of pain, and distress, and humiliation, and bereavement, and loss; but thrive and grow it shall. "The inward man [shall be] renewed day by day."

IV. THE VERY WEARING DOWN, SUFFERING, DECAYING, AND DYING OF THE BODY-LIFE ARE MADE AGENTS IN NOURISHING THE SOUL'S LIFE. St. Paul goes on from our text to say, "For our light affliction . . . worketh for us a far more exceeding and eternal weight of glory." How bright and hopeful that bruised, worn, suffering apostle always was! He even found it in his heart to glory in his infirmities, because the weaker he was, the more of Christ's power must rest on him and work through him. The outward man perishes, but he is not going to be sad or to faint about it, since the inward man is renewed day by day. And Paul says that there is such an intimate relation between these two that, by the dying of the one, the life of the other is actually furthered. Our light afflictions and our testing death are even made food for our soul's growth. We may thrive upon our very woes. Trial, toil, struggle, weariness, frailty, pain, bereavement, all the body can know of sorrow and care, are the soul's food. It lives by them. It thrives on them. It steps up toward heaven with the help of them. "Out of the eater it brings forth meat; out of the strong it brings forth sweetness."—R. T.

Ver. 17.—*The Christian estimate of affliction.* There is a passionate intensity, a kind of extravagance, in these words, which we often notice in the utterances of the noble but impulsive apostle. High feeling, strained emotion, are often helpful in our religious experiences. They lift us, as on a great wave, over the bar of difficulty. They help us in the doing of duty, and they lighten the burden of our sorrow. Our hymns and sacred poems are often the expression of such high emotions as are only felt by the best of men in their best of times; but they are an inspiration and a joy to us, though they may be beyond our actual attainment. In this way we may get gracious help through our text. The context refers to ministerial troubles, but troubles are our common human lot, and if we had to choose what form they should take for us, we should make sad mistakes. Concerning the blessings wrought by affliction we have remarkable Scripture testimonies. Moses would rather "suffer affliction with the people of God than enjoy the pleasures of sin for a season." David says, "Before I was afflicted I went astray, but now will I keep thy word." Solomon tells us that it is "better to go into the house of mourning than into the house of feasting." And the writer of the Epistle to the Hebrews says that "whom the Lord loveth he chasteneth, and scourgeth every son whom he receiveth." Our text suggests what estimate the child of God may and ought to make of afflictions, and he may judge them as regards *weight, time,* and *influence.*

I. As to their weight. He may call them "light afflictions." This is apparently untrue. Surely Job, and Jacob, and Naomi, and David, and Martha and Mary could never call theirs "light afflictions." It is truly said that "no affliction for the present seemeth to be joyous but grievous." It seems impossible to call such a catalogue of woes as is given us in ch. xi. 23—27 "light afflictions." And yet this is the deeper truth, and we may see that it is if we weigh our troubles in fair balances : (1) in the balances of our deservings; (2) in the balances of comparison with the sufferings of others; and (3) in the balances of consequences, for out of sorrow comes spiritual health. Both knowledge and faith may help us to call our affliction "light."

II. As to their time. "But for a moment." This also is apparently untrue. Joseph cannot call those weary prison years "but a moment." The captives in Babylon, worn out with hope deferred, hung their harps upon the willows because they could sing no longer. They could not call their captivity "but for a moment." And we can never call "short" those dreadful six hours of agony borne by our Lord upon the cross. And yet this also is the deepest truth. In comparison with life itself it is. Our times of suffering are few, of joy are many; they lie together in something of the proportion of streams and fields. Then, too, it is the actual fact that in our suffering times only brief moments bring unbearable pain. And it is found that the worst pain is the least remembered; it passes, and we cannot even recall it, so as to suffer it over again in imagination. And earthly suffering is truly but for a moment if it be compared with the eternity of joy into which it leads us.

III. As to their influence. "Working a . . . weight of glory." It is as important that we should be prepared for the glory as that the glory should be prepared for us. St. Paul's idea of glory is what is done by affliction in the Christian himself. And amongst the things wrought in the Christian character and life we may note these. 1. Patience—the power to be quiet and wait. 2. Trust—the full committal of our keeping to God. 3. Holiness—the deliverance from the enslaving power of evil. 4. The sanctifying of human relationships, which nothing makes so tender and so true as does our sharing in common sorrows. 5. And the renewal of Christian activity; for affliction is the time when we may seriously review the past, and make earnest resolves for the days to come.—R. T.

EXPOSITION.

CHAPTER V.

Continuation of the topic that hope is the chief support of the preacher of the gospel (vers. 1—10). Their self-sacrifice in preaching the gospel of reconciliation (vers. 11—21).

Vers. 1—10.—*The hope of the future life is the great support of our efforts.*

Ver. 1.—For. A further explanation of the hope expressed in ch. iv. 17. We know. This accent of certainty is found only in the Christian writers. Our earthly house. Not the "house of clay" (Job iv. 19), but the house which serves us as the home of our souls on earth ; as in 1 Cor. xv. 40. Of this tabernacle ; literally, *the house of the tent ;* i.e. the tent of our mortality, the mortal body. In 2 Pet. i. 13, 14 it is called *skenoma*, and the expression, "the Word became flesh and *dwelt* among us," is literally, "he *tabernacled* among us"—he wore "a tent like ours and of the same material." The figure would be specially natural to one whose occupation was that of a tentmaker. Compare—

"Here in the body pent,
Afar from him I roam,
But nightly pitch my wandering tent
A day's march nearer home."

A very similar expression occurs in Wisd. ix. 15, "*The earthly tabernacle* (γεῶδες σκῆνος) weigheth down the mind." Be dissolved; rather, *be taken to pieces.* A building. Something more substantial than that moving tenement. Of God; literally, *from God ;* namely, not one of the "many mansions" spoken of in John xiv. 2, but the resurrection-body furnished to us by him. We *have* this building from God, for it exists now, and shall be ours at the same time that our tent-home is done away with. Not made with hands. Not like those tent-dwellings at which St. Paul was daily toiling with the hands which ministered to his own necessities. In the heavens. To be joined with "we have." Heaven is our general home and country (Heb. xi. 16), but the present allusion is to the glorified bodies in which our souls shall live in heaven (comp. 1 Cor. xv. 42—49).

Ver. 2.—In this we groan. Since we have the firstfruits of the Spirit, who assures us of that future building from God, we, in this earthly tent, "groan within ourselves, waiting for the adoption, to wit the redemption of our body" (Rom. viii. 23). To be clothed upon; rather, *to further clothe ourselves with.* Here the metaphors of a tent and a garment—the "wandering tent" and the "mortal vesture of decay"—are interfused in a manner on

which only the greatest writers can venture The corruptible yearns to clothe itself with the incorruptible, the mortal with immortality (1 Cor. xv. 53). The glorified body is compared to an over-garment. House; rather, *habitation (oikētērion).*

Ver. 3.—If so be that. The verse may be rendered, "If, that is, being clothed, we shall not be found naked." The word "naked" must then mean "bodiless," and the reference will be to those whom, at his coming, Christ shall find *clothed in these mortal bodies,* and not separated from them, i.e. quick and not dead (1 Thess. iv. 17; 1 Cor. xv. 51). This seems to be the simplest and most natural of the multitude of strange interpretations with which the pages of commentators are filled. It is true that the aorist *endusamenoi*, means literally, "having clothed ourselves," and that, in taking this meaning, we should have expected the perfect participle *endedumenoi*, having been clothed. If this be thought an insuperable difficulty, we must suppose the verse to mean "If, that is, in reality we shall be found [at Christ's coming] after having put on some intermediate body, and therefore not as mere disembodied spirits." But there is no allusion in Scripture to any intermediate body, nor is any gleam of light shed on the mode of life among the dead between death and resurrection, though the Church rejects the dream of Psychopannychia, or an interval of unconscious sleep. The uncertainty of the meaning is increased by two various readings, *ei per* instead of *ei ge*, which latter expresses greater doubt about the matter; and *ekdusamenoi* (D, F, G), which would mean "if in reality, after *unclothing* ourselves [i.e. after 'shuffling off this mortal coil'], we shall not be found naked." This seems to be the conjecture of some puzzled copyists, who did not see that a *contrast*, and not a coincidence, between the two expressions is intended. If this reading were correct, it would mean, as Chrysostom says, "Even if we would lay aside the body, we shall not there be presented *without* a body, but with the *same* body which has then become incorruptible." It is quite untenable to make "clothed" mean "clothed *with righteousness*," as Olshausen does. In the Talmud, 'Shabbath' (f. 152, 2), the righteous are compared to men who keep from stain the robes given them by a king (i.e. their bodies), which robes the king deposits in his treasury and sends the wearers away (bodiless) in peace; but foolish servants stain these robes, and the king sends the robes to the wash, and the wearers to prison.

Ver. 4.—For we that are, etc.; literally, *for indeed we who are in the tent ;* i.e. in the transitory mortal body. **Do groan.** "Oh wretched man that I am! who shall deliver me from the body of this death?" (Rom. vii. 24). **Being burdened.** "The corruptible body presseth down the soul, and the earthy tabernacle weigheth down the mind that museth upon many things" (Wisd. ix. 15). **Not for that we would be unclothed, but clothed upon**; more literally, *since we do not wish to strip off (our bodily garment) but to put another garment over it.* St. Paul here repudiates the Manichean notion that the body is a disgrace, or in itself the source of evil. He was not like Plotinus, who "blushed that he had a body;" or like St. Francis of Assisi, who called his body "my brother the ass;" or like the Curè d'Ars, who (as we have said) spoke of his body as "ce cadavre." He does not, therefore, desire to get rid of his body, but to "clothe it over" with the garment of immortality. Incidentally this implies the wish that he may be *alive* and not *dead* when the Lord returns (1 Cor. xv. 35—54). **Mortality**; rather, *the mortal; that which is mortal.* **Might be swallowed up of life.** As in the case of Enoch (Gen. v. 24) and Elijah (2 Kings ii. 11), who entered into life otherwise than through "the grave and gate of death." St. Paul wishes to enter the "building from God" without having been first buried in the collapse of the "soul's dark cottage battered and decayed." He desires to put on the robe of immortality without stripping off the rent garb of the body.

Ver. 5.—**He who hath wrought us for the selfsame thing.** God prepared and perfected us for this very result, namely, to put on the robe of immortality. **The earnest** (see ch. i. 22). The quickening life imparted by the Spirit of life is a pledge and part payment of the incorruptible eternal life. The Spirit is "the Earnest of our inheritance" (Eph. i. 14; iv. 30).

Ver. 6.—**Therefore** we are **always confident**; literally, *being of good courage.* The sentence in the Greek is unfinished (an anacoluthon), but is resumed after the parenthesis by the repetition, "we are of good courage." *Always* (ch. iv. 8). **We are at home in the body.** The tent is pitched in the desert, and even the pillar of fire can only shine through its folds. Yet the tent may become brighter and brighter as life goes on,

"To me the thought of death is terrible,
Having such hold on life. To you it is not
More than a step into the open air
Out of a tent already luminous
With light which shines through its transparent folds."

(Longfellow.)

Absent from the Lord (John xiv. 2, 3). Christ is indeed with us here and always; but the nearness of presence and the clearness of vision in that future life will be so much closer and brighter, that here, by comparison, we are absent from him altogether.

Ver. 7.—**For we walk by faith** (ch. iv. 18; Heb. xi. 1; Rom. viii. 25). **Not by sight**; rather, *not by appearance; not by anything actually seen.* We do not yet see "face to face" (1 Cor. xiii. 12), but are guided by things which "eye hath not seen."

Ver. 8.—**To be absent**, etc.; literally, *to be away from the home of the body, but to be at home with the Lord.* **To be present with the Lord.** The hope expressed is exactly the same as in Phil. i. 23, except that here (as in ver. 4) he expresses a desire not "*to depart,*" but to be quit of the body without the necessity for death.

Ver. 9.—**We labour**; literally, *we are emulous.* This, says Bengel, is "the sole legitimate ambition." The same word occurs in Rom. xv. 20. **Whether present or absent;** literally, *whether at home or away from home;* i.e. whether with Christ or separated from him (as in ver. 8); or, "whether in the body or out of the body" (as in ver. 6). The latter would resemble 1 Thess. v. 10, "That *whether we wake or sleep* we may live with him." **We may be accepted of him**; literally, *to be well-pleasing to him.*

Ver. 10.—**We must all appear**; rather, *for it is necessary that we must all be made manifest;* that we must be shown in our real nature and character. The verb is not the same as in Rom. xiv. 10, which occurs in ch. iv. 14. **Before the judgment-seat of Christ.** The special final judgment is represented as taking place before the *bema* of Christ, although in Rom. xiv. 10 the best reading is "of God" (Matt. xxv. 31, 32). St. Paul might naturally use this Roman and Greek idea of the *bema*, being too familiar with it in his own experience (comp. Acts xii. 21; xviii. 12; xxv. 6; Rom. xiv. 10). **The things** done **in the body**; literally, *the things (done) by the instrumentality of the body.* Another reading (which only differs by a single letter from this) is, "the proper things of the body" (τὰ ἴδια τοῦ σώματος); *i.e.* the things which belong to it, which it *has made its own.* St. Paul, always intent on one subject at a time, does not stop to co-ordinate this law of natural retribution and inexorable Nemesis with that of the "forgiveness of sins" (1 Cor. v. 11; Rom. iii. 25), or with the apparently universal hopes which he seems sometimes to express (Rom. v. 17, 18; xi. 32). *Omnia exeunt in mysterium.* **According to that he hath done**; rather, *with reference to the things he did.* The aorist shows that all life will be as it were concentrated to one point. The Pelagians raised questions on this verse about the sinlessness of infants, etc., all of which may be left on one side, as probably nothing was more absolutely distant from the thoughts of St. Paul. Observe that each is to receive the natural issues of what he has done. There is to be an analogy between the sin and the retribution. The latter is but the ripe fruit of the former. We shall be punished by the action of natural laws, not of arbitrary inflictions. We shall reap what we have sown, not harvests of other grain (Rom. ii. 5—11; Rev. xxii. 12; Gal. vi. 7). **Whether it be good or bad.** St. Paul, who always confines himself to one topic at a time, does not here enter on the question of the cutting off of the entailed curse by repentance and forgiveness. He leaves unsolved the antinomy between normal inevitable consequence and free remission.

Vers. 11—19.—*Self-devotion of the ministry of reconciliation.*

Ver. 11.—**Knowing therefore the terror of the Lord, we persuade men.** Multitudes of texts have been torn from their context and grossly abused and misinterpreted, but few more so than this. It is the text usually chosen by those who wish to excuse a setting forth of God under the attributes of Moloch. With any such views it has not the remotest connection. It simply means, "Knowing therefore the fear of the Lord, we persuade men," either "to keep in view the same fear of the Lord as ourselves," or (reverting to his last assertion of his own sincerity and integrity in ver. 9), "that our sole ambition is to please God." The rendering, "the terror of the Lord," for the every-day expression, "the fear of the Lord," was wantonly intruded into modern versions by Beza, and has not a single word to be said in its favour. The phrase means (as always) not the dread which God inspires, but the holy fear which mingles with our love of him. To teach men to regard God with *terror* is to undo the best teaching of all Scripture, which indeed has too often been the main end of human systems of theology. *We persuade men.* Not in a bad sense (Gal. i. 10). The attacks and calumnies of enemies make it necessary to vindicate our integrity to men; but we have no need to do so to God, because he already knows us (comp. *"persuading* Blastus," Acts xii. 20). **We are made manifest unto God;** rather, *but to God we have been (and are) manifested.* He needs no self-defence from us. **Are made manifest in your consciences;** *but I hope that I have been, and am now, made manifest in your consciences.* In other words, I trust that this apology into which you have driven me has achieved its ends; and that, whatever may be your prejudices and innuendoes, before the bar of the individual *conscience* of each of you we now stand clear (comp. ch. iv. 2).

Ver. 12.—**For we commend not ourselves again unto you.** Still reverting to the charge that he was guilty of self-praise, he says that his object is not this, for it was needless (ch. iii. 2, 3). **But give you occasion to glory on our behalf.** But we speak as we have done to give you a starting-point for something to boast of on our behalf. He has already said (ch. i. 4) that the teachers and the taught in their mutual affection ought to have some ground for "boasting" (*i.e.* for speaking with some praise and exultation) of each other. The Corinthians were being robbed of this by the interested lies of St. Paul's opponents, who thought only about outward appearances. This is why he has set forth to them the aim and glory of his ministry. Nothing could be more gentle and forbearing than such a mode of stating his object. Yet for those who were sufficiently finely strung to understand it, there was an almost pathetic irony involved in it. **Which glory in appearance, and not in heart;** literally, *in face.* The grounds of their boasting, whatever they were, were superficial and external (ch. x. 7), not deep and sincere. But those who would judge of Paul aright must look into his very heart, and not on his face.

Ver. 13.—**For whether we be beside ourselves;** rather, *for whether we were mad.* Evidently some person or some faction had said of St. Paul, "He is beside himself," just as Festus said afterwards, "Paul, thou art mad," and as the Jews said of Paul's Lord and Master (John x. 20). The fervour of the apostle, his absorption in his work, his visions and ecstasies, his "speaking with tongues more than they all," his indifference to externals, his bursts of emotion, might all have given colour to this charge, which he here ironically accepts. "Mad or self-controlled—all was for your sakes." It is **to God;** rather *for God.* My "enthusiasm," "exaltation," or, if you will, my "madness," was but a phase of my work for him. **We be sober.** The word "sober" (*sōphrōn*) is derived from two words which mean "to *save* the *mind.*" It indicates wise self-control, such as was represented also by the many-sided Latin word *frugi.* It is the exact antithesis to madness (Acts xxvi. 25). What you call my "madness" belongs to the relation between my own soul and God; my practical sense and tact are for you. **For your sakes;** literally, *for you.*

Ver. 14.—**The love of Christ.** It matters little whether this be interpreted as a subjective genitive, "Christ's love to man," or as an objective genitive, "our love to Christ;" for the two suppose and interfuse each other. St. Paul's usage, however, favours the former interpretation (ch. xiii. 14; 1 Cor. xvi. 24). **Constraineth.** The word means that it compresses us, and therefore keeps us irresistibly to one object (Luke xii. 50). **That if one died for all, then were all dead.** This is an unfortunate mistranslation and wrong reading for *that one died for all, therefore all died.* What compels Paul to sacrifice himself to the work of God for his converts is the conviction, which he formed once for all at his conversion, that One, even Christ, died on behalf of all men (Rom. v. 15—19) a redeeming death (ver. 21); and that, consequently, in that death, all *potentially* died with him—died to their life of sin, and rose to the life of righteousness. The best comments on this bold and concentrated phrase are—" I died to the Law that I might live to Christ;" "I have been *crucified with Christ*" (Gal. ii. 19, 20); and, "Ye died, and your life has been hidden with Christ in God" (Col. iii. 3). When Christ died, all humanity, of which he was the federal Head, died potentially with him to sin and selfishness, as he further shows in the next verse.

Ver. 15.—**Unto themselves.** That they should live no longer the psychic, *i.e.* the animal, selfish, egotistic life, but to their risen Saviour (Rom. xiv. 7—9; 1 Cor. vi. 19).

Ver. 16.—**Know no man after the flesh.** It is a consequence of my death with Christ that I have done with carnal, superficial, earthly, external judgments according to the appearance, and not according to the heart. **Yea, though we have known Christ after the flesh.** The word for "know" is different from the one just used (οἶδα, *scio*; ἔγνωκα, *cognovi*), and may be rendered, "though we have taken note of." The whole phrase, which has been interpreted in multitudes of different ways, and has led to many different hypotheses, must be understood in accordance with the context. St. Paul is saying that he has now renounced all mere earthly and human judgments; and he here implies that the day has been (whether—which is a very unlikely view—before his conversion, when he looked on Christ as a "deceiver," or just after his conversion, when possibly he may only have known him partially as the *Jewish* Messiah) when he knew Christ only in this fleshly way; but henceforth he will know him so no more. Probably this "knowing Christ after the flesh" is a rebuke to those members of the Christ party at Corinth who may have boasted that they were superior to all others because they had personally seen or known Christ—a spirit which Christ himself not only discouraged (John xvi. 7) but even rebuked (Matt. xii. 50). To St. Paul Christ is now regarded as far above all local, national, personal, and Jewish limitations, and as the principle of spiritual life in the heart of every Christian. In the view which he took of his Lord St. Paul henceforth has banished all Jewish particu-larism for gospel catholicity. He regards Christ, not in the light of earthly relationships and conditions, but as the risen, glorified, eternal, universal Saviour.

Ver. 17.—**Therefore.** If even a human, personal, external knowledge of Christ is henceforth of no significance, it follows that there must have been a total change in all relations towards him. The historic fact of such a changed relationship is indicated clearly in John xx. 17. Mary Magdalene was there lovingly taught that a "recognition of Christ after the flesh," *i.e.* as merely a *human* friend, was to be a thing of the past. In Christ; *i.e.* a Christian. For perfect faith attains to mystic union with Christ. **A new creature**; rather, *a new creation* (Gal. vi. 15). The phrase is borrowed from the rabbis who used it to express the condition of a proselyte. But the meaning is not mere Jewish arrogance and exclusiveness, but the deep truth of spiritual regeneration and the new birth (John iii. 3; Eph. ii. 10; iv. 23, 24; Col. iii. 3, etc.). **Old things**; literally, *the ancient things*, all that belongs to the old Adam. **Behold.** The word expresses the writer's vivid realization of the truth he is uttering. **All things.** The whole sphere of being, and therewith the whole aim and character of life. The clause illustrates the "new creation."

Ver. 18.—**And all things are of God**; literally, *but all things* (in this "new creation") *are from God.* **Who hath reconciled us**; rather, *who* (by Christ's one offering of himself) *reconciled us to himself.* We were his enemies (Rom. v. 10; xi. 28), but, because he was still our Friend and Father, he brought us back to himself by Christ. **The ministry of reconciliation.** The ministry which teaches the reconciliation which he has effected for us.

Ver. 19.—**God was in Christ, reconciling the world unto himself.** This and the many other passages of Scripture which always represent the atonement as the work of the blessed Trinity, and as being the result of the *love*, not of the *wrath*, of God, ought to have been a sufficient warning against the hideous extravagance of those *forensic* statements of the atonement which have disgraced almost a thousand years of theology (Rom. v. 10; 1 John iv. 10). That God's purpose of mercy embraced all mankind, and not an elect few, is again and again stated in Scripture (see Col. i. 20). **Not imputing their trespasses unto them.** See this developed in Rom. xv. 5—8. **Hath entrusted unto us**; literally, *who also deposited in us,* as though it were some sacred treasure.

Ver. 20.—**Now then.** It is, then, on Christ's behalf that we are ambassadors. This excludes all secondary aims. St. Paul uses the same expression in Eph. vi. 20, adding with fine contrast that he is "an ambassador in fetters." **As though God did beseech you by us**; rather, *as if God were exhorting you by our means.* **In Christ's stead**; rather, *we, on Christ's behalf, beseech you.* **Be ye reconciled to God.** This is the sense of the embassy. The aorist implies an immediate acceptance of the offer of reconciliation.

Ver. 21.—**He hath made him** to be sin for us; rather, *he made;* he speaks with definite reference to the cross. The expression is closely analogous to that in Gal. iii. 13, where it is said that Christ has been "made *a curse* for us." He was, as St. Augustine says, "delictorum susceptor, non commissor." He knew no sin; nay, he was the very righteousness, holiness itself (Jer. xxiii. 6), and yet, for our benefit, God made him to be "sin" for us, in that he "sent him in the likeness of sinful flesh and for sin" (Rom. viii. 3). Many have understood the word "sin" in the sense of sin offering (Lev. v. 9, LXX.); but that is a precarious applica-tion of the word, which is not justified by any other passage in the New Testament. We cannot, as Dean Plumptre says, get beyond the simple statement, which St. Paul is content to leave in its unexplicable mystery, "Christ identified with man's sin; man identified with Christ's righteousness." And thus, in Christ, God becomes Jehovah-Tsidkenu, "the Lord our Righteousness" (Jer. xxiii. 6). **That we might be made the righteousness of God in him**; rather, *that we might become.* The best comment on the pregnant significance of this verse is Rom. i. 16, 17, which is developed and explained in so large a section of that great Epistle (see iii. 22—25; iv. 5—8; v. 19, etc.). *In him* In his blood is a means of propitiation by which the righteousness of God becomes the righteousness of man (1 Cor. i. 30), so that man is justified. The truth which St. Paul thus develops and expresses is stated by St. Peter and St. John in a simpler and less theological form (1 Pet. ii. 22—24; 1 John iii. 5).

HOMILETICS.

Vers. 1—7.—*Christian knowledge concerning the future body of the good.* "For we know that if our earthly house," etc. Two things are to be noticed at the outset. 1. *Metaphorical representations* of the body. The body is here spoken of under the figure of a "tabernacle" or a tent, and of a vestment or clothing. These two things would not be so distinct in the mind of the apostle as they are in ours, for both had the same qualities of *movableness* and *protection*. The "house" to which the apostle refers was not a building of bricks or stone, a superstructure that would be stationary, but a mere tent to be carried about. 2. The *implied necessity* of the body. Paul's language implies that the body is a clothing or protection. As a clothing, or protection, for the soul it is necessary, both here and in the other world. The soul must have an organ where-ever it is. Now what does the Christian know concerning the future body?

I. He knows it will be BETTER THAN THE PRESENT. 1. It will be directly Divine. "A building of God." The present body is from God, but it comes from him through secondary instrumentalities. The future body will come direct, it will not be transmitted from sire to son. 2. It will be fitted for a higher sphere. "In the heavens." The present body is fitted for the earthly sphere, it is of the "earth, earthy." The future will be fitted for the more ethereal, and celestial. 3. It will be more enduring. "Eternal." This body is like the tent, temporary; it has no firm foundation; it is shaken by every gust. We "perish before the moth." The future body will be eternal, free from the elements of decay. 4. It will be more enjoyable. "For in this we groan, earnestly desiring to be clothed upon with our house which is from heaven," etc. In this body we "groan, being burdened." To what pains and diseases is the present body subject! By implication the apostle states the future body will be free from all this, for all that is mortal will be "swallowed up of life." In that body there will be no groaning, no sighs or sorrows, no burden, no weight to depress the energies or to impede progress. The future body will be more fitted to *receive* the high things of God, and more fitted to *communicate* them also.

II. He knows he is now BEING DIVINELY FITTED FOR THE BETTER BODY OF THE FUTURE. "Now he that hath wrought us for the selfsame thing is God, who also hath given unto us the earnest of the Spirit." Every seed has its own body; it is the seed that makes the body; the organization does not produce the life, but the life the organi-zation. And this spiritual life in man God is now preparing to pass into a higher body. Just as the chrysalis is being fitted to struggle into an organization with higher appetencies, more exquisite in form, and with faculties that shall bear it into mid-heaven. When will you have this body? When your soul has the life-energy to produce it.

Vers. 8—10.—*The philosophy of courage.* "We are confident, I say," etc. Paul says we are courageous, or of good courage. Courage is often confounded with recklessness of life, a brutal insensibility to danger. True courage always implies two things. 1. *The existence of unavoidable dangers.* He who rushes into danger is not courageous, but reckless. Paul had unavoidable dangers: "We are troubled on every side." 2. *True convictions of being.* Ignorance of existence may make men reckless, but never courageous. What was Paul's view of life? (1) He regarded the body as the organ of himself. He speaks of it as a "house," a "tabernacle," etc. (2) The soul he regards as the personality of his being. "We that are in this tabernacle," etc. The soul, not the body, is the "I," or self. (3) He regarded death as a mere change in the mode of his being. Death changes the house and the garment; it is not the extinction of the tenant or the wearer. (4) He regarded heaven as the perfection of his being. "The house not made with hands, eternal in the heavens." The courage of which the apostle here speaks seems to have been based on three things.

I. A consciousness that his death would not ENDANGER THE INTERESTS of his being. Notice: 1. His view of the interests of being. It was being "present with the Lord." 2. His view of the bearing of death upon the interests of being. He regarded it as the flight of the spirit into the presence of the Lord. "Absent from the body, present with the Lord." A view of death this antagonistic to the ideas of *purgatory, annihilation, soul-sleep.* 3. His state of mind under the influence of these thoughts. "Willing rather to be absent from the body."

II. A consciousness that death would not DESTROY THE GREAT PURPOSES of being. It is the characteristic of a rational being that he has some purpose in life—the purpose is that in which he lives, it makes life valuable to him. To a man who has no purpose in life or has lost his purpose, life is deemed of little worth. What was Paul's purpose in life? "Wherefore we labour, that, whether present or absent, we may be accepted of him." Is not this purpose sublimely reasonable? If there be a God, does not reason teach that to please him should be the supreme purpose of all intelligent creatures? Now, Paul felt that death would not destroy this purpose. It destroys the purpose of the voluptuous, avaricious, etc.; and hence to them it is terrible. But it does not destroy the chief purpose of the Christian. In all worlds and times his chief purpose will be to be "accepted of him."

III. A consciousness that death would not PREVENT THE REWARDS of being. "We must all appear [or, ' be made manifest'] before the judgment-seat of Christ." Success, while it should never be regarded either as a rule of conduct or a test of character, must ever have an influence on the mind of man in every department of labour. Non-success discourages. Paul felt that his labour here would appear and be recognized hereafter. "We must all appear," etc. 1. Every one shall receive the recompense of labour after death. "Must all appear." None absent. 2. Every one shall receive a reward for every deed. "That every one may receive the things done in his body." No lost labour. With this consciousness we may well be courageous amidst all the dangers here and in view of the great hereafter. Dread of death is a disgrace to the Christian. "If," says Cicero, "I were now disengaged from my cumbrous body, and on my way to Elysium; and some superior being should meet me in my flight and make me the offer of returning and remaining in my body, I should, without hesitation, reject the offer; so much should I prefer going into Elysium to be with Socrates and Plato and all the ancient worthies, and to spend my time in converse with them." How much more should the Christian desire to be "absent from the body, and present with the Lord"!

Vers. 11—18.—*Man in Christ a new man.* "For whether we be beside ourselves," etc. To be "in Christ" is to be in his Spirit, in his character, to live in his ideas, principles, etc. Such a man is "a new creature."

I. The man in Christ has a new IMPERIAL IMPULSE. "The love of Christ constraineth us." Whether the "love of Christ" here means his love to us or our love for him is of no practical import. The latter implies the former; his love is the flame that kindles ours.   Now, this love was Paul's dominant passion ; it " constrained " him ; it carried him on like a resistless torrent ; it was the regnant impulse.   Two thoughts in relation to this new imperial impulse.   1. *It is incomprehensible to those who possess it not.*   " Whether we be beside ourselves, it is to God," etc.   Probably Paul appeared as mad to his contemporaries.   They saw him brave the greatest perils, oppose the greatest powers, make the greatest sacrifices.   What was the principle that moved him to all ?   This they could not understand.   Had it been ambition or avarice, they could have understood it.   But " the love of Christ " they knew nothing of; it was a new thing in the world.   Only the man who has it can understand it ; love alone can interpret love.   2. *It arises from reflection on the death of Christ.*   It is not an inbred passion, not a blind impulse, not something divinely transferred into the heart.   No; it comes " because we thus judge, that if one died for all, then were all dead."   Paul assumes as an undoubted fact that Christ died for all.   Because of this fact he concludes : (1) That the whole world were in a ruined condition: " Then were all dead."   (2) That this fact should inspire all to act with the same sacrificing spirit as Christ.   " He died for all, that they which live should not henceforth live unto themselves, but unto him."

II. The man in Christ has a new SOCIAL STANDARD.   " Henceforth we know no man after the flesh."   The world has numerous standards by which it judges men, birth, wealth, office, etc.   To a man filled and fired with love to Christ these are nothing.   He estimates man by his *rectitude,* not by his rank ; by his *spirit,* not by his station ; by his *principles,* not by his property.   Paul might have said—I once knew men after the flesh, Jew or Gentile, rich or poor, learned or ignorant ; but now I know them so no more ; I see them now in the light of the cross, sinners dead in trespasses and sins ; " Yea, though we have known Christ after the flesh," etc., I think no more of his body, but of his mind, not of his station, but of his Spirit.   The fact that this is the true standard serves : 1. As a test by which to try our own religion.   2. As a guide for us in the promotion of Christianity.   3. As a principle on which to form our friendships with men, 4. As a rule to regulate our social conduct.

III. The man in Christ has a new SPIRITUAL HISTORY.   " Therefore if any man be in Christ, he is a new creature."   In what sense can this change be called a creation ?   1. It is the production of a *new thing.*   This passion for Christ is a new thing in the universe.   2. It is the production of a *new thing by the agency of God.*   Creation is the work of God.   3. It is the production of a *new thing according to a Divine plan.*   The almighty Maker works by plan in all.

IV. The man in Christ has a NEW STANDING.   " All things are of God, who hath reconciled us," etc.   That is, all things pertaining to this new creation.   The great want of man is reconciliation to God.   Man's alienation or apostasy from his Maker is *the* sin of all his sins, and the source of all his miseries.   His reconciliation is not the means to his salvation; it is his salvation.   Friendship with him is heaven.   On the other hand, alienation is hell.   A river cut from the fountain dries up; a branch cut from the tree withers and dies ; a planet cut from the sun rushes into ruin.   Separate a soul from God its Fountain, its Root, its Centre, and it dies— dies to all that makes existence tolerable.   Such, then, is what Christianity does for us.

Vers. 19, 20.—*God's work in Christ.*   " To wit, that God was in Christ," etc.   God is a great Worker.   He is the eternal Fountain of life in unremitting flow.   He is essentially active, the mainspring of all activity in the universe but that of sin.   There are at least four organs through which he works—*material laws, animal instincts, moral mind,* and *Jesus Christ.*   By the first he leads on the great revolutions of inanimate nature in all its departments; by the second he preserves, guides, and controls all the sentient tribes that populate the earth, the air, and the sea; by the third, through the laws of reason and the dictates of conscience, he governs the vast empire of mind; and by the fourth, viz. Christ, he works out the redemption of sinners in our world. There is no more difficulty in regarding him in the one Person, Christ, for a certain work than there is in regarding him as being in material nature, animal instinct, or moral mind.   The words lead us to make three remarks concerning God's work in Christ.

I. It is a work of RECONCILING HUMANITY TO GOD.   " God was in Christ recon- ciling the world unto himself."   The work of reconciling implies two things—*enmity* on the side of one of the parties, and a *change of mind* in one of the parties. The enmity here is not on God's part—he is love; but on man's. The "carnal mind is enmity with God." Nor is the change on God's part. He *cannot* change, he *need* not change. He could never become more loving and merciful. The change needed is on man's part, and on man's *exclusively*. Paul speaks of the world being reconciled to God, not of God to the world. The "world;" not a section of the race, but all mankind.

II. It is a work involving the REMISSION OF SINS. "Not imputing [reckoning] their trespasses unto them." The reconciled man is no longer reckoned guilty. Three facts will throw light on this. The state of enmity towards God is : 1. A *state of sin*. There is a virtue in disliking some characters, but it is evermore a sin to dislike God, for he is the All-good. 2. A state of sin *liable to punishment*. Indeed, sin is its own punishment. 3. In reconciliation, the enmity being removed, *the punishment is obviated*. What is pardon? A separating of man from his sins and their consequences. This God does in Christ.

III. It is a work in which GENUINE MINISTERS ARE ENGAGED. "He hath committed unto us the word of reconciliation. Now then we are ambassadors for Christ, as though God did beseech you by us: we pray you in Christ's stead, be ye reconciled to God." Observe: 1. The *position* of the true minister. He acts on behalf of Christ, and stands in "Christ's stead." 2. The *earnestness* of the true minister. "We pray you."

From the whole we observe concerning this work : 1. That it is a work of *unbounded mercy*. Whoever heard the offended party seeking the friendship of the offender? 2. It is a work *essential to human happiness*. In the nature of the case there is no happiness without this reconciliation. 3. It is a work exclusively of *moral influence*. No coercion on the one hand, no angry denunciations on the other, can do it; it can only be effected by the logic of love. 4. It is a work that must *be gradual*. Mind cannot be forced ; there must be reflection, repentance, resolution.

Ver. 21.—*Christ made sin.* "For he hath made him to be sin for us, who knew no sin; that we might be made the righteousness of God in him." "Him who knew no sin he made to be sin on our behalf; that we might become the righteousness of God in him" (Revised Version). From this passage we gather three wonderful truths.

I. That Christ was ABSOLUTELY SINLESS. "Who knew no sin." Intellectually, of course, he knew all the sin in the world ; but he never experienced it, he was absolutely free from it. 1. He was "without sin," although *he lived in a sinful world*. Of all the millions who have been here he alone moved amongst the world and received no taint of moral contamination. 2. He was "without sin," although he was *powerfully tempted*. Had he been untemptable there would have been no virtue in his freedom from sin, and had there been no tempter there would have been nothing praiseworthy in his sinlessness. "He was tempted like as we are, yet without sin."

II. That, though sinless, Christ was in some sense MADE SIN BY GOD. "He hath made him to be sin for us." What meaneth this? 1. It cannot mean that God made the sinless One a sinner. This would be impossible. No one can create a moral character for another. 2. It cannot mean that God imputed to him the sin of the world, and punished him for the world's sin. The idea of literal substitution is repugnant to reason and unsustained by any honest interpretation of God's Holy Word. The atonement of Christ consists, not in what he said, did, or suffered, but in what he was. *He himself is the Atonement, the Reconciler.* What, then, does it mean? Two facts may throw some light. (1) That God sent Christ into a world of sinners to *become closely identified* with them. He was related to sinners, mingled with them, ate and drank with them, and was in the community, counted as one of them. "He was numbered with the transgressors." (2) That God permitted this world of sinners to *treat Christ as a sinner*. He was calumniated, persecuted, insulted, murdered. God permitted all this, and what he *permits* is, in Scripture language, often ascribed to him.

III. That the sinless One was thus made sin in order that men MIGHT PARTICIPATE IN. GOD'S RIGHTEOUSNESS. "That we might be made the righteousness of God in him." Never did Divine moral excellence or the righteousness of God shine out with such glory to man as in the sufferings which Christ endured in consequence of this connection with sinners. As the stars can only show themselves at night, and as aromatic plants can only emit their precious odour by pressure, so the highest moral virtues can only come out by suffering and battling with the wrong. What self-sacrificing love, what unconquerable attachment to truth, what loyalty to the infinite Father, what sublime heroism of love, was here exhibited in the incarnation, the beneficent deeds, and overwhelming sufferings of Jesus!

HOMILIES BY VARIOUS AUTHORS.

Vers. 1—10.—*Assurance of eternal life; faith and its effects.* Death intervenes between the present state of affliction and the glory of heaven, but death is only the destruction of the body now existing. It is not an end to bodily form and life. This is no speculation of the apostle's; it is an assurance, "for we *know*" that if this earthly tent be destroyed, it will be followed by an enduring habitation—a mansion, not a tabernacle. In the earthly body he groans, not because it is a body, but because it is flesh and blood suffering under the effects of sin, and hence he longs for the "house which is from heaven." It is a heaven for body as well as soul that he so ardently desires. To be bodiless even in glory is repulsive to his nature, since it would be nakedness. Death is repugnant. The separation of soul and body, however, is only temporary; it is not for unclothing, but for a better clothing, one suited to the capacities of spirit. If the fourth verse repeats the second verse, it enlarges the idea and qualifies it by stating the reason why he would be "clothed upon," viz. "that mortality might be swallowed up of life." And this longing is no mere instinct or natural desire, but a feeling inspired of God, who "hath wrought us for the selfsame thing." A Divine preparation was going on in this provisional tabernacle—a training of the spirit for the vision of Christ and a training of the body for the immortal companionship of the spirit. An "earnest" or pledge of this was already in possession. The sufferings sanctified by the Spirit, the longing, the animation of hope, were so many proofs and tokens of awaiting blessedness. How could he be otherwise than confident? Yea; he is "*always* confident." Though now confined to the body, yet it is *a home* that admits of affections and loving fellowships; and though it necessitates absence from the Lord and the house of "many mansions," nevertheless it is a home illumined by faith. "For we walk by faith, not by sight." The home is in the midst of visible objects that exercise our sense of sight, but our Christian walk, or movement from one world to another, is not directed by the eye, but by faith, the sense of the invisible. We know what are the functions of the eye. If we did not, the antithesis would convey no meaning. The eye receives impressions from external things, communicates them to the soul, is a main organ in developing thought and feeling, acts on the imagination and the will, and is continually adding something to the contents of the inward nature. Faith is like it as a medium of reception, unlike it in all else. Faith is not conversant with appearances. We do not see Christ in his glory; we see him (using the term figuratively) in his Word by means of the Spirit; and this seeing is faith. How do we know when we have faith? It attests itself in our capacity to see the path leading to eternal glory, and it enables us to walk therein. The path is from one home to another—from the home on the footstool to the home by the throne of Christ, and faith has the reality and vigour of a home sentiment. So strong and assuring is St. Paul's confidence that he prefers to depart and be with Christ. "At home in the body;" yes, but it is a sad home at best, and trial and affliction had begun to make it dreary to him. To die is to be with the Lord, and he was "willing rather to be absent from the body, and to be present with the Lord." Whether absent or present, at home or away from home, we labour that we "may be accepted of him." To make himself and his life acceptable to Christ was paramount to every other desire; to labour was his absorbing thought. Such an energetic soul as his must have felt that its energies were immortal. There was no selfishness in his hope of heaven, no longing to be freed from work, no yearning for the luxury of mere rest. It was to be with Christ, for Christ was his heaven. If this was his confidence, if he was labouring untiringly to be acceptable to the Lord Jesus, was he understood and appreciated as Christ's apostle and servant among men? The burden of life was not the work he did, but the obstacles thrown in his way—the slanders he had to bear, the persecutions open and secret that followed him everywhere. He thinks of the "judgment-seat of Christ." It will be a judicial inquiry into works done and "every one" shall " receive [receive back] the things done in his body." Measure for measure, whatsoever has been done here shall return to every one. The individuality of the judgment, the complete unveiling of personal character, the correspondence between the reward and the good done on earth and between the retribution and the evil done here, he brings out distinctly. This was with him a fixed habit of thought. " Whatsoever a man soweth that shall he also reap." How near the two worlds are—the growing field here, the harvest in another existence hereafter ! But observe another idea. " We must all appear," we must be *made manifest*, every one shown in his true character. Not only will there be recompense as a judicial procedure, but a revelation " in the day when God shall judge the secrets of men by Jesus Christ." St. Paul had vindicated himself again and again from the charges made against him ; but the battle was now going on, nor was there any sign of its speedy abatement. It was natural that he should have the idea of manifestation prominent in his mind, since we all think of the future world very much according to some peculiarity in our experience on earth. How engrossed, heart and soul, in his apostleship is beautifully indicated by the fact that heaven itself was the heaven of St. Paul as the apostle of Christ. The sufferings of the man are never mentioned. First and last, we have the autobiography of an apostle, and hence, looking forward to the glory to be revealed, the supreme felicity is that he will *appear* in his true character as the Lord's servant.—L.

Vers. 11—21.—*Person and ministry of the apostle further considered ; his work as an ambassador.* How was he conducting this ministry, of which he had spoken so much and had yet more to say ? It was in full view of accountability to the day of judgment. " Knowing therefore the terror of the Lord, we persuade men," adding motives to affect them, and not remaining content with arguments to convince their understandings. And in this work he now felt God's approval ; before he had declared, " we are confident," and he reaffirms it in the words, " we are made manifest unto God." Every hour he stood at the bar of his conscience an acquitted man, and this conscience was a manifestation of God. Honestly was he striving to please God, as honestly labouring to save them, and in this spirit he was ever seeking to manifest himself to their consciences. If he were a temporizer, a man-pleaser, he might adopt worldly arts and captivate them. No ; he would address their consciences ; the best in them should come to his side or he must lose them. " Savour of life unto life" or "savour of death unto death ; " no other alternative. But do not misunderstand us. Commendation is not our object. If we have, as we trust, manifested ourselves to your consciences, then let your consciences speak in our behalf, and let their voices boast in this—that we are truthful in the sight of God and man. This is the way to answer our enemies who "glory in appearance and not in heart." Suffer he would rather than be wrongly vindicated. Do it in the highest way or not at all. " Your cause " is the great interest. No doubt we seem " beside ourselves," or we may appear " sober," but you may boast of this—" it is for your cause." And in this devotion to your well-being what motive presses with weight enough to make us endure all things for your sakes ? " The love of Christ constraineth us." And wherein is this love so signally demonstrated as to embody and set forth all else that he did ? It is love in death. Looking at this Divine death, we form this judgment or reach this conclusion, that he " died for all " because " all were dead—" dead under the Law of God, dead in trespasses and sins, dead legally, morally, spiritually. Nothing less than such an atoning death for all men—so it seems to us the apostle meant—could exert on him this constraining influence. And how should this influence operate ? " They which live should not henceforth live unto themselves." The very self had been redeemed by Christ's vicarious death ; body, soul, and spirit had been bought with a price, and the price was Christ's blood ; and with such a constraining motive, the most potent that the Holy Ghost could bring to bear on the human mind, how could men live unto themselves ? If, indeed, the constraining power had its legitimate effect, only one life could result, a life consecrated to " him which died for them and rose again." If, therefore, all being dead, one died for all, that all might live in freedom from selfishness and be the servants of him who had redeemed them from sin and death, we can know henceforth no man after the flesh. The very purpose of Christ's death was that the fleshly life of sin might pass out of view (might be covered over and thus disappear from sight), and another life be entered on, a life in the redeeming Christ. Admitting that this passage presents the moral aspects of Christ's death and the obligations consequent thereupon as they act on moral sentiment, yet the fundamental idea of the apostle is that Christ stood in the stead of sinners, took their guilt upon himself, and made an offering of his life for their rescue. To strengthen this doctrine, he says that, though he once knew Christ after the flesh (as a mere man), he knew him now in a very different way. We are not to suppose that he had seen him in his earthly life, but merely that he knew of him. St. Paul, after his conversion, had an experimental knowledge of Christ as his Redeemer through the sacrificial death of the cross ; nor was there any room in his heart for moral sentiment, nor any spiritual force in Christ's teaching and example, nor ground for any trust or hope, till he as " chief of sinners " had realized the righteousness of God in the atoning blood of Calvary. Such a change was a creation. He was " a new creature," and whoever experienced this power of the Lord's death was a new creature. Old things had passed away—the old self in taste and habit, the old unbelief rooted in the fleshly mind, the old worldliness—and all things had become new. No wonder that " all things " had become " new ; " for " all things " pertaining to this change in its cause, agency, instrumentalities, " are of God." Strong language this, which sounds even yet to many as the rhetoric of excited fancy ; but not stronger than the blessed reality it represents. Nay ; words cannot equal the fact. A man may overstate his own experience of Divine grace; never can he exaggerate the grace itself. " All things are of God ; " and how is this fact manifested ? In the method of reconciliation which is God's act through Christ. " Who hath reconciled us to himself by Jesus Christ." To understand what is implied in reconciliation, we must remember that much more is involved in it than the moral state of a sinner's mind toward God. The enmity of the carnal man has to be subdued, and in this sense he is " a new creature," but the possibility of this creation rests upon an antecedent fact, viz. a changed relation to the violated Law of God. What has been done for him must take precedence, as to time, of what is done in him. We must know how God as Sovereign stands to us, and by what means the sovereignty co-operates with the fatherhood of God, before we can accept the offered boon of mercy. There must be a reason why God should pardon in advance of a reason why we should seek pardon. A principle of righteousness must be established as preliminary and essential to the sentiment of Christianity, since it is impossible for us by the laws of the mind to appreciate the power of any great sentiment unless we have previously felt it as connected with a great principle. " Whom God set forth to be a Propitiation, through faith, by his blood, to show his righteousness, because of the passing over of the sins done aforetime, in the forbearance of God ; for the showing, I say, of his righteousness at this present season : that he might himself be just, and the Justifier of him that hath faith in Jesus " (Rom. iii. 25, 26, Revised Version). There is a " ministry of reconciliation " because " God was in Christ, reconciling the world unto himself, not imputing [reckoning] their trespasses unto them." Forgiveness through Christ, the Propitiation, is free to all who believe in him. Nor are we left in doubt as to the substance of our belief. It is faith in Christ, God in Christ, the Reconciler, who pardons our sins and makes us new creatures in him. To make this reconciliation known, to demonstrate its infinite excellence as the method of grace, to show its Divine results in the very men who proclaimed the gospel, Christ had instituted the ministry, and its title was, "*ministry of reconciliation.*" Recall, O Corinthians, what I have said in defence of my apostleship. Recall my sufferings in your behalf. See the reason of it all. Whom are these factious Judaizers fighting ? Whom did those beasts at Ephesus try to destroy ? Who is this man, troubled on every side, perplexed, persecuted, cast down, dying everywhere, dying always ? This is the character he sustains, the office he fills—an " ambassador for Christ." Has he manifested himself to your consciences ? Does he look forward to the day of judgment as a day of revelation as well as a day of reward and punishment ? Know we not a man, not even Christ, after the flesh ! Behold your minister, your servant, as an " ambassador," commissioned to offer you the terms of reconciliation. " We pray you in Christ's stead [on behalf of Christ], be ye reconciled to God." Nothing remains to be done but for you to accept the offered reconciliation. And he enforces this idea by stating that he who " died for all," since " all were dead," had been made " sin for us, who knew no sin." " Holy, harmless, undefiled, separate from sinners, and made higher than the heavens ; " yet he was " made

II. CORINTHIANS.

to be sin for us," made a substitute or ransom, an offering, whereby the wrath of God was turned away.   Reconciliation is accomplished not by our repentance and confession of sin, nor by any suffering on our part, nor by any merit of our work, but altogether by the death of the Lord Jesus Christ in our behalf.   God's righteousness is thus set forth.   The plan of salvation changed nothing in the character of Almighty God. Neither his righteousness nor his love was modified integrally by Christ's atonement. " *God is righteous,*" " *God is love,*" are no truer facts now than they eternally were. What the gospel teaches is that the righteousness and the love of God have assumed special forms of manifestation and operative activity through the Lord Jesus Christ.   It is *righteousness,* not in the normal relation of Law to the original transgressor, but in an instituted relation of Law to one who took the place of the transgressor.   It is *love* as *grace,* the form of love that provided for the righteousness on which St. Paul lays such an emphasis.   It is not a change in the Law, but in the administration of Law, and the glory of it lies in the fact that the Divine government presents in this higher form the resplendent spectacle of that progression from the " *natural* " to the " *spiritual,*" which St. Paul discusses in his argument on the resurrection.   Whatever obstacles existed in the way of this sublime advance have been removed by Christ.   " *Mercy and truth* " have their existence as attributes of the Divine nature; they have " *met together.*" " *Righteousness and peace* " are not to be confounded, but they have " *kissed each other.*"—L.

Ver. 6.—"*Absent from the Lord.*"   To those disciples and apostles who were with the Lord Jesus during his earthly ministry, the separation which commenced upon his ascension must have been painful indeed.   In the case of Paul, however, the language employed in this passage scarcely seems so natural.   But we learn from the record of his sentiments what ought to be to all Christians their first thought, their governing principle, viz. their relation to Jesus Christ.   The earthly state of all such is a state of absence from the Lord—a fact not to be grieved over, but to be recognized and felt.

I. THIS ABSENCE IS NOT SPIRITUAL, BUT BODILY.   His own word is fulfilled, " A little while, and ye shall not see me."   The exclamation of his people is verified, " Him, not having seen, we love."

II. THIS ABSENCE IS APPOINTED BY DIVINE WISDOM AND LOVE.   It cannot be regarded as a matter of chance or of fate.   It is the will of him who most loves us and who most cares for us, which is apparent in this provision.

III. THERE IS A BENEFICENT PURPOSE IN THIS ABSENCE.   Such was the obvious intention of our Saviour himself.   " It is good for you," he said, " that I go away." His aim was to lead his people into a life of faith, and to excite our confidence in himself who has gone to prepare a place for us.

IV. THERE ARE CERTAIN DANGERS INVOLVED IN THIS ABSENCE.   There is danger lest, separated from our Lord, we should grow worldly and carnal, lest our love to Jesus should wax cold, lest we should magnify ourselves, lest we should be ashamed of a religion whose Head is not visibly among us.

V. YET THERE ARE COMPENSATIONS IN THIS ABSENCE.   It is intended to fortify and perfect the truly Christian character.   It will make the meeting, when it takes place, more delightful and welcome.

VI. WHAT EXERCISES ARE SUGGESTED BY THIS ABSENCE?   1. Remembrance of Christ. 2. Faith in Christ.   3. Communion with Christ.   4. Fidelity to Christ in his absence. 5. Anticipation of his speedy return.

VII. THE TERMINATION OF THIS PERIOD OF ABSENCE IS AT HAND.   Those who live until the Lord's return shall welcome him to his inheritance.   Others must be absent from Christ until they are absent from the body, when they shall be "*present* " with the Lord."—T.

Ver. 7.—*The walk of faith.*   Life is a pilgrimage which men undertake and accomplish upon very different principles and to very different results and ends.   In this parenthesis St. Paul very succinctly and very impressively describes the nature of that pilgrimage which he had adopted and with which he was satisfied.

I. THE WALK WITH WHICH THAT OF THE CHRISTIAN IS CONTRASTED.   This, which is that of the unenlightened and unrenewed, is the *walk by sight* ; i.e. by repressing the spiritual nature and walking by the light which earth offers, by the mere guidance of the senses, by the influence of society, the approval and esteem of men, by considerations drawn from earth and limited to earth. This is a course of life in which there is no satisfaction, no safety, and no blessed prospect.

II. THE CHARACTERISTICS OF THE WALK OF FAITH. Faith in itself is neutral; its excellence depends upon its object. The Christian regulates his course through this life of temptation, danger, and discipline by: 1. Faith in the existence of God, the God who possesses all moral excellences as his attributes. 2. Faith in Providence; *i.e.* in the personal interest and care of him who is called Friend and Father. 3. Faith in God as a Saviour, which is faith in Christ, the salvation of the Lord revealed to man. 4. Faith in a righteous and authoritative law. 5. Faith in ever-present spiritual aid—guidance, protection, bounty, etc. 6. Faith in Divine promises, by which the pilgrim is assured that he shall reach home at last.

III. THE ENCOURAGEMENTS TO UNDERTAKE AND TO PERSEVERE IN THE WALK OF FAITH. 1. It is the one principle enjoined throughout revelation, from the day of Abraham, the father of the faithful, down to the apostolic age. 2. The possibility of the walk by faith has been proved by the example of the great and the good who have gone before us (*vide* Heb. xi.). 3. To those who live by faith life has a meaning and dignity which otherwise cannot possibly attach to it. 4. Faith can sustain amidst the trials and sorrows of earth. 5. And faith is the blossom of which the vision of the glorified Saviour shall be the heavenly and immortal fruit.—T.

Ver. 14.—*The love of Christ.* Every quality met in the Lord Jesus which could adapt him to accomplish the work which he undertook on behalf of our human race. But if one attribute must be selected as peculiarly and pre-eminently characteristic of him, if one word rather than another rises to our lips when we speak of him, that attribute, that word, is love.

I. THE OBJECTS OF CHRIST'S LOVE. Look at his earthly life and ministry, and the comprehensive range within which the love of Jesus operates becomes at once and gloriously obvious. 1. His friends. Of this fact—Christ's love to his friends—we have abundant proof: "Greater love hath no man than this, that a man lay down his life for his friends." 2. His enemies. This is more wonderful, yet the truth of what the apostle says is undeniable: "While we were yet sinners, Christ died for us." And we cannot forget his prayer offered for his enemies as they nailed him to the cross: "Father, forgive them." 3. All mankind. During his ministry the Lord Jesus was gracious to all with whom he came into contact. His aim was by the bands of love to draw all men unto himself, that they might rest and live in his Divine and mighty heart.

II. THE PROOFS OF CHRIST'S LOVE. The great facts of his ministry and mediation are evidences of his benevolence. 1. His advent.

> "Nothing brought him from above—
> Nothing but redeeming love."

2. His ministry. He went about doing good, animated by the mighty principle of love to man. Every sickness he healed, every demon he expelled, every sinner he pardoned, was a witness to the love of Christ. 3. His death. His was the love "stronger than death;" for not only could not death destroy it, death gave it a new life and power in the world and over men. 4. His prevailing intercession and brotherly care.

III. THE CHARACTERISTICS OF CHRIST'S LOVE. 1. It is sympathizing and tender, "passing the love of women." 2. It is thoughtful and wise, ever providing for the true welfare of those to whom it is revealed. 3. It is forbearing and patient, otherwise it might often have been checked and repressed. 4. It is self-sacrificing, counting nothing too great to be given up in order to secure its ends. 5. It is faithful: "Having loved his own, he loved them even unto the end." 6. It is unquenchable and everlasting: "Who can separate us from the love of Christ?"—T.

Ver. 14.—*The constraint of Christ's love.* The apostle represents the Saviour's love, not merely as something to be admired and enjoyed, but as something which is to act as a spiritual force. He experienced it as the supreme power over his own life, and he had confidence in it as the principle which should renew and bless the world.

I. THE NATURE OF THIS CONSTRAINT. Men are influenced by many and various motives, some lower and some higher. Their natural instincts and impulses, their interests, their regard for public opinion and their ambition, the laws of the land,—these are among the admitted and powerful inducements to human conduct. But these are not the highest motives, and are unworthy of the nature and possibilities of man, unless in conjunction with something better. Even the sacred obligation of duty is insufficient. But Christ's love in his redemptive work, revealed to us in the gospel, is a moral and spiritual force of vast power. It awakens gratitude, love, devotion, obedience. It is the universal Christian motive. He who does not feel it, however correct his creed and conduct, is not in the proper sense of the term a Christian. Happy they who live under its sweet and constant constraint!

II. THE DIRECTION OF THIS CONSTRAINT. Physical power is of two kinds—it is either energy or resistance; e.g. the ocean and the dyke, the powder and the cannon, the steam and the boiler. As with physical, so with moral power. 1. Christ's love acts by way of restraint. It withholds those who experience it from self-indulgence, from worldliness, and from other sins to which men are naturally prone, and from which only a Divine power can deliver. 2. It acts by way of impulse, inducing to the imitation of Jesus in character and conduct; to obedience such as he enjoins when he says, "If ye love me, keep my commandments;" to consecration such as Paul exemplified when he said, "We live unto the Lord."

III. THE EFFICACY OF THIS CONSTRAINT. This depends upon a just interpretation of the passage. Were it our love to Christ which is imputed, this would be a feeble and vacillating motive; but it is something far greater and better, viz. Christ's love to us. The power of this motive may be seen in the life of every faithful friend of Jesus; e.g. in the apostles, as Paul, Peter, John; in the confessors and martyrs and reformers; in the missionaries and philanthropists, etc. It may be seen in the dangers braved, the opposition encountered, the persecutions suffered, the efforts undertaken and persevered in. What of noble and beautiful and beneficent conduct has not this Divine motive proved able to inspire! Greater deeds and more heroic sufferings than the love of Christ has accounted for, the annals of mankind do not record. It is to this motive that we must look for all that in the future shall bless our common humanity. What nothing inferior can effect the love of Christ will certainly prove powerful to accomplish.—T.

Ver. 18.—"The ministry of reconciliation." Every good man is a peacemaker. Both unconsciously by his character and disposition, and consciously and actively by his efforts, he composes differences and promotes concord and amity among his fellow-men. The Christian minister, however, goes deeper when he aims at securing harmony between God and man. And he purposes to effect this reconciliation, not by the use of ordinary persuasion, but by the presentation of the gospel of Christ.

I. THE CHRISTIAN MINISTRY PRESUMES THE NEED OF RECONCILIATION. 1. There is a moral Ruler and a moral law, righteous and authoritative. 2. Against this Ruler men have rebelled, they have broken the law, and thus introduced enmity and conflict. 3. Divine displeasure has thus been incurred, and Divine penalties, by which just displeasure is expressed.

II. THE CHRISTIAN MINISTRY IS AUTHORIZED BY HIM WHO ALONE CAN INTRODUCE RECONCILIATION. God is the greater, and not only so, he is the wronged, offended party. If any overtures for reconciliation are to be made, they must proceed from him. He must provide the basis of peace and he must commission the heralds of peace.

III. THE CHRISTIAN MINISTRY PROCLAIMS THE MEDIATOR OF RECONCILIATION. The Lord Jesus has every qualification which can be desired in an efficient Mediator. He partakes the nature of God and of man; he is appointed and accepted by the Divine Sovereign; he has effected by his sacrifice a work of atonement or reconciliation; his Spirit is a Spirit of peace. And in fact he has "made peace," removing all obstacles on God's side and providing for the removal of all on man's.

IV. THE CHRISTIAN MINISTRY CONSISTS IN THE OFFER OF RECONCILIATION. It is a moral and not a sacerdotal ministry; it is experimental, being entrusted to those who are themselves reconciled; it is a ministry accompanied with supernatural power, even the energy of the Spirit of God; it is an authoritative ministry, which men are not at liberty to disregard or despise; it is an *effectual* ministry, for those who discharge it faithfully are unto many the "savour of life unto life."—T.

Ver. 20.—"*Ambassadors for Christ.*" Even among the members of the Corinthian Church there were those who had offended the Lord by their inconsistency and who needed to be reconciled. How much more was and is this true of mankind at large! There is no denying the need of a gospel and of a ministry of reconciliation.

I. WHO ARE CHRIST'S AMBASSADORS? Probably the language is most justly applicable to the apostles only, inasmuch as their commission and credentials were altogether special. An ambassador owes his importance, not to himself, but to the power he represents, the message he bears. The preachers of Christ are all heralds, if they cannot be designated ambassadors. They may learn hence the dignity of their office and their personal unworthiness and insufficiency, and they may be admonished as to the imperative duty of fidelity.

II. BY WHAT COURT ARE THESE AMBASSADORS COMMISSIONED? They are the ministers of the King of heaven, and their authority is that of the King's Son. Thus their mission is one entrusted by a *superior* power and authority; and not only so, it is from an *offended* and outraged power. This appears when we consider—

III. To WHOM THESE AMBASSADORS ARE SENT. Properly speaking, an ambassador is one accredited to a power sovereign and equal to that from whom he comes. But in this case the resemblance fails in this respect, inasmuch as the ministers of the gospel address themselves to offenders, to rebels, to those who cannot treat with Heaven upon equal terms, or any terms of right.

IV. WHOSE SUBSTITUTES ARE THESE AMBASSADORS? They act "on Christ's behalf," "in Christ's stead." The Lord himself first came upon an embassage of mercy. He has entrusted to his apostles, and in a sense to all his ministers, the office and trust of acting as his representatives, in so far as they publish the declaration and offer of Divine mercy.

V. WHAT IS THE COMMISSION WHICH THESE AMBASSADORS ARE SENT TO EXECUTE? It is an office of mercy. Their duty is to publish the tidings of redemption, the offer of pardon, and themselves to urge and to entreat men that they accept the gospel and thus enjoy the blessings of reconciliation with God.—T.

Vers. 1—9.—*The two bodies of the saint.* I. THE BODY THAT NOW IS. 1. Frail. 2. Perishing. 3. Often a burden. 4. Frequently a temptation. 5. Not helpful to spiritual life. 6. Subject to many pains. 7. Debased.

II. THE BODY THAT SHALL BE. 1. *Eternal.* (Ver. 1.) Having no tendencies towards decay, no marks of coming death. A body of *life*. Stamped with the eternalness of God. 2. *Heavenly.* (Ver. 1.) The first body is of the earth, earthy; the second body is spiritual and heavenly in origin and character. Capable of heavenly joys. Fitted for heavenly service. Free from earthly weaknesses, pains, and soil. 3. *From God.* (Ver. 1.) The present body is this in a certain sense, but it has passed through the hands of the devil. The resurrection-body shall be of God and only of God, his unmarred workmanship. It shall be like the glorified body united to Deity in the person of Jesus Christ: "Who shall fashion anew the body of our humiliation, that it may be conformed to the body of his glory" (Phil. iii. 21).

III. THE SAINT'S CONDITION WHILST IN THE EARTHLY BODY. Frequently a condition of sorrow. "We that are in this tabernacle do groan, being burdened" (ver. 4). There are (1) the ordinary afflictions which befall mankind; (2) the special chastisements of God inflicted for the saint's welfare, but still painful; (3) the sense of living in a strange country, not in his own—uncongenial surroundings; (4) struggles against temptations: the presence and power of hated sin.

IV. THE SAINT'S ASSURANCE OF THE HEAVENLY BODY. 1. *Revelation.* 2. *Preparation.* "He that wrought us for this very thing" (ver. 5). 3. *The Spirit's witness.* We have the "earnest" of the Spirit, which is a pledge of the fulness of the Spirit (ver. 5). In the next life we shall be dominated by the Spirit; shall have a *spiritual* body—one pervaded by the Spirit. The apostle's confidence is strong; he says, "We *know*;" there was no uncertainty about the matter.

V. THE SAINT'S LONGING FOR THE HEAVENLY BODY. The desire is very intense especially when the lot is hard and the nature spiritual. "We groan, longing to be clothed upon with our habitation which is from heaven" (ver. 2). The paramount attraction is, however, not in the body itself, but in the fact that the union with Christ will be closer. We shall be present with the Lord—*at home* with the Lord (ver. 8). Now we walk by faith; then we shall see him as he is, and be like him. The gaining of the heavenly body will be the gain of closer access to our Lord, and will be the entering into our heavenly home, out of which we shall go no more for ever.

VI. THE SAINT'S DESIRE FOR A SPEEDY CHANGE FROM ONE BODY TO THE OTHER. (Ver. 4.) 1. The intermediate state between death and the resurrection will probably not be so perfect as that which follows. 2. There is a natural shrinking from death. "Not for that we would be unclothed, but that we would be clothed upon" (ver. 4). The apostle seems to desire what is expressed in 1 Thess. iv. 17—a *translation*, not death and tarrying for the resurrection.

VII. THE SAINT'S RESOLUTION WHETHER IN THE EARTHLY OR HEAVENLY BODY. To please Christ. This the apostle made his "aim" (ver. 9). This was his supreme ambition. He resolved to live, not to himself, but to Christ and for Christ. Note, that the life for the heavenly and earthly body is to be the same. We must do now what we hope to do by-and-by. Heavenly life in the earthly body is the preparation for the heavenly life in the heavenly body.—H.

Ver. 10.—*The judgment.* I. THE JUDGMENT IS CERTAIN. 1. It is a matter of most definite revelation. 2. It is necessary for the vindication of Divine justice.

II. CHRIST WILL BE THE JUDGE. "The judgment-seat of Christ." 1. A very solemn fact (1) for those who have rejected his salvation and his rule; (2) or who have treated his claims with neglect and indifference; (3) or who have professed to believe on him, but in works have denied him. 2. A very joyous fact for those who have loved, confessed, and served him. 3. A very impressive fact that the One who died for men will judge men.

III. ALL WILL STAND BEFORE CHRIST'S JUDGMENT-SEAT. Not one will be missing. How vast an assemblage! A great multitude, and yet no one lost in the crowd! We shall be conscious of the great number which no man can number, and yet be impressed with our own individuality. "*Each one*" will receive (ver. 10)—*one by one*. Every day we are brought a day nearer to that dread convocation.

IV. AT THE JUDGMENT-SEAT OF CHRIST THERE WILL BE A GREAT REVELATION. 1. *Of character.* 2. *Of condition.* 3. *Of life.* We shall be "made manifest." Life-secrets will cease. Successful deceptions will be successful no longer. All veils and disguises will be torn off. The world as well as God will see us as we are.

V. AT THE JUDGMENT-SEAT OF CHRIST WE SHALL RECEIVE OUR DOOM. This will be according to the deeds of our life. Will the faithful then be justified by faith? Yes; by faith *which produces works*. *Profession* will then go for very little. "Lord, Lord," will be but an empty cry. Ability to pray fluently or to preach eloquently will not come into the account. Nor the ability to look extremely pious. Nor facility of talk respecting "blessed seasons" enjoyed on earth. *What faith has wrought in us will be the question.* What our Christianity has amounted to really and practically. "A name to live" then will be nothing if we are found "dead." Upon the branch professedly united to the Vine *fruit* will then be sought. "Faith without works is dead." At the judgment it will seem very dead indeed. Yet not by the mere outward act shall we be judged. The *motive* will be considered as well as the actual deed. "Faith which worketh by love" (Gal. v. 6) will be diligently sought for. Note: 1. The distinction between good and evil will be strictly drawn at the judgment. 2. There will be degrees of reward and punishment. Some "saved as by fire;" some having an "abundant entrance;" some beaten with few stripes, some with many. It will be "*according* to what he hath done." 3. The dependence of the future upon the present. We shall receive *the things done in the body*. A remarkable expression. What we do now we shall receive then. We are now writing the sentence of the judgment! Time is *sowing*. Judgment is *reaping*. "What manner of persons ought we to be?"—H.

Ver. 14.—*The constraining influence of the love of Christ.* I. CONSIDER THE LOVE OF CHRIST. Shown in: 1. *Advent.* Relinquishment of heavenly glory. The highest place above exchanged for one of the lowest on earth. 2. *Assumption of human nature.* A vast condescension. A most striking proof of love. 3. *Life.* Miracles, acts of kindness, words, spirit. 4. *Death.* A transcendent proof. (1) Death for enemies. (2) Death at the hands of those he came to save. (3) Most painful death, (*a*) physically, (*b*) mentally, and (*c*) spiritually. " My God, my God, why hast thou forsaken me? " (4) A death the object of which was the redemption, purification, exaltation, and eternal happiness of men. 5. *Intercession.* " He ever liveth to make intercession " (Heb. vii. 25).

II. CONSIDER THE EFFECT OF THE LOVE OF CHRIST. It *constrained* the apostle—" compressed with irresistible power all his energies into one channel." " Constraineth "— its influence was *continuous.* Its power was not soon spent; rather that power increased as the love of Christ was increasingly realized. 1. *Negatively.* Not to live to himself (ver. 15). There was now a greater power operating upon him than the mighty power of self. 2. *Positively.* To live to Christ (ver. 15). The love of Christ overmastered him. He felt that through it he had been purchased with a great price, and therefore sought to glorify Christ in his body and spirit which were peculiarly his. (1) By a blameless life. (2) By seeking to show forth Christ in his character, spirit, acts, etc. (3) By submitting his will to Christ's in all things. (4) By cherishing a deep love for Christ. (5) By seeking to extend the kingdom and to increase the glory of Christ. (6) By being wholly devoted to Christ. He was wont to speak of himself as the " slave of Christ."—H.

Ver. 17.—"*A new creature.*" I. HOW THE NEWNESS ORIGINATES. 1. *The believer has died with Christ.* (Ver. 14.) Christ is his Substitute, has borne his sins, has made complete satisfaction for his guilt. By faith he is so united to Christ that what Christ has done is imputed to him. He is thus new in relation to God. He was condemned; now he is justified. 2. *The believer partakes of the life of Christ.* He is " risen with Christ" (Col. iii. 1). He has received the Spirit of Christ. Having been justified, he is now being sanctified. The likeness of the Redeemer is being wrought upon and in him by the Holy Ghost. There is thus a " new creation." The old life was a life of sin, but the new life to which he has risen is a life of righteousness. The love of Christ constrains him (ver. 14) to live, not to himself, but to Christ.

II. HOW THE NEWNESS IS MANIFESTED. In the believer's (1) spirit; (2) speech; (3) character; (4) acts; (5) plans, purposes, desires, etc. "*All things* are become new " (ver. 17). There is no part of the believer's life from which the newness should be absent. Whilst not yet perfect, manifestly a great change has taken place: " Old things are passed away " (ver. 17).

III. THIS NEWNESS FURNISHES A TEST. What have we more than our profession of Christianity? Have we been transformed; made new creatures? " Ye must be born again " (John iii. 7). Can faith save a man—faith which has a name to live, but is dead; faith which we only know a man possesses because he tells us so? We are not in Christ at all unless thereby we have become new creatures. The test is beyond appeal. The sentence of the judgment will proceed upon the assumption of its infallibility (ver. 10). *All* men in Christ become new creatures. "If *any* man," etc. A decided change takes place in the best as well as in the worst. *All* men *may* become new creatures in Christ. The vilest can be re-created equally with the most moral. This newness is not to be waited for till we enter another world. It belongs to *this* sphere in which we now are. Unless we are new creatures in this world we shall not be new creatures in another. It is on earth that " new creatures " are specially needed.—H.

Ver. 20.—"*Ambassadors of Christ.*" I. THE DUTIES OF AMBASSADORS OF CHRIST. 1. *Negative.* (1) Not to originate their message. (2) Not to think lightly of their mission. (3) Not to seek their own glory. (4) Not to aim at their own comfort and pleasure as a chief object. (5) Not to depart from their instructions. Not to add to them nor take away. 2. *Positive.* (1) To go where they are sent. (2) To communicate the mind of their Lord. (3) To defend his honour. (4) To be influenced by the welfare of his kingdom. (5) To make their Master's business pre-eminent. (6) To strive in every way to qualify themselves for their work. (7) To endeavour to do their work in the best possible way. (8) To endure loss and suffering rather than the interests of their Master's kingdom should be prejudiced.

II. THE MESSAGE OF THE AMBASSADORS OF CHRIST. 1. That God loves men. 2. That he has given Christ for men. A vast proof of love! The first step was on God's side. Whilst we were enemies Christ died for us. 3. That Christ willingly gave himself for men. The death of Christ was perfectly voluntary. 4. That by the death of Christ God has provided the means for the perfect reconciliation of the world to himself. In the death of Christ God *does* reconcile; *i.e.* he removes every obstacle to reconciliation. Justification is *fully prepared* for the sinner. Christ was made sin for us (ver. 21). He bore our sins. Our sins were imputed to him. God's justice was satisfied. Christ is made our Substitute, and this so perfectly that what we are is imputed to him, and what he is is imputed to us. He takes our sins; we take his righteousness. No hindrance to complete restoration thus remains, except hindrance which may lie in the human heart itself. 5. That God earnestly invites men to be reconciled to him. Amazing condescension! The climax of Divine love! "As though God were entreating" (ver. 20).

III. How THE MESSAGE IS TO BE CONVEYED. 1. *With courtesy.* 2. *With intense earnestness.* It is momentous. What issues depend upon its acceptance or rejection! 3. *With zealous pleading.*

IV. How AMBASSADORS OF CHRIST ARE TO BE REGARDED. 1. As speaking on behalf of Christ. 2. As declaring the mind of God.—H.

Ver. 1.—*The tent and the house.* I. THE CONTRAST EXPLAINED. The foundation of this passage is to be found in ch. iv. 18, where a contrast is drawn between "the things seen," viz. the toils and afflictions endured in the service of Christ, and "the things not yet seen," viz. the joys of resting in Christ from present labours and of receiving from him approval and reward. Pursuing this train of thought, St. Paul writes, "We are here in a tent upon the earth, surrounded, affected, and limited by the things which are seen. But this tent will be struck, to be set up no more. The things which are seen are temporal. The present conditions of our life of toil and suffering will cease, and we shall enter a house of everlasting habitation." The apostle mixes together the figures of a dwelling in which we reside and that of a garment with which we are clothed. It was not an unnatural combination of metaphors; for the haircloth tents with which Paul was familiar, and which his own hands had made, suggested almost equally the idea of a dwelling and that of a vesture. The tent is to be taken down, the clothing to be removed. The present condition of labour and trial will come to an end. What then? Things not yet seen; a building from God; a new condition of life and order of things which will be permanent. Hands of men have not provided it and cannot destroy it. It is a house where nothing fades, nothing falls to ruin, nothing decays or dies—a house eternal in the heavens.

II. THE CHRISTIAN PERSPECTIVE OF THE FUTURE. It was St. Paul's habit to regard the state after death and the state after resurrection as from one angle of vision, and to describe them together. Probably he had no idea of the long interval which was to extend through all the Christian centuries. In his first letter to the Corinthians he had said, "We shall not all sleep," as though some of that generation might not see death. But now the feebleness of his body was as "a sentence of death" in himself. He expected and even wished to die; and yet his thoughts never paused on death or even on the rest of the departed, but rushed past death to the coming of Christ and the glory to be revealed. There is a real and obvious distinction between the post-decease and the post-resurrection state; but let us not overdo distinctions between conditions of blessedness which to an apostle's eye were so intimately blended. If some of the things which belong to the ultimate state are supposed by any to belong to the proximate, no great harm is done. The future is not mapped out with the precision of a chart. It is not for definite knowledge, but for hope. St. Paul, as we have said, never paused on death, took no pleasure in the thought of being "unclothed." At the resurrection he would be clothed with a body of incorruption and immortality. Nay; before that great day of triumph over death, he knew that he would be well clothed or guarded. He would be in God' building, "clothed upon" with the house which is from heaven.

III. The mood of mind that wishes for death. St. Paul wrote this in dejection of spirit. To his sickness, which had much enfeebled him, was added at that time much anxiety about the condition of the Churches in Greece and their feelings toward himself. So his heart, as tender and sensitive as it was ardent and brave, was bruised and weary; and he fell a-thinking of death as welcome. Let the outward man perish; let the earthen vessel break; let the weary spirit escape and be at rest. A mood this into which, at one time or other, many Christians fall; but it should not be elevated into a pattern or rule, as though it were the duty of every Christian to long and sigh for death. Our holy faith requires nothing so unnatural. They who are in health and well employed ought to make the most of life—to value and not despise it. Enough that they do not forget death; and they need not fear it if they live well. We must do Paul the justice to acknowledge that there was nothing peevish or impatient in his mood. So long as there was service for him to render to the Church on earth, he was willing to abide in the flesh and to endure any toil or suffering in order to finish his course. But the mood that was on him led him to long for the finish, when he might leave the little horsehair tent on earth and be at home in God's building in the heavens.—F.

Vers. 14, 15.—*The secret of devotedness.* No one now flings a charge of madness at the sublime enthusiasm of St. Paul. He is looked on as a paragon of Christians. But, while he lived, he had no such general appreciation to encourage and sustain him. What he had above other men were not praises, but labours and reproaches. He endured all because he had in himself the mainspring of faith and the holy energy of love. Throughout this Epistle he shows his feelings and motives with the utmost candour, and in this passage tells how he came to be so enthusiastic toward God and so thoughtful and self-controlled toward his fellow-Christians.

I. The moving principle of Christian devotedness. It is the strong unchanging love of Christ to his people, assured to them by his Spirit and his Word. Paul had a fear of God, a reverence for the Law, and walked in all good conscience; but when the love of Christ was revealed to him and suffused his spirit it made a new man of him—thrilled, stirred, animated, constrained him to love and serve Christ and the Church. And as the apostle grew old and experienced, this motive lost nothing of its power. The love of Christ became to him, as it does to all experienced Christians, more and more wonderful—a Shepherd's love, that led him to die for us, and that now secures that we "shall not want;" a Brother's love, and "love beyond a brother's;" a Bridegroom's love, who gave himself for the Church and will present the Church to himself.

II. The way in which the motive acts. It is through no mere gush of feeling, but through consideration of the purpose and efficacy of Christ's death and resurrection. 1. He died for all to this intent and with this result, that all of them died. Virtually and in the estimate of God this crucifixion of the whole Church took place when Christ was crucified. In the actual realization of it it becomes true to each man as and when he looks to Christ crucified and is united to him by faith. And with effects both legal and moral. He who was married to the Law dies to the Law, and is freed from its claims, so as to be married to the risen Christ. He who lived in sin dies to sin, and may not any longer live therein. He who loved the world is crucified to it, that he may love and live to God. 2. He rose again; and all the crucified ones live by him. So they have justification, as represented by the accepted One, who has gone to the Father; and sanctification too, as separated to God in holy living and guided by the indwelling Spirit. The former manner of life is marked by self-regard. The new manner of life exchanges this for the habit of regarding Christ. So his constraining love induces his followers "to live unto him."

III. Uses of this doctrine. 1. *Let it instruct us.* Many are very ill informed on the relation of our Lord's death and resurrection to the Divine will and to human salvation; and for this reason they are much less constrained by his love than they ought to be. Study these things. Bring thought and consideration as well as emotion to the theme. The love constrains "because we judge." 2. *Let it humble us.* Has the Son of the living God so loved us, and where is our love to him?

> "Lord, it is my chief complaint
> That my love is cold and faint."

3. *Let it impel us.* What we need to overcome our moral indolence and habits of
self-pleasing is the pressure of strong convictions and motives; and we can best get
these in contemplating the love, the death, and the resurrection of Christ. This, too,
is a great security against departure from the Lord. When we know and feel little of
Christ's love we are easily tempted; but when this is in our thoughts and affections we
abhor and repel whatever might separate us from him. 4. *Let it comfort us.* We are
delivered from the wrath to come. Christ loves us. Then the Father also loves us.
Duties are pleasant, afflictions are light; to live is Christ, to die is gain.—F.

Vers. 18—21.—*Reconciliation.* Great truths hang together. When the Lord Jesus
had told Nicodemus of regeneration, he immediately proceeded to teach him salvation
through a Redeemer. So when the Apostle Paul has spoken of new creation in Christ
(ver. 17), he instantly follows it with the doctrine of reconciliation through Christ.
I. THE NEED OF RECONCILIATION. The world is not in harmony or at peace with God.
Sin has done it. On the one hand, God's displeasure is declared against the workers of
iniquity; on the other, those workers are afraid of God and alienated from him. A
great gulf yawns between God and man; and the need of reconciliation is the need
of a bridge across that chasm. Or, a great mountain is cast up between God and
man; and the need of reconciliation is the need of that mountain becoming a plain,
so that God and man may not merely approach, but unite and be at peace. "What
can be the difficulty," some exclaim, "if God desires it? Is he not omnipotent,
and can he not accomplish whatever he pleases?" But we speak of a moral obstacle,
not a physical. And, while God can certainly do what he pleases, he cannot please to
do anything but what is perfectly righteous. So there is a difficulty. It is twofold:
there is a sentence of condemnation in heaven against the transgressors of the law of
righteousness; and there is an enmity to God or a cowering dread of him in the
hearts of those transgressors on earth.
II. THE AUTHOR OF RECONCILIATION. "All things [*i.e.* all the things of the new
creation] are of God, who has reconciled us to himself." Man, the creature and the
sinner, should have been the first to seek the healing of the breach, by suing for
pardon and imploring mercy from God. But it has not been so. The initiative has
been taken by God, who is rich in mercy, and, loving the world, has provided for its
reconciliation by Jesus Christ.
III. THE METHOD OF RECONCILIATION. Messages sent from a distant heaven or
throne of God could not suffice. There was need of an authorized Messenger. So God
sent his only begotten Son. For so great a work was constituted a unique and
wonderful personality. The Son of God became man and yet continued Divine. So,
in the very constitution of his person, he brought the Divine and the human together.
And thus his relation to both parties was such as perfectly fitted him to be the
Reconciler. He loved God, and therefore was faithful to all Divine claims and prerogatives; while at the same time he loved man and was intent on securing his salvation.
1. He dealt with the difficulty on the side of eternal righteousness. He did so by
taking the room and the responsibility of the transgressors and making atonement for
them. And the hand of God was in this. "He hath made him," etc. (ver. 21).
"Made . . . sin," though he never was a sinner, and laden with it as a burden,
enveloped in it as a mantle of shame. "Jehovah laid upon him the iniquity of us all."
The issue is that we "become the righteousness of God in him." And in this is
nothing illusive or fictitious. There was a real laying of our sins on the Lamb of God,
that there may be a real laying or conferring of Divine righteousness on us who
believe in his Name. 2. He deals with the difficulty of alienated feeling. No change
is needed in the mind or disposition of God. He does not need to be persuaded to love
the world. All the salvation in Christ proceeds from his love. But the enmity of
men to God must be removed, and this is effected by the revelation of God as gracious
and propitious to sinners in Christ Jesus. When this is known and believed, the heart
turns to God and actual reconciliation is made.
IV. THE WORD OF RECONCILIATION. (Vers. 19, 20.) When St. Paul preached the
gospel it was as though God entreated or exhorted the people through his servant's
lips. He was an ambassador, not a plenipotentiary with powers to discuss and negotiate terms of peace, but a King's messenger sent to proclaim terms of free grace and

to press the acceptance of them on the enemies of the King. This embassy continues. Do not meet it with excuses and delays.—F.

Ver. 1.—*Our permanent building.* Taking the apostle's words in a general way, and not confining them to the precise topic which he has under consideration, we are taught by them that, regarding all our present things as but shadows and symbols, we need not trouble ourselves overmuch about their changing forms, or even about their passing away. All our heart and all our efforts should go out in the endeavour to bring nearer, and make clearer and fuller, the sense of our dwelling in, breathing in, working in, the unseen, the spiritual, the eternal. Our sphere is God. " In him we live, and move, and have our being." The real is the unseen. The stable and lasting is the eternal. And this view of things alone can put us in right relations with the body, and set us upon the right use of things seen and temporal. Whenever we are brought face to face with any passing, dissolving, removing, earthly thing, then God seems to call us, saying, " Remember the house not made with hands, eternal in the heavens." Take for illustration—

I. THE TENT AND THE HOUSE. No figure could be more appropriate than this for the apostle, who gained his living as a tentmaker, and was familiar with its material, its construction, and its use. We can well imagine how, as he wrought, either at weaving the rough Cilician cloth, or at sewing together the various lengths, and the holes for the poles and ropes, he would meditate on the frailty of the tent which he was thus making, contrasting it with the stable marble and stone mansions found in such cities as Corinth. In his day tents were chiefly made for travellers ; for those who journeyed from place to place, either for business or for pleasure, in districts where accommodation at inns could not be found. They had their settled homes in the great cities, and they went forth on their travels with quiet hearts, because of the cherished feeling that they had a home. They used the tent awhile, camping out in the open country ; but if the wild storm did come, and even lift and carry away the tent ; if the midnight robber did overthrow it, and seize the spoil,—the traveller might bear the hardship and the loss, in pleasant confidence that he had a home. If the worst came, it could be but the *shadow* of his home passing away ; in yonder city stood his secure dwelling.

II. THE DOCTRINE AND THE TRUTH. For doctrine is like the frail tent, and. truth is like the granite mansion that outlasts the passing ages. We cannot be too thankful for the forms in which sacred truth is conveyed to us, unfolded before us, or impressed upon us. We bless God for all holy and helpful words, full of tender and dear associations ; words of simple catechism for our childhood's weakness ; words of formal doctrine fashioned to help us when, in our youth-time, we tried to get personal hold of mysterious and many-sided truth. Let no man despise the doctrines which, like tents, have often given us their shelter and their help. And yet they are only like " earthly houses of this tabernacle." Truth is the " building of God, the house not made with hands," wherein alone human souls may find quietness from controversy or from fears. Doctrines are only symbols and shadows, the human representations of the Divine and eternal things, the unspeakable realities which yet our souls may apprehend. Within, behind, above, around, the doctrine ever dwells the truth ; and, at first, we are very dependent on the *forms* which it gains for mortal eyes and ears and minds ; but, as the soul grows, and gains its vision, its hearing, and its touch, we get loosened from our dependence on the forms, we can calmly see them change and pass. Resting in the stable house of truth, we calmly look on all transitory forms, even of doctrine, and say, " We have a building of God, a house not made with hands, eternal in the heavens."

III. NATURE AND GOD. Nature, the world of things seen—the firmament, golden-glowing, cloud-shaded, and star-sprinkled ; earth, with its vales, and hills, and flowers, and trees ; the great and wide sea—is in a very serious sense *God*. It is God manifest to our senses. Behind what is called pantheism there is a deeply poetical and spiritual truth. Nature is God seen ; God in toned picture for mortal eyes to see ; God, if we may so say, in photograph. Earth is the plate which has caught all that human eyes may see of the figure of God. Nature is the tent-symbol of the eternal *house.* The Jew called his mountains " the hills of God," because they brought to him the sense of the highness and almightiness of God. He called the splendid trees " the cedars of Jehovah," because they brought to him a sense of the stately beauty of God.

Yet nature is not really God himself, only God in expression for our apprehending, only the veil that he shines through. Therefore we turn from the shadow to the substance which throws it; from the form to the reality which it does but exhibit. And if all nature passed away, we should lose nothing. It would be but dropping the veil that we might see *the face.*

IV. OUR EARTHLY AND OUR HEAVENLY BODIES. St. Paul was plainly thinking of his body, the vehicle by means of which our souls come into contact with the world of created things. But he cherished the idea of a spiritual body, which could be the clothing and vehicle of his soul through the long, the eternal ages. Thinking of *it* he could say, "What matter if my tent-body be destroyed? I have a building of God, a house not made with hands."—R. T.

Ver. 5.—"*The earnest of the Spirit.*" The apostle has been referring to the great hope set before us in the gospel, which, as he regards it, is this, that "mortality might be swallowed up of life." That is the object of the Divine working in the believer, and of its final realization he has this "earnest," or pledge of assurance, God has given us already the "earnest of the Spirit," who is the power that alone can work out such a sublime result as our final triumph over the flesh and sin, and meetness to take our place and part in a spiritual and heavenly state. "It is because the Spirit dwells in us by faith while we are here that we are to be raised hereafter. The body thus possessing a principle of life is as a seed planted in the ground to be raised again in God's good time" (comp. the sentence in ch. i. 22 and Rom. viii. 1—11). Observe that the Holy Spirit is presented to us under many aspects and figures; no one representation of his Divine mission can exhaust his relations to us. We must see his work on one side after another, and be willing to learn from all the figures under which it is presented.

I. WHAT IS MEANT BY AN "EARNEST"? It is something offered as a pledge and assurance that what is promised shall surely be given. But it has been well pointed out that an "earnest" materially differs from a "pledge." A pledge is something different in kind, given as assurance for something else, as may be illustrated by the sacraments; but an earnest is a part of the thing to be given, as when a purchase is made and a portion of the money is paid down at once. The idea of the "earnest" may be seen in the "firstfruits," which are a beginning of, and assure the character of, the coming harvest.

II. WHAT IS THE SPIRIT AS "EARNEST" TO US NOW? St. Paul's one point here is that it is an assurance of the final victory of the higher life over the lower. We have indeed that higher life *now*, in its initial and rudimentary stages, in having the Spirit dwelling in us.

III. WHAT FUTURE IS PLEDGED IN OUR HAVING THE SPIRIT NOW? Precisely a future in which the spiritual life shall be victorious and supreme, and our vehicle of a body simply within the use of the Spirit. That is full redemption, glory, and heaven.—R. T.

Ver. 7.—*Walking by faith.* "We walk by faith, not by sight." "Walking" is a familiar Scripture term for a man's life on the earth. It seems to have been associated with the figure of life as a "pilgrimage" in the Old Testament, and as a "racecourse" in the New Testament. It is joined to another word sometimes, and our "walk and conversation" are spoken of, our "going forward" and "turning about."

I. WALK AS DESCRIPTIVE OF HUMAN LIFE. Its suitability will be seen if we notice: 1. That it is a moving on. The days of our life go by as do the scenes in a panorama. 2. It is a slow moving on, steady and regular as the clock; time moves on, bearing all its sons away. 3. It is a moving on through ever-changing scenes, as is the path of the traveller, now up the hillside, now along the dusty highway, and now through the shaded valleys, with ever-varying sights and sounds around us. 4. It is a moving on somewhere; for he who walks has some end before him or some home in view. So our human life has its goal. We pass on into the eternal, where we may find our home.

II. WALK BY SIGHT AS DESCRIPTIVE OF THE WORLDLY LIFE. "Walk by sight" does not mean "in the power of our vision," but "under the influence and persuasion of things seen and temporal." It is the one essential characteristic of the worldly man that his judgments and decisions are made, his affections are ruled, and his conduct is ordered by what may be gathered under the term " the fashion of this world." Sense-conditions determine his place. Sense-requirements command his allegiance. Sense-principles inspire his doings and decide his relations. He " walks " with a horizon no further off than yonder ridge of hills, and with no thought really bigger in his soul than " What shall we eat? what shall we drink? and what shall we enjoy? " Saying this is the saddest revelation of man's essential wrongness before the God who " made him for himself."

III. WALK BY FAITH AS DESCRIPTIVE OF THE CHRISTIAN LIFE. We are not yet face to face with the eternal realities, but faith as the " substance of things hoped for " gives us a present actual possession of those eternal things, and makes them exert their power on our " walk." Faith in the unseen and eternal can (1) cheer; (2) raise the tone; (3) bring steadfastness into our walk and conversation. The realities are revealed to faith; human sight can only see passing shadows of things.—R. T.

Ver. 10.—" *The judgment-seat of Christ.*" It is needlessly forcing language to regard this expression as referring to the general judgment of mankind. This letter is addressed to the saints, the Church at Corinth, and it may be specially instructive to keep within the limits of St. Paul's thought when he said, " For *we* "—that is, we Christians—" must all appear before the judgment-seat of Christ." Such a judgment, or appraisement, of our conduct is involved in the very idea of our mastership to Christ. He will be sure one day to take account of his servants, and this Jesus himself taught us in his parables of the talents and pounds. Christians are as stewards, men entrusted for a time with their Master's goods. They are even to be thought of as " slaves," wholly the Master's possession; and he has full power to estimate their conduct, reward faithfulness, and punish neglect and disobedience. St. Paul even loves to think of himself as the bondslave of Jesus. And the apostles long to prove so faithful in all things that they may not be ashamed, or terrified, or loth to meet their Master at his coming. " The feeling of accountability may take two forms. In a free and generous spirit it may be simply a sense of duty; in a slavish and cowardly spirit it will be a sense of compulsion." To us it should be a joy and an inspiration that our own loved Master will appraise our lives; and that, if he is true to observe our faults, he will be no less gracious to recognize what he may call our goodnesses and our obediences. The thought of his judgment can only be a terror to the rebellious, disobedient, and wilful among his servants. We notice three things.

I. LOYALTY TO CHRIST IS OUR SPIRIT. " We call him Master and Lord, and we say well; for so he is." The rule of our life is the will of our glorified and ever-present Lord. We have voluntarily given ourselves to him. To him we owe our supreme allegiance. He is to us what his queen and country are to the general who leads forth his army. We must be ever true to him; and he, and he alone, is the Lord whose approval or condemnation of our work we should seek. Because I am loyal to Christ I will care about nobody's judgment of my life until I know *his*.

II. SERVICE OF CHRIST IN RIGHTEOUSNESS IS OUR LIFE. This is the very essence of the matter. Christ is served *by righteousness*, and really by nothing else. Our place of service, our kind of service, our success in service, are quite the secondary things. The first thing is the *rightness* with which we do the service. Was the work *good?*—this it is that Christ asks. Herein Christ differs from all other masters. They can only judge the work; he judges the *character* which found expression through the work. It is that personal righteousness that Christ will search for when he judges his servants.

III. THE APPRAISEMENT OF CHRIST IS OUR EXPECTATION AND OUR HOPE. A day of final judgment is men's expectation, but not their hope. It is too often a terror to them, a thought put away in fear. Christ's judgment of his saints is our hope; it is the first day of our glory. The thought of it may make us serious and watchful, but it never can make us sad. Christ will test and try our lives. Christ will weigh us in his balances. Christ will apportion our future place. Christ will chastise if there be found evil in us, and his chastisements shall be our joy; for we too want all the evil in us found out and put away. We even glory in this coming appraisement by our Lord; for if, in subtle disguises, evil lurks in any of our secret places of heart and life, Jesus will find it out, and will not leave us until we stand in the likeness of his own spotless purity. And upon our Lord's judgment of us our future, our eternal location and work, must depend. Tested in this life, he will know what we can do; and it may be that he will give us trust of higher things, "authority over ten cities."—R. T.

Vers. 14, 15.—*The power of the Christian motive.* The life of an intelligent being must be under the sway of some chosen and cherished motive. High degrees of intelligence find their expression in the careful selection of the motive. Where the intelligence is low and untrained, we find men blindly obeying motives which the accident of the hour may have raised up, or to which the bodily passions may excite. We can look into the face of no fellow-man and say, "That man is living without a motive." The consideration of the motives that actually rule men's lives give us very sad thoughts of our humanity. They range all the distance between the animal and the Divine, but they belong for the most part to the lower levels. The entire aspect and character of a man's life may be changed by a change of his motives. A new and nobler motive will soon make a man a better man. No man ever did rise to do noble things while his motive concerned only self and self-interests. All noble lives have been spent in service to others. All the best lives in private spheres have been self-denying lives. All the heroic lives in public spheres have been the lives of patriots, the lives of the generous, the pitying, and the helpful. St. Paul was in every way a remarkable man, full of energy, consecration, self-denial, and the "enthusiasm of humanity;" and in the passage now before us he tells us what was the supporting motive, the secret strength, of it all. "The love of Christ constraineth us."

I. THE SOURCE OF THE CHRISTIAN MOTIVE. "Because we thus judge, that if one died for all, then all died in him." Apparently that life of the apostle was the life of an enthusiast. But if you used that word in any bad sense he would indignantly deny such an accusation. It was indeed a life to which he was constrained, held fast, impelled, coerced, and that by the intense love of his soul for another—a love passing the love of women. But St. Paul would most earnestly urge that this love of his was no mere passion, no mere impulse, no blind force taking sudden mastery of his heart, and crushing down and silencing thought and judgment and will. He declares it to be a love based on judgment, and strengthened by maturer judgment. If that love was first won by the gracious vision granted to him when he was nearing Damascus, it was more truly a love confirmed and established by the serious meditations and calm decisions of his time of blindness, and by the Scripture studies of his lonely days in the desert. That sober consideration took up: 1. The sadness of man's condition. "Then were all dead;" or, as otherwise read, "then all died." 2. St. Paul's judgment decided that it was quite true about Jesus Christ—he had intervened to save men by his own sufferings and death. "He died for all." Paul—or Saul, as he was then called—was nearing the fulness of manhood when he heard of the appearance of a new prophet-teacher in the land of his fathers. But all his prejudices arrayed themselves against the acceptance of him and against belief in his special commission and authority. It appeared from the reports that he was a poor man; that he came from the despised Galilean Nazareth, about which Old Testament Scriptures prophesied no such great thing; that he made himself the "friend of publicans and sinners;" that he was an unsparing foe of Paul's own sect, the Pharisees; but that at last he had been stopped in his mischievous career, and made a public example of by an ignominious and shameful death. And then one day prejudice was overthrown. Prejudice was made to see the living glory of him whom it had tried to believe was disgraced and dead. Prejudice heard the authoritative voice of the supposed impostor speaking out of the heavenly places. Prejudice was conquered; the reason, the judgment, and the heart were enthroned, and set to form a judgment concerning Christ. And what a different thing the career of the Lord Jesus became when it was soberly, thoughtfully judged! Poor was he? It was the worthy outer garb of the unspeakable humiliation of the Divine Lord to the weakness of men. It was the fit outward seeming for "Immanuel," God with us. Out of Nazareth did he come? That was only one of the thousandfold proofs that he was indeed the Messiah promised to the fathers, now in dimmer and now in clearer outlines. Friend of publicans and sinners was he? No wonder; for he well knew that the real want of men is, not the removal of diseases, or the extensions of ceremonial worship, or even the unfolding of new truths, but the pardon of sin, the cleansing away of iniquity, and the assurance, carried home to the very soul, that God loves and would save the sinner. Despised and rejected of men was he? Yes; and it must have been so. Sinful humanity could not bear the reproach of the presence of perfect virtue. The forces of evil would be sure to wrestle hard against him who came that he might cast them out and destroy them. Die, did he, a mournful, shameful death? Judgment says—There, amid the very shame of the cross, thrown up by the very darkness that lies behind it, shine forth rays of transcendent glory. There, in those hours of agony, may be seen sublime self-sacrifice, mystery of spiritual suffering, Divine sin-bearing, and the most persuasive manifestation of God's love to men. There is God "not sparing his own Son, but delivering him up for us all;" and there is God's Son "bearing our sins in his own body on the tree." On that sober judgment the apostle based his new life-motive. He set the love of that dying Saviour so high in his soul that it became from henceforth the master motive of all that he did.

II. THE WAY IN WHICH THE CHRISTIAN MOTIVE WORKS. "They which live should not henceforth live unto themselves, but unto him which died for them, and rose again." The motive works by establishing a new law for the ruling of our life and conduct. It is the *not-unto-self* law. We do not know ourselves as we really are in our carnal state if we think that is not a new law. Gratification of self is the great *unnatural* human law. The not-unto-self law is the chosen life-principle of all the good. It is the law of God, the life-rule of Jesus the Christ; and, learnt of him, it has made many a human story since then beautiful and gracious. Could it be established in all hearts, the golden age would have come, in which the unselfish King can reign for ever and ever. The only possible deliverance from the sway of the old self-law is found in the elevating of some new and inspiring love to the throne of the heart. And Jesus makes *himself* the Object of just such love. The new motive also works in another way. It gives an inner spiritual force to sustain us in the endeavour to obey the law. Love becomes to us what it is to the child. The love of the parent becomes the law of the child's life; but the love, as it dwells in the heart of the child, makes obedience easy. So our love to Christ can become the inner force by which our obedience is sustained day by day.—R. T.

Ver. 19.—*God the Reconciler.* "God was in Christ, reconciling the world unto himself." "This is the first occurrence, in the order of time, in St. Paul's Epistles, of this word 'reconcile' as describing God's work in Christ. The idea involved is that man had been at enmity and had now been atoned (*at-oned*), and brought into concord with God. It will be noted that the work is described as originating with the Father and accomplished by the mediation of the Son" (Plumptre).

I. THE DISTURBANCE WHICH CALLS FOR RECONCILIATION. This may be presented as a disturbance occurring between (1) a Creator and his creatures; (2) a King and his subjects; or (3) more worthily in this case, a Father and his children. The point of impression is, that the disturbance is in no sense due to any action or neglect of God as Creator, King, or Father, but is wholly due to the self-willed and rebellious conduct of the creatures, subjects, or children. It involved a state of enmity, a withdrawal of pleasant relations, and acts of judgment on the part of God. All these statements need illustration and enforcement. Only as the difficulty is duly estimated can the grace of the remedy be fully understood.

II. THE SIDE ON WHICH WAS THE EARLIEST DESIRE FOR RECONCILEMENT. Not man's side. The offenders did not seek forgiveness and restoration. Show that this is true (1) historically, (2) experimentally. None of us, now, are *before God* in seeking reconciliation. The offended Creator, King, and Father seeks to make both one, and break down the middle walls of partition. "God was in Christ, reconciling the world unto himself." The deep ground of redemption is God's pitying love for us sinners. We must not think that we claimed the love or that Christ persuaded God to show it. "God so loved the world as to give his only begotten Son." The enmity of man to him grieved him, and love found the ways in which to break the enmity, and win, by a free forgiveness, the very heart of the offenders.

III. THE WAYS IN WHICH GOD EFFECTS THE RECONCILEMENT. All are summed up in Christ. He is the Agent through whom God practically carries out his reconciling purpose. We may gather all the ways under two heads. 1. God reconciles by removing the hindrances. 2. God reconciles by persuading the offenders. For both Christ is the Agency. He takes "the handwriting of ordinances that was against us out of the way, nailing it to his cross." He could say, "I, if I be lifted up, will draw all men unto me." Plead, in conclusion, that God's reconciling mercies, embodied in Christ Jesus, ought to be a mighty persuasion on us to yield ourselves to him. They should say in our hearts, "Be ye reconciled to God."—R. T.

Ver. 21.—*The Sinless counted as a sinner.* We give but the bare outline of a course of thought on this subject, because it is so suggestive of controversial theological topics, and can be treated from the points of view of several distinct theological schools.

I. CHRIST AS A SINLESS MAN. What proofs of this have we? And how does such sinlessness separate him from man and ensure his acceptance with God?

II. THE SINLESS CAN NEVER, IN FACT, BE OTHER THAN SINLESS. Neither God nor man can be deceived into regarding Christ as a sinner. No exigencies of theology may make us speak of God as regarding Christ as other than he was.

III. THE SINLESS CAN TAKE, AS A BURDEN ON HEART AND EFFORT, THE SINS OF OTHERS. Show fully in what senses this can be done.

IV. WITH SIN THUS ON HIM, A SINLESS MAN MAY SUBMIT TO BE TREATED AS IF HE WERE HIMSELF A SINNER.

V. WHEN THE SINLESS MAN THUS TAKES THE SINS OF OTHERS ON HIM HE BEARS THE SIN ALTOGETHER AWAY. Jesus took up the matter of our sin that it might be a hindrance and trouble to us no more for ever.—R. T.

EXPOSITION.

CHAPTER VI.

The methods and conditions of an apostolic ministry (vers. 1—10). Appeal to the Corinthians to reciprocate his affection and separate themselves from evil (vers. 11—18).

Ver. 1.—**We then, as fellow-workers.** Continuing the entreaty of ch. v. 20, he adds, "But as [his] fellow-workers we also exhort you." The "also" shows that he does not rest content with merely *entreating* them (δεόμεθα), but adds to the entreaty an exhortation emphasized by a self-sacrificing ministry. "Fellow-workers *with God*" (1 Cor. iii. 9). **Beseech.** The word is the same as that rendered "beseech" by the Authorized Version in ch. v. 20, and it should be rendered "exhort:" "God exhorts you by our means; we therefore entreat you to be reconciled to God; yes, and as Christ's fellow-workers we exhort you." **That ye receive not.** The word means both passively to receive and actively to accept as a personal boon. **The grace of God.** To announce this is the chief aim of the gospel (Acts xiii. 43; xx. 24). **In vain;** that is, "without effect." You must not only accept the teaching of God's Word, but must see that it produces adequate moral results. It must not, so to speak, fall "into a vacuum (εἰς κενόν)." "He," says Pelagius, "receives the grace of God in vain who, in the new covenant, is not himself new." If you really are in Christ you must show that you have thereby become "a new creation" (ch. v. 17). The branches of the true Vine

must bear fruit. (For the phrase, "in vain," see Gal. ii. 2; Phil. ii 16.) What the grace of God is meant to effect is sketched in Titus ii. 11, 12.

Ver. 2.—**For he saith;** that is, "God saith." The nominative is involved in the "*fellow*-workers," so that this is hardly to be classed with those rabbinic methods of citation found also in Philo, which deliberately omit the word "God" as the speaker, and use "He" by preference. **I have heard thee,** etc. The quotation is from the LXX. of Isa. xlix. 8, and is meant to express the necessity for receiving the grace of God, not only efficaciously, but at once. The "thee" in Isaiah is the Servant of Jehovah," the type primarily of Christ, and then of all who are "in Christ." **In a time accepted;** literally, in the Hebrew, *in a time of favour.* It is the season of grace, before grace has been wilfully rejected, and the time for judgment begins (Prov. i. 24—28). **The accepted time;** literally, *the well-accepted opportunity.* St. Paul in his earnestness strengthens the force of the adjective. The same word occurs in ch. viii. 12; Rom. xv. 16, 31.

"There is a deep nick in Time's restless
    wheel
For each man's good."

(Chapman.)

Now. No doubt St. Paul meant that, as long as life lasts, the door of repentance is never absolutely closed; but it is probable that he had specially in view the nearness of the advent of Christ. Compare the stress laid upon the word "to-day" in Heb. iii. 7, 8, and "at least in this *thy day*" (Luke xix. 42).

Ver. 3.—**Giving no offence in anything.** An under-current of necessary self-defence runs through St. Paul's exhortation. The participle is, like "fellow-workers," a nominative to "we exhort you" in ver. 1. *Offence.* The word here is not *skandalon*, which is so often rendered "offence," but *proskopē*, which occurs here alone in the New Testament, and is not found in the LXX. It means "a cause of stumbling." *Proskomma*, a stumbling-block, is used in 1 Cor. viii. 9. **Be not blamed.** When any just blame can be attached to the minister, the force of the ministry of reconciliation is fatally weakened. (For the word, see ch. viii. 20.)

Ver. 4.—**Approving ourselves**; rather, *commending ourselves*. He is again referring to the insinuation, which had evidently caused him deep pain, that *he* was not authorized to preach, as his Judaic opponents were, by "letters of commendation" (ch. iii. 1—3) from James or from the elders at Jerusalem. His credentials came from God, who had enabled him to be so faithful. **As the ministers of God** (1 Cor. iv. 1). The article should be omitted. **In much patience.** Christ had forewarned his apostles that they would have much to endure, and had strengthened them by the promise that "he that endureth to the end shall be saved" (Matt. x. 22). **In afflictions.** This word, as we have seen, is one of the haunting words in ch. i. 4—11. **In necessities.** St. Paul was poor, and was often in want (Acts xx. 34). **In distresses.** The same word which occurs in ch. iv. 8. It means "extreme pressure" (literally, *narrowness of space*), and is a climax of the other words.

Ver. 5.—**In stripes** (comp. ch. xi. 23—28). The stripes were of two kinds—from Jewish whips and Roman rods. But of the five scourgings with Jewish whips not one is mentioned in the Acts, and only one of the three scourgings with Roman rods (Acts xvi. 23). Nothing, therefore, is more clear than that the Acts only furnishes us with a fragmentary and incomplete record, in which, as we gather from the Epistles, either the agonies of St. Paul's lifelong martyrdom are for some reason intentionally minimized, or else (which is, perhaps, more probable) St. Paul was, as his rule and habit, so reticent about his own sufferings in the cause of Christ that St. Luke was only vaguely, if at all, aware of many scenes of trial through which he had passed. **In imprisonments.** St. Paul was frequently in prison, but St. Luke only tells us of one of these occasions (Acts xvi. 24)—at Philippi; the Roman imprisonment and that at

Cæsarea were *subsequent* to this Epistle. **In tumults.** These were a normal incident of St. Paul's life, both up to this time and for years afterwards (Acts xiii. 50; xiv. 19; xvi. 22; xvii. 4, 5; xviii. 12; xix. 28, 29; xxi. 27—39; xxii. 22, 23; xxiii. 9, 10; xxvii. 42, etc.) The word *akatastasiai* might also mean "insecurities," *i.e.* homelessness, wanderings, uncertainties (comp. 1 Cor. iv. 11); but New Testament usage seems decisive in favour of the former meaning (ch. xii. 20; 1 Cor. xiv. 33; Jas. iii. 15). **In labours** (ch. xi. 28; 1 Cor. iv. 12; xv. 10; Acts xx. 34; 1 Thess. ii. 9; 2 Thess. iii. 8). **In watchings.** "Spells of sleeplessness" were a necessary incident of such a life; and an eminently nervous nature like that of St. Paul is rarely capable of the habitual relief of sound sleep. Hence he again refers to this in ch. xi. 27. His "sleeplessness" was sometimes the necessary result of labours "night and day" (Acts xx. 31; 1 Thess. ii. 9, etc.). **In fastings.** St. Paul never inculcates the practice of voluntary fasting as a duty (for the reading in 1 Cor. vii. 5 is more than dubious); but it is probable that he found it personally useful at times (Acts xiii. 2, 3; xiv. 23; ix. 9). The nine forms of suffering hitherto mentioned—three general, three specific, and three voluntary—are all *physical* sufferings borne with "much endurance."

Ver. 6.—**By pureness**; rather, *in pureness*, as the preposition is the same. He now gives six instances of special gifts and virtues. The "pureness" is not only "chastity," but absolute sincerity (1 John iii. 3; ch. iv. 2; 1 Thess. ii. 10). **By knowledge.** The knowledge is the true knowledge of the gospel in its fulness (Eph. iii. 4). In his depth of insight into the truth St. Paul was specially gifted. The word *gnosis* had not yet acquired the fatal connotations which afterwards discredited it. **By long-suffering** (2 Tim. iii. 10; iv. 2). The patient endurance of insults, of which St. Paul shows a practical specimen in this Epistle, and still more in Phil. i. 15—18. **By kindness.** "Love suffereth long, and is kind" (1 Cor. xiii. 4); "Long-suffering, kindness" (Gal. v. 22). **By the Holy Ghost.** To the special gift of the Spirit St. Paul attributed all his success (1 Thess. i. 5; Rom. xv. 18, 19). **By love unfeigned;** which is the surest fruit of the Spirit, and the best of all spiritual gifts (ch. xii. 15; 1 Cor. viii. 1; xiii.; Rom. xii. 9, etc.).

Ver. 7.—**By the word of truth.** St. Paul now passes to the more specific endowments of the true teacher (comp. ch. ii. 17; iv. 2; 1 Cor. ii. 4; Gal. ii. 5). **By the power of God**; literally, *in power of God* (ch. iv. 7; 1 Cor. ii. 4; iv. 20). "For the kingdom of God is not [only] in word, but in power."

By the armour of righteousness. Here first the preposition "in" (ἐν) is changed for "through," "by means of" (διά). *Armour;* rather, *arms.* **On the right hand and on the left.** That is, both by offensive weapons and a defensive panoply (ch. x. 4; Eph. vi. 11—17; 1 Thess. v. 8).

Ver. 8.—**By honour and dishonour;** rather, *by glory and dishonour.* There is no need to change here the meaning of δ.ά, "by means of," to "through," *i.e.* "amid." The honour and dishonour are alike means which contribute to the commendation of the ministry. Of our Lord some said, "He is a deceiver," while others said, "He is a good man" (John vii. 12); and the dispraise of some is the highest praise (Matt. v. 11). Compare with the whole passage 1 Cor. iv. 9—13, where we see that "abuse," "insult," and "slander," constituted no small part of the apostle's daily trial. **By evil report and good report.** The beatitude of malediction (Luke vi. 22; 1 Pet. iv. 14). St. Paul had deliberately abandoned the desire to win the suffrages of men at the cost of undesirable concessions (Gal. i. 10). **As deceivers.** The Jews called Christ "a deceiver" (*mesith,* i.e. a deliberate and misleading impostor), Matt. xxvii. 63; John vii. 12. This is an illustration of the "evil report," and in the Clementine homilies, a century later, St. Paul, under the disgraceful pseudonym of "Simon Magus," is still defamed as a deceiver. **And yet true.** There is no "yet" in the original, and its omission gives more force to these eloquent and impassioned contrasts.

Ver. 9.—**As unknown;** literally, *as being ignored; as those whom no one cares to recognize.* **And yet well known.** "And becoming fully recognized." "Recognized" by God (1 Cor. xiii. 12), and ultimately by all good men (ch. xi. 6), though they might be contemptuously ignored by men. **As dying** (ch. i. 9; iv. 10, 11). **Behold.** The word calls attention to what seemed like a daily miracle. The paradox of the Greek tragedian—

"Who knows if life be death, and death be life?"

which seemed so supremely amusing to Aristophanes and the wits of Athens, became a familiar fact to the early Christians (Rom. viii. 36; 1 Cor. xv. 31; Eph. ii. 5, 6; Col. ii. 13, etc.). **As chastened.** The daily Divine education of suffering (Ps. cxviii. 18).

Ver. 10.—**As sorrowful, yet alway rejoicing.** The early Christians always insist on "joy" as one of the fruits of the Spirit (comp. Matt. v. 10—12), and especially joy in the midst of grief and anguish (Rom. v. 3; xiv. 17; 1 Thess. v. 16, "Rejoice always"). The best proof that this was no mere phraseo-

logy, but an amazing and new *charism* granted to the world, may be seen in the Epistle to the Philippians. It was written when St. Paul was old, poor, deserted, imprisoned, in danger of immediate death, and apparently in the lowest deeps of forsaken sorrow; yet the spontaneous key-note of the whole Epistle is, "I rejoice; rejoice ye" (Phil. iv. 6, 12). **As poor.** The word means even "paupers," and describes a very literal fact. St. Paul, for Christ's sake, had suffered "the loss of all things" (Phil. iii. 8). **Yet making many rich.** Not by getting collections for them (which would be a most unworthy antithesis, though it is strangely accepted by Chrysostom and others); but "by imparting to them the true riches, in the form of spiritual gifts, and the teaching of the gospel" (comp. Jas. ii. 5). **Possessing all things;** rather, *as having nothing, and fully having all things.* The verb means "possessing all things to the full." For "all things are ours" (1 Cor. iii. 21, 22).

Vers. 11—18.—*An appeal to the Corinthians to reciprocate his love for them, and separate themselves from evil.*

Ver. 11.—**Corinthians!** A rare and very personal form of loving appeal, which occurs nowhere else in these Epistles (comp. Phil. iv. 15). **Our mouth is open to you.** St. Paul has evidently been writing in a mood of inspired eloquence. The fervour of his feelings has found vent in an unusual flow of beautiful and forcible language. He appeals to the unreserved freedom with which he has written as a reason why they should treat him with the same frank love. **Our heart is enlarged.** After writing the foregoing majestic appeal, he felt that he had disburdened his heart, and as it were made room in it to receive the Corinthians unreservedly, in spite of all the wrongs which some of them had done him (comp. ch. vii. 3, 27). On the antithesis of the *mouth* and the *heart,* see Matt. xii. 34; Rom. x. 10.

Ver. 12.—**Ye are not straitened in us.** Any narrowing of the sympathy or straining of the relations between us does not rise in any way from me. (For the verb, see ch. iv. 8.) **Ye are straitened in your own bowels;** rather, *in your own hearts.* Any tightening or pressure of the feelings which should exist between us rises solely from your own hearts. Enlarge and open them, as I have done, and we shall once more love each other aright. The verb has already occurred in ch. iv. 8 ("distressed"). *Your own bowels.* It is to be regretted that the Authorized Version adopted the meaningless and often rather incongruous word "bowels" for the Greek word σπλάγχνα used in its Hebraic sense of "feelings," "affections"

(Cant. v. 4; Isa. xvi. 11). This literalism is always out of place, and especially in Philem. 7, 12, 20.

Ver. 13.—**Now, for a recompense in the same.** He begs them to give him "a reward in kind;" in other words, he wishes them to be as frank with him as he has been to them. **As unto my children.** And therefore, as a spiritual father, I may surely ask for sympathy. St. Paul uses the same metaphor in 1 Cor. iv. 14; 1 Thess. ii. 11. **Be ye also enlarged.** Treat me as I have treated you (comp. "Be as I am," Gal. iv. 12).

Ver. 14.—**Be ye not unequally yoked together with unbelievers.** Ewald, followed by Dean Stanley, Holsten, and others, thinks that here there is a sudden dislocation of the argument, and some have even supposed that the section, ch. vi. 14—vii. 1, is either an after-thought written by the apostle on the margin of the Epistle after it was finished; or even an interpolation. The latter view has arisen from the unusual expressions of the section, and the use of the word "Belial," and the command of Greek shown by the varied expressions. There is no adequate ground for these conjectures. Every writer is conscious of moods in which words come to him more fluently than at other times, and all writers of deep feeling, like St. Paul, abound in sudden transitions which correspond to the lightning-like rapidity of their thoughts. It is doubtful whether the readers would not have seen at once the sequence of thought, which depends on circumstances which we can only conjecture. Probably the alienation from St. Paul had its root in some tampering with unbelievers. Such might at any rate have been the case among the Gentile members of the Church, some of whom were even willing to go to sacrificial feasts in heathen temples (1 Cor. viii.—x.). "Unequally yoked" is a metaphor derived from Lev. xix. 19 and Deut. xxii. 10, and is the opposite of "*true yoke-fellow*" (Phil. iv. 3). **What fellowship;** literally, *participation* (Eph. v. 6—11). **Unrighteousness;** literally, *lawlessness* (1 John iii. 4). It was a special mark of heathen life (Rom. vii. 19). **Light with darkness.** This antithesis is specially prominent in Eph. v. 9—11 and Col. i. 12, 13, and in the writings of St. John (John i. 5; iii. 19; 1 John, *passim*).

Ver. 15.—**Concord;** literally, *harmony* or *accord.* The word does not occur elsewhere in the New Testament or in the LXX. The adjective *sumphōnos* occurs in 1 Cor. vii. 5. **Christ with Belial** (see 1 Cor. x. 21), *Belial.* Here used in the form *Beliar*, as a proper name, because no Greek word ends in the letter *r.* In the Old Testament it does not stand for a person, but means "wickedness" or "worthlessness." Thus

in Prov. vi. 12 "a naughty person" is *adam belial.* "A son of Belial" means "a child of wickedness" by a common Hebraism (Deut. xiii. 13; Judg. xix. 22). And hence, since Belial only became a proper name in later days—

"To him no temples rose,
No altars smoked."

Perhaps, as has been conjectured, this clause, which contains two such unusual words, may be a quotation. It is, however, no ground of objection that Belial does not occur elsewhere in St. Paul, for until the pastoral Epistles he only uses *diabolos* twice (Eph. iv. 27; vi. 11). **What part, etc. ?** This is not, like the other clauses, an illustration, but the statement of the fact itself which "has come in amidst the lively, sweeping flow of the discourse." **With an infidel;** *i.e.* with an unconverted Gentile.

Ver. 16.—**What agreement.** The word means "unity of composition." This is the fifth synonym which St. Paul has used in this clause—μετοχή, κοινωνία, συμφώνησις, μερὶς, συγκατάθεσις. The verb συγκατάθημι occurs in Luke xxiii. 51. St. Paul in this chapter shows an almost unwonted command over the Greek language. **With idols** (Matt. vi. 24; 1 John v. 21). **Ye.** "We" is the reading of א, B, D, L. Ewald, without sufficient ground, makes it one of his arguments for regarding this section as interpolated (comp. ch. v. 21). **Are the temple of the living God.** The indwelling of the Holy Spirit in every Christian heart, which is the distinguishing result of the new covenant, was very prominent in the thoughts of St. Paul (1 Cor. iii. 16; vi. 19; Eph. ii. 21, 22; 1 Tim. iii. 15; comp. 1 Pet. ii. 5; Heb. iii. 6). **As God hath said.** The quotation is altered slightly from the LXX. of Lev. xxvi. 12. But in this and the next verses we have "a mosaic of citations" from this passage and Exod. xxix. 45; Isa. lii. 11; Ezek. xx. 34; 2 Sam. vii. 14; comp. Jer. xxxi. 9; Isa. xliii. 6. This mode of compressing the essence of various quotations into one passage was common among the rabbis. **In them.** In the original Hebrew this means "among them" (Exod. xxix. 45; Lev. xxvi. 12). since the *indwelling* of God by his Holy Spirit belongs only to the new covenant.

Ver. 17.—**From among them;** *i.e.* from among the unbelievers. **Touch not the unclean thing** (Lev. xi. 8, etc.; Isa. lii. 11). **I will receive you** (comp. Ezek. xx. 34). These promises to Israel are naturally transferred to the ideal Israel, the Christian Church.

Ver. 18.—**And will be a Father unto you.** These reminiscences are sufficiently near to 2 Sam. vii. 8—14; Isa. xliii. 6; Jer. xxxi. 9, to render needless the supposition that they come from any apocryphal book (Ewald) or Jewish hymn (Grotius). **Saith the Lord Almighty.** The phrase, not elsewhere used by St. Paul, is taken from 2 Sam. vii. 8 (LXX.). The epithet indicates the certain fulfilment of the promises. *Pantokrator*, for "Almighty," is used in the LXX. for "Lord of sabaoth," and in the New Testament only occurs elsewhere in the Apocalypse.

HOMILETICS.

Vers. 1, 2.—*The grace of God received in vain.* "We then, as workers together," etc. There are three topics here for meditation.

I. A SUBLIME MISSION. "Workers together with him." What is the grand work in which God is engaged and in which we can co-operate? He is engaged in numerous works—works of creation, government, conservation, in which we can have no hand. The work here is evidently the work spoken of in the preceding chapter—the work of reconciling man to himself, the work which he does in Christ. Now, all genuine ministers co-operate with him in this; their grand endeavour is to bring alienated souls into friendship with him. Blessed partnership this.

II. A SOLEMN POSSIBILITY. "Receive not the grace of God in vain." The grace of God here evidently refers to the offer of this reconciliation. This may be looked upon objectively or subjectively. Objectively it is the gospel, which is called the "gospel of the grace of God;" subjectively it is personal Christianity. It may be received "in vain" in two forms. Many have the offer of reconciliation and reject it, and to them the offer has been received "in vain." It is possible for those who have personally experienced it to lose it. The free agency of man, the exhortations of the Scriptures, and the facts of apostasy—as in the case of David, Peter, etc.—show the possibility of losing this. No greater calamity can happen to a man than to receive this "grace in vain;" hence the earnestness of the apostle.

III. A SUPREME OPPORTUNITY. "For he saith, I have heard thee in a time accepted, and in the day of salvation have I succoured thee: behold, now is the accepted time; behold, now is the day of salvation." To use the words of a modern writer, "There is, so to speak, a 'now' running through the ages. For each Church and nation, for each individual soul, there is a golden present that may never again recur, and in which lie boundless possibilities for the future. The words of the apostle are, as it were, the transfigured expression of the generalization of a wide experience, which tells us that 'there is a tide in the affairs of men.'"

Vers. 3—8.—*The highest office injured by its officer.* "Giving no offence in any thing," etc. Paul was engaged in the highest office—the office of *reconciling men to God;* in this he was a co-worker with the Infinite, and here he refers to—

I. AN EVIL TO WHICH MINISTERS OF THE GOSPEL ARE LIABLE. The evil referred to is bringing blame upon the ministry. "Giving no offence in anything, that the ministry be not blamed." So perverse is man that he often degrades some of the highest offices he is called to sustain. There are merchants that degrade commerce, doctors that degrade medicine, judges that degrade justice, statesmen that degrade legislation, kings that degrade the throne; but, what is worse far, there have been ministers who have degraded the ministry, and there are such still, ignorant men, intolerant men, worldly men, unspiritual men, blatant dogmatists. Ah me! how the pulpit is often degraded!

II. AN EVIL WHICH MUST BE AVOIDED AT ANY COST. See what Paul did and suffered to avoid this stupendous evil. "But in all things approving ourselves as the ministers of God, in much patience, in afflictions, in necessities, in distresses," etc. Mark: 1. How he suffered in order to maintain the honour of the ministry. "Afflictions," "necessities," "distresses," "stripes," "imprisonments," "tumults," "labours," "watchings," "fastings," etc. 2. How he wrought in order to maintain the honour of the ministry. By "pureness," "knowledge," "long-suffering," "kindness," etc. He learned to labour and to wait. "Neither count I my life dear unto myself, so that I might finish my course with joy, and the ministry, which I have received of the Lord Jesus, to testify the gospel of the grace of God." The ministry in these days is too often degraded into a trade, a profession, a medium for the gratification of the vanity;

ambition, and the greed of men. The millions have come to call churches and chapels "preaching-shops." One of the greatest trades carried on in this commercial age is, perhaps, the trade in the gospel.

Vers. 9, 10.—"*Things are not what they seem.*" "As unknown, and yet well known," etc. Against misrepresentations and slanders, Paul, in the context, vindicates his apostolic authority, and proclaims at the same time the unworldly principle which animated both him and his fellow-workers. These words present to us the two opposite sides of a good man's life—the secular and the spiritual. The side revealed, as seen by man, and the side in the sight of God.

I. To THE SECULAR EYE HE WAS UNKNOWN; TO THE SPIRITUAL WELL KNOWN. "As unknown, and yet well known." The world has never yet rightly interpreted and understood the real life of a genuine disciple of Christ. To the world, Paul appeared an ignominious fanatic. John says, "The world knoweth us not." The world does not understand self-sacrificing love, the animating, shaping, directing principle of a godly man's life. It understands ambition, greed, revenge, but not this. Hence men in every age, so far as they have come under the rule of this "new commandment," have been regarded as monsters unworthy of life. This explains martyrdom, ay, and the crucifixion of Christ. But, though thus unknown to men, they are well known to others. 1. Well known to *Christ.* "I know my sheep." Christ knows all his disciples. 2. Well known to *heavenly spirits.* They are famous in heaven. At their conversion heaven rejoiced, and over every step of their subsequent history heaven watches with a loving care.

II. To THE SECULAR EYE HE WAS DYING; TO THE SPIRITUAL HE WAS LIVING. "As dying, and, behold, we live." To worldly men Paul appeared as mortal as other men; with a frame scourged by persecution, shattered by perils, wasted by labour and want, he was nothing but a dying man. His contemporaries knew that he would soon run himself out, and mingle with the dust of all departed men. But *spiritually* he was living. "Behold, we live." The soul within that dying body of his was living a wonderful life—a life of Christly inspiration and aims, a life of communion with heaven; a life destined to become more sunny, vigorous, and beautiful with every aspiration and act. Living is not *body-breathing*, but *spirit-acting*, acting according to the Divine laws of our constitution.

III. To THE SECULAR EYE HE WAS MUCH TRIED; TO THE SPIRITUAL HE WAS NOT DESTROYED. "Chastened, and not killed." The word "chastened" here refers, I think, to his various scourgings, suffered in the synagogues and elsewhere. To worldly spectators he, with all his wounds, would appear a dead man; but he was spiritually alive. The hardships and the strifes did not touch his soul; his spiritual purposes, enjoyments, and hopes were not killed. Spiritual life is unkillable; like certain plants in the vegetable kingdom, which have their germs or roots so deep down in the soil, and so thoroughly mixed up with it, that, though you cut down the trunk, or pull up the roots from the earth, their life will break out again.

IV. To THE SECULAR EYE HE WAS VERY SORROWFUL; TO THE SPIRITUAL HE WAS ALWAYS REJOICING. "As sorrowful, yet alway rejoicing." As if Paul had said, "Under our sufferings, we seem to be very cast down and sad; dreary, degraded, and wretched does our life seem to the worldly men around us." So it often is with the life of a Christian man. But, on the spiritual side, a truly godly man is "always rejoicing," rejoicing in a good conscience, rejoicing in a stream of pure and noble thoughts, rejoicing in a consciousness of Divine favour.

V. To THE SECULAR EYE HE WAS VERY POOR; TO THE SPIRITUAL HE WAS WEALTH-GIVING. "As poor, yet making many rich." Paul and his colleagues were poor; they had suffered the loss of all things. Yet spiritually they were not only rich, but made others rich. 1. The highest work of man is to impart spiritual riches to his brother man. 2. Worldly poverty does not disqualify a man for the discharge of this sublime mission.

VI. To THE SECULAR EYE HE WAS DESTITUTE; TO THE SPIRITUAL HE WAS ENORMOUSLY RICH. "Having nothing, and yet possessing all things." Nothing of this world's good, yet "possessing all things," not legally, but *morally.* Christliness gives us an interest in all things. "All things are yours."

Do not estimate life by appearances—things are not what they seem. Christliness with poverty, persecution, and suffering, is infinitely to be preferred to wickedness with the whole world at its command.

Vers. 11—13.—*Genuine Christian love.* "O ye Corinthians," etc.   Notice—

I. ITS POWER. What does it do? It enlarges the heart. "Our heart is enlarged." The heart means the whole spiritual nature, and this spiritual nature is capable of indefinite expansion and Christian love, and nothing else can effect this. A man's intellect may be expanded by ideas, but his heart, out of which are "the issues of life," only by love. What a difference between the heart of a miser or a bigot to the heart of a Paul, a Howard, or a Fénelon! Selfishness contracts the soul into a grub, love expands it into a seraph. Therefore "covet earnestly the best gift," that is, love.

II. ITS IRREPRESSIBILITY. "Our mouth is open unto you." A large heart is so full of loving sympathies and aims that speech becomes a necessity. "Out of the abundance of the heart the mouth speaketh." The language of love is the language of nature, the language of eloquence, the language of inspiration.

III. ITS HUNGER. What does it hunger for? "Ye are not straitened in us, but ye are straitened in your own bowels ['affections,' or 'hearts']," etc. Paul states that their hearts towards him were "straitened," or narrow, compared with his to them. He entreats them to be "enlarged," and thus "recompense" or return his affections. Love, by a necessity of its nature, hungers for a return of its affections from the object on which it is bestowed. Paul did not ask them for their money, or their patronage or praise, but simply for a return of the love which he had for them.

Vers. 14—18.—*Unequally yoked.* "Be ye not unequally yoked," etc. Observe here three things.

I. THERE IS AN ESSENTIAL SPIRITUAL DIFFERENCE BETWEEN THOSE WHO ARE TRULY CONVERTED TO CHRISTIANITY AND THOSE WHO ARE NOT. The line of demarcation is broad and conspicuous. The difference is the difference: 1. Between "righteousness and unrighteousness." 2. Between "light and darkness." 3. Between Christ and Satan. "What concord hath Christ with Belial?" 4. Between faith and infidelity. "What part hath he that believeth with an infidel?" 5. Between the "temple of God" and the "temple of idols."

II. NOTWITHSTANDING THE SPIRITUAL DIFFERENCE, THE CONVERTED ARE IN DANGER OF BEING ASSOCIATED WITH THE UNCONVERTED. Hence the command, "Be ye not unequally yoked together with unbelievers." Also the command, "Come out from among them." Alas! we find such association in almost every department of life— in the matrimonial, the commercial, the political, etc.

III. FROM SUCH AN ASSOCIATION IT IS THE DUTY OF THE CONVERTED TO EXTRICATE THEMSELVES. "Wherefore come out from among them," etc. Observe two things. 1. The *nature* of the separation. "Come out from among them." It must be: (1) *Voluntary.* Not to be driven out, but you must break away from all the ties that bind you. Agonize to enter the "strait gate." (2) *Entire.* "Touch not the unclean thing." Sin is an *unclean thing*—unclean in its essence, its phases, and its influences. 2. The *encouragement* to the separation. "I will receive you, and will be a Father unto you, and ye shall be my sons and daughters." As a Father, what does God do for his children? (1) He *loves* them. His love is the fountain of all the love in the universe. All the love that human parents have for their children is but one drop from the boundless ocean. (2) He *educates* them. Who teaches like God? He teaches the best lesson, in the best way, for the best end. He educates the whole soul, not for temporal purposes, but for ends spiritual and everlasting. (3) He *guards* them. Human parents can only guard the bodies of their children. This Father guards the soul—the conscience from guilt, the heart from impurity, the intellect from error, etc. (4) He *provides* for them. The best of human parents can only provide for their children a few supplies for their bodies, and that for a time only. This great Father provides for the soul, and provides for ever. "He is able to do exceedingly abundantly above all that we ask or think."

HOMILIES BY VARIOUS AUTHORS.

Vers. 1—10.—*Appeal growing out of the foregoing argument.* The grace of God had been manifested in the reconciliation of which he had been treating; and this reconciliation had its period, or season, special as to its character and advantages. Everything has relation to time. Life has infancy, childhood, youth—successive eras. Nature has her seasons. It was now God's receiving-time, a dispensation of mercy, an acceptable time, a day of salvation. So sensible was St. Paul of this fact that he, as a co-worker with God, pressed the exhortation on the Corinthians not to neglect the grace of God freely vouchsafed in this auspicious time. Good influences were conspiring in their favour; "receive not the grace of God in vain." It was a co-working period. Out of the turmoil, the strife of tongues, the collisions within the Church and without, doctrines were emerging into clearer view, and, as doctrines were better understood, duties would be more faithfully discharged. Had not these Corinthians been revived and strengthened of late? Had they not heeded his affectionate warnings and purified the Church? It was a season for continued and enlarging co-working, the Holy Spirit and the Church combining in an effort, peculiarly desirable then, to extend Christ's kingdom. And what was he doing to this end? For his part he was studious to put no stumbling-block in the way of others, lest the ministry be reproached. That was the prudence which wards off evil. It has grave duties. It is vigilant, able to see the approach of danger and measure the extent of the peril. It is prompt to act in a precautionary manner. Yet this was only one part of a co-worker's duty. On the other hand, then, he was intent on commending himself to their confidence and affection, and by what means? The portraiture of St. Paul as a co-worker is now presented. Previously to this he had sketched himself (see ch. ii., iii., iv.) in certain specific relations, such for instance as an "able minister," and as one who carried his treasure in an "earthen vessel;" but it was now his purpose to delineate himself and his experience with reference to a particular end. To be a co-operator, patience is the first virtue required. He speaks, therefore, at the outset, of "much patience," and assuredly he did not mistake the basic position of this great quality. He mentions nine forms of suffering which have been regarded by some commentators as constituting three classes, viz.: afflictions or general calamities, necessities, distresses, the leading idea being pressure, or "narrow straits;" *then* stripes, imprisonments, tumults, referrable to the popular excitement against him as a preacher; and *lastly*, labours, watchings, fastings, as indicative of ministerial experience. In all these things patience was exercised, keeping him steadfast, enabling him to endure, and preserving his mind in the peace of Christ. It is a description of one whose body was open on all sides to the invasions of pain as the infliction of opposition and malice; and again, of one whose mind had anxieties and sorrows originating in its own sense of responsibility. Body wrought upon mind, mind upon body. Under these conditions the co-worker had to proceed with his task—patience, "much patience," being the cardinal excellence of his character. But, further, the co-worker speaks of purity, knowledge, long-suffering, kindness, endowments of the Spirit, sincere love; and again, he speaks of the word of truth, how he worked with God's power, and fought also with an armour of righteousness, right hand and left hand engaged in the conflict. Just here the mind of St. Paul reacts from its subjective state, the enumeration of his moral virtues is suspended, and the idea of conflict brings back the "afflictions" alluded to (ver. 4). Nearly all his transitions occur in one of two ways, either as the immediate product of a physical sensation or as the result of some exciting thought, having its source in his train of reflection. At the instant when the image of battle comes before him, the co-worker has the doctrine and morality of the gospel to defend against fierce, vindictive, mighty assailants. The honour of his position and the glory of Christ as the Captain of his salvation are at stake. Sword and shield are in hand, and for what is he fighting and how? "Armour of righteousness" is very expressive. The great truth was present in his mind, foremost as a restraint as well as an impulse, the truth so ably argued in the previous chapter that we are "made the *righteousness* of God in him." Give the ethical philosopher all the credit he deserves; honour the moralist who strives to protect society from immorality; and yet it is very obvious that a man who feels himself set for the defence of the "righteousness of God" as manifested in Christ stands on ground infinitely higher than the mere philosopher and moralist. This cannot be denied; such a man has a spirit, a motive, an end, far remote from the others, and peculiar to the sphere he fills. What the apostle fights for is *righteousness*. And how is he fighting? It is important that we should see his temper, his tactics, his whole method of conducting the campaign. Men who ostensibly fight for righteousness are not always righteous fighters. "I will not trust in my bow, neither shall my sword save me," said one of the psalmists. "Make haste to help me, O Lord my salvation," was David's prayer. "Ye know not what manner of spirit ye are of," were the words of Jesus when the "sons of thunder" wished to call down fire from heaven on the Samaritan village. Michael the archangel, in contention with the devil, "durst not bring against him a railing accusation." A bad spirit is not allowable even towards Satan, nor can an archangel go beyond "The Lord rebuke thee." Now, the apostle speaks of himself as fully armed for offensive and defensive warfare. And the fight goes on amid honour and dishonour, praise and cheer from friends, hostility and contempt from enemies; by evil report and good report; vilified as a deceiver, but yet a true man; as unknown ("obscure nobodies") to men, but known to God; as dying, and behold, out of perils, life springs renewed and enlarged; chastened as a discipline needed for a spiritual warrior who was meantime in everything a co-worker with Christ; a sorrowful man in the estimation of many, but in reality always rejoicing; poor, working with our own hands for a living, but making many rich in spiritual blessings; and, finally, *having nothing*, and yet—glorious paradox—possessing in Christ *all things*.—L.

Vers. 11—18.—*His warmth of affection; anxiety of the apostle lest the grace of God be received in vain.* The ruling thought of the chapter is twofold. St. Paul, the ambassador, is a fellow-worker with God in Christ, and as such he is deeply concerned that the Church at Corinth should not fail to use its means and opportunity for salvation then within reach. A critical period had come in its history, and he saw it very clearly. What so sagacious as love? what love so abounding as his? "O ye Corinthians," out of the depths of my heart, the heart just described—out of its purity, knowledge, long-suffering; "O ye Corinthians," by my kindness, by the Spirit of God in me, by love unfeigned; "O ye Corinthians," amid my chastenings from God and my afflictions from men;—whom I have besought not to receive the grace of God in vain, once more I pray you hearken. "Our mouth is open unto you, our heart is enlarged." Only a very large and roomy nature could have entertained the thoughts and feelings, could have suffered, could have passed through the experiences which had just been described; but various and multiplied as were that heart's burdens and tribulations, it had ample space for his brethren at Corinth. "Ye are not straitened in us [no narrow place you occupy in our affection], but ye are straitened in your own bowels [narrowness in your love for us]," the word "bowels" being used to express the seat of the feelings. "For a recompense [return of love] . . . be ye also enlarged," and he asks this as a father seeking affection from his children. A sudden break occurs in the movement of thought. Did the use of the word "children" quicken a feeling akin to parental solicitude? Or did the sorrows he was undergoing in behalf of this Church at Corinth, a moment before so vividly pictured, give him a new insight into the dangers surrounding its members? Or was he recalling the supreme truth in his theology, the atoning death of Christ, and the righteousness that came to us and became a part of us? One in whose mind associations gathered so very rapidly and suggestions arose with such spontaneous vigour would probably feel the sudden return of the ideas and images on which he had been dwelling. A peculiarity with him is this partial development of a thought on its first appearance in his intellect. A similar law is traceable in his emotional nature. There is a second production, and this "aftermath" is very valuable. The subject under consideration (vers. 14—18) had engaged attention in the First Epistle, and he now reverts to it under the apprehension that these Corinthians, who were particularly exposed to the "evil communications" that "corrupt good manners," might receive the grace of God in vain. If there had been a strong reaction against the Judaizing party in the Corinthian Church, that may have introduced unusual hazards as to

Gentilism. Reactions, no matter how wise and truthful in themselves, always involve more or less danger. Facts are distorted, truths are mixed with prejudices, and the victory is our victory. Generally, indeed, only when time has befriended our infirmities and given us an opportunity to recover from reactions are we put in an attitude to see and judge with entire fairness. But, whatever the impulse at the moment on St. Paul's mind, his words are surcharged with energy. Question hastens after question. "Unequally yoked together with unbelievers" is the trumpet-note of alarm. What the union was he does not specify. It may have been promiscuous intercourse with heathens, or participation in idol festivals, or mixed marriages. Whichever it was, it was unequal yoking, a very ill-devised union; and under how many aspects did it deserve condemnation? The heart of the evil is exposed; could righteousness have fellowship with unrighteousness, light commune with darkness, Christ have concord with Satan, believers have part with infidels, the temple of God agree with idols? Metaphors multiply, as they commonly do with him when excited. By their profession of Christ they were pledged to depart from all iniquity, especially all associations that might revive their former Gentile tastes and habits, most especially those social usages which identified them with idolatry. Quoting twice from the Old Testament (Leviticus and Isaiah), he shows what the true religion demanded of its subjects in its earlier stage under Moses and its later under the prophets, in both cases separation from a world given over to heathenism. Only by means of this line of demarcation between them and the corruptions of society would God acknowledge them as his people, walk in their midst, and be a Father unto them. "Touch not the unclean thing." It was the language of Judaism from her tabernacle in the wilderness, from her temple in Jerusalem, and now reaffirmed and emphasized anew and with most solemn intensity by Christianity. St. Paul saw that history repeats itself. Not otherwise were it history. The peril of the gospel was precisely that which had wrecked Judaism. From this point of view it is profitable to re-read this earnest chapter. Chrysostom and others have spoken of its lofty eloquence. Stanley, Robertson, Webster, and Wilkinson have taught us to appreciate the breadth of its ideas and the classical force of its diction. It is a chapter of warning from the memorials of the past, as that past demonstrates most signally the jealousy of God's rule over men. On the one hand, we have the terrible fascinations of that spirit of idolatry which in some form or other is the besetting sin of the human race, the innate disposition to supplant Jehovah, the fatal surrender to "the god of this world," never so blinding as when he makes men as gods unto themselves. On the other hand, we have the visible symbols of God's presence among his people in the temple and its institutions, and further, the proof of the Spirit's power in their hearts, his actual indwelling and sanctifying agency. Yet this grace may be received in vain. The higher the gift, the more freedom in its use. No sooner has the apostle set forth the fact that God was in Christ recovering the world unto himself, than the magnitude of the risk presses on his attention. The risk was altogether in man. It was a risk, moreover, in the Christian man who had received grace and might lose its influence. Law had been violated, but Christ, as the eternal Son of God, had expiated the guilt, and by faith we accepted him as the Divine Reconciler. Man's responsibility had utterly failed under Law; would it fail under grace? If it did, there was an end of hope, since there remaineth no other sacrifice for sin. St. Paul was aware of the local circumstances that enhanced the dangers of the Corinthians. The style of the appeal recognizes this fact. Let it not be forgotten, however, that, while men as men have these local surroundings, Christianity deals with man as man, and, accordingly, the warning is addressed to us not to receive the grace of God in vain. Our probation goes on in the midst of contingencies; temptation and trial are things most completely shut out from ordinary modes of calculation, and no prophetic eye reads our future. Yet this very sense of uncertainty is the most merciful of all providential arrangements. It is a source of great power. Except for its keen sensitiveness, our liability to evil would be far greater. Apprehension acts in two ways— it constantly reduces the amount of evil existing; and again, it fortifies us to resist the evil that remains. Now, Christianity operates in both these modes. With the latter only have we now to do. The problem for every individual Christian is the efficiency of grace in his resistance to Satanic influence. So far as the Scriptures teach us on this subject, Jesus Christ had no temptations save those which Satan offered; and, while we have no warrant to say this of believers, we may safely affirm that it is the reconciled man in Christ, "made the righteousness of God in him," who is the object of Satan's sharpest assaults. To destroy the power of grace in the child of God is his unceasing effort. Now, this grace is received through two great channels—the conscience and the affections. St. Paul is referring continually to these organs of spiritual activity, and hence, we infer, that he would have his converts most earnest at these points. Conscience must be enlightened by the gospel and directed by the Spirit. It must be a conscience of that righteousness we have in Christ and through Christ, external to us as the ground of justification, internal to us as the regenerating and sanctifying work of the Holy Ghost. "For the law of the Spirit of life in Christ Jesus hath made me free from the law of sin and death." But this sense of righteousness in the conscience must act likewise in the affections, or it cannot be "the law of the Spirit of life." If, then, St. Paul commended the gospel "to every man's conscience in the sight of God," was he content to rest here? "O ye Corinthians, . . . our heart is enlarged." Open your hearts, open them freely, open them as mine is opened unto you. If they would thus realize the righteousness of Christ, they could not receive the grace of God in vain. It is here, while speaking of the enlarged heart, that he appeals to them as his children. "Be ye also enlarged." Here we see how grace is lost; the heart, instead of expanding, is narrowed and cramped. Ministers must preach the gospel of love; and, to do this, they must be lovely in spirit and conduct. Christians must accept the grace of the gospel in hearts that enlarge, so that growth in loveliness may develop strength of character in its most enduring form. Just at this point backsliding sets in. No man's conscience begins to be blinded till his heart begins to be narrowed. Sympathy is checked; openness of feeling arrested; giving to charitable objects abated; cordiality of intercourse with ministers and members of the Church supplanted by fault-finding, prejudice, and censoriousness; and then conscience becomes careless, then inert, then callous, and grace dies in the soul. The enlarging heart is the secret of growth. Nor is there any growth so beautiful as this in itself and so inspiriting as an example to others. Its *fellowship* is with souls that are its kindred in Christ; its *communion* with that wisdom and purity symbolized by light; its *concord* with him who took upon himself our nature that we might bear his image; its *part* or share is in the possession of holiness; and its capacity is a *temple*, or habitation, of which "God hath said, I will dwell in them, and walk in them."—L.

Ver. 1.—"*Workers together.*" One who is sent upon a mission, who fills the office of an ambassador, is evidently one who, however he works, does not work alone. He is the representative of the court from which he is sent, by which he is accredited. When the apostle thought of his life-mission, especially when he thought of its difficulties, it was natural that he should recall to his own mind the fact that God, who had commissioned him, was working with him and giving efficacy to his labours. And, in writing to others, it was appropriate that he should remind them that they had to deal, not merely with a fellow-man, but with a fellow-man who was supported and authorized by Divine wisdom and grace.

I. GOD WORKS. He not only wrought the earth and the heavens, which are "the work of his fingers:" he follows his work of creation by the unceasing work of providential care, government, and oversight. The laws of nature are the ways in which God works. And the spiritual realm is his highest and noblest sphere of operation, in which he is carrying out his holy purposes.

II. MEN, WHEN THEY WORK SUCCESSFULLY, WORK WITH GOD. Take two illustrations. The husbandman toils through all the changing seasons of the year, and in his ploughing, sowing, and reaping depends upon the processes of nature, *i.e.* works along with God. The physician studies the human frame, and, when it is diseased, seeks its recovery to health through co-operation with the laws of the various organs and tissues of the body, and succeeds only by working with God. So is it in the spiritual sphere. The preacher of Christianity makes use of God's truth and relies upon God's Spirit; any other method must involve failure and discouragement.

III. HUMAN LABOURERS WORK IN SUBJECTION TO THE DIVINE LORD. There is no equality in this fellowship. God can dispense with any man's services, however great, wise, and good he may be. No man can dispense with the counsel and the aid of

Heaven. 1. In the recognition of this lies the labourer's strength. 2. And the dignity attaching to his position and office, which is not personal, but ministerial. 3. And the responsibility of all for whose welfare the Christian labourer toils. Such are bound to consider, not the human minister merely, but the Divine Lord, whose servant and messenger he is.—T.

Ver. 2.—*The acceptable time.* As an ambassador for Christ, Paul used both authority and persuasion in urging his readers and hearers to take advantage of the opportunity afforded them of reconciliation with God through Jesus Christ. And he very naturally and justly pressed upon them an immediate attention to the summons, the invitation of Divine grace. There are reasons why delay should be avoided, why acceptance should be unhesitating.

I. THE BLESSING. This is set before us in two lights. 1. On the *Divine* side, we observe that God is ready both to hear and to succour. To hear the cry of those in danger, the petition of those in want. To succour those who are in present distress and who are unable to deliver themselves from their afflictions. 2. On the *human* side, we observe that men may be accepted and reconciled, that they may be delivered and saved. The salvation here proffered is spiritual and eternal.

II. THE OPPORTUNITY. It is not for us to speculate as to God's reasons, so to speak, for limiting the day of grace and of visitation. We have to deal with the fact that there is a period during which the blessings of salvation may be sought and secured. The first advent of our Saviour may be fixed as the *terminus a quo* of this period, the second advent as the *terminus ad quem.* During the Christian era, the dispensation of the Holy Spirit, the gospel is preached to all men, and the invitation is freely offered to those who need to apply, with the assurance that their request shall not be refused.

III. THE APPEAL. The blessing is great and adapted to the case of the sinner; the opportunity is precious and not to be despised without guilt and folly. What, then, follows? Surely the appeal is powerful and timely; it deserves the immediate attention of all to whom the gospel comes. 1. The conditions are such that they may be at once fulfilled. The call is to obey God, to believe in Christ, to repent of sin, to live anew. 2. Nothing can be advanced to justify delay. Delay is unreasonable, dangerous, and foolish. To neglect the appeal would be to defy and displease God. 3. Those of every age and condition are alike placed in this position of privilege and of responsibility.—T.

Ver. 4.—"*Ministers of God.*" Man is not meant to be a law or an end unto himself. He finds the true secret of his being, who lives, not unto himself, but unto his Lord. To take employment under a wise and holy Master, to engage in a spiritual service, to look up daily for direction and for blessing, to aim at the glory of the Eternal,—this is the true vocation and the true happiness of man. Paul found his strength for labour and his consolation in suffering, not in anything personal, but in losing and merging himself in his Lord and King.

I. THE MASTER. Our Lord has bidden us call no man master, by which he directs our attention to the fact that we receive our instructions for duty and our revelations of truth, not from human, but from Divine authority. God is, to those who accept service under him, a wise, just, forbearing, considerate, and liberal Master. In him we find one free from all imperfections of knowledge, and all flaws of character, such as must be expected in all human governors.

II. THE SERVICE. In its outward aspects this varies in different cases, so that the life-work of no two men is quite the same.

> "How many serve! how many more
> May to the service come!—
> To tend the vines, the grapes to store,
> Thou dost appoint for some;
> Thou hast thy young men at the war,
> Thy little ones at home."

III. THE OBLIGATIONS OF SPIRITUAL SERVANTS. 1. Obedience. This is indispensable. The vow which Christians take is that they will be the Lord's servants to obey him.

2. Fidelity. The allegiance due to the Divine Lord must, upon no consideration, be transferred to another; his cause must not be betrayed. 3. Readiness to suffer in the path of devotion. The context shows us that this was an element in Paul's conception of true ministry.

IV. THE RECOMPENSE. 1. This is entirely of grace; the purest and the best have no claim to it. 2. Success in ministry is the true servant's best reward. 3. With this is conjoined approval on the Master's part. 4. And the recompense is imperishable and immortal.—T.

Ver. 7.—"*The armour of righteousness.*" There was something soldierly both in the nature and in the life-course of the Apostle Paul. His resolution, courage, fortitude, capacity for endurance, fidelity to his spiritual Commander, were all high military qualities. We do not wonder that he made in his writings use so frequent and so effective of the warrior's life. The Christian's career, and much more emphatically the apostolic career, appeared to him one large campaign. Hence his reliance upon "the armour of righteousness on the right hand and on the left."

I. THE CHRISTIAN'S NEED OF SPIRITUAL ARMOUR. 1. His foes are many, active, vigilant, formidable, untiring. 2. The warfare to which he is called is accordingly perilous and serious. 3. His own natural resources are utterly inadequate for his defence.

II. THE NATURE OF THE CHRISTIAN'S SPIRITUAL ARMOUR. 1. It is not physical, or carnal, but moral. 2. It is described in one word as "the armour of righteousness," as opposed to fraud and cunning and iniquity of every kind. 3. It is adapted to the several necessities of the welfare. *Vide* Eph. vi., where the several weapons are enumerated and described.

III. THE PURPOSES WHICH THE CHRISTIAN'S ARMOUR EFFECTS. 1. The right hand of the warrior wields the sword; and this is the emblem of the weapon of *attack* which the Christian grasps—even "the sword of the Spirit," which is the Word of God. 2. The left hand of the warrior holds the shield, which is the symbol of that mighty principle of faith, which is the *defensive* weapon used by every soldier in the spiritual warfare, with which he quenches the fiery darts of the evil one.

IV. THE RESULTS OF THE WARFARE WAGED BY THE CHRISTIAN THROUGH THE USE OF HIS SPIRITUAL ARMOUR. 1. To himself, security and honour. He is delivered from his foes, and he fights the good fight of faith. 2. To his cause, victory. Righteousness is destined to conquer; there is no uncertainty as to the issues of the holy war. 3. To his Commander, great and growing renown, as his foes are vanquished and his kingdom is consolidated and extended.—T.

Ver. 16.—*A temple of God.* The temple at Jerusalem, built for the glory of Jehovah, and honoured by him as his dwelling-place and shrine, was as edifice quite unique. No material structure can with justice be said to have replaced it; for, when the old dispensation passed away, all local and material sanctity vanished, and a spiritual dispensation surpassed as well as abolished the glory that had been. The body of Christ was the temple of God, and when that had been taken down, the only temple which remained was the spiritual edifice, built of living stones and inhabited by the Holy Spirit of God.

I. THE RESPECTS IN WHICH THE CHRISTIAN CHURCH IS THE TEMPLE OF THE LIVING GOD. 1. Christians are separated from the world around. As the temple as Jerusalem was different from all other edifices, so the spiritual society designated the Church is distinct from the common and secular associations which men form for their own convenience, advantage, or pleasure. 2. In this spiritual temple the living God makes his chosen dwelling-place. The Lord loved the gates of Zion; he revealed his glory in the Shechinah-cloud; he was sought and found in his sanctuary. In like manner the Eternal chooses the hearts of his people for his congenial abode, where he makes himself known, and especially reveals his holiness and his grace. 3. The Church is the scene of worship; there praise, prayer, and sacrifices of obedience are offered to God and accepted by him.

II. THE PECULIAR CHARACTERISTICS OF THE CHRISTIAN CHURCH AS THE TEMPLE OF GOD. 1. It is holy. 2. It is universal, extending throughout the world, and including within it men of every race and of every condition.   3. It is enduring.   For, whilst the individual members disappear from sight, those who quit the Church militant do so only to join the Church triumphant.   And whilst human societies, organizations, and states pass away, this Divine society loses nothing of its glory, but lives from age to age.   4. It is growing,   Every several stone built into it adds to its majestic proportions, and prepares for its final completeness; it "groweth an holy temple unto the Lord."

III. The practical obligations laid upon all the members of the Church in respect of their incorporation in the spiritual temple.   1. They are called upon to uphold the dignity of their calling and position.   2. And to maintain that purity which is their distinctive quality—to be "separate, and to touch no unclean thing."   3. And to seek the consolidation and unity of the spiritual edifice.   4. And at the same time to strive after its enlargement and ultimate completeness.—T.

Ver. 18.—*Father and children.*   No human relation is close enough and no human language is strong enough to set forth the union which subsists between God and his people.   They are the temple, he is the Deity inhabiting, inspiring, and glorifying the sacred and spiritual edifice.   Nay, he is the *Father*, and they the sons and daughters whom he has adopted and whom he loves.

I. The natural basis of this relation between God and his people.   This has ever been recognized by the thoughtful and pious.   Even heathen philosophers and poets could say of themselves and their fellow-men, " We also are his offspring."   Created by his power, sustained by his bounty, cared for by his wisdom and goodness, the children of men are also the children of God.

II. The redemptive elevation of this relationship.   The old covenant contained intimations of the Divine fatherhood, as is apparent from the language of the text.   But it was in the gospel of our Lord and Saviour Jesus Christ that this truth was fully realized.   " Ye are all the children of God through faith in Jesus Christ."   The Spirit of adoption makes and seals the true believers in Christ as members of the Divine family.   It is to his fellow-Christians that the Apostle John exclaims, " Beloved, now are we the children of God."   It is in the case of those who are born anew of water and of the Spirit that the relation in question is made unmistakably evident ; the spiritual features of the Father are, so to speak, reproduced, and the subjection and obedience of the children evinces their sacred kindred.

III. The innumerable proofs of God's fatherhood.   God is not satisfied simply to be called our Father; he feels and acts like a Father.   He provides for his children all that is necessary for their spiritual well-being and happiness, supplies their wants, directs their steps, defends them from danger, comforts them in sorrow.   And, above all, he assures them an abode in his own—in the Father's—house, where they shall for ever enjoy the blessedness, the fellowship, the glory of a sacred, secure, and everlasting home.   Thus both in this world and in the world to come the gracious Parent justifies his Name and fulfils his promises.

IV. The expected response of filial love and obedience.   Alas! how often is this withheld, or very partially and inadequately rendered!   Yet in the hearts of God's true children there resides a principle which impels to childlike love and service.   God has a right to his children's reverence and service, gratitude and love, devotion and consecration.   "If I be a Father," he asks, "where is my honour? "   Nothing that we can do can ever sufficiently express the sense we ought to cherish of the infinite love and pity, forbearance and generosity, of our heavenly Father.   It is for his children to witness to his faithfulness, to hallow his Name, to cherish his revelation, and to do his will.—T.

Ver. 2.—*" Now . . . now."*   I. God has provided a salvation for men.   This salvation (1) is in Christ ; (2) is to be obtained by repentance and faith ; (3) embraces justification and sanctification ; (4) results in present joy, holy and useful life ; and (5) in these in far higher degree, and eternally, in heaven.

II. The opportunity for securing this salvation is limited to the present.   1. *The present age.*   2. *In an individual to his brief life on earth.*   No unsaved one can afford to waste any time ; no saved one will want to.   Salvation is so great a matter that it should be sought instantly. To miss it is to miss everything. If we get nought but this, we should see to it that we get this. "Seek ye *first* the kingdom of God and his righteousness" (Matt. vi. 33).

III. TENDENCIES TO PROCRASTINATE ARE OFTEN STRONG. Such pleas as the following have power with not a few : (1) there is time enough ; (2) after temporal matters are arranged we can attend to spiritual ; (3) pleasure must be tasted, after that seriousness ; (4) it will be easier to repent and believe " to-morrow." This reflects the human view, and the *Satanic* (for Satan is a great advocate of delay). The Divine is otherwise : "*Now* is the acceptable time ; behold, *now* is the day of salvation."

IV. THE PERILS OF DELAY. 1. Life may be cut short speedily and suddenly. 2. Painful sickness prior to death may render attention to spiritual concerns practically impossible. 3. Desire for salvation may pass away. 4. The heart may be fatally hardened. 5. The Spirit may cease to strive. "God is not mocked."

V. THE SINFULNESS OF DELAY. 1. What an insult to God ! 2. What a return for the love and sacrifice of Christ ! 3. What a pernicious example ! 4. What an injustice to ourselves !

VI. THE DIVINE URGENCY. When Paul is intensely earnest in this matter it is because God makes him so. It is the Divine mind declared by a servant. And so of all faithful ministers ; their voices are echoes of the voice of God. Christ on earth cried, " Repent." " Wherefore even as the Holy Ghost saith, To-day if ye will hear his voice, harden not your hearts" (Heb. iii. 7, 8). The Divine message of salvation is pressed upon the instant attention of those to whom it is delivered. We cannot wonder at the urgency of God, for : 1. God knows the tendencies of our nature. 2. God knows what loss of salvation involves.—II.

Vers. 3—10.—*Not hindering the gospel.* I. PAUL'S GREAT ANXIETY NOT TO HINDER THE GOSPEL. He preached the gospel faithfully and with utmost earnestness, but : 1. He guarded anxiously against lessening the effect of his preaching by his conduct. 2. He realized that life speaks as well as verbal utterance. 3. That what is built up by the lip is often pulled down by the life.

II. PAUL'S EFFORTS TO AVOID IN LIFE AND CONDUCT THAT WHICH MIGHT HINDER THE GOSPEL. He sought not to give offence in anything (ver. 3). He dreaded proving a stumbling-block to his hearers. So in every way he endeavoured to commend himself as a true minister of God, and thus to advance the cause which he had at heart. Illustrated : 1. *In his endurance of trial and suffering.* Here he exhibited amazing patience and fortitude. (1) *In those of a general kind.* Afflictions, necessities, distresses. Of these he had a large share. Ministers, especially very active and devoted ones, must be prepared for a like experience. (2) *In those inflicted by enemies.* Stripes, imprisonments, tumults. These were largely occasioned by his faithfulness to the gospel. He was so faithful to the gospel that he would bear these in such a spirit as to further advance that gospel among men. That which his enemies intended as a check he would transform into a help. (3) *In those of voluntary origin.* Labours ; working with own hands for support, and toiling in the ministry. Watchings ; sleepless nights in travel, peril, and sickness occasioned by exposure or excessive effort. Fastings ; " foodlessness "—he was often hungry when, if less devoted, he might have had abundance. 2. *In the conduct of his ministry and life.* (1) *Pureness.* Chaste living. Disinterestedness. Singleness of motive. (2) *Knowledge.* Knowledge of gospel truth, and this sincerely conveyed to hearers. A minister is often a hinderer through ignorance, especially through spiritual ignorance. But Paul sought to be thoroughly furnished, so that he might not retard but help forward the truth. To teach others he felt that he himself must be taught, and he was as diligent a learner as a teacher. Paul was well acquainted in every way with the gospel which he preached. (3) *Long-suffering.* Patient submission to wrongs. Not quick to retaliate. The pulpit may be irritable as well as the pew. (4) *Kindness.* Gentleness. Courtesy. Benevolence. A kindness which ever meant usefulness. (5) *In the Holy Ghost.* Showing in all utterance and conduct that he was under the influence of the Divine Spirit. (6) *Love unfeigned.* A ministry of true love is a ministry of real power. To call our hearers, as some are very fond of doing, " beloved," is one thing ; to have them truly in our hearts is another. (7) *The Word of truth.* Ever preaching the truth as it is in Jesus. Not proclaiming human theories, but Divine revelations. Holding to the "one thing," and not carried about by every wind of doctrine. The weathercock preacher may be amusing, but he will do little to advance the gospel. (8) *The power of God.* Upon this Paul relied. To this he submitted himself. He humbled himself into nothingness, that God might work through him and be all in all. He gave the praise of everything accomplished to the great Worker. And God specially honoured him by manifesting his power in and through him. Some ministers are too strong and great to accomplish anything. They can do without the power of God; they do without it, and then they *do nothing* except hinder the gospel. (9) *The armour of righteousness on the right hand and on the left.* He was clad in the whole armour of God (Eph. vi. 13). Offensive and defensive. Himself justified and accepted and living in holiness; and weapons in his hand by which he smote evil wherever he saw it. 3. *In the maintenance of consistency and integrity under specially trying circumstances.* Whether he was held in honour or dishonour, whether subject to good report or evil, he strove to be ever the same, to preach the same gospel, to manifest the same spirit, to live the same life. His life and ministry were not dependent upon surroundings. 4. *By not succumbing to adverse circumstances.* (1) Though branded as a deceiver, he convinced the candid that he was true and sincere. (2) Though unknown in true character by many, his faithful persistent ministry and life made him well known to multitudes, and won their high regard. (3) Though chastised by enemies and dying daily, his heroic spirit continued its hold upon God, and he was not overborne. (4) Though sorrowful as to outward lot, his inward condition enabled him ever to rejoice, and his joy found constant expression and was a powerful tribute to the gospel. (5) Though poor and outcast, he laboured so zealously in the gospel that many were made rich. (6) Though seeming to have lost all possessions, he could and did lay claim to everything. In the spirit of his own words to the Corinthians, "All things are yours" (1 Cor. iii. 21). Such conduct, spirit, life, bore the most powerful testimony to the gospel. *Paul himself* was a great sermon which, under God, shook the world. What Paul *was* is to-day one of the mightiest witnesses for Christianity.—H.

Vers. 14—18.—*Unequal yoking.* Intimate associations ought not to be formed by the people of God with the ungodly. The reference is, no doubt, to Deut. xxii. 10.

I. How THIS MAY BE DONE. 1. *In religious fellowship.* The apostle had occasion to warn the Corinthians against fellowship with idolaters. We may be attracted by a religious community in which the truth is not found or in which it is greatly obscured or distorted. 2. *In marriage.* With believers the religious question should be a prime question. Alas! it is often no question at all. Religious inequality is most frequently esteemed as the dust of the balance, and less than that. Consent is asked of the earthly father, but the heavenly Father is too commonly forgotten altogether. Marriages too often are not made in heaven, and that is why they have so little heaven about them. The ill-assorted union does not lead so much to Paradise as to misery and the divorce court. 3. *In friendships.* There is often much unequal yoking here. A wise man chooses his friends with care, but a fool takes them haphazard or on mere "liking." The power of a friendship is great, for good or for evil. Believers should choose friends who will help, not hinder, and friends who will be friends for ever, and not severed at the grave. 4. *In business.* Partnership in commerce is a yoke which brings men very close together. They must have very much in common; their lives must run in very much the same channel; their actions must largely agree. Or, if not, their union will be disunion, and the issue, quarrels first, and perhaps bankruptcy or worse next. How often a child of God has lived to rue the day when he entered into partnership with a child of the devil!

II. WHY THIS SHOULD NOT BE DONE. 1. *Unreasonable in itself.* Consider what believers and unbelievers are. (1) The one, "righteousness" (ver. 14)—lovers of holiness, striving for its fuller possession. The other, "iniquity"—the heart alienated from God, loving sin and walking in it, though possibly exterior gloss may obscure inward defilement. (2) The one, "light" (ver. 14)—illumined by the Holy Ghost, shone upon by the "Light of the world"—possessing a knowledge of the truth, children of the day. The other, "darkness"—the true light rejected or ignored, subjects of error, preparing themselves for "the outer darkness." (3) The one, in Christ (ver. 15)—members of his body, his disciples, his ransomed people. The other, followers of Belial, the children of the wicked one, serving him daily. (4) The one, the temple of God (ver. 16), consecrated to God, God dwelling in them. The other, the temple of idols—of the idols of sin, made into gods. God in the one, the devil in the other. How can such opposites as these be united? Why should righteousness seek alliance with iniquity? Can light and darkness walk together? Can Christ and Belial be on terms of concord? How can temples of God and temples of vilest idols be brought to agreement? 2. *Extremely perilous.* How many have found this! In marriage, for example. What misery, loss of peace, loss of holiness, loss of everything most prized once, have followed upon an unequal alliance! The life has been utterly ruined and lost. Some marry in order to convert; but we should always convert people before we marry them. The peril applies to all cases of unequal yoking. The evil generally triumphs because the good has robbed itself of power by taking a false step. 3. *Expressly forbidden by God.* The Divine Word is emphatic: "Come ye out from among them, and be ye separate, saith the Lord, and touch no unclean thing" (ver. 17). This is a Divine *command* which we dare not set aside. This is Divine *wisdom;* our wisdom may not accord with it, but if so, our wisdom is assuredly folly. This is Divine *love,* purposing to save us from misery and loss. 4. *A most gracious promise for the obedient.* The resolve not to be unequally yoked may sometimes seem to entail large sacrifice. If we lose something, this is what we gain. God says: (1) "I will receive you" (ver. 17). We shall be with God. We shall have God. Though we may lose the creature, we shall gain the Creator. God will be gracious to us if others are ungracious. If the stream fail, we may resort to the Fountain. Here is the warrant for doing so. (2) "And will be to you a Father" (ver. 18). We may lose the earthly father, who may have singular views respecting our "prospects;" we shall have a Father above. If we are obedient, God will reveal himself in the tenderest and most loving guise. If God be our Father it must be well with us whatever betide. (3) "And ye shall be to me sons and daughters" (ver. 18). Note, "daughters" are specially mentioned. These have frequently to endure much when "unequal yoking" is resisted. We shall be "children of God." Then we shall be "heirs of God, and joint-heirs with Christ." Sweet, indeed, are the fruits of obedience. We may lose much; let us never imperil *this.*—H.

Ver. 2.—"*Now.*" Before Christ came, religious privileges were with Israel. The Gentiles walked in darkness through "times of ignorance." But with Christ came tidings of great joy to all people. And when the Holy Spirit fell on Gentiles as well as on Jews who heard the gospel, it was evident that a new age had come. This is the "acceptable year of the Lord," and is the dispensation of grace intended to continue till the second coming of Christ. It is the world's great opportunity. So it is on the large scale; but when we take groups of men and individuals, the scale of time is proportionally reduced. Nations miss opportunities which may never return. Congregations have a bright season, a time of visitation, which may come to a lamentable end. The Lord may withdraw his favour; may even fight against an unfaithful Church with the sword of his mouth. Shorter still is the day of salvation for the individual.

1. THE VALUE OF OPPORTUNITY. In affairs of this life it is fully recognized. It is the dictate of worldly wisdom to wait for and to seize the fit occasion. Does a speculator watch for a rising market? or a capitalist look out for a good investment? or a politician aspire to office? Such men keenly watch their opportunities and must not let them slip.

> "There is a tide in the affairs of men
> Which, taken at the flood, leads on to fortune;
> Omitted, all the voyage of their life
> Is bound in shallows and in miseries;
> And we must take the current when it serves
> Or lose our ventures."

All this is quite as true of spiritual advantage. There is an opportunity to be seized, a tide to be taken at the flood. There is a day which must become the birthday of the soul, the peace-day of the conscience, or loss will be suffered—eternal loss. There is an emergency on which all the future secretly depends, and which, if one let slip, he may wring his hands and curse his folly, but will never find a remedy.

II. INDICATIONS OF OPPORTUNITY. The favourable day for spiritual life is not so easily recognized as that of worldly advantage. In external aspect it is as other days. A preacher may speak to you whom you have often heard and not heeded. The view of truth which is to carry you captive may be one which has often been pressed on you to little purpose. But somehow you are moved; you catch the urgency of *now*; and you listen and believe as you never listened or believed before. So that common day becomes a beginning of days and a spiritual epoch to you. There are, however, indications or hints of a critical time which watchful spirits may perceive. Often it is preceded by sickness, sorrow, or disappointment, making one more thoughtful and more wistful about the things unseen. Or there springs up, one hardly knows how, a sense of inward weariness and want. Conscience is uneasy, and the heart cannot rest. Then some word in season falls on the ear, or looks out of a book or a friend's letter. These things indicate opportunity. Miss it not. Embrace the gospel at once. Receive not the grace of God in vain.

III. PENALTY OF MISSING OPPORTUNITY. The wasted day can never be recalled. Lost property may be recovered; lost friendships regained; but the lost year never comes back. It was a sign of wisdom in the young Roman emperor that he grieved when a day had been wasted. *Perdidi diem!* But such tasks as he had in hand might still be accomplished by redoubled diligence on the morrow. Not so with him who wastes the day of salvation. *Perdidi vitam!* The day of grace neglected is followed by the night of doom.

IV. THE APPEAL FOR IMMEDIATE COMPLIANCE WITH THE GOSPEL. 1. *Let gratitude move you.* The God of grace calls you to him; not exacting his rights and dues from you as his creature and his subject, but with open hands extending pardon and countless benefits for time and eternity, freely. "Now then," exclaimed an old English preacher, "what is more suitable to ingenuous gratitude than to embrace the season of God's bestowing so free a favour? Surely the least we can do is to accept of that God that accepteth of us; of him who is full of beauty and rewards, while we have nothing to bring to him but deformity and beggary." 2. *Let a proper self-regard move you.* Why should you lose your own soul? Why will ye die? It is more pleasant for the preacher to speak as from the gate of heaven; but it is necessary to cry aloud sometimes as from the mouth of hell. Turn ye! Get you back! Seek the Lord, and do it now!—F.

Ver. 10.—*Sorrow and joy.* The apostle's experience is in some degree known to many Christians. The apparent paradox of simultaneous grief and joy is to them a fact of sober consciousness.

I. SORROWFUL. Not querulous, but bruised and sad. The course of the world rushes past us, and we sit down with our pain or grief. We are chastened. And not without reason. 1. We must take our share of the troubles common to mankind. Spiritual life carries with it no exemption from the usual cares and losses of the present state. To bring about such exemption would require a multiplication of miracles without any sufficient reason. If famine come upon a land, or war, or pestilence; if a railway train or a passenger steamship be wrecked,—there can be no discrimination between the good and the bad in the common catastrophe. Indeed, it is questionable whether a special immunity from pain and grief accorded to spiritual men might not do serious harm to religion, by giving strong temporal inducements to worldly men to cover themselves over with a thin coating of godliness. And there are sorrows which no personal qualities can ward off. Some troubles are inherited; others come from the mishap or misconduct of a relative or of a partner in business. And the sickness and death of those who are dear to us must bring us grief. Man is born to trouble. 2. We find in the discipline of sorrow some of the best lessons and impulses of the Christian life

> " Night brings out stars ;
> So sorrow shows us truths."

And conformity to Christ is gained in suffering with him, working out a deeper patience and keener moral sensibility.

II. YET ALWAYS REJOICING. The Man of sorrows had joy in his Father's love; though it is his affliction that is made prominent in the account of his state of humiliation. There was also a joy set before him, and in this he now sits at the right hand of God. As his followers, we too have joy now amidst sorrow, and fulness of joy set before us. *Always.* Not sorrowing always, but always rejoicing. It cannot mean any ecstatic emotion, for that cannot be habitual; the excessive strain would break the springs of feeling. But we may be always glad and satisfied and triumphant in our Lord. Not only is this possible to the sorrowful; it seems to be fullest and strongest in them. Remember Paul and Silas singing in the dark dungeon with their stripes unwashed. Samuel Rutherford in prison at Aberdeen, and Madame Guyon in prison at Vincennes, tasted the same gladness. The latter said, "My heart was full of that joy which thou givest to them that love thee in the midst of the greatest crosses." This can be understood only by those who have some real acquaintance of heart with the Lord Jesus, and know what treasures his people have in him—unsearchable riches, unerring wisdom, precious atonement, prevailing inter-cession, helpful sympathy, victorious strength, and everlasting love. Genius often shows the combination of a pensive vein, a tenderness, a pathos, with a healthy elastic hopefulness, nay, with a joyfulness robust as in a man, yet simple and playful as in a child. But we speak of what is better than even genius—the grace of God. This can make even very ordinary people both gentle and brave, tender and strong, patient in sorrow, and constant in joy. "The meek shall increase their joy in the Lord, and the poor among men shall rejoice in the Holy One of Israel."—F.

Ver. 13.— '*Be ye enlarged.*" The apostle had specially in view the increase of joy. But we may use the exhortation to commend the enlargement of Christian people as respects head and heart and hand.

I. BE ENLARGED IN YOUR THOUGHTS. No doubt there is a dangerous breadth or laxity; but there is also mischief in the opposite direction, in narrowness. Good people are apt to become the slaves of their own phraseology, and to insist on their own traditions of expression and definition as exclusively safe and orthodox. Christian truth appears to be with them quite a narrow ledge of stone shaped to their liking, whereas it is a broad firm rock that does not submit itself to men's measuring-lines. Never follow a narrow-minded religious teacher. He is sure to be opinionative and monotonous. And even when he lodges a truth in the mind, he gives it the effect of a prejudice. Be enlarged in the comprehensive and manifold wisdom of the Bible. Dare to give yourself room in the far-reaching thoughts and words of God. Especially seek to be enlarged in your estimate of Jesus Christ. Only by degrees was any sufficient knowledge of him attained by those who "companied with him" on earth. They loved him from the first and often wondered. They tried by questions to peer into his mind, but could not make him out. They were surprisingly slow in their appre-hensions, till he opened the Scriptures to them after his resurrection, and the Holy Spirit fell on them after his ascension. And now, though the Holy Spirit is with us, his teaching is not received all at once by disciples, and they need more and more enlargement. It is the mark of a growing Christian that in his view Christ increases; the mark of a great Christian that to him Christ is very great. Augustine, Bernard, Leighton, Rutherford, Owen, Martyn,—were these great Christians? And what had they in common? Large and admiring thoughts of Christ.

II. BE ENLARGED IN YOUR SYMPATHIES. Narrow hearts are even more mischievous and unchristian than narrow heads. It is confessedly difficult for one who may have received little mental culture, or has been early imbued with strong prejudices, to gain breadth of view; but there is no excuse for any one who, while naming the name of Jesus, and professing to know the love of God, retains a peevish and contracted heart. We have said "professes to know the love of God," because, when this love is really "shed abroad by the Holy Spirit," it must tend to expand the affections and sym-pathies. Argument will not do it. Admonition cannot produce the effect. Love only kindles love, and so imparts a larger kindness and more delicate sensibility. Love cries shame on harshness and envy, spreads brotherly kindness, disposes to forgiveness of wrong and a kindly construction of motives, covers a multitude of sins. Have sympathy with all good objects, though you cannot actually help all. Take the part of right-hearted men. A great Christian is one to whom the Lord has given "largeness" of heart. Paul, Chrysostom, Bengel, Baxter, Whitefield, Chalmers,—were these great Christians? And what had they in common? Great hearts, large generosity of soul, the capacity of loving much, and of enlisting the love and sympathy of others for worthy objects.

> "The truly generous is the truly wise,
> And he who loves not others lives unblest."

III. BE ENLARGED IN LABOURS AND GIFTS. A grudging hand and indolent temper in the Church go with a narrow spirit; but where mind and heart are enlarged in Christ, the hands will be found ready to every good enterprise and open in giving up to the measure of ability.—F.

Vers. 14—18.—*Separation.* St. Paul wished to see the Corinthian brethren enlarged, enlivened, and encouraged. But this was not to be by the easy and unprincipled method of ignoring all distinctions and binding together incongruous materials and moral opposites. The exhortation, "Be ye enlarged," must be taken with this, "Be ye separate;" and charity must go hand in hand with purity. The contrasts expressed in this passage were very apparent in ancient Corinth, where the Christians, as saints, were openly separated from the heathen worship and heathen vices around them. A similar state of things may be seen now at mission stations in populous heathen cities. The Christians turn away from the temples, disown the priests and soothsayers, disregard the festivals, and have nothing any more to do with idols. They may still maintain family and social intercourse with the heathen, because conversion, as St. Paul explains, does not break family ties, or change the station in which one is when "called," or drive Christ's followers "out of the world." But they may not be unequally yoked with non-Christians or profane persons in Church fellowship. The distinction cannot be made so palpable where all society has accepted the Christian name as when and where the Church is in sharp contrast with a powerful heathenism. Yet in principle the distinction insisted on by St. Paul must be maintained, else the strength of the Church as a spiritual institution is sapped, and a compromising spirit enters which destroys the glory of Christ. To carry out the principle in actual Church discipline is confessedly difficult; but the Church has a right to expect that her overseers will prevent the admission of scandalous persons; and individual professors of the Christian faith should not claim Church fellowship without examining themselves as to the side on which they stand with reference to the five points of contrast indicated in this text. 1. *Between righteousness and iniquity.* This takes us at once into the region of conscience and moral conduct. The Christian should be a righteous man. He may not lie, or cheat, or overreach, or take unfair advantage of another, because to do so would not be right or righteous. The rogue and the worker of iniquity are as heathen men, and not fit for Christian fellowship. 2. *Between light and darkness.* This points to the mental and moral environment as affecting thought, feeling, and action. It is a mode of expression common with St. Paul, as may be seen in other Epistles. The Christian is a child of the light and of the day. Darkness, on the contrary, is the covering of the heathen world; and its works are unfruitful and shameful. 3. *Between Christ and Belial.* Abstractions are left, and the leaders of two conflicting hosts are set in opposition. A Christian is "of Christ," as the Lord whom he obeys and the pattern which he follows. On the other side is a man of Belial, or the follower of a worthless and profligate spirit. So this contrast has reference to disposition, and excludes every false and wicked person from Christian fellowship. 4. *Between the believer and the unbeliever.* This takes us to the question of religious persuasion and conviction. A Christian is a believer on the Son of God. In this lies the secret of his life, strength, holiness, and patience. A man without faith is no more fit for fellowship in the Church than a heathen. To him the trials and triumphs of the life of faith are alike unknown. 5. *Between the temple of God and idols.* The Church is the living temple of the living God, the holy temple of the holy God. The individual Christians are stones in that temple, and must be in harmony with its sacred character and use. What agreement has it with idols? If the Jew would have thought it a horrible profanation to set up a graven image in the temple at Jerusalem, much more should Christian minds abhor the setting up of idols of selfishness, covetousness, or sensuality in that better temple which is now the habitation of God in the Spirit. So much of incompatibilities and contrasts. Then the apostle, who did not address himself to the heathen, bidding them stand off, but wrote to the Christians, urging them to avoid entanglement with the heathen, gave them a charge from the Lord, and enforced it by a gracious promise. (1) *The charge.* "Wherefore come out from among them." The Christians were not to leave Corinth, but to hold their positions and preserve their callings in that city, while scrupulously avoiding the contamination of idolatry and vice. So should we continue in the world, yet not be conformed to it or love it; should do our part in our generation, yet separate ourselves from all that is unjust or unholy. "Touch not the unclean," under which category comes, not mere licentiousness, but all that is unhallowed, and so out of harmony with the purity of God. (2) *The promise.* "I will receive you," etc. (vers. 17, 18). Such was the promise made to King David in regard to his posterity (2 Sam. vii. 14); and it is extended to all the household of faith. From the sure belief of this promise we may derive strength and resolution to keep the rule of separation. Are we to be openly acknowledged as the sons and daughters of the Lord God Almighty? What, then, have we to do with iniquity, with darkness, with Belial, with unbelief, with idols? The best-known Christians are not always the best. They may have some striking quality or rare endowment, or may have reached by favour some conspicuous post. But the best are those men and women who most fully and consistently obey the holy calling. How sweet is fellowship with such Christians, and how stimulating! It is good to be yoked together with them under Christ's yoke which is easy, and his burden which is light. It is good to be builded together with them in the temple of the living God. It is good to be joined as brothers and sisters in the same family, and call the Lord Almighty our Father. The friendship of the world, the alliance of the sons of Belial, the communion of the unclean,—what are these to the dignity of the people of God and the family affection of his children?—F.

Ver. 2.—"*The accepted time.*" This text immediately follows upon the full declaration of the truth in Jesus, the free offers of Divine mercy, and the earnest pleadings of ch. v. St. Paul understood well that there was this sad and strange tendency in men— they are ever disposed to shift into the future the most serious duties of life. In the time of disease they will not send for the doctor until they absolutely must. They put off making their wills until the very power to make them is gone. How is the tendency to be explained? It is one of the forms in which man's hopefulness expresses itself. The future always seems to be richer and better than the present; though, when that future is reached, it very seldom realizes our hope. It is, however, a mischievous form of hopefulness if it lifts us off from the performance of present duty. Then it becomes procrastination, "the thief of time."

I. THE INCOMPARABLE ADVANTAGES OF TIME PRESENT. The "*now.*" By this term is properly meant that moment in which any duty stands right before us. Observe: 1. Its security. We have it; it is here; it is ours. The only thing in all the world that is or ever can be ours. The only sphere for the activity of our will. We "act in the living present." Nothing really belongs to us except that which we have at this moment. The past is gone. The future may never come. When we put off duty to the future, we deal with something that is not our own. We have no future until God gives it to us and makes it present. We have only the *now*, and on it may hang eternity. 2. Its peculiar suitability for action. Because the whole nature is aroused, awakened, interested, prepared, and action can be taken so easily and so heartily, *now*. You can never again be sure of the same interest, and, if neglected duties do *ever* get done, they must push into the place of some other duty, and push it aside. *Now* we have the assistance of all aiding impulses. We are helped by an awakened conscience, by deep emotions, and by the urgings of the Divine Spirit. Now is the time of our opportunity. Illustrate by the boats waiting for a wave to help them ashore. How the men watch, and at last say, "*Now, now!*" as they bend to the oar! The times when the claims of Christ come home to us are just such times; then why not now be flooded over all hindrances and difficulties unto the harbour of salvation?

II. THE SERIOUS PERIL INVOLVED IN THE NEGLECT OF TIME PRESENT. Notice: 1. The insecurity of the return of such another opportunity. Others we may have, but this precise one will never come again. There is only one round of seasons in each life. Spring-time never comes but once, with its encouraging assurance, "They that seek me early shall find me." Summer-time and autumn-time come but once, and by-and-by we may have to wail, and to say, "The harvest is past, the summer is ended, and we are not saved." 2. The burdening of life with the sense of unfulfilled duty. That may indeed be made an impulse to higher activity, but usually it presses as a hopeless hindrance. 3. The injury done to our moral nature by resisted spiritual influences. There is a disease whose special feature is the ossification of the heart, the turning of its flexible walls into hardness and bone. It is the disease which they suffer from— in its spiritual form—who neglect the golden opportunities offered them in the time present. Illustrate by the man on the *Royal Charter*, who was on the stern half when the vessel broke in two, and had but a moment in which to leap for dear life. Yet how men resist the claims of God to their immediate attention! Some wilfully put off the matter, deliberately finding excuses for delay. Surely no other proof of human depravity is needed than this. Men will hang their immortality on the thread of life, and even dally with the offered mercy of their God. But some honest hearts may be in real difficulty as to the claims of Christ upon them *now*. They think they are too young, or that they have not been anxious long enough; or they are waiting for a deeper sense of sin, or, it may be, for more faith. But all these are subtle ways in which we show our desire to manage our own salvation. If we were really willing that Christ should save us, we would be quite willing that he should save us *now*.—R. T.

Vers. 3—10.—*The holy power of character.* The subject occupying the attention of the apostle is the "ministry of reconciliation;" the preaching of the gospel of the grace of God unto the forgiveness of sins and restoration of man to the Divine favour. This ministry has been entrusted to him. He had, indeed, no "letters of commenda-tion" to rely on, as had some other teachers, but he could appeal to the character of his ministry, to the sufferings he had endured in fulfilling it, and to the Divine bene-dictions which had rested upon it. He does, in a sense, commend himself; but how? He looks back on his life of labours and sufferings, and challenges comparison. Can others, with their letters of commendation, point to anything like this? Dean Stanley divides the means by which the apostle commended himself into four classes: (1) from "patience" (or endurance) to "fastings," referring to the bodily sufferings of the apostle; (2) from "pureness" to "love unfeigned," referring to the virtues, that is, the manifestations of the Divine presence in St. Paul; (3) from "by the word of truth" to "by evil report and good report," referring to the means whereby he was enabled to prove himself to be a true minister of God; and (4) the remainder, relating to the acceptation in which the apostles were held, and its contrast with the reality. St. Paul's personal appeal presents for our consideration the importance of securing for the gospel a favourable hearing through the consistency and gracious beauty of the character of those who proclaim it. Its spiritual efficiency directly depends on the *character* of its ambassadors. The three following subjects need careful treatment:—

I. The preacher of the gospel must show its power on his own character and life. Illustrate by a man offering an infallible remedy for a skin-disease, from which everybody could see he was still suffering. The gospel is life for dead souls, and he who preaches it must be himself "alive unto God." The gospel is healing for sin-sick souls, and he who proclaims it must be able to tell his own experiences of the Balm of Gilead. The gospel provides a regeneration of character, and what it can do for men we expect to see in the men who commend it to us. As a fact, the men who show the power of the gospel in themselves are the men who alone can wield the power of the gospel on others. The preacher must be an ensample of them that believe.

II. As examples of the Christian spirit, ministers may expect unusual testings. These come in several ways: (1) in the bodily strain which a Christian ministry involves; (2) in the more anxious and careful self-culture which the ministry demands; (3) in the fatigues and perils which come in carrying out the ministry; and (4) in the difficulties found in dealing pleasantly with all kinds of men. To these should be added those direct dealings of God with his servants, by means of which he prepares them for service, sharpens and furbishes their swords for his war. Even "fiery trial" is not strange for those who have to stand in the chief places of influence. They must have a large experience, if, in measure like their Lord, they are to be fully " touched with the feeling of men's infirmities."

III. THEIR EXPERIENCES WILL GIVE THE TRUE POWER TO THEIR PUBLIC PLEADINGS. Illustrate in the case of the Apostle Paul, who could not have written such letters if he had not passed through such trials. Experience is the secret of power. It gives the tone of tenderness and sympathy to a minister's work. It gives confidence in speaking of the comforting and sustaining power of Divine grace. It is the true power on our fellow-men to be enabled to speak to them of " that which we have heard, which we have seen with our eyes, which we have looked upon, and our hands have handled, of the Word of life." But if all this be, in high degrees, true of the recognized ministry, it is true of all who seek to influence others for God and goodness. The world which we long and strive to save very properly asks of us this most searching question, " What has this gospel done *for you*? "—R. T.

Ver. 12.—*Where are men straitened?* The apostle, in an intense outburst of feeling, had just said, " O ye Corinthians, our mouth is open unto you, our heart is enlarged." He was referring to that opening of his ministry, and disclosure of his love for them, which filled the previous part of the chapter. And so he is led to ask from them a worthy response. He would have his love quicken love. He wanted it to break down the barriers and enmities and prejudices which were so sadly limiting the confidence of the Corinthians in St. Paul. So he pleads with them, " Ye are not straitened in us ; " there is no limit of our love to you ; " but ye are straitened in your own bowels," your own affections, which are sadly kept in bondage by your passions and prejudices and antipathies ; by misrepresentations of me and my doings, and the influence of unworthy teachers. Then he urges them to break the bonds, to be enlarged, and to let their hearts express the love they feel. What they needed in their spiritual life was breadth and expansiveness of affection. There is suggested by the apostle's words a series of contrasts between—

I. THE LIMITED IDEAS AND AFFECTIONS OF MEN. Who are straitened by ignorance, imperfect character, prejudice, false sentiments, readiness to misjudge and to impute bad motive, etc.

II. THE BROAD IDEAS AND AFFECTIONS OF APOSTLES. Who see in men souls to be redeemed unto God, and, labouring for men's spiritual and eternal well-being, can rise above the smaller occasions of difference and separation.

III. THE SUBLIME IDEAS AND AFFECTIONS OF GOD IN CHRIST. Who would have all men saved ; who loved the world ; whose love found expression in self-sacrifice ; and whose invitations now are sent to whosoever will. No man is straitened in God. " When my father and mother forsake me, then the Lord will take me up." In his heart and home there "yet is room." Men are straitened, limited, in themselves, not in God, not in the gospel, not in Christian teachers. They forge, and fix on, their own bondages.—R. T.

Ver. 14.—*Christian friendships.* The Bible would not be a complete book, adequately representing all phases of human life and experience and associations, if it contained no instance of close, personal, sacrificing friendship. But we have the very beautiful illustrative case of David and Jonathan. Christianity would not meet us at every point of our need if it had not something to say about the *choices*, the *changes*, and the *claims* of friendship.

I. ON THE CHOICES OF FRIENDSHIP. Our friendships are not always gained by choice ; they are sometimes determined by outward circumstances ; sometimes by felt affinities ; and sometimes they are started by some impressive or generous deed. But friendship ought always to be put to the decision of our will, seeing that it bears so directly on our character and on our life. It sounds chilling to the freshness and warmth of our love to say that we must *decide* who is to be our friend, and put into careful consideration the qualities and habits and probable influence upon us of the person towards whom we are drawn. Yet, surely, as we would not trust our property to a man whom we did not know, or our child to an education that we had not carefully selected for him, so we would not give our hearts to one whom we were not sure that we might fully trust. Moreover, as Christians, we guard against the approach of evil in every form, and nothing will more directly affect our Christian spirit than the influence of an unworthy friend. He may be a scoffer. He may be one whose sneer at all we love and seek may hurt and wound us far more than the scoffer's open speech. He may be an indulgent pleasure-seeker, whose disposition will be sure to nourish the worldliness and self-loving of our spirit. And, on the other hand, few things will help us more than a well-chosen Christian friendship. Many a doubt is scattered by the contact of a friend's faith, and many a sliding step is steadied by the influence of a friend's firmness. Two things lie at the basis of a worthy and lasting friendship, viz. a certain felt sympathy and a certain recognized equality.

II. ON THE CHANGES OF FRIENDSHIP. Sometimes friendships are broken through changeableness of disposition. Others are broken by the wrong-doing or unfaithfulness of one of the friends. And at other times friendships are broken by the rude, rough hand of death.

III. ON THE CLAIMS OF FRIENDSHIP. All associations of men together bring claims and responsibilities. If we have the privilege of a loving friendship, it claims from us two things. 1. Unfailing confidence in our friend. And this involves openness one with the other. Close natures, that can keep secrets, seldom know the full joy of friendship. 2. Mutual self-sacrifice, readiness to spend our best for our friend, and to put forth our best efforts in his behalf. Foote well says, " Be thankful if God has given you a sympathizing friend, one who can share with you your deepest griefs, who is one with you in all your interests for time and for eternity, whose heart answers to your heart. This is one of God's best gifts; be thankful for it and use it right, for he may deprive you of it, and leave you grieving,—Would I had prized it more! It is a most sweet and blessed fellowship; use it—use it for the high ends of mutual, spiritual good, and the Divine glory."—R. T.

Ver. 17.—*Christian relations with the world.* This verse is a partial quotation from Isa. lii. 11, which reads, "Depart ye, depart ye, go ye out from thence, touch no unclean thing; go ye out of the midst of her; be ye clean, that bear the vessels of the Lord." The first reference of these words is to the captives in Babylon, who were thus counselled to prepare for their return to Canaan, and to see to it that they carried back with them none of the evils of the idolatrous land in which they had so long sojourned. " The local and historical meaning has for the apostle passed away, and the ' unclean thing' is identified with the whole system of heathenism." Since we are counselled to be separate from the world, it will be well for us to understand what is properly meant by "the world." Some have thought that they were called to separate from the world of creation, and compel themselves to find no interest in field, or flower, or song, or the thousandfold charms of nature. Others have thought that " the world " must mean the mass of humanity, and so a true religious life could only be lived in convent or hermit-cell. Others, again, think that " the world" must mean the common scenes and pleasures of life, and that we can only live for God by resisting every pleasure and severing ourselves from every form of personal enjoyment. But " the world," in the New Testament sense, is not a thing or a set of things, but a spirit and disposition—it is *worldliness.* It is none of these things, but it may be *in them all.* It is all these if we persist in having them without God. This green earth, with its vales and hills, apart from God, is just " the world." But with God, seen as God's, it is no longer "the world; " it is the footstool of the eternal throne, the dwelling-place of the Divine majesty, the garment of the all-glorious King. The mass of humanity, without God, is just " the world; " but in the light of God's relation, it is the Father's family, the Father's school. The common cares and pleasures of life are filled with an infinite meaning and importance when they become the testing-scenes out of which God purposes to bring his children, "faultless in the presence of his glory." Whether a thing is worldly or not depends simply on this—Can you see God in it? To the Christian man God is in everything, and if he finds anything into which he cannot bring the thought of God, then he calls that worldly and shrinks from it. The " world " is that act, that scene, with which we feel the cherished thought of God does not harmonize. It is heaven where God *is ;* it is earth where he *is not ;* it is hell where he will not come.

I. THE CHRISTIAN MUST BE IN THE WORLD. He cannot, he may not, get free from outward and physical relations. His present sphere of life and duty is earthly; and his Master did not pray that his disciples should be taken " out of the world."

II. THE CHRISTIAN NEED NOT BE OF THE WORLD. In the sense of adopting its principles or its maxims, yielding to its fashions or seeking its ends.

III. THE CHRISTIAN MAY BE ABOVE THE WORLD. In the sense of having a Divine life, which masters worldly principles, resists worldly influences, and even makes him a quickening and healing power on the world, as Christ himself was. This is expressed in plain terms by the apostle, in Rom. xii. 2, " Be not conformed to this world : but be ye transformed by the renewing of your mind." The separation from the world is not to be effected by any mere watching of our acts and habits. Let us realize the higher transformation in the renewal of our minds, and we shall find it easy to reach a true nonconformity to the world. He who glorifies God in the spirit will be sure to glorify him in the body too. He who is daily more renewed in mind will most readily discover, in practical details, what is the "good, and acceptable, and perfect will of God."—R. T.

Ver. 18.—*Proving sonship by obedience.* Then—if ye fulfil my commands in separating yourselves from the unclean thing, then I " will be a Father unto you, and ye shall be my sons and daughters, saith the Lord Almighty." The thought to which we now direct attention is that a merely abstract relationship is of very little value apart from the fulfilment of those duties which are involved in the relationship. It is a very little thing for a man to stand in the abstract relation of a citizen to this great country. It is a very great thing for a man to fulfil, nobly and cheerfully, the duties of citizenship. It is a very little thing to stand in the mere relation of a husband, a father, and a master. It is a great thing indeed that we are earnestly striving to meet the responsibilities and fulfil the duties that belong to those relationships. So the name of a " son of God" will save and bless no man apart from the spirit of a son manifested and proved in an obedient, humble, devoted, and faithful life. Only the obedient sons can have the comforting sense of the Divine fatherhood.

I. THIS WAS TRUE OF CHRIST, THE FIRSTBORN SON. God said of him and to him, " This is my beloved Son, in whom," evidently meaning, in whose obedience, " I am well pleased." Each of the relations in which men stand to each other has some one thing which is its essential characteristic. The essential of kingship is the spirit of judgment. Of fatherhood, is loving authority. Of motherhood, is self-denying affection and service. Of sonship, is obedience. Whatever other expressions childhood may find, all are worthless if there be no obedience. I have no right to the name of a son, save as I obey. I show, I prove, my sonship in this—that I obey. We take, then, the life of the Lord Jesus Christ, and seek it for the signs of what we know to be the very essence of sonship, and we receive surprising impressions of the completeness of his obedience. Jesus when a boy gained and settled the principle of life : " Wist ye not that I must be about my Father's business?" Painting and poetry gain truest insight of his spirit when they represent him dutifully working at the carpenter's bench. When weary at the well of Sychar, he was beyond the interest of earthly food; "his meat and his drink were to do the will of his Father." And when the sorrows of an awful conflict and agony were gathering thickly over him, he could utter the perfect devotion of a Son, saying, " I have glorified thee on the earth : I have finished the work which thou gavest me to do." Watching that life of cheerful, hearty, loving obedience, who of us is not prepared to say—We know now what it is to be a son or a daughter of the Lord Almighty? Let us not, however, fail to observe that the obedience of his sonship was not a mere *series of acts;* it was that series of acts instinct with the cherished *spirit of obedience,* done in the freeness of the will, under the impulse of holy affections and resolves. A life full of obedient acts will no more make a real sonship than a wealth of apples, tied on, will make a fruitful tree. They must be the genuine utterances of the soul's life of obedience.

II. THIS IS TRUE OF US, THE YOUNGER SONS. " Now are we the sons of God." " Ye shall be my sons and daughters, saith the Lord Almighty." What is the value of a right without fitness; of a title without preparation to fulfil its claims; of the name of a son without the spirit and obedience of the son? " If any man have not the Spirit of Christ"—that is, the sonlike spirit of Christ—"he is none of his." "If ye be sons, God hath sent forth the Spirit of his Son into your hearts." How, then, are we proving our sonship? Are we breaking free from the old worldly bondages? Are we separating ourselves from all unclean things? Are we perfecting holiness in the fear of God? Can God meet our daily practical obediences of his will by saying, "I will be a Father unto you"?—R. T.

EXPOSITION.

CHAPTER VII.

Conclusion of his appeal (ver. 1). The apostle's feelings towards them (vers. 2—4). Explanation of the objects of his last letter, and expression of his joy at the good results it had brought about (vers. 2—16).

Ver. 1.—Having then these promises. The promises of God's indwelling and fatherly love (ch. vi. 16—18). **Dearly beloved.** Perhaps the word is added to soften the sternness of the preceding admonition. **Let us cleanse ourselves.** Every Christian, even the best, has need of daily cleansing from his daily assoilment (John xiii. 10), and this cleansing depends on the purifying activity of moral effort maintained by the help of God's grace. Similarly St. John (1 John iii. 1—3), after speaking of God's fatherhood and the hopes which it inspires, adds, " And every man that hath this hope *in him purifieth himself* even as he is pure" (comp. Jas. iv. 8). **From all filthiness;** rather, *from all defilement.* Sin leaves on the soul the moral stain of guilt, which was typified by the ceremonial defilements of the Levitical Law (comp. Ezek. xxxvi. 25, 26). The word used for "filth" in 1 Pet. iii. 21 is different. **Of the flesh and spirit.** From everything which outwardly pollutes the body and inwardly the soul; the two being closely connected together, so that what defiles the flesh inevitably also defiles the soul, and what defiles the spirit degrades also the body. Uncleanness, for instance, a sin of the flesh, is almost invariably connected with pride and hate and cruelty, which degrade the soul. **Perfecting holiness.** This is the goal and aim of the Christian, though in this life it cannot be finally attained (Phil. iii. 12). **In the fear of God.** There is, indeed, one kind of fear, a base and servile fear, which is cast out by perfect love; but the fear of reverential awe always remains in the true and wisely instructed Christian, who will never be guilty of the profane familiarity adopted by some ignorant sectarians, or speak of God "as though he were some one in the next street" (Heb. xii. 28; 1 Pet. iii. 15).

Ver. 2.—Receive us; rather, *open your hearts to us; make room for us* (comp. Mark ii. 2; John ii. 6). It is an appeal to them to get rid of the *narrowness* of heart, the constricted affections, of which he has complained in ch. vi. 12. **We have wronged . . . corrupted . . . defrauded no man.** The "no man" in the original is placed first, and this emphatic position, together with its triple repetition, marks St. Paul's insistence on the fact that, whatever his enemies might insinuate, there was *no single member* of their Church who could complain of injury, moral harm, or unfair treatment from him. Clearly he is again thinking of definite slanders against himself. His sternness to the offender may have been denounced as a wrong; his generous sanction of broad views about clean and unclean meats, idol-offerings, etc., may have been represented as corrupting others by false teaching (ch. ii. 17) or bad example (ch. iv. 2; 1 Thess. iv. 6); his urgency about the collection for the saints (ch. xii. 16; Acts xx. 33), or his assertion of legitimate authority, may have been specified as greed for power. The verb *pleonektein* is often used in connection with other verbs, implying sensuality. It is difficult for us even to imagine that St. Paul had ever been charged with gross immorality; but it may have been so, for in a corrupt atmosphere everything is corrupt. Men like Nero and Heliogabalus, being themselves the vilest of men, openly declared their belief that no man was pure, and many in the heathen world may have been inclined to similar suspicions. Of Whitefield, the poet says—

"His sins were such as Sodom never knew,
And calumny stood up to swear all true."

We know too that the Christians were universally charged with Thyestean banquets and promiscuous licentiousness. It is, however, more natural to take *pleonektein* in its *general* sense, in which it means "to overreach," "to claim or seize more than one's just rights" (see ch. ii. 11). In 1 Cor. ix. 1—6 he is defending himself against similar charges, as also in this Epistle (v 12; vi. 3; x. 7—11; xi.; xii., *passim*). For similar strains of defence, see those of Moses and of Samuel.

Ver. 3.—I speak not this to condemn you. "Not by way of condemnation am I speaking." My object is to maintain the old love between us; what I say, therefore, is merely to defend myself, not to complain of you (comp. 1 Cor. iv. 14). **I have said before.** He has not said it in so many words, but has implied it in ch. iii. 2, 3; vi. 11—14. **Ye are in our hearts.** So he says to his beloved Philippians, "I have you in my heart" (Phil. i. 7). **To die and live with you.** Similarly he tells the Thessalonians that he was ready to give them even his own life (1 Thess. ii. 8). This is no mere conventional expression of deep affection, like Horace's, "Tecum vivere amem, tecum obeam libens;" nor is it the description of some compact for life and death like that of the Theban Band. It has the deeper meaning which was involved by the words "life" and "death" on the lips of a Christian (ch. iv. 11.; vi. 9). And one whose life was, for Christ's sake, a daily death, naturally mentions death first.

Ver. 4.—**Boldness of speech.** St. Paul feels that he may address them with perfect frankness and openness (ch. iii. 12). **My glorying of you.** "My boasting on your account" (ch. i. 14; v. 12; viii. 14; comp. 1 Cor. i. 4—7). **I am filled with comfort.** "I have been filled with the consolation." "Consolation" is the word which occurs so frequently in ch. i. 3, 4. **I am exceeding joyful.** "I superabound in my joy" (ch. ii. 2—14). **In all our tribulation.** The clause belongs to both the preceding clauses. Joy in the very midst of affliction was an essentially Christian blessing (Phil. ii. 17).

"Thou shalt have joy in sadness soon;
   The pure calm hope be thine
Which brightens the Eastern moon,
   When day's wild lights decline."

(See ch. vi. 10; Gal. v. 22; Rom. xiv. 17; John xv. 11.)

Ver. 5.—**For, when we were come into Macedonia.** "For *even* when we came." The word "affliction" reminds St. Paul to resume the thread of the narrative which makes this letter almost *like an itinerary.* He has spoken of his trials in Ephesus (ch. i. 8) and in the Troad (ch. ii. 12, 13), and now he tells them that *even* in Macedonia he was no less troubled and agitated. **Our flesh had no rest.** *External* troubles assailed him as well as inward anxiety. "Had" seems here to be the best reading (B, F, G, K); not "has had," which may be borrowed from ch. ii. 13. *Rest ;* rather, *remission, respite.* **But we were troubled on every side;** literally, *but in everything being afflicted.* The style, in its picturesque irregularity, almost seems as though it were broken by sobs. **Without were fightings, within were fears.** "From without battles, from within fears." No light is thrown on these "battles." The Acts of the Apostles has no details to give us of this brief stay

in Macedonia. The "fears" were doubtless still connected with anxiety as to the reception of Titus, and of his First Epistle (ch. xii. 20).

Ver. 6.—**Who comforteth those that are cast down.** "The Comforter of the humble comforted us, even God." The word "humble" has in classical Greek the sense of "mean," "abject." Pride, not humility, was the virtue even of Stoic morality. Christ was the first to reveal the beatitude of lowliness (Matt. xi. 29; Luke i. 52). Doubtless the word still retained some of its old associations, and had been used of St. Paul in a disparaging sense (ch. x. 1). But he whom his opponents accused of so much egotism, ambition, and arrogance, meekly accepts the term and applies it to himself. God (ch. i. 4). "The God . . . of consolation" (Rom. xv. 5). **By the coming of Titus.** This was the cause of that outburst of joy in ch. ii. 13, 14, which passage here finds its explanation. The absence of Titus from the Acts is another proof of the fragmentariness of that book. It is evident that he was an ardent, able, active fellow-worker, and most beloved friend of the apostle (Gal. ii. 1, 3; 2 Tim. iv. 10; Titus i. 4; iii. 12). We learn most about him from this Epistle.

Ver. 7.—**And not by his coming only.** The mere fact of Titus's arrival cheered St. Paul, because Titus seems to have been of a strong and cheery temperament. St. Paul, partly because of his infirmities, was peculiarly dependent on the support of human sympathy (1 Thess. iii. 1—8; Phil. ii. 20; 2 Tim. iv. 4; Acts xvii. 15; xxviii. 15). It was not, however, the mere arrival of Titus which cheered him, but still more the good news which he brought, and which partially lightened his anxieties. In all probability this letter was written almost immediately after the arrival of Titus, and while the joy caused by his presence was still glowing in the apostle's heart. It is characteristic of the seclusion of an austere life that St. Jerome supposes the cause of the apostle's distress to have been that Titus was his interpreter, and that in his absence he could not preach! **Your earnest desire.** Your yearning to see me once more. **Mourning;** rather, *lamentation* (see ch. ii. 12). They were aroused to lament their past "inflation" (1 Cor. v. 2) and remissness. **Your fervent mind toward me.** This rendering well expresses the kindling affection implied by the word *zēlos.* **So that I rejoiced the more.** More than he had even anticipated could be possible; or, as the next verse may imply, all the more because of his past anguish (ch. ii. 4).

Ver. 8.—**With a letter;** rather, *with my Epistle.* Probably the First Epistle, though some suppose that the allusion is to a lost intermediate letter. **I do not repent, though I did repent;** better, *I do not regret it.* Every one has experienced the anxiety which has followed the despatch of some painful letter. If it does good, well; but perhaps it *may* do harm. The severity was called for; it seemed a duty to write severely. But how will the rebuke be received? Might we not have done better if we had used language less uncompromisingly stern? As St. Paul thought with intense anxiety that perhaps in his zeal for truth he may have irrevocably alienated the feelings of the Corinthians, whom, with all their grave faults, he loved, a moment came when he actually regretted what he had written. He himself assures us that he had this feeling. Those who try all kinds of fantastic hypotheses and tortuous exegesis to explain away this phrase as though it were inconsistent with St. Paul's inspiration, go to Scripture to find there their own *a priori* dogmas, not to seek what Scripture really says. The doctrine of inspiration is not the fetish into which it has been degraded by formal systems of scholastic theology. Inspiration was not a mechanical dictation of words, but the influence of the Holy Ghost in the hearts of men who retained all their own natural emotions. **For I perceive,** etc. There are various ways of taking this clause. Nothing, however, is simpler than to regard it as a parenthetic remark (for I see that that Epistle, though it were but for a time, saddened you). **Though** it were **but for a season.** (For the phrase, see Philem. 15; Gal. ii. 5.) He means to say that their grief will at any rate cease when they receive this letter, and he can bear the thought of having pained them when he remembers the brevity of their grief and the good effects which resulted from it.

Ver. 9.—**Not that ye were made sorry.** They might have drawn this mistaken conclusion from his remark that he "rejoiced" when he heard of their "lamentation" (ver. 7). **After a godly sort;** literally, *according to God;* i.e. in a way which he would approve (Rom. viii. 27). **In nothing.** Not even when we rebuked you, and caused you pain.

Ver. 10.—**For godly sorrow,** etc. "For the sorrow which is according to God worketh out a repentance unto salvation which bringeth no regret." Sin causes regret, remorse, that sort of repentance (*metameleia*) which is merely an unavailing rebellion against the inevitable consequences of misdoing; but the sorrow of self-reproach which follows true repentance (*metanoia*, change of mind) is never followed by regret. Some take "not to be regretted" with "salvation," but it is a very unsuitable adjective to that substantive. **The sorrow**

of the world. Here sorrow for the loss, or disappointment, or shame, or ruin, or sickness caused by sin; such as the false repentance of Cain, Saul, Ahithophel, Judas, etc. **Death.** Moral and spiritual death always, and sometimes physical death, and always—unless it is followed by true repentance—eternal death, which is the opposite of salvation (Rom. v. 21).

Ver. 11.—**For behold,** etc. The effects produced by their repentance showed that it was "according to God;" for it brought forth in them "the fruits of good living to the honour and glory of God." **Carefulness;** rather, *earnestness, active endeavour.* **Yea what.** There is an untranslatable energy about the original Greek. The same use of ἀλλὰ (Latin, *immo vero*) in a climax is found in 1 Cor. vi. 11. **Clearing of yourselves;** literally, *apology, self-defence,* addressed to me through Titus. **Indignation.** Against themselves for their neglect. **Fear.** Of the measures which I might take, if I came to you "with a rod" (1 Cor. iv. 21). **Vehement desire.** Longing that I should return to you (see ver. 7). **Zeal.** To make up for past remissness. **Revenge.** Judicial punishment of the incestuous offender. The "apology" and "indignation" referred to themselves; the "fear" and "yearning" to the apostle; the "zeal" and "judicial retribution" to the offender. **In all** things. His summing up is, "In every respect ye approved yourselves to be pure in the matter." Whatever may have been your previous carelessness and connivance, the steps you took on receiving my letter vindicated your character. **In this matter;** rather, *in the matter.* It is quite in accordance with St. Paul's usual manner that "he speaks indefinitely of what was odious" (1 Thess. iv. 6).

Ver. 12.—**Wherefore, though I wrote unto you.** "So then, even if I *did* write you," namely, about that matter. **For his cause that had done the wrong,** etc. My object in writing was not to mix myself up with the personal quarrel. I had in view neither the wronger nor the wronged, directly and primarily, but wrote for the sake of the whole Church (1 Cor. v. 1, 2; vi. 7). **Nor for his cause that suffered wrong.** Apparently the father of the offender (1 Cor. v. 1). **Our care for you,** etc. Among the diversity of readings in this clause, which seem to be still further confused by mere mistakes of copyists, the best supported reading is "your care for us" (B, C, E, K, L, and various versions, etc.). The Sinaitic manuscript has "your care for yourselves." The variations have partly risen from the apparent strangeness of the remark that his letter had been written in order that their care for him might be manifested *to themselves;* in other words, that they might learn from their own conduct the reality of their earnest feelings for him. He has already spoken of this "earnest care" of theirs (ver. 11), but not in quite the same sense. Certainly, however, the reading followed by our Authorized Version, even if it be a correction, furnishes a more natural meaning (comp. ch. ii. 4), and the other may have arisen from a clerical error.

Ver. 13.—Therefore we were comforted, etc. Since my Epistle secured the result of manifesting your true feelings towards me, "we have been comforted." The Revised Version and many editions put the stop here, and continue (reading δὲ after ἐπὶ), and in addition to our consolation, abundantly the more did we rejoice at the joy of Titus, because his spirit has been refreshed by you all. Exceedingly the more. In the Greek this is expressed by double comparatives (comp. ch. xii. 9; Phil. i. 23). Was refreshed; rather, has been (and is) refreshed. The same verb is used in 1 Cor. xvi. 18; Philem. 7, 20.

Ver. 14.—I am not ashamed. The due rendering of the tenses brings out the sense much more accurately. "Because if I have boasted anything to him on your behalf, I was not put to the blush;" in other words, "One reason of my exceeding gladness was that you fully justified that very favourable picture of you which I had drawn for Titus when I was urging him to be the bearer of my letter." Is found a truth; literally, proved itself to be a truth. Here again there is a most delicate reference to the charge of levity and unveracity which had been brought against him (ch. i. 17). I always spoke the truth to you; but I might well have feared that, in speaking of you to Titus, my affection for you had led me to overstep the limits of perfect accuracy. But you yourselves, by proving yourselves worthy of all I said of you, have established my perfect truthfulness, even in the only point where I might have thought it doubtful. Nothing could exceed the tact and refinement, the subtle delicacy and beauty, of this gentle remark.

Ver. 15.—His inward affection. The same word which is so needlessly rendered "bowels" in ch. vi. 12. More abundant. His love for you has been increased by his recent visit. With fear and trembling. On this Pauline phrase, see 1 Cor. ii. 3.

Ver. 16.—I rejoice therefore. The "therefore" concludes the whole paragraph, but is omitted in many manuscripts. I have confidence in you; literally, I am bold in you, i.e. I feel courage about you. The phrase in 2 Thess. iii. 4 expresses a calmer and less hazardous trust.

HOMILETICS.

Vers. 1—4.—A minister's address to his people. "Having therefore these promises," etc. In these verses the apostle exhorts the Corinthians to two things.

I. TO THE PURSUIT OF SPIRITUAL PURITY. "Having therefore these promises, dearly beloved, let us cleanse ourselves from all filthiness of the flesh and spirit, perfecting holiness in the fear of God." He seems to regard the attainment of spiritual purity as consisting in two things. 1. Getting rid of the wrong. "Let us cleanse ourselves from all filthiness of the flesh and spirit." Perhaps the reference to "filthiness" here referred especially to the idolatry and unchastity which was so prevalent in the Corinthian Church. All sin is "filthiness," and cleansable; it is not nature, it is a stain on nature; it is not something inwrought into the very texture of our being, otherwise it could not be cleansed away. It is no more ourselves than the soil on the white robe is the robe. It can, it should, it must, be washed out, that we may appear "without spot or wrinkle." 2. Attaining the right. "Perfecting holiness in the fear of God." Holiness implies the consecration of our entire nature, flesh and spirit, body and soul, to the Divine will, and this requires habitual, solemn effort in "the fear of God." Now, the grand end of Christ's mission to the world is to produce this purity in man. "Having therefore these promises" (viz. the promises in the last verse of the preceding chapter, which are in substance the promises of the gospel), this spiritual purity should be struggled for. "The grace of God hath appeared to all men, teaching them that, denying ungodliness and worldly lusts," etc. The supreme desire of every true minister of the gospel is that his people shall become pure.

II. TO REGARD HIM WITH AFFECTION. "Receive us [open your hearts to us]," etc. He grounds his claim on their affection: 1. On the fact that he had done harm to none. "We have wronged no man, we have corrupted no man, we have defrauded no man." This is said, no doubt, in answer to some of the charges which his enemies had brought against him—said in self-vindication. He had "wronged no man," done injustice to none; he had "corrupted no man" in doctrines or morals; he had "defrauded no man," he had availed himself of no circumstance in order to extort from them money or power. A grand thing this for a minister to be able to say to his people without any fear of contradiction, and in the sight of God. 2. On the fact that he *loved* them. "I speak not this to condemn you: for I have said before, that ye are in our hearts to live and to die with you." Although I might "condemn" you, I still love you; you are so strong in my affections that I will not only visit you, but would live and die with you, if my mission would allow. 3. On the fact that he *rejoiced in the good* that was in them. "Great is my boldness of speech toward you, great is my glorying of you: I am filled with comfort," etc. Thus he commends himself to their affection. It is self-commendation, it is true; but who else could commend him? There were none greater than he living. There is no egotism in his self-commendation.

Vers. 5—7.—*The good tried and comforted.* "For when we were come into Macedonia," etc. Here we have—

I. A GOOD MAN GREATLY TRIED. "For when we were come into Macedonia, our flesh had no rest, but we were troubled on every side; without were fightings, within were fears." In ch. ii. 13 he refers to one circumstance that troubled him on his way to Macedonia. "I had no rest in my spirit, because I found not Titus my brother." He had come from Troas full of excitement and agitation, fully expecting to meet with Titus, who would convey to him some information concerning the Church at Corinth, which would allay his intense anxieties. But he was disappointed. What the other particular troubles were that he refers to here, the "fightings without" and "fears within," we know not; but well we know that everywhere in the prosecution of his apostolic mission he met with trials—great, varied, and most distressing. The best of men in this life are frequently "cast down." There are many things that "cast down" the spirits of good men. 1. *The prosperity of the wicked.* Asaph felt this. "My feet had almost gone, my steps were well-nigh slipped," etc. 2. *The triumphs of wrong.* Fraud in trade, corruption in politics, errors in science, moral filth in popular literature, blasphemies, sectarianism and cant in religion. What noble souls are depressed here in England with these things! 3. *The non-success of Christly labour.* How many preachers of spiritual thought, disinterested love, inflexible loyalty to truth, are subject to depressing moods on account of the little success apparently resulting from their arduous and self-denying toils! Often, like Elijah, they feel inclined to retire into the caves of solitude; like Jeremiah, who resolved " to speak no more " in his Name, and like One greater than either or all, who wailed out the words, "I have laboured in vain, and spent my strength for nought."

II. A GOOD MAN DIVINELY COMFORTED. "Nevertheless God, that comforteth those that are cast down, comforted us by the coming of Titus." God is a Comforter. No one requires higher qualifications than a true comforter. He must have a *thorough knowledge of the sufferer*, know his constitution, and the causes of the complaint; his diagnosis must be perfect. He must possess the necessary *remedial elements*; he must have the antidote at *command.* He must also have the *tenderest sympathy*; an unsympathetic nature can never administer comfort, whatever the extent of his knowledge or the suitableness of his means. God has all these qualifications in an infinite degree. Hence he is the Comforter. God comforted Paul by sending him Titus. 1. *The appearance* of Titus was comforting. The advent of his young friend was as the rising of the morning sun in the dark heavens of his spirit. God comforts man by man. Moses was comforted in the wilderness by the unexpected visit of his father-in-law Jethro (Exod. xviii. 7). Hannah was cheered in spirit by the talk of old Eli (1 Sam. i. 18). David, dejected in the wood, had his heart strengthened by Jonathan (1 Sam. xxiii. 16). 2. *The communication* of Titus was comforting. "And not by his coming only, but by the consolation wherewith he was comforted in you, when he told us your earnest desire, your mourning, your fervent mind toward me; so that I rejoiced the more."

CONCLUSION. Learn : 1. That Christianity in its highest form does not exempt from the trials of life. A more Christly man than Paul perhaps never lived. Yet how great his trials! 2. That the vicarious sufferings of love are amongst the most depressing. The more love a man has in him in this world of affliction and sorrow, the more, by the law of sympathy, will he endure. Paul now suffered for the Corinthians. 3. A genuine disciple of Christ carries comfort into the house of his distressed friend. Young Titus carried comfort into the saddened home of the Apostle Paul.

> "He who hath most of heart
> Knows most of sorrow; nor a thing he said
> Nor did but was to him at times a woe,
> At times indifferent, at times a joy.
> Folly and sin and memory make a curse
> Wherewith the future fires may vie in vain,
> The sorrows of the soul are graver still."
>
> (Festus.)

Vers. 8—11.—*Godly sorrow.* "For though I made you sorry," etc. Three remarks here concerning the godly sorrow that was wrought on the minds of the members of the Corinthian Church.

I. IT WAS PRODUCED BY A FAITHFUL REPROOF OF WRONG. There were, as we have seen, certain evils more or less prevalent in the Church at Corinth, such as schism, idolatry, unchastity, and abuse of the Lord's Supper. These so affected the mind of the apostle that his letter abounded with strong reproof. Concerning the reproofs he administered to them, two facts are noteworthy. 1. *They caused him much pain.* "For though I made you sorry with a letter, I do not repent, though I did repent." Men, more or less malign in their nature, take pleasure in dealing out reproaches and reproofs, but to those whose natures are of the genial and the generous type, few things are more painful than the administration of reproofs. Paul no doubt felt it so; still it had to be done. Loyalty to his conscience and his mission demanded it. A loving nature recoils at the idea of giving pain to any one. 2. *They were administered with the tenderest affection.* In almost every reproving sentence contained in his letter there beats the pulse of affection, and it is evermore this love that invests reproof with a heart penetrating and melting power. With the tenderest love ministers should always reprove, admonish, and exhort.

II. IT WAS ESSENTIALLY DIFFERENT TO THE SORROW OF THE WORLD. "Now I rejoice, not that ye were made sorry, but that ye sorrowed to repentance," etc. Great is the difference between godly sorrow and worldly sorrow. 1. The one is *selfish*, the other is *generous*. In the former the man regrets having done the wrong thing simply on account of inconvenience to himself; in the latter the anguish is in the wrong itself. 2. The one results in future *regret*, the other in future *joy*. All the sorrow that an ungodly man has felt will lead to some deeper, darker, more terrible distress. 3. The one leads to *ruin*, the other to *salvation*. See the results of worldly sorrow in Cain (Gen. iv. 12); in Saul (1 Sam. xxxi. 3—6); in Ahithophel (2 Sam. xvii. 23); in Judas (Matt. xxviii. 3—25). See godly sorrow in the prodigal son (Luke xv.); in Peter (Matt. xxvi.); in the converts on the day of Pentecost (Acts ii. 44—47).

III. IT WROUGHT GREAT RESULTS IN THE SOUL. It wrought: 1. *Solicitude.* "What carefulness it wrought in you!" Careful to resist the wrong and pursue the right. 2. *Deprecation.* "What clearing of yourselves!" How anxious to show your disapproval of the evil of which you have been guilty! 3. *Anger.* "What indignation!" Indignation, not against the sinner, but against the sin. This is a holy anger. 4. *Dread.* "What fear!" Dread, not of suffering, but of sin; not of God, but of the devil. This fear is, indeed, the highest courage. He who shrinks from the morally wrong is the truest hero. 5. *Longing.* "What vehement desire!" What longing after a better life! All these expressions mean intense earnestness, and earnestness, not about temporal matters, which is common and worthless, but about spiritual matters, which is rare and praiseworthy. Genuine repentance is antagonistic to indifference; it generates earnestness in the soul, it leads to the most strenuous efforts, to the most vehement cries to Heaven. "Sorrow in itself," says F. W. Robertson, "is a thing neither good nor bad; its value depends on the spirit of the person on whom it falls. Fire will inflame straw, soften iron, or harden clay; its effects are determined by the object with which it comes in contact. Warmth develops the energies of life or helps the progress of decay. It is a great power in the hothouse, a great power also in the coffin: it expands the leaf, matures the fruit, adds precocious vigour to vegetable life; and warmth, too, develops with tenfold rapidity the weltering process of dissolution. So, too, with sorrow. There are spirits in which it develops the seminal principle of life; there are others in which it prematurely hastens the consummation of irreparable decay."

Vers. 12—16.—*Church discipline.* "Wherefore, though I wrote unto you," etc. The subject of these words may be regarded as that of Church discipline; and two general remarks are suggested.

I. CHURCH DISCIPLINE SHOULD BE EXERCISED FOR THE GOOD OF THE WHOLE CHURCH. "Wherefore, though I wrote unto you, I did it not for his cause that had done the wrong, nor for his cause that suffered wrong, but that our care for you in the sight of God might appear unto you." The particular individual referred to here, on whom Paul calls discipline to be exercised, was the incestuous person (1 Cor. v. 1). The apostle here states that this was done, not merely for the offender's sake, nor indeed for the sake of the person whom the offender had injured (viz. his father, whose wife he had taken as his own). His object in writing was, not merely to chastise the one and to obtain justice and redress for the other, but that "our care for you in the sight of God might appear unto you." He had a larger aim; it was to prove to them how much he cared for their spiritual *purity and reputation.* Punishment should not only be for the reformation of the wrong-doer, but as an example to others. The unhealthy branch should be cut off for the sake of the tree's health and growth. All true chastisement for wrong aims, not only at the good of the offender, but at the good of the community at large.

II. WHEN THE GOOD OF THE CHURCH IS MANIFESTED THEREBY IT IS A JUST MATTER FOR REJOICING. "Therefore we were comforted in your comfort: yea, and exceedingly the more joyed we for the joy of Titus, because his spirit was refreshed by you all." The Church was improved by Paul's disciplinary letter. Of this Titus had assured him, for they had "refreshed" his "spirit" during his visit among them. Their improvement, too, justified the high testimony which he had given Titus concerning them. "For if I have boasted anything to him of you, I am not ashamed," etc. The love of Titus for them was increased by the discovery of it. "His inward affection is more abundant toward you." Thus the godly sorrow which they manifested on account of that which was wrong amongst them, was in every way satisfactory to him; it gave him comfort, it greatly refreshed the spirit of Titus, increased his affection for them, and inspired the apostle himself with confidence and with joy.

HOMILIES BY VARIOUS AUTHORS.

Ver. 1.—*An exhortation to perfection.* "Having therefore these promises," which the apostle had just mentioned (ch. vi. 16—18), what were the Corinthians expected to be? "Sons and daughters" of the Father, God in Christ. But the condition was, "Be ye separate, touch not the unclean thing, and I will receive you." There was a character involved ("sons and daughters"); there was something to be done ("come out from among them, and be ye separate"); then "I will receive you." St. Paul is specific in his appeal: "Let us cleanse ourselves from all filthiness [defilement] of the flesh and spirit, perfecting holiness in the fear of God." The enlarged heart, of which he had been speaking and would soon speak again, has a tender voice, addressing them as "dearly beloved." Nothing magisterial appears; he is one of them—"Let *us* cleanse ourselves;" nor has he any doubt of their ability to do this thing. Separation from old associations, changes in customs and habits, call for firm resolution and self-denial; but he is well assured that God makes no promise without giving ample strength for the accepting party to comply with the terms offered. If the promises embraced every good connected with their relation to God as a Father, then they must be like God in Christ; they were to entertain no views of God, except as God in Christ, but were to reverence, love, serve him in this one single and complete relationship. The ground, motive, impulse of action, were to spring from this consideration—God in Christ as a Father. If so, the righteousness of Christ was not only to be the reason of their justification before the law of rectitude, but they were also to have that righteousness as a property of personal character. By nature they were far gone from righteousness; they were defiled, born in sin; grace had already been communicated to renew their evil character; he had written to them as "washed, sanctified, justified," in the "name" of Christ, and by "the Spirit of our God." As yet the work was only begun. Much was to be done. Sinful tendencies were in them which had never come under the eye of consciousness. Enemies lurked within and without, of whom they were unaware. Imperfect as they and he were, they must go on to perfection. Strength consisted in putting forth strength, to be stronger. First of all, this perfection was to be sought by purifying themselves from evil. What an amount of corruption still remained was seen in the fact of the filthiness in the flesh and spirit. Each part of our complex nature was vitiated, and each combined with the other in opposing the progress necessary to attain holiness. There were vices of the animal man. There were vices of the moral man. And there were vices resulting from the union of the two, so that a thorough and complete cleansing was required. "All filthiness;" no matter of what class or kind, hereditary or acquired, local as respected the wickedness of Corinth, or general as belonging to the human family, the wrong-doing among you from the Judaizers, from the free-thinkers, from all your ambitious partisanships,—"cleanse" yourselves from "all filthiness," whether of the "flesh" or the "spirit." This was the negative side of a great and imperative duty, not all, but much, and very much, since, until this were done, they could take no direct steps towards perfection. Observe now that gross bodily sins were not the only lusts. Tempers and dispositions were just as urgent as passions and appetites in seeking unlawful enjoyments. Reflect on this point. "The spirit in us *lusteth* to envy." Inordinate affections led to transgression. Nay, they often excited the body to wicked indulgences. Physical organs are frequently torpid; they are aroused by images in the intellect, and stimulated by an impure imagination; and, furthermore, after these organs, because of age or over-gratification, have little or no originating force, and are well-nigh worn out, the recollections of past pleasures kindle the expiring embers into a flame. Thus, indeed, depravity assumes its most licentious forms. For it is not the animal man that is the chief or the most dangerous factor in this sort of iniquity. The intellectual and moral man descends into corporeal abuses, and then it is these temptations are strongest. In many of these sins there is an element of sentiment supplied by an unholy imagination, which makes them far more tyrannical and debauching than they would be otherwise. And hence it is not the beastly possibility in man that is the greatest danger, but the Satanic agency brought to bear on the body by means of the spirit. It is the devil of the spirit that is the devil of the body. A terrible conjunction this, and yet it is not a common spectacle. Ordinarily the incipient stage of vice is a bodily evil merely. It is a matter of blood and nerves. Not such does it remain long. Satan knows his citadel, and hastens to its occupancy. While it does continue, a man may be reasoned with; he is open to shame, conscience may be reached, and concurrent motives made operative on his feelings, but when physical vice allies itself with spirit, men "glory in their shame," and are "taken captive by Satan at his will." In the final outcome there is but one will, and it is Satan's will. Much more than this cleansing from the "filthiness of the flesh and spirit" is necessary, if "these promises" are to be fully realized. Therefore he adds, "perfecting holiness in the fear of God." Here we have the positive side of that experience which is demanded of those who are the "sons and daughters" of God in Christ. It is *inward* holiness. Under the Law, beasts were clean and unclean; things, vessels, places, were externally holy; emblems and symbols of purity abounded; manners, customs, domestic and national usages, were so ordered as to impress on the senses the difference between good and evil. Under the gospel, spiritual holiness is demanded. The circumcision is of the heart, not of the flesh; the sanitary idea of the human body, so frequently set forth in the Old Testament, is changed into that of the body as the temple of the Holy Ghost; and hence, no sooner does the Lord Jesus begin to unfold the constitution of the new kingdom in the sermon on the mount, than he speaks directly to the heart. Righteousness must exceed the righteousness of scribes and Pharisees. Impure thoughts are forbidden. Passions that have no outward voice utter their sinfulness in the ear of God; and feelings that escape not into visible acts are realities in the light of eternity. Inasmuch as the cleansing was a purification of body and spirit, St. Paul argues that the sanctification, begun in regeneration, was to continue, body and spirit sharing together the Spirit's influence. Neither the one nor the other was to be lost sight of; neither part of the work was to be carried on in a way detrimental to perfect unity; neither was to be exaggerated at the expense of the other. But as body and spirit had been redeemed by Christ's blood, so were both to be hallowed by the indwelling of the Holy Ghost. Throughout St. Paul's Epistles there run these two leading ideas—the sanctification of body and of spirit; and if, at times, the idea of the former is prominent, and then, at other times, the idea of the latter, we must recollect that this variation was necessary to the full presentation of his subject. Great truths are not to be vividly seen except in great moods, and great moods are not habitual, but occasional. Now, this mode of displaying his subject by a rotation of its aspects exposes the apostle to misconception. The ascetic takes him in one mood of thought, dominant at the moment, because of the nature of his argument. The mystic takes him in another. And they both do him injustice, the ascetic by laying an undue stress on bodily mortifications, the mystic by extravagance in spiritual abstractions. St. Paul is always true to his theology. He never loses his balance, never exalts spirit at the expense of body, never forgets that body is mated with spirit under an economy of permanent neutrality. Hence the argument for inward holiness, that cleansing of spirit and flesh which proceeds from the Holy Ghost in the conscience and heart, and works from the centre and seat of vitality through all the organs of life. It is *growing* holiness. Growth is the law of existence. The body grows until it attains its physical development, say from twenty-one to twenty-five years of age in men, and then another and much higher growth sets in, that of intellectual and moral adaptiveness to the mind, whereby the nerves, the ganglia, the brains, are brought into closer union with thought, volition, sensibility. But it is in religious life that growth is most perceptible—a growth in the fear of God, a filial and tender fear, that is jealous of its sense of sonship, and ever watchful lest it grieve the witnessing Spirit. There is an increasing delight in the discharge of duty, in taking up the daily cross, in practising self-denial, and especially in a clearer view of the ground and reason of self-denial. How the Scriptures grow upon us, the exercises of the closet, the Holy Communion, the fellowship of Christians! And, as we advance, we feel more and more the evil of sin as it is in itself. " Against thee, thee only, have I sinned, and done this evil in thy sight." This psalm, the most profoundly heart-searching and personal of the psalms, is nevertheless most representative of that sense of sin which forgets all else in the thought of an offended God. In that bitterest hour of David's life, his home, other homes, a nation's homes, involved in his terrible transgression, there is the one overwhelming reflection, " *Against thee!* " The growing Christian sees the innate quality of sin, its deep-seated hold, its presence in the life-blood of his old nature, and learns from thence to perfect holiness, by realizing, as far as may be, the holiness of God. " By studying the character of Christ and imitating his example, this Divine holiness defines itself to his mind and engages his affections. " Looking unto Jesus " is the secret of his growth. He looks to him as the " Author " of his faith; how long ago it was! How feeble then! What gracious forbearance! The bruised reed not broken, the smoking flax not quenched! And the " Author " is the " Finisher; " for he is " the same yesterday, and to-day, and for ever." Law changes into love, and love advances from one degree of strength and beauty to another, from one relation of life to another, from one victory to a victory still greater, the holy ideal rising before him and assuming new glory, and yet, as it retreats to a loftier height, drawing him towards itself with a stronger charm. " Blessed are the pure in heart." It is far on in the Beatitudes; but it is there, thanks to God, it is there as an attainment. The pathway to it is very clearly marked out, the successive steps, the preparatory agencies, the gradual advances, the blessedness of poverty of spirit, of mourning, of meekness, of hungering and thirsting after righteousness, of mercifulness. One may know what progress he is making towards it, and this is the great thing to be known. Milestones along the road record the onward tread and assure the pilgrim of the certain goal. " Blessed are the pure in heart: for they shall see God."—L.

Vers. 2—7.—*Appeal for affectionate relations between himself and the Corinthians;*

sorrow and consolation. The rendering of ver. 2, Revised Version, is full of vigour. "Open your hearts to us: we wronged no man, we corrupted no man, we took advantage of no man." Room in their hearts for whom? Room for him who had violated no rights, led no one astray, acted fraudulently in nothing towards any person, so that he challenges their confidence to the full. But had he not done this before, and that very earnestly? Had he not done it again and again? Yes; but his enemies had their head-quarters at Corinth; they were untiring, ever inventing new scandals, ever increasing in zealotry, for his overthrow. Now, it is a matter of interest to understand St. Paul's motive in this frequent and vehement defence of himself. From the outset his position had been singular. Not one of the original twelve who had "companied" with the Lord Jesus, a converted persecutor and blasphemer, an apostle called to an exceptional apostleship, and placed in the forefront of that battle which was to liberate Christianity from Jewish thraldom, and preserve it from Gentile corruptions. It was inevitable that the man and the apostle should be subjected to a most critical and severe inquisition. Yet how wonderfully was this overruled! Only think of the *spiritual biography* that has grown out of this painful necessity of his attitude before the Church. Somewhat of this kind of writing we have in the Old Testament, particularly in the Book of Job, in the Psalms, and in Ecclesiastes, but nothing as to depth, variety, profundity, compass of experience, such as we have in St. Paul's Epistles. In the latter we see the Christian consciousness in its early realizations, and that too in all its important aspects. For what is there in the struggles of the "new creature" with the "old Adam"? What is there in outward conflict we have not here in exactness of detail? No finer illustration of this could be given than the Second Epistle to the Corinthians. Was he simply giving his spiritual history? Nay, indeed, but writing a typical biography of the human heart under the training of the Holy Ghost. This is its distinctive merit—the portraiture of the human soul forming and shaping in the image of Christ for eternal glory. Such a mirror was needed. Of what avail a standard of doctrine without a standard of experience? Of what utility a knowledge of duties, and yet entire ignorance of the legitimate results of precepts carried into practice? From his pen we have Christianity as a system of truths; from the same pen, Christianity in personal consciousness; and the two are so wrought together and interblended, that we are no more at a loss to understand what Christianity is as an inspiration of life than a revelation of Divine wisdom. Follow the man in this chapter. Do you admire manly boldness? There it is in that second verse. Are you touched by delicacy and tenderness? You have them in the third verse: "I say it not to condemn you: for I have said before, that ye are in our hearts to die together and live together." Is this commonplace sentiment? Is this the language, the air, the spirit of a persecuted hero of the world? Match it if you can. "*To die together and live together*"—this would be poetry, if it were not that rarer thing, the most impassioned and exalted prose. "In our hearts;" there they abide to die and live together. If he had written to them, it was not to condemn, but to save them. Inclined to find fault and harshly criminate? Far from him a censorious temper. "Great is my boldness of speech towards you;" and why bold? "Great is my glorying on your behalf;" and why glory? The glad spirit, free once more from its oppressive burden, cannot repress its exultation. "*My* boldness," "*my* glorying;" just before "*we*" and "*us*" and "*our*," the personal intensity bursting forth. "I am filled with comfort, I overflow with joy in all our affliction." Such a heart authenticates itself instantly to our confidence and love. To doubt its truthfulness would be treachery to our own instincts. We all love a fervent lover. However cold and constrained our temperament, there is something divinely contagious in a spirit like St. Paul's; and, for the sake of humanity, "great" is our "glorying" on his "behalf." If, then, we find him in the next verses (5—7) referring to his individual solicitudes, we may be sure that this has its place in the development of Christian doctrine, going on in the history of the Church. Instead of being an insight into the private heart of the apostle only, it is likewise a most trustworthy record of religious experience, to which we may come for instruction and help when burdened by cares and anxieties. Unable to remain in Troas, because of his deep concern to hear from Corinth, he passed into Macedonia; but there was no relief from the pressure. "We were troubled on every side." His whole nature shared the suffering of the mind, his "flesh had no rest," and the sorrow reached such an extent that he sums it up in the condensed expressions, "without were fightings, within were fears." Things had put on their darkest look. Yet in that very hour consolation was near by. Titus came with good tidings from Corinth, and, in his opportune arrival, St. Paul sees the good hand of God. The statement is given in an emphatic form. At first it is he "who comforteth the lowly;" and then *even God* "comforteth us by the coming of Titus;" and how happy Titus himself was! The visit to the Corinthians had been a blessing to his young friend, and this added much to his joy, for he participated in "the consolation wherewith he was comforted in you." Grace to others is often grace, and the richest grace, to our own souls. And in this instance we can easily understand how a man with St. Paul's quick sympathies entered into the experience of Titus. A delicate task had been assigned to his youthful companion, and it had been managed with success. Added to his intense pleasure growing out of the favourable change at Corinth was the gratification from the skill and efficiency of Titus's mission. One pictures the scene of the meeting, the narration, the questions asked and answered, the frequent interruptions of the story by the sudden outbreaks of the listener's emotion, the happy exclamations, and the surprise increasing as the detail of incidents progressed to the completion of the history. Had not St. Paul a valuable helper now? Was not God giving him a co-worker precious to his heart? Could he not see the future Titus, the same who was afterwards to be associated so closely with him, and to whom he would write a pastoral letter? Those were gracious hours, and he might well say, "I rejoiced the more," since he was not only greatly cheered by the "earnest desire," the "mourning," the "fervent mind" of the Corinthian brethren towards him, but was confirmed in the impression that Titus was to be a valuable auxiliary in the work now enlarging on his hands, and daily getting to be more complicated.—L.

Vers. 8—16.—*True repentance and its effects; ministry of Titus.* There are reactions from our highest moods. There are reactions from our wisest deeds. Nor can it be otherwise under the present constitution of our nature. That St. Paul should have had these reactions was perfectly natural, the more so as his temperament made him liable, in an unusual degree, to their occurrence. If they did not appear in his writings we should be surprised, nor could their absence be explained but on the supposition that he was an exception in this respect to the ordinary laws of mind, and particularly to those laws as seen in men of his class. Some persons think it very strange that he should say, "Though I made you sorry with a letter, I do not repent, though I did repent." What was his inspiration, they ask, if he could "repent" of writing his former Epistle to the Corinthians? Whatever he meant by "repent," he did not mean moral self-reproach, nor indeed any permanent state of mind, but simply a transient emotional condition, due probably to excess of nervous sensibility. His inspiration from the Holy Ghost was the inspiration of a man. It did not set aside his temperament. It was in perfect harmony with the characteristics of his intellect, and quite likely intensified those characteristics as related to his physical peculiarities. Who has not had these seasons of experience in which things that were very clear a few days before have been suddenly darkened? Judgments were then formed, committals made, promises given, that now seem unwise or even rash; and how gladly would we undo what was done!—and that too in matters which were entered on after long and earnest deliberation, and which proved in the sequel to be eminently fortunate. Are the arguments that led us to certain conclusions less valid now than then? No; the arguments are the same, but nerves and brain are not in the same state, not in the same vigorous tension, and, consequently, we do not see the truth and the grounds of the truth as we did when we were in fuller possession of ourselves. The logic of nerves and brain is a very wayward and fitful thing, and a very different thing from the logic of the intellect. Pascal says, in the 'Pensées,' "To have a series of proofs incessantly before the mind is beyond our power." Now, in the instance under review, St. Paul would have been more or less than man not to have undergone precisely this temporary reaction. Ill health, an unusual combination of exciting circumstances, dangers of an extraordinary sort threatening the Church, a new and most promising sphere of labour and by far the greatest that had opened in his ministry overcast with sudden gloom, Titus still absent, suspense wearing upon a fortitude taxed already to the uttermost; what a lack of the human and of the genuine manliness of the human, if he had felt no uneasiness, no misgivings, no rebound! It was not weakness, but weakness struggling into strength, that led him to say, "I did repent." Let us take comfort from the apostle's human nature and the grace manifested in its infirmities. Companionship in weakness aspiring to get the victory is very precious to honest souls. Men are never wanting to teach us the ideals of life. What is needed far more is to have traced in a distinct manner the progress of the soul towards perfection. Who in this respect can compare with the Apostle Paul? Who has delineated the Christian consciousness in all its various moods, in all its alternations, in its baffled endeavours, in its victorious strength, and done it in such a natural way that the lowliest heart feels at home in his fellowship and finds no language of its own so much its own as the words in which he tells how he sorrowed and how he rejoiced? Lest they should misunderstand his joy by supposing that he had any pleasure in their pain, he explains (ver. 9) why he was happy. They had "sorrowed to repentance." Instructed by the doctrinal truths he had unfolded in the First Epistle, moved by his entreaties, made conscious of their delinquencies, made ashamed of their gross inattention to discipline, they had repented of their backslidings and reformed their evil doings. A "godly sorrow" had they shown, and could anything "godly" be deplored? Least of all, could a "godly sorrow" over envy and jealousy, over strife and schismatic partisanships, over vices tolerated in the bosom of the Church—could such a sorrow be regretted? It was "godly," indeed, for it had wrought out its true nature and was known by its fruits. Of course he gave it a doctrinal form, and, for all time, thus reads one of the most vital and solemn of all Christian verities: "Godly sorrow worketh repentance to salvation not to be repented of." Well might he claim that they had received "damage in nothing." It was all gain, infinite gain. Notice the development of the thought. A true repentance is from God. Christ said that the Holy Spirit should come to rebuke "the world of sin, and of righteousness, and of judgment." It is not our idea of sin, but God's idea, that enables us to realize what sin is, and this proceeds from the Spirit. Think of it as we may, study its consequences, feel its enormity as far as we can, look at the paradise it blighted, read its records on the earth, picture the hell it has created; this is not that sense of the guilt of sin which leads to repentance. Not what sin is in our sight, but what it is in God's sight, determines the estimate of the penitent. And just in the degree that this initial process is from the illumination and under the guidance of the Holy Spirit, in that same degree is the work genuine and profound. Large allowance must be made for individuality of character. Modes of thinking, habits of feeling, education and circumstances, must be taken into consideration, since men are very thoroughly personal when God comes to deal with their souls. Nevertheless, the truth cannot be stated too strongly, that repentance is a "godly sorrow" only so far as the Holy Ghost is concerned in the work. And, further, it is salutary. It works no "damage." Now, at this point, the apostle confesses that he had been anxious, and certainly there was ground for anxiety. To rebuke men for their sins is the most difficult and the most hazardous of all the functions devolved on a minister of the gospel. Happy the minister who can say that he has not done "damage," some time in his career, in this particular. But in the present case all had turned out well. The censure, the exhortation, the personal lovingness, he had put into his letter, had blended in one gracious influence, so that conscience had witnessed to conscience, heart to heart, energy on their part to decision and resoluteness on his part, and a result most blessed to him, to Titus, to the Church, had been effected. It was not the sorrow of the world that "worketh death." Instead of that, it had wrought life, a renewed and most hopeful life, a change so glorious that it would never be repented of. But he would particularize. If the repentance had been "godly," and therefore without "damage," he would show them the full meaning of these words. "Behold this self-same thing." He would arouse their attention and concentrate thought on this manifestation of God's mercy. To see it they must look within. What a transformation! Lately so careless, so insensible, so puffed up, even the Holy Communion shockingly abused; what save a "godly sorrow" could bring about a radical change? It was a sorrow to humble them, not to "damage" them. It was not the sorrow of the world, mortifying to pride and vanity, intensifying to selfishness, driving to desperation, and arming the soul in deadlier hostility to goodness. The proof of all this was at hand. *Carefulness;* activity and diligence in ferreting out evils and extirpating them. *Clearing of themselves;* anxiety to get rid of the stain on their Church character, and stand fair with the apostle. *Indignation;* not only against the incestuous man, but that feeling of self-vexation which arises when we see the folly and evil of our conduct. *Fear;* lest a heavier punishment should come from God than that already experienced. *Longing;* fervent desire to do better. *Zeal;* industrious effort in discharging their duties, and especially such duties as concerned Church discipline. *Avenging* the wrong done by punishment so as to evince their sincerity of amendment. *Yea;* repeated in every item, specified that each element of the sentence might maintain its proper degree of force. Finally, his hearty commendation; *in every respect,* approving themselves to be right-minded in this matter. A word of justification for himself follows. Not for the sake of him who had done the wrong, nor for his sake who had suffered the wrong, had he written, but that their earnest care in his behalf might be manifested and his apostleship honoured. In the name of God he had called them to repentance, and they had promptly hearkened to the Divine message. Once more the power of the gospel had been vindicated, and " therefore we have been comforted." Throughout the affair he had been intensely personal, but had he been actuated by selfishness, or had any element of selfishness mixed with his motives, this personal intensity could not have assumed the form presented in his conduct. Yet in that hour of gladness there was an uppermost joy. A beautiful touch of nature it is when he says that he " joyed the more exceedingly " on account of his young associate Titus, " because his spirit was refreshed by you all." The long-continued trouble seems over now. The unrest, the fightings without and the fears within, Ephesus and Troas and Macedonia, pass out of presence, and the only spectacle left in the horizon of vision is Paul the apostle standing firmly on the historic soil he has won for Christ, with Titus at his side, in whose blooming spring-time his eye reads the harvest not far off. "O ye Corinthians, our heart is enlarged." Can he express his gratification too often, too freely? Once again, "I rejoice therefore that I have confidence in you in all things."—L.

Ver. 1.—*Holiness.* It is too customary for religions of human origin and authority to lay stress upon merely external and ceremonial purity. Many such religions pay not the slightest attention to the higher claims of morality. Now, Judaism used all its ceremonial cleansings as means for developing the idea of true morality. And Christianity is emphatically a religion of holiness. This appears from considering the unique and sinless character of Christ, the spirituality of his teaching; and further, from the atonement he has made for sin, and the provision for true purity made in the dispensation of the Holy Spirit.

I. THE NEGATIVE VIEW OF HOLINESS. The text assumes that man's state is naturally impure, that his heart is defiled and polluted by sin, that his life is stained and dyed with its moral blackness. Hence the admonition to cleanse: 1. From all filthiness of the flesh. There was a special reason why this should be made prominent in addressing the Corinthians, inasmuch as not only was their city celebrated for its licentiousness, but the Church itself had tolerated a flagrant case of immorality. The sins of the flesh are indeed the especial fault of those who have lately been rescued from the corruptions of paganism; yet we shall mislead ourselves if we suppose that, in any state of civilization or Christian privilege, men are free from temptations to offences of this kind. 2. From all filthiness of the spirit. Our Lord himself has been careful and faithful to warn against these; the heart may sin as well as the body. In fact, it is the heart that needs to be the first and chief seat of purification.

II. THE POSITIVE VIEW OF HOLINESS. The expression is noticeable, "perfecting holiness." Such language implies: 1. That there are degrees of moral purity, and that it is expected of the Christian that he should go forward, from one stage to another, conquering sin, achieving new degrees of virtue, and leaving infirmities behind. 2. It is implied also that this is to be the result of effort. No sanction can be found here for that quietism which represents holiness as acquired without effort, struggle, and conquest. 3. Yet it is to be understood that in this process we stand in need of the gracious influences of the Holy Spirit, whose distinctive work is a work of sanctification.

III. THE CHRISTIAN MOTIVES TO HOLINESS. They are represented here as two. **1.** The fear of God, by which we understand a reverence for his holy character, respect for his holy Law, and a proper dread lest we should by disobedience incur his displeasure and indignation. 2. The promises of God. The promises here adduced are indeed sufficient to animate us to the most ardent efforts. The favour and indwelling of the Eternal, his most tender representations of his fatherhood, and his assured consideration and treatment of us as his beloved children,—these surely are promises which should and will exercise a mighty influence over the heart and urge to a cheerful and consecrated obedience.—T.

Ver. 3.—"*In our hearts.*" The strong personal feeling which breathes throughout this Epistle is at its strongest here. Paul claims to occupy a very close and tender relation to these Corinthians; however they may feel towards him—and he acknowledges that they have shown respect to his authority and have caused him joy—he holds them very dear. "Not merely are you," he seems to say, "on our lips, not merely are your names upon our pen, not merely do we keep you in memory; 'ye are *in our hearts* to die together and live together.'"

I. HOW TO ACCOUNT FOR THIS AFFECTIONATE INTEREST. The feeling here described is appropriate in the case of all Christian ministers in relation to those placed in their spiritual charge. 1. The *general* reason: Christ's friendship towards his people is the model and the motive of the friendship which obtains among them mutually. There is something distinctively Christian in sentiments and relations of this kind. Not kindred, not interest, but fellowship in Christ, constitutes the bond of union. 2. The *special* reason: labour and suffering deepen interest and strengthen and hallow love. The apostle had toiled for these Corinthians, had exposed himself to danger on their behalf, had suffered anguish of spirit through their unspirituality and folly. Hence the tender interest, resembling maternal affection, which he cherished towards them. 3. The *personal* reason. Many of the members of this congregation had come to love their evangelist, to regard him as the minister of God to their souls; and he had found in their devotion a rich reward for all he had done for their good. Those who would benefit their fellow-men spiritually and lastingly must have them "in their hearts." This will give a zest, a vigour, to all efforts for their good.

II. IN WHAT RESPECT TO TRACE THE RESULTS OF THIS AFFECTIONATE INTEREST. If the heart be the very spring of action, the true explanation of conduct, it may be expected that the minister who has his people in his heart will be by that fact powerfully affected in his ministerial life. 1. Such a minister will leave no labour unaccomplished which may tend to the good of his people. Much occurs to deject the zealous servant of God; and, as a mere matter of duty, it will often be hard for him to persevere in his endeavours. But, prompted by love, he will not grow weary or hopeless, but will persevere in his faithful efforts and sacrifices. 2. Such a spiritual labourer will be either distressed or cheered by the treatment with which he may meet from those to whom he ministers. We may be indifferent as to the conduct of some of our acquaintances; but those who are in our hearts must needs give us either satisfaction and comfort or anxiety and grief. Let all hearers of the gospel, all members of the Church, consider how deeply their action must affect the hearts of God's servants. 3. The true minister hopes to enjoy the society of his people in the heavenly state. So closely are pastor and flock united, that in heart, in feeling, they may be said to "die together" as well as to "live together." The saved are to those who have been helpful in their salvation their joy and crown of rejoicing in the world of glory.—T.

Ver. 5.—*Fighting and fears.* The course of the apostle was one remarkably varied; sometimes prosperous, sometimes adverse. At the time when he wrote this Epistle he looked back upon a period of trouble, contention, and opposition, and upon experiences of suffering and disappointment. His nature was not one to pass through life unmoved; he was sensitive to all influences. And at Ephesus, at Troas, and in that Macedonia from which he was now writing, Paul had endured much which was fitted to harass and depress his mind. Never was affliction more comprehensively summed up than in the language he here employs—" without, fightings; within, fears."

I. THE TROUBLES WHICH ASSAIL THE CHRISTIAN WORKER FROM WITHOUT. 1. Opposition to his doctrine. This Paul experienced, and this every servant of Christ must expect, both from open enemies of Christianity and from false brethren who corrupt the truth. 2. Persecution. That the apostle was exposed to this, the record of his life abundantly proves; and, in the first age, as at many subsequent periods, such experience was common. Thus the Master suffered, and thus his servants must expect to suffer like him.

II. THE TROUBLES WHICH ASSAIL THE CHRISTIAN WORKER FROM WITHIN. What were the "fears" to which St. Paul refers? We can but conjecture. 1. Fear lest there had been a want of wisdom, or devotion, in the services undertaken. 2. Fear lest the work of the Lord should have suffered through any insufficiency on the part of the worker. 3. Fear lest at last the labourer should fail of acceptance and approval.

III. THE SUPPORT AND CONSOLATION PROVIDED FOR THE CHRISTIAN WORKER TO SUSTAIN HIM UNDER THESE TROUBLES. 1. The testimony of a good conscience, that, however imperfectly and inadequately the service has been rendered, it has yet been rendered in sincerity. 2. The assurance that an overruling Providence has remarked and has permitted all that has taken place, even to the temporary discouragement of the toiler for Christ. 3. The conviction that in such trouble the servant has had fellowship with his Lord. 4. The hope and expectation that light affliction will work out an exceeding and eternal weight of glory.—T.

Ver. 6.—*The Comforter of the lowly.* We are accustomed to think of the apostle as the soldier of the cross, the hero of the spiritual war. And this is just. Nevertheless, we should not forget that he had a human heart, with human susceptibilities and cravings; that he knew what it was to be weary, disappointed, and sorrowful, and what it was to be consoled, encouraged and elated. This Epistle represents him as bitterly distressed by the conduct of the Corinthian Christians, and yet as truly comforted by the tidings brought by Titus and by the brotherly fellowship and sympathy of his youthful colleague.

I. THE NEED OF COMFORT. This is owing to the fact that Christian people and Christian workers are sometimes among the downcast, the lowly, the depressed. It is a permitted experience of human life, and there are reasons, some of them obvious enough, why the faithful and zealous servant of Christ should not be exempt from such feelings. It may be necessary, in order to keep him humble, to preserve him from self-confidence, to cherish within him a spirit of dependence upon Divine assistance.

II. THE AUTHOR OF COMFORT. This view which the apostle here takes of God may to some seem derogatory to his dignity. But it should rather be regarded as setting God's character in an admirable and attractive light. If God has made the human heart such as it is, if he has appointed its varied experiences, it cannot be beneath him to minister to that nature which is his own handiwork, to overrule to highest ends those circumstances which his wisdom has created. He has delighted to reveal himself to his people as a God of consolation, especially when their hearts have been most sore and their cry most piercing.

III. THE MEANS OF DIVINE COMFORT. These means accord with the nature with which the Creator has endowed us, and are none the less honouring to his wisdom because they are often of the simplest kind. The case of Paul illustrates this. 1. The presence and brotherly kindness of a friend is consolatory to the afflicted; *e.g.* the coming of Titus. 2. The good tidings that reach the downcast cheer the soul; *e.g.* good news concerning the Corinthian Church. 3. The assurance of affection and sympathy on the part of those whose welfare is sought (*vide* vers. 7—9).—T.

Ver. 10.—*Sorrow and repentance.* There is only one way to avoid sorrow, and that is to avoid sin. Even then sympathy will awaken sorrow on account of the sin of others. But so long as there is evil in this world, so long will it be a world of anguish and of tears. It is not the sorrow which is to be regretted, but the sin which is its cause. "They that lack time to mourn lack time to mend."

I. THE SORROW OF THE WORLD. The ungodly may sorrow because they have sinned. But observe: 1. What are the *characteristics* of this sorrow. When the irreligious are rebuked and chastened for their wrong-doing, their vanity is wounded, their anger is excited, their resentment is aroused, they are vexed because they lose the favour of their neighbours or suffer in reputation. 2. The *issue* of this sorrow is death; instead of being profitable, it is deleterious, drawing the thoughts away from the moral heinousness of sin, and confirming the sinner in courses whose only end is spiritual death.

II. THE SORROW WHICH IS GODLY. 1. This is occasioned by the recognition of the sin as an offence against the Divine Law. "Against thee, thee only, have I sinned." 2. And by the feeling that sin is a grief to the Divine heart. As a tender child grieves to hurt his father's spirit, so a truly sensitive nature is pained in the very pain of Christ. 3. And *by* the knowledge that human sin brought the holy Saviour to the cross. 4. And is heightened by the knowledge that privileges have been abused and grace defied.

III. THE REPENTANCE TO WHICH GODLY SORROW LEADS. It is a change of mind and purpose; a turning away from the error, the folly, the unbelief of the past, a turning away from temptation and from the society of the sinful, a turning to God as he has revealed in Christ his infinite mercy and loving-kindness. Especially is this repentance that "which bringeth no regret." He who comes out of bondage into liberty can never rue his choice.

IV. THE ULTIMATE ISSUE OF TRUE REPENTANCE. This is salvation, which contrasts with that death to which worldly sorrow leads. Such is the appointment of Infinite Wisdom. And he who studies this process must acknowledge that, to a true and eternal salvation, there can be no other path than the path of repentance and of faith.—T.

Ver. 13.—*Refreshment of spirit.* The very decidedly personal character of this Epistle is the occasion of its bringing before the reader some topics to which otherwise his attention might not be directed. The writer, his friends and colleagues, Timothy and Titus, the several persons in the Corinthian Church alluded to, the community which was called upon to take action,—all seem to live before us. Human feelings appear in the light of Christian truth, privilege, and duty. The experiences of the heart are represented as hallowed and elevated by the principles of spiritual religion. Titus is depicted as visiting Corinth, as received with respect, and as obeyed with alacrity, and consequently as cherishing a deepened affection for the Corinthian Christians, as rejoicing because of their attitude of spirit and their united action, and, in fact, as refreshed in spirit by his visit to them.

I. THE SPIRIT'S NEED OF REFRESHMENT. This may arise from : 1. Weariness in labour. One may become weary *in* the work when not weary *of* it. 2. Disappointment in efforts made for the good of others. When energy and self-denial have done their best, and no results have followed, or at all events none have become apparent, the spirit is sometimes saddened and dejected. 3. Opposition, whether from the world without or from professed brethren, produces a most disheartening effect upon the sensitive nature.

II. THE POWER OF TRUE CHRISTIAN FELLOWSHIP TO REFRESH THE SPIRIT. It does this in many ways. 1. It brings home the conviction that the Christian labourer is not alone. He may be disposed to lament, as Elijah did, that he is left alone in the world; but it is not so, and there are occasions upon which he realizes this. 2. It sometimes takes the form of appreciation of services rendered on behalf of the brotherhood. The pastor finds that his visits have been valued; the preacher that his word has been a living seed in hearts of which he had thought there was but little that was good ; the admonition awakens confessions, acknowledgments, resolutions, which were but little expected. 3. United exercises of praise and prayer react upon the weary soul ; listlessness, discouragement, disappear ; the whole nature is braced by Heaven-born energy for new and happier service.—T.

Ver. 1.—*The promises of God an incentive to holy living.* I. CONSIDER THE DIVINE PROMISES. 1. *How numerous they are.* Some are specified in preceding verses. Divine promise is, however, found in all parts of the Scripture. The crown of revelation is thickly studded with the pearls of promise. God encourages his people by multiplying promises to them. 2. *How varied.* There are promises suited to every condition—for joy, sorrow, sickness, health, penury, prosperity, weakness, strength. We change greatly in experience, but in every new condition we find a promise appropriate to it. The manna of promise covers the path of pilgrimage. 3. *How needful to us.* For our support, guidance, comfort, encouragement, happiness, advance. God's promises are our rods and staffs. Were it not for such upholdings, we should soon sink in the mire. 4. *How precious.* What promises are like unto these? How can we compute the value of that which is invaluable? Divine promises are things by themselves. Nothing could compensate for their loss. Of such value are they that only a God is rich enough to bestow them. 5. *How faithful.* What reliance may be placed upon them! They are all " yea " and " amen " in Christ (ch. i. 20). Promises, indeed, are easily obtained from men, but what men fail in is fulfilment. But the word of Jehovah cannot be broken. His promises are precious, but they are not more precious than sure. 6. Divine promise culminates in such special promises as those given in preceding verses (ch. vi. 16—18): God's engagement to dwell within us; God's continuous adoption of us, whereby we are ever his sons and daughters. If these things be ours, then all things are ours.

II. CONSIDER THE LIFE TO WHICH THESE PROMISES SHOULD LEAD. 1. *Sins of the flesh should be discarded.* If we are God's, our body is the temple of God (ch. vi. 16). Such a temple must be kept pure. Such sins as intemperance, gluttony, lust, etc., must be renounced by the child of God. We are to glorify God in our bodies (1 Cor. vi. 20). Many forget how truly they may do so. Sins of the flesh are defilements of the flesh. If we defile the temple of God, God will not bless us, but curse us (1 Cor. iii. 17). It is not enough to be pure within, we must be pure without also. Our whole being must be consecrated to God and ruled by his laws. 2. *Sins of the spirit must be renounced.* Such sins as pride, malice, wrath, envying, falsehood, idolatry, impure conceptions, etc. Many cleanse the exterior only; they whiten the sepulchre, but trouble not about the dead bones within. Many are quite satisfied with external piety; God is not. Note: Sins of the spirit lead to sins of the flesh, and *vice versâ.* 3. *We are to seek complete holiness.* We are to cleanse ourselves from " all " defilement. We are to " perfect holiness." We are not to be easily satisfied with ourselves. 'Tis not enough to do a little and then rest. The statue must be finished; it is begun that it may be completed. The ideal set before us is a high one. Like the painter, the poet, the orator, we must strive to realize this ideal. We are not to rest until all things have become new. 4. *All should be done in the fear of God.* Our duty to God must influence us more than our own happiness or the welfare of others. True life is a life which is *full of God.* " The fear of the Lord is the beginning of wisdom," and the fear of the Lord runs throughout the truly wise life. Much righteousness is society-satisfying righteousness; social sanction takes the place of Divine; our fellows become our god. In our righteousness we must seek to please and satisfy God. Fear of God's disapprobation will spur us to sterner efforts. 5. *Earnest effort on our part is necessary.* The apostle says, " Let us cleanse ourselves." Many wait for God when God is waiting for them. Our salvation is ascribed to God; nevertheless, we are enjoined to work it out; and our efforts to work out our salvation are the evidence that God is working in us. All cleansing of our life is voluntary on our side; and there is no high spiritual life without *striving.*

III. CONSIDER WHY GOD'S PROMISES SHOULD LEAD TO SUCH A LIFE. 1. *Gratitude.* This is a life well pleasing to God. He in his promises has done how much for us! What is our " reasonable service " ? 2. *The fulfilment of the Divine promises is conditional upon our seeking to live the new life.* Newness of *living* is the evidence of newness of *condition.* God's promises are made to God's people, or to those who sincerely desire to be his people; but if we do not walk in righteousness we have evidently believed in vain. We are then only of the *nominal,* not the *real,* Israel; and the promises are for the latter, not the former. The nominal Jews lost their privileges because they possessed only nominal piety. All God's promises are conditional. If we are not fruit-bearing trees, we must expect not to be cared for, but to be cut down. The promises of God are not for any save those who walk in his fear and love.—H.

Vers. 2—4.—*Christian affection.* I. HINDERS WRONG-DOING. Paul had many reasons for not in any way injuring the Corinthians, but his love for them was certainly one. He loved them too well to wilfully do them any evil. As true love to God leads to obedience to Divine commands and abstention from injuring the Divine kingdom, so love to men leads us to consult their interests. We should love men too well to harm them. This check of love is very beautiful as well as very powerful. It is love, after all, that rules the world; only, alas! it is largely love of self and love of sin.

II. Leads to faithful utterance. The apostle was very outspoken to the Corinthians because of his great love for them. His love rendered silence impossible. If we love our brother much we shall not suffer sin upon him. Blindness and dumbness towards the sins of our brethren are cruelty, not kindness. If we find it practically impossible to admonish the erring, it is not because we love them so much, but because we love them so little. Ministers and teachers should have great boldness of speech. A house-dog is no good unless he barks. A surgeon who never uses the knife deserves few patients. Faithful speech is a true child of the chief of the graces.

III. Should be very intense towards believers, especially towards our spiritual children. The only manacles of the children of God are golden ones. Believers can be truly knit together by love alone. The cement joining together the living stones of God's house is love. Churches without love are scandalous spectacles to the world, dens of misery in themselves, and hateful in the sight of God. But love can make a happy family out of otherwise incongruous elements, and a holy family out of elements still marked by imperfections. A particular affection should be cherished towards those whom we have led to Christ. Paul's affection for his spiritual children was remarkable; yet not greater than ours ought to be. If we love such greatly, we can do much for them; our love to them and special relation will give us power over them. They will need guidance, counsel, possibly admonition. A great love for them will prompt to great efforts on their behalf. Paul's love made him cleave to his converts; they were in his heart "to die together and live together" (ver. 3).

IV. Should be strong enough to bear a great strain. It is very likely to be subjected to this. So easy is it to love when we are loved, deferred to, obeyed, courteously treated; so difficult otherwise. But apostolic love could bear this test (see ch. xii. 15). We are apt to love *ideal* persons, or to suppose that the real persons of our affection have ideal excellences. Love is tested when we discover the many imperfections in the objects of our affection; but love ought to bear the test. Profitably may we remember that, if we see faults in others, they probably see not a few in us.

V. Will often triumph over opposition. If you want to conquer men, love them. Persist in loving the unlovely. Some hearts may not yield even to love, but nothing is likely to bring them so near to yielding. There is mighty power in love. But it must be real, solid, test-bearing, abiding. Paul's great power was love-power.

VI. Brings much joy to those exercising it. It has its pains, but these are chastened. It is the unloving heart which is the unrejoicing heart. Especially is the joy great when this love is reciprocated or begins to triumph. Paul's cup ran over when the Corinthians yielded to his love. He could say, "I overflow with joy in all our affliction" (ver. 4). God is love, and God lives in unsullied bliss. If we were more like God in love we should be more like God in joy. The atmosphere of heaven is love; if we breathe this atmosphere on earth we experience heavenly delight.

VII. Fits us for usefulness. A less loving apostle than Paul could never have done Paul's work. The greatest teacher the world has ever seen was the One who had most love. Love drives us to usefulness and qualifies us for it at the same time. If we would be more educated for Christian service, let us labour to take a higher degree in the university of love. The world wants Christian workers whose hearts are full of apostolic, yea, of Christ-like, love.—H.

Vers. 5—7.—*Ministerial sorrows and their alleviation.* I. Much sorrow is often the portion of ministers of Christ. Arising from various causes, such as: 1. *Bodily weakness.* Some seem to forget that ministers have bodies at all. Certainly many expect them at all times to be ready for their duties. Ministerial work is very trying to bodily strength. And ministerial work is exceedingly painful in bodily sickness and infirmity. Here many ministers bring much sorrow upon themselves by carelessness as to the body. In some Churches it might be a good thing to appoint a deacon whose special function should be to see that the pastor took sufficient open-air exercise. 2. *Mental weariness.* The mind soon tires. The Lord's servant has often to do his work with a flagging brain. Great sorrow is felt when the need of work is seen and the capacity not possessed through exhaustion. 3. *Mental depression.* "Fears within." Sometimes experienced in the very midst of success. When under adverse circumstances, it becomes indeed a Marah of bitterness. 4. *Church troubles.* A Church, carefully planted with prayers and tears and toil, threatened with ruin or with severe injury. Factious opposition—"fightings without." Misrepresentation; ingratitude; division. 5. *The inconsistencies of believers.* The true pastor deeply loves his spiritual children, and can say, "I have no greater joy than to hear that my children walk in truth" (3 John 4). But when they go astray, when they dishonour the cause to which they belong, his anxiety becomes intense and his grief profound; when they grow careless, idle, worldly; when the prayer-meetings and more spiritual gatherings are neglected; when no spirit of zeal burns in their hearts or is manifested in their lives. 6. *The callousness of the impenitent.* When the wave of his own earnestness beats upon the rock of carnality, and is dashed back, leaving the rock as hard and cold as ever. When the very heart of a man is nearly preached out of him, and yet no sign follows. 7. *The opposition of men of the world.* The sneer of the sceptic, and his insidious efforts. The open or covert endeavour of ungodly men to hinder the progress of the truth. 8. *Personal difficulties, doubts, and temptations.* The minister has his own spiritual life to care for, and whilst it might easily be concluded that his special work is pre-eminently favourable to that life, the fact is that ministerial labours involve very special temptations, and that much grace is needed to preserve a spiritual tone. The minister, too, is the favourite target of Satan and of the followers of Satan. These troubles are cumulative. Many, and sometimes all, press at the same time; and yet the all-responsible work of the ministry has to be carried on under such conditions. Well may one cry, "Who is sufficient for these things?"

II. NOTE SOME ALLEVIATIONS OF MINISTERIAL SORROW. 1. *Conviction of the Divine approval.* The faithful minister often has this joy, and may always have it if he will. This is enough to make any man brave in peril, and to cheer any man in heaviest sorrow. This was one of Paul's sheet-anchors. 2. *A good conscience.* If conscience does not condemn, we may pluck up our courage. Still, a man must not conclude too easily that he is faultless. There are some over-contented, non-successful ministers who are a bane to the Church. 3. *Realization of the grandeur of the work.* The soul sinks when this is lost sight of or obscured. The soul rises when the service of Christ is seen in a clear, true light. 4. *Evidences that labour is not in vain.* God sends some Titus with good news. Conversions, causing joy in the presence of the angels of God, cause joy also in the pastor's heart of hearts. Here is infinite compensation for all toil, anxiety, and suffering. 5. *Suitable response of those under charge when appealed to.* Paul's joy was largely caused by the Corinthian response to the First Epistle. When the inconsistent give up much of their inconsistency under pastoral admonition; when the worldly become more spiritual; when the indifferent become earnest;—then the under-shepherd is made glad indeed. 6. *The anticipation of the Master's commendation at last.* Paul ever had regard to "the crown of righteousness." If we can but please our Master, everything else must be a matter of comparative indifference.

Applies to some extent to all Christian workers. All such are "ministers," and in their degree share in ministerial joys and sorrows.—H.

Vers. 8—15.—*Marks of true penitence.* I. TRUE REPENTANCE IS IN CONTRAST WITH THE SORROW OF THE WORLD. It is the fruit of "godly sorrow" (ver. 10). It is sorrow "after a godly sort" (ver. 9), or "according to God." It makes us see sin as *against God.* It is *coming to the mind of God* as to sin. It leads to salvation—to eternal life. It is never the subject of regret, but of thankfulness. The sorrow of the world is not because of sin, but because of its penal consequences. It issues in death because it still holds to the sin. It is a regret that sin in any stage should be so painful. *It would reform hell by banishing its pains, not its wickedness.*

II. IT INVOLVES DEEP SOLICITUDE. (Ver. 11.) Opposed to prior indifference. The Corinthians had regarded their sin as of little importance, but now they feel far otherwise towards it. So unrepentant men boast that they have sinned so little. Job said, "I abhor myself, and repent in dust and ashes." When true penitence is begotten in the heart, the time for carelessness in respect of sin has gone, and the time of carefulness has come. Sin is no longer a light matter, but one most momentous and urgent.

III. RENUNCIATION OF THE EVIL. Thus the Corinthians sought to clear themselves (ver. 11). Before, they had connived; now, they repudiated. True repentance involves a desire to be separate from the sin. The evil thing is renounced. To hold to the evil, whilst we profess to repent of it, is to demonstrate that we do not repent at all.

IV. DETESTATION OF THE EVIL. (Ver. 11.) We may renounce what we still love, but in true penitence the mind is enlightened, the true nature of sin is perceived, and the soul ceases to love and begins to loathe it. Sin is detested, and self is detested because self has sinned. The soul is roused against sin; there is "indignation."

V. FEAR. (Ver. 11.) 1. Of the Divine wrath. 2. Of again sinning.

VI. DESIRE FOR RESTORATION. (Ver. 11.) 1. To the approval of righteous men. 2. To peace with conscience. 3. Above all, to the favour of God.

VII. ZEAL. (Ver. 11.) 1. In immediately taking a right course. 2. In seeking to remedy the effects of sin. 3. For God's honour.

VIII. CONVICTION THAT SIN DESERVES PUNISHMENT. (Ver. 11.) A sense of justice is aroused. It does not seem wrong for the sinner to be punished then, but right. Hearts unstirred by true penitence carp at and question sin-penalties. But "godly sorrow" gives to sin a tongue crying loudly for wrath. When sin is rightly apprehended it becomes an evil for sin *not* to be punished. This applies to ourselves; we condemn ourselves. This applies to others; we feel that they ought to be condemned. "Yea, what avenging!"

IX. A HUMBLE, TEACHABLE SPIRIT. (Ver. 15.) Godly sorrow breaks down pride. The Corinthians before had found fault with the teaching of Paul himself. Now they are willing to be taught by one of his disciples.—H.

Vers. 9—11.—*Two kinds of sorrow.* Reproof works well when it induces sorrow toward God and issues in repentance. But of sorrow there are two kinds.

I. THE SORROW OF THE WORLD. 1. *Its nature.* It is regret for worldly loss, or, if for faults and sins, it is for them as bringing worldly discredit. It is vexation, not for wrong done, so much as for damage incurred, credit spoilt, advantage missed, pride wounded. 2. *Its issues.* It works death. It wears the mind, sours the temper, fills the breast with discontent, takes away all zest of exertion, chokes the heart with resentment and chagrin. It actually kills; a rankling annoyance or shame tends both to embitter and to shorten life. There are more than is commonly believed dying of vexation; as Spenser has it—

"Dying each day with inward wounds of Dolour's dart."

II. SORROW ACCORDING TO GOD. 1. *Its nature.* It springs from a sense of sin in the light of God, and in relation to his Name, Law, and glory. It is the grief of a mind that has learnt to honour, observe, and follow the Lord, and therefore mourns for sin as committed against heaven and in his sight. See the sorrow of the world in King Saul, who, when he was reproved by the prophet, admitted, "I have sinned;" but immediately added this request to Samuel, "Yet honour me now." See the sorrow according to God in King David, who, when he was reproved by a prophet, said, "I have sinned against Jehovah," and then prayed the fifty-first psalm, saying, "Hide thy face from my sins." 2. *Its result.* It works "repentance to salvation," otherwise described as "repentance toward God" and "repentance unto life." The sorrow does not exhaust itself in emotion, but induces a change of mind, a turning from sin to God, and so from death to life. And such repentance will never be regretted. St. Paul had regretted his first letter, but now did not regret it, since he learned the good effect it had produced. A minister of Christ may have to speak sharply to men about their sins. He may have to regret that he evaded such duty or spoke smooth things, but not that he brought trouble to the consciences of sinners or godly sorrow to their hearts. And many a hearer of the Word may have to grieve that he was deaf to reproof, but none that he listened to it and mourned for his sin. No one will ever regret that he repented toward God. 3. *Its further issues and evidences.* The moral earnestness which was connected with sorrow according to and repentance toward God showed itself thus at Corinth. "What carefulness it wrought in you!" What diligence! Blessed is the reproof, healthy is the sorrow, which puts a stop to trifling, and makes us face the reality and feel the seriousness of living in God's sight. We must not then excuse our faults or count them unavoidable, but set about the correction of them with all diligence. "Yea, what a clearing of yourselves!" What solicitude to be right with God! "Yea, what indignation!" What lively abhorrence of evil! "Yea, what fear! yea, what longing desire!" What anxiety to satisfy the apostle, or any servant of God who has brought our sins home to our conscience, that we are and mean to be what he would approve! Thus the effect of godly sorrow is to make the heart tender and affectionate as well as pure. "Yea, what zeal" in reformation! "Yea, what revenge!" What holy severity against sin! When a sinner, charged with his offences against God, stands on his defence, he is fertile in excuses. The sin was a little one; or the motive was not bad; or the provocation or temptation was great; or the circumstances almost compelled him; or he did it without thought; or he did as others do. But when he is convinced of the Holy Ghost and moved with godly sorrow, he has no plea, and does not wish to have any excuse pleaded for him. He wants rather to have revenge upon his sin, and abhors himself on account of it, repenting in dust and ashes. There is no peace for his conscience but in the sin-purging blood of Jesus Christ. When the believer (and this rather than the other is the case which this text suggests) is reproved for grave inconsistency, moral earnestness is roused within him. Not that he is bound to accept the strictures and rebukes of ill-natured and censorious persons who call it faithfulness to find fault freely with their neighbours. But let a righteous man smite him, and he takes it as an excellent oil. As his fault is shown to his conscience, he scorns to excuse it. He breaks off the sin by righteousness, and that with a sort of sacred indignation, not against the reprover, but against the thing reproved. Indeed, a sorrow God-ward for one fault works a repentance for all sin. As Gurnal says, "One spot occasions the whole garment to be washed. A careful man, when he findeth it rain in at one place, sends forth the workmen to look over all the roof. So should the discovery of one fault lead to a general renewal of self-examination and repentance; and sorrow for one sin should rend the heart for all sins."—F.

Ver. 1.—*The practical power of the promises.* The Apostle John gives a very similar counsel. In 1 John iii. 3 he says, "And every man that hath this hope in him purifieth himself, even as he is pure." Our hope is based upon the promises; and the promises which the apostle has been recalling to mind are (1) the indwelling of God; (2) his free reception of us; and (3) his fatherhood and our sonship, with all the love and care and keeping which these involve (ch. vi. 16—18). St. Paul argues in this way—Because you are saved, because you have entered into such a state of privilege, because you are covered by such "exceeding great and precious promises," therefore be in earnest to cleanse yourselves from all evil, watch over all the various forms of conduct, and seek to tone and purify every expression of the life. The expression, "filthiness of the flesh and spirit," needs explanation. St. Paul evidently had in mind the immoralities which are associated with idolatry, and which the Corinthian Church had treated too lightly when brought into their midst by the incestuous member. Writing of the apostle's association with Corinth, Archdeacon Farrar says, "There was one characteristic of heathen life which would come home to him with overwhelming force, and fill his pure soul with infinite pain. It was the gross immorality of a city conspicuous for its depravity even amid the depraved cities of a dying heathenism. Its very name had become a synonym for reckless debauchery. . . . So far from acting as a check upon this headlong immorality, religion had there taken under its immediate protection the very pollutions which it was its highest function to suppress. It was to the converts of this city that he addressed most frequently, and with most solemn warning and burning indignation, his stern prohibition of sensual crime. It was to converts drawn from the reeking haunts of its slaves and artisans that he writes that they too had once been sunk in the lowest depths of sin and shame. It is of this city that we hear the sorrowful admission that in the world of heathendom a pure life and an honest life was a thing well-nigh unknown." Distinguishing between the flesh and the spirit, though these are so subtly related, we may say, "The outward defilement is caused by sins of the *flesh*, or bodily part of man; the inward by those of the *spirit*, such as pride, unbelief, or the like." Dealing comprehensively with the topic suggested by the passage, we may show—

I. THE VARIETY OF THE PROMISES. They are found scattered throughout the sacred

Word, and taking every variety of form. They are sometimes: 1. Involved in the Divine dealings with individuals. 2. At other times they are embodied in doctrinal truths, and found as soon as we try to give those truths practicable applications. 3. And at other times they are words which come to us with the seal of the experience of good men through all the ages. In all God's gracious dealings, as well as in all God's gracious words, lie hid precious and inspiring promises for all who can read aright.

II. THE ADAPTATION OF THE PROMISES. As life advances it comes to us with a great and blessed surprise, that we never pass into circumstances and conditions for which precise promises have not been provided. They are manifestly suited just *for us*, and for just the *conditions* in which we, at any given time, are placed. It seems as if they were fashioned and sent for us and to us.

III. THE ESSENCE OF ALL THE PROMISES. This is given in the promises which St. Paul has been impressing on the Corinthians. It is God's *fatherliness*. All promises are the assurance of our acceptance with God, our sonship with God, and the expression of the love and the faithfulness with which he fulfils his fatherhood. At the heart of every promise lies this declaration, " I will be a Father unto you."

IV. THE MORAL INFLUENCE OF THE PROMISES. They set us upon seeking to be what God would have us be. Assuring *strength* they set us upon *endeavour*. Or, to put the matter in relation to the previous division of the subject, realizing the fatherliness of our God, we are set upon seeking to be true and faithful " sons and daughters " —pure sons of the holy Father, obedient sons of the King-Father, loving sons of the loving Father, very sensitive to the things that are unworthy of him, and very earnest in the endeavour to put them wholly away from us.

V. THE COMFORTING POWER OF THE PROMISES. This may be added to complete the treatment of the subject, though it is not the point set forth prominently by the apostle, and is a familiar topic. The true comforting, however, of God's promises only can come to those who carry out the Christian duties, walk worthily of the Lord, and need grace and upholding and cheer in their Christian conflict.—R. T.

Ver. 1.—*Our great life-work.* " Perfecting holiness in the fear of God." The former clause of the verse indicates one side of Christian duty—the putting away of sin ; this presents the other side—the putting on of holiness. We must " put off the old man, which is corrupt, according to the deceitful lusts." We must " put on the new man, which, after God, is created in righteousness and true holiness." Melvill says, " At present the believer is like the marble in the hands of the sculptor ; but though day by day he may give fresh touches and work the marble into greater emulation of the original, the resemblance will be far from complete until death. Each fresh degree of likeness is a fresh advance toward perfection. It must then be that when every feature is moulded into similitude, when all traces of feebleness and depravity are swept away for ever, the statue breathes, and the picture burns with Deity,—it must be that then we ' shall be filled.' We shall look on the descending Mediator, and as though the ardent gaze drew down celestial fire, we shall seem instantly to pass through the refiner's furnace, and, leaving behind all the dishonour of the grave, and all the dross of corruptible humanity, spring upwards an ethereal, rapid, glowing thing—Christ's image, extracted by Christ's lustre." The apostle had been speaking of the temple, and of Christians as Divine temples, and so his idea of " holiness " was chiefly " consecration," "separation unto God," "entire devotement to God." Treating the perfecting of holiness as a continuous work, to which the whole of the Christian life and effort must be given, we consider—

I. THE INITIAL STAGE. The *winning* of holiness. There is some danger of confusing justification with sanctification. The distinction between the two may be simply expressed if we say that a man must be *set right* before he can *go right*. Regeneration is the setting of our will right with God. Justification is the setting us in the right standing with God. These stand at the very threshold of the holy life, and there is no entrance to it by any other way. Regarded from another point of view, the act of solemn personal decision for God and consecration to his service is the winning of holiness, the beginning of the godly life.

II. THE CONTINUOUS STAGE. The beginning is a frail and feeble thing. Good so far as it goes, and full of hopefulness ; but needing growth, culture, perfecting. In

New Testament Scriptures the word "perfect" stands for "whole," "entire," in opposition to "one-sided," to imperfect developments of parts, to monstrosities; and so it is suggestive of the many-sided forms in which the perfecting of holiness must be carried on. The Christian has to win *holiness* in thought, expression of thought in word, in conduct, in relations. He is even to keep before him this unattainable ideal, "Be ye holy, even as I am holy," saith the Lord. And the perfect holiness is no merely cleaned surface, whitened free of all old stains of sin and self; it is that whitened surface painted all over with the infinite grace and purity and goodness of the Lord Christ. It is being free of the old image, but it is also being changed into *his* image. Whether the "perfect holiness" has ever been attained by any man while he dwelt among the shadows of the earthly can never be known, for the best of men will say to their dying days as did David, "My goodness extendeth not to thee, only to the saints that are in the earth." Enough for us to know that it is a lifelong pursuit, the cry of the soul as long as the soul can cry, the endeavour of the life so long as the life endures. Only when passed through shall we know that we are holy; and then "he that is holy may be holy still."

III. THE INSPIRATION OF THE ENDEAVOUR AFTER HOLINESS. "In the fear of God." With the ever-present thought of him who is revealed as the "consuming fire." The fear of offending God, and the desire to please God, are necessary elements in the process of sanctification. F. W. Robertson says, "We cannot do without awe; there is no depth of character without it. Tender motives are not enough to restrain from sin."—R. T.

Ver. 4.—*A minister's joy in tribulation.* The intensity of the apostle's language is explained by the intensity of his feelings in relation to the Corinthians. He loved them greatly, and was ready to make any sacrifices for them. And he was proportionately grieved when the news came, through Titus, of the way in which evil men were trying to destroy his character and his influence. The tribulation he here refers to is chiefly this mental distress and the bodily suffering which it involved. His great relief in circumstances of so much distress was that the Corinthian Church, as a whole, had received his first letter in a right spirit. He could be joyful in this, even amidst his tribulation. Two points may receive illustration.

I. THE TRIBULATION COMES FROM ANXIETY CONCERNING SPIRITUAL WELL-BEING. Precisely this is the minister's sphere. His interest is in the moral and spiritual condition of those who are set in his charge. But this is the most serious and overwhelming of all burdens that can be laid upon a man's heart and effort. If we estimate what the due maintenance and culture of our own spiritual life involves, we may understand how great is the anxiety of Christian ministers who watch over souls as well as watch for souls. Illustrate by Samuel Rutherford's intense expression of feeling, "God is my witness that your salvation would be two salvations to me, and your heaven two heavens to me." Show what a strain upon nervous constitutions the pressure of the ministry becomes in these our days.

II. THE JOY COMES FROM DUE RESPONSE MADE TO EFFORTS FOR SPIRITUAL WELL-BEING. Compare other expressions by apostles : *e.g.* "I have no greater joy than to hear that my children walk in truth;" "What is our joy or crown of rejoicing? Are not even ye in the presence of our Lord Jesus at his coming? For ye are our glory and our joy." The minister has, in the culture of spiritual life, to use truth, warnings, threatenings, as well as comfortings and inspirings; and his joy is ever this—his people are open-hearted to receive, are humble enough to regard what he may say, and earnest enough to obey. No earthly joy is like that which they know who help their brethren to truth and purity and God.—R. T.

Vers. 9, 10.—*Godly sorrow; or, the sorrow that is after the will of God.* Reference is to the distress which the more spiritual members of the Corinthian Church felt on the receipt of St. Paul's first letter. He had written severely, and, after sending his letter, almost regretted that he had expressed himself so strongly; but he now felt thankful to hear that they had so well responded to his appeals, and sorrowed unto repentance and putting away of the evil in a manner that would be so certainly approved by God. "The series of emotional words in ver. 11 represent the apostle's

estimate of what he had heard from Titus.   There was (1) *earnestness* where there
had been indifference to evil, and even approval of it (1 Cor. v. 2); and this was shown
(2) in the *vindication* of their conduct which they had sent through Titus; and (3) in
their stern 'indignation' against the offender; (4) in their fear, partly of the supernatural chastisement which St. Paul had threatened, partly of the judgment of God
which was against such things; (5) in the *longing* to have him once more among
them, which mingled with their fear; (6) in their new *zeal* for the law of purity; (7) in
their actual *vengeance*, i.e. their sentence of condemnation passed upon the offender."
"The apostle rejoiced, not that the Corinthians sorrowed, but that they sorrowed unto
repentance.   Sorrow has two results—it may end in spiritual life or in spiritual death;
and in themselves one of these is as natural as the other.   Sorrow may produce two
kinds of reformation : a transient or a permanent one; an alteration in habits, which,
originating in emotion, will last so long as that emotion continues, and then, after a
few fruitless efforts, be given up; a repentance which will be repented of; or again,
a permanent change which will be reversed by no after-thought—a repentance not to
be repented of."   Beza says, "The 'sorrow of the world' is the certain way to desperation, unless God prevent it, as appears from the horrid examples of Cain, Saul,
Ahithophel, and Judas; but the written tears of David give the clearest example of
the other kind of sorrow."

I. The distinction between remorse and repentance.   The word "remorse"
has in it the figure of "biting back," and it means going over our sins in thought, with
a keen gnawing regret at having done them, but without any softened feelings such as
belong to the penitent.   Remorse is exactly that "sorrow of the world" which worketh
death.   Repentance is that humble, regretful spirit which sets a man ready to receive
and to value the Divine forgiveness.

II. The tests of genuine repentance in the individual.   They are : 1. Mental
distress.   2. Humility and self-abasement.   3. Confession without attempt at excuses.
4. Earnest seeking of Divine forgiveness.   5. Resolute putting away of the evil.   6.
Keen watchfulness over the circumstances that involve temptation to the sin.   7. And
an attitude of simple and unquestioning obedience to the will of God, and submission
to whatever judgments on the sin it may please him to appoint.   "Sorrow has done its
work when it deters from evil.   In the sorrow of the world the obliquity of the heart
towards evil is not cured; it seems as if nothing cured it; heart-ache and trials come
in vain; the history of life at last is what it was at first.   Sorrow avails only when the
past is converted into experience, and from failure lessons are learned which never are
to be forgotten."

III. The tests of genuine repentance in a Church.   These more especially
are dealt with in the passage before us.   Bengel says that the six results mentioned by
the apostle fall into pairs.   The first two relate to their feelings towards themselves,
the next to their feelings towards the apostle, the last to their feelings towards the
offender and his offence.   The tests we notice are (1) clearings, earnest efforts to put
away the wrong, and to show that they had no complicity in it, and would make no
excuses for it; (2) anxiety for each other, that the membership may be quite purified,
and no brother cherish even a secret sympathy with the wrong; (3) discipline on the
wrong-doer, by at least a temporary removal of him from the Church fellowship.   The
penitence of a Church will also find expression in united acts of confession and humiliation, and in prayer for Divine forgiveness and restoration.   Perhaps much too little is
made in these days of the united acts of the corporate Church life.   There is a befitting
Church penitence, a proper godly sorrow of a community, when, by any evil of its
members, such a community has become defiled.—R. T.

Ver. 12.—*Apostolic cares.*   "Our care of you in the sight of God might appear unto
you."   The apostle always used the persuasion of his affection, whenever it was
possible, rather than the force of his apostolic authority.   Elsewhere he pleads thus :
"Not that we have dominion over your faith, but are helpers of your joy."   And he
speaks of "that which cometh upon me daily, the care of all the Churches."   We
may compare the care of a wise and faithful mother for the well-being of her children,
and the burden of thought and interest which they are to her every day.   The apostle's
care concerned three things.

I. PURITY. Of this he was supremely zealous. Christians must be seen to differ essentially from pagan idolaters. Immorality and uncleanness were directly associated with heathenism, and were even consecrated by idolatrous religions; but there must be no possibility of questioning that the Christian Church was "called *unto holiness*." "Every member must know how to possess his vessel in sanctification and honour." There must be no "touching of the unclean thing."

II. EDIFICATION. Security for the Christian lies in continuous growth. This, indeed, is the law of all life. When a thing ceases to grow it begins to die. The growth or upbuilding of the plant is St. Paul's supreme anxiety; and he evidently feared that the Corinthians must have been neglecting their spiritual culture, seeing they could suffer such evils to come in amongst them. Fungus-growths only attack trees in which the vitality is lowered.

III. WITNESS. St. Paul expects the Churches to make positive and active testimony to all around them. That witness can only be a fitting one and a powerful one as the Church is kept pure. So St. Paul is moved with so much anxiety for the clearing of the Corinthians. He wants the light that shines from them on all the heathen world around to be a pure light, clear, white, in no way dimmed, and therefore he can rejoice that they have so fully responded to his supreme *care* on their behalf.—R. T.

Ver. 16.—*Apostolic confidence ;* or the fulness of the *restoration* man may make to follow on his forgiveness of his fellow-men. "I rejoice, therefore, that I have confidence in you in all things." F. W. Robertson says, "We learn from this the value of explanations. Had St. Paul left the matter unsettled, or only half settled, there never could have been a hearty understanding between him and the Corinthians. Whenever there is a misunderstanding between man and man, the true remedy is a direct and open request for explanation." This sentence closes the apostle's reference to a very painful subject; he wishes it now to be put quite away, out of thought, and so he assures the Corinthians that no relic of suspicion or fear is left in his mind; he restores them fully to his affection and esteem; he has "confidence in them in all things." Now, in this complete restoration of the Corinthians to favour we see that man may be the shadow of God, and his forgiveness and full reconciliation may help his fellow-men to realize the fulness of the restoration which God gives to the penitent. He puts our sins behind his back. He casts them into the depths of the sea. He separates them from us as far as the east is from the west. He remembers them no more against us for ever. He blots out our transgressions as a cloud, and our iniquities as a thick cloud. The figure of our God is the father in the parable of the prodigal son, who brings the penitent and forgiven son into the old place at the family table, dresses him in the son's robes, and gives him such a welcome as will show the sad past to be all forgiven and forgotten. It should be a serious thought to us that men may take their ideas of God's dealing with them from the manner of *our* dealing with them. If they find that we cannot forgive and forget, and wholly restore confidence, it will be very hard for them to believe that God can. Three points of man's dealing with man, especially of the Christian man's dealing with his fellow-Christian, may be taken as representing God's dealings with us. In these we may be ourselves examples of God.

I. MAN WITHDRAWING CONFIDENCE BECAUSE OF CHERISHED SIN. God never passes by sin, and we must not. Every Church member should be quickly sensitive to the inconsistencies and sins of his fellow-members. If the sin is kept and cherished there ought to be withdrawal of confidence, for whenever his people cherish sin there is a cloud passes before God and hides his face from them.

II. MAN ENDEAVOURING TO INFLUENCE FOR THE PUTTING AWAY OF SIN. Falling into transgression ought to set our brothers upon our Christian love and effort. Erring brothers must not be left to go in their evil ways. Illustrate from St. Paul's efforts to bring the incestuous man to repentance. Too often Churches are more eager to exercise discipline than to attempt recovery, and labour to secure repentance. "Ye that are spiritual restore such a one in the spirit of meekness."

III. MAN RESTORING TO CONFIDENCE WHEN THE SIN IS PUT AWAY. This we have illustrated in the hearty words of the apostle. Speaking of Newman's sentence, "A true penitent never forgives himself," F. W. Robertson says, "A false estimate of the gospel of Christ and of the heart of man! A proud remorse does not forgive itself the forfeiture of its own dignity; but it is the very beauty of the penitence which is according to God that at last the sinner, realizing God's forgiveness, does learn to forgive himself." And help to this "self-forgiving" we can render if we show to the sincere penitent the heartiness of our forgiveness and restoration.—R. T.

EXPOSITION.

CHAPTER VIII.

Liberality shown by the Macedonian Churches (vers. 1—5). He is sending Titus to receive their contribution for the Church of Jerusalem, and he invites them to give according to their power (vers. 6—15). Recommendation of Titus and the other delegates (vers. 16—24).

These two chapters (viii. and ix.) form an independent section of the Epistle. The *plural* alone ("we") is used throughout; participial and unfinished constructions abound; the style is a little embarrassed; and various words, such as "grace," "blessing," "righteousness," "simplicity," occur in somewhat unusual shades of meaning. All this arises: 1. From St. Paul's natural delicacy in alluding to pecuniary subjects. 2. From a desire to conciliate the Corinthians, while at the same time he cannot conceal from them a little apprehension that they were rather more forward and zealous in words than in deeds. Their large promises had led him to speak of them in a way which seemed unlikely to be justified by the fulfilment. He was thus more or less under the influence of conflicting emotions. Out of patriotism (Rom. ix. 3) and compassion, and an effort to fulfil an old pledge (Gal. ii. 10), and a desire to conciliate and, if possible, win over the affection of the Jewish Church—which had been much alienated from him by differences of opinion and by assiduous calumnies—and from a wish to show that his Gentile converts were faithful and loving brethren (Rom. xv. 31), he was intensely anxious that the contribution should be a large one. This feeling is apparent, not only throughout every line of this appeal, with the solemn topics which it introduces, but also in all his other allusions to the subject (Rom. xv. 26; 1 Cor. xvi.; Acts xx. 22; xxi. 4, etc.). On the other hand, he was careful lest he should seem to have even the most distant personal aims, and lest he should lay on his Gentile converts a wholly unfamiliar burden.

Ver. 1.—**We do you to wit**; rather, *we make known to you*. The phrase is like the modern "I wish to inform you." In this and the next chapter St. Paul, having fully spoken of the joy which had been caused to him by their reception of his first letter, and having said as much as he then intended to say in answer to the charges insinuated against him, proceeds to give directions about the collection for the poor saints at Jerusalem. He had already spoken of it (1 Cor. xvi. 1—4), but feared that they were behindhand, and now sends Titus to stimulate their zeal. The style throughout is brief and allusive, because he had already, in various ways, brought this matter fully before them. Throughout this section he shows in a remarkable degree the tact, courtesy, high sense of honour, and practical wisdom which were among his many gifts. The "but" with which the chapter begins in the original is St. Paul's ordinary formula of transition, as in 1 Cor. vii. 1; xii. 1; xiii. 1, etc. (For the phrase, "we inform you," see 1 Cor. xii. 3; xv. 1.) It is one of numberless incidental proofs of the genuineness of this group of Epistles—the Epistles of the second great missionary journey—that the same words, phrases, and thoughts constantly recur in them. **The grace of God** (see next note). **Bestowed on the Churches of Macedonia**; rather, *which is being bestowed in the Churches*. St. Paul wants to tell the Corinthians how extremely liberal the Macedonians have been, since it was his custom to stir up one Church by the example of another (ch. ix. 2); but he begins by speaking of their generosity as a proof of' the grace which they are receiving from the Holy Spirit. *The Churches of Macedonia.* The only Macedonian Churches of which we have any details in the New Testament are those of Philippi, Thessalonica, and Berœa. They seem to have been peculiarly dear to St. Paul, who was attracted by their cheerfulness in affliction and their generosity in the midst of want.

Ver. 2.—**In a great trial of affliction**; rather, *in much testing of affliction*; i.e. in an affliction which put to the proof their Christian character. "They were not simply afflicted," says St. Chrysostom, "but in such a way as also to become approved by their endurance." (For the word rendered "trial," see Rom. v. 4, and in this Epistle, ch. ii. 9; ix. 13; xiii. 3.) "Affliction" seems to have befallen the Churches of Macedonia very heavily (1 Thess. i. 6; ii. 14), chiefly through the jealousy of the Jews, who excited the hatred of the Gentiles (Acts xvi. 20; xvii. 5, 13). **The abundance of their joy.** Another reference to joy in sadness (see on ch. vii. 4). There is not the least necessity to understand the verb "is" or "was" after this clause. "The abundance . . . abounded" is indeed a pleonasm, but is not at all unlike the style of St. Paul. He means to say that their joy overflowed their affliction, and their liberality overflowed their poverty (Mark xii. 44). **Their deep poverty**; literally, *their pauperism to the depth;* their abysmal penury. Though they were βαθύπτωχοι, they showed themselves in generosity to be βαθύπλουτοι. Stanley refers to Arnold's 'Roman Commonwealth,' where he mentions that the provinces of Macedonia and Achaia, which had suffered greatly in the three civil wars, appealed successfully to Tiberius for a diminution of their burdens. The gift of the Macedonians was like the widow's mite (Luke xxi. 3, 4, where similar words occur—*perisseuo, husterema*). **Of their liberality**; rather, *of their singleness of purpose* or *simplicity* (Eph. vi. 5). The "grace" and single-heartedness to which he alludes *showed* themselves in liberality.

Ver. 3.—**They were willing of themselves.** "Of their own accord," as in ver. 17. The verb in the original is energetically omitted, with the "they gave" of ver. 5. St. Paul does not mean that the notion of making the collection *originated* with them (ch. ix. 2), but only that they displayed a voluntary energy in carrying it out.

Ver. 4.—**Praying us.** The entreaties came from them, not from me. **That we would receive.** These words are almost certainly an explanatory gloss. The translation then is, "begging us for the grace of participation in this ministration to the saints." They were so willing in the matter that they entreated me, as a favour (χάρις), to allow them to have a share in this contribution, because it was to be given to the saints, that is, the suffering poor in the Church of Jerusalem. This Church suffered from chronic poverty. Even the Jewish population were liable to famines, in one of which they had only been kept alive by the royal munificence of a proselyte, Queen Helena, of Adiabene. The Christians would, of course, suffer even more deeply, because they were drawn from the humblest classes and had fewer friends. This was one of the reasons why, as an act of common humanity, it was incumbent on the Gentile Christians to help them (Acts xi. 29; Rom. xv. 25, 26). St. Paul had already brought the subject to the notice of the Corinthians (1 Cor. xvi. 1—4).

Ver. 5.—**Not as we hoped**; rather, *not as we expected.* They were so poor that it was

impossible to expect much from them, but they surpassed my expectations in every way. The Church of Philippi, perhaps under the influence of Lydia, was remarkable for generosity, and was the only Church from which St. Paul would accept any personal help (Phil. ii. 25; iv. 15—18). **First.** "They gave *themselves* to the Lord, which is the best of all, and they gave themselves as helpers to us also—by the will of God." (For a similar use of "and" to imply a matter of less importance, see Acts xv. 28.) The phrase, "by the will of God," implies a thanksgiving to God for the grace which enabled them to give themselves to him, and their goods to his saints. Being "a peculiar people," they naturally showed themselves "zealous of good works" (Titus ii. 14). *First* (Rom. i. 16; ii. 9, 10).

Ver. 6.—**Insomuch that.** Their liberality encouraged me so greatly that I exhorted Titus to return to Corinth once more, and see whether he could not receive some proof that you were equally liberal. The remarks that follow are full of delicate reserve, but under their exquisite tact and urbanity we can perceive that the Corinthians had *talked* very loudly about their contributions, and had promised with great zeal, but had shown themselves somewhat slack in redeeming their promises. **We exhorted Titus.** It is curious that this word is constantly used of the missions of Titus (ver. 17; ch. xii. 18; 1 Cor. xvi. 12). **As he had begun.** "That as he inaugurated (this collection), so he would also complete towards you this gracious work also." Among other works of grace which Titus might complete by returning to them from Macedonia was the kindly collection which he had begun to set on foot in his previous visit (ch. xii. 18).

Ver. 7.—**Therefore**; rather, *but.* In the following verses to ver. 15 he tells them his wishes about this collection. He desires them to show generosity among their other graces (ver. 7), not by way of command, but that they may emulate others and show their love (ver. 8) by following the example of Christ (ver. 9). And by acting thus they would prove the sincerity of their former promises (vers. 10, 11), especially as he did not wish them to give more than they could justly spare by way of reciprocity (vers. 12—15). **As ye abound in every thing, in faith, etc.** Perhaps "by faith," etc., "St. Paul," says Grotius, "knew the art of the orators to move by praising." This method of conciliating attention is technically called *proparaitēsis.* The praise was, of course, sincere, though, no doubt, it was expressed with the generosity of love (see 1 Cor i. 5). **And in your love to us.** The Greek is more emphatic, "and by the love from you in us;" *i.e.* by the love which streams from you, and which I feel in myself. **In this grace also**; namely, the grace of Christian liberality.

Ver. 8.—**Not by commandment.** St. Paul felt an honourable sensibility which prevented him from straining his authority by *urging* the Corinthians to give of their substance. Among Gentiles such contributions towards the needs of others — the result of unselfish compassion—were all but unknown. **The forwardness**; *i.e.* the ready zeal. **The sincerity**; more literally, *the genuineness.*

Ver. 9.—**The grace of our Lord Jesus Christ.** The word "grace," as in vers. 4, 6, 7, here means "gracious beneficence." **Though he was rich** (John xvi. 15; Eph. iii. 8). **Became poor.** The aorist implies the concentration of his self-sacrifice in a single act. **By his poverty.** The word " his" in the Greek implies the *greatness* of Christ. The word for "poverty" would, in classical Greek, mean "pauperism" or "mendicancy." Dean Stanley (referring to Milman's 'Latin Christianity,' v. bk. xii. c. 6) points out how large a place this verse occupied in the mediæval controversies between the moderate and the extreme members of the mendicant orders. William of Ockham and others, taking the word "poverty" in its extremest sense, maintained that the Franciscans ought to possess *nothing*; but Pope John XXII., with the Dominicans, took a more rational view of the sense and of the historic facts.

Ver. 10.—**And herein I give my advice**; *and in this matter I offer an opinion* (*only*). **For this is expedient for you.** It is more to your advantage that I should merely suggest and advise you about the matter than command you. **Who have begun**; rather, *seeing that you formerly began.* The verb is the same as in ver. 6. **Not only to do, but also to be forward**; rather, *not only to do, but also to be willing.* The "to do" is in the aorist, the "to be willing" in the present. We should naturally have expected a reversed order, "not only to be willing, but also to put in action." There must be a strong touch of irony in the words, unless we interpret it to mean "not only to make the collection, but to be willing to add yet more to it." Perhaps in the "to be willing" lies the notion of "the cheerful giver," "the willing mind" (ch. ix. 7; 1 Tim. vi. 17—19). **A year ago**; rather, *since the previous year;* i.e. last year (ch. ix. 2). They had probably begun to collect in the previous Easter, and it was now soon after Tisri, or September, the beginning of the Jewish civil year.

Ver. 11.—**Now therefore perform the doing** of it, etc.; "but now complete also the actual work, in order that, as was the readiness of the willing, so may be also the completion according to your means." **Out of that which ye have.** This, and not "out of your

ability," is probably the right reading, as we see from the next verse.

Ver. 12.—**For if there be first a willing mind**, etc. "For if the readiness is forthcoming, it is acceptable," etc. In other words, God considers not *quantum*, but *ex quanto;* not the magnitude of the gift, but the proportion which it bears to the means of the giver.

Ver. 13.—**And ye be burdened**; literally, *for not that there may be relief to others, but to you affliction.* In other words, I have no wish that you should *distress* yourselves to set others at ease. You must not suspect me of Jewish proclivities which would lead me to impoverish you to provide luxuries for the Christians at Jerusalem. Others refer it to the Macedonians: "I do not wish to burden you, but the Macedonians, who are poor, have contributed, and if you join them in this good work now, they may help you hereafter." But there is no hint of this anywhere.

Ver. 14.—**But by an equality**, etc. The verse, like so many in this chapter, is expressed very elliptically: "But by a reciprocal fairness in the present case, your superabundance to their lack, that also their superabundance may be in proportion to your lack, that there may come to be reciprocal fairness." St. Paul may possibly be thinking of the reciprocity of spiritual and temporal benefits, as in Rom. xv. 27; but if so he leaves the thought unexpressed. The application of the text to "works of supererogation" (Art. XIV.), as forming a fund at the disposal of the hierarchy in the way of indulgences, pardons, etc., is a singular perversion. The passage has been pointed out by Dean Stanley as one which indicates a *possible* acquaintance with the writings of Aristotle.

Ver. 15.—**As it is written** (Exod. xvi. 17, 18, LXX.). The reference is to the gathering of manna.

Ver. 16.—**Which put**; rather, *which giveth.* The zeal is *continuous.* **The same earnest care.** The same in the heart of Titus as in my own.

Ver. 17.—**The exhortation.** My request that he would undertake this task. **Being more forward.** Because he was more earnestly zealous than I had ever ventured to hope, he went spontaneously. (On the word *authairetos,* see ver. 3.)

Ver. 18.—**The brother, whose praise is in the gospel.** The phrase means, "whose worth is praised wherever the glad tidings are preached." There can be no reference to any of the four written Gospels, for they were not in the hands of Christians till a later date; nor did the word "gospel" acquire this significance till afterwards. From Acts xx. 5, it is somewhat precariously inferred that

St. Luke is meant. Others have conjectured Barnabas, Silas (who are out of the question), Erastus, Mark, a brother of Titus, etc. St. Luke is not unlikely to have been selected as a delegate by the Church of Philippi; but further than this we can say nothing. St. Luke was not a Macedonian by birth, and any Macedonian (*e.g.* Aristarchus, Sopater, Secundus, Epaphroditus) seems to be excluded by ch. ix. 4. Paley notes it as curious that the *object* of St. Paul's journey to Jerusalem, which is so prominent in this group of Epistles, is only mentioned indirectly and incidentally by St. Luke (Acts xxiv. 17) in the Acts of the Apostles.

Ver. 19.—Chosen. The word (literally, *chosen by show of hands*) implies a popular vote (comp. 1 Cor. xvi. 3, 4). This brother was not only widely known and valued, but also specially selected for this task. To travel with us. "As our fellow-traveller." The word occurs in Acts xix. 29. With this grace. The better reading is "in:" "in this matter of kindness." To the glory of the same Lord. The word "same" should be omitted. And declaration of your ready mind. The best reading is "our," and the clause should be rendered, *to further the glory of the Lord and our readiness.*

Ver. 20.—Avoiding this. The object in sending Titus and the brother was to cut away the possibility of blame and suspicion. The word "avoiding" (*stellomenoi*) literally means "furling sail," and then "taking precautions." It may, however, mean "making this arrangement" (see 2 Thess. iii. 6). Too much stress has been laid on St. Paul's "use of nautical terms" (Acts xx. 20; Gal. ii. 12, etc.). They belong, in fact, to the very phraseology of the Greek language. That no man should blame us (see ch. vi. 3). St. Paul here sets a valuable and necessary example to all Christians who are entrusted with the management of charitable funds. It is their duty to take every step which may place them above the possibility of of suspicion. Their management of the sums entrusted to them should be obviously and transparently business-like and honourable. St. Paul taught this behaviour both by example and by precept (Rom. xii. 17; Phil. iv. 8). There is such a thing as a

foolish and reprehensible indifference to public opinion (1 Pet. ii. 12). Yet with all his noble carefulness, St. Paul did not escape this very slander (ch. xii. 18). In this abundance. The word, which occurs here only, means literally "succulence," but in the LXX. the adjective means "rich" (1 Kings i. 9). It here implies that the sum which had been collected by St. Paul's exertion was a large one.

Ver. 21. — Honest things. The word "honest" means "honourable" (Rom. xii. 17; Prov. iii. 4, LXX.). Not only in the sight of the Lord. Such precautions would be unnecessary if others were not concerned, for God knows our honesty (ch. v. 11). But also before men. Although the text "avoid all *appearance* of evil" should be rendered "avoid every species of evil," the mistranslation conveys a wise lesson. "In a field of melons," says the Chinese proverb, "do not stoop to tie your shoe;" for that will *look* as if you wanted to steal one of the melons.

Ver. 22.—Our brother. It is impossible to conjecture with any certainty who was the brother thus warmly eulogized. Clement, Epænetus, Apollos, Luke, Zenas, Sosthenes, Trophimus, and Tychicus have all been suggested. Stanley conjectures that the two who accompanied Titus were the Ephesians Tychicus and Trophimus (Acts xx. 4; xxi. 9; 2 Tim. iv. 12; Eph. vi. 21; Titus iii. 12; Col. iv. 7).

Ver. 23.—Whether any do inquire of Titus; literally, *whether about Titus*, or, *as to Titus*; i.e. "if I speak about Titus." (For the phrase, comp. ch. i. 6, 8; 2 Thess. ii. 1.) Titus, long afterwards, was delegated on a similar mission to Crete (Titus i. 1—5; ii. 15). My partner and fellow-helper concerning you; rather, *my associate* (Philem. 17) *and, as regards you, my fellow-worker.* Messengers; literally, *apostles.* The word is used in its original and untechnical sense of delegates (Phil. ii. 25; Rom. xvi. 7). The glory of Christ. Men whose work and worth redound to Christ's honour (Gal. i. 24).

Ver. 24.—Of your love. Not only of your love "to me," but of your brotherly love in general. And of our boasting. Show to the Church that my boasting of you was justifiable.

HOMILETICS.

Vers. 1—9.—*Genuine beneficence* (1). "Moreover, brethren, we do you to wit of the grace of God," etc. The subject of these words is *genuine beneficence,* and they suggest certain general truths concerning it.

I. THAT ALL GENUINE BENEFICENCE IN MAN IS FROM GOD. "Moreover, brethren, we do you to wit of [we make known to you] the grace of God." All that is loving and generous in all moral beings is from one Source, and that is God. He is the primal Font whence all flows. Wherever you see love, in young or old, rich or poor, cultured or rude, you see an emanation from and a reflection of the Eternal. As you may see the ocean in a dewdrop, you may see God in every throb of affection in human souls.

II. THAT IN SOME MEN IT IS MORE STRONGLY DEVELOPED THAN IN OTHERS. According to St. Paul, the "Churches of Macedonia" displayed it in a remarkable degree. It would seem from what Paul says concerning the beneficence of the Macedonian Churches that it was: 1. *Self-sacrificing.* "How that in a great trial of affliction the abundance of their joy and their deep poverty abounded unto the riches of their liberality." It would seem from this that they could ill afford—as the phrase is—to render any help in the way of property to others, and yet their contributions "abounded unto the riches of their liberality." 2. *Spontaneous.* "They were willing of themselves." They were not pressed into it by outward appeals. The only pressure was from love within. 3. *Earnest.* "Praying us with much entreaty that we would receive the gift." Instead of giving because they were besought by others to do so, they themselves besought the reception of their gifts. They might have presented plausible reasons for withholding their contributions to this charity. They might have pleaded *distance,* and said, "Jerusalem is a long way off, and charity begins at home." They might have pleaded *lack of personal knowledge,* and have said, "We are utterly unacquainted with any of these saints at Jerusalem;" or they might have pleaded their own affliction or poverty. But instead of that, they earnestly seized the opportunity to render what help they could. 4. *Religious.* "And this they did, not as we hoped, but first gave their own selves to the Lord, and unto us by the will of God." "This means," says a modern expositor, "of course, that they had done what was far beyond his hopes. And here the point lies in the fact that they gave, not their money only, but themselves, their time, thought, energy, primarily to Christ as their Lord, and then to the apostle as his minister. And this they had done because they allowed the will of God to work upon their will." Consecration of self to God is at once the cause and virtue of all our gifts to men. Unless we give ourselves to God, all our gifts to men are morally worthless.

III. THAT THOSE IN WHOM IT IS MOST STRONGLY DEVELOPED MIGHT BE URGED AS AN EXAMPLE TO OTHERS. Paul here holds up the beneficence of the Macedonians as an example to stimulate the charity of the Corinthians. It would seem that the Church at Corinth had, through the influence of Titus, commenced a subscription for the poor at Jerusalem, and that Titus was about to return in order to obtain larger contributions. The charity of the Macedonian Churches Paul quotes as an example in order to help forward the work. His argument seems to be this—You have the advantages of the Churches at Macedonia in many things; you "abound in everything," you are wealthy, they are poor; your endowments are greater than theirs, your "faith, and utterance, and knowledge," and "in your love to us;" this being so, "See that ye abound in this grace also;" see that you excel in your contributions to this charity. It is wise and well to hold up the good example of others to stimulate men to a holy emulation. The good deeds of other men are amongst the Divine forces to purify and ennoble our own characters.

IV. THAT THE HIGHEST EXAMPLE OF IT WE HAVE IN THE LIFE OF JESUS CHRIST. "For ye know the grace of our Lord Jesus Christ," etc. Christ is the supreme Model of philanthropy. 1. *His philanthropy was self-sacrificing.* "Though he was rich, yet for your sakes he became poor." Observe: (1) He was rich in material wealth before he came into the world. It is of material wealth that the apostle is speaking. (2) His existence on earth was that of material poverty. "The foxes have holes," etc. (3) He passed voluntarily from one stage to another. "For your sakes he became poor." Of all the myriads of men that have appeared on this earth, and that will appear, he alone had the choosing of his circumstances, and he chose poverty. 2. *His philanthropy aimed supremely at the promotion of spiritual wealth.* "That ye through his poverty might be rich." Rich spiritually. Great is the difference between spiritual wealth and material. (1) The one is absolutely *valuable,* the other is not. (2) The one is essential to *happiness,* the other is not. (3) The one is *within the reach of all,* the other is not.

Vers. 10—15.—*Genuine beneficence* (2). "And herein I give my advice," etc. In these verses there is a continuation of the subject presented in the preceding passage, viz. *genuine beneficence.* And there are three further remarks suggested concerning this all-important subject.

I. It is the embodying of the beneficent desire in contributions for the good of others. "Herein I give my advice [judgment]: for this is expedient for you, who have begun before [who were the first to make a beginning], not only to do, but also to be forward a year ago. Now therefore perform [complete] the doing of it; that as there was a readiness to will, so there may be a performance [completion] also out of that which ye have." They had shown the will to contribute, for they had "a year ago" commenced their subscriptions. Now Paul exhorts them to go on and complete the work. "As there was a readiness to will, so there may be a performance." The mere generous will is good in itself, but is not enough; it requires to be embodied in deeds. Every good desire requires embodiment: 1. *For our own sake.* It is only as our best desires are translated into deeds that they give solidity and strength to our character. In words and sighs they die away; they are like the morning dew. A good desire in itself is like the raindrop on the leaf of the tree; it may excite admiration as it glistens like a diamond in the sun, but it is soon exhaled, and probably does no good to the tree. But when embodied in a generous deed it is like the raindrop that penetrates the roots and contributes some portion of strength to all the fibres. A charity-sermon delivered with the eloquence of a Chalmers may excite in the congregation the beneficent idea, almost to a passion, but, unless that passion takes the form of a self-denying act, it evaporates and leaves the congregation in a worse state than the preacher found it. 2. *For the sake of others.* It is generous deeds that bless the world. They go where ideas cannot penetrate, into the hearts and consciences of men; they work silently and salutarily as the sunbeam.

II. The contributions of beneficence are only virtuous as they spring from a generous desire. "For if there be first a willing mind, it is accepted according to that a man hath, and not according to that he hath not." The doctrine is this, that the disposition of the heart, not the doings of the hand, constitute the essence of moral character. This is the Divine method of estimating human conduct. "The Lord judgeth not as man judgeth," etc. The motive is the soul of the deed. "Though I bestow all my goods to feed the poor, . . . and have not charity, it profiteth me nothing." Do not judge the desire by the effort, but judge the effort put forth by the desire. The poor widow would have made munificent contributions, but she could only give a "mite;" but in that mite there was more value than in all the amount in the temple exchequer. Some have the means to do good and not the heart, and some have the heart but not the means. The former are grubs in the universe, the latter are angels. There are deeds done *in* the body, seen of God, infinitely more numerous and essentially more valuable in most cases than deeds done by the body.

III. The contribution of others cannot supersede the obligation of ours, but may supplement their deficiencies. 1. *It is not a substitute.* "For I mean not that other men be eased, and ye burdened." It behoves every man to contribute to the extent of his riches, to the good of others. If one man gives a thousand it does not relieve me from my obligation to contribute what I can. 2. *It is a supplement.* "But by an equality, that now at this time your abundance may be a supply for their want." It is the duty of all to contribute. Some have the ability to contribute a hundred times the amount of others; let their large sums go to supplement the deficiencies of their poorer brethren, so that there may be "an equality." Thus the old Scripture will be illustrated, that "he that had gathered much had nothing over; and he that had gathered little had no lack."

Vers. 16—24.—*Stimulating men to beneficent actions.* "But thanks be to God," etc. The verses under notice present to us the subject of *stimulating men to efforts of beneficence*, and three remarks are suggested concerning this occupation.

I. It is a work that requires the highest order of Christian men. We find here that not only Paul employs himself in it with all his loving earnestness and logical power, but he engages Titus also, and a "brother" with him of such distinction that his "praise is in the gospel throughout all the Churches." To excite men to beneficent enterprises is pre-eminently a Christian work. Christianity is the mother of all philanthropic labours and institutions. Christian piety is a fountain whence all the myriad streams of human beneficence that circulate through all the districts of human life proceed. To stimulate this beneficence in men is the highest ministry on earth, and for it men of the most distinguished character and faculty are required. No man is too great for it, and but few men are equal to its successful discharge.

II. It is a work deserving the gratitude of all. Paul refers to: 1. The gratitude of those who *had been excited* to beneficent efforts. "But thanks be to God, which put the same earnest care into the heart of Titus for you." It is implied that Titus conferred on them an immense favour in stimulating them to generous deeds. No man can render us a greater service than by taking us out of ourselves and inspiring us with a genuine concern for the interests of others. It is not he who gives me a good thing, *but who stimulates me to do a good thing*, that is my greatest benefactor; for it is "more blessed to give than to receive." In giving we become God-like, and therefore we ought to thank the man most devoutly who evokes within us the spirit of true charity. Instead of endeavouring to avoid appeals to our benevolence, we should hail them and thank our Maker for them. 2. The gratitude of those who have *effected* the excitement. Paul says, "Thanks be to God, which put the same earnest care into the heart of Titus for you." (1) There is no office *higher in itself* than this. This is the work for which Christ came into the world, the work for which he established the Christian ministry. The aim and tendency of the gospel are to drown the selfish *ego* in the sunny tide of universal charity. The love of Christ constrained men to feel that they should not henceforth live to themselves. (2) There is no office more *useful* than this. Success in this means ruin in all that is ruinous to souls in human history, ruin to selfishness and all its fiendish brood. Well, therefore, may those who are engaged in such a work thank God for the distinguishing honour to which they have been called. Paul says nothing here about the gratitude of those on whom the excited beneficence has bestowed its favours—the beneficiaries. He seems to take it for granted that they ought and would be thankful; that they ought to be admits of no doubt, but that they always are cannot be asserted. Ingratitude, alas! is one of the reigning sins in human life.

III. It is a work exposed to the suspicions of worldly men. The apostle seems to have been afraid that the contributions that would flow from stimulating the beneficence of the Corinthian Church would occasion the allegation that they were participating in them, and so obtaining some personal advantage. Hence, to guard against the possibility, he gets the Churches to choose from amongst them some men of the best reputation, whom he calls "messengers of the Churches," and Titus, and perhaps Luke, in the administration of the charity, and thus "providing for honest things, not only in the sight of the Lord, but also in the sight of men." Dishonest men have existed in all ages, and the more dishonest men are, the more suspicious. Paul here guards himself against all scandalous imputations. He had great respect for his own reputation, so much so, that one at times, in reading these Epistles, is well-nigh astonished that a man so great in nature and sublime in character should think so much about the opinions of others.

HOMILIES BY VARIOUS AUTHORS.

Vers. 1—6.—*Christian liberality in the Macedonian Churches.* Grace prepares the way for grace. Denial of self in one direction leads to cross-bearing in other forms. Duty is a spirit, not a mechanical thing; a life, and not a mere performance. If the Corinthians had shown such a "godly sorrow," they would now be eager to demonstrate their renewed Christian strength by a more faithful regard to all obligations. Carefulness, zeal, vehement desire, had characterized their repentance, and these would not expire with the occasion that had called them into exercise. Deep feeling is quiet feeling, and therefore permanent, and deep feeling is always the mark of true penitence. St. Paul had confidence in his Corinthian brethren, and it was a large-hearted trust; "confidence in you in all things." The "all things" is the *nexus* between the seventh and eighth chapters. So then he proceeds to speak of the liberality of the Macedonian Churches preparatory to urging on them the duty of benevolence. Observe his manner. If he states a doctrine, he illustrates it. If he teaches a duty, he gives an example. Never so abstract as to neglect the practical side of life, never so intent on action as to lose sight of the determinative principle, he reminds one of Lord

Bacon's remark, that the highest order of mind is that combining most fully the abstract and the practical. The example of these Macedonian Churches was well worthy of imitation. Macedonia had been overrun by armies, and we all know how armies devastated countries in those days and stripped the inhabitants of their wealth. St. Paul speaks of their "great trial of affliction," the losses and persecutions they were enduring, and yet they had "abundant joy," that could only be represented by its filling the depth of their poverty and overflowing in "the riches of their liberality." No common poverty was theirs—"deep poverty;" and no ordinary love was theirs, but a very profound and tender love. "This sentence is completely shattered in passing through the apostle's mind" (Stanley). How much more is unsaid than said in the marvellous words, "Their deep poverty abounded unto the riches of their liberality"! Two things are taught us. 1. The inspiration of a joyous influence. Duty, motive, impulse, all exalted into Christian happiness. "Rejoice evermore." Such joy is a glorious power. Let us not make a mistake here. Fine feelings, exuberant emotions, loud hallelujahs, the thrill and shout and ecstasy, may deceive us. If they exhaust themselves in sensational excitement, they do deceive us, and that most awfully. Joy as a fruit of the Spirit is a giving joy, a sacrificing joy, a joy in the cross by which we are crucified to the world and the world unto us. 2. And we learn that even "deep poverty" is no obstruction to helping others. It often hinders us from doing what we would; but in the estimate of the Lord Jesus, the heart of this matter is in the "could," not in the *would*. "She hath done what she could." Capacity is always a mystery. It surprises us ever, and more and more, and in nothing is it so surprising as in the charitable heart with small means at its command. The glory of giving is in the quality of love, and it never fails to find something to bestow. "She of her penury hath cast in all the living that she had." If this poor widow could spare "two mites," who can plead depth of poverty? Notice that St. Paul emphasizes the depth of poverty in the Macedonian Church. If it had been simply a case of poverty, the example would not have been so instructive, and, accordingly, we find the apostle citing his cases from such as had to make sacrifices of personal comfort in order to aid those poorer than themselves. So that while in the Acts of the Apostles we hear of "possessors of lands or houses" selling them and laying the prices at the feet of the apostles, this fades from view in the tragic deaths of Ananias and Sapphira. But the image of the poor widow returns to us in the Epistles, with many suggestions as to the class of persons who do the most of the steady Christian giving. What is further noteworthy is the apostle's description of the self-moved generosity of these Macedonians. "Willing of themselves." Liberality is not a common virtue, and self-induced liberality is its rarest form. Men wait to be urged, begged, entreated; special occasions set are for special efforts; fine speakers are engaged; and the whole system of giving, or very much of it, proceeds on the habitual reluctance of giving for the support of the gospel. As to spontaneousness in this matter, who thinks of it, who trusts it? Now, we do not suppose that all religious people in the apostolic age were like these Macedonians. We know they were not. Yet, consider this fact, viz. they were the persons held up as shining examples of what liberality ought to be in the Church of Christ. And this accords precisely with the incidents mentioned concerning Mary of Bethany, and the poor widow and her mites, and the disciples after Pentecost who disposed of their property to help the poor. It was cordial and voluntary action, no external agency operating to give inducements. Without pressing this point too far, we must say that whatever utility belongs to the machinery of collecting funds for Church uses (and this seems to be necessary), it is nevertheless clear enough that spontaneous liberality is the truest, noblest, surest, mode of cultivating this grace in our hearts. So, unquestionably, the apostle thought. With what a glow he writes! "According to their power;" nay, it was more than this, for they went "beyond their power [beyond their means];" and so earnest was their purpose that they prayed the apostle to receive their gifts and let them share the grace and fellowship of ministering to the saints. No doubt many of these men found life a hard struggle, and for them, in more senses than one, "without were fightings, within were fears." Yet they deemed it a privilege to give; they coveted earnestly the best gift, which was the gift of giving; they prayed "with much entreaty" that they might participate in a work which was most blessed. To let such an opportunity slip was more than they could bear. And this conduct exceeded his expectations; for they had given themselves first to the Lord Jesus, and then, anxious to show their affection for the apostle, had given themselves in this special matter to him. Heart and property; what a consecration! What a page in *spiritual biography!* Out of "deep poverty;" what chorus of voices ever rose like this, pleading that these Macedonians might be permitted to share the grace of ministration! "The short and simple annals of the poor" have added much to our English literature, nor is it extravagant to claim that this is one of the most praiseworthy marks of that distinctive genius which has signalized its excellence in so many departments of poetry and fiction. But do we realize our indebtedness to the Bible for this beautiful and humanizing element in English literature? Here, in this single chapter from the Apostle Paul, what a touching picture of Christian poverty, surrendering means it could ill afford to spare, and doing it "with a self-dedication which involved a complete renunciation of all personal interests" (Kling)!—L.

Vers. 7—15.—*Appeal to the Corinthians.* A wise use had been made by the apostle of the example of the Macedonians. He had not appealed to pride, vanity, or any selfish feeling, but had simply presented a remarkable case of Christian philanthropy. Robertson very properly remarks, "Had the apostle said, 'Be not beaten by those Macedonians;' had he called natural prejudices into play—a Corinthian to yield to a Macedonian!—then all the evil passions of our nature had been stimulated." Emulation is a true principle, and may be a religious principle. The danger lies, not in the thing itself, but in its abuses, and particularly in the encouragement which it may afford to false rivalry and jealousy. In a large measure, the spirit and conduct of others make the social atmosphere we breathe, nor can we live in the world without contact with it. Goodness assumes its most attractive forms in noble examples, and, except for these, our own ideals, if they existed at all, would be very imperfect. Consistently, then, with his purpose of stimulating the Corinthians to seek a high degree of Christian excellence, the apostle sets before them in most vivid colours the liberality of the Macedonian Churches. Titus had begun, and he would have him "finish in them the same grace also." Men are channels of Divine influence to our souls, and, as such, should be acknowledged in their work. St. Paul saw God's blessing on the labours of his young friend, and he would not deprive him of the honour of completing the task. He stood out of his way, encouraged his efforts, and lent him a fatherly hand in furtherance of his undertaking. This sympathy with young men is one of his characteristic qualities, and it is worthy of warm admiration. Many an elderly officer in the Church might heed it to great advantage. Titus should have all the credit. Let the brethren at Corinth heartily second his exertions in behalf of the poor saints at Jerusalem. If they abounded "in everything, in faith, and utterance, and knowledge, and in all diligence," and in their love for the apostle, let them "abound in this grace also." The *quality* being pure, *quantity* was a favourite idea which he never lost an opportunity to urge. "Abound" and "abundant" flow freely from his pen. "Not by commandment" was this written. Free hearts, joyous impulses, could alone be recognized in this enterprise of humanity. This was the value of example, it was a sympathetic influence; and hence his reference to "the forwardness of others," which would test the "sincerity of their love." What a great truth is taught here, and that too so incidentally as to escape the attention of all save those who make the cultivation of discernment a constant duty! Noble examples are Divine tests; they prove, as we have said, the depth and activity of our sympathies, and in this respect supply the means of a discipline otherwise lacking. "Forwardness of others;" study its meaning. God commissions the leaders. Vast enterprises are never born of masses, but of individuals; apostles first, and then Churches; Bunyan, and two centuries of literature for the poor and illiterate; Watts and the sacred poets following; Raikes and Wesley; Martyn and Judson; successors multiplied because of their "forwardness." Having dwelt on the example of the Macedonians, the transition is easy to the Divine Exemplar. A single verse reminds them of "the grace of our Lord Jesus Christ," the surrender of his eternal glory, the riches of his Godhead's state, the extent of the abnegation, the earthly poverty assumed, and all for their sakes, that "through his poverty" they "might be rich." The supreme consideration must be kept in full view. Of the Macedonians he had spoken; of the "great trial of affliction," of their "deep poverty," and how it abounded "unto the riches of their liberality." Whence came this power? A new heart had been given to poverty, so that now, though its means were meagre, its social position unhonoured, its claims to influence set at nought, yet it had achieved wonders such as had never been thought possible. Macedonia had stretched out her arms of blessing to distant Jerusalem, and Gentiles and Jews long alienated were now one in the holiest of brotherhoods. It was due to the grace of Christ. It was his Spirit reproducing itself in the lives of believers. And therefore he had cited their conduct; but most of all let them remember the one great sacrifice of the incarnate Christ. Years subsequently we have in another Epistle (Phil. ii.) a similar train of thought. Age was upon him then, and life was drawing to a tragical close at Rome. Yet then, as now, then and now as throughout his ministry, the grace of the Lord Jesus was the one thought that inspired all other thoughts. It is still "advice." "Advice" is better than "commandment." They had begun the work of the collection, complete the task; they had a "readiness to will," let the effort be consummated. And, again, an important principle is brought to their notice. Was not "advice" sufficient? Would not an *opinion* be strong enough without a command? Yea, indeed, for a year ago the Corinthians had made a start in this matter. A willing mind is the first thing; grace begins here, and if this willing mind gives all it can, it is accepted of God, according to what "a man hath, and not according to that he hath not." Mark the solicitude of the apostle as to the education of this sentiment of giving. He cannot think of it as a thing to which they must be constrained, and, accordingly, he acknowledges the largest freedom, only it must be Christian freedom. Motive must have free play. Conscience must advance into affection, or conscience is stunted. Sensibility must be self-impelled. Nor must any conclude that he wished to oppress them that others might be relieved, "but only to establish between Jewish and Gentile Churches a reciprocity of aid in time of need" (Dr. Farrar). To establish an "equality" was his object. Do not mistake his meaning. Political, social, natural equality was utterly foreign to his thought and purpose. No revolutionist, no anarchist, no leveller, was he in any sense, in any degree, but simply the advocate of such an equality as should be produced by the sentiment of Christian liberality in the distribution of gifts. That equalizing influence was not to proceed from an arbitrary law nor from force-work of any sort. It was to be spontaneous, each man a judge for himself, and the superabundance in one place was to supply the deficiency at another place, so as to secure an abundance for all. Reference is made to the manna in the wilderness. If one gathered more manna than the allotted supply, it was sent to those who had not collected enough, so that the necessities of all were met. This was the law of Judaism as between Hebrew and Hebrew, and the spirit of this law, fifteen centuries afterwards, reappears in a letter to the Corinthians. History in one portion of the world and among one people becomes prophecy in another portion and among another people. Prophecy, in turn, becomes a new history. And to-day, A.D. 1884, thousands in Europe and America are acting on this equalizing sentiment in the use of their property.—L.

Vers. 16—24.—*Prudential management; care to avoid blame.* St. Paul has given us many sketches of himself, especially much insight into his varying moods; and in these chapters (vii. and viii.) he interests us in the character of Titus. The section opens with thanksgiving to God, who has inclined the heart of his young friend towards the Corinthians and awakened his zeal in behalf of their welfare. No doubt it had occurred to Titus to undertake the project of collecting for the Jerusalem Church, but he had not broached the subject to the apostle. It lay quiet in his heart, doing the Spirit's work, expanding and strengthening his purpose, yet nursed in silence. "While I was musing, the fire burned." St. Paul had presented the matter to him and found him willing, ready, and zealous to enter on the task. "More forward [more earnest], of his own accord he went unto you." Two brethren of reputation had been chosen by the Churches to accompany Titus, and the three travellers, having this loving embassy in hand, would manifest "this grace," so that they and he as co-workers in the ministration would glorify God. Not enough for the apostle to honour Christ in the gifts alone, but he would enhance the glory by the manner of doing the work. The way of performing it should be exceptional, impressive, and great-hearted, and thus the very mode of the act should prove a blessing as well as the thing done. For this course another reason existed. Appearances should always be consulted. No one can afford to put himself above them, to neglect, and still less to despise, them. Circumstances have their laws, and they must be obeyed. The contribution was " abundant," and he would take all possible precaution in the administration, lest the enemies of his apostleship should invent and propagate some new slander about him. The inspired man, the ambassador, the pioneer of a new Europe, was not ashamed to practise the lowly code of common sense and put a very strong emphasis on prudence. Hence his extreme caution. Blameless in the sight of God, he would be blameless in the eyes of men. And now a commendation of our brother, and a special word in behalf of Titus, " my partner and fellow-helper," not forgetting to say " partner and fellow-helper concerning you," and to exhort the Corinthians to make good his boasting to the Macedonian Churches on their behalf. So ends this admirable chapter. Is it not a beautiful pendant to that lamp which, for eighteen hundred years, in the thirteenth chapter of First Corinthians, has hung out its blaze of splendour before the world?—L.

Ver. 5.—*Dedication.* If it seems strange to us that a large portion of an inspired Epistle should be occupied with directions as to a charitable collection which was going forward at the time, it should be remembered that Christianity introduced into human society new and more powerful principles of benevolence, and further, that the new and Divine revelation was one which laid the foundation for this as for all human duties in the character and action of God himself.

I. THE PRIMARY AND ALL-IMPORTANT DEDICATION IS THAT OF THE WHOLE PERSONAL NATURE UNTO THE LORD. 1. This appears when it is recollected that the Lord has first given himself for us. His sacrifice thus becomes the ground of our consecration. 2. Our very constitution, taken in connection with our natural relation to our Lord, points to such a dedication. " No man liveth unto himself." Our " chief end is to glorify God." 3. This spiritual consecration is pre-eminently acceptable to God. His demand is, " Give me thine heart." Every gift which does not flow from this is vain and worthless in his sight.

II. THE DEDICATION OF SELF TO THE LORD SHOULD BE FOLLOWED BY THE DEDICATION OF SELF TO THE LORD'S PEOPLE. Paul looked for the brotherhood, the confidence, the co-operation of his converts, and indeed of all Christian people whom Divine providence might bring into contact with him. The Corinthians apparently wished to be personally associated with him in the ministration to the Judæan Christians who were in poverty, and their wish was a source of satisfaction and joy to him.

III. TRUE CHRISTIAN CONSECRATION INVOLVES THE GIFT OF PROPERTY TO THE LORD'S CAUSE. It is sometimes objected against calls for liberality that God cannot be enriched by our giving. This is true, yet God's people may receive advantage, and Christ has shown us that what is done for his people is done for himself. As most people value their possessions, their generosity is a proof of the sincerity of their love and the reality of their consecration.

> " How can I, Lord, withhold
> Life's brightest hour
> From thee; or *gathered gold,*
> Or any power?
> Why should I keep one precious thing from thee,
> When thou hast given thine own dear self for me?"

T.

Ver. 8.—*Sincere love.* In giving liberally towards the collection made for the poor Christians of Judæa, the Corinthians showed their love to the objects of their charity, to the apostle to whose appeal they responded, and also to the unseen Lord and Saviour by whose desire and for whose sake they befriended the least of his brethren.

I. LOVE TO CHRIST IS THE MIGHTIEST OF ALL SPIRITUAL PRINCIPLES. Human life abounds with evidence of the might of love; every family, every society, has some exemplifications of the power of love to overcome difficulties, to prompt to exertion, to sustain under self-denial. And all Christendom in every age has shown that love to

Christ is an unrivalled motive to holiness, to patience, to benevolence. The hymns of the Church's literature, and the gifts and labours recorded in the Church's annals, are alike proof of the vitality and efficacy of Christian love.

II. The profession of love to Christ is not always accompanied by the reality. The early disciples were admonished to "love unfeigned," were warned, "Let love be without dissimulation." Doubtless in all ages there have been those who have deceived themselves, and have imagined that they loved Christ, because they have felt some glow of admiration towards him, but who in time of trial have made it manifest that they had no depth of love. Weighed in the balance, they are found wanting. The soul is brought face to face with its own weakness and worthlessness, inconsistency and treachery.

III. The Lord Jesus tests in many ways the sincerity of his people's profession of love. 1. By his bodily absence from them, which shows whether they have an attachment to their professed Lord which can abide even though not fostered by sight and constant personal intercourse. 2. By permitting rival powers and persons to invite the supreme affection of the heart. These, though they cannot satisfy, may please, and the Lord of all suffers their attractiveness; for the love which cannot abide amid rival attractions is poor indeed. 3. By his demand that we should surrender what is dear to us, if to retain it conflicts with our supreme attachment to Christ. The young ruler was subjected to this test. In some form it comes to many. Feigned love will then go away, even though it go away grieved. 4. By our necessary and probationary contact with an unloving world. In the presence of the unspiritual and unsympathizing, the sincerity of the Christian's love is often sorely tested. 5. The trials and sufferings of life not only exercise the faith, they test the love, of the professed follower of Jesus. The storm proves whether the vessel is seaworthy or not. 6. By enjoining upon his people obedience to commandments which are contrary to our natural inclinations. Love can vanquish even the attachment to a "darling sin." 7. Love is tested when it is invited to direct itself towards others also, for Jesus' sake. Who can love Christ, and yet hate his brother, for whom Christ died?—T.

Ver. 9.—*The condescension of Christ.* According to the teaching of the New Testament, human kindness should be based upon Divine benevolence. Such is the import of this wonderful parenthesis—a jewel which the inspired writer drops by the way and passes on.

I. Christ's native riches contrasted with his voluntary poverty. 1. His proper rightful wealth is apparent, not only from his nature as the Son of God, but from his evident command, during his earthly ministry, of all the resources of nature. Bread, wine, money, he could multiply or create; the earth and the sea obeyed his will; diseases and demons fled at his bidding. 2. His poverty was not compulsory; it was a "grace." We see it in his incarnation, in which he emptied himself of his glory; in his ministry, passed in a lowly and all but destitute condition of life; in his refusal to use his power for selfish ends; in his cheerful submission to a shameful death. Compare the glory which he claimed to have had with the Father before the world was, with the homelessness and poverty of his life and the desertion and ignominy of his death, and his "grace" appeals to every just mind, to every sensitive heart.

II. Our native spiritual poverty contrasted with our acquired spiritual wealth. 1. Our natural destitution is undeniable; by sin we have lost our possessions, our inheritance, our powers of acquisition, and are left resourceless and friendless. Apart from the interposition of Christ, and where Christianity is unknown, such is still the state of man. 2. Christ's humiliation was for the sake of man's spiritual enrichment. Only by condescension, compassion, and sacrifice could man be reached. Thus he drew near to us, and imparted to us of his own true and Divine riches, of knowledge, of righteousness, of favour, and of glory. 3. By Christ's mediation all things are ours. God, giving Christ, gives with him all good things. "I have all things and abound," is the testimony of every right-minded and appreciative disciple of Christ. The history of the Church is the history of the enrichment of the race; and this in turn is the pledge and promise of the inestimable and inexhaustible riches of eternity.—T.

Ver. 12.—*The rule of acceptance.* Justice is distinctive of all the demands and of all the proceedings of the providence of God. Often, as in the case before us, the righteousness of the principles of the Divine government is so apparent that no question can possibly be raised concerning it.

I. THE GENERAL PRINCIPLE HERE PROPOUNDED. It is that the requirements of God correspond to the possessions of man. 1. What men have, they have received from the undeserved bounty of their Creator. This holds good with regard to property and to talents and opportunities. 2. An account is expected from every man by him who is the Judge and sovereign Lord of all. We are to some extent and in some matters accountable to our fellow-men, but for everything to him in whom "we live, and move, and have our being." 3. The rule according to which the supreme Governor will judge mankind is one of absolute rectitude—"according to that a man hath." The feeble man will not be expected to have done the work of the strong; the dull man the work of the genius; the peasant the work of the prince; nor the beggar to have given with the generosity of the millionaire. But each must answer for that which has been entrusted to himself. In all things the disposition, the spirit, the endeavour, will be taken into account; "if there be first the ready mind"—"if the forward zeal be at hand." Such is the universal condition of Divine acceptance and approval.

II. THE SPECIAL APPLICATION OF THE PRINCIPLE HERE DEDUCED. 1. In the matter of gifts there is scope for moral culture and watchfulness. Unless liberality be shown upon definite principle, it will most likely not be shown at all. There is need of watching against selfishness and avarice. 2. It is well for every Christian to anticipate and apply beforehand the Divine principle—to judge himself, that he may not be judged by God; to put to himself the question, "How much owest thou unto thy Lord?" 3. Especially should the inspired rule of liberality be observed by those who are prospering in the world. As means increase, let gifts be enlarged. The Judge cannot accept from the wealthy the gifts which were approved when offered by the poor.—T.

Ver. 21.—*Things honourable.* It might have been supposed that the apostle would have considered himself superior to the considerations here adduced. His life was so completely unselfish, so obviously governed by higher than interested principles, that it seems as if he might have taken it for granted that no suspicion could attach to his personal administration of the alms to be forwarded to Judæa. Probably others thought thus; few, if any, could have suspected Paul of fraud and misappropriation. But he judged himself by a standard which was applicable to all Christian agents, a standard which every wise man, experienced in the ways of the world, will do well to adopt as his own.

I. THE RULE OF CONDUCT HERE PROPOSED. 1. Things honourable are things actually good, admirable, beautiful, in themselves. The word in the original denotes primarily this. What things are morally excellent and praiseworthy, let these things be done. 2. Things honourable are things reputable and approved. It is especially prudent to be very careful and scrupulous, and very open, in the administration of public money, and so to act that there may be no opening for slander or misrepresentation. And the same rule applies to other departments of conduct. It should not be a prominent motive with us to secure men's approval, yet our conduct should be such as to secure that approval, and even to command it. 3. Things honourable may best be provided by endeavouring to realize the inquisitive inspection of men and the all-searching gaze of the omniscient God.

II. THE MOTIVES URGING TO THE PRACTICAL ADOPTION OF THIS RULE. 1. It will tend to the satisfaction and peace of our own conscience. 2. It will tend to the honour of the religion we profess, when it is seen to be, not a cloak for covetousness, but an impulse to disinterestedness and a principle of integrity. 3. It will be for the glory of God. Actions done in his sight and at his command, from the motive of his love, and with the hope of his approbation, are the actions which the Christian should aim consistently and constantly to perform, in all positions and in all relations of life.—T.

Ver. 23.—*The appreciation of fellow-labourers.* Anxious as Paul was that a generous contribution should be sent to Judæa for the relief and assistance of the poor Christians in that province, he was equally anxious that the *mode* in which this contribution was transmitted should be open and above all suspicion of carelessness or misappropriation. Hence he secured that Titus and two others should be appointed as trustees, so to speak, of the fund, to take charge of it and to carry it to the destined quarter. Of these three Christian men Paul speaks in terms of notable commendation. He terms them—

I. HIS OWN ASSOCIATES. The expressions used with this intent are three in number. 1. They are *partners*, engaged in the same work, under the same Master, and with the expectation of a similar reward, with himself. 2. They are *fellow-workers*, each having his own faculty, his own implement, for labour, but all co-operating to the one end. 3. They are *brethren*; i.e. bound together by a personal tie, a spiritual kindred, in the Christian family and household of faith. These expressions involve a deep and lasting attachment, such as should unite those who are engaged in one and the same service rendered to the one great Master.

II. MESSENGERS OF THE CHURCHES. The expression in the original is very strong. They are apostles; *i.e.* sent forth by the congregation as their representatives and plenipotentiaries. This gives a special dignity to the office and work of accredited servants of the body of Christ, and therefore of Christ himself.

III. THE GLORY OF CHRIST. There is something mystical, something difficult to expound, in this epithet. It certainly implies that these faithful men were exalted to a position of very high honour, and were looked upon as related very closely to the Lord himself. Certainly it was to the glory of the Redeemer that a new principle of benevolence was introduced into human society, impelling the Gentile of Europe to display a practical interest in the welfare of the Jew of Palestine. Here was exhibited a moral glory radiating from Christ himself, before which the world might well bow down in wonder, admiration, and reverence.—T.

Vers. 1—7.—*A pattern of charity.* The charity commended is that of the Macedonian Churches.

I. THEY GAVE UNDER VERY UNFAVOURABLE CIRCUMSTANCES. 1. *They were in much affliction.* (Ver. 2.) This might have suggested special care of themselves rather than of others. Suffering often produces selfishness. Our pain often prevents us from realizing the pains of others. 2. *They were in deep poverty.* (Ver. 2.) How *could* they give? Charity must begin at home, and does not "deep poverty" demonstrate that it must end there? How inconsiderate, and indeed absurd, to ask *them* to give! Was it not *their duty* to be provident? to hold some reserve in store against possibly worse times? *No people talk more of duty than those who intend to violate it.* The Macedonians saw the high duty of charity, and nobly performed that duty.

II. THOUGH AFFLICTED AND POOR, THEY GAVE LARGELY. (Ver. 3.) Their danger was not that they might give too little, but that they might give too much. "Beyond their power." Affliction and poverty combined could not cramp their large-heartedness. Many ask how little they can give; the Macedonian Christians asked how much. A modern curse of the Church is small giving. There are too many threepenny-bit Christians.

III. THEY GAVE VOLUNTARILY. (Ver. 3.) Compulsory kindness is of little worth. And there are other compulsions than physical. "Voluntary offerings" are often anything but voluntary.

IV. THEY GAVE WITHOUT URGENT APPEAL. They gave "of their own accord." They did not require the importunities of a "collection sermon." They required only to know of the need; the charity was spontaneous.

V. THEY BEGGED FOR THE PRIVILEGE OF GIVING. (Ver. 4.) They *longed* to help, and supplicated for a share of the good work. Giving, to them, was a privilege—a gain, not a loss. Giving was not a thing to be avoided, but a thing to be sought. Perhaps they remembered the words of the Lord, "It is more blessed to give than to receive." Had they given in an assembly it would not have been necessary to have the collection in the middle of the meeting to avoid a stampede and empty plates at the close. Much giving of to-day is not an illustration of charity, but a burlesque of it.

VI. THEY GAVE WITH MUCH JOY. (Ver. 2.) They reaped the firstfruits of charity at the time of the seed-sowing! Such are the wonders of spiritual agriculture. The grudging giver defrauds no one so much as himself. To miss the joy of giving is to miss how much! There are few luxuries so sweet as the luxury of charity.

VII. THEY GAVE THEMSELVES AS WELL AS THEIR MONETARY CONTRIBUTION. (Ver. 5.) 1. *To the Lord*. They solemnly dedicated themselves and their belongings to the Most High. 'Twas easy for them to surrender a part when they had surrendered the whole. We give haltingly because we do not believe the Scripture which saith, "Ye are not your own." Our gifts cannot be acceptable to God if we withhold ourselves or parts of ourselves. 2. *To the apostle*. As to a servant of their Lord. For service. When they surrendered themselves to God they did not surrender themselves to idleness, but to activity. Many present to God a mass of indolence. Some consecrated people seem consecrated to do nothing. The Macedonian conduct exceeded the apostolic expectation, not the Divine. This was what God expected, and what he expects from us. It was " by the will of God " (ver. 5).

PRACTICAL. 1. Here is an example for us. Though we abound in faith, utterance, knowledge, earnestness (ver. 7), yet if we have not this practical love we are no better than " sounding brass" (1 Cor. xiii. 1). 2. We can attain to this only as the Macedonian Christians attained to it, by " the grace of God " (ver. 1). We do not want more money in our pockets, but more grace in our hearts. God can work this work in us. Let us commit ourselves into his hands, that this miracle may be wrought in us also.—H.

Ver. 9.—*The great Example of benevolence.* Consider—

I. HOW RICH THE SON OF GOD WAS. 1. *In possessions.* All things were made by him. All things were his. Not this world only, but all worlds. Not one race of creatures, but all races and orders. 2. *In power.* Omnipotence untrammelled and unrepressed. 3. *In homage.* (1) The adoration of the heavenly hosts; and (2) their perfect obedience to every command and wish. 4. *In the love and fellowship of the Father.* 5. *In purest happiness.*

II. HOW POOR HE BECAME. 1. *In condition.* (1) The Godhead veiled in humanity. (2) The Divine power restricted. (3) The God of joy transformed into the Man of sorrows. 2. *In circumstances.* (1) At his birth. His cradle a manger. An outcast; no room for him in the inn; a foreshadowing of the whole earthly life. (2) At Nazareth an artisan, earning bread by the sweat of his brow, standing thus so closely to fallen Adam. (3) As a preacher, dependent upon casual charity. (4) As a traveller, journeying in penury. (5) For his triumphal entry, dependent upon strangers. (6) As a prisoner, stripped of the little he possessed. " They parted my garments." (7) His dying bed, a cross; his last resting-place, a borrowed tomb. 3. *In surroundings.* (1) Instead of homage, mockery and insult. (2) Few friends. One of these a traitor, and the remnant faithless at the supreme moment. (3) Heaven darkened to him. " My God, my God, why hast thou forsaken me?"

III. THIS MARVELLOUS TRANSFORMATION AND ITS CAUSE. 1. *It was purely voluntary.* *He* gave himself. " No man taketh it from me . . . I lay down my life " (John x. 18, 15). 2. *It was prompted by love.* " Ye know *the grace*," the spontaneous, unmerited love. The compulsion was the compulsion of compassion and affection. 3. *It had for its object the enrichment of men.* (1) Men were poor. (*a*) Always dependent. (*b*) Through sin, had forfeited all title to things bestowed by God, all title to the Divine favour, all title to brighter prospects. (*c*) Thus were poor deservedly. (2) Through Christ's poverty men are made rich. Those who are redeemed by Christ lose the poverty which is inseparable from sin, and : (*a*) Gain holiness. (*b*) Become partakers of the Divine nature. (*c*) Receive the adoption of children and become heirs of God. (*d*) Become inheritors of the heavenly kingdom. (*e*) Obtain present and future joy. (*f*) Become sharers in the glory which Christ for a while set aside. " The glory which thou hast given me I have given unto them " (John xvii. 22).

IV. CHRIST IS HERE OUR EXAMPLE. 1. If Christ did this for us, how ready we should be to do what lies in our power for others! In doing it to them, we show our love to him. 2. How small our sacrifice must be compared to his! 3. Self-sacrifice makes us like Christ. He not only said, " It is more blessed to give than to receive ; " he himself tasted this blessedness. And he gave *what?* He gave *himself* for us.—H.

Vers. 10—15.—*Things that belong to charity.* I. To WILL. 1. *Charity must be voluntary.* No one can make us will. We can be made to *give*, but such giving is morally worthless. God loveth a cheerful giver, because a cheerful giver is in all certainty a voluntary giver. The "voluntary system" is not *one* form of charity; it is the *only* form. Unless we willingly give, the less said about our charity the better; *for we have none!* 2. *The "willing" must be rightly prompted.* True charity means heart-love. The coin is base unless it bears this stamp. Though it may pass current amongst men, God will arrest and condemn it. Motives in giving should be carefully studied; not others' motives, but *ours!*

II. To DO. Some are charitable in *intention*, not in *action*. Fruit trees are sometimes destitute of fruit, but to those thus symbolized there is but little encouragement in the fate of that barren tree which confronted Christ as he walked from Bethany to Jerusalem. Charity must be spiritual, but it must be practical also. Our *love* will never feed the hungry nor clothe the naked; and if our love does not prompt us *to do*, it is of less value than a mote in the sunbeam. Faith without works is dead, and charity without works is dead, buried, and rotting in its grave.

III. To GIVE ACCORDING TO OUR ABILITY. (Ver. 12.) Not according to what others give. We are apt to give according to the ability of somebody else. Perhaps when we judge of our own ability we had better ask God to help us. There are two occasions when a man's possessions are apt to dwindle—the one when he makes out his income-tax return, and the other when he is asked for a subscription. We need much grace rightly to estimate our own resources. Charitable appeals are apt to derange the laws of arithmetic and to lead to astonishing results.

IV. To GIVE JUDICIOUSLY. 1. *The needs of any case should be carefully considered.* Not to make them *less* than they are, but to know them *as they are*. To give to undeserving cases is not only to waste our substance, but to do a vast amount of mischief. 2. *We are not required to impoverish ourselves that others may be enriched.* (Ver. 13.) Though, if we had tendencies in this direction, perhaps we should not be travelling away from our Master's example (ver. 9). Our danger probably lies in being content with the impoverished condition of others. But the object of charity is not that the poor should be made rich and the rich poor. 3. *An equality is to be aimed at.* (Ver. 14.) As to believers especially we should remember that they are members of the same faith, and should seek to make their condition equally healthy with our own. But our charity should not be restricted by the limits of "the household of faith." One has well said, "Our luxuries should yield to our neighbour's comforts, and our comforts to his necessities." This seems Paul's conception, who explains what he means by "equality" in the expression following: "Your abundance being a supply at this present time for their want, that their abundance also may become a supply for your want" (ver. 14); and he illustrates it by reference to the manna given to Israel in the wilderness (Exod. xvi. 18). How far from approach to this equality is the giving of many! 4. *We must not so give as to check the exertions of those whom we help.* Paul does not apprehend that so undesirable a result will follow the charity which he recommends; he anticipates that the poor may become so rich as to help those now helping them. Unwise charity hinders, not helps, the recipient. Pauperism is a poor harvest to reap. Still we must see that this argument is not unduly pressed. It is to be a *protector*, it is not to be a *murderer*, of charity.—H.

Ver. 18.—*An enviable reputation.* I. A GREAT CHARACTER IS BETTER THAN A GREAT NAME. The brother referred to here is unnamed; a better mark than a name is put upon him. A great name may be inherited; may be won by a merely fortunate conjunction of circumstances; may be unmerited; may have no moral excellence associated with it. A great character must be earned. A great name blesses one's self; a great character, others.

II. THE APPROBATION OF HOLY MEN IS VERY PRECIOUS. The applause of a fallen world may be reckoned at a cheap rate. Mere popularity is quite in contrast with the praise of all the Churches. That men who love Christ, and who thus have corrected tastes, can see in us what is lovely should cause us to be deeply thankful to God, who has wrought this good thing in us. When the approval is widespread and general among such, it becomes correspondingly precious. The praise of God, indeed, is what we should strive after; but this may be expressed by the lips of his children.

III. REPUTATION "IN THE GOSPEL" IS MOST TO BE DESIRED. This was the reputation of the brother alluded to by Paul. It was in the sphere of the gospel that he had obtained his renown. And this is the very highest sphere. How can we make known the gospel? How can we exalt it in the estimation of men? How can we show forth its excellences in our lives? These should be supreme questions with us. Reputation in arms, art, science,—what are these compared with reputation in the gospel? What can arms do for men, or art, or science, compared with the gospel? The gospel presents the most magnificent arena for human life and achievement.

IV. Opinion is tested by trust. Here is a test of men's words. Will those who praise us put confidence in us? It was so with the brother in question (ver. 19). The friends who praised him trusted him with *money*, and this is an extreme form of trust with most men. They praised him for a piety which extended to the secularities of life. His gospel ruled the money-bag. We want more pounds-shillings-and-pence religion. If our piety does not make us uncorrupt in practical life, we had better cast it to the dogs, for it is only fit for them.—H.

Vers. 20, 21.—*Ministerial carefulness in money matters.* I. Strictest honesty is, of course, essential. How can a man preach this common Christian virtue if he lacks it himself? How can his ministry in spiritual things be blessed if he is tainted with the slightest dishonesty in things carnal? What peace of conscience can he possess if he knows that herein he is faulty; and without peace in his own conscience how can he minister in the gospel of all peace? Those who bear the vessels of the Lord must be clean. What a fearful condemnation will be theirs who, whilst expatiating upon the preciousness of heavenly treasure, are all the while dishonestly grasping the treasure which perishes!

II. Strictest honesty is not sufficient. A servant of God may be perfectly innocent, and yet by carelessness may give occasion to some to denounce him as guilty. It is not only needful to do right, it is needful *to appear* to do right as well. Whilst no man should be content with satisfying men apart from God, a wise man will not rest content with satisfying God and his own conscience, but will recognize the importance of not giving a handle for reproach to those amongst whom he lives. Prudent, indeed, was the apostle when he resolved to " take thought for things honourable, not only in the sight of the Lord, but also in the sight of men " (ver. 21). Through lack of such wisdom on the part of ministers: 1. *Many a ministerial reputation has been wrecked.* The lie has been believed, and has been believed because it has been corroborated by unwise conduct. A lie thus strengthened is very attractive to many minds. Lies need no help on our part. It is often easier to make a man believe the barest lie than to make him believe the barest truth. It has been quaintly said, " A lie will travel round the world before truth has finished putting on its boots." 2. *Powerful ministers have been rendered impotent.* 3. *Churches have been greatly injured.* The shadow falling upon the minister has spread its darkness over the Church. 4. *Many have become prejudiced against the gospel.* 5. *Much dishonour has fallen upon the Name of Christ.* Christians dare not be careless; they carry with them the honour of their Master. It is not a question about being careless of *our own* name; the matter affects *his* Name. No man can afford to despise popular opinion in such a matter as this. If a false accusation has been brought without occasion given, that accusation will have the elements of weakness in it, and may generally be successfully repelled; but if occasion has been given, the honest man furnishes evidence of his own dishonesty, he forges the chain wherewith he is bound, he signs his own condemnation. Public men have many enemies. Ministers are the targets of the devil, and often of the devil's children. Great wisdom do they need to walk so that they shall not unwittingly furnish their adversaries with a weapon against themselves and their cause. This applies, of course, not only to money matters, but to all matters. 'Tis the utmost folly to present our own sword to the foe. If we fall, let it be by our enemy's weapon, not by our own.—H.

Ver. 23.—*What true Christian workers are.* I. They are the glory of Christ. 1. *They are the monuments of the triumph of Christ.* They are " saved " to some purpose. Many assert that they are " saved," but they cannot discover, neither can any one else, *unto what* they are saved. They seem to be saved unto *nothingness*, and in this sense to have experienced a singularly complete redemption. But the active, devoted Christian proves the reality of his faith by works following. Christ has not only triumphed over the judgment and heart, but over all powers, which are now willingly dedicated to his service. 2. *They resemble Christ.* Christ was pre-eminently a *worker.* He "went about doing good;" they seek to do so. He practised self-denial and endured suffering that others might be benefited; they strive to imitate him. 3. *They exalt Christ.* They desire that his kingdom may be extended over the earth. Whilst they labour for others, they do this out of their love for him. He is *first,* all else second. The exaltation of Christ is their supreme wish. Their mission is to speak well of his Name wherever they go. 4. *Christ delights in them.* They are the fruitful trees which he loves. He cursed the barren tree, but these he blesses. They are the faithful servants of the absent Lord. He loves not idlers who filch the name of "servant;" but those who are servants indeed his soul rejoices in. He glories in these, for they show forth his praise.

II. THEY SHOULD SEEK FULLY TO REALIZE THEIR HIGH CALLING. 1. The dignity of Christian work is not always perceived as fully as it should be. It is *infinitely* superior to all other work. 2. Nor its privilege. Were this adequately realized, what alacrity there would be in entering upon Christian service! As it is, alas! almost force has to be employed in some cases. 3. Nor its responsibility. 4. Nor how much the work done is affected by the life lived.

III. THEY SHOULD BE HIGHLY ESTEEMED. They are the instruments through which God works. They are the means employed by him for the building up of the kingdom of Christ. They are the special representatives of Christ upon earth. They should be (1) encouraged, (2) helped, (3) honoured.—H.

Ver. 5.—*Praiseworthy Churches.* Praise from St. Paul was worth having. He was a serious man, who could not pay empty compliments, and having a high sense of the Christian calling, he would never think of praising a Church merely to please the people or ingratiate himself with them, if he had not judged it worthy of commendation. Here are two marks of a Church on which the grace of God has been bestowed.

I. CONSECRATION OF ITS MEMBERS TO THE LORD JESUS CHRIST. Before they made their contribution to the relief of the poor saints elsewhere, the Macedonian Christians "gave their own selves to the Lord." Though poor and afflicted, happy were they and generous, because their conversion was thorough, and their devotion to Christ hearty and unfeigned. By profession all Christians give themselves to the Lord; but alas! in some cases it is a mere profession. Not every one so believes and lives as to entitle him to say, "I am my Lord's, and he is mine." This, however, is the true ideal. "Thy people shall be freewill offerings in thy day of power." And without this spirit in its members no Church is strong or pleasing to Christ, no matter how venerable its history, how admirable its constitution, or how well conducted its services.

II. SUBJECTION TO APOSTOLIC GUIDANCE BY THE WILL OF GOD. Some of the Macedonian Christians gave themselves to St. Paul as his companions and assistants in missionary labour. Such were Sopater, Secundus, Aristarchus, and Epaphroditus; of whom the first was a Berœan, the second and third were Thessalonians, and the fourth was a Philippian. But these choice men were only favourable specimens of the Churches to which they belonged, and which were pervaded by reverence for the apostle and gratitude for his labours. Every true Church of Christ must be apostolic. It must stand on the apostolic testimony and doctrine, follow apostolic direction and practice, and both inhale and exhale the spirit of apostolic devotion to Christ. Of the history and writings of the apostles enough is extant to guide and comfort every Church that is, like those of Macedonia, ready to learn of an apostle by the will of God. We are "built on the foundation of apostles and prophets." On the twelve foundations of the wall of the holy city are inscribed the names of the twelve apostles of the Lamb.

EXHORTATION. Follow those of Macedonia. Give yourselves to the Lord, and then to the apostolic word and fellowship. Present yourselves a living sacrifice.—F.

Ver. 9.—*Amazing love.* The insertion of this compact statement of our Saviour's love and self-devotion for our sakes into an exhortation to love and liberality in the Church, illustrates the habit of St. Paul's mind to revert often to central truths, and take his motives and arguments directly from Christ and the cross. "Ye know the grace of our Lord." But consider what you know, that it may influence your disposition and conduct; for nothing is more common than to hold known truth so loosely and carelessly in the mind that it is as though it had never been known or were quite forgotten.

I. THE SAVIOUR'S WEALTH. Of the riches of his pre-existent glory who can adequately speak? Who can tell the wealth of Divine power and dignity and love in the Word which was with God and was God—all the angels of God his servants, all the works of God full of his praise? But this is not a subject on which to dilate. It is above the reach of our comments and illustrations. Read John i.; Col. i.; Heb. i.

II. THE SAVIOUR'S IMPOVERISHMENT. (Comp. Phil. ii. 5—11.) Our Lord's participation of the Divine essence was not, could not, be surrendered. But the form of God could be and was laid aside. The form cannot be without the being and nature; but the being and nature may dispense with the form. So the Son of God in his grace toward us assumed the form of a man, and that in low estate—the form of a servant. He accepted a lowly human rank, with no attendants on his person but such as followed him in love, and no house of his own wherein to lay his head at night. In wisdom, indeed, and all that constitutes moral wealth and dignity, Jesus of Nazareth was rich; but in earthly station and treasure he was poor, and poor by choice. See him in youth in the carpenter's house, eating the bread of the working man with cheerfulness. In the little town there must have been many a piece of furniture, and on the farms and vineyards around many a tool, which had been under the human hands of the Son of God. See him on foot on the rough roads of Palestine, while others rode past on horses and mules. See him in the days of his ministry dependent on any who pleased to minister to his necessities; at last deserted by his friends and insulted by his foes—despised and rejected of men. Truly he became poor.

III. THE SAVIOUR'S GRACE. "For your sakes he became poor, that ye through his poverty might be enriched." In this short statement the whole work of substitution and redemption is implied. You are enriched through his poverty, blessed because of his suffering, accepted by reason of his rejection, reconciled through his death. It is evident that the riches thus secured to those that believe are not treasures of this world, but of the same order with the riches which the Saviour laid aside for a season. They receive the privilege of sonship with God, and therefore also the heirship of all things with Christ Jesus. The Son of God became man, and a poor man, that they, being men, and poor men, might be owned as sons of God. Dwell upon the riches in redemption, regeneration, forgiveness, justification, adoption, sanctification, comfort, patience, the earnest of the inheritance now, and the inheritance itself at his coming. And all because he became poor for your sakes. You get sweetness out of sorrow, glory out of shame, strength from weakness, wealth through poverty, and life through death.

IV. THE PRACTICAL INFLUENCE OF CONSIDERING THE SAVIOUR'S GRACE. 1. Not to raise a foolish admiration of poverty for its own sake. At one time this text was cited in support of lazy beggary. The mendicant friars quoted it, insisting that the Lord himself was a mendicant, and that this must be the most holy and Christ-like state. Great schoolmen debated this, and papal bulls dealt with this notion. Such questions we can no longer discuss with seriousness. Property is not to be abandoned by Christians, but wisely administered. The rich and the poor are to continue together in the Church, each condition having its own duties and its own attendant temptations. 2. To set our hearts on the true riches—faith and good works, a calm conscience, and affections set on things above. He is rich who has a patient spirit, a pure heart, a heavenly mind, and a hope of glory. 3. To live and give that others may be blessed. Be generous in service and gifts to the Church and the poor. Be willing to communicate, ready to distribute. Otherwise do not allege that you have the grace of our Lord Jesus Christ. You have not felt the constraint of his love or the beauty of his example.—F.

Ver. 12.—*Readiness accepted.* It is characteristic of St. Paul that, when dealing with specific questions of duty, he laid down principles of much wider application. Thus, while the immediate topic was a collection for the relief of poor saints, and he acknowledges the liberality of the Corinthians, the apostle takes occasion to explain the value of "readiness," *i.e.* a disposition stretching forward to serve God and the Church, and not needing to be dragged forward by importunity. This is acceptable to God, the supreme Lover and spontaneous Giver of every good and perfect gift. What he regards is not the amount of the gift laid on his altar, but the disposition which gives promptly and gladly according to the resources at its command. Now, this principle is of wide application. It will prove all kinds of service. God is pleased with those servants of his who have a ready mind. An apt but misleading phrase is sometimes heard—"taking the will for the deed." Too often it is used as an excuse for shirking duty or withholding gifts. Two things must be kept in mind—

I. GOD DOES NOT ACCEPT INTENTION OR GOOD WILL INSTEAD OF THE DEED WHEN IT IS WITHIN ONE'S POWER TO PERFORM. And God looks behind the excuses that a covetous or indolent heart puts forward, and knows the absolute fact regarding what each man has or has not, can or cannot do. In giving to the poor or for the propagation of the gospel, one may obtain praise of men by bestowing a large sum in answer to an urgent appeal; but he has no praise from God if his contribution has been reluctant, or if it does not bear a fair proportion to the resources at his disposal. Sometimes one cannot give as much as formerly or as much as his neighbours, and therefore prays to be excused from giving anything, expressing a hope that the will may be taken for the deed. But it will not be so taken. He is required to give according to what he has, not what he has not. And the willing offering is just as acceptable to God as a gift a thousand times as large from a man a thousand times as rich. So also in regard to personal service. How many who call Jesus "Lord," when any definite piece of Christian work is proposed to them, put it aside, alleging that they have no turn for it or no time for it! So they stand all the day idle. Because they cannot serve with great ability or in a conspicuous station, they do nothing, and simply wish well to the cause of God and of righteousness. But empty good wishes are cheap and little worth, and God will not in such cases take the will for the deed. He who employs two talents with a willing mind will be commended in exactly the same terms as his fellow-servant who has had five. And let him who has only one beware of hiding it in the earth. Men are very apt to take gifts from Christ, but not the gift of his "yoke." They are also not unwilling to own their faults, but do not mend them— merely raise a sort of foolish protest against their own weakness. In like manner they hear with much satisfaction of the efforts made to purify and reform society, but personally they take no trouble about it, devote no time or pains to such endeavours. The hard work of philanthropy they complacently leave to others. Many act in the same way in regard to the expense incurred in a good cause. They are quite proud of the large sums raised in their church, and of the free-handedness of their country. But they do not give. They blandly wave their best wishes over the gifts of others. But where there is power to do something for the good cause, God will not accept a wish for the deed. Where there is power to give, he will not accept a smile for a gift.

II. WHERE GOOD WILL SHOWS ITSELF IN DEEDS OR GIFTS, GOD LOOKS NOT SO MUCH ON THE AMOUNT OF THE OFFERING AS ON THE HEART OF THE DOER OR GIVER. It is the *prothumia*, the readiness of disposition, which pleases him. He loves the earnest worker and the cheerful giver. He approves that doer of the Word who does not need to be coaxed and pressed to undertake some part of Christian service, and that giver who, instead of waiting to be solicited, seeks out the objects most worthy of help, and makes his offering with a simplicity and a spontaneousness which greatly enhance the gift. In fact, while God does not accept the will for the deed from those who are able to do, he always accepts the will in the deed, and is pleased with the evidence of a ready mind. King David was not permitted to build a temple to Jehovah; but it was well that it was in his heart to do so (1 Kings viii. 18), and the preparations which he made for the work are recorded with honour (1 Chron. xxix.). The women who prepared spices and ointments for the dead body of Jesus Christ were not allowed to carry out their purpose, for before they reached the sepulchre he had risen; but their readiness of mind was pleasing to the Lord, and they got something better to do than anoint a corpse. They were made the first preachers of his resurrection (Luke xxiv. 10). The men who had followed Jesus were more slow of heart. They brooded over the disappointment of their hopes about the Messiah's kingdom, and the dark storm of odium which had broken on their Master and on his cause. So they had no thought of an early visit to the sepulchre. But the women thought less of the cause and more of the Master. And so with their ready mind they got the highest honour. Learn that the secret of happiness and usefulness lies in having the same ready mind, fastened, not so much on this piece of work or that, as on the Lord himself, for or to whom all Christian work is to be done. You may not get outlet for your readiness in the way that you planned or expected, but you will get outlet and employment for it; and God will accept it according to what it is, not according to its apparent success. Man looks on the outward appearance, but the Lord looks upon the heart.—F.

Ver. 1.—*The model Churches of Macedonia.* By these we are to understand the Churches at Thessalonica, Philippi, and Berœa. There is a sense in which we speak of the Church of Christ as *one*, and also a sense in which we speak of it as *many*. It is correct to say, "the Church," and it is also correct to say, "the Churches." All who love the Lord Jesus Christ, and have surrendered their will and life to his ruling, and have made open profession of their devotion to him, make together the one catholic and apostolic Church, and may properly be thought of as a whole, as the members of the one body of Christ; but as these are located in various places, as they unite for purposes of fellowship and worship in different spheres and different buildings, they may be spoken of as Churches. The answering terms, which help to explain those on which we are dwelling, were used by our Lord, who spoke of his many *folds* and his one *flock.* St. Paul might with equal truthfulness have spoken of the *Church* in Macedonia, but he probably desired to direct attention to the special circumstances of each individual community, in order to bring out forcibly the remarkable character of their generosity and self-denial. He sets before us for our consideration this fact, that, just as a Christian man's conduct and character may make him a model to others, and a gracious power upon them, touching and quickening into power that spirit of emulation which dwells in various strength in us all, so an individual Church, or a set of Churches, may act with a nobility, a generosity, and self-denial that should make them an inspiring model to other Churches. We consider in what ways the Macedonians became a model to the Corinthians.

I. A MODEL AS THE OBJECTS OF DIVINE GRACE. "We do you to wit of the grace of God bestowed on the Churches of Macedonia." By "grace" here we are to understand the special *favour* of God, and the precise "gifts" with which they were endowed. The disposition and the power to give is to be regarded as a divinely bestowed talent or trust, and as a special sign of the Divine favour. The gift of benevolence, charity, generosity, is as truly a Divine trust or bestowment as the gift of healing, of preaching, or of tongues. And, like all other Divine gifts, it is dependent on recipiency, preparedness to use such gifts aright. Divine bestowments on Churches are never made at hap-hazard, upon any kind of favouritism, or in the exercise of any so-called *sovereignty.* Neither Churches nor individuals can get free from the responsibility of being *ready to receive.* The loving and thoughtful spirit of the Philippians, and the studious openness of the Berœans, and the suffering experiences of the Thessalonians, prepared them to receive this special grace of God unto generosity and brotherly charity. Illustrate and impress this point, that nowadays Churches lack "grace" because they are not in attitudes and moods fitting them for its reception. We are not straitened in God, in God's provisions, or in God's willingness, but we are sadly straitened in ourselves, in our unreadiness and unfitness to receive. Of God it is said, "He giveth more grace;" but of us it must be said, "Ye have not because ye ask not, or because ye ask amiss." Illustrating how God delays his bestowments until there is the fitting attitude for their reception, the Prophet Hosea (ii. 21, 22) represents God as saying, "It shall come to pass in that day, I will hear, saith the Lord, I will hear the heavens, and they shall hear the earth; and the earth shall hear the corn, and the wine, and the oil; and they shall hear Jezreel." When all unite to cry for the refreshing rains, then, and only then, shall the windows be opened, and grace in copious showers descend.

II. A MODEL AS RESPONDING TO DIVINE GRACE. For the grace may come, and be neglected or misused. Compare the expression St. Paul uses concerning himself (1 Cor. xv. 10): "By the grace of God I am what I am: and his grace which was bestowed upon me *was not in vain*; but I laboured more abundantly than they all: yet not I, but the grace of God which was with me." It is a great and ever-working law that all Divine gifts that are unused or undervalued will be taken away or lost. The one condition of the renewal and enlargement of grace is that we have faithfully responded to the grace we have had. We retain the gift of preaching only by preaching, and the gift of charity only by the exercise of generosity and self-denial. The remarkable thing about the Macedonian Churches, the thing which made them a model to other Churches, was that they so nobly responded to the grace that rested upon them, and acted in so earnest and self-sacrificing a manner. So often Churches have more grace than they follow out, and so they lose the grace. The grace abounds, but the response to the grace is set under unworthy limitations.

III. A MODEL AS SELF-DENYING. The apostle notices two things which might reasonably have excused the Macedonians from sharing in the contribution. 1. Their persecution, and the anxieties and distresses which it had brought them. 2. Their poverty, for the Church was not gathered from the rich ; the poor of this world were made " rich in faith." So their large and generous gifts were a delightful surprise, and a testimony to the power of Christian principle upon them. Christian motive mastered worldly considerations; and their gifts became peculiarly acceptable to God, because upon them rested the Christly stamp of self-sacrifice. St. Paul commends, in these Macedonians, just what our Lord commended when he directed attention to the poor widow who cast two mites into the treasury—" all her living."

IV. A MODEL AS THOROUGHLY EARNEST IN GENEROUS SCHEMES. St. Paul dwells, in a very delighted way, upon their *willingness* and their *earnestness*. It was not merely that they gave, but that they gave in such a hearty way, so cheerfully, under the sway of such high motives, and with such evident warmth of affection for himself. If it is true that " what is worth doing is worth doing well," it is especially true of the Christian duty of brotherly kindness as finding expression in self-denying gifts. The great blessing of a gift is the spirit in which it is made. The value is taken away when it is given grudgingly. God loveth—and so do men—the cheerful, willing giver.—R. T.

Ver. 5.—*The religion of association must be made personal.* One of the words in this passage is evidently used in an unfamiliar sense. " Hoped " means " expected," " anticipated." The verse is connected with the collection for the saints at Jerusalem, and is part of the apostle's endeavour to inspire the Churches of Achaia to nobler endeavour by the example of the Churches of Macedonia. The text expresses the deeply religious character of the Macedonian gift. As St. Paul saw it, it was no mere gift, it was the expression of consecrated and devoted hearts. They gave themselves, and *then* their gifts. They gave themselves *in* their gifts. We dwell now, not on the charity, but on the expression, " gave their own selves to the Lord," which suggests for consideration the *personal character* of saving religion.

I. ALL OF US ARE, IN OUR MEASURE, RELIGIOUS. There may still be godless audiences, such as Whitefield gathered at the fairs, or Wesley and Hill at the mouths of colliery pits. But in the ordinary assemblies in our Churches there is not a man, woman, or child who is not, in some degree, religious. They are religious (1) as belonging to a Christian country; (2) as baptized into mystical relations with the Church of Christ; (3) as by acts of formal worship making Christian profession; or (4) as variously related to Christian families. But the question comes again and again before us—Is our kind and degree of religion satisfactory ?

II. IN TOO MANY CASES OUR RELIGION IS WHOLLY MATTER OF ASSOCIATION. 1. We are members of a Christian home, and share in the religion of the home. And this is, for the children, an every way beautiful and hopeful beginning of religious life. 2. We are affected by the tone of the spheres we occupy. Illustrate by young people in situations, where they join in family worship and in attendance at the house of God ; also by the influence of Christian friendships. 3. We are swayed by our near relationship with those who are godly, as in the case of the husband and wife. But the question comes—Is this *all* our religion ? Is it enough ? Is it saving ? Can any reliance be placed upon it ? Will it stand in the coming testing-day ? It is so far good. It is a favourable breeze catching the sails, but it is not safety in the harbour. It is the angel's voice in our ear crying, " Flee for thy life ; " it is even the angel's hand on our arm, as on the arm of Lot; but it is not safety in Zoar. There is a familiar old saying that "Hell is paved with good intentions;" it might have been with "good associations." Such associations are good if they are used as helps, but not if they are relied on as sufficient. They are only evil if they are allowed to hinder personal anxiety. Religion is personal or it is nothing.

III. God, by his providence and by his Word, is ever urging us to make religion personal. Providence breaks up our associations. A time comes when the child passes into manhood or womanhood, and must learn to go alone. Then changes and testing-times come, which show what the religion of association has been worth. Illustrate by the child going to boarding school; the youth to business; the assistant changing his situation; the man or woman going through times of sorrow. In each God is wanting to lead the soul to personal religion. God's preached Word, with its various persuasions, is ever bearing on the same point. It is a singling out of the individual; a two-edged sword to the individual; a pressure of the personal claims of God on the individual. Its voice is, "Thou art the man;" "To you is the word of this salvation sent." It labours to secure a personal decision for Christ, a giving of "our own selves to the Lord." Is, then, your religion yet no more than the religion of your home and associations? And is your manhood come, your womanhood come? Remember that you are *not saved*, only associated with salvation. This is the question which should set you upon anxious self-searchings, "Dost thou believe on the Son of God?" It is not enough to be *close by* salvation, to be even on its doorstep. Enter in. Strive to enter in. Strive to enter in *now*.—R. T.

Ver. 9.—*The poverty that made others rich.* The question is often asked—Which gives most pleasure to us—the faculty of memory, which vivifies the past, or anticipation, which brightens the future? The answers we make at once depend upon, and become revelations of, character. The apostle in this passage is using the faculty of memory; he is recalling what is known respecting the Lord Jesus Christ. He is treating of the grace of self-sacrificing liberality and generosity; and of this Christ is the most illustrious and glorious example. We hold the memory of a twofold exchange on the part of the Lord Jesus—(1) from riches to poverty; (2) from poverty to riches; but here the apostle contrasts Christ's exchange from riches to poverty with our exchange, through Christ, from poverty to riches, and this is the double exchange on which we propose to dwell.

I. The first exchange. *Christ*—from riches to poverty. Christ's riches may be treated under the headings (1) rank; (2) wealth; (3) pleasure. Or we may say that he was rich (1) in his Divine nature; (2) in the infinite love and acceptance of the Father; (3) in the adoration of all holy beings; (4) in possession of all the wealth and joy of heaven. Christ's poverty, which was a comparative thing, may be brought out by presenting such contrasts as (1) God—man; (2) son—servant; (3) at home—homeless; (4) rich—empty; (5) happy—suffering. He became poor by (1) giving up the wealth of heaven; (2) in his birth as a poor man's child; (3) in his lowly station as one of the common people; (4) in his death-time of sorest humiliation. Such a condescension in incarnation had never before been conceived. It surpasses thought. It is the exceeding great mystery which the eternal ages will not fathom. It is " so great love;" it is "what manner of love."

II. The second exchange. *We*—from poverty to riches. By our poverty we need not understand our earthly conditions, seeing that poverty is but a relative thing, and depends upon the degree in which a man matches his circumstances. The man who has little and wants little is not poor; the man who has little and wants much is the man who can alone be called " poor." Our real poverties are the conditions to which we have reduced ourselves by our sins. See how much we have thus lost, so that we are become poor indeed. (1) Lost harmony with the world; (2) lost peace within; (3) lost brotherhood with men; (4) lost fellowship with God. Then what are the riches we attain through Christ Jesus? They are riches for the souls, which are our real selves; they are not any mere riches of circumstances. They consist in (1) the smile and favour of God; (2) the love of a living and Divine Friend; (3) the prospect of an eternal glory. Or we may say that we become rich (1) in the hope that Jesus brought; (2) in the words that Jesus spoke; (3) in the love to us that Jesus showed; (4) and in the salvation that Jesus secured. But no human words càn exhaust our riches in Christ Jesus.

III. THE CONNECTION BETWEEN THESE TWO EXCHANGES. "*For your sakes.*" The one exchange was made in order to accomplish the other. To bless us Christ must condescend to become one of us. Illustrate by the missionary making himself a Chinaman, and living all alone among the people that he might reach them with the gospel message. Or by the Moravian missionary, giving up friendship, love, and hope, to enter the lazar-house and try to teach and save the lepers. And what did Christ do for us when he had thus humbled himself to take our nature on him? It is said that "he went about doing good," and that was his way of making everybody rich with (1) blessings; (2) truth; and (3) salvation. And St. Paul appeals to the Corinthians and to us, saying, "Ye know the grace." But *do we know?* Have we felt the persuasion and attraction that are in such "love Divine, all love excelling"?—R. T.

Ver. 12.—*Willing minds putting value on gifts.* "First a willing mind." The apostle has been calling to mind the resolve which the Corinthian Church had made a year previously. They had determined to join in the collection that was being made for the poor and suffering saints at Jerusalem. It seems that the disturbed state of the Church and the delay of St. Paul's visit had led to the forgetfulness of this resolve, and little or nothing had been done in relation to it. The apostle now brings the matter again before them, reminds them that there was at one time the *willing mind,* and he seems delicately to suggest to them that it would be a beautiful way of testifying to the restored relations between himself and them, if they would revive this collection, carry the matter through, and give him the joy of carrying their gifts to the poor Jerusalem saints, in whom he was so deeply interested. He was thus led to dwell upon the importance, before God, of the spirit in which gifts are made. They ought to carry our hearts to him, just as the old Mosaic sacrifices carried the hearts of the worshippers. Gifts have voices which God can hear, and he reads our hearts by the help of them. Two points are here suggested.

I. MAN ESTIMATES GIFTS BY THEIR MONEY VALUE. A fair enough standard in view of the institutions that have to be sustained and the work which has to be done. The Church needs large gifts, and is compelled to ask for quantity. She needs the devotements of the rich, and is not wholly wrong in trying to raise ever higher the standard of Christian gifts for Christian uses. But the money estimate of gifts needs to be set under most careful limitations. It fails to take account of the relative circumstances of the givers. A pound is a pound, whoever may give it; but the rich man passes it over, and knows that it will not involve his going without any one thing that he wishes to have. The poor man hands it over, and knows it means wearing the threadbare coat a few months longer, or going without some personal gratification. In really worthy scales that poor man's pound weighs heavy, for there is added to it that self-denial which is, in God's sight, of great price. Man cannot discern or rightly appraise *motives.* The business principle too often wholly sways men in their Christian and Church relations, and men are accepted by the largeness of their contributions rather than by the largeness of the love with which they contribute.

II. GOD ESTIMATES GIFTS BY THEIR WILL VALUE. "If there be first the willing mind, there is acceptance." God seeth not as man seeth. Man looketh on the countenance; God looketh on the heart. Man appraises the value of the thing; God reads the state of the will and the purpose of the heart. Illustration may be taken from the large gift of Barnabas to the early Church. God accepted it because it was the expression of a willing mind. The gifts of Ananias and Sapphira were smaller; they were not, however, refused on this ground, but only because the will was wrong and the motive mixed and bad. The "amount" of a gift is quite as important in the sight of God as in the sight of man, because a great gift alone can express the willing mind of a man with great means. God judges proportions. He only desires to see Christian love triumphing over disabilities, and making the rich, who cling to riches, splendidly generous, and the poor making the "poverty which had consumed them even to the very bottom" (ver. 2) yield noble and self-denying contributions. With God the question is—How much did your heart give? It is a second thing, with him, to ask—How much did your hand give? But he does expect the heart and the hand to honourably act together, the hand honestly expressing what the heart feels.—R. T.

Ver. 21.—*Honest before God and man.* Comp. Prov. iii. 4, which, in the Greek Version reads, " Write them upon the table of thine heart, and thou shalt find favour. Provide things honest in the sight of God and man." This may be treated as a general precept, applicable to all Christian people; or it may be regarded as a reminder of the care which the apostle had taken that, in the administration of money affairs, he should not be misunderstood or blamed.   Consider—

I. THE COUNSEL AS APPLIED TO THE APOSTLE HIMSELF. As a fact he had been jealously providing for honest things, and doing everything possible in order to secure the due checking of the gifts and safety of the stored money. Calvin says, " He was not so satisfied with himself as to think it unworthy of his dignity to avoid calumny." Dean Plumptre says, " In this case, had the apostle had only the judgment of God to consider, he could with a pure conscience have taken up the money to Jerusalem by himself. But he had to consider that men were judging him, and might suspect him, and therefore he insisted on having his accounts audited." F. W. Robertson says, " In this is to be observed St. Paul's wisdom, not only as a man of the world, but as a man of God. He knew that he lived in a censorious age, that he was as a city set on a hill, that the world would scan his every act and his every word, and attribute all conceivable and even inconceivable evil to what he did in all honour. It was just because of St. Paul's honour and innocence that he was likely to have omitted this prudence." Archdeacon Farrar indicates the kind of things that were said about the apostle by his Corinthian enemies, which made such an earnest self-vindication absolutely necessary. He represents them as saying that St. Paul was " half demented, and yet there was some method in his madness which showed itself partly in self-importance and partly in avarice, both of which were very injurious to the interests of his followers. What, for instance, could be more guileful and crafty than his entire conduct about this collection which he was so suspiciously eager to set on foot ? He had ordered them to get up a subscription in his first letter, had, in answer to their inquiries, directed that it should be gathered, as in the Galatian Churches, by a weekly offertory, and had, since this, sent Titus to stimulate zeal in the matter. They dared to insinuate that all this was only a cunning device to hide his real intentions, and give him a securer grasp of their money." Give in detail the arrangements made by the apostle to secure the due safety and auditing of the collection; and urge that all who have responsible positions in relation to Christian monies should show a similar anxiety to " provide things honest."

II. THE COUNSEL AS APPLIED TO CHRISTIAN GIVING. Those who give must give only that which is honourably their own. The man who is in debt must pay his debts before he gives. The man who has family claims is bound to make adequate provision for them before he gives. To use the familiar proverb, " A man must be just before he is generous." When this rule is neglected, a man's gifts can neither be acceptable to God nor right in the sight of his fellow-men.—R. T.

EXPOSITION.

CHAPTER IX.

Encouragement to the Corinthians to fulfil their promises by giving speedily (vers. 1—5), amply (ver. 6), cheerfully (ver. 7), and thereby earn God's blessing (vers. 8—11) in a cause fruitful of blessed consequence (vers. 12—14). He concludes the subject with a heartfelt thanksgiving (ver. 15).

Ver. 1.—**For.** This word shows that he is continuing the same subject, and therefore excludes the supposition that this chapter is a separate letter or fragment. No doubt, however, the express mention of the collection after he has been practically writing about it through the whole of the last chapter looks as if he had been interrupted, or had left off dictating at the end of the last verse. Such breaks must often and necessarily have occurred in the dictation of the Epistles, and doubtless help to account for some of their phenomena. Perhaps, on reperusing the last paragraphs before resuming the subject he observed that, after all, he had not directly mentioned the contribution, and therefore explains that he thought it superfluous to do so. **To the saints.** The poor Christians of Jerusalem (ch. viii. 4). **Superfluous.** Because the subject had been already fully brought to their notice by himself and by Titus.

Ver. 2.—**I boast of you;** literally, *I am boasting.* The tense shows that he is writing from Macedonia, probably from Philippi (ch. viii. 24). **Achaia** (see ch. i. 1). **Was ready a year ago;** *has been prepared since last year.* **Your zeal hath provoked very many;** literally, *zeal from you hath stimulated the majority.* "Zeal *from* you" means zeal which emanated from the Corinthians and aroused emulation in others.

Ver. 3.—**But.** Though it is needless to *write* to you about this collection, I sent the brethren to make sure that all I had said about you might be justified by reality. **In this behalf;** *i.e.* about this matter (comp. ch. iii. 10), or, as we might express it, "in this direction." He seems to have felt more uncertainty about their liberality than about other matters (ch. vii. 4).

Ver. 4.—**They of Macedonia;** rather, *Macedonians;* i.e. any friends from Macedonia (Acts xx. 4). Shall Achaians have to blush before Macedonians? **We, that we say not ye.** Nothing can exceed the delicacy of this touch. St. Paul asks them to be ready with their contributions for *his* sake, not for their own; that *he* may not have to blush for his generous words respecting them, whereas really the discredit would be simply theirs. **Confident boasting;** rather, *confidence.* The reading "of boasting" is not genuine here. For the word *hypostasis* in the sense of "confidence," see ch. xi. 17; Heb. iii. 4. The use of the word to represent the "Persons" of the Blessed Trinity is later. The other sense of the word, "substance" (or underlying base of attributes), is found in Heb. i. 3.

Ver. 5.—**That they would go before unto you.** The triple repetition of the word "before" shows how earnest St. Paul is in the matter. The Corinthians had promised largely; it was evident that there had been, or that there was ground for fearing that there might be, some slackness of performance. St. Paul was so unwilling to have seemed inaccurate in what he had said about them in Macedonia that he wished to give them ample notice before the Macedonian delegates arrived. **Your bounty, whereof ye had notice before;** *your previously promised blessing-bounty;* literally, *blessing.* The mere word should have acted as an inducement to generosity. See the use of the word to express a generous gift in Gen. xxxiii. 11; Judg. i. 15, etc. (LXX.); Eph.

i. 3. In this sense it resembles the Hebrew *berachah* (Josh. xv. 19, etc.). **As** a matter of **bounty, and not as** of **covetousness;** *as a blessing, and not as an extortion;* i.e. as a free gift of your own, and not as something which I had wrung from you, or "got out of you" (ch. vii. 2; xii. 17, 18). It is less likely that the word *pleonexia* refers to the "parsimony" of the Corinthians, as though the *smallness* of their gift would show their greed for large gains.

Ver. 6.—**But this** I say. The Greek only has "But this." The ellipse can hardly be "I say." It is an accusative used absolutely —"as to their." Compare "But one thing" (Phil. iii. 14). **Shall reap also sparingly.** In the Greek the more emphatic order is "sparingly also shall reap." The metaphor of the harvest implies that the more generous the gift the richer will be the return; and that "withholding more than is meet" will only tend to poverty (Prov. xi. 24, 25; xix. 17; xxii. 9). (For "sowing" and "reaping" in this connection, comp. 1 Cor. ix. 11.) **Bountifully;** literally, *with blessings;* Vulgate, *in benedictionibus* (comp. Gal. vi. 7, 8). Bountifulness blesses both him that gives and him that takes.

Ver. 7.—**In his heart.** The heart must not only go with but anticipate the hand. **Grudgingly;** literally, *from grief* (Exod. xxv. 2; Rom. xii. 8). **A cheerful giver.** The phrase is from the addition to Prov. xxii. 8, which is found in the LXX.; except that "loveth" is substituted for "blesseth." Compare "He that showeth mercy, with *cheerfulness*" (Rom. xii. 8). The rabbis said that cheerful kindness, even if nothing was given, was better than a morose gift.

Ver. 8.—**To make all grace abound toward you.** God can give you such abundant gifts that you will not feel the loss of a generous contribution to his service. **Sufficiency.** The word *autarkeia* (1 Tim. vi. 6) in the Stoic philosophy was used for the perfect independence which enabled a man to stand alone. The term is here softened and Christianized to express the contentment which arises from the full supply of all our needs by God. The affirmations of the original are as emphatic as language can make them. They express that the man who places all his trust upon God will be "perfect and entire, lacking nothing" (Phil. iv. 11, 19).

Ver. 9.—**As it is written.** The quotation is from the LXX. in Ps. cxii. 9. **He hath dispersed abroad.** He has been a large and generous giver. **The poor.** The word here used is *penēs*, which does not occur elsewhere in the New Testament. It means moderate and honourable poverty, whereas in classical Greek *ptocheia* implies disreputable pauperism and mendicancy (comp. ch.

viii. 9). **His righteousness.** Meaning here his good deeds. The word is often rendered "pity" by the LXX. (*eleēmosunē*, from which word comes our "alms"), and this word occurs as a synonymous reading in Matt. vi. 1. **Remaineth for ever.** Because—

"Good deeds never die.
They with the sun and moon renew their light,
For ever blessing him that looks on them."

Ver. 10.—**He that ministereth.** The verb used is *epichorēgein*, to furnish abundantly. At Athens a *choragus* was one who furnished a chorus, and as this was a *leitourgia* (or "public service"), involving great expense, and often discharged with extreme munificence, the verb came to imply "provide abundantly." St. Paul may (so to speak) have "picked up the word" at Athens. **Seed to the sower** (Isa. lv. 10). **Both minister.** The true reading almost certainly is "*will* both supply bread for food, and *will* multiply your seed for sowing, and *will* increase the fruits of your righteousness" (see Isa. lv. 10, LXX.). **The fruits of your righteousness** (Hos. x. 12, LXX.). In "righteousness," as in all things else, it is God only who "gives the increase" (1 Cor. iii. 10).

Ver. 11.—**To all bountifulness;** rather, *to all simplicity*, or "singleness of heart" (ch. viii. 2). **Through us.** We are the agents in collecting and distributing your gifts (ch. viii. 19, 20). **Thanksgiving to God.** From the recipients of your single-hearted generosity.

Ver. 12.—**For the administration of this service.** The word "liturgy," here rendered "service," is used in the same connection in Rom xv. 27. Generally it means "religious service" (Acts xiii. 6; Phil. ii. 17; Heb. x. 11). Here it more resembles its classic sense of "a public office discharged for the good of the state," such as undertaking the office of a *choragus* (see ver. 10). **Not only.** St. Paul is anxious to emphasize the *religious* side of the contribution fully as much as its *philanthropic* object. **Is abundant.** It *overflows* as it were in the form of thanksgivings to God.

Ver. 13.—**By the experiment of this ministration;** rather, *by the test (of your love)*

furnished by this ministration (ch. viii. 2). **For your professed subjection;** literally, *for the submission of your confession to the gospel of Christ.* **And for your liberal distribution unto them;** rather, *and for the simplicity of your fellowship towards them.* A large contribution would prove two things; namely, (1) that the Corinthians showed due subjection to the truths and duties which they theoretically accepted as resulting from the gospel; and (2) that they were united to their Jewish-Christian brethren and to all others in single-hearted fellowship. It is very doubtful whether *haplotēs* ever means "liberality," and *koinōnia* is here better understood of "communion" than of "communication." **Unto all men.** For if the Corinthians behaved with such brotherly kindness to the once-despised Jews, who were now their Christian brethren, they would be not likely to refuse fellowship with any others.

Ver. 14.—**And by their prayer for you.** These words are joined by our Authorized Version with "glorifying God." The saints at Jerusalem would, in consequence of the proved sincerity of the Corinthians, glorify God with thanksgiving for their faithfulness and kindness, by prayer for them. The Revisers take the clause with the following participle, "while they themselves also, with supplication on your behalf, long after you by reason of the exceeding grace of God in you." This is the only right view of the construction. **Long after you for the exceeding grace of God in you;** literally, *yearn for you because of the grace of God which overabounds to you.*

Ver. 15.—**Thanks be unto God.** Nothing ever seems so much to disburden the full heart of St. Paul after deep emotion as an utterance of thanksgiving (Rom. vii. 25; ix. 5; xi. 33; 1 Cor. xv. 57; Gal. i. 5; 1 Tim. i. 17). The thanksgiving here is like a great sigh of relief. The subject of it is perfectly general. It is not a mere "Amen" uttered, as it were, by St. Paul at the end of the thanksgivings of the saints at Jerusalem which he has been presupposing; but an offering of thanks to God for the issues of grace in general, all summed up in one act of "inestimable love" (John iii. 16; Rom. vi. 23; xi. 33; Eph. iii. 19).

HOMILETICS.

Vers. 1—5.—*Paul's directions for collecting the contributions of the Corinthian Church.* "For as touching the ministering to the saints," etc. The work of collecting was entrusted to Titus and a brother whose praise was "throughout all the Churches," and probably to other Christians more or less distinguished. Concerning the collecting of their subscriptions, three things are observable in Paul's own conduct.

I. HE RECOGNIZED THEIR MERITS. "For as touching the ministering to the saints, it is superfluous for me to write to you: for I know the forwardness of your mind, for which I boast of you to them of Macedonia that Achaia was ready a year ago; and your zeal hath provoked very many." He gives them full credit for what they had already done. They had so much cheered him some months before with the readiness with which they had entered into his beneficent enterprise, that he had boasted of them to those of Macedonia and Achaia, and he assures them that their zeal had stimulated, or " provoked very many." We may be assured that Paul not only credits them for what they had done, merely as a matter of policy or politeness, but as a matter of justice. It is right that goodness in others should be recognized wherever found, and that we should with a hearty frankness praise them that do well. This is a duty sadly neglected.

II. HE RESPECTED THEIR REPUTATION. " Lest haply if they of Macedonia come with me, and find you unprepared, we (that we say not, ye) should be ashamed in this same confident boasting." The apostle knew human life and the circumstances that influence it, and he apprehended that, had the members of the Corinthian Church been called upon suddenly, without any previous advice, to complete the beneficent work into which they had entered so readily some twelve months before, they might not be able on a sudden either to do justice to their own reputation or to justify the high praise he had given them. The reputation of Christian men should always be sacredly respected. Reputation is social power; deprive a man of this, and he is powerless in society; deprive a Church of this, and you leave it as infirm as a merchant without credit. Respect for the reputation of good men is the duty of all. No man can deprive me of my character, but he may of my reputation, and without my reputation my social influence is *nil*.

> " The purest treasure mortal times afford
> Is spotless reputation ; that away,
> Men are but gilded loam or painted clay."
> (Shakespeare.)

III. HE STUDIED THEIR CONVENIENCE. " Therefore I thought it necessary to exhort the brethren, that they would go before unto you, and make up beforehand your bounty," etc. " Every one knows," says Robertson, " how different is the feeling with which we give when charity is beforehand, from that which we give when charitable collections come side by side with debts and taxes. The charity which finds us unprepared is a call as hateful as that of any creditor whom it is hard to pay. Paul knew this well ; he knew that if the Corinthians were taken unawares their feelings would be exasperated towards him with shame, and also towards the saints at Jerusalem, to whom they were constrained to give. Therefore he gave timely notice." Special duties have times and seasons. There are moods of mind, and passing circumstances so unfavourable as to render their discharge almost impossible, hence men's conveniences have to be studied. The apostle, in recognizing merits, respecting reputations, and studying conveniences, should be taken as an example by all Christian ministers in dealing with their people.

Vers. 6—15.—*The way and worth of genuine beneficence.* " But this I say, He which soweth," etc. Our subject is—*The way and worth of genuine beneficence.*

I. THE WAY OF GENUINE BENEFICENCE. What is the method of its operations? How does it develop itself? 1. *Bountifully.* " But this I say, He which soweth sparingly shall reap also sparingly ; and he which soweth bountifully shall reap also bountifully." The apostle does not intimate, still less dictate, the amount of contribution he required, but what he requires is bountifulness. Nothing niggardly or from restraint, but with a full, open, generous heart. A man may give bountifully who only subscribes a mite, and niggardly who subscribes his ten thousand pounds. In the fifth verse Paul says, " The same might be ready, as a matter of bounty, and not as of covetousness." 2. *Deliberately.* " Every man according as he purposeth in his heart, so let him give." A spurious charity gives from impulse or pressure. There is a species of eloquence which extorts money, which the giver regrets as soon as he has parted with it. Genuine charity acts not thus ; it forms a generous purpose, and from that purpose it acts, as love always acts, on the universe. 3. *Cheerfully.* " Not grudgingly, or of necessity." There are those who part with their contributions as if they parted with their life-blood. They have been wrung from them, and they groan when they are gone. Genuine charity acts not thus; its greatest happiness is in giving. In sooth, he who gives reluctantly never truly gives at all. "God loveth a cheerful giver." His own happiness is in giving; he rejoices in the happiness of the creation, and to be happy there must be giving.

II. THE WORTH OF GENUINE BENEFICENCE. The most valuable thing in the universe is genuine, practical love, or charity. 1. It is a most valuable thing in its *issues*. (1) It confers happiness on the man who practises it. Every act of it is to him a seed of life, a seed which in his own soul, as in a garden, will germinate and grow, and will produce fruits, delectable to the moral tastes, and strengthening to the moral powers of the soul, imperishable fruit. The more of these deed-germs he sows, the more abundant the harvest. "He which soweth sparingly shall reap also sparingly, and he which soweth bountifully shall reap also bountifully." He will be "blessed in his deed;" in truth, there only is blessedness to be found. (2) It ensures the blessing of the Almighty. (*a*) He sees that the man of charity shall lose nothing by his contributions. "God is able to make all grace abound toward you; that ye, always having all sufficiency in all things, may abound to every good work." The God of goodness sees that no man shall be really injured by his goodness. "In all thy gifts show a cheerful countenance, and dedicate thy tithes with gladness. Give unto the Most High according as he hath enriched thee; and as thou hast gotten, give thee with a cheerful eye. For the Lord recompenseth, and will give thee seven times as much" (Ecclus. xxxv. 9—11). (*b*) He sees that his beneficent deeds shall be blessed for ever. "His righteousness remaineth for ever." A good deed is a seed that will go on multiplying for ever. Beneficence, after all, is righteousness. (3) It alleviates the distress of mankind. "For the administration of this service not only supplieth the want of the saints, but is abundant also by many thanksgivings unto God." What hushes the sorrows of the distressed, heals the wounds of the afflicted, relieves the poverty of the indigent, dispels the darkness of the ignorant, etc.? Practical beneficence. It is, indeed, through this that God helps the world to rise from its fallen condition of guilt and misery. (4) It is promotive of universal worship. "Whiles by the experiment of this ministration they glorify God for your professed subjection unto the gospel of Christ." And "which causeth through us thanksgiving to God." The tendency of practical beneficence is to turn the world to the universal worship of the one God, the Source of all good. 2. It is a most valuable thing in *itself*. "Thanks be unto God for his unspeakable gift." What is the "gift" here? Undoubtedly charity, or practical love. Has Paul here a special reference to Christ? Be it so. The value of that gift was the love which it expressed, incarnated, and diffused. The gift of love is the highest gift. The greatest thing in the universe is mind, the greatest thing in mind is love, and the greatest element in love is practical philanthropy.

HOMILIES BY VARIOUS AUTHORS.

Vers. 1—5.—*Reference to his former argument; its completeness; why he resumes the subject.* Reviewing the reasoning on the duty of Christian beneficence, the apostle concluded that he had expounded the subject in a manner so clear and explicit as to make any addition "superfluous" on the score either of logic or of appeal. Recall the argument for a moment, and see if he was not justified in this opinion. The appeal was for the poor of the Church at Jerusalem. Macedonia was depressed and sorely troubled, Achaia was internally agitated by Judaizers and free-thinkers; and between this upper and nether millstone the young Churches were well-nigh ground to powder. St. Paul himself was greatly afflicted. But he had strong faith in Christ and in human nature under the influence of Christ's grace, and having this confidence he was hopeful, resolute, and courageous. Macedonia had done nobly. Corinth would not fall below the standard he had set for their generosity. Full of heart, he presses the claim of the occasion, but his zeal and anxiety never betray him into using a false motive or into pushing a true motive too far. The "rod" is not threatened. All through, the appeal is to the best elements of our nature, for he recognizes, as "the sacred writers constantly recognize, the fact that the freest and most spontaneous acts of men, their inward states and the outward manifestations of those states where good, are due to a secret influence of the Spirit of God which eludes our consciousness. The believer is most truly self-determined when determined by the grace of God" (Hodge). We have seen that the apostle never loses sight for a moment of the one inspiring motive—the love of Christ towards us and his Divine sacrifice in our behalf. Equal with God and infinitely blessed, he left his glory, assumed our flesh took its infirmities, bore its sins, endured its shame and humiliation, and expiated its guilt. The abnegation was so complete that he depended on the Holy Ghost for wisdom, fortitude, and strength. A man of prayer, he sought the Spirit's aid on every occasion, and was so dependent as to say, "I do nothing of myself." Every adventitious help was set aside; loneliness and sorrow were his self-chosen lot; and he made himself the poorest of men, that he might show how supremely he rested upon the Father in his mediatorial work. But poverty and sorrow were not thus borne for their own sake, nor, indeed, was it the circumstances of his lot, but the lot itself, that marked the greatness of his condescension. The argument of St. Paul is directed to one point, viz. what Christ was and what he became, so that the contrast between his earthly position and that of other men is not so much as hinted at, but the whole force is thrown upon the contrast as to his being "rich" and becoming "poor," that we "through his poverty might be rich." On this basis Christian beneficence was founded. Christian "equality" was a natural sequel. For this was, in the order of Providence, the one specific and preeminent sphere in which Christian conscience and affection and humane impulses would most fully and freely combine to glorify God in Christ. On no other ground could a Church be a spiritual *human* community, and hence the stress laid on human virtues sanctified by the grace of Christ. There is emulation; how he exalts it! There is imitation; how he emphasizes it! There is prudence; what an excellence it is to protect our good from being spoken of as evil! After such a presentation of gospel truth and its effective enforcement, he might well say that it was "superfluous" to write concerning "the ministering to the saints." One bright spot had all along lingered on that murky horizon; "Achaia was ready a year ago; and your zeal hath provoked very many." Men who are backsliding in religion do not lose their hold all at once on the Christian virtues. Happily for us, some of these virtues are stronger than others, and these act as a breakwater against the incoming surges of temptation. One or more qualities exist in us that are more receptive of grace than other qualities, and they are specially resistant of decay. As in physical disease life would often succumb were it not that some organs have so much more functional vitality than others, so in religious life, a single vigorous principle or sentiment may save us from spiritual death. So it was with the Corinthians. Despite of their corruptions, they had one redeeming excellence, viz. the "forwardness" of their "mind" in this benevolent enterprise of helping the poor saints in Jerusalem. God honoured this trait of their character. Many a virtue had gone down under the pressure of worldliness and carnality. This survived, and it was capable of being evoked into healthy and energetic action. St. Paul knew his opportunity. He saw the good in these erring brethren. If he had not, he could never have seen the evil. And seeing the good so clearly, he recognized it and laboured for its immediate development in a very earnest form. The true growth would choke out the weeds, and to this he directed his wise husbandry. Every way the prospect was encouraging. Yet he would make assurance doubly sure. He had boasted of the Corinthians. If they should not be ready in time with the collection, "we [too delicate to say, 'ye'] should be ashamed in this same confident boasting." On this account he sent Titus and the deputies to "make up beforehand" their bounty. It must be "bounty," not a matter of "covetousness." Postponing the work might open the way for selfishness to suggest reasons for less giving. Love of money might have a sudden quickening. Risks were numerous when men believed that the heart of to-day would be the heart of to-morrow. Satan was mightier at some times than at others, and Christian men were not always quite themselves. "Make up beforehand." The right thing was ennobled by doing it at the right time, and the right time was now. "Withhold not good from them to whom it is due, when it is in the power of thine hand to do it." Debts of love mature when the heart is first warmed by the Spirit. Putting off invites covetousness. "Beforehand" is the watchword of the bountiful soul.—L.

Vers. 6—9.—*Correspondence between Christian sowing and reaping.* There was nothing of chance or luck in the operations of beneficence. It was a transaction with God, who had instituted certain laws for its government. 1. As to the law of proportion. If they sowed sparingly, they reaped sparingly; if bountifully, they reaped bountifully. This was natural law. It was also spiritual law. If the law met them everywhere, addressed the senses and the soul, and enforced itself both in providence and grace, surely they could not but give very profound heed to a principle which was so amply illustrated. 2. As to the spirit of giving. The law was spontaneity of sentiment—" according as he purposeth in his heart, so let him give;" and again, it was cheerfulness of feeling—not "grudgingly, or of necessity; for God loveth a cheerful giver." On this aspect of giving, the apostle had delivered his mind without reservation. Freedom here was scrupulously insisted on. To be Christ-like it must be wholly self-directed. It must be born directly of the Spirit. Vast and indeed sacred as human agency is, there are seasons when the Spirit bids it retire, and he takes the soul into his solitary communion. 3. The element of recompense is stated. "God is able to make all grace abound toward you." Blessings used rightly would bring other and larger blessings. Benevolent contributions were disciplinary. The act was educative. If a man gave because of his love to Christ, if he gave willingly and cordially, if he gave freely, then he was being trained as a giver, and of course was, in this particular, a growing man. Any sort of arrested development in goodness is bad enough, but this checking of progress in charity is peculiarly harmful. Worldliness rushes back with an overwhelming current. Avarice, denied its food for a time, has a voracious appetite. And, therefore, the very urgent need of growth in this sentiment, which the apostle argues in a manner uncommonly forcible. Spiritual blessings are assured. "All grace abound toward you." Temporal blessings are promised. "Always having all sufficiency in all things, may abound to every good work." There was to be an "*all sufficiency,*" an overflowing measure on God's part, so as to furnish the means or resources for continued and enlarged benevolence, or otherwise the growth would stop. "Every good work" has a very broad signification. We take it to mean a very wide and generous activity in kind deeds, an "enthusiasm," not for "humanity," but for Christ in humanity, and a desire and a purpose expanding in the ratio of new blessings, spiritual and temporal, to pour forth its heart in ministration to others. "God is able." Yet we must not forget that he never resigns his Divine sovereignty in a promise or to a promise, but is infinitely wise and considerately tender in the administration of providential blessings. To elucidate his meaning, St. Paul quotes from Ps. cxii. 9, "He hath dispersed, he hath given to the poor, his righteousness endureth for ever." The rule is that God gives us what we have in order that he may give us more. There is a future in everything, a future in every seed, a future in every dollar honestly made, a future in every blessing God bestows. But it is for him alone to order this future, so as to "make all grace abound" in us, and to enable us to "abound to every good work."—L.

Vers. 10—15.—*Unity in nature and grace; manifold results of beneficence; thanksgiving.* St. Paul had spoken in the sixth verse of the law of the spiritual harvest—proportion of reward in reference to quantity, so much sowing followed by so much reaping. But there is another law—a grain of corn or wheat produces many grains. In some instances hundreds of seeds come from one seed. Seeds multiply seeds, and the harvest of a county may sow a large territory. Nothing in the vegetable kingdom is on a stinted scale. Omnipotence touches a clod of earth, and in a few months it is transformed into bread; but this is not all the wonder, for that clod has yielded far more than it received. Thus it is that, in the physical world, labour becomes accumulative, producing over and above its own wants a vast surplus, which goes to feed those who are unable to work. Not abundance but superabundance is the lesson nature teaches. We make enough to supply necessities, comforts, and luxuries; enough to meet artificial wants; enough to compensate for impotence, idleness, and dissipation; enough to allow for a waste that can scarcely be computed. So it is in spiritual things. The productive power is immensely rewarded. This striking correspondence was in his view when St. Paul said, "He that supplieth seed to the sower and bread for food, shall supply and multiply your seed for sowing, and increase the fruits of your righteousness"

(Revised Version). The fact is always grander than the figure, and hence we may believe that the fruits of righteousness will infinitely surpass the work done. Observe now that this was a present thing as well as a future thing. Just then a gracious influence was spreading through the Churches and uniting them in closer fellowship by reason of a common interest in behalf of Jerusalem. And, furthermore, they should be " enriched in everything to all bountifulness," no lack of seed for sowing, fruits of righteousness abounding, and especially their liberality should cause thanksgiving to God. This idea of thanksgiving fills a large space in his mind. It becomes in the twelfth verse " many thanksgivings." What joy would it bring to Jerusalem! How far would the glad tidings spread! Not only for the pecuniary aid afforded, but for this new and cheering evidence of their obedience unto the gospel of Christ, what praise would ascend to God! If we could transfer ourselves into the position of these early Christians and enter into their feelings, especially those of the Jerusalem Church, we should realize the apostle's meaning where he lays such a stress on the results of this Gentile beneficence. But we can hardly approximate this state of mind. The loneliness of the saints at Jerusalem, the large sacrifice of property after Pentecost, the loss of employment because of professing faith in Christ, the destitution and suffering that had befallen them, the growing disturbances with Rome, the increase of bitter strife among the Jews, the darkness with its prophetic woes descending on the doomed city, parties becoming more and more virulent in their antagonisms to one another, and amid it all, the " poor saints " subjected to all sorts of insult and grievance, give us but a general idea of the misery and wretchedness they were enduring. It was all very real to St. Paul. No such earthly reality as Jerusalem occupied his intellect and heart. Was he looking forward to the day (as Stanley suggests) when he should stand in the holy city and witness the gratitude of the Church for this great benefaction? Likely enough; but whether so or not, it is certain that his soul overflowed with joy. It was a grand proof of brotherhood between Jewish and Gentile Christians. It was a perfecting link in the chain that was to bind them together. It was a blessed testimony to the divineness of the gospel. Contemplating the gifts, he rises in a moment to the Divine Gift, and exclaims, "Thanks be unto God for his unspeakable Gift! "—L.

Ver. 2.—*The contagion of zeal.* The interest which Christians living in distant lands learned, under apostolic guidance and by the spiritual tuition of the indwelling love of Christ, to take in one another's welfare, was an evidence of the introduction into humanity of a new moral power, a principle of universal love and brotherhood. It is very instructive to see the congregations of Macedonia and of Corinth rivalling one another in the benevolent enterprise of relieving the wants of the mother Church at Jerusalem. Paul evidently encourages this beneficial emulation.

I. ZEAL IN CHRISTIAN BENEVOLENCE IS IN ITSELF GOOD. The languid and unemotional, the cold and calculating, however they may pride themselves upon their justice and reasonableness, are not the people who do the good, the benevolent work of the world. It is good to be zealously affected in a good cause.

II. THE CONTAGIOUSNESS OF ZEAL IS FOUNDED UPON THE SOCIAL NATURE OF MAN. We are members one of another, and it is not desirable, it is not possible, for any person, for any community, to be indifferent to the welfare of others. And the conduct of each has some influence upon the conduct of others. It is not easy to be zealous when all around are unconcerned and inactive, whilst, on the other hand, the spectacle of zealous devotion and self-denial is stimulating and encouraging.

III. THIS EMULATION MAY BE CARRIED TO A PREJUDICIAL EXTENT. It cannot but be acknowledged that emulation may lead to ostentation. Who can question that the motive of some givers to charitable and religious institutions is impure? One wishes to excel another, for the pleasure of triumphing over him, or of cutting a more important figure in the eyes of his fellow-men. And thus the true motive is lost sight of, and a moral injury is wrought.

IV. YET IT IS WELL TO FEEL THE FORCE OF A GOOD EXAMPLE AS A PRACTICAL MOTIVE TO ZEALOUS SERVICE. We may learn from the case of others what may be done where there is consecration, self-denial, and prayerful effort. Our apathy may be rebuked, our flagging benevolence revived. It is when the coals are not only kindled, but put together, that the fire burns clear and bright, and gives forth its genial warmth.—T.

Ver. 6.—*Sowing and reaping.* This is one of those natural analogies which are common to all languages and to all ages. There is sowing and reaping in the history of the individual; the moral bias of his youth may determine the direction of his after life. There is sowing and reaping in the experience of a Christian community; its founders may impart to it an impulse the consequences of which shall be discernible in distant generations. And in this passage the apostle reminds his readers that giving is a kind of sowing, and that, as the husbandman reaps as he has sown, so shall it be in the experience of all benefactors. The liberal shall reap abundantly; the grudging and sparing shall gather a slender crop.

I. THE LAW OF CORRESPONDENCE BETWEEN SOWING AND REAPING IS A JUST LAW. It is an appointment of a God of righteousness. It is in harmony with the principles of his government. Its maintenance is evidently productive of the welfare of Christian society.

II. THIS LAW IS ONE THE OPERATIONS OF WHICH WE CAN IN SOME MEASURE TRACE. 1. It may be observed that illiberality stunts the spiritual stature of the giver, whilst generosity promotes his growth. There is noticeable in large-hearted and generous natures an expansion which is its own reward; a happy disposition, a constant satisfaction in the result of gifts and efforts; a width of view which removes such from the petty and miserable emotions of envy, jealousy, and suspicion. 2. In connection with this it may be remarked that the treatment of the generous by others is in itself a rich reward. The liberal man is honoured, appreciated, loved. Small services, slight tokens of respect, are offered him which are evidences of deep feeling, and which cannot be received without gratification. It may be left to observation whether the reverse of this picture is not equally just—whether the mean, selfish, and niggardly do not suffer personal deterioration; and whether they do not receive from their neighbours a merited contempt.

III. THERE ARE OPERATIONS OF THIS LAW WHICH IT IS BEYOND OUR POWER TO TRACE. If we believe that the results of earthly labour extend into the future eternity, what a solemnity does this conviction impart to the principles upon which we are accustomed to act! The labours of the evangelist, the teachings of the pastor, the gifts of the supporters of religion, all bear fruit in the world to come. The nature and the measure of the harvest are largely determined by the way in which the field is tilled and sown in time. A motive this to that diligence and devotedness which is commended in the text by the inspired apostle. Only sow liberally, and by all waters, and, even if you sow in tears, it is promised that you shall reap in joy.—T.

Ver. 7.—"*A cheerful giver.*" Paul here supports his appeal for liberality by a quotation from Old Testament Scripture. The words are almost literally those of the Septuagint Version of the Book of Proverbs. If the most powerful and practical motive to benevolence and especially to almsgiving is that which comes from the incarnation and from the cross of Christ, still all revelation enjoins and commends a virtue which is always beneficial to the giver, even when the advantage to the recipient is questionable.

I. GOD HIMSELF IS A CHEERFUL GIVER. There is no grudging in his benevolence. If he shows mercy, he delights in mercy. If he gives, he gives with open hand and smiling face.

II. CHEERFULNESS IN THE GIVER ENHANCES TO THE RECIPIENT THE VALUE OF THE GIFT. "One may give with his hand and pull it back with his looks." Some benevolent characters give with such a grace that those who receive at their hands think more of the giver than of the gift. Even a trifle in such case is more welcome than a handsome donation from an unsympathizing and uninterested donor. A foreign scholar waited upon a theological professor in London, who was a man well known for his exquisite grace and suavity of manner, to lay before him his position as one of peculiar destitution. That he was assisted, and assisted generously, is certain; but as he left the house he was heard to break forth into the exclamation, "Oh, the *modus*, the *modus*, the *modus*!" i.e. the manner of the giver in the bestowal of his liberality.

III. CHEERFULNESS IN THE GIVER REACTS UPON HIS OWN SPIRITUAL NATURE. He who gives coldly, ungraciously, and grudgingly, is none the better for the act. But the ready, liberal, and cheerful giver is a happier and a more truly Christian man, because of the spirit in which he has discharged a duty and rendered a service.

IV. THERE IS A SPECIAL RECOMPENSE ASSURED TO THE CHEERFUL GIVER. "The Lord loveth him." The Lord sees his own character reflected in that of his servant; he witnesses in the generous and unselfish spirit the fruit of the redemption wrought by his Son, and of the fertilizing operation of his own gracious, free, and beneficent Spirit.—T.

Ver. 8.—*Abounding grace and abounding service.* Christianity does not come to men, saying, "This is pleasant," or "This is expedient," or "This is what society expects from you, and therefore do it." It comes saying, "This is what God does, and what God requires you to do." It lays the basis for human duty in Divine acts. So with liberality, as in this passage.

I. THE ABUNDANT RESOURCES GOD PUTS AT THE DISPOSAL OF THE CHRISTIAN. 1. Men are at their best estate altogether dependent, having in themselves nothing. but want, weakness, and sin. 2. All grace is in God; he has both the power and the disposition to supply every want. It is his nature to bestow; he is the God of grace. 3. His grace not only gives, it *abounds* to us. The gift of his Son is the proof of inexhaustible love. So with the gift of his Spirit. In fact, in the gospel there is a generosity of bestowment; no withholding and no grudging. 4. Christians, as his people, are thus partakers of Divine sufficiency. "All things are yours;" such is the deed of gift in which the heavenly Father places at the disposal of his family all the resources of his nature and liberality. 5. The liberality of God extends through every stage of individual life, and through every period of the Church's history. His bounties and favours are as the leaves of the forest, the waves of the sea, the stars of the sky— unnumbered and innumerable.

II. THE CORRESPONDING REQUIREMENTS AND EXPECTATIONS OF GOD FROM HIS PEOPLE. Religion consists of two parts—what God does for us, and what God demands from us. 1. It is taken for granted that the Christian life consists in "good works;" that the disciple of Christ is naturally a worker, whose energies and possessions are to be consecrated to God in his Son. Gifts, services, sympathy, speech, aid,—such are the manifestations of the spiritual life which the Lord of all desires and beholds. 2. Here is implied a relation between God's works and those of his people. His abounding gifts are to be regarded as (1) the example of ours; (2) the means of ours, for we can only give others what he has given us; (3) the measure of ours, as liberal and generous; and (4) the motive to ours, inasmuch as we are constrained by the love of God and by the cross of Christ.—T.

Ver. 11.—*True enrichment.* The encouragement which the apostle here addresses to the Corinthian Christians, in order to stimulate their liberality, is appropriate to all professed followers of the Lord Jesus. Paul urges that the liberal helper of others is in every respect the wealthier and happier for his generosity. It is not the highest motive, but it is sound and powerful and effective.

I. THE HUMAN NEED OF SUCH ENRICHMENT. Impoverishment is the lot of multitudes; but whilst many are deeply sensible of their temporal needs, it is too often the case that, with regard to spiritual possessions, they boast that they are rich and increased with goods, and know not that they are poor. In fact, we have nothing which we have not received from the free bounty of him who is the Giver of all.

II. THE DIVINE AUTHOR OF SUCH ENRICHMENT. The God of nature supplies the need and relieves the poverty distinctive of our bodily and physical state. The God of grace provides liberally for the wants of the soul, saying to his child, "Son, thou art ever with me, and all that I have is thine."

III. THE VARIETY AND PLENITUDE OF THIS ENRICHMENT. "In everything," says the apostle. He appears to teach that, as a general rule, it is the ordinance of Providence that the way of liberality should be the way of prosperity. All have known fortunate and wealthy niggards; and all have known generous men who have come to poverty; but such cases are the exception. And if generosity is the way to temporal abundance, a liberal spirit is sure to acquire virtues and excellences. Faith, hope, and love,—all are cultivated in the exercise of liberality; progressive enrichment is the recompense of a large heart and open hands.

IV. THE HUMAN AND EARTHLY RESULT OF THIS ENRICHMENT. This is increase of liberality; the more the generous man receives from God, the more he helps his fellow-men.

V. The ultimate result of this enrichment. Thanksgiving will be rendered to God, both by the liberal who are enriched, by the grateful recipients of their abundant bounty, and by all who witness the fruit of the Spirit and the evidences of the power of the Saviour's love.—T.

Ver. 15.—*The unspeakable gift.* The gifts of the Corinthians to their poor brethren in Judæa were welcomed, acknowledged, approved. But every Christian duty and service led the mind of the apostle up to Christ himself. Earthly gifts suggested to his mind that Gift which is heavenly and supreme.

I. God's Gift to man. 1. The Lord Christ is emphatically *the* Gift of God. He was sent by the Father, and his mission was a proof of the Father's interest and love. All gifts beside are pale and poor, by reason of the splendour and the beauty of this. 2. The Lord Christ is the *unspeakable* Gift of God; *i.e.* so rich and wonderful as not to be capable of a full description. Observe: (1) Its intrinsic value. Could God himself give a more precious treasure than the Son of his love? He is "the Pearl of great price." (2) Its adaptation to the needs of those to whom it is given. Christ is the Gift of bread to the hungry, of water to the thirsty, of freedom to the slave. Spiritual good was what man needed; and it was what came to man by Christ. (3) Its infinite train of blessing. We are told that "all things" are placed at the disposal of those from whom God has not withheld his Son. And this doctrine is one which experience supports. The innumerable blessings which have come into the world with the gospel are a proof that the language of Scripture is not exaggerated.

II. Man's gratitude to God. 1. It is often wickedly withheld. Our Lord was despised and rejected of men when he was upon earth; and there are still multitudes who are insensible to his preciousness, and who take no part in the grateful praises of his Church. 2. It is offered by appreciative hearts. They who have gratefully accepted the boon, who have tasted and seen that the Lord is good,—they are forward to acknowledge the liberality and the loving-kindness of the great Giver above. 3. It is openly and joyfully expressed by those who feel it. Hymns of grateful praise; a loving witness to the world of the Divine pity and kindness; gifts to his cause, which are accepted as offered to himself; deeds of cheerful and holy obedience;—such are the means by which the redeemed and spiritually enriched may show forth their gratitude for the Gift which is unspeakable.—T.

Ver. 2.—*The contagion of charity.* I. An indisputable fact. Man is imitative, even in generosity. Example is often potent when appeal falls flat. Many do not see that they can afford to give until others in similar circumstances demonstrate the possibility. Men do not like to be outdone in good works; a friend's beneficence is a spur to our own.

II. A suggestive fact. When we give we often think only of the direct good which our contribution will effect, but much other good may follow. Our charity may be stimulative. Should lead us: 1. *To give promptly.* Delayed gift may be in time for the special object, but may be too late to induce others to give in time. Our charity must have time to work; some people take hints slowly. *Bis dat, qui cito dat,* is true in more ways than one. 2. *To give liberally.* We may curtail the charity of others. On the other hand, a liberal gift may draw forth liberal responses. 3. *To give joyfully.* If we give with evident gladness, others may desire to share our happiness. Joyful giving is more contagious than any other, since all men naturally crave for joy. 4. *To give to suitable objects only.* We may misdirect the charity of others. There is not a little *responsibility* attaching to benevolence. Some seem to think that, if they give, it is little matter how or to what they give.

III. A comforting fact. The truly liberal are often distressed because they can give so little. But small gifts may have large issues. The small rudder directs the great ship. The little weight often turns the scale. Our gift, of little value, may call forth large help from those wealthier than ourselves. This is likely if men see that, though we give little, we give as much as we can.

IV. A useful fact. To be made use of according to the example set by Paul. A legitimate instrument for moving sluggish natures. Whilst we may be silent respecting our own charity, we may often profitably speak of the charity of others.—H.

Ver. 7.—*The cheerful giver*. I. How THE CHEERFUL GIVER GIVES. 1. *Bountifully.* His cheerfulness ensures liberality. It is the grudging giver who gives but little. But he who gives with gladness will desire much of that gladness. And he who sows bountifully reaps bountifully, and that without waiting, for he has at once a great harvest of joy. 2. *Willingly.* No compulsion is needed. He runs eagerly in the flowery and fruitful path of charity. He is not driven by the stings of conscience or by a desire to stand well with his fellows. His heart is enlisted, and the service he renders is hearty. 3. *Joyfully.* It is not a pain to him to give, but a pleasure. Some give their money to the needy as they give their teeth to the dentist; and often the disposition to give totally disappears on the threshold! But the cheerful giver *enjoys* giving. It is a delight to him. How giving is transformed in character when this is so! The same thing, how different to different natures! When we have learnt to love giving, what a pure joy we experience! Before, it was but the carcase of Samson's dead lion, but now we gather most luscious honey by handfuls. We miss a most heavenly joy if we miss the gladness of giving.

II. GOD'S REGARD FOR THE CHEERFUL GIVER. What God thinks of us is the all-important question. Now, the cheerful giver approves himself to the Most High. And not with cold approbation does God behold him. "God *loveth* a cheerful giver." God loves this kind of giving, and he loves the one who thus gives. A grudging giver is peculiarly offensive to God. It is so monstrous that, when God has *lent* us so many things, we should hesitate to return to him the few for which he asks. But when we have as much joy in returning as we had in receiving, he is well pleased. And when we rise still higher and believe truly that "it is *more* blessed to give than to receive," we please him the more. The cheerful giver resembles God, for God is a cheerful Giver;—how bountifully and how willingly he has endowed us! Here are incentives to cheerful giving—that we please God, secure the love of God, and become like God.

III. GOD'S PROMISE TO THE CHEERFUL GIVER. A promise of great prosperity (vers. 6, 8—10). The short-sighted always judge that giving means losing, and that saving means gaining; but "There is that scattereth, and yet increaseth; and there is that withholdeth more than is meet, but it tendeth to poverty" (Prov. xi. 24). And our Master said, "Give, and it shall be given unto you" (Luke vi. 38; see also Mark x. 29, 30). If we want to get little we must give little. The niggardly farmer gets a scanty crop. In God's providence those who are benevolent are commonly largely blessed in earthly things. Approving themselves to God, they are the subjects of his special care; "And God is able to make all grace abound" unto them (ver. 8). If those who give money do not always get more money, they always get much of what is far better than money. The distinct promise of God is that they shall be blessed and prospered. What *form* the blessing and prosperity shall take will be gladly left to God by the devout spirit. Often an increase of the means of charity results. God gives us more that we may give more. Having wisely used our talent, he entrusts us with further riches (see vers. 8, 10, 11).

IV. THE INFLUENCE OF THE CHEERFUL GIVER. 1. *He convinces men of the reality of religion.* (Ver. 13.) Men appreciate such a test of piety as this. Words they are apt to reckon at a cheap rate, but spontaneous and joyful liberality staggers them. Cheerful giving is to be ranked amongst the evidences of Christianity. 2. *He causes men to thank and to glorify God.* (Vers. 11—13.) What is *the origin* of Christian benevolence? is a question suggested to the minds of those blessed by it. And this inquiry terminates in God. As he has implanted charity in his people's hearts, he is clearly entitled to the praise. Aided believers naturally bless God that he has inclined his stewards to minister to their needs, and magnify his grace which has produced such fruitfulness in human hearts. The cheerful giver has a wider and more powerful influence than sometimes he suspects.

V. THE GIFTS OF MEN TO THE CHEERFUL GIVER. 1. *Their prayers.* (Ver. 14.) What is the price of prayer! What a valuable return for the expenditure of mere gold! If we secure the earnest, loving, believing prayers of those to whom we minister, we shall be greatly enriched. The "prayer of a righteous man availeth much"

(Jas. v. 16). Men are willing to give much if their friend will but speak for them to the sovereign; but the cheerful giver is often spoken for to the King of kings. 2. *Their love.* (Ver. 14.) Love is not to be lightly estimated; it is spiritual gold, much more precious than material. A man is rich if his treasury is well stored with the love of his fellows. The love of good men especially is a large recompense. Here we have the love of man and the love of God promised to those who delight in mercy and in helpfulness to the children of want.—H.

Ver. 15.—*The Gift of gifts.* Undoubtedly the gift of the Lord Jesus Christ. Paul has been speaking of the lesser gifts of saints. Now he rises to God's supreme Gift. Consider—

I. THE GIVER. God. Who could *give Christ* but God? We must not forget that God gave Christ. Many do, and form the erroneous notion that, whilst Christ is their friend, God is their enemy. Redemption is of the whole Deity. "*God* so loved the world," etc. Note: the Giver was a God (1) unworshipped, (2) unserved, (3) unloved, (4) grievously sinned against, (5) defied in the very act of giving. It was whilst we were yet sinners that Christ came to redeem us. "Herein is love, not that we loved God, but that he loved us, and sent his Son to be the Propitiation for our sins" (1 John iv. 10).

II. THE GIFT. 1. *A gift.* (1) A free gift. Nothing was given in exchange. Men *had nothing* to give. (2) A voluntary gift. Prompted by Divine compassion and love. (3) An undeserved gift. Men deserved condemnation, not Christ. (4) A continuous gift. Christ is not ours merely for a time. He is ours *for ever and ever.* He is the saint's everlasting inheritance. 2. *An unspeakable gift.* (1) In value. The most costly of gifts. The pearl of great price. The treasure discovered in the fields of heaven. Who can estimate the value of such a gift as this? If God had given a thousand worlds or all the angelic hosts, he would have given less. (2) In splendour. Consider the *graces, powers,* and infinite *excellences* of Christ. His presence made heaven glorious. (3) In efficacy. This gift fully met our need. How fully we yet know not, for now we are looking through a darkened glass. All our known wants are supplied by the Redeemer, and the vast catalogue of wants as yet unknown to us. Through him we are pardoned, cleansed, sanctified, adopted, and through him we shall at last be brought into the great home above.

III. THE RECIPIENTS OF THE GIFT. 1. *Human beings.* Christ was given to the human race, not to the angelic, nor to the merely animal. How greatly honoured is mankind! If Christ was given to men, what a future must be before those who receive this gift! 2. *Fallen human beings.* Man, "made a little lower than the angels," soon fell much lower, and *then* the gift came. A marvellous return for man's apostasy! When the cry of humanity was for sternest punishment, Heaven's response was "Jesus of Nazareth." Well may we exclaim, "Oh the depth of the riches both of the wisdom and the knowledge of God! how unsearchable are his judgments, and his ways past tracing out!" (Rom. xi. 33).

IV. APPROPRIATE GRATITUDE. Paul cries, "Thanks be to God;" and well he may. How can we thank God enough for such a gift as this? What would be our state if this gift had not been bestowed?

> "Love so amazing, so Divine,
> Demands my soul, my life, my all."

Throughout eternity we shall praise God for the gift unspeakable. Now let us praise him with: 1. *Lip.* Tell out our gratitude. Suppressed praise is indecent. We should desire all the world to know how thankful we are. 2. *Heart.* The tongue in this matter must be moved by the spirit, or it will not make sweet music in the ear of God. The gift came from the heart of God: let our thanksgiving come from the heart also. 3. *Active service.* What are we willing to *do* to show our gratitude? Paul was so subdued by the "unspeakable gift" that he loved to call himself "*the slave* of Jesus Christ;" and he counted no toil too severe to show his thankfulness. 4. *Life.* Our whole being and existence should constitute a psalm. This is the true "psalm of life." Every power should be pressed into the service. As this gift is ever the supreme blessing in our life, we should ever be praising God for it.

Terrible thought! The unspeakable Gift may be rejected! What unspeakable folly, what unspeakable guilt, what unspeakable condemnation, must follow!—H.

Ver. 8.—" *Always.*" Let us not take our standard of Christian life and experience from our own hearts, or from the customary piety which shows itself around us. The Lord requires and expects of us constancy—a life regulated by the steady action of principle, and animated daily by faith, hope, and love. Alas! how many are unsteady in his service! How their light flickers! how their faith wavers! how their convictions and affections fluctuate! This is so common that it seems to be regarded as inevitable. Vacillation and inconstancy are supposed to be not so much sins as very pardonable infirmities. But is constancy, while theoretically right, practically impossible? When called to maintain a steady tenor of Christian life and conduct, may we say, *Non possumus?* What says Reason? And what says Holy Writ?

I. We ask the question of Reason, as a fair judge of the nature of things. Physical life is maintained in us by certain natural processes which never cease from the moment of birth to the moment of death. The lungs play always, and the heart beats always. We call these automatic movements, as being not dependent on our volition. They continue when we are fast asleep. But moral and spiritual life rises above mere automatism, and requires for its continuance and growth a succession of moral volitions, a steady and well-directed purpose. Now, is this state of the will possible? Reason will answer that it is the proper habit of a healthy and vigorous mind. Weak minds are obstinate or fickle; dull minds are stolid and monotonous; but those that are strong and intelligent have a steady moral pulse, a wise tenacity of purpose, and a careful balance of temper and will. It is the most rational, healthy, and happy condition of man to believe firmly what he believes, and to maintain an even tenor of conduct in harmony with his belief. George Herbert is right to praise the man of constancy, who

> " Doth still, and strongly, good pursue ;
> To God, his neighbours, and himself most true."

II. We ask the question of Holy Scripture. Does it admit excuses for inconstancy? or does it assume and require that men who believe in God should live to him always? David said, " I have set the Lord always before me." No doubt this is absolutely true only of the great Son of David, of whom the Spirit of prophecy spake in the sixteenth psalm, as St. Peter taught on the day of Pentecost. But of all that was most worthy in the career of the poet-king of Israel this was the sustaining principle ; and of his character this formed the sacred charm, that he constantly kept his eyes upon God. In great deeps of sorrow, in dens and caves of the earth, in exile, in peril by the sword, among temptations of ambition, tumults of war, cares of government ; in the obscurity of his youth, in the sudden promotion and the stirring adventures of his early manhood ; in all the publicity of his later years, in " that fierce light which beats upon a throne ; "—always and everywhere the son of Jesse looked to God, and sought to walk in the light of his countenance. Alas! he looked off, and sinned grievously. We find no perfect example but that of the Man Christ Jesus, the Son of David, who maintained a constant obedience to, and therefore a constant communion with, God (see John viii. 29 ; xi. 42). In the midst of incessant occupations and in the face of frequent "contradiction of sinners against himself," he found it possible to look always to the Father in heaven, and do always the Father's will. So he knew that the Father heard him always. Now, every one admits that the life of Christ is, in its principles and motives, the supreme model for the life of Christians. But the force of the admission is sadly weakened for any practical purpose by the prevailing impression that actual conformity to so perfect a Pattern is not to be expected of any one. Let us take the example of a servant of Christ. It will not be disputed that we may and should emulate the attainments and experience of St. Paul. Now, he had extraordinary vicissitudes in the course of his ministry, and does not conceal from us the changing moods of his mind—now depressed and sorrowful, now bold and enthusiastic. But as respects the main current of his life and service, Paul was, ever after his conversion, gloriously consistent. In love to God, in zeal for Jesus, in fidelity to the gospel, in care for the Churches, in abhorrence of sin, in esteem of holiness, in vigilant resistance to the devil, and in tender affection for the saints, he was always the same, and wavered not. Accordingly we find the word "always" often used in regard to his own spiritual experience and missionary life (see Acts xxiv. 16 on conscience; ch. ii. 14 on the career of a missionary; ch. iv. 10 and v. 6 on sufferings and joyful hope). What a living sacrifice to God was this apostolic man! What singleness of purpose he had, what integrity of heart, what constancy, in serving the Lord always! Why may not similar constancy be shown by us? God is able to make all grace abound toward us. And all the injunctions for Christian life given in the Holy Book assume that we are to be always and wholly the Lord's. Our speech should be "always with grace, seasoned with salt." Our prayers should be offered up alway; and in active service we should be "always abounding in the work of the Lord." The proper season for piety is always. Labour sometimes, study sometimes, recreation sometimes, sleep sometimes; but the fear of the Lord always, and the life of faith always. No day of the week, no hour of the day, without the Lord. This is not bondage: it is the best liberty. This is not being "righteous overmuch." It is simply to order our character and conduct habitually by the highest aims and models set before us. It is the aspiration of the meek and lowly, not of the proud. It is the path of the just, which shines more and more until the perfect day.—F.

Ver. 2.—*Forwardness in good works.* Very remarkable is the tenderness, consideration, and delicacy of feeling with which St. Paul addresses the better, the more spiritual, part of the Church at Corinth. He was very anxious that they should stand well in the matter of the collection, and therefore he had sent messengers to collect their gifts; but he gives them notice of their coming, and heartily expresses his confidence in the ready and willing mind of these Corinthian saints. In such expressions "there was no subtle policy; there was no attempt to get at their purses by their weak side. St. Paul was above such means. It was natural, instinctive, real delicacy; and yet it was the surest way of obtaining what he wished, and that which the deepest knowledge of the human heart would have counselled. For thereby he appealed, not to their selfish, but to their most unselfish, feelings. This is a great principle—one of the deepest you can have for life and action. Appeal to the highest motives; appeal, whether they be there or no, for you make them where you cannot find them. Let men say what they will of human nature's evil, a generous, real, *unaffected* confidence never fails to elicit the Divine spark." Consider—

I. ST. PAUL'S CONFIDENCE IN THEIR GOOD-HEARTEDNESS. "I know the forwardness of your mind." 1. So far as tidings had reached him, and so far as he knew their Christian disposition and character, he felt sure that they were thinking rightly about the matter, cherishing proper sentiments concerning Christian brotherhood and charity, and the duty of the strong to bear the infirmities of the weak. This would be the matter of first importance to the apostle, for mere gifts are of no more acceptableness to God nowadays than mere sacrifices were in older days. God reads hearts and motives, and accepts the *spirit* of generosity and brotherly kindness which may find expression through gifts. So God could send this gracious message to David, "Thou didst well that it was in thy heart." 2. The Corinthians also planned to meet the apostle's wishes. There had been consideration and consultation and united endeavour to form good schemes for the regular devotement of gifts, for the storing and the ingathering of the moneys. In such signs of thought and care and wise arrangement St. Paul could but unfeignedly rejoice. 3. It seems that the Corinthians had actually made a good and hopeful beginning. They had been "forward" in advance of other Churches; to use a familiar figure, they had "taken time by the forelock." This the apostle could not fail to regard as a most encouraging and hopeful sign of earnestness, as well as of the preparedness to act upon principle rather than upon mere impulse and excitement.

II. ST. PAUL'S USE OF THEM FOR THE INSPIRATION OF OTHERS. "For which I boast of you to them of Macedonia." Probably St. Paul had been setting their example before the Churches of Macedonia previous to his receiving news of the trouble at Corinth over the incestuous member, and the disturbance of the Church by St. Paul's personal enemies and traducers. Show that whenever a Church of Christ, or a Christian individual, affords prominent illustration of any grace or duty, they properly become, in such matters, models and examples for the inspiration of others. All who attain above an average level in Christian living ought to be used for the permanent raising of the average. It is a somewhat difficult question, how far lesser motives, such as emulation and rivalry and ambition to be topmost, may be appealed to in Christian life and work. Certainly it must be admitted that they can only be secondary motives, buttresses of a building that is well founded on the one great motive of loyalty and love to Christ.

III. St. Paul's fears lest they should come short of his hope. "His boasting of them might be in vain in this behalf." He was very properly anxious "lest haply if they of Macedonia come with me, and find you unprepared, we (that we say not, ye) should be ashamed in this same confident boasting." The ground of fear was the influence which the troubles and conflicts through which the Corinthian Church had been passing would have upon such a matter of external interest. Churches whose peace is disturbed are seldom found zealous in good works. The energy of the Church which is turned into dissension and strife is taken from its proper spheres of growth, witness, and charity. But St. Paul had further cause for his fears. Enemies at Corinth were so earnestly endeavouring to undermine his authority and destroy his influence that it seemed likely the Church would throw up this collection for the Jerusalem saints as a merely Pauline affair, with which they had better have nothing to do. The apostle opposes this malign influence by his delicate pleading, and by sending messengers who would testify that the collection was a matter of public concern, not one of personal interest to the apostle, and not one which was left in his hands. It was the united contribution of the Gentile Churches to the mother Church in her distress, and the matter was wholly under the regulation of those Churches. Impress how important is manifest clean-handedness for all who have to do with Church moneys. No man must blame us concerning the gifts which we administer.

IV. St. Paul's anxiety to secure the practical results of right feeling. He had been made glad by the report which he had received concerning the more spiritually minded Corinthians. They had received his reproofs and counsels with right feeling. They had cleared themselves of all complicity with the doings of the unworthy member; and the apostle felt that now all that was needed, as a sign of their right-heartedness, was the resumption of this collecting scheme. If they would earnestly take that up and carry it through, in a generous and self-denying way, it would be the all-sufficient and outward proof that they had come well through the stormy and troubled periods of their Church history.—R. T.

Ver. 5.—*Covetousness.* "As a matter of bounty, and not as of covetousness." Dean Plumptre translates, "as a work of *your* bounty, and not of *my* claims upon your purses." The Revised Version renders, "and not of extortion," but putting the word "covetousness" in the margin. The Greek of the word "covetous," signifies "to have more," and it signifies (1) one who has more than enough; (2) one who desires more than enough of whatever kind; and (3) one greedy after money. But these do not precisely express the thought which is in the word as employed in Scripture. Covetousness is that exaggerated consideration for *self* which makes it possible, not only to neglect the interests of others, but even to injure others to secure a man's own ends. It is the desire to get and to hold for self, which shuts up a man's hand and heart so that he cannot give to others. We suggest for treatment—

I. The covetous spirit. Distinguish between covetous acts, and the covetous spirit which may be cherished in such a way as to utterly spoil acts which men may call acts of liberality. It is "covetousness," the self-seeking spirit, concerning which St. Paul is anxious, and this is a form of spiritual evil to which we are all more exposed than we think. The most painful exemplification of it is found in Judas Iscariot. Its subtle and mischievous workings in him can be clearly traced. The examples of Achan, Demas, etc., may also be given. "It is not necessary to describe at any length the sin which the Word of God brands under the name of 'covetousness,' and always associates with whatever is most offensive and most vile, 'the root of all evil,' by bad pre-eminence, 'idolatry.' We assume its existence. It will not be denied. Its spell is upon all. It is the abuse and perversion of a great law of man's nature—the law which teaches him to aspire heavenward and Godward; or of a law not less primary—the law of self-preservation. It is the ruling passion of nearly all men, of all tastes and times. 'Take heed, and beware of covetousness,' said the All-wise; and though his Word teems with such warnings against the sin, men have not been warned. At one time men call it 'the great queen-regent of the world;' at another, 'the all-consuming cancer' of the Church; at another, her 'deadly upas;' at a fourth, 'a fatal opiate;' while others assure us that, at the best, man is only the heir of a vault or the lord of a grave. Yet vain are all such exposures. Though it creeps stealthily upon man like grey hairs or dropsy, the conquests of covetousness continue far wider than those of Alexander. The monarch and the menial are alike its slaves. The phlegmatic are covetous because this freezing sin specially suits their nature; the earnest, because it stimulates; the licentious, because it can pamper; the ambitious, because it can exalt; the stupid, because it compensates for dulness. Prosperity fans it, and adversity cannot quench it; men willingly bow down before it, as the tyrant summoned them of old to bow before another idol" (W. K. Tweedie, D.D.).

II. ITS RELATION TO THE CHRISTIAN CHARACTER. It is always and necessarily injurious, and, wherever willingly cherished, not only imperilling the finer and more delicate features of character, but even destructive of it root and branch. For the very essence of Christian character is the love of Christ, which takes us out of ourselves, and absorbs us with concern for him; and the love of others, for Christ's sake, which sets us upon making their interests superior to our own. Covetousness may linger in the holes and caves of Mansoul while Immanuel is its King, but where covetousness reigns Christ cannot; or, to put it in other words, it is absolutely impossible to raise a Christian character upon a foundation of covetousness, and this spirit will but exert itself to daub and spoil the whole picture of the Christian graces.

III. ITS HINDRANCE TO CHRISTIAN GIVING. 1. By preventing the reception of a due impression of cases of need. Covetousness hardens, deafens, and blinds. 2. By compelling its victim to form a false estimate of his ability. 3. By deceiving a man through the presentation of unworthy excuses.—R. T.

Ver. 7.—*Cheerful givers.* Those to whom giving is no forced service, no painful duty, no grudgingly yielding to command, but the joy of their life, the thing which brings them their keenest and purest pleasure. We need only suggest the sources whence such cheerfulness will come. Dean Plumptre points out that in this sentence we have a distinct echo of Prov. xxii. 8, as it stands in the Greek Version: "He that soweth wicked things shall reap evils, and shall complete the penalty of his deed. God blesseth a cheerful man and a giver, and shall complete [in a good sense] the incompleteness of his works." "Cheerfulness in visits of sympathy, in the daily offices of kindness, in the life of home, in giving instruction or advice,—all come under the head of that which God approves and loves. So, the greatest of Greek ethical teachers (Aristotle) had refused the title of 'liberal' to the man who gave without pleasure in the act of giving. The pain he feels proves that, if he could, he would rather have the money than do the noble action."

I. CHEERFULNESS THROUGH THE MOTIVE OF GIVING. Which is that thankfulness and love to him who was God's great saving Gift to us, which kindles in our hearts the joy unspeakable.

II. CHEERFULNESS THROUGH THE PLEASURE OF GIVING. For our Lord read human hearts aright when he said, "It is more blessed to give than to receive."

III. CHEERFULNESS THROUGH THE HOPE OF BLESSING BY GIVING. Our giving meets and supplies needs; it tends to lift off burdens and to soothe sorrows. It is glad work to find ourselves, in a sinful and a sorrow-stricken world, healers, comforters, and saviours. No joy is like the joy of wakening joy in others.

IV. CHEERFULNESS THROUGH THE SENSE OF DIVINE APPROVAL ON GIVING. "God *loveth* the cheerful giver," and when he loves, there is for us his uplifted countenance, his acceptance, and his smile.—R. T.

Ver. 8.—*God's ability and man's.* Even in the early Church, the first Church of the apostles, there was need of money. In the first Council it was resolved to send a general direction to the Churches that they should "remember the poor." The Apostle

Paul was deeply interested in a collection, which he set on foot throughout the Churches he had founded, on behalf of the poor saints at Jerusalem, and his last journey to the holy city was occasioned by his earnest desire to present these "alms and offerings of the Gentiles" with his own hands to the apostles and elders. This text is directly connected with the matter of money, of Christian giving for Christian uses, which we properly regard as still one of the first duties, as it is certainly one of the highest privileges, of the Christian Church. St. Paul had been boasting in other places of the willingness, the heartiness, and the liberality of the Church at Corinth; but in consequence, perhaps, of the interruption of his relations with them, he feared that they would hardly come up to the account which, in his trustfulness, he had given of them. He therefore sent on before him collectors, who were to gather their stored gifts together, and he reminds them again of those considerations by which he had already urged them to a noble liberality. "Give," he says, "according to the generous purposings of the heart that is made tender and thankful by the sense of God's saving love. Remember, 'he that soweth bountifully shall reap also bountifully.' Let your giving be a 'matter of bounty, not as of covetousness.' 'God loveth a cheerful giver.' And God is able to give all temporal good to you, so that, having sufficiency for all your own needs, you yet may be able to distribute generously. And did not the Lord Jesus lay down for all his people this most comprehensive principle, 'It is more blessed to give than to receive'? And did he not illustrate, in his own uttermost self-sacrifice, the glory of his own great principle? Verily the beatitude of God rests on those who *give!*" This is the first connection of the passage before us, but it broadens its reach beyond the money and the giving. It covers and hallows all the features and expressions of our religious life. Wheresoever we may be, whatsoever we may have to do, whensoever needs arise, the sound of this assurance comes to us, quieting all fears, and stilling the heart to peace and rest. There is a gracious power in the word "all," repeated as it is again and again in the verse. The word seems designed to drive away every lingering doubt. "All grace," "all sufficiency," "all good."

I. GOD'S ABILITY, AND ITS CONDITION. Nothing that is not an absurdity in the statement is beyond God's power. Much has been made of the contention that God cannot put two things into the same place at the same time, or that he cannot make the addition of two and two make five, or make two parallel lines ever meet. But, in view of the essential conditions of human thought and human language, these things are absurdities, and not impossibilities; and it is no limitation of the Divine omnipotence to say that God cannot do what is absurd in the very statement. "He is able." We feel the truth of this in the world of nature. Sky and earth and sea proclaim that he is "able." Who can listen to the wild storm, hear the mighty winds bowing the great trees, and the thunder-echoes rolling from hill to hill, and the breakers plunging against the guardian cliffs, and not reverently say, "He is able"? Who can feel how the gentle spring sunshine warms the wintry air and the chilled ground, tenderly touching every life-germ in bud and seed and plant, and wakening life and hope and beauty all around, and not lovingly say, "Verily thou art able"?

"O spirit of the strong things and the gentle, thou art able."

But nature is outside us. We may watch the omnipotent workings, but we want to ask this: "Do *we* come within the all-powerful grasp?" Admit all we may about our "free-will," nevertheless, of ourselves, of body, soul, circumstances, can we say, "He is able"? Yes; in him we "live, and move, and have our being." Our circumstances are his overruling. Our souls are his inbreathing. He in whom we trust *can* do all things. We are continually crushed by being compelled to say, "I cannot;" but the feeble limited creature steadies its tremblings by leaning on One who can. "Then Job answered the Lord, and said, I know that thou canst do everything, and that no thought can be withholden from thee." But we long to know this—What can the almighty God really be to us? Can he come right into the spheres of our life and work? and is he able to make all grace abound to us there? Can he "supply all our need out of his riches in glory by Christ Jesus"? Into the shadow of his fatherhood may we run, since our "heavenly Father knoweth what things we have need of before we ask him"? That is the ability of God concerning which we need to gain such deep and satisfying impressions. As a redeemed son of his, is he able to find all the grace

I need; able to meet me at every point; able to give the grace according to the day; able to adapt himself to all the changes and fluctuations of my moods and circumstances? The little child brings all her broken dolls and damaged toys to her father; she is perfectly sure that, however dreadful the damage may be, "father can mend it." And the sweet confidence dries up the tears. But the little thing never stops to consider how strong the father-arms are or how skilful his fingers; she only reads his power by the light of his love; and she is quite sure that he will try, and her trust says that he will succeed. What can God do for us, his blood-bought children? He can breathe on us the spirit of a holy contentment. He can inspire us with zeal unto all good works. He can strengthen us for all noble enterprise. He can make the mountains of difficulty before us lie level as a plain. He can so prosper and bless us that very thankfulness shall urge us to generous and noble deeds. "I cannot indeed, but God can:" let us learn to say that, and then this will be our glorying—"Here, there, yonder, in this and in that, in the light and in the dark, I can, through him who strengtheneth me." There is a condition upon which the ability of God alone can come to us. We must gain and keep the *receptive mood*, which includes the humble, obedient, and trustful spirit.

II. MAN'S ABILITY AND ITS EXPRESSION. For we also are "able to abound unto every good work." Sometimes we are deeply impressed with the feebleness, the imperfection, of the best that we can do. But when we estimate that work of grace which God, the All-merciful, is carrying on in the world—so silent, yet so mighty; so long, and yet so surely triumphant at last; so rich in long-suffering patience; so quick to take up and use a thousand trifling influences, sanctifying even a passing word and a gentle look to its gracious ends,—then it seems wonderful that, in so great a matter, we should be "co-workers with God," and that the rich streams of Divine grace should even flow to others through us. With the grace of God *we can* do all things. In the renewed man there is ability. God makes him mighty, and uses him to "pull down the strongholds." God shows him what great things he can suffer, and what great things he can do, for his Name's sake. In full harmony with the Christian humility and dependence we may gain this sense of Christian ability. We want the inspiration of the conviction settled deeply into our souls—"I can." We need the cheer that comes to every man when God says to him, "Thou canst." We are weak, depressed, hesitating; we touch things with a trembling hand; we faint before the first difficulty, so long as we say to ourselves, "I cannot." With the "all sufficiency" we can abound to every good work.—R. T.

Ver. 10.—*God's rewards for liberal souls.* This verse may be read in a sentence: "The liberal soul shall be made fat." F. W. Robertson's passage in reference to this is so characteristic of him, and so wise and suggestive, that it cannot be withheld. He says, "In the particular instance now before us, what are the rewards of liberality which St. Paul promises to the Corinthians? They are (1) the love of God (ver. 7); (2) a spirit abounding to every good work (ver. 8); (3) thanksgiving on their behalf (vers. 11, 12, 13). A noble harvest, but *all* spiritual. Comprehend the meaning of it well. Give, and you will not get back again. Do not expect your money to be returned, like that of Joseph's brethren in their sacks' mouths. When you give to God, sacrifice, and know that what you give *is* sacrificed, and is not to be got again, even in this world; for if you give, expecting it back again, there is no sacrifice: charity is no speculation in the spiritual funds, no wise investment, to be repaid with interest either in time or eternity! No, the rewards are these: Do right, and God's recompense to you will be the power of doing more right. Give, and God's reward to you will be the spirit of giving more; a blessed Spirit, for it is the Spirit of God himself, whose life is the blessedness of giving. Love and God will pay you with the capacity of more love, for love is heaven, love is God within you." Setting out the various forms in which Divine rewards come to liberal souls, we notice—

I. TEMPORAL PROSPERITY. However true it is that this was associated with goodness only under the Old Testament economy, it is still found that the liberal soul makes friends, wins love, and so secures actual temporal advantages.

II. HUMAN LOVE. It is our best earthly treasure, and it comes in response to our power to give. The dearest relationships of human life are the rewards of them that can give. And Job reminds us how the good man, the gracious man, gets his reward in the love of the poor whom he seeks to bless (Job xxix. 11—17).

III. Soul-culture. For it is a steadfast law of soul-life, that it cannot grow by keeping; it can only grow by giving, expending. The law of receiving more grace is this—we must use up, in good generous deeds, the grace that we have.

IV. Power to do more good. See the extract from F. W. Robertson given in the introduction to this homily.

V. Divine favour. Which must include those rewards of the heavenly world which now escape our apprehension, because they can only be presented to us in material forms and figures. T. Binney says, "Beneficent acts, right in spirit and principle, though they may be forgotten by the doer—who may not let his ' left hand know what his right hand doeth '—are not forgotten by him to whose will they have an ultimate respect, and by whom they are received as a sacrifice. They have a relation to God, and are regarded by him long after they have been accomplished and have passed away from the memory of man. They do not terminate with their being finished and done with here, or, so to speak, with the immediate pleasurable impression on the Divine mind. That impression is retained and prolonged. He to whom they rise up as incense gives to them, as it were, a substantial embodiment in the upper world—lays them up there as valuable treasure belonging to his children, and thinks of and surveys them with satisfaction and complacency."—R. T.

Ver. 15.—*The unspeakable Gift.* This can refer to none other than the Lord Jesus Christ, who himself said, in such a striking way to the woman of Samaria, "If thou knewest the *gift of God*, and who it is that saith to thee, Give me to drink; thou wouldest have asked of him, and he would have given thee living water" (John iv. 10). In Jesus Christ "dwells all the fulness of the Godhead bodily." And "God so loved the world, that he gave his only begotten Son" (comp. Rom. v. 15; vi. 23; Heb. vi. 4).

I. Christ is a Gift. This is but reminding us that salvation is altogether of grace. We in no sense can be said to have *purchased* Christ. Nor did any merit of ours attract him. Nor by any power of ours did we win him. God pitied us in our lost estate, and *gave* his Son. A priceless Gift indeed, seeing that it includes: 1. Pardon. 2. Peace. 3. Eternal life.

II. Christ is God's Gift. This reminds us that salvation is a Divine work. We read of the "grace of God" and the "gift by grace." And "when there was no eye to pity and no arm to save, his own arm brought salvation." Salvation is said to be of God to show us: 1. It is not some human scheme. This is the essential difference between Christ's salvation and all other salvations. They are human devices—philosophies or religions; this is Divine intervention, arrangement, and revelation; God's power directly working in God's way. It is indeed God himself saving men. To trust in any merely human redemption schemes is like hoping to save a drowning man with a rope that is too short. 2. To give us right views of God. Man's usual thought of God is that of an offended King or stern Judge. But the unspeakable Gift reveals the higher truth that God is *love*, and the gift being that of a Son unfolds the sublime fact that God is Father. So we know God through his gift.

III. Christ is an unspeakably precious Gift. This reminds us that salvation is priceless. It is beyond all possibility that we could speak worthily (1) all the glory of Christ himself; (2) all the sorrow Christ went through; (3) all the needs which Jesus can meet; or (4) all the love that Jesus feels. The apostle felt overwhelmed with the thought of it, and spoke of the "love of Christ, which passeth knowledge."

IV. Christ is a Gift offered for our acceptance. It suffices no man to know that this Gift has come; nor to know that others have received it to the joy and rejoicing of their hearts. No man can offer worthy heart-thanksgiving for this Gift until he has personally accepted it, sufficiently proved it, and can speak for himself of the pricelessness of it. The law is this: "He that *hath the Son* hath life." And he can " thank God for his unspeakable Gift."—R. T.

EXPOSITION.

CHAPTER X.

With this chapter begins the last great section of the Epistle (ver. 1—ch. xiii. 10), which contains an impassioned vindication of the apostle's position as compared with that of his opponents. It is so much more vehement and severe than the former part of the Epistle, and the whole style and tone of the Epistle at this point change so completely, that many have supposed that this is in reality another letter, and some have even identified it with the letter alluded to in ch. vii. 8—12. There is no trace of external evidence in favour of this view. It is much more probable that St. Paul would here have ended his letter but for fresh information given him by Titus, or the arrival of some new messenger from Corinth, from whom he learnt the bitter way in which his enemies spoke of him. The most flagrant offender seems to have been one teacher from Jerusalem (vers. 7, 10, 11, 12, 18; ch. xi. 4). This man and his abettors and other party opponents spoke of St. Paul as mean in aspect (vers. 1, 10), untutored in speech (ch. xi. 6), bold at a distance and cowardly when present, a man of mere human motives (ver. 2), and not quite sound in intellect (ch. xi. 16, 17, 19). They had been introducing new teaching (ch. xi. 4), and had shown themselves boastful (ver. 7), insolent, rapacious, violent (ch. xi. 20, 21), intrusive (ver. 15), and generally dangerous in their influence (ch. xi. 3), which had succeeded in alienating from St. Paul the minds of many (ver. 18; ch. xi. 8, 20; xii. 13, 14). Such accusations and such conduct now roused the deep indignation of St. Paul, and his *Apologia pro vitâ suâ* is mainly given in these chapters.

Plunging at once into his subject, with a solemn appeal, he declares his apostolic power (vers. 1—8), and that he will exercise it in person as well as by letters, in answer to the taunt of his opponents (vers. 9—11). He then shows that his estimate of himself is formed on very different methods from those of his adversaries (vers. 12—16),

and that he referred all grounds of boasting solely to the judgment of God (vers. 17, 18).

Ver. 1.—**Now I Paul myself.** The words, as Theodoret says, express the emphasis of apostolic dignity. He is going to speak of himself and for himself. "I, the very Paul, with whose name you make so free." The conjecture may not even be impossible that this portion of the letter may have been written with his own hand. Perhaps he began without any intention of writing more than a few concluding words, but he was carried away by his feelings, and the subject grew under his hands (comp. Gal. v. 2; Eph. iii. 1; Philem. 19). **Beseech**; rather, *exhort*. **By the meekness and gentleness of Christ.** The conduct which he is obliged to threaten might seem incompatible with this meekness and gentleness (Matt. xi. 29, 30). It was not *really* so, because even Christ had been compelled at times "to burst into plain thunderings and lightnings." Still, severity and indignation were not in themselves after the inmost heart and will of Christ, though human perversity might compel love itself to assume such tones. He entreats them, however, not to force him to stern measures. *Gentleness.* The word *epieikeia* means "fairness, forbearance, sympathetic consideration for others," or, as Mr. Matthew Arnold prefers to render it, "sweet reasonableness" (see Acts xxiv. 4; Phil. iv. 5; Jas. iii. 17; 1 Pet. ii. 18). **Who in presence,** etc. Here, and in many similar passages of this section, he is evidently adopting or quoting the actual taunts of his adversaries. In modern times the words would be enclosed in inverted commas. **Base**; rather, *humble* (see note on ch. vii. 6; xii. 7). **Being absent am bold.** The charge, if true, would have been the mark of a coward; and it naturally awakens an indignant echo in the language of St. Paul.

Ver. 2.—**I beseech** you. The "beseech" is here right (*deomai*). The "you" is not in the Greek, but is rightly supplied. It rests with them to avert the necessity of personal severity, and he entreats them to do so (comp. ch. xiii. 2, 10; 1 Cor. iv. 21). **Against some.** He leaves these undefined till the vehement outburst of ch. xi. 13, 14. **As if we walked according to the flesh** (see note on ch. v. 16). To say this of St. Paul was to charge him with being insincere and not disinterested

Ver. 3.—**We walk in the flesh.** St. Paul does not disclaim the possession of human infirmities, but maintains that such trials and temptations were not the guiding force of his life. **We do not war after the flesh.** His *campaigns* (Luke iii. 14) were fought with spiritual weapons. The metaphor is a constant one with St. Paul (ch. ii. 14—16; 1 Cor. ix. 26; Eph. vi. 10—17, etc.).

Ver. 4.—**Weapons** (see ch. vi. 7; Rom. vi. 13). **Not carnal.** He did not rely on the mere "arm of flesh," or on earthly sword or panoply. **Mighty through God;** literally, *powerful for God;* i.e. either (1) powerful for the cause of God, or (2) powerful in *his* estimate. **To the pulling down of strongholds.** The word for "pulling down," which implies the entire clearance of an obstacle, is only found in the New Testament in this Epistle (vers. 4, 8; ch. xiii. 10). The word for "strongholds" is found here alone. These "fortresses" were the opposition aroused by factious and hostile partisans, and he hoped to subdue them by the strong exercise of apostolic authority (1 Cor. iv. 21; v. 1—5). Dean Stanley suggests a reminiscence of the hundred and twenty *Cilician* fortresses pulled down by Pompey; but I think that these general allusions are often pressed too far.

Ver. 5.—**Casting down.** This agrees with "we" understood, not with "weapons." **Imaginations;** rather, *disputations,* or *reasonings.* **Every high thing that exalteth itself;** rather, *every height that is exalted.* **Against the knowledge of God** (see 1 Cor. xv. 34). There, however, we have passive ignorance, here active opposition. **Bringing into captivity.** When the fortresses are razed, their defenders will be taken prisoners, but for a beneficent end. **Every thought.** Even intellectual result. The word (*noēma*) is not common in the New Testament. It occurs five times in this Epistle (ch. ii. 11; iii. 14; iv. 4; x. 5; xi. 3), but elsewhere only in Phil. iv. 7.

Ver. 6.—**Being in a readiness;** *i.e.* being quite prepared. My sternness of purpose is ready, but my hope is that it may not be called into action. **To revenge;** rather, *to do justice upon.* In any case, in this infliction of justice, whatever form it might take, he would only be an *agent* of God (Rom. xii. 19). **When your obedience is fulfilled.** St. Paul is confident that he will overcome the mazes of those opposed to him, and win them to Christ's obedience; but if there were any who should obstinately refuse to submit, they must be reduced to submission by action, not by words.

Ver. 7.—**Do ye look on things after the outward appearance?** Like many clauses in this section, the words are capable of different interpretations. They might mean, (1) as in the Authorized Version, "Do you judge by mere externals?" or, (2) "You judge by things which merely lie on the

surface!" or, (3) "Consider the personal aspect of the question." The Authorized Version is probably right (comp. John vii. 24). **If any man.** Perhaps alluding to some party ringleader. **That he is Christ's.** If a man holds this in an exclusive and partisan sense (1 Cor. i. 12). Some manuscripts (D, E, F, G) read, "a slave of Christ." **Of himself.** The true reading is probably ἐφ', not ἀφ', but in either case the meaning is, "by his own fair judgment." **Even so are we Christ's.** In a true and real sense, not by external knowledge and connection (which he has already disclaimed), but by inward union. This he proceeds to prove by the fact that he was the founder of their Church (vers. 13—18); that he had always acted with absolute disinterestedness (ch. xi. 1—15); that he had lived a life of toil and suffering (ch. xi. 21—33), and that he had received special revelations from God (ch. xii. 1—6).

Vers. 8—11.—*Assertion of his intentions.*

Ver. 8.—**Should boast.** In this section St. Paul is thoroughly *haunted* by this word. The fact that a word could thus possess and dominate over his style and imagination shows how deeply he was moved. The Corinthian Church, with its inflated factions and their fuglemen, reeked with boasting, and St. Paul is driven, with utter distaste, to adopt in self-defence language which, to the uncandid and indiscriminating, might seem to wear the same aspect. The word, which is unfrequent in other Epistles, occurs eighteen times in these chapters alone. Other haunting words are "tolerate," "bear with" (ch. xi. 1, 4, 19, 20), and "senseless," "fool" (ch. xi. 16, 19; xii. 6, 11); see note on ch. i. 3. **Somewhat more;** *something more abundantly.* **For edification, and not for your destruction;** *for building you up, not pulling you down.* The word *kathairesin* is from the same root as the verb in ver. 5. **I should not be ashamed;** rather, *I shall not be ashamed.* No shame shall ever accrue to me from my "boast" being proved false.

Ver. 9.—**By letters;** rather, *by the letters.* He had certainly addressed *two* letters to them (1 Cor. v. 9).

Ver. 10.—**Say they;** literally, *says he.* The phrase may, indeed, imply "it is said" (*on dit*); but it may refer to one main critic and opponent (comp. vers. 7, 11). Perhaps it would have been wiser and kinder if no one had reported to St. Paul all these subterranean calumnies and innuendoes. **Weighty and strong.** This could not be denied, considering the immense effect which had been produced by his first letter (ch. vii. 7). **His bodily presence is weak.** This is usually taken to mean that St. Paul's personal appearance was unprepossessing

(Gal. iv. 1). This, indeed, we should infer from many other passages (1 Cor. ii. 34; Gal. iv. 13, 14), and as a natural result of his "stake in the flesh." It is, too, the consistent though late tradition respecting him (see my 'Life of St. Paul,' ii. 628). Here, however, the words may mean no more than that "he adds nothing to his cause by being present in person, since he shows vacillation and want of energy." **Contemptible**; rather, *despised* (see 1 Cor. ii. 3, 4).

Ver. 11.—**Such a one.** A formula used to avoid mentioning a special name (see note on ch. ii. 7). **Such** will we be; rather, *such are we.* The verb is not expressed, but it would have been if the future tense had been intended. In this verse St. Paul is not saying what he would do hereafter, but is rebutting with calmness and dignity the false charge that he was in any way different when absent from what he was when present.

Ver. 12.—**We dare not.** They are in this respect of self-praise much bolder than I. **Make ourselves of the number, or compare ourselves**; literally, *judge ourselves among or judge ourselves with.* There is a play on the words, like the Latin, *inferre or conferre,* or the German, *zurechnen oder gleichrechnen.* **That commend themselves.** The verb rendered "commend" is that from which is derived "the *commendatory* letters" (ch. iii. 1) at the arrogant and intrusive use of which he had glanced already. St. Paul is once more rebutting the charge of self-commendation (ch. iv. 2; v. 12; vi. 11). **But they measuring themselves . . . are not wise.** The clause is difficult; for (1) to compare ourselves with others in order to learn what we can and cannot do is usually accounted wise; (2) some manuscripts and editions, omitting οὐ συνιοῦσιν ἡμεῖς δὲ, render, "But we ourselves (αὐτοὶ), measuring ourselves by ourselves, and comparing ourselves with ourselves, will not boast above measure;" (3) some, for συνιοῦσιν (they are not wise) read συνίουσιν (with ourselves, who are not wise). The reading, however, of the Authorized Version is undoubtedly right, and most probably the rendering also. The meaning is that the little cliques of factious religionists, never looking outside their own narrow circles, became inflated with a sense of importance which would have been annihilated if they had looked at higher standards. Hence they thought themselves at liberty to intrude and lay down the law and usurp a claim to infallibility which there was nothing to justify. Such conduct is the reverse of wise. It is a mixture of selfishness, Pharisaism, and conceit, and there have been abundant examples of it among religious parties in all ages. St. Paul, on the other hand, keeps within his own measure, because he has learnt to adopt larger and loftier standards.

Ver. 13.—**Will not boast of things without our measure.** This might be rendered, "will not indulge in these immeasurable boastings;" but ver. 15 points to the sense, "we will not glory beyond our measure." **Of the rule**; i.e. of the measuring-line. I will keep to the province and limit which God has assigned to me in my proper measure. St. Paul declines the favourite office of being "other people's bishop (ἀλλοτριο-επίσκοπος)" (1 Pet. iv. 15). **Hath distributed**; rather, *apportioned.*

Ver. 14.—**As though we reached not unto you.** In including you within the reach of our measuring-line, we are guilty neither of presumption nor of intrusion. Your Church is a part of our legitimate province and range of work (Acts xviii. 1, 4). **We are come as far as to you**; rather, *we anticipated others in coming to you;* "we were the first to come as far as unto you." To St. Paul belonged the undisputed glory of having first introduced the gospel into the regions of Macedonia and Achaia.

Ver. 15.—**That is, of other men's labours.** Not to thrust himself obtrusively into spheres of labour which legitimately belonged to others was a part of St. Paul's scrupulously chivalrous rule (ch. iii. 10; Gal. ii. 9; Rom. xv. 20). It contrasted with the usurping arrogance of these Jerusalem emissaries. **When your faith is increased**; rather, *increases* or *grows.* He delicately implies that their lack of faith prevents the extension of his labours. He could not leave in his rear an unstormed fortress of opposition to the gospel. The spread of the gospel *depends on them.* **We shall be enlarged by you according to our rule abundantly.** The Revised Version renders it more clearly, "We shall be magnified in you according to our province unto further abundance."

Ver. 16.—**In the regions beyond you.** Even to Rome and Spain (Rom. xv. 19, 24, 28).

Ver. 17.—**But he that glorieth,** etc.; literally, *he that boasteth,* etc. (see note on 1 Cor. i. 31; Jer. ix. 24).

Ver. 18.—**But whom the Lord commendeth** (comp. 1 Cor. iii. 13, 14; iv. 5; Prov. xxvii. 2).

HOMILETICS.

Vers. 1, 2.—*Self-vindication.* " Now I Paul myself beseech you," etc. Paul, as we have frequently intimated, had detractors in the Corinthian Church, men who sought to gain power by calumniating him. We are not in possession of all the calumnies. Paul knew them all. Throughout these two Epistles we find him constantly on the defensive; here again we find him standing up for himself. In his defence he manifests—

I. A STRONG DESIRE TO DEAL WITH THEM IN THE SPIRIT OF CHRIST. " Now I Paul myself beseech [entreat] you by the meekness and gentleness of Christ." He seems to shrink from the idea of so defending himself as to act contrary to the mild and gentle spirit of Christ. Whatever I say in my defence, I would say in the spirit of him " who, when he was reviled, reviled not again." Thus we should always act, even in reproving others and defending ourselves; in all we should be actuated and controlled by the spirit of Jesus Christ. No reproof will go so thoroughly home to the heart of the offender as that which breathes and echoes his spirit.

II. A KNOWLEDGE OF THE CONTEMPTUOUSNESS WITH WHICH HIS DETRACTORS REGARDED HIM. " Who in presence am base [lowly] among you, but being absent am bold [of good courage] toward you." This does not seem to be the estimate he forms of himself, but the character which his slanderers had given him. In ver. 10 it is so stated : " For his letters, say they, are weighty and powerful; but his bodily presence is weak, and his speech contemptible." It would seem that they spoke somewhat thus—How bold and courageous this man is in his " letters; " but how mean and contemptible in his appearance and conduct ! He here intimates that when he comes amongst them he would be " bold " and courageous. They shall know that I am no coward, and with indomitable fearlessness I shall administer the necessary rebuke.

III. A DREAD OF EXERCISING SEVERITY TOWARDS THEM. " But I beseech you, that I may not be bold when I am present with that confidence, wherewith I think to be bold against some, which think of us as if we walked according to the flesh." It is the characteristic of a great soul, especially of a great soul inspired with the spirit of Christ, to shrink from inflicting pain on any heart. Yet when duty calls it must be done.

Vers. 3—6.—*The true soldiership.* " For though," etc. The passage leads us to notice the *weapons* and *victories* of a true soldiership.

I. THE WEAPONS OF TRUE SOLDIERSHIP. The apostle states two things concerning these weapons. 1. *They are not carnal.* The word " carnal " here may be regarded as standing in contradiction to three things. (1) To miraculous agency. Miracles, though employed at first, are not the regular weapons by which Christianity fights her battles. (2) To all coercive instrumentality. The civil magistrate now for fifteen centuries has sought by exactions and penalties to force Christianity upon the consciences of men. Such weapons disgrace and misrepresent it. (3) To all crafty inventions. In nothing, perhaps, has the craftiness of men appeared more than in connection with the profession of extending Christianity. What are the tricks of rhetoric, the assumptions of priests, and the clap-trap of sects but craft? 2. *Though not carnal, they are mighty.* " Mighty through God." (1) They are mighty through God because they are his *productions.* Gospel truths, the weapons of which the apostle speaks, are God's ideas, and those ideas are mighty—mighty with truth and love. (2) They are mighty through God because they are his *instruments.* God goes with his ideas and works by them.

II. THE VICTORIES OF TRUE SOLDIERSHIP. What are the victories ? 1. *They are mental.* Paul is speaking about *imaginations* and things pertaining to mind. They are not over body. There is not any glory in destroying the bodily life of man. The lion, the bear, a poisonous gust of air, will excel man in this. The victories of a true soldiership are over *mind.* And indeed you do not conquer the man unless you conquer his mind. If there be a future world, then the men you slay upon the battlefield may hate you in the great eternity with a profounder hatred than ever. 2. *They are corrective.* These victories do not involve the destruction of the mind nor any of its native faculties, but certain evils that pertain to it. What are they? (1) The evil fortifications of the mind. "The pulling down of strongholds." What are they? Prejudices, worldly maxims, associations, passions, habits; behind these "strongholds" the mind entrenches itself against God. (2) The corrupt thinking of the mind. "Casting down imaginations." The word "thinking" comprehends this, for the faculty which we call imagination thinks as well as the intellect. It is against evil thinkings, therefore. (3) The antitheistic impulses of the mind. "And every high thing that exalteth itself against the knowledge of God." Every feeling and passion that rises against God. These are the victories of true soldiership. 3. *They are Christian.* They "bring into captivity every thought to the obedience of Christ." Thought is everything to man. Now, the work of a true soldier is to bring this fontal force into entire subjection to Christ.

Ver. 7.—*Paul's special power.* "Do ye look on things after the outward appearance?" These words point to two evils.

I. JUDGING FROM APPEARANCE. "Do ye look on things after the outward appearance?" or that "are before your face." The teachers at Corinth who were opposed to the apostle prided themselves on their external advantages, and regarded themselves as superior in appearance, rank, and manners to Paul. They judged from appearance. This judgment led them to regard Paul as their inferior. But was he inferior? Was he not, in all that is intrinsically excellent, in mental capacity, in spiritual knowledge, in Christly enthusiasm, and supernatural power, their superior, the very prince of the apostles? Men judged Christ by the "outward appearance," and how false, wicked, and pernicious their judgment turned out to be! The only true test is the fruit. "By their fruits ye shall know them;" fruits, not actions—which often misrepresent the character of the soul—but productions that are the natural, complete, and spontaneous outgrowth and expression of the leading moral principles of man's life. Because men judge from "the outward appearance," wolves in society pass for sheep, paupers for princes, devils for saints, churls for philanthropists, etc.

II. ARROGATING SUPERIOR CHRISTLINESS. "If any man trust to himself that he is Christ's, let him of himself think this again, that, as he is Christ's, even so are we Christ's." Whilst there were those in the Corinthian Church who said some of them were of Paul, of Apollos, of Cephas, there were some who said they were of Christ. They wished to be regarded as superior to all, as knowing more of Christ, being more intimate with him, having a stronger claim upon him. It might be that some of the members of this party had (not like Paul) been with Christ while on earth, had talked with him, walked with him, feasted with him, and of this they would boast. But thousands could boast of this who had no vital fellowship with Christ. There always have been men in Churches who have arrogated superior piety. I have known not a few, not distinguished by any spiritual nobleness, who were accustomed to speak of him as "*my* Christ," "*my* Saviour," "*my* Redeemer," implying that he was more to them than to others.

Vers. 8—10.—*God's gift of special power to man.* "For though I should boast," etc. These verses present to our attention *God's gift of special power to man.* The "authority" of which the apostle here speaks was, in all probability, a supernatural endowment. Such an endowment he both claimed and manifested (see Acts xiii. 8—11; xiv. 8—10; xv. 9—12). Having this power he was superior even to the ablest of his censors in Corinth, and he felt that should he "boast somewhat" of this there was no reason for him to be ashamed. The words suggest three remarks concerning such special gift of power to man.

I. IT IS UNDER MAN'S CONTROL. Paul's language seems to imply that he might or might not use his "authority" or power; it did not coerce him; it did not make him a mere instrument; it did not overbear his will or infringe in any way his freedom of action. God has given exceptional power to some men—to Moses, Elijah, Elisha, Peter, etc.; but in all cases it seemed to leave them free—free to use it or not, to use it in this direction or in that. The Maker and Manager of the universe respects evermore the free agency with which he has endowed his rational and moral offspring.

We may enslave ourselves, but he will not. He will always treat us as responsible for all we do.

II. ITS GREAT DESIGN IS USEFULNESS. "The Lord hath given us for edification, and not for your destruction." He gives power to men, not to pull down, but to build up. Usefulness is the grand end of our existence. We are formed, not to injure, but to bless our fellow-creatures. Whatever endowments we have, be they ordinary or transcendent, all are given by our Maker to promote truth and virtue and human happiness through the world. Alas! how extensively men pervert these high gifts of Heaven!

III. IT IS NO PROTECTION FROM MALICE. Though Paul was thus so distinguished by signal endowments, he was nevertheless the subject of bitter envy and cruel slander. "For his letters, say they, are weighty and powerful; but his bodily presence is weak, and his speech contemptible." Did the supernatural power with which some of the old Hebrew prophets were endowed shield men from the malice of men? How were Moses, Elisha, and Elijah treated? The fact is, the higher gifts a man has the more he is exposed to the malice of others; the more distinguished a man is in gifts and graces, the more he will arouse among his contemporaries the spirit of detraction and hate. It was so with Christ himself.

Vers. 11—13.—*The false and true method of estimating men.* "Let such a one think this, that, such as we are in word by letters when we are absent, such will we be also in deed when we are present. For we dare not make ourselves of the number, or compare ourselves with some that commend themselves: but they measuring themselves by themselves, and comparing themselves among themselves, are not wise. But we will not boast of things without our measure, but according to the measure of the rule which God hath distributed to us, a measure to reach even unto you." In these verses we have two subjects worthy of notice.

I. THE FALSE AND TRUE METHOD OF ESTIMATING THE CHARACTER OF OTHERS. "Let such a one think this, that, such as we are in word by letters," etc. 1. To judge by *public report is a wrong method.* It would almost seem that there was a general impression in Corinth that not only was Paul's "bodily presence" somewhat contemptible, but that his letters were not a fair representation of himself, that they displayed an elevation and a heroism of which the writer was destitute, and from this general impression he was judged and considered to be something of a boaster and charlatan. How common it is for people to judge those they have never seen by general report! But a miserably false standard of judgment is this. Not unfrequently have I received impressions concerning a person whom I have never seen, which a subsequent personal acquaintance has completely dispelled. As a rule, the public estimate of men, both in Church and state, is most fallacious and unjust. 2. To judge by *personal knowledge is the true method.* "Let such a one think [reckon] this, that, such as we are in word by letters . . . such will we be also in deed when we are present." The meaning of this seems to be—Wait until I come amongst you, and you will find that I am true to the character of my letters, that I will act out their spirit. A man's own letters, even when rightly interpreted, will not give a free and a complete idea of the author. The author is greater than his book, the man greater than his productions. One hour with an author will give me a better idea of him than I could obtain from all the productions of his pen, however voluminous.

II. THE FALSE AND TRUE METHOD OF ESTIMATING OUR OWN CHARACTERS. 1. The *false* method is *comparing our own character with the character of others.* "Measuring themselves by themselves." This the Corinthians seem to have done, and this, perhaps, is the general tendency of mankind. We judge ourselves by the characters of others. When we are accused we are prone to say we are not worse than So-and-so. A false standard this, because: (1) The mass of mankind are corrupt. (2) The best of men are more or less imperfect. (3) There is only One perfect character—Jesus Christ. In these words Paul indicates: (*a*) That it is a *terrible* thing thus to judge ourselves. "We dare not [are not bold enough to] make ourselves of the number." Truly it is a terrible thing, for it leads to fearful issues. (*b*) That it is an *unwise* thing thus to judge ourselves. Those who compare themselves with others "are not wise," or are "without understanding." 2. The *true* method is *judging ourselves by the will of God.*

"According to the measure of the rule which God hath distributed to us." Though the apostle by the expression, "rule which God hath distributed," *primarily refers to the Divine limits of his apostolic work,* as will appear again, the "rule" applies also to his personal character. God's will is the standard or canon by which all characters are to be determined.

CONCLUSION. "Search me, O God, and know my heart: try me, and know my thoughts: and see if there be any wicked way in me, and lead me in the way everlasting."

Vers. 14—18.—*The true sphere of human usefulness and the source of human glory.* "For we stretch not ourselves beyond our measure, as though we reached not unto you: for we are come as far as to you also in preaching the gospel of Christ: not boasting of things without our measure, that is, of other men's labours; but having hope, when your faith is increased, that we shall be enlarged by you according to our rule abundantly. To preach the gospel in the regions beyond you, and not to boast in another man's line of things made ready to our hand. But he that glorieth, let him glory in the Lord. For not he that commendeth himself is approved, but whom the Lord commendeth." Here are two subjects for meditation.

I. THE TRUE SPHERE OF HUMAN USEFULNESS. 1. It is a sphere in which we are placed by *Divine appointment.* Paul teaches that his sphere of labour in Corinth was according to the Divine will. "We stretch not ourselves beyond our measure [overmuch], as though we reached not unto you." As if he had said, "I am not come to Corinth merely by my own inclinations, or as a matter of impulse or caprice, or as an intruder. I am come here by the will of God. I am licensed by him to this sphere." 2. The consciousness that we are in this sphere is a *just reason for exultation.* "Not boasting of things without our measure." As if Paul had said, "My boasting, or my exultation, is not that I have entered into the sphere of other men's labours, but that I am in the sphere to which I have been divinely commissioned." The opponents of Paul, in Corinth, boasted of the influence they had gained in the Church which he himself had founded by his self-sacrificing labours, and whose members owed, either directly or indirectly, their conversion to him; whereas his rejoicing was that he was doing the work of God in the *sphere to which he had been sent.* 3. It is a sphere which *widens with our usefulness.* Although Paul felt that Corinth was the sphere to which he had been sent, he knew that the field would be widened according to his spiritual success. "Having hope, when your faith is increased [that as your faith groweth], that we shall be enlarged [magnified] by you according to our rule [province] abundantly." The increase of their faith would lead to an enlargement of his sphere of labour. *The true method of extending the sphere of labour to which we have been sent is by the multiplication of our converts.* Each soul which a minister brings to Christ enlarges the field of his usefulness, enables him to break up new ground still further on.

II. THE TRUE SOURCE OF HUMAN EXULTATION. In what did Paul exult or "boast"? 1. Not in *crediting himself with the labours of other men.* He did not "boast in another man's line [province] of things made ready to our hand." How common it is for men to credit themselves with the labours of others! We find this in every department of labour. In literature there are plagiarists, in scientific discoveries and artistic inventions there are unjust claimants, and even in religion one minister is often found to claim the good that others have accomplished. Paul was above this. The genius of Christianity condemns this mean and miserable dishonesty. 2. Not in *self-commendation.* "For not he that commendeth himself is approved." That conscience approves of our conduct, though at all times a source of pleasure, is not a true source of exultation; for conscience is not infallible. Conscience sometimes deceives. What, then, was his true source of exultation? "He that glorieth, let him glory in the Lord." "God forbid that I should glory, save in the cross."

HOMILIES BY VARIOUS AUTHORS.

Vers. 1—7.—*Change in the Epistle; spirit of his defence.* No one can fail to notice the change in the tone of the Epistle which appears in this chapter. Every thoughtful reader of St. Paul knows how abrupt his transitions frequently are, and how rapidly he digresses from his main point to something incidental to his topic. His mental associations are governed by two distinct laws—first, by ideas exciting feelings which lead him to diverge from his main line; and next, by emotions arising from some occult source that vary his action of intellect. In this instance there may have been a pause in writing after he had finished the subject of the collection. Naturally a reaction would set in. One of his excitable temperament could not have been relieved of oppressive solicitude, as he had been by the return of Titus, nor given such an expression to his joy as we have in ch. viii. and ix. without subsequent exhaustion of nervous energy. If, meantime, news came to him of the renewal of Judaizing zeal at Corinth, and of some sudden accession of strength to the party so inflamed against him, we can readily see why his indignation should be aroused. To have his hopes dashed in this way, in such a conjuncture and by such unscrupulous opponents, would put a terrible strain on a nature organized as sensitively as his, all the more so since a new era seemed about dawning in the history of the gospel. Europe and Asia appeared ready to join hands most heartily in the work of evangelizing the world, and, just at this most auspicious period, to witness a fresh outbreak of discord was the severest of trials that could have befallen him. Whatever the cause, it was a sad thing for this noble spirit to be sorely chafed in an hour when it was rallying from an unusual depression and girding itself for special endeavours to cement the Asiatic and European Churches closer together. Here, in the very heart of Achaia, were agents from the Judaizing party at Jerusalem, who appear to have become more jealous than ever of his growing influence, and were heated to fiercer hostility against the apostle because of the recent triumph of his authority. While he was exerting every nerve to help the Church in Jerusalem, men from that very community were working in Corinth to disparage his ministry and undermine his personal character. It was shocking ingratitude. In itself it was rankling jealousy; in its connections, base partisanship. At that moment the interests of Christianity hung on the precise work he was doing. The liberal gospel he was preaching, the gospel of free grace and of equal honour and privilege to Jew and Gentile, was attesting its Divine excellence in the "exceeding grace of God" manifested by means of the abounding charity of Macedonia and Achaia. And yet all the promise and hope of this inspiring movement were thrown into the utmost peril by these fanatical zealots. Had he not felt this wrong keenly and resisted it courageously, he would have shown a want of manliness; for no character can have force that lacks indignation when its own integrity and a great cause identified with that integrity are ruthlessly assailed. It is under such circumstances that the true man appears in the way his sense of injustice operates. Quite as plainly the wise leader will display himself in the perception of what the emergency requires and in the decision with which his measures are executed. Now, the apostle is before us again as a study in this particular aspect of his character and ministry. Much as we have learned of him, something remains to be seen, and we may feel assured that the additional insight will amply reward us. The first utterance of his soul enkindles our admiration. Wronged, vilified, St. Paul appeals to the Corinthians "by the meekness and gentleness of Christ." It is not "we," but "I Paul," for he was the person singled out for these malicious attacks and he would reply from his own heart. It is not that sort of "meekness and gentleness" which craft and conventionality often assume to hide their art and malignity. It is the spirit of Christ, the meekness which acts by turning inwardly upon the mind and soothing its faculties, and the gentleness that exhibits itself in outward tranquillity. St. Paul cannot speak of these except as Christ's virtues. They are his; they have his life; they take their power and beauty from him. "I Paul myself"—his individuality emphasized in an unusual manner—"beseech you," at the instant when the lion was more likely to show itself in human nature than the lamb, that it may not be necessary for me to exercise my authority over these offenders. If, as my enemies say, I am base in presence among you and bold only when absent, I pray you not to let this matter go to such an extremity that I shall have to use "the rod." When one's courage has been challenged and his heroism derided, it is extremely hard for a brave man like St. Paul to forbear. But had he not said, "Love suffereth long and is kind"? Words were things to him and here was the proof of love, side by side with the irony that was not to be concealed. Would he announce an inflexible determination to punish? No; further discipline might be needful for him, further forbearance might be desirable in the case of his assailants; and all he ventured to affirm was, "I *think* to be bold against some." Who were the "some"? Evidently those who impeached his motives and openly reviled his ministry. How does he describe them? By the thoughts they entertained of him as an apostle. "They think of us as if we walked according to the flesh," referring to a course of conduct "determined by the fear of men or the desire of pleasing men, and hence a personal bearing disgraced by cowardice or servility. The human nature referred to was therefore one enfeebled, not merely from the want of Divine support, but from sin" (Lange's 'Commentary'). Such an opinion respecting the apostle indicates clearly enough the evil source whence it sprang. It happens often that the judgments we pronounce on others are most true in application to ourselves, and, unawares, we have disclosed what our own hearts are in estimating outside parties. A politician who is always charging other politicians with being demagogues is generally a demagogue himself, and the man who never hesitates to apply the epithet of a liar to others is quite sure to be a liar himself. But how does St. Paul meet the charge of being carnally minded in his high office? "Though we walk in the flesh [live a corporeal life], we do not war after the flesh," or "according to the flesh," the contrast being in the words "in" and "according." And forthwith he proceeds to show the difference between walking in the flesh and warring according to the flesh. A warrior he is, an open and avowed warrior—a warrior who was to cast down imaginations and every high thing that exalteth itself against the knowledge of God, and bring into captivity every thought to the obedience of Christ; a warrior too who would punish these Judaizers if they continued their disorganizing work; but a prudent and considerate warrior, deferring the avenging blow till "I am assured of your submission" (Stanley) "that I may not confound the innocent with the guilty, the dupes with the deceivers." What kind of a *preacher* he was he had shown long before; what kind of an *apostle* he was among apostles as to independence, self-support, and resignation of official rights in earthly matters, he had also shown; further yet, what kind of a sufferer and martyr he was had been portrayed. Step by step he had gone on with this faithful unfolding of himself, giving the most unique spiritual biography in the world of literature, and that too on no preconceived plan. How many aspects of his character had been sketched! The man as ambassador, representing the majesty of a glorified King, and labouring to reconcile a world to his Divine sceptre; the man as co-worker with all the blessed ministries of earth and heaven; the man as philanthropist sharing the poverty of his countrymen in a far-off city; and now the man as warrior, leading on his hosts to battle against alien spirits; —what a wide activity, how minute, how full, how varied, how comprehensive! At no point does this personal narrative draw its interest from self alone. Self is always subordinate. The biography interweaves with a history that infinitely transcends all private fortunes and all earthly affairs, and is nothing less than the history of providence in the development of Christian doctrine coincident with the work of the Holy Ghost in glorifying the ascended Christ of the Father. "Casting down imaginations." The reference is to reasonings or disputings of the natural man in the pride of his intellectual power. Yet they are *imaginations*, the products of the imaging faculty, the fond conceits of creative ingenuity. All these were religious beliefs or connected in some way with them, so that what the apostle said at Athens was true elsewhere: "I perceive that in all things ye are too superstitious." Men who held these beliefs were earnest supporters of them and were always ready to defend their tenets. No matter in what province or city he preached the gospel, these disputants appeared. It was a battle on all occasions, and hence a battle figure, "casting down," or the destruction of bulwarks. Philosophy, art, manufactures, trade, husbandry, seamanship, military life, domestic life, statesmanship, were all intimately associated with these religious beliefs. Paganism occupied the ground. Or, if Judaism had found lodgment over the empire at every prominent centre of industry, it was the Judaism that had crucified Jesus of Nazareth. So then there was battle everywhere. The "wisdom of the world" and of "the princes of the world," backed by social influence and civil authority, was arrayed against the gospel. In the land of its birth, Christianity had nothing to show but a few Galilean fishermen, with a community of poor disciples, and behind these a malefactor's cross. In the lands to which it came on its mission of grace, it summoned men to repent of sin, to practise self-denial, to become new creatures, to abandon idolatries that were in league with lust and cruelty, and, in lieu thereof, accept a faith which demanded a pure heart and a holy morality. It could only make its way by " casting down imaginations," by telling men that they were deluded by sophistries, and further by destroying " every high thing " that exalted itself against the knowledge of God communicated to man by the revelation of the gospel. No compromise could be allowed ; every thought was to be brought into " captivity " to the " obedience of Christ." What *captivity* meant they fully understood. It was a military word, and he uses such terms that they might have clear and vivid ideas of Christianity as a war, and nothing less than an exterminating war, on whatever stood opposed " to the obedience of Christ." The " weapons " he used were not " carnal." All the world knew his weapons. He made no disguise of them. Boldly, constantly, in every place, he proclaimed Christ, the Power of God and the Wisdom of God, nor had a mob occurred, nor had perils gathered about him, nor had Roman officers interfered for his protection, except on the single issue of preaching Christ crucified. No heathen would charge him with using carnal weapons. Philosophers of Athens, inhabitants of Lycaonia, Demetrius and his workmen at Ephesus, would make no such accusation against his ministry. Only the Judaizers had done this thing. Let them understand that these weapons were " mighty through God to the pulling down of strongholds." Neither a false Judaism nor a colossal idolatry could offer any effective resistance to the gospel. Let these Judaizers know that his weapons were " mighty through God," and that in due time he would show " a readiness to revenge all disobedience." And let the Corinthian Church look deeper than the " outward appearance." To construe his manner of " meekness and gentleness " into imbecility and cowardice was not truth, but falsehood. And whence came this evil way of judging ? Not from themselves, but from some wrong teacher who professed to have external advantages in favour of his teaching. Let that conceited man know that, if he is Christ's, so also am I.—L.

Vers. 8—11.—*Continuation of his defence.* What he had just claimed was no more than other apostles claimed. If he were to boast in stronger terms of the authority the Lord had conferred upon him, there would be no risk of personal shame by his overstating the matter. Power had been given, not for their destruction, but for their edification. It is his favourite figure once more—*edification*, building up, and that power should be used for this object. To terrify them by letters was not his aim ; edification, not destruction, led him to write. By the admission of his enemies, the letters from him were " weighty and powerful." On the other hand, his " bodily presence " was " weak," and his " speech contemptible." This is the only notice we have in the New Testament of an apostle's personal appearance. Had it occurred in the case of St. Peter or St. John, we should have been surprised, but it falls in naturally with the order of events and the play of circumstances connected with St. Paul's apostleship. His call, position, and career were singular ; the individuality gives a colouring to the minutest details of his life ; and accordingly, as he was subjected to an exceptional kind and degree of criticism, even his bodily infirmities came under inspection and were made matters of public notoriety. By itself, this reference to his appearance would not attract more than a passing notice. Yet it has a broader meaning, since it serves to illustrate the fact that nothing about him escaped the closest scrutiny. Enemies in the Church, enemies out of the Church, officials, centurions, proconsuls, procurators, find something in the man to study, and their opinions of him come into the public thought of the day. The plan of Providence, we may infer, was that St. Paul should be well known, thoroughly well known, and that we should hear from both sides—friends and foes—all that could be known of him, even to his " presence " and " speech." He thought the matter of sufficient importance to recognize it so far as to say that, what he was in his letters, he would be in his deeds. Beyond this he has no concern about it.—L.

Vers. 12—18.—*Limits and labours.* Was the apostle a great letter-writer only ? So his enemies had declared ; but he would not put himself among those who had no higher standard of what they ought to be than what they were, nor would he compare himself with such men. Instead of measuring themselves by a Divine rule, these persons thought it enough to measure themselves by themselves or by others; and this mode of judgment, originating in self and ending with self, was without understanding. Yet there was a measure, and he acknowledged it whenever he thought or spoke of himself. If he referred to his labours, if he enumerated his sacrifices, if he cited his sufferings, it was not with any human standard in view, but in the sight of God and with respect solely to the sphere of activity to which God had appointed him as an apostle. Had he come to Corinth? Corinth had been given him of God as a field of apostolic effort. "The surveyor's chain" had laid off the territory, and he had traversed Macedonia and Achaia only because Providence had assigned the ground to him, and the Holy Spirit had inspired him to undertake the task. "As far as to you;" so far in the warfare of the West the campaign had extended, so far had he gone in the great fight of *pulling down strongholds*, and in demonstrating that the *weapons were not carnal*, but *mighty through God*. If he had reached Corinth as a place within the boundaries of his province, would he pause there? Was this the outer line of the vast battle-field? He hoped not. There he was only waiting till another territory had been marked out, and he should hear the signal to arise and possess the land. Was he looking across the sea of Adria and wondering when he should visit Rome? And when would that glad opportunity come? But one thing was clear to him just then, and this was that, if the faith of the Corinthians were increased, he would have his own heart enlarged, and be further endowed and qualified for apostolic labour. One moment, a glance at the Judaizers and their presumptuous occupancy of fields delegated of God to him (ver. 15), "not boasting of things without measure, that is, of other men's labours;" the next moment, a thought of new work so soon as the Church at Corinth should recover from its troubles and he should find it safe to leave them. Already his heart was burning to preach the gospel in the regions beyond Corinth, and "not to glory in another's province in regard to things ready to our hand." Observe how often this last idea recurs: ver. 13, "We will not boast of things without our measure;" ver. 14, "We stretch not ourselves beyond our measure;" ver. 15, "Not boasting of things without our measure;" ver. 16, "Not to boast in another man's line of things [see Revised Version, above] made ready to our hand." Two things here are noteworthy. 1. The apostle is willing and ready to wage the holy war in new territories. He is not tired of fighting the Lord's battles. Nor is he afraid of greater and more numerous enemies. Probably his eye was on Rome. If God will, he shall go further West. His weapons have been tried and proved. He himself has been tested. Grace has been sufficient. Cast down, he has not been destroyed. Dying, he has lived. The promises of God have been *Yea* and *Amen* to his soul, nor could any experience happen that would not bring the strength and consolation of Christ to his heart. How much he had lived and how rapidly! What years had been compressed into each year! Before the dilating eye of intellect, what vistas had spread afar in the light that brightened towards the perfect day! And then the blessed realizations, ability increasing perpetually, and capacity growing even faster so as to supply fully the expanding spheres of ability, consciousness of self enlarging as self in Christ, deep opening into deep, wonder springing afresh from wonder, and, with every victory gained by the weapons of his warfare, a larger assurance that, if he had been "mighty through God" at Ephesus and Corinth, he should be mightier still "in the regions beyond." Here is a most useful lesson to teach us what we are slow to learn, namely, that no natural endowments, no amount of culture, no inspiration of knowledge, no miracles wrought in his behalf, can set aside the necessity of Christian experience, a personal work of grace in the soul, a profound sense of that work as from the Holy Spirit, in the case of one called to the highest office of minis-tration. 2. We see how we are, as Christians, "members one of another." Although St. Paul was so highly endowed and so remarkably successful in the apostleship, yet he depends on the Church at Corinth for his *enlargement* to the work opening before him in Europe. "We shall be *enlarged* by you." This was conditioned on their conduct. If their divisions were healed, their false teachers silenced, their energies set free from exhausting strife and concentrated on building up Christ's kingdom, would Corinth and Achaia be the only gainers? Nay; he himself would be liberated from restraints that clogged his feet. A fresh impulse would be given his apostleship. A new current of life would flow from their hearts into his heart, for it was not his working nor any other apostle's working, but the co-working, the hearty union of Church and apostles, the co-operation of the "diversities of gifts," the oneness of the mystical body of Christ, by which the world was to be evangelized. The schism that had been threatened between the Asiatic and European Churches was in a fair way to be arrested. Jewish and Gentile believers were getting reconciled to the peculiarities of each other; the collection for the mother Church at Jerusalem was doing much to effect this most important unity. Yet this is not before him now. Nor does he allude to the singular advantages of Corinth as to geographical location and commercial opportunities. Situated on a narrow strip of land between northern and southern Greece, and connected with two seas by its harbours of Lechæum and Cenchreæ, it was a great emporium of trade for the East and West, and hence offered extraordinary facilities for the diffusion of Christianity. No doubt St. Paul felt that it was a centre of commanding influence. But he was extremely cautious as to using local motives, and in the present case he made no allusion to them. What occupied his whole thought was the increase of grace among them as a Christian community, and to this he looked for a happy furtherance in his contemplated missionary tour. If they were revived and consecrated anew to Christ, he knew well that, when obstacles were thrown in his future pathway, when persecutions even fiercer than those already undergone came upon him, they would afford him sympathy and assistance while getting foothold in "the regions beyond." Obviously a prevailing idea in his mind was that Christianity must have a central home in every great section of country, and thence draw its human supplies during its conquests of outlying territory. And he longed for the Corinthian brethren to attain a richer experience of grace, so that they might magnify his office. Instead of being independent of their fraternal support, the stronger he felt himself the more he leaned on their sympathies. Heaven never gets so close to a man that earth does not get closer also. How the blessed Jesus leaned on his friends in the Passion week! How he needed the chosen among them to watch with him in the garden for *one hour*! The weary days of the apostle had not yet come, and his soul was having glorious visions of apostolic work, but amid it all, the pressure of uncertainty was upon his hope, and he would gladly hasten away from the present scene of anxiety just as soon as Providence permitted. We can enter into his solicitudes. We can imagine how Kirke White felt when he wrote the closing lines of the 'Christiad':—

> "O thou who visitest the sons of men,
> Thou who dost listen when the humble pray,
> One little space prolong my mournful day!
> One little lapse suspend thy last decree!"

And we can realize Dr. Arnold's emotions when he made the last entry in his diary: "Still there are works which, with God's permission, I would do before the night cometh; especially that great work, if I might be permitted to take part in it." So too we can form some conception of St. Paul's anxiety to widen the field of his ministrations. But he could not go alone; the heart of the Corinthian Church must go with him; and he must wait till they were sufficiently "increased" in "faith" to enter on the future enterprises of his universal apostleship. How humble in his greatness! Not what St. Paul accomplished, but what God accomplished in him, was his boast and commendation. This was his strength and glory, and therefore, "He that glorieth, let him glory in the Lord."—L.

Ver. 4.—*Spiritual weapons.* The Apostle Paul was naturally of a combative, soldier-like disposition. Before his conversion this temperament displayed itself in opposition to the cause of truth, to the Church of Christ. After his conversion his warfare was directed against the error, sin, and evil that afflicted and cursed mankind. As a soldier of Christ he fought a good fight and gained an honourable reputation. In the text we have, upon his own authority, the acknowledgment and explanation of his victories.

1. THE NATURE OF THE WEAPONS CHRISTIANITY EMPLOYS AND SANCTIONS. It is evident from this and other passages that Paul did not place his main reliance upon the miraculous and supernatural powers which he possessed, and sometimes wielded.

1. Carnal weapons are disclaimed; *e.g.* the appeal to force of arms or of law; the

appeal to the superstitious fears of men; the address to interest and selfishness, in the use of worldly policy and craft. 2. Spiritual weapons are relied upon. The truth of God, the gospel of Christ,—this was the arm in which inspired apostles were wont to trust. 3. These weapons are mighty. In fact, there are no means of combating error and sin, of promoting the cause of truth and righteousness, so powerful as those which are taken from the armoury of the New Testament. They are "mighty through God," *i.e.* their power is of Divine origin, the Holy Spirit accompanying them to the souls of men.

II. THE EFFICACY OF THE WEAPONS WHICH CHRISTIANITY EMPLOYS AND SANCTIONS. 1. They are mighty to *demolish*. As in warfare fortresses and cities are taken by a victorious army, and are then demolished, razed to the ground, so when the religion of Jesus went forth, conquering and to conquer, it attacked and brought low every high thing that exalteth itself against the knowledge of God. Thus sin, ignorance, error, superstition, vice, crime, bigotry, malice, were again and again vanquished by the victorious energy of the gospel. 2. They are mighty to *subjugate*. Captivity was the common lot of the conquered foe. And as *thoughts* are the motive power of life, the gospel attacked these; and rebellious, disobedient, indifferent, ungrateful thoughts were captured, and, by the gentle but mighty force of Divine truth, were brought into subjection to Christ, whom to obey is liberty, peace, and joy.—T.

Ver. 5.—*The captivity of the thoughts.* Spiritual warfare is represented as leading to spiritual victory, and this as involving spiritual captivity. As the Roman general, having vanquished his foe and taken multitudes of prisoners, reserved his captives to grace his triumph, so the apostle, commissioned by Christ, regards himself as contending with all lawless and rebellious forces, and as resolved with Divine help to bring all such forces into subjection to his great Commander and Lord.

I. THE FORCES WHICH ARE BROUGHT INTO CAPTIVITY. Christianity does not contend with physical powers, does not aim at the mere regulation of outward and bodily acts. It strikes at antagonists far more powerful than any which are dealt with by the powers of this world. *Thoughts*, i.e. the desires and purposes of the souls of men,—these are the foes with which the spiritual religion of the Lord Jesus contends. Disobedient thoughts, selfish thoughts, worldly thoughts, murmuring thoughts,—these it is that the religion of the Lord Jesus assails. These are the source and spring of all the outward evils that afflict and curse mankind. If these can be mastered, society may be regenerated and the world may be saved.

II. THE SUBJECTION AND SUBMISSION INTO WHICH THESE FORCES ARE TO BE BROUGHT. 1. It is to the obedience of Christ, the rightful Lord of thoughts and of hearts, that the spiritual forces of humanity are to be rendered subject. A grand future is in this view opened up before humanity. The Son of man is King of man; and he will then ascend his royal throne when men's hearts bow loyally before him, acknowledge his unique spiritual authority, and offer to him their grateful and cheerful allegiance. 2. It is a willing captivity into which human thoughts will be led. In this it is utterly unlike the subjection from which the metaphor is taken. Not brute force, but the convincing authority of reason, the sweet constraint of love, the admired majesty of moral excellence, secure the submission of man's nature to the control of the Divine Lord 3. It is a lasting captivity, not temporary and brief. Whom Christ governs he governs for evermore. Time and earth cannot limit his empire. His kingdom is an everlasting kingdom.—T.

Ver. 8.—*Apostolic authority.* Paul had to contend with difficulties, not only from without, but also from within, the Churches. There were rivals to his authority and claims. It happened that sometimes these rivals met with a certain measure of success. And this drove the apostle into the assertion of his rightful position and demands.

I. THE SOURCE OF APOSTOLIC POWER AND AUTHORITY. 1. It was not in himself, in any personal gifts and qualifications, that this power lay. Paul was indeed by nature a highly gifted man; but he laid no stress upon his abilities. He was by education a man of learning and culture; but he did not rely upon his knowledge for his influence. 2. It was not in any human commission that Paul confided. A king commissions an ambassador; a university confers a degree and right to teach; a Church licenses and authorizes a ministry. But the apostles were forward to declare that they had not received their commission from man. 3. It was by the Lord Jesus himself that the apostles were empowered and appointed to fulfil their high office. If Paul was the latest thus to be commissioned, none the less did he receive his authorization from the Divine Lord himself.

II. The scope and purpose of apostolic power and authority. 1. As negatively described, it was not for casting down, for destruction. The power of the warrior is too often employed for this end. And even religious leaders and rulers—popes, defenders of the faith, and others—have too often bent their energies rather to destroy than to save. The apostle had occasion sometimes to threaten that he would put forth his power to silence and crush the rebellious. But he had no delight in "casting down," neither did he regard this as the ultimate end of his ministry. 2. As positively described, it was for edification. We must understand by this the rearing of the structure of Christian doctrine, and at the same time the building up of Church life. And as doctrine is intended to produce results in character, and as every true Church is built up of renewed natures and holy lives, obviously edification is a moral and personal process.

Application. Apostolic power and authority give an assured basis for the faith of a Christian believer and for the teaching of a Christian minister. For the foundation is laid, not by human ignorance, but by Divine wisdom.—T.

Ver. 10.—*Letters, weighty and strong.* In this passage St. Paul records the impression which, according to his adversaries, was made by his personal presence and by his epistolary writings. Although the reference is to the feeling at Corinth as a result of his First Epistle to the Church in that city, the language applies to the apostle generally as a minister discharging his ministry by the pen. There was nothing commanding in Paul's appearance, and there were in his delivery some drawbacks to the impressiveness of his speech; but with regard to his letters, there was no room for difference of opinion. They were masterpieces, and their effectiveness was undeniable. In what does this effectiveness consist?

I. St. Paul's Epistles abound in vigorous reasoning. It is sufficient to refer to the First Epistle to the Corinthians in order to establish this assertion. On a doctrinal question such as the resurrection of the dead, on a practical question such as that connected with the sacrificial feasts, he proved himself a master of argument. As Christianity is a religion appealing to the intelligence, it has been wisely ordered that in its authoritative documents there should be much reasoning which commends itself to the wisest understanding and the soundest judgment.

II. St. Paul's Epistles abound in manifestations of the finest feeling. Far from sentimental, the apostle was yet a man of tender affections, of emotional suscepti- bilities. Take, for example, the panegyric of charity in his First Epistle to these Corinthians. Take the personal references to his friends and fellow-labourers, to be found in most of his letters. Many readers or hearers, who were not capable of appre- ciating his argumentative power, would feel deeply the appeals to their best and purest sentiments. If we feel thus now, at this distance of time, and when imagination is necessary in order to throw ourselves into the circumstances in which these letters were written and read, how much more must this have been the case when all was fresh and recent!

III. Paul's Epistles have proved their power by the practical results they have produced. They were not written to be approved and admired, but to convince, to persuade, to induce to prompt and cheerful action in compliance with their counsels. And this result followed these documents when first perused. And every age attests their moral authority, and proves that their weight and power are still undiminished.—T.

Ver. 17.—*Glorying in the Lord.* Boasting is universally denounced as a petty and a vulgar fault. Yet it is a fault not uncommon. It imposes upon the unthinking and the unwary, but it awakens the suspicion and the distrust of those who have a larger experience of life. But in the region of spiritual service, boastfulness is a serious offence, not only against society, but against God himself. The apostle protests against it, and in this verse exhibits the true remedy.

I. Men are tempted to glory in themselves. What men have they are in danger of over-estimating, and thus taking credit to themselves when no credit is due. Some glory in natural endowments, strength of body, or mental ability. Some in the accidents of birth or of fortune. Some in their position in society, etc.

II. From this temptation to boastfulness spiritual labourers are not free. Some religious teachers, preachers, writers, officials, pride themselves upon their "gifts," and the esteem in which they are held; boast of their credentials, their learning, their acceptance. If the persons to whom the apostle referred were the first, they were certainly not the last, of this order of men.

III. The only admissible glorying is glorying in the Lord. 1. Christians may glory in the Divine grace to which they owe their spiritual position. This they do when they ask—What have we that we did not receive? Who hath made us to differ? 2. Christian ministers may glory in opportunity of service and in the Divine bestowal of ability for its fulfilment. The apostle felt that the Head of the Church had put honour upon him in commissioning him as the messenger of life to the Gentiles, and in qualifying him for a mission so sacred and glorious. Every bishop, pastor, and evangelist may well acknowledge the condescension of the Eternal in counting him faithful and putting him into the ministry. 3. All true labourers may glory in their success by attributing it to the Divine Author. Paul had abundant reason of this kind for glorying. He needed no letters of commendation; his own converts were epistles witnessing to his faithfulness and zeal, known and read of all men. Joy and thanksgiving, glorying and congratulation, may justly follow when Heaven has smiled upon the labourer's toil, and has suffered him not only to sow, but also to reap.—T.

Ver. 18.—*Commendation, human and Divine.* A good man's difficulties do not always come from avowed adversaries. It sometimes happens that those who are professedly upon his side trouble and harass him. So the Apostle Paul found it, for he had to complain of perils among false brethren, and he frequently had to contend with the undermining influence of those who disparaged his ability and authority, and asserted and praised themselves.

I. The vanity of self-commendation on the part of Christian labourers. 1. Such a habit is a flaw in personal character. True dignity and self-respect dictate modesty in estimating one's self and reticence in speaking of one's self. 2. It has an injurious effect upon the ministry. They who commend themselves in words are not likely to commend themselves in deeds. The estimation in which others hold them is probably in inverse ratio to that in which they hold themselves. 3. It is displeasing to the Lord and Judge of all, who regards the lowly and meek and raises them up in due time.

II. The Lord himself commends and will commend his faithful servants. He is not unjust; he is not ungenerous; he is not unmindful.

> "All works are good, and each is best
> As most it pleases thee;
> Each worker pleases when the rest
> He serves in charity;
> And neither man nor work unblest
> Wilt thou permit to be."

1. This commendation is bestowed here and now. In the success of the labourer is evidence of the approbation of the Master. 2. Hereafter shall be a public and pronounced commendation. In the day of account those who have done their Lord's will shall be accepted. "Then shall every man have praise of God."

III. It is not the self-commended, but the commended of the Lord, who endure the test and come out from it approved. Work is put to the proof; and not only the work, but the workman, is thus submitted to a decisive trial. If it be asked—Who stand the test, and are brought out with honour and acceptance? the answer is—Not the boastful, the self-confident, those who are loud in their own praise; but those who, by patient continuance in well-doing, by diligent devotion to the service of the Lord, secure his commendation. Such shall abide in the judgment, and shall receive the recompense of reward.—T.

Ver. 1.—" *The meekness and gentleness of Christ.*" How different was Christ to (1) the anticipations of the chosen people! (2) the heathen conceptions of deity!

I. THE MEEKNESS OF CHRIST. Illustrated in : 1. *His lowly birth.* The manger prefigured the whole life. 2. *His humble station.* Highest in heaven, lowliest on earth. 3. *His obedience to Joseph and Mary.* Obedience was new to him. He was *the Ruler*, and yet he submitted to be ruled. 4. *His manual toil.* The Jews looked for a conqueror and saw a carpenter. 5. *His endurance of scorn and insult.* Scorn and insult were much more to him than they ever can be to us. Remember he was the adored of heaven! 6. *His earthly poverty.* He possessed all things, and yet had nothing—not even a place where to lay his head. 7. *His bearing before the Sanhedrim, Pilate, Herod, the soldiers, etc.* How little and mean they must have seemed to him! and yet he did not crush them. 8. *His submission on the cross.* The infinitude of meekness! Nothing could transcend this. This was the culmination of a meekness which shone throughout the marvellous earthly life.

> " Ride on, ride on in majesty ;
> In lowly pomp ride on to die;
> Bow thy meek head to mortal pain ;
> Then take, O Christ, thy power and reign."

9. *His burial.* He went, not only to death, but to the grave. He lay in a borrowed sepulchre.

II. THE GENTLENESS OF CHRIST. Exhibited in : 1. *His treatment of children.* How immortal have those words become! how typical they are of the Christ-heart, "Suffer the little children, and forbid them not, to come unto me" (Matt. xix. 14)! 2. *His conduct towards the poor, the sick, the bereaved, the penitent.* What compassion and tenderness! "A bruised reed shall he not break" (Isa. xlii. 3). 3. *His words.* "He shall not cry, nor lift up, nor cause his voice to be heard in the street" (Isa. xlii. 2). Well might they marvel at the gracious words which proceeded out of his mouth. 4. *His forbearance towards his disciples.* Few things illustrate his gentleness more strikingly than this. How much had he to bear from those nearest to him! How gentle he was to the impulsive, blundering, often almost insolent, Peter ! How gentle even to Judas ! 5. *His dealing with sinners.* Except to the hopelessly hardened, upon whom gentleness would have been thrown away, and to whom it would have been an evil rather than a good. His general attitude towards the sinful is expressed by those memorable words, "Take my yoke upon you, and learn of me; for I am meek and lowly in heart: and ye shall find rest unto your souls" (Matt. xi. 29). 6. *His care of his mother.* History has no more touching incident than that at the cross, "Woman, behold thy son!" (John xix. 26).

III. THOUGH SO MEEK AND GENTLE, CHRIST WAS FULL OF POWER AND MAJESTY. No student of his life can question this; enemies and friends alike confess it. Force and noise are not synonymous. Silent forces are often mighty. To be meek is not to be weak. Simplicity, tenderness, humility, are marks of the truly great. These flowers grow upon the top of the mountain. A man who is ever anxious to "assert himself" usually shows how very little he has to assert.

IV. THOSE WHO BEAR CHRIST'S NAME SHOULD PARTAKE OF CHRIST'S NATURE. It is for us to be meek and lowly followers of the meek and lowly Jesus. When the apostle would be most forceful to the Corinthians, he claimed for himself these attributes of his Master. We are strongest when we are most like Christ. We shall *be* better, *live* better, *worship* better, *work* better, if we possess the "meekness and gentleness of Christ."—H.

Ver. 4.—" *Our weapons.*" I. THEY ARE FOR USE IN THE GREATEST OF ALL CONFLICTS 1. Not a physical conflict. These are poor, of comparative unimportance, often very contemptible, can effect little. 2. Not for the destruction of men. What labour, thought, skill, genius, are expended by man for man's destruction ! 3. Not a mere mental conflict. Intellectual battles are not chief. 4. A spiritual conflict. 5. A conflict in which the honour and glory of the Eternal are contended for. 6. A conflict in which man's highest interests are sought. 7. A conflict against evil in every form.

II. THEY ARE HERE DESCRIBED. 1. *Negatively.* They are not carnal. (1) They are not physical. Physical weapons have often been used in the cause of religion, but always by mistake. Peter's blunder in cutting off the ear of Malchus has had many repetitions. (2) They are not carnal, for they are not of man. The apostle did not carry on his conflict by using (a) cunning and trickery in order to secure converts. Some unwisely think that, if converts be obtained, it is no matter how. But Paul desired to "strive lawfully" (2 Tim. ii. 5). (b) Nor did he rely upon human eloquence. He came not with "wisdom of words" (1 Cor. i. 17). (c) Nor upon human reason. Philosophical subtleties he discarded. He had a revelation, and, whilst willing to demonstrate to human intelligence that this *was* a Divine revelation, he then employed *it*, and hoped for victory only as the Divine Spirit blessed his efforts. The apostle *preached the gospel* by his words, by his deeds, by his spirit, by his life; and using these weapons he relied pre-eminently upon that supreme weapon, Divine power, to secure the victory. 2. *Positively.* Carnal weapons seem strong. They impress men. Paul's weapons, which are ours, are apt to excite ridicule on the part of fleshly men, who judge by outward appearance. But the apostle contends that these weapons are mighty. They have done what all others have failed to do. (1) They cast down strongholds. By these Satan is hurled from his seats, from his fastnesses in the hearts of men. (2) They triumph over sceptical human philosophies and false religions (ver. 5). This is the conflict between truth and error. Truth *has* won. Truth *will* win. Though these are high things exalted against the knowledge of God (ver. 5), they find something higher and mightier in the gospel and in the accompanying power of God. They are but Dagons; before the ark they must fall. (3) They make captive human thought (ver. 5). Illustrated in a true conversion. Thought is then dominated by Christ—no more a boastful foe, but a servant, a captive. The wise man becomes a fool that he may be truly wise (1 Cor. iii. 18). Pride, boastful and arrogant in the realm of human thought, is smitten—smitten to the death. (4) They are mighty before God. *Through* God, but also *before* God, *i.e.* in his judgment. They come from his armoury. They are specially fashioned by him for this strife.

III. WE SHOULD RELY ONLY UPON THESE WEAPONS IN THE GREAT CONFLICT. Our strength is here. There are many temptations to use others. *The devil loves to furnish us with weapons wherewith to attack his kingdom!* With what strange weapons has the Church fought! No wonder the strife has so often gone against her. With what weapons are *we* fighting?

IV. WE SHOULD SEEK SKILL IN THEIR USE. 'Tis not enough to have good weapons, we must know how to employ them. The best weapons are the worst in unwise hands. We must enter the military school of Christ.—H.

Ver. 7.—*Judging from appearances.* I. A VERY EASY WAY OF JUDGING. A sound judgment often involves hard labour. Many jump to conclusions because the jump is so easy and so soon over. But a judgment lightly got may generally be lightly valued. Few things are more difficult than forming accurate judgments. The importance of correct judgment is, however, so all-important that we should spare no pains to secure it.

II. A VERY COMMON WAY OF JUDGING. Surface-judgments are popular. Many people are fatally prejudiced by appearance, whether good or bad; of the former they will hear no blame, of the latter no praise. We need remember this when we estimate human judgments generally.

III. A VERY PERILOUS WAY OF JUDGING. It leads to constant errors and evils. Note one or two. 1. *Gentleness is mistaken for weakness.* This was the case with the apostle. That which was kindest and best in him was esteemed a fault. 2. *The physical and external are over-estimated.* The voice, manner, appearance, language of a preacher are unduly regarded. The "outward appearance" often goes for much more than the inward grace and power. 3. *The flashy and dazzling are more esteemed than the solid and weighty.* Sensational religion triumphs in the realm of shallow judgment. 4. *The religious life suffers in comparison with the worldly.* The deep, quiet, permanent joys of the former are unconsidered. The pleasures of the latter are thought to be *as great as they seem*: a fatal blunder. 5. *God's dealings with us are misunderstood.* He is often kindest when he seems most unkind. God's "No" is often a far greater good than God's "Yes" could be; but a hasty superficial judgment does not perceive this. We often complain most when we have most cause to bless. 6. *The more striking forms of*

Christian worship and work eclipse other and more important. The shallow judgments of Corinth were all for speaking with tongues. "Prophecy" was little accounted of. "Giving money" is often attractive when true charity is not. The grand choral service is more popular than quiet consistent living. To be a "great preacher" is the object of ambition rather than to be a real teacher of men. 7. *Christ was rejected and is to-day by those who judge according to the outward appearance.* He is "a root out of a dry ground" to such; they have no spiritual insight. The Gospels which speak of him are full of inconsistencies to those who will not examine them. Yea, the Bible itself, which is one revelation of him, must be rejected by these weak surface-judges. But what said he? "Judge not according to appearance, but judge righteous judgment" (John vii. 24).—H.

Vers. 12—18.—*Boasting, wrong and right.* I. WRONG BOASTING. 1. *That we excel some others.* We are very apt, like some at Corinth, to compare ourselves with certain around us. This is measuring by a false standard, and measuring by a false standard is likely to lead to enormously erroneous results. The question is not whether we excel others, but whether we have attained to the measure for which God created and endowed us. The true measuring-rod is not found in the stature, physical, mental, or moral, of our fellows; the true measuring-rod is held in the hands of the Almighty. If a man were to judge of himself by comparing himself with a mouse or a molehill, we should say he was a fool; and the apostle says, "They themselves, measuring themselves by themselves, and comparing themselves with themselves, are without understanding" (ver. 12). It has been said, "The one-eyed is easily king among the blind." 2. *That we possess what we are destitute of, and that we have done what we have not done.* Wrong boasting is the twin brother of downright lying. The false teachers at Corinth boasted of gifts which they did not possess, and took to themselves the credit of other men's labours. It is astonishing what powers of appropriation the boastful spirit possesses. When a man once gets addicted to vain-glory it is useless to attempt to predict to what excesses he will be led. He clears the barriers of truth as though they were straws. What he is, is what he can persuade people to think him; what he has done is what he can by any means induce them to credit. The braggart knows no restraint. His parish is the world—the worlds of fact and fiction rolled into one, and he is as much at home in the one as in the other. His domain has only one boundary—the credulity of his listeners. 3. *That the praise of our good actions is to be ascribed to us.* This strikes at the root of wrong boasting. A boasting which robs God must be of the devil. The man who knows himself knows that there is no good thing in him. If he finds anything good he immediately concludes that it did not spring from himself, and he looks about for the originator and owner. It is only the very bad who think themselves very good. If we are disposed to take the praise of our good actions to ourselves it is strong evidence that these actions were not really *good.* "Good" actions cannot be done by those who are so utterly out of true relation to God.

II. RIGHT BOASTING. This is boasting or glorying in the Lord (ver. 17). We may boast of God, and the more boastful we are in this direction the better. There will be no danger of running to excess; after we have boasted to our utmost we shall have fallen far short of the truth. Alas! few things are more uncommon than this boasting in God. Fallen human nature finds it easier and more reasonable to boast of the mud-puddle than of the crystal ocean—of the dim rushlight than of the glorious sun. 1. *We may well boast of the Divine perfections.* Here we shall find an inexhaustible subject. The glories of our God will exhaust our powers of glorying. Whilst carnal men applaud their little gods, the saints may well extol Jehovah. "Who is a God like unto our God?" we may proudly cry. Pride becomes one of the chiefest virtues when it is centred in God. Christians are not half boastful enough in the right direction, and twice too boastful in the wrong. Shame upon us that we boast so little of our God! 2. *We may well boast of the great redemptive work of God.* So loud should be our boasting as to make all men hear it. Here the perfection of God finds highest and most beautiful expression. Here each Person in the adorable Trinity works a matchless work of grace and power. Upon us especially, since we are the subjects of redemption, rests the burden of boasting respecting it. This is our peculiar province of glorying. Of all creatures in the universe we are bound to this service. If *we* were silent, surely the stones would cry out. As God has wrought this great thing for us, we must never let men or God hear the last of it! What a subject for boast! Where is there aught that can for a moment compare with it? Boast, ye Christians, of redeeming love till all your powers of boasting fail. 3. *We may well boast of God's work in us and through us.* (1) In us. When we joyfully recognize that we are growing in grace we must exult in the God of all grace. This thing is not of us, but of him. To him must all the praise be accorded. The "old man" within us is the child of our fall and our folly; the "new man" is God's special creation. Clearly should we realize this, and concentrate all our boasting in him from whom this "unspeakable Gift" (which is "Christ in us") emanates. Humility and abasement in respect of ourselves; boastfulness in respect of him who has wrought the marvel in us. (2) Through us. To depreciate what is accomplished through us is but *lying humility.* Paul was not guilty of it. It is professedly abasing ourselves and really abasing God. When the work accomplished is undoubted, the only right course is to glory to our utmost in the God who has accomplished it. We must reserve no praise for ourselves, since we have deserved none; all the praise must be his. We need care, however, when glorying in God for what he has accomplished through us, lest, whilst ostensibly praising him, we should be covertly praising ourselves. There is a mouth of hell which lies near the gate of heaven. We must guard against feeding conceit by supposing that we are of ourselves instruments so fit that God could not have so well performed the work through others; or that through personal merit we are favourites of God, and that therefore he has specially wrought his will through us; or that, having been so honoured, we may now hold our heads high. Whilst extolling God we must abase ourselves; whilst boasting in him we must refuse to glory in the least in the unworthy instrument. That he has so greatly distinguished what was so greatly unworthy should but deepen and intensify our humility.—H.

Ver. 4.—*Holy weapons.* One style of weapon for one kind of conflict, another for another. For the common battle-field, cannon and rifle with their horrid din, the bayonet, and the sword. For contests of opinion, weapons of argument and intellectual precision—writings, lectures, and debates. For successes in the sphere of spiritual thought and life, spiritual weapons mighty through God. St. Paul was much addicted to the use of military metaphors. To him a zealous missionary was a good soldier of Christ; a well-equipped and disciplined Christian was a man armed in the panoply of God. His own course of service in combatting errors and publishing the truth of the gospel was as the march of a warrior, nay, of a victor, triumphing in every place. So he regarded both the ordering of things within the Church and the aggression of the Church on the world around as parts of his military duty, in which he was bound to war, but not according to the flesh. There is still need to make war. On every side are obstinate hindrances to the gospel of grace, and to the health and peace of the Church. The most formidable of these are in the region of thought and feeling; strongholds of prejudice and self-righteousness, and entrenchments of unbelief. And those who propagate the gospel, and guard the purity and peace of the Church, must surmount those obstacles, or pull down those strongholds, so as to lead away the convictions of the delivered ones as happy captives to the obedience of Christ.

I. NOT BY CARNAL WEAPONS OR ANY FORM OF PHYSICAL COACTION. Though St. Peter drew his sword to defend his heavenly Master, he was bidden at once restore it to its sheath. When Pontius Pilate interrogated our Lord about his being King of the Jews, he received for answer, "My kingdom is not of this world: if my kingdom were of this world, then would my servants fight." Extremists have inferred from this language that the followers of Christ may not, in any circumstances, wield a weapon of war; but this is mere folly. The subjects of the kingdom of Christ are also for the time subjects of an earthly kingdom also, or citizens in an earthly community, and have the same natural and civil rights as other men, and the same warrant and obligation to defend them. They may not delight in war; but even to that dire extremity they may proceed if there be no other way to keep order and secure justice and liberty. To do otherwise would be tamely to surrender the earth to the most unscrupulous and aggressive of its inhabitants. But weapons of worldly warfare do not advance that spiritual power which is the highest of all; nor is it permitted to use them for direct furtherance of Christ's kingdom of the truth. This, of course, condemns all forms of persecution; and when we say, "all forms," we mean, not merely imprisonment, pillage, and death, but the imposition of civil disabilities, or social and educational penalties, or any abridgment of political rights. On all such coercive measures the gospel frowns. Equally inadmissible is the use of misrepresentation. Those "pious frauds" which have been practised and propagated for the supposed glory of God have been very carnal weapons. So are all the misleading phrases and cajoleries by which it is still attempted to draw men into adherence to some form of religion without conviction of the understanding or real allegiance of the heart.

II. But by weapons that are after the mind of Christ. See the catalogue of such weapons as they had been used by St. Paul at Corinth: "In pureness, in knowledge," etc. (ch. vi. 6, 7). Come honour or dishonour in this world, good report or evil, with such weapons must all the soldiers of Christ be content in the warfare to which they are called. The strongholds they assail may make a formidable resistance, but nothing is gained by changing the spiritual weapons for the carnal. They are mighty in God's sight and in God's strength. Paul knew them to be so. With them, though he was but one man and a man reproached and afflicted, he had pulled down many strongholds and won many victories. It is not a simple question of conversion. The truth has many a struggle in the heart after conversion as well as before. When Jericho fell, the holy war of Israel was well begun; but there still remained many holds and fenced cities to be taken. So, when the first opposition is surmounted, and a sinner yields to the power of the saving truth as it is in Jesus, much is gained, but not everything. The work of grace has to be pressed further ere every thought is brought into captivity to the obedience of Christ. Little worldly stir or éclat attends the warfare of which we speak, but it awakens in heaven and through all the heavenly kingdom the liveliest interest and the noblest joy. There are shouts and Te Deums there, when evil is defeated and pulled down in the world, in the Church, in the breast of the individual man; when sinners repent; when rebels submit to God; when thoughts that were lifted up in scorn are cast down at the feet of Jesus, and affections that sin had beguiled and the pride of life enchanted, are fixed on truth, on duty, and on the things which are above.—F.

Ver. 1.—" *The meekness and gentleness of Christ.*" It is important to notice that this chapter begins a new section of the Epistle. St. Paul has hitherto been addressing the better, the more spiritual, portion of the Corinthian Church; but now he turns to the section that impugned his authority, misrepresented his conduct, and spoke evil things of himself. Olshausen says, "Until now Paul has addressed himself preeminently to the better-intentioned in the Christian Church; but henceforth he addresses himself to those who had sought to lower his dignity and weaken his authority by representing him as weak in personal influence," as well as in bodily strength and consistency of purpose, "although courageous and full of self-commendation in his letters." Dean Plumptre says, "The stinging words which Titus has reported to him vex his soul. He speaks in the tone of the suppressed indignation which shows itself in a keen incisive irony. The opening formula is one which he reserves as emphasizing an exceptionally strong emotion (see Gal. v. 2; Eph. iii. 1; Philem. 19)." Conybeare indicates that the party with which St. Paul now deals was the Christian section of the Judaizing party—a section which, throwing off all authority, even though it was apostolic, declared that they received Christ alone as their Head, and that he alone should communicate truth directly to them. There is some ground for the supposition that "they were headed by an emissary from Palestine, who had brought letters of commendation from some members of the Church at Jerusalem, and who boasted of his pure Hebrew descent, and his especial connection with Christ himself. St. Paul calls him a false apostle, a minister of Satan disguised as a minister of righteousness, and hints that he was actuated by corrupt motives. He seems to have behaved at Corinth with extreme arrogance, and to have succeeded, by his overbearing conduct, in impressing his partisans with a conviction of his importance and of the truth of his pretensions. They contrasted his confident bearing with the timidity and self-distrust which had been shown by St. Paul. And they even extolled his personal advantages over those of their first teacher; comparing his rhetoric with Paul's inartificial speech, his commanding appearance with the insignificance of Paul's 'bodily presence.'" Conybeare gives a translation of vers. 1 and 2, which effectively expresses the spirit in which the apostle began his pleading with this malicious party. "Now I, Paul, myself exhort you by the meekness and gentleness of Christ—(I, who am mean, forsooth, and lowly in outward presence, while I am among you, yet treat you boldly when I am absent)—I beseech you (I say), that you will not force me to show, when I am present, the bold confidence in my power, wherewith I reckon to deal with some who reckon me by the standard of the flesh." Archdeacon Farrar says, "There is (in these closing chapters) none of the tender effusiveness and earnest praise which we have been hearing, but a tone of suppressed indignation, in which tenderness, struggling with bitter irony, in some places renders the language laboured and obscure, like the words of one who with difficulty restrains himself from saying all that his emotion might suggest. Yet it is deeply interesting to observe that the 'meekness and gentleness of Christ' reigns throughout all this irony, and he utters no word of malediction like those of the psalmists." By the term "meekness" we are to understand the habit of putting self aside, which was so characteristic of Moses, and the supreme grace of the Lord Jesus. By the term "gentleness" is not meant "softness of manner," but "fairness," "considerateness of the feelings of others." It indicates the habit of mind that is engendered by the practice of regarding the rights of others as well as our own. Meekness and gentleness belong to those *passive graces* which it was a great part of our Lord's mission to exemplify, to set in prominent place, and to commend. Bushnell speaks of the sublime efficacy of those virtues which belong to the receiving, suffering, patient side of character. They are such as meekness, gentleness, forbearance, forgiveness, the endurance of wrong without anger and resentment, contentment, quietness, peace, and unambitious love. These all belong to the more passive side of character, and are included, or may be, in the general and comprehensive term, "patience." "These are never barren virtues, as some are apt to imagine, but are often the most efficient and most operative powers that a true Christian wields; inasmuch as they carry just that kind of influence which other men are least apt and least able to resist." Considering St. Paul's naturally sensitive and impulsive temperament, it must have cost him much effort and prayer so to restrain himself that he could speak, even to such active enemies, with the "meekness and gentleness of Christ."

I. THE MEEKNESS OF CHRIST IN ST. PAUL. The word seems unsuitable for him unless we give it the proper meaning, which is—not self-assertive, willing to bear quietly, more anxious for others than for self. St. Paul was not even anxious, first of all, for his own imperilled reputation. The honour of Christ was involved in his self-vindication, and for Christ's sake he undertook it.

II. THE GENTLENESS OF CHRIST IN ST. PAUL. Save to hardened scribes and Pharisees, our Lord ever spoke softly and persuasively, or, at most, reproachfully. He, in his considerateness for others, would not break the bruised reed, or quench the smoking flax. And nothing is more striking in the Apostle Paul than the gentlemanly delicacy with which he considers the feelings of others. His hand trembles when it holds the rod. And the words of reproof and reproach break forth from a grieved and troubled heart. F. W. Robertson says, "He vindicated his authority because he had been meek, as Christ was meek; for not by menace, nor by force, did he conquer, but by the might of gentleness and the power of love. On that foundation St. Paul built; it was the example of Christ which he imitated in his moments of trial, when he was reproved and censured. Thus it happened that one of the apostle's 'mightiest weapons' was the meekness and lowliness of heart which he drew from the life of Christ. So it ever is; humility, after all, is the best defence. It disarms and conquers by the majesty of submission. To be humble and loving—that is true life."—R. T.

Ver. 3.—*In the flesh, but not of it.* "For though we walk in the flesh, we do not war after the flesh." This expression recalls the corresponding words of our Lord, with which we may assume that St. Paul was familiar. Addressing his disciples during those closing hours of communion with them in the "upper room," Jesus had said, "If ye were of the world, the world would love his own: but because ye are not of the world, but I have chosen you out of the world, therefore the world hateth you." And, in his sublime high-priestly prayer, Jesus spoke thus: "They are not of the world, even as I am not of the world. I pray not that thou shouldest take them out of the world, but that thou shouldest keep them from the evil." The thought expressed in the passage now before us seems to have been a cherished one with the apostle. He enlarges upon it in writing to the Romans (viii. 4—9). He speaks of "us, who walk not after the flesh, but after the Spirit." He explains that "to be carnally minded is death; but to be spiritually minded is life and peace." And he firmly declares, "So then they that are in the flesh cannot please God. But ye are not in the flesh, but in the Spirit, if so be that the Spirit of God dwell in you." By "living *in* the flesh" we are to understand simply our possessing this fleshly, bodily nature, with its frailties, limitations, and infirmities. By "living, or warring, *after* the flesh," we are to understand neglecting the higher dictates of the higher spiritual nature, and living as though the desires of the body were the only ones that needed satisfying. But the precise thought of the apostle here may be that he will not be moved against the evil party at Corinth by those natural feelings of indignation which their conduct towards him had aroused, but will reprove and exhort only upon the great Christian principles, and only in the Christly spirit. Self shall not rule even his warfare with such unreasonable foes. Christ shall rule.

I. THE CHRISTIAN POSSIBILITIES OF OUR FLESHLY CONDITION. "We walk in the flesh." God is pleased to set us in this human body, to give us this vehicle of communication with other men and with the surrounding world; and it is possible for us to win this body for Christ, to possess and rule it so that all its powers shall be used, and all its relations sustained, only in Christly service. In fact, the work of human life may be spoken of as this—winning our bodies and our life-spheres for Christ. Our bodies, our fleshly natures, include (1) natural faculties, such as eating and drinking; (2) passions, affecting the relationship of the sexes; (3) mental emotions; and (4) powers of acquiring knowledge. It is possible to dominate the whole machinery of the body with the sanctified and Christly will.

II. THE LIMITATIONS OF OUR FLESHLY CONDITION. It is not a merely dead machine that we have to move by the force of the regenerate life. Nor is it a machine in full efficiency and repair. If the figure may be used, the body is a machine of too limited capacity for the work which the renewed soul wants done; and even taking it for what it is, it is sadly out of repair, rusted and worn, so that we have continually to complain that "we cannot do the things that we would." Illustrate in St. Paul's case. The body would have so affected him, if he had yielded to it, that he could not have been noble towards his traducers at Corinth. The body would have urged a passionate reply. So we find the body such a drag upon the high and holy aims, purposes, and endeavours of the soul, that we are often saying, "O wretched man that I am! who shall deliver me from the body of this death?"

III. THE CHRISTIAN MASTERY OF FLESHLY CONDITIONS. This is precisely the discipline of life. Christ wins our soul. Christ regenerates our will. Christ assures us of his own spiritual presence as our inspiration and strength; and then seems to say, "Go forth, win your flesh, your mind, your body, your associations, for me, so that henceforth no fleshly ends are sought, and no carnal, self-seeking tone rests on any of your doings and relations." It is inspiring to find how fully St. Paul could enter into Christ's thought for him, but it is comforting to observe how very near he was to failure in his endeavour to gain the mastery over self, again and again. Through much tribulation and conflict only can any one of us gain the mastery of the spirit over the flesh.—R. T.

Ver. 5.—*Captivity of thoughts for Christ.* Probably the apostle makes special reference to the confidence of Christians at Corinth in their learning and philosophizing; "to the efforts of human reason to deal with things beyond it, the best corrective of which is, and always will be, the simple proclamation of God's message to men." But our thoughts are the springs of action, as well as the means of acquiring knowledge; so they may be treated in a comprehensive way.

I. THE IMPORTANCE OF OUR THOUGHTS. "As a man thinketh in his heart, so is he." Note: 1. The defiling power of cherished evil thought. 2. The inspiring and ennobling power of cherished good thought. 3. The relation of thought to (1) conduct, (2) culture,

(3) associations. Right thoughts make openness to God, give graciousness to our conversation, enable us to be considerate of and helpful to others. As we must keep the fountain pure, if the stream is to run sweet and clear, we must recognize the supreme importance of taking heed to our thoughts.

II. OUR RESPONSIBILITY FOR OUR THOUGHTS. On this point a sentiment prevails which greatly needs correction. It is assumed that we cannot help thoughts coming up before us, and that they may be the suggestions of our soul's spiritual enemy, and so we cannot be held responsible for them. This is one of those half-truths that are oftentimes more mischievous than downright error. We are not responsible for the mere passing of thoughts, as in a panorama, before our mental vision; but we are responsible for what we select of them for consideration; we are responsible for what we cherish. We are further responsible for the *materials* of our thought, and for the circumstances in which we place ourselves, so far as they may suggest thought. Therefore we have the counsel so earnestly given us, "Keep thy heart with all diligence, for out of it are the issues of life."

III. THE SECRET OF CONTROLLING OUR THOUGHTS. That secret is made up of parts. It includes: 1. The full surrender of our will to Christ, so that he may rule all our choices and preferences, even the very choices of our thoughts. 2. The cherished consciousness of Christ's living presence with us gives tone and harmony with him, to all our preferences. 3. The culture of mind, disposition, and habits, which involves the resolute putting away from us of all associations and suggestions of evil. 4. The freeness of access to God in prayer for strength whenever temptation seems to have an overcoming power. 5. The occupying of heart, thought, and life so fully with the things of Christ that there can be no room for evil. There is no more practical way of mastering doubting, sensual, corrupt thought than by turning at once to good reading or engaging at once in works of charity. While we pray to God to "cleanse the thoughts of our hearts by the inspiration of his Holy Spirit," we must also remember that the apostle teaches us to make personal efforts of watchfulness and good endeavour, and so "bring into captivity every thought to the obedience of Christ." In every age sincere hearts have prayed the psalmist's prayer: "Search me, O God, and know my heart: try me, and know my thoughts: and see if there be any wicked way in me, and lead me in the way everlasting."—R. T.

Ver. 7.—*Mistaken judgment by appearances.* "Do ye look on things after the outward appearance?" In the mind of the apostle was, no doubt, the evident disposition of the community at Corinth to "attach undue weight to the outward accidents of those who claimed their allegiance rather than to that which was of the essence of all true apostolic ministry." Bold and forward men, who make great boasting and pretension, whose appearance and manners are taking, often do incomparable mischief in Christian Churches. So easily are people carried away with the "outward appearance." The Divine teaching on this subject is given in connection with Samuel's visit to the house of Jesse, for the selection and anointing of Jehovah's new king. Samuel looked on the stately figure of Eliab, Jesse's firstborn, and said to himself, "Surely the Lord's anointed is before him. But the Lord said unto Samuel, Look not on his countenance, or on the height of his stature; because I have refused him: for the Lord seeth not as man seeth; for man looketh on the outward appearance, but the Lord looketh on the heart." Plutarch says, "We ought to be candid enough to extol the merits of him who speaks, but not suffer his address to lead into incaution; to regard his talents with pleasure, but investigate strictly the justness of his reasonings; not to be influenced by the authority of the speaker, but to scrutinize accurately the grounds of his argument; the orator's subject should be considered rather than his eloquence admired."

I. THE OUTWARD APPEARANCE OUGHT TO EXPRESS THE INWARD FACT. Outward and inward should be in perfect harmony. They should be related as are *thought* and *word*. A man's words should clearly, precisely, worthily, express to men his thought. And so his outward appearance should exactly correspond with his inward condition. Only then can a man be "sincere." We speak of a man as being "always the same." He can only be so if he will let what he really is find due expression in his life. The consciously sincere man makes no show. Without restraint he lets the life speak freely what message it pleases. The life of the Lord Jesus Christ is so sublimely attractive, because we feel that it was through and through true ; and whatever were its appearances they were but manifestations of his life.

II. THE OUTWARD APPEARANCE IS OFTEN UNTRUE TO THE INWARD FACT. Of this the familiar illustration is taken from the usual description of the fruit grown near the Dead Sea, and called "apples of Sodom." Beautiful to all appearance, but dry and unpleasant to the taste. Hypocrisy is real " part-acting," representing ourselves to be other than we are. It is a very subtle form of sin, especially in what are called " civilized times," when so much depends on " keeping up appearances." Illustrate in relation to house, dress, society ; and show that it may even concern personal religion. The assumption and the show of piety are not always faithful transcripts of the heart's love and devotion. But sometimes the outward appearance is untrue by being *below* the reality. This seems to have been the case with St. Paul. His insignificant appearance, and his modesty and considerateness of manner, gave little indication of the force that was in him, or the bold and valiant defence of the truth which he could give upon occasion. So the outward appearance may be unworthy of the inward, without being wrongfully so ; unworthy by reason of infirmity, and not of hypocrisy.

III. THEREFORE WE ARE ALWAYS BOUND TO TEST THE IMPRESSIONS MADE BY OUTWARD APPEARANCES. " Prove all things ; hold fast that which is good." The testings can often be done (1) by patient waiting; (2) by observing the *whole* of a man's conduct ; (3) by comparing our impressions with those made on others' minds ; (4) by the standards given us in Holy Scripture ; (5) by cultivating our own sensitiveness to that which is truly Christ-like. In order to find unworthy men out, and in order to esteem aright good men, we must go beyond their form, feature, and outward show, and we must know *them.* St. Paul will bear thoroughly knowing.—R. T.

Ver. 16.—*The gospel for the regions beyond.* "To preach the gospel in the regions beyond you" (comp. Rom. xv. 19—24). The apostle, filled with the true missionary spirit, was longing to be free from the care of Churches already founded, so that he might be free to go again upon his journeyings, and preach the gospel in Western Greece, in Rome, and even away in distant Spain. St. Paul was first and chiefly a missionary. The genius of the missionary is a Divine restlessness, a constant impulse forward into new spheres, a passion for finding some one else to whom the gospel message might be told. The men who settle down in Churches situated in heathen districts are ministers and pastors and clergymen ; they cannot properly be called missionaries, since these are men who are always hearing a call from " regions beyond," saying, " Come over and help us."

I. MISSIONARY WORK AS HERALDING A MESSAGE. The word for " preaching " properly means " heralding "—going forth to make a royal proclamation. Explain the work of the Eastern herald. He would go through the land, and, wherever he could find people, deliver the king's message. We need a fuller and worthier impression of the gospel, as the royal proclamation of the King of kings, entrusted to us for delivery to " all the world," to " every creature."

II. HERALDING WORK AS TEMPORARY. It is done when the message is declared and delivered. The herald—as a herald—has no more to do there; he must pass on his way. There is abundant work left behind for others to do ; but his is over. And we are told that the gospel heralds will not have gone all over the world when the kingdom shall come. So we need fear no lack of work for missionaries and heralds.

III. HERALD'S DUTY TO FIND REGIONS BEYOND. A glance at the map of our world will show what vast masses of mankind have never heard of the true God, the redeeming Son, and the eternal life. We rejoice that, especially in Africa and China, the Christian Church is showing that it keeps the true missionary idea, and is ever reaching out to " regions beyond."—R. T.

Ver. 17.—*Man's only true glorying.* " But he that glorieth, let him glory in the Lord." The apostle used the simpler and stronger word, " boasteth." Dean Plumptre complains of the besetting weakness for variation which characterized our English translators. And oftentimes force of utterance is gained by dwelling on a word, even at the peril of tautology. Reference is made, no doubt, to the boastings of this leader of the party at Corinth that was antagonistic to St. Paul, and also to the accusation which this man made against the apostle, that he was always boasting of his authority, his superior knowledge, and the great things he had done. St. Paul firmly urged the distinction between glorying in what a man is or in what a man has done, and glorying in what God has made a man to be and in what God has done by him. The first kind of boasting is wrong and dangerous. "Let him that thinketh he standeth take heed lest he fall." The other kind is right, is honouring to God, and may be our proper form of testifying for him. There is then a *sin* of boasting, against which we require to be duly warned. And there is a *service* of boasting which may, under certain circumstances, be our most effective mode of resisting evil and witnessing for God. On the whole, however, it may be fully urged that a man's *life*, rather than his *lips*, should do all his boastings for him. These distinctions may be further elaborated and illustrated.

I. Glorying in what we are is always a sign of Christian weakness. A man had better not even think about himself, but put all his effort into higher attainments in the Divine life. There is danger for us when we find that we have anything in ourselves to talk about or to glory in. All the finest and most delicate Christian graces are so fragile that they break with a touch, so sensitive that they fade if we only look on them. Do not even think about what you *are;* fill your thoughts with what you *may be,* what you *may become,* in the grace and strength of Christ. Christian progress stops as soon as we begin to boast. He that is satisfied with his attainments falls from the Christian ideal, which is this, "Not that I have already obtained, or am already made perfect; but I press on, if so be that I may apprehend that for which also I was apprehended by Christ Jesus" (Phil. iii. 12, Revised Version). Show the peril that lies in habits of introspection and self-examination with a view to finding subjects of self-satisfaction. And also of meetings in which Christians are encouraged to boast of religious feelings and experiences. The text suggests an altogether "more excellent way." "Let him that glorieth glory in the Lord."

II. Glorying in what we have done puts Christian humility in peril. Because it directs men's thoughts to *us,* sets them upon praising *us,* and so lifts up our minds, gives us undue notions of our own superiority and excellence. When he gains the applause of an unthinking multitude, Nebuchadnezzar can forget himself, and, in uttermost pride, cast God wholly away, and say, "Is not this great Babylon, which *I* have builded?" Boastfulness of our doings is always perilous. God does not need it, since he knows all about it. And man does not need it, for he can see the doings well enough without our telling. "Let thine own works praise thee." Let thine enemies praise thee. Let thy friends praise thee. But if you would keep fresh the great grace of humility, never *praise yourself.*

III. Glorying in what God has done for us and by us is always inspiring and healthy. Such was the glorying of the apostle, and such are the narratives of labour given us by great missionaries. All true records of our life-work should lead men to say, "What hath *God* wrought?"—R. T.

EXPOSITION.

CHAPTER XI.

An Apostle driven against his Will into a Semblance of Boasting.

An apology for the "foolishness" of boasting (vers. 1—4). He is not afraid of comparisons (vers. 5, 6). He will not recede from his despised practice of teaching gratuitously (vers. 7—15). A second apology, drawn from the outrageous conduct of his opponents (vers. 16—20). His privileges, life, and labours (vers. 21—33).

Ver. 1.—**Would to God**; rather, *would that I* (comp. 1 Cor. iv. 8). **You could bear;** rather, *ye would bear.* **In my folly**; rather, *in a little foolishness.* Namely, in this foolishness of boasting. "Fool" and "folly" are here haunting words (ch. i. 16, 17, 19, 21; xii. 6, 11). The article (*the* i.e. *my* folly) is omitted in א, B, D, E. **Bear with me.** It is better to take this as an indicative. It would be meaningless to pass from an entreaty to a command. On the other hand, "Nay, ye do really bear with me" was a loving and delicate admission of such kindness as he had received from them.

Ver. 2.—**For.** This gives the reason why they bore with him. It was due to a reciprocity of affection. **I am jealous over you.** The word implies both jealousy and zeal (ch. vii. 7; ix. 2). **With a godly jealousy**; literally, *with a jealousy of God.* My jealousy is not the poor earthly vice (Numb. v. 14; Ecclus. ix. 1), but a heavenly zeal of love. **For I have espoused you**; rather, *for I betrothed you;* at your conversion. I acted as the paranymph, or "bridegroom's friend" (John iii. 29), in bringing you to Christ, the Bridegroom. The metaphor is found alike in the Old and New Testaments (Isa. liv. 5; Ezek. xxiii.; Hos. ii. 19; Eph. v. 25—27). **To one husband** (Jer. iii. 1; Ezek. xvi. 15). Our Lord used an analogous metaphor in the parable of the king's wedding feast, the virgins, etc. **That I may present** you. The same word as in ch. iv. 14. The conversion of the Church was its betrothal to Christ, brought about by St. Paul as the paranymph; and, in the same capacity, at the final marriage feast, he would present their Church as a pure bride to Christ at his coming (Rev. xix. 7—9).

Ver. 3.—**I fear.** Even now he would only contemplate their defection as a future dread, not as a present catastrophe. **Lest by any means**; *lest haply* (ch. ii. 7; ix. 4). **As the serpent beguiled Eve.** St. Paul merely touches on the central moral fact of the temptation and the Fall (Gen. iii. 1—6). He enters into no speculation about the symbols, though, doubtless, like St. John (Rev. xii. 9; xx. 2), he would have identified the serpent with Satan (comp. ch. ii. 11 and Wisd. ii. 23). **Through his subtlety.** The word means "crafty wickedness." It is used in ch. xii. 16, and is found in ch. iv. 2; Luke xx. 23. **Your minds**; literally, *your thoughts* (ch. ii. 11). **Should be corrupted** (comp. Col. ii. 4—8; 1 Tim. iv. 1). **The simplicity.** The apostles always insisted on this virtue, but especially St. Paul, in whose Epistles the word (ἁπλότης) occurs seven times. **That is in Christ**; rather, *that is towards* (literally, *into*) *Christ;* as Cranmer rendered it, "The perfect fidelity which looks to him above."

Ver. 4.—**He that cometh.** Apparently an allusion to some recent and rival teacher. **Another Jesus.** The intruder preaches, not a *different* Jesus (ἕτερον) or a different gospel (comp. Gal. i. 6—8), but ostensibly the same Jesus whom St. Paul had preached. **Another spirit . . . another gospel**; rather, *a different spirit* (ἕτερον) *. . . a different gospel.* The Jesus preached was the same; the gospel accepted, the Spirit received, were supposed to remain unaltered. **Ye might well bear with** him. This is not without a touch of irony. You are all set against me; and yet the new-comer does not profess to preach to you another Jesus, or impart a different Spirit! Had he done so, you might have had some excuse (καλῶς) for

listening to him. Now there is none; for it was I who first preached Jesus to you, and from me you first received the Spirit.

Ver. 5.—**For.** It cannot be that you received this rival teacher as being so much superior to me; *for*, etc. **I suppose.** Again, like the Latin *censeo* or *opinor*, with a touch of irony. **I was not a whit behind**; *in no respect have I come short of.* **The very chiefest apostles.** The word used by St. Paul for "very chiefest" is one which, in its strangeness, marks the vehemence of his emotion. It involves an indignant sense that he had been most disparagingly compared with other apostles, as though he were hardly a genuine apostle at all. Yet he reckons himself to have done as much as the "above-exceedingly"—or, as it might be expressed, the "out-and-out," "extra-super," or "super-apostolic," apostles. There is here no reflection whatever on the twelve; he merely means that, even if any with whom he was unfavourably contrasted were "apostles ten times over," he can claim to be in the front rank with them. This is no more than he has said with the utmost earnestness in 1 Cor. xv. 10; Gal. ii. 6. There is no self-assertion here; but, in consequence of the evil done by his detractors, St. Paul, with an utter sense of distaste, is forced to say the simple truth.

Ver. 6.—**Rude in speech**; literally, *a laic in discourse;* see ch. x. 10 and 1 Cor. ii. 13; and, for the word *idiotes*, a private person, and so "one who is untrained," as contrasted with a professor, see the only other places where it occurs in the New Testament (Acts iv. 13; 1 Cor. xiv. 16, 23, 24). St. Paul did not profess to have the trained oratorical skill of Apollos. His eloquence, dependent on conviction and emotion, followed none of the rules of art. **Yet not in knowledge.** Spiritual knowledge was a primary requisite of an apostle, and St. Paul *did* claim to possess this (Eph. iii. 3, 4). **We have been thoroughly made manifest among you in all things.** This would be an appeal to the transparent openness and sincerity of all his dealings, as in ch. iv. 20 and xii. 12; but the best reading seems to be the active participle, *phanerösantes* (א, B, F, G), not the passive, *phanerothentes.* The rendering will then be, *In everything making it* (my knowledge) *manifest among all men towards you.*

Ver. 7.—**Have I?** literally, *or have I?* An ironical exception to his manifestation of knowledge; "unless you think that I committed a sin in refusing to accept maintenance at your hands." It is clear that even this noble generosity had been made the ground for a charge against the apostle. "If he had not been conscious," they said, "that he has no real claims, he would not have preached for nothing, when he had a perfect right to be supported by his converts" (1 Cor. ix. 1—15). **Abasing myself.** The trade of tentmaker was despised, tedious, and mechanical, and it did not suffice to provide even for Paul's small needs (Acts xviii. 3; xx. 34). **That ye might be exalted;** namely, by spiritual gifts (Eph. ii. 4—6). **The gospel .., freely.** Some of them would feel the vast contrast between the words. The gospel was the most precious gift of God, and they had got it for nothing. Compare the fine lines of Lowell—

"For a cap and bells our lives we pay,
    Bubbles we earn with our whole soul's
    tasking;
'Tis only God who is given away,
'Tis only heaven may be had for the
    asking."

To be a free and unpaid missionary was St. Paul's pride (ch. xii. 14; 1 Thess. ii. 9; 2 Thess. iii. 8, 9; Acts xx. 33).

Ver. 8.—**I robbed;** literally, *I ravaged*, or *plundered.* The intensity of St. Paul's feelings, smarting under base calumny and ingratitude, reveals itself by the passionate expression which he here uses. **Other Churches.** The only Church of which we know as contributing to St. Paul's needs is that at Philippi (Phil. iv. 15, 16). **Taking wages.** The expression is again impassioned. It is meant rather ironically than literally. Literally it means *rations* (1 Cor. ix. 7).

Ver. 9.—**And wanted.** The aorist shows that this sad condition of extreme poverty was a crisis rather than chronic. Yet even at that supreme moment of trial, when from illness or accident the scanty income of his trade failed him, he would not tell *them* that he was starving, but rather accepted help from the Philippians, who, as he knew, felt for him an unfeigned affection. It is needless to point out once more how strong is the argument in favour of the genuineness of the Acts and the Epistles from the numberless undesigned coincidences between them in such passages as those to which I have referred in the foregoing notes. **I was chargeable to no man;** literally, *I did not benumb you.* The word *katenarkēsa,* which occurs only here and in ch. xii. 13, 14, is ranked by St. Jerome among St. Paul's *cilicisms,* i.e. the provincial expressions which he picked up during his long residence at Tarsus. *Narkē* (whence our *narcissus* and *narcotic*) means "paralysis," and is also the name given to the *gymnotus,* or electric eel — in Latin, *torpedo,* the cramp-fish—which benumbs with the shock of its touch. "I did not," he indignantly says, "cramp you with my torpedo-touch." Perhaps in a less vehement

mood he would have chosen a less picturesque or technical and medical term. **That which was lacking to me the brethren which came from Macedonia supplied;** rather, *for the brethren, on their arrival from Macedonia, filled up my deficiency.* This must have been the *third* present which St. Paul received from Philippi (Phil. iv. 15, 16). These brethren from Macedonia accompanied Silas and Timotheus (Acts xviii. 5). **And so will I keep myself** (ch. xii. 14).

Ver. 10.—**As the truth of Christ is in me.** The strength of St. Paul's feelings on the subject has already been expressed in 1 Cor. ix. 15. We have a similar appeal in Rom. ix. 1. The "as" is not in the original, but evidently the words are meant for a solemn asseveration—"The truth of Christ is in me, that," etc. **No man shall stop me of this boasting;** literally, *this shall not be stopped as concerns me.* The verb means literally, "shall be fenced," and with that tendency to over-elaboration which is frequent in commentators, some suppose that St. Paul referred to the projected wall across the isthmus of Corinth, etc. But the same word is used for simply stopping the mouth in Rom. iii. 19; Heb. xi. 33. **In the regions of Achaia.** He would not apply the rule to Corinth only, but seems to have felt the need for the utmost circumspection, and for cutting off every handle for suspicion or slander among these subtle, loquacious, intellectual Greeks. He could act more freely among the more frank and generous Macedonians.

Ver. 11.—**Wherefore?** He cannot tell them the real *ultimate* reason, which is their whole character and nature. **Because I love you not?** He has already assured them of his deep affection (ch. vii. 2; comp. xii. 15).

Ver. 12.—**Occasion;** rather, *the occasion.* **Wherein they glory, they may be found even as we.** "These new teachers boast to you how disinterested they are. Well, then, I have proved myself to be equally disinterested." But the words apparently involve a most stinging sarcasm. For these teachers were *not* in reality disinterested, though they boasted of being so; on the contrary, they were exacting, insolent, and tyrannical (ver. 20), and did *not* preach gratuitously (1 Cor. ix. 12), though they sneered at the apostle for doing so. Being radically false (vers. 12, 13), "while they were," as Theodoret says, "openly boasting, they were secretly taking money," and therefore were *not* "even as we."

Ver. 13.—**For such are false apostles.** This, with 1 Thess. ii. 14—16 and Phil. iii. 2, is one of St. Paul's most passionate outbursts of plain speaking. "Now at length," says Bengel, "he calls a spade a spade."

They were "false apostles" (Rev. ii. 2), because a true apostle delivers the message of another, while these cared only for self (Rom. xvi. 18). **Deceitful workers.** Workmen who cheat their employers (ch. ii. 17; iv. 2). **Transforming themselves.** The verb is the same as in 1 Cor. iv. 6 and Phil. iii. 21, and does not occur elsewhere in the New Testament.

Ver. 14.—**Even Satan . . . angel of light.** This is one of Satan's devices (ch. ii. 11). The allusion may be to the temptation (Matt. iv. 8, 9); or to the appearances of Satan with the angels before God in the Book of Job (ii. 1); or perhaps to the Jewish *hagadah*, that the "angel" who wrestled with Jacob was in reality Satan.

Ver. 15.—**Whose end shall be according to their works.** Whatever their fashion (*schēma*), they shall be judged, not by what they *seem*, but by what they *are*, as shown by their *works*.

Vers. 16—33.—*Apology by contrast.*

Ver. 16.—**I say again.** St. Paul evidently feels an almost invincible repugnance to begin to speak of his own works. He has twice swerved away from the task (ch. x. 8; xi. 1, 6) to speak of collateral topics. Now at last he begins, but only (to our grievous loss) to break off abruptly in ver. 33, before the story of his past sufferings has been much more than begun. **A fool . . . boast.** Here, again, we have the two haunting words of this section (see note on ver. 1; 1 Cor. xv. 36; xiii. 3). "Boast" occurs sixteen times in these three chapters alone. **That I**; rather, *that I also.*

Ver. 17.—**Not after the Lord.** "Boasting," or what might be stigmatized as such, may become a sort of painful necessity, necessitated by human baseness; but in itself it cannot be "after the Lord." There is nothing Christ-like in it. It is human, not Divine; an earthly necessity, not a heavenly example; a sword of the giant Philistine, which yet David may be forced to use. **Confidence;** *hypostasis*, as in ch. ix. 4, where exactly the same phrase occurs.

Ver. 18.—**After the flesh** (see note ch. x. 3; comp. Phil. iii. 4). **I will glory also.** But, as Robertson admirably observes, he "does not glory in what he has *done*, but in what he has *borne*."

Ver. 19.—**Seeing you yourselves are wise;** *ye gladly tolerate the senseless, being intellectual* (comp. 1 Cor. iv. 10). The irony would be very scathing to those whose minds and consciences were sufficiently humble and delicate to feel it.

Ver. 20.—**For ye suffer, if a man bring you into bondage.** The verse gives us an unexpected and painful glimpse of the enslaving (Gal. ii. 4), greed-loving (Matt. xxiii. 14; Rom. xvi. 18), gain-hunting

(1 Pet. v. 2, 3), domineering (3 John 9), and even personally violent and insulting character of these teachers; whom yet, strange to say, the Corinthians seem to take at their own estimate, and to tolerate any extreme of insolence from them, while they were jealously suspicious of the disinterested, gentle, and humble apostle. **If a man devour you.** As the Pharisees "devoured" widows' houses (Matt. xxiii. 14). **Take of you;** rather, *seize you;* makes you his captives. The verb is the same as "caught you," in ch. xii. 16. **Smite you on the face.** They must have brought their insolence with them from Jerusalem, where, as we see, not only from the details of our Lord's various mockeries, but from the accounts of the priests in Josephus and the Talmud, the priests made free use of their fists and staves! The fact that so many of the converts were downtrodden slaves and artisans would make them less likely to resent conduct to which they were daily accustomed among the heathen. Neither Greeks nor Orientals felt to anything like the same extent as ourselves the disgrace of a blow. That sense of disgrace rises from the freedom which Christianity has gradually wrought for us, and the deep sense of the dignity of human nature, which it has inspired. Christ had been so smitten, and so was Paul himself long afterwards (Acts xxiii. 2), and he had to teach even Christian bishops that they must be "no strikers" (1 Tim. iii. 3; Titus i. 7). The "syllogism of violence" has, alas! been in familiar use among religious teachers in all ages (1 Kings xxii. 24; Neh. xiii. 25; Isa. lviii. 4; Matt. v. 39; Luke xxii. 64; 1 Cor. iv. 11).

Ver. 21.—**I speak as concerning reproach, as though we had been weak.** The sense is uncertain, but if with the Revised Version we render it, "I speak by way of disparagement," the verse may be understood as an ironical admission that, if absence from these violent and self-assertive proceedings be a sign of weakness, he has been weak. He proceeds to correct the ironical admission in the next clause. The meaning can hardly be, "I admit the disgraces I have suffered" (comp. ch. vi. 8), because he is speaking of the Corinthians, not of himself. **I am bold also.** If they derive their right to this audacious and overweening line of conduct from any privileges of theirs, there is not one of these privileges which I too may not claim.

Ver. 22.—**Hebrews.** In the strictest sense those who still understood and spoke Aramaic, not Hellenists of the dispersion, who no longer knew the sacred language. (For the use of the word, see Acts vi. 1; Phil. iii. 4.) **Israelites.** Jews, not only by nation, but in heart and feeling (see John i. 48; Acts ii.

22, etc.; Rom. ix. 4; xi. 1). **The seed of Abraham.** Alike literally and spiritually (see John viii. 33—53; Rom. ix. 7; xi. 1). It may seem strange that St. Paul should have found it necessary to make this statement; but his Tarsian birth and Roman franchise may have led to whispered innuendoes which took form long afterwards in the wild calumny that he was a Gentile who had only got himself circumcised in order that he might marry the high priest's daughter (Epiphan., 'Hær.,' xxx. 16).

Ver. 23.—**I speak as a fool.** Not merely as before *aphrōn*, but *paraphronōn*, "I speak as a madman." It is downright insanity on my part to enter into this contest of rival egotism. The verb does not occur elsewhere in the New Testament; the substantive is used of "downright infatuation" in 2 Pet. ii. 16. **I am more.** I may claim to be something beyond an ordinary servant of Christ (comp. ch. xi. 5). This is the "frantic" boast which he proceeds to justify in a fragment of biography which must ever be accounted as the most remarkable and unique in the world's history. And when St. Paul lived the life was, as Dean Stanley says, "hitherto without precedent in the history of the world." No *subsequent* life of saint or martyr has ever surpassed St. Paul's, as here sketched, in self-devotion; and no previous life even remotely resembled it. The figure of the Christian missionary was, until then, unknown. **In labours more abundant**; literally, *more abundantly*. The best comment is 1 Cor. xv. 10. **In stripes above measure.** The expression is partly explained in the next verse. **In prisons.** St. Clement of Rome says that St. Paul was imprisoned seven times. The only imprisonment *up to this date* recorded in the Acts is that at Philippi (Acts xvi. 23). The imprisonments in Jerusalem, Cæsarea, and Rome all took place later. He says later, "The Holy Ghost witnesseth in every city that bonds and imprisonment await me" (Acts xx. 23). **In deaths oft.** He alludes to the incessant opposition, peril, and anguish which make him say in 1 Cor. xv. 31, "I die daily" (comp. ch. iv. 11; Rom. viii. 36). With the whole passage we may compare ch. vi. 4, 5.

Ver. 24.—**Five times.** Not one of these Jewish scourgings—which yet were so severe that the sufferer often died under them—is mentioned in the Acts. This paragraph is the most striking proof of the complete fragmentariness of that narrative, marvellous as it is. On the circumstances which probably led to these Jewish scourgings, see 'Life of St. Paul,' exc. xi.; and comp. Acts xxii. 19; xxvi. 11; Matt. xxiii. 34. The question arises—Was St. Luke entirely unaware of all these scenes of anguish and daily martyrdom? Had St. Paul, in his humble reticence, never cared to speak of them? or were the Acts only intended for a sketch which made no pretension to completeness, and only related certain scenes and events by way of specimen and example? **Forty stripes save one** (Deut. xxv. 3). On this instance of Jewish scrupulosity, and for all that is known of the *rationale* of Jewish scourgings, see 'Life of St. Paul,' *ubi supra*.

Ver. 25.—**Thrice was I beaten with rods.** This alludes to scourgings inflicted by Gentile magistrates with the *vitis*, or vine-stick, of soldiers, or with the fasces of lictors. Only one of these horrible scourgings, which likewise often ended in death, is narrated in the Acts (xvi. 22). We do not know when the others were inflicted. In any case they were egregious violations of St. Paul's right of Roman citizenship; but this claim (as we see in Cicero's various orations) was often set at nought in the provinces. **Once was I stoned.** At Lystra (Acts xiv. 19). **Thrice I suffered shipwreck.** Not one of these shipwrecks is narrated in the Acts. The shipwreck of Acts xxvii. took place some years later. **A night and a day I have been in the deep.** An allusion, doubtless, to his escape from one of the shipwrecks by floating for twenty-four hours on a plank in the stormy sea. We have no right to assume that the deliverance was *miraculous*. The perfect tense shows St. Paul's vivid reminiscence of this special horror. "In the deep" means "floating on the deep waves." Theophylact explains the words ἐν βυθῷ to mean "in Bythos," and says that it was a place near Lystra, apparently like the Athenian *Barathrum* and the Spartan *Cæadas*—a place where the bodies of criminals were thrown. The word does not occur elsewhere in the New Testament.

Ver. 26.—**In journeyings often.** In those days and in those countries journeys were not only perilous and fatiguing, but also accompanied with many severe hardships and discomforts. **In perils of waters**; rather, *of rivers.* In all countries which, like parts of Greece and Asia Minor, abound in unbridged mountain torrents, journeys are constantly accompanied by deaths from drowning in the sudden rush of swollen streams. **In perils of robbers.** Then, as now, brigandage was exceedingly common in the mountains of Greece and Asia. In **perils from** mine own **countrymen**; literally, *from my race.* These are abundantly recorded in the New Testament (Acts ix. 23, 29; xiii. 50; xiv. 5, 19; xx. 3, etc.; 1 Thess. ii. 15, 16; Phil. iii. 2) **From the heathen.** They were generally *instigated* by the Jews (Acts xvi. 19—39, xvii. 5; xix. 23—34, etc.). **In the city.** As at Damascus, Jerusalem, Philippi, Thessalonica, Berœa, Ephesus, etc.—"in every city" (Acts xx. 23). **In the wilderness.** As, for instance, in travelling through the wild waste tracts of land between Perga and Antioch in Pisidia, or thence to Lystra and Derbe; or over the mountain chains of Taurus to the cities of Galatia. **In the sea.** Storms, leaks, pirates, mutinies, etc. **Among false brethren.** The word only occurs elsewhere in Gal. ii. 4.

Ver. 27.—**In weariness and painfulness;** literally, *in toil and travail* (1 Thess. ii. 9; 2 Thess. iii. 8). **In watchings;** literally, *in spells of sleeplessness* (Acts xx. 34). **In hunger and thirst** (ver. 8; 1 Cor. iv. 11; Phil. iv. 12). **In fastings often.** It is not clear whether this refers to voluntary fastings (ch. vi. 5; Acts xxvii. 9) or to general destitution short of the actual pangs of hunger. **In cold and nakedness.** St. Paul's ideal, like that of his Master Christ, was the very antithesis of that adopted by the wealthy, honoured, and full-fed Shammais and Hillels of Jewish rabbinism, who delighted in banquets, fine garments, pompous titles, domestic comforts, and stationary ease.

Ver. 28.—**Those things that are without.** The adverb thus rendered *parektos* only occurs in Matt. v. 32; Acts xxvi. 29. It may either mean "trials that come to me from external and extraneous sources (*quæ extrinsecus accedunt*) or things in addition to these (*præterea*), which I here leave unmentioned." The latter meaning is (as St. Chrysostom saw) almost certainly the correct one. **That which cometh upon me.** The word thus rendered is either *episustasis* (J, K), which means "hostile attack" or "tumult," as we talk of "a rush of trouble or business;" or *epistasis* (אַ, B, D, E, F, G), which may imply "halting, lingering thoughts; "attention," and so "anxiety" (comp. Acts xxiv. 12, where there is the same various reading). **Of all the Churches.** No doubt he is thinking of his own Churches, the Churches of the Gentiles (Col. ii. 1).

Ver. 29.—**Who is weak, and I am not weak?** See, by way of example, 1 Cor. viii. 13; ix. 22; Rom. xiv. 21. Instead of stiffly maintaining my own prejudices, I am always ready to make concessions to weak brethren. **Who is offended, and I burn not?** That is, "who is ever caused to stumble without my burning with indignation?" In other words, "Is not the intensity of my sympathy whenever any scandal occurs an addition to the trials of my life?"

Ver. 30.—**If I must needs.** If boasting is forced on me as a moral necessity (δεῖ). **The things which concern mine infirmities.** After all, St. Paul cannot keep up even for a few verses anything which can be regarded as "boasting after the flesh" (ver. 18). Practically his boasting has been only of those

afflictions which to others might sound like a record of disgraces, but which left on him the marks of the Lord Jesus. His hairbreadth escapes were to him, as Bossuet said of the wounds of the Prince of Condé, "marks of the protection of Heaven."

Ver. 31.—**The God and Father of our Lord Jesus Christ.** This solemn asseveration does not seem to be retrospective. It is used to preface what was perhaps intended to be a definite sketch of the most perilous incidents and trials of his life, which would have been to us of inestimable value. This awful attestation of his truthfulness was necessary, (1) because even the very little which we do know shows us that the tale would have been "passing strange;" and (2) because his base and shameless calumniators had evidently insinuated that he was not straightforward (ch. xii. 16). (On the phrases used, see ch. i. 23; 1 Cor. xv. 24; Eph. i. 3.)

Ver. 32.— **In Damascus.** (For the incident referred to, see Acts ix. 22—25.) **The governor;** literally, *the ethnarch.* This is obviously the title given to the commandant of the city (whether an Arabian or a Jew), left in charge by Aretas. The word does not occur elsewhere in the New Testament, but is found in 1 Macc. xiv. 47; Josephus, 'Ant.,' xiv. 7, § 2. **Under Aretas the king.** Hareth, the Emîr of Petra, father-in law of Herod the Great. He had either seized the city during his war with Herod, to avenge the insult offered to his daughter by Herod's adultery with Herodias; or it may have been assigned to him by Caligula. His relations with Damascus are confirmed by coins (see 'Life of St. Paul,' exc. viii.). **Kept . . . with a garrison;** literally, *was guarding.* It is said in Acts ix. 24 that *the Jews* did this; but they could not in any case have done it without leave from the ethnarch, and *qui facit per alium, facit per se.* **Desirous to apprehend me.** Both words are a little stronger in the Greek—"determining to seize me."

Ver. 33.—**Through a window.** A "little door," or lattice in some house which abutted on the wall. **In a basket** (comp. Josh. ii. 15; 1 Sam. xix. 12). The word used by St. Luke in Acts ix. 25 is *spuris*, which is a general name for a large basket. The word here used is *sarganē*, which is defined by Hesychius to be a basket of wickerwork, but which may also mean a rope-basket. This particular incident, no doubt, seems to be less perilous and trying than many which St. Paul has already mentioned. We must, however, remember that escape from a window in the lofty wall of a city guarded by patrols was very perilous, and also that such a method of concealment was very trying to the dignity of an Oriental rabbi, such as St. Paul had been. Further, it is clear that St. Paul only mentions this as the earliest incident in a long line of perils which it had been his original intention to recount. But at this point he was interrupted, and laid aside his task of dictation—an incident which has not unfrequently had its effect in literature. When next he resumed the Epistle, he was no longer in the mood to break through his rule of reticence on these subjects. He had played "the fool" and "the madman," as he says of himself with indignant irony, enough; and he proceeds to speak of other personal claims which he regards as more important and more Divine. Of all "chapters of unwritten history," not one is more deeply to be regretted than the one which we have thus lost.

HOMILETICS.

Vers. 1—4.—*Inviting men to Christ the supreme object of preaching.* "Would to God ye could bear with me a little," etc. The purpose and spirit of this chapter are the same as the preceding one. The apostle proceeds against the charges which they had brought against him, and the same breeze of irony breathes through all. These verses seem to be his defence against the charge of his foolish boasting, "Would to God," or rather would that ye could "bear with me a little in my folly," or better, in a little foolishness. What I have said already you say is foolish boasting; be it so, bear with me whilst I proceed in the same strain of self-vindication; tolerate me a little further. It has been observed that no less than five times in this chapter does the expression "bearing with," or "burden," occur, and the word "folly" eight times; and the inference is that the expressions refer to something which he had heard of some of their remarks concerning him. Paul here seems to claim their continued attention on two grounds.

I. THE GREATNESS OF THE WORK HE HAD ACCOMPLISHED AMONGST THEM. "For I am jealous over you with godly jealousy: for I have espoused you to one husband, that I may present you as a chaste virgin to Christ." He had "espoused," or united them, to Christ, as the bride to the Bridegroom—a relationship the most sacred, close, tender, and lasting. To unite men in *supreme affection* and *supreme purpose* is the grand work of the Christian minister, and what work on earth is so sublimely beneficent and glorious as to make men *one* with Christ? It is impossible to make men one with a creed or a Church, and were it possible it would be to the last degree undesirable. But to make men one with Christ is at once most *practical* and *urgent*—practical because God has established an infallible method, and urgent because souls disconnected from Christ are in a guilty and ruined condition.

II. THE DREAD WHICH HE HAD LEST THAT WORK SHOULD BE UNDONE. "But I fear, lest by any means, as the serpent beguiled Eve through his subtlety [craftiness], so your minds should be corrupted from the simplicity that is in Christ." It would seem from this that the *union of souls to Christ is not absolutely indissoluble*, that a separation is possible; and, in truth, were it not so, man would with the union lose his freedom of action, and would become a mere instrument. Angels fell from their primitive holiness, our first parents from innocence, and Peter for a time from connection with Christ. The holiest creature in the universe is conscious of a power by which he could break away from his orbit of purity and obedience; otherwise he would have no sense of personal virtuousness. The apostle here seems to ascribe the *possible dissolution of the marriage of souls to Christ to Satan*, whom he here represents as the "serpent," implying his belief at once in the *personality*, *moral maliciousness*, and *mighty spiritual influence* of this superhuman intelligence. See how he does this. 1. *By insidiously corrupting the mind.* "I fear, lest by any means, as the serpent beguiled Eve through his subtlety, so your minds should be corrupted from the simplicity that is in Christ." There can be no union between a soul morally corrupt and impure, and Christ. The moment those who are united to Christ become corrupted, the union is at an end; the rotten branch falls from the trunk. So Satan's work is to "corrupt," and thus undo the grandest of all works. This he does insidiously, or craftily, just as he dealt with Eve (Gen. iii.). How craftily this huge enemy of souls pursues his soul-corrupting work! "Beware of his devices." 2. *By the agency of false teachers.* "For if he that cometh preacheth another Jesus, whom we have not preached, or if ye receive another spirit, which ye have not received, or another gospel, which ye have not accepted, ye might well bear with him." There is but one absolute Christ, but as many subjective ones as call themselves Christians, and not a few of the *subjective* ones are pernicious caricatures of the true Jesus of Nazareth. These are preached, and the preaching of them corrupts souls and fulfils the purpose of the devil. There is as much difference between the Christ of the Gospels and the Christ of the creeds, as there is between the cedar growing in Lebanon and that cedar reduced to its primitive elements in the laboratory of the chemist; in the one form beautifully attractive, in the other hideously repulsive. Such Christs were preached in Corinth. Paul, perhaps, specially refers to some one who was preaching " another Jesus," and ironically he intimates that such preachers they tolerated. " Ye might well bear with him." As if he had said, "Such men who are doing the work of the devil ye would tolerate."

Vers. 5—12.— *The highest knowledge and the noblest generosity.* " For I suppose I was not a whit behind the very chiefest apostles. But though I be rude in speech, yet not in knowledge; but we have been thoroughly made manifest among you in all things. Have I committed an offence in abasing myself that ye might be exalted, because I have preached to you the gospel of God freely? I robbed other Churches, taking wages of them, to do you service. And when I was present with you, and wanted, I was chargeable to no man: for that which was lacking to me the brethren which came from Macedonia supplied: and in all things I have kept myself from being burdensome unto you, and so will I keep myself. As the truth of Christ is in me, no man shall stop me of this boasting in the regions of Achaia. Wherefore? because I love you not? God knoweth. But what I do, that I will do, that I may cut off occasion from them which desire occasion; that wherein they glory, they may be found even as we." Few things in human life are more distasteful than egotism or vanity. There are those in society whose chief delight is to parade their own imaginary merits and distinctions. We are wrong, however, if we regard the man who sometimes speaks about himself as an egotist. When a man is denied virtues which he knows he possesses, and charged with faults of which his conscience tells him he is not guilty, he is bound by the laws of his nature to stand up in self-defence. Every man is justified in fighting for his moral reputation, which is to him more precious than gold, and dear to him as life itself. This is just what Paul does here and in many other places in his letters to the Corinthians. He had slanderers at Corinth. Here he says, " For I suppose [reckon] I was not a whit behind the very chiefest apostles." Two facts are here indicated which warranted his boasting.

I. He felt that, though he had not rhetorical accomplishments, HE HAD THE HIGHEST KNOWLEDGE. " Though I be rude in speech, yet not in knowledge." He was not trained in all the rhetorical parts of Grecian oratory, his periods were not polished, his sentences were not tuneful, and, perhaps, his utterances lacked flow and his voice music. This he seems to have felt; but what of that? He had the highest " knowledge." What is the grandest oratory without true knowledge? Clouds of golden splendour without water for the thirsty land. Paul's knowledge was of the highest kind. He knew Christ; he knew what Christ was to him; what he had done for him, as well as what he was in himself and in his relation to the Father and the universe. This is the science of all sciences; the science of which all other sciences are to it the mere leaf, or stem, or branch, of which this is the root. " This is life eternal, to know thee the only true God, and Jesus Christ, whom thou hast sent." " I count all things but loss for the excellency of the knowledge of Christ Jesus my Lord."

II. He felt that, though he consecrated himself to their highest interests, he RECEIVED FROM THEM NO REMUNERATION. What trials he endured for them! what perils he braved for them! what labours he prosecuted for them (see vers. 24—27)! All this was done and endured for what? Not for selfish ends, not for worldly gain. " Have I committed an offence in abasing myself that ye might be exalted, because I have preached to you the gospel of God freely?" Why did he not receive remuneration at their hands? Nay, why did he reject it? (1) Not because he did not need such a recompense. "And when I was present with you, and wanted, I was chargeable to no man." He was dependent upon such contributions for his subsistence. He had received them at Thessalonica before his first visit to Corinth. (2) Not because he did not love them. " Wherefore? because I love you not? God knoweth." It would have been a *gratification* to those whom he had spiritually saved, to have made some secular recompense for his labours, but he denied them this gratification, not because he did not love them. Why, then, did he reject their secular help? 1. *To furnish in his own life a proof of the benevolent terms of the gospel.* " I preach to you the gospel of God freely." The gospel is a free gift of God, and I present it to you as a free gift. The gospel should never be preached as a *means of livelihood* or for filthy lucre. 2. *To silence the tongue of his slanderers.* No doubt his enemies at Corinth sought in every way to degrade the apostle. The false apostles, no doubt, boasted that they did their work there as benefactors disinterestedly and without pay. Had Paul taken payment he would have given them some ground for boasting of their generosity. 3. *To compel his enemies by his example to act from generous impulses.* " That they may be found as we are." " Notice," says Mr. Beet, " the bitter irony of these words. Paul's opponents boasted their disinterestedness whilst making gain of the Corinthians, and eagerly watched him to detect self-enrichment, that they might boast of their own superiority. These have been the tactics of demagogues in all ages. But Paul resolved to refuse just recompense for real and great benefits, that thus by his example he may compel those who boasted their superiority to come up to his own level of working without pay, so that when his conduct and theirs are investigated, they may be found to be as disinterested as he was."

CONCLUSION. Truly that man might well exult who feels that, however deficient in mere verbal learning, he possesses the highest knowledge—the knowledge of Christ; and who also feels that he is rendering to men the highest service from kindly generous impulses without a desire for fee or reward, giving freely to men what God has given freely to all—the gospel of Jesus Christ.

Vers. 13—15.—*Self-misrepresentation.* "For such are false apostles, deceitful workers, transforming themselves into the apostles of Christ. And no marvel; for Satan himself is transformed into an angel of light. Therefore it is no great thing if his ministers also be transformed as the ministers of righteousness; whose end shall be according to their works." Three thoughts are suggested by these words.

I. MAN HAS THE POWER OF MISREPRESENTING HIS CHARACTER TO OTHERS. Naturalists tell us of animals which have the power to appear what they really are not. Some feign sleep and death. Be this as it may, man has this power in an eminent degree— he can disguise himself and live in masquerade. Hence our Saviour speaks of " wolves in sheep's clothing." In fact, throughout all circles and populations those who appear to be what they really are have ever been in a miserable minority. As a rule men are not what they seem.

II. IN THE EXERCISE OF THIS POWER MAN CAN INVEST EVIL WITH THE HIGHEST FORMS OF GOOD. The " false apostles," to whom reference is here made, seem to have done so. Paul speaks of them as " deceitful workers, transforming themselves into the apostles of Christ. And no marvel; for Satan himself is transformed into an angel of light." *The worse a man is the stronger the temptation he has to assume the forms of goodness.* Were corrupt men to show the state of their hearts to their contemporaries, they would recoil from them with horror and disgust, and they would be utterly unable to enjoy social intercourse or to transact their worldly business. As a rule, the worse a man is the more strenuous his efforts to assume the habiliments of virtue. Selfishness robes itself in the garbs of benevolence, error speaks in the language of truth. Hence it does not follow that a man is a true apostle or minister of Christ because he appears in the character. Some of the worst men on the earth have been deacons and priests, occupied pulpits and preached sermons. " No marvel," says the apostle; " for Satan himself is transformed into an angel of light." Hence it behoves us all to look well into the real moral character of those who set themselves up as the representatives of Christ and the teachers of religion. " Beloved, believe not every spirit, but try the spirits whether they are of God : because many false prophets are gone out into the world."

III. HE WHO EXERCISES THIS POWER IN THIS WAY RENDERS HIMSELF LIABLE TO TERRIBLE PUNISHMENT. " Whose end shall be according to their works." Of all characters the *hypocrite* is the most guilty and abhorrent. More terrible and more frequent were the denunciations Christ hurled against such than against the voluptuary, the gross sensualist, or the sordid worldling. " Woe unto you, scribes and Pharisees, hypocrites!" etc. (see Matt. xxiii. 13—33). As such are the greatest sinners, such will have the most terrible end; the "end shall be *according to their works*." They will reap the fruit of their own doings.

CONCLUSION. Learn: 1. The duty of *self-truthfulness*. Let us seek to be such true men, so true to self, society, and God, that we may have no temptation whatever to play the hypocrite or to appear to others what we are not.

> "To thine own self be true,
> And it must follow, as the night the day,
> Thou canst not then be false to any man."

2. The duty of social *caution*. Do not let us estimate men by their appearances, and take them into the circle of our confidence and friendship merely on account of what they appear to be. Often those whose outward garb is the most holy are inwardly the most corrupt, who outwardly move as angels of light are inwardly the greatest devils. Let us learn to take off the mask, to disrobe corruption of its external robes of purity, and to give neither our trust nor our sympathy until we are convinced that they have truth in the "inward parts."

Vers. 16—19.—*Man talking about himself, and the limitation of apostolic inspiration.* "I say again, Let no man think me a fool; if otherwise, yet as a fool receive me, that I may boast myself a little. That which I speak, I speak it not after the Lord, but as it were foolishly, in this confidence of boasting. Seeing that many glory after the flesh, I will glory also. For ye suffer fools gladly, seeing ye yourselves are wise." Observe here—

I. MAN TALKING ABOUT HIMSELF. Paul had said a good many things about himself. Here again he takes up the subject, and his language suggests: 1. That the world is disposed to regard *such talk as foolish*. "Let no man think me a fool [or, 'foolish ']." In this he recognizes the tendency of men to regard such self-reference and self-talk as weak and unwise. So in truth unsophisticated men do. When they hear a man talking about himself he impresses them with a sense of his folly. Inwardly they say, "What a fool that man is to be talking about himself!" It must be confessed that *generally* it is a very foolish thing—few things are more foolish. 2. That such conduct *may become a duty*. Paul felt it such an urgent obligation at this time that he begs them to bear with him. "Yet as a fool receive me, that I may boast myself a little." He was on his defence, and he felt that such self-references as he made he owed to himself, to the Christians at Corinth, and to the cause of his Master. Hence he seems to say, "Though you regard me as a fool whilst I thus talk about myself, yet do hear me." 3. That to attention to such talk about himself the apostle *had a special claim*. "Seeing that many glory after the flesh, I will glory also. For ye suffer fools gladly, seeing ye yourselves are wise." As if he had said, "The false apostles amongst you talk about themselves; they boast of their merits and achievements, and you listen to them. I have a special claim to your attention because of the proofs of my apostleship amongst you."

II. THE LIMITATION OF APOSTOLIC INSPIRATION. "That which I speak, I speak it not after the Lord, but as it were foolishly, in this confidence of boasting." As if he had said, "I do not talk of myself by 'commandment;' I have no special commission from Christ." How frequently does the apostle, in his communications to the Church at Corinth, guard against the impression that everything he wrote was divinely inspired! Indeed, in one case he indicates an imperfection of memory. "I baptized also the household of Stephanas: besides, I know not whether I baptized any other" (1 Cor. i. 16). "I know not." What, an inspired apostle not knowing what he had done, forgetting the religious ordinances he had celebrated! In his letter to Timothy he himself says, "Every Scripture inspired of God is also profitable for teaching," implying that all Scripture is not inspired. It is for us to find out which the inspired ones are, to separate the human from the Divine. Whatever agrees with the character and the teaching of the Spirit of Christ we may rest assured is inspired of God. Who but God himself can tell the enormous amount of injury that has been done to sacred truth by the dogma of verbal inspiration, regarding all the imprecations of David, all the reasonings of Job's three friends, and even the utterances of Satan himself, as inspired by Heaven? The Scriptures *contain* the word of God, but they are not the word of God; the casket is not the jewel, the shell is not the kernel. This by a devout and earnest study we must find out for ourselves.

CONCLUSION. The subject teaches: 1. That we must not *shrink from the discharge of a duty, however painful.* Paul, as a humble and modest man, felt it a very painful thing to talk about himself. His native modesty shrank from it; yet, though he would be considered a "fool," he did it. 2. That we must *study the Scriptures with a discriminating judgment.* We must penetrate through the "letter" that is human and reach the "spirit" that is Divine. "Open thou mine eyes, that I may behold wondrous things out of thy Law."

Ver. 20.—*A picture of religious impostors.* "For ye suffer, if a man bring you into bondage, if a man devour you, if a man take of you, if a man exalt himself, if a man smite you on the face." This verse suggests five things concerning religious impostors.

I. THEY ARE TYRANNIC. "For ye suffer [bear] if a man bring you into bondage." The reference is undoubtedly to those described in ver. 13, who were false teachers in Corinth. They were enslaving the souls of men with their dogmas and rites. False teaching always makes men spiritual serfs. Heathens are slaves to their priest, fanatics are slaves to their leader, papists are slaves to their pope. True teaching makes men free men. Spiritual bondage is infinitely worse than physical or political. A man's body may be in chains, yet he may be free in spirit; but if his spirit is enslaved, he himself is in captivity. The work of a false teacher is always to subdue souls to himself; the work of the true, to win souls to Christ. Even conventional Christianity is enslaving.

II. THEY ARE RAPACIOUS. "If a man devour you." False teachers devour widows' houses. They teach for money, turn temples and churches into shops. They shear the sheep instead of feeding them. Greed is their inspiration.

III. THEY ARE CRAFTY. "If a man take of you [taketh you captive]." The expression "of you" is not in the original. The idea to me seems to be—if a man takes you in, deceives and entraps you. This is just what religious impostors do— they "take men in," they cajole men, and make them their dupes.

IV. THEY ARE ARROGANT. "If a man exalt himself." It is characteristic of false teachers that they assume great superiority. With this they endeavour to impress men by their costume, their bearing, and their pompous utterances. They arrogate a lordship over human souls.

V. THEY ARE INSOLENT. "If a man smite you on the face." This is the last form of outrage; no greater insult could be offered to a man. The religious impostor has no respect for the rights and dignities of man as man. With his absurd dogmas and arrogances he is everlastingly smiting men on "their face," on their reason, their consciences, and their self-respect.

Vers. 21—33.—*Pauls' avowal of his advantages and his history of his trials.* "I speak as concerning reproach," etc. The two subjects for thought that stand out conspicuously in these verses are Paul's manly avowal of his distinguished advantages and his historic sketch of his extraordinary trials.

I. HIS MANLY AVOWAL OF HIS DISTINGUISHED ADVANTAGES. There are three advantages which he here touches upon. 1. *His superior character.* "I speak as concerning reproach [by way of disparagement], as though we had been weak." Hitherto I have spoken of myself as if all the disparaging things you have said of me were true. The idea of Paul's language here seems to be this: "I have been speaking of reproach or disgrace, as if I was weak, *i.e.* as if I was disposed to admit as true all that has been said of me, as reproachful or disgraceful, all that has been said of my want of qualifications for the office, of my want of talent, my dignity of character, my folly. In all this I have been speaking ironically. I am superior to all; I am not ignorant, but learned; I am not foolish, but wise; not greedy, but generous; not proud, but humble; not ignoble, but dignified." How far his character transcended that of his traducers, history shows. 2. *His superior ancestry.* "Are they Hebrews? so am I. Are they Israelites? so am I. Are they the seed of Abraham? so am I." His traducers, the false teachers, were, it would seem, Jews; probably boasted of their descent, and certainly implied that Paul was a mere Hellenistic Jew, born at Tarsus. If they gloried in their descent, so could he; the blood of Abraham quivered in his veins, he was a lineal descendant of the man who wrestled with Jehovah and prevailed, an Israelite. 3. *His superior apostleship.* " Are they ministers of Christ? (I speak as a fool) I am more." They called themselves " ministers of Christ," and belonged, perhaps, to the party in the Corinthian Church who said they were " of Christ "—Christites. But he was more an apostle of Christ than they were. Of this he was conscious. In touching this Paul says, " I speak as a fool," or as one beside myself. Here his great soul seems to flash out in the fire of indignant irony. There is an egotism here, say some. True, but it is a just, manly, necessary egotism.

II. His HISTORIC SKETCH OF HIS EXTRAORDINARY TRIALS. He was scourged "five times," in " prisons frequent " and in " deaths oft," thrice "beaten with rods," once "stoned," " thrice suffered shipwrecks," in "perils in the sea" and on land, midst foes and friends, in the "wilderness" and in cities, tried by " weariness and painfulness, in watchings often, in hunger and thirst, in fastings often, in cold and nakedness." Besides all this, he refers to the trials that came "daily" upon him in "the care of all the Churches." The Churches were dear to his heart, and all the dissensions, heresies, unchastities, immoralities, that appeared from time to time in the Churches would carry anguish into his heart. Why he should refer in the last verse to the event that happened at Damascus, when he was let down "through a window in a basket," has been a puzzle to commentators. But as it was amongst his first trials as an apostle, it, perhaps, made the greatest impression on his mind. The trials here sketched indicate several things. 1. *The mysteriousness of God's procedure with his servants.* One might have thought that the man inspired with supreme love to God, and receiving a commission from him, involving the salvation of souls, would have had his way made clear and safe and even pleasant for him; that in his path no enemy should appear, no peril should threaten, no pain should be endured, that all things would be propitious; that he who embarked in such an enterprise as Paul's would sail in a bark absolutely secure, under a sky without a cloud, with every billow and every breeze propitious. But not so. The more important the Divine work entrusted to a man, and the more faithful he is in its discharge, the more trials will embarrass and distract him. For an explanation of this we must await the great explaining day. 2. *The unconquerableness of Christly love in the soul.* What stimulated Paul to embark in such an enterprise as this? What urged him on through innumerable difficulties and dangers? What bore him up under distressing and ever-thickening trials? Here is the answer: " The love of Christ constraineth me." This is the love that is unconquerable and all-conquering, the love that makes the true hero. 3. *The indelibility of the impressions which trials produce.* The trials in this long catalogue, so varied and tremendous, had long since transpired, but they were fresh in Paul's memory. Each one stood before the eye of his memory in living reality. It is a law in our nature that our trials make a deeper impression on us than our mercies. Why should this be so? Because they are the exceptions, not the rule. 4. *The blessedness which the memory of trials rightly endured produces.* In Paul's case it did two things. (1) It generated sympathy with the woes of others. " Who is weak, and I am not weak? who is offended, and I burn not?" No man can sympathize with the trials of others unless he has passed through trials himself. The sufferings that Christ endured qualified him to sympathize with the woes of the world. He who hungers for sympathy in his sufferings will go in vain to the man who has never suffered. (2) It inspired the soul with true rejoicing. " If I must needs glory, I will glory of the things which concern mine infirmities." The reminiscence of the trials he had endured, the foes he had encountered, the perils he had braved, in the cause of Christ were now for him subjects for congratulation and glorifying. They had exerted such a beneficent influence on his character, and were endured in such a noble cause, that he rejoiced in them. In declaring all this Paul makes a solemn appeal for its truth. " The God and Father of our Lord Jesus Christ, which is blessed for evermore, knoweth that I lie not."

HOMILIES BY VARIOUS AUTHORS.

Vers. 1—6.—*Relations of the apostle to the Corinthians; ground of anxiety.* How shall we read this chapter? To read it aright it is certain that we must do more than exercise the understanding on its contents; more than treat it as an argument intended to set forth a definite conclusion; and, especially, more than a defence, on any private grounds, of St. Paul's character and conduct. First of all, a general view of the situa tion is necessary. In this large, growing, and influential city, a bond of connection between Asia and Europe, a medium through which the most prominent agencies of the day operated over a very broad surface,—in this active and aspiring city a Christian Church had been founded by St. Paul on his first visit. It was an era in his apostleship. Of Greek intellect and habits, he had learned enough at least to give a special bias to his style of preaching. Thrown among a population of Jews, Romans, Greeks, and adven- turers from every quarter of the globe, he found a degree of skill and prudence necessary in the management of his work that had not been required in any previous stage of his career. Shrewd money-lovers were all around him; he would practise his trade and support himself. Aquila and Priscilla had stood faithfully by his side and cheered his toil. He preached in the synagogue, trouble came, and he transferred his work to the house of Justus. A vision from God assured him of help and protection, and one of its fulfilments occurred when Gallio drove the apostle's persecutors, the turbulent Jews, from "the judgment-seat," and, in the subsequent tumult, "cared for none of these things." But it was more than an era in his ministry. It was an epoch in the history of the gospel. There had been something like a repetition of Pentecost. None of the outward symbols, and yet a mighty descent of the Holy Ghost in the number and variety of gifts. If the great Pentecost had been followed by sad lapses in the cases of Ananias and Sapphira, even by lying unto the Holy Ghost whose dispensation had just been inaugurated, could it be wondered at that disorder, misrule, heart-burnings, strife, immoralities, had sprung up as tares among the wheat in this luxuriant harvest? It was Corinth out and out. It was the excitable emporium in one of those ferments, good and evil intermixed, which have happened at intervals in the history of the Church. To check the unhealthy excitement, to purify the Church from corruption, to suppress rivalries and animosities between parties, St. Paul had put forth all his wisdom, energy, and fidelity, and, in large measure, had succeeded. At this point, a closer view of the situation becomes necessary. Looking at St. Paul as the apostle to the Gentiles, we see at once the significance of his relation to the Corinthian Church. Humanly speaking, he had fought here his greatest battle and had won a grand victory. Where was there a Church potentially of such promise? Where such an array of brilliant endowments? Where such a manifoldness and plenitude of captivating gifts? Here, in the very city where the Jews had required a sign and the Greeks had sought after wisdom; here, in the very metropolis of Achaia, where learning and culture and Jewish traditions were so strongly entrenched behind wealth and social influence, he had chosen to lay a peculiar and profound stress on "the foolishness of preaching." And the Christ crucified had suddenly revealed himself as the Christ glorified, had refulfilled his promise of the Holy Ghost, and a glorious Pentecostal season had been granted to Corinth. It was the miracle of all the miracles in his career. How personal it was to him as the apostle to the Gentiles is obvious. It was akin to the demonstration made before Jerusalem and her Sanhedrim in behalf of the twelve; and if that event gave St. Peter a commanding attitude at once, only second to that, if indeed second, was this outpouring of the Holy Spirit as an attestation from Christ the Lord of the special ministry of St. Paul. Amid these signs and wonders dissension and bitter strife had appeared at Corinth. Most alarming of all, Judaizers had come from Jerusalem to assail St. Paul's authority and destroy his influence. They had been zealous, unscru- pulous, persistent, malignant. At every point they had attacked him, and they had a sufficient following to make the apostle apprehend serious damage. The persecution, he had hoped, was checked if not ended. But it had broken out anew, and that, too, while writing this Second Epistle. It was a severe blow. He was not prepared for it. Could it be possible that his work here was to be undone, or, if not that, to be arrested by these unprincipled adversaries? Corinth was the key to the vast citadel of the West; should he lose it from his hand? It is in the light of these facts that we must read this eleventh chapter. And if we find him making a most vigorous and determined effort to reinstate his authority over the disaffected portion of the Corinthian Church, let us remember that it is not Paul as an individual, but St. Paul as an apostle—*the* apostle to the Gentiles—who pleaded for a cause far dearer to him than reputation, honour, or life itself. It was not a party, however strong, but the Church he needed in his future work. The opening verse of the chapter indicates his sense of the embarrassing position. "Would that ye could bear with me in a little foolishness, nay indeed bear with me." To commend himself to them by this frequent recital of his labours and sufferings must have been exceedingly painful to one of his sensibility. Only as a duty to his apostleship and to them could he do it, and hence he says, "I am jealous over you with godly jealousy." The figure introduced is expressive of love and purity: "For I have espoused you to one husband, that I may present you as a chaste virgin to Christ." But what is the actual state of the Corinthian Church? Is it making ready for presentation as a bride to the Bridegroom when he shall appear in his glory? There is ground for his jealousy: "I fear, lest by any means, as the serpent beguiled Eve through his subtlety, so your minds should be corrupted from the simplicity that is in Christ." Deception is plainly stated as the danger threatening them—no ordinary danger, for it had an infernal origin, one that had been successful even with Eve in Paradise; and as these new teachers were using just such insidious arts, he warns them lest they fall into the snare. The character to be maintained was virginal purity; the end to be kept in view was that Christ's betrothed Church might be worthy of her Lord at the marriage supper; the peril was the deceitfulness of agents who, under the mask of instructors and authoritative guides, were acting in the interest of Satan; and the enforcement of the warning was the success of the serpent as Satan's instrument in beguiling Eve. If Eve could be deceived in her purity, how great the danger to this chaste virgin! The "subtlety" had lost none of its persuasive arts; thorough the deception then, thorough would it be now, if they hearkened to these false teachers. To supplant the gospel by the Law, to sink the Christian Church in the Jewish Church, to rob him of his disciples and degrade them into the slaves of Pharisaic superstitions already in their dotage,—this was the mercenary aim of these emissaries of Satan. Such they were, as he would presently show. And what were the evidences of imminent danger? If this new preacher come to you preaching another Christ, another Spirit, another gospel, how would you receive him? Would you refuse to hear him? Nay; you would "bear with him," dallying with temptation, blinded, fascinated, opening your hearts to the "subtlety" of the "serpent." On this account he was unhappy. The chaste virgin should listen to no hints of another love. Aside from such conduct, as most evil in itself, what consistency had it with their relation to him as their apostle? He it was who had espoused them to Christ as the Bridegroom, and therefore his jealousy lest they should be "corrupted from the simplicity that is in Christ." The passage is very difficult to understand, and we are by no means sure that we have caught the true meaning. But these seem to be the main points, viz.: 1. St. Paul claims that he has espoused them to Christ, and that he was anxious to present the Church as a chaste virgin to him. 2. There was great danger of their losing this virginal purity. 3. If this purity were lost, it would be through the subtlety of Satan acting by means of human agency. 4. This agency threatened the Corinthians even now, some of whom were inclined to reject his authority and become the disciples of these arrogant and self-sufficient teachers. 5. His authority was indisputable. "Not a whit" was he "behind the very chiefest apostles," and this had been demonstrated most signally by his apostolic labours in Corinth. "Rude in speech," according to the Grecian standard of rhetoric, but "not in knowledge;" so that if some of the Corinthians went after another preacher with a different Christ and Spirit and gospel, and would "bear with him" and "might well bear," it would be in contempt of him who had been "made thoroughly manifest" among them as "not a whit behind the very chiefest apostles," and that, too, "in all things." "Bear with him," the new teacher, weaning you away from your former love? Then "bear with me a little in my folly: and indeed bear with me." If you accede to his claims who comes to you with such a novel, presumptuous, and overbearing manner, then surely you can tolerate me in the *little folly* of lowering myself to a comparison with him. I condescend to it for your sakes and for my own. The equal of any apostle, I let myself down to this folly, and "would to God ye could bear with me" in it!—L.

Vers. 7—12.—*Questions asked and answered.* His enemies had charged that, if he were an apostle, he would have claimed a support from the Corinthians. Instead of that, he had worked at his trade as a tentmaker, and done what he could to gain a livelihood. It had been used against him. Was it, then, beneath the dignity of an apostle to labour with his own hands? What his right was to a maintenance he knew and they knew. But he had waived this right for reasons most satisfactory to himself. Had he committed a sin in this voluntary abasement that they might be exalted by his preaching gratuitously the gospel of God? Was this at variance with his statement that he had been "thoroughly made manifest" among them "in all things," and was not "a whit behind the very chiefest apostles"? In coming to Corinth, and while labouring there, he had "robbed other Churches," and what he lacked in sustaining himself had been supplied from Macedonia. This was done that he might not be "burdensome" unto them. Would his opponents say that he would claim remuneration for the future, or that he was running up a debt against them? Nay; the future shall be as the past. "So will I keep myself." Speaking in accordance with Christ's truth in him, he would avow a fixed determination that this boasting should never be denied him in Achaia. But would they misinterpret this language and accuse him of wanting kind feelings towards them? "God knoweth." To be suspected of such a motive would do him wrong, since he meant it to be a proof of the sincerity and earnestness of his ministry in their behalf. No one should charge him with selfishness; he would be disinterested in all the services rendered to Corinth, that he might "cut off occasion from them" who were always eager to find or make an "occasion" against his apostleship. Had he, then, descended from the ordinary level of the apostolic office, and abased himself, that the Corinthians might be exalted by a special proof of his disinterested love? Further than this, he would protect the Church against these money-loving partisans, who, while standing in a hostile attitude towards him and his work, were looking after their own sordid interest, and intent on making a gain of godliness. "Wherein they glory, they may be found even as we." It was the spiritual intelligence of love. It was the prudence of sanctified worldly experience; and the wisdom of the serpent and the harmlessness of the dove were never more happily blended.—L.

Vers. 13—15.—*Character of these teachers.* Indications of a marked change in the apostle respecting these intruders at Corinth appear in the tenth chapter. Recent circumstances had aroused his attention to their acrid and persistent hostility as directed against him and the spiritual welfare of the Church. From the first he had not misjudged them. Under all their specious arts he had detected a low and carnal spirit, calculated to affect these volatile Corinthians and obstruct the progress of his ministry. Meantime they had increased in boldness and audacity, and assailed him with more impetuous virulence. Evidently, then, there was a growth in his convictions as to their mischief-making power, and of late these convictions had become very strong. The growth is apparent both in his thought and feeling, and in such a mind as St. Paul's it could not be long in reaching his will and shaping itself in a resolute purpose to put down the evil. So long as it was mainly a personal vexation, he had borne it patiently; but the hour had come when, while true to "the meekness and gentleness of Christ," he must show "the rod." Very clearly is the military attitude of his mind exhibited in the previous chapter. He speaks of "weapons," of their might to overthrow "strongholds" and "cast down imaginations," and of his readiness at the proper moment "to revenge all disobedience." This deepening intensity finds utterance in the paragraph now under consideration. Unable to repress his feelings any longer, he gives them expression in the most forcible form his language could assume as it regarded the religious pretensions of these men. They are "false apostles, deceitful workers, transforming themselves [by their own act] into the apostles of Christ." Looking at the matter from St. Paul's point of view, nothing worse could be said of them. What his description involved quickly appears. "No marvel;" how could there be any room for surprise? It was characteristic of him, the great adversary, to send just such "apostles;" for "Satan himself transforms himself into an angel of light." Perfectly natural; sender and sent are one; and the union is seen in the transforming power. No great thing if "his ministers" should so fashion themselves as to seem "ministers of righteousness." And having stated who and what they were, he announces their future doom: "whose end shall be according to their works." We see now why he mentioned his fear in the opening of the chapter, and referred to Eve as led into sin by the subtlety of the serpent, and we see also why he spoke of their bearing with these hypocrites. Hitherto some of the Church had been deceived by the plausible devices of these persons. But he had opened their eyes to the danger, and, if they continued to listen to these ministers of Satan, they themselves would be willing dupes and participants in their guilt "whose end shall be according to their works." The passage has a deep spiritual meaning. It shows us the great power of Satan in adapting himself to circumstances and using means suited to times and occasions. It shows him versatile, adroit, untiring in inventiveness as well as in energy, and able to impart to others this transforming or fashioning power which he pre-eminently possesses. Not only does the Pauline theology recognize the inherency of sin in our nature, but in addition thereunto it recognizes a mighty agent who employs the utmost skill and a prodigious strength of will and passion to call out and direct this indwelling evil. And it shows this Satanic agency working in the Church, and even counterfeiting the apostleship. The passage is full and explicit. Its force cannot be evaporated in rhetoric; its truth is the sternest reality in most earnest speech. A critical occasion had arisen, one of momentous interest in the history of Christianity, one that presented a turning-point in St. Paul's career, and he met this occasion by exposing the diabolical source of their conduct. From his course of action we may learn a very useful lesson. His way of dealing with sin looked to a personal agent beyond the sinner—one with the sinner and yet distinct and separate, and this agent exerting his tremendous ability in exciting all the latency of evil as unconscious to the sinner, and with it all his conscious susceptibility, so as to accomplish his eternal ruin. Too often with us this Satanic power in men is not duly estimated. In trying to save men, we should remember from whom we are delivering them, and what an awful hold Satan's tyranny has upon their souls. As a practical fact, this is a matter of vast importance. And, accordingly, we find the Lord Jesus impressing on the apostles that the Holy Ghost was not only to convince the world of "sin" and of "righteousness," but also of "judgment"—"because the prince of this world is judged." How else, indeed, could the work of *conviction* be consummated? Precisely here the Spirit perfects his gracious office as the Divine Convincer; and precisely here we must labour with all diligence and prayerfulness in order to convince men that they are by nature the subjects of this prince, and that only Christ, who has "judged" him, can deliver them from his bondage. No closeness of contact with man as mere man will meet the requirements of the case. It is man, the servant of sin because the slave of the devil, with whom the preacher of the gospel has to do, and unless he realize as far as may be the fearful import of Christ's words, "Ye are of your father the devil," it is not likely he will co-operate with the Holy Ghost in bringing men to that depth and thoroughness of repentance which go far to determine the stability and worth of future Christian character. Depend upon it, our danger at this point is real and serious. What is the human nature with which we are struggling in the daily endeavours of thought and in special sabbath efforts, praying, wrestling, agonizing, that it may be rescued from unbelief and restored to its Father? Inspiration is never content to portray it as merely far gone from original righteousness, dead in trespasses and sins, but the very phraseology takes its deepest import from ideas and images originally associated with Satan. If detached from Satan, such terms as "subtlety," "blindness," "deceitfulness," "bewitched," "craftiness," "beguiled," "wiles," "snares," "captivity," "bondage," would lose the peculiar force which always accompanies them in the Scriptures. And with this use of language the spirit of the New Testament accords when its writers are setting forth human depravity in its special relations to Christ's mediatorial work. Is Judas about to negotiate for the betrayal of Jesus of Nazareth? "Satan entered into him." Is St. Peter over-confident, proud of his devotion to Jesus, full of daring? "Simon, Simon, behold, Satan hath desired to have you, that he may sift you as wheat." St. John: "He that committeth sin is of the devil." St. Peter: "Your adversary, the devil." St. James: "Resist the devil." St. Paul: "Recover themselves out of the snare of the devil." Surely, then, this uniform tenor of scriptural language, coupled with Christ's most emphatic declaration as to man's incapacity to see Satanic agency in its true light except through the convicting office of the Holy Ghost; surely, we say, this should impress us very deeply as to the urgent need of making prominent in our preaching and teaching the fact of

Satan's enormous power over the human soul. Time was when this truth was felt far more profoundly than now, or at least when it filled a much larger space in pulpit thought and Christian literature. And the fruits of it appeared everywhere, not only in a higher order of religious sentiment, but in the amenability of folly and vice to that moral fear which no community can afford to lose. Wickedness abounded then, as now, and yet wickedness was open to the probing of its conscience and to the disturbance of its sensibilities, nor did it commonly have the complacent hardness and the defiant attitude towards the solemn hereafter which it now wears as its familiar aspect. Communities had convictions then on moral and religious subjects, but only sections of communities (speaking generally) have such convictions now. Men of convictions were sure of an audience. Savonarola could not but be heard. Luther had an intense realization of an evil spirit; less of it would have made him less of a reformer. Milton and Bunyan, the two names that Englishmen would choose as the finest representatives of English genius and manhood in the literary spheres they filled, wrote as men who realized that Satan was something more in the affairs of the world than a subject for artistic treatment. We have come to the closing quarter of the nineteenth century, and within the century the land of Luther has given us 'Faust' with Mephistopheles, and the England of Milton and Bunyan has gives us 'Festus' with Lucifer. Insensibly to itself, the pulpit has caught the effeminate spirit of the age, and it discusses sin much more than it grapples with Satan in sin. "For this purpose the Son of God was manifested, that he might destroy the works of the devil." If the most tender and loving soul among inspired thinkers could lay such an emphasis on this truth, assuredly there is a way for this doctrine to be strenuously preached, free from every taint of extravagance and morbid imagination. Depend upon it, when we throw this doctrine into the background of set purpose, or when we let it lapse from our grasp by casual infirmity, we have nothing left but a fragmentary Christ and a depleted ethical Christianity.—L.

Vers. 16—20.—*Comparison of himself with his opponents.* The weapons of his warfare were not carnal, and yet he must use, under protest and with undissembled humiliation, the weapons of his enemies. Boasting was their favourite art. Would they think him a fool? Let him not be so considered. If, however, they would regard him in this light, nevertheless he must "boast a little." Only he would pray to be heard by the Corinthians, but, at the same time, he wished it understood that he was speaking as a man, not as an apostle. "That which I speak, I speak it not after the Lord, but as it were foolishly, in this confidence of boasting." St. Paul is careful to state when he speaks from his own mind, and he is equally concerned to let his readers know that, if others boasted from mean and selfish motives, he boasted in a very different spirit from theirs. "Many glory after the flesh," referring to his adversaries, and "I will glory also," but not as they do. "After the Lord" and "after the flesh" are contrasted, and yet in doing this (boasting), if he imitated the *manner* of these "false apostles, deceitful workers," there was nothing *false* or *deceitful* in his conduct. What he boasted of was *matter of fact;* and then he remarks, continuing the ironical vein in which he had been arguing, that the Corinthians were well able to bear with his foolishness, since they *suffered fools gladly,* seeing that they were *wise.* "Wise," verily. Then he cites what they had endured from these new teachers. Where was their freedom? They had been brought into "bondage"—moral and ecclesiastical submission to tyrannical rulers. Where was their self-protection against imposition and craftiness, their discernment of men and motives? They had been taken in, captured, *devoured,* by these designing men. Where was their self-respect? These "fools," whom they suffered "gladly," had exalted themselves and humiliated a Church abounding in special endowments. Where, finally, was their manliness? They had borne insolence, personal ill treatment—had been *smitten on the face.* Such was his arraignment of these "false apostles," such his indictment of those Corinthians who had allowed themselves to be dominated by these insulting pretenders. Such, too, was the background for a vivid picture now to be sketched.—L.

Vers. 21—33.—*What St. Paul was and what he had suffered as an apostle of Christ.* If, indeed, the standard of strength which the deceiving ministers of Satan had set up among them were a correct one, then he must say that he had been *weak* in his inter-course with them on his visit to Corinth. He had not abused them as slaves, nor been avaricious, nor offered them insults. Yes; he must admit that they were strong and he weak, they wise and he foolish, and he confesses the shame he felt. The sharp irony is now dropped, and he proceeds to show what reasons he had for genuine boasting. If he had to vindicate his claims against these men who had transformed themselves into " ministers of righteousness," it was extremely abasing, but he would be bold (boastful), since there was no escape from the painful task. And, as we shall see, he would do it with great deliberation, item by item, the points clearly made, and only such points as were capable of easy verification.

I. As TO NATIONALITY. These Judaizers, seeking to prop up a sinking theocracy by means of a perverted Christianity, and putting a most inordinate and carnal estimate on their prerogatives as members of an elect race, had made on this score a very earnest appeal to the Corinthians, and especially to the converted Jews. "Are they Hebrews?" By this general race-title the chosen people had been early known, and it was still in vogue. If they are Hebrews, St. Paul says, "so am I." Again, "Are they Israelites?" That name was derived from Israel, the name given to Jacob after wrestling with the angel at Peniel, and designated, originally, the union of the tribes as one community under Jehovah's rule, and set apart to bear witness against all idolatry. "Israelite" carried in its import a reference to the nation as representative of the Divine unity, and was, therefore, distinctively religious. St. Paul responds again, "So am I." Finally, as to nationality. "Are they the seed of Abraham? so am I." One by one the honourable distinctions are mentioned, closing with the highest—a son of Abraham, and in them he claims equality with these pretentious teachers. There was an evident reason for this mode of procedure. No one suspected his devotion to the Gentiles and his zeal in behalf of the apostleship of the uncircumcision. But there were prejudices, strong and bitter, against him on his supposed want of fealty to his nation, and hence his anxiety to show on all occasions that he prized his blood and loved his people. We see from our standpoint that he was an *ideal* Jew, the truest and most sagacious Jew of his age; and yet it was a memorable part of his discipline, and a main factor in his fortunes, to be subjected to all sorts of vexations and persecutions on the ground of disloyalty to his nation. Other uses he subsequently made of these and similar facts, giving them an enlarged application (Phil. iii.), and directing them with exclusive intent to objects then engaging his thought; but, at present, he only individualizes far enough to prove that the "false apostles" had no advantage over him as to national ties.

II. As TO THE MINISTRY OF THE LORD JESUS. Do these men claim to be Christ's ministers? Whatever they might assume to be in this regard, *he* (speaking as one beside himself) "was more." And what evidence shall he give of the fact that he *was more*? Shall he point to his wonderful successes? "He proceeds to mention, as the reason for his pre-eminence, no illustrious achievements or wonderful results he had accomplished, but difficulties, troubles, conflicts, perils" (Kling). Could more be condensed in the same number of words than he compresses in one short verse? The " more" means " in labours more abundant, in stripes above measure, in prisons more frequent, in deaths oft." But he will furnish particular illustrations of the statement just made. His own countrymen head the list, for " of the Jews five times received I forty stripes save one," thrice was he " beaten with rods," once stoned, thrice ship-wrecked, " a night and a day in the deep." Yet this is only a partial account, and he offers other instances of his superior devotion as a minister of Christ. There were his frequent journeys, and what a history of perils!—perils of waters, perils of robbers, perils by his own countrymen, perils by the heathen, perils in the city, perils in the wilderness, perils in the sea; did not this enumeration exhaust the sad experience? Nay; one pictures him pausing at this point and falling into a mood of most touching reflection. To one who loved the name of brother in Christ as he did, who recalled how Ananias had come to him at Damascus and addressed him as " Brother Saul," and who remembered how often it had cheered him to be recognized and honoured as a brother in the ministry, what could be more oppressive to his spirit than to write at the last, " perils among *false brethren*"? Thus closes the account of perils. Have his sorrows all been catalogued? The outward sufferings have been generalized in classes of peril and in forms of physical torture.   Enough has been said to make good his claim to pre-eminence in affliction for the cause of Christ.   Outside of the duties he was discharging as the Lord's servant, not one of these evils had befallen him.   It was the cross of Christ, and only the cross, which had brought all these upon him.   But he had more to say.   A man of feeble health, of acute nervous sensibility, struggling with disease and infirmity; who among us can enter into all he meant by "weariness and painfulness, watchings often, hunger and thirst, fastings often, cold and naked-ness"?   It is only a rude outline; imagine the details.   But what were details to him?   The rapid summation shows why he writes.   Artistic eff ct offers him no temptation.   Literary motives are impossible to his imagination and tastes.   The eagerness of his spirit, approaching a topic most dear to his soul, hurries him to "the care of all the Churches."   Ah! that was something transcendent.   *Daily* it came upon him amidst weariness, painfulness, and other ills, and *daily* it came as a crowd pressing upon him with anxieties beyond utterance.   Sympathy is incapable of complete expression.   It cannot make itself known.   It can only make itself felt, and therefore contents itself with hints.   "Who is weak," sympathy asks, "and I am not weak?"   And who is overcome by temptation (made to stumble), and I burn not?   The sympathetic man is now deeply moved, and his heart breaks forth, "If I must needs glory, I will glory of the things which concern mine infirmities [my weakness]."

III. THE TRUE NATURE OF HIS BOASTING.   Examine this fragment of St. Paul's biography, and what do you find as the shaping thought?   It is the idea of suffering as expressive of human infirmity.   Suffering for a moral purpose is continually kept before the mind, and, agreeably to that end, it is suffering that not only humbles its subject in a spiritual point of view, but humiliates him in the eyes of the world.   Hence the conclusion to which he brings the mournful narration, "If I must needs glory, I will glory of the things which concern my weakness."   No doubt it seemed very strange to many that he should boast of these things, but this was its justification.   Had it not appeared as "folly," it would not have vindicated him against the malicious taunts of his adversaries; for it is exactly such a "folly" as identifies his life and experience with the "foolishness" of the gospel, the preaching of Christ crucified, on which, at the outset, he had laid a very distinctive stress.   Boast he must to meet the low state of intellect and spirituality in those of the Church who had fallen under the influence of these self-aggrandizing "apostles."   Boast he would in defence of himself, of his motives and intentions.   Yet, while stooping to such a worldly method, he would do so in no carnal spirit, but as one who had a profound sense of his own unworthiness.   What did the Jewish world think of his apostleship?   Let the five times "forty stripes save one" answer.   What did the Roman world think of it?   The thrice "beaten with rods" was the reply.   No allusion is made to his having been a "blasphemer" and "persecutor," for this had no bearing on the question at issue.   It is a contrast throughout of himself with the "deceitful workers."   And, finally, to make the contrast as perfect as possible, he refers to "the care of all the Churches" among the Gentiles.   This point reached, he shows why he had made these concessions to the folly of certain Corinthians, and his true heart exclaims, "If I must needs glory, I will glory of the things which concern my weakness."   Here, then, we have the first distinct appearance of one among those great thoughts that we find frequently in various forms in his subsequent writings—*the idea of glorying in his infirmities.*   Not enough is it for him to accept it as a burden and tolerate it as a thing providentially ordained to be borne.   From this hour he enters on a higher experience, for he has learned to cherish a sentiment as well as find a duty and a principle in his infirmities.   He will welcome them, he will press them to his heart as a treasure, he will "glory" in them.   And if, hereafter, we shall often listen to his exultation when he rejoices in tribulation and glories in the cross, we can revert to the time and circumstances that first made this experience an era in his career.   No wonder that he appeals with such solemnity to God for the truths asserted.   It is a moment of impassioned thought which brings the past most vividly before his eye, and lo! the opening scene in a long series of afflictions for the gospel.   There it was—the far-off Syrian city of the Damascenes, and the beginning of that persecution which the Jews had continued so unrelentingly.   And there, too, it had been announced to Ananias in a vision that the Lord had made Saul of Tarsus "a chosen vessel" unto himself, and would show him "how great things he must suffer." Straightway the revelation of sorrow began, for the stay at Damascus was interrupted by a conspiracy of the Jews, and he sought refuge in Arabia. All the intervening years had been years of suffering, the first link of the unbroken chain forged by the hatred of the Jews at Damascus, the last up to this period forged by the same hands at Corinth, and the issue of his experience was that he had learned to glory in his weakness.—L.

Ver. 4.—*A different gospel.* That the apostle was pained, distressed, and mortified by the partial success with which the false teachers, his opponents, had met at Corinth, is very obvious from his bitter and sarcastic language. He reproached the Corinthians that, indebted as they were to his labours, and grateful as they had shown themselves for the benefits conferred upon them through him, they were nevertheless ready to forget the lessons they had learned and the teacher they had revered, and to allow themselves to be led away into false and delusive doctrines.

I. That is a different gospel which proclaims another Jesus. The Judaizing teachers acknowledged that Jesus of Nazareth was the Messiah, but they seem to have represented him as merely human, as merely a prophet, as destitute of Divine claims upon the faith and reverence of men. The form of error changes, whilst the substance remains. In our own day there are public teachers who commend Jesus to the admiration and the imitation of men, but who ridicule or despise the notion that he is the one Saviour, that he is the rightful Lord, of humanity.

II. That is a different gospel which breathes another spirit than that of the New Testament. The Judaizers taught the doctrine of the letter, the doctrine of bondage to the Law. In this their religion was contradictory to the religion of Jesus, of Paul, of John, who upheld the religion of liberty, who taught that the heart inflamed with Divine love will itself prompt to deeds of obedience, who discountenanced the merely formal and mechanical compliance with the letter of the Law, as altogether insufficient. In our own day there are those who láy all stress upon the form, upon that which is external and bodily ; these proclaim a "different gospel."

III. That is a different gospel which neglects to offer the free salvation of God to sinful man. Whether this be the consequence of a defective view of man's sinful condition, or of a failure to enter into the glorious counsels of Divine compassion, or of an unworthy desire to retain a priestly power in their own hands, the result is that, if there be anything that can be called a gospel, it is a different gospel. In truth, there is but one gospel—that which is the power of God unto salvation to every one that believeth, a gospel which is worthy of all love and of all acceptation.—T.

Ver. 7.—*Gratuitous ministry.* It has been usual for all communities who possess religious ordinances and organizations to set apart an order of men to officiate as the representatives of the people generally, and to maintain them either by voluntary offerings or by public provision. The Lord Jesus sanctioned the maintenance of the Christian ministry by his general principle, "The labourer is worthy of his hire." And no one has more vigorously vindicated the right of spiritual teachers and preachers to live at the expense of those whom they benefit than has the Apostle Paul. Yet for himself, as the text and context prove, he was determined to waive this right, and to preach the gospel of God for nought. Why was this ?

I. The principle of gratuitous ministry is the benevolence and sacrifice of Christ. Of our Lord Jesus we know that, though he was rich, yet for our sake he became poor, that he had not where to lay his head, that he had no possessions in this world which was yet his own. The spirit of the Master has in a greater or less measure penetrated the disciples. They have felt the force of the appeal, "Freely ye have received, freely give." No other religion has a supernatural power mighty enough to overcome the selfishness and self-seeking so characteristic of human nature.

II. The aim of gratuitous ministry is the salvation of men. It is not expected that men should labour without fee or reward in order to supply the ordinary bodily and social wants of their fellow-men. The apostle preached at Corinth amidst weakness, weariness, discouragement, and ingratitude, because he sought the spiritual welfare of the population of that wealthy, intellectual, but profligate city. His heart was moved by the spectacle of vice and idolatry which encumbered him on every side, and, being in possession of the true and only remedy, he sought to bring it within the reach and urge it upon the acceptance of all.

III. THE SPECIAL PURPOSE OF GRATUITOUS MINISTRY IS TO REMOVE THE MINISTRY ABOVE THE SUSPICION OF INTERESTED MOTIVES. It is upon this that the Apostle Paul in this passage lays such stress. There were professing Christians who were ready enough to bring the charge of covetousness against the apostle of the Gentiles, and so to undermine his credit and authority. There was one way in which such designs might be surely and conclusively defeated, and, although this was a way involving self-denial to himself, Paul adopted it. He laboured with his hands, he accepted help from the poor Christians of Macedonia, so that he might hold himself altogether free from any suspicion of working at Corinth for the sake of anything he might receive from the Corinthians. Herein he exemplified his own axiom, "All things are lawful, but all things are not expedient."

APPLICATION. 1. Learn the wonderful and unique power of the Christian religion, which alone is capable of vanquishing the sinful selfishness of human nature. 2. Learn the importance of so acting as not to leave room even for suspicion or calumny to injure Christian character and cripple Christian usefulness.—T.

Vers. 13—15.—*Hypocrisy.* Like his Divine Master, the Apostle Paul, although compassionate to the penitent, was severe with the hypocritical. The vehement language he here uses with reference to his opponents and detractors is not to be attributed to personal resentment, but to a stern and righteous indignation against those who sought to undermine his just influence, and so to hinder the progress of his gospel.

I. THE MANIFESTATIONS OF HYPOCRISY. 1. What these hypocrites professed to be: "ministers of righteousness," and "apostles of Christ." They posed as such, and with many of the guileless and unwary they passed as such. As far as profession, pretension, and language went, all was well. 2. What they really were: "false apostles," and "deceitful workers." They had no real grasp of Christian truth; they gave no real evidence of Christian principle; they consequently could do no real spiritual work for the good of the people.

II. THE MOTIVE OF HYPOCRISY. Some characters seem to find a pleasure in dissimulation and deception for their own sake; but usually the motive is (1) to gain influence over others, and enjoy their respect and support; and (2) in this way to exalt themselves and secure their own selfish ends.

III. THE GREAT PROTOTYPE OF HYPOCRISY. This is to be found in Satan himself, who "fashioneth himself into an angel of light." It is the wont of the tempter, the adversary of souls, to proceed by fraud, to invent specious pretexts for sin, and to give to vice the semblance of virtue. It is wise to bear in mind that, whilst we have sometimes to resist the devil and his open assaults, we have at other times to be wise as serpents, that we may "not be ignorant of his devices."

IV. THE DISCOMFITURE AND EXPOSURE OF HYPOCRISY. Hypocritical teachers of religion and pretenders to authority may for a time escape detection by their fellow-men, and may for a time be suffered by an overruling Providence to lead astray, if possible, the very elect. But the day is coming which shall test every man and shall try every man's work. The earthly course of the hypocrites may be according to their words, according to appearances. But their "end shall be according to their works." By these they must be judged, and, since these are evil, by these they shall be condemned.—T.

Ver. 23.—*Ministers of Christ.* It was not congenial to St. Paul's nature to boast. He would have preferred to keep himself in the background, that his Lord might be prominent and might attract the attention and the admiration of all men. But his apostolic authority and consequently the value of his life-work, the credibility of his doctrines, the soundness of the Churches he had founded, were all at stake. As to his national position, that was comparatively immaterial. But the great question was this—Was he, or was he not, a true minister of Christ? His adversaries made great pretensions; he had no choice but to overwhelm them with his own unrivalled credentials: "Are they ministers of Christ? . . . I more!"

I. TRUE MINISTERS ARE APPOINTED BY CHRIST. Whatever be the human, the ecclesiastical agency by which men are summoned to, prepared for, employed in, the ministry of the gospel, all true Christians are agreed that the real appointment is by the Divine Head of the Church. It is he who, from the throne of his glory, places one minister in this position, and another in that, holding the stars in his right hand.

II. TRUE MINISTERS ARE WITNESSES TO CHRIST. It was Paul's justifiable boast " We preach not ourselves, but Christ Jesus the Lord." His ministry had for its one great theme the character, the life, the sacrifice, the redemption of the Divine Saviour. A ministry which, professing to be Christian, is concerned with anything rather than with Christ, discredits and condemns itself. Inadequate as is all human witness to our Lord, it is required to be sincere and outspoken.

III. TRUE MINISTERS ARE FOLLOWERS OF CHRIST. Upon this the apostle lays great stress. His own ministry was, in many of its circumstances, a copy of his Lord's. His labours, privations, and sufferings were all akin to those of the Lord whose spirit he shared, and in whose steps he trod. The outward circumstances of the ministerial life may vary, but the temper and aim must ever be those of the Divine Master.

IV. TRUE MINISTERS LOOK FOR THEIR REWARD TO CHRIST. Had the apostle expected an earthly recompense for all he undertook and underwent, bitter indeed would have been his disappointment. But he and every faithful minister must have one supreme desire and aim—to receive the approval and the acceptance of the Divine Lord himself.—T.

Ver. 23.—*Labours and prisons.* This is one of those passages which enable us to institute a comparison between the Book of the Acts and the apostolic Epistles. It is true that some of the circumstances alluded to in the context have nothing corresponding with them in St. Luke's narrative. But this exception proves the independence of the documents, whilst the coincidences, which are numerous and striking, confirm our faith in the authority and validity of both.

I. THE VARIOUS ENDURANCES INVOLVED IN THE APOSTOLIC LIFE. 1. *Labours* abounded, both of body and of mind; almost incessant toil was continued throughout long years. Journeyings, preaching, writing, were a constant strain upon his whole nature. 2. *Hardships, sufferings, perils,* and *persecutions* were even more painful to endure. There are many, especially in the prime of life, to whom toil and effort are congenial; but none can do other than shrink from pains and imprisonments. Paul's enumeration of his privations and afflictions shows how deep an impression they had made upon his nature.

II. THE AIM OF THE APOSTOLIC LIFE IN VIEW OF WHICH THESE EXPERIENCES WERE CHEERFULLY ACCEPTED. His purpose was, not his own exaltation, but the spread of the gospel and the salvation of his fellow-men. His benevolent heart found in the extension of that kingdom, which is "righteousness, peace, and joy in the Holy Ghost," an object worthy of all his devotion and all his endurance.

III. THE MOTIVE OF THE APOSTOLIC LIFE. If it be asked—How came St. Paul to voluntarily engage in a service which involved experiences so bitter? there is but one solution of the problem, but that is a sufficient and satisfactory one : "The love of Christ constrained" him. No inferior motive can be relied upon for the production of such results.

IV. THE PRACTICAL ADVANTAGES ACCRUING TO MANKIND FROM THIS APOSTOLIC LIFE. 1. It has an *evidential* value. Why should such a man as Saul of Tarsus have lived a life of obloquy, poverty, and suffering? Is any other explanation credible than this —that he knew and felt that he was witnessing to the truth? 2. It has a *moral* value, both in the beneficent results of the ministry and in the illustration afforded of the power of the gospel and of the Spirit of Christ to raise a true Christian above the control of influences and interests merely earthly and human.—T.

Ver. 28.—*Anxiety for the Churches.* Bodily labour and even suffering are sometimes felt to be less oppressive than mental anxiety and care. The Apostle Paul was familiar with all alike; and in his case a peculiarly sensitive and sympathetic nature caused him to feel more keenly and constantly than others might have done the pressure of daily anxiety for the welfare of the converts he had made and the Churches he had founded.

I. THE REASONS FOR ANXIETY WITH REGARD TO THE CHURCHES. 1. Their immaturity.

They had been in existence but a few years, and were subject to the natural disadvantages of youth and inexperience. They needed diligent watching and tender, fostering care. 2. Their exposure to the insidious efforts of false teachers. Some of these sought to lead the Christians of the first age back into Judaism, others strove to introduce licence and lawlessness. 3. Their constantly recurring needs. Some needed the visits of evangelists or the appointment of pastors. Others needed the instructions or counsels which circumstances might render appropriate.

II. The practical promptings of apostolic anxiety. We see the evidences of Paul's sincere solicitude for the Churches in: 1. His frequent visits, by which he brought his personal influence to bear upon those whose welfare he sought and who naturally looked to him for help. 2. His Epistles, full of clear statement, convincing reasoning, earnest persuasion, and faithful warning. 3. His selection and appointment of devoted fellow-labourers to assist him in the superintendence and edification of the youthful communities. 4. His fervent prayers, which abounded on behalf of all in whose spiritual well-being he was interested.

III. The profitable lessons of apostolic anxiety. 1. A general lesson of mutual interest and sympathy. Who can read this language without feeling to what an extent it enforces the scriptural precept?—"Look not every man upon his own things, but every man also upon the things of others." 2. A special lesson of mutual helpfulness as the duty and privilege of all who occupy positions of influence and authority in Christ's Church. Some forms of Church government tend rather to isolate Christian communities than to draw them together. This tendency may be happily counteracted by compliance with the precept implicitly contained in this declaration of the apostle.—T.

Vers. 2, 3.—*Pastoral anxiety.* How little understood by most believers! What strange notions many form of ministerial experience! To not a few the pastor appears a monarch with a minimum of duties and cares, and whose lot has thus fallen in singularly easy and pleasant places. But what a heavy burden is carried by the most prosperous minister! He who seems to be surrounded by all that can make his ministry cheering and his life happy is agitated by a host of disquieting thoughts and pressed upon by innumerable anxieties. So was it with that amazingly successful minister, the Apostle Paul. Following his line of thought, we may gain some knowledge of a true pastor's experience.

I. The pastor's earnest desire. 1. *That his testimony may not be ineffective.* Sorely burdened is that pastor's heart whose words seem to fall to the ground. He has a great object in his earnest appeals; if these fail, his strength has been spent for nought, his life fails. To preach on and on, and yet to see no spiritual result, strains his heartstrings till they threaten to snap. Hope deferred makes the heart sick, and, if the people of his charge are merely interested or amused by his preaching, he cries, "Woe is me!" 2. *That those to whom he preaches may be truly converted.* He desires that they may be united to Christ as a bride to her husband (ver. 2). He is not satisfied with their thinking or speaking well of Christianity, or with their outward observance of religious duties; his longing is for their real redemption and for their thorough consecration to Christ. If he be faithful, he aims to attach them, not to himself, but to his Master. His joy is full only when they are married to Christ, and live as those who are no longer their own. For this he longs, prays, labours, agonizes. 3. *That at last they may appear in holiness before Christ.* "That I might present you as a pure virgin to Christ" (ver. 2). The true pastor desires, not only that his people should start in the Christian race, but that they should continue, and at last attain to the "crown of righteousness." Flash-in-the-pan conversions please none but fools. Pastoral anxiety is largely the anxiety of watching development. The man of God has the toil and care of building up spiritual life. He counts that labour lost, so far as the objects of it are concerned, which has no abiding effects. The merest flash of thought will reveal the multitude of disappointments certain to crowd upon his soul.

II. The pastor's constant dread. This dread is lest his converts should fall away. Lest it should be made evident that the good seed has, after all, fallen upon the wayside, or into stony places, or amongst destructive thorns. He remembers: 1. *The power of the tempter.* Perhaps, like Paul, he calls to mind the fall of Eve, and remembers how much the children are like their mother. He feels the power of temptation in himself; he sees others fall; he wonders whether his own converts will yield. They are his crown of rejoicing when they stand fast; his crown of thorns when they fall. 2. *The weakness of the human heart.* He remembers the old nature still within them —their infirmities, their tendencies to trust to their own strength. They seem to be easy prey for the devil. 3. *The subtlety of false human teachers.* So many other gospels besides the true will be preached to them—adroitly contrived, it may be, to pander to the carnality still remaining within them. Called by seductive names—bearing the name of Christ possibly, and yet inimical to his kingdom and person. Philosophies falsely so called, and philosophers as full of confidence and conceit as of emptiness, and yet presenting to shallow judgments the appearance of the fulness of wisdom.

III. THE PASTOR'S JEALOUSY. 1. *A watchful jealousy.* He will have to give account of the souls entrusted to his care, so dares not be careless. He loves his flock, and therefore watches over it. He watches for the approach of peril, if peradventure he may avert it. He jealously scrutinizes all influences affecting his charge. His Master is the shepherd; he is the watch-dog. 2. *A warning jealousy.* His keen feelings lead to solemn admonitions when needed. He barks, and, when occasion arises, even bites; faithful are the wounds of such a friend. A short shrift is the desert of a pastor who is but a dumb dog. Pity it is if our feelings are so fine that we cannot rebuke men to save them from perdition. Silver bells are all very well for seasons of festivity, but when the fire blazes forth we must swing lustily the rough alarm-bell in the turret. He is a poor surgeon who is too tender-hearted to use the knife. If we love people very much we shall be willing to hurt them that we may heal them. An unwarning jealousy is not worth a farthing a bushel. It is a poor sham. 3. *A godly jealousy.* (Ver. 2.) (1) Jealousy which centres in *the welfare of others* rather than in gratification at their attachment to the minister of Christ. (2) Jealousy which is concerned pre-eminently with the honour of God. The falls of professed Christians bring dishonour upon the cause of Christ. (3) Jealousy wrought in the heart by God himself. A right feeling, since God has given it place in the pastor's heart. (4) Jealousy which allies with God. Leading to prayer, communion with God, dependence upon him in every strait.—H.

Vers. 7—12.—*Misinterpretation.* I. OUR BEST ACTS MAY BE MISINTERPRETED. Acts of the greatest nobility and unselfishness have often been. The world's greatest benefactors have tasted the bitterness of being misunderstood. 1. We should not judge of our acts by man's estimate of them. 2. We should not be surprised by any interpretation put on them. 3. We should not be dismayed by any interpretation. 4. We should rejoice that we have a higher, wiser, and more impartial tribunal than the human. Our Master said, " Woe unto you when all men shall speak well of you! " (Luke vi. 26)—a pregnant warning to those who live upon the approval of men!

II. MISINTERPRETATION SHOULD NOT HINDER US FROM CONTINUING IN A RIGHT COURSE. 1. We have not to give account to men, but to God. 2. To change our conduct might not avoid misinterpretation, but rather give occasion for it (ver. 12).

III. MISINTERPRETATION MAY BE MET AT SUITABLE TIMES BY EXPLANATION AND JUSTIFICATION OF CONDUCT. 1. It is well to take away occasion for misinterpretation. Misinterpretation, like martyrdom, should not be courted. Both should be borne heroically when they meet us in the path of duty. 2. It is often well to show that misinterpretation is misinterpretation. We should not forget that misinterpretation may (1) injure our usefulness; (2) injure those who misinterpret us; (3) bring dishonour upon Christ. In this matter we have need to be wise as serpents and harmless as doves.—H.

Ver. 14.—*A very beautiful angel.* I. A STARTLING FACT. We learn from Paul that the most sable of Ethiopians can change his skin and the fiercest beast of prey throw off his warning garb. The blackest devil can appear as the brightest angel. This is, indeed, a transfiguration, the most marvellous of transformation scenes. As an angel of wisdom Satan appeared to Eve; as an angel versed in theology, to Christ, glibly crying, " It is written." Satan *was* an angel of light. He thus knows well how to play the angel. Herein is he to be feared. It is not the ugly devil we need dread so much as the pretty devil. The old Scotchman's comment on the horned and hoofed Satan of a celebrated picture of " The Temptation " is full of point : " If that chiel cam' to me in sic an ugly shape, I think he wud hae a teuch job wi' me too."

II. An explanation of some mysteries. 1. *The power of temptation.* Men frequently fall before *white* temptations rather than *black* ones. Satan is an adept at whitewashing the sepulchre. The voice that calls us to sin sounds often more like the voice of an angel than the voice of a devil. The great adversary *transforms his temptations* as well as himself. 2. *That wrong often seems much like right.* Satan is a clever editor. 3. *That folly often seems wisdom.* A most dexterous counsel is the devil ; as we listen to him, folly is evidently wisdom, and wisdom certainly folly. His splendid intellect overmasters ours when we cope with him alone.

III. An impressive warning. 1. *To ever be on our guard.* We need have our wits about us whilst we have such an enemy about us. To be careless in such peril would be suicidal. Our guard should be severe ; none should be admitted within the gates but proved friends. 2. *Not to judge by appearances.* Our tendency is to do so, and *therefore* the devil transforms himself. " There is a way which seemeth right unto a man, but the end thereof are the ways of death " (Prov. xiv. 12). We must get below the surface of things. We must *take pains* to ascertain the right and the good. Every trap is baited, and the fool who concludes that there can be no difference between a bait and a meal, is soon caught. 3. *To seek true wisdom and discernment.* Conceit in our own unaided powers is just what delights the devil, and he often preaches to us an angelic discourse upon the pleasing theme of our wonderful faculties, before demonstrating our unutterable folly and weakness. We need know that we are know-nothings. Self-distrust baulks Satan. When a man is on the pinnacle of pride he can easily deal with him, but when he is in the valley of humility and self-abnegation the enemy gets sorely perplexed. Let us empty ourselves of the wind of conceit and self-sufficiency, that God may fill us with his own wisdom. 4. *To ever abide with Christ.* Thus alone can we be truly safe. Here alone shall we secure the victory. Christ overcame the devil when he spake least like a devil, and, if we are truly *with Christ,* no disguise of Satan shall deceive us, and no might of his shall overthrow us. The cross of Christ is Ithuriel's spear, which, touching the tempter, reveals him in his true character.—H.

Vers. 23—33.—*Apostolic experiences on earth.* I. These experiences, as narrated here, assume a gloomy character. 1. *Painful.* (1) *Bodily suffering.* Excessive toil, prison privations, scourgings, stoning, shipwrecks, a night and day in the deep, sleeplessness, coldness, foodlessness, nakedness. (2) *Mental suffering.* (*a*) Persecution from Jews as well as Gentiles. His "own countrymen" hated him more fiercely than any. (*b*) Hostility of false brethren. Peculiarly painful to such a noble nature as Paul's. (*c*) Anxieties respecting the numerous Churches. (*d*) Acute sympathy with the weak and hindered ones (ver. 29). 2. *Perilous.* What a catalogue of perils in ver. 26 ! how extreme the one instanced in vers. 32, 33 ! how pathetic and suggestive the expression, " in deaths oft " (ver. 23) ! Paul lived on the margin of the next world. Of him was it peculiarly true that he knew not what a day would bring forth.

II. Much of the painful and perilous experience of the apostle arose from his marvellous zeal and enterprise. He might have avoided not a little by : 1. *Being only moderately active.* That delightful "mean" coveted by so many— it was too *mean* for Paul ! 2. *Being more compliant.* If he had been a man of *expediency,* and not, as he was, a man of *principle.* If he had bent to the storm ; but he intended that the storm should *bend to him,* or rather to those God-truths which he proclaimed. 3. *Placing God's honour in the second place.* The servant was persecuted so vindictively because he would talk so much of his Master. It was not *Paul* that Jew and Gentile hated so much, but Christ ; but where Paul was there men could hear of nothing but the contemned Nazarene. 4. *Loving himself more than a perishing world.* It was a question which should suffer, Paul or the world ; Paul said, " I will." *In his sphere* he thus imitated his Lord, who, though he was rich, for our sakes became poor.

III. No suffering or peril succeeded in damping the apostolic ardour. How keen must have been his love for Christ and for his fellow-men ! Ever before him he had the future exaltation of Christ and the "saving some." We have here a marvellous triumph of mind over matter, and a still more marvellous one of spirituality over carnality. The life of the apostle was so vigorous that he could bear to die daily.

What little aches and pains stop us! An avalanche of grief and trial failed to arrest Paul!

IV. IT WAS ONLY WHEN SUBJECTED TO GREAT PRESSURE, AND THEN ONLY UNDER PROTEST, THAT THE APOSTLE ALLOWED HIMSELF TO DWELL UPON THIS PERPETUAL MARTYRDOM. He rejoiced in it; yet he did not like to speak about it. He almost calls himself a fool for doing so. The martyr has sometimes sullied his crown by pride; but the apostolic affliction seemed strangely sanctified to him. Some are *not great enough* to suffer much for Christ. God does not allow it. It would make them so intolerable that prayer would ascend on all hands for their transference to a world where they would have a humble opinion of themselves. Paul went through all the privation, anguish, peril, catalogued here, *and came out from it with the spirit of a little child.*—H.

Ver. 3.—*The simplicity in Christ.* "So your minds should be corrupted from the simplicity that is in Christ." Some manuscripts read, "simplicity and chastity." By the term "simplicity" is first meant "singleness of affection," "single-minded devotion to Christ," and the word is used in connection with the marriage figure of vers. 1, 2. It should be remembered that, in the East, the time of espousal is regarded as sacred, and any infidelities during the time of espousal are treated as adulteries are after marriage. In St. Paul's conception the Church is the espoused bride of Christ, and he had been the means of arranging the espousal in the case of the Church at Corinth. "What the apostle now urges is that it is as natural for him to be jealous for the purity of the Church which owes its birth to him, as it is for a father to be jealous for the chastity of the daughter whom he has betrothed as to a kingly bridegroom." The older theocratic figure of idolatry as adultery, which so often appears in the books of the prophets, should be compared with this. The term "simplicity" may, however, be more full and suggestive to us, and mean singleness of devotion to Christ, entireness of service to him, unmixed love for him. F. W. Robertson says that the expression, "the simplicity of the gospel," is constantly mistaken. "People suppose simplicity means what a child or a ploughman can understand. Now, if this be simplicity, evidently the simplicity of the gospel was corrupted by St. Paul himself; for he is not simple. Who understands his deep writings? Does one in a thousand? St. Peter says there are things hard to be understood in St. Paul's Epistles. We often hear it alleged as a charge against a book, a lecture, or a sermon, that it is not simple. If we are told that what we are to preach must be on a level with the most inferior intellect, so that without attention or thought it may be plain to all, we are bound to disclaim any obligation to do this; if it is supposed that the mysteries of God, of which we are the stewards, can be made as easy of comprehension as an article in a newspaper or a novel, we say that such simplicity can only be attained by shallowness. There must be earnestness, candour, patience, and a certain degree of intelligence, as well as a sort of sympathy between the minds of the preacher and his hearers, and there must be a determination to believe that no man who endeavours to preach the gospel will deliberately and expressly say what he knows to be false or wrong. 'Simple' means, according to St. Paul, unmixed or unadulterated."

I. THE PLACE OF CHRIST IN THE CHURCH. It is as unique as that of the husband in relation to the wife. A place that can know no rivalry. Christ is Head, Lord, Husband. "One is your Master, even Christ, and all ye are brethren." The old testimony is renewed for the Christian spheres, "Hear, O Israel, the Lord your God is *one Lord.*" "One Lord, one faith, one baptism." No earthly teachers may push into his place. No claim of Judaic ceremonies may spoil the trust in and devotion to him. "Him first, him midst, him last, him all in all." The bride has but one Husband, even Christ.

II. THE SPIRIT OF THE CHURCH TOWARDS CHRIST. It is that full loyalty which follows upon setting our whole affection on Christ, and which finds expression in all loving submissions and obediences. It is precisely set before us by the great apostle when he says, "To me to live in Christ." "I live, yet not I, but Christ liveth in me."

III. THE TEMPTATIONS TO WHICH THE CHURCH IS EXPOSED. Answering to the disloyalty of a wife. And such temptations may take forms of subtlety, like those presented by the serpent to Eve. In every age there are things which tend to take the mind and heart from Christ. Nowadays it is worldliness, self-indulgence, the beautiful in art, and the fascination of scientific knowledge. We want now to love and serve so many things much and Christ a little, and still the old message sounds forth, " If a man forsake not all that he hath, he cannot be my disciple." St. Paul counted " all things loss for Christ," and would have nothing—Mosaic rite, human philosophy, or aught else—come between him and his one Lord.—R. T.

Ver. 4.—*One Jesus, one Spirit, one gospel.* Evidently St. Paul recognized a vital distinction between the Christ whom he preached and the Christ preached by the teachers of the Judaic party. The Christ whom he preached was the " Friend and Brother of mankind, who had died for all men that he might reconcile them to God." The Christ whom they preached was the " head of a Jewish kingdom, requiring circumcision and all the ordinances of the Law as a condition of admission to it." St. Paul could see no gospel, no good news, in such a Christ as that. By " another Jesus " we may understand Jesus otherwise presented ; "another spirit " is something opposed to the spirit of liberty in Christ from Mosaic ordinances ; and by " another gospel " the apostle means something different from the good news of God reconciled to faith. " His gospel was one of pardon through faith working by love ; theirs was based on the old Pharisaic lines of works, ritual, ceremonial and moral precepts, standing in their teaching on the same footing." Here St. Paul makes distinct claim to be the authorized teacher of the truth, and we consider this claim.

I. THE SENSE IN WHICH APOSTOLIC TEACHING WAS FINAL. In relation to this modern opinion differs from the older opinion, and therefore the subject needs to be treated with extreme care and prudence. When the generally received doctrine of inspiration was that known as the *verbal* theory, which affirmed the direct communication from God of every word of Scripture, the apostles were regarded as inspired for every detail of Gospels and Epistles, and appeal to their expressions was regarded as final. We now more clearly see that they were inspired to guide men's thoughts, but not to fetter them, or force them into precise moulds. The apostles do fix the lines along which Christian thought may safely run, but they leave full room for the diversities and idiosyncrasies of men to find free expression. They make a firm stand, and plainly show the boundaries of Christian thinking, but within the lines they leave us free. We properly use our own cultured Christian judgment—in the leadings of the Holy Ghost —upon the value of their arguments, and the precise applications of their counsels. And this appears to us quite consistent with a becoming reverence for these divinely endowed men, and necessary to that personal leading of the Holy Ghost, which we are permitted to realize as well as they. God's truth for the race can be set within no permanent bonds, even though men may call them apostolic.

II. THE LIMITS WITHIN WHICH DIVERSITY CAN BE PERMITTED. 1. There can be no dispute with regard to the great Christian *facts.* 2. There can be no attempt to alter the supreme position of Christ in his Church and relation to his Church. There is nothing so essentially Christian as the truth of the direct relation of the soul to Christ, a relation that is independent of doctrine, creed, ceremonial, or priesthood, though these all have their place. 3. There are great foundation truths and principles which may be stated in simple and comprehensive terms, but outside of which, or contrary to which, Christian thought cannot safely run. None may take from us our " liberty in Christ," but we may wisely " hold fast the form of sound words."

III. THE WAYS IN WHICH APOSTOLIC TEACHING MIGHT BE IMPERILLED. Unfold and illustrate the following ways. 1. By overloading it with the old. 2. By overstraining it to fit the new. 3. By applying it in a spirit that is out of harmony with its principles. 4. By the pressure of the peculiarities of men who are strongly self-willed. 5. By translating the claims into the things we should *like* to do, rather than into the things which we *ought* to do. 6. By permitting the common philosophy and sociology of men to give tone to the Christian revelation, rather than to make Christianity tone them.

IV. THE TESTS BY WHICH SUCH PERVERSIONS OF APOSTOLIC TEACHINGS MIGHT BE DISCOVERED. The all-sufficing tests of any teaching, under the influence of which we may come—whether it be teachings of the pulpit or of the press—are these. 1. Is it in harmony with the first truth of the Christian revelation—the fatherhood of God ?

2. Does it uphold the honour, and the supreme administrative rights in souls, of the Lord Jesus Christ?   3. And does it practically tend towards the things that are pure, and true, and holy, and good?   Everything godly is helpful to godliness.   In conclusion, argue this point—Can we still safely receive truth upon the authority of men?   and if so, are there any limitations under which such reception is properly placed?   And are we still open and exposed to the persuasions of self-interested or self-deluded teachers?   We have to find out for these times in which we live what is the secret of "holding fast the faith once delivered to the saints."—R. T.

Vers. 10, 21—30.—*Apostolic boastings.*   This is a most reproachful passage, and the intensity of St. Paul's feeling can only be accounted for by some knowledge of the bitter and shameful treatment he was receiving from the antagonistic Jewish party at Corinth. Archdeacon Farrar, in a very vivid and forcible manner, presents the kind of things that were being freely said at Corinth about the apostle.   " He had shown feebleness in his change of plan; his personal appearance, feeble and infirm, did not match the authoritative tone of his letters; his speech had nothing in it to command admiration ; he threatened supernatural punishments, but he did not dare to put his threats to the proof.   What right had he to claim the authority of an apostle, when he had never seen the Christ in the flesh?   Was it certain that he was a Hebrew, a Jew of the pure blood of Palestine, or even that he was of the seed of Abraham?   Who was this Paul, who came without credentials, and expected to be received on the strength of his everlasting self-assertions?   Was there not a touch of madness in his visions and revelations?   Could he claim more than the tolerance which men were ready to extend to the insane?"   "Conceive all these barbed arrows of sarcasm falling on the ears, and through them piercing the very soul, of a man of singularly sensitive nature, passionately craving for affection, and proportionately feeling the bitterness of loving with no adequate return ; and we may form some estimate of the whirl and storm of emotion in which St. Paul began to dictate the Epistle."   As a rule, *boastings* are only evil both for him who boasts and for those who hear the boasting; but no rule is without exception, and there are times when a man is absolutely driven to boasting—it is the one thing that he can do, and that he ought to do.   It becomes the plain duty of the hour.   A man may never boast until he is thus driven to it, and then his boastings will have their foundation in his humility.   The apostle's boastings had direct reference to the accusations made against him.

I. THERE WERE BOASTINGS OF HIS JEWISH BIRTH AND RIGHTS.   These had been assailed.   He was a foreign-born Jew, and the Palestine Jews rather looked down upon all such.   It was easy to raise prejudice against the apostle on this ground.   He therefore pleads the facts of his pure birth, his Pharisaic relationships, his Jerusalem training, and his manifest Jewish sympathies.   He was proud of the fact that no Jew could plead superior Jewish birthrights to his.   So far he did but boast of facts of his life that were beyond his own control.

II. THERE WERE BOASTINGS OF SUFFERINGS BORNE IN MINISTERING FOR CHRIST. See vers. 21—30, the most amazing catalogue of woes ever written.   One wonders how so frail a body could have endured them all.   But even this record we feel is holy boasting, for one can but feel that, under all the intensity of the utterance, there is a great sadness of heart in being thus compelled to speak of such things.   He never would have said one word about them had it not been that attacks upon his apostleship meant dishonour to Christ, and mischievous hindrance to Christ's work.   St. Paul never would have boasted if he had not thus been compelled to boast for *Christ's sake.* And this is the one law for us.   Never put self in the front unless so putting self will glorify our Master.   We may even boast if it is clear that our boasting will serve him.—R. T.

Ver. 14.—*Satanic subtleties.*   "Satan himself is transformed into an angel of light." This expression suggests that the Judaic party at Corinth laid claim to some angel manifestations or revelations, and set these off against St. Paul's claim of apostolic inspiration and authority.   He really asserts here that they are deluded.   It is not Divine revelations which they have received.   These things in which they boast are Satanic subtleties and transformations, by which they are deceived and ensnared.

There may, however, be a reference to what was so evidently in St. Paul's mind—the serpent's deception of Eve (ver. 3). The mode in which reference is made to the incident in the garden of Eden suggests to us that St. Paul thought the serpent put on some form of beauty, or that he, in a very subtle way, explained his superior wisdom and intelligence by the fact that he fed on the fruit of that forbidden tree.

I. THE SATANIC POWER OF DISGUISE. Illustrate the very various ways in which evil is made attractive. Apply to the temptations of vice and self-indulgence, to mental error, to religious wanderings and backslidings. He said a great thing, who, knowing much of the evils of Christian and Church life, exclaimed, "We are not ignorant of his [Satan's] devices."

II. SUCH POWER ILLUSTRATED IN RELIGIOUS LEADERS. Such as Joe Smith, the Mormon leader. All who seek to delude men for self-seeking ends are really Satanic; they are doing Satan's work. According to the standpoint of the preacher, it may be shown that the methods by which men are deluded still are (1) mental, (2) ritual, (3) moral. Therefore we have the very earnest advice, " Prove [test and try] all things; hold fast that which is good."—R. T.

Vers. 23—30.—*The evidential value of sufferings borne for Christ's sake.* Recall Paley's use of the labours and sufferings of the early Christians as an argument for the truth of Christianity. Carefully observe under what limitations such an argument must be set. There have been martyrs of all sorts of opinions. Men intense on any subject are usually willing to bear much for its sake; and the enthusiast or fanatic does not shrink from giving his life for his faith, though his faith may be unreasonable or absurd. We can only go so far as to say that willingness to bear suffering proves—

I. PERSONAL SINCERITY. Men's hearts must be in that which they will maintain at cost of toil, sorrow, disability, and pain. Christianity must be true to the man who can die for it; but it is not therefore proved to be absolutely true.

II. A DIVINE CALL OR COMMISSION. It is *one* of the indications of such a call. Not sufficient if it stands alone, but very helpful as a buttress to other arguments and considerations.

III. THAT THERE IS A FINE MORAL STRENGTH CULTURED BY CHRISTIANITY. This, perhaps, is its chief value. The noble endurance illustrates Christianity, and shows what the almighty grace in it can do. That must be worthy, and it may be Divine, which nerves men to such heroic labour, such patient submission, and such triumphs over ills and death. So, when kept within due limits and carefully combined with other considerations, the sufferings and martyrdoms of the Christian saints become an evidence of the Divine origin of Christianity.—R. T.

EXPOSITION.

CHAPTER XII.

The revelations vouchsafed to him (vers. 1—6). The counteracting "thorn in the flesh" (vers. 7—10). One more apology for glorying (vers. 11, 12). His disinterestedness (vers. 13—15). Indignant refutation of the charge that he had made gain of them through the agency of subordinates (vers. 16—18). Caution and warnings (vers. 19—21).

Ver. 1.—**It is not expedient for me doubtless to glory.** This rendering follows the best-attested reading; but it is at least doubtful whether, instead of δεῖ or δὲ, the ironic δὴ of K, M, and the Greek Fathers is not the true reading. In mere vowel variations, especially in passages where the meaning does not lie on the surface, the diplomatic (external) evidence is less important. If St. Paul wrote δὴ, it means, " of course it is not expedient for me to boast." **I will come**; *for I will come;* if the reading of D is correct. In that case it is hardly possible to define the counter-currents of feeling which caused the use of the conjunction. **Visions and revelations.** The word used for " visions " means presentations perceived in a state which is neither sleeping nor waking, but which are regarded as objective; " revelations " are the truths apprehended as a result of the visions. *Optasia,* for " visions," only occurs elsewhere in Luke i. 22; xxiv. 23; Acts xxvi. 19 (comp. Gal. ii. 2).

Ver. 2.—**I knew**; rather, *I know.* **A man.** St. Paul speaks in this indirect way of himself (see vers. 5, 7). **In Christ** (1

Cor. 'i. 30). To St. Paul every true Christian was a man whose personal life was lost in the life of Christ. **Above fourteen years ago.** The note of time is very vague. If we are *at all* able to identify the vision alluded to, it must have been the vision in the temple, referred to in Acts xxii. 17, which was, roughly speaking, "about fourteen years" before this time. The vision on the road to Damascus had occurred about twenty years earlier than the date of this Epistle. **Whether in the body,** etc. A powerful description of the absorption of all conscious *bodily* modes of apprehension. In their comments on these verses, many commentators enter into speculations which seem to me to be so entirely arbitrary and futile that I shall not even allude to them. St. Paul's bodily and mental state during this vision is familiar to all who know the history of Oriental and mediæval mysticism. **Caught up** (Ezek. xi. 24; Acts viii. 39; Rev. iv. 1, 2). **Into the third heaven.** It is most unlikely that St. Paul is here in any way referring to the Jewish *hagadoth* about seven heavens. The expression is purely general, and even the rabbis did not expect to be taken *au pied de la lettre*. Hence all speculations about first, second, and third heavens are idle and useless. Even as late as the Clementine writings in the middle of the second century, an attempt is made, in reference to this passage, to disparage St. Paul by sneering at visions as a medium of revelation, on the ground that they may spring from self-deception; and this rapture of the "bald hook-nosed Galilean" to the third heaven is also sneered at in the 'Philopatris' of the pseudo-Lucian. Yet how modest and simple is St. Paul's awestruck reference to this event, when compared, not only with the lying details of Mohammed's visit to heaven, but even with 'the visions of St. Theresa or Swedenborg!

Ver. 4.—Into Paradise. Here, again, we encounter long speculations as to whether Paradise is the same as the third heaven; whether St. Paul is referring to two visions or two parts of one vision. Such questions are clearly insoluble, and I leave them where I find them. We shall never understand this passage otherwise than in the dim and vague outline in which St. Paul has purposely left it. All that we can know from the New Testament about Paradise must be learnt from this verse and Luke xxiii. 63 and Rev. ii. 7, and it is extremely little. **Unspeakable words.** A figure of speech called an oxymoron. Utterances (or "things") incapable of utterance. **Not lawful for a man to utter.** How futile, then, must be the attempt to guess what they were, or on what subject!

Ver. 5.—Of such a one. These are legitimate subjects of "boast," because they are heavenly privileges, not earthly grounds of superiority. **Except in my infirmities** (ch. xi. 30).

Ver. 6.—I forbear; literally, *I spare;* i.e. I refrain from boasting. **Should think of me;** literally, *that no man should estimate concerning me beyond what he sees me (to be), or hears at all from my own lips.* If he were to tell them more of his revelations, he might encourage them to think more of him than he deserves or wishes.

Vers. 7.—10.—*The thorn in the flesh.*

Ver. 7.—Lest I should be exalted above measure; literally, *that I may not be over-exalted.* It was necessary to show St. Paul that he only held the treasure in an earthen vessel. **There was given me.** Even God's afflictions are meant for gifts. **A thorn** (*skolops*). The more usual meaning is, as Hesychius says, "a sharp stake" ('Sudes,' Tert.). Hence the word *skolopizō,* I impale or crucify. St. Paul's agony was an impalement or crucifixion of all sensual impulses and earthly ambitions. **In the flesh.** There have been endless conjectures as to the exact nature of this painful and most humbling physical affliction. It is only by placing side by side a great many separate passages that we are almost irresistibly led to the conclusion which is now most generally adopted, namely, that it was acute and disfiguring ophthalmia, originating in the blinding glare of the light which flashed round him at Damascus, and accompanied, as that most humiliating disease usually is, by occasional cerebral excitement. It would be impossible here to enter into the whole inquiry, for which I refer to my 'Life of St. Paul,' i. 214—226. **The messenger of Satan;** rather, *an angel of Satan.* By way of comment, see Matt. xxv. 41; Luke xiii. 16; Job ii. 7; Rev. xii. 7, 9. **To buffet me.** The verb is derived from *kolaphos,* a slap *on the face,* and would be suitable to such a disfigurement as ophthalmia (ch. x. 10).

Ver. 8.—For this thing. In reference to this or "to him," the angel of Satan. **The Lord.** That is, Christ (1 Cor. i. 3). **Thrice** (comp. Matt. xxvi. 44).

Ver. 9.—And he said unto me. The original is much more forcible: "And he *has* said to me." **Is sufficient for thee.** A similar phrase, though in a very different context, occurs in Deut. iii. 26. **My strength is made perfect in weakness** (comp. ch. iv. 7; Phil. iv. 13; 1 Cor. ii. 3—5). The verse contains a paradox, which yet describes the best history of the world. The paradox becomes more suggestive if, with א, A, B, D, F, G, we omit "*my.*" **May rest upon me**; literally, *may tabernacle over me.* The compound verb occurs here alone, but the simple verb and the substantive occur in similar meanings in John i. 14; Rev. vii. 15; xxi. 3 (comp. ch. v. 1).

Ver. 10.—I take pleasure in; *I am content to bear them cheerfully* (ch. vii. 4; Rom. v. 3). Strong; rather, *powerful, mighty.* The resemblance to Philo ('Vit. Mos.,' Opp., i. 613, "Your weakness is might") is probably accidental (see 1 Cor. xv. 54; Col. iii. 4).

Ver. 11.—A fool (see ch. xi. 16). For I ought. The "*I*" is emphatic. You compelled me to become senseless in boasting of myself to you, whereas *I* ought to have been commended by *you.* To have been commended. The verb gives one more side allusion, not without bitterness, to the *commendatory* epistles of which his adversaries boasted (ch. iii. 1; v. 12; x. 12—18). The very chiefest apostles. The same strange compound, "out-and-out apostles," is used as in ch. xi. 5; comp. Gal. ii. 6.

Ver. 12.—The signs of an apostle. St. Paul always claimed to have attested his mission by spiritual and miraculous gifts (Rom. xv. 19; Acts xv. 12).

Ver. 13.—I was not burdensome. The same word as in ch. xi. 9. Forgive me this wrong. There is an exquisite dignity and pathos mixed with the irony of this remark.

Ver. 14.—The third time I am ready to come to you. He had been ready *twice* before, though the second time his actual visit had been prevented by the scandals in their Church. That the visit which he now contemplates is a third visit, and that there was an unrecorded second visit, is a needless and improbable inference from this passage. Be burdensome (see ver. 13). Not yours, but you (1 Thess. ii. 8).

Ver. 15.—Spend and be spent; rather, *spend and be outspent,* or *spent to the uttermost* (Phil. ii. 17).

Ver. 16.—But be it so, I did not burden you. The "I" is emphatic. It is shocking to think that, even after Paul has so triumphantly cleared himself from the disgraceful charge of trying to make gain out of the Corinthians, he should still be obliged to

meet the slanderous innuendo that, even if he had not personally tried to get anything out of them, still he had done so indirectly through the agency of Titus. Being crafty, I caught you with guile. He is here quoting the sneer of his enemies (see what he has already said in ch. i. 12; vii. 2). The word used for "being" means "being by my very nature."

Ver. 17.—Did I make a gain of you, etc.? The same verb as in ch. ii. 11. It means "to overreach," "to take unfair advantages."

Ver. 18.—Titus. This refers to the first visit of Titus. He was now on the eve of a second visit with two others (ch. viii. 6, 18, 22). A brother; rather, *the brother.* Who it was is entirely unknown. Perhaps Tychicus (Titus iii. 12). In the same Spirit; namely, in the Spirit of God.

Ver. 19.—Again, think you that we excuse ourselves unto you? The best reading is not *palin,* again, but *palai,* long ago. This word with the present is an elegant classical idiom, and means, "You have, perhaps, been imagining all this time that I am pleading with you by way of self-defence. Do not think it! You are no judges of mine. My only object is to speak before God in Christ, not to defend myself—since I need no defence so far as you are concerned—but to help in building you up, by removing the falsehoods that alienate you from me."

Ver. 20.—Such as ye would not (see 1 Cor. iv. 21). Debates. "Discords," "quarrels." Strifes. "Party-intrigues," "factious and emulous rivalries" (Rom. ii. 8). Backbiting. Detractions, talkings *against* one another. Swellings. Inflated conceit, pompous egotism (1 Cor. iv. 6, 18, 19; Col. ii. 18). Tumults. Disorderly excitement (ch. vi. 5; 1 Cor. xiv. 33; comp. 1 Cor. xiii. 2, 10).

Ver. 21.—Humble me among you; rather, *in my relation to you.* Many which have sinned already, and have not repented; rather, *who have sinned before and did not repent.* Many had sinned (1 Cor. vi. 12—20); some only had repented.

HOMILETICS.

Vers. 1—5.—*Apostolic piety and psychology.* "It is not expedient," etc. These verses present two subjects of thought.

I. APOSTOLIC PSYCHOLOGY. The words reveal certain ideas which Paul had concerning the human mind. He had the idea: 1. *That whilst here it is capable of existing separate from the body.* "Whether in the body, I cannot tell; or whether out of the body, I cannot tell." If he had been certain that the soul could not exist whilst here apart from the body, would he have spoken thus? And who is not conscious of the mind having experiences in which the body does not participate? Paul speaks of himself as entering regions far away. (1) The "*third heaven.*" The Bible speaks of three heavens. (*a*) The atmospheric. There the clouds travel and perform their functions.

(*b*) The starry. There the sun, moon, and stars appear. (*c*) The heavens that lie beyond the heavenly orbs; where God and his holy angels are supposed to have their special residence. Up to this "third heaven" Paul was caught. (2) *Paradise*. "Caught up into Paradise." The word here denotes some place in the universe distinguished in beauty and fruitfulness. Paul regarded it possible for the soul to go away into those distant regions of supernal brightness and beauty. Who has not been conscious of being borne far away from the body on the wing of thought? 2. *That whilst here it is capable of receiving extraordinary revelations apart from the body.* "Heard unspeakable words." Things of the soul may be unutterable either from *necessity* or from *impropriety*. The deepest things of the heart are unutterable in any language. Perhaps what Paul saw and heard in the spirit was neither possible nor proper to communicate. There are but few of us who have not received impressions of distant things. We are often caught away to distant scenes, and see and hear extraordinary things. 3. *That whilst here it may exist apart from the body and the man not know it.* "Whether in the body, I cannot tell." He was so charged with spiritual things that he had lost all consciousness of matter and his relations to it. The man whose soul is flooded with the higher elements of being does not know for the time whether he is "in the body" or "out of the body." 4. *That wherever or however it exists it constitutes the man.* "I knew a man in Christ." That which had these wonderful revelations he regarded as the *man*. To the apostle the body was the costume of the man, which he put on at birth and took off at death. In fact, he regarded the body as his not him, the soul as himself.

II. APOSTOLIC PIETY. There are three things concerning piety here. 1. *Humility.* That the man of whom Paul here speaks is himself scarcely admits of a doubt. Why should he speak of himself in the third person? It is because of that modesty of nature which is ever the characteristic of a truly great soul. Humility is an essential attribute of piety. 2. *Christism.* "A man in Christ." To be in Christ is to live in his ideas, character, spirit, as the atmosphere of being. He who lives in the spirit of Christ becomes a man. 3. *Transport.* His soul was borne away in ecstasy. The time when the revelation occurred is specified—"fourteen years ago." Strange that he did not speak of it before. Piety has its hours of ravishments, ecstasies, and transfigurations.

Vers. 6—10.—*Soul-schooling.* "For though," etc. These words teach us several things concerning soul-discipline.

I. THAT THE EXERCISE OF SPIRITUAL DISCIPLINE IS EXPEDIENT FOR THE BEST OF MEN. Paul required it. He says, "Lest I should be exalted above measure." 1. *Pride is a great spiritual evil.* This is implied in the discipline with which the apostle was now visited. "To be exalted above measure [or, 'overmuch']" is, of course, to be proud, and to be proud is to be in a position inimical to soul-progress. 2. *Good men have sometimes great temptations to pride.* Paul's temptation seems to have arisen from the "abundance of the revelation" of which he speaks.

II. THAT THE MODE OF SPIRITUAL DISCIPLINE IS SOMETIMES VERY PAINFUL. Paul was visited with a "thorn in the flesh." What the thorn was is a question for speculation; our object is practical. Two things deserve notice here. 1. *That suffering stands connected with Satan.* This painful dispensation was a "messenger from Satan." The great original sinner is the father of suffering. 2. *Both suffering and Satan are under the direction of God.* He uses them as his instruments for good. Satan himself is the servant of the Holy One.

III. THAT THE MEANS OF SPIRITUAL DISCIPLINE ARE SOMETIMES MISUNDERSTOOD. Paul prays to be delivered from that "thorn in the flesh" which was sent for his good, and he does so frequently—"thrice." Notice: 1. *The ignorance which sometimes marks our prayers.* We often pray against our own interests. There are some blessings which are positively promised by God, such as pardon for sin, etc., for which we may pray incessantly; and there are others which we may esteem desirable, but which are not promised. These we must seek in submission to his will. 2. *The kindness of God in not always answering our prayers.* He knows what is best. The great Father may refuse the cry of his children for toys here, but he will give them estates in the great hereafter.

IV. THAT THE SUPPORTS UNDER SPIRITUAL DISCIPLINE ARE ALWAYS ABUNDANT. "My grace is sufficient for thee: for my strength is made perfect in weakness." Observe : **1.** The *nature* of the support. "Strength." What matters the weight of the burden if the strength is equal to bear it with ease? 2. The *principle* of the support. "Grace." It comes, not from merit, but from grace free and unbounded. 3. The *influence* of the support. "Most gladly therefore will I rather glory in my infirmities, that the power of Christ may rest upon me." "Rest upon me." Spread over me like a tent to screen me from the scorching sun. "I glory in my infirmities." The cup may be bitter, but it has curative virtues. Tempests may toss, but those storms will purify the atmosphere round the heart and bear us away from scenes on which our hearts are set. All prayer is answered when the mind of the suppliant is brought into cordial submission to the Divine will.

Vers. 11—21.—*Paul's state of mind concerning his past and prospective connection with the Church at Corinth.* "I am become a fool in glorying," etc. These verses throw light upon Paul's state of mind, both in relation to his *past* and *prospective* connection with the Corinthian Church.

I. HIS STATE OF MIND CONCERNING HIS PAST CONNECTION WITH THE CORINTHIAN CHURCH. 1. He remembers the *ill treatment which forced him to speak with apparent boastfulness of himself.* "I am become a fool [I am become foolish] in glorying; ye have compelled me: for I ought to have been commended of you: for in nothing am I behind the very chiefest apostles, though I be nothing." Dean Plumptre's remarks tend to illustrate Paul's state of mind. "The verse opens with a somewhat thrilling abruptness, 'I am become insane—it was you who compelled me.' The words are partly ironical, partly speak of an impatient consciousness, that what he had been saying would seem to give colour to the opprobrious epithets that had been flung at him. The passage on which we now enter, and of which we may think as begun after a pause, is remarkable for the production in a compressed form of most of the topics, each with its characteristic phrase, on which he had before dwelt. The violence of the storm is over, but the sky is not yet clear, and we still hear the mutterings of the receding thunder. He remembers once more that he has been called insane, that he has been taunted with commending himself, that he has been treated as 'nothing' in comparison with those apostles extraordinary, who were setting themselves up as his rivals. 'I,' he says, with an emphatic stress on the pronoun, 'ought to have had no need for this painful self-assertion. You ought to have acknowledged my labour and my love for you.'" 2. He remembers *the work which he had done amongst them, and which raised him above all the apostles.* "Truly the signs of an apostle were wrought among you in all patience, in signs, and wonders, and mighty deeds." Paul possessed supernatural power and wrought supernatural results in their midst. Of this they must have been aware and could not deny. Referring to his ministry there he says elsewhere, "My speech and my preaching was not with enticing words of man's wisdom, but in demonstration of the Spirit and of power" (1 Cor. ii. 4). In this respect he was, therefore, not only not behind "the very chiefest apostles," such as Peter, James, and John, but immeasurably superior to the false teachers, his traducers. Can a man who was conscious of such power as this be charged with egotism in proclaiming it in the presence of his detractors? Does he become "a fool in glorying"? Nay, nay, a wise man. 3. He remembers that for his labours amongst them *he had not sought any temporal assistance.* "For what is it wherein ye were inferior to other Churches, except it be that I myself was not burdensome to you? forgive me this wrong." Probably it had been insinuated by his traducers that Paul cared less for the Churches at Corinth than for those at Macedonia, because he had maintained his independence and sought no gifts. He seems to intimate that this was some disadvantage to them, and he asks their forgiveness. And, indeed, it seems to me it is a spiritual disadvantage to any Church not to contribute to the support of its minister; for there is more good in giving than in receiving.

II. HIS STATE OF MIND CONCERNING HIS PROSPECTIVE CONNECTION WITH THE CORINTHIAN CHURCH. 1. *Here are loving resolves.* "Behold, the third time I am ready to come to you; and I will not be burdensome to you: for I seek not yours, but you." We have no record of a second visit, but this does not disprove its existence; for no doubt there **is** more omitted of Paul's history than recorded. He resolves that in this third visit he would not be burdensome to them, but pursue the same conduct of independency towards them as he had done all along, taking nothing from them, but giving to them. " I seek not yours, but you." Act as a father generally acts towards his " children," "lay up" for them, not they for him, and gladly spend and be spent for them. And all this, whether they love him or not. What noble generosity breathes in all these resolves! 2. *Here are painful memories.* " I did not burden you: nevertheless, being crafty, I caught you with guile." This, again, is ironical. You say that, although I made no demand on your purses for myself, I want a collection for the " saints," and that out of that collection I will craftily take what I want. He seems to fling back upon them their accusation of his being crafty and catching them "with guile." " Did I make a gain of you by any of them whom I sent unto you? I desired Titus, and with him I sent a brother. Did Titus make a gain of you? walked we not in the same spirit? walked we not in the same steps?" Nay, neither they nor he had ever sponged on them, but had maintained their high independency. In saying this he deprecates the idea that he was amenable to them for his conduct, but to God only. "Again, think ye that we excuse ourselves unto you? we speak before God in Christ: but we do all things, dearly beloved, for your edifying." Thus, in the prospect of visiting Corinth once more, most painful memories of his traducers arose. 3. *Here are anxious apprehensions.* "For I fear, lest, when I come, I shall not find you such as I would, and that I shall be found unto you such as ye would not." His tender nature seemed to shrink at the supposition of the old evils still rampant there. " Lest there be debates, envyings, wraths, strifes, backbitings, whisperings, swellings, tumults." He was too brave a man to dread perils, or toils, or death. "None of these things moved " him, but from such evils as "strifes," " envyings," " wraths," " backbitings," "whisperings," " swellings," " tumults," "uncleanness," "fornication," " lasciviousness," his pure and pious nature shrank with horror. The great thing to be dreaded is sin. It is the " abominable thing," the soul-destroying devil of humanity.

CONCLUSION. 1. Do not *judge any minister by the opinions of his brethren.* Paul was the best and the most useful of men, but the opinion of his brethren was that he was the worst and the most pernicious. 2. Do not *cease in your endeavours to benefit men because they calumniate you.* The worst men require your services most, the " whole need no physician." 3. Do not *sponge upon your congregation.* Do not seek theirs, but them. Do not study how to increase your pew-rents, swell your collections and offertories, but how to increase the spiritual intelligence, freedom, and true blessedness of the people. 4. Do not *cower before anything but sin.* Sin is the Apollyon of the universe.

HOMILIES BY VARIOUS AUTHORS.

Vers. 1—6.—*Supernatural communications as evidences of his apostleship.* The old question as to his apostolic authority, which had recently been revived in a most exciting form, was not yet disposed of, and he must now discuss it in another aspect. So far as external circumstances were concerned, had not the prophetic declaration to Ananias been fulfilled?—" I will show him how great things he must suffer for my Name's sake." And, furthermore, he had proved that his own state of mind, the inward being of his soul, had corresponded with his call to suffer. The flesh had been subdued. Years of growth had brought him to a stage of experience that allowed him to speak of glorying in his infirmities. But he would now turn to another branch of experiences, viz. " visions and revelations of the Lord." Glorious as these exaltations were, they would see that, while they were exceptional in certain respects, yet they fell in with the providential discipline of his life, and opened the way for *a keener sense of his infirmities by* " a thorn in the flesh." All along St. Paul has been painfully aware that his enemies were using these infirmities to his official disparagement. Painfully, we say, for it is obvious that he was sensitive to the disadvantages under which he appeared before the public. " Humble," "rude in speech," " bodily presence weak," " speech contemptible," were things that had some foundation in fact. Of course, his adversaries exaggerated them, but the apostle could not escape instinctive feeling, and at times acute feeling, touching this matter. This, however, was only one source of depression. A fuller account of his sufferings, physical and mental, than he had ever given had just now been presented, and the conclusion of it was that his bodily disadvantages as a speaker, his low repute as a public teacher, his constant endurance of pain and solicitude, had resulted in his realizing the fact that this very weakness was his strength. Could "visions and revelations" be entrusted to him—such visions and revelations—and he not be humbled by Divine direction? The more-glorious the revelation, the greater the necessity for him to be reminded, and most painfully reminded, that the treasure was committed to an "earthen vessel." Witness the following: a man fourteen years ago— the memory of it still vividly present as a reality of to-day—such a man, whether in the body or out of the body it was impossible to tell, elevated to the third heaven, and hearing "unspeakable words not lawful for a man to utter." "Fourteen years ago" the fact now first divulged, and yet the fact alone; the secret disclosures still a secret and personal to the man alone; and the sanctity such that it would be profanation to make the contents of the communication known. "Caught up to the third heaven, caught up into Paradise," face to face with the Lord Jesus in his mediatorial glory; and there, the senses laid to rest and the' body forgotten and the spirit opened to receive instruction and inspiration, the man taught what he was to be and what he was to do as the servant on earth of his Divine Master. Of this man, as a man in Christ, he would boast; of himself in the flesh and subject to its infirmities, he would not boast save of his weakness. Under grace, what a debtor was he to these humiliations! Intellectual pride and vanity, spiritual pride and vanity, pride and vanity as a Jew to whom the God of the fathers had manifested himself—how could these be kept down except by mortifications of the flesh? If, nevertheless, he were to boast of these revelations, he should do it truthfully. Suppose, then, that he should make this boast; who would be able to transfer himself into the proper attitude of a listener? It would not be *weakness*, but *power*, the observer would see. "I forbear," and I shrink from it, lest the contrast between this *power* and my visible *weakness*, this *glory* and my present *humiliation*, be too great for any man to bear.—L.

Vers. 7—10.—*Need of humility and the means appointed to secure it.* If the Lord Jesus passed from the baptism in the Jordan, and the dovelike descent of the Holy Ghost upon him, to the solitude of the wilderness and the assaults of the tempter; if he came down from the mount of transfiguration to witness the failure of the disciples to heal the lunatic boy, and to give expression to his sorrow in the words, " O faithless and perverse generation ! " etc.—it is not surprising that an apostle should be sorely tried after his exaltation. New endowments must have new tests. New and larger grace must be immediately put on probation, since there are many probations in this one probation that have eternal issues. "Lest I "—this man in Christ, who fourteen years ago was prepared by special revelation for the toil and trial of his Gentile apostleship— "lest I should be exalted above measure;" and what was the danger? "The abundance of the revelations." Against that danger he must be fortified. If new endowments and new graces are instantly put on trial, and the conditions of life's general probation changed, then, indeed, a new check to guard against abuse of increased gifts must not be lacking. The man is not precisely the same man as before, nor is he in the same world that he previously occupied. Accessions of outward advantages, such as wealth and social position, are full of risks, but accessions of inward power are far more perilous. To preserve St. Paul from self-glorification, there was given him " a thorn in the flesh." First of all, the revelations were as to the fact itself to be kept a secret, and this was a means of humility, but the thorn in the flesh was added. What it was we know not, but it was a bodily infirmity that caused him much suffering. "This is significant. It is of the very nature of thorns to be felt rather than seen, and to appear trifling evils to all but those directly stung by them " (Dr. Bellows). It was " a messenger of Satan," though this does not imply that it was not under God's direction. The idea is that this "angel of Satan " was an impaling stake that produced severe and continued pain, and the reason therefore is twice stated, "lest I should be exalted above measure." So, then, it was not as an apostle, but as *the apostle* to the Gentiles, that he was specially afflicted. Pain is instinctively resisted as an enemy to the activity, comfort, and pleasure of life. Naturally, therefore, St. Paul felt that it would interfere with his energy and happiness, and, of course, the Satanic side of the torture would be uppermost in his thought. The evil in pain is what we see first. If this were not realized, it could not be an affliction. Hence he prayed thrice to the Lord that it might depart from him. But his prayer was denied. At the same time, the promise was given—a promise worth far more than the removal of the pain—"My grace is sufficient for thee : for my strength is made perfect in weakness." The thorn was to continue—a lifelong suffering in addition to his other infirmities was to be fastened upon him, a special and grievous suffering. Yet, while it had to remain a sad memorial, not of his exaltation, but of human frailty in connection with great endowments, there was an assurance direct and specific of sustaining grace. Along with that a most important truth was taught him, namely, that the perfection of strength is attained through the consciousness of our utter weakness. First, then, the evil of pain ; next, the good of pain under the agency of God's grace;—this is the method of providence and grace, for the two are one in the Divine purpose. Alas! had the prayer of those sensitive nerves of his been literally answered, what a loser would he and we have been! How much of his power would have vanished with the pain! How many thoughts and emotions that have cheered the afflicted and inspired the weak to be heroic, would have been unknown! Such Epistles as the apostle wrote (to say nothing of his other services to the world) could never have been written under the ordinary experience of the ills of life. All men have thorns in the flesh, for there is no perfect health, no human body free from ailments. But in St. Paul's case the thorn was a superaddition to existing infirmities. Nor is it difficult for us to see how this particular infirmity, sanctified by the Spirit, was specially adapted to guard him at a most exposed point. Inasmuch as he was the object of a peculiar and violent opposition, he was singularly liable to the temptation of over-asserting himself and his merits, the more so as his enemies took delight in taunting him with his personal defects as to manner and appearance. The safeguard was provided where it was most wanted. Such, in fact, was his own view of the matter : " Most gladly therefore will I rather glory in my infirmities, that the power of Christ may rest upon me." " My infirmities," he argues, " instead of being the hindrance they would be if left to themselves, are helpers, since they are the occasions of grace, and this grace *rests* upon me, *i.e.* abides continually. The thought is precious ; it must be repeated. " Therefore I take pleasure in infirmities," etc. ; for the power of Christ had been imparted to him with such fulness as to transform pain into pleasure so far as his spiritual nature was concerned. The body continued to suffer, the humiliations were increased, but his soul was filled with Christ as the Christ of his pains and sorrows, and thus he had the victory, not only over physical misery, but over all pride and vanity that might have sprung up " through the abundance of the revelations." Glorious words are these: " When I am weak, then am I strong." Notice the clear view St. Paul has of the Divine hand in his thorn in the flesh. If he is perfectly assured of the abundance of the revelations, if he can locate the scene in Paradise, if he realizes the sanctity of these disclosures in the " unspeakable words," he is just as certain that the thorn " was given " him. He knew it was a " thorn," and he knew whence it came. He acknowledged God in it, and, in this feeling, prayed thrice for its removal. Christians often fail at this point. They doubt at times whether their afflictions come from God. Some Christians cannot be induced to believe that their sufferings are sent from above, and they see in them nothing more than evil casualties. But if they fail to recognize God in the sorrow, they will not find him in the joy of his blessed promise, " My grace is sufficient for thee." It was not merely the " thorn " that St. Paul had to endure. This was a source of pain, and it aggravated, doubtless, his other physical infirmities, and, in turn, was augmented by them. But we must not forget the state of mind such an affliction naturally produced—the surprise that it should follow such wonderful signs of God's favour as had been vouchsafed in the " abundance of the revelations," the temptation to a rebellious spirit and the occasion for unbelief it would furnish. A literal answer to his prayer was refused ; a spiritual answer was granted. The " grace" bestowed was " sufficient," not only to bear the pain as a peculiar addition to his "infirmities" already existing, but to enable him to " glory " in it ; and the providence of it was specially manifested in the power it had given him to be patient, forbearing, humble, in the late trouble with the Corinthians. O Christians, who are called to a lifelong discipline in the school of suffering, think of the measure implied in the *sufficient grace!* Sufficient for what? Sufficient, not only to glory in pain and infirmity, but to glory "most gladly."—L.

Vers. 11—15.—*Recurrence to the former argument.* The intense feeling of St. Paul indicates itself by not continuing on one unvarying level. From the climax just reached he reverts to what had been previously discussed in ch. x. and xi. These reverberations are very characteristic of the man as a thinker, and they show how closely, in him, temperament was allied with intellect. If aroused, he never became artificial or unnatural, but was then most true to his organization. In the verses before us he resumes his ironical vein: "I am become a fool in glorying;" but not of his own accord, for "ye have compelled me." The disaffected party at Corinth had not respected his just claims, had not "commended" him, and they had failed in this matter when he had demonstrated that he was "in nothing behind the very chiefest of the apostles"— the same idea expressed in ch. xi. 5, adding in this instance, "though I be nothing." Was he thinking of the abundant revelations with which he could not have been entrusted save on the condition of a thorn in the flesh? Only a brief utterance, yet very sincere—"though I be nothing." It was safe for such a man in his impaled situation to dramatize the "fool," but he hastens to serious work and mentions that "the signs of an apostle" had been wrought among them. His language is full and earnest; "truly," "in all patience," "signs and wonders and mighty deeds," no lack, no irritating haste, no deception, number and variety and extraordinary power all provided for. Despite of the accumulation, the magnitude, the unimpeachable quality of these Divine evidences, God among you of a truth, Christ honouring his servant and his servant's work, ye Corinthians, or some of you, have not "commended" me! In what respect were ye inferior to other Churches? Look at Macedonia, look at Asia; wherein were you less favoured than they? They commended me; what have you done to exemplify your sense of my apostleship? I remember but one thing in which ye were "inferior"—and the irony is keen now—I remember that I preached the gospel gratuitously, so as not to be "burdensome to you;" and this is your acknowledgment, this your *commendation* of my course! What a mistake my disinterestedness was! What a "fool" in my goodness! "Forgive me this wrong!" Despite of it all, I am not weaned from Corinth. "The third time I am ready to come to you." Though my self-denying conduct has been used to bring me into contempt, I shall repeat it without any abatement, for "I will not be burdensome to you." And now his heart swells as he says, "I seek not yours, but you"—words that he bequeathed to the admiration of ages; for was he not their spiritual father? If, at the bidding of natural instinct, children were not to lay up for the parents, but the parents for the children, then it became him to provide for his spiritual children. But was this all that his love had to promise? Nay; what means he had or might have should not only be freely used in their behalf, but he would give his faculties, his heart, his whole self, to advance their well-being. "Signs of an apostle" had been wrought at Corinth, "wonders and mighty deeds," but the signs of a sublime moral manhood rise before us when he declares, "I will very gladly spend and be spent for you." Will this avail? "If I love you more abundantly, am I loved the less?"—L.

Vers. 16—19.—*Forestalling false criticism.* What limit is there to the carping skill of envy and hatred! Some of this Judaizing party might say that, under cover of disinterestedness, he had acted cunningly in the matter of the collection for the poor saints at Jerusalem. Was this so? Did the deputies make a gain of you? Did Titus abuse his position? One spirit, Christ's spirit, animated us, for we all "walked in the same steps." Think you that this has been said for self-justification? Do we excuse ourselves? Fears were oppressing him, fears that he would mention presently. Can it all be in vain? Assurances of fatherly regard, assurances of a willingness, ay, of a gladness, in giving all he had and all he was, even life itself, to their service and interest; would they pass for nought? And were there both history and prophecy in the melancholy words, "The more abundantly I love you, the less I be loved"? The fervent appeal, the protracted argument, the action and reaction, the irony and the profound sincerity, the grieved tenderness, the sad ingratitude, the memory of noble self-sacrifice, gather into the climax, "We speak before God in Christ." There, at that bar of judgment, he makes the solemn avowal, "We do all things, dearly beloved, for your edifying." Once more he would conciliate, nor should this long and impassioned outburst come to a close without calling God in Christ to witness his deep-felt affection for these ungrateful Corinthians.—L.

Vers. 20, 21.—*Expression of his fears.* Why had he just spoken with so much earnestness? Why had St. Paul brought facts to their notice which he had never used in addressing his Churches? Why had he referred to that extraordinary event in his career, when he had been ushered into the secret chambers of Paradise and permitted to hear things which were not to be told? Why a revelation to be unrevealed? It was to teach the rebellious and evil-disposed among the Corinthians that he was Christ's apostle to them, and, as such, charged with maintaining the order, peace, and purity of the Churches entrusted to his oversight. Very tenderly had he appealed to the Corinthians, and now, having called God, even God in Christ, to witness the depth and sincerity of his love for them, he would entreat them not to drive him to extreme measures. To exercise stern authority gave him no pleasure. The greatest thing in an apostle was love, and he wished to restore harmony and prosperity to the Church by means of forbearance and affectionate counsel. Therefore he had pleaded so fervently; therefore he had condescended to boasting; therefore he had told them more of his infirmities than his enemies knew; therefore he had gloried in those things which these very men used to alienate his own spiritual children by putting contempt on him and his office. Fears he had, lest when he should come to Corinth, he should not find them such as he wished, and fears too that he would have to act in an apostolic way not agreeable to them, so that on their meeting together each party would be disappointed in the other. Hope he had, and so he speaks doubtingly. But the fatherly heart is overloaded with apprehensions and "lest" is thrice employed, for he would not conceal these apprehensions. What a dark list of vices and sins is spread out in the last two verses! If he should have to confront these evils, he will not find them such as he would and they will find him such as they would not. First comes the catalogue of moral evils such as originated in the factious spirit so rife in Corinth, viz. strife, jealousy, wraths, factions, backbitings, whisperings, swellings, tumults. These things would require discipline. But, moreover, he feared the sensual wickedness which had such a hold on Corinth. For he might have to deal with gross offenders, men who had committed sins of "uncleanness and fornication and lasciviousness," and had not repented. Such a state of things would grieve him. Disappointed and afflicted by a blight like this falling on his labours in the ministry of the gospel, he tells them, "My God will humble me among you." To avoid these distressing results, to restore peace and spiritual prosperity to a Church rent by faction and disgraced by immorality, he had written and laboured and prayed. If all failed, "my God will humble me among you."—L.

Ver. 2.— "*A man in Christ.*" When we consider what man is, and who Christ is, the conjunction seems wonderful indeed. Yet, when apprehended, this union appears one fraught with richest blessings for him who is the inferior and dependent member. The thought was one familiar to the apostle; himself "a man in Christ," he spoke of others who were "in Christ before" himself, and he designated Christian societies, "Churches in Christ Jesus."

I. THE NATURE OF THE UNION THUS DESCRIBED. 1. The Christian is grafted "in Christ" as a graft in a tree, joined to him as a branch to a vine. The union is thus a vital union, and is to the Christian the means and the occasion of spiritual life. 2. The Christian is accepted "in Christ," *i.e.* in the Beloved. For Christ's sake the Christian is received into Divine favour. The Saviour is in this capacity a Representative, a Mediator, an Advocate. 3. The Christian is incorporated "in Christ" as the member in the body, and has a new function to discharge in consequence of this relationship. 4. The Christian is hidden "in Christ" as the traveller in the cleft of the rock, as the voyager in the ark, when "the Lord shut him in." 5. The Christian dwells "in Christ" as in a house, a home appointed for him by Divine wisdom and goodness.

II. THE IMPORTANCE AND ADVANTAGES OF THIS UNION. 1. As is apparent from considering the position of those who are *out of* Christ. For such, where is safety, where is a law of life, where is a prospect for immortality? For to be out of Christ is to be without God, and so without hope. 2. From considering what in this life they possess who have Christ and are in him. Whilst, so far as the bodily life is concerned, they are in the world, they are in spirit in the Lord, and thus partake a higher nature and existence than belong to earth and to time. 3. From considering the imperishable character of this union. To be "in Christ" now is to be "with Christ" for ever. To those who are in him there is no condemnation now, and from him there shall be no separation hereafter. The visions which Paul beheld, and the declarations he heard when he was caught up into the third heaven, were to him, and may be to us, an earnest and promise of immortal union. Therefore "Abide in him."—T.

Ver. 5.—*Glorying in weaknesses.* It is not to be wondered at that Paul boasted; the wonder is that, instead of boasting of the extraordinary visions he had experienced, the extraordinary commission he had received, the extraordinary success which had followed his labours, he boasted of what other men would have concealed or have lamented—his own infirmities, disadvantages, and troubles.

I. THE WEAKNESSES IN WHICH THE APOSTLE GLORIED. 1. His own bodily infirmity was especially present to his thoughts, when using this language. Whatever this was, whether general ill health or some special malady, as of the eyes, it was naturally distressing to himself, as it prevented him from doing his work with the ease and pleasure which he might have experienced had he possessed health and vigour of body. 2. The contempt he met with from some amongst whom he laboured was to Paul no cause of mortification, but cause of rejoicing. Let men despise him; if he was able to serve and please his Master, that was enough. 3. The hardships and privations and persecutions he endured in the fulfilment of his ministry were matter of glorying. In these he took pleasure, contrary as such a fact was to ordinary human experience.

II. THE GROUND OF THE APOSTLE'S GLORYING IN HIS WEAKNESSES. 1. There can be no doubt that the deepest ground lay in Paul's sympathy with his Divine Lord. The humiliation and obedience unto death of the Lord Jesus in order to secure man's salvation became a new source of inspiration, in the direction both of human action and of human suffering, and Paul was crucified with Christ unto the world. He bore about with him in the body the marks of the Lord Jesus, and of this he justly boasted. 2. Personal weakness was the occasion of the reception of new and spiritual strength. For Christ made his own grace sufficient when his servant's strength was gone. And by a sublime paradox the apostle learned that, when he was weak, then was he strong. And thus the very infirmities which seemed to disqualify for service became the occasion of the communication of such spiritual power and aid as rendered the apostle more efficient and successful in the service of the Lord.—T.

Ver. 9.—*Sufficient grace.* Perhaps there is no verse in Scripture which has brought more strength and comfort to the hearts of Christ's people than this. The explanation of its preciousness and its power is to be sought first in the spiritual, the revealed truth which it communicates, and secondly in the fact that it is the record of personal experience. There is an instinctive persuasion in the human mind that the experience which has been realized by one is possible to another. The grace which was actually bestowed upon Paul does not seem inaccessible to the feeble, the tempted, the overburdened Christian who cries to Heaven for help.

I. THE NEED FOR THIS SUFFICIENCY. 1. The manifold duties, the severe temptations, the varied sorrows and troubles, incidental to the Christian life. There are difficulties and trials common to the Christian with all men, but there are others peculiar to him, arising from the higher view he takes of life, both as a personal discipline and as an opportunity for serving and glorifying God. 2. The conscious insufficiency of human resources. This, indeed, accounts for the universal practice of prayer, frequent or occasional, deliberate or spontaneous. Men feel their utter helplessness in the presence of the demands of life, and therefore they call upon God. Much more keenly does the follower of the Lord Jesus realize his need of a higher than human aid. Conscious that only Divine grace has reconciled him to God, he daily acknowledges his dependence upon the same grace for the maintenance of his spiritual life and usefulness.

II. THE GROUND OF THIS SUFFICIENCY. 1. The divinity of the Saviour. Can we imagine any other than Christ using this language, "*My* grace is sufficient"? It is becoming, it is possible, only to him who possesses Divine resources, who is spiritually present with all his people. 2. Christ's mediatorial position. This involves the possession and the disposal of whatsoever is necessary for the spiritual welfare of those whom the Lord Jesus saves. Accepted as our Representative, he has received gifts for men; and it is in the fulfilment of his mediatorial office that he imparts to each individual disciple and friend the specially needed grace. 3. The spiritual dispensation over which the Lord Jesus presides. He is Head over all things unto his Church. He distributes to every man severally as he will. His Spirit is the Spirit of truth, of holiness, of power.

III. THE EVIDENCE OF THIS SUFFICIENCY. 1. The personal experience of Paul as recorded in this passage. He tells us here, not only what Christ promised, but what he performed. He was perfectly satisfied with the course he had taken. He did not find his own personal weakness and insufficiency a barrier to his efficiency and usefulness. What he lacked, his Lord supplied. 2. The recorded experience of all who have trusted to the same Divine Source of all-sufficiency. There is no discordant note in the song of grateful, affectionate adoration which fills the Church of the Redeemer. All his people have known their own demerits, their own powerlessness, and all have known the sufficiency of their Lord. And every Christian has reason to acknowledge—

> "And when my all of strength shall fail,
> I shall with the God-Man prevail."

T

Ver. 12.—*Signs of apostleship.* The evidences of deep feeling, which are manifest throughout this Epistle, are very prominent in this passage. There were special reasons why a sensitive man like Paul should lay to heart the treatment with which he met from the Corinthians. Considering what he had done among them and for them, he felt it hard that empty pretenders should be preferred to himself. And he was convinced that, in disregarding his authority, these members of the Corinthian congregation whom he had in view were doing injustice to his ministry among them. For all the proofs of a Divine commission had been exhibited in his ministry in their city. He appeals to—

I. MIRACULOUS EVIDENCES OF APOSTLESHIP. Upon due occasion the apostle did not hesitate to bring forward and adduce as proofs of his commission the supernatural gifts which had been bestowed upon him. How could he have publicly made such a claim as this in an authentic letter, unless the Corinthians, friendly and inimical, were ready to witness to the truth of his language? It would not be fanciful to discriminate among the terms which Paul in this passage applies to these miraculous evidences. Observe that they are designated: 1. *Powers*, as pointing to the heavenly and Divine source to which they must needs be traced. Whether exercised in controlling nature, in healing disease, or in inflicting punishment, they bore upon their very presence the evidences that they were of superhuman origin. 2. *Wonders*, as fitted and indeed intended to awaken the interest, the inquiry, the amazement, of all beholders. Wonder may be useful in leading to such reflection, such emotion, as may surpass itself in value. 3. *Signs*, as indicating the authority of those at whose prayer or command these marvels were wrought "among" the Corinthians.

II. THE MORAL EVIDENCE OF APOSTLESHIP. Nowhere in the New Testament is the portent placed above the spiritual. Christ's mighty works answered their purpose when they prompted the exclamation and inquiry, "What manner of man is this!" And in Paul's character there was seen an evidence of apostleship far more convincing and far more instructive than the most marvellous deeds which he performed. He justly claims to have exhibited *patience*, both in his continuing to work for the Corinthians and to interest himself in them notwithstanding their ingratitude, and in his tender and brotherly treatment of them with a view to their restoration to entire sympathy with himself.—T.

Ver. 15.—*Ministerial devotion.* Paul rejoices and boasts that, however the Corinthians may misunderstand him, he cannot be accused of having acted towards them in a mercenary spirit. Disinterestedness at all events he must claim, and they must concede. They are the debtors, not he. He is the parent who lays up for the children. This he does cheerfully, and is resolved that he will do in the future as in the past. His determination is to spend and to be spent for their souls.

I. A SINCERE PROFESSION. Had Paul been a stranger to his correspondents he could not have used such language as this. But he was well known to them, having lived and laboured in Corinth, working with his own hands for his maintenance, and putting forth every effort for the spiritual enlightenment and salvation of the citizens. 1. The minister of Christ *spends* for the enrichment of his people's souls. He has "treasure," though in earthen vessels. He has "the true riches" committed to his keeping. His aim is to bestow the choicest and most precious blessings upon the spiritually necessitous. All he has he longs to part with. 2. The minister of Christ is willing *to be spent* for his people's souls. Labour often involves suffering. Bodily powers may be exhausted ; even the mind itself may give way under the strain of a toilsome, emotional, prolonged ministry. The missionary may sink beneath the burden of climate, of unrequited toil, of persecution. Every faithful minister must lay his account, not only with effort, but with self-denial and self-sacrifice.

II. AN ARDENT APPEAL. The Revisers adopt a rendering of the latter part of this verse which harmonizes with what we may well believe to have been the sentiment of the apostle. 1. Paul has proved the abundance of his love ; and every true minister, animated by the love of Christ and by pity for souls, has shown himself to be a true lover and friend of his fellow-men. 2. Shall it, then, be the case that those whom the Christian minister loves, and whose welfare he seeks, shall be indifferent and ungrateful ? It is sometimes so ; the very faithfulness and earnestness of the minister may occasion the aversion of those who desire that he should "prophesy smooth things," and leave them to their sinful pursuits and pleasures uninterrupted. Yet the affection and devotion of spiritual workers deserve a very different return.—T.

Ver. 19.—*Edification.* The strain in which this portion of the Epistle is written may, the writer is conscious, mislead some readers. It displays a good deal of personal feeling ; it reproaches those who have not shown themselves amenable to rightful influence and authority ; it reveals a wounded heart. Some readers may misinterpret these signs and infer that the apostle regards himself as on his defence, as excusing and vindicating himself, as asking that the best construction possible may be forbearingly put upon his conduct. But all this is erroneous. Paul's one great aim is, not his own vindication, but, on the contrary, the edification of those to whom his Epistle is addressed.

I. IN WHAT DOES EDIFICATION CONSIST ? 1. It has respect to those who are already built upon the one Foundation—Christ. The minister of Christ, like other workmen, must begin at the beginning. When men receive the gospel, then, and only then, are they in a position to be "edified." 2. It consists in the building up of the Christian character in the case of individuals. The resemblance to Christ is what is mainly to be sought. 3. And in the formation of solid and serviceable Christian societies, all of which are parts of the holy temple which is being reared to the glory of God.

II. BY WHAT MEANS IS EDIFICATION PROMOTED ? 1. The means divinely appointed and approved are moral and spiritual. All employment of mechanical or political agency to secure such an end is to be condemned, as both inappropriate and useless. 2. Personal agency is that which the New Testament exemplifies and which experience approves. Living spirits, full of love and sympathy, are divinely qualified to engage in such a work as this. 3. The presentation of truth, the addressing of language of encouragement and promise, of admonition and rebuke,—these are emphatically the scriptural methods of edification. Of all these abundant and very instructive examples may be found in this very Epistle.

III. WHAT PURPOSES DOES EDIFICATION SUBSERVE ? 1. The welfare, the highest spiritual development and happiness, of those who are edified. 2. The impression thus made upon the world by the presence in the midst of it of a Divine temple reared with human souls. 3. The honour and glory of the heavenly Architect himself.—T.

Vers. 1—4.—*Apostolic experiences in heaven.* I. THE APOSTLE HAD A HEAVENLY EXPERIENCE DURING HIS EARTHLY LIFE. His earthly experience was, very largely, dark and sorrowful ; but amidst the darkness appears this brilliant flash of heavenly light. 1. *He gives us this experience as an actual fact, and as such we must receive it.* It was a reality to him. He records it that it may come before us as a reality, not as a mere fancy or illusion. 2. *It furnished him with an opportunity of contrasting man's treatment and God's.* In the closing verses of the preceding chapter we have a catalogue of Paul's tribulations, many of these occasioned by human perversity and enmity. *Men* treated Paul evilly; *God* gave him this special and marvellous heavenly experience!

II. THE CHARACTER OF THIS EXPERIENCE. 1. *A real entrance into the heavenly world.* Paul has no doubt about this. His only doubt is whether he was in the body at the time. He most distinctly conveys that there was a removal of his spirit into another sphere; he is not sure whether his body accompanied his spirit. There could not have been a doubt as to whether he was " in the body " if his experience had been a mere trance or any special influence brought to bear upon his mind. There was a *removal*, but whether of body and spirit, or of spirit alone, the apostle cannot declare. We may note the apostolic *belief* that *conscious life is possible to us when we are* "*out of the body.*" The apostle did not know whether his experience was of this order, but he evidently recognizes this order of experience as *possible*. We may note further that the apostle regarded heaven or paradise as a *place* as well as a *state*. " Third heaven " and " paradise " seem to be used synonymously—" third heaven " indicating the realm in which God's glory is pre-eminently manifested. The rabbins taught the existence of seven heavens, but it is not probable that Paul refers to their notions. 2. *An entrance effected by God.* It was not by the apostle's merit or power; it was by a Divine act—he was " caught up." Admittance to the heavenly world is in the hands of God; if we enter, then God must effect the entrance for us. Christ, *the Way*, is given to us by God. 3. *Astonishing visions.* Paul *saw* much (ver. 1). 4. *Wonderful revelations.* He *heard* much. " Unspeakable words," understood by him, but not to be repeated on earth. Possibly they would not have been intelligible to any who had not participated in the heavenly experience. Our curiosity craves to know what Paul saw and heard, but our needs do not demand it. We have the *speakable* words of the gospel, which, rightly received, will prepare us to hear by-and-by the " unspeakable words " of heaven and to behold the heavenly glories.

III. THE OBJECT OF THIS EXPERIENCE. 1. *To encourage the apostle in his many labours and sufferings.* Christ took his disciples up into the mountain and was transfigured before them; then he brought them down into the world of men to toil and to endure. 2. *To quicken his faith in the unseen.* Great natures doing great works have often great trials of faith. A big devil always comes against a big Christian. 3. *To speed him onward to the final rest of God's people.* He was a much-loved child; the Father showed him special favour. 4. *That others to whom the experience should be recounted might participate in the benefit.* The experience was for us as well as for the apostle. From us its special features are largely hidden; but *it* is revealed to us, and *this* knowledge may well encourage us in the earthly service, quicken our faith, and hasten our footsteps towards the glories beyond the veil.

A general lesson may be learnt from the event that those who have special trials and sorrows experience also special comforts and helps.—H.

Ver. 7.—*The thorn in the flesh.* I. WHAT WAS IT ? 1. *In itself.* There have been almost infinite conjectures. As to the *figure:* some prefer a " goad for the flesh," a sharpened stake; others, a rankling thorn; others, a stake on which offenders were impaled or the cross to which they were fastened. As to the *reality:* evil suggestions; fiery darts of Satan; some prominent adversary; some painful bodily affection, weak eyesight, defective speech, carnal cravings; whilst a bold imaginationist has had the temerity to suggest a termagant wife! Possibly the precise nature of the affliction is concealed that no one may say, " Ah, that is not *my* trouble." It was very grievous to the apostle whatever its precise nature. 2. *As Satan was concerned in it.* Paul recognized Satan's hand (see Job ii. 7; Luke xiii. 16). It was used of Satan to annoy, pain, depress, and harass Paul, and with the hope that it would hinder his great work. Satanic malice rejoiced in the anticipation that it might prove the last straw upon the camel's back. Paul interfered much with the devil's kingdom; it is no wonder that the devil sought to interfere with him. Satan can afford to leave some people alone; but if we faithfully attack his kingdom and his rule we may expect reprisals. Yet Satan is but a fool after all, and constantly overreaches himself. One has well said, " The devil drives but a poor trade by the persecution of the saints—he tears the nest, but the bird escapes; he cracks the shell, but loses the kernel." 3. *As allowed by God.* God's hand was in it as well as Satan's. This is so with all our tribulations; in one aspect they are messengers of Satan, in the other messengers of God. *All depends upon which message we listen to.* Paul's thorn in the flesh was God's teacher of humility. There was danger that the extraordinary revelations made to the apostle might foster pride. Human nature is intensely susceptible to this temptation. Those who enjoy remarkable favours often experience remarkable affliction. The ship in the high wind needs plenty of ballast. When we build high we must also build low—the lofty building requires a deep foundation. It is well for us that God is not merely indulgent. God will not allow us to become spoilt children.

II. THE APOSTLE'S RESTLESSNESS UNDER THE AFFLICTION. Paul was very human. He would not have been so could he have borne this additional trouble with indifference. Remember his other troubles. If this special affliction seemed likely to hinder his life-work, how keenly would he feel it! 'Tis hard to dance in chains. Heavy labour tries the healthy; how exceedingly burdensome to the sick! Yet he did not grumble, or make himself a nuisance, or find fault with God, or sit down in despair. It was said of him once, "Behold, he prayeth;" it may be said of him again.

III. HIS PRAYER. 1. *In his distress he betook himself to the mercy-seat.* Like Hezekiah, he spread the matter before the Lord. Affliction should drive us *to*, not *from*, God. And we should come to *pray*, not to *complain*. The throne of grace is sometimes turned into a bar of judgment, at which men arraign God. When some strange experience comes upon us we should *ask concerning it* in the audience-chamber. 2. *He prayed to the Lord Jesus.* This seems evident from ver. 9, "that the strength of Christ may rest upon me." The servant's difficulties may well be submitted to the Master. Christ had directly appointed the apostle; to Christ, therefore, Paul brings his seeming hindrance. Whilst usually we pray to the Father in the Name of Christ, we may at other times pray to Christ himself. 3. *He prayed with importunity.* There was no mistaking his earnestness. As Christ in Gethsemane prayed "the third time," so thrice did this Christ-like apostle knock at heaven's gate. He went on knocking until he got a response. Many in prayer want nothing, ask nothing, get nothing. Some are so polite that they dread lest they should disturb God, and knock so lightly and daintily that it would require a microphone to make the sound audible. Others ring and run away. The apostle stood at the gate till he was answered. Such holy boldness delights God instead of affronting him. 4. *He prayed definitely.* (1) For "this thing." Some pray for everything in general, and therefore get nothing in particular. (2) That it might depart. Here, perhaps, he went too far. If our troubles were sent away, our best friends might be sent away. The counterpart of "a thorn in the flesh" may be "grace in the spirit." It is a good thing that it does not rest with us to send away or to retain; we should often send away the good and draw to ourselves the injurious and evil.

IV. THE ANSWER. 1. *A true answer, yet not what was looked for.* (Ver. 9.) Such a prayer, offered in such a manner, was certain of a response, but not of the response anticipated. God often answers our prayers by not answering them. We get what we *want*, not what we *wish*. We dictate our prayer; God dictates the answer. Generally *we do not ask enough*—the apostle did not; to take away the thorn was small compared with sanctifying its presence. To eject the devil's messenger was poor compared with transforming it into a ministering spirit. 2. *A lesson of faith.* Paul's faith must transcend his feeling. He must lay hold of Christ with more tenacious grasp; he must believe that Christ can use this trouble for high purposes. Perhaps as he looked to Christ with stronger faith he could realize that, as great purposes were accomplished by the many thorns in the flesh of Christ (he was *crowned* with thorns), so the one thorn in his flesh should not prove unfruitful. Grapes might be gathered from this thorn. 3. *A definite assurance.* There was a *basis* for the faith demanded, as *there always is*. "My grace is sufficient for thee" (ver. 9). Christ engages to bear him through; can he believe this? The Lord's resources are boundless; they are *our* resources when strong faith binds us to their possessor. My "grace" may mean my "love," which secures all things needful for my servants; or the aid of the Holy Spirit, which will prove sufficient for every exigency. 4. *An intimation of purpose.* There was no *mistake* in sending or allowing the "thorn in the flesh." Prayer becomes blasphemous when it proceeds upon the assumption that God has made a blunder! The thorn in the flesh was the stem upon which the flower of the Divine glory was to blossom. The " messenger of Satan " would be made a herald proclaiming the power of Christ. The apostle's flesh was to be a battle-field on which Christ would triumph.

V. THE ISSUE. A new thought has been given to Paul—Christ's glory will be enhanced. At once he begins to glory in this infirmity, " Most gladly " (ver. 9), or most *sweetly ;* it became a delight of the highest kind. What he wanted to lose he now wants to keep. *With* the thorn in the flesh he can become, as he could not without it, the dwelling-place of the power of Christ. It is enough if through his humiliation Christ may be exalted, if through his suffering Christ may be glorified. Many are more than content with being *resigned* under suffering; to submit they think is a mark of highest grace. But the apostle is far beyond this. He can " take pleasure " (ver. 10) in troubles, because through his troubles the power of Christ is more strikingly and impressively exhibited.—H.

Ver. 11.—*Much, yet nothing.* I. THE APOSTLE'S CLAIM. A large claim, put strongly. Paul claimed to be on a perfect equality with the leading apostles. Unwillingly he referred to this matter, which might *look like* self-glorification ; but when the occasion came, his utterance was full and unmistakable. There is nothing derogatory in magnifying our office, the evil lies in magnifying ourselves in it. It is not conceitedness but righteousness to assert for ourselves what God has already asserted for us. Paul felt that he must not lightly esteem, or allow others to lightly esteem, a high office conferred upon him by God, and an office in which God had signally witnessed to his efforts. Paul speaks about " the signs " of an apostle ; the interesting question arises— What were these signs ? We may note the following :—1. Knowledge of the gospel derived by immediate revelation from Christ (Gal. i. 12). 2. Being specially under the influence and teaching of the Divine Spirit, so as to be able to announce truth with authority (1 Cor. ii. 10—13; xii. 8, 29 ; xiv. 37). 3. External manifestations of Divine favour sanctioning claim to the apostleship. 4. Continued faithfulness to the gospel (Gal. i. 8, 9). 5. Success in preaching the gospel (1 Cor. ix. 2). 6. Power of communicating the Holy Ghost by imposition of hands (Acts viii. 18). 7. Power of working miracles (ver. 12 ; Rom. xv. 18, 19). 8. Holiness of life (ch. vi. 4). Such of these as could be exhibited to the Corinthians, had been, and there was one respect in which his readers would scarcely contest Paul's claim, and to this with his accustomed dexterity the apostle refers. If founding great Churches was a mark of great apostleship, what an apostle Paul must have been to found such a Church as the Corinthian (ver. 13) ! This was a perfectly sound argument, but it was an *argumentum ad hominem* of a singularly happy character. There was only one thing lacking, and here the apostle blends irony with pathos—" I myself was not a burden to you : forgive me this wrong " (ver. 13). For reasons given elsewhere in the Epistle, he had resolved not to derive any part of his temporal support from them. They might esteem this a slight. Had they lived in later days they would have counted it a virtue!

II. THE APOSTLE'S ACKNOWLEDGMENT. Paul's humility is marvellous. Yet it was not one whit greater than it ought to have been. The " thorn in the flesh " (ver. 7) has accomplished a gracious work. Paul has at the same time the clearest view of the Divine power and glory, and of his own insignificance and impotence. He does not take to himself for a moment what was not of himself. Note in ver. 12 he says, not " *I* wrought," but " *were* wrought "—*he distinguishes between God and Paul !* We have a beautiful insight into the apostle's mind. He has risen too high to deck himself in plumes stolen from his Lord. Though divinely endowed, strikingly witnessed to in his labours, beyond question the pre-eminent apostle, he says, " I am *nothing.*" We wonder not that God used such a man. We magnify God's grace in him. Truly the promise had been amply fulfilled, " My grace is sufficient for thee " (ver. 9). Our pride is our folly—it drives God out and lets the devil in. We cannot be great because we will be so great. The bag is full of wind, so that it cannot be filled.

III. LEARN : 1. *Humility becomes us.* It became Paul. If he had so lowly an estimate of himself, how little should we think of ourselves! Even if we are " great men," we are very small men compared with him. 2. *Humility is reasonable.* It is not fiction, but fact, to say that we are *nothing*. Pride is based on *a lie*. 3. *Humility is generally associated with large usefulness.*—H.

Ver. 15.—*Self-expenditure.* I. A SPLENDID ILLUSTRATION OF CHRISTIAN SERVICE. The apostle is carried beyond the thought of giving some time, or strength, or property, for his beloved Corinthians; he expresses his perfect willingness *to give himself*. He will not count it a grief, but a gladness, to *expend himself* for them. Whilst many find great difficulty in giving a little for others, the apostle seems to find none in giving all. Here we have: 1. *Whole-souled devotion.* Nothing can transcend the apostle's offer. And the voluntariness and the joy of the devotion place it in the first rank of excellence. 2. *Earnest desire for welfare.* The love of Paul for the Corinthians could not have been more forcibly expressed. Men gauge our love for them by what we are willing to give up for them; when we are willing *to give up ourselves* for them, they cannot but be convinced of our sincerity. 3. *Indication of the importance of Christian work.* For nothing else in the world would Paul have willingly spent himself. But Christian service more than justified the self-sacrifice. In his judgment nothing could compare with it for a moment. We may remember that in all departments of life we can render Christian service; spheres of labour become insignificant and mean only when Christian service is excluded from them. 4. *A striking imitation of Christ.* Paul has caught his Master's spirit. His Lord laid down his life for him; he will now lay down his life for his Lord. Christ "*gave himself.*" The Lord's servant is most fitted to do his Lord's work when he is most like his Lord. 5. *A secret of success.* When we labour for Christ in such a spirt as this we are certain to prosper. Failure is the child of half-heartedness and selfishness. Christ honours an entire consecration to his service.

II. SELF-EXPENDING CHRISTIAN SERVICE PROMPTED BY A HIGH MOTIVE. The apostle was willing to spend himself for *the souls* of the Corinthians—" and be spent for your souls" (New Version). In this labour he was seeking at the same time the highest glory of God and Christ, and the truest welfare of men. These objects unite in Christian service, which aims pre-eminently to do good to *the souls* of men. The saving and perfecting of souls redounds supremely to the glory of the Divine Being, whilst it secures the highest good for humanity. So dominated was the apostle by the desire to do good to the souls of men, that what is usually a very strong motive for action, viz. the love of others for us, was quite swept away. He declares that he will expend himself for the Corinthians, though this strongest indication of his love to them should produce a decreasing love for him on their part. The *disinterested* character of true Christian service is here very strikingly displayed. It was by such self-expenditure as that of Paul's that early Christianity won its triumphs; it is for such self-expenditure that later Christianity pathetically calls. God is always thoroughly in earnest, but men are not. When men become so then "the arm of the Lord is revealed."—H.

Ver. 2.—"*A man in Christ.*" St. Paul spoke of himself. Once he had been out of Christ, though in a legal fashion very religious. But he gave up his legality when he found Christ. He looked to him for help, fled to him for defence, and thenceforward lived in him as a new creature. It is the best short description of every believer.

I. CHOSEN IN CHRIST. (Eph. i. 4.) We put this first, because this must come first in the Divine order and in the very nature of things. But man does not begin with any knowledge of this as affecting himself. He grounds his faith, not on the secret purpose, but on the revealed good will of God to all in the gospel. It is after he has believed that he learns gratefully to trace his own calling and salvation, in common with that of all his fellow-believers, to the gracious choice and purpose of God. Then, as the seventeenth Article of the Church of England expresses it, " The godly consideration of predestination and our election in Christ is full of sweet, pleasant, and unspeakable comfort to godly persons and such as feel in themselves the working of the Spirit of Christ."

II. FREELY GRACED IN THE BELOVED. (Eph. i. 6.) The man in Christ is embraced in the favour with which God regards his beloved Son. He has redemption and reconciliation to God, unsearchable riches, spiritual blessings in heavenly places, and continual freedom of access to the Father in heaven.

III. CREATED ANEW IN CHRIST JESUS. (Eph. ii. 10.) God begins this work, as of old, by causing light to shine out of darkness.; then he introduces a new order, peace and fertile life, and this is wrought on and in every genuine Christian. "If any man be in Christ, he is a new creation." And therefore he does what is right, not by a continual strain and effort against nature, but spontaneously and naturally, because he has a clean heart and a right spirit.

IV. ESTABLISHED IN CHRIST. (Ch. i. 21.) He who comes to Christ under the drawing grace of the Spirit of God abides in him by the same Spirit, so as to imbibe his wisdom, experience his support, and learn what consolation there is in him, and what comfort of love. So God confirms and establishes his people in Christ, making good to them his promises, anointing them, sealing them, and giving "the earnest of the Spirit" in their hearts. This is much more than being settled in one's religious opinions and habits. It is the staying of the mind on Christ. And usually it is reached through conflicts and sufferings that compel the soul to grapple more firmly the reality of Christ and the security of Divine promises in him, just as trees rocked by the winds strike their roots the more widely and deeply into the ground (see 1 Pet. v. 10).

V. APPROVED IN CHRIST. (Rom. xvi. 10.) Establishment relates to faith, knowledge, and comfort; approval refers to service. Labour for the Lord ought to be rendered in the Lord, i.e. in virtue of union with him, and by the power derived from such union. But as there are gradations of faith and love among true Christians, so also there are degrees of diligence and thoroughness in service; and some servants are more approved than others, and shall have a more full reward. Oh to serve so as to have our Master's smile upon us now, and to be openly accepted of him at his coming as good and faithful servants!

VI. PERFECT IN CHRIST JESUS: COMPLETE IN HIM. (Col. i. 28; ii. 10.) There is all-perfect resource in our Lord. But all have not attained. There are babes in Christ, not perfect or mature; let them go on to fuller stature and strength. It is an object to be desired and worked for, that every believing man may be presented perfect in Christ Jesus, i.e. ripe and mature, not crude or ill-developed in the Christian character.

VII. ASLEEP IN JESUS. (1 Cor. xv. 18; 1 Thess. iv. 14, 18.) If we are Christ's, death is ours. It cannot do us hurt or separate us from the love of God. For a man who is in Christ, the whole state of death is brightened by the love and faithfulness of the Lord. Blessed are the dead who die in him. Sweetly sleep the labourers who, when their day's work for Jesus is ended, fall asleep in him.

> " Oh, never doleful dream again
> Shall break the happy slumber when
> 'He giveth his beloved sleep.' "

F.

Vers. 7—9.—*An instructive experience.* Like all true saints, Paul was modest about his own experience. He did not write down his heavenly rapture and what followed it, till fourteen years had passed, and then he wrote it only because he felt compelled to prove to the Corinthians that even "in visions and revelations of the Lord" he surpassed the false apostles as much as in labours and sufferings for Christ. Never did Christian tell an experience more useful and strengthening to the Church.

I. AFFLICTION THE ANTIDOTE TO PRIDE. We do not speak so much of the natural pride of men over personal advantages of body or mind, over rank or riches, as of that subtle pride which is apt to creep into the heart after a great influx of spiritual light and joy. One may be exalted overmuch on account of the clearer vision of heavenly things or the near access to the Lord which he has enjoyed. But there comes a timely affliction or rebuke, not merely to correct pride if it is indulged, but to anticipate and prevent its rising. "Lest I should be exalted." The wise man accepts this as a kindness from God. "There was given to me a thorn in the flesh."

II. PRAYER THE ANTIDOTE TO DESPONDENCY. "I besought the Lord thrice." When one is cast down, worldly-wise friends can only bid him cheer up, cast off dull care, etc. But the resource of the Christian is to pray to the God of his life. And prayer must be repeated. The Saviour prayed thrice before the angel from heaven appeared to strengthen him. Paul prayed thrice before the answer of grace and peace fell upon his fainting soul.

III. Christ's grace that sweetens all. He knows well the piercing of thorns, the fiery darts, and the "blast of the terrible ones," and he can have compassion. He did not, indeed, see fit to relieve his servant Paul at once of his distress, but assured him of compensative grace and sustaining strength; and so the apparent evil was turned into a blessing, the pain and sorrow into joy. Be of good comfort, O believers! Against your own felt weakness set Christ's strength; and against all malice of Satan and his messengers set Christ's sufficient grace.—F.

Ver. 1.—*Visions and revelations.* "I will come to visions and revelations of the Lord." The apostle had been dwelling on his personal experiences. He had been compelled by the evil things that were said of him to refer to his own life, conduct, and sufferings for Christ's sake, in self-vindication. He would, however, not have spoken one word about these things if the honour of Christ had not been bound up with his claim to apostleship. He had now said everything that needed to be said about himself; and it was every way pleasanter and healthier to turn away from his own doings and sufferings, and to fix his heart and his thoughts upon what God had done for him. Upon the Divine visions and revelations given to him he in great part rested his apostolic claim. To him an apostle was, just what a prophet of the olden time had been, a man who had direct and personal communications with the Lord Jesus, and received instructions immediately from him. For such instances in St. Paul's career, see Acts ix. 4—6; xvi. 9; xviii. 9; xxii. 18; xxiii. 11; xxvii. 23; Gal. ii. 2; and the scenes recorded in the chapter now before us. This claim to direct revelation the enemies of St. Paul denied, and laughed to scorn his pretensions as the indications of insanity. Dean Plumptre tells us that "in the Clementine Homilies—a kind of controversial romance representing the later views of the Ebionite or Judaizing party, in which most recent critics have recognized a thinly veiled attempt to present the characteristic features of St. Paul under the pretence of an attack on Simon Magus, just as the writer of a political novel in modern times might draw the portraits of his rivals under fictitious names— we find stress laid on the alleged claims of Simon to have had communications from the Lord through visions and dreams and outward revelations; and this claim is contrasted with that of Peter, who had personally followed Christ during his ministry on earth. What was said then, in the form of this elaborate attack, may well have been said before by the more malignant advocates of the same party. The charge of insanity was one easy to make, and of all charges, perhaps, the most difficult to refute by one who gloried in the facts which were alleged as its foundation—who did see visions and did 'speak with tongues' in the ecstasy of adoring rapture." Compare the expression, "whether we be beside ourselves," in ch. v. 13. When the particular visions came to which reference is made in the passage before us cannot certainly be known. St. Paul only aids us by referring to the time as "about fourteen years ago." The suggestion we prefer is that they were granted during the time of his fainting after the stoning at Lystra, and were the Divine comfortings of that hour of sorest peril and distress (Acts xiv. 19).

I. Visions and revelations are agencies which God has always used. They do not belong to any one age. We have no right to say that they are limited to ancient times. There have always been the true and the counterfeit; but the true should not be missed or denied because the false have been found out. There are good gold coins, or men would not trouble to make spurious sovereigns. Fanaticism deludes its victims into imaginary visions, but souls that are kin with God, and open to him, can receive communications from him. Illustrate from all ages, *e.g.* Noah, Abraham, Jacob, Joseph, Moses, Joshua, Gideon, Samuel, David, Isaiah, Joseph (the husband of Mary), aged Simeon, Zacharias, etc. So in the Christian age we find visions granted to Cornelius, Philip, Peter, and John, as well as Paul, and traces of prophets, such as Agabus, and even of prophetesses. St. Paul's visions were probably of the nature of a trance; the mind being absorbed in contemplation may be prepared to receive Divine revealings. It is right to subject all claims to visions to careful scrutiny, and the things communicated to men at such times must be tested by their harmony with the written revelation; but we need not refuse to recognize the truth that God has direct relations to souls now as certainly as in past ages. Both truth and duty may still be directly revealed.

II. They come to certain prepared individuals. Not to masses, not to Churches, not to meetings. The vision is for individuals, who are thus made agents in the communication to men of the Divine thought and will. F. W. Robertson says, "To comprehend the visions we must comprehend the man. For God gives visions at his own will, and according to certain and fixed laws. He does not inspire every one. He does not reveal his mysteries to men of selfish, or hard, or phlegmatic temperaments. He gives preternatural communications to those whom he prepares beforehand by a peculiar spiritual sensitiveness. There are, physically, certain sensitivenesses to sound and colour that qualify men to become gifted musicians and painters; so, spiritually, there are certain strong original susceptibilities (I say *original*, as derived from God, the origin of all), and on these God bestows strange gifts and sights, deep feelings not to be uttered in human language, and immeasurable by the ordinary standard. Such a man was St. Paul—a very wondrous nature, the Jewish nature in all its strength. We know that the Jewish temperament fitted men to be the organs of a revelation. Its fervour, its moral sense, its veneration, its indomitable will, all adapted the highest sons of the nation for receiving hidden truths and communicating them to others."

III. They come on particular occasions. By the law of Divine economy, only when they are the precise thing demanded, the only agency that will efficiently meet the case.

IV. They come in graciously adapted forms. Heard voices sometimes, at other times dreams, ocular visions, symbols, trances, and mental panoramas. Close by showing that, because the modern mode is direct to souls, immediate to the shaping of men's thoughts, and not through symbols, or dreams, or visions, we need not lose the conviction that, upon due occasions still, God gives to some amongst us insight and revelation of his truth.—R. T.

Ver. 7.—*Satan's messenger; or, the thorn in the flesh*. It would be a grave mistake to make this description of St. Paul's affliction the basis of any argument for the personality or agency of Satan. He does but use the familiar Jewish figure of speech, which may or may not embody for him any doctrine concerning Satan. The figure is most strikingly used in the introduction to the Book of Job; but the following other passages illustrate how familiar it was to the Jewish mind: Luke xiii. 16; Acts x. 38; 1 Cor. v. 5; 1 Thess. ii. 18; 1 Tim. i. 20. "These are enough to prove that, while men referred special forms of suffering of mind and body, chiefly the former, to the agency of demons, they were prepared to recognize the agency of Satan in almost every form of bodily calamity." No single description of Satan can cover the entire Scripture representation of him, but one aspect presented by it has not been duly considered. He is sometimes regarded as the agent, or executor, of the Divine purpose in physical calamity, and even in moral testings through temptation. We may think of an angel of temptation as well as of an angel of death. We may not even think of Satan as in any sense acting independently. He, too, comes fully within the Divine rulings and *over*rulings. What the nature of the apostle's affliction or temptation was cannot be certainly known from his descriptions of it. Many explanations have been suggested. Lightfoot summarizes them thus: (1) a bodily ailment of some kind: (2) some opposition encountered from his enemies, or suffering endured; (3) carnal longings; (4) spiritual trials, doubtings, etc. Archdeacon Farrar thinks the "thorn" must have been some physical malady, and suggests epilepsy, of which he says, "It is painful; it is recurrent; it opposes an immense difficulty to all exertion; it may at any time cause a temporary suspension of work; it is intensely humiliating to the person who suffers from it; it exercises a repellent effect on those who witness its distressing manifestations." But he adds that there can be no doubt that St. Paul also suffered from ophthalmia, and that this disease fulfils in every particular the conditions of the problem. Dean Plumptre favours the idea of corporeal rather than mental suffering, and says, "Nor need we be surprised that this infirmity—neuralgia of the head and face or inflammation of the eyes, perhaps in some measure the after-consequences of the blindness at Damascus—should be described as 'a messenger of Satan.'" Another suggestion has been made which is fresh and interesting, and worthy of very patient consideration. Professor Lias writes, "Our last alternative must be some defect of character, calculated to interfere with St. Paul's success as a minister of Jesus Christ. And the defect which falls in best with what we know of St. Paul is an infirmity of temper.   There seems little doubt that he gave way to an outbreak of this kind when before the Sanhedrim, though he set himself right at once by a prompt apology (Acts xxiii. 2—5).   A similar idea is suggested by St. Paul's unwillingness to go to Corinth until the points in dispute between him and a considerable portion of the Corinthian Church were in a fair way of being settled.   In fact, his conduct was precisely the reverse of that of a person who felt himself endowed with great tact, persuasiveness, and command of temper.   Such a man would trust little to messages and letters, much to his own presence and personal influence.   St. Paul, on the contrary, feared to visit Corinth until there was a reasonable prospect of avoiding all altercation.   In fact, he could not trust himself there.   He 'feared that God would humble him among them' (ch. xii. 21).   He desired above all things to avoid the necessity of 'using sharpness,' very possibly because he feared that, when once compelled to assume a tone of severity, his language might exceed the bounds of Christian love.   The supposition falls in with what we know of the apostle before his conversion (Acts vii. 58; ix. 1).   It is confirmed by his stern language to Elymas the sorcerer (Acts xiii. 10), with which we may compare the much milder language used by St. Peter on a far more awful occasion (Acts v. 3, 9).   The quarrel between St. Paul and St. Barnabas makes the supposition infinitely more probable. The passage, Gal. iv. 13, 14, may be interpreted of the deep personal affection which the apostle felt he had inspired in spite of his occasional irritability of manner.   The expression (Gal. iv. 20), that he 'desired to be present with them, and to change his voice,' would seem to point in the same direction.   And if we add to these considerations the fact, which the experience of God's saints in all ages has conclusively established, of the difficulty of subduing an infirmity of temper, as well as the pain, remorse, and humiliation such an infirmity is wont to cause to those who groan under it, we may be inclined to believe that not the least probable hypothesis concerning the 'thorn,' or 'stake,' in the flesh is, that the loving heart of the apostle bewailed as his sorest trial the misfortune that by impatience in word he had often wounded those for whom he would willingly have given his life."   Whatever the form of the trial may have been, we note—

I. ST. PAUL'S THOUGHTS ABOUT IT. These may be unfolded and illustrated generally, in relation (1) to Christian culture; (2) to Christian work, and especially (3) in relation to peril of spiritual pride.   St. Paul saw clearly that the humiliation came "through the abundance of the revelations;" and "lest he should be puffed up beyond measure."

II. ST. PAUL'S LESSON LEARNED FROM IT. It was mainly this—that the mission of suffering may be continuous through life.   It may be the point of God's dealing with us that he does not sanctify us by sudden, occasional, and severe afflictions, but by calling us to bear a lifelong burden of disability or frailty.   Troubles of this kind cannot be removed in response to prayer, because to remove them would be to check the sanctifying process.   God, in sending a temporary affliction, may have a temporary end in view, and so, when that end is duly reached, the affliction may be removed.   But if the work of our sanctification is, in the Divine wisdom, to be wrought by a continuous life-pressure, then the response to our prayer can only be this: " My grace is sufficient for thee."   Dean Stanley points out that " St. Paul's sufferings were to him what the mysterious agony that used at times to seize on Alfred, in the midst of feast and revel, had been to the saintly and heroic king, a discipline working for his perfection."—R. T.

Ver. 9.—*Sufficient grace.* The following incident from John Bunyan's experience may serve to introduce this subject.   One evening, as Bunyan was in a meeting of Christian people, full of sadness and terror, suddenly there " brake in " upon him with great power, and three times together, the words, " My grace is sufficient for thee; my grace is sufficient for thee; my grace is sufficient for thee."   And " Oh, methought," says he, " that every word was a mighty word unto me; as 'my,' and 'grace,' and ' sufficient,' and ' for thee,' they were then, and sometimes are still, far bigger than others be."   The great practical question for us, in our endeavour to live the godly life, is not—What have we to bear? but—What strength have we for the bearing?   God's help never comes first to a man in his *circumstances,* but always first *in him.*   The grace given is grace helping *him* in the circumstances. So the Christian often knows that he is helped when those around him can see no signs of the helping. God's promise from the olden time is this, "As thy day so shall thy strength be." In all our relations with human trouble, our attention is directed to the removal of the trouble itself or the change of the circumstances which occasioned the trouble. We move the pain-wearied sufferer into a position of greater ease. We soften and smoothe the pillow for the aching head. We offer temporary help to the man distressed in business. But God does not promise any man that he will alter his circumstances or altogether relieve him from his trouble. The economy of life is arranged, in the Divine wisdom, for the greatest good of the greatest number, and consequently some of those circumstances which bring trouble to Christian hearts cannot be altered without involving injury to others. God "strengthens with strength in the soul." To him body and circumstance are secondary things; souls are of the first importance, and bodies and circumstances gain their importance by their influence on souls. Inward strength to bear is a far higher provision than any mere mastery of the ills and troubles of the life. A man is never lost until he has lost heart. But if God supplies inward strength we never shall lose heart, and so we never shall be lost. Outwardly a man may be tossed about, worn, wearied, lost, wounded, almost broken, and yet inwardly he may be kept in perfect peace; his mind may be stayed on God; he may be "strong in the Lord, and in the power of his might." We may say of this "sufficient grace" that it is—

I. ADAPTED. We are to conceive of the grace of God, not as a great mass, a quantity of which is duly measured out to meet our need, but rather as a treasury of various kinds and various colours, from which may be obtained just those threads that will match our circumstances and repair the disasters into which we have fallen.

II. TIMELY. Here we require to distinguish between what we think to be timely and what *God* thinks to be timely, remembering that God never delays, but is never hurried. He waits for the moment of extremity. "When the tale of bricks is doubled, then comes Moses." And it should also be shown that we may not look for some particular grace and help to-day, which God knows will only be required to-morrow. The very charm of "sufficient grace" is that it is precisely the thing for the occasion." Those who are looking for kinds of grace for which they have no immediate and pressing needs will be in danger of missing the gracious provisions which their Lord is ever making for them. The way between earth and heaven is a ladder—Jacob saw it—and the angels came up and down it. We cannot reach the top by looking up; only by putting our feet up one round after another. And God is willing to be ever close beside us, holding us with his hand and strengthening us for each uplifted step.

III. ABUNDANT. That is assured in the fact that it is the grace of *God*, who is able to do exceedingly abundantly for us above all that we ask or think. The man with "sufficient grace" is *efficient* to all work, whether it be *bearing* or *doing*. He is *nowhere* alone; grace is with him.—R. T.

Ver. 9.—*Glorying in infirmities.* In introduction should be given some high and noble instances of triumph over disease, pain, or disability, in doing philanthropic and Christian work; *e.g.* Baxter, Robert Hall, H. Martyn, C. Pattison, F. W. Robertson, etc. Show that, while bodily strength may be consecrated to God's service, it is also true that physical weakness may serve him, and a man's very frailty glorify his Lord. This may be further opened out by showing how—

I. IT BEARS UPON HUMILITY. The grace which is the necessary completion and final adornment of Christian character. The grace which puts on Christian fruitage all the bloom. Humility is won by the pressure of God's hand upon us.

II. IT NOURISHES DEPENDENCE ON GOD. "When I am weak, then am I strong." This is the Christian paradox. Such dependence is not easy; it is one of the things to which experience of failure and frailty alone can bring us. He is fitted for life and for heaven who from his deep heart says, "I cannot, but God can."

III. IT CULTIVATES CHARACTER. We know that physical weakness bears directly and continuously upon temper, disposition, and virtue. Afflictions never test us, never bear upon the whole culture of character, as does continuous pain or frailty. "As the outward man perishes, the inward man is renewed day by day."

IV. IT KEEPS A MAN OPEN TO God. By its constant reminder of the need of God. The frail man proves the preciousness of prayer. F. W. Robertson most forcibly says of prayer, "The true value of prayer is not this—to bend the eternal will to ours, but this—to bend our wills to it." Frail, ever-suffering Paul laboured "more abundantly than they all," and astonishing still is the soul-work that can be gotten out of feeble men and women—with God's grace.—R. T.

Ver. 16.—*Caught with guile.* "Nevertheless, being crafty, I caught you with guile." This expression occasions serious difficulty to the exegete. It may be that St. Paul is referring to the accusation made against him that, being a crafty man, he had caught the Corinthians with guile. He repudiates altogether such a charge, and pleads, as a sufficient proof of his guilelessness, that no man could say he had ever used his official position to make personal gains. Archdeacon Farrar says, "Being confessedly one who strove for peace and unity, who endeavoured to meet all men half-way, who was ready to be all things to all men if by any means he might save some, he has more than once to vindicate his character from those charges of insincerity, craftiness, dishonesty, guile, man-pleasing, and flattery which are, perhaps, summed up in the general deprecation which he so indignantly rebuts, that 'he walked according to the flesh,' or in other words, that his motives were not spiritual, but low and selfish." He paraphrases the sentence taken as our text thus: "But stop! though I did not burden you, yet 'being a cunning person, I caught you with guile.' Under the pretext of a collection I got money out of you by my confederates! I ask you, is that a fact?" A possible insinuation of the Corinthians is hereby anticipated and refuted; and we need not treat the statement of the text as any acknowledgment by St. Paul that he had adopted any guileful schemes. No man could have been more thoroughly genuine, more honourably straightforward. The subject for our consideration may be treated under three divisions.

I. THE IDEA OF "CAUGHT WITH GUILE" THAT IS INADMISSIBLE IN CHRISTIAN WORK. 1. Anything approaching to "doing evil that good may come" is inadmissible. 2. So is any altering or qualifying the fundamental truths, claims, and duties of the gospel. 3. So is any kind of action that is immoral, or of which the morality is even doubtful. Illustrate by some of the guileful principles enunciated by the Jesuit fathers, and so mercilessly exposed by Pascal in the 'Provincial Letters.' Sincerity and simplicity are first virtues in Christian workers; both the man and his labours must be such as can be searched through and through. Guile, as the world understands the term, must not be once known among us, as becometh saints.

II. THE IDEA OF "CAUGHT WITH GUILE" THAT IS ADMISSIBLE IN CHRISTIAN WORK. In the sense of adaptation to capacity it is an essential feature of Christian service. This may sometimes appear to the onlooker as guile. In teaching children or uneducated people, truth has to be simplified, to be set in figure and parable, and broken up into parts and pieces, and such guilefulness St. Paul recognizes as valuable. He fed the people with "milk" when he knew that they were unfit to receive "strong meat" of truth. Our Lord himself was guileful in this good sense, for at the close of his intercourse with his disciples he said, "I have many things to say unto you, but ye cannot bear them now." It may also be shown that there is a "quick-wittedness" and skilful seizing of opportunities, which are gifts finding honourable spheres in the Christian Church.

III. THE IDEA OF "CAUGHT WITH GUILE" THAT NOBLE-MINDED MEN SHRINK FROM EMPLOYING. Such are the various sensational devices of modern revivalism. The masses are to be caught with the guile of trumpet, and drum, and dress, and excited meetings. We need not say that such things are inadmissible, because they are not morally wrong. But where there is a full sympathy with the Divine Lord, who "did not strive, nor cry, nor cause his voice to be heard in the streets," all such guilefulnesses cannot but be painful. Anything approaching to an *advertising* of the gospel or the preachers of the gospel grieves the sensitive feeling of all who know that the gospel needs no such introductions, but is itself God's power unto salvation to every one that believes. Our "yea" had better be simple "yea;" with no blast of trumpet or roll of drum let us tell men of the life there is for all in Christ our living Saviour; and let our only guile be *adaptation.*—R. T.

Ver. 21.—*The humbling of God's ministers.* "I fear . . . lest, when I come again, my God will humble me among you." "There is something almost plaintive in the tone in which the apostle speaks of the sin of his disciples as the only real 'humiliation, which he has to fear." The following points will be readily worked out and illustrated according to the experiences of the preacher:—

I. SUCH HUMBLINGS COME FROM SEEMING FAILURES. Compare our Lord's distressful reproach of Capernaum and other towns on the shores of the lake of Galilee. See also St. Paul's trouble over the failure of the Galatians from their primitive faith: "O foolish Galatians, who hath bewitched you?" etc.

II. SUCH HUMBLINGS COME FROM STRIFE AND DIVISIONS. As illustrated in the Corinthian Church (see 1 Cor. ii.). Such strife may arise from (1) false teaching; (2) masterful individuals, who make parties; (3) misunderstandings; (4) exercise of necessary Church discipline.

III. SUCH HUMBLINGS COME FROM INDIVIDUAL BACKSLIDINGS. There is no sadder phase of experience for Christian ministers than the spiritual and moral failure of their converts, and of those whom they have most fully trusted in Christian life and work. So often men fall into temptation and are overcome in their middle life. When ministers look for the ripest fruitage, then there is blight and death; wealth, pleasure, vice, smite and kill the soul, and the pastor weeps over the toil of life that seems to have been all in vain. St. Paul spoke of the Corinthians as "his glory and joy;" and the things which he goes on to mention in this verse put shame on his work, for the gospel call is "not unto uncleanness, but unto holiness." And ministers spend their strength for nought if those who believe are not "careful to maintain good works."—R. T.

EXPOSITION.

CHAPTER XIII.

CONCLUDING APPEALS AND EXHORTATIONS.

Ver. 1.—**This is the third time I am coming to you.** I have thrice formed the intention, though the second time I had to forego my plan (ch. i. 15—17). **In the mouth of two or three witnesses.** The quotation is from Deut. xix. 15. It has been explained as a reference to *examinations* which he intended to hold on his arrival at Corinth. It is much more probable that St. Paul is representing his separate visits as separate *attestations* to the truths which he preaches. Ver. 2.—**I told you before;** rather, *I have told you before.* **As if I were present, the second time.** The meaning seems to be, "You must understand this announcement as distinctly as if I were with you, and uttered it by word of mouth." **And being absent now I write;** rather, *so now being absent.* The verb "I write" is almost certainly an explanatory gloss. **And to all other;** rather, *and to the rest, all of them.* Namely, to those who, though they may not have fallen into gross sin, still rejected St. Paul's authority, and said that he was afraid to come in person. **I will not spare** (ch. i. 23; iv. 19, 21). Ver. 3.—**Of Christ speaking in me;** rather, *of the Christ who speaketh in me.* **Which;** rather, *who.* **But is mighty in you.** The spirit of Christ, in spite of all their shortcomings, had not deserted them (see 1 Cor. i. 6, 7; ii. 4).

Ver. 4.—**For though.** The "though" should be omitted. **Through weakness;** literally, *out of weakness;* i.e. as a result of that human weakness of our nature which he took upon him, and which rendered him liable to agony and death (ch. viii. 9; Phil. ii. 7, 8; 1 Pet. iii. 18; Heb. ii. 10—18). **But we shall live with him . . . toward you.** This thought of participation alike in Christ's humiliation and his glory, alike in his weakness and his might, was very familiar to St. Paul (ch. iv. 10—12; Eph. i. 19, 20), Here, however, the following words, "toward you," *i.e.* "with reference to you," show that the life of which he is thinking is the vigorous re-establishment of his spiritual authority in Christ over the Church of Corinth. Ver. 5.—**Prove your own selves.** In other words, "test your own sincerity." **Jesus Christ is in you.** To this truth—that the body of every Christian is a temple of the Holy Spirit of Christ—St. Paul returns again and again (Gal. ii. 20; iv. 19; Eph. iii. 17; Col. i. 27). We find the same truth frequently in St. John (John xv. 4, 5; 1 John iii. 24, etc.). **Except ye be reprobates.** The Greek word *adokimoi*—from the same root as the verb "to test"—means tried and found to be worthless. "*Reprobate* silver shall men call them, because the Lord hath rejected them" (Jer. vi. 30). The word is found almost exclusively in St Paul (ch. xiii. 5, 6, 7; Rom. i. 28; 1 Cor. ix. 27; 2 Tim. iii. 8; Titus i. 16). The only other passage of the New Testament where it occurs is Heb. vi. 8; and the reader must not read Calvinistic horrors into an expression which gives no sanction to them.

Ver. 6.—That we are not reprobates. My power and faithfulness will be tested as well as yours, and I hope that it will stand the test.

Ver. 7.—Approved (*dokimoi*). The opposite of "reprobates." **Though we be as reprobates**; rather, [*I pray*] *that ye may do what is excellent, and that we may be as reprobates.* This is one of the intense expressions which, like Rom. ix. 3, spring from the earnest and passionate unselfishness of St. Paul. His anxiety is for them, not at all for himself. *As reprobates;* i.e. in the judgment of men (comp. Rom. ix. 3).

Ver. 8.—**We can do nothing against the truth.** I am powerless against anything which is true, real, sincere; I can exercise *no* power except in the cause of the truth. Be true to the gospel, and you will be mighty and I shall be powerless, and (as he proceeds to say) I shall rejoice at the result.

Ver. 9.—**When we are weak, and ye are strong** (comp. 1 Cor. iv. 8—10). *Strong;* "powerful" (ch. x. 4). **We wish**; rather, *we pray.* **Your perfection**; rather, *your perfect union;* "the *readjustment* of your disordered elements." A similar word occurs in Eph. iv. 10, and the verb in ver. 11; 1 Cor. i. 10; 1 Thess. iii. 10, etc. It is also used in the Gospels for "mending nets" (Mark i. 19, etc.).

Ver. 10.—**I should use sharpness.** The word rendered "sharpness" is an adverb, like our "abruptly" or "precipitately." The only other passage of the New Testament where it occurs is Titus i. 13; but the substantive *apotomia* occurs in Rom. xi. 22 for "severity."

Ver. 11.—**Finally, brethren, farewell.** His concluding words are marked by great gentleness, as though to heal the effects of the sharp rebuke and irony to which he has been compelled to have recourse. The word may also mean "rejoice" (Phil. iii. 1; iv. 4). **Be perfect** (see note on "perfection" in ver. 9). **Be of one mind**; literally, *think the same thing* (Phil. ii. 2; 1 Pet. iii. 8; 1 Cor. i. 10; Rom. xii. 16, 18). **Be at peace** (Eph. iv. 3).

Ver. 12.—**Greet one another.** The verb, being in the aorist, refers to a single act.

When the letter had been read in their hearing, they were, in sign of perfect unity and mutual forgiveness, to give one another the kiss of peace. **With a holy kiss** (see on 1 Cor. xvi. 20; comp. 1 Pet. v. 14).

Ver. 13.—**All the saints**; namely, **in** Philippi or Macedonia.

Ver. 14.—**The grace of our Lord**, etc. This is the only place where the full apostolic benediction occurs, and is alone sufficient to prove the doctrine of the Trinity. St. Paul seems to feel that the fullest benediction is needed at the close of the severest letter. **With you all.** The word "all" is here introduced with special tenderness and graciousness. Some have sinned before; some have not repented; yet he has for them all one prayer and one blessing and one "seal of holy apostolic love."

The superscription, though of no authority, may here correctly state that the letter was written at Philippi, and conveyed thence to Corinth by Titus and (possibly) Luke (see ch. viii. 16—22).

These are the last recorded words addressed by St. Paul to the Corinthian Church. The results produced by the letter and by his visit of three months (Acts xx. 2, 3) were probably satisfactory, for we hear no more of any troubles at Corinth during his lifetime, and the spirit in which he writes the letter to the Romans from Corinth seems to have been unwontedly calm. He had been kindly welcomed (Rom. xv. 23), and the collection, about which he had been so anxious, seems to have fully equalled his expectations, for as we know (Rom. xvi. 18; Acts xx. 4), he conveyed it to Jerusalem in person with the delegates of the Churches. We gain a subsequent glimpse of the Corinthian Church. Some thirty-five years later, when a letter, which is still extant, was addressed to them by St. Clement of Rome, they were still somewhat inclined to be turbulent, disunited, and sceptical (see 'Ep. ad Cor.,' iii., iv., xiii., xiv., xxxvii., etc.); but still there are some marked signs of improvement. About A.D. 135 they were visited by Hegesippus (Eusebius, 'Hist. Eccl.,' iv. 22), who spoke very favourably of them, especially of their obedience and liberality. Their bishop, Dionysius, was at that time exercising a widespread influence (Eusebius, 'Hist. Eccl.,' iv. 23).

HOMILETICS.

Vers. 1—14.—*Paul's epistolary farewell to the Corinthians.* "This is the third time I am coming to you," etc. This chapter concludes Paul's letters to the Corinthians. There is no evidence that he wrote a word to them after this. The letters had evidently been a task to him. To a man of his tender nature no duty could be more painful than that of censure and reproach. Nothing but a sense of loyalty to the holiness of Christianity could have urged him to it. No doubt he felt a burden rolled from his heart, and a freer breath, when he dictated the last sentence. He was now to visit them for the third time, determined to execute the discipline that might be required, earnestly hoping at the same time that, when he was once more amongst them, the necessity for such discipline would not appear. In this concluding chapter we find words of *warning, exhortation, prayer, comfort,* and *benediction.*

I. WORDS OF WARNING. He warns them of a chastisement which he determined to inflict upon all offenders, both in doctrine and conduct, against the gospel of Christ. Four things are suggested here concerning the discipline he intended to prosecute. 1. *The discipline would be righteous.* " In the mouth of two or three witnesses shall every word be established." Here is a rule quoted and endorsed by Christ (Matt. xviii. 16), an axiom of the Jewish Law and a natural dictate of judicial policy. What he probably means to say, is, "I will not chastise any without proper evidence. I will not trust to rumours or surmises ; I will test every case myself, so that justice shall be done. Therefore the true need not fear, the false alone need apprehend." 2. *The discipline would be rigorous.* " I told you before, and foretell you, as if I were present, the second time ; and being absent now I write to them which heretofore have sinned, and to all other, that, if I come again, I will not spare." He had threatened this in his former letter (1 Cor. iv. 13—19), in which he had also indicated severity (1 Cor. v. 5), and spoken of " delivering them to Satan "—an expression which probably means not only excommunication, but the infliction of corporal suffering. The blindness of Elymas and the death of Ananias and Sapphira are instances of the power of the apostles over the body of men. This chastisement would be dealt, not only to the notorious incestuous person often referred to, but to " all other ; " he would " spare " none. " I will not spare." A more terrible chastisement know I not than entire excommunication from the fellowship of the good. 3. *The discipline would demonstrate the existence of Christ in him.* " Since ye seek a proof of Christ speaking in me." " They had called in question his apostolic authority, they had demanded the evidence of his Divine commission. He says he would now furnish such evidence by inflicting just punishment on all offenders, and they should have abundant proof that Christ spoke by him." He could have given this proof sooner, but he acted in this respect like Christ, and was content to appear " weak " amongst them, in order that his power might be more conspicuously displayed. " For though he was crucified through weakness, yet he liveth by the power of God. For we also are weak in him, but we shall live with him by the power of God toward you." " The thought," says Dean Plumptre, " that underlies the apparently hard saying is that the disciples of Christ share at once in their Lord's weakness and in his strength. We, too, are weak, says the apostle, we have our share in infirmities and sufferings, which are ennobled by the thought that they are ours because we are his, but we know that we shall live in the highest sense in the activities of the spiritual life, which also we shall share with him, and which comes to us by the power of God. This life will be manifested in the exercise of our spiritual power towards you and for your good." In the case of the truly good, in all weakness there is strength, and the weakness one day will disappear and the strength be manifest.

II. WORDS OF EXHORTATION. " Examine yourselves." Self-scrutiny is at once a duty the most urgent and the most neglected. Hence the universal prevalence of self-ignorance. Even men who know a very great deal of the world without are ignorant of the world within, the world of worlds. 1. *The momentous point to be tested in self-scrutiny.* " Whether ye be in the faith." Not whether you have faith in you, for all men are more or less credulous, and have some kind of faith in them ; but whether you are " in the faith." The faith here is the gospel, or rather the Christ of the gospel ; whether you are in Christ, in the character of Christ. Intellectually and morally, all men are living in the characters of others. The grand thing is to be in the character of Christ, in his principles, sympathies, aims, etc. 2. *The momentous conclusion to be reached by self-scrutiny.* " Know ye not [emphatic] your own selves, how that Jesus Christ is in you, except ye be reprobates ? " If you are in the faith, you are in his character, and he is in your life ; nay, your life itself. Should you find you are not in the faith, ye are " reprobates," counterfeits, spurious, not genuine ; tares, not wheat ; hypocrites. Here, then, is a work for every man to do—" examine " himself, introspect, scrutinize, decide, and thus know his real moral condition.

III. WORDS OF PRAYER. "Now I pray to God," etc. For what does he pray? Not for his own reputation or himself. As if he had said, "I am not anxious about my own standing amongst you." He prays for two things. 1. *That they should be kept from the wrong.* "Now I pray to God that ye do no evil." "Do no evil," nothing inconsistent with the character and teaching of Christ. "Cease to do evil, learn to do well." 2. *That they should possess the right.* "Not that we should appear approved, but that ye should do that which is honest, though we be as reprobates." "We pray not that *we* may gain a reputation as successful workers in your eyes or those of others, but that *you* may do that which is nobly good (may advance from a negative to a positive form of holiness), even though the result of that may be that we no longer put our apostolic supernatural powers into play, and so seem to fail in the trial to which you challenge us."

IV. WORDS OF COMFORT. "We can do nothing against the truth." There are two comforting ideas here. 1. *That truth is uninjurable.* "We can do nothing against the truth." Let the "truth" here stand for Jesus, who is the "Truth," the great moral Reality incarnated, all that is real in doctrine and duty embodied in him; who can injure such? Man can do much against *theories* of truth, *conventional manifestations* of truth, *ecclesiastical representations* of truth, *verbal revelations* of truth. The more he does against these, perhaps, the better; but he can do nothing against "the truth," its *essence.* Man may quench all the gas-lamps in the world, but he cannot dim one star. The great ethical and doctrinal truths embodied in the life and teaching of Christ are imperishable, they live in all religions. Men can destroy the forms of nature, level the mountains, dry up the rivers, burn the forests, but can do nothing against the imperishable *elements* of nature, and these elements will live, build up new mountains, open fresh rivers, and create new forests. You can do nothing against the truth. 2. *That goodness is unpunishable.* "For we are glad, when we are weak, and ye are strong: and this also we wish, even your perfection." It is unpunishable: (1) Because it is goodness. The best of men are too "weak" in authority to punish those who are "strong" in goodness. And in truth there is no authority in the universe, even God himself, to punish goodness. The stronger a man is in goodness, the weaker the power to chastise him. Hence Paul wishes to find them "strong" in goodness when he comes amongst them. He wishes this because goodness is their "perfection," or restoration. The way to paralyze all penal forces is to promote the growth of goodness. (2) Because it is restorative. "Therefore I write these things being absent, lest being present I should use sharpness, according to the power which the Lord hath given me to edification, and not to destruction." Its destiny is "edification," not "destruction;" building up, not pulling down. Moral goodness is the restorative power in the universe.

V. WORDS OF BENEDICTION. "Finally, brethren, farewell. Be perfect, be of good comfort, be of one mind, live in peace; and the God of love and peace shall be with you." His benedictory words imply: 1. *Be happy.* "Farewell," which means rejoice. To be happy they must be "perfect," "of good comfort," etc. 2. *Be blest of God.* "The grace of the Lord Jesus Christ, and the love of God, and the communion of the Holy Ghost, be with you all."

HOMILIES BY VARIOUS AUTHORS.

Vers. 1—4.—*Announcement of his purpose; Christ's power in him and in his apostleship.* About to visit the Corinthians "the third time," he informs them very distinctly what they had to expect. In the words of the Old Testament Law, he says, "In the mouth of two or three witnesses shall every word be established." The strength of his resolution to punish impenitent offenders is declared—"I will not spare." A crisis was at hand, and he was fully prepared to meet the issue. He refers to the main source of all the trouble, viz. the disparagement of his office as Christ's apostle. Everything had been done by the Judaizers to put contempt on him and his official position. The forbearance he had shown, the patience under repeated and aggravated provocation, his deeds of self-denial, Christ's testimony to the greatness of the work done among them, had all been misconstrued and turned to his injury. Even his infirmities, the defects of personal appearance, his conscientious avoidance of the least worldly art in his ministry, had been used to his disadvantage. Craft, falsehood, malignity, had followed him with persistent steps. Neither his private nor public life had escaped prying eyes and slanderous tongues. A man in feeble health, his strength constantly over-taxed, infirmities growing beyond his years as well as with his years, labouring to support himself, and thus making heavy drafts on his bodily powers, he had these ills daily augmented by annoyances and vexations from those who sought to come between him and his Churches. To undo his work was their aim and ambition. They hated him officially, they despised him personally, nor could they rest while he had friends to cheer him on in his labours. What is most noticeable is the utter blindness of these persecutors to the wonderful tokens of God's presence with him. It is to this fact he alludes in the words, "Since ye seek a proof of Christ speaking in me." Remember, it was in this Corinth, where these turbulent spirits were most industrious to overthrow him, that Christ had given the most numerous and remarkable evidences of the favour bestowed on his apostle as the apostle of the Gentiles. "Seek a proof," to our ears sounds most strangely. "Signs and wonders and mighty deeds," and yet "seek a proof of Christ speaking in me"! It is well that there was an antecedent history, a fourfold history but one biography, and that this biography of the Lord Jesus opens to us a full view of man's capacity to disbelieve where Divine manifestations are concerned. "If they have persecuted me, they will also persecute you." So the Lord Jesus had foretold; so St. Paul had realized. And now, in the closing hour of writing this Epistle, the apostle identifies his condition with that of Christ in the days of the flesh. Years before, the great fact had occurred of which these recent facts were no more than exemplifications. Taking upon himself the lowly form of a servant and submitting to every kind of privation and sorrow, putting himself as to his circumstances in extreme contrast with his power and never exercising this power except under the agency of the Holy Ghost, men treated him, Son of God, Son of man, as one in their hands, over whom and his earthly destiny they had entire control. "He was crucified through weakness." He could have been crucified in no other way. The sole condition under which this event was possible is here stated, viz. *weakness.* The weakness was assumed voluntarily by him because it was necessary to the work of redemption. "Yet he liveth by the power of God." Even in the grave his body was treated as though men had it under mastery. Roman procurator and Jewish Sanhedrim held it as their own, and stationed a military guard at the sepulchre where his corpse, still their prisoner, lay till the third day ended the mystery of his weakness. Then came the triumph "of the power of God." Authority felt it and was abased. To its degradation it added the infamy of a lie, and to the lie the infamy of a money bribe. Guilt felt it and acknowledged its impending curse in the return of innocent blood as vengeance on its head. Sad as this hour was to St. Paul, his faith was never firmer. Had he not said just before, that if he should have to "bewail many which have sinned already, and have not repented," he should accept the humiliation as a holy discipline? "My God will humble me among you." One had gone before him in weakness. But his Leader in trial would be his Leader in triumph. "For we also are weak in him." It is not our weakness. It wears a human look, speaks human words, trembles with human sensibility, sighs with human pathos, yearns for relief with human desires. Nevertheless it is a fact, "we also are weak *in him.*" The weakness we share is that of the God-Man, the weakness of the Divine incarnation, so that we walk according to our small measure in the footsteps of him who "himself took our infirmities and bare our sicknesses." "But we shall live," not in the resurrection, but in the day when we come to Corinth and vindicate our authority, "we shall live with him by the power of God *toward you.*" Then, indeed, you who have taunted us as "weak and contemptible," shall see and know that this risen and exalted Christ is Christ in us, "the power of God toward you." Do you then "seek a proof of Christ speaking in me"? I shall come with "the power of God" and the "proof" shall be given.—L.

Vers. 5—10.—*Self-examination recommended; supremacy of Divine truth.* Proof of his apostleship had been the demand of the disaffected portion of the Corinthians; "but *prove* your own selves" is St. Paul's exhortation. "Examine not me, but yourselves, whether you are truly in the faith; put yourselves to the proof concerning

Christ's presence with you which you seek in me" (Conybeare and Howson). No one can help seeing how natural this advice was to the apostle, and how suitable to these noisy and fault-finding Corinthians. On the one hand, St. Paul was a man whom casual observers could easily misunderstand. His temperament, his habit of introversion, his intense self-consciousness, exposed him to constant misconception. Again, he was a born leader of men. Such a leader as he could not escape a severe probation while acquiring the ascendency to which he was predestined. Leaders who adapt themselves unscrupulously to times and circumstances gain a quick mastery. Leaders that shape contingencies to their high purposes and bring men into sympathy with a lofty ideal in their own souls must have creative genius, and exert it under sharp and continual opposition. To this class of leaders the apostle belonged. Furthermore, his position was unique by reason of the fact that his apostleship necessarily placed him between the two great rival forces of the age, Judaism and Gentilism. To show what the Law meant as a Divine institution; to show what Gentile civilization and culture meant as a long-existing providence; to harmonize as far as might be the truths in each; in brief, to mediate between their claims as widely organized economies, and put them on common ground as it respected Christianity and its supreme authority, and do away with the distinction of Jew and Gentile as to the conditions of salvation;—this was the most difficult task ever committed to a man. Owing to its intrinsic character, it brought him at every turn in contact with prejudices and passions which justified themselves in the one case by the miracles of Jehovah, in the other by the prescripts of government, and in both by the venerable sanction of ages. What wonder, then, that his career as a public man among public men was specialized quite as much by systematic and vindictive misrepresentation as by a success unequalled in the influence exerted over the thought and morals of the world! On the other hand, look at these young Christian communities, situated often wide apart and unable to strengthen each others' hands, planted in the midst of peoples hostile to their creeds and still more to their virtues, and dependent in most instances on the nurture of a single apostle; look at them in a state hardly more than inchoate,— and can we be surprised that they were in some cases the subjects of intestine disturbance, nay, of violent commotion? "Not many wise men after the flesh, not many mighty, not many noble," were "called;" but the "weak things of the world," "base things, and things despised," were "chosen," for the most part, as the original materials of that edifice which was to show in its proportions, its symmetry, its permanence, the workmanship of the Hand unseen. The "called" and the "chosen" were eventually to vindicate the wisdom of the call and the choice. Let us not overlook, however, the disadvantages inseparable at the time from the crude elements that constituted the early Churches. Without dwelling on these at length, suffice it to say that they were imperilled by a corrupt Judaism on the one side, and a most corrupt paganism on the other, the agencies and influences of which sought them as a prey to their lust of avarice and ambition. Now, the Church at Corinth was notably in this state of exposure. Gallio, the Proconsul of Achaia, had protected St. Paul against the fury of the Jews, and the Greeks had used the occasion to wreak their vengeance on the Jews. Retaliation was the order of the times. Baffled by a Roman official, insulted and beaten by a mob of Greeks, the Jews were not likely to forget the apostle, and we can imagine with what zest they would enjoy the zeal of the Judaizing emissaries, and how they would diligently foment the efforts made for his disgrace in Corinth. To what extent this was carried by the Jews as a body we can only conjecture. Certain it is, however, that for several years Corinth was the seat of a most active and uncompromising warfare on St. Paul. Once more, and finally, he comes before us in the passage under notice in an attitude unmistakably stern and authoritative. Is Christ in you, he asks the Corinthians, or are ye reprobates? Prove yourselves, apply the test, find out whether or not you are in Jesus Christ and share his spirit, and if you cannot stand the test, know then that you are reprobates. He expresses the hope that they will not find him a reprobate (unapproved or spurious) if they put him to the test of exercising his authority. Yet he trusts that the test of his power will be avoided, and prays that they may "do no evil." If they should act as he prayed they might, then there would be no necessity for him to demonstrate his authority, and, in that happy event, he would appear "unapproved," *i.e.* not tested as to the display of his power. Welcome such unapproval! It would be in exact conformity to the spirit and end of his apostolic administration, which was in accordance with the truth of the gospel and designed to show forth that truth. What is the test of a great and wise ruler? The test is the uselessness of a punishing power (except in extreme cases and as an ultimate resort), because his subjects govern themselves. Such was the apostle's argument. Nothing against the truth, all for the truth, Christ the Truth; this was the beautiful summation in which he rested. If this should apparently exhibit his weakness, what a glorious weakness it would be! Apostolic judgment made needless by self-government; what could be a grander testimony to the truth and excellence of his work among them? Then, verily, they would be strong. "Perfection" in the order and unity of the Church, "perfection" of individual character, was the object of his prayer, and hence this Epistle. Whoever teaches Christianity as God's truth cannot fail to teach much else besides. These verses are maxims of infinite wisdom. What man in authority, what statesman in the affairs of a nation, what father at the head of a family, what office-holder in the Church, if he would bear his faculties so meekly and be thus "clear in his great office," would not be a providence of instruction and helpfulness in the world! Decay of reverence for law begins in decay of reverence for men who administer the law. Unhappily enough, this decline in reverence for law is one of the growing perils of the age. It is peculiar to no form of government. It is spreading everywhere as an atmospheric evil, and threatening like an epidemic to travel round the globe. Power to build up, not to destroy; this is St. Paul's idea of power divinely bestowed. And accordingly we see what a blessed discipline it was to him personally and officially; and having accomplished this result in his own soul, it is not remarkable that it achieved its ends in this distracted and corrupted Church at Corinth.—L.

Vers. 11—14.—*Parting tenderness.* If ever great principles of government were subjected to the severest of ordeals, it was in the instance which has been under review. If ever personal qualities and official prerogatives were inextricably mixed in pending issues, and those issues diffused over a vast surface, it was in this affair at Corinth. If ever the chief actor in the interest of tranquillity and social purity had to fight a battle absolutely single-handed and alone, it was St. Paul's fortune in this struggle to save a community from degradation and destruction. We have seen what he endured when endurance was probably harder than at any period of his life. What aids he summoned in these critical hours, what recourse he had to the past, what account he gave of the "thorn in the flesh" and its uses in his work, we have seen in the progress of this interesting section of his career. Most of all, we have seen how the man and the apostle, the tentmaker and the preacher, the liberal Jew and the sagacious Christian, were most happily interblended in the rarest harmony and unity while doing the work of pacification and reformation. And now that he comes before us, in the last expression of himself as to this weighty controversy, it is ennobling to see how finely poised he is, and what anxiety he has "lest, being present," he should be compelled against all his prayers and hopes "to use sharpness according to the power which the Lord had given him." That miraculous gift was his as the apostle of Christ, but it was for "edification, and not to destruction." At the cost of personal humiliation, he would be "glad" if the Corinthians were "strong," and he "weak." How like his Master he was! "Thinkest thou that I cannot now pray to my Father, and he shall presently give me more than twelve legions of angels?" Had he waved his hand, Jerusalem would have been darkened by the wings of gathering angels for his rescue; but he was to be crucified in "weakness" that the "power of God" might be the more gloriously manifested in his resurrection. Power denied in one of its uses, to be more signally displayed in another and higher use, was the lesson St. Paul had learned of his dying Lord. "I am crucified with Christ," said he on a subsequent occasion; but he shares that crucifixion word in one of its most painful forms by withholding the exertion of authority to punish his enemies till all other means had been exhausted. He preached Christ "the Wisdom of God," no less than Christ "the Power of God." Under circumstances of extreme hazard, reputation and influence and future success trembling in the balance, flesh and blood supplying clamorous reasons for a self-asserting course and the swift riddance of a most vexatious trouble, he abides with heroic fortitude by Christian principle in its demands for self-crucifixion, and makes everything yield to magnanimity in his ardent desire for the "perfection" of the Church at Corinth. All this is admirable as a mere matter of congruity in respect to the laws of art. But it leaves the domain of art and rises to a realm infinitely more exalted when he comes before us "apparelled in celestial light," and completes the impression of one

> "Whose high endeavours are an inward light,
> That makes the path before him always bright."

Nothing in the apostle's life more became him than the tenderness in the parting words of this Epistle. "Finally, brethren, farewell." There have been throes of spirit during the birth of this Epistle, moments of vehemence, outbursts of indignation and menace; but they are over now. The sun sets in a sky that the storm has purified, and the last beams glide through an atmosphere of holy stillness. "Be perfect," or, be perfected, making up what ye lack; "be of good comfort," taking encouragement and hope from your trials that God would overrule them for your happiness; "be of one mind," by suppressing all selfishness and partisanship and cultivating unity of interest; "live in peace," so that your outward life bears witness to the fact that ye have "one mind." So shall the "God of love and peace be with you." Let not the sign of your union in Christ as members of his Church be forgotten, and, accordingly, "greet one another with a holy kiss." Macedonian brethren salute you. And now, acknowledging with profoundest reverence the Holy Trinity, "in place of his own salutation, he gives us finally that precious benediction which has acquired such a liturgical use in every age and in every part of the Christian world" (Lange). *Grace, love, communion,*—these three, and each blessing and all the blessedness for every one, friends and enemies, since they are, in this touching moment, "brethren" to his heart. "The grace of the Lord Jesus Christ" in the fulness of his mediatorial office, "the love of God" the Father revealed through that grace, and the "communion of the Holy Ghost" as the effect of the "grace" and the "love" in their fellowship with God and one another, "be with you all. Amen."

It pleased God to make St. Paul his own historian during the memorable period to which this Epistle belongs. No one was competent to this task, not even St. Luke, with all his skill and insight as a writer, and his close relations to the apostle. The inner life of the author was to be set forth with a force and vividness never equalled in sacred literature; and we were to have a section, and a most important section, of the New Testament as a Scripture of a private soul. For, indeed, the Holy Spirit would not limit the wonders of inspiration to the narration of outward events. Great as those events were in the midst of changes going on in the Roman empire, "the mingling and confusion of races, languages, and conditions," of which Dean Milman gives so eloquent a description ('Latin Christianity'), and vast as was the influence of the gospel in slowly transforming that "heterogeneous mass of a corrupted social system" by "instilling feelings of humanity," and giving "dignity to minds prostrated by years, almost centuries, of degrading despotism," it yet was vital to the purpose of the written Word that we should have the record of a human soul in the most typical period of its perplexity and conflict, and under just such circumstances as identified it most nearly with the sharpest trials of manly intelligence and courage. It is St. Luke who describes the one class of occurrences. Only a St. Paul was qualified for the other; and in the Second Epistle to the Corinthians he does this most interesting work. At no point are we left in dimness or obscurity as to what he felt and purposed. Every moment, as the eye follows his path, we see the end to which his steps are tending. "Faint, yet pursuing," often thwarted, often thrown back, often sorely embarrassed, without the lights of past experience, without the helps of brother apostles, alone and unbefriended, he had to solve those problems of Church order and discipline which involved all the future administrative policy of Christian communities. Throughout the struggle we accompany him. We know what he thought, and why. We mark his wisdom, earnestness, and fidelity. In the variety of his moods, in exaltation and depression, in the alternate predominance of very unlike states of consciousness, we find him the same man as to his ruling principle and aim, the same when he threatens and beseeches, the same when he unmasks "false apostles," that he is in prayers for peace and brotherhood. It was a most energetic and exciting portion of his career. But the man's heart is the chief interest as illustrative of the cardinal doctrines of grace. True, we have invaluable contributions to theological truth, expositions of rare profundity and insight, contrasts between the Law and the gospel never surpassed in this favourite department of his intellectual work, references to the body that throw a new light on its relations to mind, and directions as to practical benevolence which cover the whole range, in this particular, of Christian obligation.   Yet these are enhanced in value by the fact that the spirit of an intense living personality is ever present.   We lose nothing of the logic and philosophy, nothing of the force in the historical allusions, nothing of the charm of metaphor and similitude.   At the same time there runs through everything the subtle influence of an individual soul, so that the strength which throbs in doctrinal arguments is from a heart all alive with sensibility.   " Men," says Foster (' First Essay on a Man's writing Memoirs of Himself'), " carry their minds as for the most part they carry their watches, content to be ignorant of the constitution and action within, and attentive only to the little exterior circle of things to which the passions, like indexes, are pointing."   Not so St. Paul.   Temperament, disease, special circumstances in his position, made him in an unusual degree a self-observing man.   In this Epistle we have the richest fruits of his self-knowledge.   Most of all, we see the meaning of that discipline of affliction by means of which the life of Christ in the soul is perfected.   And we see, too, how our private history is far more than a personal concern, and widens out in connections no one could have foreseen.   " A thorn in the flesh " becomes a part of St. Paul's public character ; incidents that historians and philosophers and poets would have passed by as of little meaning, take on a most impressive significance, and endear an Epistle, great on other grounds and great as a work of art, to the struggling and sorrowing heart of every Christian.—L.

Ver. 4.—*Weakness and power.*   It must have been very painful to the sensitive and benevolent mind of the apostle to have written thus to any congregation of Christians, especially to a congregation so intimately connected with him as was this at Corinth. The whole society was to blame for suffering the Judaizers and the questioners of St. Paul's authority ; when they should have taken the part of their spiritual benefactor, and have indignantly resented the slights and misrepresentations which they tolerated. In the prospect of visiting Corinth, the apostle requires that the people shall put themselves to the test and shall give a proof of their reformation; otherwise, he will be compelled to give them a proof of his supernatural power and thus to silence calumny and opposition.

I. THE WEAKNESS OF CHRIST IS SHARED EVEN BY HIS SINCEREST AND MOST FAITHFUL FOLLOWERS.   1. In the Lord Jesus were, both in his person and in his ministerial career, many circumstances of humiliation.   His helpless childhood; his subjection to hunger, thirst, and weariness; his liability to pain ; his endurance of death, are instances of the former.   His submission to calumny and insult, to betrayal and desertion, to hatred and rejection, are proofs of the latter.   2. Now, our Lord himself forewarned his disciples that they should share their Master's lot.   Paul certainly took up the cross. The thorn or stake in the flesh, the feeble body, the scourgings and imprisonments which he was called upon to endure, were not regarded by him as accidents and misfortunes, but rather as proofs of true discipleship, as participations in the sufferings of the Lord. And this is the light in which all followers of the Lord Jesus are justified in regarding the endurances and calamities which befall them in treading in his steps and in executing his commission.   It is the moral glory of Christianity that it dignifies the sufferings of those who partake their Leader's spirit in self-denying endeavours for the salvation of their fellow-men.   Such servants of the Divine Master may well " glory in infirmity."   Their wounds are the honourable scars telling of the severity of the conflict in which they have been engaged.

II. THE POWER OF GOD WHICH WAS UPON CHRIST SHALL BE DISPLAYED IN THOSE WHO, SHARING THE MASTER'S SERVICE, SHARE ALSO HIS WEAKNESS.   Paul was content that men should perceive the weakness manifest in the crucifixion of the Redeemer; but he preached to them a risen, reigning, and glorified King.   The resurrection and ascension of Christ were both proofs of the acceptance of the Son by the Father, and they were an inspiriting omen of the approaching victory of the cause for which Jesus deigned to die.   From the throne of might and dominion, possessed of all authority, the victorious Lord governs his Church on earth, and secures its safety and well-being.

St. Paul felt himself entrusted with abundant means of maintaining his spiritual authority as the "ambassador of Christ." He might possess marks of the dying of the Lord Jesus ; but he wielded a might which no foe could resist. Let all faithful servants of Jesus and true soldiers of the cross be encouraged by the reflection that their Commander is omnipotent, and that he must reign until every foe is beneath his feet.—T.

Ver. 5.—"*Prove yourselves.*" The apostle, before closing his Epistle, turned round upon his detractors. They had been questioning his authority and disparaging his claims, and he had been defending himself and asserting his apostolic rights. But was this as it should be? How was it with themselves? They were very anxious to test him, to compel him to verify his claims. Why should not they be asked whether their own position was assured, whether their own professions were justifiable? Let them examine, test, and prove themselves! The exhortation is one by which all professing Christians may profit.

I. The importance of self-proof. This appears from the unquestionable fact that men generally are disposed to take too favourable a view of themselves, their own character, their own services, their own importance to the Church or the world. Illusion often becomes delusion. That which is nearest at hand, and which might be supposed, because most accessible, to be best known, is often judged with the least fairness and justice. Yet if we form a false estimate of ourselves, how disastrous the consequences may be!

II. The method and spirit of self-proof. 1. There should be perfect candour. 2. The examination should be carried on as under the eye of the omniscient and all-searching God. 3. The standard by which we judge ourselves should be the high and infallible standard of God's own Word. 4. There should be no attempt to exalt self by depreciating others.

III. The consequences of self-proof. 1. The process may reveal what is altogether unsatisfactory and lamentable. He who tests himself thoroughly may come to the conclusion that his life is all wrong from the very foundation. If this is so, it is well that it should be known, that a new basis for the moral life may be laid in the truth and righteousness of God himself. 2. The process may yield results partly gratifying and partly regrettable. If so, while there will be reason for gratitude and encouragement, there will be a call to repentance, reformation, and improvement. For a man to know his faults and errors is the first step towards what is better and nobler.—T.

Ver. 8.—*Invincible truth.* Paul boasted that he could do all things, *i.e.* through Christ who strengthened him. Let his adversaries rage and threaten, he had no fear. He would assert his authority, exercise his power, and reduce the proudest opponent to helplessness. For the truth's sake, for the gospel, there was nothing which he was not able to achieve. But if those whom he chided should submit, should return to their fidelity, not to him only, but to the gospel, then he was powerless to harm them. Nay, in such a case he was with them, on their side. Such appears to be the explanation of this grand utterance occurring in this connection.

I. The powerlessness of man when in opposition to the truth of God. 1. The avowed enemies of the truth have failed in their attacks upon it, whatever have been the resources upon which they have drawn, the arms upon which they have relied. Persecution has raged first against Christianity itself, and then against its purer representation in days of reformation. With what result? The blood of the martyrs has ever been the seed of the Church. "Truth, like a torch, the more it's shook it shines." 2. The false, hypocritical friends of the truth have never succeeded in exterminating it. Their efforts have often been insidious, and have often corrupted and ensnared individuals and even societies. But the pure truth of God has survived, whilst these attempts have again and again been foiled.

II. The strength of those who work with and for the truth of God. 1. Their natural feebleness does not hinder the victory of the cause which they embrace. The ignorant, the poor, the young, the feeble, have done and are still doing great things for the gospel. As at first, so now, God chooses "the weak things of the world to confound the mighty." 2. The efficiency of the truth depends upon its Divine origin and source.

"If God be for us, who can be against us?" Wherever God's truth is proclaimed, there God's Spirit works and God's power is felt. 3. The efficiency of the truth lies in its harmony with the nature and constitution of man. With the use of this divinely tempered implement the divinely prepared soil of humanity may be rendered fruitful in great results. *Magna est veritas, et prevalebit.*—T.

Ver. 11.—"*Live in peace.*" The Christian religion ever represents all true peace among men as taking its beginning in peace with God. This first creates peace of conscience, and then issues in harmony and concord in civil and ecclesiastical society. There can be no doubt that the apostle is here enjoining mutual good will, kindness, and amity.

I. CHRISTIAN PEACE IS IN CONTRAST TO THE ENMITY WHICH IS NATURAL TO SINFUL MEN. "Whence come," asks the inspired writer—"whence come wars and fightings among you?" And the answer is that they may be traced to the lusts which are inherent in depraved human nature. In a more primitive state of society, mankind are actually and almost normally at war. In more civilized society, hatred, malice, envy, etc., prevail, and produce disastrous results, although the worst outward manifestations may be restrained.

II. CHRISTIAN PEACE IS OFTEN VIOLATED IN THE SOCIETIES WHICH ARE NAMED AFTER THE PRINCE OF PEACE. How signally this was the case with the Church at Corinth these Epistles make abundantly manifest. It was distracted by party spirit, by schism, by factions. Christ was "divided" in his body and members. And in this respect the example set at Corinth has, alas! too often been followed. The abode intended for peace has too often been converted into a scene of strife.

III. FELLOWSHIP WITH CHRIST IS THE ONLY MEANS FOR RESTORING OR PRESERVING CHRISTIAN PEACE. Interest is not sufficient; external authority and advice continually fail. But if Christ be enthroned in each heart and in the society at large, then conflicts will be hushed and the peace of God prevail. Hence the need for all those exercises of prayer and meditation by which this truly Christian grace may be promoted.

IV. CHRISTIAN PEACE IS A CONDITION OF CHURCH PROSPERITY. Work and warfare are inimical. If there be strife, the vitality must needs be low, the witness must needs be marred, the work must needs suffer in all finer quality. On the other hand, harmony conduces to co-operation as well as to devotion. The world cannot fail to feel the effects of the presence and the testimony of a united and harmonious Church.—T.

Vers. 12, 13.—*Salutation.* Among the various features which distinguish these apostolic documents from ordinary treatises must be noticed the prominence they attach to social greetings. The personal element mingles very beautifully with the doctrinal and the practical. The apostle's theme may have been absorbing, but he usually, in bringing an Epistle to its close, refers to the individuals by whom he is himself surrounded—his companions and colleagues, and to such as were known to him among the community he is addressing.

I. UPON WHAT CHRISTIAN GREETINGS ARE BASED. They differ from common every-day salutations in this, that they are not mere forms, and are not exchanged as a matter of course. They presume a common relation to, a common interest in, the Divine Saviour. The vital union of Christ's people to himself involves an inter-communion of sympathy amongst themselves.

II. IN WHAT CHRISTIAN SALUTATION FINDS EXPRESSION. 1. In words and in messages of spiritual friendship, in the case of those who are absent from one another. It is thus proved that distance does not sunder hearts, that the spiritual family, dispersed through many places, is nevertheless but one. 2. In the primitive Churches the Christian greeting took the form of the "holy kiss." In this a common social usage was sanctified by a new and higher meaning. The custom was one which in some Churches was retained for centuries. The kiss of peace, brotherhood, and love was felt to be the appropriate symbol of the new and all-pervading sentiment of Christian kindness.

III. WHAT PURPOSES CHRISTIAN GREETINGS SUBSERVE. We may trace several very useful practical ends secured by them. 1. They are evident tokens of the wide diffusion of the Saviour's spiritual presence. It is because Christ is with and in his Church that the living members of this Church, pervaded by one Spirit, show true unity and love. 2. They remove the distressing feeling of isolation from which Christ's people may in many circumstances grievously suffer.   3. They are an anticipation of the confidential and affectionate fellowship which is (next to the presence of the Redeemer) to be expected as the highest joy of the heavenly state.—T.

Ver. 14.—*Benediction.*   When we remember what just cause of complaint Paul had against many members of the Corinthian Church, we cannot but regard this concluding benediction as an evidence of his large-hearted charity.   There is no exception; his benevolent wishes and earnest intercessions are for *all.*   And what fulness and richness of blessing is this which the apostle here implores!

I. TRUE BLESSING DOES NOT CONSIST IN EARTHLY ENJOYMENTS OR EVEN IN HUMAN FELLOWSHIP.   Men's good wishes usually relate to these advantages, and as far as they go they are good, and may be very good.   But the apostle took a higher view of the possibilities of human nature and life.

II. TRUE BLESSING CONSISTS IN THE CONSCIOUSNESS OF A DIVINE RELATIONSHIP.   The three Persons of the Trinity are all concerned in the best and happiest experiences of the pious soul.   It is a lofty view, it must be admitted, this which the apostle takes of religion, but not therefore unreasonable.   It is all the worthier as evincing the interest of the Creator in the spiritual well-being of mankind.

III. TRUE BLESSING ASSUMES A DISTINCTIVELY CHRISTIAN FORM.   This is apparent from the remarkable fact that in this solemn formal language the Lord Jesus occupies the foremost place.   Harmonious this with the Saviour's saying, "No man cometh unto the Father but by me."   The Mediator brings us into relation of sonship towards the Father and of participation in and with the Divine Spirit.

IV. TRUE BLESSING RESIDES IN THE REVELATION TO CHRISTIANS OF THE EMPHATICALLY BENIGNANT ASPECTS OF THE DIVINE CHARACTER.   Observe that "favour," "love," and "communion" are here put forward as those attributes and relations in which it is chiefly desirable that the Eternal should manifest himself to his finite and dependent creatures.

V. TRUE BLESSING IS THE SUBJECT OF MUTUAL CHRISTIAN INTERCESSION.   It is noticeable that, not only is this incomparable boon to be sought by each devout soul for itself; we have the example and the authority of the apostle for including it among the objects sought in intercessory supplications.   Hence the appropriateness of this language for use at the close of devotional services.—T.

Ver. 4.—*The death and resurrection of Christ contrasted.*   I. THE FORMER WAS THROUGH WEAKNESS.   1. *Christ assumed a nature which was capable of crucifixion.* Who could crucify *God?*   But the God-Man might walk in weariness and weakness to Golgotha.   What a pathetic consideration that Christ voluntarily chose a nature which was subject to suffering and death!   2. *Christ repressed his innate power.*   (1) *His Divine power.*   Thus he laid down his life; no man took it from him.   But a flash of that power, and the cross would never have been reared.   But a word from his lips, and his persecutors would have been dead men.   But then the gospel would never have been told to man; so *for man* omnipotence became impotence.   (2) *His human power.* Man-power as well as God-power was discarded.   There was *no* resistance.   He became "as a sheep before her shearers."   He voluntarily became the weakest of the weak that he might be strong to redeem.   Learn here that repression is often a triumph.   Not always does the putting forth of power mean success.   It is sometimes our wisdom to sit still, to submit, to be silent.

II. THE LATTER WAS IN POWER.   1. *A marvellous event.*   What a contrast between the first day and the third!   How mighty men seem on the former! how unutterably impotent on the latter!   How weak Christ seems on the one! how omnipotent on the other!   2. *Demanding Divine energy.*   This power was not of man.   Man stands completely helpless at the grave.   Here his boastings are silenced.   But the Author of life can restore life.   The Divine power manifested in our Lord's resurrection we find sometimes ascribed to God the Father (Eph. i. 20), sometimes to the Son (Mark xiv. 58); "I and my Father are one" (John x. 30).   3. *Complete.*   (1) Christ arose in perfect power.   The cross and the grave left no marks of weakness upon him.   His omnipotence was untainted.   (2) He has reigned since in power above.   (3) He works in power to-day on earth through his Word and Spirit.

III. THE DEATH AND RESURRECTION OF CHRIST, THOUGH IN CONTRAST, ARE IN CLOSE ASSOCIATION. They are in point of time. A few hours only separated the weakness of the cross from the power of the restoration. But there is real dependence also. In a certain sense the one was the natural result of the other. Without so perfect a crucifixion there could not have been so triumphant a resurrection. Christ was perfect alike when he was in weakness and when he was in power. Had there been any less "weakness" in the death, there had been less "power" in the resurrection. The humiliation was, in its order, as truly glorious as the exaltation. So with us—if we are abased with Christ here we shall be glorified with him hereafter. We have the cross—*must* have the cross—if we would have the crown.—H.

Ver. 5.—*Self-testing.*   I. MANY ARE FOND OF TESTING OTHERS WHEN IT IS MORE NEEDFUL FOR THEM TO TEST THEMSELVES. "Beginning at Jerusalem" is beginning at the right place. "Know thyself" was a very wise exhortation. To ascertain the shortcomings of others is more pleasant, but not so profitable, as to ascertain our own. The matter of *first* importance to us is, not whether our neighbour's scales are true, but whether ours are. Men are singularly unselfish in some directions—in the directions of giving advice and passing condemnatory judgments.

II. THE TEST WHICH WE APPLY TO OTHERS WE SHOULD BE ABLE TO STAND OURSELVES. Paul was not what the Corinthians thought he ought to be, because they were not what they ought to have been. A blind man is a poor judge of colours. The beam must be taken out of our eyes before we shall be able to see clearly. An unclean man denouncing uncleanness is no very edifying spectacle. If we warn men against getting into the mire, they will expect us to come out of it. If we would be leaders, we must *lead.* "Come" is much more potent than "go."

III. THERE IS ONE POINT UPON WHICH WE SHOULD BE MOST DESIROUS OF TESTING OURSELVES. This is—whether we are "in the faith." Men test themselves frequently, but generally upon points of secondary importance. This is the question of questions. 1. *Do we truly repent of sin?* Do we grieve over evil as that which has been done *against God?* Do we hate it, loathe it, desire to be freed from it? 2. *Have we a living faith in the Lord Jesus Christ?* Do we gratefully receive him as our Redeemer, and believe that his blood cleanses *us* from all sin? Have we *come to God* by Christ and obtained his forgiveness? 3. *Is the vitality of our faith demonstrated by the fruits of holy living?* If our faith is not accompanied by works, it is no faith—we are "reprobates" still, and hypocritical reprobates into the bargain. If we are "in the faith," we shall be subject to God, striving daily to do his will, living and labouring to please him and to extend his glory in the earth. We may still be very imperfect, but, having been "born again," we shall walk in "newness of life."

IV. HOW WE MAY TEST OURSELVES UPON THIS VITAL POINT. 1. *By prayerful self-examination.* Prayer must come into this examination of ourselves because God must come. We need Divine help to aid us in knowing ourselves. 2. *By comparing head, heart, and life with God's Word.* In the Scriptures we have declared what those "in the faith" *believe, feel, do.* 3. *By pressing home the question—Is Christ in me?* "If any man hath not the Spirit of Christ, he is none of his" (Rom. viii. 9). We are in the faith if the Lord of the faith is in us.

How earnestly should we examine ourselves! How restless should we be until we enter into the rest which comes from knowing that we are truly in the faith!—H.

Vers. 11, 12.—*A beautiful farewell.* I. RECOGNITION OF BROTHERHOOD. In his letter the writer had been compelled to insist much upon his apostleship, but he now wisely and graciously stands upon common ground. He was compelled to magnify his office, but he was too good and too great to magnify himself. Amongst men there is a natural craving for equality; we resent a fellow-creature attempting to lord it over us. And in the realm of religion we have ever need to remember "all ye are brethren." What a poor fool a great man seems when he swells and struts in his miserable pomposity and conceit! he is *not* great—no one can persuade us that he is great—he is extremely little. How much greater our great men would be if they would not be so great ! One might imagine, sometimes, that our Lord had commanded those who would be chief to imitate turkey-cocks; but he said they must become **as** little children.

II. GOOD WISHES. "Farewell," or "Rejoice." All joy to you, all prosperity, all happy and profitable experience. Not a few of them had ill wishes for him; he had nothing but good wishes for friends and foes. This was a very real *fare well*. Upon our lips it often means too little—in fact, it has become but the barest signal for separation; but coming from Paul's heart it was full of earnest meaning. Possibly in his thought it took the form of " Rejoice in the Lord," as in Phil. iii. 1. Everything of value in the eyes of Paul was "in the Lord." And there is no real faring well unless we are in Christ.

III. LOFTY AND GRACIOUS DESIRES. 1. *For spiritual growth.* "Be perfected." Correct the evils which I have pointed out. Reform yourselves. Seek to become more like your Lord. Strive to get rid of the "old things," and to become new in Christ. Rest not as long as any sin abides within you. This was desiring for them the very highest good. This was a practical suggestion of the way in which they might "fare well." 2. *For comfort.* "Be comforted." Paul's heart was tender towards them. They had caused him great, discomfort; he desires their consolation. He had, indeed, wounded them himself in administering stern but necessary rebuke—but faithful were the wounds of such a friend; and now he desires that these wounds may be healed, trusting that the lancet has done its work. Note: he does not say, "Be comforted, be perfected," but "Be perfected, be comforted;" true comfort comes only as we strive for true holiness. The quickest way to bring comfort to men is to seek to make them better. To comfort men *in* sin is devil-like; to comfort men by bringing them *out of* sin is God-like. 3. *For unity.* "Be of the same mind." Disunited, they would be miserable and weak; united, they would be happy and strong. When we are drawn nearer to Christ we shall be drawn nearer to the brethren; if we quarrel with the members we shall soon quarrel with the Head. The Church has to fight united foes; union should not be the monopoly of the servants of the devil. 4. *For peace.* "Live in peace." Let peace be continuous, uninterrupted. Disunion will lead to civil war, and how can Christians fight the devil if they are fighting one another? If we have peace with God we should live in peace with his children, and be at war only with Satan and sin. 5. *For love.* Conveyed by the exhortation to "salute one another with a holy kiss." Union is not enough; peace is not enough; there must be heartfelt affection between the people of God. This is the only true basis of union and peace. An armed truce is sometimes worse than open battle. We must not "tolerate" the brethren—we must *love* them. A "Toleration Act" is a blasphemy against Christ.

IV. A STRENGTHENING PROMISE. "The God of love and peace shall be with you." What Wesley said in death is true for all life, "The best of all is—God is with us." "If thy presence go not with me, carry me not up hence" (Exod. xxxiii. 15). If we have God with us, what can we lack? Perhaps we may regard this promise as *conditional*. If you sincerely strive to be holy, united, loving, God will abide with you; otherwise, he will depart. Like Israel of old, you may become desolate through carnality and hardness of heart. But if you desire to live in love and peace, the God of love and peace will presence himself with you. You must be workers together with him; from him you get desires for love and peace; but you must cultivate these, and be true and earnest in your religious life. It has been well said, "God's presence produces love and peace, and we must have love and peace in order to have his presence; God gives what he commands; God gives, but we must cherish his gifts."—H.

Ver. 14.—*The benediction.* These words have become the universal sanctuary utterance of the Christian Church. As Paul wrote them, how real and full of meaning they were! Now, alas! they have too much degenerated into a mere signal for terminating public worship, anxiously anticipated by the weary—an empty appendage, for which might adequately be substituted a bare announcement, "The meeting is over." Yet how beautiful is this benediction! how suggestive! how full of teaching! It is a summary of Christianity, a revelation of the Trinity and of the great threefold Divine work for human redemption and exaltation.

I. THE MATTER OF THE BENEDICTION. 1. *"The grace of the Lord Jesus Christ."*

(1) Remark the title. *Lord*—the Divine One and the Master. *Jesus*—the Saviour and the Man. *Christ*—the Anointed of God, the long-promised Messiah. A trinity of qualification. (2) The grace. The favour, and all that the favour of such a Being involves. The blessings of Christ's rule as Master, of his redemption as Saviour, of his boundless resources as the Divine Messiah. If we are the objects of his favour, how inestimably rich we are! 2. "*The love of God.*" The apostle has just spoken of God as the God of love (ver. 11)`; now he desires for the Corinthians the love of this God of love. The riches of Divine love are the Christian's portion. Here is specially referred to the love of God as our *Father*. It was through the Father's love that the Saviour was given, but it is through the Saviour's work, and our participation in it, that we enter into the enjoyment of the love of God as the love of our Father. This is the covenanted love of God; his special fatherly affection for those who have become, through Christ, his sons and daughters. Thus "the grace of the Lord Jesus Christ" is made to precede "the love of God." 3. "*The communion of the Holy Ghost.*" The *participation* in the Holy Ghost. This we enjoy through Christ (Gal. iii. 13, 14). Who can estimate the value of this? The great work of sanctification, the constant effective teaching of the truth, preservation in times of spiritual peril, comfort in sorrow, ability to carry on Christian work,—all these depend upon our participating in the Holy Ghost. "Quench not the Spirit" (1 Thess. v. 19). If in aught we hinder the Divine Spirit's working within us, in that measure we become spiritual suicides.

II. The extent of the benediction. It is for all Christians; it is not for any special order or class, but for every individual. Some privileges were associated with the apostleship, some with certain of mark and power in the early Church, but the privileges which are of supreme value have ever been the common heritage of God's people. Some smaller favours may be for the few, the greatest are for the many.

III. How may we come under this benediction? A very important question. To be beyond its reach must be to be in peril and misery. As it is for all the people of the Lord, those must become the people of the Lord who would share in its blessings. If we are willing to be blessed, God is willing to let this benediction rest upon us. By the way of repentance and faith and sincere striving to do the Divine will we pass from under the curse and abide under the benediction.—H.

Ver. 5.—*Self-examination.* I. Points on which self-examination is required. They relate to your connection with Jesus Christ—whether he is in you and you are in the faith. It is assumed that the word of faith has been preached; then follows the question—How does this Word affect or influence you? It is easy to hear it and give it a formal assent—but this is not enough. Are you really in the faith? Does the truth compass you about and impress itself on all your views, motives, and principles of action? If so, Christ is certainly in you. He dwells in your heart by faith, and by his Spirit vitalizes and purifies your spirit.

II. The kind of evidence needed. The thing is not to be assumed, but proved. There is a mode of proof which onlookers may read and estimate. It is that which appears in your temper, demeanour, and actions. If men see good fruit in you, they infer that you are a good tree. But self-scrutiny must go into the matter more deeply. Onlookers see actions, but not the motives from which they spring. Some of your words and deeds they know, but not all of them, and not your actuating dispositions. Examine yourselves by the double test of the inward and the outward life. Review your motives and secret desires, as well as the current of your tempers and the tenor of your lives.

III. The difficulty of conducting this examination. 1. *In the nature of the case.* Genuine self-knowledge is perhaps a rare attainment. The moment we go beneath the surface and try to probe the hidden things of the heart, we find ourselves among intricacies hard to unravel—a review of motives, the detection of half-motives, and the analysis of transient thoughts and feelings as respects their moral complexion and significance. We are in a labyrinth of plans, wishes, imaginations, passions, caprices, and principles. One motive lurks behind another, one current of desire flows beneath another. And feeling, when subjected to analysis, ceases to be feeling, and it is only the recollection or the shadow of it which you can examine. 2. *Through the delusions of self-esteem.* Men shrink from a severe self-examination, lest the resul·

should be mortifying, if not alarming.   And even so far as they go, they are influenced by a desire to think hopefully of their own state, and to apply to themselves easy and partial tests.   Like a teacher who is partial to a particular scholar and asks him only those questions which he is sure to answer, or an unjust judge who gives ear only to the side that he favours, every man is apt in self-examination to be biased in his own favour and to dwell on his best points as though they formed the whole staple of his character.   3. *From exaggerated self-distrust.*   Some minds are morbidly sensitive, and do not so much examine as torment themselves.   They cannot own what Christ has done for them, through fear of presumption.   And their self-judgment is hindered by over-caution and a dejection mistaken for humility.

IV. THE WAY TO REACH THE TRUTH ABOUT YOURSELVES.   The Lord must be asked to preside over and direct the examination.   It is he who looks upon the heart, and so it is he who can give you an insight into your real selves.   Begin with the prayer in Ps. cxxxix. 23, 24.   The Spirit of the Lord then shows you what you are by means of the lamp of the Word.   And with such guidance you ought to know whether you are the Lord's or no.   But you must yourselves watch as well as read and pray.   It is a good rule to note the significance of little things, in which the mind is less on its guard and so more freely reveals its bent.   A physician watches slight symptoms in order to detect and cure disease.   A judge takes note of small incidents in a case, and shows the jury how, on the combination of these, the verdict of guilt or innocence must turn. So also should he act who would diagnose or judge himself; though, on the other hand, one must not lay all the stress on minor points, but should rest the main conclusion on broad and comprehensive grounds.

V. THE CONDITION OF THOSE WHO CANNOT BEAR THE TRIAL.   "Disapproved."   There is no verdict of "not proven."   Those who name the Name of Christ are approved or disapproved.   Leave not your relation to Jesus Christ in doubt.   Repair to him who can solve your doubt and give you the good part that shall not be taken away.—F.

Ver. 11.—" *The God of love and peace.*"   Love is the nature, and peace the very element, of God.   Whatever the detached indications of severity under his sway, whatever the calamities permitted or the penalties inflicted by God, there is love in, over, and under all.   Whatever the trouble or turmoil in parts of creation, at the centre of the universe there is a perfect peace.   It is the conviction of this which makes our Christian faith so powerful both to calm and to satisfy the soul.   We can endure much if we have for our Friend and our eternal Portion the God of love and peace.

I. THE INITIAL KNOWLEDGE OF GOD.   You become in your heart acquainted with God through the faith of the gospel.   You hear and believe that he loves, and is so far from desirous that any should perish, that he has made provision in Jesus Christ for eternal life to all who confide in his Name.   So you repent of your enmity to him and turn to the God of love.   Not only so.   The gospel, while a revelation of love, is also a message of peace.   " God was in Christ reconciling the world to himself."   Hearing this, you perceive that God is not pursuing you with an angry countenance and a terrible dart, but regards you with a face of sublime compassion and good-will, and bids you fight against him no more, but become his friend.   So you repent of your alienation and turn to the God of peace.   And all is changed in you.   You also love.   You also are in peace.

II. PROGRESSIVE FRIENDSHIP WITH GOD.   In order to abide with God, you must grow in those moral qualities which in their perfection make up his character.   Thus you are to dwell in love, and to make peace.   1. *Dwell in love.*   What notion can a hard-hearted, uncharitable man form of God ?   Faith needs love in order to the higher attainments of holy knowledge and holy fellowship.   Only he who dwells in love dwells in God.   The Divine Word is sweet to him.   The Divine purposes are all good in his eyes ; for love enters into the secret of love, and by a touch of sympathy recognizes its presence and strength.   2. *Cherish and make peace.*   A quarrelsome Christian, a former of party, a fomentor of strife,—how can he know the God of peace ?   St. Paul by no means shrank from controversy, and made no truce with error or evil ; but what a peacemaker he was in the Church !   How impressive his appeals to the Corinthians to be of the same mind and at peace among themselves !   It brings God into the heart to arrange disputes, to forgive offences, to bury prejudices, and to exhibit and foster brotherly kindness in the Church. It is the dove that was made a symbol of the Spirit of God; and that is a bird which flees away from noise and tempest. So it is in the quiet heart, and in those Churches where the brethren are at peace with one another, that the Spirit of the God of peace, the Comforter, will dwell.

III. DEFEAT OF THE FLESH AND THE DEVIL. 1. *Hatred is a work of the flesh.* Love is part of the fruit of the Spirit; and he who is born of the Spirit ought to smile at provocation and forgive injury and even love his enemies, because the God whom he serves is love, the Father of whom he is begotten is merciful. 2. *Discord is a work of the devil.* And in breathing a spirit of mutual consideration and concord over his people, the God of peace bruises Satan under their feet (Rom. xvi. 20). He brings order out of confusion, and crushes the hissing serpents of dissension and malignity under the feet of his saints.—F.

Ver. 4.—*" Crucified through weakness."* This is a very characteristic view of the crucifixion of our Lord. St. Paul never dwelt upon it complacently, as we do. There is no trace of his having ever elaborately described it, or endeavoured to move the feelings of his hearers or readers by the persuasions of his Lord's dying distresses. The Crucifixion was a painful subject to him. It was Christ's time of weakness. The apostle always seems to hasten away from that theme to what he can glory in, even Christ, the risen One, the living One, who now can save. Dean Plumptre explains the expression taken as our text thus: " *For even he was crucified.* St. Paul seems to see in Christ the highest representative instance of the axiomatic law by which he himself had been comforted, that strength is perfected in infirmities. For he too lived encompassed with the infirmities of man's nature, and the possibility of the Crucifixion flowed from that fact as a natural sequel." Professor Lias says, " Our Lord assumed our human nature with all its infirmities (Heb. ii. 10—18; iv. 15; v. 2, 3), and although they were the result of sin. He bore all those infirmities, death itself included. And then he shook them all off for ever when he rose again ' by the power of God.' "

I. CHRIST WAS BODILY WEAK. We may fairly assume that our Lord had a healthy body; but it was subject to ordinary human infirmities. He felt fatigue, hunger, thirst, need of sleep; and spiritual work exhausted his nervous system as it does ours. We may even assume that his must have been a nervously sensitive body, since this is found to be the characteristic of all highly intellectual and all highly spiritual men and women. It will be easy to show how St. Paul would feel a special sympathy with the Lord Jesus in all this, since his too was a frail, sensitively organized body. Those who are easily depressed, readily affected by outward circumstances, and conscious of physical frailty, seldom realize how near to them in sympathetic experience comes the Lord Jesus Christ, and, after him, the great apostle of the Gentiles.

II. CHRIST WAS SOUL-STRONG. And therefore he could go through all the lot which God appointed for him, even though that included the bitter and terrible experiences of the Crucifixion. The soul-strength St. Paul thought of as *Christ living* in the very midst of his weakness and suffering. His idea may be thus expressed: " We too are weak; we have our share in infirmities and sufferings, which are ennobled by the thought that they are ours because they are his; but we know that we shall live in the highest sense, in the activities of the spiritual life, which also we share with him, and which comes to us by the power of God; and this life will be manifested in the exercise of our spiritual power towards you and for your good." Reference is to the present *ministry* and not to the *hereafter-time.* If Christ's weakness was, like St. Paul's, frailty of body, he might rejoice that Christ's strength was *soul-strength*, and, like his, the strength of God made perfect in weakness.—R. T.

Ver. 5.—*Self-examination.* " Examine yourselves, whether ye be in the faith; prove your own selves." This is without question a necessary and practically important Christian duty. But the forms it takes and the estimates of its value differ according to the tones and peculiarities of Christian life and feeling in each age. When prominence is given to doctrine, and conflicts rage round precisions in the expression of opinion, self-examination is neglected, and, as a rebound, is unduly cultivated by the pietistic few. When feeling rather than truth is cultivated, and religion is conceived as a mood of mind rather than as a body of doctrines, self-examination is set forth prominently as one of the essentials of Christian living. It must also be added that self-examination has always been urged by the priesthood as an agent in preserving for such priesthood the control of men's thoughts, opinions, conduct, and life. Recognizing its importance, but carefully avoiding exaggerations in reference to it, we notice—

I. WHAT IT MAY PROPERLY CONCERN. 1. *Conduct.* This may include (1) our mode of performing our ordinary life-duties; (2) the character of our relationship with others; (3) the wise use of our opportunities of usefulness; (4) the helpful occupation of our leisure hours; (5) and the worthy meeting of our life-responsibilities. 2. *Opinion.* St. Paul here enjoins a proving or testing of opinion, so that a man may know whether he is "holding fast the profession of his faith without wavering;" "holding fast the form of sound words." 3. *Feeling.* So far as this is related to the *motive* of conduct, and gives inspiration and character to the expressions of Christian life. Self-examination of feeling with a view to confidence of our state and satisfaction in our progress and attainment is always perilous and often ruinous. Watching frames and feelings is the most enervating thing a Christian can do. It never can culture humility; it often, in a very subtle way, nourishes spiritual pride and severs the soul from the simplicity of its dependence on Christ. It brings a false satisfaction in feeling right, or a needless distress in feeling wrong. It clouds the Christian life with hindering and weakening depressions, or it brings an extravagant joy which is really joy in self, not joy in God.

II. WHEN SHOULD IT BE UNDERTAKEN? Only occasionally, and under special pressure, such as comes with times of conscious weakness and failure; or times when error is being freely taught; or times when the Christian morality is imperilled; or times when the changes of life are bringing to us fresh responsibilities. St. Paul commends the duty in a special form in relation to the Communion of the Lord's Supper. And many Christian people have found special times of self-examination useful—at the New Year, at birthdays, etc. Where there is a natural tendency to morbid introspection the seasons should be very infrequent. Where the active side of Christian life is over-developed, the times for self-examination may safely be multiplied.

III. IN WHAT SPIRIT SHOULD IT BE CONDUCTED? There should be (1) great seriousness; (2) earnest prayer for a spirit of sincerity and faithfulness; (3) careful avoidance of any desire to test themselves by any human standards; (4) anxiously cherished dependence on the leadings and teachings of God the Holy Ghost; and (5) firm resolve to turn the conclusions of our self-examination into principles and directions for the guidance and the improvement of our practical life of godliness. Compare the psalmist, who prays, "Search me, O God," before attempting to search himself.

IV. HOW MAY THE POSSIBLE EVILS OF IT BE COUNTERACTED? 1. By making Holy Scripture the standard according to which we test ourselves. 2. By making conduct rather than feeling the subject of our review. 3. By turning the results of the examination into prayer for more grace. 4. By persisting in seeing the things that we may have to rejoice in, as well as those which we may have to groan over. 5. And by regarding the Lord Jesus Christ—and none but he—as our Model of the *interior*, as well as of the exterior, Christian life.—R. T.

Ver. 5.—*Who are the reprobates?* Essentially such as have not Christ in them. Those whose experience and conduct are *not* sufficient to prove the indwelling presence and sanctifying power of the living Christ. The word "reprobate" signifies those who have been *tried and found wanting.* Illustrations of the use of the term may be found in Rom. i. 28; 1 Cor. ix. 27; 2 Tim. iii. 8; Tit. i. 16; Heb. vi. 8. The subject may be effectively introduced by a description of the scene in Belshazzar's palace, with the mystic handwriting on the wall. Then it may be shown how the term may gain its application to—

I. INDIVIDUAL CHRISTIANS. Some such St. Paul refers to by name, as Alexander, Hermogenes, Demas, etc. Compare Peter's finding Simon the Sorcerer wanting. Individuals may be reprobate (1) intellectually, by accepting false and dishonouring doctrine; (2) morally, by yielding to temptations of self-indulgence, vice, or crime.

II. CHURCHES. This may be illustrated by the searching addresses sent by the glorified Christ to some of the seven Churches of Asia. The principles of the search may be effectively applied to modern Churches.

III. PASTORS. These fail from the pastoral ideal generally after they have failed from the private Christian ideal. Shepherds are reprobates when they neglect their duty to their flock; when they feed themselves and not the flock; when they see the wolf coming, and flee; and when they fail duly to honour the chief Shepherd before the flock. Illustration may be taken from the experiences of the City of Mansoul as figured by John Bunyan, in his 'Holy War.' Reprobates, such as are here dealt with, are recoverable by penitence, humiliation, and heart-return to Christ.—R. T.

Ver. 11.—*Final counsels.* What should the godly minister most desire for his people? All his best wishes for them can be gathered up in the word "unity." And the terms here used embody the idea of unity. And this was the supreme want of the Corinthian Church, which had been so broken up by (1) party feeling, (2) false teachings, (3) immoral members. As this subject has been so often taken as a theme for sermons preached at the close of ministries in particular places, we only give an outline from the point of view which regards *unity* as the central idea of the passage.

I. PERFECT. That is, exactly fitted together; a whole.

II. OF GOOD COMFORT. This would only come by the removal of the jealousies and envyings, which spoiled the unity and the brotherhood.

III. OF ONE MIND. Giving up individual preferences and peculiarities, so that they might agree together, think and plan the same things.

IV. LIVE IN PEACE. Or show that thoughtfulness for others which is the great secret of the peaceful life.

Upon such unity as the apostle thus commends the Divine benediction is sure to rest.—R. T.

Ver. 14.—*The Christian benediction.* This is the closing sentence of a long letter. Letters bear the stamp of the age in which they are written. Their modes of beginning and ending, and their forms of salutation, are characteristic of nations and periods. This closing benediction may be compared with those of other Epistles. The most simple form is "Grace be with you," and this we find in Colossians, 1 and 2 Timothy, Titus, and also in the Epistle to the Hebrews. A somewhat fuller but still very simple form is this: "The grace of our Lord Jesus Christ be with you all." This is found in Romans, Philippians, and 1 and 2 Thessalonians. The Epistle to the Galatians closes thus: "Brethren, the grace of our Lord Jesus Christ be with your spirit." Philemon ends in a similar way. In Ephesians there is a peculiar form: "Grace be with all them that love our Lord Jesus Christ in sincerity." Comparing St. Paul's mode with that of the other apostles, we find similarity with distinctive differences. St. Peter closes his First Epistle thus: "Peace be with you all that are in Christ Jesus;" and his Second Epistle thus: "But grow in grace, and in the knowledge of our Lord and Saviour Jesus Christ." St. James has no greeting; nor has John, except to his Third Epistle, and there it is simply, "Peace be to thee." Jude closes with a doxology. From this comparison it appears that the Christian benediction, in its simplest form, is the wish that "grace" may be with the Church. The point of it lies in the word "grace," and in the ideas that St. Paul attached to the word "grace," and to its "being" or "continuing" with the believers.

I. THE MEANING OF THE TERM "GRACE." It must be distinguished from the word "graces," as meaning the special gifts and endowments granted to the early Church. As used in the singular number, it sometimes means the free favour and love of God as shown to us in our salvation by Christ. Then the full expression is, "the grace of God, and the gift by grace" (Rom. v. 15). A characteristic instance of this use of the word may be found in Titus ii. 11, 12. St. Paul, however, uses the term in quite another sense. He often means by it what we should call the *state of grace*, that condition of privilege and relation, that favour and acceptance with God, into which we are brought by Christ and in which we stand—a state of justification and acceptance; a state of rightness with God through faith. This state of favour he calls "grace." Illustrative references may be made to Rom. v. 1, 2; Gal. i. 6; Phil. i. 7, and also to a striking passage in 1 Pet. v. 12. It seems that the Lord Jesus Christ is regarded as the model or representative of this state or standing of acceptance and favour with God. The Father himself testified to it, saying, "This is my beloved Son, in whom I am well pleased." Christ declares it to be his abiding state, "I do always the things that please him." He was the perfect, obedient Son, in his trust, and love, and devotion, and obedience, and freeness of communion with the Father, giving us the very model and illustration of the state of rightness, of grace and favour, into which he brings us. St. Paul's burden of benediction is "grace," and he sometimes means by it the state of favour and acceptance with God into which we are brought by faith. Now, this state of grace is so thoroughly that in which Christ himself stands, and it is so manifestly the state into which we can only be brought by him, that it may properly be called the "grace of the Lord Jesus," or the "state of grace of the Lord Jesus." Sometimes this state is viewed on the side of the Spirit that brings us into it, and then it is called the state of *faith*; at other times it is viewed on the side of the privilege that belongs to it, and then it is called the state of *grace*. Reading St. Paul's benediction in the light of these explanations, it may run thus: "May you enjoy and enter yet more fully into that state of grace and favour with God which Christ has, by his sonship, and which you have, in measure also by yours : that state of grace, I mean, which consists in these things—an ever-deepening sense of the love of God, and feeling of the impulse of that love; and an abiding consciousness of the communion of the Holy Ghost, whereby ye are sealed."

II. THE CHRISTIAN STATE OF GRACE OR FELLOWSHIP WITH GOD. Surely no fact could be presented that is more calculated to fill our hearts with the "joy unspeakable" than this. No principle of Christian steadfastness can be of more practical value than this. If any one thing more than another is the burden of the Epistles, it is the right of the believer in Christ. In multiplied ways the apostle seems to say—Realize your sonship; enter into your privilege; use your right of access; live as restored and accepted ones; seek to know the spirit of your new state; lift yourselves up to meet the responsibilities resting on your privilege. Ye receive "now the end of your faith, even the salvation of your souls." "Now are ye the sons of God." Yet surely this is not the thought which, as Christians, we most readily cherish. Too often we encourage uncertainty as to our spiritual status; we hope that all will be well at last; we walk under clouds of doubt, and very feebly welcome even the salvation which God grants. The higher Christian life takes in simple trust, not only Christ, but all the status, rights, and privileges that come to us in Christ. It loses its fears, buries its questioning, and rejoices in having "passed from death unto life." If any longing for a more earnest religious life has been started in any of our hearts; if for our own cold lifeless souls we have been led to pray, "O Lord, revive thy work in the midst of the years!"—then let us be assured that the beginning of better things is this—Enter into, possess, and enjoy your full rights in Christ; not your own rights, but Christ's, which are made yours on believing. Believe that you have been brought into, and do now stand in, a state of grace and favour with God, accepted by him in the Beloved. For assurances of present salvation and privilege, see Rom. viii. 1, 14—17; Eph. ii. 12, 13, 18—22; 1 Pet. ii. 5, 9, 10; 1 John iii. 1, 2, etc. But how is such a sense of our standing in Christ to be won? Faith—trust—is the answer. Trust is the attitude of our souls which God demands. Trust in his Son Jesus Christ, who "of God is made unto us wisdom, righteousness, sanctification, and complete redemption." Simple, entire, perfect trust. Taking Christ as he is offered—as our "all in all," not for deliverance only, but also for standing and sanctification. United with Christ, his rights become ours. We are sons with God. We stand in the state of favour with God in which Jesus, the perfect Son, who is our life, stands.—R. T.

HOMILETICAL INDEX

TO

THE SECOND EPISTLE OF

ST. PAUL TO THE CORINTHIANS

---◆◇◆---